VIVA-FACTS ON FILE
ENCYCLOPEDIA OF SOCIETY AND CULTURE IN THE ANCIENT WORLD

Volume I • A–C

Editor in Chief
Peter Bogucki

Viva Books

New Delhi | Mumbai | Chennai | Kolkata | Bangalore | Hyderabad | Kochi | Guwahati

First Indian Edition 2010

VIVA BOOKS PRIVATE LIMITED

- 4737/23 Ansari Road, Daryaganj, New Delhi 110 002
  E-mail: vivadelhi@vivagroupindia.net, Tel. 42242200
- 76, Service Industries, Shirvane, Sector 1, Nerul, Navi Mumbai 400 706
  E-mail: vivamumbai@vivagroupindia.net, Tel. 27721273, 27721274
- Jamals Fazal Chambers, 26 Greams Road, Chennai 600 006
  E-mail: vivachennai@vivagroupindia.net, Tel. 28290304, 28294241
- B-103, Jindal Towers, 21/1A/3 Darga Road, Kolkata 700 017
  E-mail: vivakolkata@vivagroupindia.net, Tel. 22836381, 22816713
- 7, Sovereign Park Apartments, 56-58, K. R. Road, Basavanagudi, Bangalore 560 004
  E-mail: vivabangalore@vivagroupindia.net, Tel. 26607409, 26607410
- 101-102 Mughal Marc Apartments, 3-4-637 to 641, Narayanguda, Hyderabad 500 029
  E-mail: vivahyderabad@vivagroupindia.net, Tel. 27564481, 27564482
- First Floor, Beevi Towers, SRM Road, Kaloor, Kochi 682 018, Kerala
  E-mail: vivakochi@vivagroupindia.net, Tel: 0484-2403055, 2403056
- 232, GNB Road, Beside UCO Bank, Silpukhuri, Guwahati 781 003
  E-mail: vivaguwahati@vivagroupindia.net, Tel: 0361-2666386

www.vivagroupindia.com

Published by arrangement with
Facts on File, Inc.
132 West 31st Street
New York 10001
USA

ISBN : 978-81-309-0929-5 (Set of 4 Volumes)

Published by Vinod Vasishtha for Viva Books Private Limited, 4737/23, Ansari Road, Daryaganj, New Delhi-110 002. Printed and bound by Sanat Printers, Kundli-131 028, Sonepat, Haryana.

Contents

Volume IV

Advisers and Contributors

EDITOR IN CHIEF

Peter Bogucki
Associate Dean for Undergraduate Affairs,
School of Engineering and Applied Science
Princeton University

ADVISORY BOARD

Lisa R. Brody
Assistant Professor of Art
Queens College, City University of New York

R. Hunt Davis
Professor Emeritus of History and African Studies
University of Florida

Leo Depuydt
Associate Professor of Egyptology
Brown University

Paul R. Goldin
Associate Professor of East Asian Languages
and Civilizations
University of Pennsylvania

Eloise Quiñones Keber
Professor of Art History
Baruch College, City University of New York

Amelie Kuhrt
Professor of Ancient Near Eastern History
University College, London

Daniel Potts
Edwin Cuthbert Hall Professor of
Middle Eastern Archaeology
University of Sydney

CONTRIBUTORS

Saheed Aderinto is a Ph.D. student at the Department of History, University of Texas at Austin. Some of his most recent publications include "Prostitution and Urban Social Relations" and "Policing Urban Prostitution: Prostitutes, Crime, Law and Reformers in Colonial Nigeria" in *Nigeria's Urban History: Past and Present* (2006) and "Discrimination in an Urban Setting: The Experience of Ijebu Settlers in Colonial Ibadan, 1893–1960" in *Inter-group Relations in Nigeria during the 19th & 20th Centuries* (2006). His writings have also appeared in *IFRA Special Research Issue, Ethnic and Third World Review of Books, African and Asian Studies Journal,* and *The Encyclopedia of Prostitution and Sex Work* (2006).

Olutayo Charles Adesina, Ph.D., teaches at the Department of History, University of Ibadan, Nigeria. He is the author of "The Underground Foreign Exchange Market in Ibadan during Devaluation" in *Money Struggles and City Life: Devaluation in Ibadan and Other Urban Centres in Southern Nigeria, 1986–96* (2002) and "Teaching History in Twentieth Century Nigeria: The Challenges of Change" in *History in Africa: A Journal of Method*, vol. 33 (2006).

David Otieno Akombo, Ph.D., teaches music education and world music at Wabash College of Indiana. He is the author of *Music and Healing across Cultures* (2006).

Francis Allard, Ph.D., teaches in the Department of Anthropology at Indiana University of Pennsylvania. His research interests include the archaeology of early China and Mongolia. He has contributed articles to *Archaeology of Asia* (2005) and *Beyond the Steppe and the Sown: Proceedings of the 2002 University of Chicago Conference on Eurasian Archaeology* (2006).

Miguel Arisa is finishing his doctoral studies in art history at the Graduate Center, City University of New York. He teaches at Technical Career Institutes and is a regular lecturer at the

Cloisters and a docent at the Metropolitan Museum of Art, New York.

Mariam F. Ayad, Ph.D., teaches graduate-level classes on Egyptian language and literature at the University of Memphis, where she is the assistant director of its Institute of Egyptian Art and Archaeology. Her main research interests focus on the role of women in ancient Egyptian temple ritual and the selection and transmission of funerary texts in post–New Kingdom Egypt. Her book on the God's Wife of Amun is under contract with Routledge.

Heather D. Baker, D.Phil., is a researcher at the University of Vienna, Austria, specializing in Babylonian history, society, and culture. She has published widely on Babylonian and Assyrian history and is writing a book to be titled *The Urban Landscape of First Millennium BC Babylonia.*

Robin Barrow, Ph.D., FRSC, is professor of philosophy of education at Simon Fraser University, Canada. His most recent books include *Plato* (2007) and *An Introduction to Moral Philosophy and Moral Education* (2007). He is the author of *Athenian Democracy* (2001) and *Greek and Roman Education* (1996).

László Bartosiewicz, Ph.D., D.sc., teaches archaeozoology at the Loránd Eötvös University in Budapest (Hungary) and the University of Edinburgh (United Kingdom). He is the author of *Animals in the Urban Landscape in the Wake of the Middle Ages* (1995) and principal author of *Draught Cattle: Their Osteological Identification and History* (1997) and has published more than 200 scholarly articles.

Kirk H. Beetz, Ph.D., emeritus, has published over two dozen books and more than 900 articles. His books span topics from endangered mammal species to children's literature, including *Exploring C. S. Lewis' "The Chronicles of Narnia"* (2000). His recent writings have focused on the history and culture of ancient Japan.

Craig G. R. Benjamin, Ph.D., teaches world and ancient Eurasian history at Grand Valley State University. He is the coeditor of vols. 2 (1998), 4 (2000), and 6 (2002) in the Brepols Silk Roads Studies series and the author of *The Yuezhi: Origin, Migration and the Conquest of Northern Bactria* (2007).

Uffe Bergeton, Ph.D., is in the Ph.D. program in the Department of Asian Languages and Cultures at the University of Michigan. He is the author of *The Independence of Binding and Intensification* (Ph.D. dissertation, University of Southern California) and various articles on theoretical phonology and syntax.

Amy Hackney Blackwell has degrees in history from Duke University and Vanderbilt University and a J.D. from the University of Virginia. Her books include *Mythology for Dummies* (2002), *LSAT for Dummies* (2004), *The Everything Irish History and Heritage Book* (2004), and *Essential Dictionary of Law* (2004). She has contributed to the *Encyclopedia of World Nations and Cultures* (2006), *Alternative Energy* (2006), and *Chemical Compounds* (2006).

Christopher Blackwell, Ph.D., teaches classics at Furman University. He is the author of *In the Absence of Alexander: Harpalus and the Failure of Macedonian Hegemony* (1999) and various protocols and software applications for building digital libraries, and he serves as technical editor for the Center for Hellenic Studies of Harvard University.

Amy Bogaard, Ph.D., teaches prehistory and archaeobotany at the Department of Archaeology, University of Nottingham, United Kingdom. She is the author of *Neolithic Farming in Central Europe* (2004).

Peter Bogucki, Ph.D., is an archaeologist who is associate dean for undergraduate affairs of the School of Engineering and Applied Science at Princeton University. He has studied prehistoric settlements in Poland and has a particular interest in the spread of farming in Europe. He is the author of *The Origins of Human Society* (1999) and the editor (with Pam J. Crabtree) of *Ancient Europe 8000 B.C.–A.D. 1000: An Encyclopedia of the Barbarian World* (2004).

Larissa Bonfante, Ph.D., professor of classics at New York University, is the author of several books on Etruscan and early Roman culture as well as publications on ancient dress and nudity, including *The World of Roman Costume*, coedited with Judith Sebesta (1994).

Charlotte Booth is a Ph.D. student at the University of Wales, Swansea, and teaches Egyptology for Birkbeck College and other institutions in the United Kingdom. She is the author of *People of Ancient Egypt* (2007), *The Hyksos Period in Egypt* (2005), and *The Role of Foreigners in Ancient Egypt* (2005).

Lisa R. Brody, Ph.D., teaches Greek and Roman art history at Queens College, City University of New York. Her research interests include Greek iconography and cult, ancient lamps and their decoration, children in antiquity, and representation of ethnicity in Greco-Roman art. She compiled the revised edition of David Sacks's *Encyclopedia of the Ancient Greek World* (2005) and is author of *Aphrodisias III: The Aphrodite of Aphrodisias* (2007).

David Brown, Ph.D., is researching the interactions of the pre-Islamic astral sciences of Mesopotamia, Greece, India, Egypt, Iran, the western Semitic world, and China at the Free University of Berlin. He is the author of *Mesopotamian Planetary Astronomy-Astrology* (2000) and *The Interactions of Ancient Astral Science* (forthcoming).

Deborah N. Carlson, Ph.D., teaches in the Nautical Archaeology Program of the Department of Anthropology at Texas A&M University. She also directs the Institute of Nautical Archaeology's shipwreck excavation of a Roman marble carrier off the Aegean coast of Turkey at Kizilburun and is preparing the final publication of the Classical Greek ship excavated by the Institute of Nautical Archaeology at nearby Tektas Burnu.

Jeffrey S. Carnes is associate professor of classics at Syracuse University. He is the author of *The Uses of Aiakos: Pindar and the Aiginetan Imaginary* (forthcoming) as well as articles on Greek lyric poetry, gender studies, literary theory, and Plato.

Julia Marta Clapp is pursuing her doctorate in art history at the Graduate Center, City University of New York. Her research interests include modern and pre-Columbian Latin American art.

Wendy E. Closterman, Ph.D., teaches ancient history and Greek at Bryn Athyn College. Her research focuses on Athenian burial and funerary ritual. She is the author of "Family Members and Citizens: Athenian Identity and the Peribolos Tomb Setting" in *Antigone's Answer: Essays on Death and Burial, Family and State in Classical Athens*, edited by C. Patterson (forthcoming).

Leah A. J. Cohen is an independent writer and editorial consultant with a master's degree in geography from the University of Florida. She specializes in Africa area studies and food security. She was a senior author for the *Encyclopedia of African History and Culture*, volumes 4 and 5 (2005).

John Collis is professor emeritus in the Department of Archaeology, University of Sheffield, where he taught for over 30 years. He has had a major role in the development of university and professional training in archaeology in Britain, and is secretary of the European Association of Archaeologists' Committee on Training and Education. He is author of several books and excavation monographs, including *Digging Up the Past* (2004) and *The Celts: Origins, Myths and Inventions* (2004).

Constance A. Cook, Ph.D., directs the Asian Studies program and teaches Chinese language and literature courses at Lehigh University. She is the author of *Death in Ancient China: The Tale of One Man's Journey* (2006) and coeditor of *Defining Chu: Image and Reality in Ancient China* (1999).

Susan Cooksey, Ph.D., is the curator of African art, Harn Museum of Art, University of Florida.

Justin Corfield, Ph.D., teaches history and international relations at Geelong Grammar School, Australia. He is the co-author of *Historical Dictionary of Cambodia* (2003) and has written extensively on Asia, Australia, and European colonial history.

James A. Corrick, Ph.D., is a full-time editor and writer with 25 books to his credit. His most recent titles are *The Early Middle Ages* (2006), *The Byzantine Empire* (2006), and *The Renaissance* (2007).

Arden Decker is a Ph.D. candidate in the history of art at the Graduate Center, City University of New York. Her research interests include Mesoamerican art as well as modern and contemporary art of Mexico.

Leo Depuydt, Ph.D., teaches Egyptology at Brown University and is curious about everything relating to ancient Egypt in its Near Eastern and Mediterranean context, especially the area's languages and history. He wrote *Civil Calendar and Lunar Calendar in Ancient Egypt* (1997) and *The Other Mathematics: Language and Logic in Egyptian and in General* (2007).

Haig Der-Houssikian, Ph.D., is professor emeritus (2003), linguistics, at the University of Florida, Gainesville. His research and publication interests are in morphology, Creolization, and sub-Saharan Africa.

Christine End, M.A., works on the Giza Archives Project at the Museum of Fine Arts, Boston. Her main interests of research are Middle Kingdom funerary iconography, material culture, burial practices, and mummification. As a researcher and illustrator, her work has appeared in Egyptological publications and documentaries.

Linda Evans, Ph.D., specializes in ancient Egyptian art at Macquarie University, Sydney, Australia. She recently completed her doctoral dissertation on the representation of animal behavior in Egyptian tomb paintings and has published several papers on the role and depiction of animals in the ancient world. She has also contributed chapters to *Egyptian Art: Principles and Themes in Wall Scenes* (2000), *The Encyclopedia of Animal Behavior* (2004), *Egypt: The Land and Lives of the Pharaohs Revealed* (2005), and *Historica* (2006).

Stephen M. Fabian, Ph.D., is an anthropologist and currently teaches seminars on religion, myth, and ritual at Princeton University. He is the author of *Space-Time of the Bororo of Brazil* (1992), *Clearing Away Clouds: Nine Lessons for Life from the Martial Arts* (1999), and *Patterns in the Sky: An Introduction to Ethnoastronomy* (2001).

Erin Fairburn is a graduate student in the Department of Egyptology and Western Asian Studies at Brown University. She has contributed to *The City and Urban Life* (forthcoming).

Alessia Frassani is a Ph.D. candidate at the Graduate Center of the City University of New York. Her research interests in-

clude the art and civilizations of ancient Oaxaca and issues surrounding the cultural interaction between the Old and New Worlds.

Markham J. Geller is professor of Semitic languages at University College London, in the Department of Hebrew and Jewish Studies. He has recently published a text edition of cuneiform medical texts, *Renal and Rectal Disease Texts, Babylonisch-assyrische Medizin* VII (2005).

J. J. George is working on his Ph.D. at the Graduate Center, City University of New York. His research area is pre-Columbian art and architecture.

Wolfram Grajetzki, Ph.D., wrote his dissertation at the Humboldt University of Berlin and has taught Egyptology there. He has excavated in Egypt and Pakistan and was principal archaeologist and author for the online learning project Digital Egypt for Universities (University College London). He is preparing the catalogue of Egyptian coffins in the Fitzwilliam Museum, Cambridge. His publications include *Burial Customs in Ancient Egypt* (2003) and *The Middle Kingdom in Ancient Egypt* (2006).

Lyn Green, Ph.D., has taught at several Canadian universities and for the Royal Ontario Museum. She has contributed to several encyclopedias, including *The Oxford Encyclopedia of Ancient Egypt* (2000) and the *Encyclopedia of the Archaeology of Ancient Egypt* (1999) as well as *The Royal Women of Amarna* (1996). Currently she is devoting her time to her duties as president of the Society for the Study of Egyptian Antiquities, which has over 400 members and subscribers internationally, and to writing.

Angela Herren, Ph.D., teaches pre-Columbian art and architecture as an assistant professor in the Department of Art and Latin American Studies at the University of North Carolina at Charlotte. A specialist on painted manuscripts from central Mexico, she completed a 2005 dissertation entitled "Portraying the Mexica Past: A Comparative Study of Accounts of Origin in Codex Azcatitlan, Codex Boturni, and Codex Aubin."

David B. Hollander, Ph.D., teaches ancient history at Iowa State University. He is the author of *Money in the Late Roman Republic* (2007).

Brooke Holmes, Ph.D., is an assistant professor of classics at the University of North Carolina, Chapel Hill. She is at work on a book about the symptom in early Greek medicine and classical Greek literature.

Michael Allen Holmes is a freelance editor and writer who recently contributed to *Shakespeare for Students*, 2nd edition (2007). He has also written an unpublished novel.

John W. Humphrey, Ph.D., is professor of Greek and Roman studies at the University of Calgary. A veteran of many seasons of archaeological excavation in Turkey and Greece, he is the author of *Greek and Roman Technology: A Sourcebook* (1998, with J. P. Oleson and A. N. Sherwood) and *Ancient Technology* (2006).

Keith Jordan, M.Phil., is a Ph.D. candidate in pre-Columbian art history at the Graduate Center of the City University of New York. He is currently finishing his doctoral dissertation, entitled "Stone Trees Transplanted? Central Mexican Stelae of the Epiclassic and Early Postclassic and the Question of Maya 'Influence.'"

Amr Kamel is an Egyptologist in the Rare Books and Special Collections Library at the American University in Cairo, Egypt.

David Kelly is an instructor of English writing and literature at Oakton Community College in Illinois. He has written over 100 published literary analyses and wrote the instructor's manual for the *Exploring Poetry* computer program. His short fiction has been published in *The Rockford Review, Grub Street*, and *The Iconoclast*, among other places.

Panagiotis I. M. Kousoulis, Ph.D., is a lecturer in Egyptology at the Department of Mediterranean Studies of the University of the Aegean. He is the author of *Moving across Borders: Foreign Relations, Religion and Cultural Interactions in the Ancient Mediterranean* (2007) and *Ancient Egyptian Demonology: Studies on the Boundaries between the Demonic and the Divine in Egyptian Magic* (2007).

Philippa Lang teaches ancient science and related subjects, with research interests in ancient medicine and philosophy, in the Classics Department of Emory University, Atlanta. She is the editor of *Re-Inventions: Essays on Hellenistic and Early Roman Science, Apeiron* special issue vol. 37 (2004).

Russell M. Lawson, Ph.D., is associate professor of history and chair of the Division of General Studies at Bacone College in Oklahoma. He is the author of *Science in the Ancient World* (2004), *The Land between the Rivers: Thomas Nuttall's Ascent of the Arkansas, 1819* (2004), and *Passaconaway's Realm: John Evans and the Exploration of Mount Washington* (2002, 2004).

Anne Mahoney, Ph.D., teaches Greek and Latin linguistics and literature at Tufts University. She is the author of *Plautus: Amphitryo* (2004) and *Roman Sports and Spectacles: A Sourcebook* (2001). She is also the editor of revised editions of *Allen and Greenough's New Latin Grammar* (2001), *Morice's Stories in Attic Greek* (2005), and *Bennett's Essentials* (2007).

Susan Malin-Boyce, Ph.D., serves as deputy director of the Regime Crimes Liaison Office, Mass Graves Investigation

Team, in Baghdad, Iraq. She has contributed to *Ancient Europe 8000 B.C.–A.D. 1000: Encyclopedia of the Barbarian World* (2004) and to publications addressing Early and Late La Tène settlement in Bavaria, Germany.

Renee McGarry is a student in the Ph.D. program in art history at the City University of New York Graduate Center. Her research interests include Aztec sculpture of the natural world and religious manuscripts from the post-Conquest period.

Paul McKechnie, D.Phil., is a senior lecturer in classics and ancient history at the University of Auckland, New Zealand. He is the author of *First Christian Centuries: Perspectives on the Early Church* (2002) and *Outsiders in the Greek Cities in the Fourth Century B.C.* (1989).

John M. McMahon, Ph.D., teaches at Le Moyne College in Syracuse, New York, where he directs the classics program. He is author of *Cave Paralysin: Impotence, Perception and Text in the Satyrica of Petronius* (1998) and numerous articles on the intersection of ancient literature and natural history. His most recent work includes nine entries in the forthcoming *Biographical Encyclopedia of Astronomers* (2006).

Jianjun Mei, Ph.D., teaches the history of science and technology at the University of Science and Technology Beijing. He is the author of *Copper and Bronze Metallurgy in Late Prehistoric Xinjiang: Its Cultural Context and Relationship with Neighbouring Regions* (2000).

James E. Meier, Ph.D., is assistant professor in the Department of Humanities and Social Sciences at Central Florida Community College. He is a contributor to the *Encyclopedia of African History and Culture* (2005).

Francesco Menotti, Ph.D., is a lecturer in European prehistory at the Institute of Prehistory and Archaeological Science, Basel University, Switzerland. He is the author of *Living on the Lake in Prehistoric Europe* (2004).

Melissa Moore Morison is associate professor of classics and classical archaeology at Grand Valley State University. She has extensive experience in archaeological fieldwork in Greece, Turkey, and the United States. Her research interests include Roman provincial archaeology, Greek and Roman pottery, and ceramic technology.

Penny Morrill, Ph.D., teaches pre-Columbian and early colonial Mesoamerican art at Hood College, Frederick, Maryland. She has an essay, "The Queen of Heaven Reigns in New Spain: The Triumph of Eternity in the Casa del Deán Murals," in a Brill anthology, *Woman and Art in Early Modern Latin America* (2006). She has authored several books on modern Mexican silver: *Mexican Silver: 20th Century Handwrought Silver Jewelry and Metalwork* (4th ed., 2007), *Silver Masters of Mexico: Héctor Aguilar and the Taller Borda* (1996), and *Maestros de Plata: William Spratling and the Mexican Silver Renaissance*, a catalog for a traveling exhibit (2002–2004).

Julian M. Murchison, Ph.D., teaches in the Department of Sociology and Anthropology at Millsaps College. His work in cultural anthropology examines the intersections of medicine and religion in East Africa. He recently published a chapter examining stories about a cure for HIV/AIDS in *Borders and Healers* (2005).

Caryn E. Neumann, Ph.D., teaches history in Ohio Wesleyan University's Black World Studies Department. She is a former managing editor of the *Journal of Women's History.*

Emily Jane O'Dell, is a Ph.D. candidate at Brown University and has taught at Brown University in both the Department of Egyptology and Ancient Western Asian Studies and the Department of Literary Arts. She has been the chief epigrapher of the Cairo-Brown University Abu Bakr Epigraphic Survey in the western cemetery of the Great Pyramids in Giza, Egypt, for the past five years.

Simon O'Dwyer is founder and researcher for Prehistoric Music Ireland, author of *Prehistoric Music of Ireland* and prehistoricmusic.com, and contributor to *The Encyclopedia of Music in Ireland* and *The Encyclopedia of Ireland.* He has published four papers for the International Study Group on Music Archaeology.

Penelope Ojeda de Huala is a Ph.D. candidate in art history at the Graduate Center of the City University of New York, where she studies pre-Columbian to contemporary art of Latin America. Her research focus is Guatemala and Peru, particularly the enduring thoughts and practices of indigenous cultures as manifested in art.

Michael J. O'Neal, Ph.D., is a writer who lives in Moscow, Idaho. He is a frequent contributor to reference and educational books, including *Lives and Works: Young Adult Authors* (1999), *The Crusades* (2005), and *America in the 1920s* (2006).

Dianne White Oyler, Ph.D., teaches African history at Fayetteville State University. She is the author of *The History of the N'ko Alphabet and Its Role in Mande Transnational Identity: Words as Weapons* (2005) as well as articles in the refereed journals *Research in African Literature, the Mande Studies Journal*, and the *International Journal of African Historical Studies.*

Katie Parla is an art historian and archaeological speleologist working in Rome and Naples as a docent leading didactic seminars of archaeological sites. She consults for the History

Channel and will appear in their 2007 series *Cities of the Underworld* as an expert on underground Rome and Naples.

Marie Passanante is a doctoral candidate in the Department of Egyptology and Ancient Western Asian Studies at Brown University.

William H. Peck teaches at the College for Creative Studies, Detroit, and the University of Michigan, Dearborn. He was for many years the curator of ancient art at the Detroit Institute of Arts and is at present a member of the Brooklyn Museum excavations in Egypt at Karnak. He is the author of *Drawings from Ancient Egypt* (1987) and numerous contributions to reference books and encyclopedias on the ancient world.

David Petechuk is a freelance writer specializing in educational texts focusing on the sciences, literature, and history. The former director of publications for the health sciences at the University of Pittsburgh, he is the author of *The Respiratory System* (2004), *LSD* (2005), and *Health & Medical Issues Today: Organ Transplantation* (2006).

Mark Anthony Phelps is taking a leave after teaching continuously since 1994 (primarily at Drury University, in five different departments) to finish his dissertation at the University of Arkansas entitled "Sewage from the Orontes: Roman Elite Attitudes toward Ecstatic Religion in the 3rd and 4th centuries C.E." This degree in ancient Mediterranean history augments his graduate degrees from Harvard and Johns Hopkins in Hebrew Bible and ancient Near Eastern languages and cultures. His research interests reflected in his writings are widely eclectic, spanning Paleolithic to contemporary society and including the disciplines of archaeology, linguistics, cultural anthropology, physical geography, historical geography, classical history, ancient Near Eastern history, medieval history, modern history, religion, and biblical history.

Jen Piro is a Ph.D. candidate in anthropological archaeology at New York University. Her dissertation research focuses on the development of pastoral economies in Early Bronze Age Transcaucasia.

Karen Radner, Ph.D., is lecturer in ancient Near Eastern history at University College, London. She specializes in the Assyrian Empire and is the author of *Die neuassyrischen Texte aus Tall Seh Hamad* (2002), *Das mittelassyrische Tontafelarchiv von Giricano/Dunnu-sa-Uzibi* (2004) and *Die Macht des Namens: Altorientalische Strategien zur Selbsterhaltung* (2005).

Judith A. Rasson, Ph.D., teaches in the Department of Medieval Studies, Central European University, Budapest (a post-graduate American-accredited university). Her research interests lie in southeastern Europe (especially the countries of the former Yugoslavia) and focus on Neolithic and historic archaeology and ethnographic material culture.

Kelly-Anne Diamond Reed, Ph.D., teaches ancient Egyptian history and archaeology at Villanova University's Department of History. She is investigating early Egyptian funerary rituals and burial customs.

Duane W. Roller is professor of Greek and Latin at Ohio State University. Trained as an archaeologist, he has over 30 years' experience in field archaeology in numerous Mediterranean countries. He is the author of *The Building Program of Herod the Great* (1998), *The World of Juba II and Kleopatra Selene* (2003), and *Through the Pillars of Herakles* (2006) as well as many other publications in history, classics, and archaeology.

Kelley L. Ross, Ph.D., teaches philosophy at Los Angeles Valley College. He specializes in Kantian epistemology, metaphysics, and ethics, with emphasis on members of the Friesian tradition—Jakob Fries, Leonard Nelson, Rudolf Otto, Sir Karl Popper, and others. Since 1996 he has been the publisher and editor of the online philosophy journal *Proceedings of the Friesian School, Fourth Series.*

Edward M. W. A. Rowlands, M.Phil., has research interests in Mycenaean political geography, trade, and religion.

Lucas G. Rubin, Ph.D., develops master of science programs for Columbia University. He was previously administrator of the university's Center for Archaeology, where he managed multiple excavations and projects. His research and scholarship have focused on fires and firefighters in ancient Rome.

Michael M. Sage, Ph.D., teaches classics and ancient history in the Classics Department at the University of Cincinnati. His main areas of study are historiography and military history. He is the author of *Cyprian: A Biography* (1975) and *Warfare in Ancient Greece: A Sourcebook* (1996).

Rick Schulting, Ph.D., is a lecturer in scientific and prehistoric archaeology at the University of Oxford. His current research interests lie in understanding the Mesolithic-Neolithic transition in western Europe, emphasizing the use of radiometric dating and stable isotope analysis, and in skeletal evidence for interpersonal violence in earlier prehistoric Europe.

David R. Sear, a fellow of the Royal Numismatic Society in London and the American Numismatic Society in New York, has authored an extensive range of numismatic books over the past four decades, aimed at collectors and students of ancient Greek, Roman and Byzantine coinage. He has been a resident of Los Angeles for the past 25 years and operates a research service authenticating ancient coinage. His

numerous publications include *Roman Coins and Their Values* (1964; rev. ed., 2000–2005), *Byzantine Coins and Their Values* (1974, rev. ed., 1987), *Greek Coins and Their Values* (1978–1979), and *The History and Coinage of the Roman Imperators, 49–27 B.C.* (1998).

Robert Shanafelt, Ph.D., teaches courses in anthropology, religion, and Africana studies at Georgia Southern University. He has published a number of articles on different aspects of life in southern Africa, among them, "Crime, Power, and Policing in South Africa" in *Democratic Policing in Transitional and Developing Countries* (2006).

Alison Sheridan, Ph.D., is head of early prehistory in the National Museums Scotland, Edinburgh, specializing in the British and Irish Neolithic and Bronze Age. Exhibition work includes *Heaven and Hell—and Other Worlds of the Dead* (2000), for which she was lead curator and book editor. Other books include *From Sickles to Circles* (with A. M. Gibson, 2004) and *Vessels for the Ancestors* (with N. M. Sharples, 1992).

Spyros Siropoulos is senior lecturer of Greek philology and history at the Department of Mediterranean Studies, University of the Aegean, Greece. He has published various articles in three books: *Unlike a Woman: Gender and the Social Function of the Athenian Tragedy* (2003), *The Goat's Skin: The Other Side of Alexander the Great's Power* (2003; in Greek with English summary), and *The Things after Alexander: The Centrifugal Potencies of the Hellenistic Kingdoms* (2005, in Greek).

Bradley Skeen, M.A., has taught at the University of Minnesota, Webster University, and Washington University. He is a specialist in magic, religion, and philosophy in late antiquity and has contributed to research in that field in *Die Zeitschrift für Papyrologie und Epigraphik*, among other journals.

Christopher Smith, D.Phil., is professor of ancient history at the University of Saint Andrews in Scotland. He is the author of *Early Rome and Latium: Economy and Society c 100–500 B.C.* (1996) and *The Roman Clan: From Ancient Ideology to Modern Anthropology* (2006) as well as editor of several collections of essays, including *Trade, Traders and the Ancient City* (with Helen Parkins, 1998); *Sicily from Aeneas to Augustus* (with John Serrati, 2000), and *Religion in Archaic and Republican Rome and Italy: Evidence and Experience* (with Edward Bispham, 2000). He is engaged in work on Roman historiography and oratory.

Nancy Shatzman Steinhardt is professor of East Asian art and curator of Chinese art at the University of Pennsylvania. She is author of *Chinese Traditional Architecture* (1984), *Chinese Imperial City Planning* (1990), *Liao Architecture* (1997), and *Chinese Architecture* (2002) and more than 60 scholarly articles.

Tom Streissguth is a freelance author, editor, and journalist who has published more than 70 nonfiction and reference books. His most recent titles include *Clay v. United States, Genghis Khan's Mongol Empire, Library in a Book: Hate Crimes, Eyewitness History: The Roaring Twenties,* and the *Greenhaven Encyclopedia of the Middle Ages.*

Ananda Cohen Suarez is a Ph.D. student at the Graduate Center of the City University of New York, specializing in pre-Columbian and colonial Latin American art history. She is particularly interested in cross-cultural encounters, vernacular religious art, and manuscript production in the early colonial Americas.

Frank J. Swetz, D.Ed., is professor emeritus of mathematics and education, Pennsylvania State University. His research interests focus on cultural and societal impact on mathematics learning and teaching. Among his recent books are *Legacy of the Luoshu: The 4000 Year Search for the Meaning of the Magic Square of Order Three* (2002) and *Teaching Mathematics to Children* (2003).

John Thorburn, Ph.D., is associate professor of classics at Baylor University, where he teaches a variety of subjects dealing with the classical world. He has published on Greek tragedy, Greek comedy, Greek and Roman history, and a variety of ancient subjects. He is the author of *The Alcestis of Euripides* (2002) and the *Facts on File Companion to Classical Drama* (2005).

Alain Touwaide, Ph.D., is a historian of sciences in the Department of Botany of the National Museum of Natural History at the Smithsonian Institution (Washington, D.C.). He has extensively published on the history of medicine in the Mediterranean world from antiquity to the Renaissance. Recently, he coedited the volume *Visualizing Medieval Medicine and Natural History, 1200–1550* (2006).

Francesca C. Tronchin, Ph.D., teaches Greek and Roman art and archaeology at Ohio State University. Her primary area of research is Roman domestic decor and issues of eclecticism in ancient sculptural displays.

David K. Underwood, Ph.D., teaches Western humanities, art history, philosophy, and Latin American studies at the University of South Florida in Tampa and at Saint Petersburg College in Clearwater, Florida. He is the author of two books and several articles and essays on Iberian and Latin American art and architecture.

David Vallilee is an independent scholar.

Frans van Koppen, M.A., teaches Akkadian at the School of Oriental and African Studies, London. He contributed to *The*

Ancient Near East: Historical Sources in Translation (2006) and *The Babylonian World* (forthcoming).

Lawrence Waldron, M.F.A., is an associate professor and doctoral candidate at the City University of New York, specializing in non-Western fields of art history and culture. He has presented and published various articles on the art and culture of the pre-Columbian Caribbean and Southeast Asia.

Ezekiel A. Walker, Ph.D., teaches African and world history at the University of Central Florida. His forthcoming book is entitled *Growth, Crisis and Transformation in the Cocoa-Farming Economy of Southwestern Nigeria* (2007).

Peter S. Wells is professor of anthropology at the University of Minnesota. His publications include *The Barbarians Speak: How the Conquered Peoples Shaped Roman Europe* (1999), *Beyond Celts, Germans and Scythians: Archaeology and Identity in Iron Age Europe* (2001), and *The Battle That Stopped Rome: Emperor Augustus, Arminius, and the Slaughter of the Legions in the Teutoburg Forest* (2003).

Jacqui Wood is an archaeologist and authority on prehistoric cooking and the lifestyles of prehistoric Europeans. She runs her own excavation in Cornwall, England.

Ronald Young, Ph.D., teaches in the Social Sciences Department at Canterbury School in Fort Myers, Florida. His teaching and research interests are in the area of Latin American Studies. In addition to numerous reference articles, he is presently working on a general history of Colombia to be published by Greenwood Press.

Katharina Zinn, M.A., is writing her Ph.D. dissertation on ancient Egyptian libraries and archives at the University of Leipzig, Germany. She works in a project on scarabs in the Fitzwilliam Museum, Cambridge (United Kingdom) and a project on Middle Kingdom Reliefs from Lisht in the Princeton University Art Museum. She has published articles on the organization of collective wisdom as well as multilingualism in ancient Egypt.

List of Illustrations

VOLUME III

VOLUME IV

List of Maps and Primary Source Documents

MAPS

VOLUME I

VOLUME II

VOLUME III

VOLUME IV

PRIMARY SOURCE DOCUMENTS

VOLUME I

VOLUME II

VOLUME III

VOLUME IV

Preface

Welcome to the *Encyclopedia of Society and Culture in the Ancient World*, a four-volume set that provides comprehensive coverage of the ancient world from prehistory through the fall of Rome in 476 C.E. For coverage after that point, readers are urged to consult our companion set, the *Encyclopedia of Society and Culture in the Medieval World*, which covers the period from the fall of Rome to the start of the Renaissance.

SCOPE AND ARRANGEMENT OF THE SET

The *Encyclopedia of Society and Culture in the Ancient World* contains 69 separate entries, each devoted to a specific cultural or societal topic. Of these 69 entries, 14 comprise "major" topics with longer, more in-depth coverage than the standard entries. The entries are arranged in alphabetical order by topic; readers may consult the Contents page for a listing of these topics.

Each entry includes a discussion of the topic from the perspective of the following centers of civilization:

- Africa
- Egypt
- The Middle East
- Asia and the Pacific
- Europe
- Greece
- Rome
- The Americas

Readers will note that there is some overlap in this list: Egypt is part of Africa, of course, just as Greece and Rome are part of Europe. However, because the civilizations of ancient Egypt, Rome, and Greece are so often studied separately, we decided to treat them as such in this encyclopedia. Entries devoted to Europe will thus not discuss Rome and Greece, while those devoted to Africa will not discuss Egypt.

In addition, we understand that the term *Middle East* has not traditionally been used to refer to the ancient regions of the Levant (Israel, Jordan, parts of Syria, the Palestinian Authority, and Lebanon), Anatolia (Turkey), Armenia, Persia (Iran), and Mesopotamia (Iraq and parts of Syria). However, some educators and scholars, especially those involved in comparative history, are beginning to adopt the term when discussing this region. We decided to use the term *Middle East* for this encyclopedia in light of that increasing usage.

ENTRY DETAILS

Each entry begins with an introductory essay that outlines the major developments on a given topic in the ancient world. Following that introduction are separate essays on the topic from the perspective of the named centers of civilization. At the end of the main text of each entry is a list of "see also" references to related entries, followed by a further reading list of books, articles, and Web sites on the topic.

OTHER ELEMENTS

In addition to the main text, the encyclopedia incorporates sidebars on topics that do not fit neatly into the central discussion as well key primary source excerpts scattered throughout the set. These primary source documents appear at the end of many entries. Our goal in identifying and including these primary sources is to facilitate additional comparative study between cultures on a given topic. Readers may consult the List of Primary Source Documents in the front matter for a guide to the individual sources found in the encyclopedia. The set also features more than 250 maps and illustrations. The front matter lists these maps and illustrations.

Aside from detailing the maps, illustrations, and primary source documents, the front matter includes a section about the set's advisers and contributors and a general introduction to the ancient world by Dr. Peter Bogucki of Princeton University, who served as the editor in chief of the encyclopedia. At the back of the set, readers will find a glossary of key terms, a general bibliography, a chronology by region, and a general subject index.

ACKNOWLEDGMENTS

In addition to Dr. Peter Bogucki and the members of the advisory board, we wish to thank the more than 100 scholars, journalists, and writers who contributed to this work. At Facts On File, Claudia Schaab provided essential guidance throughout the project. A special note of thanks is due to Paul Halsall, who operates the Internet History Sourcebooks. This Web site supplied many of the primary source documents included in the encyclopedia.

—Neil Schlager and
Marcia Merryman Means,
Project Managers

Introduction

The story of the ancient world spans the globe and covers vast amounts of time. It is the largely overlooked story of the tremendous diversity in human experience, ranging from the ice age societies whose way of life is so remote from ours to the citizens of Greece and Rome whom we easily recognize from history books. During the 2 million years since we became human, members of our species have settled every corner of the earth and organized their lives in countless different ways. The articles in this encyclopedia will provide you with an overview of the various ways in which people lived in the past and point to sources where you can find more information about the topics that interest you.

To learn about the modern world, all we have to do is look around, travel, read, or watch a video about what we cannot see. But we cannot travel back in time to see what life was like several thousand or several hundred thousand years ago. We cannot hear an ancient Roman speak, nor can we meet a Stone Age hunter in Siberia. We have to rely on researchers to piece together many different bits of evidence to come up with a picture of past life. A lot of the pieces are missing. Many people say that it is like putting together a jigsaw puzzle, but it is a puzzle in which most of the pieces are missing and, worse, there is no picture on the box.

The people who study the humans of the past call themselves various names. *Archaeologists* excavate and study the physical traces of past societies, called sites and artifacts, while *physical anthropologists* study the remains of ancient humans to learn about their evolution, health, and genetics. Researchers who study both the archaeology and the physical anthropology of the earliest humans are called *paleoanthropologists. Historians* and *epigraphers* study the texts and monuments of ancient civilizations, while *historical geographers* examine the ways in which past societies interacted through exploration and trade. *Paleobotanists* and *archaeozoologists* study the remains of the plants and animals that were used by ancient people, while *geologists* study events in the earth's history that may have affected the lives of nearby people. Many other fields of research also contribute to our understanding of how people lived in the past.

SOURCES OF INFORMATION ABOUT THE ANCIENT WORLD

Scholars who study the ancient world have many sources of information to reconstruct life in the past. The most important categories are ancient sites, ancient artifacts, and ancient texts, supplemented by information on the ancient environment and climate. These are the pieces in the jigsaw puzzle that researchers must fit together.

Sites

Ancient sites are the locations where human activity took place in the past. Since there are many different types of human activities, there are diverse types of sites. The most important are settlements, burials, and ceremonial sites, but any location where ancient people performed some activity and left traces behind can be considered an archaeological site.

Settlement sites are probably the most common form of ancient site, for they are the locations where people lived. These can range from Stone Age caves to the residential parts of cities such as Athens and Rome. All settlement sites have characteristics in common that are of special interest to archaeologists. The first special characteristic of most settlement sites is that people built structures of various types. In the Stone Age cave they might have built a hearth by digging a pit and lining it with stones, while in larger settlements they built houses and other domestic buildings, along with storage pits, barns, and other necessary structures. The other important feature of settlement sites is that people create a tremendous amount of rubbish, and this rubbish contains a lot of information for archaeologists. In addition to the broken tools, pots, and other equipment of daily life, it also contains animal bones and charred seeds that provide information on the ancient diet.

Burials and cemeteries are another important category of ancient site. The skeletons of ancient people impart information about their diet and health, and the ways in which they were buried can tell a lot about how the society was organized. Sometimes burials are found within settlements, while at other times they are located in separate cemeteries. The corpses may have been buried intact, or they may have been cremated. Some burials are in simple pits, while others are in elaborate tombs. In many societies it was traditional to bury objects with the corpse that reflected the individual's status in life, while in other societies little or nothing is found in the tomb other than bones.

Another important type of site is the ritual or ceremonial site, sometimes called a "monument." Stonehenge in England is perhaps the most famous, but other examples include the mounds in Ohio that are shaped like animals when viewed from the air, the Nazca Lines in Peru, and the Sphinx in Egypt. While we do not know the exact purpose such monuments served, it is clear that they were not primarily the locations of settlements or cemeteries, though these sites may have been located nearby.

Finally, any location of ancient human activity qualifies as an archaeological site. These might include roads, boat landings, or even the boats themselves, buried in the mud. In Boston subway construction found the remains of an ancient fence that was used for catching fish by Native Americans around 2000 B.C.E. At high tide water and fish would pass over it, while at low tide the water would flow out and leave the fish stranded. This is an unusual and important type of site. Ancient sites are everywhere, and many more await discovery under our feet.

How Sites are Found and Studied Archaeologists are often asked how they find ancient sites. With the exception of well-known sites that are visible above the ground, like Stonehenge or the Mayan pyramids, the most common way that sites are discovered is by accident. A farmer plows up a stone ax, people digging a foundation find an ancient burial, a road construction crew discovers a prehistoric settlement—many sites have been uncovered by ordinary people who have the good judgment to alert scholars who can properly study the site. Sometimes, researchers search for sites using aerial photography or other scientific methods of detecting buried structures, and these techniques have also been very successful in discovering undisturbed sites.

When a site is found, it normally has to be excavated, which means digging away the soil to expose the structures, burials, and other finds and then measuring their exact location and documenting the discovery with drawings, photographs, and videos. This is the activity that most people associate with archaeologists, though it is only part of their job. It has to be done very carefully, because the act of digging up a site destroys it, even if the finds are removed or restored for display. For that reason, archaeological excavation must be done by trained and experienced investigators who know the proper techniques. Sites that are above the ground still need to be measured and mapped as a way to understand their original size and their position in the landscape.

Archaeologists use many different techniques to determine the age of the remains that they find on sites. The most important scientific technique is carbon-14, or radiocarbon, dating, which is based on the decay of a radioactive isotope of carbon that is absorbed by living plants and animals and its measurement in charcoal, bones, and other organic remains. Carbon-14 dating is effective for artifacts between about 1,000 and 60,000 years old. For artifacts dating to before that time other methods are employed, depending on the circumstances. A very precise method of dating involves the counting of tree rings on sites where wood is preserved, and tree-ring chronologies that cover the last several thousand years have been established in many parts of the world. Archaeologists and ancient historians also can use artifact styles to date sites, especially when these styles can be correlated with historical events for which dates are known.

Artifacts

Archaeological sites generally contain the objects made by ancient people and left behind as rubbish or as deliberate deposits in burials or simply lost. Researchers call these objects "artifacts," which refers to any portable object made by humans. If you look around you, you can see many types of artifacts. Those that are made from plastic, metal, and glass will probably still be around, if only in a landfill, in a thousand years, but those made from paper, leather, cotton, or wool probably will have decayed. On ancient archaeological sites, investigators usually find artifacts that might be made from stone, pottery, bone, or metals like bronze and iron if those were used by the ancient society. They might have served as tools, containers, ornaments, or symbols of rank. In very wet or very dry conditions wood, cloth, and netting might also be preserved.

Artifacts are studied closely by archaeologists and historians of the ancient world. First they are classified by material, form, and decoration. Then they are compared with other artifacts from other sites to see whether they are unusual or fit into a broader pattern of style shared throughout the region. Scientists also study the physical composition of artifacts to find trace elements that might point toward the source of the raw materials or which might show that the artifact was used for a specific purpose. For example, one of the most important recent breakthroughs in prehistoric Europe was the discovery of traces of fats associated with dairy products on pottery fragments, showing that animals were used for their milk as early as 5000 B.C.E.

Documents

Toward the end of antiquity in many parts of the world people began to express themselves using systems of symbols to represent sounds, things, people, or ideas. Some systems of writing are tied to spoken language, such as the scripts used in the ancient Near East and the Mediterranean world; others, such as the hieroglyphs of Egypt and Mesoamerica, represent people, places, and objects and the relationships among them. Some writing systems are not understood, such as the script used in the ancient civilization of the Indus Valley.

While documents may seem to provide very clear descriptions of ancient life, they need to be regarded with some caution. The ability to write was usually limited to a tiny fraction of the population in any ancient society, so the writing tells their story from their viewpoint, which naturally can be expected to be biased. The majority of the population had no representation among the literate, and thus they are known to us only through their sites and artifacts. Documents also may describe only a limited range of activities, such as royal histories or mercantile transactions, and usually they do not include discussions of everyday life.

Environmental Data and Geography

Finally, scholars study information about the ancient environment, which would include pollen and seeds that reflect ancient vegetation and climate; animal bones to see what animals people hunted and herded; geological cores to study events such as volcanic eruptions; and lines scraped into rocks that show the advances and retreats of glaciers, which show when the climate warmed and cooled. Small creatures such as snails are very sensitive to changes in climate, and thus researchers study how the numbers of different species changed over time to track changes in the environment around a site.

Understanding the environment and climate in which ancient people lived enables researchers to comprehend why settlements are located in particular places, how agriculture and stock herding developed, what major events in the earth's history had an effect on human activity, and many other important aspects of ancient life. Although people could respond to changes in the environment and climate in many different ways, knowing the earth's history during the past two million years is important for grasping the variation in ancient ways of life.

AN OUTLINE OF WORLD PREHISTORY AND ANCIENT HISTORY

Although the scholars who study the ancient world focus on many different questions to guide their research, these questions can be grouped into several big areas. The following sections represent an attempt to delineate the matters that concern many researchers and at the same time to give a very broad summary of the story of the ancient world. The entries in this encyclopedia illuminate many aspects of these topics.

Early Humans and Ice Age Society

After archaic humans developed from their hominin ancestors two or more million years ago in Africa, they spread to Asia and Europe. On all three continents they lived in mobile foraging bands. Palaeoanthropologists debate whether they actually hunted or rather scavenged the carcasses of dead animals, using stone hand axes and flakes. In Eurasia the ice age climate had a profound impact on their distribution and settlement. They developed the ability to make fire, probably between one million and 500,000 years ago, as shown by hearths at sites like Gesher Benot Ya'acov in Israel that are about 780,000 years old. Early humans also learned to organize sounds into language. Between 200,000 and 100,000 years ago, anatomically modern humans emerged in Africa and spread to Europe and Asia.

Human Dispersals

Modern humans at the end of the last ice age made more elaborate stone tools and also had a capacity for symbolic expression, most vividly presented in the cave paintings in France and Spain between 30,000 and 15,000 years ago. They also colonized Australia, probably around 60,000 years ago, and the Americas, at least by about 15,000 years ago. Thus by about 10,000 years ago every continent except Antarctica was settled. The mammoths and other large animals that were found in ice age environments disappeared, replaced by the wild animals that we know today.

Adaptation to Modern Climate

The end of the last ice age and the appearance of "modern" environmental conditions across the Northern Hemisphere and Southern Hemisphere led to many changes to human society. Rising sea levels cut off the Americas from Asia, so there was no further known contact between the Old World and the New World until the time of the Vikings and Christopher Columbus. The replacement of migratory herd animals such as reindeer by territorial forest animals like deer at temperate latitudes meant that people began to settle down and stay longer in one spot. They began to build substantial houses and to cross water bodies in dugout canoes.

Spread and Adoption of Agriculture

One of the major consequences of settling down was the use of certain very productive wild plants such as wheat, barley, rice, and maize. Repeated human harvesting had the effect of domesticating these plants, enabling people to cultivate them to produce large quantities of edible food. Domestication took place at different times in different places: around 11,000 years ago in the Near East, about 9,000 years ago in China, and between 10,000 and 6,000 years ago in Central America, for example. In parts of the Near East and Asia people changed their relationships with animals, particularly cattle, sheep, goat, and pigs, from one of hunting to one of herding. Animals became livestock, which provided a continuous source of meat and also eventually milk, wool, and power for pulling carts and plows. From its core areas agriculture eventually spread to become the primary way that people in most parts of the world obtain their food.

Differentiation in Status, Power, Wealth

With agricultural surpluses and settlement in villages came opportunities for individuals and households to acquire more social status, political power, and wealth than their neighbors. Such social differentiation into elites and commoners, or patrons and clients, characterizes the later millennia of prehistory in many parts of the world (but not everywhere). At first, the differences were temporary and were not passed along from one generation to the next. Later, we often find that the children of elites inherited their parents' social status. Anthropologists often refer to small societies with hereditary social ranking as "chiefdoms." While chiefdoms did not occur everywhere, it does seem that they emerged in many parts of the world toward the end of prehistoric times.

Ritual Landscapes

Along with differences in status and power came the development of monuments and ceremonies meant to demonstrate and reinforce social relationships. Sometimes these monuments and ceremonies are connected with tombs that commemorate ancestral ties, while elsewhere they are connected with cosmology and religion. Many sites are mysterious and defy attempts to explain them. It is clear that their significance extends beyond the individual sites to their surrounding landscapes, where there are additional monuments and ritual structures. Thus archaeologists speak of "ritual landscapes" that held tremendous significance for ancient people.

The Rise of Civilization

In many parts of the world, civilizations led by kings and royal dynasties developed. Many early civilizations were based in cities with large populations, such as those in Mesopotamia, while in others, such as Egypt and Central America, the rulers lived in royal precincts with their retainers, and most of the population lived as farmers in the countryside. Tribute flowed from the commoners to the elites. Many early civilizations developed the formal administrative structures and bureaucracy that are characteristic of states. Some, like the Romans and Assyrians, sought to expand their territory by conquest, thus becoming empires.

Interaction between Civilizations and their Neighbors

Scholars are not interested only in states and empires by themselves but also in how they interacted with their neighbors, who may not have had such complex forms of organization. The classic example is the relationship between the Greeks and Romans and the people living outside their civilizations, which they called "barbarians," yet every civilization has to contend with the people outside their borders. The relationship may be complex. The outsiders might willingly provide important goods and even services, but they may also pose a threat to the civilization if they are belligerent. The rise and fall of civilizations in the ancient world is very much the story of their relations with the peoples beyond their frontiers.

With this background about the ancient world, you are now welcome to explore the articles in this encyclopedia.

—Peter Bogucki

Entries A to C

A

► adornment

INTRODUCTION

In modern life people in developed countries spend billions of dollars on personal adornments, including clothing, jewelry, makeup, hair-care products, and perfumes. It is tempting to believe that people who lived in ancient, simpler times, when mere day-to-day survival was their paramount concern, did not give in to the temptations of vanity. This belief would be incorrect. Throughout the world the archaeological record shows that people who lived thousands of years ago devoted considerable attention to their personal appearance and found numerous ways to adorn themselves. Of course, the extent and variety of this personal adornment varied with rank and social class in much the same way it does in modern life. Royalty and people of high social rank probably adorned themselves in much more luxurious ways than did the poor or members of lower classes. Not only could they afford the materials they needed for personal adornment; they also used such adornments as markers of their social class. Sometimes the adornments had religious significance as well.

Often, too, items of adornment had a more practical significance. In ancient times the world's population tended to cluster close to the equator, where climates were mild and people did not have to protect themselves from the bitter cold of more northerly regions. The trade-off, however, was that many ancient peoples were often exposed to extremely dry air and to intense sunlight. As a result, they took steps to protect and moisturize their skin using makeup made of a variety of substances, all with a view to restoring the skin's moisture. Typically, as civilization developed, men were outdoors more than women, so they tended to have deep tans that protected them from the sun; women, on the other hand, spent more time indoors, so they needed more skin protection from both cosmetics and clothing when they ventured out.

The evidence that suggests a concern with personal adornment is found principally in tombs and artwork, though in some cases, such as ancient Greece, there is a written record of efforts people made to adorn themselves. Archaeologists, though, have discovered numerous artifacts in tombs that existed entirely for purposes of personal adornment, and surviving artwork shows people who used makeup, jewelry, clothing, and other items to enhance their personal appearance.

Most of these items were made from materials that were at hand, though as trade developed, the wealthy came to value imported materials as a symbol of status. Common materials used to create items of personal adornment included bone, shells, wood, precious metals such as gold and silver, other metals such as copper, and semiprecious stones, including, for example, jade. These materials were made into beads, necklaces, hair clips, rings, bracelets, necklaces, ankle bracelets, and similar items. Cosmetics were made primarily from plant materials, and spices were used for perfumes and lotions and for bathing. Henna, a dye still used in the 21st century, was often used as a hair dye. Throughout the world it was also common for people to use natural dyes to tattoo themselves. Among archaeological remains are also found such items as mirrors, tweezers, and similar cosmetic tools that would have been used particularly by women.

AFRICA

BY SUSAN COOKSEY

Most of what we know about African adornment in the ancient period is from archaeological evidence. Although a few objects such as beads have been found, the major sources of information are depictions of figures wearing various types of decoration. Even though few actual objects have been unearthed and many of the early representations of adornment items are difficult to decipher, we can hypothesize that most were made of natural materials. These probably included plant fibers, grasses, bark, wood, seeds, seed pods, roots, and leaves and animal hides, fur, feathers, bone, sinew, claws, horns, eggs, shells, and teeth. The earliest known forms of personal adornment—drilled ostrich shells—were found at the Kenyan site of Enkapune Ya Muto and date to 40,000 years ago. Shell beads have been used throughout many regions of Africa for both decoration and exchange.

Petroglyphs on cave walls in north-central Africa include images of male and female figures wearing various items of adornment. A cave painting in the region of Tassili n'Ajjer, done with white, red, and black pigments, depicts a large female figure with horns who appears to be running or dancing. In this painting that dates to 8000–6000 B.C.E., the figure has rows of dots on the torso and legs that may represent body painting, scarification, or tattooing. The horned figure also is wearing armbands and a rear apron made of long strands that appear to be fiber or hair. She has cuffs at her ankles, knees, elbows, and wrists with small random dots that may be multiple strands of beads, knotted fibers, or painted designs. Other figures in the painting have helmets and belts that seem to be made of shells.

In the Tsaisab Gorge in the Brandberg Mountains of Namibia in southern Africa, archaeologists have found rock paintings showing figures with body adornment. In one of these paintings, all of which date from 2000 to 1000 B.C.E., figures are depicted in a long procession. Rows of dots are painted on their heads, ankles, and knees that may represent beaded jewelry made of ostrich shell. Ostrich-shell beads are made from small sections of shell that are rounded to form flat white beads through which a hole is drilled so they can be sewn to a leather strip or strung on a thread.

Approximately 600 terra-cotta sculptures, many of which are adorned figures, have been found at Asinda Sika near Niamey, Niger. Dating from 200 to 1000 C.E., they include an elaborately ornamented male equestrian figure who has marks on his cheeks and forehead that may be scarification marks. Such facial marks may have signified his status or his ethnic identity. Large spiked bangles on his forearm are similar to armlets made of iron found on skeletons in Asinda Sika tombs. The equestrian figure also has crossed bandoliers on his chest and several choker necklaces. The pattern on these adornments suggests that they were made of either beads or braided fibers.

A great number of terra-cotta figures with various kinds of adornments were found in north-central Nigeria in the Jos Plateau region. They are a product of the Nok culture, named for the Nok Valley where many of the sculptures were found, an area between the Niger and Benue rivers. Through thermoluminescence testing, these figures have been dated to 500 B.C.E. to 500 C.E. Nok figures vary in style according to where they were found, but they all have elaborate headdresses, hairdos, jewelry, and garments. Male figures have various types of hairdos and hats as well as distinctive and diverse forms of facial hair, including beards and mustaches. Among the hairstyles are long strands of hair hanging down their cheeks, upswept hairdos bound by bands, lobed hairdos with holes that may have been adorned with feathers, various types of buns, and ringlets.

Nok figures are also depicted wearing necklaces, collars, girdles, armbands, and anklets that may be multiple strands of beads. One small Nok figure of a kneeling man wearing many beaded strands is perforated with holes on the head and waist and may have been a pendant. A terra-cotta head has a trilobed hairdo with a band on the forehead that may represent a beaded headband, braided fiber, or iron chain. The beads depicted on the terra-cotta sculptures were probably made of quartz, as hundreds of quartz beads were found at Nok sites. The beads were made by placing the quartz pieces in a stone groove and grinding them into cylinders. Holes were then drilled in the cylinders with an iron tool.

Beginning in the first millennium B.C.E. and up to 300 B.C.E. there were thriving communities in the region of Asmara in Eritrea. These communities are referred to as Ona, after the site Ona Gudo. Archaeologists have excavated numerous artifacts of glass, stone, and ceramic, including beads, earlobe plugs, and lip plugs. The stone beads, made from chlorite, come in a variety of shapes. The lip plugs and earlobe plugs are ceramic and stone. One type of plug was made from soft black stone and has an incised surface. One lip plug resembles a type found in the eastern Sudan in the Atabi region, dating to the fourth millennium B.C.E. Similarly shaped glass ear and lip plugs were found in excavations of Axum, a powerful kingdom in nearby Ethiopia that arose in the latter part of the first millennium B.C.E.

EGYPT

BY EMILY JANE O'DELL

The ancient Egyptians adorned their bodies with jewels, perfumes, lotions, makeup, and a variety of hairstyles for aesthetic, health, and symbolic reasons both in life and in preparation for the afterlife. Both men and women in ancient Egypt took great care to moisturize and perfume their bodies, and they had various tools and palettes to help them create certain hairstyles and apply makeup.

There is no one hairstyle particular to ancient Egypt. Hairstyles changed with time, and different people in the same period were known to wear different hairstyles, based on personal taste, fashion, sex, age, and social standing. Priests were required to shave their heads and whole bodies for ritual purification. However, other ancient Egyptians cropped their hair short or shaved it to fit their heads in wigs, to keep them cool in the heat, and to keep lice at bay. Small children had their heads shaved except for the so-called sidelock of youth, a long, side ponytail. Hairdressing tools were carved from bone or ivory and were used as metal hairpins and combs and to help curl, braid, and attach tresses of hair as extensions with the aid of beeswax and resin.

The upper class and royal family wore wigs of human hair reinforced with vegetable fibers. The hair of mummies, including those in the Royal Mummy Room in the Cairo Museum, has helped scholars piece together the various hairstyles, wigs, and hair colors of the ancient Egyptians. Gray hair was rare, for hair could be dyed with juniper berries and other plants. Hair loss and wrinkles could be combated with advice from medical texts.

One decorative element that continues to confound Egyptologists is the cone-shaped objects or headdresses that banqueters wear in reliefs from the Eighteenth Dynasty onward (after ca. 1550 B.C.E.). Although the symbolic meaning and practical use of these cones remains contested, it is generally assumed that they contained beeswax or perfume of myrrh along with wax, animal fat, or tallow. While they may have been used to combat the dryness of natural hair and wigs, their presence seems to be confined to party celebrations, suggesting that they may have been intended to be purely cosmetic and aromatic.

The ancient Egyptians took great care to clean, moisturize, and perfume their skin. Some of the body scrubs they concocted contained natron (a sodium carbonate–based cleansing agent), salt, honey, and animal fat and vegetable oils. Ancient Egyptian perfume did not utilize alcohol as a base; instead, Egyptians used a base of oils and fats that they infused with the scents of a multitude of plants, as displayed in tomb reliefs and Greco-Roman texts. Plants that may have been used for perfumes include the henna plant, the lotus, and the Madonna lily. In addition, it appears that ancient Egyptians used cinnamon, herbs, spices, carob, juniper, cedar, and resins that contained myrrh, frankincense, laudanum, and galbanum.

The ancient Egyptians are known for their use of kohl, a darkening cosmetic applied in the way we apply eyeliner today. It was not restricted to the living; it was also placed on statues of the gods and goddesses and on the deceased. Kohl was aesthetically pleasing but also may have helped reflect the rays of the sun and alleviate inflammation around the eyes by repelling insects that carry disease and cause infections. Kohl came in a variety of colors, such as black, taken from the bluish-gray lead ore galena, and green, which was derived from malachite. Kohl was placed on the eyes with a small stick of ivory, bronze, stone, glass, or wood both below the eye and above, on the eyelid. The ancient Egyptians also decorated their lips and cheeks with lip color and rouge

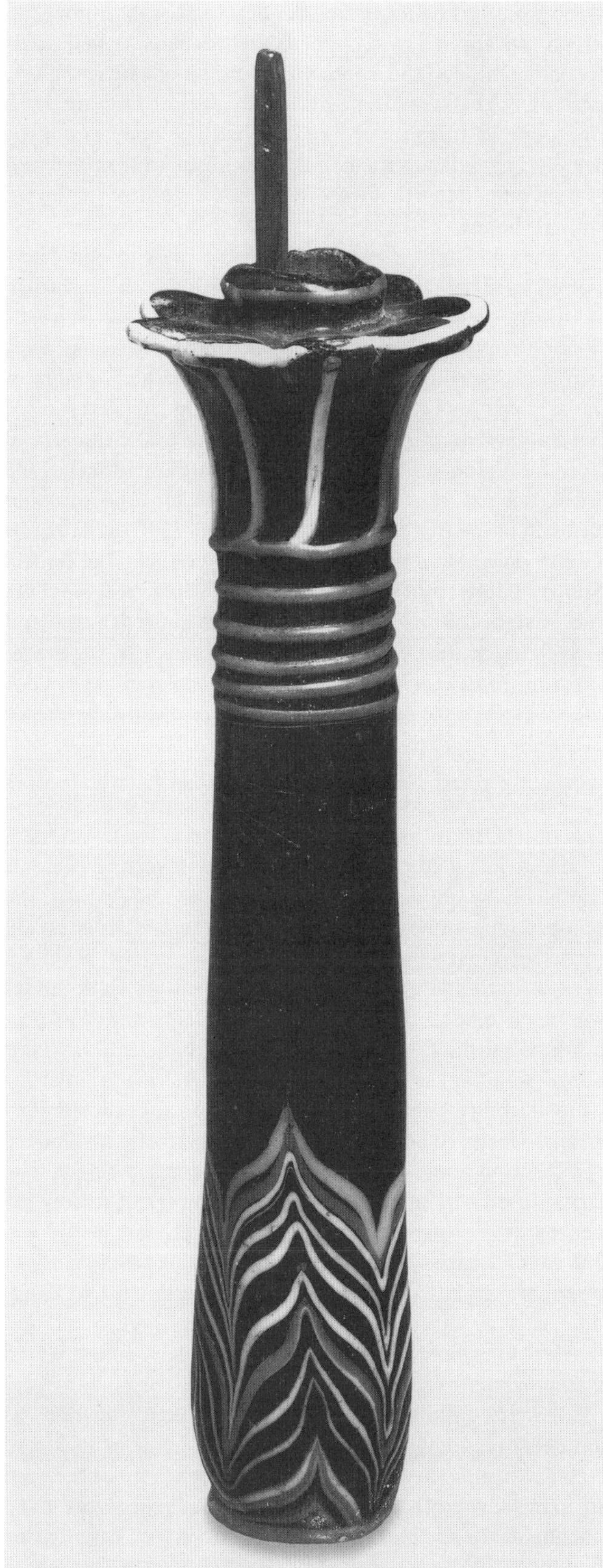

Glass kohl tube in the form of a palm column, from the Eighteenth Dynasty in Egypt (© The Trustees of the British Museum)

made from red ocher or henna combined with animal fat, which was applied to fingernails and toenails as well. Cosmetic containers and spoons were made of faience, glass, stone, clay, and wood in whimsical shapes and varying sizes. One popular form for the spoons had the body of a slender young woman as the handle. Cosmetics were mixed and ground on palettes that were frequently decorated in playful animal shapes.

Ancient Egypt is renowned for the colorful and finely crafted jewelry that was placed on images of deities and worn by royalty; men, women, and children all wore jewelry. Jewelry came in a variety of forms, such as rings, bangles, hairpins, arm cuffs, earrings, amulets, and beads. The high quality of the semiprecious stones and craftsmanship signaled the social class and wealth of its wearer. Jewelry was also traded and given for diplomatic reasons and to appease and influence the public, such as when the rulers Akhenaten (or Ikhnaton) and Nefertiti of the Eighteenth Dynasty (1550–1307 B.C.E.) threw jewelry down from the Window of Appearances, the central palace window from which the pharaoh would greet his court and foreign visitors. Jewelry was present in predynastic and early dynastic times, as evidenced, for example, by the bracelets from King Djer's (r. third century B.C.E.) tomb at Abydos as well as a type of pendant that was worn mostly by officials in the Old Kingdom (ca. 2575-2134 B.C.E.).

It is no secret that the ancient Egyptians favored gold. For those who could not afford gold, craftsmen used the process of gilding to make objects like faience, wood, and steatite look like gold. Silver was not found in such abundance and had to be imported from the Near East and Aegean. The semiprecious stones used included turquoise, lapis lazuli, carnelian, amazonite, amethyst, malachite, calcite, obsidian, hematite, red and green jasper, and serpentine. These stones were used to fashion beads, amulets, pendants, and inlay pectorals. Glass, however, was not manufactured until the New Kingdom (after ca. 1550 B.C.E.). Faience was very popular for its malleability, color variation, and glazed appearance. Jewelry also featured flowers, shells, seeds, and ivory. A standard combination of red, green, and blue had arisen for royal jewelry in the Old Kingdom, but other members of society experimented throughout the rest of the pharaonic period (ca. 332 B.C.E.) with different colors and styles. A set of standard visual archetypes and designs crystallized in the Old Kingdom, such as the bee and falcon, lotus and papyrus, and text that would usually be a name of a king or deity accompanied by hieroglyphic signs.

Jewelry fulfilled more than an aesthetic function, as amulets were thought to provide good health, good luck, and stability in this life and the next. Most jewelry was believed to magically protect parts of the body. Perhaps the most phenomenal examples of jewelry from ancient Egypt come from the Middle Kingdom (ca. 2040–1640 B.C.E.) burials of the princesses Sithathoriunet (at Illahun) and Sithathor and Mereret (at Dahshur), which showcase a variety of bracelets and collars along with an exquisite gold diadem.

THE MIDDLE EAST

BY TOM STREISSGUTH

In prehistoric times the Mesopotamians were farmers and herders living in the fertile plains between the Tigris and Euphrates rivers. Their attire was simple and unadorned by jewelry and other personal effects. As the first cities were raised in Sumer (ca. 3000 B.C.E.), in southern Mesopotamia, trade with outsiders along the rivers and seacoasts allowed the import of stone and metal, resources not found in the region, and the gathering of wealth and possessions that marked high status. Social divisions emerged, while a centralized government gave rise to an aristocracy surrounding the kings and the priesthood. High status was shown by wearing more elaborate, ceremonial clothing decorated with embroidery and fringe and tassels at the neck and bottom hem and dyed with bright colors mixed from minerals and oil. Precious stones sometimes were woven into the clothing; in ceremony men of high status also carried swords, seals, and staffs, symbols of their authority.

Throughout Mesopotamia a great variety of personal adornments has been found in excavated cities, settlements, and graves. The most common item is a small bead, of clay, shell, or stone, which was strung onto leather and used in adornments of the head and neck, or sewn directly into clothing or footwear. Mesopotamian artisans developed great skill in drilling and stringing beads, even in the hardest stones and densest metals. Bead strings were the earliest mark of status and are commonly found in the most ancient gravesites and settlements of the Middle East. They often were used as a medium of exchange; in this time before the minting of coins, beads could be collected on their strings and easily unstrung or attached as people bought and sold their food and household goods.

The Mesopotamians also used pins and brooches to fasten clothing about the shoulders. (The most common item of clothing was a long mantle that hung from the neck and shoulders and was fastened on the left side of the body, leaving the right arm free.) Artisans worked these pins into long cylinders with one end shaped into a spherical head. Hairpins made of flattened and rolled metal were used to decorate the hair and hold plaits and braids on top of the head, a favored style. Small rings of metal were suspended from the hair locks and plaits. Headbands made of thin metal, some of simple design and some very elaborate, were worn around the forehead and tied in the back with a thin cord of string or leather. Royalty wore crowns worked in silver and gold, which covered the sides and back of the head like a finely woven metal helmet. Unadorned and undressed hair was a mark of the lower classes and slaves.

Men and women of the upper classes wore a great number of personal adornments, including amulets, ankle bracelets, necklaces, earrings, and seals. Artisans decorated these pieces with precious stones, including obsidian, turquoise, shell, serpentine, agate, jasper, and carnelian, a stone imported from India. A favorite blue stone, lapis lazuli, was imported from the mountains of modern-day Afghanistan and worked into rings and necklaces. Gold was pounded into thin leaf and used as a setting, often shaped into leaves, cones, and abstract geometrical forms.

Some larger items of adornment allowed artists the space to depict the gods and spirits, or favorite scenes from myth. Pectorals were small plates sewn together, suspended from the neck and worn on the chest or over the abdomen. Pectorals (also used as body armor) and belts most commonly were worn by men, while both sexes wore armbands around the upper arm and bracelets on the forearm near the wrist. The Mesopotamians also wore knee rings, ankle rings, toe rings, and finger rings. The cylinder seal, which was originally meant to mark documents and possessions, later developed into a personal accessory. The seals were made of clay, ivory, bone, or stone and engraved with a geometric pattern, a symbol of high office, or a scene from mythology. They were hung about the neck and provided the wearer with protection and good fortune.

Gold lion, used as a fabric ornament; found at Persopolis, Persia (modern-day Iran) (Courtesy of the Oriental Institute of the University of Chicago)

ANCIENT KOHL

The traditional black eye cosmetic known as kohl has several millennia of history, stretching back into the ancient kingdoms of the Near East and Egypt. Men as well as women used many different forms of eye makeup in Mesopotamia. It was a status symbol, indicating wealth and enough leisure time to care for and decorate the face. Makeup of different colors lengthened the eyebrows, accented the eyelashes, and rimmed the upper and lower eyelids to give a striking appearance.

In all times, painting the eyes with protective minerals also had a practical use: It warded off diseases of the eye that are still common in the dry desert climate of the Near East. Galena, a common ingredient of kohl, served as a disinfectant; it deterred flies and also provided some protection from the sun. Eye makeup also was believed to provide the wearer with psychic protection, warding off bad spirits and imparting good fortune.

Small glass tubes used to hold eye cosmetics are among the first glass objects of any kind. The tubes were made of silica, mined from quartz sand, and sodium carbonate, a substance made from the ashes of plants, which lowers the melting point of quartz. These tubes held galena or green malachite, which could be applied separately on the upper and lower eyelids. Later ingredients were antimony, lead, ocher, ash, malachite, and burnt almonds, mixed in various portions. The Akkadian word for galena, *guhl,* was the original source of the word *kohl.*

Men wore their hair long, with some going bearded, some clean shaven, and others shaving only the upper lip. Women braided their hair, wrapping a single braid around the head, fastening it with a pin, and adorning it with a headdress on special occasions. They also made use of wigs and extensions to achieve the desired long and thick appearance. Both men and women wore headgear, most often in wool felt or linen. There were rounded, square, and conical caps worn by courtiers, soldiers, officials, and common citizens. In Persia of the Achaemenid dynasty (sixth century B.C.E.), prominent headgear indicated social position. Only Persian kings, for example, had the right to wear high turbans. Distinctive ribbons were worn by the king and the princes; royal officials and courtiers also had turbans and hats that showed their rank.

With bathing a relatively rare event, the Mesopotamians used a variety of oils and ointments to keep the body fresh and sweet smelling and to protect their faces from damaging sun and dry winds. On the occasion of a solemn religious ceremony, powdered minerals were applied to the face and around the eyes. Plant gums and resins, including cedar, myrrh, frankincense, lavender, thyme, rose, aloe, and cypress, were burned and mixed with vegetable oil (often sesame, olive, or almond) or rendered animal fat, to use as ointments and perfumes. Mesopotamian women distilled henna from a plant and used it to color their hair, hands, and nails.

Women also used mascara, lipstick, and face powder, applied with the tip of a reed; red or yellow ocher were the most common ingredients,. By an Assyrian law passed in about 1200 B.C.E., women of the upper classes were permitted to go about veiled, but the veil was prohibited to slaves and prostitutes. Originally a sign of high status, this custom spread to the rest of society and throughout the Middle East in the millennia to come.

ASIA AND THE PACIFIC

BY AMY HACKNEY BLACKWELL

In ancient China jewelry indicated a person's social status; the more expensive and elaborate the jewelry, the richer the wearer was considered to be. Most people wore earrings and amulets, charms used to ward off evil; they could be made of gold, silver, and stones such as jade, bone, or clay. Women wore headdresses made of gold or silver. Men fastened gold or silver pins on their hats. Most graves of the ancient Chinese contain pieces of jewelry owned by the dead person.

Because women dressed in long robes that hid the shapes of their bodies, they concentrated on decorating their faces, hands, and feet. Women spent a great deal of time on their makeup. They used powder to whiten their faces, rubbed red pigment on their cheeks and lips and gold makeup on their foreheads, and drew dots on their cheeks. Chinese people were very interested in eyebrows. They believed that only men should have natural eyebrows. Women shaved off or plucked out their eyebrows and drew them back in a more flattering shape. They used a black pigment made from a metal ore, charcoal, or ink. They might then paste designs between their eyebrows; plum blossoms were popular. They worked their hair into elaborate designs, the taller and more unique the better, and decorated their heads with combs and kerchiefs.

Jade was a common jewelry material; people started carving it as early as 12,000 years ago. By the time of the Zhou (1122–256 B.C.E.) and Han (206 B.C.E.–220 C.E.) dynasties jade carving was a highly developed art. Craftsmen made jade into bracelets, rings, pendants, and other objects—some of them elaborately carved. They fashioned jade into charms that had symbolic meanings and were meant to bring luck to the wearer; for example, a dragon charm was said to impart status and power to the wearer, and a butterfly could bring longevity.

Fans were the quintessential Chinese accessory. No upscale ensemble was complete without one. Dancers at the emperor's court raised fan manipulation to a high art form. Fans could be made with bird feathers, paper, wood, or silk and were delicately perfumed. Silk was the first luxury fabric. Chinese people were wearing silk at least 3,000 years ago; at first only royalty could wear it, but soon it spread to the nobility and others concerned with showing their status. Silk provided the background for the elaborate embroidery that still decorates Chinese items today. The first known Chinese embroidery dates to about 1600 B.C.E. By the time of the Han Dynasty embroidery covered nearly every piece of cloth in the homes and on the bodies of the nobility. Women embroidered cloth with a vast range of images, including landscapes, wild animals, and geometric designs.

The ancient Chinese used scented gums and resins as incense and to anoint dead bodies, though in the earliest days they did not perfume themselves. They scented rooms to induce particular moods, choosing their incense based on the effect they wanted to achieve. In the early centuries of the Common Era, they made ample use of perfumes, scenting their bodies, clothing, ink, paper, and cosmetics. Scents could be made from Chinese camphor, Indian cinnamon, and sandalwood and from gum resins, ginger, nutmeg, and other spices from all over Asia.

People in the Indus Valley started making jewelry about 5,000 years ago. The habit of making and wearing jewelry quickly spread throughout India. At first Indian people made necklaces and bracelets out of beads of polished stone, clay, or shells. Around 1500 B.C.E. they began working with gold, making earrings, necklaces, bracelets, and other adornments. Women wore the majority of jewelry, often wearing several bracelets and necklaces at once to indicate their wealth and status. They also might wear rings, pins, and headbands of gold. Around 300 B.C.E. people in India began mining diamonds and other gems and incorporating them into jewelry. Indian people did not bury jewelry with their dead but instead passed it down to surviving family members.

Indian women used many cosmetics. The *Kama Sutra,* a manual written between 100 and 600 C.E. and describing

Jade ornament of four discs carved from a single jade pebble, from China, Eastern Zhou Dynasty, fifth century B.C.E. (© The Trustees of the British Museum)

methods for attracting lovers, suggests that women tattoo themselves and use makeup on their faces, nails, and bodies. They colored their eyelids with a dye made with antimony, a poisonous heavy metal. They colored their faces and arms with yellow saffron powder.

Henna, a paste that leaves red stains on the skin, was a popular cosmetic substance in ancient India and in other parts of Asia. Some historians believe that henna originated in ancient India about 5,000 years ago, though others think that it was brought to India from Egypt. Henna decorations appear in cave paintings in the Deccan in western India and in Sri Lanka, dating to the fourth or fifth century C.E. Indian people mixed henna with other plant substances, such as tea, coffee, or lemon, to make a paste and applied it to their hair to redden it. They also used it to draw elaborate designs on their bodies, especially for such special occasions as weddings. Henna stains can last for several weeks, until the upper layer of the skin wears off. The hands and feet were the most popular places to draw henna designs, partly because the stains last the longest on those areas of the body.

The art of making gold jewelry traveled with Hindu traders from India to Southeast Asia about 2,000 years ago. They landed in western Thailand, where the Mon people of the area learned the techniques and became expert goldsmiths in their own right. Early Mon jewelry looks very much like Indian jewelry of the time. Goldsmithing spread to the Khmer and Tai people to the east; they also made necklaces, earrings, and bracelets in the Hindu style. Pacific Islanders had limited materials with which to make jewelry. They made their adornments out of locally available materials, such as shell, feathers, bone, and wood.

Japanese adornment in ancient times was not nearly as elaborate as it became in later periods, and it usually had a practical purpose. Before 300 C.E. men and women wore clothing made of hemp, with loose belts that they tied in an attractive fashion. Between 300 and 500 C.E. the Japanese people began wearing robes made of silk, likewise fastened with decorative belts. These belts gradually evolved into the obi, a long, elaborately embroidered strip of cloth used to tie robes around the waist. The only jewelry Japanese people wore in ancient times were small pieces of jade carved into a comma shape and worn on a necklace. They buried these pendants with their dead. The Japanese did not begin working with incense until the fourth century C.E. They quickly developed incense into an art form, using it to set moods in rooms or to prepare the ambiance for ceremonies, but they did not regularly use perfume on their bodies until the eighth century.

EUROPE

BY CARYN E. NEUMANN

It is difficult to determine the types of adornment used in ancient Europe because much of the evidence did not survive the passage of time. Adornment included belts, brooches, crowns, hairstyles, and tattoos as well as perfumes and often served both ornamental and practical purposes. It also typically reflected class divisions. Many adornments, such as jewels and perfume, were available in only small quantities, and this rarity limited their use to the nobility.

Hairstyles are perhaps the simplest form of adornment. The Frankish kings in the second century wore their hair long, whereas the rest of the men in the royal court and other male subjects had short hair. Among the Celts, both sexes preferred long hair, which women wore in braided pigtails. Men apparently shaved all facial hair, preserving only mustaches. Among other groups, evidence of styles is lacking, though long hair appears to have been common for both men and women. On the other hand, perfume is one of the most complex forms of adornments, since the scent needs to be long lasting. Perfumes based on floral scents have been popular since ancient times.

Tattooing has been a European practice since Neolithic times (7000–2000 B.C.E.) but the purpose of tattoos at that period in history is not always clear today. Pict (from the Latin *pingere* for "painted folk") warriors, active in present-day Scotland and noted in Roman literature in the third century C.E. colored their bodies with woad, a type of blue dye, before going into battle; this habit made them look terrifying to the Romans. The Picts may have turned themselves blue to intimidate their foes, to secure the protection of the gods, or to obtain some other advantage. Tattoos among Europeans often were animal designs, perhaps to give the wearers the attributes of the animals. The Picts were famously tattooed (or scarified, that is, cut or scratched) with elaborate dark blue woad designs. Germanic, Celtic, and other central and northern European tribes were also heavily tattooed, according to surviving accounts.

Belts were found at every level of ancient society because they had both ornamental and practical purposes. Distinctive belts served as insignia of high civil or military status. Beginning in the fourth century C.E. in Gaul and Germany, belts were buried in graves with their owners, since they expressed ideal status and were thought to protect their wearers. The wide belts of women found in Celtic graves have one or more leaves of beaten bronze, with geometric ornaments. In other parts of Europe gem-bedecked gold belts were offered along with swords as precious gifts and tribute. In Ireland belts sometime had hollowed spaces for holding relics or amulets.

Brooches in antiquity were also not simply ornamental items but frequently were employed to join pieces of clothing. However, most examples show some form of decorative elaboration, either through being made of showy metals like copper or gold or by being engraved or decoratively enlarged and used as a setting for gems. The Celts adorned themselves with copper and bronze bracelets and brooches of a style that has remained popular even in modern times.

Celtic jewelry is especially distinctive and has been well preserved through the ages. Highly imaginative representations of the human form, including both the head and full body, are found on Celtic jewelry. Geometric designs known as Celtic knots and representations of flora and fauna were also popular. Celtic knots are complete loops with no end or beginning, possibly to ward off evil spirits. These intricately patterned knot designs undoubtedly had some significance, but those meanings changed from tribe to tribe and location to location. Celtic jewelry with animal patterns is similar in construction to Celtic knots, but the cords terminate in feet, heads, tails, and other animal elements. The animal designs reflect Saxon and Pict traditions of abstract beast forms. Much of Celtic jewelry was made of bronze, the preferred metal of this culture.

Crowns in ancient times were more exclusive. They served as symbols of rulership, as rewards, and as offerings in public and private ceremonies. Crowns ranged from ephemeral circlets of grass, leaves, and flowers to permanent insignia made of gold and gems. Their shapes also varied, from wide bands to diadems, tiaras, and ribbons. The type of crown used depended upon the ritual context and the wearers.

Various types of jewelry could be found throughout Europe. The Gauls had enameled torques, anklets, and rings, which men wore on their left hands and women pushed only halfway onto their fingers. They also wore fibula, or clasps something like safety pins, with metal disks or openwork decorations. The fibula increased in size over time and was sometimes decorated with emblems. Much European jewelry was enhanced by gems. Amber, a stonelike substance composed of fossilized tree resin from the Baltic Sea coastline, may have been among the first substances used solely for decorative purposes. It was used extensively in ornaments in Europe from Paleolithic times (dating to as recently as 8000 B.C.E. but stretching back much longer). Nordic, Germanic, Celtic, and Slavic tribes all incorporated amber into their culture, with craftsmen fashioning the amber from its shapeless natural state into such personal adornments as beads and disks for the elite classes.

Other ornaments were made of tortoiseshell. The removable outside layer of a seagoing turtle's shell, tortoiseshell was used by cultures with access to sea turtles. The shell of the

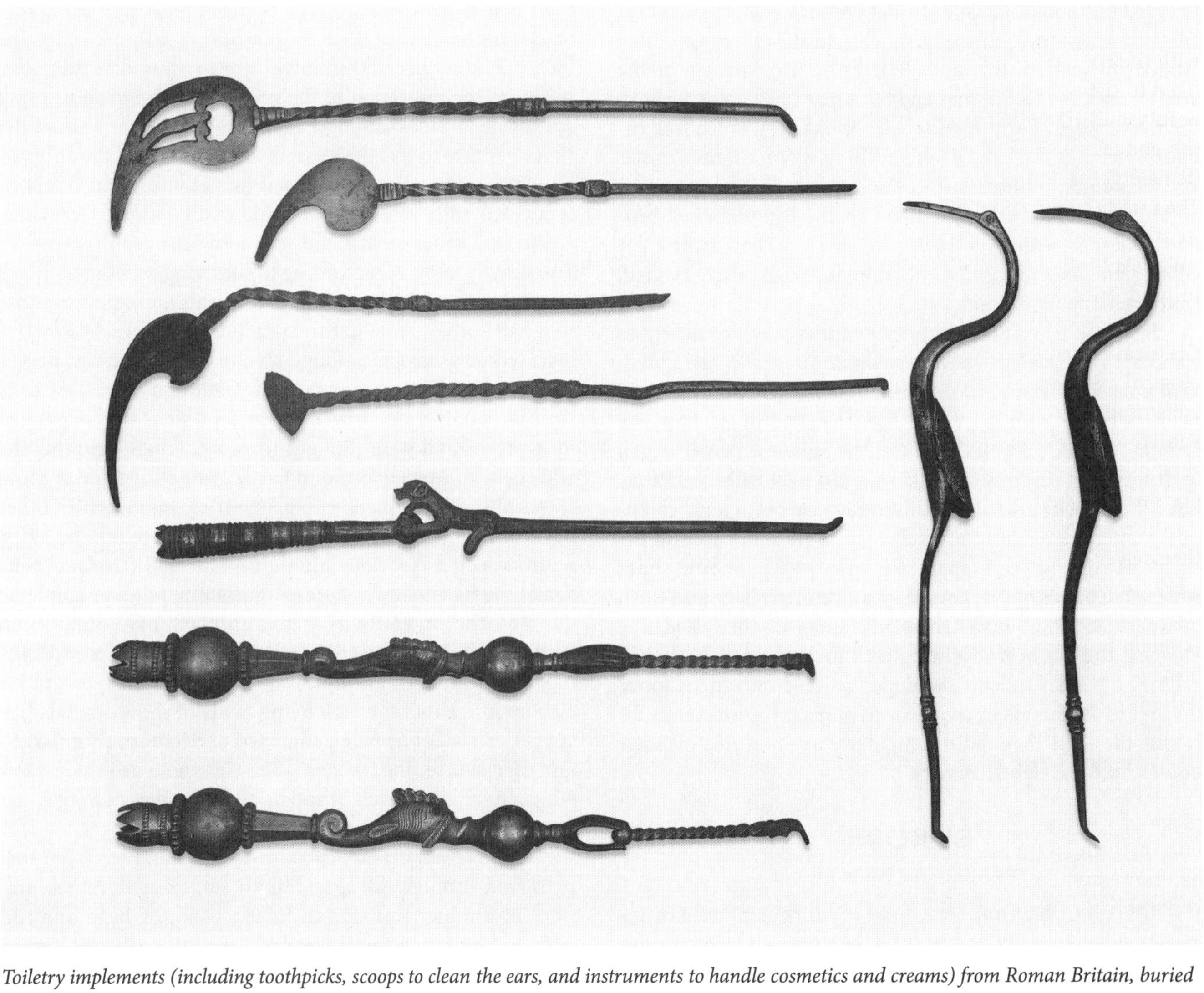

Toiletry implements (including toothpicks, scoops to clean the ears, and instruments to handle cosmetics and creams) from Roman Britain, buried in the fifth century C.E. (© The Trustees of the British Museum)

green turtle was used in the Mediterranean, while loggerhead turtle shell had a northerly distribution. The high cost of the small tortoiseshell ornaments made them a luxury item limited in use to only the wealthy members of society. The Gauls were known to favor bold colors and used garnets in jewelry and other adornment. Gauls also preferred coral and enamels as decorative stones. Coral was often associated with lucky amulets, and workers even tried to imitate its color in enamel, a completely Celtic industry. Gaul craftsmen also made rings and bracelets from jet and ignite.

The use of adornment sharply diminished after the fourth century of the Common Era. The art of cutting gems declined rapidly, as did the use of amber. By the fifth century the only continuous jewelry-making practice within Europe was the cutting of garnets for cloisonné, or raised enamel work set into a metal background.

GREECE

BY SPYROS SIROPOULOS

It has been said that the fifth century B.C.E. was the age of vanity. This is what the thousands of beautiful statues, painted with lifelike colors, spread all around Athens signify. Greeks liked to see beauty around them. They certainly appreciated beauty and thought naught of enhancing it. In mythology the goddess of love, Aphrodite, was adorned by the Horae (female goddesses of the seasons) as soon as she was born. Then when Hera, the first lady of Olympus, needed to seduce Zeus to avert his attention from the battlefield of Troy, she called Aphrodite to make her up and help her with a beautifully adorned garment.

Adornment was popular among the Athenians of the Classical Period (480–323 B.C.E.), especially women. Archaeological excavations have unearthed a great number of artifacts used by the women of classical Athens, which are very similar to items used by women today. Among these are tweezers, pliers, mirrors, jewelry, and other means of enhancing one's natural beauty.

The Greeks knew nothing of soap. In order to clean themselves they used lead carbonate made of pure soda (ore); a solution of potash, made of wood ash (useful also for washing clothes); or a special clay, consisting of silica with chalk (*kimolia* in Greek). Even today the island of Kímolos in the heart of the Aegean Sea is famous for producing a light stone, rich in soda, called *kimolia*. For washing their hands, the ancient Greeks also used a kind of paste.

Women powdered their faces with a fine white powder called *psimythion*. In the fifth century B.C.E. Athenians thought much of women who stayed indoors and gave no reason for talk of them in public. Of course, only aristocratic women had no reason to go out to work in the sunshine, and thus a white complexion was associated with women of aristocracy, a detail often depicted in vase paintings from the same period. Women also liked to use red rouge for their cheeks and wore high shoes, to appear taller. The courtesans known as hetaerae

Greek marble head, from about 350 B.C.E., showing headdress of snail-shell curls (© The Trustees of the British Museum)

used the white color of carbonic lead and the red powder of a plant's roots, as well as dyeing their eyebrows.

The use of makeup was sometimes frowned upon, however. The philosopher Plato (ca. 428–347 B.C.E.) complained that using makeup was "harmful and deceptive" (*Gorgias*). Even the fifth-century B.C.E. playwright Euripides, in his tragedy *Medea*, seems to associate adornment and vanity with destruction. Planning to take revenge on her adulterous husband, Jason, Medea offers to his future bride, the princess of Corinth, fine veils and a golden headband, anointed with some kind of poison. Death finds the ignorant princess while she admires herself in front of the mirror.

Perfumes were bought from a *myropoleíon* ("perfumery"), and they were of animal or plant origin, usually imported. A woman selling perfumes to a slave girl is depicted on one side of a *pelike* (a ceramic container for storing liquids) dating to about 460 B.C.E.; on the other side we see the girl carrying the small perfume jar home to her mistress. Perfumes were used by men, too, especially at symposia and wrestling halls, but it was considered disreputable for a man to sell perfumes.

However, there are cases when loans for establishing perfumeries by men are discussed by orators in court.

The length of hair varied from area to area. Spartan men wore their hair short, while Athenian men wore their hair long when they were young. Written and pictorial evidence attests to a tendency to curl hair—men did it too. Athenian women parted their hair in the middle and drew it back into a chignon. They never let it loose, except on the occasion of special celebrations and festivals. They cut their hair only when they were mourning, but slave women and hetaera wore their hair short.

Curling was so popular for men that they frequented professional hairdressers. One terra-cotta statuette from Boeotia from around 550 B.C.E. shows a man sitting on a hairdresser's chair, covered in a long towel that protects his clothes from falling hairs, while the hairdresser stands behind him holding scissors over his head. Not only women but men also used to lift and hold their hair in a kind of pug held by golden hairpins that either looked like cicadas or sounded like cicadas as they walked. Dyeing of hair was not unknown. Facial hair was common for grown men in Athens, though they preferred to be clean shaven, especially in the years after Alexander the Great (356–323 B.C.E.), who was famously clean shaven. His successors continued the fashion.

Women cared much about smooth skin. Depilation with the aid of a blade and special creams or the burning of hairs with the aid of a lamp was very common. Women of the upper classes often wore a kind of hairnet or tight scarf called *kekrýfalos*. From vase paintings we infer that this scarf pulled the hair from the forehead to the back of the neck and then pushed it forward. An ornament called a *diadema* added height to the forehead.

Golden and silver earrings, necklaces, rings, and bracelets have been made since the beginning of civilization. Many such findings come from the Minoan Period (2600–1450 B.C.E.) and the Archaic Period (680–480 B.C.E.). Stone inlay was rare, but men wore stone rings to be used as seals. Women often wore jewelry around their calves too. Heavy chains and pendants, popular in the Archaic Period, gave their place to thin coils and chains of linked wire and thin foil formed into petals and rosettes in the Classical Period. Bracelets were worn not only around the wrist but also between the elbow and shoulder, when that part of the arm was bare. Women pierced their ears for earrings, which were heavy and complex in the Mycenaean Period (1600–1100 B.C.E.) and took the form of light metal disks with a hole in the middle in the Classical Period.

ROME

BY ALAIN TOUWAIDE

Perfumes and cosmetics, which were much used in Greece, were not so common in the early Roman world. As time passed, their use spread, such that as early as 189 B.C.E., according to the Roman writer Pliny, a law banned so-called

Gold coin of the Roman emperor Marcus Aurelius, set in a gold ring, dating to 167 C.E. (© The Trustees of the British Museum)

unguenta exotica ("luxury unguents"), as they were seen as a corrupting influence causing Roman citizens to deviate from the traditional "*mos romanum*" ("Roman way") of a more austere character. Nevertheless, the use of cosmetics and perfumes became more common with the transfer of Greek culture to Rome, particularly after the defeat of Greek troops in Pydna in 168 B.C.E., the presence of Greek hostages in the capital, and the arrival in a constantly increasing number of Greek physicians, technicians and others.

Perfumes in the Roman world reached their zenith under the empire (from 27 B.C.E. onward) with an extensive body of specialized literature on medicine and hygiene in general and also specifically on cosmetics. Among the writings focusing on cosmetics is a small booklet, *Medicamina faciei feminae* (Women's Facial Cosmetics) by Ovid (43 B.C.E.–17 C.E.). The most famous and most specialized work on the topic was a volume by a disciple of Socrates, Criton (ca. 100 C.E.), now lost but which supposedly contained four books; it is known to the modern world only in fragments.

Perfumes were made of rare vegetal essences from the Near East, such as balsam, cardamom, and canella, as well as strongly odoriferous Mediterranean species, such as iris, saffron, and violet, together with gums and resins and, in some cases, such animal substances as musk and beaver glands. All such substances were soaked in olive oil, which had been treated to condense and separate out the fat component. They also included a fixative (moss, for example) and, for some, such colorants as saffron or ocher. The process of their production is described in *De odoribus* (On Perfume) by Theophrast (ca. 372–ca. 286 B.C.E.). One of the most famous perfumes was the so-called *koufi*, from Egypt, made of a wide range of substances. Because of the rarity of the ingredients, these perfumes were extremely costly and very much sought after. They were contained in small glass vials in the shape of fruits.

Cosmetics were aimed primarily at bodily hygiene. They were made mainly of perfumed lotions to be applied to the entire body several times a day. They also included a wide range of makeup products for women. On skin previously cleaned with a lotion, women applied mineral powders of different colors: white lead (which, in fact, was extremely harmful to the skin), chalk, and "Melian earth" (that is, earth from the island of Melos) for a pale color; *rubrica* and *purpurissum* for a touch of red; *stibium* (in fact, a derivative of lead) to make eyelashes and brows black. Various works on drugs and medicine, particularly *De materia medica* (The Materials of Medicine) by Dioscorides (ca. 40–ca. 90 C.E.), include an infinite range of recipes for the aesthetic treatment of wounds, scars, and other imperfections of the skin—not only to treat them but also to erase their possible traces. They were often made of caustic vegetal substances that eliminated the first layer of the skin, not without provoking problems due to excessive abrasion. Ancient Latin texts also describe cold creams for the skin, which were used to alleviate wrinkles and to make the skin soft.

Mouth hygiene was particularly important to ancient Romans. The *Compositiones* (Prescriptions) of the physician Scribonius Largus (fl. first century C.E.) describes toothpastes made of a pasty base, to which were added abrasive substances of a mineral nature (to clean the teeth) together with tasty vegetal products to refresh the mouth. Hair care was also important. Baldness was a major complaint, and medical texts list numerous vegetal and animal substances supposedly capable of regenerating hair. (In fact, they provoke a higher influx of blood to the scalp.) From the third century C.E. on, when recipes were listed in medical texts in detail, formulas against baldness always appeared first. All kinds of perfumed substances were applied to the hair, and it was colored either black or blond with vegetal and mineral products. Men's hair, which was rather long, was dressed in early Roman times in a way very similar to the Greek style. The fashion trended toward shorter hair starting in the first century C.E. Women wore a rather simple hairstyle during the time of the Roman Republic, from the fifth century B.C.E. until the first century C.E. During the period of the Roman Empire that followed, however, they adopted extravagant styles dominated by the court. Later, from the second century C.E. on, simplicity made a comeback.

Personal adornment was completed with jewelry, even though extravagant jewels had been prohibited as early as the Twelve Table Law (the foundation of Roman Republic law, drawn up in about 451–450 B.C.E.). A short-lived prohibition against a woman's right to own gold or wear elaborate clothing was instituted in 215 B.C.E. in the Lex Oppia (abolished in 195 B.C.E.). Nevertheless, the wearing of jewelry had a long tradition in the Mediterranean (dating back at least to the third millennium B.C.E.) and was widely diffused in Roman society, as the vestiges excavated at Pompeii, for example, testify. Women usually wore bands in their hair, earrings, neck chains, bracelets and arm rings, and rings on the index finger. A particular case was gem rings, used as seals. The luxury of Roman adornment was sharply criticized by the first Christian apologists, who saw in it a sign of decadence that was rightly to be punished by God.

THE AMERICAS

BY JULIA MARTA CLAPP

Our knowledge of the objects that peoples from ancient American civilizations used to adorn themselves is largely dependent on findings at burial sites as well as on information deduced from paintings and sculptures. Many ancient American peoples were skilled metalworkers, and silver, gold, and copper were used frequently to great effect in addition to bone, jade, wood, and shell. The purposes of ancient adornment were often as an indicator of social rank and as part of religious rituals. Excavations from other ancient cultures, such as the ancient Egyptians, have yielded evidence of the use of cosmetics, both by depictions of made-up faces and the remains of cosmetics vessels. Unfortunately, in the ancient Americas no such evidence exists, owing partly to the relative lack of painted documents or sculpture. Any claims about the use of cosmetics at this point would be speculative and without significant material evidence.

Certain features are nearly omnipresent in Mesoamerican culture as early as the Olmec (1500 B.C.E.–400 B.C.E.). Stela 3, from the Olmec site La Venta (1200 B.C.E.–400 B.C.E.) in what is now Mexico, shows a ruler wearing a headdress so elaborate and tall that it nearly doubles the wearer's height. Also notable from this era is the documentation of facial hair:

Jade pectoral of the Olmec culture (Mexico), showing large holes in the earlobes, where earplugs would be placed (© The Trustees of the British Museum)

Stela 3 has been dubbed "Uncle Sam" for its pointy beard. The early to middle preclassic Olmec Wrestler from Veracruz also has a beard and moustache, as does one of Los Danzantes (The Dancers) from Monte Albán, Mexico.

Other figural sculptures (sculptures that represent human beings) reveal still other kinds of bodily ornamentation that must have been practiced during this period. First and foremost are the holes left for earspools and lip plugs, which are larger than traditional pierced jewelry and require stretching of the skin. For example, a preserved wooden mask from the Olmec culture has stylized, rectangular ears with large holes in the lobes, indicating the use of earplugs during this period. One figure of a man from the Nayarit region of western Mexico (400 B.C.E.–150 C.E.) has bands around the upper arms and large rings in the nose and ears and a relatively elaborate hairstyle.

Of particular interest during this time in Central America was the harvesting and sculpting of jade in Costa Rica, particularly during the period 300 B.C.E. to 700 C.E. Ornamental objects in general—and jade, in particular—delineated social rank at a time when such distinctions were gaining importance in Central America. Personal adornment carried with it not only socioeconomic significance but religious importance as well. The first group in Mesoamerica to work jade was the Olmec, in the first or second millennium B.C.E. It is unclear whether jade working began indigenously in Costa Rica (ca. 500 B.C.E.) or as a result of intercultural contact (or some combination of the two). During the initial period (500 B.C.E.–300 C.E.), Costa Ricans carved pendants of jade, which may have been strung with beads. At the site of La Regla on the Gulf of Nicoya, archaeologists found a jade pendant and wooden beads that were likely strung together (ca. 500 B.C.E.).

The use of jade in Olmec cultures yielded some particularly interesting and beautiful objects. One jade pendant is in the form of a winged figure, though the wings are schematic and difficult to associate with a particular bird or beast. The pendant has holes, which would have allowed it to be attached to a ruler's headband.

Burial sites of the Chavín culture (900 B.C.E.–200 B.C.E.) in what is now Peru offer insight into the adornment practices of ancient Andean peoples. At these sites archaeologists have found bone hairpins used to fix hairstyles and mantles (some with beads affixed to them), stone beads, earplugs made of wood (some with white shell attached to them), beaded necklaces of stone and shell, and a necklace with gold discs embossed with a serpentine design.

In the middle to later part of the Chavín civilization, as in other ancient American civilizations, these ornaments served to indicate the wearer's social status. As they are today, items crafted with precious material and fine technology were prized. At a burial in Chongoyape, Peru, archaeologists found gold ornamental items, such as headbands, beads entirely in gold, pottery beads encased in gold, headdresses, rings, and pins. Metalworking was common in the Americas, especially using gold and silver in South and Central America.

At the Hacienda Almendral near Chongoyape, archaeologists discovered decorated gold crowns and earspools. Crowns were formed into a cylinder shape similar to an upside-down bucket. The gold was either molded or pressed into both abstract patterns and faces of people or animals. The ear flares had decorations similar to elaborate sun rays extending outward from the circular base. Another clue to the practices of hair grooming during this period is linked to the presence in the burial of tweezers, which may have been used by men to remove facial hair.

Burial items were deeply symbolic and significant, and the placement of the objects as well as their quantity and material were meaningful. One burial included a body with a quartz crystal in its mouth, which was of importance in terms of its placement and the value this civilization placed on quartz. Archaeologists also have found fascinating artifacts in the burial sites of rulers in Paracas, Peru (750 B.C.E.–100 C.E.). In addition to clothing and headbands, the sites also contained wigs made of human hair.

Some of the most spectacular examples of ancient Andean ornamental craftsmanship came from the site of Sipán, Peru (early Moche culture, 100 C.E.–700 C.E.). Sipán had three tombs filled with extraordinary examples of Andean gold work. In Tomb 3 (known as the Tomb of the Old Lord), archaeologists discovered a necklace made of 10 gold "spider" beads. The back of each bead was formed by a concave disc and the front of a human head with a spider body, with thin strands of gold forming the legs and web.

The Hopewell Indians of North America (ca. 200 B.C.E.–400 C.E.) left burial sites that also provide modern-day archaeologists and anthropologists with indications of what ancient American adornment looked like. In Hopewell burials archaeologists have discovered earspools, which often were made of copper, a costly material commonly used in jewelry. Earspools also were made of silver, sometimes in conjunction with copper, providing a contrast in color. Because ancient American cultures were deeply steeped in symbolism, the circular shape of the earspool probably was meaningful. The presence in a burial of more earspools than the deceased was capable of wearing indicates that their mere inclusion was significant. They would have testified to the social status of their owner.

Other copper items found at burial sites were bracelets and beaded necklaces. Copper was combined with leather to create what is known as a headdress but which more closely resembles a contemporary skullcap or ski cap. The leather was fashioned to fit over the skull to the ears, and a curved copper plate decorates the front middle portion of the headdress. In addition to copper beads, the Hopewell made necklaces of marine conch shells and beads in the shape of animals and birds.

See also ART; CERAMICS AND POTTERY; CLOTHING AND FOOTWEAR; DEATH AND BURIAL PRACTICES; FESTIVALS; HEALTH AND DISEASE; LAWS AND LEGAL CODES; METALLURGY; RELIGION AND COSMOLOGY; SACRED SITES; SOCIAL ORGANIZATION; TRADE AND EXCHANGE.

FURTHER READING

Cyril Aldred, *Jewels of the Pharaohs* (London: Thames and Hudson, 1978).

Sue Blundell, *Women in Ancient Greece* (Cambridge, Mass.: Harvard University Press, 1995).

Richard Corson, *Fashions in Makeup: From Ancient to Modern Times* (London: Peter Owen Publishers, 2004).

Antonio d'Ambrosio, *Women and Beauty in Pompeii* (Los Angeles: J. Paul Getty Museum, 2001).

Mikhal Dayagi-Medeles, *Perfumes and Cosmetics in the Ancient World* (Jersusalem: Israel Museum, 1989).

Giuseppe Donato and Monique Seefried, *The Fragrant Past: Perfumes of Cleopatra and Julius Caesar* (Rome: Istituto Poligrafico e Zecca dello Stato, 1989).

Bernard Fagg, *Nok Terracottas* (Lagos: Nigerian Museum/London: Ethongraphica, 1977).

Joann Fletcher, *Oils and Perfumes of Ancient Egypt* (New York: Harry N. Abrams, 1999).

Mary G. Houston, *Ancient Egyptian, Mesopotamian, and Persian Costume* (Mineola, N.Y.: Dover Publications, 2002).

Julie Jones, ed., *Jade in Ancient Costa Rica* (New York: Metropolitan Museum of Art, 1998).

Mary Ellen Miller, *The Art of Mesoamerica: From Olmec to Aztec*, 3rd ed. (London: Thames and Hudson, 2001).

Anne Paul, *Paracas Ritual Attire: Symbols of Authority in Ancient Peru* (Norman: University of Oklahoma Press, 1990).

Clare Phillips, *Jewelry: From Antiquity to the Present* (New York: Thames and Hudson, 1996).

Elizabeth Riefstahl, *Toilet Articles from Ancient Egypt* (Brooklyn: Brooklyn Museum, 1943).

Phyllis G. Tortora and Keith Eubank, *Survey of Historic Costume: A History of Western Dress* (New York: Fairchild Publications, 1994).

Monica Blackmun Visoná, Robin Poyner, Herbert M. Cole, et al., *A History of Art in Africa* (New York: Abrams, 2001).

Alix Wilkinson, *Ancient Egyptian Jewellery* (London: Methuen, 1971).

► agriculture

INTRODUCTION

For most of human history people survived as hunter-gatherers. Hunter-gatherers fed themselves by hunting game, including fish, seafood, and birds (as well as birds' eggs) and by foraging for plant foods that grow wild, including fruits, berries, roots, leafy vegetables, rice, grains, and the like. Hunter-gatherers lived in small nomadic bands, meaning that they moved from place to place in search of food, especially as the seasons and weather conditions changed.

Because the ancient world was sparsely populated, hunting and gathering were successful ways of finding food much of the time. Populations did not have to compete with one another for territory and the foodstuffs it might contain. Further, the food supplies of a territory usually did not run out because of too much consumption; if they did, the band of people could simply move on to another territory.

As the world became more populated, however, it became less and less practical for roving bands of hunter-gatherers to move about at will. One band of hunter-gatherers often found itself in competition with another for food, leading to conflict. Growing numbers of people meant that food supplies in a territory could quickly become used up. Furthermore, hunting and gathering were extremely uncertain ways to obtain food. Early peoples were dependent on what they could find when they could find it, but such factors as drought, monsoon rains, and temperature extremes made the availability of food supplies inconsistent over time. Furthermore, early hunter-gatherers had no way of storing and preserving food. The result was often famine and starvation.

A major development in the history of humankind was the advent of agriculture—not just as a way of providing food but as a way of life. In roughly 7000 to 6000 B.C.E. humans began to trade their lives as hunters and gatherers for the more settled life of agriculturalists, though hunting and gathering did not disappear. By learning to plant, cultivate, harvest, and store crops, particularly important crops such as wheat, barley, and legumes (beans), people could provide themselves with a greater variety of food. They were no longer dependent entirely on what was locally available at a given time but could supplement their diets with other plant foods as well as with animal foods, such as goats, sheep, cattle, chickens, and, in some parts of the world, dogs.

Additionally, they could make use of by-products from agriculture for other purposes. The straw left over in the fields after a grain crop was harvested was used to give strength to mud bricks used in the construction of homes. Hides could be used for their leather, and such animals as sheep could be sheared to provide clothing, fabrics, and similar goods. Domesticated animals provided manure used to fertilize fields; in the case of sheep, goats, and cattle they also supplied milk. In turn, milk could be used to make cheese and butter. Chickens and other fowl provided meat and eggs as well as feathers that could be used in such items as bedding. Little went to waste on an ancient farm.

Agriculture enabled people to store and preserve food for the lean times. In such places as ancient Egypt, for example, farmers were able to grow a year's worth of grain, perhaps more, which then could be stored throughout the year and distributed to people as it was needed. This ability to store and preserve food evened out many of the ups and downs of food availability, reducing the threat of famine and starvation. The result was longer life expectancies, improved health, and the growth of populations. Adding to population growth was the fact that women, no longer having to move about in search of food, could bear and raise more children, who then were able to provide labor in the fields.

Perhaps most important, agriculture resulted in a more sedentary way of life. In modern times, the word *sedentary* has a negative connotation. It implies lack of physical activity, perhaps to the point of laziness. Historians, though, use the word to refer to settled cultures that did not move about as nomads. Once people began to settle in villages and hamlets that were surrounded by their farming plots, cities began to grow. The growth of cities, in turn, gave rise to governments, institutionalized churches, art and architecture, trade and manufacture, and all the other characteristics of more modern civilizations.

Moreover, because farmers in outlying regions could produce a surplus of food, not everyone in the community had to be involved in agriculture. Surplus food meant that the community could support a class of civil servants, architects, engineers, soldiers, priests, artists, poets, and crafts workers, all of whom provided goods and services that enhanced the quality of life for their neighbors. As people gathered in larger towns and cities, they developed a sense of community and were able to bring individual points of view to public discussion, leading to more formalized belief systems, systems of government, economic and trade networks, public works, and the like. None of this would have been possible without the development of agriculture.

Agriculture, though, was not just a matter of sticking seeds into the ground and waiting for food to appear on the table. As agricultural systems became more complex and as the number of mouths to feed grew, people looked for ways to control their environment in order to maximize their food output. In many parts of the world, for example, rainy seasons were followed by drought, and the annual flooding of rivers was followed by a period of receding waters. In some parts of the world, particularly around the equator, the climate was desertlike.

As a result, humans put their ingenuity to work to develop dams, canals, sluices, waterwheels, and other engineering feats that enabled them to control and store water for use during the dry season. In turn, the ability to control water gave rise to systems for supplying drinking water and sewage systems for cities. Some people turned their attention to experimenting with different types of seeds to increase the variety and yield of their crops, in effect becoming the world's first experimental scientists. Still others focused their attention on developing tools that made agriculture more efficient. Early tools consisted of such items as simple wooden blades for cutting and stones for grinding grain. In time, agriculturalists developed more sophisticated cutting and grinding tools that enabled them to increase their output. Development of these tools provided the technology for tools used in other endeavors, such as the construction of palaces, temples, and other public buildings.

AFRICA

BY AMY HACKNEY BLACKWELL

Agriculture arose independently in many locations throughout the world, and each time it was the result of people's manipulating plants and animals that already lived around them. In Africa this process happened numerous times in different locations. Africa's geography prevented the smooth transmission of crops and livestock from place to place. As a result, people on the continent never had the chance to develop large agricultural civilizations such as those in Mesopotamia.

Egypt was the first place agriculture appeared in Africa, arising about 6000 B.C.E. as traders from the Near East ventured into the Nile River valley, bringing crops with them. Near Eastern agriculture traveled as far as the Ethiopian highlands but could not move farther into the continent, owing to geographical and climatic barriers. Hunter-gatherers in the area just south of the Sahara domesticated livestock starting about 3000 B.C.E. but did not begin growing crops for another thousand years or so. Between 2000 B.C.E. and 1 C.E. people living south of the Sahara developed several different kinds of crops, depending on climatic conditions; people in West Africa grew rice and yams, while people in the Sahel grew drought-resistant grains.

Farming and herding did not travel south of the Serengeti until about 1 C.E.; eastern Africa around Kenya and Tanzania was home to the tsetse fly, which caused sleeping sickness, deadly to both humans and cattle. As cattle evolved resistance to the disease, farmers and herders began moving south into southeastern Africa, bringing African crops with them. People in this area gradually adopted some Asian crops as well, importing them from Indian traders. The southward progress of agriculture continued to be very slow; domesticated crops did not arrive in South Africa until the 17th century, and they came with European sailors, not overland.

AFRICAN GEOGRAPHY: AN OBSTACLE TO AGRICULTURE

Africa's geography presented a major obstacle to the spread of agriculture. Africa is a large continent with a wide range of climatic conditions. Its longest axis runs from north to south and crosses the equator, which means the various parts of Africa are very different from one another. The length of days varies depending on distance from the equator; this is important, because many plants grow well only in days of a particular length. For example, at the equator days are about the same length year-round. Far south of the equator, in South Africa, days are long in summer and short in winter. Plants that thrive at the equator may not succeed in South Africa. Seasons are different in different places as well; summer in North Africa is winter in South Africa. Tropical eastern Africa experiences the monsoons of the Indian Ocean. Rwanda is mountainous and has its own climate. By contrast, agriculture spread quickly through the Middle East and Asia because the Eurasian continent stretches from east to west on roughly the same latitude. Plants that grow in southeastern Turkey will also grow in Spain or Iran. Rice that grows in western China will also grow in Japan and India.

The Near East is close to Africa, so it would seem that agriculture would have quickly moved from there to Egypt, but in fact agriculture entered Africa a good 1,000 years after it traveled to Europe around 6000 B.C.E. The Sinai desert was

View of rice fields in the Malagasy Republic of southern Africa (© Board of Regents of the University of Wisconsin System)

the first obstacle; most people did not want to venture into it. The Sahara was another enormous impediment. Central Africa is full of dense rain forest and mountain ranges, both of which present difficulties to travelers. Middle Eastern crops grew well in the Nile River valley, with its stable climate and regular flooding. They also grew well in other locations with climates similar to that of the Near East, such as the Ethiopian highlands. They did not, however, grow well in Sudan, which has periodic monsoons. The Sahara likewise did not provide a suitable climate for Near Eastern grains. South Africa has a climate suited to Near Eastern grains, but it was so far away that no one could get there from North Africa.

As a result of these geographical limitations, agriculture did not spread readily through Africa, as it did through Europe and Asia. People domesticated plants and animals, but they did so in isolated pockets and independently of one another. This domestication also happened much later in Africa than it did in Eurasia; scholars believe that Africans did not domesticate their own grains until 2000 to 1000 B.C.E.

Nile River Valley

The Nile River valley was the first place agriculture appeared in Africa. The Nile is a very long river, flowing more than 4,000 total miles through eastern Africa. The White Nile begins in Rwanda and flows north through Tanzania, Lake Victoria, Uganda, and Sudan. The Blue Nile starts in Ethiopia and flows through Sudan as well. The two tributaries meet in Sudan and flow north through the desert into Egypt. People lived all along the length of the river. Thousands of years ago they lived as hunter-gatherers, hunting wild animals, fishing in the river, and gathering the many wild plants that grew in the river valley. The Nile River valley has a very regular annual flood schedule. The Nile overflows its banks every summer, and the flooding reaches southern Egypt by the middle of August and the Mediterranean about a month later. This flooding wets the soil along the length of the river for about two months, creating a moist environment for plants.

Agriculture traveled south down the Nile River valley between 6500 and 5500 B.C.E. People living in the Near East had started growing plants for food about 8000 B.C.E. Travelers venturing southwest into Egypt brought agricultural techniques with them, and these practices gradually made their way south into Africa. By 5000 B.C.E. the Nile River valley was populated by people living off domestic crops and livestock. They also made pottery similar to that of the Near East. Near Eastern agriculture traveled as far as the highlands of Ethiopia, where the climate was similar to the climate where the plants and animals had first been domesticated.

Sub-Saharan Africa

The Sahara is now a desert that grows bigger every year. Few people venture into it, and no one farms it. In prehistoric times, however, the Sahara was very different; it was fertile enough to be one of the places where humans developed agriculture. Scholars are not sure whether people living in Africa invented agriculture or learned of agriculture from foreigners; archaeologists have not studied African history nearly to the extent that they have in other parts of the world. Nevertheless, it seems entirely possible that humans could have independently domesticated crops in the Sahara and Sahel.

Between 5000 and 2000 B.C.E., the Sahara had greater rainfall than it does now. Parts of it had so much rainfall that the areas were among the most fertile environments in Africa. The Sahel, the grassy area south of the Sahara, extended farther north and covered the areas that are now the southern and central parts of the Sahara desert. During the rainy season these grasslands became marshy in places, and seasonal lakes appeared. Hunter-gatherers lived on the shores of these lakes, gathering wild plants, fishing, and hunting the animals that came there to drink.

Africans domesticated cattle before they domesticated plants. Starting around 3000 B.C.E., people in the southwestern Sahara began to herd cattle. Most scholars believe that these cattle had come from domesticated cattle in the Near East that had traveled into Africa with herders in search of pastures. Other historians think that Africans caught and domesticated wild cattle living in the area. In any case, by 2000 B.C.E. numerous people in East Africa lived off their cattle herds, consuming meat and milk. The climate in the Sahara was starting to get drier around that time, and it was impossible to cultivate grain. Cattle became central to the economy there. People also herded goats, but cattle were much more important to them. They lived in villages with several houses made of mud and sticks, and they made pottery and traded with neighboring villages.

Around 2000 B.C.E. the Kintampo people of present-day Ivory Coast and Ghana began herding and trading sheep and goats in addition to cattle. They started growing pearl millet and extracting oil from oil palms around 1,500 B.C.E. At about this time agriculture began spreading slowly throughout central and southern Africa. People in the area had lived as hunter-gatherers, but they gradually began settling down and farming instead. These people were of the group called the Bantu. Bantu people started growing crops in the Lake Victoria region between 500 and 250 B.C.E.

In the first century of the Common Era people in modern-day Kenya, Malawi, Zambia, and Mozambique started cultivating African crops, including pearl millet, finger millet, and sorghum, and raising cattle, sheep, chickens, and goats. During the first five centuries C.E. people living on the Kenyan coast began trading with people sailing from India and Southeast Asia. They adopted Southeast Asian crops, such as bananas, yams, and taro, which grew equally well in the East African climate. During this period people living in wet coastal areas began settling in villages, feeding themselves with their crops. People in the drier inland regions continued to live as herders.

Agriculture and domestic animals did not reach the northern parts of South Africa until the late fifth century C.E. Farmers and herders could not settle farther south, across South Africa's Fish River, because their crops could not grow in South Africa's Mediterranean-like climate. Agriculture did not reach South Africa until Europeans arrived in ships in 1652, carrying with them European crops that could thrive in the local climate. Agriculture's progress southward through the continent was quite slow, mainly because Africa itself presented so many geographical difficulties. In addition to the problems of terrain and adapting plants to new climates, pests such as the tsetse fly devastated populations of cattle and herders. Herders stayed north of the Serengeti Plain from 2000 B.C.E. until 1 C.E., by which time new breeds of livestock had evolved that could cope with the southern conditions. Humans had to adapt their trading economies as well; because travel was so difficult, different tribes rarely met and had to learn how to communicate with one another.

The people who adopted agriculture began raising several types of crops and animals at once. They grew sorghum, pearl millet, and finger millet, and they raised cattle, sheep, goats, and chickens. They began to work with iron as well, as the technology spread through the continent. As agriculturists took over the landscape, groups of hunter-gatherers were pushed to the margins. The Khoisan Bushmen were forced into the Kalahari Desert and South Africa, where they took up sheep herding. The jungle peoples of the Congo region continued to hunt and gather wild plants deep in the forests. The Bantu people themselves never formed the large civilizations that appeared in other parts of the world. They had villages and trading networks and cultural traditions, but they did not build cities or develop advanced technologies.

North Africa

North Africa's climate and geography are very different from those of sub-Saharan Africa. Although the desert begins within a few miles of the sea, the area along the Mediterranean coast is fertile and flat. Phoenicians traveling from Lebanon colonized North Africa from Libya to Morocco between 1000 and 600 B.C.E. People living in the area farmed Near Eastern crops, such as wheat, for export to other areas. Carthage became the center of the North African trading empire in the fifth century B.C.E. Rome took over much of Cathage's territory after the Punic Wars, fought with Rome, forming a new province in northern Tunisia in 146 B.C.E. This province encompassed some 5,000 square miles of the most fertile part of North Africa. The land there became Roman public land, and the government leased it out to grain farmers, who grew wheat for export to Rome. North African estates were vast. Most of the land was in the hands of a few absentee landowners, although there were also more modest estates owned by locals. Scholars believe that about half a million tons of wheat left Carthage annually. Carthage became the second-largest city in the Mediterranean on the basis of its agricultural exports. By the second century B.C.E. North Africa was also exporting olive oil, figs, grapes, and beans. North Africa continued to supply grain to Rome until the end of the Roman Empire.

The main agricultural challenge in the region was lack of water. All African farmers had to irrigate their crops, and they invented elaborate systems to transport water to their fields. In areas with narrow rivers and flat lands, farmers dug canals and built dikes to channel and contain water. Every year large numbers of people worked together to clear canals of debris and repair damage to structures. In the areas closest to the sea farmers had to ensure that saltwater did not enter into their irrigation structures and kill their crops.

In areas where fields lay above the level of floods, farmers had to use mechanical systems of irrigation. One irrigation device was the *shaduf*, or *shadoof*, a device that lifted water in a container. It consisted of a wooden or stone frame with a long horizontal pole affixed to a hinge at its top. A farmer would tie a bucket or skin bag to one end of the pole and attach a stone or clay weight to the other end. If the device was balanced correctly, it was very easy for the farmer to lift the bucket or bag of water from a body of water and swing it over to an irrigation ditch that flowed into a field. Although irrigating a field with a *shaduf* was less work than carrying water by hand, it was still slow and laborious; one *shaduf* could irrigate about an acre a day.

During the Hellenistic Period two more advanced irrigation devices appeared. One was the Persian water wheel known as a *saqiya*. This device was a large wheel with buckets attached to its perimeter. An ox or donkey turned it to raise water from a river or pond and transfer it to an irrigation ditch. The Archimedean screw, or Egyptian screw, was a device that raised water by means of a large screw inside a pipe attached to an inclined plane. The lower end of the screw was placed in a body of water, and laborers turned the screw by hand. As it turned, it collected and raised water and then dumped it out at the top. Both the *saqiyah* and the Archimedean screw were large and expensive devices, out of the reach of most small farmers. Only large landowners could afford to use them.

African Crops

Africans south of the Sahara domesticated several crops that are not widely grown in other continents. All the African grains are annuals, plants that complete their life cycles in one year. Unlike the grains domesticated in the Near East, however, African grains all show a strong tendency to cross-pollinate. Near Eastern grains will pollinate themselves, which results in seeds that produce offspring just like their parents, a desirable trait for a crop. African grains will cross-pollinate with wild grains and produce plants that are very little like their parents. This probably made it much more difficult for African farmers to domesticate crops than it was for people in the Near East and Mesopotamia. They would have had to grow their crops far away from patches of wild grains that might contaminate the fields.

The main African grains were sorghum, pearl millet, and African rice. Africans also domesticated yams, oil palms, cowpeas, and groundnuts. Sorghum and pearl millet were domesticated in the dry areas of the Sahel. Rice and yams grew better in the wet regions of the forest-savanna border in West Africa. In Ethiopia people domesticated two unique grains, finger millet and tef. Sorghum is a grass grown for its grain. People made it into couscous (a grainlike type of pasta) and porridge, which they ate with vegetables and sauces. Sorghum straw was used as a building material, mixed with mud to form bricks for walls. Sorghum is highly resistant to drought, an advantage in the dry climate of the sub-Saharan region. People were gathering wild sorghum for food about 6000 B.C.E. It was domesticated in the Ethiopian highlands of Africa around 1000 to 500 B.C.E.

Pearl millet is another drought-resistant grain. It grows wild in the region, and people evidently started gathering it more than 8000 B.C.E. It produces small seeds and is currently grown worldwide both as food for humans and as fodder for animals. Millet contains about 11 percent protein, about the same as wheat. It does not rise like wheat, so it cannot be used to make leavened bread. People generally grind it into flour to make into flat bread or boil it into porridge. Pearl millet probably was first domesticated in the southwestern Sahara, in what is now Mauritania and northern Ghana, around 1000 B.C.E. In addition to making pearl millet into porridge, couscous, or unleavened bread, people also used the stalks of the plants for building. Pearl millet traveled from Africa to India around 1500 B.C.E., and it became a staple crop there as well.

African rice is very similar to Asian rice. The ancestor of African rice resembles the wild rice of Asia and is closely related to it. Ancient wild African rice grew in holes in the ground that filled with water during the rainy season and dried out in the dry season, a similar environment to that in which Asian rice evolved. African rice became the staple crop in West Africa, where people boiled it and ate it with vegetables and meats. African rice was domesticated in West Africa near the Niger River around 200 C.E.

Yams are tubers or roots that grow underground. People prepare them like potatoes, boiling or roasting the flesh; certain substances in yams can cause illness if the yams are not cooked before they are consumed. A single yam can grow up to seven feet long and weigh 150 pounds. They have thick skins and brown or pink interiors. They can be stored for several months without spoiling, which made them an attractive crop for tropical climates, where the heat and dampness of the wet season quickly spoiled grains. They were especially common in West Africa.

Oil palms grow in West Africa. People domesticated them to harvest their fruit, which grows in clusters; each fruit consists of an oily seed surrounded by oily flesh. They pressed the fruit to extract the oil. Palm oil is high in calories and vitamin K, which made it a valuable addition to African diets. Animals can eat the meal left over from extracting the oil.

The cowpea is a type of bean. There are several varieties of cowpeas today; the best known are black-eyed peas and crowder peas. The cowpea plant can tolerate drier weather than other beans, such as those domesticated in the Americas. It grows well in poor soils, can thrive in some shade, and is good for improving soils by adding nitrogen to it. Africans used the cowpea to correct the soil in their fields in between crops of millet or sorghum. Cowpeas appear to have been domesticated in West Africa between 2500 and 600 B.C.E.

Groundnuts are legumes related to peanuts with pods that ripen underground. They originated in West Africa, where they added protein to people's diets. The most common means of preparation was boiling. Like cowpeas, groundnuts were domesticated in West Africa sometime between 2500 and 600 B.C.E.; historians do not know more precisely when this happened.

Ethiopia, in eastern central Africa, developed its own unique agricultural products. Tef is a grain that is similar to millet, though tef contains more amino acids and minerals and therefore is a more complete food than millet. It grows well in the dry climate of the region, though it also grows well in waterlogged soil. Insects do not eat it, so they are not a problem during growing or storage. Cooks ground tef into flour to make flatbread or boiled it to make porridge. Ancient farmers also fed tef grain and stalks to their cattle and used the stalks to reinforce their mud bricks. Tef was domesticated some time before 1 C.E., most likely in western Ethiopia. It was probably more difficult to domesticate than wheat. Tef seeds are small, which makes it difficult to sow them evenly and to find them on the ground once they are sown. Because tef fields grow unevenly, farmers have always had to weed them by hand.

EGYPT

BY MICHAEL J. O'NEAL

Thousands of years ago, before the existence of Egyptian civilization, the regions of North Africa that surround the Nile River were fertile grasslands and woodlands, providing farmland and grazing land for communities of people. Historians estimate that around 3500 B.C.E., however, the environment in these grasslands began to change dramatically, perhaps because of overgrazing of the land, and eventually the region turned into desert, primarily the Sahara. Looking for a place where they could grow crops and keep herds of farm animals, people migrated into the area around the Nile River, forming small settlements beginning in about 3000 B.C.E. Because Egypt then and now has almost no rainfall, the Nile, which flows northward from Lake Victoria in Uganda, became the central feature of Egyptian agriculture, as well as of the Egyptians' cultural and religious life.

The region's very earliest settlers relied primarily on hunting, fishing, and foraging. They produced food, including limited crops, only for personal consumption. They were unable to store food, so food production was limited by the seasons. The development of more organized agriculture in many senses led to the rise of Egypt as a nation, for it was only through the agricultural surpluses that farmers produced that Egypt was able to take part in trade and support a class of rulers, soldiers, scholars, civil servants, and others who made the existence of the state possible. Further, by growing crops that could be stored, the Egyptians could maintain a steady supply of food throughout the year. This enabled the population of ancient Egypt to expand dramatically, because famine became far less common. Without the Nile River, the world's longest river at 4,037 miles, ancient Egypt could not have existed as a nation.

THE FLOODPLAIN

The Nile River was surrounded by a fertile strip of land that provided the ancient Egyptians with most of their material needs. Immediately adjacent to the banks of the river was the floodplain. Each year, this land flooded with rising waters from the Nile, which was fed by water from monsoon rains in Ethiopia, far to the south. In an average year, the water would rise about 27 feet during a period called *akhet*, or the inundation, which ran roughly from July to December, with the flooding reaching its peak in late September and then beginning to recede in October. During this period, the land was flooded, and farm animals were moved to higher ground. The flood waters provided not only moisture for growing crops but also large amounts of fertile silt—that is, tiny particles of soil that were carried and left behind by the water when it receded. This silt was rich in nutrients, and it was in the waterlogged silt that the Egyptians planted their crops. The soil was so rich that it was black, causing the area often to be referred to as the Black Land.

In addition to the floodplain were higher elevations around the river. These areas of low desert did not become flooded, so they were not used extensively for crops. They were used primarily for hunting and burial of the dead. At still higher elevations away from the river were sparsely inhabited desert regions. In these areas, dates and grapes were cultivated. Traveling caravans passed through the desert, and the dates and grapes were often picked up and used to trade with other regions in North Africa and beyond. Water for these crops had to be laboriously transported from the river.

WATER MANAGEMENT

Growing crops in the floodplain was not simply a matter of allowing the water to recede and then sowing seed. The ancient Egyptians relied on a complex system of locks and dams to control, contain, store, and distribute the water. They built dams at right angles to the water's flow, forcing the water into large basins that covered some 1,000 to 4,200 acres of ground. These basins were lined with clay to prevent the water from seeping into the ground. The water in the basins was then diverted by a system of dikes into canals, where it flowed where it was needed. Keeping this system of dikes and canals in working order was an ongoing task. Each year every Egyptian (and most took part in agriculture) had to move on average about 23 cubic yards of soil to keep the canals and dikes working properly.

Wooden model of a man plowing with oxen, from the Middle Kingdom of Egypt (© The Trustees of the British Museum)

Overall, about 5 million to 8.4 million acres were flooded in this way. Construction of these dams, dikes, and basins occurred over a thousand years, so that by about 2000 B.C.E., the entire region bordering both sides of the Nile each year became a checkerboard of flooded basins during the high-water season and beyond. Water was regarded as property held in common, so the basins were also connected by sluices (canals with gates) so that it could be drawn for use upstream whenever there was not enough water downstream.

On average, the river rose 27 feet during the flood season. In some years, though, the river's rise would be less, sharply reducing the amount of water and silt and therefore the area available for crop cultivation. In these years, famine could result. On the other hand, in some years the water rose higher than 27 feet. The result was chaos, as people and farm animals could lose their lives as they scrambled to find higher ground. In modern times, the floodwaters of the Nile are controlled by the Aswān Dam. Construction of the dam was begun in 1902 and completed in 1988.

Planting

Planting usually began in December, after the waters had receded enough for work to begin. This period of receding waters was called *proyet* or *peret*, meaning "the emergence," when the ground emerged from the water. The period December through March was the coolest season of the year. It was during this time that crops germinated and grew (unlike many other regions of the world, where crops are grown during the warmest months).

Unlike the soil in such places as the American Midwest, which has to be turned over with heavy plows, the light alluvial silt in which the ancient Egyptians planted their crops had only to be broken up on the surface. (*Alluvial* describes deposits of soil on a floodplain or anywhere it collects next to a body of water.) For this purpose the Egyptians used plows that were light in weight and connected to the horns of oxen or even cattle. These draft animals were driven by a person, often children, with a stick. The plows were generally made of wood, although some had bronze blades. Sometimes draft animals were not available, so people pulled the plows or used short-handled wooden hoes to break up the surface of the soil; these hoes were so short that the work was backbreaking.

One important tool was the *shaduf* (also spelled *shadouf* or *shadoof*). This was a tool for irrigation that was originally developed by the ancient Sumerians. It was made of a long branch or pole on an upright frame. At the long end of the pole hung a skin bag, a bucket, or even a reed basket coated so that it would hold water. At the short end of the pole was a weight, typically a stone. This weight served as a counterweight to the bucket when it was filled with water. The operator lowered the bucket into the water and then easily raised it out with the help of the counterweight. He then swung the pole to carry the water to where it was needed, often an irrigation canal. Thus, the floodwaters continued to irrigate crops even after the river receded. Estimates are that a farmer could move about 660 gallons of water each day with the *shaduf.*

The planting of crops at this point was relatively easy. The farmer simply walked over the ground with a bag of seed, sowing the seed as he walked. Frequently, the farmer would then drive a herd of goats, cattle, or sheep over the ground. In this way the seed was pressed into the soil so that birds were not able to eat it. The ancient Egyptians grew a variety of crops in this way. The most common crops were grains. (In many older texts, readers are likely to find the word *corn* used to refer to these grain crops. To Americans, *corn* refers to the yellow vegetable found on cobs, but in earlier eras it was a general word for *grain.*) One was emmer wheat, though the Egyptians stopped growing this crop after the Romans took over the area. Other varieties of wheat were grown as well. Barley was grown for use in beer and in baking, though this crop became less important after the Romans invaded and replaced beer with wine as the favored beverage.

Other crops included flax, used to make ropes and cloth; papyrus reed, used to make such products as boats, paper, rope, sandals, and various household goods such as mats); and the castor oil plant, from which oil was pressed. Also grown were vegetables, though typically in smaller plots for consumption by the farmer and his family. Fruits included melons, pomegranates, dates, figs, and grapes. An enormous number of bees provided honey used in desserts.

In addition to crops, the ancient Egyptians relied on livestock for food. Some of this livestock, including oxen and donkeys, was used to help with the work of plowing and harvesting. Later, around 1600 B.C.E., camels and horses were imported from Asia for similar purposes; camels were unknown in Egypt during the time of the pharaohs. Otherwise, the Egyptians also kept sheep, pigs, goats, ducks, and cattle for consumption as well as for hides and milk. Dried animal dung was put to use in cooking fires.

Harvesting

The dry season began in March and continued to July. This period was called *shemu* (also *shomu*), meaning "the drought." Harvesting usually occurred in May or June and sometimes in April, before the next flood began. Grains were harvested using sickles made of wood that was cut and glazed to form a sharp edge; by Roman times sickles made of iron were becoming more common.

Large estates made use of traveling harvest teams, who began their work early in the season and followed the maturing of crops downriver as the season progressed. (The Nile flows north into the Mediterranean Sea, so *downriver* means in a northerly direction and *upriver* refers to a southerly direction.) Because harvesting involved a great deal of work in a relatively short period of time, nearly everyone participated. Livestock was then allowed to graze in the fields to eat the stalks left behind. Also, poor people often followed harvesters, hoping they could scavenge some bits of grain for themselves.

After the grain was cut with sickles, it had to be bundled. Sometimes the bundles were loaded onto the backs of donkeys, but often they were carried in sacks suspended from poles, each pole carried by two men. The grain was then taken to a dry place to undergo a process called *parching*, or drying out the grain so that it did not later get moldy or rot. There, the threshing process would begin. Workers spread the grain, still on its grassy stems, in a fenced or otherwise contained place where the ground was packed hard and first carefully cleaned. Donkeys then trampled it. In some places cows performed this job. This trampling helped separate the grain from the chaff, or the seed coverings and other debris that is not eaten.

During the next step in the harvesting process, called winnowing, workers used large forks, like pitchforks, to scoop up the straw, leaving behind mostly grain. The straw was kept for use in the production of mud bricks, which were strengthened by the inclusion of the straw. Using sieves made of palm leaves and reeds, workers—usually women at this stage—sifted the materials to further separate the grains from the remaining smaller bits of chaff. Finally, the grain was ready to be stored in granaries for later consumption.

The fields of ancient Egypt were highly productive, particularly considering that crops were grown without benefit of modern tools or fertilizers. Records show that at that time an acre of land could yield nearly 4,200 pounds. Total production could range as high as 2.8 million tons, though 2.5 million tons was the production for a typical good year. This amount of grain fed a population during the New Kingdom (1550–1070 B.C.E.) that has been variously estimated from as few as 2 million to as many as 5 million people. During bad harvest years, production fell to as low as about 1.5 million tons.

One period of dryness demonstrates the vital importance of the Nile and its annual flooding in the life of the ancient Egyptians. Late in the third millennium B.C.E., Egypt suffered a period of great political instability. The royal families were feuding, and questions arose about the proper succession of kings. Then, around 2134 B.C.E., the Eighth Dynasty fell. In the resulting power vacuum, local nobles seized control of the land in their areas and gained command of portions of the king's army. Although in theory

HYMN TO HATHOR: THE EGYPTIAN AGRICULTURAL CYCLE

About two miles southeast of the town of Dendera, Egypt, is the Dendera Temple complex, which features one of the best-preserved temples in all of Egypt. Covering about 430,000 square feet, or nearly 10 acres, it has become a major tourist attraction. The main temple in the complex is the Hathor Temple, dedicated to the goddess Hathor, whom the Egyptians regarded as the mother-goddess of the world and the patron of, among other things, the sky, the sun, music, dance, and the arts. The dates of construction provided in the texts inscribed on the temple range from 54 B.C.E. to 64 C.E.; it was built on the site of an earlier temple from the Middle Kingdom (ca. 2140–1640 B.C.E.).

Hathor's name means "house of Horus," referring to the night sky and therefore the god of the sky, Horus, who was the son of Osiris. As a mother-goddess, Hathor had been considered in earlier centuries as symbolic of the Milky Way, which the ancient Egyptians believed was the milk that flowed from a celestial cow. Thus, as far back as 2700 B.C.E., Egyptians worshipped her as a cow deity. She was also known by the name Mehturt (also spelled Mehurt, Mehet-uret, and Mehet-Weret), a name that means "great flood," again in reference to the Milky Way. However, because the Egyptians saw the Milky Way as a waterway on which the gods could travel, they came to associate it with the Nile River. Hathor, then, was believed to be responsible for the yearly flooding of the Nile. In this way, she also became associated with motherhood, for the breaking of the amniotic sac as a signal that a woman is about to give birth was thought of as analogous to the flooding of the Nile, with the "birth" of the crops that would grow after it receded.

Archaeologists discovered a hymn to Hathor when they refurbished the Dendera Temple complex. This hymn, inscribed on the Hathor Temple, makes clear her connection with Egyptian agriculture. Hathor is said to "cause the flood flowing downriver in its season." To farmers, Hathor caused "the watered earth to close over the seed when its right time has come," making men to "work it in joy."

Egypt retained a ruling monarch, in practice these nobles ruled Egypt, often causing suffering among their people. Much of this instability came about because of a long period of dryness. The people were starving, and in response many became violent. Peasants revolted and seized property from landowners, turning them into servants. Order was restored to the country beginning in about 1900 B.C.E., when Amenemhet I took power and began a new dynasty. It is likely that much of this instability would not have occurred had it not been for the famine caused by low flooding of the Nile.

Amenemhet and his followers believed that Egypt had suffered famine and instability because it had been abandoned by the gods. This abandonment was the result of the injustice and cruelty of previous dynasties. Amenemhet resolved to rule more justly. In particular, he acknowledged that common people and not just nobles could enjoy an afterlife and meet the god Osiris after they died.

Osiris

The ancient Egyptians did not see agriculture as merely a physical process. For them, agriculture was an expression of the will of the gods in their daily lives. One of these gods was Osiris, who represented a number of elements of Egyptian life, including the Underworld. Beyond that, Osiris was the god of vegetation and the earth. The year's dry period represented the death of Osiris, who was reborn when the Nile flooded and crops grew.

According to legend, Osiris was the son of Nut and Geb, Egypt's original king, and he took the throne when Geb gave it up. His brother was Seth, and his sister was Isis, to whom he was married. At the time he took the throne, Osiris saw that the land of Egypt was backward and primitive, inhabited by barbarous cannibals. In an effort to bring civilization to the Egyptians, he traveled among them, teaching them about agriculture.

A major myth surrounds Osiris. According to ancient texts, Osiris traveled to other lands to bring them the benefits of civilization. While he was gone, his brother Seth plotted to take over the throne. He and a band of conspirators later murdered Osiris, placed his body in a coffin, and cast the coffin into the Nile. After much searching, Isis found the body, but Seth then tore the body into pieces. He scattered the pieces throughout Egypt, but Isis found them. After she reassembled them, Osiris was magically reborn and lived long enough to father a new king. After his death, he was king of the afterlife, where he admitted people to a fertile, green land.

In time, the life, death, and rebirth of Osiris became symbolic of the cycle of the seasons in Egypt. His death represented the receding of the Nile and the dry season; his rebirth represented the flooding and the growth of crops. This cycle of death and rebirth was also seen as symbolic of the sun, which daily "dies" and then is "reborn" the following day. Further, Osiris's battle with Seth came to be seen as symbolic of the eternal struggle between the green, fertile area around the Nile and the surrounding harsh deserts.

To celebrate Osiris, the Egyptians held annual festivals. A festival called the Fall of the Nile was a period of mourning; during this festival the Egyptians brought gifts to the banks of the Nile and expressed their grief. When the river flooded again, another festival to Osiris celebrated the event, commemorating Isis's location of his body. Shrines to Osiris were thrown into the river, and priests officiated at celebrations signifying that Osiris's body had been located again. The Egyptians also believed that Osiris entered a person's body when he or she ate the vegetables of his creation. Isis became a model of womanhood, who taught women to weave cloth and grind grain.

Administration

Agriculture in ancient Egypt was a highly organized activity. Most people were involved in agriculture in some way. Nobles and wealthy people often owned the land that was farmed and supervised the activities of farmers, who worked the land in exchange for shelter and food. Because land was owned privately (though, in theory, it was owned by the gods and therefore by the pharaoh as the gods' representative), some landowners became wealthier than others, and class divisions inevitably came about, sometimes leading to conflicts such as boundary disputes that had to be resolved. In other cases, people rented land from wealthy landowners, paying them with a percentage of their crops. The Egyptian government also enlisted people to work on the dikes, canals, and other components of the irrigation system. This work was in effect a type of tax called corvée, or unpaid labor exacted in place of taxes by a governmental authority, usually for public works.

The economic system of ancient Egypt was a command economy, that is, an economy controlled and directed by the state. The state employed a large class of scribes, surveyors, inspectors, and supervisors to manage agricultural activity. For example, keeping track of land boundaries was difficult, because the Nile River valley flooded each year, changing the contours of the land, so surveyors had to be employed each year to remeasure and mark out fields with stones. An oath had to be taken that the boundary was correct: "I swear by the great god that is in heaven that the right boundary stone has been set up."

Establishing boundaries was important, because the output of each field determined how much tax, in the form of a percentage of the crops, the landowner or farmer had to pay to the government. The amount of this tax varied, with higher taxes assessed on the most fertile land, a smaller amount on higher and less productive land, and a still smaller amount on the highest and least productive land. Generally, it is estimated that the tax amounted to about 10 percent of output, usually assessed as a number of bags per unit of land. The bureaucrats who measured and surveyed the fields also assessed the tax and were responsible for collecting the grain, storing it in local and regional granaries, and distributing it as needed throughout the year.

Ancient Egypt experienced dry periods, when the Nile did not rise as much as it did in other years and agricultural output was reduced. In general, though, the Nile Valley produced an abundance of food. This surplus enabled the state to support traders, merchants, craftsmen, civil servants, priests, an army, scribes, and others who contributed to the rise of Egyptian civilization. Without this surplus, people would have been limited to subsistence agriculture, or agriculture that provided just enough food for a family to stay alive. Further, the abundance of grain enabled ancient Egypt to engage in trade with neighboring regions. By trading its surplus of grain, the nation was able to acquire many commodities, including lumber, metals, precious and semiprecious stones, minerals, and the like.

Horticulture

The word *agriculture* refers to the cultivation of major crops such as grains, usually grown in large fields and harvested a single time at the end of a growing season. In contrast, the word *horticulture* is used to refer to the cultivation of flowers, fruits, vegetables, and ornamental plants, usually in smaller family plots of ground. Because these plots were not irrigated in the same way as the fields were in ancient Egypt, water typically had to be carried in by hand. Also, because the soil was poor without the silt carried by the flooding Nile, it had to be fertilized. Some families kept pigeons in cages and used the birds' droppings to fertilize their gardens.

The ancient Egyptians devoted considerable energy to horticulture. The earliest record of a private garden dates to 2200 B.C.E. The ground surrounding nearly every home had trees that were thought to be the dwelling places of spirits and gods. Additionally, the Egyptians cultivated flowerbeds; if space was limited, they grew flowers in pots or troughs. Flowers included poppies, cornflowers, irises, jasmine, chrysanthemums, ivy, mandrakes, mallows, lotus lilies, and larkspurs. Families grew fruit such as dates, as well as oil-bearing trees such as the baq, or horseradish tree. Grapes were a popular crop, used in making wine. Vegetables and herbs such as lettuce, cabbage, cucumbers, radishes, beans, leeks, garlic, dill, chickpeas, and lentils were routinely grown for family consumption. The flower gardens attracted bees, so honey was a staple in the ancient Egyptians' diet. Many gardens had ornamental ponds with fish.

The ancient Egyptians also made use of trees, shrubs, and other plants that grew wild. These plants were used to produce dyes as well as wickerwork, including sandals, mats, baskets, and similar items. In marshlands the Egyptians found papyrus used to make not only paper but also amulets thought to have magical powers. Bouquets of papyrus symbolized joy and victory.

THE MIDDLE EAST

BY AMY HACKNEY BLACKWELL

Agriculture first appeared in the Near East. The world's first agricultural societies appeared between 8000 and 6000 B.C.E. in an area called the Fertile Crescent, which stretches over 1,200 miles from the Mediterranean coast of Israel and Lebanon to the Zagros Mountains in Iraq and Iran. Climate change made agriculture possible. At the end of the last ice age in about 11,000 B.C.E. the climate in the Fertile Crescent grew warmer and wetter. This improved growing conditions for many local grains and other plants. Grasslands and forests expanded, increasing the available habitats for both animals and humans. The local grazing animals became more plentiful along the edges of woodlands; the most common game animals were wild sheep and goats, two species of gazelles, onagers (wild donkeys), aurochs (wild cattle), and several kinds of deer. Small mammals and waterfowl also thrived in the improved climate. Wild grasses such as einkorn wheat, wild emmer, and wild barley grew more abundant. These local plants and animals served as the raw materials that humans domesticated.

Humans had been in the area for thousands of years. They lived as hunter-gatherers, feeding themselves by gathering wild plant foods and killing wild animals. The increased availability of wild cereals and wild animals for meat allowed them to expand their populations throughout the Fertile Crescent. Groups of humans tailored their lifestyles to local conditions. In the eastern part of the region, hunter-gatherers moved up and down the mountains, depending on the season. In the spring they pursued herds of wild sheep and goats up to higher elevations, harvesting wild grasses along the way. In the winter they moved to lower elevations along with their game animals. In the more temperate zone of the western Mediterranean, groups of hunter-gatherers lived in permanent settlements, harvesting the more than 40 species of wild plants that grew around them and hunting and trapping local animals. These settlements were the precursors to the permanent agricultural settlements established in the next two to four millennia. Humans did not switch from hunting and gathering to settled agriculture instantly. The transition took centuries and occurred at different times in different places throughout the region.

Fertile Crescent Crops

The Fertile Crescent was an ideal location for developing agriculture. Its climate was characterized by long, hot, dry summers and wet winters that rarely got too cold. The seed-bearing plants that grew there just after the last ice age were perfect for cultivation. They were annuals, which meant they completed their life cycles in one year; because the plants' lives were so short, they put all their energy into making many big seeds and little into making stalks or leaves. They were productive enough even in their undomesticated state to allow hunter-gatherers to live in permanent settlements largely supported by wild plants. They were easy to cultivate because they did not have complicated fertilization requirements.

The Fertile Crescent had a large number of wild grains suitable for human consumption, all of them nutritious and high in calories. Eight separate crops launched human agriculture in this area. Historians call them the eight founder crops. They included three grains: emmer wheat, einkorn wheat, and barley; four legumes: lentils, peas, chickpeas, and bitter vetch; and flax, a fibrous plant that furnishes the raw material for linen. Historians know little about the domestication of the legumes and flax but have found a great deal of information on the domestication of the grains.

The grains were the first cultivated plants. Emmer wheat, einkorn wheat, and barley are all grasses that are so-called edge species in the wild, growing naturally on fine-grained soil at the edges of woodlands at high elevations. All three of them appear to have been domesticated in a relatively short period of time, between 8000 and 7800 B.C.E. Emmer was first cultivated around Jericho in the Jordan River valley and near Damascus in present-day Syria around 7800 B.C.E. Einkorn wheat grew throughout the Anatolian Peninsula, and hunter-gatherers are known to have harvested it between 9000 and 8000 B.C.E. Farmers were cultivating it near Damascus and Jericho around the same time as they were domesticating emmer.

Barley grew wild throughout the entire Fertile Crescent. Archaeologists have found evidence of domesticated barley near Damascus and Jericho between 7800 and 7600 B.C.E., and it is clear that farmers of the time were gradually selecting barley types to maximize yields. Wild barley has two rows of grains on its heads. The earliest farmers grew this type of barley, but by 7500 B.C.E. they were also growing a denser type of barley with six rows of grain per head. Farmers in other areas did not manage to produce the denser six-rowed barley and continued to grow the two-rowed type along with emmer and einkorn.

Grains soon became the staple of Fertile Crescent diets, furnishing the majority of calories for agricultural peoples in the region. In addition, grains kept well in the dry climate of the region, providing a steady supply of food year-round. People ate wheat by grinding it into meal and cooking it as bread or porridge. Legumes were also an important food source. Lentils and peas were domesticated around the same time as grains. Both grew wild in the Fertile Crescent, and hunter-gatherers had been gathering them long before they were domesticated. Wild peas and lentils grow in pods that usually explode to spray the seeds outward, but some mutant pods do not. Humans selected these nonpopping pods as the most desirable because they kept the peas and lentils conveniently packaged until they could be picked. Peas and lentils are high in protein, keep for a long time when dried, and can be cooked quickly by boiling.

The First Agricultural Settlements

The first places in the world where humans deliberately planted seeds in order to harvest their crops in the future were isolated to a small area called the Levantine Corridor, a six- to twenty-five-mile-wide corridor along the Jordan River extending from the Damascus basin to Jericho and neighboring sites. Each of these sites had a high water table and high water supply. Early farmers had no irrigation systems and so conditions had to be optimal for them to succeed. As of 8000 B.C.E. people were clearly collecting wild grasses to eat their seeds. They already had the equipment used to process grains: flint sickles for harvesting, flat grinding stones, and bowls.

Cuneiform tablet recording barley rations given to workers and their families at the temple of the goddess Bau, about 2350–2200 B.C.E., from Tello (ancient Girsu), southern Iraq (© The Trustees of the British Museum)

At the site called Netiv Hagdud in Israel, archaeologists have found evidence of the first steps toward genuine agriculture. Some 9,800 years ago a single type of domesticated two-rowed barley appeared along with the wild grains people continued to harvest. This is the earliest known example of people deliberately transitioning from gathering to cultivation. Archaeologists are not sure exactly why people began settling down and cultivating crops, but they believe it was tied to a growing population that made it harder for people to wander from place to place without running into competitors. As for what inspired people to begin experimenting with putting seeds in the ground, that, too, is unknown. Once people settled in one place and built structures, they naturally developed rules for running their new social structure. They had time to make tools to facilitate gathering of plant foods and were not constrained by the need to move them.

The earliest farmers were Stone Age people; they did not know how to work metal into tools so they made tools out of stone, bone, wood, and clay. Ancient farmers at first dug the soil with pointed wooden sticks called digging sticks. These were soon replaced by hoes with stone blades and wooden handles. As farms grew larger, farmers began using wooden plows to churn up the soil; plows could dig much deeper than hand tools. The first plows were pulled by humans; after about 6000 B.C.E. people began using oxen to pull plows. Farmers harvested their crops with sickles made of stone. They stored seeds and dried beans in containers made of baked clay. In order to eat grain, people had to grind it into meal or flour, which could be made into flat bread. Grinding wheat was extremely laborious work, done entirely by women. They used a device called a quern, a primitive mill made of a flat piece of stone. They would place a handful of wheat on the quern and crush it with another stone.

Domesticating Animals

Long before they began domesticating animals, humans had contact with wild animals that they hunted and trapped for meat and leather. Sheep and goats in particular were abundant in the region, and both of them are known to have been domesticated in the Fertile Crescent by around 8000 B.C.E. Pigs and cattle followed suit about 2,000 years later, around 6000 B.C.E. In choosing animals to domesticate, people observed the habits of the mammals that shared their environment. They noticed which animals were incurably dangerous or bad-tempered. They also noticed which animals had a dominance structure that could be manipulated. Dogs, horses, pigs, and sheep all follow leaders and care about their rank within their group. Humans substituted themselves for animal leaders and, after several generations of selective breeding, soon had domesticated animals.

Sheep and goats became the first domestic animals, because they share several characteristics not held by other local large mammals that were equally populous, such as gazelles or onagers. Sheep and goats are fast growing and easily fed on local vegetation. They are herd animals that imprint on leaders, meaning that an entire group of animals will imitate the actions of the animal they accept as their leader. In this way they could be trained to follow humans. They do not mind living in crowded conditions with limited mobility. They are relatively easy to tame. Humans began taking over herds as their own, persuading the animals that they were their leaders, herding them to and from pastures, and manipulating the populations to maximize human interests. They had already been following herds for millennia, going up and down mountains with goats and sheep, so they knew a great deal about herd behavior. Once they had taken possession of the herds, people furthered their advantage with selective techniques. They killed off aggressive animals or poor milkers and allowed the animals with more desirable traits to live and breed.

Archaeologists know that animals were domesticated between 8000 and 6000 B.C.E. The numbers of sheep and goat bones have been found to increase dramatically in more recent layers at archaeological digs. Domesticated animals of this period are smaller than their wild counterparts, partly because people eliminated the larger and more aggressive males and partly because the beasts did not eat as much as they did in the wild. Another reason for the smaller size of bones is that domestic herds contain many more females than males; herders wanted animals that could produce milk and young and that were less likely to attack them, so they kept females and slaughtered young males. Sheep were domesticated primarily in the area that is now Lebanon, southeastern Turkey, northwestern Syria, and southwestern Iran. Sheep needed good pastures and hilly grasslands to survive, so they did not thrive in other parts of the Fertile Crescent. Goats, on the other hand, are not as particular, and were domesticated throughout the Near East.

Another domestic animal that soon became common was the pig. Wild pigs ranged throughout the region. Although pigs do not live in herds, they have a dominance structure that allows humans to take control of them. They eat anything, grow quickly, and produce large litters frequently. Pig bones from about 8,000 years ago show the same decrease in size seen with sheep and goats, indicating that they were under human management. It appears that pigs were domesticated in the central part of the Fertile Crescent, modern Lebanon, Syria, and eastern Turkey and spread to other parts of the region already domesticated. They never became as common as sheep or goats. Cattle also appear in the archaeological record. These cattle were bred from the large and dangerous aurochs, wild cattle that roamed the region and had been hunted for thousands of years. Smaller cattle bones appear in the Fertile Crescent about 6000 to 5000 B.C.E.

Societal Changes following the Introduction of Agriculture

Once humans had learned the basics of agriculture and animal husbandry, their lives changed dramatically. Domesticating plants and animals allowed humans to feed more people with available resources. Farmers could feed between ten and 100 times more people than hunter-gatherers could do with the same amount of land. This was because they had concentrated edible plants in the available space, removing all competing plants that would decrease the available food. Livestock could make land more productive by adding manure to the soil to function as a natural fertilizer. Domestic animals also supplied people with milk and eggs and meat, and they helped humans cultivate larger plots of land by pulling plows. When animals were no longer useful for labor or the production of milk and eggs, people used their bodies, eating all the edible portions and using everything else for nonfood items, such as leather and bone tools. Agriculture and livestock furnished the raw material for cloth as well.

Growing crops forced people to stay in one place. Hunter-gatherers typically moved around frequently, and they had to be able to carry all their possessions with them every time they moved. In particular, mothers had to carry their young children. As a result, hunter-gatherer mothers could have only one baby every four years or so, spacing their births so that they never had to carry more than one child at a time.

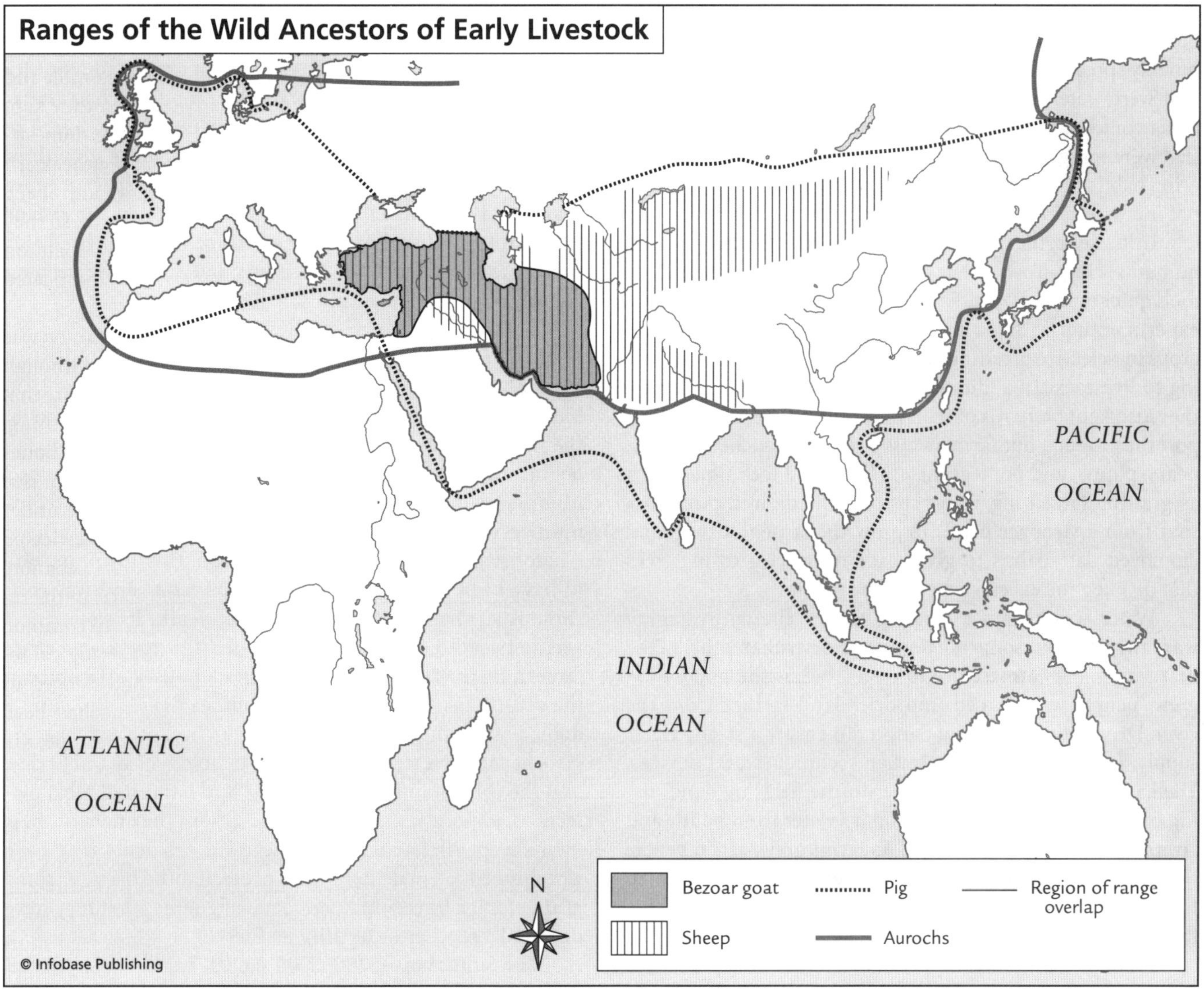

People in the ancient Middle East began domesticating wild sheep and goats around 8000 B.C.E. and wild cattle and pigs around 6000 B.C.E.

Farmers, on the other hand, could live in the same place year after year and did not have to worry about transporting young children long distances. Societies that settled down in one place were able to shorten their birth intervals from four years to about two. This meant that each woman could have more children than her hunter-gatherer counterpart, which in turn resulted in rapid population growth among farming communities. An increased population was actually an advantage to agricultural societies, because farming required large amounts of human labor.

Between 8000 and 4000 B.C.E. most settlements of the region resembled one another. They were all located near a source of water. They contained a number of houses built of mud bricks. The settlement was surrounded by wheat or barley fields and animals were pastured beyond them. Most people could not read and spent their days handling their basic needs: farming, hunting, cooking, hauling water, and tending children. Life in farming communities was guided by the agricultural calendar, with festivals and other events tied to agricultural events such as the harvest. Agricultural equipment gradually improved. People had started farming by hand, using stone or metal tools to work the soil. The invention of the wooden plow around 4000 B.C.E. made this job easier, and employing animals to pull the plow helped farmers produce even more crops.

Not all societies perfected every agricultural technique at once. Some regions specialized in growing one or two kinds of wheat. Others concentrated on herding goats. Regardless of which agricultural methods they used, however, communities did not depend entirely on agriculture for their sustenance. People continued to gather wild foods such as wild legumes, oats, wild alfalfa, and canary grass. They caught and ate fish, shellfish, turtle, migratory waterfowl, and other waterbirds. They continued to hunt gazelle, wild pigs, aurochs, and onagers. Agriculture supplemented their diets but did not necessarily dominate it. The cultivation of plants quickly spread from areas with a good water supply to regions that were watered only by sporadic rainfall, but these latter areas could not produce much in the way of crops. In areas that were marginal for agriculture, people kept up their gathering habits for thousands of years, and their populations did not increase as rapidly as those in more fertile regions.

In these fertile regions agriculture dramatically altered human society. Towns that could produce large amounts of food quickly grew larger. Farmers improved their techniques, experimenting with grains and developing more productive crops by selective breeding. They also applied selective breeding to livestock. In addition to growing wheat and legumes, they also kept orchards of fruit trees; dates were the most important product, but farmers also grew apples, cherries, figs, pears, plums, and pomegranates. They used techniques such as grafting (attaching a branch from the desired plant to a root from a stronger plant) to grow the strongest trees and employed date palms to give shade to lower-growing trees that disliked the excessive heat of the region.

Water was always a limiting factor. The entire region was fairly dry, but some portions were drier than others. The first settlements arose close to rivers, but as the population grew, people were forced into drier land farther from the river. Drought was always a danger. To ensure a steady water supply, farmers invented irrigation techniques and devices. The earliest farmers carried water to the fields by hand, using baked clay containers to scoop up water from ponds and rivers and transport it to crops. As farms grew larger, people began digging irrigation ditches to direct water from rivers to their fields. They also dammed rivers to prevent water from flowing downstream.

Farmers built several types of machines to help with the task of moving water from its natural sources to their fields. The *shaduf* (also spelled *shadoof*) was a counterweighted device that used leverage to lift water. It consisted of two upright posts made of wood and a wooden crosspiece with a weight on one end and a bucket on the other. The weight made it easy for farmers to lift water from ponds or wells and swing it up to their fields or irrigation ditches. Around 300 B.C.E. large farms began using more complicated devices such as the *saqiyah* and the Archimedean screw (also called Archimedes' screw). The *saqiyah* (also spelled *sakia* or *sakieh*) was a large wheel with buckets attached to its circumference and turned by oxen or donkeys. The buckets filled with water when they were submerged and then poured the water out into a pipe or other device that allowed it to flow where it was needed. The Archimedean screw consisted of a pipe placed on an inclined plane, with the lower end in the water. Inside the pipe a large screw turned, raising water as it moved; the water poured out of the top of the pipe into an irrigation ditch or channel.

Developments in irrigation increased agricultural productivity and heightened the need for food storage. Eventually farmers developed methods of storing grain. Agricultural surplus has many advantages for those who can store it; it can stave off famine in lean years, and it means that not everyone must work at farming. A successful agricultural community can support people who do not produce foods, such as craftsmen, scholars, soldiers, priests, bureaucrats, and rulers. The rise of agriculture was thus accompanied by the growth of towns and eventually cities. In a city there was space to store grain, and the inhabitants gradually developed the means to control and distribute it; kings and scribes facilitated this process, kings by making decisions and scribes by keeping records of grain storage and distribution.

Ancient Agricultural Societies

Agriculture spread throughout the Middle East; by 7500 B.C.E. people were cultivating crops throughout Anatolia, the Levant, Mesopotamia, and Persia, and grain crops were beginning to make inroads in Pakistan and the Caucasus Mountains. One ancient Near Eastern agricultural community was Çatalhüyük, a large settlement in southern Anatolia, near modern Konya, Turkey. This town appears to have been first settled around 7500 B.C.E. and was continuously inhabited for thousands of years. Its population was between 8,000 and 10,000 when the town was at its largest. Its residents lived in mud-brick houses with holes in the ceiling that served as both a source of ventilation and a door; people climbed ladders to get in and out. Archaeologists have found storage bins used to hold wheat and barley, and the inhabitants also grew peas and harvested local pistachios, almonds, and fruits. In addition, they herded their own sheep. Archaeologists believe the residents may have worshipped a female deity who protected the harvest; some grain storage bins contained female figurines that may have depicted a mother or fertility goddess.

The Sumerians (5200–2000 B.C.E.), based in the city of Sumer in southern Mesopotamia, developed the first major agricultural society. Sumerian farmers were constantly plagued by lack of water. The region received only about five inches of rain per year, and, thus, farmers had to invent ways of getting water to their fields. They dug canals and reservoirs and built dams. The Tigris was prone to flooding, and the canals required constant maintenance to remove silt and repair banks. Once a year, however, the farmers deliberately flooded their fields by opening the canals; this was to wet the soil in preparation for sowing. After the water drained back out, they released cattle into the fields to stomp out weeds and fertilize the ground with their manure. They used oxen to pull plows to break up the earth and then raked it to smooth it out before sowing their grain. During the fall farmers reaped their grain with stone or bronze sickles and bound it into sheaves before threshing and winnowing it to separate the grain from the straw and chaff. In addition to wheat and barley, Sumerians grew other crops, including lentils, chickpeas, onions, leeks, as well as garlic and lettuce.

As their population grew, Sumerians became an urban people; by 3000 B.C.E. nearly 90 percent of Sumerians lived in cities. Because of the limited water, settlement was concentrated on riverbanks. The population grew steadily but remained concentrated in the same areas because it was impossible to farm land more than a few miles from the river. Towns grew into cities, and the people of the cities developed governments that organized farming and food distribution. Most Sumerian people had to spend part of the year farming, but they did not own their own farms. They were working for their city, which oversaw all aspects of agriculture, from irrigation to sowing to harvest. The city also stored and distributed grain to its citizens. Sumer's communal agricultural form was successful enough to create an extensive empire based on its flourishing agriculture. The farmers produced such a surplus that the society could support a large army. The Sumerian Empire eventually encompassed some 21 known cities, each ruled by its own priest or king.

The farmers' practice of flooding the fields yearly gradually made the soil around Sumer get too salty for wheat. Toward the end of the Sumerian Empire they could grow only barley, which tolerates higher salinity. Eventually the region became too saline for successful agriculture, and the empire collapsed around 2000 B.C.E. By the Bronze Age (3500–1200 B.C.E.) agriculture supplied the majority of the food for residents of the ancient Near East. Some nomads depended largely on their herded sheep or goats, but most people lived in or near cities or towns and had to grow food to survive. During the Bronze Age people throughout the Middle East began using bronze to make farming implements. This was an improvement over the stone tools of the Neolithic Period. Bronze plows in particular were much more efficient than earlier wooden and stone plows.

The Bronze Age was characterized by the rise of city-states. Following the example of the Sumerians, societies organized themselves around cities and agriculture. The famous empires of the ancient Middle East—the Assyrians, Babylonians, Hittites, Hyksos, Persians, Parthians, and Israelites—were all founded on agriculture. They competed with one another for farm space and access to water, which are still points of contention in the region today. Governments in the region regulated irrigation very closely. The Iron Age began around 1200 B.C.E. People had already started working iron in Anatolia by the 14th century B.C.E., and iron became more prevalent than bronze throughout the region. Much iron was worked into weapons, but iron farming implements became common as well. Iron plows especially helped increase production. Farms grew smaller again as large cities disappeared during times of drought, such as the three-century-long drought that ended the Akkadian civilization around 2200 B.C.E.

The Persian Empire arose in Iran starting in 648 B.C.E. Persia, like most of the Middle East, was plagued by constant water shortages. Most years it received between four and eight inches of rain. In order to prevent this scant rainwater from evaporating, Persian engineers created a system of underground tunnels called *qanats* (also called *kareez*) that channeled water from water sources to the fields. The emperor Darius (r. 522–486 B.C.E.) encouraged research into irrigation and agriculture by rewarding skilled innovators. The government regulated irrigation systems and encouraged experimentation with new crops, introducing crops such as alfalfa, rice, pistachio, and sesame into various parts of the Persian Empire.

Agriculture continued to improve during the classical Greek and Roman periods. People had by now domesticated a larger variety of crops, including almonds, walnuts, grapes, and olives. Letting fields lie fallow from time to time improved the fertility of the soil. Under the Romans, wealthy landowners began creating large estates worked by slaves and running them as businesses. During the Roman Empire slaves from all over Europe and the Middle East went to Rome and then brought Roman agricultural techniques and crops back to their homelands. Many agricultural products were exported from the Middle East to Rome. These included wines, nuts, onions, and fruits such as the plums from Damascus and the dates from Jericho; nonfood exports included linen from Palestine and wool from Damascus.

ASIA AND THE PACIFIC

BY AMY HACKNEY BLACKWELL

Agriculture first appeared in China in about 6500 B.C.E. Although the Fertile Crescent of the Near East is generally credited with being the first place where agriculture arose, about 8000 B.C.E., China was not far behind. Just as wheat spread from the Middle East into Europe and brought with it cultural changes, rice spread through Asia. Although rice was not the only crop domesticated in Asia, it was by far the most important. Rice helped China grow into a well-organized, technologically advanced, and populous civilization while neighboring countries were still inhabited by hunter-gatherers using stone tools. People throughout the entire Asia Pacific region eventually acquired agriculture for themselves; however, the Chinese remained the dominant culture, thanks in part to their head start in growing rice.

ASIAN CROPS

Asians domesticated several staple crops and grew them throughout the Asia Pacific region. Rice, by far the most important staple, is a grassy plant with edible seeds. It comes in many varieties and can be grown almost anywhere, though most varieties thrive in water. To eat rice, people first remove the outer hull and possibly the bran as well, producing white rice. This milling process removes many of rice's nutrients, making it a source of calories and little else. People generally prepare rice by boiling it, though it can also be pounded into flour to make sticky dumplings. Rice originated in China and quickly spread throughout Asia, where it became the staple cereal of many people's diets. Today more than half the world's population eats rice as its main food. The people of

China, Japan, Southeast Asia, and India have all grown and consumed vast quantities of rice for thousands of years.

Millet, a grain that produces small seeds, is currently grown worldwide both as food for humans and as fodder for animals. Millet contains about 11 percent protein, about the same amount as wheat. It does not rise like wheat, so it cannot be used to make leavened bread. People generally grind it into flour to make flat bread or boil it into porridge. Millet was first domesticated in China around the same time as rice.

A leafy plant that grows from a tuber, taro is much like a potato. People grow taro mainly for its root, though they eat the leaves as well. Taro plants, also called elephant ears, look like caladiums, which are common garden plants. Taro was one of the first plants to be cultivated, and it is still grown throughout Southeast Asia and the Pacific islands. Its ancestors grow wild in much of tropical Asia, and tubers are easy to propagate by cutting them into pieces and burying them. Taro needs a steady supply of water, but most of the region has ample rainfall. Taro root is very starchy; people eat it mainly for calories. It also contains some fiber, vitamin B_6, and manganese. Taro must be cooked before eating, because the raw plant can damage the stomach and intestines. Generally, ancient people boiled it into a kind of porridge. Taro leaves are full of vitamins and supplied many necessary nutrients to peoples' diets.

Asian nations grow a huge variety of fruits and vegetables, many of which were domesticated thousands of years ago. In tropical areas people long ago cultivated bananas, oranges, coconuts, breadfruits, durians, mangoes, papayas, lemons, grapefruits, sago palms, cucumbers, and jackfruits, as well as many others. In China people grew mustard greens, daikons, numerous beans, snow peas, eggplants, cabbage plants such as bok choy, and melons. These vegetables and fruits added color and nutrients to an otherwise bland and nutrient-poor diet composed mainly of starches.

The soybean has been grown in Asia for many centuries. People first grew soybeans not for food but as a nitrogen-fixing crop; they grew the plants and then plowed them back into the fields to prepare the soil for other crops. Around the first century C.E. people discovered methods of fermentation and used those to form soy into a variety of food products, such as miso, soy sauce, and tofu. After that discovery, soy became an important source of protein for many people in China, Korea, and Japan. Asian people from ancient times to the present have obtained most of their calories and nutrients from vegetable foods. Animal protein in the ancient world came in large part from domestic pigs and chickens, which provided both eggs and meat. People also caught fish and hunted for wild birds and other game. In some areas people ate rodents and insects.

The Origins of Agriculture in China

Agriculture in China developed independently in two very different locations. Farmers domesticated rice along the Yangtze River in southern China between 6500 and 4500 B.C.E. During approximately the same time period, farmers in northern China concentrated on the cultivation of millet on the banks of the Yellow River.

The Yangtze River runs through the southern part of China and enters the Pacific Ocean near the site of the modern city Shanghai. The Yangtze basin is warm and wet and has a stable temperate to subtropical climate. Rain falls year-round, though about half of the annual rainfall occurs in the three months of summer. The lowlands around the river become inundated with shallow water every summer, and this water drains away by autumn. Major floods, droughts, cold snaps, and other extremes of weather are uncommon. Such a temperate climate made the Yangtze basin an ideal location for early experiments in agriculture.

The first farmers had to work with plants that already grew in the area. Wild rice existed throughout southern China and Southeast Asia before it was cultivated. Archaeologists and botanists have tried to identify the wild ancestor of modern rice, but they have had only limited success; rice has been so widely cultivated and moved so far across Asia that it is impossible to tell which ancient grain was its ancestor. There are still annual (living only one year) and perennial (living several years) varieties of rice growing in South Asia, and scientists have based their theories about the domestication of rice on these plants.

Modern wild rice varieties live in places that flood yearly. They start growing when the land is covered with shallow water, up to about 18 inches deep. When the rainy season ends, they release their seeds, which scatter on the drying ground and lie dormant until the floods arrive the next year. The earliest cultivated types of rice, then, were plants that grew in the border zone between land that was permanently dry and land that was always covered with water.

Ancient people lived as hunter-gatherers, hunting for wild game and fish and gathering wild plant foods. Wild rice was one of the foods they collected and ate. They would have noticed the life cycle of the rice plant, following the progress of its growth through the yearly floods. Farming probably resulted from attempts to increase the area on which wild rice grew. Historians believe that people built circular dams to trap floodwaters, flooding land that had previously stayed dry and allowing rice to grow there. They would break down the dams at the end of the wet season to let the ground dry and permit the rice seeds to germinate. They might have further increased the rice crop by scattering wild seeds they had collected elsewhere inside the artificially flooded area. The next step was the deliberate harvesting and sowing of the seeds that grew in these enclosures, sometimes called *rice paddies*.

The oldest-known site of rice cultivation was Pengtoushan on the Liying Plain; scientists believe its inhabitants were growing rice around 6400 B.C.E. Hangzhou Bay, just south of the mouth of the Yangtze, was the site of a large society that grew up around rice cultivation about 4500 B.C.E. People grew rice and other aquatic crops in the lowlands. They lived in houses built of reeds and clay placed atop mounds to keep them out of the floods. They kept domestic dogs, pigs, and water buffaloes. They made agricultural tools out of wood and the bones of their animals; for example, they constructed shovels with wooden handles and blades made from water buffalo shoulder blades. Growing rice was very labor intensive, and most of the people in the settlement would have spent much of their time sowing rice, tending plants, and harvesting grains. Upriver a collection of lakes formed the center of the settlements of the Hubei Basin. These towns arose between 4000 and 3000 B.C.E. The people there used stone sickles to harvest rice, which was then stored in ceramic bowls.

While southern Chinese farmers were domesticating rice, their counterparts in northern China were conducting their own experiments with millet. The Yellow River is north of the Yangtze and is separated from it by the Qin Ling Mountains. The land surrounding the Yellow River is buffeted by the cold, dry winds blowing east from the Central Asian plains. The climate is harsh and unstable, prone to droughts and unexpected violent floods. Summer rains are unreliable, and winters can be severe. The plants native to this region were drought-resistant grains adapted to growing with little rainfall. Hunter-gatherers in the area knew these grains and had been collecting them as food for centuries. In addition to grains, they collected walnuts, hazelnuts, berries, acorns, and dates, and they caught fish and killed deer.

Two species of millet, broomcorn and foxtail, both of which need little water to survive, were chosen for cultivation in northern China. Archaeologists know that people were deliberately growing millet, because the settlements they have excavated are too large to be anything but agricultural communities and because they have found many millet grains on the sites. The earliest evidence of millet agriculture is that of the Peiligang culture in northern China. These people lived near the Yellow River starting about 7000 B.C.E. By around 4500 B.C.E. the Peiligang people were living in oval-shaped towns surrounded by protective ditches. Within this enclosed space families lived in circular houses with thatched roofs arranged around a central square. They stored their food in pits and kept animals in enclosures in the main plaza. Dead people were buried outside the town. Society was organized according to kinship, and the year's work was planned according to the agricultural calendar. This pattern of social organization continued unaltered in rural China up until well into the 20th century. Millet was never as dominant a grain as rice, but it did spread to Japan by 4000 B.C.E. and Korea by about 3000 B.C.E.

Asian Animals

Domesticated animals were important to the ancient people in both northern and southern China because they offered a reliable source of protein and could provide labor as well. The earliest evidence for the domestication of chickens comes from the Yellow River region about 5400 to 5200 B.C.E. Pigs appear at archaeological sites in the same area at about the same time. Some historians have suggested that domesticated pigs could have been brought to China from Mesopotamia, but others think it more likely that native pigs were domesticated independently in China by Chinese people. Water buffaloes seem to have been domesticated as draft animals in the Yellow River basin about 4500 B.C.E. Their use had spread to Southeast Asia by 1500 B.C.E.

Consequences of Agriculture

Once humans had learned the basics of agriculture and animal husbandry, their lives changed dramatically. These changes in Chinese life had major implications for people throughout Asia over the next several millennia. Farming had several advantages over hunting and gathering. Domesticating plants and animals allowed humans to feed more people with available resources. Domestic animals supplied people with milk, eggs, meat, fertilizer in the form of manure, and labor, pulling plows so that humans could cultivate more land. Crops and livestock also provided humans with nonfood items such as leather, feathers, and fabrics. Growing crops allowed people to stay in one place, instead of forcing them to move about regularly in pursuit of food as hunter-gatherers did. Farming women had babies more often than hunter-gatherer women, which resulted in rapid population

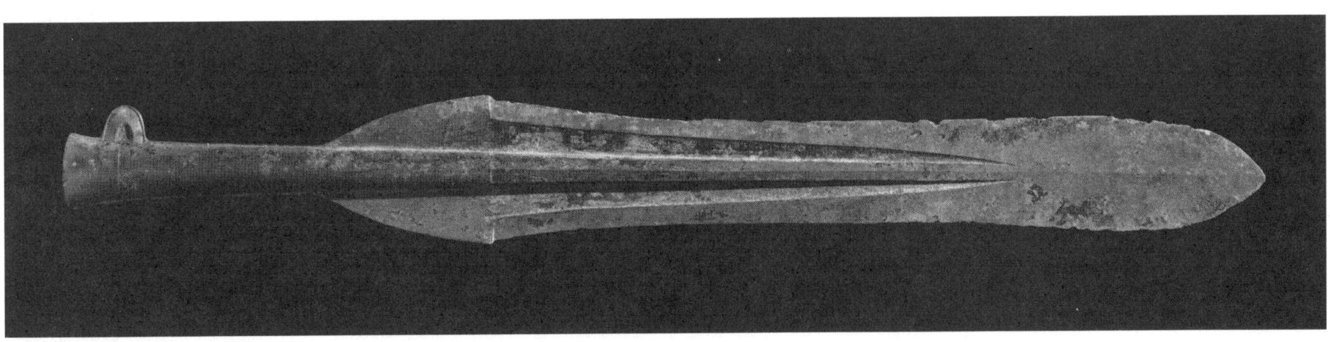

Ritual spear blade from Japan, from the Yayoi Period (ca. 300 B.C.E.–300 C.E.), made for burial in a ceremony thought to have been connected with agriculture (© The Trustees of the British Museum)

growth. More people meant more labor to work on farms and, hence, larger harvests.

Larger harvests in turn made for greater security. Agricultural surplus could stave off famine in lean years, and it meant that not everyone had to work at farming. A successful agricultural community could support people who did not produce foods, such as craftsmen, scholars, soldiers, priests, bureaucrats, and rulers. The rise of agriculture was accompanied by the growth of towns and eventually cities, as well as the development of increasingly elaborate belief systems and organized religion.

The early invention of agriculture in China gave the Chinese many advantages over people in neighboring countries, which resulted in China's coming to influence or dominate much of the Asia Pacific region. Rice quickly became the main cultivated grain throughout southern Asia. Rice did not travel on its own; it was carried by Chinese people who moved into Southeast Asia around 4000 B.C.E. It arrived in Thailand between 3000 and 2000 B.C.E. People were growing rice in Mahagara, India, on the upper Ganges about 1500 B.C.E., while the earliest known rice cultivation in the Philippines dates to about 1400 B.C.E. In Japan and Korea people began growing rice in about 1000 B.C.E. Archaeologists have found rice in a cave in Celebes, Indonesia, that was probably grown during the first century C.E.

Chinese culture became the standard against which all other regional cultures compared themselves. Korea and Japan not only adopted rice farming from China but also borrowed its system of writing. The modern Japanese language contains a large portion of Chinese words and characters, a relic of China's cultural conquest. Modern people from Thailand, Burma, and Laos are descended from southern Chinese ancestors. The previous occupants of the region, hunter-gatherers of different ethnic groups, were almost entirely eradicated.

Southeast Asia, India, and the Pacific Islands

Once humans had mastered agriculture, increasing populations led them to investigate other lands. Over the course of about 5,000 years, people managed to spread agriculture through the entire Asia Pacific region. Scientists are not sure that rice cultivation was the first form of farming to reach Southeast Asia. Southeast Asians have long grown a variety of roots and tubers, including taro, arrowroot, and yam, as well as fruits such as coconut, sago palm, citrus, banana, breadfruit, and jackfruit. No one knows exactly when these crops were domesticated. Some historians believe that agriculture arose independently in the region long before rice cultivation arrived around 3000 B.C.E. and that the first domesticated crops were replaced by rice farming. They theorize that roots and trees are plentiful in Southeast Asia and that they are easier to cultivate than rice and other grains, so it makes sense that people should have started farming them before rice arrived with the Chinese.

Scientists have found evidence of rice cultivation in Thailand that dates from 3000 to 2000 B.C.E. at the sites Ban Chiang and Non Nok Tha. The rice grains found at these sites are larger than the grains of wild rice, a common sign of domestication. The settlements themselves appear to have been permanent, and there are many ceramic and metal objects in graves, indicating a well-established society. Throughout Southeast Asia people modified the land to grow their crops. They terraced hills to make flat surfaces that would not erode. They dug drainage canals. They cut down trees and burned underbrush to make room for crops.

India received agriculture from both east and west. The earliest agricultural societies in India clustered around the major rivers, the Indus and the Ganges. The people of the Indus valley began cultivating Near Eastern grains such as emmer wheat and barley as early as 5000 B.C.E.; they also began growing cotton and lentils around the same time. Additionally they domesticated cattle, which became the main measure of wealth in their society. Along the Ganges, people began cultivating rice around 1500 B.C.E., and rice culture gradually traveled south through the subcontinent.

Most of the Indian subcontinent was subject to annual monsoons, which brought nearly all of the year's rainfall in a single season. Although in some areas the soil retained enough water from the monsoon to sustain crops year-round, in most of the region farmers had to use artificial irrigation, especially canals. Floods and droughts were perennial problems. Some years the monsoons did not bring much rainfall; in other years they brought far too much.

In New Guinea people began experimenting with agriculture around 7000 B.C.E. This makes New Guinea one of the few locations in the world where agriculture arose independently. Historians believe that humans invented agriculture in several places; the Fertile Crescent of the Middle East and the rivers of China are two of the most significant cradles of agriculture. Agriculture spread from these places as people moved around, bringing along with them seeds, tools, and expertise. In a few places, however, people invented farming by experimenting with wild seeds or roots and gradually domesticating them, creating plants that could grow only with human assistance. New Guinea is one of the places where this happened. Native New Guineans had no contact with the rest of Asia, so external agricultural techniques could not be brought in. The island was home to several wild plants that lent themselves to agricultural experimentation. Although most people on the island in the eighth millennium B.C.E. lived as hunter-gatherers, early farmers had begun growing bananas, nuts, grasses, and green vegetables. They also grew breadfruit, sugarcane, yam, taro, and other roots. Root vegetables that survived in the hot, wet climate predominated.

New Guinea has several natural limitations that prevented farmers from growing other major crops, notably grains. No grains like wheat or barley are native to the island, so farmers had no opportunity to domesticate them. New Guinea also lacked large mammals; thus the human residents had nothing to domesticate. This meant that they had to depend on wild animals such as fish for protein. As the population of New Guinea grew, people came to subsist entirely on the food they grew. The local landscape could not support many hunter-gatherers. Taro made up the bulk of the local diet, but it contains almost no protein and few other nutrients. This locally grown diet was deficient in many ways and caused children to grow up malnourished. New Guineans ate small rodents, frogs, spiders, and insects in an effort to consume some protein; they even ate the bodies of their dead, but these measures could not make up for a general lack of nutrients.

Over the years humans traveled by boat to the far-flung islands of the Pacific. They started with the islands closest to the mainland, near southern China and Southeast Asia. Taiwan had human inhabitants by 3500 B.C.E. and Java by 2000 B.C.E. Borneo was inhabited by 1600 B.C.E. In 1200 B.C.E. people settled in Samoa. Pacific peoples made it to Hawaii and Easter Island by 500 C.E. Wherever humans settled, they adapted their agricultural practices to local conditions. The staple crops of most Pacific islands were those of New Guinea: taros, yams, bananas, coconuts, breadfruits, and other tropical fruits and vegetables. To augment their diet, many Polynesian islanders kept domestic dogs as a source of meat.

Australia was the only large landmass that humans failed to turn to agricultural production. It has an extremely dry climate, infertile soil, and unpredictable extremes of weather. No suitable wild plants grew there for humans to domesticate. None of Australia's large mammals were amenable to domestication; kangaroos are notoriously dangerous, and the other large marsupials that lived in Australia during the last ice age all became extinct soon afterward. Aboriginal Australians did modify their environment by burning it from time to time, which drove out game animals and made some edible grasses and ferns grow better, but they did not sow and harvest their own crops. These techniques were a way of maximizing the foods they could collect as hunter-gatherers, which remained the way of life for Aboriginal Australians into the 20th century.

EUROPE

BY AMY BOGAARD

Farmers across Europe face a wide range of climatic conditions. Mild winters and hot, dry summers characterize southern regions bordering the Mediterranean; harsh winters and hot summers are typical in central Europe; and the Atlantic coastline experiences moderate seasonal shifts. Climatic differences underlie broad regional contrasts in crops. Plants that cannot withstand frosty winters (such as chickpeas and olive trees) are confined to the Mediterranean region, while hardier crops (such as barley, rye, and oats) can be grown in the far north. The timing of farming tasks is also related to climate. The winter rainfall of the Mediterranean encourages farmers to sow their crops in the autumn, while the long, cold winters of northern Scandinavia necessitate later sowing, in the spring.

Climatic conditions alone, however, do not dictate which crops to grow or when and how to sow them. Nor do they determine the amount of care taken to tend crops throughout the growing season, the area of land planted, and so on. Rather, a series of social factors, reflecting the particular nature of a society, come into play. One factor is the relationship between the producers and the consumers of crops: Do farmers grow crops for their own use or for others who do not farm? A related factor is land ownership: Is land held communally, divided up by family, or controlled by an elite few? Available labor, patterns of settlement, culinary tradition, and ideology are also important factors. Study of early agriculture in Europe is thus concerned not only with adaptation to diverse environments but also with changing social conditions. In some cases, new social formations emerged through constraints and opportunities introduced by the farming way of life.

The Emergence and Spread of Agriculture in Europe

The earliest agriculture in Europe appeared around 9,000 years ago (ca. 7000 B.C.E.) in the Aegean, on the eastern side of the Greek mainland and on the island of Crete. The early emergence of agriculture in the Aegean reflects its proximity and environmental similarity to the area of the Near East, where agriculture and herding began. This area is known as the Fertile Crescent: an arc of grassland and open oak-pistachio woodland curving round from the Mediterranean coast in the west (modern Israel, Jordan, Lebanon, Syria, and southeast Turkey) to the Zagros mountain range in the east (northern Iraq and Iran). By 8000 B.C.E. agriculture and herding were established in the Fertile Crescent and on the nearby island of Cyprus in the eastern Mediterranean.

Cultivation of a range of crops (cereals, such as wheat and barley; pulses, such as lentils and peas; and flax or linseed) and herding of animals (sheep, goats, pigs, and cattle) were linked practices that spread together from the Near East to Europe. The crops that formed part of this package complement one another in terms of nutrition (cereals and pulses together providing complete protein, for example) and ecology (allowing rotation of crops on the same land). Similarly, the grazing preferences of sheep, goats, and cattle target different components of vegetation, while pigs consume a variety of settlement waste. It appears unlikely, on current evidence, that any members of this original set of Neolithic crops and livestock were domesticated independently in Europe.

Agriculture and herding spread into Europe by two major routes: a land route that followed river valleys up the Balkan Peninsula and into central Europe and a maritime route along the northern Mediterranean coast. Farmers along these two routes emphasized different types of cereals: Those on the land route grew mainly the hulled wheats einkorn and emmer, while those on the Mediterranean coastal route focused on naked wheat. By around 6000 B.C.E. these dispersals had reached the Great Hungarian Plain of central Europe and southern Italy in the western Mediterranean; 500 years later farming and herding had spread as far as southwestern Germany and the Iberian Peninsula. By around 5000 B.C.E. farming and herding were practiced all along the Mediterranean coast and across much of the European interior. After a pause of about 1,000 years, agriculture was eventually adopted in southern Scandinavia, the Atlantic fringe of western Europe, and the British Isles. This conspicuous halt in the spread of agriculture probably reflects the tenacity of local hunter-gatherer communities and their way of life in resource-rich coastal environments, though climatic factors may also have played a role. Farming did not reach some regions of northern Europe until the first millennium C.E.

Scholars are divided on the question of whether agriculture and herding spread as a consequence of the movement of people or as novel practices imparted from one group to another. A combination of the two processes is a strong possibility, but in either case the nature of agricultural and the nature of herding practices are equally important for understanding these early farming communities. These everyday routines subsequently shaped the development of later prehistoric communities.

As new practices that spread together into Europe, early farming and herding were closely associated from the outset. The most common domesticated animal of the early Neolithic in the Near East and in adjacent parts of southeast Europe (Greece and the Balkans) was the sheep. The zooarchaeologist Paul Halstead has pointed out that sheep are particularly suitable for integration with farming, since they provide manure for maintaining soil fertility and are used to graze fields of unripe cereals in order to regulate crop growth. Halstead developed a model of small-scale, labor-intensive farming for Neolithic Greece that incorporates manure from livestock and rotation between crops as well as careful tilling, weeding, and watering during the growing season. This model, which has relevance across Neolithic Europe, has largely replaced earlier theories based on the idea of shifting cultivation, or slash-and-burn (short-term cultivation on newly cleared forest soil, followed by a shift to new plots due to soil exhaustion). Current zooarchaeological and archaeobotanical evidence from various parts of Europe suggests that early farming was of a sustainable type, relying on high inputs of time and effort to create small but very productive cultivation areas, in some ways resembling gardens. Early European agriculture, therefore, was more akin to horticulture (small-scale cultivation of diverse garden crops) than to the large-scale cultivation of grain crops that is dominant in Europe today.

Viewed from above, the landscapes of Neolithic Europe would appear largely to have retained the extensive woodlands that developed after the end of the last ice age. Early farming communities were largely confined to areas with fertile, easily tilled soils. The small scale of cultivation did not require extensive clearance, and nearby woodland was carefully managed to provide a renewable source of firewood and timber.

The crop and livestock package that initially spread to Europe was altered as it passed from the Mediterranean climate of mild, wet winters and hot, dry summers to the frosty, harsh winters of central Europe. These changes are visible as a reduction in the number of original Neolithic crops from the Near East, since certain crops (such as chickpeas) could not be grown successfully in colder climates, and as a general shift from sheep to cattle, which are better adapted to colder climatic conditions. New additions to the original crop spectrum also began to appear: The opium poppy, native to the western Mediterranean, was probably exploited for both its oil-rich seeds and its narcotic properties.

Although agriculture continued to play a major role in Neolithic communities of central and western Europe, there are archaeological indications that it was increasingly supplemented by more intensive use of livestock, in particular for dairy products. Zooarchaeological data on cattle-culling patterns (the ages at which male and female animals were slaughtered) and recent analysis of organic residues on pottery suggest that milking was practiced in various parts of central and northwestern Europe during the earlier Neolithic.

Milking is one example of the exploitation of secondary products from animals: resources that can be extracted repeatedly during the animal's lifetime, such as milk, wool or hair, and muscle (draft) power for pulling a sledge, plow, or cart. As early as the seventh millennium B.C.E. on Crete (at Neolithic Knossos) there is evidence for the use of cattle as draft animals, which leaves characteristic deformations and wear patterns on certain parts of the skeleton. Early cattle traction in Crete, and probably elsewhere in Europe, focused on cows—female animals kept into their advanced years for the purpose of reproduction and milking and not specifically raised and bred for the purpose of pulling a cart or a plow. These early draft cattle, therefore, were not the powerful ox teams of later times, and their impact on the nature of farming was limited, though they would have spared human labor to an appreciable degree.

A detailed snapshot of Neolithic farming life in central Europe is provided by Hornstaad-Hörnle, a village on the western shore of Lake Constance in southwest Germany and one of many prehistoric lakeshore villages in the Alpine Foreland (the foothills of the Alps). Ten years after the first houses were built (in 3915 B.C.E., according to tree-ring dating), the village burned down shortly after harvest time, preserving large amounts of stored crops in each house. These household crop stores, along with similar tool kits found in each dwelling, suggest that each family produced its own food. Farming tools recovered at the site included angled wooden digging sticks and the remains of a sieve for removing weed seeds and chaff from the threshed and winnowed crop. Weed seeds found as occasional contaminants in the crop stores indicate effective and careful tillage and high fertility, as would be expected in small-scale intensive cultivation located near the settlement. It appears that cereals were harvested by cutting with a harvesting knife about a hand's breadth below the cereal ear and spread out in the roof space of each house for drying. After threshing outside the village, the crop would be processed for food preparation on a daily basis. Carbonized lumps of cereal-based food were found, including porridge-like food of ground wheat grains and bread of finely milled flour. Botanical remains in preserved human feces indicate that people ate a combination of cereals and wild plant foods.

The clear example at Hornstaad-Hörnle of what the anthropologist Marshall Sahlins called the domestic mode of production (production by the household for its own use) provides insights into the social consequences of early agriculture in Neolithic Europe. Households undoubtedly cooperated in certain activities, and similarity of house layout and size reflects relative equality between families. Nevertheless, imbalances in household production must have occurred, and there is evidence of differences between houses in access to rare goods, such as copper objects. The very insistence on house uniformity may have functioned to discourage emerging inequalities and tensions between families. Under certain conditions, such tensions led to new social formations in the Bronze and Iron Ages.

Agriculture in the Bronze and Iron Ages

The European Bronze Age (ca. 2200–800 B.C.E.) and the Iron Age (ca. 800 B.C.E.–100 C.E.) occupy a shorter chronological span than the Neolithic Period, which stretched back some 5,000 years earlier. The quickening pace of economic and social change, however, makes these episodes crucial to an understanding of early agricultural development in Europe.

The most dramatic change occurred in that part of Europe where agriculture had the longest history: the Aegean. Halstead has charted the emergence of increasingly complex society from the early agricultural villages of the Greek Neolithic. Social advantages gained by the most successful farmers eventually led to the formation of an elite social stratum in the late Neolithic Period and Bronze Age. Furthermore, the growth of larger settlements encouraged more efficient means of cultivating larger and more distant fields. Harnessed to a simple plow, powerful teams of oxen are capable of tilling soil at a much faster rate than is possible by hand and hence can produce large-scale surplus—that is, far more food than is needed by those carrying out the farming tasks. In parallel with ox-drawn plow agriculture, large-scale herding of wool-bearing sheep developed to produce woolen textiles for exchange. Other surpluses included luxury products, such as wine and olive oil–based perfume. All of these developments are reflected in the earliest European written records to have been deciphered fully—the Linear B tablets of the Late Bronze Age Mycenaean palaces, mostly preserved in destruction layers of the 13th century B.C.E. These surplus-oriented systems emerged under special conditions, however; elsewhere in the Aegean, beyond the sphere of the palaces, small-scale intensive agriculture of the Neolithic type continued.

Agricultural features generally associated with the Bronze Age in Europe include the use of animals for muscle power, transport, wool, and dairying; the diversification of the seed-crop spectrum with spelt wheat, millet, and broad bean; and the establishment of olive, vine, and fig cultivation in the Mediterranean. Horse bones are increasingly common on archaeological sites of this time period, and decorated bridle pieces suggest that horses played an important role in social display. Aspects of the radical social change seen in the Aegean Bronze Age developed elsewhere in Europe, visible most clearly in the emergence of elaborate elite burials. This trend toward increasingly complex society was based in part on the ability to produce and mobilize agricultural surpluses. The introduction of bronze and, later, iron tool making had a direct impact on agriculture. Metal sickles could be used to bring in the harvest more efficiently than previous methods of collection by hand or with stone sickles—an important development, making larger scale cultivation and harvesting more feasible.

A general phenomenon of Bronze Age Europe, visible in different ways from the Aegean to Britain, is expansion of the agricultural landscape to include increasingly marginal areas with thinner, poorer soils. This marginal colonization may have had diverse local causes, but its environmental consequences were often dramatic. In Britain, for example, upland clearance for cultivation and herding, evidenced by pollen records and clearance cairns (piles of stones cleared to make way for cultivation), accelerated the formation of heath and moorland areas that persist to this day. Many of these landscapes were eventually abandoned for agriculture owing to

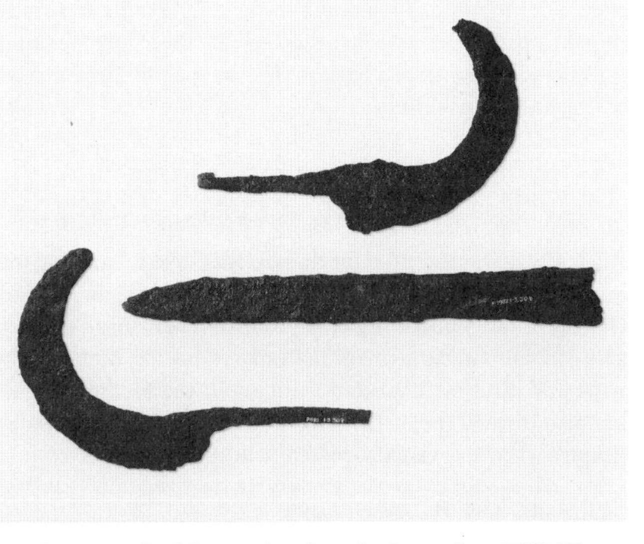

Iron farming tools of the Iron Age, from the Stantonbury Hill hillfort, Somerset, England (© The Trustees of the British Museum)

deteriorating soil conditions, leaving behind preserved field systems, such as the Dartmoor Reaves in Devon, England.

Social change during the Iron Age is reflected in the construction of hill forts across much of Europe. Hill forts reflect the accumulation of wealth chiefly by elites through long-distance exchange in materials as well as the collection and storage of local agricultural surplus, indicated by storage pits containing substantial deposits of charred grain. The Iron Age elite were also interested in acquiring exotic food and drink. Archaeological evidence indicates that they obtained wine and drinking paraphernalia from the Mediterranean sphere as well as the domestic chicken, introduced from southern Asia via the Near East.

Agriculture in the Roman Period

The Roman period offers an abundance of ancient commentary on agricultural matters (especially Cato, Varro, Columella, and Pliny the Elder) and a wealth of archaeological evidence, extending from the agricultural hinterland of Rome itself to its eastern frontier provinces in the Balkans and its westernmost province of Britain. A number of agricultural innovations are associated with the Romans, including the introduction of a heavier plow, the asymmetrical plowshare (capable of turning the soil to one side), and the coulter (added to make a preliminary vertical cut in advance of the plow). All of these introductions made it easier to cultivate heavier soils. Expansion of arable farming to new ground also involved the introduction of water mills for irrigation or drainage.

With the disintegration of the Roman Empire, improved farming methods and government-led developments in agricultural organization largely disappeared, to reemerge in different forms under new political regimes in medieval times. Other Roman practices, such as the widespread grafting of fruit trees and use of new varieties, may have continued in some areas. Across much of the European countryside, however, older methods of farming using simple tools and traditional techniques reasserted themselves. These local farming traditions can be traced back to the Europe's earliest farmers of the Neolithic Period.

GREECE

by David B. Hollander

Agriculture was essential for the ancient Greeks. Farming was both the fundamental basis of their economy and for much of Greek antiquity about the only profession befitting a respectable citizen. Greek farmers not only produced high-quality wine and olive oil, exported throughout the Mediterranean, but also formed the armies that defeated the mighty Persian Empire when it invaded Greece in 490 and 480 B.C.E.

Sources on Agriculture

Despite agriculture's importance, ancient written sources describing Greek farming practices are difficult to find. Columella, a Roman agricultural writer of the first century C.E., knew of many Greek authors who wrote on the subject, but nearly all of their works are now lost. The ones we still have tend to be moral, poetic, or botanical writings, not technical manuals. Hesiod's *Works and Days*, written around 700 B.C.E., is one of the earliest and best sources still available. This poem provides valuable information about the working of an Archaic Greek farm and the times that various tasks had to be completed during the year. Xenophon's *Oeconomicus* (*The Estate-Manager*), written more than 300 years later, consists primarily of a conversation between Socrates and a wealthy Athenian named Ischomachus about the management of a farm household. Ischomachus describes his practices to Socrates, who concludes that farming is the best profession for an Athenian man to pursue, since farmers produce food and are the most willing and able to defend the city-state.

Theophrastus, a philosopher of the fourth century B.C.E., wrote two botanical treatises, *De causis plantarum* (*On the Causes of Plants*) and *Historia plantarum* (*History of Plants*), both of which contain much useful information about Greek agriculture. Theophrastus also produced an amusing, if stereotypical brief, character study of the Greek farmer, whom he describes as boorish and unsophisticated. Theocritus, a poet of the third century B.C.E. from Syracuse, invented the genre of bucolic poetry, in which life in the countryside is described in idealized form. A number of his *Idylls* survive, and they tend to feature herdsmen relaxing and singing songs in pleasant rural surroundings. From Greek estates in Ptolemaic Egypt a different type of evidence has emerged: account books and other documents related to the management of large farms. These texts, though often fragmentary and difficult to read, provide valuable information concerning what was grown, who worked on the estates, and how much they were paid.

Archaeology has also begun to provide some information concerning Greek agriculture, despite a continued preference for urban over rural sites. With respect to the study of ancient farming, the most important archaeological tool is survey archaeology, in which a team of archaeologists walks over and examines large areas of land for surface traces of ancient activity. This process can reveal evidence of ancient farmhouses and villages, thus enabling the archaeologists to build up a picture of settlement and land use. Aerial photography and remote sensing technology, such as soil resistivity testing (using changes in the electrical resistance of the soil to detect the remains of structures hidden beneath the ground), can accomplish some of the same ends, though it is the fragments of pottery found in surface surveys that allow archaeologists to date newly discovered sites. The excavation of such rural sites as farmhouses has also yielded important information about Greek agriculture. One problem that archaeologists face in studying Greek farming is that many of the tools used in agriculture were made of wood and have not survived.

The Development of Greek Agriculture

Agriculture arrived in Greece during the sixth millennium B.C.E., well before the earliest known Greeks, the Mycenaeans, built their great palaces in the middle of the second millennium. The Mycenaean kingdoms operated centralized economies in which the products of agriculture were gathered in by the palaces and then redistributed as needed to the subject population. This system collapsed along with Mycenaean civilization around 1200 B.C.E. In the unsettled conditions of the Dark Age that followed, the population of Greece declined dramatically, the economy deteriorated, and Greeks came to rely more heavily on livestock than on agriculture to supply them with food.

The eighth century B.C.E. saw a revival of Greek fortunes. The population increased, and land soon became scarce. The desire of many Greeks to have their own farms probably contributed to the boom in colonization that lasted down to the beginning of the fifth century. During this period an ideology linking landownership and agriculture to citizenship and virtue began to emerge. In the Classical Period (fifth and fourth centuries B.C.E.) and later some Greek philosophers argued that farmers were a city-state's best defenders and most prudent citizens. Agriculture continued to be highly regarded during the Hellenistic Period (323–31 B.C.E.). The new Greek kingdoms in Asia and Egypt encouraged the further development of agriculture through experimentation and scholarship. The Roman conquest of the eastern Mediterranean over the course of the last two centuries B.C.E. seems to have brought about no substantial changes in the practice of agriculture there.

Geography and Climate

Before a discussion of specific farming practices, it is necessary to consider briefly the geography and climate of Greece, since the nature of the land and the weather dictated where and how farming could be done. Greece is a very mountainous country, and much of it was not well suited to agriculture. Terracing—building walls along the sides of hills to create flatter farmland and prevent soil erosion—seems to have been a common practice among ancient Greek farmers. The best farmland, like that in Messenia in the southwestern Peloponnese, was extremely valuable. The Spartans conquered Messenia in the eighth century B.C.E. and used its rich lands to support their totalitarian military system. Unfortunately, much of the textual evidence for Greek farming comes from Athens, whose territory, Attica, had some of the poorest farmland in the region. What crops could be grown and when and how they should be cultivated, varied, sometimes considerably from place to place. Thus it is difficult to generalize about Greek agriculture.

The Greek climate is quite variable both from year to year and from region to region, especially with respect to rain. Although springs supplied some water for agriculture, there were few rivers or streams capable of supporting irrigation, so most farms depended on rainfall. This made farming an unpredictable and risky proposition. It was better to have many widely scattered plots of land rather than one big one; with fields spread over a relatively large area, a farmer could be confident that at least some of his plots would yield a good crop in any particular year. If, on the other hand, a farmer had one large plot of land and there was insufficient rain to support the crops he was growing, he could face famine or bankruptcy. Summers in Greece tend to be warm and dry. while the winters are relatively mild and wet. Because irrigation was usually not an option, most crops were grown in the winter rather than the summer. Wheat was sown early in the fall and harvested in May and June of the following year. If, however, the winter crops failed, one could sow quick-growing plant varieties in the spring.

Marble statue of Demeter (carved ca. 350 B.C.E.), Greek goddess of fertility who governed the cycle of the seasons and the growing of grain (© The Trustees of the British Museum)

Crops

The main Greek crops were the olive, the grape, and grain (barley and wheat). These three crops are often referred to as the "Mediterranean triad," since they were staple foods of many people living in the Mediterranean basin. Nevertheless, the Greeks supplemented their diet with a variety of foods, such as figs, apples, pomegranates, peas, beans, lentils, turnips, cabbage, dates, and plums. As Greek traders and conquerors ventured farther afield, they imported new crops such as the peach, which was introduced to Greece in the second century B.C.E. The Greeks seem to have preferred eating wheat over barley, but wheat required much more water to grow; thus, many farmers had no choice but to grow barley. They cultivated several varieties of barley, which was hardier than wheat and grew well in poor soils. The Greeks were aware of the importance of crop rotation; they also knew that some crops could reinvigorate the soil, as could periodically leaving fields fallow.

The olive was an important source of fat but was also grown to produce soap, perfume, and fuel for lamps. Olive trees require a considerable investment of time, money, and labor. They must be grown from cuttings rather than seeds so that the plant does not revert to its wild state, and they must be pruned annually. It could take many years for a new plantation to reach full production. The trees required weeding as well as hoeing around their bases to drive the roots down into the soil. This practice made the trees more resistant to drought. Apparently as a natural defense against drought, olive trees produce a good crop only every other year. These fluctuations in crop size are a regional phenomenon, since all the trees in a given area face roughly the same climatic conditions. Olives ripen in October and are harvested through the winter. They must be treated before becoming edible. Greek olive oil was traded throughout the Mediterranean, and the oil produced in certain regions such as Attica became especially popular. Jars of Athenian olive oil were given to the winners of some competitions at the greater Panathenaea (a quadrennial festival celebrated at Athens).

Wine was the staple drink of the ancient Greeks. Vineyards, like olive groves, required a lot of labor: weeding, pruning, and tilling the soil around the vines to drive down the roots (again, drought resistance was of critical importance). Stakes, trellises, and trees were used to support the growing vines. In Greece the grapes would be harvested in the early fall, and laborers would press the grapes and store the juice for fermentation. The wine of certain Aegean islands, such as Cos and Chios, was in particularly high demand. Even though they produced their own vintages, the Romans imported considerable quantities of Greek wine into Italy. Most Greeks would consume wine every day, though it was normally mixed with water. The symposium, a fundamental Greek institution, was a drinking party at which aristocratic men enjoyed wine while socializing, playing games, and listening to music and poetry.

Pastoral Agriculture

In addition to growing crops, the Greeks also practiced pastoral agriculture, keeping cows, sheep, goats, and pigs. Cows were a good source of labor in addition to meat. Cattle were expensive, and most people would have been unable to eat meat except when cattle were sacrificed at religious ceremonies. Cow's milk was apparently not used, but their hides were an important product. Sheep provided wool (the primary fabric for Greek clothing) and meat, and their milk was used to make cheese. Goats also were a source of meat and milk for cheese. Herds often grazed on the marginal land unsuited for farming. Some shepherds would move their herds to mountain pastures in the summer, when the lowlands became dry and fodder was harder to come by. This practice is called transhumance. The summer pasturelands were sometimes in border areas, and competition for these regions could lead to war with neighboring city-states. Pigs were kept for meat and also sometimes sacrificed. Some Greeks raised poultry for eggs, meat, or sacrifice. Beekeeping was also important. Honey sweetened many dishes, preserved food, could be mixed with wine, and was an ingredient in some medicines. Throughout antiquity wild game was hunted, and wild herbs and nuts were gathered to supplement the Greek diet.

Labor

Some animals were kept for their labor rather than as a source of food. Horses were not widely used in agriculture both because they were too expensive (considerable amounts of land would have been needed for cultivating their fodder) and because the proper type of harness had not yet been invented to exploit their labor in plowing fields. Oxen, donkeys, and mules performed the heavy work, since they required less food than horses and were physiologically better suited to the available harness technology. Donkeys and mules also live longer than horses and so were a better investment. Since mules are the product of a male donkey and a mare—and must be nursed by the mare—most farmers would have had to purchase them rather than raise their own.

On most farms people did the bulk of the labor. Poorer farmers worked the land themselves, while those who could afford to own slaves assigned them to perform various agricultural chores. In some Greek communities slaves formed a major part of the workforce. The Spartans, for example, had effectively enslaved both some of the population of Sparta as well as many of the neighboring Messenians. These slaves, known as helots, worked the land for their Spartan masters and were required to turn over to them a large quantity of produce. Other city-states, such as Syracuse, and some Cretan communities developed similar systems of exploitation. In some times and places estate owners would hire free laborers to work on their farms either on a regular basis or at times of peak demand such as during harvest times. Unfortunately, the upper-class Greek writers tended to look down on all labor performed for wages as demeaning and servile. Hence there is little evidence of such practices. Tenancy was another option for those possessing large tracts of land. Landowners could lease parcels of land to tenants who would farm the land and pay them a rent, usually a portion of their harvest.

Agricultural Tools

Greek farmers used a variety of tools to cultivate their crops, but most of them, constructed of wood or iron, deteriorate considerably over time and so rarely appear in the archaeological record. Among the most important tools were plows that were fitted with bronze or iron plowshares and used to break up the earth prior to the sowing of seeds. Hoes helped those engaged in weeding, while sacks and baskets held seed grain for sowing the fields. Harvesters used iron sickles to cut down the stalks of grain, which they would then bind together in sheaves and transport to the threshing floor. Either livestock or a sledge could be used to remove the hulls from the grain. Then the grain would be tossed in the air to separate out the chaff, and mills would grind the grain into flour. Olive and vine cultivation also required specialized equipment, such as baskets to hold the grapes and olives, mills to crush olives, and presses to extract the oil or grape juice. Such equipment could be expensive, and operating a vineyard or olive grove constituted a major investment.

Landholding

There is little firm evidence for the size and distribution of landholdings. The study of Greek colonies and the remarks made by the philosopher Aristotle (384–322 B.C.E.) on the subject suggest that, ideally, land was to be divided into a relatively large number of small plots owned by individual citizens. Aristotle claimed that farmers of moderate means made the best citizens, since they had enough land to support themselves but were not rich enough to have much leisure time. Under such circumstances, Aristotle believed, farmers would not allow politics and excessive public meetings distract them from their work. Furthermore, great disparities in landholdings often led to civil war in Greek city-states. Such conflict was thought to be among the greatest evils that could afflict a community. Relative equality of wealth among citizens would ensure tranquility. Unfortunately, the Greek practice of bequeathing property equally among all sons and the inherently risky nature of agriculture meant that even if a community's land was at first evenly divided among its citizens, that situation was unlikely to last long.

Farmers who were unlucky and suffered a string of poor harvests would have to borrow money, going into debt to continue cultivating their land. Some might be able to pay off those debts eventually, but many were not. Such farmers were forced to sell part or all of their land to their more successful neighbors. For some, even the sale of their land was not enough to pay off their debts, and they found themselves sold into slavery. The Athenian politician Solon faced just such conditions in 594 B.C.E. when, as archon, or magistrate, he was chosen to mediate a dispute between debtors and creditors. In this position of power he addressed the situation by canceling debts, freeing enslaved citizens, outlawing debt bondage, and reorganizing the city-state's constitution. In many cities and on many occasions throughout Greek antiquity, poor and indebted citizens demanded the cancellation of debts and the redistribution of land. Similar movements were successful, but others met with violent repression. On the other hand, farmers who were fortunate enough to have high yields were able to invest the profits, lending money or food to their neighbors. If those neighbors were unable to pay off their loans, their creditors could seize their property as collateral. Farmers with more land were less likely to suffer in times of drought, since they could store or sell the surplus food they had accumulated. Thus rich farmers tended to get richer as the poor got poorer.

At Sparta there seems to have been an increase in the size of individual landholdings during the fifth century B.C.E. At the same time, Spartan women came to own a larger portion of the land through inheritance. Since citizenship and military service were tied to landholding at Sparta, the size of the Spartan army and citizen body (both exclusively male preserves) began to decline at this point. In the fourth century the Spartans were unable to field the large, highly trained armies with which they had once fended off the might of the Persian Empire and dominated the neighboring Greek communities. In 369 B.C.E. the valuable lands of Messenia were wrested from Spartan control and became independent. In the third century B.C.E. the kings Agis IV and Cleomenes III attempted to revive Spartan power in part by canceling debts and redistributing land to create a larger and more equal pool of citizens. Their efforts ultimately failed.

From the fourth century B.C.E. onward much of Greece saw the same trend in landholding that Sparta had experienced. In general, fewer people came to own more land. Urbanization increased, as did the gap between rich and poor. These trends led to the development of new pools of manpower, which the Hellenistic monarchs of Egypt and Asia exploited to hire mercenaries and administrators. From the late fourth century onward the great kings of the Seleucid, Antigonid, and Ptolemaic dynasties lured poor Greeks to their kingdoms with grants of land confiscated from the indigenous populations. This practice drew off a substantial part of the free poor of mainland Greece, though many still remained behind to demand debt cancellation and the redistribution of land. Thus revolution became a persistent fear among the wealthy in the Hellenistic era. At the same time, as fewer people owned farmland and more and more people lived in cities, nostalgia for the countryside developed. The rural-themed works of poets such as Theocritus reflect this increased yearning for a now idealized rural life.

Warfare and Agriculture

Farmland was a regular target in Greek warfare. Invading armies needed to travel light and so would ransack farms and storehouses in enemy territory for food. Often armies sought to damage their enemies by destroying the crops growing in the fields as well as olive groves, vineyards, and farmhouses. Olive trees and vines were difficult to destroy. The real toll on the countryside from warfare was financial, as it took money to rebuild structures and replace lost stores of seed grain, wine, and oil as well as damaged equipment. War forced farmers to spend their savings or borrow and thus pushed many into debt, enabling richer neighbors to acquire their land. During the Peloponnesian War between the Athenians and the Spartans (431–404 B.C.E.), Sparta and her allies invaded Attica repeatedly and did considerable damage to the Athenian countryside. Their attacks sought to do economic damage to the Athenians and also provoke them into leaving the protection of their walls and fight an infantry battle (in which the Spartans would have a considerable advantage). Such tactics were common throughout the ancient world.

Religion

The main Greek crops were all associated with particular gods. Dionysus was the god of wine, while Athena was credited with the olive tree. Demeter was the goddess of grain and agricultural fertility, and her sanctuary at Eleusis in Attica was an important cult center from the Archaic era down to the Roman Empire. People came from all over Greece and beyond to be initiated into the "Eleusinian mysteries" at the sanctuary of Demeter and her daughter Kore (also known as Persephone). There were religious festivals associated with all the main events in the agricultural cycle. Many farmers offered "first fruits," or food from the harvest, to the gods each year. At Athens all farmers had to give a small portion of their barley and wheat crops to Demeter. Some temples even owned their own land and leased it out to generate income to pay their operating expenses.

ROME

by Amy Hackney Blackwell

A vast and efficient system of agricultural production was essential to Rome's success as an empire. The staple ingredients of Roman cooking were olive oil, wine, and wheat. Producing these basic foodstuffs occupied more than 30 percent of the total workforce. The Italian countryside, Sicily, Sardinia, North Africa, and Egypt were all cultivated to keep food on Roman tables. Romans brought home foods from foreign lands and in return left some of their favorite crops in far-flung provinces. A complex governmental bureaucracy managed the distribution of grain to citizens to avoid famine and riots. Over the centuries of Roman history, agricultural enterprises progressed from small farms to larger businesses worked by slaves to the precursor of the medieval tenant farmer system.

Roman Writings on Farm Management

Marcus Porcius Cato (Cato the Censor) (234–149 B.C.E.), wrote one of the best-known works on Roman agriculture, *De agri cultura* (ca. 160 B.C.E.). Cato was born to a peasant family in Tusculum, and although he had a lengthy career in the army and the Roman government, he devoted a great deal of his time and energy to the subject of farm maintenance and domestic economy.

Cato believed that a farm should be run as a business. In *De agri cultura* he provides directions on all aspects of farming. Cato assumed that the farmer reading his manual would be an absentee landlord who lived in Rome and made only occasional trips to his farm. The farm's daily operations would be handled by a slave overseer and his wife, who would manage a large staff of slaves. Whenever the farmer arrived at the farm, Cato directs that he first greet his household gods and then go around the property. Having assessed the situation, he would then meet with the farm's manager to discuss operations. The farmer should always seek the highest profit. He should hold his olive oil until the price was high and then sell it. He should sell livestock as soon as the animals became too old to work; likewise, old tools, carts, or slaves should be sold without sentiment. Cato was himself known for frugality; he disapproved of frivolity, and he believed that the farmer should always sell more than he bought.

De agri cultura contains detailed instructions for all types of farming jobs. Cato explains how to build a farmhouse and an olive press. He describes grape culture and wine production. He mentions other fruits that might be profitable for a farmer in Italy. He also includes a list of recipes for preserving food produced on the farm. These recipes were intended to help the farm be self-sufficient and produce surplus items for sale. Cato also provides recipes for cheesecakes, pastries, medicines, and special wines. Some of the wine recipes suggest ways, such as by adding seawater to make local wines taste like more fashionable vintages from Greece. Cato also describes the use of spices in making olive relish and other snacks.

Cato lived fairly early in the Roman period, but subsequent writers proved just as interested in matters of family farms. Wealthy Romans often owned property in the country, and they liked to farm it, both for profit and as a matter of fashion. Many people enjoyed serving their dinner guests with food that had come straight from their family farm. The poet Juvenal (ca. 55–ca. 127 C.E.) mocked fashionable Romans who bragged about the fresh meat and produce served in their homes.

Government Policies on Grain

Feeding Rome's people required a vast amount of grain. Wheat does not grow in cities. By ancient standards Rome and its environs covered a large area and housed a large urban population that could not grow food to feed itself. Rome therefore relied on imports of grain from North Africa,

Spain, Egypt, Sicily, and Sardinia. This grain needed to arrive on a regular basis and be available at a reasonable price—both uncertain propositions in the ancient world. The government therefore stepped in to help. A large portion of the governments of both the republic and the empire was dedicated to getting this bread to Roman tables.

In order to prevent famines and the peasant revolts that could accompany them, the Roman government created a system to provide wheat to all citizens. This began under Gaius Gracchus, who in 123 B.C.E. passed a *lex frumentaria*, or grain law, that provided each citizen grain at a subsidized price. In 58 B.C.E. Clodius Pulcher made grain free to all citizens. Administering this enterprise required a large bureaucracy of officials to keep track of distributions. An elected official monitored the grain imports that arrived in Rome's port, Ostia, and saw to the proper distribution of the supply. The free grain was immensely popular, and by the time of Julius Caesar (100–44 B.C.E.) some 25 percent of Rome's population was receiving it. For financial reasons, both Caesar and the emperor Augustus (63 B.C.E–14 C.E.) had to reduce the number of people receiving the grain dole. Despite these difficulties, the free distribution of grain continued until the end of the empire.

Rome furthered its agricultural needs through the use of *ager publicus*, or public land. When a community or a foreign possession rebelled and was subdued, the government would claim a portion of its territory, usually a third, for public use. The best-known *ager publicus* was the rich land around the city of Capua in southern Italy, which Rome's government took after Capua rebelled several times. In 59 B.C.E. Caesar distributed this land to Pompey's veterans, the soldiers who had fought in Pompey's army during the civil war. There was *ager publicus* in every Roman province, both overseas and on the Italian peninsula. Some of this land was given to Roman colonists, and the state held other portions of it. The censors (magistrates) leased land to those who requested it, typically favoring those who wanted to run large estates. Generals would give away plots of public land to their soldiers after concluding military campaigns. Most recipients of plots of public land used them for agriculture, building small farms for their own families or running large estates if they held enough acreage. During the empire most of the *ager publicus* was eventually incorporated into the emperor's own estates.

Roman Crops: Wheat

Romans grew mainly wheat and barley. The barley was used chiefly as fodder for animals, while wheat was the primary energy source in the Roman diet. In the earliest days of Rome, the wheat was most commonly cooked into porridge, but by the time of the republic baked bread was more common and formed the bulk of most meals. This transition in culinary habits went along with a change in agricultural preferences; as people began to eat more bread, farmers replaced husked species of wheat (suitable only for boiling) with wheat that did not have a husk and could be baked. These new "naked" species of wheat included durum wheat, now used to make pasta, as well as the types of wheat still used in modern bread.

Roman Crops: Olives

Olives were tremendously important to ancient people. They ate cured olives as a vegetable, but the oil from the olives was more significant. Olive oil was the principal or even the only source of fat in many people's diets and a good source of nutrients, such as vitamin E. People also used olive oil as a skin moisturizer and a cleaner; instead of cleaning themselves with soap, they would rub themselves with olive oil and scrape it off. Olive oil could also be burned in lamps.

Olives grow wild in the Mediterranean region, so they were readily available to ancient farmers. The ancient Greeks improved the cultivation of olives, and the Romans took their techniques and varieties to Italy and throughout the Mediterranean. Olive farmers grew the trees in groves; olives could grow in areas where grain could not, allowing farmers to take advantage of more land. Olive trees thrive on drought and are not particular about soil quality. They can live for hundreds of years.

Romans knew of at least 27 different varieties of olive. They used grafting to combine hardy rootstocks with productive trees, grafting cultivated olive cuttings onto fig tree stocks or wild olive cuttings onto cultivated olive tree stocks. Once trees reached a productive size, they were kept small and fruitful by yearly pruning done by slaves. Slaves also did most of the olive harvesting, an operation that required a great deal of labor because every tree branch had to be beaten with sticks to loosen the olives.

Most farmers did not grow only olives; an olive grove was typically just one component of a larger establishment that might include several other crops. Olives typically bear a crop every other year, but harvests can be erratic, so it made sense for farmers to diversify their holdings. Cato's ideal olive grove, for example, included a shepherd, a swineherd, and a herd of 100 sheep; the pigs ate the material left over from making olive oil, and the sheep ate the grass under the trees so that slaves did not have to weed. To make oil, slaves crushed the olives in a large stone press. The oil flowed out through openings at the bottom of the press and could be collected in fired clay jars. To eat the olives themselves, people cured them by soaking in a salt solution for several weeks or by packing in salt. This treatment removed the olives' natural bitterness and preserved them.

In his handbook, Cato describes an ideal olive plantation; this farm was run by a slave overseer and his wife and was worked by five slaves, three ox drivers, one donkey driver, a swineherd, and a shepherd. It covered 160 acres of land and had its own oil press, so oil could be made on the premises. The size of this establishment and the time it took olive trees to mature (15 years) made olive cultivation difficult for small farmers. On the other hand, olive trees live up to 1,000 years, so an established olive grove could be very valuable. For a wealthy landowner olive farming could be quite profitable. Cato writes that the average profit was 6 percent on invested capital.

Roman Crops: Grapes

Wild grapes grew throughout the ancient Mediterranean. Humans were cultivating grapes in the Middle East and in Minoan Greece long before the Romans arrived on the scene; the Greek authors Homer and Hesiod both mention wine in their writings. Before the start of Rome, Etruscans in northern Italy and Greek colonists in southern Italy grew grapes and made wine. By the second century B.C.E. Romans were maintaining and investing in vineyards throughout the Mediterranean, and grapes had become a more profitable crop than grain. The government was quick to notice that the wine industry was extremely profitable, and as early as the fourth century B.C.E. Rome had passed laws protecting local growers from foreign wine imports. By 150 B.C.E. Rome had begun exporting wine to the provinces; the wine sent to Gaul was traded for slaves who came to Italy to work the large vineyards.

The source for most Roman knowledge on viticulture came from a work that was written in Carthage and was translated into Latin in 146 B.C.E. Ancients knew of many different species of grape. Grape plantations could include other fruits and vegetables, but as time went on farmers specialized in vines exclusively. Cato describes an ideal vineyard: It required 66 acres of land and was managed by a slave overseer, his wife, sixteen slaves, two oxen, three donkeys, and a large amount of equipment.

Starting a new vineyard was a complicated and time-consuming process. Before planting the vines, the farmer ploughed the fields, did any necessary terracing, and created an irrigation system. He then planted the new vines and tied them to stakes or trees for support. After planting, he would dig the ground in the entire vineyard to loosen the soil and allow water to reach the roots and then cover the dirt with manure for fertilizer. As the vines grew, the farmer would remove the young sterile shoots to nurture the productive parts of the plant. Once the grape crop was ripe, the farmer tied up the vines and watered the whole field thoroughly before harvesting. Vines could live for many years but eventually would die and have to be replaced. Good vines were valuable, and farmers had to guard their fields against thieves. Farmers also surrounded fields with walls or fences for protection.

The grapes had to be picked by hand. Once grapes were harvested, slaves would crush them to extract their juice, either by using a wine press or by stomping on the grapes with their feet. Then the new wine was left to ferment. Ancient Roman winemakers used many of the techniques that are still employed by winemakers today. To create sweet wines, they would leave the grapes on the vine well into autumn to develop natural sugars. Weak wines were aged in large clay containers buried underground. Robust wines fermented in the open air, where the sun, rain, and other elements helped them develop flavor. Vintners added honey or spices to wines for flavoring and as preservatives. Once the wine was finished, the vintner poured it into large clay jars called amphorae and either stored it to age it or sent it away for sale. It was much easier to transport wine by sea than by land, so most vineyards were located near the coast or on rivers.

Other Crops

In addition to wheat, grapes, and olives, Romans grew a number of other plants. Beans, chickpeas, and lentils were the main sources of protein in most people's diets. Farmers grew numerous vegetables to eat fresh or to preserve. The most common vegetables included onions, garlic, radishes, celery, asparagus, carrots, beets, and zucchini. Typical fruits included figs, grapes, dates, apples, pears, mulberries, peaches, apricots, and cherries. Walnuts and almonds were popular nuts. Roman cooks loved to add herbs and spices to food, so farmers grew a range of them: oregano, cumin, coriander, fennel, lovage, rue, and silphium, or asafetida, the resin of a plant related to fennel. Roman farmers did not grow either tomatoes or potatoes, which are New World vegetables. Farmers also kept chickens and other fowl for their eggs and meat, and they raised some goats and sheep for their milk and wool. Italy's terrain is not good for growing large livestock, so few farmers would have kept herds of cattle.

Honey was the most common sweetener, so many farmers kept bees. The Greeks had already been keeping bees for centuries, and the Romans continued their work in selecting breeds of bees and maximizing honey production. A single beehive could produce between six and 18 pints of honey every season. Romans sought out honey from the best areas, which included Sicily (especially the area near Syracuse), Liguria, and the south of Spain. They also imported honey from Rhodes, Cyprus, several regions of Greece, and Syria. The Roman authors Virgil and Varro both wrote about the practical details of beekeeping.

Types of Farms

The most common type of farm was known as a villa. This traditional farm was located in a rural area and consisted of a house, stables, and workshops with a central courtyard. The author Varro describes villas in some detail in his writing. Villas were usually maintained by slaves for an urban owner, but small farms owned by their residents were also common and were built according to the same structure.

Life on a farm was fairly simple, with none of the glamour that went with living in Rome. A farmer and his wife who owned their own small farm had jobs to keep them busy from morning until night. They had to till fields, sow crops, weed, fetch water, and occasionally guard their plants from thieves. At harvest time they had to gather all the crops and process them, threshing the grain and drying or preserving any vegetables they could not eat fresh. Farm wives would spin their own thread and weave their own cloth to make clothing. During lengthy military campaigns the wives of soldiers would be forced to run the farms themselves for months or years while their husbands fought in distant wars.

During the early Roman Republic farmers began to specialize in particular crops and to run their farms as businesses. Agriculture became even more widespread and productive during the late republic and early empire. Large estates called *latifundia* began to appear in the early second century B.C.E. as wealthy Romans took over the *ager publicus*. Large villas, with their wealthy landlords and body of slave laborers, quickly became more prosperous than the smallholdings owned by local residents. Wealthy owners had the money to experiment with new crops and breeds of animals, and they had the economic weight to dictate prices. As a consequence, large numbers of small farmers lost their farms. The slaves who worked the *latifundia* were often prisoners taken in war. Conditions for these slaves were notoriously bad because slaves were cheap and plentiful, so landowners had no reason to treat them well.

The *latifundia* system was prominent until about 100 C.E., when slave labor became more expensive and landowners moved toward a system that used tenant farmers, a precursor of the medieval system of serfs tied to the land. Large farms ceased to be profitable. Gradually the landowners broke them down into smaller plots of land tilled by tenant farmers, peasants who were bound to the land. During the heyday of large estates, small farmers had made little technological progress and continued to use ancient cultivation techniques, but now landowners ensured that their tenants improved their techniques to keep the farms productive. German and Asian prisoners of war who worked Roman farms learned Roman techniques and tooke them back to their home countries. Agricultural practices of the late empire laid the foundation for the medieval system of tenant farming.

Agricultural Practices

Almost all ancient agricultural work was performed manually, without even the use of oxen or mules. Farmers had to till their fallow fields constantly to prevent the incursion of weeds, and they did this work with hoes. Plots of arable land in Italy were small and rocky. Large, flat fields were quite rare, so plows were impractical, though they did exist and were occasionally used to break up rough soil.

Italy had a wide range of soil types, and Roman farmers created a variety of different tools to suit different conditions. They invented hoes with multiple tines to make the soil finer; footrest spades to help them till deeply; and several kinds of sickles, such as the balanced sickle and the "spitted" sickle, which helped the user collect harvested crops. Roman farmers also made great improvements in devices to lift water. During the empire farmers in Gaul began using a reaping machine called a *vallus*, which was pulled by an animal and used to cut off the heads of wheat stalks and drop them in a container. Many of these tools were made of iron instead of the bronze that was popular in earlier days, allowing Roman farmers to produce many more crops than their predecessors.

Most threshing was done by hand, the farmers hitting the grain with sticks to separate the grain from the straw. Sometimes farmers had animals walk on the harvested stalks to thresh them. Wealthier farmers occasionally used a device called a *tribulum* to thresh grain; this device, also used by the Greeks, consisted of a heavy board with flints or small wheels on its underside and was dragged over the stalks to remove the wheat kernels.

The Greeks had pioneered many agricultural techniques, such as using manure for fertilizer, choosing crops based on soil type, and rotating crops. By rotating two or three different types of crops, they managed to keep fields in continuous cultivation without needing to let fields rest when they were depleted of nutrients. Roman farmers adopted these practices as well.

Imports and Exports

Rome depended on its many provinces to supply it with grain and other crops. Sicily, Sardinia, North Africa, and Egypt all produced vast amounts of wheat for Rome at different times in Rome's history. Sicily and Sardinia were important sources of grain throughout Roman history. Both islands are mountainous but fertile; Sicily's warmer climate makes it especially suited to agriculture. Sicily was located near the center of the Mediterranean, making it a crossroads for all ancient traffic and a magnet for conquest. The Greeks colonized it in the eighth century B.C.E. and used it as a point of trade with Corinth, Rhodes, North Africa, and Italy. Carthage gradually claimed most of the island, but by 211 C.E. Rome had taken all of Sicily for itself. The Romans decided that Sicily would be best used for growing wheat. Much of Sicily's land was divided into *latifundia* worked by slaves on behalf of owners back in Rome. Conditions were deplorable, and slaves revolted many times; some of the most serious revolts occurred in 135–132 B.C.E. and 104–100 B.C.E. Under the empire the *latifundia* system continued in Sicily even as it declined in the rest of Europe, and Sicily remained an important source of Roman grain.

Sardinia was wilder than Sicily. The Greeks seem never to have colonized it. Carthage took it in the sixth century B.C.E. but did not make any progress toward pacifying the natives. Rome took the island from Carthage in 238 B.C.E. and turned it into a colony together with nearby Corsica, which was less fertile. The Roman government and people never thought much of Sardinia or the Sardinians and looked on the island purely as a source of grain. It continued to supply grain to Rome until the end of the empire.

North Africa also supplied a vast amount of grain to Rome's tables. Rome took over much of Carthage's territory after the Punic Wars (a series of three wars fought between Rome and Carthage between 264 and 146 B.C.E.), forming a new province in northern Tunisia in 146 B.C.E. This province encompassed some 5,000 square miles of the most fertile part of North Africa. The land there became Roman public land, and the government leased it out to grain farmers, who grew wheat for export to Rome. North African estates were vast. Most of the land was in the hands of a few large absentee land-

Section of the facade of a Roman aisled barnlike building on a villa estate in the parish of Meonstoke, Hampshire, England, dating to the early fourth century C.E. (© The Trustees of the British Museum)

owners, though there were also more modest estates owned by locals. Scholars believe that about half a million tons of wheat left Carthage annually. The province of Carthage's capital city (also called Carthage) became the second-largest city in the Mediterranean on the basis of its agricultural exports. By the second century B.C.E. North Africa was also exporting olive oil, figs, grapes, and beans.

All African farmers had to irrigate their crops, and they invented some elaborate systems of getting water to their fields. The simplest forms of irrigation were ditches dug from rivers to fields and dams to hold the water in place, but African farmers also used machinery to move water mechanically. The *shaduf* was a seesaw-like device consisting of a bucket attached to a long counterweighted pole on top of a frame; the weight opposite the bucket allowed farmers to lift water easily and swing it over to an irrigation ditch. The Archimedean screw was a large screw in a tube resting on an inclined plane. The bottom of the tube sat in water, and as the screw turned, it lifted the water up and out of the top of the tube. The *saqiya* was a type of water wheel turned by donkeys or oxen.

Rome took over Egypt in 30 B.C.E., after Augustus defeated Marc Antony and Cleopatra at the battle of Actium. Augustus annexed Egypt as a Roman province. This event caused Egypt's fortunes to plummet. Augustus considered Egypt his own personal estate and exploited it at the expense of its inhabitants. Most of the country's land was turned over to agriculture, and Egypt ended up growing a large portion of the grain eaten by Romans. Egypt also supplied Rome with papyrus, a reed used to make paper.

Over the next three centuries this agricultural exploitation resulted in the loss of farmland and declining fortunes for Egypt. Only after the Romans left did Egypt's farmers reorganize their properties.

Roman provinces had their own agricultural specialties that they exported to the capital. Crete was the best source for herbal medicines. Spain and Gaul made the best *garum*, a sauce that was made by fermenting fish in salt and that was used to flavor most Roman dishes. Romans also exported their own plants to other countries. Roman soldiers and colonists missed their wine, lentils, and olives, and so they attempted to plant their own favorite foods wherever they went. Grapes did so well in Gaul (France), Germany, and Spain that wines from those regions began to be popular with Romans during the imperial period. Even distant Britain, which the Romans occupied from 43 to 410 C.E., acquired Roman crops; celery, cilantro, fennel, carrots, pears, peaches, mulberries, and many other plants that now grow there were brought by the ancient Romans.

THE AMERICAS

BY AMY HACKNEY BLACKWELL

Historians do not know much about early agriculture in the Americas. The earliest farmers did not leave written records of their farming practices. To discover what crops were grown and when, scholars have to look for evidence of crops at archaeological sites, digging for fossilized seeds and attempting to date them through various scientific processes. There is currently a fair amount of disagreement among historians of agriculture as to when early Americans began farming, what they grew, and how crops spread through the Americas. Some scholars believe that the first American farmers grew corn in the highlands of Mexico around 4000 B.C.E. Others insist that agriculture began much earlier, perhaps as early as 8000 B.C.E., in the lowland forests of Central America and northern South America. At present there is not enough evidence available to answer any of these questions conclusively.

Despite the scholarly disputes, it is known that Americans did grow crops in ancient times and that they were certainly farming by 4000 B.C.E. Agriculture seems to have arisen independently in four separate areas: the Andes, Middle America from northern Panama to central Mexico, the Southwest of the United States, and the Eastern Woodlands of the United States In the Andes, from central Ecuador south to Chile, people began farming between 3500 and 2000 B.C.E. People in Mexico are believed to have started farming corn about 4000 B.C.E. and soon added beans and squash to their crops. The cultivation of corn traveled north to the Southwest of the present-day United States by 2000 B.C.E. Farmers in the Eastern Woodlands started cultivating a few local crops around 2000 B.C.E. but did not engage in large-scale agriculture until corn appeared there in the first century C.E.

The Americas, like Africa, were a less-than-ideal environment for the development and spread of agriculture. Unlike the Middle East, Europe, and Asia, the Americas do not have many native wild grains suitable for domestication. Teosinte, the probable ancestor of corn, was not nearly as easy to domesticate as wheat in the Middle East or rice in Asia. The Americas also lie along a north-south axis, as opposed to an east-west axis like Eurasia. Plants tend to be adapted for particular latitudes; they can move from east to west fairly easily because climate and day length remain the same, but they cannot move as easily from north to south because climate and day length change too much. In addition, the mountain ranges that run north to south in the Americas separated the east coasts from the west, preventing easy east-west transmission of crops. As a result, agriculture in the Americas was slow to develop and travel through the continents, and American civilizations never reached the level of development achieved by those in Eurasia.

THE TRINITY: CORN, BEANS, AND SQUASH

Humans developed agriculture in the Americas long before Europeans arrived and long before the famous three New World civilizations of Maya, Aztec, and Inca arose. The staple crops of these societies were corn, beans, and squash. These three crops were so ubiquitous and so often found together that historians have christened them the "trinity." Combining the three ingredients made for a balanced diet; the corn supplied energy, the beans provided protein, and the squash furnished other nutrients.

The trinity is very old. Historians have found numerous caves in Mexico that were inhabited by about 4000 B.C.E. Within these caves are traces of corn, beans, and squash. The residents of these caves lived primarily as hunter-gatherers; in the caves, archaeologists have found many bones of wild animals, such as deer and rabbit, as well as traces of pine nuts, hackberries, and other wild plants. Wild ancestors of squash, beans, and corn grew in the area, and the cave dwellers certainly gathered and ate them, but scientists have analyzed the remains in the caves and determined that some of the corn, beans, and squash were definitely domesticated. Corn, or maize, was the foundation of the trinity. It provided the bulk of calories in the form of carbohydrates. Transforming corn from its wild ancestor into the cultivated version took a long time; it was much more difficult than the process of domesticating wheat in Mesopotamia, mainly because the wild ancestor of corn is so drastically different from the domesticated version.

Modern corn is probably descended from a plant called teosinte. No one knows exactly how this transformation occurred. Teosinte, in fact, looks almost nothing like corn. Corn grows as a single stalk with many ears on it; each ear has multiple rows of seeds. Teosinte, in contrast, is a grass with many stalks, each of which contains several spikes with single rows of seeds. Hunter-gatherers could have used these seeds, but wild teosinte is not an impressive source of food. It grows throughout Mexico, Guatemala, and Nicaragua. There are five different species, some of which are annual (completing their life cycle in one year) and others perennial (living several years). Archaeologists believe that two of the annual species that grow in the Tehuacán valley in Mexico were probably the ancestors of corn. The first primitive cobs of what appears to be domestic corn grew between 2700 and 2600 B.C.E. near inhabited caves in the Tehuacán valley. The inhabitants were still hunter-gatherers who moved about with the seasons, but they grew a small crop of corn to give themselves a little food security.

This early corn was nothing like the large ears grown today. It had tiny ears with small kernels and resembled a modern crop known as Argentine popcorn. Its ears were only slightly bigger than those of teosinte. Nevertheless, scientists know this corn was domesticated, because it had kernels that could not release themselves from the cob; it could be reseeded only when humans removed the kernels and planted them. Cob sizes increased; between 500 B.C.E. and 1 C.E. cob length doubled in size.

Corn gradually spread through the Americas. The same small, primitive corn appeared in northern South America 1000 B.C.E., near the Pacific coast in Ecuador between 1200 and 800 B.C.E. and along the Orinoco River in Venezuela about 800 B.C.E. People in the southwestern United States were growing corn by about 1000 B.C.E. Small-kerneled corn reached the mountains of Peru by 450 C.E. Corn was not initially a staple of most peoples' diets; historians believe that much of the earliest domesticated corn was used to brew beer. As the years went by, however, corn provided an increasingly larger share of the calories of many American diets. Corn can be eaten whole, from the cob, but it was most important dried, which made it a source of food that could be stored year-round. People used stone mills to grind it into cornmeal and made this meal into flat bread or porridge. Corn is not an especially nutritious grain because it lacks two essential amino acids (the building blocks of proteins). Early Americans solved this problem by adding ashes to cornmeal to increase the niacin content and by combining corn with beans.

Beans form the second component of the trinity and supplied the protein that corn lacked. Lima beans appear to have been domesticated first, followed by the beans now called common beans, which include navy, kidney, and red beans, among many others. Ancient common beans evolved into the more than 100 types of domestic beans known today. Common beans and the lima beans were all widely cultivated in the Americas long before Europeans arrived. Scientists can tell that the beans were domesticated because, just as with domesticated corn, these beans cannot expel their own seeds; humans must do that in order to plant the next crop. Beans appear to have been domesticated later than corn. Historians had long theorized that corn and beans were domesticated simultaneously, but that does not now seem to have been the case.

Mexican and Andean Americans domesticated lima beans independently of one another. Historians currently believe that people in the Andes may have started growing lima beans around 2000 B.C.E. Earlier research into this area led to speculation that humans may have domesticated limas around 5600 B.C.E., but these dates are now considered inaccurate. The Andean lima was a large-seeded variety. It had spread along the Pacific coast of Chile and Peru by about 400 B.C.E. The smaller-seeded Mexican lima bean appeared later, around 800 C.E. Large-seeded lima beans predominated at higher altitudes, while small-seeded varieties grew at lower altitudes. Lima beans are high in protein and fiber; people ate them fresh or dried them to save for later. They cooked dried beans by boiling them.

To trace the ancestry of various types of common beans, scientists have analyzed the protein content of domestic and wild beans in Mexico, Central America, and South America. They discovered that common beans were domesticated twice, in two different places. One type of bean was domesticated in Mexico, and another type was domesticated in the Andes. The earliest known domestic common beans were grown about 300 B.C.E. in Mexico. Common beans, similar to lima beans, provided necessary protein to ancient diets, especially when combined with corn. Common beans keep well when dried, so people could count on eating them year-round.

Squash formed the third component of the trinity. Humans cultivated several varieties of squash that still exist today as acorn, spaghetti, and patty pan squashes; pumpkins; and zucchini. Green and yellow squashes came from the eastern United States, and orange pumpkin squashes came from Mexico. Historians know little about the process by which humans domesticated squashes. Some experts believe squash cultivation may have occurred simultaneously with corn cultivation, perhaps around 3000 B.C.E.

Mesoamerican Civilizations

Agriculture facilitated the rise of the great Mesoamerican civilizations, which built large cities with complex bureaucracies and religions. The Olmec lived on the coast of the Gulf of Mexico between 1500 B.C.E. and 400 C.E. They worshipped a rain god, a sign that rain was extremely important for growing their crops. The city of Teotihuacán, near modern Mexico City, was inhabited from 150 B.C.E. to 750 C.E. In its heyday it was the size of Rome. Its inhabitants also worshipped a weather deity, a fanged storm god who would release the rains to grow the crops of corn, beans, squash, and peppers.

The Maya, a civilization that lasted from about 1800 B.C.E. to the 17th century C.E., had a vast empire that encompassed parts of Guatemala, Mexico, Honduras, and Belize, with several regional capitals. Their kings and bureaucrats oversaw a large population of citizens, most of them farmers. To feed the population, Mayan farmers maintained vast permanent plantings that included raised fields, terracing, canals, and other irrigation systems. The raised fields and the canals were constructed together; when the farmers dug out the canals, they dumped the excess dirt onto the fields. This provided the crops with a steady source of water and kept them away from floods. The canals were a valuable food source, too; farmers allowed wild turtles and fish to live in them and caught them for meat. The Mayan priests maintained a complex calendar that helped farmers keep track of the solar year. This calendar told farmers when to plant their crops and when to harvest them. It helped farmers plan their year so they could produce the best possible crop.

Despite the fact that about 70 percent of the Mayan people worked as farmers, Mayan farming never produced the vast surpluses of grain that farmers in other areas achieved. The damp climate made it difficult to store corn for more than a year. The Maya had no domestic animals to help them plow and instead had to do all their work by hand. Corn, the largest crop, contains little protein, and the Mayan diet had few other protein sources; as a result, most people were malnourished.

The Andes: Quinoa, Potatoes, Llamas, and Guinea Pigs

People living in the Andes mountains of Peru developed their own crops and domestic animals suited to their dry climate and high altitude. They cultivated two crops not grown elsewhere, the potato and the grain quinoa. They also domesticated three animals: the llama, the alpaca, and the guinea pig. Andean Americans ate many types of wild potatoes; there is fossil evidence that people consumed wild potatoes as early as 10,000 B.C.E. in Chile. Potatoes were domesticated between 2000 and 1200 B.C.E. The people of the Andes cultivated four types of potatoes, one of which became the common potato eaten all over the world today. People of the Andes also cultivated the sweet potato. Archaeologists have found evidence of domestic sweet potatoes dating to about 2000 B.C.E. The sweet potato spread throughout the tropical portions of the Americas and was a staple of the Caribbean diet by the time Columbus arrived.

Quinoa is a grain that produces edible seeds. People began cultivating it from 2000 to 3000 B.C.E. It grows well in dry soils at high elevations and is quite hardy. Quinoa contains a complete set of amino acids, which meant that people did not have to combine it with a legume to get their necessary protein. It also contains fiber, iron, magnesium, and phosphorus. People boiled it like rice and ate it as a cereal.

Llamas and alpacas are four-legged animals related to camels. Their wild ancestors, the guanaco (for the llama) and the vicuña (for the alpaca), lived in herds with dominance hierarchies, making them easy for humans to domesticate. The process of domestication occurred gradually between 5000 and 2500 B.C.E. People used llamas and alpacas for both wool and meat. They also used llamas as pack animals on the high mountain paths. Historians believe humans may have domesticated llamas and quinoa simultaneously. Llamas eat wild quinoa and pass the seeds onto the ground in their manure. When people began herding wild llamas and shutting them in enclosures at night, the llamas' manure would have contained both seeds to grow quinoa and natural fertilizer to help them germinate. After a successful crop of quinoa started growing, the farmers would move the llamas to another corral. The quinoa grew inside the enclosure, safe from grazing llamas.

The guinea pig was the third domesticated animal of the Andes. Hunter-gatherers between 5500 and 10,000 B.C.E. consumed a great deal of wild guinea pig meat. Between 2500 and 5000 B.C.E. people began keeping guinea pigs in their settlements to save the trouble of hunting them and ensure a steady supply of meat. Guinea pigs were ideal candidates for in-home domestication. They reproduce rapidly and prolifically, they eat table scraps, and they like to live in close quarters.

Southwestern United States

Agriculture first appeared in the southwestern region of the present-day United States about 1000 B.C.E. People living in caves in the mountains of New Mexico were growing corn and squash around 800 to 1200 B.C.E. Beans arrived slightly later, around 400 B.C.E. The tools and pots found with the fossilized remains of corn and squash indicate that the cave dwellers were not colonists from Mexico but instead local hunter-gatherers who made occasional trips south of the Rio Grande and returned home with seeds. Once agriculture arrived in the region, southwestern Americans adopted it quickly. Some historians believe these people had already domesticated some local seed crops such as little barley, amaranth, or chenopod, which prepared them for larger-scale agriculture with corn. Scholars agree it was certainly possible that foragers had discovered these local seeds and begun growing them deliberately, but so far no one has found changes in the forms of these local seeds that would indicate domestication.

The people of the Southwest managed to create farming practices that succeeded in a variety of environments and at different elevations, adapting their agriculture to local landscapes and wild animals. Early southwestern farmers lived in circular houses in small settlements. They kept their corn in underground storage pits and spent much of their time tending crops and grinding corn, which became an increasingly important portion of their diet as the centuries went by. Nevertheless, they continued to gather such wild plants as cactus, mesquite, grasses, pinyon, and agave. They hunted mountain sheep, mule deer, and pronghorn antelope. Agriculture did not become the primary means of sustenance for southwestern Americans until about the first century C.E. One reason this transformation took so long was the problem of irrigation. The southwestern United States has little rainfall, and it was a constant challenge to keep crops alive in the arid environment. The earliest farmers used groundwater to irrigate their crops; they planted their fields near springs and lakes and counted on the high water table to keep the plants alive. Later farmers built irrigation canals and dams to hold water until they needed it for their fields.

Eastern United States

The Native Americans who lived in the eastern United States invented agriculture independently of those who lived in the Southwest. They domesticated their first plants between 2500 and 1500 B.C.E., focusing on local seed plants. The four so-called founder crops of the eastern United States were sunflowers, sumpweed (a plant related to the dais and, grown for its seeds), goosefoot (related to spinach), and a small squash that provided seeds. This squash was the predecessor of the modern acorn squash and summer squashes.

All four of these crops were highly nutritious, comprising 17 to 32 percent protein, compared with wheat's 8 to 14 percent. Both sumpweed and sunflower seeds are high in oil content, providing healthy fats with dense concentrations of calories and vitamins. Despite their nutrition, though, these four crops could not sustain communities that survived solely by farming. All of the crops had disadvantages that discouraged farmers. Sumpweed, for example, is related to ragweed and causes hay fever and skin rashes; it also smells bad. None of the founder crops could produce anything like the agricultural surplus of wheat or corn. (Wheat comes from the Middle East and Europe and did not arrive in the Americas until it was carried across the ocean by European settlers during the 16th century. Consequently, Americans of that period continued to support themselves mainly by hunting wild game and gathering wild plants.)

Between 500 and 200 B.C.E. the eastern tribes began cultivating three more seed crops: knotweed, maygrass, and barley. All three of these plants have very small seeds that do not yield nearly the harvest volumes of major grains such as wheat. Although people supplemented their diets with these new grains, they still had to rely on wild food sources for most of their nutrition and calories. Would-be farmers had no other options. They could domesticate only those plants that already grew in the area, and none of the native species of the eastern United States lent itself to agriculture in the way wheat and barley did. Otherwise, however, conditions in this region were excellent for farming; the soil was rich and the water supply ample. The climate was pleasant and encouraged the growth of many plants. The people living in the region knew their local plants and did what they could to domesticate them. The Hopewell culture that existed in Ohio from 200 B.C.E. to 400 C.E. supported itself in large part with locally domesticated crops, but within the region there were simply not the resources needed to expand agriculture, so most societies remained small groups of hunter-gatherers.

Mexican crops did not reach the eastern United States until after 1 C.E. Corn arrived around 200 C.E., but it was not until 1100 that American Indians began growing the nutritious Mexican trio of corn, beans, and squash. In many areas these three Mexican crops replaced local crops entirely. At that time the human population increased rapidly, as it typically does when societies settle down and adopt an agricultural lifestyle. People began building the larger towns that traditionally accompany the advent of large-scale agriculture.

Farming Implements

All ancient American civilizations were Stone Age civilizations, meaning that they used stone to make most of their tools and had not yet discovered how to use metals. They also used wood and bone to make handles and tools, clay to make pottery, and straw to make baskets. The earliest American farmers used pointed sticks to dig the soil. As they became more expert at farming, they made more complicated tools such as hoes, usually with long wooden handles and stone blades tied on with leather cords. These implements were designed to make long days in the fields more comfortable and efficient, eliminating the need for farmers to get down on their hands and knees to work the soil. People probably used woven baskets to collect their crops at harvest time, and they stored dried corn and beans in clay containers. One important agricultural device was a kind of mill called a quern, a flat stone used for grinding corn. A person would place a handful of corn on the quern and use another stone to crush it into dust. This was a very laborious process, and women in ancient American agricultural societies typically spent many hours every day grinding corn.

An Absence of Domestic Animals

Aside from Andean llamas, alpacas, and guinea pigs, as well as dogs in North America, Americans did not domesticate mammals. The Americas did not have any large mammals that could be used to plow fields. People had to do all the plowing and tilling by hand. As a result, American farmers tended to grow many plants in single fields, letting bean plants twine up cornstalks, for example; in contrast, wheat farmers in the Middle East and rice farmers in Asia tended to dedicate single fields to one grain crop.

See also BUILDING TECHNIQUES AND MATERIALS; CALENDARS AND CLOCKS; CERAMICS AND POTTERY; CHILDREN; CITIES; CLIMATE AND GEOGRAPHY; CRAFTS; DEATH AND BURIAL PRACTICES; ECONOMY; EMPIRES AND DYNASTIES; EMPLOYMENT AND LABOR; FESTIVALS; FOOD AND DIET; GOVERNMENT ORGANIZATION; HEALTH AND DISEASE; HOUSEHOLD GOODS; HUNTING, FISHING, AND GATHERING; ILLUMINATION; INVENTIONS; METALLURGY; MIGRATION AND POPULATION MOVEMENTS; NATURAL DISASTERS; NOMADIC AND PASTORAL SOCIETIES; OCCUPATIONS; RELIGION AND COSMOLOGY; RESISTANCE AND DISSENT; SETTLEMENT PATTERNS; SLAVES AND SLAVERY; SOCIAL ORGANIZATION; SPORTS AND RECREATION; STORAGE AND PRESERVATION; TOWNS AND VILLAGES; TRADE AND EXCHANGE; WAR AND CONQUEST.

Egypt

Hymn to the Nile, ca. 2100 B.C.E.

Hail to thee, O Nile! Who manifests thyself over this land, and comes to give life to Egypt! Mysterious is thy issuing forth from the darkness, on this day whereon it is celebrated! Watering the orchards created by Re, to cause all the cattle to live, you give the earth to drink, inexhaustible one! Path that descends from the sky, loving the bread of Seb and the first-fruits of Nepera, You cause the workshops of Ptah to prosper!

Lord of the fish, during the inundation, no bird alights on the crops. You create the grain, you bring forth the barley, assuring perpetuity to the temples. If you cease your toil and your work, then all that exists is in anguish. If the gods suffer in heaven, then the faces of men waste away.

Then He torments the flocks of Egypt, and great and small are in agony. But all is changed for mankind when He comes; He is endowed with the qualities of Nun. If He shines, the earth is joyous, every stomach is full of rejoicing, every spine is happy, every jaw-bone crushes [its food].

He brings the offerings, as chief of provisioning; He is the creator of all good things, as master of energy, full of sweetness in his choice. If offerings are made it is thanks to Him. He brings forth the herbage for the flocks, and sees that each god receives his sacrifices. All that depends on Him is a precious incense. He spreads himself over Egypt, filling the granaries, renewing the marts, watching over the goods of the unhappy. . . .

Where misery existed, joy manifests itself; all beasts rejoice. The children of Sobek, the sons of Neith, the cycle of the gods which dwells in him, are prosperous. No more reservoirs for watering the fields! He makes mankind valiant, enriching some, bestowing his love on others. None commands at the same time as himself. He creates the offerings without the aid of Neith, making mankind for himself with multiform care.

He shines when He issues forth from the darkness, to cause his flocks to prosper. It is his force that gives existence to all things; nothing remains hidden for him. Let men clothe themselves to fill his gardens. He watches over his works, producing the inundation during the night. The associate of Ptah . . . He causes all his servants to exist, all writings and divine words, and that which He needs in the North.

It is with the words that He penetrates into his dwelling; He issues forth at his pleasure through the magic spells. Your unkindness brings destruction to the fish; it is then that prayer is made for the [annual] water of the season; Southern Egypt is seen in the same state as the North. Each one is with his instruments of labor. None remains behind his companions. None clothes himself with garments, The children of the noble put aside their ornaments.

The night remains silent, but all is changed by the inundation; it is a healing-balm for all mankind. Establisher of justice! Mankind desires you, supplicating you to answer their prayers; You answer them by the inundation! Men offer the first-fruits of corn; all the gods adore you! The birds descend not on the soil. It is believed that with your hand of gold you make bricks of silver! But we are not nourished on lapis-lazuli; wheat alone gives vigor.

A festal song is raised for you on the harp, with the accompaniment of the hand. Your young men and your children acclaim you and prepare their [long] exercises. You are the august ornament of the earth, letting your bark advance before men, lifting up the heart of women in labor, and loving the multitude of the flocks.

When you shine in the royal city, the rich man is sated with good things, the poor man even disdains the lotus; all that is produced is of the choicest; all the plants exist for your children. If you have refused [to grant] nourishment, the dwelling is silent, devoid of all that is good, the country falls exhausted.

O inundation of the Nile, offerings are made unto you, men are immolated to you, great festivals are instituted for you. Birds are sacrificed to you, gazelles are taken for you in the mountain, pure flames are prepared for you. . . .

Men exalt him like the cycle of the gods, they dread him who creates the heat, even him who has made his son the universal master in order to give prosperity to Egypt. Come (and) prosper! Come (and) prosper! O Nile, come (and) prosper! O you who make men to live through his flocks and his flocks through his orchards! Come (and) prosper, come, O Nile, come (and) prosper!

From: Oliver J. Thatcher, ed., *The Library of Original Sources*. Vol. 1: *The Ancient World* (Milwaukee: University Research Extension , 1907), pp. 79–83.

Asia and the Pacific

Hymn to Goddess Earth, ca. 600 B.C.E.

1. Truth, greatness, universal order [rita], strength, consecration, creative fervor [tapas], spiritual exaltation [brahma], the sacrifice, support the earth. May this earth, the mistress of that which was and shall be, prepare for us a broad domain!

2. The earth that has heights, and slopes, and great plains, that supports the plants of manifold virtue, free from the pressure that comes from the midst of men, she shall spread out for us, and fit herself for us!

3. The earth upon which the sea, and the rivers and the waters, upon which food and the tribes of men have arisen, upon which this breathing, moving life exists, shall afford us precedence in drinking!

4. The earth whose are the four regions of space, upon which food and the tribes of men have arisen, which supports the manifold breathing, moving therein, shall afford us cattle and other possessions also! . . .

7. The broad earth, which the sleepless gods ever attentively guard, shall milk for us precious honey, and, moreover, besprinkle us with glory! . . .

11. Thy snowy mountain heights, and thy forests, O earth, shall be kind to us! The brown, the black, the red, the multi-colored, the firm earth, that is protected by Indra, I have settled upon, not suppressed, not slain, not wounded.

12. Into thy middle set us, O earth, and into thy navel, into the nourishing strength that has grown up from thy body; purify thyself for us! The earth is the mother, and I the son of the earth; Parganya is the father; he, too, shall save us! . . .

17. Upon the firm, broad earth, the all-begetting mother of the plants, that is supported by [divine] law, upon her, propitious and kind, may we ever pass our lives! . . .

19. Agni (fire) is in the earth, in the plants, the waters hold Agni, Agni is in the stones; Agni is within men, Agnis [fires] are within cattle, within horses. . . .

22. Upon the earth men give to the gods the sacrifice, they prepared oblation; upon the earth mortal men live pleasantly by food. May this earth give us breath and life, may she cause me to reach old age!

23. The fragrance, O earth, that has arisen upon thee, which the plants and the waters hold, which the Gandharvas and the Apsaras have partaken of, with that make me fragrant: not anyone shall hate us! . . .

25. That fragrance of thine which is in men, the loveliness and charm that is in male and female, that which is in steeds and heroes, that which is in the wild animals with trunks [elephants], the luster that is in the maiden, O earth, with that do thou blend us: not any one shall hate us!

26. Rock, stone, dust is this earth; this earth is supported, held together. To this golden-breasted earth I have rendered obeisance.

27. The earth, upon whom the forest-sprung trees ever stand firm, the all-nourishing, compact earth, do we invoke.

28. Rising or sitting, standing or walking, may we not stumble with our right or left foot upon the earth!

29. To the pure earth I speak, to the ground, the soil that has grown through the brahma [spiritual exaltation]. Upon thee, that holdest nourishment, prosperity, food, and ghee, we would settle down, O earth! . . .

36. Thy summer, O earth, thy rainy season, thy autumn, winter, early spring, and spring; thy decreed yearly seasons, thy days and nights shall yield us milk. . . .

42. To the earth upon whom are food, and rice and barley, upon whom live these five races of men, to the earth, the wife of Parganya, that is fattened by rain, be reverence! . . .

46. The serpent, the scorpion with thirsty fangs, that hibernating torpidly lies upon thee; the worm, and whatever living thing, O earth, moves in the rainy season, shall, when it creeps, not creep upon us: with what is auspicious (on thee) be gracious to us! . . .

52. The earth upon whom day and night jointly, black and bright, have been decreed, the broad earth covered and enveloped with rain, shall kindly place us into every pleasant abode! . . .

53. Heaven, and earth, and air have here given me expanse; Agni, Sûrya, the waters, and all the gods together have given me wisdom. . . .

59. Gentle, fragrant, kindly, with the sweet drink [kîlâla] in her udder, rich in milk, the broad earth together with [her] milk shall give us courage! . . .

62. Thy laps, O earth, free from ailment! Free from disease, shall be produced for us! May we attentively, through our long lives, be bearers of bali-offerings to thee!

63. O mother earth, kindly set me down upon a well-founded place! With (father) heaven cooperating, O thou wise one, do thou place me into happiness and prosperity!

From: Max Müller, ed., *Sacred Books of the East*. Vol. 42: *Hymns of the Atharva-Veda*, section 12:1, translated by Maurice Bloomfield (New York: Oxford University Press, 1897).

Rome

Cato: On Agriculture, *excerpt, ca. 150* B.C.E.

. . . Perform the vow for the health of the cattle as follows: Make an offering to Mars Silvanus in the forest during the daytime for each head of cattle: 3 pounds of meal, 4½ pounds of bacon, 4½ pounds of meat, and 3 pints of wine. You may place the viands in one vessel and the wine likewise in one vessel. Either a slave or a free man may make this offering. After the ceremony is over, consume the offering on the spot at once. A woman may not take part in this offering or see how it is performed. You may vow the vow every year if you wish. . . .

. . . Before harvest the sacrifice of the *porca praecidanea* [the hog offered in sacrifice before the harvest] should be offered in this manner: Offer a sow as *porca praecidanea* to Ceres before harvesting spelt, wheat, barley, beans, and rapeseed and address a prayer, with incense and wine, to Janus, Jupiter, and Juno, before offering the sow. Make an offering of cakes to Janus, with these words: "Father Janus, in offering these cakes, I humbly beg that thou wilt be gracious and merciful to me and my children, my house and my household." Then make an offering of cake to Jupiter with these words: "In offering this cake, O Jupiter I humbly beg that thou, pleased by this offering, wilt be gracious and merciful to me and my children, my house and my household." Then present the wine to Janus, saying: "Father Janus, as I prayed humbly in offering the cakes, so wilt thou to the same end be honored by this wine placed before thee." And then pray to Jupiter thus: "Jupiter, wilt thou deign to accept the cake; wilt thou deign to accept the wine placed before thee." Then offer up the *porca praecidanea*. When the entrails have been removed, make an offering of cakes to Janus, with a prayer as before, and an offering of a cake to Jupiter, with a prayer as before. After the same manner, also offer wine to Janus and offer wine to Jupiter, as was directed before for the offering of the cakes and the consecration of the cake. Afterwards offer entrails and wine to Ceres."

From: G. Goetz, ed., *De Agri Cultura* (Leipzig, Germany: Teubner, 1922). Republished in *Cato and Varro: On Agriculture*, translated by W. D. Hooper and H. B. Ash (Loeb Classical Library, 1934).

FURTHER READING

E. N. Anderson, *The Food of China* (New Haven, Conn.: Yale University Press, 1990).

Graeme Barker, *Prehistoric Farming in Europe* (Cambridge, U.K.: Cambridge University Press, 1985).

Peter Bellwood, *First Farmers* (Malden, Mass.: Blackwell, 2005).

Amy Bogaard, *Neolithic Farming in Central Europe* (New York: Routledge, 2004).

Andrew Dalby, *Cato: On Farming/De Agri Cultura* (London: Prospect, 1998).

Jared Diamond, *Guns, Germs, and Steel* (New York: Norton, 1997).

André Dollinger, "Hymn to Hathor: The Egyptian Agricultural Cycle." Available online. URL: http://nefertiti.iwebland.com/texts/hathorhymn.htm. Downloaded on August 7, 2006.

Stephen L. Dyson, *The Roman Countryside* (London: Duckworth, 2003).

Paul Erdkamp, *The Grain Market in the Roman Empire* (Cambridge, U.K.: Cambridge University Press, 2005).

Peter J. Fowler, *Farming in the First Millennium* A.D.*: British Agriculture between Julius Caesar and William the Conqueror* (Cambridge, U.K.: Cambridge University Press, 2002).

Victor Davis Hanson, *The Other Greeks: The Family Farm and the Agrarian Roots of Western Civilization* (New York: Free Press, 1995).

Victor Davis Hanson, *Warfare and Agriculture in Classical Greece* (Berkeley: University of California Press, 1998).

Catherine C. Harris, "Ancient Egyptian Agriculture," *Tour Egypt Monthly* 2, no. 7 (July 1, 2001). Available online. URL:

http://www.touregypt.net/magazine/mag07012001/magf5.htm. Downloaded on August 7, 2006.
Cho-Yun Hsu, Xu Zhuoyun, and Jack L. Dull, *Han Agriculture: The Formation of Early Chinese Agrarian Economy, 206 B.C. – A.D. 220* (Seattle: University of Washington Press, 1979).
R. Douglas Hurt, *Indian Agriculture in America: Prehistory to Present* (Lawrence: University of Kansas Press, 1996).
Signe Isager and Jens Erik Skydsgaard, *Ancient Greek Agriculture: An Introduction* (London: Routledge, 1992).
Jules Janick, "Ancient Egyptian Agriculture and the Origins of Horticulture." Available online. URL: http://www.hort.purdue.edu/newcrop/history/egypt/egyptpaper.pdf. Downloaded August 7, 2006.
Franklin Hiram King, *Farmers of Forty Centuries; or, Permanent Agriculture in China, Korea and Japan* (Whitefish, Mont.: Kessinger Publishing, 2004).
Bruce D. Smith, *Rivers of Change: Essays on Early Agriculture in Eastern North America* (Washington, D.C.: Smithsonian Institution Press, 1992).
Bruce D. Smith, *The Emergence of Agriculture* (New York: Scientific American Library, 1995).
K. D. White, *Country Life in Classical Times* (Ithaca, N.Y.: Cornell University Press, 1977).

► architecture

INTRODUCTION

Architecture is a human activity that combines a number of fields, including art, design, geometry, engineering, construction, and materials science (the science that studies the properties of materials, including, for example, their strength and durability). Architects draw on their knowledge of these fields to create structures for human use. In the ancient world these structures included not only homes but also a great many public buildings, including temples, tombs, government buildings, pyramids, granaries, theaters, athletic stadiums, and the like.

Archaeologists have few remains of prehistoric architecture to study, primarily because the earliest human-built structures were built with nondurable materials, so they have disappeared. The earliest architecture was a haphazard affair and consisted of homes that were built with whatever materials lay at hand. Thus, depending on local geography, prehistoric peoples built their shelters out of such materials as reeds, mud bricks, poles, logs, stones, or animal hides, or they found shelter in caves. These structures tended to be temporary because the earliest peoples were hunter-gatherers, so they moved about from place to place in search of food. There was very little "architecture" involved, and little attention was paid to the aesthetic qualities of the structure. The structure served a purely functional purpose—that of keeping out the wind, rain, and snow while providing the inhabitants with at least a minimal level of safety and security and storage for their few belongings.

True architecture did not develop until people began to lead more settled lives, staying in one place long enough to make the construction of more permanent and aesthetically pleasing buildings worthwhile. Only when people turned to agriculture rather than hunting and gathering for their food did they begin to gather in ever-larger communities, forming the first hamlets, then larger towns, and finally cities where architecture flourished.

Thus, the development of agriculture had a profound affect on architecture. People gathered in communities began to develop more formalized belief systems, giving rise to organized religions and the temples where those religions were practiced. Further, because so many of the buildings found in places like Greece, Rome, and the Americas were so immense, they often took generations to build, requiring a settled, stable population of workers. Surplus food supplies, made possible only with agriculture, supported a class of priests as well as others who provided to city dwellers the fruits of civilization. Included would be poets and dramatists, who needed theaters for the production of their work.

Also included were classes of bureaucrats and civil servants, who ran the affairs of the community out of public buildings. The emergence of hereditary royal families gave rise to magnificent public buildings erected to demonstrate the power of the ruling class, and elaborate tombs, including the immense pyramids of ancient Egypt and Central America, ensured that royalty and members of the upper classes enjoyed a smooth trip into the afterlife. As society became more socially stratified, meaning that upper and lower classes of people developed, architecture became a way for the upper classes to design and build magnificent homes and villas that became a symbol of their status.

Architecture also provided more practical structures. For the military it supplied fortifications and walls along borders. For farmers it provided granaries, barns, and similar structures. For the upper classes, it furnished cookhouses, privies (toilets), bathhouses, gardens, terraces, and similar structures that enhanced the quality of life. Architects also learned to construct and position buildings in a way that in the 21st century would be called "environmentally friendly." As firewood became more and more scarce because of the growth of cities and populations, architects learned to take advantage of the sun to provide warmth.

Architecture drew on the skills of numerous people. An architect had to design a building in a way that guaranteed it would last. He had to understand the properties of the materials he used to ensure that they were suitable for the building. As time progressed and as contact and trade between cities and empires developed, builders gained access to a wider variety of materials. Where stone was used, miners had to quarry, cut, smooth, and transport immense blocks. Builders had to organize masses of laborers to assemble the building, devise techniques for lifting heavy materials into place, and take care of such everyday chores as keeping track of the budget; in many cases they had to oversee slaves, making sure that they were fed and housed.

As architecture became more developed, builders had to understand such elements as drainage systems, and in time they learned to incorporate such features as arches, vaulted ceilings, domes, and so on. Stonemasons were highly skilled artisans who carved stone ornaments, including statues, that became part of the structure, and other artists painted murals and frescoes that enhanced the aesthetic appeal of the structure. City planners learned to arrange buildings in a way that increased their usefulness. For example, as cities grew and trade between cities and kingdom developed, architects arranged buildings in clusters surrounded by fortified walls and gates, to protect the population from marauders who might seize the city's wealth. Because it was not possible to move large amounts of earth, buildings had to be arranged around natural features of the terrain.

Because architecture was a community pursuit that required large numbers of workers and vast sums of money, most of the buildings that survive from ancient times were palaces for royalty, temples, or tombs. Royal palaces were a testament to the power and authority of the king or other ruler, and because they were as magnificent as temples, they served to remind the people that the ruler derived his authority from the gods. Temples were large and elaborate, much like the mosques and Christian churches built during the medieval period, to become a focus of worship for the particular god or goddess in whose honor the temple was built. Building such temples in parts of the world was considered a religious act. Tombs took many forms, in particular that of pyramids, but these pyramids and other public structures often served—or may have served—other purposes, such as those of scientific and astronomical observatories and calendars.

AFRICA

BY MICHAEL J. O'NEAL

Studies of the architecture of ancient Africa tend to feature most prominently that of ancient Egypt, located on the north of the continent adjacent to the Sahara Desert. The remainder of the continent, particularly in the context of discussions of ancient life, is generally referred to collectively as "sub-Saharan Africa," or that part of Africa that lies south of the massive Sahara Desert.

Because of a lack of written records and because the kingdoms and nations of sub-Saharan Africa in general never achieved the prominence or lasted as long as ancient Egypt, not a great deal is known about the architecture of this vast region. Much of the architecture has disappeared, leaving archaeologists with fragments and ruins, often just foundations, to study. Often they are required to make inferences about ancient African architecture on the basis of limited evidence. Then, too, many ancient architectural sites were lost when the Great Aswān Dam was constructed on the Nile River, flooding vast tracts of land to form Lake Nasser. Nonetheless, archaeologists have discovered a number of intriguing monuments, ruins, and, in some cases, intact structures that provide insight into the architectural skills of the ancient Africans.

Much of the architecture of sub-Saharan African was strongly influenced by that of the Egyptian dynasties. Just as ancient Egypt was the home of towering obelisks (a towering pillar that rises to a point), royal tombs, palaces, and the pyramids, so can similar structures, or their remains, be found in other parts of Africa as the influence of Egypt spread and grew. Influences can also be traced back to the Carthaginians and the Middle East.

ETHIOPIA

The early history of Ethiopia, sometimes called Abyssinia, is dominated by the kingdom of Axum. The kingdom originated in about the second century B.C.E. and reached the height of its power from the fourth through the seventh centuries C.E. Axum controlled most of modern-day Ethiopia as well as parts of Egypt, the Sudan, Eritrea, and parts of the Middle East, and its influence rivaled that of the empires of the Egyptians, Greeks, Persians, and Byzantines. It was a major trading nation, serving as a link between Asia and the Mediterranean region. It was also the first African state to issue its own coins. Archaeologists have uncovered the ruins of reservoirs, temples, and cities that attest to the influence of the kingdom, including the ruins at Yeha, a pre-Axumite kingdom. But perhaps the most intriguing remains from ancient Axum are its black granite obelisks.

Yeha lies in a remote part of what is called the Tigray region, several hours by car from the city of Axum. Visitors are willing to make the trip to see the remains of the Temple of the Moon, built in about 500 B.C.E. While little is known about the people who built the temple, the ruins themselves are striking. The roof and upper stories are missing, but the remains are nearly 40 feet tall. The inward-reclining walls are made of sandstone blocks that fit together with near-perfect precision; ancient Africans believed that the temple could be filled with water and not a single drop would leak out, despite the fact that no mortar was used to connect the blocks.

Axum is regarded as the successor kingdom to Yeha in that part of Ethiopia. The most prominent architectural site in Axum features its obelisks, carved beginning in about 400 C.E., which were among the tallest stone monuments in the ancient world. The largest one, which has fallen and lies on the ground in six pieces, would have stood nearly 110 feet high. The tallest standing obelisk is about 78 feet tall.

Archaeologists have long been puzzled by the carvings on this and other nearby obelisks. Although the obelisk was carved out of a single block of stone, it is covered with carvings that give it the appearance of having 13 stories, each "floor" with its own "windows" carved into the stone. At the base are carvings of "doors," which even have locks and door knockers carved into them. Archaeologists are not certain about the purpose of the obelisks. That they were erected near tombs suggests that they may have been built as memorials to dead kings and queens and may have represented stairways to heaven for the kingdom's rulers. In common with obelisks throughout the ancient world, they may have served as gigantic sundials, enabling people to tell time as the obelisk's shadow grew shorter and longer and changed position with the movement of the sun.

The tallest standing obelisk was recently returned to Ethiopia. Prior to World War II, Italy invaded Ethiopia, and the Italian dictator Benito Mussolini ordered the obelisk to be dismantled and taken to Italy. For many years the Ethiopian government asked the Italians to return it. Their request was finally granted, and in April 2005 the obelisk was loaded onto cargo planes and returned to its rightful home.

The Cathedral and the Ark of the Covenant Another archaeological site from the ancient kingdom of Axum is located just a few hundred yards away from the obelisks. Two Christian churches, both dedicated to Saint Mary of Zion, are enclosed in a walled compound. Between the two churches are the ruins of an ancient temple. According to legend, the area had been a swamp infested with evil spirits, but God came to the aid of the local people, who descended from the nearby hills and threw dust on the site to drive out the spirits. On this site were built shrines, and around these shines the kingdom of Axum gathered.

Then, in 331 C.E., Axum's king Ezana (whose reign began ca. 330) was converted to Christianity. In 372 he ordered the construction of a magnificent cathedral, the oldest Christian church in sub-Saharan Africa. The church was destroyed by Muslim invaders in the 1500s but has since been rebuilt. A Portuguese explorer, writing in the early 1500s, left behind a detailed description of the church, with its five long naves, vaulted ceiling, a choir, painted walls, and two surrounding walls. A major historical mystery surrounds the site. That such a massive church would be built in an area so distant from the center of the Christian world has suggested to some scholars that the church was built for a specific purpose: to house the Ark of the Covenant.

The Ark was a gold-lined chest. According to the Old Testament, the prophet Moses placed the stone tablets inscribed with the Ten Commandments into the Ark. In the centuries that followed, the Ark was the source of mysterious power. After it was moved from Mount Sinai, where Moses received the Ten Commandments, it was originally housed in the Holy of Holies, a chamber in the Jewish temple in Jerusalem. It later disappeared, and for generations historians, treasure seekers, archaeologists, and others have tried to find it. (The search for the Ark even formed the basis for one of the *Indiana Jones* movies.) Some believe it is housed in a mysterious "treasury" that is part of the cathedral site at Axum, where it has been guarded for many centuries.

Some scholars have theorized that the Ark is in Ethiopia because it was stolen and taken to Axum by Menelik, the son of Axum's most famous historical figure, the Queen of Sheba. According to this theory, the queen traveled to Jerusalem to meet King Solomon because she wanted to see firsthand the results of his architectural skills, particularly the temple of Jerusalem. While she was there, she became pregnant by King Solomon, and after she returned to Ethiopia she had a son. Years later, her son left Ethiopia to be with his father but was driven out of Jerusalem by the jealousy of the city's elders. He left the city in the company of a number of the elders' firstborn sons, and according to this theory, either Menelik or the sons took the Ark with them. An alternate theory is that centuries later the Jews hid the Ark in Egypt to protect it from invaders. Later, after the kingdom of Axum converted to Christianity, church officials moved the Ark to Axum, where it has remained for 1,700 years. However, this is pure speculation, as no one has uncovered the Ark at Axum (or anyplace else, for that matter).

The City, Palaces, and Homes Archaeologists have uncovered and in many cases tried to reconstruct Axum's royal palaces and the homes of some of the kingdom's wealthy citizens. These structures consisted of tall pavilions mounted on high foundations. These foundations show that Axumite architecture favored walls that were not long and straight. Rather, the walls were indented at regular intervals along their length, creating recesses and salients (projecting segments of the wall) on the inside. Evidence suggests that most of these buildings were one or two stories tall.

Some of these buildings were of considerable size. The royal palace, called Ta'akha Maryam, is the largest that has been excavated. It measures nearly 400 feet by more than 260 feet. The pavilion in the center had nine rooms, all with roofs supported by columns and floors covered with flagstones. The palace also featured a central peristyle (an open area or courtyard surrounded by columns) and a number of four-columned porticoes, or porches, with elaborate floral carvings at the octagonal bases.

This style was favored because the walls were made of loose, irregular rock bound together with mud. The "in and out" design of the walls made them stronger and allowed them to expand and contract with changes in temperature. The walls also featured an architectural device called a rebate, a continuous rectangular recess along the top or bottom edge of the face of stonework. Sitting atop each of these rebates was a flat stone that formed a small shelf. The purpose of these rebates was to help rainwater run off the surface of the mud walls, making them last longer. Further, they strengthened the walls and added an element of ornamentation. The walls were also strengthened by the use of granite blocks at each of the corners; sometimes an entire row of granite blocks was used, and granite was also used for features such as columns, capitals, stairways, and the like. In some buildings, wooden beams were used to give strength. These beams typically projected from the building at the ends.

These structures were surrounded by more modest homes, giving them privacy and helping to defend them from intruders. The larger buildings had carved pedestals made of granite, with capitals at the tops of columns. Flooring and paneling were made of marble, and the homes had drainage systems and even brick ovens. In palaces, the kings dedicated thrones to the gods, including Mahrem, Meder, Beder, and Astar, and inscribed them with narratives of war.

The architecture of more common domestic buildings varied. Remains have been found of small round huts made of clay, with cone-shaped thatched roofs. Thatch may have been the most common roofing material, and it may even have been used on palaces and the homes of the wealthy. Other dwellings were rectangular with roofs supported by beams. Because only fragments of ruins have been found (except for foundations, which are more extensive), archaeologists have to make inferences from limited evidence about these and other matters.

The Pyramids of Nubia

The region called Nubia lay in the Nile River valley south of ancient Egypt. Most of what was Nubia is in modern-day Sudan, and a small portion lies in modern Egypt. The earliest inhabitants of the region were nomads, but by the beginning of the Dynastic Period of ancient Egypt (2920 B.C.E.), Nubia was an important trading center that provided Egypt with gold, ebony, ivory, exotic animals, and slaves.

As trade with Egypt increased, the region's power grew, but during the Middle Kingdom (2040–1640 B.C.E.) Egypt expanded into Nubia, which the Egyptians called Kush. The region remained politically disorganized until the first in a series of three kingdoms was established. The first, called the kingdom of Kerma, lasted from about 2400 to 1500 B.C.E. Kerma's kings accumulated enough power to build large walls, tombs, and other structures. During the New Kingdom, Egypt expanded farther into Nubia and built a new capital at Napata, which lasted from 1000 to 300 B.C.E. and was powerful enough to conquer Egypt, with its kings ruling Egypt as the Twenty-Fifth Dynasty (770–712 B.C.E.). After the Egyptians pulled out of Nubia, its capital centered on Meroë, which lasted from about 300 B.C.E. to 300 C.E.

In modern times a team of Swiss archaeologists excavated Kerma, the oldest African civilization other than Egypt. They found remains of a temple built of mud brick in about 2000 B.C.E. and funerary temple built in about 1600 B.C.E. The researchers have discovered tombs that were essentially manmade hills some 100 feet wide and 50 feet tall. Inside excavators discovered numerous skeletons, suggesting that when a ruler died he took a number of his followers with him into the afterlife. In one royal tomb were found the skulls of 4,500 cattle that analysis showed were brought from throughout the kingdom. Surrounding the city were monumental walls, with at least a two-mile stretch of military fortifications.

It was during the period when Napata was the center of the Nubian region that builders embarked on a program of pyramid building. This program continued into the Meroitic Period, beginning in 590 B.C.E., when the capital was Meroë. At three sites in the region are some 223 pyramids that functioned as tombs for royalty. The earliest ones were built at a site called el-Kurru, and they include the tombs of King Kashta, his son Piye (who assumed control of most of Egypt), three of his son's successors (Shebaka, Shebitku, and Tantamani), and 14 queens. Unlike the practice of the Egyptians, who built much larger pyramids for kings than for queens, the Nubian pyramids for queens are only slightly smaller than those built for kings. The pyramid of Piye has been removed, but its foundation trench has been found, as well as 19 steps leading to a burial chamber cut into the bedrock below and covered with a corbelled masonry roof. (In a corbelled roof the masonry is set in courses, or layered rows, so that each course overhangs the previous one, forming a false vault or arch.) The tomb of Piye's successor, Shebaka, has a vaulted ceiling.

Later pyramids were built at Nuri after Taharqa, one of the last kings of the Twenty-Fifth Dynasty, moved there. His pyramid is much larger than the others, measuring about 170 feet square at the base and rising to as much as 160 feet high. This pyramid has the distinction of having been built in two stages. The first stage was covered with smooth sandstone. Over it was built a second, larger pyramid, but the earlier-phase portion projects out above the ruins of the later phase. The whole was surrounded by a nearby wall. The underground chambers of Taharqa's pyramid are elaborate. The pyramid is entered by an eastern trench, with three steps down to a door with a molded frame and a cavetto cornice (a concave molding shaped like a quarter circle). Through the doorway is a tunnel that opened into a large chamber with six large pillars. The pillars separated the burial chamber into a central nave and two side aisles, and each of these three segments has a vaulted ceiling. In addition to Taharqa, some 21 kings were entombed at Nuri, along with some 52 queens and royal princes. The pyramids for these rulers were built according to a consistent plan, and they were all larger than the pyramids at el-Kurru. Each has a chapel on the east side, along with a stela (a decorated stone slab) and relief decorations showing the king before the gods.

The largest Nubian pyramid site is at Meroë, located about 60 miles north of Khartoum. At this site, at least 40 kings and queens were buried over a period of about 600 years until 350 C.E. The site at Meroë, sometimes characterized as the largest archaeological site in the world, is divided into the South Cemetery, the North Cemetery, and the West Cemetery; the North Cemetery was built when the South became too crowded, and the West Cemetery was built for less important royal persons. The pyramids, made of sandstone, range in height from about 30 to 100 feet. Stripes of raised masonry framed each triangular side of the face the pyramids where they came together, and the corners of the upper fourth of the pyramids were rounded. As usual, a chapel was built against the eastern side. The early Meroitic pyramids were stepped, but those built later in the period were smooth, with wedge-shaped casing blocks positioned along each course. The core of these later pyramids tended to be poorly built with rubble.

The Nubian pyramids differ markedly from those of ancient Egypt, though the pyramids of the pharaohs probably inspired Nubian builders. Like the pyramids of Egypt, they are built with stepped stone layers, or courses, but they are not as tall, ranging in height from about 20 to 100 feet, and they have a much smaller "footprint," meaning that they do not take up as much ground—usually an area of about 25 feet square. They are much more steeply pitched, rising at an angle of about 68 to 70 degrees, so they appear more pointed compared with the Egyptian pyramids. At the base of the pyramids are small temples.

Mention should be made of another Meroitic site, the temple at Faras. Faras became an important town in the Meroitic kingdom in the third century C.E. On the west bank of the Nile stood a temple constructed during the reign of the Egyptian pharaoh Tutankhamen (r. 1333–1323 B.C.E.) as well as a chapel to the Egyptian god Hathor cut into the rock and probably built during the reign of Egyptian pharaoh Thutmose III (r. 1479–1425 B.C.E.) and enlarged under Tutankhamen and Ramses II (r. 1290–1224 B.C.E.). Today only ruins remain. The symmetrical temple included a square courtyard with a portico on two sides and two rows of columns. It also included a hypostyle hall with a sanctuary and 12 columns. (A hypostyle hall is one with a flat ceiling supported by columns.)

The Stone Pillars of Namoratunga

In southern Ethiopia and northwestern Kenya was a community of people called the Borana. Near Lake Turkana in Kenya archaeologists have studied a cluster of 19 magnetic stone pillars. These pillars are referred to as Namoratunga, a word that means "stone people" in the local language. Writing on the stones is markedly similar to writings found at other archaeological sites and thus indicates that the pillars were constructed in about 300 B.C.E.

What is intriguing about these pillars is that they seem to form an ancient calendar. The Borana developed a lunar calendar that was based on the positions and movements of seven stars or star groups in conjunction with the moon. The result was a calendar of 354 days and 12 months, with a leap month added every three years. The modern names of the stars and star clusters are Triangulum, Pleiades, Aldebaran, Bellatrix, Orion's Belt, Saiph, and Sirius. According to Borana reckoning, a new year began when a new moon was observed in conjunction with Triangulum, the next month began when the new moon was seen in conjunction with the Pleiades, and so on. Each day had its own name, but since there were only 27 day names, the Borana started over when they arrived at the end of the list.

Astronomers and archaeologists have noted, though, that some of these stars and star clusters are invisible to the naked eye when they are too close to a new moon. Some researchers suggest that the 19 Namoratunga pillars were intended to mark the positions of these stars. Using statistical analyses, archaeologists have determined that there is only a small chance that the pillars could have marked the rising of the stars by chance. For them, this is strong evidence that the cluster of pillars was an astronomical observatory and hence a calendar.

EGYPT

BY MICHAEL J. O'NEAL

Historians credit the ancient Egyptians with teaching humankind how to build. By trial and error over many centuries, the Egyptians learned how to design and build structures such as palaces, temples and temple gates, courtyards, and pyramids as well as homes. Until the rise of Egyptian civilization, people lived in makeshift structures made from whatever materials were locally available, including mud bricks. These structures did not last very long, so the communities in which they were built tended to be impermanent.

After the Egyptians, people constructed cities and homes that were fixed and settled. This led to a greater sense of homeland, of a specific place where people could remain permanently and develop the fruits of civilization. Permanent construction kept people in one place over a long period of time, as a structure was begun in the reign of one king and then continued during the reign of one or more of his successors. In many cases, by the time the structure was completed a century or more after it was begun, it was time to begin expanding or refurbishing it, so construction was an ongoing activity. The most famous architectural wonders of ancient Egypt are the pyramids, many of them located on the Giza Plateau and "guarded" by the Sphinx.

Probably the most recognizable element of ancient Egyptian architecture is the chain of some eighty pyramids and pyramid-like structures that stands like a row of mountains along the west bank of the Nile River. All are on the west bank because they were probably used primarily as tombs and the Egyptians buried their dead west of the Nile, in the direction of the setting sun. Although most are within about fifty miles of Cairo to the north, others can be found near Aswān to the south. Some were never completed, and most had to be dug out of the desert's shifting sands by explorers and archaeologists. Most were constructed during the Old Kingdom, from about 2685 to 2180 B.C.E., and during the Middle Kingdom, from about 2125 to 1648 B.C.E.

The Step Pyramid at Saqqara

The oldest surviving stone structure in the world is the Step Pyramid at Saqqara, the first pyramid to be constructed. It was built for the pharaoh Djoser sometime after 2700 B.C.E., during the Third Dynasty. It is called the Step Pyramid because its six tiers, each one smaller than the one beneath it, give the pyramid the appearance of a flight of stairs. The Step Pyramid represented a major shift in Egyptian architecture. This was essentially the first major building constructed of stone rather than mud brick. Further, the complex system of tunnels and chambers that lie beneath the pyramid itself suggest a major leap forward in the design and construction of buildings. Many archaeologists believe that the pyramid underwent changes in design over time. It appears to have begun as a simple mastaba, a flat-roofed tomb with sloping sides. Later it was enlarged, and tiers of stone were added. At one time there were only two tiers, then four, and later six.

Although historians do not know much about Djoser, they do know a fair amount about the person who designed and oversaw the construction of the Step Pyramid. His name was Imhotep, and in later centuries he came to be regarded as a legendary figure, one who was almost godlike. It is known that he was Djoser's principal adviser as well as a scientist, physician, astrologer, sage, and poet. He founded a school of architecture that transformed Egyptian building from a collection of crude huts made of mud brick and thatch into a nation of lavish temples and palaces that were designed to last forever. His work provided the inspiration for Fourth Dynasty builders to construct the pyramids. An ancient Arab proverb states, "All things dread Time, but Time dreads the Pyramids."

The Step Pyramid consists not just of the pyramid itself. It also includes a complex of structures. The complex was originally surrounded by a limestone wall 34 feet high and 5,397 feet in length. This wall contained an area of about 37 acres with a number of buildings, terraces, and carved facades. In fact, many of the architectural elements of the complex are the first known examples of these elements. They include its colonnades (row of columns), porticoes (porches), hypostyles (the rooflines of a building resting on a row of columns), life-sized statues, and various types of moldings and cornices (the ornamented crowns of a structure, such as a column). The Step Pyramid itself is 197 feet tall and was constructed with almost 12 million cubic feet of stone and clay.

Other early pyramids include the pyramid for King Sneferu at Dashur, which was built around 2600 B.C.E. This pyramid is often referred to as the Bent Pyramid because about midway up there is a bend that makes it look as though the pyramid is bulging out. This bend was probably the result of a construction mistake, showing how difficult it was to make the sloped sides of a pyramid meet precisely at the top. The pyramid at Meidum is also attributed to King Snefru. Although this pyramid is slightly less than 300 feet tall, it sits on elevated ground, so it can be seen for miles around.

The Pyramids at Giza

The most prominent of the pyramids are those at Giza, built on a 1-mile-square plateau about 10 miles west of Cairo. From the top of nearly any building in Cairo, one can see this cluster of six pyramids, three large and three small. The ancient Greeks regarded this group as one of the Seven Wonders of the World. Over a period of perhaps 10 to 20 years during the 25th century B.C.E., King Khufu (sometimes referred to as Cheops, the name ancient Greek historians gave him), built the largest of the pyramids, the Great Pyramid. His successor, King Khafre (written as Chephren by the ancient Greeks) had a somewhat smaller pyramid built, though from a distance it looks as large as the Great Pyramid because it sits on higher ground. The third large pyramid was built by King Menkure (or Mykerinos to Greek historians). Menkure had the three smaller pyramids at Giza erected for his queens.

The Great Pyramid at Giza is an architectural wonder. It occupies a site of some 13 acres—about seven city blocks—and it is level to within a small fraction of an inch. It was constructed of two and a half million stone blocks ranging in weight from 2 tons to 70 tons, with an average of 2½ tons. It is estimated that the Great Pyramid weighs 6.5 million tons. Over the period of construction, 100,000 blocks per year, or 275 per day, had to be cut, smoothed, and put in position—no mean feat, given that the pyramid consists of 201 levels that rise to a height of 485 feet. Originally, the Great Pyramid, covered with limestone, had a smooth, polished appearance. During the 14th century, however, the limestone was stripped off for use in buildings in Cairo; many of these buildings, made in part with limestone from the Great Pyramid, still stand.

The Great Pyramid appears to be solid, but in fact it contains a labyrinth of passageways and rooms. One passageway, called the "descending passage," enters the pyramid about halfway up and leads down to a chamber 600 feet directly beneath the apex. Angling off from this passageway is another, the "ascending passage," that leads up to the Grand Gallery, a room that is 28 feet high and 157 feet long. This gallery leads to the King's Chamber, where an empty sarcophagus (coffin) was found in the ninth century. The ceiling of this chamber consists of just nine stone blocks that together weigh about 400 tons. Another passageway leads to what is called the Queen's Chamber, so called because its ceiling is peaked, a common feature in queens' tombs during this era.

Considerable mystery has surrounded the question of why the pyramids at Giza were built. The usual explanation is that they were built as tombs for the pharaohs. No bodies or other objects typically included in tombs have been found in them, because over the centuries treasure hunters looted the pyramids. Nonetheless, most archaeologists agree that the principal purpose of the pyramids was to provide a home during the afterlife for the pharaohs. The Egyptians believed deeply in the concept of the afterlife. They believed that in addition to the physical body each person had a *ka*, a kind of replica or double of the body (not to be confused with the *ba*, or soul). According to the pharaohs, the *ka* did not die with the body—or at least it did not have to. It could survive if the deceased's body was protected from hunger, violence, and decay. To avoid decay, the body was mummified, that is, cleaned, wrapped, and treated with chemicals, and then buried in a human-shaped coffin. The function of the pyramids was to protect the body from hunger and violence. Because the pyramids were so tall and massive, with a complex system of shafts and chambers, they protected the body from intruders. Further, the chambers in the pyramids could be filled with jars of water, food, tools, and other objects to help the deceased on his or her journey into the afterlife.

Some historians, though, offer competing theories about why the pyramids were built. They believe that the pyramids were constructed for political purposes. The pharaohs saw the need to unite the competing tribes of Upper and Lower Egypt, so the pyramids became a massive public-works project to give people pride in the nation's accomplishments. Some of the pyramids' blocks of stone even contain inscriptions from the workers, with names like "Enduring Gang" and "Vigorous Gang," suggesting that work groups took part in healthy competition over the work.

The pyramids have given rise to eccentric, if not fantastic theories. Some people believe that the pyramids are cursed, because a disproportionate number of archaeologists and others have died from illness or accident after working in them, and many other have suffered rashes, fevers, nausea, weakness, and other physical problems. Scientists, though, offer more prosaic explanations for these occurrences: that the sealed pyramids could house fungi or bacteria that cause illness or that the researchers could have been exposed to poisonous herbs, plants, or scorpions or to excessive amounts of radiation from uranium in the pyramids' chambers.

The Sphinx

One of the most recognizable statues in the world is the Great Sphinx of Giza. The Sphinx, depicting the body of a lion and the head of a man, is the largest statue in the world made out of a single block of stone. It is believed to have been carved sometime during the third millennium B.C.E., most likely during the Fourth Dynasty (from 2723 to 2563 B.C.E.) Many historians believe that the head depicts King Khafre, and the Sphinx may have been built under Khafre's orders. The Sphinx is immense at 260 feet long, 20 feet wide, and 65 feet tall. It faces to the east and may have been built as a guardian for the pyramids on the Giza Plateau that lie behind it. An adjoining temple was constructed using blocks weighing up to 200 tons that were cut out during the carving of the Sphinx.

Tombs

The ancient Egyptians revered the pharaohs as gods, so they built elaborate and permanent tombs to ensure that the pharaoh enjoyed a prosperous afterlife. In the earlier centuries of the Old Kingdom (roughly 2700 to 2200 B.C.E.), tombs for royalty consisted of simple mastabas. These tombs were not decorated in any way. It was not until the Third and Fourth Dynasties that pyramids were built to serve as tombs for the pharaohs. The Fourth Dynasty pyramids were built without decorations as well. Not before the Fifth Dynasty of the Old Kingdom were pyramids decorated, and they were more modest in size. The decorations consisted largely of hieroglyphic writing. This writing was intended to give the deceased instructions on how to have a safe journey to the afterlife.

The most elaborate tombs were built during the New Kingdom period (roughly 1600 to 1100 B.C.E.) in the Valley of the Kings and the Valley of the Queens. These tombs were built deep underground, primarily to hide them from tomb robbers. Robbery was a problem, for the tombs contained treasures such as vases, jewelry, gold masks, and similar items, often made of gold. These tombs were decorated with detailed paintings depicting the journey to the underworld. The most famous of these tombs is that of King Tutankhamun, better known to the world as King Tut. Tutankhamun was a relatively minor king who died young after ruling for only about nine years, probably in about 1325 B.C.E. Little is known about his life. His tomb was discovered near Luxor, Egypt, in 1922 by the archaeologist Howard Carter. The find remains significant not because the tomb itself was very elaborate—the tombs of other kings hold more interest for archaeologists—but because robbers had never discovered it, so archaeologists recovered about 3,500 items from the tomb. Since then exhibits of these objects have toured the world.

Temples

In modern life, the word *temple* is used most often to refer to a house of worship. In ancient Egypt, however, buildings that were called temples often served a number of purposes. Some were "mortuary temples," built to commemorate a dead king or to serve as a permanent residence for his soul, such as the so-called *ka* temples. Others were built primarily for political purposes. The temples at Abu Simbel, including one to Nefertari (1300–1250 B.C.E.) and one to her husband, Ramses II (1302–ca. 1210 B.C.E.), seem to have been built primarily to remind neighboring countries to the south of Egypt's greatness. Another class of temples, called Sed festival temples, was built to celebrate the king's jubilee. Others had several purposes, such as serving as administrative centers and fortresses. Even those that had primarily a religious purpose were not "houses of worship" like today's churches and temples. They were thought of more as houses for the gods and were built to serve the symbolic needs of these gods. People, though, did not necessarily assemble in the temples for any kind of organized worship conducted by priests.

Heliopolis Unfortunately, many of the temples of ancient Egypt are lost. Historians and archaeologists know about them primarily from surviving records or in some cases from ruins that indicate the size and overall shape of the temple. One example of a lost temple is that at Heliopolis, one of the three major cities of ancient Egypt (after Thebes and Memphis). Heliopolis, now covered by the suburbs of Cairo, was an important center for learning. In particular, it was a center for the study of astronomy, and its high priest was even referred to as the Chief of Observers (of the heavens). It is known that Heliopolis was the site of a magnificent "sun temple," or temple devoted to the worship of the sun gods Atum and Re-Horakhty as the source of all creation.

Archaeologists theorize that other sun temples built during the Fifth Dynasty were probably modeled after the one at Heliopolis. They know that six such temples were built, but to date only two have been discovered. One of these temples, at Abu Ghurob, was built by Niuserre, the sixth king of the Fifth Dynasty. This temple was constructed on a mound and surrounded by a limestone wall. At the eastern edge of the surrounding desert was a large pavilion with an elevated passageway leading to a terrace. Inside, at the upper end, was a gate that led to a paved courtyard 250 feet across and 330 feet long. Additionally, the temple had a large rectangular podium that was exposed to the sun. Its sides sloped inward, and the structure was built out of limestone on a base of granite. On top of the podium was a limestone obelisk, or a tapered pillar with a pyramid at the top (similar to the Washington Monument in Washington, D.C.). This obelisk symbolized the sun god. An immense alabaster altar, built of a single huge circular block of stone, lay to the east of the obelisk. A small chapel was located at the base of the obelisk. At the sides of the entrance were two large basins and two stela (stone slab or pillar) made of granite.

Obelisks

Obelisks, or tall tapered columns with pyramid-shaped caps, were a common feature of ancient Egyptian architecture. The temple at Heliopolis began the trend, and most temples built afterward featured obelisks, typically one on either side of a temple gate. In some cases, a single obelisk, representing the creative power of the sun, was built in the center of a temple. Most weighed hundreds of tons, and little is known about how they were transported or put in place. The largest surviving obelisk, weighing 1,000 tons, was never completed and still lies in the quarry near Aswān.

The Temple at Karnak

The world largest religious structure is the temple at Karnak, located just north of the city of Luxor. Karnak is a modern name; at the time of its construction it was called Ipet-sut, a name that means "The Most Sacred of Places." While much of the temple is damaged, parts of it remain intact, and it is one of the most popular tourist sites in Egypt. It is possible that the Temple of Ptah in Memphis was larger still, and numer-

Facade of the Great Temple of Abu Simbel (Courtesy of the Oriental Institute of the University of Chicago)

ous other temples in the Nile Delta region, now entirely lost, may also have been larger.

Karnak is actually a temple complex consisting of three main temples and several smaller outer temples. It occupies a site 247 acres in size and was built over a 1,300-year period beginning in about the 16th century B.C.E. Enclosed by tall brick walls are the three chief temples dedicated to the gods Amun (the sun god), Montu (the war god), and Mut (the mother goddess). The Great Temple of Amun, the major feature of the complex, was built during the reign of Ramses II.

Also considered a masterpiece of architecture is the Hypostyle Hall, begun during the reign of Ramses I, continued during the reign of Seti I, and finished by Ramses II. The hall is noted for its immense architraves (beams that extend across the top of columns, forming the lowest part of the entablature, the usually decorated area above the tops of columns). It is also noted for its windows with stone latticework. The ceiling is 82 feet high and supported by 12 columns. The walls are painted in earth tones; throughout are reliefs that depict scenes symbolic of creation. Covering the outer walls of the hall are pictures of battle scenes. In the courtyard outside the hall is a 70-foot obelisk erected by Tuthmose I and a 97-foot-tall, 320-ton obelisk erected by Hatshepsut, best remembered in ancient Egyptian history as the woman who challenged the notion that only men could be kings.

The Temple at Edfu

One of the chief attractions of Edfu, a small city on the west bank of the Nile River, is the temple built to the sun god Horus. Although in many respects the temple is not especially beautiful, it holds a great deal of interest for historians because it is the most completely preserved and intact of all the ancient Egyptian temples. It was built during the Ptolemaic dynasty—the ruling period of the Greek family that controlled the region from 305 B.C.E. to 30 B.C.E. (and the most famous member of which was Queen Cleopatra). The temple itself was built over a period of time stretching from 237 B.C.E. to 57 B.C.E.

The temple is approximately 450 long, 260 feet wide, and 118 feet tall. It features columns, halls, stairs and a ceiling that are still largely in their original state, including the colors and decorations. In the courtyard stand statues, and there are two obelisks at the temple's entrance. Archaeologists are also interested in the remains of the ancient town that lie only steps away from the temple, including monuments that document the history of Edfu as an important provincial town.

Homes

Virtually no homes survive from ancient Egypt. Archaeologists, however, know a great deal about ancient Egyptian homes, because when a homeowner died, a model of his home was often placed in his tomb, especially if the person was wealthy. Archaeologists have also excavated a village called Deir el-Medina. This was the village that housed the workmen and their families as they constructed and decorated the rock tombs in the Valley of the Kings and the Valley of the Queens. While the homes themselves did not survive, archaeologists have been able to learn much about the size and layout of homes from the ruins.

Typically, homes were square and consisted of sleeping quarters and a living area. Kitchens were usually outside in the yard and often included a baking oven made of clay. The outside yard was also used as a shop for craftwork and as a pen for livestock. Many homes had storage areas underneath for food. Depending on how wealthy the family was, there could be a granary, stables for horses and livestock, and a threshing area where grain for baking and beer brewing could be produced. Inside walls were often painted with murals that depicted scenes from daily life. Of course, wealthy people had more lavish homes. They often occupied estates that included beautiful courtyards, gardens and ornamental ponds with fish, trees to provide shade, and a shrine to the gods. The insides of their homes typically featured high ceilings, intricately painted walls, and tall pillars.

Most homes had niches that held statues of gods and goddesses. Thus, a woman who wanted to bear a child might have a niche with a statue of the cat goddess Bastet, regarded as the goddess of fertility, or Taweret, the goddess who protected pregnant women. In general, homes were sparsely furnished. Again depending on the wealth of the homeowner, there might have been a bed made of a woven mat placed on a framework, a table for eating, and low stools for sitting; few chairs had backs. When an occupant bathed, he or she typically stood on a limestone slab while servants doused the bather with water; the water ran to a bowl below, which was later emptied by hand. Toilet needs were met in much the same way; waste was flushed with water to a container below or sometimes directly into the sand outside.

THE MIDDLE EAST

BY DAVID PETECHUK

The known history of advanced architecture in the ancient Near East dates back to around 3500 B.C.E. and can be traced to the Sumerians, who established a highly developed civilization in this area. The Sumerians also developed one of the oldest monumental architecture styles, called the ziggurat, a pyramid-shaped tower featuring a temple at the top. Despite the many different types of peoples who lived in the ancient Near East over the years and the constant shifting of centers of political power, the architecture of ancient Mesopotamia shows a certain amount of continuity or cultural uniformity of style.

What is known today about Mesopotamian architecture has been gathered from archaeological studies, ancient texts describing building practices, and pictorial representations of structures. For example, the Sumerians invented the cylinder seal to keep records of rulers who built various edifices and also, at times, to document building construction and rituals associated with the building process. Cylinder seals are cylinder-shaped stones carved with decorative designs and engraved. These seals were used for a variety of purposes, including as a signature, to confirm a receipt, and to mark building blocks. They remained in general use throughout the area until the first millennium B.C.E. Some of the most notable cylinders providing architectural information about ancient Mesopotamia come from the late third millennium B.C.E. during the rule of King Gudea of Lagash (ca. 2150–2100 B.C.E.), who built the temple of Ningishzida and the temple of Geshtinanna. Although they did not normally contain information on common architecture and building practices, Sumerian cylinder seals have also recorded that houses in marshlands were built of reeds instead of the commonly used mud-baked brick made from local clay.

Most scholarly interest and available data on Mesopotamian architecture have focused on monumental buildings, such as temples and palaces. Temples represent the most enduring architectural monuments of the land, reflecting that culture's focus on serving and honoring the gods they worshipped. Less is known about houses and other structures, primarily because little stone was available for building and these mud-brick buildings deteriorated quickly or were routinely destroyed, with new structures built over the same sites.

ZIGGURATS

The most ancient and impressive monumental architecture of ancient Mesopotamia can be traced back to the Sumerians and is called a ziggurat. The name comes from the Akkadian word *ziqqurratu*, which means "height" or "pinnacle." These ancient towers were stepped structures that archaeologists believe served primarily as the bases for temples to the Mesopotamians' various gods. Archaeologists have also found that the process of building one of these structures was considered a religious act, which included frequent offerings to the gods and required that each worker contributing to its construction be a good and honest person.

Ziggurats evolved from the ancient Mesopotamian practice of building temples on platforms resting above the floodplain and providing a solid foundation on the damp soil. These platforms, or plinths, which date back to the Ubaid Period (ca. 6000–3800 B.C.E.), were built of mud brick, as were most structures in southern Mesopotamia because of the lack of wood or stone. During the third millennium B.C.E. the platforms became larger and higher. Eventually the decision was made to build temples that rose higher above the ground by constructing them on stepped, or terraced, platforms. This design may have stemmed from the practice of building on top of older temples and constructions. These platforms were completely solid throughout and allowed the ancient architects, who knew little at the time about how to keep tall, hollow structures standing, to build taller structures. The Mesopotamian equivalent of Egypt's pyramids, ziggurats were common in cities throughout Mesopotamia by approximately 2000 B.C.E.

In addition to the practical origins of ziggurats, archaeologists have developed several theories about social or philosophical underpinnings of ziggurat construction. For example, some new inhabitants came to Mesopotamia from a mountainous region in modern-day Iran, and archaeologists believe that ziggurats may represent a reconstruction of old mountain temples. Other theories include ziggurats as structures symbolic of a "cosmic mountain" from creation myths or as a bridge between the earth and heaven. This last theory is partly attributable to the ancient Tower of Babel described in the biblical book of Genesis, in which builders proclaim they will build a tower to "reach unto heaven." There is little doubt that ziggurats were potent symbols. For example, some researchers theorize that trees and gardens were planted on ziggurats to make them represent a mountain that was visited by God and was meant to be climbed by the priests for ceremonial worship.

A typical ziggurat construction included a square or rectangular base, with the most common sizes being around 164 by 164 feet or 131 by 164 feet. Archaeologists also estimate that ziggurats were often 150 feet or higher, such as the one built over an older structure by Nebuchadnezzar II (ca. 605–561 B.C.E.), which had seven terraces, stood 231 feet high, and remains standing at 172 feet. One of the best-preserved ziggurats comes from the city of Ur in what is now Iraq. It had a base of 150 by 200 feet and reached a height of approximately 75 feet. The outer walls of early ziggurats seldom included architectural decoration such as moldings and cornices. Instead, the occasional adornment consisted only of depressions in or projections of brick that were alternately curved and rectilinear.

To allow people to ascend to the tops of ziggurats, about half the structures included stairs or a spiral ramp or path leading to each successive level, or concentric platform. The rest have no visible means of ascent. The temple towers were built with sloping walls believed to have been planted with trees or shrubs to make gardens. In addition, the Mesopotamians incorporated a unique technique that made normally straight, horizontal lines in buildings slightly curved, or convex, which made the overall structure seem softer or less rigid, especially when viewed from a distance. They were so accomplished at this technique that the human eye cannot easily discern the curve. Ziggurats were a prominent construction in Mesopotamia until around 500 B.C.E. and stretched from Babylonia in the south to Assyria in the north.

A notable ziggurat is the Choga Zanbil ziggurat, which rivaled the pyramids of Egypt in character and dimensions. It was built at the city of Dur-Untash by King Untash-Gal around 1250 B.C.E. The complex included three temples or places of worship and a number of courtyards that were paved with bricks. Glazed, kiln-fired bricks that gave off a metallic glimmer of blue and green extensively covered the ziggurat's walls. The design of ziggurat and temple included ivory mosaics and wooden doors decorated with opaque glass mosaics. In its current state the ziggurat towers 82 feet above the plain; it is believed to have been 170 feet tall when first built.

Because it was restored at a much later date by King Nabonidus (r. 556–539 B.C.E.), one of the best-preserved ziggurats found in Mesopotamia was one built at the city of Ur by Ur-Nammu (ca. 2112–2095 B.C.E.). Constructed to honor the moon god, Nanna, it contained three stages, or platforms. The first rectangular platform measured approximately 205 by 141 feet. The entire ziggurat has been partially reconstructed to a height of about 36 feet. The structure's core was of mud bricks—unbaked bricks made of fine straw and clay and dried in the sun—which were then surrounded with more water-resistant baked bricks made of clay in a compressed mold. As was the tradition, almost all of these baked bricks were stamped with the name of the ruler, in this case Ur-Nammu. The exterior bricks were inclined to form a slope and included regularly spaced, flat buttresses (supports). The exterior walls on this ziggurat also included "weeper holes," which were small gaps between the bricks that allowed moisture to evaporate from inside the structure. Vertical mud-brick drains were also built on the ziggurat's sides to drain rainwater. The ziggurat included three converging ramps in the first stage and a central stairway to the second stage. The access to the third stage is unknown, but it was probably another central staircase.

Temples

Although archaeologists have no concrete evidence that a temple sat on top of the ziggurat at Ur, they know many ziggurats did serve as the base for temple buildings. Temples were also built on platforms or at ground level. One of the earliest known temples is a small square building uncovered at Eridu that dates back to ca. 5500 B.C.E. In addition to an offering table, it includes a niche and platform, most likely the resting place of a religious statue.

Most of the temples on top of ziggurats from the first period of Mesopotamian civilization, called the Protoliterate Period (ca. 3800–3000 B.C.E.), have been lost to time. Archaeologists have judged their appearance primarily on facade ornaments discovered at places such as Tell el-Ubaid, the ancient site that gave its name to the Ubaid Period. Most of the early ziggurat temples were small, single-roomed shrines, some measuring 80 by 40 feet. The ziggurat temples, like the bases, were made of mud brick and included some ornamentation, such as alternating buttresses and recesses built into the outside walls. Eventually they were designed with a long central sanctuary and various chamber rooms flanking both sides.

A good example of Protoliterate architecture is the White Temple (ca. 3200 B.C.E.) that sat atop the 40-foot-tall Anu Ziggurat at Uruk, which was named after the primary god, Anu. The temple itself measured 61 by 16 feet, indicating that it was meant for use by a small number of people, such as priests and perhaps certain important personages. The outer walls were whitewashed and contained niches and buttresses typical of the temple architecture at that time. The building contained a *cella*, or central hall, and a stepped altar.

The temples' corners typically faced the cardinal points of north, south, east, and west, unlike the Egyptian pyramids, whose sides face the cardinal points. Although these began as modest structures, over time they were better planned and contained more intricate architectural designs. For example, during the Early Dynastic Period (ca. 3000–2350 B.C.E.) interior wall ornaments included a patterned mosaic of terracotta cones within the walls with the exposed ends covered in bronze or brightly colored. A temple in Uruk included similarly decorated brick columns, some of which were free standing. Facade ornaments were commonly used to break the uniformity of the outer brick walls. These include wooden columns covered in patterned mosaic stone or shell, copper-sheathed bands with decorations, and copper-covered lintels with designs, such as animals. In the Dynastic Period several of the most important temples were patterned after what is called a temple oval, an immense oval platform with a separate wall built around the platform and temple.

During the Neo-Sumerian Period (ca. 2100–2000 B.C.E.) many temples were built in the form of the *broad-cella*. In this architectural design the broad and shallow central hall could be approached only through a series of rooms or courts and surrounding halls. These courts and halls were typically laid in various floor plans designed to hinder access to the altar or statue of a god. Sometimes spaces were arranged around an axis that helped ensure that most worshippers glimpsed the deified ruler only from afar. Few, if any, of the common people could enter the main hall and approach the statue of the local deity.

Palaces

While much is known about the early ziggurats, considerably less is known concerning the early Sumerian palaces and other secular buildings. Archaeologists have discovered that as far back as the third millennium B.C.E. Mesopotamian notables lived in large complexes that often included lavish decorations. A Mesopotamian palace complex found at Ur included numerous courtyards and sanctuaries, a banquet hall, and burial chambers. These complexes were associated with the temples and shrines of the times and may have included facilities for workshops and storehouses.

Like most structures in southern Mesopotamia, the palaces were built out of mud brick and on platforms. Some were eventually built atop ziggurats. While little has been found to shed light on the earliest Mesopotamian palaces, archaeological excavations at Kish, today the site of Tall al-Uhaimer in Iraq, have shown that the buildings dating back to before 2000 B.C.E. included brick columns and simple, austere facades. Most palaces and other buildings probably had flat roofs supported by the trunks of palm trees. Nevertheless, architectural historians believe the ancient Sumerians also knew how to make a simplified support system known as the corbelled arch and corbelled vaulting. The arch form uses

The ruins of Persepolis (in modern-day Iran), the seat of the Achaemenian Empire of Darius I in the fifth and sixth centuries B.C.E.*; terrace, throne hall, and palace are visible.* (Courtesy of the Oriental Institute of the University of Chicago)

segments of stone or brick jutting out of a wall to span a space, such as a door or other opening. The corbelled vault uses the same technique to support the building's roof. Ancient Sumerian architects also may have made common use of dome construction, as indicated by tombs found at Ur.

According to some observers the Neo-Assyrian Period (ca. 1000–626 B.C.E.), when the Assyrian Empire ruled over much of Mesopotamia, represents the high point of Mesopotamian architecture. Assyrian architecture was heavily influenced by ancient Mesopotamian architecture from the south, which had spread north as civilization expanded from the Sumer in southernmost Babylonia to Akkad in northern Babylonia and eventually to far-northern Assyria. However, unlike southern Mesopotamian architecture, Assyrian architecture also incorporated stone, which was more readily available in the region. As a result, Assyrian palace walls typically included sculptured and colored stone slabs called orthostats. These monumental vertical slabs were also used to line gates and entryways. The Assyrians also used a technique to make polychrome (multicolored) glazed bricks.

The palace complex of King Sargon II (r. ca. 722–705 B.C.E.) at his capital city of Dur Sharrukin, now Khorsabad, Iraq, was built within the city's inner citadel. Made of thick, mud-brick walls without windows, the palace featured doors opening onto internal courtyards of different sizes, including the Grand Entrance Court and the State Court. The throne room was situated between the State Court and a smaller court for women and children. Overall, the palace featured more than 200 courts and rooms, including public rooms, the king's apartments, and a freestanding, seven-level ziggurat with a temple complex. The vast palace complex covered approximately 1,000 acres, and many of the rooms and courtyard walls were covered with intricately sculpted decorations on stone slabs. For example, on the facade of the northern part of the palace Sargon II is shown welcoming a high official. Other sculpted walls depicted the king's military and civic accomplishments.

King Sennacherib, who ruled Assyria from about 705 to 681 B.C.E., decided to build the largest and most elaborate Assyrian palace ever known, which he referred to as the "Palace without Rival." Built on a platform close to the

Teblitu River, whose course Sennacherib had changed to accommodate his building site, the king's palace incorporated mud-brick stone and precious materials, including ivory and cedar brought from the forested mountains of Lebanon. It included large columns of bronze or cedar. The walls were lined with slabs of gypsum alabaster brought from Assyrian quarries and used because the soft stone was more easily carved than other types of stone in the area. The doorways included stone statues of human-headed winged bulls and lions as guardians on either side. Smaller statues were also used to help support columns. In addition, numerous stone reliefs of spirits and animals decorated the palace walls and were meant to protect the king from evil. The palace contained more than 70 halls and chambers, most lined with stone panels depicting the king's many accomplishments.

During the short-lived Neo-Babylonian Period (ca. 625–539 B.C.E.) builders combined both northern and southern architectural approaches and methods, including the polychrome glaze popular among the Assyrians. The Chaldeans, who made enameled baked bricks by applying a colored paste before baking, used these bricks for the exterior of their palaces and temples, often completely covering the faces of the structures with them. Their success in producing these bricks is evidenced by the fact that the remains of the brilliant blue, white, black, yellow, and red enameled bricks have maintained their brilliancy to modern times. Some of the bricks included floral designs and animal figures. The inside of the Chaldean palaces were also heavily decorated with murals. Another decorative technique applied to the inner walls was a thick layer of clay stucco, in which dry cones of baked clay were buried within the wall. The cones were visible on the wall's surface at regular intervals and covered with various colors. In addition, the cones' heads were separated by colored geometrical lines.

During the Persian Empire (ca. 538–331 B.C.E.) many of the Mesopotamian techniques were still being used in Near Eastern architecture. By this time, however, the Persians had incorporated the extensive use of columns, as evidenced by the famous complex of palaces at Persepolis (518–460 B.C.E.), in which the throne room alone had 100 columns. Founded by Darius the Great, who reigned in Persia from 521 to 486 B.C.E., the palace was not completed until approximately 100 years later by Artaxerxes I, who reigned from 464 to 424 B.C.E. One reason construction took so long was that the construction of buildings could not even begin until a complex platform was completed, a technically difficult project because it was inserted into an irregular and rocky mountainside. The palace complex was designed not only as a seat of government but also as a showplace and center for receptions and festivals. The northern part of the palace was meant primarily for officials and included the Hall of the Apadana, the Throne Hall, and the Gate of Xerxes. The rest of the complex included the Palaces of Darius and Xerxes, the Harem, the Council Hall, and other such facilities.

By the time of the Sassanians, who can be traced back to around 250 B.C.E., architects began using rough-hewn stone to construct their palaces. At places like Firuzabad and Sarvestan the palaces featured triple aivans, which were huge, open-air entrance halls that led to reception halls, beyond which were situated the monarch's residential quarters. The Sassanians also made extensive use of stucco, which accounts for the loss of architectural remains of these triple aivans, whose existence is based on period literature. Also worth mentioning is the Palace of Shapur I, who ruled from 241 to 272 C.E. Found at Ctesiphon, southeast of the modern city of Baghdad, the palace features the largest single-span arch in the world.

Houses

The earliest known dwellings in Mesopotamia consisted of round, mud-wall huts sunk into the ground with an entrance and a hearth. In what was the northern region of Mesopotamia archaeologists have discovered huts dating to the ninth millennium B.C.E. sunk into the ground with stone pillars made out of plaster. Many houses connected to the Marsh Arabs and their reed culture were also built of tall reeds. These reeds were staked into the ground in two parallel rows with their tops tied together and covered with matting. A similar, more complex technique is still used in rural sections of modern Iraq.

Outside the marshlands, however, houses were built of mud bricks and mud plaster. Typically, house construction varied according to the socioeconomic status of the occupants. The poorer people lived in single-story houses of reinforced mud brick with floors of packed earth or mud bricks. These houses were sometimes merely circular huts supported by a center post. As building techniques progressed, however, those higher on the socioeconomic ladder had much grander living quarters that were two and sometimes even three stories high.

Based on archaeological excavations at Ur, the typical "upper-middle-class" home of around 2000 B.C.E. was multistoried and built around an open-air courtyard, which allowed light to enter the windowless rooms. Typical ground-floor areas included a kitchen with a fireplace, a long, narrow reception room where guests were received, a chapel with an altar, and a tomb under the pavement or ground. The open-air yard probably included storage sheds or stalls for sheep, goats, and other domestic animals. The home's second story was reached by stairs, sometimes leading to a wooden balcony supported by columns. This balcony usually extended around the entire central courtyard, and the second floor usually consisted of bedrooms. Despite this luxurious space for that era, a ladder was often used so that people could sleep on their rooftops on hot summer nights. The roofs were buttressed with timbers packed with mud. Eventually these houses also included a bathroom just off the courtyard. For most houses the bathrooms were small enclosures with a central drainage hole paved on each side with bricks where people would place their feet and squat.

Contributions to Architecture and the Hanging Gardens

Architecture in the ancient Near East was advanced by the region's various rulers for dual purposes. The earliest of the larger buildings were devoted primarily to religious expressions. But large ziggurats and palaces also provided rulers with the opportunity to showcase their power and achievements.

Over time Assyrian kings, among others, began to use architectural design and city planning to further their concerns with warfare and trade. For example, cities were often circled with heavy walls and powerful gates. In one city built during King Sargon II's reign, the main gate was designed as a fortress built over the city wall with the primary citadel rising over the wall at the city's rear. Later the Babylonians borrowed from this approach to build royal palaces over the city walls. During the Neo-Babylonian Period architects designed a fortification around that city that included a double line of walls and a moat that was fed by the Euphrates and through which boats could enter the city under gatehouse bridges.

Considering the materials readily available to the ancient architects of the Near East, architects at the time revealed a high standard of originality and design. For example, the use of the dome can be traced back to mud huts built in Mesopotamia at around 4000 B.C.E. Later, the Sassanians made a major contribution to world architecture through their propagation of the dome on squinches (small arches built across the interior angle of two walls) above a square hall.

The Mesopotamians are also credited with developing the arch, and the earliest-known keyed arch was unearthed at Nippur, which is known as the ancient holy city of Mesopotamia and dates back at least to 2200 B.C.E. It is only through the use of keyed arches that architects could make large openings in walls and buildings. The Mesopotamians' use of brick led them to develop the pilaster and the column as well as frescoes and enameled tiles. Another example of architectural advancement included the *bit-hilani*, a portico entrance hall built with a stairway approach that is flanked by pillars, developed by the Hittite civilization ca. 1600 B.C.E.

A discussion of ancient Near East architecture would not be complete without mention of the fabled Hanging Gardens of Babylon, one of the Seven Wonders of the Ancient World. Although no concrete evidence of their existence has been uncovered, archaeologists believe they were probably built by Nebuchadnezzar II along the banks of the Euphrates River to please a wife or concubine who had lived in the lush mountain areas and was made homesick by the sun-baked plains of southern Mesopotamia. Interestingly, written accounts of the Hanging Gardens do not come from Mesopotamia but from foreigners who had visited Babylon or heard of the gardens. According to the Greek geographer Strabo (ca. 62–24 B.C.E.), writing in the first century B.C.E., the structure "consists of vaulted terraces raised one above another, and resting upon cube-shaped pillars. These are hollow and filled with earth to allow trees of the largest size to be planted. The pillars, the vaults, and terraces are constructed of baked brick and asphalt." This green, forested, artificial mountain was described by the Greek historian Diodorus Siculus (ca. 90–30 B.C.E.) as being 400 by 400 feet and reaching more than 80 feet in the air. Some accounts indicate that the structure, which was probably similar to a ziggurat, may have been as high as 320 feet.

ASIA AND THE PACIFIC

by Michael J. O'Neal

Architecture has often been referred to by the fanciful phrase "concrete music," suggesting in a poetic way that pleasing architecture makes more permanent the beauty of music that would otherwise disappear. Because architecture, at least during ancient times, was a collaborative effort involving many architects, builders, and craftsmen, it came to express the vision and values not just of an individual architect but also of the culture that shaped that vision and those values. That ancient architecture is the expression of a culture rather than of a person makes it of particular interest to historians and archaeologists.

Nowhere is this truer than with the architecture of ancient Asia, particularly China and India, where architecture combined function with great attention to form, beauty, and harmony with the environment. Because portions of large numbers of buildings and other structures from these and other Asian countries have been preserved throughout the centuries, architectural historians have detailed insight into the designs, materials, construction techniques, and functions of ancient Asian architecture. What they have found is a great degree of adaptability, as architects were able to use materials and methods that were available to them in their particular regions of the world.

Any tour of the architecture would begin in China, which produced one of the world's oldest and most accomplished civilizations. Indeed, the influence of ancient Chinese architecture was felt throughout Asia in such countries as India, Korea, Japan, and Thailand.

Architecture of Ancient China

The construction of a building in ancient China began with the principles of feng shui, a term that means "wind" (*feng*) and "water" (*shui*). Feng shui consists of a set of principles that can be difficult for westerners to understand, though in modern life many westerners have been trying to incorporate these principles into the design, construction, and furnishing of their homes and even offices.

Feng shui is rooted in the ancient Chinese worldview that sought harmony and balance between the opposing forces of nature and between the physical environment and humans. The principles of feng shui were applied to the

Panoramic view of West Lake in Lin'an (modern Hangzhou), China, showing the curved roof feature thought to guard against evil spirits (Freer Gallery of Art, Smithsonian Institution, Washington, D.C., Gift of Charles Lang Freer)

selection of a building site, the design of the building, its construction, and the decorations both inside and outside. In contrast to Western architecture, which represented human conquest over the environment and separated the environment from human spaces, Chinese architecture stressed living in harmony with the heavens and the earth. Not only were individual buildings planned according to the principles of feng shui, but entire cities were laid out according to these principles as well.

The process began with a feng shui practitioner, a kind of diviner, who selected the most favorable site for a building or burial site. The diviner would apply principles from a number of different systems of thought. One of the most prominent systems included the concept of yin and yang, essentially opposing masculine and feminine principles. Another was called *wu xing,* a complex system of thought that saw nature as a series of cycles in which the five elements of nature existed in harmony with one another—water in winter, wood in spring, fire in summer, and metal in the fall, with earth dominating the transitional periods between these seasons. Finally, *bagua,* another highly complex system of thought, focused on changes in the natural cycle over time. *Bagua* (pronounced "ba-gwa") helped the feng shui practitioner identify the nine areas of a home or building that corresponded with prosperity, fame and reputation, relationships, family, health, creativity and children, skills and knowledge, career, and helpful people.

The diviner would then try to achieve the most favorable chi (pronounced "chee"). Once again, the concept is difficult for westerners to grasp. In the Western scientific view of nature, at least until the findings of 20th-century physics, matter and energy were generally thought of as two different things. In Chinese thought they are considered in many respects the same. While the word *chi* is usually translated as "energy," it also refers to the notion of matter on the verge of becoming energy and energy on the verge of materializing. The concept of chi was used in ancient Chinese medicine to refer to the vital life forces of the body. More generally, it referred to the most basic element of the physical world.

Ancient Chinese architects applied the same principles to construction that ancient Chinese healers applied to the body. The goal was to site a building in a way that achieved the most harmonious chi while avoiding evil chi. The diviner would focus on five fundamental elements of the physical world: *long* (dragon), *xue* (cave), *sha* (sand), *shui* (water), and *xiang* (orientation, in the sense of which direction something faces). These elements are self-explanatory except for "dragon," which in ancient China was regarded as one of Twelve Symbols of Sovereignty. In this sense, the dragon symbolized the natural world and its ability to transform and adapt. Two dragons together but facing opposite directions were symbolic of yin and yang. The dragon was also a sign of royalty and thus of power.

To make a structure harmonize with nature, it was believed that the best way to orient it was facing southward toward a river or lake with a hill at its back to the north. In one major respect, this orientation had a practical function, for it shielded the structure from cold north winds. In laying out a city, a major goal was to locate the city's central axis, often using mountain peaks to create a line that gave the city harmony and balance.

Three specific principles therefore dominated the form of ancient Chinese architecture. The first was that a building was to be symmetrical and balanced, in the same way that chi represented symmetry and balance in nature and in the human body. This meant that if a building were divided in half along a central axis, the two parts would be mirror images of each other. The second principle was that roofs were to be held in place by columns rather than walls. This allowed builders to incorporate a greater view of the landscape; the view from inside was not blocked by solid walls that enclosed the space and separated it from nature, and a more natural flow of energy from outside to inside could be maintained.

Finally, the roofs themselves were to be curved rather than straight. This principle reflected the ancient Chinese belief that curves repelled evil spirits, while flat roofs allowed evil spirits to enter the building. This principle explains why most ancient and traditional Chinese buildings have something of a curved, swooped appearance, rather than the appearance of boxes, triangles, and other geometric shapes characteristic of Western architecture. One of the chief innovations of ancient Chinese architecture was development of the corbel bracket. A corbel is any kind of projecting support that extends outward from a building's roofline. The corbel can be decorated, and it was the use of corbels on ancient Chinese buildings that gave the roofs their distinctive style.

The most dominant form of architecture that survives from ancient China is imperial architecture, referring to structures associated with ruling dynasties. Rulers, of course, had access to immense funds to build huge mausoleums (tombs) and palaces, and they could command the efforts of literally thousands of architects and builders as well as slaves and prisoners of war to perform the actual labor. Although many ancient buildings in China were constructed of stone and even of metals, most were constructed with wood, which was plentiful. But because wood is a nondurable material, most of the ancient structures archaeologists have studied exist only in ruins. In many cases, archaeologists have only foundations to study.

Tombs and mausoleums were prominent structures in ancient China. For many centuries Chinese imperial rulers constructed elaborate tombs and mausoleums for themselves, and these structures are scattered about China since different dynasties ruled from different capital cities. Employing the principles of feng shui, they typically backed these structures up against hills and mountains, with the entrance looking out over a plain. Usually, a prominent feature was a *Shendao,* meaning "the Sacred Way." This was a broad, long entrance leading to the tomb. Guarding the tomb would typically be rows of statues of humans and animals. Along with the tomb would be other elaborate structures designed to enhance the dignity and power of the deceased.

Before arriving at his tomb, however, an ancient Chinese ruler would occupy a royal palace. As noted, these and other structures in ancient China were often built with wood, so they employed massive beams and posts that transferred the weight of the structure to the ground. The earliest such structures were painted primarily to protect the wood from the elements, but over time painting became much more elaborate, colorful, and decorative. One of the most famous palace complexes in China, built for the emperor Qin Shi Huang more than 2,000 years ago during the Qin Dynasty (221–207 B.C.E.), is called the Epanggong Palace. (*Gong* was the Chinese word for palace, though depending on the context it could also mean simply "home.") The complex's Front Palace was immense, capable of holding many thousands of people and covering an area of about 861,000 square feet. (By comparison, a football field, including the end zones, covers 57,600 square feet.) Another prominent set of palaces included those of the Western Han Dynasty (202 B.C.E.–9 C.E.), collectively referred to as Weiyanggong, which had some 40 palaces within an area measuring just 6.8 miles across.

Much of the imperial architecture of ancient China incorporated the number 9, which had special meaning. According to the principles of yin and yang, yin represented even numbers, while yang represented odd numbers. Odd numbers were thought of as masculine, while even numbers were considered feminine. To display their power (and masculinity), ancient Chinese emperors insisted on designs that incorporated 9, the largest odd number less than 10, and its multiples. Thus, for example, ancient temples and palaces were often built with nine sections, and gates were often built with various materials, including lumbar and stone, arranged in nine columns and nine rows. Another common feature on ancient Chinese palaces was the depiction of dragons and phoenixes. These figures were totems, or personal emblems, and they represented the emperor and his wife or consort. Columns, screens, walls, and other elements were painted or carved with representations of dragons and phoenixes.

Of nearly equal importance in ancient China were temples and other structures with religious significance, such as pagodas. It is estimated that during the Northern Wei Dynasty (386–535 C.E.), some 30,000 temples were built throughout China under orders from the emperor. Many of these temples were built with as much splendor as imperial palaces, and many were built in a shape that resembled that of a mushroom, suggesting the concept of rapid growth.

Like palaces, temples were extremely symmetrical, with the building balanced on a central axis and facing south. On the flanks of the temple proper were annexes and other buildings, again constructed with great symmetry and balance. Temples typically included an elaborate gate, a "heavenly king hall," and a library, as well as more practical elements such as dormitories, kitchens, dining halls, and rooms for receiving visitors. Also prominent in China are some 3,000 existing pagodas, which were built with various materials, including wood, stone, brick, iron, and bronze. Some of these pagodas are as high as 130 feet. Most are multistoried, and they were built as religious shrines, memorials, or temples. In many cases a temple was constructed below the pagoda.

One of the most famous Chinese architectural achievements is the Great Wall of China, the world's longest artificial structure at nearly 4,000 miles. However, the Great Wall that exists today is only one of five different walls built by the Chinese. The first, made primarily of rammed earth, was built during the Qin Dynasty in 208 B.C.E. Very little of this first wall remains intact, though archaeologists have discovered remains of it along with the remains of watchtowers constructed along its length. The wall was not built as a single project; rather, construction was a matter of joining together a number of regional walls primarily to mark China's northern boundary at the time. Most of the laborers who built the wall were slaves, prisoners of war, and political prisoners, and it is estimated that up to a million of them died during the wall's construction, giving the wall the nickname "the long graveyard." A second wall, built during the Han Dynasty (202 B.C.E.–220 C.E.) during the first century B.C.E., was constructed in a similar way. It, too, has largely disappeared. The Great Wall that remains a tourist attraction in China was built under the Ming Dynasty over a 300-year period beginning in the 14th century.

Architecture of India

Historians and archaeologists use the phrase *Indian architecture* to refer to the architecture not just of the nation of India but of the entire Asian subcontinent as well, including the modern-day nations of Bangladesh, Pakistan, and Sri Lanka. In ancient times, and even in modern life, these nations shared a culture and religion that gave rise to a common architecture.

The history of Indian architecture begins in the Indus Valley (roughly corresponding to the modern Indian state of Punjab) when, some 5,000 years ago, people migrated into the area and found a fertile, hospitable land. Archaeologists have discovered the remains of cities that were laid out with a degree of planning that would put to shame many modern cities, with defensive walls and streets arranged in a regular octagonal pattern, making it easier for carts laden with food and other materials to make turns. The remains of numerous houses have been found. These houses were built around a central courtyard that afforded privacy while also allowing light to enter the rooms constructed around it. The courtyard also provided a cool place for the family to gather during hot spells, yet it held warmth during colder weather. Long before the ancient Romans developed plumbing systems, the cities of the Indus Valley had sewage and drainage systems.

Roughly 3,500 years ago the cities of the Indus Valley, most prominently Mohenjo Daro, fell to nomadic Aryan invaders from the northwest. These invaders drove out the indigenous people, but rather than occupying their cities, the invaders preferred to live in forest hamlets. Although little of their architecture survives intact, archaeologists have studied ruins and have determined that the simple architecture of the Aryans influenced Indian architecture for many generations. Much of what is known about the architecture of this age, called the Vedic Age (ca. 1500–ca. 600 B.C.E.), is preserved in the ancient texts, the Vedas, that later formed the basis of Hinduism. It is known that the Aryans built homes with the abundant materials that lay at hand, including lumber and bamboo thatch. Their homes were circular and domelike, though later the homes expanded into a more rectangular shape. In time Aryan villages developed into small cities divided into quadrants and intersected by two main streets at right angles to each other. One quadrant was for the city's citadel, which guarded it from outsiders. A second was residential, a third was for merchants, and the fourth was for tradesmen.

A third phase of Indian architecture is associated with the rise of Buddhism. The connections between Buddhism and architecture, though, provide an interesting case study in the links between religion and other elements of a culture. During the Vedic period and up to about 500 B.C.E. the teachings of the Vedas had an impact on virtually every aspect of people's lives. The rigid caste system separating the social classes of India emerged, and religion consisted primarily of pure ritual. At about this time two major religious reformers rose. One was the Buddha, or Siddhartha Gautama, who was born in 563 B.C.E. and founded the Buddhist religion. The other was Mahavira, the date of whose birth is uncertain but whose life probably overlapped that of the Buddha. Mahavira was the founder of Jainism, another major Indian religion and one that has many features in common with Buddhism. In both instances, the new emphasis was on the nature of the soul rather than on ritual observances.

Both of these key religious figures attempted to reform Vedic culture by lessening some of the emphasis on ritual. Buddhism turned out to be the religion that had the wider appeal, and it won the support not only of the region's mercantile classes but also of the king, Asoka the Great (r. ca. 273–232 B.C.E.), who declared Buddhism the state religion. Under Asoka, funds were provided to build monasteries throughout the region. Further, because the Buddha himself was the closest thing to a god among Buddhists, his relics became scattered throughout the land. The key point is that these religious developments gave rise to much of the architecture that developed in the Buddha's wake.

Accordingly, throughout India a large number of shrines were built in honor of the Buddha, many of them little more than piles of rocks purporting to contain a relic of the Buddha. In time, however, the people began to believe that these shrines needed to be improved, which gave rise to more elaborate stupas, or spherical configurations of stone, that reflected the growing influence of Buddhism. These stupas could be found throughout the country, and people visited them as shrines.

By about the second century B.C.E., though, the influence of Buddhism began to wane. India's rulers were returning to the teachings of the Vedas, and they found the Vedic caste system more congenial to their notions of power. After the reign of Asoka the Great and the decline of two major Indian ruling dynasties (the Kushans in the north and the Andhras in the south), Indian art and architecture underwent a severe decline. Buddhism, however, by no means disappeared. Merchants continued to support Buddhism, and they supplied most of the funds that allowed Buddhist monks to establish monasteries and centers of learning.

One of the most important of these centers was Sanchi, located near the modern-day city of Bhopal in India. Sanchi survives as a major pilgrimage site for modern Buddhists and as a tourist attraction for people the world over. The stupa at Sanchi is a domelike structure with a surrounding path and topped with a finial called a *harmika.* (A finial in this context is an ornamental projection from the top of a wall or column.) The domed shape of the stupa reflects the shape of the universe, and the *harmika* represented the Bodhi tree where the Buddha achieved enlightenment.

In addition to the main stupa are a number of other buildings that serve the needs of visitors and the monks who travel to the site to meditate and do penance. One, called the *vihara,* consists of cubicles, or cells, arranged around a central courtyard. These drab cells evolved from the caves in which monks had lived in previous centuries. Another, called the *chaitya,* was a set of halls that could be used when the main outdoor stupa could not because of bad weather.

One of the interesting elements of the *chaitya* is that they were built in a manner similar to older Vedic architecture, but in stone rather than in wood. Thus, the *chaitya* have barrel-shaped vaulted roofs, entrances shaped like horseshoes, and railings. Archaeologists speculate that the craftsmen who built the structure were reluctant to give up the techniques they had used for building wooden structures when they turned to the use of stone. In fact, much of the cave architecture of ancient India, such as the caves at the city of Karle, look in most ways as though they have been carved out of wood, right down to the "joints" that were carved into the stone. Other early temples, such as the modest temple at Tigawa near modern-day Jabalpur, use a great deal of stone, including a stone slab for the roof, giving the temples an almost cavelike quality, though much of the stone is intricately carved.

These and similar structures were precursors to an era marked by the construction of magnificent Buddhist temples under the reign of the Gupta Dynasty, which reached the height of its power in about 400 C.E. During this period builders turned away from their "wood carving" approach to stone and began to employ techniques more suitable for stone and masonry construction. This gave rise to a style of architecture that was radically new. Until this time Indian architecture had been relatively simple and impermanent. The earliest Indians worshipped in the open, then in buildings constructed with reeds and bamboo, then in wooden post-and-beam buildings, and finally in stone stupas. Under the Gupta Dynasty, though, architects began to develop the core principles that led to more magnificent temples during the later medieval period.

One early Gupta temple is a small Shiva temple in the Jhansi district of India, in the town of Deogarh. (A Shiva temple was one dedicated to the Hindu god Shiva.) One noteworthy characteristic of this temple is that above the central worship area was erected a raised, pyramid-shaped structure that is estimated to have been 40 feet tall (much of the temple is lost). The temple also has four porticoes, or covered porches, one facing in each compass direction. The temple is also of interest because of the elaborate carvings on the exterior pillars.

Architecture of Ancient Korea

Archaeologists have discovered the remains of Korean civilization dating back to the fifth millennium B.C.E. Among the remains are those of homes. The earliest homes on the Korean Peninsula were pits in the earth. Later homes used earthen walls with thatched roofs, and still later homes were made of logs.

Among the architectural sites that have been excavated is that of the city of Choson, which emerged in the fourth century B.C.E. and survived to the third century C.E. There archaeologists have uncovered the remains of colonial headquarters buildings and tombs. Most of the official buildings were constructed of brick and wood, and their roofs were tiled. Tombs include the Tomb of the Painted Basket, a wooden structure with a single chamber and a large number of treasures. Tombs of kings and members of the upper classes have also been found in Koguryo, Kungn ae-song, and Pyongyang, which served as district capitals. In about 18 B.C.E. the city of Paekche was founded, and it, too, is the site of numerous building sites and tombs. Prominent among the city's sites was a central pagoda with an entrance gate, a main hall, and other rooms laid out along a central axis, reflecting the influence of Chinese architecture.

Ancient Architecture on the Pacific Islands

Not a great deal is known about the architectural achievements of the peoples who inhabited the four major regions and some 25,000 islands that make up Oceania: Australasia (including Australia and New Zealand), Micronesia (including Guam, the Mariana Islands, and the Marshall Islands), Melanesia (including Fiji, New Guinea, Indonesia, and the Solomon Islands), and Polynesia (including Samoa, the Cook Islands, and Tonga). Settlement of these islands was a slow process over long periods of time, as people had to travel from far-flung locations by boat. Most of the region's architectural record dates back, at the earliest, to about 500 C.E. However, the remains that do exist demonstrate an ability on the part of Oceanic peoples to adapt their architecture to their environment, using wood, coral, lava rock, reeds, and other materials that happened to be at hand on a particular island.

EUROPE

BY JAMES A. CORRICK

Ten thousand years ago the people of Europe lived a nomadic life as they followed game and searched for other food. These hunter-gatherers established temporary camps from which to hunt, fish, and forage. Their dwellings were as temporary as their camps and were easily assembled from materials found at hand, such as the wood and bark of trees, stones, and animal hides. These early shelters were the beginning of European architecture.

Tents and Huts

The most common shelters for early Europeans were tents that were fashioned in a variety of shapes—circular, oval, rectangular, and square. Whatever the shape, each tent had a wooden frame from which hides hung to form walls. Sometimes stones were placed along the bottom of the hide walls to hold them in place. European hunter-gatherers also built wooden huts, which had the same variety of shapes as tents. The walls were wooden poles or stakes covered with bark, reeds, or hides in order to add further protection from wind and rain. Entry was through an opening left in the wall, which was sometimes small and sometimes large. Some huts had stone foundations, while others built along riverbanks or lakeshores rested on platforms of brushwood, stone, or moss that served as protection from the often wet and marshy ground.

These tents and huts were generally small, probably meant for a single family. Some circular tents and huts in Scotland, for instance, were 13 feet in diameter, about the size of a small modern bedroom. A few larger structures did exist to house more people. Early Europeans would connect together two small tents with a long, hide-covered passageway to make a larger tent or to construct long huts up to 80 feet in length.

No matter the size, the interior of a tent or hut was not divided but rather formed a single dwelling space, one area of which was used for sleeping, another for cooking. If a shelter did not sit on a platform, its floor was often sunken and either left bare or covered with clay, bark, or brush. There was no chimney, and smoke escaped through entryways, gaps in the walls, or openings left in hut roofs and tent tops.

Settling Down

Agriculture appeared in Europe around 7000 B.C.E., and the migratory hunter-gatherers eventually became settled farmers and transformed their temporary shelters into more permanent buildings. This process took several thousand years to complete. By 2000 B.C.E. individual farmsteads and farming communities existed throughout ancient Europe. Within them were homes, barns, storage sheds, workshops, and cookhouses, sometimes all in the same structure but often in separate buildings.

Although elaborations and variations were eventually made to the design of these structures, the basic features remained constant throughout the ancient period. Some ancient Europeans who came under the influence of Greece and Rome, particularly those living in regions conquered by the Romans, adopted all or part of their architecture. However, even in Roman-controlled Gaul (roughly modern-day France), Iberia (present-day Spain and Portugal), and Britain (modern-day England), the more traditional architecture of ancient Europe remained the preference of many.

Building Shapes and Sizes

The buildings of ancient Europe were commonly either circular or rectangular. Both kinds of structures were found all over the continent, although a specific region generally favored one design over the other. Thus many of the people of central and northwestern Europe built rectangular structures. Elsewhere, the circular house, or roundhouse, predominated, as it did in Britain even into the period of the Roman conquest in the first century of the Common Era.

The square was also a popular shape, and some oval-shaped structures existed. In northern France during the fifth millennium B.C.E. some buildings were shaped like trapezoids, which have only two sides parallel, unlike rectangles that have all four sides parallel. Again unlike the rectangle, in which each side is the same length as its parallel partner, in the trapezoid one of the parallel sides is shorter than the other. The size of a building generally depended on its use: A house was larger than a storehouse, and a home meant for several families was larger than one intended for a single family. Accordingly, roundhouses varied in size from 15 to 70 feet across.

Rectangular buildings also varied in size. Small square buildings were 15 feet on a side, while larger rectangular structures averaged lengths of 100 feet. The latter were known as longhouses; they first appeared in central Europe sometime after 5500 B.C.E. and eventually spread to western and northern Europe, where they remained in use through the early centuries C.E. Longhouses were not only long, ranging from 33 feet to 246 feet in length, but they were also narrow, between 16½ and 23 feet in width. An average-sized longhouse could accommodate 20 to 30 people, either a large extended family or several smaller families, as opposed to smaller houses meant for a single nuclear family.

House Exteriors

Both circular and rectangular buildings served people as homes. Some of these ancient European houses had foundations of stone or wooden beams. River- and lakeside structures often sat on platforms supported by sturdy wooden posts a few feet or yards high; thus they were high enough to be above normal flood levels. A few houses in Italy actually were set on platforms erected over water, with supports for these platforms being as much as 30 feet in length, taller than many modern homes.

Most houses—indeed, most buildings of any kind—of ancient Europe, whether circular or rectangular, had wooden walls, though those in regions with few trees were made of stone and those in dry regions of bricks of dried mud. A few of the timber structures were log cabins, similar to those later favored by many American pioneers. More commonly, however, timber houses had walls of wattle stretched between upright posts and covered with daub for weather proofing. Wattle was made from vertical bundles of reeds or wooden stakes through which thin rods of wood were woven horizontally, while daub was a mixture of soil and clay along with grass, straw, animal hair, or dung. Dried daub was both hard and weather resistant. The upright posts were set at the corners of rectangular houses and evenly spaced around the circumference of roundhouses. The walls frequently had a coat of whitewash, made by crushing limestone or seashells and mixing with water. Whitewashing was both decorative, giving the exterior a glossy white appearance, and practical, since it further protected the walls from the effects of weather.

Rising from the top of the walls of most ancient European buildings were pitched roofs (typically two sided and sloped), which ascended at steep angles of 45 to 55 degrees and were generally covered in thatch, peat, or turf. Pitched roofs were needed because they allowed rain and snow to slide off rather than collecting on and possibly collapsing the roof. Some roofs had eaves, which were roof edges extending beyond the walls so that dripping water or falling snow would not damage the walls.

A roundhouse's pitched roof was cone-shaped, rising to a peak. On rectangular structures one side of the roof might have been raised higher than the other, or the roof might have been double-pitched, that is, having two halves, each of which angled down from a central beam running the length of the house. At either end of the house, the two roof halves and the top of the end walls formed a triangle. This triangle might have been covered by further roofing or filled in with gables, triangular pieces of wood or wattle that rose from the tops of the end walls. Houses in parts of southern Europe, where conditions were drier and warmer, often had flat roofs, since water and snow accumulation was not a serious problem. Many of these roofs had an outer covering of dirt that often supported a rooftop garden.

For thousands of years most houses lacked windows and had only one doorway. After 800 B.C.E., however, houses with several entrances appeared. In Britain, for example, roundhouses of the last centuries B.C.E. and the first century C.E. had a main door that was flanked by two smaller entryways. Halfway around the circle was another large entrance. The main entrances, perhaps for religious reasons, faced east and west.

The entryway might or might not have had some sort of covering. In some ancient European homes entryways were left open or hung with a hide curtain. In Bulgaria in the sixth millennium B.C.E. a screen just inside the door provided privacy by blocking the view of anyone looking in from the outside. Many later houses, however, had wooden or wattle doors that pivoted on stone pins. The large entryways of British roundhouses in the ninth century B.C.E. had double doors. Some entryways were sheltered from rain and snow by a porch, a rectangular wooden frame with wattle walls and a flat or pitched roof. The porch was used at times to house animals such as pigs. Occasionally, to keep heavy rain, melting snow, or other groundwater from running into the house's interior, the bottom of the door did not reach the ground, and a step was provided to make entry easier. If the floor was dug below ground level, steps inside led down.

House Interiors

Inside ancient European houses the roof poles and rafters were left visible. Floors were often dug down a foot or more. They were made of beaten earth or were covered with animal skins, clay, paving stones, or wooden planks. Sunk into the floors of some buildings were clay- or stone-lined pits for storage. A rare house even had a shallow basement with a clay coating or stone lining. The interior walls were occasionally painted, as in German houses of the fourth millennium B.C.E., in which red and white zigzags streaked across a yellow background. If the walls were thick enough, as they were in some houses in Britain and Scotland, cupboards, shelves, and benches were cut into them.

Many houses, particularly in the early agricultural period, had a single room. In small rectangular buildings and in most roundhouses, the room space was empty. However, many rectangular structures had several roof-supporting posts—sometimes in rows, sometimes staggered—breaking up the floor area. Buildings that lacked these posts had roofs that were fully supported by their frames, which in turn were supported by the walls. Among roundhouses, only the largest had roofs heavy enough to require support posts, and even they had a large, central, unbroken space because the posts, numbering 12 or more, were placed around the border of the room a few feet from the inner wall. Some roundhouses did have a central post that rose up to the roof and to which roof poles connected, but most of the floor area still remained free.

Commonly, in larger rectangular and circular houses partitions of wattle stretched between the support posts to divide the interior into two or more rooms. In a two-room house one room was used for cooking and activities such as weaving and tool making and repair, while the other was for sleeping. In buildings with many rooms the front chamber was a combined reception area and workroom, while other chambers served as a kitchen–dining room and one or more bedrooms.

In northern Scotland a special class of stone roundhouses, known as wheelhouses, had rooms formed by piers, stone supports that projected from the wall and ran from floor to roof to give the latter support. The piers also formed the walls of the rooms, each of which faced an open central space. These houses also had a stone hallway leading from the entryway into the house's center. The house's name comes from the wheel-like appearance of its interior: The house wall was the wheel rim, the piers were the spokes, and the central room was the hub.

Many homes housed more than just people. In regions with hard winters one room would contain stalls, mainly for cattle. In Scotland in the last centuries B.C.E. the space along the walls of roundhouses was sunken and paved with stone, probably as a pen for animals. Frequently one or more rooms had a loft, a partial second floor that was reached by ladder from the ground floor. Lofts had plank floors covered with wattle and made excellent places to keep food away from both domestic and wild animals. A few houses even had a complete second story. The same houses in Scotland that had paved sunken areas had a second floor supported by posts that served as the building's living quarters.

Without windows and often with only a single entryway to let in sunlight during the day, house interiors were quite dim, particularly in rooms partitioned off from the door. In a longhouse, for instance, which had its door at one end of the building, much of the interior was dark. The end farthest from the door was thus used for food storage and for housing livestock, the middle section for eating and sleeping, and the door's end for all activities requiring light.

Since chimneys did not exist in ancient European houses, the home's entryway allowed smoke from fires for cooking and heating to escape. Smoke also escaped through the roof. Much of the roofing material, such as thatch or turf, was porous enough to allow smoke to seep out. However, it was not porous enough to let rain in, at least as long as the angle of the roof's pitch was great enough to allow water to flow off rather than through the roof.

Farmsteads

Many ancient European houses stood on isolated farmsteads, often the home of a single nuclear or extended family. The farmhouses varied greatly in size, ranging from a small roundhouse to a large longhouse. Surrounding the house, although in no particular pattern or order, were other structures that served a variety of purposes. Some were to house or pen animals. Farmsteads that raised cattle often supplemented or replaced the farmhouse stalls with a byre, or cattle stable. Many farms also had pens made of wattle for pigs, goats, and sheep, which in winter might have been housed in the human residence or in a barn. In terms of design and construction, byre and barn would have been like the main house, though probably smaller, particularly if the human dwelling was a longhouse.

In addition to animal enclosures, farmsteads had a number of storage facilities for wheat, barley, oats, and other grains. Early farmsteads dug pits that were then sealed with clay and covered with dirt. Beginning around 800 B.C.E. these pits were replaced by small storehouses, or granaries. Each wattle-walled granary, many of them rectangular even on farmsteads where the main structures were roundhouses, sat on a wooden platform supported by four to nine posts. The posts kept the stored grain out of the reach of animals.

A farmstead might also have had a cookhouse and a workshop for pottery making, weaving, and tool production and repair. Small buildings for storing tools and other equipment were sometimes present as well. There might even have been additional living quarters if the main house proved too small to accommodate a farmstead's human population. To keep domestic animals from wandering off, some farmsteads were fenced with a stone wall or a wooden palisade, which is a fence made of upright stakes. Many, however, were unfenced, relying on a ditch dug around the perimeter to keep the animals in. Beyond the fence or ditch were the fields for growing crops.

Village Buildings

Along with solitary farmsteads, ancient Europe had many villages, some of which may have started as single farmsteads. Much the same sort of structures that were found on the farmsteads also were found in the villages, except in larger numbers. Thus there were houses, storehouses, byres, barns, and workshops. The houses of individual villages were often very similar to each other in size and design. For example, the houses in a village in Switzerland in the 18th century B.C.E. were small, rectangular buildings 13 to 16 feet long. All had wooden plank walls, and most had stone foundations.

Some communities even standardized their houses, as did a village in Poland in the eighth and seventh centuries B.C.E. This village had rows of two-room houses; each row shared a single roof covered with reeds, and all the houses were the same size. The walls and floors were split logs, with clay and moss corking any gaps in the walls. One of the two rooms was a large common room for working, cooking, and eating, while the smaller one was a bedroom. Each house had a loft and a front porch.

Other ancient European communities displayed a range of houses of varying sizes, the smallest having only one room and the largest having several. The larger homes may have belonged to more prosperous villagers, or they may simply have been the residences of large families. Some ancient European houses were markedly different from the rest found in their villages. This difference may have indicated that their occupants were important members of their communities. In Britain in the second century B.C.E., for example, a number of houses, known as courtyard houses, probably belonged to prosperous or influential villagers. Each house had a rectangular, paved courtyard surrounded by a stone wall. Built into the wall were rooms, some of which were living quarters and others of which were for animals and storage. Some courtyard houses also had underground chambers.

House of the Chief

Some courtyard houses may have been the homes of village chiefs. Although few ancient European villages had special houses for their leaders, such dwellings did exist. A chief's house was not a palace, which ancient Europeans did not have. Instead, it was often the largest house in a village, frequently had more auxiliary structures associated with it than other homes, and sometimes was set apart from the rest of the village, either by being located a short distance from other homes or by being surrounded by a palisade.

In the sixth century B.C.E. central European village chiefs lived in compounds surrounded by double palisades, or a fence within a fence. In each compound was a smithy for metalworking and a large wooden house with a stone wall along one side. The chiefs' houses sometimes contained as many as four rooms. The doorway gave entry to a large central room where the chief probably conducted business. Off to one side was a large bedroom, and off to the other were a kitchen and a smaller bedroom.

Later, during the first century B.C.E. in Germany, at least one palisaded chief's compound included granaries and many animal stalls, indicating that much of the food production was under the chief's control. The compounds also enclosed small workshops in which villagers forged bronze and iron tools and weapons; made pottery and leather goods; and manufactured items out of wood, bone, and antler.

The *Broch*

In addition to being large and set apart, a chief's house was sometimes physically different from the homes of other villagers. One house located in France in the latter centuries B.C.E. had one end that was semicircular and may thus have belonged to a village leader. Among the most distinctive of chief residences was found in Scotland from the first century B.C.E. to the second C.E. Known as a *broch*, this structure was a stone tower, of which some five hundred were built. Surrounding it were the houses of the rest of the village. Despite *broch* being Scottish for "borough" or "fortified place," the structure was not a military post or fort but a fortified house, akin to the castles of the Middle Ages and the home of the local chief.

The *broch*'s wall, 15 feet or more in thickness, was actually two walls, which converged toward one another as they rose to a height that could exceed 40 feet. With some *brochs* the two walls sat atop a single solid wall; with others, they began at ground level. Passageways with wooden floors ran between the walls and were probably used for storage. The double-walled construction made for good insulation from the harsh northern winters. The *broch*'s entryway was a large tunnel that could be closed off with a heavy wooden door fastened by wooden bars. Beyond the door was a chamber, perhaps meant to house guards, and a stairway that led up to the wall passages. Tower interiors ranged in size from 18 to 40 feet in diameter. Built against the inside wall were several wooden or stone rooms, or cells, whose own walls sometimes contained cupboards and windows that looked out on the *broch*'s interior. Some *brochs* had a walled courtyard inside.

Public Halls

In some ancient European villages, chiefs may have presided over village meetings, feasts, and other community activities in a public hall. Exceptionally lengthy longhouses, such as the 148-foot ones of central Europe, may have been such community halls. A different kind of longhouse found in Scotland, Britain, and northwestern and central Europe may also have been a village hall. These buildings differed from the usual longhouse in having rounded corners and being twice as wide, at about 40 feet. The interior was divided into rooms with partitions, and animals were apparently kept in stalls in some of these structures. It is also probable that, despite their communal nature, one or more families lived in these halls.

Religious Buildings

It is also possible that these halls were used for religious ceremonies. If so, they were among the few buildings that functioned for worship in ancient Europe, whose people preferred outdoor sacred sites. Occupying Romans did build temples, but these were for their own use. Only on the island of Malta between 3600 to 2500 B.C.E. did large temples appear in ancient Europe. Built in groups of two, three, or four, these temples had walls made of limestone covering a core of dirt and broken rock. A large entryway led into a central passage, off of which were three to six semicircular chambers. Floors were covered with crushed limestone or paved with stone. At least one temple had stairs leading to the roof, which was probably flat and made of clay-coated wood. Another temple had red-painted walls. Other religious structures in Europe for the next several thousand years were generally simpler affairs than those of Malta. Some villages had a shrine that was a house set apart from the rest and left vacant except for human and animal figurines.

In the last centuries B.C.E. and the first centuries C.E. the Celts built both shrines and temples. A Celtic shrine built during this period was a small structure with a pitched roof and gables supported by posts. The structure lacked walls and was surrounded by a palisade and a ditch, across which was a wooden bridge. More elaborate were circular, stone Celtic temples found in southern France. Influenced by Greek architecture, each temple had a colonnaded portico, a porch with regularly spaced columns. The portico surrounded a *cella*, or sanctuary. The latter always towered over the portico and was paved with stones arranged in geometric shapes.

GREECE

by Michael J. O'Neal

For generations of tourists, a visit to Greece has meant touring architectural ruins in Athens and other sites throughout the country. Even those who have never visited Greece are likely to recognize the names of some of the most famous sites, such as the Parthenon, for these buildings are tangible reminders of the beginnings of Western civilization. Greek builders inspired and taught the later builders of the Roman Empire (31 B.C.E.–476 C.E.); the Romans copied Greek architecture extensively, and many of their surviving buildings provide insight into the methods and materials of Greek architects. Indeed, much of what archaeologists know about Greek architecture comes from their knowledge of later Roman architecture. Still today, modern buildings are sometimes built in the Greek Revival style, suggesting that they copy many of the features of ancient Greek architecture.

Interestingly, the architects of ancient Greece were not regarded as artists, as prominent architects in modern times are. An architect was seen as a combination of skilled tradesman, contractor, and builder. The state—or sometimes a wealthy individual—hired an architect to complete a building project. He designed the building, hired the necessary laborers, acquired the materials, and kept track of the budget. In many instances, the name of the architect is not even known. Only later, during the Hellenistic Period from the fourth century into the first century B.C.E., did architects come to be thought of as artists in their own right.

The Roots of Greek Architecture

The ruins that survive date primarily from the late Classical and the Hellenistic periods of Greek culture. Historians cite the Persian Wars (480–448 B.C.E.) as the beginning of the Classical Period of Greek art, which extended to the death of Alexander the Great in 323 B.C.E. The Hellenistic Period began with Alexander's death and extended to about the first century B.C.E. Like Greek civilization generally, though, Greek architecture did not spring out of nowhere. The centuries before the Classical Period are called the Archaic

Period, which began in roughly 600 B.C.E. During the Archaic Period and the earlier part of the Classical Period, structures were built primarily with mud brick, clay, and wood. These materials are not very durable, so virtually nothing remains of them, nor are there any surviving written descriptions of them. Only in the Classical Period did architects and builders begin to use more durable stone so that many of their buildings survive, at least in part.

Archaeologists, though, have excavated sites from earlier Bronze Age civilizations around the Aegean Sea, including such sites as the cities of Knossos, Mycenae, and Troy. (Bronze Age refers to the period in history beginning in about 3000 B.C.E. when bronze, an alloy of tin and copper, was widely used for tools and other purposes.) These were the very earliest civilizations that can be called Greek, flourishing from about 3000 to 1200 B.C.E. The first of these, the Cycladic culture, rose during the Early Bronze Age (about 3000–2200 B.C.E.). The second was that of the Minoans, who flourished from about 2700 to 1450 B.C.E. on the island of Crete. The third, the Mycenaean, rose during the Late Bronze Age, from about 1600 to 1200 or 1100 B.C.E. and provided the setting for such literary works as the epics of Homer. The Mycenaeans occupied an area of the Greek mainland south of what would become Athens. Surviving from each of these civilizations are remains of structures that give archaeologists clues about the roots of Greek architecture.

One of the most famous of these sites is Knossos, a city on the island of Crete. Archaeologists believe this site was the political capital of the Minoan culture. It was discovered in 1878 by an amateur archaeologist, who began excavating it then. In 1900 a British archaeologist purchased the entire site, and with the help of a team of archaeologists he excavated and began reconstructing the palace of Knossos. Further study revealed that humans began inhabiting the site in about 7000 B.C.E. The population grew until it numbered from 5,000 to 8,000 people in the years 1900–1600 B.C.E. The community's central building, both for religious and administrative purposes, was the palace. Archaeologists' best guess is that the palace was built sometime between 1700 and 1300 B.C.E.

The palace is a wonder of ancient architecture. It occupies a site of some six acres and comprises 1,300 rooms. Among them are storage rooms that contained numerous large vases (called *pithoi*) used for food storage. Beneath the storage rooms were holes used to store valuables. The five-story-high palace also had running water and a sewage system. Its porticoes (porches) and airshafts provided ventilation and allowed the building to catch sea breezes to remain cool during the hottest weather. The plaster walls of the palace were decorated with numerous frescoes. These frescoes were in a state of decay and were reconstructed by Piet de Jong, a 20th-century artist who specialized in fresco reconstruction. The Throne Room has an alabaster throne that was built into the wall and flanked by carvings of mythological animals.

At the end of the Bronze Age, architecture in effect "disappeared" from ancient Greece. It reemerged during the seventh century B.C.E. It was at about this time that Greek civilization began to flourish. Greece became more prosperous, and a more urban culture developed. This gave rise to cities and the buildings that filled them.

Features of Greek Architecture

Most ancient Greek buildings were either cube shaped or had a rectangular footprint. Public buildings, such as temples, were constructed primarily of limestone, an abundant building material in ancient Greece. Architects would probably rather have built using marble, but marble was expensive, hard to transport, and not readily available; the only marble available had to be transported from Mount Pentelus and Attica or from a few of the Greek islands. Marble was used, though, for decorative and structural components in some of the most important buildings, including the Parthenon.

Most buildings were flanked with a colonnade, or a row of columns. Sometimes the colonnade was just at the front entrance, but other times it was on all four sides. Many buildings, too, had a portico, or a covered porch supported by columns. In general, Greek buildings did not have arches or domed roofs, so all the buildings had a squarish appearance; only later did the Romans add arches and domes to their buildings. Roofs consisted of wooden beams covered with tiles, usually made of terra-cotta, or unglazed clay. (Terra-cotta, meaning "burnt earth," is the material used to make modern flowerpots; the word also refers to their brownish-orange color.) Some buildings were roofed with marble tiles.

A common feature of Greek buildings was their low-pitched roofs. (The Greeks did not have to worry about snow building up on roofs, so the roofs did not need a steep pitch, or angle, for snow to fall off.) At each end of the building was a pediment, or a triangular area under the angle of the roofline. Pediments were typically filled with stone statues. Many buildings, too, featured an entablature. This term refers to a horizontal row of stone blocks under the roof between the tops of the columns that supported the building. The entablature provided an "easel" for sculptors, who carved friezes on them, or sequences of carvings that often told a story. These friezes often alternated metopes and triglyphs. A metope was simply a pictorial panel; a triglyph was a group of three projecting vertical blocks that separated the metopes.

Forms of Greek Architecture

A theater could be found in nearly every Greek town of any size. These theaters were used not only for dramatic performances but also for official meetings. The origins of Greek drama lay with religious ceremonies, but by about the sixth century B.C.E. drama came to be regarded as one of the highest forms of art, and the plays of such dramatists as Sophocles (ca. 496–406 B.C.E.), Aeschylus (525–456 B.C.E.), and Euripedes (ca. 484–406 B.C.E.) are still performed throughout the world. The theaters were typically built into a hillside with tiered seating arranged in a semicircle. Behind the stage area was a low building used for storage and as a place where the

FROM ANCIENT GREEK HISTORY TO ROMAN MYTHOLOGY

A widely known story from Roman mythology is that of Daedalus and his son, Icarus. Icarus flew too close to the sun with wings his father had made. The sun melted the wings, and Icarus fell to his death. This myth has a strong connection with the palace at Knossos.

After the spread of the Roman Empire, the legend grew up that the palace, because of its large number of rooms and confusing layout, was the labyrinth King Minos had built to house the Minotaur. The story goes as follows. Minos, the king of Crete, boasted that the gods would grant him anything he wished. He believed that the sea god Poseidon would give him a magnificent bull if he offered an appropriate sacrifice of one of his own bulls. When a white bull miraculously emerged from the sea, Minos sacrificed a bull to Poseidon, but the bull was inferior. Poseidon was annoyed, so he caused Minos's wife, Queen Pasiphaë, to fall in love with the white bull. To consummate her love for the bull, she enlisted the support of Minos's chief builder and architect, Daedalus. Daedalus's solution was to build a wooden cow into which Pasiphaë could be lowered. Later, to everyone's horror, Pasiphaë gave birth to a creature that was half-man and half-bull, called the Minotaur.

Minos was eager to hide this evidence of his wife's infidelity. He consulted with the oracle at Delphi, which counseled him to build a labyrinth where he could hide the Minotaur. That labyrinth, according to Roman myth, was the palace at Knossos. Later, Minos's son was killed by the Athenians, leading to war between Crete and Athens. With the help of the god Zeus, Minos won the war. To put an end to the conflict they were losing, the Athenians agreed to provide Minos with seven stalwart young men and seven maidens every nine years. These people would be sent into the labyrinth, where they would be consumed by the flesh-eating Minotaur. Eventually, the Athenian hero Theseus killed the Minotaur with help from Minos's daughter, Ariadne.

Minos later learned that Daedalus had helped Pasiphaë in her wickedness. In anger he imprisoned Daedalus and his son, Icarus, in the labyrinth, but Pasiphaë got them out. Daedalus and Icarus wanted to flee Crete, but they knew that doing so would be impossible, for the king had all the harbors watched. Accordingly, Daedalus made wings out of feathers that were held together with wax so the two could fly away. He and Icarus flew north, but Icarus was so intoxicated with his ability to fly that, despite his father's warnings, he flew too near the sun. The wax in his wings melted, and he fell to his death in the sea near an island that was named Icaria in his honor.

actors could dress. The theater at Epidaurus is one of the best-known Greek theaters, and it survives almost entirely as it was when it was built beginning in the fourth century B.C.E.

Greek towns of any size were also likely to have a gymnasium, often with an attached *palaestra,* or facility for training in wrestling and boxing. The *palaestra* had a fairly standard architectural style. Surrounding a rectangular open-air court were colonnades. Adjoining rooms served a variety of functions, including bathing, storage, and socializing. One of the most famous surviving *palaestrae* can be found at Olympia as part of the original site of the Olympic Games. The famous arena at the University of Pennsylvania in Philadelphia is called the Palestra, named when it was completed in 1927 by one of the university's professors of Greek.

Other common architectural forms include the *tholos.* This was a circular building used for religious purposes. The *tholos* at the city of Delphi, built to honor the goddess Athena in about 380 B.C.E., is one of the best examples. The *propylon* was a porchlike structure that typically served as an entrance to the grounds of a temple; one of the best preserved is the *propylon* at the Acropolis in Athens, built from 437 to 432 B.C.E. The *bouleuterion* was a council chamber found in many towns that also served as a courthouse. Finally, the *stoa* was a narrow hallway often found in the commercial districts of Greek towns. The *stoa* consisted of a narrow hall with an open colonnade, where merchants would set up shops. In Athens the Stoa of Attalus has been completely restored.

Many of the best surviving examples of Greek architecture are temples. These temples, though, did not serve the same function as modern-day churches, temples, or mosques. Generally, the altar was placed outside in a sacred area called the *temenos.* The temple itself served more of a storage function for offerings made to the local god, artwork, and a treasury. Inside the temple was a *cella,* or an inner room or sanctuary that housed the statue of the local god and was typically surrounded by a row of columns. The most famous example of a surviving temple is the Parthenon in Athens, built from 447 to 432 B.C.E.

Orders of Greek Architecture

Archaeologists, architects, and art historians have identified three main orders, or styles, of ancient Greek architecture. These styles can be seen on modern buildings, including those in the United States. Government buildings, courthouses, and even homes, many of them built in the early years of the United States, incorporated the Greek orders, in large part because Greek architecture for early Americans symbolized the birth of democracy. Wanting to incorporate democratic ideals into American life, early American architects tended to copy the Greek orders.

As these styles evolved, the goal for Greek architects was to find pleasing proportions. They wanted to ensure that each part of the building was proportioned in relation to the other parts to achieve a perfect form. Thus, they constantly experimented with these forms. In earlier centuries the forms were fashioned primarily out of wood; during the Classical Period stone was the favored building material. Since many buildings had religious significance, the Greeks wanted them to last forever and have the ability to withstand earthquakes. Because so much depended on the buildings' supports, a great deal of attention was paid to the columns. These columns consisted of a number of parts; from bottom to top, they included the pedestal, base, shaft, and capital. Resting on the capital was the horizontal architrave (a beam that extends across a row of columns). Above the architrave was the frieze carved on the entablature, and on top of that was the cornice, or projecting moldings that allow rainwater to flow off the top of the building.

The first of the orders, the earliest to develop (in about the seventh century B.C.E.), is called the Doric, a term the Greeks themselves used in the belief that this style of architecture descended from the more ancient Dorian culture. The ancient Romans regarded the Doric style as the most masculine. The distinguishing features of this style are that the columns are thick and sturdy and the capitals, or the tops of the columns, are plain. The ancient Greeks believed that a man's foot was one-sixth his height, and they used this proportion in Doric columns. The Doric style of architecture can be seen in the Parthenon in Athens, the Temple of Hera at Paestum, and the Temple of Apollo in Corinth.

The second order of Greek architecture was the Ionic, which developed about a century later. Its distinguishing features are that the columns are more slender, about eight times the width at the base, and the capitals are ornamented with spiral scrollwork called volutes. The Romans thought of the Ionic style as more feminine, with the scrollwork representing a woman's hair and the vertical fluting (concave, semicircular grooves) of the column representing the folds of her gown. The Greeks themselves saw this distinction. The Ionic style was prevalent in regions that were urban and sophisticated. The people saw this style of architecture as refined and elegant. In contrast, the people in regions where the Doric order predom-

The theater at Epidaurus, Greece (Alison Frantz Photographic Collection, American School of Classical Studies at Athens)

inated were more rural; they preferred what they considered the sturdier, more "manly" Doric style. They resisted Ionic architecture because they saw it as symbolic of the dominance of Athens over the other city-states of Greece. A good example of the Ionic style is the Temple of Apollo at Didyma with its 122 enormous columns (only two of which survive).

The Doric and the Ionian are regarded as the two main styles of Greek architecture. A third order, though, called the Corinthian, emerged from the Greek city of Corinth. This style was an evolution of the Ionic, for it features columns that were even longer and slimmer than Ionic columns. The distinguishing feature was elaborate and detailed carvings on the capital. These carvings were of the leaves of the acanthus, a plant that grew in the Mediterranean region. Because the Corinthian style was more detailed and "fancy," it came to be associated with luxury and wealth. The reason the Corinthian style is not considered a major style of Greek architecture is that few buildings in Greece adopted the style. Later, though, it was commonly used in Roman buildings, including the Pantheon.

Ancient Greek Homes

Because the houses of ancient Greece were generally built with inferior materials, archaeologists do not have very many complete or nearly complete houses to study. The generalizations they make about Greek homes are pieced together from contemporary descriptions and from the remains of housing sites that have been excavated. These sites are found primarily in Athens and the northern Greek city of Olynthos. One exception is a house that has been excavated in the town of Vari, located southeast of Athens. This is the best-preserved house archaeologists have had to work with, and while it was a farmhouse, evidence suggests that houses in the cities were similar.

These sites provide evidence in the form of floor plans. Also, the remains of artifacts provide evidence of the use to which rooms and areas of the house were put. For example, the existence of a drain suggests that an area was used as a bathroom, while chips of a substance like marble suggest that an area was used as a workshop by a stonemason.

A number of factors influenced the design and construction of Greek homes. In Athens many houses were irregularly shaped because the streets of ancient Athens were extremely narrow and crooked. In earlier centuries people had built crude homes on sites that gave them access to water and that followed the natural contours of the land. Later, when Greek civilization was at its height and new homes were being built over the old ones, little effort was made to impose more order on the layout of the city.

Further, efforts were made to build housing in places near to where Athenians worked. Thus, many homes were built in and around the industrial district of the city. The streets were made of hard-packed earth, sometimes covered with gravel. Water was brought in by conduits carved in the rock or sometimes by terra-cotta pipes, though water often had to be carried to the home from public fountains. The remains of many cesspools have been found, suggesting that waste was removed by channeling it into these pools. In some places, drainage ditches were constructed; some were simply conduits carved into rocks, but some were elaborately constructed with floors, walls, and even slab ceilings.

Greek houses tended to be of poor quality. Even the better homes were made primarily with stone and mud, not the limestone that was used for public buildings. The foundation of the house consisted of irregularly shaped rocks that were simply piled in place. The exterior walls were made with mud brick, sometimes coated with lime. These walls were thin and rickety—so much so that burglars, rather than coming through doors or windows, simply knocked holes in the walls to gain entry; in fact, a common Greek word for *burglar* literally meant "wall digger." In some cases, the thickness of the surviving foundation suggests that the house might have been of two stories. While most homes, especially those built before about 500 B.C.E., were small, in later years larger and more luxurious homes were built. Many were built in the countryside, where wealthier Athenians would go in the summer to escape the city's heat, as well as the smells, insects, rats, and disease caused by garbage piling up in the streets.

An almost universal feature of Greek houses was that they were built around a central open courtyard. Rooms were adjacent to the courtyard on all four sides, though the homes of poorer people generally consisted of just one room divided by partitions. Many had a veranda that provided shade and protection from the rains. The interior walls were generally coated with whitewashed plaster, and the homes of wealthier people were decorated with frescoes. Either animal skins or reed mats covered floors of hard-packed earth, and small stones were often used to create mosaics on the floors. Small windows were positioned close to the ceilings to admit light but keep out the heat of the summer sun. Roofs were generally made of terra-cotta tiles over wood. Wood, though, was expensive and hard to obtain. Only the wealthy could afford wooden shutters over the windows and wooden doors; when people in the countryside fled during outbreaks of war, they often took their wooden doors and shutters with them.

Another feature of Greek homes was that many had separate quarters for men and women. Greek husbands believed that their wives and daughters had to be shielded from public view. Thus, if they could afford to do so, they constructed homes with a separate area for women either at the back of the house, away from the street, or on the second story. This area was called a *gynaikeion.* Similarly, men had their own quarters, called the *andrôn,* typically located on the north side of the house, which stayed cooler. Many men used this area of the house to entertain male friends.

Few examples of what could be called apartment houses have been found. A notable exception is the port town of Piraeus, where apartment blocks called *synoikiai* were occupied by the poor and foreigners. These apartments, though, were often death traps because of earthquakes and fires.

ROME

BY FRANCESCA C. TRONCHIN

The remains of Roman architecture are enormously varied, from the most humble one-room home in Pompeii to impressive amphitheaters in Rome, France, and North Africa. Like Greek buildings, the surviving Roman structures have had considerable influence on architecture in the Western world and beyond. Although a great many Roman structures survive, the record geographically favors the architecture of the city of Rome itself. The eruption of Mount Vesuvius in the year 79 C.E. not only destroyed the cities of Pompeii and Herculaneum but also preserved a great number of private houses as well as public and religious buildings. These sites offer a very good picture of what Roman cities looked like, but only for the earliest phases of the Roman Empire. Other regions like North Africa, the Middle East, and central Europe are helping to complete the picture of Roman architecture, both in the heart of the empire and in its far-flung provinces.

In addition to the archaeological evidence, some ancient texts reveal a good deal about Roman buildings and their design. One written resource in particular—the *Ten Books on Architecture* by Marcus Vitruvius Pollio—is a very useful tool in the study of Roman structures, engineering, decoration, and even city planning. Vitruvius was an architect and an engineer living in the first century B.C.E., and he dedicated his comprehensive treatise to the emperor Augustus. While Vitruvius's writings are very helpful, he primarily described the state of architecture in his own time and a few centuries before. To learn about later periods in Roman building, one must look again to the physical remains as well as to a few surviving pieces of ancient texts by writers in later periods.

Vitruvius was, like most Roman architects, more than simply a designer of buildings; he was also an engineer and was knowledgeable about landscape design and art. Although Roman architects were skilled in a great many areas, few of their names survive to our day. In antiquity it was more important that the name of the person who commissioned and paid for a building be preserved, rather than the name of the person who designed and constructed it. Vitruvius, among other ancient writers on architecture, described the importance of symmetry, harmony of forms, durability, utility, and beauty in buildings. These are principles that can be observed in many surviving Roman structures.

Although Roman designers borrowed heavily from Greek architecture, they made considerable contributions in construction and style. The arch and vault were perfected by the Romans. Concrete was essentially discovered in the Roman period and exploited by the architects of the time. The Romans also introduced new building types like the amphitheater, bath, and apartment building (called an *insula* in Latin). The Markets of Trajan in Rome, built between 110 and 112 C.E., could be regarded as the first multistoried shopping mall in the world.

DESIGN AND MATERIALS

Among the earliest building materials in Roman Italy were mud brick and tufa, a local volcanic stone. Both eventually fell out of use for the most part, but for different reasons. Tufa was a sturdy and readily available stone, but it was not well suited to the kind of fine decorative carving favored by Roman architects. Mud brick had been used for millennia throughout the Mediterranean region, but it is only a semi-permanent material. The kiln-fired bricks that came into use during the first century B.C.E., in conjunction with concrete, proved to be much more durable; many of the Roman buildings that survive are made of this combination of fired bricks and concrete. Eventually travertine (a type of marble from quarries close to Rome) became an important material for Roman buildings. With the discovery of beautiful and pure white marble in northwestern Italy during the life of Julius Caesar (100–44 B.C.E.), builders came to favor that type of stone for luxurious buildings in Rome and elsewhere. In various parts of the Roman Empire different building materials were exploited because of their availability as well as their suitability to the local climate.

The earliest Roman buildings were frequently decorated with terra-cotta statuary, evidence of a strong relationship to the Etruscan civilization of central Italy. Vitruvius describes the reliance of Roman architecture on Etruscan design. Not only did the Etruscans use terra-cotta statues on their buildings, but they gave their temples a strong focus on the front of the building as well. This design is very different from that favored by earlier Greek architects, and it came to be adopted by Roman builders.

Like much of Roman art, Roman architecture was eclectic. Designers borrowed styles from both the Etruscans and the Greeks, and many architects working in Rome just before the days of the empire (beginning in the first century B.C.E.) and shortly afterward were Greek or of Greek descent. The Romans used innovative materials such brick and concrete throughout the empire, but they almost always used Greek architectural forms to decorate building exteriors. For example, the facade of the Colosseum—Rome's monumental amphitheater—is decorated with columns in the Greek Doric, Ionic, and Corinthian orders. (The "orders" made up an organizational system of Greek architecture.) Beginning in the second century C.E. materials and styles showed an Eastern influence, such as with the importation of Proconnesian marble from modern-day Turkey and in the use of various architectural details native to other Eastern provinces.

The Roman architects combined Greek, Etruscan, and other design elements in new and original ways, as in the Temple of Portunus in Rome. The building has the Etruscan features of a high supporting platform, a porch with columns, and a focus on the front of the building. The freestanding columns at the front and half-columns at the sides and back, however, show a reliance on Greek examples. The combination of different forms gave the temple its distinctly Roman flavor.

Concrete—a mixture of lime, volcanic ash, stones, a binding agent, and water—had been in use on a minor scale in Mesopotamia, but Roman architects perfected the material. Concrete had advantages over previous architectural materials, such as cut stone, in that it was exceedingly strong and flexible and was faster and cheaper to construct. The Romans' first use of concrete dates to the late third century B.C.E. Concrete allowed Roman architects to improve upon a feature that had been used by the Greeks and Etruscans: the arch. The arch is a highly stable structure that transmits and bears weight very effectively. Arches can accommodate a wider span than more traditional architecture, which uses simple vertical and horizontal supports, and the strength of concrete allowed for even wider spans. The use of poured and shaped concrete to create arches imparted a greater flexibility of form as well. When arches are extended, they create a barrel vault, like a semicylindrical ceiling over a corridor.

Roman architects used concrete and the structures of the arch and barrel vault to create new types of buildings. The Sanctuary of Fortuna Primigenia at Palestrina in central Italy is an early example of the creative and complex use of concrete vaults. The Pantheon in Rome, however, is perhaps the most spectacular example of concrete construction. It was the largest dome in the world until modern times. The Pantheon survives almost completely intact, allowing visitors to gain an exceptional sense of occupying an ancient space.

Although visitors to Rome and other ancient Roman cities in modern times see large sections of brick-faced concrete walls that still stand, in antiquity these walls were frequently covered with other materials, usually to give a richer appearance. Stucco was often employed to cover the walls and could be enhanced with thin layers of the fine plaster that was a suitable surface for fresco painting. Both interior and exterior walls could be plastered and painted. In more costly buildings, thin slabs of marble and other stones were used to cover the concrete walls and therefore give the illusion that the entire building was made of more expensive materials. White marble was particularly popular for these panels, probably because of the associations with more ancient and venerable Greek buildings (which were actually made of solid marble in many cases). The emperor Augustus is said to have boasted that he transformed the city of Rome from a brick one to one made of marble. This statement is partly true, since a great many buildings were constructed in the city during Augustus's reign, frequently faced in white marble.

Colored marble was also popular for revetment panels (decorative think slabs of stone) as well as entire columns and pavements for floors. These stones came from all corners of the Roman Empire. Yellow stone veined with purple came from Tunisia, green "serpentino" from southern Greece, red-purple porphyry from Egypt, and the Phrygian white and purple stone from what is now Turkey. These colored stones, in combination with glass and terra-cotta, could also be used in small cubes, or tesserae, to make mosaics. Mosaics were used as beautiful and durable floor coverings in private homes and public buildings alike.

Roman Temples

The Romans most frequently worshipped their gods and goddesses at temples. Roman cities were full of small and large temples, which could also be dedicated to deified emperors. Most Roman temples were rectangular in plan; stood on a high, stepped podium; and had one entrance at the front of the building. A columned porch, topped by a pitched roof (two sided and sloped) and pediment (the triangular section just below a sloped roof, which sometimes contained sculptural decoration), drew attention to the doorway. This is a departure from the design of Greek temples, which typically had colonnades (rows of supporting columns) along all four sides, creating the illusion that no particular side was more important than the others. The interiors of Roman temples were occupied by statues of a deity as well as expensive gifts that had been dedicated to the god or goddess. Some temples were round in plan, also with a single entrance.

The Pantheon, constructed between 118 and 125 C.E., is the quintessential example of this kind of temple. Dedicated to the 12 major Roman gods, the Pantheon is entered through an impressive porch supported by enormous granite columns. The domed interior of the Pantheon alludes to the canopy of the heavens and the orb of the world. In the eastern part of the empire, especially after the second century C.E., temple design became even more innovative. The Temple of Venus at Baalbek (in modern-day Lebanon) combines traditional aspects such as the high podium and single entrance with a scalloped roofline and unique five-sided Corinthian column capitals.

The Forum

Every Roman city had at its heart a forum. This was a place for commercial, legal, political, and religious activity. A forum was essentially an open plaza, usually in the center of a town. The open space was usually a rectangle marked by colonnades or porticoes (covered entrances or walkways) on three sides, with a major temple occupying one of the short sides of the plaza. The forum was frequently decorated with commemorative statues of military and political leaders and other historic monuments. Arches, sometimes celebrating military triumphs, could stand as monumental portals into the forum. Arches celebrating the various victories of the emperors Augustus, Tiberius, and Septimius Severus stood in the main forum in Rome. Porticoes provided shade for visitors to the forum, who met friends and business associates there for meetings. Administrative and political buildings like the Senate house and record building were also located in the main forum of a city.

Basilicas were multipurpose buildings common in the Roman forum. A basilica was usually a long and narrow rectangular structure with a wide central aisle and narrow side aisles separated by rows of columns. Magistrates and

Engraving of the Roman Colosseum by Antoine Lafréry (© The Trustees of the British Museum)

judges could preside over trials or other business on a raised platform at one end of the interior, called a tribunal. Court cases would be heard in basilicas, though less-important trials could be carried out in the open space of the forum itself. In some cases, as in the Basilica Julia in Rome's main forum, small shops occupied the front section of the ground floor.

In the main forum of a Roman city, a major temple stood at the short end of the oblong open space of the plaza. This placement focused visitors' attention on the temple. The temple was usually dedicated to three of the major gods in Roman religion: Jupiter, Juno, and Minerva. Other temples could also be present in a forum, especially if they were dedicated to the protective deity of the city or to a deified emperor.

The Architecture of Entertainment

Some of the greatest innovations of the Roman architects were the buildings designed as entertainment venues: baths, theaters, and amphitheaters. Although Greek builders had constructed their own baths and theaters, the Romans improved upon their forms and monumentalized them. The amphitheater, used for gladiatorial combat and hunts, is a Roman invention.

The ritual of visiting a bath in the Roman world was significant. It was not merely a place to clean oneself; it also allowed visitors to exercise in the *palestra* (an open space for ball games, stretching, and running), have a massage, meet with friends or colleagues, read a book, stroll in a landscaped garden, or hear a concert. Some luxurious private homes had bath suites, but most Romans visited a public bath. Many cities had more than one bath; Pompeii had at least four at the time of its destruction. One of the largest bath complexes ever built was the Baths of Caracalla in Rome, constructed in the early third century C.E. The site measures 390 by 740 feet, just slightly smaller than Giants Stadium in New Jersey.

Most baths had three main rooms, named for the temperature of the environment: a *frigidarium* for a cold-water dip, a *tepidarium* for a swim in warm water, and a *caldarium* for a hot bath. A *laconium*, like modern saunas, offered a steamy place to sit and work up a sweat. Bath buildings were usually arranged symmetrically with the hot, warm, and cool rooms in a row. The *caldarium* would be situated closest to the furnace that was used to heat the entire structure. The floors and walls of many baths were heated by a hypocaust. In this system, the floors were raised on small brick piers and hot air was directed into the open space. Public and private baths alike were usually sumptuously decorated with multicolored marble revetments, elaborate mosaics, and statuary. A Roman bath should not be confused with a latrine; these public restrooms were situated in many parts of a city and were not always associated with a bath building.

While both Greek and Roman theaters were used for theatrical performances, they were very different in design. Greek theaters were typically cut into a hillside to accommodate the sloped seating area; Roman ones were freestanding, thanks to the use of concrete vaulting. The earliest Roman theaters were only temporary, erected for religious festivals. These short-lived structures, however, could be quite elaborate, like the one erected by Marcus Aemilius Scaurus in 58 B.C.E. Although it was dismantled after a month of use, it could hold 80,000 spectators and was made of at least two kinds of marble. Roman theaters resembled Greek theaters with their tiered seating, but they had a semicircular orchestra (the place where the actors stood) instead of a circular one. The stage building behind the orchestra and facing the audience in a Roman theater was usually elaborately decorated with columns and statues in niches. The theaters at Orange in France and Mérida in Spain are very well preserved and represent the standard type of Roman theater.

Domestic Architecture

Ancient Roman homes were almost as varied as modern dwellings. Some members of the lower classes lived in a single room or a dimly lit apartment in an *insula*, an apartment building. The wealthiest Romans enjoyed vast estates with many different types of structures as well as fountains, gardens, and bath suites. Much of the city-dwelling population lived in a *domus*-style (single family) house, of which Pompeii gives us many examples. In middle- and upper-class houses decoration played a significant role, and frescoes, statuettes in marble and bronze, and mosaics frequently created a sumptuous atmosphere.

The *domus* was very popular in Roman Italy but less so in the provinces. Vitruvius describes the origins of the *domus* as well as its typical plan and types of rooms. The *domus* probably grew out of the designs of Etruscan homes, but Roman architects experimented with new and borrowed forms, elaborating on the earlier forms. *Domus* structures were like modern townhouses in that groups of these homes could occupy an entire city block, and they shared walls. There was a strong focus on the interior of the house, as few windows could be opened up to the exterior. The circulation of light and air was a major concern for the designers of the *domus*, and the houses incorporated a number of innovative features that allowed for the illumination and ventilation of interior spaces. Since artificial lighting in the ancient world was largely created by the use of oil lamps with open flames, many architects attempted to bring as much natural light into the house as possible, for fires were frequent and could be devastating in densely populated cities. Elaborate wall paintings enlivened the interiors of these buildings with images from classical mythology, landscapes, cityscapes, or imitations of marble revetments. Floor mosaics, either patterned or with figural scenes, also adorned Roman homes. The *domus* frequently had more than one story, as evidence from Pompeii and Herculaneum demonstrates.

A typical *domus* was entered through a narrow doorway followed by a hall called a *fauces* (Latin for "throat" or "jaws"). Once in the *fauces*, a visitor was often presented with an axial view through the house. Many homes in Pompeii and Herculaneum preserve this vista from the front door through rooms called an atrium and a *tablinum* and on toward a garden in the rear of the house. The atrium was an important room, used for the display of portraits of family members and the reception of guests. A rectangular opening in the roof of the atrium—a *compluvium*—admitted light into the house and directed rainwater to a shallow pool (*impluvium*) below. The rainwater could be stored in an underground tank and used for cooking and cleaning. Although allowing rain into the home seems strange, it was essential in a time when indoor plumbing was rare or nonexistent. (Eventually many Roman cities came to have quite sophisticated water systems that allowed for running water in private homes.)

Four to six small bedrooms called *cubicula* opened into the atrium from the sides. *Alae* (Latin for "wings") were open rooms off the atrium that had a number of purposes, frequently serving as storage or work spaces. At the far end of the atrium was the *tablinum* that could be likened to a "home office," where the head of the household met with colleagues and clients. Beyond the *tablinum* was the more private area of the home, which frequently included a porticoed landscaped garden with statuary and fountains as well as a *triclinium*, or dining room. The *triclinium* takes its name from the Greek words meaning "three couches," referring to the ancient use of couches, instead of chairs, for dining. The rooms beyond the *tablinum* functioned as reception and entertainment areas for guests. A Roman *domus* usually had a very small kitchen (sometimes with an adjacent latrine) with wood-fired stoves and braziers (a type of grill). Vitruvius describes a symmetrical and axial *domus*, but a great number of variations on this plan exist, demonstrating a variety of personal needs and tastes of the homeowners. The use of a peristyle—a garden surrounded by columns—as well as beautiful decoration inspired by more ancient works of art are two examples of the Greek influence on Roman domestic architecture, alluding to the highly decorated public spaces of Greek cities.

Although many Romans must have enjoyed the relative luxury of living in a beautifully decorated and spacious *domus*, the vast majority of urban residents lived in an *insula*. These multistoried structures were prevalent in large and densely populated cities like Rome and Ostia. *Insulae* were usually about four stories high, opened on to a multifunctional courtyard, and comprised individual units that were rented by the residents. The Insula of Diana at Ostia (built around 150 C.E.) is an interesting example of this building type; the ground-floor apartments were well appointed and large, while the units on the upper floors were smaller, some having only a single room. The most desirable apartments were on street level rather than up several flights of stairs. Most *insulae* were dark and uncomfortable, judging from the ancient written descriptions of them. Authors report the cooking odors of other tenants, rats' and pigeons' nests, leaky roofs, and noisy neighbors. The only latrine in the building was on the ground floor, near the entrance to the *insula*. Fires were common in these apartment buildings, especially because most residents did their cooking on braziers in the hallways of the building. Concrete construction and strict building codes in some cities alleviated some of these dangers.

At the other end of the spectrum of domestic architecture from the *insula* was the villa. While some villas were simply large, but modest farmhouses, many were the luxury estates of the very wealthy. Most Roman elites would have more than one home, and villas in the countryside and at the seaside were very popular. The structure of an extra-urban or suburban villa varied greatly throughout the empire but was generally spacious and well decorated. Some villas included smaller versions of the amenities found in cities, like baths, theaters, and libraries. The villa of the emperor Hadrian at Tivoli outside Rome was, in fact, like a small city enriched by pools, gardens, covered walking paths, and at least one temple. Although it was commissioned by Hadrian in the first quarter of the second century C.E., it apparently served as a villa for later emperors who enjoyed all its luxuries and tranquility outside the busy city of Rome.

Other emperors constructed impressive and grandiose villas within the city, which were actually urban palaces. Domitian, who ruled from 81 to 96 C.E., commissioned the architect Rabirius to build a three-part complex on the Palatine Hill in Rome. Like many villas, the palace was multifunctional and included spaces for entertainment, official business, and residential use. The public wing of the palace even included a basilica where Domitian could preside from an elevated tribunal under a vaulted niche.

Later Influence

The remains of Roman architecture have been enormously influential in Western culture. Many of the government buildings and memorials in Washington, D.C., for example, exhibit distinctly Roman forms and decoration. This long afterlife of Roman style and structure is well deserved, for the ancient architects created new types of structures, improved and expanded upon the use of various materials, and combined the influences of other cultures into a useful and attractive architectural vocabulary.

THE AMERICAS

BY JULIA MARTA CLAPP

The geographical regions of North, Central, and South America are distinguished by profoundly diverse climates. Ancient Andeans lived in arid areas and tropical ones, at sea level and in mountainous areas. The region known as Mesoamerica included wetlands and dry land, civilizations located at high altitudes and those positioned near bodies of water. Mound builders in North America lived in the flat, temperate climate of what is now the eastern United States. Ancient American architecture is both specific to its environmental conditions and universal among varying peoples and eras.

For ancient Americans, religious ritual was at the center of cultural life, and this was reflected in their architecture. Many of the structures that remain are public buildings, plazas, and temples where ceremonies and rituals were performed. The construction, decoration, and even cardinal orientation of these buildings were symbolically related to religion and cosmology. The importance of symbolism cannot be overstated in ancient American culture.

The Olmec

The region known as Mesoamerica included the southern half of present-day Mexico and extended approximately to present-day Costa Rica. Generally recognized as the oldest civilization in Mesoamerica, the Olmec lived in Mexico along the southern coast of the Gulf of Mexico. Far less is known about the Olmec than about later groups. Some estimates locate the birth of the Olmec civilization possibly as early as 1500 B.C.E., but there remains some variation in the group's dating. Its decline is generally located at 400 B.C.E., spanning the Early and Middle Preclassic eras.

The earliest Olmec cities were San Lorenzo (1500–1200 B.C.E.) and La Venta (1200–400 B.C.E.). At Olmec archaeological sites, evidence remains of housing and royal compounds as well as ceremonial and civic structures. While La Venta and San Lorenzo are best known for their spectacular colossal heads made of basalt, there is also evidence of great architectural structures. San Lorenzo has remains of both grand and modest housing structures, which indicate that Olmec society—not unlike much of Mesoamerica—was profoundly hierarchical. Houses were constructed by assembling pole-and-thatch systems to create walls and roofs, which is similar to modern-day techniques used in the area. The Olmec also constructed buildings with compacted earth.

Archaeologists have discovered what is now known as the Royal Compound, an elite residential area for Olmec rulers. The compound's Red Palace included a workshop where stone sculpture was produced. The Red Palace features basalt roof supports, gravel floors, and mud walls. For unknown reasons, the workshop ceased production in about 1200 B.C.E., but the compound contains the remains of much sculpture. Archaeological research uncovered a collection of basalt stones that, based on their shape, are believed to have once formed an aqueduct to the Royal Compound. It is possible that the aqueduct was used to bring fresh water to the city's inhabitants. The construction of the aqueduct as well as monolithic sculpture suggests that the Olmec were quite advanced in the fields of mathematics and engineering. Because pre-Columbian Mesoamericans did not use horses as beasts of burden, basalt stone was moved solely by human effort from the neighboring Tuxtla Mountains. Basalt, therefore, would have been used only for elite buildings or other monuments of particular sociopolitical importance.

Throughout pre-Columbian Mesoamerica, civilizations also engaged in what is commonly referred to as an ancient ballgame, which was played on a large, outdoor rectangular court, with high walls along either side. The ball was made of rubber, which was abundant along the Gulf Coast. An ancient example of what is believed to have been a ball court remains at San Lorenzo.

The Olmec city of La Venta rose in prominence with the decline of San Lorenzo and had a relatively large population until its own decline. The city's layout seems to have been divided into two halves, partitioned by the Central Plaza. As ritual practice was central to Mesoamerican public life, it is likely that the Central Plaza was the site of such practice and was therefore the heart of Olmec life at La Venta. The city's most impressive monument is the Great Pyramid (also known as Complex C), a stepped pyramid located near the Central Plaza. Rising about 105 feet above the ground, the Great Pyramid is larger and reflects more impressive engineering than other monuments of its era. Archaeologists have not determined its purpose, though scholars have put forth at least two possibilities. First, the building may be a funeral monument, storing remains or offerings (similar to the pyramids of the ancient Egyptians). Second, the pyramid might have served as a site for ritualistic ceremony. This theory is supported by the discovery of two several-ton, monolithic thrones on the south side of the building. Archaeologists also found other stone monuments near these thrones, which at some point were intentionally destroyed and buried in a ritualistic act.

Another significant discovery at La Venta was Tomb A, which was made of basalt stone carved into numerous six-foot-tall columns. These were then arranged tightly like dominoes. Marking the entrance to the tomb were five more columns that leaned diagonally against the horizontal stones. Packed mud and flagstones covered the earthen floor inside the tomb. Beneath the flagstones were burial offerings.

Other architectural complexes at La Venta contain similar mounds and plazas whose functions remain unknown, as well as a ball court, ruler residences, ritual areas, and stone monuments. The Olmec remain largely mysterious to current-day scholars; many of their buildings, sculptures, and monuments were damaged or destroyed during the civilization's downfall, and all have been vulnerable to several millennia of erosion in the Gulf Coast's tropical climate.

Teotihuacán

Teotihuacán was the largest, most powerful city in pre-Columbian Mesoamerica. It was located in the Teotihuacán Valley, about 25 miles from modern-day Mexico City, and covered eight square miles. Its population was perhaps as much as 200,000 people during its peak, placing it among the top 10 largest cities in the world during its time. Teotihuacán was occupied to a degree during the Early Preclassic Period (1800–1200 B.C.E.), but the bulk of its building activity occurred centuries later. Teotihuacán's greatest structures were completed before 300 C.E. (the Classic Period), contemporary with the early Maya. Surrounding its central structures were living compounds of varying sizes.

Teotihuacán was designed on a grid system, the centerpiece of which was the Avenue of the Dead, a boulevard extending several miles across the city. Much city planning, especially that of the Avenue of the Dead, probably took place between 150 and 200 C.E. The Pyramid of the Moon stands at one end of the Avenue of the Dead, against the backdrop of the inactive Cerro Gordo volcano. Its position in front of the volcano is strategic, as its massive presence (700 feet long and 200 feet tall) echoes that of the Cerro Gordo, suggesting a spiritual relationship between man-made structures and the land. Many Mesoamerican pyramids were designed to imitate the natural form of mountains. The Pyramid of the Moon, which was rebuilt several times during the era of Teotihuacán, also has at its base evidence of another pyramid as well as an open courtyard.

Teotihuacán's oldest structure, the Pyramid of the Sun (constructed between about 50 and 125 C.E.), is located along the eastern side of the Avenue of the Dead. One of the largest structures in pre-Columbian Mesoamerica at over 200 feet tall, the Pyramid of the Sun has five levels and an enormous staircase. Builders constructed the pyramid in several phases, the second of which was around 225 C.E. The pyramid was built over a cave that had been formed by a lava tube; the cave is 330 feet in length (with portions enlarged by human effort) and located 20 feet beneath the pyramid. The cave's floor was covered with basalt stones and its walls with mud. Inside the caves archaeologists have discovered U-shaped troughs similar to the aqueducts at San Lorenzo and which likely served a similar purpose. Caves are extremely important in pre-Columbian Mesoamerican origin myth, so the Pyramid of the Sun's location is particularly significant and would have been directly linked to religious practice in the city. It was arguably the religious and sociopolitical heart of the city—the most important building in Teotihuacán.

At the other end of the Avenue of the Dead, 2 miles south of the Pyramid of the Moon, is the Ciudadela complex, constructed in about 150–300 C.E. The Ciudadela's plaza is roughly 144,000 square feet, and it houses the relatively small Temple of the Feathered Serpent. This temple is distinguished primarily by its *talud-tablero* construction, a style of architecture that is characterized by a system of sloping and vertical surfaces. Archaeologists have speculated that the *talud-tablero* method of construction may have been developed several centuries earlier in nearby Tlaxcala, where *talud-tablero* buildings have been dated to 300–100 B.C.E. While Teotihuacán's architectural influence has been widely noted

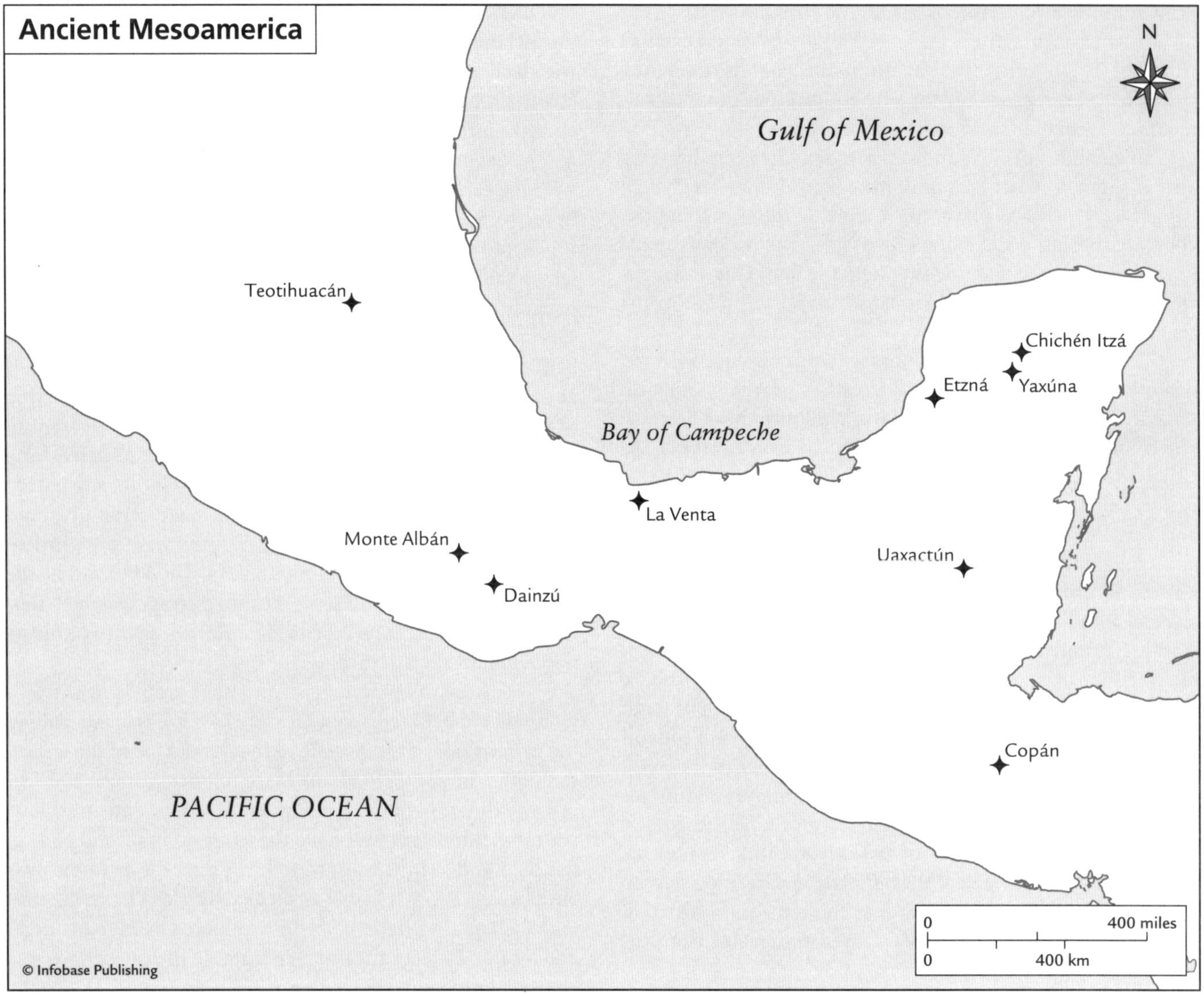

Major architectural sites in ancient Mesoamerica include La Venta, Monte Albán, and Teotihuacán.

in other cities, particularly those of the Maya, it is important to remember that the city was also influenced by others.

The temple is dedicated to Quetzalcoatl, the feathered serpent deity who remained vital to Mesoamerican spiritual life through the time of the Aztecs. The Temple of the Feathered Serpent features more decoration than the Pyramids of the Sun and Moon. Its facade is ornamented by continuous scaly reptile carving that wraps around all six levels and by large protruding heads of various beasts. The temple commemorates warfare, and evidence of human sacrifice—practiced widely in Mesoamerica—has been found at the foot of the temple.

Other architectural remains have been found at Teotihuacán, and they have enabled archaeologists to create a relatively complete portrait of the layout of the city. Teotihuacán boasts residential complexes and large open plazas. The city also has preserved murals, mostly containing religious or moral content, that were painted on the horizontal facades. The feathered serpent encircling the Pyramid of the Feathered Serpent was painted as well.

The Maya

The Mayan civilization of Mesoamerica is believed to have begun around 500 B.C.E., though it is best known for its Classic Period art and architecture of 250 to 650 C.E. In the Preclassic Period the Maya were also active builders, as settled community life requires buildings for domestic, ceremonial and civic activity. Among the buildings that characterize Mayan architecture are pyramid temples, housing complexes and plazas, as well as the ball court, which the early Maya built with sloped sides. Overall, these structures adapted to the variable landscape and were organized in a less systematic way than other Mesoamerican cities, which were based upon the grid system. For example, as Teotihuacán's rational planning was similar to that of contemporary New York City, Mayan urban planning was more akin to the winding cities of old Europe. Furthermore, the Maya created no standardized or universal design among their disparate cities; architectural style arose from local preferences. However, because they built with sensitivity to their environment, cities with similar ecological conditions did tend to resemble one another. Mayan architecture did not distinguish greatly between buildings' functions, and buildings probably served more than one purpose.

Also noteworthy in Mesoamerican architecture was the Maya's use of corbeled vaulting, a system in which the stones of two opposing walls are laid horizontally with increasing proximity until they meet in an inverted V-shaped arch. It is interesting to note that the corbeled vault was also in use by the ancient Mycenaeans in Greece. Stone was not the only building material; the Maya also constructed flat roofs with wooden beams and stucco. It is important to remember that any ancient Mesoamerican building was constructed solely through human labor, so stone blocks of all sizes were quarried, gathered, and placed atop pyramids without the help of animals or modern machines. Many early Mayan buildings were constructed by the use of projecting supports that were inserted into fitted openings. Onto this framework the Maya applied stucco to decorative effect, often in the form of large gods' heads.

One of the most notable Early Preclassic Mayan edifices is known as Structure EVII, at Uaxactún. Structure EVII is a six-level pyramid whose facades correspond to cardinal directions. It was the largest of three pyramids that formed the "E-Group." Each side has several staircases: One is central and reaches the top level, and it is flanked by narrower, shorter staircases and enormous carved masks. Structure EVII was probably used for ceremonial or ritualistic purposes, and its position in relation to the sun also indicates that it functioned as a sort of sundial.

Staircases are a hallmark of Mayan architectural design, and later temples boasted extremely tall staircases that required no small degree of athleticism to mount. In addition to the more characteristic staircases, the archaeologist Charles Suhler discovered a Late Preclassic Mayan platform with a curious staircase in the city of Yaxúna, which is about 12 miles from the famous Mayan site Chichén Itzá. The means to ascend Structure 6E-120 were buried within the building: a series of internal corridors and chambers that ultimately yielded a trapdoor leading to the apex of the structure. This style, which endured throughout the Classic Period, is significant. It has led archaeologists to conclude that for the Maya, the process of ascending a structure was at least as important as arrival at the top. In other words, the Maya placed ritualistic significance on the act of ascension.

The triumvirate arrangement of the E-Group pyramids was common in Early Classic Mayan architecture, and it is seen again at Uaxactún in a different grouping. The A-Group was built early in Uaxactún's history, and it was a relatively simple arrangement of three. Over the course of 500 years, this basic assembly was greatly expanded upon, ultimately resulting in an extravagant complex in the Late Classic Period.

Oaxaca

The Valley of Oaxaca in Mesoamerica has a rich architectural history that dates back to the 14th century B.C.E. and culminates with the great civilization of Monte Albán. The most commonly excavated buildings have been housing structures, which in the period of 1150–850 B.C.E. were constructed with wattle and daub, in which a wooden lattice structure is covered with packed mud, clay, and other materials. This method was also used during the Neolithic (7000–2000 B.C.E.) in Western Asia, Central Europe, and North America. Around 900 B.C.E. builders in this era made simple pyramids in the forms of platforms made of (and filled with) earth. These constructions had several layers and a staircase.

Home to the Zapotec, Monte Albán began its development in the Middle Preclassic around 500 B.C.E. and reached its apogee during the Classic Period, finally coming to an end concurrent with the Maya (ca. 900 C.E.). The most significant early structure from the earliest settlement at Monte Albán is a stone platform that housed what is now known as the Temple of the Danzantes (dancers), so named for its decorative carvings of loose-limbed figures. About 140 large blocks of stone were carved with the *danzantes* and arranged as part of the temple. Another set was incorporated as part of another structure at Monte Albán, which is called Building or Mound J. Art historians have recently reinterpreted the *danzantes* as prisoners of war, leading to the conclusion that the Temple of the Danzantes was a war memorial.

Building J was also built during the Preclassic Period, probably sometime between 150 B.C.E. and 150 C.E. Two sides of this stone-faced structure meet to form a westward-pointing triangular shape that is similar to an arrowhead. Scholars now believe that owing to its orientation Mound J held astronomical significance. The building also incorporates inscriptions and date symbols carved in stone in the Zapotec language, which provides insight into this early culture. Also during this period Monte Albán developed a system of standardization of buildings, in which various building functions yielded particular design.

Around the time that the hilltop city of Monte Albán was coming into being (ca. 500–150 B.C.E.), neighboring Oaxacan cities, such as Monte Negro, exhibited architectural practices that were seen in early Monte Albán as well. The buildings at Monte Negro were multichambered and reflected the hierarchy of society in their grandness and complexity. They boasted column supports, wattle-and-daub and adobe construction, courtyards, and drains. Other cultures also used adobe during this time, including the ancient Sumerians and Babylonians.

South America

The west coast of South America is home to what are known as Andean cultures, including pre-Inca civilizations such as the Chavín (900–200 B.C.E.), Paracas (600–175 C.E.), and Moche (100–600 C.E.) cultures. The ecological environment on the west coast of South America is varied and intense, with extremely dry areas as well as dense, tropical zones. Traces of human activity have been located as early as 10,000 B.C.E. in this part of South America. The Preceramic Era (3000–1800 B.C.E.) saw the first evidence of architectural endeavors. As did Mesoamericans, Andean people during this period created temples and plazas, which were often reworked over time. An example of such expansion is found in the city of Kotosh (settled ca. 2450 B.C.E.), which is northeast of modern-day Lima. Architecture at Kotosh is characterized by mound buildings, which were topped by small stone temples, such as the Temple of the Crossed Hands, which includes adobe reliefs of two crossed arms.

Community effort in building was important in Pre ceramic Andean culture, in contrast to that of the ancient Egyptians, who are believed to have used forced labor to build their monuments. In Andean culture, community identity was central to cultural tradition, so building labor was not compulsory. This makes the endeavors of this early period especially astonishing, considering their organization and accomplishment. This ethos of community remained part of Andean culture throughout pre-Columbian times.

The architecture of this period was characterized by circular or rectangular open-air plazas, which reiterate the importance of Andean community life. The site of Salinas de Chao features rectangular platforms, terraces, and plazas (some of which were underground), generally made of stone, bound by mortar, and covered with clay. Two plazas now called Unit A and Unit B had stairs leading from the complex to a subterranean plaza, as well as incised and painted clay friezes on its walls.

The largest Preceramic site, called El Paraíso, dates to ca. 2000 B.C.E. Its complexes are built with 100,000 tons of stone, which is a particularly astonishing feat of construction. El Paraíso has two buildings that are situated parallel to each other at opposite ends of the plaza. There is also a large complex called Unit 1, which has been excavated and explored. The complex has 16 rooms and a red-painted chamber of unknown purpose.

In the first millennium B.C.E. the Chavín culture created great platforms that had relief carving. Cerro Sechín, a site on a granite hill at Sechín Alto, boasts a platform of 12 stories that is dated between 1700 and 500 B.C.E. and was expanded until about 200 B.C.E. The platform was completed in a series of several phases that gradually increased in size and complexity. It included a wall of stone and clay, granite slabs, columns, and a system of aqueducts to conduct water. Granite slabs that surround the structure are carved with figures of mutilated warriors that have been linked thematically (though not with historical evidence) to the *danzantes* of Monte Albán. It is possible that Cerro Sechín's symbolic significance was similar to that of other war monuments of the ancient Americas.

The site Chavín de Huántar is one of the greatest of the Chavín Period. The site's location is strategic and advantageous, as it sits near two rivers and two mountain passes, near the coast and near the jungle. The Old Temple is built in the form of the U-shape, which was characteristic of Chavín architecture. It contained rooms and passageways (some hidden), air ducts, and a sunken platform that would have accommodated several hundred people. The temple's Sunken Circular Court has a wall of stone slabs with finely carved jaguar and human figures. The jaguar, which sometimes assumed human characteristics, is an important and pervasive motif in early art of South America and Mesoamerica. Also impressive are the more than 40 monolithic heads that protrude from the upper walls of the temple. The temple is built around a lancelike sculpture called the Lanzón, which is one of the site's earliest-dated objects. The carved figures and the Lanzón were symbolic and related thematically to the rituals that took place at the temple.

The Ica Valley has provided evidence of architectural developments from the Paracas culture. At Animas Bajas archaeologists have found rectangular mound structures that contained many rooms, ramps, and earthen foundations covered with adobe bricks. As with many buildings and sites in the ancient Americas, there is evidence of remodeling and expansion. Other sites in the area include housing terrace units made of adobe or stone brick.

The later Paracas site of Animas Altas shows a more sophisticated architectural program, also including walled fortification. Major monuments found at the site are 13 large mounds constructed of two levels with rooms, storage units, patios and corridors. These are built over an earth foundation on which adobe bricks are stacked and bonded with adobe mortar; occasionally, grassy materials fill the spaces between the bricks. Some of the walls at Animas Altas have been decorated with low-relief carving of mythological creatures, incorporating both serpentine and catlike features and references to birds and water. All of these characteristics would have had religious or cosmological significance to the inhabitants of this area.

North America

Little is known about different varieties of ancient architecture in North America. In the region now called the eastern United States, most of the structures archaeologists have identified were burial mounds. This tradition lasted for more than two millennia in North America. In the era 5500–3000 B.C.E. in the lower Mississippi area, the earliest mound structures were in present-day Louisiana. The Watson Brake Mound Group (3900–3300 B.C.E.) comprises 11 earthworks connected by a terrace and plaza. They are constructed of earth and have a conical shape.

The largest and most elaborate earthen mounds of the second millennium B.C.E. are found at Poverty Point (1730–1350 B.C.E.), which overlooks the Mississippi River floodplain in northeastern Louisiana. This structure was more complex than the hill-like mound structures built elsewhere. Schematically, its design resembles an amphitheater: It is a semicircular structure formed of six concentric, 100-foot-wide earth platforms divided by five 35-foot-wide radial passages between. Archaeologists believe that housing structures were built on the platforms. Another type of mound was built slightly northeast of Louisiana at Sapelo Island in Darien, Georgia. The Sapelo Island Shell Rings are large, enclosed circular mounds built of oyster and other oceanic shells. This is one of several similar structures and dates to about 2170 B.C.E.

The Adena culture (1000–100 B.C.E.) also built conical burial earthen mounds. They were composed of packed earth upon foundational buildings, and they sometimes included wooden tombs. This period was characterized by an increased importance placed on funeral ceremony and also trade. The emphasis on burial is especially seen in the Hopewell culture (200 B.C.E.–400 C.E.) of modern-day Ohio. This culture built circular or elliptical burial earthen mounds similar to those created by the Mississippian cultures nearly a millennium later. In fact, resemblance between the two cultures led the Mississippian mounds to be misidentified as Hopewellian until relatively recently.

The western Anasazi during the Basketmaker II Period (560 B.C.E.–700 C.E.) built rock-shelter sites in the last few centuries B.C.E. Archaeologists have found small settlements with hearths and storage spaces as well as burial and storage chambers lined with stone slabs.

See also ART; ASTRONOMY; BORDERS AND FRONTIERS; BUILDING TECHNIQUES AND MATERIALS; CALENDARS AND CLOCKS; CITIES; CLIMATE AND GEOGRAPHY; DEATH AND BURIAL PRACTICES; DRAMA AND THEATER; EMPIRES AND DYNASTIES; FAMILY; FESTIVALS; HOUSEHOLD GOODS; HUNTING, FISHING, AND GATHERING; ILLUMINATION; LITERATURE; MIGRATION AND POPULATION MOVEMENTS; MILITARY; NATURAL DISASTERS; NOMADIC AND PASTORAL SOCIETIES; RELIGION AND COSMOLOGY; SACRED SITES; SCIENCE; SETTLEMENT PATTERNS; SOCIAL ORGANIZATION; SPORTS AND RECREATION; STORAGE AND PRESERVATION; TOWNS AND VILLAGES; TRADE AND EXCHANGE; WRITING.

FURTHER READING

James C. Anderson, *Roman Architecture and Society* (Baltimore: Johns Hopkins University Press, 1997).

Dieter Arnold, *The Encyclopedia of Ancient Egyptian Architecture*, trans. Sabine H. Gardiner (Princeton, N.J.: Princeton University Press, 2003).

Kenneth Briggs and Janet Briggs, *Ziggurat: How Ur Gave Birth* (Langhorne, Penn.: Chora House Press, 1998).

Ching-Hua Ju and Hua-Liang Peng, *Ancient Chinese Architecture*, 10 vols. (New York: Springer, 1998).

John R. Clarke, *The Houses of Roman Italy* (Berkeley, University of California Press, 1991).

Somers Clarke and R. Engelbach, *Ancient Egyptian Construction and Architecture* (Mineola, N.Y.: Dover Publications, 1990).

Rodolfo Fattovich, "The Development of Urbanism in the Northern Horn of Africa in Ancient and Medieval Times." Available online. URL: http://hometown.aol.com/_ht_a/skipbdahlgren/sdahlgren/fattowich.pdf. Downloaded on December 1, 2006.

Henri Frankfort, *The Art and Architecture of the Ancient Orient*, 5th ed. (New Haven, Conn.: Yale University Press, 1996).

Peter Garlake, *Early Art and Architecture of Africa* (New York: Oxford University Press, 2002).

Jeff Karl Kowalski, ed., *Mesoamerican Architecture as a Cultural Symbol* (New York: Oxford University Press, 1999).

George Kubler, *The Art and Architecture of Ancient America* (Baltimore: Penguin Books: 1962).

Helen Leacroft, *The Buildings of Ancient Mesopotamia* (Reading, Mass.: Addison-Wesley, 1975).

Seton Lloyd, *Ancient Architecture: Mesopotamia, Egypt, Crete, Greece* (New York, N.Y.: Harry N. Abrams, 1974).

Alexander G. McKay, *Houses, Villas, and Palaces in the Roman World* (Baltimore: Johns Hopkins University Press, 1998).

Mary Ellen Miller, *The Art of Mesoamerica: From Olmec to Aztec* (London: Thames and Hudson, 2001).

Mary Ellen Miller, *Maya Art and Architecture* (London: Thames and Hudson, 1999).

William N. Morgan, *Precolumbian Architecture in Eastern North America* (Gainesville, University Press of Florida, 1999).

Donald Preziosi and Louise A. Hitchcock, *Aegean Art and Architecture* (New York: Oxford University Press, 2000).

Ingrid D. Rowland and Thomas Noble Howe, *Vitruvius: Ten Books on Architecture* (New York: Cambridge University Press, 1999).

W. Stevenson Smith, *The Art and Architecture of Ancient Egypt* (New Haven, Conn.: Yale University Press, 1999).

John W. Stamper, *The Architecture of Roman Temples* (New York: Cambridge University Press, 2005).

Rebecca Stone-Miller, *Art of the Andes: From Chavín to Inca* (London: Thames and Hudson, 1995).

Bindia Thapar, *Introduction to Indian Architecture* (North Clarendon, Vt.: Tuttle, 2005).

Mark Wilson-Jones, *Principles of Roman Architecture* (New Haven: Yale University Press, 2000).

► art

INTRODUCTION

Ancient human beings around the world painted on rocks. The purposes of these ancient rock paintings are not known. Archaeologists often suggest that they were religious works, because religion has been one of the most powerful motivators of artists. Perhaps the depictions of animals, humans, hunts, and war were intended to make hopes into reality. It was common in ancient cultures to believe that art was more than mere representation of something concrete, that an artistic depiction of something made it actual fact. That is, the act of creating art was simultaneously the creating of reality. For instance, the depiction of a bird actually created a real bird in the world. Thus, the depictions of hunts could be attempts to make successful hunts reality.

This supernatural interpretation of ancient art—whether paintings or statues—makes sense of some but not all depictions. It does not account for the portrayal of a gored man on a European rock wall, of people dancing on Saharan rock sides, or of beings that are half animal and half human found in Egypt, Africa, and the Near East. Some African rock art was used during initiation rites to tell young people about their responsibilities as adults. In Inner Mongolia the rock paintings may have done no more than list the kinds of wild game found in an area. In Australia aborigines know what their ancient paintings mean: They are stories of creation and the arrival of humans in Australia, and the aborigines can translate the paintings for outsiders.

In addition to painting stone, ancient artists sculpted it. Many of the earliest artworks that archaeologists have found are small stone carvings of humanlike figures. Stone sculpture has usually been carved either fully in the round or in relief. In reliefs, carved figures project from a flat background. Egyptians and Kushites, from south of Egypt, were masters of relief carving, illustrating military victories or interactions between gods and humans on stone walls. These carvings featured stylized figures that appear flat to modern eyes but which were seen by ancient viewers to represent several perspectives of a figure. Reliefs were popular in the Near East and the Roman world for depicting military victories; the Romans developed the triumphal arch, which celebrated a great military leader with reliefs showing his victories.

The Egyptians may have been the first to create life-sized metal statues, dating to about 3500 B.C.E. Copper, a component of bronze, tends to hold bubbles, but it often can be found in nuggets; in Europe and northwestern North America it was sometimes pounded into shape, beginning in about 4000 B.C.E. in North America and perhaps later in Europe. Wherever people learned how to make it, bronze became the preferred metal for art, because it holds its shape better than other metals, even iron.

Another early medium for artistic expression was ceramics. It is not known how early people began making ceramics, but it dates back to at least the period of the last great ice age. Decorating ceramic vessels seems a natural activity for people, because human beings tend to like to have beauty in their lives. Thus, early ceramics often took on attractive shapes and were often painted. Advances in the technology of firing clay led to the development of glazes, which required high temperatures to melt. Glazes added luster to ceramics. Ancient pottery was not always intended to have practical uses such as storing grain or for carrying water. For instance, almost everywhere, people made ceramic figures, usually small. The figures sometimes served religious purposes such as acting as spiritual guardians for graves or as substitutes for human sacrifices. In many cases ceramic figures were toys, often in the shapes of animals and carts.

Wood was certainly used for sculpture in the ancient world, but wood decays, leaving mostly objects of more durable substances such as stone and ceramics; a few ancient pieces survive, typically in dry climates. Written records tell of marvelous wooden sculptures in ancient India, and wood has long been favored for sculpture in Africa; both regions, however, have climates and insects that rapidly destroy wooden art. As with pottery figures, wooden carvings often were used for supernatural purposes, such as representing gods, but they also took the form of well-carved furniture, and wood was a favored medium for making dolls.

Glassmaking seems to have been intended originally for the making of jewelry. Glass beads, in particular, were very highly valued throughout the ancient world, with certain colors of glass sometimes being more highly valued than gold. Especially prized glass beads could travel through trade for thousands of miles, allowing archaeologists to use the ones they find to trace commerce among ancient peoples. Eventually, glass became a medium for household objects, and glassmakers became skilled at creating everyday objects such as vases and lamps into art objects such as dishes that looked like grapes or candlesticks that looked like vines.

A technique used to decorate objects was painting. Ancient peoples painted almost anything, probably because they loved color. Where a modern artist might leave a marble sculpture or bronze sculpture its natural color, ancient artists would paint the marble or bronze. The desire to create a painting for its own sake probably occurred very early among ancient artists, but aside from rocks, their paintings were usually on perishable materials such as wood, bark, bamboo, and silk. This means that a vast part of humanity's artistic history has been lost because the ancient paintings decayed or were destroyed. Sometimes the paints themselves contained acids that could eat through whatever was under the paint. From time to time, the paint lost flexibility as it dried and flaked away. For many ancient cultures art historians find only traces of paints that serve as clues as to the colors artists used. Occasionally, researchers get lucky, because in dry areas such as Egypt paint can survive in dark places, or ancient artists found a way to paint with durable colors, as the ancient Chinese did with lacquer.

Whatever form it took, ancient art was an expression of what ancient people valued and can tell modern people something about what the ancient people were like. In some cases, art is all that is left of a culture that passed from history thousands of years ago. The complexity of much ancient art speaks of people who were as complicated as modern people, and their work is sometimes unsurpassed by later artists.

AFRICA

BY KIRK H. BEETZ

ROCK ENGRAVING AND PAINTING

The earliest art to be found in Africa is on rocks. Dating the earliest rock art is difficult, but the oldest examples probably date to between 27,500 and 25,000 B.C.E. These pieces are found in eastern and southern Africa and were the work of the San, sometimes called the Bushmen, who still populate parts of southern Africa. Their ancient paintings are found in caves and areas sheltered by tall rocks. The ancient San had a rich assortment of mineral pigments: white, black, red ocher, blue, yellow, and green.

Their paintings seem to have been mostly for ritual purposes, especially for coming-of-age rituals for youngsters in early puberty. The youngsters would be shown illustrations of their history, religious beliefs, and duties, and they would be told what behavior was expected of them as men or as women. The paintings often feature depictions of the eland, a large antelope, which was held sacred by the San. Outstanding examples of ancient San art are found in caves in Namibia, where the oldest paintings are found, and in Zimbabwe and South Africa.

In Namibia paintings probably accumulated over thousands of years, with styles varying from full-bodied depictions of people to impossibly thin, knobby characterizations. Both men and women and boys and girls are represented. They carry spears and bows and are usually unclad but sometimes wear belts and possibly loincloths. The modern African passion for body ornaments seems to date back to these earliest paintings, because portrayals of people wearing body paint, bangles on the arms, and bracelets are common. The figures sometimes wear masks. In paintings found in KwaZulu-Natal, South Africa, the elands are huge, dwarfing the human figures. The humans vary in form from stick figures to broad-chested men and wide-hipped women. More recent rock paintings, perhaps from the early years of the Christian era, show a profusion of plants as well as humans and animals. Often the paintings are high off the ground—too high for a San adult to reach—but archaeologists do not know what the San used to help them reach so high.

Rock etchings and paintings of abstract designs, perhaps dating from 5590 to 2280 B.C.E., are found in Malawi and Zambia, but they do not appear to be San paintings and at present archaeologists have no idea who created them. There are ancient rock paintings of people and wildlife in Burkina Faso, Cameroon, Mali, Nigeria, and elsewhere in Africa south of the Sahara, but the cultures that painted them have yet to be identified. The best-known rock art in Africa probably is found in the Sahara, dating from 8000 to 3000 B.C.E. The art is found throughout the Sahara, from the west coast to the Nile River. It seems as though no large rock was left untouched by the ancient artists, and more than 40,000 etchings and paintings have been found. The art can be divided into periods based on style, subject matter, and carbon dating: Hunter Period (pre-6122 B.C.E.), Roundhead Period (6122–5095 B.C.E.), Herdsmen Period (5095–2780 B.C.E.), Horse Period (2780–600 B.C.E.), Camel Period (600 B.C.E. and later). Some datings put the end of the Herdsmen Period and the start of the Horse Period at 1500 B.C.E.

Many people are captivated by the Saharan rock etchings and paintings because they depict a Saharan environment that is very different from today's ever-growing desert. The painters lived in a Sahara that had many rivers and streams and much rain and was therefore lush with life. Animals flourished. The paintings show both dark-skinned and light-skinned people, often mixing together. Mineral pigments, charcoal, and burned bone were used to create such colors as white, black, red, yellow, purple, and green. The paintings show rituals, community activities, hunting, wars, and dancing. People usually are portrayed realistically, although during the Roundhead Period figures with circular or oval heads were common; they may have been wearing a kind of headdress that held hair in a net, or they may have been wearing masks. By about 6500 B.C.E. the wet era of the Saharan regions had peaked and thereafter declined. Lush wetlands became grasslands. By 3000 B.C.E. the Saharan peoples were being forced out of their lands by desertification, and the Egyptians fought fierce wars against peoples from the west called Libyans, who were seeking to occupy the farmlands of Egypt.

It is unclear how much the rock art of the Sahara influenced African art south of the Sahara. The spiral image common in African art appeared in the Sahara in about 6000 B.C.E. and may have spread from there. The spiral usually consists of a dark line twisting out from a central point. It also shows up in jewelry as wound wires. Sometimes, especially when carved or represented in ceramics, its outward end is given the head of a snake. In some African cultures the spiral signifies eternal life. When worn as a pendant, it can represent the wish for a long life for the wearer. It also may represent the eternal existence of the soul when included in burial objects.

Many of the problems in tracing influences of the early Saharan artists stem from the climate of Africa and its cultural history. Outside of the Sahara and some areas in the south, Africa is wet. Most African art has been rendered in wood, but in tropical Africa wooden objects rot in fewer than 50 years; some African cultures have made it a regular part of their lives to replace wooden objects every few decades. Moreover, few ancient Africans had written languages, and for the few that did have writing, the writing has not yet been interpreted. In addition, many African cultures have migrated often during the past 5,000 years, and only recently have anthropologists started reconstructing the paths of those migrations.

Given Africans' ancient passion for jewelry, it would be reasonable to assume that gold, which does not corrupt like most other metals, would preserve some of the history of their art. But Africans have a long tradition of melting old gold jewelry to make new gold jewelry, and many of the gold artifacts left in graves have been looted. Thus historians do not have a consistent record of art objects to trace the development of cultural art traditions; there is little written record describing the art that no longer exists; and when ancient African art objects are found, the people living near the objects are not necessarily the culture that made them and have little

Petroglyph of animals and people at Tassili, Algeria, in North Africa (© Board of Regents of the University of Wisconsin System. Photographer: Jeanne Tabachnick)

idea of who did. This means that the history of the art of ancient Africa is very fragmented and incomplete.

Nubia

Nubia is a term often used to lump together several different cultures that occupied a region just south of ancient Egypt. Second to Egypt, this region is where the most African art has been found. The earliest sculpture dates from about 4000 B.C.E. and comes from just south of ancient Egypt. It consists of clay figures, including a small, fat female figure, which may be a fertility figure. A large clay head of a hippopotamus that appears to have been broken off a bigger figure suggests that the early Nubians made large sculptures as well as small ones. When Egypt expanded its influence southward, this ancient Nubian culture moved southward, probably to get out of the way. By 2600 B.C.E. it seems to have been in decline, because of Egypt's military pressure. After about 2600 B.C.E. there is a gap to about 1900 B.C.E. in the archaeological record for Nubia; at one time this was thought to represent a different culture from the earlier one, leading to the early culture's being called A group, the middle or missing culture B group, and a culture starting in 1900 B.C.E. C group. At present these three groups are thought to be illusions, and archaeologists believe that from 4000 B.C.E. to about 900 B.C.E. there was one continuous culture, with the supposedly missing group being one whose ancient relics archaeologists have not yet found but may find someday.

Between 2150 and 1900 B.C.E. Nubian culture just south of Egypt may have mixed with a culture from farther south, forming the kingdom of Kerma, named after its capital city, which was beside the Nile River. Numerous ceramic figures have been found from the Kerma culture of 1900–1550 B.C.E. Figures tend to be small, in the 3- to 5-inch range. They depict humanlike forms with animal heads and what may be fertility goddesses with broad hips and thick thighs. The figures are carved with patterns of lines and dashes that may represent body paint. Most figures have lines around their necks, and some have dots across their chests that suggest jewelry. Breechclouts, a strip of cloth that hangs between the legs from a waistband, seem to be the common garb. There are also depictions in ceramics of animals that may have symbolized religious ideas.

By 1650 B.C.E. Kerma had extended its dominion nearly to the first cataract (rocky outcrop) on the Nile River, north of where the Aswān Dam is today. Between 1504 and 1492 B.C.E. the pharaoh Thutmose I invaded Kerma, sacked the capital city, and continued hundreds of miles south beyond Kerma's lands, seizing much of the rest of Nubia. Only in the far south of Nubia did the Nubian culture survive. The Egyptians built huge monuments, such as the temple at Abu Simbel, using enslaved Nubians, to remind Nubians who were their masters. Only in 1070 B.C.E. did Egypt withdraw from Nubia.

Kush

In about 900 B.C.E. a kingdom the Egyptians called Kush was founded in Nubia. Its capital was the city of Napata, which was beside the Nile River in what had been the south of the Kerma kingdom but was near the northern limits of the new kingdom of Kush, which extended far to the south, encompassing most of the White Nile and Blue Nile rivers. In 712 B.C.E. Kush conquered Egypt, establishing the short-lived Twenty-Fifth Dynasty of Egypt. During this period Kushite artists blended Egyptian art styles into their own. When large buildings were constructed, sculptors created large reliefs (carvings with figures projecting out from a flat background) depicting gods the way the Egyptians did, with human bodies and animal heads, wearing Egyptian-style black wigs but Kushite clothing. Some reliefs portray kings wielding swords and others show prisoners taken in war. The Kushite carvings of people are notably chunkier than Egyptian carvings, with heavier legs and broader shoulders, resulting in a style influenced by Egypt but uniquely belonging to Kush. In the 700s and 600s B.C.E. Kushite bronze statues were exceptionally sophisticated, portraying people realistically. Small sculptures still have color on them, showing that they were painted realistically.

In 663 B.C.E. Kush was forced out of Egypt by an invasion into Egypt from Assyria. In 593 B.C.E. Egypt invaded Kush, sacking Napata. The kings of Kush moved their capital south to the city of Meroë, and there they reigned from about 590 B.C.E. to 350 C.E.; Nubian art flourished. Meroë is located on the Nile River south of where the Atbara River flows into the Nile and lies on an ancient north-to-south trade route. It is famous for its more than 60 steep pyramids marking the tombs of Meroite kings. Many of them were 50 to 100 feet in height when new, though ones built in the last 200 years of the kingdom were about 13 feet in height.

Although the royal tombs were looted by grave robbers, the robbers occasionally missed spectacular golden jewelry. Some bracelets feature inlaid glass in abstract designs or in depictions of a four-winged goddess. Egyptian influence can be seen in the clothing of some of the figures and in beads shaped like scarab beetles. Rings are elaborate, sometimes wide enough to cover two or three upper knuckles. Small figures of animals may have represented gods meant to protect the dead, and snakes were probably symbols of the Meroite kings and queens.

Meroite sculptors had contact with Greek and Roman sculptors as well as Egyptian ones, and they incorporated Greek and Roman styles into their own, creating freestanding sculptures in sandstone. A bust of the deceased from a Meroite tomb from 100 to 200 C.E., in the Sudan National Museum in Khartoum, shows the mixture of influences and its unique result, with hair tied down in rows, a Greek-like pose, and an Egyptian-like nose but with slitlike eyes that are African in style, as well as an overall composition of features identifying the figure as a Meroite and no one else. Another example is the Venus of Meroë from the 100s to 200s C.E. She is missing most of her legs but still is almost a yard in length. She shows the influence of Roman sculpture in her body proportions and gives the appearance of soft plumpness. She was painted a reddish brown.

Axum

To the southeast of Kush, in the highlands of Ethiopia, a nation arose out of the mixing of Sabeans from southwest Arabia and local Africans in about 500 B.C.E., and they spoke and wrote in the Sabean language. The city of Axum was built on trade, shipping African goods off to the Near East and the rest of Asia and importing goods from the Near East and southern Asia. It was a major trading center by the dawn of the Christian era; by 350 C.E. it was capital of a kingdom that included Yemen and Meroë. When the nation converted to Christianity at about that time, Christian images influenced its art.

Stone sculptures from as early as 1500 B.C.E. have been found in the area of the city of Axum. One of a lion, in the National Museum of Ethiopia in Addis Ababa, is covered with Sabean inscriptions, indicating that Axum had a long cultural history before its emergence as an empire in East Africa. By the 400s B.C.E. Axum was producing sculptures in stone in its own national style: Human figures were stiff, with stylized faces rather than portraits of individual people, and altars were marked by the symbols of the gods they served.

The most impressive of Axum's sculpture began to be carved in the 300s C.E. These were stelae, or large upright stones carved with images, the tallest of which was 108 feet high; the tallest still standing is 22 feet high. More than 200 stelae have been found. They were carved to look like tall buildings, with doors at their bases and upper stories with windows and columns. From a distance they appear to be actual buildings. They were built to mark tombs. An older tomb built to resemble a house stands near some of the stelae, and it is possible they evolved out of earlier, smaller imitation houses. The stelae show some influence from Arabian and Indian sculpture. Other works from the 300s to 500s C.E. are Christian symbols such as silver crosses.

West Africa

Westward across Africa from Nubia and Axum, in Nigeria at a tin mine at the village of Nok, stone tools and pieces of ceramic sculptures were found in 1928: a human head, a monkey's head, and a foot. Apparently, the tools and sculptures had been washed into a gully by rain, and the sculptures had been broken apart in the process. The heads showed signs of having been broken off from larger sculptures. In 1943 more ceramic heads were found, mostly by accident. In the late 1950s these sculptures were identified as being from one culture located near the Niger River in a 60,000-square-mile area. This culture was dubbed Nok, after the village where its artifacts were first found.

Exactly when the Nok culture flourished is uncertain, with its beginning being placed either in the 700s B.C.E. or the 500s B.C.E. It seems to have ended in the 200s C.E. The origins of Nok culture are likewise uncertain. Some historians believe the Nok were influenced by people from the Sahara, either nomads or possibly Romans. Others suggest a movement westward of the arts and skills of Kush, especially during the period when Meroë was the capital of Kush. It is possible that the Nok people developed their art on their own.

Nok sculptures are so far the earliest sculptures in the round found in sub-Saharan Africa, meaning that they are fully three-dimensional and are modeled on all sides. A head that was being used on a scarecrow in the village of Jemaa in 1943 now resides in the National Museum in Lagos, Nigeria. It dates from the 400s B.C.E., and it could be either a man or a woman. Its hair is pulled back in tight rows, even over its ears. Its eyebrows appear to be woven into tight lines. The lips are full, and the nose is broad and flattened. It is broken off at the neck. Enough sculpted body parts have been found to indicate that the head was attached to a complete, life-size body. Its pupils, nostrils, and mouth have holes that probably were made to allow moisture to escape during firing (baking at high heat).

There is much variety in Nok sculpture. There are bearded men with tall headgear and bare-breasted women with high foreheads and heavy, ponderous bands of necklaces. Some figures are crude and barely recognizable as humans, while others are well proportioned and detailed. The Nok made many small figures that are less than two feet in length. These figures include depictions of humans sitting or kneeling as well as animals. Sculptures of monkeys appear to have had religious or magical importance. Archaeologists speculate that the figures were once parts of tombs or rested on wooden altars that decayed; they believe that water eventually washed away many of the ancient sites, so that most Nok art is not found where it originally was made. Some archaeologists believe that the Nok culture did not disappear but instead moved from Nigeria to the southeast, becoming the Yoruba culture, known from the late Middle Ages. Other archaeologists disagree with this view, believing the Yoruba culture to be separate from the Nok.

Much of the history of African art is no more than frustrating hints of what may have existed. For instance, the kingdom of Wagadu may have existed in West Africa from the Atlantic Ocean eastward to rivers that flowed into the Niger River, possibly in the 200s to 100s B.C.E. There are a few accounts of Wagadu kings dressed in fabulously colorful robes and of people wearing beautiful jewelry, yet no remains of the Wagadu have been found. The Wagadu kingdom was succeeded by the kingdom of Ghana, which was described by Arabs in the Middle Ages but which arose around 1 C.E. The Ghanians sculpted ceramic snakes, which featured in their creation stories.

South of the kingdom of Ghana in the region of the Volta River lived the Akan-speaking culture, which survives in modern times. The ancient Akans were probably animists, people who believe that the universe is full of spirits and that plants, animals, and even inanimate objects can have spirits. Their culture arose during the first millennium B.C.E. It is possible that they made ceramic busts of people and that by 500 C.E. they were making gold jewelry.

Farther south, on the African coast at the Niger River delta, were the Igbo-Ukwu people, for whom a small number of relics have been found. In about 500 B.C.E. the Igbo-Ukwu people learned to smelt copper. They eventually mastered the making of bronze, perhaps learning this skill from Berber traders from the Sahara. Almost nothing is known about the Igbo-Ukwu, except that they made metal sculptures in a style uniquely their own and that by about 800 C.E. they were making exquisitely detailed pots and small busts. A pendant of a human head, in the National Museum in Lagos, has scarification on its scowling face. Scarification is the deliberate scarring of skin to create decorative patterns. Especially mysterious is the carefully detailed and assembled bronze sculpture of a leopard skull, also housed in the National Museum in Lagos.

Central and Southern Africa

South of Lake Chad lived the Kanem-Borno culture. Agriculture began in the region in about 1,000 B.C.E., which probably marks the beginning the Kanem-Borno culture. The Kanem-Borno people made ceramic vessels about four feet in height for storing grain and for burying people as well as pottery for everyday use. They made numerous ceramic sculptures of humans and animals. The human sculptures may have been used in ancestor worship. The animals include sheep, cattle, and antelopes. Dating is uncertain for these sculptures, though one of a sheep may be from the 500s C.E. It is not known when the Kanem-Borno people learned to cast metal, but early examples of jewelry of brass and iron show they had mastered the lost-wax technique. (In this technique clay is molded around a wax sculpture, the clay is heated until the wax melts, molten metal is poured into the empty mold, the metal cools, and the mold is broken to reveal the metal sculpture.) They manufactured beads of quartz and glass. For much of central and southern Africa, ancient art is either lost, probably because it was made of wood or has yet to be discovered.

Jewelry

It seems that Africans universally have loved wearing jewelry. In Africa every part of the body can have jewelry, and even in Africa's earliest art people are portrayed wearing jewelry. Egyptians were famous throughout ancient Asia for their beads, and Africans south of the Sahara imported beads from Egypt. The oldest African-made glass beads probably came from South Africa, but the date is uncertain. By about 300 B.C.E. Africans wore a wide variety of beads: glass ones from Egypt or ones they made themselves, clear and carnelian quartz ones, ones made from seashells, and ones made of polished ceramics. By 300 C.E. Africans were importing beads from Europe, the Near East, and India. The beads were often balls, but they could be rectangular, diamond-shaped, or shaped like animals—just about any shape.

Beads were woven into men's and women's clothing and often into their hair. They sometimes symbolized good health or prosperity but mostly were valued for their beauty. Beads often were set into jewelry, and glass beads in Nubia were set into bracelets so they glittered from any angle. The metals gold, silver, bronze, brass, copper, tin, and iron were used by different cultural groups to create jewelry. The type of metal usually depended on its availability. Gold was typically the most-prized metal; in West Africa, however, silver was preferred because it symbolized purity—gold was thought to be impure. For anyone studying the history of jewelry, there will always be the frustration caused by the African custom of melting down old jewelry, especially gold jewelry, to use the metal to make new jewelry. This tradition means that sculptures showing people wearing jewelry and jewelry placed in graves are often the only sources of information about what ancient Africans wore.

Jewelry often identified a person's place in society. The size and weight of an anklet sometimes expressed a woman's wealth. In the Congo ivory or bone jewelry with human heads with three points sticking out would indicate that the wearer was a king. Jewelry had practical value. For example, hairpins could be made of metal or ivory; they would hold sometimes elaborate hairdos in place, and their length could speak of a wearer's social status.

Perhaps as ancient as the Nok culture are leg ornaments in the shape of snakes. Worn lengthwise and usually made in bronze, the ornaments are bars with coils and snake heads, and modern cultures wear them to ward off real snakes. Bronze bracelets shaped like snakes have been excavated near the Cross River in Nigeria. Anklets, armlets, and bracelets in the shape of coiled rope have been found throughout central Africa. Some items weigh several pounds and probably were worn only to show the wearer's status.

EGYPT

BY MICHAEL J. O'NEAL

The ancient Egyptians had no word for *art*. Artists were mindful of the aesthetic properties of their creations, but they had no abstract word that was understood as art, and no one thought of their creations as art in the modern sense of the word. When they created items, they did so almost always with either a practical or religious purpose in mind. Practical items, like bowls and other vessels, were used in the home for everyday purposes. Religious art commonly depicted gods and goddesses as well as the pharaohs, who were seen as divine. It was created to serve a spiritual purpose, most often to honor the gods, to ensure a continuous connection between the physical and spiritual worlds, or to help a deceased person on his or her way into the afterlife.

Egyptian artists worked within a limited range of subject matter. Ancient Egyptian culture valued conformity rather than individualism, so there was little room for innovation, experimentation, or personal idiosyncrasies—features usually thought of as characteristic of art. Most forms of artwork, especially larger pieces, were produced by teams rather than individuals. That said, the best, most artistically pleasing objects that survive from ancient Egypt feature carvings and paintings that seem to be present solely because they are beautiful. In other words, they are works of art.

ARTISTIC CONVENTIONS

Ancient Egyptian artists adhered strictly to a set of rules and conventions. These rules did not change dramatically over a period of three thousand years. Painting and drawing made use of simple lines and shapes and broad areas of color. Male figures were always darker than female figures (perhaps reflecting the fact that women stayed indoors more than men and thus were not burnished by the sun). The size of a figure reflected its relative importance; men were always larger than women, and the pharaoh was always larger than the other figures and equal in size to the gods. Pharaohs were always shown with their symbols of power, and other symbolism was strictly maintained: blue represented the Nile River, red symbolized power, and yellow represented the sun (and hence the sun god). Commoners were always portrayed with either two left or two right feet. Depictions of animals, too, were symbolic; for example, a falcon's head represented the sky god Horus, and a jackal's head represented Anubis, the god of funeral rites. By adhering to these rules, Egyptian artists created a sense of order and continuity. Rarely did Egyptian art attempt to create an impression of chaos, despair, or other dark elements of life.

In portraying the human form ancient Egyptian artists made use of what is called the canon of human proportions. They started with a square grid that, for standing figures, included 18 "units." Two were used for the face, 10 for the area from the neck to the knees, and six from the knees to the bottom of the feet. For seated figures a 14-square grid was used. This way of proportioning the human body remained remarkably consistent throughout Egyptian history and was used to guide the artist not only in making statues but in creating paintings and relief work as well.

THE ORIGINS OF EGYPTIAN ART

This history of ancient Egyptian art began millennia ago, long before the time of the pharaohs, the great temples, and the pyramids. In the Nile River valley archaeologists have discovered late Stone Age cliff drawings created by the valley's first inhabitants that date back to the eighth millennium B.C.E. These drawings show scenes from everyday life, including wild animals, hunting, herds of domesticated animals, and boating. Archaeologists have also discovered such items as pottery and carved stones and ivory, often placed in graves. Also discovered have been small statues of animals and people. Sometimes the figures of people had grotesquely large genitals, suggesting that these pieces were part of rituals surrounding a fertility cult.

Later, during the Predynastic Period, or the centuries immediately before Egypt was united under the rule of the pharaohs during the Dynastic Period, painted scenes on pottery became more common. Also, artists began to practice some of the artistic forms that became common in Dynastic Egypt. Many of the art objects they created were for ceremonial purposes, including knives with ivory handles, palettes (vessels made of stone or wood and used for various purposes), and maces (ceremonial staffs). These objects, often used as votive offerings (gifts made for the gods), played an important role in religious rituals, and their possession helped define the status of a person in the social order.

Many of these kinds of items have been found in and around the temple at Hierakonpolis. In fact, this temple and its environs have been a treasure trove for archaeologists and art historians. A partial list of "firsts" and "onlys" from this temple includes such large structures as the first tomb cut into stone, from about 3100 B.C.E.; the earliest painted tomb, depicting a funeral procession; the earliest preserved royal palace, from about 2900 B.C.E.; and Egypt's earliest temple, dating to about 3400 B.C.E. Notable statuary includes the oldest life-size statue of a human; the earliest large-scale metal statuary, including a life-size statue of the Sixth Dynasty (2323–2150 B.C.E.) king, Pepi I, and his son; and the oldest known stone statue of a named person, King Khasekhemwy of the Second Dynasty (2770–2649 B.C.E.). The first mummies, from about 3600 B.C.E., also come from this temple, as do Egypt's earliest masks, made of pottery; the oldest-known cult image, a golden hawk head of the god Horus; and the largest flint knives made in Egypt, along with huge bowls, maces, and other items. There are a number of other interesting items, including the earliest surviving house in Egypt, from about 3600 B.C.E.; the first preserved beard; Egypt's earliest beer brewery; and the first evidence of hair extensions and henna hair dye.

Painting

Most of the painting that survives from ancient Egypt is found on pottery and stonework. Paintings have been found on relief stonework, but many paintings have also been found on flat stone. Unfinished paintings have given art historians clues about how painters worked. Evidence suggests that skilled draftsmen marked out the areas to be painted by making sketches with red paint and then making corrections with black paint. In the Middle Kingdom (2140–1640 B.C.E.) painters began to use a system of grid lines to plan out the composition—in representing humans, the canon of human proportion referred to earlier. These grids would then aid the painter in maintaining proportions as the painting was sketched in. Sometimes the lines were etched in using a straight edge, but often they appear to have been done with red chalk lines made with a string that was stretched tightly and then snapped against the surface (in the same way that modern builders "snap lines" on the floor when marking out the interior walls of a house under construction).

Once the plan of the composition was in place, artists made a sketch using fine brushes, similar to the brushes used for writing. Brushes were made with reeds cut at an angle and split to produce bristles. To apply the paint, more substantial brushes were made with fibrous wood. A typical brush was made of twigs that were tied together; the ends were then pounded to break the fibers into bristles.

Pigments were made from local minerals that could be found in the deserts surrounding the Nile River valley. White paint was made with gypsum (calcium sulfate), "whiting" (calcium carbonate), or huntite, a chalky white compound of calcium and magnesium. Soot and charcoal were used to produce black, and iron oxide (rust) produced a range of yellows and browns. Various other minerals, including realgar (arsenic sulfide), orpiment (arsenic trisulfide), jarosite (potassium sulfate and iron sulfate), azurite (copper carbonate), and malachite (also copper carbonate), were mixed to produce other colors, including blues, greens, reds, and yellows. Many of these compounds are unstable in light, and the colors have faded over the centuries.

Most surviving painting can be found on the walls of tombs and temples built at the behest of royalty, though similar work was increasingly part of private tombs and houses beginning in the Eighteenth Dynasty (1550–1307 B.C.E.). The Egyptians believed that painted scenes in tombs would help ensure the continuity of life. In temples they believed paintings preserved the memory of the accomplishments of the pharaohs and, by depicting rituals, would serve as a visual record that would ensure that important rituals were later performed. While many examples of fine relief painting could be cited, art historians often point to the painting found in the tomb of Mentuhotep II (r. 2061–1991) at Dayr al-Bahri and to the carvings found in the shrine to Sesostris I (r. 1971–1926) in Karnak as particularly superior examples.

One feature of ancient Egyptian painting that strikes modern viewers is the lack of three dimensions. Most later painting, beginning in Renaissance Europe, creates the illusion of a third dimension, depth, by arranging the elements of the composition and altering their size so that some are in the viewer's foreground and others in the background and objects themselves have a sense of depth. Egyptian painters, in contrast, remained happy with flat, two-dimensional paintings and drawings. Further, more modern painting creates the sense that the objects are viewed from a single perspective. An Egyptian painting, in contrast, employs multiple perspectives.

Modern viewers, too, are often struck by a kind of oddity in the way human figures are represented in Egyptian painting. Rather than giving the figures naturalistic poses, the paintings seem almost to be made of a collection of parts. Thus, for example, the head might be in profile, but with a full "frontal" view of an eye. The shoulders may then be rendered frontally, but the legs and buttocks may again be in full profile.

No discussion of painting would be complete without mentioning the illumination of papyrus manuscripts. Papyrus is a form of paper made from the reeds of papyrus plants. Beginning in about the Eighteenth Dynasty, artists started to include small drawings and paintings on official and religious documents. Among the best examples of this type of work are the illuminations of the Book of the Dead by a scribe named Ani in the Nineteenth Dynasty (about 1250 B.C.E.).

Banquet scene, fragment of wall painting from the tomb of Nebamun, Thebes, Egypt, Eighteenth Dynasty, around 1350 B.C.E. (© The Trustees of the British Museum)

Sculpture

Because sculptures are made of stone or other durable materials such as ivory, many from ancient Egypt survive intact. Most sculptures were created for one of two purposes. One was to be placed in tombs, and the other was to serve as a votive offering in temples. Overall, the purpose was not realistic representation; particularly in the case of tomb art, it was expected that no one would ever see it. Rather, the purpose was to preserve an idealized image of the individual in death when he or she stood before the gods. Accordingly, the emphasis was on idealized types rather than individual portraiture.

Egyptian sculptors worked with a variety of materials. Generally, sculptures were made with soft stone. The most easily obtained was limestone, which could be found in the cliffs on both sides of the Nile River. Other soft stones included alabaster (calcite), sandstone, graywacke (a dark gray sandstone sometimes mixed with bits of quartz or feldspar), and schist (a crystalline rock that can easily be split along parallel planes). Egyptian sculptors also worked with harder stone, including basalt, granite, granodiorite (a granular rock with characteristics of both quartz and granite), diorite (a crystalline rock containing a number of minerals), and quartzite (a type of sandstone). Sculptors shaped softer stone using stone tools and copper chisels. Harder stone was shaped by hammering it and using abrasives made from still-harder stone.

Whichever type of stone the artist used, it was often covered in plaster and painted; in some cases it was painted without plastering. Frequently, though, the stone was left unpainted because of its color symbolism: black stone symbolized the life-giving silt left behind by the flooding of the Nile; reds, golds, and browns represented the sun; and green represented vegetation and the emergence of new life.

Sculpture included not only statuary but also relief carved into the surface of stone. Relief work was of two types. In raised relief, the background is cut away, leaving the figures standing out from the surface of the stone. (A modern coin is a good example of raised relief.) In sunk relief, the opposite is done: the background is left as it is, and the figures are carved into the stone. Typically, the outside walls of a temple or tomb used sunk relief, where sunshine and shadow had the effect of enhancing the figures. In contrast, interior walls more commonly used raised relief.

Wood was also used for sculptures, though most of the wood had to be imported. Some common woods included tamarisk, acacia, and the wood from fig trees as well as a variety of pine from Syria. Wood was shaped with knives and adzes and polished with rubbing stones. Some pieces were made with single chunks of wood, but many were made with pieces or strips that were joined. Sometimes the wood was painted, but often it was left in its natural state, especially if the quality of the wood was high.

Metal, too, was a common medium, especially arsenic bronze (an alloy of arsenic and copper) in the Old Kingdom (2575–2134 B.C.E.) and bronze (an alloy of tin and copper) beginning in the Middle Kingdom. Gold and silver were highly valued. Although today gold is regarded as the more precious metal, in ancient Egypt silver's rarity made it the more precious metal compared with gold, which was used extensively.

During the Old Kingdom some characteristic types of statuary began to emerge. One of the most common was that of a man standing with his left leg advanced slightly forward. Another common form was a seated man. While fragments of wooden statues of the first type survive from the city of Saqqara and date to the First Dynasty (2920–2770 B.C.E.), more impressive examples include a statue of King Djoser of the Third Dynasty (2649–2575 B.C.E.) in the temple complex at Saqqara and the statue of King Menkaure II and Queen Khamerernebty of the Fourth Dynasty (2575–2465 B.C.E.) from the pyramid complex at Giza. During the Old Kingdom the convention of "frontality" was established. This term refers to the convention of always having the figure facing to the front, even if the figure is in motion, perhaps walking. Many sculptures were housed in enclosed niches and alcoves, so it made sense to have the figure face to the front so that viewers could see the face and interact with the figure more readily.

During the Middle Kingdom sculpture became more realistic, and many statues from this period appear to be portraits rather than idealized types. Many portray royalty, including such figures as Sesostris III and Amenemhet III. Sculptors during this period began to use the sphinx—with the body of a lion and the head of a king—to create an image of the pharaoh as the protector of Egypt. The most dramatic example is the huge Sphinx on the Giza Plateau, the site of the Great Pyramid. Another good example is the statue of Amenemhet II. In addition to royal figures, some statuary appears to have been commissioned by private individuals. Many of these pieces show the figure seated, standing, or in many cases squatting and often wearing a cloak. Some of the statues are entirely cubical, with the figure portrayed with his or her knees drawn up. These types of statues are called block statues.

During the New Kingdom (1570–1070 B.C.E.) the art of sculpture rose to new heights. Art historians regard many of the statues that survive from this period as among the most accomplished works of art the ancient world produced. Again, many of the statues were created to honor a pharaoh. Particularly well known are the statues of Hatshepsut and Thutmose III. Hatshepsut, an 18th Dynasty pharaoh, remains famous in part because she was a woman. In order to legitimize her rule, she dressed as a man and was even known to wear a false beard. Her statue, housed at the Metropolitan Museum of Art in New York City, is clearly that of a powerful ruler, with all the trappings of authority rather than the subordinate, domesticated woman most often portrayed in Egyptian art.

New Kingdom pharaohs commissioned a number of so-called colossal sculptures. Many of these extremely large sculptures were housed in funerary temples. Perhaps the best known is the colossus of Ramses II, located now in a special museum built to house it near the village of Mit Rahina in Egypt. Although the statue is unfinished, modern sculptors and art historians remain in awe of the work. It portrays the pharaoh lying down. Even without feet, the statue is nearly 34 feet long and carved out of a single block of limestone. Modern artists point out that even with mechanized carving, grinding, and sanding tools, creating a statue that achieves the anatomical perfection of the Ramses statue would today be a long, painstaking process. They marvel, then, at the ability of teams of Egyptian artists to achieve the results they did using far less sophisticated tools.

A pair of statues inspiring similar awe can be found in Thebes at the entrance to a mortuary temple built by Amenhotep III, an Eighteenth Dynasty pharaoh. Both of these statues of Amenhotep III are 75 feet tall and carved out of single blocks of stone. These works are called the Colossi of Memnon because the ancient Egyptians associated the statues in legend with King Memnon, the son of Eos. Because of a crack in the stone, one of the statues emitted a soft moan when it warmed in the morning; according to the legend, this sound was Memnon greeting his mother. (Later the Romans attempted to "fix" the stone, and the sound was no longer heard.)

The Amarna Period

Generalizations about the reliance of Egyptian artists on fixed conventions and rules do not apply strictly to the Amarna Period, during and just after the reign of Akhenaten in the late Eighteenth Dynasty, in the mid-1300s B.C.E. The period is called Amarna, from El-Amarna, the name of a modern city that has been built over the site of a new capital city Akhenaten had built in dedication to the sun god. Scholars conclude that art in Egypt changed because the nation was in a state of turmoil during Akhenaten's reign. He was very much a religious and social revolutionary, and he violated many of the conventions that had dictated the behavior of the pharaohs for centuries. After his death Egypt returned to normal, and the aberrations of Amarna Period art disappeared.

Amarna Period art was different because it conveyed more of a sense of motion and vitality than conventional Egyptian art. Instead of being posed formally, figures were often portrayed in motion. Figures appeared in groups, and depictions of the pharaoh and his family were naturalistic and informal. For some reason a great deal of attention was paid to the portrayal of hands and feet, right down to the details of the fingernails. Many of the representations of Akhenaten himself, as well as others from the period, strike the modern viewer as bizarre, with elongated heads, distended bellies, and thin limbs. Representations of his queen, Nefertiti, suggest that she wielded as much power as her husband, in part because images of her were the same size as those of Akhenaten.

Other Arts

Pottery was not considered an art form in ancient Egypt. Although there are examples of pottery with human or animal figures, and a few were made in the form of animals, most of the surviving pottery was purely functional. Historians know that during the Eighteenth and Nineteenth Dynasties, floral designs appeared on high-quality pottery, but none of this pottery survives.

Egyptian artists did, however, exercise their skills on a type of pottery called faience. The term is used to refer both to the materials from which the piece is made and to the piece itself. In ancient Egypt faience consisted of silica made of sand, crushed quartz, or sometimes crushed pebbles in water. Lime was added to make the materials adhere, and ground copper provided color. After the piece was formed, it was coated with a mixture of soda, lime, and silica. Most of the pieces that survive are a rich blue-green because the coating also contains copper, though other pieces are black, brown, red, yellow, and white. The piece was then fired in a kiln to produce a glassy surface. Faience was used to produce a range of items, including scepters, bowls, beads, amulets (a charm against evil), scarabs (beetles used as charms), goblets, and small statues. It was also used to make decorative tiles, such as those found in the Step Pyramid of Djoser at Saqqara. One of the most famous pieces of faience is a blue hippopotamus nicknamed "William" in the New York Metropolitan Museum of Art.

The ancient Egyptians were accomplished jewelers. Although they did not use precious stones such as diamonds, they used a wide range of semiprecious stones, including agate, turquoise, lapis lazuli, feldspar, garnet, jasper, amethyst, and carnelian. Bracelets were found in the tomb of Djer, a First Dynasty king, and from the Fourth Dynasty came bracelets belonging to Queen Hetepheres. The most spectacular jewelry, however, dates from later dynasties, including the collection of jewelry belonging to Queen Ahhotep of the 18th Dynasty and the large collection found in the tomb of King Tutankhamen ("King Tut") of the Eighteenth Dynasty.

Glassware was known during the Predynastic Period, but it did not become an independent form until the 18th Dynasty. Glass was used to make small vessels, such as cups and flasks, as well as for beads and amulets. Glass thread was often applied to the objects for decoration, and some had gold rims. Glass was also used as an inlay. Perhaps one of the most widely recognized pieces of ancient Egyptian art, the funerary mask of King Tutankhamen, is made of gold with colored-glass inlay.

Artwork was produced with a number of other materials as well. The ancient Egyptians were accomplished metalworkers, and many pieces made of copper and bronze survive. These include jugs and bowls, as well as metal statues. Some were made by pounding the metal, while others were made from castings. One of the most famous pieces of metalwork is the life-size statue of King Pepi I from the Sixth Dynasty, made of pounded copper plates affixed to a wooden core. Gold, more easily found in ancient Egypt than silver, was widely used for many purposes, including jewelry, vessels, furniture, and inlay, and it was frequently pounded into thin gold leaf for decorative purposes. Again, the most impressive display of gold objects comes from the tomb of King Tutankhamen.

Among less durable materials, wood was used not only for statues but also for cabinetmaking and furniture. In the tomb of King Tutankhamen, archaeologists found a wooden chest with an ivory veneer and 33,000 pieces of ebony and ivory inlay. Ivory and bone were also used to produce small statues, often of creatures such as grasshoppers and gazelles.

THE MIDDLE EAST

by Tom Streissguth

Ancient Mesopotamia comprised different ethnic groups and cultures located along the Tigris and Euphrates rivers in what is modern-day Iraq and parts of what are now northeastern Syria and eastern Turkey. In this region archaeologists have discovered remains of human habitation dating back more than 100,000 years. The ancient Mesopotamians were among the first to develop farming, build an urban civilization, and create a distinctive artistic style.

Historians classify Mesopotamian art by periods named after important excavation sites and kingdoms, with the earliest being the prehistoric sites of Hassuna, Samarra, and Halaf, all preceding 5000 B.C.E. Following these eras are the Ubaid (fifth millennium B.C.E.), Uruk and Jemdat Nasr (4000–2900 B.C.E.), Early Dynastic (2900–2340 B.C.E.), Akkadian (2340–2100 B.C.E.), Babylonian (1900–1600 B.C.E.), Assyrian (1400–612 B.C.E.), and Persian (to 637 C.E., the date of the Islamic conquest of Mesopotamia). Many of these periods overlap according to location, and many have subcategories covering more specific times and places. Excavations of Mesopotamian cities at different levels reveal a constant flux as local dynasties conquered, rose, and fell from power and as sculptors, painters, metalsmiths, and jewelry makers learned new methods and styles to apply in their work.

The Gods and Spirits of Mesopotamia

Despite many wars and political upheavals, ancient Mesopotamian art has distinctive and constant themes. The gods of Sumer (in southern Mesopotamia) and Akkad (near what is now Baghdad in Iraq), each with their particular attributes, symbols, and familiar groups of demons and spirits, are found across the millennia in the work of Mesopotamian artisans. Each major city had its patron deity, which was depicted in ceramics and sculpture and featured in temples decorated with statues and paintings of the god. Some of the more important Mesopotamian gods were the sky god, Anu, worshipped in Sumer; the fertility goddess, Inanna, of Uruk; Nergal, the god of the underworld; and Ishtar, a goddess associated with the planet Venus, love, and war. There were also gods of the moon (Sin) and of the sun (Shamash). These deities were shown in anthropomorphic (human) form, along with important symbols of their power and attributes.

Shamash, for example, is shown near a disc representing the sun. Sin appears near a crescent symbolizing the moon, and the goddess Ishtar is depicted with an eight-pointed star. The water god, Er, is most often shown with streams flowing from his shoulders or from a jar. Adad, the god of storms, appears with a lightning bolt and stands on the back of a bull. A goddess of healing, Gula, was associated with the figure of a dog. The messenger of the gods, Ninshubur, holds a staff in his hands, and Nusku, the god of fire, holds a lamp or flame. Marduk was the principal god of Babylon. He was originally a god of the earth and of agriculture, and he appears with a spade in the shape of a triangle. Assur, the god of the powerful realm of Assyria, wears a horned headdress and a staff or spear as a symbol of his office.

Mesopotamian artists also relied on a large repertoire of minor spirits, usually taking the form of a familiar animal. Lions were a favored species and appear winged, half-human, and with their maned heads atop the form of a powerful bird with long talons. Bulls are shown with their horns and often in the form of half-man, half-bull. Other familiar animals are snakes, turtles, scorpions, sheep, goats, and horses. The evil goddess Lamashtu, daughter of Anu, had the head of a lioness, the ears of a donkey, and the feet and talons of a bird. Lamashtu commonly stands on top of a donkey, holds a pair of snakes in her hands, and nurses a pig or a dog.

Prehistoric Art

Clay figurines in a rounded female form date to the early Neolithic Period (10,000-3,000 B.C.E.) and are the earliest works of art from Mesopotamia. These were found in great number at Hassuna, a site that gave its name to a period of art dating to about 5800 B.C.E. Statuettes and household vases carved in clay and alabaster have been uncovered in graves near Samarra, which lent its name to the following period, of the late sixth millennium B.C.E. These figures were decorated with stone necklaces and shells for eyes. Samarran artisans also created new geometric, human, and animal forms for use on their finished pottery. Halaf works, from 5300 B.C.E. to about 4500 B.C.E., display religious symbols, such as a double ax head and the stylized head of an ox.

The first cities of Mesopotamia were built in the plains between the lower Euphrates and Tigris rivers, the region known as Sumer. Trade and a centralized government brought about the invention of cuneiform writing, in the form of angular marks made with sharpened reeds (*cuneus* in Latin) on wet clay tablets. Sumerian palaces were decorated with elaborate friezes, horizontal wall paintings that depicted royal processions and mythological scenes.

Art of the Sumerians

During the Uruk Period, named for an important Sumerian city, sculptors began working in new materials and giving their figures a larger and more lifelike appearance. Using a flat wall or a finished ceramic piece, they carved away the smooth surface to create geometric or figurative art in a technique known as bas-relief. Artists of this time began moving away from conventional shapes and styles to give their figures individual characteristics and emotions. Nevertheless, Mesopotamian art remained two dimensional, with the human body and animals portrayed in flat profile against a patterned background, as in the wall paintings of ancient Egypt.

The famous Warak vase, found at the site of Uruk, is carved of alabaster and shows four different designs on parallel horizontal bands known as registers. The bottom band shows a row of barley and palm plants, and above is a line of rams and ewes. At the next level appears a procession of men carrying jugs and baskets, and at the top is a lord or king attended by servants and a temple priestess. The Warak vase displays the dedication of the Sumerians to Inanna, the goddess of fertility and of the fruit of the land. It also serves as a textbook example of Mesopotamian pictorial style, in which a scene or story is depicted in registers against a flat, stylized background and in which figures are given importance according to their size, position, and the detail of their clothes and adornment.

Metalsmiths of this time began mastering new techniques of casting and shaping copper, bronze, silver, and gold. The lost-wax process allowed artists to form a desired figure out of wax, surround it with clay, and then fire the clay to melt the wax. The result is a hollow, hardened clay mold into which molten metal is poured; after the metal cools and hardens, the mold is broken away to reveal the finished piece. Mesopotamian smiths brought the art of lost-wax casting to a very high level, creating jewelry, statuettes, and other objects that could also be etched and engraved in minute detail.

In the Uruk era the Sumerians raised stepped temples known as ziggurats, used to bring the kings and priests closer to the gods of the heavens. The ziggurats served as symbols of the power and wealth of the kings who raised them. The exterior walls were elaborately decorated with horizontal friezes, and the interior featured paintings of scenes from mythology and religious symbolism. The Sumerians also gave detailed attention to the burial of their monarchs. The Royal Cemetery at the city of Ur has provided archaeologists with the largest single treasure of ancient Mesopotamian art in existence. Nearly two thousand graves were unearthed at this site in the 1920s, many of them containing valuable worldly goods meant to accompany kings and queens to the afterlife: jewelry in gold, lapis lazuli, carnelian, and other semiprecious stones; gold and silver crowns and other personal adornments; bowls of alabaster and silver; and thousands of cylinder seals. The fabulous Great Lyre found at Ur is made of bitumen and lapis lazuli, and it displays the head of a bearded bull cast from a large mass of solid gold.

The cylinder seal emerged during this time as a practical tool as well as an important artistic medium. A seal was a small, carved cylinder that could be rolled across a wet clay tablet or sheet of papyrus to show possession or to record a document or transaction. A seal was made of stone, fired clay, bone, or ivory; when rolled across a document, it left a long rectangular impression showing a simple geometric design, banqueting scene, religious symbols, or a god or gods in a variety of aspects and poses.

Artists of the Early Dynastic Period that followed Uruk worked in a familiar style in their statuary, paintings, and cylinder seals. Statuettes from a temple site at Tell Asmar were given very large eyes, which were originally inlaid with semiprecious stones; the eyes symbolized fervent devotion of ordinary worshippers to the god of the temple. Square stone plaques attached to the temple walls showed banquet scenes in bas-relief. Historical scenes of battle and victory were carved into stelae, freestanding blocks of stone that carried inscriptions, proclamations, or human figures. Sculptors also carved portraits in stone of kings, scribes, and administrators, each with individual expressions and features.

King Gilgamesh of Uruk, who reigned in Sumer around 2500 B.C.E., became the central hero of the Epic of Gilgamesh, a poem of 3,000 lines that survives as one of the world's oldest works of literature. For the next two millennia the Gilgamesh epic provided artists of the region abundant subject matter in their sculpture, paintings, and cylinder seals.

Akkad and Babylon

The conquest of Mesopotamia by King Sargon in 2340 B.C.E. established the Akkadian Dynasty. Sumerian cities declined in importance as Sargon united the northern and southern regions of Mesopotamia for the first time. The art of Mesopotamia also underwent important changes. Humans and animals gained prominence by being set against plain backgrounds, rather than serving as simply another useful motif in a repeating pattern. Seal and jewelry engravers showed much greater skill in bringing out realistic features of the head, face, and body and in depicting lifelike emotions. The stelae and bas-reliefs of the Akkadian Dynasty honored the achievements of their kings, who are shown engaging in battle, taking prisoners, and driving their enemies from the field. Artists began using diorite, an extremely hard gray stone that could be polished to a glossy sheen, for their monumental sculptures. Akkadian metalsmiths skillfully cast sculpture and vases in silver, copper, and gold, and they created ceremonial weapons and tools that carried symbols of the ruler and the gods.

Human-headed winged bull from the palace of King Sargon II (721–705 B.C.E.) at the Assyrian capital Dur-Sharrukin (modern-day Khorsabad, Iraq) (Courtesy of the Oriental Institute of the University of Chicago)

The Kassite Dynasty that rose in the 16th century B.C.E. is best known for a series of *kudurrus,* or boundary stones, which became an important medium for commemorative inscriptions and in which the figures of the gods were replaced by familiar emblems.

The fall of Akkad ushered in a period of weak political control but important artistic advances in Mesopotamia. Artists mastered the human form, rendering movement with great realism and decorating the body with elaborately designed and draped clothing. The reign of Hammurabi of Babylon, which lasted from 1792 to 1750 B.C.E., left as its most enduring monument a code of laws carved into a tall, diorite stele, which as both a social and artistic artifact has become the most famous single work of ancient Mesopotamian art. In the Stele of Hammurabi, the king stands before the sun god, who presents a ring and staff to the king as symbols of his sovereignty. French archaeologists unearthed the stele at Susa, in what is now Persia, where the ancient Elamites had taken it after the conquest of Babylon in the 12th century B.C.E.

Assyria

As Babylon grew weaker, the realm of Assyria rose in northern Mesopotamia and spread its authority over the mountains of Asia Minor and the valleys of the Tigris and Euphrates. The kings of Assyria ordered the carving of enormous bas-reliefs to celebrate their military victories and their rule of much of the Middle East. Made from marble and limestone, these friezes were placed along the walls of temples and palaces, in throne rooms and hallways, and in staircases and reception halls.

One of the largest groups of wall reliefs survived at monumental buildings raised by King Ashurnasirpal II (r. 884–859 B.C.E.) at the royal city of Nimrud. In these horizontal slabs the king is shown hunting, battling, and winning victories with the blessing of the gods. Foreigners are shown humbly bearing tribute, while inscriptions recount the king's name and titles and his many conquests. In all these works the sculptors achieved great detail in clothing and in the rendering of faces and limbs. Assyrian artists also celebrated the kings' achievements with freestanding obelisks (large pillars), which were decorated on all sides, and marked their conquests with carvings in natural rock located at the physical limits of the empire.

Monumental sculpture and reliefs also survived at the palace of Sargon II at Khorsabad and of Sennacherib (who reigned from 704 to 681 B.C.E.) at Nineveh, the last Assyrian capital. Archaeologists of the 19th century uncovered nearly two miles of wall reliefs within 70 different rooms at Sennacherib's enormous palace, which was burned by a conquering army and then buried by new construction that took place in the following centuries. The subjects, as in the other Assyrian sites, were processions of tribute and military campaigns, with inscriptions on the walls recounting the victories of the king.

Under the later Assyrian kings, wall paintings replaced friezes in stone in many monuments and public buildings. Colored pigments were mixed and applied to whitewashed plaster on interior spaces, while glazed and painted bricks were used on exterior surfaces. These paintings depicted hunting and battle scenes, royal parades and processions, symbols of the king and the gods, mythological beasts, and various repeated geometric and abstract designs. The Ishtar Gate, an entrance to the city of Babylon, dates to about 575 B.C.E. and was built during the reign of Nebuchadnezzar II. The gate was made of tiles fired in a deep blue glaze and decorated with bas-reliefs of bulls and dragons. A Processional Way, which began at the gate and led to the city's royal palace, showed a series of lions carved in relief.

Persian Dynasties

The Achaemenid Dynasty of Persia conquered Mesopotamia in the sixth century B.C.E. The Achaemenids claimed to be the heirs of the mighty Assyrians and drew on the monumental style of Assyria in their palaces and temples. At the palace of Susa, built by the Achaemenid King Darius I, artists rendered human-headed lions underneath a winged disk in bas-relief on the palace walls, made from glazed, multicolored bricks. At Persepolis large friezes depicted processions of courtiers and men bearing tribute to the king. Colossal animals—bulls and griffins and other mythological beasts—were carved in stone or cast in bronze to guard the entrances to the palace.

In 331 B.C.E. the Macedonian general Alexander the Great defeated King Darius III of Persia at the Battle of Guagemela. Alexander died in Babylon a few years later, but his victory over the Achaemenid ruler ushered in the Seleucid Dynasty, founded by his general Seleucus. The Seleucids reigned for less than a century in Mesopotamia, while the gods and myths of the Greek world were taken up by the region's sculptors and metal engravers. Very few complete works of art survived, as sculptures in bronze were later melted down and their scarce metal recovered for new works. Seals of the time showed Greek gods and Seleucid rulers as well as important symbols such as the anchor and horse head, the personal emblem of Seleucus.

The Parthians overthrew the Seleucid Dynasty in the middle of the third century B.C.E. They were followed by the Sassanian Dynasty, which was established in 224 B.C.E. and endured until the Islamic conquest of Mesopotamia in 633 C.E. The palace at the Sassanian capital city of Ctesiphon in central Mesopotamia is best known for elaborate decoration in stucco on the interior walls. Colorful floor mosaics found in Sassanian palaces portrayed women dancing, making music, and weaving garlands. The art of metalsmithing also reached a zenith during the dynasty, which left behind no paintings and very few portraits in sculpture, while lifelike portraits of the rulers, imitating a style introduced by the Macedonians, were created for coins of the realm. Sassanian artists mastered the art of detailed engraving in a variety of techniques, including chasing, embossing, and cloisonné enameling, applied to silver and gold cups, bowls, ewers, plates, and dishes. They used as their subjects the royal banquets, hunting scenes, and mythical beasts that were ancient traditions in Mesopotamia. The elaborate, repeated designs and borders of Sassanian art in stone and metal had a strong influence on subsequent Islamic art. Sassanian artistic style also traveled to the Byzantine Empire, which survived the fall of Rome in Eastern Europe and Asia Minor, and to central Asia and China.

ASIA AND THE PACIFIC

BY KIRK H. BEETZ

Indian Painting

The earliest paintings in India are probably ones found on large stones and rock faces, mostly in central India, in the region of the city of Bhopal. They depict humans and animals and are all thought by archaeologists to have been painted after 5500 B.C.E. The earliest ones show people as stick figures wearing only loincloths and animals that sometimes have abstract designs on their bodies. The humans appear to be hunting the animals with spears and bows and arrows. Later rock paintings show humans riding horses and wielding swords and shields. The innards of animals are sometimes depicted, a style also found in rock paintings in faraway Borneo and Australia.

Few other paintings in India and southern Asia survive from before the 200s C.E. because surfaces such as wood and silk and other fabrics, which were used for painting, decay quickly in wet climates and are subject to destruction by fire. In India the second-earliest surviving paintings are found on walls in cave temples at Ajanta; they are fragmentary because much of the paint has peeled off over the centuries. Cave X of Ajanta houses the earliest painting that dates from the first century B.C.E. It depicts the life of the Buddha and is so richly presented that the mural suggests that painting had become a highly sophisticated art form much earlier in history. Much better preserved are paintings in Cave I from the 400s C.E. In these paintings, human beings and gods are sometimes serene, sometimes joyful, and always surrounded by activity, suggesting that life is an enterprise rich in spiritual and physical pleasures that people who set free their inner vitality can enjoy.

Indian Sculpture

The roots of Indian arts probably reach back to the Harappan civilization of the Indus River region (ca. 2600–ca. 1500 B.C.E.). Metal casting emerged early in Harappan culture, perhaps 2300 B.C.E., and it was already highly developed, suggesting that the Harappans learned how to make bronze and other metal figures from Mesopotamians. Most Harappan castings have been found in the ruined city of Mohenjo Daro. Perhaps the most spectacular artifact is the copper image of a young woman housed in India's National Museum in New Delhi. Dating from before 1750 B.C.E., she is 5½ inches tall, missing her feet, and clad only in bangles and a necklace. She features the wide nose and thick lips typical of the Harappans and may represent a dancing girl. She is in a relaxed, languid pose, as if waiting for something, and the figure presages the graceful ancient Indian style to come.

The Harappan culture began to decline between 1900 B.C.E. and 1800 B.C.E. After its fall to natural disasters and an Aryan influx around 1500 B.C.E., the primary influences on Indian art were remnant Harappan populations southeast of the Indus River and the Greeks. The Aryan tribes that invaded the Harappan lands in the Indus Valley spread through northern India. Little remains of Indian art from about 1500 B.C.E. to about 500 B.C.E., though Indian writings indicate that the period was a colorful one for the arts. Perhaps most artworks were made with perishable materials such as wood, which rapidly decayed in India's wet environment.

A new sculptural tradition began in India from the influence of a Hindu prince named Siddhartha Gautama. Born into the warrior caste (one of four social divisions in India), Siddhartha lived from about 563 to about 483 B.C.E., and he became known as the Buddha. He traveled through the northeastern kingdoms, urging people to forsake their desires, and he formed the first Buddhist order of monks. At first Buddhist sculptures focused on symbols, but in the 200s B.C.E. artists began sculpting realistic portraits of the Buddha, starting an artistic tradition that would shape much of the art and taste of Asia and the Pacific.

In 326 B.C.E. Alexander the Great conquered much of northwestern India. He brought with him Greek culture, including artists. In 321 B.C.E. a general of the Nanda Dynasty, Chandragupta Maurya, overthrew the Nanda government and defeated the Greek state that had been created by Alexander in the northwest of India. The Maurya Dynasty (321–185 B.C.E.) featured great empire builders in its first three rulers, who expanded their nation to cover most of the Indian subcontinent, but in 261 B.C.E., Chandragupta's great-grandson Asoka had a crisis of conscience after seeing the misery his conquering had caused, converted to Buddhism, and made his nation a pacifist state. Thereafter its power and territory waned, yet the Mauryans initiated a great age of stone sculpture.

Greek-style sculpture was immensely popular, especially for portraits, and Greek sculptors found ready work in the

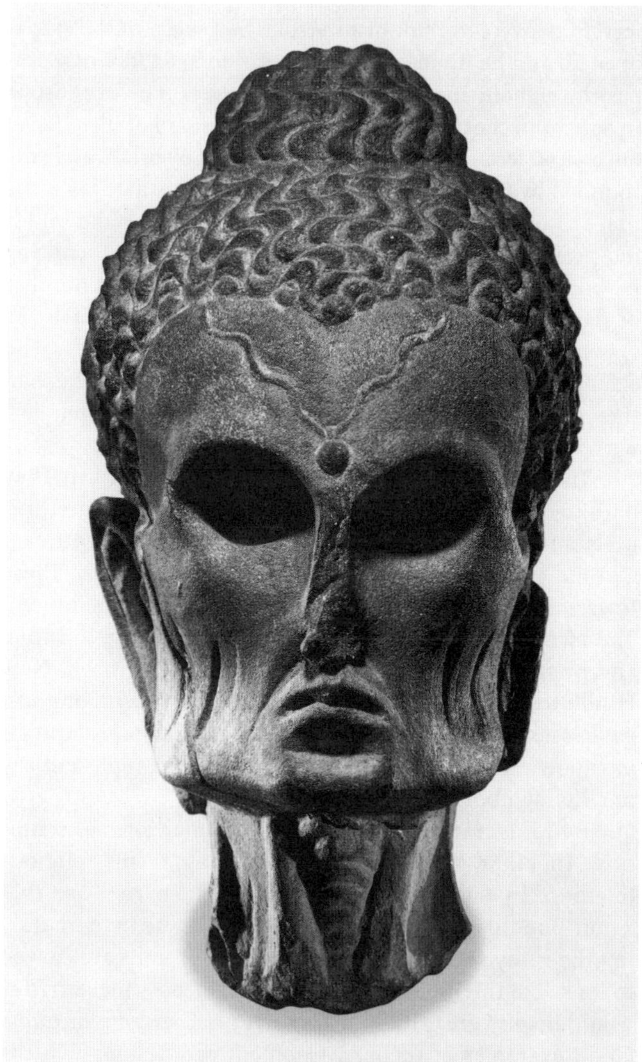

Schist head of the fasting Buddha, from Rawalpindi District, Gandhara, Pakistan, second to third century C.E. (© The Trustees of the British Museum)

Maurya Empire. In India, Greek artists would carve standardized torsos of men and women, leaving off the heads, and would later supply heads when orders for individual portraits were made. Thus were made numerous portraits of wealthy Indians that had identical Greek bodies. Indian-style sculptures were also common, especially for public works. Such an example from about 200 B.C.E. is in the Patna Museum. It is a depiction of a *yakshi*, a female spirit that protected the wealth of the earth. At 5 feet, 4 inches tall, it has a lifelike height, but its curves are exaggerated, creating fluidity in its pose and suggesting it might step forward, alive. Its clothing and other physical features are done in fine detail, and it glistens with Mauryan gloss, a smooth, highly polished shiny surface that was unique to the Maurya Era.

The Buddha's death sparked another kind of sculpture that came into full flower during Asoka's reign. Burial hemispheres of dirt, called *stupas*, had been in use on a small scale for the interment of important people, but the Buddha's ashes were divided into eight large stupas after his death. A fervent convert to Buddhism, Asoka had seven of the stupas opened, and he divided the remains among 84,000 new stupas throughout India. The finest of these is the Great Stupa in Sanchi in central India. Originally a mound of dirt 25 feet tall and 60 feet across, the dirt was covered by bricks and surrounded by temples and gates. The stone gates date from the first century B.C.E., and they mark the end of the major building period for the shrine. Sculpting the stone as if working in wood, artists adorned the gates with a dazzling number of figures so that the pillars and crossbeams appear to be crawling with life, including graceful figures of women who exemplify inner vitality. Indians loved depictions of life, and their architects believed that no public building was complete without depictions of women.

Thus, for Indians buildings became works of art. They built towers abounding with sculptures of trees, plants, animals, and stones, making the entire structure a sculpture on a grand scale that was meant to emulate mountains. These towers represent a Buddha-like climb to enlightenment. The ascendancy of Buddhism did not last for long in India, and by the 100s C.E. Hinduism was reasserting itself. New Hindu towers were adorned with sensuous images of gods, goddesses, nature spirits, and people, usually naked and almost always graceful and lively; these towers represent the phallus, symbolizing creative power.

Buddhism inspired another spectacular form of sculpture. In Bihar, near Nepal, Asoka displayed his religious tolerance by having rooms carved into huge rocks so that a non-Buddhist sect of ascetics could meditate in them during the rainy season. The interiors of the rooms are carved to look like the interiors of wooden, thatched houses. They would inspire great Buddhist structures elsewhere in India. Good examples of their development can be found in the Western Ghats mountain range, where thousands of rock structures were carved into the mountainsides and cliffs. The first structures were Buddhist monasteries, begun in 150 B.C.E. These were followed by temple complexes, carved by iron tools into rock faces, with one temple having a hall 124 feet long. The main structural elements were made to look like wood, as if the monastery or temple were wooden. The walls were carved with scenes of the Buddha's life and teachings. Dancers, preachers, kings, and bodhisattvas were depicted on pillars and walls as well. Bodhisattvas were people who could have ascended to oneness with God but who chose to put off their salvation to help other human beings reach nirvana—a state of blessedness or union with the godhead. As Hinduism returned to dominance in India, caves were carved to become Hindu temples where even lower castes would worship. They feature lush statues of nature deities, often monumental in stature. At Elephanta Island a three-faced statue of the god Shiva from the 500s C.E. is 17 feet tall and situated so that light from the entrances to the cave falls directly on the faces.

The Indian style of sculpture, especially when connected to the Buddhist or Hindu faiths, spread throughout Indochina and eventually to the main Indonesian islands, reaching Java in about the 700s C.E. The Indian painting style also spread, though surviving examples in Indochina tend to date from the 1200s C.E. In the 100s and 200s C.E. Buddhist evangelists brought Indian sculptural and painting traditions to China, which already had a well-established painting tradition of its own.

Chinese Painting

The earliest known paintings in China are from Inner Mongolia. Consisting of mineral pigments drawn on stone, they are on large rocks and sheer rock faces, all in the open; none so far have been found in caves. The paintings depict animals and stick-figure people, and they include elephants—creatures that became extinct in the area before 8000 B.C.E. Such rock paintings continued to be created among illiterate peoples in this region until about 200 B.C.E. They may have been created to give the painters magical powers while they were hunting, or they may have had more prosaic uses, such as telling travelers the kinds of game that could be found nearby.

Lacquer at first came from the resin of the lacquer tree (*Rhus verniciflua*), yielding a glossy black paint that was highly durable. During the Shang Dynasty (ca. 1500–ca. 1045 B.C.E.), Chinese painters began experimenting with pigments in lacquer to give it color, and vivid yellows, reds, and browns still survive. Archaeological finds suggest that lacquer may not have come into widespread use until the Warring States Period (453–221 B.C.E.). From the 400s B.C.E. on, lacquer was used for decorative art on chests, furniture pieces, walls, doors, and other household surfaces. This must have made homes brightly colorful during the Warring States Period and the ensuing Qin Dynasty (221–207 B.C.E.) and Han Dynasty (202 B.C.E.–220 C.E.). Surviving paintings depict animals and mystical beasts such as dragons, usually in highly stylized forms more interesting for their symmetrical patterns than their verisimilitude.

Paintings of other sorts were common, especially on silk. By the end of the Zhou Dynasty (ca. 1045–256 B.C.E.) there were tens of thousands of silk paintings, but only one from the Zhou survives, dating to the 400s B.C.E. Housed in the Beijing Historical Museum and known as Lady with the Phoenix, it was discovered in Changsha and is about eight by twelve inches. In it, an elegantly robed woman in profile looks at a dragon and a phoenix.

The invention of paper in the 100s C.E. significantly affected Chinese art. Paper expanded a painter's artistic possibilities beyond silk by being cheaper and firmer. Calligraphy was regarded as a fine art and often became part of paintings, uniting into a form of storytelling that was created on paper scrolls. On a scroll a single figure or landscape could be depicted as if in motion, with the unrolling of the scroll showing someone standing and turning around or showing the passage of time in a single setting. Combined with the calligraphic art, by the 400s C.E. scrolls had become short moving pictures, telling tales about the Buddha, tales from mythology, or even tales drawn from contemporary life.

Chinese Calligraphy

Chinese writing inscribed on bones and turtle shells that were used to foretell the future is known from as early as the Shang Dynasty. Even in the 1500s B.C.E. Chinese writing was taking the form it has today, creating a writing tradition that has been unbroken for 3,500 years. Chinese is written in ideograms, characters that represent an idea or thing. These began as small pictures representing objects such as trees or houses; then such characters were combined to suggest new ideas. During the Han Dynasty and thereafter, scholars were held in high esteem because they knew 40,000 to 50,000 individual characters.

Early in the Han Dynasty calligraphy came to be regarded as an art form. Calligraphers used brushes lightly dipped in very black ink that they mixed themselves to paint characters on silk, bamboo, and wood. Their work was taken so seriously that their brushes and bars of black pigment became works of art themselves. Pigment came in beautifully embossed sticks, and the grinding of such beauty to make ink impressed on the calligrapher the importance of his putting the destruction of the stick to good use. Calligraphers developed styles of their own and learned how to express emotions with the way they stroked their brushes—firm or careless, fine or crude, long or short. A form called *cursiv* developed, in which the calligrapher's strokes blended from one ideogram (written symbol) down to the next in a constant flow. The invention of paper revolutionized calligraphy by providing an inexpensive surface that held ink well. It allowed nearly any educated person to practice calligraphy, and some calligraphers became famous for their styles.

The artist Wang Xizhi (321–379 C.E.) was China's greatest calligrapher. His preface "Lanting Lu" for a book of poetry, *Meeting at the Orchid Pavilion*, is considered to be the pinnacle of Chinese calligraphy. It was written in flowing semicursive characters that melded ideas and ideograms into images that its readers loved passionately. The emperor Taizong (r. 626–649 C.E.) revered this work so much that he wanted to have it with him in the next life, and he had it buried with him. Only copies remain.

Chinese Sculpture

The history of Chinese stone sculpture is sketchy. There are stone carvings associated with the ancient rock paintings, and such carvings that depict people wearing masks date from about 3500 B.C.E. During the early Shang Dynasty tombs were sometimes decorated with carved stone or ceramic tiles portraying people, such as guardians to ward off enemies and entertainers to make the next life pleasant. Many tomb sculptures survive from the Han Dynasty. These were relief carvings in stone. Relief carvings have figures projecting out from a flat background. In the Han reliefs, the figures themselves are slightly flattened. These relief sculptures show scenes from everyday life and objects such as peasants and fish. There are many scenes of people and animals during hunting.

The most spectacular tomb sculpture predates the Han Dynasty by several years and was not in stone, but in ceramic. The tomb of Qin Shi Huangdi (r. 221–210 B.C.E.) in Shaanxi province has about 7,000 life-size figures of soldiers, though as yet 80 to 90 percent of the tomb remains unexplored. Although there seems to have been a set pattern underlying the sculpting of each figure, the soldiers are individualized with details such as improperly buttoned jackets and different sorts of personal jewelry. Each face and head is unique, as if every figure were modeled after a real-life person.

Monumental public sculpture began in the 400s C.E. Buddhism had been introduced to China in about 65 C.E., and by the 400s it had become a major part of Chinese culture. Sculptures of Buddha in the 400s resembled the Indian style of sculpture, with figures having Indian features and the serene grace typical of Indian depictions of human figures; the garments shifted from Indian ones to ones typically worn by the Chinese. An example of this is the great 45-foot-tall Buddha Amitabha from about 460 C.E. found in the Yungang Caves in Shanxi province. His massive stone features are still not Chinese, but he wears clothing typical of a Chinese man of the 400s.

Chinese Decorative Arts

Elaborate decorations on the sides of pots, kettles, and chalices indicate that the decorative arts were already well advanced when people of the Shang began working with bronze, suggesting a highly developed art of wood carving, with the wooden works now being lost. The decorations on bronzes featured abstract images such as crisscrossed patterns and bumpy surfaces, but they also had images of animals and mythical creatures that were usually rendered in a symbolic style that often make them difficult for modern observers to interpret. Eyes could be whorls, faces could be represented twice on two sides of a pot, and wings could be depicted with sharp S-shaped swirls. These images indicate that the Shang had a well-known and complex system of symbols that would be readily recognized by those who used the bronzes. The Shang bronze sculptors often combined realistic images with abstract or symbolic images; the ram's head was especially popular for decorating kettles and storage vessels.

The Shang was a warlike culture, expanding territory through conquest, and it is therefore not surprising that along with making extraordinarily beautiful household bronzes, they made decorated weapons. The most elaborate weapons tended to be sacrificial axes. The Shang practiced human sacrifice, usually by beheading. When a military or civic leader died, his servants would be ritually executed and interred with him to serve him in the next life. The axes used were specially made for the purpose and could feature molded human faces, engraved decorations, and openings for mouths or other facial parts such as ears.

The people of the Zhou Dynasty were a technologically less advanced group from the west who overthrew the Shang Dynasty in 1045 B.C.E. At first, the Zhou seemed to have employed the same bronze makers as had the Shang. Even so, there was a notable shift in style. The Zhou bronzes of the 1000s B.C.E. were often constructions of multiple castings, with images exploding into three-dimensional space. The Smithsonian Institution in Washington, D.C., has an outstanding example of a pot from the late 1000s B.C.E. with handles arcing up and out, heads thrusting out of its sides, and a chaos of images rendered on several vertical layers of castings. By the end of the 900s B.C.E. Zhou bronzes became mostly plain and utilitarian, leading some historians to believe that advanced casting techniques had been lost, perhaps with the dying off of the last generation of Shang artisans.

During the late Zhou (ca. 600–221 B.C.E.), an era of warfare, fine detail in bronzes made a comeback, possibly signaling influence from cultures to the west that reintroduced advanced bronze-casting techniques. At first, blocky vessels seem to have been preferred, with symbolic animal faces and thick, upraised lines in decorative, often leafy, patterns. By the end of the Zhou, bronzes of extraordinary complexity and beauty were again being produced, and casters were playing with three-dimensional space with the surety of masters of their craft. An outstanding example produced during the late Zhou resides in the Hubei Provincial Museum. It is a drum stand about 21.25 inches in circumference at its base; the base is a platter with an attached cylindrical post that bears the weight of the drum. Around that post and filling the platter are writhing dragons, their bodies and limbs driving out into space in myriad angles. Graceful and full of motion, it is a high point in the art of casting bronze and represents the sort of detail and skill of the best bronzes of its age.

Arts in Oceania

In Australia the native peoples have painted on exposed rocks since ancient times; their images tell creation stories and relate their history. Stone Age peoples did not survive long enough to be able to explain their art to modern historians; too often, when such civilizations have survived, modern people have not been interested in their culture. For instance, people arrived at Easter Island in the 400s C.E. and began carving small sculptures; eventually, after hundreds of years, they began erecting mammoth statues along the edges of their island. In the 1800s C.E. most of the Easter Islanders were shipped away to Peru as slaves, resulting in the deaths of those who knew what their written language and their sculptures meant.

Australia offers a special chance to learn about Neolithic art from people who still paint in the ancient ways. Thus it is known that large blocks of stylized images actually tell stories, with creation stories being common. Many rocks feature images of hands, made by placing a hand against the surface of a rock and then blowing pigment around it. In the late 20th century similar handprints were found in remote caves and rock surfaces in Borneo, suggesting a possible continuity in artistic practice from people who migrated to Borneo and then on to other islands before eventually reaching Australia. Painted with the handprints in Borneo are elongated figures of humans and large images of animals that are so detailed that they must have taken days to paint. A few of these paintings have been dated between 10,000 B.C.E. and 8000 B.C.E. In both Australia and Borneo there are animal images that, like ones found in India, depict their insides as well as their outsides.

Japan, Korea, and Southern Asia

What survives of ancient Japanese art is pottery. On the island of Kyushu pottery shards dating to 12,000 B.C.E. have been discovered. During the Jomon Era (13,000–300 B.C.E.) the inhabitants of the Japanese islands made elaborately shaped vessels. During the Yayoi Era (300 B.C.E.–300 C.E.) the Japanese made *haniwa*, ceramic figures varying in height from about four inches to seven inches. They were usually figures of people wearing their everyday garb, sometimes holding the tools of their trade. They were set upright in the ground, surrounding graves; sometimes hundreds of them encircled a large tomb. Archaeologists think that they represented spirits that would guard graves against evil. They are notable for the way in which posture or facial expression gives each one a unique individuality.

Koreans and peoples along the southern edges of China tended to adopt Chinese styles and art forms. Most of what is presently known of ancient Korean art comes from its ceramics. The cups, plates, and serving dishes from ancient Korea show that their makers were well schooled in Chinese techniques, especially in the use of glazes. They also made ceramic figurines as burial goods and as toys.

Much of the rest of southern Asia was divided between Chinese and Indian influences. For instance, some of the

Nanyue of the Yangtze River migrated south into North Vietnam after China conquered their country in 333 B.C.E. and brought with them Chinese tastes, but the natives were related to the peoples of Indonesia and were influenced by India. The kingdom of Funan was centered on the Mekong Delta from the 100s to 500s C.E. By the 300s C.E. it included central Cambodia. The archaeological finds of Funan include temples and statues in the style of India.

Asia Pacific Jewelry

Determining what ancient Oceanic jewelry may have been like involves more speculation than hard evidence. Stone Age peoples survived not only in Australia but also in places like New Zealand and Papua New Guinea long enough to leave for study recently made jewelry. Necklaces, bracelets, and anklets made of pig or shark teeth strung together with animal sinews or string made from palm leaves were common. In Indonesia wood, seashells, and metal would be combined to create headgear, necklaces, and bracelets that were supposed to protect warriors in battle and cure sickness. Beads of glass and quartz were popular, especially in the Philippines, where beads sometimes represented supernatural powers.

In much of ancient Asia beads were valued decorative elements. In Japan they had magical powers and were important components of rituals. Still, jewelry in general was not important to the Japanese. The opposite was true in India, where beads and other decorations were highly esteemed. A single bead of glass of a rare color could be worth as much as a precious gem in India. According to Hindu tradition, jewels had divine attributes, and even the gods worshiped gems. For instance, Indra worshiped rubies and Vishnu worshiped sapphires. India had rubies, sapphires, emeralds, and diamonds in abundance; in fact, India was the world's only source of diamonds until the gem was discovered in Brazil in the early 1700s C.E. Gems were incorporated into all kinds of Indian jewelry. Turquoise, a valued mineral, was imported from the Himalayas.

Ancient Indians loved wearing jewelry. The Harappans wore toe rings and anklets of gold and silver. Neck rings were common. These were made of solid bars of gold, silver, copper, or other metals that were bent, or they were composed of wires that were tightly wound together, ropelike. During much of the period from 500 B.C.E. to 500 C.E., only members of India's two highest castes, the priests and the warriors, were allowed to wear gold and silver, but this did not discourage members of lower castes from wearing jewelry made of other metals.

During the Six Dynasties period in China (220–589 C.E.), women took to wearing silver bracelets. Rings often had settings with gems, with various stones that held mystical properties. For instance, a jade ring was said to recognize the soul of its owner, and if lost would find its way back to him or her.

EUROPE

BY KIRK H. BEETZ

Europe of the Last Great Ice Age

The earliest dated European art forms are paintings from caves in southern France. These paintings date from 32,000 to 30,000 B.C.E., during the last great ice age. Other seemingly related paintings in caves from France and Spain date as recently as 15,000 B.C.E. The world of these ancient artists was very different from the modern one. All of Scandinavia and much of northern Europe were covered by a giant glacier that was so heavy it pressed Scandinavia down below sea level. Most of Britain was covered by a glacier, and it was connected by land to the rest of Europe.

The people who lived in this environment were scattered in small groups. They were hunter-gatherers, meaning that they lived from hunting wild animals and gathering wild edible plants. Their cave paintings depict bison, deer, rhinoceroses, mammoths, and horses—the creatures they hunted. These animals are depicted in profile (from the side). This format allowed the artist to show all parts of the animal: head, body, tail, and all four legs. Throughout the era of ice age paintings, artists took pains to be sure that all parts of animals showed. Even dead animals were shown in profile, lying on the ground as if seen from directly above. The animals are depicted not only with precision but also with a vibrant sense of life, showing a mature artistic style that indicates that people began painting far earlier than the earliest paintings yet discovered.

These cave paintings are found deep underground. To get to them sometimes requires crawling around stalagmites and stalactites (spikelike mineral deposits) or large fallen stones and through narrow passages. The artists illuminated their caves with stone lamps filled with flaming animal fat, and they brought meals with them so that they could spend hours at their work. To reach high surfaces of rock walls or ceilings, they built wooden scaffolds, cutting holes high in the rock to insert branches to hold up the scaffolding. They used stones to smooth out the rock surface for their paintings, though they often tried to include the natural bumps and cracks in the rock surface in their compositions. For certain parts of their pictures, they used flint to first carve lines into the rock. For instance, the bristling hair of bison would be cut first and then filled with colored pigment. The artists mixed pigment with animal fat for painting, or they put pigment into their mouths and blew it onto the rock.

Ice age painters' practice of working very deep inside caverns has led to much speculation by archaeologists and historians. Because a great deal of art has been inspired by religious beliefs, many archaeologists believe that creating the paintings deep in the ground represented access to a supernatural world: Even tens of thousands of years later, Greeks and Romans believed that caves led from the world of the living to the world of the dead. Many ancient peoples believed

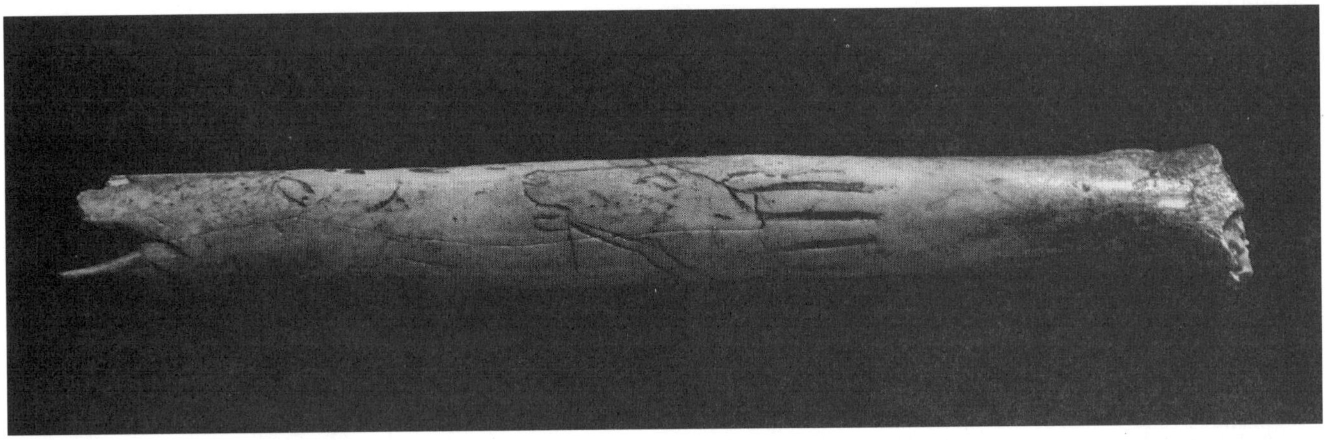

Bird bone engraved with animal heads, Late Magdalenian, dating to about 10,500 C.E., from the cave of Courbet, Penne-Tarn, France (© The Trustees of the British Museum)

that art had a transforming power—that the act of painting made whatever was depicted actually happen. Thus, paintings that show hunting are thought to have been created to make a successful hunt become reality. In some of the caves, paintings of animals show signs of having been struck repeatedly, as if by the points of spears, suggesting a ritual in which the hunt is made real by attacking the paintings.

On the other hand, the paintings may have had other purposes, and the paintings deep in caverns may have been the only ones found because they were out of the way of erosion by nature and humans. Paintings on rocks outside caves and paintings near the entrances of caves could have been destroyed by wind, rain, and vandalism. Those that have been found are fragile; even exhaled human breath damages them, so others may have existed in profusion only to be worn away over 15,000 to 30,000 years. The paintings could have served as lists of game available in a region or as part of initiation rites for young people, like many works by the San (or Bushmen) in southern Africa.

The paintings of human beings in the caves also are puzzling to archaeologists. Among the brilliantly detailed animal figures are ones of men who are graceless stick figures. On occasion they appear to be hunting; on other occasions they may be dancing. In the Lascaux Cave in France is a painting from 15,000 to 13,000 B.C.E. of an apparently wounded or dead man, placed between a rhinoceros and a disemboweled bison. He seems to be wearing a mask of a bird. The only way to know he is male is from his prominent penis. Why are the men portrayed so badly, while the animals are portrayed so beautifully? The answer is as yet unknown.

The problem becomes more complicated when the portraits of women are considered. Many small stone carvings of women from the same era as the early paintings have been found. They have been dubbed Venuses by archaeologists, in humorous reference to the Roman goddess of love and beauty. The Venus of Willendorf from Austria, dating from 28,000 to 23,000 B.C.E., is the most famous of these figures. She is carved from limestone and is only a little more than four inches high. Her stomach, breasts, and thighs are huge, but her arms are small, with her hands resting atop her breasts. Her head is covered by a cap or elaborately curled hair, so that her face does not show. This sculpture may be a fertility symbol, with the breasts and stomach representing a woman's ability to create new life.

There are other depictions of women, and many, like the Venus of Willendorf, are artistically superior to the depictions of men. In the Musée d'Aquitaine in Bordeaux, France, is a relief carving (with the figure projecting out from a flat background) of a woman from 23,000 to 20,000 B.C.E. She is about 18 inches tall and is depicted from the front. Like the Venus of Willendorf, her face is obscured by what may be locks of hair, and her breasts, stomach, and thighs are large. Unlike the Venus of Willendorf, she has well-proportioned arms. In her right hand she holds aloft a bison's horn. She is better detailed than the depictions of men from her era. These Venuses suggest that their sculptors may have been from a matriarchal society or perhaps that women controlled the religious practices.

In addition to creating the earliest-known paintings and rock sculptures, the ice age peoples of Europe appear to have created the earliest clay sculpture. In a cave at Ariège, France, are two clay bison, modeled in relief. They each are about two feet in length and date from about 12,000 B.C.E. Like their painted counterparts, they are in profile and in the same graceful style.

MESOLITHIC: 9000–4000 B.C.E.

By about 9000 B.C.E. Europe was warming, and the glacier over Britain had disappeared; Scandinavia, however, was still under a glacier, and Britain was still attached by land to the rest of Europe. Mammoths and rhinoceroses no longer lived in Europe, and reindeer had moved northward, followed by the ancestors of the Lapps, who eventually would populate northern Finland. Some of the major cultural groups that would figure in the later history of European art had begun to form, each belonging to two major language groups: the West Mediterraneans in the Iberian Peninsula, where Spain and Portugal are today, and the Indo-Europeans, who began somewhere north of the Black Sea or southeast of the Baltic Sea and migrated eastward and westward, occupying all of central and northern Europe as well as much of Asia.

Both the West Mediterranean peoples and the Indo-European peoples were inheritors of the artistic legacy of ice age Europe, but the direct line of development of art is easier to see in Iberia. There are not as many paintings and other art works known from 9,000 to 4,000 B.C.E. as from earlier, perhaps because a matriarchal religious system changed or perhaps because Europeans had other preoccupations, spending their energies using new tools such as stone saws and working at new technologies such as dugout canoes. With the loss of some of their largest prey, people may have had to spend more time hunting than earlier, thus diminishing the time they had to create art. Perhaps the spreading out of the European population over new lands revealed by the retreating glaciers diminished the sort of interplay among groups that would have stimulated new ideas in art. There were only about 75,000 people in all of Europe.

Still, in Spain are rock paintings that incorporate new detail in the portrayals of men. The most famous is a rock painting in Castellón, Spain, sometimes called the Marching Warriors, though they could be dancing. They have noses, lips, and beards, and the leader wears a feathered headdress. They carry spears and bows. The painting dates from 7,000 to 4,000 B.C.E. Much has been made of the resemblance between this painting and the rock paintings of the Sahara of the same era, and it is possible that some of the Saharan painters and the West Mediterraneans were part of a single cultural group.

In about 6500 B.C.E. people in the Balkans and Greece began practicing agriculture. Some historians view this event as the beginning of an invasion of Europe by people from the Near East, who eventually conquered the areas through central Europe to northern Europe, replacing the people already there. A more likely possibility is that the idea of agriculture spread through Europe. Even though they were still living primarily by hunting and gathering, Europeans were already a mostly settled people who lived in small villages. The spread of agriculture brought with it new trade routes, and with those trade routes came an exchange in artistic ideas.

For instance, in what is now Hungary, in the 5000s to 4000s B.C.E., people made ceramic stamp pendants that could emboss symbols and images in clay, an idea that probably came from Syria. The symbols, consisting of lines and curves, may have served as charms. They also sculpted ceramic human and animal figures and what may be phallic symbols. None of these sculptures is unbroken, making it hard to tell how detailed they may have been. A sign that people were adopting a more sedentary way of life, staying in one location, comes from clay models found in Bulgaria, dating from 5,000 to 2,000 B.C.E. These depict household furniture such as chairs and couches. Their purpose is unknown, but they may represent a tradition of toy making.

Late Mesolithic and Neolithic: 4000–2000 B.C.E.

By 4000 B.C.E. the Indo-Europeans occupied most of central and eastern Europe, northern Europe, southern Scandinavia, and most of Britain, which was no longer attached by land to the rest of Europe. The West Mediterraneans still occupied Iberia and some of southern France. This era saw special creativity in the manufacture of household wares. For instance, a pot from the 3000s B.C.E., found in Hungary, looks like two bowls placed lip to lip and fused, with the stem of the top lid open and a face etched into it. The bowl is decorated with zigzags, straight lines, crosshatching, and other designs, perhaps representing clothing for the body of the face or perhaps simply intended to please the eye. It may have been meant for use in religious rites, but it may simply reflect the human tendency to beautify even everyday objects.

Romania has proved a rich site in sculpture from the 3000s B.C.E. Its figurines tend to be female and spare in appearance, with sharp angles. Many female figures also were produced in Ukraine during the 3000s B.C.E. Two ceramic figures of a woman and a man were found in a grave in Cernavodă, Romania. Although they are nearly abstract, they seem very human. The woman is fat in the stomach and thighs, with small, sharply angled breasts; a long neck; a circular head with impressions for eyes; a flat nose; and a pursed mouth. The man is seated on a small stool, his knees high, with his elbows pressed into his thighs and his hands pressed into his cheeks. His head is more oval than the woman's, with the same sort of eyes, nose, and mouth. They come across as ordinary people at rest, both looking a little weary. They represent a tradition of geometrical sculpture that would survive until the era of classical art.

Between 3000 and 2500 B.C.E. the Únětice culture in what is now central Poland learned to make bronze by combining tin and copper. This development did not occur until about 2300 B.C.E. in Greece and the Balkans, 1800 B.C.E. in Britain and Iberia, and 1500 B.C.E. in southern Scandinavia. Bronze would give artists an important new medium for their sculptures.

Bronze Age: 2000–500 B.C.E.

By about 2000 B.C.E. the Indo-Europeans had come to dominate Europe. Within Europe they had fragmented into the Celts of central Europe, the British Isles, and Iberia; the Germanic peoples, possibly from the east, occupying southern Scandinavia; the Slavs of northeastern Europe; the Italics of southern Europe; the Illyrians of the Balkans; and the Thracians of eastern Europe. Of these groups, the Celts would develop the most distinctive style of art. The most important outside influence on Indo-European art came from Mycenae, Greece, in about 2000–1200 B.C.E. Mycenaean art has been found in northern Europe, and northern European art has been found in Mycenae. One of the most interesting paintings of the era is a mural from the Mediterranean island of Thera in the 1500s B.C.E. that depicts what appears to be a boat from Scandinavia.

Numerous rock paintings and carvings from 2000 to 500 B.C.E. were created in Scandinavia, by Germanic peoples sometimes called Nordic by anthropologists. These paintings and carvings have been found in Norway, Sweden, and Denmark, and they number in the hundreds of thousands. The artworks appear on broad rock faces. First they were carved by using an unknown tool to punch chips out of the surface. In the earliest examples a color lighter than the rock was added into the carved lines, giving the figures greater definition. In later examples ocher—a mineral with iron oxide, colored red, brown, or yellow—was added into the lines. The subject matter is varied, showing people dancing, hunting, and even making love, but pictures of ships predominate. The interest in ships is indicative of oceangoing trade, perhaps into the Mediterranean, which would help explain the Mycenaean influence in Britain and northern Europe as well as central Europe. Among the rock carvings from the first century B.C.E. are studies of chariots, depicting various kinds of harnesses, and of spoked wheels, sometimes apart from the pictures of the chariots. In European art of the period wheels with spokes often represented the sun. Chariots often indicated the presence of an elite warrior class.

By 1500 B.C.E. Mycenaean metalwork, especially in copper and gold, had spread across western Europe. A scepter buried with a British chieftain duplicates one found in Mycenae, dated at about 1600 B.C.E. Mycenaean armor was in central Europe by the 1500s B.C.E. and may have influenced the development of helmets and body armor among the Celts. Golden cups from about 1500 B.C.E. that imitate Mycenaean styles and techniques for working gold have been discovered in Britain and in far northwestern Germany. The spread of Mycenaean influence in Europe cannot be explained fully by oceangoing traders and must have included overland trade routes. The Mycenaeans set up trading posts in the Balkans and perhaps farther north to Germany, and they had trading posts in Britain. When the Mycenaean culture abruptly ended in about 1200 B.C.E., their traders may have been stranded in those trading posts, and their artists may have ventured into central Europe to find employment. They brought with them their techniques for metalwork, which may help to account for the flowering of Celtic metal sculpture that followed.

The Celts loved jewelry, and Celtic sites that have not been plundered yield a rich assortment of jewelry. Beads were well loved, and even Egyptian glass beads have been found not only in central Europe but also as far as northern Germany, probably imported into Europe through trade routes established by the Mycenaeans. A necklace from Britain from 1500 to 1000 B.C.E. shows the use of shale beads and faience beads. Faience is brightly colored glazed pottery. Bones and antlers also were worked, mostly for decoration. Amber was mined in Jutland in modern Denmark and exported throughout Europe, where it was used to make beads and strung on necklaces. Eastern Europe, especially Hungary and the Czech Republic, has yielded bracelets and pendants from 1500 to 1000 B.C.E., many with designs that echo Mycenaean ones, yet some show the intricate interlacing of curves and lines as well as the three-pointed swirls, which would set apart Celtic art.

It is in metal that Celtic art from this era fully captivates the imagination. Much of the metalwork seems to have served ritual purposes, sometimes given in sacrifice to a local god. For the Celts the world was full of gods; lakes, rivers, mountains, stones, and more had their own gods. This means that rivers such as the Thames in England have yielded finely sculpted gold and bronze. Early examples that hint at what was to follow come from the Únětice culture, from what is now eastern Germany. They produced armlets (bands worn around the arm), earrings, beads, and pins of gold from 1500 to 1000 B.C.E. Their designs were simple, sometimes just a winding of strands of gold into circles of wire to form tightly wound beads. Even so, there are hints of what would come. For example a grave in Germany has yielded an armlet from about 1500 B.C.E. that has lines along its length and a twisting design between the lines, somewhat like a simple version of the twisting and looping of lines in later Celtic armbands and torques (neck rings).

Of particular interest are the many model cart sculptures of the era. The earliest ones tend to be ceramic. For instance, in the National Museum in Belgrade, Serbia, is a three-wheeled wagon pulled by what look like ducks, dating to the 1300s B.C.E. Archaeologists find this cart interesting because of the three wheels, which indicate experimentation in the design of carts; from the point of view of art, the interest is in the ducks, which are portrayed only from the breast up, and the very plain human-shaped figure, which may represent a god. The sculptor emphasized the basic shapes of his or her subjects without providing details. The theme of waterbirds pulling a cart seems to have been an important one in the Balkans. From Romania circa 800 B.C.E., but housed in Naturhistorisches Museum in Vienna, is a bronze four-wheeled cart with a cauldron in the middle. It is surrounded by abstractions of ducklike birds, facing forward and backward in continuous lines. Housed in the same museum is a bronze four-wheeled cart from the 700s B.C.E. found in Bosnia and Herzegovina. This wagon is carrying the birds instead of being pulled by them. There are two ducks, with one as a receptacle and the other riding on its back and capping the receptacle. The birds were cast in multiple pieces and then fused together by hammering, and they are more realistic than the earlier pieces.

From Denmark, from about 1300 B.C.E., comes a bronze sculpture well known to both archaeologists and art historians: the Sun Wagon. It has six wheels with spokes. At that time these could have represented the movement of the sun. On a wire chassis (the framework attached to the wheel axles) are a horse and disk. The disk is elaborately decorated with swirls and circles. Some of the gold leaf that covered its sides remains. The horse is recognizable as a horse, but it is a flow of curves not found in real horses. Its surface was carved with lines representing a mane and harness. The sculpture was broken, probably deliberately, before it was buried; it was customary at the time to break objects before offering them as sacrifices. An even more spectacular model wagon comes from southern Austria from 650 B.C.E. It may be the pinnacle of European art of the era. On the cart stands a tall, slim woman holding on her head a shallow bowl, perhaps where incense was burned. Less than half her size are men standing and on horseback, and among them are deer with large, tall antlers. All are depicted in a fluid style that seems to be the logical descendant of the earlier carts. The depiction of carts by European sculptors would continue into the era of the Roman conquest, with the images becoming more realistic.

Iron Age: 500–50 B.C.E. and the Roman Conquest

Historians often record 500 B.C.E. as the peak of Celtic European culture. The Celts dominated almost all of Europe. Their society was dominated by warriors, who believed that killing, looting, and enslaving others were honorable pursuits. They were constantly at war either against non-Celts, such as the Slavs or the Etruscans, or among themselves. Their art from this era is often bloody, reflecting a warrior's code of kill or die. The Celts loved art and were ostentatious in their displays of jewelry. The number 3 was a magical number to them, and their jewelry often features three-pointed swirls, as well as very intricate interlaced patterns of lines.

It would be a mistake to say they were not influenced by art from other cultures, but their artists absorbed the techniques of others and then worked them into their own Celtic traditions. Thus, even when their sculptures began to shift from the abstract forms found in their model carts to the realism of classical art, they continued to incorporate their own ideas of what made for natural forms. To the Celts almost everything they saw had a living vitality, and this vitality was seen in the graceful curves of plants and animals. The apparent geometric designs on pottery, full of sweeping curves and sharp angles with nothing in particular represented, were to the Celtic artist a depiction of the complexity and vitality of the natural world. What may look like three-pronged swirls to an outsider looked like the sun coursing across the sky to the Celt. Their twining together of lines that never seem to end was an expression of the eternal movement of life.

The Celts of central Europe also made representational art, either carving in the realistic manner of the Greeks and Romans or making ceramic images for use in temples and public buildings. It was customary for Celtic warriors in central Europe to cut off the heads of their enemies and display them. In Roquepertuse in southern France one such display still exists, now decayed. It is a sanctuary with tall stone pillars which have skull-shaped niches in them, in which were placed skulls, a few of which remain. In about 200 B.C.E. real heads began to be replaced by sculptures of heads. These stone and ceramic pieces were not portraits in the sense of detailed accuracy. The sculptors emphasized the outstanding features of their subjects such as thick lips, a bushy moustache, curly hair, or a long nose. When the Romans invaded Gaul in 58 B.C.E., under the leadership of Julius Caesar, they would see these sculptures side-by-side with real severed heads in monuments built to celebrate warriors and warfare.

Iron Age to the End of the Roman Empire: 50 B.C.E.–476 C.E.

Although Celtic and Germanic artists learned to create works in the classical manner of the Greeks and Romans, they never lost their love of ornamentation and of the intricate, flowing lines of Celtic art. Long after they had absorbed the Roman way of life—speaking Latin and thinking of themselves as Roman people—traits of their ancestral culture lingered. For instance, they continued to wear thick-barred armlets. These became the rings that early medieval German poets described—the rings of power that would inspire the idea of magical rings in J. R. R. Tolkien's classics *The Hobbit* and *The Lord of the Rings* in the 20th century. To the Celts and Germans the giving and receiving of armlets symbolized the bond between lord and follower. In Scandinavia the elaborate swirls and intertwining of lines endured into the era of the Vikings.

In 312 C.E. Rome's Emperor Constantine I (r. 306–337 C.E.) converted to Christianity, ending centuries of persecution of Christians. In much of Europe, Christianity already had been taking hold, but Christianity did not sweep through Europe when it became the official religion of the Roman Empire. Yet it became a profound influence on European art. One form in which Christian art excelled was the illustrated manuscript. Copies dating from the Roman era are very rare, but others from the 500s and 600s C.E. survive and have been widely reprinted in the 20th and 21st centuries. They look like ancient Celtic art. The three-pointed swirls, intricate interlacing of lines, and interweaving of vines are notable in European Christian manuscripts, whether they are copies of the Bible or biographies of saints.

The Celtic cross remains a popular image. It typically consists of a Christian-style cross with a circle around the spot where the vertical and horizontal bars meet. The circle is the ancient Celtic symbol of the sun, adapted to decorate sculpture for the new religion and perhaps adding a touch of the traditionally supernatural, which would be recognized by Celtic viewers. Sculpted stone versions survive in much of Europe. On these would be carved traditional Celtic designs or figures representing a biblical passage or Christian story.

The images and subjects found in ancient European art continued to be explored by artists in later eras. From the graceful bison of cave art to abstractions of human and animal shapes, to the stylish and dynamic geometrical designs of the Celts and Germans, artists have continually reused, reinterpreted, and further developed the art forms and styles begun by ancient artists.

GREECE

BY MICHAEL J. O'NEAL

It would be difficult to overstate the influence of ancient Greek art, particularly sculpture, throughout the world. Greek art inspired the artists of the later Roman Empire, and the influence of Greek art spread, through the conquests of Alexander the Great in the third century B.C.E., to the Middle East, central Asia, Southeast Asia, and the Far East. In the West, Greek art, with its high degree of technical perfection and its interest in the human form, inspired many artists of the European Renaissance, and that influence extended into at least the 19th century.

Very little painting survives from ancient Greece for the simple reason that paintings, unless stored and cared for properly, deteriorate over time. The ancient Greeks painted primarily on wooden panels, which had fallen into a state of near total decay by the fourth century C.E. In contrast, pottery and sculpture are created with more durable materials, so art historians have many examples of ancient Greek sculpture and pottery to study. The Greeks, though, regarded painting as an important art form. The works of one painter of the fifth century B.C.E., Polygnotus of Thasos, were held in particularly high esteem for hundreds of years, but none of his paintings survive. Otherwise, the only surviving Greek painting can be found on the walls of tombs and on terra-cotta pots. Copies of a few paintings from the Roman era exist, but they tend to be of poor quality.

The history of ancient Greek art is conventionally divided into three periods: the Archaic, the Classical, and the Hellenistic. Together these three periods span about a thousand years. During the Archaic and into the Classical Periods, sculptors and potters were regarded less as artists than as craftsmen who went through apprenticeships to learn their trades. In fact, the ancient Greek word *tekhni* is usually translated as "art," but it is the word from which the English word *technique* comes, suggesting that these artists were at the time thought of primarily as craftsmen. Only later, during the Hellenistic Period, did sculptors and painters come to be thought of as artists, in the same category as dramatists and poets.

THE ROOTS OF ANCIENT GREEK ART

Ancient Greek art had its roots in the art of earlier Bronze Age civilizations in the region around the Aegean Sea. Little was known about these civilizations until archaeologists excavated sites at such cities as Knossos, Mycenae, and Troy, which were cultural centers during the Bronze Age. These civilizations flourished from about 3000 to 1200 B.C.E. The first, the Cycladic culture, arose during the Early Bronze Age (about 3000–2200 B.C.E.). Craftsmen during this period, working in small walled villages, produced decorated pottery, silver jewelry, and marble sculptures. These sculptures represented the human form and often were used as grave offerings. Art historians regard this sculpture as the very earliest produced by a Greek civilization.

The second Bronze Age culture was that of the Minoans, who flourished from about 2200 to about 1800 B.C.E. on the island of Crete. These people constructed buildings and palaces, and their artwork included vases and frescoes found on homes and public buildings. This artwork is noteworthy for its vivid colors, dynamic figures that seem to be in motion rather than static, and the development of more three-dimensional figures, having more of a sense of depth rather than being flat.

The third ancient culture, the Mycenaean, flowered during the Late Bronze Age, from about 1600 to 1200 B.C.E. The Mycenaes occupied an area of the Greek mainland south of what would become Athens. The Mycenaes produced decorative art, ceramics, and painted weapons and vases, often depicting battles and hunting scenes. Their artwork was more geometric than that of the Minoans and is considered a foreshadowing of later Greek Archaic and Classical Period art because the geometric designs resemble those of later Greek art. The Mycenaes unexplainably disappeared after about 1200–1100 B.C.E.

THE ARCHAIC PERIOD

Art historians date the start of the Archaic Period of Greek art at about 1000 B.C.E. The period extended to roughly the time of the Persian Wars (480–448 B.C.E.), a series of conflicts between Persia and several Greek city-states. Most of the art that survives from this time is in the form of sculpture, pottery, gem engraving, and coin design. The number of coins from this period is small; coins were not used until about the seventh century B.C.E. and were not in common use until about the fifth century B.C.E.

The pieces that survive from the Archaic Period represent only a small percentage of the work that the early Greeks produced. In the early years of Christianity sculptures of Greek pagan gods from this period and later were burned or otherwise destroyed as a way of rooting out pagan beliefs. During the Middle Ages, Greek statues made of marble were burned in order to create lime, and bronze statues were melted down for their metal for use in such items as weapons. Many sculptures that survive were buried and later found or else went down with ships at sea as they were being transported from their original sites to countries in Europe and recovered in recent centuries.

Art historians divide the history of archaic pottery into five periods, each with a unique style. The first is called protogeometric. During this period potters began to put abstract geometrical designs on their pots. This trend continued into the geometric period, which began roughly in 900 B.C.E. After this time geometrical designs were common features on pots, and by the late geometric period (about 750 B.C.E.) the practice was universal. During these three periods the pots had a natural light color, though they were decorated with substances that turned black when the pot was fired in a kiln. The "black figure" period began in the seventh century B.C.E, followed by the "red figure" period in about 530 B.C.E. These terms refer to changes in the coloration of pots. During the black figure period the background of the pot was red, and the figures depicted on it were black. In the red figure period the reverse was the case: The background was black, and the figures were red.

During these two later periods potters moved away from abstract geometrical designs; as their skills developed, they began to include pictures of human figures on their pots. Many of these figures were gods and goddesses, but other pictures were of battles, hunting forays, heroic and legendary people, and horses. Much of the pottery also depicts erotic themes. Some of the pottery is signed, but art historians tend to identify particular artists by their themes (for example, "the Achilles painter," referring to the Trojan War hero) or by where their works are currently located (such as "the Berlin Painter").

While a good deal of pottery survives from the Archaic Period, pots are more fragile than statues, so art historians have far more statuary to study than pottery. Even so, only a small percentage of Greek sculpture survives. Like pottery, little sculpture was produced for purely decorative purposes. Most was commissioned by the state or by wealthy individuals, and most was used for offerings in temples or as memorials or grave markers.

The dominant form of sculpture was the *kouros*, a figure of a standing male nude. Less important, though still common, were *kore*, or representations of standing female nudes. The prevalence of these statues reflects the Greek belief that the human form provided an elevated subject for art, and most showed young men and women in their physical prime (even when they were used as grave markers for the elderly). Since Greek gods and goddesses had human forms, sculpture could capture an ideal of beauty, nobility, and other virtues, and a particular sculpture could represent either a god or an athletic champion. This concern with secular, or nonreligious, themes and the beauty of the individual human form laid the foundation for much of Western thought and art over the following millennia.

The *kouroi* and *korai* were carved according to a kind of formula. The body is rigid, and the figure's hands and arms are held to the sides. Most have a mysterious smile. The pose is from the front, with the left foot slightly forward. Part of the reason for this stylized form was the chiseling techniques the artists used. They carved the statues from marble using point chisels, which made artistic innovation and subtlety of design difficult. It also concentrated the force of the sculptor's hammer blows, crushing the stone's crystals and giving the sculptures an opaque, or cloudy, appearance.

The Classical Period

Art historians cite the Persian Wars as the beginning of the Classical Period of Greek art, which extended to the death of Alexander the Great in 323 B.C.E. This period is known primarily for its exquisite statuary, both in stone and bronze. Statuary from this time had a wider range of uses than it did during the Archaic Period. In particular, it decorated the interior of public buildings, such as the Parthenon in Athens. Many of these buildings had pediments, or triangular spaces at the gable ends of pitched roofs. Statues were often placed in those pediments to fill them in and give them visual appeal.

Hermes with the Infant Dionysus by Praxiteles (Alison Frantz Photographic Collection, American School of Classical Studies at Athens)

The Elgin Marbles, named after the Englishman Thomas Bruce, the seventh earl of Elgin, who transported them to his homeland, are a major artistic treasure from this time. Also called the Parthenon Marbles, they include statues from the Parthenon's pediments and marble panels called metopes on which battle scenes were carved. (A metope is a flat panel that is part of a tryglyph; a tryglyph is a raised ornamental structure that consists of three raised vertical bands with metopes between them.) Also included are parts of a frieze—a horizontal band of carved stone, typically depicting a progression of events and figures and running along the top of a wall—from the interior of the temple. The originals that survive include 524 feet of frieze, 92 panels, and 17 statues. While experts disagree about the meaning of the frieze, many believe that it depicts the procession that was held every four years in connection with the Panathenaic Games, which in turn were held in connection with a larger religious festival, the Panathenaia.

Classical Greek statuary is famous for its extraordinarily high degree of precision and technical perfection. During the Archaic Period, the *kouroi* and *kourai* were rigid and stylized. The sculptors seemed to have worked from a pattern so that many of the statues are similar in appearance. None of the figures were in natural poses, and none of the sculptures seem to have captured either motion or emotion.

The classical Greek sculptors took the art form to new heights. They came to celebrate the human form for its aesthetic beauty. Even when they were depicting the gods and goddesses, they gave to the figures perfectly proportioned human forms, right down to the details of the fingers and hands. The poses of their figures were more natural, and the subjects' poses in general had more variety. The statues are more fluid and realistic, and many of the figures seem to be in motion rather than held rigidly. While the statues of the Archaic Period seem almost two-dimensional, those of the Classical Period are more three-dimensional, bursting with energy and movement. On the other hand, the figures depicted by most of the Archaic Period sculptures were smiling, if only faintly. During the Classical Period most of the figures have solemn expressions. This feature reflected the Greek ideal of emphasizing reason and logic rather than emotion.

Art historians believe that the emphasis on depicting the human form reflected in art the same concerns that preoccupied Greek philosophers of the era: studying and observing the natural world in order to explain it. Historians generally believe that these developments in philosophy and art reflected the emergence of democratic institutions in Greece during this time period. The *kouroi* were the products of an aristocratic society; the sculptures of the Classical Period were the products of a society in which people were more equal. For this reason, many of the sculptures of the Classical Period depict real people. Historians believe that the statues of the heroes Aristogeiton and Harmodius in Athens, erected to celebrate the end of earlier Greek tyranny, may be the first-ever public statues of real people. Also, many cemetery statues depict the deceased rather than idealized figures.

Classical Greek sculptors are the first Greek sculptors that historians know by name, at least in some cases. One of the most prominent was Phidias (ca. 493–ca. 430 B.C.E.). After the general Pericles defeated the Persians and assumed power in 449 B.C.E., he named Phidias superintendent of public works in Athens and made him responsible for beautifying the city. Phidias also supervised the design and construction of the Parthenon. He produced two of the most famous works of the Classical Period. One was the statue of Zeus at Olympia, one of the Seven Wonders of the Ancient World. This work, considered his masterpiece, showed the god Zeus seated on a throne. His flesh was carved in ivory, and his tunic was made of gold. The figure of Zeus himself was 42 feet high, filling the entire height of the temple. Phidias's other masterwork was his Athena Parthenos, one of three statues of the goddess Athena on the Athenian Acropolis. This statue, made of gold and ivory, was 38 feet high. Both of these sculptures are now lost. They were destroyed by fire after they were taken to Constantinople (modern-day Istanbul), though copies and descriptions exist.

Another prominent classical sculptor was Praxiteles (ca. 400–ca. 330 B.C.E.), best known for his female nudes, especially the now-lost Aphrodite of Knidos. His model for these nudes was probably a courtesan named Phryne, with whom he may have had a romantic relationship. His sculptures are famous because they were carved and polished in a way that makes the light bounce off them, giving them a shimmering, almost lifelike appearance. He was also one of the first sculptors to give his figures curly hair. Praxiteles created what artists and art historians call the "Praxitelean curve." This term refers to a sensuous, almost erotic posing of the model to create the illusion of a living, seductive figure. Later artists copied the curve, which can be seen in Hermes with the Infant Dionysus (housed at the Olympia Museum in Greece).

The Hellenistic Period

The Hellenistic Period of Greek art began roughly with the death of Alexander the Great in 323 B.C.E. and ended in the first century B.C.E. Alexander's death marked a key turning point, for during the years 336 to 323 B.C.E. he extended the Greek Empire through conquest. Most of these conquests were eastward, so Greek influence extended to such places as Persia; Egypt; the kingdoms that occupied modern-day Afghanistan, including most prominently the kingdom of Bactria; and India. The influence flowed in the other direction as well: Greek art was influenced by forms of artistic expression from these other countries. While formerly Greece had been a collection of relatively isolated city-states, after Alexander the entire Mediterranean region was alive with commerce, travel, and cultural exchange.

Hellenistic art can be distinguished from classical art by its greater boldness and sense of experimentation. While artists did not entirely abandon the rules from the Classical Period, they created their own conventions through art that was more dramatic and that portrayed a wider range of human emotion; a good example is the bronze Boy Jockey (now in the National Archaeological Museum of Athens), recovered from a shipwreck off the Greek coast. The statue—of a nearly life-size boy riding a horse—captures in new ways a sense of tension, energy, and movement. One of the world's most famous sculptures, housed in the Louvre Museum in Paris, is the Winged Victory at Samothrace, also called the Nike of Samothrace, an 8-foot-high statue created by Pythocritos of Rhodes in about 190 B.C.E. (*Nike* means "victory" and is the name of a Greek goddess, and Samothrace is a Greek island.) Unfortunately, the statue is missing its head and arms, but some observers believe that the damage in a strange way enhances the sculpture, creating a sense that the figure, with its intricately carved robes, is almost floating in space.

The sculptors of the Hellenistic Period retained the earlier interest in figures of gods and goddesses, but they also turned to more human themes, giving their figures a mysterious smile or an expression of surprise. Many of the statues from this period are erotic and sensual. Common figures included Aphrodite, the goddess of love, beauty, and sexual passion (known in Roman mythology as Venus); Pan, the half-man, half-goat god of the woods who, according to myth, had affairs with many nymphs; and various satyrs (any god of the woods noted for love of unrestrained revelry). Among this type of sculpture is the famous Venus de Milo, is an 80-inch-high marble sculpture once thought to have been created by Praxiteles but now believed to have been created by Alexandros of Antioch sometime around 130–90 B.C.E. Although the statue's arms are missing, visitors to the Louvre in Paris continue to be amazed by the beauty of the figure depicted, with its perfect proportions and the Praxitelean curve.

Coins

Although coins are not typically thought of as "art," art historians take an interest in ancient Greek coinage for two reasons. One is that a large number of coins survive from the period, so they are available for study. The other is that Greek artisans exhibited considerable skill in crafting coins, giving art historians insight into Greek craftsmanship and aesthetics—particularly because coins were made by hand one at a time.

In making a coin, a craftsman carved the image for one side in reverse into iron or stone and then carved the image for the other side into another block. After the silver or gold was heated to the melting point, it was placed between the two blocks, and the top block was struck with a hammer. (For this reason, coins are still said to be "struck" when they are manufactured.) This punched the images onto the coin. The fact that many Greek coins are technically perfect is testimony to the high degree of artisanship craftsmen brought to coin making.

Coins developed in China and India in about 600 B.C.E., but in the Greek Empire, they emerged at roughly the same time in the kingdom of Lydia (now in western Turkey). In common with other forms of Greek art, historians divide the history of Greek coinage into the archaic, the classical, and the Hellenistic. Archaic coins were relatively crude, consisting initially of lumps of gold or silver with geometric designs, though in time flat coins were developed. Later, coins became more sophisticated and included an image of a god or goddess as well as animal symbols.

By the Classical Period, Greek coinage had achieved greater technical proficiency, and the aesthetics of Greek coins were more pleasing. During this period, many of the conventions of coinage still in use today were developed. On one side of the coin were images of gods, goddesses, or heroes. On the other were symbols, such as the owl that symbolized Athens. Also, inscriptions were engraved on the coins for the first time. During the Hellenistic Period, Greek influence spread into such areas as Egypt, Iran, Syria, and as far as India. Many of these kingdoms began producing their own coins, and in some cases the coins were mass-produced. Gold came to be used more frequently than silver. While many of these coins lacked the artistic qualities of classical coins, many also represented the highest level of the coin maker's art, and some were quite large. What distinguishes Hellenistic coinage from that of earlier periods was the inclusion of the images of living persons on coins. While this practice was frowned upon in Athens, many surviving coins from other regions in the realm, especially Syria and Egypt, contain magnificent portraits of their rulers.

Jewelry

Ancient Greek jewelry not only reflected the love of beauty but also was connected with important moments in people's lives. Jewelry was given as gifts at birth and marriage, and much surviving jewelry was buried in tombs. Throughout a person's life, jewelry was worn in honor of the gods.

Most Greek jewelry was made with gold or silver, though some was made with semiprecious stones and cheaper materials, such as bronze or clay. Some early Greek jewelry was cast in molds, but most was made by hammering sheets of metal to the desired thickness and then soldering the pieces together. Most such pieces of jewelry had a design on the surface produced with a variety of techniques, including repoussé. This process creates a relief on the surface by hammering or pressing on the reverse side. Other techniques included granulation (using tiny granules of metal to create a decoration), engraving, and filigree (decorations created with fine wire). Wire was often used to connect the pieces of such objects as necklaces.

ROME

BY WILLIAM H. PECK

The history of Roman art is derived from two important sources: actual works of art that have been preserved by chance or rediscovered by archaeology and the writings of ancient authors. Abundant examples exist of some of the art forms practiced by Roman artists and craftsmen, but it is to the literary sources that we must turn to learn about traditions, techniques, and personalities. Of these sources Pliny the Elder (Gaius Plinius Secundus), who lived and wrote in the first century C.E., is by far the most important writer on arts and crafts. His *Natural History* contains detailed information on almost every aspect of the arts as practiced in his time.

The art of ancient Rome developed from two important roots. The first was the artistic tradition of the Etruscans, who occupied the northwestern part of the Italian peninsula and flourished from the eighth century B.C.E. to the rise of the Romans. The second major influence was the art of the Greeks, with which the Romans came into contact through the Greek colonies in southern Italy and on the Greek mainland itself.

Etruscan art provided a base that was mainly concerned with realistic representation, whereas Greek art contributed ideas of idealism and perfection. The combination of the two gave Roman art its distinct style.

Roman art went through several historic phases, which closely follow the history of Rome itself. During the Republic (509–27 B.C.E.) the arts of Rome were highly dependent on Etruscan models, attitudes, and techniques, particularly in portraiture. As the Roman Empire developed, the arts took on a distinctive character that can be recognized as an outgrowth of Etruscan art but with added characteristics derived from Greek influences. In the third period, called "Late Antique" (roughly 300–600 C.E.), art forms assumed new styles and character, reflecting the changes in the fortunes of the Empire and the addition of new attitudes and religious beliefs.

Much of Roman art was meant to be essentially propaganda, in the service of the state and the rulers. The word *propaganda* is used today mainly in the negative sense of misinformation, but in a broader definition it means information intended to convey a special point of view. This was the purpose of a great deal of the art of the Romans; it celebrated the qualities the Romans accepted, especially as demonstrated by the accomplishments of a strong emperor or a victorious military leader. As a consequence, Roman art provided a mirror and inspiration for a strong government and state.

The various art forms employed by Roman artists and craftsmen included sculpture, painting, plaster and mosaic work, pottery, metalwork, weaving, jewelry making, woodworking, and glassmaking. Of these mediums, sculpture is the best-known art for us today, partly because of the widespread use of statues for propaganda purposes but also due to the chances of preservation. Roman sculpture was made in a large variety of materials, ranging from marble and other kinds of stone to bronze, copper, and even silver and gold, as well as terra-cotta (fired clay). Wood was also used but is seldom preserved. Of all these materials, the most important works were done in bronze, an alloy of copper and tin. Bronze statues frequently were copied in marble, and it is in those versions that many famous compositions have come down to us, because the metal originals were often melted down for other purposes.

The Etruscan heritage on which Roman art was founded is particularly evident in terra-cotta, a material favored by the Etruscans. Clay images were used extensively for the decoration of temples and other buildings. The Etruscans were also very able workers in bronze and passed this tradition on as well. However, the Roman artists used techniques and materials in their own way for decoration, information, and votive purposes. Sculpture is generally divided into two major types. Sculpture "in the round" involves three-dimensional statues meant to be seen from all sides; sculpture "in relief" includes designs carved against a flat background. The first requires the artist to visualize how the work will be seen as the observer moves around it. With the second the artist must be able to suggest roundness and depth in a shallow space. Both types were used by the Romans for appropriate purposes. Three-dimensional statues decorated public areas and private dwellings. Relief sculpture enlivened the surfaces of buildings and monuments.

Portrait Art

The Roman use of realism in portraits lets us see the ancient Romans as they saw themselves, or at least as they wanted to be seen. During the time of the Republic portrait sculptors attempted to be very realistic. The portrait of the typical paterfamilias (male head of the household), for example, while intended to show him as a strong personality who shared with his family the Roman virtues of wisdom, strength, steadfastness, and loyalty, might convey these desirable characteristics and indicate experience and achievement by depicting him at advanced age, often bald and wrinkled. With growing influence from the arts of classical Greece came more of an attempt to create an ideal and somewhat ageless vision of the individual. A good example is the statue of the emperor Augustus created around 20 B.C.E. and found at the villa of his wife Livia at Primaporta in Rome. In this sculpture the figure and likeness of the emperor are idealized to suggest that he is not an ordinary person but has qualities that associate him with the gods of Rome and make him more than human. (In fact the Julio-Claudian family traced their line back to the goddess Venus/Aphrodite.) A similar example is the equestrian statue of Marcus Aurelius (161–180 C.E.) that depicts the emperor as a philosopher-king rather than as a conquering military commander. This idealization in the arts was learned or copied from Greek art; even the pose of the statue of Augustus imitates a Greek original. The love of Greek customs and art was especially strong under the emperor Hadrian (117–137 C.E.), an ardent admirer of Greek culture who encouraged the imitation classical style.

The Romans continued to look to Greece, particularly Greece of the fifth century B.C.E., for inspiration and for models in the arts. They imported Greek art and even Greek artists to decorate their public buildings and homes. A favored practice was the copying of famous originals to adorn homes and gardens, much as one might have a copy of a famous painting on the wall today. This penchant resulted in numerous Roman copies that today give us our only knowledge of the lost Greek originals. One example of such a lost original is the Venus Genetrix type, an image of Aphrodite adapted by the Romans. It is known from more than 70 preserved copies or variants, suggesting that it was very famous in the Roman world.

Many portraits of famous Romans have been preserved, particularly of the emperors and their families. We can recognize the nobility of Augustus or the decadence of Nero in the images made of them because of the abilities of artists to capture such qualities in addition to surface appearances. Portraiture is probably one of the greatest art forms developed by the Romans. It also exemplifies the combination of Etruscan and Greek sources that came together to influence Roman art.

ROMAN COPIES OF GREEK ORIGINALS

In almost every museum that has a collection of Greek sculpture many of the labels will say "Roman copy after a Greek original." As Rome grew powerful in the Mediterranean world, the ruling classes aspired to become cultured and knowledgeable about art, literature, and the other aspects of a civilized people. This cultural ambition resulted in an admiration of Greek art, particularly the art of the fifth century B.C.E., and led to the serious collecting of Greek art on a grand scale.

The Romans had several ways to satisfy the demand for sculpture to decorate the houses and villas of the well-to-do. First, actual Greek works, purchased or looted, were exported to Rome literally by the boatload. Underwater archaeologists have found countless examples in the sea as well as in the port of Athens, where the artworks were lost in the process of being shipped. Second, Greek sculptors were brought to Rome, either as slaves or as free operatives, to produce their sculpture locally. Third, copies of famous works by artists of great reputation were ordered and produced for the Roman market by the thousands.

Greek artists such as Phidias, Polyclitus, and Praxiteles were famous in their time, and individual works by them were well known throughout the Greco-Roman world. Since these works usually stood in temples or public places, it was impossible to acquire the originals, but copies were considered a good substitute.

Most of the famous pieces of sculpture were cast in bronze, and only a few have survived. Most of the copies for the Roman art trade were carved from marble. The difference in material necessitated small changes in the composition. A bronze statue could stand securely on its own legs with little chance of breaking, but stone copies needed additional support around the legs. This fact helps to explain much of the drapery, tree stumps, small animals, and other additions found in the Roman copies. Copyists took other liberties as well. If the original was considered too revealing of the female form, a more modest arrangement of the draperies might be employed. To fit in with a particular placement or arrangement, the whole composition might be reversed so that the figure gestured with the left hand instead of the right. Copies could also be made in different sizes. The Roman collector could choose the size best suited for his house or garden.

We have knowledge of many famous works of art only from the copies commissioned by Roman collectors. In some cases there are dozens of examples based on the same well-known original that was destroyed or lost long ago.

Relief carving was used to embellish the interior or exterior of buildings, the surfaces of monuments such as the triumphal arch and tombs, as well as smaller structures such as altars and sarcophagi (stone containers for the dead body). Relief sculpture could consist of compositions made up of figures and decorative devices of plants, fruit, and other symbols. The Ara Pacis (Altar of Peace, made around 13–9 B.C.E.) of the emperor Augustus is an example of the use of figural decoration while depicting a procession of members of the imperial family and servants in a stately composition. The decoration of the Arch of Titus (around 81 C.E.) uses relief to commemorate a significant historical event, the sacking of the Jewish Temple of Jerusalem and the removal of the temple treasure.

From some of the ancient authors we know that, in addition to sculpture, painting was an important art form. Paintings on canvas or on wood panels from Roman times have seldom been preserved, and this much-respected art has almost totally disappeared, so this is one instance where we must turn to the written evidence. Pliny the Elder describes paintings exhibited in the Roman Forum as well as the unusual example of a colossal 120-foot-high painting commissioned by Nero, naturally of himself. Pliny also tells us that realistic portraits attracted a great deal of interest and caused considerable discussion and comment.

Some panel paintings found in the dry climate of Egypt may give us an idea of the Roman painting tradition. When the Romans occupied Egypt, it became common to put a painted portrait, rather than a modeled mask, over the face of a mummy. In these mummy portraits, painted in wax pigments on thin wood panels in a very realistic manner, some evidence of the painting styles of the Romans during the time of the Empire has been saved for history.

Wall Painting

In contrast to the scarcity of original Roman portrait painting, many examples of paintings on the walls of public buildings and private houses have survived. It is important to remember that this kind of wall painting was intended as a kind of interior decoration and often followed a set formula or pattern. It generally employed the technique called *fresco*, painting on the plaster of a wall when it is still wet or "fresh." The major advantage of this method is that the painting becomes a permanent part of the wall.

The subjects of wall painting often included views of gardens and vistas of elaborate buildings, creating the illusion that the room was open to pleasant scenery. Roman houses had few real windows, and wall images of this kind helped to lessen the feeling of confined spaces. The greater part of fresco painting, however, was simple color and geometric shapes, intended to add variety to the rooms it decorated. In some cases it imitated varicolored stone to suggest a richer and more expensive effect. Roman wall fresco painting gives us a great deal of information about the artistic taste of the people whose houses it decorated.

The artists who specialized in wall painting were organized with a master craftsman as the lead designer and assistants to accomplish the more routine tasks. There is historical evidence that a "figure painter" was paid more than the ordinary wall painter. There is also evidence that Roman painters used pattern books for repeated decorative designs and types. The technique of fresco painting required that the plaster be applied to the walls in sections, only as much as the painters could decorate in a single day. The materials used, in addition to the lime plaster, were mainly natural pigments. These included chalk white, carbon black, and earth colors such as red and yellow ocher. Blue had to be specially produced from a copper compound. The use of natural materials has contributed to the permanence and preservation of the paintings.

From archaeological evidence we can trace the development of Roman wall painting from the second century B.C.E. to about the fourth century C.E. Styles changed with popular taste. At Pompeii, where many examples were preserved when the town was buried in 79 C.E. by the volcanic eruption of Vesuvius, it is possible to distinguish four styles. Not all scholars agree on the historical sequence, but the "four styles of Pompeian painting" form a basis for the general study of the art form. The first style consisted of a combination of paint and plaster, imitating stonework, often brightly colored. The second style kept some of the imitation stonework but added fanciful views of imaginary architecture with the intention of suggesting illusions of depth. In the third style the illusions of architecture became less important, and images on the walls were treated more like surface decoration, even when they represented landscapes. The fourth style reverted to an emphasis on fantastic architecture and illusionist spaces and became even more elaborate.

In addition to fresco painting, interior walls were often further ornamented with plaster decoration. This work often imitated relief carving in stone and served to make interiors even richer in appearance. Decorative plasterwork was a highly skilled craft, used in the embellishment of buildings as important as Nero's palace in Rome, the Domus Aurea (Golden House).

Mosaic

Mosaic was another important art form used in the decoration of architectural spaces. The Romans especially favored it because it added color and interesting compositions to floors in a much more durable material than rugs or carpets. It was not only hard wearing but also easy to keep clean. Mosaics consist of small pieces (tesserae) of stone, or sometimes ceramics or glass, set in a cementlike matrix. The stones were generally of natural colors, collected from many different sources. The designs of mosaic floors might be simple geometric patterns, scenes of daily life, illustrations from Greek and Roman mythology, or special themes such as the seasons or months of the year. In some cases mosaics were made in imitation of famous paintings. Usually, the subject of figural decoration was selected to suit the purpose of the building. For example, the designs in Roman public baths were often compositions with Neptune, god of the sea, surrounded by mermaids and mythical sea animals. At Ostia, the seaport of Rome, mosaics in an area of commercial offices depict the various kinds of business and trade carried out. The subject matter of a domestic mosaic floor could suggest the cultural interest or special occupation of a householder.

Some exceptional mosaics were made as small wall decorations. Usually composed of very small pieces of stone, they approach the art of painting in their detail and realism. Some of these wall pieces are compositions of familiar objects that would today be called "still lifes." Depicting bottles, glasses, fruit in baskets, and similar items arranged in interesting groupings, they suggest the skill of the mosaic makers as well as of the painters who probably originally designed them.

Ceramics and Metalworking

Pottery or ceramics, the art of working with clay, has been a necessary and important craft in almost every civilization and culture. In the ancient world pottery took the place of many materials in use today, such as glass and plastic. Efficient ceramic manufacture was especially crucial to the Roman economy, because vital products such as olive oil and wine were shipped in clay containers. In addition to the simple containers made for cooking, eating, storage, and shipment, the Romans developed several art forms based on clay. Small statuettes or figurines made from molds were popular as decorative and religious objects. They included carefully detailed and brightly painted representations of gods and goddesses or even favorite athletes and gladiators. Useful items such as clay oil lamps were made by the hundreds of thousands, but they were often enhanced with interesting designs. Probably the most important type of ceramic ware made in Roman times was the pottery called Arretine ware, made in the region of modern Arezzo. This type took advantage of a kind of fine red clay that lent itself to the production of cups, plates, and bowls with fine designs, made in figured molds. Arretine ware was imitative of designs made in silver and may have been a substitute for the more expensive material. Often these clay vessels were stamped to designate the maker and even the individual craftsman responsible for the design, suggesting that Arretine ware was special enough for the artist-designers to take pride in their work.

Roman craftsmen were particularly skillful in making objects of metal. In part this was one the traditions learned from the Etruscans, who had been famous as metalworkers throughout the ancient world. Roman bronze workers created objects ranging from colossal statues to simple pots and

Roman terra-cotta relief showing an Egyptian scene set on the Nile, from the first century B.C.E. (© The Trustees of the British Museum)

pans to weapons and armor. Many different household objects found in the ruins of Pompeii and nearby Herculaneum (also destroyed in the great Vesuvian eruption) evince the widespread use of bronze for such items. It is very informative to see the variety of metal objects used in everyday life: containers, serving implements such as pitchers and ladles, scales for weighing food and other materials, tools and medical instruments, and even small stoves for hot water. These may be classified as crafts objects rather than works of art, but they were often designed to be decorative as well as useful. Tables, chairs, beds, and accessories such as lamp stands were made either completely of bronze or with bronze parts or fittings. This wealth of material attests to a well-developed and resourceful metal industry.

The armies of ancient Rome, as well as the combatants in the frequent gladiatorial games, required a vast amount of arms and armor, usually made of bronze but occasionally of silver or even gold for special ceremonial uses. This military gear ranged from swords and spears to beautifully decorated body armor and helmets. The metal craftsmen who worked in the imperial armories were highly skilled in making practical protective pieces as well as "parade" armor meant only for display. Helmets and arm guards made for the gladiators were often as thick as boiler plate and provided excellent protection in the arena.

Specialized metalworkers dealt with the luxury crafts in gold and silver. They produced splendid table services and display pieces for the aristocracy and the wealthy. Highly skilled craftsmen made matching sets of ware and utensils decorated with scenes from mythology and embellished with garlands of grapevines, olive branches, and other plant forms. These opulent sets required the ability to adapt metalworking techniques to creating a high level of careful detail.

Another specialized area of metalworking was coinage. During the sixth and fifth centuries the Greeks had developed the design and production of coins to a high degree of art. Under the Roman Republic and Empire the specialized artistic design of coins continued. The materials were gold, silver, and bronze and other alloys. The art was in the cutting of the dies from which the coins were struck. The images were mainly of the emperor, his family, and other important persons, as well as symbols of state and representations of myth. Roman coins are not only miniature works of art but contain considerable historical information.

Others Arts and Crafts

Few examples of the art of woodworking have been preserved, but from depictions in wall painting, representations in relief carvings, and a scant few remains, we know that the craft was used extensively in furniture making. Similarly, few products of the art of weaving survive. The climate of Italy and much of Europe has prevented the preservation of garments and other woven materials, so we must rely on the pictorial evidence in paintings, relief carvings, and mosaics. However, garments preserved from parts of the Roman Empire, such as Egypt, give us an idea of textile decoration. Materials used were cotton, linen, and wool. Design devices included colorful borders and appliqués, so the impression we have from sculpture of Roman attire as colorless is not completely accurate. Colorful cottons from India and silks imported from China have been found in the oasis caravan city of Palmyra in the Syrian desert, further attesting to a general interest in richly decorated dress during the time of the Roman Empire.

Roman craftsmen excelled at the art of jewelry making. In part this was one more tradition inherited from the Etruscans. Over the centuries the Etruscans had evolved a highly developed jewelry industry exhibiting great artistry and technical skill. They were especially expert in working gold. Among other techniques they developed was granulation, a method of applying tiny balls of gold in patterns on a plain surface. Roman jewelry makers continued to use methods invented by the Etruscans and took them to an even higher degree of accomplishment. In addition to working in gold and silver, they were skillful at engraving stones to be set into rings, bracelets, earrings, and necklaces. Where today these gemstones would probably be diamonds, rubies, and emeralds, the ancient jewelers used semiprecious stones such as carnelian, agate, and quartz. The designs might include images of the gods and goddesses, scenes from mythology, and the name or motto of the owner. The art of the cameo in glass or multicolored stone was also highly developed. Elaborate profile portraits were often done in this technique, which required great skill in design and execution.

Not all jewelry or objects of personal adornment were made of precious metals. One of the most characteristic objects used by Roman men and women alike was the fibula, a broach that served to fasten a cloak or other garment. The fibula was like a large safety pin with spring action and a clasp, but it was often decorated with designs so that it became an object of art in its own right.

Some of the great achievements of Roman artists and craftsmen were in the art of glassmaking. Glass was not a new invention—it had been produced in some parts of the ancient world for centuries—but the methods of making *blown* glass did not become well known until the first century B.C.E. Roman craftsmen excelled in the manufacture of all sorts of vessels and containers in glass—jars, bottles, plates, bowls, inkwells, and even such specialized objects as baby feeders. The forms employed ranged from simple undecorated shapes to elaborate and fanciful showpieces. Glass was mainly freeblown but also blown in molds to give it designed shapes and surface decoration. Cameo glass was produced by coating one color of the material with another, then grinding away parts of the surface to make a design. Some examples of complicated glassmaking that survive are evidence of a highly developed working tradition in a material that challenged the imagination of the artisans to great heights of creativity.

The arts of Rome reflected the accomplishments and aspirations of the Roman people. The artistic traditions evolved with the development of the Roman state from its beginnings in the Republic to the height of Empire and its eventual decline. The values of republican Rome are best illustrated by the severe portraits of distinguished personalities of the time. The attitudes of the ruling elite during the greater expansion under the Empire are shown by the return to forms that imitate Greek styles and by the flourishing decorative arts. With the division of the Empire in the fourth century and the advent of Christianity, the arts, particularly sculpture, underwent changes that reflect the social situations of the time.

The Arch of Constantine (312–15 C.E.) illustrates these changes, being decorated with reliefs salvaged from previous reigns as well as work from the time of Constantine himself. The reused pieces are in the traditional styles reflecting the influences of the Greeks and Etruscans. The new compositions are in a style that can be characterized only as more schematic and less realistic. They depict the emperor and his court, but in graphic contrast to earlier representations such as that of Augustus and his entourage on the Ara Pacis, the Arch of Constantine shows the ruler and courtiers in stiff frontal views. The art of Rome had once again adjusted to the needs of its time. The interest expressed was not in realistic or ideal representation but in information conveyed in the most direct and diagrammatic fashion possible.

THE AMERICAS

BY ARDEN DECKER

Ancient North America

The most significant cultural activity of ancient North America took place in a region now known as the American Woodlands, which extends from the Hudson Bay to the Gulf of Mexico and from the eastern Great Plains to the Atlantic coast. While evidence suggests that the creation of utilitarian objects dates back to the Paleo-Indian Period

(13,000–8000 B.C.E.), regional cultural traditions first arose in the Late Archaic Period (3000–1000 B.C.E.). From utilitarian to ceremonial objects the American Woodland cultures laid the foundation for a tradition of distinct and sophisticated art forms.

Mostly utilitarian items were created by the Early and Middle Archaic Woodland cultures (8000–3000 B.C.E.). Items such as mortars, pestles, axes, and knives were made from stone and copper. Ceremonial objects and ornaments of minimal design also began to be produced. The first significant art forms in North America—mostly portable carved stone objects—were made by the Woodland peoples of the Late Archaic. While they continued the tradition of stone tool making, they also made many ornamental objects out of highly polished precious stones, such as beads and pendants. Such ceremonial objects as simply shaped smoking pipes and flutes made from luxury materials became more prevalent.

Poverty Point (1600–1300 B.C.E.), in northeastern Louisiana, was the largest and most influential site of this period. Numerous ceremonial, burial, and ornamental objects were created there, including the first known human figures in North America. These figurines of men and women would have been hand-molded out of clay and then fired. At the Great Lakes burial site known as Glacial Kame (1500–1000 B.C.E.), a uniquely shaped object called the sandal-sole gorget (an ornamental collar named for its sandal-like shape) made its appearance. These ornaments were carved from shell and often featured small relief carvings of animals. At Glacial Kame and the nearby Red Ocher site, unique bird-shaped atlatls (throwing devices used to propel spears) with large, popping eyes have been found, which suggest the importance of imbuing functional objects with a sense of design.

By the time of the Early Woodland Period (1000 B.C.E.–100 C.E.), regional communities had made developments in agriculture, ceramic production, and the burial of the dead and had become even more sedentary. This period was marked by growth in the practice of mound building. The Adena burial sites of the central Ohio River valley are the most complex. Here mound building became more monumental and complex, as did burial caches. Fine utilitarian and ornamental objects made from luxury materials were buried with the dead. Along with these objects, some late Adena burial mounds contained stone pallets incised with highly stylized designs. Of particular note are the ceremonial smoking pipes found in association with later Adena complexes. Instead of being confined to a simple, tubular shape, these pipes incorporate zoomorphic (animal-like) and human figures as part of their design or as the whole. This advancement greatly influenced the carving practices of the later Woodland cultures.

Many of the key objects of the Middle Woodland Period (200 B.C.E.–400 C.E.) were created by the Ohio Hopewell culture. While the Ohio Hopewell culture is best known for highly sophisticated mound building (ranging from geometric or curvilinear designs to zoomorphic forms), they did engage in small-scale artistic production of particular importance. The Ohio Hopewell began carving two-dimensional animal and human cutouts from copper, shell, and mica. They also made human figurines from fired clay. Ornamental objects like breastplates, headdresses, and cymbal-shaped earspools (circular ear ornaments that are hollow at their centers and worn by being placed within a hole in the earlobe) decorated with animal designs also were created. They developed the platform pipe, in which the traditional tubular pipe was modified to include a curved platform base with a carved bowl on top. Quite often these pipes displayed highly naturalistic renderings of bears, birds, wolves, and other animals. Many Hopewellian characteristics appear in objects created in contemporary and later Woodland sites, indicating that the Ohio Hopewell tradition played an essential role in the development of artistic production in this period.

Another significant region of artistic activity in the Middle Woodland Period arose in Alabama. The Copena complex (100–600 C.E.) developed a distinct brand of pipe design in which the entire pipe takes on the shape of an animal, bird, or other creature. Evidence of these great pipes has been uncovered as far as the Ohio River valley, again signaling a widespread exchange of cultural practices in the Middle Woodland Period.

Ancient Mesoamerica

While evidence of human activity in Mesoamerica dates back to at least 8000 years B.C.E., it was not until around 1500 B.C.E. that the most significant early center of culture arose in Central America with the Olmec. This early culture set the stage by establishing the artistic production that all subsequent cultures would follow. Monumental sculpture, portraiture, images of supernatural deities, and semiprecious stone objects were the key art forms developed by the Olmec and shared by all ancient Mesoamerican cultures.

The Olmec culture developed along the Gulf Coast of Mexico around 1500 B.C.E. Sometimes referred to as the "mother culture" of Mesoamerica, the Olmec developed many of the crucial stylistic elements that become characteristic of Mesoamerican art. The earliest Olmec site is San Lorenzo, a complex, man-made center of civilization established south of what is now Veracruz, Mexico, in the Early Preclassic Period (1500–1200 B.C.E.) Significantly, the well-known monumental stone colossal heads were created here. These giant heads are entirely three-dimensional (sculpted in the round). They probably depict important Olmec rulers and provide early evidence of portraiture. While the heads share many similar features (deep-set eyes, wide nose, full lips), they are also each slightly different.

The second most significant Olmec site is La Venta, near the border of what are now the Mexican states of Tabasco and Veracruz. Founded during the Middle Preclassic Period (1200–400 B.C.E.), La Venta also produced impressive examples of monumental art. In addition to colossal heads, there are large stone altars that actually functioned as ruler thrones. These thrones depict a ruler seated in a niche connected to a rope attached to captives who are carved in relief on the sides of the object. This imagery probably indicates the ruler's earthly and supernatural powers.

Also of note is the appearance of the stela form of monumental sculpture, where a large stone slab is decorated with relief carvings to commemorate an event or person. Relief carvings are created by cutting a design into stone and then removing the background to make the design stand out. Often depicting rulers, deities, or both, stelae became one of the most distinguishing art forms in Mesoamerica. Stelae functioned as records of events and have provided significant information concerning Mesoamerican history, society, and religion. The Olmec carved smaller objects in the form of supernatural beings in jade and greenstone. One example is the werejaguar, a supernatural figure marked by its almond-shaped eyes, upturned lip, pug nose, and cleft head. The features of the werejaguar reappear throughout Mesoamerican art.

Other unique artistic developments are found outside the Olmec center. Highly naturalistic male and female figurines were made at Xochipala (in modern-day Guerrero) and Tlatilco (north of Mexico City) and lifelike ceramic baby figures at Las Bocas (in central Mexico). Cave painting also began during the Middle Preclassic Period. One example found at Oxtotitlan depicts a ruler in the guise of a bird deity. While Olmec cultural production was varied, a clear emphasis was placed on rulers and supernatural beings. Despite the dominance of the Olmec for many centuries, the culture eventually collapsed sometime before 100 B.C.E. for reasons still unknown.

The Zapotec culture arose within the Oaxaca valley region during the Late Preclassic Period (400 B.C.E.–150 C.E.). A key Zapotec site, Monte Albán, features impressive examples of monumental architecture and art. Of particular importance is the Temple of the Danzantes, which is named for its numerous incised stone slabs featuring dancing figures. The dancers are male captives who bear physical evidence of their captors' power and brutality; they all have their eyes closed, symbolizing their death, and are stripped nude as a form of humiliation. Each dancer also has a scrolling motif emanating from the genital area as a sign of mutilation. Given the abundance of dancers (numbering at least 300), the Zapotec rulers clearly wished to express their dominance and power, but not all of their art production focused on such issues. The Zapotec also created ceramic and jade objects that demonstrate the influence of the Olmec. Indeed, pieces of Olmec jade have been found at Monte Albán and throughout later sites, providing further evidence of the Olmec's prestige and influence.

An entirely different artistic tradition developed in western Mexico during the Late Preclassic. Unaffected by activities taking place elsewhere in Mesoamerica, the cultures of western Mexico produced a style of ceramics unlike any other. In Colima unique ceramic vessels in the shape of hairless dogs were created. Often wearing human masks, the Colima dogs display an unusually high degree of charm and naturalism. The Nayarit engaged in an entirely different form of ceramics, creating unusual scenes of human figures placed in architectural settings. From ball courts to domestic houses, the Nayarit ceramic scenes provide an unprecedented view of daily life in Mesoamerica. This area is known for their unusual, nonfunctional ceramic art works, which was their primary form of artistic production.

Many important cultural developments of the early Maya also occurred during the Late Preclassic Period—in the highlands of Chiapas, Mexico, and Guatemala; along the Caribbean coast; and in the Petén region of northern Guatemala. The highland sites of Izapa in Chiapas and Kaminaljuyú in what is now Guatemala City produced objects that bear the mark of Olmec influence, but they developed stylistic programs all their own. The importance of stelae as markers of rulers, deities, and events evolved with the development of glyphs and an iconographic, or symbolic, program. Images on early Maya stelae primarily emphasize the mythical and supernatural (such as the water god Chaak, the mythical World Tree, and the bird deity), though ruler stelae do appear at Kaminaljuyú. These stylistic developments set the stage for the Maya to become one of the most sophisticated cultures in the world.

The most important and influential center of civilization in all of ancient Mesoamerica was Teotihuacán. Located in the Valley of Mexico, it became a powerful urban center of commerce and cultural activity during the Early Classic Period (150–650 C.E.). At its height it is estimated that the city's population reached as high as 125,000 inhabitants. Teotihuacános expanded upon the existing pantheon of Mesoamerican gods to develop a synthesized and complex visual program. This culture produced monumental art and architecture as well as ceramics, ceremonial and burial objects (like censers, adornments, and figurines), and intricate masks. Many monumental stone sculptures were created at Teotihuacán, such as a large depiction of Chalchiuhtlicue (the water goddess, also called the Great Goddess, an important deity in this culture). Not all of the sculpture produced at Teotihuacán was monumental in size. Many extraordinarily detailed figurines in various poses have been found. Also large, brightly colored ceramic urns with human and animal elements were created from mass-produced elements. Numerous beautiful death masks have been found at Teotihuacán, which demonstrate an emphasis on craftsmanship.

Caves and mountains were essential components of Teotihuacán's religion, because it was from these locations that water flowed and life was generated. This concept informed much of the art produced there, particularly with respect to the prevalence of the Great Goddess. The most unusual and striking contributions made by Teotihuacános to the history of art were their advancements in mural painting. Brightly painted and intricate murals would have decorated the walls of Teotihuacán's buildings. Many of these murals seem instructive, in that they depict processional scenes of figures in profile carrying ceremonial implements like incense bags and maguey spines for bloodletting. The only figures that were depicted frontally were gods. The most well-known example of this may be seen in the murals in the Tepantitla apartment complex: The Great Goddess is portrayed amid an abundance of water and plants, which she brings to the people. From her head grow plants and insects. She is flanked by two figures in profile that make offerings to the goddess. Below the Great Goddess flows water from a mountain that carries many small figures with speech scrolls flowing from their mouths, presumably out of happiness. Clearly, the emphasis in this mural is on life and abundance.

Ancient South America

Social development took place throughout the South American coast and along the Andes mountain ranges, extending from modern-day Venezuela and Colombia south toward the north of Chile. The most significant cultures of the Andean region formed in modern-day Peru. With sharp contrasts in the ecological climates of these areas, from the desert coasts, fertile waters, tropical forests, and mountainous highlands, it is perhaps not surprising that much of these cultures' artistic output is marked and shaped by contact made between the irrigational coastal groups and the migrant and farming peoples of the highlands. Despite the diverse influences from the natural landscape, much of ancient Andean art centers on issues of universality, duality, the supernatural realm, or human life.

Evidence of textiles in South America dates back to the Lithic Period (10,000–3000 B.C.E.). Although these first textiles did not yet feature patterns or artistic elements, they provide us with the longest continuous historical record of textiles ever found. Along with new technical developments in textile arts, in the Preceramic Period (3000–1800 B.C.E.) the important concepts of duality, multiplicity, and transformation began to be incorporated into textiles. At the coastal Andean site of Huaca Prieta, in the Chicama Valley, the development of such fiber arts may be traced. More than 9,000 twined cotton scraps have been found there, featuring complex images and polychrome patterns. Specifically, they depict strange and fantastical images, such as double-headed birds and crabs with legs turning into snakes. Images that embody transformation and duality are central to all later Andean arts. Jewelry, feather work, mirrors, and female effigy figures also have been discovered at Preceramic Period sites.

As society grew, so did a more sedentary, agricultural lifestyle. This led to the beginnings of monumental sculpture and wall murals during the Initial Period (1800–800 B.C.E.). At the site of Moxeke in the Casma Valley, near Peru's northwest coast, colorfully painted, monumental adobe sculptures were created in association with the site's main pyramid. Once placed along the structure's platforms, there are now only several remaining fragments, including two severed torsos and one decapitated head. Painted in blue, white, and pink with heavy, black incised lines, the figures are heavily modeled. Although their identities are unknown, the figures suggest the grisly power of the Moxeke rulers.

The largest ceremonial site in all of the Americas was Sechín Alto (1800–900 B.C.E.), also in the Casma Valley. As this coastal site was near Moxeke, the art and architecture had much in common with this earlier culture, including the depiction of gruesome acts of decapitation and dismemberment. The central focus of Sechín is the walled temple complex called Cerro Sechín or Sechín Hill. The wall comprises more than 300 large granite monoliths incised with images that make up a long procession of warriors and victims. Alternating images of decapitated heads, dismembered bodies, abstract spinal columns, and victorious warriors all move toward the north entrance of the complex. The images are composed of deeply beveled (cut at a slant) lines to create the outline of the body, while the smaller interior details are created with shallow incisions. The victims are indicated by their contorted mouths, closed eyes, and unkempt hair, which all indicate their deaths and humiliation. While it is unknown if this procession represents a historical event or mythological story, the important use of art as political propaganda is evident. Like the Moxeke adobe sculptures, these monoliths suggest the awesome power of the Sechín elites and signal the arrival of conflict and conquest in Andean society.

The first major artistic development of ancient South America was the Chavín style, which emerged during the Late Initial/Early Chavín Period (900–500 B.C.E). The Chavín arose in the north of Peru, where they united and synthesized the developments of earlier cultures into their own unique style. Chavín artistic production included monumental sculpture, ceremonial objects, textiles, gold work, and various types of portable art. All monumental stone Chavín art was done in relief carving. Major Chavín monuments focus on uniting the natural elements and on duality in relation to the totality of the universe, a central concept of Andean thought. This style is characterized by complex, obscure images that allow the viewer to perceive alternate realities. Often described as hallucinatory, artworks of this period often feature transforming deities, animals, and shamans.

The Chavín Period is most often discussed in two phases; the Early Chavín is marked by the development of the Chavín de Huántar site and the construction of the Old Temple. Chavín de Huántar probably functioned as a sacred oracle and ceremonial center where priests would consult and perform rituals. Most of the religious cult activities took place in the Old Temple, with ceremonies performed by and for the elite class and not for society at large. The specificity of place, function, and audience greatly affected the design of their art. This is readily seen in one of the key artworks from the Early Chavín period—the Lanzón or Great Lance.

The Lanzón, named for its blade shape, is a monolithic stone sculpture that featured prominently within the Old Temple's sunken court. The Lanzón originally was placed within a cruciform-shaped gallery inside the center of the temple. The gallery's shape represented the four cardinal directions and therefore marked the location as a world center.

The Lanzón acted like a supernatural channel, in that it was placed in the center of this space rooted in both the ground and the ceiling. The Great Lance is a misnomer, as the shape actually refers to digging sticks used in the highlands for farming and not to a blade. The shape of the work suggests that the Lanzón refers in some way to plentiful crops and the survival of the people. The supernatural deity stands with the right arm up and left arm down, as a sign of uniting the heavenly and the earthly. In typical Chavín style, the Lanzón is incised with round eyes, flat nose, upturned mouth with large fangs, and clawed feet. The entire deity is covered with small repeating elements that perform dual functions and may be read in two ways, thus challenging the viewer's perception. This technique of using one set of lines to create two images is called contour rivalry. For example, on the deity's belt, fanged mouth bands with eyes may be interpreted as faces in either direction.

The second phase of Chavín art, known as the Early Horizon/Late Chavín Period (500–200 B.C.E.), focused on the New Temple addition in Chavín de Huántar. Monumental stone works centering on themes of transformation and fertility continued to be produced and become more synthesized, as is exemplified by the Raimondi Stela. This monumental work carved in diorite presents a complex dual image using contour rivalry. When looking at the stela in the upright position, the viewer sees a standing agricultural deity known as the Staff God. The deity displays eyes with pendant irises, a fanged mouth, and clawed feet. In either hand, the figure holds two staffs composed of snakes, faces, and vegetation. From the deity's head grows an enormous headdress. Yet when the stela is inverted, the viewer is confronted with an entirely different image. The headdress now forms a series of supernatural animal faces growing out of one another and charging down toward the earth. This stela exemplifies the Chavín culture's extraordinary facility for expressing the concept of duality.

Portable art also made up a large portion of Late Chavín artistic output. Ceramics, cut shells, textiles, gold work, obsidian, drug paraphernalia, and weaving tools have been found in association with the site of Chavín de Huántar. Of particular note is the use of gold to create wearable art, such as pectorals (breast coverings), crowns, masks, or appliqués.

During the period from 200 B.C.E. to 600 C.E. South American art continued to evolve among the Paracas, Nazca, and Moche peoples. In what is now Peru's Ica region, located along the southern coast of the central Andes, the Paracas peoples developed some of the most sophisticated, unique aesthetic systems to date. They became nearly obsessed with the detailed process of creating their works, mostly in ceramics, textiles, and gold. Thanks to the arid, desert climate in which the Paracas lived, many examples of their work have been preserved. Paracas art demonstrates an avid interest in color, repetition, curvilinear forms, and geometric patterns and often features animals and colors indicative of the region. This obsession with process and detail became one of the key characteristics of later Andean art, particularly among the Inca. The primary deity featured in both Paracas and Nazca art is a monkey-like figure with round eyes and a grin on his face. This deity is often engaged in the act of head-hunting, an essential component of Andean culture. It was believed that the act of decapitation allowed the captor to retain any power or energy the captive possessed. The victim's power could then be added to that of the aggressor.

The people living near the Nazca River, southeast of Ica, also made textiles and ceramics of extraordinary quality. But the Nazca are perhaps best known for their enormous earth drawings or "geoglyphs." Utilizing geometric principles and simple survey techniques, the Nazca created their lines by moving the darker top layer of earth away to reveal the lighter layer underneath. These large-scale drawings found in the desert most often depict abstract images of birds, animals, anthropomorphic (humanlike) figures, plants, and geometric designs, which may be seen in their entirety only from an aerial perspective. Many of these same designs are echoed in the painted ceramics of the Nazca. While the geoglyphs have long puzzled archaeologists and art historians, they probably served a ritual purpose, one that reinforced the Nazca's relationship to their unique landscape. Many theories on the meaning of the Nazca lines have been formulated, from astronomical associations to indications of water sources, but it is clear that the lines were intended to be viewed solely from the celestial realm.

Moche is a term used to describe the culture, people, and kingdom that developed along Peru's northern coast at this time. The Moche peoples are now best known for their ceramics, but they also created textiles and engaged in metallurgy. Their ceramic output consists primarily of portrait heads of rulers as well as ancestor figures and supernatural animal-headed deities. Moche ceramics are all stylized, though they are rendered in a naturalistic, three-dimensional style. They are typically limited to a color palette of cream and red. While their ceramics do portray supernatural beings, the Moche mostly were concerned with the human world, a unique characteristic of this culture.

See also ADORNMENT; ARCHITECTURE; BORDERS AND FRONTIERS; BUILDING TECHNIQUES AND MATERIALS; CERAMICS AND POTTERY; CHILDREN; CLIMATE AND GEOGRAPHY; CLOTHING AND FOOTWEAR; CRAFTS; DEATH AND BURIAL PRACTICES; FESTIVALS; GENDER STRUCTURES AND ROLES; GOVERNMENT ORGANIZATION; HOUSEHOLD GOODS; HUNTING, FISHING, AND GATHERING; LAWS AND LEGAL CODES; LITERATURE; METALLURGY; MIGRATION AND POPULATION MOVEMENTS; MINING, QUARRYING, AND SALT MAKING; MONEY AND COINAGE; NATURAL DISASTERS; OCCUPATIONS; RELIGION AND COSMOLOGY; SACRED SITES; SEAFARING AND NAVIGATION; SOCIAL ORGANIZATION; SPORTS AND RECREATION; TEXTILES AND NEEDLEWORK; TOWNS AND VILLAGES; TRADE AND EXCHANGE; WAR AND CONQUEST; WEAPONRY AND ARMOR; WRITING.

FURTHER READING

John Boardman, *Greek Art,* 4th ed. (London: Thames and Hudson, 1996).

France Borel, *The Splendor of Ethnic Jewelry: From the Colette and Jean-Pierre Ghysels Collection*, trans. I. Mark Paris (New York: Harry N. Abrams, 1994).

Richard Brilliant, *Roman Art from the Republic to Constantine* (London: Phaidon, 1974).

David S. Brose, James A. Brown, and David W. Penney, *Ancient Art of the American Woodland Indians* (New York: Harry N. Abrams in association with the Detroit Institute of Arts, 1985).

Dominique Collon, *First Impressions: Cylinder Seals in the Ancient Near East* (London: British Museum Press, 1987).

Roy C. Craven, *Indian Art: A Concise History*, rev. ed. (New York: Thames and Hudson, 1997).

Digital Arts and Sciences, *Ancient Egyptian Art* (CD-ROM) (San Francisco, Calif.: Chronicle Books, 1995).

Abeer El-Shahawy and Farid Atiya, *Funerary Art of Ancient Egypt* (Cairo, Egypt: American University of Cairo Press, 2005).

Gabriele Fahr-Becker, ed., *The Art of East Asia* (Cologne, Germany: Konemann, 1999).

Fergus Fleming, *Heroes of the Dawn: Celtic Myth* (New York: Time-Life Books, 1996).

Mark D. Fullerton, *Greek Art* (New York: Cambridge University Press, 1999).

Miranda Green, "The Sun Gods of Ancient Europe." In *The Sun: Symbol of Power and Life*, ed. Madanjeet Singh (New York: Harry N. Abrams, 1993).

George M. A. Hanfmann, *Roman Art: A Modern Survey of the Art of Imperial Rome* (New York: W. W. Norton, 1975).

John Henderson and Mary Beard, *Classical Art: From Greece to Rome* (New York: Oxford University Press, 2001).

George Kubler, *The Art and Architecture of Ancient America: The Mexican, Maya, and Andean Peoples*, 3rd ed. rev. (London: Penguin Books, 1984).

Jean-Pierre Mohen and Christian Eluère, *The Bronze Age in Europe*, trans. David Baker and Dorie Baker (New York: Harry N. Abrams, 2000).

Robin Osborne, *Archaic and Classical Greek Art* (Oxford, U.K.: Oxford University Press, 1998).

Esther Pasztory, *Pre-Columbian Art* (New York: Cambridge University Press, 1998).

Nancy H. Ramage and Andrew Ramage, *Roman Art: Romulus to Constantine*, 4th ed. (Upper Saddle River, N.J.: Pearson Prentice Hall, 2005).

John Malcolm Russell, *Sennacherib's "Palace without Rival" at Nineveh* (Chicago: University of Chicago Press, 1991).

Rebecca Stone-Miller, *Art of the Andes: From Chavín to Inca* (New York: Thames and Hudson, 1996).

Richard F. Townsend, ed., *The Ancient Americas: Art from Sacred Landscapes* (Chicago: Art Institute of Chicago, 1992).

Richard F. Townsend, ed., *Hero, Hawk, and Open Hand: American Indian Art of the Ancient Midwest and South* (New Haven, Conn.: Yale University Press in assoc. with the Art Institute of Chicago, 2004).

Susan Walker, *Roman Art* (Cambridge, Mass.: Harvard University Press, 1991).

Mortimer Wheeler, *Roman Art and Architecture*, rept. ed. (New York: Thames and Hudson, 1985).

Richard H. Wilkinson, *Reading Egyptian Art: A Hieroglyphic Guide to Ancient Egyptian Painting and Sculpture* (London: Thames and Hudson, 1994).

Leonard Woolley, *The Art of the Middle East Including Persia, Mesopotamia, and Palestine* (New York: Crown Publishers, 1961).

► astronomy

INTRODUCTION

Astronomy was probably the first science that ancient peoples pursued. They looked heavenward and recognized that the objects they saw in the sky seemed to move with great regularity. The sun rose each morning and set each evening, and the moon appeared in predictable patterns. They also noticed that stars seemed to form groups that had particular shapes, such as the Big Dipper. From these observations, they tried to infer the cosmology (the branch of thought that deals with the origins of the universe) they lived in.

In time, ancient peoples began to understand that they could use this regularity for their own purposes. They noticed, for example, that they could predict the shortest day of the year, knowing then that the days would become longer, and lengthening days signaled the start of the growing season. They could use this information to predict, for example, when rainy and dry seasons would arrive. Since prehistoric people attributed natural phenomena to the will of the gods, they came to attach their astronomical observations to religious beliefs. Thus, the harvest at the end of the growing season, when the sun was lower in the sky, was as much a religious event as it was an agricultural one. Similarly, a momentous event such as an eclipse, the appearance of a comet, or the appearance of a supernova (making a star visible for the first time) was believed to be the manifestation of will of the gods. Such events could create great fear among people.

Astronomy served a number of purposes other than just to mark the passage of time or tell farmers when to plant. Kings and other rulers encouraged astronomers to study the regularity of the heavens. In this way they could predict events, demonstrate their divine knowledge, and retain their power. In this vein, horoscopes and zodiacs enabled shamans, priests, and others to "predict" events based on the movements of the stars, similarly giving them authority and power while at the same time making life a little less uncertain for people.

Astronomy and architecture were also strongly connected. Architects used astronomy to site the foundations of buildings, and in turn buildings, because of their orientation to the sun, moon, star constellations, the points of the equinoxes and solstices, and the like, could be used as astronomical observatories. They could also function as calendars by marking, for example, the summer solstice or the autumn equinox. It is believed that many ancient stelae, or upright stone slabs or pillars, were also used for astronomical purposes. Modern archaeologists are often amazed at the precision with which ancient builders sited their buildings; the four sides of the Great Pyramid at Giza (Egypt), for example, are oriented precisely north, south, east, and west.

Early astronomy was not an exact science, primarily because trigonometry had not yet been discovered. The ancient Greeks developed trigonometry, which deals with the relationships between angles and distances. Only then were early astronomers able to make increasingly accurate observations of the stars and predictions of their movements. In time, early astronomers began to compile star catalogues, mapping the heavens in the same way they tried to map the earth.

AFRICA

BY TOM STREISSGUTH

The astronomical lore and knowledge of ancient Africa are still largely a mystery to archaeologists. Several sites of astronomical significance have been excavated, but their true purpose is still unknown. With no written records to consult, historians must carefully examine each site—with its alignments of standing stones and markings—and speculate on how these "observatories" may have been used.

In ancient Africa the brightest objects of the night sky were important for the purposes of navigation and timekeeping. These objects include the moon, the Milky Way, the constellation Orion, the planet Venus, the stars Sirius and Canopus, and the star cluster known as the Pleiades. Observation of the sky may have also served more utilitarian purposes. On the frontier between the Congo and Uganda, a lunar calendar dating to 6500 B.C.E. has been found in the form of the Ishango bone. The bone has a series of notches carved into it that kept track of the 28-day cycle of the moon's phases. The Batammaliba people in Togo and Benin built their houses so that they were aligned with the course of the sun at the equinoxes—the days of spring and fall when the lengths of day and night are equal. In the kingdom of Kush, established in about 1000 B.C.E., pyramids raised near the capital of Meroë have their fronts facing the eastern rising of Sirius, a star that was also important to the astronomers of ancient Egypt.

Observatories in the form of stone megaliths (groups of enormous stones that form a structure) arranged to indicate the positions of the stars and other bright objects have been discovered in Zimbabwe, Togo, Kenya, Sudan, and Benin. The oldest such site in Africa lies in the Nabta Basin of southern Egypt. Here stone megaliths weighing up to one and a half tons were raised in a circle 12 feet in diameter. Archaeologists have dated the circle to the fifth millennium B.C.E., a date that makes it the world's oldest astronomical observatory.

Nabta was once the site of a shallow lake and a settlement of herders who migrated through the region when it was much more temperate and fertile than it is now. On the western edge of the settlement, the inhabitants shaped and raised the large stones, aligning two groups of stones along a north-south axis while pointing another to the rising of the sun at the summer solstice, the day on which the sun reached its northernmost point in the sky. In this arid region the solstice signified the return of annual rains and the life-giving flooding of the Nile River.

A similar group of stones known as the Namoratunga II circle was found in a remote region of northwestern Kenya. This arrangement of 19 basalt stones was used as a calendar by the Borana, a people of northern Kenya and southern Ethiopia who reckoned their days and months using seven prominent stars and their positions relative to the moon. At Great Zimbabwe, a city raised by the Karanga people, a series of pillars and other structures are enclosed within a thick, high wall. Patterns in the wall indicate the position of the sun at the solstices.

A vast system of more than 1,000 stone circles and monuments also exists in Gambia and Senegal, covering an area of 15,000 square miles. Each circle has as many as 24 stones, reaching up to seven feet in height. Archaeologists date the circles to as early as the fifth century C.E. and believe them to be burial sites. However, the careful alignment of the stones also suggests that they may have been used as astronomical observatories. Another mysterious set of more than 70 standing stones was excavated in the 1960s near Bouar, a town of the Central African Republic. These stones were raised around 500 B.C.E., according to radiocarbon dating of artifacts found nearby.

With scarce physical evidence, historians must also draw on contemporary traditions for clues to the astronomical knowledge of ancient Africa. Along the coasts of Africa, sailors and fisherman orient themselves using prominent stars, such as Sirius and the Orion constellation. The Bozo people of Mali carefully observe the Pleiades star cluster and time the season of fishing in the Niger River when the Pleiades disappear from the night sky.

Another people of Mali, the Dogon, have developed remarkable insight into Sirius, the brightest star of the sky. In Dogon lore Sirius has a companion star, known as po tolo, which is associated with a small white grain known as *fonio.* This companion star is small, white, and very dense, with a mass that holds all other stars of the sky in their place. Po tolo circles Sirius every 50 years, and the Dogon hold a regular ceremony to celebrate this event. In fact, the nature of Sirius as a binary star with a dense, "white dwarf" companion known as Sirius B, which is invisible to the naked eye, was not established by modern astronomers until the 20th century and the era of the modern telescope.

EGYPT

BY LEO DEPUYDT

The term *astronomy* implies a level of complexity that Egyptian astronomy does not exhibit. Because Egyptian astronomy was relatively unsophisticated, the designation

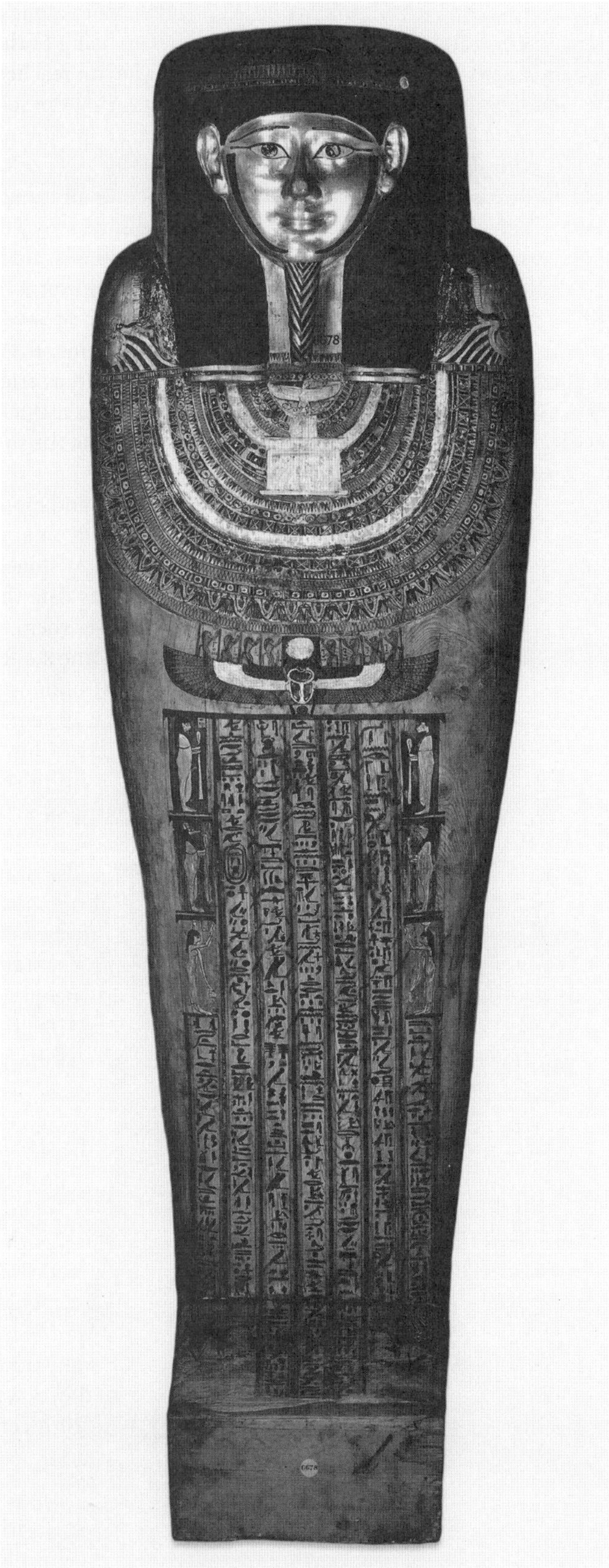

Inner coffin of the priest Hornedjitef, Thebes, Egypt (third century B.C.E.); the coffin lid interior is decorated with figures relating to astronomy. (© The Trustees of the British Museum)

systematic observations of the sky might be more suitable than *astronomy.* Then again, astronomy has a historical dimension. Before it became complex, it had to be simple. A full appreciation of astronomy involves a proper understanding of where the subject was at every stage of its evolution, even in its small beginnings.

One reason that Egyptian astronomy could not have been truly scientific is that trigonometry had not yet been discovered. The Greek astronomer Hipparchus discovered it in the second century B.C.E. Trigonometry relates angle and distance to each other. In observing the sky, one cannot measure the distance between the zenith (the point in the sky right above us) and a point on the horizon or between a point on the horizon and a certain star. In trigonometry it is not the distances themselves that matter but the relation between distances and angles. The numbers of trigonometry are mostly irrational, meaning that they cannot be expressed in fractions featuring whole numbers. Without such irrational numbers, a true scientific astronomy is impossible. Nowhere in hieroglyphic writing is there a trace of irrational numbers.

Ancient Egyptian texts and images are replete with references to the night sky and what happens there. Strictly speaking, these texts and images are not astronomical. Still, they, too, contribute to our understanding of how Egyptians viewed the night sky. They were understandably fascinated by the disks of light and the twinkling dots, even if they did not understand their true nature. As a result, they interpreted the movements in the sky in terms of tales populated by divine characters. Among the earliest such interpretations are the texts inscribed on the walls of the inner rooms of the pyramids dating to the third millennium B.C.E. It is no longer possible to reconstruct fully what these authors saw and why they saw it in the star sky, just as it is not clear why someone sees a certain shape in a certain cloud. This may account for the frustrating incomprehensibility of much of the so-called Pyramid texts, a collection of ancient Egyptian religious texts. A remarkable section in the Pyramid texts is the Cannibal hymn. The contents of this hymn are unique in Egyptian literature. There is mention of slaughtering firstborn children, slitting throats, eating organs, cooking body parts, using victims for kindling, and lighting fires with thighs. On the surface, there is no way of interpreting its contents charitably, yet the hymn may be nothing more than a description of how the sun dims the light of the stars—that is, eats the stars, so to speak—when it rises in the morning. In fact, much of the texts found in pyramids appear to concern an effort to interpret the movements of the stars.

The best represented type of early-period astronomical text is the so-called star clock. Star clocks, of two main types, are found in tombs. The first type appears on the insides of coffin lids dating to about 2100–1900 B.C.E. In this type, the year is subdivided into 36 intervals of 10 days, for a total of 360 days. Twelve stars are listed for every 10-day period, one each for every hour of the night. The second type of star clock is found on the walls of subterranean rock tombs dating to the 12th century B.C.E. In this type, the year is subdivided into 24 intervals of 15 days, also for a total of 360 days. Thirteen stars are listed for every 15-day period, one for each of the 12 hours of the night plus an additional star for what is called the night's "beginning."

The first type of star clock may be called "diagonal," because stars shift exactly one position every 10 days in the table of columns and lines every 10 days. The second type is then "broken-diagonal." This type is not laid out in tables, but if one reconstructs the tables, the stars shift, on average, more than one position for every 15-day period. Star clocks, found only in tombs, have been interpreted both as calendars and as clocks, but they may well be neither. It was customary to adorn tombs with representations of what life had been like on the earth, and therefore star clocks probably do not do more than evoke the changing positions of the stars over the course of a year. They served for the deceased as a recollection of what life had been like on the earth and of what it might again be like in the afterlife.

At a later period, from about 500 B.C.E. onward, Egyptian astronomy began to exhibit the influence of Babylonian and Greek astronomy. Horoscopes and zodiacs were imported from Mesopotamia from about 100 B.C.E. onward. Among astronomical texts dating to this time is the papyrus Carlsberg 9, kept in Copenhagen. The text is written in Demotic, which is a stage in the development of the Egyptian language. Carlsberg 9 has often been called the only Egyptian mathematical-astronomical text, but the sole and simple aim of the numbers in the text seems to be to distribute 145 lunar months of 29 days and 164 lunar months of 30 days (which total 9,125 days) over 25 Egyptian years of 365 days (which also total 9,125 days) in a certain optimal pattern of alternation of 29-day and 30-day months.

It is a matter of controversy whether the Egyptian star names can be successfully matched with modern stars. Some believe they can. Others, including the present writer, believe they cannot. But everyone agrees that the star named *sopdet* in ancient Egypt refers to Sirius.

THE MIDDLE EAST

BY DAVID BROWN

Clay seals dating to the fourth millennium B.C.E. in Mesopotamia depict stars with gods. The Sumerians identified major deities of their pantheon with the brightest heavenly bodies. For example, Utu was the sun god, Nanna the moon god, and Inana the planet Venus. The cuneiform script preserves the close connection between gods and asterisms (stars or planets). The sign for "asterism" in cuneiform script consists of three *dingir* signs, where *dingir* means "god" or "divinity." The *dingir* sign itself, meanwhile, depicts a star.

In later classical Sumerian literature Jupiter and Mars are identified with the gods Šulpae and Nergal. By about 1700 B.C.E. the Mesopotamians had identified the five planets now known as Mercury, Venus, Mars, Jupiter, and Saturn. In both the Sumerian and the Akkadian languages the term for these bodies means "wild sheep asterism," rather picturesquely designating the planets' "wandering" nature against the background stars.

The Mesopotamians did not merely identify asterisms with major gods but also treated them as agents of those gods. They believed that the behavior of the stars carried messages the gods wished to impart to humankind, and the decoding of these messages developed into an elaborate art of "astral divination." In other contexts some stars or groups of stars were thought to rain down direct influence and imbue substances or situations with special potency. This concept, too, formed an important part of the intellectual endeavor of some Mesopotamians, and we identify it as "astral magic."

Cuneiform tablet with observations of Venus, neo-Assyrian, seventh century B.C.E., Nineveh, northern Iraq (© The Trustees of the British Museum)

Astral divination involved encoding the phenomena of the heavens into omens and associating them with events on earth. Thus, eclipses were thought to signify that the king might die if appropriate magical countermeasures were not invoked. Omens of this sort are also known from about 1700 B.C.E. Given that signs in the heavens are visible to all, it is not surprising that they were thought to offer comments on the king, the land, or the state, and not on private individuals. Not until the configurations of the heavens at the moment of any individual's birth could be determined was it possible for astral divination to enter the private domain to any great extent.

From the Old Babylonian Period (2000–1600 B.C.E.) to around 700 B.C.E. no surviving sources can be classified as "astronomical," if by this term we mean the prediction or calculation of celestial configurations at a given moment. There are, however, compositions in cuneiform that elaborate numerically on certain idealizations as to the movement of the heavens. Most famously, one of the 70 tablets of the celestial omen series known by its opening words as *Enūma Anu Ellil* ("When the gods Anu and Ellil . . .") is devoted exclusively to the lengths of time for which the moon and sun are visible throughout the year. Nevertheless, the lengths of time are derived from assumptions as to the ideal length of the month (30 days) and of the year (360 days), the ratio of the longest to the shortest day (2:1, where the reality is closer to 3:2), and so forth. This tablet (number 14) represents a very poor model of the actual behavior of the heavens, but despite appearances its purpose was astrological, not astronomical—hence its place in the great omen series. It provided a set of ideal times against which the real behavior of the heavens could be compared and interpreted. In short, if observed reality cohered with the ideal, that boded well; otherwise, it boded ill. Compositions such as Enûma Elishl, the creation epic of the cult of the main god of Babylon, Marduk, further show that the ideals employed in celestial divination were those ascribed to the universe as it was believed to have been when the gods first formed it.

By around 700 B.C.E. astral divination had become a large industry, with expert scholars employed directly by the Assyrian kings and the great Marduk temple of Babylon taking detailed records of successive ominous phenomena. We are well informed about this period because large numbers of the scholars' letters to their kings were discovered in the ruins of Nineveh. It has been suggested that competition among scholars for royal favor led them to attempt to *predict* forthcoming celestial configurations ominous to the king. They did so by studying the long records of dated ominous configurations, such as eclipses or the heliacal rising (the first appearance in the east directly before sunrise) of the planets, and eliciting the intervals at which such configurations recur. There is no reason to assume that astronomy came about because of a desire to regulate the calendar or for intellectual interest, as has often been assumed in the past.

Relatively rapidly the Assyrian investigators discovered a characteristic interval between eclipses of the same type, amounting to 223 months exactly, or 6,585 days and about 8½ hours, on average. There is some evidence of attempts to model the variation of the interval about that mean as early as the eighth century B.C.E. In the seventh century B.C.E. scholars identified intervals, expressed in years, at which the planets exhibit the same phase (such as opposition or heliacal rising) in more or less the same place on the ecliptic. For example, they found that Jupiter is in the same phase at the same place in the sky every 71 years. They also discovered the means by which the length of the month, very ominous to the Mesopotamians, could be determined. The methods derived depended on summing the intervals between sunrise and moonrise and sunset and moonset recorded some 18 or 18½ years earlier. It was only very recently that the rationale behind these methods became clear to modern scholars and revealed that the ancients must have carefully scrutinized their records of such lunisolar intervals in order to extract these periodicities. Truly, bookwork lies behind the world's oldest astronomy.

If astronomy was invented to service royal astral divination, the democratization of deriving interpretations from the sky led to its first and greatest transformation. Babylon had become the home of astral science with the demise of Assyria around 612 B.C.E., but with the arrival of the Persians in 539 B.C.E. it ceased to be a capital. It appears that the scholars who had been making astronomical predictions for their kings turned to the private market. Where celestial divination derived interpretations from visible phenomena, private astrological predictions were based on the calculated locations of all the planets, be they above or below the horizon, at a given moment (usually the moment of the subject's birth). The zodiac was probably invented around 500 B.C.E. as a way to provide a framework for those calculated locations, and it is to this time that we should date the earliest private birth astrology, though the earliest known actual birth chart or "proto-horosocope" dates to 410 B.C.E.

Calculating planetary locations at a given moment represented a new challenge for the Babylonian astronomers, one they met by interpolating between locations of the phases, determined from the database of observations and characteristic periods. In due course they derived means to calculate planetary locations and the details of eclipses without constant recourse to the database of observations. These database-independent methods constitute the high point of cuneiform astronomy and are found in tablets unearthed in Babylon and Uruk. They reached their most advanced state around 200 B.C.E. after centuries of evolution. Thereafter, these wonderful methods reappear along with zodiacal astrology in the Egyptian, Greco-Latin, Iranian, and Indian worlds.

ASIA AND THE PACIFIC

BY MICHAEL ALLEN HOLMES

Most of the advances in the scientific study of the heavens in ancient eastern Asia were achieved by the people of China, where astronomical truths were sought largely to refine the understanding of astrology. Kings, in fact, restricted such study to scholars under royal employment, in hopes of maintaining a sure hold on power that was often secured through accurate predictions. Into medieval times ordinary citizens were punished for possessing or using objects associated with the measurement of celestial bodies or with divination based on such measurements. The importance ascribed to the study of astronomy is reflected in the fact that the Chinese recorded a number of observations before either the Greeks or the Babylonians.

In general, the ancient Chinese classified astronomical events into two categories: predictable and unpredictable. Predictable events included the shifting of the phases of the moon and the rotation of the constellations around the North Star. Unpredictable events of particular note included the wandering of the planets (whose orbits were long undetermined in geometric terms), the appearance of comets, and instances of sunspots, which were especially observable when dust storms in northern China screened the sun's glare. A great deal of attention was paid to these unpredictable events, which wise men, particularly those in the service of rulers, interpreted in order to extract cosmic meaning.

Knowledge regarding predictable events, then, was valued largely for its providing the frame of reference against which unpredictable events occurred. The origins of an imperial almanac, which served as a register of these predictable events, are so ancient as to be obscure. The almanac delineated the annual astronomical cycle, including the lengths of the months (which were based on the phases of the moon and thus varied from year to year) and the dates of the equinoxes (the two times of the year at which the sun crosses the equator and day and night are of relatively equal length) and solstices (the times of year when the sun is at the greatest distance from the equator and the day is either at its shortest or at its longest, depending on the season). The year began at the winter solstice, when the yang force—a Chinese conception associated with warmth, among other qualities—was at its nadir. Since the winter solstice often proved to be a cloudy day, its date was calculated based on that of the summer solstice, which was determined through the measurement of the shadow of an 8-foot stone pillar. The length of the year was estimated to be 366 days until the fourth century B.C.E., when the figure was revised to 365¼ days; further corrections were made continually thereafter.

According to legend, basic star charts were first compiled sometime before 1000 B.C.E. by a shaman named Xian, who identified the Big Dipper, among other constellations. The revolution and rotation of the Big Dipper around the North Star, rather than the movement of the sun, provided the basis for many Chinese astronomical computations. Records still exist of the star charts compiled in the fourth century B.C.E. by the early astronomical observers Shi Shen and Gan De—whereas charts compiled by Timocharis (ca. 320–260 B.C.E.), of Greece, have never been found. Much later, in the fifth century C.E., Qian Lezhi incorporated the findings of his three regional predecessors into a single chart, coding their findings with the colors white, red, and black.

Covered jar, from the second to first century B.C.E., China; the scene is of a blue beast (the star Sirius) with bared fangs lunging at a mounted archer (the adjoining constellation, Bow). (Copyright the Metropolitan Museum of Art)

Comets, eclipses, and supernovae (explosions of stars) were seen as especially momentous astronomical occurrences. Records of comets are more extensive in China than in anywhere else in the ancient world, and these records provided the original basis for determining the orbit of Halley's comet, which was sighted in China first, in 240 B.C.E. Records of eclipses extend back even further in time, as inscriptions were found on oracle bones— animal bones that were used for divination—dating back to the Shang Dynasty, which ended around 1045 B.C.E. Thus, Chinese records predate Babylonian ones by some seven centuries. Starting in the third century B.C.E. eclipses were carefully registered. Supernovae, which are stellar explosions that can make distant stars visible to the naked eye for the first time, were referred to as inexplicable *new stars* or *stranger stars*.

The Chinese made a number of advances in the design of astronomical equipment. The Han Dynasty, which lasted from the second century B.C.E. to the second century C.E., witnessed the invention of a star-mapping tool called the *armillary sphere*, a fixed set of rings demarcating the sectors of the sky. The ring representing the skyward extension of the equator, dubbed the *Gauge of the Red Road*, was particularly important, as it allowed for increased accuracy in the measurement of the paths of the sun and moon; the astronomer Geng Shouchang, who lived during the first century B.C.E., is credited with the invention of the equatorial ring. In the first century C.E. an even more important ring was added: one denoting the ecliptic, or the path taken by the earth around the sun, allowing for even greater accuracy in measurement taking and prediction making, especially with regard to eclipses; this ring was dubbed the *Gauge of the Yellow Road*. Overall, Chinese astronomical predictions never equaled those of the Greeks, whose geometry was more refined.

One of the most renowned Chinese astronomers was Zhang Heng, who lived in the second century C.E. and was also a poet. He is widely credited with the invention of the first comprehensively functional armillary sphere, featuring rings representing the equator and the ecliptic as well as a meridian, circling the earth over the poles, and a horizon. The accuracy of this sphere, which was a yard in diameter and was dubbed the *Gauge of the Enveloping Sky*, allowed a fourth-century astronomer named Yu Xi to discover the fact that the equinoxes occurred some 20 minutes earlier every year, a process called the *precession of the equinoxes*. (This process was actually first discovered by the Greek Hipparchus around 120 B.C.E.) Zhang Heng is also presumed to have built the first orrery, a smaller armillary sphere combined with representations of other bodies in the solar system, all of which moved in accordance with reality using water power. This smaller sphere was a prototype for modern clockwork.

Advances in astronomy were also achieved in ancient India, though on a less definitive scale. One known fact is that during the rule of the Guptas, in the fourth and fifth centuries C.E., the number of days in the year was calculated with accuracy exceeding that attained by the Greeks. Otherwise, generally speaking, scientific knowledge was recorded in such elaborate Sanskrit that the sharing—and further developing—of that knowledge was somewhat hindered. Other Asian and Pacific cultures, including those in Japan, Korea, Southeast Asia, and Australia, are known to have amassed knowledge of the stars, particularly of the appearances of constellations, over the millennia. However, little concrete evidence exists to demonstrate how far back into ancient times this knowledge existed.

EUROPE

BY STEPHEN M. FABIAN

Hesiod, a Greek poet-farmer of the seventh century B.C.E., provides a calendar that weds productive human activity to astronomical observations. "At the time when the Pleiades, the daughters of Atlas, are rising," he says, "begin your harvest, and plow again when they are setting. The Pleiades are hidden for forty nights and forty days." Recorded two centuries after he lived, Hesiod's *Works and Days* combines astronomy with mythology, religion, the cycles of flora and fauna, farming and sailing, and the celebration of holidays, indicative of astronomy's integration into ancient cultures. But Hesiod's ability to use accurate observations of celestial events, such as the heliacal rising of the Pleiades (their first appearance near sunrise after a period of invisibility due to proximity to the sun), and their timing with important tasks must be the result of years—even generations—of careful sky watching. This and other evidence suggest a long prehistoric European tradition of systematic astronomical observations that were the basis for successfully coordinating and synchronizing human activity with the perceived natural and cosmic cycles engendering life, power, and fecundity.

The roots of European astronomy run deep. The archaeologist Alexander Marshack interprets the crescent-shaped and circular carvings on an eagle's wingbone from the Dordogne Valley, France (ca. 30,000 B.C.E.), as tallies recording the synodic—or lunar phase—cycle. While Marshack's interpretations remain the subject of controversy, researchers have found precise astronomical alignments among many of the hundreds of megalithic ("large stone") constructions—including mounds and passage tombs, single standing stones (menhirs), and stones in rows, circles, and other geometric patterns—of Neolithic peoples from the Mediterranean to Ireland and the North Sea built between 4500 and 2000 B.C.E.

The Scottish engineer Alexander Thom visited and made measurements at many of these sites in the middle decades of the 20th century. His main postulates include a standard megalithic unit of measure (for example, the "megalithic yard"), and he theorizes that this unit of measure allowed for the precise layout of features (such as Pythagorean triangles), that these features often incorporated astronomical alignments to the rising and setting positions of important celestial bodies, and that such layouts functioned to mark off important events and periods of time which included a standardized megalithic year and even allowed for eclipse prediction. Scholars continue to debate Thom's specific claims, but his work and that of others make it indisputable that astronomy was significant to life in ancient Europe.

The oldest reliably dated megalithic site with a precise astronomical alignment is that of Dissignac in Brittany, France (4500 B.C.E.). Its main feature is a mound with two passage tombs, one of which is oriented so that the rising December solstice sun shines directly down the 7-meter passage to illuminate the rectangular burial chamber. Another important passage tomb is the mound and site of Newgrange (ca. 3000 B.C.E.) in Ireland. There the light of the rising December solstice sun penetrates approximately 20 meters to the burial chamber via its main passage and a "roof box" feature above it. The mound at Newgrange also is surrounded by rings of stones, many of which are engraved, and some scholars interpret astronomical relevance in the iconographic (symbolic) features of these stones, their placement, and the effects of their shadows, such as the shadow cast on the December solstice from a stone of one ring onto a three-leafed spiral design of another stone directly at the tomb's entrance.

Some Neolithic Europeans seem to have been particularly interested in marking the extreme positions of the moon. At Callanish, in the Outer Hebrides of Scotland (third millennium B.C.E.), for example, a burial mound is ringed by a stone circle from which emanate apparent avenues to east, south, and west as well as to the north-northeast. This last avenue, in its southerly direction, is oriented to the moon's southernmost setting point (major standstill), a point to which it would return only once every 18.6 years. Thom identified the site as a "lunar observatory" based on his measurements there, and the site's lunar significance is enhanced through its association by the archaeologist Aubrey Burl with a description made by Diodorus of Sicily (first century B.C.E.) of a circular temple said to be dedicated to the moon and its divine visitation every 19 years.

Site location and orientation are no more important than at Crucuno (probably built around 3000 B.C.E.), a site in Brittany that is a rectangle of stones with sides oriented exactly to the cardinal directions with lengths of precisely 30 and 40 megalithic yards and therefore a diagonal of 50, the classic Pythagorean dimensions. The diagonals themselves align precisely to the rising and setting of the December and June solstice suns, a phenomenon possible in the Northern Hemisphere only at this latitude (47.5°N). Crucuno's stunning combination of astronomical alignments with cardinal orientation as well as its ideal geometric and numeric proportions is a strong case for ancient European sophistication in coordinating cosmic features into the cultural landscape.

The most famous megalithic site of Europe associated with astronomy is Stonehenge on England's Salisbury Plain, whose numerous features represent several major building phases between approximately 3000 and 1500 B.C.E. Stonehenge has been called an astronomical observatory and is associated with a computational device for predicting eclipses, but many claims are disputed. Its least controversial alignment is that of the main avenue in conjunction with its trilithon (two large vertical stones supporting a horizontal stone) and bluestone horseshoes, past the Heelstone, to the June solstice sunrise. The astronomer Gerald Hawkins suggests that the site's circle of 56 Aubrey holes (a ring of debris- and chalk-filled pits that encircles the stone monument portion of Stonehenge and is associated with the site's earliest building phase) functioned in an elaborate tally system for predicting eclipses, but there is little corroborating evidence to support this computational scheme.

Still, the interest of ancient Europeans in making and utilizing precise and complex astronomical observations should not be underestimated. A recently unearthed and somewhat controversial artifact from Germany known as the Nebra sky disk furthers this association. Dated to approximately 1600 B.C.E., the bronze disk is inlaid with golden symbols that have been interpreted as the sun or full moon, crescent moon, and stars, including the Pleiades. The artifact also is associated with an enclosure atop a hill known as the Mittelberg ("Central Hill"), which is associated with astronomical observations. Since it was not excavated using proper archaeological methods, the authenticity of the sky disk has been questioned, though microscopic analysis suggests that it is genuinely ancient.

Without the confirming evidence of written records from the era, interpretations of archaeological remains of ancient Europe must remain speculative, but the mounting data indicate that ancient Europeans were interested in and skilled at observing the sun (especially solstices and equinoxes), moon (including its standstill positions), and prominent stars (notably for their heliacal rise). Even in the absence of writing—as Hesiod's orally transmitted poetry reveals—astronomical observations are recorded in hand-worked devices, such as the Nebra disk, and alignments of cultural features to orient people in time and space, to organize their productive and ritual activities, and to integrate and synchronize them within the flow of natural and cosmic forces.

GREECE

BY TOM STREISSGUTH

The mythology of gods and heroes accounted for what the ancient Greeks observed in the heavens until the advent of geometry. The Greek astronomers replaced the ancient legends with a system of mathematical logic created not by remote gods but by philosophers. In this way the natural world, including the sun, moon, and the mysterious lights of the night sky, could be understood as a consistent, harmonious system rather than as arbitrary chaos or the whim of a deity.

The earliest Greek astronomer of renown was Thales of Miletus (ca. 625–ca. 547 B.C.E.), who lived in a colony of Ionia on the eastern shores of the Aegean Sea. According to tradition, Thales predicted a solar eclipse of May 28, 585 B.C.E., and, in this way, helped the warring Medes and Lydians reach a cease-fire. He used a mathematical system of predicting eclipses from Babylonia, which relied on the saros (eclipse) cycle of every 18.6 years.

While written records and observations of Babylonia formed an important foundation for Greek astronomy, the Greeks went further to create more complex blueprints for the structure of the universe. Anaximander of Miletus (ca. 610–ca. 545 B.C.E.) held the sun as the highest and farthest body in the heavens, followed by the moon, the stars in their fixed positions, and the planets. Like nearly all the Greek astronomers who followed him, Anaximander was a geocentrist: He believed that the earth lay fixed, at the center of the universe.

Pythagoras, a philosopher of about 500 B.C.E., created concepts and theorems that could be applied universally to observations of the natural world. He recognized that the earth is a sphere—the perfect geometrical shape—and determined that the orbit of the moon was inclined, or tilted, to the plane of the earth's equator. The Pythagorean sect of southern Italy saw in nature a symmetrical structure, with all things having an underlying unity of form, based on numbers, ratios, and proportions.

Observed nature is not always symmetrical, however, and later Greek thinkers had to account for many strange anomalies. For the astronomer, the most serious was retrograde motion: The earth's orbit relative to that of the planets occasionally makes it appear that the planets are moving in reverse. Eudoxus of Cnidus (ca. 400–ca. 347 B.C.E.) tackled this problem while proposing a geometrical model for the motion of the heavenly bodies. He believed in simple circular motion, as did the Pythagoreans, but added two spheres that were concentric—sharing the same center point—and nested within each other. The planets moved along the edges of these spheres, which rotated in opposite motion. The smaller, planetary sphere was inclined to the larger sphere, which lay on a different axis. This arrangement explained the apparent motion of the planet backward and forward in the sky.

Aristotle (384–322 B.C.E.) refined the system of Eudoxus, proposing that the motion of each of the heavenly spheres has an effect on the others. Aristotle confirmed the belief in a spherical earth by observing that earth's shadow on the moon during lunar eclipses is curved. Of all the Greek philosophers, Aristotle had the strongest influence on medieval astronomers, who imitated his elaborate schema to explain all observable phenomena—including the earth and stars, planets, sun and moon, and the four basic elements of water, air, fire, and earth.

The varying distances of the stars, planets, sun, and moon—shown by their changing brightness—could not be explained by spheres and perfect circular motion. More sophisticated geometric models of the universe were required. Using the Pythagorean theorem and the geometry of Euclid (fl. ca. 300 B.C.E.), Aristarchus (ca. 310–230 B.C.E.) measured the ratio of distances to the moon and sun, showing that the sun was farther from the earth than was the moon. He also proposed a heliocentric, or sun-centered, universe, an idea counter to the prevailing wisdom that placed the earth at the center of the universe. Aristarchus explained the apparently fixed position of the stars as a result of their great distance from the earth. The planets in his system moved around the earth in an eccentric orbit, with the earth located off the orbit's center. This arrangement accounted for the varying speeds and brightness of the planets.

By comparing the length of shadows at two distant locations in Egypt, Eratosthenes (276–194 B.C.E.) of Alexandria came up with a fairly accurate measure of the earth's circumference. He also calculated the distance of the sun and the moon and the 23.5-degree tilt of the earth toward the plane of its orbit around the sun. Apollonius of Perga (ca. 262 B.C.E.–ca. 190 B.C.E.) introduced a theory of epicycles. The planets moved on a circle, or epicycle, whose center moved about a greater circle known as the deferent. In his book *The Sand Reckoner*, the mathematician Archimedes of Syracuse (287–212 B.C.E.) calculated the diameter of earth's orbit and that of the sun and used this ratio to determine the diameter of the universe.

Hipparchus (ca. 190 B.C.E.–ca. 120 B.C.E.) was an astronomer and mathematician of Nicaea, in Asia Minor. He proposed mathematical theorems for the motion of the sun and moon; created a system of brightness magnitudes for the stars; compiled a star catalogue; built a celestial globe; and discovered precession, the movement of the axis of a rotating body. Hipparchus was the first to divide the circle into 360 degrees, which allows astronomers to map the heavens and geographers the earth. Many consider Hipparchus to be the greatest of all the Greek astronomers, but only one of his books survives. By contrast, Claudius Ptolemaeus (Ptolemy) of Alexandria (ca. 90–ca. 168 C.E.) earned the highest renown of all Greek astronomers. Ptolemy wrote an important work of observations, theories, and calculations known in Greek as *Mathematike Syntaxis* and more familiarly by the Arabic-derived name *Almagest* (The Great Book). This 13-book treatise drew on Greek and Babylonian astronomy as well as observations that Ptolemy himself made over a span of 40 years.

The *Almagest* was first translated into Latin in the 12th century by Gerard of Cremona. The book gives a mathematical theory of the motion of the sun, moon, and planets. The sphere theory propounded by Aristotle was used by Ptolemy as the basis for his description of the epicycles of the spheres. Ptolemy compares observations of the solar equinoxes and solstices with those of Meton and Hipparchus and gives a precise measurement of the length of the seasons. Ptolemy postulated a spherical universe, at the center of which lay the spherical, fixed, and unmoving earth. The planetary spheres contained, in ascending order from the earth, the moon, Mercury, Venus, the sun, Mars, Jupiter, Saturn, and the stars.

Ptolomy's *Almagest* also contains a star catalogue updated from that of Hipparchus and listing 1,022 stars and 48 constellations. The star-mapping techniques described the stars as points on a grid, a system that he later extended to earthly locations in other books. Ptolemy's system of a 360-degree globe, further divided into minutes and seconds, could also be applied to earthly locations—what is known at present as latitude and longitude. This system of location was later used in his book *Geographia*. The *Almagest* was the standard scholarly text on astronomy until the 16th century in Europe. Ptolemy's geocentric universe was accepted by European and Arab astronomers for more than 1,000 years after his death, until it was replaced by the heliocentric system devised by Copernicus.

Alexandria remained the center of Greek astronomy, philosophy, and mathematics after the time of Ptolemy. Writers created commentaries on the works of past astronomers and helped preserve their theories. Theon of Alexandria (ca.

335–ca. 405 C.E.) wrote commentaries on Ptolemy's *Almagest* and was the father of Hypatia, the first well-known female mathematician. Marinus of Neapolis (ca. 450–ca. 500 C.E.) speculated on the nature of the Milky Way, arguing that it could not be a collection of very faint stars, a theory that dated back to the fifth century B.C.E.

ROME

BY JOHN M. MCMAHON

Scientific astronomy did not occupy as important a position in Rome as it held in Greece, but knowledge of the heavens remained a major factor in the intellectual, social, cultural, and political life of the Roman world. Early contact with Etruscan civilization in Italy and later with Hellenistic Greek civilization in the Mediterranean influenced attitudes toward astronomy throughout the Roman period. The Romans' own practical nature, which favored applied knowledge over theoretical science, largely determined the role astronomy played. Roman writers often included astronomical subject matter in literary works, and by recording the discoveries of the Greeks, Roman technical writers ensured that scientific astronomical knowledge reached both Roman readers and those of later ages.

During their earliest history the Romans incorporated the monthly lunar cycle into a formal calendar, a concept that may have originated with the Etruscans. Made up of 10 months (March through December), it had an unnamed period of time during the winter. King Numa Pompilius (ca. 715–ca. 672 B.C.E.) added two additional months, January and February, to fill the gap. Since the annual solar cycle is not compatible with a purely lunar calendar, numerous adjustments to the Roman civil calendar were made over the centuries. Finally, in 46 B.C.E. Julius Caesar (100–44 B.C.E.), advised by the Greek astronomer Sosigenes, refashioned the Roman calendar by basing it on the sun's apparent yearly motion.

Roman farmers incorporated knowledge of the heavens into agricultural activities and relied on recurring seasonal events in the sky to indicate appropriate times for plowing, sowing, and harvesting. These times were marked by the observable annual rising or setting of specific stars and constellations, which were noted on a *parapegma*, or "star calendar." Cato the Elder (234–149 B.C.E.) refers to such information in his *De agri cultura* (*On Agriculture*). The writings of later authors on farming practices, such as Varro (ca. 40 B.C.E.) and Columella (ca. 60 C.E.), reveal the transition from the use of astronomical information to the Julian civil calendar.

In the Roman world at large other practical applications of astronomical information were common. Seafaring and navigation, a major component of trade and commerce, necessarily depended on astronomical principles and a familiarity with the starry sky. Among a variety of astronomically oriented instruments developed by Greek science during the Roman period, such as the astrolabe (a two-dimensional working model of the heavens) and the celestial globe, sundials were by far the most commonly used. These instruments came in a wide range of sizes and applications, both public and private. Surviving examples of the latter indicate that some were even designed for use as portable personal timepieces. Public sundials were also set up, the most famous being the enormous Horologium Augusti of the emperor Augustus in Rome's Campus Martius, which served as a political as well as calendrical monument.

During a period of close cultural assimilation in the seventh and sixth centuries B.C.E. the Romans adopted from the Etruscans the practice of observing the heavens to ascertain the will of the divinities, to interpret past events, and to predict future ones. In accordance with carefully prescribed rules, the visible sky was divided into specific regions to determine what celestial occurrences might mean for human affairs. Such traditional practices became an essential part of Roman religious and civic custom. The tendency to recognize in the movements of the heavenly bodies an influence on people's lives became common in the Roman world with the spread from the East of the pseudoscience of astrology. Manilius (early first century C.E.) composed an entire didactic poem (a poem meant to instruct the reader) on astrology called *Astronomica* (Astronomical Matters), and many leading figures were believers in the efficacy of astrology.

From the third through first centuries B.C.E. the Romans were increasingly exposed to a more purely scientific approach to astronomy through their expansion into the Greek cultural sphere. This contact occurred first in southern Italy and Sicily and subsequently on mainland Greece and in Asia Minor, long the home of thriving centers of learning. An important Roman from this period was Sulpicius Gallus, who wrote a work on astronomy based on Greek sources. His scientific knowledge of mathematical astronomy was such that, as an officer in the Roman army in 168 B.C.E., he predicted a lunar eclipse before the battle of Pydna.

Intercultural contact with the Greek world also introduced to the growing Roman intellectual class those philosophical and literary elements associated with knowledge of the heavens. The foremost example of this process was the *Phaenomena* (Appearances) by Aratus (ca. 315–240 B.C.E.), a lengthy didactic poem based on the earlier work of the astronomer Eudoxus (ca. 400–ca. 350 B.C.E.). Combining astronomical subject matter with Stoic philosophy, Aratus proposed that the orderliness of the heavens was evidence of divine intent in the universe. The *Phaenomena* became very popular throughout antiquity and greatly influenced a number of Roman authors, including Cicero (106–43 B.C.E.) and Ovid (43 B.C.E.–17 C.E.), both of whom wrote Latin versions of the poem. On the other hand, the Roman poet Lucretius (ca. 94–55 B.C.E.) enlisted astronomy in support of Epicurean philosophy, which he expounded in his work *De rerum natura* (*On the Nature of Things*).

The Latin literary tradition also includes astronomical material, with Roman writers adapting it to their own cultural and social contexts. The poet Virgil (70–19 B.C.E.) bases parts of his *Georgics* on the Greek agricultural poem *Works and Days* of Hesiod (late eighth century B.C.E.), a major source for early Greek observational astronomy. Political elements appear in the *Georgics* as well. For example, Virgil suggests that the origin of the constellation Libra derives from cosmic support for the emperor Augustus. Ovid, too, incorporates into his epic *Metamorphoses* elements from the account of the beginnings of the universe in Hesiod's *Theogony*. A number of tales in Ovid's works also recount instances of catasterism, the transformation of a mortal into a star, constellation, or other celestial object. This concept was not restricted to myths, for at the very end of the *Metamorphoses*, Ovid describes the ascent of Julius Caesar's spirit as a comet, known as the Sidus Iulium ("Julian Star"). Ovid also wrote in praise of astronomers in his *Fasti* (Festivals), a poem explaining the myths associated with the traditional Roman calendar.

Popular handbooks of astronomy appear during the Roman period. While many were in Greek, such as that of Geminus (ca. 110–40 B.C.E.), the *De astronomia* (Concerning Astronomy) of Hyginus (early first century C.E.) was an important Latin work. In addition to outlining the basics of astronomy, the author retells from Greek sources the myths related to the constellations. Vitruvius (late first century B.C.E.) includes an account of the heavens in his work on architecture. Another important figure was Pliny the Elder (24–79 C.E.), whose second book of the *Naturalis historia* (*Natural History*), preserved for later ages valuable information about the scientific astronomy of the day.

THE AMERICAS

BY J. J. GEORGE

Most ancient American cultures paid attention to what was happening in the sky. The periodic cycles of the sun, moon, stars, and planets, being reliable and predictable, allowed for the development of the calendar. Broadly speaking, astronomy was one area that contributed to a greater Mesoamerican cosmology, and subsequent uses helped define and order such areas as agriculture, site orientation, astrology, myth, shamanism, divination, and even warfare. Our best astronomical data come from successful early agricultural cultures in Mesoamerica—the Olmec of the Gulf Coast of Mexico (1500–400 B.C.E.), the Zapotec of the Valley of Oaxaca at Monte Albán (600 B.C.E.–900 C.E.), and the inhabitants just outside the Basin of Mexico at Teotihuacán (1 B.C.E.–650 C.E.). The Classic Period Maya (200–900 C.E.), building upon earlier Mesoamerican thought, established the clearest astronomical record. Astronomy in the ancient period focused on horizon and zenith events of the rising and setting sun, moon, planet Venus, and star cluster Pleiades and on the sacred four cardinal directions.

The beginnings of the Mesoamerican calendar signified the first concrete astronomical achievement. A carved stela, or upright stone, from La Mojarra on Mexico's Gulf Coast (150 C.E.), exhibits in hieroglyphic form the beginnings of a solar 365-day calendar. When used in tandem with a unique 260-day sacred calendar (called the Tzolkin), like a system of interlocking cogwheels, this stela established everything in the Mesoamerican world, from agricultural rites to ritual and religious ceremonies to feasts and the inauguration of New Year. This stela also records a hieroglyph for Venus as well as a date that correlates with a visible solar eclipse. The Mayans later developed an extraordinarily accurate Venus table as well as an eclipse table that accurately predicted the occurrence of those celestial events.

Mesoamerican site orientation, the layout of a particular ritual site or city across the landscape, often had astronomical significance. For example, a structure referred to as Building J at Monte Albán strongly suggests an astronomical relationship. Building J is unique in that it is roughly pentagonal (with a "pointer" side and a stairway side) and set considerably askew (nearly 45 degrees) from the general site orientation. Recent research suggests that Building J aligns with another building (Building P) to form a sightline that extends to the horizon point where the rising star Capella announces the solar zenith passage.

Similarly, Building J aligns with a neighboring site, Caballito Blanco, which has a similar skewed building. A straight line between the two coincides with the sunset position on the horizon on the day of the solar zenith passage, when at local noon the sun is directly overhead and casts no shadow of perfectly vertical structures. In the opposite direction the line marks the sunrise azimuth on the morning after the antizenith (nadir) passage, when the sun is directly below at local midnight. It has been suggested that Building J was a calendar temple, a structure that embodied numerology and astronomy and permitted Mesoamericans to create their interlocking calendars.

By 550 C.E. Teotihuacán, northeast of modern-day Mexico City, was the sixth-largest city on the planet, with an estimated population between 125,000 and 250,000. The Aztecs later called Teotihuacán the place where time began and centered their origin myths there. Astronomical alignments were used at Teotihuacán for overall site orientation and to orient more specific dates related to agriculture and the sacred calendar. The overall orientation of its grid pattern falls within what is often referred to as the 17-degree family of orientations, a group of orientations widely distributed throughout Mesoamerican sites with axes typically 15 to 18 degrees clockwise from the cardinal directions.

Punctuating the grid of Teotihuacán is a large, flat-topped pyramid called the Pyramid of the Sun (a second pyramid on the site is called the Pyramid of the Moon; both names are attributed to the later Aztec) and a ceremonial structure called the Ciudadela, both skewed approximately 15.5 degrees and

16.5 degrees clockwise from the cardinal directions, lining up with certain mountain peaks that could have been used as natural markers of sunrises and sunsets on significant dates. These dates were necessary for predicting important seasonal changes and for efficiently scheduling corresponding agricultural activity. For example, in the first century C.E. these alignments would have recorded sunrises on February 11 and October 29 and sunsets on April 30 and August 13. The intervals from February 11 to October 29 and from August 13 to April 30 are exactly 260 days, again coinciding with the 260-day sacred calendar. The 260-day period is also tied to the human gestation period, the time from the first missed menstrual flow to birth, thereby connecting the functional aspect of the calendar to the birth cycle as well as to agriculture, ritual, and urban planning.

The astronomical record for North and South America in the ancient period suffers from a lack of hard data. Data for later periods are much more convincing. Some evidence does suggest, however, that ancient North American mound builders used the star group Pleiades as a celestial template for particular clusters of conical mounds in the Midwest, such as burial mounds and earthworks at Poverty Point, Louisiana (1600–1300 B.C.E.); Adena burial mounds in Ohio, Kentucky, and West Virginia (1000 B.C.E.–200 C.E.); and Hopewell mounds in southern Ohio (200 B.C.E.–400 C.E.). The Pleiades were important, especially in northeastern North American latitudes, because their horizon cycle corresponds to the limits of the frost-free zone and thus helped define the growing season once agriculture became common.

The medicine wheels left by the nomadic Indians of the Great Plains are thought to have astronomical significance, though the exact use is unclear. Medicine wheels are enigmatic large patterns of linear stone alignments, many of which have the appearance of a spoked wheel. Often the spokes, or rays, point to the horizon and mark points of the summer solstice sunrise, the winter solstice sunrise, or the rise of the star Sirius. Various examined sites, such as those at Majorville in Alberta, Canada, and Moose Mountain in Saskatchewan, show evidence of use dating back to 2500 B.C. Many of the medicine wheels are thought to exist from later periods.

In South America a clearer data record exists for the Inca (1438–1534 C.E.) than it does for earlier cultures, such as those at Chavín de Huántar (900–200 B.C.E.), Paracas (600–175 B.C.E.), and Nazca (1–700 C.E.). The most suggestive early astronomical possibility comes from the Nazca culture, which created the Nazca Lines with some possible astronomical significance in mind. Shaman imagery on textiles from the Paracas culture suggests at least an affinity for connecting the earth and the heavens through visual iconography, or symbolism. Architectural remains at Chavín de Huántar show a solar east-west axis that conflates architecture, human ritual, and cosmological associations. A corresponding north-south axis is suspected, thereby symbolizing all four cardinal directions. More research needs to be undertaken to establish a clearer record for the relationship of astronomy to these sites.

See also AGRICULTURE; ARCHITECTURE; CALENDARS AND CLOCKS; CITIES; CLIMATE AND GEOGRAPHY; DEATH AND BURIAL PRACTICES; HUNTING, FISHING, AND GATHERING; INVENTIONS; LITERATURE; NUMBERS AND COUNTING; RELIGION AND COSMOLOGY; SACRED SITES; SCIENCE; SEAFARING AND NAVIGATION; WEIGHTS AND MEASURES; WRITING.

THE NAZCA LINES

First located in the 1920s from aerial reconnaissance, the Nazca Lines have prompted debate, speculation, and confusion over what exactly they represent. Created by the Nazca culture (1–700 C.E.) across a 130-square-mile swath of desert tableland on the central Peruvian coast, the lines are made by displacing dark stones from atop lighter ones. Created over many hundreds of years, the more than 1,000 miles of lines consist of overlapping, radiating lines and trapezoids and immense figures of animals, humans, plants, and objects (including a monkey, a dog, a killer whale, lizards, birds, a tuber, geometric figures, and even a fantastic figure often referred to as the Martian). The span of a hummingbird image is greater than the length of five jumbo jets. One line goes perfectly straight for 13 miles.

Theories have linked the lines to pilgrimages, water rituals, astronomical alignment, ceremonial walkways, and religious activity tied to ensuring a good harvest. Modeling the lines with the aid of computerized mapping in reference to celestial positioning has shown that twice as many astronomical alignments show up than would be expected from pure chance. Furthermore, prominent archaeoastronomists (scholars who combine astronomy and archaeology to study ancient civilizations) have used computer analysis to show that many lines point to the sun's position on the horizon during the time of year when the rains begin.

The immensity of the lines prevents them from being viewable on the ground, automatically orienting them to the celestial world above, where a shaman, or holy man, in bird form might have been the intended audience. Although their overall meaning is still debated, most theories involve the idea of repeated ritual action. Where some of the rituals are tied to water and thus to agriculture and seasons, simply by raising one's head one connects the lines at one's feet to the horizon and eventually to the rising sun and stars.

The Middle East

"The Reports of the Magicians and Astrologers of Nineveh and Babylon," excerpts, ca. 2500–670 B.C.E.

II. Omens from the Horns of the Moon

When the Moon's horns face equally, there will be a secure dwelling for the land. When at the Moon's appearance [its horns] are pointed, the king. wherever his face is set. will rule the land (or) wherever he presses on will overcome. From Irasshi-ilu, the king's servant, the greater.

When at the Moon's appearance its right horn is long and its left horn is short, the king's hand will conquer a land other than this. When the Moon at its appearance is very large, an eclipse will take place. When the Moon at its appearance is very bright, the crops of the land will prosper. When the day is long according to its calculation, there will be a long reign. The thirtieth day completed the month. In Elul an eclipse of Elam. From Nergal-etir. . . .

V. Various Omens from the Moon

When the Moon disappears, evil will befall the land. When the Moon disappears out of its reckoning, an eclipse will take place. (The Moon disappeared on the twenty-fourth day.) When a halo surrounds the Sun on the day of the Moon's disappearance, an eclipse of the left side of the Moon will take place.

In Kislev a watch was kept for the eclipse, the halo surrounding the Sun and the disappearance of the Moon (being the causes of the watch for an eclipse in Kislev) having been observed. May the king, my lord, know, and may he rest happy! From Irasshi-ilu, the king's servant (the greater).

VI. Omens from Halos

Last night a halo surrounded the Moon, and Jupiter and Scorpio stood within it. When a halo surrounds the Moon and Jupiter stands within it, the King of Akkad will be besieged. When a halo surrounds the Moon and Jupiter stands within it, there will be a slaughter of cattle and beasts of the field. (Marduk is Umunpauddu at its appearance; when it has risen for two (or four?) hours it becomes Sagmigar; when it stands in the meridian it becomes Nibiru.) When a halo surrounds the Moon and Scorpio stands in it, it will cause men to marry princesses (or) lions will die, and the traffic of the land will be hindered. From Nabu-mushesi.

When a halo surrounds the Moon, and Regulus stands within it, women will bear male children. From Nergal-etir. . . .

When the greater halo surrounds the Moon, that land will be enlarged, destructions will surround men. When it surrounds and Cancer stands within it, the King of Akkad will prolong life. When Regulus stands within it, women will bear male children. When the greater halo surrounds the moon and is thin, there will be a giving of years to the king. (A great halo has surrounded it and has remained for many nights and is uninterrupted.) From Shapiku, of Borsippa. . . .

IX. Omens from Stars

. . . . Venus is appearing at sunset in the Tropic of Cancer: this is its interpretation. When Venus appears in Sivar, there will be a slaughter of the enemy. When Venus appears in the Tropic of Cancer, the King of Akkad will have no rival. Five or Six days ago it reached Cancer. This is its interpretation. When Venus approaches Cancer there will be obedience and welfare in the land: the gods will have mercy on the land. . . . The crops of the land will prosper; the sick in the land will recover. Pregnant women will perfect their offspring. The great gods will show favor to the sanctuaries of the land, the houses of the great gods will be renewed. From Shumai. . . .

Mercury is visible with Mars at sunset; it is ascending to Shugi. There will be rains and floods. When Jupiter appears at the beginning of the year, in that year its crops will prosper. From Nadinu.

XV. Omens from Eclipses

On the fourteenth an eclipse will take place. It is evil for Elam and Aharru, lucky for the king, my lord; let the king, my lord, rest happy. It will be seen without Venus; to the king, my lord, I say, "There will be an eclipse." From Irasshi-ilu, the servant of the king (the greater).

To the king of countries, my lord, thy servant, Bel-usur. May Bel, Nabu, and Shamash be gracious to the king, my lord! An eclipse has happened, but it was not visible in Asshur; this eclipse passed the city

(continued)

(continues)

Asshur, wherein the king is dwelling; now there are clouds everywhere, so that whether it did or did not happen we do not know. Let the lord of kings send to Asshur, to all cities, to Babylon, Nippur, Erech, and Borsippa; whatever has been seen in those cities the king will hear for certain. . . . The omen for an eclipse happened in Adar and Nisan; I send all to the king, my lord, and they shall make . . . ceremony for the eclipse. Without fail let not the king omit to act rightly. The great gods in the city wherein the king dwells have obscured the heaven and will not show the eclipse; so let the king know that this eclipse is not directed against the king, my lord, or his country. Let the king rejoice!

From: R. Campbell Thompson, "The Reports of the Magicians and Astrologers of Nineveh and Babylon." In *Assyrian and Babylonian Literature: Selected Transactions, with a Critical Introduction,* by Robert Francis Harper (New York: D. Appleton and Company, 1904), pp. 451–460.

Greece

Ptolemy: Tetrabiblos, *excerpt, second century* C.E.

Book I

4. Of the Power of the Planets

The active power of the sun's essential nature is found to be heating and, to a certain degree, drying. This is made more easily perceptible in the case of the sun than any other heavenly body by its size and by the obviousness of its seasonal changes, for the closer it approaches to the zenith, the more it affects us in this way. Most of the moon's power consists of humidifying, clearly because it is close to the earth and because of the moist exhalations therefrom. Its action therefore is precisely this, to soften and cause putrefaction in bodies for the most part, but it shares moderately also in heating power because of the light which it receives from the sun.

It is Saturn's quality chiefly to cool and, moderately, to dry, probably because he is furthest removed both from the sun's heat and the moist exhalations about the earth. Both in Saturn's case and in that of the other planets there are powers, too, which arise through the observation of their aspects to the sun and moon, for some of them appear to modify conditions in the ambient in one way, some in another, by increase or by decrease.

The nature of Mars is chiefly to dry and to burn, in conformity with his fiery color and by reason of his nearness to the sun, for the sun's sphere lies just below him.

Jupiter has a temperate active force because his movement takes place between the cooling influence of Saturn and the burning power of Mars. He both heats and humidifies; and because his heating power is the greater by reason of the underlying spheres, he produces fertilizing winds.

Venus has the same powers and tempered nature as Jupiter, but acts in the opposite way; for she warms moderately because of her nearness to the sun, but chiefly humidifies, like the moon, because of the amount of her own light and because she appropriates the exhalations from the moist atmosphere surrounding the earth.

Mercury in general is found at certain times alike to be drying and absorptive of moisture, because he never is far removed in longitude from the heat of the sun; and again humidifying, because he is next above the sphere of the moon, which is closest to the earth; and to change quickly from one to the other, inspired as it were by the speed of his motion in the neighborhood of the sun itself. . . .

8. Of the Power of the Aspects to the Sun

Now, mark you, likewise, according to their aspects to the sun, the moon and three of the planets experience increase and decrease in their own powers. For in its waxing from new moon to first quarter, the moon is more productive of moisture; in its passage from first quarter to full, of heat; from full to last quarter, of dryness; and from last quarter to occultation, of cold. The planets, in oriental aspects only, are more productive of moisture from rising to their first station, of heat from first station to evening rising, of dryness from evening rising to the second station, of cold from second station to setting; it is clear that when they are associated with one another they produce very many variations of quality in our ambient, the proper force of each one for the most part persisting but being changed in quantity by the force of the stars that share the configuration.

From: Ptolemy, *Tetrabiblos*, translated by Frank Egleston Robbins (Boston: Harvard University Press, 1940).

Rome

Petronius: "The Banquet of Trimalchio," extract from The Satyricon, *60* C.E.

Our applause was interrupted by the second course, which did not by any means come up to our expectations. Still, the oddity of the thing drew the eyes of all. An immense circular tray bore the twelve signs of the zodiac displayed round the circumference, on each of which the Manoiple, or Arranger, had placed a dish of suitable and appropriate viands: on the Ram ram's-head peas, on the Bull a piece of beef, on the Twins fried testicles and kidneys, on the Crab simply a crown, on the Lion African figs, on a Virgin a sow's haslet, on Libra a balance with a tart in one scale and a cheesecake in the other, on Scorpio a small sea-fish, on Sagittarius an eye-seeker, on Capricornus a lobster, on Aquarius a wild goose, on Pisces two mullets. In the middle was a sod of green turf, cut to shape and supporting a honeycomb. Meanwhile an Egyptian slave was carrying bread around in a miniature oven of silver, crooning to himself in a horrible voice a song on wine and laserpitium. . . . Seeing us look rather blank at the idea of attacking such common fare, Trimalchio cried, "I pray you gentlemen, begin; the best of your dinner is before you." . . .

The second course had now been removed, and the company being merry with wine began to engage in general conversation. Our host then, lying back on his elbow and addressing the company, said, "I hope you will all do justice to this wine; you must make the fish swim again. Come, come, do you suppose I was going to rest content with the dinner you saw boxed up under the cover of the tray just now? 'Is Ulysses no better known?' Well, well! even at table we mustn't forget our scholarship. Peace to my worthy patron's bones, who was pleased to make me a man amongst men. For truly there is nothing can be set before me that will nonplus me by its novelty. For instance the meaning of that tray just now can be easily enough explained. This heaven in which dwell the twelve gods resolves itself into twelve different configurations, and presently becomes the Ram. So whosoever is born under this sign has many flocks and herds and much wool, a hard head into the bargain, a shameless brow and a sharp horn. Most of your schoolmen and pettifoggers are born under this sign."

We recommended the learned expounder's graceful erudition, and he went on to add: "Next the whole sky becomes Bull; then are born obstinate fellows and neatherds and such as think of nothing but filling their own bellies. Under the Twins are born horses in a pair, oxen in a yoke, men blessed with a sturdy brace of testicles, all who manage to keep in with both sides. I was born under the Crab myself. Wherefore I stand on many feet and have many possessions both by sea and land, for the Crab is equally adapted to either element. And this is why I never put anything on that sign, so as not to eclipse my horoscope. Under the Lion are born great eaters and wasters, and all who love to domineer; under the Virgin, women and runaways and jailbirds; under the Scales, butchers and perfumers and all retail traders; under the Scorpion, poisoners and cutthroats; under the Archer, squint-eyed folks, who look at the greens and whip off with the bacon; under Capricorn, the 'horny-handed sons of toil'; under Aquarius or the Waterman, innkeepers and pumpkin-heads; under Pisces, or the Fishes, fine cooks and fine talkers. Thus the world goes round like a mill, and is for ever at some mischief, whether making men or marring them. But about the sod of turf you see in the middle, and the honeycomb a-top of it, I have a good reason to show too. Our mother Earth is in the middle, round-about like an egg, and has all good things in her inside, like a honeycomb!"

From: Petronius, *The Satyricon*, translated by Alfred R. Allinson (New York: Panurge Press, 1930).

FURTHER READING

Anthony F. Aveni, *Ancient Astronomers* (Montreal: St. Remy Press, 1993).

Anthony F. Aveni, *Stairways to the Stars: Skywatching in Three Great Ancient Cultures* (New York: Wiley, 1997).

Anthony F. Aveni, *Skywatchers of Ancient Mexico*, 2nd ed. (Austin: University of Texas Press, 2001).

Anthony F. Aveni, *Empires of Time: Calendars, Clocks, and Cultures*, rev. ed. (Boulder.: University Press of Colorado, 2002).

Arthur Berry, *A Short History of Astronomy: From Earliest Times through the Nineteenth Century*, rpt. ed. (New York: Dover Publications, 1961).

Marshall Clagett, *Ancient Egyptian Science: A Source Book*. Vol. 2: *Calendars, Clocks, and Astronomy* (Philadelphia: American Philosophical Society, 1995).

Theony Condos, *Star Myths of the Greeks and Romans: A Sourcebook* (Grand Rapids, Mich.: Phanes Press, 1997).

James Cornell, *The First Stargazers: An Introduction to the Origins of Astronomy* (New York: Scribner, 1981).

Kevin Cuff, *African Skies* (Berkeley: Lawrence Hall of Science Holt Planetarium, University of California, Berkeley, 1997).

David Ewing Duncan, *Calendar: Humanity's Epic Struggle to Determine a True and Accurate Year* (New York: Avon, 1998).

James Evans, *The History and Practice of Ancient Astronomy* (New York: Oxford University Press, 1998).

Thomas L. Heath, *Greek Astronomy*, rpt. (Mineola, N.Y.: Dover Publications, 1991).

Michael Hoskin, ed., *The Cambridge Illustrated History of Astronomy* (Cambridge, U.K.: Cambridge University Press, 1996).

Wayne Horowitz, *Mesopotamian Cosmic Geography*. Mesopotamian Civilizations 8 (Winona Lake, Ind.: Eisenbrauns, 1998).

Hermann Hunger and David Pingree, *Astral Sciences in Mesopotamia* (Leiden, Netherlands: Brill, 1999).

David H. Kelly and Eugene F. Milone, *Exploring Ancient Skies: An Encyclopedic Survey of Archaeoastronomy* (New York: Springer, 2005).

Ulla Koch-Westenholz, *Mesopotamian Astrology: An Introduction to Babylonian and Assyrian Celestial Divination*. CNI Publications 19. (Copenhagen: Museum Tusculanum Press, 1995).

Edwin C. Krupp, ed., *In Search of Ancient Astronomies* (Garden City, N.Y.: Doubleday, 1977).

Otto Neugebauer and Richard A. Parker, *Egyptian Astronomical Texts* (Providence, R.I.: Brown University Press, 1960–1969).

Erica Reiner, *Astral Magic in Babylonia* (Philadelphia: American Philosophical Society, 1995).

Francesca Rochberg, *The Heavenly Writing: Divination, Horoscopy, and Astronomy in Mesopotamian Culture* (Cambridge, U.K.: Cambridge University Press, 2004).

Clive Ruggles, *Ancient Astronomy: An Encyclopedia of Cosmologies and Myth* (Santa Barbara, Calif.: ABC-CLIO, 2005).

Helaine Selin and Sun Xiaochun, eds., *Astronomy across Cultures: The History of Non-Western Astronomy* (Dordrecht, Netherlands: Kluwer, 2000).

Ivan Sprajc, "Astronomical Alignments at Teotihuacán, Mexico," *Latin American Antiquity* 11, no. 4 (2000): 403–415.

Christopher Walker, ed., *Astronomy before the Telescope* (London: British Museum Press, 1996).

Ray A. Williamson, ed., *Archaeoastronomy in the Americas* (Los Altos, Calif.: Ballena Press, 1981).

B

► borders and frontiers

INTRODUCTION

At first, people may have had no concept of borders anywhere in the world. The world's human population was so small and the available land so big that peoples of different cultures could settle among each other with so much space between them that they did not care that the others were there. Even when cities began and central governments formed, it was possible that people would know they were no longer on their native land only when they bumped into settlements of people belonging to another culture.

As human populations expanded, controlling food supplies became important. It is possible that the first borders were just boundaries between farms, perhaps marked by stones. With the beginning of large public works projects, such as irrigation canals, groups of people formed a mutual interest in protecting what they built and the lands on which they all worked. Territory that remained wild became frontiers between communities but lacked defined borders.

Perhaps the first borders formed around trade routes. That trade routes could define a frontier was common in the ancient world. Control of trade routes could bring in wealth in the form of tariffs charged to traders and could stimulate a local economy through trade with other peoples. Building forts on trade routes and ignoring much of the rest of the land was also common in ancient times. The fortifications on borders suggest that the borders were intended to keep people out; this, in turn, suggests that borders originally were reactions to warfare and invasion.

Probably more than any other ancient culture, the Romans were concerned about borders. In most of the world people defended towns or cities, but the Romans developed the idea of defending borders that were far from cities and trade routes. In so doing, they could hope to prevent enemies from reaching their cities. The emperor Augustus (r. 27 B.C.E.–14 C.E.) tried to establish clear borders that cartographers could map, using natural barriers such as rivers.

Many cultures used natural barriers such as rivers, mountain ranges, and deserts for borders. These were not perfect, because enemies could cross rivers, scale mountains, and endure thirst, but a river crossing could be defended, and mountains and deserts could kill would-be invaders. Even so, these natural barriers required watching, and people crossing them would be considered outsiders and potential threats. Sometimes natural barriers were unavailable or there were not enough to mark clearly defined, defensible borders. Thus, marking borders with fortresses was often done. For example, the Great Wall of China was a long fortification that defined China's northern border and helped protect the Silk Road, a major trade route.

Much of the world still had ill-defined borders when the Western Roman Empire fell. In much of Africa the idea of borders took root only when Europeans arrived during the Renaissance era. In China the northern border was defined by the Great Wall and a vast desert, but the southern border was vague, because of dense forests and native populations that resisted China's rule. In the ancient Americas territory between the frontiers of cities was often claimed by no one. Thus, creating borders was not a universal desire among ancient peoples. Instead, borders may have developed out of a desire to protect territory where natural resources were too scarce to be shared, to protect trade routes, or to protect a nation's wealth and population from raiders.

AFRICA

BY JUSTIN CORFIELD

The borders and frontiers of many of the civilizations in Africa were ill defined until the colonial period, and even then discrepancies between treaties often occurred. In terms of North Africa, the Egyptians, the Numidians, the Carthaginians, and subsequently the Romans were able to establish frontiers to their lands largely with small garrisons in isolated oases astride trade routes. Tariffs were generally collected on entry into a particular city rather than across any given frontier. Some writers of the ancient world speak of a borderless world—"one world"—especially in relation to the period of Alexander the Great (336–323 B.C.E.) and again for the Roman Empire.

Until the emergence of larger kingdoms, most of society was organized into states centered on cities or towns, with their surrounding hinterland supplying produce to them. Most of these larger settlements were located in rich, arable areas. A few others appear to be located on land trade routes. Certainly two of the routes across the Sahara appear to terminate in the ports of Lixus (modern-day Larache, Morocco) and Oea (modern-day Tripoli, Libya). The former is set in good agricultural land, but the latter had little arable hinterland, though even this might have been enough for Carthaginian farmers, using slave labor, to construct aqueducts.

During the ancient period the dual system of land tenure arose, which existed in much of North Africa until the establishment of the European colonial empires in the 19th century. Essentially the boundaries of cities were clearly defined, often by walls or fortifications, and land within them was available for purchase or rent with a system of land tenure not too different from that operating in many of those countries today. However, in the countryside, even though the land occupied by an individual farm might be defined, with no accurate cadastral service, that is, a register of ownership of land, the fullest extent of any kingdom or empire tended to be defined in terms of the presence of army garrisons placed in particular far-flung small settlements to ensure the easy collection of taxes and the maintenance of law and order. As a result, the areas that paid taxes to a particular ruler were within his borders, often leaving the southern boundaries of Carthage, Numidia, and Roman North Africa ill defined.

Gradually, the Egyptian Empire and the empires of Carthage and subsequently Rome tended to fix boundaries of provinces and install provincial governors who were in charge of dispensing justice as well as collecting taxes within their area of authority. To achieve this objective, provinces, and hence borders, had to be more clearly defined than they had hitherto been. Most literature exists for the Romans, who certainly built forts in the desert in Tripolitania (modern-day western Libya). In addition, there also seem to have been large numbers of fortified farmhouses, probably occupied by *limitanei* (soldier-farmers).

Although the Romans originally took over and absorbed the lands of the Carthaginians, maintaining Mauretania as a client state, in 42 C.E. they annexed Mauretania, and within two years it was divided into the two provinces Mauretania Tingitana and Mauretania Caesariensis. During the first century there was significant Italian migration to Mauretania, leading to more lands being opened to agriculture and the borders of the existing chieftains being more closely delineated. In the 210s, during the reign of Septimus Severus, the only African-born emperor of Rome, there was a reduction in trade throughout the whole Roman Empire and consequently an economic slump in North Africa, which saw the reduction of Roman influence over the more distant Saharan outposts. However, during the later periods of the Roman Empire maps tended to show more details connected with the East African coast, including coverage as far south as Cape Delgado, south of Zanzibar, possibly on account of traders returning with new information.

The descriptions of the different tribes in North Africa noted by the fifth century B.C.E. Greek historian Herodotus show that society was organized by clan groups following different customs but that there was clearly no physical barrier from one community to another. Indeed, rather than groups being divided by rivers, many tribes were located astride them. The problem was further exacerbated by the nomadic tribes that operated in the Sahara and in parts of central and southern Africa. Because the area was very sparsely populated, for the most part the borders of one area were to remain undefined until recent times, when primarily European cartographers took an interest in Africa.

However, in some areas the frontiers of particular groups can be clearly ascertained. Work by the anthropologist Patrick Munson in Sudan has shown that farmers in the Tichit-Walata part of the Sudan from 1000 B.C.E. had tended to congregate in fortified cliff-top villages, clearly showing that protection from attack was more important than access to fertile arable land. The settlement of Tin Hinan in the Hoggar, nearly 1,000 miles south of Algiers, excavated in 1926 and again seven years later, showed the importance of fortifications there to protect the local people from marauders during the first century B.C.E.

On the east coast of Africa, at Port Durnford (in modern-day South Africa), in 1912 a fortress was discovered that enclosed five acres, obviously showing the need of the people there to be able to withstand a substantial siege. Inland, even before the massive stone buildings of Great Zimbabwe were constructed in the ninth century C.E., there were smaller efforts to centralize power. These kingdoms were probably defined by the areas from where tax revenue, often the form of cattle, was raised and where men were available for conscription.

At Jenne-jeno, in what was then known as Ghana but is now modern-day Mali, remains of a large settlement (covering 60 acres by 450 C.E.) has been excavated. Houses made from mud sustained a large town on ground slightly higher than the plains that surround the site. The thin walls show that there seems to have been little danger of internal conflict. However, the entire site is surrounded by a wall that measures about 10 feet wide at the base and runs for slightly more than one mile. Although two Roman or Greek beads have been found there, it seems likely that any trade would have been through intermediaries.

EGYPT

BY MARIE PASSANANTE

The borders of ancient Egypt remained remarkably stable for such a long-lived civilization, largely because Egypt was a country defined by natural borders. It occupies the long section of fertile land lining the Nile Valley that stretches from the Mediterranean Sea in the north down to Elephantine, near modern Aswān, in the south. On the east and west the Nile Valley is adjoined by harsh deserts. The greatest fluctuations to the Egyptian borders occurred during the three Intermediate Periods, times of political upheaval that took place after the Old Kingdom (2575–2134 B.C.E.), Middle Kingdom (2040–1640 B.C.E.), and New Kingdom (1550–1070 B.C.E.). During and after these periods, Egypt was divided internally among rival Egyptian dynasties (First Intermediate Period, 2134–2040 B.C.E.), among Egyptian dynasties and a group of foreigners called the Hyksos (Second Intermediate Period, 1640–1550 B.C.E.), and among Egyptian dynasties and Libyan tribes as well as invaders from Kush in the south (Third Intermediate Period, 1070–712 B.C.E.).

The Egyptians used several terms when referring to their borders. The term *tash* was applied to a physical, politically defined border, such as the border between Egypt and Nubia in the south. *Wepet-ta* literally means "the horns of the Earth." It was applied to limits of Egyptian domination in the south. The term *khent-hen-nefer*, translating to "the frontier region of the last fortification," also referred to the southern border. It was used with reference to the region bordering Egyptian territory. This region was not officially part of Egypt but was still under Egyptian control.

The Mediterranean Sea borders Egypt on the north. Few nations attempted sea travel before 1500 B.C.E.; their ships were designed mostly for river travel and were not sturdy enough for the sea. The northern border of Egypt was relatively secure and did not need to be as heavily fortified as the south and the edges of the delta. South of Elephantine was the land of Nubia. As well as being a major source of gold and the only source of goods from Africa, Nubia was home to a potentially dangerous people who could—and did—threaten the security of the Egyptian state. From the Old Kingdom to the New Kingdom, Egypt engaged in extensive military activity directed against Nubia in order to retain control of this important area. The southern border of Egypt was set at the first cataract of the Nile, the mythical source of the Nile. Elephantine was established here as a frontier town and as a base for trading with

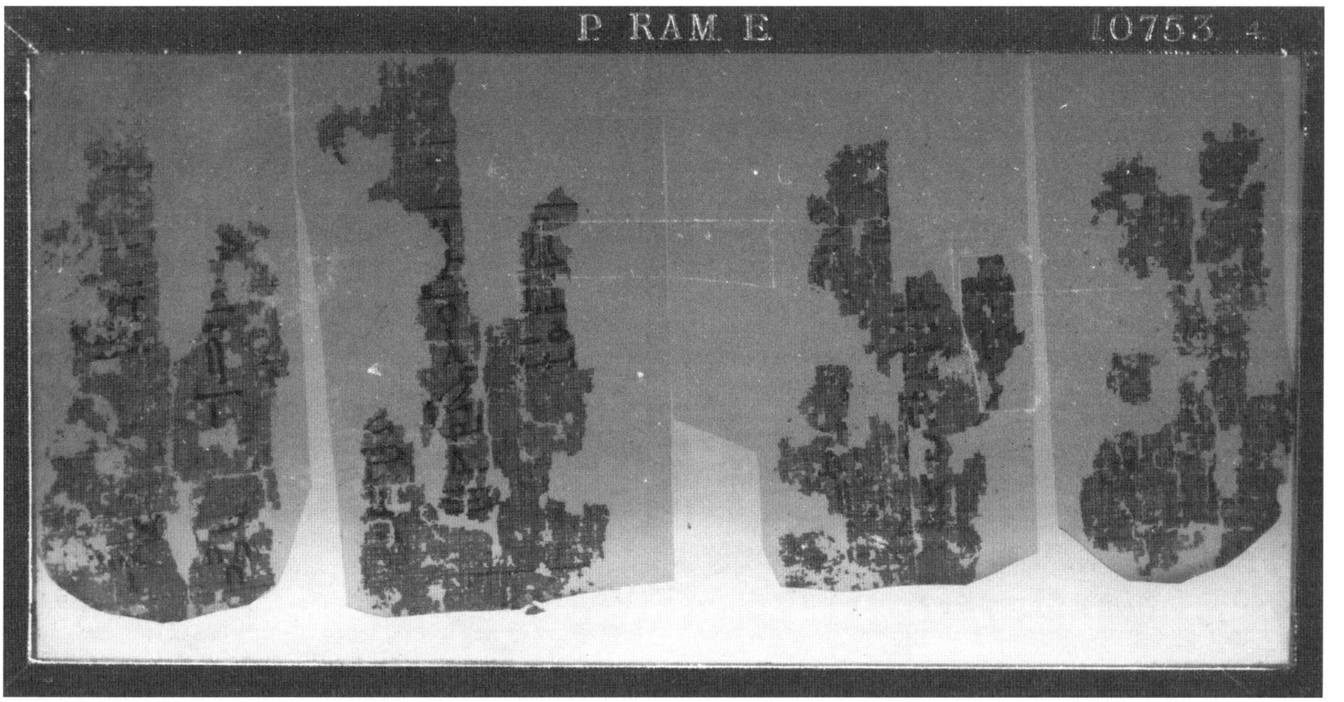

The Semna dispatches, administrative documents from an Egyptian outpost, from Thebes, Egypt, Twelfth Dynasty (© The Trustees of the British Museum)

Nubia in the Old Kingdom. Several settlements were established south of Elephantine to control the frontier, including the town at Buhen at the second cataract.

In the Middle Kingdom, two series of fortresses were built along the Nile to protect Egyptian interests in the south. The first series of forts was built to the north of the second cataract and includes the fortress at Buhen. These forts were completed by the end of the reign of Sesostris I (r. 1971–1926 B.C.E.). The second set of forts—at Semna, Kumma, Uronarti, Shelfak, and Askut—was built south of the second cataract by Sesostris III (r. 1878–1841 B.C.E.). Between Semna and Uronarti there is also a fortified brick wall almost three miles long. Sesostris III left inscriptions declaring Semna to be the border of Egyptian control. The inscriptions announced that no Nubian was allowed to pass Semna either by land or by water, with the exception of Nubian traders and envoys; Nubian traders were allowed to travel as far as Iken, just south of the second cataract. The control of the region between Elephantine and Semna was entrusted to the governor of Elephantine, who held the titles Great Controller of Nubia and Overseer of all Foreign Lands.

The kings of the New Kingdom increased the zone of influence and built forts from Semna to the fourth cataract. South of the fourth cataract, Thutmose III (r. 1479–1425 B.C.E.) built a fort at Napata and left an inscription delineating the boundary of the Egyptian Empire. The length of the Nile from Edfu, north of Elephantine, down to Karoy, the region beyond the fourth cataract, was entrusted to the leadership of the viceroy of Kush. The viceroy acted on the king's behalf in Nubia, protecting the trade routes and leading the Egyptian army against Nubian rebellions when necessary.

In the east, along the length of the Nile Valley, the desert was uninhabitable by a sedentary civilization. However, the eastern desert was populated by the nomadic Medjay, whose numbers were insufficient for a major invasion of Egypt, yet they were independent enough to be considered a minor threat. Beyond the eastern desert lies the Red Sea and the Arabian Peninsula, which is largely uninhabited. The only point in the east where Egypt was vulnerable to attack was the eastern edge of the delta, where a frontier region was recognized from the Mediterranean to the Gulf of Suez. The Middle Kingdom pharaoh Amenemhet I (r. 1991–1962 B.C.E.) built a fortress there called the Walls of the Ruler as a base for trading and mining expeditions into Sinai. The eastern delta was a heavily trafficked area, as it was the entrance point for the caravan route to Palestine. The road from Egypt to Palestine was called the Ways of Horus and was protected by a series of fortresses. In the New Kingdom, Avaris, the former capital of the Hyksos, was transformed into a military stronghold.

As in the east, the greater part of the western border was protected by an extensive desert. Also as in the east, the most vulnerable spot was at the western edge of the delta. New Kingdom Egypt saw an increase in attacks from the west. As a result, a line of fortresses was built along the edge of the delta, most likely by Ramses II (r. 1290–1224 B.C.E.). The fort marking the westernmost point of Egyptian occupation was called "The Fortress of the West."

THE MIDDLE EAST

BY KIRK H. BEETZ

During the 7000s B.C.E. nomadic peoples gradually settled in Mesopotamia and domesticated crops such as wheat and barley. Their territory was defined by two great, meandering rivers that flowed across the Near East and into the Persian Gulf, the Tigris and the Euphrates. At first the settlements were small, and there was little concept of *borders*. As settlements grew during a population boom enabled by secure farming techniques, some became city-states.

The settlements dug irrigation ditches to draw water from the rivers into farmlands; rain was rare, however, and without rain to leech out salts left from the irrigation water, lands became ever less fertile, requiring that more and more land be farmed to feed the growing population. This meant that during the Uruk Period of roughly 4300–3100 B.C.E., farmlands of different Sumerian cities began bumping into each other. By then the notion of land ownership was well established, with property owners identifying their boundaries with large stones. However, ownership of territory by a city's people was hard to establish, because there were no defensible frontiers. Further complicating the situation were nomadic tribes that would loot the food and wealth of a city or would move into a region of land and settle, creating pressure on nearby cities by competing for natural resources.

During the Early Dynastic Period of the Sumerian culture (2900–2334 B.C.E.) competition for land frequently resulted in warfare. City administrations had been run by a chief administrator, who could be overruled on city policy by a council of civic leaders that in turn could be overruled by a vote of the people. Success in war required strong leaders, and chief administrators who were notably successful gradually became kings, though their power was still tempered by the will of the voters. Cities came to define their territory as having at their core an urban land area; during the 2000s B.C.E., walls were built around these central urban areas. Around the walled city would be homes and intensively cultivated land, the outer limits of which constantly expanded. Then there was a sphere of influence that included villages protected by the central city and a frontier that was disputed by other cities.

In 2334 B.C.E. Sargon I became king of the city-state Kish, and he may have been the ruler who began the doctrine of constant territorial expansion in order to protect territory already held. Without defensible frontiers, any territory was open to invasion. To many rulers in the ancient Near East the best way to secure territory was to push the frontier out as far as possible; this created a perpetual state of conquest, because protection of newly won lands meant conquering the neighbors of those lands. To help hold together his ever-expanding kingdom, Sargon I created a cult of personality, in which he became synonymous with the city-state and claimed to be the lover of the goddess Ishtar. The kingdom he created was called Akkad, after the name for Agade, its now-lost capital city. The territory of the empire was defined primarily by trade routes, along which the Akkadian government would build fortresses to protect travelers, and it was primarily along trade routes that Akkad directed its aggression. Sargon I and his successors extended the Akkadian Empire into Anatolia and Iran, but eventually it became too big to protect, and nomads invaded along its breadth, causing the empire to collapse in 2193 B.C.E. Still, Sargon left as a legacy the concept of a nation composed of many cities.

Another big step in thinking about borders and frontiers came with the Hittite Empire of about 1650–1205 B.C.E. The Hittites settled in Anatolia in about 2000 B.C.E. and established Hatti, a nation that, like others in the Near East, had a nebulous territory determined more by cultural influence than by well-defined borders. In 1344 B.C.E. King Suppiluliuma I established discipline in its government and ordered the government's policies. In 1335 B.C.E. Egypt's pharaoh Akhenaten died, and Egypt's politics became muddled, giving Suppiluliuma the opportunity to seize lands held by Egypt in the Levant.

In 1285 B.C.E. Egypt's Ramses II tried to recover the lost Egyptian territory, and he and the Hittite ruler Muwattali II met in battle at Kadesh in Syria; both sides claimed victory, but Ramses II nearly lost his life, and the Hittites actually extended their territory southward. After that, Egypt slowly regained territory until the two sides ended their conflict in 1258 B.C.E. with a peace treaty that was recorded and copies of which still exist. In it, the nations carefully defined a border that demarcated the frontiers of each country. Although some portions of national borders were still vague as late as the Persian Empire of 559–330 B.C.E., the trend was toward defined borders and treaties that recognized where they were.

With the completion of the invasion of the Greeks under Alexander the Great in 326 B.C.E., some portions of national borders were still vague, and the creation of clearly defined borders in the Near East became a must. At Alexander's death the Near East fragmented into small states ruled by Alexander's generals. One of these generals, Seleucus I, succeeded in uniting most of the Asiatic territories Alexander had conquered into the Seleucid Kingdom (ca. 312–ca. 174 B.C.E.). One of his achievements was to create clearly defined borders among the states and between the Seleucid Kingdom and its neighbors. In about 174 B.C.E. Mithridates I of the Parthian Empire, originating in Iran, conquered most of the Seleucid Kingdom.

The Parthian Empire endured attacks on both its western and eastern frontiers, and the fighting in the east was so persistent that a clear border was difficult to maintain. In the west former Greek states had clearly defined borders left from the Seleucid Kingdom. In 100 B.C.E., western Parthia shared borders with Armenia, Edessa, and the remnant of the Seleucid Kingdom in Syria as well as smaller states, each with a well-established territory and clearly defined borders. Rome was able to pick off these states one at a time and absorb them into the empire, beginning in 101 B.C.E. with the takeover of small Cilicia in Anatolia.

Babylonian boundary marker from about 978-943 B.C.E., Sippar, southern Iraq (© The Trustees of the British Museum)

The structure of well-defined borders served Rome well. Borders enabled Rome to seize individual provinces within the Parthian Empire on the pretense that it was extending itself only to the next border to the east and no farther. Parthia played this game as well, and states in northern Mesopotamia and Syria shifted back and forth between the two countries until 273 C.E., by which time Rome had reorganized its eastern holdings into new provinces that included a chunk of the Parthian Empire north of the Euphrates River. In about 300 C.E. Constantine created the Eastern Roman Empire, known as the Byzantine Empire (ca. 300–1453 C.E.), and established its Near Eastern border with a new province called Oriens. When the western empire ended in 476 C.E., the border established by Constantine I for the eastern empire remained intact.

ASIA AND THE PACIFIC

BY MICHAEL ALLEN HOLMES

Nations and states as defined in modern terms, with explicit boundaries often demarcated by lines of latitude and longitude, did not exist in Asia and the Pacific region in ancient times. Also nonexistent was the means for making maps that could have recorded boundaries. While cartography using parallel lines running north to south and east to west was developed as early as the third century, standardized, widely distributed maps would not have been available to the masses in ancient times. In turn, borders were not necessarily viewed as fixed, and from India through Southeast Asia to China the extents of city-states and kingdoms were ever in flux.

The most immediate ancient borders, then, were fortifications surrounding towns and cities, which in northern China appeared as early as Neolithic times, over 4,000 years before the Common Era, when simple ramparts were constructed with compacted earth. Over the centuries, these walls grew higher and more expansive, indicating communities' needs to defend themselves from invaders. Within the larger states that developed, as often coinciding with geographic regions, a fief ruled locally was known as a *feng*, literally referring to its earthen boundaries. Meanwhile, stone walls were also being constructed, particularly to the north, to prevent incursions from the nomadic horsemen-warriors who were the forefathers of the Mongols and other peoples.

Modern eastern-central China, excluding Tibet, the northwest, and southern expanses, was unified in 221 B.C.E. with the rise to power of the Qin Dynasty. Accordingly, the Qin emperor Prince Zheng, who became known as Shi Huangdi, or "First Emperor," is said to have overseen construction that connected many of the northern walls to produce the Great Wall. Some historians doubt, however, that the Qin walls were seamlessly interconnected and that it makes sense to speak of a single "Great Wall" in Qin times. These walls were supplemented and rebuilt sporadically over the centuries and, including all of its various branches, came to span some 4,500 miles by the Ming Dynasty, beginning in the 14th century C.E. Its utility ultimately proved marginal, as successful invasions were eventually conducted by the northern warriors.

Aside from the historically spectacular Great Wall, borders in the ancient world were largely defined by geographical formations that more naturally provided defense and limited the transportation of both peoples and their belongings. In the region of China the Gobi Desert, consisting of formidable swaths of both sand and rock, impeded travel to the north, especially on foot, beyond the Great Wall. Similarly, the Tarim Basin, consisting largely of the Taklamakan Desert, and surrounding marshlands, restricted travel to the northwest, while to the west, the Tibetan Plateau naturally isolated its own inhabitants. Through the Qin Dynasty and into the Han Dynasty, which lasted from 206 B.C.E. to 220 C.E., armies undertook incursions into the southern forestland and jungle beyond, much of which was subject to violent monsoons, nominally extending the Chinese border to the daunting waters of the South China Sea. Since the land and its peoples were difficult to conquer, the Chinese state incorporated the region only in that the emperor declared this intention; many borders would have been defined thus in ancient times.

The only other ancient Asian kingdom rivaling China in size was India, with the two great regions separated by Tibet and the extremely high and vast Himalayas. The Himalayas extend some 200 miles from north to south and, like the Great Wall at its inception, 1,500 miles from west to east. Meanwhile, the Kirthar and Sulaiman ranges to the northwest, which merge into the Hindu Kush to the north, effectively sealed India off from mass incursions from the Middle East and Central Asia. To the south, the Western and Eastern Ghats prevented unhindered maritime access by way of either the Arabian Sea or the Bay of Bengal.

Whatever borders existed within the Indian subcontinent in ancient times are little known, inasmuch as few historical records survive from antiquity. Throughout India, apart from the mountainous margins, the countryside is mostly flat, and the majority of rivers are narrow enough to make crossings manageable. Thus, prehistoric kingdoms were established and reestablished constantly, with no specific landmarks serving as permanent borders. The disparate kingdoms centered on the Indus and Ganges river valleys were united for the first time in 324 B.C.E. by Chandragupta Maurya, who was perhaps inspired by the failed attempt at conquest of the region by Alexander the Great in 326 B.C.E. When the Maurya Dynasty ended in 185 B.C.E., borders within India returned to a state of flux for some 500 years. While Greco-Bactrian, Persian, Scythian, and various barbarian invaders breached India's natural borders throughout this period, they were typically absorbed into Indian culture and life, essentially leaving the region's outer borders intact. Northern India was again unified with the advent of the Gupta Empire in 320 C.E.

Other regional kingdoms in ancient times were smaller in scale and even more geographically isolated; consequently both the definition and defense of their borders were generally of little concern. One entity found in the third century C.E. in Southeast Asia, covering modern Cambodia and southern Vietnam, left no historical records of its own but was referred to as Funan by the Chinese; it may have been either a state or simply a collective of ports, as the thickly forested terrain would have made regional unification impractical. Southeast Asia was populated by several bronze-using civilizations, including the Khmer and Cham; other complex cultures have been discovered archaeologically and are not known to us by name. Similarly, while people are known to have used advanced sailing techniques to reach and occupy islands throughout the Pacific for millennia, the isolation of individual islands meant that significant states did not come into existence until much later in history. On the islands of modern Japan as well, while people long inhabited the more arable valleys, the abundant mountains served to inhibit interaction and cooperation among tribes. By the third century C.E. small states had come into existence, but even the largest occupied only a loosely defined portion of the southernmost Japanese island, Kyushu. The first significant Japanese court did not appear until the sixth century C.E.

EUROPE

BY KIRK H. BEETZ

Most of the territory of ancient Europe consisted of unsettled wild lands. The practice of agriculture probably came to Europe from the Near East, passing through Anatolia in modern Turkey, the Balkans, and then north and west throughout Europe, ending in southern Sweden, with all the people farther to the north remaining hunter-gatherers. By 4000 B.C.E. almost all of Europe had adopted agricultural ways. It was a period in which different cultures could mix with only rare conflicts. Thus people could move among settlements in Europe with little hindrance. This would continue to be the case until about 2500 B.C.E., but by then what is now called the megalithic culture had begun to change how Europeans regarded territory.

The culture that built the megaliths was probably the first to establish anything recognizable as a single group's territory. The word *megalith* means "large stone," and the megalithic people built huge stone monuments such as Stonehenge in England. In about 3000 B.C.E. Europeans north and west of the Alps and all the way south through Portugal began building burial chambers constructed of stones that were often 13 feet in height. These impressive burial chambers could have been built by large families or clans as ways to let other people know that they claimed the nearby territory and were showing their claim by burying their dead in a tomb that could be seen for miles.

By about 2000 B.C.E. burial chambers for only one person were being built, indicating that a tomb was honoring a leader, perhaps a chief or a priest. Other megalithic structures such as Stonehenge were being erected not only to mark burials but also for worship. These building projects involved transporting stones weighing several tons for many miles, probably by boat along the Atlantic coast of the Continent and the west coast of Britain and both coasts of Ireland. Planning and building such huge projects required the cooperation of hundreds of people over long periods and probably involved the cooperation of several villages, all part of a chiefdom that ruled over hundreds of square miles of land. Such interaction suggests recognition that one group of people could own territories consisting of many villages.

In southern and eastern Spain ca. 2340 B.C.E. people began building fortresses. Tin was mined in southern and eastern Spain, and tin was one of the two metals required for making bronze, the other being copper. Of the two metals, tin was the harder to find, and merchants from the Near East would sail all the way to Spain to trade for it. To protect their tin mines and themselves, the peoples of the region built walls and towers of stone. These structures meant that they were claiming territories for themselves.

In the 600s B.C.E. Carthage, a city on the coast of North Africa southwest of the island of Sicily, began conquering the southern coast of modern Spain. By 264 B.C.E. the Carthaginians controlled almost all of Spain's trade in tin. From 237 to 218 B.C.E. they conquered the land north, beyond the Guadalquiver River in southern Spain and along Spain's east coast to the Ebro River, displacing Celtic tribes. On the east coast in 218 B.C.E. they conquered the town of Saguntum, an ally of Rome, and this conquest started the Second Punic War (218–201 B.C.E.) between Carthage and Rome. When Rome invaded Spain, the Romans found two kinds of Celtic peoples: one still in the process of shifting from nomadic lives to living in towns and cities and the other living settled urban lives in Carthaginian territory. At the end of the war, Rome made its newly won Spanish territory into the province Hispania, using the Pyrenees mountain range as its northern border.

North of that border was Gaul, which was populated by Celts. *Celt* is the name given to the majority of Europeans by the Greeks; the Romans called them Gauls. Anyone speaking one of the Celtic languages is called a Celt (pronounced "Kelt"). The Celts originated in either central Asia or central Europe. They were a violent people ruled by warriors. Individual Celtic tribes often held ill-defined territories in which farmers worked to serve the warriors. Other tribes packed everything they owned onto large carts pulled by horses and traveled across the land. They routinely waged war against each other and raided territories for loot and slaves. In 390 B.C.E. Celts raided Italy and sacked the city of Rome. When Julius Caesar (100–44 B.C.E.) set out to conquer Gaul in 58 B.C.E., Rome already controlled portions of the region in modern-day southern France and northern Italy, with borders through the Alps and along the headwaters of several southern rivers.

In central France, Caesar found many Celts living in towns and cities made of wood, and there were some small kingdoms with ill-defined frontiers. To defy Rome, in 52 B.C.E. some of these kingdoms united under one of the kings, Vercingetorix—perhaps the first time they had thought of themselves as one people; however, they were defeated at the town of Alesia. In the north, near the Rhine River, Celtic tribes still tended to be nomadic, organizing themselves around the carts that carried their possessions when they traveled. To Caesar, the Rhine was a natural border. To the north of the river lived another ethnic group of people, the Germans. Caesar believed that the Germans were migrating into northern Europe from Asia. Some historians contend that the Germanic peoples developed within Europe, perhaps in modern-day Poland, but in general they have much in common with ancient central Asian tribes. They were territorial, and they had small realms that they called kingdoms. During Caesar's time they took control of southern Scandinavia, forming many small kingdoms. It was Caesar and Rome who introduced the concept of fixed borders to central and northern Europe.

The Germanic tribes that lived outside the Roman Empire were constantly at war with each other, and they sometimes banded together in small kingdoms for self-defense. Along the southern coast of the Baltic Sea there were several kingdoms that became fairly stable in the 500s C.E., but in the modern Ukraine they had difficulty establishing stable borders because of attacks from nomads such as the Scythians and from displaced peoples such as the Huns, who had been forced out of central Asia by the Chinese. Some Germanic tribes wanted to settle in Roman territory because behind Roman defenses they would be protected from invaders from Asia, but within the empire's borders Germanic tribes swept through Europe, looting and killing. By 395 C.E. borders in Roman Europe had lost most of their meaning and the new Germanic overlords struggled to establish clearly defined national borders. Much of the history of Europe after 476 C.E. involves almost unending wars to create and protect national frontiers.

GREECE

BY JEFFREY S. CARNES

Until the time of Alexander the Great (356–323 B.C.E.), ancient Greece was not a single political entity but was instead composed of a large number of individual city-states (poleis)—well over one thousand of them, according to the best modern estimates. As such, Greece may have had more borders than any other known civilization. These borders may be classified broadly as internal (with other Greek-speaking poleis) and external (with non-Greek civilizations).

Borders between Greek poleis were typically defined by the natural features of the landscape: rivers, mountains, and coastlines. (In addition to the numerous poleis on islands, cities in mainland Greece were often on the coast, as were virtually all of the numerous Greek colonies spread throughout the Mediterranean.) Borders between cities could also change in accord with political developments. For instance, as Athens took over the surrounding smaller communities in its region of Attica (including Piraeus, which became Athens's seaport, and the village of Marathon, site of a famous battle against the Persians in 490 B.C.E.), they were incorporated as political divisions known as *demes* rather than as independent cities, usually maintaining their former boundaries.

When it was necessary to mark borders, boundary stones known as *horoi* were used. Some still exist and are similar in size and form to the boundary markers used to delineate the space of a public place, such as the agora (marketplace) or temple precincts. As with many aspects of Greek life, boundaries had a minor religious significance: Boundary stones were under the protection of Zeus Horios, or Zeus of the Boundaries. (Such epithets were common for the major Greek gods; hence, Zeus Xenios, responsible for protecting *xenoi*, or strangers.) Given the general competitiveness of Greek culture, border disputes must have been fairly common, but little direct evidence of them remains. On some occasions disputes were serious enough to require the appointment of neutral commissioners, known as *horistai*, to settle them.

Borders were not normally guarded except in times of war: The ancient world lacked the elaborate system of routine border controls found in modern nations. Since war, however, was a more or less constant threat during certain periods, fortresses might be established at certain key points to control access to one's territory. Warfare was often directed at depriving one's enemies of the materials necessary to conduct a war, so cross-border raids were extremely common. During the Peloponnesian War (431–404 B.C.E.), Spartan incursions forced the Athenians from outlying districts to retreat behind

Dedication by Alexander the Great to Athena Polias, around 330 B.C.E., from Priene, Asia Minor; this was one of several dedications Alexander made in the course of his travels while extending the boundaries of the Greek world. (© The Trustees of the British Museum)

their city walls, which were designed to guard only Athens and its port of Piraeus. In addition, one of the key incidents of the later part of the war was the Spartans' seizure of Decelea, at the northern edge of Athenian territory, and their construction of a fortress there, in effect giving them partial control of their enemy's borders. Border controls could be tight enough to cut off the flow of goods in case of wartime embargo: Characters in Aristophanes' *Lysistrata* complain that the war has deprived them of access to such luxuries as eels from nearby Boiotia.

As for external borders, population pressures, political upheaval, and the generally poor quality of soil in mainland Greece led to the frequent founding of colonies, starting in approximately 750 B.C.E. and continuing for more than two centuries. As a result, Greek frontiers were constantly shifting, and Greek speakers shared borders with virtually all the peoples of the Mediterranean: Lydians, Medes, and Persians (among many others) in Asia Minor; Scythians along the Black Sea; Etruscans and various Latin peoples (including Romans) in Italy; Carthaginians and Sicels in Sicily; and Gauls in the south of France. Alexander's conquests expanded the Greek world still further, bringing Greeks into contact with lands as distant as Afghanistan and India.

Frontiers had a strong hold on the Greek popular imagination. Border areas and hinterlands were where the norms of human culture were subject to reversal and where the "otherness" of strangers could extend to the barbaric and the monstrous. Various cities, including Crete and Sparta, had rituals that involved sending young men out to the frontiers of the polis to take part in rites of passage, which could involve behaviors (thieving, deception, ritualized pederasty) that were normally excluded from the city itself.

The best-known example of the strange fascination of frontier regions is the array of odd and semihuman peoples encountered by Odysseus during his wanderings, ranging from the relatively normal (but socially inept) Phaeacians to the monstrous and cannibalistic Cyclops Polyphemus. Yet peoples less fantastic than these were widely believed to exist just beyond the frontiers of the known world. Among these were the Amazons, an all-female tribe who were everything that Greek women were not supposed to be: independent, nomadic, sexually and militarily aggressive. Always located on the very edge of the known Greek world, the Amazons were an embodiment of the notion that the edge of this world was the edge of civilization itself. In fact, the supposed location of the Amazons moved eastward, starting from Asia Minor and winding up in the Caucasus Mountains: As the border of the known world moved, the Amazons moved with it.

ROME

BY TOM STREISSGUTH

The Roman Empire, the largest realm of ancient history, began as a village spread across the hills near the Tiber River in central Italy. The Romans established a republic after deposing their last king, Tarquin, around 509 B.C.E. Upon turning back an invasion from the north by the Celts in 390 B.C.E., the Romans began the conquest of the Italian peninsula. They expanded their control north to the Po River and south to the Greek colonies along the Mediterranean. The Roman frontiers, as well as private estates and city limits, were marked by boundary stones sacred to the god Terminus. An elaborate ceremony accompanied the placement of these stones. During the annual festival of Terminalia, at the end of the Roman year on February 23, the stones were cleaned, and the blood of sacrifices poured on them to renew their protective powers.

During the third and second centuries B.C.E., the growing republic clashed with Carthage, a North African empire, in the Punic Wars. After the last of these conflicts ended in 146 B.C.E., the Romans established their first overseas colonies in Sicily, Spain, Sardinia, Corsica, and Numidia (modern Tunisia). Roman armies then subdued Macedonia, southern Greece, Asia Minor, and the rest of North Africa, the province of Asia (Syria), and Gaul (France) in the first century C.E.

With the conquest of Gaul by Julius Caesar, at the Battle of Alesia in 52 B.C.E., Rome's frontier extended to the English Channel and the Rhine River, which served as natural barriers against the Germanic tribes to the east and north. The Roman provincial governors allowed local commerce and culture to continue without interference, using these territories as sources of revenue and buffers against the barbarian tribes beyond. To encourage cooperation in the frontier territories, Rome held out the promise of citizenship to all outsiders who served in the Roman armies.

Under the first Roman emperor, Augustus, who reigned from 27 B.C.E. to 14 C.E., Rome expanded to the Sahara in North Africa, the forests of Germany, the Atlantic coast of Gaul and Hispania (Spain), the Danube River in the northeast, and the Red and Black seas in the east. The defeat of a Roman legion in Germany's Teutoburg Forest in 9 C.E. persuaded Augustus to end any further expansion of the empire and station his legions behind these natural frontiers.

Rome reached its greatest extent during the second century C.E., when the emperor Trajan conquered Dacia, pushing the northern frontier of Rome beyond the Danube. Trajan's successor Hadrian strengthened the frontiers with forts, walls, and earthen ramparts in Britain and along the Rhine. A network of roads, originally built to carry the legions into enemy territory, extended to the empire's farthest limits. The vast network of roads—more than 50,000 miles—symbolized a superior civilization, highly skilled in engineering and capable of mustering armies of laborers to meet its needs. Local subjects were taxed to maintain the roads and levied to build them when the legions first arrived. The roads allowed the fast movement of armies as well as trading caravans, messengers, and private mail carried between the capital and the major cities out to the frontiers.

Roman fortifications were strategically placed along the frontiers. They were laid out in a quadrilateral, with a ditch surrounding the perimeter and earth thrown up behind it to form a rampart. On top of the rampart was a palisade of timber or stone. The camps were divided into three main areas, centering on the *praetorium*, the tent of the commander, where the symbolic banners were kept safe. In front of this structure was the *praetentura*, where the elite troops camped closest to the entrance; at the rear was the *retentura* for the common troops and cavalry. A principal gate cut into the rampart faced the enemy, with secondary gates sometimes built at the rear and sides. The largest forts covered as much as 50 acres, included quarters for civilians and slaves, and housed an entire legion of about 5,200 soldiers. Smaller outposts, signaling stations, watchtowers, and temporary camps protected laborers, travelers, and smaller campaigning forces, who would abandon these quarters at the end of the fighting season.

Where the threat of attack was constant, Roman engineers raised continuous physical barriers. Hadrian's Wall and the Antonine Wall in northern Britain protected Roman colonies against the troublesome Picts, who attacked from their homeland in what is now Scotland. In Germany the Roman *limes*, running nearly 400 miles, was raised in the first century, after the Roman defeat in the Teutoburg Forest. It was a rampart of earth and stone, which was more a boundary marker than a defensive structure, since not even Rome could raise a wall strong and long enough to guard the entire Rhine frontier. Watchtowers and small forts were placed at regular intervals along the *limes* but were not always manned.

Tribes living outside the border stones and walls found Roman territory, with its wealthy towns and farming estates, a most inviting target. The long frontier could not be guarded at every point, so Rome began hiring *auxilia* (mercenaries) from the local population to beef up the army. In the second century, however, Germanic tribes overran the Danube frontier—a preview of the full-scale invasions to follow as the empire weakened over the next three centuries. In the third century civil unrest in Rome prompted the emperors to pull back from the Rhine-Danube frontiers, leaving the northern frontiers exposed. As Goths, Vandals, Franks, Burgundians, and Huns raided Roman territory in northern Europe, fortifications were abandoned, and hundreds of Roman towns were raided and pillaged.

In 293 the emperor Diocletian divided the empire in half. The western half continued to be ruled from Rome, with Maximian as emperor. The eastern half had its capital at Nicomedia, where Diocletian ruled. In 324 the emperor Constantine shifted the capital to Byzantium. This former Greek town, on the narrow straits between the Aegean Sea and the Sea of Marmara, thrived as the western empire weakened and Rome's European provinces suffered increasing violence and administrative chaos. In 410, the Vandals stormed down the Italian peninsula and sacked Rome itself. In 476 the Germanic chieftain Odoacer deposed the last western Roman emperor in his palace at Ravenna, Italy. Historians traditionally have marked this event as the fall of the western empire.

THE AMERICAS

BY J. J. GEORGE

Maps and timelines of the ancient Americas that outline spatial and temporal borders are becoming more defined through research and exploration. Culture area borders as clearly defined as the contemporary border between the United States and Canada or Mexico were unknown. The sweeping arcs and circles that most maps use to delimit the ancient cultures of the Americas are largely arbitrary, but nonetheless instructive. For the people who lived within them, defining these areas and then defending them proved to be a subtle political or economic maneuver, though defensive architecture, battles, and skirmishes often added clarity and definition.

A frontier generally designates a physical margin, fringe, or outer boundary—more of a zone than a line—dividing peoples. It is also the division between settled and uninhabited parts of one nation, state, or culture area. Since the North American landscape during much of the ancient period comprised vast swaths of variable terrain traversed by hunter-gatherer bands and some semisedentary groups, it can be said that much of the land was frontier. Similarly, in Mesoamerica and South America, early settled agrarian culture areas were small in comparison to the total landmass, and often a substantial frontier existed between contemporaneous cultures. When those cultures came into contact, the notion of borders became relevant.

Borders symbolize aspects of nationhood and identity construction and are linked to state building. Factors that ultimately define borders include natural topographic limiters or barriers (mountains, rivers, or forests, for example); competition for space, resources, or power; the relationship of a dependent periphery to a central core; trade; tribute; migration; warring; and, on a broad scale, climate change. New technologies allowed for expansion into previously uninhabitable areas. Any combination of these factors contributed to the classification and continuous redefinition of borders throughout the Americas.

By 300 C.E. the Inuit of the far arctic north had settled at Birnirk, in what is today Barrow, Alaska, where they maintained a subsistence pattern based primarily on maritime resources such as whale and seal. Scarce resources and a changing climatic environment necessitated group cohesion for survival. Later, having mastered the technology necessary for surviving the harsh climate, a period of expansion ensued. This time of ferment meant that new groups were coming into contact. War and trade, instead of subsistence, became the focus of innovation, sometimes expressed aggressively across informal borders in order to procure goods meant for survival. Farther south the frontier between Inuit and Aleut populations on the Alaska Peninsula was relatively resource-poor and acted as a buffer zone between two relatively richer zones. The boundary remained stable over a long period of time until the Thule culture—because of environmental change, increased technological efficiency, or population pressures—was finally able to penetrate the boundary.

Along the Northwest Coast raiding and warfare were the primary forms of interaction. Three-thousand-year-old remains of human skeletons excavated in Prince Rupert Harbour, British Columbia, show a high rate of injury among males. Numerous fortified sites have been found, some of which are thought to be true villages, indicating at least that some understanding of borders was coming into existence. Since borders are intrinsically tied to notions of ownership, possession, and power, it is not unusual to find fortified sites adjacent to areas of resources. Notably, along the Northwest Coast the earliest sites that suggest a more sustained sedentary or non-nomadic lifestyle, with a greater commitment to principles of defense, are found beside rivers with rich salmon runs, a primary food staple for the area.

Between 200 B.C.E. and 400 C.E. some Hopewell Indian complexes as far east from their Illinois and Ohio "centers" as eastern Pennsylvania and New York are thought to have been assumed into a Hopewellian culture, representing daughter communities or colonies derived from one or the other center. The exact nature of the relationship is unclear. Gathering disparate villages under an umbrella classification to define the spatial aspects of a culture does not necessarily establish or define a border, though it does indicate broader spheres of influence or interest that are suggestive of transparent borders and frontiers with a limited political, economic, and territorial association.

Between 1500 B.C.E. and 300 B.C.E. the early Mesoamerican Gulf Coast settlements attributed to the Olmec civilization acquired the marks of town planning, with regular site orientations and large-scale constructions. An emerging nobility, established channels of commerce and communications, the construction of monumental architecture, and a significant population in the thousands supported by a large area of peripheral settlements all imply a form of political economy and integrated local and distant polities. These are conditions that precipitate the establishment and control of border areas. The monumental carved heads of the Olmec, sculpted from basalt rock gathered from the Tuxtla Mountains, are further evidence of established relations and regional economies that transcend defined borders.

Farther south, in Mexico's Valley of Oaxaca, three converging valleys and their surrounding alpine environment defined the generic borders of the earliest sustained villages. Around 1400 B.C.E. a regional network of small villages with a total population suspected to be around 500 defined the early settlement. By the period referred to as Monte Albán I (500–300 B.C.E.), a population thought to be about 17,000 clustered at the hilltop civic-ceremonial center of the same name, with as many as 50,000 at the surrounding sites. The increased proportion of populations living on the far periphery may have been related to defensive concerns and border control. Through the periods of Monte Albán II and Monte Albán III, by about 450 C.E., more sites were built in defensible positions, and several of these sites still have evidence of standing fortified walls. They may have been located there simply as administration centers or as centers for traffic monitoring, though they strongly suggest a mechanism for frontier maintenance in their aggressive, forward placement and defensive architecture.

The topography of Andean South America provides some of the most extreme physical markers for natural borders and frontiers. The landscape moves rapidly upward from a coastal desert cut through by rivers to the high alpine environments. These natural obstacles to easy migration provided obvious borders and frontiers and helped define areas of settlement. By 4000 B.C.E. settlements based on the rich maritime environment along the coast had been established. Between 1 and 700 B.C.E. the Recuay culture, a highland culture composed of a large number of independent polities, shared its borders with the Moche culture, a lowland coastal entity, and the two were known to have expansionist tendencies. In response to intensive competition with Moche neighbors, Recuay settlements were founded along ridgetops, which served as defenses, and were sometimes fortified with moats, restricted access, perimeter walls, and parapets. On its side, Moche pottery testifies to warfare, with its common themes of warriors, weapons, and trophy heads. Despite natural geographic buffers, the Moche and the Recuay fought over and defended their borders while continually trying to expand them.

See also AGRICULTURE; BUILDING TECHNIQUES AND MATERIALS; CITIES; CLIMATE AND GEOGRAPHY; DEATH AND BURIAL PRACTICES; ECONOMY; EMPIRES AND DYNASTIES; EXPLORATION; FESTIVALS; FOREIGNERS AND BARBARIANS; GENDER STRUCTURES AND ROLES; GOVERNMENT ORGANIZATION; HUNTING, FISHING, AND GATHERING; MIGRATION AND POPULATION MOVEMENTS; MILITARY; MINING, QUARRYING, AND SALT MAKING; NOMADIC AND PASTORAL SOCIETIES; RELIGION AND COSMOLOGY; ROADS AND BRIDGES; SACRED SITES; SEAFARING AND NAVIGATION; SETTLEMENT PATTERNS; SLAVES AND SLAVERY; SOCIAL ORGANIZATION; TOWNS AND VILLAGES; TRADE AND EXCHANGE; TRANSPORTATION; WAR AND CONQUEST.

FURTHER READING

John Baines and Jaromír Málek, *Cultural Atlas of Ancient Egypt*, rev. ed. (New York: Facts on File, 2000).

Richard E. Blanton, Stephen A. Kowalewski, Gary M. Feinman, et al., *Ancient Mesoamerica: A Comparison of Change in Three Regions* (Cambridge, U.K.: Cambridge University Press, 1981).

Alexander Cunningham, *The Ancient Geography of India* (Varanasi, India: Bhartiya Publishing House, 1975).

Antonio Di Vita, Ginette Di Vita-Evrard, and Lidiano Bacchielli, *Libya: The Lost Cities of the Roman Empire* (Cologne, Germany: Könemann, 1999).

Hastings Donnan, and Thomas Wilson, ed., *Border Approaches: Anthropological Perspectives on Frontiers* (Lanham, Md.: Anthropological Association of Ireland, 1994).

Hastings Donnan and Thomas M. Wilson, *Borders: Frontiers of Identity, Nation and State* (Oxford UK: Berg Publishers, 1999).
Nic Fields, *Rome's Northern Frontier A.D. 70–235: Beyond Hadrian's Wall* (Oxford, U.K.: Osprey Publishing, 2005).
Edith Hall, *Inventing the Barbarian: Greek Self-Definition through Tragedy* (New York: Oxford University Press, 1989).
John Haywood, *The Penguin Historical Atlas of Ancient Civilizations* (New York: Penguin, 2005).
Julia Lovell, *The Great Wall: China against the World, 1000 B.C.–2000 A.D.* (London: Atlantic, 2006).
Magnus Magnusson, *Archaeology of the Bible* (New York: Simon and Schuster, 1977).
Bill Manley, *The Penguin Historical Atlas of Ancient Egypt* (London: Penguin Books, 1996).
Fergus Millar, *The Roman Empire and Its Neighbours,* 2nd ed. (London: Duckworth, 1981).
J. R. V. Prescott, *Political Frontiers and Borders* (London: Unwin Hyman, 1987).
Michael Roaf, *Cultural Atlas of Mesopotamia and the Ancient Near East* (New York: Facts On File, 1990).
Richard J. A. Talbert, ed., *Atlas of Classical History* (New York: Macmillan, 1985).
Bruce Trigger, *Nubia* (London: Thames and Hudson, 1976).
Sir Mortimer Wheeler, *Rome beyond the Imperial Frontiers* (London: Bell, 1954).
C. R. Whittaker, *Rome and Its Frontiers: The Dynamics of Empire* (New York: Routledge, 2004).

► building techniques and materials

INTRODUCTION

In a modern city a common sight is that of towering cranes that reach high into the sky to lift building materials to the tops of huge, multistoried buildings under construction. In cities, small towns, and rural areas, the sound of tractors, bulldozers, and backhoes, along with electric saws and drills, pneumatic hammers, and the engines of massive trucks, accompanies the construction of roads, bridges, houses, public buildings, and the like.

In a world in which these labor-saving tools are so common, even indispensable, it seems almost impossible to understand how ancient people built many of the structures that define their civilization for modern-day historians and archaeologists. Yet build them they did, using whatever materials were available to them and working out construction techniques that enabled them to erect some of the most magnificent structures the world has ever seen. Lacking the tools and materials so common in the 21st century, they had to rely on their ingenuity as well as on massive teams of laborers (often slaves), to muscle local materials into usable and permanent structures.

Prehistoric peoples relied on whatever materials were at hand. In some regions it was common to build structures such as houses out of reeds, grasses, thatch, clay, mud, bark, bamboo, stones, or wooden poles and beams. A common early building technique is called wattle and daub. *Wattle* refers to a lattice wall constructed with small, flexible tree branches woven together. Once the wall was complete, a daub made of mud, perhaps strengthened with ground-up straw, was smeared over it, like plaster. Also common among early peoples were earth mounds, typically used as burial sites.

As people began to gather in cities and as civilization became more complex and advanced, early builders began to use a wider variety of materials and to devise building techniques that allowed them to create more elaborate structures. As it is today, wood was a common building material in forested regions, but wood is nondurable and especially vulnerable to moisture, so modern scholars have very few examples of wooden structures to study. Further, when some regions of the world became deforested as populations grew, builders had to turn to other types of building materials, particularly stone. In many cases, this stone was joined with cement and covered with a layer of adobe, limestone plaster, or some other substance.

Stone is heavy, making it hard to transport, so builders typically relied on the type of stone that was locally available. In some regions it was sandstone and in others marble, granite, or some other stone. Using primitive hand-held cutting tools, miners quarried the stone, dressed it (that is, cut into shape, trimmed, and smoothed), and then transported it to the building site. Where possible, as in ancient Egypt, builders used water power to transport the stone.

At a building site builders relied on a number of tools to ensure that their buildings were level and square and that walls were perpendicular to the ground. These included such tools as plumb bobs and various other contrivances that gave them level, perpendicular lines. Water troughs were also commonly used to find a level line. Levers, pulleys, and ropes, along with a good deal of manpower and the work of horses or oxen, were used to lift materials into place. In some cases, such as the pyramids of ancient Egypt, large ramps were constructed to raise the materials; sometimes these ramps were almost as much of a construction project as the building itself.

AFRICA

BY KIRK H. BEETZ

Most ancient Africans used clay, rushes (a type of plant), wicker, grass, bamboo, or tree bark when building. Stone was used for construction primarily in the northeast and east of Africa. Elsewhere in Africa stone was rarely used for anything but altars in shrines, and then it tended to be used as it was found and left uncut.

The majority of Africans lived in huts. These were usually windowless, with the only opening being a doorway. As a result, interiors were smoky from the open cooking fires or clay ovens. Huts were most often circular but could be oval. Their walls were made of clay that had probably been dug up and transported by women. These clay walls were built up in circular layers, first a bottom one of perhaps eight inches high, with an opening for the doorway. The next layer would then be spread on top of the first.

In northwestern, sub-Saharan Africa, the walls curved inward, layer by layer, giving the finished structure a dome-shaped roof. Elsewhere in Africa the houses were topped by thatch. These thatched roofs were usually conical, with the thatch hanging over the top edge of the clay wall. In some areas the roof might be made of wood, but again forming a cone.

Sometimes walls had frameworks of wattle, or poles intertwined with branches. The wattle would be covered inside and out with clay. In areas where clay was hard to find, walls were made of tree bark or woven rushes. Such walls seem to have been most often constructed in grassy areas that were drier than Africa's rain forests. The herdsman culture of the Sahara grasslands of 5095–2780 B.C.E. built huts of wicker with grass roofs.

Many materials used in ancient African building were not durable. Buildings disappeared quickly if they were not maintained. For instance, wood decayed rapidly in the moist regions of Africa, and in the drier regions voracious termites ate it away. Even clay bricks eroded from wind and rain. Such erosion left many ancient buildings little more than melted heaps. One building material that does manage to endure is stone, although even it is subject to erosion. Cultures that used stone are likely to have had some building remains survive. Most use of stone in southern and western Africa dates from the Middle Ages and later, but in northeast Africa at least two cultures from the ancient era built in stone. One was the kingdom of Kush, and the other was Axum.

Kush was a Nubian kingdom, to the south of ancient Egypt. Its principal building materials were reeds, wood, clay, and stone. Most Kushites lived in houses made of reeds, probably laid over a wooden framework. Their homes tended to look like rounded cones, with the reeds of the walls gathered together at the top. Even now, ceramic finials are popular in Africa, and these reed houses seem to have had ceramic finials shaped like pots on their peaks. (A finial is a decorative object placed on the peak or corner of a roof.)

In Kushite cities and towns, houses were made of durable sun-dried brick or fired brick that was less durable and would erode quickly in rain. The houses consisted of complexes of huts that served as rooms. There would be an outer wall with only one door in it, and along the inside wall were about five

Wattle framework being filled with red mud, a construction technique used in ancient times, from Zambia (© Board of Regents of the University of Wisconsin System)

brick huts. Each hut, or room, opened onto a central courtyard where most of the home's activities took place. Kush was founded around 900 B.C.E., and for some two hundred years, brick was the favored building material for palaces, temples, and other important buildings.

The Kushites were heavily influenced by the Egyptians, and one Egyptian building device in particular facilitated a shift to using stone for major construction. This device was the *shadoof*, a long, wooden pole that pivoted on a post near its middle. Heavy stone blocks would be placed in a basket that hung from ropes at one end, and a counterweight was placed on the other end to swing the basket upward. The *shadoof* had its limits: It could not lift stones that weighed several tons, like those found in monumental Egyptian structures, but it could lift stones weighing hundreds of pounds. It is still in use in eastern Africa.

Sandstone was favored in Kushite buildings. The Kushites were skilled rock carvers. They imitated Egyptian techniques using wooden mallets and metal chisels to carve pillars and decorations on walls. They hollowed out impressive cisterns, tanks cut out of rock to hold water. The most famous structures in Kush are the pyramids where kings and members of the royal family were buried. While they are not as large as many Egyptian pyramids, they do sometimes top one hundred feet in height. To achieve this height, ramps made of piled rubble were built perpendicular to one side of a pyramid, and rectangular stones were dragged up to within several feet of where they were to be set and then hauled the rest of the way by a *shadoof*. It is not clear whether the stones were fully dressed before or after they were set in place, but given the evenness of the slopes of the sides of these pyramids, the dressing was probably completed afterward. Although special care was taken in the building of tombs for royalty, good workmanship was shown in the graves of ordinary people also. These graves were lined with bricks, and a shelf was built within the graves on which the corpses were placed.

The Kushites took great pains in the making of their doors. Ancient visitors described wooden doors that were carved with images of gods, kings, and their people. Palace doors were made of ebony inlaid with ivory. Gold foil was applied by hammering it onto images on the doors. Gold was also used for images on walls and pillars, making the walk along a corridor to the palace doors one of constant glitter.

For over a thousand years, the people of Kush built impressive structures, but sometime before 350 C.E. their government collapsed, probably from a combination of overgrazing the land, loss of trade contacts with Europe and the Near East, relentless raiding by desert nomads, and pressure from Axum, a city in northern Ethiopia that had developed into a kingdom. Axum was influenced by African, Near Eastern, and Indian cultures, because it was a focus of trade between Africa and Asia. The Axumites lived in communities built of brick and stone. Their houses were blends of influences, often featuring columns like those found in southern India. When using stone, they built their walls with uncut rock with dressed and smoothed rocks for doorways.

EGYPT

BY KIRK H. BEETZ

The earliest Egyptians were probably subsistence farmers who were squeezed into the region of the Nile River as the surrounding deserts expanded during a long period of climate change. Their homes were probably huts made of dried mud. By the end of the Predynastic Period in about 3000 B.C.E., geography and climate had left Egypt with four abundant building materials: mud, reeds, straw, and stone. It is likely that Egyptians also built structures of wood, but these seem to have been primarily temporary buildings set up for special events and then taken down. For most of its history Egypt needed to import wood for large construction projects from Nubia and farther south as well as from the Levant.

The manufacture of mud bricks is described in the book of Exodus in the Bible, and the process changed little during ancient Egypt's long history: Mud was tamped into rectangular molds and left out in the sun to dry. To make the bricks more cohesive, chopped straw was often added. The result was a building block that could be made in large quantities quickly. Its disadvantage was that it wore out quickly; rains and winds could destroy a building of mud brick in a couple of decades. More durable than sun-dried bricks were fired bricks. At first the bricks were roasted in open fires, but this made for uneven baking. Tougher, more enduring building blocks were produced when eventually kilns were built for firing them. Until the era of Djoser, king from about 2630 to about 2610 B.C.E., mud bricks were Egypt's primary building material whether for small homes or massive public works; even obelisks were originally stout piles of mud bricks. As late as the New Kingdom of 1550–1070 B.C.E., mud bricks were still used for building the tombs of most commoners.

The first Egyptian stone construction known is a floor of granite for a tomb at Abydos, about 100 miles north of Thebes, probably for a king of the Second Dynasty (2770–2649 B.C.E.). Even though there were supplies of limestone nearby, the granite had been shipped down the Nile for the purpose. The stone blocks were not well dressed, only roughly squared, and they were poorly fitted together. A revolution in building with stone began with Djoser's tomb at Saqqara. At first it was going to be a typical mastaba, or underground tomb carved down into rock and topped with a square masonry platform. Sometime during its building, Djoser or his chief architect, Imhotep, decided to expand the structure above the ground. First a step that was lower than the walls of the mastaba was built around it, and then smaller mastabas were built on top of one another, forming steps that may have represented a ladder for ascending to heaven. These were built with local limestone, roughly dressed and coated with finely smoothed limestone blocks from Tura, an ancient site for quarrying thought to have had the finest stone. The stones were not the massive sort used in the Great Pyramid but were smaller than a human being; the Egyptians were experimenting with the stones as they built, seeing what they could do. Now known as the Step Pyramid, it was surrounded by a temple complex of stone and mud brick.

Not only tombs but also temples became signs of the power of Egyptian rulers, who built them even in the far reaches of the empire. But spreading out big building projects across the landscape created logistical and labor problems for the builders. Most ancient Egyptian public works projects were carried out by volunteers. Typically, they would donate their labor for part of the year to work on such structures as giant pyramids. Only a small group of people would work on construction projects all year round, among them, architects, foremen, engineers, specialized artisans, and those who served them, such as physicians who repaired their injuries and bakers who supplied them with bread. A small town built for full-time workers on the Great Pyramid of Khufu has been uncovered near the pyramid. It has individual homes, places for eating, supply areas, and shops, mostly built out of mud bricks. The main avenue that bisected the town was probably covered.

In the outer reaches of the empire, it may have been hard at times to find enough volunteers or local people to conscript for the building of monuments. For instance, the famous Great Temple of Ramses II at Abu Simbel, with the colossal statues on its facade (ca. 1270 B.C.E.), has within it depictions of Nubian slaves working to build it. Even so, later accounts of the use of tens of thousands of slaves to build the Great Pyramid of Khufu, from about 2551 to about 2528 B.C.E., are erroneous; most of the public construction was done by volunteers, by people paying their taxes with their labor, or by conscripts who were paid for their labor.

The Nile may have looked like a highway filled with giant stones during and after the era of Khufu. Granite or limestone blocks would be quarried at sites along the river. Workers would hack at rock, forming a narrow trench into which wooden stakes would be pressed; the stakes would be soaked and, as they expanded, would crack the rock. This technique was used for stones ranging from 200 pounds to 60 tons, for stones intended for bearing weight to long, tapering ornamental obelisks. The stone would be placed on sleds made of wood and reeds; the ground in front of the runners would be wetted down, making the ground slippery, while teams of men hauled at ropes, pulling the stones to the river. The blocks would be slid onto reed boats built specifically for ferrying stone. Special docks were built near the individual sites of construction, and the stones would be hauled by sled to the building site. At some sites, such as the Giza Plateau, basic limestone could be quarried nearby, but special stones such as granite or the Tura limestone used for outer facings had to come via the river.

Ramps for raising stones have been found at the Medūm pyramid built by Snefru (r. 2613–2589 B.C.E.) and beside an unfinished pylon at the temple at Karnak (on which construction began in the 16th century B.C.E. and proceeded through the reigns of 30 pharoahs). Exactly how the ramps were structured is not known, but they were used to haul even huge stones up and into place. Egyptian masons would then coat the top of a row of stones with mortar, not to hold them together but to act as a lubricant to ease the sliding of the next row of stones onto them. Once in place, the stones would be fully dressed by carvers so that they would fit together tightly.

HOW TO BUILD A PYRAMID WHEN ONE HAS NOT BEEN BUILT BEFORE

When King Djoser ruled Egypt, the tombs of kings were mastabas. These tombs were mostly underground, carved into solid rock, and had a couple of long stairways, with chapels, storage rooms, and a place for the sarcophagus. Aboveground would be a rectangular or square area composed of sloping walls filled in with mud brick. Perhaps the inspiration to make the mastaba of Djoser more impressive came from the ancient tradition that said that a deceased king would climb a stairway into the afterlife. The ancient Egyptians gave credit to Djoser's chief administrative officer, Imhotep, for what happened.

First he had the outer wall of the mastaba surrounded by another, lower wall and had the space between the two walls filled in. It made the original mastaba look more impressive and may have served to brace the first mastaba's walls for what came next. A platform was erected atop the mastaba, and another smaller platform was built on top, giving the tomb four steps and making it a step pyramid.

Imhotep decided to make the pyramid higher, but its base was probably not going to tolerate more weight being placed on it. Instead of adding another level onto the top, Imhotep shifted construction to the side of the pyramid. He built outward about half again the length of one side of the bottom step. Then stone was leaned against the side of the pyramid and built outward to form steps that were level with the original steps. Each level was now much wider than it had been. When this new construction was even with the fourth level of the original pyramid, the top level had as much surface area as had the original plain mastaba and could now bear more weight.

With more weight possible, two more levels could be added atop the original top step. The visible levels were faced with white limestone and polished. The smooth, white limestone walls shone in the sunlight. At 200 feet high and with a base of 393 by 467 feet, the Step Pyramid of Djoser dominated the land for miles around.

Wooden scaffolding would eventually be built to give sculptors and painters access to the outer walls. In the case of the pyramids at Giza, granite stones were set on the outsides of the pyramids, carved until they formed smooth slopes to the tops of the pyramids, and then polished so that they shone brightly in sunlight, while displaying carved images and glyphs.

THE MIDDLE EAST

BY JAMES A. CORRICK

The building materials used in Mesopotamia, Persia, and the rest of the ancient Near East were reeds, wood, stone, and mud bricks. Reeds, harvested along the banks of the Tigris, Euphrates, and other rivers, were commonly used because houses could be built quickly and cheaply from them. A reed house began with a circle of holes for a round structure or two parallel lines of holes for a rectangular one. The builder then pushed bundles of tightly tied tall reeds into each hole and pulled together the bundles opposite each other, tying them at the top to form the roof that was then covered with a mat woven of reeds. More mats were hung in the openings left for doorways.

Unlike reeds, trees were scarce in much of the Near East, particularly in Mesopotamia, and wood was not generally used to construct houses or any other buildings. Instead it was reserved for door frames, doors, roofs, supports for roofs, and paneling. Mesopotamia used stone, as did the rest of the Near East, but more rarely because it had few sources of the large stones needed for construction. Stone was used to make city walls, building foundations, and floor paving. It was less often used for the walls of buildings. The Persians, who had a readier source of stone, used it to make stairs, doorways, window frames, and columns, many of which stood 65 feet high. They sometimes carved whole building elements out of a single stone block, as they did with the great stone staircase in Persepolis.

Even the Persians did not use stone for building walls, however—not even for their palaces. Like the Mesopotamians and other ancient Near Easterners, they constructed building walls from brick. Indeed, of all the building materials of the ancient Near East the most common was brick formed from mud. Mud brick was quick and easy to make as well as to use. In the heat of Near Eastern summers, bricks had the added advantage of absorbing and radiating that heat very slowly. Thus brick buildings, particularly those with thick walls, remained relatively cool. Mud bricks were made from river mud or clay that was mixed with either sand or finely chopped straw to give added strength. At first individual bricks were shaped by hand. These handmade bricks were either cigar shaped or bun shaped. Although shaping bricks by hand would continue, after 2700 B.C.E. many Mesopotamians began to use rectangular molds, which formed bricks that were twice as long as they were wide.

The brick makers either pressed the mold down into a mass of prepared mud or filled the mold up with mud. Be-

Clay foundation peg, the first Dynasty of Lagash, around 2400 B.C.E. from Bad-tibira, southern Iraq (© The Trustees of the British Museum)

ginning around 2700 B.C.E. Mesopotamians began manufacturing plano-convex bricks. A mold would give a brick a flat bottom and flat sides (planes). The top, however, bulged or curved out, forming a convex surface. It was this convex surface that faced out and became the exterior wall of a structure. The plano-convex brick was confined to Mesopotamia, and even there this shape was mostly abandoned after 2400 B.C.E. Mesopotamian brick makers after that time scraped off any excess mud, making every surface a flat plane. This technique would be used by all other Near Eastern brick makers, including the Persians.

Once shaped, a brick was removed from the mold to dry and harden. The hardest mud bricks were those baked in ovens. However, it was easier to let bricks dry in the sun, the trade-off being that sun-dried bricks were not as strong as oven-baked ones. Once dried, by whatever method, the brick was ready for use, primarily in building walls. Brick walls were built up one horizontal layer, or course, at a time. Each course had to be cemented to the course under and over it, using any one of a number of methods. Workers could simply press wet bricks together and let them harden in place. More commonly they used mortar, a moist substance that adhered the courses to one another when it dried. The most usual mortar in the Near East was clay or mud mixed with straw or grit. In Mesopotamia another common mortar was bitumen, a black, sticky petroleum material that seeped up from the area's underground oil deposits. Bitumen and other mortars were also used as plaster coverings for brick constructions. Mud bricks, even baked ones, needed protection from sun, wind, and rain. Plastering them once a year protected them from disintegrating over time.

Walls made of stone were also built in courses and were often cemented together with mortar. One form much favored by the Phoenicians did not use mortar but rather stones shaped into equivalently sized rectangles that fitted tightly together. Then the blocks were laid in courses in which groups of three of four stones had their ends facing out of the wall while other groups had their long sides exposed. This alternation of the ends and sides of wall stones increased the wall's stability and helped prevent its collapse. Another method of stabilizing both stone and brick walls was to add buttresses that kept heavy walls from collapsing under their own weight. Although buttresses take a variety of shapes, in the ancient Near East they were flat pillars of brick or stone that projected out from a wall. The buttress transferred the outward force that the wall's weight exerted down into the ground.

Walls could also crumble under the weight of a building's roof. However, by resting the rafters that supported the roof on buttresses, builders could partially relieve the wall of carrying the load. Walls could also be weakened by being pierced with openings for doors and windows. The absence in Mesopotamia and other parts of the Near East of wood or stone to reinforce window frames and doorjambs also meant the absence of full support for the wall above. Consequently, windows were often kept small and narrow, a single brick's width, for instance. By carving windows out of single blocks of stone, the Persians were able to increase the size of these window openings for their public buildings. The stone frame provided the necessary strength to hold up the brick wall above it.

Doors also were made as small as possible. Some early Near Eastern houses even had doors so low and set so narrowly that people crawled through them to reach the interior. Larger doors became possible through reinforcement. Builders placed two upright posts, or jambs, on either side of the opening and then laid a beam of wood or a stone, known as the lintel, across the top of the jambs. The lintel transferred the weight of the wall above the door down to the jambs. An exceptionally large doorway or the gateway in a city wall would have buttresses against either side as added bracing. Lintels were not sufficiently strong to bear the weight of large expanses of wall. They would break under such weight. Thus for entryways in large walls, Near Eastern builders used the arch, which was invented in Mesopotamia by the Sumerians in the fourth millennium B.C.E.

The most common type of arch in the ancient Near East was the corbeled arch. A corbel is a brick or block of stone that sticks out of a wall and on which another building element, a rafter or a beam for example, rests for support. In a brick corbeled arch—most made of brick—the object being supported was another brick. This second brick would itself stick out over the end of the first brick. On top of the second brick a third brick was laid, also projecting beyond its support. As one overlapping brick was added to another, gradually the side of the arch rose, looking much like a series of brick steps. From the other side of the entryway, another brick staircase rose to meet its counterpart, forming the apex of a triangle.

ASIA AND THE PACIFIC

BY KIRK H. BEETZ

Little is known about what ancient peoples of Oceania built. Many lived in caves even into the modern age, and others probably lived in huts made of branches and sticks. On Easter Island, where people arrived around 400 C.E., there is evidence of such huts, but most of the people lived in caves they dug in the slopes of the island. For much of eastern Asia, little has been uncovered for Neolithic structures, probably because they were either temporary or built from perishable materials, principally wood.

In the prehistoric era the peoples of the Indian subcontinent and Southeast Asia built domed homes of mud, and their tombs for local leaders were typically large mud domes called *stupas*. When the Buddha died in 483 B.C.E., his cremated remains were divided among eight stupas, but in 260 B.C.E., King Asoka opened seven of these stupas and divided the remains among 84,000 stupas throughout most of India. One of these is the Great Stupa in Sanchi in central India, which still stands. Its mud dome was eventually blanketed by bricks without the use of mortar.

Although it is known that Indians used wood for building many structures, superseding the use of mud in the north early in recorded history, little is known about the ancient wooden structures because they did not survive long enough. Heavy rains and humidity made wood rot quickly. Still, a little is known about early wooden buildings from surviving temples carved in stone. In about 150 B.C.E., in the Western Ghats mountain range along the west coast of India, rock carvers expanded caves that initially had been homes for religious ascetics, creating spectacular temples and monasteries. The ceilings of some of these temples are arched, and representations of wooden beams have been carved into them. The carvings show many small wooden beams fitted together to form arches, resembling a technique used in ancient China at that time. Iron axes with flat edges were used for the initial dressing of the stone, and fine tools of iron and stone were used for carving images.

The Indians used the post-and-crossbeam technique, in which two or more posts are set in the ground in a row and beams are laid across their tops to bear the weight of a roof or higher floor while leaving openings that could be filled by walls or doors. When building with bricks or small stone blocks, they used the corbeling technique to create openings in free-standing stone structures, such as towers. A corbeled opening is an arch shaped like an upside down *V* of steps, in which blocks are set with one end projecting outward and the other end held in place by the weight of blocks piled on it. Because they have no mortar to hold them together, the blocks are prone to shifting from the effect of earthquakes or erosion of their foundations, sometimes causing the structures to collapse. When building tall stone structures such as gateways, Indians first constructed an outer framework of bamboo that crisscrossed to make squares up which workers could climb.

Corbeling without mortar created problems for ancient builders that they did not fully solve. Most of Indochina and Indonesia imitated Indian building techniques. In the region of modern Cambodia, the Funan kingdom of the first through sixth centuries C.E. imitated Indian construction techniques, but their tall brick buildings would fall down. Later Funan and Angkor (802–1432 C.E.) builders in the region of modern-day Cambodia used sand to even out the foundations of their buildings, but water would wash away the sand, and towers would tilt and eventually crumble. They tried to solve that problem by hollowing out stones at the bases of buildings and inserting timbers buried in the ground to stabilize tall structures, but in the wet climate the timbers would rot, and the walls and towers would fall. These ancient builders and those in Java tried using dowels of iron for holding stones in place, but they required maintenance; iron would rust and fall apart and then so would walls.

In China, around 4000 B.C.E., the Yellow River culture built homes that were circular, with timber walls shored up on the outside by mounds of dirt and conical thatched roofs that peaked in the middle. This basic structure spread to much of eastern Asia, and circular houses were still being built on the island of Honshu in the 200s C.E. As the Yellow River culture encountered cultures from the south and north, building protective structures became as important as building homes. During the Shang Dynasty (ca. 1500–ca. 1045 B.C.E.) towns were surrounded by walls of tamped dirt. On the northern frontiers, during the Zhou Dynasty (ca. 1045–256 B.C.E.), some small feudal provinces built long walls to deter nomadic northern tribes from invading. In 214 B.C.E. the emperor Shi Huangdi began to have these various walls connected into the Great Wall. The inner part of the wall was filled with debris, while stones were laid for the outer parts of the wall. This technique became common for building fortifications in China.

Even though the Great Wall is justifiably renowned, the great genius of Chinese architecture came not in the building of the wall but rather in creating techniques of construction that could be applied to monumental structures and to tiny homes and that were versatile enough to be adapted to different building materials according to availability. Thus, in northen China golden loess from desert areas was used for bricks, which were combined with wood to build structures; in central China stone would be combined with wood; and in southern China stone would be combined with bamboo as well as wood. All builders followed basic practices developed by the time of the emperor Shi Huangdi: Foundations would be excavated and filled with unhewn stone, bamboo or timber frameworks would be created for workers to climb, posts would be set in the foundation to bear most of the weight of the structure, and walls would bear little or no weight.

The posts would often have to bear immense weight, especially from roofs tiled with earthenware. On the top of a post, Chinese workers would place struts, usually of wood, that spread out upward like upturned legs; on their ends would be laid crossbeams or more struts spreading out, and the pattern would be continued as high as needed to reach the bottom of the floor above or the roof; the effect was to draw the weight of a building into the posts. This method resulted in buildings that had posts throughout their interiors, often set close together; provided the posts were sturdy, builders could place almost anything they wished onto a structure, which resulted in majestic pagodas, imposing palaces, shops, and houses for rich and poor.

The ancient Chinese used corbeling for their arches. This resulted in sometimes awkward public works, especially bridges, which tended to have tall, steep arcs that were very hard for people and carts to traverse while burdened. Even as the Great Wall was being built, Chinese engineers were borrowing from the technique of post and crossbeam to lay sturdy stone bridges. The stone beams were as long as 70 feet and weighed as much as 200 tons; these beams were smoothed with iron axes, dragged to riversides, lashed across several boats abreast, and floated into place during flooding season inland or the annual high tide near the sea. Even during the late Shang Dynasty, builders used primarily stone tools, with bronze being reserved for weapons and household goods such as pots. By the end of the Zhou Dynasty iron was commonly used for axes and picks as well as for woodworking tools.

Chinese building techniques were imitated in Japan and the region of modern Thailand, and they spread to the west and southwest as the Chinese Empire grew. The homes of most Japanese were made of wooden walls and thatched roofs and were round or oval. In Korea and northern Vietnam, Chinese building techniques arrived with the migration of Chinese beginning during the Zhou Dynasty, with Koreans becoming masters of the craft of building by the 200s C.E. and carrying their skills first to the Japanese island of Kyushu in the 300s and Honshu in the 400s.

EUROPE

BY JUDITH A. RASSON

People throughout prehistory used locally available building materials that were assembled in different ways with little alteration beyond basic shaping. They did not use building materials that required many steps in preparation, such as roof tiles, which had to be fired before they could be used. The people of the Paleolithic cultural period (in the Pleistocene geological period, which ended about 8000 B.C.E.) were nomadic hunters, relying only on wild animals and plants for food. To find food, they moved from place to place several times during the year. Conveniently located caves provided campsites, but elsewhere they built shelters. The structures they built did not require a great deal of investment in labor or materials.

Archaeologists think that they used animal skins to make tents or sometimes piled pieces of shrubs against a framework of saplings to make shelters. Examples of temporary dwellings have been found in France and Ukraine, among other places. What they have in common is stones or other heavy objects encircling the floor, probably used to hold the walls in place, and poles supporting a roof. The covering of the roofs is not known for sure; it may have been branches or skins. In France (at Terra Amata, dating to about 36,000 B.C.E.) stones outlined the tent or hut and poles around the edges and in the center supported a roof of some kind. At the Paleolithic site of Mezhirich in Ukraine (dating to 13,000 B.C.E.) lower jaws of mammoths were nested together to form the floor and tusks held up the roof.

Later, after climatic changes at the end of the Pleistocene, people began to control the breeding of plants and animals for food instead of relying only on wild foods. Domesticated plants and animals characterized the economy of the Neolithic and the subsequent Bronze and Iron Ages (broadly, 7000 B.C.E–500 C.E.). Relying on domesticated food resources meant that people settled in villages, where they lived all year round. They needed to construct buildings that were more substantial and usually larger than earlier buildings and would last longer than a tent or brush shelter.

The main building materials of the Neolithic, Bronze Age, and Iron Age were wood and shrubs (brush, slender branches, planks, and posts), stone, clay, plant materials such as chaff and straw, and sod (in some areas). The way raw materials were used and the shapes and sizes of structures varied across Europe. All the raw materials were used without further processing other than shaping. People throughout Europe took advantage of local resources to construct a wide range of buildings.

Stone was not generally used for walls unless wood was scarce, as in the area around the Neolithic settlement of Skara Brae in Scotland (dating to 3100–2500 B.C.E.), which was wind swept and mostly treeless. Stone was the main building material; even the furniture was made of stone. Houses were dug into the ground and had an inner and outer wall of dry-laid sandstone slabs with earth packed between them. Earth also covered the roofs; the beams may have been made of driftwood. On Dartmoor in England granite was abundant, and during the Bronze Age natural slabs were set upright in circles to form walls. The roofs were probably made of wild shrubs like heather or straw or perhaps pieces of sod. During the Iron Age in Ireland underground chambers (called *souterrains*) lined with stone were built below wooden structures. Even when stone was used, it was dry-laid; mortar, which starts with a chemical reaction, was not used until Roman times.

Wood in many forms was a common building material in prehistory. Hard, durable tree trunks of oak or ash often served as the main posts of the structural framework. Smaller withes, or slender branches, of flexible wood such as hazel filled in the walls, often as wattle. Clay mixed with chaff or other fine-textured vegetal material was used as daub, or plaster, for the walls. The added organic materials left tiny openings in the clay so it would dry and also reduced the weight a bit. The walls were built directly on the ground surface or in foundation ditches. There were no separate foundations, so eventually the posts and walls decayed, leaving only the post holes and ditches. Much of the information archaeologists have about prehistoric building materials was preserved when the buildings burned down, preserving impressions of wood and other plant material in the remaining mud plaster.

In Central and Eastern Europe during the Neolithic and Bronze Age, wooden posts dug into the ground formed the framework of structures. The walls were made of wattle thickly plastered with daub, most often made from clay mixed with chaff. Straw was used to thatch the roofs. Houses built in this way are known from numerous sites: in Germany (the Neolithic site of Köln-Lindenthal), Poland (the Neolithic settlements of Brześć Kujawski and Olszanica), Hungary (Neolithic site of Herpaly), Serbia (Neolithic settlements of Vinča, Divostin, and Selevac), and elsewhere. Similar construction techniques continued in use during the Bronze Age (at settlements such as Százhalombatta Földvár in Hungary) and elsewhere throughout the region.

Wonderful preservation of building materials is found in hundreds of so-called lake-dwelling settlements occupied from 4000 to 500 B.C.E. (the Neolithic, Bronze, and Iron Ages) scattered on both sides of the Alps from France to Greece (most famously in Switzerland). Because the sites are waterlogged, wood and other perishable materials are well preserved and show a range of uses. Wooden posts were driven into the ground to support the house. Covered with saplings and branches, this became a foundation for a wooden floor; the structure's framework was also of wood. The walls were made of wattle and the roof was probably of reeds or straw. Similar materials were used in Ireland during the late Bronze Age and Iron Age to construct artificial islands called crannogs. Tree trunks were driven into the mud of a lakebed to create a stable base, which was then covered with stones and peat. Dwellings and other structures were then built on this platform.

Besides being used for plaster, the earth itself could be part of structures. Large ditches were sometimes dug around settlements throughout Europe during the Bronze and Iron ages, usually interpreted as defensive and defining the territory of the settlement, and perhaps also serving to confine domestic animals. The earth dug out of the ditch was usually piled up next to the ditch in a bank or berm or rampart. This made the ditch seem even deeper.

It was mainly during the Iron Age that sod or turf was used to build structures by cutting it into slabs like bricks and stacking them up to form walls. Turf slabs could also be used to make roofs if they were laid over a strong wooden framework; this was done because they became heavy after soaking up water when it rained. This building material was used extensively in Scandinavia during the Iron Age, but it is also known from the United Kingdom. Elsewhere in Europe during the Iron Age wood, wattle, and daub continued to be the main building materials.

GREECE

BY CHRISTOPHER BLACKWELL

Archaeological excavations in Crete, beginning with those of Sir Arthur Evans in the late 19th century, have revealed the earliest buildings in the Greek world. The lowest excavated levels at the Cretan palace of Knossos, dating to around 7000 B.C.E., suggest structures with stone foundations and walls of mud bricks that had been sun-dried but not baked in an oven or furnace. On top of these ruins the monumental palaces of the Bronze Age (second millennium B.C.E.) were built. These structures combine finely worked walls, built of limestone and gypsum blocks shaped by masons who would "sign" blocks using unique marks, with rubble walls built of unevenly shaped stones, which were often the leftover remains of earlier structures that had been destroyed in this earthquake-prone area.

These walls were frequently plastered over and covered with frescoes. The walls defined rooms—often kept small so as to survive earthquakes—and served as retaining structures, creating terraces that allowed the palaces to sprawl over large, hilly areas. Wooden columns supplemented the stone walls in supporting ceilings that covered rooms and open-air colonnades. There is evidence of wooden beams inserted horizontally in the fabric of stone walls; these may have served as shock absorbers to protect the otherwise brittle walls during earthquakes.

During the latter third of the second millennium B.C.E., the Mycenaean Greeks of the Peloponnesus favored large, strongly fortified settlements. These are notable for their megalithic constructions—immense blocks of stone, roughly shaped and stacked without mortar or with only a thin layer of clay. Some of the blocks in the walls of the palace at Mycenae measure 26.25 feet in every dimension. The ancient Greeks of centuries later believed that the mythical giants called Cyclopes must have built them, and this style of construction is still called Cyclopean. These immense stones lie in regular courses, forming so-called ashlar walls. Inside their corridors, the upper levels of stone project inward, each slightly farther, until the two walls meet and lean into each other; this technique, also used to create large domed chambers, is called corbel vaulting.

The period after the collapse of the Bronze Age civilizations until the reemergence of literacy in the eighth or seventh centuries B.C.E. is known as the Greek dark ages. Construction from this period is much more modest, with sites such as Lefkandi in Euboea (the long island along the eastern coast of Greece) and Smyrna (modern İzmir, Turkey) yielding the remains of simple mud-brick structures. These show evidence of thatched roofs supported by wooden poles. Even the Temple of Apollo Daphnephoros ("Laurel-bringing Apollo") in Eretria was, during the mid-eighth century, a small building (26.25 feet by 19.6 feet) of wood and brush.

By the Archaic Period (seventh to sixth centuries B.C.E.) and the Classical Period (fifth to fourth centuries B.C.E.), deforestation had made wood scarce in Greece, so much so that wooden structures were remarkable. A character in Plato's *Critias* says of Greece in the early fourth century, "There are some mountains that now have nothing but food for bees, but they had trees not very long time ago, and the rafters from those felled there to roof the largest buildings are still sound."

The monumental architecture of the Classical Period, therefore, was constructed mainly of limestone, trachite (a kind of sandstone), and marble. For economic reasons, buildings in any area would tend to use local stone. The ancient travel writer Pausanias notes this when he describes the temples and public buildings of Athens as being built mainly from Pentelic marble that had been brought from Mount Pentelicon just to the east of Athens. Stone blocks were fitted and joined with wooden or metal clamps, and important buildings had roofs of terra-cotta tiles.

The buildings of the Athenian Acropolis are the most famous representatives of Classical Greek architecture. They suggest an aesthetic of gleaming white marble, but this idealized vision is a mistaken one resulting from an accident: In antiquity, these buildings were painted in bright colors that have wholly worn away with time. Large buildings were invariably built using post-and-lintel construction, with upright columns supporting horizontal blocks of stone. The strength of stone lies in its capacity to withstand compression, not in its capacity to flex; when the horizontal beams (the "lintels") had to extend across a wide gap, the weight of the roof or upper floor would cause them to crack because they could not flex. So any large building would need many internal columns to support the roof. In many Classical Period Greek buildings, the internal elements, less visible from the outside, would be made of common limestone, with more costly marble used only for external elements.

The masons used bronze and iron tools, with wooden mallets to shape the stone. Very rough shaping could be done by driving wooden wedges into cracks. When these wedges were soaked with water, they would expand and break off pieces of stone. Transporting large blocks of stone was laborious. Because the rigid chest-reinforcing harness for horses was not to be invented until well into the second millennium C.E., only oxen had the chest strength needed to drag heavy loads unaided, and their speed was limited to barely more than one mile per hour. Transportation by sea involved more risks, but it was cheaper and faster. The only famous exporter of marble was an island, Paros, the source for Parian marble.

The blocks for these marble buildings were roughly shaped in the quarry and finely shaped, or dressed, at the building site. Columns were constructed by stacking many drums of stone on top of one another. Each drum had a hole through its center; these holes would be lined up in the finished columns and then filled with molten metal to provide rigidity. Fluting, which consisted of vertical grooves, was cut into the columns after they had been entirely assembled.

Stones were lifted using the simple but sound principles of leverage, which were famously identified and described by the Greek mathematician Archimedes during the third

Dolphin fresco in the queen's megaron (reception hall) at Knossos, the capital of Minoan Crete (Alison Frantz Photographic Collection, American School of Classical Studies at Athens)

century B.C.E. but had been well known long before then. Workers would raise blocks slightly with wooden levers, place wooden supports underneath, and repeat until the stone was high enough to move into place by sliding it over wooden rollers.

There were variations and innovations in the basic techniques of post-and-lintel structures in stone. Most notably, the historian Thucydides reports that the Temple of Athena Chalkioikos in Sparta was lined in bronze (*chalkioikos* means "bronze-house"); the bronze was melted down from weapons the Spartans captured during a battle at Aphidna.

In the Hellenistic Period (323–31 B.C.E.) building techniques did not change fundamentally, with the main innovations being aesthetic flourishes (often combined with cost-saving measures), such as the use of colored stone, marble veneers over cheaper limestone construction, or bricks covered with plaster painted to look like marble.

ROME

BY TOM STREISSGUTH

The craft and science of architecture made important advances in Roman times. Roman leaders considered public buildings as personal monuments to themselves, legacies of their power and benevolence. For this reason, many imposing structures were raised in the Roman cities, and Roman architects enjoyed wide renown and lucrative patronage. The early Roman builders borrowed their construction techniques from the Greeks and from the Etruscans of northern Italy. The Etruscan arch, adopted by the Romans in the third century B.C.E., marked an important advance over the post-and-beam construction traditional to the Greeks. The first arches were corbeled—made up of horizontal courses of stone, overlaid slightly as the courses rose higher and extended across a limited space. Later arches were true arches, made of stone that was cut and fitted to produce a regular semicircle.

The Roman discovery of *caementum* (cement), in approximately the second century B.C.E., made possible not only the longevity but also the more grandiose scale of Roman buildings. *Caementum* was made of three parts sand and one part burnt lime, mixed with a volcanic ash known as pozzolana. The ash helped the mixture dry quickly and evenly into concrete and also made it waterproof. Builders often added a rubble of small stones and broken brick to the mix to strengthen it. Concrete was impervious to fire and weather, and it bore more weight than stone. It was also more abundant and easier to handle than stone, which had to be laboriously cut, transported, raised into place, and fitted. Concrete allowed walls to support heavier loads and gave builders more flexibility in designing interior spaces.

Simple leveling devices, including the *chorobates* and the *groma*, ensured precise alignment of foundations, walls, and piers. The *chorobates* was a long, narrow wooden bench, with plumb lines hanging near both ends. The plumb lines were

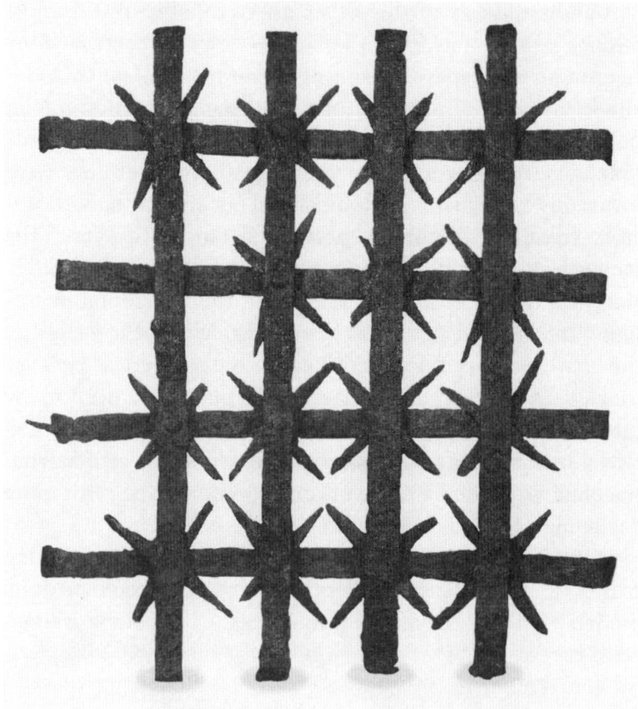

Iron window grill, Roman Britain, late third or fouth century C.E. (© The Trustees of the British Museum)

precisely matched to a vertical line marked on the bench supports. To ensure the measure, the surveyor checked a small trough of water or oil on top of the *chorobates*; if the water line was straight, the device lay horizontal. The surveyor then sighted along the top of the device to a distant ranging pole to mark position and height. To align vertical surfaces, Roman builders used the *groma*, a wooden crosspiece suspended from a pole. Plumb lines hung from the four ends of the crosspiece. The surveyor verified that the lines hung a matching distance off the ground and then sighted along the plumb lines to ensure that a distant wall or pier (vertical support) was at a perfect right angle to the ground.

Once a site was surveyed and marked out, builders raised wooden frames to begin construction. *Caementum* could be poured into frames of nearly any size and shape. The drying concrete was faced with stones of tufa, a soft and porous volcanic rock. Different facing patterns went in and out of style over the course of Roman history. The earliest style was the *incertum* wall, in which tufa stones were placed randomly into the concrete. Reticulum walls had regularly shaped blocks, a technique begun at the end of the first century B.C.E. Dressed stones, commonly of tufa or travertine (limestone), were joined to the concrete in the *quadratum* wall. In later years, marble, porphyry, and alabaster were also used to face Roman buildings.

Finished stone walls were given a film of stucco, which could be decorated with painted signage or simple geometric designs. Interior spaces in both private homes and public buildings, displayed fresco paintings of mythological or pastoral scenes or of more utilitarian pictures, giving visitors a hint at the profession or business at hand. Floor mosaics, employing colored tiles placed into concrete floors, grew popular after their introduction from Greece in the first century B.C.E. In the early empire, brick facing was a fairly uncommon technique, as the sun-dried (unfired) brick cracked easily from weather and stress. Later, kiln-drying techniques made bricks harder and stronger. Vast brickyards on the outskirts of Rome provided the basic facing material that endured until the Western Roman Empire's decline and fall in the fifth century C.E.

During the empire, cement mixed with a lighter ash known as scoria allowed the Romans to construct larger and loftier interior spaces. For their public baths and consecrated temples, such as the Pantheon, the Romans designed slender arches over entrances and raised domes and half-domes over interior spaces. A series of regularly spaced arches over a rectangular hall provided the frame for a barrel vault, while intersecting arches framed the groin vault. Stronger concrete walls could also be pierced with large window spaces, which, in this era before sheet glass, were commonly filled with wooden latticework.

The expanding empire raised a great variety of large public buildings, including markets, baths, temples, meeting halls, palaces, and such outdoor structures as hillside terraces, aqueducts, racecourses, amphitheaters, watchtowers, and speaking platforms. The arch and vault, along with concrete, gave architects great flexibility in the design of these structures and in the floor plans of large homes and *insulae*, or apartment blocks. Thousands of these massive Roman structures have endured more than two millennia, while modern concrete buildings, which are raised on skeletons of steel beams and slender iron bars, begin wearing out in a few decades.

Under the emperor Augustus, the first great public baths and theaters as well as multistory *insulae* were built in the city of Rome. In 64 C.E., however, a massive fire destroyed entire neighborhoods, and thousands of buildings had to be demolished. The emperor Nero passed new building regulations to prevent another such disaster. Building height was limited to seven stories, and all buildings were required to have porticoes (a colonnade, or row of columns, supporting a roof) for easier access to upper stories. Private homes had to keep fire buckets and equipment handy, and no common walls were allowed—all new Roman buildings had to be freestanding.

The gradual decline of the later empire degraded Roman construction and architecture. Late-empire architects replaced scoria and pozzolana with pumice, a weaker bonding material. There were few design innovations, and builders had to rely on inexpensive materials. Without the resources to maintain and repair buildings or to replace those lost to fire, war, or earthquake, Roman cities grew more chaotic and public buildings smaller and plainer. The great public structures, such as the Colosseum and the Pantheon, became public meeting halls, storage yards, useful stone quarries, and finally empty monuments to Rome's past glory and engineering genius.

THE AMERICAS

BY ARDEN DECKER

Much of what is known of early building practices centers around the movement and shaping of the natural landscape. Everyday buildings were usually created from perishable materials, so it is architecture of a more monumental nature that has provided archaeologists with much of what they understand about building techniques and materials in ancient times. Adobe bricks, mud, clay, stone, and perishable materials made up the majority of building materials for all ancient American cultures.

In ancient Mesoamerica the wattle-and-daub building technique was one of the simplest and most prevalent methods used. A wood latticework (wattle) was covered in a mixture of clay, mud, and straw (daub) to create a structure. Posts were added for houses that would have been covered with thatched roofs and sometimes with plaster. During the Late Preclassic period (400 B.C.E.–150 C.E.) the simple wattle-and-daub style of housing became larger, incorporating cut stone and plaster. The development of columns during this period allowed for the construction of larger enclosed rooms.

More monumental structures, such as platforms and temple pyramids, were also made using this method. Platforms from the Early Preclassic period (1800–1200 B.C.E.) have been found at San José Mogote, in the Oaxaca Valley of Mexico, which were made using wattle and daub and then faced with bun-shaped adobe brick. Such platforms would have served as bases for large-scale public buildings. However, adobe brick was used less often as the working of stone became more and more sophisticated. At the early Mayan site of Nabké, in the Petén (present-day Guatemala), this sophistication was carried forward with the development of apron moldings (joint stones that slightly hang over the bottom stonework of a wall), which allowed cut stones to be secured to walls that were growing ever higher and steeper, which would be exploited by later Mayan centers.

The Early Preclassic site of San Lorenzo (dating to around 1700–1200 B.C.E.), located on the Gulf Coast of Mexico, was built on a large, man-made platform constructed from excavated, existing earth as well as imported filler materials. Measuring 3,937 feet by 1,969 feet and standing 164 feet high, this is the first example of large-scale construction in Mesoamerica. Such a structure would have required large forces of organized labor. The platform pyramid style of construction would reach mammoth scale at Teotihuacán, Mexico (around 100 C.E.). For the Pyramid of the Sun, the first major structure built here, nearly 30 million baskets of dirt and rubble were hauled to the site. The final structure was finished off with a layer of mud and volcanic gravel that was then covered with a layer of plaster and faced with stone. Teotihuacán apartment complexes, built on top of raised platforms, were constructed out of adobe and stone and then covered with plaster.

As in Mesoamerica, building materials used by the ancient Andeans ranged from simple structures made from perishable materials to monumental structures built from stone and adobe. During the period from around 3500–2000 B.C.E. more permanent domestic and ceremonial structures began to be created out of stone and clay or stone and adobe.

At the Chavín site called Cerro Sechín, in northern Peru (ca. 800 B.C.E.), a style of temple construction developed. After a platform had been created from excavated earth, the temple itself was built using a series of cone-shaped adobe bricks that were arranged in rectangular form and then filled in with mortar. The cones were laid out point to point so that their round circular bases would form a roundel pattern on the wall. This created a flat, smooth wall surface. The structure was then covered by a wood or straw roof. Some structures were also faced with stone. This building technique would be continued after the Chavín culture declined.

Ancient Andean burial mounds and other monumental structures were built primarily of adobe brick. The large burial tombs of such north-coast cultures as the Moche (ca. 300 C.E.) consisted of low platforms as well as large adobe mounds. In the Moche site Huaca del Sol, near the northern coast of Peru, more than 143 million molded adobe bricks were laid in columns to create a burial mound. On the south coast the burial mounds and temples were smaller but still utilized adobe.

The earliest North Americans, like the Mesoamericans, built structures primarily from ephemeral materials, but there is evidence that they used more permanent building techniques. Pit houses were the earliest style of building in North America; they began to be built about 4300 B.C.E. Round or oval-shaped pits would be dug into the earth, providing at least one wall of the structure, and mud-covered vertical poles supplied the framework. The roof was made of perishable materials supported by a single crossbeam or by posts. Variations on the pit house were created in numerous periods throughout ancient North America.

Perishable structures would have been built above ground as well. Some were round and contained internal hearths for winter use, while in the summer, rectangular structures without hearths would have been occupied. On the Northwest coast the construction of large, rectangular, wooden plank houses dates back to around 1100 B.C.E. These structures would have required a great deal of communal labor to build and were most likely reused throughout many generations.

The North Americans also built monumental structures out of the existing landscape. Impressive mounds were constructed over burial and ceremonial sites and would have required carrying massive amounts of soil to the site with the aid of baskets and simple tools. One of the earliest great examples of mound building is found at "Poverty Point" in modern day Louisiana (dating to ca. 1500 B.C.E.) Here, six semicircular ridges, divided into segments measuring 9.8 feet high and 131 feet wide, were constructed from excavated earth to form a horseshoe shape. Mound sites would become larger and more elaborate in later cultures, taking on more complex geometric and curvilinear shapes. These ceremonial structures demonstrate the North American people's propensity for building on a monumental scale.

See also ARCHITECTURE; ART; BORDERS AND FRONTIERS; CERAMICS AND POTTERY; CITIES; CLIMATE AND GEOGRAPHY; DEATH AND BURIAL PRACTICES; EMPIRES AND DYNASTIES; EMPLOYMENT AND LABOR; FOREIGNERS AND BARBARIANS; HOUSEHOLD GOODS; HUNTING, FISHING, AND GATHERING; ILLUMINATION; METALLURGY; MINING, QUARRYING, AND SALT MAKING; NATURAL DISASTERS; NOMADIC AND PASTORAL SOCIETIES; RELIGION AND COSMOLOGY; ROADS AND BRIDGES; SACRED SITES; SETTLEMENT PATTERNS; TOWNS AND VILLAGES; TRANSPORTATION.

FURTHER READING

Jean-Pierre Adam, *Roman Building: Materials and Techniques* (London: Routledge, 2005).

Susan Toby Evans, *Ancient Mexico and Central America: Archaeology and Culture History* (London: Thames and Hudson, 2004).

Brian M. Fagan, *Ancient North America: The Archaeology of a Continent*, 3rd ed. (London: Thames and Hudson, 2000).

Ron Fisher, Norman Hammond, Anne Nottingham Kelsall, et al. *Builders of the Ancient World: Marvels of Engineering* (Washington, D.C.: National Geographic Society, 1986).

Gwendolyn Leick, *A Dictionary of Ancient Near Eastern Architecture* (London: Routledge, 1988).

Richard Ernest Wycherley, *How the Greeks Built Cities* (New York: Norton, 1962).

C

► calendars and clocks

INTRODUCTION

An old proverb defines the difference between ancient and modern life by saying that early people had time but no watches and busy modern people have watches but no time. As the proverb pertains to ancient peoples, it is only partly true. While ancient peoples did not have tools for measuring time that rival the modern atomic clock, they were vitally interested in the passage of time and developed numerous ways of measuring it. In doing so, they became the world's first astronomers, using the movements of the heavenly bodies to keep track of time.

Prehistoric peoples tended to rely on the moon and stars rather than the sun to mark the passage of the seasons and to define the year. In ancient Africa, for example, early peoples devised a calendar based on the movements of various star groups in conjunction with the phases of the moon. These types of calendrical systems are called lunar calendars (as opposed to solar calendars). Throughout the world, people observed the phases of the moon and used them to define months and seasons. In some cases, such as ancient Rome, the agricultural seasons were used to structure the calendar, giving rise in Rome to a calendar of ten months. Only later were calendars devised that relied on the movement of the sun. In some cultures both lunar and solar calendars were used, often making the calendrical system complex and hard to understand. Solar calendars were used principally for civil purposes, while lunar calendars were used mainly for religious and ritual purposes. It was the ancient Egyptians who worked out the fact that the year is 365¼ days long.

Ancient peoples were concerned with the passage of the seasons, for the seasons determined when crops needed to be planted or when people could expect the arrival of a rainy or dry season. Historians believe that many public monuments, including burial pyramids, were positioned to mark the arrival of the summer or winter solstice or the spring or autumn equinox. A passageway, for example, might have been constructed in a pyramid in such a way that the sun's rays are focused straight into the passage at the time of the spring solstice.

Most ancient peoples were not interested in accurate timekeeping throughout the day. It was enough to have a rough idea of what time it was by observing the passage of the sun throughout the sky. Most ancient cultures used primitive sundials, often consisting of nothing more than a stick placed in the ground. The shadow cast by the stick marked the passage of time. Later, more formal sundials were built, and the ancient Greeks spread the use of sundials and water clocks throughout the Mediterranean region. Some public monuments may have served as sundials as well. These include obelisks, or tall, tapered structures capped with a pyramid (similar to the Washington Monument in the U.S. capital). The stela, or a stone slab or monument positioned vertically, may also have served as a public sundial.

AFRICA

BY MICHAEL J. O'NEAL

While ancient Africans in general had little interest in measuring the hours and minutes of the day, they needed to mark the passage of the seasons. To that end, they developed an

View of the royal tombs at Meroë, ancient city of northeastern Africa in present-day Sudan; the entrances face east, toward the rising star Sirius, a positioning that suggests that they served as a type of calendar. (Courtesy of the Oriental Institute of the University of Chicago)

expertise in astronomy, for the progression of days, months, seasons, and years represents the movement and rotation of the earth in relation to the sun and moon. Archaeologists who study these matters refer to their field of inquiry as archaeoastronomy. These scholars are interested in archaeological evidence of astronomical observations that ancient societies made to keep track of time.

One of their major findings was the discovery of a calendar system used by the Borana of southern Ethiopia and northwest Kenya. The Borana, ignoring the sun, developed a calendar regulated by seven stars and star groups observed in conjunction with the phases of the moon. In 1978 archaeologists discovered at a site near Lake Turkana in Kenya a cluster of 19 stone pillars. The name of the site is Namoratunga, meaning "stone people." Writing carved on the stones provides evidence that the pillars date to 300 B.C.E.

The Borana measured time using a 354-day lunar year with 12 months; they did not keep track of weeks. Every three years a leap month was added so that the lunar years remained consistent with the 365-day solar year. The Borana relied on seven stars or star groups: Their modern names are Triangulum, Pleiades, Aldebaran, Bellatrix, Orion's Belt, Saiph, and Sirius. The new year began when a new moon was observed in conjunction with Triangulum; the next month began when the new moon was seen in conjunction with the Pleiades, and so on. The Borana had names for only 27 days of the month, even though the month could be as long as 30 days; when they arrived at the end of the list after 27 days, they started over with the name at the beginning of the list.

Astronomers and archaeologists, though, have struggled with how the Borana knew that the specific star systems were near the moon, because some of these stars cannot be seen when they are too close to a new moon. Some researchers believe that the 19 Namoratunga pillars were intended to mark the positions of these stars, allowing the stars' placement in the sky to be known even when the stars themselves could not be seen clearly. Using statistical analyses, archaeologists have determined that the possibility is less than a half a percentage point that the pillars could have marked the stars' locations by chance. For them, this is strong evidence that the cluster of pillars was an astronomical observatory and hence a calendar.

Structures that function like calendars have also been found in other parts of ancient Africa. In central Sudan the kingdom of Kush flourished from about 1000 to 100 B.C.E. The area features numerous pyramids, similar to the pyramids found in ancient Egypt. The entrances to these pyramids face east, directly at the rising star Sirius. This positioning suggests that they served as a type of calendar. In numerous places in Tanzania archaeologists have discovered cave drawings of precisely drawn circles. The circles are concentric and exactly spaced. The number of circles ranges from one to 29 or 30—numbers that suggest some connection with the lunar cycle.

Little is known about timekeeping in ancient Africa. Like most cultures throughout the world, the ancient Africans probably kept track of time throughout the day with some sort of basic sundial. A sundial can consist of little more than a stick placed in the ground. When the sun rises, the stick casts a shadow that points toward the west. As the sun rises higher in the sky, the shadow becomes progressively shorter until noon, after which the shadow begins to lengthen and point toward the east. In fact, a stick is not even necessary. A tree or any other vertical object would serve the same purpose.

One of the earliest forms of the sundial was the obelisk, a tall, tapered, four-sided monument with a pyramid at the top. (In the United States, the Washington Monument in the nation's capital is an obelisk.) The ancient Egyptians built the continent's first obelisks in about 3500 B.C.E. While these monuments served various purposes, they also helped the community keep time by functioning as massive sundials. Over the following centuries, similar obelisks were built in other parts of Africa.

One of the most famous of these obelisks was in the kingdom of Axum in northern Ethiopia. The precursors of this kingdom were established as early as 500 B.C.E., and the region quickly emerged as a major trading center, a gateway between east and west. Axum's influence spread throughout much of northeast and east Africa and the Arabian Peninsula. Prior to the Christian era in Ethiopia, a number of towering obelisks were constructed, including one that is 78 feet tall and weighs over 100 tons. The obelisk was in the news in the early 2000s because it had been looted and taken to Italy by the Italian dictator Benito Mussolini when Italy occupied Ethiopia in the 1930s. In April 2005 the Italian government returned the obelisk to its home.

Other types of timekeeping devices were developed and spread throughout North Africa during the centuries when the region was under Greek control, beginning in the fourth century B.C.E. In such countries as Syria, smaller sundials had a plate that marked the hours and a gnomon, or "shadow maker," that cast a shadow that moved with the passage of the sun. Under the influence of the Greeks, water clocks, which measure time by the regulated flow of water, became common in North Africa starting in about the fourth century B.C.E.

EGYPT

BY LEO DEPUYDT

In 45 B.C.E. Julius Caesar instituted the Julian calendar that we still use in modern times. Pope Gregory XIII slightly modified it by decree in 1582 C.E., and it is therefore now known as the Julian-Gregorian calendar. This calendar offers a kind of continuity from 45 B.C.E. down to the present time that makes the study of calendars of little concern to historians of the Middle Ages or the French Revolution. Calendrics demands a much higher degree of attention and energy from historians concerned with the time before the birth of Christ than it does from later historians.

In the history of humanity the ancient Egyptians were the first to notice that the year is close to 365 days long and also to put that number into calendrical practice. What is more, they were ahead of everyone else in this respect by 2,000 to 3,000 years. The Babylonians, the Greeks, the Hebrews, and others all regulated daily life by the moon. So did the Romans until the fifth century B.C.E., when they switched to a complex calendar that exhibits peculiar vestiges of lunar time-reckoning. The sole division of 365 days that is positively recognizable in ancient sources is a year of 12 months of 30 days plus five added days. This structure was known in antiquity as the "civil" calendar. This continuous cycle is often praised for its simplicity, as if it is a work of genius. One wonders about the historical circumstances in which this simple structure was created, presumably in the early third millennium B.C.E. Not a shred of evidence has survived about these circumstances. It is not known, for example, how the number 365 was obtained.

The civil calendar is pseudo-lunar, because the length of its months is close to, but not quite the same as, the average length of real lunar months, which is a little more than 29.5 days. The civil calendar is pseudo-solar, because the length of its year is close to, but not quite the same as, the average length of the solar year, or the year of the seasons, which is about 365.2422 days long. Because the civil year, at 365 days, is about a quarter day shorter than the solar year, the Egyptian calendar shifts in relation to the seasons. It falls behind in relation to the solar year and the seasons by about one day every four years. This means that a given day, for example, the Egyptian New Year's Day, which at a given time fell in summer, would slowly recede into spring, then winter, fall, and again to summer, returning to the original point after about 1,460 years. This motion in relation to the solar year is commonly described as wandering, hence the term *wandering year* for the Egyptian 365-day year.

All this does not mean that there was no lunar time-reckoning at all in ancient Egypt. Lunar time-reckoning was used marginally in religious life, for instance, in order to regulate services in the temple. Lunar calendars cannot differ from one another in many ways. One way is the position of the first month of the lunar year inside the solar year. In that respect, no evidence contradicts the following hypothetical scenario. Earlier on, the first lunar month began in the summer around the time in July when the star Sirius rose again early in the morning after it had been invisible for about two months. The rising of Sirius was the lunar calendar's anchor. As the civil year wandered, the rising of Sirius came to coincide with the civil new year in about 1300 B.C.E. At that point, the lunar calendar switched anchors from the rising of Sirius to the civil new year. Civil calendar and month names were henceforth attached to one another by a naming procedure in a kind of double-helix calendar, winding its way through time. A civil month was given the same name as its lunar twin, that is, the lunar month beginning in it. This double civil-lunar calendar system therefore exists purely by virtue of specific assignments of names. Ancient Egypt thus knew two calendars, the dominant 365-day calendar, usually called the civil calendar, and the somewhat marginal lunar calendar. By contrast, past research on ancient Egyptian timekeeping is characterized by a proliferation of postulated calendars. Then again, there is no conclusive evidence for the existence of more than two calendars at any one time in Egyptian history.

Much discussion on calendars has revolved over the decades around the two problems of the month names. Egypt had both a nonlunar calendar—that is, the civil one—and a lunar calendar. It comes as no surprise that the two problems of the month names have everything to do with the relationship between these two calendars. The first problem is that the last month can be named as if it were the first, namely, *opener of the year* or *birth of Re*, which are also names for New Year's Day, the quintessential beginning. The second problem is that a feast could sometimes be celebrated on the civil day 1 following the civil month with the same name, as if a feast called January were celebrated on February 1.

The two problems of the month names came about as the result of two actions by ancient calendar makers. First, calendar makers transferred month names from the lunar calendar to the civil calendar. As a result, the name of the first lunar month—the month inside which the civil new year fell—was rolled backward in time onto the 12th and last civil month, resulting in the awkward circumstance that the last civil month was named as if it were the first civil month. Second, calendar makers transferred the names of feast days from the middle of lunar month X, that is, from the full moon, to day 1 of the civil month, because that civil day 1 fell inside lunar month X. The name of the feast day at full moon was the same as the name of the entire lunar month X. As a result of the first action, the name of lunar month X was rolled back onto the civil month preceding the civil day 1 that had received the same name owing to the second action. Consequently, it was indeed as if a feast called January was celebrated on February 1.

Clocks were not in any kind of regular use in ancient Egypt, even if a small number of water clocks, sundials, and related devices have been preserved. The rise of mechanical clocks dates to the Middle Ages, in the 13th and 14th century C.E. Before mechanical clocks, people's lives were not normally guided by numbered subdivisions of the day. The daily course of the sun, the yearly succession of the seasons, and the agricultural cycle sufficed as markers of time. For most people most of the time, there was no need to count the days or to watch clocks. Life was much simpler then.

THE MIDDLE EAST

BY DAVID BROWN

Some mythological texts composed in ancient Mesopotamia describe great lengths of time in terms of a round number of years, but what was a year to a scribe? Years were counted from one seasonally or sidereally recurring event to another, and there is no evidence in cuneiform sources that the small difference between a seasonal (or equinoctial) and a sidereal (or stellar) year was remarked upon. An equinoctial year is the period between one spring equinox, when day and night are of equal length, and the next. A stellar year marks one 360-degree rotation of the sun. The two lengths are slightly different. Nevertheless, around 150 B.C.E. cuneiform scholars determined lengths of the year that are close to both. The Greek astronomer Hipparchus at about the same time was seemingly the first to note and quantify that difference.

More generally, though, years were defined in terms of lunations, the intervals from new moon to new moon. One year was defined as either 12 or 13 lunations. The seasonal names given to the months of the calendars used during the course of the third millennium B.C.E. indicate that from the earliest times the year was characterized by its seasons. An attempt was made to insert an extra month into the calendar about every three years to ensure that the beginning of the first month of the year coincided roughly with the vernal equinox, the date in spring when day and night are of equal length. A lunation lasts either 29 or 30 days, with slightly more than half lasting 30. Because 12 lunations fall some 11 days short of the length of aʃ year, without the addition (known as intercalation) of an extra month, the start of each month would fall ever earlier in the year, and the agricultural activities described by their names would soon occur within inappropriately named months.

A rule-of-thumb intercalation of one extra month every three years was employed in most areas of Mesopotamia and periods of history. During the course of the second millennium B.C.E. the names assigned to the months by the people of

Fragment of a basalt water clock, from Tell el-Yahudiya, Egypt, Macedonian Dynasty, around 320 B.C.E. (© The Trustees of the British Museum)

Nippur came to be those most commonly used. The astrological Mul.Apin tablets, which date to this period, refer to the intercalation and to rules used to determine when it should take place. They also associate the equinoxes and solstices with the heliacal rising of certain stars—that is, their first appearance after a period of absence from the sky in the east directly before sunrise—thereby equating the sidereal year with the equinoctial. One reference in a classical Sumerian composition know as *The Farmer's Instructions* states: "When the constellations in the sky are right, do not be reluctant to take the oxen force to the field many times." This suggests that the stars had long been used to determine the time of the year.

Not until the seventh century B.C.E., however, is there any evidence that the months and years were put into any form of systematic arrangement, leading to what is termed a regulated calendar. This regulation was connected with the rise of astronomical prediction. The most accurate of the schemes devised by Mesopotamian scholars for regulating the numbers of months and years was also the longest lasting. During the first half of the first millennium B.C.E. it was noted that 19 years last almost exactly as long as 235 lunations. Multiplying 19 by 12 yields 228, which is 7 less than 235. Therefore, this scheme implies that 7 of those 235 months are intercalary. The Mesopotamians distributed those intercalations in a particular manner throughout the 19 years while adhering to the age-old tradition of inserting them after either month 12 or 6. Before long, people other than astronomers were making use of this relationship, including the governmental authorities (who used it in dating contracts and the like.) The scheme was adopted in 503 B.C.E. by the Persians and in the late fifth century B.C.E. by the Athenians, who used an identical formula attributed to a scholar named Meton. The scheme is often referred to today as the Metonic cycle. The Macedonians reconciled their calendar with the Babylonian 19-year scheme before 323 B.C.E., and the Parthians continued to use it when they acquired hegemony over Babylonia. The 19-year scheme appears in Indian sources of the second or third centuries C.E. It perhaps arrived with zodiacal astrology from Roman Egypt, Parthian Iran, or China, where a 19-year scheme had been in use for some centuries.

From the third millennium B.C.E. the year is sometimes said to comprise 12 months of 30 days each, or 360 days. This is an idealization, useful both in administration and divination. It simplified calculations and provided the basis for a series of further idealizations as to the behavior of the heavenly bodies, against which their real behavior could be compared and interpreted. Thus the span of 360 days is not an estimate of the length of the year, for providing such information was not the aim of the texts in question. The Mul.Apin tablets give a length of 364 days for the year. Again, this probably does not represent the level of accuracy prevalent at that time. A year of 364 days is used in West Semitic circles in the first millennium B.C.E. because it amounts to 52 weeks of seven days and therefore fit with cosmological ideas common to this area. In Mesopotamia increasingly accurate values of the length of the year in terms of days and smaller units are found in the astronomical texts beginning around 700 B.C.E.

Days were measured from sunset to sunset. In the astronomical texts a further "day," defined as 1/30th of a mean lunation, was employed to facilitate calculations. Lengths of time shorter than a day were measured in both seasonal and nonseasonal units. Watches (such as that used by a village to guard against intruders)—three at night and three during the day—varied in length depending on the time of the year. There is some evidence of the use of seasonal time units in compositions found in Nineveh and in the "proto-horoscopes" found in Babylonia.

Far more common, though, was the use of units that did not vary with the time of year. Prime among these was the UŠ, defined as 1/360th of a day. Its origin lies in the observation of the similarity of the sun's daily and annual motions, for the UŠ is to the day as the day is to the (ideal) year. Given the sun's daily revolution, 1 UŠ amounts to 1/360th of a revolution and is the ancestor of the modern degree. The UŠ is used as a unit of time and celestial displacement in Mul. Apin. From early in the first millennium B.C.E. the intervals between the culminations of the members of a certain group of stars—meaning the point at which the stars appear directly overhead—were given in terms of their mutual displacement. That these displacements were understood as time intervals is confirmed by their direct equation with weights of water collected from a constant-head water clock, where the water flows out without emptying the clock, since enough other water flows in to keep the head constant. No examples of Sumerian water clocks still exist, but descriptions of them appear in mathematical texts of the early second millennium B.C.E.

Herodotus, in the fifth century B.C.E., wrote that the Greeks adopted the gnomon (a vertical stick that casts shadows and is thus used to tell time) from the Mesopotamians. The Mul.Apin tablets do describe some form of time measure involving shadows, though there is no direct evidence for the use of sundials in ancient Mesopotamia. Time intervals were most commonly measured with the water clock, supplemented by the use of culminating stars at night. In India are examples of the sinking water clock, a bowl with a hole in the base. The bowl sits on the surface of a reservoir and gradually fills until it sinks. A possible example of a sinking water clock from Nimrud, dating to the eighth century B.C.E., is in the British Museum in London.

ASIA AND THE PACIFIC

BY AMY HACKNEY BLACKWELL

Ancient Asians constructed elaborate calendar systems based on the cycles of the sun and moon. The people of China and India both created calendars that kept track of solar cycles, the moon's movement around the earth, and the movements of the stars, especially the stars corresponding to the 12 zodiac signs. These calendars probably started as a means of tracking the seasons so that farmers would know when to plant and harvest their crops. Both the Chinese and Hindu calendars are still used today.

The Chinese calendar was supposedly invented by the first legendary ruler of China, Huang Di, who is said to have reigned from 2698 to 2599 B.C.E. Although various calendars were in use over the centuries, Chinese tradition says that the first year of the first calendar cycle was either 2637 B.C.E. or 2697 B.C.E. under the Gregorian calendar system (the system used in the United States today). The Chinese calendar runs in cycles, or epochs, of 60 years. Chinese years are numbered from one to 60; after 60 years, a new epoch begins and the count starts over. If the calendar began in 2637, the current cycle is the 78th 60-year cycle; if the calendar began in 2697, the current cycle is the 79th.

The most ancient Chinese dates are impossible to verify because the first few centuries of calendar keeping were somewhat flexible. The year had 12 months based on the movements of the moon and the sun, but people constantly had to adjust the calendar to keep up with the seasons, adding one or even two months as needed. The first generally accepted specific date is in 841 B.C.E. (The Chinese kept dates before then, but we do not know what they were.) The first month started around the time of the winter solstice; if an extra month was needed to put the seasons back in sync with the calendar, it was added at some point during the year. Instead of calling years by their numbers, the Chinese typically marked dates by the year of the current ruler's reign.

In 484 B.C.E. the Chinese invented a more precise calendar with 365¼ days. The Qin Dynasty instituted the use of this calendar throughout China in 256 B.C.E. It still needed an extra month from time to time in order to keep the months stable. In 104 B.C.E. Emperor Wu of the Western Han Dynasty established new rules to govern the calendar; these rules are still used today. Under these rules the solstice generally occurs in the 11th month. The first day of a new month begins at midnight on the day of the new moon. Each year has 12 months, and every third year has an extra month that can fall after any month; the extra month shares the number of the month that precedes it. Each month corresponds with one of the 12 signs of the zodiac. According to the Gregorian calendar, the Chinese New Year occurs at a different time every year.

The Chinese zodiac added another layer of complication to the calendar. The 12 zodiac signs are rat, ox, tiger, rabbit, dragon, snake, horse, sheep, monkey, rooster, dog, and pig. Every Chinese year is assigned one zodiac sign; for example, 2006 was the year of the dog. The cycle repeats itself every 12 years. Each day is divided into 12 hours, each of which corresponds to two Western hours. Each of the 12 hours is labeled with one of the zodiac signs. The Chinese also divide the day into 100 equal parts, each of which roughly corresponds to 15 Western minutes. For the most part, people in ancient days told time by the position of the sun and the shadows it cast on the ground. Accurate mechanical clocks were not invented during the ancient period, but people did use sundials made of bamboo or other materials. These could be very accurate at determining the days of the winter or summer solstice; the sundial's shadow would be shortest at the winter solstice and longest at the summer solstice.

Many Asian nations adopted the Chinese calendar system. In Japan, for example, the emperor Kōtoku decided in 645 C.E. that the nation would begin the practice of naming periods of time for the current emperor. The Korean calendar was taken directly from the Chinese calendar and recognized the Chinese New Year. According to tradition, the calendar began counting with the year 2333 B.C.E., the year in which Korea was supposedly founded. Most Asian cultures adopted the Chinese zodiac system, occasionally substituting animals that seemed more appropriate to them; for example, Vietnam and Thailand placed a cat in the fourth position, and Japan inserted a wild boar in place of the pig.

The Hindu calendar of India was invented in Vedic times, between 1300 and 1500 B.C.E. The Vedas, the main scripture of Hinduism, describe the cycle of the calendar. The Vedic calendar began with the spring equinox, the day at the end of winter when night and day are of the same length. The year is based on the length of time it takes the earth to circle the sun. The calendar is both a solar calendar, based on the earth's movement relative to the sun, and a lunar calendar, based on the moon's movement around the earth. The solar calendar has 12 months, each corresponding to a sign of the zodiac. Each month has between 29 and 32 days, determined by the length of time the constellation of stars associated with a particular zodiac sign remains in the path of the sun across the heavens. The 12 months are also defined by the portion of the earth's orbit around the sun, called the *rashi*. The calendar also has lunar months, based on the cycle of the moon. When the lunar calendar falls out of sync with the *rashi*, or solar months, an extra month is added to the lunar calendar. The combination of lunar and solar months is known as a lunisolar calendar. The first day of the first year of the Hindu calendar is said to be January 23, 3102 B.C.E. The calendar runs in 60-year cycles, or epochs. Each year has a name, and the names start over when a new epoch begins.

The Vedic calendar has a very complicated approach to daily timekeeping. Each day is a *tithi*, or lunar day, but because a day is measured by the length of time it takes the angle between the sun and the moon to increase a specified amount, a day can range from 19 to 26 hours in length. Each Hindu month is divided into 30 *tithi*, which are further divided into two groups of 15 days. These divisions are meant to keep the month in step with the phases of the moon.

Most ancient people did not have clocks, instead noting the positions of the sun, moon, or stars to furnish a rough idea of the time. The earliest clocks were water clocks, containers made of stone or metal. Water was set to drip at a constant rate into such a container and gradually filled it; markings in the container indicated how much time had passed by the time the water level reached them. Other water clocks were bowls with small holes in the bottoms;

people put them in larger containers of water and they gradually filled and sank.

One of the earliest water clocks discovered in Asia was bronze basin water clock dating to the Han Dynasty (202 B.C.E.–220 C.E.). It contained several wooden arrows carved with lines; as water flowed out of the basin, the arrows sank, allowing the viewer to tell how much time had passed by markings on the arrows. Starting around 300 C.E. Chinese artisans began making more elaborate and accurate water clocks, using multiple basins to hold water and floating arrows. Some of these clocks could ring bells to mark the hours. Others were attached to astronomical devices that showed the positions of the stars and planets.

EUROPE

BY AMY HACKNEY BLACKWELL

The earliest European systems of keeping time were based on the movements of the sun and the moon. Stone Age people as early as 30,000 years ago appear to have kept track of days by making notches in bones. Rituals were timed according to the phases of the moon, and the new moon was a common time for celebrations. People observed the natural changes that happened to plants and animals at particular times and remembered them from year to year. Some ancient people probably named the times of the year according to events that took place in particular seasons, such as "deer time," or "bird-migration time."

In prehistoric times people built megalithic, or large stone, structures in western and northern Europe, some of which may have functioned as primitive solar calendars. One of the most famous such sites is Newgrange in Ireland, a tomb that was built in about 3200 B.C.E. Newgrange consists of a passageway leading to a subterranean burial chamber containing several side chambers. The entrance to the tomb is constructed so that every year at the winter solstice the rising sun shines through a slit over the entrance and illuminates the main burial chamber for 17 minutes. When Newgrange was built, the light would have fallen directly onto a spiral design on the far wall.

Other Stone Age sites in Ireland were also designed to catch the sun on particular days of the year. The tomb at Dowth catches the light of the setting sun at the winter solstice. The tomb at Knowth has an eastern-facing passage that catches the light of the rising sun on the spring and autumn equinoxes, the two days each year when day and night are of equal length. Knowth's western-facing passage catches the light of the setting sun on the same days. Stonehenge, a circle of giant stones built in England between 2700 and 1500 B.C.E., also appears to have been constructed to catch sunlight on specific days. Sunlight shines on the center of the monument on the day of the summer solstice, and similar phenomena happen at the equinoxes.

Ancient people kept track of the seasons for various reasons but mostly to know when to plant or harvest their crops. The Celtic and Germanic people who lived in Europe in ancient times also used calendars to help them plant and reap, but they appear to have been more interested in keeping track of days for ritual purposes. Holidays fell on the winter and summer solstices and the spring and autumn equinoxes, and ancient European calendars were designed to identify these days. Druids, the priests of the Celtic world, used calendars to plan festivals—one in each quarter of the year. Because each festival fell on either an equinox or a solstice, they needed to know when these days would occur. Some scholars believe that Celts began using calendars as early as 800 B.C.E. The most famous Celtic calendar is the first century C.E. Coligny calendar, found in France in 1897 and dated to the first century C.E. The calendar's letters and numbers were carved in Latin letters on a bronze tablet. The tablet depicts a five-year cycle that contains exactly 62 months.

The Coligny calendar, a similar calendar found nearby at Villard d'Heria, and the writings of the Romans Julius Caesar and Pliny the Elder have provided historians with the means of reconstructing the Celtic calendar system. The Celtic calendar was lunisolar, which means that it tracked the movements of both the earth around the sun and the moon around the earth. Julius Caesar (100–44 B.C.E.) noted that the Gauls kept track of time by counting nights, not days. The Celtic calendar based its months on the cycles of the moon, though no one knows whether months began at the new moon or the full moon. Each month was divided into two halves, or fortnights; the first half was 15 days, and the second half was 14 or 15 days, alternating by month. The 30-day months were considered lucky, and the 29-day months were thought to be unlucky. The lunar year was 354 or 355 days long. To keep the year in sync with the earth's orbit around the sun, or the solar year, Celts added a 13th month every two and a half years. Scholars believe that each new year began on the autumn equinox.

As the Romans gained power, they spread their calendars through Europe. Before 46 B.C.E., people in Spain and other parts of Europe under Roman domination used the old Roman calendar. This calendar had 12 lunar months, adding up to 355 days in a year; the Roman priests would periodically insert an extra month between February and March to put the calendar back in line with the seasons. The decision of whether to add the extra month was entirely up to the discretion of the priest in charge, and some priests did not bother to add the month for several years in a row. The calendar became quite confusing, especially for people who lived some distance from Rome, and most people using the system never knew what date it was.

The Gauls and Germans gradually adopted the Julian system created by Julius Caesar in 46 B.C.E. Under this calendar, a year was 365 days long, with an extra day added to February every four years. The year was divided into 12 months, and each week consisted of seven days, with both months and days named after gods. The Julian system was virtually identical to the modern Gregorian calendar. The Germans and

SEVEN OR EIGHT DAYS A WEEK?

Ancient Romans did not use weeks. They marked points in the month by naming specific days (calends, ides, nones) after phases of the moon. They also counted market intervals, but market days were eight days apart, not seven. Europeans north of the Mediterranean did not count weeks either, instead letting the moon guide them from night to night. These systems worked well for centuries, so why did people switch to a seven-day week?

The answer comes from a combination of astrology and Christianity. Ancient Babylonians invented a seven-day week in 700 B.C.E. They chose the number seven because they knew of seven planets (five modern planets plus the sun and moon) and believed that each day was controlled by one of these heavenly bodies. They named each day after a planet. By the fourth century C.E. many Romans had adopted this seven-day system, substituting the names of their own gods for the Babylonian ones. These names are still visible in three English day names: "Sun" day, "Moon" day, and "Saturn" day.

When the Roman emperor Constantine converted the Roman Empire to Christianity in 313 C.E., he had to decide when to celebrate the Sabbath. In 321 he issued an edict declaring an official seven-day week, with the Sabbath on Sunday. Everyone then knew when they were supposed to rest and worship.

The seven-day week gradually spread through the empire over the next couple of generations. Europeans beyond the reach of the empire took longer, but even they eventually adopted the seven-day week as the primary unit of time. By the fifth century even Anglo-Saxons in Britain were using the week, but they renamed four days after their own gods. The day that the Romans had named for the war god Mars became "Tuesday," named for the heroic Germanic god Tiw. The day the Romans had named for Mercury became "Wednesday," after the god Wodin. The following day, named for Jupiter by the Romans, became "Thursday," for the god Thor. The day the Romans had named for Venus became Friday, for the goddess Frigga.

Gauls adapted the system to their own uses, but they renamed the months and the days of the week after their own gods.

Ancient Europeans did not spend much time worrying about the time of day. They might use sundials to give themselves a rough idea of the time, but they had no mechanical clocks, and, like most ancient peoples, they saw no need for minute-to-minute precision in timekeeping. As the Romans infiltrated the continent, Gauls and Germans adopted Greek and Roman technologies, such as the sundial and the water clock. A sundial was a flat disc with an upright piece oriented in such a way that the sun's light created a regular pattern of shadow over the course of a day. Romans brought sundials with them to Gaul and Britain, installing them in their home gardens. After the Romans left, the Europeans kept their timepieces; early medieval monastery gardens often contained sundials installed according to the Roman practice.

The water clock was a device that allowed people to keep track of time by measuring the regular flow of water into a stone or metal vessel. The water dripped at a constant rate and gradually filled the container; markings in the container indicated how much time had passed when the water level reached them. This was especially useful for timing the hours of the night, when the sun was not available to provide visual clues. Water clocks could at best provide only a rough estimate of the time, and they had to be refilled constantly with water in order to work at all. Still, they could provide more information about time than mere astronomical observation. For example, when Julius Caesar visited Britain in 55 B.C.E., he used a water clock to determine that the nights there were longer than those on the Continent. Water clocks were valuable objects in ancient times; often a town would acquire a single water clock for the entire community.

GREECE

BY TOM STREISSGUTH

An accurate measure of the year was important for ancient societies concerned with the best times for planting and harvesting, for observing annual religious festivals, and for recording their own history. Early methods for counting the days, however, were not precise enough to match the true solar year, meaning that calendars gradually went out of phase with the seasons. The Greek writer Hesiod (ca. 700 B.C.E.), in his poem *Works and Days*, advises tillers of the soil to reckon planting and harvest times by the first appearance of stars in the night sky. After Hesiod's time the Greeks developed a more artificial system, a lunar calendar of 12 months with an "intercalary" 13th month inserted when needed to make up days missing from the lunar year. Calendars changed somewhat from one Greek city to the next; each had its own method of figuring the precise length of the year and the time to impose the extra month.

Athens, the dominant city of ancient Greece, left behind the calendar most familiar to historians. The months of Athens had 29 or 30 days, alternating from one month to the next. Each month was divided into three shorter periods. The first 10 days were those of the "waxing moon." The second period was simply named by the consecutive numbers, from the 11th to the 19th, and the final 9 or 10 days were counted in reverse order from tenth to the first—the days of the "waning moon." The final day of a 29-day month, for example, was the "second waning moon," while that of a 30-day month was the "first waning moon."

The first month of the year, Hekatombion, arrived with the summer solstice (other city-states began the year at different times). Hekatombion was followed by Metageitnion, Boedromion, Pyanepsion, Maimakterion, Poseidon, Gamelion, Anthesterion, Elaphebolion, Munychion, Thargelion, and Skirophorion. The intercalary month was known as "second Poseidon" and came after the month of Poseidon. This calendar results in a year of 354 days, plus the intercalary month. The Athenians figured their calendars in eight-year cycles, with the extra month added in the second, fifth, and eighth years. This system was further corrected in 432 B.C.E. by the astronomer Meton (fl. fifth century B.C.E.), who noted that every 19 years the phase cycles of the moon match the cycles of the solar years. Meton proposed a 19-year calendar cycle in which there were 235 months; 125 of them were "complete" 30-day months, and 110 of them were "deficient" 29-day months. The month containing every 64th day became a deficient month, and that day was omitted; there were nine intercalary months.

As Greek measurement of the heavens and the sun grew more precise, astronomers came up with lengthier calendar cycles. In the fourth century B.C.E. Calippus (ca. 370–ca. 300 B.C.E.) suggested a change to a 76-year cycle, which would have been a total of one day shorter than the Metonic cycle. The astronomer Hipparchus (ca. 190–ca. 120 B.C.E.) proposed a 304-year cycle of 3,760 months. These refinements were never publicly adopted; they would have meant complex record keeping and would have made little practical difference to everyday citizens. A second "conciliar" calendar divided the year into ten *prytaneis*, marking the term of office of the *prytany*, or council chairman, elected from each *phylai*, or tribe. (Until 307 B.C.E. there were ten phylai in Athens.)

The Athenians and other Greeks named their years according to the leader in power (the designation "B.C.E." not being in use before the time of Christ). Starting with the Alexandrian writers of the third century B.C.E. historians adopted the four-year cycle of Olympiads to date events. They cited the number of the Olympiad, counting from the first (in the year we know as 776 B.C.E.), followed by the Olympiad year—first, second, third, or fourth ("zero" was unknown in the ancient world). The Greeks counted Olympiads to be 49 or 50 months apart, as different city-states inserted intercalary months at different times.

The confusions of the lunar calendar and the intercalary months prompted Julius Caesar, a leader of Rome, to appeal to the Alexandrian Sosigenes to come up with an accurate solar year. Sosigenes, who is mentioned only in the book *Natural History* of the Roman writer Pliny the Elder, devised the Julian calendar, with a year of 12 months and a leap year including an extra day every four years. This calendar has survived with a slight modification made in 1582 under Pope Gregory XIII, who suspended the leap day every 400 years to put the calendar more precisely in line with the solar year of approximately 365.25 solar days.

The ancient Greeks first measured time with the sundial, which the historian Herodotus (484–ca. 425 B.C.E.) claimed had originated in Babylonia. A Greek sundial held a vertical gnomon (indicator), which cast the sun's shadow on a flat surface. Later sundials used the inside of a bowl or a circular depression made in stone or earth. Eleven lines marked out the hours, with the first hour beginning with the sunrise and the last ending at sunset. Sundials grew more complex and precise as different hour lines were marked for different seasons of the year.

According to the biographer Diogenes Laertius, writing in the third century C.E., the sundial gnomon was the creation of Anaximander of Miletus (ca. 611–ca. 546 B.C.E.). Anaximander also fit the indicator into a simple and portable wooden instrument made of two pieces of wood set at right angles. By casting the sun's shadow on its vertical piece, the gnomen marked the passage of the sun and the progress of the day. The instrument also held markings showing compass directions and could predict solstices and equinoxes.

Another instrument used to measure time was the clepsydra (literally "water thief"), a spherical or cylindrical vessel made of stone or clay. An aperture at the bottom of the vessel allowed water to escape at a slow, constant rate and fill a receiving vessel positioned underneath. As the water level rose in the receiving vessel, the passing hours were indicated by a series of horizontal lines on its inner surface. Unlike sundials, clepsydras could be used day or night and on sunny or cloudy days. The best-known example of a Greek water clock is the Horologion of Andronicus, or Tower of the Winds, built in the marketplace of Athens in the first century B.C.E. Water from the nearby Acropolis supplied the Horologion, which had a 24-hour time indicator as well as sundials to show the time of day and the seasons of the year.

ROME

BY DAVID KELLY

The original Roman calendar system, developed in the seventh or early sixth century B.C.E., was based on an agricultural cycle, not on the lunar cycle; as a result, it had 10 months, for a total of 304 days. Each new calendar year began in March, at the vernal equinox. It had 10 months, six with 30 days each and four with 31 days. This is why the Latin names of the months of our calendar do not correspond to their positions. The ninth month is called September, even though that word means "seventh" in Latin. In the same way our 10th month is called October, which to the Romans meant "eighth"; "November," the 11th month, translates to "ninth"; and December, our 12th month, comes from the Roman word for "tenth." After December the 61 days remaining in the earth's revolution around the sun were not counted, since the calendar was based on the agricultural cycle, the Romans had no need to measure the winter months.

Early Roman calendars kept pace with the sun by periodically adding a month of 27 days after February, at the discretion of the *pontifex maximus*, a priest who was appointed by the emperor and often wielded his control over the calendar for political reasons. By the sixth century B.C.E. the Romans changed to the 12-month calendar, with a total of 355 days per year. This still was not in accordance with the earth's revolution around the sun, which was later measured as taking 365.25 days per year, but it was close. By the time of Julius Caesar (100–44 B.C.E.), the calendar was about three months ahead of the earth's natural revolution around the sun.

The Julian calendar, instituted in 46 B.C.E., revised the calendar into what has become the standard for Western civilization. Starting in January of 45 B.C.E. the year was established at 365 days, with an extra day added every fourth year. The Julian calendar was out of sync with the earth's revolution by only about 11 minutes each year. Since Caesar's time, the only significant change has been the Gregorian calendar, commissioned by Pope Gregory XIII in 1582: It removed 10 days that year and included provisions to keep extra days from building up in the future by removing three days every 400 years. This was accomplished by skipping leap year in years that are divisible by 100 (but not by 400), so that February of 1700, 1800, and 1900 did not have the extra leap-year day added, while February of 2000 did. The Julian calendar was so influential, though, that it was still followed in Britain until 1751.

Romans did not count the days continuously through the month until it ended. Instead, they broke the month into three separate sections. The first day of each month was Kalands; the Nones, originally the day on which the moon reached its first quarter phase, was the designation for the seventh day of some months (March, May, July, and October) and the fifth day of the rest; and the Ides, based on the time of the full moon, was the 15th day of those same months and the 13th of the others. Days were measured counting up to the next demarcation. The third of March, for instance, would be "5 before Nones March" (*V ante diem Non. Mar.*): the Romans counted inclusively, so their tally would include the number they were counting toward. The 10th of March would be "6 before Ides March" (*VI a.d. Ides Mar.*), and the 20th of March would be "12 before Kalands April" (*XII a.d. Kal. Apr.*).

Ancient Romans were quite familiar with many of the methods we use today to measure time, even though they did not feel the need to be as precise about time as we are in the modern world. The Romans did not divide the day into 24 equal hours but instead divided it into two halves, with 12 night hours and 12 day hours. The duration of these hours varied as the year changed, except at the two equinoxes, when day and night are the same length. In winter, when the days are shorter, a daytime hour could be as short as 45 minutes, while in the middle of the summer, when daylight lasted longest, a daytime hour could be as long as one and a half of our hours. In addition to being affected by the seasons, the lengths of sunlight hours also varied across the Roman Empire according to one's longitudinal position.

In the Roman day "first hour" was the hour following sunrise. "Midday" was the sixth hour after sunrise, "12th hour" the hour before sunset, and midnight the sixth hour of the night. Hours were marked with sundials or, in wealthy households, with water clocks. Anything occurring before midday was referred to as ante meridiem, which is used today by its common abbreviation "A.M."; anything after midday was called post meridiem, or "P.M." While this system of dividing the day was consistent across the empire, the Romans were far less skillful at measuring units of time within an hour. At first there was no attempt to measure time in shorter increments than the hour. In 263 B.C.E. the first sundial was brought to Rome from Sicily, as part of the treasure gained in the first Punic War (264–241 B.C.E.). It was not calibrated for the Roman sun and was therefore unreliable. Eventually someone realized that the problem was not just with the Sicilian sundial, constructed for a different latitude, but indeed with all sundials, which could not be adjusted for accuracy as the earth changed its position relative to the sun during the year.

In 159 B.C.E. the water clock was imported from Greece. This clock measured time according to how much water dripped through a narrowed opening in a measured span. Because it did not rely on the sun, a water clock's measurement could remain constant throughout the year. This benefit, however, was also a weakness: without any universal source such as the sun for reference, it was very unlikely that the time measurements of any two water clocks were consistent with each other. Ancient Rome was instrumental in devising a calendar that could follow the earth's revolution around the sun, but the Romans were never very accurate about measuring units of time within the days.

THE AMERICAS

BY ANGELA HERREN

Many inhabitants of the ancient Americas developed sophisticated methods of marking time based on careful observation of natural and astronomical phenomena. While the archaeological record in North America provides no evidence of calendar and clock use, simple farming began around 100 B.C.E., suggesting a basic knowledge of seasonal cycles. In Mesoamerica and South America the alignment and orientation of many pre-Hispanic buildings and archaeological sites acknowledge the rotation and movements of the sun, moon, and stars. Painting, sculpture, and portable arts often reflected ritual activities designed to promote success in seasonal agriculture. In ancient Mesoamerica the Maya and their predecessors developed sophisticated 260-day and

365-day calendar counts. Integral to daily life, these complementary calendar systems spread throughout Mesoamerica and dictated agricultural, ritual, and social activities until the arrival of the Spaniards in the 16th century C.E.

The first inhabitants of the Americas who crossed the Bering Strait land bridge approximately 10,000 to 12,000 years ago, after the last ice age, surely possessed a basic understanding of the movements of the sun. However, the region's first farmers, around 2000 B.C.E., necessarily developed a more acute interest in seasonal climate changes as they cultivated important staple crops like maize, beans, squash, and tomatoes. Early settlers created ritual centers oriented to the cardinal directions, and several early Mesoamerican structures mark the summer and winter solstices.

For example, the Old Temple at the highland Andean site of Chavín de Huántar dates to the late Initial Period (ca. 900–500 B.C.E.) and forms part of a cardinally oriented ceremonial center. A U-shaped structure typical of coastal Andean sites, the Old Temple turned away from the other buildings at the settlement and faced the rising sun in the east. Archaeologists discovered that darker stones set within the patio floor emphasized the east-west trajectory of the sun and the processional movement of participants in temple rituals. This patio also contained a sunken circular court.

Relief carvings of shamans in human and jaguar forms line the walls of this court, echoing human movement through the space. The entrance to the Old Temple on the east side of the building led to a dark, windowless, and labyrinthine interior. Set within a cruciform space at the center of this structure, a 15-foot-high monolithic stone sculpture of a Chavín deity marked the intersection of the four cardinal directions and a fifth vertical dimension, making it an axis mundi, or center of the world. As the Andean scholar Rebecca Stone-Miller notes, the wedge shape of the sculpture probably references the shape of the local highland foot plow. Obeisance to this supernatural deity ensured successful planting.

The Nasca Lines, created by the Nasca people who inhabited the Ica and Nasca Valleys of the Andean coast around 1–700 C.E., may also mark astronomical and seasonal events. Created by brushing away darker, oxidized stone to reveal the lighter earth beneath, the Nasca Lines create trapezoids, radial lines, and outlines of the forms of humans, plants, animals, and other objects. Comprehensible only from an aerial view, the Nasca Lines cut straight lines across mountains and valleys, revealing forms on an immense scale. Archaeological remains indicate ritualized use of the lines. Studies suggest that the Nasca Lines point to the sun's position on the horizon at the start of the rainy season and that the lines may run parallel to streams that traverse the plain.

In Mesoamerica, buildings that mark astronomical phenomena and a complex calendrical system developed in the Late Formative and Proto Classic periods (400 B.C.E.–250 C.E.). Mound J at Monte Albán, a small observatory that points to bright stars during the zenith passage of the sun, is one of the oldest chronographic markers and may contain some of the earliest recorded dates in Mesoamerica.

Early inhabitants of Mesoamerica in Guatemala and the Mexican regions of Veracruz and Chiapas devised several methods of keeping time. The oldest, a 260-day calendar, marked the intersection of a continuous and repeating cycle of 20 day names and 13 numbers. As the day signs and numbers meshed together, it took 260 days to arrive back at the original configuration. Painter-scribes recorded this information in almanacs, and diviners used the calendar to interpret the future. Each day name carried positive or negative associations with a supernatural entity. Diviners called in after the birth of a child assessed the nature of his or her birth date, renaming the child on a more auspicious day as necessary. The 260-day calendar probably derived from the nine-month human gestation period.

A 365-day solar calendar came into use shortly thereafter. This calendar consisted of 18 periods of 20 days. Each period had a name and associated number. Ancient Americans considered the five days remaining at the end of this count unlucky and dangerous. People avoided activity during this time and viewed them as unfortunate birth dates. Known as the Vague Year, the solar year calendar lacked leap days and eventually wandered through the seasons, necessitating moveable feasts or periodic adjustments of the associated festivals. Mesoamericans used the 260-day and 365-day calendars concurrently and kept track of the intermeshing of these two cycles. Every 52 years the two calendar counts completed a full cycle, or calendar round.

While the calendar round completed every 52 years and then started over, the development of the Long Count or Initial Series allowed records of a much longer span. The Long Count posited a starting point, or zero date, equivalent to the European date of 2 August 3114 B.C.E. Units of time measured the amount of time elapsed since that point. According to the Maya system, time was recorded in units of 400 years, 20 years, single years, 20 days, and single days. These five numbers appeared on monuments and architecture in a specific order, with the largest numbers first. The Maya used a vigesimal system, or a system based on units of 20, the number of fingers and toes on a person. In the Long Count system, all years equaled 360 days. These dates appear carved on stone monuments and portable objects, and painter-scribes may have recorded the calendar counts in native paper manuscripts like those in use in the 16th century.

No clocks from the ancient period of the Americas exist, but early inhabitants may have noted the position of the sun in the sky and the movement of shadows around the everyday objects that surrounded them.

See also AGRICULTURE; ARCHITECTURE; ART; ASTRONOMY; CLIMATE AND GEOGRAPHY; FESTIVALS; NUMBERS AND COUNTING; RELIGION AND COSMOLOGY; SACRED SITES; WRITING.

FURTHER READING

Anthony Aveni, "Pre-Columbian Images of Time." In *The Ancient Americas: Art from Sacred Landscapes*, ed. Richard Townsend (Chicago: Art Institute of Chicago, 1992), pp. 49–59.

Anthony Aveni, *Between the Lines: The Mystery of the Giant Ground Drawings of Ancient Nasca, Peru* (Austin: University of Texas Press, 2000).

E. J. Bickerman, *Chronology of the Ancient World*, 2nd ed. (Ithaca, N.Y.: Cornell University Press, 1980).

Bonnie Blackburn and Leofranc Holford-Strevens, *The Oxford Companion to the Year: An Exploration of Calendar Customs and Time-Reckoning* (New York: Oxford University Press, 2000).

John Britton, "Treatments of Annual Phenomena in Cuneiform Sources." In *Under One Sky—Astronomy and Mathematics in the Ancient Near East*, ed. John Steele and Annette Imhausen (Münster, Germany: Ugarit Verlag, 2002): 21–78.

Mark E. Cohen, *The Cultic Calendars of the Ancient Near East* (Bethesda, Md.: Capital Decisions Ltd., 1993).

Laurance R. Doyle and Edward W. Frank, "Astronomy of Africa." In *Encyclopaedia of the History of Science, Technology and Medicine in Non-Western Cultures*, ed. Helaine Selin (Dordrecht, the Netherlands: Kluwer, 1997).

Robert K. Englund, "Administrative Timekeeping in Ancient Mesopotamia," *Journal of the Economic and Social History of the Orient* 31 (1988): 121–132.

Sharon Gibbs, *Greek and Roman Sundials* (New Haven, Conn.: Yale University Press, 1976).

Robert Hannah, *Greek and Roman Calendars: Constructions of Time in the Ancient World* (London: Duckworth, 2005).

Hermann Hunger and David Pingree, *Mul.Apin: An Astronomical Compendium in Cuneiform* (Horn, Austria: Verlag Ferdinand Berger and Soehne, 1989).

B. M. Lynch and L. H. Robbins, "Namoratunga: The First Archaeo-astronomical Evidence in Sub-Saharan Africa," *Science* 200 (1978): 766–768.

Edward M. Reingold and Nachum Dershowitz, *Calendrical Calculations* (Cambridge, U.K.: Cambridge University Press, 2001).

E. G. Richards, *Mapping Time: The Calendar and Its History* (New York: Oxford University Press, 2000).

Alan E. Samuel, *Greek and Roman Chronology: Calendars and Years in Classical Antiquity* (London: Taylor and Francis, 1972).

Duncan Steel, *Marking Time: The Epic Quest to Invent the Perfect Calendar* (New York: J. Wiley, 2000).

► ceramics and pottery

INTRODUCTION

The making of ceramics arose independently in several different parts of the world. It seems that for every culture that learned to make ceramics, the first ceramics were functional: They were vessels for carrying liquids or grain, containers for storage, pots for cooking, pitchers for pouring, cups for drinking, or utensils used in cooking or eating. It is a sign of a universal desire to have beauty in one's life that pottery that was both decorative and functional came to predominate in the world's ancient cultures. The earliest designs on pottery seem to have had no other purpose than to beautify. Potters employed whatever materials they had at hand to color their pottery, using red, yellow, brown, and black probably because those colors could be made out of minerals or, in the case of black, out of charcoal.

Ancient ceramics were of three kinds: unfired, partially fired, and fired. Firing involves baking a clay object in high heat to dry and solidify it. Unfired pottery was usually dried in sunlight, which had significant limitations. One was that pottery making had to be seasonal, because wet weather would destroy wet pottery and cloudy skies would prevent sunlight from drying the clay. Another limitation was that sun-dried clay did not hold together well. The clay would crumble and fall apart with use.

Partially fired pottery is usually of clay that was fired literally in an open fire. How ancient potters discovered the technique of firing is not known, though it is often guessed at. It is possible that early potters learned about firing after accidentally dropping clay into a fire; alternatively, they may have used pots for boiling water or cooking stews and discovered that the bottom parts of the pots hardened, kept their shapes better than the bottoms of unfired pots, and were more durable than unfired bottoms. Examples of partially fired pottery are found in almost every ancient pottery-making society.

Fired pottery was the most desirable kind of ceramics. It held its shape better than unfired or partially fired pottery, which invited potters to experiment with the shapes of their products. Thus, with fired pottery come works of art such as human, animal, and plant figures. The earliest attempts at complete firing probably involved covering pottery completely with fiery wood and ash in an open fire. Sometime during the 3000s B.C.E. the vertical kiln was invented. It was heated at the bottom, and heat rose up out of the top; pottery was placed in a chamber over the heat. Temperatures between 850 and 1300 degrees Fahrenheit could be reached, but the flow of heat meant that the pottery would be unevenly baked. Another important development in the third millennium B.C.E. was the invention of the potter's wheel, which allowed potters to work faster and to shape wet clay as it spun. The Romans invented a horizontal kiln, and such a kiln was in use in China by 200 B.C.E., achieving temperatures over 2100 degrees Fahrenheit. This advance allowed for the development of porcelain in the 700s C.E.

AFRICA

BY KIRK H. BEETZ

The skills for making ceramic objects were not developed equally in ancient Africa. In northeastern Africa, where the potter's wheel was imported from the Near East, the manufacture of pottery became as sophisticated as anywhere in the world. Nearly all the rest of Africa, however, knew nothing of the potter's wheel until Arabs or Europeans introduced it during the Middle Ages. Without the potter's wheel, pottery was made by molding with the hands or by laying ropes or slabs of clay on top of each other. Very often, the results were coarse and rough, but several African cultures developed techniques for creating polished, beautiful work.

Exactly who did the work is hard to determine. In most modern African societies working with clay falls almost entirely to women. Women dig the clay from quarries, transport it, and then shape and fire it. Usually, they do this at home as just one of several chores performed during a day. In some places it is known that women gathered together to create manufacturing centers, which they managed like businesses, selling their wares not only among their own people but to outsiders as well. It is likely that most ancient African ceramics were made by women.

Also difficult to determine is the cultural origin of ancient African ceramics. It is fairly safe to assume that pottery found in Nubia was made by one of the cultures that existed there, but throughout most of Africa ancient pottery often has no cultural context. For instance, the Nok culture (500–300 B.C.E.) in Nigeria is known almost entirely by its ceramics, pieces of which were washed into gullies, where they were found by miners. These fragments are magnificent, but because floods carried them to where they were found, it is not known either who made them or where they were made. (They are called "Nok" because their pottery was first collected at a mine near a village named Nok.)

Many ethnic groups that lived south of Egypt were called Nubian. Dating their earliest pottery has been difficult, but a

Kerma ware pottery beaker, from Kerma, Sudan, about 1750–1550 B.C.E. (© The Trustees of the British Museum)

clay sculpture of a female found just south of Egypt has been dated to 4000 B.C.E. Animal figures found farther south are nearly as old. Vessels found near Khartoum may date to 2950 B.C.E., which would mean that Nubians developed some skills for making ceramics before they were influenced by Egyptians. Until 2600 B.C.E. Nubian ceramics manufacturing seems to have remained independent of Egyptian influence. The vessels made from 3000 to 2600 B.C.E. are painted with red geometric patterns on their outsides. Inside they are black. This black was probably achieved by mixing graphite with tree resin, a formula used elsewhere in Africa. The vessels are polished smooth, probably by being rubbed with a stone, a technique that was also used farther south, in eastern Africa.

There is a gap in the archaeological record for Nubia from 2600 to 1900 B.C.E. Some archaeologists once thought this meant that a different culture moved into Nubia in 2600 B.C.E., but most now believe that the culture continued without break to 1550 B.C.E. and that the relics for the missing years have not been found as yet. From 1900 to 1550 B.C.E. come not only vessels but also numerous human figures, often abstract, portraying both young people and adults. Usually no more than five inches tall, these figures had designs etched into them, after which they were fired and polished smooth.

The most interesting ceramics in the Nubian kingdom probably belong to Kush, which existed from about 900 B.C.E. to 350 B.C.E. and actually ruled Egypt from about 780 to 664 B.C.E. The artisans of Kush were proud of their association with Egypt and used Egyptian images and styles in their work. In 590 B.C.E. the Kush kings moved their capital south to Meroë, in southern Nubia, and ceramics from here are often called Meroitic. From the 100s to 300s C.E. there seem to have been several schools of Meroitic ceramics, including pottery made with and without the use of wheels. Some art historians think they can even identify individual artists, one of whom is the Antelope Painter, known for vivid paintings of antelopes on vases.

Southeast of Nubia was the city of Axum, which built a kingdom that lasted from the first century to the ninth century C.E., based on trade with the Near East and Far East. Its people were both African and Sabean; the Sabeans were from the southern Arabian kingdom of Sheba, where Yemen is today. They made both plain ceramic vessels and vessels with complex designs that were abstract or depicted plants and animals, using primarily the colors black and red. They also made small animal and human figures.

Nubian ceramic manufacturing techniques seem to have spread west and south in Africa. It is possible that Nubians fleeing war may have made their way as far west as Nigeria, where they may have influenced the Nok potters. Their pottery making flourished from about 500 B.C.E. to about 200 C.E. They made human figures, now existing only in fragments because they were broken long ago in floods.

The heads of their figures were sometimes spherical and sometimes elongated and were made in the manner of pots, to which features such as ears, noses, and lips were added

WHAT CERAMICS CAN TELL US ABOUT ANCIENT AFRICA

In many parts of Africa ceramics are all that remain to tell us about ancient cultures, but what they can tell us has limits. For example, the pottery of the Nok culture of about 500 B.C.E. to 200 C.E. reveals a sophisticated artistic sensibility without telling us why the Nok created these beautiful portraits of people and animals. We know that they probably liked to wear jewelry, because their figures wear necklaces, earrings, and bracelets. The features on these figures are similar to those of people native to modern Nigeria, so it is likely that they were not descended from North Africans, such as Carthaginians or from Greeks, Romans, or Egyptians. Still, this does not exclude them from being of mixed ethnic ancestry, as were the people of Axum.

The Nok ceramics inspire speculation, such as the notion that the figures belonged to shrines that were washed away in floods, since Nok pottery was deposited in gullies by flowing water; without more information, this remains no more than an educated guess. The men and women depicted in the figures are sometimes so well portrayed that the figures seem to be portraits of real people: The figures could be representations of kings and queens or even portraits of ordinary people who paid artisans to make the pottery.

Sometimes a simple piece of pottery can tell much about its culture. In the Aegyptisches Museum in Leipzig there is a small sculpture of a cow from Nubia (ca. 1990–1550 B.C.E.). It resembles the rock paintings of cattle found in the Tibesti Massif in northern Chad, dating from 5095 to 2780 B.C.E. This resemblance indicates to archaeologists that the cattle in Nubia may have been descended from the cattle herded by the lost peoples belonging to the era when the Sahara was grassland, rather than desert. This, in turn, suggests that ancient Nubian culture was influenced by or was descended from the culture of ancient Saharan herders.

before firing. Hair, head, torso, and other body parts were made separately and then fitted together using "keys," or grooves cut into the clay into which a projection fits, with a V-shape fitting into a V-shape groove. The surfaces of the figures were polished. To the northwest of Nigeria, in Mali, ceramic figures from 2010 to 1670 B.C.E. have been found with pottery intended for daily household use. The artifacts are associated with the western Sudan culture that may have been related to the Saharan grassland cultures. The pottery was incised with lines and dots. Little is known about these artifacts.

Much of central and southern Africa is now inhabited by the Bantu-speaking culture that began spreading through Africa in the last couple of centuries B.C.E. Some of these people settled in an area beside Lake Victoria stretching westward. Their pottery is called Urewe ware, named for the region in which it was discovered, and it was made from about 200 to 500 C.E. The bases of Urewe vessels had indentations, perhaps so they could be carried on the head. The potters added designs that look like bumps, and they etched in lines, usually horizontal. The lips of the vessels tend to bend outward and then turn under and in on themselves.

EGYPT

BY ERIN FAIRBURN

Pottery in ancient Egypt first appears in the archaeological record throughout the Nile River valley in the Predynastic Period (around 3800 B.C.E.). Pottery is the predominant artifact from that point on. Two types of clay were used to make pottery in the ancient Nile River valley, marl and Nile silt. Nile silt was formed from sediments deposited during the annual flooding of the Nile and would have been relatively easy to obtain, especially following the inundation, when deposits would settle on the surface. Marl clay appears in proximity to the limestone and shale formations near the Nile, stretching from the area of modern Cairo south. Marl is very dense and stonelike and has to be mined in underground works.

The preparation methods for the two types of clay would probably have varied very little. The first step might have been to purify the clay. Then the clay would be soaked in a pit of water to soften it. The softened clay would next be mixed by trampling. Humans trampled silt clays, but animals were probably used for marls. The person treading the clay would remove any bits of impurities found underfoot. Next, the trampled clay would be taken from the pit and placed on the floor, where workers would wedge it, a process of stamping on it that removed air pockets and any remaining impurities. An optional final step was tempering the clay to improve consistency and strength by adding foreign substances such as sand, hair, ash, chopped straw, or ground-up quantities of old pottery.

After the clay had undergone this preparation, it was finally ready to be formed into pottery. Vessels could be created by modeling, coil building, molding, and throwing. Handmade pottery was the most common, and the earliest Egyptian pottery was made by the hand techniques of modeling or coil building. Modeling was achieved by working a lump of prepared clay with the hands, using tools to build up the sides, usually a paddle of wood and an anvil, a stone, or a round piece of clay. The technique was to hold the anvil inside the vessel and beat the outside with the paddle. Coil-built pottery is made by laying rolled lengths of clay, formed into rings, on top of each other. The sides could be smoothed out with a paddle and anvil. The best-known coil-built pottery from ancient Egypt is the black-topped red ware from the Predynastic Period. A molded vessel is created by pressing clay into a hollow mold or by pressing it over a form, which was the most common method for creating molded pottery in ancient Egypt. It was used to create bread molds employed to bake specially formed loaves. Molds were also used to create lids for canopic jars (jars that held the entrails of mummies) and certain New Kingdom (1550–1070 B.C.E.) pottery forms, including popular vessels depicting the god Bes, protector of women in childbirth.

Pottery could be produced on a turning wheel, which was a rotating stand that gave easier access to all sides of the vessel placed on it. It was turned by hand and probably could not achieve sufficient speed to throw a vessel. Thrown vessels were created on a stand either with a flywheel that was turned with a baton or a kick wheel that the potter kicked. The rate of speed it achieved allowed the potter to build up a vessel's walls purely by hand, which made for a more regular shape. Throwing was the predominant method used in vessel formation in ancient Egypt, although several techniques were often used on a single vessel.

After a vessel was formed, it had to dry. When it had turned to a so-called leather-hard, or semidry, state, various decorations could be applied. When the vessel had dried completely and after any decoration had been applied, it was fired. As there is little evidence for open firing in ancient Egypt, it can be assumed that kiln firing was the predominant method used by ancient potters, especially since a number of kilns are known. Updraft kilns, with a lower chamber for fuel and an upper chamber with a chimney-like feature for stacking vessels, could produce a high, constant temperature, reducing the risk of incomplete firings. When stacked upside down on a vented floor above the heat source, the vessels would bake simultaneously from inside and outside. These kilns could reach temperatures of 1650 to 1830 degrees Fahrenheit; 1110 degrees was sufficient for firing Nile silt vessels, but 1290 degrees was needed for marl vessels.

How pottery was used is often very difficult to determine. Labels listing contents, scientific analysis of residues left inside vessels, and charring or other visible post-firing processes help determine their function. Pottery can generally be divided into two classes, domestic and nondomestic. Domestic vessels were used in the preparation and consumption of food. They were generally made of coarse-tempered clays and bore little or no decoration. Nondomestic vessels, often used for funerary, ritual, or decorative purposes, were frequently made of finer textured clays and were more likely to be decorated.

Several types of decoration were used on ceramics in ancient Egypt, often more than one on a single vessel. Burnishing (rubbing smooth) and applying slips (thin clay used for coatings) were common techniques for domestic and nondomestic vessels; dry vessels were treated in these ways before firing.

Painted pottery group of cattle, from el-Amra, Egypt, about 3500 B.C.E. (© The Trustees of the British Museum)

These techniques were utilized on many forms throughout the history of Egyptian ceramic production. Modeling of the vessel wall was frequently done in Egypt. The clay of the wall would be manipulated by hand, often to create human or animal forms out of either the entire vessel or portions of the wall. Sometimes modeled elements, often depicting animals, were attached to the rim or shoulder of a vessel. Incision and fenestration were decorative techniques employed on leather-hard vessels and were more likely to be used for nondomestic wares. Using the former technique, designs would be cut into the clay with a reed or knife; with the latter, sections of the vessel would be cut out in various patterns.

Throughout the history of pottery production in Egypt, painting was a major method of decoration. Paint commonly had ochre (red and yellow), charcoal (black), manganese (black), or cobalt (blue) bases. Paint was applied with fingers or with reed brushes either before or after firing. Painted vessels became most popular during the New Kingdom, when "blue-painted" and polychrome decorations began to appear on nondomestic wares. Ships were common images on Predynastic and Protodynastic pottery of the late fourth millennium B.C.E. Flora and fauna were popular motifs all through the era of Egyptian pottery production. Human figures were popular on early painted vessels, and returned to fashion beginning in the New Kingdom.

THE MIDDLE EAST

BY TOM STREISSGUTH

In Mesopotamia, the "land between" the Tigris and Euphrates rivers, the abundant red clay could be shaped by hand or on a potter's wheel, hardened over a flame, glazed, and painted. This earthenware pottery was used for preserving and storing food, such as grain, oil, beer, water, and wine, and for drinking vessels, plates, statuary, writing tablets, and seals. As one of the most durable objects of antiquity, pottery also serves as a valuable tool for modern archaeologists. The distinctive styles and colors used in different eras allow historians to date surrounding homes and streets found at the same level with remnants. The shape and size of pottery also give strong clues as to how it was made and used; its thickness testifies to its method of transport. (Thin-walled storage pottery, for example, traveled by boat, and thus reveals a civilization in contact via overseas trade with foreign lands and cultures.)

The earliest Mesopotamian pottery, from the site of Hassuna and dating to 7000 B.C.E., was hand-shaped, lightly fired, unglazed, and simply decorated with lines incised into the surface. Later designs included painted geometric forms, such as rectangular lozenges and zigzag lines. Halaf pottery (5900–5300 B.C.E.) from northern Mesopotamia is sometimes dubbed "fineware" because of the smooth surfaces that allowed potters to apply white slip (thin, watery paint) as a ground for red or black paint, mixed from oxidized ores, on the finished product. Charcoal was used to produce black paint; ground gypsum produced white paint.

Ceramic bowl with abstract decoration, from Tall-i-Bakun in modern-day Iran (Courtesy of the Oriental Institute of the University of Chicago)

Halaf pottery carried a wide variety of geometric motifs; animal forms, such as birds, leopards, deer, and rams' heads; and depictions of feasting, ceremonial processions, and other human activities. Artisans of the Halaf Period also produced ceramic figurines that may have been used in religious ceremonies or as votive objects in the home. These statues display exaggerated female features with clothes and adornments painted on their surfaces.

The pottery of the Ubaid culture (5300–4000 B.C.E.) originated in southern Mesopotamia and gradually spread to the north as well as to Persia (modern-day Iran) and the Arabian Peninsula. Ubaid objects—drinking cups, storage jars, bowls, and plates—were made of darker clay, and they often had a brown or green tint. Simple household pots were roughly shaped and undecorated and were provided with small lugs or knobs on their sides, which allowed them to be easily carried. A distinctive feature of higher-quality Ubaid vessels is a wide rim that flares out from the vessel's mouth. Some Ubaid ceramics were the first to be produced on potter's wheels, which allowed the making of larger and more symmetrical forms that could be turned out at a much faster rate. Clay figurines from this period are much slimmer than those of the Halaf era and have more elaborate clothing and adornments.

The Uruk culture of the fourth millennium B.C.E. was the first to mass-produce pottery on a wheel. The production of pottery moved from the household into the hands of professional artisans, who turned out storage vessels by the thousands for the use of traders and merchants. Most of these industrial pieces went unpainted, but ceramic artists had developed cedar oil as a painting medium. Cobalt was ground down and mixed in the medium to produce a blue pigment, copper could be added for green, and antimony produced yellow. In the city of Uruk clay was also used to manufacture writing tablets. To keep records, pictographs (figures used in a kind of picture writing) were pressed into the still-wet clay with a cylinder seal or a pointed stick.

Pottery of the Jemdet Nasr era originated around 3200 B.C.E. Jemdet Nasr jars are thick and painted in black or dark red. During this period clay seals also came into use throughout Mesopotamia (though archaeologists have discovered seal impressions from as early as the Halaf Period). Seals are small, engraved, cylindrical objects, one to two inches in length; they were also made of silver, bone, ivory, or semiprecious stone. The seals had a variety of designs and were rolled over tablets or bricks while the clay was still wet. They left a permanent, rectangular image in the clay. Engraved with images of the gods, symbols of office, or simple geometric designs, they served to authenticate records, agreements, and official documents. Later cylinder seals became items of jewelry, acting as talismans and amulets that provided the wearers with protection and good luck.

At this time clay tablets came into widespread usage for cuneiform writing, a wedge-shaped script. The tablets were incised with a reed or stick (*cuneus* in Latin) while still wet and then baked and used to keep records for trade or government functions related to the storage and movement of grain, weapons, and money. During the Uruk Period the need for record keeping arose as cities were built and people gathered under a central authority. Pictographic symbols represented commodities, while simpler designs indicated numbers.

In the second millennium B.C.E. ceramic art developed further in the Mesopotamian kingdoms. Drinking vessels were delicately shaped into abstract and animal forms that were provided with shiny glazes in a variety of colors. Painted pottery and ceramic animal figurines were everyday objects in the home. Bulls symbolized masculinity; rams and stags were given elaborate sets of horns. Female figures showed wide and rounded hips and hands held to the breasts, a symbol of fertility. Statuettes of gods and spirits were also shaped from clay and used as votive figures, guardians of the hearth and home.

By the time of the Assyrian Empire (1813–609 B.C.E.), pottery was a large-scale industry throughout Mesopotamia. Potters set up large workshops, fired their wares in massive stone kilns, and incised their work with distinctive marks and stamps. There was a wide variety of standard shapes for bowls, jugs, beakers, and plates; a distinctive blue glaze was applied that became the hallmark of Assyrian ceramics.

The fall of Nineveh, the capital of Assyria, in 612 B.C.E., brought the rise of the Achaemenid Persian Empire in Mesopotamia. Under the Achaemenids and the later Parthian and Sassanid empires, pottery artisans achieved a very high level of skill in shaping and painting clay. Vessels appeared in all manner of abstract, animal, and human forms, some very complex and others downright whimsical. As models, the ancient Persian artisans favored horned mountain goats and deer, domestic livestock such as cattle and sheep, camels (symbolizing wealth), and horses (symbolizing speed and power). Graceful handles appeared on drinking cups and jugs; spouts emerged from unlikely places, often along the side or even at the base. Historians speculate that the many twin-spouted drinking vessels found in ancient Persian cities may have been used in wedding ceremonies or in rituals that sealed treaties and agreements by drinking from a common vessel. Ceramic workshops also produced sarcophagi and funerary urns in which to bury the dead and, for the living, monumental sculptures designed for the walls of palaces and religious shrines.

ASIA AND THE PACIFIC

BY KIRK H. BEETZ

The oldest-known ceramics in Asia are found on the island of Kyushu in Japan, where pottery discovered in a cave has been carbon-dated to 12,000 B.C.E., an era in the grip of an ice age that lowered sea levels enough to connect Kyushu by dry land to Korea. The era from 13,000 to 300 B.C.E. is the Jomon Period, during which the primary way to make ceramic vessels, whether small cups or burial urns large enough for a human corpse, was to wind ropes of clay in a circle, one atop another. The ancient ceramics were elaborately decorated with designs impressed into the clay or created by adding ridges of clay to the side of the pottery, making images of trees, animals, and supernatural figures as well as abstract designs. Painting pots and other ceramic objects probably did not begin until late in the Jomon Period, when potters depicted images of everyday life on their creations.

During the Yayoi Period (300 B.C.E.–300 C.E.) numerous *haniwa* figures were made. *Haniwa* were representations of people and animals that surrounded graves and burial mounds, warding off evil spirits who might disturb the dead. Some of these figures may have been used as toys. Although they were quickly made, with sometimes hundreds being used for one burial, they nevertheless tended to be expressive, with the human figures showing emotions such as anger or happiness. It was also during the Yayoi Period that the potter's wheel was introduced to Japan. During the 400s C.E. many Korean artisans moved to the islands of Kyūshū and Honshu, bringing with them new skills. Korean potters introduced a kiln to Japan that became very popular, sometimes scores of them covering whole mountainsides. The kiln was erected on a slope, a long, brick tube pointing upward; pots were placed in it and a fire lit at the bottom end, while the heated air flowed up through the kiln's tube. Potters learned the special quirks of individual kilns and just where to place a particular ceramic object to fire it the way they wanted it to be fired.

Ceramics appeared in the Harappan culture in the Indus River region in the northwest of the Indian subcontinent about 2300 B.C.E. Harappans used potter's wheels to produce large jars that they painted with elaborate designs of animals and plants. They also made bowls and other dishes, including goblets with pointed bottoms that would be stuck into the ground to hold them upright. Harrapans created many small figures, some of which seem to be gods but others of which may have been toys.

In the Hindu culture that followed the Harappans, the story was told of how the god Shiva wanted to marry Sati but lacked a pot for the ceremony, so he created the first man and woman, potters, to make him one. Yet there is a long gap in information about Indian arts from 1500 to about 500 B.C.E. Pottery was certainly made, but it is mostly pieces of plain housewares that remain. Indian potters made items for burials and for religious occasions. They had an exceptional period of creativity in the 200s to 400s C.E., during which they created terra-cotta sculptures that rivaled stone sculptures for both gracefulness and delicacy of facial expression.

The earliest Chinese ceramics have proved difficult to date, but they may predate 5000 B.C.E. The earliest ceramic pots were black, with clay twisted to look like rope pressed on the outside as decoration before firing. Cultures such as the Banpos of 4865 to 4290 B.C.E. on the Yellow River painted their vessels, usually in black over a red surface. The images were sometimes inspired by nature, resulting in stylized depictions of people and plants. Alternatively, they could be intended just to please the eye; these images consisted of crisscross patterns or loops and would often feature the interplay of black and red in which the eye could be fooled into perceiving the red as the outer color. In about 2500 B.C.E. the Longshan culture, which existed in modern Henan, Shandong, and Shaanxi provinces from 3200 to 1800 B.C.E., revolutionized the making of earthenware in the Asian Pacific region by introducing the potter's wheel, probably imported from the Near East, thereby freeing both hands to shape clay. As early as 2400 B.C.E. various cultures living in central and eastern China were making toys out of clay as well as small images of people and deities to be included in burials.

Pottery jar with dragon handles, from China (fourth to third century B.C.E.), made to imitate a more expensive bronze vessel (© The Trustees of the British Museum)

The Shang Dynasty (1500–1045 B.C.E.) brought forth the invention of stoneware, which was hard and waterproof, and that came about when Shang potters learned how to mix clay that could be fired at about 2100 degrees Fahrenheit. They also learned to glaze ceramics. A glaze is a glasslike coating that seals the surface of a ceramic object and decorates it. During the Zhou Dynasty (1045–256 B.C.E.) potters made ceramic tiles for roofs, consisting of half-cylinders perhaps patterned after the shape of split bamboo. Some Zhou potters applied tinfoil to their creations, while others applied lacquer. During the Han Dynasty (202 B.C.E.–220 C.E.), lead glazing was introduced, probably from the Near East. This glazing melted at relatively low temperatures, making it cheaper to produce than other glazes. During the period of the Six Dynasties (220–589 C.E.), Chinese potters experimented with glazes and clays, laying the basis for the development of porcelain.

When China established the colony city of Lolang in Korea in 108 B.C.E., Chinese technology filtered through the Korean peninsula. Korean ceramic vessels tended to have three legs, which made them less likely to tip over than four-legged pots with uneven legs, and they were glazed green similar to those of the Han Chinese. From about 18 B.C.E. until unification of Korea in 676 C.E., potters made black or dark gray, finely decorated pots, and figurines of people and animals for burial goods and toys. When the Han potters of China began making white ceramics, Korea started producing extraordinarily beautiful decorated white ceramics that would develop into porcelain, establishing Korea as an important center of porcelain manufacture from the Middle Ages to the present.

Little is known about the ceramics of ancient Indochina. Cambodians began making pottery with brown glazes around 500 C.E., but in the region of Thailand, pottery making may not have begun until the 1200s C.E. The potter's wheel was not to be found in ancient Oceania, although pottery was introduced to Samoa and other islands before the first century B.C.E. The Philippines appear to have followed Chinese patterns of manufacturing pottery by about the first century B.C.E., but the peoples of Indonesia seem mostly to have imported pottery from China and Korea rather than manufacture it.

EUROPE

BY ALISON SHERIDAN

Ceramic pyrotechnology—the transformation of a flexible raw material (clay) into a rigid, if fragile end product—first appeared in Europe around 24,000 B.C.E. in the form of figurines found at the cave of Dolní Věstonice in the Czech Republic and a few other sites in central and eastern Europe. However, this seems to have been an isolated phenomenon and not the beginning of an unbroken tradition. Its next appearance was not until the early to mid-seventh millennium B.C.E. in early farming communities in the eastern Mediterranean and southeast Europe. By 4000 B.C.E. it had spread across almost all of Europe.

The spread of this technology related closely to wider changes in people's lifestyles, especially the shift to using domesticated plants and animals for food instead of relying on wild resources. In most areas these changes involved the emergence of permanent or semipermanent settlements—a way of life suited to the use of fragile ceramics. However, pottery was not exclusive to farming communities: Along the northern fringe of Europe during the sixth millennium B.C.E. fisher-gatherer-hunter groups learned from their farming neighbors to the south how to make pottery. They used this knowledge to create items suited to their lifestyle, including shallow dishes that acted as lamps for burning the oil from seals and whales and pointed-based pots for cooking. Traces of fish stew have been found in one such pot from a submerged settlement at Tybrind Vig in Denmark.

The flexibility and versatility of clay gave it uses in almost every aspect of life in prehistoric Europe. Its main usage was as vessels and utensils for preparing, serving, and consuming food and drink, but it was also formed into other kinds of containers, including urns and graves for the dead and vessels for transporting trade goods. Various manufacturing processes used ceramics (for example, as molds and crucibles for metalworking), and ceramic ovens are known from several parts of Europe, including the Orkney Islands off Scotland. Fired clay served as a building material in the warmest and driest parts of prehistoric Europe. The many other uses of ceramics in prehistoric Europe include jewelry, items connected with belief systems (such as figurines, models, and cult objects), toys, writing tablets and seals, and musical instruments such as whistles and even drums.

The methods of preparing, working, and firing clay varied greatly, as did the organization of ceramic production. At the most basic level, nonspecialist (but often highly skilled) individuals hand-built pottery, firing it rapidly in a bonfire or firing pit, for use by the family or residential group. This was the norm for much of the period in question. Potting skills

Buccero ware water jug, Etruscan, about 550-500 B.C.E., from Chiusi, Tuscany, Italy (© The Trustees of the British Museum)

were handed down through the generations. At the other end of the spectrum was the factory-based, wheel-thrown, kiln-fired commercial mass production of pottery as seen in various parts of the Roman Empire. Every variant between these extremes is found in prehistoric Europe.

There are many examples of small-scale, specialist pottery production for elite use as prestige items. These include some of the Bell Beakers of Copper Age Europe (around 2800–2300 B.C.E.), the Early Bronze Age high-status pottery of the Argaric culture in southeast Spain (early second millennium B.C.E.), and the Late Bronze Age graphite-coated and tin-inlaid pottery of south-central Europe (ninth and eighth centuries B.C.E.).

Specialist production on a larger scale is seen from around the mid-second millennium B.C.E. in the eastern Mediterranean, for example in Minoan Crete, Mycenaean Greece, and Cyprus. Such production was not only for local elite use but also for exchange or trade: sophisticated networks of contacts linked the east Mediterranean with other parts of the Mediterranean and with the Near East, ensuring the flow of many kinds of goods. Techniques of pot building included the use of the potter's wheel, often in conjunction with coil building or other methods. In coil building, rolled lengths of clay are formed into rings, one atop the other.

The trend toward large-scale, specialist production reached its peak during the first millennium B.C.E. in the form of Etruscan, Greek, and Roman pottery. Trade and other mechanisms took Greek and Roman pottery far from its places of manufacture, including into the hands of the elite in other parts of Europe. Local potters then emulated the sophisticated techniques used to make these imported pieces. This was how the technique of "throwing" pottery on a wheel spread across parts of Europe around 500 B.C.E.

Modern analytical techniques reveal much about the manufacturing methods, function, origin, and significance of prehistoric European pottery. Advances in the study of pot contents have allowed archaeologists to detect invisible traces of dairy products, meat, fish, resins, oils, and even the remains of cabbage or related plants. This technique is shedding important new light on the diet and methods of food preparation of ancient Europeans. In Britain it has revealed the use of "secondary" products such as milk around 3900–3500 B.C.E., much earlier than previously suspected. It has also shown that in England and Wales around 3000–2500 B.C.E. certain kinds of pots seem to have been preferred for cooking pork, while others were used for cooking beef.

Analytical techniques can also provide details about decoration and other surface treatments, ranging from what fibers made up the cords that were impressed into the surface of a pot to detailing methods of coating used to produce a specific surface color or texture. Analysis of the stone fragments employed as filler to stop rapid-fired vessels from exploding during firing can reveal whether pottery production was locally based or not. This technique has shown that the particularly good clays of the Lizard Peninsula in southwest England were used to make pottery that then traveled long distances during the Neolithic and Bronze Ages. We can also gain insights into prehistoric European belief systems by considering the kinds of objects made (for example, figurines) and the methods of manufacture (such as the use of recycled ancestral vessels as filler in new pots).

GREECE

BY SPYROS SIROPOULOS

Pottery surpassed its practical uses and became an art in Greece in the Bronze Age (1500–1050 B.C.E.), but there are signs that clay was worked five thousand years earlier. Archaeological excavations have come up with artifacts that indicate experimentation with clay as early as the Neolithic Period, between 6800 and 6500 B.C.E., though the general use of clay is in dispute.

Extensive manufacture and use of clay vessels characterize the Neolithic Period from 7000 to 5800 B.C.E. Decoration is very simple, mostly consisting of geometric forms in red (lines and triangles) incised on the surface of the pots, which often mimic objects such as reed baskets and leather sacks. Techniques and patterns varied greatly in different areas of Greece. In Thessaly and western Macedonia pots were decorated with human forms. On mainland Greece pots with incisions of white material were discovered. Monochrome ceramics prevailed in the Peloponnese, and decoration was not important. In Crete ceramics with incised and dotted decorations were found, while in western Greece there are indications of a connection with the Adriatic thanks to the presence of impressed ceramics, decorated with a kind of stamp. Stamping was done by using nails, seashells, or other objects to imprint a design on the surface of the pot, which was of very simple shape.

By 3000 B.C.E. bronze began to be used in Greece. Two great civilizations developed, one on the island of Crete, called the Minoan (after the mythical king Minos), and the

Terra-cotta statuette of a lady in a swing, from Agia Triada, Herakleion (Alison Frantz Photographic Collection, American School of Classical Studies at Athens)

other one in Mycenae, in the Peloponnese. The Bronze Age there ended in about 1200 B.C.E. Despite the introduction of bronze, clay was still used to produce a number of household goods, an example of which is a beautiful *hestia* (cooking stove), now kept at the Museum of Nauplia (Peloponnese, Greece), dating to 2600–2300 B.C.E. Clay objects were also made to accompany the dead in their tombs. Discoveries of numerous clay idols dating from 1380 to 1100 B.C.E. hint at the fact that clay sculpture might have been used almost exclusively for worship.

In the 1900s archaeological excavations on Crete brought to light some 3,000 clay tablets inscribed with two scripts, called Linear A and Linear B, respectively. Linear A was used by the Minoans around 1750 B.C.E., but this early form of writing has not been deciphered yet. Minoans also added inked Linear A inscriptions to stone and terra-cotta vessels. At the site of Phaestus archaeologists came across a most peculiar object: a clay disk decorated with imprints (stamps made with seal stones on wet clay) on both sides. The meaning of the 45 symbols puzzles scientists still.

Linear B tablets were found on Crete and also at Pylos and Mycenae on the Greek mainland. Most of them date to 1400–1150 B.C.E. Linear B was deciphered in 1952 by the British architect and cryptographer Michael Ventris. These clay tablets are the earliest evidence of the use of written language in the history of Greece.

During the Archaic Period (600–480 B.C.E.) the two main pottery-making techniques were the black-figure technique (invented in Corinth but perfected in Athens) and the red-figure technique. In black-figure vase painting a black coating was applied on lighter, reddish-orange clay. This coating was not color but rather a refined essence of the same clay. The details were incised with a sharp object that drew away the black coating from the surface before the vessels were fired. Sometimes white or reddish color was added later. The most celebrated artifact of this period is the so-called Amphora of Nessos (dating to 610 B.C.E. and now kept at the Archaeological Museum of Athens). This vessel marks the beginning of a series of black-figure-style works by great Athenian potters, some of whom are known by nicknames and others by conventional names (for example, Painter of the Gorgons, from a vessel of 600–590 B.C.E.). Cleitias and Ergotimos are perhaps the two most famous representatives of the early Attic black-figure style, and then Nearchus, an artist from the second quarter of the sixth century B.C.E. The names that prevail in the third quarter of the sixth century B.C.E. are those of Lydos, the Amasis Painter, and Exekias.

Around 525 B.C.E. the so-called Andokides Painter, named after the potter he worked with in Athens, used the red-figure technique for the first time. Figures maintained the reddish color of clay, while the background of the scene was painted black, as were all the details of the faces and every decorative detail of the vessels. This technique adds more volume to forms, and details are more distinctively depicted through the use of various size brushes. Red-figure vase painting begins to approximate painting.

During the 30 years of Pericles' leadership of Athens (450–420 B.C.E.), a new style developed, called *totally free* or *beautiful rhythm*. The compositions are freer, sometimes figures appear in three-quarter profile, and coatings are used for indicating depth or shadows. The Achilles Painter, the Cleophon Painter, the Eretria Painter, and Polygnotos are some of the most famous artists of this time. At the same time, a new technique appeared: painting of vessels with dull red and black paint on a white ground. This technique was gradually limited to the *lekythos*, a vessel used to store olive oil for the anointing of the dead in preparation for burial or as a burial offering. A freer style developed later (420–390 B.C.E.), with scenes from daily life and domestic or ritual activities.

Ceramics of the Hellenistic Period (323–31 B.C.E.) do not have the aesthetic quality of the red-figure style of the Classical Period. The most characteristic Hellenistic vessels are certain *skyphoi* from Megara, an ancient city in Attica. These deep, two-handled cups feature embossed decoration, usually mimicking plants. Other styles appear, such as the so-called Western Klitys style (vessels with simple linear or plant decoration, in white and yellowish coloring on a dark glazed surface), the Gnathia style (with female heads, cupids, birds, musical instruments, and discs on the surface), and the Hadra style (with black tinning on a yellowish coating and multicolored painting on white coating).

ROME

BY MELISSA MOORE MORISON

Pottery is the most common artifact found on ancient Roman archaeological sites—hardly an accident, since ceramic objects played an important role in every aspect of Roman life. The Romans cooked and served their food in ceramic vessels, used lamps made of clay to illuminate their houses at night, constructed their homes and temples with brick and ceramic roof tiles, and often used ceramic urns to preserve the ashes of the deceased. Sturdier than objects made of glass, wood, or metal, ceramic artifacts like these easily survived over time and thus provide archaeologists and historians with important information about the daily lives of the Roman people. Specialists divide Roman ceramics into categories based on function. The primary categories include vessels related to food transport, cooking, and table service; lamps; bricks and tile; and ritual objects, such as incense burners and cinerary urns (used to hold the ashes of the dead).

Amphorae were large clay containers (3 to 5 feet long) used for shipment of important commodities such as olive oil, wine, condiments, and grain. Amphorae were produced in several regions of the Roman Empire, including Spain, North Africa, France, Italy, Greece, Turkey, and the Levant. Each region produced amphorae of characteristic colors, sizes, and styles. However, all amphorae shared a characteristic shape

Amphora from Pompeii, Italy (© The Trustees of the British Museum)

directly related to their function as transport containers. In order to function effectively as containers for food, amphorae also needed to be watertight, thick, strong enough to withstand the stresses of maritime shipping, and large enough to contain between 5 and 10 gallons of liquid. It was also necessary to produce amphorae in standardized sizes and shapes, so that large numbers of them (often up to 3,000) could be loaded efficiently into the cargo holds of ships.

The production of amphorae therefore presented a significant technological challenge. For this reason, amphorae were usually made in specialist workshops located near the harbors from which trade goods were shipped. Potters in each region developed specific clay "recipes" based on their understanding of the relative strengths of different clays and mineral additives. Assembly-line techniques were also employed, with one craftsman producing the top half of a vessel, another producing the lower half, and another joining the halves and adding handles and so on. Amphorae are very important indicators of trade patterns and other economic structures. The presence of a Spanish olive oil container on a small farmstead in Jordan, for example, or the discovery of a North African wine jar in a fortress in Britain says a great deal about the extent of trade, the movement of goods, and the consumption of food within disparate provincial populations.

The Romans employed several specialized ceramic vessels for cooking. Roman cooks, like modern chefs, could choose from a wide variety of pots and pans designed to optimize the success of different cooking techniques. Herbs, vegetables, and soft cheeses were ground and mixed in the *mortarium*, a heavy bowl with sharp stone fragments embedded in its interior surface. The *olla* (or *aula*) was a deep, round-bottomed vessel used for boiling stews or porridge. One could fry or sauté fish in a shallow-angled pan with a nonstick surface (*patera* or *patina*) whereas the *patella*, a deep, straight-sided pan, was most suitable for baking casseroles (which were much-loved and characteristically Roman dishes). Grills for cooking meat were also regularly made from clay, as was the *clibanus*, a portable oven for bread baking. These vessels, in various sizes, made up a standard "set" found in most Roman households across the empire.

Beyond the standard cookware repertoire, cooks throughout Italy and the provinces also owned other vessels that reflected regional preferences in food preparation. Archaeological analysis of how cookware sets vary provides important information about Roman food preferences across the empire. Casseroles, for example, are found in relatively small quantities in provinces without a strong Roman colonial presence, as the dish is used for a specialized form of cooking most popular in Italy itself that only rather slowly became popular in other parts of the Mediterranean. Most cookware was produced in local workshops, and only a small number of ceramic cooking vessels were exported beyond regional markets. While metal versions of these objects were available, they were more expensive than the standard ceramic vessels and are less commonly found.

Tableware includes all vessels intended for food service and dining, from pitchers and platters to small cups and plates. Many Roman tableware vessels were decorated with bright red slip and intricate designs in raised relief. These designs consisted of simple geometric patterns; images of fish, birds, and plants; early Christian iconography, or symbols and images; elaborate mythological scenes; and workshop trademarks. Vessels decorated in this style are often referred to as *terra sigillata*.

Terra sigillata vessels were first produced in Italy in the first century B.C.E. Unlike amphorae and cookware, which were thrown by hand on a potter's wheel, *terra sigillata* objects were made in molds in large factories. Clay molds were created in the desired shape, and decorative patterns were cut into the interior of the molds. When the molds were complete, they could be used to make hundreds of standardized cups, bowls, plates, and platters very rapidly. Soft, wet clay was pressed firmly into a mold and smoothed so that the exterior of the finished vessel would exhibit the desired pattern in raised relief. Once the clay was dry, the vessel was removed from the mold, coated with red slip, and finished with a decorative base and handle while the mold was immediately used to create another vessel. Thousands of such vessels were fired at once in massive kilns shared by several related workshops. Most of the potters at the large *terra sigillata* factories in Italy (and, later, in France) were slaves.

By the first century C.E. Italian *terra sigillata* was widely exported to the large urban centers of the Roman provinces as well as the military garrisons on the frontiers, where standard table services, including cups, bowls, and plates, were issued to army units. *Terra sigillata* vessels were so popular that they were widely emulated in other regions of the empire. In the course of the second and third centuries C.E. production centers in Turkey, Syria, the Levant, and North Africa produced vessels of such beauty and high quality that they rapidly superseded the Italian products in popularity. Less elaborately decorated or plain tableware was also widely produced for local markets; each province of the Roman Empire had its own distinctive tableware suite reflecting local taste.

THE AMERICAS

BY RONALD YOUNG AND MICHAEL J. O'NEAL

Ceramics and pottery played an important role throughout the ancient American world. While all major civilizations in the Western Hemisphere produced ceramics in some form, the most advanced examples technically and artistically were produced by the great civilizations of Mesoamerica and the Andean region. Two principal characteristics marked ceramics and pottery throughout the hemisphere. First, American cultures built ceramic works by hand, for the potter's wheel was unknown in the Americas. Second, all ancient Americans decorated their ceramics with pigment or with slip, or clay thinned with water to a liquid consistency and used as a coating to produce a finer finish.

In North America, Native American groups in what is now the eastern United States produced ceramics extensively. Historians refer to these tribes collectively as the Eastern Woodlands, or sometimes just Woodlands, tribes. Included among them are such well-known tribes as the Iroquois and the Chippewa, along with a large number of smaller tribes that lived sedentary lives in the forested regions east of the Mississippi River. Some of the earliest pottery in North America may have been produced in the region around modern-day Georgia and South Carolina beginning in about 2500 B.C.E. From there it spread to the north, west, and south, so that by about 1200 B.C.E., the Woodlands tribes throughout the southeastern United States were making storage and cooking vessels out of fired clay.

The development of fired vessels and pottery was a major innovation, often referred to by historians as the "container revolution." Until the development of clay pottery, Native Americans had stored seeds, grains, and other food products in woven baskets and gourds, where they remained susceptible to spoilage by moisture. Such pottery as the people were able to produce, usually made from soapstone, was easily broken during transportation. But with the development of sturdier, more durable fired pottery that was glazed and therefore waterproof, people were able to store materials much more efficiently over longer periods of time. They could store not only agricultural products but also such foodstuffs as shallow-water seafood, giving their diets much greater variety. Further, the ability to store seeds contributed to the development of horticulture, which in turn gave rise to crop manipulation. All of these developments played a major role in the transition from earlier hunting and gathering to a more settled agricultural way of life.

Pottery was used for purposes other than cooking and food storage. The Hopewell culture, referring to the peoples who lived along the Mississippi and Illinois rivers (200 B.C.E.–400 C.E.), also used fired pottery for burial purposes. The pottery of the Hopewell peoples was elaborately decorated and made use of the so-called coiled pottery technique. In making a coiled pot, the potter rolled and squeezed wet clay into coils, or long segments roughly the thickness of a pencil. The clay was then wound into circles and the coils stacked one atop the other and pressed into a smooth container on the inside.

Feline-head ceramic bottle from Peru, ninth to fifth century B.C.E. (Copyright the Metropolitan Museum of Art)

The people of ancient Mesoamerica—modern-day Mexico and Central America—produced excellent pottery. During the Formative Period (1800 B.C.E.–150 C.E.) most of the basic pottery shapes could be found in ancient Mexico, including bowls, neckless jars, long-necked bottles, and spouted trays. People of the Formative Period often decorated their ceramics by covering them in black, brown, red, or white slip and sometimes polished them by rubbing with a smooth pebble. Some ceramics were plain, while others were decorated with simple geometric patterns. People of ancient Mexico also used "negative" painting, in which they painted a design with hot wax and then dipped the pot in a colored pigment. In the firing process the wax melted away, leaving the design in the original color.

During the Classic Period (150-650 C.E.) Mexico saw the growth of urban centers with large pyramids and temples. Ceramics were used frequently in the rituals carried out in these temples. Chief among the cities was Teotihuacán. While the people of Teotihuacán produced technically advanced ceramics, their early works were aesthetically dull. They later developed a polychrome style of decoration, covering pots in a brown or black slip, which was then scraped away to show a dark body, itself sometimes painted in with cinnabar. Teotihuacán also developed a stucco technique in which artists covered pots with plaster, carved a design, and filled in the design with colored clay. This type of ceramic was fragile and impractical, but it was highly regarded at the time.

The ceramics of Teotihuacán influenced the early work of the Classic Maya (250–650 C.E.). After about 600 C.E. the Maya developed a decorative technique that used brilliantly colored pigments, and they fired their ceramics at lower temperatures. These ceramics were aesthetically pleasing but less durable than those made by the older methods. The Maya decorated their ceramics with hieroglyphs, animal images, and ceremonial scenes.

In South America the most developed civilization emerged in the Andes on the western side of the continent. The Chavíns were among the earliest of the Andean peoples, flourishing from about 900 to 200 B.C.E. They produced gourd-shaped pots in white or beige, sometimes decorated with a red inlay and topped with a stirrup handle that allowed for easy carrying, drinking, and pouring. Such stirrup handles would become a trait of later Andean people, particularly the Moche peoples. The Chavíns often covered their ceramics with a resinous paint to make them waterproof. They also used "negative" painting and incised decoration.

Later, the Moches, who flourished from about 100 to 600 C.E., created sophisticated works of art, especially mold-made pottery known for its highly naturalistic forms. Moche potters used a molding technique to produce stirrup-spout bottles, handle bottles, whistling bottles, jars, and many other forms. Moche vessels, such as fine-quality water jars with stirrup spouts, bear portrait heads of individuals, animals, plants, buildings, and supernatural beings. The unique forms and representations of Moche ceramics have made them one of the most widely recognizable forms of pre-Hispanic art in South America. Although clay was the predominant medium of the Moches, copper, silver, and gold also were important in Moche art.

Painted lively scenes on Moche pottery provide visual descriptions of their complex rituals and daily activities. For example, Moche ceramics depict humans, animals, and deities in highly detailed, realistic activities such as hunting, fishing, burials, sacrifices, healing rites, the presentation of goblets between high-ranking individuals, combat, and other ceremonies.

See also AGRICULTURE; ART; BUILDING TECHNIQUES AND MATERIALS; DEATH AND BURIAL PRACTICES; EMPIRES AND DYNASTIES; FOOD AND DIET; HOUSEHOLD GOODS; HUNTING, FISHING, AND GATHERING; ILLUMINATION; METALLURGY; MINING, QUARRYING, AND SALT MAKING; MUSIC AND MUSICAL INSTRUMENTS; STORAGE AND PRESERVATION; TRADE AND EXCHANGE; WRITING.

FURTHER READING

Dorothea Arnold and Janine Bourriau, *An Introduction to Ancient Egyptian Pottery* (Mainz, Germany: Verlag Philipp von Zabern, 1993).

J. D. Beazley, *The Development of Attic Black-figure*, rev. ed. (Berkeley: University of California Press, 1986).

Janine Bourriau, *Umm El-Ga'ab: Pottery from the Nile Valley before the Arab Conquest* (Cambridge, U.K.: Cambridge University Press, 1981).

Donald Brown and David Brown, eds., *Roman Crafts* (London: Gerald Duckworth, 1976).

Robert J. Charleston, ed., *World Ceramics* (New York: McGraw-Hill, 1968).

Joaquim Chavarria, *The Big Book of Ceramics: A Guide to the History, Materials, Equipment, and Techniques of Hand-Building, Molding, Throwing, Kiln-Firing, and Glazing Pottery and Other Ceramic Objects* (New York: Watson-Guptill, 1992).

Emmanuel Cooper, *A History of World Pottery*, rev. ed. (Radnor, Pa.: Chilton, 1981).

Emmanuel Cooper, *Ten Thousand Years of Pottery* (Philadelphia: University of Pennsylvania Press, 2000).

Roy C. Craven, *Indian Art: A Concise History* (New York: Thames and Hudson, revised 1997).

Gabriele Fahr-Becker and Chris Murray, eds., *The Art of East Asia* (Cologne, Germany: Konemann, 1999).

Ian Freestone and David Gaimster, eds., *Pottery in the Making: World Ceramic Traditions* (London: British Museum Press, 1997).

Alex Gibson, *Prehistoric Pottery in Britain and Ireland* (Stroud, U.K.: Tempus, 2002).

Werner Gillon, *A Short History of African Art* (New York: Penguin Books, 1984).

Kevin Greene, *Roman Pottery* (Berkeley: University of California Press, 1992).

John W. Hayes, *Handbook of Mediterranean Roman Pottery* (Norman: University of Oklahoma Press, 1997).

Elizabeth Moignard, *Greek Vases: An Introduction* (London: Bristol Classical Press, 2006).

Paul T. Nicholson and Ian Shaw, *Ancient Egyptian Materials and Technology* (Cambridge, U.K.: Cambridge University Press, 1999).

Daniel P. Potts, *Mesopotamian Civilization: The Material Foundation* (Ithaca, N.Y.: Cornell University Press, 1997).

C. F. Vafopoulou-Richardson, *Ancient Greek Terracottas* (Oxford, U.K.: Ashmolean Museum, 1991).

Michael Vickers, *Ancient Greek Pottery* (Oxford, U.K.: Ashmolean Museum, 1999).

Sarah Underhill Wisseman, "From Pots to People: Ceramic Production in the Ancient Mediterranean." In *Ancient Technologies and Archaeological Materials*, ed. S. U. Wisseman and W. W. Williams (Langhorne, Pa.: Gordon and Breach Science Publishers, 1994).

► children

INTRODUCTION

The life of a child was extremely uncertain and difficult in the ancient world. First, a child had to be born alive. But in the absence of the knowledge and technologies of modern medicine, large numbers of children were stillborn or died shortly after birth. Then the child had to survive. Historians estimate that 25 percent of newborns the world over did not survive their first year, dying from respiratory problems, diarrhea (and the dehydration it caused), infectious diseases, and starvation. Even if children survived their first year, dangers still lay in wait, and larger numbers failed to survive to age 10. Meanwhile, life expectancy for adults was low, and many women died during childbirth, so a child faced the danger of losing one or both parents, making the chances of the child's survival slim.

The child had to be reasonably healthy and well formed to grow to adulthood. In most ancient cultures people did not have the resources to care for sick people who could not fend for themselves when necessary. A common practice was for sick or deformed infants to be left to die, often in forests or deserts. The word *foundling*, referring to a baby who is "found" and raised by another, attests to the prevalence of this practice.

Few children went to anything that resembled a school, though in some ancient cultures, such as Greece and Rome, young boys were often taken away at an early age for training in the responsibilities of citizenship, including military training; in ancient Sparta boys were regarded as the property of the state from the age of seven. For the most part, though, children stayed at home with their parents. Toys were few, though some archaeological evidence for toys has been found. Few parents attached much sentimental value to their children. Children were a resource, and from an early age they were taught the skills they needed to help them and other members of their clan or tribe survive, including hunting, herding, and farming. Boys worked out of doors at these tasks, and it was expected that a boy would follow his father's occupation. Girls were taught domestic chores such as cooking.

In modern life children are thought to be the sole responsibility of their parents, though parental authority can be delegated to teachers in schools. In many ancient cultures, in contrast, children were thought of as the responsibility of the entire community. Early peoples lived in extended clans, not only with parents but also with grandparents, uncles, aunts, and cousins. Often these cultures were matrilineal, meaning that descent was traced through the female rather than the male line. In this type of culture, the responsibility for training children in the values of the community belonged to the community as a whole.

If children survived all these hardships, they were ready for initiation into adulthood. Usually at around the age of puberty boys—and somewhat less often girls—were subjected to initiation rites that identified them as adult members of the society. Often these rites involved some sort of arduous task; typically, the child was segregated from the rest of the community during the initiation. The child who successfully completed the initiation became a full-fledged member of the adult community.

AFRICA

BY MICHAEL J. O'NEAL

Generalizations about children and child rearing in ancient Africa are difficult to make. The continent of Africa is and was home to hundreds of ethnic groups, each with its own customs and traditions. Thus, to talk about "African" children and child rearing is misleading. Further, the lack of written records from ancient Africa makes it difficult for historians and archaeologists to make with confidence precise statements about children and child rearing. They know, however, that in modern times African communities continue to follow many of the same customs and to practice many of the same rituals they did many centuries ago.

The history of children and child rearing in Africa begins millions of years ago. Research by archaeologists and geneticists strongly suggests that the human species originated in Africa. The earliest "hominids," the *Australopithecines*, emerged in Africa some four to six million years ago. Among the earliest archaeological evidence are the "*Australopithecine* footprints" found near Laetoli, Tanzania. The footprints are those of an adult and child, made about 3.5 million years ago.

The concept of "childhood" as it is understood today was probably unknown in ancient Africa. Thousands of years ago human behavior was in large measure dictated by the simple goal of survival. Mates tried to produce as many offspring as possible during the woman's childbearing years, with the hope that some would survive to adulthood (when they could reproduce). Beyond mere survival the purpose of child rearing was to teach youngsters how to be human—that is, how to function with one another in a social group in order to hunt, forage, grow crops, and perform other functions necessary to survival. In particular, children early on were taught the value of collecting food, taking it back to the community, and sharing it with other family members.

Because of the importance of food gathering, mothers learned to fashion slings so that they could carry their infants while foraging. Indeed, the child's ability to survive depended heavily on a mother's ability to carry the child long distances until he could walk as well as on her ability to provide food. Further, her survival and that of her offspring depended on spacing the birth of children, in some instances as much as four or five years apart. Otherwise, the mother would be tied down with nursing infants and unable to look for food. It was also important for the mother to maintain ties with her own brothers and sisters and those of her mate. Doing so provided her and her children with protection and a community that taught children the skills they needed to survive. Most ancient African cultures were probably matrilineal, meaning that descent was traced through the mother's ancestors rather than the father's. The father often gave the child a name, but the matrilineal clan name remained an important part of the child's identity.

The concept of community in child rearing was important to ancient Africans. Every adult in the community shared in the task of raising children and teaching them not only physical skills (hunting, foraging, growing crops, tool making, cattle herding, and the like, depending on the economy of the particular community) but also social skills, leadership, conflict resolution, and the like. A common modern proverb that expresses this concept is "It takes a village to raise a child." This proverb, though, has many different variations from throughout Africa: "A child does not grow up only in a single home," "A child belongs not to one parent or home," and others. Skills tended not to be specialized, for specialization would have made the tribe—typically 30 to 100 people—dependent on the skills of one person at a period of time when life was precarious. Thus, children were early on taught the arts of cooperation. They often learned these lessons through community storytellers, who preserved and transmitted tales that promoted the values of the group over the individual. Children—and

Boys kept in seclusion in an initiation camp in Angola, southern Africa; such rites date back to ancient times. (© Board of Regents of the University of Wisconsin System)

adults—spent a great deal of time with their "age sets," or people who were roughly the same age. At an early age children were responsible for labor. Boys as young as six or seven would, for example, help with herding or other farming activities; girls were responsible for fetching water, caring for younger children and the sick, cleaning, helping their mothers in the fields, and food preparation.

A key development for the ancient African was initiation into adulthood. Initiation rituals can be found in cultures throughout the world. They mark the passage of males or females from childhood to the duties and responsibilities of adulthood. An example is the traditional initiation ritual for boys among the Xhosa, a Bantu-speaking people in modern-day South Africa, whose ancestors arrived there some 1,500 years ago. Boys were isolated in a special hut built for the purpose of keeping them away from the community. Elders provided them instruction, and they lived frugally for a period of weeks or months. Perhaps the harshest part of the initiation was the *abakweta* ceremony, during which the boy was circumcised. Boys used white clay to whiten their bodies and wore a white blanket. The color white protected them from evil. They also wore traditional masks, hats, and reed skirts. All of these items, along with the hut, were burned on the completion of the process, to signify that the boys had cast off the past. The elders then herded the boys to the river, often beating them along the way. The boys plunged into the river to wash off the clay and emerged on the opposite riverbank as men. They were then painted with red ochre, and their fathers gave them new clothes or new blankets. These types of ceremonies were not limited to boys. When they reached puberty, girls, too, often underwent similar practices, as happened in the Sande society among the Mende people of West Africa. While the girls lived in huts, older women would instruct them in the duties and responsibilities of marital life. When they emerged from the hut, the community would hold a celebration.

EGYPT

BY KELLY-ANNE DIAMOND REED

At birth an Egyptian child was given his or her name; according to Egyptian religious belief, a person could not exist without a name. The name was as integral to the individual as his or her body or soul. Usually the mother named the child, and the name could be associated with physical attributes or the family's occupation or ethnic origin; it might also derive from an ancestor. Some names also reflected wishes or exclamations, for example, the name Mersure, which means "May the god Re love him."

There was a high rate of infant mortality in ancient Egypt. Families that had five surviving children might easily have lost three others. It is thought that 20 percent of pregnancies were not carried to term, another 20 percent of newborns died within the first year, and 30 percent of children did not make it to their sixth year of life. Support for these figures derives from the abundance of children's graves dating to ancient Egyptian times. Numerous spells were employed to aid in childbirth and keep the newborn safe. That the well-being of their children was of great importance to most parents is evident in the countless magical objects and amulets for the protection of children that have been found.

Newborns were always breast-fed, since there was no substitute for breast milk. Normally, the mother would be the one to nurse, but a wet nurse might be employed if there was a problem with the mother's milk supply. In the New Kingdom (ca. 1550–1070 B.C.E.) it was common for women of high rank to act as wet nurses for the royal family and to be paid well for their services. Nursing often continued until the child reached the age of three. It was the women who were responsible for rearing children, sometimes with the help of female servants.

Information about childhood and about children in general derives mainly from Egyptian tomb scenes, statuary and figurines, and text sources. In Egyptian art children are depicted as smaller than their adult counterparts, but they are not properly proportioned, nor are they always anatomically correct. Children are frequently shown wearing the "sidelock of youth," possibly a marker of a child who had not yet reached puberty. Children often had their heads shaved, except for this thick lock of hair on the side of the head, gathered with a tie. In the Old Kingdom (ca. 2575–2134 B.C.E.), children were generally depicted nude until the age of puberty. In the Middle Kingdom (ca. 2040–1640 B.C.E.), they were more commonly illustrated with clothes, similar in style to that of their parents. In the New Kingdom children were illustrated both clothed and unclothed.

It is difficult to confirm whether Egyptian children had toys. Archaeologists have encountered many items that have the character of toys; however, the Egyptians also had many small models of boats, houses, people, animals and the like, usually carrying religious significance and often buried with the dead for their use in the afterlife. Such miniature magical and religious paraphernalia could be confused with toys. When found in settlement areas (as opposed to sacred sites and burial locations), these artifacts are assumed to be toys. It is also possible that the two functions overlapped—children might have played with religious items. Games were especially popular among Egyptians. They played a board game called Senet, an ancestor to our game of backgammon, and another, similar one called Twenty Squares. Tomb scenes confirm that children enjoyed wrestling, ball games, racing, swimming, and dancing.

The Greek historian Herodotus (ca. 484–420 B.C.E.) states that the Egyptians used circumcision for hygiene purposes; however, it may also have had a religious association. This act was not performed at birth or shortly thereafter but instead near a boy's 14th year, marking the transition to puberty. From the Late Period (ca. 712–332 B.C.E.) onward, priests were circumcised as a purification rite. This would seem to indicate that the practice was not universal and that not all boys were circumcised. A scene from the Sixth Dynasty (ca. 2323–

Game of Senet from New Kingdom (© The Trustees of the British Museum)

2150 B.C.E) tomb of Ankhmahor at Sakkara, the necropolis at Memphis, may show a priest circumcising a boy with a curved flint knife, though this scene may instead depict a ritual shaving. Egyptian mummies show evidence of circumcision. The Greek historian Strabo (ca. 63 B.C.E.–21 C.E), who wrote in Roman times, claims that the Egyptians also practiced female circumcision, but this has not yet been confirmed through examination of surviving female mummies.

The main education of Egyptian boys came in the form of an apprenticeship under their fathers. Boys belonging to the elite class were sent to scribal school. Scribal students often copied literary works, which has led to the preservation of numerous documents of "wisdom literature," or texts of an instructional or philosophical nature. Because wisdom literature was set up as guidance from father to son on how to behave and how to live one's life, it has been assumed that the majority, if not all, official scribal students were boys. Boys belonging to the upper echelons of society received a broader training, often involving the study of mathematics. It is not known whether girls received any sort of formal education. Letters dating to the New Kingdom are considered by some scholars to be evidence that at least some women were literate. Not surprisingly, young girls learned from their mothers how to take care of household duties. Theban tomb scenes also show girls serving food and drink at banquets.

Children of the poorer classes had to work from an early age. Around the mortuary complex and tomb of Khasekhemwy, the last king of the Second Dynasty (2770–2649 B.C.E.), children's footprints were found in the mud plaster, indicating that they, too, worked on its construction. Fathers were anxious for their sons to take over their jobs, and the boys learned their father's trade as apprentices. Likewise boys and girls would have worked alongside their parents in the fields. For the children of the poorest class, a childhood as we know it did not exist.

Children looked after their parents later in life. Evidence from Deir el-Medina, a village near Thebes that was home to craftsmen who worked on the tombs in the Valley of the Kings and the Valley of the Queens, indicates that an aging father would give his post to his son and, in turn, the son would provide for his father. Children were not forced to look after their aging parents, but if they did not, they could be prevented from receiving their inheritance.

THE MIDDLE EAST

BY KAREN RADNER

The purpose of a marriage in the ancient Near East, including Mesopotamia and Persia, was to produce children. For Mesopotamia specifically, children were a necessity for any family, as the continuation of the bloodline guaranteed survival for all ancestors. Children were expected not only to provide for their parents in old age but also to perform memorial service to commemorate the dead of the family, thereby keeping their essence alive. Not to have children was therefore extremely awkward, and if the situation could not be helped with the assistance of prayer, magic, and medicine, a couple had the option to adopt a child or to use a surrogate mother to produce an heir. With high mortality rates among pregnant women and babies, the birth and the survival of a child were always considered a divine blessing; many people bore names that reflected their parents' joy in having had them, often referring to dead siblings whom they had replaced. For example, the meaning of the name of the Assyrian king Sennacherib (r. 704–681 B.C.E.), the Old Testament's rendering of Sin-ahhe-eriba, means "The god Sin has replaced the (dead) brothers."

As the French historian Philippe Ariès first recognized in 1960, the idea of childhood as a distinct phase of human life is a modern Western concept, developed as late as in the 17th century. It is therefore not surprising to find it a concept alien to the cultures of the ancient Near East, including Mesopotamia and Persia. There is no specific term for "children," from birth to adolescence, and this fact is best reflected in Near Eastern art, where children are simply depicted as miniature adults, without any evidence for a special dress code or hairstyle and without any attempt to emphasize a childlike physique, other than simply showing them to be of small size. Good examples of this can be found in the reliefs from Sumerian temples of the mid-third millennium B.C.E. as well as from Assyrian royal palaces of the ninth to seventh centuries B.C.E.

Only young children, up to the age of four years, were perceived as different from the rest of humankind: In art they are shown as bald and naked and usually in closest proximity to their mothers. While there is no general word for *child*, there are specific terms referring to babies and toddlers. Babies were called "he of the milk" or "she of the breast," referring to the fact that they were breast-fed; the available sources as well as ethnographic comparisons, derived from the study of contemporary cultures in Africa and Asia, suggest that babies were weaned relatively late, at the age of two years or even later. The word used for *toddlers* refers to the termination of breastfeeding and means literally "separated one," indicating that they were no longer physically inseparable from their mother. Babies and toddlers were normally never parted from their mothers: Slave sale contracts, for example, show that mothers were sold together with their young offspring, and administrative lists, enumerating the workforce of large institutions such as temples and palaces, list mothers with their small children; both text types date to ca. 2200 to 100 B.C.E.

A group of texts that were used to calm down a crying baby shows that this was thought to be as great a challenge to Mesopotamian parents as to modern ones. One such text that was found in a library in the city of Assur, the capital of ancient Assyria, begins like this: "He who lived in darkness, where it is not bright, came out and saw the light of the sun. Why is he weeping so that his mother cries, so that the goddess Antu sheds her tears in heaven?" While the texts are called magical incantations, invoking the help of the gods, they may well have worked also as simple lullabies, as they were chanted rather than just spoken.

A female demon called Lamashtu, mentioned in Assyrian and Babylonian ritual texts of the second and first millennium B.C.E., was thought to prey on pregnant women, young mothers, and babies, and amulets depicting this monstrous creature were used to ward her off. When a baby's mother died, a wet nurse had to be found quickly to provide milk for

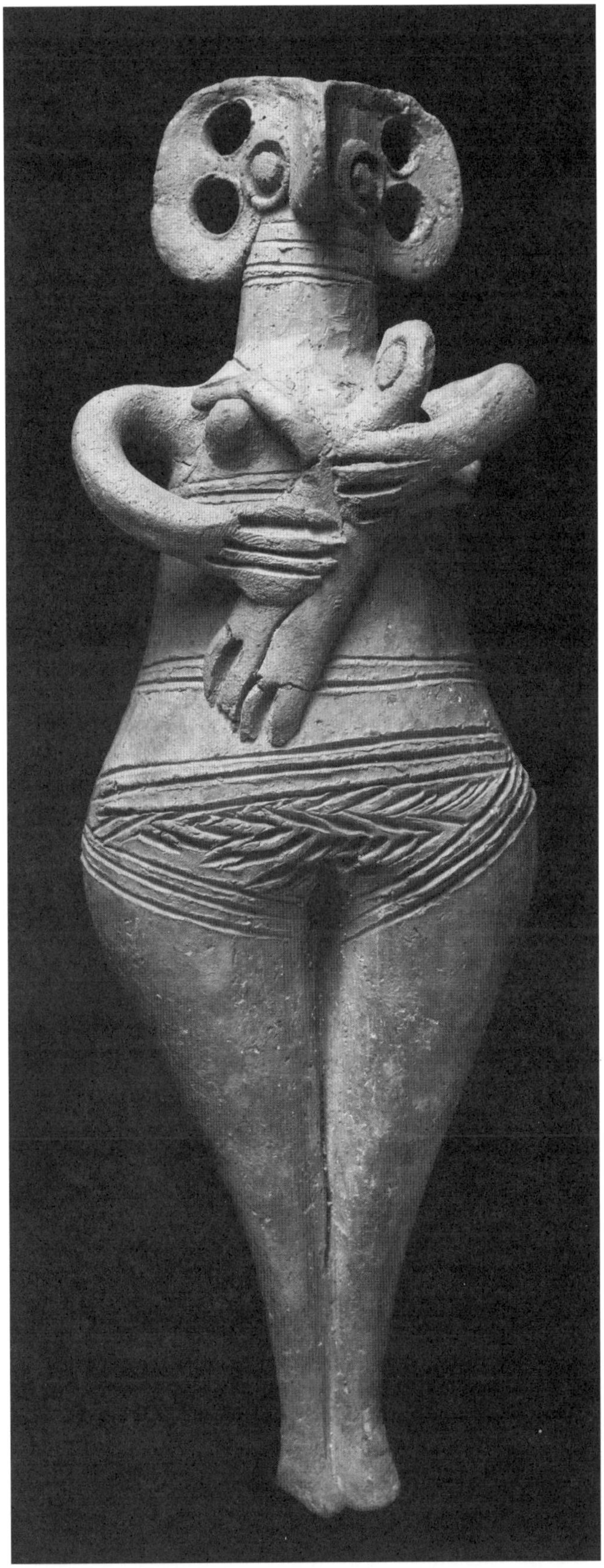

Terra-cotta figurine of a woman with a child, Cyprus (1450-1200 B.C.E.) (© The Trustees of the British Museum)

the child. With the mother alive, wet-nursing seems to have been less common, though the fact that some wet-nursing contracts survive is clear evidence that the practice was well established. Moreover, in Mesopotamian prayers and temple inscriptions from the third to the first millennium B.C.E., the bond between a goddess and her adorant is often likened to that of a wet nurse and her charge: The comparison is meaningful only in a society accustomed to this intimate and nurturing relationship between a woman and a child that is not her own.

Once toddlers reached an age when they could be instructed to perform simple tasks without the need for ongoing supervision (typically at the age of four years), they were treated as adults. This is best demonstrated by the fact that we find them listed as individuals in rosters of temple dependents and similar administrative texts; the crucial factor was not a person's age in years but his or her physical ability. Hence, a boy of 10 who was small for his age could find himself at work with children several years his junior, while his physically more developed contemporary would work alongside grownup men. If concessions were made to the working conditions of children, it was not because as children they would automatically enjoy privileged treatment but because anybody with a weaker physique, including the aged or disabled, was eligible for adjustment.

Most children were educated at home, and it is important to note that education and work went hand in hand. Girls learned from their mothers all the many skills expected to be mastered by women, such as spinning, weaving, sewing, laundering, cooking, and baking, while boys were usually instructed in their father's trade: Hence, a smith would teach his son how to refine and work metal, a stonemason would train his son in the different stone-working techniques, and a scribe would instruct his son how to read and write the cuneiform script and also how to prepare writing materials. In this way, specialized knowledge and skills were passed through the generations within family networks.

There was no compulsory school attendance in the ancient Near East. Still, the ability to read and write was an advantage for the sons and, to a far lesser extent, also the daughters of the urban elite, who were typically predestined to follow the family tradition and take on a role in government and administration. A number of satirical compositions shed light on the schooldays of these students and mock their often strained relationship with their teachers, who are referred to as "master" or "father." Many, if not most, kings received formal schooling; some, such as Shulgi of Ur (ca. 2000 B.C.E.) and Ashurbanipal of Assyria (r. 668–ca. 630 B.C.E.), even proudly referenced their high level of education in the inscriptions that celebrated their accomplishments, by recording them for posterity on public monuments. As shown by a scolding letter of the crown prince Ashurbanipal's sister Sherua-etirat to his young wife, at the time in her teens, a good school performance was considered essential also for a future queen: "Why don't you write your paper [literally, "clay tablet"] and do your homework? For if you don't, people will say: Is this really the sister of the royal princess Sherua-etirat? You are, after all, married to the crown prince of Assyria."

ASIA AND THE PACIFIC

BY KIRK H. BEETZ

In Asia and the Pacific during ancient times, most children lived harsh lives. In some cultures—among the aborigines of Australia, for example—children appear to have had more free time than in other societies. Elsewhere in the region, however, children had to work hard beginning at a young age to help their families survive. Early in the Stone Age, about 6000 B.C.E., some peoples in central and northern Asia began following herds of game such as reindeer, linking their survival to the welfare of the herd animals; certain groups of people continued that way of life throughout ancient times. Children in these families were expected to learn to care for the animals, and as soon as they could walk they would begin participating in the work of their nomadic existence.

In societies based on pastoral nomadism children were expected to care for horses and domesticated cattle, sheep, and goats. With the development of horseback riding both girls and boys learned to ride early, and their initiation rites at puberty usually required them to display feats of horsemanship by participating in races, by capturing or herding domesticated animals, by hunting, or by displaying fighting skills.

By the second millennium B.C.E., throughout China and India, agricultural societies were settling near rivers and floodplains. Nearly all these societies practiced human sacrifice, often using children. Throughout southern Asia, east of India, children were bought to be ritually murdered in sacrifice to a goddess of fertility so that crops, especially rice, would grow abundantly. This practice continued in Burma into the 20th century.

In the early agricultural communities children were expected to learn the skills of their parents, nearly every task needed for survival. A child would learn to gather wood, make ovens, craft pottery, tan animal hides, sew, and develop any other necessary skill. As communities grew more settled, people began to specialize. The future life of children was generally determined by what their parents did: Peasant children were to be peasants, potter children were to be potters, and noble children were to be nobles. Most were peasants. From 1500 to 500 B.C.E. children of the rich and powerful had beautiful clothes, were taught by tutors, and played with finely crafted toys. From the Harappan civilization of the Indus valley of 2300 B.C.E. in India and in China from before 1500 B.C.E., small objects have been found that may have been toys: little clay animals such as horses with thick, stubby legs from ancient India and clay tigers from Asia. These items suggest that even poor children had time to play. However, throughout most of Asia children were most often victims: In India they were war trophies to be sold into slavery; in China they were frequently slaughtered by the thousands by victorious armies; in India and southern Asia poor families often sold their children into slavery.

Lives for children in China, at least, began to change significantly for the better in 415 B.C.E., when one Confucian Chinese governor introduced a moral code to govern social behavior. At the beginning of the Han Dynasty in 202 B.C.E. Confucianism became official state policy, and in 145 B.C.E. Governor Wen Weng of Shu, where modern Sichuan is, set up schools for boys from throughout the province; so effective were his graduates that the Han government established an educational system that encouraged the most able boys to attend school and better their lives by competing for government jobs.

As another way for children to escape the grinding poverty of peasant life, beginning in the first century C.E. girls and boys could be given to Buddhist monasteries or convents at about five to eight years of age. They would be given simple robes and have their heads shaved, symbolizing their renunciation of worldly desires. Such children would have worked hard, but they probably ate regularly and, in many cases, were taught to read; as adults, they could even gain community influence and help their families.

In India religious and secular education were combined. When boys were initiated into manhood, a symbolic rebirth of the spirit, they would be sent to gurus, or spiritual teachers, to study sacred Hindu texts, mathematics, and medicine and other sciences. This would happen at age eight for boys born into the priestly caste, at age 11 for those born into the ruler and warrior caste, and at age 12 for those of the worker and farmer caste. However, those of the laboring caste and the untouchables were excluded. Some boys were sent to schools at Buddhist monasteries; these were so popular during the Gupta Dynasty of 240–550 C.E. in what is now India that one in Nalanda had more than 10,000 students. Girls were taught at home, usually by tutors and mostly in arts such as painting, singing, and literature as well as in home economic skills, including weaving and supervising servants. Girls were usually married by age 16, but boys did not finish their studies until age 18 and typically married later.

ENTERTAINMENT, EUROPEAN STYLE

In ancient Europe most children were illiterate. For entertainment they listened to stories. On long winter nights everyone in a community would gather around a fire in the woods or in a lodge and listen to a poet creating scenes from history and myth. These stories were about the things that interested European peoples: the gods who controlled the weather and human events, heroes fighting battles, dwarfs and dragons, kings and lovers. The stories gave people a sense of identity and continuity. The plots and characters were usually familiar, but the actual words varied from telling to telling, as the poet chose episodes to embellish in the moment. Poets worked entirely from memory. No one wrote down European folktales and poems until the eighth century C.E. at the earliest, and even then stories appeared in many different versions, making it impossible to identify "definitive" tales.

Many of these stories still exist today, some as a result of an oral tradition that continued through the medieval and modern period and some because they were written down by medieval monks. The Tain Bo Cuailnge (pronounced "toyn bo cooley"), or "Cattle Raid of Cooley," is an Irish epic telling of the rivalry between a king and queen based in part on the size and quality of their respective herds of cattle. This story introduces the fearsome Irish hero Cúchulainn (pronounced "coo-hoo-lin"). The people of Germany told stories of their gods, such as the fierce war god, Thor, and the wise father of gods, Wodin. The Gauls' stories also featured a large cast of deities, some of them borrowed from their Roman neighbors. Like the ancient Greeks, other Europeans also honored poets who could tell long tales of adventure, heroism, and love. Poets could visit any community with impunity; though many Europeans were warlike and violent, they welcomed those who offered them entertainment.

EUROPE

BY AMY HACKNEY BLACKWELL

Not much is known about childhood in ancient Europe aside from what was recorded by Greek and Roman authors. Childbirth was dangerous; many women died giving birth, and many infants died during or soon after birth. A newborn who survived birth but whose mother died stood a fair chance of dying as well from lack of a mother's care. Even if baby and mother both survived the birth, the baby's parents might not keep her. Parents frequently abandoned unwanted infants, leaving them in the countryside to die; they were especially likely to abandon illegitimate children, deformed children, and girls.

Most mothers breast-fed their infants. Women who could afford to do so, such as the nobility, would sometimes hire wet nurses to feed their babies. Women in ancient times typically nursed babies for about two years, a practice that had the effect of spacing births because nursing can decrease fertility. Rates of infant mortality were high. Children less than two years of age were vulnerable to numerous sicknesses, and ancient Europeans had no reliable remedies for them. Many babies died of diarrhea or respiratory ailments. Scholars estimate that more than one-quarter of all babies died before they were a year old. Of those children who survived infancy, another third died by the age of 10. This was true throughout Europe.

European children lived with their extended families; households often included a husband, wife, children, grandparents, and aunts, uncles, and cousins. Children wore smaller versions of the clothes their parents wore, mainly long tunics and wool cloaks. They lived in houses made of stone or timber and mud with thatched roofs. They spent their evenings listening to folktales and participated with the adults in frequent feasts and festivals. Children did not have their own rooms or even their own beds. They slept on the mud floor wrapped in animal skins, huddled with their parents and siblings for warmth.

Most European societies of the time had no schools or other institutions for children, so children would have spent most of their time at home, playing and learning home skills or assisting their families with work around the house or farm. Farming families tried to have as many children as possible, because their labor would be needed for cultivation and keeping livestock and because those who did not survive to adulthood needed to be replaced. Most Europeans worked on their farms raising grain, cattle, pigs, sheep, hens, and geese. These tasks included sowing wheat, harvesting grain, and preparing fields for the next season; milking cows, goats, and sheep; making milk into butter and cheese; spinning wool into thread, dyeing it bright colors, and weaving it into cloth; and hunting in the forests. Girls would have concentrated on homebound tasks that other women performed, learning to cook, grind grain, bake bread, and weave. Boys would have helped their fathers and uncles with their daily work, such as plowing, hunting, and occasionally building houses. When boys were old enough, they might learn a craft such as metalwork. Boys also would have learned how to fight with swords and other weapons. If they were wealthy, they learned to ride horses.

Many noble Celtic families sent their children to live with other noble families as foster children. The most common arrangement was for a child to live with the family of his mother's brother. A child would spend several years living with his foster family and usually formed very strong bonds with his foster parents and siblings. These ties were valuable in a warlike society where allies could mean the difference between victory and defeat in battle.

Childhood was harsh and dangerous for ancient European children. Cold, hunger, and illness were constant threats, and wild animals could snatch them away. A child's parents sometimes died—the father in war or the mother in childbirth or both of them from disease. Unless someone else, such as a relative, took in the child, his fate was uncertain. There was always the chance that a child's parents would abandon her even after infancy if times were hard and food supplies were low; fairy tales of foundlings have their root in ancient stories of parents leaving children alone in the woods to meet whatever fate awaited them. The ancient Celts and Germans lived a rough existence and had no resources to waste on the weak or sickly. They often traveled through the wilderness, wandering from one place to another without a permanent home, and they could not afford to carry useless people with them. The Romans observed that when the Gauls were on the march, they would kill their old people and anyone who could not care for himself, which included children.

Ancient European children also faced the risk of kidnap or capture in war. Slavery was a common practice in ancient Europe. Saint Patrick of Ireland (386–493 C.E.) spent seven years of his youth as a shepherd slave after being kidnapped from his wealthy family's home in Britain around 400 C.E. Many of the slaves who worked in Greece and Rome came from central and northern Europe. When Romans defeated a tribe in battle, they typically sold all the surviving women and children into slavery; in this way many European children found themselves in Rome, performing menial labor for Roman families. For some children this proved a wonderful opportunity; Roman masters and mistresses sometimes educated their slaves and treated them as family members. In other cases slavery was a dreadful existence of starvation, rape, beatings, and sometimes death at the hands of a cruel master.

GREECE

BY AMY HACKNEY BLACKWELL

The Greeks wanted children. Children were legally bound to take care of parents when the parents grew old; in the absence of any other provision for old-age care, children were essential. Many infants did not survive birth, however, and many women died during or after childbirth from bleeding, exhaustion, or infection. An infant who survived birth without a mother was in danger of dying from lack of maternal care unless another woman took him in and raised him. When a baby was born, the midwife would announce the sex and then examine the baby to see if he was healthy. If the parents decided to keep their child, they celebrated the baby's birth on the fifth day of life, publicly acknowledging the child as a family member and naming the baby in a ceremony called the *amphidromia*.

Parents did not always choose to raise the children they produced. Resources were limited, and parents who lacked food, money, or opportunities could not always afford to keep all their children. If a baby seemed sickly and unlikely to survive or if the baby was not the desired sex, usually male, the parents might decide to abandon the infant, leaving it out in the countryside to die. In most of Greece the father could decide whether to keep the child regardless of what the mother thought. In Sparta the city's elders chose which infants would be raised to adulthood. Historians do not know the percentage of Greek babies that were abandoned, but the ones most susceptible to this practice were girls, illegitimate infants, deformed infants, and the babies of slaves. Occasionally strangers would keep and raise foundling children, but usually the infants died. Greek literature sometimes mentions the exposure of infants; the most famous infant to be saved from this fate was Oedipus, the hero of Sophocles' trilogy of plays that includes *Oedipus the King*.

The natural way to nourish infants was for their mothers to breast-feed them, a practice that was encouraged in the belief that a mother's own milk was the best food for her child. Still, nursing was considered tiring, and mothers were supposed to refrain from sexual intercourse while they were nursing a baby, a prohibition that made the practice unappealing to many parents. In reality, then, many mothers who could afford the expense hired wet nurses to breast-feed their babies. Wet nurses were women who had recently given birth themselves, were producing milk, and breast-fed babies other than their own. Some of these women were slaves who lived with the family, but others did it purely for economic reasons, receiving wages for the service.

Mortality rates were high among infants and children. Perhaps one-quarter of babies died before the age of one. Another third of children died between the ages of one and 10. Doctors had no effective remedies for diarrhea, respiratory infections, and other common sicknesses, which killed many children. Children also died from accidents, fires, and attacks by wild animals.

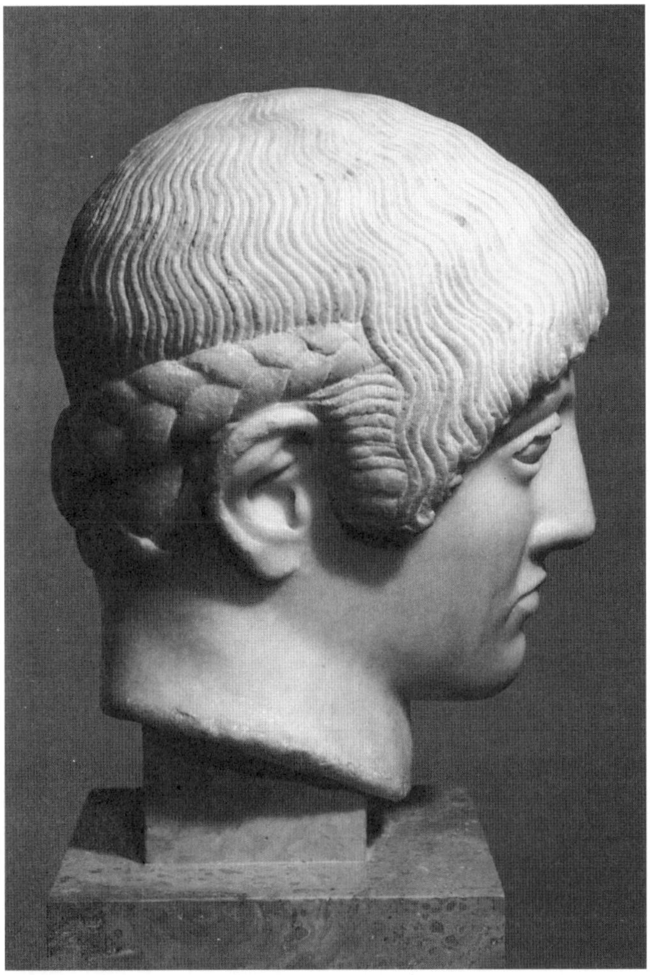

Profile of a Greek boy (Alison Frantz Photographic Collection, American School of Classical Studies at Athens)

Young children of both sexes stayed home with their mothers until they were about six years old. Most Greek adults seem to have liked their children and enjoyed seeing them grow up. Plato describes the play of children in his *Laws* and praises it as an excellent means of forming personality. Scholars know that Greek children had toys because they have found pictures of playthings on Greek vases and actual toys in Greek graves. These included rattles for infants, rolling carts, balls, hoops, toy animals, swings, and seesaws. Girls had dolls and dollhouses complete with miniature furniture. Children also played games; ancient authors have described blindman's buff, catch, dice, and prisoner's base. Many of these games were accompanied by traditional songs, similar to modern children's games such as London Bridge.

Both boys and girls dressed in simple tunics. Many children wore good-luck charms around their necks; bells were especially popular because they could amuse the child and were believed to ward off the evil eye, or bad luck. In literature many abandoned infants are identified by the unique charms they wear.

Around the age of six or seven boys began their educations. In Athens they were enrolled in hereditary organizations called phratries when they were still quite young. These organizations served as an extension of the family, handling community affairs and resolving disputes among members. Every Athenian citizen had to belong to one, and participating in the activities of phratries gave Athenian boys important early training in the affairs of the city. In addition to engaging in their civic duties, Athenian boys attended elementary schools, where they learned reading, writing, arithmetic, music, poetry, dance, gymnastics, and general physical education. Parents paid for school; there was no public education. Discipline was strict and corporal punishment common. Students competed in periodic public contests to show what they had learned.

In Sparta children were considered the property of the state from the age of seven. Young boys left home and moved into public schools called *agoge*, which were primarily concerned with training soldiers. Spartan schools were hard on their young pupils; boys were given only a cloak to wear, winter or summer, and were encouraged to become tough and violent. Spartan girls trained with boys in athletic feats such as running or gymnastics; this was considered essential preparation for their future duties as mothers of Spartan soldiers.

Girls in most of Greece spent their childhoods at home, in the company of their mothers and other women. They learned the skills they would need as adults, such as spinning and weaving. Girls as well as boys attended school, though they did not necessarily study the same subjects. When boys reached their late teens, various ceremonies marked their entry into manhood. Before they became adults, many boys became the lovers of men; this was considered entirely proper and good training for young boys. Girls married in their teens and were considered adults at that point. Many girls conducted rituals on the day before their weddings to mark this change in their status, but there were no specific public ceremonies to commemorate their transformation into women.

ROME

BY AMY HACKNEY BLACKWELL

In ancient Rome children were valued as the best means of supporting their parents in their old age and the only means of carrying on the family name. Childbirth was very dangerous to mothers and babies. Ancient midwives and physicians did not understand the mechanisms of birth very well and had few useful treatments to offer mothers. Many infants died during or after birth, and any women died during or after childbirth from bleeding, exhaustion, or infection. If a baby's mother died in childbirth, the father or other caretaker would have to find a wet nurse to feed the child, or the baby would be at risk of dying as well.

When a baby was born, the midwife would determine the sex and then examine the baby to see if it was healthy. If the parents kept the child, they celebrated its birth on the eighth day of life in a purification ceremony called the *lustratio.* If the baby was sickly or deformed or if it was a girl, the parents might decide to abandon it in the countryside to die. An ancient law attributed to Rome's legendary founder Romulus directed parents to keep all male offspring and the first born of their girls, but most people disregarded these old laws and did not abandon their female children.

Mothers were encouraged to breast-feed their infants. The physician Soranus of Ephesus (fl. second century C.E.) recommended that mothers breast-feed their own children because this provided the best food for the baby and strengthened the bond between mother and child. In practice, many mothers with the resources to do so hired wet nurses to nurse their babies. Soranus provided detailed advice on selecting a wet nurse, suggesting that the nurse not drink wine and that she live with the family. He advised breast-feeding a baby exclusively for six months and then gradually introducing foods until the child was weaned at about two years of age.

A high percentage of Roman babies and children died. Scholars believe that about 25 percent of infants died before their first birthdays. Of those children who survived the first two years of life, another third died before the age of 10. Respiratory illnesses, gastrointestinal diseases, accidents, fires, and violence killed large numbers of children.

Children of both sexes were under the authority of their fathers or other male relatives. The father, or paterfamilias, technically had the power of life or death over his children, though in the days of the Republic (509 B.C.E.–ca. 27 B.C.E.) and Empire (ca. 27 B.C.E.–476 B.C.E.) almost no father exercised this right. Both boys and girls spent their early childhoods in the home nursery in the care of women. Mothers sometimes

Roman rag doll made of linen, rags, and papyrus and dating to the first to fifth century C.E. (© The Trustees of the British Museum)

raised the children themselves, but many mothers employed slaves as caretakers for their young children. Corporal punishment was a common means of enforcing discipline.

Boys learned what they would need to know as men—the sons of craftsmen were taught their fathers' crafts, and the sons of farmers learned farming and animal husbandry. Sons of nobility went to school or studied at home with tutors called pedagogues, who were usually slaves owned by the family. Schools were informal by modern standards; many teachers simply set up portable desks on street corners or in town squares and taught their students amid the hubbub of the marketplace. Boys studied grammar, mathematics, geography, history, and law as well as Greek, the language of educated people in the ancient world. All boys had to learn the basics of warfare, such as swordplay, in preparation for their military service. On festive occasions boys dressed in a special toga called the toga praetexta, bordered in red or purple to mark the boy's juvenile status. All boys wore a necklace called a bulla, a chain with a pouch containing protective amulets. Boys became adults in a ceremony conducted at the age of 16, at which point they exchanged the toga praetexta for a simple white toga called the toga virilis.

Girls spent much of their time at home, learning female skills such as weaving and sewing. They also went to school or studied with pedagogues, though female education was not considered as important as male education. Girls, like boys, wore the bulla necklace; they stopped wearing it when they married. They also wore the toga praetexta on special occasions. Girls did not undergo a ceremony inducting them into adulthood. They married at about the age of 18; younger girls certainly married, but it was often considered improper.

Both boys and girls played roles in Roman religion. Children could hold priesthoods and were in fact desired for these positions because of their purity. The young Julius Caesar (100 B.C.E.–44 B.C.E.) was appointed *flamen dialis*, chief priest of Jupiter, when he was about 13 years old. Because the *flamen dialis* had to be married, Julius Caesar wed a young girl when he took office; she served as his female counterpart, the *flaminia dialis.* Vestal virgins, the priestesses who cared for the sacred flame of the hearth goddess, Vesta, entered service at the age of seven or eight and spent the next 20 years or so performing their duties.

The Roman nobility especially valued their children, both boys and girls, as necessary players in maintaining the family's status. Boys were raised to uphold family honor. Girls were taught from an early age that their duty was to marry whomever their fathers selected as husbands for them, with the understanding that this choice would be dictated by financial and political needs and not by romantic inclination. Despite this apparently callous attitude toward offspring, there is ample evidence that Roman parents loved their children and wanted them to enjoy their childhoods. Ancient vases depict toys, and ancient writers wrote about children's games. Funeral inscriptions often mention children, and parents who lost children sometimes held elaborate funerals for them.

THE AMERICAS

BY ANGELA HERREN

Little information exists on the role of children in the ancient Americas. In the past archaeological studies focused on adult roles in society; however, some recent scholarship addresses the social experience of children in the ancient period. These studies rely on archaeological evidence and early forms of artwork that may represent infants and children. Some scholars caution that the concept of childhood is a social construct. Like their descendents, ancient Americans probably welcomed children into the world, training them early to perform tasks appropriate to their gender, but did not conceive of childhood as a distinct period in one's life. Rather, children gradually assumed the responsibilities of adulthood, probably marrying a few years after the onset of puberty. While men generally engaged in agricultural production, hunting, and other activities, women typically cared for children, prepared food, maintained the home, wove textiles, and in some cultures were responsible for ceramic production.

In South America the Paracas (ca. 700 B.C.E.–200 C.E.) and Nazca (ca. 1–700 C.E.) cultures interred many children in their burial grounds on the southern coast of Peru. Twentieth-century excavations along the sandy desert coastline found the remains of children among the hundreds of mummy bundles buried in shallow shaft tombs. The bodies, placed in a fetal position within a basket and wrapped in layer upon layer of cloth, generally show that the children experienced malnutrition or died from childhood diseases. The children wore textiles sized to fit their small bodies, and some burials included figurines or toys in the layers of their bundle. Archaeological evidence indicates that early cultures experienced a much higher infant mortality rate than is true today, and the average life expectancy for adults was 37 or 38 years old.

While few clues exist about childhood experience in North America, skeletal remains and artwork from Mesoamerica and South America indicate that many cultures practiced cranial deformation, compressing and shaping the skull of a newborn infant with boards or mats to achieve an aesthetically pleasing

Olmec figure of a baby (ceramic, cinnabar, and red ochre) 12th to ninth century B.C.E., Mexico (Copyright the Metropolitan Museum of Art)

profile. There is such evidence in the region of the Andes. The distinctive results of skull compression could signal the beauty, status, or ethnic group of the individual and may have had religious or ritual purposes as well. Neonatal head shaping did not seem to result in neurological damage.

Some evidence suggests that child sacrifice, a documented practice in the later Inca Period (ca. 1400–1500 C.E.), also occurred in ancient South American cultures. At times, ancient societies offered children in sacrifice to deities believed to control natural phenomena; adults considered children the most precious and pure gift they could present to the gods. In 1995 the archaeologist Steve Bourget discovered the bones of 42 male adolescents of the Moche culture (ca. 1–700 C.E.) embedded in a sacrificial plaza near a ceremonial structure called the Huaca de la Luna on the northern coast of Peru. This excavation marked the first discovery of large-scale sacrifice at a Moche site. The skeletal remains showed many healed fractures, indicating that the boys participated in combat activities in the years before their deaths.

Archaeological studies indicate that ancient Mesoamericans also practiced both cranial deformation and occasional child sacrifice. Practitioners of child sacrifice in Mesoamerica probably sought to venerate water deities to ensure adequate seasonal rains for farming or to appease deities in times of drought or famine. Some studies suggest that children chosen for sacrifice suffered from illness; ancient Mesoamericans may have viewed them as chosen by the gods for this honor. Skeletal studies indicate that some sacrificed children suffered from infection due to dental caries.

The Olmec, a culture that began to establish ceremonial centers along the Gulf Coast of Mexico around 1500 B.C.E., often represented infants or figures with infantile aspects in their artwork. Hollow ceramic figures depict the splayed legs and chubby limbs of infants. Flattening at the back of the head on these and other figures documents cranial deformation also found on skeletal remains. In addition, many ceramic baby figures have crossed eyes. The Olmec and later Maya cultures interpreted crossed eyes as a sign of beauty and elegance and induced the effect by hanging a bead in front of the child's eyes.

Many sculptural forms combine corpulent infantile bodies and crying Olmec "baby faces" with supernatural or jaguar attributes. The resulting figure, referred to as a *werejaguar*, probably functioned as a representation of a deity. Some scholars argue that this association derives from Olmec belief that young children were closer to the supernatural world in their early years, before they learned to speak.

The Olmec also took a special interest in representing birth anomalies in sculptures. One finds numerous figurines representing dwarfs, hunchbacks, and club-footed or pigeon-toed individuals. The Olmec believed that people who were born with unusual physical traits possessed supernatural abilities. The Olmec infant cults surely viewed the small stature of dwarfs as a link to the world of their deities.

Like their descendents, the ancient Maya welcomed children and may have turned to Ix Chel, goddess of childbirth, to promote fertility. Soon after birth the infant's parents applied a pair of flat boards to the back of the head and the forehead. Left in place for several days, the device created a permanently flattened forehead, signaling beauty and status. Like the Olmec, the Maya admired and induced crossed eyes. Just as some families today pierce the ears of female children, the Maya pierced the ears, lips, and nasal septum of boys and girls to hold ornaments. Mothers cared for male and female children until the age of four; by four or five years of age male children began to train with their fathers.

See also AGRICULTURE; ART; CLOTHING AND FOOTWEAR; DEATH AND BURIAL PRACTICES; ECONOMY; EDUCATION; EMPLOYMENT AND LABOR; FAMILY; FESTIVALS; FOOD AND DIET; GENDER STRUCTURES AND ROLES; HEALTH AND DISEASE; HUNTING, FISHING, AND GATHERING; LITERATURE; MILITARY; NOMADIC AND PASTORAL SOCIETIES; OCCUPATIONS; RELIGION AND COSMOLOGY; SETTLEMENT PATTERNS; SLAVES AND SLAVERY; SOCIAL ORGANIZATION; SPORTS AND RECREATION; WAR AND CONQUEST.

The Middle East

The Advice of an Akkadian Father to His Son, ca. 2200 B.C.E.

Do not set out to stand around in the assembly. Do not loiter where there is a dispute, for in the dispute they will have you as an observer. Then you will be made a witness for them, and they will involve you in a lawsuit to affirm something that does not concern you. In case of a dispute, get away from it, disregard it! If a dispute involving you should flare up, calm it down. A dispute is a covered pit, a wall which can cover over its foes; it brings to mind what one has forgotten and makes an accusation against a man. Do not return evil to your adversary; requite with kindness the one who does evil to you, maintain justice for your enemy, be friendly to your enemy.

Give food to eat, beer to drink, grant what is requested, provide for and treat with honor. At this one's god takes pleasure. It is pleasing to Shamash, who will repay him with favor. Do good things; be kind all your days. . . .

My son, if it be the wish of a ruler that you belong to him, if you are entrusted with his closely guarded seal, open his treasure house and enter it, for no one but you may do it. Uncounted wealth you will find inside, but do not covet any of that, nor set your mind on a secret crime, for afterwards the matter will be investigated and the secret crime which you committed will be exposed.

Do not speak ill, speak only good. Do not say evil things, speak well of people. He who speaks ill and says evil—people will waylay him because of his debt to Shamash. Do not talk too freely; watch what you say.

Do not express your innermost thoughts even when you are alone. What you say in haste you may regret later. Exert yourself to restrain your speech.

Worship your god every day. Sacrifice and pious utterance are the proper accompaniment of incense. Have a freewill offering for your god, for this is proper toward a god. Prayer, supplication, and prostration offer him daily, then your prayer will be granted, and you will be in harmony with god.

From: Internet History Sourcebooks. Available online. URL: http://www.fordham.edu/halsall/.

Asia and the Pacific

Confucius: Analects, *excerpt, ca. 479–221* B.C.E.

. . . Mang I asked what filial piety was. The Master said, "It is not being disobedient."

Soon after, as Fan Ch'ih was driving him, the Master told him, saying, "Mang-sun asked me what filial piety was, and I answered him, 'not being disobedient.'"

Fan Ch'ih said, "What did you mean?" The Master replied, "That parents, when alive, be served according to propriety; that, when dead, they should be buried according to propriety; and that they should be sacrificed to according to propriety."

Mang Wu asked what filial piety was. The Master said, "Parents are anxious lest their children should be sick."

Tsze-yu asked what filial piety was. The Master said, "The filial piety nowadays means the support of one's parents. But dogs and horses likewise are able to do something in the way of support; without reverence, what is there to distinguish the one support given from the other?"

Tsze-hsia asked what filial piety was. The Master said, "The difficulty is with the countenance. If, when their elders have any troublesome affairs, the young take the toil of them, and if, when the young have wine and food, they set them before their elders, is THIS to be considered filial piety?"

From: *The Analects of Confucius*, translated by James Legge (Oxford, U.K: Clarendon Press, 1893).

Greece

Herondas (Herodas): The Third Mime *excerpt, ca. third century* B.C.E.

[A mother, Metrotimé, brings her truant son Cottalos to his schoolmaster, Lampriscos, to receive a flogging.]

Metrotimé. Flog him Lampriscos, across the shoulders, till his wicked soul is all but out of him. He's spent my all in playing odd and even; knucklebones are nothing to him. Why, he hardly knows the door of the Letter School. And yet the thirtieth comes round and I must pay—tears no excuse.

His writing tablet, which I take the trouble to wax anew each month, lies unregarded in the corner. If by chance he deigns to touch it, he scowls like Hades and then puts nothing right but smears it out and out. He doesn't know a letter till you scream it twenty times. The other day his father made him spell "Maron"; the rascal made it "Simon": dolt I thought myself to send him to a school! Ass-tending is his trade!—Another

(continued)

(continues)

time we set him to recite some childish piece; he sifts it out like water through a crack, "Apollo"—pause,—then "hunter!"

[The poor mother goes on to say that it is useless to scold the boy; for, if she does, he promptly runs away from home, to sponge upon his grandmother, or sits upon the roof out of the way like an ape, breaking the tiles, which is expensive for his parents.]

Yet he knows the seventh and the twentieth of the month, whole holidays, as if he reads the stars; he lies awake o'nights dreaming of them. But, so may yonder Muses prosper you, give him in stripes no less than—

Lampriscos [briskly]. Right you are, here, Euthias, Coccalos, and Phillos hoist him upon your backs. I like your goings on, my boy! I'll teach you manners! Where's my strap, with the stinging cow's tail?

Cottalos [in terror]. By the Muses, sir,—not with the stinger?

Lampriscos. Then you shouldn't be so naughty.

Cottalos. O, how many will you give me!

Lampriscos. Your mother fixes that.

Cottalos. How many, mother?

Metrotimé. As many as your wicked hide can bear.

[They proceed with the flogging]

Cottalos. Stop!—That's enough!— Stop! Lampriscos. You should stop your ways.

Cottalos. I'll never do it more, I promise you.

Lampriscos. Don't talk so much, or else I'll bring a gag.

Cottalos. I won't talk,—only do not kill me,—please!

Lampriscos [at length relenting]. Let him down, boys.

Metrotimé. No—eather him till sunset.

Lampriscos. Why, he's as mottled as a water snake.

Metrotimé. Well, when he's done his reading, good or bad, give him a trifle more, say twenty strokes.

Cottalos [in agony]. Yah!

Metrotimé. [turning away]. I'll go home and get a pair of fetters. Our Lady Muses, whom he scorned, shall see their scorner hobble here with shackled feet.

From: William Stearns Davis, ed., *Readings in Ancient History: Illustrative Extracts from the Sources*. Vol. 1: *Greece and the East* (Boston: Allyn and Bacon, 1912–1913), pp. 255–257.

Rome

Plutarch: "The Training of Children," ca. 110 C.E.

Children ought to be made to abstain from speaking filthily, seeing, as Democritus said, words are but the shadows of actions. They are, moreover, to be instructed to be affable and courteous in discourse. For as churlish manners are always detestable, so children may be kept from being odious in conversation, if they will not be pertinaciously bent to maintain all they say in dispute. For it is of use to a man to understand not only how to overcome, but also how to give ground when to conquer would turn to his disadvantage. . . .

Add we now to these things some others of which children ought to have no less, yes, rather greater care; to-wit, that they avoid luxurious living, bridle their tongues, subdue anger, and refrain their hands. . . . To begin with the last: some men there have been, who, by opening their hands to take what they ought not, have lost all the honor they got in the former part of their lives. So Gylippus the Lacedaemonian, for unsewing the public money-bags, was condemned to banishment from Sparta. And to be able also to subdue anger is the part of a wise man. Such a one was Socrates; for when a hectoring and debauched young man rudely kicked him, so that those in his company, being sorely offended, were ready to run after him and call him to account for it, *What,* said he to them, *if an ass had kicked me, would you think it handsomely done to kick him again?* And yet the young man himself escaped not unpunished; for when all persons reproached him for so unworthy an act, and gave him the nickname of *Laktistes*, or the kicker, he hanged himself. The same Socrates—when Aristophanes, publishing his play which he called *The Clouds*, therein threw all sorts of the foulest reproaches upon him, and a friend of his, who was present at the acting of it, repeated to him what was there said in the same comical manner, asking him withal, *Does not this offend you, Socrates?*—replied: *Not at all, for I can as well bear with a fool in a play as at a great feast. . . .*

These things, you will perhaps say, are very difficult to be imitated. I confess it; but yet we must endeavor to the utmost of our power, by setting such examples before us, to repress the extravagancy of our immoderate, furious anger. For neither are we able to rival the experience or virtue of such men in many other matters; but we do, nevertheless, as sacred interpreters of divine mysteries and priests of wisdom, strive to follow these examples, and, as it were, to enrich ourselves with what we can nibble from them.

And as to the bridling of the tongue, . . . if any man think it a small matter or of mean concernment, he is much mistaken. For it is a point of wisdom to be silent when occasion requires, and better than to speak, though never so well. And, in my judgment, for this reason the ancients instituted mystical rites of initiation in religion, that, being in them accustomed to silence, we might thence transfer the fear we have of the gods to the fidelity required in human secrets. Yes, indeed, experience shows that no man ever repented of having kept silence; but many that they have not done so. And a man may, when he will, easily utter what he has by silence concealed; but it is impossible for him to recall what he has once spoken. And, moreover, I can remember infinite examples that have been told me of those that have procured great damages to themselves by intemperance of the tongue. . . When Ptolemy Philadelphus had taken his sister Arsinöe to wife, Sotades for breaking an obscene jest upon him lay languishing in prison a great while; a punishment which he deserved for his unseasonable babbling, whereby to provoke laughter in others he purchased a long time of mourning to himself. Much after the same rate, or rather still worse, did Theocritus the Sophist both talk and suffer. For when Alexander commanded the Greeks to provide him a purple robe, wherein, upon his return from the wars, he meant to sacrifice to the Gods in gratitude for his victorious success against the barbarians, and the various states were bringing in the sums assessed upon them, Theocritus said: *I now see clearly that this is what Homer calls purple death, which I never understood before*. By which speech he made the king his enemy from that time forwards. . . .

Besides all these things, we are to accustom children to speak the truth, and to account it, as indeed it is, a matter of religion for them to do so. For lying is a servile quality, deserving the hatred of all mankind; yes, a fault for which we ought not to forgive our meanest servants.

From: Oliver J. Thatcher, ed., *The Library of Original Sources*. Vol. 3: *The Roman World* (Milwaukee: University Research Extension Co., 1907), pp. 370–391.

FURTHER READING

Traci Ardren and Scott R. Hutson, *The Social Experience of Childhood in Ancient Mesoamerica* (Boulder: University Press of Colorado, 2006).

Elizabeth P. Benson and Anita G. Cook, *Ritual Sacrifice in Ancient Peru* (Austin: University of Texas Press, 2001).

Jean Bottéro, ed., *Everyday Life in Ancient Mesopotamia* (Baltimore, Md.: Johns Hopkins University Press, 2001).

Mark Golden, *Children and Childhood in Classical Athens* (Baltimore, Md.: Johns Hopkins University Press, 1993).

Rosalind M. and Jac. J. Janssen, *Growing Up in Ancient Egypt* (London: Rubicon Press, 1990).

Lynn Meskell, *Private Life in New Kingdom Egypt* (Princeton, N.J.: Princeton University Press, 2002).

Sarah B. Pomeroy, *Families in Classical and Hellenistic Greece* (New York: Oxford University Press, 1999).

Beryl Rawson, ed., *The Family in Ancient Rome: New Perspectives* (Ithaca, N.Y.: Cornell University Press, 1987).

Beryl Rawson, ed., *Marriage, Divorce, and Children in Ancient Rome* (New York: Oxford University Press, 1996).

Sobonfu E. Somé, *Welcoming Spirit Home: Ancient African Teachings to Celebrate Children and Community* (Novato, Calif.: New World Library, 1999).

Marten Stol, "Private Life in Ancient Mesopotamia." In *Civilizations of the Ancient Near East*, ed. J. M. Sasson (New York: Charles Scribner's Sons, 1995).

Marten Stol, *Birth in Babylonia and the Bible* (Groningen, Netherlands: Styx, 2000).

► cities

INTRODUCTION

One of the basic problems in the study of ancient cities is defining what makes a settlement a true city and not a town or village. Some archaeologists use population to make this determination, with 40,000 to 50,000 inhabitants making for a true city. By that definition, the Mesopotamian settlement of Uruk, when it was ruled by Gilgamesh in about 2700 B.C.E., would have been a city because it had about 50,000 residents. Yet the requirement that a city have that many people would exclude most other Mesopotamian settlements that are called "cities." Elsewhere, the Indus River valley settlements of Harappa and Mohenjo Daro, the biggest settlements in their part of the world, might not qualify as cities. The large communities of the Maya (600 B.C.E.–1521 C.E.), and those of the Shang Dynasty (ca. 1500–ca. 1045 B.C.E.) of China in the might not meet the criterion either.

Another approach to defining the nature of a city is by the settlement's social organization. Are the people living lives apart from one another, organizing themselves more like a cluster of villages than a unified community? Such a settlement might not be a city. On the other hand, if the city has the equivalent of a public works department, would it be a city? If there were public employees who repaired streets, lighted lamps at night, or kept the sewers clear, would that imply a civic government and therefore a city? Still, a settlement of 1,500 people might well have people in charge of lighting lamps at night and maintaining irrigation ditches or sewers. Is such a settlement a village with public employees, the beginning of a city, or a true city? Perhaps public maintenance of common ground sets a city apart from other settlements.

Another way of defining what makes a true city is by its construction. When archaeologists discuss Mohenjo Daro, they almost inevitably note that it was designed to be a city. It streets were laid out in a grid. Its sections were defined by brick walls. It had sewers with manholes for people to enter in order maintain them. Perhaps its construction of public streets and buildings made it a city. The ancient Romans believed that to be true. When the Romans designed a city from the ground up, they made sure that it had public buildings. To the Romans, the city of Rome had become a city when King Tarquinius Priscus (r. 616–578 B.C.E.) built the first Roman Forum. That public structure made Rome a city. In ancient Mesopotamia a wall around a city served the same purpose. To Mesopotamians, that wall defined the sacred grounds of their city.

In addition to the question of what makes a settlement a city, archaeologists have long debated why cities arise in the first place. At present, the most common explanation is that ancient people banded together for agricultural reasons. This explanation has logic. In the 7000s B.C.E. people settled in the land surrounding the Tigris and Euphrates rivers to farm wheat and barley, but most of the region had too little rain to raise crops, so they dug channels out of the rivers to irrigate their fields. To dig irrigation canals required that many people work together, which may have necessitated a central government to organize them and direct their work. It also may have been more convenient for people to live in close proximity rather than scattered in villages, so that they could easily gather together for their work and share in its benefits.

There are alternatives to the view that agriculture prompted the beginning a cities. One alternative is presented by Eridu in Mesopotamia. At present, Eridu is the earliest-known city. Archaeologists have found at the very lowest level of Eridu, beneath which is only sand, a small shrine. If archaeologists are correct that the first structure at Eridu was a small shrine, then it would appear that people gathered into a community at Eridu not to farm but to live on sacred ground. This would suggest that they gathered together first and then found a way to irrigate their land near their sacred place. The motivation for creating the city would therefore be spiritual, not agricultural. Given that the Mesopotamians regarded their cities as sacred, perhaps many of their cities began as spiritual places. Thousands of years later Romans took pains to make sure their cities were on sacred land, which suggests the spiritual motivation was important for many centuries.

Another possible reason for creating a city would be mutual protection. Sometime between 10,000 and 8000 B.C.E. people built high and thick stone walls and an intimidating stone tower at Jericho. Even that early some people needed defenses to protect themselves, their property, their harvests, or their sources of water. Jericho's ancient walls required the efforts of many people working together to build them. Did people gather together in large communities to better protect themselves from other people? Walls protecting cities were almost universal in the ancient Near East, were common in the region of China, and eventually show up as wooden palisades in northern European settlements before 700 B.C.E.

Yet another motivation for creating cities may have been trade. It seems that everywhere in the world people began trading resources before they made cities. A city might arise on a trade route where people gathered together to share the benefits of foreign goods. The city of Rome arose at the best place for travelers to cross the Tiber River in Italy. Romans had to build defensive walls because many people wanted to take that crossing from them by force. In North Africa cities arose to take advantage of the trade in salt and copper; the sites of the cities sometimes corresponded with the only place for travelers to get fresh water for many miles in the surrounding desert.

All this suggests that as one reads about the ancient cities of the world, one delves into one of the greatest mysteries of human nature. Why do we gather in cities? How do we know when we have a true city? Is there even such a thing as a "true" city? Just asking such questions while studying ancient cities may give one greater insight into one's place in the world and the part one plays in one of the greatest dramas of human history, the building of cities.

AFRICA

BY JAMES E. MEIER

Cities emerged at very early dates in some regions of Africa, especially in the Nile River valley and along the North African coast. However, in general terms the development of cities lagged significantly in Africa, particularly in sub-Saharan Africa. Irrespective of their date of establishment, cities in ancient Africa invariably arose in those areas with especially favorable agricultural conditions or where opportunities for exploiting local, regional, and international trade networks existed at the crossroads of traditional overland routes or along major river networks or coastlines. Cities also tended to be located in zones with high levels of rainfall and fertile soils and sometimes close to abundant deposits of precious and semiprecious minerals.

Despite some notable instances of the early formation of cities, relatively few important African cities arose before approximately the 10th and 11th centuries C.E. At about that time, as highly centralized states with advanced degrees of economic specialization began to take root, many cities were established. Yet most African cities that are occupied today were established only in the late 19th and early 20th centuries, during the period of European colonial conquest. As the overwhelming majority of Africans retained their ties to the land, cultivating crops, fishing, hunting, and raising domesticated animals, urban populations remained low well into the 20th century. Africa's relatively poor soils, harsh climates, and lethal disease environments meant that most of the continent's inhabitants historically dedicated the greater share of their energies to subsistence in the context of a rural setting.

Conceptualizing Cities and Urbanization in Africa

The study of cities and the process of urbanization in Africa has long been complicated by a lack of agreement about definitions. Specifically there is no universally accepted set of criteria for what constitutes a city proper, as opposed to a town, village, kingdom, or other type of political and social entity. In part, consensus has proved elusive owing to the misapplication of a Western model of what warrants the designation of city. Scholars of many different disciplines have often been guilty of seeking out those characteristics that commonly appeared among cities in the West or among the great metropolises of the ancient world outside Africa. However, many indigenous African cities developed differently and displayed features unlike those found elsewhere in the world, owing to the contingencies of culture, social organization, systems of livelihood, ecology, and climate.

The lively debate about African urbanization has been fraught with a strong European ethnocentric bias. Owing to the close association that is often made linking cities to high civilizations and vice versa, many Western scholars, believing that Africans were backward peoples incapable of high civilization without the benefit of outside influence, have been reluctant to confer the status of civilization upon early African societies, even those boasting complex and highly urbanized structures. Since many scholars have approached the study of Africans and their societies with preconceived, stereotypical, and possibly racist views, they assumed a skeptical position in crediting the creation of cities, most notably those of pharaonic Egypt and the medieval site of Great Zimbabwe, to Africans. Typically, they attributed the construction of cities and massive engineering feats to the contributions of Arabs, Asians, and Europeans.

Overall, Western scholars have underestimated the degree of urbanism present in ancient Africa. The limited number of ancient cities that archaeologists have uncovered may partly reflect the general failure to unearth African cities of the distant past in areas outside archaeological zones of high visibility and where the building materials were primarily mud and thatch. The siting of archaeological research in Africa, which has concentrated mainly in the Nile Valley, the Ethiopian plateau, the Swahili coast, the West African savanna, and Great Zimbabwe, has been unevenly applied. Many cities and states remained undisturbed, most notably in Central Africa.

The Western conceptualization of what cities are and what they are not has typically hinged upon certain criteria, foremost among them the development of a system of writing and the erection of monumental architecture. Monumental structures might include stone or mud walls, timber stockades, palace complexes, burial mounds, or obelisks (an extremely large tapering pillar that ends in a pyramid). Seemingly, the study of ancient cities in Mesopotamia and Mesoamerica validated this approach. Although there were cities in the Nile River valley that fulfilled these criteria, great cities of venerable origins in other regions of Africa, where knowledge was retained and transferred to successive generations through oral, not written, methods, would be unfairly disqualified, as would cities that erected impermanent structures owing to the unavailability of or lack of necessity for permanent materials. Clearly, definitions of the kind widely accepted by Western archaeologists, geographers, political scientists, and historians did more to obscure than to elucidate the nature and dynamics of African cities.

Despite the problematical nature of employing broad universal criteria in discerning which population centers are cities and which towns, several useful markers and features were generally present in African cities. Most basically, African cities were the loci of dense concentrations of population, with a large percentage of residents relying upon an economic pursuit other than farming as their principal means of livelihood. Normally, political, commercial, and religious elites were centered in cities and constituted a centralized authority that exerted adequate power to control the community's agricultural surplus and to command labor for public works projects. As elsewhere in the world, African cities served as centers of far-flung trade networks and as political capitals (of provinces, kingdoms, and empires) and often evolved into centers of learning, scholarship, and religious worship. Additionally, they were characterized by social stratification and craft specialization. In Africa cities did not exist in isolation; they were intimately tied into their immediate hinterlands, in large part through their markets, which provided opportunities for farmers, pastoralists, artisans, and market traders and stimulated agricultural production in the surrounding countryside.

Notable Early African Cities

Ancient African cities are often difficult to locate by modern archaeologists, given the propensity of Africans historically to use organic building materials that suffer rapid decomposition. This factor, combined with a long-standing bias toward focusing their studies on architectural remains constructed of stone, has meant that archaeologists still know little of those cities where stone-built structures were not erected. That Africans constructed few cities of stone ought not to be cause for surprise. The relative absence of catastrophic storms and the warm or temperate climates of most African environments do not warrant using materials of an especially durable or well-insulated nature. Palm fronds, thatch, mud, and adobe served admirably as the standard materials of construction.

The modest number of ancient African cities that archaeologists have discovered to date has contributed to the facile assumption of Western scholars that Africa trailed behind Asia, the Middle East, and Europe in terms of its degree of civilization. It might therefore be instructive to examine some of the most noteworthy examples of cities that were established at early dates in Africa.

Africa's earliest cities developed in the Nile River valley. Around 5000 B.C.E., at about the same time that Africans succeeded in domesticating plants and animals, permanent settlements began to appear along the Nile. Egyptian cities emerged as early as 4000 B.C.E. as centers for provincial administration, religious worship, defense, and organization of the redistribution of food in times of drought. Egypt's neighbors to the south also benefitted from the Nile River. Owing to the rich soils along the banks of the Middle Nile and its role as a natural conduit for transportation and communication, some of the earliest cities beyond Egypt's borders sprang up here as early as 2500 B.C.E. When the Egyptian state nearly collapsed during the First Intermediate Period (2134–2040 B.C.E.), the city of Kerma, in Upper Nubia just south of the third cataract of the Nile, capitalized on this weakness and emerged as an important center for the exchange of goods between the Lower Nile Valley and inland Africa. It achieved its greatest height in the period 1785–1552 B.C.E., when the Hyksos, an ethnically mixed group of possibly Asiatic peoples, conquered Egypt. By 1500 B.C.E. a resurgent Egypt extended power over Nubia but again withdrew with the collapse of the New Kingdom (1070 B.C.E.). The independent Kingdom of Kush took root, ruled by locals and centered at the capital city of Napata.

Napata may have been occupied by as early as the 15th century B.C.E. and became a religious center of great importance both for Egypt and Kush from the ninth century B.C.E. Kush came to dominate much of the Nile Valley from the first cataract into the central Sudan, with Napata functioning as its political and economic capital. Napata's first temples may have already been built in the eighth century B.C.E., and even after the seat of political power for the Kingdom of Kush was transferred to Meroë farther south, Napata remained the kingdom's religious capital, where kings were crowned. Napata was sacked by Egyptian forces in 593 B.C.E. and again by the Roman army in 23 B.C.E.

The Kushites retreated south to Meroë, which can be reached by a direct route across the desert from Napata. Evidence of Meroë's occupation dates to the 10th century B.C.E. As the capital of Kush from the sixth century B.C.E. to the fourth century C.E., Meroë became a vital center of ironworking and trade, particularly during the first two centuries C.E., when it flourished. Situated 160 miles north of the confluence of the Blue and White Nile, Meroë became the leading trade center spanning the Red Sea and the Mediterranean world. It exported ivory, gold, copper, ebony, slaves, animal skins, and feathers. It also had ample access to iron ore and hardwood timber, which proved vital in its rise as one of ancient Africa's great sites of iron production. Meroë was also in a tropical rainfall region, and its hinterland was a rich agricultural zone capable of feeding a large urban population. It had more available land than Napata, where the Nile was narrower and the floodplain less expansive, providing insufficient agricultural land to support a large urban population.

The remains of temples, tombs, cemeteries, and monumental statuary found in both Napata and Meroë provide suggestive evidence that both cities had populations of great size and were sophisticated capitals. Meroë developed its own unique cursive script, which has not yet been deciphered. Even employing the flawed criteria of Western archaeologists, Meroë was undoubtedly a notable African city. Although Rome invaded Nubia in 23 B.C. and conquered Napata, Meroë eluded the same fate, and its prosperity was quickly restored. The Kingdom of Meroë began to decline by 300 C.E., and the city was probably invaded by Axum in 350 C.E., during the reign of the great Axumite king Ezana, who ruled from 330 to 356 C.E. and was instrumental in spreading Christianity throughout the region.

Axum's role in delivering the coup de grâce to Meroë was the culmination of a long-standing commercial rivalry between the two states. Axum had been founded in the sixth century B.C.E. by migrants from the Saba region of southern Arabia. It grew and prospered from the first century C.E. until its gradual decline in the seventh century. It became the dominant power in northern Ethiopia owing to its proximity to the Red Sea and the Gulf of Arabia and its successful exploitation of the trade between the Indian Ocean and the Mediterranean. In particular, trade ties with the eastern Roman Empire provided an important stimulus for Axum's economy. Its exports included ivory, jewelry, frankincense, myrrh, rhinoceros horn, animal hides, gold dust, tortoiseshell, and slaves. Axum's population reached upwards of 10,000, and the city could boast not only brisk international trade but also a written language and monumental structures in stone. Axum's gigantic granite funerary stelae, which were built as early as 300 C.E., have attracted intense scholarly scrutiny. The tallest stelae (inscribed stone pillars), measuring 108 feet high and weighing between 550 and 700 tons, were the world's largest such monuments built with dry stone. In additional to their tremendous size and craftsmanship, they represent a remarkable engineering feat, not least because they were erected without the benefit of mortar.

The Swahili Coast is located along the east coast of Africa, from Mogadishu (in Somalia) down to northern Mozambique. Swahili culture was the product of a unique blend of African traditions mixed with Arab and Islamic influences. In *The Periplus of the Erythraean*, a sailor's handbook written by an Egyptian Greek in the first century C.E., the author describes how East Africa traded with other nations in Arabia, the Persian Gulf, and Asia. In time these coastal cities drew visitors and migrants from those same regions. The Swahili population was concentrated in the cities that dotted the Swahili Coast and the offshore islands. Trade with the Indian Ocean world was well established probably no later than 600 C.E., long before Islam made inroads among the coastal peoples.

West African cities of size existed even before the opening up of the trans-Saharan trade on a significant scale and the penetration of Islam. The site of Jenne-jeno (in present-day Mali) on a floodplain of the Niger River provides clear evidence of an urban center before the Christian era. The city was founded in approximately 250 B.C.E. and flourished between the second century B.C.E. and the 15th century C.E. Already by 200 C.E. it probably had a population of 4,000, which was later to swell to between 10,000 and 25,000. Its prosperity was the result of the active trade its merchants plied as they capitalized on the movement of goods along the Niger. It was close to large deposits of gold and copper and enjoyed the added advantage of being protected by marshes largely impenetrable to outside invaders. Fishing and intensive agriculture on the fertile floodplain contributed to its thriving population.

Other West African cities were founded at an early date but assumed the status of great cities only later. In the savanna and forest lands of Nigeria, the Yoruba and Edo peoples built large urban centers surrounded by earthen walls and earthworks. Most notably, the Yoruba city of Ile Ife was probably established as early as the fourth century B.C.E. in southwestern Nigeria, but it emerged as a large and powerful city only in the 10th century C.E.

The Hausa city-states of Kano, Zaria, Katsina, and Gobir in northern Nigeria were founded possibly as early as the fifth century C.E. Tapping into the lucrative caravan trade that linked neighbors to the west (the West African states of Mali and Songhay) and east (Kanem-Bornu) with Mediterranean ports on the coast of North Africa, they acquired great wealth and grew dramatically in size, but scholars know little of these city-states before the 16th century.

Carthage, a port city founded by the Phoenicians ca. 800 B.C.E., developed into a unique civilization that was variously Semitic, Mediterranean, and African in its origins. By the sixth century B.C.E. it dominated the entire North African coast. Two centuries later it controlled much of the western Mediterranean world and extended its influence even beyond the Strait of Gibraltar, reaching Britain in the north and sailing down the coast of West Africa. Its immense wealth and power eventually brought it into conflict with the Roman Republic. Three costly conflicts with Rome between 264 and 146 B.C.E., known as the Punic Wars, ultimately resulted in the Roman conquest and destruction of Carthage. Of its population, which may have exceeded 700,000, only 50,000 inhabitants remained alive by the end of the Third Punic War.

After it was destroyed and razed, Carthage was resurrected in 122 B.C.E. by the Romans and renamed Colonia Junonia. This city too was destroyed, but in 29 B.C.E. Caesar Augustus rebuilt it, naming it Colonia Julia Carthago. Carthage declined after the third century C.E. All told, Rome built an impressive urban society along the North African coast, with as many as 500 cities and a population of nearly two million inhabitants. Roman rule ended in North Africa with the invasion in 429 C.E. of the Vandals, who were conquered in turn by the Byzantine Empire in 534 C.E.

EGYPT

BY DAVID PETECHUK

Egypt was once believed to be a "civilization without cities," but archaeological explorations over the past several decades have shown otherwise. Settlement excavations in Egypt have revealed that towns and cities date back at least to 3500 B.C.E. The cities were essentially regional capitals connected to smaller towns that made up various administrative districts. It would be many centuries, however, before Egypt would develop cities as they are thought of today.

Although it was home to one of the most ancient civilizations in the world, Egypt has kept the secrets of its ancient settlements and cities relatively hidden. Part of the reason is that people generally lived along the fertile riverbeds, especially along the Nile River. As a result, they also lived near shifting floodplains. Because houses and most other buildings—other than the stone temples and tombs—were built of mud brick, recurring floods and the changing course of the Nile in ancient times have destroyed the bulk of these dwellings. Furthermore, the Egyptians usually built directly on top of previous buildings and settlements because of the scarcity of good building sites. Consequently, much of Egypt's ancient cities—such as Heliopolis, which is largely buried under the urban expansion of Cairo, and Thebes, where the current city of Luxor rests—remain inaccessible to archaeological research.

URBANIZATION

The people who lived in the Nile River valley of Egypt before 5000 B.C.E. were primarily hunters and gatherers. The oldest-known farming village existed about 15 miles outside present-day Cairo from about 5000 B.C.E. to 4000 B.C.E. With a population believed to be between 1,300 and 2,000, it included residential areas, work facilities, and public areas. As villages and settlements grew, however, the rural community

Ancient Egyptian city of Sesebi; the buried remains of the city wall and a temple and mounds covering houses are visible. (Courtesy of the Oriental Institute of the University of Chicago)

and environment would remain an integral part of the new urban complexes, serving essentially as extensions of the towns. In fact, many farmers and workers lived within the villages and settlements and worked in the nearby fields.

The early development of villages was based on a variety of factors, including security, economics and trade, administrative demands, religious cult influences, and political motives. For example, archaeologists believe that the village of Maadi was established around 3500 B.C.E. as a trade link between southern Egypt and the Levant, an ancient and large geographical region in southwestern Asia. Archaeologists have found silos and cellars, huts, and various other storage facilities along with assorted other items.

Most of the early settlements were little more than small villages or hamlets built on the edge of floodplains. Composed primarily of fragile huts, these hamlets were established around every mile along the Nile River, with the primary considerations for building being nearness to a waterway and high ground above the floodplains. According to historians and archaeologists, two factors led to the development of urbanization: a reduction of Nile flood discharge and an increased demand for trade goods by a growing population.

In addition to shrines and temples, a common feature of many Egyptian towns was the enclosure wall. Archaeologists consider the development of these walls as marking the separation from a time of scattered farming villages that predominated in the Predynastic Period (before ca. 3000 B.C.E.) and the more compact towns that primarily developed during the Early Dynastic Period (ca. 2920–2575 B.C.E.). Among the most noted of these towns, both of which began in the Predynastic Period, are Naqada, which sat on the west bank of the Nile downstream from ancient Thebes, and Hierakonpolis, between the current cities of Cairo and Aswān.

Hierakonpolis is one of the largest Predynastic sites found by archaeologists and is believed to have been established around 3500 B.C.E. It included houses, temples, administrative buildings, and artisan areas. The houses were interlocking and built along narrow, irregular or seemingly unplanned streets. To date, archaeologists have discovered that some planning seems to have gone into the town but that it took place after the initial establishment because the innermost segments of Hierakonpolis are irregularly laid out. This early "city" also included a religious district and an area where artisans manufactured linens, stone vessels, baskets, beer, and other items in demand at the time. A stone wall surrounding the site was built around 3300 B.C.E. or possibly a bit later. Hierakonpolis is believed to have been abandoned around the time of the Middle Kingdom (ca. 2040–1640 B.C.E.)

Early Town Planning

The primary urban area in ancient Egypt by around 3000 B.C.E. was the city of Memphis, which had a population at its peak of 30,000 to 40,000 and served as the capital city of Egypt after administrative districts had been unified under a single theocratic dynasty. Built by the First Dynasty (2920–2770 B.C.E.) pharaoh Menes near the entrance to El Faiyûm (an area separated from the Nile Valley by a ridge and containing a large lake called Birket Qārūn), the city served as a place of consolidated power for the first kings of

Egypt. The city also sat at the meeting points between the Nile Delta and the Nile River valley, making it a good marketplace that could be taxed and controlled. Unfortunately, little is known about the actual city itself, as much of the remains of early Memphis are situated beneath thick alluvial deposits from the Nile and below the water table. However, recent archaeological excavations and new technologies are beginning to shed light on this ancient city. For example, archaeologists have found that the city shifted eastward over its history because of the shifting course of the Nile and encroaching sand dunes.

While Egyptian towns and cities seemed to have little planning underpinning their initial development, archaeologists have discerned some attempts at a rational approach to building urban areas. For example, the ancient city Kahun, which was founded by Sesostres II (r. 1897–1878 B.C.E.) and unearthed by Sir Flinders Petrie in the 1880s, is a workers' town for the builders of the pyramid of Seostres II and was conceived as an administrative area inhabited by those who served the local pyramid cult, a funerary cult that acted to sustain the king in the afterlife. Inhabitants included priests, officials, and craftsman as well as the farmers who worked the agricultural land surrounding the city.

Following digs by Petrie and others, archaeologists found that the strict internal planning was undertaken for Kahun, whose population has been estimated at between 3,000 and 10,000. Kahun and other similar towns were developed primarily to support the royal cult by providing a living for those responsible for the cult's operation. In addition to celebration of religious ceremonies, inhabitants of Kahun were also primarily concerned with agriculture and construction.

A walled town built near the modern town of El-Lahun, Kahun's interior was divided into two sections by another wall. While the residents of different classes generally were not separated in ancient Egyptian towns and cities, Kahun included a wealthy residential area that contained houses with 60 to 70 rooms, making them as much as 50 times bigger than the houses of those living in the other part of the city. Careful planning went into Kahun's streets, with a system of parallel and cross streets. Alleys, where the workers lived, often ended in a cul-de-sac. The town's main street, which led to the palace, was approximately 30 feet wide, whereas streets and alleys were much smaller, often only 3 to 5 feet wide. Stone channels ran down the middle of the streets for drainage, and archaeologists believe that Kahun contained several large granaries. Overall, the city was densely built with mud huts and streets covering the landscape, leaving little room for large gardens, which Egyptians loved.

An example of a different kind of city planning can be found in the capital city of Akhenaton, which is now known as Amarna. Built by Akhenaton (also known as Ikhnaton and, early in his reign, as Amenhotep IV) during the Eighteenth Dynasty (1550–1307 B.C.E.), the city is situated about 365 miles south of Cairo along the Nile River in a natural amphitheater between two imposing cliffs. In designing the city, planners created many public open spaces that included planted trees and gardens for some of the inhabitants. Built without an enclosure wall, Akhenaton included a large open area in the center of the city where temple complexes for the cult of the creator god Aton were situated. The city's main road ran north to south, with the Great Palace and king's residential palace located on the western side of the road and facing the Nile and the temple complexes located on the eastern side of the road. The central part of the city also included administrative and industrial buildings, such as those used for baking. Residential areas of various sizes were situated to the north and south of the central area. Clusters of houses indicated the existence of distinct neighborhoods. Unlike Kahun and other Middle Kingdom cities, Akhenaton's streets were irregularly laid out.

Specialized Settlements Surrounding Cities

In addition to the major towns and ancient cities, Egyptians also built numerous specialized villages and towns in close proximity to them. Integral to ancient Egypt's larger towns and cities was the workers' village. Worker's' villages can be traced back to the Fourth Dynasty (ca. 2575–2465 B.C.E.) and are often associated with the building of the pyramids. One such site northwest of present-day Cairo, called Abu Ghalib, was twice the size of Kahun. The discovery of a rectangular grid uncovered during archaeological excavations indicates that the city was carefully planned.

In fact, workers' villages appeared to be well-organized settlements, each with its own economic administration separated from the nearby larger city or town. For the most part, workers' villages contained larger residential sites for administrative officials and many small, nearly identical residences for the workers. The smaller units were inhabited by both skilled and unskilled laborers and their families.

A prime example of the workers' village is one that was located at the edge of the desert about three-quarters of a mile east of Akhenaton. It contained 73 identical houses and one slightly larger for a total population of approximately 300 to 400 people. The workmen generally lived in small, barracks-like dwellings of approximately 650 square feet. In dwellings with a second floor, the living space expanded to approximately 1,100 square feet. The residents of such homes often included animals. Many of the houses included hearths shaped like keyholes and jars sunk into the floor. The long, narrow streets of the village were laid out parallel to each other and were approximately 6½ feet wide. Within this walled workers' village, houses took up almost the entire area. In addition to residences, the village included an area for the delivery of goods from the city (including water, since the village had no wells), a guardhouse, and quarry sites later turned into rubbish pits. In addition, the village had animal pens for livestock that were not housed with the workers. There is also some evidence that vegetable gardening took place within the town.

One of the best-known workers' villages of ancient Egypt is the village of Deir el-Medina, where workers on the Theban royal tombs in the Valley of the Kings lived. Founded under the reign of Eighteenth Dynasty ruler Thutmose I (r. 1504–1492 B.C.E.), the village was surrounded by a 21-foot mud-brick wall. Over the course of its 500-year habitation, the village was occupied initially by unskilled workers who lived in about 60 houses. As the work on the tombs increased, so did the size of the village, which eventually grew from 60 households to approximately 120 within an area of about 60,000 square feet. In addition to size, the socioeconomic makeup of the village changed in that its inhabitants soon included relatively affluent workers, such as masons, painters, and sculptors. Overall, houses varied in size from 430 square feet to 1,300 square feet, with the larger structures containing three big rooms, a kitchen, a yard, and underground cellars for storage. The homes typically contained wall niches for statues of gods. The village was abandoned after the last of the royal tombs were built during the reign of Ramses XI (r. 1100–1070 B.C.E.).

Temple Towns and Districts

The relationship between towns and temples was a fundamental aspect of ancient Egyptian life. Often the temple served as the central location for the eventual development of cities, such as Memphis and Thebes. During the New Kingdom (ca. 1550–1070 B.C.E.), settlements surrounded the temples and included domestic dwellings and industrial facilities.

A good example of the importance of temple towns and how later larger towns or cities built up around them is a temple site that existed on the west bank of Thebes in an area called Medinet Habu. Traced back to the Eleventh Dynasty (ca. 2140–1991 B.C.E.), the site contained a small shrine that was rebuilt and expanded under the reigns of Hatshepsut (r. ca. 1473–1458 B.C.E.) and Thutmose III (r. ca. 1479–1425 B.C.E.). During the reign of Ramses III (r. ca. 1194–1163 B.C.E.) a larger temple complex was built around the older temple buildings. The larger complex included temples, administrative buildings, workshops, storehouses, a garden, and a funerary palace. Beyond the wall surrounding the great temple were residential houses, stables, orchards, and a stockyard. Encompassing the entire site was a complex fortification system of walls, towers, and a moat. This walled city contained two entrances. The eastern gate facing the Nile River was several stories high and decorated with scenes denoting the king's authority. There was also a heavily fortified western gate facing the desert.

By the Twentieth Dynasty (ca. 1196–1070 B.C.E.) Medinet Habu served as an administrative center for the area, and the housing areas once restricted to temple staff were soon inhabited by the general population. During this time the Great Girdle Wall that surrounded the complex was destroyed, perhaps during fighting with nomadic peoples. Rebuilt during the Twenty-First Dynasty (ca. 1070–945 B.C.E.), the complex then included small, closely packed houses on the eastern side and larger villas with gardens on the west. Although the cult of Ramses III was eventually abandoned sometime during the Twenty-First Dynasty, the area remained a focal point for religious practices and subsequently led to rebuilding and continued habitation through the Coptic Period (ca. 400–800 C.E.) of Egypt.

For the most part, temple districts were planned better than most of the early cities and towns. Individual temples were laid out symmetrically with surrounding walls, sometimes nearly 40 feet thick. Streets and avenues were designed to be wide, sometimes up to 16 feet, to accommodate processions and other religious activities. Unlike most streets in towns and cities, temple streets often were paved.

Initial planning of temple districts included a large open space around the temple, but as the population grew, houses were eventually built right up to the temple walls, which also served as a strategic place to make a last stand in case of attack. An interesting phenomenon concerning temple sites is that as houses around the temple were continually rebuilt over the older houses through the years, the temples themselves remained standing and often appeared to be sunk into the ground. The larger cities of Memphis and Thebes had a number of temple complexes that were at one time separate but eventually were interconnected by large avenues beginning around the 18th Dynasty.

Fortress Settlements

Another form of specialized city was the fortified settlement, with some of the best known dating to the Middle Kingdom. Fortified settlements were also built in the northeast and northwest, where they helped protect borders from various invaders and mass immigration. Archaeologists have traced the existence of fortified settlements at least as far back as 2160 to 2040 B.C.E. A chain of fortified settlements known as the "Walls of Princes" was completed under Amenemhet I (r. ca. 1991–1962 B.C.E.). Various other fortress complexes were also built with functions such as supplying and protecting river traffic. One of the largest fortress settlements of ancient Egypt was excavated at Buhen, which is about 155 miles south of present-day Aswān. Built over an Old Kingdom site facing the Nile, the fortress was surrounded by a mud-brick enclosure that had walls 26 to 30 feet high and sometimes as thick as 16 feet. The enclosure also included external towers and was surrounded by a ditch and another brick-paved parapet wall. Water was provided from the Nile via a stone passage. In addition to an entrance facing the Nile, the fortress had a western entrance facing the desert.

The interior of the fortress was planned with a grid pattern of streets with rectangular buildings made of brick. Initial residents of the fortress included soldiers and their families as well as government officials who oversaw the treasuries and state granaries. Also inhabiting the fortress where interpreters, scribes, and craftsmen. Eventually, rotating troops and officers were replaced by a permanent settlement of soldiers and others within the fort. Much like the temple towns or districts, this site and others like it eventually developed into towns and cities that included residential areas and temples. The site was populated until around 1552 B.C.E.

The Royal Cities

By the time of the New Kingdom onward, most of the specialized towns or cities had been linked via geography and economics to larger urban centers that included extensive temple complexes, ceremonial palaces, residencies, and prominent cemeteries. In addition to the temples, these urban areas were held together by the kingship, which required massive workforces, thus providing the foundation for larger cities.

Within the ancient Egyptian capital cities, the royal palaces were enclosed and separated from the rest of the capital. The palaces housed the pharaoh's primary family and servants, along with secondary wives, concubines, and numerous children. Typically, the location of capital cities in Egypt shifted with changing rulers. As a result, royal residential palaces existed in numerous cities, including Akhenaton, Heracleopolis, Avaris, Napata, and Saïs.

Relatively few excavations have been able to uncover the most ancient aspects of these cities. As a result, little is known about them. Conjecture based on their functions, however, indicates that they all had a large and extremely diversified workforce and often included a large population of people who relocated, such as when palace authority was moved from one city to another. While the population of provincial capitals and towns has been estimated at about 1,400 to 3,000 people, royal capitals were much larger; Akhenaton was estimated to have a population of 20,000 to 30,000 people. Likewise, Memphis, which housed the first known royal residence, and Thebes may have achieved populations of 30,000 to 40,000 during their peaks.

Alexandria

The city of Alexandria is perhaps the best known of Egypt's ancient cities. Alexandria's fame can be traced to its rapid growth into an intellectual, cultural, economic, and political metropolis. Its mystique also comes from its magnificent history. Founded in 331 B.C.E. by Alexander the Great (356–323 B.C.E.), it was made the capital of Greco-Roman Egypt and quickly became one of the greatest cities of the classical Greek Hellenistic world. Legend has it that Alexander initially laid out his plans for the city using lines of grain, since he had no chalk or other writing materials available.

Like contemporary Alexandria, ancient Alexandria is northwest of the Nile Delta and inhabits a narrow strip of land between Lake Mariut and the Mediterranean Sea. When Alexander came to the site of a small, ancient Egyptian village called Rhakotis, which dates to the 13th century B.C.E., he admired it for its natural beauty and its location between Greece and the rest of Egypt. He quickly decided that the site would be an ideal regional capital. Although he was the founder of Alexandria, Alexander did not live long enough to see a single building constructed on the site; he was later buried there.

Alexandria was built by the Greek architect Dinocrates of Rhodes under the supervision of Alexander's viceroy, Cleomenes, who oversaw its continued initial development. Growth of the city would thrive under the first three Ptolemies, who ruled much of the Egyptian part of the vast empire once conquered by Alexander. Ptolemy I (r. 304–284 B.C.E.) set out to make Alexandria the cultural and intellectual capital of the known world. Ptolemy II (reigned 285–246 B.C.E.) focused much of his efforts on building Alexandria, including construction on what would become the Royal Library of Alexandria. Ptolemy III (r. 246–221 B.C.E.) was a strong supporter of the sciences, which also contributed to the city's fame. Under these three men, Alexandria became the center of commerce among Europe, Arabia, and the Indian East. It grew so fast in successive generations that in a mere 100 years it was the largest city in the world. According to the census in 32 B.C.E., which was conducted three hundred years after Alexandria was founded, the city remained a major metropolis with 180,000 adult citizens, rivaling Rome in population at that time. Among the numerous exceptional achievements made under the rule of the first three Ptolemies were the Pharos Lighthouse, one of the seven wonders of the ancient world, and the Royal Library of Alexandria, known as the Mouseion. The Heptastadion Dike that connected the island of Pharos with the mainland was also built at this time and served additionally as a double harbor to the city.

Alexandria thrived primarily because it fulfilled the several functions intended for it, which included initially serving as a Greek city-state and as the capital of Egypt. In addition to fulfilling these functions, Alexandria's greater reputation was as a center for world trade and learning. One of its earliest inhabitants included the noted Greek mathematician Euclid (ca. 325–ca. 265 B.C.E.).

Because of the city's multiple functions, people from various lands came to it and intermingled on the streets, creating a population that included Egyptians, Macedonians and Greeks, Nubians, Persians, Indians, and perhaps the largest number of Jewish residents in any large city of the era. As a result, Alexandria was the basis for growing international business efforts. For example, an ancient maritime loan contract for importing incense included twelve partners of at least seven different nationalities. Likewise, scholarly life in ancient Alexandria was international in nature. Greek scholars, intellectuals from the Mediterranean, and numerous others embarked on various academic pursuits. In turn, scholars from Alexandria also traveled abroad, thus fostering international scholarship and a growth of scientific thought in the region. In fact, the Royal Library of Alexandria was one of the largest and most noted in the world at that time. It was subsequently destroyed by a fire or fires of unsure origins.

Alexandria's cosmopolitan environment was noted by Greek poet Herodas (ca. third century B.C.E.), who asserted that a person could find nearly anything in Alexandria, including "wealth, . . . power, prosperity, glory, shows, philosophers, gold, youth, the temple of the Adelphoi, the generous king, Mouseion, wine, all the good things you may desire, and women more numerous than heavenly stars who could compete in beauty with the goddesses who sought the judgment of Paris." Alexandria was annexed by the Romans around 80 B.C.E. and once again began to regain its notoriety and splendor, which had diminished through wars and conflicts, both external and internal, during the reigns of the later Ptolemies. During this time Alexandria served as a central granary of Rome. Later, in about the third century C.E., Alexandria became noted as a center of Christian theology and church government, but only after Saint Mark, who first introduced Christianity to the region, was martyred there in the first century C.E. Nevertheless, many of the early Christian church leaders, such as Clement, Origen, Arius, and Athanasius, were Alexandrians or had adopted the city as their home.

THE MIDDLE EAST

BY DAVID K. UNDERWOOD

The Near East, known today as the Middle East, is a region generally defined by archaeologists as that part of Southwest Asia that stretches from Iran in the east to the coast of the Mediterranean and Aegean seas in the west. The cities of the ancient Near East are located in four distinct subregions: Anatolia (modern-day Turkey), Persia (Iran, mostly west of the Zagros Mountains), the Levant (including Israel, Jordan, Palestine, and Syria), and Mesopotamia (Iraq). Many of the earliest and most important urban sites are found in Mesopotamia, which means "land between the rivers" in Greek and refers to the floodplain and sometimes fertile stretch of land between the Tigris and Euphrates rivers. In antiquity the southern part of Mesopotamia, between modern Baghdad and the Persian Gulf, was generally known as Sumer. The northern part, or upper Mesopotamia, was home to the Semitic cultures of the Akkadians and the Assyrians. Because of the low levels of rainfall in the region, especially in the southern lowlands, the growth of cities in ancient Mesopotamia depended on the development of intensive, irrigation-based agriculture.

NEOLITHIC SETTLEMENTS

It was not until the fourth millennium B.C.E. that there emerged, in Sumer, an "urban revolution" and the first true cities as opposed to towns. But the earliest traces of the move toward urbanization go back to the Neolithic Period and the agricultural revolution (ca. 8000 B.C.E.), when the domestication of plants and animals made possible a more settled lifestyle and the growth of villages and towns. Archaeological findings at such sites as Jericho, in modern-day Palestine, suggest that urbanization and its elements were under way there as early as 8000 B.C.E. Jericho had a significant, 10-acre settlement of mud-brick houses protected by impressive stone fortifications with a circular tower (28 feet tall and 33 feet in diameter at the base).

Another unique example of an early experiment in urban living is Çatalhüyük in Anatolia, where excavations have revealed a flourishing Neolithic culture (ca. 7000–5000 B.C.E.) that built its wealth from a regular trade in obsidian, a glass-like volcanic stone used for making tools with fine cutting edges. The curious absence of a street plan at Çatalhüyük is a product of the peculiar arrangement of the houses, which adjoin one another and have "entrances" through the roofs instead of doors. The advantages of such a system would appear to be a heightened sense of communal living and defense, not to mention a greater structural stability than would be afforded by freestanding walls of mud-brick and timber frames. A number of richly decorated interior spaces in the town seem to reflect a ritual or ceremonial purpose and have thus been called "shrines" by excavators. These decorations include wall paintings (some with hunting-related narrative scenes and one of the first "landscapes" in history), animal heads, *bucrania* (bovine skulls), and bulls horns (symbols of masculine virility), adjacent to plaster reliefs of female breasts (symbols of female fertility) projecting from the walls. The overall impression of Çatalhüyük at its height is of a prosperous Neolithic settlement with several of the material and artistic foundations of a proto-urban culture, but still more of a town than a city.

CITIES AND CIVILIZATION

The question of how to distinguish large towns from the earliest cities remains a problem for modern archaeologists. (Jericho's estimated population in 7500 B.C.E. was only about 2,000.) It seems clear, however, that the rise of the first cities is inseparable from the problem of how to define "civilization." The solution seems to lie in the equation of cities with a higher level of social organization and material culture, as defined by ten characteristics or criteria of civilization observed in early Mesopotamian cities, the most important of which were writing, the exact sciences, and a socioeconomic hierarchy.

The primary characteristics of civilization all relate to social organization: settlement in cities, specialization of labor, concentration of surplus production, class structure, and state organization (government). The secondary characteristics relate to material culture and reflect the impact of the primary characteristics: monumental public works (especially architecture and hydraulic engineering for irrigation), long-distance trade for precious resources, monumental artwork reflecting religious or governmental power, writing and record keeping, and math and science (especially geometry and astronomy). The significance of these categories lies in the fact that the earliest cities of the ancient Near East, especially in Sumer, possessed all of these characteristics. To this list should be added the invention of the wheel, the early use of basic metals and alloys (especially bronze), and a certain population size, perhaps between 7,000 and 20,000 people.

The weakness of such materialistic theories of civilization is ironically also revealed by the earliest cities of the ancient Near East, which were primarily ritual centers with a religious and ceremonial function, and not major economic magnets of surplus production. Still, the early development of such ritual sites as Eridu in Sumer (ca. 5000 B.C.E.) no doubt depended on the management of a surplus by an elite class of temple priests serving theocratic rulers in an increasingly stratified and hierarchical society. The growth of such ritual centers with "temple economies" would culminate in the formation of independent Sumerian city-states (eventually about 12), each of which would develop under the protection of a different Mesopotamian deity. The religious and ritual nature of the ancient city thus cannot be overestimated: The basic function of the city and its populace was to ensure the blessings and support of the deities, who were understood to control everything from the seasons to the course and flow of the two life-giving rivers, the Tigris and the Euphrates.

Eridu and Mythical Origins

The importance of polytheistic religion and myth as the driving force behind the development of the ancient city is nowhere better seen than in Eridu, the mythical place of origin not just for the Sumerians but for all of civilization. For the Mesopotamian people, Eridu represented the prototype for the idea of the city as a sacred place. It was here, according to the myth elaborated by the Babylonians, that the god Marduk created not only the world and humankind but also the first city from the primordial marshland. He did so by spreading mud upon a reed frame to form a platform for a temple (the god's abode), to be placed on a mound of dry land surrounded by the swampy water of a lagoon called the *abzu*. Eridu's unique geographic position at the edge of the marshes and the alluvial river plain of southern Sumer (15 miles south of Ur) parallels its symbolic function as a transitional space where land and water came together to form a human civilization made possible by the gods. The *abzu* became synonymous with the religious core of the city.

Eridu was not only the cult center of the gods of freshwater but also, according to traditions recorded in texts going back to the fourth millennium B.C.E., the oldest shrine and most sacred city. Its very first building, a small and primitive chapel of sun-dried mud-brick, dates to 4900 B.C.E., but there is little evidence of monumental buildings beyond temple structures, among them, a ziggurat, or temple tower. As in the city of Uruk, later temple structures reveal the use of limestone, sandstone, and gypsum for wall structures and clay cone mosaics covered with thin copper plating for the decoration of the main temples. But Eridu never really became a fully functioning city or a center of political or economic power with its own kings; its importance was primarily symbolic, as a sanctuary and a holy place where land and water were brought together by the gods to enable humanity to take the first steps toward civilization.

Uruk and the Urban Matrix

The first site in the ancient Near East to demonstrate the basic elements of a fully functioning city with both political and ceremonial components was Uruk, the biblical Erech, known to the Arabs as Warka. The Sumerian word for city was *uru*, which may have been the root for the Latin *urbs* and thus the origin of our modern term *urban*. Uruk has often been considered the "mother of cities" because of its

Panels with striding lions, Neo-Babylonian, during the reign of Nebuchadnezzar II (r. 604–562 B.C.E.), when Babylon reached its full glory as a city; this relief of a lion is one of a series of striding lions that lined the most important city street, the Processional Way, and guided ritual processions from the city to the temple. (Copyright the Metropolitan Museum of Art)

great antiquity (going back to the fifth millennium B.C.E.), its impressive size (3.4 square miles—bigger than Athens in the fifth century B.C.E.), and its provision of a matrix or pattern for future urban development. Possessing the earliest, largest, and most numerous monumental buildings in Mesopotamia, dating mostly from the fourth to the first millennium B.C.E., Uruk was the birthplace not only of monumental Sumerian architecture and planning but also of the cuneiform writing system (revealed on clay tablets and cylinder seals, engraved seals used to make impressions on clay) and a government bureaucracy with centralized, theocratic control. Representing the first phase of Mesopotamian urbanization, known as the Uruk Period (4000–3100 B.C.E.), Uruk appears to meet the basic criteria for both the first city and the first civilization of the ancient Near East.

Uruk's somewhat experimental urbanism is characterized by large, multifunctional buildings with diverse plans, arranged with a concern for open and fluid space and apparently designed for ease of access and circulation. Accurate description of individual buildings at any given point in time is complicated, however, by the tendency for later structures to cover over those of the earlier building phases, which were sometimes deliberately preserved or expanded upon. The most important structures date from the Uruk Period or later and are concentrated on the two largest mounds: Eanna (precinct of the goddess Inanna), which is the oldest and central part of the ruin, and Kullab (precinct of the sky god An), the western and highest mound, dominated by a towering ziggurat.

Excavations on the Eanna mound reveal that new materials and building techniques were used beginning with the Middle Uruk Period (ca. 3400 B.C.E.), most notably clay cone mosaics for wall decorations and especially imported limestone for foundations and walls, which tended to be both tall and thick—as in the Stone Cone Temple and the somewhat later Limestone Temple of Eanna. The most famous Uruk building, the White Temple, stood on a tall, archaic ziggurat—a sort of man-made mountain—towering high above the Kullab mound. The ziggurat and White Temple were dedicated to the sky god An, the father of all the gods. The temple takes its name from the coating of white gypsum plaster that covered its massive walls. Much of Uruk architecture thus conspicuously breaks with the local tradition of building with basic mud-brick that was favored both before and after the Middle Uruk Period.

At Uruk we find the prototypes for a wide variety of Mesopotamian temple designs. The basic plan was roughly symmetrical, consisting of a central rectangular or T-shaped chamber, possibly vaulted, with flanking corridors or attached rooms, some of which also opened to the outside. Within this basic formula, there was considerable variation in the layout, apparent function, and dimensions of the structures. A notable feature, especially on Eanna, is the tendency to arrange the buildings at different angles around large, open terraces faced with monumental colonnades of massive semicircular, engaged pillars decorated with mosaic patterns. The spatial arrangement and structural system used at Uruk thus foreshadow those of the great terraces and temples of ancient Egypt and Greece.

Despite the archaeological excavations that provide basic information about the site, we actually know very little about life in Uruk. For instance, there is no evidence of residential quarters, graves, or commercial buildings or neighborhoods. The most important urbanistic episode in the city's history concerns the construction of its famed ramparts, undertaken during the Early Dynastic Period (first half of the third millennium B.C.E.), when the city was at its height, with a population of about 50,000. The walls extended about miles around the site and stood more than 23 feet tall. The tablets of the Gilgamesh epic credit Gilgamesh, king of Uruk, with this undertaking and describe the wall, "the likes of which no one can equal," as having "a foundation of baked brick" and being "as straight as an architect's string." This wall protected not only the sacred precincts of the gods and their pious worshipers but also the growing population of a place described by Mesopotamian poets as a festive city of singing and dancing, with a "population of beautiful and voluptuous women, women with luxuriantly curly hair and available women in general." The late Babylonian poem *Erra*, for example, talks about Uruk as a "city of prostitutes, courtesans, and call-girls," deprived of their husbands by Ishtar, who becomes associated with the rising "mother goddess" of Uruk, Inanna, and a cult of free love that witnessed erotic adventures in the city's streets and possibly even the institution of "sacred prostitution." The libidinous energy of Uruk looks forward to the infamous licentiousness of Babylon and the likes of modern Amsterdam.

Akkad, Ur, and the Rise of the Mesopotamian Capital City

The continuing importance of the cult of the goddess Inanna for the development of Mesopotamian cities is clearly illustrated in a famous literary text, *The Curse of Agade*, written ca. 2000 B.C.E. The text deals with the rise of the city of Agade (Akkad) as the center of a successful international trading empire and the great capital of a powerful centralized state founded by the Akkadian king Sargon, who ruled from 2340 to 2284 B.C.E. Although the site of the city has not yet been identified, there is ample evidence of its existence and greatness in written documents and cuneiform inscriptions found at other sites and dating back to the third millennium B.C.E. The imperial state forged by Sargon during his 56-year regime incorporated all the formerly independent Sumerian city-states, including Uruk, whose impressive walls were no challenge to the military might of the Akkadians. Sargon's Akkad, believed by some experts to lie somewhere beneath modern-day Baghdad or in its vicinity, was the first city in ancient Mesopotamia to function as the true capital of a state and an empire.

Like Akkad, Ur became the capital of a powerful centralized state with grandiose city walls, rich furnishings, and an extensive religious precinct. It is the site of two of the most impressive archaeological discoveries of antiquity: the monumental ziggurat of King Ur-Nammu (partially restored in the late 1970s) and the famous cemetery unearthed by the British archaeologist Leonard Woolley and a joint expedition of the British Museum and the University Museum of Philadelphia from 1920 to 1934. The interest in the site had been intensified by the discovery of ancient tablets that identified the city as Ur of the Chaldees, the biblical home of Abraham. The most impressive finds of the expedition were the 16 tombs identified as elite or "Royal Graves" because of the wealth and quality of the objects found in them and because of the unique arrangement of the main body alongside those believed to have been servants, ritual attendants, and possibly sacrificial victims.

The richness of the finds was unprecedented in Mesopotamian history: objects of gold, bronze, ivory, and semiprecious stones, and a wide variety of tools, weapons, headdresses, and hair ornaments. The most famous objects found were the remains of a decorated harp or lyre with the head of a golden bull wearing a beard of lapis lazuli and the Standard of Ur, the sound box of a string instrument decorated with shell and lapis lazuli inlays, showing scenes of war and peace on either side. We cannot say for certain that the cauldrons and goblets found in the tombs were used for the ritual mass poisoning, an interpretation that has been much popularized. What is clear from the remains is that there were more women than men buried in the cemetery and that the feminine ornaments and decorative objects found were used to define an increasing level of cultural and political status for many of the women found buried at Ur.

This apparent rise in the status of women officials at Ur was accompanied by the emergence of an efficient state administration that enforced monopolies on the most important commodities (linen and wool cloth), implemented a new calendar and standardized measures with accounting based on the use of silver rods, and regulated activities as diverse as cattle raising, date-palm horticulture, and advanced irrigation and large-scale architectural engineering. The two best examples of engineering advancements are the city's massive walls and the monumental Ziggurat of Ur-Nammu (ca. 2113–2096 B.C.E.), which was part of the temple precinct dedicated to the moon god Nannar. The city walls were constructed with an innovative type of standardized brick, called planoconvex because it was flat on the bottom and rounded on the top. The main advantage of this new form was that the bricks could be laid more quickly, without mortar or a skilled labor force. It also was more conducive to the construction of rounded corners and curving walls.

The monumental dimensions of the main buildings at Ur indicate the use of a highly organized and disciplined but unskilled labor force, one of the main ingredients of an imperial civilization. The religious precinct at Ur also demonstrates this tendency toward greater monumentality. The entire area stood on a huge platform reinforced by heavy brick walls, 24 yards thick and 8.7 yards tall. The ziggurat itself was a three-layered structure that stood within its own enclosure, occupying only a part of the precinct. On the southeast side was a large building called the Gipar, which functioned as the main residence of the high priestess of the city and of the goddess Ningal, the spouse of the moon god Nannar. The Gipar offers further testimony of the powerful role played by female gods and priestesses in the history of Mesopotamian cities. But ultimately Ur and its empire, like Akkad, would fall into decline. This process was described in a text entitled *Lamentation over the Destruction of Ur*, which, like the *Curse of Agade* upon which it was modeled, emphasized the power of the gods over humans and the endless cycle of rebirth and destruction.

Ashur, Nineveh, and the Assyrian Empire

The Akkadian imperial achievement set the stage for the emergence of the Assyrians, a Semitic people who built great palace-fortress complexes and a militaristic empire on the limestone plateau of northern Mesopotamia, beginning around 1365 B.C.E., under the leadership of King Ashur-uballit I. The ceremonial capital of the empire was Ashur, situated on a cliff overlooking the Tigris, from which point it commanded a lucrative Anatolian trade in tin and Babylonian textiles. The official religious center of the Assyrians, the city was dedicated to the god Ashur and became the sacred burial place of Assyrian monarchs, especially after 879 B.C.E., when King Ashurbanipal II moved his capital to Calah (Nimrud), itself soon to be eclipsed by the emergence of Nineveh as the administrative and residential capital of the empire.

The rise of Nineveh as the last official capital of the Assyrians began in 705 B.C.E. with King Sennacherib's decision to move his administration and palace there from the palace-fortress complex of Dur Sharrukin (Khorsabad), which had been established by Sargon II to escape associations with the old capital Nimrud. Achieving a population of some 120,000 at its height, Nineveh would remain the capital of Assyria until it was sacked in 612 B.C.E. Located amidst the sprawl of modern-day Mosul, Iraq, the site of Nineveh was a roughly rectangular enclosure with a massive wall about 7.5 miles in length.

The palace, conceived as both royal residence and government headquarters, was only part of the extensive urbanistic undertaking sponsored by Sennacherib, the purpose of which was to transform Nineveh into a world-class royal city. Especially noteworthy was his pragmatic planning, involving not only the widening of streets and squares but also the provision of parks, orchards, and advanced hydraulic engineering to guarantee a fresh water supply for the city. It has even been suggested by some scholars that the famous Hanging Gardens, one of the Seven Wonders of the Ancient World, were more likely found in Nineveh than in Babylon. The subsequent creation in Nineveh of the first great cuneiform tablet library of the ancient Near East, founded by Ashurbanipal (r. 668–627 B.C.E.), demonstrates clearly that Assyrian capitals were both the hubs of military administration and royal government as well as the cultural and symbolic centers of multinational empire.

Nippur, Babylon, and the Cultural Metropolis

Just as the emergence of cities had depended on the specialization of labor within an evolving hierarchy of functions and classes, so too did the growth and spread of urban culture throughout the ancient Near East depend on the rise of a small group of elite centers of specialized, "symbolic" cultural production and religious privilege. Foremost among these were Babylon, the first great cultural metropolis of the ancient world, and Nippur, an academic city of scribes and higher learning. Although it was not the capital of a political or military empire, Nippur commanded its own kind of cultural power and religious prestige as the major center of Sumerian text production with a sizable "scribe quarter" and as the locus of an extensive religious precinct with a temple economy that employed hundreds of thousands of people in the service of the god Enlil. Its growth unimpeded by the presence of a secular government, Nippur was well known for the ethnic diversity of its population and came to acquire a reputation as a city where peoples of diverse backgrounds could come together to live peacefully and intelligently. Nippur thus stands as the paradigm of the "cultural" city and multicultural place, where the priorities of urban life involved much more than the wealth generated by a specific trade relationship or the politics of a particular dynasty.

The endurance of the cultural metropolis is best illustrated by the case of Babylon and the Babylonians, whose civilization flourished for centuries, despite multiple foreign invasions and changes of political regime. The city of Babel of biblical fame was decadent, corrupt, and very worldly, but in fact it was here that the Bible was first written down, something that would not have been possible in a less-tolerant environment. Babylon probably became a large city as late as the 19th century B.C.E., after the collapse of the Third Dynasty of Ur, and a world power by the 14th century B.C.E., when it covered an area of about three square miles, with broad, straight streets and a diverse population that spoke Aramaic. It was the Neo-Babylonian Empire (625–539 B.C.E.) that triumphed over the Assyrians and became the main power of the ancient Near East. King Nabopolassar undertook the reconstruction of the great ziggurat, a project continued by his son Nebuchadnezzar, who also developed the great Processional Way of Marduk (ca. 605 B.C.E.) and the Ishtar Gate, now housed in partial reconstruction in a German museum. In 539 B.C.E. Babylon was taken over by the Achaemenid Persians under Cyrus II. When Alexander the Great defeated the Persian king Darius in 331 B.C.E., he chose Babylon as the capital of his empire and, upon his death, left it under the control of one of his Macedonian generals, Seleucus I. During the Roman Period, Babylon fell into decline and became a provincial town on the outskirts of the Roman Empire.

The City as a Forum for Empire and Power Politics

The decline of Babylon saw the rise of the Persian Empire and its best-known palace complex, Persepolis, begun by King Darius I in 518 B.C.E. and further developed during the subsequent reigns of Xerxes and Artaxerxes I. This Aachemenid site was defined by a vast terrace, some 40 feet high, measuring 1,500 by 900 feet in area, and originally topped by a mud-brick wall about 50 feet high. The complex was approached by a wide, gently graded stairway protected by a gatehouse with monumental sculptures of bulls and human-headed bulls, recalling the earlier *lamassus* (human-headed winged bulls) of Assyrian palaces. The interior of the complex featured a spacious audience hall, a throne hall, and the famous Hundred-Column Hall, all of which made extensive use of square spaces and distinctively carved columns and pillars, some topped with human-headed bull capitals. The great stairways leading to the terraces and platforms on which these structures stood were decorated with bold carvings of a great procession of tribute bearers, which effectively modeled (or mirrored) the expected behavior of the human subjects entering the imperial precinct. Like the Assyrian palace-complexes, Persian sites like Persepolis were essentially imperial centers that sought to promote the ceremonial and prestige of the emperor and his court. The Persians' manipulation of dramatic spatial sequences and the political potential of architectural sculptures, however, appear to have taken the propagandistic message of a vainglorious empire to even greater heights.

Polytheistic theocracy, with its temple economy and demanding ceremonial ritual, may have been the major driving force behind the initial growth of the ancient Near Eastern city, but over time there emerged a surprising and irrepressible diversity of form, function, and cultural personality among individual cities, as typified by places as diverse as Babylon and Persepolis. This diversity has both challenged and ultimately reinforced the region's prevailing religious and political conservatism. It is this very duality—of attempting to uphold traditional religion and politics in the face of the multicultural diversity and modernization that would appear to destabilize it—that makes contemporary Near Eastern cities so dynamic and fascinating.

ASIA AND THE PACIFIC

by Nancy Shatzman Steinhardt

The date assigned as the beginning of urbanism in Asia and the Pacific varies from region to region. Group settlement in extended families or larger units, in which certain aspects of hunting, gathering, or planting may have been shared, predated the formation or construction of cities in Asia, often by millennia. Urban settlement also occurred in all parts of Asia before writing appeared, so that the dates assigned to cities have been derived from archaeological evidence. Based on excavations and the analysis of their data, it is believed that the first cities in Asia were in China. Urbanism developed next in South Asia, particularly Pakistan, followed by Southeast Asia and, finally, Korea and Japan.

China's Most Ancient Cities

Not only are China's cities the oldest in Asia, but they also most readily lend themselves to definition. The Chinese word for city, *cheng*, is the same as the word for wall, and evidence of Chinese walls is at least as old as the evidence of cities. The first-known walled settlement in China is a Neolithic village of the sixth millennium B.C.E. in Li County in Hunan Province. An earthen wall 19.5 feet wide at the base that narrowed to about 5 feet at the top, roughly rectangular in shape, enclosed an area of 35,888 square yards. A ditch associated with the wall was also discovered. Several thousand miles to the north, in Aohanqi, Inner Mongolia, a ditch, but without any remains of a wall, enclosed a settlement of 28,700 square yards. Its date was determined by carbon-14 testing to be between 6200 and 5400 B.C.E. Houses in the Aohanqi settlement were arranged in rows. Remains of a cemetery dated to the mid-seventh millennium B.C.E., associated with a residential settlement but with no evidence of a wall or ditch, have been found in Wuyang County in the province of Henan. By the fifth millennium B.C.E. a settlement in Shaanxi Province included houses of at least three sizes, three cemeteries, a pottery workshop, and animal pens.

Walled settlements of the fourth millennium B.C.E. have been found in every region of China. A nearly circular wall surrounded by a moat enclosed a settlement in Zhengzhou, Henan. Also circular, enclosed by both wall and moat, was Chengtoushan, in Li County. At 95,680 square yards in area, it is more than twice as large as any other settlement known in Asia at the time. Both Zhengzhou and Chengtoushan had walls that were made using the rammed earth technique, associated with Chinese wall construction for the next four thousand years. (In the rammed-earth technique, walls are constructed of earth mixed with sand, gravel, and clay. The dampened material is poured into a form and then compacted, and the process is repeated until the desired height is reached.) By the fourth millennium B.C.E. Chinese cities were defined by walls, moats, residential architecture, cemeteries, and sometimes workshops.

It has been said that China experienced an urban revolution in the third millennium B.C.E., which was still nearly a thousand years before China entered the Bronze Age or had a written language. Cities from this period were huge in comparison to earlier times, sometimes between 1,195,990 and 3,587,970 square yards and serving a population that spread as many as 60 miles in either direction. It has been estimated that medium-size cities served a population of between 1,250 and 3,750 households, whereas the largest cities may have serviced as many as 50,000. Wall shapes appear to have become predominantly quadrilateral, in contrast to the more circular configurations found in the fifth and fourth millennia B.C.E.

Jade ritual reaping knife, from Henan province, northern China, during the Erlitou Period (17th-16th centuries B.C.E); a large number of items made of such materials as bronze, jade, lacquer, and bone attest to a complex urban life at this site. (© The Trustees of the British Museum)

More than 50 walled settlements from this period have been uncovered along the Yellow and Yangtze river valleys.

This was also the time when great houses appeared, structures so large compared with other dwellings that they are believed to have filled palatial or ceremonial functions. Some of the most impressive evidence of urbanism in the third millennium B.C.E. in China is associated with the Neolithic culture known as Longshan. Longshan has been identified in eight Chinese provinces, but its most impressive cities are in Shandong. In Yanggu County, Shandong Province, a walled enclosure of approximately 236 miles has been found. China's most famous Longshan city is at Chengziya, in Zhangqiu County, Shandong. Dated to about 2600 B.C.E., the city had a wall that enclosed an irregular rectangle roughly 1,460 by 1,772 feet. Several Longshan city remains suggest that many walls existed in single cities. At Lianyungang, in Jiangsu Province, a Longshan city with inner and outer walled areas has been identified. By about 2500 B.C.E. a city in Pingliangtai, Henan, had a system of pottery drainpipes. (Their use is contemporary with a drainage system in the ancient Indus Valley civilization city of Mohenjo Daro in Pakistan.) A long avenue divided Pingliangtai into two sections, a feature that would be present in some Chinese cities for the next several millennia.

Also by this time, it is believed that ceremonies were a part of urban life. There was a distinct group of people in the society who performed rituals and a group of craftspeople who made ritual objects. Much of the evidence of ritual comes from the Neolithic site Niuheliang, in Liaoning Province, dated to about 3000 B.C.E., which is an example of the Hongshan culture. The focal points of ritual at Niuheliang included a large, high mound, more than 23 feet of which remains; a structure named the Female Spirit Temple for the pieces of female statues uncovered there; stone platforms; and burial mounds beneath which were objects made of jade and other expensive materials. In southern China at Yushan in Yuhang County, Zhejiang Province, near the city of Shanghai, ritual altars and jade objects that attest to ceremonies as part of urban life in the fourth and third centuries B.C.E have been excavated.

By the middle of the third millennium B.C.E., China was composed of numerous city-states, most of them walled and some with several walls. Often a walled enclosure called an enceinte was the hub of activity of a larger region, but rarely was the territory within the jurisdiction of a city-state more than 62 miles in any direction. The city-states are believed to have had a ruling elite and economies based on agriculture, supplemented by stock breeding and fishing. There was a division of labor, meaning that builders of city walls and ritual architecture ate food grown or gathered by others.

The most importance evidence of urbanism in China of the second millennium B.C.E. is along the Yellow River valley in North China. This was the time, before the middle of the second millennium, when writing appeared in China, though some believe pictographs were used in the third millennium B.C.E. China entered its Bronze Age early in the second millennium, even before the official beginning of China's first great historic period, the Shang Dynasty (1500–1045 B.C.E.). According to literary sources, Shang was preceded by the Xia Dynasty. Most historians believe that this dynasty began before the age of Neolithic cultures ended in China.

Cities of Bronze Age China

A city that may well date to the Xia Period was excavated at Erlitou, near Luoyang in Henan. Large palatial complexes, bronze vessels, bronze plaques inlaid with turquoise, and remnants of jade, lacquer, bone, and pottery excavated at Erlitou attest to the complexity of urban life there, even though no wall remains have been uncovered.

North of Erlitou in Yanshi County is a city dated to about 1600 B.C.E. Sometimes it is referred to as Shixiangguo, named after a drainage ditch that ran through it. Consisting of an outer wall with an inner wall sharing its southern boundary and the southern part of its western boundary, the city measured 1,356 by 1,870 yards. Its outer wall was more than twice as thick as the inner one and was surrounded by a moat 65½ feet wide. Seven gates provided access to the outer city, and wide boulevards ran through it. Several palaces, large ritual sectors for animal offerings, pottery workshops, and a drainage system were among the urban features.

It has been surmised that Erlitou was the first of seven capitals from which the Shang kings ruled. There is little doubt that the Shang city at Zhengzhou was one of those capitals. Certainly the city was the most important urban center in the first half of the Shang Dynasty. Its main outer wall measured just short of 4 miles, and parts were as wide as 98 feet at the base. A little over 16 feet of wall have been uncovered south and west of the main wall, suggesting either that this was a significantly larger city or that it had many sections. The wall was made of pounded layers, lined by wooden planks, a technique introduced to China in Neolithic times. The largest palace foundation uncovered so far is 21,528 square feet.

Cities that were not capitals flourished in many parts of China during the Shang. Two of the best excavated have been found at Panlongcheng (near Wuhan, Hubei) and Gucheng (in Yuanqu County, Shanxi). At Panlongcheng a gate and two main buildings, believed to be a palace complex, stood in the northeast of the squarish city wall, which measured about 951 by 853 feet on each side. Contemporary with the capital at Zhengzhou, the city is important evidence that a similar level of urbanism was present in the Yellow and Yangtze river valleys by about 1400 B.C.E. The four wall segments of the city at Gucheng measured between 1,102 and 1,312 feet. The base of the wall was less than half the thickness of the wall at Zhengzhou, but portions along the south and west were doubled. The area believed to be the palace was roughly in the center of Gucheng.

Shang China's most important city was Yinxu, northwest of the city of Anyang, in Henan. It spanned about 14 square miles on either side of the Huan River. Excavation has occurred there almost every year since the late 1920s. Among the remains are more than 3,000 tombs, 2,200 sacrificial burials, and about 200 residential foundations, along with thousands of artifacts in bronze, bone, ivory, jade, stone, pottery, and horn as well as a few fragments of painting. A rectangular Shang wall has been found at Anyang, but the most important part of the settlement is at Xibeigang, west of the walled area. Xibeigang was the location of the royal cemetery, with at least 13 large-scale tombs dated from 1250 B.C.E. or slightly earlier until 1046 B.C.E. Much of the residential architecture lay in yet another area, just north of the village of Xiaotun and south of the walled enclosure. Xiaotun is the site of the important tomb of Lady Hao, consort of King Wu Ding, who ruled in the 12th century B.C.E.

From Yinxu through the rest of Chinese history, the names of all primary capitals, their dates, and their rulers are known. Between 1045 and 256 B.C.E., the period of the Zhou Dynasty, China's main capitals were near Xi'an and Luoyang. Hundreds of other walled cities were built during this period as well. The first part of the Zhou, sometimes known as Western Zhou (1045 B.C.E.–771 B.C.E.) because its capital was in the western of the two locations, had two capitals, Feng and Hao, located southwest and northeast of each other, about 7½ miles southwest of Xi'an. Ten building foundations, more than a thousand tombs, and caches of bronze goods have been excavated in the area of the two cities.

The most important capital of the second half of the Zhou Dynasty, known as the Eastern Zhou (770 B.C.E.–256 B.C.E.), is one of China's most famous ancient cities. Wangcheng, literally "ruler's city," part of a larger city in the environs of Luoyang, is described in the "Kaogongji (Record of Craftsmen)" section of the *Rituals of Zhou*, a book that describes imperial and official rites and ceremonies of the Zhou Dynasty. The text sets forth a prescription for an idealized city, square in shape with three gates at each side from which three-lane thoroughfares run through the city. The only interruption to those streets is the centralized palace area. It includes the ruler's hall of audience, temples to the ancestors and to soil and grain, and markets. This idealized city plan may never have been achieved, but the description has been viewed as a standard against which all later Chinese imperial cities are compared.

Besides the major capitals, each of the states contending for power in the first millennium B.C.E. built at least one capital. More than 100 state capitals from this period have been excavated. Among the most famous is the city at Qufu, in Shandong Province, where Confucius taught around 500 B.C.E. Its plan may have followed the prescription for a royal city in the *Rituals of Zhou*. Like Qufu, other cities of major states of the Zhou, including Linzi, capital of the state of Qi in Shandong; Xiadu, capital of the state of Yan, just south of Beijing in Hebei province; Handan, capital of the Zhao state in Hebei; and Houma, capital of Jin in southern Shanxi Province, all had walled palatial sectors and at least one more walled area either adjacent to or surrounding the palace-city.

China's First Imperial Cities

China's first emperor, Qin Shi Huangdi, who unified existing states in the formation of his empire in 221 B.C.E., built his national capital northeast of the early Zhou capitals Hao and Feng. Remains of palaces and countless other foundations have been uncovered, as well as pits that contained thousands of life-size warriors to guard the emperor in the afterlife. However, the outer boundary of the capital at Xianyang has not yet been determined.

Like their Zhou predecessors, the two great capitals of Han China—the earlier capital in the west, Chang'an, of the Western Han (202 B.C.E.–9 C.E.) and the later capital in the east, Luoyang, of the Eastern Han (25–220 C.E.)—are known through extensive documentation and equally extensive excavation. Chang'an is probably best known for the irregular shape of its outer wall: only the eastern boundary is a straight line. About 16 miles in perimeter, the length corresponds fairly closely to the 62 *li* (a Chinese unit of distance that varied over time) recorded in texts. The wall was between 39 and 52 feet at the base and rose more than 39 feet. The one accommodation to the ideal prescription for a city described in *Rituals of Zhou* was the presence of three gates on each side. From them emanated eight major streets, none stretching the full expanse of Chang'an in any direction.

More unusual was the presence of six palaces, five inside the walls and one beyond the western boundary. The palaces occupied most of the space inside the walls, and probably the placement of city walls was a response to the positions of palaces. Largest was Changle palace, a little over 2 square miles and built on the ruins of a palace from Qin times (221–207 B.C.E.). Weiyang palace, opposite it on the western side of Chang'an, was almost 2 square miles. Between them was an armory. Excavation and theoretical reconstruction have been conducted at each palace site. Extensive excavation has also been undertaken in the southern suburbs, the location of an ancestral temple complex that consisted of 11 individual halls and other ritual structures. Nine mausoleums for emperors and empresses spread north of the Wei River, north of Chang'an, and four more royal tombs lie in the southeast. Kilns, bronze foundries, and a mint were located in the market area in the northwestern area of Chang'an within the city walls. The population of Chang'an during the Han Dynasty was nearly 250,000.

Although its population was twice that of Chang'an and its shape more regular, the Eastern Han capital at Luoyang was less than half the size of the earlier capital. The nearly rectangular city, whose eastern and western walls, compared with the lengths of its northern and southern walls, were proportionately 3:2, had 12 city gates, 10 major street segments, and two palaces. The palaces were not used simultaneously. Like Chang'an, Luoyang had ritual structures for the same ceremonies and sacrifices in its southern suburbs. Luoyang, with its two palaces, should be viewed as a transitional imperial city in Chinese history, whereas Chang'an was largely a city of palaces. After Luoyang, all Chinese capitals would have only one palace area. Moreover, beginning with the Eastern Han capital of Luoyang, all palace sectors would be positioned along a central north-south axis. Both Chang'an and Luoyang would be the locations of China's most important imperial cities for nearly a millennium following the fall of the Han in 220 C.E.

A strong economy and commerce throughout the country gave rise to important cities outside the capitals in Han China. Some of them, such as Linzi and Handan, had their roots in cities of the Zhou Dynasty. Others, also with earlier building periods, such as Nanjing in Jiangsu Province, Hefei in Anhui, and Chengdu in Sichuan, have remained important Chinese cities since the time of the Han Dynasty. Han military commands spread across the empire, beyond China's borders, and some cities built strong walls and defense systems that resembled castle towns of medieval Europe.

Ancient Cities of South and Southeast Asia

After China, remains of the most significant urban activity in Asia or the Pacific in ancient times can be found in South Asia, particularly in Pakistan and Afghanistan. In Baluchistan, Afghanistan, at the site of Mehrgarh, there is evidence of settlement in the seventh millennium B.C.E. Domestication of animals occurred in the sixth millennium, and within the next 2,500 years pottery and objects of stone and metal were produced. These developments set the stage for the Indus Valley's first true cities, represented by the largest ones, Mohenjo Daro and Harappa. In India the city of Dholavira, in Gujarat, developed at the same time.

Both Mohenjo Daro and Harappa have been known since excavations of the 1920s. More recently, Kalibangan, about 87 miles southeast of Harappa, has emerged as an important urban center. All three cities flourished during the period from about 2600 B.C.E. to 1099 B.C.E. The most striking feature of the cities was the orthogonal arrangement of streets. In other words, major streets were oriented on a grid that ran north-south or east-west. It is believed that builders first studied the movements of the sun and stars and then designed their cities based on them. There is evidence of massive walls and gates at both Mohenjo Daro and Harappa, but the cities are better known for high, wall-enclosed mounds on which buildings were raised. The highest mound, at Mohenjo Daro, rose 39 feet. Unlike the main streets, the mounds were not oriented to the four cardinal directions. Main streets were as wide as 236 feet, with narrower lanes dividing the spaces between the main streets into quadrilaterals. Both Mohenjo Daro and Harappa were situated beside rivers, the former near the Indus and the latter near a tributary of the Indus, a waterway called Ravi. Indus Valley cities had sophisticated drainage, bathing, and sanitation systems, including wells, reservoirs, and cisterns (a receptacle for holding liquids, such as rainwater. The bathing areas were separated from lavatories. Many houses had private wells, but there were also public wells in the cities. Mohenjo Daro and Harappa were each approximately 3 miles in circumference, Mohenjo Daro slightly larger.

Harappa was marked by a large central depression, believed to have been a tank or reservoir. If this was a public space, it was not the only one. Indus Valley cities had large public buildings and great baths. Southwest of the great bath of Mohenjo Daro, beyond the outer city wall, was a large building elevated on a mound. It has been identified either as a great hall, perhaps for ritual use, or a granary. About 98 feet south of Harappa was a mound with its own houses, drainage system, and baths. This may have been a rest stop for travelers. Mud brick was the main construction material of Indus Valley cities, with wood being the next most common building material. It is believed that artisans who specialized in one material or the other worked together in city construction.

Ban Chiang, in northeastern Thailand, is the most important Neolithic and Bronze Age settlement in Southeast Asia. It is dated to about 3600 B.C.E. to 200 C.E. Bronze production in Ban Chiang is believed to have occurred by the mid-second millennium B.C.E., consistent with that of China but more than a thousand years before evidence of a Bronze Age in the rest of Thailand.

Urbanism in Northeast Asia

Although Korea and Japan enjoyed long Paleolithic and Neolithic periods, urbanism was not part of them. There is no evidence of cities during either Japan's or Korea's Bronze Age. Korea's earliest walled cities may have been constructed as military commands of Han Dynasty China. In Japan, where the Bronze Age flourished well into the Common Era, there is little evidence of urbanism through the first several centuries C.E. It is probable that cities came about in Japan as a result of influences from continental East Asia, either from Korea or China, and that cities were first constructed as late as the sixth century C.E. City walls were built even later in Japan. Still, by the end of ancient times, cities flourished in every part of Asia. Soon thereafter, cities reached the Japanese islands in the Pacific.

EUROPE

BY JOHN COLLIS

Between 58 and 51 B.C.E. Julius Caesar conquered Gaul (modern France, Belgium, and parts of Holland, Germany, and Switzerland). In his detailed account of the Gallic Wars he talks about large defended sites that on occasion he had to attack; indeed, he spent a winter at one of them, Bibracte, composing his memoirs. Though he sometimes uses the word *urbs* (city) to describe these places, the term he normally uses is *oppidum*, meaning "defended place" or simply "town." Among the sites he lists are some that are still towns today: Geneva, Besançon, Paris, Bourges, Orléans. Others are now deserted hilltops like Bibracte (Mont Beuvray, in Burgundy), which was abandoned a couple of generations after the conquest for the more accessible Augustodunum (Autun).

Many of the sites mentioned by Caesar have been identified; they are characterized by massive ramparts, usually a single bank and ditch, surrounding areas of 100 to 1,000 acres, mostly on hilltops or promontories that could be easily defended. Caesar describes these ramparts, which he calls *murus gallicus* (Gallic wall). They consisted of several layers of timbers laid out in a rectilinear grid with iron spikes nailing them together where they crossed. The spaces between the timbers were filled with rock and soil, and the front and back were revetted (faced with a material that gives support) with walls of drystone (stones fitted together without mortar) through which the timbers protruded; an earthen ramp ran behind. Caesar notes that these barriers were resistant to fire, ramming, and sapping (excavating). Some 40 sites, including Mont Beuvray, have produced ramparts approximating Caesar's description, mainly west of the Rhine but also as far east as Manching in Bavaria. Caesar mentions other types of ramparts; one, with a massive earthen bank and wide ditch, was common in northern and central France, often replacing a *murus gallicus*.

Many sites not mentioned by Caesar have also been identified, not only in Gaul but east of the Rhine in areas he never reached: southern and central Germany, the Czech and Slovak republics, and Austria and Hungary. In these areas, however, the usual rampart is an earthen bank revetted in front by wooden posts, with the gaps filled by drystone walling.

Finds from these sites show that they were being constructed from the late second century B.C.E. onward, though some in central Europe may date to as early as 180–150 B.C.E. There had been a long tradition of constructing defended sites in temperate Europe extending back to the fourth millennium B.C.E., but the *oppida* tend to be much larger than these early sites, implying a higher level of social organization. Farther north, in Poland, northern Germany, and Scandinavia, urban sites did not appear until the late first millennium C.E. The *oppida* also contrast with the defended sites on the Mediterranean coast in southern France and eastern Spain, which were much smaller and more closely spaced, more like "city-states" than the "tribal" states that produced the *oppida*.

Before the *Oppida*

Although the *oppida* are often called the "earliest towns north of the Alps," they did not appear from nowhere; sites with urban characteristics existed as early as the sixth century B.C.E. in western Europe. In 600 B.C.E. refugees from the Greek city of Phocis founded the colony of Massalia (modern Marseilles) near the mouth of the Rhône in southern France. Trade linking the developing civilizations of Greece and Italy with central and western Europe had started earlier, but it expanded rapidly after the foundation of the colony, and fine pottery from mainland Greece, wine amphorae (large pottery jars for shipping and storing liquids and other goods) from southern France, bronze vessels from Italy, and other luxury goods turn up on a number of trading sites that were established along the main river routes leading into the interior. Bronze buckets from northern Italy are found as far north as southern Sweden.

The major route led northward along the Rhône and its tributaries the Saône and the Doubs. At Lyons, where the Rhône meets the Saône, a major settlement has been identified on the banks of the Saône. A bit farther south, at Vienne, a similar settlement was established where land routes between the upper Loire and northern Italy crossed the Rhône. Bragny lies on the Doubs, near its confluence with the Saône, controlling the route that leads northeast up to the Middle Rhine and the headwaters of the Danube. Although these sites seem mainly to have been ports for river traffic, Bragny was also involved in producing iron and bronze goods, and a site on the Dürrnberg in Austria was associated with salt mining, although its inhabitants engaged in other industries as well.

The most spectacular evidence for this trade system, however, comes from farther inland, from sites controlling the headwaters of rivers that lead away from the Rhône valley toward the Atlantic, the Baltic, and the heart of Europe. The Heuneburg, in southern Germany, overlooks the point at which the Danube becomes navigable; Asperg, near Stuttgart, controls the Neckar, a tributary of the Rhine; in France, Mont Lassois overlooks the upper Seine and Bourges the confluence of two tributaries of the Loire. At most of these sites there is a small central hill fort; at the site of the Heuneburg the fort was defended by a wall made of sun-dried brick with bastionlike towers, features unknown at this period anywhere else outside the Mediterranean area. Inside, a thriving settlement produced metal objects and other goods, and surrounding it a concentration of other settlement areas likewise engaged in industry and trade, as the imported Mediterranean artifacts show.

What makes some of these sites stand out are the exceptionally rich burials under massive tumuli (artificial hills or mounds of earth or stone). The Hohmichele at the Heuneburg, Hochdorf at Asperg, and Vix at Mont Lassois are the richest prehistoric burials from central or western Europe, featuring large wooden chambers, four-wheeled vehicles, rich gold objects, and spectacular imported luxury goods like, at Vix, a bronze vessel for mixing wine that stands nearly five and a half feet high. These graves are presumed to be those of "chieftains" who controlled and grew wealthy from the trade in goods gathered locally as tribute and "gift exchange." Bourges is more enigmatic; the settlement is richer than the others in terms of the quantity of imported goods, but it lacks the exceptionally rich burials, and a central defended site has yet to be identified. The site consists of a cluster of areas of occupation, with extensive evidence of industrial activity, especially bronze production, manufacturing brooches and other ornaments. The site seems to have been occupied for only a short period in the late sixth and the fifth centuries B.C.E., perhaps three or four generations.

These developments toward urbanization were short-lived. The very rich burials disappeared, and Mediterranean imports into temperate Europe became scarce. Mont Lassois and the Heuneburg had already been abandoned soon after 500 B.C.E. Bourges and Asperg may have survived until as late as 400 B.C.E., but the trading systems had collapsed, one factor being an economic downturn in southern France, perhaps owing in part to the political conflicts at that time in the Mediterranean among the Etruscans, Carthaginians, and Greeks as well as the unrest in northern Italy caused by the Gallic colonization.

In the third century B.C.E. the economic situation in temperate Europe revived. Although renewed contact with Italy (Etruria and Rome) was one element in the revival, it played only a partial role, as imported wares such as fine pottery remained rare until the second century B.C.E., when there was an enormous upsurge in imported goods, especially amphorae manufactured at sites on the west coast of Italy such as Pompeii, Cosa, and Albinia. These turn up by the thousand in central France; their main contents were wine, but they were also used for other goods such as olive oil and *garum* (fermented fish paste). From the third century coinage was also adopted, mainly based on Greek prototypes. Initially only gold was used, but by the second century lower-value coins of silver and bronze appeared, allowing lower levels of transactions and perhaps also the appearance of market exchange alongside the traditional gift exchange and barter.

This surge in economic activity led to the establishment of settlements that in some cases were the direct predecessors of the *oppida*, in that they were abandoned when the population moved to nearby hilltop sites, as in the cases of Levroux, Basel, and Breisach. These early sites were much bigger than normal farming settlements or hamlets, usually at least 25 acres in size, and they stand out not merely for their exotic imported goods but also for the presence of a range of industries working materials such as iron, bronze, glass, shale, and bone to produce weapons, tools, and ornaments. A few of these sites, like those of the fifth century, lie on major trade routes (Basel and Breisach on the Middle Rhine, Manching on the Danube), but most seem rather to have been administrative or market centers (Levroux and the newly discovered site of Bobigny in the northern suburbs of Paris).

In central Europe the sites seem more industrial in nature, as at Mšecke Žehrovice in Bohemia, which specialized in making shale bracelets that were widely traded, as well as iron from local ore. Clearly some inhabitants of these sites were artisans and possibly traders, and at Manching small wooden houses showing evidence of various industries cluster along the main east-west road paralleling the Danube. But Levroux and Manching also had fenced enclosures like those found on the later *oppida*, and they seem to have been farms that also engaged in industrial production; they are usually interpreted as the residences of a rich farming elite who were becoming increasingly important in these societies. None of these sites have rich burials like those of the sixth century. The cemetery at Bobigny, while wealthy for its period (male burials with weapons, a couple of imported Italian pots), does not have the rich gold objects or high-status imports found in earlier burials, and the cemetery as Basel seems positively poor.

One site stands out as exceptional: Aulnat, just east of Clermont-Ferrand in the Auvergne of central France. Like the other sites, it is not on a major route; instead it sits on very rich agricultural land. It is a concentration of areas of dense occupation covering an area measuring at least one and a quarter miles by a third of a mile by the late second century B.C.E. Despite its large size, it reflects the general pattern of the other settlements, with a range of industries (minting of gold and silver coins, working of bronze and iron, manufacture of glass and bone objects, and probably production of textiles). In its early phases, in the late third century B.C.E., imported items were rare—some coral as inlay for brooches and a few fine vessels and cooking utensils. This was followed by the upsurge in the second century B.C.E. of importation of wine amphorae and fine pottery.

There is also a structure identified as a shrine, with associated offerings (notably the burial of a horse with its gear). There are many burials and small cemeteries scattered around the settlement, though again the very richest contain only items such as swords, and none are very rich by Iron Age standards. But for this area we have documentary evidence from Greek authors such as the ethnographer Poseidonius. He relates how the Arverni (after whom the Auvergne is named) were the most powerful state in Gaul in the second century B.C.E., controlling an area "from the Rhine to the Atlantic" and extending into southern France. Their king Luernios was described as the "richest man in all Gaul" and his son Bituitos, after the defeat by the Romans of his army in southern France in 123 B.C.E., was paraded in Rome in his chariot "of gold and silver." Aulnat seems to have been the center of this powerful state.

The Foundation of the *Oppida*

Several of the open sites were direct predecessors of the *oppida*, as they were abandoned at precisely the time when new defended sites were established on nearby hills: Basel, Breisach, Levroux, and Aulnat. Only at Manching did the open site itself go on to become a defended site. There the open settlement had continued expanding until, by the time a *murus gallicus* rampart was placed around the site around 120 B.C.E., it was nearly a mile in length, enclosing some 1,000 acres. Almost the whole area, which included a port site on the Danube, was densely occupied.

For most of the *oppida*, however, we do not know where the population came from. There will probably be more open settlements discovered, especially underlying modern towns. But in some *oppida* we are probably seeing the nucleation of people from many smaller settlements of a nonurban nature—in short, the deliberate foundation of a city where none had existed before. This, of course, implies a central organization capable of making the decision to found a new site, with the vision and knowledge of what was needed and the political, legal, and economic power to sustain the settlement once it was established. Caesar refers to the "tribes" of Gaul as *civitates,* a word best translated as "states," and he talks about ways in which the states held meetings to govern their affairs (for example, the *senatus* of the Aedui or the popular gatherings of the Treveri), the election of magistrates (such as the elected chief magistrate of the Aedui), and the collection of taxes (for instance, the auctioning of the right to gather tolls from the traders among the Aedui).

The reasons for this abrupt change in settlement pattern, from open to defensive positions, is not clear, especially in central Europe, where we have no information on events from the written sources for the early second century when the *oppida* were founded. The dates for southern Germany, Switzerland, and France of around 120 B.C.E., however, correspond closely to the Roman invasion of southern Gaul in 125–123 B.C.E. and the defeat of the Arverni. With the collapse of the major coalition, there may have been a power vacuum that led to conflict by new competing powers. By the time Caesar arrived 60 years later, although the Arverni were still a major force, they had been eclipsed by the Aedui based in Burgundy and the Sequani to the east in the Franche Comté.

Not all of the *oppida* succeeded; some sites were founded and their defenses constructed, but we have little evidence for much occupation of them. In some areas, especially in western France, *oppida* were not established at all, even in places where we have evidence for major open settlements. So the pattern is not uniform.

Within the *oppida* there was considerable difference in the types of houses, indicating that the population covered the whole range of the society. At the top of the hierarchy were fenced enclosures containing a number of buildings, some of which seem to have been for agricultural purposes (stables, barns, and granaries) and others for industrial activities such as iron- and bronzeworking, coin production, as though some aspects of production were under close elite control. At Mont Beuvray one or two of these enclosures evolved, first into large timber houses and then, after the Roman conquest, into luxurious stone houses with courtyards, mosaic pavements, heating systems, and elaborate painted walls, comparable to the best Mediterranean houses. These were clearly the residences of the aristocrats who formed the leading groups within the oligarchic states that Caesar describes.

There are also industrial areas with small buildings such as those along the main street at Manching. The best preserved are those excavated at Mont Beuvray, initially built in timber but again, after the conquest, reconstructed in stone, indicative of an independent and increasingly wealthy artisan class. At Mont Beuvray the houses seem to have been of two stories, with double rooms on the ground floor, one of which was devoted to industry (the casting of brooches, forging of iron tools and weapons, production of glass ornaments, objects with enamel inlay, and so on). It is less easy to identify public areas such as market squares. Some of the sites had temples, but temples are more a characteristic of the countryside in Gaul, where sanctuaries that were to continue into the Roman period started appearing from the fourth century onward.

Although many of these sites evolved into permanent settlements, in some areas they were inhabited for only a generation or two. This is most clear in the Aisne Valley in northern France and in the Auvergne, where we can identify series of sites, one succeeding the other; in the Auvergne parts of the earlier sites did continue to be occupied. The large open settlement at Aulnat was completely abandoned at the end of the second century B.C.E. in favor of a hilltop site at Corent, centered on a religious enclosure. Although the temple remained in use, the majority of the population moved to a more low-lying site at Gondole overlooking the river Allier, and this, too, had a ritual area just outside the defenses, where pits containing skeletons of men and horses have been uncovered. By the time Caesar arrived, the center of population was on a nearby hilltop, the site of Gergovia, which he besieged unsuccessfully. This site, too, was abandoned a couple of generations after the conquest in favor of the nearby town of Augustonemetum, though the temple site continued in use. Clearly the shifting of the town required considerable expense and resources, and the reasons for these shifts are unclear. It was more common for the sites, once founded, to continue in use, and many Roman towns in Gaul, both provincial capitals and smaller centers, are now known to have pre-Roman origins.

Other Areas

The coastal areas of southern France and eastern and southern Spain had been subject to colonization first by the Phoenicians (for example, at Cadiz, though some settlements were little more than small intermediary trading centers with few urban characteristics) and then from 600 B.C.E. by the Greeks, most notably at Massalia (Marseilles) and Emporion and Rhode (Ampurias and Rosas, in northwestern Spain) which in their turn established their own colonies. The model for all these sites was the "city-state" controlling only a small amount of territory and mainly reliant on the sea for its external contacts.

These sites were certainly one factor that led to urbanization among the native peoples labeled as Ligurians and Iberians; a plethora of defended sites developed in the hinterlands of foreign colonies as well as along the river Guadalquivir in central southern Spain, though they certainly were not set up in the image of the Greek sites. They were mainly defended sites on hilltops surrounded by impressive drystone walls with projecting towers to allow cross fire, as at Entremont in Provence. However, certainly in southern France, the internal structure was very different from the colonial sites—lacking, for instance, the massive public buildings and temples that dominated Greek cities.

The road system, often rectilinear, was designed to give access to blocks of houses that were generally very uniform in plan, with rarely more than a couple of rooms on the ground floor, though there is evidence that most had a second story. The only cult sites were unpretentious, incorporated into the blocks of domestic buildings and seemingly dedicated to hero or ancestor cults rather than a pantheon of gods. The enclosed areas varied considerably, from small villages to sites of several acres, but show nothing like the massive size of the *oppida* of central Gaul. By the time of the Roman conquest, when we start to gain information about the administrative units, they were generally small. Although some of these sites developed into major cities such as Nemausus (Nîmes) under Roman rule, many of them were not urban; rather they were a nucleation of the total population, with little evidence of smaller settlements around. Naturally, these sites were also centers of industrial and trading activity.

The Iberian Peninsula was complex, with almost the full range of types of societies found elsewhere in Europe, from major foreign colonies such as Ampurias, Cartagena, and Cadiz to communities based in small hill forts in the north and northwest. In the Iberian-speaking areas there is evidence for defended sites—for instance, in the Ebro Valley—as early as the Late Bronze Age (2800–700 B.C.E.), but only from the seventh century onward did complex defended sites appear in numbers in eastern and southeastern Iberia. Some of these were comparable to those in southern France, with towers and ramparts on stone footings. Some of the earlier sites, such as Cortes de Navarra and Cabezo de Monleón, consist of a series of almost identical conjoined houses with little sign of social differentiation, but by the sixth to fifth centuries at sites such as Puente Tablas near Jaén there are more elaborate houses with several rooms around a courtyard, indicative of a more complex society.

In the immediate hinterland of Ampurias, the 27-acre urban site of Ullastret, dating to the fifth century B.C.E., was enclosed by a massive stone wall with towers. In size these *oppida* are comparable to those in southern France. Inland, however (for instance, around Ávila), there are massive sites more like those of central France: Ulaca, whose double enclosures encompass about 200 acres, and La Mesa de Miranda, which in its final stage enclosed about 70 acres. Even within one tribal area there are very different patterns of settlement.

In Britain there is a group of sites labeled by archaeologists as *oppida*, but they are very different from the continental sites. They date somewhat later, from the late first century B.C.E. to the middle of the first century C.E. Several of them, such as Colchester, Saint Albans, and Silchester, developed into major Roman towns after the Roman conquest in the 40s C.E. They are characterized by linear boundaries or "dikes" that cut off large expanses of land, in the case of Colchester roughly 8 square miles, in which various activities were concentrated. We know that Colchester, the ancient Camulodunum, was the "capital" of the "king of the Britons" Cunobelin, who controlled much of southeast England in the period before the Roman conquest, and his gold coins bear the name of the site. It included a port area that shows evidence of industrial activity, such as coin and pottery manufacture, and of extensive trade with the Roman Empire. There is also a temple enclosure, some probable royal burials under large tumuli, and a possible royal residence.

GREECE

BY TOM STREISSGUTH

To the ancient Greeks the city (polis) was the hallmark of civilization. The city provided the Greeks with an identity, with culture, and with the means to live well. Urban manners, arts, trade, and government—along with their language—marked the Greeks as civilized, in their own eyes, and not as barbarian outsiders.

While a Greek "nation" did not yet exist, Greek cities were the basic geographical, political, and social units. Every Greek citizen first identified himself with his family and clan and then with the city to which he belonged. He lived as the member of that city, no matter where he resided or moved, with his citizenship permanently conferred by birth. When voyaging abroad, he called himself by his given name, his father's name, and by the city where he came from. He fought and died for the polis, if called on to do so, and aspired to serve it as a civic leader.

The ancient Greeks gave much thought to the form of the city. While their philosophers and mathematicians sought perfect forms in the natural world, their town planners strived to build a logical system of streets, districts, and public places. The Greek city was renowned for its orderliness and sense of proportion as well as the civic pride displayed in the form of buildings, monuments, temples, schools, theaters, and other structures that served the public interest.

EARLIEST SETTLEMENTS

The Greek world of the Mycenaean Age (to about 1200 B.C.E.) had no towns of any large size. It was a farming society ruled by kings who lived within palace complexes of homes, barracks, and markets. These strongholds relied on the surrounding farms for their sustenance; trade took place from harbor to harbor, and many coastal settlements also relied on piracy. During the Bronze Age in Greece (to about 1050 B.C.E.), farmers lived on communally owned land within extended families. The *genos*, or family, lived in or near a stronghold raised for their mutual defense. The families associated themselves with a tribe, whose members shared a common founding myth and ancestor and who belonged to a single religious cult.

The families of the tribe shared a meeting place and market center near their defensive stronghold, which was also known as an acropolis, or "high city." The acropolis was situated on the crown of a hill, usually near a harbor but some distance from the shore to protect against raids from the sea. Beneath the acropolis was the agora, or marketplace, where the people could meet to buy and sell their livestock, tools, weapons, and crops. Although home industry provided most of life's necessities, only craftsmen had the needed skill and equipment to forge good weapons and tools, to cast jewelry or armor, or to paint pottery with scenes of the gods and heroes. Workshops and forges raised near the agora provided access to the marketplace and to traders who bought and sold goods across the seas. Nearby forests and public quarries provided raw materials for construction, for pottery, and for iron and bronze forging.

Permanent settlements grew near the agoras and fortifications. The first large Greek towns were built on the island of Crete and in Ionia (the islands of the eastern Aegean and the nearby coast of Asia Minor), the most prosperous region of the early Greek world. The Ionian cities, including Miletus and Smyrna, had the essential ingredients for successful towns: an extensive hinterland that provided food, wine, and oil as well as a market for crafts such as pottery and tools. The cities of Ionia also lay astride busy trade routes between the Aegean, the Black Sea, Egypt, and the Levant.

In the early Greek cities regular blocks shared unpaved streets that led from the town gates to central public squares. The houses had several rooms, with some rising two stories in a wing set back from the street. Alleys separated the blocks and provided drainage for rainwater and wastewater. In the outer districts and in smaller settlements, haphazard, unpaved lanes meandered among the private homes and workshops.

From the beginning of the Archaic Period (ca. 600 B.C.E.) and the earliest Greek writing, many Greek settlements became entirely self-sufficient, their inhabitants having the skills or the wealth to live independently off the land. In contrast to farming settlements, these towns gave rise to distinct social divisions. At the top was an urban aristocracy, men who were responsible for civic affairs, for lawmaking, for settling disputes, and for leadership in war. The members of this class held full membership and rights in the city. Women, children, and foreigners did not hold the privileges of the citizenry; slaves—most gathered by war and piracy—had no legal rights whatsoever and could be disposed of in any manner their owners saw fit.

By the process of *synoikismos,* several villages unified themselves into a polis, or city-state. The most significant such event in Greek history was the confederation of several villages in Attica, a peninsula of southern Greece, to form the polis of Athens, an act that by the city's tradition was carried out by its founder-king, Theseus. Other leading city-states were Thebes, Sparta, and Corinth; Delos and Rhodes were prominent island-states in the Aegean region. In some places this unification took place without a physical center, and so the polis could simply mean a political alliance among extended families or villages. But in most cases cities had such a center, as well as a gymnasium or school, public halls, a theater, a temple, and water delivered through public fountains. The city reserved to itself the authority to mint coins, to regulate the calendar, to keep standard weights and measures, and to set down the proper timing and duration of religious festivals. Grain inspectors, superintendents of the markets, and port overseers watched over commerce. A city might depend for its existence on the export of its marble, silver, wine, timber, or flax; to keep careful control over trade in this item was the difference between success or failure, wealth or starvation.

The Innovations of Hippodamus

The architect Hippodamus of Miletus is the first-known city planner in Greek history. According to historical tradition, Hippodamus created the orthogonal (rectangular) pattern of streets that came into vogue during the Classical Period (starting in the fifth century B.C.E.). In fact, Hippodamus was not the first to create a regular street grid, but he did apply his philosophy of the ideal city to his Ionian hometown, thereby setting a standard for new Greek towns raised in the centuries to come.

In the ideal city of Hippodamus, the citizens of the polis were divided into artisans, farmers, and soldiers, while the land consisted of religious, public, and private zones. He carried this tripartite division to Miletus, which was rebuilt in 479 B.C.E. after its destruction by a Persian army. Hippodamus laid out three main sections, divided by the city's two harbors. The central agora and public buildings were raised in a low-lying precinct, while the city's theater was built into the side of a hill overlooking the main harbor; on the other side of the harbor was a temple dedicated to the goddess Athena (at the smaller harbor, known as the Lion Harbor, stood a temple of Apollo). A highway linking the city to sacred precincts in the countryside led away from the wall at the southern edge of the city. After it was rebuilt by Hippodamus, Miletus grew to a population of 100,000, one of the largest cities of ancient Greece, and boasted three large covered markets, one of them made of fine marble and surrounded by galleries two stories tall.

The renown of Hippodamus spread to Athens, which had become the wealthiest city of the Greek world. Athenian leaders invited Hippodamus to lay out the streets of the new harbor town of Piraeus, near Athens, as well as the colony of Thurii in southern Italy. The Hippodamian plan was imitated, or applied by him personally, at Olynthus in Macedonia, at the city of Rhodes, and at the town of Priene. The rectangular grid, and the idea of specialized precincts carefully laid out within that grid, became a convention throughout the Greek world, even on hilly ground and mountain slopes where the terrain made surveying and construction on such a plan difficult.

Public and Private Buildings

The cities of ancient Greece grew by absorbing nearby settlements and by commerce, which earned money and attracted foreign traders and fortune seekers. By proving their merit, these outsiders could win citizenship, granted by a vote in the public assembly. Wealthy rural landowners also built homes in the city to enjoy its services and entertainments, to conduct business in the agora, and take

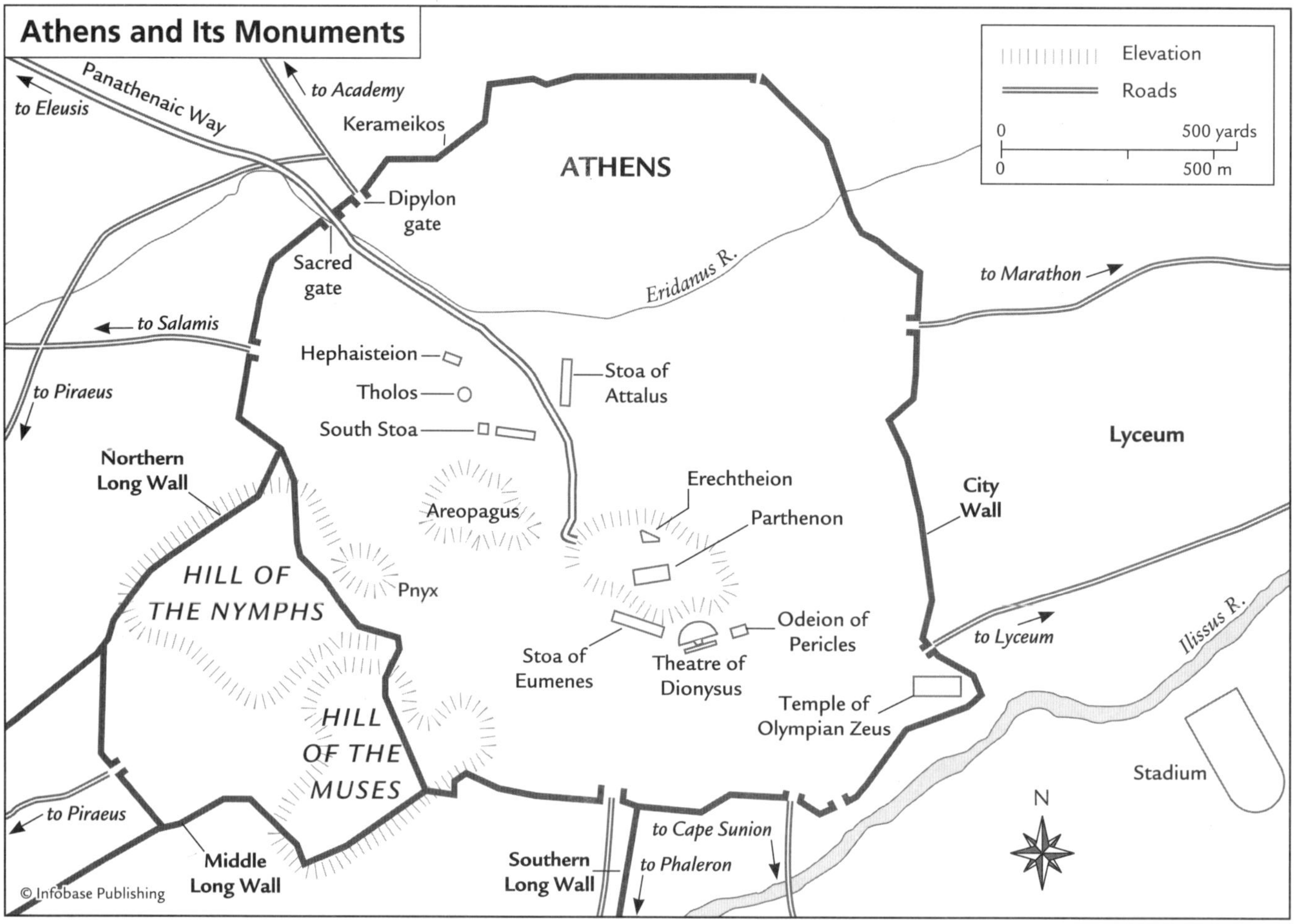

Ancient Athens reached its zenith in the fifth century B.C.E., when its population numbered around 300,000, of whom 40,000 were citizens.

part in city government, which was considered a right and duty of every citizen.

Civic leaders regulated their city's physical layout by controlling the height of buildings and the width of streets and by restricting certain activities to particular zones. The agora remained the central meeting place or town square in addition to being the center of public commerce. Surrounding the agora were one or more stoas, long and low buildings with shops and arcaded walkways for the use of the public. The stoa provided shelter from the elements and served the public as a meeting place.

The *bouleuterion* was a place for the meeting of the boule, or city council, whose members arranged themselves on tiers of seats set around a central platform for speakers. The *prytaneion* was the ancient Greek city hall, which held the offices of the executive committee known as the *prytaneis* as well as offices for the magistrates who received state guests and ambassadors. The symbolic heart of the city, the *prytaneion* was home to a sacred flame, which was always kept burning. Some cities had a *tholos*, a circular building used for public ceremonies, such as sacrifices and state banquets, and for meetings and meals of the *prytaneis*.

An important function of the city was to provide pleasant occupation for a citizen's leisure time. A *balaneia* was a public bath that held bathtubs made from stone or glazed terra-cotta brick, set in rows, and with running water that could be heated over a fire. An *odeion* was a roofed hall used for musical performances. The earliest Greek theaters consisted of wooden benches set into a hillside in a semicircular layout. From the fourth century B.C.E. on, theaters grew to rival the agoras as places of public assembly. The finest had several dozen tiers of raised seats built in stone or marble, often with an expansive view of a valley, harbor, or city from above.

Gymnasia were public buildings raised for education of the young. The gymnasium had an open courtyard for physical training, a running track, and a colonnaded hall similar to a stoa, with rooms for instruction and for public speaking. A palaestra was a building for athletic training, with small changing rooms surrounding a central courtyard. The stadium was a running track, with banked sides for the use of spectators.

Private homes were small and simple, built of dried brick or cob, a mixture of wet clay and straw. They were built separately, though many large Greek cities had tenement blocks. The front entrance of the home faced south, with a small entrance hall beyond which was an enclosed central courtyard. Living rooms were at the back of the home, arranged around a portico or courtyard; separate servants' quarters, kitchens, and reception halls were also situated around the ground floor. Finer homes had bathrooms as well as second-story galleries over the porticoes, where separate women's quarters were located. City homes were furnished with beds, chests, tables, chairs, carpets, and tapestries and were provided with clay and metal drinking vessels and storage jars. Walls were whitewashed and sometimes painted with geometric designs. The homes of the wealthy displayed wall frescoes and mosaic floors.

New Cities Abroad

During the fifth century B.C.E. the polis of Athens reached the height of its power and prosperity. About 40,000 citizens belonged to Athens, among a total population of about 300,000. Sparta held far fewer citizens but included a large number of serfs and slaves and a group of autonomous people who lived in the city's vicinity; altogether the Sparatan city-state included about 250,000 people.

As the cities of Greece grew, overpopulation prompted overseas colonization. Greek colonists built new cities on the coasts of the Black Sea, in Sicily, on the Adriatic Sea, in North Africa, and Egypt. Greek town planning in Magna Graecia, in modern-day southern Italy, had a strong influence on republican Rome. A Greek polis was first and foremost a body of citizens, and if it moved overseas to a colony site, the colonists still identified themselves as members of a city. They were dependent on their homelands for goods and trade, for protection from coastal raids and pirates, and for the masons, carpenters, and other tradesmen who could provide essential services in the new territory.

The conquests of the Macedonian general Alexander the Great (r. 336–323 B.C.E.) in the fourth century B.C.E. spread Greek culture and cities into western Asia, from Egypt to the Levant to Afghanistan. New Greek towns and camps were raised where Alexander's armies had passed, and in defeated foreign capitals Greek temples, columns, statuary, and public buildings appeared as monuments to Greek civilization.

As his most enduring monument Alexander envisioned a trading city on the Mediterranean shores of Egypt, at a sheltered point between Lake Mareotis and the island of Pharos. After Alexander's death in Babylon in 323 B.C.E. and under King Ptolemy I (r. 323–285 B.C.E.), Dinocrates of Rhodes laid out the city of Alexandria on the site of a small fishing village, Rhakotis. The new town had two main avenues, 200 feet wide and lined with colonnades, running north-south and east-west. The side streets crossed at right angles, in the Greek fashion. The city had abundant fresh water drawn from Lake Mareotis, as well as street gutters that drained into subterranean canals that lay underneath every street.

Alexandria prospered as the capital of Ptolemaic Egypt. A flourishing center of Greek learning and culture, which endured long after the conquest of Greece proper by the Romans, the city boasted impressive monuments, including the tomb of Alexander, the lavish royal palaces of the Ptolemaic kings, a monumental temple known as the Serapeion (also spelled Serapeum), a museum, and the Library of Alexandria,

THE DECLINE OF THE CITY-STATE

Rivalries among the Greek cities worsened in the fifth century B.C.E. as populations rose, trade routes grew more crowded, and the Persian Empire threatened invasion and conquest. The Peloponnesian War set Athens and her allies against a federation led by Sparta, and it forced all other Greek cities to choose sides. The war brought widespread death and destruction and ended the dominance of Athens over the Greek world. It prepared the Greeks for nationhood—and for the end of the independent city-state.

In the semibarbarous northern realm of Macedon, the ambitious King Philip II (r. 359–336 B.C.E.) aspired to lord it over a weakened Athens and the entire Greek world. He seized the gold and silver mines of northern Greece and raised allies to work for his own interests in all the major cities to the south. Thebes allied with Athens to resist the Macedonians, but the Greeks were soundly defeated at the Battle of Chaeronea in 338 B.C.E. Leading one wing of the Macedonian troops in this battle was Philip's 17-year-old son, the future Alexander the Great.

Chaeronea marked the end of Greek resistance to Philip of Macedon. Soon after the battle, he organized the League of Corinth to fight the Persians, who remained a constant threat. Each member of the league was allowed to keep its own constitution, but a national assembly began meeting at Corinth, and Philip raised a new Greek army, under his personal leadership, by levying troops from all the corners of the Hellenic world.

Although Philip was assassinated in 336 B.C.E., his goal of uniting all the Greeks under a Macedonian dynasty was realized by Alexander, a brilliant military tactician. Philip's young heir traveled to Corinth, where representatives from all the major Greek cities hailed him as their nominal king. He took the reins of the national army and, when the city of Thebes rebelled against him, besieged the city and burned it to the ground. The traditional, independent city-state of Greece, an institution dating back a millennium, grew obsolete under Alexander's reign and the subsequent conquest of Greece by the Romans.

the most famous and largest library of the ancient world, which held more than 200,000 books. Alexandria attracted a Mediterranean melting pot of Greeks, Jews, Phoenicians, Egyptians, Arabs, and many other nationalities. Textile, furniture, pottery, glassware, and papyrus industries flourished; Alexandria also served as Rome's principal Mediterranean grain port.

To handle the trading fleets that called at Alexandria, the city had two large sheltered harbors divided by the Heptastadion, a dike that ran nearly a mile from the mainland to the island of Pharos. At night the ships were guided by the tall lighthouse known as the Pharos of Alexandria, one of the seven wonders of the ancient world. The east harbor was known as the War Harbor and the west harbor as the Merchant Harbor. A canal linked these harbors with Lake Mareotis, from which another canal ran to the Nile River.

As a city, Alexandria was surpassed only by Rome in its reputation as a center of trade, learning, and culture. The city endured long after the fall of the Western Roman Empire, though most Alexandrian monuments vanished after Egypt was conquered by the Arabs, and the capital moved to Cairo, the basic layout of the city survived and is still in evidence. More important, the political institutions of the Greek city had a lasting influence in Europe, where citizenship is still prized and democratic government remains the ideal.

ROME

BY KIRK H. BEETZ

Ancient Romans regarded their cities as essential statements of what it meant to be a Roman. They built their cities to be centers of politics, commerce, and culture and, in newly conquered territories, to draw native peoples into the Roman way of life to the point that their ways were indistinguishable from those of Roman citizens. Indeed, where Roman cities took hold, even outside Italy, after a few generations the local people were often declared Roman citizens, with the same rights and responsibilities as citizens born in Rome.

The first Roman city was Rome itself. Ancient Roman historians placed the founding of Rome in 753 B.C.E., but modern archaeology has found graves in Rome dating at least a century earlier. Rome began as a small village on Palatine Hill, one of the famed "seven hills" of later Rome, overlooking the Tiber River. The settlers were probably Latins, an ethnic group that populated central Italy. Archaeological evidence indicates that another village on a nearby hill merged with the one on the Palatine, beginning an expansion that would produce the greatest metropolis of its time.

According to Roman accounts the brothers Romulus and Remus (probably Etruscans, the dominant military and commercial power in the area) settled in what was to become Rome, and Romulus founded the city. To the Romans, a city was not a true city unless it rested on sacred ground. Romulus laid out the town's dimensions by plowing a square around Palatine Hill, leaving gaps for gates. (Because of this legend, Romans considered the Palatine the true Rome, the center of the city's spirit.) Wherever the ground was plowed, diabolical spirits from within the earth supposedly could rise to the surface. Thus people were forbidden to cross the ground Romulus had plowed; they could enter Rome only through gates. For ancient Romans anyone who entered a city over the plowed ground rather than through a proper gate had to be killed in order to save the city from ill fortune brought by the diabolical spirits. Romulus killed his brother Remus because Remus jestingly jumped over the plowed ground.

In building new cities, Romans traditionally engaged in a ceremony based on Romulus and his plow. After first checking for signs from the gods that the site was acceptable to them, the chief builder, while wearing a toga, used a bronze plow pulled by two white cattle, one male and one female, to cut a square or rectangular perimeter for the city, lifting the plow over the areas where the gates were to be. Walls were built around the outside of the plowed ground. (The walls could be serious structures for defense, but in secure areas they were often more for show, forming a statement that within them was a sacred Roman city.)

Every city that Romans built from scratch was oriented north-south and east-west as marked by two main roads. The north-south road was called the *cardo* and the east-west road the *decumanus*, and they crossed in the center of the city. It is not known why the *cardo* and *decumanus* were so important—possibly they had religious significance—but they were among the first things a city designer laid out, even before plowing the sacred barrier. In Rome building and rebuilding gradually covered over its original *cardo* and *decumanus* roads, and as the city's relations with the rest of the world grew, several other major roads radiated out from it into the countryside.

The Romans borrowed some of their rituals for founding a city from the Etruscans, including the creation of a *mundus*, a circular pit dug near the center of the city. Here again communication with the earth's diabolical spirits was possible. The *mundus* was covered with a stone slab, on which offerings such as food were left. Three times a year the slab was removed, giving the spirits access to the city, and on those days no business of any kind was conducted, because it would be doomed to failure. In Rome the *mundus* was occasionally paved over and seems to have been moved a few times to accommodate the city's growth.

THE CAPITOL AND THE FORUM

Essential to any Roman city's spirituality was its capitol, usually located in the center of the city. The capitol—the name comes from the Latin word for "head"—was not a governmental complex in the modern sense but contained temples dedicated to deities important to the city. Rome had three temples in its capitol, one dedicated to the chief god, Jupiter; one to his wife, Juno; and one to Minerva,

Roman silver coins, 275–260 B.C.E., depicting the founding twins of the city of Rome, Romulus and Remus (© The Trustees of the British Museum)

goddess of wisdom. All capitols were built on high ground; Rome's was on the Capitoline Hill. If there was no natural high ground, a platform was built to raise the capitol above the surrounding area. Residents believed that the gods represented in the temples were their city's protectors, and that they could only protect what they could see from the capitol.

In conquered territories a city's capitol might hold temples to local gods, with their names changed to those of Roman deities. For instance, in the cities of former Phoenician colonies the Romans conquered in North Africa, they built capitols with temples dedicated to the god Baal but changed Baal's name to Saturn. Beginning with Augustus Caesar (r. 27 B.C.E.–14 C.E.) Roman emperors themselves began to be declared gods, and capitols throughout the empire began to include temples to the emperors and members of their families who had been declared gods, such as Augustus's wife, Livia. In some parts of North Africa all the old temple gods were replaced by emperor-gods, perhaps because the armies of the emperors offered more obvious protection than did the old gods.

These practices led to conflict in some colonial cities such as those in Palestine, where Jews worshipped only one god and were forbidden by their faith to worship any others. To the Romans no city was protected from evil without a capitol on high ground, and they seem to have had trouble understanding why anyone would object to such a thing, especially when they were willing to let the local people worship whatever gods they preferred, if perhaps under the names of Roman gods. The process of Romanizing people included acclimating them to Roman ways of worship, and it worked almost everywhere, but not in Palestine.

Besides the capitol, every Roman city had another public area that was in some ways even more important: the forum. This was the center of civic life, the place where vital news first circulated and where citizens debated the key issues of the day. It was the heart of any Roman city. The typical forum was a rectangular, flat open space, usually paved, of varying size from city to city, and bordered by the buildings for the city's basic institutions. The forum did not originate with the city of Rome; earlier examples have been found in southern Italy, perhaps influenced by the ancient Greek agora (literally "marketplace" but extended to mean an open meeting place in a city). But the famed Roman Forum was the model for all that followed.

The Roman Forum was established in a marshy valley near the Tiber. In its early days it was plagued by mosquitoes and the diseases those insects carried, and the river sometimes flooded it. Between 616 and 579 B.C.E. King Tarquin had a canal dug to drain the area; in the 100s B.C.E. this canal was covered and became a sewer. At first people seem to have built homes haphazardly around the Forum, and apartment houses called *insulae* ("islands") were crowded together. The Forum itself was always kept clear and was reserved for pedestrians only.

Forums generally had colonnades on one or more sides, often with shops selling food or other goods. Nearby buildings commonly included a basilica and a curia. The basilica was a rectangular open building with a flat roof. Rome had one of the largest, the Basilica Julia, its floor area only slightly smaller than a football field. The basilica was primarily a market space for private businesses, but it often included a dais called a "tribunal," where courts of law held session. The curia was a hall where senators had their meetings. Senators tended to be from the social elite, mostly aristocrats. During the Roman Republic (509–27 B.C.E.) they were the primary governing body of the city and its empire. In cities other than Rome the curia housed meetings of officials who functioned much like senators for these localities.

Fountains and Public Baths

To the Romans no city was truly a city without enough water to meet the basic needs of its population. First and foremost this meant water to supply public fountains, from which anyone could gather it for free. Fountains became standard parts of a Roman city, and in Rome itself they were everywhere. Next there had to be enough water for people to bathe daily in the public baths. Public baths were built in every Roman city and were considered to be part of what made a city livable. Even small cities had several such baths. (Although it was not the norm, some private homes also had baths. When an earthquake hit Pompeii in 62 C.E., its public baths were too damaged to be used; one of the city's many enterprising businesswomen, Julia Felix, found a way to profit by charging people to use her private bath.) Some city governments also charged for use of the public baths, but the fee was usually small; a city could expect unrest, even violence, if people did not have access to bathing facilities.

Public baths were called *thermae*, from the Greek word for "heat," because some of the pools in them were heated. Typically a Roman bather disrobed in a room provided for the purpose and then dived into a large pool of cold water and swam its length. Next he or she bathed in one or more heated pools smaller than the cold pool; in large baths there were several of these pools, varying from tepid to very hot. Furnaces outside the building heated water that ran through pipes under the bottoms of the pools, warming them in turn. From the warm pool the bather went to a steam room and, after working up a good sweat, often returned to the cold pool for a final swim.

The baths were not merely for bathing; they were social centers. Big *thermae* had several large rooms set apart from the pools, and here Romans conducted business, met with friends, or simply rested. The Roman business day usually ended at about 4 P.M., and the bathhouses quickly filled with people who had finished work. People of all ages and both genders mixed freely, unclothed or nearly so (though it was customary to set aside certain times when only women were allowed in the baths, perhaps so they could comfortably relax without sexual pressures from men). *Thermae* were supposed to be open all hours of the day, and having the furnaces go out at any time was considered a major inconvenience and even cause for government inquiry.

If a city's water supply exceeded what was needed for the fountains and public baths, some of it might be piped into private homes. The pipes were usually of lead. Water was first piped into private homes in Rome about 146 B.C.E. For the most part, however, only wealthy or at least middle-class people could afford this amenity, not only because the plumbing was expensive but also because cities usually charged for water used in this way. Another limiting factor was the water pressure. Although it was sufficient to feed low-lying fountains, the water pressure in Rome and other cities was never great enough to raise piped water above the ground floor of a home or other building.

Theaters and Amphitheaters

Romans expected a true city to provide entertainment, including theatrical offerings of singing, dancing, and plays. Beginning in the 400s B.C.E. Roman theaters were made of wood and were temporary, taken down after the performance In the 200s Romans began building stone theaters in their cities, and whenever a new city was planned, a spot for the theater was included. Almost every Roman city had a theater with seats arranged in a semicircle facing a broad stage, although Rome itself did not have a permanent theater until 55 B.C.E. At its height Pompeii had only 12,000 residents, including slaves, but its theater could hold 5,000 people.

On the other hand, an amphitheater was not essential to a Roman city, although many city plans made room for one. The most famous is the Colosseum in Rome. Built in 75–80 C.E., it was a massive structure that featured many of the best traits of Roman architecture. An amphitheater, with its spectacular events, such as chariot races and gladiatorial combats, was meant to serve an entire region, not just a city. In fact, some amphitheaters were built in open land away from cities, drawing audiences from the countryside. The amphitheaters had rows of stone benches. Seating was separate for different classes of society, with the best seats reserved for the emperor in the city of Rome and for the regional governor or chief administrator in other cities.

The amphitheater was not a Roman idea, but one borrowed from southern Italy. Yet Rome made the amphitheater an instrument of government. It served to pacify the public with entertainments, helped indoctrinate native peoples into the Roman way of life, and through its battles and human sacrifices inured audiences to violence and warfare. Most Roman men were expected to serve long terms in the army or navy, and the cruel entertainments of the amphitheater helped prepare them for the horrors of battle.

Roman Cities Abroad

Wherever Romans conquered, they built new Roman cities or added a strongly Roman touch to existing towns. In some cases the new cities were intended largely for the Roman soldiers themselves. The Roman government encouraged its soldiers to settle in conquered territories and built cities specifically for them because the retired soldiers would be tough, tenacious, and hard workers who could ably defend the city from attack and build its economy.

North Africa had many such cities. An example is Timgad (Thamugadi), built in 100 C.E. for retired soldiers in Numidia (in present-day Algeria). It was laid out in a strict grid with its eastern and western gates opening on significant trade routes. Within its walls were a forum, basilica, market, and baths, but somewhat unusually its capitol was placed outside the wall. As the city grew, perhaps reaching 15,000 people, it added several baths outside the city walls.

In North Africa the Romans also built cities at the sites of existing Phoenician towns. Leptis Magna (in modern-day Libya) was a Phoenician colony that became part of the Roman Empire in 46 B.C.E. It gained fame as the birthplace of Emperor Septimius Severus (193–211 C.E.) and may have had a population of 12,000. Timgad and Leptis are examples of the different fates of Roman cities after the fall of the Western Roman Empire. Timgad survived because it was on an important trade route. Without Roman engineers to maintain its once splendid harbor and without the empire's market for its goods, Leptis Magna faded and was abandoned during the Arab invasion of the 500s C.E.

During its long existence the Western Empire itself contained had many examples of cities that became successful showcases for Roman life. In what is now Germany, Trier (the Roman name was Augusta Treverorum) began as a military camp under Augustus and was made a city between 41 and 54 C.E. It was laid out as grid, but its wall curved with the contours of the Moselle River. London (Londinium) was founded in 43 C.E. and grew to 45,000 people before, for various reasons, its population began declining in the 200s C.E.

Population and Problems

To Roman city planners the ideal city would have no more than 20,000 residents, and thus they designed new cities to hold no more than that. In a new city the initial residents, perhaps just soldiers and their families, might number only a few thousand. When a city filled up, the hope of the Romans was to build another several miles away, thus keeping each city to a size thought to be comfortable. This is one reason Roman cities seem to be everywhere in the lands that fell within the empire's borders—they were part of a continuous process of managing populations, and the building of them was not expected ever to end. Even so, some cities had exploding populations simply because they were ideally located for commerce or to be seats of government, and they drew so many people to them that the cities sprawled beyond their walls. One example was Lyons, in modern-day France. Under its Roman name of Lugdunum its population reached 200,000.

Rome itself provided the greatest example of out-of-control population growth. Even by 509 B.C.E. it had a population of 40,000, and during the first century B.C.E. that number reached a million. The city's original plowed circumference had to be redone outside the new city limits, with new outer walls built, but this was hardly the only problem associated with mushrooming population growth. Rome had become a place with many tenements and, in the old quarters, narrow streets. During his reign Augustus attempted to bring some order to the situation through massive building projects and a reorganization of the city into 14 regions, each with its own administrator appointed by the emperor. He created a police department to battle a crime wave, and he organized a fire department. Every Roman city was vulnerable to fire, and large portions of Rome had burned on several occasions. The duties of Rome's fire department were mainly to organize bucket brigades (there was never enough water pressure for fire hoses) and to knock down buildings around a blaze to prevent its spread.

Augustus assigned to his son-in-law Marcus Agrippa the administration of many of Rome's building projects, and Agrippa also expanded and added to the city's aqueducts, increasing the flow of water by two to four times. Other public projects undertaken by Augustus were the dredging of the Tiber, which was filling with silt, and personally overseeing the distribution of food to the city's poor. Caring for the poor became institutionalized in the empire, with some cities even setting aside a covered area near the forum where homeless people could gather to stay out of bad weather.

Inside a Roman City

A traveler entering the typical ancient Roman city first passed through an enormous stone gateway. The Romans built grand gates to impress visitors with the feeling of entering sacred ground that was set apart from the ordinary world outside. Once within the gates, the traveler would notice the many small touches that enhanced life in a Roman city. The streets would be paved with either stone or brick and would be wide enough for two carts to pass each other with room enough left for a third cart. Most people walked wherever they needed to go in the city, whether for business or pleasure, and great care was taken to protect pedestrians. Streets had raised stone along their sides to prevent carts from straying onto the sidewalks, and sidewalks were everywhere, even among the residences of the poor. In commercial and residential areas alike the sidewalks were covered, either by roofs or by overhanging balconies. In some cities the law required homeowners to provide cover over the sidewalks adjacent to their buildings. There were also crosswalks consisting of rows of large, flat-topped stones set less than a stride apart, on the top of which pedestrians stepped. (The crosswalks also helped to slow traffic, rather like ancient speed bumps, because carters had to maneuver their wheels around the stones.)

A Roman city was typically laid out in a grid pattern of streets and was either square or rectangular. This was not a rigid practice; Roman city planners accommodated the local terrain, working around variations such as hills and valleys. Once the essential elements of forum, capitol, basilica, curia, and the theater were mapped, neighborhoods were laid out, usually divided into sections for the upper class, middle class, craftsmen, and the poor. If the city had been built around or next to an existing settlement, that area was often left untouched, and its passages were not part of the grid pattern. These sections tended to become the homes of the working poor.

Planners were careful to leave open spaces for hotels, shops, taverns, parks, and gardens. Parks and gardens were important aspects of the Roman city, which typically devoted about one-third of its total space to them. The gardens might harbor vineyards, orchards, or farms generating produce for the local markets. The parks ranged from places intended for exercise to quiet spaces where people could simply relax among flowers and trees. As some cities prospered, drawing more residents than they could comfortably house, civic leaders had to struggle to preserve such areas from developers who would fill open nooks and crannies, as well as marshes and hillsides, with apartment houses three or four stories high with small rooms. Made hastily of brick, these buildings often collapsed because of poor construction.

Toward the center of the city the visitor would discover many shops offering local and imported goods and might perhaps stop in at a *thermopolium*, many of which were scattered throughout the city, with clusters near the forum and the theater. These establishments served hot wine that was kept warm in tubs set into the top of a counter; customers could also buy snacks or a meal. People went to a *thermopolium* for much the same reasons they might visit a bar today, including to meet friends, business associates, or members of the opposite sex.

In contrast to the many public venues, homes in a Roman city were designed for privacy. Walls facing the street had only small windows or none at all. The focus of the interior of the house was the atrium, an open, courtyardlike central area where a family did most of its living and entertaining. An atrium was usually covered except for a large square opening in the center that let in air, sunlight, and rain. Directly beneath the opening would be a square tub to catch and store the rainwater. Much of the atrium consisted of soil planted with bushes, flowers, and trees. In early Roman houses the atrium opened at the back onto a space for growing food. By the first century B.C.E. atriums were usually closed on all sides and surrounded by rooms. The rooms tended to be small cubicles intended for sleep, study, preparing meals, and such crafts as weaving or woodworking.

The Roman home provided privacy and the city at large a sense of community. Thus it was that Roman city builders hoped to create the ideal urban environment by fulfilling public spiritual and physical needs while making space for individual lives.

THE AMERICAS

BY J. J. GEORGE

Urban settlements originated during the social transformation of simple nonhierarchical farming societies into class-stratified states. While cities, towns, and villages were prominent features in all of the Americas in the ancient period, only a handful could properly be called cities, even according to the most basic definition. Determining all the criteria is a matter of debate among scholars; thus, classifying a city is a fluid matter. Although many basic features were shared, settlements in the Americas showed a high degree of variation in size, function, and layout.

Part of the difficulty in analyzing cities is that *cities, urban society*, and *urbanization* are often left undefined, leading to overlap and confusion. Since there is no uniform agreement on what makes a city, one question is whether demography (the statistical study of populations, especially with reference to size, density, and distribution) or function (a definite end or purpose) is more important in defining and analyzing ancient towns and cities. From a demographic perspective a settlement with a large, dense population is evidence of social and economic complexity accounting for great diversity in ethnicities, classes, occupations, and activities. The Mexican city of Teotihuacán (1–650 C.E.) represents the ideal city in this scenario. From a functional perspective, which defines cities as settlements whose institutions affect a much greater hinterland, often for religious and ritual purposes, a Mayan site such as Tikal in northern Guatemala, of about the same time period as Teotihuacán, would be considered a city.

Characteristics of Cities and Urbanization

Cities are typically political, economic, and religious centers for surrounding territory and the focus for a wider range of specialized production and services than are found elsewhere in the region. As true as it is today, a city represents a central core of activities within which a greater and more diverse range of activities take place. According to the archaeologist V. Gordon Childe, a 20th-century urban theorist, definitions of "city" include the site as the head of a hierarchy of settlements that performs unique functions for a regional society for its time. A city is a permanent settlement within the larger territory occupied by a society, considered home by a significant number of residents whose activities, roles, practices, experiences, identities, and attitudes differ significantly from other members of the society who identify most closely with *rural* land outside such settlements. Cities are large settlements with many urban functions that affect a large hinterland, whereas towns are smaller settlements with fewer urban functions affecting a smaller region. In all of the definitions, size and sociopolitical complexity alone are not adequate criteria for defining a city, though it does seem that a population of at least a few thousand seems necessary to qualify a settlement to be urban and thus a city.

The hierarchy of settlements comes in various sizes and with varying functions. Major capitals, political towns, hilltop ceremonial zones, fortresses, administrative centers, regal-ritual sites, mercantile cities, and sites whose political status is unknown represent different classifications according to type and function. A major capital will obviously show a greater level of urban complexity than a fortress, whose primary role is singularly defensive. Consequently, the urban texture of a hilltop fortress is limited and coarse by comparison and its social function more abbreviated. Considering its defensive nature, it can also be assumed that the occupants of a fortress site are primarily concerned with the business of defense, thereby limiting the overall social fabric to a narrower field of participants compared with what a larger general center might show.

Growth and complexity were constantly evolving urban traits throughout the ancient period, such that by 250 C.E., in Mesoamerica especially, the following political structures had developed, in this order: regional economic centers, elite classes, administrative centers, true urban centers, and some form of state structure. This last classification type, the achievement of some form of state-level society, presents a unique conundrum for defining the qualities of a city, because city and state are often tied together in a kind of circular redundancy, such that one scholar will say that there cannot be a city without a state, and another scholar will say that there cannot be a state without a city. Thus, the questions become these: In the absence of a so-called state, is a large, complex urban settlement necessarily a city? And if a city is, in essence, responsible only for itself and is not bound to its hinterlands by political, economic, or militaristic terms, is it then a self-sustaining state, a city-state, or still just a city?

Similarly, if there is a necessary correlation between city and state, is there a corresponding relation between city and civilization? What qualities of civilization, if any, are necessary for the development of a "city"? Suggestions presented by scholars include monumental public architecture, art styles involving artistic representations in many media, development of practical sciences and means of recording (astronomy, accounting systems, and, often but not always, writing), populations of a relatively great size and density often but not always including localized areas of great density, differentiations of the populations into a number of more or less distinguishable social classes ordered in hierarchical fashion, a concentration of natural and human resources for public enterprise, and extensive trade. The question of civilization is intimately tied to definitions of culture, and culture is a defining quality of cities.

Features of Cities in the Americas

Cities in and of themselves are a fairly recent phenomena. As late as 1900 C.E. there were only 16 cities in the world with populations in excess of 1 million, and 100 years earlier only 17 cities in Europe had populations over 100,000. A clear view of the nature of cities in the Americas in the ancient period is complicated by a lack of written texts and the fact that many urban centers were only then emerging. Although many settlements would not satisfy a strict urbanist's criteria for a city, many achieved city status in the broader sense of civilization. Urban settlements everywhere varied in terms of size, social composition, economic institutions, administration, religious institutions, and urban planning and layout, and each settlement needs to be examined individually. The examples mentioned here—San Lorenzo, Teotihuacán, Monte Albán, Tikal, Pukara, Tiwanaku, and Moche— reflect the variety and range of cities in the Americas.

It should be noted that weak and insufficient data plagues much analysis of North American sites prior to the 18th century and that nothing resembling the level of complexity found farther south in Mexico and in the Mayan civilization had developed by the time the Europeans arrived in the 15th century. Most North American indigenous settlements of this period are more properly classified in the spectrum of towns, villages, village clusters, ceremonial centers, burial mound sites, or camps.

Mesoamerican Cities

The earliest example of a Mesoamerican urban center is San Lorenzo, an Olmec site that occupies a long ridge above surrounding riverine lowlands in Mexico's Gulf Coast region. First settled around 1500 B.C.E., it covered 1,235 acres, had a population of several thousand residents, and exhibited all the major urban characteristics. It is generally defined as a regal-ritual city, an urban center with highly developed ritual functions but modest populations; relatively weak, decentralized rulership; and limited economic functions. One reason for San Lorenzo's preëminence during this period is its choice of site: high enough to remain dry during the worst floods; close enough to fertile farmlands; easily defendable; near to freshwater springs and other natural resources such as sandstone, hematite, and limestone; and, owing to its location, exercising control over important river and land transportation routes. Prominent features include a great earthen platform complex honeycombed with an elaborate drainage system and perhaps laid out in a zoomorphic, or animal-like, shape. Colossal carved stone heads made of basalt from the Tuxtla Mountains 60 miles away, some weighing as much as 20 tons, indicate a level of complex coordination and centralized authority.

Teotihuacán (ca. 1 B.C.E.–650 C.E.) is the standard by which all other ancient American cities are judged. Located 40 miles north of contemporary Mexico City, Teotihuacán was the largest and most complex urban development in the Americas until the rise of Aztec Tenochtitlán in the 14th century C.E. By 600 C.E. Teotihuacán was the fifth-largest city in the world, with a population estimated at 125,000. Its design was based on a central grid plan, sometimes referred to as the Mexican imperial plan, aligned along a major north-south axis called the Avenue of the Dead. The primary architectural features of the site are two massive flat-topped pyramids called the Pyramid of the Moon and the Pyramid of the Sun, as well as a ceremonial structure toward the southern end of the site called the Temple of Quetzalcoatl contained within an area called the Ciudadela (or Citadel). Overall, the city's development and its architectural expressions are a symbol of power.

Teotihuacán is the clearest example of a city in both functional and demographic terms. It was a large, densely populated urban environment with highly specialized economic, social, ritual, and ceremonial activities. Its influence spread far outside its own borders not only through trade and exchange and religious influences but also through military aggression and occupation. Teotihuacán's influence in the development of a greater Mesoamerican tradition cannot be underestimated. Its influence can be traced throughout Mesoamerica by the presence of its signature *talud-tablero* ritual architectural style, recognizable in profile as a series of horizontal platforms sitting on sloping panels and finished with fine plaster. This style shows up throughout Mexico and in the Mayan areas of Guatemala, including the sites of Kaminaljuyu, a highland Maya site; Monte Albán, in the Valley of Oaxaca; Cholula, in the Valley of Puebla; and Tikal, the major lowland Maya site in Guatemala's northern Petén jungle region. These are but a few primary urban settlements under Teotihuacán's influence.

Urban planning at Teotihuacán included an internal drainage system composed of a vast system of subterranean canals that flowed into a central canal, administrative and ceremonial buildings aligned along the Avenue of the Dead, congregational plazas at the Pyramid of the Moon and the Ciudadela, elite residential complexes ranging in size from 5,900 square feet to 39,000 square feet, and districts for workers and foreigners on the periphery believed to have been specific to specialized craftsmen, including obsidian carvers, figurine makers, stonecutters, and jewelers. One of the foreigner's districts was called the Oaxaca Barrio because it was supposed to include only individuals from Oaxaca. More than 500 craft workshops and 20,000 rectangular single-story residential compounds existed at Teotihuacán.

Farther south in the Valley of Oaxaca the settlement of Monte Albán (ca. 500 B.C.E.–900 C.E.) developed gradually and rose to become the principal Zapotec capital city. Settled at the conjunction of three valleys, the region was divided into three branch communities oriented toward agricultural production, pottery manufacture, and the extraction of salt. One suggestion is that Monte Albán rose as a center to coordinate the various sites in the valley and gradually developed its administrative, economic, social, and ritual functions into those of a major urban center. Primary settlement at Monte Albán is generally broken down into periods or phases noted as I, II, IIIa, and IIIb, with population and influence fluctuating through the centuries. Long after it diminished as an urban center, which some have linked to the fall of Teotihuacán to the north, it remained a ritual pilgrimage site and an active burial site. It was abandoned as a functioning city in the 10th century as power shifted to other Zapotec settlements in the valley, such as Mitla.

Development at Monte Albán focused on a hilltop site about a thousand feet above the valley floor with the population concentrated on the habitable terraces beneath the hilltop. The layout focused on a civic-ceremonial center atop the hill with multiple structures most often referred to as mounds flanking and framing a central plaza. The North and South Burial Mounds punctuate the ends of the plaza's ceremonial core and, along with the periphery mounds, form a kind of ceremonial way that recalls the Avenue of the Dead at Teotihuacán, albeit much smaller. A ball court, stone slabs covered in bas-relief, slabs with hieroglyphics including some evidence of a ritual 260-day calendar, and pottery produced on a large scale all suggest the greater cultural complexity indicative of true cities.

Pottery vessel of the storm god, Teotihuacan, Mexico (150 B.C.E. to ca. 700 C.E.); the god was portrayed frequently in stone and murals, suggesting that he was an important god in the city's pantheon. (© The Trustees of the British Museum)

In the Maya territory, Tikal is often referred to as the greatest city of the Classic and Epiclassic periods (usually defined as 150–900 C.E.). Set in a dense jungle in the north of Guatemala, Tikal probably achieved full city status late in the Classic Period. The rise of Tikal is thought to have led to the fall of another community called El Mirador as villages and communities came into increased contact with one another and began vying for resources, control, and influence. It seems likely that El Mirador fell to Tikal as elites attempted to consolidate their power and range of influence until Teotihuacán became interested in the area's resources and exportable goods, including cacao, honey, salt, beeswax, and medicinal herbs. The influence of Teotihuacán at Tikal was secure by 360 C.E. thanks to a ruler referred to as Curl-Nose in hieroglyphic inscriptions found at the site. Curl-Nose was apparently a collaborationist ruler who accepted military and political advisors from Teotihuacán, which gave Tikal an edge over rival Mayan centers and allowed for further expansion.

Architecture and urban planning at Tikal featured massive stone temples, funerary monuments, acropolis structures, great plazas, a residential or administrative complex consisting of small courtyards, the Great Plaza, a possible market area, a sweat bath, a ball court, stone sculpture that includes great chronographic (timekeeping) markers, memorials to ancestors, and bureaucratic structures. All Maya architecture was composed of elevated platforms and corbel-vaulted chambers organized in a variety of configurations. The similarity of all the building structures has made it difficult to differentiate between their functions. At its height Tikal was home to 40,000 inhabitants and its nuclear area alone included more than 3,000 separate structures and some 200 stone monuments.

Sometime in the fifth century C.E. the people of Teotihuacán began to pull back from their frontier positions. Their sudden departure seems to have upset development at a number of Mayan sites, with some areas plunging into open revolt suggesting civil war. Not until around 650 C.E. was Mayan civilization able to reorganize and function once again. Tikal continued for a couple hundred more years before its eventual collapse.

South American Cities

In South America all areas show vast numbers of archaeological sites, indicating widespread population since 8000 B.C.E., though relatively few have been fully excavated. Only the Peruvian cultures seem to have attained a complex level of civilization. Of the ancient Peruvian cultures, the cities of Pukará, Moche, and Tiwanaku (also spelled Tiahuanaco) stand apart.

The north coast Peruvian settlement of Moche (100–600 C.E.), evidently the capital of the Mochica state, comprised two huge adobe structures called the Huaca del Sol and the Huaca de la Luna, an immense plaza, and an extensive residential zone. The Huaca del Sol was a terraced platform that measured 1,100 by 500 feet at its base and rose to 130 feet. Trash heaps at its summit suggest that it may have served as elite living quarters. More than 143 million adobe bricks were used in the construction, many with identifiable markings indicating the individual mason's hand. The Huaca de la Luna consisted of a massive, terraced multiroom complex. Moche was traditionally regarded as an immense ceremonial center and thought to lack a substantial population. Recent excavations, however, revealed a residential zone able to accommodate a sizable population density.

The site of Pukará, which lies 75 miles northwest of the northern shore of Lake Titicaca, high on the altiplano (a high plateau), had a brief but important florescence between 200 B.C.E. and 300 C.E. Pukará's buildings were adobe on stone foundations. Its main structure was a temple, built on an artificial terrace and consisting of a rectangular sunken court. An extensive residential area lay in the plain below the acropolis. Beyond the southern end of the lake, at an altitude of 12,600 feet above sea level, Tiwanaku was a major settlement with a central core of monumental structures occupying an area of 125 acres surrounded by an extensive residential zone; the whole site covered 1½ square miles. Population estimates range from 30,000 to 70,000 people.

True urbanism happened at Tiwanaku because of balances in herding and agriculture that gave rise to surpluses. Extensive irrigation projects reclaimed fields for planting; as much as 200,000 acres were irrigated. By 100 C.E. monumental stone architecture was being built. There was no mistaking the power in the stone city the Tiwanakans built as their center. The principal buildings are a giant stepped mound called the Akapana and a semisubterranean temple called the Kalasasaya surrounded by a moat that limited entrance and public use and separated the sacred from the profane. Excavations of the Akapana revealed numerous burials, one of which has been called the High Priest-Puma Shaman because it showed a seated man holding a puma effigy. For this reason it is believed the Akapana was a monument to shamanic transformation. (Shamans were believed to mediate between the world of spirits and the world of the living and to take on various forms.) These structures stood adjacent to another low flat temple called the Puma Punku. Reconstructing the exact look of Tiwanaku is an impossible task because it has been constructed, reconstructed, plundered, and rebuilt numerous times over 2,000 years. Tiwanakan dominance spread considerable distances as they tried to export religion and import foreign products. Like Teotihuacán, Tiwanaku influenced societies far outside its own boundaries.

See also AGRICULTURE; ARCHITECTURE; ART; ASTRONOMY; BORDERS AND FRONTIERS; BUILDING TECHNIQUES AND MATERIALS; CLIMATE AND GEOGRAPHY; CRAFTS; DEATH AND BURIAL PRACTICES; ECONOMY; EDUCATION; EMPIRES AND DYNASTIES; FAMILY; FOREIGNERS AND BARBARIANS; GOVERNMENT ORGANIZATION; HOUSEHOLD GOODS; ILLUMINATION; INVENTIONS; METALLURGY; MIGRATION AND POPULATION MOVEMENTS; MILITARY; MONEY AND COINAGE; OCCUPATIONS; RELIGION AND COSMOLOGY; ROADS AND BRIDGES; SACRED SITES; SCIENCE; SETTLEMENT PATTERNS; SLAVES AND SLAVERY; SOCIAL COLLAPSE AND ABANDONMENT; SOCIAL ORGANIZATION; SPORTS AND RECREATION; STORAGE AND PRESERVATION; TOWNS AND VILLAGES; TRADE AND EXCHANGE; TRANSPORTATION; WAR AND CONQUEST; WRITING.

FURTHER READING

David M. Anderson and Richard Rathbone, eds., *Africa's Urban Past* (Oxford, U.K.: James Currey, 2000).

Françoise Audouze and Olivier Buchsenschutz, *Town, Villages, and Countryside of Celtic Europe* (London: Batsford, 1991).

John Collis, *Oppida: Earliest Towns North of the Alps* (Sheffield, U.K.: Department of Prehistory and Archaeology, University of Sheffield, 1984).

Graham Connah, *African Civilizations: An Archaeological Perspective*, 2nd ed. (Cambridge, U.K.: Cambridge University Press, 2001).

Catherine Coquery-Vidrovitch, *The History of African Cities South of the Sahara: From the Origins to Colonization*, trans. Mary Baker (Princeton, N.J.: Markus Wiener, 2005).

Barry Cunliffe and Simon Keay, eds., *Social Complexity and the Development of Towns in Iberia: From the Copper Age to the Second Century* AD (Oxford, U.K.: Oxford University Press, 1995).

Denise Dersin, ed., *What Life Was Like on the Banks of the Nile: Egypt 3050–30* BC. (Alexandria, Va.: Time Life Books, 1996).

William M. Ferguson and Arthur H. Rohn, *Mesoamerica's Ancient Cities* (Niwot: University Press of Colorado, 1990).

Ron Fisher, Norman Hammond, Ann Nottingham Kelsall, et al., *Builders of the Ancient World: Marvels of Engineering* (Washington, D.C.: National Geographic Society, 1986).

Michael Haag, *Alexandria: City of Memory* (New Haven, Conn.: Yale University Press, 2004).

Richard J. Harrison, *Spain at the Dawn of History: Iberians, Phoenicians, and Greeks* (London: Thames and Hudson, 1988).

Jonathan Mark Kenoyer, *Ancient Cities of the Indus Valley* (Karachi, Pakistan: Oxford University Press, 1998).

Richard M. Leventhal and Alan Kolata, eds., *Civilization in the Ancient Americas: Essays in Honor of Gordon R. Willey* (Albuquerque: University of New Mexico Press, 1983).

Gwendolyn Leick, *Mesopotamia: The Invention of the City* (London: Penguin, 2002).

Thomas O'Neill, "Pompeii: City Sealed in Time." *Splendors of the Past: Lost Cities of the Ancient World* (Washington, D.C.: National Geographic Society, 1981).

E. J. Owens, *The City in the Greek and Roman World* (New York: Routledge, 1992).

Jeremy A. Sabloff, *The Cities of Ancient Mexico: Reconstructing a Lost World* (New York: Thames and Hudson, 1989).

Chris Scarre, *The Penguin Historical Atlas of Ancient Rome* (New York: Penguin Group, 1995).

Thurstan Shaw, Paul Sinclair, Bassey Andah, et al., eds., *The Archaeology of Africa: Food, Metals, and Towns* (London: Routledge, 1993).

Nancy S. Steinhardt, *Chinese Imperial City Planning* (Honolulu: University of Hawaii Press, 1990).

Eric P. Uphill, *Egyptian Towns and Cities* (Princes Risborough, U.K.: Shire Publications, 1988).

Marc Van de Mieroop, *The Ancient Mesopotamian City* (Oxford U.K.: Clarendon, 1997).

► climate and geography

INTRODUCTION

In modern life, technology enables people to adapt the environment to their needs. If farm fields are dry, electric-powered or gas-powered pumps allow farmers to irrigate. If the temperature is too high, electricair-conditioning cools the air in people's homes and offices; if the temperature is too low, furnaces provide heat. In contrast, ancient peoples had to adapt their needs to the environment. Obviously, they could modify their environment in simple ways, such as by building a fire to provide warmth. But overall much of the history of ancient peoples was determined by their physical environment and their efforts to adapt their lives to the physical conditions that surrounded them.

One major problem ancient peoples faced, however, was climatic change, which disrupted societies and sometimes forced the migration of people. An area that was wet and fertile during one era could become dry and desertlike in a later era, as happened in parts of Mesoamerica, the region that comprises the southwestern United States, Mexico, and Central America. Meteorological events in one part of the world could cause climatic change in another part of the world, raising or lowering temperatures, increasing or decreasing rainfall, or touching off violent storms. Further, catastrophic events could wreak havoc with a people. A volcanic eruption, for example, could not only wipe out a population but also change the physical environment for survivors and for those living in neighboring regions. Similarly, earthquakes could destroy settlements and change the face of the earth for nearby settlers. Drought could lead to famine and population depletion.

Africa, in particular, has been subject to climatic swings. During parts of its ancient history, Africa was cool and dry, primarily as a result of the last ice age, when ice pushed southward and covered much of what is now Europe. Later, Africa became much warmer and moister, leading to monsoon rains. Later still, temperatures dropped again, and weather patterns dried out. These changes, which were not unique to Africa, led to changes in vegetation, sometimes turning forests into deserts and deserts into forests. After the advent of agriculture, such climatic shifts required Africans to adapt the crops and farming practices to the new conditions. They also contributed to African history in major ways. When the continent dried out, the Nile River became essentially the center of civilization. It also led to conflict between nations as they struggled for resources to support their people.

Ancient peoples were driven by their need to find ways to adapt to their environment. One of their primary needs, of course, was fresh water. Accordingly, early peoples tended to form settlements along the banks of rivers or adjacent to lakes, but living in these types of regions posed special problems. People in Asia and Oceania, where oceans were nearby, were subject to cyclones and tsunamis, and people in such places as ancient Egypt were dependent on the annual flooding of the Nile River along which they lived. In time, people learned to harness at least some of the natural forces that surrounded them. The ancient Egyptians, for example, developed a complex and highly sophisticated system of irrigation and water management, storing the floodwaters of the Nile for later use in irrigating their crops. The ancient Romans, too, developed sophisticated plumbing systems, with canals, dikes, and the like to manage water flow.

Temperature was also a critical environmental factor, but ancient peoples discovered that they were highly adaptable to temperature extremes, unlike some other species. The earliest settlers of the Americas, who probably crossed from Asia to Alaska along a land bridge that is now covered by the Bering Sea, found themselves in an inhospitable environment, with bitter subzero temperatures and large amounts of snow and ice. Their descendants migrated to desert regions of the American Southwest and Mexico, where they faced hot, dry conditions, with temperatures often exceeding a hundred degrees. And their descendants migrated farther south to cold and forbidding regions of South America.

At the same time, human beings discovered that they were also able to adapt to widely different elevations. The people of the Pacific islands lived essentially at sea level. The early inhabitants of the Andes range in South America discovered that they could adapt to elevations well over 10,000 feet, where the air is thin and their lungs had to expand to take in more oxygen. In time, humans, because of their adaptability, were able to occupy virtually every niche in the ecosystem, including mountains, forests, grassy steppes, deserts, tropical islands, and every region between. In doing so, they adapted their tools, technologies, and ways of life to the climate and terrain.

A major consideration for ancient civilizations was travel and transport. In an age of effortless air travel, it is easy to forget that geography and natural barriers were formidable obstacles as people tried to immigrate to new regions or simply to follow food supplies. The early Romans, for example, were unable to cross the mountains that divided Italy from the rest of Europe, though in time they were able to do so and expand their empire farther to the north. Later, they found that major rivers in northern Europe blocked their expansion in that direction, allowing the tribes that would eventually overrun Rome to settle and amass on the empire's northern border. Geographical obstacles also inhibited contact between peoples. In the Andes of South America the forbidding terrain left the communities that settled there isolated from other groups of people. By remaining isolated, they were unable to learn from other people, in contrast to other civilizations that enriched themselves by contact with others. Similarly, the Pyrenees Mountains cut off the people of the Iberian Peninsula from contact with other Europeans.

To solve the transportation problem, many early peoples settled along bodies of water. The Egyptians used the Nile to travel up and down much of the African continent, and various civilizations in such places as Mesopotamia and China navigated the rivers for trade and cultural contact. Using boats and rafts, these people were able to obtain goods—spices, salt, foodstuffs, ores, precious metals, fabrics, lumber—that were unavailable at home. Of course, one of the main reasons that the ancient Greeks and then the ancient Romans were able to extend their influence over a wide geographic region was that they controlled the Mediterranean Sea. (It is worth noting that *Mediterranean* means "middle of the world.") Like other peoples, including many Asians and especially Pacific islanders, geographical conditions made the Greeks and Romans excellent boat builders and mariners.

AFRICA

BY LEAH A. J. COHEN

Many systems (such as the celestial systems that dictate the movement of the earth around the sun and around its own axis) have driven climate change in Africa over the span of Earth's four-billion-year existence. Since most of these systems change very slowly (cycling on the scale of tens of thousands to millions of years), many of the systematic conditions that have affected climate change in Africa during the past 10,000 years have remained relatively similar.

The Geography and Topography of Africa

Africa's physical geography has been a key factor in its climatic conditions over this period of time. Africa is a large expanse of land, covering 11.7 million square miles. It is the second-largest continent (behind Asia) and represents 20 percent of the world's land. This is relevant to the study of climate in Africa, because land that borders large bodies of water tends to show less variation in temperature than areas at the same latitude (the east-west global location) that are landlocked. In other words, locations near the center of large continents (such as Africa) have much wider climate variability than locations at the same latitude that receive the same amount of solar radiation (sunlight) but are near large expanses of water. Because Africa is a large, consolidated landmass, much of the continent does not benefit from the tempering effect of water. Thus (all else being equal) temperatures inland in Africa tend to be either higher or lower than those on the coastlines.

Africa's major lakes include Lake Victoria, bordering Kenya, Tanzania, and Uganda (East Africa); Lake Tanganyika in western Tanzania (East Africa); Lake Malawi in western Malawi (southern Africa); and Lake Chad bordering Niger, Chad, Nigeria, and a small part of Cameroon (western Africa). Paleoclimatologists (scientists who study past climatic conditions on Earth) have learned a great deal about past climate change by collecting lake-bottom sediment cores from these and other African lakes. Sediment cores are samples of sediment taken using a long cylindrical tube that is driven into the lake bottom and closed, so that the layers of sediment, which represent different time periods, are preserved for the purposes of research. The data collected from sediment core sampling and other research techniques are set to a timeline using at least one of a variety of dating methods. The most commonly employed method for dating sediment core layers is radiocarbon (or carbon-14) dating.

The topography of Africa is varied, with lowlands, highlands, mountains, and valleys, but in general the continent of Africa is a large plateau. Africa is not known for an abundantly mountainous landscape. Its two tallest mountains are

Grass, sand, and volcanic formation in the Sahara, southern Algeria (© Board of Regents of the University of Wisconsin System. Photographer: Jeanne Tabachnick)

Mount Kenya at 17,058 feet and Mount Kilimanjaro at 19,340 feet, both in East Africa. The main reason that Africa has a relatively small percentage of mountainous landscape has to do with Africa's placement on the tectonic plate system. The African plate is moving toward the northeast, pushing into the Eurasian plate and separating from the Arabian plate. Since only the northern and eastern edges of the African continent are near the edges of the much larger African tectonic plate (which extends far into the Atlantic Ocean) upon which it sits, there is relatively little volcanic activity throughout the rest of the continent.

The major mountain ranges formed well before 10,000 years ago as a result of the movement patterns of the African tectonic plate. These mountainous regions are on the northern and eastern sides of the continent and include the mountains that divide eastern and central Africa and the Atlas Mountains in northwestern Africa. The other areas of Africa are not subjected to tectonic plate pressure or separation and therefore are not particularly mountainous. Mountains often have great effects on local weather conditions. In eastern Africa (Tanzania, Kenya, and Ethiopia) the climate is much drier than it is directly on the western side of the central mountains that divide central and eastern Africa, owing to the rain-shadow effect. Moist air comes from the west and when it hits the mountains, it is forced to rise; as it rises, it cools and is not able to hold the moisture, which produces rain. Thus, once this air reaches the other side of the mountains, it is no longer moist, creating a much drier climate in eastern Africa.

The other major land features of Africa are the Sahara (which dominates the northern region of Africa, running west to east) and the Kalahari and Namib deserts (which dominate southern Africa). The Sahel is an east-to-west band of semiarid savanna that separates the dry Sahara environment from the lush and moist tropical forests of central Africa.

African Humid Period

At the start of the Holocene geologic epoch (10,000 years ago to the present), Africa had emerged from a long period of dry and cool temperatures associated with the last major ice age. Evidence from sediment cores from many of Africa's lakes, ice cores from Mount Kilimanjaro in East Africa, and animal and plant fossil records show that much of Africa (including the present-day Sahara region) was more humid during the first part of the Holocene than it is today. This period is known as the African Humid Period, which lasted from approximately 11,000 years ago to 4,000 years ago (though there have been numerous minor swings between humid and dry conditions during this generally humid period).

The African Humid Period can be explained in part by the earth's place within the overarching celestial cycles during this time period. Specifically, the increased moisture and warmth in Africa are associated with variation in the amount of solar radiation hitting the earth's surface during the Northern Hemisphere summer. About 10,000 years ago the amount of solar radiation during the summer was approximately 8 percent higher than it is today, because the Northern Hemisphere summer solstice occurred at the point when the earth is closest to the sun rather than at the point when the earth is farthest from the sun (as is the case today).

Effect of the Intertropical Convergence Zone on African Climate

The rainfall that is driven by increased solar radiation (and temperatures) is associated with a zone near the equator called the Intertropical Convergence Zone. Africa's global position during the past 10,000 years (straddling the equator) places much of the continent between the northern Tropic of Cancer and the southern Tropic of Capricorn, firmly within the Intertropical Convergence Zone, the intersection between two of the earth's major surface wind systems: the southern and northern trade winds. These two major winds systems are known as the Southeast Trade Winds (also referred to as the southern monsoon winds), which travel from west to east and pick up moisture as they move over the Atlantic Ocean, and the Northeast Trade Winds, which travel down from the northwest across the northern Atlantic Ocean. The intersection of these wind systems is associated with a wide swath of low pressure that is driven by solar heating. In the zone in which these trade winds come together, the low pressure lifts the moist air around the equator, which results in abundant rainfall when the moist air cools as it is lifted higher in the atmosphere and is forced to release moisture. The rain associated with the Intertropical Convergence Zone falls over Africa near the equator as the winds move east across the Sahel, just north of the equator and just south of the Sahara.

The location of the low pressure that is associated with the Intertropical Convergence Zone corresponds approximately to the latitude at which sunlight falls perpendicularly to the land's surface (when the sun is directly overhead, a time also known as the equinox). Since the latitude at which the sun strikes perpendicularly changes seasonally, so does the positioning of the Intertropical Convergence Zone and therefore the region of Africa that receives monsoonal rainfall. In modern times in the Northern Hemisphere summer, the latitude at which sunlight strikes the earth perpendicularly is at or around the Tropic of Cancer (23.5 degrees north of the equator); conversely, the low pressure associated with the intersection of the trade winds is found at or around the Tropic of Capricorn (23.5 degrees south of the equator) in the Southern Hemisphere summer. The north-south oscillation of the Intertropical Convergence Zone is primarily driven by the tilt of the earth and the seasons. Since this zone and the low pressure and rains associated with it move north to south twice in a year, the regions surrounding the equator in Africa experience two rainy seasons each year.

Since the swath of the Intertropical Convergence Zone and the intensity of its rainfall over Africa have varied over time, the landscape in this area has also varied. Relative dryness or wetness shaped the ecological landscape, supporting expansion of forest areas (which require more moist conditions) in the areas of wetter periods and expansion of more drought-resistant open vegetation, such as grasslands or desert ecosystems, during drier periods. The border between the Sahara (arid desert) and the Sahel (semiarid savanna and grasslands) has shifted north and south over time as a result of either more or less rainfall, which is associated with more or less solar radiation reaching the earth.

Impact of the Humid Period on African Ecosystems

About 10,000 years ago, increased moisture from the Atlantic monsoonal rains (partly attributed to increased solar radiation in the Intertropical Convergence Zone) created tropical rainfall conditions in parts of the Sahel and Sahara in northern Africa. Some estimates place rainfall up to 50 percent higher in selected areas of Africa compared with that in modern times. Evidence shows a northward movement of vegetation from the Sahel into the Sahara and an expansion and thickening of forests, such as the Zambezi woodlands and the area around Lake Victoria (East Africa) during this humid period. Areas of the Sahara were even flooded at times. The rain forests of Ghana expanded from 9,000 to 15,000 years ago (after having completely dried out during the last ice age).

Lake-bottom sediments used for researching past climate change show that lake levels were high in central and eastern Africa, including those of water bodies in Kenya's Rift Valley and the upper part of the White Nile River, which originates from Lake Victoria (in East Africa), and the Niger River, inner Niger delta, the Senegal rivers (all in West Africa). Lake Chad, which during high times borders present-day Niger, Chad, Nigeria, and Cameroon (western Africa), occupies a very shallow basin, allowing for enormous variability in the area covered by water with changing depth. This lake is believed to have covered approximately 186,400 to 248,550 square miles 6,000 to 12,000 years ago (compared with 885 square miles in 2003). During this humid period areas of today's more arid Sahara were more densely populated, as people (and animals) moved out of the flooded areas of the inner Sahel into the more moderately wet and hospitable regions of the outer Sahel and farther north in the present-day Sahara regions.

Pollen samples from ice or sediment cores provide valuable evidence of plant type and volume and can paint a picture of vegetative cover and rainfall for a particular moment in history. Such samples from sediments in the dry desert region of eastern Libya have confirmed the presence of *Typha* and *Cyperaceae* (wetland plant families) about 9,700 years ago. Paleoclimatologists use the properties of these and other plants and animals from the present day to draw conclusions about past climate. For example, we know from present-day species of *Typha* and *Cyperaceae* that they are wetland plants; however, little is known about how ancient vegetation (those species that do not exist today) resisted drought or flooding.

The evidence paints an overall picture of increased warming and wetness across Africa over time, but the picture is fragmented both spatially and geographically. Climate-change data are not available for all locations or for each year. Furthermore, there is variability in the climatic conditions of particular regions during the general period of increased humidity. For example, there is no evidence that the desert areas of present-day Libya and western Egypt (northern Africa) also experienced a much more vegetated state. South Africa provides data that indicate a general warming trend with increasing moisture in some areas, but data from southern Africa's Kalahari and Namib deserts indicate more severe dryness. Evidence from Lake Tanganyika, an extremely deep lake in the Rift Valley, shows a reduction in forest cover in the surrounding area around the same time.

Some parts of Africa experienced a more minor dry period (compared with the last major ice age) again around 7,500 to 8,000 years ago. Ice cores from glaciers on Mount Kilimanjaro that also have been used to reconstruct the details of past climatic conditions show a brief but intense drying period some 8,300 years ago. In many areas of Africa there was another period of increased moisture until about 4,000 to 5,000 years ago. This humid period was apparently much shorter in the area north of the Algerian Sahara than in the central mountains. During this last humid period, areas south of the Sahara were often flooded, and the waters of Lake Chad, the Niger River, and the Senegal rivers were at record-high levels. Ice cores from Mount Kilimanjaro date this period of increased moisture to 5,200 years ago and associate it with cooler temperatures (rather than warm temperatures, which often seem to be associated with increased moisture in African climate history).

End of the Humid Period

About 4,000 to 5,000 years ago the temperatures started to drop again, and conditions became much drier. Vegetation began to change as forests shrank and sand dunes formed in the Sahara. The glaciers on Mount Kilimanjaro retreated. Animals and people migrated out of the inner Sahara to escape the increasingly dry hostile conditions. Data recovered from caves and cliffs in eastern Libya that show a gap in evidence of human occupation some 5,000 years ago have been compared with other climate data and have indicated increased dryness there. It is thought that humans migrated out of the area at the onset of drought conditions.

Cave paintings and human settlement remains from Mauritania (in northern Africa) suggest that humans migrated from farther north to this area around 4,000 years ago in an attempt to escape the onset of drier conditions. There is also evidence of the dispersal of cattle from the drier areas of western and northwestern Africa around 3,700 years ago and from the Sudan and Niger 4,000 to 4,500 years ago. Water levels lowered in the areas of present-day Ghana, Sudan, Ethiopia, and Uganda. This period, referred to as the First Dark Age, includes a severe 300-year drought in tropical Africa that began about 4,000 years ago. Starting some 5,000 years ago, many of the lakes in southern Africa also began gradually drying out, and about 2,000 years ago the forests of present-day Senegal and those surrounding Lake Chad had been depleted, causing a change in the composition of species inhabiting the area. Evidence of the start of this cooler drying period is also present in data from other tropical areas around the world, suggesting a global change in climate.

As the Sahara dried out, the Nile River valley, along with the area encompassed by the Tigris and Euphrates rivers, became a center for human civilizations. The Nile, at 4,146 miles long (8,671 kilometers), is the longest river in the world. It also has experienced predictable flooding through centuries, which has provided relief during dry periods for humans and animals living in the surrounding area. Annual floods continually renew the soils with a deposit of fertile silt on a continent characterized by very old soils that have over time lost many of the nutrients that support productive agriculture.

Humans have migrated to the Nile Valley many times throughout history during periods of harsh climatic conditions. Many scientists have found data, for example, that point to bursts in population and social development in this region during periods of drought in the Sahara. Fossil records of flora and fauna provide information on the presence and migration patterns of humans, domestic animals, and wild animals as well as data on vegetative cover. These data have been used to date major migrations into and out of today's Sahara that coincide with evidence of extreme conditions in the Sahara. Migrations out of the Sahara, associated with the environmental pressure of drought, may have contributed to increased conflict over hospitable land, such as the wars between the Egypt and Libya in about 1200 B.C.E.

Traditionally, migration has been a survival strategy commonly used by social groups in Africa to deal successfully with climate changes. For those peoples that did not migrate during periods of increased dryness in Africa, adapting livelihood strategies was essential. As a result of drought conditions around 4,000 years ago, livelihood activities such as pastoralism in East Africa and agriculture in West Africa, including the use of specific techniques such as terracing and dams, expanded as people adapted to the different environmental conditions. Other data reflect that during drought conditions in Africa from 1200 to 2100 B.C.E. some Saharan communities developed and extended mining activities in order to trade for food with communities to the south.

Africa's unique geography and global climatic context jointly have affected specific regions of the continent differently during ancient times. Resulting changes in ecosystems led to variations in human settlement and activity patterns during this time period. These shifting patterns did not occur in a vacuum but were part of a larger-scale system of global variation in geography and climate.

EGYPT

BY KELLY-ANNE DIAMOND REED

Egypt is located in the northeast corner of the African continent, its nearest modern neighbors being Libya to the west, Sudan to the south, and Israel to the northeast. The Gulf of Aqaba and the Red Sea lie to the east, and the Mediterranean Sea is to the north. The country occupies 386,650 square miles and is the 12th-largest country in Africa. The modern border between Egypt and Sudan lies just north of the second cataract of the Nile River. In the Predynastic Period (5000–3100 B.C.E.) or Early Dynastic Period (ca. 3000–2575 B.C.E.) the border lay at Gebel el-Silsila, where the limestone banks in the north give way to sandstone in the south. For most of antiquity the border lay at the first cataract, though on various occasions the Egyptians pushed farther south to expand their territory. In the New Kingdom (1550–1070 B.C.E.) the southern border of Egypt reached past the fourth cataract.

LANDSCAPE AND CLIMATE

The habitation of the Nile Valley began in Paleolithic times. By 15,000 B.C.E. there were many Paleolithic sites in the desert near the valley edge. In the Neolithic Period (ca. 5500–5000 B.C.E.) more people entered Egypt to enjoy the wild game, water, and pleasant climate. These people were wanderers and gatherers, not food producers. Some fruits, seeds, and roots could be found in the wild. The first settlements appeared around 5000 B.C.E.; the settlers could not go far from the water supply and settled near the Nile and in the Faiyûm, a large, fertile depression in Libyan Desert. It is generally thought that over time there was a gradual lack of rainfall and an increase in desert, which in the end led to a scarcity of game. In Neolithic times there was greater movement of people west of the Nile, especially in the north. It is quite likely that it was agriculture that anchored them there. Irrigation began only after the population could no longer survive on the food of the naturally inundated land.

The Egyptian landscape can be broken up into two main parts: the delta in the north and the Nile Valley in the south. The Nile River was, and still is, the heart of Egypt. Without this river Egyptian civilization might never have developed in the dry desert climate of northeast Africa. The Nile Valley and the Nile Delta are known as Upper Egypt and Lower Egypt, respectively. The term *Middle Egypt* is also sometimes employed to describe the region between the Faiyûm in the north to the modern city of Asyut in the south. Upper and Lower Egypt are two very distinct regions, both geographically and culturally. The delta and the valley cover approximately 13,000 square miles. The majority of the ancient Egyptian population lived in this region.

The Egyptian climate is hot and arid. In Cairo (ancient Memphis) the summer can reach temperatures as high as 95 degrees Fahrenheit and then as low as 45 degrees Fahrenheit in the winter. The climate is hotter the farther south one goes. In Aswān the temperature can rise as high as 107 degrees Fahrenheit in the summer. There is rarely rain or even clouds in Egypt and hardly any rainfall in the Nile Valley; in the delta there can be from 4 to 8 inches of rainfall per year. The city of Cairo averages five rainy days per year, usually between November and January. Because of this lack of rainfall the ancient Egyptians were entirely dependent on the Nile inundation for the survival of their crops.

Measuring 4,189 miles, the Nile is the longest river in the world. It flows from south to north and empties into the Mediterranean Sea. In the south the Nile is formed by the confluence of the White Nile (the parent stream), the Blue Nile near Khartoum, and the Atbara some 200 miles north. The White Nile originates in Lake Victoria, and the Blue Nile originates in the mountainous region of northern Ethiopia, the Ethiopian Highlands. The Nile proper then hits the Mediterranean Sea some 1,700 miles away.

Just north of Khartoum the Nile is interrupted by the sixth cataract, the first of a series of six. A cataract is a rocky outcrop that produces rapids when the water runs over it. The fifth cataract is located in the Bayuda Desert, north of where the Atbara merges with the Nile. The fourth cataract is found near Gebel Barkal. The third cataract is just north of Kerma. The second cataract is found near the ancient site of Buhen. The first cataract marked the ancient boundary between Egypt and Nubia, located just south of the island of Elephantine.

NUBIA

The geography of Nubia is important for understanding ancient Egyptian culture. Aside from the fact that this territory was often dominated by the Egyptians, the natural resources that the Egyptians took from Nubia enriched their kingdom and gave them various means with which to prosper. The name Nubia is derived from the word *nwb*, meaning gold. Between the first and second cataracts was Lower Nubia. This was a relatively poor region with very little cultivable land, since the desert cliffs often came right to the river's edge. Lower Nubia was repeatedly being absorbed into the ancient Egyptian territory. The ancient Egyptians regarded Nubia as rightfully theirs and exploited it for its natural resources, used it as a corridor to retrieve exotic African goods, and recruited men for the Egyptian army and police force.

The Egyptians had penetrated into this southern land as early as the Early Dynastic Period, as evidenced by the rock inscriptions and reliefs located in the area of the second cataract. During the Old Kingdom (ca. 2575–2134 B.C.E.) King Snefru brought back to Egypt 7,000 Nubian captives and 200,000 head of cattle, according to the Palermo stone, which records events from the first five dynasties. Additionally, the Egyptians built a fortress at Buhen, which may be interpreted as their having control over the region. During the First Intermediate Period (ca. 2134–2040 B.C.E.) the Egyptians lost hegemony over the area, despite the fact that there were very few settled people. They regained control of the area in the Middle Kingdom (ca. 2040–1640 B.C.E.) and erected a series of enormous mud-brick fortresses to control the gold extraction and drive back the Nubians. The Second Intermediate Period (ca. 1640–1532 B.C.E.) also marks a period of Nubian independence; in fact, at this time the kingdom at Kerma was thriving. With the advent of the Eighteenth Dynasty (ca. 1550–1307 B.C.E.) there was renewed domination of the area, reaching as far south as Kurgus, past the fourth cataract. The Egyptian presence in this area was important for later Egyptian history because the culture that emerged from the Upper Nubian site of Napata was later responsible for the Twenty-Fifth Dynasty (770–712 B.C.E.) in Egypt proper. At this late point, some of the ancient Egyptian customs and traditions were dying out, and the Nubian Dynasty helped to reestablish them. The Napata-Meroitic Empire remained in existence until the fourth century C.E.

Upper Egypt

The Nile Valley, or Upper Egypt, is long and narrow, and the width nowhere exceeds 13 miles. At some points the floodplain is very thin, and the rocky cliffs of the eastern desert hit the water's edge. At other points the cultivable land is more substantial. The ancient Egyptians called this area *kemet*, or black land, in reference to the color of the soil. They contrasted this with *deshret*, or red land, which referred to the desert. The boundary between these two areas is very abrupt. One can actually stand with one foot in the vegetation and the other foot in the desert.

The summer monsoon rains, occurring in Ethiopia between the months of June and September, trigger an increase in the water levels of the Blue Nile. In the past this caused an inundation in Egypt between July and October. The inundation occurred earlier in the south and later in the north. In Cairo the river was at full height around the end of September. The Nile remained high for another two weeks, and then the water began to subside. The Nile was at its lowest in April. Any part of the land that was not inundated by the Nile was desert. The Nile waters brought tons of soil and rock fragments, which would have washed over the riverbanks. This annual event left fresh layers of silt on the floodplain, making the soil fertile. This rich soil made the use of fertilizer unnecessary since new soil was being deposited annually. There was much variation in the water amount and the dates of its deposition on the surrounding land. A low Nile would have had a drastic effect on the ancient culture, possibly leading to famine. This situation, however, is no longer the case in modern Egypt.

Since the 1830s a series of dams have been erected that allow for perpetual irrigation between Sennar in the south and the apex of the delta. Due to the construction of the Aswān High Dam, the course and pattern of the Nile inundation have changed considerably since ancient times. The dam was finished in 1971, and with its completion Lake Nasser was created and Lower Nubia destroyed. Between 1934 and 1960 the population of Egypt grew to almost 28 million inhabitants. This growth proved to be too much for the available agricultural land. Because of necessity the decision was made to build a dam that would span the entire width of the Nile. This dam prevents the annual inundation from occurring in Egypt proper and allows for consistent irrigation patterns and constant agriculture. These circumstances prevent observation of the seasonal patterns that would have existed earlier; historical documents need to be relied upon in order to determine the old flood patterns. Because the Nile's course has changed over time, some of the ancient monuments, which originally lay on the banks of the Nile, now appear to be floating in the desert with no means of access from the waterway.

The inundation was extremely important to the ancient Egyptians—so important that they worshipped it in the form of the god Hapy. The inundation is not to be confused with the river itself, which was called *itrw*. The ancient Greek philosopher Herodotus remarked that "Egypt is the gift of the Nile." The Egyptians even created their calendar based on the stages of the Nile's transformation. The Egyptian year was divided into three seasons: *akhet* (inundation), *peret* (growing season), and *shemu* (drought season). The names of the seasons were associated with the stages of the inundation. The inundation began in July with the peak water levels occurring in the middle of August. The inundation did not completely overflow the banks but instead ran off through channels into the fields beyond the riverbanks. The banks of the Nile would have been raised so as to prevent the flooding of nearby villages. These channels, or canals, were then blocked off in order to keep the water for future use. The dikes would then be cut when necessary. However, even up to the end of the 19th century the river at times would have overflowed and flooded the surrounding areas, except for the roads that were raised above it. When the waters had receded in October or November, the farmers plowed their fields and laid their seed. In the months from January to April the crops matured. The main crops were barley, emmer, einkorn and spelt.

It is possible that the employment of these canals dates back as early as the Predynastic Period, as evidenced by the macehead of King Scorpion (ca. 3150 B.C.E.). The area of cultivable land was increased in New Kingdom times by the invention of the *shaduf*, an irrigation tool, and increased again in Ptolemaic times with the advent of an animal-powered waterwheel (*sakkia*). With improved methods of agriculture more land was cultivated, and the marshy areas disappeared. The reduction in marshy land is one of the reasons for the extinction of the papyrus plant, which used to grow in the marshy delta regions.

The Nile also functioned as the primary mode of transportation. If people wanted to travel north, they could go with the flow of the Nile. If they wanted to travel south, then they would simply hoist their sails, since the wind blew south. When looking at ancient Egyptian nautical depictions, the modern scholar can discern which way the boat was traveling simply by noting whether the sails were up.

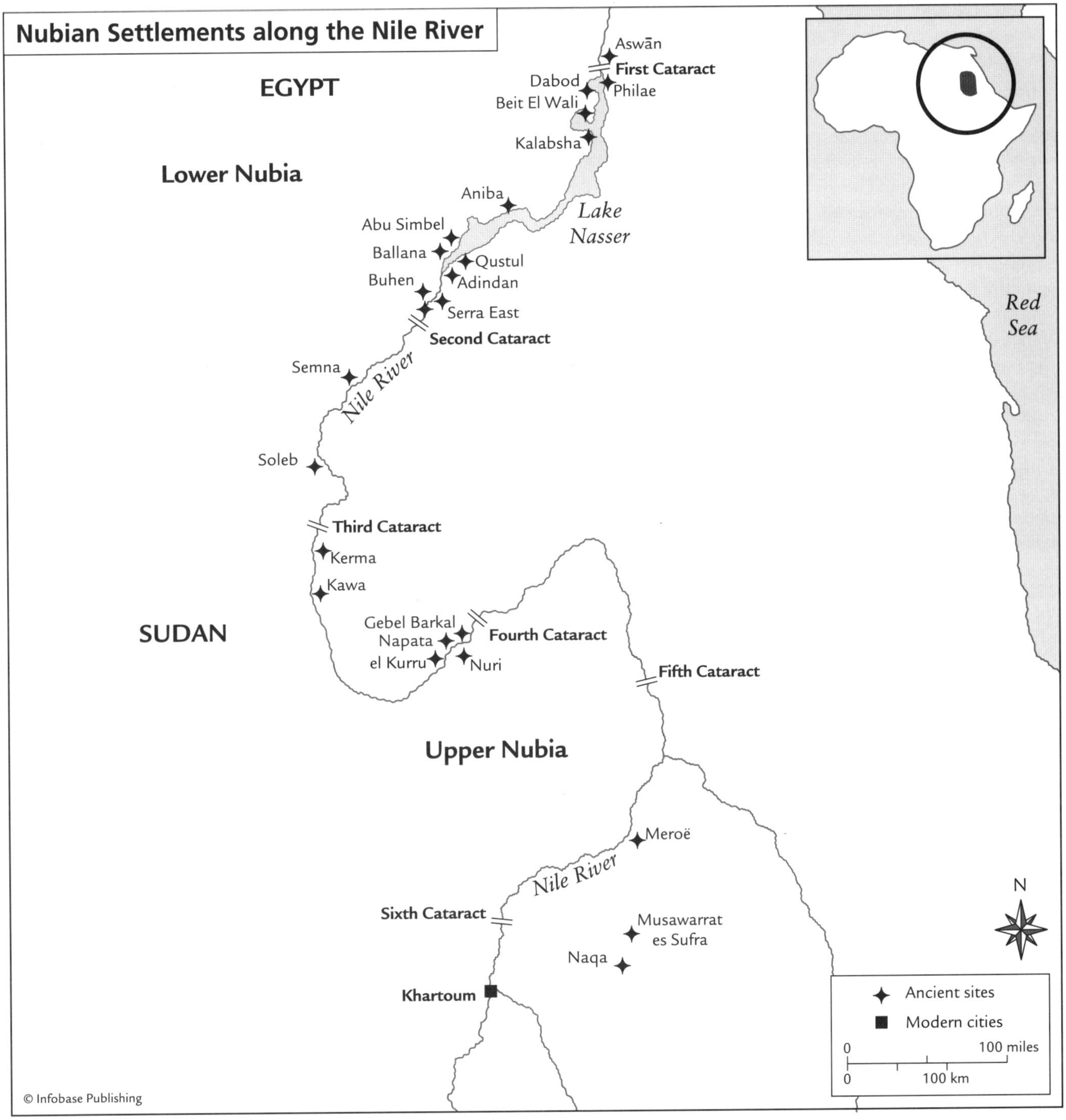

As the Sahara dried out between 3000 and 2000 B.C.E., the Nile River valley became a center for human civilizations, including those in ancient Nubia.

With the invention of the Nilometer the Egyptians could record the river levels and attempt to predict their crop yields. A Nilometer consisted of a series of steps that were used to mark the height of the Nile inundation as well as regular water levels. Surviving Nilometers exist at the sites of Philae, Idfu, Isna, Kom Ombo, Dendera, and Aswān. In Cairo there is also an Islamic Nilometer from about 705–715 C.E., which may have been built on the site of a Pharaonic Nilometer.

Lower Egypt

The ancient capital of Memphis (modern Cairo) sits at the apex of the Nile Delta. The delta, or Lower Egypt, is wide and marshy and quite different in appearance from the Nile Valley. There are also many lakes and patches of low, salty ground. These landscape differences may be the reason that the ancient Egyptians distinguished between the Two Lands. The area of the delta creates a fertile triangle that is shaped like the Greek letter delta. In ancient times there were five major branches of the Nile that flowed into the Mediterranean Sea: the Damietta, the Rosetta, the Canopic, the Sebennytic, and the Pelusiac. Now there are only two: the Damietta in the east and the Rosetta in the west. It is possible that a rise in the ground level of the eastern delta caused the other branches to dry up. Despite the fact that the delta contained many waterways, there was not much available land more fertile than that in the Nile Valley. Much of the area was marshy and too wet to farm, but it did contain wildlife and fish. Many of the archaeological sites located in the delta cannot be fully explored owing to the high water table. It is thought that the delta played a fundamental role in the earliest periods, especially in the religious sphere. Unfortunately, the material evidence does not fully reveal the area's importance. The delta was an important region because of its agricultural potency as well as its proximity to the Mediterranean Sea and to the Near East.

Ancient Provinces

The ancient Egyptians divided Egypt into nomes, or provinces. Upper Egypt had 22 nomes, and Lower Egypt had 20, equaling 42. The nomes in Lower Egypt developed much later than those of Upper Egypt. The area occupied by the Faiyûm and the western oases were not organized according to this scheme. One way that the size of the individual nomes can be reconstructed is through a list of their lengths along the Nile recorded in the kiosk of King Sesostris I (r. ca. 1971–1926 B.C.E.) at Karnak. Each nome had a capital city and a nomarch who ruled the nome. Some capitals changed over time, and others are still uncertain. Each nome had its own symbol, and standards were used in Upper Egypt to make such identifications. Over time new titles emerged, and certain localities became known by such designations as the "ibis nome."

An auxiliary region, called the Faiyûm, was located to the west of the Nile Valley and south of Memphis. This area measured about 4,633 square miles and created a fertile depression in the Libyan Desert. The Faiyûm was consistently inhabited, and archaeological remains date back to around 8000 B.C.E. Some of the remains date to as recently as the Christian Period (641 C.E.). During the Paleolithic Period this depression consisted of a salt lake, which eventually changed into Lake Moeris (modern-day Birket Qārūn). Lake Moeris is linked to the Nile by the Bahr Yusef Canal, which diverges westward north of Asyūt. In Pharaonic times the water level was lowered, and it was used to irrigate the surrounding land for agriculture. It is thought that an area of 174 square miles was gained during the reclamation projects of the Middle Kingdom. This area was increased in Ptolemaic times (ca. 304–30 B.C.E.) to approximately 463 square miles and was used for agriculture. At this time the Faiyûm was one of the most prosperous areas in Egypt.

Oases

The oases in the western desert running from north to south are as follows: Siwa, Baharīya, Farafra, Dakhla, and Khārga. They were settled by the Egyptians, but in ancient times this area was known as Libya. Siwa Oasis is located about 348 miles west of Cairo and was first settled in the Twenty-Sixth Dynasty (ca. 664–525 B.C.E.). This site is famous for the oracle that was visited by Alexander the Great. The Baharīya Oasis was another fertile depression, located about 124 miles west of the Nile. This site was founded earlier than Siwa and contains remains from the New Kingdom. Farafra Oasis is the smallest of the major Egyptian oases. It is located about 186 miles west of modern Asyūt. So far no Pharaonic archaeological remains have been discovered there; however, the site is mentioned in Old Kingdom sources, and by the time of the New Kingdom it was known as a Libyan settlement. The Dakhla Oasis is located even farther south, about 186 miles west of Luxor. This site is of interest because it has Old Kingdom settlement remains, which testify to the expansive control the Egyptians held in the Libyan Desert at this time. Khārga Oasis is the largest of the major Egyptian oases. It is located only 108 miles west of Luxor. The Pharaonic remains are scarce, but what is left dates to the Ptolemaic period. These oases were held only in times of strong government. They were valuable because they produced grapes and dates, acted as caravan posts for long journeys, and functioned as outposts for dealing with the Libyans. Additionally, this area is where thieves fled to escape the law and where exiles were banished. Some scholars have called it the Egyptian Siberia.

Alexandria, the Sinai, and the Near East

The city of Alexandria, located at the western end of the Mediterranean coast of Egypt, was an important city in the Ptolemaic Period. It was founded by Alexander the Great and was established on a less important ancient Egyptian town called Rakote. Alexandria was a prosperous, cosmopolitan city that replaced Memphis as the capital of Egypt. The coastal region west of Alexandria is where the majority of the Libyan population resided. This area was also home to a series of forts built by Ramses II (r. ca. 1290–1224 B.C.E.) as far as 210 miles west of Alexandria. The Ptolemies pushed all the way to Cyrenaica (about another 400 miles west).

The Sinai, a peninsula lying between the Mediterranean Sea and the Red Sea, was also important for the Egyptians. The Wadi Maghara and Serabit el Khadim are two of the main Egyptian sites in the Sinai. It was by way of three main routes through the eastern desert that the Egyptians traveled to the Red Sea and ultimately to the Sinai. These routes also gave access to various quarries located in the eastern desert. The Egyptians would have had to cooperate with the local nomadic populations in these regions. As far as is known, the Egyptians navigated the Red Sea in order to trade with the Sinai and Punt, whose exact location remains unknown.

The Great Temple at Abu Simbel on the banks of the Nile; the Nile is the heart of Egypt and without it Egyptian civilization may never have developed in the dry desert climate of northeast Africa. (Courtesy of the Oriental Institute of the University of Chicago)

The proximity of the Near East to Egypt's northeastern border also played a primary role in the development and evolution of Egyptian culture. Connections between these two regions were established as early as the Predynastic Period. Evidence of trade in the Old Kingdom can be seen in the Lebanese cedar used to make King Khufu's (r. ca. 2551–2528 B.C.E.) boat. In the Middle Kingdom the Egyptians traded with the Near East, mainly through the port of Byblos located on the Mediterranean coast, north of modern Beirut. Official Egyptian seals have been found in Israel, Syria, and Turkey. Royally sponsored trade activities reached as far as Ugarit in the north, and objects from Minoan Crete have been found in Egypt. Local trade took place between the people of the eastern delta and those living in the region that is now southern Israel. Similarities existed in the material cultures of these two populations. In the New Kingdom the Egyptian military held parts of the Near East for over 200 years; this situation was repeated in the later periods.

Natural Resources

The natural resources that were available to the Egyptians in antiquity are quite impressive. The northern part of the Nile Valley is made up of limestone; beginning in Gebel el-Silsila the sandstone comes down on both sides of the Nile and replaces the limestone all the way into Sudan. Limestone is a softer stone, and the Nile has been able to carve some of it away, thus creating a broader floodplain in the north. Such is not the case with the sandstone in the south. The Egyptians used both limestone and sandstone for construction. There were many resource sites within easy reach. Schist could be found between Qena and Quseir, quartzite came from Gebel Ahmar, alabaster came from Hatnub, and granite was quarried at Aswān. Although some of the resources were nearby, others required large-scale expeditions, such as greywacke in the Wadi Hammamat and gold in the Nubian mines. The Egyptians also mined copper, turquoise, malachite, and amethyst in the eastern desert and the Sinai. There is no evidence that the Egyptians themselves conducted the mining operations in the Sinai; they most likely had a local crew working for them.

The Wadi Natrun in the western desert was the source of natron, which was used for mummification and purification rituals. Above all Egypt acquired a wealth of gold through its mining activities along the Nile in Nubia and in Nubia's eastern desert. Aside from gold, Nubia also supplied Egypt's hard stone: pink and black granite, diorite, and porphyry, all of which were much desired by the Egyptians. From the natural resources, the Egyptians were able to produce and trade faience, glass, gold, jewelry, precious and semiprecious stones, linen, papyrus, and stone vessels. They used these natural resources to trade with their neighbors for other commodities that they lacked, like timber from Lebanon, lapis lazuli from Afghanistan, and ebony, ivory, various spices, and incense from Africa. Furthermore, the Nile itself provided the material for making pottery and mud-bricks, two essentials for everyday life.

In ancient times Egypt's culture prospered in relative isolation. To the north was the Mediterranean Sea; to the west were mountains with the desert running almost all the way to the Atlantic Ocean; to the south was Lower Nubia, where six cataracts blocking the Nile from Aswān to Khartoum made it impossible to navigate; and to the east rocky cliffs and desert gave way to the Red Sea. The only area that was left vulnerable was the corridor in the northeastern delta that met with the Sinai and led to the Near East. The Egyptians made great attempts at securing this defenseless point. Although this seclusion allowed an independent culture to flourish and postponed the invasion of Egypt, it was through this northeastern corridor that the Assyrians, Persians, and Macedonians would eventually enter Egypt.

THE MIDDLE EAST

BY AMY HACKNEY BLACKWELL

Historical events in ancient times were greatly influenced by climate and proximity. People who lived in areas with good climates and fertile soil had a much easier time thriving than those who lived in areas in which daily living was more difficult. People who lived close to centers of civilization were more likely to come in contact with that civilization, exchanging learning and trading goods, than those who lived on mountaintops or on distant islands where no visitors ever came. In the ancient Near East a combination of water sources and drought forced people to master agriculture and band together in cities; these activities in turn resulted in the creation of some of humanity's first centers of civilization.

The world's very first agricultural societies appeared between 6000 and 8000 B.C.E. in an area called the Fertile Crescent, which stretches 1,200 miles from the Mediterranean coast of Israel and Lebanon to the Zagros Mountains in Iraq and Iran. Climate change made agriculture possible. At the end of the last ice age, about 11,000 B.C.E., the climate in the Fertile Crescent grew warmer and wetter. This change improved growing conditions for many local grains and other plants. Grasslands and forests expanded, increasing the available habitats for both animals and humans. Good living conditions allowed human populations to grow and fill the ancient Near East.

MESOPOTAMIA

The Tigris and Euphrates rivers define the area known as Mesopotamia, which has long attracted human settlers. Both rivers originate in Turkey. The Euphrates, south of the Tigris, flows through Syria before entering Iraq's northwest corner. Several large tributaries flow into the Tigris from the eastern mountains, including the Khabar, the Great Zab, the Little Zab, and the 'Uzaym. The Tigris and the Euphrates meet 115 miles before they jointly reach the Persian Gulf. Both the Tigris and the Euphrates are prone to flooding and changing their courses. The upper reaches of both rivers are rough, unpredictable, and difficult to travel by boat. People living in the area never adopted either river as a major trade route, though some intrepid merchants did transport goods on wooden rafts from Anatolia to the cities in lower Mesopotamia.

The area southeast of the modern city of Baghdad is a broad, flat delta. Just above the point where the Tigris and Euphrates meet is a large marshland. Northeast of Mesopotamia are the high Zagros Mountains. These form a physical boundary between fertile Mesopotamia and points east. The Zagros Mountains were home to forests of oak, maple, pistachio, and hawthorn trees. Many wild animals lived there, including sheep, goats, and gazelles. To the south and west of Mesopotamia are deserts. There is also a sizable desert between the Tigris and Euphrates north of the modern cities of Hīt and Sāmarrā.

Mesopotamia has always been dry and prone to violent extremes of weather. Rain falls between December and March, but even then only a few inches fall each year. More rain falls in the mountains. The prevailing winds in this area are a dry cool wind blowing from the north and the warmer sirocco from the southeast. Summers are very hot, reaching temperatures of 120 degrees Fahrenheit, and winter temperatures are cold but not devastatingly so. This pattern has varied slightly over the past 10,000 years, with some periods in the ancient world being slightly wetter than others, but lack of water and unpredictable weather have always defined life in the region.

The population of the area first started to grow around 5800 B.C.E., when the climate suddenly improved after a brief "mini ice age" that afflicted all of Europe and Mesopotamia and lasted for about 400 years, starting in 6200 B.C.E.. Scientists believe that Mesopotamia may have received about 25 percent more rain then than it does in modern times, and more of the year's rain may have fallen in the summer, making it more useful to farmers. The annual floods of the Tigris and Euphrates were higher then, too, providing farmers even more water. The climate changed, however, around 3800 B.C.E. For the next thousand years Mesopotamia and the entire eastern Mediterranean region were afflicted by a severe drought. Rain stopped falling in the summer, and when it did fall, it arrived too late to water crops.

From that time onward Mesopotamians relied almost entirely on their two rivers to provide water for their crops. The

Tigris and Euphrates overflowed their banks every spring, fed by melting snow in the Anatolian highlands. These annual floods were a mixed blessing. They provided necessary water for fields, but they were unpredictable; some years they arrived with such force that they swept away entire villages. Mesopotamians spent much of their effort containing the waters of the rivers, building levees to keep the overflowing rivers within their banks. Some years the floods were much lower than in other years, or they arrived later than expected, causing farmers to lose their crops. Sometimes the rivers changed course, leaving towns high and dry. Farmers had to control water flow in order to water their crops reliably. People living close to the river banks could use groundwater or floodwater to grow plants, but people farther away had to dig irrigation canals or build dams to harness water for their own fields.

As the droughts continued in the centuries after 3800 B.C.E., it became harder for people to live in the countryside away from the rivers. People clustered on the river banks in settlements that gradually turned into cities. Cities provided the only means of keeping large numbers of people alive in the arid environment. All food had to be grown in a small area just beside the river, and water had to be allocated and dispensed carefully to make the most of the small amount that was available. City officials organized farming and irrigation, stored food to prepare for droughts, and dispensed carefully rationed portions of grain to residents. By 3100 B.C.E. about 80 percent of Mesopotamians lived in cities. Sumerians and Babylonians constantly negotiated and fought with one another over scarce water resources.

Though these cities provided some protection against climatic fluctuations, they were extremely vulnerable to catastrophes. The Sumerian city of Ur died as a result of one such catastrophe. Ur was a huge city on the Euphrates. In 2200 B.C.E. a major volcanic eruption somewhere in the Northern Hemisphere sparked a major drought that lasted for 278 years and affected the entire Mediterranean world. Snow stopped falling in Anatolia, and as a result the Tigris and Euphrates stopped flooding. The city found it increasingly difficult to grow enough food for the population. At the same time nomads who had lived in the countryside moved into the cities in an effort to feed themselves. The combination of overpopulation and lack of food was disastrous for the government; by 2000 B.C.E. it had collapsed, and most of Ur's population was dead or dispersed into the countryside in a quest for water and food. By 1900 B.C.E. the rains had returned, and farming once again became possible. Nevertheless, water shortages remained a perennial problem, as they do to this day.

Levant

The Levant is a common name for the part of the Near East that includes Israel, Lebanon, Jordan, Palestine, and Syria; it is bounded by the Mediterranean Sea, the Taurus Mountains, the Arabian Desert, and Mesopotamia. Most of the region is hilly, except for the Mediterranean coastal plain. The climate is Mediterranean, with long, hot, dry summers and cool, rainy winters. Winters are usually not very cold, but snow can fall in the mountains. Many types of plants and animals lived there in ancient times, including sheep, goats, migratory birds, date palms, and olive trees. Lebanon was famous for its cedar trees, the wood of which was coveted throughout the Mediterranean region.

The Levant has a warm climate and fertile soil, but it has always been plagued by lack of water. Much of the area is desert. The Jordan River is the largest river in Israel; humans have always lived near it to take advantage of its water, and they have often fought over it. The largest body of freshwater in the area is the Sea of Galilee, a freshwater lake that lies several hundred feet below sea level in modern Israel. Many fish lived in this lake, and many of the humans who lived around it worked as fishermen.

One of the area's largest bodies of water is the hypersaline (extremely salty) Dead Sea. The Dead Sea is almost nine times as salty as the ocean. It was salty in ancient times as well and was one of the world's first tourist attractions. The biblical king David took vacations there, as did King Herod the Great. The Dead Sea's waters were of no use for agriculture, but local people did extract minerals from the waters to sell as fertilizer or as ingredients in making Egyptian mummies.

The Levant was located in the center of the ancient world and was prone to being occupied and fought over as a result. Its Mediterranean coastline made it desirable to traders who carried goods between Greece, Rome, Egypt, Mesopotamia, and the Persian Empire. It was surrounded by large powers, including Greece, Rome, Egypt, Mesopotamia, and the Persian Empire, and most of them marched through it or occupied it at one time or another. Anyone walking to or from Egypt passed through the Levant; these passersby included numerous armies. A road along the shore, which the Romans called the Via Maris (sea road, or way of the sea), linked Egypt with the northern empires; it was built long before the Romans arrived to name it, probably during the Bronze Age.

Persia

Persia occupied the area that is now called Iran. It was to the west of Mesopotamia and separated from it by the Zagros Mountains. The Zagros Mountains run along the Gulf of Oman and the Persian Gulf up to Armenia and Pakistan, a fertile but mountainous area. Central Persia consisted of a large, flat plateau surrounded by mountains. It was inaccessible and saline, covered with salt marshes and salt flats, and very few people ventured there in ancient times. Northern Persia is also lined with mountains, the Elburz and Talish mountain ranges, which extend eastward to modern Afghanistan. The area near the Caspian coastline is flatter. Iran's modern eastern border is another series of mountains that form a boundary between Iran, Afghanistan, and Pakistan; in the heyday of the Persian Empire, however, Persia included this mountain range in its territory, and Persian territory extended all the way to the Indus River.

Persia's climate was and is characterized by extremes of temperature. Some of the world's highest modern temperatures have been recorded in the central plateau, reaching highs of 132 degrees Fahrenheit. Winter temperatures are below freezing; mountainous areas have the coldest temperatures. Most of the country is quite dry; the central plateau receives almost no rainfall. Some parts of Persia have long been subjected to periodic violent windstorms.

The most fertile area of Persia in ancient times was along the coast of the Caspian Sea. This part of the country received by far the most rain and has always had the highest human population of the region. The Caspian lowlands were heavily forested with many kinds of trees, including orange, lemon, date, fig, pomegranate, willow, and oak. Animals native to the area included Persian gazelles, onagers (wild donkeys), many types of goats and sheep, porcupines, badgers, partridges, and pheasants. The Caspian Sea itself was a rich source of food, such as white fish, herring, and the valuable sturgeon.

Persia was located at a crossroads between Asia and Europe. By the fifth century B.C.E. Persians were regularly trading with their neighbors in India, Mesopotamia, Greece, and Egypt. They built and maintained a road from Susa, on the Tigris in Mesopotamia, all the way to Smyrna, the modern Aegean city of İzmir, Turkey, principally to facilitate royal communication throughout the empire but also to permit easy trade with the West. This road was called the Persian Royal Road.

On the other side of Persia, traders from China and India frequently appeared with silks, jade, and other Asian goods. Alexander the Great opened a route through Persia and brought eastern traders all the way to Europe. By the first century B.C.E. there was an established trade route running from China to Rome; this trade route is known as the Silk Road. The Silk Road ran through Persia just south of the Caspian Sea and followed the Persian Royal Road to the Mediterranean. From there traders could take ship or walk overland to the Aegean coast of Turkey, Egypt, northern Black Sea ports, Rome, North Africa, and Spain. Traders carried goods in caravans of carts and pack animals, such as camels and donkeys, selling Chinese and Central Asian goods to people in the West and bringing Western goods back to Asia. By the first century C.E. Romans were regularly trading with merchants in China, Sri Lanka, India, and Southeast Asia, all of whom transported their goods through Persia and the Near East.

Arabia

South of Mesopotamia and the Levant lies the Arabian Peninsula. It has coasts on the Red Sea, the Persian Gulf, and the Indian Ocean. Almost all of this vast expanse of land is desert. The climate is extremely dry and excessively hot, and very few people lived in it in ancient times. The few who did were experts at water conservation. The Arabians of the ancient world clustered on the coasts of the Red Sea and the Persian Gulf.

Arabia was of interest to ancient Greeks and Romans chiefly because its coasts provided convenient ports for trade with India. Greeks and Macedonians traded with Arabs who brought goods from India and the southern Arabian Peninsula (modern Yemen and Oman) overland by camels; major trade routes ran from Yemen to Medina and from Petra to Syria. During the early empire sailors mastered the weather patterns caused by the monsoons in the Indian Ocean, and from then on most trade with India was done by sea.

Anatolia

Anatolia is the region that today forms the large Asian portion of the nation of Turkey. The western parts of Anatolia are very close to Europe, and during ancient times these regions were the main point of cultural exchange between Asia and Europe. People traveling from Mesopotamia, Persia, the Levant, or Egypt went either overland through Anatolia or in ships, hugging the southern Anatolian coast.

Anatolia is a giant peninsula with coastlines on the Black Sea, the Sea of Marmara, the Aegean Sea, and the Mediterranean Sea. The Mediterranean coastline is pocked with coves and bays that are virtually indistinguishable from one another and hence difficult to navigate. In ancient times these coves and bays made ideal hideouts for notorious pirates, such as the pirates who kidnapped Julius Caesar in 75 B.C.E. The island of Cyprus lies in the northeast corner of the Mediterranean, in the angle formed where the Anatolian peninsula meets the Levant. The Aegean coastline is also rocky and full of islands just offshore. Both the mainland coast and the islands attracted large numbers of human inhabitants in ancient times; Lesbos, Kos, Smyrna, and Ephesus are all in this area. The area was not good for growing grain, but residents took advantage of other opportunities, such as shipbuilding, marble quarrying, and trade.

The Dardanelles form a strait between the Aegean and the Sea of Marmara. They were a prime strategic location in ancient times; the ancient city of Troy was built on a hill overlooking the southern entry to the straits. The Bosphorus was another strategic strait, running between the Sea of Marmara and the Black Sea. The ancient city of Constantinople was built on the southern point of the Bosphorus. The area south of the Sea of Marmara was fertile and proved an ideal location for agriculture. This fertile plain included the area east of the Bosphorus and the western Anatolian Black Sea coast; the ancient kingdom of Bithynia occupied these areas. The eastern part of the Black Sea coast was somewhat isolated from the rest of Anatolia by its steep coastlines.

The Anatolian plateau itself is high and surrounded by mountains. The northern mountains, called the Pontus Mountains, parallel the Black Sea coast. The Taurus Mountains parallel the Mediterranean coast. Central Anatolia is situated between these two mountain ranges. To the east of the plateau the Taurus and Pontus ranges meet, creating the highest peaks in the region; Mount Ararat is the highest point in Anatolia. The Tigris and the Euphrates both originate in this region and are fed by snowmelt from the mountains. Southeast of the mountains the terrain slopes down to Syria.

The most fertile parts of Anatolia are the Mediterranean coastal plain and the area south of the Sea of Marmara. These regions and the area on the Aegean coast all have a Mediterranean climate, with long, hot, dry summers and cool, wet winters. Crops from these areas included grapes, olives, citrus fruits, figs, and wheat. Central Anatolia has a much harsher climate, with very cold winters and more rain and snow than coastal regions. In ancient times much of Anatolia was covered with forests. Cyprus was also heavily forested, and ancients used its forests for timber. Natural rock structures within the Anatolian plateau lent themselves to interesting housing arrangements; many people in Cappadocia lived in caves that had formed naturally in the rocks. People who lived in central Anatolia typically made their living by trading in some local substance. For example, the settlement of Çatalhüyük (first colonized about 7500 B.C.E.) was built near a large deposit of obsidian, a volcanic rock used to make tools in the ancient world; its economy was entirely based on the obsidian trade, which residents sold to Syrian and Mediterranean traders. Despite the existence of trade routes, people living in the Anatolian plateau tended to be isolated from one another and from the larger Mediterranean civilization.

Human settlement surrounded the Black Sea and extended into the region between the Black Sea and the Caspian Sea. This region was the home of the ancient kingdoms of Pontus, Colchis, and Armenia; Colchis was considered the legendary source of the Golden Fleece and the destination of Jason and the Argonauts (a mythical story involving heroes searching for treasure, plus love, betrayal, and murder). Colchis was situated on a plain east of the Black Sea, but aside from that flat area, the region is rugged and mountainous. The Caucasus Mountains have a cold climate. The mountains, the dense forests, and the harsh weather combined to make the region northwest of Anatolia inaccessible to most travelers. As a result, the people who lived there tended to be isolated from one another and from the larger ancient world.

The Black Sea Deluge Theory

The body of water that is now known as the Black Sea has not always been a body of saltwater. After the last ice age it was the Euxine Lake, a vast freshwater lake that may have had no physical connection to the Sea of Marmara. Its surface was about 450 feet below the level of the Mediterranean Sea. The lake's shores were fertile and full of wild game, and the climate was mild. Humans settled on the shores of the lake, farming, hunting, and raising animals.

Around 6200 B.C.E. the giant Laurentide ice sheet in Canada began to melt; as it melted, it fed icebergs into the Atlantic Ocean. This event caused the planet's overall temperature to drop, resulting in a mini ice age that lasted about 400 years. Anatolia and the Levant became much drier; farmers could no longer count on being able to grow their crops. Numerous inland settlements were abandoned as people moved closer to Euxine Lake. When the warm, wet weather returned around 5800 B.C.E., the population on the lake's shores increased.

Around 5600 B.C.E. the lake changed. According to a modern theory, a massive flood turned the Euxine Lake into the Black Sea in about two years' time. Rising sea levels in the Atlantic raised sea levels in the Mediterranean, which fed into the Sea of Marmara. The land separating the Sea of Marmara from the much lower Euxine Lake was thin and narrow. One day the water started lapping over the edge. This trickle of water eroded away some earth, allowing more water to flow downhill. Within days saltwater was rushing from the Sea of Marmara into the Euxine Lake. The water level of the Euxine rose six inches per day. Within two years the Euxine Lake's surface was at the same level as that of the Mediterranean, and the water was no longer fresh but was instead brackish. The villages that had lined the shores of the lake were completely inundated.

This theory, sometimes called the Black Sea deluge theory, is now the topic of much debate. Many people believe that this event, if it happened, could have been the historical inspiration for the story of the Biblical flood and Noah's ark. What appear to be ancient buildings and freshwater snails have been discovered about 300 feet below the surface on Turkey's Black Sea coast. These items date to about 5000 B.C.E., providing evidence to support the theory. Some geologists, however, insist that water flowed between the Black Sea and the Sea of Marmara for thousands of years before the deluge supposedly happened.

ASIA AND THE PACIFIC

BY AMY HACKNEY BLACKWELL

Asia and the Pacific region encompass an enormous area, from the Arctic to the Antarctic and from the Ural Mountains to the eastern Pacific Ocean. This area includes all imaginable variations of climate and geography, from the highest mountains on earth to some of the flattest floodplains, from extremely wet environments to places with no rainfall at all. The Asian continent has several large river systems, many of them originating in the Himalayas. The whole area is affected by monsoon patterns in the Indian Ocean and cyclones that form in the Pacific.

The Asian landmass includes a large coastline on the Indian and Pacific oceans surrounding a huge central landlocked area. The coastal areas, including India, China, and Southeast Asia, all fostered early civilizations that developed around rivers; the Yangtze, the Yellow, and the Indus River valleys were home to some of the earliest agricultural civilizations in Asia. These regions had good climates and ample water, which allowed their residents to build towns, grow large populations, and create culture and technology, including writing. Coastlines facilitated travel and exchange of goods and culture. The east-west axis of the continent made it easy for people to transport agricultural products and techniques from one place to another.

Central Asia

The region west of Persia (modern Iran) and the Caspian Sea encompasses a variety of terrains. The southern coast of modern Pakistan lies along the Arabian Sea. Just north of the coast is the Central Makran Range. The central area is a large, flat plateau. Most of this area is extremely dry with almost no rainfall. To the west the Indus River flows south from the Himalayas. The river creates an extremely fertile valley that was a center of human settlement in ancient times. The Hindu Kush Mountain Range runs through northern Pakistan and most of modern Afghanistan. These mountains are high and snow covered, and they prevented ancient people from moving freely in this area. The same mountain chain continues north into modern Tajikistan and Kyrgyzstan. This entire region is prone to earthquakes.

The Caspian Sea coast drew ancient human settlers who caught fish, such as sturgeon, in its waters; the northern coast where the Volga River enters the sea was especially attractive. To the west of the Caspian Sea and north of Persia lies a huge, flat area of deserts and steppes. The Amu Darya River crosses this region from the Pamir Mountains to the Aral Sea, a large body of freshwater. Aside from this water, this area (modern Turkmenistan and Uzbekistan) has been arid desert with little rainfall for many centuries. The ancient Chinese Silk Road passed through this region, going north of the mountains to the southeastern end of the Caspian Sea in Persia. North and northeast of the desert is a large area of grassland pocked with small lakes and salt flats. The Syr Darya River flows from the Kyrgyz Range to the Aral Sea; in ancient times, it had a wide, well-watered delta that could support agriculture.

India

The Indian subcontinent is a giant triangular peninsula that juts southward into the Indian Ocean. The Arabian Sea forms its west coast, and the Bay of Bengal lies to the east. Narrow mountain ranges called Ghats run down both coasts, the Eastern Ghats in the east and the Western Ghats in the west. Between the Ghats and the ocean are fertile, wet coastal plains.

The Thar Desert lies to the east of the Indus River; though historians are not sure exactly when it formed, it was certainly a dry, rocky desert by ancient times. The Ganges River runs from west to east across northern India and drains into the Bay of Bengal. The river drains a large, flat area that has very fertile soil, is easily irrigated, and has been intensively farmed and densely populated for thousands of years. The Brahmaputra River joins the Ganges just above the delta. It flows through the Assam valley, one of the wettest and most fertile places on earth.

The Himalayas, the Thar Desert, and the Indian Ocean rule India's climate. The mountains block cold winds from central Asia, keeping winters warm in India south of the Himalayas. The Thar Desert attracts rain-bearing clouds that bring the seasonal monsoon. The monsoon is a wind pattern that follows the same course every year; the Indian monsoon blows out of the Arabian Sea in early summer, causing heavy rains on the subcontinent after about June 1, and reverses direction in the fall, taking the rain with it. The monsoon rains can also be dangerous, causing floods and thunderstorms. Ancient farmers did their best to time plantings with the monsoons. Although the monsoon rains were generally predictable, some years they came later or failed entirely, devastating crops. Droughts plagued India as they did most of the ancient world. The people looked to their kings to end droughts by placating the gods. One ruler, Chandragupta, abdicated his throne in 301 B.C.E., hoping to end a drought by dedicating his life to prayer; he is said to have fasted to death.

All of India was fairly accessible to the outside world. The northeast was close to Persia, facilitating commerce as well as cultural and religious exchange with the Middle East. It was also vulnerable to invasion from northern cultures, including the Persians and the Scythians, because of its proximity to central Asia. The southern part of the subcontinent was well positioned to trade with other ancient empires, especially once sailors mastered sailing with the monsoons around the first century C.E. The Dravidian people of southern India used this ability to trade with the Middle East and even the Roman Empire, sailing around Arabia to get close to the Mediterranean. Many Indians emigrated east from south India during the first 500 years C.E., settling in Thailand, on the Malay Peninsula, and in Indonesia, and even reaching as far as Taiwan or the Philippines.

Himalayas

The Himalayas lie to the north of the Indian subcontinent. The southern edge of the range stretches 1,500 miles northwest to southeast from the Hindu Kush to the headwaters of the Brahmaputra River. The Himalayas are the world's highest mountains; 14 of the peaks, including Mount Everest, are over 26,427 feet high. The Indus, the Ganges, the Brahmaputra, and the Yangtze rivers all originate in the Himalayas. The Himalayas were formed by the collision of the Indo-Australian plate with the Tibetan plateau; this geological plate has been moving slowly northward for the past 70 million years and keeps the Himalayan region geologically active. Earthquakes were common in ancient times. Ancient peoples in the Himalayas and India certainly experienced earthquakes; ancient texts such as the Vedas (perhaps written around 3000 B.C.E.) often mention them and suggest supernatural causes.

The terrain of the Himalayas varies more by altitude than by latitude. The lower slopes of the southern Himalayas are fertile lands with deciduous forests. Above this area is a region called the Terai belt, an area of clay, sandy soils, and seasonal floods that turn the terrain into marsh. Indian rhinoceros were plentiful here in ancient times. Above the Terai is a zone of rocky soils and subtropical pine and broadleaf forests. Next come temperate broadleaf and mixed forests, and above them subalpine conifer (trees with needles for leaves) forests. Several glaciers run through the upper Himalayas; these glaciers periodically drop chunks of ice, which can create extremely rugged terrain.

The mountains affect the climate throughout Asia, blocking winds from every direction. Cold northern winds cannot reach India, keeping India warm. In turn, India's monsoon cannot reach Mongolia, keeping Mongolia dry and possibly accounting for the formation of the Gobi and Takla Makan deserts. The Himalayas themselves have harsh weather, which limited human settlement.

The mountains formed a barrier to the intermingling of peoples. Ancient people did most of their traveling on foot, and it took a great deal of time and effort to climb slopes and find mountain passes. Consequently, few people traveled between India and China. Nevertheless, the Chinese Silk Road passed through the Himalayas, going through the Nathu La Pass between China and Tibet and the Jelep La Pass between Tibet and India. Merchants used this road to transport Asian merchandise to Persia and points farther west.

China

North of the Himalayas is the huge, high plateau of Tibet. This region is covered with lakes created by glaciers. Winters in Tibet can be very cold and snowy, and the rugged terrain kept the area sparsely populated and ensured that the people living there were isolated from other areas. North of Tibet is the Takla Makan Desert, a sandy, barren area. East of the Takla Makan is the larger Gobi desert, which extends north into Mongolia.

Eastern China is much wetter and more fertile. Many rivers run from west to east, originating in the Tibetan highlands or the Himalayas and emptying into the Pacific. These include the Pearl, the Hai, the Yangtze, and the Yellow rivers. China has coasts on the Gulf of Tonkin, the South China Sea, the East China Sea, and the Yellow Sea.

The Yangtze River in southern China is China's longest river. It begins in the Tibetan Plateau and enters the Pacific Ocean near the site of the modern city of Shanghai. The Yangtze basin is warm and wet and has a stable temperate to subtropical climate. Rain falls year-round, though about half of the annual rainfall occurs in the three months of summer. The soil is very fertile, making this area one of the first places that humans domesticated plants, starting around 8000 B.C.E. The river had become a major transportation route by the first century B.C.E.; ships could sail 600 miles upriver from the ocean, allowing foreign imports to reach well inland. Many cities rose up on the river's banks; one of the most important was modern Nanjing, built around 500 B.C.E. The Yangtze was wide and difficult to cross, making it an effective boundary between ancient kingdoms.

The Qin Ling Mountains north of the Yangtze divide northern and southern China. North of these mountains is the Yellow River valley. The land surrounding the Yellow River is buffeted by the cold, dry winds blowing east from the central Asian plains. The soil here is fertile, and early humans domesticated crops here as well, starting around 8000 B.C.E. For centuries the Yellow River region was richer and more populated than the Yangtze River valley, despite the Yangtze's warmer climate; the Yangtze gained prominence starting in the Han Dynasty between 202 B.C.E. and 220 C.E.

Summer rains in the Yellow River region are unreliable, and winters can be severe. The climate is harsh and unstable, prone to droughts and unexpected violent floods, both of which killed millions of people over the centuries. China was afflicted with numerous severe droughts during its ancient history. Writings from the sixth century B.C.E. mention techniques for coping with drought and methods of praying for rain, some of them suggested by the philosopher Confucius. Rulers also put a great deal of work into holding back floods.

Northeast China, called Manchuria in the 20th century, was heavily forested in ancient times. The climate in this region varies widely from season to season. Summers are very hot and rainy, as Pacific rain blows in from the southeast. In the winter winds blow from the northwest, bringing Siberian cold; the winds are dry, so little snow falls.

The Korea Peninsula juts southeast into the ocean from northeast China. It is separated from China by the Yalu River and a mountain range. North of Korea is the Sea of Japan; south of it is the Yellow Sea and Korea Bay. The Korea Strait separates Korea from Japan. Korea's climate is similar to that of northeast China, with warm, wet summers and cold, windy winters. Northeast Korea is mountainous, but the rest of the peninsula consists of flat, fertile plains. Rivers flow southwest from the mountains, providing water and floodplains suitable for rice cultivation.

Siberia and Mongolia

Siberia stretches all the way across the northern portion of Asia from the Ural Mountains to the Pacific. Eastern Siberia consists of grasslands with some marshy areas. The central Siberian plateau has a number of lakes. The ground in northern Siberia is permafrost, earth that never thaws, even in the summer. The northern coastline of Siberia lies along the Arctic Ocean. Siberia has always been known for its harsh climate and extreme winters, which have discouraged settlement. Few people aside from some nomadic herders attempted to live there in ancient times. The land is covered with ice and snow for half the year, most of the rivers and lakes are frozen for months at a time, and winter temperatures in modern times reach minus 90 degrees Fahrenheit.

Japan

Japan is a chain of islands stretching along the Pacific coast of mainland Asia from just south of Sakhalin Island in the north to Okinawa in the south. Although the archipelago contains around 3,000 islands, four large islands make up the main body of Japan. These are Hokkaidō, Honshū, Shikoku, and Kyūshū. All of Japan is mountainous and experiences frequent earthquakes; several volcanoes were active there in ancient times. Most of Japan was covered with forests.

Hokkaidō is the northernmost island of the chain and has the coldest climate. The Sea of Okhotsk lies off its northeast coast, and it is separated from the island of Sakhalin (now part of the Russian Federation) by a narrow strait. This strait was one of the two main points of entrance to Japan in ancient times. Hokkaidō has the highest mountains in Japan. It was heavily forested in the past, making it difficult for people to travel in the interior.

Honshū is the largest island with a range of latitudes. Its western coast is on the Sea of Japan, and its east coast is on the Pacific Ocean and the Philippine Sea. The western side of Honshū receives winter winds from the northwest; it has colder weather and receives more snow than the eastern side. The central mountains have a mountainous climate, with cold, snowy winters and hot, humid summers as well as a large temperature difference between night and day. On the Pacific coast summers are hot and humid, and winters are warmer than in the west; the central mountains block the western winds, so this region receives its weather from the Pacific to the southeast. All of Honshū is covered with mountains except for the low-lying marshy area where the city of Tokyo was founded. Mount Fuji, Japan's most famous volcano, is in central Honshū.

The southern islands of Kyūshū and Shikoku have warm, wet climates. The islands that stretch south from Kyūshū are even warmer and wetter, with a subtropical climate. They are at particular risk of tropical storms and typhoons (tropical cyclones). Southwestern Kyūshū is separated from Korea by a narrow strait; this was the other spot where people entered the islands from mainland Asia.

The ample rainfall and fertile volcanic soil made most of Japan a good place to grow rice and other crops, though the mountains and forests did present obstacles to travel and agriculture. Geographical isolation, however, slowed the development of Japanese culture. Japanese people did not learn about agriculture until around 300 B.C.E. and did not appear in contemporary histories until the first century C.E. Japan's separation from mainland China affected cultural practices; Japanese people adopted Chinese culture and writing as their own, but they transformed them into something completely different.

Mainland Southeast Asia

Mainland Southeast Asia lies on a peninsula south of the southeastern part of China. This area includes the modern countries of Myanmar, Thailand, Laos, Vietnam, Cambodia, and Malaysia. The Gulf of Tonkin and the South China Sea lie off the east coast of Vietnam. The Gulf of Thailand lies to the south of Thailand and Cambodia and to the east of the Malaysian isthmus. To the west of Southeast Asia are the Andaman Sea and the Bay of Bengal. The extensive coastline gave ancient people easy access to the sea, and they became expert sailors, sailing to islands south and east of the mainland. Southeast Asian societies also traded with India, and Southeast Asian ports often served as middle stages for the transport of goods between India and China; trade was vigorous during the first five centuries C.E.

Several rivers flow through this region. The Irrawaddy flows south from the northern mountains of Myanmar and empties into the Bay of Bengal; its delta is large, fertile, and well watered, making this area a prime location for human settlement. The Mekong River originates in the mountains of southern China, flows through northern Myanmar, and crosses Laos, Thailand, and Cambodia before reaching southern Vietnam, where it creates a vast delta before emptying into the ocean. In ancient times this delta was one of the most productive agricultural regions in all Asia. The upriver stretches of the Mekong flow through mountainous terrain, creating rapids and waterfalls; the lower stretches are more placid and easily navigable. The Red River flows from China to northern Vietnam, where it also forms a fertile delta near the modern city of Hanoi.

This region has a tropical climate, with warm weather year-round except in the mountains. The monsoons affect the weather, creating an annual rainy season; ancient farmers and sailors relied on the predictable weather and winds. Because of its proximity to China, the region was readily colonized by Chinese people moving southward. These Chinese brought with them agriculture, which was easily adapted to the Southeast Asian climate and terrain, and their own culture, which local people quickly adopted.

Indonesia, New Guinea, and the Philippines

South of mainland Southeast Asia lies maritime Southeast Asia, a huge collection of islands between Asia and Australia. Most of these islands are mountainous but have fertile soil and ample rainfall to grow crops. People living in these areas adapted the landscape to create fields; they dug terraces on many hillsides to create flat fields for their rice and other crops.

The sea was essential to the dissemination of culture and trade. Whether these islands were heavily populated and developed complex civilizations depended very much on how close they were to the mainland and to one another. Generally the closer a location was to China, the more likely that it would be exposed to Chinese culture and agriculture. The remoter islands never acquired much technology in ancient times. Java and the Philippines were densely populated and had some educated residents; Borneo and Sulawesi were not.

The Strait of Malacca separates Malaysia from the Indonesian island of Sumatra. Sumatra is a large island, mountainous on its southern side and flat everywhere else. The Indian Ocean lies to the south of Sumatra. To the west of Sumatra is the island of Java; the Java Sea lies to its north. To the east of Java lie the islands of Bali, Lombok, Sumbawa, Flores, Timor, and many others.

This region is part of the Pacific "ring of fire," a chain of active volcanoes that circle the Pacific Ocean. The volcano Krakatoa is one of the most famous. It lies in the straits between Java and Sumatra. The Javanese *Book of Kings* describes an event that may have been a 416 C.E. eruption of Krakatoa, though geologists are not sure this happened. Krakatoa seems more likely to have erupted in 535 C.E., disrupting the global climate for several years.

To the east of the Indonesian archipelago lies New Guinea, a giant island. New Guinea is very mountainous. Although it has a tropical climate, the hilltops can be cool. The terrain is extremely rugged, and travel through the interior is difficult. As a result, people living there in ancient times tended to be isolated from one another, to the point that islanders developed numerous different languages that were all mutually unintelligible.

OCEANIA

The Pacific Ocean is home to numerous islands. These islands were gradually populated during ancient times, as people set out from their homes in boats. Over the years humans traveled by boat to the far-flung islands of the Pacific. They started with the closest islands and moved from there farther afield. Samoa was settled around 1200 B.C.E.; Hawaii and Easter Island were much later, around 500 C.E.

The island group called Micronesia lies to the east of the Philippines. The Marshall Islands lie east of Micronesia. East of Papua New Guinea are the Solomon Islands, Vanuatu, Nauru, and New Caledonia. Farther east are Fiji, Samoa, Tonga, Kiribati, the Cook Islands, Tahiti and French Polynesia, the Marquesas Islands, and Pitcairn Island. Hawaii lies far to the north of these, and Easter Island far to the east.

Pacific islanders were expert seafarers. Boats were the only way to travel among the islands, and people regularly set out in outrigger canoes for voyages that lasted several days. They navigated by the stars and the sun. They also used boats at home for fishing. People could not inhabit new islands without food; when they went on voyages of settlement, they brought with them their agricultural and hunting habits, adapting them to local conditions. This practice did not always result in balanced or adequate diets. Many groups of islanders were extremely isolated from outside influences and hence developed their own unique cultures.

AUSTRALIA AND NEW ZEALAND

Australia is a continent south of Indonesia and New Guinea. It is separated from Asia by the Arafura Sea, the Timor Sea, and the Torres Strait. The Indian Ocean lies to its west, the Southern Ocean to its south, and the Tasman Sea, Coral Sea, and Pacific Ocean to its east. The Great Barrier Reef, a giant coral reef, runs over 1,200 miles along the northeast coast.

The continent is mostly flat. The majority of the mainland consists of several plateaus of limestone with some highlands in the coasts and in the very center. The Nullarbor Plain on the southern coast is one of the flattest places on earth. The Simpson Desert in the eastern central area has numerous salt basins. A chain of mountains called the Great Dividing Range runs along the eastern coastline. The Australian Alps

MICRONESIA, MELANESIA, AND POLYNESIA

The islands of the South Pacific are divided into three groups: Micronesia, Melanesia, and Polynesia. The native populations of these island groups look very different from one another. Melanesians have dark skin and tightly curled dark hair and resemble Australian aborigines. Micronesians have dark skin, somewhat lighter than that of Melanesians, and straight or wavy dark hair. Polynesians are taller than Micronesians and Melanesians; they have light skin, straight or wavy dark hair, and Asian facial features. How these ethnic populations arose where they did is very much a function of geography.

Melanesia ("black islands") lies south of Micronesia. It includes Papua New Guinea, Fiji, Vanuatu, and the Solomon Islands. Melanesia was first populated around 38,000 B.C.E. by dark-skinned people who traveled there from Southeast Asia. These people probably descended from humans living in Java (in Indonesia) at least a million years ago, giving them time to evolve features typical of people living in the tropics, such as dark skins. Micronesia ("small islands" in Greek) lies in the western Pacific northeast of Australia. This region was also colonized by dark-skinned people from Asia around 28,000 B.C.E.

Polynesia ("many islands") is a much bigger region to the east of Micronesia and Melanesia. It was populated much later, between 1600 B.C.E. and 500 C.E. Polynesia's population came from China. (Historians refer to these people by their language group, Austronesian). The Austronesian people had a fertile homeland and mastered agriculture early, allowing them to spread out from their homeland. They moved into Taiwan and Southeast Asia and displaced the native populations there; they then built boats and started sailing east.

The peoples of Melanesia were firmly ensconced in their homes, with solid agricultural systems, and they managed to keep their homelands despite the invasion of technologically advanced Austronesian invaders. New Guinea's forbidding geography helped isolate its natives and preserve their ethnic features. Micronesians seem to have mixed more with the Chinese. Polynesia, however, had no native inhabitants, so the Austronesian colonists furnished all ethnic stock. For this reason, Polynesians look East Asian.

lie in the southeast corner. The island of Tasmania lies south of this area; its mountainous terrain is a continuation of the Australian Alps. Tasmania is covered with temperate rain forest. East of the mountains is a narrow coastal plain that receives regular rainfall.

Because of its extreme isolation, Australia did not see an influx of settlers in the ancient period. Its aboriginal inhabitants apparently arrived over land bridges attached to Southeast Asia more than 40,000 years ago; the bridges were covered by water soon thereafter, and Australia's human population evolved by itself. The only exception was the region of the Torres Strait and Queensland, both close to Indonesia and New Guinea; the people here had more contact with Asia and were culturally different from the aborigines.

Australia's climate presented major difficulties to human settlers. Aside from the eastern and northern coastal areas, most of the land is desert; it receives little or no rainfall, and there are very few sources of water. Aboriginal people learned techniques for surviving in the desert, but these required great ingenuity. Agriculture was impossible on most of the continent, owing to the dryness and the poor soil. Northern Australia has a tropical climate similar to that of neighboring New Guinea and Indonesia. It has rain forests, mangroves, and other woodlands; in ancient times the rain forests on the Cape York Peninsula contained a huge number of plant species.

New Zealand is an archipelago formed by a pair of large islands and numerous small ones 1,250 miles to the southeast of Australia, separated from the Australian continent by the Tasman Sea. New Zealand extends about 1,000 miles from northeast to southwest. Both islands are mountainous and volcanic. Most of the land was covered with forests in ancient times. New Zealand was home to many unique plants and animals that evolved in isolation from other species. The climate is temperate; the southern island is wetter and cooler than the northern island.

EUROPE

BY PETER BOGUCKI

The study of ancient European society depends on an understanding of the ancient environment. Archaeology, especially prehistoric archaeology, is very closely related to environmental science and geography, and archaeologists work closely with the botanists, climatologists, and geologists who provide information about the ancient environment. The environment, which includes climate, vegetation, fauna, drainage, and soils, provided prehistoric peoples with resources for economic and social development but also placed constraints on their activities.

MAJOR DIVISIONS OF EUROPE

The two environmental zones that have the most relevance for ancient Europe are the Mediterranean evergreen zone and the temperate deciduous forest. A third major European environmental zone, consisting of the northern boreal coniferous forest of northern Scandinavia and European Russia and the treeless zones of northern Scandinavia, did not figure prominently in the major developments of European prehistory.

The Mediterranean evergreen zone encompasses most of the regions that are now Greece, Italy, and Spain along with the southern coast of France and the Adriatic coast of Croatia and Albania. The vegetation is the result of an arid summer and winter rain. The vegetation in this zone must retain foliage in the winter in order to grow, and its deep roots and thin leaves reduce evaporation during the summer drought. Today only remnants of this natural vegetation remain, owing to grazing and agriculture.

The temperate deciduous forest encompasses most of western, central, and eastern Europe, including the British Isles and southern Scandinavia up to about latitude 60 degrees north. Its vegetation consists primarily of broad-leaved trees, such as oak, elm, linden, alder, and beech, that grow in the summer and shed their leaves in the winter. In modern times only small tracts of the primeval European deciduous forest remain, surrounded by farmland, industry, and towns.

KEY REGIONS

Within Mediterranean and temperate Europe are several geographical zones that had particular significance for ancient European societies. At many points during the last 10,000 years, these regions had distinct cultural personalities but were not so separate from their neighbors that connections could not be perceived as well. Greece, including Crete and the islands of the Aegean all the way to western Turkey, was one such area with a distinctive cultural personality during later prehistoric times. A distinctive sequence of prehistoric cultures culminated in the civilizations of the Bronze Age and Classical Greece (480–320 B.C.E.).

Italy, including Sicily, forms another distinct unit of cultural geography when linked with the coastal areas of Croatia and Albania across the Adriatic Sea, though the Apennine spine of Italy divides this area even further. A sequence of prehistoric cultures culminated in the Etruscan and Roman civilizations.

The Iberian Peninsula, cut off from continental Europe by the Pyrenees Mountains, is the third major subdivision of Mediterranean Europe. Although the prehistoric societies of this region did not culminate in urban civilization, their artifacts and settlements have a very distinctive character that reflects their distance from the other societies of both Mediterranean and temperate Europe.

The mountain systems of central and eastern Europe, the ranges that make up the Alps and the Carpathians, were of significance for prehistoric society in temperate Europe insofar as they formed barriers that needed to be crossed and that in turn separated other geographical zones from each other. "Ötzi," the famous frozen and mummified man found in the Alps in 1991, was attempting such a crossing. Later these ranges were also important as areas for the acquisition of raw materials, such as copper and salt, as well as for their lush upland pastures in their foothills.

The arc of the Carpathians encloses a bowl known as the Carpathian Basin, which is the territory of modern Hungary and adjacent areas. Part of this area is covered by open grassland, the Great Hungarian Plain, while elsewhere there are fertile floodplains. The Danube River runs through this area on its way to the Black Sea while the Tisza is an important tributary that attracted prehistoric settlement in its drainage.

East of the great curve of the Carpathians stretch the grasslands of Ukraine and southern Russia that form the western end of the vast Eurasian steppes. Since it occupies much of the area north of the Black Sea, this region is also called the Pontic steppe. The valleys of the major rivers that drain through this region—the Dniester, the Dnieper, and the Volga—were forested, but the areas between them were dry, cold grasslands. These natural grasslands provided rich grazing lands for livestock-herding peoples in prehistoric times and were also the region in which the horse was first domesticated.

The hills of central Europe contain the headwaters of many of the major European rivers, including the Danube, the Rhine, the Elbe, the Oder, and the Vistula. Among these hills are basins filled with very fertile soil called loess, which was deposited by winds during the ice age. Beginning with the earliest farming settlements, these basins were centers for prehistoric settlement throughout later prehistory. Flint outcrops in the hills were the source of raw material for stone tools.

North of the uplands is the North European Plain, which stretches from Holland across northern Germany and Poland into the Baltic states and Russia. The North European Plain was shaped by the ice age glaciers, either having been covered by ice or being buried in the sand and gravel that were deposited by melting ice in front of the advancing and retreating ice sheet. Sandy outwash plains, gravel and clay ground moraine, marshy hollows, small ponds and large lakes, and meandering streams characterize this flat area.

The Atlantic facade is the part of Europe whose environment is closely linked to the Atlantic Ocean. Western and northern France, Britain and Ireland, and much of the Benelux countries are all part of this zone. The sea provides not only the weather but also food, and the prehistoric inhabitants of this region were at home on the coast and on the water. Straits such as the English Channel and the Irish Sea were easily crossed with watercraft. Interior regions benefited from the rain and from the proximity of the sea as well.

The final geographical zone of temperate Europe with particular significance for ancient societies is southern Scandinavia, which encompasses modern Denmark, the southern third of Sweden, and the extreme southern tip of Norway, along with the Baltic islands of Gotland, Öland, and Bornholm. Southern Scandinavia, like the North European Plain, was also shaped by glaciers, but in addition it has a strong maritime influence from the North Sea and the Baltic Sea. Numerous estuaries and bays were locations for prehistoric fishing settlements while interior regions of Denmark and southern Sweden contained fertile plains. Gotland, in the middle of the Baltic sea, has its own distinctive character and a rich archaeological record reaching back to Stone Age seal hunters.

Ancient Climate and Environment

The prehistoric environment in these regions was far different from that of the present day. From the mid-19th century, scientists—geologists and botanists foremost among them—have been able to reconstruct the prehistoric environment. Analytical tools are continually improved, so there is still much that can be learned about the prehistoric environment in Europe.

The principal sources of data on the prehistoric environment come from landforms and sediments, their composition and structure, and the pollen and other biological elements they contain. Since much of Europe was shaped by glaciers and their meltwater, geologists can trace their advance and retreat through the relic landforms they left behind, like moraines and eskers. Other landforms are formed through erosion, which in turn can indicate increased rainfall. River terraces show ancient water levels and episodes of sedimentation and downcutting. The sizes of particles in sediments can reveal information about their transport and sorting.

One of the most important tools for the study of the ancient environment is pollen analysis. Each species of plant produces pollen that has a distinctive shape. The pollen is then blown away from the plant and eventually settles out of the atmosphere. When it falls into lakes and bogs, it sinks to the bottom, accumulates among the sediments building up, and is preserved. Botanists are able to extract cores from the sediments and study the range of pollen types and their quantity present in each layer. In this way they can reconstruct the vegetation around the lake or bog based on the proportions of different types of pollen. Broad regional changes in vegetation can also be traced on the basis of a sufficient number of samples. Changes in vegetation can also be correlated with changes in climate.

The scientific tools for the study of prehistoric environments would be of only limited value if there were not a means of dating them. Carbon-14 (radiocarbon) dating is the principal tool available to scientists to obtain dates from ancient sediments or pollen cores. This technique, developed in the late 1940s and improved dramatically in the 1980s, works best for samples between 48,000 B.C.E. and 1000 C.E. It involves the fact that the radioactive form of carbon, an isotope known as carbon-14, is absorbed by plants and the animals that eat them. When such organic remains are found, it is possible to measure how much carbon-14 remains and determine the age of the organic substance and the sediments in which it was found. The dates derived from carbon-14 cannot be expressed in precise years but are given in ranges of years within which the actual date lies.

Valuable information both for studying ancient climate and for dating comes from tree rings. Ancient timbers and old trees dredged from rivers or preserved in waterlogged sediments can be sampled to examine their growth rings. Thin rings indicate poor growing conditions, most often correlated with low rainfall and summer temperatures, while thick rings appear when the growing conditions are good. Patterns of thick and thin rings can be matched from one timber to another, and regional sequences of growth rings can be built up. Scientists have been able to develop over much of temperate Europe tree-ring sequences that cover thousands of years. Dates obtained from tree rings are often to an exact year or even season. For example, all the timbers used in a Bronze Age ceremonial monument on the coast of eastern England popularly known as "Seahenge" were cut in 2049 B.C.E., probably in the spring or early summer.

These are only a few of the techniques used for reconstructing the prehistoric environment. Recently ice cores from Greenland have provided important evidence that bears on the environment of ancient Europe. Land snails in ancient soils can show whether the landscape was forested or open. Computer modeling of ancient climates has revealed potential periods of increased rainfall and winds.

The End of the Ice Age

The environment and geography of ancient Europe are very much the product of the ice age, known as the Pleistocene. Even in areas that were not covered by ice, the presence of the ice sheets and the tundra and other periglacial conditions that extended in front of them influenced almost every corner of the continent. For example, the loess that fills the basins in the hills of central Europe and covers vast parts of the Carpathian Basin was deposited by winds sweeping up soils on the desolate unvegetated parts of western Europe and dropping it hundreds of kilometers to the east. Even Mediterranean Europe felt the presence of the ice in the form of colder temperatures and lower sea levels.

The ice sheets advanced and retreated many times over the course of the Pleistocene. Four major advances and retreats were punctuated by many minor ones. Although humans have inhabited parts of Europe since at least 700,000 B.C.E., this discussion traces the environmental changes during the final millennia of the Pleistocene and during the Holocene, the period of modern conditions during which we live today.

Around 17,000 B.C.E. the large ice sheet that had covered northern and parts of central Europe for thousands of years began to retreat from its maximum advance. The ice front ran in a line southeast from the North Sea across Denmark and northern Germany, reaching its southernmost point in southwestern Poland and then northeast across Belarus and Russia. Smaller glaciers were found in the Alps and in the Scottish Highlands. The ice retreated in fits and spurts, leaving debris and moraines in its wake across northern Europe. Except for mountain glaciers in northern Scandinavia, the

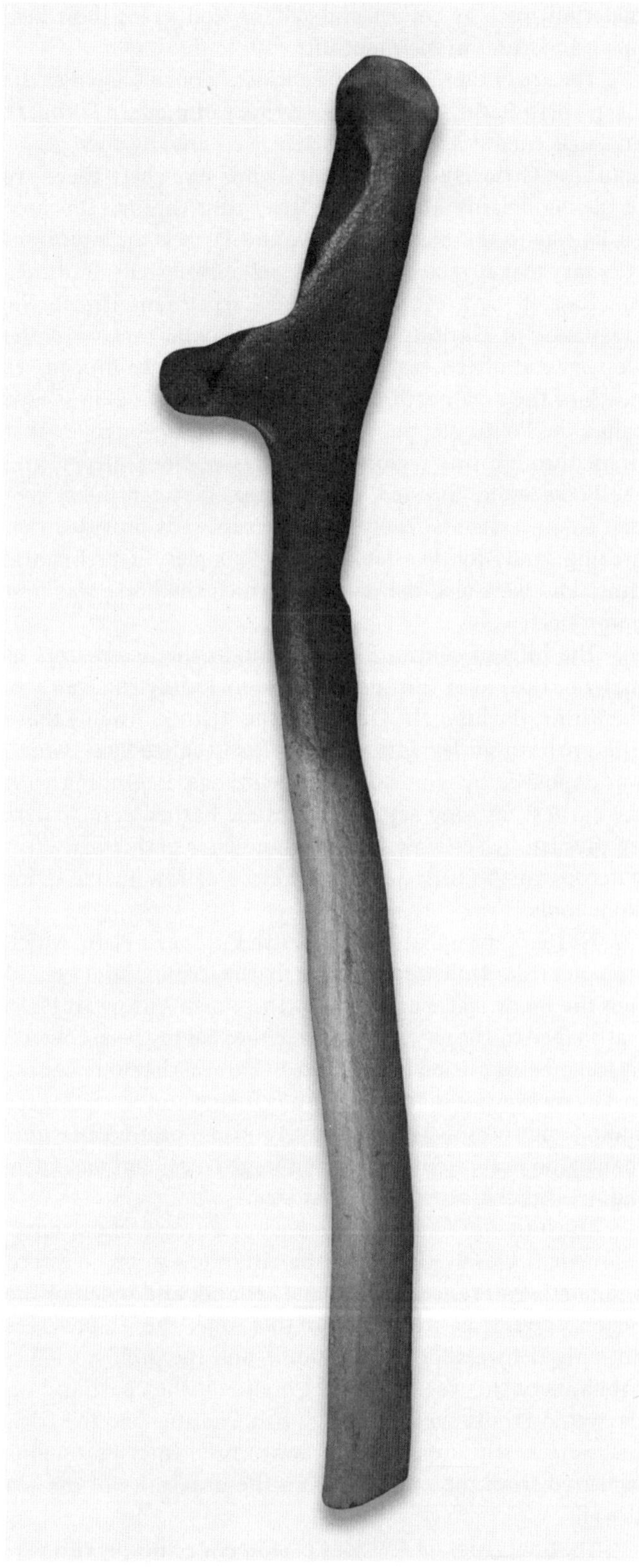

Ax made from reindeer antler found at Earls Barton, Northamptonshire, England, dating to about 8,500 B.C.E. and characteristic of similar items from Denmark, the Netherlands, and Germany; this is one of several finds that links Britain to Europe at the very end of the last ice age, when sea levels were still low and there was dry land between Britain and Europe. (© The Trustees of the British Museum)

Pleistocene Ice Sheet of northern Europe was almost completely melted by about 7000 B.C.E.

The melting of the glaciers meant that large amounts of water were released into the oceans, dramatically affecting sea levels and coastlines. The phenomenon of rising and falling sea levels is known as eustasy. Postglacial eustasy caused sea levels to rise over 100 meters, drowning the continental shelves of North America and Europe. In the Mediterranean, the northern Adriatic sea, which had been a large plain, was inundated. The entrance to Cosquer cave in southern France with its spectacular ice age paintings made between 25,000 B.C.E. and 17,000 B.C.E. is now just over 120 feet below the surface of the Mediterranean, whereas it was once high above the water.

In northern Europe eustasy had even more dramatic effects. In 8000 B.C.E. Britain was connected to the continent by a vast land bridge across the southern North Sea. It was possible for hunter-gatherers to walk from Poland to Yorkshire, getting wet only when they had to swim across the rivers. Over the next 5,000 years, rising sea levels inundated this terrain, creating the English Channel (which was previously a large Atlantic bay) and the current coasts of the North Sea. Recent research using seismic data produced by oil exploration has enabled archaeologists at the University of Birmingham to map a remarkable drowned landscape with river channels and hills, essentially the western end of the North European Plain.

In Scandinavia, which had borne the greatest burden of the Pleistocene ice sheets, another force was at work to counteract eustasy. Released from the weight of the ice, the earth's mantle rebounded upward, a process known as isostasy. The effects of isostasy are best seen in northern Denmark and in central and northern Scandinavia. In the northernmost reaches of Sweden, land is now about 820 feet higher than it was before the ice melted, and it is still rising. Near Stockholm, Neolithic sites far inland were previously on the coast, and hunter-gatherer shoreline sites are now 262 to 295 feet above sea level. Bronze Age rock carvings made on coastal boulders are now 82 to 98 feet above the water level.

The European vegetation and climate changed dramatically as the ice sheets retreated, for the tundra and other periglacial landscapes that lay before the ice front also moved northward. Warm and cold periods alternated during the last stages of the ice age. A rapid increase in temperature about 12,000 B.C.E., followed by general warmth, was suddenly interrupted by a sharp cold period, known at the Younger Dryas, about 9000 B.C.E., when tundra again characterized the landscape across the North European Plain and northern England. After about 600–700 years the climate warmed up again, and around 8300 B.C.E. a transition to an essentially modern climate and vegetation occurred across much of Europe. This transition marks the beginning of the postglacial period known as the Holocene.

As the ice sheet retreated northward, the reindeer herds that roamed the periglacial landscapes of western and central Europe also moved northward. The establishment of the Holocene forests brought the forest fauna that characterized later European prehistory, including red deer, roe deer, brown bears, beavers, wild horses, wild cattle, and wild pigs. Fish were abundant in the lakes and streams while flocks of waterfowl and solitary forest birds populated their preferred habitats. Along the coasts shellfish and seals were abundant. The result was an extraordinarily rich menu of resources for the hunters and gatherers who lived in these forests, known to archaeologists as Mesolithic societies. The change was not nearly so dramatic in Mediterranean Europe, but rising sea levels made it possible to take advantage of fish and shellfish that had previously been far offshore.

The Holocene Climatic Optimum

The onset of warmer temperatures resulted in the growth of forests across temperate Europe, first birch and later pine. By about 7000 B.C.E. the first oaks, elms, and hazel began to appear. During the millennium that followed, a type of woodland, known as "mixed oak forest" but whose primary constituent was linden, appeared throughout much of temperate Europe. In the Mediterranean zone, broad-leaved deciduous trees still dominated the woodland, although the typical evergreen forests and shrubs that characterize modern vegetation in this area were beginning to appear.

During the Holocene the climate became progressively warmer such that between 6000 and 5000 B.C.E. it reached what is called the Postglacial Climatic Optimum. Summer temperatures averaged about 2 degrees warmer than they are today, and the winters were very mild, yet abundant rainfall resulted in lush vegetation. Such favorable climatic conditions were a major factor in the spread of farming across much of temperate Europe, resulting in the introduction of domesticated plants and livestock. The climate of Mediterranean Europe, however, appears to have cooled off somewhat at the same time, according to recent evidence.

Cooler, Moister Climate

A sharp cold period called the Piora Oscillation, during which glaciers in the Alps again advanced significantly, brought the Postglacial Climatic Optimum to an end between 4000 and 3000 B.C.E. The climate of temperate Europe remained warm and dry between about 3000 and 1000 B.C.E. but then became progressively cooler and moister. By 700–500 B.C.E. temperatures were much lower than even 500 years earlier, though the weather in the British Isles remained relatively mild, and everywhere north of the Alps was much wetter and windier. Then the climate warmed again, such that the first few centuries C.E. were milder.

During these final millennia of prehistoric Europe the environment was irrevocably modified by human settlement, cultivation, and stockbreeding. Just after 4000 B.C.E. agriculture was introduced to Scandinavia and the British Isles, and by 3000 B.C.E. its spread throughout Europe was virtually complete. Once the most fertile lands were colonized, farming spread to poorer quality soil, which the invention of the plow made it possible to cultivate.

Deforestation

The most visible effect of cultivation and stockherding was the cutting of the forest for fields, pastures, construction material, and firewood. This deforestation appears in the pollen record as a dramatic and unnatural drop in the amount of tree pollen and a simultaneous increase in the amount of grass pollen. The ribwort plantain (*Plantago lanceolata*) flourishes in pastures, and its abundance in pollen samples from 4000 B.C.E. onward across temperate Europe reflects the high degree of deforestation. Deforestation in turn promoted soil erosion. When the climate turned wetter around 500 B.C.E., increased sediment deposition, or alluviation, occurred in valleys.

Blanket Bog Formation

In Ireland and parts of Britain the removal of the forests by early farmers caused soil nutrients to be washed away, making the soils more acidic. Heather and rushes grew on the acid soils, and in areas of poor drainage the acidity inhibited the decomposition of dead vegetation, which formed peat. Layer upon layer of peat accumulated over the next several millennia, burying entire landscapes. The field walls and house remains of early farmers at the Céide Fields in northern County Mayo in Ireland that date to 3500 B.C.E. were subsequently covered by blanket bog over the last 5,000 years, preserving them for archaeologists.

During the later part of European prehistory, resources that had very localized sources came into widespread demand. Key among these were metal ores, especially the copper and tin needed to make bronze, which came into use around 2500 B.C.E. Copper comes from sources in the Balkans, the Alps, Wales, and southwestern Ireland, while tin has a much more limited distribution. Cornwall and Iberia were most often mentioned as its sources. Since copper and tin have to be smelted together to make bronze, it was necessary for people to mine the ores and then transport them to the same location.

Gold was extracted from placer deposits in streams and then hammered to make ornaments. The goldwork of the Late Neolithic in southeastern Europe, most notably found at the Varna cemetery, and of the Bronze Age in Ireland, is truly remarkable. Even more noteworthy is that much of it was deliberately buried in graves or in ritual deposits in bogs.

Later in prehistory, around 800 B.C.E., iron came into widespread use, though bronze continued to be used extensively. Iron ores are more widely distributed and easily mined, but smelting the iron from its ore requires high temperatures and the addition of carbon and limestone to the furnace to complete the chemical reaction. Iron manufacture was thus technically more advanced than bronze production, despite the fact that the raw material is easier to obtain.

Another commodity that was widely in demand in prehistoric Europe was salt, which was used for food preservation. Along the coasts and near salt springs, salt was produced through evaporation. When prehistoric people found deposits of rock salt, they mined them. Some of the most famous Iron Age salt mines, dating between about 800 and 500 B.C.E., are found at Hallstatt, near Salzburg in Austria. The shafts and tunnels of the Hallstatt mines reached deep into the mountain, and artifacts found nearby reflect trade networks that stretched from the Baltic to the Mediterranean.

Among the materials obtained in exchange were amber from the Baltic and coral from the Mediterranean. Amber is fossilized pine resin, and it is still abundant along the coasts of Poland and Lithuania even today. Another Mediterranean substance highly desired by the Iron Age chiefs of central Europe was wine, for grape cultivation and fermentation had become major agricultural activities in the warmer parts of Europe by the last millennium B.C.E.

The demand for copper, tin, salt, gold, amber, and coral as well as agricultural products, tools, and weapons led to the establishment of regular trade routes. Wagons pulled by oxen and horses, and large watercraft that could cross open bodies of water, were crucial in sustaining the trade connections between the communities of prehistoric Europe. Large boats built from planks, like the one discovered near Dover in 1992, crossed between the continent and the British Isles. Along with the goods, people and ideas also moved.

Such was the world that the Romans encountered when they extended their empire into temperate Europe. The Roman historian Tacitus (ca. 56–117 C.E.) described the Iron Age geography of temperate Europe in his book *Germania* and of the British Isles in *Agricola*, although his information was not generally based on firsthand knowledge. A key geographical boundary in Europe at this time was the Roman imperial frontier, which ran roughly from the mouth of the Rhine to the mouth of the Danube and across the neck of the British Isles just below Scotland. Yet the rest of Europe was not ignorant of the Roman world. The spectacular gold artifacts that date to about 400 C.E., found in Sweden, were made from gold coins brought back by Scandinavian mercenaries who had served in the Roman army.

GREECE

by Christopher Blackwell

The ancient Greek world had the mainland peninsula, the site of modern Greece, at its center, surrounded by the Mediterranean Sea and including a cloud of islands to the east and west. The sea to the immediate west of the peninsula was known as the Ionian Sea, between the southern end of the Adriatic and the Mediterranean itself; to the east was the Aegean Sea. The Gulf of Corinth divides the peninsula almost in half, east to west, bounded on the east by the Isthmus of Corinth and opening on the west to the Ionian Sea, separating northern Greece from its southern territory, the Peloponnese.

Because water has a specific heat at least four times greater than land—that is, it takes on heat and gives up heat four times less readily—seas have a moderating effect on temperature. In territories around the Mediterranean, one consequence of this effect is to make latitude less significant in terms of climate and temperature than proximity to the sea. Greek cities near the coast enjoyed similar climates, whether they were far to the south in Crete or far to the north in Thrace. But inland areas might differ in climate greatly from coastal areas at the same latitude. So the city of Corinth, close to the sea both to its east and west, had a very different climate from Delphi, less than a hundred miles inland but farther from the water.

The Mediterranean world enjoys mild, wet winds from the Atlantic Ocean to the west during the winter and dry, relatively cool winds from the northeast during the summer; the ancients called these latter winds the Etesian winds (the Greek historian Herodotus, for example, in his discussion of the climate of Egypt). Long, hot, and dry summers, followed by mild, wet winters, provided long growing periods, which suited grains, olives, and fruit (olives and figs, especially).

This climate probably accounts for the location of the earliest great civilizations of the Greek world, the Minoan and Mycenaean civilizations of the Bronze Age (the third and second millennia B.C.E.). The remains of these cultures show that they flourished in coastal areas of the mainland and on the Greek islands. Food was plentiful there, both agricultural produce and seafood—the wall paintings and pottery found in Bronze Age settlements on Crete and in the Aegean islands feature many scenes of sea life and fishing. The large, open-air palaces of the Minoans suggest that those people took full advantage of the mild climate, spending their time largely outdoors. Classical Greek architecture, too, reflects the climate. The great temples of Athens and Olympia, for example, have very little room inside them; they were intended not to contain worshippers but to be the centerpiece for outdoor rituals.

Ancient culture profited from this climate and geography. The sea provided easy travel, and closely spaced islands made navigation easy. Thus, Greeks could mingle with each other and with the peoples of the civilizations to the east and south—Babylonians, Assyrians, Persians, and Egyptians. The mild weather encouraged public congregations outdoors, in marketplaces and in parks. So the Stoic philosophers got their name from meeting in public colonnades, or stoas, and Plato's famous school of philosophy, the Academy, got its name from the park in which the philosophers met, the Akademe at Athens.

Highlands and Lowlands

A spine of mountains runs the length of the Greek peninsula, from north to south, from the northern highlands between Macedonia (in the northeast) and Epirus (in the northwest), including Mount Olympus, down through Phocis (the site of the famous sanctuary of Apollo at Delphi, on the slopes of Mount Parnassus), and reemerges south of the Gulf of Corinth to form the highlands of Arcadia in the Peloponnese. These mountainous regions have a climate similar to that of the more northerly parts of continental Europe—including regular snowfall in the winter months. These mountain ranges are the result of the intersection of tectonic plates, whose regular shifting makes the whole of the Greek world subject to earthquakes, accounting for the volcanic activity in the Aegean.

The majority of the population of Greece has always lived in the lowlands, near the coast, but both mountains and coastal plains played an important role in the lives of the people of ancient Greece. The mountains, less prone to drought in winter, provided grazing for livestock, mostly smaller animals like sheep, pigs, and goats, but cattle as well. Shepherds, goatherds, and swineherds would pasture their flocks in the mountains during the summer and bring them down to the plains, near the inhabited areas, during the winter. The nomadic life of these pastoral workers led to their status as both "insiders," important members of the community, and "outsiders," living at the margins of communities, a status that plays an important role in the literature of ancient Greece. Figures such as Eumaeus, the "noble swineherd" of Homer's *Odyssey*, and the shepherd of Sophocles' *Oedipus the King* provide insights into the workings of dysfunctional communities by virtue of the characters' marginal status.

The mountains were forested, providing fuel for heat, timber for building houses and ships, and other important forest products, such as oak tannin, used for curing hides into leather. As the population increased, though, during the first half of the first millennium B.C.E., overuse of this resource led to deforestation. By the fourth century B.C.E. ancient writers were commenting on the relative scarcity of wood. A character in Plato's *Critias* says of Greece in the early fourth century that "there are some mountains which now have nothing but food for bees, but they had trees no very long time ago, and the rafters from those felled there to roof the largest buildings are still sound." This scarcity of timber affected the shipbuilding industry especially—the famous "cedars of Lebanon" became an important import during the Classical Period.

The coastal lowlands hosted most of the population and most of the land for growing crops. While the mountains provided animal products—meat, milk, and leather—the lowlands provided grains, fruits and vegetables, and olives, whose oil was not only an important source of fat and calories for the ancient Greeks but also a source of light when burned in lamps, hygiene when used as soap, and mechanical lubrication.

Geography and Travel by Land

There are no navigable rivers in Greece. In antiquity a few rivers could convey boats a short distance from the sea, but Greece had nothing equivalent to the Seine, the Danube, the Volga, or the Mississippi, comfortable thoroughfares for travel and communication. Those rivers that existed were narrow and shallow, and tended to swell to raging torrents during the rainy winter and spring, as snow melted off the mountains, only to dry to trickles or dry up altogether during the dry summer. This lack of rivers, combined with the mountainous terrain, made commerce and communication by land extremely difficult and expensive. Travel by land tended to hug the coasts, moving north and south along the Ionian and Aegean coasts and east and west along the coast north of the Gulf of Corinth. This restriction of land travel to a few routes helps explain why battles occurred in the same places, century after century. Thermopylae, for example, a site where the north-south road from Boeotia and Thessaly passes through a narrow pass between the mountains on the west and the sea on the east, was the site of battles between Greeks and Persians in the fifth century B.C.E., among Greeks in the fourth century B.C.E., and between Romans and Seleucids in the second century B.C.E. During the Roman Empire the main Roman roads bypassed the Greek peninsula altogether, passing to the north.

The Ionian Sea

Along the western coast of the Greek peninsula, the Ionian Sea offered the least hospitable waters for travel. Close to the coast, protected by the chain of islands just off Epirus, the sea offered relatively predictable winds—blowing toward the land during the day and blowing out to sea at night. The islands offered many protected harbors, and there was easy entry to the protected waters of the Gulf of Corinth.

But to the west, beyond the single chain of islands off the coast, there are no islands between Greece and Italy and none south between the Peloponnese and Africa. To the north the Ionian Sea joins the Adriatic where the latter narrows, like a funnel, between the heel of Italy and what is now Albania. Because of this narrow passage between the seas, the same Etesian winds that brought cool, dry summers could whip up sharp storms in the channel. The passage between Italy and Greece, between Greek Corcyra (modern Corfu) and Italian Brundusium (modern Brindisi), was notoriously dangerous, both because of these sudden storms and because ships would lose sight of land, both to the east and to the west, at the midpoint of the passage.

A letter from the Roman Cicero to his friend Tiro, written in November 50 B.C.E., illustrates the fickle nature of the sea here, which could afford an easy passage or sudden death. Cicero wrote in *Epistulae ad familiares* (Letters to Friends), "At Corcyra we were detained by bad weather till the 15th. On the 16th we continued our voyage to Cassiope, a harbor of Corcyra, a distance of 120 *stades* [about 12 miles]. There we were detained by winds until the 22nd. Many of those who in this interval impatiently attempted the crossing suffered shipwreck. On the 22nd, after dinner, we weighed anchor. Thence with a very gentle south wind and a clear sky, in the course of that night and the next day we arrived in high spirits on Italian soil at Hydrus, and with the same wind next day—that is, the 24th of November—at 10 o'clock in the morning we reached Brundisium."

The Aegean Sea

The Aegean Sea, to the east of the Greek peninsula, is more hospitable. The Etesian winds are predictable out at sea during the summer, and the inshore and offshore breezes during the day and night are predictable near the coast. The many islands of the Aegean serve to reduce fetch, the distance wind travels over water unimpeded, reducing the maximum size of waves. The eastern coast of Greece is protected for a long stretch by the island of Euboea, and that coast, as well as the coasts of the many islands, provides innumerable protected harbors. The dry summer ensures good visibility by day and night for navigation (which was not a highly developed science among the Greeks of antiquity).

Storms, when they did arise, could be treacherous, producing sharp, unpredictable waves in the shallow waters and arising without much evident warning in the landlocked sea. Ships at sea could find themselves being blown downwind toward a lee shore, which often was rocky and steep. During the rainy, and windier, winter months the ancient Greeks regarded the sea as mostly impassible. The festival of Dionysia at Athens, for example, which was that city's occasion to show itself off to people from the rest of Greece, was held in March, specifically because that month marked the beginning of the "sailing season." But despite the unfriendly winter months, the Aegean served as a crossroads of commerce between the Greeks and the peoples of Asia and Africa. Greeks have been famous for their trade by sea, from Odysseus of Homer's *Odyssey* to the Onassis dynasty of the present.

Epirus (Northwestern Greece)

Epirus was the northwestern territory of Greece, west of the Pindus Mountains. It enjoyed heavy rainfall and was known in antiquity for its rich forests and ample pasturage for grazing livestock. Dodona, a flat plateau, in Epirus was the site of a famous sanctuary of Zeus, who was said to utter oracles from within an oak tree. According to Homer's *Odyssey*, the hero Odysseus's wealth was largely in the form of livestock, which grazed on the mainland, in Epirus and Amphilochia, just to the south, while the hero's own home was on the island of Ithaca.

Macedonia (Northeastern Greece)

To the east of the Pindus Mountains was Macedonia. High and rugged in the west, it descended to fertile plains near the Thermaic Gulf, which opens into the northwest Aegean. Macedonians were looked on as only semicivilized by the southern Greeks during antiquity, but by the end of the fifth century B.C.E. the people of Macedonia had embraced high Greek culture. The Athenian poet Euripides retired to the Macedonian court, and 50 years later Philip II hired the philosopher Aristotle to tutor his son, Alexander. To the south of Macedonia was Mount Olympus, almost 9,600 feet high, whose summit, often wrapped in clouds, was the mythological home of the Greek gods.

Thessaly, Phocis, Boeotia (Central Greece)

South of Mount Olympus, on the east coast of Greece, was Thessaly. Homer calls this territory "Horse-rolling Thessaly," and its flat, grassy plains were among the relatively few areas conducive to raising horses and training cavalry. The soil of Thessaly, carried down as sediment by snowmelt from Olympus, was extremely fertile, and in antiquity Thessaly was an exporter of food. Between Thessaly and the area to the south, Boeotia, the mountains came close to the sea, near the gulf of Magnesia, forming a narrow pass through which ran the main road. This pass was also the site of geothermal springs, giving it the name *Thermopylae*, or "Hot Gates."

Boeotia, the territory of the ancient cities of Thebes and Plataea, was ringed by mountains, including Mount Helicon to the west, site of an important cult of the Muses, the nine daughters of Zeus and patronesses of the arts. Poetry associated with this cult claims that the Muses taught the art of singing to the rustic farmer Hasid, making him an epic poet and entrusting him with agricultural and theological wisdom. Boeotia was fertile, although its climate tended toward extremes of heat in the summer and damp cold in the winter. Its main city, Thebes, was the home of the poet Pindar, the site of many of the myths that are the subject of Greek tragedy, and a great military power during the fourth century B.C.E. under the generals Epaminondas and Pelopidas. To the south of Thebes was Plataea, long an important ally of Athens, farther to the south, and famous for its participation in the Greco-Persian Wars at the beginning of the fifth century B.C.E.

West of Boeotia, in the high mountains around Mount Parnassus, was the territory of Phocis, site of Delphi. The ancient Greeks considered Delphi to be the center of the world, the site where Apollo spoke to humans through his oracle. The sanctuary at Delphi was considered a possession of all Greeks, was governed by an international council, and contained treasuries belonging to many individual cities, in which were stored the gifts that those cities had dedicated to the god. Even non-Greek nations sent gifts to Apollo, most notably King Croesus of Lydia, whose lavish dedications are described in Herodotus's history.

Attica (the Southeastern Mainland)

The southeastern corner of the Greek peninsula, north of the Isthmus of Corinth, was Attica, the region around the city of Athens. Originally a region of many independent cities, the ancient Greeks claimed that the legendary king Theseus united the area into a single unified political entity with Athens at its head. Attica is bounded by the sea to the east and south. It connects with Boeotia to the north. To the west is Eleusis, once an independent city but said to have been conquered by Theseus. Farther to the west is Megara, a neighboring state and often an enemy of Athens. Just offshore to the south are the islands of Salamis, the site of the great victory of the Greeks over the Persian fleet in the 480s B.C.E., and Aegina, another Athenian possession.

The Peloponnese (the Southern Peninsula)

The southern peninsula of Greece, the Peloponnese, is connected to the northern mainland by the Isthmus of Corinth, whose principle city, Corinth, was an important center of trade. There is a canal across the Isthmus today, but in antiquity any commerce moving between east and west by sea would have either to make the (potentially dangerous) passage around the south of the Peloponnese or to stop at the Isthmus, unload cargo, and have the ships dragged across the land on rollers. This enterprise was profitable for the Corinthians, not least because the crews of these ships would be tempted to spend money in the city. Likewise, all north-south commerce by land, between the northern mainland and the Peloponnese, had to pass through Corinth. The Isthmus lies between the Gulf of Corinth to the west and the Saronic Gulf to the east. Immediately to its south is the area of the Argolid, named for its principal city of Argos.

The Argolid, site of the palace of Mycenae, was an important center during the Bronze Age. Another Bronze Age settlement on the coast, just across the Saronic Gulf from Athens, was Troezen, legendary birthplace of the Athenian king Theseus. The Argolid in antiquity was mostly self-sufficient, with access to the sea, fertile plains, and mountainous pasturelands to the west, as was its southern neighbor, Laconia, the region that included the ancient city of Sparta and the territory of Messenia. The Spartans, famous for their rigorous lifestyle and warlike abilities, had by the Classical Period reduced Messenia to a client-state, its population little more than slaves for the Spartans. As was often the case among ancient Greek cities, Sparta was regularly at war with its neighbor Argos, as Athens was with Megara.

The central Peloponnese, Arcadia, was isolated. High and rocky, far from the sea, it was a relatively sparsely inhabited land of forests and pastures, and the mythological home of wild spirits of the mountains. The main city of Arcadia was Megalopolis, in the south, closest to the sea, on the river Pamisus, which drained the high Arcadian plateau. To the west of Arcadia were Elis and Olympia. The latter was the site of the Olympic Games, in honor of Zeus, an international event founded in 776 B.C.E. and held every four years until closed by Theodosius, the Christian emperor of Rome, in 393 C.E. The games at Olympia are now the most famous of these ancient festivals, but there were many such events in antiquity: the Nemean Games in the Argolid, the Isthmian Games at Corinth, and the Pythian Games at Delphi in Phocis.

The Ionian Islands

The islands of the Ionian Sea offered protected ports; the western coast of Greece did not. So, most trade between the mainland of Italy and Greece came through the islands of Cephallenia, Zacynthus, Corcyra, and Ithaca. The island of Corcyra, modern Corfu, was especially prosperous. Its active trade to the east and west, combined with its high rainfall, led it to have the densest population of any area in ancient Greece. Corcyra was the site of a vicious civil war during the 430s B.C.E. that was one of the sparks which ignited the conflict between Athens and Sparta known as the Peloponnesian War.

The other islands of this area share similar characteristics. They are rocky and good for grazing, with easy access to the mainland, close by to the east. Ithaca was said to be home of Homer's hero Odysseus, though a precise identification between the real island and its poetic counterpart is impossible. Cephallenia was famous in antiquity for its pine forests, of which nothing remains today.

The Aegean Islands

The islands of the Aegean were even more inviting to settlement, combining the most attractive elements of the Mediterranean climate, the diversity of mountains and coastal plains in close proximity, with easy access abroad by sea. Aegina at the mouth of the Saronic Gulf, controlling access to the Argolid in the Peloponnese, Corinth on the Isthmus, and Megara and Attica on the mainland, was an early power until it came under Athenian control in the sixth century B.C.E.

The long island of Euboea, very close off the eastern coast of the mainland, was another early power in the Greek world. During the eighth century B.C.E. the cities of Lefkandi and Eretria sent out trade and settlements as far as Asia Minor and Sicily. By the Classical Period, however, Euboea had receded in importance after the rise of cities like Athens and Thebes.

The group of islands known as the Cyclades, because they form an uneven circle at the south end of the Aegean, is actually a continuation of the mountain range that runs down Euboea and across Attica. The islands of Naxos, Páros, Ándros, Delos, Syros, and Melos all possessed rich quarries of stone (which could be transported by sea much more easily than stone from landlocked quarries) as well as gold and silver. The islands' position in the path of trade between Greece, Asia, and Egypt ensured their prosperity.

The island of Thera (modern Santorini) was the site of prosperous settlement during the Bronze Age but was largely destroyed by a volcanic explosion during the 15th century B.C.E., an event, with the inevitable earthquakes and tsunamis radiating from it, to which many scholars point as the cause of the decline of Minoan civilization.

South of the Peloponnese the islands of Cythera and Anticythera form stepping stones from the Greek peninsula to the large island of Crete. Ships sailing from Greece could reach Crete without ever leaving sight of land, and Crete's coastline offers many safe harbors on the north side. The same is not true south of Crete; the island's southern shore is much less convoluted, and there are no islands for almost 200 miles southward toward the shores of Egypt and Libya.

Crete, then, was unified with the Greek world not only in climate but in culture and was the site of the earliest civilization of people speaking a language recognizable as Greek. Crete was legendary in antiquity as the home of King Minos, who was said to have ruled over a maritime empire and extracted tribute from Athens. It was for Minos that the Athenian inventor Daedalus built the labyrinth at Knossos.

The Islands of the Asian Coast

East and north from Crete the islands of Kasos and Carpathus form two more stepping stones toward the large island of Rhodes, which is within sight of the mainland of Asia Minor, near what is now southwestern Turkey, and was the territory of Caria in antiquity. Caria, and the city of Halicarnassus, was the birthplace of the historian Herodotus, who came to Athens to compose his ethnographic account of the peoples of the Greek world and the conflict between the Greeks and the Persians. Along the coast of Asia Minor, in the eastern Aegean, were the large, prosperous, and often powerful islands of Lesbos and Chios. These were prosperous in agricultural products and in culture, enjoying their ethnic relationship with the Greeks of the mainland and constant contact with the many peoples of Asia.

The deforestation noted in antiquity was not the only significant factor changing the ecology and environment of the Greek world since antiquity. Under Byzantine and Turkish rule, cultivation of both grapes and olives increased, since these were valuable export crops during the period of Roman rule and afterward. Both of these crops have deep taproots that do little to hold soil in place. The practice of polyculture, planting other crops amid the vines and olive trees, held erosion at bay for a time but increased grazing of goats among vineyards and orchards led to the loss of a vast amount of rich topsoil. The dry, rocky landscape of exposed limestone evident in Greece today would have seemed very unfamiliar to a Greek of the sixth century B.C.E.

Erosion also caused the silting up of the mouths of rivers, and erosion from southern Russia, into the Black Sea and thence into the Aegean, has altered coastlines. The city of Pella, Alexander the Great's capital in Macedonia, used to be accessible by boat from the Mediterranean but today is shallow and choked with boulders. A modern visitor to Thermopylae, to take another example, might wonder why this place was called a pass. Today the sea is several miles from the old coastal road while in the fifth century B.C.E. waves would have broken at the base of the roadbed.

ROME

by Amy Hackney Blackwell

The location of Rome combined a pleasant climate with good soil and other important advantages. The city was built on the Tiber River where it met with the smaller Anio (Aniene) River. Situated near the center of the Italian peninsula and close to the Adriatic coast, Rome was well placed to control both the peninsula and, ultimately, the lands surrounding the Mediterranean.

Rome was a hilly city. The ancient town was built on top of a hill on the east bank of the Tiber near a point where the river could be easily crossed because of an island in the middle of the stream. Before the founding of Rome itself, people lived in the area in smaller hilltop settlements; archaeologists have found evidence of towns dating to 1000 B.C.E. People built their homes on the hills for defense against attackers. These settlements gradually grew and spread into one another to cover the famous Seven Hills of Rome, an area that makes up about 4 percent of the modern city. The Seven Hills were the Palatine (traditionally believed to be the hill on which the legendary Romulus founded Rome), the Aventine, the Capitoline, the Quirinal, the Viminal, the Esquiline, and the Caelian. The lowlands between the Seven Hills were marshy in ancient times, but the residents had drained the marshes by the time Rome was known as a city.

Rome has a Mediterranean climate, with long, hot, dry summers and cool, wet winters. The climate appears to have been warmer in ancient times than it is today. The hot summers contributed to diseases in the densely populated city. Food-borne gastrointestinal diseases spread easily. The Tiber is a relatively short river, though it is the third-longest in Italy. It flows about 250 miles from its origin at Mount Fumaiolo in the Apennine Mountains to its mouth in the Tyrrhenian Sea. On its way it curls through the modern provinces of Tuscany and Umbria. After Rome the Tiber continues another 15 miles to the Tyrrhenian Sea. The Aniene meets it in the city. The Tiber and the Aniene provided Rome with two necessities: transportation and fresh water.

In its early days Rome had water adequate for its population from the Tiber and from local springs and wells. By the fourth century B.C.E., however, the growing city had to import some of its water from elsewhere. Romans began building aqueducts to bring water from distant streams. Many aqueducts took water from the Aniene River or its tributaries and brought it to locations in central Rome. One of the most famous was Acqua Marcia aqueduct, which transported water from the Aniene to the Capitoline Hill; it was known for water of high quality. (The city's sewers emptied directly into the Tiber, which somewhat disqualified it as a source of drinking water.)

Rome itself was too far from the sea to be a port. For shipping it used Ostia, the port city at the northern mouth of the Tiber. Romans believed that Ostia was founded by their fourth king in the seventh century B.C.E. Ostia was originally built to defend Rome from attackers sailing up the Tiber, but the port quickly took on much more commercial than military importance. River access from Ostia to Rome was easy, and most of Rome's grain and other goods imported from Mediterranean locales passed through Ostia on their way to the city. Starting with Tiberius, several emperors improved Ostia to better equip it for both shipping and military purposes. So much business passed through Ostia that the city became quite prosperous; some 50,000 people lived there in the second century C.E. When the empire ended, Ostia faded away, partly from lack of shipping and partly because the Tiber had gradually filled with silt over the centuries and had become unnavigable.

By the second century B.C.E. Rome either controlled or wanted to control all of Italy, which was already home to numerous peoples, such as the Etruscans. Italy occupies a long peninsula running northwest to southeast into the middle of the Mediterranean Sea. The peninsula resembles a high-heeled boot with the heel pointing to western Greece and the toe not quite touching Sicily. The Italian peninsula is mainly mountainous; only about a third of the land is flat. The largest flat area in Italy is the plain around the Po River in northern Italy. There were also marshlands in various areas, such as the Pontine Marshes that lay between Rome and Capua (a city north of Naples). When people settled in Italy, they clustered in locations where travel and agriculture were easy. Water transport on rivers and along the coastline was easier than land transport, so many settlements arose on rivers and near the sea.

Italy has an extremely long coastline relative to its land area. The total coastline is about 4,600 miles long. To the north of Corsica is the Ligurian Sea, which has its coast along the northwestern corner of Italy. The Tyrrhenian Sea lies along its southwestern coast, bounded by the islands Corsica, Sardinia, and Sicily. Southeast of the sole of the boot is the Ionian Sea. Along the northeast coast lies the Adriatic Sea. Italy's long coastline provided locations for numerous ports. Puteoli, on the north side of the Bay of Naples, was a major port for grain shipped from Egypt. Tarentum was a port city situated in the sole of the Italian boot. Like many southern Italian cities it was founded by Greeks. Brundisium, modern Brindisi, on the Adriatic coast in southern Italy, was the main port for embarkation to Greece and points east. The famed road known as the Appian Way went from Rome to Brundisium. The coastline also furnished spots for vacation homes for wealthy Romans who spent their summers at the seashore away from the heat and humidity of the crowded city.

The Apennine Mountains run from northwest to southeast down the center of the peninsula. Rocky but not as steep or rugged as the Alps, they never impeded traffic through the countryside nearly as much as high mountains like the Alps did. Well-traveled roads such as the Appian Way were built right over numerous hills. Nevertheless, people whose homes were separated from Rome by mountains found themselves culturally isolated from the city; Roman authors talk of the different diets and habits of people in the countryside. The physical barrier imposed by the mountains did have an advantage, however: it kept attackers from being able to march quickly across the entire peninsula. If Italy was attacked on one coast, the mountains would keep the attackers on that coast long enough for Rome to assemble its defenses.

The Apennines split Italy into two main geographic zones. The western side of the peninsula had fertile soils with ample phosphates and potash (minerals that enhance soils for plant cultivation) and easily navigable rivers such as the Tiber and the Arno. The east side had rivers that were narrow or dry in summer but swelled to floods in winter, carving gullies through the hillsides. The soil there was less fertile, and there was less of it: the mountains were closer to the sea and the flat coastal plain was narrow, in some places only about 20 miles wide. Throughout ancient times more people settled in the west than in the east.

The Po Valley in northern Italy was the largest patch of flat land on the peninsula. Before the Romans settled on the Po, the region was mostly marshland. These marshes helped deter the Carthaginian general Hannibal's invasion in 218 B.C.E., but they also made it difficult for Romans to live there because the ground was too wet to build roads and farms and the swamps incubated diseases such as malaria. During the first centuries B.C.E. and C.E. Romans developed techniques to drain swamps, using canals and dikes to channel and contain water. Rome's immediate vicinity was drained by the censor (a top government official) Marcus Aurelius Scaurus in 109 B.C.E. The emperor Augustus (r. 27 B.C.E.–14 C.E.) continued draining the area, intending to turn it into farmland. After the land was drained, the Po Valley became the richest agricultural area in the empire. The surrounding region was heavily forested with oaks and other hardwoods. The acorns from the oaks furnished ample fodder for a thriving pork industry. Much of the meat eaten in ancient Rome came from this area.

The length of the peninsula isolated north from south, resulting in the emergence a variety of cultures and languages throughout Italy before the rise of Rome. Southern Italy, especially the "heel" region called Apulia, was particularly isolated from events in Rome. Greeks settled in Apulia before the Romans conquered it in the third century B.C.E. Even during Roman times Apulia was never densely populated.

Italy's mountains included several active volcanoes, some of which remain active today. The most famous is Vesuvius, near Naples. Vesuvius erupted in 79 C.E., inundating the cities of Pompeii and Herculaneum with lava and ash. Mount Etna in Sicily erupted from time to time, including one eruption in 396 B.C.E. that was said to have prevented the Carthaginians from attacking the city of Syracuse and another in 251 C.E. that supposedly coincided with the martyrdom of the Christian saint Agatha. Ancient authors place Etna in many myths; the Cyclops (a one-eyed monster who appears in Homer's *Odyssey*) and the god of the forge, Hephaestus (Vulcan in Roman myth), both supposedly kept blacksmith shops beneath Etna. The Aeolian islands north of Sicily had several very active volcanoes, including Stromboli and Vulcano; these also were said to be the physical locations of mythical events. The presence of volcanoes was a sign of geological instability, and Italy suffered numerous earthquakes.

To the north of the Italian peninsula lay the Alps, a major but not insurmountable barrier to travel and attack. In summer travelers regularly crossed the mountains on foot trails, which were in use throughout the ancient period. Crossing the Alps in the winter was considered an extreme measure and required extensive preparation; when Julius Caesar brought his soldiers across the Alps to suppress the Gauls in the winter of 52 B.C.E., contemporary observers considered it evidence of brilliant generalship and courage. Regardless of season, Romans preferred to avoid the Alps entirely by traveling along the flatter coastline of Liguria. The Alps never entirely prevented attacks from the north, but they hampered and weakened invaders. For example, when Hannibal crossed the Alps to attack Rome in the autumn of 218 B.C.E., his passage through the mountains impressed the Romans but cost him about half his army and most of his war elephants.

The Italian peninsula had more climatic variation than the city of Rome. Coastal regions shared Rome's Mediterranean climate, with hot, dry summers and cool, wet winters. Southern areas were warmer than northern ones. The Adriatic coast had colder winters and hotter summers than the Tyrrhenian coast. Rainfall in most of the Italian peninsula was low and could be erratic; winter could bring severe rainstorms, but then no rain would fall at all during the summer, precipitating droughts. The Apennines had mild winters and hot summers. The climate in the Po Valley was semicontinental, with long, cold winters and warm, humid summers. The Alps in northern Italy had mountain weather, with warm summers and cold, snowy winters.

Mediterranean Sea

Italy's long coastline and many ports gave Rome access to the entire Mediterranean world. By the time of the empire, Rome controlled the whole Mediterranean shoreline. In ancient times travel was much faster by sea than by land. It was easier to ship large items by sea than to haul them overland; marble, for example, cannot easily be dragged over rough countryside in a wagon, but it moves quite nicely on a boat. A Roman army in Greece could sail to Egypt much faster than it could march.

In the immediate neighborhood, Sicily was so close to Italy as to be almost attached to it. From Sicily it was a short sail to Carthage and North Africa. Sardinia and Corsica were not as close but were still readily accessible. Sailing around the coastline that is now the French Riviera took travelers to Spain. To the east Greece was a quick voyage across the Ionian Sea. From there Roman travelers could make their way through the Aegean to ports in western Asia Minor or even voyage through the Sea of Marmara into the Black Sea. They could also sail along the southern coastline of Anatolia to ports in Asia Minor or in the Levant. By continuing to hug the coastline, sailors could go as far as Egypt.

The Mediterranean presented many challenges to seafarers. It was large enough that they were often out of sight of land and had to navigate by other means than coastal sightings. The winds were fickle, and it was almost always necessary to supplement wind power with human rowers. The weather was notoriously changeable, especially in winter;

winter travel could mean seasickness at best and shipwreck at worst.

Sicily, Sardinia, and Corsica

Sicily is a large island southwest of Calabria (the toe of the Italian boot. It is separated from Italy by the Strait of Messina, which is not quite 2 miles wide. This strait has always had rough waters; a natural whirlpool forms there and caused many shipwrecks of ancient sailors attempting to sail between Sicily and Calabria. This whirlpool and its accompanying rocks may have given rise to the legend of Scylla and Charybdis, two nautical obstacles faced by the hero Odysseus in Homer's *Odyssey*. Despite the dangers of the Strait of Messina, however, Sicily has always been fairly accessible by sea. It had several ports, notably the formerly Greek port of Syracuse in the southeast.

Sicily's location in the center of the Mediterranean made it a popular target for kingdoms looking for good colonies. Phoenicians, Carthaginians, and Greeks all lived there before the Romans took over the island in 242 B.C.E. Sicily has fertile soil and warm, sunny weather, ideal for growing grain. As a result Rome used it for centuries to supply grain to the city. The warm climate also attracted rich landowners who built sumptuous villas; one of the best preserved is the Villa Romana del Casale, built near Piazza Armerina in the fourth century C.E. and known for its elaborate mosaics.

Sardinia is a large island due west of the Italian peninsula across the Tyrrhenian Sea. Phoenicians traded with Sardinians beginning around 1000 B.C.E., and the island became a Carthaginian province around 500 B.C.E., but it was too remote for Carthage to administer effectively. Rome took Sardinia from Carthage in 238 B.C.E. Sardinia has a cooler climate than Sicily but equally fertile soil, and it, too, was a source of grain for Rome. Most of Sardinia's interior is mountainous. The mountains prevented Roman culture from spreading efficiently among the native people; Sardinians revolted frequently, and the geographical restrictions of the island made it impossible to entirely subdue them. The mountains contain many deposits of iron, copper, lead, and silver, all of which the Romans mined; mineral riches and agriculture made some areas of Sardinia quite prosperous.

Corsica, an island north of Sardinia, is considerably smaller than its southern neighbor. Etruscans and Carthaginians occupied it before Rome took it over around 231 B.C.E. Corsica's interior was mountainous and wild, and Rome never exercised complete authority over the people who lived there. Corsica's climate and landscape were conducive to forestry and shipbuilding but not to most forms of agriculture.

Climate and the Empire

Some historians believe that climate change was partly responsible for Rome's expansion from Italy into Europe, and then for the decline of the Western Roman Empire. Rome began to grow powerful while Europe's climate went through a warm period, and it fell when the climate suddenly grew colder several centuries later. Much of the empire's stability was due to Rome's ability to grow crops throughout its territory.

During the fourth century B.C.E. Italy was not especially warm and Rome was not particularly powerful. Celts raided Rome from the north in 390 B.C.E., marching straight down the peninsula through the Apennines. It seemed that they meant to settle in Italy. By 300 B.C.E., however, the Celts had moved back north. Historians believe that this retreat was necessitated by warmer weather that arrived in Europe during the fourth century B.C.E. As temperatures rose, the Mediterranean climate zone moved north as far as Burgundy in France. Celtic crops and living habits were based on a colder, wetter European climate, so the Celts returned north to find more amenable conditions.

The Romans moved into southern Europe in the wake of the Celts and established Roman-style farms growing wheat, millet, grapes, and olives. By 200 B.C.E. Mediterranean weather had reached southern France, and Rome had taken over that land. Rome created its first European provinces in the regions that had suddenly acquired a Mediterranean climate, Gaul and Spain.

Cisalpine Gaul ("Gaul on this side of the Alps") lay south of the Alps and north of the Apennines, in today's northern Italy; it encompassed the fertile Po Valley. During the Republic, this region was not considered part of Italy. The Rubicon River formed the border between Cisalpine Gaul and Italy. It was a symbolic as well as a physical border. To protect Rome from coups by its own military, Roman generals were forbidden by law from crossing the river with a standing army. When Julius Caesar took an army across the Rubicon in 49 B.C.E., all Romans knew that he had declared civil war.

Transalpine Gaul ("Gaul across the Alps") occupied the area that is now called France, from the Mediterranean French coast to the Pyrenees, north and west to the Atlantic and the English Channel, and east to the Rhine River. Its native inhabitants were Celts, many of them called Gauls. Between 300 B.C.E. and 300 C.E. Gaul had ample fertile soil for crops and a pleasing climate, and Romans found it an ideal location for agricultural villas.

Southwest of Transalpine Gaul lay Spain, which Rome took from the Carthaginians in 206 B.C.E. Romans used Spain to produce wheat, olive oil, wine, and metals. The hot, dry Spanish climate resembled that of Italy and thus was ideal for growing Roman crops. There were two main routes between Rome and Spain. Armies and merchants could walk along the Mediterranean coastline of eastern Spain and the French Riviera to northern Italy and vice versa; along the way, they might stop in seaside towns esteemed for their seafood and scenery. Faster, but riskier at certain times of year, was sending men and goods by sea; the weather during the Mediterranean winter made sailing dangerous. Most large shipments of cargo traveled by boat simply because it was so much more difficult to transport them along the rough terrain of the coastline. Spain's eastern coast had numerous port cities. The southern city of Cordoba, located on the river Baetis, was also accessible by water.

To the south of Italy, directly across the Mediterranean, lay North Africa. Its proximity to Sicily and Italy made for easy travel from one place to the other. North African peoples had occupied Sicily before Rome took it, and Carthage, in what is now Tunisia, was geographically close enough—barely 100 miles by sea from Sicily—to present a military threat. All of North Africa, including Egypt, was also close enough to be an ideal location for Roman farms and military installations. During the Roman Republic and the Roman Empire much of Rome's food came from North Africa and Egypt. The climate was warm and sunny most of the year; during the 500-year period between 200 B.C.E. and 300 C.E. the weather was especially warm, making the region extremely productive, even despite its perpetual water shortages. Roman troops were often sent to North Africa to subdue local people and consolidate Roman control of the area. Roman generals also based troops there during Roman civil wars, such as those involving Julius Caesar in the mid-first century B.C.E.

By the time of the empire, the warm weather zone had reached northern France. During the first two centuries B.C.E. Roman landlords created large-scale farms in northern Gaul, producing cereals for cities and military installations. The well-being of Roman civilization depended on the government's ability to grow food in its northern territories; this made it possible to feed the armies and citizens who maintained order in the more far-flung provinces.

Rome's more northerly territories, Germany and Britain, never received the attention or the level of Roman control that the more southern possessions did. This neglect was due to a combination of geographic distance from Rome and a colder climate. Germany lay north of the Alps and east of the Rhine. It was densely forested and had a colder climate than Italy, making it unsuitable for Mediterranean agriculture. Britain was separated from Europe by the English Channel, so Romans could only reach it by sailing. The sea voyage was difficult and dangerous and proved a substantial disincentive to settlement. The sheer distance of Britain from Rome also made it difficult to govern the province. Britain's climate was much colder and wetter than that of the Mediterranean, and Mediterranean crops did not thrive there.

The warm period persisted until about 400 C.E., when conditions suddenly grew cooler and wetter. The Mediterranean zone moved back south into Italy, and southern Europe ceased to be suitable for Roman agriculture. At this point it became clear how much the Roman Empire had relied on the climate to sustain its control of Europe. Britain and Germany were the first regions to be abandoned. Gauls and Germans began encroaching from the north again as the warm climate band crept south. By the late 400s the Mediterranean climate zone had moved entirely south of the European continent; Mediterranean crops continued to thrive in North Africa, but Italy itself now had a colder continental climate. Romans could no longer withstand the attacks of Gauls and Germans, and the Western Roman Empire fell apart, at least in part the victim of climate change.

THE AMERICAS

BY AMY HACKNEY BLACKWELL

In the Americas difficulty of travel and isolation from other cultures kept people from developing large civilizations until well after the ancient period. Humans came to Alaska from Siberia during an ice age between 18,000 and 13,000 B.C.E. By 10,000 B.C.E. they had reached the southern tip of South America and inhabited all parts of both American continents. By 8000 B.C.E. the climate had warmed considerably all around the world, the passage between Asia and the Americas was blocked, and Americans lived separately from humans on other continents until Europeans crossed the Atlantic in ships in the 1400s.

ALASKA

Humans moved into the Americas sometime between 18,000 and 13,000 B.C.E. They appear to have traveled from Siberia across the Bering Strait to what is now Alaska, though whether they walked across a land bridge, paddled in boats, or combined the two methods is a matter of debate among scholars. In any case, the first place humans inhabited in the Americas was western Alaska. Western Alaska has a long coastline on the Bering Sea. Many inlets and bays lie along the coast. The Yukon River empties into the sea in southwestern Alaska, creating a wide delta. To the east the Aleutian Islands stretch in an arc westward across the northern Pacific Ocean. Early settlers probably stayed in these areas, fishing and hunting as they had done in Siberia.

Northern Alaska is very cold. The Brooks Range of mountains runs from east to west, south of the northern tundra. North of Alaska is the Arctic Ocean. People living in this region had to adapt to long winters during which the sun almost never appeared. The ground is permafrost, never thawing even in summer, and agriculture is impossible. Central Alaska is heavily forested and is home to many wild animals. The Alaska Range runs along Alaska's southern coast, which is pocked with glaciers and fjords. This coastal area has rich fisheries that attracted human settlers who already had the skills needed to live there.

The weather in Alaska can be very bad. The winters are long and cold, even in the southern areas. Many of Alaska's rivers stop flowing entirely in the winter. The western and southern coasts have cool summers and cold winters. Fog and storms on the ocean are common, especially in winter; these weather phenomena killed many ancient sailors and kept others from going to sea in the winter.

NORTHERN NORTH AMERICA

From Alaska humans walked into what is now Canada's Yukon region. This area is cold, forested, and mountainous. The northern Rocky Mountains begin in northwestern Canada and run down the western coast. To the east of the mountains, the Great Plains begin. The northern plains are pocked with glacial lakes. The climate in this region is harsh, with cool summers and cold, snowy winters. During the last ice age this region was completely covered with snow and ice. Historians believe that around 11,500 B.C.E. an ice-free corridor opened in the western part of the region, allowing people to travel south into what is now the United States. By 10,500 B.C.E. the region was much warmer, and plants and animals had returned.

Much of northeastern Canada is part of the Canadian Shield, a region of thin soil on top of bedrock; it consequently cannot support much agriculture. The climate is cold and snowy, and the land is heavily forested. Hunter-gatherers lived mainly by hunting the ample wildlife in the region. Southeastern Canada, including the Appalachians and the region surrounding the Great Lakes and the Saint Lawrence River, has more fertile soil and a more hospitable climate than northern Canada. In ancient times the region was covered with mixed evergreen and deciduous forests. The northernmost portions of Canada, Baffin Island, and Greenland all have Arctic climates with year-round snow and ice. The only people to settle there were those who knew how to survive in such conditions.

Western North America

Several mountain ranges run north to south in the Pacific Northwest. Inland from these mountains is a broad plateau that climbs gradually to the Rocky Mountains. The Pacific Ocean just offshore is rich in fish and shellfish that supported large communities of ancient humans. The region has ample rainfall, especially on the coast. In ancient times this region was heavily forested; some of its trees, notably redwoods and sequoias, were among the largest in the world.

The coast of what is now California has historically been quite dry. The climate there was stable from the end of the ice age until about 2000 B.C.E. and then began cycling through wet and dry periods characterized by droughts that lasted a century or more. People began settling in the region around 3000 B.C.E., during a period of good weather and high food production. When the climate became unpredictable 1000 years later, the people adapted to less productive fisheries and forests. Droughts and storms plagued the inhabitants of the region for the rest of the ancient period.

What is now the southwestern United States is much warmer and drier than the Pacific Northwest. Like the Pacific Northwest several mountain ranges run north to south, paralleling the Pacific coast; these mountains continue southward to what is now Mexico. Rainfall has always been low, and much of the region is desert. Ancient farmers had to devise means of maximizing the available water. One strategy was to maintain family networks in different regions; rainfall varied from place to place, so households in wet areas could help others in places where the rains failed. Central American agriculture appeared in this region around 1000 B.C.E., brought by people moving north on foot from Mexico. The area that is now Arizona and New Mexico had a rough landscape with many mesas and steep-walled canyons created by water and wind erosion. The early people of the area took advantage of this natural landscape by creating homes called pueblos in the cliff faces.

The Rocky Mountains form the highest mountain chain in North America. The Rockies are high, steep, and cold in winter, when they could be a nearly impassible obstacle for people on foot. Many animals lived in the mountains, and ancient hunters went there for seasonal hunts but then returned to their homes on the plains.

The Great Plains are an enormous grassland or prairie east of the Rocky Mountains stretching from modern Canada to central Texas. Many animals lived there in ancient times, including giant herds of bison. The climate could be harsh; summers were very hot, and winters could bring multiple blizzards and heavy snowfall.

Eastern North America

The Mississippi River has long formed a boundary between the modern western and eastern United States. It drains the entire region between the Rocky Mountains and the Appalachians. The Mississippi by itself is the second-longest river in North America. When the length of its tributary the Missouri River is added to it, it becomes by far the longest. All the major rivers in central North America flow into the Mississippi; they include the Illinois, the Ohio, and the Arkansas Rivers. The Mississippi empties into the Gulf of Mexico in what is now Louisiana. The river has long been a major transportation artery for people with boats; it presents some challenges for sailors but is fairly easily navigable with primitive watercraft. The river is quite wide, especially in its southern reaches, and was very difficult for ancient people to cross. The river's width is one reason that Central American agricultural practices and crops did not reach eastern North America until after 1 C.E., long after they were common in Mexico and the Southwest. In ancient times the river flooded regularly and was prone to changing course unexpectedly. The river deposits silt at its mouth; these deposits create the Mississippi delta, an ever-changing landscape of marsh and extremely fertile soil.

The Great Lakes are five large freshwater lakes on the border between modern Canada and the United States. They are connected to one another by narrow rivers, and the easternmost lake, Lake Ontario, drains into the Saint Lawrence River. These large contiguous waterways allowed ancient people to move about the region more quickly than they could have moved overland. The climate in the Great Lakes region is fairly cold, and some portions of the lakes freeze in winter. The lakes themselves attract heavy snow. The lakes absorb heat in the summer, cooling summer temperatures and then warming autumns as the waters release heat back into the air. The land around the lakes is fertile and good for agriculture.

The Appalachian Mountains stretch from what is now eastern Canada down to northern Georgia. They are fairly low, gentle mountains and in ancient times were heavily forested with many different species of trees. They also had a large population of wild animals, both carnivores and herbivores. They form a physical barrier between the eastern and western portions of the region; walking through them was difficult, though by no means impossible. The highest mountain in the chain is Mount Mitchell in North Carolina. The higher elevations have colder temperatures than the lowlands to the east and west.

The southern coast of what is now the United States lies along the Gulf of Mexico. This region has fertile soil and warm temperatures, though it has always been prone to hurricanes in the late summer and autumn. In fact, researchers have found that hurricanes struck the Gulf Coast much more frequently between 1500 B.C.E. and 1000 C.E. than they do today. The region was heavily forested in ancient times, and the forests were full of wild game animals. The Gulf of Mexico itself supported many fish and shellfish. The gulf has gentler tidal patterns than the larger oceans and is more easily navigated in small boats.

Caribbean

The Caribbean region lies to the southeast of North America and north of modern Venezuela in South America. It consists of an arc of islands that run from the Bahamas and Cuba in the northwest to Trinidad and Tobago in the southeast. The only way to travel from island to island in ancient times was by boat. People who lived on the islands tended to be very isolated from other cultures. It appears that humans colonized the Caribbean from South America and moved northward. The first evidence of humans on the islands was found in Trinidad, just off the coast of Venezuela, and dated to about 5000 B.C.E. The journey from the mainland to Trinidad would have been very short, unlike the voyages to more distant islands, which would have required sailors to leave sight of land and navigate ocean waters.

The Bahamas are low, flat islands in shallow water. Most of the other islands of the Caribbean have more variation in elevation. Modern Cuba and Hispaniola contain a mix of hills and flat plains. Puerto Rico and Jamaica are hilly, as are most of the islands in the Lesser Antilles, the chain of islands forming the eastern boundary of the Caribbean chain. Many of these islands are volcanic in origin, and some of them contain volcanoes that are active to this day. Eruptions and earthquakes were common occurrences in ancient times.

The Caribbean climate ranges from subtropical in the Bahamas to tropical in the southernmost reaches. The islands supported lush vegetation and thick forests that were home to many species of animals, including some unusually small birds and snakes and other animals unique to the islands. The oceans around the islands teemed with fish and shellfish. Coral reefs lay just offshore of most Caribbean islands, attracting fish and other marine life to their rich habitats. Hurricanes presented one of the greatest risks to people living in the islands. A hurricane could completely destroy towns and kill thousands of people in a single day.

Mexico and Central America

Mexico and Central America were home to several large civilizations. The Olmec lived on the coast of the Gulf of Mexico between 1500 B.C.E. and 400 C.E. The city of Teotihuacán, near modern Mexico City, was inhabited from 150 B.C.E. to 750 C.E. The Mayan Empire encompassed parts of what are now Guatemala, Mexico, Honduras, and Belize, and lasted from about 1800 B.C.E. to the 17th century C.E. All of these civilizations supported themselves by farming, and all worshipped rain gods, a sign that they were preoccupied with receiving enough rain to nourish their crops.

Modern Mexico lies south of the main North American continent. Two-thirds of Mexico is mountainous. The Sierra Madre Occidental and the Sierra Madre Oriental are the main ranges; they run north to south and have an average elevation of 10,000 feet. They were formed by volcanic activity, and many of them were active in ancient times. The Pacific Ocean lies to the west and the Gulf of Mexico to the east of Mexico.

Mexico's climate varies depending on altitude, latitude, and distance from the ocean. Warm areas, including the coastal zones, southern Mexico, and the Yucatán, have mean temperatures of about 80 degrees Fahrenheit, though they can reach 120 degrees Fahrenheit. The central region has mean temperatures of about 60 degrees Fahrenheit. Rainfall is low throughout Mexico except in the southern Gulf Coast area (modern Tabasco). El Niño activities affect weather patterns on the Pacific coast, and hurricanes sometimes batter the Gulf Coast. In ancient times about two-thirds of Mexico was covered with forests; numerous types of plants and animals lived there in various ecosystems.

Central Mexico is covered with rolling hills and valleys; the soil in the valleys is generally much more fertile than that on the hillsides. Many of the hills are former volcanic cones. Mexico City, the former Aztec capital, is located in the southern part of this area. A wide coastal plain lies along most of Mexico's eastern coast. The Yucatán peninsula juts north into the ocean between the Gulf of Mexico and the Caribbean Sea. The Yucatán is very hilly. It lacks major rivers. In ancient times this region was covered with seasonal tropical forests; it received rain between May and October but also experienced some dry times in the spring. The region experienced periodic droughts when little rain fell for many years; these droughts seem to have occurred every 200 years or so. No major rivers supplied water to the region, so the Maya had to depend on rain.

The Yucatán has ample freshwater underground, but this is not always accessible to humans. Much of the Yucatán is underlaid with subterranean sinkholes called cenotes, and the Maya dug wells to reach the freshwater contained in these. Lack of water and hilly terrain forced people to build rainwater reservoirs, construct irrigation systems, and dig terraces on hillsides for their crops. Historians believe that rainfall fluctuated in the area during the ancient period. From 5500 to 500 B.C.E. the region was relatively wet, followed by about 250 years of drought. The Classic Maya civilization arose during another period of high rainfall between 250 B.C.E. and 125 C.E. Another drought between 125 and 250 C.E. led the Maya to abandon some of their settlements, such as El Mirador. Large portions of the Maya population died out during dry periods, only to be built back up when the rains returned.

The Maya who lived in this region became very skilled at maximizing their use of available water. In much of the southern Yucatán the ground is made of porous limestone; water runs straight through the rock into the ground here, and people could not make use of it for crops. In this area people dug holes in the limestone and plastered their bottoms to create artificial reservoirs. Even during wet times Maya faced food problems; the humid climate made it difficult to store corn for any length of time, so they could never build up a surplus of food to stave off famine in years of bad harvests. Throughout the region people lived in small city-states positioned on watersheds, which gave them the flexibility to handle sudden droughts.

South of the Yucatán the mountains continue through modern Guatemala, Honduras, and northwestern Nicaragua. The distance between the Pacific and the Caribbean Sea is narrower here than in Mexico. A number of rivers flow through this area, and it has several large lakes, notably Lago de Nicaragua. This region was covered with forests in ancient times. It is wetter than Mexico; the coastal regions have a wet, tropical climate, though the highlands are cooler and drier. Most rain falls between April and October. Hurricanes have always been a danger here.

From modern Costa Rica to the point where modern Panama joins northern Colombia the land forms a narrow S-shaped pattern. In this region the Pacific coast lies to the south of the land, and the Caribbean Sea lies to the north. The mountains continue to run down the center of the isthmus with swampy lowlands on the coasts. The climate is warm and wet. The climate and the range of habitats made this region a hospitable home for thousands of species of plants and animals, many of which were good sources of food.

Andes and Western South America

The Andes Mountains run the entire length of the western coast of South America. The name *Andes* comes from a Quechua (a local Indian language) word meaning "high crest." At 4,400 miles long, the Andes chain is the longest mountain range in the world. The Andes are the second-highest mountain chain, after the Himalayas; Mount Aconcagua (22,841 feet) in modern Argentina is the highest mountain in the Americas. The Andes range is about 150 to 200 miles wide along most of its length, except in Bolivia, where it is about 400 miles wide. Most of the tallest peaks are covered with snow year-round. The snow line varies from north to south. The southernmost peaks have very low snow lines and permanent glaciers. The snow line in the central Andes of Chile and Peru is actually higher than that of the tropical Andes; the wetter climate in the north allows for more snow to fall.

The Andes harbor several active volcanoes. The most famous is Cotopaxi, which assumed its current shape about 3000 B.C.E. This geothermal activity heats underground water, which comes above ground in numerous hot springs. The Galapagos Islands, about 1,000 miles west of Peru on the equator, were also formed by volcanic activity.

The Andes in the north begin in Colombia, Venezuela, and Ecuador. In this area they exist as two parallel mountain ranges, currently called the Cordillera Occidental (Western Rope) and the Cordillera Oriental (Eastern Rope). The Caribbean Islands of Aruba, Bonaire, and Curaçao are actually part of the range, with most of their landmass submerged. Two branches of the chain border either side of Lake Maracaibo. The Maracaibo lowlands of western Venezuela are flat and swampy and have never attracted much human settlement.

The Central Andes lie in modern Peru, Chile, and Bolivia. The snow line begins at about 15,700 feet. The western portion of the mountain range is quite dry, though the eastern mountains toward the Amazon region receive fairly heavy rainfall, over 100 inches a year in modern times. A flat coastal plain lies between the western mountains and the Pacific Ocean. The climate here is normally very dry but is greatly affected by periodic El Niño events, which can cause large amounts to fall all at once. At high elevations temperatures do not vary much over the course of the year but can change drastically from day to night, dropping from 75 degrees Fahrenheit to 32 degrees Fahrenheit in a matter of hours. Rivers on the east side of the Andes drain into the Amazon, and rivers on the west drain into the Pacific. Lake Titicaca, one of the highest lakes in the world, lies in the Andes on the modern border between Peru and Bolivia.

Between 1500 B.C.E. and 500 C.E., the Lake Titicaca region had higher rainfall than it does now. Between 300 and 500 C.E. Lake Titicaca was higher than today, making agriculture easier. The area around Lake Titicaca was a fruitful habitat for the people of Tiwanaku, a civilization that flourished in southern Peru and northwest Bolivia starting around 400 B.C.E.; by 650 C.E. it had a large population. Rainfall was unpredictable, so the people of the region used the fluctuating waters of Lake Titicaca to water crops in raised fields. A centralized bureaucracy helped the people organize themselves enough to cope with the harsh climate. The Tiwanaku civilization eventually died out during a major drought starting around 1000 C.E.

Travel in the Andes was extremely difficult and had to be done almost entirely on foot at high altitudes. Andean peoples evolved large lungs and thicker blood that helped them make the most of their oxygen-poor air. They also chewed coca leaf, a drug that helped them metabolize their food and function better in the thin air. The physical difficulty of traveling to and from the mountains kept Andean people from trading or engaging in cultural exchange with other South Americans. Water shortages were a constant problem, and people developed complicated irrigation techniques to water their crops. The steep slopes of the mountains made it difficult to grow crops; people learned to cut terraces into the mountainsides to create flat fields.

In ancient times the mountains of the central Andes were covered with forests. The trees were adapted to the climate and altitude and included unique species, such as the queñua and the yagual. The southern Andes run through modern Argentina and Chile down to the Tierra del Fuego. Chile's coast contains numerous fjords, islands, ice fields, and glaciers. Snow cover in this area gets progressively higher toward the south; in the Tierra del Fuego, the snow line can be below 1,000 feet. The terrain and climate discouraged much human settlement in ancient times.

Tierra del Fuego is separated from mainland South America by a narrow strait, now called the Strait of Magellan. There appears to have been a land bridge or glacier between the island and the mainland around 8000 B.C.E., which would have allowed human settlers to walk there. The climate is cold and stormy, and the terrain is rocky. The mountains feed glaciers into the ocean. Only three species of trees are native to the area. In ancient times agriculture was impossible due to poor soil and harsh climate, so humans in this area lived by hunting and fishing.

Amazon and Northeastern South America

The Amazon River and its basin dominate northeastern South America. The river originates in the Andes and is fed by numerous tributaries. Most of the tributaries are difficult to navigate in the mountains because of their numerous waterfalls and rocky rapids. Outside of the mountains, however, the Amazon experiences very little change of elevation along its length, and it is fairly easy to navigate. The Amazon and its tributaries were the main means of traveling through the region before the advent of airplanes and helicopters and the building of modern roads.

The Amazon is 6 miles wide in some places. About 400 miles from the ocean, it narrows to about a mile wide but about 200 feet deep; the water flows very quickly there. Closer to the mouth the river overflows its banks regularly. The mouth of the river encompasses a wide area of outlets and land about 207 miles wide. The Amazon does not have a delta. A tidal bore, or wave that travels from the ocean upriver, prevents silt from accumulating at the mouth.

The Amazon drains a huge area. The Amazon basin contained about seven million square miles of rain forest in ancient times. This rain forest was extremely dense and difficult to travel through. The river supports a huge variety of wildlife, including river dolphins, carnivorous piranha, giant snakes, and a number of edible fish, crab, and turtle species. The rain forest also harbors a plethora of species of plant and animal, both beneficial and dangerous to human occupants. In ancient times few people lived deep in the rain forest. Those who did lived mostly as hunter-gatherers, though some practiced slash-and-burn agriculture, a method of farming in which farmers cut down vegetation and burn it to create fields for crops. The soil in most of this region is not especially fertile and cannot sustain permanent agriculture; the slash-and-burn technique allowed farmers to exploit the fertility of an area and then move on to allow it to recover over many years.

Northeast of the Amazon is the Rio São Francisco, which was also used as a major transportation artery. South of the Amazon the Paraná River flows into the Rio de la Plata. The origin of the Paraná lies in the Pantanal, a giant marshland just west of the modern southwestern border between Bolivia and Brazil. The Pantanal experiences annual floods during the rainy season of December to May. This flooding made the land very fertile and suitable for agriculture, much as the Nile's annual floods made Egyptian agriculture possible.

Southwestern South America

The Pampas is a large fertile plain encompassing nearly 300,000 square miles in modern northern Argentina and southern Brazil. The name Pampas comes from a Quechua Indian word meaning plain. The area was almost entirely grassland before humans began cultivating it, but since then it has been used very successfully for agriculture. The soil is rich, and the rainfall is moderate (about 39 inches per year) and steady throughout the year, with no particular rainy or dry seasons, though more rain falls in summer than in winter. Rainfall is heaviest in coastal areas and lighter near the mountains to the west. Winters are cool, and summers are warm and humid.

The landlocked Gran Chaco region lies in modern northwestern Argentina, Paraguay, Bolivia, and a small piece of southwestern Brazil. This area is very dry and hot. Western Gran Chaco has almost no vegetation; in the east the main plants are thorn bushes and grasses. The land is almost entirely flat. Ancient humans in this region lived as hunter-gatherers because of the difficulty of growing anything.

Patagonia is the area encompassing the southern half of Argentina and all of southern South America, including some portions of the southern Andes. Most of Patagonia is a flat or hilly plateau, rising in abrupt terraces toward the mountains. The western portions are forested with southern beech and other deciduous trees and evergreens. The eastern portion contains some rain forests and bogs in areas of high rainfall. Eastern Patagonia is grassland. Humans lived there as hunter-gatherers starting about 8000 B.C.E.; by 1000 B.C.E. people were cultivating crops in the eastern plains.

See also AGRICULTURE; ARCHITECTURE; BORDERS AND FRONTIERS; BUILDING TECHNIQUES AND MATERIALS; CITIES; ECONOMY; EMPIRES AND DYNASTIES; EMPLOYMENT AND LABOR; EXPLORATION; FOOD AND DIET; GOVERNMENT ORGANIZATION; HEALTH AND DISEASE; HUNTING, FISHING, AND GATHERING; LANGUAGE; METALLURGY; MIGRATION AND POPULATION MOVEMENTS; MINING, QUARRYING, AND SALT MAKING; NATURAL DISASTERS; NOMADIC AND PASTORAL SOCIETIES; ROADS AND BRIDGES; SEAFARING AND NAVIGATION; SETTLEMENT PATTERNS; SHIPS AND SHIPBUILDING; SOCIAL ORGANIZATION; STORAGE AND PRESERVATION; TOWNS AND VILLAGES; TRADE AND EXCHANGE; TRANSPORTATION; WAR AND CONQUEST.

Africa

Strabo: Geography, *excerpt on Africa, ca. 22 C.E.*

The country deep in the interior is called Tenessis [modern-day Eritrea]. It is occupied by those Egyptians who took refuge from the government of Psamtik III. They are surnamed Sembritae, as being strangers. They are governed by a queen, to whom also Meroë, an island in the Nile near these places, is subject. . . . From Meroë to this sea is a journey of fifteen days for an active person. Near Meroë is the confluence of the Astaboras [modern Atbara], the Astapus [the White Nile], and of the Astasobas [Blue Nile]. . . .

Far in the interior was a place called Endera [modern Axum], inhabited by a naked tribe [the Gymnetae] who use bows and reed arrows, the points of which are hardened in the fire. They generally shoot the animals from trees, sometimes from the ground. They have numerous herds of wild cattle among them, on the flesh of which they subsist, and on that of other wild animals. When they have taken nothing in the chase, they dress dried skins upon hot coals, and are satisfied with food of this kind. . . . Further still towards the south [near modern-day Addis Ababa] are the Cynamolgi, called by the natives Agrii, with long hair and long beards, who keep a breed of very large dogs for hunting the Indian cattle which come into their country from the neighboring district, driven there either by wild beasts or by scarcity of pasturage. . . . Next to the harbor of Antiphilus is a port called the Grove of the Colobi (or the Mutilated), the city Berenice of the Sabae, and Sabae a considerable city; then the grove of Eumenes.

Above is the city Darada, and a hunting-ground for elephants. . . . The district is inhabited by the Elephantophagi (or Elephant-eaters), who are occupied in hunting them. When they descry from the trees a herd of elephants directing their course through the forest, they do not then attack, but they approach by stealth and hamstring the hindmost stragglers from the herd. Some kill them with bows and arrows, the latter being dipped in the gall of serpents. The shooting with the bow is performed by three men, two, advancing in front, hold the bow, and one draws the string. . . . The nomads call the hunters Acatharti, or impure.

Above this nation is situated a small tribe—the Struthophagi (or Bird-eaters), in whose country are birds of the size of deer, which are unable to fly, but run with the swiftness of the ostrich. Some hunt them with bows and arrows, others covered with the skins of birds. . . .

Bordering on this people is a nation blacker in complexion than the others, shorter in stature, and very short-lived. They rarely live beyond forty years; for the flesh of their bodies is eaten up with worms. Their food consists of locusts, which the south-west and west winds, when they blow violently in the spring-time, drive in bodies into the country. The inhabitants catch them by throwing into the ravines materials which cause a great deal of smoke, and light them gently. The locusts, as they fly across the smoke, are blinded and fall down. They are pounded with salt, made into cakes, and eaten as food. Above these people is situated a desert tract with extensive pastures. It was abandoned in consequence of the multitudes of scorpions and tarantulas, . . . which formerly abounded to so great a degree as to occasion a complete desertion of the place long since by its inhabitants.

Next to the harbor of Eumenes, as far as Deire and the straits opposite the six islands, live the Ichthyophagi, Creophagi, and Colobi, who extend into the interior. Many hunting-grounds for elephants, and obscure cities and islands, lie in front of the coast. The greater part are nomads; husbandmen are few in number. . . .

There are three islands which follow in succession, the island of Tortoises, the island of Seals, and the island of Hawks. Along the whole coast there are plantations of

(continued)

(continues)

palm trees, olive trees, and laurels, not only within, but in a great part also without the straits. There is also an island called the island of Philip; opposite to it inland is situated the hunting-ground for elephants, called the chase of Pythangelus; then follows Arsinoë, a city with a harbor; after these places is Deire, and beyond them is a hunting-ground for elephants. From Deire, the next country is that which bears aromatic plants. The first produces myrrh, and belongs to the Icthyophagi and the Creophagi. It bears also the persea, peach or Egyptian almond, and the Egyptian fig. Beyond is Licha, a hunting-ground for elephants. There are also in many places standing pools of rain-water. When these are dried up, the elephants, with their trunks and tusks, dig holes and find water. . . .

The mode of life of the Ethiopians is wretched; they are for the most part naked, and wander from place to place with their flocks. Their flocks and herds are small in size, whether sheep, goats, or oxen; the dogs also, though fierce and quarrelsome, are small. . . . They live on millet and barley, from which also a drink is prepared. They have no oil, but use butter and fat instead. There are no fruits, except the produce of trees in the royal gardens. Some feed even upon grass, the tender twigs of trees, the lotus, or the roots of reeds. They live also upon the flesh and blood of animals, milk, and cheese. They reverence their kings as gods, who are for the most part shut up in their palaces.

Their largest royal seat is the city of Meroë, of the same name as the island. The shape of the island is said to be that of a shield. Its size is perhaps exaggerated. Its length is about 3000 *stadia*, and its breadth 1000 *stadia*. It is very mountainous, and contains great forests. The inhabitants are nomads, who are partly hunters and partly farmers. There are also mines of copper, iron, gold, and various kinds of precious stones. It is surrounded on the side of Libya by great hills of sand, and on that of Arabia by continuous precipices. In the higher parts on the south, it is bounded by the confluence of the rivers Astaboras [modern Atbara], Astapa [the White Nile], and Astasobas [the Blue Nile]. On the north is the continuous course of the Nile to Egypt, with its windings, of which we have spoken before.

From Strabo, *The Geography of Strabo* trans. H. C. Hamilton and W. Falconer (London: H. G. Bohn, 1854–1857).

Asia and the Pacific

Pliny: Natural History, *excerpt on India, ca. 77* C.E.

And it will not be amiss to set out the whole of the voyage from Egypt, now that reliable knowledge of it is for the first time accessible. It is an important subject, in view of the fact that in no year does India absorb less than fifty million sesterces of our empire's wealth, sending back merchandise to be sold with us at a hundred times its prime cost. Two miles from Alexandria is the town of Juliopolis. The voyage up the Nile from there to Keft is 309 miles and takes 12 days when the midsummer trade winds are blowing. From Keft the journey is made with camels, stations being placed at intervals for the purpose of watering; the first, a stage of 22 miles, is called Hydreuma; the second is in the mountains, a day's journey on; the third at a second place named Hydreuma, 85 miles from Keft; the next is in the mountains; next we come to Apollo's Hydreuma, 184 miles from Keft; again a station in the mountains; then we get to New Hydreuma, 230 miles from Keft. There is also another old Hydreuma known by the name of Trogodyticum, where a guard is stationed on outpost duty at a caravanserai accommodating two thousand travelers; it is seven miles from New Hydreuma. Then comes the town of Berenice where there is a harbor on the Red Sea, 257 miles from Keft. But as the greater part of the journey is done by night because of the heat and the days are spent at stations, the whole journey from Keft to Berenice takes twelve days. Traveling by sea begins at midsummer before the dogstar rises or immediately after its rising, and it takes about thirty days to reach the Arabian port of Cella or Caned in the frankincense-producing district. There is also a third port named Mokha, which is not called at on the voyage to India and is only used by merchants trading in frankincense and Arabian perfumes. Inland there is a town, the residence of the king of the district, called Sapphar, and another called Save. But the most advantageous way of sailing to India is to set out from Cella; from that port it is a 40 days' voyage, if the Hippalus is blowing, to the first trading station in India, Cranganore not a desirable port of call, on account of the neighboring pirates, who occupy a place called Nitriae, nor is it specially rich in articles of merchandise; and furthermore the roadstead for shipping is a long way from the land, and cargoes have to be brought in and carried out in boats. The king of Muziris, at the date of publication, was Caelobothras. There is another more serviceable port, belonging to the Neacyndi tribe, called Porakad; this is where king Pandion reigned, his capital being a town in the interior a long way from the port, called Madura; while the district from which pepper is conveyed to Becare in canoes made of hollowed tree trunks is called Cottonara. But all these names of tribes and ports or towns are to be found in none of the previous writers, which seem to show that the local conditions of the places are changing. Travelers set sail from India on the return voyage at the beginning of the Egyptian month Tybis, which is our December, or at all events before the sixth day of the Egyptian Mechir, which works out at before January 13 in our calendar—so making it possible to return home in the same year. They set sail from India with a southeast wind and after entering the Red Sea continue the voyage with a south-west or south wind.

From: Internet History Sourcebooks. Available online. URL: http://www.fordham.edu/halsall/.

Greece

Pausanias: Description of Greece, *Book I: Attica, second century* C.E.

[1.1.1] On the Greek mainland facing the Cyclades Islands and the Aegean Sea the Sunium promontory stands out from the Attic land. When you have rounded the promontory you see a harbor and a temple to Athena of Sunium on the peak of the promontory. Farther on is Laurium, where once the Athenians had silver mines, and a small uninhabited island called the Island of Patroclus. For a fortification was built on it and a palisade constructed by Patroclus, who was admiral in command of the Egyptian men-of-war sent by Ptolemy, son of Ptolemy, son of Lagus, to help the Athenians, when Antigonus, son of Demetrius, was ravaging their country, which he had invaded with an army, and at the same time was blockading them by sea with a fleet.

[1.1.2] The Peiraeus was a parish from early times, though it was not a port before Themistocles became an archon of the Athenians. Their port was Phalerum, for at this place the sea comes nearest to Athens, and from here men say that Menestheus set sail with his fleet for Troy, and before him Theseus, when he went to give satisfaction to Minos for the death of Androgeos. But when Themistocles became archon, since he thought that the Peiraeus was more conveniently situated for mariners and had three harbors as against one at Phalerum, he made it the Athenian port. Even up to my time there were docks there, and near the largest harbor is the grave of Themistocles. For it is said that the Athenians repented of their treatment of Themistocles and that his relations took up his bones and brought them from Magnesia. And the children of Themistocles certainly returned and set up in the Parthenon a painting, on which is a portrait of Themistocles. The most noteworthy sight in the Peiraeus is a precinct of Athena and Zeus. Both their images are of bronze; Zeus holds a staff and a Victory, Athena a spear. . . .

[1.1.4] The Athenians have also another harbor, at Munychia, with a temple of Artemis of Munychia, and yet another at Phalerum, as I have already stated, and near it is a sanctuary of Demeter. Here there is also a temple of Athena Sciras, and one of Zeus some distance away, and altars of the gods named Unknown, and of heroes, and of the children of Theseus and Phalerus; for this Phalerus is said by the Athenians to have sailed with Jason to Colchis. . . . Twenty stades away is the Coliad promontory; on to it, when the Persian fleet was destroyed, the wrecks were carried down by the waves. There is here an image of the Coliad Aphrodite, with the goddesses Genetyllides (Goddesses of Birth), as they are called. And I am of opinion that the goddesses of the Phocaeans in Ionia, whom they call Gennaides, are the same as those at Colias. On the way from Phalerum to Athens there is a temple of Hera with neither doors nor roof. Men say that Mardonius, son of Gobryas, burnt it. But the image there to-day is, as report goes, the work of Alcamenes. So that this, at any rate, cannot have been damaged by the Persians.

From: Internet History Sourcebooks. Available online. URL: http://www.fordham.edu/halsall/.

FURTHER READING

Sigmar Bortenschlager and Klaus Oeggl, eds., *The Iceman and His Natural Environment: Palaeobotanical Results* (New York: Springer, 2000).

Brian Fagan, *The Long Summer: How Climate Changed Civilization* (New York: Basic Books, 2004).

Heidi H. Jacobs, Michael L. LeVasseur, Kate Kinsella, et al., *Asia and the Pacific: Geography/History/Culture* (New York: Pearson Prentice Hall, 2004).

Keith J. Kirby and Charles Watkins, *The Ecological History of European Forests* (New York: CAB International, 1998).

Pak Sum Low, ed., *Climate Change and Africa* (New York: Cambridge University Press, 2005).

Bill Manley, *The Penguin Historical Atlas of Ancient Egypt* (New York: Penguin, 1996).

Alan Moorehead, *The White Nile* (New York: Harper, 1960).

John Harris Paterson, *North America: A Geography of the United States and Canada*, 9th ed. (New York: Oxford University Press, 1994).

Norman J. G. Pounds, *An Historical Geography of Europe; 450 B.C.–A.D. 1330* (Cambridge: Cambridge University Press, 1973).

Neil Roberts, *The Holocene: An Environmental History*, 2nd ed. (Malden, Mass.: Blackwell Publishers, 1998).

Richard J. A. Talbert, *An Atlas of Classical History* (New York: Macmillan, 1985).

Charles Watkins, *European Woods and Forests: Studies in Cultural History* (New York: CAB International, 1998).

► clothing and footwear

INTRODUCTION

Very little is known about clothing in ancient times. There are few original garments that have survived the passing of the ages. Those that remain in existence are mostly from dry regions in the Near East. There are almost no examples of clothing from Europe. Hints about the dress of ancient people have to be taken from depictions of clothing in art and written sources as well as studies of the disintegrated remains found at burial sites. Psychologists and sociologists have attempted to identify the motivations that prompted people to dress themselves. Clothing is not essential for survival in every part of the world, particularly in warm regions, but there were several basic reasons for dressing. Clothing was worn for protection, for decoration, out of modesty, and to denote status. Ancient people apparently wore clothing for all of these reasons.

The earliest clothes were animal skins and pieces of plants, such as leaves and bark. The garments of the ancient world, with a few exceptions, were draped. The basic form of much ancient clothing was a length of square, rectangular, or semicircular fabric draped to create a variety of styles, each of which was distinctive and characteristic of the particular culture and period within that culture. These draped garments were fastened together, when fastening was required, by pins or threads. Heavier garments were required in northern regions for protection against cold weather, while lighter-weight fabrics were used in southern regions. By the start of the Common Era, European peoples dressed chiefly in wool and linen, while Asian civilizations preferred silk and cotton clothing.

Ancient people dressed in loincloths, skirts, tunics, shawls, cloaks, and veils. The skirt, in the ancient world, was a garment that began at the waist and hung loosely around the body. Skirts were worn by both men and women and varied in length. The loincloth was a length of cloth wrapped in any of several ways to cover the genitals. The tunic was a simple, one-piece, and typically T-shaped garment, cut with an opening for the head and arms. Tunics were usually long enough to cover the trunk and were made in as many different lengths as skirts. Shawls were rectangles, squares or ovals of fabric that were commonly combined with skirts or tunics. These ranged from pieces that covered only the upper body to larger pieces that could be wrapped to make a complete garment. The veil was a smaller rectangle that covered the head and, sometimes, part of the upper body. It was worn exclusively by women. A cloak, worn outdoors, was a capelike garment tied or pinned around the shoulders. Sandals were the most common type of footwear, with boots popular in colder climates. Fancy materials and certain colors, such as purple among the Romans, were often restricted to the elite classes. Decorations often indicated status or military rank.

AFRICA

BY JUSTIN CORFIELD

The dress throughout Africa during ancient times varied considerably with the climatic conditions and the status of the people. Many Egyptian, Greek, and Roman accounts and images describe the North Africans. There are also records and images from the travels of Egyptians, Carthaginians, Greeks, and Romans. Archaeological remains have been recovered from elsewhere in Africa. From this evidence it is clear that yarn spinning and weaving were done throughout most of ancient Africa.

Rock art from the Atlas Mountains (modern-day Morocco) dating from as early as 6000 B.C.E. shows people dressed only in loincloths. Over time, trade led to many changes. The clothing of Greeks and Romans in northern Africa was similar to the clothes they wore elsewhere in the Mediterranean region. The standard item of clothing for a man was a tunic, and a woman wore either a simple or a pleated dress. Although Greeks and Romans always wore belts, the Carthaginians probably did not, possibly because of the extreme heat in Carthage and other parts of North Africa during the summer. Evidence of this style of dress is in the play *Poenulus* by Titus Maccius Plautus (254–184 B.C.E.). The character Milphio challenges a Carthaginian merchant, "Hey, you there without a belt, why have you come to this city?" The Romans used a belt to hold a purse for their coins, and it is likely that the Carthaginians used moneybags strapped to their wrists or on a cord around their necks.

Most Carthaginians dressed modestly, covering most of the body. Because the nights were cold, many Carthaginians wore cloaks, and several cloak clasps have been found in Carthaginian graves. Many Carthaginians also regularly wore hats, and it seems to have been one feature that differentiated free men from slaves, who were often bare-headed. Carthaginian women wore dresses similar to those worn by Greeks, often with heavy embroidery. Shoes were similar to those worn by the Greeks, with men wearing leather sandals. Carthaginian soldiers dressed in the Greek fashion with a plumed Thracian-style helmet, breastplate, and tunic colored red for officers and purple for men of the noble cavalry. In battle Carthaginians wore high open-toed boots. Most of the infantry, the men who made up the Carthaginian citizen spearmen, were barefoot in battle.

The clothing of Numidian and Mauritanian rulers tended to imitate Carthaginian and then Roman clothing. Many of the subjects wore simple, short tunics that allowed movement and exposure to the sun. The cavalry tended to wear a loose, unbleached singlet, or loose shirt, held at the shoulders with two brooches. Some men also wore a strip of leather or wildcat fur around their heads. When horsemen were riding, the lower part of the tunic was pulled up, leaving most of the legs exposed. They did not use footwear. It seems likely that these fashions were also followed in Cyrenaica, in modern-day Libya. The Libyans who fought in the Carthaginian army tended to wear very short tunics made of soft red leather, later called Morocco leather. Many images of Simon of Cyrene show a black man wearing long, loose-fitting robes helping Jesus on the day of the Crucifixion. According to the Greek historian Herodotus (ca. 484–430/420 B.C.E.), some women in Libya wore a bronze ring on each leg, while others wore leather bands around their ankles.

In the Sahara loose tunics similar to those worn by Carthaginians seem to have been favored by the merchants who followed the ancient trade routes through central Africa. Even the Romans in North Africa wore a hooded woolen garment known as a *birrus*, similar to the burnoose, a one-piece hooded cloak worn by Arabs. Most of the people crossing the Sahara, men and women, wore headscarves and possibly dyed their robes bright colors, making their dress little different from that of the Tuareg people of modern-day West Africa. People in the desert often wore a cloth over the face, giving them the nickname "men of the blue veil." Excavations of graves at the monument to the early Tuareg leader Tin Hinan show that Morocco leather was used in clothing. Herodotus describes a competition in Ethiopia involving the stringing of a bow, at the end of which a scarlet robe is awarded, indicating that the color was unusual in the area at the time. At Meroë, in Sudan, small fragments of textiles dating from the ancient period are cotton, showing the importance of this material in clothing of the region.

Farther south, in modern-day East Africa, there are no surviving descriptions of ancient clothing. Diogenes (ca. 320 B.C.E.), whom the geographer Ptolemy (fl. second century C.E.) suggests visited modern-day Kenya, makes no mention of clothing or lack of clothing of the local people. The dress may have been little different from that in Nubia at the time and probably was similar to the cotton garment worn by traditional Masai today. These cloths were often brightly colored and worn over one shoulder, leaving the other parts of the body bare. Few of these peoples would have worn shoes, though it is possible that some people might have worn sandals imported from other regions. It also seems probable that the dress of the Bantu of southern Africa and of tribes such as the Khoikhoi and the San would have changed little from ancient times to the early 20th century. In Madagascar, though most clothing was made from cotton, wool was worn in the south, and silk, obtained from Asia, was worn in the northeast.

Petroglyph of a human figure wearing a loincloth, from the Sahara Desert at Tassili, Algeria, North Africa (© Board of Regents of the University of Wisconsin System. Photographer: Jeanne Tabachnick)

In West Africa several surviving terra-cotta figurines from Nok, on the Benue plateau of modern-day Nigeria, survive. First discovered in 1928, these objects date from the fifth century B.C.E. They show people with beaded hair but wearing very little except a small, tight loincloth, occasionally seeming to be a piece of rolled cloth or rope. There are suggestions that this was the style of the artwork of the Yoruba people of Nok, who were keen to emphasize the detail of hairstyles.

EGYPT

BY CARYN E. NEUMANN

The wealth of ancient Egyptian works of art, ordinary objects, and written records that have survived through the ages has provided scholars with a fairly good picture of Egyptian clothing and footwear. Egyptian civilization existed at about the same time as the civilizations of the Mesopotamian region, but the warmer climate in Egypt led to creation of a clothing style very different from that of those civilizations.

The Egyptians, like many ancient peoples, initially dressed in animal skins. Quite early they developed the art of tanning and dressing leather. Even after cloth had been developed, the Egyptians continued to use leather for clothing, particularly for belts and shoes. More so than the Greeks and Mesopotamians, the Egyptians dressed in linen. Egyptian dress relied on linen because it kept the wearer cool in a hot climate. The basic style of clothing complemented the natural lines of the body. The preference for one fiber and a consistent style is typical of ancient civilizations. Egyptians used wool for many garments but often used linen underneath the wool clothing. The Egyptians also apparently originated the practice of interweaving linen with wool, probably to take advantage of the softer properties of linen. The Egyptians were noted for fine embroidery. In the later period of their civilization the Egyptians embroidered with gold thread made of beaten and rounded strips of metal. Overall, the Egyptian style of dress involved more luxurious fabrics and styles than the style of contemporary civilizations in other regions.

The Egyptians had a style that was essentially timeless. They dressed in the same fashions for thousands of years. The basic garment worn by men of the Old Kingdom (2575–2134 B.C.E.) was a white loincloth, or *schenti,* that was wrapped around the body several times and held in place by a girdle, or wide belt, that kept the *schenti* fitted closely around the hips. The type of fabric and amount of fabric in the *schenti* indicated status. The garment was made of linen for the pharaohs and priests, but common people dressed in leather or woven vegetable fibers. Wealthier Egyptians had their *schentis* decorated with gold thread. Decoration was also achieved by rounding one end of the fabric to form a diagonal line across the front, by pleating the end or by placing decorative panels at the front. Paintings indicate that some men wore a network of fabric, possibly leather, over the *schenti.*

People of both sexes in the Old Kingdom wore wide collars decorated with embroidery and beads. Women wore white linen, tubelike, tight-fitting dresses held in place by two straps. The straps might or might not have covered the nipple. The dresses were highly decorated with embroidery, painted designs, appliqués, leather, beadwork, or woven patterns.

Only important men wore a *schenti* that was decorated. The common people did not drape a large amount of material and used a simpler design that reflected their relatively insignificant social standing. Lower-caste women wore tunics. Slaves and dancing girls either went naked or dressed in a small loincloth held up with a narrow waistband. As is typical of every Egyptian period, in the Old Kingdom children either dressed like adults or went naked. Some artwork shows girls wearing a belt at the waist. After beginning school, boys dressed in the *schenti.* Girls went naked until puberty, when they adopted adult garb.

In the Middle Kingdom (2140–1640 B.C.E.) men wore the *schenti* and added a linen cape knotted on the chest. A short version of the cape sometimes exposed the midriff, and a long version was tucked into a skirt or was belted. Some cape fabrics were very sheer. The skirts were elongated, sometimes reaching to the ankle, but workers, soldiers, and hunters wore shorter versions. A double skirt, the under layer opaque and the outer layer sheer, appeared in the Middle Kingdom and was worn into the New Kingdom (1550–1070 B.C.E.).

Pharaohs and priests of the Middle Kingdom wore pleated linen skirts, occasionally with a leopard or lion skin as a shawl. Animal skins were reserved for the most powerful members of Egyptian society because of a belief that wearing the skin of a fierce beast magically transferred the animal's powers to the human. Soldiers wore a loincloth, leather apron, and linen breastplate. The linen was folded in a manner to deflect attacks. For women, the Old Kingdom style of dress extended into the Middle Kingdom.

By the time of the New Kingdom increased trade brought new clothing styles to Egypt. Longer tunics, similar to those worn in Mesopotamia, appeared. These garments were worn over loincloths and skirts or underneath skirts. Both men and women dressed in a *kalasiris.* This linen tunic, made of transparent gauze, had a design at the base and was worn over a loincloth. Some tunics were seamed at the sides, and some had either short or long sleeves made separately and then sewn on. The *kalasiris* might cover the body so snugly as to restrict movement or might be worn very loosely. It might have a band over one shoulder, or it might reach up to the neck. A *kalasiris* could be short, as working people wore to allow greater movement, or long, as worn by the wealthy. The material of a *kalasiris* was either woven or knitted and typically was pleated. In one variation the fabric was arranged so that the pleats fell in different directions at different points on the body. A girdle usually was worn with a *kalasiris.* If no girdle was worn, the rectangular shape of the material was altered so that it narrowed at the shoulders. A woman's *kalasiris* would be more ornately embroidered than a man's and often was pleated with batwing sleeves. It became fashionable for women to use only one shoulder strap, leaving the other

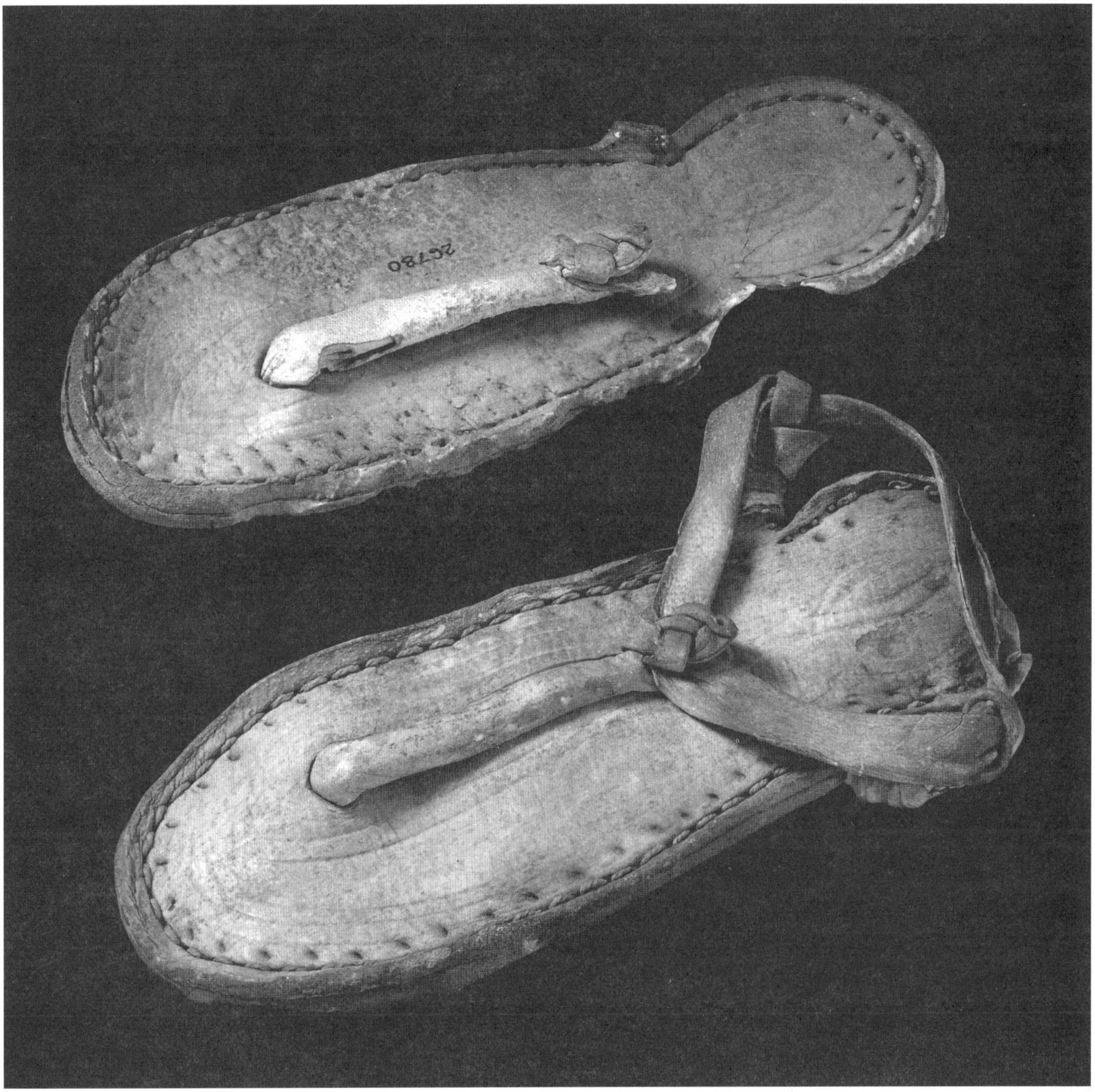

Pair of child's leather sandals from Thebes, Egypt, New Kingdom (© The Trustees of the British Museum)

shoulder bare. In the New Kingdom every color except black was used for clothing.

Footwear was initially unusual in Egypt. Good terrain and a warm climate made footwear unnecessary. Only priests wore sandals, which consisted of leather, papyrus, or wooden soles held on by straps. These sandals gradually were adopted by the general population. Both men and women wore the same design. Wealthier people wore more elaborate sandals with jeweled ornamentation. Children probably went barefoot.

THE MIDDLE EAST

BY CARYN E. NEUMANN

The Sumerians, Babylonians, Persians, and Assyrians of the ancient world had the same consistency in dress over the centuries and the same preference for draped materials as other ancient peoples. Unlike their contemporaries the Egyptians, the people of the Near East developed clothing that suited a range of climates from the cold of high altitudes to the hot, dry desert regions.

Mesopotamia produced so much wool that it became one of the region's chief exports. Accordingly, wool was the preferred fabric for clothing. Wool cloth was produced for domestic use and traded to other regions, as ancient records indicate. Linen has been discovered in archaeological excavations, and flax is occasionally mentioned on clay tablets, but linen was clearly less important than wool. Evidence of details of Mesopotamian dress comes largely from visual materials such as seals, statues, tombs, and wall paintings.

Sumerian civilization existed from 3500 to 2500 B.C.E. In that era both men and women wore sheepskin skirts with the fleece still attached. Length varied according to the physical tasks performed by the wearer and the status of the wearer. Servants and soldiers wore shorter skirts, while royalty dressed in long skirts. The skirts apparently wrapped around the body. If it was long enough, the fabric was passed up under a wide, padded belt and over one shoulder. Cloaks made of animal skins, leather, or felt were worn over the upper part of the body. Children typically dressed as adults did or, if they were very young, went naked. Men, women, and children typically went barefoot.

Babylonian civilization extended from about 2500 to 1000 B.C.E. The slow rate of change in ancient fashion means that it is difficult to distinguish between late Sumerian and early Babylonian clothing styles. However, dress gradually increased in complexity. While men's and women's clothing continued to have similar elements, the trend was toward greater distinctions in dress according to gender.

By the time of the Babylonians skirts were no longer made of sheepskin and were woven from wool. Soldiers wore skirts with fringed decoration around the lower edge and often wore shawls with the skirts. The center of the shawl was placed across the left shoulder, with ends crossing the chest and carried back to be knotted over the right hip. Soldiers wore helmets of leather or metal with horn-shaped decoration. They wore simple sandals when rough terrain made foot covering necessary. Civilian men wore a skirt, loincloth, or tunic.

Wealthier members of Babylonian society, including the nobility, wore a draped square of fabric about 118 inches wide and 56 inches long. The fabric was fringed or had woven or embroidered edging. The men wore turban-like hats with a small brim or padded roll at the edge. As did soldiers, men wore sandals when traveling through rough terrain. There is evidence that men, possibly only royalty, sometimes were leather shoes imported from cold, mountainous regions. The toes of these shoes were curved upward and adorned with a pompon. Babylonian women wore garments that covered the entire body. They dressed in skirts with short capes cut with an opening for the head or in tunics with openings for the head and arms. Wealthier women wore sandals, though bare feet were common.

The Assyrians dominated Mesopotamia from about 1000 to 600 B.C.E. They adopted Babylonian costume, and a clear break between the late Babylonian and early Assyrian styles cannot be seen. While they wore Babylonian-style dress, the Assyrians added their own decorations. Woven or embroidered patterns were used in the dress of royalty and nobility. In about 700 B.C.E. the Assyrian king apparently introduced cotton, but there is no evidence that the new fabric was used by the Assyrians. Wool remained the preferred fabric. Persian clothing was similar to the Assyrian style. Persian textiles were often decorated with golden clothing ornaments such as gold plaques with loops on the back to allow for attachment to cloth.

At some point the Assyrians abandoned the skirts preferred by the Sumerians and Babylonians and began wearing tunics. Ordinary Assyrians wore a tunic that ended above the knee. It was worn with a belt and showed little decoration. Soldiers wore a knee-length tunic with a corset of mail armor and a wide belt. The mail was probably made by sewing small metal plates onto leather or heavy cloth. The corset might cover only the upper torso, particularly for soldiers on horseback, or the entire torso. Soldiers additionally wore helmets that came to a peaked point at the back of the head. In the late Babylonian and Assyrians periods women began wearing veils. The veils, which either covered the face or hung over the hair on either side of the face,

Two Assyrian court officials from the reign of Sargon II (721–705 B.C.E.), wearing ankle-length robes ornamented with squares and trimmed with fringe and beads and sandals (Courtesy of the Oriental Institute of the University of Chicago)

indicated marital and social status. Free, married women wore veils, while slaves and prostitutes did not. A concubine was allowed to wear a veil only when she accompanied a wife. The Assyrians and Persians wore sandals with thick or thin soles, depending on the intended use. Closed shoes were available, though they were not common, and high boots were worn by soldiers on horseback.

As is typical of the clothing styles of many civilizations, royals dressed more elaborately than ordinary people. Royalty wore a floor-length tunic under several long, fringed shawls. The weight and draping of the numerous shawls probably inhibited movement to such an extent that simpler dress was probably worn for everyday activities such as hunting. The clothing was heavily decorated with either embroidery or weavings. The specific garment worn by the king on any given day was determined by priests. The Assyrians believed that some days were more favorable than others, and the priests settled on the appropriate attire, fabric, and color for each day. On some unfavorable days the king was not permitted to change clothing. Assyrians wore high, brimless hats, and the king wore the tallest hat. The king also wore a false beard to supplement his own beard. Children had little status in Assyrian society and probably were dressed as cheaply and minimally as possible.

ASIA AND THE PACIFIC

BY KIRK H. BEETZ

Factors that govern types of clothing are climate, the availability of resources for making cloth, and the wealth of the people wearing the clothing. Pictures drawn on rock faces by the Australian aborigines suggest that throughout their long history they wore either loincloths made of animal skin or nothing at all. In Oceania males typically wore no clothing, and women wore skirts of grass or leaves. Both men and women went barefoot, which made sense given the warm climate in which they lived.

In eastern and northern Asia the nomadic peoples wore animal skins, with loincloths being the primary garment for both men and women. In cold regions a simple tunic was worn sometime before recorded history; it consisted of a rectangle of animal hide with a hole cut in it to facilitate pulling the garment over the head. This tunic could be bound at the sides and probably evolved into a warm jacket. Throughout Asia, from the Yellow River south and including India, loincloths were all that everyone but the rich and powerful wore. As late as 100 B.C.E. men and women in Japan wore only loincloths while going about their everyday work. In most of Indochina loincloths were all that was worn by peasants, and they were also the basic garments in India until the Muslim invasion in the 1700s C.E.

The region that is now China has the earliest remains of clothing in Asia and the Pacific, where shoes made of straw from about 5000 B.C.E. have been found. By 2000 B.C.E. the many ethnic groups in the region were making shoes from animal hide. By the end of the Zhou Dynasty (256 B.C.E.) most Chinese were wearing shoes made of silk interwoven with grass fibers, nettle cloth, or hemp. Such shoes were durable enough that soldiers could wear them even while marching. But by 85 C.E. silk was in such short supply that commoners had taken to walking barefoot. Before 1550 B.C.E. the Chinese developed the *san* and the *ku*. The *san* was a jacket; it could be padded with straw to provide warmth in cold weather. The *ku* were trousers. Until the first century B.C.E. most clothing of poor Chinese, which included almost everyone, was made from hemp, a plant with tough fibers. Linen, made from flax, slowly overtook hemp as the preferred fabric. The ancient Chinese shunned wool because they associated sheep with barbarian shepherds, which made wool disgusting to them.

Silk fabric had been developed in the Yellow River area, perhaps about 1900 B.C.E., and it was the preferred cloth of the rich because of its durability, shine, and ability to hold colorful dyes. For the rich, silk was usually made into robes. By 200 B.C.E. the emperor of China was expected to wear robes of different colors for different seasons, to encourage the gods to change the seasons in a reliable order. During the Han Dynasty of 202 B.C.E. to 220 C.E., the *ju* became standard wear. Known in the West as the mandarin shirt, it had a stiff collar; it remained common into the 1900s C.E. The *chun* also became common. It was a skirt with pleats and was worn instead of trousers. During the Han era, it became illegal for poor people to dress well; they were forbidden to wear robes, silk, or colorful patterns.

Silk reached Korea and Japan probably in the first century C.E., with Chinese geographers of the third century recording that the Japanese made a very high grade of silk cloth that was coveted by Chinese merchants. Before 200 C.E. the ancient Japanese invented the zori, the forerunner of modern-day "flip-flops." Zoris were sandals of wood or woven grass with a grip that fit between the big and second toes and straps that extended back over both sides of the foot. In about 500 C.E. the Japanese created the *kataginu*, a vest with broad, stiff shoulders that became popular with swordsmen because it gave their arms freedom of movement. Korean footwear tended to follow the fashions of China, with Koreans in the north more likely to wear Chinese-style shoes and Koreans in the south more likely to go barefoot.

The people of the Philippines tended to follow the clothing customs of the peoples of Oceania, but in 2000 B.C.E. they began weaving cloth and therefore sometimes had more choices in clothing than others in Oceania. At first using bark, they later learned to grow hemp, cotton, and flax, which they used mostly for loincloths, though shirts and blankets became common, perhaps in the first century B.C.E. To the southwest, an independent tradition of clothing and footwear developed in India. It was a tradition of colorful fabrics that tended to be lightweight and worn loosely, appropriate to warm weather. In India and southern Asia the loincloth remained the principal and often the only article of clothing for ordinary people at work, but it was also used as an undergarment for occasions outside of work.

Perhaps the earliest garment known from India is the sari, which was in use by 3000 B.C.E. It is a piece of cloth about 10 feet in length that is wrapped around the body in various patterns. As fashion dictated, it could be tight or loose, and it could be wound in elegant patterns for special occasions or wound loosely to give freedom of movement for work. It was made either from cotton or silk and was worn primarily by women. Also ancient is the *uttariya*, worn by both men and women. Perhaps as old as the sari, the *uttariya* was a scarf used to cover the upper body and could be made from bark, hides, or silk, though it was usually cotton.

Somewhat later the *lungi* developed. This cloth, worn by both men and women, was wrapped around the waist and tucked in, resulting in a skirt that stopped above the knee for work and at the ankle for formal occasions. It was usually made of cotton but was sometimes silk and more rarely wool. Similar to the *lungi* was the dhoti, which probably developed before 1000 B.C.E. Wrapped similarly to the *lungi*, the dhoti looked more like loose, short trousers that ended above the knee and was worn by both men and women. These garments were typically worn alone, with women generally remaining bare-breasted in everyday life until the Muslim invasion.

For warmth Indians often wore the *chadar*, which predates 200 C.E. and is still worn in modern times. It was used mostly in northern India and was made of heavy cloth, usually cotton, about 10 feet long and 3 feet wide and acted as a blanket or shawl that could give the upper body protection from the cold. Another somewhat heavy garment was the purdah, imported from Assyria in about 1000 B.C.E. It was adopted in some Hindu communities and was worn only by women, covering their entire bodies and restricting their movements. It was intended to symbolize the loss of all social rights of women by making them nonentities.

By and large the Indians preferred freedom of movement and color in their clothing, and they preferred the same for their feet. They began wearing jewelry on their feet before 2500 B.C.E. but tended to be barefoot. In the first century C.E., *khapusa* were invented. They were knee-high boots worn in the mountains of northern India as protection from the cold, and they were probably a style imported from nomads in central Asia. They tended to be made of animal hide and were decorated in colorful patterns. In the 200s C.E. *chappals* became common. These were sandals made of animal hide, with straps over the big toe and the upper foot.

EUROPE

BY AMY HACKNEY BLACKWELL

Clothing in ancient Europe was simply made and functional. Sewing and tailoring techniques were not advanced, and most people made their own clothing. Most people across Europe dressed in simple tunics and untailored cloaks that varied in design according to regional climate. Few ancient people had extensive wardrobes; many of them had one set of clothing and wore it day after day for months or years.

One of the earliest examples of European clothing is that worn by the well-preserved frozen body of a man found in 1991 in the Alps. It was estimated that the man had died before 3000 B.C.E. His entire ensemble was perfectly designed for keeping a person warm in the Alpine climate. It contained no cloth at all, possibly because Europeans at that time did not make cloth. The man wore deerskin moccasins attached to wooden frames that probably functioned as snowshoes. Historians believe that the man may have stuffed hay into the shoes as insulation. Above the shoes, fur leggings were tied with leather thongs. The man wore a loincloth made of goat hide sewn into shape and fastened around the waist with a belt. On his chest he wore a knee-length shirt made of goat hide that may or may not have had sleeves. Over his shoulders he wore a cloak woven of grass. His hat was made of brown bear skin and tied under the chin.

As they began to raise sheep and settle down in villages, people perfected techniques of making thread and weaving cloth. Most Celtic and German clothing was made of wool. Sheep thrived in the European climate, and Celtic people kept herds of them for meat, milk, and wool. The Celts also made clothing of linen, much of which was imported from regions to the south. Europeans occasionally used silk thread to embroider their garments with patterns such as meanders or swastikas (a symbol that had no racist meaning in ancient times). The silk probably came from China, and people may have unraveled old silk garments to use the thread. The Celts who lived in Hallstatt, near Salzburg, Austria, between 1200 and 500 B.C.E. practiced advanced weaving techniques. They wove cloth in various patterns, including stripes, checks, and twills. Archaeologists have found stamps that people may have used to decorate their clothing with dye.

By the time of the Roman Republic (510–27 B.C.E.) most Europeans were wearing cloth garments, with leather and fur pieces sometimes being added for warmth. Few ancient Celtic or German garments have survived. The Romans, however, spent centuries fighting with and then living with Celts and Germans, and they wrote detailed descriptions of their clothing. One of the first things Romans noticed about Gauls was that they dressed in brightly colored patterned or checked cloth. These patterns were known as plaids, or tartans. The Celts and Germans were experts at dying their woolen thread with natural dyes made from plants. They used plants such as madder to make red dye, weld to make yellow, and woad to make blue. The people wove threads into patterns that looked just like modern Scottish tartans. Different tribes became identified with particular patterns. Linen does not take dye well, so most linen remained its natural light color.

Most ancient European garments required minimal sewing. Cloaks were often not sewn at all but were worn as lengths of cloth straight off the loom. Celts and Germans shaped sleeves and made trousers, but they also made simple tunics that required only a piece of cloth, pins at the shoulders, and a belt at the waist. To sew, people used needles made of iron, bronze, or bone and thread of wool or linen. During the late Iron Age (500 B.C.E.–1 C.E.) Celtic clothing resembled Greek clothing. The Celts in continental Europe had long traded with Greeks, and they knew what Greek people wore. Celts made cloth out of wool or linen. Celtic women dressed in long-sleeved tunics covered with another tunic called a chiton by Greeks. The tunic sometimes was belted at the waist. Men wore tunics with long or short sleeves.

Celtic men often wore breeches or pants under their tunics. Pants came in various styles: wide, narrow, or wide at the top and narrow below the knee. Both sexes wore clothing with ornate decorations. They added fringes to hems, embroidery to cuffs and collars, and sometimes sewed on beads. They used colored wool to embroider on linen and white linen to embroider on colored wool. Men and women also wore a pouch at the waist to hold personal items. Before Celts went into battle they styled their hair with lime to make the hair stand up in spikes, and they also bleached their hair blond. Especially courageous Celts sometimes went into battle naked except for sandals and a gold necklace called a torque. According to the Greek philosopher Aristotle (384–322 B.C.E.), Celtic children were accustomed to nakedness from an early age. Aristotle wrote that to make children tough, parents had them go around in minimal clothing in cold weather.

German clothing was similar to that of the Celts. Because of their colder climate Germans also wore heavier clothing made of leather and fur, such as fur-lined capes and trousers. The historian Tacitus (ca. 56–120 C.E.) wrote that some primitive German tribes wore only rough animal skins. The Romans considered the German and Celtic habit of wearing trousers barbaric. Romans never wore pants. Clothing styles across the rest of Europe followed the basic styles of the Celts and Germans. People in Ireland wore a long linen tunic called a *léine*. It had long sleeves or was sleeveless and was usually decorated with embroidery around the hem, cuffs, and neckline. Women wore a longer tunic than that of men. People who did outdoor labor wore shorter tunics than people who did not. On top of the tunic, people wore a cloak or shawl, usually fastened at the shoulder with a pin. This woolen shawl was often woven of wool in bright colors and decorated with embroidery and gold or silver thread.

Throughout Europe people used clothing to show their status. The armor of noble Celtic and Germanic warriors was more elaborately decorated than that of ordinary men. Nobles wore helmets made of bronze or iron instead of the plain leather of common soldiers. The wealthiest men wore chain mail, which was very expensive. The Celtic torque was a mark of elite status, as was elaborate jewelry, especially of gold. In general, the clothing of noble people was more finely made and more ornately decorated than that of common people. In some areas linen was considered a finer fabric and was reserved for the wealthy, while peasants were forced to wear rougher wool cloth.

Ancient Europeans often went barefoot, but in the winter shoes were a necessity, and throughout the Continent shoes were a mark of status. Some shoes were of a very simple design, just a rectangular piece of leather with holes punched in the sides. The wearer threaded a leather thong through the holes, wrapped the leather around the foot, and drew it tight as if it were a drawstring bag. More meticulous shoemakers cut the leather to the shape of the foot and sewed portions of it to help it keep its shape. Many Celts borrowed the shoe design of the Roman soldiers, attaching a carefully designed piece of leather to a hobnailed sole. This shoe was tied on with leather thongs.

GREECE

BY CARYN E. NEUMANN

As numerous surviving statues and painted vases show, clothing among the ancient Greeks varied little from century to century. From the tenth to the first centuries B.C.E., both men and women dressed similarly in draped material of wool or linen and in sandals. This largely unchanging Greek costume gave a sense of stability and permanence.

Ancient Greeks first dressed in a simple, woolen, thickly woven sleeveless tunic known as an *exomis*. The *exomis* evolved into the chiton, a woolen rectangle of seamless cloth open on the right side, fastened on the left, and held in place with two belts, the top one wider than the other and between which the wearer made a wide tuck of cloth. Without a belt this tunic hung loosely and served as a night garment. Lengthened, the tunic was worn as a ceremonial costume; it also replaced the short tunic in winter. The chiton was woven in varying sizes according to its intended use and the height of the wearer. Usually the opening over the right thigh was closed by a few stitches. The shoulder was fastened with threads of the cloth, which formed natural, strong fastenings, or the two upper corners of the rectangle of cloth were simply knotted together. Women wore an ankle-length version of the chiton. The cloth was always draped, never shaped or cut. Children generally dressed in the same manner as adults of the same sex or, if they were young enough, went naked. Only slaves wore breeches, which were regarded as barbarian dress fit only for foreigners.

The woolen fabrics preferred by the Greeks shows their resistance to the luxurious fabrics, such as silk, preferred by the peoples of the East. The early Greeks, however, were influenced by other civilizations. The same groups that shaped Greek architecture shaped Greek dress. The Dorians, from Illyria, invaded Greece in about 1200 B.C.E. and introduced the Doric tunic. In the sixth century the Greeks came into contact with the Ionians of Asia Minor and adopted their finer linen style of dress.

The Dorians gave the Greeks a wide woolen cloak, the himation, and its military derivative, the chlamys. The Doric tunic, which measured about twice the width of the wearer from elbow to elbow, was basically a folded oblong of material

Caryatids from the Porch of the Maidens at Erechtheion, a temple on the north side of the Acropolis at Athens; the maidens are dressed in the simple tunic called the peplos. (Alison Frantz Photographic Collection, American School of Classical Studies at Athens)

that was folded again, placed around the body, pinned at the shoulders, and often worn with a girdle. The himation, made of a single six-by-nine-foot piece of cloth, swathed the body without fixed fastenings and was often worn under a tunic. The poor sometimes wore only a himation. The *tribon* was similar to the ordinary himation except that it was typically brown or black and tattered. It was worn to demonstrate poverty and contempt for earthly vanities. In Athens the *tribon* also was worn by advocates at the bar.

Women wore a long tunic known as a peplos. The peplos was basically a shawl completely open down one side, usually the left. The open peplos was not normally belted at the waist, but Greek women made a closed peplos by seaming together the two free edges of the garment instead of leaving them open to the thigh. They folded up the edge of the garment, shortening it to waist length, and used the flap to cover the head or veil the face. Spartan girls wore short tunics, slit at the sides, to make it easier to compete in athletic events.

The use of wool kept most garments in a tonal range of off-whites, but ordinary people seem to have worn lighter-colored tunics and cloaks in dark colors, such as rust reds and reddish brown. Color distinguished the costume of warriors, and the chlamys was generally decorated with bands of color, either along the upper edges on the neck and shoulders or down the side seams. The borders had patterns of flowers or geometric designs. Youths in earlier times wore black tunics, and those in later centuries wore white.

Linen was introduced to Greece by the Ionians. The Ionic linen tunic had more elegant drapes than a woolen tunic. Often pleated, the Ionic tunic was so long that the extra material was pulled through the waistband to give a bloused effect. Unlike the Doric tunic, the Ionic one did not require fastening pins. Women dressed in Ionic style wore brilliant colors, known as flowered colors, including greens. It became fashionable for women to wear a ground-length tunic with a peplos on top. The peplos either hung loose to just below the waist or was worn longer and fastened with a girdle. An alternative, known as a *diploidion*, was a piece of material left very long in front and folded at the shoulders so that an extra flap of material fell to waist level. Women from all parts of Greece and a few men wore a *tarentine*, a white gown so thin that the body was visible through it.

The Greeks usually went barefoot, wearing shoes only as protection or for special occasions. Sandals worn by both sexes were fastened with light leather throngs that left the foot almost bare. Soles were made of cork or leather and occasionally studded with nails. Closed shoes fit either foot and had elevated soles that added height to the wearer. A binding was fastened to the sole and passed between the big toe and the second toe, divided into two and passed through a latchet, or a narrow leather strap, to secure the sole of the shoe to the foot. The two bands were criss-crossed high on the legs and then fastened. Greek women, who rarely left the house, wore only sandals in public. By the fourth century B.C.E. shoes had become more elegant, often red with yellow-edged soles.

A variety of hats were worn by Greek men and women to protect them from the blazing sun of the region. Hunters and travelers wore wide-brimmed hats. The petasos was a flat, cylindrical head covering worn by young men. Women wore a similar round, semiconical head covering called a *tholia*.

The simplicity of Greek dress influenced the people who came into contact with the Greeks, especially the Romans. Greek dress reflected the ancient habit of wearing tunics, and the styles and patterns preferred by the Greeks spread throughout the ancient world.

ROME

BY LARISSA BONFANTE

Garments in ancient Rome were made of wool or linen. In the time of Alexander the Great, in the 300s B.C.E., cotton was introduced, as was silk, which was always an extravagant luxury. Wool was woven in a great variety of textures, weights, and colors, from the sturdy dark cloth of slaves' tunics to the fine purple wool of imperial togas. Linen, much of which was imported from Egypt, was usually left in its natural color and could be extremely fine-woven.

The basic dress of Roman male citizens, which visually distinguished them from Greeks wearing rectangular mantles, was the woolen toga, a mantle with rounded borders like the earlier Etruscan *tebenna*, a shorter semicircular woolen mantle. With the toga were worn boots or *calcei*, formal laced shoes worn with the toga outside the house. Working men wore their tunics belted. Unlike the Greeks, who normally wore sandals everywhere, the Romans wore them only indoors.

Again unlike the Greeks, Roman men did not exercise in the nude. They shared the universal taboo against appearing naked in public, though in their art they represented youthful male figures in an idealized "nudity as costume," adopting the Greek artistic convention. They did strip in the public baths, but when they exercised or had to be free of clothing to work, they wore a type of loincloth, called a *subligaculum* or a *campestre* because it was worn for military exercises in the Campus Martius.

Citizens and slaves, male and female, old and young wore shirts or tunics of various lengths, materials, and colors. Greeks and lower-class Romans also wore a plain rectangular woolen mantle called a pallium, which could double as a blanket in cold weather. Roman women wore linen tunics that were longer and wider than those of men, but this garment was basically unchanging in shape, being made up of one or more rectangular pieces of cloth, which were sewn, buttoned, or pinned at the shoulders; belted at the waist; and draped on the body, creating pleasing folds. The *stola*, which looked much like a slip with thin straps, was worn over the tunic from at least the time of Augustus (63 B.C.E.–14 C.E.) by the Roman *matrona*, or married woman. The outer garment of women was a rectangular mantle (*palla*). Only young girls and disreputable women wore the toga.

Otherwise, Roman women's clothing did not have the same varieties and distinctions as those used to mark the status of men. A higher-class woman depended on the elegance, color, and luxury of her garments, her jewelry, and her hairstyle to set her apart. Women's sandals, normally made of leather, had straps arranged in a variety of styles and attached to soles of various heights and ranged from the sturdy, simple styles of working women and slaves to the luxurious, extravagantly decorated footwear of sophisticated Roman ladies. Women athletes or entertainers wore a sports costume consisting of short pants and brassieres; this was probably the underwear of women, which was usually not visible.

Babies were swaddled in strips of cloth or went naked, depending on weather and other circumstances. Children were not distinguished by gender before they reached adolescence. Until then, whether slave or freeborn, they all wore simple narrow tunics and sandals. Both freeborn boys and girls wore rounded togas. Over the tunic the boy wore the characteristic toga praetexta, decorated with a purple-red stripe at the border, which was meant as a good-luck charm to keep him safe. For a boy, the formal rite of passage marking the change from childhood to adulthood took place sometime between his 15th and 17th year, at which time he laid aside his purple-bordered toga and put on the plain white toga virilis of an adult, full-fledged Roman citizen.

The equivalent rite of passage for girls was the wedding. As was the case with boys, a formal change of dress marked a girl's initiation into womanhood and her new status as a married woman. Just as the boy laid aside his toga praetexta, the girl put aside her dolls and toys and her toga before the wedding. As in many cultures, the bride's wedding costume was traditional and symbolic. The night before the wedding, she slept in a narrow, white tunic, like a boy's, and wore a yellow hairnet, both of which she had woven herself. Her wedding dress was tied with a square knot, the Hercules knot, and her hair was dressed in a special, primitive style. It was parted with a spear and twisted or braided on top of her head in a kind of bun made up of six braids or coils. Her head was then covered with a flame-colored, yellow veil and a wreath of flowers and herbs.

Roman culture, more than any, used dress to mark a person's status, rank, and wealth. Social roles were fluid, and perhaps for this reason they had to be visually recognizable. The son of a freedman, or former slave, was a full-fledged Roman citizen, with all the rights and privileges of a freeborn citizen, including wearing the toga. The color, decoration, and manner of wearing a toga indicated various roles or ranks. A plain toga distinguished an adult male from a boy, who needed the magical protection of a purple-bordered toga praetexta. This purple-bordered toga worn by a man, on the other hand, meant that he held one of the highest important Roman offices, a curule magistracy. The dark toga pulla was worn by mourners. The priests pictured on the famous altar Ara Pacis in Rome wore traditional leather hats with a peak or apex, and their togas were draped in front in a semicircular shape. The triumphal toga, purple in the early days and later decorated with gold, became the imperial costume. Ritual gestures were rigidly observed: when citizens carried out a religious ritual, they covered their heads with their togas; another ritual gesture involved wrapping the toga tightly around oneself.

The costume and hairstyle of the important public priesthood of the vestal virgins resembled those of brides; they also covered their hair with veils and added woolen fillets, or ribbons. From the time of Augustus, a woman's marital status was visually marked by her *stola*. There are literary references indicating that the toga rather than the *stola* was worn by prostitutes and adulteresses.

THE AMERICAS

BY JULIA MARTA CLAPP

Because it was made of perishable or delicate materials, such as woven textiles, leather, and feather work, little clothing of the ancient Americas has survived, especially from tropical or wet climates. Archaeologists and art historians have hypothesized about ancient American dress on the basis of evidence from a few burial sites that contained salvageable clothing. Art and artifacts from the era also provide clues. Complicating the issue is that some figures, especially in Mesoamerican art, are depicted nude or in clothing that is represented abstractly and is difficult to interpret.

Excavations in the Valley of Mexico have uncovered remains at the site of Tlatilco, which was settled in about 1300 B.C.E. Figurines at such burial sites wear clothes that differ by sex. The attire is rendered in a simple manner that makes it challenging to recognize. Anthropologists have speculated that the female sculptures wear a form of grass skirt and that the male sculptures wear loincloths.

Little is known about the Olmec (1500–400 B.C.E.), who occupied the wetlands of the southern Gulf Coast of modern-day Mexico. Because the land was tropical and wet, textiles have not survived. The Olmec are a relatively unknown culture compared with later and better-researched civilizations such as the Maya and the Aztec. Limited knowledge of Olmec clothing comes from sculpture of the era. Figures are depicted in animal costumes, such as a figure in one Olmec mural in the Oxtotitlan Cave, Guerrero, Mexico, that wears a birdlike costume with a scalloped-edge cape. It is unknown, however, whether this representation is symbolic or is representative of the actual dress of religious leaders.

In the realm of ordinary daily attire, a figurine of a seated woman found in a tomb at the Olmec city of La Venta (occupied 900–400 B.C.E.) has a ridge carved across her folded legs that seems to indicate a skirt. Male figures in works such those in a monument found at Potrero Nuevo, Veracruz, wear what appear to be simple loincloths. Outside the Olmec heartland, in the modern-day Mexican state of Guerrero, archaeologists have found a wall painting in the Juxtlahuaca cave. The figure in the painting wears jaguar skins on his arms and legs, a red-and-yellow striped tunic, and a feather headdress. Other findings of the Olmec period are figures wearing varying elements of dress for an ancient ball game that was an important ritual throughout pre-Columbian Mesoamerica. Early representations of the Maya also support the findings that center on forms of skirts or loincloths. A Mayan incised stone from about 100– 400 C.E. shows a figure wearing a patterned skirt and leg coverings in addition to extensive jewelry and other adornment.

In South America people of the early Chavín civilization (900–200 B.C.E.) did not wear constructed, or sewn, clothes. They wore large cloths wrapped as mantles or skirts, a practice that continued in the Andes even after the incorporation of shaped or sewn clothes. Burial excavations have unearthed belts, sandals, and caps from the Chavín era. Excavations of ruler burials from the Paracas civilization (600–175 B.C.E.) give a limited amount of information on ancient South American dress. Because the burial sites contain the remains of deceased elite, not common, people, the items found may not be typical. In addition, the garments buried with a person might not have been the garments he or she wore in daily life. The articles of clothing found may have been ceremonial, produced for daily life, or made for burial.

Many of the items found by archaeologists continue to be worn by Andean people. One such garment is the mantle, which is a large, rectangular cloth arranged around the neck and over the shoulders. The cloth would have been woven

Pottery figures of a drummer and a woman and child, Tala-Tonalá style, Jalisco, Mexico 300 B.C.E. to 300 C.E.; the woman is wearing earplugs, a necklace, and a typical wrap skirt, while the man wears the same ornaments and a mantle over one shoulder. (© The Trustees of the British Museum)

with a pattern or embroidered. The woven patterns and embroidery were not simply ornamental but told important facts about the wearer, such as social status and family lineage. Weaving was an important cultural tradition in the Andes that flourishes in modern times. The weavers are known for their skill in creating complex, often abstract designs that require intensive planning and labor. The tradition of Andean weaving and embroidery began with the early civilizations.

Also found in ruler burials were ponchos, large pieces of cloth with slits cut into them so that the garments could fit over the head. An elaboration on the poncho was the tunic, which was sewn up the sides. Skirts were of the wraparound style and often were embroidered. Some people of the Paracas era wore rectangular loincloths with two ties pulled between the legs and fastened around the waist. Excavated examples of loincloths were not decorated except for the border.

Little is known about clothing and footwear in ancient North America.

See also ADORNMENT; ART; CHILDREN; CLIMATE AND GEOGRAPHY; DEATH AND BURIAL PRACTICES; FOREIGNERS AND BARBARIANS; GENDER STRUCTURES AND ROLES; MILITARY; NOMADIC AND PASTORAL SOCIETIES; OCCUPATIONS; RELIGION AND COSMOLOGY; SLAVES AND SLAVERY; SOCIAL ORGANIZATION; SPORTS AND RECREATION; TEXTILES AND NEEDLEWORK; TOWNS AND VILLAGES; TRADE AND EXCHANGE; WEAPONRY AND ARMOR.

FURTHER READING

Francois Boucher, *20,000 Years of Fashion: The History of Costume and Personal Adornment* (New York: Harry N. Abrams, 1987).

Thomas Hope, *Costumes of the Greeks and Romans* (New York: Dover, 1962).

Mary G. Houston, *Ancient Greek, Roman, and Byzantine Costume and Decoration* (London: A and C Black, 1931).

Sara Pendergast and Tom Pendergast, *Fashion, Costume, and Culture: Clothing, Headwear, Body Decorations, and Footwear through the Ages* (Detroit: Thomson Gale, 2004).

Judith Lynn Sebesta and Larissa Bonfante, eds., *The World of Roman Costume* (Madison: University of Wisconsin Press, 1994).

Marion Sichel, *Costume of the Ancient World* (London: Batsford Academic and Educational, 1980).

Phyllis G. Tortora and Keith Eubank, *Survey of Historic Costume: A History of Western Dress* (New York: Fairchild Publications, 1994).

Anne Paul, *Paracas Ritual Attire* (Norman: University of Oklahoma Press, 1990).

► crafts

INTRODUCTION

When archaeologists study ancient sites, including the remains of villages and individual homes, one of the things they look for is evidence of occupational activity. In particular, they look for the remains of tools and materials that might have been used in the production of crafts. Among the materials can be precious metals, other metals (such as copper, iron, and lead), semiprecious stones, glass, ceramics, and stone shards, as well as tools used for cutting, carving, grinding, sanding, polishing, and the like. Any of these materials can provide evidence that a family or group of people were involved in the production of crafts.

The earliest humans were highly dependent on the crafts items they could make themselves with whatever materials were at hand, typically wood, stone, shells, bones, antlers and horns, and the like. Most of these crafts would have served entirely practical purposes. Examples include arrow and spear points for use in hunting, pottery to hold water and food, primitive cooking utensils, and similar items. Occasionally, too, archaeologists find carved items that may have had religious significance, including amulets (or charms), small statues, and other objects to which their owners might have attached spiritual significance.

As human civilization advanced, the production of crafts progressed as well. While the earliest humans had to be generalists in the production of crafts, producing anything they needed to make their lives more livable, people in later eras began to specialize in crafts production, creating objects that were not only useful but beautiful as well. They typically passed their skills down to their descendants, who continued the family tradition of crafts production. Some of these specializations would have included metalworking (including coin making), woodworking, glassmaking, stonework, the production of fabrics, and so on. Even such persons as brewers and vintners (winemakers) could be considered crafts workers. Some of these craftspersons would have been involved in the building trades. Some, for example, became experts in thatching roofs, while others became stonemasons who carved ornamental stonework for public buildings and monuments. Others would have focused on metalworking for farming, producing implements for plowing and harvesting, or they might have specialized in pots, bowls, cups, and other household items.

Still other crafts workers devoted their attentions to jewelry and other items used for personal adornment. Some worked with metals, including both precious metals like gold and silver and ordinary metals like copper and iron. Others learned to make glass objects, turning glass into beads, amulets, and other objects. In ancient Egypt, for example, many people were skilled in the production of faience, a glasslike material that consisted of a paste made of quartz crystals that was then glazed. Faience was used in a variety of applications, including not only jewelry, pots, and bowls but also walls and floor tiles. Among Native Americans, beadwork and leather crafts were particularly important.

The expansion of trade opened new opportunities for crafts workers. They were no longer limited to materials they could find locally. Particularly as trade to the Far East and Africa grew, crafts workers in Europe, the Middle East, and around the Mediterranean Sea had access to precious gemstones, ivory, exotic hardwoods, new types of minerals and stones, silks, fabric dyes, pigments, and mother-of-pearl. Trade contact also exposed crafts workers to new technologies and techniques, enriching crafts production for all.

AFRICA

BY KIRK H. BEETZ

It is possible that ancient Africa's greatest achievements in crafts involved perishable materials, such as wood and reeds, with only rare traces of those materials surviving to the present. Thus, ancient crafts are represented mostly by ceramics and metal artifacts. Most early African metalwork was in copper, tin, or bronze. Copper by itself was hard to work with, and making it keep its shape during casting was a problem with which ancient African metalworkers struggled, but combining copper with tin made bronze, and bronze held its shape well. In Nubia, the land south of Egypt, bronze was at first used for casting bowls and other vessels. Bronze gradually replaced stone for use in weapons, with spears still being tipped with stone as late as 900 B.C.E., when the kingdom of Kush arose.

The Kushites cast bronze using clay molds that were probably sculpted by hand, instead of by the lost-wax method that involved sculpting a figure out of wax and shaping a mold around it. The National Museum in Athens, Greece, has a bronze casting of the Kushite king Shabaka, who was also pharaoh of Egypt (ca. 716–ca. 702 B.C.E.). The artifact shows the skill that Kushite bronze casters had attained: Shabaka's face is an individual portrait taken from life, and the body is well defined and proportioned. Kushite casters made even such everyday objects as bowls and pitchers decorative. For example, the British Museum has a handle shaped like a girl, probably for a pouring vessel, such as a pitcher, from the 400s–200s B.C.E. Bronze was used for religious practices, with the most unusual perhaps being the legs of beds on which the dead were laid in their graves.

The Kushites cast in other metals besides bronze. They made silver objects with the same fine skill as their bronzes, including realistic human images on such objects as silver mirrors. They developed ironworking in about the 600s B.C.E., perhaps after being exposed to the iron weapons of the Assyrians when the Assyrians drove them out of Egypt in about 656 B.C.E. The monarchs of Kush moved their capital from Napata to the city of Meroë, far south along the Nile River, in about 590 B.C.E. The area of Meroë is rich in iron ore, and a few archaeologists have suggested that Meroë became a great iron-manufacturing center. But of the city's iron-smelting furnaces the earliest so far discovered date to around 370 B.C.E., and it is likely that before then the Kushites imported iron ingots from the Near East. After 370 B.C.E. Kush may well have exported iron ingots to other parts of Africa.

Another significant center for smelting iron was in the region of modern Nigeria, where a mysterious people called the Nok lived from ca. 500 B.C.E. to ca. 300 C.E. The Nok are named for the village where some of their pottery was first found. By 300 B.C.E. the Nok had iron-smelting furnaces. Some archaeologists think that the Nok learned to smelt iron from Berbers who brought the technology south from Phoenician colonies in North Africa or from Kushites who migrated to the west, but the existing evidence largely suggests that the Nok developed smelting of iron independently. How they did so is unknown.

Trade in metals was extensive in ancient Africa. Metal may have been in use in the ancient land of Ghana, about 100 miles north of modern Ghana, from 1000 B.C.E. to 500 C.E. There were copper mines in modern Niger, in central Africa, that may have supplied copper to much of central and eastern Africa. The Bantu-speaking peoples who began expanding through Africa from central Africa in the last 200 or so years B.C.E. worked with copper. They probably worked metal inside their houses, and they seem to have favored copper. They wound copper wire into bracelets, made copper beads, and even made copper money, shaped into crosses. If they were like the Bantu-speaking people of later eras, their metalsmiths were highly regarded members of the community and were credited with having supernatural powers.

Trade in materials that could embellish the body were common. The magnificent metal jewelry of Africans is representative of this practice. In addition to metal, glass beads were traded extensively and were popular in most of Africa in ancient times, but at present evidence for local manufacturing of glass in Africa dates no earlier than the medieval era. In ancient Africa glass came from Egypt, Rome, and India.

Other crafts are harder to identify because of the perishability of materials. The oldest wooden object may be a vessel from about 1000 B.C.E. found in a cave in southern Kenya. It is shaped like vessels used by modern cattle herders to carry milk and may indicate a cultural tradition for the area that is mostly lost because wood usually decays rapidly in the area. Masks, which are an important part of the culture of much of Africa, were usually made of wood, and archaeologists must make do with depictions of masks in stone and ceramic figures, mostly from northeastern Africa.

In Kush wood was used for footboards of burial beds as well as for doors and probably other objects. Kushite doors to important buildings were wondrous, often made of ebony, carved with geometric and realistic figures, inlaid with ivory, and embellished with bronze or gold. Magnificent doors were made well into the modern era in eastern Africa, especially in cities and towns that traded with people from Asia. Furniture of any kind came late to much of Africa, especially western Africa, where chairs were first seen when Europeans brought them. In Kush furniture tended to imitate Egyptian forms, with wooden headrests being common.

Basketry seems to have been important in most of Africa, but as with wooden objects, most surviving indications of the types of basketry are found in ceramics and on stone images. Many designs for ceramic vessels seem to be imitations of forms of baskets, and there is logic to this practice. Even in modern times people make baskets that are watertight and can be used to carry liquids; it is not surprising, then, that ancient Africans created pottery designed like baskets. In Africa basketry has had other significant uses besides carrying or holding objects. The walls of houses were sometimes made entirely of woven reeds. In modern Chad there are farming communities in which not only houses but also the walls surrounding family compounds are woven, preserving a skill that developed in ancient times. Thus, some of the crafts of historical times offer clues to the craft of ancient times, helping to fill in the gaps among the metal and ceramic remains of ancient African cultures.

EGYPT

BY ERIN FAIRBURN

The type of crafts found and the way crafts were made help researchers flesh out the practices of daily life. Objects made by Egyptian craftsmen were often prestige items, and the materials used and quality of workmanship can indicate the social ranking of their owners. Egyptian craftsmen made items in stone, metal, wood, glass, faience, and basketry, among other materials. Stone was used for a variety of objects, including jewelry, amulets, and tools, and the use of stone for vessels was common from the earliest times. Different types of stone, most of which were found near the centers of production, were used in the creation of vessels. The exteriors were shaped with stone tools and smoothed and finished with stone and quartz sand, and the interiors were probably drilled.

Stone vessels were produced in a number of forms. Stone bowls and jars were common throughout ancient times and were the most common types seen until the New Kingdom (1550– 1070 B.C.E.). Alabaster, diorite, gneiss, limestone breccia, and porphyry were popular materials for vessels in the Predynastic Period (5000–3100 B.C.E.) and Early Dynastic Period (2920–2770 B.C.E.). Modeled vessels of blue anhydrite, often decorated with monkeys or ducks, came into fashion during the Middle Kingdom (2040–1640 B.C.E.) and Second Intermediate Period (ca. 1640–1532 B.C.E.). Diverse forms were created in the New Kingdom. Kohl tubes and applicators, often made of alabaster, were very popular types of stone objects from this period on. (Kohl was a cosmetic preparation often used to darken the eyelids and rims.)

Metals were worked into tools, figurines, jewelry, and sculpture in Egypt, but they were also used to create vessels, which were almost invariably hammered, rather than cast. Metal was likewise used for model tools, cylinder seals (used to stamp impressions into clay), mirrors, and *ushabtis*, or small figurines that were buried with the dead to accompany them into the underworld and work for them in the afterlife. Most Egyptian metal products were made of a copper alloy, silver, or gold. Not many examples of metal craft survive, perhaps because they were reused or melted down in later periods. However, a silver box lid is known from a Predynastic context, and a copper ewer and basin date to the Second Dynasty (2770–2649 B.C.E.). Silver vessels were found in the el-Tod treasure dating to the Middle Kingdom, and silver was used for a number of decorative vessels in the New Kingdom.

Egyptian craftsmen created objects from such native woods as acacia, tamarisk, and sycamore beginning in the Predynastic Period. They also used imported woods such as cedar, ash, elm, and oak from North Africa and the eastern Mediterranean region as early as the First Dynasty (2920–2770 B.C.E.). Native woods could be utilized in woodworking, but they are of generally poor quality; imported wood was preferred if longer pieces were required. Wood was joined using variations on butt, miter, or mortise and tenon joints. Furniture and wooden objects could be finished in a number of ways. Wood was often plastered to even out any imperfections and create a surface on which to apply gilding or paint. Pieces were sometimes inlaid with decorative woods like ebony as well as with the nonwooden materials of ivory, faience, glass, or precious stones. Veneers of decorative wood were used on some furniture. Varnish was sometimes applied to pieces in the New Kingdom, and beeswax was used to seal painted pieces.

In the Predynastic Period carved wood relief panels have been found in tombs of private individuals, 11 of them in the tomb of Hesire, a high official during the reign of the pharaoh Djoser. From the Old Kingdom (2575–2134 B.C.E.) there is furniture of the royal mother Hetepheres, which included a canopy frame, two armchairs, a bed frame, headrest, chest, and carrying chair. A diverse variety of wooden chests appear at this point. Stools and boxes are seen with great frequency in Middle Kingdom and New Kingdom contexts. Little furniture is preserved from the Late Period (712–332 B.C.E.), though cabinetry became a highly developed form by the Graeco-Roman Period (332 B.C.E.–395 C.E.). Royal furniture, such as that of Hetepheres and Tutankhamen, was similar in form to that of private domestic furniture but of better quality and workmanship.

Faience is a unique material that had been developed by the Predynastic Period. It is a composite of crushed quartz or sand mixed with lime and plant ash or natron (a sodium compound), which is glazed and fired. Glazing was usually accomplished by including an alkali in the core material, which would crystallize on the surface as it dried and then melt, becoming glassy, upon firing. Because of copper inclusions the finished product is often a bright blue-green, though Egyptians developed techniques that created a wide spectrum of glaze colors, from opaque white to violet.

Faience was used in the Old Kingdom in the production of molded figurines of both humans and animals. Tens of thousands of blue-green glazed tiles were found in the chambers beneath the step pyramid of Djoser (r. 2575–2551) at Saqqara. Figures of hippopotami and hedgehogs were popular during the Middle Kingdom, as were vessels decorated on both the inside and the outside. The range of colors increased during the New Kingdom, as seen on the polychrome tiles of

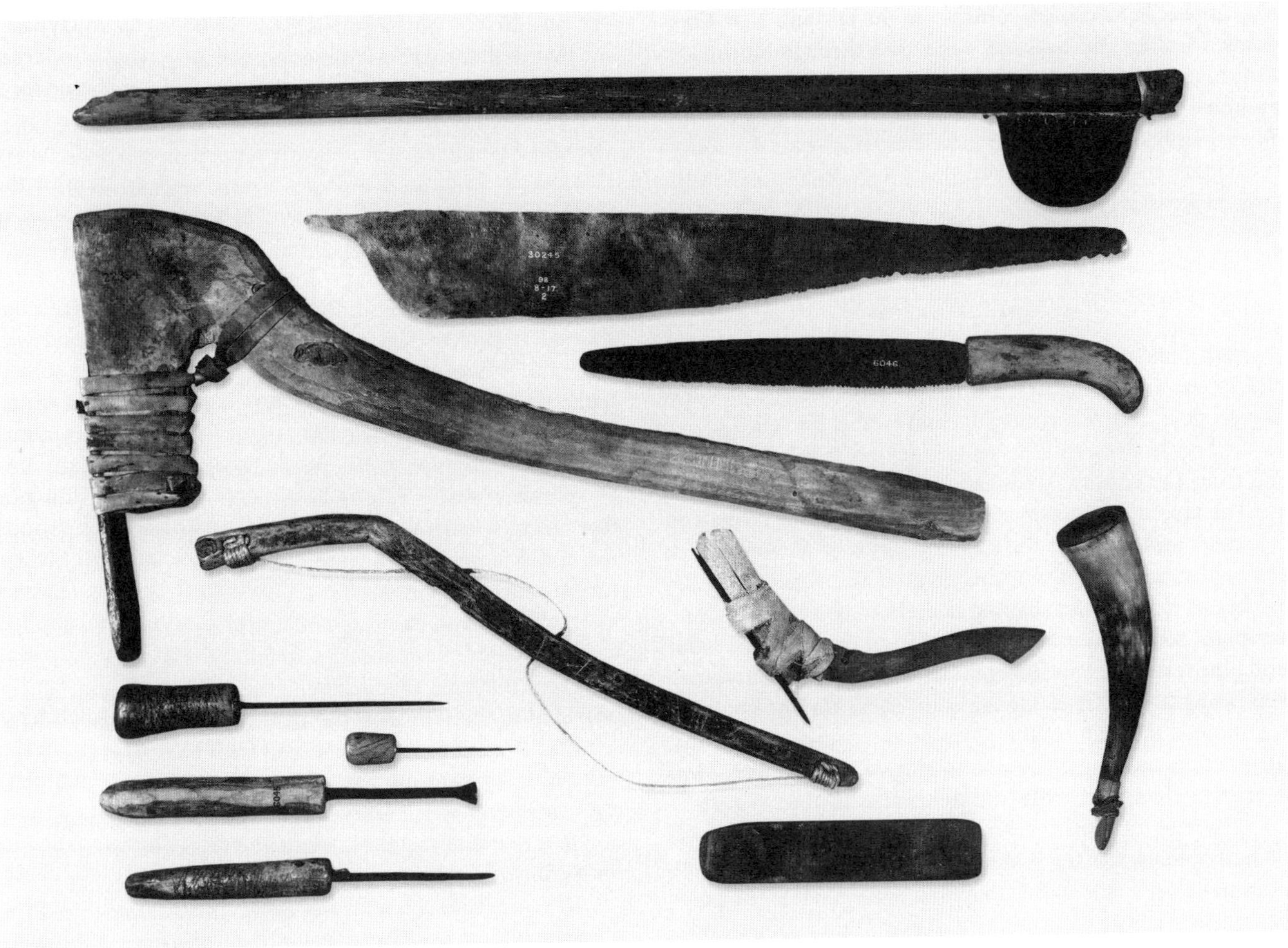

Group of bronze tools for woodworking, from Thebes, Egypt (New Kingdom, around 1300 B.C.E.) (© The Trustees of the British Museum)

the period depicting cartouches (oval or oblong decorations framing a ruler's name), hieroglyphs, and human figures. Bowls and chalices were common vessel forms. In the Twenty Sixth Dynasty (ca. 664–525 B.C.E.) *ushabtis* and model *sistra* (musical instruments of the percussion family) became increasingly popular forms.

Little glass is found in Egypt before the New Kingdom, and research indicates that what has been found was probably imported. Because glassmaking appears as a fully formed industry early in the New Kingdom, it is possible that foreign glassmakers were brought to Egypt to develop a native industry. Regardless of who produced New Kingdom glass, this period was the peak of Egyptian glass production. Production was in full swing and highly developed by the reign of Thutmose III (r. 1479–1425 B.C.E.) A number of workshops are known from the New Kingdom, especially from the palace of Malkata, near Thebes, and from Amarna. Glass production was on the decline by the late Twentieth Dynasty (1196–1070 B.C.E.) and continued on a reduced scale from that time.

During the New Kingdom several techniques were used to create glass objects. Vessels were almost entirely core-formed, or shaped around a center rod; they could also be mold-made. Glass could be worked like stone using a technique known as cold cutting, with the glass being chipped away and sculpted with a hammer and chisel. Molding and cold cutting were often combined to create glass sculptures in the round, a unique practice in the ancient world. Core forming was slowly replaced by blowing as the most common vessel-making technique in the Graeco-Roman Period.

Nets, bags, baskets, and matting were created by ancient Egyptians out of a limited range of materials, usually palm leaves and grasses but occasionally reeds and rushes. Basketry has been found in some quantity at certain sites. Additional information can be gleaned from mud impressions that were often made when old matting or basketry pieces were incorporated into building materials for new constructions as a means of reinforcement.

Several techniques were used to create basketry in ancient Egypt, but coiled basketry predominated from Prehistoric until Ptolemaic times. In the Predynastic Period matting was incorporated into housing. Throughout the Dynastic Period bed frames and chair seats were woven with matting. Twined bags appear to have been common in the Old and New Kingdoms. Matting and basketry were used throughout the Dynastic Period in both domestic and funerary contexts. Coiled basketry continued in Ptolemaic times, but plaiting became a commonly used technique as well, especially for decorative containers and fans. Sewn-plait mats were widespread in the Graeco-Roman Period.

THE MIDDLE EAST

BY TOM STREISSGUTH

Ancient Mesopotamia was a land of fertile soil and little else in the way of natural resources. Base metals, precious stones, gold and silver, marble, and timber were all scarce in the Fertile Crescent, the semicircle of fertile land stretching from the eastern Mediterranean coast of the Levant to the Persian Gulf. But as trade increased along the rivers and seacoasts and between the growing cities of Mesopotamia, the Levant, and Egypt, artisans began making use of a wider variety of materials in shaping household objects, tools, and weapons. Silver and iron ore arrived from Anatolia; the cedar and pine forests of Palestine provided timber, and lapis lazuli was brought west from Afghanistan. These trading contacts, maintained through seagoing vessels and overland caravans, fostered the sharing of new technologies, and the spread of Mesopotamian craft styles and techniques to other regions.

The rise of urban civilization stimulated the growth of new manufacturing industries. While farming was the dominant occupation of Mesopotamian villagers, the cities became a focus of labor, money, and trading activity. Independent merchants bought and sold goods, while the taxes collected from craft workshops in turn contributed to the region's political and military power. The city of Ur, for example, drew vast revenues from trade in its textiles, which were renowned throughout the Middle East. Mesopotamian kingdoms conquered through military power but prospered through trade in their finished goods, which were produced by private workshops and then exchanged for the raw materials they lacked.

The first crafts of the region drew on the few easily available natural resources. Red clay dug from riverbeds was shaped and fired, creating useful pottery and brick, which went into basic construction and the paving of city streets. Mesopotamian marshlands provided material for floor mats, for baskets, for shoes, and for house construction, in which wooden frames were filled in with thickly woven reeds. Baskets, used to carry fruits, nuts, grains, and fish, were woven from reeds and fiber—the precursor to the carpet and textile industries of the Middle East—and waterproofed with bitumen. Basket weavers worked in a variety of techniques, interweaving the material in a coiled basket or "twilling" it in diagonal strips. The size and shape of the finished piece depended on the pliability and thickness of the material used. These perishable materials survive only in the form of small fragments, some dating to 7000 B.C.E. Houses in the southern marshlands were also made from cut and woven plants, a technique that survives to modern times. Artisans also used woven plant materials to produce boats and small furniture.

For their farming tools and their weapons, the Mesopotamians first replaced stone with copper, an unalloyed metal that occurs in natural deposits. Copper remained the principal metal of tools and weapons as late as the fourth millennium B.C.E. The use of copper was later displaced by the discovery of bronze (a more durable alloy of copper and tin). Weapon smiths crafted knives, axes, daggers, and body armor out of bronze before turning to iron, a much harder and more durable substance that, at first, was collected from meteorites. By 1200 B.C.E. iron smelting was coming into wider use throughout the Middle East, though Mesopotamian ironworkers had to import the raw ore from distant regions.

Timber was as rare as iron in Mesopotamia, meaning that wooden furniture was a scarce luxury item. Because wood deteriorates with time and weather, authentic furniture from the region is very uncommon, and archaeologists have to depend on painting and sculpture to learn how it was made and used. Basic wooden furniture was often combined with reed matting. Wooden benches, beds, and cabinets were provided to the homes of the wealthy. These pieces were assembled from sawn timber, joined with pegs, and decorated with mosaics, paintings, and marble or ivory inlay. The most elaborate items were reserved for Mesopotamian kings, who saw to it that any city they conquered was carefully searched for its finest furniture, a prized spoil of war.

The most skilled artisans worked in the new medium of glass, which was first developed in northern Mesopotamia in the early second millennium B.C.E. Glass vessels were made by core forming, in which a core of stone or coal was placed into molten glass around a core. The thin layer of

Stone bowl, from Khafajeh, Iraq, Early Dynastic Period, about 2600–2400 B.C.E. (© The Trustees of the British Museum)

cooling glass was then wrapped with extra glass fibers. The glass itself was made by heating silica-bearing sand and soda ash, which created a clear vitreous substance as it cooled. Glassmakers decorated their wares with designs gently carved into the cooling material. They used familiar colors that imitated semiprecious stones: copper and cobalt dyes produced blue colors, manganese produced purple, and lead and antimony produced yellow. Glassblowing techniques that originated in Syria in the first century B.C.E., under the Romans, quickly spread to Mesopotamia and throughout the empire.

Glassmakers and all other skilled artisans held a respected place in Mesopotamian societies. The Code of Hammurabi recognizes the class of *amelu*—citizens of full rights and high status, in which were included royalty, government officials, landowners, aristocrats, and craftsmen. Craft workers commonly followed the profession of their ancestors, but they were also developed through a system of apprenticeship. Boys were often adopted into the family of an artisan and given a full course of training, after which they were free to establish themselves as independent professionals.

To the east, the wealthy Persian Empire founded in the sixth century B.C.E. fostered the work of skilled artisans in stone, metal, and ceramic. Monumental sculpture and painted friezes decorated the mammoth palaces of Persepolis and Susa, the seat of power of the Persian rulers. The wealthy of ancient Persia decorated their bodies with heavy gold and silver jewelry. Their homes and palaces held furniture crafted from cedar imported from Lebanon and Anatolia. Potters used great creativity in fashioning drinking cups, bowls, and jars in imaginative shapes, many inspired by mythological creatures and tales. Persian craftsmen made use of a variety of abstract shapes as well, beginning a tradition in the visual arts that would survive the fall of the empire and continue in the Parthian, Sassanian, and Islamic realms of later times.

ASIA AND THE PACIFIC

BY KIRK H. BEETZ

Along the Indus River metal casting emerged early in the Harappan culture, perhaps in about 2300 B.C.E. Harappans made household goods, such as bowls and cups, from bronze and copper, and they made small depictions of animals, some of which may have been religious symbols and others toys. Harappans had a large inventory of symbolic graphs whose meaning remains unknown, which they used on seals carved in steatite (also known as "soapstone"), probably in imitation of Near Eastern seals. Harappan seals included portraits of gods and realistic portrayals of animals. Two famous Harappan seals are the image of a rhinoceros in the National Museum of Pakistan and the image of a Brahman bull in the British Museum. The rhinoceros stands firmly on four legs and has an elaborately carved hide; its proportions are lifelike. The Brahman bull is also well proportioned and stands firmly; it is an image common among Harappan remains and is most likely representative of the status Brahman bulls would have later in Hindu culture.

The Harappan civilization began to decline by about 1900 B.C.E. and was overrun by northern nomads in about 1500 B.C.E. These nomads, called Aryans, began the Vedic culture in India, a culture with a caste social system. The Sudra caste included the craftspeople, who were supposed to serve the higher castes. The crafts of carpentry, stonemasonry, metalworking, basket weaving, and garland making were usually hereditary. Over time large extended families were

THE MYSTERY OF SHANG BRONZE CASTINGS

The Chinese Shang Dynasty bronze casters made molds out of several parts that fit together like pieces of a puzzle. Molds were made of clay. A mold had a base on which the other pieces were set. The base had openings for molten bronze to be poured in and for hot gases to escape. The base would actually become the top when the metal was poured in, but it contained the part of the mold that would form the base of the object.

The central core of the mold was a solid piece. It provided the shape for the inside of whatever was being cast. In the case of an eating vessel, it might be shallow for a serving plate or deep for a soup bowl. It could be carved with symbols or depictions of animals or people. It was the core that allowed a Shang bronze caster to produce an object as completely decorated on the inside as the outside.

There might be several outer parts to the mold, but there had to be at least two so that the mold could be opened to release the bronze object without breaking the mold. The outer pieces were shaped to fit around the core while allowing space for the molten metal to flow in. The interiors of the outer parts of the mold would be carved with the images that were to be displayed on the outside of the bronze object. It is possible that no Shang bronze was without carved decorations.

The pieces would be put together using notches as guides so that the outer ones did not touch the core. After the metal cooled, the pieces could be pulled apart. The seams that formed where the outer pieces joined together would be filed or sanded to match the surface—except, in the late Shang, some bronzes were cast using this method that had no seams to file, sand, or polish. How these seamless bronzes were produced remains a mystery.

Bird head made of stone, thought to be from the first millennium B.C.E., Papua, New Guinea; the image may represent the head of the cassowary, an ostrichlike bird regarded as a supernaturally powerful animal endowed with magic powers. (Copyright the Metropolitan Museum of Art)

devoted to a single craft, sometimes taking up an entire area of a town or city. By the 200s B.C.E. craftspeople were settling outside cities in entire villages devoted to one particular craft. Craftspeople often formed guilds that protected their members and collected money for public works, as well as setting the standards of workmanship that craftspeople had to meet. The leaders of the guilds usually became the leaders of those villages that were devoted to one craft.

Indian carpenters employed foresters to find trees to use as lumber. Before the foresters would cut down any tree, the carpenters would apologize to the god who lived in the tree and ask for forgiveness. Carpenters helped construct buildings, and they also made furniture, primarily beds. Few Indian homes had much furniture, because people sat on the floor most of the time, but they did have beds. Homes often had small cabinets made of wicker, which were the work of basket weavers. Basket weavers made bowls and baskets from grass, flexible branches, or bamboo. Basket weavers were usually women, and they often worked alone, at home. Sometimes they worked for a big manufacturer, bringing their finished work to a warehouse to be paid. When women of the three higher castes had to work for such manufacturers because they needed to earn money, the master of the warehouse was forbidden to look at them or speak of anything other than work, or he would be fined.

Blacksmiths made household goods such as water vessels, as well as weapons. It has yet to be established when Indian blacksmiths learned to make steel, but they made very durable steel weapons. Whereas blacksmiths pounded their goods into desired shapes, metal casters used molds. They were responsible not only for practical goods, such as plain cups and serving dishes, but also for decorative bronzes cast with images of gods and goddesses, plants, and animals.

Garland making was the work of both men and women who shaped and wove garlands out of flowers and stems. A wealthy person had to have a fresh garland every day, so garland makers tended to live near cities, where the rich were likely to be. They had homes with small plots of land on which they grew the exotic flowers they used. It took three years for a new garden to begin producing flowers that could be made into garlands and sold.

In ancient China most of what can be learned about craftspeople comes from archaeological research. The products of metalworkers are the best known because of the durability of metal. Working with copper probably began before 2100 B.C.E. Bronze came into use for toys, burial images, and vessels in the Yellow River region in the 1600s B.C.E. and was an important medium for artistic expression at the beginning of the Shang Dynasty (ca. 1500–ca. 1045 B.C.E.). During the Shang Dynasty, bronze was used for water vessels, for grave goods such as decorated bowls to honor ancestors, and for works of art. The Shang typically cast bronze by pouring molten metal into molds that were cut in halves, so that they could be separated to be used again. This usually left visible seams on the sides of bronze objects, but by the last century of the dynasty the Shang became so skilled that the seams could not be seen.

Ironworking came into prominence in the 500s B.C.E., when metalworkers learned how to build kilns that could heat to 2,800 degrees Fahrenheit. Iron was more brittle than bronze, but it was easier to make than bronze, which required hard-to-find tin. Chinese nobles preferred to use bronze weapons and shields, leaving iron ones for the peasants in their armies. But the primary use of iron was for agricultural instruments such as plows.

Little wooden furniture survives from the Shang Dynasty, but examples survive from the Zhou Dynasty (1045–256 B.C.E.). Peasants could not afford furniture. The rich owned wooden chests, tables, and couches decorated with lacquer paintings. The makers of furniture tended to cluster in cities near where the wealthy buyers of their work lived. Little is known of their lives, but they probably were independent workmen, whereas metalworkers often worked in large factories, manufacturing tens of thousands of ordinary objects. During the second half of the Han Dynasty (202 B.C.E.–220 C.E.) even peasants commonly owned metal objects, such as cooking pots and frying pans.

Little is known of the crafts of the Asian islands and Oceania prior to 500 C.E., when Japanese metalwork becomes common. Knowledge of metalworking was carried by Koreans to the Japanese Islands, perhaps in the 200s C.E., when the Japanese still used stone for most objects, even swords. Basket weaving was quite likely important throughout southeastern Asia and the islands, but almost nothing is known about the weavers or their products.

EUROPE

BY MICHAEL J. O'NEAL

Compared with the ancient empires of Greece, Persia, and Mesopotamia, Europe remained relatively undeveloped until the arrival of the Roman Empire in the first century B.C.E. and, later, the advent of Christianity. At the dawn of history much of Europe was covered with ice, so the population was sparse at best. Only after the ice receded in about 8000 B.C.E. did people move into the region, where they found fertile ground for crops and an abundance of game. They survived purely by means of what they could raise and grow for their own use, settling in widely separated hamlets that consisted of low huts and barns for their livestock. There the ancient Europeans developed crafts that made their lives at least slightly more comfortable. Because the passage of time is kinder to stone than it is to other, less-durable materials, the archaeological record consists largely of examples showing that the ancient Europeans worked with stone to form such objects as tools (primarily for cutting), arrowheads, and spear points as well as pottery for food and water storage. Less commonly found are examples of craft items made of ivory, bone, and wood.

In discussions of ancient European peoples the terms *Celt* and *Celtic* are often used. In modern life these terms typically refer to the people of Ireland, but historians use the words more generally to refer to the peoples who migrated into Europe, probably about 3000 B.C.E., from the steppes of central Russia. Early on they settled in Hungary and Romania, but in time they moved on to Italy, France, Switzerland, Germany, the Iberian Peninsula (Spain and Portugal), the Balkans, and Poland. Later still, they settled the British Isles. For centuries the Celts were the dominant people of the European continent.

The ancient Romans regarded the Celtic peoples to the north as crude "barbarians." The Roman writer Polybius wrote, "Their lives were very simple, and they had no knowledge whatsoever of any art or science." In fact, the Celts developed a great deal of sophisticated technology, including crafts production. They became especially adept at metalwork, and one of their major achievements was the substitution of the more durable iron for bronze. The ancient Celts invented such items as chain-mail body armor, the plowshare (that is, the plow's blade), handsaws, and chisels, and they were the first people to put iron shoes on horses. Tombs found throughout southern and eastern Europe contain large numbers of craft items, including cups, bowls, jewelry, helmets, horse gear, and the like. The famous Agris helmet, found in western France in 1980, is a magnificent piece made of iron with gold plating, silver rivets, and decorative stripes, along with inlay made of coral. The ancient Celts were also skilled at leatherwork.

Archaeologists refer to two periods of Celtic dominance on the Continent. The first is the Hallstatt Period (1200–500 B.C.E.), referring to a small town not far from Salzburg, Austria, which is still the site of huge salt mines. The remains of a great many craft items have been found in the region, most of it relatively unsophisticated metalwork. The other period was the La Tène, named after a metalworking site in Switzerland. The La Tène began in 480 B.C.E. and lasted until the Romans entered the picture in about 1 C.E., and historians regard it as important because of the flowering of craftsmanship and technology in the region at this time. One of the distinguishing characteristics of the La Tène culture was the use of a great deal of ornamentation and decoration on craftwork, particularly metal. Much of this ornamentation was based on plant and animal forms, though a lot consisted of purely geometric designs; it is believed that La Tène craftsmen used geometric compasses to inscribe decorative elements on their work. In addition to iron the La Tène craftsmen worked extensively with gold and, to a lesser extent, silver.

Art historians identify three distinct styles of La Tène craftwork. One they refer to as the vegetal style, referring to the use of decorative plant motifs. The second is the sword style, referring to sharply geometric designs inscribed on such items as sword scabbards. The third is the plastic style, referring to the three-dimensional depiction of objects, primarily on jewelry. The La Tène craftsmen were skilled not only at metalworking but also at "fired" crafts, that is, those that used fire in the making, such as inlay work, enameling, glass, and pottery. Finally, some examples of woodwork survive. Unused timbers of up to 40 feet long have been found, along with a variety of woodworking tools, including lathes, adzes, and saws. La Tène woodworkers produced wooden bowls and turned tool handles on lathes, but their most noteworthy achievement was the construction of ships and land vehicles. An important craft was that of the wheelwright, who constructed wheels made of wood that were then bound by iron "tires." La Tène wheels were more soundly constructed and durable than any wheels the Roman Empire ever produced for its famous chariots.

The Celts were not the only cultural and linguistic group to occupy Europe. In addition, various Germanic tribes dominated Scandinavia and northern Germany, including the Angles, Vandals, Burgundians, Danes, Norwegians, Goths, and Saxons. The development of crafts among these Germanic tribes in many respects paralleled that of the Celts. During the Bronze Age (2800–700 B.C.E.) the early Germanic tribes worked primarily with bronze, but later these tribes worked with iron. Archaeological findings include pots and bowls, tools, and various ornamental items.

In the late centuries before the beginning of the Common Era, the Celts lost power on the Continent. In the north they were overrun by the Germanic tribes, and in the south they were under pressure from the expanding Roman Empire, which imported its technologies and craftwork into the regions it conquered. The Celts found themselves isolated on the British Isles, the only place in Europe where they continued to flourish. They carried with them the craft traditions they had learned on the Continent, continuing to work with bronze, silver, gold, and enamel as well as with iron and wood. After the advent of Christianity, craftwork was directed to the production of objects of religious significance, including such items as chalices and crosses.

GREECE

BY SPYROS SIROPOULOS

The appreciation of craftsmanship by the Greeks is evident in the fact that one of their supreme gods was Hephaestus, the craftsman-god, responsible for the construction not only of weapons (such as the famous armor of Achilles or the thunderbolts of Zeus) but also of various objects for daily use, such as tripods and statues. In addition to Hephaestus, the goddess Athena was the protector of craftsmen; not only was she wise, she was also an expert in ceramics, weaving, and woodworking. In the National Museum of Berlin there is a red-figure vessel (with red figures on a black background) dating to the fifth century B.C.E., on which Athena is depicted finishing up with great care the clay molding of a large horse, while woodworking tools hang behind her.

The economy of almost all Greek cities depended mainly on farming, fishing, small industry, and trade. However, during the height of the fifth century B.C.E. the Athenians established an almost civic way of life, meaning that many people turned away from farming for a living. A new cast of skilled craftsmen developed, practicing special skills necessary for the well-being of the polis, or city-state, and its citizens. Not all professions enjoyed the same respect, and not all workers were considered worthy of being free citizens. Manual labor was frowned upon, considered something only slaves or *metics* ("resident aliens," who did not enjoy citizenship) did. For free citizens only professions such as the practice of medicine, rhetoric, or sculpting, painting, and teaching were considered appropriate.

In Sparta it was inconceivable for freeborn citizens to work and be paid for working, but this was not true everywhere. In Corinth, for example, people respected and honored craftsmen and manual labor. The *Republic* of Plato (ca. 427–347 B.C.E.) is a valuable source of information about the kinds of crafts and professions that developed within an organized city. In the *Republic*, Socrates and Adeimantos discuss a great number of the crafts and professions necessary for the smooth functioning of the civic mechanism. Equally useful is an excerpt from *Pericles*, written by the Roman Plutarch (ca. 46–120 C.E.), in which the statesman Pericles, the leader of the Democratic Party in Athens during the fifth century B.C.E., names all the crafts and professions necessary for the construction and decoration of the Acropolis.

It seems that glassmaking was passed from Egypt to Greece via Crete, where findings date from the second millennium B.C.E. The earliest glass objects were beads. Various vessels begin to appear about 1500 B.C.E. Some fine artifacts of dark blue glass, in imitation of lapis lazuli, are found in Mycenae. Glassworkers adapted techniques used by potters and metalworkers, modeling molten glass around a core of hardened glass and pressing it into open molds to produce inlays, small vases, jars, and bowls. A more complex process was the heating and fusion of preformed rods of glass.

Not much glass survives from Greece during the Archaic (600–400 B.C.E.) and Classical (480–323 B.C.E.) periods, and it seems that pottery was the craft used to provide tableware. Small vases found in Greece, made by the sand-core technique are dated to the sixth century B.C.E., but their origin is unknown. (In the sand-core technique threads of molten glass were wound around a shaped core of sand. After the glass hardened, the sand was removed.) It was not until the Hellenistic Period (323–31 B.C.E.) that glassmaking became more common, when the invention of glassblowing in the first century B.C.E., probably in Syria, made work simpler for glassmakers.

Baskets were a very functional item of daily use, the oldest preserved artifacts dating to the Mesolithic Period (8000–4000 B.C.E.). Basket making takes skill but only simple tools, such as a knife, a needle, and a pair of pliers. In Classical Greece, lower-class women or *metics* would supplement their income by constructing baskets and bags, mats, rugs, and other items using weaving, plaiting, or coiling techniques. Materials varied from reed, cane, rush, and sisal fiber to ashwood splints. Baskets were used by traders in the market, fishermen, and even miners. A vase of the sixth century B.C.E. from Corinth shows miners loading baskets with clay from a pit, while younger slaves pull the baskets up with ropes.

The construction of weapons was not the only task of metalworkers. A number of items for daily use, for farming, hunting, fishing and other work, were constructed by freeborn citizens or *metics* with the help of slaves. Vase paintings often depict a tall shaft for melting metals. Blasts of air were introduced at the back by hand, while the mass of wrought iron was extracted at the base. The most common fuel was charcoal. Iron was especially difficult to work; the furnace had to be broken in order to extract the wrought iron, so it could be used only once.

Woodworkers skilled at sawing, joining, and finishing produced a wide variety of useful and ornamental objects, from jewelry boxes to furniture. Woodcarving, a quite different craft, produced objects such as bowls, toys, and other items that could be created from a piece of wood with only a saw, a mallet, files, gouges, and sandpaper. Even items used in worship were constructed from wood. A red-figure cup by Epictetus (fl. 520–500 B.C.E.) shows a youth adding the final details to a wooden herm. A herm is a statuette of the god

Hermes, usually placed at house gates or as a marker on roads. An impressive finding is the wooden *xoanon*, a simple statue, from the island of Samos, dating to the seventh century B.C.E. *Xoanons* were cult objects venerated for the deities that they represented. Only a very small number of these fragile statues survive, mostly from waterlogged sites that preserved the wood.

A variety of materials were used for the construction of furniture throughout the centuries. Homer (ca. 900–800? B.C.E.) describes bedsteads, chairs, and footstools with inlays of gold, silver, and ivory in the palaces of Mycenae. Marble and stone thrones were reported, and their remains were discovered at the palaces of Knossos, in Crete, and at the palace of Pylos. Less-durable materials were used during the Classical Period, and so our knowledge of Classical Period furniture and cabinetry comes mainly from written descriptions and representations in art. Already by the sixth century B.C.E. carving wood on a lathe, a technique called *turning*, was introduced and, together with curving techniques, enabled skilled craftsmen to construct a variety of forms, the principle ones being the *klismós* (chair), a light construction for domestic use, without arms; the *threenýs* (footstool), in various shapes and sizes; the *thrónos* (throne), a more elaborate high-backed chair for special occasions; the *trápeza* (table), small in size, oblong or circular; the *cline* (couch), used for sleeping as well as for reclining upon during banquets; and the *lárnax* (chest), for storing clothes and bedding.

ROME

BY KIRK H. BEETZ

In Roman society there were senators, knights, members of the third estate (or common people), and slaves. Craftspeople were either members of the third estate or slaves. They tended to form guilds, but guilds were not meant to protect their members or to set standards of workmanship. Instead, they were intended to be meeting places where members could gather and mix comfortably together, without worrying about paying the required courtesies to members of the upper classes. Although one might find a guild in a Roman city or town that encompassed all the area's metalworkers, it was more likely that there would be separate guilds for those who worked in copper, tin, bronze, brass, or iron. A single guild might take over an entire block in a city, with its members living in rooms behind or above their shops, but shops could be located almost anywhere in a city. Craftspeople often rented ground-level rooms in other people's homes. As Rome grew in population, the demand for crafted goods increased. Thus, over time, a few shops in a town could multiply into dozens, even hundreds.

Blacksmiths were found in every town and city and almost every village. They not only made new items but also repaired old ones. They often sat on low stools while they worked, using hammers to shape sheets of metal against a solid stone table. They made iron pieces for joints on carts, parts of bridles for horses, and weapons; bronze pieces for utensils, pots, pans, and chamber pots; and copper and tin pieces for cups and bowls. Almost any man who was not rich had to know how to hammer copper sheets into basic tools. Thus, blacksmiths learned to make complex and specialized metal objects that ordinary people could not make. They seldom smelted their ore themselves, instead purchasing ingots. Metal was usually smelted near where it was mined, using kilns designed to make a powerful updraft of air that provided the oxygen needed for high heat. Blacksmiths often enhanced the metal they received by reworking it with hammering and heat. For example, they could toughen iron by softening it with heat, mixing it with carbon from charcoal, and then hammering it, turning and folding it on itself, hammering again, and so on until it was several compressed layers of iron mixed with carbon. Blacksmiths were often specialists in one kind of metal or even in one kind of tool, such as medical instruments. Although they worked their ingots with large tongs and hammers, they used small hammers of different sizes and shapes, as well as pliers of varying sizes, to shape and squeeze their metal.

Some stonemasons worked in the actual rock quarries. They used metal tools to carve out stones of the shape and size they wanted. They took such care in this work that when the stones were removed from the quarry, they needed little further dressing. They used metal hammers, chisels, and picks,

Steatite vase (Alison Frantz Photographic Collection, American School of Classical Studies at Athens)

as well as a mason's square that was usually metal but could be wooden, for making corners square. The stones would go to homebuilders or, in the case of marble, to stonemasons who specialized in carving statues and columns. Statues were usually painted. Although stonemasons often went to construction sites for their work, they also might keep shops that sold small decorative items or markers for tombs. Although modern-day people regard the statues as art, the ancient Romans usually did not. Creating images to decorate buildings or the interior of the home was considered just a routine part of the stonemason's work. Types of stone would by chosen for different types of work. For instance, hard stone would be used for building aqueducts and walls intended to bear heavy weight, whereas soft were preferred for sculptures to decorate the interiors of room. Marble was often used for carving because it was soft but held its shape well but not for its looks, because it would be painted.

Woodworkers were probably found in every city, town, and village, because their products were in great demand. They seldom cut their own trees. Instead, they purchased wood brought out of local forests or imported from other lands. A European Roman woodworker was prosperous if he could afford to purchase wood from Africa; furniture made of African wood sold for high prices. Woodworkers used tools probably purchased from blacksmiths: saws, augers for drilling holes, chisels, and hammers. They needed to know how to shape and fit metal fastenings for constructing furniture.

Romans made exceptionally fine glass. There were important glassmaking centers throughout the Roman Empire in Italy, Egypt, Syria, and northern Gaul. Egyptians, in particular, were famous for the unusual colors of their glass. The town of Aquileia on the Adriatic Sea in Italy was an important center for manufacturing glass. When the town was sacked by Huns in 452 C.E., the people fled to islands in the lagoon, founding Venice, where the skills of their craftspeople helped keep glass making alive after the fall of Rome.

Roman glass was made from sand, lime, and sodium bicarbonate. These would be mixed together in a vessel, probably made of stone, and heated in a kiln that may have been a duplicate of one used for heating ceramics. At first, glass objects were made using three different techniques: One was to pour molten glass into a mold the way metal was cast. Another was to coat a stone or wooden shape with molten glass. The third was to layer not-yet-hardened warm glass in strips, slowly building up the sides of jugs or other vessels somewhat the way strips of clay were used to build the sides of a ceramic pot. Molded glass was often carved to depict chariot races or other exciting scenes.

Then, in the first century B.C.E., glassmakers in Syria invented glassblowing. This involved taking molten glass out of a furnace on a hollow tube through which the glassmakers blew air to inflate the cooling glass. By twisting, lifting, and lowering the tube, the blowers could make glass objects of different shapes. In addition, glassblowing was fast, enabling glassblowers to manufacture many simple objects, such as bottles, quickly. Glass factories developed, with many blowers working together not only to create a variety of glass objects but also to make enough quantities to mass-market them. Thus the Roman Empire had a profusion of glass objects for everyday use that were affordable to almost anyone.

This ordinary glass for bottles and other household objects was usually bluish green, but glass could be mixed with pigments to create other colors. Roman windows were often made out of wooden screens with glass panes in the spaces, allowing light in but not the weather. Bathhouses sometimes had large skylights made of glass that allowed sunshine in but kept out cold winds. Glass jugs came in a variety of curvaceous shapes that pleased the eye, and molded glass often was cast to make jars shaped like fruit or animals.

THE AMERICAS

BY ANANDA COHEN SUAREZ

The ancient inhabitants of the Americas produced crafts ranging from the utilitarian to the ritual. Crafts of the ancient world are generally defined as objects hand made of natural materials such as wood, metal, or plants. They often possessed a dual significance, serving basic human needs as well as having associations to a cultural belief system. Crafts were produced in many different cultural, social, and economic contexts, from households in rural areas to highly specialized workshops in large cities. Many crafts, particularly those of such perishable materials as plant fibers and wood, have not survived. The unequal preservation level of these objects in the archaeological record means that secondary evidence, such as tools associated with crafts manufacture or painted depictions of crafts, helps to provide information about them.

Present-day craft production among indigenous communities throughout the Americas offers critical ethnographic evidence of ancient traditions whose technique and form have survived the test of time. Baskets, metal ornaments and tools, wooden and bone implements, and other utilitarian goods can be found in all regions of the continent but with much variation in appearance as well as in cultural significance. A great deal of cultural interchange existed in the ancient Americas, increasing in intensity as societies became sedentary. Thousands of different cultural groups coexisted in the vast territory now known as the Americas, each with their own histories and distinct cultural practices that influenced the appearance, mode of production, and function of their particular craft items.

Around 10,000 B.C.E. hunter-gatherers began to populate North America, Mesoamerica, and South America, traveling in bands and settling in different locations depending on the time of year. These were all preceramic cultures that domesticated squash and pumpkin, used to make gourds for transporting water and food. The sites of Guila Naquitz in central Mexico and the Tamaulipas caves in northeastern Mexico provide some of the earliest surviving evidence of craft production in the Archaic Period (7000–1800 B.C.E.). At Guila Naquitz archaeologists found bone awls and needles, copper bells, wooden digging sticks and weapons, finely woven basketry, and even fragments of sandals. Given the extreme dryness of these particular caves, they provide ideal conditions for the preservation of very fragile and perishable artifacts. At the Tamaulipas caves, ground stone tools for processing food, chipped stone tools and weaponry, along with coiled baskets, nets, and woven floor mats crafted out of maguey fibers were found.

The Andes, encompassing modern-day Peru and Bolivia as well as parts of Chile, Ecuador, Venezuela, and Colombia, witnessed a rich and complex history of craft production, extending from the Lithic Period (10,000–3000 B.C.E.) up to the present day. During the Lithic Period the inhabitants of the Andes developed diverse utilitarian craft, such as nets for catching fish, textiles, and simple undecorated baskets made of plant fibers as well as stone tools for hunting and food processing. Some well-preserved archaeological sites have yielded wooden earplugs, gourds with simple carved designs, and wooden bowls.

North America's indigenous inhabitants began to create beautifully executed basketry as early as 4500 B.C.E. In the region now known as the southwestern United States and northern Mexico, baskets were made from a variety of plant fibers, including yucca and willow wood. In eastern North America there is evidence of continuous human occupation since about 10,000 B.C.E. The North American Archaic Period roughly coincides with that of Mesoamerica and South America's Lithic Period, lasting until about 1000 B.C.E. The first evidence of metalwork produced in the Americas, in the form of simple copper spear points and bells, comes from Archaic Period archaeological sites.

With the advent of agriculture in Mesoamerica, the Andes, and throughout the United States, populations became less mobile and settled into communities ranging from small villages to major urban centers. As communities settled, craft specialization developed, meaning that a distinct group of craftspeople and artisans emerged. In Mesoamerica throughout the Formative (1800 B.C.E.–150 C.E.) and the Classic (150–650 C.E.) periods, craft objects appear in increasing abundance, many associated with sedentary life. Wooden digging sticks for planting and wooden spindles used in conjunction with ceramic spindle whorls (circular parts of spindles, used to rotate the spinner) for spinning cotton and maguey fibers into thread can be found. Baskets appear to have declined in importance as ceramic vessels rapidly became one of the most common features of sedentary life. Functional items used in food preparation, such as certain specialized tools used to grind corn, occupied a central place in domestic life. Surviving luxury goods tend to consist of ceramics and objects made of obsidian and precious stone, but evidence suggests that objects of perishable material such as feathers, wood, and cloth were widely produced and disseminated.

Although in Mesoamerica metallurgy had yet to play a significant role in craft production, artisans in the Andes began to produce large quantities of portable goldwork as a form of tribute for the first major urbanized pilgrimage center, Chavín de Huántar (900–200 B.C.E.). There are examples of repoussé vessels (shaped or ornamented by hammering on the reverse side), masks, and headgear with finely executed geometric designs and symbolic representations of deities. The Moche culture, which dominated the north coast of Peru from about 100 to 600 C.E., developed specialized systems of craft production, with workshops producing fine copper and gold decorative objects such as ornate earspools, necklaces, bracelets, and hammered shields. *Spondylus* shells, imported from Ecuador, were worked into objects of ritual significance frequently found in Moche funerary contexts. They took on a number of different forms, sometimes left in their natural state and other times fashioned into small sculptures, incorporated into mosaics, or crafted into beads.

Archaeological evidence of basketry abounds in North America as the region emerged from the Archaic Period; in fact, the period from 100 B.C.E. to 700 C.E. in the American Southwest is known as the Basketmaker for the presence everywhere of this cultural product in the archaeological record. Basket making was traditionally performed by women. Different basket designs and decorative motifs might distinguish the hand of the maker or signify the particular family, region, or cultural group within which the basket was produced. The discovery of engraved stone tablets at several Middle Woodland Period (300 B.C.E.–1000 C.E.) archaeological sites in the eastern United States provides further insights into ancient North American craft production. Archaeologists believe the tablets were probably used for printing decorations on cloth or other perishable materials.

Although they were made from the same basic materials, crafts produced throughout the ancient Americas had a diversity of forms, decorations, and functions. Climate, geographical location, access to natural materials, and human needs and desires mostly determined this variation. The basic large-scale continuities across the Americas are a common preceramic material culture, the development of crafts associated with sedentary life, and the rise of domestic and institutionalized craft specialization. With the development of cities, chiefdoms, and empires from the middle of the first millennium until European contact, however, crafts began to diverge widely from their shared cultural foundations and took on ever more varied forms to satisfy the needs of increasingly complex and stratified societies.

See also ADORNMENT; AGRICULTURE; ARCHITECTURE; ART; BUILDING TECHNIQUES AND MATERIALS; CERAMICS AND POTTERY; CITIES; CLIMATE AND GEOGRAPHY; CLOTHING AND FOOTWEAR; DEATH AND BURIAL PRACTICES; ECONOMY; FOOD AND DIET; GENDER STRUCTURES AND ROLES; HOUSEHOLD GOODS; HUNTING, FISHING, AND GATHERING; ILLUMINATION; INVENTIONS; METALLURGY; MINING, QUARRYING, AND SALT

MAKING; OCCUPATIONS; RELIGION AND COSMOLOGY; SACRED SITES; SHIPS AND SHIPBUILDING; SLAVES AND SLAVERY; STORAGE AND PRESERVATION; TEXTILES AND NEEDLEWORK; TRADE AND EXCHANGE; TRANSPORTATION; WEAPONRY AND ARMOR; WEIGHTS AND MEASURES.

FURTHER READING

Barb Aston, *Ancient Egyptian Stone Vessels: Materials and Forms* (Heidelberg, Germany: Heidelberger Orientverlag, 1994).

J. D. Cooney, *Catalogue of Egyptian Antiquities in the British Museum IV: Glass* (London: British Museum, 1976).

Ilay Cooper and John Gillow, *Arts and Crafts of India* (London: Thames and Hudson, 1996).

George Wharton James, *Indian Basketry*, 2nd ed. (New York: Dover, 1972).

Geoffrey Killen, *Ancient Egyptian Furniture*, vol. 1 (Warminster, U.K.: Aris and Phillips, 1980).

Geoffrey Killen, *Ancient Egyptian Furniture*, vol. 2 (Warminster, U.K.: Aris and Phillips, 1994).

Paul T. Nicholson and Ian Shaw, *Ancient Egyptian Materials and Technology* (Cambridge, U.K.: Cambridge University Press, 1999).

P. R. S. Moorey, *Materials and Manufacture in Ancient Mesopotamia—The Evidence of Archaeology and Art: Metals and Metalwork, Glazed Materials and Glass* (Oxford, U.K.: B.A.R., 1985).

P. R. S. Moorey, *Ancient Mesopotamian Materials and Industries: The Archaeological Evidence* (New York: Oxford University Press, 1994).

G. M. A. Richter, *The Furniture of the Greeks, Etruscans and Romans* (London: Phaidon Press,1966).

Philip Steele, *Clothes and Crafts in Roman Times* (Milwaukee, Wis.: Gareth Stevens, 2000).

Rebecca Stone-Miller, *Art of the Andes from Chavín to Inca*, 2nd ed. (London: Thames and Hudson, 2002).

► crime and punishment

INTRODUCTION

Crime was dealt with harshly in the ancient world. Early human settlements had no legal codes, courts, prisons, or other systems for dealing with crime, so most often crime was punished by family retribution. If someone committed a crime against another person, that person's clan would hunt down the perpetrator and mete out punishment. Crime was always a personal matter. Because there were no nation-states, there was no such thing as a crime against the state or "society." The victim of a crime was always a person.

The world's earliest legal code, developed in Mesopotamia, specified particular punishments for particular types of crime. While historians know about the existence of this code, no record of the code itself survives. However, the later Code of Hammurabi, also from Mesopotamia, provides historians with a comprehensive legal code developed by a king for his people. Historians are particularly interested in the prologue to the legal code, which outlines its rationale and moral underpinnings. Hammurabi was one of the first rulers to see punishment not just as a form of retribution but also as a deterrent to crime. His code was also the first to incorporate the notion of "an eye for an eye," a phrase later used in the Bible to refer to the notion that a punishment should be proportional to the crime committed.

Early legal codes were also developed in China and India. These codes were harsh by modern standards. In China, for example, five forms of punishment were typically carried out. Tattooing and disfigurement served to identify the person as a criminal, but still harsher punishments included castration, mutilation, and death. Often, the manner of death differed for different sorts of crimes, also a common practice later under the Roman Empire.

Punishment could also vary by a person's social class or, in the case of India, caste. While the Code of Hammurabi purported to treat all people equally, in practice people of higher social classes often did not face the same harsh punishments that people of lower classes did; in fact, crimes were defined differently depending on the social classes of the perpetrators and victims. In India the caste of a person often played a major role in the harshness of a person's punishment.

Ancient Greece was the source of the modern jury system. Until then, legal codes and administration were dictated by kings or a king's delegates. The ancient Greeks, however, devised the first system in which citizens took part in hearing cases and meting out punishment. The ancient Romans were the first to distinguish between private crimes, such as assault and burglary, and public crimes, such as treason and bribery.

Prisons were not common in the ancient world, though ancient Assyria had some fairly large prisons. Convicted criminals were swiftly punished in a variety of ways, including beating, having arms or hands cut off, or being put to death by various means, including hanging and crucifixion. Another common form of punishment was exile, meaning that a criminal was forced to leave the community. Sometimes criminals were sold into slavery, and sometimes they were abandoned in remote areas, where they faced death by starvation or attack by wild animals.

AFRICA

BY SAHEED ADERINTO

Conceptualizations of crime vary from one part of Africa to another and from one time to another. An act that constitutes a criminal offense in one culture might be permitted in another culture; an act treated as a criminal offense today might have been condoned in the past and vice versa. As African societies moved from one period to the next in the course of their history, perceptions of crime, its control, and the punishment of offenders changed. Any analysis of the history of crime requires a critical understanding of the socioeconomic, cultural, political, and other changes a society experienced in succeeding decades and centuries.

Ancient African societies were made up of the living, the ancestors or gods, and the generation unborn. The living deified and worshipped the ancestors as god and goddesses because of their roles in protecting and enhancing the welfare of the community. Criminal offenses were not only against the living but also against the ancestors. The place of the ancestors in the day-to-day activities of the living is evident in light of the fact that the ancestors were responsible for laying the foundation of the community, its values, culture, and sanctions. Their demise did not represent their detachment from the society, and because they were chiefly responsible for having made the laws, antisocial behavior was an offense against them as well as against the living. Among the Asante of present-day Ghana "private offenses" (*efisem*) are those that emerge as a result of social, political, and economic relations solely among the living, while "public offenses" (*oman akyiwade*) are those that involve the entire community, including the ancestors. Regarding this second category, the living must make sure that laws are enforced and criminals are punished, to avoid incurring the wrath of the ancestors.

Criminal codes as we have them today did not exist in ancient Africa. African criminal laws were based on fundamental teachings that were deeply interwoven with several aspects of culture and custom. A criminal offense was an act that breached basic moral teachings or flouted customs. For example, the unwritten moral codes of most societies frowned upon stealing and adultery. For stealing, however, the actual loss of someone's property to theft carried less weight than the effects of the criminal's disobedience on the society's morals. Adultery was a criminal offense because it involved breach of the trust between husbands and wives. The spiritual vows men and women exchanged during marriage rites made adultery a serious form of antisocial behavior.

African criminal or legal systems also included taboos. Indeed, it is difficult to differentiate between taboos and laws, because both are integral parts of Africa culture. The list of taboos is endless. There were taboos that governed when crops should be planted and harvested, when fishing should be done, what parts of the community people ought not venture into, which animals must not be killed, and so on. Among the Yoruba of present southwestern Nigeria it is sacrilegious to hunt game in ancestral forests. This type of forest is preserved for religious and cultural purposes. Forests, rivers, and mountains are the abodes of the gods. In such places activities that were not spiritual or religious in nature were thought to be a breach of cultural beliefs and sanctions.

How was crime detected in ancient Africa? In most African societies there were gods or cults associated with crime, and when a criminal act was committed without apprehension of the perpetrator, the entire community assembled at the village shrine, where oaths were taken to reveal the offender. It was believed that the gods were capable of striking and killing offenders immediately after such oath takings. Sometimes the offender died after several weeks of sickness. In cases where the criminal was apprehended without the help of deities, the chief or ruler of a community determined the offender's punishment.

The gravity of the offense played a significant role in determining the type of punishment meted out. Among the Akan-speaking people (Ghana) offenses such as stealing were punishable by banishment from the community. In virtually all African societies crimes like murder were punishable by death. If an offense was closely connected to disobedience of a deity, the offender might be sacrificed to appease the god. Antisocial elements could be sold into slavery. Not all offenders were killed or banished. In some communities, such as among the Masai of East Africa, adulterers were made to pay fines in the form of cattle.

Private prosecution of offenders also took place in some parts of Africa. Magico-religious methods of punishing offenders included placing charms on property that caused thieves to be paralyzed or die after stealing it. Charms (*juju*) of this nature can also prevent people from committing crimes, for instance, by making a stealable commodity less attractive to the potential thief. Husbands also placed charms on their wives to punish other men who had sex with them.

EGYPT

BY DAVID PETECHUK

Most of what is known about ancient Egyptian law, crime, and punishment comes from funerary documents and court manuscripts, as well as some other ancient writings. Drawing on these sources, historians believe that the earliest Egyptians probably had developed a sophisticated view of right and wrong within the context of crime and punishment. They had a comprehensive system of law that addressed crimes ranging from murder and theft to grave robbing and even necrophilia, erotic interest in the dead. According to most accounts, Egyptian law was first unified under King Menes (ca. 2925 B.C.E.), who united Upper and Lower Egypt.

As in most ancient cultures, the final authority on all disputes was the king—in Egypt, the pharaoh—who was considered a living god and as such was the ultimate judge and lawmaker. Intertwined with the Egyptian judicial philosophy was Maat, the goddess who represented the ideals of law, order, and truth. In an attempt to live up to the ideals embodied by Maat, the pharaohs and those to whom they delegated authority in matters of crime and punishment were expected to view everyone, except for slaves, as equal under the law. Nevertheless, as in most societies, there were differences, both subtle and overt, in how the judicial system treated people from different social classes. For example, a noble convicted of a crime requiring the death sentence might be allowed to commit suicide, whereas others were executed.

The most serious cases of crime in Egypt were decided by the pharaoh or a special delegation that he appointed. In rare cases, divine oracles made decisions, often for crimes or transgressions involving the temples and the gods. Because Egyptians viewed the objects in Egyptian tombs as sacred,

Papyrus with part of the "Tale of the Eloquent Peasant" from Egypt, around 1800 B.C.E.; a major literary text of the Middle Kingdom, this is the story of crime and its punishment in a way that questions social and divine justice. (© The Trustees of the British Museum)

they considered tomb robbery one of the most heinous crimes. Tomb robbers became so rampant and bold that they even began robbing the graves of the pharaohs during the rule of Ramses IX (ca. 1131–1112 B.C.E.). Death was generally the penalty for tomb robbing. One man, believed to be a grave robber from the Twenty-Fifth Dynasty (which began around 700 B.C.E.), is reported to have been buried alive. Most crimes against the government resulted in execution, as did most murders, whether committed by a free citizen or a slave. The death penalty was also administered for perjury, which the Egyptians viewed as irreverence toward the gods as well as a crime against society.

Nevertheless, some historians believe that Egypt made relatively little use of the death penalty, at least in comparison with other ancient cultures. Part of the reason may be that Egyptians considered disgrace and designation as a "nonperson" to be a harsher penalty to endure than death. (Sometimes brands or cuts were used as visible signs of dishonor.) Furthermore, a dead person could not serve the pharaoh or government. Considering that those disgraced could regain their honor and lost rights only by performing heroic or valiant deeds, an individual punished with disgrace could ultimately prove beneficial to society.

In addition to death and disgrace, Egyptian law meted out a variety of other punishments, with beatings being among the most common. Many punishments were barbaric by modern standards. Mutilation—especially cutting off the nose, ears, hand(s), or tongue—was a common punishment for a variety of crimes. For example, a woman caught in adultery had her nose cut off, not only as punishment but also to destroy her attractiveness and thus prevent her from committing the crime again or enticing a man into adultery. As in most ancient cultures, women often suffered more severe penalties than men. A man caught in adultery with a married woman received a beating as a penalty, usually a thousand strokes with a stick. However, if a man raped a freeborn woman, he was castrated.

Despite the harshness of many penalties, Egypt possessed some concepts of basic human rights. For example, when a pregnant woman received the death penalty, she was not executed until her child was born, because the Egyptians considered the child guilty of no crime and therefore not to be punished for the mother's misdeed. Pharaoh Bocchoris (ca. 717–712 B.C.E.) suppressed the use of bondage or imprisonment for debtors.

The Egyptians also had some unusual concepts of certain crimes and unique penalties for dealing with them. For example, parents convicted of murdering their child were not put to death, because they were considered to have given life to the child. Instead, they were punished by having to hold the baby's dead body in their arms for three consecutive days and nights, a penalty designed to evoke repentance and deter them from committing the crime again. For a time the Egyptians also tried dealing with the exploding problem of common theft (excluding theft involving tombs or temples) in a unique way. They set up a system in which thieves had to register with a "captain of thieves" and report all the goods that they stole, which the robbed person could then ransom for one-fourth of the value. Despite this attempt to control theft and restitution, it is believed that other punishments for theft predominated throughout ancient Egypt's history, including death, fines, and various corporal punishments.

While confinement was not a common form of punishment for free citizens of Egypt, prisons did exist, dating to the Middle Kingdom Twelfth and Thirteenth Dynasties (ca. 1991–1640 B.C.E.). The prison population was made up mostly of servants and foreigners; for citizens penalties such as public beatings, fines, or execution predominated. Some temple depictions of prisons show decorative rows of panels that contain the name of a conquered country or people, with the heads and shoulders of bound prisoners above the panels. Each panel is attached to a rope, and the pharaoh is depicted as holding all of the ropes. Historians believe that the Egyptian prisons were generally operated in an orderly manner and kept relatively clean.

The influence of Egyptian laws related to crime and punishment was wide ranging. For example, the Greek Solon, who became lawgiver in Athens in 594 B.C.E., visited Egypt and is believed to have adopted some Egyptian views on crime and punishment, including the idea of applying the same punishment prescribed for a crime to someone who falsely accuses another of that crime. The Greek idea of idleness as a crime may also have come from Egypt, where free citizens had to declare in writing how they made a living and could be put to death for making a false declaration or for being in an illegitimate business.

THE MIDDLE EAST

BY DAVID PETECHUK

The world's oldest surviving legal codes and laws come from Mesopotamia. The first known legal code, the Code of Urukagina, dates to 2350 B.C.E., and the region probably had legal prescriptions for centuries prior to this code, which was developed by and named after a ruler of Lagash. Before the Code of Urukagina, laws designating crimes and their punishment were probably based on the customs of the people and prevailing ideas of right and wrong. Although customs and laws transmitted orally served their purpose, as Mesopotamian cities and kingdoms grew and literacy spread, laws were put into writing to reduce vagueness or public discord about exactly what constituted a crime and what should be the punishment.

As with most ancient cultures, punishments for crimes were often severe. For example, a document dating to around the time of the Code of Urukagina notes that both thieves and adulteresses had their names inscribed on rocks, which were then used to stone them to death. Although the Code of Urukagina is the oldest-known legal code, an actual text has never been found, and its existence is known only through references in other ancient writings. The oldest legal code recovered dates to time of Ur-Nammu, who ruled the Sumerian city of Ur from 2112 to 2095 B.C.E. Of the code's decipherable segments, approximately 40 statements focus on crimes and punishment. Monetary fines and the death penalty were the primary punishments for crimes and were established in a manner that the reflected the social conventions of the times. For example, deflowering a virgin wife of another man resulted in a death sentence. However, if the woman was only a slave to a man, the penalty was only five shekels of silver. Murder was punishable by death, but physical wounds inflicted on another were punished with a monetary fine, partly because prison was seldom used as a means of long-term punishment.

The jewel of ancient Mesopotamian law is the Code of Hammurabi. Established in the 18th century B.C.E., it is the earliest surviving record of an entire code of laws proclaimed by a king to his people. What makes the code especially exciting to historians is that it includes the entire prologue explaining moral and spiritual rationalization for the laws. Hammurabi, who ruled Babylon from 1795 to 1750 B.C.E., states that his goals are to punish severely those who are evil and to protect those who are weak. Nevertheless, many of the laws were based on social status, with harsher penalties inflicted for crimes committed against the upper class while the same crime against someone from the lower class usually garnered a much less severe punishment. Hammurabi, however, kept in mind that lower social status meant lesser ability to pay fines. As a result, poor people usually had to pay lower fines than their rich counterparts. Overall Hammurabi's code applied various penalties to the population according to three classes: *amelu* (patrician), *muskinu* (free non-landowner), and *ardu* (slave).

The most significant aspect of Hammurabi's codes for crime and punishment is his establishment of the law of retribution, known in legal language as *lex talionis* and popularly familiar as the biblical law of "an eye for an eye." For example, historians believe that before Hammurabi, monetary fines for causing bodily injuries were deemed sufficient largely because injuries to private individuals were not considered crimes against the state or society in general. Hammurabi, however, set more severe penalties for physically harming another person, such as cutting off the hand of a son who struck his father. His rationale for these harsher penalties may have stemmed not only from the concept of *lex talionis* but also from a belief that fines and lesser punishments alone were not enough to ensure that his people obeyed the laws.

Hammurabi's comprehensive set of codes guided by *lex talionis* covered a wide range of crimes, such as bearing false witness. The penalty for someone falsely accusing another of crime was to suffer the punishment assigned to that crime. So if a man falsely accused another of murder, the accuser would be executed instead. Other examples include cutting off a surgeon's hand when his work resulted in the death or loss of a limb of a patient and the execution of a builder or his son if a building collapsed and killed its owner. Cases dealt with in this manner also included crimes involving slavery, sexual offenses, assault and bodily injuries, murder, theft, and debts.

As for the death penalty, ancient Mesopotamian laws required death for a wide range of crimes, including the illegal buying of a slave from a minor, selling or receiving stolen goods, false claim to another's possessions, disorderly conduct in a tavern, and the practice of magic. While the means of execution for these crimes was often not specified, other crimes resulted in specific types of execution. Hanging was the punishment for many crimes, among them burglary, obliterating a slave's brand, and a woman's seeking to have someone murder her husband. Other forms of execution included burning when convicted of incest with one's own mother and drowning for certain cases of adultery, rape, and bigamy.

The Code of Hammurabi greatly influenced the legal system throughout the Near East and Persia for several centuries, including the dominant rule of the Assyrians until around 500 B.C.E. As a result, the predominant form of punishment remained corporal and, other than death, included severe beatings of up to 100 blows, forced labor, and various types of mutilation, such as cutting off the tongue. Similarly, in ancient Persia, under the rule of Darius I (r. 522–486 B.C.E.), the penalty for attacking and severely injuring or killing someone was five to 200 lashes of the whip. For the most severe crimes, usually crimes against property, the state, or the king or his family, death by impalement was a typical punishment. (Little information is available concerning punishments for ordinary crimes in Persia.)

Throughout the Middle East, an ordeal was often assigned to prove guilt or innocence. For example, a popular test from the time of Hammurabi was to throw the accused into the Euphrates River. If the current brought the person to shore, he or she was not guilty. Drowning, on the other hand, proved guilt. (It appears that the art of swimming was little known at the time.)

As in most ancient societies, imprisonment was a relatively secondary form of punishment (though the Assyrians are known to have had some exceedingly large prisons for the times). Imprisonment was primarily for lesser crimes, such as debt, bribery, tax evasion, and smuggling; offenders largely remained in prison until they could pay off their debts or fines. Long-term prisoners were usually foreigners or prisoners of war who were subsequently used for forced labor.

ASIA AND THE PACIFIC

BY DAVID PETECHUK

Asia and the Pacific are endowed with a vast and varied cultural heritage, and much of the region's history concerning crime and punishment remains unknown and is not easily synopsized outside India and China. In China, which boasts one of the oldest legal traditions, laws focusing on crime and punishment originated from ancient moral teachings that were eventually written into legal codes. Many of the first laws formulated in ancient China date to the Zhou Dynasty (ca. 1045–256 B.C.E.) and were divided into various rituals designed to punish criminals and deter others from committing crimes.

The *Shan shu (Book of History)*, primarily composed of recorded sayings of the governors in the Shang Dynasty (ca. 1500–1045 B.C.E.) and the Zhou Dynasty, describes the earliest of China's "five penalties": tattooing, disfigurement, castration, mutilation, and death. For example, pickpockets received brands on their arms for their first two offenses, while a third offense probably resulted in a more severe punishment. Death was the penalty for armed robbery. One of the most basic laws of ancient China was that children should obey and honor their parents; thus, for example, a girl found guilty of insulting her parents was strangled. Beating with a bamboo stick was a common but, for the times, relatively mild punishment for a variety of crimes. Because of the Chinese belief that the head is the noblest part of the body, decapitation was considered particularly shameful and was used to punish murder and a number of other serious crimes. A Han Dynasty (202 B.C.E.–220 C.E.) legal code included more than 1,000 articles on capital punishment and decapitation.

The first known complete Chinese written law dates to the fifth century B.C.E. and outlined six basic areas of law. The Law of Theft focused on property crimes against the landlord class; the Law of Banditry pertained to rebellions and personal injuries; the Law of Miscellaneous Affairs was associated with state affairs; the Law of Verdict dealt with the logic and rules behind increasing or reducing punishments; the Law of Arrest and the Law of Prisons centered on those facets of the justice system. These laws, later called the "Law Classics," covered everything from major crimes such as murder to lesser offenses such as roguery, getting over city walls, gambling, and lewdness, and they influenced how subsequent dynasties down to modern times dealt with crime and punishment.

Culturally, linguistically, and ethnically diverse, India was one of the cradles of civilization. Nevertheless, because of the lack of written records, historians know little concerning ancient India's approach to crime and punishment. According to some sources, during the sixth and seventh centuries B.C.E. criminals were seldom if ever put to death but were rather fined for various crimes. However, by the time Chandragupta Maurya (r. 321–297 B.C.E.) came to power laws were harsher, and the death penalty and mutilation were common punishments.

The Manusmriti, or Laws of Manu, the most authoritative and best-known legal text of ancient India, combines the beliefs of Hinduism with law. It first appeared sometime between 200 and 100 B.C.E. and was derived from ancient religious texts and authoritative commentaries on these texts. As such, the Manusmriti provided ethical counsel as well as commentaries on law. The laws were thought to reflect the values of India's Hindu priests and clearly distinguished between civil wrongs, which primarily related to disputes over money and wealth, and criminal offenses involving sins such as theft and murder. Some historians believe that the laws described by the Manusmriti may not have been enforced diligently but rather provided an ideal of what the laws should represent. In fact, only a few chapters focus on crime, justice, and punishment.

Overall the Manusmriti divides crimes into 18 categories, such as nonpayment of debts, sale without ownership, nonperformance of agreements, disputes between owners of cattle and their servants, boundary disputes, assault and defamation, theft, robbery and violence, and adultery. For physical assault, various punishments were applied in ancient India, based largely on the perpetrator's caste, or social class. For example, a man of low caste who assaulted a man of higher caste often had a limb cut off as punishment. (The Laws of Manu identified places on the body where punishment could be inflicted, including the sexual organs, belly, tongue, hands, and feet.) While property damages were settled through fines, acts of violence were seen as the worst crimes imaginable and were severely punished. The Laws of Manu viewed punishment as an extremely important tool for controlling people and keeping them within their castes, thus ensuring that inferior people would not take the place of their superiors.

Laws in ancient India and the handing out of punishments were administered by the kings, who in turn were advised by various ministers and learned Brahmins (members of the highest of the four Hindu *varnas*, or social divisions, which also included, in order of importance, the Kshatriayas, or warriors; the Vaisyas, or merchants; and the lowest class, Sudras or workers). Judges were appointed to determine punishments. At the village level a committee of five or more members, called the village *panchayat,* was in charge of dealing with criminals. The Laws of Manu had a lasting influence on India and were even revived during the modern British colonial era.

Little is known about ancient principles of crime and punishment in other parts of Asia and the Pacific. For example, Japan was sparsely populated prior to 200 B.C.E., when a culture that used iron tools began to replace the hunters and gatherers who populated the island. According to ancient Chinese records, the people who lived in what is now Japan did not commit theft, and violations of the law or customs were handled by a family member. This authority figure was ultimately responsible for establishing retribution against a family for crimes committed by any of its members. In some cases the offender's entire family was executed as a strong signal to others not to commit crimes. Interaction with China and its peoples probably influenced Japan's early approaches to crime and punishment.

EUROPE

BY MICHAEL J. O'NEAL

As is commonly the case, historians have little direct evidence about crime and how it was punished in ancient Europe. The primary obstacle is the absence of written records. In some cases, archaeologists have found inscriptions on monuments that deal with matters of law, crime, and punishment, but these inscriptions tend to be fragmentary and of little help. In Scandinavia rock carvings have been found that shed faint light on ancient Scandinavian law, but historians are uncertain about their meaning.

Missing from the record of ancient Europe is any kind of systematic legal code. Through most of the ancient period crime and punishment were matters dealt with through custom rather than any prescribed body of law. While local custom differed from region to region, early European societies operated under similar principles, suggesting that the various branches of local law descended from a common Indo-European source. Some ancient European legal principles, particularly those of the Celts, probably date back to the Early Bronze Age (roughly 1800–1600 B.C.E.) and perhaps even earlier. Others date to later periods, primarily as a result of trade and cultural contact with the Greeks and, later, the early Romans.

An overarching principle of ancient European law was the preeminence of the family, with the senior male at its head. Prior to the development of nation-states and the rise of empires and ruling dynasties, legal traditions were a matter of family ties. A person's identity was taken from the clan to which he belonged. The head of the family had absolute sway over the individuals belonging to it. In this respect, a family was a bit like a corporation, with its own rules and procedures and an ongoing existence after the death of its head. Crime, then, was a breach of the rights and privileges not just of the individual victim but of the family as well. Accordingly, it was common for the family to impose its own brand of "frontier justice" on offenders, for the concept of a legal code, police forces, jails, courts of law, procedures for conducting trials, and the like were unknown. The result was often blood feuds.

The written record becomes more complete after the spread of the Roman Republic and the Roman Empire in the centuries before the start of the Common Era. Such classical figures as Caesar, Tacitus, and Pliny wrote about aspects of law in some of the far-flung areas of the empire, including Gaul (modern-day France), Spain, and later England. Julius Caesar (100–44 B.C.E.), for example, wrote extensively about legal matters in Gaul, which he learned about firsthand because of his participation in the Gallic wars beginning in 58 B.C.E. In time, as the Romans imposed their legal system on their colonies, legal codes developed that represented a blend of Roman and local law. After the advent of the Common Era and the beginning of the spread of Christianity, ecclesiastical law became a third ingredient that influenced the legal practices of the European nations.

According to Caesar, the ancient Celts recognized such crimes as murder, robbery, and theft, as well as other, more specific laws, such as usurping the authority of a king. A principle that ran through ancient European law was the distinction between public crimes and private crimes. Public crimes were those committed against the state; the victims of private crimes were individuals. While the state prosecuted crimes against the state, individual victims, or their families, had to pursue legal remedies on their own if they were victims of a crime. The process began with a plaintiff making an appeal to whoever was responsible for enforcing the law. Among the Celts, this person would often have been a Druid, a priestlike figure who was believed to have legal wisdom. In others, it may have been a public official or a noble whose patronage the injured party enjoyed. Often it became the obligation of the injured party to "distrain," or seize, the offender. The parties then assembled to swear oaths that they would give truthful accounts of the events in question. Witnesses, kinsmen, and other supporters of each party swore similar oaths. Monetary pledges were frequently given to ensure that the parties would appear for the hearing.

At the hearing, a judgment was rendered. If the accused was found guilty, punishment was imposed. Because there were no prisons in ancient Europe, other means of punishment had to be used. One of the most common was the monetary fine. Sometimes fines were simply a form of restitution to the victim or his family. Other fines were regarded as more of an "honor price," a way of restoring the honor of the victim. The amount of these fines often differed depending on the rank of the victim. Another common form of punishment was banishment from religious sites and rituals, a punishment the ancient Celts and Germanic tribes found particularly severe. In some cases the death penalty was invoked, but death was not a common form of punishment.

The Germanic tribes of northern Europe used the ordeal as a way of determining the guilt or innocence of an accused criminal. The ordeal was based on the religious belief that God would not allow an innocent person to be convicted nor allow a guilty party to go free. While the ordeal remained a common practice after the spread of Christianity, it had its roots in pre-Christian Germanic practice. It was used when other forms of evidence were not available and descended from the more ancient practices of the Babylonians, Jews, and other cultural groups that also used the ordeal. The practice was used among the Germanic tribes and spread with the spread of the Roman Empire into Gaul, Italy, and the British Isles—although the Romans themselves never used the ordeal.

One of the most common ordeals was the duel. Again, the belief was that God determined the outcome of the duel based on the guilt or innocence of the parties. Only free men could take part in duels, with free women required to appoint a substitute. Another practice that had its roots in ancient Germany was the ordeal by fire. In some cases the person had to carry a red-hot bar of iron in his hands; in others he had to walk over burning coals or across a row of red-hot plowshares. Success in doing so was a sign from God of innocence. A similar ordeal was to force the accused to reach into a cauldron of boiling water and withdraw a stone at the bottom; if the accused was innocent of the crime, his bandaged arm would heal in three days. Alternatively, the accused's hands and feet were bound and he was hurled into a body of cold water. If he floated, he was innocent, but if he sank, he was guilty. In addition to several other types of ordeals was the oath. The belief was that if the accused took a solemn oath of innocence but was in fact guilty, God would punish him with death for committing perjury.

GREECE

BY DAVID PETECHUK

Although no comprehensive collection of ancient Greek laws has survived to modern times, historians believe that before approximately 700 B.C.E., Greece had no official laws or punishments for crimes. Prior to this time, retribution for various crimes was often carried out by individuals. For example, when someone was murdered, the victim's family members were likely to reciprocate by killing the murderer, which often led to extended blood feuds between families. The Greek poet Homer (ca. 850 B.C.E.), author of the *Iliad* and the *Odyssey,* also indicated in his writings that it was up to individuals to settle disputes over property, possessions, and other claims. They usually did so by fighting among themselves. Homer also suggested that in some cases people could appeal to a third party over a dispute or crime—for example, to a king, leaders of the community, or ordinary people gathered together as a group for the express purpose of judging a specific case.

Established universal laws and punishments for crimes began to appear in Greece about the middle of the seventh century B.C.E., with the evaluation of crimes and punishments based primarily on oral laws. Because of the development of Greek city-states, each of which had their own laws, historians have found it difficult to provide a comprehensive overall picture of crime and punishment in early Greece. Nevertheless, a generalized picture has been developed based on Athenian law and procedures, which included the establishment of the Council of Areopagus by the seventh century. (Areopagus means "rocky hill" and is the name of a site northwest of Athens where the council met.) The Council of Areopagus, which was made up of a group of nine elders who served as magistrates called archons, was in charge of both conducting trials for serious crimes, such as murder and tyranny, and setting the punishment based on individual cases.

The first known instance of laws being put into writing was in 621 B.C.E., when Draco, (or Drako) the lawgiver had existing oral laws transcribed onto *axones*, or wooden tables or rollers, none of which survive today. At that time Draco made distinctions between crimes such as murder and accidental homicide. Nevertheless, almost every crime was punishable by death, from the serious crimes of murder and treason to what modern society would consider minor infractions, such as stealing food. Draco also made exile from Athens a potential punishment for murder committed by citizens. It is from Draco's name that the term *draconian* originated, to signify excessively harsh rules, leadership, and punishment. Part of the reason for mandating severe punishments for even minor crimes was that Greek religious and philosophical thought considered almost all forms of misconduct to be sacrilegious, an outrageous violation of something held sacred. As a result, a crime, no matter how minor it might appear, could bring the wrath of the gods down upon the entire populace.

In 594 B.C.E. the aristocrat Solon became the appointed lawgiver in Athens. Partly in an attempt to address public dissatisfaction over laws and punishments for crimes, Solon set out to revise the laws and institute new punishments for various crimes. He not only overturned most of Draco's death penalties but also gave the common people a more substantial role in the justice system, making it possible for even the poorest citizens to serve on a panel of judges that determined the outcome of cases and meted out punishments. In addition, all male citizens could bring charges against people and appeal verdicts they believed were unjust.

Under Solon's new laws, most penalties for crimes involved monetary payments. For example, a person convicted of rape was fined 100 drachmas or, according to other sources, staters—two denominations of money in ancient Greece. Likewise, fines for adultery with a free woman that took pace in her family's house (including her father's or brother's houses) was also 100 drachmas but was reduced to a fine of 50 drachmas if it took place somewhere else. Fines for theft varied according to what was stolen and its value.

Solon also established new laws that defined specific deeds as crimes, including the mistreatment of children, slander, and male prostitution. Other common crimes in ancient Greece included bribery of the magistrates, which resulted in the death penalty if the briber was convicted, and the theft of statues and monuments erected at Olympia and Delphi in honor of major Greek figures, such as political and military leaders and Olympic athletes. Some unusual Greek crimes included causing damage to the stump of a sacred olive tree and idleness, which prevented a person from supporting himself and his family and was punishable by death before the penalty was eventually reduced to a fine by the fifth century B.C.E.

Despite the appearance of a greater judiciousness in establishing laws covering crimes and punishments, penalties often remained severe. For example, death remained a potential penalty for a statesman who misled the Athenian assembly. In a noted case, the wealthy Athenian and military commander Miltiades was charged with this crime by Xanthippos in 489 B.C.E. for his failure to fulfill his promise of victory in a military expedition against the island of Paros. Although he was convicted, Miltiades died in prison from a war wound before his sentence was carried out. Exile was also considered a severe form of punishment in ancient Greece, because citizenship within a city-state came with many privileges that the exiled person forfeited.

Several ancient sources have noted that the ancient Greeks did have prisons. Nevertheless, long imprisonment probably was not a typical form of punishment. Imprisonment for crimes probably was rare and usually temporary until a punishment, such as death, exile, or a fine, was decided upon. Historians believe that most prisoners kept for any extended time were debtors who owed money to the state. However, the prisons were not draconian in nature. According to historians, prisoners were generally allowed freedom of movement, and restraints, such as chains, were used only occasionally.

From the writings of Greek philosophers and historians, it is clear that the ancient Greeks developed a sophisticated notion of the role punishment should play for various crimes. Their concepts of justice and punishment moved beyond the idea that punishments should be applied merely for retribution and to appease the gods. Instead, the Greeks viewed punishment for crimes as an example to deter others and as a means of correction so that those who were punished became better people unlikely to repeat their misdeeds.

Roman law was officially introduced to Greece following Rome's conquest of Greece in 149 B.C.E. Nevertheless, many Greek laws concerning crime and punishment remained in effect. In fact, Greek law and custom greatly influenced the development of Roman law. For example, in both systems, theft from a temple was punishable by death, but only Roman authorities had the power to execute criminals.

ROME

BY TOM STREISSGUTH

Roman law originated in the ancient customs of the kingdom and the Roman Republic, established among the farming villages along the banks of the Tiber River. The first written Roman law—in fact, the first surviving Roman writing of any kind—is the Lex Duodecim Tabularum, or the Law of the Twelve Tables, of 450–449 B.C.E. At the prompting of the plebeians, or commoners, the leaders of Rome convened a committee of 10 men—the *decemvirs*—to create this code. The intention was to reframe in a more just form the unwritten, customary laws that heavily favored the patricians, enshrine the new laws in writing in a public place, and make them a cornerstone of the Roman Republic. To that end, the laws of the Twelve Tables were set up on bronze tablets in the Roman Forum and enforced by Rome's two elected consuls, who served as the chief law-enforcers of the realm.

A MOST HUMILIATING DEATH

To the Romans, the worst form of execution was crucifixion: the killing of a condemned prisoner on a cross or stake. The Romans first encountered crucifixion as practiced by the Carthaginians of North Africa. Reminded of their own custom of tying or nailing criminals to a tree and allowing them to die without food or water, the Romans adopted crucifixion as a punishment for slaves, pirates, thieves, and mutinous rebels. (A Roman citizen of high birth guilty of serious crimes was beheaded, allowed to commit suicide, or permanently exiled.) Mass executions of the defeated were common after civil unrest or rebellion; after the slave revolt led by Spartacus in 71 B.C.E., 6,000 prisoners were crucified along the Appian Way between Rome and the town of Capua.

A prisoner to be crucified was stripped, scourged nearly to death, and forced to carry the cross to his place of execution. He was then nailed or roped to the cross, which was made of a *stipes* (upright) and *patibulum* (crosspiece). The traditional cross was built in the shape of a letter T; the Romans sometimes attached the *patibulum* beneath the top of the *stipes,* in what became known as the Latin cross. By one tradition, a sign giving the crimes or the name of the prisoner was attached to the top of the cross.

The victim of a crucifixion could die of suffocation, shock, loss of blood, or dehydration. The death could take several days; to hasten death, the Romans broke the prisoner's legs, forcing the body's collapse and a rapid death through asphyxiation. The worst dishonor of crucifixion was in the fact that the body was left on the cross after death, to be consumed by vultures or wild animals, and not afforded a proper burial. The practice of crucifixion was central to the tradition of Christianity, which held its founder to have been executed in this brutal manner. For this reason, the emperor Constantine, the first Roman leader to convert to Christianity, discontinued the practice during his reign in the early fourth century.

The Twelve Tables prescribed the death sentence for a variety of crimes. A debtor unable to repay after 60 days could be killed by his creditor. Writers of slanderous or insulting songs could be clubbed to death. Accepting a bribe or committing fraud was also a capital crime. Those bearing false witness in court were flung headfirst from the Tarpeian Rock, a cliff near the center of Rome that served as the city's place of public execution. Anyone suffering injury could exact "an eye for an eye" but could also agree with the aggressor on monetary compensation for the injuries. In all, the Twelve Tables set out eight different forms of punishment: a fine, fetters, flogging, retaliation in kind, civil disgrace, banishment, slavery, and death.

Patricians still benefited from prejudice in the law, as the punishment of crimes often depended on the offender's social standing. Under the Roman Empire, established by Augustus in 27 B.C.E., *honestiores* were distinguished from *humiliores*. The former were aristocrats, soldiers, and those holding public office; the latter were everyone else. For the *honestiores*, the usual sentence for serious crimes was exile and the confiscation of property; for the *humiliores*, death or slavery was the more common consequence of a guilty verdict. Only *humiliores* could be crucified, tortured, or publicly whipped.

The Romans also distinguished between public and private crimes. Public crimes were those committed against the state, including perjury, bribery, espionage, and treason. Such crimes were more severely punished than private ones throughout Rome's history. Private crimes were those against individuals, including indebtedness, theft, murder, and assault. A robber surprised in the act could be legally killed by the injured party. A Roman who committed assault, however, could simply pay a fine, and aristocrats sometimes amused themselves by openly breaking a "private" law and blithely paying a few coins to those they had injured or insulted. In this case the victim had no recourse to the justice system.

In the fourth century B.C.E., the judicial duties of the consuls passed to the praetor. The praetor was the head of the judicial branch of government and responsible for the state's legal decisions. He appointed judges to hear cases; he also had the power to pronounce sentence and to fix the amount of damages in cases involving theft or fraud. By custom the praetor announced new laws and procedures at the beginning of his term, a practice that supposedly prompted him to enforce the laws impartially. Criers wandered the city and the Forum to announce the edicts of the praetor, whose laws were also inscribed on public tablets. Although the praetor was supposed to uphold the law equally for patricians and plebeians, juries were nonetheless composed of Roman aristocrats (who, it was asserted, had the sense of honor that would guarantee fair decisions).

Capital punishment became more common under the Roman Empire than during the Roman Republic. The usual method of execution in Rome was beheading. Crucifixion was reserved for noncitizens and for crimes considered extremely dangerous to public order, such as the rebellion of a slave or anyone's inspiring a revolt against Roman authority in the provinces. The bodies of executed criminals were commonly left exposed in public for the education of the citizens. A special sentence was reserved for vestal virgins, priestesses responsible for keeping the sacred fire of Vesta burning in the center of Rome. The vestals were to abstain from sexual conduct of any kind; if found guilty of impurity, the offender was buried alive.

Drawing by Michelangelo of the Crucifixion of Christ and two thieves; crucifixion was a punishment for crimes against public order and for noncitizens. (© The Trustees of the British Museum)

Some criminals were sentenced to take part in gladiatorial contests, where they were left to their own devices to face skilled combatants; others were left bound in the wild and at the mercy of the elements and animal predators. Sentences of perpetual labor in the Roman quarries or slavery on a seafaring galley were also very common. Roman prisons were never the convicted criminal's final destination; they were used only to detain criminal suspects and those sentenced to death.

The praetor could commute a death sentence, order the demolition of a home, or impose permanent exile on those found guilty of a crime. In these cases the state also confiscated the guilty party's property. By ancient custom the accused were presumed innocent until proved guilty, but anyone who committed suicide to avoid a public trial and a sentence was believed to be confessing his guilt, and his property was immediately forfeited.

Within the family, the father had the authority of judge, police, and executioner. He could put a rebellious son to death or sell his children into slavery. He could punish a son or daughter who married someone the father opposed. A Roman family also had the right to put a deformed child to death if at least five neighbors agreed.

During the empire dozens of new laws were set down by the emperors, who had the power to decree anything with the force of law at their own whim. Under Constantine (r. 306–337 C.E.), Rome officially adopted Christianity, and subtle changes began in the criminal laws. Adultery and homosexuality were made punishable by death, which was carried out by beheading, drowning, or burning. All imperial pronouncements from the time of the emperor Hadrian to that of the emperor Justinian, as well as the edicts of the praetors, were collected by Justinian in the Corpus Juris Civilus, promulgated in the sixth century C.E. This law code was revived in the 11th century and became the basis of law and jurisprudence on the European continent down to the present time.

THE AMERICAS

BY ARDEN DECKER

There is little to no written or other evidence to suggest how societies dealt with crime and punishment in the ancient Americas. Because of this lack of information, nothing definitive can be gathered about the region's ancient legal or court systems.

See also EMPIRES AND DYNASTIES; GOVERNMENT ORGANIZATION; LAWS AND LEGAL CODES; MONEY AND COINAGE; RELIGION AND COSMOLOGY; SLAVES AND SLAVERY; SOCIAL ORGANIZATION; TRADE AND EXCHANGE.

The Middle East

The Code of the Assura (Assyrians), ca. 1075 B.C.E., excerpts

I.7. If a woman bring her hand against a man, they shall prosecute her; 30 *manas* of lead shall she pay, 20 blows shall they inflict on her.

I.8. If a woman in a quarrel injure the testicle of a man, one of her fingers they shall cut off. And if a physician bind it up and the other testicle which is beside it be infected thereby, or take harm; or in a quarrel she injure the other testicle, they shall destroy both of her eyes.

I.9. If a man bring his hand against the wife of a man, treating her like a little child, and they prove it against him, and convict him, one of his fingers they shall cut off. If he kiss her, his lower lip with the blade of an axe they shall draw down and they shall cut off. . . .

I.12. If the wife of a man be walking on the highway, and a man seize her, say to her "I will surely have intercourse with you," if she be not willing and defend herself, and he seize her by force and rape her, whether they catch him upon the wife of a man, or whether at the word of the woman whom he has raped, the elders shall prosecute him, they shall put him to death. There is no punishment for the woman.

I.13. If the wife of a man go out from her house and visit a man where he lives, and he have intercourse with her, knowing that she is a man's wife, the man and also the woman they shall put to death. . . .

I.15. If a man catch a man with his wife, both of them shall they put to death. If the husband of the woman put his wife to death, he shall also put the man to death. If he cut off the nose of his wife, he shall turn the man into a eunuch, and they shall disfigure the whole of his face.

I.16. If a man have relations with the wife of a man at her wish, there is no penalty for that man. The man shall lay upon the woman, his wife, the penalty he wishes.

I.18. If a man say to his companion, "They have had intercourse with they wife; I will prove it," and he be not able to prove it, and do not prove it, on that man they shall inflict forty blows, a month of days he shall perform the king's work, they shall mutilate him, and one talent of lead he shall pay.

I.20. If a man have intercourse with his brother-in-arms, they shall turn him into a eunuch.

I.21. If a man strike the daughter of a man and cause her to drop what is in her, they shall prosecute him, they shall convict him, two talents and thirty *manas* of lead shall he pay, fifty blows they shall inflict on him, one month shall he toil. . . .

I.32. If a woman be dwelling in the house of father, but has been given to her husband, whether she has been taken to the house of her husband or not, all debts, misdemeanors,

(continued)

(continues)

and crimes of her husband shall she bear as if she too committed them. Likewise if she be dwelling with her husband, all crimes of his shall she bear as well. . . .

I.40. If the wives of a man, or the daughters of a man go out into the street, their heads are to be veiled. The prostitute is not to be veiled. Maidservants are not to veil themselves. Veiled harlots and maidservants shall have their garments seized and 50 blows inflicted on them and bitumen poured on their heads. . . .

I.47. If a man or a woman practice sorcery, and they be caught with it in their hands, they shall prosecute them, they shall convict them. The practicer of magic they shall put to death.

I.50. If a man strike the wife of a man, in her first stage of pregnancy, and cause her to drop that which is in her, it is a crime; two talents of lead he shall pay.

I.51. If a man strike a harlot and cause her to drop that which is in her, blows for blows they shall lay upon him; he shall make restitution for a life.

I.52. If a woman of her own accord drop that which is in her, they shall prosecute her, they shall convict her, they shall crucify her, they shall not bury her. If she die from dropping that which is in her, they shall crucify her, they shall not bury her.

I.55. If a virgin of her own accord give herself to a man, the man shall take oath, against his wife they shall not draw nigh. Threefold the price of a virgin the ravisher shall pay. The father shall do with his daughter what he pleases.

I.57. In the case of every crime for which there is the penalty of the cutting off of ear or nose or ruining or reputation or condition, as it is written it shall be carried out.

I.58. Unless it is forbidden in the tablets, a man may strike his wife, pull her hair, her ear he may bruise or pierce. He commits no misdeed thereby. . .

From: Internet History Sourcebooks.
Available online.
URL: http://www.fordham.edu/halsall/.

Asia and the Pacific

Kautilya: The Arthashastra, excerpt, ca. 250 B.C.E.

Book IV, Chapter 11, Death with or without Torture

When a man murders another in a quarrel, he shall be tortured to death. . . . When a man hurts another with a weapon, he shall pay the highest amercement; when he does so under intoxication, his hand shall be cut off; and when he causes instantaneous death, he shall be put to death. When a person causes abortion in pregnancy by striking, or medicine, or by annoyance, the highest, middlemost, and first amercements shall be imposed retrospectively. Those who cause violent death either to men or women, or those who are in the habit of often going to meet prostitutes, those who inflict unjust punishment upon others, those who spread false or contemptuous rumors, who assault or obstruct travelers on their way, who commit house-breaking, or who steal or cause hurt to royal elephants, horses, or carriages shall be hanged. Whoever burns or carries away the corpses of the above offenders shall meet with similar punishment.

When a person supplies murderers or thieves with food, dress, any requisites, fire, information, any plan, or assistance in any way, he shall be punished with the highest amercement. Sons or wives of murderers or thieves shall, if they are found not in concert, be acquitted; but they shall be seized if found to have been in concert.

Any person who aims at the kingdom, who forces entrance into the king's harem, who instigates wild tribes or enemies against the king, or who creates disaffection in forts, country parts, or in the army, shall be burnt alive from head to foot. If a Brahman does similar acts, he shall be drowned. Any person who murders his father, mother, son, brother, teacher, or an ascetic shall be put to death by burning both his head and skin; if he insults any of the above persons, his tongue shall be cut off; if he bites any limb of these persons, he shall be deprived of the corresponding limb. When a man wantonly murders another, or steals a herd of cattle, he shall be beheaded. . . . When a person breaks the dam of a tank full of water, he shall be drowned in the very tank. . . . Any man who poisons another and any woman who murders a man shall be drowned. Any woman who murders her husband, preceptor, or offspring, sets fire to another's property, poisons a man, or cuts off any of the bodily joints of another shall be torn apart by bulls, no matter whether or not she is big with child, or has not passed a month after giving birth to a child. . . .

Any person who insults the king, betrays the king's council, makes evil attempts against the king, or disregards the sanctity of the kitchens of Brahmans shall have his tongue cut off. When a man other than a soldier steals weapons or armor, he shall be shot down by arrows; if he is a soldier, he shall pay the highest amercement. He who castrates a man shall have his generative organ cut off. He who hurts the tongue or nose of another shall have his fingers cut off. . . .

From: Kautilya, *Kautilya's Arthashastra,* 2nd ed., trans. R. Shamasastry (Mysore: Wesleyan Mission Press, 1923).

Rome

The Twelve Tables, ca. 450 B.C.E., excerpt

Table VIII.

2. If one has maimed a limb and does not compromise with the injured person, let there be retaliation. If one has broken a bone of a freeman with his hand or with a cudgel, let him pay a penalty of three hundred coins If he has broken the bone of a slave, let him have one hundred and fifty coins. If one is guilty of insult, the penalty shall be twenty-five coins.

3. If one is slain while committing theft by night, he is rightly slain.

4. If a patron shall have devised any deceit against his client, let him be accursed.

5. If one shall permit himself to be summoned as a witness, or has been a weigher, if he does not give his testimony, let him be noted as dishonest and incapable of acting again as witness.

10. Any person who destroys by burning any building or heap of corn deposited alongside a house shall be bound, scourged, and put to death by burning at the stake provided that he has committed the said misdeed with malice aforethought; but if he shall have committed it by accident, that is, by negligence, it is ordained that he repair the damage or, if he be too poor to be competent for such punishment, he shall receive a lighter punishment.

12. If the theft has been done by night, if the owner kills the thief, the thief shall be held to be lawfully killed.

13. It is unlawful for a thief to be killed by day....unless he defends himself with a weapon; even though he has come with a weapon, unless he shall use the weapon and fight back, you shall not kill him. And even if he resists, first call out so that someone may hear and come up.

23. A person who had been found guilty of giving false witness shall be hurled down from the Tarpeian Rock.

26. No person shall hold meetings by night in the city.

Table IX.

4. The penalty shall be capital for a judge or arbiter legally appointed who has been found guilty of receiving a bribe for giving a decision.

5. Treason: he who shall have roused up a public enemy or handed over a citizen to a public enemy must suffer capital punishment.

6. Putting to death of any man, whosoever he might be unconvicted is forbidden.

From: Oliver J. Thatcher, ed., *The Library of Original Sources.* Vol. 3: *The Roman World* (Milwaukee: University Research Extension Co., 1901): pp. 9–11.

FURTHER READING

Ilias Arnaoutoglou, *Ancient Greek Laws* (London: Routledge, 1998).

George B. N. Ayittey, *Indigenous African Institutions* (Ardsley-on-Hudson, N.Y.: Transnational, 1991).

Richard A. Bauman, *Crime and Punishment in Ancient Rome* (London: Routledge, 1996).

R. S. Betai, *Evolution of Law and Crimes in Ancient India* (New Delhi, India: Bharatiya Kala Prakashan, 2003).

James Henry Breasted, trans. and ed., *Ancient Records of Egypt*, vol. 1, *The First through the Seventeenth Dynasties* (Urbana: University of Illinois Press, 2001).

John A. Crook, *Law and Life of Rome* (London: Thames and Hudson, 1967).

Israel Drapkin and Thorsten Sellin, *Crime and Punishment in the Ancient World* (Lexington, Mass.: Lexington Books, 1989).

M. Rama Jois, *Ancient Indian Law: Eternal Values in Manu Smriti* (New Delhi, India: Universal Law, 2002).

L. W. King, *The Code of Hammurabi* (Kila, Mont.: Kessinger, 2004).

Wilfried Nippel, *Public Order in Ancient Rome* (Cambridge, UK: Cambridge University Press, 1995).

R. P. Peerenboom, *Law and Morality in Ancient China: The Silk Manuscripts of Huang-Lao* (Albany: State University of New York Press, 1993).

Edward M. Peters, "Prison before the Prison: The Ancient and Medieval Worlds." In *The Oxford History of the Prison: The Practice of Punishment in Western Society,* ed. Norval Morris and David J. Rothman (New York: Oxford University Press, 1995).

O. F. Robinson, *The Criminal Law of Ancient Rome* (London: Duckworth, 1995).

A. H. Sayce, *Babylonians and Assyrians: Life and Customs* (Boston: Adamant Media, 2000).

Joyce Tyldesley, *Judgment of the Pharaoh: Crime and Punishment in Ancient Egypt* (London: Weidenfeld and Nicolson, 2000).

Russ VerSteeg, *Law in Ancient Egypt* (Durham, N.C.: Carolina Academic Press, 2002).

VIVA-FACTS ON FILE
ENCYCLOPEDIA OF SOCIETY AND CULTURE IN THE ANCIENT WORLD

Volume II • D–K

Editor in Chief
Peter Bogucki

Viva Books
New Delhi | Mumbai | Chennai | Kolkata | Bangalore | Hyderabad | Kochi | Guwahati

First Indian Edition 2010

VIVA BOOKS PRIVATE LIMITED

- 4737/23 Ansari Road, Daryaganj, New Delhi 110 002
  E-mail: vivadelhi@vivagroupindia.net, Tel. 42242200
- 76, Service Industries, Shirvane, Sector 1, Nerul, Navi Mumbai 400 706
  E-mail: vivamumbai@vivagroupindia.net, Tel. 27721273, 27721274
- Jamals Fazal Chambers, 26 Greams Road, Chennai 600 006
  E-mail: vivachennai@vivagroupindia.net, Tel. 28290304, 28294241
- B-103, Jindal Towers, 21/1A/3 Darga Road, Kolkata 700 017
  E-mail: vivakolkata@vivagroupindia.net, Tel. 22836381, 22816713
- 7, Sovereign Park Apartments, 56-58, K. R. Road, Basavanagudi, Bangalore 560 004
  E-mail: vivabangalore@vivagroupindia.net, Tel. 26607409, 26607410
- 101-102 Mughal Marc Apartments, 3-4-637 to 641, Narayanguda, Hyderabad 500 029
  E-mail: vivahyderabad@vivagroupindia.net, Tel. 27564481, 27564482
- First Floor, Beevi Towers, SRM Road, Kaloor, Kochi 682 018, Kerala
  E-mail: vivakochi@vivagroupindia.net, Tel: 0484-2403055, 2403056
- 232, GNB Road, Beside UCO Bank, Silpukhuri, Guwahati 781 003
  E-mail: vivaguwahati@vivagroupindia.net, Tel: 0361-2666386

www.vivagroupindia.com

Published by arrangement with
Facts on File, Inc.
132 West 31st Street
New York 10001
USA

ISBN : 978-81-309-0929-5 (Set of 4 Volumes)

Published by Vinod Vasishtha for Viva Books Private Limited, 4737/23, Ansari Road, Daryaganj, New Delhi-110 002. Printed and bound by Sanat Printers, Kundli-131 028, Sonepat, Haryana.

Contents

Volume IV

Advisers and Contributors

EDITOR IN CHIEF

Peter Bogucki
Associate Dean for Undergraduate Affairs,
School of Engineering and Applied Science
Princeton University

ADVISORY BOARD

Lisa R. Brody
Assistant Professor of Art
Queens College, City University of New York

R. Hunt Davis
Professor Emeritus of History and African Studies
University of Florida

Leo Depuydt
Associate Professor of Egyptology
Brown University

Paul R. Goldin
Associate Professor of East Asian Languages
and Civilizations
University of Pennsylvania

Eloise Quiñones Keber
Professor of Art History
Baruch College, City University of New York

Amelie Kuhrt
Professor of Ancient Near Eastern History
University College, London

Daniel Potts
Edwin Cuthbert Hall Professor of
Middle Eastern Archaeology
University of Sydney

CONTRIBUTORS

Saheed Aderinto is a Ph.D. student at the Department of History, University of Texas at Austin. Some of his most recent publications include "Prostitution and Urban Social Relations" and "Policing Urban Prostitution: Prostitutes, Crime, Law and Reformers in Colonial Nigeria" in *Nigeria's Urban History: Past and Present* (2006) and "Discrimination in an Urban Setting: The Experience of Ijebu Settlers in Colonial Ibadan, 1893–1960" in *Inter-group Relations in Nigeria during the 19th & 20th Centuries* (2006). His writings have also appeared in *IFRA Special Research Issue, Ethnic and Third World Review of Books, African and Asian Studies Journal*, and *The Encyclopedia of Prostitution and Sex Work* (2006).

Olutayo Charles Adesina, Ph.D., teaches at the Department of History, University of Ibadan, Nigeria. He is the author of "The Underground Foreign Exchange Market in Ibadan during Devaluation" in *Money Struggles and City Life: Devaluation in Ibadan and Other Urban Centres in Southern Nigeria, 1986–96* (2002) and "Teaching History in Twentieth Century Nigeria: The Challenges of Change" in *History in Africa: A Journal of Method*, vol. 33 (2006).

David Otieno Akombo, Ph.D., teaches music education and world music at Wabash College of Indiana. He is the author of *Music and Healing across Cultures* (2006).

Francis Allard, Ph.D., teaches in the Department of Anthropology at Indiana University of Pennsylvania. His research interests include the archaeology of early China and Mongolia. He has contributed articles to *Archaeology of Asia* (2005) and *Beyond the Steppe and the Sown: Proceedings of the 2002 University of Chicago Conference on Eurasian Archaeology* (2006).

Miguel Arisa is finishing his doctoral studies in art history at the Graduate Center, City University of New York. He teaches at Technical Career Institutes and is a regular lecturer at the

Cloisters and a docent at the Metropolitan Museum of Art, New York.

Mariam F. Ayad, Ph.D., teaches graduate-level classes on Egyptian language and literature at the University of Memphis, where she is the assistant director of its Institute of Egyptian Art and Archaeology. Her main research interests focus on the role of women in ancient Egyptian temple ritual and the selection and transmission of funerary texts in post–New Kingdom Egypt. Her book on the God's Wife of Amun is under contract with Routledge.

Heather D. Baker, D.Phil., is a researcher at the University of Vienna, Austria, specializing in Babylonian history, society, and culture. She has published widely on Babylonian and Assyrian history and is writing a book to be titled *The Urban Landscape of First Millennium BC Babylonia.*

Robin Barrow, Ph.D., FRSC, is professor of philosophy of education at Simon Fraser University, Canada. His most recent books include *Plato* (2007) and *An Introduction to Moral Philosophy and Moral Education* (2007). He is the author of *Athenian Democracy* (2001) and *Greek and Roman Education* (1996).

László Bartosiewicz, Ph.D., D.sc., teaches archaeozoology at the Loránd Eötvös University in Budapest (Hungary) and the University of Edinburgh (United Kingdom). He is the author of *Animals in the Urban Landscape in the Wake of the Middle Ages* (1995) and principal author of *Draught Cattle: Their Osteological Identification and History* (1997) and has published more than 200 scholarly articles.

Kirk H. Beetz, Ph.D., emeritus, has published over two dozen books and more than 900 articles. His books span topics from endangered mammal species to children's literature, including *Exploring C. S. Lewis' "The Chronicles of Narnia"* (2000). His recent writings have focused on the history and culture of ancient Japan.

Craig G. R. Benjamin, Ph.D., teaches world and ancient Eurasian history at Grand Valley State University. He is the coeditor of vols. 2 (1998), 4 (2000), and 6 (2002) in the Brepols Silk Roads Studies series and the author of *The Yuezhi: Origin, Migration and the Conquest of Northern Bactria* (2007).

Uffe Bergeton, Ph.D., is in the Ph.D. program in the Department of Asian Languages and Cultures at the University of Michigan. He is the author of *The Independence of Binding and Intensification* (Ph.D. dissertation, University of Southern California) and various articles on theoretical phonology and syntax.

Amy Hackney Blackwell has degrees in history from Duke University and Vanderbilt University and a J.D. from the University of Virginia. Her books include *Mythology for Dummies* (2002), *LSAT for Dummies* (2004), *The Everything Irish History and Heritage Book* (2004), and *Essential Dictionary of Law* (2004). She has contributed to the *Encyclopedia of World Nations and Cultures* (2006), *Alternative Energy* (2006), and *Chemical Compounds* (2006).

Christopher Blackwell, Ph.D., teaches classics at Furman University. He is the author of *In the Absence of Alexander: Harpalus and the Failure of Macedonian Hegemony* (1999) and various protocols and software applications for building digital libraries, and he serves as technical editor for the Center for Hellenic Studies of Harvard University.

Amy Bogaard, Ph.D., teaches prehistory and archaeobotany at the Department of Archaeology, University of Nottingham, United Kingdom. She is the author of *Neolithic Farming in Central Europe* (2004).

Peter Bogucki, Ph.D., is an archaeologist who is associate dean for undergraduate affairs of the School of Engineering and Applied Science at Princeton University. He has studied prehistoric settlements in Poland and has a particular interest in the spread of farming in Europe. He is the author of *The Origins of Human Society* (1999) and the editor (with Pam J. Crabtree) of *Ancient Europe 8000 B.C.–A.D. 1000: An Encyclopedia of the Barbarian World* (2004).

Larissa Bonfante, Ph.D., professor of classics at New York University, is the author of several books on Etruscan and early Roman culture as well as publications on ancient dress and nudity, including *The World of Roman Costume*, coedited with Judith Sebesta (1994).

Charlotte Booth is a Ph.D. student at the University of Wales, Swansea, and teaches Egyptology for Birkbeck College and other institutions in the United Kingdom. She is the author of *People of Ancient Egypt* (2007), *The Hyksos Period in Egypt* (2005), and *The Role of Foreigners in Ancient Egypt* (2005).

Lisa R. Brody, Ph.D., teaches Greek and Roman art history at Queens College, City University of New York. Her research interests include Greek iconography and cult, ancient lamps and their decoration, children in antiquity, and representation of ethnicity in Greco-Roman art. She compiled the revised edition of David Sacks's *Encyclopedia of the Ancient Greek World* (2005) and is author of *Aphrodisias III: The Aphrodite of Aphrodisias* (2007).

David Brown, Ph.D., is researching the interactions of the pre-Islamic astral sciences of Mesopotamia, Greece, India, Egypt, Iran, the western Semitic world, and China at the Free University of Berlin. He is the author of *Mesopotamian Planetary Astronomy-Astrology* (2000) and *The Interactions of Ancient Astral Science* (forthcoming).

Deborah N. Carlson, Ph.D., teaches in the Nautical Archaeology Program of the Department of Anthropology at Texas A&M University. She also directs the Institute of Nautical Archaeology's shipwreck excavation of a Roman marble carrier off the Aegean coast of Turkey at Kizilburun and is preparing the final publication of the Classical Greek ship excavated by the Institute of Nautical Archaeology at nearby Tektas Burnu.

Jeffrey S. Carnes is associate professor of classics at Syracuse University. He is the author of *The Uses of Aiakos: Pindar and the Aiginetan Imaginary* (forthcoming) as well as articles on Greek lyric poetry, gender studies, literary theory, and Plato.

Julia Marta Clapp is pursuing her doctorate in art history at the Graduate Center, City University of New York. Her research interests include modern and pre-Columbian Latin American art.

Wendy E. Closterman, Ph.D., teaches ancient history and Greek at Bryn Athyn College. Her research focuses on Athenian burial and funerary ritual. She is the author of "Family Members and Citizens: Athenian Identity and the Peribolos Tomb Setting" in *Antigone's Answer: Essays on Death and Burial, Family and State in Classical Athens*, edited by C. Patterson (forthcoming).

Leah A. J. Cohen is an independent writer and editorial consultant with a master's degree in geography from the University of Florida. She specializes in Africa area studies and food security. She was a senior author for the *Encyclopedia of African History and Culture*, volumes 4 and 5 (2005).

John Collis is professor emeritus in the Department of Archaeology, University of Sheffield, where he taught for over 30 years. He has had a major role in the development of university and professional training in archaeology in Britain, and is secretary of the European Association of Archaeologists' Committee on Training and Education. He is author of several books and excavation monographs, including *Digging Up the Past* (2004) and *The Celts: Origins, Myths and Inventions* (2004).

Constance A. Cook, Ph.D., directs the Asian Studies program and teaches Chinese language and literature courses at Lehigh University. She is the author of *Death in Ancient China: The Tale of One Man's Journey* (2006) and coeditor of *Defining Chu: Image and Reality in Ancient China* (1999).

Susan Cooksey, Ph.D., is the curator of African art, Harn Museum of Art, University of Florida.

Justin Corfield, Ph.D., teaches history and international relations at Geelong Grammar School, Australia. He is the co-author of *Historical Dictionary of Cambodia* (2003) and has written extensively on Asia, Australia, and European colonial history.

James A. Corrick, Ph.D., is a full-time editor and writer with 25 books to his credit. His most recent titles are *The Early Middle Ages* (2006), *The Byzantine Empire* (2006), and *The Renaissance* (2007).

Arden Decker is a Ph.D. candidate in the history of art at the Graduate Center, City University of New York. Her research interests include Mesoamerican art as well as modern and contemporary art of Mexico.

Leo Depuydt, Ph.D., teaches Egyptology at Brown University and is curious about everything relating to ancient Egypt in its Near Eastern and Mediterranean context, especially the area's languages and history. He wrote *Civil Calendar and Lunar Calendar in Ancient Egypt* (1997) and *The Other Mathematics: Language and Logic in Egyptian and in General* (2007).

Haig Der-Houssikian, Ph.D., is professor emeritus (2003), linguistics, at the University of Florida, Gainesville. His research and publication interests are in morphology, Creolization, and sub-Saharan Africa.

Christine End, M.A., works on the Giza Archives Project at the Museum of Fine Arts, Boston. Her main interests of research are Middle Kingdom funerary iconography, material culture, burial practices, and mummification. As a researcher and illustrator, her work has appeared in Egyptological publications and documentaries.

Linda Evans, Ph.D., specializes in ancient Egyptian art at Macquarie University, Sydney, Australia. She recently completed her doctoral dissertation on the representation of animal behavior in Egyptian tomb paintings and has published several papers on the role and depiction of animals in the ancient world. She has also contributed chapters to *Egyptian Art: Principles and Themes in Wall Scenes* (2000), *The Encyclopedia of Animal Behavior* (2004), *Egypt: The Land and Lives of the Pharaohs Revealed* (2005), and *Historica* (2006).

Stephen M. Fabian, Ph.D., is an anthropologist and currently teaches seminars on religion, myth, and ritual at Princeton University. He is the author of *Space-Time of the Bororo of Brazil* (1992), *Clearing Away Clouds: Nine Lessons for Life from the Martial Arts* (1999), and *Patterns in the Sky: An Introduction to Ethnoastronomy* (2001).

Erin Fairburn is a graduate student in the Department of Egyptology and Western Asian Studies at Brown University. She has contributed to *The City and Urban Life* (forthcoming).

Alessia Frassani is a Ph.D. candidate at the Graduate Center of the City University of New York. Her research interests in-

clude the art and civilizations of ancient Oaxaca and issues surrounding the cultural interaction between the Old and New Worlds.

Markham J. Geller is professor of Semitic languages at University College London, in the Department of Hebrew and Jewish Studies. He has recently published a text edition of cuneiform medical texts, *Renal and Rectal Disease Texts, Babylonisch-assyrische Medizin* VII (2005).

J. J. George is working on his Ph.D. at the Graduate Center, City University of New York. His research area is pre-Columbian art and architecture.

Wolfram Grajetzki, Ph.D., wrote his dissertation at the Humboldt University of Berlin and has taught Egyptology there. He has excavated in Egypt and Pakistan and was principal archaeologist and author for the online learning project Digital Egypt for Universities (University College London). He is preparing the catalogue of Egyptian coffins in the Fitzwilliam Museum, Cambridge. His publications include *Burial Customs in Ancient Egypt* (2003) and *The Middle Kingdom in Ancient Egypt* (2006).

Lyn Green, Ph.D., has taught at several Canadian universities and for the Royal Ontario Museum. She has contributed to several encyclopedias, including *The Oxford Encyclopedia of Ancient Egypt* (2000) and the *Encyclopedia of the Archaeology of Ancient Egypt* (1999) as well as *The Royal Women of Amarna* (1996). Currently she is devoting her time to her duties as president of the Society for the Study of Egyptian Antiquities, which has over 400 members and subscribers internationally, and to writing.

Angela Herren, Ph.D., teaches pre-Columbian art and architecture as an assistant professor in the Department of Art and Latin American Studies at the University of North Carolina at Charlotte. A specialist on painted manuscripts from central Mexico, she completed a 2005 dissertation entitled "Portraying the Mexica Past: A Comparative Study of Accounts of Origin in Codex Azcatitlan, Codex Boturni, and Codex Aubin."

David B. Hollander, Ph.D., teaches ancient history at Iowa State University. He is the author of *Money in the Late Roman Republic* (2007).

Brooke Holmes, Ph.D., is an assistant professor of classics at the University of North Carolina, Chapel Hill. She is at work on a book about the symptom in early Greek medicine and classical Greek literature.

Michael Allen Holmes is a freelance editor and writer who recently contributed to *Shakespeare for Students*, 2nd edition (2007). He has also written an unpublished novel.

John W. Humphrey, Ph.D., is professor of Greek and Roman studies at the University of Calgary. A veteran of many seasons of archaeological excavation in Turkey and Greece, he is the author of *Greek and Roman Technology: A Sourcebook* (1998, with J. P. Oleson and A. N. Sherwood) and *Ancient Technology* (2006).

Keith Jordan, M.Phil., is a Ph.D. candidate in pre-Columbian art history at the Graduate Center of the City University of New York. He is currently finishing his doctoral dissertation, entitled "Stone Trees Transplanted? Central Mexican Stelae of the Epiclassic and Early Postclassic and the Question of Maya 'Influence.'"

Amr Kamel is an Egyptologist in the Rare Books and Special Collections Library at the American University in Cairo, Egypt.

David Kelly is an instructor of English writing and literature at Oakton Community College in Illinois. He has written over 100 published literary analyses and wrote the instructor's manual for the *Exploring Poetry* computer program. His short fiction has been published in *The Rockford Review*, *Grub Street*, and *The Iconoclast*, among other places.

Panagiotis I. M. Kousoulis, Ph.D., is a lecturer in Egyptology at the Department of Mediterranean Studies of the University of the Aegean. He is the author of *Moving across Borders: Foreign Relations, Religion and Cultural Interactions in the Ancient Mediterranean* (2007) and *Ancient Egyptian Demonology: Studies on the Boundaries between the Demonic and the Divine in Egyptian Magic* (2007).

Philippa Lang teaches ancient science and related subjects, with research interests in ancient medicine and philosophy, in the Classics Department of Emory University, Atlanta. She is the editor of *Re-Inventions: Essays on Hellenistic and Early Roman Science*, *Apeiron* special issue vol. 37 (2004).

Russell M. Lawson, Ph.D., is associate professor of history and chair of the Division of General Studies at Bacone College in Oklahoma. He is the author of *Science in the Ancient World* (2004), *The Land between the Rivers: Thomas Nuttall's Ascent of the Arkansas, 1819* (2004), and *Passaconaway's Realm: John Evans and the Exploration of Mount Washington* (2002, 2004).

Anne Mahoney, Ph.D., teaches Greek and Latin linguistics and literature at Tufts University. She is the author of *Plautus: Amphitryo* (2004) and *Roman Sports and Spectacles: A Sourcebook* (2001). She is also the editor of revised editions of *Allen and Greenough's New Latin Grammar* (2001), *Morice's Stories in Attic Greek* (2005), and *Bennett's Essentials* (2007).

Susan Malin-Boyce, Ph.D., serves as deputy director of the Regime Crimes Liaison Office, Mass Graves Investigation

Team, in Baghdad, Iraq. She has contributed to *Ancient Europe 8000 B.C.–A.D. 1000: Encyclopedia of the Barbarian World* (2004) and to publications addressing Early and Late La Tène settlement in Bavaria, Germany.

Renee McGarry is a student in the Ph.D. program in art history at the City University of New York Graduate Center. Her research interests include Aztec sculpture of the natural world and religious manuscripts from the post-Conquest period.

Paul McKechnie, D.Phil., is a senior lecturer in classics and ancient history at the University of Auckland, New Zealand. He is the author of *First Christian Centuries: Perspectives on the Early Church* (2002) and *Outsiders in the Greek Cities in the Fourth Century B.C.* (1989).

John M. McMahon, Ph.D., teaches at Le Moyne College in Syracuse, New York, where he directs the classics program. He is author of *Cave Paralysin: Impotence, Perception and Text in the Satyrica of Petronius* (1998) and numerous articles on the intersection of ancient literature and natural history. His most recent work includes nine entries in the forthcoming *Biographical Encyclopedia of Astronomers* (2006).

Jianjun Mei, Ph.D., teaches the history of science and technology at the University of Science and Technology Beijing. He is the author of *Copper and Bronze Metallurgy in Late Prehistoric Xinjiang: Its Cultural Context and Relationship with Neighbouring Regions* (2000).

James E. Meier, Ph.D., is assistant professor in the Department of Humanities and Social Sciences at Central Florida Community College. He is a contributor to the *Encyclopedia of African History and Culture* (2005).

Francesco Menotti, Ph.D., is a lecturer in European prehistory at the Institute of Prehistory and Archaeological Science, Basel University, Switzerland. He is the author of *Living on the Lake in Prehistoric Europe* (2004).

Melissa Moore Morison is associate professor of classics and classical archaeology at Grand Valley State University. She has extensive experience in archaeological fieldwork in Greece, Turkey, and the United States. Her research interests include Roman provincial archaeology, Greek and Roman pottery, and ceramic technology.

Penny Morrill, Ph.D., teaches pre-Columbian and early colonial Mesoamerican art at Hood College, Frederick, Maryland. She has an essay, "The Queen of Heaven Reigns in New Spain: The Triumph of Eternity in the Casa del Deán Murals," in a Brill anthology, *Woman and Art in Early Modern Latin America* (2006). She has authored several books on modern Mexican silver: *Mexican Silver: 20th Century Handwrought Silver Jewelry and Metalwork* (4th ed., 2007), *Silver Masters of Mexico: Héctor Aguilar and the Taller Borda* (1996), and *Maestros de Plata: William Spratling and the Mexican Silver Renaissance*, a catalog for a traveling exhibit (2002–2004).

Julian M. Murchison, Ph.D., teaches in the Department of Sociology and Anthropology at Millsaps College. His work in cultural anthropology examines the intersections of medicine and religion in East Africa. He recently published a chapter examining stories about a cure for HIV/AIDS in *Borders and Healers* (2005).

Caryn E. Neumann, Ph.D., teaches history in Ohio Wesleyan University's Black World Studies Department. She is a former managing editor of the *Journal of Women's History.*

Emily Jane O'Dell, is a Ph.D. candidate at Brown University and has taught at Brown University in both the Department of Egyptology and Ancient Western Asian Studies and the Department of Literary Arts. She has been the chief epigrapher of the Cairo-Brown University Abu Bakr Epigraphic Survey in the western cemetery of the Great Pyramids in Giza, Egypt, for the past five years.

Simon O'Dwyer is founder and researcher for Prehistoric Music Ireland, author of *Prehistoric Music of Ireland* and prehistoricmusic.com, and contributor to *The Encyclopedia of Music in Ireland* and *The Encyclopedia of Ireland*. He has published four papers for the International Study Group on Music Archaeology.

Penelope Ojeda de Huala is a Ph.D. candidate in art history at the Graduate Center of the City University of New York, where she studies pre-Columbian to contemporary art of Latin America. Her research focus is Guatemala and Peru, particularly the enduring thoughts and practices of indigenous cultures as manifested in art.

Michael J. O'Neal, Ph.D., is a writer who lives in Moscow, Idaho. He is a frequent contributor to reference and educational books, including *Lives and Works: Young Adult Authors* (1999), *The Crusades* (2005), and *America in the 1920s* (2006).

Dianne White Oyler, Ph.D., teaches African history at Fayetteville State University. She is the author of *The History of the N'ko Alphabet and Its Role in Mande Transnational Identity: Words as Weapons* (2005) as well as articles in the refereed journals *Research in African Literature, the Mande Studies Journal*, and the *International Journal of African Historical Studies.*

Katie Parla is an art historian and archaeological speleologist working in Rome and Naples as a docent leading didactic seminars of archaeological sites. She consults for the History

Channel and will appear in their 2007 series *Cities of the Underworld* as an expert on underground Rome and Naples.

Marie Passanante is a doctoral candidate in the Department of Egyptology and Ancient Western Asian Studies at Brown University.

William H. Peck teaches at the College for Creative Studies, Detroit, and the University of Michigan, Dearborn. He was for many years the curator of ancient art at the Detroit Institute of Arts and is at present a member of the Brooklyn Museum excavations in Egypt at Karnak. He is the author of *Drawings from Ancient Egypt* (1987) and numerous contributions to reference books and encyclopedias on the ancient world.

David Petechuk is a freelance writer specializing in educational texts focusing on the sciences, literature, and history. The former director of publications for the health sciences at the University of Pittsburgh, he is the author of *The Respiratory System* (2004), *LSD* (2005), and *Health & Medical Issues Today: Organ Transplantation* (2006).

Mark Anthony Phelps is taking a leave after teaching continuously since 1994 (primarily at Drury University, in five different departments) to finish his dissertation at the University of Arkansas entitled "Sewage from the Orontes: Roman Elite Attitudes toward Ecstatic Religion in the 3rd and 4th centuries C.E." This degree in ancient Mediterranean history augments his graduate degrees from Harvard and Johns Hopkins in Hebrew Bible and ancient Near Eastern languages and cultures. His research interests reflected in his writings are widely eclectic, spanning Paleolithic to contemporary society and including the disciplines of archaeology, linguistics, cultural anthropology, physical geography, historical geography, classical history, ancient Near Eastern history, medieval history, modern history, religion, and biblical history.

Jen Piro is a Ph.D. candidate in anthropological archaeology at New York University. Her dissertation research focuses on the development of pastoral economies in Early Bronze Age Transcaucasia.

Karen Radner, Ph.D., is lecturer in ancient Near Eastern history at University College, London. She specializes in the Assyrian Empire and is the author of *Die neuassyrischen Texte aus Tall Seh Hamad* (2002), *Das mittelassyrische Tontafelarchiv von Giricano/Dunnu-sa-Uzibi* (2004) and *Die Macht des Namens: Altorientalische Strategien zur Selbsterhaltung* (2005).

Judith A. Rasson, Ph.D., teaches in the Department of Medieval Studies, Central European University, Budapest (a post-graduate American-accredited university). Her research interests lie in southeastern Europe (especially the countries of the former Yugoslavia) and focus on Neolithic and historic archaeology and ethnographic material culture.

Kelly-Anne Diamond Reed, Ph.D., teaches ancient Egyptian history and archaeology at Villanova University's Department of History. She is investigating early Egyptian funerary rituals and burial customs.

Duane W. Roller is professor of Greek and Latin at Ohio State University. Trained as an archaeologist, he has over 30 years' experience in field archaeology in numerous Mediterranean countries. He is the author of *The Building Program of Herod the Great* (1998), *The World of Juba II and Kleopatra Selene* (2003), and *Through the Pillars of Herakles* (2006) as well as many other publications in history, classics, and archaeology.

Kelley L. Ross, Ph.D., teaches philosophy at Los Angeles Valley College. He specializes in Kantian epistemology, metaphysics, and ethics, with emphasis on members of the Friesian tradition—Jakob Fries, Leonard Nelson, Rudolf Otto, Sir Karl Popper, and others. Since 1996 he has been the publisher and editor of the online philosophy journal *Proceedings of the Friesian School, Fourth Series.*

Edward M. W. A. Rowlands, M.Phil., has research interests in Mycenaean political geography, trade, and religion.

Lucas G. Rubin, Ph.D., develops master of science programs for Columbia University. He was previously administrator of the university's Center for Archaeology, where he managed multiple excavations and projects. His research and scholarship have focused on fires and firefighters in ancient Rome.

Michael M. Sage, Ph.D., teaches classics and ancient history in the Classics Department at the University of Cincinnati. His main areas of study are historiography and military history. He is the author of *Cyprian: A Biography* (1975) and *Warfare in Ancient Greece: A Sourcebook* (1996).

Rick Schulting, Ph.D., is a lecturer in scientific and prehistoric archaeology at the University of Oxford. His current research interests lie in understanding the Mesolithic-Neolithic transition in western Europe, emphasizing the use of radiometric dating and stable isotope analysis, and in skeletal evidence for interpersonal violence in earlier prehistoric Europe.

David R. Sear, a fellow of the Royal Numismatic Society in London and the American Numismatic Society in New York, has authored an extensive range of numismatic books over the past four decades, aimed at collectors and students of ancient Greek, Roman and Byzantine coinage. He has been a resident of Los Angeles for the past 25 years and operates a research service authenticating ancient coinage. His

numerous publications include *Roman Coins and Their Values* (1964; rev. ed., 2000–2005), *Byzantine Coins and Their Values* (1974, rev. ed., 1987), *Greek Coins and Their Values* (1978–1979), and *The History and Coinage of the Roman Imperators, 49–27 B.C.* (1998).

Robert Shanafelt, Ph.D., teaches courses in anthropology, religion, and Africana studies at Georgia Southern University. He has published a number of articles on different aspects of life in southern Africa, among them, "Crime, Power, and Policing in South Africa" in *Democratic Policing in Transitional and Developing Countries* (2006).

Alison Sheridan, Ph.D., is head of early prehistory in the National Museums Scotland, Edinburgh, specializing in the British and Irish Neolithic and Bronze Age. Exhibition work includes *Heaven and Hell—and Other Worlds of the Dead* (2000), for which she was lead curator and book editor. Other books include *From Sickles to Circles* (with A. M. Gibson, 2004) and *Vessels for the Ancestors* (with N. M. Sharples, 1992).

Spyros Siropoulos is senior lecturer of Greek philology and history at the Department of Mediterranean Studies, University of the Aegean, Greece. He has published various articles in three books: *Unlike a Woman: Gender and the Social Function of the Athenian Tragedy* (2003), *The Goat's Skin: The Other Side of Alexander the Great's Power* (2003; in Greek with English summary), and *The Things after Alexander: The Centrifugal Potencies of the Hellenistic Kingdoms* (2005, in Greek).

Bradley Skeen, M.A., has taught at the University of Minnesota, Webster University, and Washington University. He is a specialist in magic, religion, and philosophy in late antiquity and has contributed to research in that field in *Die Zeitschrift für Papyrologie und Epigraphik*, among other journals.

Christopher Smith, D.Phil., is professor of ancient history at the University of Saint Andrews in Scotland. He is the author of *Early Rome and Latium: Economy and Society c 100–500 B.C.* (1996) and *The Roman Clan: From Ancient Ideology to Modern Anthropology* (2006) as well as editor of several collections of essays, including *Trade, Traders and the Ancient City* (with Helen Parkins, 1998); *Sicily from Aeneas to Augustus* (with John Serrati, 2000), and *Religion in Archaic and Republican Rome and Italy: Evidence and Experience* (with Edward Bispham, 2000). He is engaged in work on Roman historiography and oratory.

Nancy Shatzman Steinhardt is professor of East Asian art and curator of Chinese art at the University of Pennsylvania. She is author of *Chinese Traditional Architecture* (1984), *Chinese Imperial City Planning* (1990), *Liao Architecture* (1997), and *Chinese Architecture* (2002) and more than 60 scholarly articles.

Tom Streissguth is a freelance author, editor, and journalist who has published more than 70 nonfiction and reference books. His most recent titles include *Clay v. United States, Genghis Khan's Mongol Empire, Library in a Book: Hate Crimes, Eyewitness History: The Roaring Twenties,* and the *Greenhaven Encyclopedia of the Middle Ages.*

Ananda Cohen Suarez is a Ph.D. student at the Graduate Center of the City University of New York, specializing in pre-Columbian and colonial Latin American art history. She is particularly interested in cross-cultural encounters, vernacular religious art, and manuscript production in the early colonial Americas.

Frank J. Swetz, D.Ed., is professor emeritus of mathematics and education, Pennsylvania State University. His research interests focus on cultural and societal impact on mathematics learning and teaching. Among his recent books are *Legacy of the Luoshu: The 4000 Year Search for the Meaning of the Magic Square of Order Three* (2002) and *Teaching Mathematics to Children* (2003).

John Thorburn, Ph.D., is associate professor of classics at Baylor University, where he teaches a variety of subjects dealing with the classical world. He has published on Greek tragedy, Greek comedy, Greek and Roman history, and a variety of ancient subjects. He is the author of *The Alcestis of Euripides* (2002) and the *Facts on File Companion to Classical Drama* (2005).

Alain Touwaide, Ph.D., is a historian of sciences in the Department of Botany of the National Museum of Natural History at the Smithsonian Institution (Washington, D.C.). He has extensively published on the history of medicine in the Mediterranean world from antiquity to the Renaissance. Recently, he coedited the volume *Visualizing Medieval Medicine and Natural History, 1200–1550* (2006).

Francesca C. Tronchin, Ph.D., teaches Greek and Roman art and archaeology at Ohio State University. Her primary area of research is Roman domestic decor and issues of eclecticism in ancient sculptural displays.

David K. Underwood, Ph.D., teaches Western humanities, art history, philosophy, and Latin American studies at the University of South Florida in Tampa and at Saint Petersburg College in Clearwater, Florida. He is the author of two books and several articles and essays on Iberian and Latin American art and architecture.

David Vallilee is an independent scholar.

Frans van Koppen, M.A., teaches Akkadian at the School of Oriental and African Studies, London. He contributed to *The*

Ancient Near East: Historical Sources in Translation (2006) and *The Babylonian World* (forthcoming).

Lawrence Waldron, M.F.A., is an associate professor and doctoral candidate at the City University of New York, specializing in non-Western fields of art history and culture. He has presented and published various articles on the art and culture of the pre-Columbian Caribbean and Southeast Asia.

Ezekiel A. Walker, Ph.D., teaches African and world history at the University of Central Florida. His forthcoming book is entitled *Growth, Crisis and Transformation in the Cocoa-Farming Economy of Southwestern Nigeria* (2007).

Peter S. Wells is professor of anthropology at the University of Minnesota. His publications include *The Barbarians Speak: How the Conquered Peoples Shaped Roman Europe* (1999), *Beyond Celts, Germans and Scythians: Archaeology and Identity in Iron Age Europe* (2001), and *The Battle That Stopped Rome: Emperor Augustus, Arminius, and the Slaughter of the Legions in the Teutoburg Forest* (2003).

Jacqui Wood is an archaeologist and authority on prehistoric cooking and the lifestyles of prehistoric Europeans. She runs her own excavation in Cornwall, England.

Ronald Young, Ph.D., teaches in the Social Sciences Department at Canterbury School in Fort Myers, Florida. His teaching and research interests are in the area of Latin American Studies. In addition to numerous reference articles, he is presently working on a general history of Colombia to be published by Greenwood Press.

Katharina Zinn, M.A., is writing her Ph.D. dissertation on ancient Egyptian libraries and archives at the University of Leipzig, Germany. She works in a project on scarabs in the Fitzwilliam Museum, Cambridge (United Kingdom) and a project on Middle Kingdom Reliefs from Lisht in the Princeton University Art Museum. She has published articles on the organization of collective wisdom as well as multilingualism in ancient Egypt.

List of Illustrations

VOLUME II

VOLUME III

VOLUME IV

List of Maps and Primary Source Documents

MAPS

VOLUME I

VOLUME II

VOLUME III

VOLUME IV

PRIMARY SOURCE DOCUMENTS

VOLUME I

VOLUME II

VOLUME III

VOLUME IV

Entries D to I

D

death and burial practices

INTRODUCTION

Death in the ancient world had many similarities to death in any other era. While bodies were burned, buried, or left in the open, survivors grappled with ideas about what it meant to be human. The history of death involves not only the disposal of remains but also the emotion of grief and the breaking of bonds between people.

Ancient cultures lacked the means to preserve intact bodies. Especially in warm climates, decomposition set in quickly, with the body emitting a stench by the fourth day. Accordingly, quick disposal of remains was needed for sanitary as well as aesthetic reasons. Ways of physically removing the dead from the living have changed very little during the course of human history, with earth burial and cremation preferred in ancient times as the basic form of funeral. In Asia followers of Zoroastrianism believed that preliminary exposure to flesh-eating animals in an open space was the only acceptable way of disposing of a body. No other means of disposal avoided desecrating the revered elements of fire, earth, and water. Subsequent collection of the bones was recommended but not required. Most other people sought to avoid animal intrusion. Near Eastern people were known to place bodies in a cave and close the opening with rocks to keep out carrion-eating animals. For Christians dismembering of bones ran counter to the hope of the resurrection of the flesh. Muslims outlawed the pre-Islamic Arabian practice of animal sacrifice at the gravesite and preferred level graves.

Some cultures extensively prepared bodies and delayed burial until their cultural rituals were complete. Many cultures washed and dressed the body, and women were typically responsible for this duty. Mummification was the preferred way of handling elite human remains in Egypt and all remains in some American cultures. The Chinchorro people of present-day Chile placed stylized masks on mummified remains of all members of their society, including babies. They kept the dead among the living for a period of time, perhaps as a comfort for the bereaved.

Death among the pagan ancients in the Mediterranean apparently did not involve any metaphysical agony. In the scant pieces of literature that have survived the ages, there is no evidence of tortured thought or psychological malaise. Salvation was associated with the deliverance of the soul from the bindings of the body, the acquisition of ordinary and supernatural benefits, and sometimes with the securing of a better fate in the hereafter. Even tragic situations, such as the death of a child, did not necessarily bring humans closer to the divine. Many Greeks and Romans either sank into despair or appear to have accepted the limits of human existence. In sharp contrast, early Christians radically departed from pagan beliefs by sanctifying human remains and building monuments over the dead. They ignored the pagan taboo against burying the victims of plagues and the corpses of strangers, which came out of a fear of catching the disease that had killed these people. Meanwhile, Muslims avoided funerary monuments as a vain custom. Death is the one constant in every culture in every period. Ancient death and burial practices showed concern for both sanitation and cultural taboos.

AFRICA

BY ROBERT SHANAFELT

Africa provides evidence of some of the world's oldest burials and mortuary rituals. At a site containing some of the oldest human remains, near Herto, Ethiopia, the skull of a child from 160,000 years ago was found to be so polished that it must have been repeatedly handled, probably in a ritual-like way. At the other end of the continent, at Border Cave, between South Africa and Swaziland, excavations uncovered what may be one of the earliest intentional burials that also dates back tens of thousands of years. There the remains of an infant were found together with a shell ornament; some of the child's bones had been stained with the red ocher. Archaeological evidence suggests that individuals continued to be buried in caves and rock shelters throughout South African prehistory.

Ocher (a powdery form of iron-rich earth or clay that can be used as a pigment) and other materials such as shells have served as mortuary goods and for other ceremonial purposes for thousands of years in much of Africa, continuing up into contemporary times. Red ocher is of great ritual significance both in life and in death. Typically mixed with fats and then smeared on the face or body—whether of a living person or a corpse—it results in a glossy, bright red sheen. Because of the association of the color red with blood, the pigment is often linked with life and fertility.

In all of Africa, Egypt is most famous for its ancient pyramids and the tombs where mummies are found, but it is not the only place on the continent where there are elaborate pyramids and burial monuments. The rulers of Egypt's 25th Dynasty were Nubians who hailed from what is Sudan today, and they built their pyramid gravesites in their homeland. The Nubians continued these practices even after losing control of the Egyptian part of their empire. For example, at the city of Meroë, capital of the kingdom of Kush (ca. 800–ca. 350 B.C.E.), members of the ruling families were buried beneath stone or brick pyramids in tombs hewn from solid rock. At an even earlier period the royal tombs of Kerma, topped with

Pyramid of a king, thought to be Adikhalamani Tabirqa, in Meroë, Sudan. (Courtesy of the Oriental Institute of the University of Chicago)

great mounds, some as much as 100 feet wide and 45 feet high, showed the power and prestige of the rulers.

During the fourth and fifth centuries B.C.E. in Axum, a city and kingdom in highland Ethiopia, gravesites of rulers were marked with some of the world's tallest obelisks, monolithic pillars up to 100 feet high. During this time the practice of erecting obelisks and granite tombs for leaders held sway in numerous settlements extending from the Ethiopian highlands to the Red Sea coast.

Other parts of Africa have thus far shown less evidence of great tombs for the deceased in antiquity. One reason may be that social stratification and kingship developed later in these other areas, and consequently there was less focus on building costly structures to provide special honors for elites. Elaborate monuments and precious grave goods are rarely associated with the ordinary members of society. Rather, they are associated with nobility, kingship, and accumulated wealth. However, new discoveries continue to be made in Africa. For example, archaeologists have recently documented dramatic burial sites in Niger. Located primarily in the northern part of the country, these finds include stone chambers beneath massive conical mounds, some of them standing more than 45 feet tall.

Cremation is another possible way of dealing with the dead, and there is early evidence of this practice in Africa. For example, along the Rift Valley in western Kenya the famous archaeologists Mary and Louis Leakey excavated a Late Stone Age cave site known as the Njoro River Cave that dates to around 1200 B.C.E. There they found a number of cremated remains as well as funeral offerings that had also been partially burned, including elaborately decorated wooden vessels, baskets, beads, shells, and semiprecious stones that were probably strung together and worn as jewelry. The Njoro find is exceptional, however; for reasons that are unclear and that probably vary greatly from one culture to another, cremation appears never to have been very common in Africa.

Much remains to be discovered about the death and burial practices of prehistoric Africa, especially among non-elite levels of society. From what is known from more recent practices and religious beliefs, however, it is very unlikely that the dead of typical families in antiquity were disposed of without ceremony or community involvement. Throughout Africa the burial of the dead is a community matter, and there is great concern with honoring and maintaining a proper relationship with the spirit of one's ancestors.

EGYPT

BY KELLY-ANNE DIAMOND REED

Much of our information about the death and burial customs of the ancient Egyptians comes from surviving illustrations of their tomb scenes. No tomb shows all the episodes of a complete burial, but from an assortment of them we can reconstruct the typical funeral. The elaborateness of individual ceremonies and the quantity and richness of the tomb furnishings of course varied with the wealth of the deceased's family.

Upon the death of an ancient Egyptian the body was taken from the home and transported to the tent of purification (*ibw*) for a ritual cleansing and then to the embalming workshop (*wabet*) for mummification. Both were probably located in the cemetery, either near or attached to the tomb. The purpose of the *ibw* was to purify the body before the rituals that inducted the deceased into the world beyond. Everything used in these ceremonies had to be ritually pure, and certain ceremonies were done behind closed doors with only the initiated allowed to attend.

Before the invention of artificial mummification, the ancient Egyptians buried their dead in the ground. Egypt's hot dry climate evaporated the moisture in the body and left it dry. In the Predynastic Period (ca. 5000–3100 B.C.E.) the body was wrapped in an animal skin or linen and placed in a shallow grave. By the end of the Early Dynastic Period (ca. 2920–2575 B.C.E.) royal graves were deeper and lined with materials such as sun-dried mud bricks or wood. Often there was also a superstructure. The coffin gave further protection. All of these protective measures prevented the body from drying and eventually led to a new method of preservation, owing to the need for an eternal body according to Egyptian religious beliefs. Thus mummification was invented, aimed at preserving the body in a dry condition mainly by using a chemical salt known as natron. The details of the mummification process varied over time. By the New Kingdom (ca. 1550–1070 B.C.E.) the procedure took 70 days. The ritual of preservation was later interpreted as imitation of the god Osiris, who died and came back to life.

From the embalming workshop the body embarked on a ritualistic voyage or pilgrimage. In the Old Kingdom (ca. 2575–2134 B.C.E.) the ceremonial voyage went to cult centers in the Nile Delta, but in the Middle Kingdom (ca. 2040–1640 B.C.E.) and New Kingdom the destination was Abydos, the most sacred place of the Osiris cult, which had become popular near the end of the Old Kingdom and influenced the funerary rituals. Once the cortege arrived on the west bank of the Nile (west being associated by the Egyptians with death), the body was hauled to the tomb on a sledge pulled by either men or oxen. The sledge also carried the so-called canopic chest containing the four canopic jars, which held the deceased's liver, stomach, lungs, and intestines.

The funeral procession consisted of relatives and other mourners, servants who carried the burial goods, and priests. Sometimes two women impersonated the goddesses Isis and Nephthys, who mourned their brother Osiris in the myth. In the older tradition the *mww*-dancers, who may have represented the ancestors of the ruler (there are many theories about the identity of the *mww*-dancers, would have met the procession at the cemetery. Boxes, baskets, furniture, jewelry, sandals, writing boards, and other items were buried with the deceased. Additional rituals took place before the body was deposited into the tomb. A special lector priest read funerary

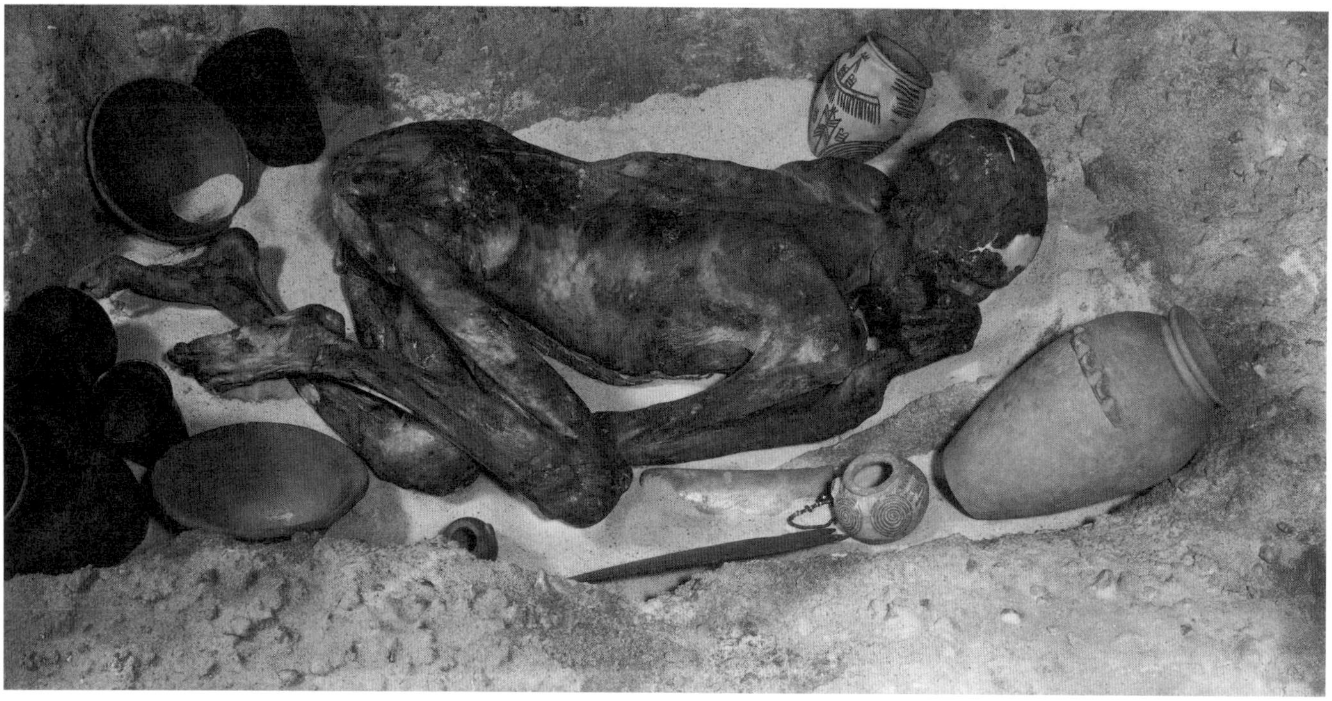

A reconstructed Predynastic Egyptian grave pit from about 3400 B.C.E. at a time before mummification, when bodies were placed directly in shallow desert graves, where they did not decay. (© The Trustees of the British Museum)

texts from a papyrus, the Opening of the Mouth ceremony took place (supposedly restoring the faculties of the deceased so that he could be reborn in the hereafter), and offerings were made. Once the body was placed in the tomb, the footprints were swept away. An ancient Egyptian narrative, "The Story of Sinuhe" (ca. 1800 B.C.E.), provides a detailed account of an ancient Egyptian funeral: "A funeral procession is made for you on the day of burial; the mummy case is of gold, its head of lapis lazuli. The sky is above you as you lie in the hearse, oxen drawing you, musicians going before you. The dance of the *mww*-dancers is done at the door of your tomb; the offering-list is read to you; sacrifice is made before your offering-stone."

Tomb architecture developed over time. The first superstructure was a mastaba, a stone shell (in Arabic the word *mastaba* means "stone bench"), rectangular in shape, its walls sloping so that the area of the roof was less than that of the base. The first step pyramid was built for King Djoser (r. ca. 2630–2611 B.C.E.) at Saqqara by the architect Imhotep in the Third Dynasty (ca. 2649–2575 B.C.E.). It appears that the step pyramid originated as a mastaba. It eventually developed into a true pyramid by the addition of an outer facing, as can be seen in the pyramid at Medūm built either by Huni (r. ca. 2599–2575 B.C.E.), the last king of the Third Dynasty, or by his son Snefru (r. ca. 2575–2551 B.C.E.), the first king of the Fourth Dynasty (ca. 2575–2465 B.C.E.). The most famous pyramid site is Giza, where Khufu (r. ca. 2551–2528 B.C.E.), Khafre (r. ca. 2520–2494 B.C.E.), and Menkure (r. ca. 2490–2472 B.C.E.), the son, grandson, and great-grandson of Snefru, respectively, built their pyramid complexes. Khufu's monument is known as the "Great Pyramid" because it is the largest one surviving.

It was at this time that the formal pyramid complex emerged, consisting of the pyramid itself, a mortuary temple, a valley temple, and a causeway down to the Nile. Sometimes there were subsidiary burials of queens or important officials, or boat burials. Most of the pyramids of the Fifth Dynasty (ca. 2465–2323 B.C.E.) are at Abusir; they are much smaller than those of the Fourth Dynasty. Pyramids were constructed until the Thirteenth Dynasty, and there are a few Seventeenth Dynasty examples from Thebes as well. Beginning in the New Kingdom a hidden valley on the west bank of Luxor, called the Valley of the Kings, was chosen as the burial spot for the kings. There they carved their tombs out of the mountain.

Royal tombs were built of stone to survive for eternity; for this reason scholars have more information about them than about the tombs of the lower classes. Private people of high rank were buried in mastabas in the Old Kingdom and later in rock-cut tombs. Simple pit graves continued to suffice for the poorest classes throughout Egyptian history.

THE MIDDLE EAST

BY KAREN RADNER

The ancient Mesopotamians usually buried their dead, either beneath their houses or in graveyards. The bodies were often laid to rest in stone or clay sarcophagi (coffins) or, most frequently, in one or two large pots. Above-ground grave markers were rare; memorial monuments inside temples have been found but had no physical connection to the burial. Cremation was uncommon, not because of a perceived need to preserve the body intact but because of the forbidding costs of building large fires in a virtually woodless environment. The Achaemenid kings of Persia were laid to rest in free-standing tombs and rock tombs cut into the imposing cliffs near the royal palaces of Persepolis. In contrast to the hidden Mesopotamian graves, these burials were highly visible and hint at a rather different role of death and funerary care in Persian society.

Spectacular recent finds of the royal tombs from the Middle Bronze Age (ca. 2000–1600 B.C.E.) palace at Qatna in Syria and the tombs of several Assyrian queens of the ninth and eighth centuries B.C.E. beneath the royal palace of Nimrud in northern Iraq have caused sensations in the archaeological world, but the most famous ancient Near Eastern burial ground remains the cemetery of Ur in southern Babylonia, excavated in the 1920s. This site, adjoining the central temple, was used for more than half a millennium, from about 2600 to 2000 B.C.E., for thousands of burials. The vast majority of the bodies were interred in simple pits—although often with very rich grave goods—but 16 burials from the mid-third millennium B.C.E. occupy multichambered stone tombs at the bottom of shaft graves. This group of graves is known as the Royal Cemetery of Ur. Its best-known resident is Queen Puabi, whose identity was revealed by an inscribed cylinder seal found with her body. Puabi and the other main occupants of the shaft graves were not buried alone but with many other bodies, male and female, evidently as part of opulent sacrifices that also included vehicles with their draft animals, luxury objects such as musical instruments and furniture, and food and drink. One such mass burial contained the bodies of 74 men and women.

Today most scholars agree that in life these people were the attendants of the main occupiers of the graves. They died during ceremonies conducted at the funerals of members of the ruling elite. As drinking bowls were found close to their bodies, it is thought that they took poison. While no writings that could shed light on this practice survive from that time, literary texts from the beginning of the second millennium B.C.E. describe the burials of Mesopotamian rulers. Most important, a Sumerian composition today known as "The Death of Gilgamesh" mentions how the favorite wife, junior wife, singer, cup bearer, barber, and attendants of this mythical hero-king of Uruk lay down with him in death. The grave goods are described as meeting gifts and presents for the gods of the netherworld, and this idea is also prominent in other textual sources.

Ancient Mesopotamian texts allow considerable insight into the mythology of death. Death was seen as the inevitable fate of all humans. The Epic of Gilgamesh, the best known of these texts, exemplifies the impossibility of escaping physical death even for a man like Gilgamesh, who is two parts divine and only one part human. The funeral ceremony enabled the dead person's spirit to voyage properly into the netherworld. Without it a spirit would wander the world of the living, lost and increasingly dangerous. Consequently, the loss of a dead body—for example, to the enemy on a battlefield as in the case of Sargon II, king of Assyria (r. 721–705 B.C.E.)—was a catastrophe that demanded rituals to calm the restless and malicious spirit. The responsibility for the funeral rested with the family of the deceased, as did the ensuing care for the dead, consisting offerings of food and drink to the ancestors and the evocation of their names. Although cemeteries existed, the most common form of burial was in tombs underneath the family home and accessible to it.

Contacts between the living and their dead were not limited to funerary duties but could also provide insight into the future. The netherworld was where the sun god, on his daily cycle through the universe, spent the night. Hence it was the source of the new day and, implicitly, of all forthcoming events. The inhabitants of the netherworld were therefore privy to future knowledge, and contacting them by necromancy (conjuring of the spirits of the dead in order to communicate with them) could offer that knowledge to the living.

The netherworld mirrored the world of the living and was imagined as a city surrounded by fortified and gated walls. This "Land without Return," as it was called, was ruled by a queen, Ereshkigal, and her consort, Nergal, the god of pestilence and destruction. They were assisted by the vizier Namtar and the judges of the netherworld, among them Gilgamesh and his friend Enkidu as well as the historical king Ur-Nammu, who ruled Ur at the turn of the second millennium B.C.E. The story of how Ishtar/Inanna, the goddess of sexuality and fertility, unsuccessfully tried to wrest control over the netherworld from her sister Ereshkigal survives in two different versions, one with very close parallels in the Greek myth of Persephone: Ishtar/Inanna goes to the netherworld in order to rescue her dead lover Dumuzi, the god of vegetation. Captured by Ereshkigal, she succeeds only in striking a compromise: Dumuzi is allowed back among the living for part of the year but must return to the netherworld for the rest of it, thus defining vegetation's cycle of demise and renewal. In the other version of the story Ishtar/Inanna has another motivation, the ambition to rule over the innumerable dead, but like death itself, the queen of the dead cannot be defeated.

The concept of the dying god who returns to life featured prominently in the Near Eastern mythology of death. This ultimate sacrifice of a deity was presented as an integral part in the creation of humankind, as the dead god's essence was added to the clay from which humans were formed to be servants to the gods. Originally, therefore, humans were immortal, and mortality came about only through a later decision of the gods: As humankind became numerous and their constant hubbub a nuisance, the divine creators sent a flood to destroy them. Appreciating the value of the few survivors, the gods then conceived mortality as a countermeasure to unchecked human propagation. Thus death from old age and disease came into existence.

ASIA AND THE PACIFIC

BY CONSTANCE A. COOK

The earliest human burials in Asia are found in caves occupied as much as 25,000 years ago in Southeast Asia, such as in peninsular Thailand. The very early burials are random and unclear in nature, but beginning in about 8000 B.C.E. people here began burying their dead in circular pits, their bones sometimes marked with red ocher. Regular burial grounds with grave goods, often in caves used earlier as habitations, became common in this region around 3000 B.C.E. and log coffins just before the start of the Common Era. Cremation first appeared in the northern Indus valley in 1900 B.C.E., after the decline of the predominant Harappa cultures (ca. 2500–2000 B.C.E.), whose dead were buried in wooden or brick coffins and surrounded with pottery vessels.

The 45,000-year-old Niah cave complex in Sarawak, Borneo, represents the most ancient burial style, although the period of greatest activity dates to around 4,000 years ago. In the earliest chronological layer of these cave burials, rain-forest foragers buried their dead inside logs, in wooden coffins, or simply wrapped in a shroud—a basic burial style perpetuated throughout much of Asia. Later, in Sarawak and elsewhere in island Southeast Asia and the Pacific, bodies were sometimes partially burned and placed in ceramic or bamboo containers. At Sarawak and many other sites the bodies show evidence of being processed after their primary burial and then interred again in what are known as secondary burials. Secondary burials here and elsewhere, such as among early farming communities in China, consist of group burials. One major difference is that the secondary burials in the Niah caves were in jars. Jar burials were common for children in early northern Chinese cultures, but the primary and secondary burials of adults were in pits. The Polynesian Lapita culture of 3,000 years ago removed the skulls of their dead after decomposition and sealed them in pots. The headless skeletons and the teeth were buried in pits.

Early Neolithic (7500–6000 B.C.E.) cave sites in southern China contain burials similar to those found farther south: flexed, some with perforated skulls, and bones covered in red ocher. Bodies found in Thailand from 2000 to 1400 B.C.E. were likewise covered with red ocher but wrapped in cloth and placed supine in wooden structures with pottery and shell jewelry. There is evidence of lineage burials (burials in grounds set aside for a single lineage) and ritual feasting. Burials from 3,000 to 5,000 years ago in the Red River valley in Vietnam also have bodies wrapped in ramie shrouds and buried with pottery and beads but placed in canoes, oddly reminiscent of the Ba people's canoe burials in the cliffs near the upper Yangtze River valley of China around the same period.

Beginning in the cemeteries of the Early Neolithic farming communities in China, burials were aligned in a single direction, such as north–south or east–west. A number of communities practiced secondary burials in which the bones were reorganized into kin burial sites. Grave goods included such items as stone mortars and pestles, stone axes, and pottery tripods and bowls. Occasionally, a primary burial was marked as that of a person of importance by inclusion of ritual implements such as musical instruments—for example, flutes carved of crane bones or rattles made of tortoise shells. Many cemeteries include ash pits filled with animal and human bones, vessels, and tools suggesting sacrifice to the dead and the beginning of ancestor cults. The burial of humans as sacrifice occurred especially in building projects, such as of a tomb, house, or city wall. This practice reached its peak during the Shang Dynasty (1500–1045 B.C.E.) when large royal tombs contained hundreds of victims and the cemeteries thousands.

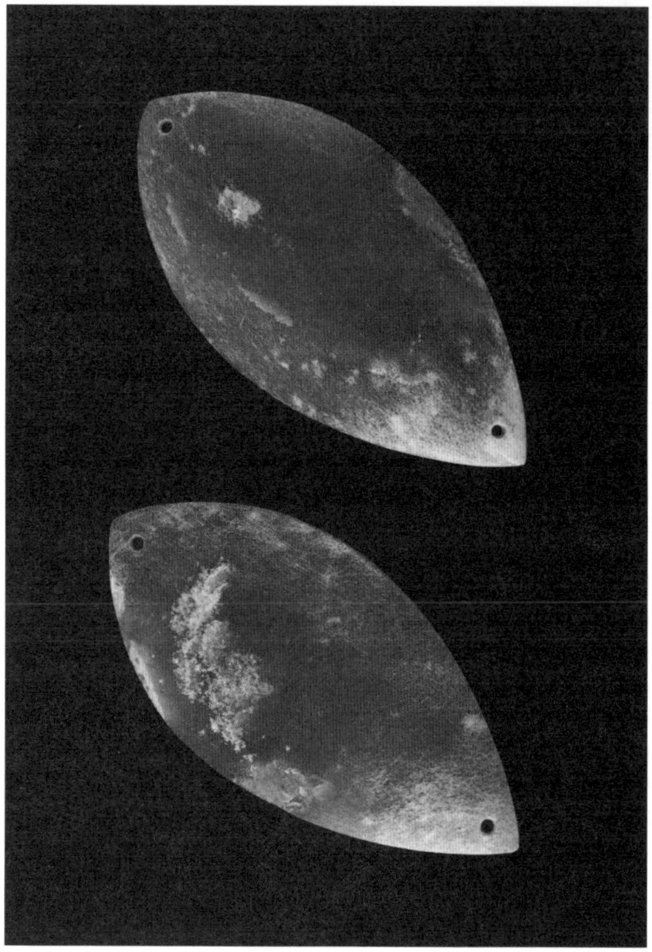

Jade eye plaques from China during the Han Dynasty (206 B.C.E. to 220 C.E.), used to cover the eyes of the dead to protect the body from decomposition. (© The Trustees of the British Museum)

By the end of the Middle Neolithic in northern China (5000–3000 B.C.E.) the majority of cemeteries clearly gave preference to males. Some primary burials began to have a "second-level ledge" for the display of mortuary feasting vessels around the bodies, which might be covered with bone or stone beads. Some jade objects and tomb decor suggest the use of astrological or cosmic symbols in rituals to contact the supernatural through spirit mediums. In Manchuria burials from the Hongshan culture (4500–3000 B.C.E.) used rock cairns (mounds of piled stones) with a central tomb surrounded by a cluster of similar but smaller tombs. Large tombs at one Hongshan site seem to have been associated with a temple filled with statues of pig-dragons and of women naked and pregnant.

Cemeteries during the Late Neolithic (3000–2500 B.C.E.) and the highly socially stratified Erlitou culture (1900–1500 B.C.E.) in the middle Yellow River valley bear many traits that would remain common in Chinese burials for millennia. The mortuary feast display became increasingly ostentatious for the elite and included exotic and highly crafted goods such as fine painted or thin-walled pottery, jade, alligator and pottery drums, stone chimes, painted wooden vessels, and accumulated stores of meat, such as whole pigs. Bodies were placed in wooden painted and lacquered coffins over a "waist pit," a pit dug into the cinnabar-covered floor of the tomb chamber under the waist area of the body and filled with dog, deer, or human sacrifices. In some tombs grave goods were placed in painted wooden chests at the foot and sides of the wooden coffin or in an outer coffin containing the inner coffin, with different categories of goods placed in each.

The Shang Dynasty saw the creation of royal mausoleums such as the complex near present-day Anyang, in Henan Province. It consisted of numerous large cruciform (in the shape of a cross) tombs originally filled with display bronzes and jades. Sacrificial victims of all ages and both genders, some intact, some headless or otherwise mutilated, were buried in all areas of the tomb and in thousands of sacrificial pits, along with an array of domestic and exotic animals. The burial of horses and chariots began during this period. Such magnificence was not seen again until the burial of the first Qin Dynasty emperor in 220 B.C.E., though by then the horses, chariots, and humans were made in miniature or cast out of clay.

After the Shang the second-level platform and waist pit became less common, but jades, jewelry, weapons, and clothing continued to be buried in or around the inner coffin. The outer coffin (a wooden chamber inside the tomb and outside the "inner" coffin or coffins) came to display, at first, a rich array of bronze cooking, eating, serving, and ritual ablution (or purification) vessels and some ritual jades, and then, by the fourth century B.C.E., fine painted lacquer vessels and statues. The statues protected the tomb from demons and aided the journey of the deceased into the afterlife. By this time, too, bamboo texts were placed in the tomb. Some listed mortuary gifts used in the funeral, and some of these gifts were buried with the dead. Other texts, including accounts of healing rituals, almanacs, administrative documents, and philosophical tracts, suggest that the occupant wanted to have these items to maintain some aspect of his mortal identity in the afterlife or perhaps to prove his rank in the world of the ancestors. Wooden, clay, or stone figurines were buried with equipment for hunting, travel, ritual ceremonies, and musical feasts.

The ancient practice of jar burials continued in Japan with the Yayoi culture (300 B.C.E.–300 C.E.), whose burials consisted of stamped-earth mounds over a coffin consisting of two large painted jars placed end to end. In some cases other jar burials radiated outward from the central burial or were placed in clusters or lines. Besides bronze daggers, mirrors, glass beads, and other items found in the jars, burial mounds hold a variety of pottery vessels and serving dishes. The earlier Jōmon people buried their dead in rows of pits in communal cemeteries marked off with stone circles or ramparts.

EUROPE

BY PETER BOGUCKI

Death was an important part of life in late prehistoric Europe. The death of a member of Neolithic, Bronze Age, or Iron Age society was often the occasion for elaborate ritual and mortuary ceremonies and the display of status and wealth, and the dead continued to be present in the everyday lives of the living. There was a remarkable range in the ways that corpses were treated and eventually buried. Archaeologists consider many characteristics of mortuary practices, or practices relating to the burial of the dead. The most fundamental is the treatment of the body itself: How was the corpse prepared for burial, and how was it buried? The two principal options for dealing with a corpse are either burial as an anatomical entity of flesh and bone or transformation into ashes through cremation. Prehistoric European societies practiced both at various times and places. In addition, some societies left bodies to decay in a ceremonial location and then gathered the defleshed bones for burial, a practice known as "excarnation."

The principal choices for burial of a body in ancient Europe was either to lay it in the grave in an extended position, with legs straight and arms at the sides or crossed over the torso, or to place it in a contracted position, lying on one side with legs drawn up to the chest and arms bent. Seated burials are also known, and occasionally bodies were placed in a grave pit without apparent consideration for how they were lying. Bodies were sometimes enclosed in coffins. Virtually nothing is known of embalming or other techniques of preparing the corpse that leave little trace on the bones and therefore no long-lasting evidence.

Graves were individual, multiple, or collective. Individual burial was most common in ancient Europe, one corpse per grave; some graves contain several or many corpses, especially if members of the same family died at about the same time. Collective burials, in which graves contain many bodies, are found from time to time, commonly at the gravesites of societies that practiced excarnation. The bones were gathered into crypts containing dozens of people; in instances of violence many bodies were buried quickly in a mass grave.

Often buried with the bodies were offerings that archaeologists call "grave goods." Sometimes these goods are lavish, in the form of finely crafted objects made from expensive materials, and sometimes they are meager or absent. Archaeologists debate the significance of grave goods. The items certainly reflect the ability of the deceased person's family and community to acquire objects and to dispose of them by burying with the corpse. The question is whether they reflect the status and rank of the deceased person or are a symbolic display by the survivors that has ritual or spiritual meaning.

Another key feature of mortuary practice in ancient Europe was the construction of mounds (also called "barrows," "tumuli," or "kurgans"), cairns (mounds of small stones), megalithic tombs (built of large stones forming chambers), or wooden structures over the grave or as crypts. Careful attention was paid to the locations of these structures in the landscape. They were often positioned where they could be viewed from afar or, in some cases, only when approached from a particular direction. Over time burial monuments accumulated in specific localities to create "ritual landscapes" of mounds and other features.

Archaeologists also debate the time at which human beings began to bury their dead in a formal, careful way. The practice dates well back into the Paleolithic Period (8,000 B.C.E. and earlier). A triple burial from Dolní Věstonice in the Czech Republic dates to 25,660 B.C.E., while at Sungir' in northern Russia, several individuals were buried around 22,000 B.C.E., some ornamented with thousands of beads. Cemeteries, specific localities devoted to repeated burials over a long time, appear during the Mesolithic Period in about 7,000–5,000 B.C.E. At Skateholm in southern Sweden about 90 people (and several dogs) were buried in a variety of positions, often with deer antlers and other artifacts, while at

Pottery cinerary urn shaped like a hut, early Italian iron age 900–800 B.C.E (© The Trustees of the British Museum)

Téviec and Hoëdic in Brittany (France), single, double, and multiple graves, some in stone cists and containing antlers, were associated with large ritual hearths.

During the Neolithic Period, burials became elaborate and diverse. Sometimes they were in cemeteries separate from settlements, as in central Europe between 5500 and 5000 B.C.E., and at other times they are found within settlements, as at sites like Brześć Kujawski and Osłonki in Poland a millennium later. Elongated mounds called "long barrows" were constructed over graves in several parts of Europe, including Poland, Denmark, Britain, and France. Some of the best-known Neolithic burials are the megalithic tombs of western Europe and Scandinavia, constructed between 4000 and 2000 B.C.E. Large stone slabs were set upright to form chambers and passages, while other large stones formed roofs; the whole construction was covered with earth or small stones. Thousands of megalithic tombs were built, usually as collective graves into which whole bodies or defleshed or cremated bones were placed on many occasions. A tomb at La Chaussée-Tirancourt in France contained the remains of more than 360 people, many of which had been rearranged during subsequent openings of the chamber. At Newgrange and other Irish megalithic tombs, cremated bones were placed in small chambers that opened off the main passage.

During the Neolithic we also see glimpses of sudden and violent death. A mass grave at Talheim in Germany contains the bodies of at least 34 men, women, and children. Many had suffered blows to their skulls from stone axes. In 1991 hikers found the frozen body of a man known as "Ötzi," or the "Iceman," in the Alps, where he had died 5,300 years earlier. His body showed evidence of a hard life, including injuries and an arrow wound, although the cause of his death is unknown.

Late in the Neolithic and into the Bronze Age, between about 3000 and 1200 B.C.E., single burials under mounds became common across much of Europe. Examples are the famous barrows of the Wessex culture, associated with Stonehenge in southern England, which contained artifacts of gold and other exotic materials. At Leubingen in central Germany, a barrow covered a timber mortuary house in which an elite person was interred around 2000 B.C.E. In Denmark around 1250 B.C.E., oak trunks were hollowed out as coffins, which preserved hair, textiles, and grave goods superbly.

Around 1200 B.C.E. the burial rite over many parts of Europe shifted to cremation, with the ashes buried in urns. Some cremation cemeteries, such as Kietrz in southern Poland, contain thousands of graves. Elsewhere bodies continued to be buried, as in the very rich so-called prince's graves in southwest Germany and eastern France, around 500 B.C.E., at sites like Hochdorf and Vix. Later in the Iron Age (1000 B.C.E.–500 C.E.) some corpses were thrown into bogs and ponds across northern Europe, where they remained remarkably preserved. These "bog bodies" were either human sacrifices or executed criminals. During the early part of the first millennium of the Common Era, the burial rites throughout

Europe were different from region to region, with skeletal burial common in some areas and cremation in others.

Ancient European mortuary practices varied dramatically over the millennia after people began to regard burial as a way of expressing a relationship between the dead and the living. Archaeologists pay very close attention to burial rites and graves, because they reflect social organization, status, and symbolism better than almost any other form of archaeological remains.

GREECE

BY WENDY E. CLOSTERMAN

Funerals were family affairs in ancient Greece. When someone died, family members took the lead in conducting all stages of the funeral; no religious official seems to have been involved. The funeral began with the *prothesis,* a ceremony in which the corpse was laid out for mourning at home. The women of the family washed the body, dressed it in special funerary clothes, and placed it on a bed, around which the family members gathered and mourned. Athenian vases portray women and children closest to the head of the corpse at this stage of the ritual, tearing at their hair, singing dirges, and crying out in distress, while the men stand near the feet raising their hands in more subdued gestures of mourning.

The next stage of the funeral, the *ekphora,* consisted of a procession transporting the corpse from the house to the gravesite. Here the men walked in front while the women followed, continuing to mourn. Exactly what rituals took place during burial is uncertain. Probably someone made a libation, a ritual pouring of wine or other liquid onto the ground. Archaeological digs near graves reveal long trenches or smaller areas of burnt soil containing animal bones and pottery normally used for dining, suggesting that a ritual meal was offered to the deceased. Whether the survivors participated in this meal is unknown, but it is clear that after the funeral the family gathered at a home for a communal meal.

Aristocratic families, especially in the Archaic Period (600–480 B.C.E.), often took advantage of the opportunities funerals offered for ostentatious display of wealth and position. It was probably for this reason that various cities passed laws curtailing some aspects of funerary display. For example, at the beginning of the sixth century B.C.E. the Athenian lawmaker Solon limited the length of the *prothesis* to one day and its location to within the house and required that the *ekphora* take place before daybreak.

The Greeks practiced both burial and cremation. Burial might be directly in the ground, in stone-lined graves, or in wooden or stone coffins. With cremation, the ashes of the deceased were placed in a vessel that was then buried in the ground. The Greeks also deposited objects in graves during burial. In addition to jewelry or other items worn by the deceased during the funeral, grave offerings might include pottery, mirrors, figurines, weapons, and toys. The amount and expense of grave gifts varied in different periods and regions.

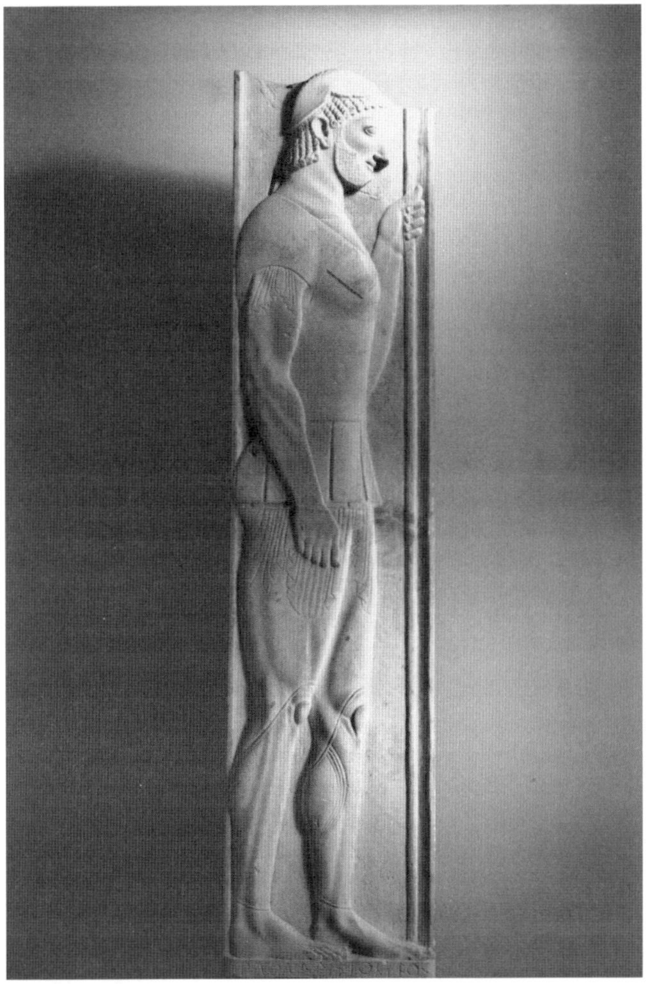

Stele of Aristion, a philosopher of Athens who died in 86 B.C.E. (Alison Frantz Photographic Collection, American School of Classical Studies at Athens)

Because the Greeks usually buried beside roads, especially those leading in and out of a town, the gravestones were visible to many people. The form of gravestones and the imagery on them differed with time and place. In Athens large vessels painted with *prothesis* and *ekphora* scenes, 3 feet or more in height, marked graves during the eighth century B.C.E. Later Athenian funerary markers no longer focused primarily on ritual but instead presented generalized and idealized images of the deceased. In the Archaic Period tombstones took the form of statues or stelae (stone slabs or pillars) carved in relief, most commonly depicting near-life-size men in their prime, sometimes as soldiers or athletes. Sculpted grave markers fell out of use in Athens for much of the fifth century B.C.E. When they returned to favor from about 430 to the late 300s B.C.E., they included depictions of women and of family gatherings.

Ritual obligations to the dead continued beyond the funeral. Athenians visited the gravesite for third-day, ninth-day, and 30th-day rites, the last of which officially marked the end of the mourning period. They continued to visit periodically afterward, including during the Genesia, an annual religious festival for the dead. Fifth-century Athenian vase paintings depict women tending graves by decorating the tombstones with ribbons or bringing offerings such as food or vases that held oil or perfume.

In addition to family-run funerals the city of Athens in the Classical Period (480–323 B.C.E.) commemorated those who died in battle each year with annual public funerals. A prominent politician gave a speech honoring the sacrifice of the fallen soldiers, and their bones were buried together by tribe.

The Greeks believed that the mythical boatman Charon ferried the deceased to the afterlife. The god Hermes, in his capacity as guide of souls, could also play a role in leading the dead. Several different views of the afterlife circulated in the Greek world. The earliest description is found in Homer's epic poem the *Odyssey* (eighth century B.C.E.). Here the dead dwell in Hades, a dark realm beneath the earth ruled by the god Hades and his bride Persephone. The dead are shadowy beings leading a tedious existence without the physical strength or mental acuity they had on earth. Everyone, whether good or evil in life, shares the same fate in Hades.

Some prescribed rites with secret components, so-called mystery religions, seem to have offered the possibility of a happier afterlife to anyone who completed the initiation. Taking place in Eleusis, near Athens, the Eleusinian mysteries for Demeter, the goddess of grain, and Kore, Demeter's daughter, attracted people from all over the Greek-speaking world from at least the sixth century B.C.E. until the fourth century C.E., when the sanctuary closed. These rites were open to anyone who spoke Greek and was not a murderer.

Mythical figures might arrive at other destinations in the afterlife. Menelaus, the king of Sparta in the *Odyssey*, found a pleasant afterlife in the Elysian Fields, and according to the poet Hesiod (eighth century B.C.E.) the heroes went to the Isles of the Blessed. Other myths tell of people who disobeyed the will of Zeus, the king of the gods, and spent their afterlife in perpetual torment. For example, the hungry and thirsty Tantalos stands in a pool of water with fruit overhead, but both food and drink move out of his reach whenever he tries for them. The Greeks do not seem to have ascribed such fates, good or bad, to ordinary mortals.

Another common belief was that the dead were present at their graves. As part of their ritual grave visits, family members might bring offerings of food and drink. Some people even placed lead curse tablets into the graves of strangers to communicate with the underworld. These tablets asked the dead to carry the message to deities of the afterlife to magically harm the person designated on the tablet.

ROME

BY TOM STREISSGUTH

During the early years of the Roman Republic, established around 509 B.C.E., Romans generally buried their dead. Cremation became more common in the late republic. By the third century C.E. funeral customs were again changing from cremation to burial. The spread of Christianity and the belief in an afterlife played an important role in this change, which was complete by the fifth century and the fall of the Western Roman Empire.

In ancient Rome many religious and social traditions were attached to the funeral ceremony, though much also depended on the status and wealth of the deceased's family. All Roman families served as guardians of their dead, dressing and otherwise preparing the body for the last rites. Personal belongings of the dead were collected for burning or burial with their owner. It was also traditional to place a coin in the mouth of the deceased in order to pay Charon, the mythical ferryman who brought the souls of the dead to the underworld. After preparation, the body was displayed so that family and friends could pay their last respects. In the case of a prominent citizen a public viewing known as a *laudatio* took place, during which a speaker recounted the deeds and virtues of the dead.

All funeral processions ended outside the city: as the bodies of the dead were believed to pollute the city's sacred precincts, cremation pyres and cemeteries always lay outside the walls. Borne on a litter, the body was followed by the family and other mourners, who often gathered at night to avoid unruly crowds. Musicians, dancers, and professional mourners sometimes took part, while members of the family, if they were well to do, might ride chariots or horses. It was customary for the members of important families to wear *imagines,* or ancestor masks, made of wax and representing members of the clan who had already passed away.

The procession ended at the cemetery and, for a cremation, at the funeral pyre. The body was then burned, along with gifts and offerings brought by mourners and the possessions of the dead. After a eulogy was given, a member of the immediate family gathered the ashes into an urn. Urns ranged from simple cloth bags or ceramic vases to more elaborate stone caskets or wood or metal chests. The urn was kept in the home, sometimes the centerpiece of a small display maintained in remembrance of the dead.

For burials the body was protected by a shroud or encased in a stone or wood coffin. To further preserve the body, it might be embalmed with gypsum. Proper burial was of utmost importance to the Romans; they believed an unburied body would be rejected by Charon and would wander forever. To allow a body to become food for birds or animals was the ultimate punishment for a criminal or traitor. Those who committed suicide by hanging themselves also sacrificed their right to a proper burial, and their bodies were left exposed to the elements.

Funeral societies known as collegia helped people prepare for their own funeral ceremonies. Individuals made contributions to their collegium, which then helped to arrange and pay for their funerals. If burial was used, members were entombed in a columbarium, an underground vault holding niches for the storage of funeral urns, which were marked by commemorative sculpture and plaques.

The poor were buried in mass graves, their bodies covered by simple shrouds or sacks. The wealthy used sarcophagi—coffins made of wood or stone—and often had elaborate tombs. Non-Christian Romans buried a wide variety of grave goods, including household items, jewelry, pottery, shoes, clothing, weapons, and even food and drink, intended to succor the dead on their journey to the next world. Images of the dead were painted on small wooden planks or carved into stone tombstones or memorials.

Elaborate mausoleums were constructed for aristocrats, with the emperors having striking monumental buildings raised to house their remains. The most famous is Hadrian's Tomb, later known as the Castel San Angelo, which still rises above the right bank of the Tiber River in Rome. Another monument, known as the Pyramid of Cestius, was built directly into the city wall at the southern edge of Rome and survives intact to this day. The pyramid, which contains a small burial chamber, was raised about 12 B.C.E., shortly after the Roman conquest of Egypt, when Egyptian monuments and religious cults were fashionable.

Christian Romans built underground catacombs, cities of the dead that protected the remains of thousands of people. The bodies were placed in sarcophagi and then set in niches in the walls of the narrow passageways. Each grave was marked by a stone slab carved with the deceased's name, age, and date of death.

The Romans believed that the dead sometimes wandered the underworld in a state of limbo. An unappeased or restless spirit, especially of someone who had died a violent or sudden death, could appear among the living to deliver important messages or warnings. To prevent such wanderings the Romans often cut off the head of the dead or weighted the body down with stones. All the same, "curse tables" created to invoke the powers of the dead to harm an enemy were common. During the Parentalia festival the spirits of dead parents are appeased with offerings made by their offspring. Romans also carried out rituals of appeasement to the dead during the Lemuria festival.

THE AMERICAS

BY KEITH JORDAN

The earliest evidence of ancient American burial rituals and the provision of grave goods to accompany the deceased into the afterlife dates beyond 8,000 years B.C.E., suggesting that these cultural traits came to the New World with the first peoples crossing from Asia. Burials from the Paleo-Indian Period (ca. 13,000–8000 B.C.E.) show a great variety of practices. At the Anzick site in Montana, ice age hunters buried two children accompanied by finely worked stone blades, bone tools, and red-ocher pigment believed to symbolize life, blood, and rebirth. At the Marmes site on the Washington coast people were cremating their dead by 8500 B.C.E. A man from a hunter-gatherer community was interred on the ledge of a sinkhole at Warm Mineral Springs, Florida, at around the same time, taking with him a tool of his trade—the shell hook of a spear thrower (a rodlike implement used to provide greater impetus for throwing a spear or similar weapon). At Spirit Cave, Nevada, an early Native American was buried in a rock shelter, wrapped in reed mats and a rabbit-fur robe, some 9,400 years before the present.

This diversity of burial practices continued into the succeeding Archaic Period (8000–1000 B.C.E.). Prehistoric peoples in Florida buried their dead in wetlands some 6,000 years ago. At about the same time the fisherfolk of the Chinchorro culture of Chile preserved the bodies of the deceased, especially children, by elaborate methods of mummification, the oldest evidence for this practice anywhere. They skinned the bodies, tied the bones together to form a frame, and sometimes removed the muscles and internal organs. The corpses were then dried and stuffed with ash, the features modeled in an ash paste, and the skin was reattached and covered with a black mineral pigment or painted red with iron oxide. Apparently, like later Andean peoples such as the Incas, the Chinchorros felt a need to preserve the dead so as to keep them a part of the community and ensure their survival in the afterlife.

In most hunter-gatherer burials in the Americas up to historical times, grave goods tended to be similar for all members of the community, consistent with a lack of marked differences in social status. Conversely, an increased complexity of funerary practices and the appearance of luxury burial

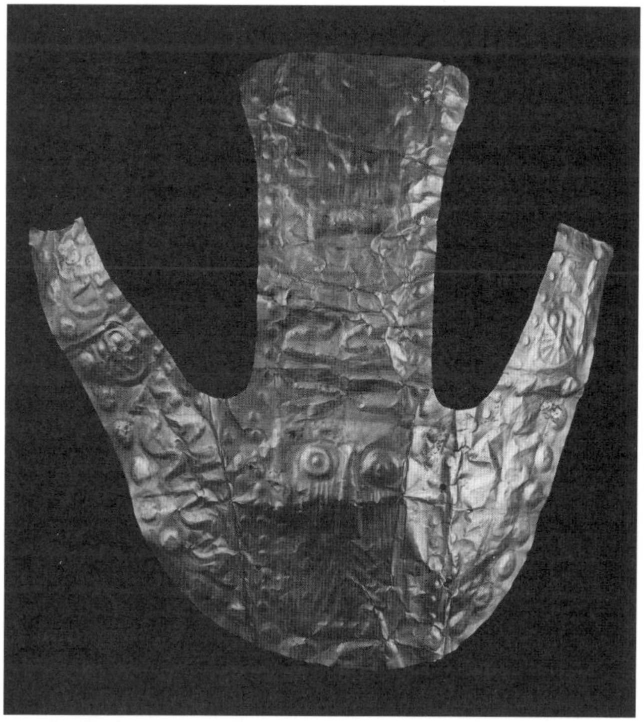

Gold diadem, found in the Camaná valley, Peru, and dating to the first century C.E.; it would have been attached to a mummy. (© The Trustees of the British Museum)

goods reserved for a few individuals reflect the development of social ranking in ancient American societies.

In what is now the eastern United States, groups practicing a mix of hunting-collecting and limited agriculture participated in the Adena and Hopewell burial and ritual complexes (ca. 1000 B.C.E.–400 C.E.). These widespread traditions focused on the practice of burying selected members of the community in artificial mounds accompanied by elaborate gifts, many obtained via long-distance trade. At Adena sites in the Ohio Valley small communities built conical mounds, some as high as 70 feet, over circular or rectangular wooden structures that covered graves lined with clay or logs. The dead were buried in the flesh, as secondary burials (meaning that the bodies had been allowed to decay to bones elsewhere before burial here), or as cremations. The mounds grew in layers as burials were added over time. The honored dead, who may have achieved their status by their abilities as traders or shamans, were accompanied by slate pendants, stone smoking pipes, and copper beads, bracelets, and breastplates.

Hopewell peoples (ca. 200 B.C.E.–400 C.E.) in Ohio and Illinois erected mounds over log crypts or charnel houses that might contain a hundred or more cremations or burials. The honored dead took with them thousands of objects, including stone pipes, copper axes and ornaments, freshwater pearls, shells traded from the Gulf of Mexico, and obsidian from the distant Rocky Mountains. At one Ohio site, the many dead interred in the mounds took with them a total of 500 copper ear ornaments for luxury adornment in the afterlife, while one individual was accompanied by 300 pounds of obsidian imported from the distant Rocky Mountains. At some Illinois sites crypts were reopened periodically for new arrivals and older remains shifted to other sections of the mound to make space.

In early agricultural villages in central Mexico of the Early Formative Period (ca. 1800–1200 B.C.E.) the dead were frequently buried under the floors of their houses, presumably to keep ancestors in contact with the living. At the same time the rise of centralized chiefdoms and states in Mesoamerica led to the creation of monumental tombs for elite figures. At the Olmec site of La Venta (1200–400 B.C.E.) on the Gulf coast of Mexico, a stone tomb covered by a clay platform contained the remains of two children, who might have been royalty or sacrificial victims—with jade jewelry and figurines, mirrors of polished iron ore, ritual bloodletting implements, and red cinnabar pigment. A crocodile-shaped stone sarcophagus at La Venta probably held an Olmec ruler, though the bones had disintegrated, leaving only the jade jewelry behind. At the Chalcatzingo site in Mexico local rulers allied to those of La Venta were laid to rest in stone crypts under their palaces

INSIDE A HOPEWELL BURIAL MOUND

Hopewell burial mounds often contain numerous burials, thousands of artifacts made from such exotic materials as Gulf coast shells, Lake Superior copper, silver, meteoric iron, freshwater pearls, and coal, along with evidence of several ceremonial constructions. For example, Mound 13 at the appropriately named site of Mound City, Ohio, a low, round pile of earth some 3 feet high and 70 feet across, was built over the remains of two successive ritual buildings. These buildings consisted of wooden poles driven into the ground and probably woven together to create an arched frame, which was then covered with sheets of bark, much like later Native American wigwams. Only the depressions left by the rotted poles survive to tell us of the buildings' shapes. The second building seems to have been a funerary shrine where the bodies of the honored dead were cremated and rituals performed. It was roughly square, measuring 40 by 42.5 feet. It contained a 4-by-6-foot crematory, identified by a depression or pit where the soil was baked by repeated fires. Four "altars"—small platforms of earth—supported groups of cremated human bones and deliberately broken objects, presumably meant to accompany the ancestors' spirits into the hereafter.

Treatment of the dead may not always have been orderly by modern Western notions. The structure also contained 13 piles of cremated remains and their associated ornaments of copper, mica, slate, and other materials, and in one central area of the floor fragmentary artifacts and cremated bones had been trampled into the earth by the feet of participants in the ceremonies. At some point before the wooden building was buried under the mound, this central space ceased to be used for rituals and its stomped-upon relics were covered with sand.

Two shallow graves had been dug into the floor, but one clearly overshadowed the other in splendor and importance. The excavators of the mound in 1920–1921, William Mills and Henry Shetrone, called the more elaborate burial the Great Mica Grave because it was completely lined with sheets of this silvery material, probably imported from the Carolinas. The 6.5-by-7-foot grave was surrounded by a raised circle of mica pieces and soil containing broken stone smoking pipes—perhaps the possessions of a Hopewell shaman—as well as ornaments of animal teeth and chunks of another silvery mineral, the lead ore galena. Within the shallow excavation the cremated remains of four people accompanied a copper ceremonial headdress. Before the whole building was entombed beneath the earth mound, a small mound was erected over the Great Mica Grave, and it, too, received a shiny covering of mica sheets.

or atop platforms, alongside similar mirrors and jade figures, beads, and ear ornaments. One ruler lay alongside the broken head of a stone statue—perhaps his portrait, ritually destroyed at his death.

Elaborate burials for ruling elites in Mesoamerica continued among the ancient Maya. At Tikal, Guatemala, kings of the Late Formative Period (ca. 400 B.C.E.–150 C.E.) were buried in vaults under stone temple platforms that served as shrines for their veneration as ancestors. Some of these tombs are decorated with wall paintings, and human sacrificial victims accompanied some rulers into the afterlife. Painted pottery (probably used for funeral feasts) and jade ornaments rested with the royal dead. (In one instance, the remains of the monarch lacked the skull and thighbones—presumably they were either taken as relics by his own people or removed as trophies by enemies on the battlefield. A stone mask might have served as a magical substitute for his missing cranium.) Later (ca. 250–550 C.E.) at Tikal the burials of kings Yax Nuun Ayin and Siyah Chan Kawil contain similar riches as well as ceramics imported from the distant city of Teotihuacán (near modern-day Mexico City). Yax Nuun Ayin, whose name means "First Crocodile," even took a sacrificed caiman into the tomb with him—perhaps a very literal emblem of his name.

At Teotihuacán a wide range of burial practices prevailed during the city's heyday (ca. 1 B.C.E.–650 C.E.). Deceased residents of palaces and apartment complexes often remained there in subfloor burials and cremations. Though royal tombs have not been identified with certainty, the great pyramids of the city may have covered the interments of its leaders. Over a hundred sacrificial victims, along with rich offerings of stone and shell weapons and ornaments, have been found beneath the Pyramid of the Feathered Serpent. These people may have been killed to accompany the now-looted burial of an absolute ruler. In the Pyramid of the Moon, recently discovered high-status burials include individuals buried in a seated posture—a Maya trait—along with Maya-style jade jewelry, further evidence of links between Maya and Teotihuacán rulers.

Many early Peruvian cultures show evidence of preserving the dead so that they could be accessible for veneration and to give advice to their descendants. In Paracas arid conditions have preserved mummy bundles buried in the late first millennium B.C.E. Paracas tombs are of two types, probably partially overlapping in time. In one type the mummy bundles were stacked up in bottle-shaped tombs cut into bedrock. In the other type the bundles occupy abandoned structures, often with what appears to be a most important burial surrounded by the remains of lower-ranked figures. The core of each bundle consists of a corpse seated in a fetal position on a basket. Layers of shrouds interspersed with grave goods—most frequently, beautifully woven and decorated clothing—surround the body. Single cloths can reach 85 feet in length. Gold jewelry, painted ceramics, and even the polished trophy skulls of enemies could also be included between layers of wrappings. Consequently the biggest bundles contain the richest burials and their numerous effects. Although the bodies are often well preserved and commonly called "mummies," their condition is the result of the extremely dry environment and not of artificial embalming techniques.

See also ART; CALENDARS AND CLOCKS; CRAFTS; CRIME AND PUNISHMENT; FESTIVALS; LITERATURE; RELIGION AND COSMOLOGY; SACRED SITES; SOCIAL ORGANIZATION.

Egypt

Herodotus: "Mummification," from The Histories

The mode of embalming, according to the most perfect process, is the following: They take first a crooked piece of iron and with it draw out the brain through the nostrils, thus getting rid of a portion, while the skull is cleared of the rest by rinsing with drugs; next they make a cut along the flank with a sharp Ethiopian stone, and take out the whole contents of the abdomen, which they then cleanse, washing it thoroughly with palm wine, and again frequently with an infusion of pounded aromatics. After this they fill the cavity with the purest bruised myrrh, with cassia, and every other sort of spicery except frankincense, and sew up the opening. Then the body is placed in natrum for seventy days, and covered entirely over. After the expiration of that space of time, which must not be exceeded, the body is washed, and wrapped round, from head to foot, with bandages of fine linen cloth, smeared over with gum, which is used generally by the Egyptians in the place of glue, and in this state it is given back to the relations, who enclose it in a wooden case which they have had made for the purpose, shaped into the figure of a man. Then fastening the case, they place it in a sepulchral chamber, upright against the wall. Such is the most costly way of embalming the dead.

If persons wish to avoid expense, and choose the second process, the following is the method pursued: Syringes are filled with oil made from the cedar-tree, which is then, without any incision or disemboweling, injected into the abdomen. The passage by which it might be likely to return is stopped, and the body laid in natrum

(continued)

(continues)

the prescribed number of days. At the end of the time the cedar-oil is allowed to make its escape; and such is its power that it brings with it the whole stomach and intestines in a liquid state. The natrum meanwhile has dissolved the flesh, and so nothing is left of the dead body but the skin and the bones. It is returned in this condition to the relatives, without any further trouble being bestowed upon it.

The third method of embalming, which is practiced in the case of the poorer classes, is to clear out the intestines with a clyster and let the body lie in natrum the seventy days, after which it is at once given to those who come to fetch it away.

From: Internet History Sourcebooks. Available online. URL: http://www.fordham.edu/halsall/.

The Middle East

Descent of the Goddess Ishtar into the Lower World

To the land of no return, the land of darkness,
Ishtar, the daughter of Sin directed her thought,
Directed her thought, Ishtar, the daughter of Sin,
To the house of shadows, the dwelling, of Irkalla,
To the house without exit for him who enters therein,
To the road, whence there is no turning,
To the house without light for him who enters therein,
The place where dust is their nourishment, clay their food.
They have no light, in darkness they dwell.
Clothed like birds, with wings as garments,
Over door and bolt, dust has gathered.
Ishtar on arriving at the gate of the land of no return,
To the gatekeeper thus addressed herself:

"Gatekeeper, ho, open thy gate!
Open thy gate that I may enter!
If thou openest not the gate to let me enter,
I will break the door, I will wrench the lock,
I will smash the door-posts, I will force the doors.
I will bring up the dead to eat the living.
And the dead will outnumber the living."
The gatekeeper opened his mouth and spoke,
Spoke to the lady Ishtar:
"Desist, O lady, do not destroy it.
I will go and announce thy name to my queen Ereshkigal."
The gatekeeper entered and spoke to Ereshkigal:
"Ho! here is thy sister, Ishtar . . .
Hostility of the great powers . . ."
When Ereshkigal heard this,
As when one hews down a tamarisk she trembled,
As when one cuts a reed, she shook:
"What has moved her heart [seat of the intellect] what has stirred her liver [seat of the emotions]?
Ho there, does this one wish to dwell with me?
To eat clay as food, to drink dust as wine?
I weep for the men who have left their wives.
I weep for the wives torn from the embrace of their husbands;
For the little ones cut off before their time.
Go, gatekeeper, open thy gate for her,
Deal with her according to the ancient decree."
The gatekeeper went and opened his gate to her:
"Enter, O lady, let Cuthah greet thee. . . ."

Now when Ishtar had gone down into the land of no return,
Ereshkigal saw her and was angered at her presence.
Ishtar, without reflection, threw herself at her [in a rage].
Ereshkigal opened her mouth and spoke,
To Namtar, her messenger, she addressed herself:
"Go Namtar, imprison her in my palace.
Send against her sixty diseases, to punish Ishtar.
Eye-disease against her eyes,
Disease of the side against her side,
Foot-disease against her foot,
Heart-disease against her heart,
Head-disease against her head,
Against her whole being, against her entire body."
After the lady Ishtar had gone down into the land of no return,
The bull did not mount the cow, the ass approached not the she-ass,
To the maid in the street, no man drew near
The man slept in his apartment,
The maid slept by herself.

The countenance of Papsukal, the messenger of the great gods, fell; his face was troubled.

In mourning garb he was clothed, in soiled garments clad.
Shamash [the sun-god] went to Sin [the moon-god], his father, weeping,
In the presence of Ea, the King, he went with flowing tears.
"Ishtar has descended into the earth and has not come up . . . ." Ea, in the wisdom of his heart, formed a being,
He formed Asu-shu-namir the eunuch.
"Go, Asu-shu-namir, to the land of no return direct thy face!
The seven gates of the land without return be opened before thee,
May Eresbkigal at sight of thee rejoice!
After her heart has been assuaged, her liver quieted,
Invoke against her the name of the great gods,
Raise thy head direct thy attention to the khalziku skin."

"Come, lady, let them give me the khalziku skin, that I may drink water out of it."
When Ereshkigal heard this, she struck her side, bit her finger,
"Thou hast expressed a wish that can not be granted.
Go, Asu-sbu-iaamir, I curse thee with a great curse,
The sweepings of the gutters of the city be thy food,
The drains of the city be thy drink,
The shadow of the wall be thy abode,
The thresholds be thy dwelling-place;
Drunkard and sot strike thy cheek!"
Ereshkigal opened her mouth and spoke,
To Namtar, her messenger, she addressed herself.
"Go, Namtar, knock at the strong palace,
Strike the threshold of precious stones,
Bring out the Anunnaki, seat them on golden thrones.
Sprinkle Ishtar with the waters of life and take her out of my presence."
Namtar went, knocked at the strong palace,
Tapped on the threshold of precious stones.
He brought out the Anunnaki and placed them on golden thrones,
He sprinkled Ishtar with the waters of life and took hold of her.
Through the first gate he led her out and returned to her her loin-cloth.
Through the second gate he led her out and returned to her the spangles of her hands and feet
Through the third gate he led her out and returned to her the girdle of her body, studded with birth-stones.
Through the fourth gate he led her out and returned to her the ornaments of her breast.
Through the fifth gate he led her out and returned to her her necklace.
Through the sixth gate he led her out and returned her earrings.
Through the seventh gate he led her out and returned to her the large crown for her head.

From: Morris Jastrow, *The Civilization of Babylonia and Assyria: Its Remains, Language, History, Religion, Commerce, Law, Art, and Literature* (Philadelphia: J. B. Lippincott, 1915).

Asia and the Pacific

A Vedic Funerary Hymn from the Rig-Veda, Book 10

1. Go hence, O Death, pursue thy special pathway apart from that which gods are wont to travel. To thee I say it who hast eyes and hearest: touch not our offspring, injure not our heroes.

2. As ye have come effacing Mrityu's footstep, to farther times prolonging your existence,
May ye be rich in children and possessions, cleansed, purified, and meet for sacrificing.

3. Divided from the dead are these, the living: now is our calling on the gods successful
We have come forth for dancing and for laughter, to farther times prolonging our existence.

4. Here I erect this rampart for the living, let none of these, none other reach this limit.
May they survive a hundred lengthened autumns, and may they bury Death beneath this mountain.

5. As the days follow days in close succession, as with the seasons duly come the seasons,

(continued)

(continues)

As each successor fails not his foregoer, so form the lives of these,
O great Ordainer
6. Live your full lives and find old age delightful, all of you striving one behind the other.
May Tvashtar, maker of fair things, be gracious,
and lengthen out the days of your existence.

7. Let these unwidowed dames with noble husbands
adorn themselves with fragrant faint and unguent.
Decked with fair jewels, tearless, free from sorrow,
first let the wives ascend unto the place .

8. Rise, come unto the world of life, O woman: come
he is lifeless by whose side thou liest.
Wifehood with this thy husband was thy portion,
who took thy hand and wooed thee as a lover.

9. From his dead hand I take the bow he carried , that
it may be our power and might and glory
There art thou, there; and here with noble heroes
may we o'ercome all hosts that fight against us.

10. Betake thee to the lap of the earth the mother,
of earth far-spreading, very kind and gracious.
Young dame, wool-soft unto the guerdon-giver,
may she preserve thee from Destruction's bosom.

11. Heave thyself, Earth, nor press thee downward
heavily: afford him easy access, gently tending him.
Earth, as a mother wraps her shirt about her child,
so cover him.

12. Now let the heaving earth be free from motion: yea,
let a thousand clods remain above him.
Be they to him a home distilling fatness, here let
them ever be his place of refuge.

13. I stay the earth from thee, while over thee I place
this piece of earth. May I be free from injury.
Here let the Fathers keep this pillar firm for thee,
and there let Yama make thee an abiding place

14. Even as an arrow's feathers, they have laid me down
at day's decline.
My parting speech have I drawn back as 'twere a
courser with the rein.

From: *The Hymns of the Rigveda*, vol. 4, trans. Ralph T. H. Griffith (Benares, India: E. J. Lazarus and Co., 1892), pp. 137–139.

Rome

Homer: The Odyssey, *Book XI: 18–50*

Odysseus speaks:

"Thither we came and beached our ship, and took out the sheep, and ourselves went beside the stream of Oceanus until we came to the place of which Circe had told us.

"Here Perimedes and Eurylochus held the victims, while I drew my sharp sword from beside my thigh, and dug a pit of a cubit's length this way and that, and around it poured a libation to all the dead, first with milk and honey, thereafter with sweet wine, and in the third place with water, and I sprinkled thereon white barley meal. And I earnestly entreated the powerless heads of the dead, vowing that when I came to Ithaca I would sacrifice in my halls a barren heifer, the best I had, and pile the altar with goodly gifts, and to Teiresias alone would sacrifice separately a ram, wholly black, the goodliest of my flocks. But when with vows and prayers I had made supplication to the tribes of the dead, I took the sheep and cut their throats over the pit, and the dark blood ran forth. Then there gathered from out of Erebus the spirits of those that are dead, brides, and unwedded youths, and toil-worn old men, and tender maidens with hearts yet new to sorrow, and many, too, that had been wounded with bronze-tipped spears, men slain in fight, wearing their blood-stained armor. These came thronging in crowds about the pit from every side, with a wondrous cry, and pale fear seized me. Then I called to my comrades and bade them flay and burn the sheep that lay there slain with the pitiless bronze, and to make prayers to the gods, to mighty Hades and dread Persephone. And I myself drew my sharp sword from beside my thigh and sat there, and would not suffer the powerless heads of the dead to draw near to the blood until I had enquired of Teiresias."

From: Homer, *The Odyssey*, trans. A. T. Murray (New York: G. P. Putnam's Sons, 1919), pp. 387–389.

FURTHER READING

Tony Allan, "Glimpses of Past Grandeur." In *The Archaeology of the Afterlife: Deciphering the Past from Tombs, Graves, and Mummies* (London: Duncan Baird, 2004).

Bernardo T. Arriaza, *Beyond Death: The Chinchorro Mummies of Ancient Chile* (Washington, D.C.: Smithsonian Institution Press, 1995).

Paul G. Bahn, *Tombs, Graves and Mummies* (London: Weidenfeld and Nicolson, 1996).

Robert Chapman, Ian Kinnes, and Klavs Randsborg, *The Archaeology of Death* (Cambridge: Cambridge University Press, 1981).

Constance A Cook, *Death in Ancient China: The Tale of One Man's Journey* (Leiden, Netherlands: Brill, 2006).

Jon Davies, *Death, Burial, and Rebirth in the Religions of Antiquity* (New York: Routledge, 1999).

Don W. Dragoo, *Mounds for the Dead: An Analysis of the Adena Culture* (Pittsburgh, Penn.: Carnegie Museum, 1963).

Robert Garland, *The Greek Way of Death*, 2nd ed. (Ithaca, N.Y.: Cornell University Press, 2001).

P. V. Glob, *The Bog People: Iron Age Man Preserved* (Ithaca, N.Y.: Cornell University Press, 1969).

Salima Ikram and Aidan Dodson, *The Mummy in Ancient Egypt: Equipping the Dead for Eternity* (London: Thames and Hudson, 1998).

Sarah Iles Johnston, *Restless Dead: Encounters between the Living and the Dead in Ancient Greece* (Berkeley: University of California Press, 1999).

Naguib Kanawati, *The Tomb and Beyond: Burial Customs of Egyptian Officials* (Warminster, U.K.: Aris and Phillips, 2001).

Dina Katz, *The Image of the Netherworld in the Sumerian Sources* (Bethesda, Md.: CDL Press, 2003).

Donna C. Kurtz and John Boardman, *Greek Burial Customs* (Ithaca, N.Y.: Cornell University Press, 1971).

Donald G. Kyle, *Spectacles of Death in Ancient Rome* (New York: Routledge, 1998).

Magdalena S. Midgley, *The Monumental Cemeteries of Prehistoric Europe* (Stroud, U.K.: Tempus, 2006).

George R. Milner, *The Moundbuilders: Ancient Peoples of Eastern North America* (London: Thames and Hudson, 2004).

Ian Morris, *Death-Ritual and Social Structure in Classical Antiquity* (New York: Cambridge University Press, 1992).

Carlos Serrano Sánchez, "Funerary Practices and Human Sacrifice in Teotihuacan Burials." In *Teotihuacán: Art from the City of the Gods*, ed. Kathleen Berrin and Esther Pasztory (London: Thames and Hudson, 1993).

Jo Ann Scurlock, "Death and the Afterlife in Ancient Mesopotamian Thought." In *Civilizations of the Ancient Near East*, ed. J. M. Sasson (New York: Charles Scribner's Sons, 1995).

Martha L. Sempowski and Michael W. Spence, *Mortuary Practices and Skeletal Remains at Teotihuacán* (Salt Lake City: University of Utah Press, 1994).

A. J. Spencer, *Death in Ancient Egypt* (New York: Penguin, 1982).

John H. Taylor, *Death and the Afterlife in Ancient Egypt* (Chicago: University of Chicago Press, 2001).

J. M. C. Toynbee, *Death and Burial in the Roman World* (Baltimore: Johns Hopkins University Press, 1971).

W. A. B. van der Sanden, *Through Nature to Eternity: The Bog Bodies of Northwest Europe* (Amsterdam: Batavian Lion International, 1996).

Emily Vermeule, *Aspects of Death in Early Greek Art and Poetry* (Berkeley: University of California Press, 1979).

James M. Vreeland, Jr., "Mummies of Peru." In *Mummies, Disease, and Ancient Cultures*, ed. Aidan and Eve Cockburn (Cambridge, U.K.: Cambridge University Press, 1983).

Richard L. Zettler, ed., *Treasures from the Royal Tombs of Ur* (Philadelphia: University of Pennsylvania, Museum of Archaeology and Anthropology, 1998).

► drama and theater

INTRODUCTION

The impulse for people to take part in performance art runs deep into human history. While early ancient peoples left behind no drama as the term is understood in modern life, archaeological evidence shows that they engaged in ritual performances, often dance, in connection with major life events. The nature of these performances was often dictated by geography. People who survived by cultivating crops, for example, took part in ritual performances connected with planting and harvesting. Those who lived in regions where they survived as hunters took part in ritual performances in connection with successful hunts. Such ritual performances also occurred to celebrate victory in battle as well as to celebrate births and marriages, mourn the dead, or ensure fertility. These early dramatic performances, however, had no plot, character development, and the like. They tended to be spontaneous expressions of the community in response to the events that defined their lives.

Much early theater had a strong religious element. Shamans, for example, often directed ritual performances. These performances, enacted out of doors, were designed to honor or appease a god. They often illustrated the culture's cosmology, or beliefs about the origin of the universe. They became a way of preserving and transmitting the culture's values and norms as well as its history, myths, and legends. In some cases, such as India, the earliest dramatic performances depicted events recorded in sacred texts. It is no exaggeration to say that in many cultures, drama and theater were the culture's history and religious "textbooks" for youngsters and others in the community.

More formalized dramatic presentations became common in ancient India, Japan, and China. These performances, which were highly ritualized and stylized and with elaborate costumes, makeup, masks, and other conventions, were often done at court for the entertainment of royalty, and Asian theatrical performances still reflect these ancient roots. In Asia, too, the arrival of roving bands of performers was often a highly anticipated event in communities.

The development of theater as the word is understood in modern times began with the ancient Greeks and Roman. While the performances of the Greeks were still highly stylized, they incorporated many of the conventions of drama that modern theatergoers expect, including costumes, sets, dialogue, character development, conflict, and a climax. Performances took place outdoors, but the theaters in which they took place resembled modern theaters, with a stage area, a backstage area, and rows of tiered seating for spectators. Playwrights competed for honors with cycles of plays, and theatrical festivals were major events. Many of the plays written by the ancient Greeks, including Aeschylus, Sophocles, and Euripides, are still performed on modern stages, and their texts, such as Sophocles' *Antigone* and *Oedipus Rex,* remain standards in the study of literature. The Greeks, too, began to distinguish between tragedies and comedies, with the comic plays of Aristophanes occupying a major place in the history of comedy. Such plays as satyr plays, with their depictions of drunkenness and debauchery, provided comic relief for more serious tragic performances. The ancient Romans continued the Greek tradition with formal theatrical productions. The Romans performed Greek plays, but in time they produced their own playwrights, including Plautus and Terence, whose comedies are still produced.

AFRICA

BY MICHAEL J. O'NEAL

The words *drama* and *theater* in modern life evoke specific responses. A person is likely to imagine a theater with a stage, lighting, and rows of seats for spectators. Dramatic productions in modern life—and among some ancient peoples as well—are based on a script, usually one written by someone other than the performers. Theatergoers bring certain expectations to a dramatic performance, expectations about how the story progresses onstage primarily through dialogue between characters. They expect to see a linear performance, where the story unfolds in a logical progression from beginning to end. They anticipate a resolution to the story that provides them with some measure of satisfaction.

Few of these expectations would apply to the drama and theater of ancient Africa, though in the absence of surviving written texts, it is difficult for historians to reconstruct the nature of ancient African theatrical performances. To do so, they often have to extrapolate backward from later times, finding the roots of later theater in the practices of ancient peoples. In some cases archaeological findings can shed light on drama as it was performed by ancient Africans.

The "stage" for an ancient African theatrical performance could be anywhere, including a private home. Most likely, however, theater was conducted in open-air venues where members of the community could gather. In some parts of Africa the baobab tree, a tree of great symbolic significance, continues to serve as a gathering place for the community. The only lighting was that provided by fires and torches for presentations after dark. The "script" for an ancient African theatrical presentation was probably in most cases largely improvised, though such scripts could be based on traditions, folklore, and legends that had been passed down through many generations.

In ancient Africa there was a close link between theater and storytelling. An important member of the community in most African societies was the storyteller, often referred to as a *griot,* who acted as a repository, a kind of living museum, for the origins, history, and genealogy of the community. Such a person would have learned mythic stories about the community and then passed them down orally in dramatic presentations to his audience. Such stories could include accounts of creation, the origins of the people, the lineages of kings, the origins of animals and the stars in the sky, and perhaps great victories that were won in battle by the community's ancestors. None of these stories would have been new to the audience. These stories were part of the shared cultural inheritance of a people, so they already knew the characters and outcome. But like modern theatergoers, they judged the quality of the performance on the level of drama and suspense that the storyteller was able to build. Sharing an unwritten text over many generations socialized people into their community and forged social bonds.

The "actors" of ancient African theater were not trained professionals but could include anyone from the community. Again, storytellers, who could craft stories and present them with dramatic flourishes, incantations, repetition, and inflections all designed to capture the attention of the audience, could be considered among the earliest actors. It is likely, however, that members of the community participated in the productions through singing and dancing. In this sense, theatrical productions took on characteristics of spontaneous community celebrations. Dance in particular was probably an important part of a theatrical performance. In the absence of a text, the movement of people to the rhythms of drums and other musical instruments allowed people to take part in their shared cultural heritage and celebrate events—a harvest, a successful hunt—with their community. Dance, music, and song, including "call and response" singing, allowed people to express and reenact the community's deepest cultural longings and beliefs and forge a sense of unity and togetherness.

The most important actors were probably shamans and other religious figures. While some drama in ancient Africa had secular purposes and themes, it is difficult to distinguish the secular from the religious in ancient African life, for daily activities almost always had some sort of religious significance. This religious significance was often tied to the seasons and the cycles of the natural world. Religious meaning was found in virtually everything, from a storm to the emergence of crops to a flood and so on. Thus, just as modern dramatists try to interpret the complexities of life by distilling them into a two- or three-hour presentation, so African shamans and diviners tried to interpret their world through religious rituals with strong theatrical elements.

A good example of this kind of ritualistic performance is provided by the San people, often referred to as the Bushmen. Archaeologists had long assumed that the oldest ritual site in African dated back to about 40,000 years ago. A recent find in northwest Botswana has pushed this date back some 30,000 years. There, archaeologists discovered a kind of cave that was carved into the rock by ancient Bushmen. The cave, along with the surrounding rock face, is a remarkable artistic achievement, for it depicts a python, reflecting the ancient Bushmen's creation myth that said that humans descended from pythons and that stream and riverbeds were made as the python crawled around in search of water. The cave, then, was a religious site, but the distinction between religious observance and theater among ancient Africans was no doubt one that they would not have recognized. Archaeologists speculate that as people visited the cave, the shaman would have retired into a secret chamber, where he could see the visitors. He then could have spoken to people, making it seem as though the words came from the mouth of the python. Two small shafts would have allowed the shaman to disappear. Thus, if archaeologists are correct, the cave took on elements of performance and theater, giving visitors a visual representation of the culture's creation myth. Numerous sacred sites such as this can be found throughout Africa. While their primary purpose was religious, the enactment of that religion was distinctly a form of theater.

Seasonal festivals, too, were an occasion for theatrical and ritualistic performance. Ancient Africans' lives were dependent on the cycles and changes of the natural world. Again, because religion imbued every aspect of their lives, ancient Africans would have seen the arrival of a harvest as an important event, a sign that the gods favored them. The modern Christmas-season festival called Kwanzaa has its roots in these types of ancient celebrations. Kwanzaa, contrary to widespread belief, is not a replacement for Christmas but rather a harvest festival. The rituals of renewal that surround Kwanzaa have their roots in ancient African harvest celebrations.

Bronze figure of Isis and Horus, from North Saqqara, Egypt, Late Period, after 600 B.C.E.; Egyptian dramas often focused on the gods and were more like morality plays; two feature Isis and Horus, respectively. (© The Trustees of the British Museum)

EGYPT

BY EMILY JANE O'DELL

Whether ancient Egypt even had a distinct dramatic form and style has been debated for many years. Egypt provides nothing in any way comparable to the archaeological and textual evidence we possess for the drama and theater of the Greeks. There are no known theatrical structures or play scripts written with the sole intention of secular entertainment. In fact, there are no dramatic scripts at all, unless one considers certain religious rituals and religious texts as blueprints for religious drama.

Neither the literature nor the tomb reliefs of ancient Egypt make any reference to the acting or theatrical profession. Since it was customary to inscribe the title or profession of a tomb's owner, the lack of evidence for an acting profession is notable and supports its nonexistence. Ancient Egypt did, however, have a rich oral tradition, and many of the myths and much of the literature were passed down orally from generation to generation. We do not know exactly how these performances and recitations of texts were organized, but it is probable that they involved a dramatic street performance of sorts. One Egyptian story in particular, "The Contendings of Horus and Seth," thought to have been written during the New Kingdom (1550–1070 B.C.E.), reads very much like a play because of its quick changes from scene to scene and because the many different characters speak to each other in a way that is highly reminiscent of play dialogue.

The question of ancient Egyptian drama's existence is complicated by how we define *drama*. Drama can take many different forms, and theatrical styles are determined and shaped by the culture, ritual, religion, language, and ceremonies from which they emerge. Thus it can be very difficult to say what constituted or did not constitute drama in one culture or another. For example, some scholars focus on religious ritual as performance. Ancient Egyptian culture was heavily steeped in religious ritual; mythology and religious beliefs and practices were inseparable from daily life. Ancient Egyptian rituals were very theatrical, taking place in dark temple rooms with incense and recitations of sacred texts. Spells were read aloud, which is theatrical in a sense, but whether it qualifies as drama is debatable; there is a difference between ritual and more traditional forms of drama that presuppose a script, actors, and predetermined stage actions.

Egyptologists do, however, call certain religious texts "dramatic texts." Known from papyri and temple walls, these texts seem to be concerned with re-creating actions of the gods from when time began. They were probably not used frequently or on a daily basis but rather at commemorative events and festivals where their purpose was to inspire the triumph of order and balance over chaos. These texts were not internally focused. They show no interest in human psychology, motivations, relationships, or emotions. These "dramatic texts" are extremely fragmentary and incomplete, which may or may not have been intentional. They would have been read and acted out by the temple priesthood both within and outside the temple buildings. One wall of the Ptolemaic Dynasty (304–330 C.E.) temple at Edfu contains such a text, known as the "Triumph of Horus." It features a linear plotline, there seem to be stage directions, and the reliefs of the different deities that accompany the text offer evidence of what the ritual reenactment may have looked like.

There are also dramatic ritual texts that celebrate the mysteries of the god Osiris. These would have been performed at Abydos, the supposed burial site of Osiris and thus the most sacred place in Egypt. The Osirian rituals were performed at Abydos from 2500 to 550 B.C.E. One papyrus has stage directions calling for two beautiful women to kneel on the ground and bow their heads. Another gives similar stage directions for the women playing Isis and Nephthys in a ritual for the temple of Osiris Khentyimentiu at Abydos. This papyrus also specifies that the women were to be virgins without any hair at all on their bodies, other than wigs, to signify purification. The papyrus shifts back and forth from first person singular to first person plural (from "I" to "we"), suggesting that sometimes one of the reciters spoke alone and other times the two spoke in unison. These virgins, holding tambourines, would read the stanzas of the text in the presence of the deities. It can be inferred that the tambourines were used to accompany this recitation.

There are other so-called dramatic texts that focus on other aspects of ancient Egyptian mythology and history. For example, the so-called Memphite Drama relates the myth of Osiris' death and resurrection and the crowning of his son Horus as his successor. The Dramatic Ramesseum Papyrus features a ceremonial play composed to celebrate the accession to the throne of Sesostris I of the Twelfth Dynasty. The text is accompanied by illustrations at the bottom of the papyrus that show the pharaoh appearing as Horus. The Egyptian Book of the Dead might also be considered a dramatic text. It is composed of many spells the dead must recite as they move through the afterlife. Many of these utterances are dramatic in form, with the gods asking questions that the dead must answer from the Book of the Dead in order to pass to the next station in the afterlife. This call-and-response format reads very much like dialogue, and one could argue that Egypt's most theatrical drama was reserved for the dead, not the living.

THE MIDDLE EAST

BY LYN GREEN

Theater as we understand it in modern Western culture does not seem to have existed in many societies of the ancient Near East. This does not mean that performance art—and especially dance—did not play an important role in these civilizations. In fact, in ancient Phoenicia one of the gods bore the name Baal Marqod, or "Lord of the Dance," perhaps because he was worshiped through dance. Dance was an important part of the worship of many other gods and goddesses as well. At different times and in different places it seems to have been more common for one sex to dance within the temples than the other. In Iron Age Israel, for example, there seem to be more mentions and depictions of women and girls dancing than of men.

Dances were also key parts of seasonal festivals associated with agriculture, where they reenacted important myths. Some dances could put the participants into a trancelike state in which they might receive religious visions. Dance was closely associated with what anthropologists call "life crisis" occasions such as birth, death, weddings, and coming of age. It was especially closely linked to sexuality and courting. From around the 15th and 14th centuries B.C.E. there are representations of naked dancing girls done in a style strongly influenced by contemporary Egyptian art. Dance was even used in magic or healing ceremonies, both in and out of the temple. Texts from ancient Mesopotamia describe personnel from the temple of the goddess Ishtar as being part of rituals in which dancers helped drive away the demons of illness and possession.

Performances in which dancers mimed important activities such as hunting or played the roles of gods or goddesses might be considered the ancient Near Eastern form of theater. One of the most common myths to be acted out seems to have been the "Sacred Marriage." This myth, which tells of the marriage of a fertility goddess, symbolizes the need to ensure a good harvest and bountiful offspring for herds and flocks. Although it may have been acted out between a high priestess and high priest or between a queen and a king, musicians and dancers were always involved in the ceremony.

Dance could also be used to celebrate great occasions such as victory in battle. On the walls of the palace of Nimrud in northern Iraq the soldiers of an Assyrian king are shown dancing to harps and drums while waving the decapitated heads of their enemies. The Old Testament contains numerous mentions of dances in honor of military victory. For example, after the escape across the Red Sea Moses' sister

Lapis lazuli cylinder seal of Sin-ishmeanni, Old Babylonian, about 19th century B.C.E., showing Sin-ishmeanni being brought into the presence of the king; the dwarf figure in the center is thought to represent a dancer in rituals or entertainments. (© The Trustees of the British Museum)

Miriam led the women in celebratory dances. Virtually all depictions of kings or other high-status persons drinking or feasting also show musicians and dancers.

Festivals and especially weddings were often the occasion for group dances. Ancient Jewish texts such as the Talmud describe men dancing before the bride at a wedding. Cylinder seals from the early third millennium B.C.E. show figures with linked hands apparently dancing in a circle, and wedding dancers in present-day Syria have been observed doing very similar dances. The arms of the figures on the cylinder seals are raised to about shoulder level, and this seems to be a common position in representations of dancers from throughout the ancient Near East. From the earliest images onward the dancers in these groups are almost always shown as being all alike in posture, stature, and dress, perhaps in order to stress the unity and equality of the performers.

One type of performer common to many ancient Near Eastern cultures was the "dancing dwarf" (a name bestowed by modern scholars). The ancient images of these performers depict male musicians who, unlike most other figures in the art of their cultures, are shown frontally. They are naked and appear very short and bowlegged. Until recently, scholars interpreted these images as depicting individuals with the genetic growth disorder known as achondroplasia, but some art historians now suggest that the bowlegs and short stature are merely artistic conventions intended to show that the men are dancing while they play their instruments. This possibility reflects the fact that there is often little distinction between musician and dancer in ancient Near Eastern art. One ivory from Bronze Age Canaan shows a woman with a tambourine dancing energetically in front of seated man of high status. Her knees are bent and her head turned to one side as the artist tries to indicate her motions. The conventions of ancient Near Eastern art made it difficult for artists to depict rhythmic movement. Other representations from ancient Mesopotamia show male dancers poised on one leg, with the other one bent, perhaps to indicate a pirouette. Other dancers, such as those shown on an ancient Hittite terra-cotta jar, are shown leaping high in the air with bent knees.

It seems that in the ancient Near East much dance was done by professionals, performing either alone or in groups. We know that in the ancient Canaanite city of Lachish dancers belonged to a guild, and performers in other cultures probably did too. These guilds would have provided training for performers. Nonprofessionals might also dance on specific occasions. At some ceremonies held by the Hittites of ancient Anatolia even the king and queen might be called upon to perform. However, it was much more common for royalty and those of status to watch than to participate. In the art of every culture of the ancient Near East from Sumer to Persia the highest-ranking individuals are often recognizable as the audience for dance of various kinds.

Dance in these ancient cultures had little in common with modern-day notions. For example, there do not seem to have been any dances where a single man and woman would dance together as they do in modern ballroom dancing. Although dancers could express themselves through their art, the goal of ancient performance was not the expression of an individual's personality but communicating group solidarity, religious belief, or social status.

ASIA AND THE PACIFIC

BY JUSTIN CORFIELD

Ancient peoples throughout the Asian and Pacific region used drama and theater to re-create the past, recount history, and explain legends. Over time these enactments became formalized into great pieces of work like the Mahabharata, the Ramayana, and the life of Buddha and other important figures. Although both the Mahabharata and the Ramayana originated in India, they were adapted throughout Southeast Asia and farther afield. Similarly, Chinese stories and Buddhist epics were used to illustrate the triumph of good over evil, with subplots offering examples of love and betrayal, battles won and lost, skill and stupidity.

Drama in the Indian subcontinent was overshadowed by the two great epics: the Mahabharata and the Ramayana. The former surrounds the clash by two groups of cousins fighting for supremacy, and includes within it the Bhagavad Gita, the most important Hindu text. The latter is about the life of King Rama and his efforts to free his wife, Sita, who is captured by demons and taken to the island of Lanka (modern-day Sri Lanka). The Mahabharata, consisting of 100,000 couplets, is about seven times longer than the Greek *Iliad* and *Odyssey* combined. Although performances of the entire Mahabharata or Ramayana took place, many groups of actors performed only the more famous scenes as they traveled from one village to another. Indian dance was also highly stylized and has been traced back to the theory put forward by the ancient Indian sage Natya Shastra of Bharata Muni in about 400 B.C.E. Written in Sanskrit, this work gives, in vivid detail, the precepts for actors and also playwrights. For the latter there are nine major *rasas* ("emotional responses") which can be used: love, anger, fear, heroism, terror, comedy, pity, disgust, and awe. However, one must always dominate any given play. The costumes, the makeup, and the types of dance are also listed precisely.

A 19th-century Indian painting depicting the climax of the epic the Ramayana, where the hero Rama defeats the 10-headed demon Ravana. (© The Trustees of the British Museum)

In China, at the court of the emperors, the theatrical performances tended to be long and formal. The Chinese opera of today, which often covers ancient stories, had its origins in about 350 C.E. but did not attain its state of refinement until perhaps 300 years later. During the Shang Dynasty (1500–1045 B.C.E.) court entertainers not only amused the emperor and his retinue but also performed ceremonies to protect the harvest and ward off evil spirits. The Imperial Music Bureau was first established by the emperor Qin Shih Huang (r. 221–210 B.C.E.) and was expanded by the Han emperor Wu Di (r. 141–87 B.C.E.). As well as being played at court for its own sake, music often provided accompaniment for theatrical performances.

Throughout the Chinese countryside bands of entertainers wandered from village to village telling stories and getting ideas for new ones. Some tombs from the Han Dynasty (202 B.C.E.–220 C.E.) are decorated with scenes of entertainers involved in acrobatics, mime, and other drama activities. As shown in Chinese classical stories, these performers were always much awaited by villages, and the roles of actors, acrobats and professional musicians in Chinese society were always highly regarded. In the Han Dynasty capital there were special horse-drawn carriages for actors. However, on the stage many actors lost most of their individuality, wearing very heavy makeup or using masks. Actors were always male, with female parts often played by young men or teenage boys. There were also groups from China's minority peoples, especially from Central Asia, who traveled the countryside telling stories of life from their point of view and introducing their customs in towns and cities throughout China. Most drama performances were accompanied by music, and it was common for groups of musicians to travel with actors.

In Southeast Asia most early drama and theater was Indian in origin, with some local variations. In Cambodia the Naga snakes would make appearances; these were supernatural beings with the attributes of both humans and snakes. While most theatrical performances drew heavily from the two Indian classics, the Mahabharata and the Ramayana, other legends were common, such as that of the birth of Cambodia through the union of the daughter of a dragon king and the Indian Brahmin Kaudinya. The Mahabharata and especially the Ramayana also proved popular in Java (in modern-day Indonesia). The Javanese variations to the story can still be seen in Bali, though the most popular theater there has long been connected with the mythological Barong, the "king of the spirits." In Southeast Asia, Vietnam was an exception because it drew more heavily from Chinese stories. Japan had similar traditions of extensive formalized performances for the court and wandering teams giving theatrical performances in towns and villages throughout the country. The earliest surviving Japanese theatrical scripts date to the 300s C.E.

Throughout the Pacific, Polynesian theater and drama often had the same themes as some of those in Asia but tended to focus more on long sea voyages, floods, the coming of "strange" peoples, and other related historical themes. In most cases these stories have come down to the present day in oral tradition. Unlike the tales of the great cultures of Asia those of the Aborigines of Australia essentially focus on the environment and geography instead of history. The Aboriginal "dreamtime" stories, which have been passed down in tribes over 40,000 years, tend to relate to providing explanations for land features. They explain how particular mountains or rivers formed, the color of natural features, and the seasons. As the oldest surviving culture in the world, the Aboriginals, with their nonhierarchical society, seem to show that the origins of drama and theater lie in something like their corroborees, festivities at which they gather, sometimes from considerable distances, to celebrate important occasions with (usually nocturnal) songs and dancing, both often having complex geographical themes.

EUROPE

BY MICHAEL J. O'NEAL

For a number of reasons very little is known about drama, theater, and performance arts in ancient Europe. One reason is the low rate of literacy among the ancient Europeans. In contrast to ancient Greece, Rome, China, and other cultures, the civilizations of ancient Europe produced few people who could read and write, with the result that literature was transmitted orally rather than in written form.

Another problem was the social disruption caused by war, conquest, and migrations. The ancient Celts, for example, migrated westward, probably from western Russia, and became the dominant culture of central Europe. The Celts, though, were conquered by the Germanic and Scandinavian peoples from the north while at the same time feeling pressure on the south from the Roman Empire, which used its power to eradicate cultures and customs in the conquered territories. (Much of what little drama and theater is known from ancient Europe existed only because of the Romans.) Under these conditions, it would be surprising if much in the way of an indigenous dramatic literature survived.

Much of what historians know, or theorize, is based on fragmentary evidence, hints, and inferences, but it is likely that performance art in ancient Europe paralleled that in other parts of the world, where the record is more complete. For example, a good deal of performance art was probably conducted as part of ritual religious observances. Among the Druids, the religion of the ancient Celts, priests and shamans controlled the ritual observances of the people and were often regarded as having magical powers. They also functioned as teachers for the community. These priests conducted ritual observances, often in conjunction with such events as the equinoxes and solstices. Like most northern cultures, the Celts saw the arrival of spring or of the shortest days of winter as important events, recognized in communal ritual celebrations (celebrations that gave rise to many modern traditions surrounding such holidays as Christmas and Halloween). It is likely that these communal celebrations took on features of a dramatic performance.

One form of performance art that probably was widely practiced was the reading or recitation of myths, legends, and epic poems. Historians know that a considerable number of such works of literature existed, though how many were written down is anybody's guess, for few texts survive and even those are mostly fragments. It is known, however, that many later European epics—from Scandinavia, the Germanic peoples, and the Celts—preserved literary traditions, characters, and story lines from centuries before. Most of these works were transmitted orally, passed down from one generation of storytellers to another. Thus it is likely that some medieval narratives were developments of narratives from the ancient world. A good example is the Edda, a group of medieval folktales from Old Norse mythology whose origins no doubt extend into the mists of the ancient past.

The role of the bard, or oral storyteller, was not acquired in a haphazard fashion. The performance of these tales, myths, and legends was conducted for the aristocracy, and the bards constituted the libraries and museums of the time, guarding the culture. Most bards underwent intensive training for their role, and over time they acquired a repertoire of tales, including tales about feasts, deaths, adventures, cattle raids, battles, and visions.

One example of a relatively complete text that may have served as the script for a dramatic performance is the *Skírnismál,* a Scandinavian love poem of uncertain date but generally believed to have been written in pre-Christian times. The poem is set in dramatic form, with dialogue between the characters. The basic plot is simple: Freyr dispatches his servant Skírnir to court for him the maiden Gerdr, the daughter of Gymir, a giant. Skírnir promises gifts, but to no avail, so he finally uses threats to persuade Gerdr to meet Freyr in the grove called Barri, where the two will be married.

Some scholars believe that the *Skírnismál* is a surviving example of a flourishing tradition of ritual Scandinavian drama from pre-Christian days. It is believed that performers created effigies of gods and goddesses for use in these productions and that two or more actors performed the speaking parts, perhaps with a narrator delivering the narrative parts of the drama. A chorus wearing animal masks may have added to the production. These plays were probably performed in temples or other sacred places, perhaps at yearly festivals. Some scholars see the *Skírnismál* and other ritual dramas as helping communities deal with the overwhelming forces of nature. For the participants ritual drama and performance would have reinforced community taboos, helped ensure a successful harvest, provided support in the cold and snow of winter, and celebrated the return of spring. In short, such performances were a kind of religious ritual to enact humans' relationship with the gods.

Dance, too, had a theatrical function. The best way historians have of studying dance from the ancient world is through pottery and artwork that depicts people dancing. It is likely that the earliest forms of dance were spontaneous celebrations of a successful hunt or marked other important occasions in the life of the community. Later more formalized dances appeared, as pictured, for example, on pottery from Romania dating to 4000–3000 B.C.E. In most cases these depictions show line or circle dances. Interestingly, in the Balkans one village dance event was called the Hora, and it still takes place in the region on Sundays. Dance may also have helped to induce trancelike states in religious rituals.

GREECE

BY JOHN THORBURN

The ancient Greeks enjoyed several kinds of dramatic entertainment, including tragedy, comedy, and satyr plays. How, why, and when such performances began is uncertain, but by the fifth century B.C.E. they were well established. Our knowledge of Greek drama comes primarily from about four dozen plays by five Athenian playwrights: the tragedians Aeschylus, Sophocles, and Euripides and the comic poets Aristophanes and Menander. Greek dramas had a religious element and honored Dionysus, best known as the god of wine, and performing plays apparently evolved from some aspect of his worship.

Besides their religious aspect, ancient theatrical performances often occurred as part of a competition. In Athens the two festivals with dramatic competitions were the Lenaia and the far larger and more important City Dionysia. At the Lenaia two tragedians, each staging two plays, competed, and two comic poets were judged based on a single play each. At the City Dionysia three tragic poets each put on three tragedies and a satyr play, whereas five comic poets each put on a single play.

The Greeks viewed performances outdoors and during the day. In the earliest times spectators might sit on the bare ground of a hillside or on temporary wooden bleachers. By the fourth century B.C.E. theaters built of stone were commonplace. They varied in size, but the Theater of Dionysus in Athens seated well over 10,000 spectators. The action of

The figure of Silenus, the mentor of Dionysus, the god of plays; the figure was placed at the front of the stage in the Theater of Dionysus, sitting at the foot of the Acropolis in Athens. (Alison Frantz Photographic Collection, American School of Classical Studies at Athens)

the plays occurred both on a rectangular stage and in front of it within the circular orchestra (literally "place for dancing"). At the rear of the stage stood a buildinglike structure, the *skene,* with one to three doors. The *skene* might represent a house, palace, military tent, or even a cave. Because the actors performed only in front of the *skene,* playwrights usually had to use a character to describe events that were supposedly occurring inside. Occasionally, though, dramatists used a wheeled platform to bring something or someone out from within the *skene.* Sometimes characters (especially divinities) appeared on the roof of the *skene* or were suspended above the stage by means of a crane called the *mechane.* Over time stages became more elevated and deeper, and the *skene* increased from one to two stories.

Music from a pipe player accompanied dramas, and the performers—all of whom were men—took roles as individual characters or members of the chorus. The Greek word *choros* means "dance," and besides speaking, chanting, or singing their lines, the chorus members also danced. Comedies had 24 chorus members; early tragedies and satyr plays had 12, but that number later increased to 15. Contrasting with the relatively large number of performers needed for a chorus, Greek playwrights usually had no more than three actors to perform all the speaking roles. Because a play might have more than three speaking parts, actors often had to play more than one. One reason that actors could perform both male and female roles is that they wore masks. Evidence from ancient sculpture and pottery indicates that these masks had lifelike features and hair. Masks for comedy and satyr plays often had humorous or grotesque touches such as highly arched eyebrows or grinning mouths.

The players wore costumes appropriate for their roles (for example, as kings, queens, warriors, or mourners). Euripides became notorious for dressing his downtrodden heroes and heroines in ragged clothing. The costumes worn in comedies of the fifth century B.C.E. must have been spectacular. During this period spectators saw choruses dressed as ants, birds, clouds, wasps, and many other improbable beings or creatures.

Tragedies rarely dealt with historical subject matter—Aeschylus' *Persians* is an exception—but instead were usually derived from mythology. Tragedians dramatized events from the lives of mythical figures such as Achilles, Agamemnon, Medea, Oedipus, and Orestes but used these mythological events as a platform for examining issues that concerned their audiences, such as war, the nature of justice, relationships between the sexes, and the relationship of human beings to the gods.

At the City Dionysia playwrights concluded their dramatic offerings with a satyr play, satyrs being creatures usually depicted as part human and part goat or horse. In satyr plays the chorus typically dressed as satyrs. Because satyrs were very fond of wine and sexual activity, the plays often relied heavily on jokes about wine and drunkenness, as well as sexual references. Our knowledge of these works is limited because only one complete satyr play (Euripides' *Cyclops*) has survived. We do, however, possess about 400 lines from Sophocles' *Trackers* and short fragments from many other satyr plays.

Comedy (from the Greek word *komoidia,* "revel song") varied more than tragedy in its subject matter and content. Comic poets sometimes put a humorous spin on mythological figures or events, but in the fifth century B.C.E. the Athenian comic poets also poked fun at local politics and politicians and at the social or intellectual trends of the day. By the end of that century, however, political and topical humor began to disappear. Aristophanes' *Ecclesiazusae* and *Plutus,* staged between 393 and 388 B.C.E., contain fewer references to actual persons than his earlier plays and also have diminished choral roles. By the end of the fourth century B.C.E. the chorus's function seems to have been reduced to performing a standard set of songs serving as mere interludes between acts.

After Aristophanes, comedy focused more on life in the Greek home. Roles became stereotyped: the worried father, prodigal son, meddling slave, innocent maiden, prostitute, braggart warrior. Again, our knowledge after the fifth century B.C.E. is limited because only one or two works, from Menander, have survived in anything resembling complete form. Still, hundreds of fragments from Menander and many other comic playwrights of the fourth century and later supplement our understanding. Additionally, we have some two dozen complete plays from the Roman comic poets Plautus and Terence, who modeled their plays on those of Menander and other poets who composed in his style.

ROME

BY KIRK H. BEETZ

Much about Roman drama and theater is unknown. Most of the plays have been lost, much of Roman drama was spontaneous and not written down, and for a long time theater buildings were temporary, erected for a particular occasion and then taken down. Roman theater began as part of festivals, usually honoring gods and goddesses but sometimes celebrating military victories. Until the development of mimes, actors were only men, who wore masks that represented the characters they played; they not only spoke their lines but sang and danced as well. Even though the performances might celebrate gods, performers soon discovered that they could win audiences with comic sketches and vulgar humor.

It is not known exactly when Greek drama began to influence Roman drama, but during the 400s B.C.E. some actors put on Greek plays, with comedies being more popular than tragedies. They performed on temporary stages that were usually made of wood, though one stage used in Rome in the first century B.C.E. was recorded as having been made of marble, glass, and wood. These temporary theaters often had no seats, and audiences had to stand, but as the performances increased in popularity, builders included benches that rose in tiers like those in Greek theaters. The stage was usually broad. In front of it was the orchestra, where choruses and musicians were placed. At its back were openings that could simulate doors to buildings. By the mid-200s B.C.E. vast painted cloth backdrops were hung over the back of the stage to indicate settings for the action. Some of these backdrops were so well done that they gave the appearance of depth for background objects, while objects in the foreground seemed to thrust out over the stage. All Roman theaters were open air until 69 B.C.E., when a sponsor of theatricals, Quintus Lutatius Catulus, added a *vela,* a linen covering forming an awninglike roof for a theater.

The works of most Roman playwrights are lost, but those of Plautus (254–184 B.C.E.) have survived. He was a former actor and failed businessman who wrote plays to earn a living. Thus he catered to the desires of the paying public as much as he could. Like other Roman playwrights he borrowed plots from Greek plays and modified them for Roman audiences. His plays were often musical comedies, filled with music and lyrics he had composed. His audiences loved the variety in his plays, which included scheming slaves, braggart soldiers, pimps, prostitutes, bossy wives, and naive lovers. So successful was Plautus that his plays were performed to the end of the Roman Empire, long after stage plays had otherwise lost their popularity.

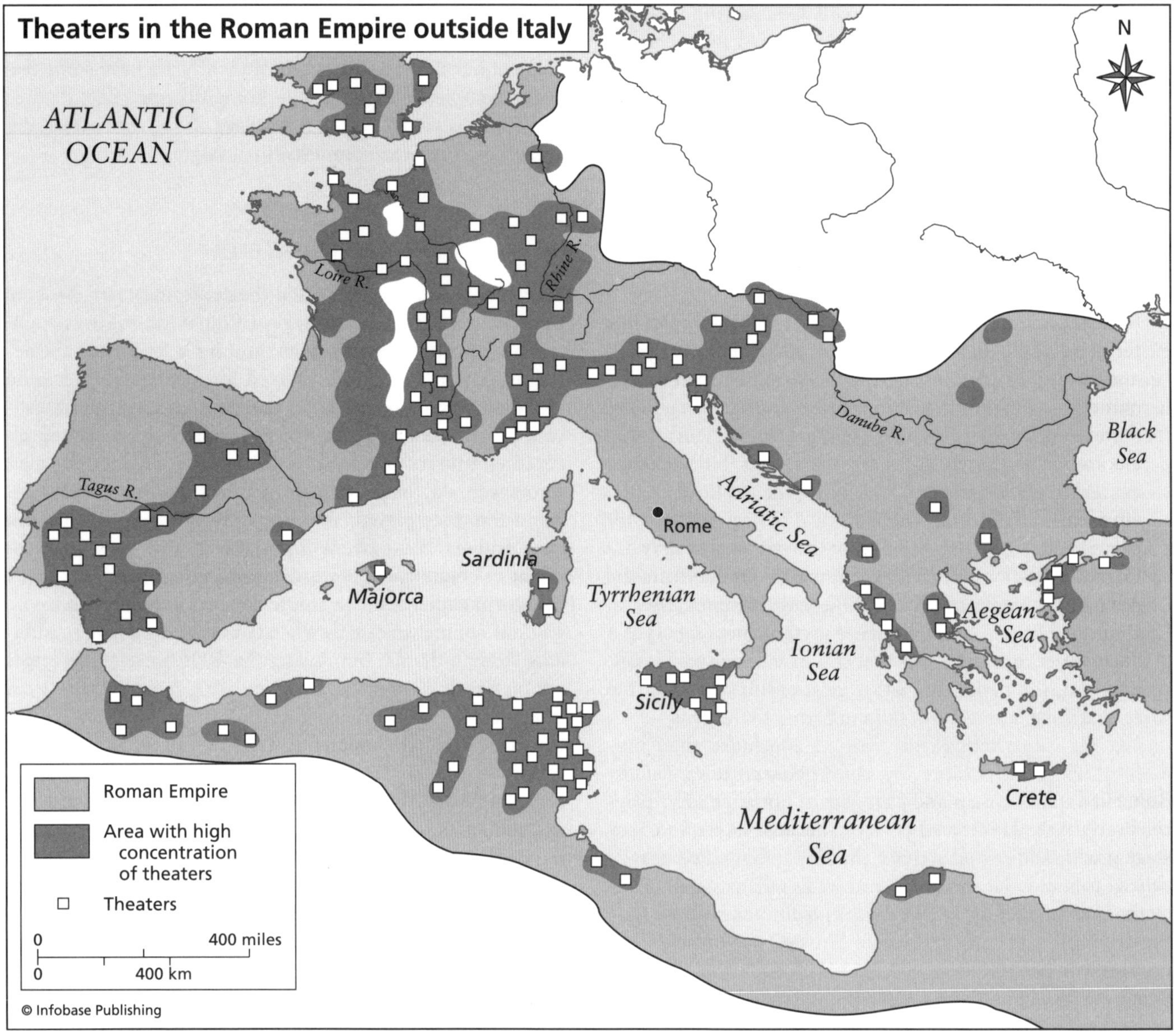

In addition to theaters on the Italian peninsula, the Roman Empire encompassed numerous theaters elsewhere in the empire.

Terence (185–159 B.C.E.) was Rome's other great writer of comedies, and all six of his plays are still complete, because monks carefully copied and preserved them throughout the Middle Ages. He came to Rome as a slave but was well educated by his owner and given his freedom. Although he was less popular than Plautus, he was admired for his understanding of human nature. Like Plautus, he borrowed from Greek sources. For Roman playwrights, using Greek settings was a matter of self-preservation. It was against the law, for example, to show Roman slaves as smarter than their masters, and the penalty for writing negatively about a living Roman citizen could be death. But with Greek sources audiences could laugh at smart slaves and other social commentary as representing Greeks, who they thought were crazy anyway.

Not much is known about Roman tragedies. Like Roman comedies they tended to be based on Greek plays, but they were more formal than the comedies. They featured actors in lavish costumes with often-grotesque masks, and they emphasized action over dialogue. The actors were held to high standards: Roman audiences often knew the plays by heart and anticipated every gesture an actor was supposed to make. They enjoyed extravagant costumes, though an entire audience reportedly fled in horror when an actor on stilts, in a long cloak, and wearing a mask of a howling face walked on stage; he conveyed terror too well.

By the time of the emperor Augustus (r. 27 B.C.E.–14 C.E.) few plays were being written, and even most of those were intended only to be read or recited, not acted. In 173 B.C.E.

THE PERILOUS LIFE OF THE ROMAN ACTOR

Much as in Hollywood or New York in modern times most actors in ancient Rome had to struggle to earn enough to live on, but a few were fortunate, becoming the equivalent of millionaires with their successful shows. Even then, however, their popularity sometimes betrayed them. Cases in point are the actors Mnester and Paris.

Mnester was not only a skilled dancer and actor but very handsome, and the emperor Caligula (r. 37–41 C.E.) forced him into a sexual relationship that became a scandal in Rome. The relationship gave Mnester high standing in Caligula's court, and it probably irritated many patricians, who resented the upstart. Yet when Caligula was murdered, Mnester was spared, probably because his acting was held in high esteem.

When Messalina, the third wife of the emperor Claudius (r. 41–54 C.E.), demanded a sexual relationship from Mnester, he at first declined. His reward was to have his lover Poppaea Sabina forced into suicide (though her daughter of the same name went on to marry the notorious emperor Nero). Mnester himself was whipped, which left scars across his back, and eventually he submitted to an affair with Messalina. When she then conspired with a consul-elect named Gaius Silius to overthrow Claudius, she and her co-conspirators were executed. Mnester gave a great performance in pleading his innocence before Claudius, who was inclined to let him go, but the patricians demanded that a commoner not be spared when aristocrats had been executed, and Mnester lost his life.

Paris was a popular name for actors, and one such actor had a love affair with Domitia, the wife of the emperor Domitian (r. 81–96 B.C.E.). Through her he gained so much power in the imperial court that he even appointed generals. Playwrights needed his approval to put on plays. It had long been the practice of the rulers of Rome to free slaves who gave good stage performances and to elevate to the aristocracy those commoners who were good actors by giving them golden rings; Paris also did these things, even though he had no authority for it. Eventually, Domitian divorced Domitia, and after several years of wielding imperial power as if it were his own, Paris was executed.

Rome had instituted a new spring festival called Floralia; the celebrations included horse races, gladiatorial combats, and stage productions that were primarily a kind of performance called "mime"—though it was far from the silent art known by that name today. By the time Rome had its first permanent theater, built by Pompey in 55 B.C.E., mimes were its main entertainment. Mimes wore no masks, and they included both men and women. They delighted audiences with their exaggerated gestures and facial expressions, and their shows also featured dancing, magic acts, acrobatics, and singing. Performances were either unscripted or followed thin story lines arranged around jokes. Their subject matter tended to be sex (actors and actresses alike were frequently naked) or parodies of current events. Mime shows were opportunities for audiences to escape their troubles, and Romans resented anyone, including the emperor, who tried to bring seriousness to the songs, dances, and pratfalls on stage.

Marble relief with two Roman theater masks—one tragic and one comic, from the second century C.E. (© The Trustees of the British Museum)

The permanent Roman theater was usually made of stone, often marble, with a semicircle of tiered seats. The first rows of seats belonged to the upper class, the middle rows to the middle class, and the back rows to the lower class. Often there were balconies to the side of the stage that were reserved for the emperor, his relatives, or other important figures. The large stage had a permanent backdrop of doors and colonnades with as many as three stories of open floors. The stage itself was heavily decorated with trees and other plants. At Pompey's theater those rooms away from the stage area had fountains, artificial waterfalls and streams, and gardens where people could rest during breaks in the entertainment or go at other times to socialize and relax.

During the reign of Augustus pantomime became popular. Usually depicting tragic myths, it was often performed to music, but as with pantomime today the actors and actresses did not speak. They were much admired for their ability to tell stories with their movements, and even everyday audiences became very sophisticated in their appreciation of the art form, able to note even slight mistakes. It was possible for the best actors to become very rich, and slaves often won their freedom with skilled performances.

Mimes, dancing, and pantomimes were performed throughout the rest of the history of the Roman Empire as essential parts of festivals and other celebrations. If a wealthy Roman wanted to become popular, he or she would pay for extravagant performances. Even after the fall of the Western Roman Empire and during the reigns of Germanic kings in Italy and much of the rest of Europe, mimes and pantomimes continued to be performed until historical records for them disappear in the 600s C.E.; they probably survived on a small scale during the Middle Ages in southern Europe.

THE AMERICAS

BY ALESSIA FRASSANI

Drama and theater are essential aspects of Native American artistic expression today. Theatrical performances are a ritual activity triggered by specific events and needs and with specific desired results. Entertainment is achieved through storytelling and special effects but is not always the ultimate goal. Ensuring the community's well-being is often a main concern. Archaeological evidence suggests that public performances in the ancient Americas embodied some of these same elements.

People of high social stature (kings and religious figures) received particularly grand rituals. To some degree ceremonial performances, in ancient America and elsewhere, were political. The more complex the social organization, the stronger was the need for cohesion among different social classes. Ceremonial behavior toward higher-ranking people served this purpose.

Shamanism, a common feature of Native American religions, played a crucial role in early drama. Shamans, through innate ability and years of training, are thought to be able to do such things as transform themselves into animals or supernatural beings. During rituals a rhythmic beating of drums and shaking of rattles, repetitive chants, dancing, and the use of elaborate costumes accompany the shaman's transformation. Shamanic rituals are thus theatrical in their very nature. Conjuring up the ancestral dead was a common purpose of such performances. Assuming the identity of a supernatural being enabled the shaman to communicate with the dead in order to resolve critical political, economic, or social issues.

Excavations all over the Americas have uncovered small figurines from ancient times. In North America the funerary sites of the Adena and Hopewell civilizations (1000 B.C.E.–400 C.E.) have yielded large numbers of ritual items shaped like animals or humans. A tobacco pipe from Newark, Ohio, for example, represents a seated man wearing a bear costume. In Native American lore bears are feared and respected and are sometimes referred to as "grandfathers." This pipe probably mourned and revered a deceased shaman-bear and testifies to the importance of animal doubles in early Amerindian rituals.

In Mesoamerica the sites of Tlatilco in central Mexico (1200–900 B.C.E.) and Colima and Nayarit in western Mexico (100 B.C.E.–200 C.E.) are famous for their abundance of small clay figurines, especially from burials, depicting dancers and musicians. The figurines, which may represent either the deceased or funerary attendants, often have richly plumed headdresses, wear jade or shell tinklers on their ankles, and hold fans or musical instruments (especially ocarinas). Typical of Colima are assemblages of warrior-dancers with helmets, weapons, and elaborate ritual armor. Effigy headdress includes crocodiles, sharks, and deities. Pacific Coast people of Mexico still wear similar costumes during annual religious celebrations.

The rich ceramic tradition of Jama-Coaque and Tumaco–La Tolita, flourishing along the Pacific coast of Ecuador and Colombia between about 600 B.C.E. and 500 C.E., produced small effigy figures that include musicians, dancers, and ritual performers. Shamans, often impersonating bats, birds of prey, or jaguars, perform fertility rituals by dancing and scattering seeds and precious stones while shaking rattles. Shells, symbols of fertility, decorate clothes and bags and may allude to the shamans' propitiatory role. The bags probably contained coca leaves, used to induce trances, or seeds to be cast ritually.

The political role of performance became more apparent in Mesoamerica and South America around the first millennium B.C.E. The Olmec civilization, flourishing between 1200 and 400 B.C.E. on the Gulf coast of Mexico, produced the earliest monumental architecture and stone sculpture in Mesoamerica. A rising elite instituted large and ambitious programs and used rituals and public spaces to legitimize their political and economic privileges.

At the Olmec site of La Venta, pyramids and platforms around large plazas created stages for open-air ceremonies that included music, singing, and dance. Stelae—vertical stone slabs carved, inscribed, or sometimes painted with commemorative information—were first created during the Late Formative Period (400 B.C.E.–150 C.E.). Often portraying rulers in full attire, they provide interesting information about the theatrical devices employed to convey the supernatural powers of these individuals. Stela 2 at La Venta, for example, shows a royal figure wearing a giant headdress with decorations probably referring to the maize (corn) plant, Mesoamerica's staple food crop, first grown on an intensive scale by the Olmec.

The Maya of southern Mexico, Guatemala, Belize, and Honduras continued the Olmec tradition of empowering rulership through public ritual performance. The emergence of elaborate public centers during the first century B.C.E. reflects the development of a more complex social hierarchical structure that had at its top the *ahaw*, a ruler able to contact the ancestors during ritual activities. Such ceremonies were a form of public memory and a means of fostering social cohesion.

At the site of Cerros, Belize, a large step pyramid rises near the Atlantic shore. Four masks in two rows flank its central stairway. Scholars believe the masks symbolize the primary forces of the cosmos, relating to cardinal directions and celestial bodies. The temple's facade was a backdrop for ritual display of the ruler's power to control natural forces. Representations of rulers in ritual attire, holding such ritual objects as spears and serpents, symbols of visionary abilities, appear on all Mayan stelae. The frontal stance, alignment of the feet, and position of the hands suggest ritual dance.

Although no stelae survive from Teotihuacán (near modern Mexico City), the most influential center in ancient Mesoamerica, murals found inside residential compounds depict fertility rituals, suggesting that here too figures with political and religious powers existed. Walls exhibit painted images of priests walking in procession. The figures, with large goggle eyes typical of rain and fertility gods, are shown scattering seeds, precious stones, and shells. Wriggly or curly shapes indicating words and chanting come from their mouths. In some cases green-plumed headdresses transform the priests into feathered serpents, while black paint around the eyes indicates visionary abilities.

Chavín de Huántar in the northern Peruvian Andes is one of the oldest and largest archaeological sites of ancient South America. Founded around 900 B.C.E., Chavín was until 500 B.C.E. the major religious center of South America, attracting pilgrims from all over the Andean and coastal regions. Its most important place for open-air ritual activity is a large U-shaped mound. Immediately in front of the entrance to this sacred place is a circular sunken plaza, accessible only via two facing stairways. Carvings on the plaza's wall provide one of the oldest depictions of theatrical performance in the Americas. Two rows of carvings show processions of feline and humanlike creatures. Curled serpents issue from their heads and waists. The men-animals blow *pututus*, traditional Andean wind instruments made from large seashells, and hold San Pedro cacti, a desert plant with hallucinogenic qualities. This last element makes clear the shamanic nature of the performance at Chavín. Together with music, dance, and songs, psychoactive substances were used to induce a trance that enabled the shaman's transformation.

See also AGRICULTURE; ARCHITECTURE; ART; CERAMICS AND POTTERY; DEATH AND BURIAL; FESTIVALS; LITERATURE; MUSIC AND MUSICAL INSTRUMENTS; RELIGION AND COSMOLOGY; SACRED SITES; SPORTS AND RECREATION.

FURTHER READING

Cora Agatucci, "African Storytelling." Available online. URL: http://web.cocc.edu/cagatucci/classes/hum211/afrstory.htm. Downloaded on January 4, 2007.

Kay Ambrose, *Classical Dances and Costumes of India* (London: Adam and Charles Black, 1950).

Martin Banham, ed., *The History of Theater in Africa* (Cambridge: Cambridge University Press, 2004).

Margarete Bieber, *The History of the Greek and Roman Theater* (Princeton, N.J.: Princeton University Press, 1961).

Jane Buikstra, Douglas K. Charles, and Gordon F. M. Rakita, *Staging Ritual: Hopewell Ceremonialism at the Mound House Site, Greene County, Illinois* (Kampsville, Ill.: Center for American Archaeology Press, 1998).

Dominique Collon, "Dance in Ancient Mesopotamia," *Near Eastern Archaeology* 66, no. 3 (September 2003): 96–105.

Eric Csapo and William J. Slater, *The Context of Ancient Drama* (Ann Arbor: University of Michigan Press, 1995).

Beryl de Zoete, *Dance and Drama in Bali* (London: Faber and Faber, 1937).

H. W. Fairman, ed. and trans., *The Triumph of Horus: An Ancient Egyptian Sacred Drama* (Berkeley: University of California Press, 1974).

Yosef Garfinkel, "The Earliest Dancing Scenes of the Near East," *Near Eastern Archaeology* 66, no. 3 (September 2003): 84–95.

Robyn Gillam, *Performance and Drama in Ancient Egypt* (London: Duckworth, 2006).

Richard Green and Eric Handley, *Images of the Greek Theatre* (Austin: University of Texas Press, 1995).

Amihai Mazar, "Ritual Dancing in the Iron Age," *Near Eastern Archaeology* 66, no. 3 (September 2003): 126–134.

Jonathan Tubb, "Phoenician Dance," *Near Eastern Archaeology* 66, no. 3 (September 2003): 122–125.

Sir Arthur Wallace Pickard-Cambridge, *The Dramatic Festivals of Athens* (Oxford, U.K.: Clarendon Press, 1953).

Sir Arthur Wallace Pickard-Cambridge, *Dithyramb, Tragedy, and Comedy*, 2nd ed., rev. by T. B. L. Webster (Oxford, U.K.: Clarendon Press, 1962).

David Wiles, *Greek Theatre Performance: An Introduction* (New York: Cambridge University Press, 2000).

E

► economy

INTRODUCTION

An economy requires that people cooperate in deciding what they value in their society. In a subsistence economy determining what is valuable may be easy: Everyone is focused on finding or creating the barest essential of life, food. In such an economy people have little time for creating luxuries or for recreation. Even so, their relationships may still be complex, because they may need to cooperate to create enough food that nobody starves, and they may need to create a hierarchy of who gets fed first and, in case of a shortage of food, who does not get fed at all. Thus, at its base, economics can be about who lives and who dies.

An agricultural economy is one that is focused almost entirely on raising crops. Such an economy can be a subsistence economy in which everything that is harvested is used each year, without a surplus. The ancient peoples of Mesopotamia, the Yellow River region in China, and Mesoamerica found ways to create surpluses of by using irrigation canals and by learning to plant two crops and have two harvests per year for such staples as wheat. Still, advanced agricultural practices brought with them new problems, especially overpopulation. Occasionally, crops would fail, and there would be a famine. Famines have killed millions of people over thousands of years along the Yellow River, and much of Mesopotamia may have succumbed to food shortages in ancient times.

One way to protect against shortages was by having a controlled economy. In a controlled economy a central authority, usually the government, dictated what was grown and what was manufactured. Ancient Egypt had a controlled economy and the Harappan civilization of the Indus river valley probably did too. The government could save surplus grain for distribution during periods in which crops failed. Another way to save crops against bad times was through taxes. For instance, in Mesopotamia and China farmers were usually required to give some of their harvests to the government. In Mesopotamia farmers sometimes donated part of their land to the government or to the temple of their city, buying favors for themselves and providing the government and temple with direct control over some agricultural resources. This created an early form of a mixed economy, partly free market for independent farmers and partly central controlled.

An advantage of a free market economy is that it can encourage even the poorest members of society to try to create surpluses of goods, because they can use those surpluses to trade for other goods. This was often threatening to ancient governments, whose social elites viewed the generation of wealth for those outside the elites as disrupting their traditional privileges. In China almost everyone was a peasant. Although broad-minded emperors occasionally tried to give peasants civil rights and ownership of land, most of the time peasants were slaves to the land. They could not leave the land unless they were conscripted into a warlord's army; if the land was destroyed, the peasants on it were destroyed as well. When Confucianism became the dominant philosophy of government in the late 200s B.C.E., peasants and craftspeople were allowed to benefit directly from their work, which disturbed the social elite so much that it was made against the law for an ordinary person to dress well.

Surpluses of food allowed for the development of specialization in the workplace. In most early societies, everyone needed to know how to do everything, from how to make bows and arrows to how to fashion a clay pot. Perhaps the earliest division of labor was between the genders, at its most simplistic a matter of one gender doing the hunting and farming, while the other dealt with producing baskets and other household goods. Even then, there was pressure to know how to do many tasks. For instance, in sub-Saharan Africa, most women made and fired ceramics at home, quarried the clay for building homes, tended gardens, and cared for children. With the burden of caring for crops every day lifted from some members of society, it was possible for them to master a manufacturing craft, such as metalworking or creating pottery.

Those who manufactured nonagricultural goods could trade their products for food. In southern Mesopotamia this became essential by about 1000 B.C.E. Even though Mesopotamia had at one time exported grains, its soil had been poisoned by salt from rivers, and increasing populations made it impossible to produce enough food to feed everyone. The Mesopotamians were able to feed themselves by trading goods made of metal to other people who had excess grain but lacked the Mesopotamians' expertise in metalworking. Ancient Mesopotamian goods were distributed throughout the Near East and into central Asia and as far east as the Indus River valley. Nonetheless, cultures that made fine manufactured goods that they could trade for food or other goods struggled with the barter economy, in which sellers had to find someone who had what they wanted and who wanted what they had to sell.

A solution to this was the cash economy. In a cash economy sellers do not need to find someone who has exactly what they want, because buyers will give sellers money, which the sellers can then use to buy what they want from other sellers. Historians and archaeologists often judge the maturity of an economic system by whether it developed a cash economy, which allowed trades to be made quickly and enabled people or organizations to accumulate enough money to invest in building factories, as happened in ancient China, or to invest in consumer goods such as houses, medical care, and good clothes.

The study of ancient economies has pitfalls for modern observers, because ancient peoples had their own cultural priorities that affected how they treated goods and trade. There is the example of the Chinese, who refused to wear wool because their barbarian neighbors were often shepherds. They denied themselves the benefit of a warm, sturdy fabric simply because they were prejudiced against people who happened to care for sheep. Among the Celts, minting coins did not always mean that they had a cash economy, because the coins were often symbols of a chief's power and were given to followers to symbolize their obligations to their chief. Even so, the study of ancient economies is one of the best ways to learn how ancient peoples valued their worlds.

AFRICA

BY MICHAEL J. O'NEAL

For thousands of millennia the concept of an economy, as the term is understood in modern life, would have been entirely foreign to Africans. "Wealth" consisted primarily of an abundance of food. "Capital assets" included only the few portable possessions that nomadic bands of hunter-gatherers could carry with them from one encampment to another. "Labor" consisted of the daily search for food by hunters, fishermen, and gatherers, who found nuts, berries, fruits, acorns, roots, and leafy vegetables. "Economic incentive" was a rumbling belly.

Money was nonexistent. "Banks" meant those who had surplus resources and were willing to share them with others. "Corporations" were formed by small tribal bands whose members worked cooperatively to find food, haul it back to the encampment, and prepare it for consumption as well as to perform other tasks, such as gathering firewood and water. "Stockholders" were those who accumulated a herd of livestock. The "price" of a good consisted of the time it took to find it and, perhaps in the case of hunting, the injuries and even deaths that resulted from tangling with wild animals.

THE EARLY STONE AGE

Until the Neolithic Revolution and the spread of agriculture, which began in roughly in 10,000–8000 B.C.E. or later in some parts of the world, the economic systems of Africa were simple. If economics can be defined as the science of scarcity—of time, money, resources, labor—then the ancient Africans combated scarcity with unceasing labor. The chief economic activity was the hunting and gathering of food. Secondary activities included finding or building shelters, storing food, maintaining fires, and caring for children. The basic units of both production and consumption were the family. About the only specialization of labor was along gender lines. Men did most of the hunting, while women did most of the gathering, though these gender roles were not strictly adhered to; women, for example, often functioned as hunters by combing shallow waters for such food items as shellfish, and men often assisted with the gathering of fruits, nuts, and so on.

What tools Stone Age Africans had for such tasks as digging and carving game were not produced by a separate class of craft workers. Individuals made their own stone tools, arrow points, and the like, though archaeological evidence shows that some of these items were often shared, suggesting that some individuals may have been seen as more skilled in making them. Land did not have to be allocated for production, for no one owned the land or claimed land-use rights. These small communities of people, who largely inhabited the savannas of East Africa until they spread out through the continent, were largely egalitarian, meaning that they shared all resources equally. Thus, food was taken back to the encampment for everyone; kills were not attributed to any one person, so the food was available to all. Moreover, no elite class laid claim to the production of others. No market economy drove the demand for and supply of food. The demand was persistent but the supply sometimes less so.

The Agricultural System

As populations spread throughout Africa and agriculture emerged as a primary way of life, the economic system had to change. Nomadic hunter-gatherers lived in a world in which no one possessed property rights to land or territory, though it is likely that groups defended territory against outsiders. The land existed as a resource for all to exploit. Systems of agriculture, in contrast, require the allocation of land. Which land is used, who uses it and for what, and when the land is used became primary considerations.

Making these considerations more important was that the amount of arable land was limited. Much of sub-Saharan Africa was covered by either dense forests or deserts, and while the Sahara was largely grassland until about 3000 B.C.E., climatic changes caused expansion of the desert, reducing the amount of land suitable for agriculture. Thus, agricultural communities, including both farmers and herders, had to settle on land that provided good soil, moderate temperatures, pasturage for livestock, and, in particular, an abundance of water. Complicating the situation was that water was in many cases available only seasonally. That is, floodplains became inundated with water during portions of the year and then dried out. All of these considerations made questions of land use and allocation important ones.

Good examples are provided by the floodplains of the Niger and Senegal River valleys, though other river valleys would have dealt with similar conditions. Along any river there were probably three areas whose use had to be allocated. One was the uplands, the areas farthest away from the river and its flooding. Here is where herds were usually pastured and people lived in permanent dwellings. Around these dwellings were gardens where women tended patches of vegetables. The primary source of water was not the river but rainfall. At lower elevations and closer to the river were floodplains, which were covered with water during annual flooding and then used for crops after the waters receded, in a type of agriculture referred to as recession agriculture; that is, crops were planted after the recession, or receding, of the floodwaters. Finally, the lowest elevations, closest to the rivers, were the flood basins. These areas tended to remain wet and boggy during longer portions of the year, in effect storing water. This was also the area exploited by fishermen and others who gathered foodstuffs such as crabs, snails, and shellfish in river shallows and lagoons. The end result was that land was allocated for use in parallel strips that followed the course of the river.

Decisions had to be made about how these units of land were used and when. Thus, for example, certain crops such as rice were suited to the flood basins, sometimes putting rice growers in conflict with fishermen. Others, including staple crops such as grains, were more suited to the floodplains, and still others were suited to the uplands. Further, as herds of livestock ate grasses on the uplands, they had to be moved to lower elevations for pasturage, but this had to occur at times when they would not trample growing crops. Thus, for example, a crop of sorghum might have been grown in the floodplain, but after the sorghum was harvested, livestock were herded in to graze after they had eaten down the upland grasses. This movement of the herd had two primary benefits. First, the livestock ate away the stubble left behind after the harvesting of the crop, at the same time churning up the ground with their hooves, making the next planting easier; second, the livestock fertilized the soil with their manure. Modern farmers use manure and fertilizer spreaders; the earliest manure spreaders were also the manure producers.

An additional consideration was that crops were planted in rotation, depending on rainfall and temperature conditions. All of these activities had to be scheduled. Complicating matters was that one of several clan lineages engaged primarily in one of these various activities. Thus, one lineage herded livestock, another fished, still another grew certain crops, and so forth, though fishermen tended to farm as well. The foundation of the system was the consultation of headmen of the various lineages, who made decisions based largely on the most efficient and productive use of the land; each headman would probably have defended the interests and privileges of his clan. One way that conflicts were avoided was through clan intermarriages; the headman of, say, a herding clan would, in general, be reluctant to encroach on the land-use rights of a farmer if that farmer was his son-in-law or brother-in-law.

In contrast to modern life, where social and economic relationships tend to be separated, these relationships in ancient Africa were often one and the same. Thus, property and goods exchanged hands through such institutions as inheritance, bride-prices, and dowries. In the absence of currencies, a bride-price paid by a groom's family to the bride's family to compensate them for the loss of her services or a dowry paid by the bride's family to the groom took tangible forms, such as cattle. Among Stone Age peoples, value existed in the things that provided a livelihood, so these things became the medium of exchange. Acquiring a small herd of livestock by marrying a woman whose father had surplus livestock enabled a young man to gain a toehold in the area's economic system.

Complementing this method of property exchange was a system of barter. Barter as a form of economic exchange is difficult in modern life except in isolated circumstances; a rural landowner might trade a load of firewood to a local farmer in exchange for a load of hay. But this type of exchange assumes that a person who has firewood and wants hay can find another person who has hay and wants firewood; difficulties increase if one or both of the goods is perishable or the parties live at a distance from one another. But economic needs during the late Stone Age were simpler, consisting of food, livestock, tools, textiles, pottery, and a limited number of other goods necessary to survival. Since most of these goods were available in the local economy, it was not hard for people to barter them in informal, day-to-day exchanges.

This type of bartering extended to services as well as to goods. Throughout much of Africa, patron-client relationships were common. This term means that influential and wealthier members of the community became patrons for those less influential or wealthy, their clients. The patron provided protection and economic benefits for the client, who in turn performed services for his patron. The result of all these social-economic relationships was an integrated economy, with different groups of people such as clans and tribes providing economic benefits not only for themselves but also for one another. Stability was ensured by interlocking systems of clan and patron-client relationships, all strengthened by marital alliances. In this way, over time, clans united into larger tribes, which in turn united into regional powers.

Not all floodplains and river valleys were alike. The Senegal River valley was narrow, about 12 miles wide. In contrast, the Niger River valley was much wider, some 60 miles wide. The result was that the various types of land along the Niger were much more widely dispersed; rather than parallel strips, the usable land took the form more of a patchwork. Further, this larger region was inhabited by various tribes who often did not maintain good relations with one another and may have spoken different languages. Intermarriage under these circumstances was not as common. Thus, conflicts over land use arose. The result was a far less integrated economy. Individual tribes and clans staked out land for their own purposes, resulting in a subsistence economy, with each tribe or clan living largely off its own produce. Along the Senegal River, the economy was more integrated, with the various clans sharing their productive capacity with one another in large part simply because they lived in closer proximity, intermarried, and spoke the same language.

Not all of Africa became sedentary during the Neolithic Revolution. Economic developments took place at different speeds in different places. In West Africa, for example, hunting and gathering persisted as a way of life far longer than it did in other parts of the continent, primarily because the people had abundant resources and therefore had no incentive to change their way of life. Also nomadic pastoralists (herders) continued to move their herds about seasonally in some parts of the continent. These pastoralists never developed any kind of sophisticated system of resource allocation or exchange. They were the loners, the independent spirits of the African economy. They were representative of a way of looking at economic systems in the sub-Sahara. While North Africa, including the empire of the ancient Egyptians, relied on a complex governmental system, with bureaucrats, assessors, surveyors, tax collectors, and the like, all controlled by a central authority, the sub-Sahara preferred local control and independence, with economic activity directed by headmen, clans, and lineages.

Mining, Metallurgy, and Trade

The kinds of problems faced by the inhabitants of the Niger River valley led to a fundamental change in the economy of that region. While the economic organizations of the Senegal River valley fostered generalists, who sustained a mixed economy of farming, herding, and fishing, the patchwork economy of the Niger River valley fostered specialization. As populations grew, it became increasingly difficult for people to meet their needs through a single economic activity. Accordingly, the Niger River valley turned more to trade and exchange. Early in the Neolithic Period, such trade took place between the various tribes that inhabited the region. In time, this trade would radiate outward to more far-flung regions. By about the beginning of the Common Era, the region was part of a trading belt that extended across the middle of Africa and linked the Sahara and regions to the east to the southern half of the continent.

With the precedent set for specialization, mining and metallurgy became important parts of the local economy. Africa was (and is) rich in iron ore. In many places, iron ore did not even have to be dug; it was visible in rock outcroppings. Interestingly, while much of the rest of the world passed through stages in which copper and then bronze were the primary metals, Africa seemed to have skipped the Bronze Age and passed directly to iron production. Iron, and later steel, changed the makeup of ancient Africa. Tools were developed that made agricultural production more efficient. With a greater abundance of food and other resources, populations increased. For growing numbers of people to meet their needs, they turned to trade with other parts of the world.

Meanwhile, iron became the mainstay of the African economy in some regions. In the Niger River area, the city of Jenne-jeno emerged as an important center of iron production. Again, the result was increased specialization of labor. Individuals mined ore, transported it, processed it by separating the iron from the ore, and turned it into weapons, plows, and other useful objects. Other individuals were responsible for cutting and hauling the enormous amounts of wood needed to stoke the fires, which were kept burning at very high temperatures. (This cutting of wood led to extensive deforestation in some areas, forcing people to abandon their settlements.) Archaeologists have found numerous remains of smithing and other iron-producing activities around Jenne-jeno and other parts of sub-Saharan Africa.

It appears that in Jenne-jeno no social elite or hierarchy of authority directed this economic activity from the top down. Rather, the economy was organized horizontally, again with lineages exercising authority over their members. The headmen of these lineages created a complex latticework of overlapping agencies and cooperative ventures that directed iron production from mining to finished products. Jenne-jeno and communities like it initiated one of the chief features of modern, urban economies: a central hub that drew people in search of economic opportunity and that provided goods and services for outlying areas in exchange for food and other agricultural products.

One peculiarity of the African iron industry, at least by modern standards, is that it was associated with religious beliefs. Iron, because of its strength, was regarded as a source of power, even virility. Iron provided weapons that could be used to conquer enemies who were still fighting with rocks and sticks. Thus, one group that often ran the iron industry was the priestly class. The making of iron was regarded as magical. Large fires were built to smelt the ore, out of which emerged a substance that enabled people to conquer both the land and their enemies. The flames, the smoke and ash, the heat, and the molten metal had a distinct otherworldly aspect. Accordingly, large numbers of rituals and taboos surrounded iron making. One taboo, in particular, was that ironworks, as spiritual centers, had to be strictly separated from households—perhaps the first known instance of zoning regulations that separated manufacturing from residential districts.

Iron was not the only metal that played a role in African economic systems. Gold, too, played a part, though gold in the ancient world did not have quite the same high value the modern world places on it. Gold is a soft metal, so its uses were restricted to luxury items such as jewelry. One of the most prominent gold-producing kingdoms of ancient Africa was Ghana, which began to flourish in about 200 C.E. Ghana's major export was gold. In fact, the word *ghana* referred to the ruler who controlled the region's gold supply and gold exports.

Ghana's rulers became wealthy because of the taxes they levied, though they did not tax gold. Rather, they taxed the salt for which gold was traded. (Salt was a vital commodity in the ancient world, used primarily for food preservation.) Thus, gold was traded for salt; taxes were paid on the salt, and the ruling class became the owners of capital that was used to finance public works projects such as roads and monuments. In some parts of Africa, including Ghana, only gold dust could be legally traded. Gold nuggets were regarded as the possessions of rulers, as a way of maintaining their status.

Ghana and Jenne-jeno, of course, were not the only centers of metalworking and trade. The Nubian kingdoms to the south of the Egyptian empire were also important centers of metalworking and trade. These kingdoms, including Kush and later Axum, occupied unique positions as links between Egypt to the north and the sub-Sahara to the south. And by being linked with Egypt, they were also linked to the Near East and the wider Mediterranean Sea. Accordingly, these kingdoms gained wealth as centers of trade, with middlemen importing and exporting goods—gold, jewelry, salt, ivory, ebony, elephant tusks, leopard skins, feathers, incense, and agricultural produce—up and down the region. Often this trade was not direct; one item was traded for another, which was in turn traded for a third, and so on until goods arrived in the hands of those who wanted them. Many products from the sub-Sahara were in high demand to the north because they were luxury goods or used in the production of luxury goods. Thus, the economic base of these kingdoms was not production, even though a certain amount of iron was produced, but rather exchange. Unlike the sub-Sahara, however, the Nubian kingdoms were ruled by powerful central authorities, modeling their Egyptian neighbors, so import-export exchanges were taxed, and the proceeds used for public works projects.

Carthage

The most dominant trading empire in North Africa was that of the Carthaginians. Carthage, a name derived from the Phoenician words for "new city," was founded in 814 B.C.E. by Phoenician traders from the city of Tyre in Lebanon. The city of Carthage, the capital of the empire, was in North Africa on the east edge of Lake Tunis, in modern-day Tunisia. Some historians believe that it was the world's second-largest city during Hellenistic times, the era when the Greek empire was at its height. It was protected by massive walls and had marketplaces, towers, a theater, a council house, an area for religious worship, a huge, elaborate cemetery, four residential areas, and, in the center, a tall citadel called the Byrsa.

The basis of Carthaginian power and empire was its massive navy and a large fleet of merchant ships. Much of the empire's trade was based on the Iberian Peninsula (Spain and Portugal), the source of large amounts of lead, silver, and tin ore. Tin ore was especially important, for numerous ancient civilizations mixed tin with copper to make bronze. Carthage's strategic location between the island of Sicily and the African coast allowed it to control the supply of tin to the east.

Nearly as important as tin were the silver mines in North Africa and Iberia. Another important commodity was a dye called Tyrian purple—a dye so valued that a pound of it was equal in value to up to 20 pounds of gold. Other important commodities included textiles (silk, wool, cotton), spices, perfumes, pottery, incense, glasswork, wood, bronze, alabaster, precious stones, plows, mirrors, cabinetry, household items (pillows and bedding, for example), slaves, and weapons. Food commodities included fish as well as a range of agricultural products.

Carthage's influence also spread southward. The empire sent caravans into the African continent, where they traded for such goods as ebony, ivory, salt, timber, gold, hides, and such animals as apes and peacocks. To the north they obtained amber from the Scandinavian countries and animal hides from Europe. In summary, the Carthaginians traded in just about every commodity that anyone wanted in the ancient world. Their efficiency in storage, transportation, and buying and selling was the source of the empire's wealth and power.

The Carthaginians introduced two important innovations on the continent. One was the auction method of exchange, and the other was the use of gold as a medium of exchange. Many of the communities that traded with Carthage feared Carthaginian sailors because of their reputation for seizing slaves. Thus, they avoided direct contact with the Carthaginian merchant fleet or caravans. Accordingly, when the Carthaginians arrived, they unloaded their goods onto, say, a beach, arranging them tidily for inspection. They then built a smoky fire to indicate their arrival and withdrew to a safe distance. The locals came down to the beach, inspected the goods, and then left behind a quantity of gold that they thought represented a fair price. The Carthaginians returned, and if they thought the price was fair, they took the gold and left; if not, they again withdrew and the locals could leave behind a greater quantity of gold if they wished. This process continued until a price had been reached, the Carthaginians accepted the gold and left, and the locals carried off the goods.

The Carthaginian economy was a command economy, directed by the ruling dynasty in Carthage. This dynasty was an oligarchy of prominent families. Transactions were taxed, creating a royal treasury used to finance the military and numerous public works projects.

Money

The development of money in Africa, as well as in other parts of the world, was closely related to taxation. Money, as opposed to coins and currency, is an abstraction. Money is defined in a number of ways: a medium of exchange, a store of value, a standard of value, a unit of account, and a means of payment. In modern life people store value by opening bank accounts or contributing to retirement accounts. In this way they can store resources for the future, when they can convert savings into groceries and other commodities. But while the modern world thinks of money as coins and currency, virtually anything can serve as money, as long as others accept it as money, it cannot be easily counterfeited, it is relatively scarce, and it holds its value over time.

In ancient Africa tangible goods were the primary form of money. Objects were priced relative to one another, so that a certain quantity of salt, for example, was regarded as equivalent in value to a certain amount of gold. African traders who formed the marketplace for goods were adept at determining these relative values. They served as middlemen who exchanged the commodities and collected a surplus that was their payment for brokering the transaction. Similarly, a cow could serve all the purposes of money, and objects were "priced" relative to cattle. In some cultures a person could pay for something with a cow and receive "change" in the form of a sheep or goat or perhaps some other commodity, such as a sheepskin. The English word *pecuniary,* referring to money, comes from the Latin word *pecus,* meaning "cattle," and the English words *cattle, chattel* (any goods or tangible property), and *capital* (in the economic sense of assets) all have the same linguistic origin. Interestingly, the modern world has similar financial instruments. While cattle are not used much as money, certain intangible things are. In 1997 the pop music star David Bowie introduced "Bowie bonds," a form of money that gave owners of the bonds a claim on future royalties from his music. While the form has changed, the basic concept of providing something of value in exchange for something else, rather than exchanging coins and currency, is little different from the practices of ancient Africa.

The problem was that the taxing authorities could use only so much salt or so many heads of cattle. Accordingly, systems of coinage developed primarily as a way to pay taxes and not as a way to facilitate barter, as is commonly believed. Secondarily, coinage was a more convenient way to pay such obligations as fines, bride-prices, and tribute to foreign conquerors; the word *pay* comes from the Latin *pacere,* meaning to "appease" or "make peace with." In ancient Africa coins were not minted out of precious metals for these purposes. The most common form of "coinage" was the cowrie shell, a brightly colored shell from warm-water gastropods (mollusks, for example) that had value because they were brightly colored and thus were used in luxury goods such as jewelry. At various times, though, other similar items were used as coinage, including feathers, metal tools, and ivory. The later Carthaginians minted coins and also used gold as a means of payment.

EGYPT

BY PANAGIOTIS I. M. KOUSOULIS

The inner structure of the ancient Egyptian state was based on three factors: economy, religion, and political ideology. These factors were closely connected in a variety of modes and expressions. The pharaoh was regarded as the earthly manifestation of the divine and the guarantor of the fertility of the land and the fecundity of the stock. The Egyptian lands were the exclusive property of the king, who divided them into agricultural domains and placed them under the control of the temple or political administration.

Although there was no word equivalent to *economy* in the vocabulary of the ancient Egyptians and nor was there a planned economic framework, the transition from a nomadic to an economic culture, the unification of Upper (South) and Lower (North) Egypt, and the formation of the political state and administration gradually led to the development and institutionalization of a working economic system.

Economic transactions and practices are documented in a variety of sources. Even from the inauguration of Egyptian political history there is evidence, from the end of the fourth and the beginning of the third millennium B.C.E., of the tripartite nature of Egyptian society (religious, political, economic) and the role of economy in it. For example, on the mace head (a ceremonial staff) of the mythological king Scorpion (Dynasty 0, ca. 3050 B.C.E.) the central scenes depict the king's efforts to render the land agriculturally valuable through the exploitation of certain techniques (seeding, harvest, tree plantings) and ritual actions (presentations to divinities).

Sources of economic information can be categorized into two principal groups. The first group includes monumental inscriptions and pictorial representations that cover almost two millennia, from the Old Kingdom through the New Kingdom (ca. 2575–1070 B.C.E.). The evidence from the Old and Middle Kingdoms is scanty and becomes much more plentiful during the New Kingdom. Such evidence includes offering and trading scenes among individuals or between the state authorities and the populace as well as transactions and gift exchanges between the state and foreign traders, diplomats, and rulers.

The second group of sources includes administrative documents and financial records from temples, tombs, or private individuals that attest to actual economic transactions. They are preserved mostly on papyrus rolls in a quite fragmentary nature, are written in hieratic handwriting (referring to an informal expression of Egyptian hieroglyphs), and include complicated technical terms. The best examples are the papyrus Abusir, which describes daily economic activities from the mortuary temple of Neferirkare, a Fifth Dynasty ruler (ca. 2446–2426 B.C.E.) at the region of Abusir (Lower Egypt), and papyrus Boulaq 18, which records 23 days of economic transactions at the Theban residence of the Thirteenth Dynasty ruler Sobekhotep II (ca. 1745 B.C.E.).

Individual economic transactions were recorded on ceramic or stone ostraca (fragments of pottery with inscriptions), such as those from workmen's village at Deir el-Medina, dating to the later New Kingdom. The ostraca include information about the prices of certain commodities. Because of the scanty and personal character of the material, though, important details, such as the date and time of the transactions or description of the traded goods, were often omitted.

In spite of these omissions, useful information concerning the basic principles and values of the ancient Egyptian economic system can be deduced. In many respects, the Egyptian economy showed several differences from our modern perspective, and it was centered on the following three principles: the principle of barter and market exchange, that of redistribution, and that of reciprocity and tributes. Tying these factors together were the centralized state authority (the pharaoh) and the religious institutions.

Price Units

One major difference from our modern economic system was the lack of coinage and true money to store and transport wealth throughout the Pharaonic Period (ca. 3050–712 B.C.E.). The import and use of money were inaugurated toward the first millennium B.C.E. by foreign mercenaries in the armies of the pharaoh. At first the native Egyptians did not recognize the value of coined money, regarding the coins merely as artistic objects in gold or silver, appreciated mainly by the metalworkers.

The Great Harris Papyrus, from Thebes, probably Deir el-Medina, Egypt, during the reign of Ramses IV, around 1200 B.C.E.; the scene is of the king making a donation of goods (including 309,950 sacks of grain and a quantity of metals and semiprecious stone). (© The Trustees of the British Museum)

The Egyptians used four units of measurement to price and trade commodities, the deben, the senyu, the hen, and the khar. These units coincided with quantities of certain commodities: weights of silver and copper or bronze and units of capacity of grain and sesame oil. More specifically, the deben was a measure of weight used mostly for copper but also for other precious material, such as gold and silver. One deben of copper weighed about 3.5 ounces. Silver and gold deben are not mentioned in the ostraca but only in the papyrus records. The ostraca were used and distributed only among the lower-class populace, while the papyri recorded mostly transactions among the high officials and the palace.

The senyu was a weight in silver equal to one-half deben, or 1.75 ounces. Its use was inaugurated during the Nineteenth and early Twentieth Dynasties (ca. 1307–1155 B.C.E.). The senyu could be used to express a value in the same column of figures with the deben. One could find in an ostracon the value of certain objects in senyu but the total of the column in deben of copper.

The hen was a measure of volume equal to half a quart or less. Its value could vary according to the substance or liquid to be measured, but generally it was regarded as equal to one deben. Finally, the khar was a measure of the volume of grain, either emmer (a type of wheat) or barley, equal to about 20 gallons, and it was valued at two deben. The khar was most commonly found as a unit of value for baskets, both because the volume of a basket was equal to its value and because baskets were inexpensive.

The ratios among the four units as well as their exact values are not fixed in the sources. For example, one document values a basket at one-quarter senyu for a volume of one-half khar. Because one khar is valued at two deben, one senyu is worth four copper of deben. In another document, though, one senyu of garment was worth five copper of deben. Weight and price, both expressed in deben, were hardly distinguishable from one another. In the Egyptian mind there was no difference at all, for the deben was not money.

Cases of inflation and price fluctuation have been recorded. Quite often, one deben of silver was valued as 100 deben of copper. This uncertainty in the value system was a strong indication that the Egyptians were not looking for monetary profit in their transactions but only the acquisition of objects. The lack of fixed prices led to the introduction and development of a unique bartering system.

Barter

Acquiring and disposing of goods was done by bargaining on a price. Although there were no fixed prices, ancient Egyptians were fairly consistent in determining how much an item was worth. For everyday goods, like food, clothes, or sandals, the cost would have been one or two deben, but bigger and more valuable items, like animals or territories, would have cost more deben. The objects were traded for goods that were worth the same amount.

Metals were used in exchanges but not as coinage. Their values, equated with their weights, were measured on a balance against stone weights. An example of the bartering method was documented in an ostracon from the village of Deir el-Medina. According to the inscription, one person wanted to buy a wooden coffin, nationally valued at 25 deben of copper. He had to exchange a set of commodities of equal value. These could have included actual copper pieces whose deben value was obtained by direct weighing on scales, various animals such as pigs or goats, or raw materials for coffin construction.

Before deciding whether to barter his product, the coffin maker examined the exchange goods to determine if they met his needs. According to the inscription, the coffin maker valued the exchange items as follows: the copper items for 8.5 and five deben, respectively; one of the offered animals (a pig) with five deben; the other animals (two goats) with three and two deben, respectively; and the two logs of sycamore tree for two deben. In total, the price of the exchanged goods was 25.5 deben, which was slightly more than the assessed value of the coffin. It seemed that this slight difference did not trouble the buyer, because he wanted the coffin and was willing to offer for it the items the seller required.

Evidence of loans has also been recorded in the Egyptian sources. Two types of loans existed: one was made with a fixed date for repayment and a penalty if that day was missed. The second type was based not on a fixed day for repayment but rather on an obligation for reciprocity between the lender and the debtor.

Redistribution and Labor

The land beneficiary and redistribution system was an important component of the ancient Egyptian economy. Under this system, the soil of Egypt was the exclusive property of the king, who could concede it to temple authorities, state officials, or the populace, according to his wish. Priests and high dignitaries were granted the use of land, but the king retained direct ownership. A careful distinction was made between the ownership of the land, a royal prerogative, and the right to gain income from land.

The beneficiary system led to the increase of the temples' territories and wealth, which gradually became hereditary. Control of the land was passed through the priestly offices, which were free from all obligations to the royal administration. It is known that in the time of Ramses III (r. ca. 1194–1163 B.C.E.) the domain of the god Amun in the ancient city of Karnak (South Egypt) controlled well over 900 square miles of usable agricultural land, along with vineyards, gardens, marshlands, quarries, and mines.

Trade relations between temples and religious centers from different regions as well as between temples and their surrounding areas or various state offices are well documented in the surviving sources. A primary source of income for a temple came from renting land to the peasant population. Another source of income was the plunder and foreign tributes the king obtained during his campaigns and delivered to the religious institutions.

Such royal benefits were used for the internal needs of the temple, redistributed in the form of rations, and given as payments for the expenses of the state and the king, in particular. The construction of major works, such as the royal tomb, cenotaph (a commemorative monument), statues, and stelae (commemorative stone pillars), was often accomplished through the wealth of the temples. This particular kind of redistributive economy flourished especially during the New Kingdom. The economic growth of the temples rendered them intermediaries between the central and local administrations. During the periods when royal power was in decline, the temples and their representatives became substitutes for the political authorities.

The redistributed economic practice was not confined to interactions between the state and the clergy. It also defined the pharaoh's working and compensational policy toward the state's workforce. The following working classes could be traced in the Egyptian socioeconomic system: scribes, administrators, officials, craftsmen, agricultural laborers, and slaves.

The first three classes were literate and formed the elite of Egyptian society. The educational institutes provided the state, temples, and administrative offices with their personnel. Scribes could also work outside large offices for high officials and state stewards. The lower level of scribes and officials may have been given a wage (in the form of various commodities, such as copper or grain) in addition to their rations, while the upper ranks lived on the rents collected from endowment lands attached to their positions. Craftsmen earned income by selling their crafts to provide tombs and mortuary temples with artifacts and artwork. Most of these items were made in small, organized workshops attached to the palaces, mortuary complexes, temples, or offices of the elite. Independent craft work was done as well; many tomb representations depict people making craft transactions in markets, an indication of the independent function of this class of labor.

The largest percentage of the Egyptian workforce was made up of farmers, usually under the directorship of a landlord and organized into households or small groups. Either they rented land from the state or priestly authorities, or land was rewarded to them through the economic principles of redistribution and reciprocation. Taxes were calculated based on their annual production. With larger estates, the owner or lessor of the land provided a large number of workers to farm the land together. These laborers were mostly soldiers or slaves who had been captured in war or during foreign campaigns abroad.

This brings us to the final working class, that of slaves. In ancient Egypt this class did not include only the stereotype of the foreigner but also everybody who was under the rulership of a superior being, divine or human. Thus, a nobleman was the slave of a lord or high official, a farmer was the slave of his landlord, and a priest was the slave of his local god. Even the pharaoh was regarded as the slave or servant of god. Slave dealing was done on a personal level, not in public or open markets. The transactions, though, had to be performed in the presence of a royal official or the local council.

Markets

The temple or political offices allocated the soil production and commodities to the populace according to each individual's needs. Surplus together with local food and homemade items could be traded at local markets. These were usually built close to road intersections or on riverbanks near harbors. The most commonly traded goods were bread, beer, fresh and dried fish, meat, and vegetables. The last two were probably surplus from the offerings to the priests in the mortuary and religious temples. Luxury goods were rarely traded in the markets. Common items offered for exchange included leather sandals, pieces of furniture, and ceramics.

Prices in the market were determined by supply and demand, though prices were sometimes fixed. State representatives supervised the prices and organization of the markets. They were also responsible for preventing raw materials and goods, which were the property of the state, from being diverted to illegal trading markets ("black markets") and for protecting customers from being cheated.

Taxation

The system of benefits and land bestowment on institutions and individuals brought to the state a great deal of income in the form of taxes, which might have included a share in the produce of the land, cattle and other products, human labor, and wealth. Temples, foreign settlements, and garrisons were major beneficiaries of tax revenues generated by the annual levy during the New Kingdom. Evidence for taxation covers the whole period of the ancient Egyptian civilization and comes from administration texts, letters, and tomb scenes.

The taxes were received in kind by the chancellor in charge of the treasuries of Upper and Lower Egypt. Taxes in grain were collected by the pharaoh's so-called overseer of the granary. Redistribution of tax revenues to their beneficiaries was handled by the palace's master of largesse. Agricultural and land taxes were estimated after the land production was measured by surveyors in the company of scribes and an inspector.

Corruption or failure in tax collection led to severe punishment. A distinctive scene in the tomb of the vizier Khentika of the Sixth Dynasty (2323–2150 B.C.E.) depicts the judgment and corporal punishment of five district governors brought before the vizier and charged with corruption in tax collection. Within the royal decrees enacted by the king Horemheb of the Eighteenth Dynasty (r. 1319–1307) is a series of laws for addressing specific abuses on the part of governmental officials and soldiers who denied their responsibility in giving taxes to the state. There were also cases of district mayors and officials who formally complained about the taxes for which they were held liable.

Foreign lands were also obliged to contribute to the annual levy if they were regarded as proper Egyptian cities after their conquest or surrender to the Egyptian authorities. They paid their taxes through gifts or tributes to the pharaoh and the state, which might consist of precious metals (gold, silver, lapis lazuli), chariots, horses, cattle, and people to labor as servants or serfs.

Reciprocity and Foreign Tributes

One characteristic aspect of the trade economy in ancient Egypt was the gift exchange. It existed in two forms: as gifts between the king and his populace and as diplomatic tributes from allies and foreign parties to the pharaoh and the Egyptian state, especially during the Middle Kingdom (ca. 2040–1640 B.C.E.) and New Kingdom (ca. 1550–1070 B.C.E.).

Donations from the Egyptian populace to the pharaoh were conceived as tributes to both the divine and political status of the king. The Egyptians offered precious objects and commodities to receive internal peace and stability from the king. This practice can be traced as far back as the Old Kingdom. For example, in the step pyramid of the king Djoser (ca. 2630–ca. 2611 B.C.E.) at Saqqara—the first monumental structure constructed exclusively from stone—several inscribed jars were found that attested to the continued practice of giving gifts to the king. Gift giving has been recorded in account papyri from the mortuary temple of the pharaoh Sesostris II (ca. 1897–ca. 1878 B.C.E.) at el-Lahun, as well as from the papyrus Abusir and historical texts from the New Kingdom.

The gift exchange was reciprocal. The king honored the offerings and repaid the donors with equally valuable gifts. For example, one Egyptian source refers to the king's gifts to his liegemen and locates the ritual at which they were distributed at the forecourt of the palace. Diplomatic gifts were offered to the pharaoh from foreign rulers as evidence of existing or prospective allies. A diplomatic gift tended to convey social connotations rather than economic value. It was received with special care by the Egyptian authorities on a specific day of the year, and the whole process was ritualized and closely connected with the celebration of the New Year's festival. The first evidence of such foreign "tribute scenes" is recorded on the walls of the funerary complex of Khnumhotep, a monarch in the region of Beni Hasan (Lower Egypt) at the beginning of the second millennium B.C.E. A caravan of Levantine men and women are shown offering to the pharaoh a special lead ore that was used by the Egyptians as eye paint.

The custom of the diplomatic gift reached its peak during the New Kingdom, when the foreign expeditions of the pharaohs led to increasing contacts with foreign lands, from Libya in the west to Nubia in the south and territories in the Near East. This aspect of economic practice is best documented in the royal correspondence between the Egyptian king and the rulers of the Near East, the so-called Amarna Letters. These are clay tablets that were found in the city of Tel el-Amarna (Upper Egypt), the ancient site of the palace of King Amenhotep IV (better known as Akhenaten). The collection consists of about 350 letters from the mid-14th century B.C.E. between the Egyptian state of the Eighteenth Dynasty and the rulers of the ancient territories in the Near East. The clay letters were inscribed in cuneiform script—the writing system used throughout western Asia at the time—and mostly in the language of Akkadian (Babylonian), the common language of international relations. The correspondence dealt with a variety of issues: alliance, strategic cases, trade, dynastic marriage, foreign gifts and tributes, quarrels between vassals, and legal and diplomatic issues.

Foreign tributes could include precious items or commodities that could not be found in the Egyptian territory. They were not just economic transactions but had diplomatic connotations, where the pharaoh was acclaimed as the major delineator of the action on behalf of the Egyptian society and in a superior position to the foreign representatives. In many cases these foreign tributes were combined with diplomatic marriages between members of the foreign and Egyptian courts. Thus, in Amarna Letter 22, the king of the Near Eastern kingdom of Mittani, Tushratta, gave his daughter to the king of Egypt to be his wife, together with precious gifts and various commodities.

THE MIDDLE EAST

BY JAMES A. CORRICK

There was no one single economy in the ancient Near East. Still, there were several factors that were commonplace. For the most part Near Eastern societies were agricultural in nature, and thus the growing of crops and the raising of animals were important economic activities. Equally common were other economic elements such as taxation, trade, and tribute from war. Prior to the fourth millennium B.C.E., however, except for agriculture, other economic pursuits were of little importance, as small farming communities were fairly self-sufficient, with their residents providing most of what they needed themselves. With the appearance of the first cities, more complex economies emerged.

Sumer

Around 3500 B.C.E. southern Mesopotamia came under the control of the Sumerians and became the site of several independent city-states, the largest being Uruk. Each of these Sumerian states had a distributive economy, one in which a central authority collected food and other goods, stored these collections, and then redistributed them according to the people's social positions or needs. The collection of food and goods was a form of taxation. In each Sumerian city administrators—priests and bureaucrats—required that each household pay this tax. Accordingly, part of what a household (which could be either a nuclear or extended family) grew, raised, or made was turned over to the city's temple and its palace, the headquarters of the secular authorities. Sumerians paid taxes on their crops and livestock, on boats they owned, on fish they caught, and even on burials of the dead. Merchants also paid import and export duties. Sumerians, however, did not pay their taxes with money, because currency did not exist anywhere in the ancient Near East until the invention of coinage in the sixth century B.C.E. Instead, taxpayers brought to the temple and palace animals, grain, dates, pottery, and cloth, among other items. Such payment is known as payment in kind.

The tax was a payment for the privilege of working the land, which belonged to the god or goddess of the city (each urban center being the home of specific deity). The representatives of the local god or goddess were the city's ruler, its priests, and its palace authorities. Although private ownership of land did exist, many of the fields and pastures were in the hands of the temple and the palace. Both the religious and secular authorities increased their holdings by purchasing land or by confiscating it from those who failed to pay their taxes.

By around 3000 B.C.E. an established system of distribution existed in the city-states of Sumer. As goods came into temples and palaces, they were placed in jars, baskets, or rooms, to which were affixed clay seals. Records of amounts were kept by placing clay counters or tokens into spherical clay containers, known as bullae, much as paper records today are placed in file folders. With the invention of writing at the end of the fourth millennium, a written record of the content of each bulla was incised or impressed onto its surface. Eventually, the written record, incised on a clay tablet, replaced the bullae.

Sumerian priests and palace officials oversaw the use to which the food and goods collected as tax were put. Some of the yield was stockpiled for times of famine, while some was reserved as seed for the next year's crop. A portion of the tax was used as offerings in religious ritual. Taxes also went toward financing the construction and maintenance of irrigation canals and public buildings. They paid for wars, which in turn brought back booty and tribute as additional revenues for each Sumerian city-state.

Additionally, some of the goods were used for trade, an important part of the economy of each Sumerian city-state. Food, which was sent to other, less productive regions of the Near East; pottery; and textiles were all important trade goods. In exchange, the Sumerian cities received stone and timber for building and metal for tools and weapons, as well as jewelry, perfumes, exotic animals, and other luxury items that became part of the personal wealth of religious and government officials or were given out as gifts to others to buy their support.

Finally, although many of the city's households produced enough food, clothing, and other goods to feed their members even after paying their taxes, others did not and depended on the collected tax to meet their needs. Among those dependent upon tax stores were a city-state's ruler, its priests and priestesses, and its government bureaucrats, along with their families. Others were craftspeople who produced

Mesopotamian stone vase dating to the late fourth millennium B.C.E, depicting animals of the first city dwellers of Mesopotamia; cattle and sheep were an important part of the economy. (© The Trustees of the British Museum)

cloth, pottery, and metal tools and weapons. The tax freed both the Sumerian elite and the craftspeople from the necessity of providing for at least some of their own needs and thus gave them the time to perform their duties and work.

Payment in kind was not the only method of settling a tax bill in ancient Sumer. There was also a labor tax. Known in modern times as a corvée, the labor obligation meant that the members of a household had to work a certain number of days in the fields controlled by its temple and palace, in digging or cleaning out irrigation canals, and in constructing public buildings. Of all the taxes, the corvée was the most burdensome. Farmers found themselves bringing in the harvest of the temple and the palace while their own crops languished in the fields. Worse still was military service that sometimes sent men away from their farms for months at a time, sometimes never to return if they were killed in battle.

Women and children, on the other hand, were employed in large weaving factories, in addition to performing agricultural labor. Textiles were a Sumerian economic mainstay, used for gifts, religious offerings, and trade items. Thus hundreds and sometimes thousands of women and children in each city-state plucked the wool from sheep and spun it, wove it, and washed the final cloth product. Women were also responsible for brewing beer from stores of grain.

The Sumerian tax burden had the beneficial effect of improving production efficiency so that the number of items a worker could produce increased. For instance, in order to turn out more ceramic bowls and pots faster, craftspeople moved from forming pottery solely by hand to using molds and potter's wheels. The rise of centers that specialized in making particular goods, such as pottery, metals, or textiles, contributed to increased production efficiency. Such centers, for example, appeared toward the end of the fourth millennium B.C.E. in the southern city-state of Uruk. To what extent these centers were set up and run by the priests and bureaucrats remains unknown. It is possible that the centers came into existence not because of official sponsorship but because they were located in areas that, unlike other regions, had access to the resources necessary for the items they produced.

By the middle of the third millennium B.C.E. the distributive economy of the Sumerian city-states centered on the great household, often referred to by the Greek term *oikos.* A great household could be a temple, a palace, or a large, wealthy estate. Each *oikos* controlled the production, labor, and consumption of its members, who unlike those of the traditional small household were not kinfolk. Small kin-based households still existed, but most of the economic activity was now in the hands of the *oikoi.*

The head of an *oikos* could be a man or a woman. These *oikoi* leaders were among the highest-ranking members of Sumerian society, and thus Sumerian kings and queens headed their own *oikoi,* as did prominent government officials and wealthy merchants. Each *oikos* had its own fields, pastures, herds, orchards, workshops, and storage depots. Each also had managers and a labor force. The latter were recruited from the large pool of city residents; by the third millennium B.C.E. some 80 percent of southern Mesopotamians are estimated to have lived in the cities. *Oikos* laborers were often specialists—farmhands, animal handlers, cooks, gardeners, brewers, potters, weavers, and metalworkers. With such material and human resources, an *oikos* was able to meet most of the needs of its members.

In exchange for this labor the *oikos* provided its members with certain basics—oil, beer, wool, and flour and, on special occasions, milk, fruit, salt, and fish. Age, gender, and the type of work determined how much an *oikos* member received. Generally, *oikos* members had to process these distributions further: thus they had to make the flour into bread and the wool into cloth. Each *oikos* also gave out plots of land to its highest-ranking members; the higher the rank, the larger the land grant. Among those eligible for land were political leaders, priests and priestesses, scribes, canal inspectors, managers, soldiers, and skilled artisans. In addition to these grants, an *oikos* also rented out land to nonmembers of the household for a share of the plot's crops.

The Spread of the Sumerian Economic System

The Sumerian city-states were not the only ancient Near Eastern societies to have a distributive economy, payment in kind, and a corvée. Indeed, by the early third millennium B.C.E. such were to be found in the growing urban centers of northern Mesopotamia and the Levant. To what extent these economic forms existing elsewhere in the region were due to other peoples having independently developed them and to what extent they were imported from Sumer is unclear. However, Sumerian traders, sometimes living in colonies next to other Near Eastern cities, had business connections throughout much of the region. It is certainly possible that these traders brought with them Sumerian economic concepts.

Another method for the export of the Sumerian economic system may have been conquest. In the early 24th century B.C.E. Sargon the Great created the Akkadian Empire, which he would rule for almost half a century. Under Sargon and his successors the empire incorporated the Sumerian city-states, northern Mesopotamia, Elam, and Armenia. The distributive economy of Sumer was already present in northern Mesopotamian cities. It may also have developed previous to conquest in such Elamite cities as Susa or been brought to the region by the Akkadians. The economy of Armenia at this time is unknown, but the later Armenia-based society of Urartu possibly had a distributive economy.

The Akkadians

The Akkadian rulers did not change the local economies of their subject cities. Instead, they required the payment of tribute, with each conquered city having to send a portion of its collected food and goods to the imperial capital of Agade in northern Mesopotamia. The collection of tribute was already an old idea by the time of the Akkadian Empire. Among the Sumerians, after a successful war against an enemy city, a victorious king brought back rich loot and later received tribute from the conquered. The king added this newfound wealth to the palace treasury, sharing some of it with high-ranking military officers and bureaucrats. Some of it was also presented to the city temple. Trade, another important part of the state income, also benefited from such conquest, as traders soon arrived to claim a piece of the city's increased prosperity, and taxes on their operations also enriched the city. Where in Sumer conquest was generally modest, often with only one city dominating another, and short-lived, frequently in terms of years, the Akkadian Empire held an extensive territory for a century and a half.

In order to manage the finances of the empire, the Akkadians introduced a common accounting practice in all their conquered territories. Accounting had to be done using the same cuneiform signs and tablets having the same shape and layout. Additionally, since payment was in kind, the Akkadians standardized weights and measures by introducing the gur. One gur was equal to about 43 gallons of barley. Valuing goods by comparing them to a quantity of barley, the most common grain that was grown in Mesopotamia, had been a longtime practice of the Sumerians. The gur would continue to be used, at least in Mesopotamia, for the next two millennia.

The Akkadians were succeeded by other states, such as the Third Dynasty of Ur and the Old Babylonian kingdom, who each in turn ruled much of Mesopotamia, north and south. No matter the state, the old Sumerian distributive economy remained in place in each Mesopotamian city. Payment in kind likewise survived, though it was supplemented by occasional payments in silver; along with weights of barley, weights of silver were used to determine the value of goods. The corvée still operated, though labor obligations were eased by the presence of slaves, who were either those captured in war or those enslaved when they failed to meet their tax payments. The *oikoi* continued to be the managers of at least local economies.

The Hittites

To the north of Mesopotamia were Anatolia and the Hittites, who appeared around 1800 B.C.E. and lasted until around 1200 B.C.E. Beginning in about 1650 B.C.E. the Hittite kingdom expanded from its central Anatolian homeland to conquer all of Anatolia, including Armenia in the west and part of the Levant. Unlike the Mesopotamians, the Hittites had few cities, and their domestic economy revolved around small, self-sufficient farming communities that provided most of their own needs and owned all farmland in common. Hittite agriculture, however, did not produce surpluses; indeed, the Hittites often had food shortages, which they made up either through tribute collected from those that they had conquered or through trade.

If the Hittites did not have food to trade, they did have metals. Mining of tin, silver, and iron were lucrative. Tin was important in the manufacture of bronze, and thus there was always a ready market for it. Enough silver was produced that the Hittites used it as a medium of exchange. Iron was a novelty item because it was almost as rare as gold, whose only source at this time was Egypt. Iron was also more for show than utility. Weapons and tools made from it at this period were no stronger than those made from bronze, and thus it was more often used to make jewelry and statutes, both of which were prized trade goods.

The Hittites acquired copper for manufacturing bronze in the same way that they acquired many of their resources: They conquered those who had it, in this case Isuwa in western Anatolia, Maintaining the army was a major expense for the Hittites, but as with other military states, an army allowed the Hittite kingdom to bring in loot from successful campaigns and to ensure that those conquered paid regular tribute, either in silver or as payment in kind. Additionally, the army could protect essential Hittite trade routes from others who might try to charge Hittite merchants a toll for use of these routes. Instead, any tolls exacted were collected by the Hittite kingdom.

Urartu

The waning of the Hittites around 1200 B.C.E. saw the emergence in Armenia of the kingdom of Urartu, which reached its height during the eighth century B.C.E. Like other ancient Near Eastern societies, Urartu had an economy that depended on agricultural production, with part of the harvest from its rich farmlands going to trade. Additionally, the mining and export of copper, silver, and iron was an essential part of the Urartu economy. Besides unworked metal, Urartu traded metal tools, weapons, and jewelry, which were esteemed for their craftsmanship as far away as northern Italy. The kingdom's economy also benefited from its geographic position, which allowed it to control the trade routes that connected northern Mesopotamia and Elam to the Mediterranean. Urartu exacted a toll in payment of kind from the traders who used these routes.

Urartu may have had a distributive economy, since its administration centers, fortresses located in a mountainous region of the kingdom, held large storage facilities for grain and wine. Conversely, rather than being redistributed, these stored goods may have been meant to feed the inhabitants of a fortress during the occasional siege by Urartu enemies. The kingdom also probably had a labor tax, since it undertook the construction of aqueducts and other large works projects using workforces, most likely made up of corvée draftees.

The Assyrians

The most persistent attackers of the Urartu mountain fortresses were the Assyrians, for whom loot and tribute played an extremely important role in the economy. From their northern Mesopotamian home the Assyrians conquered the remainder of Mesopotamia and much of the Near East in the 11th century B.C.E. For 400 years they would exact tribute from their subject peoples. Like previous conquerors, the Assyrians appear to have left much of the economic structure of their conquests in place, demanding an annual tribute, which was paid in silver or in kind and which was sent to the Assyrian capital. In some cases the collection of the tribute was in the hands of a native ruling family; the Assyrians then sent expeditions to bring the tribute to Assyria. In other instances, perhaps where the original ruling family proved resistant to paying the tribute, the Assyrians placed one of their own in charge. This governor then saw to the collection and delivery of the tribute.

Trade also was important to Assyria and may have dictated some of its expansion. More directly, through military control of much of the Near East, Assyria controlled almost all the trade routes and thus the flow of the majority of Near Eastern trade. It thus had ready access to copper, silver, wood, and other valuable resources as well as much of the luxury trade enjoyed by the Phoenician cities, which paid Assyria a handsome tribute. Proceeds from tribute and trade had to be large in order to make up for the Assyrian policy of exempting from taxation their home cities, such as Nineveh. The corvée also did not apply to the Assyrian homeland. Instead, conquered cities had to supply laborers when required as well as soldiers for the army.

The Phoenicians

Among the most lucrative tributes collected by the Assyrians was that from the Phoenician city-states, such as Tyre, Sidon, Byblos, and Arvad. Of all the ancient Near Eastern economies, that of the Phoenicians was the most dominated by trade. The stretch of the Levant coast on which the Phoenicians lived was narrow, mountains rising not far inland. Thus there was little arable land for agriculture. Importing food became a top priority of the Phoenicians in order to sustain the populations of their cities.

With several natural ports, which became the sites of their cities, and an abundance of cedar and other trees for lumber, the Phoenicians began seafaring early. With their freedom from Egyptian rule in the 12th century, they built one of the largest trading empires in history over the next five centuries. Their goods were shipped all over the Mediterranean and even into the Atlantic to the Canary Islands and Britain. To what extent these commercial ventures were private enterprises and or were state-financed is unknown. Luxury items, such as jewelry, fine cloth, and perfumes, were among their trade items, but the most highly prized were metals. Thus they brought copper from Cyprus, iron from Crete, gold and lead from Morocco, and possibly tin from Britain. All of these imports were used in trade for food and other goods, many of which were traded in their turn.

Around 950 B.C.E. Tyre bought a large agricultural area from Israel, freeing the Phoenician city from having to import food. As a result, Tyre could use its full range of trading stock to enrich itself. It quickly became the wealthiest of the Phoenician city-states and, indeed, one of the wealthiest cities in the ancient Near East. The collapse of the Assyrian state around 600 B.C.E. freed the Phoenician city-states from having to pay tribute. The respite was temporary, for within a century the Phoenicians found themselves paying tribute to a new state, Persia.

The Persians

In the early sixth century B.C.E., under the Achaemenid Dynasty, Persia subjugated an even larger area than the Assyrians, ruling over the region from Asia Minor and the Mediterranean to India. Initially, as with the Assyrians, local economic institutions of the Persian Near East remained unchanged. Indeed, in Mesopotamia, for example, the distributive economy remained unchanged, and the labor tax remained in force; likewise, the Phoenician city-states continued their profitable trading. Throughout the entire Persian domain, payment in kind for taxes continued, even though currency in the form of coinage began to appear.

The Achaemenids divided their empire into provinces, called *satrapies*. The governor (satrap) of each was responsible for collecting taxes, some of which were sent to the Achaemenid capitals (Susa, Ecbatana, and Persepolis) as tribute. The tribute payment was partially in silver and partially in kind and was calculated on the basis of the affluence of the people and the agricultural yield of each satrapy. During the reign of Xerxes I (519–465 B.C.E.), for instance, the eastern satrapy of Media was assessed a tribute of 100,000 sheep in addition to a large sum of silver. The province also had to provide enough pasture for 50,000 royal horses. The king exempted the Persian heartland from this taxation, although Persians, like residents in the satrapies, were subject to a military corvée.

Trade was also an important part of the Persian economy, and since the state contained many important trade routes, the Persians controlled much of Near Eastern trade. To make it easier for traders and their goods to move along these routes, the Persian king Darius I (r. 522–486 B.C.E.) improved the roads by straightening and maintaining them, thus increasing the amount of trade traffic. He also posted soldiers along the roads to deter bandits who preyed on trade caravans.

Agriculture saw innovations that increased productivity and thus brought in more taxes to the royal treasury. The construction of underground channels brought water from the mountains to dry regions, thus enlarging the amount of arable land. Rice, imported from India, was planted in wet areas that previously had not been usable for agriculture.

Another important economic innovation during the sixth and fifth centuries B.C.E. was banking, which now appeared for the first time in the Near East. Two banking houses, Egibi and Sons and Murashu and Sons, operated in Babylonia at this time. These and other banks extended credit in the form of loans to individuals and to businesses that needed capital to pay taxes or to finance new commercial enterprises. Loans per se were nothing new. In both northern and southern Mesopotamia, *oikoi*, particularly temples, had always loaned barley, dates, or other food to their own members when necessary. The borrower would then repay the loan in kind at the next harvest. Most of these loans had no interest, though if a borrower failed to repay a loan, the lender might add a penalty of up to 25 percent to the loan.

The banks that appeared in the Persian-controlled Near East were private organizations that operated as profit-making businesses. They not only issued loans but also engaged in real estate transactions and underwrote promising business ventures. Still, loans were at the heart of this banking business, and these loans often carried high interest rates, sometimes 20 percent a month. With such high interest, the amount of a debt could rise quickly beyond an individual's ability to repay. When a borrower defaulted on a loan, a lender could take possession of the person's property. The banker could also seize the borrower and sometimes his or her family and sell them into slavery to help recoup the loan.

Loans became a necessity for many under Xerxes I, who raised taxes steeply. The Persian king also demanded that more of each year's tribute be paid not in kind but in gold and silver. The result of these royal measures was that merchants and landowners had to take out loans to pay their taxes. Often, in order to pay the exorbitant interest rates, borrowers had to allow lenders the right to work their land or run their businesses. It was then the lenders who reaped the profits and often gained possession of their clients' assets.

With the conquest of Persia by Alexander the Great (356–323 B.C.E.), Near Eastern economies, especially those along the Mediterranean coast, came increasingly under the influence of first the Greeks and eventually the Romans. But through the last centuries B.C.E. and the first centuries C.E. ancient Near

Eastern economies retained much that had emerged from the Sumerian cities of the fourth millennium B.C.E.

ASIA AND THE PACIFIC

BY KIRK H. BEETZ

A lack of written records makes it difficult to characterize the economies of ancient Asia and the Pacific. Writing arrived late in Oceania, in many areas not until the arrival of Europeans in the 18th and 19th centuries. Japan did not begin keeping written records until the 600s C.E. In China before the Han Dynasty (202 B.C.E.–220 C.E.) merchants and shopkeepers were considered insignificant people unworthy of including in government records, and the emperor Qin Shi Huangdi tried to have all historical records of China destroyed during his reign (221–210 B.C.E.) in order to have all history begin with him. The lot of peasants was of little concern to record keepers so long as they paid their taxes and served their overlords. In India records are confused before the Maurya Dynasty (321–185 B.C.E.) because the written language of the earliest civilization, the Harappan (ca. 2600–1500 B.C.E.), has yet to be translated, and the records of the succeeding Vedic culture were mostly oral tales; modern historians are still trying to sort out who ruled when and rely mostly on archaeological evidence for information about economic development.

People throughout eastern Asia, southern Asia, and the Pacific were originally hunter-gatherers; the rain forests of southern Asia offered plenty to eat. In Australia the climate was mostly dry, but hunter-gatherers found animals to eat. In the plains of northern China and Mongolia finding food became increasingly tough because the land was becoming desert. Nonetheless, prior to the introduction of agriculture, people could hunt big animals such as horses and deer; in Siberia people took to following reindeer herds on their migrations. These ancient peoples traded with one another, with seashells being traded to inland tribes and stone tools coming from central Asia. This trade resulted in the development of a new kind of economy, one in which people could acquire goods beyond their day-to-day needs as well as tools that would enable them to create more sophisticated products for use in their own societies and in further trade.

The seashells became particularly important for economic development, because some kinds became money that could be exchanged for goods or services. In China and India this was the beginning of the cash economies that would eventually make them the economic giants of ancient eastern Asia. There was not a big leap from bartering goods to using money. Instead, the shift was gradual, and bartering never entirely disappeared, especially in rural areas. In China government officials kept track of the use of barter, using its frequency as a sign of the health of the national and local economy: The more bartering, the less healthy the economy. Thus, Han Dynasty officials were alarmed when peasants shifted away from using coins to bartering in the first century C.E.

Bronze cast coin, Maurya Empire (which at its peak stretched from Kabul in Afghanistan to Nellore, near Madras, in southern India), third century B.C.E.; the Maurya Dynasty opened extensive foreign trade routes. (© The Trustees of the British Museum)

The first significant civilizations of Asia and the Pacific had agricultural economies. An agricultural economy is one in which the wealth of the nation depends on the productivity of farming. Agriculture began in eastern Asia around 6500 B.C.E. In the Yellow River region people began growing millet. Those people sometimes grew surpluses that they could trade for goods, thus raising their standard of living through being able to own more goods than could hunter-gatherers. In this way, some people gained more wealth than others and contributed to the development of upper and lower classes in society. Exactly when the ability to trade surpluses for wealth resulted in a shift to a full cash economy is not as yet known, but archaeological evidence from Chinese Shang Dynasty (1500–1045 B.C.E.) sites indicates that it had developed a strong cash economy. It was possible for people to build factories for manufacturing metal goods and pottery, to pay workers with coins, and to sell products for coins. This development gave the Shang a more efficient economy than one based entirely on barter, which was an advantage in its competition for power with its neighbors.

SHANG DYNASTY

An economy that depends for its wealth on products manufactured in factories is called an industrial economy. In Shang China were the beginnings of industry focused on the mass production of household goods and tools, but it nonetheless still depended on agriculture for most of its wealth. The center of the early Chinese economy was the Yellow River, where the Shang Dynasty was founded. Archaeological evidence is only beginning to reveal what economic life was like before the Shang. The people of the Yellow River were farmers. To their north were nomadic hunter-gatherers; to the south was the Yangtze River basin, where people grew rice; and farther south were people who lived in vast forests. The Yellow River people had begun farming in about 5800 B.C.E., several hundred years after rice was cultivated near the Yangtze. Instead of rice, they cultivated cereals such as millet.

The Yellow River people were actually several different cultures when the Shang united them through military conquest. The Shang Dynasty was warlike, and its economy grew in part because of the booty it acquired through conquest, moving mostly westward and northward. The peasants were the mainstay of the economy, because agriculture was still the primary source of wealth, and nearly everyone was a peasant. At first peasants owned their own land and were expected to give their loyalty to whoever was king. Almost nothing was recorded of their lives; their purpose was to serve the nobility. They formed the bulk of ancient Chinese armies and sometimes were killed in such huge numbers that the Chinese economy almost certainly was affected by the loss of food production.

Trade with the outside world was limited. There must have been some, because the techniques for casting bronze and manufacturing iron came from the west via trade routes through northern India. There may have been merchants and shopkeepers, but in the Shang world they were valued even less than peasants.

Zhou Dynasty

In 1027 the king of Zhou in western China overthrew the Shang king, beginning the Zhou Dynasty (1045–256 B.C.E.). As in the Shang Dynasty, peasants accounted for nearly all of China's population, and growth in the economy was fueled primarily by conquest. Merchants and shopkeepers counted for little more than they had during the Shang era, and their activities were little recorded. Potters and metalworkers seem to have been important, and they sometimes had homes nearly as fine as those owned by nobles. Depending on the wishes of the current king and immediate overlord, peasants alternately owned their lands and had their lands taken from them.

The remains of Zhou arts and crafts indicate that they developed a strong enough economy that even poor people could exchange their extra goods for small luxuries. An excavation of the city of Jin revealed a large bronze-working complex from about 450 B.C.E. It had smelting furnaces and 30,000 clay-casting molds. At Xinglong in Hebei Province a 36,000-square-yard factory for manufacturing iron farm tools has been discovered. These sites suggest that some Zhou people were able to specialize in the manufacturing of a particular kind of product and could exchange it for food, clothing, and housing without actually growing the food, making the clothes, or constructing the housing themselves. Goods owned by the small ruling class of royalty and nobles were elaborately decorated, indicating that there were craftspeople who survived by providing finely crafted products to the wealthy, but even ordinary pots owned by peasants had some decoration to make them pleasing to the eye or to endow them with magical properties. This suggests that the peasants lived slightly more prosperous lives than they had under the Shang.

The Zhou monarchs created a feudal society; they appointed nobles to rule provinces, and the nobles swore loyalty to the king. This meant that individual provinces could vary considerably from one another in economic prosperity and the way in which they treated the people responsible for keeping the economy running: the peasants and tradespeople. In 770 B.C.E. the Zhou monarch moved his capital from the city of Xian in the far western province of Qin to Luoyang in the province of Zhou to be farther away from marauding barbarians. For this reason, the Zhou Dynasty's prestige fell so much that the nobles in the various provinces began vying for control of the country. Eventually the nation fell into ceaseless war among its provinces. This is often called the Warring States Period (4453–221 B.C.E.), during which the king had little power. At this time coins circulated widely enough to shift the economy from primarily one in which goods were bartered to one in which most goods were exchanged for money, resulting in a full-fledged cash economy.

Qin Shi Huangdi

In about 228 B.C.E. an especially brutal but clever warlord, King Zheng of the state of Qin, began a war of conquest against the other Chinese nobles. He was able to do so in part because the economy of his province was stronger than elsewhere and its food production was high. He called himself Shi Huangdi. His political philosophy was called legalist, and it meant that everybody and everything should be governed by a mercilessly strict rule of law in which anyone could be punished, no matter what his or her social status. The laws were so numerous and confusing that almost everyone broke several of them without knowing, and commoners convicted of even petty crimes were sent to work themselves to death on the Great Wall in northern China.

He founded the Qin Dynasty (221–207 B.C.E.). This dynasty expanded trade with central Asia and India. To boost the economy of the nation, the Qin Dynasty also standardized China's currency, which made trade between different regions easier. In this way the economy became more efficient, which allowed wealth to accumulate faster. In 210 B.C.E. China's weights and measures were standardized as well; consumers' trust grew, and both merchants and the government could keep track of what goods were selling well and exactly how much was being paid for goods anywhere in the country. The Qin Dynasty also improved its bureaucracy for collecting taxes, keeping better records of what was paid. With standardized weights and coins, paying taxes became simpler, but the emperor's high taxes drove peasants and craftspeople into abject poverty.

Han Dynasty

So deep was the hatred for the Qin Dynasty that when it was overthrown in 206 B.C.E. every member of the emperor's family was murdered. Of the warlords who remained, a particularly able soldier named Liu Bang defeated his rivals and established the Han Dynasty. As emperor, he was known as Gaozu. Perhaps the most immediate effect on the economy came from the lowering of taxes. Taxation had to be fair, according to the government's Confucian philosophy, and lowering taxes gave millions of Chinese the chance to improve their lives by investing money left over after paying taxes and purchasing their basic needs. This investing of money allowed people to pull their cash to develop business ventures jointly, which enabled those who could not have done so in the past to engage in trade with the world outside China.

This expansion of the Chinese economy had an effect on its neighbors, especially Japan. The merchants of the Han Dynasty pioneered sea routes, venturing along Asia's east coast; Chinese pottery was in especially high demand in the emerging civilizations to the south. To Japan, Han merchants brought silk, rice, iron, and bronze. By 200 C.E. the Japanese had become trading partners with China, exporting a high grade of silk coveted by Chinese merchants. Chinese copper coins became the only accepted money in Japan, aiding Japan's slow development toward a cash economy. In exchange for copper coins sent by China's emperor, Japanese rulers sent back tribute.

Foreign tribute was a complicated business in China; nearby foreign governments were often happy to give it to China because the Chinese government gave them valuable prestige by formally recognizing them. Furthermore, the Han custom was to send gifts back to those who sent tribute, sometimes of greater value than the original tribute. These gifts not only showed off China's economic prosperity but also encouraged local rulers to open their lands to Chinese traders. This began the great age of the Silk Road.

Silk Road

During the early Han Dynasty in northern China a nomadic tribe called the Xiongnu constantly conducted raids. The Xiongnu drove another tribe, the Yuezhi, westward and settled on China's main trade route to central Asia. In about 138 B.C.E. the Chinese emissary Zhang Qian was sent to sneak through Xiongnu territory to find the Yuezhi and form an alliance against the Xiongnu. He failed in this, but he returned to China in 126 B.C.E. with information about territories to the west. He also brought back grapevines and alfalfa.

Trading through central Asia was an important way to keep China's economy growing and healthy, by providing markets for Chinese goods. Furthermore, consumers in China were demanding foreign goods, putting pressure on the government to make trade routes secure. Using Zhang Qian's information, the Hans attacked the Xiongnu and drove them into central Asia. They continued into central Asia, where the local kingdoms were forced to agree to pay tribute to the Chinese emperor. This secured China's access to the Silk Road, which was actually several different routes that began in the city of Chang'an (now called Xi'an) in western China. These routes went through Persia to the city of Baghdad; from there the routes went to Syria and then to Mediterranean ports from which Chinese goods were shipped to southern Europe and North Africa. An important alternative route went down the Indus River and then westward by sea. The first major Chinese caravan reached Persia in 106 B.C.E.

China imported wine, which was very popular, from the Near East and Europe. Foods imported from the west included figs and cucumbers, as well as sesame and safflower oils, which were used in cooking. Roman technology went east as well, including an improved potter's wheel for the manufacturing of ceramics. China exported peaches, apricots, ginger, and basil. China also exported silk cloth, which was held in high value; the Chinese carefully guarded the secret of the making of silk. Chinese merchants brought home piles of Roman coins, and Roman leaders worried that all their gold was going to China and India.

Under the Han Dynasty ordinary Chinese prospered as they had never done before. Not only could peasants and the working poor afford metal pots and pans for their cooking, they could also purchase a varied diet of foods. Wheat and barley cakes became common. Peaches, plums, melons, onions, turnips, yams, and beans were part of the everyday diet. Spices such as basil and ginger were used in everyday cooking. The middle class of merchants, craftspeople, and shop owners could afford to add meat, especially pork and chicken, to their everyday diets.

On the Korean peninsula in 108 B.C.E., to boost China's economy by making trade with Southeast Asia more efficient, the Han government established four trading cities that served as ports for commerce from Southeast Asia, as well as from Japan, the Philippines, and Indonesia. The governors of the cities kept records of who came and went, taking special note of tribute that was being sent to the emperor. By about 300 C.E. the Koreans and Japanese were imitating Chinese customs and adopting the Chinese diet.

The Harappans

The other great economic power of eastern Asia was India. Unlike China, which had a unified national identity for most of its development, India saw the rise and fall of many kingdoms. The first Indian civilization was the Harappan of about 2600–1500 B.C.E. It built cities and towns in the Indus valley and surrounding areas, northward into modern southwestern China, eastward beyond New Delhi, and west and south along the coast from the mouth of the Indus River. The Harappans' main crop was rice, probably grown on dry ground rather than in rice paddies, and they built irrigation canals to bring water to their crops.

Their major cities were Harappa and Mohenjo Daro, both of which seem to have been designed from the ground up, with each city laid out in a checkerboard pattern of streets and having underground sewers that were accessible through manholes. Each city had a huge granary. Some archaeologists characterize the granaries as banks, where the wealth of the local community was stored. In hard economic times Harappans could make withdrawals from these banks, thus enabling the population to feed itself. The wealth the grain represented also could be invested. This most often took the form of exports; grain was traded to the Near East in exchange for consumer goods such as cookware as well as for luxury items such as decorative sculpture.

Harappan society seems to have been structured around an upper class and a lower class based on ownership of land. It may have had kings, but no palaces or other indications of royalty have been found. Some areas of the Harappans' cities and towns had large houses with big walls and spacious interiors, while other areas crowded together small houses along narrow streets. Based on differences in housing, some historians have theorized that the economy had a big division between rich and poor, with a small elite group controlling the wealth generated by the economy. Some also suggest that the division was so great that the lower class was made up of slaves of the upper class. Others speculate that the differences between social classes may have arisen from a difference between owners of large estates and owners of small farms, or they may have resulted from hereditary social status, with the upper class being nobility and the lower class peasants. In any case, the Harappans plainly had an economy advanced enough to have the means to pay people to care for the cities. Sewers, streets, walls, fortifications, and granaries were well maintained until about 1800 B.C.E., when the economy of the Harappan culture seems to have begun a decline, perhaps caused by natural disasters, invading nomads, or both.

The Harappans fueled an extensive trading empire and were well known to the Sumerians of the Near East, who called them Meluhha. Ships from the Harappans sailed to Dilmun, modern Bahrain, where they traded for goods made in the Near East. During the reign of Sumer's Sargon I (r. 2334–2279 B.C.E.) Harappan ships routinely sailed up the Tigris and Euphrates rivers to dock at major cities.

The Vaishyas and Sudras

The next city-building culture did not arise in India until the 900s B.C.E., when the nomadic Vedic people began settling, though they did not become a fully agricultural society until about 500 B.C.E. By 1500 B.C.E. some of the nomadic peoples of central and northern Asia had developed the practice of waiting until after harvest time and then raiding towns and villages to steal food and other valuables. This behavior was a constant factor in weakening the ancient Asian economies of India, China, and Korea.

By 500 B.C.E. India was divided into numerous small kingdoms. Complex economies developed in northern India, giving rise to a cash economy, meaning an economy based not on barter but on the use of money to make purchases. The Vedic culture that dominated northern India had brought with it a system of social classes that became the castes of India. Under this system the third-highest caste was the Vaishya, who were in charge of money lending, agriculture, and trade. They paid higher taxes than the other castes because one of their duties was to create wealth to give to the higher castes—the Brahmans, or priests, and the Kshatriyas, or warriors and rulers. The Vaishyas resented being third-class people and having to pay higher taxes than everyone else, so during the Maurya Dynasty many of them adopted Buddhism, which advocated social equality. The fourth caste was the Sudra, a group that included craftspeople. The men were blacksmiths, carpenters, and potters, while the women were basket makers and weavers of textiles. Perhaps either gender could have made garlands, which were important ornaments.

Farmers were of the Vaishya caste, and they led difficult lives, burdened by high taxes and usually allowed to work only small plots of land. The big estates tended to be owned by kings and temples, and they were worked by Vaishyas, who were little more than slaves. Their main crop was rice, but they also cultivated wheat, barley, and cotton mostly in northern India, and sugarcane, peas, and beans mostly in southern India. They raised sheep, cattle, and buffalo. Recognizing the importance of keeping their agricultural economies strong, Indian governments usually gave farmers seeds when the farmers needed them, and they lent farmers oxen, tools, and even money.

Large towns had public markets where farmers could sell their produce and where shops sold the products of the Sudras and goods imported by the Vaishyas. Merchants sold oil for lamps, perfumes, and spices. Some owned taverns, where government agents would spy on the patrons to see who was spending lavishly and therefore might not have paid all his taxes. The Mauryan government developed a bureaucracy devoted to keeping track of people and their wealth.

People paid for goods with gold and silver coins. Each coin was marked with a code that identified where it had been minted, which allowed governments to identify who might be minting underweight coins, which by law were supposed contain a certain weight of gold, silver, or copper. Underweight coins could cause inflation, because sellers would figure out that certain coins were underweight and would therefore demand more of them for their goods. A high number of underweight coins could cause people to lose faith in the coins, perhaps turning to bartering for their goods. This could lead to a collapse of the cash economy, which in turn would cause many businesses to go bankrupt. Governments also kept track of the movements of merchants and how they were treated. Villages, towns, and cities were expected to protect foreign merchants and sometimes were required to reimburse a merchant for the value of his goods if he was robbed by bandits while in their territories.

Indian Foreign Trade

During the Maurya Dynasty, India opened up extensive foreign trade routes. The Mauryans traded with people from the east coast of Africa, the Near East, Greece, Rome, and China. Alexander the Great's invasion of northwestern India in 326 B.C.E. made wide-ranging contacts with Western cultures. Beginning with the reign of Augustus Caesar in Rome (27 B.C.E.–14 C.E.) Indian kingdoms sent ambassadors to the Roman court, seeking to expand and protect trade relations with the Roman Empire, because the Roman Empire had become an important source of wealth, sending literally tons of gold and silver to India in exchange for goods India either produced or acquired from cultures farther east. Indian ships ranged westward and eastward, staying close to the southern Asian coast. They established trading posts on the Malay Peninsula and would land goods on the peninsula's west coast, then carry them overland to the east coast to be reloaded on ships. The island of Sri Lanka, off the southern coast of India, became famous for its big warehouses, extensive docks, and ships visiting from all over southern Asia. By charging docking fees and developing expertise in navigation, the Sri Lankans became wealthy.

With Greek and Egyptian crews, Indian merchants sailed as far as what is now southeastern China, and they traded in Java, Vietnam, Cambodia, and Thailand. On overland routes the Indians formed caravans, often consisting of the carts of several different merchants who had joined together for protection from bandits. Their caravans wended their way through the Western Ghats mountains to the west coast of India for loading onto ships or through the various roads called collectively the "Silk Road" that led northeastward to China as well as west into the Near East. In southern India this trade resulted in the development of trading empires, with governments devoted to fostering trade. How many people in southern India were reached by the wealth generated by the caravans is not known, but it seems that nearly everyone profited from the caravans by selling them food and goods or by providing them with services. So important was foreign trading that when the Roman Empire suffered an economic recession in about 170 C.E., the loss in trade lowered the standard of living of the Vaishya caste.

People in India imported and exported exotic animals, and they exported gems, metal, earthenware, and beads across Asia. This trade spread goods from many cultures across Asia, even bringing Roman pottery to Java. To Rome went spices, pearls, textiles, cosmetics, and a host of other goods. From Rome came wine, sculptures, ironware, and coins. By the end of the Maurya Dynasty, India had become one of the two great economic powers of eastern Asia, and it remained that way through wars and revolutions. The other great economic power was China.

EUROPE

BY PETER S. WELLS

Between the earliest human activity in Europe around a million years ago and the advent of writing around 200 B.C.E., we are dependent exclusively upon the evidence of archaeology for studying the economies of communities. The material evidence of archaeology enables us to examine in detail the three main categories of economic activity: subsistence (production of food), manufacturing (making of tools, weapons, ornaments, containers, and other necessary and desired goods), and trade (obtaining materials and products from other communities, through exchange). During the final centuries B.C.E., and especially with the writings of Julius Caesar (100–44 B.C.E.) about Gaul, written sources in Greek and Latin begin to complement the evidence of archaeology. During the Roman Period in Europe—the first four centuries C.E.—a number of texts refer to the economy, though little written information pertains directly to the topic.

SUBSISTENCE

Before the introduction of agriculture and animal domestication around 6000 B.C.E. in the southeast of Europe, all peoples in Europe were hunter-gatherers, or foragers. They relied on plant foods they collected in their environment, such as fruits, berries, seeds, nuts, and roots, and on animals they hunted, fished, and collected, including eggs and shellfish. Bones of animals that people hunted and scavenged are often well preserved on archaeological sites. At sites of the Paleolithic Period, or Old Stone Age, from almost a million years ago to the end of the ice age that dates to about 12,000 years ago, such finds attest to the hunting of elephants, mammoths, woolly rhinoceros, reindeer, red deer, elk, bison, horse, and numerous small mammals, as well as birds and fish. Plant food remains are much less apparent on archaeological sites than animal bones. A wide range of plants were collected, processed, and consumed by Europe's early hunter-gatherers.

During the Mesolithic Period, or Middle Stone Age, roughly 8,000 to 12,000 years ago, the warming of the earth's climate melted the glaciers that had covered the northern parts of Europe, and the tundra that had occupied much of the continent was replaced by the forests and grasslands that comprise the natural vegetation of Europe in recent times. With the great climatic changes, the megafauna—the mammoths, woolly rhinoceros, and other large mammals—became extinct, and the lands were populated by new species of animals, such as red and roe deer, wild boar, aurochs (wild

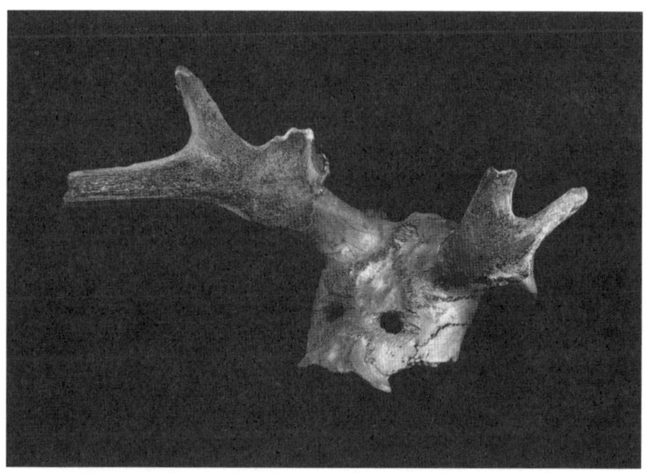

Perforated part skull and antlers of red deer dating to the Early Mesolithic, about 7,500 B.C.E., from Star Carr, Vale of Pickering, North Yorkshire, England. (© The Trustees of the British Museum)

cattle), elk, and hare. Many Mesolithic communities made great use of shellfish along the coasts of northern Europe.

Agriculture was introduced into temperate Europe around 6000 B.C.E. from the Near East, where the cultivation of wheat and barley and the raising of cattle, sheep, goats, and pigs had been established by 8000 B.C.E. Agriculture is first evident in southeastern Europe, as at Nea Nikomedeia in Macedonia, and the practice spread gradually northward and westward, arriving at the coasts of the Baltic and North seas and the Atlantic Ocean around 4000 B.C.E. The transition from hunting and gathering to agriculture was not sudden. Many communities adopted farming to supply part of their diet while maintaining their hunting-gathering practices well into the Neolithic Period.

The process of the spread of agriculture from the Near East into southeastern Europe probably involved a number of different mechanisms. We know that communities that practiced hunting and gathering, as at Franchthi Cave in southern Greece, used boats to fish the deep waters of the Aegean Sea and to trade across the sea for materials such as obsidian (a natural volcanic glass used for making cutting tools). It is likely that some such communities learned the technology of agriculture and animal domestication and acquired the seeds and animals from farming peoples on the eastern side of the Aegean Sea in what is now Turkey. Also, some farmers from that region may have traveled across the Aegean with their seed grains and animals to settle fertile valleys in the southeast of Europe.

During the Neolithic Period, Bronze Age, and Iron Age, some communities tended to rely more on agriculture and others more on livestock, depending upon local climatic conditions and soils. Archaeological evidence shows that many fruits were eaten, including apples, pears, plums, grapes, raspberries, and blackberries, but it is not clear when these plants were fully domesticated.

Technological innovations contributed to the efficiency of food production. Metal sickles came into use during the Bronze Age. Traction plows, made of wood and pulled by animals, reduced the time and energy required for planting. In the Late Iron Age, after about 400 B.C.E., metal plowshares became common, enabling farmers to cultivate heavier and more fertile soils. In addition to cereals, oil-bearing plants, including flax and gold-of-pleasure, were commonly grown, as was the broad bean.

Following the Roman conquests of about half of Europe during the first century B.C.E. and the first century C.E., there was some shift in emphasis in crops grown in the new provinces, and new, often larger, breeds of animals were introduced. But for the most part farmers in the provinces continued tending the same crops and animals they had raised during the Iron Age. Rome introduced the villa system, and this pattern was widely adopted by local landowners. The villa included a residential building in which the owner and family lived. Around that building were gardens and workshops, and beyond them fields of wheat, barley, and other cereals. Documents that pertain to subsistence in temperate Europe were written after the Roman conquest, and they describe how the villa system worked. The villa owner employed tenants who worked the land, and wealthy owners kept slaves. Villas were meant to be self-sufficient units of production. Each villa grew and manufactured what was needed by its little community, and it exported surplus produce to the urban centers to exchange for manufactured goods and luxury products. Villas varied greatly in size and wealth. Some were huge, with lavish residences decorated with mosaic floors and painted walls, and with hundreds of tenants and slaves working the fields and workshops. Others were modest, with the single family that owned the villa doing all the work.

Written documents from the Roman Period indicate that farmers had to pay tax on their produce, and the rate of taxes rose and fell with changing economic and political circumstances. Although we have no written records about taxes or tribute in the pre-Roman periods, it is likely that the political centers of the Iron Age maintained some kind of system that taxed the agricultural goods farmers produced.

In lands beyond the Roman imperial frontiers—east of the Rhine River, north of the Danube River on the Continent, and north of Hadrian's Wall in Britain—subsistence organization and practice were affected by the Roman presence but not as much as in the conquered lands. The Roman army had huge numbers of soldiers stationed along the frontiers—more than 100,000 along the Rhine and Danube rivers alone—and these troops placed a great demand on local resources for food and raw materials. Archaeological evidence shows that the Roman administrators traded for agricultural goods with peoples across the frontier. Places such as Feddersen Wierde on the northwestern coast of Germany demonstrate the effects of the Roman demand for goods from across the frontier. At that site the archaeological evidence shows an ever-increasing focus on the production of livestock during the first three centuries C.E., and at the same time an increasing flow of Roman luxury objects into the community.

Manufacturing

Among the earliest tools in Europe are those at Atapuerca in northern Spain; perhaps dating back as early as 700,000 years ago, they are called core and flake tools. Core tools are shaped by striking off flakes from the central portion of a large pebble or cobble. Flake tools are made from the flattish pieces that are knocked off. New during the Mesolithic Period, or Middle Stone Age (8,000–12,000 years ago), was an emphasis on manufacturing microliths—very small stone tools, many of which served as points on arrows. The bow and arrow was a new technology developed around the start of the Mesolithic Period as an adaptation to the hunting of the small and fast-moving animals of the forests that spread throughout Europe during the warming conditions after the end of the last ice age.

During the Neolithic Period people began to make pottery. Good potting clays are available throughout Europe, and most communities made their own pottery. Stone tools during the Neolithic Period were similar to those of earlier times, with one significant innovation. Axes made by grinding one stone against another, rather than by flaking, became common. Modern experiments show that ground stone axes are more efficient for cutting down trees and chopping wood—both activities that Neolithic farmers carried out to clear their fields and to build houses and fences—than are axes made by flaking. More efficient tools meant that farmers could spend less time on the basic tasks of managing their farms and devote more effort to generating surplus produce. Surplus might take the form of foods such as grain and meat or perhaps other goods, such as leather and wool. Surplus products might then be used to exchange for materials made by other individuals or for goods that might arrive through trade with other communities.

The farming peoples of the Neolithic Period began to manufacture textiles on a regular basis, using wool from sheep and linen from flax grown in the fields. Only under exceptional circumstances do textiles survive to be recovered by archaeologists. Complete garments made of textile fibers have been found in many submerged settlements along the lakes of circum-Alpine Europe and in some bog environments in northern regions of the continent. The widespread distribution of ceramic spindle whorls (weights attached to spindles to help them maintain momentum) and loom weights attest to the production of textiles in many communities throughout the continent. Some communities produced the textiles they needed to make clothing for their own members, while others produced surplus textiles for trade with other communities, in exchange for which they would receive materials that the other communities produced.

Metalworking in Europe began during the sixth millennium B.C.E., when copper was hammered to form beads and simple pins. By the middle of fifth millennium B.C.E. metalsmiths were casting both copper and gold to produce more substantial objects than was possible through hammering. Bronze, a copper alloy that usually was about 90 percent copper and 10 percent tin, was coming into widespread use by the middle of the third millennium for tools and ornaments, representing an important technological advance over the softer copper. Neither copper nor tin is common in Europe, and both required complex underground mining to produce. Copper mines of the Bronze Age (2000–800 B.C.E.) have been explored in the Alps of Austria, and the evidence shows that the industry was relatively large in scale and highly specialized technologically.

Small quantities of iron were being processed during the Late Bronze Age, but it was not until iron began to replace bronze as the principal material for tools that we speak of the Iron Age. In central parts of Europe this change took place around 800 B.C.E., and in northern Europe a couple of centuries later. Iron is much more abundant on the earth's surface than are copper and tin, and so much iron ore was readily available on the surface during prehistoric times that underground mining was not required in many areas. While the main advantage of iron over bronze was its greater availability, once blacksmiths had mastered the techniques of working with iron, the new metal also could yield sharper, harder, and more durable cutting implements. By the end of the Iron Age hundreds of different kinds of tools were being made of iron and of steel (an alloy of iron and carbon). Among the most common tools were knives of different kinds, axes, hammers, scythes for harvesting hay, and implements for use in woodworking, such as saws and chisels. Nails were first commonly employed for building houses and boats during the final two centuries B.C.E.

All of these tools made economic activity more efficient. Crops could be grown with less effort expended to prepare the soil and harvest the plants, and buildings and ships would be constructed faster and more sturdily. Thus, more time and energy became available for other economic activities, such as creation of surpluses for trade and engaging in trading expeditions. The overall scale of economic activity could increase, since these basic activities required a smaller proportion of a community's total resources and energy.

In the Roman Period the principal change in manufacturing was in scale, not in kind. In the politically unified landscape of the Roman Empire the production of some goods, such as pottery, could be organized on a larger scale than had been practiced earlier in temperate Europe. For example, large centers of manufacture at La Graufesenque and Lezoux in France and Rheinzabern in Germany produced great quantities of *terra sigillata,* the ornate red pottery that was favored both within the empire and outside it. In other materials also, including metal and glass, Roman Period manufacturing was carried out in greater quantities than was production in the pre-Roman context. But even with the emergence of some larger-scale industries, many of the manufactured goods that people used were still made in village or household settings.

Trade

Trade is important not only because it enables people to acquire raw materials from far away and specialized products that their own communities do not produce but also because it inevitably brings people into contact and forces them to interact. Along with goods, information passes between trade partners. Evidence shows development of active trade by the Upper Paleolithic Period (12,000–40,000 years ago). Flint of exceptional quality and shells from the seacoasts are often found on sites at considerable distances from their sources, indicating that people were either trading with groups who had access to them or traveling distances to acquire them.

By the Mesolithic Period systematic trade in amber from the Baltic Sea region is evident throughout northern Europe. With the establishment of permanent settlements and the production of agricultural and animal goods, communities had the first opportunity to generate surplus products that could be traded for other goods. From this time on people traded for a wide range of materials, including amber, coral, gold, and jet, all of which they used to make ornaments and to display their status and wealth. Trade continued in especially fine flint, as well as in some manufactured implements such as stone axes and pottery vessels.

Until shortly before the Roman conquest, we have no evidence for standards of value, such as coins. Instead of the market-based economy of today, early Europeans seem to have operated trade systems that were closely linked to social relations rather than to market exchange. Research on trade in Neolithic stone axes, for example, has shown how patterns in the distribution of these objects suggest that the objects played important roles in regulating social relations between the communities that were participating.

During the Bronze Age trade came to play an increasingly more important role in societies because many communities had to trade to acquire metal. Both copper and tin are relatively rare in nature. They occur in deposits in mountainous regions of Europe, such as the Austrian Alps and Cornwall, and not on the North European Plain, for example. Yet from the beginning of the Bronze Age on, communities all across Europe had bronze ornaments and tools. Copper mines at the Mitterberg near Salzburg in Austria show that hundreds of workers were involved in mining, smelting, and trading metal to communities throughout the continent. Along with bronze, many other materials circulated along the trade networks. Trade systems were complex and varied. Large and finely crafted items, such as swords and cauldrons, were transported great distances from their places of manufacture, while smaller and more common objects, such as decorative pins, were used near the places where they were made.

The Early Iron Age (800–450 B.C.E.) is distinguished by the appearance of trade centers, places where communities grew as a result of expanding systems of commerce. The best documented are a series of hilltop settlements, including Mont Lassois in France, the Heuneburg in southern Germany, Závist in Bohemia, and Belsk in Ukraine. At these locations communities grew to populations of perhaps 500 to 1,000, and they were actively engaged in trade with groups in different parts of Europe. Especially evident are objects that arrived into central Europe from the Mediterranean world. Greek pottery and ornaments, Etruscan bronze vessels, and branches of coral (to be cut and used for decoration on jewelry) are among the special imports that are found in considerable quantities at and around such centers during the sixth through fourth centuries B.C.E. Along with these luxury imports, more common objects circulated as well, such as bronze pins, glass beads, amber, and jet.

In the Late Iron Age, in addition to all the categories of trade goods that circulated earlier, bulk commodities came to play important roles in trade. Noteworthy are massive grindstones of basalt, quarried at different locations, such as in Bohemia and in the Middle Rhineland, and transported to still other locations where they were employed for grinding grain. In the final two centuries before the Roman conquest commerce intensified between communities in temperate Europe and the Roman world. Much of this commerce was centered on the large, city-like settlements known as *oppida,* but many Roman imports occur at other sites as well. These imports included ceramic amphoras in which wine was transported, fine pottery, coins, medicinal implements, bronze vessels, silver vessels, and glass bowls. Some communities in temperate Europe began minting coins around the middle of the second century B.C.E., and they show that exchange flourished throughout Europe during the final two centuries B.C.E.

After the Roman conquest, which divided Europe roughly into a southern and western half that belonged to the Roman Empire and a northern and eastern half that remained unconquered, many new trade goods became available to communities in the provinces, including exotic foodstuffs from the Mediterranean world. Besides wine and olive oil, these included dates, figs, olives, and the tangy sauce known as *garum* that was a great favorite among Roman diners. Mass-produced Roman pottery circulated widely, both in the imperial lands and beyond it into far northern and eastern Europe. New infrastructure contributed to the expansion and intensification of trade during the Roman Period, with large cargo ships plying the Mediterranean shores and the major rivers of Europe, roads constructed over much of the Roman provinces, and bridges built across rivers where none had stood before, such as that across the river Thames in Roman London (Londinium).

Trade across the frontier into the unconquered regions of Germany, Scandinavia, Poland, and other lands was both extensive and intensive. The imperial frontiers on the Rhine and Danube rivers were no impediment to trade, as tens of thousands of Roman-made objects found north and east of those boundaries make clear.

GREECE

BY CHRISTOPHER BLACKWELL

The ancient Greek world, from the Bronze Age in the second millennium B.C.E. through the rise of Roman dominance in the Mediterranean in the second century B.C.E., consisted of independent city-states and kingdoms, dispersed across an area that had the Greek peninsula at its center but that extended from what is now southern France through the east coast of Italy, Sicily, parts of northern Africa, the west coast of Turkey, and around the Black Sea. These thousands of communities were united by a common language, worship of a more-or-less fixed set of gods, and certain shared customs. From time to time certain states would achieve political control over larger areas—the kingdom of Mycenae during the Bronze Age, Euboea during the eighth century B.C.E., Athens during the fifth century B.C.E., and Macedonia during the late fourth and early third centuries B.C.E. Even so, it is impossible to describe a single, unified "Greece" in any meaningful sense for any period of antiquity.

The economic history of the Greek world, then, must consider different places at different periods and is limited by the available evidence. For the Bronze Age, there survive some bureaucratic records on clay tablets. For the so-called dark ages that followed, there are only archaeological remains, mainly burials. The best evidence for the Classical Period, the fifth and fourth centuries B.C.E., comes from Athens, from the speeches of Athenian orators, the writings of such philosophers as Xenophon and Aristotle, and the many inscriptions that the democratic Athenians erected to promulgate their public business. In the Hellenistic Period, after the fourth century B.C.E., the best evidence comes from Egypt, at that time ruled by Macedonian Greeks; the dry climate of ancient Egypt preserved many remains of documents written on papyrus and recording, in Greek, the day-to-day business of a complex civil administration, ruling over Egyptians but conducted mainly by Greeks and in the Greek language.

The English word *economy* derives from the Greek word *oikonomia*, a compound of the word *oikos*, "household," and the word root *nom-*, which appears in many Greek words having to do with custom, opinion, belief, order, law, and regulation. We might translate *oikonomia* as "regulation of the household." This interpretation gives some insight into the fundamentals of "economic" thinking among the ancient Greeks, which differs in important ways from the ideas that underlie modern economic institutions.

The vast majority of people in the ancient Greek world were rural peasants, living in small households and aspiring, at least, to be as self-sufficient as possible. The *oikos* of *oikonomia* does not refer to a structure but to the idea of a household; it includes all the people living together in a household, nuclear and extended family, servants, and slaves, as well as livestock, land, and any crops growing on the land. The most basic economy appears in the oldest surviving examples of texts written in the Greek, from the Bronze Age, and from Homeric poetry, from the period afterward.

Early Evidence from the Bronze Age

The oldest surviving examples of writing in the Greek language are the so-called Linear B tablets. These are clay tablets from the Greek Bronze Age (3000–1100 B.C.E.), inscribed with a script that predates the Greek alphabet. Deciphered in the 1950s, this script was revealed to be an early form of Greek, and the tablets were found to deal largely in the business of household management.

The tablets from the Bronze Age palace complex at Knossos, on Crete—over 4,000 of which have been found—contain mostly lists of material supplies. Stores of oil, wine, and grain as well as numbers of sheep and cattle—the food supply for a large, well-regulated community—were recorded and updated on clay. So certain tablets record the details of flocks of sheep: which areas they inhabited, who was responsible for them, their size, and what sort of sheep made up each flock.

More complex economic transactions appear on these tablets as well. One tablet, from Pylos in the Peloponnese (the southern peninsula of the Greek mainland), seems to record a donation of "ship bronze" to the king, from officials of various temples and other religious sanctuaries. Scholars are uncertain as to what "ship bronze" may have been, but one explanation may be that the king at Pylos demanded contributions of metal from his outlying dominions to help construct a navy. Other tablets record payments to workers, such as a tablet, also from Pylos, that records the wages for the "bath-pourers," who seem to have been paid in rations of wheat and figs.

Economics in the Homeric World

Homer's *Odyssey* describes in some detail the economic workings of the house of Odysseus. This hero left his estate on Ithaca to fight in the Trojan War, to return only after 10 years of fighting and another 10 years of wandering. While the poem is fantastic, filled with monsters, divine intervention, and mythological characters, the domestic world it describes must reflect, to a greater or lesser extent, the world familiar to the poet and his audience, during the 10th through seventh centuries B.C.E. It can thus provide some insight into the economy of a lord's estate.

Odysseus's household consisted of himself, his wife (Penelope), their son (Telemachus), and various slaves. One of these, the swineherd Eumaeus, recounts in the poem the extent of his master's wealth. This wealth is described entirely in terms of livestock: "For surely his wealth was great beyond telling. . . . he has twelve herds of cows on the mainland, the same number of flocks of sheep, the same number of pigs, and the same number of wide-roaming herds of goats, which are in the care of shepherds or pastured by strangers. Here, on Ithaca, he has eleven herds of goats grazing off in the distance, looked after by brave men."

Several kinds of economic exchanges existed in the Homeric world. The most straightforward of these, the kind most purely "economic," are trading and its more rough-edged cousin, piracy. When Odysseus arrives at various places on his wanderings, the people he meets invariably ask him, "Are you here for trade, or are you a pirate?" This question seems to reflect a new reality in the Greek world after the fall of the Bronze Age civilizations: increased economic activity across the Mediterranean, some of which was for mutual benefit (trade) and some of which was for more unilateral benefit (piracy).

The other kinds of exchange are less purely economic and are much more bound up in the social fabric. In the world described by Homer powerful people exchange gifts continually. A stranger coming to the house of Odysseus would be entertained and, upon his departure, offered gifts of material objects, such as silver bowls, shields, and gold cups. Such exchange establishes a social bond between guest and host, and the history of each gift-object was remembered and recalled forever. It was the mark of a wealthy and powerful person to give and receive such gifts. Giving precious gifts proved the wealth and status of the giver and put the receiver under an obligation.

Similar exchanges of valuable property attended marriages. The *Odyssey* suggests that a marriage involved both a dowry—payment from the family of the bride to the groom—and bride-gifts—payment from the groom to the family of the bride. The latter established the status of the potential groom; a man who could not provide valuable bride-gifts would not be considered wealthy enough to deserve the bride. The former was insurance for the well-being of the bride. The dowry was paid to the husband but did not belong to him entirely; if he should send his wife back to her family, or if she should choose to leave, the dowry would have to be repaid.

Not everyone was a lord in the community like Odysseus, of course, and there were degrees of status among the more ordinary people. These degrees may seem surprising to modern readers, however. It seems that the status of a slave was higher than that of a hired man, for example, perhaps because a slave was a full-fledged member of the household while a hired worker did not "belong" in the community. Homer also identifies a category of *demiourgoi*, "workers for the community," certain craftsmen, prophets, healers, builders, and singers of tales, who are not attached to a particular household but are nevertheless valued in the community. As the Greek world emerged from the dark ages and these household-based communities came to be organized into more structured city-states, more sophisticated economic practices and institutions came about.

Much of the literary evidence comes in the form of complaints—complaints from peasants about the oppression of the lords and from the lords about the presumption of the peasants. The poet Hesiod describes complaints about "bribe-devouring judges" who mishandled cases of inheritance, and the poet Theognis of Megara, in the sixth century B.C.E., details a complaint about how "those who previously did not know about courts and laws, but wore goatskins and held pastures outside the city" had come into political power, displacing the former lords. By the fifth century Greek society had produced enough evidence for modern scholars to describe in some detail the economic workings of a city-state, with the democratic and prosperous state of Athens providing the best evidence.

Slaves

The best early evidence for the ancient Greek economy does not appear until the Classical Period (480–323 B.C.E.), and most of that evidence comes from the city of Athens. So Athens can serve as a representative case study of the ancient Greek economy. That economy depended on slaves. They provided labor in the house, on the farm, for public works, and, in dire circumstances, even for the conduct of warfare. Slavery in the ancient world generally was not based on race but was the consequence of war or piracy. Odysseus's slave woman, Euryclea, describes how she was abducted by pirates as a child and sold into slavery. In the Classical Period it was common to sell into slavery the inhabitants of a defeated city. The children of slaves were also slaves and were often considered more reliable, never having known freedom.

The lot of slaves varied considerably. Slaves who worked in quarries or mines suffered terribly and had an extremely short life expectancy. Domestic slaves generally had an easier, but by no means easy, life. Even the most fortunate slave was still subject to the whims of the master and did not enjoy any real protection under the law. There are no accurate data on the number of slaves in Athens, and estimates vary widely. There may have been as many slaves as free Athenians, and the slaves may even have outnumbered the free by two to one or more.

No ancient writer discusses in any depth the extent to which the economy depended on slavery, though the dependence was well known. The historian Thucydides describes how, during the war between Athens and Sparta, the Spartans captured a fortress on the Athenian border, and he encourages Athenian slaves to flee there; according to Thucydides 20,000 slaves did so, damaging the ability of Athens to harvest crops and maintain public works.

Freemen

Some slaves could earn money and could hope to save enough to buy freedom. Masters could, and did, set free (or manumit) slaves in their wills. The most famous case is that of the slave Pasion in the fourth century. He was the property of a banker in Athens, and upon his master's death he became free and the owner of the bank and eventually one of the wealthiest men in Athens. Through his generous gifts to the city, he even acquired Athenian citizenship and became an associate of the most prominent people in the city. This anecdote is extraordinary and certainly does not represent the usual experience of Greek slaves, but it does reveal the fluidity of economic status during the Classical Period.

Resident Aliens

Free people who were not Athenians and yet resided in the city were an important part of the economic life of the state. These were called *metics*, or *metoikoi*, which means "resident aliens." They tended to be merchants or bankers, since as non-Athenians they could not own land. *Metics* were involved in industry, making and selling perfume and furniture; were traders in wheat, wine, or oil; and were bankers, loaning money at interest. *Metics* were acknowledged members of the community, enjoying protection of the laws, although each *metic* had to have an Athenian sponsor who would represent him in court, should the need arise. At the great festivals, when the Athenians celebrated their civic identity, the *metic* took part in the processions, a mark of formal status as part of the community. *Metics* were valuable to the community not only for the goods they brought to market and the services they may have provided but also for the taxes they paid to the city.

Women

Women in classical Athens did not enjoy political rights, could not vote, and could not hold office of any kind. An Athenian woman could be said to be a "citizen" only in the sense that her status determined the status of her children: To be a citizen of Athens during the fifth century B.C.E., one had to be a man born to an Athenian father and an Athenian mother.

Nevertheless, women were in charge of much of the fundamental economic activity that regulated daily life. Women were responsible for training and managing the slaves, ensuring that all members of the house were fed and clothed, and keeping track of the material goods and supplies of the house. In Xenophon's work *Oikonomikos*, his character Socrates states that a good wife is the partner of her husband; while he is the one who supports the family, "it is by means of the wife's economy and thrift that the greater part of the expenditure is checked, and on the successful issue or the mishandling of the same depends the increase or impoverishment of a whole estate." Xenophon expands on this philosophy as he has his character Isomachus (who is portrayed as a pompous fool) describe how he instructed his young wife regarding some of her duties: "Over those members of the household whose appointed tasks are conducted indoors, it will be your duty to preside; yours to receive the stuffs brought in; yours to apportion part for daily use, and yours to make provision for the rest, to guard and garner it so that the outgoings destined for a year may not be expended in a month."

Citizens

In Athens citizenship was limited to men born from two Athenian parents (during the fifth century B.C.E.) or to an Athenian father (during parts of the fourth century B.C.E.) or who had been granted citizenship by a vote of the democratic assembly. Economically, the most significant benefit enjoyed by citizens was the ability to own land, a right limited to citizens. In earlier centuries full political enfranchisement at Athens and in other cities was limited to citizens who met certain property qualifications, and even in the early days of the Athenian democracy certain political offices could be held only by citizens whose real property—land—yielded a certain value in crops; the citizen class of *pentekosmiomedimnoi*, the "500 bushel producers," could hold offices denied to the *thetes*, those citizens without property or with only a little.

Citizens were generally exempt from taxation, except in unusual circumstances, though the wealthy citizens were expected to support the city's finances in other ways. Citizens enjoyed full legal protection and full access to the courts. In fact, only (male) citizens had access to the courts, so when *metics* or women sought legal redress for some injury, they would have to find a male citizen willing to go to court on their behalf. Citizens could be fined by the state, and any Athenian man who had thus accumulated sufficient debt to the public treasury was prevented from holding political office and could even lose his right as a citizen, a process called *atimia*, or disenfranchisement. In the sixth century, before the legal reforms of the Athenian statesman Solon (ca. 630–ca. 560 B.C.E.), citizens who fell heavily into private debt could even be seized by their creditors and sold as slaves.

Wealth and Coinage

The most durable and esteemed form of wealth was land, and even under the democracy those Athenians who owned large tracts of land constituted a de facto aristocracy, exerting the most political influence over the affairs of the city. But during the sixth century, as trade flourished in the Greek world and as city centers grew, more and more people made their living through means other than agriculture and accumulated wealth in ways other than growing crops, raising livestock, or renting land for others to do the same. Even large landowners rarely achieved the ideal of complete self-sufficiency. Such items as tools and furniture, clothing, and luxury goods had to be brought into a house from the outside, either acquired through exchange or purchased with money.

Money first appeared in the Greek world around 600 B.C.E. in the form of coins made of electrum, an alloy of gold and silver. By the Classical Period this alloy had fallen out of favor, mainly because the ratio of gold to silver, and therefore the value of each coin, could vary and was hard for people to determine by examining the coin. Coinage in antiquity did not derive its value by any institutional guarantee, as modern money does. It was simply a convenient way of exchanging small pieces of precious metal. So the names of ancient Greek coins refer to units of weight rather than value per se. The fundamental unit, the drachma, was a unit of weight, and a drachma in Athens might weigh more or less than a drachma at Corinth. A drachma of silver would be worth much less than a drachma of gold. Certain coinages were used more widely than others, as archaeological finds indicate, reflecting perhaps the relative strength of the economies of various cities. Athenian silver drachma coins from the fifth and fourth centuries B.C.E., displaying the owl of the goddess Athena, are widely found throughout the Mediterranean world, reflecting central role of Athens in commerce during the Classical Period.

At Athens the weights of coins and their relative values were as follows: Six obols equaled one drachma, 100 drachmas equaled one mina, and 60 minas equaled one talent. There were coins that weighed an obol, coins that weighted a drachma, and (the most commonly found coin) four-drachma pieces (the tetradrachm). There were no mina or talent coins; these terms were used to describe weights of silver or gold in tallying up values.

A juror serving in an Athenian courtroom was paid three obols per day, half a silver drachma; a citizen who rowed as part of the crew of a warship in the fifth century B.C.E. was paid one drachma per day. From this information, we can conclude that a drachma per day was a reasonable wage for labor—we know from literature that the jurors tended to consist of older men, those past their laboring years, for whom half a drachma might have represented a reasonable supplement to whatever resources they were living from. A talent of silver, then, was 6,000 drachmas, or approximately 16 years' wages (at one drachma per day). The former slave-turned-banker Pasion left an estate of 24 talents' worth of silver, indicating the vastness of his wealth.

Public Finance

Greek city-states did not, as a rule, regularly tax their citizens. They did regularly impose duties on imports and exports and freely imposed taxes on noncitizens, such as the *metoikion*, the fee that each *metic* had to pay for the privilege of living in Athens. *Metics* who performed extraordinary services to the state might be granted the right of *isoteleia*, or "equal taxation," which amounted to a freedom from any fees or taxes, equal to that freedom enjoyed by citizens. During times of crisis the state could, by a vote of the assembly of citizens, impose taxes on its citizens, either calculated by head or based on the value of a citizen's property. The state had many other ways of raising funds, however. War could produce income, from treasure plundered from defeated cities, from the sale of prisoners of war into slavery, or from the sale of captured ships.

The city owned property—public lands in its own territory or in territories captured in war. This land could be leased out for grazing or farming, and the products of any mines on public land would go into the city's treasury, to be spent as the citizens saw fit. The most famous example of this practice was the discovery at the end of the sixth century B.C.E. of a vein of silver in Attica, the territory around Athens, at a place called Laurium. The initial plan for this windfall, reported to be worth about 100 talents, was to distribute it among the citizens equally—economic historians have noted this plan as evidence for the relative lack of sophistication in ancient economic thinking. Eventually, however, the citizens of Athens decided to use this new wealth to supplement their navy, a choice that proved wise a few years later when the Persian army of Xerxes invaded Greece.

Athens, which commanded a naval empire during the fifth century B.C.E., received tribute from its "allies" annually. These funds were supposedly to allow Athens to support its navy, which was to be used to defend its allies, but much of the income from this tribute went to glorify the city, being spent on the monumental building of the Athenian acropolis and on the city's own fortifications. Thucydides reports that at the height of its power, Athens received 600 talents per year in tribute.

The most remarkable source of public revenue for the ancient city of Athens, and for other cities of the Greek world, was the *leitourgia*, or institution of "liturgies." This was a system by which the wealthy citizens of the democracy were obliged to perform expensive public services from their own resources. The two most notable kinds of liturgy were the *choregia*, sponsorship of the performance of a play, either a comedy or a tragedy, during the public festivals, and the trierarchy, the private funding of a warship. The latter was extremely expensive; it could cost a talent of silver to keep a warship afloat, with a full crew, and in good repair for a year. Consequently, by the fourth century this duty was performed collectively, by groups of wealthy citizens. The benefit of liturgies for the state was obvious—costly services performed at no public expense—and the benefits for the *euergetēs*, the person performing the liturgy, were real as well. He received public acclaim as well as an enhanced reputation as a good citizen and a man of wealth and prominence. To perform some liturgies poorly, resulting in a shabby production of a play, for example, brought shame from the community; in other cases, such as fielding an ill-equipped warship, the sponsor might be liable for legal prosecution.

The raising of public money was accomplished with as little public bureaucracy as possible. At Athens the nine archons, elected public officials, oversaw a small staff of secretaries who managed duties, fees, and rents. Major taxation was handled privately almost everywhere in antiquity, from democratic Athens to Egypt under the Macedonian Ptolemies, with the state auctioning off the right to collect taxes. People who bought these rights, the so-called tax farmers, would pay a fee up front and then collect taxes from those who owed them. The stability of a state could depend on how carefully the conduct of the tax collectors was managed and how diligently the public officials ensured that no one was compelled to pay more than the law required.

Financial Services

Beginning in the Classical Period our evidence shows that financial services were offered by private banks and, very often, by religious institutions connected to particular temples. Banks and temples took deposits, offering to hold money securely on behalf of depositors. The evidence suggests that these deposits themselves did not earn interest. Banks would, however, both make and receive loans, charging interest in the former case and paying interest in the latter. The most profitable loans in antiquity were so-called bottomry loans, loans used to purchase goods to be transported by ship and sold. The return on such a loan could exceed 100 percent but could amount to nothing if the ship was lost. Loans of this sort were the basis for the banker Pasion's wealth.

These financial institutions of the Classical Period continued to evolve and under the Greek rulers of Egypt during the Hellenistic Period reached a very high level of sophistication, including such seemingly modern services as spendthrift trusts, living trusts, annuities, and giro payments (a means of monetary exchange in which ownership of a bank deposit changes hands within the record-keeping system of the bank).

ROME

by David B. Hollander

The Romans acquired and kept their empire in no small part because of their adept management of economic resources. According to Cicero, the first-century B.C.E. politician and writer, the Romans had often gone to war on behalf of merchants, but their economic policies went far beyond the mere protection of commercial interests. The Romans were masters at exploiting the resources of conquered territory though taxation, confiscation, and enslavement. They developed highly efficient systems of taxation but also of redistribution to gather in wealth from their subjects and direct it to Rome and its increasingly far-flung armies.

The study of the Roman economy presents several obstacles. First of all, it is difficult to define the nature of the economy, which, at least in the late republic and early empire, seems to have been predominantly market based but still retained some elements of reciprocity (exchange through gifts and mutual obligations) and redistribution (a centralized economic system in which goods are collected by the government and redistributed at its discretion). A second problem is that there are very few prices or other statistics for an economic historian to study. Indeed, the surviving literary sources rarely discuss economic issues at all. Third, when Roman writers discuss economic life, they tend to present a highly distorted view of it. Cicero, like most Roman elites, regarded nearly every occupation aside from farming as demeaning and dishonorable. By definition, merchants were cheats, and laborers were little better than slaves as far as upper-class Romans were concerned. Cooks, fishermen, artisans, and performers were all beneath contempt, their economic activity rarely described.

Those who would understand the Roman economy must look elsewhere for evidence, and there are several profitable sources of information. Numismatics (the study of coinage) provides one such source. The volume, quality, and denominations of the coins produced as well as their distribution on sites and in coin hoards can reveal important aspects of the circulation and use of money. Thousands of inscriptions survive, and they, along with the many scraps of papyrus recovered from Egypt and writing tablets, such as those unearthed at Pompeii and Vindolanda, often record transactions, descriptions of careers, or parts of accounts. The excavation of houses, other buildings, and even shipwrecks also show archaeologists what was traded. Together these materials present a rich, if fragmentary view of the Roman economy.

The Regal Period and the Early Republic

The evidence for the Roman economy in its first few centuries (753–300 B.C.E.) is rather poor. The tradition that the site of the city was occupied by shepherds suggests that initially Rome had a pastoral economy. The fact that the Latin word for money, *pecunia*, derives from the word for livestock, *pecus*, tends to support this conclusion, as does the fact that some early fines were imposed in terms of cattle and sheep. Nevertheless, Rome had good farmland and sat at the crossroads of two important trade routes: the Tiber River, which connected the interior of the Italian peninsula with the coast, and the river ford at Rome, which connected Latium (the territory occupied by the Romans and other Latin speakers) with Etruria (modern Tuscany), home of the wealthy and powerful Etruscans. No doubt agriculture and trade became important sectors of the Roman economy at a very early stage in its development.

Many Romans came to believe that Servius Tullius, the sixth king of Rome, created the city's fundamental economic institutions, including the census, direct taxation, coinage, the distribution of conquered land to citizens, and pay for soldiers. Servius, who allegedly reigned during the mid-sixth century B.C.E., certainly did not institute coinage (which the Romans would not begin minting until the late fourth century B.C.E.) or army pay (which other ancient sources associate with Rome's long conflict with the Etruscan city of Veii in the late fifth century B.C.E.), but some of the city's economic institutions may predate the start of the republic in 509 B.C.E. The census, regardless of its precise origins, would soon become Rome's central economic institution. At first the census seems to have been simply a survey of the wealth of Roman citizens conducted in order to assign men their appropriate military and political rights and responsibilities. Eventually, however, the censors, two magistrates placed in charge of performing the census beginning in 443 B.C.E, would wield a considerable amount of control over both the state's revenues and expenditures.

Taxation and Other Forms of Revenue

The Roman state took in revenue from a variety of sources and in a multitude of forms. The earliest tax was the *tributum*, which was assessed, when necessary, on Roman citizens, who would have to pay some percentage of their assessed wealth. As the empire expanded, however, other forms of revenue became much more important, particularly indemnity payments from defeated enemies and provincial tax receipts. For example, at the end of the First Punic War in 241 B.C.E., Carthage agreed to pay Rome 320 talents of silver a year for 10 years. Since the talent, a Greek unit of weight, was approximately 57 pounds, this payment constituted a tremendous sum of money. The treaty ending the Second Punic War in 201 B.C.E. committed Carthage to pay 200 talents of silver each year for 50 years. As their power spread to the eastern Mediterranean, the Romans continued to exact these large indemnities from defeated nations. The Treaty of Apamea, which in 188 B.C.E. ended Rome's war with Antiochus III, ruler of the Seleucid kingdom in Asia, specified, among many other terms, that Antiochus pay Rome 1,000 talents per year for 12 years.

Provinces also paid taxes, though their nature and form are often unclear. Some communities paid in coin or bullion; some paid in commodities, like grain or olive oil. There were real estate taxes, poll taxes, and taxes that required farmers to turn over a portion of their harvests. Often the Romans simply kept preexisting tax systems in place following the incorporation of new territory into the empire. *Portoria* (customs duties) were exacted at the frontiers of the empire as well as on the borders between provinces. Other taxes that were levied at various times include a 5 percent tax on the value of manumitted (freed) slaves, a 1 percent tax on sales at auction, a 4 percent tax on the sale of slaves, and a 5 percent tax on some parts of inheritances. The emperor Vespasian

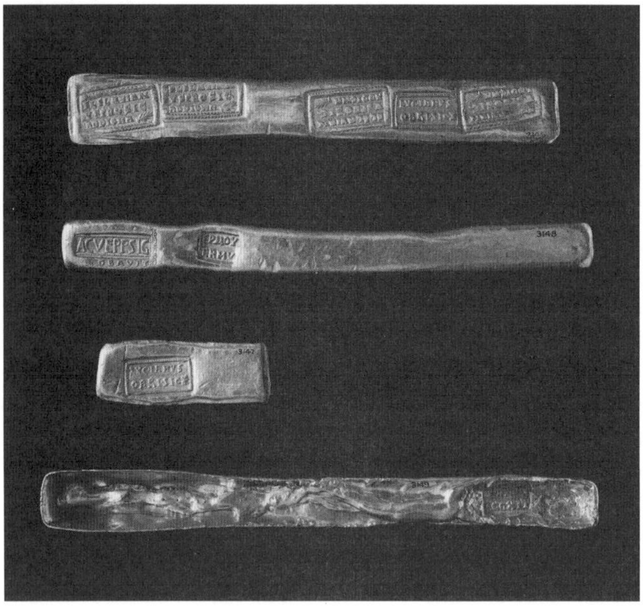

Gold bars with assayers' stamps, Roman, late fourth century C.E., *found in Egypt and Romania; at the time, taxes were payable only in gold, which was considered the most valuable metal and the one easiest to transport long distances.* (© The Trustees of the British Museum)

(r. 69–79 C.E.) even imposed a tax on Rome's urinals, since urine was sold to fullers for use in the washing of clothes. The government and its magistrates could also simply requisition both supplies and labor from Roman subjects. A provincial governor, for example, could demand food from local communities for himself and his staff or require cities to build roads or ships. This power was frequently abused, but it was difficult for provincials successfully to prosecute Roman officials. Victorious generals could also demand "gifts" of gold bullion from provincial cities.

Spoils taken in war often formed a substantial part of the state's revenues. Some of the spoils usually went to the soldiers involved in the campaign or financed the construction of a monument (usually a temple) commemorating the victory and thanking a particular god or goddess for assistance, but the rest went into the Roman *aerarium* (treasury). The spoils of war often included gold and silver coins and bullion as well as prisoners (who would be sold into slavery), livestock, and valuable works of art. It was customary for Roman generals to display some of this plundered wealth in their triumphs (victory parades held at Rome upon the conclusion of particularly successful military campaigns).

So much booty was acquired following the defeat of Perseus in the Third Macedonian War that the *tributum* was abolished for Italy in 167 B.C.E. The most notorious example of plundering in Roman history came at the end of this same conflict. The Senate decided to punish about 70 communities in Epirus (a region to the northwest of Greece along the east coast of the Ionian Sea), which had sided with Perseus. Soldiers went to the towns (which had already surrendered), collected all the gold, silver, and other valuable goods, and then enslaved the inhabitants. As many as 150,000 people were led into slavery. Proceeds from the sale of the goods and people paid for bonuses for the soldiers who had served in the war.

The expansion of the empire also brought considerable amounts of land under the control of the Roman authorities. Some of this land was redistributed to veterans or colonists, but much of it was retained and designated public land (*ager publicus*). Most such land would be used for farming or grazing herds, but mines and saltworks could also be public property and thus be subject to various forms of rent. During the republic disputes over the distribution and use of such land frequently arose and could lead to political turmoil. For example, Tiberius Gracchus's proposal in 133 B.C.E. to enforce statutory limits on individual holdings of *ager publicus* met with considerable resistance from those in possession of large tracts of such land.

Fines also generated some revenue for Rome. The Augustan historian Livy reports that in 193 B.C.E. the aediles Marcus Aemilius Lepidus and Lucius Aemilius Paulus received so much money from fines levied against grazers that they were able to build a portico and wharf at Rome in addition to placing gilded shields on the temple of Jupiter. In 189 B.C.E. aediles (public officials in charge of public works and grain) again used money from fines, this time exacted from merchants convicted of hoarding grain, to erect gilded shields and statues commemorating their actions on behalf of the people of Rome. Violations of sumptuary laws (laws designed to limit excessive consumption or use of luxury goods) could also lead to fines.

Government Expenditures

Although many aspects of the Roman government's budget must have changed over the centuries, the army almost certainly remained the single biggest expenditure. In addition to the salaries of the soldiers, who were not paid entirely in coin, there was the need for equipment, supplies, and retirement bonuses. Some payments could be made in kind, and requisitions could take care of some military needs, but cash was always essential. Rome's grain supply was another major item on the budget. Some grain was acquired through in-kind taxes (from Sicily, for example), but it was often necessary to purchase more.

Building projects could also be expensive, as were the games and shows that republican politicians and later emperors regularly put on. The maintenance of public buildings, spaces, and roads also required money. In 144 B.C.E., for example, Quintus Marcius Rex spent 45 million denarii to build and repair aqueducts. It is unclear how much money magistrates could expect to receive as allowances while governing provinces, but the sums were clearly substantial. Officials could requisition some supplies and labor, but the Romans often hired private companies to accomplish certain public ends, such as building roads or feeding the sacred geese on the Capitoline Hill. One of the main jobs of the censors was to let out such contracts for public works. They also leased public land and auctioned off the right to collect some taxes.

Tax Farming

One of the most lucrative businesses in the late republic was tax farming. Tax farmers, or *publicani*, purchased from the censors the right to collect certain taxes, ranging from the customs duties of a port to the harvest tithes of an entire province. To earn a profit, of course, the *publicani* had to collect more in revenue than they had promised to pay the Roman government. Because of the need for considerable amounts of capital to bid for such contracts and the need for big staffs to collect the taxes, the *publicani* formed large companies and even sold shares that could be traded. Although they were reviled in the provinces and even by some upper-class Romans, tax farmers came to wield considerable influence at Rome. Having bid too much for the right to collect taxes in Asia in the late 60s B.C.E., they successfully lobbied to have the sum reduced by a third. The *publicani* controlled a vast financial network and could help magistrates transfer large sums of money across the Mediterranean without physically transporting coinage or bullion. They also collaborated with governors in order to exploit the provinces fully. Corruption, provincial complaints, and the expansion of the Roman bureaucracy led to a gradual decline in tax farming under the empire.

Economic Policy and Regulation

While the Romans may not have had a sophisticated conception of their economy and the rules governing it, they did attempt to regulate certain markets and formulate what one might call economic policies. In both cases their actions were primarily reactive and driven as much by social concerns as by economic ones. Sumptuary laws provide a good illustration of this approach. In the second century B.C.E., as wealth flooded into Rome, many people began to buy foreign luxury goods and serve expensive foods at dinners. Conservative Romans believed that this trend was dangerous and attributed it to the corrupting influence of military service in the rich and exotic East. In order to combat this perceived corruption, they passed a series of laws limiting the amount of money one could spend on dinners and the types of foods one could serve. Thus, moral concerns prompted economic legislation. Interest in such laws, which seem to have been fairly ineffective, continued down into the Imperial Period. Caesar, for example, taxed or banned certain foreign luxuries and is said to have seized such goods from both the market and even the dinner tables of private homes in which they were being served. Such strict enforcement does not appear to have been the normal practice, however.

At Rome and in other communities aediles were the magistrates normally charged with (among other duties) the oversight of markets. They prosecuted those who broke market regulations and looked after the city's general food supply as well. The Roman Senate also had an important role in economic regulation. Before Clodius began in 58 B.C.E. the free grain distribution program that at times provided food for several hundred thousand Romans, the Senate arranged for the sale of subsidized grain in the city. Although the prices of basic foodstuffs seem normally to have fluctuated due to supply and demand, there were attempts to control the prices of some goods. For example, Suetonius, the imperial biographer, reports that Domitian (r. 81–96 C.E.) limited the price of eunuchs. Other measures sought to control prices by limiting production. According to Cicero, the Romans prevented the Gauls from cultivating vineyards and olive groves to protect the interests of Roman wine and olive oil producers.

The Development of the Economy in the Late Republic

The financial strain of the Second Punic War led the Romans to develop a new monetary system around 211 B.C.E. The main Roman coin became the silver denarius, which was minted in increasingly large quantities down to the end of the republic. Although some inflation occurred during this period, the growth in the money supply seems to have been balanced by an increase in monetization as more and more people came to rely on Roman coins for their transactions and as a store of wealth. Bullion and credit also contributed to the growth in the money supply, but since it is impossible to quantify the amount of bullion in circulation or the extent to which credit took the place of coin in transactions, it is difficult to estimate their significance.

The late republic witnessed a substantial increase in long-distance trade within the Mediterranean basin. Rome's newfound wealth allowed it to import many goods into Italy while continuing to export wine and other products. At the same time, Rome faced certain profound economic difficulties. An overreliance on slave labor, particularly for agriculture, led to a series of devastating slave revolts, most notably the one led by Spartacus in the 70s B.C.E. The provinces suffered too, from excessive taxation and corrupt Roman governors. Finding sufficient resources to reward Roman veterans also proved challenging.

Debt, however, more than anything else, constituted a perennial problem among farmers at the mercy of the weather, the urban plebs, and even aristocrats competing in the high-stakes and increasingly cash-intensive political arena. The Lex Poetelia Papiria, a law passed by the tribunes Gaius Poetelius Libo Visolus and Lucius Papirius Cursor in 326 B.C.E., helped ameliorate the consequences of indebtedness by outlawing debt slavery, but it could not do away with the underlying problem. Debt crises occurred frequently in the late republic and could even threaten the stability of the government. The conspiracy of Catiline, a failed plot to overthrow the state in 63 B.C.E., drew much of its support from the indebted. As dictator in the 40s B.C.E., Julius Caesar moved to solve many of Rome's economic problems. He canceled some debts while creating a new mechanism to help debtors repay their obligations. He also reformed provincial taxation, removing the *publicani* as collectors in the east. In Italy he limited the number of slaves who could work as shepherds to help prevent slave revolts.

The Development of the Economy in the Imperial Era

Under Augustus (r. 27 B.C.E.–14 C.E.), the first Roman emperor, the economy staged an impressive recovery, owing in no small part to the end of a series of disastrous civil wars. Nevertheless, Augustus did institute important economic reforms, such as giving salaries to provincial governors to prevent corruption and excessive exploitation. He took control of the finances of the army, creating a special treasury, the *aerarium militare*, to pay for retirement bonuses for soldiers. Cash sums began to replace grants of land and thus reduced anxieties concerning property rights. Many veterans were settled in colonies outside Italy, easing demand for Italian land. Augustus also reformed the management of the food supply, appointing a special official to oversee the transportation, storage, and distribution of grain at Rome. From the reign of Augustus on, the emperor's personal wealth came to play a substantial role in the state's finances. The use of Roman coins continued to spread throughout the empire, no doubt facilitating trade, but there was still no unified monetary system. Egypt had a separate system with its own special coinage, and many communities throughout the empire minted their own coins for local use. At the same time, gold coinage, first minted in quantity during the civil wars of the late republic, began to assume a larger part of the money supply, probably becoming the preferred means of exchange in long-distance commerce.

Although there were occasional crises, the Roman economy fared quite well during the first two centuries of the empire. Some emperors enjoyed sizable budget surpluses and could lavish expensive gifts on the army and inhabitants of Rome. Others emperors were less fortunate or more rapacious. They raised money through higher taxes, new taxes, or auctions of imperial property. According to Suetonius, Caligula (r. 37–41 C.E.) instituted a sales tax on food and a 2.5 percent tax on legal transactions. He may have also levied new taxes on porters and prostitutes. Although early in his reign Nero had lowered or abolished some taxes, he later became desperate for money and created a new tax on tenants and also raised funds through the manipulation of grain prices. Like many other emperors, Nero also confiscated the estates of his enemies. In the aftermath of the short-lived but destructive civil war of 69 C.E., the emperor Vespasian raised some taxes while creating new imposts as well. He was also accused of raising money by creating monopolies of some commodities and then charging inflated prices for them.

Many emperors worked to promote the economic development of the empire (although they would not have conceived of their behavior in these terms) and the welfare of their subjects. Claudius (r. 41–54 C.E.) sought to secure the city's grain supply by insuring merchants' ships, offering cash incentives for the construction of new vessels, and building a new harbor and lighthouse at Ostia, Rome's port city at the mouth of the Tiber. He also drained the Fucine Lake in central Italy, creating new farmland. Following the eruption of Vesuvius in 79 C.E., the emperor Titus (r. 79–81 C.E.) created a relief fund by appropriating the property of those who had died in the disaster and had left no heirs. Several emperors, starting with Nerva (r. 96–98 C.E.), created foundations to distribute money to poor boys and girls in Italian communities so that they could buy food.

Emperors typically financed large construction projects in the city of Rome. Vespasian, for example, began construction of the Colosseum, which his son Titus dedicated in 80 C.E. Such buildings beautified the city, but their construction and maintenance also provided jobs for the lower classes at Rome. Some emperors simply gave gifts of money to the people, and by tradition gifts of cash were occasionally made to the soldiers. Increasingly in the second century C.E. emperors would patronize other communities in Italy and elsewhere in the empire in addition to Rome. The stationing of army units in various locations in the provinces also contributed to the economic development of these regions, since soldiers had money to spend and many military supplies would be purchased locally.

In the latter half of the second century C.E. the empire began to experience economic as well as military and political difficulties. The silver coinage was repeatedly debased. (That is, its silver content was reduced.) As the intrinsic value of the coins declined, prices began to rise. Although Trajan's (r. 98–117 C.E.) conquest of Dacia and its rich gold mines in the first decade of the second century C.E. helped feed Rome's mints, precious metals seem to have been in increasingly short supply. Part of the problem was that there were few rich territories left for Rome to conquer, and it was expensive to defend what Rome already possessed. Imports, particularly from the east, also drained the empire of some gold and silver. In the first century C.E. Pliny the Elder claimed that millions of denarii were exported each year to the East to pay for spices, gems, textiles, and other luxury goods.

Although the Crisis of the Third Century, the massive breakdown of the imperial system from 235 to 284 C.E., was primarily a military and political crisis, it had severe economic ramifications. Warfare disrupted trade and the further debasement of the silver coinage brought about considerable inflation. Taxes were also raised. The empire began to recover under the emperors Diocletian (r. 284–305 C.E.) and Constantine (r. 306–337 C.E.), but economic problems persisted. Diocletian's Prices Edict of 301 C.E. attempted to deal with inflation by setting maximum prices for all goods and services. The law specified execution as the punishment for those who charged too much. The measure failed, as did Diocletian's two

At its height in 200 C.E. the Roman Empire stretched from the Rhine and Danube rivers on the north to Britain and the Iberian peninsula on the west, northern Africa on the south, and Mesopotamia on the east.

attempts to reform the currency. A reform of the empire's tax system was somewhat more successful. It created one system of taxation for the entire empire. In theory, it was more consistent and fair than the patchwork of local and regional taxes it replaced.

Constantine continued many of Diocletian's policies. He was able to introduce a new gold coin, the solidus, which was not debased and became the preferred means of exchange in late antiquity. Nevertheless, economic conditions remained grim, and the government attempted to regulate more closely the movement and professions of its citizens, creating a new class of rural serfs known as coloni while continuing to tax the population heavily to pay for the large imperial army and bureaucracy. These policies, along with a series of civil wars, left the empire ill prepared to deal with the Germanic invasions of the later fourth century C.E.

THE AMERICAS

BY MICHAEL ALLEN HOLMES AND TOM STREISSGUTH

By about 2000 B.C.E. the foundations of agricultural civilization were being laid throughout the Americas. Maize, beans, and gourds sustained many cultures in North and Central America, while South American societies relied on the potato. Economic activity beyond trade at the village level, however, did not occur on a substantial scale until the advent of political organization, which went hand in hand with expanded trading networks. Complex economic structures evolved steadily over time, leading to greater contact between regions and the sharing of technologies, resources, weapons, and tools. Barter and trade provided an essential point of contact, allowing tribes to gather scarce goods without foraging or warfare.

North America

In North America a long-distance system of exchange was developing by about 4000 B.C.E. As nomadic peoples learned to plant and harvest, they began to gather resources needed for a more settled life. They traded for goods such as obsidian, chert (a rock with characteristics of flint), turquoise, copper, silver, and the shells that served as a medium of exchange in many regions, including the coasts of the Pacific Ocean and the Gulf of Mexico. In times of drought, when crops often failed, many native North Americans relied on trade to maintain a settled life and avoid a return to a nomadic, uncertain life of hunting.

In Arctic regions the people depended on hunting almost exclusively. This life demanded constant movement to follow herds of musk ox and caribou and track the seasonal migration of seals and walrus. This lifestyle demand mobility and restricted bands to just a few individuals. Game taken in summer had to be dried and stored for the spare months ahead, particularly because people's diet consisted almost exclusively of meat. The long nights of the Arctic winter forced these groups to band together, and some historians speculate that they may have entered a state of semi-hibernation in order to survive the lack of food, heat, and light.

People of the Pacific Coast had access to a wide variety of plant and animal resources. Settled agriculture was rare, emerging only in southern California under the influence of southwestern cultures that raised maize, beans, gourds. To protect the valuable oak trees that provided acorns, the people sometimes set planned fires to burn off underbrush, which was easily ignited by lightning strikes. Areas of heavy salmon and coho runs in the Pacific Northwest allowed coastal communities to flourish. Offshore fishing was carried out in canoes; the coastal tribes also lived off seals and walrus that lived along the coast. Populations flourished where it was easy to access the sea and where streams ran perennially to their mouths.

Trade routes between the coast and the inland western regions allowed the exchange of shells, baskets, acorns, salt, fish, and clothing. Obsidian was a valued resource, and beads made of clamshells were sometimes used as a form of currency. Eastern Oregon was an important source of raw obsidian, which went into tools and spear points. By 500 C.E. the artisans of the Northwest were greatly diversifying their production of tools, fishhooks, basketry, clothing, and weapons. A highly stratified population emerged along with important signifiers of wealth and status within the clan or tribe. An abundance of food resources resulted in surpluses that came under the control of elaborate hierarchies.

In the arid Southwest a network of trails linked the desert basins and mountain valleys with the Pacific Coast. Knowledge of pottery making, irrigation, and agriculture moved along these trails, and many historians speculate that the advanced societies of Mesoamerica were an important source of goods as well as technical know-how. Large structures known as kivas served as centers for both religious activities and trading. The southwestern tribes may have also held regular market days, when traders could meet to exchange goods and information.

On the Great Plains the most important medium of exchange was the buffalo hide. The vast bison herds of the grasslands were also a source of food, clothing, shelter, tools, and weapons. In eastern North America, important exchange centers grew along the principal rivers, including the Illinois, Mississippi, and Ohio. Copper and silver were obtained from the Great Lakes region. Appalachian tribes exchanged their quartz and mica; flint was a vital resource of Illinois and Indiana; pipestone came from deposits in Ohio and Minnesota. The villages of the Hopewell culture that prospered along the Mississippi and Ohio valleys imported these raw materials and then manufactured finished goods, reexporting them throughout North America along the network of long-distance trails.

Mesoamerica

Owing to its antiquity and its absence of a substantial written record, the Olmec civilization remains shrouded in mystery. Stone figures, many of which were found buried at ceremonial sites, suggest that Olmec society revolved around a cult of jaguar worship. Rulers who derived their power from religious authority directed economic activity and physical labor, which was needed to plan ceremonial centers and obtain stone from distant sites to build structures and public sculptures, such as the colossal heads that are believed to represent rulers.

At the site of San Lorenzo, settled by about 1500 B.C.E., large gangs of workers quarried and transported massive basalt boulders from 50 miles away to raise the ceremonial heads that glorified their rulers. Basalt stone was also used to create elaborate irrigation and drainage systems. The Olmec society at San Lorenzo was divided into farmers and rulers, the latter claiming more fertile land along the banks of rivers and streams. The Olmec elite imported obsidian from distant points in Mexico and Guatemala and also obtained nodes of iron ore, which was polished to a mirrorlike surface. Sometime around 1200 B.C.E. violent events brought about the fall of San Lorenzo. The monumental heads were damaged and buried, either by outsiders or by a peasantry discontented by their subservient lot.

One of the best known Olmec centers is La Venta, an island of sand and clay surrounded by swampland in the modern eastern Mexican state of Tabasco. Among the products of corvée (forced labor) were several giant stone heads some six feet tall and a 110-foot clay pyramid. Archaeologists speculate that the pyramid, which has never been excavated, may have been used as a tomb. The priesthood at La Venta is believed to have lived in a fair degree of luxury, making them among the Western Hemisphere's first elite class. Burial sites, in some of which even infants were given riches to accompany them to the afterlife, indicate that shamanistic privileges and wealth were inherited. As religious subjects provided not only labor for the construction of temples but also food and other goods, priests ate well and wore elaborately tailored ceremonial dress.

Priests routinely buried the figures that middle-class artisans carved from stone and jade. The demand for jade probably fueled commercial relations from central Mexico to the Isthmus of Tehuantepec and as far as modern El Salvador. Other important trading goods were salt, chert, basalt, obsidian, and hard materials from which tools could be fashioned. Some luxury goods remained the property of the elite. Rubber from the Gulf Coast was made into balls used in ritual games, jaguar skins and scepters were traded among rulers, and the priestly caste dealt in jade jewelry and figurines. The elite also collected iron ore, cotton, cacao, shells, and exotic feathers, such as those from the quetzal.

With respect to the economic activity of the masses, a request for a single monolithic stone head would have required countless man-hours of peasant labor. Historians estimate that it took 800,000 man-days to raise the massive La Venta pyramid, the largest structure of its time in ancient Mexico. Thus, given the degree of domination the priesthood achieved, subjects must have been spiritually devoted or fearful of the wrath of their gods, or of the rulers themselves. The oppression of the lower classes and the system of forced labor may have brought about discontent and the violent ends met by the communities at both San Lorenzo and La Venta.

The Maya

While scattered cultures developed in the more hospitable regions of Central America throughout the centuries following the rise of the Olmec, none attained a level of societal and economic complexity comparable to the Maya. The Mayan civilization began developing around the same time as the Olmec were flourishing on the Gulf Coast, and by 300 C.E. Mayan city-states were evolving throughout eastern-central Mesoamerica. The Maya came to occupy the Yucatán Peninsula and modern Mexican land south to the Gulf of Tehuantepec, as well as modern Belize, Guatemala, El Salvador, and the western half of Honduras. As such, they found themselves in an ideal position to benefit from trade between the Olmec and other Mesoamerican cultures to the west and the remainder of Latin America to the southeast. In general, Mayan society was never explicitly unified by political means; rather, commerce served as the most significant regional unifying factor.

The regions inhabited by the Maya, particularly the tropical lowlands, were not exceptionally fertile. Water resources were relatively scant, with few rivers and lakes providing uninterrupted supplies. One early irrigation canal was constructed in Kaminaljuyú, in the southern highlands, by 700 B.C.E. Around Edzná, on the Yucatán Peninsula, a more substantial system of canals and reservoirs was developed by 100 C.E. This system spanned some 14 miles, allowed for canoe traffic, and facilitated the farming of fish. Throughout the lowlands the Maya used wells and *aguadas*, smaller reservoirs lined with clay. The *aguadas* around Tikal were substantial enough to provide water for 70,000 people over a dry period of 120 days. Underground reservoirs called *chultunes* were also carved into bedrock and into the bottoms of natural depressions, further expanding water-collection capacities.

Mayan farmers increased production by cutting ditches for drainage and raising the level of the fields with the excavated soil. To prevent the erosion of soil on sloping farmland, terraces and platforms were carved into hillsides. Household refuse was used as fertilizer to replenish the nutrients in the soil, and crops with different chemical properties were regularly rotated; beans were typically planted alongside maize, so that in the course of harvesting and replanting nitrogen produced by the beans could be extracted and used by the maize. Most basically, ancient Mayans intensified crop production through mass contributions of labor. Only stone tools were then in use, so farmers had to be more sensitive to annual climatic cycles—plants were easiest to cut at the ends of dry seasons, when they were more brittle.

Among the Maya trade in agricultural goods began as individuals and communities achieved surplus production. At first, exported crops were simply the excess supplies of foodstuffs, largely maize, which were delivered to regions lacking their own surpluses. The transportation of foodstuffs, however, was limited by the food's perishability and also by the fact that those doing the transporting would need to consume portions of the load during their journey. Historians have calculated that when traveling by land, food carriers would have been able to travel at most some 90 to 170 miles. By canoe the feasible ratio by weight of foodstuff to person would have been higher, allowing greater distances to be covered.

A number of products other than farmed foodstuffs were valued and traded in ancient Mesoamerica and beyond. Cotton and cacao beans, in particular, were major crops exported from the Mayan region. Cotton grew in fair proliferation on the relatively dry Yucatán Peninsula as well as in other locales throughout eastern Mesoamerica. Both a brown and a whiter variety were spun to form thread, which was dyed and woven into highly marketable textiles, some featuring embroidery. Cacao beans, which grow especially well in warm tropical regions where the soil is rich and the rainfall is heavy, bore particularly high economic value throughout Latin America. While they were originally used simply to brew chocolate drinks consumed by the elite classes, over time, thanks in part to their convenient size and countability, cacao beans became used as currency. Cacao beans of extraordinary quality were produced in the Soconusco lowlands, along the Pacific coastal region in modern southeastern Mexico.

An additional crop grown largely for export was hemp, derived from the agave plant, from which textiles and also sandals were fashioned. Clothes produced with hemp were almost exclusively worn by peasants, as the elite classes wore only clothes produced with finer, softer cotton. (Peasants also would have used cloth made from pounded bark.) Obsidian scrapers were used to depulp the leaves of the agave plant, especially the henequen variety, to produce rope and twine. Tobacco was another locally produced commodity that was valued both within and outside the Mayan region. Unlike in modern times, however, the tobacco was not cut and processed for mass consumption; instead, acting as a hallucinogen in its purest form, tobacco was smoked in cigars or in pipes during religious ceremonies and perhaps also served medicinal purposes. The tobacco smoke, like incense, may have also been deemed "food" fit for consumption by supernatural beings.

The extensive and accessible coasts of the Caribbean Sea and the Gulf of Mexico provided basic sustenance as well as export resources. Fishing communities near the coast used nets fitted with ceramic weights to collect lobsters, shrimp, and shellfish, while other fish were caught using nets and bone hooks. Given the abundance of marine life relative to the size of the coastal population, coastal Mayans were able to salt excesses, preserving them for as long as several years, and occasionally trade them inland. At a burial site at Lamanai, fewer than 50 miles from the coast, archaeologists determined from the skeletal remains of an elite couple that only the male had eaten seafood, such that it must have been considered a delicacy.

The salt that was used to preserve fish was also derived from the sea. One settlement, Komchén, at the northwestern tip of the Yucatán, evidently existed almost solely to facilitate the production and exportation of salt. Other sites throughout the peninsula's northern flats produced the most highly coveted salt in Mesoamerica; dubbed "white salt," it was valued enough to be shipped to the elite in the central Mexican highlands. Along the coast, seawater was collected in shallow pans, from which it evaporated under the tropical sun, leaving masses of salt behind. Elsewhere, including on the coast of the Pacific and at certain springs in the highlands, saltwater had to be boiled.

Honey was another valued commodity throughout Mesoamerica, especially because no other purely sweet substances were locally available. The Yucatán produced substantial quantities of honey, with its importance reflected in the fact that throughout the region a divine being in the form of a bee was worshipped. Hives were provided for the small, stingless bees located there in the form of tree trunks that were hollowed and filled in at the ends, with small holes drilled into the sides to allow the bees entry.

The intensification of agricultural production and the rise of export trade allowed the population density in given areas to increase. This in turn fostered the rise of large urban and ceremonial centers, where an artisanal class depended on the production of coveted goods that further fueled the trade economy. These artisans included painters, whose primary medium was ceramics; weavers, who employed both cotton and hemp; and sculptors, who worked with either stone or jade. Many of these high-quality goods were given to leaders in the form of tribute, while others were deemed valuable enough to be traded over longer distances than more commonly available commercial goods.

While the ruling classes maintained much of the administrative control over trade, middle-class merchants were responsible for most of the actual exchanges of goods and currency. Merchants conducted business at marketplaces in their home cities. Markets were likely set up in large plazas and other open spaces. Any structures that served as marketplace shelters were constructed of materials that would not have left behind any traces over the centuries, such as wooden poles and thatch.

In effect, trade heightened the power and prestige of the Mayan elite. In fact, whereas the ruling classes of the Olmec evolved primarily through spiritual and religious dominion, the royal families at the heads of Mayan cities likely attained their power by amassing and controlling wealth. Accordingly, the cities stationed on trade routes flourished as goods and wealth passed along those routes; when trade routes shifted, cities suddenly prospered or faded into regional irrelevance. The rarest and most exotic goods, such as feathers, shells, and the most elaborate garments, seem to have belonged to and been buried with noble families alone, indicating that laws may have banned the possession of such items by commoners. Likewise, only the elite would have consumed certain foodstuffs, like drinks produced with cacao beans; indeed, peasants likely would have been disinclined literally to drink what money they might have had.

Currency, which emerged at an unknown time, facilitated the exchange of goods. A trader bearing goods was no longer obligated to seek out trading partners who both wanted his goods and possessed goods that he desired. In both Central and South America, cacao beans emerged as an important form of currency. As no hieroglyphic records of financial transactions survive, details regarding the value of cacao beans are available only for the time of Spanish conquest in the 16th century. The market value of the beans may have simply been determined on a day-to-day basis by those engaged in trade. Counterfeiting did occasionally take place, with the flesh of the beans removed from the pod and replaced with soil or the rinds of avocados.

Through ancient times, certain trade routes rose and diminished in importance. With no dominant political center, haphazard and complex trade networks developed along the coasts and rivers of Central America. Good were distributed from the primary cities to the larger towns, then from the larger towns to the smaller towns, and so forth. Meanwhile, canoe trade routes to the north, particularly along the coast of the Yucatán, seem to have prospered throughout ancient times, spurred by the north–south salt trade. Trade was conducted both within the Mayan region, particularly with respect to perishable, bulky foodstuffs, and between the Mayans and neighboring cultures, especially the city of Teotihuacán, in south-central Mexico. Trading was carried out with South America via the Gulf of Ecuador, which provided both sheltered harbor and a center of exchange between the

Andean civilizations to the south and the lowlands of Central America.

South America

In South America a great variety of natural environments imposed their particular demands on the Chavín and Moche cultures that preceded the Incan empire. On the arid Pacific coast, settlement was concentrated in a series of valleys that run down to the sea from the steep Andes highlands. The mountains themselves are further divided into high plateaus known as the Altiplano and the Puna, a grassland region stretching from southern Peru into Bolivia and northern Argentina.

In these highlands little rain fell, soil was thin, and temperatures were low, and the often steep Andean slopes prevented the use of much land for planting. As a result, settlement was scattered over a large area and economic life tended to be isolated. Farming and herding went together; family groups often undertook both vocations in places where pasturage and fertile land lay close together. Some clans held land in different locations and at different elevations to exploit a greater variety of resources. They migrated from one holding to the next to cultivate and harvest crops with different growing seasons. Andean farmers also made widespread use of terraces, which extended the cultivable land and made more efficient use of the available water.

In the Andes storage was vital, and crops often failed altogether through lack of rainfall, hailstorms, and frost. Crops also had to be rotated each year to avoid depleting the less-fertile soil. Alpaca and llama provided all-purpose work animals, transporting goods on the mountain trails and providing wool for clothing and blankets and meat for storage and use in the years of crop failure. In the high Puna region, above the zone where farming is possible, these animals were essential to survival. While both men and women worked the fields, children were given the task of herding and watching the animals.

Because their agriculture was undependable, the mountain settlers acquired beans, maize, cocoa, cotton, salt, and fish by trading along the valleys leading to the seacoast.

In coastal regions, people and entire communities tended to specialize in a single type of productive activity, such as fishing, farming, or herding. Some fishing communities specialized in a certain kind of marine life. Farming along the coast was made difficult by sparse rainfall; crop fields demanded complicated irrigation systems using streams flowing down from the Andean highlands. Irrigation canals demanded large and centralized labor forces. The system gave rise to seasonal work periods; farmers worked at maintaining the irrigation works when their fields were lying fallow and unused.

See also ADORNMENT; AGRICULTURE; ARCHITECTURE; ART; CERAMICS AND POTTERY; CITIES; CLIMATE AND GEOGRAPHY; CLOTHING AND FOOTWEAR; CRAFTS; CRIME AND PUNISHMENT; EDUCATION; EMPIRES AND DYNASTIES; EMPLOYMENT AND LABOR; FAMILY; FESTIVALS; FOOD AND DIET; FOREIGNERS AND BARBARIANS; GOVERNMENT ORGANIZATION; HUNTING, FISHING, AND GATHERING; GENDER STRUCTURES AND ROLES; LABOR AND EMPLOYMENT; LANGUAGE; LAWS AND LEGAL CODES; LITERATURE; METALLURGY; MILITARY; MINING, QUARRYING, AND SALT MAKING; MONEY AND COINAGE; NATURAL DISASTERS; OCCUPATIONS; RELIGION AND COSMOLOGY; ROADS AND BRIDGES; SEAFARING AND NAVIGATION; SETTLEMENT PATTERNS; SLAVES AND SLAVERY; SOCIAL COLLAPSE AND ABANDONMENT; SOCIAL ORGANIZATION; STORAGE AND PRESERVATION; TEXTILES AND NEEDLEWORK; TOWNS AND VILLAGES; TRADE AND EXCHANGE; TRANSPORTATION; WAR AND CONQUEST; WEAPONRY AND ARMOR; WEIGHTS AND MEASURES; WRITING.

FURTHER READING

M. M. Austin and Pierre Vidal-Naquet, *Economic and Social History of Ancient Greece: An Introduction* (Berkeley: University of California Press, 1977).

Michael S. Bisson, S. Terry Childs, Philip de Barros, and Augustin F. C. Holl, *Ancient African Metallurgy: The Socio-Cultural Context* (Walnut Creek, Calif.: AltaMira Press, 2000).

Moses I. Finley, *The Ancient Economy*, 2nd ed. (Berkeley: University of California Press, 1985).

Kevin Greene, *The Archaeology of the Roman Economy* (Berkeley: University of California Press, 1986).

Edward Lipinski, ed., *State and Temple Economy in the Ancient Near East*, 2 vols. (Leuven, Belgium: Departement Orientalistiek, 1979).

J.N. Postgage, *Early Mesopotamia: Society and Economy at the Dawn of History* (London: Routledge, 1992).

Walter Scheidel and Sitta von Reden, eds., *The Ancient Economy* (Edinburgh, U.K.: Edinburgh University Press, 2002).

David Warburton, *State and Economy in Ancient Egypt: Fiscal Vocabulary of the New Kingdom* (Göttingen, Germany: Vandenhoeck and Ruprecht, 1997).

► education

INTRODUCTION

The need for the adult community to educate its youth runs deep into history. In preliterate cultures, the elders of a community educated young people in the skills they needed to survive and to be contributing members of their society. Generally, this type of education was gender specific. Boys were taught to hunt, build fires, tend fields and livestock, fight with weapons, and so on, and they often learned a trade or craft from their fathers. Girls were taught to cook, sew, take care of children, and other domestic chores. All were taught the history and values of their community through songs, legends, and stories, and all were schooled in the arts of cooperation with others, necessary for survival under usually harsh conditions. Knowledge about the world was hard won, and it was important for elders to preserve and transmit that knowledge for future generations.

In later, literate cultures more formal schooling was common, at least for boys and for members of royal and upper classes. In ancient Rome, there was a legislated system of universal education. Egypt, China, India, Mesopotamia, Greece, and Rome all had formal school systems; the oldest of these schools operated in Mesopotamia and date back some 4,000 years. In most of these schools a primary purpose was to teach literacy. Children were drilled in reading and writing, often having to learn complex writing systems based on pictographs or ideograms, such as in China. In some cultures, emphasis was placed on mathematics as well. As time progressed, some school systems allowed older students to specialize in such fields as medicine, history, astronomy, rhetoric (public speaking and argumentation), and other fields. Young people who successfully completed their education were often able to secure positions as scribes, or writers of documents for the court; as civil officials; and, in the case of those adept at mathematics, as architects and builders. Formal educational systems also became more selective, as exams were administered and students were selected for their desire and aptitude.

Early education systems, though, focused on more than career education. Formal schooling also existed to teach young people the norms, values, and proper behaviors of their culture. In ancient China, for example, students were drilled in the teaching of Confucius, the ancient Chinese philosopher. A major function of many ancient schools was the teaching of religion. In ancient India, for instance, students spent a great deal of time memorizing verses from the Vedas, the ancient Hindu scriptures. In general, students were taught about the deities that were worshiped in their religious tradition and became familiar with the basic religious texts.

School was generally not easy. In some cultures students were taken away from their homes and even communities to study in isolated schools, where they had no distractions. The conditions tended to be austere, and schoolmasters were often harsh and unforgiving. Further, much education tended to consist of rote memorization. Students had to memorize written characters, and when they studied texts, such as works of literature or scripture, they learned those texts by heart. Even the study of rhetoric often consisted of little more than the memorization of formal exercises.

AFRICA

BY DIANNE WHITE OYLER

Education in the African society and culture of the ancient world was designed to prepare children for their lives as competent, responsible, contributing adults in the community, thus prolonging the life of the community for posterity. In both preliterate societies and a large segment of literate societies, indigenous education was the norm and was controlled by the family or community leaders. In literate societies not all members of the community were literate. Those who were educated in the literate tradition also received the same primary education as those in preliterate societies but received additional formal schooling that enabled them to read and write and occupy positions as leaders in government and business.

In the preliterate community the educational leaders achieved their position by the status conferred on them from respect for the knowledge they had gained over a lifetime—by benefit of longevity. These were elders at the head of each family or clan, who worked together to govern the community. Even in the context of a community that existed as part of a larger political unit of chiefdom or kingdom, educating children remained the responsibility of the community elders. The elders taught children how to be adults. In some communities this meant being an apprentice to the parents—daughters learned how to carry gourds of water from the river and how to farm, and boys learned how to carry loads of tree branches for fuel to the compound and how to hunt. For most communities, however, there was more control over establishing what was taught as the norms of knowledge and behavior. For example, in West Africa "secret societies" and in South Africa "age grade systems" established the curriculum for boys and girls to learn the requirements of their place as adults in their communities.

For the most part, boys and girls were educated separately, with respected elders as their tutors. As early as age 10 children might be removed from the community and isolated for this intensive process, which could last three to four years. The student would leave the community as a child and return as an adult who, in some cases, had a new name. Boys learned how to be an adult hunter, husband, and father, and girls learned how to be an adult farmer, wife, and mother. This education included step-by-step instruction in a curriculum of ethnic and family history, community values and relationships, religion and cosmology, songs and dances, and acceptable behavior for all expected roles. Specialized instructions as a priest, diviner, healer, tailor, weaver, and so on were received within the family, where the new adult would learn skills that had been handed down from father to son. Alternatively, he would apprentice to another family member or a member of the community. The curriculum was delivered through oral literature, including folktales and legends that communicated the group's history, dilemma tales that honed decision-making skills, riddles and proverbs that exercised the thinking processes and taught community mores and appropriate behavior, and praise songs, stories, and dance.

When the new adults entered the community, they became members of the male or female "secret society" or "age set" because they now possessed the "secret" information of adulthood. Similarly to members of a graduating class, they had a common bond that enabled them to form significant cooperative groups for economic and social needs. While these new adults might have been ready for marriage, depending upon the community, the males were restricted for a period of time from the next step in the life cycle by the elder men, who controlled younger men's labor, but some of the new adult females married older men.

After the advent of Christianity, education in religious texts in indigenous and foreign languages and scripts became the priority for Christians as African groups converted to Christianity. The first educational institutions were monasteries and convents. The monks and nuns taught novices the scripture, giving them a religious education, and also how to read and write. King Ezana converted the kingdom of Axum to Christianity in the fourth century of the Common Era, and scripture was translated into the Ge'ez language and writing system and taught in the monasteries that became centers of education. Saint Augustine of Hippo established the first monasteries in North Africa's Maghreb region at Tagaste and Hippo, where third- and fourth-century Donatist and Gnostic Christians studied the Bible in Greek and Latin. Finally, Christian monks and traders introduced Coptic Christianity to Nubia in the fifth and sixth centuries C.E.; with conversion of the rulers and people by the seventh century, the monastic tradition continued in the teaching of its clergy.

In the ancient African world indigenous, preliterate education trained the next generation to be responsible contributing members of the community. Those who were preliterate and those who were literate lived together in the urban areas, and those who received formal schooling for jobs using literacy also received the same training as their preliterate neighbors. The two levels of instruction provided scribes with an elementary level and a secondary level of education that corresponded to an apprenticeship. Thus, scribes were educated to live in the community of their peers and to become leaders in an ever-growing civilization that required their skills.

EGYPT

BY AMY HACKNEY BLACKWELL

Most ancient Egyptian children did not go to school. For much of the ancient period, schools were rare or nonexistent. Instead, children stayed at home and helped their parents with daily tasks, in the process learning skills they would need as adults. Girls worked with their mothers, learning to weave, sew, cook, and take care of babies. Boys helped their fathers hunt, build houses, or gather wood. The sons of warriors might learn from their fathers how to use weapons. Boys and girls both worked in the fields with their parents, learning the complicated rhythms of the seasons and the Nile's flooding. Children sat with adults during religious rituals and evening storytelling, learning about their culture and religion.

Many children served as apprentices for several years, learning a craft such as metalworking, glassblowing, or embalming through practical experience. If a father practiced a craft, he would teach it to his sons starting when they were four or five years old. Many children were apprenticed to craftsmen who were not their fathers. Their parents had to pay their masters for the training. At the end of training an apprentice might have to pass a test to show that he had mastered his trade.

Some ancient Egyptian children studied academic subjects, such as reading, writing, and mathematics. The children of the Egyptian rulers were taught in the palace by tutors. The Egyptian temples ran schools for the sons of wealthy parents; students attended from the age of four to their midteens. Most students who attended school were boys. Very few girls were educated, though daughters of wealthy and noble families often did learn to read and write. A successful performance at a temple school could mean that a boy would be qualified to take a prestigious government position or to serve as an army officer. Many graduates of temple schools became scribes, professional writers who could be hired to compose documents for those who could not read or write. Educated boys might also become priests, entrusted with the rituals of Egyptian religion.

During the heyday of Egyptian rule, before Greeks entered the country, Egyptians did all their writing with a pictographic written language. A pictogram is a picture that represents a concept or an object. Egyptian pictograms are known as hieroglyphs. It took many years for students to learn all the hieroglyphs they needed to know. They also had to learn how to make paper from papyrus, a reed that grew in the marshes.

Much of the Egyptian curriculum came from volumes that are now called "books of instruction." These books contained verses of advice given by a father to his son or a king to his heir. They admonished their young readers to tell the truth, to treat others with fairness, to avoid boasting, and generally to behave with prudence and wisdom. These documents resemble the admonitions in the Old Testament book Proverbs. Students learned these lessons by copying their texts over and over until they memorized them.

Students also studied mathematics and medicine. Egyptians were very good at mathematics, using a decimal system to make the calculations they used to build pyramids and to trade with neighboring peoples. They also used mathematics to create a calendar that would allow them to predict when the Nile River would flood. Students who studied medicine benefited from the knowledge of anatomy gathered by embalmers who made mummies. They learned about incantations, prayers, and the use of amulets, or charms, to ward off evil, but they also studied the effect of diet on human health. Young doctors often specialized in particular diseases, gaining their expertise by working with older doctors.

From 332 B.C.E. until 641 C.E. Greek was the official language in Egypt. Although commoners continued to speak their native dialects, Greek was the language of education, and all upper-class Egyptians learned it. Egypt's government needed a large number of educated scribes and officials, and many Egyptians saw education as a means to social advancement. Under Greek and then Roman rule, literacy became widespread, even among peasants, who needed to read in order to engage in commerce. People moved from the country-

Granite statue of Senmut holding Princess Neferure, the temple of Amun, Karnak, Thebes, Egypt, Eighteenth Dynasty, around 1470 B.C.E.; Senmut was Neferure's tutor. (© The Trustees of the British Museum)

side to the cities, where they found more teachers and more social mobility based on education.

Egyptian education in this period was similar to education in Greece. Younger students learned reading, writing, arithmetic, music, gymnastics, and athletics. They memorized poetry, especially that of Homer. Older students might engage in specialized study of composition, philosophy, rhetoric, astronomy, history, medicine, or mathematics. In addition to classes, students were expected to compete publicly in tests of academic achievement.

Some students went to schools where they studied with groups of children of about the same age. Others studied at home with private tutors. Parents had to pay for their children's education, which meant that the poorest people could not send their children to school. Tutors were usually slaves purchased by parents to teach their children. Teachers of all sorts were held in fairly low esteem; elementary teachers received the least respect, while secondary-level teachers were somewhat more highly regarded. During this period girls studied too, though education was still less common for girls than it was for boys.

Egypt became a center of learning during the Classical Period (480–323 B.C.E.). Alexander the Great founded the city of Alexandria in 332 B.C.E., modeling it on Athens and recruiting citizens from all over the ancient world. Among the new citizens were many scholars, and Alexandria became an important destination for those seeking advanced study. One famous Alexandrian scholar was the mathematician Euclid (ca. 325–ca. 265 B.C.E.), who greatly advanced and also systematized the study of geometry. Many educated Jewish settlers came to Alexandria and taught their religion there; the Septuagint, a Greek translation of the Hebrew Bible, was written by Jewish scholars in Alexandria.

Alexandria was especially famous for its library, which was the largest collection of writing ever assembled at the time. The library had an excellent collection of texts by Homer as well as works by other famous authors and scholars. Scholars came from everywhere to read and study in the library. In ancient times it could be difficult for a student to find the works he needed to read, and texts often existed in various versions in different places, so the Alexandria library's collections were invaluable to serious students. The library functioned as an early university, its resources attracting scholars who in turn learned from one another.

THE MIDDLE EAST

BY AMY HACKNEY BLACKWELL

Ancient Mesopotamians were among the first people in the world to create schools. Archaeologists have found lists of vocabulary words dating to about 3000 B.C.E. at the Sumerian city of Uruk; this is the earliest evidence of formal schooling in the region. By 2000 B.C.E. Mesopotamians had a well-regulated school system, with scribal schools created by royal edict and students doing work in many major cities, including Ur, Uruk, Nippur, Shuruppak, and Abu Salabikh. Between 2000 and 1500 B.C.E. Mesopotamian students did enough school exercises to leave archaeologists hundreds of clay tablets containing their work with directions from and corrections by their teachers.

Mesopotamian schools had several purposes. The most basic was to create scribes by teaching children how to read and write. The government, the temples, and businesses all needed people who could read and write letters and inventories and do arithmetic. A more philosophical purpose was to create an educated, thoughtful citizenry. Mesopotamian writers are the first in the world to mention the concept of "humanity" as a condition of people who have been elevated above the animals by learning to think. Another reason to educate children was so that they could read of past events, interpret them in the present, and in their turn write down the events of their lifetimes and thus leave a record for future generations.

Sumerian schools were private, not public. Only wealthy parents, such as government officials, businessmen, scribes, priests, and military officers, sent their children to school. Almost all students were boys; the only female students were the daughters of royalty and girls being prepared to become priestesses. Still, most Mesopotamian boys and girls never went to school at all, instead spending their childhoods helping their parents and learning the tasks they would perform as adults. Schools met from sunrise until sunset, and students ate lunch at school. Students attended for several years, finishing in their teens. A school would typically contain students of many different ages and levels of academic achievement. The older students helped instruct the younger ones; they were called "big brothers." All the pupils called themselves their school's "sons."

Teachers were scholars in various fields, including mathematics, language, and surveying. They took their salaries from the fees parents paid as tuition. Parents would sometimes try to persuade teachers to give their children favorable treatment; in one ancient Sumerian school story, a lazy boy's parents invite their son's teacher to dinner and give him a ring as a present, whereupon the teacher lavishes praise upon the lad. Most schools had a disciplinary officer who beat unruly students with a stick. Infractions were similar to those in modern schools; they included speaking without permission, standing up or leaving without permission, not speaking correct Sumerian, and dressing inappropriately.

The first thing Mesopotamian students learned was the cuneiform writing system. This system was extremely complex and required readers to recognize subtle differences in patterns of tiny triangles made with a reed pen, or stylus, on clay tablets. It took years to memorize all the characters and learn to read quickly. Writing cuneiform presented its own difficulties. Students had to learn how to make clay tablets by mixing and molding the clay and how to fire the clay tablets so they hardened.

Teachers taught reading and writing by writing a sentence at the top of a tablet and requiring their students to copy it over and over. The teacher or an older student would review the work and correct it, and all the students were expected to study their day's work at home that night. The next day they had to write the previous day's lesson correctly, after which they would receive a new writing exercise. Archaeologists have found numerous clay tablets containing these exercises, including teachers' corrections; one tablet was apparently so disastrous that the teacher crossed out everything the student had written. Older boys wrote out longer texts than younger ones. Sometimes teachers gave lessons based on stories, some of them humorous. As students grew more advanced, they began reading and reciting their lessons aloud. Students might specialize in various fields, including architecture, engineering, astronomy, botany, geography, medicine, and zoology.

Mathematics was very important to Mesopotamians, who were expert architects and carefully collected and distributed their people's grain. Students practiced mathematical skills with word problems that presented situations a professional man might face, such as plotting the movements of the stars, calculating the supplies needed for a military campaign, collecting taxes, determining how many bricks were needed to build a palace, or measuring plots of land and estimating how much grain they would produce.

Sumerian schools also taught languages. Students were expected to learn Sumerian. As time went on, people stopped

Cuneiform tablet with schoolwork, Old Babylonian, about 1900–1700 B.C.E., probably from southern Iraq. (© The Trustees of the British Museum)

speaking Sumerian. but Mesopotamian students kept learning it; they used it much as Latin was used in medieval Europe, as a dead but stable language that marked people of learning. After about 2500 B.C.E. students also learned Akkadian, the language of the Akkadian people.

The ancient Jews in the Levant also developed an elaborate system of education. They believed that education was important for transmitting knowledge from generation to generation, for increasing the entire body of knowledge, and for defining culture and acceptable behavior. The three branches of education were military training, occupational skills, and religious education; the latter was generally considered the most important. Jewish people considered study to be a form of prayer. Both boys and girls were educated, and most ancient Jews were literate. Parents were supposed to teach their children the Torah at home. Children at the age of five began learning about ritual purity and how to pray. At age 10 children studied the oral law. They completed their primary education around the age of 12 or 13.

Boys in their early teens spent time at the Bet Midrash, or "House of Study," where rabbis taught them Jewish law and history, including the scriptures in Old Testament and the Talmud, the Jewish book of law and scriptural commentary. They progressed through several stages; at age 15 they were considered ready to study the works of wise Jewish scholars and at age 20 were prepared to pursue a vocation. The Bet Midrash functioned as school, place of prayer, and communal library. Teachers included scribes and Pharisees. Scribes were literate men who worked as administrative officials and teachers. The Pharisees came from the ranks of the scribes, but they were more specialized scholars, teachers, and professional writers in charge of transcribing and interpreting the Torah, the Jewish holy text. Jewish people continued to pursue education throughout their adulthoods. Thirty was considered the age at which one was mature enough to enter the ministry, and by age 50 a person was educated enough to advise others.

In ancient Persia priests called magi were trained to interpret dreams and other omens and to predict the future. The rank of magi was hereditary, so only boys born into magi families could undergo the necessary training in scripture, ritual, and astrology. One of the best-preserved accounts of education in Persia is *Cyropaedia* (*The Education of Cyrus*), the Greek historian Xenophon's fictional account of the life and education of Cyrus the Great (585–529 B.C.E.). This book recounts Cyrus's process of learning political philosophy and spreading his ideas among the Persian people. Herodotus, a Greek historian of the fifth century B.C.E., described the education of Persian boys. Noble boys spent the first five years of their lives with their mothers and then the next 15 years learning to hunt, ride, shoot arrows, and throw spears. A few learned to read and write; some of them became scribes. Although the Persians revered wise and educated men, most noble Persians restricted their philosophical education to the rudiments of ethical behavior.

ASIA AND THE PACIFIC

BY AMY HACKNEY BLACKWELL

Most children living in Asia and the Pacific region in ancient times had no formal education. They stayed at home with their parents and learned the skills they would need to function as adults. Fathers taught their sons how to hunt, build houses, and perhaps fight with weapons. Mothers taught their daughters how to make cloth, cook, sew, and tend children. Both sexes helped their parents in the fields. Children would have joined adults for storytelling sessions and religious rituals in which they learned the specifics of their culture and their own ethnic mythologies.

China developed a very complex education system during the ancient period. Much of Chinese educational philosophy was based on the teachings of the ancient thinker Confucius (551–479 B.C.E.). Confucius claimed that all people had the potential to act properly and that education was the best way to help people grow up to behave correctly. Chinese students spent years learning to read and write the Chinese script. Chinese writing consisted of ideograms, or characters—patterns of brushstrokes that represented images or concepts. Each character was painted by brush or, for inscriptions, cast with molds or incised into materials like bone or bronze. While the order of strokes was meant to be predetermined or regular, calligraphers often violated that protocol. The characters were seen as graceful images as well as written words, and beautiful handwriting was considered a valuable skill. The advantage of this system of writing was that it did not depend on spoken language for comprehensibility, so people who spoke different dialects could understand each other's writing. The disadvantage was that was difficult to learn to read and write; students had to memorize thousands of characters before they could be reasonably literate. This took many years.

The Han Dynasty emperor Wu Ti (r. 140–87 B.C.E.) founded a state educational system in 124 B.C.E. His chief purpose in educating young boys was to train them to be civil servants who could work in the government bureaucracy, creating a highly selected and trained body of government officials loyal to the emperor. (All students in China were boys. Girls could not become civil servants, and their families preferred to keep them home to work. Some girls in the nobility were instructed at home and learned to read, but they were the exception.)

Wu Ti built provincial schools all across China and founded an academy for advanced students. Admission was competitive; students had to pass a difficult examination to get in. Once students were admitted, the government provided food and housing for them. The Han Dynasty introduced a system of examinations as a way of identifying the best students on the basis of ability, rather than allowing professors to pick and choose their favorites.

Han emperors believed that the Confucian approach to education would produce a new class of educated aristocrats

Yue ware water dropper in the shape of a frog drinking from a cup, from Zhejiang Province, southern China, Six Dynasties, third to fourth century C.E.*; such items were made for the scholar's desk and used in calligraphy.* (© The Trustees of the British Museum)

who would be more loyal to the state than the hereditary nobility was. Consequently, the ancient curriculum consisted largely of Confucian philosophy and ethics. Professors were experts in the Confucian Five Classics, which included works on history, rituals, poetry, and divination (foretelling the future or discovering hidden knowledge through omens). Confucian philosophy emphasized loyalty to the state above all. Students also studied mathematics, music, and painting among other subjects.

Confucius thought that all social classes should be educated, even the poor. As a practical matter, most of the poor did not have the time or the resources to go to school, so most boys who went to school came from wealthy families. There were nonetheless many exceptions. The Han emperors set up their system to find talented boys, not wealthy boys, and this gave many poor young men an opportunity they would not otherwise have had. A number of boys from humble backgrounds did rise up through the system to take important jobs high in the governmental bureaucracy.

As Chinese culture spread throughout eastern Asia, the people in Southeast Asia, Japan, and Korea adopted Chinese educational practices. Korea, for example, created an education system during the Three Kingdoms Period (57 B.C.E.–668 C.E.) that was very similar to the Chinese system, with a heavy emphasis on Chinese classics, Confucian philosophy, and preparation for government service.

In India education was inextricably tied to religion. Hindu students were expected to learn Hindu scriptures, rites, and rituals as a preparation for higher knowledge. Every student studied with a teacher called a guru. In ancient times a guru was considered a god in human form. Students were expected to choose a single guru and stay with him until their education was complete. To study with a guru, a student would go to a *gurukula*, a sort of school that was often located in the forest, away from cities and students' families. Entering a *gurukula* was not easy; a student had to convince the guru that he was serious about wanting to study and that he was intelligent enough to learn the material. Gurus believed that there was no point in teaching those who were not interested or mentally capable of learning, and tradition forbade the acceptance of unqualified students. Once in the *gurukula*, students studied the Hindu scriptures, or Vedas, memorizing verses and reciting them in order; a student could not move on to a new verse until he had recited all the preceding verses perfectly. Although scriptures were important, students could also study practical subjects such as mathematics, medicine, music, magic, or the art of warfare.

Discipline was strict and living conditions austere; students had to observe a stringent diet, meditate, practice yoga, remain chaste, and perform menial jobs for the guru. Sometimes students traveled with the guru to perform rites. When a student finished the several-year course of study, he paid the guru for the instruction.

Almost all students in *gurukulas* were boys. Girls were not allowed to study; a few royal women were educated, but ordinary women were not. For the most part, lower-caste people were not allowed to study either; education was restricted to the upper classes. People in lower castes were allowed, however, to receive training in their occupations. Members of castes that specialized in various crafts, such as weaving, pottery, or building, would train their children in the traditional practices of their specialty. After the fifth century B.C.E. Indian students also studied Buddhism. Buddhism placed more emphasis on practical living techniques that would pave the way to enlightenment. Communities of Buddhist monks and nuns functioned as schools of Buddhism.

EUROPE

BY JUSTIN CORFIELD

Throughout Europe during ancient times there were formalized systems of childhood education involving parents, relatives, and village elders who taught lessons in farming and hunting and various other adult occupations. Indeed, education largely took the form of initiation into adulthood, and this process varied across the continent and gradually changed and adapted over time until the Romans extended their rule over much of western, southern, and central Europe.

The tradition among Celts was for boys to be handed over to "foster fathers" at the age of seven (as was the case in Ireland) to 10 (as was practiced in Scotland). The foster fathers, often uncles or longtime family friends, were then responsible for the academic, artistic, and physical training of the boys. This responsibility was regarded as a great honor, with accounts that in Ireland "five hundred kyne [cattle] and better" were often given for the training of the son of a "great man." A Celtic youth was supposed to have "four and twenty" skills. Among these skills were the "six feats of activity": hurling weights, running, leaping, swimming, wrestling, and riding a horse. There were also the "four exercises of weapons": archery, use of the javelin, use of the quarter-staff, and use of the sword and the sword and buckler. Then there were the "three rural sports": hunting, fishing, and hawking. Last there were the "seven domestic games": poetry, heraldry, diplomacy and musicianship, and four board games. Although the foster father oversaw this training, particular aspects were taught by skilled individuals; spiritual training, for example, was often performed by Druids.

Many of the skills that Celtic boys had to learn were concerned with war, and the Bronze Age in which they flourished was not only prosperous but also violent. The Germanic tribes tended to prefer boys to use the bow and arrow, while the Gauls, in the region that is now France, tended to favor the javelin. To encourage them in warlike pursuits, the Romans recorded that Celtic boys were, from a young age, served meat on the point of a sword. Many early sporting pursuits, such as tossing the caber (a pole or tree trunk) for the Picts (in Scotland) or juggling swords, were important for developing skills useful for battle, where agility rather than armor made the difference between life and death. In parts of Europe where there were no major pressures of population, skills related to hunting and trapping animals were given priority. Upon being trained, the boys would be asked to prove themselves in terms of valor and skill at arms to be acknowledged publicly as achieving adulthood.

In parts of Europe some men, especially mercenaries, had specialized occupations. The slingers from the Balearic Islands were used extensively by the Carthaginians, and Roman writers mention them in some awe and trepidation. To achieve the level of skill they had, boys on these islands were trained from an early age in the use of the sling. One writer notes that the boys were trained to hit bread with a stone and were not allowed to eat until they hit the target; it is also noted that boys were trained by their fathers, who gave them a sling as their first toy. Similarly, the Huns trained their sons from a young age to ride horses.

As the Roman Empire expanded, many well-to-do families wanted their sons to be educated in the Roman style. Many boys in towns and cities were taught by schoolmasters, who opened a room or more of their houses and tutored a number of students at the same time. Salaries were low, but there were encouragements, such as that teachers were exempted from military service by the emperor Constantine (r. 306–337 C.E.). The wealthy often used an educated slave known as a *paedagogus*, who would act as a tutor. A significant number of these slaves, especially around the Mediterranean, were Greeks.

Small schools followed an unregulated Roman system of education with rote learning of grammar as well as poetry and rhetoric, or the effective use of speech and writing. The system also involved learning how to read, often both Latin and Greek, depending on the town or city in which the school was located. The works of Homer were regularly used to teach history, to explain problems with life and morals, and also to teach rhetoric. The study of rhetoric sometimes involved repeating imaginary speeches from such historical figures as Alexander the Great, Hannibal, and Julius Caesar. Children would write on slate, with many committing information to memory, reinforcing the oral tradition used by the Celts, the Dacians, and others.

Agricola, the Roman governor of Britain from 77 to 84 C.E., brought with him from Tarsus to Britain a Greek schoolmaster called Demetrius. Other similar situations occurred. Indeed, Saint Patrick spoke some Latin from a young age. During the height of the Roman Empire the system of education, though it did not follow any set curriculum, was probably fairly uniform throughout the empire. It was not uncommon for children of the very wealthy to go to Athens or Rhodes for the best schooling available at that time. The Roman elite families certainly availed themselves of these opportunities, and it would seem likely that other rich families across the empire might have done the same.

Apart from some from wealthy families who would have had tutors, the Celts seem to have paid little attention to girls' education, which would have been conducted largely at home. It is also possible that the male Roman writers did not choose to record the education of Celtic girls, whose treatment may not have been much different from that of girls in villages in Italy. The names of very few women survive from this period, and even for those about whom much is written, such as Boudicca, who fought the Romans in Britain in 60–61 C.E., little is known about their early life and training. After the growth of the Christian church from the early fourth century, churches became places of learning, and boys (and probably a few girls) started getting their education—religious and academic—from the local priest and gradually at monasteries.

GREECE

BY CHRISTOPHER BLACKWELL

Before the fifth century B.C.E. there is little evidence for formal, organized schools in the Greek world. The education of aristocratic children would have been handled by their nurses when they were very young or by slaves, but schooling was probably left to informal instruction by peers and older mentors. In Homer's *Iliad*, we read that Achilles' father, Peleus, retained an older man, Phoenix, as a companion and tutor for the baby Achilles. Phoenix talks of teaching Achilles to eat with a spoon, and later he instructs him to play games and use weapons. Young Achilles was also said to have attended a "school" run by the centaur Chiron—the mythological nature of this schoolmaster may suggest that formal education was so rare as to seem magical, the privilege only of those aristocrats descended from gods. In the most ancient Greek world the aristocracy tended to assume that their superiority was inborn, a matter of blood and not of education.

For all Greek boys and young men in the centuries before the Classical Period (which began in the fifth century B.C.E), informal and formal athletic competitions would have been the center of their development. These games involved strength and endurance training, various foot races (including races while wearing armor), and the acquisition of military skills such as boxing, wrestling, archery, swordplay, and the use of the spear and javelin.

Before the widespread adoption of the Greek alphabet, "literary" and cultural education would have come through public rituals. The shared theology and mythology, a cultural heritage that more than anything else united the independent and scattered communities of Greek speakers, passed from generation to generation through sacrifices and festivals, each associated with a myth or in celebration of the origin of some cultural institution. Thus, Athenian children would learn of the history of their legendary king Theseus at the festival of the Deipnophoria and of the political unification of Athens at the festival of the Synoikia. Many festivals featured the performance of Homeric poetry, and all young Greeks would thereby have come to know of the legends about the Trojan War and the heroes who fought in it.

At some time, and over a period of time, before the fifth century B.C.E., the Greeks adopted a new alphabet, modified from the Phoenician alphabet, which allowed a true culture of literacy to arise and which spurred the invention of formal programs and institutions of learning. An anecdote from the fifth century B.C.E. historian Herodotus illustrates this change.

In Book 6 of his history, Herodotus describes an incident that occurred around 496 B.C.E. on the island of Chios, where a roof collapsed on a group of 120 boys as they were being taught their letters; only one boy survived. Herodotus calls this an omen, anticipating the overall political disaster that was about to befall the community of Chios, specifically an invasion by a Persian army. Herodotus mentions another disaster that happened at the same time: A chorus of 100 young men from Chios, officially sent to Delphi for a performance at a festival there, fell victim to a plague that killed 98 of them. Only two of the boys returned alive to Chios. This double tragedy serves, for us, to illustrate two parallel institutions of learning: one private and literate—an indoor school where boys quietly studied written texts—and one public and preliterate—a chorus trained to sing poetry.

In Athens during the fifth century B.C.E., we have evidence for a fully developed system of education for boys, while the education of girls seems to have continued to be a private, ad hoc affair managed, if at all, by mothers inside the home. For all Athenian boys, there was a compulsory program of public education during the years of adolescence, the *ephebeia*, designed to train young citizens of the democracy. This program included military training but also training in civic responsibility. Apart from these years, however, schooling was optional and required payment to private teachers.

Young Athenian boys learned under three kinds of teachers. A boy might begin the day with the *paidotribēs*, the gymnastics teacher, working on physical fitness and the vigorous games that formed the basis of public competition and prepared young men for war. Afterward he might go to the *kitharistēs* to study music—singing and playing the lyre, a stringed instrument like a harp. Music was considered important for teaching balance and moderation, for developing aesthetic sensibilities, and for providing a certain amount of mathematical study. And later still he might go to the *grammatistēs* to learn letters, read Homeric poetry, and study arithmetic and geometry. Apart from any examinations these teachers might give to their students, study was motivated by the prospect of festivals, at which boys would be expected to compete in games, to recite the poetry they had learned, or to dance as members of a chorus.

HOMEWORK IN ANCIENT GREECE

The dry sands of Egypt have preserved tens of thousands of documents that were part of the day-to-day lives of people. Because the ruling classes of Egypt after the fourth century B.C.E. were Greek, we have a vast number of receipts and recipes, personal letters, and business contracts written in Greek by ordinary people. Among these are school exercises from students as they learned to read and write the Greek language, the universal language of business, politics, science, and art from the fourth century B.C.E. until well into the period of the Roman Empire.

Some of these surviving exercises are extremely basic. A fragment from the fourth century B.C.E. shows a series of letters written well and clearly, followed by the same letters written in a very clumsy hand; clearly the teacher did the first row, and a beginning student tried to copy them, working on the shapes and attempting (unsuccessfully) to write between the lines scratched on the fragment.

A scrap of papyrus from the second century B.C.E. has the student's name at the top—Apollonius—and a list of the Athenian names for the months, followed by a list of the Macedonian names of the months. The writing is unsteady, and there are a number of misspellings. Other fragments show students copying the names of Greek gods and goddesses, or the names of the heroes in Homeric poetry.

After learning their letters, students went on to learn grammar. One student was set to writing the phrases "the good father," "the appropriate warning," and "the philanthropic attitude" in each of the grammatical cases of the Greek language—the teacher was clearly trying to add some moral instruction to the lesson in grammar and syntax. These fragments are a wealth of evidence for teachers and learners in the ancient Greek world, though the stories behind them—the students' successes and failures—are now lost.

Athens is not the only model, however. The poetry of Sappho (sixth century B.C.E.), from the island of Lesbos, not only shows great literary accomplishment by the poet herself but also suggests an intellectual community among the young women of Sappho's acquaintance; during the Victorian era English scholars liked to imagine that Sappho ran a prep school or finishing school for women. There is little evidence for this, but there is no denying the evidence for some formal literary training of women at that time.

In Sparta during the Classical Period girls were educated beside boys, with the whole program of education focusing on the skills necessary in a military state—athletics, gymnastics, and war games but also music, poetry, and dancing, all of which were deemed necessary for young warriors as well as for the future wives and mothers of warriors.

During the fifth century B.C.E. a number of professional intellectuals came to Athens—then the cultural, economic, and political center of the Greek world—and set themselves up as professional teachers of rhetoric and philosophy. These men were known as *sophistēs*, or sophists, and they introduced new ideas about the gods, human ethics, and the role of reason in public life. They often promised to help young men achieve prominence in the democratic state of Athens by teaching them to speak persuasively. As with most new intellectual movements, this "sophistic revolution" was met with some suspicion and often ridiculed, but it was also highly influential. Pericles, a figure who dominated Athenian politics in the middle of the fifth century B.C.E., was greatly influenced by the Sophists.

The heritage of this sophistic revolution were a number of schools of philosophy and rhetoric—Isocrates' school of rhetoric, Plato's Academy, and Aristotle's Lyceum being the most famous—and the lasting position of rhetoric, public speaking, as the centerpiece of education for wealthy young men, a movement that survived throughout the Hellenistic Period (323–31 B.C.E.) and into the Roman Empire. Indeed, long after Athens ceased to be a military or political power, it remained an intellectual center. We have a number of letters from the Roman statesman Cicero (106–43 B.C.E.), written to his son whom he sent to study in Athens. These letters confirm the lasting legacy of the Athenian model of education, and they also suggest that the challenges faced by young people going abroad for higher education, and by their parents back at home, transcend time.

ROME

BY ROBIN BARROW

In the sixth and fifth centuries B.C.E. education was a family matter. There were no schools and no formal program of study. A father had absolute legal authority over his children and took prime responsibility for their upbringing, which consisted mainly in developing character, particularly the Roman virtues of dignified bearing (gravitas), sense of duty (*pietas*), and respect for tradition (*mos maiorum*). The mother also played an influential role in the children's early years, and she went on to initiate her daughters into the customs, practices, and skills associated with a conventional female role. These skills were chiefly those suited to the running of a household. The sons would conclude their education by being apprenticed to the father's trade or, in the case of the wealthier classes, by entering military service and being inducted into the business of political life by the father or a close family friend.

Reading and writing played little or no part in education at this early date, but they had become part of the education of the families of senators and *equites* ("knights") by the end of the fourth century B.C.E. By the middle of the second century B.C.E. Roman education was increasingly influenced by Greek example. Greek tutors had been popular for some time, but now Romans began to study Greek language and culture.

The orator and statesman Cicero (106–43 B.C.E.) maintained that Rome did not have a uniform system of education; there was no centralized system, no compulsory formal schooling, no common curriculum, and no state funding (though later emperors and other wealthy individuals did sometimes endow schools and professorships). But there were schools by this date. These were generally very small and often consisted of nothing more than a small room in a tavern or even a spot in the open air. A fee-paying school was opened in the second half of the third century B.C.E., but there were a few schools of an informal nature the century before that, where payment would have been by gift or in kind, though the wealthy never ceased to employ tutors.

There was no formal requirement of attendance and no regularized curriculum even by the end of first century B.C.E., but by then students did by and large follow a basic pattern of schooling. At about the age of seven, they were taught basic literacy and numeracy by the *litterator*, being escorted to and from school by a slave. Letters were learnt by copying; once the child could form sentences, he would copy out improving phrases and sayings, such as *laborare est orare* ("to work is to pray"), intended at the same time to improve his character. Writing generally involved inscribing letters on a wax board with a *stilus* ("stylus" or "nib"). Calculation was done on the fingers, on an abacus, or in the head. At about the age of 12, the boy went to the *grammaticus* to study literature. Girls could receive a formal education but did not commonly do so; it is not clear whether boys and girls were ever taught together.

In studying literature the emphasis was on analysis and memorization, and the presumption was that the study would also be uplifting and contribute to character development. Students had to recite from chosen authors and compose commentaries on them. The material was largely poetry and initially Greek (for example, Homer). By the first century C.E., following the emergence of poets such as Virgil (70–19 B.C.E.) and Horace (65–8 B.C.E.), Romans were able to study their own literature, though Greek authors never lost their appeal.

Fragments of painted plaster, Roman Britain, first or second century c.e., *from Otford, Kent, England; these fragments from a frieze that decorated a corridor at a Roman villa are inscribed with a line from Virgil's* Aeniad, *showing widespread knowledge of classical Roman literature.* (© The Trustees of the British Museum)

At about the age of 15, students passed to the third and final stage of formal education under the rhetor. Rhetoric was first taught in the second century B.C.E., once again using Greek materials that were gradually replaced by Latin material. The rhetor taught the art of public speaking, which was important in relation to political advancement in a society that encouraged widespread debate, developed a legal system that still affects us today, and expected participation in civic affairs. In its heyday the study of rhetoric was a practical form of legal training. Romans such as Cicero and Quintilian (ca. 35–ca. 100 C.E.) wrote sophisticated treatises on the subject; Cicero, in particular, shows by his career (and in his many extant speeches) the high quality that such a training could achieve.

The study of rhetoric, however, involved a somewhat mechanistic training, consisting for the most part in a number of repeated routine exercises. For example, students were called on to argue for or against some course of action; to compose eulogies or criticisms of historic figures; to debate the merits of epigrams and other famous sayings. The student was expected to focus on selecting a suitable subject matter, arranging or organizing the argument appropriately, delivering it clearly, and adopting an appropriate tone. The study culminated in the practice of comparing imaginary speeches and presenting them to fellow students (*declamatio*). There were two kinds of *declamatio*: one (*suasoria*) involved the attempt to justify (or condemn) some course of action, usually historical; the other (*controversia*) consisted of an attempt to argue for or against a specific legal case.

By the end of the first century B.C.E. many Romans completed their education by studying rhetoric and philosophy abroad, almost invariably somewhere in the Greek world and particularly at Athens. But what started well and flourished for a while eventually went into decline under later emperors when, with political freedom being very limited, the practical significance of rhetorical ability lessened and artifice and mannerism began to overshadow substance. (Hence, today *rhetoric* is generally a critical term, suggesting a triumph of presentation over real argument).

The three stages of education outlined correspond roughly to the Greek model of schooling. However, the Romans did not share the Greek passion for either music or physical education. Generally speaking, the *litterator* and *grammaticus* were held in low repute and were poorly paid. The rhetor commanded more respect and is thought to have earned something like five times the salary of the *litterator*; a few acquired considerable fame. Holidays seem to have been quite common, taking place on festival days, market days, and any day when there was a gladiatorial show or a military triumph as well as during a lengthy summer vacation. The school day began early (often before daylight in winter); discipline was strict and included corporal punishment.

The key features of Roman education were schooling in the basic skills of reading, writing, and arithmetic; character development; and training in the art of public speaking or advocacy. In the process there was a great deal of drill, rote learning, and skill practice; the focus was on seriousness of purpose and material was chosen for its moral value rather than its intellectual interest or artistic quality, still less its entertainment value. It is perhaps sometimes difficult to see how it did so, but this system of education could produce great humanists and cultured individuals such as Cicero, Virgil, and Quintilian.

THE AMERICAS

BY ANGELA HERREN

For the ancient Americas archaeological evidence provides no indication of formalized education in schools. One can assume that parents or community members trained their children at a young age to perform the activities of daily life. Later cultures divided major tasks between the genders. Men often hunted, fished, grew crops, constructed buildings, sculpted, painted, made ceramics, and at times engaged in warfare. Women typically maintained the home, raised children, prepared food, and wove textiles. During the first millennium B.C.E. early cultures grew more complex and began to build elaborate ceremonial sites. With the stratification of society, knowledge must have become more specialized as hierarchical class distinctions between elite groups, commoners, and ritual practitioners took root. Early sculptural works and monumental constructions indicate an interest in astronomical phenomena, the cosmos, deities, genealogy, and rulership. In addition to these public monuments, ritual performances and royal ceremonies educated the populace on the history, religion, and developing power structures that provided the foundation for communal society.

Created by the Adena (ca. 1000 B.C.E.–ca. 200 C.E.) and Hopewell (ca. 200 B.C.E.–ca. 400 C.E.) cultures in the area around southeastern Ohio, the art of the Woodlands Period (ca. 1000 B.C.E.–ca. 1000 C.E.) demonstrates keen observation of nature and perhaps the development of religious practices. The Serpent Mound in Adams County, Ohio, represents one of the most striking monuments created by the Adena. A monumental earthwork, the dimensions of the serpent form measure 4 feet high, approximately 20 feet wide, and 1,254 feet long. The mouth of the serpent appears to bite an egg, while the body undulates across the landscape, terminating in a spiral form at the tail. The Adena created other earthworks depicting birds, bears, mountain lions, and various predatory animals. Such monuments may mark sacred sites and could have educated local communities on the power of these creatures or the deities they represent. Like the Adena, the Hopewell buried their dead with small artworks and effigy pipes. In their stone pipes, the Hopewell artists include certain identifying characteristics, such as beak, tail, or teeth, that make the particular species more easily recognizable. Hopewell artists must have taught their protégées how to recognize and represent these traits in the restrained naturalism so characteristic of the culture.

In South America many early ceremonial centers mark basic movements of the sun, moon, and stars; represent important cosmological concepts; and demonstrate the increased importance of shamans, intermediaries between the spiritual and mundane worlds. Shamans who directed rituals at the Old Temple and New Temple at the highland Andean site of Chavín de Huántar (ca. 900–200 B.C.E.) educated their followers on the east-west trajectory of the sun, the cardinal directions, and the axis mundi, or fifth vertical direction that connected the heavens, earth, and underworld. Art and architecture underscore themes of duality and complementarity that formed bedrock cultural beliefs, passed down through generations of Andeans.

Archaeological excavations prove that the Moche (ca. 1–600 C.E.) on the north coast of Peru practiced an important ceremony called the "Sacrifice Ritual" for hundreds of years. Moche priests and priestesses enacted their rites, educated their apprentices, and spread their practices to neighboring settlements. They recorded the protagonists, costumes, and activities of the ritual on painted ceramics and murals.

The highland site of Tiahuanaco (ca. 300 B.C.E.–1100 C.E.), near Lake Titicaca in western Bolivia, contained a ceremonial core filled with highly symbolic monuments visible to the surrounding community. One of them, a huge stone portal called the Sun Gate, depicts a relief carving of a supernatural being or shaman surrounded by bird- and human-headed attendants. Associated with the puma, this figure carries arrows and a spear thrower. The people of Tiahuanaco represented the spiritual beliefs that tied their community together in permanent stone monuments. They disseminated their ideas by copying images from ceremonial architecture in portable textiles.

Ancient Mesoamericans also used monumental sculpture, architecture, and artwork to transfer communal knowledge. Unlike contemporaries in North and South America, however, they developed pictorial writing systems and complex calendar notations to record and store information. The earliest evidence of these developments appears on carved stone sculptures and monuments.

Dating to the first millennium B.C.E. a stone block discovered in a quarry in Veracruz, Mexico, in 2006 may represent the earliest forms of glyphic, or symbolic, writing in Mesoamerica. While the glyphs remain undeciphered, they resemble forms found on art of the Olmec culture (ca. 1200–400 B.C.E.). Lightly incised glyphic marks often cover three-dimensional carved celts, or axes, and stone sculptures depicting human and animal composite figures. Many glyphs seem to represent deities or cosmological information. These art objects, often found near ritual and ceremonial structures, may indicate that Olmec villagers relied on priests or shamans to maintain and transmit spiritual knowledge on their behalf. Late Formative and Protoclassical stone sculptures from the southern Maya region (ca. 400 B.C.E.–250 C.E.) record extensive glyphic notations and calendric dates.

Priests, artists, and elite persons probably commanded the greatest knowledge in ancient Mesoamerica, training those with aptitude and interest. Commoners may have called upon these individuals to impart their knowledge when needed.

See also ARCHITECTURE; ART; ASTRONOMY; CALENDARS AND CLOCKS; CHILDREN; CRAFTS; DEATH AND BURIAL PRACTICES; ECONOMY; EMPLOYMENT AND LABOR; FAMILY; FESTIVALS; GENDER STRUCTURES AND ROLES; GOVERNMENT ORGANIZATION; HEALTH AND DISEASE; HUNTING, FISHING, AND GATHERING; LANGUAGE; LAWS AND LEGAL CODES; LITERATURE; MILITARY; MUSIC AND MUSICAL INSTRUMENTS; NUMBERS AND COUNTING; OCCUPATIONS; RELIGION AND COSMOLOGY; SACRED SITES; SOCIAL ORGANIZATION; SPORTS AND RECREATION; WEAPONRY AND ARMOR; WRITING.

FURTHER READING

Robin Barrow, *Greek and Roman Education* (London: Macmillan, 1987).

Stanley F. Bonner, *Education in Ancient Rome: From the Elder Cato to the Younger Pliny* (Berkeley: University of California Press, 1977).

Rafaella Cribiore, ed., *Gymnastics of the Mind: Greek Education in Hellenistic and Roman Egypt* (Princeton, N.J.: Princeton University Press, 2005).

Suresh Chandra Ghosh, *History of Education in Ancient India* (Delhi, India: Munshiram Manoharlal Publishers, 2001).

Frank P. Graves, *A History of Education before the Middle Ages* (Whitefish, Mont.: Kessinger Publishing, 2004).

Henri Irénée Marrou, *A History of Education in Antiquity*, trans. George Lamb (New York: Sheed and Ward, 1956).

empires and dynasties

INTRODUCTION

When people think about history, it is likely that kings and queens, emperors and empresses, as well as vast empires will soon come to mind. In empires one can often see the great sweep of history, especially when great empires extend their realms by conquering their neighbors. It is important when studying empires and dynasties to remember on whose backs the empires were built. For instance, the empires of ancient China consisted mostly of peasants who had little or no say in how they lived their lives. When there were wars to be fought, the peasants made up almost the entire military force of soldiers, and when they went away into battle, they seldom returned home. The food they produced fed the empire, and the battles they fought made emperors powerful.

On the other hand, the Zhou Dynasty (ca. 1045–ca. 256 B.C.E.) accomplished something remarkable: It created a sense of common nationhood among the many ethnic groups that lived within its territory, so that even when the empire splintered among petty warlords, everyone believed that China should be one nation. Even when barbarians seized control of parts of China, the barbarians began thinking of themselves as Chinese. During the Six Dynasties era (220–589 C.E.), when China was embroiled in many civil wars, there was an abiding belief among its people that all within China were one nation.

The success or failure of an empire can be gauged in part by how successful it was in creating among its population a sense of being one people who stand apart from others. The term *barbarian* or variants of it usually signified that one set of people were part of an empire and other sets of people belonged outside it; the outsiders were considered barbarians because they did not practice the customs of the insiders. Perhaps the world's first empire was that of the Old Akkadian Dynasty (ca. 2350–ca. 2100 B.C.E.), created by Sargon I in the Near East. It suffered from ill-defined borders and a size greater than a central government could manage at that time, but it also eventually failed because most of those within it did not see themselves as Akkadians but instead as conquered peoples, as outsiders. The rulers of the Neo-Assyrian Empire (1000–626 B.C.E.) tried resettling entire populations from their homes into parts of the empire where the rulers could keep an eye on them. When Babylon and Judah revolted and the Medes invaded in about 615 B.C.E., Assyria was full of people who did not think of themselves as Assyrian. Thus, the Assyrians were overthrown, and they had few places to hide even in their own lands.

Perhaps no one was more aware of the importance of making people feel part of their empire than were the Romans. From the time of Julius Caesar's conquest of Gaul, the Romans tended to let their conquered peoples live in peace, just as long as they paid their taxes. Human sacrifices were forbidden, but religions were mostly left alone, and wars among the peoples of the empire were forbidden, despite Rome's occasional civil wars. What Rome did was bring the benefits of the Pax Romanum, the Peace of Rome, to bear in conquered lands. There were well-built roads for communication and trade. Services on the roads included a postal system in which a letter mailed in Britain could arrive in Egypt in about four weeks. Trade along the roads was protected by soldiers in stations or forts that appeared frequently. Wealth and power could be attained by anyone who made use of Rome's opportunities, and conquered people quickly began sending their children to school to learn Latin and Roman customs, so that they could share in the wealth of the empire.

Furthermore, Romans often settled in large groups in newly conquered lands. This was crucial in the Romanization of North Africa after Rome's victory over Carthage. Roman-style cities were built from the ground up and populated by Roman soldiers, who were encouraged to marry local women. Prosperous, bustling, and exciting Roman cities made the Roman way of life very attractive, and the Romans marriages with local people made the cities seem welcoming. It was by luring people into living like Romans that the Roman Empire became the standard for civilization among its multitude of ethnic groups.

A sobering counterpoint was the German rebellion of 9 C.E. The Germans near the Elbe had been under Roman domination since about 9 B.C.E., and they were already becoming Romanized by wearing Roman clothing, speaking Latin, and following Roman laws. All this was ruined by a governor who abused the Germans, overtaxing them and brutally repressing them. The result was a rebellion in which three Roman legions were wiped out. The Romans had to withdraw. This lesson was reaffirmed in Britain, where even allies of the Romans were subjected to rape and other brutalities, and rebellion in 60–61 C.E. resulted in the killing of tens of thousands of Romans. A lighter hand in Britain later Romanized the Britons.

The practice of sharing social benefits worked in other cases. Egypt was aided by its geography, which tended to set it apart from other cultures, helping create an "us against them" mentality among all who lived there. Still, Egypt did absorb disparate peoples into its way of life. Libyans, Sea Peoples, and Semites all invaded at one time or another, and even when they lost they were sometimes allowed to settle in Egypt. They tended to adopt Egyptian culture rapidly, probably within a few generations. Even the Kushite dynasty (the Twenty-fifth Dynasty, ca. 770–ca. 657 B.C.E.) was accepted, because its rulers behaved like Egyptians and considered themselves to be part of the Egyptian culture.

Another way to judge an empire's success is by how long it lasted. The Chinese empire lasted from about 1500 B.C.E. to 1911 C.E.; the Egyptian empire lasted from before 2950 B.C.E. to 30 B.C.E. Another way to look at the success of empires is by how much they influenced later people. The Chinese empire still influences the written languages and laws of modern people. The Greeks created most of the modern sciences and empirical reasoning. The Romans have left their alphabet, their language, and their laws in numerous modern languages and legal systems. The Mesopotamians left metallurgy and the concept of national government. In terms of achieving a national identity, the Chinese are rivaled by the Mayans, who even after the collapse of their civilization remained in language, religion, and culture one people, to the present day.

AFRICA

BY MICHAEL J. O'NEAL

In ancient times much of the African continent was sparsely populated. The entire reach of the continent below the Sahara was populated largely by small nomadic hunter-gatherer tribes until about 200 years before the start of the Common Era. No one knows why the people of the sub-Saharan region remained organized in nomadic groups. The most likely explanation is that they had sufficient resources, so they had no need to turn to a more settled agricultural life. Another is that geography kept these groups isolated and protected. As a result of both these factors, the people of the sub-Sahara remained relatively immune from both invasion and migration. The result was that the sub-Saharan region was not home to any noteworthy empires or dynasties until much later.

The people of ancient sub-Sahara began to lay the groundwork for empire and more advanced civilizations during the last millennium or so of the ancient period. One of the peculiarities of ancient sub-Sahara is that it essentially skipped the Bronze Age, which played such an important role in Europe, the Middle East, and other parts of the world. Around 1400 B.C.E. the region seems to have passed directly from the Stone Age into the Iron Age. In East Africa people began to use furnaces to produce carbon steel at about this time. By about the sixth century B.C.E. people in such regions as Nigeria, Tanzania, Ethiopia, and the Great Lakes area of East Africa (which includes most prominently Lake Victoria, the world's second-largest freshwater lake in surface area, and Lake Tanganyika, the world's second-largest lake in volume of water) were also producing steel. Over the next 500 years steel technology spread throughout the continent, primarily as a result of what are called the Bantu migrations.

Bantu refers to a family of languages. These languages, the largest language family of Africa, are closely related. In the last century before the start of the Common Era, people who spoke Bantu began to migrate from north-central Africa, a process that continued throughout the first 1,000 years of the Common Era. To the south they migrated into the rain forests of the Congo. To the east they migrated to the East African highlands. This migration was no trickle. It was a flood of people who imposed their language and culture in the regions where they settled, often resulting in hybrid tongues and hybrid cultures. In time, the earliest immigrants were themselves pushed farther south and east under the pressure of new waves of migrants, continuing the process. Eventually these new people would give rise to the Great Zimbabwe civilization, sometimes called the Mwene Matapa civilization. Along with iron smelting and steel production, the Bantu migrants also spread knowledge about farming. Under their influence, indigenous peoples learned to grow such important crops as plantain, yams, and bananas.

The result was a significant growth of population as people turned from hunting and gathering to a more sedentary village life. In comparison with much of the rest of the ancient world, urban life was a late development in sub-Saharan Africa. Although there are archaeological remains of towns in Mauretania that date back almost 4,000 years, such formal settlements were an exception. But beginning in around 600 B.C.E. and over the next 800 years, the Sahel, a dry, hot savanna just south of the Sahara, became the site of numerous urban centers with large populations. Some of these included Kumbi, Gao, and Djenné, as well as the later capital of the kingdom of Ghana, Kumbi Saleh. By the early medieval period and for the next 1,000 years, these and other urban centers throughout sub-Saharan Africa became the center of important kingdoms whose roots extended back into the ancient world.

Meanwhile, the empires of the African continent lay to the north. During the ancient period the most significant of these empires was, of course, that of the Egyptians, which lasted for over three millennia and was ruled by dynasties of kings who built some of the world's greatest monuments to civilization. In addition to Egypt, three other empires of note left their mark on ancient Africa. The first was the Carthaginian Empire, which was founded in the ninth century B.C.E., reached the height of its power in the third and second centuries B.C.E., and was eventually destroyed by the Romans in 146 B.C.E. Farther south, and much earlier, was the kingdom of Kush, which reached the height of its power between 1700 and 1500 B.C.E. The third was the kingdom of Axum, which was thriving in the first century C.E.

CARTHAGE

Carthage, a name derived from the Phoenician words for "new city," was founded in 814 B.C.E. by Phoenician traders from the city of Tyre in Lebanon. (Other Phoenician settlements were also given the name Carthage, but these were all smaller towns and outposts.) Over the next centuries it grew into a large political and economic empire. As one of the major world powers at the time, it was a rival to the Roman Empire, which dominated Europe and the eastern Mediterranean. Primarily because of the strength of its navy and its trading prowess, it reached the height of its power in the third and second centuries B.C.E.

In texts the term *Carthage* can refer to both a city and a civilization. The city of Carthage, the capital of the empire, was in North Africa on the east edge of the Lake of Tunis, in modern-day Tunisia. Some historians believe that it was the world's second-largest city during Hellenistic times, or the era when the Greek Empire was at its height; only Alexandria was larger. It was protected by massive walls that were 23 miles in length. The city also had marketplaces, towers, a theater, a council house, an area for religious worship, a huge, elaborate cemetery, four residential areas, and, in the center, a tall citadel called the Byrsa. *Carthage*, though, can also refer to the civilization that spread across North Africa to dominate the western Mediterranean Sea from the border of Egypt on the east to Morocco on the west.

The roots of the Carthaginian Empire extend back to the 10th century B.C.E. and the eastern Mediterranean Sea. The Phoenicians' most important cities were first Tyre and then Sidon, but to protect their trading interests, they founded and controlled several trading posts around the region. Among them was the city of Carthage, which provided a safe harbor for ships. This network of trading cities also helped the Phoenicians protect their monopoly on natural resources used for trade. Additionally, the early Phoenicians needed funds to pay tribute to the larger empires that dominated them. They also feared that in time the Greeks would gain control of the entire region. Because the Phoenicians were few in number and their cities were small, they embarked on a project to colonize cities throughout the Mediterranean region.

Their project was successful. During the three centuries that followed its founding, Carthage became the center of the empire as Tyre declined and was eventually destroyed by the Greek conqueror Alexander the Great. Leadership of the Phoenician Empire then passed to Sidon, but in time Carthage became the most dominant city. The Phoenicians established 300 colonies in Algeria, Morocco, Tunisia, and Libya. In 509 B.C.E. Carthage signed a treaty with Rome that in essence divided the region into two spheres of influence, with Rome retaining its hold over the eastern Mediterranean. The Carthaginian Empire included not only the north coast of Africa but also important Mediterranean islands, such as Sardinia, Malta, Cyprus, portions of Crete, Corsica, and the western portion of Sicily. The Carthaginians also founded important colonies on the Iberian Peninsula (that is, Spain and Portugal), as well as the Balearic Islands, islands off the eastern coast of Spain that included Majorca, Minorca, Ibiza, and Baleares. The Carthaginians appointed magistrates who directed the activities of the colonies.

Eventually Carthage became too much of a threat to Rome. Accordingly, Rome launched a series of wars called the Punic Wars, from the Latin word for Phoenician, *Punicus*; many older history texts use the word *Punic* rather than *Carthaginian*. The First Punic War broke out in 264 and dragged on until 241 B.C.E. The outcome was indecisive. War broke out again in 218 B.C.E. The Second Punic War remains famous because of Hannibal (247–183 B.C.E.), the Carthaginian general who marched his troops from Spain over the Alps and won convincing victories against the Romans. The war ended only when the Romans invaded Carthage itself and the Carthaginians sued for peace. The Third Punic War erupted in 149 B.C.E. Unlike the First and Second Punic Wars, the Third Punic War was relatively brief. The Romans invaded, laid siege to the city of Carthage, and then finally destroyed it, killing its occupants or selling them into slavery. Thus, in 146 B.C.E. the Carthaginian Empire came to an abrupt end.

The destruction of Carthage has posed a significant problem for historians. The Romans wiped out virtually every aspect of Carthaginian civilization, razing the city and destroying its documents. Accordingly, historians have few primary documents to examine and study. These include Greek and Latin translations of Carthaginian texts, but most of what is known about Carthage comes from Greek and Roman writers, including Livy, Appianos, Plutarch, Herodotus, and others. But Rome and Greece were in competition with Carthage, so the objectivity of these sources is questionable. More information has become available as a result of recent archaeological excavations of Carthaginian sites, but much of the new information still fails to provide a clear picture. The basis of Carthaginian power and empire was its massive navy, which included up to 350 warships that continuously patrolled the Mediterranean. Additionally, Carthage maintained a large fleet of merchant ships, each capable of carrying 100 tons of goods, all protected by two large harbors. No nation would match Carthage's naval fleet in size and tonnage until 18th-century Europe. Unlike its rivals, Carthage did not typically maintain a standing army. When the empire needed to protect itself, it raised an army, such as that commanded by Hannibal, or hired mercenary armies.

Much of the empire's trade was based on the Iberian Peninsula, the source of large amounts of lead, silver, and tin ore. Tin ore was especially important, for numerous ancient civilizations mixed tin with copper to make bronze. The Carthaginians also traded for tin with Britain and possibly the Canary Islands, giving Carthage a monopoly on the tin trade and therefore on bronze. Trading rivals were eager to obtain a portion of this tin, but the Carthaginians were so bent on protecting their monopoly that ship captains would deliberately crash their ships rather than allow other nations to learn where and how to approach the rocky shores of the British Isles. Further, Carthage's strategic location between Sicily and the African coast allowed it to control the supply of tin to the east.

Nearly as important as tin were the silver mines in North Africa and Iberia. These mines were so productive that the Carthaginians were able to provide Hannibal with 300 pounds a day. Another important commodity was a dye called Tyrian purple—a product so valued that a pound of it was equal in value to up to 20 pounds of gold. Other important commodities included textiles (silk, wool, and cotton), spices, perfumes, pottery, incense, glasswork, wood, bronze, alabaster, precious stones, plows, mirrors, cabinetry, household items (pillows and bedding, for example), slaves, and weapons. Food commodities included fish as well as a range of agricultural products, such as wine, olives and olive oil, grapes, dates, nuts, and fruits. Carthage's agricultural system was so efficient that after the Third Punic War, the Romans ordered that a Carthaginian agricultural treatise written by

Mago in about 350 B.C.E. be translated for Rome's use. The Carthaginians also bred and traded prized Arabian horses. Much of Carthage's wealth came from brokering trade in these goods.

Carthage's influence also spread southward. The empire sent caravans into the African continent, where they traded for such goods as ebony, ivory, salt, timber, gold, and hides, and such animals as apes and peacocks. To the north they obtained amber from the Scandinavian countries. In summary, the Carthaginians traded in just about every commodity that anyone wanted in the ancient world. Their efficiency in storing, transporting, buying, and selling goods (they invented the auction) was the source of the empire's wealth and power.

According to legend, Carthage was founded under the leadership of Queen Elissar, sometimes spelled Elissa or Alissa. In the *Aeneid* of the Roman writer Virgil, the queen is called Queen Dido. Details of the queen's life are sketchy, but according to such sources as the Roman writer Justin, her father was King Matten, known also as Belus II or Muttoial. At his death the throne passed jointly to Elissar and her brother, King Pygmalion. She then married Acherbas, her uncle, a man of great wealth. Her brother, though, was a tyrant and wanted to gain control of Acherbas's wealth, so he killed Acherbas. Elissar escaped and founded the city of Carthage. Little is known of her subsequent fate, though according to Virgil she committed suicide.

Some details survive about the rulership of Carthage. Through most of its history the empire was ruled by an oligarchy of judges known as suffets, from the Hebrew word *shofet*, meaning "judge." (The Phoenicians were a Semitic-speaking people, meaning that their language was similar to that of the ancient Jews.) Early in the empire's history was a governing body of judges called the Hundred and Four, whose primary role was to oversee the military. Additionally, the city of Carthage was ruled by a governor.

A supreme council made up of the empire's most influential and wealthy families exercised power in the empire. Additionally, two judges with both judicial and executive powers were elected, though historians do not know whether they were elected by the people or by the council. While this oligarchy ruled the empire, Carthage had elements of a democracy, including a constitution (written about by the Greek philosopher Aristotle), workers' unions, and elected representatives. A council of elders acted in an advisory capacity. One Greek historian, Polybius, notes that the Carthaginian people had more power over their government than the Roman people had over theirs. Separate from the civil administration was a class of appointed admirals and generals.

One of the most important oligarchic families of ancient Carthage was the Barcid family, best known as tenacious opponents of the Roman Empire. The family name Barcid is an invention of historians for a family whose original name was Barca or sometimes Barcas, meaning "lightning" in the Semitic languages. According to legend, the Barcids descended from Queen Elissar, though Rome's destruction of Carthage makes it unlikely that the true origins of the family will ever be known. The Barcid family was the closest thing to a ruling dynasty that Carthage produced.

The Barcids rose to power in the third century B.C.E. They saw that the Roman Republic was expanding and foresaw that Rome could eventually eclipse Carthage and put an end to Carthage's power on the sea. Accordingly, the Barcids were the driving force behind the First Punic War and led preparations for the Second Punic War. Moreoever, they founded in Iberia a number of cities whose names still survive, including Barcelona and Cartagena, which evolved from Carthago Nova, or New Carthage.

Some of the most famous members of the Barcid family include Hamilcar Barca (270?–228 B.C.E.), a military commander during the First Punic War. Hasdrubal the Fair (?–221 B.C.E.), Hamilcar's son-in-law, followed in his father-in-law's footsteps and continued Carthaginian expansion in Iberia. Hannibal Barca was Hamilcar's son and became one of the most famous military commanders in history when he led his troops over the Alps from Spain and crushed the Roman forces in the Battle of Cannae in 216 B.C.E. His brother Hasdrubal (?–207 B.C.E.) defended Iberia in Hannibal's absence, then led reinforcements to Italy in 207 B.C.E. Their youngest brother, Mago Barca (243–203 B.C.E.), not to be confused with the Mago who wrote the agricultural treatise mentioned earlier, was also an able military commander.

Kush

In the fourth millennium B.C.E. the ancient Egyptians colonized a region around the first cataract of the Nile River. (Along its length the flow of the river's waters is interrupted by cataracts, or shallow areas with rocks, islands, and rapids. These cataracts are conventionally numbered from south to north, since this is the direction in which the Nile River flows.) This region was called Nubia, divided into Upper Nubia to the south and Lower Nubia to the north (again, because of the direction of the river's flow). Because Egypt maintained control of these regions to the south, Egyptian civilization was spread southward into the interior of the African continent. A kingdom grew up along the Nile, in the floodplain between the first and third cataracts. The Egyptians called this kingdom Kush. Thus, *Nubia* refers to the region, roughly modern-day Sudan; *Kush* refers to the people and their kingdom.

The kingdom of the Kush functioned as a major center for trade. Goods from the southern part of Africa, including gold, ebony, ivory, exotic animals, and slaves, passed through Kush on the way to points north. While at various points in their history the Kush ruled their own independent kingdom in Upper Nubia, at other points they were an Egyptian colony, and Lower Nubia remained a colony through most of its history. Throughout their history, the Kush thought of themselves principally as Egyptian, and their religion, architecture, government, and other aspects of their culture were essentially Egyptian.

As trade with Egypt increased, the region's power grew, but during the Middle Kingdom (2040–1640 B.C.E.) Egypt expanded into Nubia. The region remained politically disorganized until the first in a series of three kingdoms was established. The kingdom of Kerma lasted from about 2400 to 1500 B.C.E. Kerma's kings accumulated enough power to build large walls, tombs, and other structures. Kerma is the name of the modern city on which the kingdom was built; the name used at the time is unknown. During the New Kingdom (1550–1070 B.C.E.), Egypt expanded further into Nubia and built a new capital at Napata, which lasted from 1000 to 300 B.C.E. and which was powerful enough to turn around and conquer Egypt, with its kings ruling Egypt as Egypt's 25th Dynasty in the eighth century B.C.E. until Assyria invaded Egypt in the seventh century B.C.E.

The Assyrian invasion pushed the Kushites southward. The result was that much of their contact with Egypt, as well as with the Middle East and Europe, was closed off. In 591 B.C.E. the Assyrians conquered Napata, so the Kushites relocated their capital to Meroë. The Meroitic Kingdom lasted to about 300 C.E. Rather than focusing its attention northward, to Egypt, the Meroitic Kingdom looked southward. During the Napata and Meroitic kingdoms, the Kush embarked on a program of pyramid building that rivaled that of the Egyptians.

Establishing the chronology of Kushite dynasties has posed particular problems for historians and archaeologists. In most cases, they have to estimate dates. The principal evidence they use consists of inscriptions from tombs and pyramids. On this basis, historians have determined that the first ruler of the Napata Kingdom was Alara. He was followed by Kashta, who ruled from about 770 to 750 B.C.E. The first ruler of the Meroitic Kingdom was Aspelta, who was followed by a long succession of kings and even several queens, particularly after the start of the Common Era. Knowledge about the line of succession ends at about 355 C.E.

The most noteworthy dynasty that ruled the Kushites was the succession of monarchs who made up the 25th Dynasty of Egypt (770–657 B.C.E.). This dynasty included five Kushite pharaohs, all successors to Kashta: Piye (r. 750 to 712 B.C.E.), his brother Shabaka (r. 712–698 B.C.E.), Shebitku (r. 698–690 B.C.E.), Taharqa (r. 690–664 B.C.E.), and Tantamani (r. 664 to 657 B.C.E.). The ruling dynasties of Kush resembled those of Egypt, with several exceptions. First, the pharaohs of Kush ruled according to law rather than divine right. This law was created and interpreted by priests. The pharaoh, then, was elected from the royal family, with descent following the mother's rather than the father's line. For this reason Kush produced a number of queens, in contrast to most of the other civilizations of the world at that time.

The Meroitic Kingdom remained powerful through the second half of the first millennium B.C.E. It went through a period of decline until it was defeated and its commercial and trading power was taken over by the kingdom of Axum to the east.

Axum

The kingdom of Axum rose in power as that of the Kushites declined, and in about 350 C.E. Kush's reign as a major power in the area essentially ended when Axum conquered the Kushites. The Axumite Kingdom occupied the highlands of Ethiopia near the Red Sea, along with parts of modern-day northern Ethiopia, Eritrea, Yemen, southern Saudi Arabia, northern Somalia, Djibouti, and northern Sudan. Axum was a mixture of indigenous Kushitic-speaking people and immigrants from the southern Arabian Peninsula, who settled in the region in about 500 B.C.E.

Unfortunately, historians know little about the Axumite Kingdom. Much of what is known comes from Greek and Roman writers as well as from modern archaeological excavations. It is know that the Axumites developed their own alphabet, called the Ge'ez alphabet, and that Ethiopia, Axum's modern successor state, has one of the world's longest continuing traditions of literacy. Axum was the first African state to mint its own coins. The kingdom had large, cosmopolitan cities, including the cities of Axum, Yeha, Hawulti, Matara, Adulis, and Qohaito, which were among the most culturally advanced cities in the ancient world at that time. Axum was a crossroads for people from numerous parts of the world, including India, the Middle East, Sudan, and Egypt, and the kingdom accommodated a range of religious adherents, including Jews, Christians, and Buddhists. The Ethiopian Christian Church, created in roughly 325 C.E., when the kingdom converted to Christianity, is among the oldest Christian churches in existence.

The source of Axum's power, like that of the Kushites, was trade. The region occupied a strategic position that linked Africa with the Arabic countries, Rome, India, and later Byzantium, the capital of the Eastern Roman Empire (present-day Istanbul in Turkey). Through trade, primarily in such commodities as silk, spices, ivory, tortoiseshell, gold, and emeralds, the kingdom became immensely wealthy. With the help of a powerful navy on the Nile River and the Red Sea, Axum was able to extend its imperial power by establishing colonies throughout the region in the decades after the start of the Common Era. Axum remained a major power until the rise of Islam in the seventh and eighth centuries C.E.

The official title of the Axumite kings, found on numerous royal inscriptions, was "king of kings." While little is known about the earliest Axumite kings, it is known that they claimed to trace their lineage back to the biblical King David, King Solomon, and the Queen of Sheba. Somewhat more is known about later kings, particularly those who ruled in the centuries after the start of the Common Era, when Axum reached the height of its power. Most of this knowledge comes from coins minted during the kings' reign. Among the most important of these kings was 'Ezānā, who ruled in the fourth century C.E. and converted the empire to Christianity.

EGYPT

BY KIRK H. BEETZ

In modern works Egyptian history is subdivided into three kingdoms—Old, Middle, and New—and 31 dynasties. However, the ancient Egyptians did not divide their history into kingdoms or dynasties; instead, they recorded one continuous line of kings. The modern subdivisions are derived from those of Greek historians of the later first millennium B.C.E., who may have been inspired by Egyptian hieroglyphic lists that are now lost. Although the Greek historians made some significant mistakes, historians and archaeologists still use their list of dynasties. They also continue to use the labels *Old Kingdom, Middle Kingdom,* and *New Kingdom* for convenience, because at the end of each was a period in which the succession of kings was muddled, usually because two, three, or even more people were claiming to rule Egypt at the same time.

PREDYNASTIC ERA

Egyptians were forming large communities for cooperative farming by 5000 B.C.E. Based on artifacts discovered by archaeologists, it appears the southern part of Egypt had formed a single culture by 4000 B.C.E. This is known as the Naqâda I Period, named for an ancient settlement on the west side of the Nile River. By 3500 B.C.E. the Naqâda II Period had begun. Artifacts from that time indicate a common culture had spread from southern Egypt throughout northern Egypt. Burials indicate that by 3000 B.C.E. Egyptian society was forming an elite class. At this time they also were building small cities.

EARLY DYNASTIC PERIOD (CA. 2920–CA. 2575 B.C.E.)

Sometime between 3200 and 2900 B.C.E. Egypt was united under the rule of a single king. He was called Meni by the Egyptians of later ages and Menes by Greek historians. Menes is credited with founding the First Dynasty (ca. 2920–ca. 2770) and creating the capital city of Memphis. Supposedly, he was the king of Upper Egypt, or southern Egypt, and he conquered the kingdom of Lower Egypt, or northern Egypt. The double crown worn by Egyptian pharaohs represented a combination of the crowns of the two kingdoms, and Egyptians called their rulers dual kings. Archaeologists now believe Menes was a mythical figure and that Lower Egypt was not a kingdom when it was absorbed by Upper Egypt.

Historians continue to dispute the names of the First Dynasty kings. The first king for whom there is evidence is Narmer, who appears in written artifacts from his own time. He became king of all Egypt in about 2950 B.C.E. He either founded a dynasty of kings whose names are lost in mythological Egyptian tales, united Egypt without founding a dynasty, or founded the First Dynasty. Some historians name Narmer and Aha as two separate kings, and some assert that Aha was the legendary Menes, calling him Aha Men; others say Narmer and Aha were the same person. Before Narmer's rule, there may have been six leaders who were kings of parts of Egypt, including Ip, the legendary Scorpion King.

The kings of the First Dynasty developed a centralized government and established the belief that the king of Egypt ruled as a god on earth. All government officials derived their authority from the king, and they had to attend the king at his court periodically to show they served only at his whim. The term for king was *nyswt*. The word *pharaoh* did not come into use until late during the New Kingdom. Second in command to the king was a vizier, who during the Old Kingdom remained at the king's court.

The Second Dynasty (ca. 2770–ca. 2649 B.C.E.) had seven kings of uncertain date. Because these kings came and left quickly, some historians believe there was a civil war during the Second Dynasty, though archaeological discoveries reveal no disruptions during this time. Perhaps the number of kings is incorrect, or the kings' names represent palace coups that did not disturb the common people.

The most famous king of the Third Dynasty (ca. 2649–ca. 2575 B.C.E.) was Netjerykhet (r. ca. 2630–ca. 2611 B.C.E.), better known in later times as Djoser, meaning something like "the special one." Until Djoser's reign a king's tomb consisted of underground chambers, often carved out of solid rock, topped aboveground by a platform of mud brick called a mastaba. When the mastaba for Djoser's tomb at Saqqara was built, either he or his vizier, Imhotep, decided to make it grander. Imhotep designed the resulting Step Pyramid, Egypt's first great stone pyramid, which is built of limestone blocks and was coated with polished white limestone. The Step Pyramid is surrounded by a temple complex where spirits could roam.

OLD KINGDOM (CA. 2575–CA. 2134 B.C.E.)

The Old Kingdom consisted of the Fourth through Seventh/Eighth Dynasties. Imhotep's grand design marked the beginning of the age of the giant pyramids, the most characteristic structures built during the Old Kingdom. The foremost public work of each royal reign was the king's tomb, and Egyptians devoted parts of each year to working on its construction. Contrary to popular myth, slaves were not used. The building of a pyramid served to unify Egyptians by focusing them on a project to honor their god-king. The biggest of these works was the Great Pyramid built near Giza for Khufu (r. ca. 2551–ca. 2528 B.C.E.), a ruler of the Fourth Dynasty (ca. 2575–ca. 2465 B.C.E.).

The Fifth Dynasty lasted from about 2465 to 2323 B.C.E. and the Sixth Dynasty from about 2323 to 2150 B.C.E. The last king of the Sixth Dynasty was Pepi (or Pepy) II (r. ca. 2246–ca. 2150 B.C.E.). His was the longest reign of any Egyptian ruler, and his was the last great pyramid built on the Giza plateau. During his reign, Pepi II solidified Egypt's domination of the Nubians of the south, but the king's central authority diminished for unknown reasons.

The Greek historians mention a Seventh Dynasty, perhaps dominated by the northern city of Memphis, or Mit Rahina. Most modern historians believe that there was no Seventh Dynasty, noting the unlikely description that it had 70 kings in 70 days. The Eighth Dynasty may have lasted from about 2150 to 2134 B.C.E., with 18 or more kings.

First Intermediate Period (ca. 2134–ca. 2040 B.C.E.)

The Greeks erred in identifying two separate Ninth and Tenth Dynasties by duplicating the kings in their lists, though the Greek historians may have found the dynasties listed this way in Egyptian sources. The Ninth and Tenth were only one dynasty, lasting from ca. 2134–ca. 2040 B.C.E. Later Egyptian writings characterize this period as one of chaos, with people forsaking their old gods and proper worship. These accounts may have been written more to justify contemporary kings' absolute power rather than to provide an accurate commentary of the First Intermediate Period. However, it is known that a civil war began between the Tenth Dynasty kings of Lower Egypt and the Eleventh Dynasty kings of Upper Egypt, with an army of the Tenth Dynasty looting and desecrating tombs at the town of Abydos, north of Thebes. This attack would have been regarded as a terrible offense against religion and morality.

Modern historians are uncertain about the exact events that occurred during this civil war. Because the battles were between two different dynasties, most historians classify the first half of the Eleventh Dynasty as overlapping with the end of the Tenth Dynasty. There is also some consensus that the Theban king Mentuhotep (or Montjuhotep) II (r. ca. 2061–ca. 2010 B.C.E.) defeated the northern kings of Heracleopolis in about 2040 B.C.E., thereby reunifying Upper and Lower Egypt and establishing the relative calm of the Middle Kingdom. Other historians identify Mentuhotep I, the Theban governor Wast, as the founder of the Eleventh Dynasty, followed by Intef (or Inyotef) I, II, and III. Some believe Mentuhotep I and Mentuhotep II were the same person.

Middle Kingdom (ca. 2040–ca. 1640 B.C.E.)

After defeating the northern kings, Mentuhotep II spent the remainder of his reign strengthening the reunification of Egypt. He kept most government officials in their posts, replacing some who were not loyal to him, and his administration worked to reintegrate provinces into a single government. Mentuhotep II proved to be an exceptional administrator, and by the time of his death he had succeeded in bringing war-torn Egypt together as one nation.

The Twelfth Dynasty (ca. 1991–ca. 1783 B.C.E.) began when Mentuhotep IV (r. ca. 1998–ca. 1991 B.C.E.) was succeeded by his vizier Amenemhet I (r. ca. 1991–ca. 1962 B.C.E.). The transfer of power was peaceful. Amenemhet I was a reformer who tried to restore Egyptian government to the form it had during the Old Kingdom. He moved his residence from Thebes to the town of Itjtawy, near Saqqara, where sacred pyramids such as that of Djoser were located. Amenemhet I became an absolute ruler, and all government authority came from him. During the Middle Kingdom, beginning with Amenemhet I, eldest sons sat beside their fathers on the throne, sharing in royal authority, and wives and daughters of kings also were considered divine.

The Twelfth Dynasty was a period of great prosperity. The government pursued large public works projects, including building great tombs for kings and impressive tombs for regional governors. Beginning with Mentuhotep II, the Twelfth Dynasty's army extended Egyptian dominance in Nubia, reaching its fullest extent under Senusret III (r. ca. 1878–ca. 1841 B.C.E.), securing major trade routes into southern Africa that brought much wealth to Egypt. The last ruler of the Twelfth Dynasty was Sobeknefru (r. ca. 1787–ca. 1783 B.C.E.), a female king.

Her reign was followed by the Thirteenth Dynasty (ca. 1783–ca. 1641 B.C.E.), which was composed of a series of perhaps 33 kings, most of them with unknown names and dates. The early king Neferhotep I and others were powerful rulers of a central government, but during the middle of the Thirteenth Dynasty the kings' power waned. In the Nile Delta many small principalities became independent; their governors often called themselves kings.

Second Intermediate Period (ca. 1641–ca. 1550 B.C.E.)

The Second Intermediate Period is a confusion of dynasties that overlapped because they ruled different parts of Egypt. There was the Fourteenth Dynasty, Fifteenth Dynasty, Sixteenth Dynasty, and Seventeenth Dynasty (ca. 1641–ca. 1550 B.C.E.). Of these dynasties, only the Seventeenth Dynasty has a coherent history of kings, all ruling Upper Egypt. The Fourteenth Dynasty had 76 kings, possibly more, and the Sixteenth Dynasty had 32 or more kings. These kings probably do not represent family lineages, as Egyptian historians of the 1200s B.C.E. may have included the kings of even small territories in these dynasties. The Fifteenth Dynasty consisted of six kings of the city of Avaris, located in the northeastern Nile Delta. They were prosperous because of trade with the Near East, and Avaris was a well-defended fortress city. These kings are known as Hyksos, and historians still debate their origins. According to Egyptian records, they were Asiatic kings from the Near East who were remembered as cruel overlords.

The kings of the Seventeenth Dynasty ruled from Thebes. They saw themselves, not the Hyksos, as the true inheritors of the Thirteenth Dynasty kings and believed that Egypt should be one country. They focused on boosting the economy by freeing up trade routes that were blocked both to the north and south. The last king of the Seventeenth Dynasty, Kamose (r. ca. 1555–ca. 1550 B.C.E.), succeeded in recovering southern territory all the way to Elephantine, then known as Abu. This was just north of the region of Wawat, which was the focus of trade routes. Kamose attacked Avaris in about 1540 B.C.E. but did not breach its walls.

NEW KINGDOM (CA. 1550–CA. 1070 B.C.E.)

The 18th Dynasty (ca. 1550–ca. 1307 B.C.E.) began with Ahmose (r. ca. 1550–ca. 1525 B.C.E.), a brother (or perhaps son) of Kamose. He believed that he was the true heir to Egypt's throne and attacked Avaris possibly five different times. His army finally overwhelmed the defenses of Avaris, probably killing the last Hyksos king, Khemudy (unknown period of reign). The Hyksos used the fortified town of Sharuhen, in northeastern Sinai, southwest of Gaza, to control trade routes from the Near East into Egypt. Ahmose laid siege to Sharuhen, which fell after three years. The Egyptians massacred the inhabitants, and Egyptian dominance in the region was restored. Ahmose's son Amenhotep I (r. ca. 1525–ca. 1504 B.C.E.) was the last of the family line; a courtier, Thutmose I (r. ca. 1504–ca. 1492 B.C.E.), succeeded peacefully to the throne.

The New Kingdom was an era in which queens became corulers with their husbands, wielding both political and military power. The female king Hatshepsut (r. ca. 1473–ca. 1458 B.C.E.), the wife of Thutmose II (r. ca. 1481–ca. 1479 B.C.E.), ran Egypt during the early rule of her stepson, Thutmose III (r. ca. 1479–ca. 1425 B.C.E.). She tried unsuccessfully to have one of her daughters succeed her as king; later Egyptians believed that she had tried to upset the lawful line of kings. Other queens were very powerful, notably Nefertiti, the primary wife of Amenhotep IV (r. ca. 1353–ca. 1335 B.C.E.). In 1330 she was declared the co-king and took the royal name of Neferneferuaten (r. ca. 1330–ca. 1327 B.C.E.). Her husband was called a heretic by later Egyptians because he believed there was only one god, the disk of the sun, and changed the state religion accordingly. During the reign of Tutankhamun (r. ca. 1333–ca. 1323 B.C.E.), the old pantheon of gods was restored.

During the Eighteenth Dynasty, Egypt became one of the most prosperous nations of the ancient world. It dominated most of Nubia and expanded its influence to the east coast of North Africa. It controlled the Mediterranean coast of the Near East into Syria, as well as the Sinai. After military victories, the central Egyptian government would leave a local ruler in charge of the conquered area. This ruler was expected to follow edicts from the central government, although the local people were allowed a certain degree of autonomy in deciding their own affairs. The Egyptian government consistently required that trade routes be left open and caravans be allowed to pass unmolested; anyone who interfered with these two requirements was put to the sword. Many Egyptian military campaigns involved no fighting. Kings would lead armies all the way into Syria or deep into Nubia just to make clear that, if Egypt wished, it could crush these areas.

The Ninteenth Dynasty (ca. 1307–ca. 1196 B.C.E.) was an era of great national wealth and military power. Its kings were intelligent, strong-minded, and hard working. The word *pharaoh* came into use to describe the king. The most famous of the Ninteenth Dynasty kings is Ramses II (r. ca. 1290–ca. 1224 B.C.E.), whose reign was the second longest of the Egyptian kings; he became the model ruler for his successors. He was brash and a megalomaniac. He was also intelligent, an excellent military leader, and one of the greatest builders among Egypt's kings. His military campaigns prevented the Hittites of the northern Near East from taking control of trade in northern Palestine, and he built impressively huge monuments all over the lands he controlled. These monuments, often depicting Ramses II, were intended to show local people the power and geographical range of the Egyptian government.

The Twentieth Dynasty (ca. 1196–ca. 1070 B.C.E.) continued the strong rule of the Ninteenth Dynasty until its last 30

HATSHEPSUT, FEMALE KING

During the New Kingdom the Chief Royal Wives of the kings were partners with their husbands in ruling Egypt. Their status seems to have reflected a general social attitude in Egypt about the rights and responsibilities of husbands and wives as partners, and women and men were equals before the law. The wife of the king often ran Egypt's bureaucracy and economy. She sometimes even participated in battles, though warfare seems to have been primarily the husband's responsibility. Occasionally, a woman would become a female king, meaning she had the duties and powers of the male part of kingship.

The first such female king may have been Sobeknefru (r. ca. 1787–ca. 1783 B.C.E.), who ruled during the Middle Kingdom. The most powerful female king was probably Hatshepsut (r. ca. 1473–ca. 1458 B.C.E.), who was the daughter of Thutmose I and had been the wife of Thutmose II. When her husband died, she became the regent for her stepson, Thutmose III, but in about 1473 B.C.E. she made herself the co-king. This shift in her status was reflected in the art of the time: She was depicted wearing a beard which was a traditional symbol of kingship.

Hatshepsut was responsible for opening up new sources of trade for Egypt. In about 1460 B.C.E. she sent an expedition through the Red Sea to discover the location of Punt, with which Egypt had traded through intermediaries since the Old Kingdom. The expedition found Punt to be a region on the east coast of Africa, and it began direct trading with people in Punt. Children of chiefs from Punt were raised in the Egyptian court. Hatshepsut also established links with tribal peoples south of the kingdom of Kush, sometimes entertaining delegations from southeastern Africa in her palace. Her efforts significantly increased the prosperity of Egyptians, bringing into Egypt gold, ebony, ivory, exotic incenses, and other goods from new foreign sources.

Colossi of Ramses II and his wife at entrance to Karnak Temple; Ramses II completed this complex of temples and monuments, which was begun and developed by rulers of the Eighteenth Dynasty (ca. 1550–ca. 1307 B.C.E.) to glorify the god Amun-Re. (© Board of Regents of the University of Wisconsin System)

or so years, during the reign of Ramses XI (r. ca. 1100–ca. 1070 B.C.E.). In about 1087 B.C.E. the governor of Nubia rebelled and attacked Upper Egypt, driving all the way to Thebes. Ramses XI and his army made a vigorous counteroffensive, driving the rebel army back south of Elephantine, perhaps to the town of Miam in Wawat. Even so, Egypt did not regain control of Nubia, a land that had been part of Egypt for about 500 years, and the loss of access to southern trade routes seriously damaged Egypt's economy.

Third Intermediate Period (ca. 1070–ca. 712 B.C.E.)

Ramses XI died without an heir, resulting in the founding of the Twenty-first Dynasty (ca. 1070–ca. 945 B.C.E.). The first pharaoh of the new dynasty, Smendes (r. ca. 1070–ca. 1044 B.C.E.), was a vigorous ruler, and he led military campaigns in the Near East to enforce Egyptian dominance in that region. His successors found it increasingly difficult to hold the nation together. The Twenty-second Dynasty (ca. 945–ca. 712 B.C.E.) was founded by a man of Libyan descent, Shoshenq I (r. ca. 945–ca. 924 B.C.E.), who peacefully succeeded to the throne. The Twenty-second Dynasty saw the development of conflicts among governors of different regions, and some governors disputed the authority of the central government. Shoshenq III (r. ca. 835–ca. 783 B.C.E.) tried to maintain control of the country by appointing members of his family to be governors and giving each of them the title of king. Thereafter the family members bickered with one another and the country continued to fragment.

The last pharaoh of the Twenty-second Dynasty was Osorkon IV (r. ca. 735–ca. 712 B.C.E.), who ruled from the city of Tanis, in the Nile Delta. By this time Egypt had broken apart. The Twenty-third Dynasty (ca. 828–ca. 712 B.C.E.) ruled from the city of Leontopolis, which was at that time called Taremu, and the 24th Dynasty (ca. 724–ca. 712 B.C.E.) ruled from the city of Sais, both in the Nile Delta.

For a short time Egypt was reunited by the Twenty-fifth Dynasty (ca. 780–ca. 657 B.C.E.), which was composed of kings from Kush, the Nubian kingdom to Egypt's south. These kings followed Egyptian traditions of religion and government, and they saw themselves as Egypt's only rightful remaining royal line. The dynasty probably was established by Alura (r. ca. 780–ca. 770 B.C.E.) in the Nubian city of Napata. His successor, Kashta (r. ca. 770–ca. 750 B.C.E.), began the Nubian takeover of Egypt. Kashta's son Piye (r. 750–712 B.C.E.) led an army into Egypt to secure Thebes so that the Nubian kings could worship there. Piye continued beyond Thebes to Hermopolis, then known as Wenu, where he met the army of the Twenty-fourth Dynasty pharaoh Tefnakht (r. ca. 724–ca. 717 B.C.E.) and defeated it. Tefnakht withdrew to Sais in the Nile Delta, and Piye secured his dominance all the way north to Heliopolis, then known as On, northeast of Memphis. Local rulers swore fealty to him and he took on all the regal trappings, duties, and titles of an Egyptian pharaoh.

Late Period (712–332 B.C.E.)

The Late Period traditionally starts with the reign of Piye's successor, Shabaka (r. ca. 712–ca. 698 B.C.E.), a dynamic pharaoh who united the Nile Delta with the rest of Egypt. He and his successors tried to rule Egypt as traditional pharaohs. They defended the country's interests in the Near East, built a great fleet to patrol the Mediterranean, and constructed great public works. When Assyria became a formidable military power, the Twenty-fifth Dynasty tried to find ways to oppose it. In about 674 B.C.E. Assyria attacked Egypt and was defeated by the forces of Taharqa (r. ca. 690–664 B.C.E.), but around 671 B.C.E. Assyria attacked again, driving its way into Memphis. Taharqa withdrew into Nubia. The last pharaoh of the Twenty-fifth Dynasty was Taharqa's heir, Tantamani (r. ca. 664–ca. 657 B.C.E.), who recaptured all of Egypt before being soundly defeated by the Assyrians, who exacted cruel reprisals all the way to Thebes.

The first pharaoh of the Twenty-sixth Dynasty (ca. 672–525 B.C.E.) was Neko I (r. 672–664 B.C.E.) of Sais. He was an Assyrian puppet who was killed by Tantamani. His successor was Psamtek I (r. 664–610 B.C.E.). Although he began as an Assyrian vassal, during his long reign Psamtek I slowly rebuilt the Egyptian government. With Assyria distracted by wars elsewhere in the Near East, Egypt reoccupied part of Palestine in 630 B.C.E., and in 616 B.C.E. Psamtek's army invaded Syria. After Babylon overcame Assyrian dominance, its new king, Nebuchadnezzar II, attacked Egypt in 601 B.C.E. and again in 581 B.C.E. These invasions were repelled decisively by the pharaohs Neko II (r. 610–595 B.C.E.) and Apries (r. 589–570 B.C.E.). The Egyptian general Amasis (r. 570–526 B.C.E.) deposed Apries in 570 B.C.E., but Apries returned to Egypt at the head of a Babylonian army to reclaim his throne. He was defeated and probably killed by an army led by Amasis. Amasis and his successor, Psamtek III (r. 526–525 B.C.E.), were shrewd statesmen who won many friends in other nations, but they were outmatched by Persia.

Persia defeated Babylon in 539 B.C.E. and, when Amasis died, invaded Egypt, defeating the forces of Psamtek III. These events began the Twenty-seventh Dynasty (525–404 B.C.E.), which consisted of Persia's kings, who treated Egypt as a province of Persia. The Persian kings Cambyses (r. in Egypt 525–522 B.C.E.) and Darius I (521–486 B.C.E.) ruled somewhat benevolently, spending long periods in Egypt while behaving like traditional pharaohs; thereafter the reign of Persians in Egypt was notable for its brutality. Around 404 B.C.E. Amyrtaeus (r. ca. 404–ca. 399 B.C.E.), the ruler of Sais, succeeded in driving out the Persians. Amyrtaeus was the only pharaoh of the Twenty-eighth Dynasty.

The Twenty-ninth Dynasty (ca. 399–ca. 380 B.C.E.) and the Thirtieth Dynasty (ca. 380–ca. 343 B.C.E.) ruled an Egypt that was slowly regaining its influence in the Near East and Mediterranean. When Persia invaded in 374 B.C.E., it was defeated. When Persia invaded again in 351 B.C.E., it was defeated again, but the cost of the war nearly bankrupted the Egyptian government. When Persia's Artaxerxes III Ochus (ruled Egypt 343–338 B.C.E.) invaded in 343 B.C.E., he not only conquered Egypt but also desecrated its sacred sites. The last pharaoh of the Thirtieth Dynasty, Nectanebo II (r. 360–343 B.C.E.), briefly clung to power in Upper Egypt. He was the last native Egyptian pharaoh. The Thirty-first Dynasty (ca. 343–ca. 332 B.C.E.), known as the Second Persian Period, consisted of Persian kings (Artaxerxes III, Arses, Darius III) who were despised by the Egyptians.

Greco-Roman Period

When Alexander the Great's army drove the Persians out of Egypt in about 332 B.C.E., the Macedonian king was greeted as a hero. He cultivated his hero status by honoring Egyptian gods and following Egyptian customs, and the Egyptians gave him the status of pharaoh. When Alexander the Great died in 323 B.C.E., his empire broke into pieces, and one of his generals, Ptolemy Soter, eventually took over Egypt from the Macedonian kings and made himself Ptolemy I (r. 304–284 B.C.E.). He and his immediate successors (almost all named Ptolemy) tried to force Egypt to adopt a Greek-style culture. Ptolemy I changed the names of cities and gods to Greek ones, and he enforced laws that reduced women from partners of men, as had long been the Egyptian practice, to mere servants of men. The language of government became Greek, and using Egyptian was discouraged. As a result, the Egyptians viewed the Ptolemaic Dynasty (304–30 C.E.) with resentment.

Nonetheless, the Greek pharaohs viewed Egypt as an independent nation, and they reasserted Egypt's ancient claim to domination of Palestine. Ptolemy III (r. 247–221 B.C.E.) conquered territory all the way to Syria and Babylon, and by the end of his reign Egyptian ships ruled much of the Mediterranean. The Greek pharaohs negotiated treaties with the Nubian kingdom of Kush, thereby regaining Egypt's access to trade in both the Near East and Africa. The Greeks also introduced new farming techniques that increased the yield of crops.

Rome began to interfere in Egyptian politics when its Senate nominated Philometer to become the pharaoh, which he did under the royal name Ptolemy VI (r. 180–144 B.C.E.). In 51 B.C.E. the Senate named two coregents, Ptolemy XIII (r. 51–47 B.C.E.) and his sister and wife, Cleopatra VII (r. 51–30 B.C.E.). Ptolemy XIII was succeeded by Cleopatra's other brother and second husband, Ptolemy XIV (r. 47–44 B.C.E.), and then by her son with Julius Caesar, Ptolemy XV (r. 44–30 B.C.E.) Courtiers tried to exclude Cleopatra VII from rule, but Julius Caesar and Marc Antony championed her cause, and she became the dominant political figure in Egypt. Rather than submit to the rule of the Roman emperor Augustus, she committed suicide. With her death came the end of the Egyptian empire and its dynasties.

THE MIDDLE EAST

BY KIRK H. BEETZ

Early Settlements

By 3500 B.C.E. there were many cities in Mesopotamia, the lands around the Tigris and Euphrates rivers. Eventually, these became the city-states of Sumer. The residents of these cities spoke a common language and worshiped the same gods, and they recognized themselves as all being part of the same culture. People who lived in the cities and those who lived in land around the cities were passionate about their love for their particular city, often treating their entire city as a sacred entity with a life of its own. The cities were governed by a chief administrator, and there is evidence for the existence of city councils as well.

The invention of writing in about 3400 B.C.E. allowed city governments to become more centralized because writing gave them the means to keep track of large amounts of goods, taxes, and population. As the city-states grew, they competed with one another for good farmland, and they fought wars, for which they needed good leaders. The chief city administrators became kings, regarded as chosen by the gods to rule. Archaeologists and historians have divided ancient Mesopotamia into two geographical areas: southern Mesopotamia, which includes the lands south of Baghdad, and northern Mesopotamia.

Early Dynastic Period (ca. 3000–ca. 2350 b.c.e.)

In southern Mesopotamia the period of the early, city-based dynasties referred to in the Sumerian King List, an ancient text on clay tablets (dating to ca. 2125 b.c.e.), is called the Early Dynastic Period. Uruk (biblical Erech and modern-day Warka) grew to be some 500 acres, with a massive city wall. By 2700 b.c.e. it may have had over 50,000 residents and was ruled by King Gilgamesh, who became the mythologized hero of an early literary work, the Epic of Gilgamesh. The Sumerian King List mentions the names of many kings belonging to dynasties at various cities such as Uruk, Umma, Lagash, and Ur. By 2500 b.c.e. King Mesilim of the city of Kish established himself as the first-known lord over all the other kings of Sumer. King Eannatum of the city of Lagash overthrew the dominance of Kish around 2400 b.c.e. About 50 years later King Lugalzaggisi of the city of Umma brought all of Sumer under his rule. This was the first regional state in southern Mesopotamia that unified and held an area larger than that of a single city and its hinterland.

Akkadian Dynasty (ca. 2350–ca. 2100 b.c.e.)

The Akkadian Empire was, however, the first true empire based in Mesopotamia that ruled over an area extending beyond the borders of this region. Founded by Sargon of Akkad (r. ca. 2334–ca. 2279 b.c.e.), the Akkadian Empire at times extended from the Mediterranean to the Persian Gulf. Campaigns were conducted into the Zagros Mountains to the north and east of southern Mesopotamia as well. Sargon began as cupbearer to the king of Kish, but he established a new imperial city, Agade, which has yet to be rediscovered. Sargon I probably took power through a coup.

A grandson of his, Naram-Sin (r. ca. 2254–ca. 2218 b.c.e.), added territory to the empire from what is now western Iran and southern Anatolia, in modern-day Turkey. The more the Akkadian Empire grew, the more vulnerable its borders became and the more discontented the former city-states of Sumer were. Practically every time a new king ascended to the throne, an insurrection arose in the cities of the south. In addition, nomads from the desert and tribes from the Zagros Mountains invaded Mesopotamia. Sometime before 2100 b.c.e. the Guti from the northern Zagros took power, and the world's first empire was no more.

Third Dynasty of Ur Period (ca. 2112–ca. 2004 b.c.e.)

Eventually, Ur-Namma of the city of Ur managed to establish his rule over territory that was about one-third the size of the Akkadian Empire at its largest. He was the founder of Ur's Third Dynasty of kings. This mighty dynasty lasted for a century, but in 2004 b.c.e. the Elamites, led by their king Kindattu, conquered the city of Ur itself, ending its brief empire. The Elamites came from what is now southwestern Iran.

First Dynasty of Babylon (ca. 1894–ca. 1595 b.c.e.)

A nomadic people called the Amorites had settled in parts of Mesopotamia during the late third millennium b.c.e. Their descendants would found dynasties both in Babylon and in Assyria. The one in Assyria was founded by King Shamshi-Adad (r. 1813–1781 b.c.e.). He conquered northern Mesopotamia, but after his death his kingdom was divided between his two sons, one who was lazy and one who was foolhardy. One of Shamshi-Adad's vassals was the king of Babylon, Hammurabi (r. 1792–1750 b.c.e.), who took advantage of the foolishness of Shamshi-Adad's sons. He had already conquered the cities of Uruk and Isin, both outside Assyria's dominion, and he had proved himself an able civic leader, improving Babylon's irrigation system and constructing temples. In each city he conquered, he made a point of building temples to show the local people that he was favored by the gods.

In 1764 b.c.e. Hammurabi conquered Elam. Then, in 1761 b.c.e., Hammurabi defeated Rim-Sin of the city of Larsa, in battle and seized control of all Sumer. From 1757 to 1755 b.c.e. he conquered northern Mesopotamia. He was a clever military leader. To defeat one city—Eshnunna (modern-day Tell Asmar) along the Diyala River—instead of assaulting the city, he diverted its water supply; this caused the city to surrender. He attracted to the city of Babylon artists from throughout the Near East, who added to the city's luster as the center of Mesopotamian culture. He is famous for his code of laws, which are carved on a stone stele now in the Louvre Museum in Paris. Curiously, though Hammurabi's laws were intended to impress the gods with his good rule, they are never cited in the thousands of legal documents in cuneiform that have survived from ancient Mesopotamia.

The First Dynasty of Babylon lasted until 1595 b.c.e., when the Hittites under Mursilis I (r. ca. 1620–ca. 1590 b.c.e.) sacked Babylon. Thereafter, a people from the Sealand (the marshes of southern Iraq) took control of the south. They were followed by the Kassites, who are often thought to have originated in the Zagros Mountains of what is today western Iran.

Babylon's Kassite Dynasty (ca. 1500–ca. 1155 b.c.e.)

The Kassites appeared in Babylonia during the reign of Samsuiluna (r. 1749–1712 b.c.e.), Hammurabi's successor, who defeated their army. With Samsuiluna's consent, the Kassites settled near the Diyala River. In 1475 b.c.e. the Kassite king Ulamburiash drove the Dynasty of the Sealand out of Mesopotamia and reestablished the city of Babylon as the center of an empire, called "Babylonia." Babylonia was a major military, economic, and cultural power under the Kassite kings. It was often at war with Assyria to its north, but it was allied by ties of marriage with the ruling house of Elam to its east, with the Hittites to the north, and with the distant Egyptians in a web of diplomatic relations. In about 1154 B.C.E. the Elamite king, feeling that he was the rightful successor (through marriage and his Kassite mother's lineage) overthrew the Kassite Dynasty when his petition to ascend the Kassite throne was rudely rejected. The Elamites carried to Susa, a large site in southwestern Iran, the statues of Babylon's chief god Marduk, symbolizing Babylon's loss of independence.

A king of the Second Dynasty of Isin (ca. 1158–ca. 1027 B.C.E.), Nebuchadnezzar I (r. ca. 1124–ca. 1103 B.C.E.), drove the Elamites out of Babylonia. Isin was a city to the southeast of the city of Babylon. Nebuchadnezzar I conquered Susa and brought the Marduk statue back to Babylon, which was once again the seat of government. Nebuchadnezzar I was a patron of the arts and commissioned many literary works, especially ones about himself. His efforts to expand Babylonian control to cities in northern Mesopotamia led to retaliation by the Assyrians, who destroyed a few of the cities in Babylonia.

The Second Dynasty of Sealand (ca. 1026–1006 B.C.E.) in Babylon was begun by a former member of the Assyrian army. Little is known about Babylon from 1026 to 732 B.C.E. Apparently, a new dynasty arose, perhaps in 979 B.C.E. Its kings occasionally tried to break the dominance of Assyria. In 689 B.C.E., after King Marduk-apla-iddina II (r. ca. 700–690 B.C.E.) tried to break away from Assyria, the Assyrians sacked the city of Babylon. Marduk-apla-iddina II was a Chaldean, a Semitic tribe that had settled near the southern Euphrates River. After his defeat, Babylonians waged a guerrilla war against the Assyrians. From 654 to 648 B.C.E. Shamash-shum-ukin, the Assyrian governor of Babylonia, waged war against his rival brother, Assyria's king Ashurbanipal. After defeating the revolt, Assyria appointed a puppet, King Kandalanu (r. 648–627 B.C.E.), to rule Babylon.

Neo-Babylonian Dynasty (ca. 625–539 B.C.E.)

A Chaldean leader, Nabopolassar (r. ca. 625–605 B.C.E.), led a successful revolt against Assyria. He expanded the Babylonian Empire, and in 605 B.C.E. he sent his son Nebuchadnezzar to lead an army against Egyptian forces in Palestine. He died that year, and the ascension of his son Nebuchadnezzar II (r. 605–562 B.C.E.) marked the beginning of the Neo-Babylonian Empire. Nebuchadnezzar II successfully took control of most of Palestine, yet the Egyptians defeated him when he tried to invade Egypt in 601 B.C.E. When the kingdom of Judah in Palestine rebelled against Babylon in 587 B.C.E., the forces of Nebuchadnezzar II sacked Jerusalem. Nebuchadnezzar II repaired and rebuilt ziggurats and other public structures in his empire and built the Hanging Gardens of Babylon, supposedly to please his wife, who missed the Median mountains (in western Iran) where she had grown up.

Nebuchadnezzar II's first three successors had trouble keeping control of the throne. The last of them was assassinated. A commoner named Nabonidus (r. 556–ca. 539 B.C.E.) became king but was unpopular, and he went into exile in about 539 B.C.E. His son Belshazzar (r. ca. 539 B.C.E.) replaced him but was not fully accepted as king because his father was regarded as still king. In 539 B.C.E. Cyrus the Great invaded and put an end to the Babylonian Empire.

Elamite Dynasties (ca. 2900–539 B.C.E.)

The history of Elam is customarily divided into three eras: Old Elamite Period (ca. 2900–ca. 1500 B.C.E.), Middle Elamite Period (ca. 1500–1000 B.C.E.), and Neo-Elamite Period (1000–539 B.C.E.). During the third millennium B.C.E. the Elamites established towns in what is now southwestern Iran. Their kings ruled from the city of Susa. Elam was a vassal state of the Akkadian and later Ur III empires, but in 2004 B.C.E. Kindattu of Elam sacked Ur. In 1764 B.C.E. Hammurabi of Babylon conquered Elam, but Elam successfully rebelled against Hammurabi's son Samsuiluna.

In 1154 B.C.E. the Elamites conquered Babylon, but in about 1126 B.C.E. King Nebuchadnezzar I of Babylon conquered Elam. In the 700s and early 600s B.C.E. Elam supported Babylonian rebellions against Assyria. In about 646 B.C.E. Assyria destroyed Elam's capital city, Susa, but despite its destruction a late Neo-Elamite kingdom arose, and it was in this context that Cyrus the Great, called "king of Anshan" (the name of an ancient Elamite city and region near modern Shiraz) arose and finally claimed Babylonia in 539 B.C.E.

Old Assyrian Period (ca. 1900–ca. 1700 B.C.E.)

Assyria was a region of northern Mesopotamia, centered on the area of modern-day Mosul along the Tigris River. The first notable Assyrian king was Shamshi-Adad (r. ca. 1813–1781 B.C.E.), who built an empire partly by war and partly by diplomacy. Weaker kings of city-states voluntarily submitted to his rule in the hope that he would use his power to protect them. He left in place those kings who submitted to him, allowing them to run their territories and practice their own customs just as long as they paid their taxes to him. This made for a weak administration, and he had to constantly patrol his lands to keep them in order. His capital city was Shubat-Enlil. His sons Yasmah-Addu and Ishme-Dagan, who divided Shamshi-Adad's kingdom between them, failed to keep a strong presence in their territories, and the empire collapsed when Hammurabi of Babylon invaded it. Assyria then became a vassal state of Babylon.

Middle Assyrian Period (ca. 1390–ca. 1076 B.C.E.)

In about 1500 B.C.E. the shadowy kingdom of Mitanni was the dominant power in northern Mesopotamia, with its territory extending from the northern reaches of the Tigris River to the Mediterranean Sea; after the sack of Babylon by the Hittites in 1595 B.C.E., Assyria became a vassal state of Mitanni. In the 1300s B.C.E. Mitanni became part of the Hittite Empire, creating an opportunity for Assyria to reassert its independence under King Ashur-uballit I (r. ca. 1365–ca. 1330 B.C.E.). He established the Assyrian capital in the city of Ashur and gained dominion over several cities located near the confluence of the Great Zab River into the Tigris River. King Adad-nirari (r. ca. 1307–ca. 1275 B.C.E.) campaigned westward into the heart of Mitanni. Shalmaneser I (r. 1274-1245 B.C.E.) attacked deep into central Anatolia, securing Assyria's northern frontier.

Tukulti-ninurta I (r. 1243–1207 B.C.E.) attacked Babylonia in 1220 B.C.E. and occupied the city of Babylon until 1213 B.C.E. He adopted Babylonian titles of kingship and transported Babylonians to Ashur, resulting in a spreading of Babylonian culture. His forces drove eastward to the Zagros Mountains. His numerous building projects included a new temple of Ishtar in Ashur and a new town north of Ashur for his residence, called Kar-Tukulti-Ninurta. In 1208 B.C.E., during a palace coup, one of his sons assassinated him. His empire immediately began to fall apart.

It was Tiglath-pileser I (r. ca. 1115–ca. 1077 B.C.E.) who again pulled the Assyrian Empire together. His conquests extended south to Babylonia, northwest to the Hittite Empire, and west across the Euphrates River, through the Syrian Desert, and through Palestine to the Mediterranean Sea. The borders of his new empire were ill defined, and nomads raided the empire's territories. By about 1000 B.C.E. the Assyrian Empire had withdrawn to the territory that had been ruled by Ashur-uballit I.

Neo-Assyrian Empire (ca. 100–ca. 626 B.C.E.)

After Tukulti-ninurta I there seems to have been an unbroken line of kings who kept Assyrian cities and temples in good repair, but it was Ashur-dan II (r. 935–912 B.C.E.) who began Assyria's climb back to preeminence. He reformed Assyrian agriculture, making it more productive, and he developed a strong military to protect Assyria's frontiers. Adad-nirari II (r. 911–891 B.C.E.) developed Assyria into a military powerhouse and reconquered most of the territory held during the Middle Assyrian Period. In the 870s B.C.E. King Ashurnasripal II (r. 883–859 B.C.E.) conquered most of Syria. After the death of Shalmaneser III (r. 858–824 B.C.E.), Assyria foundered on internal conflicts and some its conquests became independent.

During the reign of Tiglath-pileser III (745–727 B.C.E.) Assyria reasserted itself. Tiglath-pileser III founded a postal service that would continue to serve later empires into Roman times. To break up hostile groups of subjects, Assyrian governments deported them to Assyrian territories, where they could be both watched and put to work. In this way, Tiglath-pileser relocated more than 200,000 people from their homelands. In 722 B.C.E. Shalmaneser V (r. 726–722 B.C.E.) was overthrown by Sargon II (r. 721–705 B.C.E.). When Babylon rebelled, Sargon II took away the sacred cult statues of the Babylonian gods, in about 711 B.C.E. In 705 B.C.E. the city of Nineveh, one of the most ancient of Assyrian cities, became Assyria's capital. When Esarhaddon (r. 680–669 B.C.E.) became king, he returned the captured cult statues to Babylon and undertook the rebuilding of shrines in the empire in an effort to build goodwill. He was succeeded by Ashurbanipal (r. 668–627 B.C.E.), famous for the immense library discovered in his palace. He was brutal and inflicted horrifying torture and suffering on victims throughout his empire, inspiring hatred of him and Assyria. In about 615 B.C.E. Babylon and Judah revolted, and the Medes invaded from the east. Ashur was leveled by the Medes, not to rise again. Nineveh fell in 612 B.C.E.; in 609 B.C.E. the last Assyrian resistance was eradicated.

Hittite Empire (ca. 1650–1205 B.C.E.)

In the third millennium B.C.E. the Hittites were one of a number of Indo-European-speaking groups living in Anatolia. In the late 18th century B.C.E. King Anitta conquered the small kingdoms of Zalpa, Hattusas and Puruskhanda and succeeded in establishing the first central Anatolian state, stretching from the Mediterranean to the Black Sea. In about 1650 B.C.E. Hattusilis I (r. ca. 1650-c. 1620 B.C.E.) made the city of Hattusas his capital, and the Hittite written record (in cuneiform) began. The Hittites were pillagers of other peoples and used their superior iron body armor and military tactics to subdue their neighbors. In 1595 B.C.E. Mursilis I (r. ca. 1620–ca. 1590 B.C.E.) led a daring raid down the Euphrates River to attack Babylon, and the Hittites sacked the city. Mursilis I was assassinated in about 1590 B.C.E., and the Hittites' warrior elite fell to killing one another. Hattusas was captured by the Kaskas, a tribe from the north. Mitanni, a kingdom in Syria, dominated much of the rest of Hatti.

Exactly when the Hittites reunified has yet to be clarified, but around 1500 B.C.E. Telipinus succeeded in restoring political, religious, and military order. Tudhaliyas I (r. ca. 1420–1400 B.C.E.) campaigned against the Mitanni in Syria, but the rise of the kingdom of Hattusas really occurred under King Suppiluliumas I (r. 1355–1320 B.C.E.), who not only retook Hattusas but also sacked Washukanni, the capital of Mitanni, during a remarkable campaign. He created a strong central government. Mursilis II (r. 1318–1290 B.C.E.) pushed the empire to its maximum size, stretching from the Aegean Sea to eastern Syria and south into Palestine.

The trade routes in northern Palestine were valued by several Near Eastern peoples, and keeping those trade routes free from bandits and marauding nations became national policy for Egypt. After fighting several battles over who should control northern Palestine, the Hittites and Egypt made a peace treaty in about 1258 B.C.E. that defined the border between them and made them allies against the Assyrians. The cause of the demise of the Hittite Empire around 1200 B.C.E. is unclear. Marauders called the Sea Peoples by modern historians but who were actually several groups of people who had been displaced from their homelands in and around the Mediterranean Sea have sometimes been credited with the fall of the Hittites, but internal troubles seem to have been more significant, and several vassal states had already succeeded in breaking free under Suppiluliuma II (after 1215 B.C.E.).

Israel

Although Palestine was dominated by Egypt for much of its ancient history, Egypt in general did not meddle in local politics. Its primary concern was keeping open and free from danger the trade routes that linked Palestinian seaports with the Near East and Egypt. Most historians believe that Hebrews settled in Palestine in about 1200 B.C.E. and that they were a nomadic people. Biblical accounts say that they left Egypt, and accounts left by Egyptians on their monuments indicate that the Hebrews had lived in Egypt in a region in the eastern Nile Delta. This was not unusual, because at other times Egypt allowed Libyan tribes and even some of the notorious Sea Peoples to settle, all of whom were absorbed into the Egyptian culture.

Palestine was a land of city-states and experienced a flow of different peoples through it. Some of the Sea Peoples who had attacked the Hittites settled in Palestine, becoming the Philistines. Wars with the Philistines and other tribes seem to have driven the Hebrews to organize their tribes into a nation. Their first king was Saul (r. ca. 1020–ca. 1000 B.C.E.), who conquered territory well north of the Sea of Galilee, much of the land around the Dead Sea, and eastward beyond the city of Ammon, but he died while fighting the Philistines. His successor, David (ca. 1000–ca. 962 B.C.E.), decisively defeated the Philistines and extended the empire of the Hebrews northward into Syria and southward to the Gulf of Aqaba, and he claimed much of the Mediterranean coastline of the region. The extent of his eastward conquering has yet to be established by archaeologists. King David conquered the city of Jerusalem and made it his capital.

David's son Solomon (r. ca. 961–ca. 921 B.C.E.) was the last to rule over a united Hebrew nation. The power of his nation was great enough to create vassal states in Syria. During his rule, the empire was a powerful economic force in Palestine. With the nation's wealth he undertook many public building projects, the most famous of which was a temple in Jerusalem. After his death the kingdom split into Israel, with its capital in the city of Samaria, and Judah, with its capital in Jerusalem. Israel lasted until around 722 B.C.E., when Shalmaneser V of Assyria destroyed it. He had the Hebrews resettled elsewhere in his empire to separate them from their homeland and relocated Mesopotamian peoples to Israel. Judah lasted until about 587 B.C.E., when Babylonia burned Jerusalem and resettled the people in Mesopotamia.

Persia

The Medes were a people in western Iran (between the Caspian and the Zagros mountains) who are spoken of in Assyrian sources and participated in the sack of Nineveh in 614 B.C.E. Although they were credited by the historian Herodotus with having a powerful empire, there is little evidence of this outside the literary sources. Indeed, the first great Persian Empire (538–331 B.C.E.), also known as the Achaemenid Empire, arose not from Median but from Elamite roots. Cyrus the Great (r. 558–529 B.C.E.), who entered Babylon in 539 B.C.E. and is credited with subsuming Media before going on to conquer Lydia, emerged from an Elamite milieu. Cyrus established a new capital at Pasargadae, not far from the ancient city of Anshan (modern-day Tal-e Malyan), northwest of Shiraz.

Cyrus was killed while campaigning near the Aral Sea in Central Asia and was succeeded by his son Cambyses II (r. 529–522 B.C.E.), who conquered Egypt in 525 B.C.E. After the death of Cambyses during the return journey from Egypt, Darius I (r. 522–486 B.C.E.) came to power. It is with him that the true Achaemenid Dynasty began, since Darius was of the house of Achaemenes, whereas Cyrus was not. Darius's conquests stretched from the Indus River valley in the east to Thrace in southeastern Europe. He reorganized the Persian Empire into 20 provinces, called satrapies, and he improved the postal system that had been created by Assyria. He built the Royal Road, extending 1,600 miles from Susa in Iran to Sardis in Lydia

Portion of a relief in the tomb of Darius I showing his throne bearers; all 28 throne bearers represent the 28 nations of his empire. (Courtesy of the Oriental Institute of the University of Chicago)

(Asia Minor) and created an efficient intelligence service. He determined how much each province could pay in taxes and then taxed half that amount. He built major palaces at the ancient city of Susa and the new capital of Persepolis.

After putting down a rebellion of Greek city-states in Asia Minor, Darius launched an attack on Athens in Greece, which had supported the rebels. His forces were defeated at Marathon in 491 B.C.E. His son Xerxes (r. 486–465 B.C.E.) campaigned against Greece in 480–479 B.C.E., but the Persians were defeated by an alliance of Greek city-states. In 401 B.C.E. a civil war broke out between the Persians of Artaxerxes II (r. 404–359/358 B.C.E.) and Greek mercenaries commanded by his brother, Cyrus the Younger. Cyrus was defeated, but the Greek mercenaries fought their way out of the Persian Empire, as recounted by Xenophon.

Seleucid Kingdom (ca. 311–ca. 140 B.C.E.)

The last Persian monarch was Darius III (r. 336–330 B.C.E.). In 336 B.C.E. Alexander the Great invaded the Near East with a well-trained army of Greeks and Macedonians. He fought a series of battles against superior numbers, first taking the cities of the eastern Mediterranean, then Egypt, Assyria—where he defeated Darius III at the battle of Gaugamela—and Babylonia and finally Iran. It took until 328 B.C.E. to secure the Persian Empire, after which Alexander conquered part of northwestern India in 326 B.C.E. He seemed to take on the role of a Persian emperor after that and had plans for an invasion of Arabia, but after an arduous overland journey through Baluchistan and eastern Iran and following the burning of Persepolis, he died at Babylon of a fever in 323 B.C.E. Thereafter, the empire he had briefly created broke into smaller kingdoms ruled by two of of Alexander's generals, Seleucus I (r. ca. 311–281 B.C.E.), who founded the Seleucid Kingdom, and Ptolemy I (r. ca. 323–285 B.C.E.), who founded the Ptolemaic Kingdom (322–168 B.C.E.). These kingdoms, centered on Syria and Mesopotamia (Seleucid) and Egypt and Cyprus and the southern Levantine coast (Ptolemaic), eventually succumbed to the superior strength of Parthia in the east and Rome in the west.

Parthian Empire (ca. 250 B.C.E.–226 C.E.)

The Parthians originally lived in what is now northeastern Iran and adjacent parts of central Asia. The kingdom of Parthia, as known from coin issues, began with the reign of Arsaces I (r. ca. 250–ca. 248 B.C.E.), whose capital was at Nisa in what is present-day Turkmenistan and after whom the dynasty is sometimes referred to as Arsacid. Mithridates I (r. 171–138 B.C.E.) conquered southwestern Iran and pushed the western frontier across most of Mesopotamia. The Arsacid kings established a more centrally located capital at Ctesiphon, near Baghdad, and for many years the Euphrates formed the border between Rome's eastern provinces and the Parthian Empire. Artabanus V (r. ca. 213–226 C.E.), the last Parthian king, was overthrown by Ardashir I (r. 226–241 C.E.) from Istakhr, near Persepolis, who established the Sasanian Empire (226–651 C.E.), Iran's last great pre-Islamic state.

ASIA AND THE PACIFIC

by Kirk H. Beetz

Harappan Civilization

Harappa and Mohenjo Daro were the two largest cities of the Harappan civilization, and both were close to the Indus River. The civilization included numerous towns and villages scattered over an area that extended from central Asia to south of the Himalayan Mountains and along the seacoast west and south of the mouth of the Indus River. Its size was enough to qualify it as a large nation for its era, 2600–1500 B.C.E. Its government is a mystery because its written language has yet to be deciphered, and the Near Eastern civilizations with which it traded give it only brief mentions in their surviving records.

In about 1900 B.C.E. natural disasters began to undermine the main Harappan cities and towns. Rivers often flooded and sometimes changed their courses, inundating cities and towns and forcing the Harappans to repeatedly repair or even rebuild them. By 1500 B.C.E. Harappa was in steep decline as its people abandoned their cities, probably because of floods and bad harvests. In about 1500 B.C.E. Aryan tribes from central Asia invaded the Indus valley and the rest of northern India. Even so, some Harappan villages and towns survived in northern India and passed on their art and religion to later generations.

Vedic India

The word *Vedic* refers to the Vedas, the oldest sacred writings of Hinduism. Passed on orally until they were first written down in the 500s B.C.E., they recount the wars of the Aryan tribes and the sources of their religious beliefs. Vedic India dates to about 1500 to 60 B.C.E. Vedic society was stratified into groups called castes. There were four principal castes: At the top was that of priests, called Brahmans; second was that of warriors and political rulers, called Kshatriyas; third was that of merchants, money lenders, and farmers, called Vaishyas; fourth was that of craftspeople, servants, and minor government officials, called Sudras. Below all these people were the people without a caste. Castes were hereditary, meaning a person's caste was the same as that of his or her parents. This social system set the pattern for the rest of India's history.

The Aryans were originally nomads who directed sheep and cattle to different grazing grounds according to the season. Some of their descendants in northern India continued to practice the old way of life into the 21st century. Most of the Vedic people began to settle down as they spread eastward and southward. By the 800s B.C.E. they had formed many small tribal territories called *janapadas* across northern India. The *janapadas* were constantly at war with one another, and the stronger ones absorbed the weaker ones until 16 were left in the late 700s B.C.E. These territories were called *mahajanapadas*. Their power extended south to the Godavari River, which flows west to east, almost bisecting India.

Magadha

One of the *mahajanapadas* was Magadha, the kingdom that would create the first Indian empire (684–26 B.C.E.). By 400 B.C.E. Magadha and another *mahajanapada*, Koshala, were conquering their neighbors. Both King Bimbisāra (ca. 543–491 B.C.E.) of Magadha and King Prasenajit of Koshala became patrons of Siddhartha Gautama (ca. 563–ca. 483 B.C.E.), who became the Buddha. When Bimbisāra died, he was succeeded by his son Ajatashatru, who spent the first few years of his reign fighting off challengers to his rule. In the meantime, one of Bimbisāra's widows died; she was a daughter of Prasenajit. Land that Prasenajit had given to Bimbisāra as a dowry was reclaimed by Prasenajit. Ajatashatru went to war to reclaim the land and was defeated. Later, Prasenajit was overthrown by his son and fled to Magadha's capital of Rajagriha, where he died of exhaustion outside the city gates. Ajatashatru swore to avenge the fallen king, and through good luck and intelligence he led a successful military campaign that put a permanent end to Koshala. Ajatashatru went on to wage war against Licchavi, a republic ruled by several thousand knights. He lost some battles, but eventually he conquered Licchavi, and he made Magadha the dominant power in northern India. Dates are very uncertain for India in the 300s, but Ajatashatru died probably sometime between 380 and 330 B.C.E.

Ajatashatru's death was followed by chaos in Magadha's government. Apparently, numerous people claimed the throne. The man who eventually made the kingdom his own was Mahapadma Nanda, who in about 424 B.C.E. founded the Nanda Dynasty, which lasted only until about 321 B.C.E. Mahapadma Nanda was the son of a barber, a member of the Sudra caste. This made him intolerable to the warriors of the Kshatriya caste, who tried to kill him. Nanda retaliated by defeating his enemies in many battles. He built an army of more than 200,000 troops and used it to establish himself as the supreme power in northern India.

India's Maurya Empire

In 326 B.C.E. Alexander the Great (356–323 B.C.E.) of Greece entered northwestern India, where he won over some Indian leaders as allies and defeated in battle those who opposed him. He was poised to battle the army of the Nandas when his own army refused to continue to fight. It is unlikely that Alexander gave up his ambition to conquer India, but he died in 323 B.C.E., before he could reasonably build a new army for a war.

By then Aggrames, son of Mahapadma Nanda, was the Nandan king. His government was very wealthy, and its riches became legendary in its time. Its taxes were high, creating resentment throughout his kingdom and making him very unpopular. Also, there was the matter of his father being a Sudra. Thus, in 321 or 320 B.C.E. one of his generals, Candragupta Maurya (r. ca. 321–ca. 297 B.C.E.), overthrew him and founded the Maurya Empire, which lasted from 321 to 185 B.C.E.

Candragupta had spent the previous few years in Greek-controlled territory, planning his revolt. He was not only a careful planner but an inspiring leader. By 305 B.C.E. he had conquered all of northwestern India, including the Indus River valley and lands to Bactria, in modern Afghanistan. He established a government bureaucracy that kept tight control of the empire's subjects. His government increased trade by building roads and improved crop yields by building irrigation systems.

He was succeeded by his son Bindusāra, who reigned from 297 to 272 B.C.E. Bindusāra conquered lands south of the Godavari River, leaving only the southern tip of India unconquered. His son Asoka, who reigned until 233 B.C.E., expended the empire farther by conquering the southeastern coastal kingdom of Kaling in 261 B.C.E. Asoka was deeply troubled by the suffering he had caused in Kaling, and this resulted in his conversion to Buddhism.

Asoka spread Buddhist values throughout his empire. He built tens of thousands of monuments to the Buddha all over the land. He reorganized the government to be less oppressive and made edicts on how government should conduct itself in a moral way. He had these edicts carved on monuments scattered about the country. Declaring that the Maurya Empire would embrace peace, Asoka assured his neighbors that he would do them no harm. He sent Buddhist missionaries into China, southeastern Asia, and the island of Ceylon. His reforms of government, his advocacy of peace, and his sending of Buddhist missionaries to foreign lands made him one of the most influential and remarkable rulers in India's history.

He had hoped to rule by moral authority rather than military authority, but this meant that after his death more militant people encroached on Mauryan territory. In 185 B.C.E., when the Maurya Empire was overthrown, its territory had shrunk to about the same as that of Magadha in 320 B.C.E. India would not see another empire until 320 C.E.

India's Gupta Empire

The Gupta Empire lasted from 320 to 499 C.E. It was founded by Chandragupta I (r. 320–ca. 330 C.E.), who was unrelated to Chandragupta Maurya. During his reign he conquered enough territory to form a new nation in the heart of what had been the Magadha kingdom. He gave himself the title Maharajadhiraja, meaning "great raja of rajas." His son Samudragupta was the great empire builder in the family. During his reign from 330 to about 380 C.E. he conquered the rest of northeastern India and drove his territory south through the eastern half of India. He established a feudal government in which he allowed some of the kings he had conquered to rule their lands while paying him tribute. Thus, he made most of central India acknowledge his supremacy over them and exacted tribute from them, but he chose not to absorb them into his empire. His government built roads that improved trade within the empire.

He was succeeded by Ramagupta, whose military ineptitude caused him to be replaced by his brother Chandragupta II (r. ca. 380–415 C.E.). By 409 C.E. he had conquered much of northwestern India and had forced the rest of northwestern India to pay him tribute. Chinese visitors recorded his reign as a golden age for the arts, while noting that most Indians had good lives. He was succeeded by Kumāragupta (r. ca. 415–455 C.E.), whose rule was weakened by a rebellion in Malwa, in central India. The next Maharajadhiraja was Skandagupta (r. ca. 455–467 C.E.), who faced an invasion by the Hunas, the Huns. During his father's reign he had put down the rebellion in Malwa, and as the Gupta ruler he drove out the Hunas. He was succeeded by his nephew Budhagupta, whose reign seems to have been brief. The Hunas returned and defeated the Gupta army, ending the Gupta Empire.

China's Legendary Dynasty

Almost nothing is known about the politics of the region of China before the Shang Dynasty (ca. 1500–ca. 1045 B.C.E.). Ancient Chinese legends say that the first Chinese king was Huangdi, also called the "Yellow Emperor." *Huang* means "august sovereign," and *di* means "high god." During the Shang and Zhou dynasties, *di* would come to mean "divine ruler." Huangdi supposedly lived sometime between the 2900s and 2600s B.C.E., with 2698 B.C.E. sometimes being asserted as the year he made himself king.

According to Chinese histories from the Han Dynasty (202 B.C.E.–220 C.E.), the first Chinese dynasty was the Xia, said to have been founded in 2205 B.C.E. This dynasty has long been thought to be a myth, but so was the Shang Dynasty until the early 20th century, when archaeologists began finding proof of its existence. In fact, one Han historian, Sima Qian of the second century B.C.E., made a list of Shang rulers that closely matches a list created by archaeologists from Shang writings, and he made a list of Xia rulers, too, so perhaps ancient Xia just remains to be discovered.

China's Shang Dynasty

Since the 1910s archaeologists have found cities of the Shang Dynasty and tombs of some of its rulers. Chinese legend says it was founded in about 1700 B.C.E. by King Tang. Modern archaeologists and historians are more comfortable with the date 1500 B.C.E. for the founding of the Shang Dynasty along the Yellow River, probably by a historical King Tang. The Shang were warlike, and they conquered territories to the north and west of the Yellow River.

By 1050 B.C.E. the Shang kingdom was remarkable. The Shang conquerors had absorbed into their kingdom a variety of different ethnic groups who spoke several different languages and had instilled in most of them the idea that they were one people, living in a kingdom given to them by gods. The cultural influence of the Shang reached south beyond the Yangtze River, north into what is now Inner Mongolia, west to the Qin Mountains, and east to the ocean. The Shang Dynasty's strong central government held the country together for centuries, but it began to weaken in the 1100s and 1000s B.C.E. because it could not keep track of its increasingly far-flung territories, and its borders were constantly fluctuating with the ebb and flow of barbarian invasions and Shang counterattacks.

China's Zhou Dynasty

During the 1100s or 1000s B.C.E. the rulers of the province of Zhou began calling themselves *wangs*, meaning "kings." There is some doubt about exactly when the Zhou overthrew the Shang Dynasty, with the earliest date being 1122 B.C.E., but the year was probably 1045 B.C.E. The Shang government had fallen into disarray, with its kingdom's provinces tending to rule themselves. Although the Zhou were not as technologically advanced as were the Shang, they had a better-disciplined military. King Wu of Zhou defeated the Shang army and sacked the capital city of Anyang.

Historians divide the history of the Zhou Dynasty into two periods: the Western Zhou, when the capital was in the city of Xian in the Qin province, and the Eastern Zhou, when the capital was in Luoyang in the province of Zhou, to the east of Xian. The Western Zhou era lasted from 1027 to 771 or 770 B.C.E. Its first monarch, King Wu, declared that the Shang Dynasty's divine energy had disappeared and that he had been chosen by the gods to found a new dynasty.

To later Chinese, the Western Zhou era was a golden age because the Zhou government maintained the peace. Instead of creating a strong central government, the Zhou monarchs solved their problems with ruling a large nation by creating a feudal system in which they appointed family members and close friends to rule dozens of small provinces. No one had a large enough province to have the manpower necessary to overthrow the government, and the Zhou Dynasty had a series of strong leaders who traveled the country with their army. The army was so magnificent when it marched that enemies were overawed by the sight of it.

During the 800s B.C.E. nomadic peoples from the west of China raided the Qin province and threatened Xian. Thus, in about 770 B.C.E. the Zhou king moved his capital east, away from the threats from barbarians. This resulted in a great loss of prestige for the king, and the rulers of provinces began ignoring the Zhou government. This began the Eastern Zhou, which historians divide into two smaller periods: the Spring and Autumn Era (722–481 B.C.E.) and the Warring States Era (453–221 B.C.E.). These names were given because the first period is covered in an ancient history book called *Spring and Autumn Annals*, and the other is covered in *The Strategies of the Warring States*.

During the Eastern Zhou the king had almost no political power and ruled only a tiny territory. He did have important ceremonial significance, and rulers of the provinces consulted him as a matter of fulfilling protocol. This protocol may have annoyed the provincial rulers, but they held their stations as rulers because they received the blessings of the king, who ruled by divine right and passed that right to them. To kill the king and be done with him would take away their own justifications for being rulers. Meanwhile, the different provinces waged war against each other.

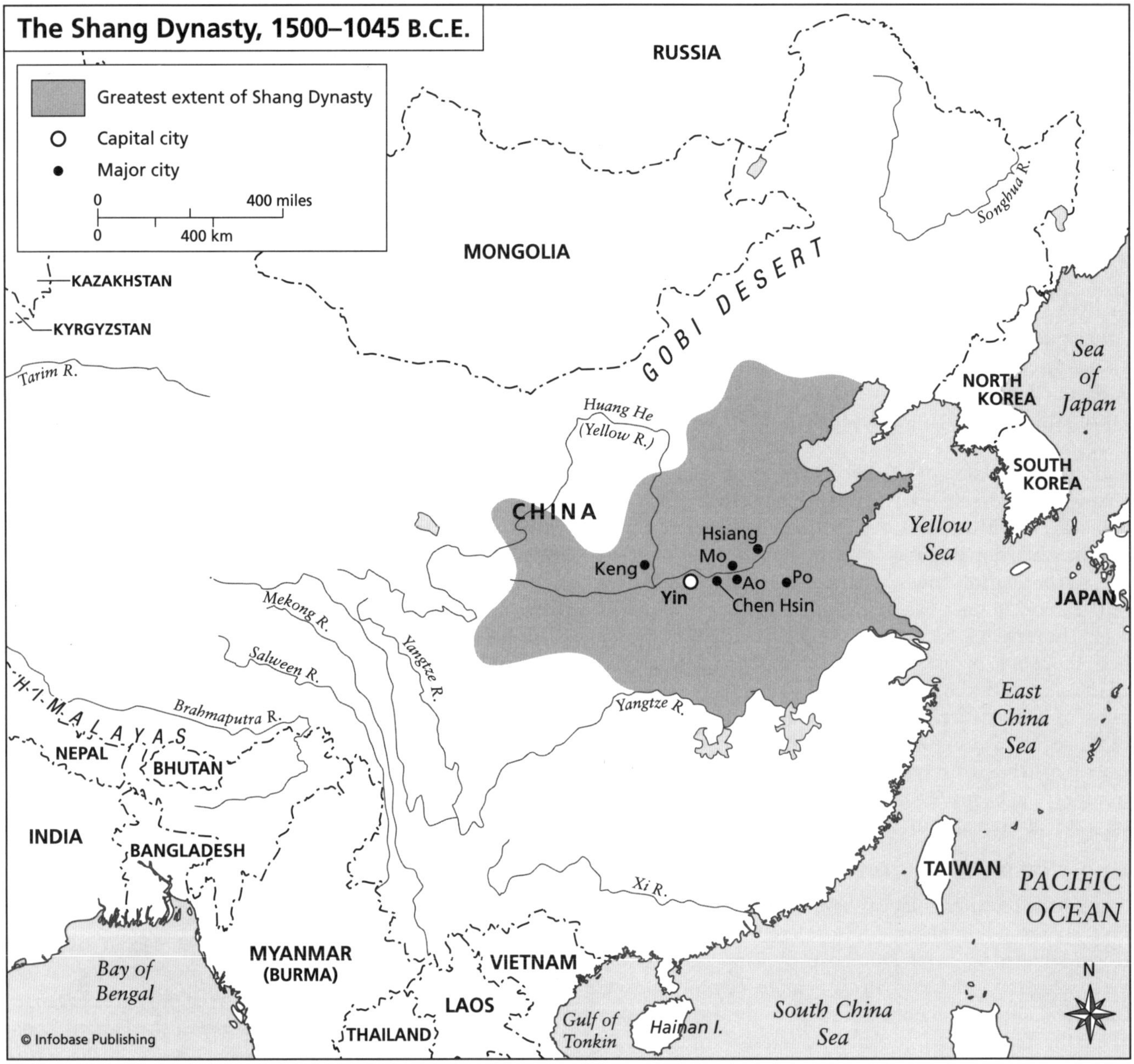

The Shang Dynasty dominated ancient China between 1500 and 1045 B.C.E.

China's Qin Dynasty

One of history's most remarkable people is the emperor Zheng (r. 221–210 B.C.E.), who ruled the Qin province from 246 B.C.E. in the west of the Zhou empire. Public works projects, such as irrigation systems, by Zheng's father and grandfather had enabled Qin to have a thriving economy, which could feed and equip a large army. They had dispensed with the tradition of using heredity to appoint public officials, instead using merit. This meant that they had an army run by able men who were often commoners who had risen through the ranks because of their accomplishments. Clever and ruthless, Zheng defeated the other provinces in battle.

In 246 B.C.E. he declared himself Qin Shi Huangdi. He chose "Huangdi" to tie himself to the mythical first king and also because *huang* outranked *wang*, because by then it meant "emperor," and *di* meant that he had the divine right to rule. *Shi* meant he was the "first" emperor of China. He ordered the destruction of historical records so that all history would begin with him as well as to eliminate what he thought was the corrupting influence of past governments. He had about 40,000 Confucian scholars buried alive to prevent their teaching about the past. He imposed the legalist philosophy of government, under which every aspect of life was governed by laws, and punishment was severe. When he died in 210 B.C.E. his government began to collapse. So loathed were Qin Shi

Huangdi and his family that when they were deposed soon after his death, every last one was executed. Qin Shi Huangdi had bragged that his dynasty would last 10,000 generations. In fact, in 206 B.C.E. the Han Dynasty took power.

China's Han Dynasty

The Han Dynasty was founded by Liu Bang (r. 206–195 B.C.E.), a commoner who had risen through the ranks to become a general. He had little idea of how to rule a country, but he had the good sense to know that to establish a stable government he had to do away with the legalist way of governing. On the advice of scholars he established Confucianism as China's governing philosophy. The precepts of Confucian philosophy were modified to make clear that everyone had to obey the emperor, but otherwise the Confucian idea that a government should serve its people rather than the other way around was made national policy. The lowering of taxes and easing of laws were popular and had the desired effect of making Liu Bang and his descendants popular for the next 200 or so years.

Trade with the outside world was expanded during the Han Dynasty, which lasted until 220 C.E. China spread southward and northwestward and extended its northern Great Wall to cover part of the so-called Silk Road, the trade routes over which China exported and imported goods to and from Europe, Rome, Persia, and India. Even peasants began to share in some of the nation's wealth. An educational system was begun in the 140s B.C.E. to teach boys Confucianism and a basic understanding of geography and the sciences. This system served to indoctrinate the barbarian provinces into the Chinese way of life, and it provided the government with a pool of people it could appoint to government offices based on their merits.

During the last 100 years of the Han Dynasty eunuchs gained control of much of the central government, and they enriched themselves and manipulated governments officials. Angry and resentful, some Han generals rebelled and slaughtered the eunuchs. One of the generals, Dong Zhuo, put the last Han emperor, Xian (r. 189–220 C.E.), on the throne. Dong Zhuo failed to control his troops, who went on a rampage in the capital city, Luoyang, sacking the city and burning government buildings, including the national library. In another age Xian might have been a great emperor, but it was all he could do just to hang on to his throne until he abdicated at sword point in 220 C.E.

China's Six Dynasties Era

The Six Dynasties Era lasted from 220 to 589 C.E. and takes its name because, except during one brief period, it was ruled in pieces by different governments. After 220 C.E. China was divided into three kingdoms: Wei in the north, Wu in the southeast, and Shu in the southwest. In 264 C.E. Wei conquered Shu, and in 280 C.E. it conquered Wu, briefly reunifying the nation under the Jin Dynasty. By 304 C.E. northern barbarians had pushed the Jin Dynasty south into the Yangtze River valley. From 304 to 535 C.E. 17 different dynasties, 14 of them non-Chinese, ruled in the north. The barbarians adopted Chinese customs and Chinese Buddhism. Throughout the Six Dynasties Era the Chinese leaders wished to reunite China under one government. It was General Sui who succeeded, establishing the Sui Dynasty in 581 C.E. and conquering most of China by 589 C.E.

Funan

Funan began as a trading city in the Mekong Delta of what is now South Vietnam. According to the Chinese of the time, an Indian merchant named Kaundinya, meaning "king of the mountain," wooed Liu-ye, meaning "willow leaf," who was a local queen, probably the leader of a tribe, perhaps a priestess. Between 100 and 200 C.E. they married and founded a royal dynasty. Funan adopted an Indian-style government and embraced Hinduism. Funan was notable for the Hindu temples it built, mostly of bricks. By conquering other tribes, by the 300s C.E. it controlled territory from Camranh Bay in the east to central Cambodia. To its north were the Chams and the Khmers. The Khmers conquered the Chams, creating the kingdom of Chen-la, which became a vassal state of Funan. In the mid-500s the Khmers conquered Funan.

Nam Viet

The ancient history of Vietnam is murky, colored by myths. In about 500 B.C.E. there was a Viet kingdom south of the Yangtze River in what is now China. The Chinese conquered it in 333 B.C.E. Many of the Viets moved southward to get out of the way of China's expansion, displacing through war a culture that may have been related to Indonesian tribes of the time. Other Viets remained in China and assimilated into the Chinese culture. In about 207 B.C.E., while Liu Bang was establishing his control of China, a Chinese general created a kingdom called "Nam Viet," meaning "Southern Viet." This kingdom reached from 40 miles south of the city of Hue in modern Vietnam to a region west of the modern city of Canton in China. In 111 B.C.E. China conquered Nam Viet, ruling it until 938 C.E., when a Viet general, Ngo Quyen (ca. 896–944 C.E.), drove the Chinese out.

Korea's Three Kingdoms

Much of ancient Korea was under no one's particular rule, and its three main kingdoms did not have clearly definable borders. These kingdoms were Silla (57 B.C.E.–935 C.E.), Koguryo (37 B.C.E.–668 C.E.), and Paekche (18 B.C.E.–660 C.E.). It was Silla that united Korea in 668 C.E. Previously, Silla ruled much of southeastern Korea, Koguryo ruled northern Korea, and Paekche ruled southwestern Korea.

Koguryo was founded by King Tongmyongsong (r. 37–19 B.C.E.) and migrants from Manchuria. After a successful military campaign by King Mich'on (r. 300–331 C.E.) in 313 C.E., Koguryo ruled much of southern Manchuria. In 612 C.E. the army of King Yong-yang under the command of General Ulchimundok decisively defeated an attacking Chinese army in a series of battles in southern Manchuria.

Paekche had been started by tribes from Manchuria that migrated farther south than had the people of Koguryo. Its first king was Onjo (r. 18 B.C.E.–28 C.E.). Paekche was heavily influenced by China, which had trading colonies in it. The kingdom sometimes needed help defending itself against Koguryo, and it was aided by the Japanese and sometimes by Silla. The first king of Silla was Hyokkose (r. 57 B.C.E.–3 C.E.). For much of its early history Silla was the weaker of the three kingdoms.

In 372 C.E. the Chinese introduced Buddhism and Confucianism to Koguryo. Buddhism's influence spread to the other two kingdoms, and the monarchs of the three kingdoms encouraged its adoption by their people, hoping that Buddhism would help their kingdoms prosper by making their societies more harmonious, as well as by repelling evil spirits. Scholars from Paekche brought Confucianism to Japan, perhaps in the late 300s C.E.

Japan

Very little is known about the rulers of ancient Japan. Although there were lists created during the Middle Ages of monarchs going back to 660 B.C.E., Japanese historians proved these to be false in the 1600s C.E. Some historians cite Jimmu as the first ruler of Japan because he is named in Japanese mythology, but he did not exist. The first ruler for whom there is any evidence is Queen Himiko. She is found in several Chinese records of her era, which note how she lived and her relationship to China. She was China's only important ally in northeastern Asia and was a valued ally of the Chinese kingdom Wei after the fall of the Han Dynasty.

Her exact dates have not been established, but Chinese records show her active for a long time; she was probably alive from the late 100s to the late 200s C.E. In 247 C.E. Himiko asked her Chinese allies for help during a period of unrest in her kingdom, and an ambassador named Zheng Zhang was sent. The Chinese record her being succeeded by a man who, in turn, was replaced by a 12-year-old girl. Like Himiko, she was a sorceress, but little else is known about the young queen. Even her name is in dispute, though it was probably Ichiyo.

During the reigns of Himiko and Ichiyo Japan moved from illiteracy toward literacy. The extensive road building that would connect the island of Honshu, north and south, probably began during their era, and they probably introduced Chinese building techniques for public buildings.

Ceylon (Sri Lanka)

It was probably the first king in Ceylon, Dutthagamani (r. second century B.C.E.), who established the capital of ancient Ceylon in the city of Anuradhapura in the northern part of the island. He and his successors were Buddhists, and they were expected by their subjects to rule according to the Buddha's teachings of modesty and compassion. They endured invasions from southern India and were ruled by southern Indian Tamils from 104 to 89 B.C.E. and again from 433 to 459 C.E. During the rule of King Dhatusena (r. 459–477 C.E.) Ceylon was famed for its large ports, huge warehouses, and cosmopolitan life.

EUROPE

BY KIRK H. BEETZ

Empires and dynasties did not emerge until relatively late in ancient Europe. An empire is a state that not only controls the territory that surrounds its capital but also seeks to expand its territory by colonization or military conquest. Thus, the leader of an empire is not just the king of his own territory but also the emperor of a much larger realm. A dynasty is a succession of hereditary rulers, a royal line. Typically in the ancient world, the rulers of kingdoms and empires passed their positions to their sons (occasionally, to their daughters) upon their deaths. In the chiefdoms, kingdoms, and small states of the Bronze and Iron Ages after about 2000 B.C.E., hereditary leadership was probably practiced, but not until the emergence of Imperial Rome and the smaller states that formed around its periphery did a true major European empire develop with its own dynasties along with the royal lines of the kingdoms that existed on its borders.

Our knowledge of empires and dynasties in ancient Europe is limited by the sources available to historians. Some modern accounts of the ancient world just skip the history of Europe outside Greece and Italy, covering most of the rest of the world without hinting at why Europe is missing. Sometimes a history of the ancient world will try to come to terms with the problem: Ancient Europeans were illiterate until the conquest by the Romans from 58 to 50 C.E., meaning that they left no written histories of themselves. What little is known of names of people and places comes from foreigners, mostly Greeks, who visited them. Thus, kingdoms may have risen and fallen, and kings and queens may have accomplished great deeds, but their names are lost to history. Archaeology can help, but without even written names, it cannot tell modern readers what the ancients called themselves or the names they had for the lands in which they lived, unless a Greek or Roman recorded the names, and surviving Greek or Roman records provide only a little of the oral history of the Celts, Germans, Slavs, and others who existed in most of Europe.

In the 1100s B.C.E. the Phoenicians began their centuries-long exploration of the Mediterranean and Atlantic coasts of Europe. They brought back home silver, tin, exotic foods, and other goods as well as information about the geography of European coasts. In about 670 B.C.E. literacy returned to Greece following a dark age after the collapse of the Mycenaean culture in about 1250 B.C.E. The Greeks adapted the Phoenician alphabet to their own language and seem almost immediately to have begun writing down everything they could remember about themselves, their politics, their religion, and their history as well as whatever they could learn about other peoples. Most of these writings have been lost, but they are sometimes quoted in later writings that have survived. There were other cultures that developed written languages, notably the Etruscans and the Romans, but most of Europe remained illiterate until conquered by Rome, and therefore much of what is known about European kingdoms and rulers comes secondhand, often from very biased Greek and Roman writers looking at other Europeans from the outside.

Etruscans

Studying the ancient Etruscans can quickly make clear the problems historians have in reconstructing Europe's past. The Etruscans had their own written language, and they were for a time the rulers of Rome. The Romans wrote many histories about themselves, so it would be reasonable to assume that there would be plenty of information about the Etruscans, yet they are still a mysterious people. Their language is strange; it does not fit with Celtic, Latin, or Greek languages, making it hard to translate. Most histories were written by outsiders—the Greeks, who regarded the Etruscans as enemies because the Etruscans had allied themselves with the Carthaginians to limit Greek trade in the western Mediterranean, and the Romans, who had fought wars against the Etruscans and typically characterized Etruscans as indolent and obese.

The empire of the Etruscans began to develop around 900 B.C.E. in Etruria, a region of northwest-central Italy. Called the "Villanovan" culture by archaeologists, it encompassed several towns and stretched from the west coast to the east coast across Italy. By 600 B.C.E. the towns had become the Etruscan League, a federation of city-states that cooperated in foreign and military affairs. Their empire extended south past Salerno, west into Corsica, north to the Alps, and east to the northwestern Adriatic Sea.

An Etruscan city-state was governed by *zilaths*, who were members of an assembly, perhaps like community elders or like Roman senators. These cities belonged to 12 divisions of the Etruscan League, each division ruled by a king. Kingships seem to have been hereditary, but succession practices are not clear. The Etruscan League also had a general assembly where the *zilaths* would meet to select a "first *zilath*," who could lead the entire league, especially during wars. These general assemblies seem to have selected the first *zilath* once a year, but some first *zilaths* were reelected several times.

A prominent Etruscan king was Porsena, ruler of the city of Clusium. When the city of Rome deposed its Etruscan king Tarquinius Superbus in 510 B.C.E., Porsena provided the army that was intended to put Tarquinius Superbus back on Rome's throne. According to Roman histories, Rome was saved by heroic stands of small groups of Roman soldiers against the advance of the mighty Etruscan army. Some historians doubt that the Roman histories tell the truth, suggesting that Porsena's army actually defeated the Romans. In any case, Porsena seems to have been regarded as one of the Etruscans' great kings. After Porsena's time Etruscan power waned while the Etruscans lost wars to Carthaginian, Greek, Roman, and Celtic rivals. The Etruscan city-sates retained their cultural identities even during Roman rule. The Etruscans received Roman citizenship in 88 B.C.E.

Noricum

Noricum was a Celtic kingdom east of the Alps and north of Italy, founded around 500 B.C.E. Under the influence of the Romans, the people of Noricum developed a stable economy and existed mostly in peace with the Romans. Not much is known about their rulers, though they seem to have followed the typically Celtic practice of appointing new kings or queens rather than having a hereditary kingship. The people of Noricum originally wore trousers but adopted Roman dress. By the time the Romans invaded Gaul, Noricum had adopted so many Roman customs and laws that it was absorbed into the empire with little disruption to its people's lives.

Gaul

Until the Germanic invasions of the fifth century C.E., the Celts were the dominant ethnic group in Europe. They were given the name Celts by the Greeks; they were called Gauls by the Romans. They had what historians call a "heroic culture," meaning a warrior culture in which great military deeds are exalted. The Gauls usually did not see themselves as a single political nation. They were divided into numerous tribes, and they were very mobile. Entire tribes of tens of thousands of people would sometimes take everything they could carry and march to settle somewhere else, sometimes pushing out the people who already lived there, who themselves would move into a new area, driving people out. This movement is how the Celts came to the Romans' attention as a danger in 390 B.C.E. Celtic tribes had been driven out of their homes and had settled in northern Italy. From northern Italy they raided into other territories, and in 390 B.C.E. they sacked Rome. This attack made them a military target for the Romans.

Most Celtic tribes were ruled by kings. The kingship was not hereditary, though the kingship tended to remain in one family. At a king or a queen's death, the elite class of the Celts, the warriors, would choose a replacement. Rulers were much more often men than women, but tales recorded by Greek writers and Roman experiences with Celtic women suggest that there were formidable women rulers among the Celts.

The Celtic tribes were forever fighting one other. When Rome's Julius Caesar invaded Gaul in 58 B.C.E., he took advantage of this Celtic trait, playing one tribe against another. Some Celtic leaders thought that they could use the Roman army to good advantage and allied themselves with the Romans in the hope of having the Romans destroy a particularly hated enemy.

Out of the Celtic tribes of southern Gaul arose Vercingetorix, a member of the Averni tribe. His father had been chief of the Averni but had been executed for being too ambitious, perhaps meaning that he had tried to become a tyrant rather than rule by the consent of the tribe's warriors. In 53 B.C.E. Celtic tribes rebelled against Caesar, and Vercingetorix had urged the Averni to join the rebellion. For this rebellion he was expelled from the tribe, yet he continued to agitate for war and drew to him many disgruntled young warriors and other warriors who were leaderless. With their assistance, he seized control of the Averni government.

The rebellion had begun under the leadership of Indutiomarus, chief of the Treveri tribe, who had led a winter attack on a Roman camp. His army was defeated, and he was hunted down and killed in 53 B.C.E. Vercingetorix's most remarkable achievement at that time was to convince many of the fractious Celts of Gaul that they should think of themselves as one people and unite to fight for their freedom, and he was made chief of the war effort. He learned in an engagement at Noviodunum that his army was no match for the Romans' superior tactics and discipline in a pitched battle, so he resorted to guerrilla warfare. He burned farmlands to deny the Romans access to food. Even so, Julius Caesar managed to track down his army and trap it in the fortified town of Alesia, where the Celts starved until they surrendered. Vercingetorix was sent to Rome, imprisoned, and publicly humiliated, and in 46 B.C.E. he was executed by strangulation.

These events did not end ambitions for the independence of Gaul. Now and then tribes would try to take a stand for Celtic freedom, but little came of their efforts until 259 C.E., when Gaul seceded from the Roman Empire. Gaul had three emperors: Postumus (r. 259–268 C.E.), Victorinus (r. 268–270 C.E.), and Tetricus (r. 270–274 C.E.). After seizing power in Gaul in 259 C.E., Postumus declared the existence of the Gallic Empire in 260 C.E. In 261 C.E. Britain, Spain, and the Germanic territories in central Europe joined Gaul as part of his empire. The Gallic emperors defeated attempted invasions by Germanic tribes from outside of Gaul. In 274 C.E. the Roman emperor defeated Tetricus's army and ended the Gallic Empire.

Among the Germanic tribes who periodically attacked Gaul were the Franks. In 418 C.E. King Pharamond (r. 418–428 C.E.) began what became the Merovingian Dynasty (418–751 C.E.). He was succeeded by Clodio (r. 428–447 C.E.), who in turn was succeeded by Merovech (r. 447–458 C.E.), for whom the dynasty is named. When the Huns under Attila attacked the city of Orleans in 451 C.E., the Franks joined the Gauls, and the Goths and the Burgundians, Germanic tribes under the command of a Roman general, rescued the city and later defeated the Huns in battle.

Merovech was succeeded by Childeric I (r. ca. 458–482 C.E.). Childeric expanded the power of the Franks in Gaul, but it was his son Clovis I (r. 482–511 C.E.) who made the power long lasting through his military prowess, his conversion to Christianity (496 C.E.), and his establishment of the city of Paris his capital. In 486 C.E. he defeated in battle Syagrius, who was the last official Roman governor of Gaul.

IBERIA

Iberia is the peninsula where Portugal and Spain are now. Iberia was settled at least 30,000 years ago by modern humans. By 5000 B.C.E. West Mediterranean peoples were migrating from the east coast into Iberia. Some ethnologists believe that descendants from both these populations still live in Iberia, especially in Portugal and the Basque provinces of northern Spain. The Greeks gave them the name Iberians. Phoenician merchants were visiting Iberia by 1100 B.C.E., and in the 700s B.C.E. the Phoenicians had colonies on the east and south coasts of Iberia. Along these coasts cities arose with their own governments, probably out of a desire to protect resources, such as tin mines, that were important in trade. These cities were ruled by warriors and priests. In the rest of Iberia people lived in small tribes that were often at war with one another.

About 750 B.C.E. the Iberian tribe the Tartessians established the kingdom of Tartessos (called Tarshish in the Bible), probably to protect their rights to copper mines in southern Iberia. By 600 B.C.E. it encompassed the lower half of the Guadalquivir River and had four cities, Osuna, El Carambolo, Niebla, and the capital, Huelva. Tartessos was not only an key source of copper but also an important way station for merchants sailing to the Atlantic coast of Europe and to Britain because its ports were on the Atlantic side from Gibralter. In the 200s B.C.E. it was conquered by the Carthaginians.

The first wave of Celtic migration into Iberia from Gaul occurred in the 800s B.C.E. A second wave followed in the 600s B.C.E. At first the Celts settled in northern Iberia, but during the second wave they spread throughout Iberia, except for the southern and eastern coasts, which remained under the control of native Iberian cities until they were conquered by Carthage in the 200s B.C.E. The Celts did not drive out the local tribes but instead mixed with them, creating a group now known as the Celtiberians. They were ruled by warriors, and the Celtiberian tribes frequently clashed with one other. In the 200s B.C.E. the Celtiberians began living in *castros*, or fortified towns.

Greeks and Carthaginians often fought over control of the western Mediterranean. In 264 B.C.E. Rome came to the aid of Greeks in Sicily, beginning the First Punic War (264–241 B.C.E.), which Carthage eventually lost. Having lost much of its influence among the Mediterranean's islands, Carthage compensated by conquering the southern and eastern coasts of Iberia. Carthage tried to conquer the Celtiberians of the interior but was mostly unsuccessful; however, through diplomacy, Carthage built alliances among the Celtiberians, allowing Carthaginians some control over events in central Iberia. During the Second Punic War (218–201 B.C.E.) the Carthaginians used Iberia as a landing ground for their armies, and for this reason Rome invaded Iberia, inflicting defeats on the Carthaginians and winning allies. Still, many Iberians resisted Roman rule, and Rome did not have complete control of Iberia until 19 B.C.E. Thereafter the peoples of Iberia adopted Latin as their primary language and adopted the Roman way of life.

The Germanic tribes the Suevi and the Vandals invaded Gaul in 405 C.E., but another Germanic tribe, the Visigoths, drove them out. They fled to Iberia. The Suevi numbered about 60,000 and chose to settle in northwestern Iberia. The Vandals conquered part of southwestern Spain, which came to be called Andalusia, in reference to the Vandals. The Visigoths were a well-organized tribe that had adopted many Roman customs. Their king Ataulphus (r. 412–415 C.E.), cooperating with the Romans, overcame the Suevi and drove most of the Vandals out of Iberia in 411 C.E. The Vandals fled to North Africa.

The Visigoths ruled Iberia as their kingdom from 412 to 711 C.E. Kingship was not hereditary. Instead, the warrior elite elected the member of the royal family whom they considered most fit to lead them. Many Visigoths became farmers, but the warriors were the nobility, serving as knights. They spoke

Latin and followed many Roman customs; although they made Iberia an independent kingdom, for diplomatic matters they acknowledged loyalty to the Roman emperor in Constantinople. The Visigoths were Arian Christians, meaning they downplayed the divinity of Jesus Christ, a practice that led to conflicts with the Roman Catholic Iberians, who believed in the divinity of Jesus Christ. In 486 C.E. King Alaric (r. 484–507) established the nation's capital in Toledo.

Britain and Ireland

The Celtic peoples of Britain and Ireland were known to the Romans as fierce savages. When Julius Caesar first led Roman troops to Britain, they were met by nearly naked warriors who waded into the ocean toward the Romans' ships to do battle. They were no match for the discipline and superior armaments of the Romans and were scattered. What Caesar later discovered was a land of petty kingdoms with fairly stable governments. He was even able to establish trade agreements that survived until the Roman emperor Claudius (r. 41–54 C.E.) invaded in 43 C.E.

When Claudius invaded Britain, the governments of southern Britain were used to trading with Romans, and a few of the small kingdoms allied themselves with Rome, believing that they would benefit from a close relationship with the Romans. The Romans viewed the Britons as savages and treated them as such. In particular, human sacrifice in religious rituals as practiced by the Druids was appalling to the Romans, who tried to end it. The Romans became cruel overlords, even maltreating their allies. Among these allies was the kingdom of Iceni. In 61 C.E. the Roman soldiers raped two Icenian girls, an act that outraged Queen Boudicca and her subjects.

Boudicca was a sorceress as well as a leader, and when she painted herself in her war colors, she was said to be terrifying. She led a revolt against the Romans that nearly expelled the Romans from Britain. A Roman legion was wiped out in one ambush. Roman settlements were sacked. The Romans were driven out of Londinium. When Boudicca's army faced that of the Roman governor Suetonius Paulinus, it probably outnumbered his forces more than 20 to one. However, the traditional Celtic fighting style of the Britons, which emphasized individual heroism, proved to be their undoing, because they attacked in an uncoordinated mass, and the Romans responded with discipline, skill, and cool efficiency. The Romans killed between 60,000 and 80,000 British warriors and drove the rest to flight. Boudicca followed Celtic tradition by committing suicide rather than being captured.

After that time the Romanized Britons always retained some independence in dress, customs, and tastes from Rome, though they loved Roman-style country villas. In 410 C.E. the Roman emperor Honorius (r. 395–423 C.E.) told the Britons that he could not help defend them. Little is truly known about what events actually followed because the few written records that have survived are short on names and dates. Germanic tribes invaded Britain. The Roman governor or perhaps a regional king may have asked Germanic mercenaries to help defend Britain from other Germans, possibly in exchange for land. The mercenaries turned on their employers, taking slaves, looting, and killing.

In the last years of the Roman Empire governorships were divided between a political governor and a military one, called a *dux bellorum*. The *dux bellorum* of Britain in the mid-400s C.E. may have been the original King Arthur, a man nicknamed Ars, meaning "bear" in the local dialect. His true name is much debated and is probably permanently lost. There is some archaeological support for one of the achievements attributed to him. Ancient chroniclers say that he defeated the Anglo-Saxons in a great battle around 460 C.E. and that thereafter were about 50 years of peace. This peaceful period seems to have occurred.

GREECE

BY CHRISTOPHER BLACKWELL

In antiquity there was no single nation known as "Greece" or even "Hellas," as the modern Greeks call their own country. Hellas was an abstract idea, and the "Greek world" described by the historian Herodotus in the fifth century B.C.E. encompassed "all those people speaking the same language, sharing the same customs, and worshipping the same gods." In the time of Herodotus this Greek world included the Balkan Peninsula, where the modern nation of Hellas (Greece) is today, and settlements in Sicily, on the coast of Italy, in southern France, along the north coast of Africa, on the west coast of what is now Turkey, and around the Black Sea in what is now southern Russia. In this area and at different times individual cities governed themselves, came together under alliances and confederacies, and enjoyed a variety of forms of government, including monarchy, oligarchy, tyranny, and democracy.

We have evidence from mythology, poetry, and archaeology for empires during the Bronze Age (3000–1100 B.C.E.), which faded before the historical period, the period for which we have written accounts. During the so-called Archaic Period (600–480 B.C.E.) a succession of dynasties of tyrants arose in assorted cities. These dynasties tended to give way to various forms of democracy during the Classical Period (490–323 B.C.E.). The latter period came to an end with the first true "empire" of historical Greece, the rule of the Macedonians Philip (r. 359–336 B.C.E.) and Alexander the Great (r. 336–323 B.C.E.). After Alexander's death Macedonian Greeks set up dynasties that ruled portions of the eastern Mediterranean world, in European Greece, Asia Minor, and Egypt, until these regions came under the power of Rome.

Bronze Age Civilizations

When Sir Arthur Evans excavated the island of Crete in the late 19th century, he uncovered the remains of a rich civilization dating from the third and second millennia B.C.E. He found large, sprawling palaces, elaborately decorated with wall paintings—scenes of dancing, games, and marine life. He also noted that these palaces lacked defensive walls. From this last fact he concluded that the long-dead inhabitants of these structures were confident in their security, and he speculated that such security must have come from a solid military command of the sea. These speculations led him to think of the legendary king Minos, who was said to have ruled the Aegean Sea and eastern Mediterranean, and he named the civilization he uncovered "Minoan." We know very little of this period apart from what archaeology can tell us, but we know that these palaces had a complex bureaucracy and great wealth.

Archaeologists have also uncovered the remains of an "empire" on the southern mainland of Greece, dating to the second millennium B.C.E. Marked by immense, strongly fortified palaces, this civilization is known as "Mycenaean," after Mycenae, one of the principal settlements of the period. Mycenae was also the home of Agamemnon, the mythological king who, according to the Homeric *Iliad* and *Odyssey*, was the chief *basileus*, or "king," of all the Greek kings who went to war against Troy. Historians are quick to point out that Homeric poetry is not history and that there is no archaeological evidence that Agamemnon was a historical figure.

Still, mythology, poetry, and archaeology tend to support each other on broad points: The cities mentioned in the *Iliad* and *Odyssey* were major settlements during the Mycenaean Period (1600–1100 B.C.E.); the king of Mycenae claims supremacy in the *Iliad* and *Odyssey*; and the network of roads between Bronze Age settlements in southern Greece seem to converge on Mycenae. It is therefore reasonable to assume that Mycenae was politically central and thus perhaps the center of something we can call an empire.

The palace at Mycenae was destroyed by forces unknown around 1150 B.C.E. During the next few centuries the Greek world entered a "dark age," so called because of the modesty of the archaeological remains and the lack of written sources. Between 750 and 700 B.C.E. the Greeks adapted the Phoenician alphabet for their own use, and the historical period began. The archaeology of this period and accounts of oral traditions written centuries later point to an empire of sorts during the dark ages. Around 800 B.C.E. Greeks from Euboea, the long island that runs along the east coast of the Greek mainland, founded a trading colony at Al Mina, in what is now Syria. Later in the eighth century B.C.E. they founded another colony near the Bay of Naples. During this period widespread finds of Euboean pottery throughout the Mediterranean suggest that the Euboean cities of Khalkís and Eretria were significant economic powers, and later accounts of a war between the two—the so-called Lelantine War that involved many other Greek cities—would suggest political and military power as well. But the Lelantine War seems to have brought an end to Euboean power, and Euboea ceased to be a political force after around 680 B.C.E.

Tyrants

In 776 B.C.E. the first Olympic Games were held in the Peloponnese, in southern Greece. This marks a clear beginning of a consciousness among Greek speakers that despite their political disunity they were in some sense a single people. The eighth through sixth centuries B.C.E. were the so-called Archaic Period of Greece, and during this period many city-states underwent political revolutions. At Corinth, Sicyon, Megara, Miletus, Mytilene, Sámos, and finally Athens, the rule of aristocratic families was overthrown, to be replaced by rule by tyrants.

According to the philosopher Aristotle, who wrote on political systems in the fourth century B.C.E., tyranny in Greece was a step away from monarchy and aristocracy and toward democracy. The common people of a city, unhappy with their aristocratic rulers, would choose a "champion" and give him (they were always men) absolute authority; this new *tyrannos* (the Greek word that gives us "tyrant") would enact economic and social reforms.

An example of this trend was the establishment of tyranny at Corinth around 650 B.C.E. This city had long been ruled by the aristocratic family of the Bacchidae. Cypselus (r. ca. 657–627 B.C.E.) himself was the son of a Bacchiad woman, Labda. When the common people of Corinth revolted against the perceived injustice of Bacchiad rule, Cypselus emerged as their champion. Ancient sources differ on the nature of his rule, with some saying that he was bloodthirsty but others noting that he never employed bodyguards, which would indicate that he enjoyed popular support. Like many tyrants, he founded a dynasty, with his son Periander (r. 627–586 B.C.E.) following him in rule. As was often the case, the second generation of a tyrannical dynasty was less benign, and ancient sources universally describe Periander's rule as one of violence and oppression. Periander passed the tyranny to his son Psammetichus, who called himself Cypselus II. This man was murdered, bringing an end to tyranny and ushering in a period of constitutional government with many democratic features.

At Athens tyranny came later, at the end of the sixth century B.C.E., after at least two close calls earlier. In 632 B.C.E. a man named Cylon attempted to set himself up as tyrant after winning fame at the Olympic Games. His efforts were thwarted by members of the aristocratic family of the Alcmaeonidae, and Cylon was murdered in a temple—a scandalous violation of religious laws that would haunt the Alcmaeonidae for centuries. Around 594 B.C.E. a period of conflict between the aristocrats and the common citizens could easily have led to tyranny, following the pattern at Corinth. But in this case both sides of the dispute agreed to allow Solon (ca. 630–ca. 560 B.C.E.), a prominent Athenian, to reform the constitution along more equitable, if not fully democratic, principles.

Then, in 546 B.C.E., Peisistratus established himself as tyrant in Athens by "taking the people into his party," according to Aristotle, and disarming the aristocrats. As with Cypselus, ancient writers disagree on the nature of Peisistratus's reign, but Aristotle states that he ruled according to the laws. Peisistratus also entertained dynastic ambitions, leaving power to his sons Hippias and Hipparchus. These men, like their father, were patrons of the arts, but this was not enough to protect them from popular ill will, and Hipparchus was murdered by Harmodius and Aristogiton in 514 B.C.E. These men were forever after hailed as the "tyrannicides," and the Athenians drove Hippias into exile in 510 B.C.E.

When the tyranny at Athens ended, the Athenians adopted a new constitution that instituted a radical democracy. At this same period the tyrannies in the Greek cities of Asia Minor came to an end due to the conquest of that territory by the Persians. The Great King of Persia, Cyrus the Great (r. 558–ca. 529 B.C.E.), established friendly puppet governments in these cities and soon came into conflict with the Greeks of Europe. There followed the so-called Persian Wars, which provided the occasion for Herodotus's great work of history, the first in the European tradition, and the first significant test of the democracy at Athens, the city that found itself playing a central role in defending the Greek world from Persian ambitions.

The Fifth Century B.C.E.

Against all reasonable expectation, the Greek cities that joined Athens and Sparta in resisting Persia were successful in defeating first the armies of Cyrus and then the massive invasion of his grandson, Xerxes (r. 486–465 B.C.E.). By 479 B.C.E. the Greeks had beaten the Persian fleet at Salamis, defeated the Persian army at Plataea, and chased down and destroyed the retreating forces at Mycale.

After the defeat of Persia, an alliance of Greek cities, including many of those on the islands of the Aegean Sea, came together for mutual defense against future Persian threats. Initially the Spartans, the preeminent military force of the day, led this coalition. But the Spartans proved to be overbearing, and Athens gradually took over leadership of this league, which came to be known as the Delian League, because its treasury was on the island of Delos.

Athens' power was based on its naval fleet, as Sparta's was based on its infantry. In 482 B.C.E., just before Xerxes invaded Europe with his army, the Athenians had discovered a rich vein of silver in their territory, at Laurium. Their initial plan was to distribute this wealth among the citizens, but a certain Themistocles (ca. 524–ca. 460 B.C.E.) persuaded his countrymen to use this treasure to build up the navy. When the Persians invaded Greece and entered and sacked Athens, the Athenians were able to evacuate to the island of Salamis, thanks to their fleet, and then to defeat the Persians at sea. With his advice thus vindicated, Themistocles assumed a position of prominence—not by virtue of any particular office, but merely by force of character and persuasion. After the Persian Wars, he planned a series of walls around the city of Athens that connected the city to its harbor. Athens was thus safe from invasion and could use its fleet to wage war and provide food from abroad in time of war.

After Athens assumed leadership of the Delian League, the Athenians gradually turned this confederacy into an empire, with themselves at its head. They persuaded the member states to cease providing ships for the common defense and simply to provide funds, which the Athenians would use to build up their own navy, ostensibly to protect all the Greeks against Persia. By the first third of the fifth century B.C.E. this "league" had become an *archē*, an "empire," and the "dues" for the common good had become tribute paid to Athens. In 454 B.C.E. the treasury of the league was moved from Delos to Athens, ending all pretence, and in 440 B.C.E., when the island of Sámos tried to excuse itself from the league, the Athenians sent military forces to enforce their rule.

The rise of Athenian power alarmed the rest of the Greeks, and particularly Sparta, which began collecting allies to oppose Athens. In 431 B.C.E. war broke out between Athens and its allies and between Sparta and its allies. This war, called by the Athenians the Peloponnesian War because Sparta was in the Peloponnese, is the subject of the historical account by Thucydides. The war lasted 25 years, though there were a few periods of truce.

The most prominent Athenian at the outbreak of the war was Pericles (ca. 495–429 B.C.E.), who was a descendant of the aristocratic Alcmaeonidae, who had ruled Athens before the time of Solon and prevented Cylon from becoming tyrant. Like Themistocles, Pericles' prominence had less to do with any particular political office than with his qualities as a leader, but his aristocratic lineage, even in Athens of the radical democracy, almost certainly added to his authority.

Pericles was most active in persuading the Athenians to rebuild the temples on the Acropolis, a building program that resulted in the monumental architecture visible there today—the Parthenon, the Propylaea, and the Erechtheum. He was also a staunch advocate for war with Sparta. The Spartans knew this, and in public debates among the ambassadors from cities of Greece, Spartans and their allies made frequent references to "the accursed" leader of the Athenians. This was a reference to Pericles' aristocratic lineage and his Alcmaeonid ancestors who had killed Cylon after the would-be tyrant had taken refuge in a temple. War between Sparta and Athens came, to the satisfaction of Pericles, but in its second year he died of the plague that devastated the urban population of the city. According to the historian Thucydides, the Athenians who assumed leadership after his death were not aristocrats but demagogues, rising to power through championing the people and playing on their prejudices, and the city's policies suffered for it.

By the end of the century the Athenians had squandered many of their advantages, having launched a disastrous expedition against Sicily in 413 B.C.E. and experienced a short-lived oligarchic coup d'état in 411 B.C.E. The Spartans, in the meantime, had begun receiving monetary and military support from Persia. The Spartans finally ambushed and destroyed the Athenian fleet at Aegospotami in 405 B.C.E. After a prolonged siege, the Athenians surrendered. The Spartans dismantled the Athenian empire, nullified the democratic constitution of Athens, and instituted an oligarchy of 30 rulers, chosen from the Athenians friendly toward Sparta.

Athenian democracy was not undone for long, however, nor was Athenian power at a permanent end in the Aegean. The Thirty Tyrants proved to be so oppressive at Athens that the Spartan general Lysander, who had instituted them in the first place, himself helped to overthrow them and restore the democracy. Athens remained an economic power in the Greek world and soon reemerged as an influential force. The rise of the city of Thebes, which allied itself with Athens, kept Sparta in check, and by the beginning of the fourth century B.C.E. Athens and Thebes had fought Sparta to a standstill in the so-called Corinthian War, Athens had reestablished an Athenian Confederacy, including many cities and islands in the Aegean, and Spartan power was fading.

Macedonia: Philip and Alexander

During the first two-thirds of the fourth century B.C.E. the main powers in the Greek world were Athens, Thebes, and Sparta, which spent these years struggling for supremacy. First, Thebes and Athens united to resist Sparta. Later, Athens and Sparta united to resist Thebes. In the 350s B.C.E. a war broke out over control of the sanctuary at Delphi, the site of a temple of Apollo. Thebes took one side of this conflict and Athens and Sparta the other. This was called the Third Sacred War, and it went on for four years without any resolution until the Thebans called for help from a new power in the Greek World: Philip, king of the Macedonians.

Philip had become king of Macedonia in 359 B.C.E. and spent the decade of the 350s unifying the small, semiautonomous principalities of northern Greece. He expanded Macedonian territory by seizing from Athens some territories in the north, including Amphipolis, which had rich gold mines. He also reformed the Macedonian military, making it a formidable fighting force. By 352 B.C.E. all the Greeks recognized that Philip's army would be decisive, and his entry into the Third Sacred War was enough of a shock to bring about a truce.

Philip settled that conflict reasonably and became increasingly involved in political affairs among the cities of the Greek mainland. In 348 B.C.E. he seized Olynthus, another territory that the Athenians considered to be theirs, causing alarm in Athens and Thebes. The Athenian orator Demosthenes (384–322 B.C.E.) gave a series of speeches to the democratic assembly urging the city to oppose Philip with all its power. In these speeches, the "Olynthiacs," the orator describes the relative strengths and weaknesses of Athens, a democracy where decisions were made collectively, comparing it with Macedonia, a military autocracy in which Philip could move and strike where and when he saw fit, with no cumbersome process of deliberation.

In 338 B.C.E. Athens and Thebes joined forces to oppose Philip's power. Their armies fought a battle at Chaeronea, near Thebes. Philip won a complete victory, with his 18-year-old son Alexander leading a unit of cavalry. For the first time since the Bronze Age, if ever, a single military power was dominant in Greece. Philip established the League of Corinth, ostensibly a kind of United Nations to manage international affairs among the cities of Greece, its charter being a Treaty of Common Peace. In reality, however, this league was the instrument of Philip's will and the means by which Macedonia exerted authority over all the cities of the Greek mainland. Philip's first plan was to expand his power and remove a significant threat by invading Asia and going to war with the Persian Empire. As plans for this invasion were under way in 336 B.C.E., Philip was assassinated, leaving rule over the Macedonians and the Greeks to his son, Alexander.

The Greeks saw this as their opportunity to throw off Macedonian rule, and once again Athens and Thebes came together to fight for their freedom. Seeing their opportunity when Alexander took his army north to put down an uprising of the Illyrians, the Greeks moved to march toward Macedonia and bring an end to the Treaty of Common Peace and the League of Corinth. Alexander proved as capable a leader as his father. He moved south faster than anyone could have expected, defeated this rebellion, and destroyed the city of Thebes. The next year, 334 B.C.E., Alexander led his Macedonian army across the Hellespont into Asia to go to war with the Persian king Darius III.

Alexander's campaigns in Asia lasted from 334 until his death in 323 B.C.E. They mark the beginning of a period when Macedonian Greeks ruled over much of the Greek-speaking world east of Sicily and over much of the Near East. After defeating Darius at Issus in 333 B.C.E., Alexander took control of Egypt in 332 B.C.E. and then all of the Persian Empire between 331 and 324 B.C.E., having marched to the Punjab in India, having sailed down the Indus River to the India Ocean, and having marched across the deserts to the former Persian capital of Susa.

Alexander seems to have sought to create a multicultural empire. Upon returning from his march to India, he arranged for the marriage of hundreds of his officers with Persian brides and sought to unify his Macedonian forces with his newly acquired Persian army. These specific plans went unfulfilled. Alexander died of a fever, leaving only an infant son, born of a Bactrian woman named Roxana, and a group of experienced and ambitious Macedonian generals. According to the historian Arrian, when asked on his deathbed to whom he would leave his empire, Alexander replied, "To the strongest." In the decades that followed, Alexander's goal for a mingling of Greek and eastern cultures in a long-lasting Macedonian dynasty was fulfilled, piecemeal, by his successors, but not without a great deal of intrigue and warfare.

The Successors, Rome, and After

Alexander had left his general Antipater (ca. 397–ca. 319 B.C.E.) behind to rule over the Greek mainland. This Antipater did with some effort, having to fight and win a war against the Spartan king Agis III and having to deal with a certain amount of Athenian intransigence. Upon news of Alexander's death, the Athenians once again made an effort for their freedom, launching a war northward against Antipater and his son, Cassander. This so-called Lamian War can be seen as the last event of the Classical Period of Greek history, the last act of an independent city-state. The Athenians lost, the Macedonians executed the most outspoken of the public orators, and Athens was never again to act as an autonomous state.

After Alexander's death, his general Ptolemy acted quickly to secure a kingdom for himself, taking control of Egypt and resisting efforts by his former colleague Perdiccas. Seleucus seized the eastern parts of the former Persian Empire around Babylon. Lysimachus took the territories north of the Aegean, in Thrace, and Antigonus (called "the One-Eyed") took the western territories of Asia Minor. Cassander succeeded his father Antipater in control of Greece. By 311 B.C.E. this new order had stabilized, and Greek-speaking Macedonians had founded dynasties that would last until the rise of Rome.

Of these new dynasties, that of Ptolemy was the most stable. Affecting the style of Egyptian rulers for millennia, these Macedonian kings and queens reused the same names, Ptolemy for men and Cleopatra—a traditional Macedonian name (Alexander the Great had a sister and an aunt named Cleopatra)—for women, and they tended to marry brothers and sisters. The line lasted from 305 until 44 B.C.E., from Ptolemy I to Ptolemy XIV and his sister, Cleopatra VII, whose alliances with Julius Caesar and Mark Antony make her the most famous member of the Ptolemaic Dynasty. Under the Ptolemies, Egypt became a center of culture and learning. The city of Alexandria, founded by Alexander in 332 B.C.E., became the focus of learning for the western world, its library boasting scholars like Euclid, the mathematician, and Aristarchus, the great editor of the Homeric poems.

Pergamum (modern-day Bergama, Turkey), which came to be ruled by the Macedonian dynasty of the Attalids in the third century B.C.E., also vied with Alexandria as a cultural center to the extent that the Ptolemies issued an embargo on the export of papyrus to Pergamum. Faced with a lack of paper for books, the scholars of Pergamum, then under the rule of Eumenes, began using animal skins: this "Pergamum sheet," or *pergamena charta* in Latin, evolved into the word *parchment*. The dynasties of Macedonian rulers made the Greek language the universal tongue of politics and commerce in the eastern Mediterranean world. This lasted long after the Seleucid, Ptolemaic, and Antigonid dynasties had fallen from power in the face of the expansion of Rome.

The patronage that the Ptolemies and Attalids showed toward scholarship helped make Greek the language of culture and learning as well. Added to this was the continued influence of Athens, which may have lost its political and military empires after the fourth century B.C.E. but continued to rule over an intellectual empire. The classical tragedies of Aeschylus, Sophocles, and Euripides; the philosophy of Plato's Academy and Aristotle's Lyceum at Athens; the histories of Herodotus and Thucydides; the oratory of Lysias and Demosthenes, all these continued to set the standard for literary art well into the Roman Empire. Roman aristocrats sent their sons to Athens to study and become cultured.

The combination of an Athenian cultural empire with the political dynasties of the Macedonian successors to Alexandria explains why Greek culture was so ubiquitous throughout the Mediterranean world. The great Roman Julius Caesar, in moments of stress, naturally spoke Greek—upon crossing the Rubicon he exclaimed a line from the Greek poet Menander, and his dying words, according to the Roman historian Suetonius, were not "Et tu, Brute?" (Latin for "You too, Brutus?") but the words "*Kai su, tekne*?" (Greek for "You too, child?"). Likewise, Saul, who became the early Christian apostle Paul, a Jew from Tarsus in Cilicia (modern Turkey) and a Roman citizen, wrote fluent Greek, as did all the Jewish authors of the books of the Christian New Testament.

Roman rule eventually absorbed these Greek dynasties or reduced them to subordinate status as client-kingdoms. But in the late third century C.E. the emperor Diocletian (r. 284–305 C.E.) split the Roman Empire into parts for more efficient governance. By the fourth century C.E. the most active site of Roman rule was in the emperor Constantine's city of Constantinople, formerly the city of Byzantium. By the sixth century the Roman Empire had given way to a Byzantine Empire that was more Greek in culture and spirit than it was Roman—in 628 C.E. the Eastern Roman Empire officially stopped using Latin terms for political offices, in favor of a return to much older Greek terms. This last empire of the ancient Greek world would last until the Turks seized Constantinople in 1453 C.E.

ROME

BY KIRK H. BEETZ

THE FIRST KINGS (CA. 753–CA. 510 B.C.E.)

The earliest years of Rome's existence are mysterious. The names of kings and when they ruled are taken from Roman historians of the first century B.C.E., whose sources may have been only oral tradition. According to the ancient Romans, the city of Rome was founded in 753 B.C.E. by Romulus, who was supposedly descended from Aenaeus, a refugee from the Trojan War.

Graves from the mid-800s B.C.E. have been found around Palatine Hill, where Rome began as a village. Also on Palatine Hill are the remains of a house dating from the 900s or 800s B.C.E., showing that the area was inhabited before the traditional date given for the founding of Rome. The traditional dates for Romulus's reign are 753 to 717 B.C.E. The reign of the next king, Numa Pompilius, was 715 to 673 B.C.E. He and his successors were probably real people, and he is remembered as a peaceful king. By the reign of Tullus Hostilius (r. 673–642 B.C.E.), Rome was growing from a village to a small town. Tullus Hostilius waged military campaigns to enlarge Rome's territory, and his successor Ancus Marcius (r. 642–617 B.C.E.) continued to expand Rome's lands until they stretched to the mouth of the Tiber River in the west.

Ancus Marcius was Sabine by ancestry, and his successor, Tarquinius Priscus, also called Tarquin I (r. 616–578 B.C.E.), was Etruscan. The Etruscans were the dominant military and political power in the region of Italy where Rome was situated. Tarquinius Priscus undertook major public works in Rome, which was expanding because of trade. The city was the best place to cross the Tiber River, and many merchants passed through it. Tarquinius Priscus drained the swamp at the base of Palatine Hill and built the Roman Forum on the newly dry land. He also built the Capitol, in which temples to Rome's patron gods would be housed, and in it he built the temple to Jupiter, Rome's chief god.

By the time of Tarquinius Superbus, meaning Tarquin the Proud (r. 534–510 B.C.E.), Rome had about 40,000 residents and had formed an aristocracy of wealthy people, called patricians. In 510 B.C.E. Sextus, a son of Tarquinius Superbus, raped an aristocrat's daughter, Lucretia. This enraged the aristocrats, and under the leadership of Lucius Junius Brutus they rebelled and threw the Tarquin family out of Rome. They established the Roman Republic, which was ruled by the Senate, composed of aristocrats. Tarquinius Superbus returned with an Etruscan army to retake Rome but was stymied by the Romans. Probably under the leadership of Brutus, Rome formed an alliance with other cities in the region; united, they defeated the Etruscans at Aricia in 506 B.C.E. and formed into independent city states.

The Republic (ca. 509–27 B.C.E.)

Although ultimate political authority rested with the Senate, the new constitution for Roman government called for two executives, called consuls, to run the government jointly for one year at a time, with an annual election of consuls by the Senate. One of the first of the early consuls was Brutus, who served in 509 B.C.E. In times of war the Senate could appoint a dictator who would rule with almost absolute power. Lucius Quinctius Cincinnatus, who was dictator in 458 B.C.E., set an important precedent by voluntarily relinquishing his power after defeating Rome's enemies, even though he could have used the army he commanded to make himself king.

Marcus Furius Camillus may have been dictator as many as five times. He may have first been declared dictator in 390 B.C.E., when Gauls sacked Rome. Perhaps he rallied the spirits of the Romans and persuaded them to rebuild their city. In 367 B.C.E. he was declared dictator when the Gauls threatened to invade Rome, again. He seems to have followed the precedent set by Cincinnatus by relinquishing his dictatorships when his tasks were done.

For the dictatorship of Quintus Fabius Maximus Verrucosus in 217 B.C.E. archaeology has found evidence to support the basic events found in Roman accounts. Fabius served as consul in 233, 228, 215, 214, and 209 B.C.E. and was named dictator in 217 B.C.E. He was sarcastically nicknamed "Cunctator," meaning the Delayer, because of his policy of avoiding direct confrontations with Hannibal's army, always trying to draw the Carthaginian army away from attacking the city of Rome. Later, after other commanders suffered disastrous losses in direct confrontations with Hannibal's forces, the nickname became one of honor, in recognition of the wisdom of his delaying tactics.

Fabius opposed the plans of Publius Cornelius Scipio, also known as Scipio the Elder. Scipio served as consul in 205 and 194 B.C.E. In 205 B.C.E. Rome was still at war with Carthage. Scipio wanted to take the war overseas by attacking the city of Carthage. Fabius and other senators regarded this plan as too dangerous, and the Senate refused to fund Fabius's military plans. Scipio went to Sicily and raised and equipped an army. In 204 B.C.E. the Senate refused financial and military support to Scipio's venture but gave its consent to his invading North Africa. Scipio succeeded in leading his forces to victory and ending the war.

An office representing the plebeians, or common people, in government had evolved, called the "tribune." Tiberius Gracchus and his younger brother Gaius Gracchus tried to use the office of tribune to reform Roman society. When the Senate blocked his reforms, Tiberius Gracchus took the matter to the popular assembly, the Concilium Plebis, which passed his reforms. He ran for reelection as tribune, and on election day he and hundreds of his supporters were murdered by followers of the Senate. Gaius Gracchus served two terms as tribune (123–22 B.C.E.) He tried to enact his brother's reforms and was mostly successful. After he was defeated for a third term, Gaius Gracchus and his supporters were set upon by henchmen of the Senate; about 3,000 of them were murdered in a day, with Gaius Gracchus either committing suicide or being murdered by bounty hunters eager to collect a reward of gold.

Powerful individual leaders gradually gathered to themselves the power to run Rome. Among them was Gaius Marius, who served as consul seven times between 107 and 86 B.C.E. He was a political and social reformer as well as a military leader, and he was willing to use the threat of his troops, who were more loyal to him than to Rome, to enforce his wishes over opposition by the Senate. Much of his work was undone by Lucius Cornelius Sulla, who was dictator from 82 to 79 B.C.E. He was a successful general who championed aristocratic dominance of society and government. He ruled with almost absolute power and condemned to death without trial thousands of people, with his soldiers enforcing terror in the streets of the city of Rome. He set a precedent for Roman military commanders by taking control of the city by military force. In an effort to shore up the privileges of the Senate, he rewrote Roman laws, placing courts under patrician control and granting patrician jurists immunity from prosecution for taking bribes. So thorough was he in restructuring Roman law that later Romans confessed that even though they disliked some of the laws, they did not know how to change them all and keep Roman society intact. Sulla chose to retire in 79 B.C.E

Julius Caesar (100–44 B.C.E.)

The next powerful figure was Gnaeus Pompeius Magnus, later known as Pompey the Great. As a military commander he had won significant victories in the Near East and had added Syria to Rome's domains. In 62 B.C.E. he entered into a contest for power against the wealthy Marcus Licinius Crassus and Gaius Julius Caesar. In 60 B.C.E. the three of them divided the rule of Rome, forming the First Triumvirate (60–53 B.C.E.). Pompey championed the rights of commoners and was immensely popular. Crassus was not only wealthy but clever, a master of the workings of government. In Caesar they faced one of history's most remarkable people: a brilliant writer, an artful propagandist, a master planner, and an outstanding military leader.

In 59 B.C.E. Caesar served as consul and then he took charge of Rome's provinces in southern Gaul, in modern southern France. He conquered most of Gaul, making the Rhine River Rome's new northern boundary. He marched into Italy with his army in 49 B.C.E. Crassus had already died, in 53 B.C.E. This left Pompey to face Caesar. Pompey formed an army near the Adriatic Sea, north of Greece. Caesar chased Pompey's army south to the city of Pharsalus, where he defeated Pompey, who fled across the Mediterranean Sea to Egypt, where he was murdered. Caesar became dictator of Rome (49–44 B.C.E.), where his popular reforms angered senators. It was clear that he could become king if he wanted to do so, but he chose to retain the institutions of the Roman Republic in order to give the outward appearance of honoring Roman traditions. On March 15, 44 B.C.E., while conducting public business, he was murdered by a group of senators.

Julio-Claudian Dynasty (27 B.C.E.–69 C.E.)

Caesar had an adopted son, Octavian (later called Augustus, 63 B.C.E–14 C.E.), who was nearly as remarkable as he was. Octavian and one of Caesar's generals, Marcus Antonius (now known as Mark Antony, ca. 82–30 B.C.E.), joined forces to fight the senators who had murdered Julius Caesar. In 42 B.C.E. their army decisively defeated the army of the assassins, and they formed the Second Triumvirate (43–36 B.C.E.), in which Octavian controlled the western part of the empire, Antony controlled the eastern part of the empire, and Marcus Aemilius Lepidus controlled the rest of Rome's North African territory. In about 36 B.C.E. Lepidus tried to overthrow Octavian but failed. He lived until 13 B.C.E., known as the incompetent member of the Second Triumvirate.

Antony became fascinated by Egypt's Cleopatra VII. She was not physically beautiful, but her exceptional intelligence and charming personality were attractive to powerful men. Her influence on Antony was resented in Rome, and her meddling in Roman politics may have been one of Octavian's motivations to go to war against Egypt in 32 B.C.E. Another motivation was that Antony had married Octavian's sister, making his relationship with Cleopatra an insult to Octavian's family. In 31 B.C.E. the Roman and Egyptian navies battled at Actium, a port on the west coast of Greece. Octavian had more ships, and Antony and Cleopatra poorly led their forces. After the Egyptians were soundly defeated, Antony and Cleopatra fled back to Egypt. In 30 B.C.E. Antony and then Cleopatra committed suicide, and the entire empire was Octavian's.

Like his adoptive father, he chose to retain the outward appearance of the Roman Republic. From 31 to 23 B.C.E. he held the title of consul. In 27 B.C.E. the Senate proclaimed him Augustus, meaning First Citizen, instead of emperor, and he made a point of appearing to consult with the Senate and government officials. Nonetheless, all knew he was emperor, and during his reign (27 B.C.E.–14 C.E.) he reshaped the Roman government into an imperial one. He sponsored massive construction projects throughout the empire and especially in Rome. He personally took on the responsibility of feeding the poor and the homeless.

When he died, he was succeeded by a successful general, his stepson, Tiberius (r. 14–37 C.E.), who had little taste for government and spent most of his reign living outside Rome. He was succeeded by Caligula (r. 37–41 C.E.), a nickname based on the name for his favorite kind of coat. He began well and had much popular support, but he was self-indulgent and cruel to a level that became intolerable to some of the patricians, who assassinated him.

The Praetorian Guard, the bodyguards of the emperor, proclaimed Claudius (r. 41–54 C.E.) emperor. He seemed an unlikely choice, chronically ill and a stammerer, but he was a strong ruler. He undertook important public works projects, such as widening the port at Rome, and he succeeded where Julius Caesar had not, by leading an invasion of Britain that resulted in bringing the southern half of what is now England into Roman domination. It is possible that he had reason to believe the young man he adopted as his successor would be a good ruler. This was Nero (r. 54–68 C.E.), who started out well. He listened to his advisers and engaged in valuable building projects, and he was popular at first. He was cruel, however, and he lost the support of the patricians. In 65 C.E. some senators conspired to kill him, but they failed. In 68 C.E. leaders in Spain and Gaul rebelled against him. Even though the rebellion in Gaul was put down, Nero had lost all support in government, and a leader from Spain, Servius Sulpicius Galba (r. 68–69 C.E.), was a dire threat. Nero committed suicide in 68 C.E.

Flavian Dynasty (69–96 C.E.)

Galba was assassinated in January 69 C.E., at the hands of Marcus Salvius Otho (r. 69 C.E.), who succeeded him. Otho was deposed by the roman legions from the Rhine, and their general, Aulus Vitellius (r. 69 C.E.), became emperor. Roman legions in the eastern empire declared General Vespasian (r. 69–79 C.E.) emperor, and those in the Danube soon followed suit. The legions from the Danube, led by General Antonius Primus, defeated Vitellius's army in September 69 C.E., making Vespasian emperor. He was succeeded by his sons Titus (r. 79–81 C.E.) and Domitian (r. 81–96 C.E.). They consolidated Rome's hold on its territories.

Adoptive Emperors (96–197 C.E.)

The Adoptive Emperors Era was one in which the Roman emperors rejected the idea of emperors being succeeded by natural-born sons. Instead, they each adopted a man they considered to be an able leader, thereby making that man next in line to the throne. Thus, Emperor Nerva (r. 96–98 C.E.) adopted a man from Spain, Trajan (r. 98–117 C.E.).

Trajan was an empire builder. The kingdom of Dacia, in present-day Romania, posed a threat to Rome. The Dacians had fought and defeated the Romans in the past. From 101 to 102 C.E. Trajan's legions fought Dacia to an apparent stalemate. Trajan tried to negotiate a settlement with the Dacian king, but the king ended negotiations in 105 C.E. Trajan invaded Dacia, overcame its army, and made it a province of the Roman Empire. From 114 to 115 C.E. Trajan conquered Armenia and much of northern Mesopotamia, adding them to the empire. His legions fought the Parthian Empire and advanced through southern Mesopotamia to the Persian Gulf, then withdrew back to northern Mesopotamia.

Trajan was succeeded by Hadrian (r. 117–38 C.E.). Rather than follow up on Trajan's gains against the Parthians, Hadrian chose to pursue peace. He had a 75-mile stone wall built across the northern frontier of Rome's territory in Britain and a 350-mile wooden one built between the Rhine and Danube rivers, each intended to keep enemies out. The purpose of the Roman army shifted from being aggressive to defensive. Historians often mark Hadrian's reign as the era in which the Roman Empire's decline began, because Roman policy had shifted from seeking out enemies and defeating them to waiting for attacks and then repelling them. This gave Rome's enemies the choice of when and where to fight.

The next emperor began the Antonine Age (138–92 C.E.). He was Antoninus Pius (r. 138–61 C.E.). Whereas Hadrian had traveled all over the empire to meet with people and discuss their problems, Antoninus Pius stayed in Italy. Through diplomacy and threats, he avoided major wars. On his death he was succeeded by two men who seem to have gotten along well with each other: Lucius Verus (r. 161–69 C.E.) and Marcus Aurelius (r. 161–80 C.E.).

In 162 C.E. the Parthians invaded the Eastern Roman Empire, and Lucius Verus led an army against them. In 165 C.E. the Roman army had penetrated to the heart of the Parthian Empire and sacked the Parthian capital, Ctesiphon. In 169 C.E. Lucius Verus died of an illness, perhaps from a plague that carried off thousands of Romans. This left Marcus Aurelius as sole ruler. He was a Stoic, a follower of a philosophical discipline in which he did not allow himself to show outward emotion or allow emotion to overcome his thinking. His personal journal, known as *Meditations*, is still studied for its wisdom. In 170 C.E. the Germanic tribes Quadi and Marcomanni crossed the Danube and attacked Italy. Rome managed to repel the invasion, and Marcus Aurelius spent much of the last decade of his reign unsuccessfully trying to expand Roman domination beyond the Danube.

He was succeeded by Commodus (r. 180–92 C.E.), who paid little attention to the day-to-day business of government. Perhaps as a consequence, government corruption grew to a level that angered the Roman public. Commodus loved gladiatorial combat and sometimes participated as a gladiator himself. He was planning to participate in New Year's gladiatorial contests when he was murdered on the final day of 192 C.E., first poisoned and then strangled.

After Commodus's death, Rome quickly went through three emperors. Publius Helvius Pertinax (r. 193 C.E.) was an elderly statesman and general who was murdered by the Praetorian Guard. Marcus Didius Julianus (r. 193 C.E.) was overthrown and killed by the general Lucius Septimius Severus (r. 193–211 C.E.). Severus faced two rival emperors. One was Pescennius Niger (r. 192–94 C.E.), whose army Severus defeated in three battles in the Near East; Niger was murdered in Antioch. The other was Decimus Clodius Septimius Albinus (r. 193–97 C.E.), who took four years to dispose of. Although he was originally from North Africa, Albinus was the governor of Britain. He had the support of much of the Senate. Severus defeated his army near Lyon, in modern France, in 197 C.E.

Severan Dynasty (193–268 C.E.)

The founder of the Severan Dynasty, Severus was from North Africa. He was married to a Syrian priestess, Julia Domna. Severus was a dynamic and aggressive leader who tried to shift the Roman Empire back to attacking its enemies rather than defending against them. From 195 to 198 C.E. he seized territory from the Parthians, founding a pair of new provinces in the captured lands, and he established a new province in North Africa while extending Roman authority southward. He tried but failed to expand Roman rule northward in Britain, to encompass modern Scotland. He left his empire to his sons, Caracalla (r. 211–17 C.E.) and Geta (r. 211–12), who was murdered by Caracalla. Caracalla granted Roman citizenship to all free men in the empire in 212 C.E.

The succeeding Roman emperors had to deal with multiple threats from within and outside the empire. From within came assassination conspiracies; from without came attacks from the Alemanni Germans across the Rhine, the Goths who had settled in Ukraine, and the Parthian Empire, now under the rule of a new Persian Dynasty, the Sassanids. In 260 C.E. Emperor Valerian (r. 253–60 C.E.) was captured and killed by the Sassanids. Valerian's son Gallienus (r. 253–68 C.E.) tried to use diplomacy to hold the empire together and stave off its enemies, but Gaul seceded to form its own nation, and provinces in the east tried to become more independent of Rome.

The breakaway nation of Gaul had three emperors: Postumus (r. ca. 258–68 C.E.), Victorinus (r. 268–270 C.E.), and Tetricus (r. 270–274 C.E.). In 260 C.E. Postumus created the Gallic Empire, and in 261 C.E. he had control of Spain, Britain, and the Germanic territories in central Europe as well as the Gallic provinces. The Gallic Empire issued coinage and held off the

Germanic tribes that wanted to loot Gaul. After about four years of war, Tetricus's reign was ended in a battle in northern Gaul by Roman emperor Aurelian (r. 270–75 C.E.).

Illyrian Emperors (268–305 C.E.)

The Illyrian emperors were primarily army officers from the Balkans. For most of their reign they tended to be murdered by their troops and replaced by another officer. The first Illyrian emperor was Claudius II (r. 268–70 C.E.), who was also called Gothicus. He defeated the Goths and drove them back beyond the Danube. His successor, Aurelian, recovered the lost territories in the east and reclaimed Gaul. Eventually Carus (r. 282–83 C.E.) invaded the Parthian Empire, and again the Romans sacked the Parthian capital, Ctesiphon.

The most important of the Illyrian emperors was Diocletian (r. 284–305 C.E.). He established elaborate royal ceremonies that kept him remote from the general populace, perhaps to lessen the opportunity for assassination. To make the Roman Empire more secure internally, he separated the military from the civil authority in the provinces, making it harder for a governor to declare himself independent of Rome. Further, he broke Rome's provinces into many smaller provinces to make sure no single province could become powerful enough to challenge the central government. To make the Roman Empire more secure externally, he increased Rome's standing army by about 100,000 troops to more than 400,000. In addition, he made sure soldiers were paid well, in full, and on time.

The Tetrarchy (284–337 C.E.)

In 285 C.E. Diocletian decided to share power because he was overwhelmed by all the work that needed to be done to preserve the Roman Empire. That year he appointed Maximian (r. 286–305 C.E.) to be a junior emperor, but in 286 C.E. he made Maximian a senior emperor, placing Maximian equal to himself. When they added two junior emperors who had separate responsibilities for the eastern and western parts of the empire, their government became a tetrarchy, meaning four rulers.

In 305 C.E. Diocletian and Maximus chose to retire, leaving governance to their junior emperors, who then became senior emperors. One of them was Constantius I (r. 305–6 C.E.). He had been in charge of the Western Roman Empire, and when he died the western provinces expected his son Constantine I (r. 306–37 C.E.) to become emperor. In 306 C.E. Maxentius (r. 306–12 C.E.), the son of Maximian, declared himself emperor. This resulted in a series of civil wars that ended the Tetrarchy and concluded in 324 C.E. with Constantine I as sole emperor.

House of Constantine (306–364 C.E.)

Constantine I became known as Constantine the Great. In 312 C.E. he invaded Italy and fought and defeated the army of Maxentius at Augusta Taurinorum, modern-day Turin, and Aquileia, modern-day Verona, but Maxentius was a tough opponent with an army that was determined to win. Before the climactic Battle of Milvian Bridge in central Italy, Constantine I had a vision of the Christian cross and heard a voice that said he would win if he carried the cross into battle, which he did. Although he waited until he was on his death bed to be baptized, he considered himself a Christian from that time on. Thousands of Christians had been slaughtered as enemies of the state during the reign of Diocletian, making Constantine's conversion very dramatic.

He agreed to allow Licinius (r. 308–24 C.E.) to rule the eastern empire, including Egypt, while he ruled the rest of North Africa as well as the western empire. In 316 C.E. Constantine I seized the Balkans and Greece, which had been under Licinius's rule. In 324 C.E. he advanced into Thrace, where he decisively defeated Licinius's army at Adrianople, present-day Edirne, and won the rest of the Roman Empire.

During his reign Constantine I strengthened the empire's army and defenses, especially along the Danube, where he built defensive earthworks. He was deeply involved in Christian affairs, even joining in theological meetings about the future course of Christianity. He built churches in Jerusalem at holy sites, such as the cave where Christ had been interred. In 330 C.E. he moved the capital of the empire to Byzantium, modern-day Istanbul, and renamed it Constantinople.

Constantine I left his empire to his sons, Constantine II (r. 337–40 C.E.), Constans I (r. 337–50 C.E.), and Constantius II (r. 337–61 C.E.), as well as to Flavius Iulius Dalmatius, the son of his stepbrother. His sons murdered Dalmatius. Constantine II was killed fighting Constans; Constans was killed by the self-proclaimed emperor Magnentius (r. 350–53 C.E.); Constantius II died of an illness. Their cousin Julian (r. 361–63 C.E.) seized power. Before Julian challenged Constantius II for the throne, he had distinguished himself with victories over Germanic tribes at the Rhine. Julian believed in the traditional Roman gods and tried to suppress the Christian faith. In 363 C.E. he invaded the Parthian Empire, but he was killed in battle.

House of Valentinian (364–395 C.E.)

In 364 C.E. the Roman Empire was divided into west and east. The west was ruled by Valentinian I (r. 364–75 C.E.), and the east was ruled by his brother Valens (r. 364–78 C.E.). In 357 C.E. the Germanic tribe the Visigoths fled the Huns into the Balkans of the empire. In 378 C.E. Valens tried to drive the Visigoths out of the empire, but he was killed and his army defeated at Adrianople. In the west Valentinian I had been succeeded by his son Gratian (r. 375–83 C.E.), who appointed the general Theodosius I (r. 379–95 C.E.) ruler of the eastern empire. In 382 C.E. Theodosius I and the Visigoths made a peace treaty that allowed the Visigoths to settle in the Roman Empire. From 394 to 395 C.E. Theodosius I ruled both east and west of the empire.

House of Theodosius (379–565 C.E.)

The Visigoths tried invading Italy in 401 C.E., during the reign of Theodosius I's son Honorius (r. 395–423 C.E.), but they were defeated in battle by Honoriuss regent Stilicho. Honorius ruled the western empire while his brother Arcadius (r. 383–408 C.E.) ruled the eastern empire. Arcadius was succeeded by Theodosius II (r. 408–50 C.E.), whose eastern part of the empire prospered. Another Germanic tribe, the Vandals, invaded the empire in 406–9 C.E., raiding all the way to the southern coast of Spain. In 410 C.E. the Visigoths again invaded Italy and sacked Rome. Honorius lost control of Spain, much of Gaul, and Britain.

In 429 C.E., during the reign of the western emperor Valentinian III (r. 425–55 C.E.), the Vandals crossed the Mediterranean Sea and invaded North Africa. In 439 C.E. they conquered Roman Carthage. That Valentinian III managed to hold together fragments of his empire was remarkable. Even more remarkable was his defeat of the army of Attila the Hun in 453 C.E. His successors became dependent on Germanic generals and kings to protect them. In 476 C.E. the last western emperor, Romulus Augustulus (r. 475–76 C.E.), was forced to resign by the dominant Germanic tribe in Italy, the Ostrogoths.

THE AMERICAS

BY J. J. GEORGE

The concepts of *empire* and *dynasty* usually imply a state-level society with organizational and administrative features tied to decision making and hierarchy. Scholars focus on different traits to establish a definition of state, and exact definitions are hard to apply. Territory, use of force, the presence of an overarching government, well-developed divisions of labor, the underlying structural features of decision making and authority, and the mechanisms that enhance and preserve the privileges of certain social groups are some of the criteria scholars focus on to classify a type of societal structure. The Americas of the ancient period was replete with social units that ranged downward from complex, hierarchical societies to intermediate units with seasonal subsistence groups coalescing at temporary villages to basic units of hunter-gatherers.

Anthropological definitions of the state as well as its material indicators in the archaeological record are closely linked to the theoretical framework in which the concept of the state is developed. Definitions that focus on political power and social classes tend to define states broadly, with many archaeological cases fitting the definition. Some scholars have even argued that the existence of social classes in and of itself is the defining feature of state organization. Other scholars have argued that the existence of any monumental construction elaborate enough to necessitate coordinated labor above the household is evidence for state organization.

Assuming that some of the basic social, economic, and political criteria defining the state are present in a given society, empires are then the result of a process of state expansion that encompasses peoples who previously had separate ethnic or state identities. Empires can express a variety of relationships and spatial forms, where distant realms may be conquered or absorbed even though the local institutions and often the local royal line are kept in place in return for fealty, tribute, or other special concessions. The opposite also may be true, whereby strong reorganizational efforts occur, including the resettlement of populations to the capital, thus dramatically altering the previously existing system of society, rulership, and authority.

RULERSHIP

Rulership in the Americas took the form of family or kin group leaders, tribal chiefs and petty princes with little authority and small domains, or powerful kings and emperors commanding tens of thousands of subjects, supervising impressive bureaucracies, and enforcing their will through military might. By 500 C.E. rulership conformed to the general pattern of early states elsewhere in the world. Kings, often thought to be divinely ordained or even godlike, were supreme, hereditary rulers of complex societies with the legitimate authority to enforce their decisions. As occupants of the highest-status position they were responsible for all state functions—administrative, military, religious, judicial, and redistributive—although the relative importance of these functions varied from one culture to another.

Dynastic rule and kingship rarely followed a strict rule of primogeniture, or the exclusive right of inheritance belonging to the eldest son. Dynastic election usually involved choosing the next ruler from a range of eligible persons, almost invariably from close relatives already in high positions of authority. However, there is also strong evidence of patrilineal descent at specific sites that suggests a dynastic genealogy of more immediate, familial succession. For example, among the later Maya it was of great importance to be able to trace one's ancestry along both patrilineal and matrilineal lines to an ancient ancestry, because society was divided into strict classes. Therefore, tracing a line of noble lineage was socially more advantageous than tracing a line with commoner roots. The situation varied, of course, as the institutions of kingship and power varied from region to region over time.

NORTH AMERICAN SOCIETIES

Direct evidence of empire and dynasty is scarce for ancient North America and generally supports sociopolitical structures more in line with hunter-gatherer societies, chiefdoms, associated villages, or interaction spheres. Although it is difficult to tell chiefdoms from empires archaeologically, the material footprint of many early North American sites suggests sociopolitical mechanisms less pervasive than an empire. It appears, then, that more localized, indigenous fluorescences were characteristic, as opposed to a centrally operated, state-supported expansion.

For example, the Adena and Hopewell cultures of the Early and Middle Woodland periods (1000 B.C.E.–500 C.E.) spread throughout the central United States over a number of sites in proximity to the Missouri, Mississippi, and Ohio river systems. There mortuary ceremonialism, the presence of earthen mounds, interregional exchange, and artistic development clustered loosely affiliated villages under an umbrella of regional extent. The lack of a centralized administrative, bureaucratic, or militaristic complex prohibited the sort of cohesive growth and expansion evidenced in empire states elsewhere. Although these mound builders apparently gathered periodically for funeral ceremonies and construction, most of the year the population was widely dispersed in small, temporary villages. Given the light trace of archaeological data and a complete absence of written history, evidence of dynastic history and major political leaders is impossible to infer. Compared with their Mesoamerican neighbors, a North American example of an empire or dynasty is virtually nonexistent in the ancient period.

The Olmec

The Olmec civilization represented the first successful kingdom in Mesoamerica, flourishing in the tropical lowlands of Mexico's Gulf Coast of modern-day Tabasco and Veracruz, a water-logged region of meandering rivers, from around 1500 to 400 B.C.E. Although the causes of the evolution from rank societies to kingdoms remains to be determined, it is clear that the subsequent flowering and spread of Olmec civilization for the next half millennium was intimately tied to the creation, display, and manipulation of monumental and portable art objects.

The Olmec had novel governmental practices based upon social stratification and kingship. Their earliest monumental sculptures included stone thrones weighing several tons and naturalistic, three-dimensional depictions of rulers, carved as either colossal heads or full figures. Between the ninth and fifth centuries B.C.E. stone carving shifted from three-dimensional forms to high- and low-relief narrative carvings, much of which is thought to portray divine kings dressed in the costume of corn deities. Other small stone statuettes are thought to depict kings in shamanic transformation. The distribution of Olmec painted pottery and figurines outside the heartland suggests not only the spread of the Olmec artistic canon but possibly also accompanying practices of governance, the nature of which is still debated. Attempts to designate the Olmec tend to shift between classification as a civilization, complex chiefdom, kingdom, state, or empire.

The major Olmec sites—San Lorenzo, La Venta, and Tres Zapotes—all contained large ceremonial structures. San Lorenzo was the largest site and was thought to yield a population of between 10,500 and 17,000 persons. Olmec public-works projects that were probably kingdom-sponsored activities include the mining, transport, and subsequent fabrication of colossal stone monuments from as far as 60 or 70 miles away; the construction of massive terraces, plazas, elite residences, platforms, and systems of elaborate stone drains; significant activities related to dragging the stones, including cutting paths through the jungle or building roads and bridges; the production of enough food for the thousands of persons necessary to transport the stones from distant workshops; long-distance trade; and the production of goods for export. It is also believed that San Lorenzo was the capital of a kingdom that had secondary centers and tertiary villages, hamlets, and special-function sites, probably administered by princes. Individual rulers, however, have not been secured from the data, nor is it known why each of the sites was eventually abandoned.

The Zapotec

Farther south, in the Valley of Oaxaca, evidence suggests that the Zapotec hilltop site at Monte Albán was the center of an empire whose imperial aspirations began around 600 B.C.E. One of the most compelling lines of evidence for its imperial conquests comes from the site itself, in the form of one of its buildings, referred to as Building J, which is shaped roughly like an arrowhead. On this building are 50 carved stone slabs depicting dead rulers of towns thought to be subjugated by Monte Albán. It is thought that these towns define the territorial limits of Monte Albán's empire. However, evidence supporting Zapotec dominance over the full range of towns has not yet been conclusively demonstrated.

An abundance of evidence is highly suggestive of Zapotec conquest and imperial influence well beyond their immediate heartland. Evidence includes the violent destruction and abandonment of local villages; the presence of objects of intimidation, including skull racks thought to be for the display of defeated warriors; village relocation, thought to reflect Zapotec-imposed resettlement for more effective agricultural production; evidence of a frontier garrison where the Monte Albán overlords were housed; the imposition of Zapotec architecture; the elimination of ceremonial facilities and trappings; and the disappearance of products previously imported from Monte Albán and elsewhere, interpreted as resulting from the termination of reciprocal exchange.

At least three models of interaction can be used to describe the political and economic interaction of the Zapotec with their neighbors following the imperial scheme. The first model suggests that the Zapotec exacted tribute from conquered polities and allowed for local political autonomy. The second suggests an economic and imperial model of exploitation under imposed, centralized Zapotec governance. The third model suggests reciprocal economic exchange in the form of intensified trade, falling short of conquest and colonization, between independent polities. Further research is necessary to clarify the exact nature of Zapotec relations to its neighbors, though current information indicates the presence of definite imperial qualities. Although it is unclear exactly why Monte Albán fell, it seems to have done so gradually and uneventfully, its authority petering out and fragmenting as other towns in the valley became settled.

Teotihuacán

No discussion of empire in the Americas is complete without a look at Teotihuacán, 40 miles northeast of contemporary Mexico City. Between 100 B.C.E. and 700 C.E. Teotihuacán rose and became an immense city. Its early growth was rapid, tied to advances in irrigation agriculture, and by the second century it covered about eight square miles with a population estimated between 60,000 and 80,000. Subsequent growth slowed and reached a maximum population of about 125,000, making it the fifth-largest city in the world for its time. Its great surge in urban growth around the turn of the millennium seems to signify the influence of strong-minded rulers. Moreover, it is about this time that virtually the entire population elsewhere in the Basin of Mexico disappeared, as people were evidently resettled in Teotihuacán. No other Mesoamerican city had such a large and dense urban concentration before the Aztec capital of Tenochtitlán in the late 1400s.

Territory under immediate Teotihuacán control by the fourth century B.C.E. covered at least 9,600 square miles, a radius of about 55 miles, though it may have reached considerably farther. Beyond the primary radius Teotihuacán probably concentrated on controlling key settlements and routes between them as opposed to controlling blocks of territory. Its immense prestige certainly exceeded its political sphere, but little is yet known about specific outposts. Teotihuacán moved to control the Valley of Morelos to the southeast, where cotton could be grown, a key resource for a textile industry and maintained a presence at Tula to the northwest, Cholula to the southeast, Cantona to the northeast on the route to the Gulf lowlands, and Alta Vista in Zacatecas. The Zapotec state, centered at Monte Albán in Oaxaca, maintained diplomatic relations with Teotihuacán, and there was even a barrio at Teotihuacán that is now referred to as the Oaxaca Barrio because it is believed to have exclusively housed craftsmen from Oaxaca.

Connections are also known to have run to southern Veracruz, Mirador in Chiapas, sites in highland and Pacific coastal Guatemala, and Belize. Connections are especially strong at Tikal in northern Guatemala and reflect the adoption of a limited number of Teotihuacán-related symbols by local elites for their own purposes. The influence of Teotihuacán at Tikal is secure by 360 C.E. thanks to a ruler referred to as Curl Nose in hieroglyphic inscriptions found at the site. Curl Nose was apparently a collaborationist ruler who accepted military and political advisers from Teotihuacán, which gave Tikal an edge over rival Mayan centers and allowed for further expansion.

The exact form of rule is unclear and might have shifted over time. Supreme political authority may not always have been strongly concentrated in a single person or lineage. A major apartment compound at Teotihuacán has been interpreted as residences of the heads of state, though it is unlike better-known royal palaces, such as those in Tenochtitlán when the Spaniards arrived. It seems to fit a pattern wherein the head of state controls fewer resources and can command construction projects less for his own glorification than for the glorification of the state, leading some scholars to suggest that rulership took the form of an oligarchic republic (one ruled by a small group), which is not necessarily democratic or egalitarian. Scholars have also suggested a corporate or collective model of leadership, which may explain why there is an apparent lack of self-glorifying rulers and consequently why dynastic history is thus far unknown. Yet most of the major constructions happened early and quickly, which indicates at least a few very powerful, able, and imaginative rulers.

Far afield the military certainly played a role in securing interests as Teotihuacán gained preeminence. Scholars disagree on the exact nature, role, and extent of the military, but it is unlikely that Teotihuacán's influence over trade would have been possible had it not been able to overcome armed resistance from rival centers. Reflecting a lack of consensus, it has been suggested both that the emphasis on war was largely symbolic and that it was very real. It has been argued convincingly that the army of Teotihuacán was highly effective, efficient, and organized. Military symbolism was adapted in the lowland Maya regions, and even though conquest of the Maya seems unlikely, the city's military prestige traveled well.

In its last century the population of Teotihuacán declined significantly. Many factors might have contributed to the decline, including a failure to adapt to new styles of government, commerce, or religion developing elsewhere; a lack of income from conquests; crises from outside threats or rulers; and possibly environmental problems. The state itself was largely destroyed by fire, especially in the central part of the city. It is unknown who was responsible for the destruction, but its focused and selective results suggest to some scholars that it was an inside job. One theory proposes that a combination of dissident insiders and members of surrounding societies who had gained power could have defeated a weakened and no longer well-led city.

The Maya

The Maya created the most sophisticated civilization of ancient America. Their achievements in art, architecture, writing, astronomy, and calendrical notation were unsurpassed. Maya civilization developed along several lines that are continuously redefined and debated. Although development varied from site to site over time, by 150 C.E. many criteria of urbanism were present, including relatively higher population density than the surrounding countryside, a stratified society, nonfarming occupational specializations, formalized religion, markets, and a bureaucracy or civil service supported by a social surplus. The levels of organization necessary for these developments indicates the complexity of regional centers and state-level society,lthough they appear to have lacked the highly centralized structures typical of imperial centers. By the end of the Late Formative Period and the beginning of the Classic Period, around 150 C.E., a number of Maya sites had become large and complex, including Tikal and Mirador, and dynastic histories were recorded in combination with the advanced Maya practice of writing.

In early Classic times population growth continued, and competition among neighboring centers increased. Concentrated urban development converted regional market and administrative centers to cities. Similarly, social structural changes took place that shifted lineage heads to hereditary aristocracy. A basic feudal system developed with an aristocracy based on control of land and water and the labor to work it. By about 350 C.E. Tikal was one of the largest and best-organized centers, probably in some form of alliance with the outside imperial influence of Teotihuacán. It appears that Tikal had moved far beyond its feudal political system to more a centralized bureaucratic state, somewhat along the lines of Teotihuacán. At its height around 750 C.E. the population of Tikal reached approximately 72,000.

Dynastic lineage is known at Tikal, because ceremonial elite burials and monumental stone stelae commemorating rulership are evident in the material record. Beginning in 376 C.E. Tikal witnessed a succession of uniquely named rulers that favor the notion of lineality, with an unbroken chain of parent-child links over 11 generations. (The beginning of the lineage according to one source is as follows: Jaguar Paw, Curl Nose, Stormy Sky, Kan Boar, Bu. 160, Jaguar Paw, Bu. 195, Man from Southeast, and so on.) It is possible, therefore, that there were actual ruling lineages, and succession would have been restricted to members of a particular ruling lineage, which would favor a sociopolitical structure of rule by hereditary dynasty.

Succession at Tikal favored the patrilineal line, where the office in question passes to the son of the previous holder; in some instances, however, authority transferred through the woman's side even though a woman was never a ruler. This happened when there were no patrilineal heirs (sons or brothers) available. It appears that this happened at Tikal at least four times in the 11 documented successions, in which case the favored transition seemed to favor the husband of the daughter of the previous ruler. Ultimately, most likely the result of necessity, the rulers of Tikal were willing to suspend the rules of patrilineal succession in favor of orderly succession. Tikal maintained a prominent role in the hierarchy of Maya centers until its collapse around 900 C.E.

The Intermediate Area

The so-called Intermediate Area, comprising most of Ecuador, highland and coastal Colombia, western Venezuela, and Central America east of Honduras, is a region of vast environmental diversity. There was little in this area comparable to architecture on the scale of Tikal or the urban complexity of Teotihuacán, though the population achieved a high level of artistry in craft production, particularly in ceramics and metallurgy. The level of sociopolitical organization did not match anything to the north or south, and small chiefdoms of a tribal level probably developed in small villages; small chiefdoms may have developed in coastal Ecuador as early as 2200 B.C.E. More complex societies, such as at La Tolita in Ecuador and San Agustin in the highlands of southern Colombia, developed between 400 B.C.E. and 200 C.E., though evidence of any dynastic history is absent and the prospects of empire far off.

The Andes

The central Andes region comprises modern-day Peru, western Bolivia, northern Chile, and Ecuador. It includes rugged mountains, highland grasslands, low forests, and some of the world's driest deserts. It is a particularly difficult region in which to succeed, yet the earliest and most advanced civilizations in South America managed to develop and flourish in this region. Atypical in comparison with their Mesoamerican neighbors, in western South America monumental architectural construction precedes state development. Nonstate societies are fully capable of amassing sufficient labor to build large monuments, usually through religious means. The Inca civilization, typically held as the supreme example of the South American empire model, did not evolve until the 15th century. Some scholars, however, favor a definition of empire in which a major center or capital is supported by other cities, a definition that would disqualify the Inca because of the absence of cities, despite the fact that they controlled and administered territory—militarily, politically, economically—stretching more than 3,000 miles. This example is cited to reinforce the idea that not all definitions and models are equally applicable, especially in the ancient period, and that the South American example offers its own possibilities. Nevertheless, true empires did not exist in the ancient period, even though at least two early civilizations, Chavín and Moche, provide examples that correlate with imperial tendencies.

Agriculture began in the Andean highlands of Peru by 5500 B.C.E. At the beginning of the fourth millennium B.C.E. all peoples in South America lived in small hunting, gathering, and horticultural camps or, on rare occasions, in semipermanent villages. On the coast there is evidence of nonegalitarian societies that did not rely on agriculture for a significant portion of their diet, practically unknown in other regions of the world. The consensus in the literature is that the Late Preceramic Period (until about 2000 B.C.E.) represents at most the development of ranked society typical of simple chiefdoms. No single site was the center of a regional polity. Andean sociopolitical development at this time may have had more in common with the interaction spheres of the North American Hopewell and Adena, with a network of chiefdoms linked in alliance and exchange relationships.

By the Early Horizon (800–200 B.C.E.) along the north coast of Peru, Chavín de Huantár was the apparent center of an interaction network and stylistic diffusion, which some archaeologists have interpreted as a marker of some form of interregional social or political integration. The widespread distribution of the Chavín style poses the same sort of problem as does the occurrence of Olmec figurines and ceramics in the highlands of Mexico. What degree of social, economic, political, or ideological unification is represented by the rapid diffusion of an art style? It is generally thought that the spread of Chavín art was a reflection of the expansion of a religious cult.

Moche is the name given to the site, river valley, culture, style, and state that dominated the north coast of Peru for the first 600 years C.E. The site of Moche comprised two enormous adobe structures, the Huaca del Sol and the Huaca de la Luna. The former was the largest structure in the Americas, constructed of roughly 130 million adobe bricks. Much information on the Moche is known through the iconography of painted pottery and murals, including the division of society into specialized classes reflecting rulers, nobles, priests, warriors, slaves, messengers, servants, hunters, fishermen, and farmers. Marked differences in wealth can be inferred from the grave goods that accompany burials, suggesting a stratified society, and scenes on painted pots offer clear proof of hierarchical organization. Images of warfare, prisoner sacrifice, and portraits of important individuals leave little doubt that the Moche were a highly militarized people led by strong individuals.

The Moche mounted an expansive conquest campaign around the fourth century C.E. over neighboring valleys and subordinated those areas to the state. While the Moche clearly had a firm grip over state organization, uniting several valleys under one administrative network, the lack of expansive trade, interaction spheres, or control of distant lands, as in other empires, such as Teotihuacán and the later Inca, largely prohibit defining the Moche as an empire even though they clearly had imperial designs. Similarly, evidence from realistic portrait vessels hints at a dynastic form of authority, but lacking further coordinating data the images remain isolated and enigmatic reminders of a once-burgeoning state. There is evidence of great floods followed by extensive droughts that not only may have interrupted what was a campaign for imperial rule but also may have lead to the collapse of the Moche. At the same time the Wari Empire, the first true empire of the Andes, was growing. Although there is no evidence that the Wari conquered the Moche, their presence on the outer boundaries may have contributed to the Moche collapse around 600 C.E.

See also AGRICULTURE; ARCHITECTURE; ART; ASTRONOMY; BORDERS AND FRONTIERS; CALENDARS AND CLOCKS; CERAMICS AND POTTERY; CITIES; CLIMATE AND GEOGRAPHY; CRAFTS; CRIME AND PUNISHMENT; DEATH AND BURIAL PRACTICES; ECONOMY; EDUCATION; FOOD AND DIET; FOREIGNERS AND BARBARIANS; GENDER STRUCTURES AND ROLES; GOVERNMENT ORGANIZATION; HUNTING, FISHING, AND GATHERING; LANGUAGE; LAWS AND LEGAL CODES; LITERATURE; METALLURGY; MIGRATION AND POPULATION MOVEMENTS; MILITARY; NATURAL DISASTERS; NOMADIC AND PASTORAL SOCIETIES; RELIGION AND COSMOLOGY; RESISTANCE AND DISSENT; ROADS AND BRIDGES; SACRED SITES; SCANDALS AND CORRUPTION; SETTLEMENT PATTERNS; SOCIAL COLLAPSE AND ABANDONMENT; SOCIAL ORGANIZATION; SPORTS AND RECREATION; TOWNS AND VILLAGES; TRADE AND EXCHANGE; WAR AND CONQUEST; WEAPONRY AND ARMOR; WRITING.

Africa

The Selection of Aspelta as King of Kush, ca. 600 B.C.E.

Now the entire army of his majesty was in the town named Napata, in which Dedwen, Who presides over Wawat, is God—he is also the god of Kush—after the death of the Falcon [Inle-Amon] upon his throne. Now then, the trusted commanders from the midst of the army of His Majesty were six men, while the trusted commanders and overseers of fortresses were six men. . . . Then they said to the entire army, "Come, let us cause our lord to appear, for we are like a herd which has no herdsman!" Thereupon this army was very greatly concerned, saying, "Our lord is here with us, but we do not know him! Would that we might know him, that we might enter in under him and work for him, as It-Tjwy work for Horus, the son of Isis, after he sits upon the throne of his father Osiris! Let us give praise to his two crowns." Then the army of His Majesty all said with one voice, "Still there is this god Amon-Re, Lord of the Thrones of It-Tjwy, Resident in Napata. He is also a god of Kush. Come, let us go to him. We cannot do a thing without him, but a good fortune comes from the god. He is the god of the kings of Kush since the time of Re. It is he who will guide us. In his hands is the kingship of Kush, which he has given to the son whom he loves. . . .

So the commanders of His Majesty and the officials of the palace went to the Temple of Amon. They found the prophets and the major priests waiting outside the temple. They said to them, "Pray, may this god, Amon-Re, Resident in Napata, come, to permit that he give us our lord, to revive us, to build the temples of all the gods and goddesses of Kemet, and to present their divine offerings! We cannot do a thing without this god. It is he who guides us. Then the prophets and the major priests entered into the temple, that they might perform every rite of his purification and his censing. Then the commanders of His Majesty and the officials of the palace entered into the temple and put themselves upon their bellies before this god. They said, "We have come to you, O Amon-Re, Lord of the Thrones of It-Tjwy, Resident in Napata, that you might give to us a lord, to revive us, to build the temples of the gods of Kemet and Rekhyt, and to present divine offerings. That beneficent office is in your hands—may you give it to your son whom you love!"

Then they offered the king's brothers before this god, but he did not take one of them. For a second time there was offered the king's brother, son of Amon, and child of Mut, Lady of Heaven, the Son of Re, Aspalta, living forever. Then this god, Amon-Re, Lord of the Thrones of It-Tjwy, said, "He is your king. It is he who will revive you. It is he who will build every temple of Kemet and Rekhyt. It is he who will present their divine offerings. His father was my son, the Son of Re, Inle-Amon, the triumphant. His mother is the king's sister, king's mother, Kandake of Kush, and Daughter of Re, Nensela, living forever, He is your lord."

From: Schäfer, *A History of Ancient Aethiopian Kingship* (London, 1905), pp. 81–100.

The Middle East

The Legend of Sargon of Akkad, ca. 2300 B.C.E.

1. Sargon, the mighty king, king of Akkadê am I,
2. My mother was lowly; my father I did not know;
3. The brother of my father dwelt in the mountain.
4. My city is Azupiranu, which is situated on the bank of the Purattu [Euphrates],
5. My lowly mother conceived me; in secret she brought me forth.
6. She placed me in a basket of reeds; she closed my entrance with bitumen.
7. She cast me upon the rivers, which did not overflow me.
8. The river carried me; it brought me to Akki, the irrigator.
9. Akki, the irrigator, in the goodness of his heart lifted me out;
10. Akki, the irrigator, as his own son brought me up;
11. Akki, the irrigator, as his gardener appointed me.
12. When I was a gardener, the goddess Ishtar loved me,
13. And for four years I ruled the kingdom.
14. The black-headed peoples I ruled, I governed;
15. Mighty mountains with axes of bronze I destroyed.
16. I ascended the upper mountains;
17. I burst through the lower mountains.
18. The country of the sea I besieged three times;
19. Dilmun I captured.
20. Unto the great Dur-ilu I went up, . . .

21 I altered. . . .

22. Whatsoever king shall be exalted after me,
23. . . . .
24. Let him rule; let him govern the black-headed peoples.
25. Mighty mountains with axes of bronze let him destroy;
26. Let him ascend the upper mountains;
27. Let him break through the lower mountains.
28. The country of the sea let him besiege three time.;
29. Dilmun let him capture;
30. To great Dur-ilu let him go up.

From: George A. Barton, *Archaeology and the Bible*, 3rd ed. (Philadelphia: American Sunday-School Union, 1920), p. 310.

Greece

Herodotus: "On the Kings of Sparta," ca. 430 B.C.E. (The History of the Persian Wars, Book 6, 56–60), extract

These are the royal rights which have been given by the Spartans to their kings, namely, two priesthood—of Zeos Sparta and Zeos Uranios—and the right of making war against whatsoever land they please, and that no man of the Spartans shall hinder this right, or if he do, he shall be subject to the curse; and that when they go on expeditions the kings shall go out first and return last; that a hundred picked men shall be their guard upon expeditions; and that they shall use in their goings forth to war as many cattle as they desire, and take both the hides and the backs of all that are sacrificed. These are their privileges in war, and in peace, moreover, things have been assigned to them as follows: if any sacrifice is performed at the public charge, it is the privilege of the kings to sit down to the feast before all other, and that the attendants shall begin with them first, and serve to each of them a portion of everything double of that which is given to the other guests, and that they shall have the first pouring of libations and the hides of the animals slain in sacrifice; that on every new moon and seventh day of the month there shall be delivered at the public charge to each one of these a full-grown victim in the temple of Apollo, and a measure of barley-groats and a Spartan "quarter" of wine; and at all the games they shall have seats of honor specially set apart for them. . . .

The kings alone give decision on the following cases only, that is to say, about the maiden who inherits her father's property, namely who ought to have her, if her father have not betrothed her to anyone, and about public ways; also if any man desires to adopt a son, he must do it in presence of the kings: and it is ordained that they shall sit in council with the elders, who are in number twenty-eight, and if they do not come, those of the elders who are most closely related to them shall have the privileges of the kings and give two votes besides their own, making three in all.

These rights have been assigned to the kings for their lifetime by the Spartan state; and after they are dead horsemen go round and announce that which has happened throughout the whole of the Spartan land, and in the city women go about and strike upon a copper kettle. Whenever this happens so, two free persons of each household must go into mourning, a man and a woman, and for those who fail to do this great penalties are prescribed. . . . A certain number of the *perioiki* are compelled to go to the funeral ceremony: and when there have been gathered together of these and of the helots and of the Spartans themselves many thousands in the same place, with their women intermingled, they beat their foreheads with a good will and make lamentation without stint, saying that this one who had died last of their kings has been killed in war, they prepare an image to represent him, laid upon a couch with fair coverings, and carry it out to be buried. Then after they have buried him, no assembly is held among them for ten days, nor is there any meeting for choice of magistrates, but they have mourning during these days.

When the king is dead and another is appointed king, this king who is newly coming in sets free any man of the Spartans who was a debtor to the king or to the state; while among the Persians the king who comes to the throne remits to all the cities the arrears of tribute which are due.

From: Fred Fling, ed., *A Source Book of Greek History* (Boston: D. C. Heath, 1907), pp. 63–66.

FURTHER READING

John Baines and Jaromír Malék, *Atlas of Ancient Egypt* (New York: Facts On File, 1980).

Stanley Mayer Burstein, ed., *Ancient African Civilizations: Kush and Axum* (Princeton, N.J.: Marcus Wiener Publishers, 1998).

China's Buried Kingdoms (New York: Time-Life Books, 1993).

Nigel Davies, *The Ancient Kingdoms of Peru* (New York: Penguin Group, 1998).

Simon Goodenough, *Citizens of Rome* (New York: Crown, 1979).

Julian Granberry, *The Americas That Might Have Been: Native American Social Systems through Time* (Tuscaloosa: University of Alabama Press, 2005).

Gene Gurney, *Kingdoms of Europe: An Illustrated Encyclopedia of Ruling Monarchs from Ancient Times to the Present* (New York: Crown, 1982).

Gene Gurney, *Kingdoms of Asia, the Middle East and Africa: An Illustrated Encyclopedia of Ruling Monarchs from Ancient Times to the Present* (New York: Crown Publishers, 1986).

Joyce L., Haynes, *Nubia: Ancient Kingdoms of Africa* (Boston: Museum of Fine Arts, 1994).

John Haywood, *The Penguin Historical Atlas of Ancient Civilizations* (New York: Penguin Group, 2005).

Stephen Howe, *Empire: A Very Short Introduction* (New York: Oxford University Press, 2002).

Serge Lancel, *Carthage: A History*, trans. Antonia Nevill (Oxford, U.K.: Blackwell, 1995).

Bill Manley, *The Penguin Historical Atlas of Ancient Egypt* (New York: Penguin, 1996).

Colin McEvedy, *The New Penguin Atlas of Ancient History*, 2nd ed. (New York: Penguin Books, 2002).

Chris Scarre, *The Penguin Historical Atlas of Ancient Rome* (New York: Penguin Books, 1995).

Linda Schele and Mary Ellen Miller, *The Blood of Kings: Dynasty and Ritual in Maya Art* (New York: George Braziller, Inc., 1986).

► employment and labor

INTRODUCTION

Among the most ancient civilizations "employment" or "labor" as an institution would have been an entirely foreign concept. The daily goal of early peoples was to ensure survival by having enough to eat. Accordingly, most labor involved the search for or production of food. Other chores were probably done communally, such as the building of huts for shelter or the construction of a boat or raft. In agricultural societies it would have been impossible for one person or one family to carry out the labor-intensive tasks necessary for agricultural production. Thus, ancient societies learned to pool their efforts in such public works projects as terracing agricultural land, building canals and dikes, irrigating fields, and draining swamps. As civilizations advanced and as farmers were able to produce surplus food, systems of employment and labor became more organized and advanced. In time specializations developed, including architects, stonemasons, plasterers, and sculptors. Meanwhile, a peasant class continued to produce food.

"Labor" was not something that was particularly valued in the ancient world. Laborers frequently occupied nearly the lowest rung of the social order, and because they often lacked skills, they were not held in high esteem. In some societies, such as ancient Greece and Rome, slaves and prisoners of war provided most of the physical labor. In ancient Egypt slave labor may have been used to construct such monuments as the pyramids. Additionally, large numbers of workers would have been involved in the quarrying, cutting, and transportation of the stones used to build the pyramids and other stone monuments throughout the world.

As urban societies became more complex and sophisticated, additional job categories began to emerge: mechanics, carpenters, artists, weavers, bakers, butchers, fishmongers, pottery makers, clothes washers, barbers, physicians, and even candy makers. Women might have found employment as seamstresses, and in places like ancient Rome they also found work as prostitutes.

In most cultures educated workers who could read and write were employed as civil servants, tax collectors, accountants, scribes (writers of documents, such as legal documents), directors of public works, and the like. Those involved in trade and commerce had to be able to keep accounts, so they needed a background in mathematics, and workers had to be organized for the storage and transportation of goods. Others became artists, astronomers, or priests. Much like today, education was a way for people to acquire the skills they needed to avoid backbreaking manual labor.

The earliest workers were not paid for their work. Rather, they were entitled to their share of food and other commodities. Over time systems of barter were developed to compensate people for labor. In ancient Egypt, for example, copper was used as a unit of measurement for valuing goods, and such commodities as grain, oil, and fish were "priced" relative to copper. In turn, workers were compensated with commodities according to their value measured by copper. Later still, systems of currency, including coins but also paper money and even money made with leather, were used to compensate workers. In ancient Rome salt was highly valued because it was used in food preservation. The Roman Empire mined a considerable amount of salt, and salt was often used as a form of payment. The modern word *salary* is derived from the word *salt*.

AFRICA

BY KIRK H. BEETZ

The earliest peoples of Africa were hunter-gatherers, and most of what is known about them comes from paintings on rocks in southern Africa and the Sahara. The purpose of many southern rock paintings may have been to illustrate adult behavior for youngsters during their initiations into adulthood and, therefore, may be depictions of everyday behaviors. For instance, paintings show people in small boats fishing with spears, and others depict humans hunting animals with bows and arrows as well as spears, labor that grown-ups would have been expected to do.

In general, in a hunter-gatherer society everybody has to be able to do all tasks, because an individual person's survival may depend on his or her being able to identify food plants, hunt animals, make tools and pots, weave baskets, and so on. Anthropologists by and large believe that specialization in particular tasks occurred only when people developed agriculture and began making enough surplus food to allow some people to forgo producing food so that they could focus on a specific job. In this case, many African societies did not allow for distinct jobs because the San (or "Bushmen") and the small-statured groups that have been termed Pygmies who occupied most of central and southern Africa until after the 200s C.E. were hunter-gatherers until the 20th century.

Each individual was responsible for the well-being of everyone else in their nomadic group. Although disabled people and the elderly were cared for, everyone else was expected to contribute to the work of staying alive. There was a division of labor between men and women, with men hunting animals, which often took them far from home, and the women and children searching for plants to eat. The manufacturing of vessels and utensils for cooking might have been done by either gender, with actual preparation of meals at the base camp being the responsibility of women and children. Men prepared their own meals while on the hunt. The San traded with other people, so that San in an area rich in clay would make pottery to trade with others who might have woven baskets or made other basic goods.

For most of Africa the big change in this way of life came with the invasion of the Bantu-speaking people from West Africa. The Bantu speakers may have included descendants of people who had lived in the Sahara when it was a fertile grassland before 3000 B.C.E., migrating south as the Sahara dried and bringing with them the knowledge of how to care for herding animals, such as cattle, goats, and sheep, and of how to raise cereal crops. Rock paintings from the Sahara date back to about 27,500 B.C.E. and reveal the development of the ancient Saharans from hunter-gatherers to herders in 5095 B.C.E. and then to adopting a horse-based culture in 2780 B.C.E. and beyond. This evolution meant that their descendants among the Bantu speakers would have had a division of labor into different jobs and would have had customs regarding employment and labor.

Even without writing, their rules about employment were complex by the time they began making substantial inroads on the ancient territories of the San and the so-called Pygmies. People were bound to one another by family, clan, village, and personal obligation. Becoming an employee was considered a personal obligation in which labor was exchanged for training, goods, or money. At first the Bantu speakers were slash-and-burn agriculturalists, but they slowly changed from that practice to a more renewable form of agriculture. The first step toward renewable agriculture may have begun in the 200s C.E. when several hundred Bantu speakers migrated up the Congo and established farms. Their success attracted others, who became farmhands. The manufacture of iron was well known to them, and ironmasters set up business and attracted apprentices. This growth in employment represented an increase in prosperity and, with it, a rise in disputes over the proper distribution of wealth among employers and employees. To resolve labor disputes, both employers and employees consulted female shamans, a priestess skilled in magical arts.

Women were usually the ones who conducted trade among the Bantu speakers. Their knowledge of trading made them experts in the value of goods and, therefore, probably in the value of labor. In that context, having female shamans, whose religious status put them in positions of authority, settle labor disputes seems natural. It is likely that the shamans put their judgments in supernatural terms, with certain labor practices angering supernatural forces or drawing bad luck. The shamans would have settled questions of how much someone was to be paid, how long an employee had to work for his or her boss before becoming free to work elsewhere or to set up his or her own business, and who owned which part of a business.

In eastern and northeastern Africa complex civilizations arose, partly because of influences from Asia. The most significant nations were Karmah (ca. 1900–ca. 1550 B.C.E.), Kush (ca. 900 B.C.E.–ca. 350 C.E.), and Axum (ca. 500 B.C.E.–ca. 900 C.E.). Little is known about employment and labor in these cultures, even though Kush and Axum left written languages. The languages have yet to be translated, leaving inscription written in foreign languages as the only readable records. Karmah did a lively business in logging and animals skins, with its products being traded to Egypt. Karmah had metalsmiths, jewelers, cabinetmakers, and potters. Somewhat more is known about Kush because of its extensive contacts with Egypt.

Farming was the most important industry in Kush, because Kush's sovereignty depended on having its own, secure supply of food. Most of its wars were fought against nomads who tried to steal crops and livestock. Caring for Kush's fields was shared labor, with families or clans cooperating in the use of water, especially during the dry growing season when the pouring of water from the Nile into irrigation ditches had to continue day and night. Cooperative families probably did this in shifts.

Kush's economy had to be intricate, and from about 700 B.C.E. to about 250 C.E., it was probably equal in complexity to the economies of Egypt and Near Eastern countries. Scribes and priests were the elite workers in Kush, though the laws governing their behavior are not known. For a time during the 600s B.C.E. some priests could order a king to commit suicide, and the king would do so. In about 590 B.C.E. a king had those priests slaughtered, ending their political ascendancy, though later priests remained important in religious life and were in general well paid.

Axum was built on trade between Africa and Asia, with contacts extending to India and perhaps to China. Its society was a mix of ethnic groups that formed a unique culture. Axum had intricate laws governing trade, mostly to make sure that people did not cheat one another, and it seems that there were specialists in the laws who were in charge of what traders did in Axum's ports and marketplaces. Axum had complex businesses that employed many people. Construction workers and scribes seem to have been particularly important, but until the written language of the Axumites can be translated, little about its employment and labor practices prior to the medieval era is likely to be known.

EGYPT

BY CHARLOTTE BOOTH

In ancient Egypt it was common for people to work to sustain their families or to increase their personal wealth. A monetary system was introduced by Alexander the Great in 332 B.C.E.; before this time wages were paid in produce or services. Goods, however, were given a relative value according to weight or volume. For example, grain was measured by the unit kher, which was roughly equivalent to 20 gallons, and the unit deben, a little over 3 ounces of copper, was used as a general value for many items.

Most of the available information regarding wages and income are records from Deir el-Medina, the village of the royal workmen at Thebes. These records show the middle-class residents were paid three times that of an ordinary field hand. The workmen at Deir el-Medina would have worked eight-hour days and had one day off in 10. Despite this long workweek, these people were able to take as many days off as they needed for a variety of reasons, including making libations (offerings) at tombs of relatives, illness, and arguments with spouses. These absentee records have been discovered at the site and are very enlightening regarding the lives of the villagers. In addition to their wages, the workmen were provided with housing, firewood, fish, vegetables, water, and oil—all the essentials of daily life. There was also a resident doctor at the village to deal with ailments; the doctor's services were paid for by the state. Within the community itself the income levels varied depending on responsibility and status. Foremen were paid the highest rate at 7½ kher of grain per month; ordinary workmen were paid 5½ kher; scribes earned less than half the foremen's wages at about 3¾ kher; porters were paid the lowest wage at 1¼ kher.

There were also extra rations awarded to the workmen by the king, as a reward for their labor. During the reign of Merneptah (r. 1224–1214 B.C.E.) some of these extra rations were noted by the scribe Anupemheb, who recorded 150 donkey loads of provisions brought to the village, consisting of 9,000 fish, a large amount of salt for drying, and 10 oxen ready for slaughter. Such extra rations would have provided enough for a few meals per person. Also recorded were four donkey loads of beans and sweet oils, eight donkey loads of barley malt (enough for four pints of beer per person), 9,000 loaves of bread (enough for 150 per household), and eight donkey loads of natron used for soap.

An average family of 10 members would consume 5½ kher of grain per month, so many of the workmen would have earned enough to live on but may have had little left over for the market. For the richer members of the Deir el-Medina society, their wages and additional rations would have been enough to feed their families and also would have provided some excess that could be used for purchasing other goods.

It was, however, possible to earn money outside the working environment, and many of the workmen at Deir el-Medina earned additional income. For example, the scribe Harshire adorned three coffins for a songstress of the deity Amun, for which he received 329 deben of copper. Another workman, Bekenwernero, received 91 deben for an order of coffins, beds, chairs, boxes, and tables. Excess wealth would, therefore, have depended on personal initiative and the willingness to make salable goods. These spare goods would then be taken to market by both the men and women. In the Theban tombs of Ipuy and Kenamun, market scenes depict men and women seated under canopies selling their goods, which include linens, sandals, and foodstuffs. The marketplace was visited so frequently that some villagers from Deir el-Medina invested in huts and chapels near the river on the east bank so that they could stay overnight rather than make the journey back. Although there was no currency, everything would have had a relative value that was of common knowledge to Egyptians. Household goods, livestock, and even servants would have been exchanged for an equivalent value of copper within a barter system.

It would have been difficult for a simple workman at Deir el-Medina or a field hand elsewhere to save enough to make expensive purchases, as 5½ kher of grain, more than many people earned in a month, would be equal only to a small amount of purchasing power—enough, for example, to buy a simple wooden chair. The workmen of Deir el-Medina were supposed to get paid on the 28th day of each month, but on some occasions these payments were late. In Year 29 of Ramses III there were six months of delays. The workmen went on strike, making protests at the funerary temples of Thutmose III, Ramses II, and Seti I, where the grain stores were situated. One text describes this event: "It is because of hunger and because of thirst that we come here. There is no clothing, no ointment, no fish, no vegetables. Send to Pharaoh our good Lord about it and send to the vizier, our superior that sustenance may be made for us." In this instance the workmen received their rations, but later that same year Djhutymose, a village scribe, had to go with two bailiffs to collect the grain rations himself from the local farmers and the temples, as the rations again had not arrived.

Although the ancient Egyptians have a reputation for slave labor, the evidence suggests that there was a positive employment program with health care and a bonus scheme. There was also the possibility of making extra income after work hours, ensuring that the workmen were well fed and had opportunities to acquire wealth.

THE MIDDLE EAST

BY TOM STREISSGUTH

As the people of the ancient Near East tamed wild cattle, sheep, goats, and pigs, their society changed from a nomadic life of hunting and gathering to farming. Their most important occupations were raising livestock and growing crops, mainly wheat and barley. Hunting wild game became the privilege of the nobles and royalty, while fishing became the occupation of the lower classes. In the rivers and along the seacoasts of Persia, Arabia, and the Levant small vessels made of wood or reeds served as fishing trawlers. In coastal areas and river valleys fish provided a vital source of protein to supplement the daily fare of grains, vegetables, and fruit.

Mesopotamia remained a largely agricultural land, even as cities and urban society developed on its plains and river valleys. Mesopotamian farmers settled and lived in one place throughout the year. They had to build homes and villages, collect their harvests, and bring their produce to market. Because rainfall was scarce, they also had to assure a steady water supply to their fields. This meant building irrigation dikes, ditches, and canals to draw water from the two main rivers of the region—the Tigris and Euphrates—and their tributaries. Irrigation works demanded central planning and collective labor, giving rise to more complex systems of government and a ruling class of government officials.

The annual cycle of farming began with the spring rains. Farmers allowed their fields to flood with the rains and with water directed from the rivers. Bulls and oxen were released to roam in the fields to stamp down weeds and fertilize the ground, after which plows, picks, and mattocks were used to break apart the soil and prepare a seedbed. In the fall the crops were harvested. The farmers cut sheaves of grain, threshed the grain stalks to separate the heads of the plants, and then winnowed the grain to separate edible portions from the chaff. The grain was stored and allowed to dry and then ground into flour in mills. The work of milling grain was carried out by humans and strong draft animals, who dragged heavy stones across the grain to pulverize it.

The work of the farmer followed an annual calendar, attuned to the growing season and to the regular spring floods. Survival became less precarious, though famine was still an ever-present danger in years of poor harvests. The rise of a market economy also allowed farmers to trade their produce for needed tools and land. The Mesopotamians became cultivators and traders and lost their former attributes of nomadism and skill in the hunt. Gradually, the Mesopotamian plains saw the rise of an urban civilization. Cities grew at strategic river crossings, at trading ports, and at market towns. People who moved into the cities began to specialize in artisanal crafts, such as pottery and tool making. In the Uruk III–IV Period (3300–2900 B.C.E.) of Mesopotamian history, new occupations emerged: baker, brewer, jewelry maker, brick maker, and weapons smith.

In the Hittite realm of Anatolia farmers raised grains, fruits, vegetables, and livestock, including cows and goats for milking. Oxen helped with plowing, horses pulled chariots, and mules helped carry goods to market. Hittite craftsmen had a ready supply of copper and iron ore as well as gold and silver deposits. Most metalsmiths, weavers, and stone carvers worked in the service of the king or lived within a temple precinct. Throughout the Near East the growing demand for luxury goods—jewelry, fine clothing, and other adornments—provided a market for artisans and their apprentices. In Persia and the Levant the difficult craft of glassmaking rose to new heights as artisans developed techniques of molding and coloring glass. Syrian glassmakers learned how to shape and score (decoratively cut) finished glass in the eighth century B.C.E. By the first century C.E. they had discovered glassblowing, which allows the artisan to create thin-walled vessels in a great variety of shapes and sizes.

As the cities grew in Mesopotamia and Persia, government began to levy workers for road building and the construction of palaces and monuments. For farmers and many city dwellers work became an obligation owed to the state for a fixed number of days every year. The labor corvée was a heavy burden, as it often took the head of a family away from his home. To avoid unrest, the corvée often took place in winter, after the harvest but before the plowing and planting season of spring. Forced laborers worked grain fields owned by the state, the produce of which was meant for armies or for state warehouses. They dug irrigation works and removed the river silt that was constantly clogging the canals. They helped build royal palaces, city walls and, in Mesopotamia, the stepped temples known as ziggurats. In the 10th century B.C.E. King Solomon of the Israelites decreed monumental construction projects for his army of 30,000 laborers, who had to work four months out of every year. Throughout the Near East the wealthy classes were usually exempt from the corvée, or they were able to replace their work with taxes paid in money or goods. However, by one of the law codes of Hammurabi, the king of Babylon (r. 1792–1750 B.C.E.), a commoner attempting to escape a labor corvée was subject to the forfeit of his lands and property.

The work of women remained largely domestic. Women ground grain and spun flax and wool to make clothing. Many wives of landowners and the wealthy had a large staff of laborers to run their households. These servants spun clothing, made pottery, prepared food and drink, cooked and cleaned, and handled the management of lands and urban estates. In the Hittite realm independent women worked as millers, weavers, and innkeepers. They attended to childbirth as midwives or entertained royalty as musicians, dancers, or singers.

In the Near East regular wages were paid to laborers in the form of grain or silver. A system of training or apprenticeship prepared workers for skilled jobs. Some workers were bound by labor contracts to a period of work, and, at the end of their service, they were rewarded with grants of land. Others paid their taxes through work or borrowed money against their labor. Their loan was considered paid when the work was completed. In Persia and Babylon slavery became a more important means of providing labor to the state and to wealthy households. Slaves were subject to the tyranny of their owners; there were no laws regarding their treatment. There was a very limited commercial trade in slaves, but captured fugitives, refugees from foreign countries, convicted criminals, and prisoners of war often were forced into slavery. The slave could be freed from his status after a period of time or for merit, but escape from slavery was very rare. There was no refuge in foreign countries, and anyone found harboring a runaway was subject to arrest, the loss of their property, and execution.

ASIA AND THE PACIFIC

BY DAVID KELLY

The records of social and economic interactions in the nations of ancient Asia vary greatly. Records of the activities of many Pacific Islanders, for instance, were kept only after westerners began to arrive in the 18th century. In contrast, much more is known about China and India for millennia before the Common Era began.

By late in the third millennium and into the second millennium B.C.E., China already had well-established divisions of labor. Cities were separated into sections where different economic functions dominated. Some areas were devoted specifically to religious and ceremonial functions, but in industrial sectors skilled workers fabricated goods, both practical and decorative, out of such materials as clay, jade, bronze, and bones. A merchant class was also well established, and young men from the lower classes were able to enter this class through apprenticeships.

A turning point in the economic growth of China was the start of the Zhou Dynasty near the end of the second millennium B.C.E. Farming was organized under a semifeudal system not much different from the feudal system that was to appear in Europe centuries later. The first ruler of the Zhou Dynasty (ca. 1045–256 B.C.E.) was King Wu Wang, who claimed that his authority was granted by God under the Mandate of Heaven, a claim that future Chinese emperors were to invoke. Land was owned by nobles, who doled it out to serfs in exchange for a percentage of the harvest. Similarly, the means of production, such as the smelting process that provided bronze for making tools and weaponry, was directed by nobles. Most of the items used in daily life were produced in individual households and were therefore not subject to barter.

The vast majority of Chinese peasants during the Zhou Dynasty were farmers or soldiers, but by the time the dynasty ended in 256 B.C.E. China had also developed a complex governmental bureaucracy. In this feudal society land was controlled by a number of territorial princes, who collected taxes from the peasants who did the actual farming on the land. The transfer of wealth that taxes required spurred the use of money for exchange, so that a distant centralized state could reap the benefits of labor without being burdened with amassing goods from all over its lands.

The later Qin Dynasty (221–207 B.C.E.) and Han Dynasty (202 B.C.E.–220 C.E.) was a period of great prosperity. Many people were employed by a large bureaucracy that controlled the economic activities of China's 36 districts. Labor became more efficient with the introduction of standardized weights and measures, roads, and even axle widths for wheeled vehicles. During the short-lived Qin Dynasty, hundreds of thousands of laborers were used to construct the first of China's great walls to keep out invaders and a massive mausoleum for the emperor. During the Han Dynasty the country underwent great economic expansion as well as an expansion of trade and commerce along the so-called Silk Road, which extended all the way to Europe. This expansion provided opportunities not only for merchants and traders but also for the many thousands of craft workers that provided goods for trade. Farm laborers were given better tools with the expansion of the Chinese iron industry. These processes continued during the subsequent Three Kingdoms Period (220–263 C.E.) and the Jin Dynasty (265–420 C.E.), though a series of military crises and internal instability worsened the condition of Chinese workers.

During the Han Dynasty, Emperor Wu Di (140–87 B.C.E.) designated Confucianism as China's official philosophy and code of ethics of the state. Confucianism focused on three elements that directly affected areas of employment and wages. One was the teaching of moral precepts to the uneducated. The second was the establishment of a clear social hierarchy. The third was that those who held prominent social positions must behave in a way that provided proper examples for the rest of society. The social hierarchy Confucius had in mind permitted movement through the ranks of society. By passing an examination, a person could become a government officer, with the potential to gain wealth and honor. Initially, the exam was offered to those who were summoned to the capital because the emperor had heard of their moral excellence, though over the centuries it became more open to anyone.

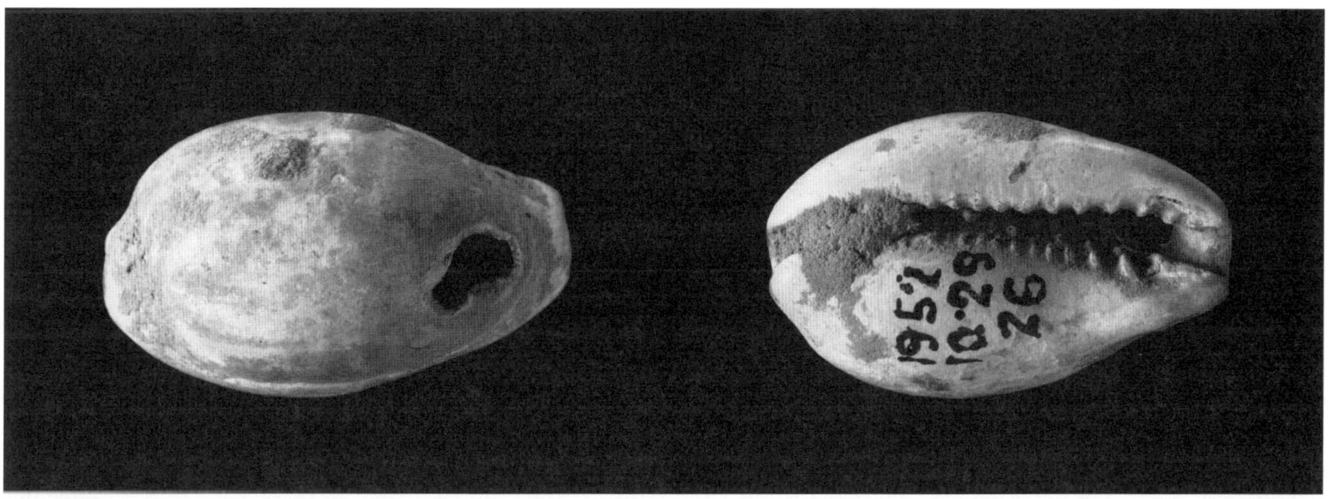

Cowrie shells, the earliest form of money in China, Shang and Zhou dynasties, 16th to eighth centuries B.C.E. (© The Trustees of the British Museum)

This system both offered possible social advancement and institutionalized the government bureaucracy.

In contrast to China's extensive recorded history, there is no reliable record of Japanese development before 400 C.E. From the first signs of civilization in 10,000 B.C.E. to the cultivation of rice that began in the Yayoi Period starting around 300 B.C.E., Japan was in a Neolithic phase, characterized by tribes of hunters and gatherers who shared chores and responsibilities related to basic sustenance. There is evidence of the use of pottery in this period but no evidence that the making of pottery was specific to any one group of dedicated professionals. At the start of the Yayoi Period, Japan was made up of hundreds of tribes, with chores within each tribe divided equally among its members. By the end of the period, however, a large class of advanced potters was making pottery on wheels. Iron was being used to produce tools and weapons, and bronze was being used to make weapons, bells, mirrors, and similar objects—all requiring classes of trained workers. In agriculture village labor was becoming more varied, with villagers weaving cloth and constructing buildings. Landowners gained wealth through the efforts of rice growers in irrigated lands.

As the tribes bonded together over centuries, forming alliances against each other, military professionalism came into existence. The Kofun Period that began in 250–300 C.E. and extended into the sixth century was marked by a central government, with regional control in the hands of families or clans, called *uji*. The *uji* were frequently identified as members of professions, such as religious *uji* or military *uji*. The growth of the clan structure created the need for subsidiary workers, called *be* or *tomo*, to work for the families. The people in this category were on the lower rungs of the labor ladder; sometimes foreigners but more often skilled Japanese laborers, they provided valuable services to the lords. Below this class was a class of common laborers and slaves who were acquired in warfare to do unskilled work.

The centralization of government services that gave Japan a stable system for workers had already been in effect in India for hundreds of years by the time that the Kofun Period emerged. The Indus Valley civilization, which flourished from 3000 to 1600 B.C.E., had a thriving economy in which people worked as farmers, herders, metalsmiths, and traders. They also worked on public works projects, building streets, drainage systems, and waterworks. The caste system, which divided people into social classes based on birth and which arose from Hinduism, created classes of workers, leading to division of labor and the development of the apprentice system for training workers.

The Maurya Empire came to power in India in 312 B.C.E., when the country was a collection of warring states that taxed workers and conscripted them into armies. Mauryan culture was organized under principles laid out in the Arthashastra, a treatise on statecraft generally attributed to a minister of Chandragupta Maurya, who founded the dynasty. In the Arthashastra rules are laid out that provided stability to the merchants, farmers, and traders who made up the civilian economy. They were freed from the oppressive taxes that had been levied on them by multiple governing bodies when the country was fragmented, and a unified economy across India allowed for increased productivity, as workers were able to move freely from district to district. One distinct benefit Mauryan culture had was that of privately held corporations, which pooled capital to create trade, craft, and artisan businesses with more international power than the family-oriented businesses that had been traditional for the country. The later Gupta Empire (240–550 C.E.) continued the expansion of trade and was a kind of golden age of Indian culture. The productivity of the country's labor force created surplus wealth that supported writers, poets, craft workers, artisans, architects, scientists and mathematicians, and philosophers.

Many of the smaller countries of the Asian mainland followed the social and economic pattern of China, with whom they had been trading for centuries. While China and the surrounding countries that it influenced (Vietnam, Cambodia, and Korea, for example) supported a steadily growing bureaucracy that, in turn, supported a centralized government, the social structures of the Pacific Island countries was less complex. While the islands, like China, tended toward large populations, they were confined to limited geographical terrain, which meant a greater population density than on the mainland.

The remotest of the islands in the Oceanic region, between Asia and America, were colonized by people from Southeast Asia in about 2000 to 1500 B.C.E., relatively late compared with the thousands of years in which civilization had already spread across Asia, but their populations grew quickly. The resulting societies tended to be as stratified as the society established in China, but they were less complicated. There were still rulers and tax collectors and tradespersons and peasants. The vulnerability of the island nations, however, tended to drive the citizenry toward the protection of the government that controlled the military. While mainland nations were ruled by governments that conquered their citizenry and imposed taxation on them, the island nations tended toward more close-knit, cooperative, and voluntary support of their leaders.

EUROPE

BY MICHAEL J. O'NEAL

The concepts of employment and labor, as they are understood in the modern world, were in many respects unknown in ancient Europe. In early hunter-gatherer societies, the chief occupation of nomadic tribal cultures was finding food. Any additional goods that people had—clothing, pots, tools—they probably produced themselves, though some bartering for goods took place, and services were provided by the family, clan, or community as a whole. The basic economic unit was the family, clan, and tribe, so there were no businesses, no commerce or trade, no large public works. In this type of economic system, no one was "employed" in the modern sense of the word, though daily life demanded "labor" just to ensure survival and protection from the elements.

In was not until the advent of agriculture, with the more settled communities that could support it, that anything like employment and labor began to emerge. Even then, however, the concept of hiring a worker to perform labor in exchange for a wage was largely unknown. Most people were farmers, growing their own crops or tending their own livestock, and again the family was the basic economic unit, with most goods being produced in the home. The development of agriculture, though, enabled communities to produce food surpluses that could be stored for the future. This enabled communities to begin to support a class of nonagricultural workers, including civil servants, priests, artisans, and the like.

Meanwhile, the work of the community proceeded. Ground had to be tilled; ditches dug; swamps drained; grain stored; livestock tended; fabrics woven, dyed, and turned into clothing; salt and ore mined, shoes sewn, barrels manufactured, the dead buried, and primitive roads built. By about the second century B.C.E. coinage was introduced, creating the beginnings of a money economy. But until then and even afterward, the economy was based on barter and in-kind transactions.

Roughly several hundred years before the beginning of the Common Era, further specialization began to take place. The Celts, in particular, began to develop an economic system and to engage in trade, primarily with the Roman Empire and the civilizations around the Mediterranean Sea. Accordingly, there emerged a more specialized class of crafts workers, who produced pottery, glasswork, and particularly metalwork, some of it for trade. Archaeological remains from northern and north-central Europe include a large number of metal objects—not just domestic goods, such as wine flagons and bowls, but also swords, scabbards, helmets, and other objects used in war. These metalworkers were adept at using not only bronze and iron but also gold and silver. A highly valued artisan was one who could make "prestige goods" for the nobility, allowing them to enhance their power and status. These goods included clothing and weapons. One highly valued craft was that of the wheelwright. The Celts were skilled carriage makers, and their wheelwrights produced wooden wheels bound with a hooped iron "tire" that were highly durable, making transport much easier.

In some parts of ancient Europe communities were a beehive of economic activity. Particularly in the Celtic Hallstatt community, in and around modern-day Austria, archaeological findings show that communities would have been alive with the hammering of smiths, the grinding of grain on millstones, the clatter of looms, and the mining of salt (a valuable commodity used for food preservation). Not only did the salt have to be mined from deep within the earth, but it also had to be stored, brought to a usable degree of concentration, baked in oven, packaged, and shipped. All of this shows a high degree of organization, with large numbers of laborers carrying out the necessary tasks. In the same region nearly every Celtic town was the site of a metal foundry and smelting forge, as well as slag heaps, suggesting the mining of ore and the production of metal was a widespread activity.

In some areas of ancient Europe land was regarded as communal property, so farmers could, for example, graze their livestock anywhere. No one person was regarded as the owner of the land. In much of early Europe, however, there emerged something like the feudal system of the Middle Ages. Historians often use the phrase "embedded economy" to refer to the system of production and land ownership that prevailed among the ancient Celts. In Celtic civilization a class structure emerged, consisting at the top of tribal chiefs, followed by the warrior nobility and then a class of craftsmen and artisans and, finally, the peasantry. While the aristocracy did not own the land, livestock, and so forth, they were entitled to receive a share of the community's production. In return, the aristocracy provided common people with protection, primarily from neighboring tribes.

The closest institution to employment is referred to as clientage. The source of wealth in ancient Europe came from warfare (and seizure of an enemy's goods and means of production), trade, and agriculture. One way that the aristocracy accumulated wealth was by acquiring clients. These clients were obligated to provide services for their noble patrons. These services could include fighting or the production of prestige goods, either through manufacture or trade; wine was such a valuable prestige good that a slave would sometimes be exchanged for a single flagon of wine. In exchange, nobles provided their clients with protection. Sometimes a noble could gain a client from another tribe, often by forging personal alliances with nobles in the tribe. In effect, the patron-client relationship was a sort of barter system in which labor and other services were provided in exchange for protection. These patron-client relationships were often more powerful than the ties of kinship and clan. In some instances, entire communities became clients, under the patronage of other, more powerful communities.

GREECE

BY CHRISTOPHER BLACKWELL

In the mythological history of ancient Greece, labor was accomplished by gods. Homer reports that the walls of Troy were built by the god Poseidon, and the Greeks assumed that the massive walls of Mycenae, whose blocks of stone measured 10 feet on a side, were constructed by the work of Cyclopes. In the historical period, the period for which we have evidence about real people doing real work, beginning (perhaps) with Hesiod's epic poem *Works and Days*, from the seventh century B.C.E., we can see evidence that ancient attitudes toward labor had very little in common with "labor" as discussed by modern economists.

There is no evidence for anything like modern unions or guilds. We do not hear of labor strikes, and for the most part labor was not considered in any way noble or admirable. The ideal life, as presented in literary sources, was one that did not involve manual work in any capacity—all such work being done by slaves. When work was necessary, it was reputable only in the context of agriculture on one's own land. So the poet Hesiod urges diligence and constant effort but on a privately held farm. His audience is assumed to be other landowners, however small and meager their holdings may have been. Other laborers appear in *Works and Days* but only as less-than-admirable tools that the independent farmer might hire, or buy, to support his own efforts.

There seems to have been among the ancient Greeks no distinction between a person and the person's labor. The consequence of this was a failure to distinguish in any meaningful way between wage labor and slavery. An employer was not buying merely the labor of a worker but in effect the worker himself, making the laborer nothing more than a temporary slave. Accordingly, there are passages in ancient literature where it seems that a wage laborer actually maintained a lower status than a slave. A slave was permanent property, after all, and enjoyed a place in the household; a slave's person was valuable and worth protection. A wage laborer had no fixed place in the community and, when the task for which he was hired came to completion, was no longer valuable.

The social and economic crises that afflicted many communities during the sixth century B.C.E. were reflections of this failure to distinguish between wage labor and slavery. Small farmers increasingly fell into debt to more wealthy landowners, having borrowed seed or money to buy seed in times of poor harvests. Since, in a largely premonetary economy, the small farmers had nothing of value with which to repay their creditors, they repaid them by mortgaging sections of their farms; the debtor would then, in a following year, continue to work that land, but the proceeds from its harvest belonged to the creditor. With even less produce for himself, the small farmer was likely to continue in this spiral of debt until the majority of his farm was worked for the profit of the creditor, making the debtor, in his own eyes and in the eyes of the community, a virtual slave, selling his own labor to another. The resolution to this state of affairs, in many Greek cities, was revolution and the institution of popular tyrannies and ultimately to enact democratic reforms.

There had to be, of course, members of the community who were not independent farmers, and even in the Homeric poetry of the Greek dark ages we find an acknowledgement of their worth. These were the "public workers," certain craftsmen, prophets, healers, builders, and singers of tales who were not attached to a particular household but whose labor, or at least the results of whose labor, benefited the farmers and their households.

Nonagricultural labor was always necessary, of course, as people needed manufactured goods, ores from mines, woven clothing, and luxury items. There were, therefore, various "industries" in any Greek community. Only rarely, however, did they employ paid workers. Furniture pieces, ships, pottery items, weapons, perfumes, and the like were the products of "workshops," small local enterprises under the control of a master and staffed by slaves. The father of the orator Demosthenes, for example, died in the early fourth century B.C.E. and left as part of his estate two workshops, one manufacturing swords and knives and employing 32 slaves and the other a furniture shop employing 20 slaves. Such industry contributed useful implements to the local markets—swords and furniture—and generated wealth to the owner, Demosthenes' father, and presumably to the people who sold ivory, iron, and wood to the owner. But this kind of industry did not create wealth in the modern economic sense, since it did not employ anyone. The slaves earned no income, and so the financial benefit to the community of either of these workshops was much less than, for example, a bicycle shop in a small town, which might support its owner, but also provide incomes to several employees, who would in turn contribute to the economy in other ways.

During the fifth century B.C.E. the city of Athens undertook an enormous project of public building, funded by the tribute paid to Athens by its "allies," the cities and islands of the Aegean under Athenian domination. Inscriptions detailing the work on the temples of the Athenian Acropolis survive and show that, in this enormous community effort, the labor of slaves, resident aliens, and citizens was employed nearly equally. What is most remarkable is that laborers seem to have been paid the same, regardless of whether they were citizen, foreigner, or free.

The inscription noting wages paid for the workers who cut the flutes in the columns of the Erechtheum in 409 B.C.E. records these figures for workers cutting channels in one column: "Onesimus, a slave belonging to Nikostratos: 16 drachmas, 4 obols; Eudoxus from Alopeke [a citizen]: 16 drachmas, 4 obols; Kleon [perhaps a foreigner]: 16 drachmas, 4 obols; Simon [foreigner] who lives in Agryle: 16 drachmas, 4 obols; Antidotus, a slave of Glaukos: 16 drachmas, 4 obols; Eudikos [status unknown]: 16 drachmas, 4 obols." All told, of the architects, secretaries, guards, masons, sculptors, carpenters, and all the laborers who are recorded as having built this temple, 24 are known to have been citizens, 42 to have been resident aliens, 20 to have been slaves, with 21 whose status remains unknown.

Citizens, foreigners, and slaves alike were paid the same rate, and it seems that all these laborers were paid the same wage of one drachma per day, regardless of whether they were sculptors working on the statuary of the temple's frieze, sawyers making wooden scaffolding, architects, or guards. More than any other evidence, this serves to demonstrate that while "work" was necessary and known to have a certain value, "labor" as a concept—something that built wealth, that was itself a commodity with greater or lesser value according to the circumstances, the demand, the supply, and the skill involved—was largely absent from ancient Greek economic thinking.

ROME

BY KIRK H. BEETZ

Not much is known about employment and labor during the era of Rome's first kings (ca. 753–ca. 510 B.C.E.). By the reign of Tullus Hostilius (r. 673–642 B.C.E.) Rome seems to have developed an aristocracy, the patricians, and commoners, the plebeians. A key moment in the history of labor in Rome occurred during the reign of Tarquinius Priscus (r. 616–578 B.C.E.), who drained a swamp beside the Tiber River and built Rome's Forum on it. A rectangular open space, the Forum had a marketplace on one side, where farmers and craftspeople could sell their products. A basilica, or place of public assembly, was built at one end of the Forum. In the basilica laborers could find work.

During the Roman Republic (509–27 B.C.E.), Rome developed a large class of unemployed people, who gathered along one side of the Forum under a shelter the city provided for them. There they collected free food from the government and sometimes found work as unskilled labor. Throughout its existence the Roman Empire had a large number of unemployed people, probably because of slavery. Slavery affected all aspects of Roman society. Slaves served in households as nannies, cooks, and other servants. On farms they held every working position, and slaves were often in charge of large farming estates, doing all hiring and firing and directing all tasks for their owners. The effect of slaves on Roman society was primarily destructive. Among the patricians, they made for lazy owners who were unprepared for leadership or hardship. They took jobs that would otherwise have gone to free citizens who needed the employment. Further, slavery took away the incentive for Romans to be innovative. For example, when the steam turbine, called an *aeolipyle,* was invented in the first century of the Common Era, it languished because it was seen as a mere labor-saving device, and it was easier just to have slaves do the labor instead. Given how the steam turbine revolutionized European culture in the 1800s C.E., the *aeolipyle* could have given the Roman Empire an enormous technological lead over its rivals in the ancient world.

Slaves had no civil rights in Rome. Their owners could kill them, torture them, and abuse them without penalties. Slaves could earn money, but that money belonged to their owners. However, it was customary to allow slaves to save their own money and to allow them to use that money as their own, even to purchase their own businesses. Until the end of the 300s C.E. Rome's wars brought large numbers of slaves into the empire, so replacing a slave was usually easy. Thus, freeing slaves was common. According to custom, however, the former owner of a slave was still responsible for the freed slave's welfare and was expected to be accountable for the freed slave's debts.

In every form of employment slaves competed with free people. Sometimes they were more respected than wage earners, who were usually treated with contempt. Roman cities and towns were divided into areas of rich and poor, with tradespeople and crafts workers having their own sections. Those who owned their own businesses lived in well-kept areas. Wage earners lived in squalid areas of narrow streets with one-room homes and small apartments. When a Roman city was built on the site of a conquered village or town, the wage earners lived in the old barbarian part of the city. They were regarded as filthy and smelly, unfit for mingling in society. As such, they formed a permanent underclass that existed throughout the empire at all times. Wage earners sometimes rebelled against their maltreatment, and their riots were feared by other Romans.

There was a hierarchy among Rome's laborers. At the bottom were town criers and undertakers, who were forbidden by law to hold public office. At its top were construction workers and musicians. In the middle were mechanics, artists, bakers, weavers, among others. Barbers were feared because their iron razors were difficult to control and could cut. Clothes washers were avoided because the chemicals they used not only made them permanently smell awful but gave them skin diseases. Physicians fell into two categories, one being wage earners, who had to go visit patients, and the other consultants, to whom patients had to come. Greeks were generally regarded as crazy and immoral, but Greek doctors were well respected.

Marble relief of Jason the physician and patient, Roman, second century C.E.; Greek doctors were especially respected in Roman society, and all doctors were exempt from paying taxes. (© The Trustees of the British Museum)

All doctors were excluded from having to pay taxes. Roman laws dealt more harshly with laborers than with other Romans. Where a patrician might be fined for stealing, a laborer could expect to be whipped and sentenced to years of hard labor.

Wage earners tried to compensate for their low status in society by establishing their own institutions, called collegia. Collegia were formed by people with related skills, such as fishmongers, butchers, perfumers, auctioneers, interior decorators, and candy makers. The collegia gathered dues and spent the money to buy a meeting hall as well as food and drink. The collegia served primarily to provide dinners at which the members could gather and enjoy one another's company. The elected leaders of the collegia were held in high esteem by members.

Women could participate in many forms of employment. Male commoners were expected to serve 20 years in Rome's military, which in time of war left many jobs to be done by women. Even women from the wage-earning class tended to be educated, and they worked as secretaries, teachers, and doctors. They also worked as hairdressers, seamstresses, and midwives. When desperate, as they often were, they worked as prostitutes.

During the Roman Republic and the early years of imperial rule, wage earners were often paid with coins, but their employers were expected to feed them too. Milk, cabbages, and vegetables were given to laborers. Sometimes they were paid in kind, meaning that for their services they were paid with other services, perhaps the cleaning of a coat exchanged for repairing masonry. During the second century B.C.E. Rome developed a cash economy: Almost all buying and selling was done with money. Inflation ate away at the value of money, and in 301 C.E. the emperor Diocletian tried to stem inflation by fixing prices and wages by law. The best-paid workers were clothes washers and teachers, who were paid by the item of clothing or by the student. Carpenters and stonemasons could earn fifty denarii (roughly 50 American dollars) per day. Farm laborers earned half that amount. Scribes were paid per 100 lines.

Coins lost their value during the final three centuries of the Roman Empire, becoming smaller and having less and less real silver in them. During his reign, Constantine (r. 307–337 C.E.) regularized Rome's money and brought back the use of large silver coins. After his reign, money became increasingly hard to find, and laborers took payment in the form of goods for their services. Taxes on them became so high that many throughout the empire had to pay the government with their children, who became government-owned slaves. By the time Germanic kings put an end to the Western Roman Empire, wage earners were little more than slaves themselves, and they were mostly glad to be rid of the empire.

THE AMERICAS

BY MICHAEL ALLEN HOLMES AND TOM STREISSGUTH

Historians have a limited understanding of the systems of employment and labor that existed in ancient America. Records are scant and in many places were kept on perishable material, such as wood or bark. The Maya used hieroglyphic or ideographic texts painted on ceramic vases or inscribed on stone, but these writings deal with political or religious rather than practical matters. Still, certain conclusions regarding the manner in which people worked for and with each other have been gleaned from archaeological research.

As the ancient Native Americans settled the deserts, plains, and woodlands of North America, the division of labor followed the demands of available local resources. On the Great Plains, for example, hunters worked together to cull massive herds of bison. In the hunt for game, the bow and arrow replaced spears and stone points around 400–500 C.E. Archaeologists have discovered many buffalo jumps, where hunters ran bison herds over cliffs and then gathered the carcasses at the base. One such buffalo jump, in Alberta, Canada, was used for more than 7,000 years.

The development of agriculture demanded a more settled and sedentary life. The tasks of raising village homes and longhouses were taken up in a cooperative manner by large clan groups. Among many tribes it was the task of women to plant and harvest maize and other edible plants, while the men's duty was to hunt. In eastern North America fishing and the gathering of edible coastal shellfish became important occupations. Wherever competition for territory and available resources gave rise to armed conflict, Native American tribes developed a class of warriors, whose occupations were tracking, raiding, and using weapons, such as clubs, spears, and bows.

In the Olmec society of Mexico, systems of hired labor developed between roughly 1000 B.C.E. and 300 B.C.E. Apart from agricultural production, labor was performed largely at the direction of the priestly class, allowing for the construction of temples as well as the carving and transportation of massive stone heads. One of the most fruitful Olmec settlements has been La Venta, an island in modern eastern Mexico. Giant heads weighing as much as 40 tons were carved from basalt found at least 80 miles away. Workers dragged the heads along land to the nearest river and then floated them aboard massive rafts. The painstaking work of transporting, carving, and raising the heads demanded the use of skilled artisans and large gangs of common laborers.

The Maya built their largest, most complex structures fairly early in their overall development as a society, in about 600 B.C.E. Mayan city-states never attained widespread centralization and unification. Nevertheless, dominant cities arose where platforms and temples stood 100 feet high; the Danta complex of El Mirador, in the central Petén lowlands, was over 200 feet tall. Between 300 and 50 B.C.E. the Maya built a system of canals and reservoirs around Edzná, on the western Yucatán, which served some 1.75 square miles of farmland.

Archaeologists have concluded that the Maya developed important work specializations, including architects, stonemasons, plasterers, and sculptors, with priests and even astronomers contributing oversight to building efforts. Historians generally assume that laborers were not employed for wages but were obligated—and perhaps perfectly willing—to provide their services as tribute to the religious and royal figures at the heads of their communities. While the most substantial coordinated labor efforts were performed at the behest of the nobility, individuals were undoubtedly occasionally employed on incidental bases. Members of the middle class could have employed peasants for such tasks as carrying goods, paying them with cacao beans. Labor would also have been bartered among peasants. Women might have exchanged hours of labor in such tasks as weaving, while men would have assisted each other in building homes.

The city of Teotihuacán, in central Mexico, an urban settlement serving much of the surrounding region, features some of the most impressive feats of peasant labor found in ancient America. Construction of the Pyramid of the Sun began around 100 C.E. and lasted at least a century. The pyramid stood some 250 feet high, with a base of more than 700 square feet. Nearby is the Pyramid of the Moon, standing almost 140 feet tall. Laborers moved more than 1 million cubic meters of brick and rubble to fill the interior of the Pyramid of the Sun. Artisans and sculptors decorated both pyramid complexes with fresco paintings and monumental sculpture. The rulers of Teotihuacán levied thousands of workers from the surrounding countryside to raise these monuments.

The Chavín of the Peruvian Andes were one of the earliest advanced societies of South America. By the ninth century B.C.E. they had developed a settled agriculture as well as industries producing textiles, pottery, and metalworking in gold, silver, and copper. They gathered and traded stone, wood, fish, shell, and pottery. In the arid lands near the Pacific coast, fishing was an important occupation. In the highlands the Chavín developed large villages and ceremonial centers. Highly skilled masons and sculptors were employed in the raising of ceremonial pyramids and other religious structures. The mining of obsidian, a hard and useful volcanic rock, also became an important occupation.

The Moche followed the Chavín culture and flourished at the beginning of the Common Era. They worked as farmers in the Andean valleys. They were highly skilled pottery artisans who pioneered the use of molds to mass-produce vases, jugs, and drinking vessels. Large labor gangs and masons raised two adobe temples, known as the Pyramids of the Sun and Moon, near the coast. The Moche are also known for their irrigation systems, which were built to canalize sparse groundwater and rainfall for agriculture. A long period of heavy rain and flooding in the sixth century, however, permanently disrupted Moche civilization.

See also AGRICULTURE; ARCHITECTURE; ART; ASTRONOMY; BUILDING TECHNIQUES AND MATERIALS; CERAMICS AND POTTERY; CHILDREN; CITIES; CRAFTS; CRIME AND PUNISHMENT; ECONOMY; FAMILY; FOREIGNERS AND BARBARIANS; GENDER STRUCTURES AND ROLES; HOUSEHOLD GOODS; HUNTING, FISHING, AND GATHERING; LITERATURE; MIGRATION AND POPULATION MOVEMENTS; MINING, QUARRYING, AND SALT MAKING; METALLURGY; MONEY AND COINAGE; NOMADIC AND PASTORAL SOCIETIES; OCCUPATIONS; ROADS AND BRIDGES; SLAVES AND SLAVERY; SOCIAL ORGANIZATION; TEXTILES AND NEEDLEWORK; TOWNS AND VILLAGES; TRADE AND EXCHANGE; WAR AND CONQUEST; WEAPONRY AND ARMOR; WEIGHTS AND MEASURES.

FURTHER READING

M. M. Austin and P. Vidal-Naquet, *Economic and Social History of Ancient Greece: An Introduction* (Berkeley: University of California Press, 1977).

Moses I. Finley, *The Ancient Economy*, 2nd ed. (Berkeley: University of California Press, 1985).

Charles Gates, *Ancient Cities: The Archaeology of Urban Life in the Ancient Near East and Egypt, Greece, and Rome* (London: Routledge, 2003).

Simon Goodenough, *Citizens of Rome* (New York: Crown, 1979).

Jac Janssen, *Commodity Prices from the Ramessid Period: An Economic Study of the Village of Necropolis Workmen at Thebes* (Leiden, Netherlands: Brill, 1975).

Leonard Lesko, ed., *Pharoah's Workers: The Villagers of Deir el Medina* (Ithaca, N.Y.: Cornell University Press, 1994).

Martin A Powell, *Labor in the Ancient Near East* (New Haven, Conn.: American Oriental Society, 1987).

► exploration

INTRODUCTION

In prehistory exploration and the migration of peoples were essentially one and the same. People lacked the means of exploring their world, and life was a daily struggle for survival, so exploration, as the term is understood in the 21st century, was a low priority. Most of the world was unpeopled, however, and much of the history of the world in ancient times was the history of migrations as people spread out and settled new lands, often to follow food supplies. As the glaciers from the north receded, people expanded into what is now Europe to find an abundance of game and fertile lands.

Perhaps one of the best examples is the Americas, whose human population was zero until some hardy Siberian hunters crossed the land bridge connecting Siberia and Alaska in search of game. In time, members of their community followed and began to make their way south through North America, into Mexico and Central America, and finally to the southern tip of South America. The people who undertook these arduous migrations were explorers, but unlike the great explorers of the 14th and 15th centuries, they did not return to their homelands bearing new knowledge about the world. Only later, when the great civilizations of Mesoamerica flourished, did people make an effort to explore outward. But even then their primary goal was to secure and expand their borders rather than to seek new knowledge of contact with new civilizations.

In Asia, too, exploration had ulterior motives. For some, exploration took place mainly with a view to expanding religious awareness. Primarily, though, the Chinese were interested in exploring trade routes. They explored southward and westward, eventually reaching central Asia. The earliest of these explorers returned with such things as seeds for new plants, and in time trade for Chinese silk developed between the two regions. Considerable exploration was done by the adventurous souls who set out in boats to migrate from island to island in the Pacific.

Perhaps the earliest true explorers were the ancient Greeks and Romans, probably because of their location in a sea that allowed travel by ship. The Greeks, in particular, exhibited a curiosity about lands beyond their boundaries, and numerous accounts exist of travels to such far-flung locations as the west coast of Africa, Britain, and the eastern Atlantic. In the other direction the Greeks explored such regions as India and Turkey. One prominent name in the history of geography and exploration was that of Ptolemy, a second-century Greek who compiled the first maps that located places by latitude and longitude. Ptolemy's maps, however, showed that the Greeks had not yet circumnavigated Africa, for he showed southern Africa as connected with China.

In and around the Mediterranean Sea most of the early exploration was done by the Greeks. After the Roman Empire absorbed the Greeks, little remained to be done, at least in that part of the world. What exploration the Romans did as they relentlessly expanded their empire west, north, and east was motivated by a desire for military conquest and to establish trade routes. Exploration more for its own sake took place primarily in Africa. After the Romans conquered the Carthaginians in the second century B.C.E., a number of Romans undertook exploration of the west coast of Africa and of sub-Saharan Africa.

AFRICA

BY MICHAEL J. O'NEAL

Archaeological evidence, which always remains open to new findings and new explanations for old findings, shows that the first humanlike species developed in Africa perhaps 5 million years ago. In 1974 in the Hadar region of Ethiopia, archaeologists unearthed "Lucy," the earliest-known ancestor of humans, whose fossilized skeleton is about 3.18 million years old. Through a process of continual evolution the species *Homo sapiens sapiens*—modern humans—developed in Africa some 150,000 to 200,000 years ago, though quite similar ancestor species had existed for some 400,000 years before that.

Modern geneticists—that is, scientists who study genetics, the branch of biology that explores the origins, variations, and heredity of organisms—are keenly interested in the emergence and spread of humans. Using DNA evidence, they have tentatively identified the genetic group of the first humans who emerged in southeastern Africa at the very dawn of the species. From there humans evolved into two further major groups. One was the San, or Khoisan, of southern Africa, commonly called the Bushmen. The other group was that made up of the small-statured people sometimes referred to as the pygmies of central Africa. Roughly 60,000 years ago some of these humans migrated into the Arabian Peninsula and then into Asia. Meanwhile, the related species known today as Neanderthals (*Homo neanderthalensis*) had occupied parts of Europe, but in time *Homo sapiens* spread there as well and outcompeted the Neanderthals, who disappeared.

The earliest humans in African formed nomadic tribes. As these hunter-gatherers searched for food and other resources, they became the first explorers of the African continent. In the process they located resources they could use not only to ensure their own survival but also for trade. They built cities and transportation networks and thus created some of the world's oldest civilizations. But while historians know much about the end results of their explorations, they know little of the process of exploring. The absence of any kind of written records is the chief obstacle. Much of the history of the movements of African peoples is preserved orally by griots, or storytellers, who retain and pass along their knowledge of the ancestry of African peoples, including those who left their tribes in search of new horizons.

Thus, the world's first explorers were Africans, though none of their names survive in history textbooks. Modern people have to use their imaginations to envision the earliest explorations of their world by humans in Africa. Some of this exploration was no doubt motivated by simple human curiosity, the need to know what lay over the horizon, on the other side of a mountain range or river. Other exploration was doubtless driven by necessity as homelands became depleted of resources, natural disasters forced people to find new homes, or one group drove out another, so that explorers had to be sent out to discover a new place to live. Whatever the motivations, *Homo sapiens* in time spread out from its origins in southwest Africa to settle every inhabitable continent of the world.

Although history does not record the names of these early explorers, it does record those of some later ones, particularly from the Carthaginian Empire. The Carthaginians were named for their capital city, Carthage, on the Mediterranean north coast of Africa in what is today Libya. The Carthaginians were actually Phoenicians, a people originally from the region around modern-day Lebanon who became one of the most active seafaring and trading nations of the ancient world. Eventually the Romans conquered Carthage in the Punic Wars, so called because *Puni* was the Roman name for Carthaginians. The final defeat came in 146 B.C.E., but long before then the Carthaginians had explored a great deal of Africa and Europe.

The most important of Carthage's explorers was Hanno, often called Hanno the Navigator to distinguish him from a later political figure, Hanno the Great. The dates of Hanno's life are uncertain, but he is believed to have lived sometime between 633 and 530 B.C.E. At some point in this time frame

Carthage's rulers sent Hanno on a voyage of exploration. He commanded a fleet of 60 ships, each propelled by 50 rowers, and explored the west coast of Africa as far south as the Gulf of Guinea and modern-day Sierra Leone. Aboard his ships he also carried numerous colonists, who established cities along the west coast of Morocco.

Hanno documented his journey in a tablet that was housed in a temple in Carthage. Later the Greeks translated the tablet under the title *The Voyage of Hanno, commander of the Carthaginians, round the parts of Libya beyond the Pillars of Heracles, which he deposited in the temple of Cronus.* ("Pillars of Heracles" refers to the promontories on either side of the Strait of Gibraltar, the opening from the Mediterranean to the Atlantic.) Some historians question the accuracy of the translation—for example, they doubt that Hanno actually took along as many as 30,000 colonists—though others believe that it is reasonably accurate. In it Hanno noted details of his journey. Perhaps one of the most interesting was his encounter with what he called "hairy women," which some historians believe may have been gorillas. He also encountered the hippopotamus, or "water horse" (*hippo* being the Greek for "horse" and *potamus* for "water" or "river").

Another Carthaginian explorer was Himilco (the Greek version of his Phoenician name, Chimilkât). Virtually nothing is known about Himilco's background or personal life, but around the middle of the fifth century B.C.E. he became the first navigator from the Mediterranean region to explore the northwestern coast of Europe. The text that records his adventure does not survive, but the Roman naturalist Pliny the Elder mentions it in his *Natural History,* and so does the later Roman poet Avienus. Himilco apparently made contact with people Avienus calls the Oestrumnides, who perhaps lived in Brittany. He probably made the voyage for trade purposes, specifically to acquire tin that could be used in the making of bronze. According to legend, Himilco's account described a harrowing journey, complete with sea monsters. Historians believe that he fabricated details such as this to deter Carthage's rivals, the Greeks, from exploring the region themselves. His voyage, though, provides yet another example of the Carthaginian genius for exploration.

EGYPT

BY AMR KAMEL

Throughout their long history, the Egyptians were confident that Egypt was the heart of the world, where "god (Amun) established the land of Egypt first," before all other lands. To its inhabitants, Egypt was always the only place where it was worthwhile to live; all foreign territories lay somewhere on an uncertain and not very attractive edge of the world. Foreign lands were depicted as a three-peaked desert mountain ridge with a strip of green at its foot. The latter represented their ideal country—the Nile Valley. The same symbolism expressed the idea of order (the green strip of Egypt) and chaos (the desert ridge).

Thus, the Egyptians saw no reason to explore the bleak wilderness beyond their borders either out of curiosity or for science. Moreover, their literature frequently asserts that the dangers that one might face abroad, particularly lions and Near Easterners ("Asiatics"), greatly outweighed any justification to venture that far. A text from the Twelfth Dynasty (1991–1783 B.C.E.) describes traveling to Asia as a sufficient reason for an emissary to will his belongings to his children before leaving.

This attitude dominated the Egyptian mentality throughout the empire's history. It is apparent in official religious and royal texts, even with respect to countries with which Egypt enjoyed good economic or political relations. Thus, not much information is contained in Egyptian literature about exploration in the modern sense. However, the Egyptians did sometimes write descriptions and make drawings with abundant topographical details of the places they visited or discovered abroad. Texts give a careful description of several ethnic groups they encountered in Nubia or the Near East, including the social mores of these peoples, which typically the Egyptians thought strange.

These descriptions came in the form of travel accounts, which dealt mainly with trade, warfare, and diplomatic activities, composed by teams of skilled scribes or painters, who traditionally accompanied Egyptian expeditions to foreign lands in the Near East and in Nubia, especially during the New Kingdom (1550–1070 B.C.E.). The earliest-known example preserved in art comes from the Fifth Dynasty (2465–2323 B.C.E.) mortuary temple of Sahure at Abusir. The temple's decorations include a scene depicting what was likely the safe return home of an Egyptian trading expedition with exotic goods sent under royal patronage to visit far-off Byblos on the eastern Mediterranean coast. The oldest written account of an encounter was carved on the external walls of a late Old Kingdom (2575–2134 B.C.E.) tomb-chapel in Aswān. The tomb's owners held the title "head of translators," reflecting their understanding of local dialects in the areas they visited when they conducted several official voyages to explore, or literally "open," the southern territories of Nubia.

Another important account was that of Harkhuf, a Sixth Dynasty (2323–2150 B.C.E.) governor of Elephantine (Aswān) who was responsible for Egyptian interests in Nubia. Harkhuf, who traveled four times to Nubia, mentioned in his inscription the first royal assignment, which was to "open a way to this foreign country" and "bring back from there all sorts of beautiful and rare gifts." His inscriptions refer to three additional trips, literally to "fulfill a horizontal mission" to an unnamed area, that he took alone. Few topographical details of these territories were recorded. Nevertheless, Harkhuf reported a clash between the ruler of Yam and some Libyans, and his role in stopping it.

The first full description of a territory outside of Egypt appears in the story of Sinuhe, from the Twelfth Dynasty. The story describes Palestine, where the author had spent much of his life after his flight from Egypt immediately after the assassination of Amenemhet I (r. 1991–1962 B.C.E.). He describes it as "as a good land, called Yaa," with "more wine than water." Along with describing the area's bounty, he wrote that the area's ruler made him chief of a tribe. Sinuhe spent many years with the ruler of Upper Retjenu and adopted the appearance, dress, and way of life of a local ruler. However, all failed to bring him happiness. Eventually, at the end of this tale, Sinuhe realizes that death is approaching, and he returns to Egypt at the king's explicit request. He is forgiven and essentially reborn as a true Egyptian after being purified, almost ritually, of all the marks of foreignness acquired during his years in Palestine.

From the New Kingdom the most splendid narration about foreign lands described a voyage to the land of Punt. It is considered to be an ethnographic record, even though the land of Punt was first noted in the Old Kingdom. The voyage was documented in reliefs on the walls of Queen Hatshepsut's (r. 1473–1458 B.C.E.) mortuary complex at Deir el-Bahri in pictures with a few captions explaining the place and the characters. The Egyptian artist carefully portrayed the Puntites, with red skin and facial features similar to Egyptians, long or bobbed hair, goatees, and kilts. These same reliefs show the Puntites as a settled people, with houses on stilts. The meticulously recorded flora and fauna suggest that the land was located in Eritrea or coastal Sudan, though scholars continue to debate this.

From the same period the Egyptian scribes who accompanied Thutmose III (1479–1425 B.C.E.) during his military campaigns into West Asia depicted them in the two chambers to the rear of his festival temple at Karnak. Egyptologists refer to these chambers as the "Botanical Garden" because of their depiction of 275 different types of plants, which are shown complete with their root systems. Adorning these walls appear to be genuine botanical specimens, thus making the chambers the world's oldest herbal garden. Also illustrated are at least 52 animals, including 38 birds, a few of which are unique to Egypt, including the darter, the diver, and the great spotted cuckoo. Also prominently represented in the Botanical Garden are several head of cattle of the two-tailed and three-horned variety. Such oddities may be simple flights of creativity or, perhaps, farmyard oddities.

The Greek historian Herodotus mentioned an expedition sent by the pharaoh Necho II (r. ca. 610–595 B.C.E.), with the aim of sailing around Africa. This maritime expedition was apparently conducted by Phoenician sailors, presumably using their ships and not Egyptian ones. Although the circumnavigation of Africa was an important event, it remains obscure whether or not this voyage was completed; some scholars believe the expedition probably had more to do with the king's naval policy rather than with a quest for knowledge.

THE MIDDLE EAST

BY KIRK H. BEETZ

As is often the case for ancient exploration, archaeologists and historians know that exploration took place, but the names of the explorers are rarely known, and the details of what they did and when are hazy. For the ancient Near East, exploring commenced the moment human beings left Africa and began spreading throughout the world. They may have been looking for food, fleeing a drought, or just wanting to see what was beyond the horizon.

Probably searching for food, nomads seem to have passed through Mesopotamia constantly before people settled down into farming communities. From about 3500 B.C.E., when Sumerian city-states flourished, to about 625 B.C.E., when the Neo-Babylonian dynasty arose, Mesopotamians worshipped their cities as holy places, and they loved their cities. This practice may have tended to pull people toward their homes and to discourage exploration, yet some did explore. Their reasons for exploration were spiritual, commercial, political, and military. They also explored to achieve personal glory and to satisfy the common human desire to discover what is over the next hill.

One of the folk beliefs that persisted in the Near East was that a land where people lived forever lay to the far east. One of the world's first great literary works, the Epic of Gilgamesh, tells of a true historical figure, Gilgamesh, who ruled the city of Uruk in about 2700 B.C.E. It tells about how Gilgamesh left his home to seek answers to fundamental aspects of human existence, especially why human beings are mortal. The story tells of his making a physical journey across strange lands to find the answers, and it probably reflects the idea of making spiritual pilgrimages that would have involved exploration. Perhaps contact with the Harappan civilization (2600–1500 B.C.E.) in the Indus River valley was first made by pilgrims seeking the land of immortality.

On the other hand, explorers may first have sought out the Harappans because of Harappan trade goods that were finding their way into the Near East through intermediaries, especially Arabian traders. People seeking out direct contact with such cultures as the Harappans to the east may have been motivated by a desire to skip the middlemen and thereby import goods less expensively. Indeed, the potential for finding new trading partners would have combined adventure with profit. Those who ventured into strange lands would have brought back with them tales of unusual peoples. It may have been such tales that inspired Sargon I (r. ca. 2334–2279 B.C.E.), founder of the Akkadian Empire, to conquer lands along trade routes. One could argue that he was just trying to monopolize trade, but he took an excursion into Anatolia during which he looted but did not absorb new territory into his empire, and the purpose of the excursion was probably primarily to explore—to find out whether there was anything worth conquering. Much later in history, from 336 to 326 B.C.E., Alexander the Great conquered his way across the Near East partly so that he could see the edge of the world, which supposedly lay to the east, beyond India. Like Sargon I's venture into Anatolia, Alexander's conquest was a form of military exploration.

Another form of exploration occurred when people wanted to escape bad economic times or to find work. Entire tribes of people migrated from the north, the east, and the south into Mesopotamia in the hope of finding a place to settle where they could prosper as the Mesopotamian city-states did. Skilled artisans could leave their homes and follow the trade routes, hoping to find a place where their handiwork would be rewarded. For example, Jewish metalworkers, beginning in the 500s B.C.E., searched the Near East and perhaps beyond to find work. Jewish metalworkers were especially valued and found new homes from Egypt to as far east as Iran. Their search for employment had begun in 586 B.C.E., when the Babylonian Empire had deported the people of Judah to Mesopotamia. After Persia's Cyrus the Great (r. 558–529 B.C.E.) conquered Babylon in 539 B.C.E., he told the Jews that they could return to Judah, but many remained in their new homes in distant lands, where they prospered.

Governments of the ancient Near East were often torn between a desire to keep their populations focused on their homes and on their duties to the government and a desire to know what opportunities lay beyond their territories. Theirs was a dangerous world, with wars for seizing loot, conquering territory, and achieving glory resulting in destroyed cities and enslaved peoples. By the time of Sargon I, exploring unknown lands was becoming a necessity for survival. Governments would send explorers to travel into unfamiliar territories to learn about customs, trade, and other governments. Nomadic peoples often explored in order to find places to settle within the territory of a nation, as the Kassites did in the late 1700s B.C.E., when they moved into Babylon's lands.

The most impressive feat of government-sponsored exploration may have occurred in about 600 B.C.E. Over the centuries Egyptian governments had sent expeditions into the Sinai and south into sub-Saharan Africa to seek sources of geological deposits of metal, especially gold, and to discover sources for trade goods valued in Egypt. In about 600 B.C.E. the Egyptian pharaoh Necho II (r. 610–595 B.C.E.) commissioned the Phoenicians to send an expedition to discover how big Africa actually was. The explorers sailed south through the Red Sea, past Punt on the east coast of Africa, and then disappeared. Three years later they sailed east through the Strait of Gibraltar, having circumnavigated Africa.

The Phoenicians were great explorers. In the 2000s B.C.E. people in the northern Levant began trading with the rest of the Near East and Egypt. From 1100 to 800 B.C.E. the Phoenicians of the northern Levant established trading posts first on Cyprus, then on Crete, and then in southern Greece and the northern Aegean, yet most Phoenician trade was by land. In the 1100s B.C.E. the Phoenicians sailed westward, trying to find new opportunities for trade. They even sailed out of the Mediterranean to Cornwall in Britain and south along the west coast of Africa, where they established trading colonies. On the south coast of the Iberian Peninsula, now Portugal and Spain, they found sources of tin and silver. On the northern coast of Africa, Phoenician explorers found a good harbor, and between 814 and 714 B.C.E. they founded the city of Carthage there.

FABULOUS VOYAGES OF THE PHOENICIANS

The ancient Phoenicians sailed to Cornwall in Britain, to the Azores, to the Canary Islands, and even around the western hump of Africa into the Gulf of Guinea, where they found crocodiles and gorillas. In the 900s B.C.E. they sailed three times a year to the mysterious Ophir for King Solomon of Israel, bringing home exotic treasures, notably peacocks, suggesting that Ophir may have been in India. Yet one voyage stands out in ancient records: the one that circumnavigated Africa in about 600 B.C.E.

The Phoenicians were very experienced in voyages of discovery by the time Necho II of Egypt commissioned them to discover the full extent of Africa. They built ships of wood, usually cut from their extensive cedar forests. Some were large 100-foot-long cargo ships with a length-to-width ratio of 2.5 to 1. Others were sleek and swift. Both types of ships could sail the oceans, usually staying close to coastlines. It was probably in a sleek, swift ship that the Phoenicians sailed south in the Red Sea to start their great voyage.

The Phoenician explorers brought seeds with them, probably knowing from past experience that the seeds might be needed. When autumn came, they went ashore and planted crops. After harvesting the crops, they continued onward. They planted and harvested each year of their voyage. The Greek historian Herodotus recorded that the voyagers said that when they sailed westward around the southern end of Africa, the sun was to their right, meaning to the north. Living north of the equator, as the people of the Mediterranean did, meant that the sun crossed the sky to the south; from south of the equator, the sun would appear to cross to the north. The way for the Phoenician explorers to have noticed this phenomenon was to have sailed, as they claimed, south past the equator and then westward around the southern tip of the continent, when the sun would be to the north, on their right. It took them three years to circumnavigate Africa and enter the Mediterranean from the west and sail to Egypt.

Another group of impressive seagoing explorers was the Arabs. They lived mostly on the Arabian Peninsula. They became the great middlemen of southern Asia and explored along the coast of Africa, establishing trade relations with eastern Africa. They also ventured eastward, reaching southern India and Ceylon (now Sri Lanka) in the 500s B.C.E. When the Roman Empire wanted to explore southern Asia and find new trading opportunities, the Arabs, as well as the Egyptians, were the people they chose for their crews.

ASIA AND THE PACIFIC

BY MICHAEL ALLEN HOLMES

Much of the exploration that took place in Asia and the Pacific in ancient times was motivated by desires for military conquest, enhanced trade, and religious enlightenment. On the Indian Subcontinent the early influx of Aryans, who arrived in waves from the north sometime between 1500 and 1300 B.C.E. (in what historians alternately describe as "invasions" and "migrations"), accounted for the importation of much of the foundations of future Indian culture, such as the language of Sanskrit. The Aryans themselves in time fully integrated with the darker resident populations of the valleys of the Indus and Ganges rivers. Much later, Buddhist missionaries proved responsible for much of the Indian peoples' exploration of outlying lands. Siddhārtha Gautama (563–483 B.C.E.), the Buddha himself, essentially wandered throughout, rather than explored, portions of the Indian Subcontinent, especially into the northeastern region now known as Bihar. That region was named after the forest in which the Buddha reached enlightenment, as its hillsides grew dotted with the ascetic stone dwellings of the many monks who were inspired by and followed the Buddha's teachings.

Later, in 250 B.C.E., the Mauryan emperor Asoka, who made sweeping efforts to spread the Buddhist affection for love and peace throughout India, held the Third Great Council of Buddhism in Pataliputra (now known as Patna), in the northeast. Afterward devout Buddhists began traveling well beyond the Indian Subcontinent, first to what are now Myanmar and Sri Lanka and later throughout Southeast Asia. By the first century C.E. Buddhism had spread along the central Asian silk trade route into China; similarly, Buddhist notions, if not the nominal faith and philosophy themselves, traveled northwest through Gandhara toward the Middle East, possibly inspiring the mythology surrounding the life of Jesus Christ. Overall, Indian rulers' and peoples' relative disinterest in exploration can largely be explained by the widely established ideal of a life of simplicity.

In China among the first frontiers breached in the name of exploratory interests were those in the north and northwest. In 139 B.C.E. the Han emperor Wu Ti (r. 141–87 B.C.E.) appointed a courtier named Chang Ch'ien both to subdue the nomadic peoples to the north and to secure the trade route into central Asia. In particular, Chang Ch'ien sought to ally the northwestern Yueh-chih tribe with the Han Empire against the feared Hsiung-nu of the north. However, in traversing the northwestern deserts and grasslands in attempting to make contact with the Yueh-chih, Chang Ch'ien was captured by the Hsiung-nu. Adapting to the circumstances, he lived with the Hsiung-nu for 10 years, marrying and even raising a family, before finally escaping and resuming his mission.

Stucco head of a monk, said to be from Hadda, Gandhara, fourth to fifth centuries C.E.; Buddhist missionaries were responsible for much of the exploration of outlying lands performed by Indian peoples in ancient times. (© The Trustees of the British Museum)

Chang Ch'ien thence traveled farther than any Chinese emissary had before, reaching Fergana, then Bactria, located in modern Afghanistan and Uzbekistan, where he discovered the Yueh-chih living peacefully. After finally traveling as far as Sogdiana, also in modern Uzbekistan, Chang Ch'ien returned home to report on what he had seen, bringing back various theretofore unknown seeds and plants. The Han then essentially took control of the trade routes and extended their empire as far as Chang Ch'ien had traveled, securing a means of exporting their widely coveted silk, among other goods. Chang Ch'ien is as renowned in Eastern history as are such explorers as Marco Polo and Ferdinand Magellan in Western history.

Much of ancient Chinese exploration was, in fact, carried out during the reign of the Han Dynasty, from 202 B.C.E. to 220 C.E., when territorial expansion was a priority. To the northeast, military colonies, termed *t'un-t'ien*, were set up in Manchuria and Korea. Often, where Han exploration led to encounters with hostile peoples, the dynasty at once made peace and increased commerce by presenting gifts; silk, in particular, proved an invaluable commodity. Mongoloid peoples first crossed the Korea Strait to the islands of Japan in the second and first centuries B.C.E., when they found such tribal peoples as the Ainu, who may have been primitive

Caucasians who had arrived there centuries earlier by way of Siberia. Here, as with the Aryans exploring as far as and moving into India, the Mongoloid peoples' integration with the local populace accounted for substantial cultural developments. Mongoloid horsemen from northeastern Asia made exploratory and invasive forays throughout Asia and as far as the Roman Empire after the dissolution of the Han Dynasty; some of these warriors made their way to Japan, further reorienting society there.

Occasional Chinese ventures into Japan provided much of the evidence of the extent to which prehistoric civilization had developed there. One traveler noted in 238 C.E. that the small states that had come into existence on the Japanese islands were ruled by sorceresses, with much of the internal political structures arranged in matriarchal fashion. Another Chinese explorer noted the Japanese people's naturalistic habits, as they reportedly subsisted largely on raw vegetables and forwent footwear. Thus, exploration in this direction served primarily to increase knowledge of regional cultural differences.

Southern exploration, led largely by Ma Yuan (14 B.C.E.–49 C.E.), "Tamer of the Waves," went only as far as the dense forests and barbaric peoples there would allow; the demons and ghosts said to inhabit those regions especially inhibited would-be conquerors. Although the South China Sea was reached, making possible travel by ship to the Gulf of Siam, the Java Sea, and the Bay of Bengal, the coastal waters were especially treacherous, and the Chinese ventured along these maritime routes far less frequently than did foreign vessels. Nevertheless, the ports established there likewise allowed for increased trade, with Persian and Sinhalese merchant ships depositing gems, drugs, and hardwoods and departing with porcelain, musk, and slaves. Those Chinese who did set out returned with coconuts and ambergris from Nicobar and with saffron, sandalwood, and ivory from India. Thus, in many ways, Han exploration led more to the enrichment of the empire than to its actual territorial expansion; as the dynasty grew satisfied with its economic situation and as further excursions, over unfriendly seas and land alike, threatened more substantial costs, outward exploration came to a halt.

With regard to the islands of Southeast Asia and the Pacific, exploration by Chinese peoples beginning as early as 3000 B.C.E. led to the region's initial inhabitation. After traveling by sea to the northern reaches of the Philippines, peoples migrated southwest to Borneo and Sulawesi around 2500 B.C.E. and then farther southwest to Sumatra and east to Irian Jaya around 2000 B.C.E. Sometime around 1500 B.C.E. more capable seafarers ventured out to central Pacific islands from the Philippines and other eastern points on Indonesia and Papua New Guinea.

EUROPE

BY KIRK H. BEETZ

For thousands of years European tribes and nations were exploring new lands to find places to live. People continued to do this even after the fall of the Western Roman Empire in 476 C.E. One way such explorations happened was recorded by Greek historians from the oral history of the Celts. According to the Greek written history, in the late 300s B.C.E. a Celtic tribe lived along the southern Danube River. Times were very hard for them, and crops were failing. Their children were dying, probably from malnutrition as well as disease. Their leaders failed to do anything worthwhile to improve the lives of the people; even the warriors, the elite of the society, looked for leadership instead of providing it. A woman named Onomaris declared that she would accept the thankless task of leadership.

First, she decided that the tribe had to move to better land, dividing the tribe's food, animals, tools, and weapons among the families according to how much each family would need for a long journey. Onomaris and her people did not know where they were going, but this would have seemed normal to the Celts who heard and retold the story, because the peoples of Europe often left their homes and moved as a group to find new lands. In the case of Onomaris and her people, they encountered rivers and swamps, and they sometimes had to fight hostile people. Eventually, they encountered an unclaimed place where they could farm the land, and they settled there, finding peace and good times. Exactly where they went is unclear; migrations from Onomaris's region tended to head eastward at that time, but north and south were also possibilities. Any tribe that moved as Onomaris's did would have to be prepared to fight people in their way and to carry what they needed.

Another reason for exploration was commerce. Among the earliest explorers in Europe who are known to modern historians were the Mycenaeans, who prospered in the Aegean region during the 1000s B.C.E. until their civilization collapsed in about 1200 B.C.E. In search of minerals, they explored the Balkans, central Europe, and northern Europe, finding metal ores and amber, which they traded with decorative goods such as glass beads they had brought from Egypt. Their presence as traders and their trading posts in Europe probably made Europeans curious about the origin of the Mycenaeans' wealth.

Among those who wanted to know were probably the Nordic peoples of southern Scandinavia. These people spoke a Germanic language and were loosely organized into tribal groups. They left a great deal of rock art, both carvings and paintings, of their boats, which resemble the later Viking ships with long bodies and oarsmen in rows on each side of the vessel. The prows do not seem to have the carved dragon heads typical of the Vikings longships, but they rise in the same graceful curve as Viking prows. Following the collapse of the Mycenaeans, little of their written literature was preserved, but some of the culture's artwork survived. A mural on the island of Thíra, in the Cyclades islands in the southern Aegean, hints at what Scandinavian explorers may have achieved. Painted in the 1500s B.C.E., it depicts the island's port, with tall houses, docks, and boats propelled by sails and oars. Among these boats is one that looks like a Nordic boat.

The Scandinavians were restless people, exploring along the coasts of the Baltic Sea and the North Sea. It is probable that they sailed south along the coast of continental Europe or out to Britain as well. Their motives were probably similar to those of the Vikings centuries later: They looked for new places to live and prosper, they looked for rich lands to loot, and they wanted the glory of discovering new lands. Sailing all the way to the Mediterranean would have taken great daring, but if they did as the Phoenicians usually did and stayed close to the coastline, they would have eventually discovered places to land and trade as well as the source of Mycenaean commerce. They may have also reached the Aegean by an overland route. There are only hints of what the ancient Scandinavians achieved because they were an illiterate people; however, they may have traveled as the Vikings did during medieval times, who would row or sail along a river until it became too shallow, then haul their longboats overland to another river and continue their journey.

Aggression was another motive for exploration. The Germanic and Celtic peoples of Europe were warrior cultures, and warriors were the elite social class. For the Celts, war was a matter of earning honor. The taking of booty was often a secondary consideration. On the other hand, war was sometimes viewed as a necessity, as one tribe needed to move from bad lands and dangerous circumstances to good lands and safety. Sometimes they seemed to explore alone or in small groups into territories where there might be a military weakness on which they could capitalize.

The Greek-Syrian explorer Posidonius (ca. 135–ca. 51 B.C.E.) lived among the Celts and noted that he was treated fairly well as an outsider. He had no merchandise to trade, which made him less interesting to his hosts than he might have been, but he was made a guest at meals given by chiefs and served as a curiosity for other visitors. He was not expected to behave like the Celts. Other explorers did not necessarily fare so well. By Posidonius's era, Germanic people were regarded with suspicion by Celts because the Germanic peoples often made war on the Celts. On the other hand, Celtic explorers from other tribes could find themselves guests and would be expected to give accounts of the lands they had visited. Such Celtic explorers were frequently restless young men sent abroad by their elders before they could make trouble for the rulers of their tribes. Singly or in small groups, these young men might kill, loot, or steal, or they might find a chief who wanted them to join his or her retainers. Among the Germanic peoples, this process was common as well, with chiefs taking in newcomers who pledged themselves to their service. This practice would later be part of the premise for the epic *Beowulf.*

While at times welcomed, a Celtic explorer could expect to be looked upon with suspicion, especially if it was plain that he was not a trader. When caught, spies would often be challenged to combat, with their severed heads being adding to the collections of those who killed them. Often young explorers were very unwelcome because the local tribal leaders already had too many hot-blooded young warriors to worry about, and the young explorers would be chased away. Still, for these voyagers, their journeys offered adventure, new and exciting experiences, and the chance to win honor in the service of the chiefs they met.

GREECE

BY CHRISTOPHER BLACKWELL

The earliest Greek explorers were the anonymous men and women who sailed off the coast of the European mainland and settled the islands of the Aegean Sea, eventually building the Bronze Age civilizations that archaeologists have found on Crete and neighboring islands. From there, early explorers made contact with the vastly more ancient civilization of Egypt as well as the empires of Asia Minor.

The earliest literary evidence for exploration is the Homeric *Odyssey*, a work of fiction and fantasy but one that reflects a resurgence of travel by sea at the end of the Greek dark ages around 800 B.C.E. Odysseus, on his 10-year journey home from the Trojan War, finds his way to Sicily, the Aeoliae Insulae (modern-day Lipari Islands), and other more obviously mythological locations. Through incidental details in this poem, it is possible to see past the fiction to a historical reality that involved adventurous Greeks going abroad to new places for trade and war. When Odysseus meets people on his journeys they invariably ask him, "Are you here for trade, or are you a pirate?" as if these were the two most likely professions of a stranger met on the beach.

During the eighth and seventh centuries B.C.E. trade between Greek cities and the rest of the world expanded greatly. Greek pottery is found throughout the Mediterranean and as far north in Europe as Sweden, although who brought it there is unknown. What is known of ancient Greek exploration has to be sifted from fragmentary accounts of voyages, some perhaps historical and some almost certainly fictional, that appear in works of authors who may have lived centuries after the events they describe. But accounts of journeys were common enough to be a named genre, *periplous*, meaning "voyage of discovery." The earliest is a narrative known to the Greeks of a voyage by Hanno, a Greek-speaking Carthaginian navigator from North Africa (in modern Tunisia). Around 480 B.C.E., when the Greek world was involved in its great war with Persia, Hanno journeyed past the Straits of Gibraltar (which the ancients called the "Pillars of Hercules") and into the Atlantic. This journey took him down the western coast of what is now Morocco. He records founding settlements of Carthaginians at Essaouira (formerly Mogador) and Agadir, and traveling south past Lixus. He also mentions seeing volcanoes and describes gorillas.

Another "voyage of discovery," known to the Greeks of the fifth century B.C.E. was that of Scylax, who was satrap, or governor, of the Caryanda, part of the Persian Empire of Darius the Great (r. 522–486 B.C.E.). Scylax is said to have sailed down the Indus River from near the Karakoram Range of modern Pakistan to its mouth, and to have come to the area of the Suez.

In the second half of the fourth century B.C.E., Alexander the Great's invasion and conquest of Persia ended in a march of discovery from the area of modern Syria and Turkey, through what is now Iraq and Iran, bringing him to Bactria, Sogdiana, Samarqand, and ultimately to the Indus River and the ends of the Punjab in India. At this point his Macedonian army, who had walked thousands of miles and fought many battles, refused to go further, and Alexander took them on a forced march back west, which entailed a grim passage of the Gedrosia Desert.

At the end of the fourth century B.C.E. the Greek explorer and navigator Pytheas of Massilia (modern-day Marseille) wrote *About the Ocean*, which recounts his journey west and north, from Gades (present-day Cádiz) in southern Spain, up the Spanish coast, past the mouth of the Loire river (near modern-day Nantes), and to the Cassiterides (the "Tin Isles," the modern British Isles), and particularly to Belerium (modern Cornwall), an important center for trading tin. Copper and tin made bronze, and of the two elemental metals tin was much rarer in the Mediterranean world. Pytheas is believed to have circumnavigated Britain and recorded other lands that scholars have tentatively identified as Norway, the Vistula River (in modern-day Poland), and an island in the North Sea that may have been Helgoland, which Pytheas reported as being rich in amber.

Euhemerus of Messene, also from the late fourth century B.C.E., was a famous author of the literature of exploration. Euhemerus served under the Macedonian Cassander, who ruled in European Greece after the death of Alexander the Great in 323 B.C.E. Euhemerus's account of a voyage to islands of the Indian Ocean, including perhaps Sri Lanka, was popular and widely quoted by later authors, such as first century B.C.E. historian Diodorus Siculus. Although the writings of Euhemerus are based on real knowledge of Indian islands that may reflect the work of more authentic explorers, they are regarded as entirely fictional.

Because Alexander's conquests left Macedonians in charge of pieces of the former Persian Empire, which stretched from the Aegean to India, knowledge of the eastern parts of the world became much more readily available to the Greeks. Alexander had left Sibyrtius as governor of Gedrosia, in the east of his conquered territory, and Sibyrtius sent one Megasthenes as an ambassador to India. Megasthenes met with Candragupta (r. ca. 321–ca. 297 B.C.E.), founder of the Maurya Empire in northern India, and returned to write of his travels in a work entitled *Indika*.

Even under the Romans, many of the fundamental works of geography and books about exploration that provided geographical data were written in Greek by Greeks. For example, the Greek historian Polybius, who served with the Roman general Scipio during the Second Punic War in the second century B.C.E., accompanied Scipio on an exploratory voyage into the Atlantic Ocean. Also during the second century B.C.E. the historian and geographer Agatharchides of Cnidus wrote of his voyage around the Red Sea, with descriptions of Arabia and Ethiopia. The historians Diodorus Siculus and Aelianus as well as the geographer Strabo, all of whom lived in Rome and wrote in Greek, relied heavily on Agatharchides' work for their own.

Ptolemy (also known as Claudius Ptolemaeus), considered one of the greatest ancient geographers, lived during the second century C.E. His treatises cover mathematics and astronomy, but he is most famous for his massive *Geography*, the first work to use latitude and longitude to identify the locations of places. For his description of lands to the east, Ptolemy relied heavily on Marinus of Tyre, about whom little is known except that he wrote during the first century C.E. and that he provided a cultural and geographical description of the "Seres," the ancient Greek term for the Chinese. Ptolemy also mentions a certain businessman from Damascus named Maes or Titianus, who claimed to know overland routes for travel to China, thus perhaps anticipating Marco Polo by over a thousand years. Ironically, the most significant error in Ptolemy's *Geography* can tell us much about ancient exploration. His maps show a large landmass connecting southern Africa to China, depicting the India Ocean as an enclosed sea. In a work as thoroughly researched as his, Ptolemy's error is convincing proof that no ancient Greek or Roman by the second century C.E. had circumnavigated Africa.

ROME

BY DUANE W. ROLLER

The Romans had no sense of exploration for its own merits; the Latin word *exploratio* refers to a military reconnaissance. But since the Roman world expanded over vast territories and since there were trade and commercial contacts throughout much of the Eastern Hemisphere, almost by accident the Romans were able to explore large regions, though inevitability as a by-product of political or mercantile interests.

In their early years the Romans made no addition to geographical knowledge. Their expansion from the fourth into the first century B.C.E. throughout Italy, into the western Mediterranean region, and eventually into the Greek world did not reach any areas previously unknown to Mediterranean cultures. Roman exploration actually began with their destruction of Carthage in 146 B.C.E. At this time the Romans acquired the cultural heritage of their defeated enemy and learned about a wide range of Carthaginian exploration into areas previously unknown to the Romans: down the west coast of Africa (and perhaps around the continent), into sub-Saharan Africa, and along the Atlantic coasts as far as the British islands.

Roman curiosity led Scipio Aemilianus (ca. 185–129 B.C.E.), the conqueror of Carthage, to commission his adviser, the historian Polybius (ca. 200–118 B.C.E.), to investigate. Polybius made a number of trips, going down the West African coast as far as the tropics and across France to its north-

The Dream of Scipio, *by Raphael; Scipio was the Roman conqueror of Carthage, the destruction of which initiated Roman exploration.* (© The Trustees of the British Museum)

west corner. He also inquired of the western Greek states such as Massilia (modern-day Marseille) what there might be of interest beyond the limits of Roman knowledge. Although both Carthaginians and Greeks tried to divert the Romans from involvement in the west—the results of their own explorations were considered state secrets—the Romans did learn about the Atlantic coast, and it became part of their cultural understanding.

In northwestern Europe, Greeks had explored the British Isles, the Baltic region, and parts of the Arctic and Scandinavia. Romans added little to this, though the North Sea coast, bypassed by the Greeks, was examined with great difficulty in the Julio-Claudian Dynasty (27–68 C.E.): Repeated maritime disasters led to a feeling that the Atlantic coasts were of no interest. Nevertheless, this completed ancient Roman knowledge of the coast from the West African tropics to the interior Baltic area. The amber trade from the Baltic acquainted the Romans with several routes across northern Europe, especially the connections between the northern affluents of the Danube River, such as the Morava River, and the systems of the Oder and Vistula rivers, explored by a Roman merchant in the 50s C.E. Romans remained only vaguely aware of the farther side of the Baltic and Scandinavia.

Interior Africa had first been penetrated from the Mediterranean in early Greek times, and the routes up the Nile River or across the Sahara had been known since at least the fifth century B.C.E. The east coast was understood as far as Zanzibar. In the first century C.E. the Romans contributed significantly to the exploration of central Africa. The question of the source of the Nile was part of this interest, having been a topic of curiosity since at least the sixth century B.C.E. and not solved until modern times. Greeks had long tangled with the issue, but attempts to follow the Nile upstream had gone barely beyond the lower cataracts. Juba II, the Romanized king of Mauretania from 29 to 25 B.C.E., believed that the river began in northwest Africa and published his proof, tracing its course across northern Africa, while admitting that it ran underground for some distance. Bizarre as this theory seems, it was still accepted in the 19th century.

Around 60 C.E. Roman officers moved up the Nile for a planned invasion of Ethiopia by the emperor Nero (r. 54–68 C.E.), reaching the marshes in present-day southern Sudan and hearing reports of the lakes beyond. A traveler named Diogenes, perhaps a generation later, moved inland from the vicinity of Zanzibar and saw or heard about the high mountains of central Africa, providing the name Mountains of the Moon, and he was also aware of the lakes around the source of the Nile. But the actual source itself remained elusive until the 19th century, and there was no further exploration of Africa in classical antiquity. Roman trade items and coins reached the southern parts, but the Romans seemed unaware of the interior south of a line from Zanzibar to Cameroon.

To the east the journey of Alexander the Great (356–323 B.C.E.) had brought India, and the routes to it, into Mediterranean knowledge, though details such as the size and shape of the Arabian Peninsula continued to be refined in the Roman period. In the first century C.E. Sri Lanka, known since the fourth century B.C.E., was examined in detail, and a Roman trading post was established at Arikamedu on the east coast of India around 50 C.E. In the following century the Bay of Bengal was explored by a certain Alexander, who may have gone as far as the Cambodian coast; by late in the century a Roman trading post may have existed at Oc-èo in the Mekong Delta.

China had been known since Greek times as the origin of silk; the name of the region first appears in Greek accounts (as "Thina") of around 50 C.E. There is no evidence that Mediterranean peoples actually reached China until around 100 C.E. The one definitive record of Roman contact with China is in 166 C.E., when an embassy from the emperor Marcus Aurelius Antoninus (r. 161–180 C.E.) reached China and was recorded in Chinese records as a mission from An-Tun. From that time there were sporadic contacts and frequent trade in both directions.

Through trade routes the Romans were aware of parts of central Asia east of the Caspian Sea, though little was added to the knowledge existing since the late fourth century B.C.E. Routes north from the Black Sea to the Baltic region had also long been known, but otherwise Siberia lay completely outside ancient knowledge. Japan and southeastern Asia were similarly unknown to the Mediterranean world. Existence of the Western Hemisphere had long been presumed, largely on the basis of geographical symmetry, and much fantasy literature was written about the existence of a western continent. This was an inspiration to the European explorers of the Renaissance, but there is no evidence of European contact with the New World until Viking times, although the mid-Atlantic islands such as the Azores and Madeiras had been known since their Carthaginian discovery.

THE AMERICAS

BY J. J. GEORGE

At a site in Midland, Texas, the skull of a woman lacking facial bones was found protruding from sand in a windblown depression. Snail shells found in a layer of earth below her yielded a carbon 14 date of about 11,000 B.C.E. Artifacts found with her resembled Folsom-style objects and were dated to about 8000 B.C.E. Folsom, along with Clovis, are two of the earliest American cultural patterns. Scientists have suggested that the woman probably died there between 9000 and 10,000 B.C.E. In central Mexico at a place called Tepexpán the skeleton of a man was found in late Pleistocene sediment and dated 9000–8000 B.C.E., but the excavation was poorly reported. Chemical tests nonetheless confirmed the date. In the 1930s the archaeologist Junius Bird excavated a few skeletons from a South American site called Palli Aike in Patagonia. Bird discovered sloth and horse bones in an overlying deposit and a fishtail point deposit in an underlying lava deposit. Carbon 14 dates for these items ranged between 9000 B.C.E. and 8700 B.C.E. Are these the remains of some of America's early explorers?

Ultimately, the idea of exploration in the ancient Americas presents a peculiar conundrum. On the one hand, the period's defining quality is exploration, when one considers exploration's relation to migration. As new peoples arrived in the Americas and diffused south, eventually reaching the southern tip of South America, their very existence was a form of exploration. On the other hand, the idea of exploration in a more familiar form, such as the maritime expeditions of Captain James Cook, Ferdinand Magellan, and Christopher Columbus or the overland exploration of the western United States by Meriwether Lewis and William Clark, in the name of colonization or science or Manifest Destiny, was virtually unknown until much later.

Exploration is a defining aspect of American migration and settlement and has its beginnings at Beringia, the name assigned by geologists for the continuous landmass that once connected Siberia and Alaska and offered a broad highway to the Americas not only to early humans but also to the animals they hunted. The traditional theory says the first North Americans were big game hunters on foot, following large animals such as the extinct mammoth. During the last glacial episode (10,500–11,000 years ago), when much of the earth's water was locked up in frozen glaciers and water levels worldwide were much lower, the landmass was as much as 1,000 miles wide. The present geographic proximity of Alaska and Siberia is itself suggestive of an easily overcome barrier; only 56 miles of water separates the two landmasses. In the winter the strait often freezes and it is possible to walk across the ice. It is generally agreed that the diffusion of the earliest peoples crossed into the Americas via this passage.

Once in Alaska, however, the early explorers would have encountered a nearly impenetrable barrier to southward progress—the same glacial advances that lowered sea levels and revealed Beringia also covered Canada and northern

America in two massive ice sheets. The western ice sheet is called the American cordillera, and the eastern is called the Laurentia. At certain times these two sheets met, and at other times a narrow corridor opened, stretching to Alberta, Canada, and there opening to the northern plains. There is much disagreement still about whether it would have been possible to traverse what certainly would have been an inhospitable environment between massive glaciers.

While an inland route of exploration would have served a cold-adapted population best, it would not have been the only option available. When the land bridge was submerged, prehistoric peoples could have walked across the ice pack in winter or paddled across in small boats in summer. The Norwegian explorer and archaeologist Thor Heyerdahl, among others, has shown the extraordinary exploratory possibilities of seafaring among prehistoric peoples. He established the feasibility of contact via an ocean crossing between South America and the South Pacific. Archaeological evidence in Australia, Melanesia, and Japan indicate that boats were in use as far back as 25,000 to 40,000 years ago. However, any signs of an exploratory route along the Pleistocene coastal shelf is now submerged; consequently, there is no direct archaeological evidence to support a Pacific coastal migration route. It is also possible that populations crossed the 56 miles of the Bering Strait via boat when it was submerged and then continued south along the coast, a theory now growing in popularity.

Regardless of the route, highly mobile populations arrived and diffused as far as Patagonia in what appears to be an extremely abrupt period of time. This area of investigation is still contested; few agree on when and where the earliest explorers and settlers arrived and under what conditions. These hunter-gatherer societies slowly filled in the continents, eventually establishing sedentary or semisedentary patterns based on resource utilization. By approximately 4000 B.C.E. increased density and intensification of resource exploitation, characterized by pastoralism and agriculture, defined the period. Few areas remained without human populations. However, why some areas developed agriculture and domestication and some remained hunter-gatherer is still debated.

In South America, for example, during the Late Holocene (5,000 years ago to the present) the area from contemporary Venezuela and Colombia to central Chile and from the coast to the Andean cordillera was defined by agriculture and pastoralism, producing more than 80 percent of all food. In Amazonia, the area including most of contemporary Brazil and the drainage of the Amazon, Orinoco, and Paraná river systems, between 20 percent and 80 percent of food was produced. And in the southern portion, dominated by Patagonia, a hunter-gatherer system was maintained.

Similarly, between 4,000 and 6,000 years ago, back at the point after the original entrance into North America, the Inuit explored the top of the globe, pushing east as far as Greenland. Subsequent cultural efflorescences and declines, and population expansions and contractions, from the standpoint of exploration, meant that people were continually on the move, populating new territory and sometimes repopulating previously occupied land. Given the great amount of time that passed, these populations might have had no idea if they were the first to explore an area.

Increasingly sedentary civilizations led to development of ceremonial centers and ultimately to cultures with greater density and more complex social, political, and economic structures. As civilizations advanced, exploration took on a different form, based in part on trade and exchange. Likewise, as states grew and empires arose, exploration developed into a form related to war and conquest in the interest of securing and expanding borders, spreading state-supported religious ideals, and procuring objects or materials of significant value.

See also AGRICULTURE; ART; ASTRONOMY; BORDERS AND FRONTIERS; CERAMICS AND POTTERY; CITIES; CLIMATE AND GEOGRAPHY; EMPIRES AND DYNASTIES; FOREIGNERS AND BARBARIANS; GENDER STRUCTURE AND ROLES; HUNTING, FISHING, AND GATHERING; LANGUAGE; LITERATURE; MIGRATION AND POPULATION MOVEMENTS; MILITARY; NOMADIC AND PASTORAL SOCIETIES; ROADS AND BRIDGES; SEAFARING AND NAVIGATION; SETTLEMENT PATTERNS; SHIPS AND SHIPBUILDING; SOCIAL COLLAPSE AND ABANDONMENT; SOCIAL ORGANIZATION; TRADE AND EXCHANGE; WAR AND CONQUEST.

FURTHER READING

M. Cary and E. H. Warmington, *The Ancient Explorers* (Baltimore, Md.: Penguin Books, 1963).

James C. Chatters, *Ancient Encounters: Kennewick Man and the First Americans* (New York: Simon and Schuster, 2001).

John Haywood, *The Penguin Historical Atlas of Ancient Civilizations* (New York: Penguin Group, 2005).

Jona Lendering, "Hanno." Livius: Articles on Ancient History. Available online. URL: http://www.livius.org/ha-hd/hanno/hanno03.html. Downloaded on January 9, 2007.

R. B. Parkinson, *The Tale of Sinuhe and Other Ancient Egyptian Poems: 1940–1640 B.C.* (Oxford. U.K.: Griffith Institute, Ashmolean Museum, 1997).

Heather Pringle, *In Search of Ancient North America: An Archaeological Journey to Forgotten Cultures* (New York: John Wiley and Sons, 1996).

Duane W. Roller, *Through the Pillars of Herakles: Greco-Roman Exploration of the Atlantic* (London: Routledge, 2006).

F

► family

INTRODUCTION

Throughout most of the ancient world the family was the basic unit of social organization. "Family" included not just the nuclear family of mother, father, and children but typically a much more extended family of aunts, uncles, cousins, and, if they survived to an old age, grandparents. The responsibility for raising children was often shared by members of the extended family. Typically, too, a family considered itself part of a much more extended clan of people who were linked by blood or marriage. In places like ancient Europe it was not uncommon for clans to be at odds with one another and engage in extended feuds. In some cultures, such as that of the Chinese, ancestor worship was practiced as a form of religion and as a way for people to remain linked to the wisdom of those who had gone before them.

Marriage in the ancient world was primarily a social, political, and economic institution. Rarely did modern concepts of romantic love play any role in the formation of a marriage and family, and marriage was usually regarded as a contractual arrangement rather than an expression of love. In the ancient world, for example, it was common for grooms to pay a bride-price to compensate a family for the loss of a daughter; alternatively, it was common for the bride's family to pay a dowry to the husband as a way of compensating him for, in effect, taking the girl off of the family's hands and promising to support her.

Marriages were often arranged as a way of linking the resources of two families, and it was not uncommon for husbands to be considerably older than their brides; the older husband had resources that enabled him to support his wife and family, and the younger bride had years of fertility to help ensure the birth of children and the survival of the family name. Further, marriages were arranged according to social class, with the bride's parents, in particular, doing everything possible to ensure that the husband-to-be was of the right class. This was particularly true in ancient India, where people were unable to marry members of a different caste. Before the advent of Christianity in some parts of the world, though, polygyny, or the practice of a man's having two or more wives, was common. Divorce, too, was relatively common in the ancient world.

Most ancient cultures were male dominated. In ancient Rome, for example, the concept of *paterfamilias,* whereby the father was the source of authority in the family, was common. In most other cultures women were regarded as inferior or subject to their husbands. Their primary role was the production of children, specifically a healthy male heir; in some cultures, babies who were not healthy were left to die. If the woman and child survived childbirth, the woman's role was to raise the children and maintain the home, performing such domestic chores as cooking and cleaning. Most ancient cultures were "patrilocal," meaning that at marriage the woman left her family and moved in with her husband and his family.

AFRICA

BY SAHEED ADERINTO

The family in Africa is as old as the history of human existence on the continent. The agricultural revolution that took place on the continent some 5,000 years ago led to the development of a sedentary lifestyle, domestication of animals and crops, and the formation of organized societies, which took the form of villages and larger human settlements. The typical African family in ancient times was both a social/cultural and production unit. It was a social unit because all individuals belonged to a family, which served as a vehicle for socialization and cultural assimilation. The family therefore integrated people into the culture of the entire community. As a production unit, all members of a family were collectively involved in tilling the land and producing agricultural products. Farm produce was consumed collectively, while excesses were sold in exchange for other goods the family lacked.

As in most ancient cultures, marriage was needed for families to be established. Marriage was a compulsory rite of passage. All individuals were expected to get married and form their own families. Conditions that prevented people from marrying were rare. Marriage was a union not just of a woman and man but of two families, clans, and sometimes villages and empires. Naturally, new families were established from preexisting ones, and the link between the old and the new was important for generational continuity. Thus, the Karanko of Sierra Leone had a proverb: *Soron i la ko yolke*, meaning "One's birth is like a chain." Only through family formation could humans guarantee generational continuity because the African race would have been wiped out of existence without marriage, procreation, and family organization.

The most prevalent type of family in ancient Africa was the extended family. An extended family consists of numerous families that descend from a single ancestor. Most extended families, often made up of several generations, lived in compounds, with different huts belonging to individual families. New family compounds were established when members of an extended family migrated to another part of the town or an entirely new settlement. The history of several communities in Africa is therefore replete with references to migration. Also, new communities, which later developed into large human settlements, were sometimes founded by migratory families. Among the Yoruba of southwestern Nigeria, some families were exclusively responsible for producing the king because the oral history of the community indicates that their forefathers were responsible for establishing the community and laying the foundation of its culture and tradition.

The family played a significant role in determining the social, economic, and political status or standing of an individual within the larger community. In both theory and practice, an individual's behavior represented the attitude and general character of the family. The reason for this is simple: The family was a vehicle for socialization. All members conformed to certain modes or patterns of behavior that had been laid down by the family's founders or ancestors. Human socialization began with the family, which molded its members in important ways. A Yoruba saying, *Ile la tin ko eso r' ode* ("Charity begins at home"), indicated that the household molded and determined the public attitude and disposition of an individual. The oral history of African peoples is replete with references to families that are boastful, polite, humane, aggressive, or antisocial.

While the family served as the primary and basic unit of socialization, the well-being of the entire community was measured by the stability of its numerous families. Families marked by tension and crises risked neglect. Contracting a marriage was more difficult, and a person's social and economic standing in the larger community was threatened. Community-oriented opportunities, such as becoming chief, were limited.

All families were traditionally headed by the oldest male, because most African societies are patrilineal. Also, ancient African societies were predominantly gerontocratic, meaning that the oldest men and women were expected to guide and lead the community because of their wealth of wisdom, which comes with age. Again, among the Yoruba the oldest man who looked after the day-to-day activities of the extended family was called the *Olori ebi,* or "the head of the family." It was also the role of the head of the family to reduce friction among family members. Most families held regular meetings to discuss the family's affairs. The head of the family was the custodian of the family's heritage. He organized the family's affairs in accordance with the rules and regulations laid down by the ancestors. All these rules and regulations were parts of larger unwritten traditions and customs transmitted orally from one generation to another.

Most families had cults of gods and goddesses they worshiped daily, weekly, or yearly. The origins of some of these cults are obscure, but what is clear is that they were associated with the history of the family's ancestors or founders. Interfamily relations served as the vehicle for the dispersal of ancestral worship. The worship of some gods and goddesses spread from one community to another through family migration. Sometimes, other families borrowed or adopted gods that belonged to another family, or entire communities worshiped of the deities of the ruling family.

The family was also a unit of production and distribution. One of the major purposes of family formation was the need for helping hands on farms. Polygyny, or the practice of taking more than one wife, guaranteed large households when manpower was needed for agricultural production. The size of families was significant in determining an individual's status. Chieftaincies were sometimes conferred on people who could prove that they had a large household.

Not all families derived means of survival and livelihood from agriculture. Some were artisans such as wood carvers and blacksmiths. Some were entertainers, while others were diviners and healers. The skills required in these professions were transmitted from one generation to another. The endogamous nature of African families, where marriage took place within the tribe or clan, ensured that skills were passed from one generation to another within the family and was a significant factor in the survival and resilience of most ancient crafts.

Aristocratic families had slaves as members. In most cases, these slaves were bought and integrated into the family for the purpose of agricultural production. Theoretically, slave owners had the power to kill or sacrifice them to the gods. A female slave could be made a wife of her master, making the slave and her offspring free.

EGYPT

BY KELLY-ANNE DIAMOND REED

Ancient Egyptian society was structured around the family unit. The purpose of marriage was procreation and maintaining the family. Egyptian wisdom literature, or texts that contain instructions or philosophical dialogue, regularly speaks of a man prospering, establishing a house, finding a wife, and having children as ideal. In the Pharaonic Period marriage is sparsely documented, with no mention of any formal ceremony that recognized marriage. It is clear, though, that the idea of a household permeated society and that the woman entered into the household of the man. From this point on, the man and woman lived together. Very few texts testify to the idea of "giving a wife" in marriage, so a man may have found a wife in a variety of ways.

Among royalty diplomatic marriages took place. This arrangement either created an alliance between two separate kingdoms or indicated submission on the part of the ruler who provided the daughter. Likewise, father-daughter and brother-sister marriages were common within the royal family as a way of preserving the bloodline and maintaining political power.

Evidence is more common for divorce than it is for marriage. Marriage contracts, which concentrated on the property rights of each partner but did not, despite their name, comment on the ceremony of marriage, specified grounds for divorce. These grounds included the wife's infidelity or infertility, the man's dislike of the wife, or his desire to marry another woman. It is known that around 500 B.C.E. a wife could initiate a divorce, possibly on the grounds of her husband's infidelity. It is not known whether the Egyptians knew the difference between impotence and infertility in men. Regardless, women were always blamed for the inability to conceive a child. Both men and women were able to remarry after a divorce.

Men belonging to the elite class, including royalty, could take more than one wife if they could afford to do so and if the wives could contribute to the household. Because most women could, by working either in the fields or with textiles, it may have been more profitable to have more than one wife.

Papyrus marriage contract between the priest Pagosh and Teteimhotep, from Assiut, Egypt, Ptolemaic Period, 172 B.C.E. (© The Trustees of the British Museum)

In essence, one could create a free workforce. Little evidence points to polygynous relationships among middle- and lower-class populations. However, little information exists about the lower classes in general, so men from all classes may have had the option of having more than one wife at a time. No evidence shows that women could have more than one husband at the same time.

Related to the topic of divorce is adultery. Many ancient Egyptian sources suggest that men had access to women other than their wives. Some tomb scenes show children who are not biologically related to the wife; that they appear in the tomb scenes demonstrates that they were not seen in a negative light. The idea of illegitimacy did not seem to exist, though it was taboo to have intercourse with another man's wife. Literary works suggest that the punishment for doing so was death, primarily because then the paternity of a child could be in doubt. In turn, it was not socially acceptable for a wife to have intercourse with other men. The paternity of a child was important, because a family's assets would eventually be passed on to the children. This was also the case with the inheritance of the mother, but the maternity of a child was never an issue.

Once a man and woman resided together (or were married), they began to have children as soon as possible. A Twelfth Dynasty gynecological papyrus indicates that the ancient Egyptians knew how to conceive a baby but probably not the biological details. This same document reveals how the Egyptians found out if a woman was pregnant, how they tried to prevent miscarriages, their methods of birth control, and how they predicted the sex of an unborn child. Small anthropomorphic jars—that is, jars whose shapes have human characteristics—have been found that are thought to have contained the oil pregnant women rubbed on their skin to prevent stretch marks or to relieve the itching of the belly as it expanded through pregnancy.

Surviving literature provides many suggestions about where birth took place—in a room of the house, on the roof, in the courtyard, in the garden, or in a confinement pavilion made of plant material. Pottery shards from Deir el-Medina and paintings from Amarna show illustrations of this pavilion-like structure, which may have also been used for the mother's confinement after birth. The mother was to remain in seclusion for 14 days, according to one document.

At Deir el-Medina are other structures often called birthing beds. These beds often feature feminine iconography, including depictions of the deities Bes and Taweret, who were associated with pregnancy and childbirth. Historians differ in their interpretations of the beds' intended purpose. Some believe that mothers gave birth in them. Others have noted that the placement of the structure in the first room of the house would not suit this function. Likewise, these were permanent structures, but they would have been used only once a year at most, suggesting a different function. Another possibility is that this was where the mother was secluded after birth.

Childbirth was a precarious event. The infant mortality rate was high, and thus many magical spells were employed to help ensure the safe arrival of the newborn. Over 150 apotropaic wands—that is, wands having the power to ward off evil or bad luck—have been found that bear protective phrases regarding children. There is also evidence for adoption in ancient Egypt. The legal details are unknown, but the adopted child would have had access to the adoptive parents' inheritance and, in turn, would have been responsible for their burial and funerary cults.

THE MIDDLE EAST

BY KAREN RADNER

Tens of thousands of clay tablets recording legal contracts and letters give historians considerable insight into the lives of well-to-do urban families in ancient Mesopotamia, and the information matches that to be gained from the far-less-plentiful source material available for the other regions of the Middle East, including Persia. The spacious town houses of big cities such as Babylon, Sippar, and Assur did not house just nuclear family units (father, mother, and children) but also extended families that encompassed at least three generations. Family names, however, are found only from the late second millennium onward and only in the Babylonian cities. These family names were either professions such as "Baker," "Smith," or "Potter" or else the names of famous ancestors, such as the prominent scholar Sinleqiunninni, the compiler of the Epic of Gilgamesh, or the antediluvian sage Enmeduranki.

At the core of the household was the married couple, who lived in the husband's ancestral home. Normally the husband was considerably older than his bride, as men often married only after coming into their inheritance, that is, after their father's death. Women, in contrast, usually married as soon as they reached sexual maturity. Marriages were often not arranged by bridegrooms themselves but by their fathers. The new couple then lived at the groom's parental home, under his father's authority. The bride officially had no say in her marriage arrangement; the groom or his father reached an agreement with her father or, if he was deceased, the male relative under whose care she lived, usually a brother.

Marriage was expensive. The bride's family had to provide a dowry, which the groom's family was obliged to match with gifts. The occasion was celebrated with a lavish feast. As part of the wedding ritual the bride formally left her own family's home and entered the groom's house, severing links with her birth family and becoming a member of her husband's family. This included worshipping her husband's household gods and providing memorial service to his ancestors. The sharp divide between the husband's family and the wife's family was reflected also by the separate terms for maternal relatives, clearly distinguishing them from the paternal ones.

Divorce was possible, with the wife (and her dowry) returning to her birth family, but children stayed in the husband's care. The most common reason for divorce, though,

Scarab stamp seal and impressions, in lapis lazuli, depicting Ishtar, the Babylonian goddess of love, fertility, marriage, and childbirth. (Courtesy of the Oriental Institute of the University of Chicago)

was the couple's failure to have children, specifically a male heir to continue the family line. In most such cases, however, the couple did not seek a divorce. Divorce was costly because of the need to return the bride's dowry and often to provide additional compensation. It was also an inconvenience because it disrupted the amicable connection between the groom's and the bride's families. Thus, couples often found other ways to produce an heir. One alternative was for the husband to take a second wife, a decision that required the consent of his first wife. Another was to find a surrogate mother, to be chosen by the wife, who was considered the mother of the child. The most common and easiest option was to adopt.

In the Akkadian language, the word for family literally means "nest," illustrating the ancient Near Eastern concept of marriage and family life: Above all, the family centered on creating and bringing up offspring, since children were the focal point of the family and guaranteed its survival into the future. The mortality rate of babies and young children was very high, and children were considered gifts from the gods, their conception and well-being the subject of many prayers.

A typical family setup consisted of the head of the household, his wife, the husband's widowed mother, the husband's younger unmarried brothers and sisters, the couple's children, and a number of slaves, mostly women and some of them with children, usually fathered by the husband. These children, too, were slaves but could be made legitimate by adoption, often providing a solution to the lack of an heir when the wife could not conceive or carry a pregnancy to term or bore only girls. Otherwise legitimizing the children born by a slave to her master was unusual, though possible.

All members of the extended family were dependent on the head of the household, and this dependency implied that he was entitled to sell or pledge not only the slaves but also any other member of his family whenever he wished to do so. This right, however, was exercised only in extreme situations, typically bankruptcy. Slaves born into a household usually spent their entire lives there, and selling one of them often implied that the family was in dire straits. The manner of treatment of members of his extended family was at the discretion of the head of household. Certain slaves were not treated much differently from legitimate relatives, and some masters arranged marriages for male slaves, who were very likely their natural sons.

Polygyny, having two or more wives, was practiced in the ancient Near East. While the kings of Mesopotamia and Persia commonly had more than one wife as a way to guarantee the succession to the crown, evidence suggests that the practice of polygyny was limited, certainly because of the expense involved. Meanwhile, cohabitation with slave women who were not considered legitimate wives was common and probably standard practice for the average head of household of an urban family.

Many women died during a pregnancy or in childbirth, and widowers were normally quick to marry again. Widows, on the other hand, typically stayed single if there was a male heir. If that boy was too young to succeed his father immediately, his mother could act as his legal guardian. According to surviving testaments, the wife's position in these circumstances was elevated to that of "father and mother." A widow without children, however—most likely a young, only recently married woman—could also return to her birth family's house or else remain in her husband's home under the authority of his brother(s).

Historians know far less about conditions in the countryside. Many families living on rural estates as farmers were slaves. They belonged either to wealthy households in the cities or to institutions such as temples and palaces. The available information comes largely from institutional archives, and from these rosters of personnel historians learn little more then the basic family setup, which corresponds to that of the urban elites but without slaves: a couple with their children living with the husband's widowed mother and his unmarried siblings.

ASIA AND THE PACIFIC

BY MICHAEL ALLEN HOLMES

Family life in ancient Asia has been difficult to reconstruct based on archaeological records, for customs governing relationships can rarely be determined by the inspection of artifacts and objects. Written records, meanwhile, generally address the activities of royalty or of gods and goddesses, likewise revealing little of life among common people. As a result, much of what is known about ancient familial attitudes comes from knowledge about the spread and rise of religious philosophies.

Confucius (551–479 B.C.E.), whose Chinese name is K'ung Futzu, meaning "Master Kong," exerted extraordinary influence over the cultures of the East. In his philosophy Confucius focused on devising a system of ethics that all morally upstanding persons were to live by. While much of Confucianism specifies social rituals to be performed during certain times or on certain occasions (for example, the period of mourning to be observed after the death of a parent), the philosophy is rooted in broader principles, with attitudes such as righteousness and empathy highly valued. While Confucianism developed into various schools, particularly after Confucius's death, by the third century B.C.E., filial piety, or the child's respect for parents, was largely seen as the foremost of all virtues. During the Han Dynasty, from 202 B.C.E. to 220 C.E., Confucian beliefs were incorporated into the state religion because rulers looking to maintain widespread cultural unification found Confucianism's dictates regarding social behavior perhaps particularly appealing.

Related to the Confucian ideal of filial piety was the domestic worship of ancestors. Even before the time of Confucius, the Chinese people believed that the spirits of the deceased lingered in the afterlife and determined the fates of their descendants. For this reason, the Chinese people made—and in modern times still make—offerings of food, drink, and other items to their ancestors, often at shrines set up in their homes. In ancient times royalty and the wealthy were particular generous toward their ancestor spirits, presenting their gifts in elaborate bronze vessels. A king might ask his forebears to bestow good fortune not just on himself but on his subjects as well, such as through the provision of a good harvest or luck in battle.

In association with ancestor worship, fathers taught their children to respect ancestors fully and eternally; no man or woman would want to be ignored as a spirit. Thus, the young universally complied in serving their parents, and even the rich performed menial tasks for their parents, such as patching articles of clothing, rather than delegate those tasks to servants. Overall, the practice of ancestor worship and Confucian teachings about the primacy of family largely determined the extent to which unconditional and oft-demonstrated love has dominated the home lives of the Chinese.

A final prominent characteristic of Chinese domestic life in ancient times was the subservience of women. While little evidence exists about precisely how peasants arranged family matters, the lives of courtly men and women were often recorded in works of art and writing, such as *Admonitions of the Instructress to the Court Ladies*, dating from the fourth century C.E. Women were obligated to be dutiful, yielding, reverential, and humble; a precept of the time read, "A husband is Heaven, and Heaven cannot be shirked." Further, women were often denied education and exposure to the outside world, limiting their intellectual development and ensuring their future treatment as inferior. Although the historical origins of the practice are uncertain, Chinese women historically were literally given to men in arranged marriages and sent off to live with the husband's family.

In India the family had similarly sacred importance, as established by the love-based doctrines of Buddhism and as solidified by the popularization of Hinduism through the reign of the Guptas (240–550 C.E.). Many of the values and traditions of Hinduism, such as dharma, karma, and the transmigration of souls, were in fact first presented and advocated by Buddhists. Regardless, the Hindu caste system, which assigned people to a hierarchy of social categories, served to cement existing familial practices, for the caste system itself was maintained through indoctrination carried out within individual families.

While founded in love and respect, the institution of the Indian family, as in many other cultures, was a patriarchal one from as early as 1000 B.C.E. Within an extended family, the words spoken by the eldest males were essentially law, and these patriarchs were treated almost as gods. As in China, through arranged marriages a woman was brought to live with the extended family of her new husband. Within a family, brothers and cousins alike—both referred to with the same word, *bhai*—supported each other in all respects, sometimes even sharing a wife. Such fraternal unity was reinforced throughout Indian history by the moral teachings found in ancient texts like the Sanskrit epics Mahabharata and Ramayana.

In accord with the patriarchal tradition, women in ancient India were largely relegated to secondary roles. The code known as the Laws of Manu, which was developed probably between 200 B.C.E. and 200 C.E., legalized the notion that women were inferior to men, with fathers, husbands, and sons successively offering "protection." If a Hindu husband was himself wholly immoral, even to the extent of committing adultery, his wife was nevertheless expected literally to worship him. In fact, a woman was expected to obey her husband even if he commanded her to perform acts that would be degrading or self-destructive. Whether supervised, guarded, or confined outright, women were essentially the possessions of the men in their family. Further cultural expectations dealt specifically with reproduction and the bearing of children: Child rearing (along with constant attention to the husband) was specifically termed the obligation of women, and if no children were produced, the husband was within his rights to find another wife.

Women did retain a greater degree of power in certain isolated societies in ancient Asia. In South India, in fact, families have long been arranged matrilineally, presumably as far back as ancient times. Although even less is known about family structures in ancient Japan, because historical records developed much later, Chinese travelers wrote that in southwestern Japan in 238 C.E., society was arranged in matriarchal fashion. States were then under the rule of sorceresses; women, in fact, maintained rulership in Japan periodically until the eighth century C.E.

EUROPE

BY AMY HACKNEY BLACKWELL

Archaeological evidence provides relatively little information on the specific details of family structure in prehistoric

Europe. Archaeologists believe that during the Paleolithic and Mesolithic, society was organized into bands of perhaps several dozen individuals connected by loose kinship bonds. Subsequently, with the spread of agriculture beginning in about 7000 B.C.E., societies were organized into households, presumably occupied by members of a single family that included several generations, though we do not know the precise composition of each residential group. Such households were the fundamental social units throughout later prehistoric times.

Textual sources, despite their imperfections, confirm that ancient Europeans lived in extended family groups. Several generations of relatives would live in households together, along with their servants, if they were members of the social elite. The most important social unit was the clan, which formed part of a larger tribe. European peoples tried to keep wealth within their clans by marrying relatives to one another. When a German or a Celtic man married, he paid the bride's family a bride-price, a fee in the form of animals or goods that compensated them for the loss of their daughter. This bride-price often consisted of a herd of cattle, but among the Germans it could include a pair of yoked oxen, a saddled warhorse, a shield, a lance, and a sword. A German bride would present her husband with weapons as well. These gifts were meant to symbolize that the couple were partners in war and in work.

The Roman historian Tacitus described his impressions about Germanic family life in his *Germania.* He wrote that young men and women did not engage in romantic escapades before marriage and that both sexes married relatively late, after they had reached their full growth. He praised the chastity of Germanic women, claiming that all women entered marriage as virgins and remained committed solely to one husband for life. According to Tacitus, adultery was rare; if a wife committed adultery, her husband would cut off her hair, strip her naked, and drive her through the village with a whip. Modern historians, however, believe that many ancient Europeans did not especially value sexual fidelity or modesty. Ancient couples did live together without being married, and men often kept concubines. Polygamy was common among ancient European groups.

Celtic people recognized several legally defined forms of marriage. All types of marriage were designed to ensure that resulting children would be cared for; the permanence of the union was not the primary consideration. Some couples declared their intention to marry through handfasting, or engagement; if they had sex before the end of the engagement, they were automatically considered married. Some couples entered into temporary marriages that would dissolve at a prearranged time. A couple could agree to a union in which the man was allowed to visit the woman at her home with the consent of her family, but this union was not a true marriage. In another kind of union the man visited the woman at home without the knowledge of her family.

There were several types of formal marriage, distinguished by which partner brought property into the union. Women could own property and keep it after marriage; a woman who owned property in her own right had more power than one with no property. Marriages involving property were usually arranged between partners of similar social

IRISH MYTHICAL COUPLES

Irish myths contain numerous depictions of married couples and lovers. The women in these stories come across as tough and outspoken, and they are as sexually aggressive as men. Ireland's great prose epic the *Táin bó Cúailnge*, or *Cattle Raid of Cooley*, is mainly about a domestic dispute. A married couple, the husband Ailil and the wife Medb (Maeve), get into an argument over which one of them owns the most property; the dispute escalates into a nationwide war over a bull. Medb considers herself her husband's equal in war and wealth, bargaining with neighboring kings for military aid against her husband and even promising them her own "friendly thighs" as payment. She rides to battle and strikes fear in the hearts of all her enemies.

Another mythical wife, Derdriu, is promised in marriage to the old king Conchobar, but when she meets the handsome young hero Noisiu, she runs off with him. When Conchobar kills Noisiu, Derdriu sings a heartbreaking song of lament in which she praises her lover's beauty, courage, and generosity. She never smiles again. Conchobar, piqued at her lack of interest in him, decides to share her with a neighboring king. Rather than submit, she leaps out of a chariot and smashes her head to bits on a stone.

When the Irish hero Cuchulainn meets the girl Emer, the first thing he does is peer down her dress and remark, "I see a sweet country. I could rest my weapon there." She is not at all offended but refuses to submit to his advances until he performs a series of tasks she sets him—killing a hundred men at every ford on a river, striking down three groups of nine men with a single stroke, and going without sleep for half the year. Until he does these deeds, she will not have him.

In Irish mythology, Irish heroines are tough even when they are pregnant. In one story, the goddess Macha takes human form and marries a man. He is so proud of her legs that he forces her to run a race against the king's chariot when she is nine months pregnant. She ties with the chariot but goes into labor at the finish line. As she gives birth, she curses the audience, announcing that the descendants of the men who heard her scream would suffer the pain of labor at their most desperate moments.

class. Celtic husbands had to pay a bride-price to the family of the bride. The bride kept a portion of this bride-price, which was considered her property while she was married. If the marriage ended through the husband's fault, the woman kept her portion of the bride-price. If the wife were to blame for the end of the marriage, the husband took the property back. Celtic women were allowed to reject prospective husbands and were not forced to marry men they did not want.

As Christianity spread through Europe in the 300s and 400s, Europeans adopted some Christian marital practices. They stopped allowing marriages between close relatives, such as cousins, and discouraged unmarried couples from living together. Divorce was common among ancient Europeans and carried no social stigma. A woman was allowed to divorce her husband if he failed to support her, lied to her, struck her, became impotent, or slept with another woman. A man could divorce his wife for being unfaithful, stealing, shaming him, performing an abortion on herself, or smothering her infant.

Ancient people had no effective means of contraception, so women typically bore many children during their lives. Most women gave birth assisted by female family members or midwives; the ancient Germans and Celts did not have effective doctors. Ancient Europeans did not understand the mechanisms of birth and had few useful treatments to offer mothers. They could instruct women on breathing techniques, and they spent much of their energy reassuring and encouraging the mother. They could not, however, perform surgery, such as cesarean sections, without killing the woman. Many women and infants died in childbirth. If a newborn's mother died, the father quickly had to find a lactating woman to act as a foster mother or a wet nurse to feed the baby.

Ancient Europeans did not make a significant distinction between legitimate and illegitimate children. Fathers acknowledged the children of concubines, though they might not grant these children the same status as their children by official wives. Some ancient Europeans practiced infanticide, abandoning or killing newborn infants they did not want to raise. During peacetime Celts and Germans lived in small settlements containing several houses and surrounded by farmed fields, yielding enough food to feed the immediate clan members. The women and older family members handled most of the home needs, tending the fields and cattle.

Children grew up among many relatives who all lived close to one another. Each German household was headed by a man who had power over the other members; he decided who would live where, who would marry whom, and which infants to raise. Children were not heavily supervised; Tacitus described Germanic children as "naked and filthy." The entire clan was responsible for raising all the clan's children. The relationship between uncles and nephews was especially strong; men took particular care of the sons of their sisters. Children often went to live as foster children in the homes of relatives, especially their uncles.

Warfare was a family affair. Young men learned the art of war from their fathers and uncles. The men within a clan held ranks based on their skill at fighting and on their leadership ability. Family members stood by one another in battle and were bound to avenge the deaths of kinsmen. Chiefs would choose young male relatives to march next to them everywhere, both during battles and in more peaceable activities. Relatives defended one another in fights; young men who allowed their older male relatives or chiefs to die were dishonored. Wives and children were expected to cheer for their men as they marched to battle and to treat their men's wounds. Family honor was extremely important. European peoples readily entered into feuds with other clans over insults or murders, but they also readily ended them after a suitable payment of cattle.

GREECE

BY CHRISTOPHER BLACKWELL

No word in the ancient Greek language corresponds closely to the English word *family*. The Greek *genos* (the root of such English words as *genealogy* and *genetics*) refers to a tribe, or widely extended family. The fundamental unit of Greek domestic life was the *oikos*, or "household," consisting of all the people who lived together. Some were bound by kinship, but others, such as slaves, were bound by social, legal, or economic ties.

The legal and traditional head of the *oikos* was the senior man. He was the *kurios*, the legal lord of the household, with power over and responsibility for all its members. The senior woman of the household, usually the wife of the *kurios* but sometimes his mother or sister, tended to have day-to-day responsibility for the food supply and cooking, making and mending clothing, arranging for domestic chores, caring for infants, educating the younger male children and all the female children, and training and disciplining the slaves.

Households tended to be patrilocal, meaning that when a man and woman married, the woman moved into the man's household. Consequently, while the household often contained many members related by blood (aunts, uncles, grandparents), they were more often related to the man of the house than to the woman. Marriage involved the transfer of a woman from one *kurios* to another, usually from her father to her new husband. In most Greek communities laws governed this process, because the institution of marriage affected inheritance and the citizen status of children. Thus it was a concern of the whole community. For example, in Athens during the fifth century B.C.E. the law forbade marriage between an Athenian citizen man and the daughter of a noncitizen. (Women did not formally enjoy citizenship, even under the democratic constitution of Athens.)

Marriage often involved the exchange of gifts, sometime in two directions. A potential husband offered bride gifts to his potential father-in-law, which served to establish the suitor as economically and socially suitable. The future father-in-law, in turn, promised a dowry, a certain amount of property that accompanied his daughter into marriage. The dowry was, after the marriage, available to the new husband for his use but nevertheless belonged in a certain sense to the wife. If the husband divorced her, or she divorced him, the dowry was to be repaid to her father.

Weddings were religious ceremonies, in most Greek communities involving a triad of goddesses. Artemis was invoked, as the goddess overseeing a young woman's transition from girlhood to womanhood. So, too, were Hera, the goddess overseeing the institution of marriage, and Aphrodite, responsible for the sexual and erotic aspects of marriage. Weddings usually took place at the house of the bride's father, ending with a public procession to the husband's house; the procession was often accompanied by a crowd of celebrants shouting bawdy jokes. At the husband's house was a ceremony of *katachusma*, a "uniting" of the bride with the new household. This ceremony was also used when new slaves were brought into a house, which may shed some light on assumptions about marriage. The age of marriage differed in different communities, but the general practice was for young women to marry between the ages of 16 and 23 and men to marry in their 20s or 30s. Marriages between much older men and much younger women were relatively common.

Childbirth was generally left in the hands of women, either relatives of the mother-to-be or midwives. Male doctors seem to have been involved only rarely, though the ancient medical writers, all of whom were male, left some treatises on childbirth. Soranus, writing in the first century C.E., describes childbirth as taking place on a birthing chair or on a hard bed (the latter when the woman was too weak to sit). Given the limits of ancient medical knowledge, his treatise is responsible and humane, emphasizing the importance of breathing, of having the midwife reassure the mother, and of taking care not to embarrass the mother. Estimates vary as to how many women died in childbirth, ranging from a high of 25 of every 1,000 women to a low of five of 20,000. The figure surely varied according to the prosperity of the family, if only because more prosperous women would likely be better fed and therefore stronger.

After a baby was born, the midwife laid it on the ground to assess its health and vitality. If it was deemed worth rearing, it would be given to the mother or a wet nurse for feeding. Later, sometimes days later, the father displayed the baby to the members of the household, thus acknowledging it as legitimately his. If a baby was not deemed worth rearing, or if the husband refused to accept it, it might be exposed, that is, left outside to die or be taken away. There is no good evidence regarding how frequently infants were exposed. The practice figures frequently in literature, which may reflect how common it was but also may reflect merely a cultural anxiety about the practice.

Mothers generally breast-fed their children themselves, for this was considered the duty of a responsible woman of the house and most wholesome for the child and the mother's

Fragment of an archaic Greek stelae, with the heads of a mother and child. (Alison Frantz Photographic Collection, American School of Classical Studies at Athens)

relationship with it. Soranus recommended the hiring of a wet nurse when the mother could not produce enough milk or was too sick or exhausted to nurse her baby herself. The status of a wet nurse could vary, but evidence suggests that wet nurses could be valued members of the family. An Athenian woman of the fourth century B.C.E. named Hippostrate had this inscription carved on the tomb of her wet nurse: "I loved you while you were alive, nurse, I love you still now even beneath the earth, and I shall honor you as long as I live."

Divorce was possible, at the initiation of either a husband or wife. The community of Gortyn, a small city in Crete whose laws survive on an inscription from the 450s B.C.E., required that in cases of divorce a wife retained all property she brought into the marriage, as well as half of any profits or proceeds that came from that property, with provisions for judgment in the case of disputes. Existing children remained in the father's household in cases of divorce. Children born to a woman after she was divorced were to be brought to the father; if he accepted them, they would be reared in his household, but if he rejected them, the mother was free to rear them or expose them herself.

After the death of either spouse, the survivor was free to remarry. In the case of a widowed woman, she brought her own property into her new marriage, but any property she had held in common with her former husband belonged to her children from the first marriage. Through inscriptions on tombs ancient Greeks would sometimes try to speak to a dead spouse or praise them to passing strangers. One such inscription, from Athens in the fourth century B.C.E., contains a dialogue between husband and wife: "Farewell, tomb of Melite; a good woman lies here. You loved your husband Onesimus, and he loved you back. You were the best of wives, and he mourns your death. You were a good wife." And the wife's reply: "And farewell to you, my dearest man; love my children."

ROME

BY AMY HACKNEY BLACKWELL

The family was the most important unit in Roman social organization. Every Roman belonged to a family, and a person's ancestry was considered of great importance. Families were tracked along male lines; children took their fathers' names. Romans knew the details of their mothers' families as well. Kinship of any sort was considered a strong bond, and family members were expected to help their relatives when possible.

The head of a family was the paterfamilias. This was usually the father or grandfather of the family, who held a power called *patria potestas* over all his descendants, male and female. The paterfamilias technically had the power of life or death over his children; this power to kill children was rarely exercised during the republic and the empire, except in the case of newborn infants. The paterfamilias had to give consent for his children to marry; anything his children earned technically belonged to him. A young man could leave the *patria potestas* only if his paterfamilias freed him, either by dying or by deliberately releasing him. A young boy could become a paterfamilias through the death of his father, or a young man could remain under the authority of his paterfamilias even after he had become a husband and a father himself.

Girls were always under the authority of a male. A girl's father or paterfamilias had control over her actions until she married, but at that point her husband gained authority over her. If her husband died, her son or uncle or another male relative would become paterfamilias and keep control of the family. Roman women did, however, retain some rights. Depending on the details of her marriage contract and domestic situation, a Roman woman could retain some control over her own dowry and could transact business on her own. Some women ran prosperous businesses with their husbands' consents.

Marriages were often made for political or economic reasons; romantic considerations were often irrelevant. A paterfamilias would decide whom a woman would marry and would handle all arrangements of her property for her. Young men also had to follow the desires of a paterfamilias in choosing a bride. Roman women typically married for the first time around the age of 18. Men married later, in their late 20s or early 30s, after they had spent some time in military service and had established a career. June was the most popular month for weddings. A bride dressed in a white tunic and wore a flame-colored scarf and shoes. The wedding took place in the bride's father's house. After the ceremony and the feast, the bridal party walked in procession to the groom's house, where the groom carried the bride over the threshold.

There were several different types of marriage. *Confarreatio* was the oldest style of marriage; it could be contracted only between two patricians (members of the Roman nobility), and it put the bride entirely under her husband's control, or *manus*. It was very difficult to dissolve through divorce. By the time of the Roman Republic (509–27 B.C.E.) other forms of marriage contracts that were easier to end and that gave women more independence had become much more common, except among priests, who were required to marry *confarreatio*. A bride was expected to bring a dowry to the marriage; this property usually remained hers if she divorced.

Divorce was easy, unless the couple was married *confarreatio*. Either partner could end the marriage simply by informing his or her spouse that the marriage was over. Augustus (r. 27 B.C.E–14 C.E.) introduced the practice of using written documents to prove that a wife had committed adultery, but for the most part no formal procedure was necessary to end a marriage. Children usually stayed with their father after their parents divorced. Roman men were often absent from the home for extended periods while they went off to wars or conducted business overseas. They expected their wives to maintain the home while they were gone.

Romans wanted children to carry on their names and care for them in their old age. Though they preferred biological children, they did not hesitate to adopt children from relatives or friends if they could not produce their own. People sometimes adopted children for political reasons as well; adults could even have themselves adopted if they needed a particular name or social class for some political purpose.

Most women gave birth assisted by female family members or midwives, though occasionally male doctors helped with difficult labors. Many women died during or after childbirth from bleeding, exhaustion, or infection. Many infants also died during the birth process. If a baby survived birth, the father or paterfamilias could decide whether to keep the child. If he decided not to keep it, the child would be left outside to die. Historians do not know what percentage of Roman babies were abandoned, but it is known that people were much more likely to expose girls, illegitimate children, deformed infants, and the children of slaves than they were to expose boys, legitimate children, or children of well-to-do families. If the parents kept the child, they celebrated its birth on its eighth day of life in a purification ceremony called the *lustratio*.

Mothers might breast-feed their own infants, or they might hire wet nurses to nurse the babies for them. Many people believed that women should not have sexual intercourse while they were nursing babies because it would harm their milk, so some wives hired wet nurses so that they could resume relations with their husbands. Women also knew that breast-feeding could delay the next pregnancy; some chose to breast-feed their own babies for this reason. Wet nurses might live with the family, or they might come to the house for regular feedings. Babies were nursed for two years or so, with solids gradually introduced during this period.

About one-fourth of Roman babies died of various illnesses before the age of one, but young children were not the only people at risk of sudden death. Romans of all ages were prone to dying of various illnesses for which there were no treatments as well as of accidents and injuries from war. Roman families were not surprised when their members died young. Despite this fact, there is ample evidence that Romans found the deaths of their loved ones just as tragic as modern people do. They spent a great deal of money on elaborate funerals, hiring actors to portray dead family members in a procession through the city streets.

Both boys and girls of wealthy people spent their early childhood in the home nursery in the care of women. They usually slept in the nursery until they were about 12 years old and could be given rooms of their own. Poorer children slept in much closer quarters, all inhabitants of a dwelling sharing a room. Many wealthy mothers employed slaves as caretakers for their young children. Corporal punishment was a common means of enforcing discipline.

THE AMERICAS

BY ANGELA HERREN

While we know little about family life in ancient North and South America, archaeological evidence gives us some indication of how communities developed. Studies of residential groupings suggest that families of the ancient Americas began to shift from nomadic to sedentary lifestyles with the development of agricultural practices. Many families lived in small villages or hamlets, and some larger populations with elaborate communal civic and religious spaces developed.

In the four corners region of the American Southwest, the area where Colorado, Utah, Arizona, and New Mexico meet, a lifestyle of hunting and gathering prevailed for the first millennium B.C.E. The ancestors of the Hohokam, Mogollon, and Anasazi peoples fished the streams and rivers and hunted elk, deer, antelope, rabbits, and other local animals. Seasonal gathering of nuts, berries, cacti, and other flora rounded out the early diet. In the first centuries C.E. the cultivation of maize and squash began to supplement the indigenous diet, and "pit house" villages sprang up around these agricultural areas. For example, the Mimbres people, a branch of the Mogollon culture of southwestern New Mexico, began establishing pit-house villages of 10 to 15 households around 200 C.E. Over the next thousand years more permanent architectural forms developed, and many of these early settlements expanded into communities of 200 to 300 people as local populations grew and additional families adopted a more sedentary lifestyle.

In ancient South America most families lived in small hamlets and villages, but larger residential settlements grew up around some of the more elaborate ritual centers. Like later Andean cultures, early societies probably maintained a moiety structure, divided into two separate, unequal but complementary parts. Families engaged in activities appropriate to their position in a stratified society.

At Chavín de Huántar, a highland site that flourished between 900 and 200 B.C.E., Andean families survived by hunting deer, herding llamas, and growing important staple crops like maize and potatoes. In addition to subsistence activities, many families contributed labor and artistic skills that led to the construction and decoration of the site's Old Temple (900–500 B.C.E.) and New Temple (500–200 B.C.E.). As society turned increasingly to Chavín's deities to maintain their subsistence economy, most families probably engaged in communal ritual activity to some extent.

The necropolises, or cemeteries, of Paracas culture (ca. 700 B.C.E.–200 C.E.), discovered along the south coast of Peru, provide information about the stratification of Andean society. Twentieth-century excavations along the sandy desert coastline revealed hundreds of mummy bundles buried in shallow shaft tombs. Paracas communities placed the body of a deceased family member in a fetal position within a basket and wrapped it in layer upon layer of textiles. The quality of the textiles, the size of the mummy bundles, and the goods and offerings wrapped in the bundles indicate a strong social hierarchy. Groupings of individuals in burial may indicate familial or social relationships.

As they had at Chavín de Huántar, early Andeans built residential structures near important ceremonial buildings at the site of Moche (ca. 1–600 C.E.) on the north coast of Peru. Between two large mud-brick pyramids known as the Huaca del Sol and Huaca de la Luna, archaeologists unearthed a series of housing compounds. Plazas and streets connected the patios and rooms where Moche families lived and worked. Moche ceramics depict the basic forms of housing. Using construction techniques still employed today, the Moche built adobe structures as well as simple houses of matting supported by poles. Using a naturalistic representational style, the Moche created tens of thousands of ceramic vessels that document many aspects of Moche life. Images of women weaving, male and female copulation, and childbirth may represent some aspects of daily family life.

The highland site of Tiahuanaco (ca. 300 B.C.E.–1100 C.E.) contains one of the largest residential groupings of the ancient Americas. Archaeologists estimate populations as high as 30,000 to 60,000. Most families lived outside the moat that surrounded Tiahuanaco's ceremonial core. Only the highest political and religious practitioners occupied the city center. Excavations indicate that during the period of around 400–1100 C.E., residential neighborhoods, like the ceremonial core, were oriented to the cardinal directions. Archaeologists theorize that Tiahuanaco society consisted of three classes: a governing group of lineages composed of warrior elites who held political and religious offices; a middle class of artisans, who worked as retainers of the ruling lineages; and a commoner class of farmers, herders, and fishers, who sustained the economic system.

Early Mesoamericans practiced settled agriculture as early as around 2000 B.C.E. and developed more complex societies in the first millennium B.C.E. During the first 500 years C.E. small settlements grew, interacted with one another, and gave rise to bustling urban cities like Teotihuacán. Beginning about 1500 B.C.E. the Olmec began establishing major centers at the Gulf Coast sites of San Lorenzo, La Venta, Laguna de los Cerros, and Tres Zapotes, a region often referred to as the Olmec "heartland." Archaeological studies indicate that families typically lived in small wattle-and-daub houses with thatched palm roofs, similar to those built near these sites today. They clustered their houses around a central patio, where the community performed various tasks and grew maize nearby. At the larger sites, like San Lorenzo, excavations have revealed more elaborate housing complexes inhabited by the ruler, his family, and attendants. Like the palaces of the elite, these residences occupied a prime location very close to the ritual center. Olmec culture was far-reaching, and families also lived in rural villages in central Mexico and surrounding regions.

Early inhabitants of the Pacific coastal region, the ancestors of the Maya, established some of the first settled communities in the Maya area between 2000 to 1000 B.C.E. Over the next millennium societies in this region developed political and social complexity, with the emergence of Maya civilization between ca. 400 B.C.E. and 100 C.E. Many families practiced swidden, or slash-and-burn, agriculture and settled at early sites like Izapa, Kaminaljuyú, Takalik Abaj, El Baúl, Uaxactún, Tikal, El Mirador, and Cerros.

Our knowledge of West Mexico during the ancient period comes primarily from objects recovered from shaft tombs. A variety of ceramic vessels, figurines, and objects found in the modern Mexican states of Colima, Jalisco, and Nayarit, as well as near the Mezcala River, provide valuable information about West Mexican architecture, spiritual beliefs, and society. In Nayarit many tombs contained pairs of male and female ceramic figures that may have accompanied married couples in the tomb. The painted slip on the figures details the elaborate accoutrement of the matching costumes, and the pairs often hold musical instruments.

Early inhabitants of Teotihuacán, a central Mexican site that flourished ca. 150–600 C.E., laid out their city on a grid plan with residential compounds of various sizes flanking the elaborate pyramid structures of the ceremonial core. Walls surrounded each residential compound with a single entry offering access to the many dwellings within. Each grouping included three shrines and a platform for ritual activities. Consistency in materials and structure suggests state-sponsored building. The most elaborate apartment complexes contained painted fresco murals depicting warfare, deities, and sacrifice. Populations have been estimated as high as 125,000.

See also AGRICULTURE; ART; ARCHITECTURE; BUILDING TECHNIQUES AND MATERIALS; CHILDREN; CITIES; CLOTHING AND FOOTWEAR; CRAFTS; EDUCATION; EMPIRES AND DYNASTIES; GENDER STRUCTURES AND ROLES; HEALTH AND DISEASE; HUNTING, FISHING, AND GATHERING; LAWS AND LEGAL CODES; LITERATURE; MIGRATION AND POPULATION MOVEMENTS; OCCUPATIONS; RELIGION AND COSMOLOGY; SETTLEMENT PATTERNS; SLAVES AND SLAVERY; SOCIAL ORGANIZATION; TEXTILES AND NEEDLEWORK; TOWNS AND VILLAGES; WAR AND CONQUEST.

The Middle East

A Collection of Contracts from Mesopotamia, excerpts, ca. 2300–428 B.C.E.

VIII. Marriage

Contract for Marriage, Reign of Shamshu-ilu-na, ca. 2200 B.C.E.

RIMUM, son of Shamkhatum, has taken as a wife and spouse Bashtum, the daughter of Belizunu, the priestess (?) of Shamash, daughter of Uzibitum. Her bridal present shall be _____ shekels of money. When she receives it she shall be free. If Bashtum to Rimum, her husband shall say, "You are not my husband," they shall strangle her and cast her into the river. If Rimum to Bashtum, his wife, shall say, "You are not my wife," he shall pay ten shekels of money as her alimony. They swore by Shamash, Marduk, their king Shamshu-ilu-na, and Sippar.

Contract for Marriage, Thirteenth year of Nebuchadnezzar II, 591 B.C.E.

Dagil-ili, son of Zambubu, spoke to Khamma, daughter of Nergal-iddin, son of Babutu, saying: "Give me Latubashinni your daughter; let her be my wife." Khamma heard, and gave him Latubashinni, her daughter, as a wife; and Dagil-ili, of his own free will, gave Ana-eli-Bel-amur, a slave, which he had bought for half a mana of money, and half a mana therewith to Khamma instead of Latubashinni, her daughter. On the day that Dagil-ili another wife shall take, Dagil-ili shall give one mana of money unto Latubashinni, and she shall return to her place—her former one. [Done] at the dwelling of Shum-iddin, son of Ishi-etir, son of Sin-damaqu.

IX. Divorce

Contract for Divorce, Third year of Nabonidus, 552 B.C.E.

NA'ID-MARDUK, son of Shamash-balatsu-iqbi, will give, of his own free-will, to Ramua, his wife, and Arad-Bunini, his son, per day four *qa* of food, three *qa* of drink; per year fifteen *manas* of goods, one *pi* sesame, one *pi* salt, which is at the storehouse. Na'id-Marduk will not increase it. In case she flees to Nergal [i.e., she dies], the flight shall not annul it. [Done] at the office of Mushezib-Marduk, priest of Sippar.

From: George Aaron Barton, "Contracts." In *Assyrian and Babylonian Literature: Selected Transactions*, with a Critical Introduction by Robert Francis Harper (New York: D. Appleton and Company, 1904), pp. 256–276.

The Middle East

Herodotus: Excerpt from The History of the Persian Wars, *ca.* 430 B.C.E.

I.196: Of their customs, whereof I shall now proceed to give an account, the following (which I understand belongs to them in common with the Illyrian tribe of the Eneti) is the wisest in my judgment. Once a year in each village the maidens of age to marry were collected all together into one place, while the men stood round them in a circle. Then a herald called up the damsels one by one and offered them for sale. He began with the most beautiful. When she was sold for no small sum of money, he offered for sale the one who came next to her in beauty. All of them were sold to be wives. The richest of the Babylonians who wished to wed bid against each other for the loveliest maidens, while the humbler wife-seekers, who were indifferent about beauty, took the more homely damsels with marriage-portions.

For the custom was that when the herald had gone through the whole number of the beautiful damsels, he should then call up the ugliest—a cripple, if there chanced to be one—and offer her to the men, asking who would agree to take her with the smallest marriage-portion. And the man who offered to take the smallest sum had her assigned to him. The marriage-portions were furnished by the money paid for the beautiful damsels, and thus the fairer maidens portioned out the uglier. No one was allowed to give his daughter in marriage to the man of his choice, nor might any one carry away the damsel whom he had purchased without finding bail really and truly to make her his wife; if, however, it turned out that they did not agree, the money might be paid back. All who liked might come even from distant villages and bid for the women. This was the best of all their customs, but it has now fallen into disuse. They have lately hit upon a very different plan to save their maidens from violence and prevent their being torn from them and carried to distant cities, which is to bring up their daughters to be courtesans. This is now done by all the poorer of the common people, who since the conquest have been maltreated by their lords and have had ruin brought upon their families.

From: Herodotus, *The History*, trans. George Rawlinson (New York: Dutton and Co., 1862).

Asia and the Pacific

Kautilya: Excerpt from the Arthashastra, ca. 250 B.C.E.

Book III, Chapter 2, Concerning Marriage and Women

Marriage is the basis of all disputes. The giving in marriage of a virgin well adorned is called "*Brahma*-marriage." The joint performance of sacred duties by a man and a woman is known as "*prajapatya*-marriage." The giving in marriage of a virgin for a couple of cows is called "*Arsha*-marriage." The giving in marriage of a virgin to an officiating priest in a sacrifice is called "*Daiva*-marriage." The voluntary union of a virgin with her lover is called "*Gandharva*-marriage." Giving a virgin after receiving plenty of wealth is termed "*Asura*-marriage." The abduction of a virgin is called "*Rakshasa*-marriage." The abduction of a virgin while she is still asleep and intoxicated is called "*Paisacha*-marriage." Of these, the first four are ancestral customs of old and are valid on their being approved of by the father. The rest are to be sanctioned by both the father and the mother; for it is they that receive the money paid by the bridegroom for their daughter. In case of the absence by death of either the father or the mother, the survivor will receive the money-payment. If both of them are dead, the virgin herself shall receive it. Any kind of marriage is approvable, provided it pleases all those that are concerned in it.

Means of subsistence or jewelry constitutes what is called the property of a woman. Means of subsistence above two thousand shall be endowed in her name. There is no limit to jewelry. It is no guilt for the wife to make use of this property in maintaining her son, her daughter-in-law, or herself, whenever her absent husband has made no provision for her maintenance. In calamities, disease and famine, in warding off dangers and in charitable acts, the husband, too, may make use of this property. . . . On the death of her husband a woman, desirous to lead a pious life, shall at once receive not only her endowment and jewelry but also the balance of the marriage-price due her. If after obtaining these two things she remarries another, she shall be caused to pay them back together with interest on their value. . . . If a widow marries any man other than of her father-in-law's selection, she shall forfeit whatever had been given to her by her father-in-law and her deceased husband. . . . No woman shall succeed in her attempt to establish her title to the property of her deceased husband after she remarries. If she lives a pious life, she may enjoy it. No woman with a son or sons shall after remarriage be at liberty to make free use of her property; for that property of hers, her sons shall receive. . . .

If a woman either brings forth no live children, or has no male issue, or is barren, her husband shall wait for eight years before marrying another. If she bears only a dead child, he has to wait for ten years. If she brings forth only females, he has to wait for twelve years. Then, if he is desirous to have sons, he may marry another. . . . If a husband either is of bad character, or is long gone abroad, or has become a traitor to his king, or is likely to endanger the life of his wife, or has fallen from his caste, or has lost virility, he may be abandoned by his wife.

Book III, Chapter 3, The Duty of a Wife

Women, when twelve years old, attain their majority, and men when sixteen years old. If, after attaining their majority, they prove disobedient to lawful authority, women shall be fined fifteen *panas*, and men twice the amount. A woman who has a right to claim maintenance for an unlimited period of time shall be given as much food and clothing as is necessary for her, or more than is necessary in proportion to the income of her maintainer. . . . Women of refractive natures shall not be taught manners by using such expressions as "You, half-naked!; you, fully-naked; you, cripple; you, fatherless; you, motherless." Nor shall she be given more than three beats, either with a bamboo bark or with a rope or with the palm of the hand, on her hips. Violation of the above rules shall be liable to half the punishment levied for defamation and criminal hurt. The same kind of punishments shall be meted out to a woman who, moved with jealousy or hatred, shows cruelty to her husband. . . .

A woman who hates her husband, who has passed the period of seven turns of her menses, and who loves another, shall immediately return to her husband both the endowment and jewelry she has received from him, and allow him to lie down with another woman. A man, hating his wife, shall allow her to take shelter in the house of a beggar woman, or of her lawful guardians or of her kinsmen. . . . A woman, hating her husband, cannot divorce her husband against his will. Nor can a man divorce his wife against her will. But from mutual enmity divorce may be obtained.

From: Kautilya, *Kautilya's Arthashastra*, 2nd ed., trans. R. Shamasastry (Mysore, India: Wesleyan Mission Press, 1923).

Europe

Tacitus: Excerpt from Germania

Marriage Laws. Their marriage code, however, is strict, and indeed no part of their manners is more praiseworthy. Almost alone among barbarians they are content with one wife, except a very few among them, and these not from sensuality but because their noble birth procures for them many offers of alliance. The wife does not bring a dower to the husband, but the husband to the wife. The parents and relatives are present and pass judgment on the marriage-gifts, gifts not meant to suit a woman's taste, nor such as a bride would deck herself with, but oxen, a caparisoned steed, a shield, a lance, and a sword. With these presents the wife is espoused, and she herself in her turn brings her husband a gift of arms. This they count their strongest bond of union, these their sacred mysteries, these their gods of marriage. Lest the woman should think herself to stand apart from aspirations after noble deeds and from the perils of war, she is reminded by the ceremony which inaugurates marriage that she is her husband's partner in toil and danger, destined to suffer and to dare with him alike both in peace and war. The yoked oxen, the harnessed steed, the gift of arms proclaim this fact. She must live and die with the feeling that she is receiving what she must hand down to her children neither tarnished nor depreciated, what future daughters-in-law may receive and may be so passed on to her grandchildren.

Thus with their virtue protected they live uncorrupted by the allurements of public shows or the stimulant of feastings. Clandestine correspondence is equally unknown to men and women. Very rare for so numerous a population is adultery, the punishment for which is prompt, and in the husband's power. Having cut off the hair of the adulteress and stripped her naked, he expels her from the house in the presence of her kinsfolk and then flogs her through the whole village. The loss of chastity meets with no indulgence; neither beauty, youth, nor wealth will procure the culprit a husband. No one in Germany laughs at vice, nor do they call it the fashion to corrupt and to be corrupted. Still better is the condition of those states in which only maidens are given in marriage and where the hopes and expectations of a bride are then finally terminated. They receive one husband, as having one body and one life, that they may have no thoughts beyond, no further-reaching desires, that they may love not so much the husband as the married state. To limit the number of children or to destroy any of their subsequent offspring is accounted infamous, and good habits are here more effectual than good laws elsewhere.

From: Tacitus, *The Agricola and Germania*, trans. A. J. Church and W. J. Brodribb (London: Macmillan, 1877), pp. 87ff.

FURTHER READING

M. M. Austin and P. Vidal-Naquet, *Economic and Social History of Ancient Greece: An Introduction* (Berkeley: University of California Press, 1977).

George Ayittey, *Indigenous African Institutions* (New York: Transnational Publishers, 1991).

Karen Olsen Bruhns and Karen E. Stothert, *Women in Ancient America* (Norman: University of Oklahoma Press, 1999).

Confucius, *The Analects of Confucius*, trans. Arthur Waley (New York: Vintage Books, 1989).

Jack Goody, *The European Family: An Historico-Anthropological Essay* (Oxford, U.K.: Blackwell Publishers, 2000).

Rosalind M. Janssen and Jac. J. Janssen, *Growing Up in Ancient Egypt* (London: Rubicon Press, 1990).

M. R. Lefkowitz and M. B. Fant, *Women's Life in Greece and Rome* (Baltimore, Md.: Johns Hopkins University Press, 1982).

Lynn Meskell, *Private Life in New Kingdom Egypt* (Princeton, N.J.: Princeton University Press, 2002).

Arthur Phillips, *Survey of African Marriage and Family Life* (Oxford: Oxford University Press, 1953).

H. K Schneider, "Kinship and Lineage Amongst the Yoruba," *Africa* 25 (October 4, 1955): 352–374.

Jo-Ann Shelton, *As the Romans Did*, 2nd ed. (New York: Oxford University Press, 1998).

Marten Stol, "Private Life in Ancient Mesopotamia." In *Civilizations of the Ancient Near East*, ed. J. M. Sasson (New York: Charles Scribner's Sons, 1995).

festivals

INTRODUCTION

Ancient peoples were highly dependent on their natural environment. Rather than conquering it, they usually learned to find ways to make peace with it and try to understand their place within the natural world. Many of the festivals ancient peoples took part in served the purpose of reflecting their cosmology, or understanding of the origins and structure of the world.

Throughout the ancient world, festivals of various sorts were held in conjunction with natural events. In colder northern climates, for example, the course of people's lives was dictated by the cycle of the seasons, and even in warmer climates, cycles of flooding and dry seasons dictated many activities. Thus, many festivals were held to celebrate such events as the solstice in spring and fall and the equinox in summer and winter. Because many early calendars were structured according to the moon and its phases, many festivals were held in conjunction with a new moon. Major life events, such as the initiation of children into the adult community, were also a cause for celebration and festivals. Some early harvest festivals in the fall evolved into Halloween, and the roots of many modern-day Christmastime celebrations extend back to ancient winter festivals. The beginning of May, when warmer weather signaled the opportunity to start planting, was also a common time for festivals.

Many ancient festivals had religious motivations. Just as people were dependent on the cycles of nature, so, too, they believed that their fates depended on the will of the gods. It is no surprise, then, that many ancient festivals were organized and run by priests and religious leaders to give honor to a particular god or group of gods or to celebrate events in the community's shared mythological history. Some festivals, for example, were motivated by the desire for fertility as a way of ensuring the continuity of the community, so people set aside time to pay homage to a fertility goddess. In some cultures, such as that of ancient Mesopotamia, the purpose was to demonstrate the divine right to rule of kings by structuring the festival to show the role of kings as intermediaries with the gods. Throughout much of the world these gods and goddesses were local; that is, a particular deity might have been worshiped only in a local community rather than throughout the larger region.

Festivals served other purposes as well. Much as they do in the 21st century, they gave workers time off from labor, and they brought people together to help them forge a sense of community. By allowing behavior that would otherwise be frowned on (such as drunkenness), they served as a social safety valve, giving people a chance to "blow off steam." Just as in modern life festivals are often held in connection with sports and the arts, so, too, were festivals held in connection with sporting events in ancient Rome, and Greece was the source of the Olympic Games. Theater was also a time for festivities, with theatrical festivals held in ancient Greece and the Americas.

AFRICA

BY ROBERT SHANAFELT

In the ancient world festivals were generally special occasions for celebration and public commemoration of particular deities or religious ideals based on the calendar and the season of the year. Ancient Egypt had numerous festivals; less is known about ancient festivals in other African traditions, though the celebration of Jewish and Christian festivals in Africa goes back to antiquity. In all cases, it can be difficult to tell the precise origins of religious festivals because they involve sacred myths and oral traditions where other sources of objective evidence may be lacking.

In many instances, historians have to extrapolate backward from modern African festivals to their ancient roots. A good example is Kwanzaa, a modern African celebration that takes place during the Christmas season in the West. Kwanzaa is thought by some to be a replacement for the Christian traditions of Christmas, but this belief is incorrect. Kwanzaa is, in fact, a harvest festival, as reflected in the Swahili origin of the name, *matunda ya kwanza*, meaning "first fruits of the harvest." Thus, Kwanzaa is a seasonal celebration that has been practiced by Africans for thousands of years.

Ethiopia's Timkat festival, which has deep roots in tradition, is one festival about which much is known. Although it is a celebration of the Christian holiday of Epiphany (January 6), at which time the three kings brought presents to the newborn Jesus, it is also connected to the belief that the Ethiopian Orthodox Church is the guardian of Judaism's Ark of the Covenant, the chest that holds the Ten Commandments. The belief is that the ark is hidden at the site of the Church of Our Lady Mary of Zion, built over the ruins of a temple constructed by the ancient Axumite kingdom. While a great deal of uncertainty surrounds the fate of the ark, many people believe that it was stolen from the temple in Jerusalem by Menelik, the son of Axum's most famous historical figure, the Queen of Sheba, and deposited at the remote Christian outpost. During this festival thousands of white-clad worshippers parade through the streets carrying crosses as well as replicas of the holy object.

History, tradition, and sacred myth also come together in the annual Olójó festival held in the Nigerian city of Ilé-Ifè. Although historians date the origin of the city to later times, in Yoruba traditional accounts the world actually began at Ilé-Ifè, and the city continues to be at its center. As it is practiced in contemporary times, the Olójó festival is a festival of renewal, in which the king renews the power of the god of war and the goddess of wealth and fertility. The ceremony is highlighted by a ritual procession led by the Ooni, or king, of Ilé-Ifè and his entourage. The two end points of the procession are the shrines to the divinities, where offerings are made to ensure the political and economic well-being of the people.

A number of contemporary black African peoples claim Jewish decent. They practice Jewish customs, including Jewish rituals such as circumcision, which are traditionally celebrated during community festivals. Until recently, these claims were often not taken literally and certainly not thought to represent genetic realities that go back to antiquity. However, genetic evidence is starting to validate at least some of these claims. For example, a certain lineage of the Lemba of South Africa has been shown to descend from the Cohen ancestral line, the Kohanim, a line of descent traditionally ascribed to Jewish priests. In Ethiopia a group called Beta Israel also trace their roots to Judaism. They lived with their traditions for hundreds of years, but thousands immigrated to Israel in the 1980s. The Jewish feast days and festi-

Ethiopian Orthodox priests at festival of Timkat, celebrated since ancient times. (© Board of Regents of the University of Wisconsin System)

vals they respect include New Year, Yom Kippur, Sucot, and Passover. They also had a special day to celebrate the Torah, which involved bowing and making offerings on hilltops near their homes.

In southern Africa there is cultural continuity between scenes depicted on ancient rock paintings and the religious traditions of the people known as the Khoisan, or Bushmen. Although it is hard to say if their ceremonies fit the category of a festival, rock paintings dating back thousand of years shows their ancestors engaged in what appear to be ritual dances and hunts. Some paintings show scenes reminiscent of contemporary rituals. One interpretation is that the rock paintings were commemorations of trance states experienced by shamans during particularly important ritual occasions.

EGYPT

BY MARIAM F. AYAD

Festivals, or periodically occurring religious celebrations, were an integral part of life in ancient Egypt. The Egyptian word for festival was *heb*. Text and iconographic (pictorial) evidence provides us with details concerning the nature, timing, and duration of such celebrations. While a few were civic in nature, most Egyptian festivals were associated with the cult of a specific deity. In ancient Egypt each temple was dedicated to the cult of a specific god, or group of gods, such as the temple of Amun at Karnak, the temple of Hathor at Dendera, and the temple of Horus at Idfu.

Temple representations indicate that boat processions were an integral component of celebrating some of the major Egyptian festivals. Enclosed within a shrine, the cult statue of the deity would be carried out of the temple by priests. Because lay people had limited access to the inner halls and sanctuary of the temple, cult festivals became occasions for oracles. Supplicants would place their yes-or-no questions to the god. Forward motion of the shrine indicated a positive outcome. The evidence suggests that nonroyal officials took part in religious festivals both as priests and as festival leaders.

In an Egyptian temple, texts inscribed on the walls and doorways of the temple describe religious services performed for the benefit of its divine occupant. Such texts include not only hymns, prayers, and liturgies but also detailed lists of festivals or feasts associated with the temple. Often referred to as festival calendars, these lists provide organized and detailed accounts of the cultic and liturgical activities performed in the temple. Such calendars were probably copied from liturgical papyrus rolls kept in the temple archives. Dating to the Old Kingdom, the earliest known festival calendar is inscribed on the walls of the Fifth Dynasty sun temple of King Niuserre (ca. 2450 B.C.E.). Private tombs of the Old Kingdom also included brief feast lists.

Temple calendars indicate that the Egyptians celebrated annual festivals. Whether a festival lasted for one day or for several days, each had a fixed date within the Egyptian civic calendar, occurring on the same day, or over the same period, every year. Festival calendars also include brief accounts of the major religious events celebrated within the confines of a particular temple.

Wep Renpet (New Year's Day) was celebrated on the first day of the civic calendar (first day of the first month of the year, or first month of Akhet, day 1). This festival marked the New Year and celebrated the notions of rejuvenation and rebirth.

The festival of Wagy was originally a lunar festival that was celebrated on the 18th day of the first month of the civic calendar (first month of Akhet, day 18). This festival was funerary in nature, but evidence for it comes from both major cult centers and private tombs. From the Fourth Dynasty (2575–2465 B.C.E.) onward, this festival is included in feast lists inscribed in private tombs. Because the civic and lunar dates for this festival did not always coincide, the Egyptians eventually celebrated this festival on two separate occasions: once on its firmly set date within the civic calendar and at another time according to its actual lunar date.

The Opet festival, which was first celebrated in the reign of Hatshepsut of the Eighteenth Dynasty (ca. 1470 B.C.E.), lasted up to 27 days during the Twentieth Dynasty (ca. 1196–1070 B.C.E.). This New Kingdom festival took place in the second month of the civic calendar. The Opet festival included a procession during which the pharaoh-elect traveled to the temple of Amun at Luxor, where he would receive emblems of kingship from his divine father. During the course of this festival the pharaoh was identified with Horus, the divine ruler of the living, and was officially crowned as king of Egypt. Because of its importance in asserting the power and divinity of the Egyptian king, this festival held special significance in royal ideology and was closely supervised by state officials.

The festival of the god Sokar, or Choiak, was celebrated during the fourth month of the civic year. This ancient festival was dedicated to the cult of Osiris, the divine ruler of the afterworld. This festival, which was included in Old Kingdom private feast lists, linked Osiris both to the city of Memphis and to the god Sokar. Originally celebrated over a period of six days, this festival lasted for almost an entire month during the Late Period (712–332 B.C.E.). Since the Egyptian civic calendar comprised three seasons of four months each, the feast of Sokar served as a celebratory conclusion to the first season of the year (Akhet, or Inundation). By day 26 of the Sokar feast, Osiris was considered officially dead, and a period of four days marked by intense sadness and mourning followed.

Nehebkau was a festival celebrated on the first day of the fifth month. Similar to a New Year's Day festival and occurring just five days after the festival of Sokar, this feast became another occasion to celebrate rebirth. In the interim five-day period, the king, who was identified with Osiris in his death, was reborn as the living Horus. Because the concepts commemorated during this festival were very similar to those celebrated on the first day of the civic year, this festival shared many rituals with the Wep Renpet festival, the original New Year Day's celebration.

The festival of Min, the god of fertility, was celebrated at the beginning of the harvest season (Shemu); the festival of Min occurred in the ninth civic month. The date of this predominately agricultural festival was set according to the lunar calendar. During the course of this archaic festival, the king would harvest the first sheaf of grain and would ritually act as the provider and sustainer of his people.

The Beautiful Feast of the Valley was enacted during the 10th month of the year. Dating to the Middle Kingdom (ca. 2040–1640 B.C.E.), this Theban festival became very important during the New Kingdom. A major part of celebrating this festival involved a boat procession during which the statues of the divine Theban triad Amun, Mut, and Khonsu were ferried across the Nile to the temple of Hatshepsut at Deir el-Bahri on the western bank of the Nile. Because the city of the dead was also located on the western bank, this festival became an occasion to visit the tombs of deceased family members.

Because festival calendars are primarily preserved on temple and tomb walls, it should come as no surprise that the extant evidence is biased toward official religious celebrations, providing us with very little information on nonreligious civic festivals. One very important noncultic festival was a royal jubilee celebration, known as the Heb-Sed festival. Celebrated throughout the Dynastic Period, the Heb-Sed festival is first mentioned on ivory tags dating to the reign of King Den of the First Dynasty (ca. 2900 B.C.E.) and may have originated in a predynastic tradition. During the course of this celebration the king performed a series of physically strenuous rituals, possibly to prove his virility. While in theory the Heb-Sed was celebrated every 30 years, the evidence suggests that Egyptian rulers may have held it more frequently. Representations of the Heb-Sed festival are found in the sun temple of Niuserre, in the tomb of Kheruef at Thebes, in the temple of Amenhotep III at Soleb in Nubia, in the temple of Akhenaten in East Karnak, in the Twenty-second Dynasty (945–712 B.C.E.) temple of Osorkon II at Bubastic, and from the Twenty-sixth Dynasty (664–525 B.C.E.).

THE MIDDLE EAST

BY KAREN RADNER

In the ancient Near East there was no working week culminating in a fixed Sabbath or Sunday to provide time for rest and relaxation as well as worship. Instead, the course of daily life was interrupted by various festivals that were part of the cultic calendar, the schedule of interaction between a community and its deity. The importance of religious festivals to structure time is made most obvious by the fact that many month names are actually the names of festivals, for example, the Sumerian month name Ezem-mah-Nanna, "Great Festival of the Moon God," or the Akkadian month name Kinunum, "Brazier Festival" (celebrated at the advent of winter).

Festivals were those occasions when the gods met with the public, not just with the specialized personnel who served them on a daily basis. At the core of every festival lies an encounter with the divine, and those who together met with the deity gained a strong sense of group identity from the event.

In the third millennium B.C.E., in the period of early city-states, every city had its own distinctive calendar. This calendar reflected the individual schedule of each city's local deity, starting every year anew with the celebration of the new year, when the god bestowed his blessing on his people. Although the beginning of the year was often celebrated in early spring, the various city-states did not celebrate at the exact same time. In the northern Mesopotamian city of Ekallatum, for example, the New Year festival took place in autumn. Only with political unification came the merging and synchronization of these local calendars. Typically, the cultic calendar of the royal dynasty's city of origin was imposed on the entire country, while the most prominent festivals of regional centers were integrated into this calendar. As late as in the seventh century B.C.E. we have evidence that the Assyrian king not only participated in the New Year festival at the imperial god Assur's temple at the city of the same name, the cultic capital of Assyria, but also celebrated the New Year festival at Kalchu, in the temple of the god Nabû, and at Arbīl, in the temple of the goddess Ishtar.

The king's prominent role in all important festivals is the legacy of the personal union between political leader and high priest in the early city-states. It was the obligation of vassals personally to attend the main festivals of their overlords or at least to send a high-ranking deputy. The same was expected of allies, and from the diplomatic correspondence found at Amarna we know that Kadashman-Enlil I, the king of Babylon, felt slighted that Amenophis III of Egypt had not invited him to join him in celebrating his "great festival," in all likelihood the Sed festival, a sort of royal jubilee.

While those festivals that took place in a yearly cycle were closely connected to and reflected by the calendar, there are other festivals that were celebrated less often, for example, in a seven-year cycle, such as the Zukru festival to commemorate the dead of the Syrian city of Emar, or at entirely irregular intervals, such as the funeral of a king or the installation of a new high priestess after the demise of her predecessor. Some of these festivals could take several or even dozens of days, as we know from surviving texts that describe the programs for the events. It is not surprising to find that it is often the irregular festivals that are documented in this way: Their schedule was laid down in writing so that future generations would be guaranteed to hold the celebration in the correct way; an exact liturgy, down to the songs to be sung and the prayers to be recited, needed to be followed, as any mistake would have upset the meeting with the divine, with possibly fatal consequences for the community. As members of the elite, including rulers and priestly personnel, could reasonably hope to live to old age, many decades could pass before a royal funeral or an investiture ceremony was necessary. Hence, the installation of the high priestess of the storm god's temple at Emar is one of the best-known Near Eastern festivals. The event, as it was celebrated in the second half of the second millennium B.C.E., took nine days and involved the participation of the residents of the entire city, who selected one of their daughters to be given to the god as his human consort.

While the number of those who could enter the temple and meet with the god or goddess in his or her shrine was always restricted, the general public had the chance to come into contact with the divine when, as was an important part of many festivals, the deity left the temple on a procession through the city or even the country. The deity did so in the form of a statue and traveled by chariot or on a boat. So important was the moment when the god left the shrine that a series of omens was recorded that forecast the future from the way the statue looked or "acted" at that particular time. The divine statue on its vehicle provided the focal point, but the procession consisted of many participants: Priests, musicians, and singers formed the human entourage, together with attendants, who steered and protected the divine means of transport. The god often found himself in the company of other deities who partook in his festival. While the procession in itself was an important element of the festival, the outing would often lead to a particular destination, such as a garden residence, a game park, or another temple, where the deity was to undertake elaborate activities, such as hunting expeditions or wedding ceremonies; we probably should imagine this practice as a form of ritual drama, possibly similar to early Greek theater.

With the processions being the most public part of the festivals, the communion of selected individuals, as the representatives of their entire community, with the god in the privacy of the temple was at the heart of every celebration. The meeting was accompanied by sacrifices, consisting of food, drink, and incense; the community, or at least parts of it, benefited from these sacrifices because these provisions were in turn distributed in the form of public feasts. As the sacrifices included luxury food, such as wine, meat, and fruit, festivals were also occasions when the general populace had a chance to enjoy these otherwise rare treats.

Hence, ancient Near Eastern festivals served a variety of purposes. For the community, festivals strengthened the group's identity and provided public entertainment, holidays from work, and the opportunity to encounter the divine; for the leaders of the community, festivals served to legitimize and highlight their role as the intermediaries between the divine and the people.

ASIA AND THE PACIFIC

by Michael Allen Holmes

Throughout Asia many ancient festivals had origins in the natural world. As early agriculture rooted peoples in homelands, communities flourished not just because of individual efforts but also because of the intensified labor of extended family, friends, and neighbors. Meanwhile, humans became more dependent on the cooperation of nature—and more endangered by its caprices, as droughts, floods, and brutal winters could all lead to great loss of life. Festivals allowed communities both to recognize the powers of nature and to cement the social ties that allowed them to persevere through difficult times.

In ancient China most festivals featured some form of dancing. During the Shang Dynasty (ca. 1500–ca. 1045 B.C.E.) kings would dance to avoid incurring the wrath of the demons believed to cause droughts. During the ensuing Zhou Dynasty, lasting until 256 B.C.E., kings welcomed barbarians into their courts for the performance of dances. The men waved around the tails of yaks and also rods with pheasant feathers attached to the ends, likewise driving away destructive spirits. Among the masses in the Sichuan region during the Han Dynasty (ca. 202 B.C.E.–220 C.E.) general feasts and revelry grew so popular and disruptive that the government had to restrict such activity to designated festival times.

Popular Chinese festivals revolved around the changing of the seasons. The end of winter and beginning of spring were celebrated with particular vigor, amplifying widespread feelings of joy and renewal. Festivals at this time of year featured offerings to earthly spirits as well as human-oriented rites related to mating and fertility. The Chinese New Year, also known as the Spring Festival, generally occurred on the day of the second new moon after the winter solstice, thus falling during this celebratory time. While various changes to the time of the New Year were made by various rulers, the New Year was oriented as it currently stands by Emperor Wu in 104 B.C.E.

Another seasonal celebration still held is the Mid-Autumn Festival, which has several other names, including the Mooncake Festival. Falling in the middle of the eighth lunar month of the Chinese calendar (usually aligning with late September and the autumnal equinox), when the moon is especially bright, this festival is a celebration of the year's harvest. The general worship of the moon in China has been traced back through the second millennium B.C.E. During the Zhou Dynasty moon worship centered on the Mid-Autumn Festival.

An ancient Chinese festival unrelated to nature is the Duan Wu Festival, also known as the Dragon Boat Festival, commemorating the death of Qu Yuan (ca. 340–278 B.C.E.). Qu Yuan was said to be a patriotic minister from the state of Chu who was exiled by his deceived king. After long wandering and writing poetry near his hometown, he waded into a river and committed suicide when he learned that his state had been overrun by the state of Qin. Local people searched for his body in boats while scattering rice as an offering to his spirit until his spirit told his friends that a river dragon was eating the rice and that they should wrap it in silk. The honoring of Qu Yuan's death and the search for his body evolved into a tradition of dragon boat racing, held on the fifth day of the fifth lunar month.

In India many festivals over time focused on events of a mythical or religious nature, similar to Christian festivals in the Western world. Since the major Sanskrit epics are among the earliest surviving writings from the Indian subcontinent, the precise origins of festivals cannot necessarily be attributed to specific aspects of the annual cycle. Also, in certain parts of India seasonal changes were not nearly as prominent as they were throughout more northerly Asian regions.

The most prominent ancient Indian festivals, which in modern times are celebrated as Hindu festivals, serve as commemorations of mythical and sacred events. The majority of these events are narrated in the ancient Sanskrit epics Ramayana and Mahabharata, the former dating from roughly the third century B.C.E., the latter from a less certain date in ancient times. Both of these texts are considered not only great mythological epics but also compilations of much ancient philosophy and wisdom. Given the ancient origins of these epics, the festivals associated with events described in them have presumably been celebrated since ancient times. Some Indian festivals evolved from the more ancient recognition of the seasonal cycles.

Holi, also called the Festival of Color, occurs on the full-moon day falling in late February or early March and features carefree springtime revelry. The name is derived from a mythical event in which Holika was burned to death when her father, the king of the demons, tried to set fire to her brother, a devotee of Lord Vishnu. To commemorate the flirtatious playfulness of Lord Krishna, whose mother used color to darken the face of his fair-skinned consort Radha, Indians celebrate Holi by throwing colored powder and water at each other. The festival is understood to have originated in the agricultural celebration of the arrival of spring and its variegated colors.

Diwali, also known as the Festival of Lights and usually falling in October or November, is generally regarded as a celebration of the victory of good over evil. Specifically, in the Ramayana, Lord Rama returned victorious from a war with Ravana, a demon king, on this day. Upon his return, people lit lamps to reveal paths in the darkness. Also, in accordance with the Mahabharata, Diwali commemorates certain events associated with the goddess Shakthi and Lord Krishna's wife. Diwali celebrations generally involve lighting lamps and lanterns and sharing time with family and friends. In much of India, Diwali marks the opening of the New Year. The festival of Dussehra, also called Dasara and occurring roughly a month earlier, is closely related to Diwali, as it marks the day on which Rama actually killed Ravana. Other significant Indian festivals mark the birthdays of Lords Ganesha, Krishna, Rama, and Hanuman.

EUROPE

BY AMY HACKNEY BLACKWELL

The people of Europe celebrated festivals that marked the seasons dividing the year. There were eight main points of celebration. The summer and winter solstices (the longest and shortest days of the year, respectively) and the spring and autumn equinoxes (the days in the spring and fall when night and day are the same length) marked the year's turning points and were occasions for feasts and parties. The other four were festivals that did not fall on solstices or equinoxes and thus were usually scheduled for the full moon between these events. The Celtic calendar used both solar and lunar cycles, so dates for such festivals varied from year to year. Ancient Europeans divided the year into two halves, the dark winter half and the bright summer half. The festivals known as Samhain and Beltane in Ireland (but celebrated under other names throughout ancient Europe) marked the dividing lines between these two halves of the year.

The Celtic year began at the end of autumn and the beginning of winter, around October 31, when Celts celebrated the final harvest. This festival was known as Samhain in Ireland. On this date the spirits of the dead were said to walk the earth to visit their old homes. Gods were also believed to roam about the dwellings of the living, intent on doing harm. People lit large bonfires to honor the dead and protect themselves from evil spirits wandering the land. Young men lit torches and ran around the boundaries of their farms to protect their families and property from evil spirits. Families put out the fires in their homes and used flames from the communal bonfires to rekindle their hearths; they tried to keep these same fires lit for the entire year. Because the line between the living and the dead was blurred at this time, Druids believed that Samhain was the best possible time to predict the future.

Tribes gathered at this festival to hold political discussions, horse races, and markets, and to exchange spouses. Animal sacrifices were common, as people killed and ate animals fattened during the summer. In some areas of Gaul (modern-day France) and Germany people dressed in animal costumes and paraded about. In Roman Gaul this harvest festival blended with the Roman festival Feralia. People celebrated Feralia by leaving food on the graves of their ancestors and decorating their homes with apples. This autumn festival gradually transformed into the modern festival Halloween.

Ancient Germanic and Norse peoples celebrated a winter solstice festival called Jól, or Yule. Historians believe this name may have come from the Anglo-Saxon word for "yellow," possibly derived from sun shining off the snow or perhaps from the festival's purpose of bringing back the sun from the depths of the cold, dark northern winter. The festival occurred on or around December 21, the shortest day of the year. The significance of the winter solstice has considerable antiquity, as seen in the construction of the megalithic tomb at Newgrange around 3000 B.C.E., where the sunrise on December 21 shines directly down the entrance passage into the burial chamber. People celebrated with feasts, especially with roast pig, which may have been a sacrifice to the god Freyr. They decorated their homes with branches of holly and mistletoe and burned special oak logs in the fires; they kept these traditions after converting to Christianity in the medieval period. The ancient Germans also honored sacred trees at this time by sacrificing and killing male animals and slaves and hanging them from the tree branches. This practice may have influenced the custom of decorating trees for Christmas.

Imbolc was the ancient festival marking the end of winter. It was traditionally celebrated on the full moon halfway between the winter solstice and the spring equinox, which fell around February 1. This was the date on which people began to milk their ewes (female sheep), which gave birth around this time. Days began to grow visibly longer at this time, and people marked the coming of spring by lighting large numbers of candles and lamps. The Mound of the Hostages in Tara, Ireland, appears to have been constructed to identify the date of Imbolc; it is aligned to catch the rising sun that morning. Irish people continued to observe Imbolc after converting to Christianity, transforming the festival into Saint Bridget's Day.

The first day of spring fell on the spring equinox, around March 21. Celtic people traditionally sowed their crops on this date. Ancient Germans believed that their fertility goddess Ostara mated with the sun god on the spring equinox; her son Jól, or Yule, was born on the winter solstice. Ancient Europeans celebrated the return of spring around May 1, on the full moon between the spring equinox and the summer solstice. In Ireland this festival was called Beltane. At this point people celebrated the return of life to the soil and the beginning of the planting season. People lit enormous bonfires out of sacred wood and drove their animals past them to protect them through the summer. They decorated their houses with branches of hawthorn, the tree of hope and protection. This festival was particularly popular with young lovers, who gathered flowers, danced around maypoles, and spent the night in the forest cavorting with one another. Leaping over fires was believed to bring luck to all who did it, from pregnant women hoping for smooth deliveries to travelers embarking on journeys. This tradition was preserved in Germany as the May Day festival.

The summer solstice, or midsummer, fell around June 21. This was the longest day of the year, with a very short night; in the far north the sky hardly darkened at all on midsummer. Stonehenge in England is aligned precisely to catch the light of the rising sun on Midsummer's Day. This was an occasion for giant bonfires, dancing, games, and outdoor feasts. In some areas people walked their domestic animals around the bonfires to bless them.

The harvest festival, called Lughnasa in Ireland, fell on the full moon between the summer solstice and autumn equinox, usually around August 1. It was named after the

Celtic god Lugh, the god of the sun and agricultural fertility. The harvest season began at this time and lasted until the end of October. In some areas the beginning of the harvest was marked by gathering wild berries; if the berries were plentiful, crops would be too. Young people participated in games of athletic skill; horse racing naked was a popular sport in Ireland.

The autumn equinox fell around September 21 and marked the beginning of autumn. Numerous ancient stone structures were designed to catch the light of the rising sun on this date. The Druids celebrated the equinox by burning a large wicker figure that represented the plant spirit; some scholars believe that this custom was the origin of Julius Caesar's belief that Druids practiced human sacrifice.

GREECE

BY CHRISTOPHER BLACKWELL

Every ancient Greek community celebrated a number of festivals, *heortai*, throughout the year. These were simultaneously religious and social events. Festivals honored various gods but also provided occasions for members of a community or members of various communities to come together in celebration. There were other religious events during the year, recurring rituals of various kinds, and public sacrifices. Festivals stand out, however, because they were decidedly enjoyable occasions, never somber or grim, as certain other rituals might be.

Some of the oldest festivals had to do with the cycles of the agricultural year and were associated with divinities of the earth and the environment. The Mysteries celebrated at Eleusis, near Athens, honored Demeter and marked the end of winter. Citizens of Athens celebrated plowing with the Proerosia, planting with the Thesmophoria, and harvesting with the Anthesteria. Other festivals marked periods of transition in human life, particularly transitions during childhood and from childhood to adulthood. Athenian boys were initiated into the community at the festival of the Apaturia. This took place in the autumn at each of the small subcommunities of Attica. The three days of this festival included the Dorpia, a dinner feast ringing in the festival; a sacrifice to Zeus and Athena (the patron goddess of Athens); and the Koureōtis, the final admission of the young men into the community. Boys would participate in this festival at least three times during their childhood: first when they were small children; again when they entered the "*ephebate*," a period of military instruction for adolescents; and finally when they married.

Athenian girls were initiated into the community at the festival of the Brauronia, named after its location at a sanctuary in the town of Brauron near Athens, also called the Arkteia, or "bear festival." Celebrated in honor of the goddess Artemis, this festival involved Athenian girls between five and 10 years old who dressed as bears and gathered to perform dances. Scholars disagree on the meaning of this ritual, but many think it was an occasion to celebrate the "wildness" of young girls, who would eventually be "tamed" by marriage and take their position as women of the community.

Some festivals were purely local, specific to a small village or town. Others emphasized the relationship among towns, united into the larger political entity of the city-state, or polis. Athens, which was a political unity of the city of Athens with the many towns of the territory of Attica, celebrated this coming together, or *synoikism*, during the festival of the Synoikia and celebrated its unity and greatness at the Panathenaea, or All-Athens festival. The latter festival, in honor of the goddess Athena, began with a procession, or *pompē*, through the city; the procession involved all members of the community, including children, unmarried young men and women, soldiers, and resident aliens. During this festival the married women of Athens would present a new cloak, or *peplos*, to the statue of Athena in the Parthenon, having woven the garment collectively during the year.

The most famous of festivals among the ancient Greeks were the "agonistic" festivals, featuring competitions. These competitions fell into two categories: Gymnastic festivals had athletic competition, and musical festivals, having to do with the Muses, had competitions in poetry or drama. The most famous gymnastic festival was that in honor of Zeus, held at Olympia in the Peloponnese every four years beginning in 776 B.C.E. This festival, open to participants throughout the Greek world, featured competitions in foot racing (including a race in which runners wore bronze armor), chariot racing, boxing and wrestling, and weight lifting. So important was this Olympic festival that warring states regularly called a truce to enable participants to travel to Olympia safely. Other festivals of athletic competition were the Nemean Games, held in honor of Heracles; the Pythian Games, held in Delphi in honor of Apollo; and the Panathenaic Games, held in Athens.

Of the musical festivals, the most famous were the dramatic festivals at Athens, the occasion for the production and performance of tragedies and comedies. There were two main dramatic festivals celebrated by the Athenians, the Dionysia and the Lenaea. The Dionysia was celebrated in the spring, timed to coincide with the opening of the sailing season on the Aegean Sea, after the unpredictable storms of winter had passed. This festival was the occasion for Athens to show itself off to the rest of the Greek world, and it was open to all Greeks. During the period of Athens's naval empire, in the fifth century, their "allies," subject states, sent representatives bearing annual tribute, which was presented to the city of Athens in a public ceremony during the festival.

The focus of the Dionysia was the Theater of Dionysus, which was at once a theater and a temple. The democratic government of Athens arranged for public funding of plays, both tragedies and comedies. Each play was acted by two or three professional actors and a trained and choreographed chorus of citizens. Plays competed for prizes, with a panel of judges awarding prizes for best play, best actor, and so forth. A comic playwright would compete with a single play, but tragedians submitted four plays, a trilogy of tragedies, and a so-called satyr play. The Dionysia ran for five or six days.

The Lenaea took place in midwinter and was a smaller and more intimate festival for Athenians alone. There is evidence that slaves could attend performances at the Lenaea and even act in the plays. It is not clear whether women were allowed to attend plays at either of the major dramatic festivals. At both of these festivals and at other festivals throughout the Greek world, there were competitions in other kinds of poetry and music, especially choral singing and dancing, reciting Homeric epic, and performing on the double flute and the kithara.

Festivals generally served to reinforce community, through a shared enjoyment of art, through eating and drinking, and by means of other activities. Some festivals emphasized drinking, with drunkenness serving as a release. Others invited people to invert normal social roles, allowing slaves to order their masters around or men to dress in women's clothing. Some emphasized the shared history, real or mythological, of a community, such as the Oschophoria and the Deipnophoria at Athens, which involved reenactments of events in the mythology of Theseus, the legendary king of Athens.

After the fourth century B.C.E., during the Hellenistic Period, new festivals arose in parts of the Greek world, in honor of (and sponsored by) the dynastic monarchs who then held power over large territories; one such festival was the Ptolemeia, in honor of the Macedonian Ptolemies, the dynasty that ruled Egypt after the third century B.C.E.

ROME

BY AMY HACKNEY BLACKWELL

The ancient Romans celebrated numerous festivals, or *feriae*. These festivals served both as occasions to honor gods and as days off from work, since most businesses closed for the occasion. Rome's many priests and legal officials fixed the dates for festivals on the calendar. Some festivals had set dates, but others moved around from year to year. Many Roman festivals had their origins in older cultures and religions. Many of them also form the basis for modern seasonal and religious festivals.

Some festivals occurred on specific dates, but others were set monthly according to the phases of the moon and other signs. Every month had significant days. The first of the month, called the Kalends, was considered sacred to the goddess Juno. It was meant to coincide with the new moon. The fifth or seventh day of the month was called the Nones, and on this day the priest would announce that month's festivals. The Ides, sacred to Jupiter, occurred in the middle of the month and ideally coincided with the full moon. Priests set festivals to occur during the second half of the month because it was easier to track the moon's phases then.

The Bona Dea, or Good Goddess, was a goddess worshipped only by women, who considered her responsible for their fertility and the safe development and birth of their children as well as the fertility of the earth. She was often depicted wreathed with vines next to a jar of wine and a holy snake. Every year the wife of the consul or of the pontifex maximus (chief priest) and the vestal virgins (priestesses of the hearth goddess, Vesta) held a party to celebrate her feast day. The wealthiest women in Rome attended this party, where they drank wine that they called "milk"; an ancient and largely disregarded law forbade women to drink wine, so calling the wine "milk" was a way to acknowledge this law while disobeying it. In 161 B.C.E. Publius Clodius Pulcher, a man, dressed as a woman in order to sneak into the Bona Dea party. The Roman women panicked when they discovered this, fearing that all childbirth that year would be cursed.

The Magna Mater was the Great Mother goddess, also called Cybele. People believed that she made plants and animals grow and celebrated her festival in the spring. One festival in her honor involved cutting down a pine tree and placing it in her temple.

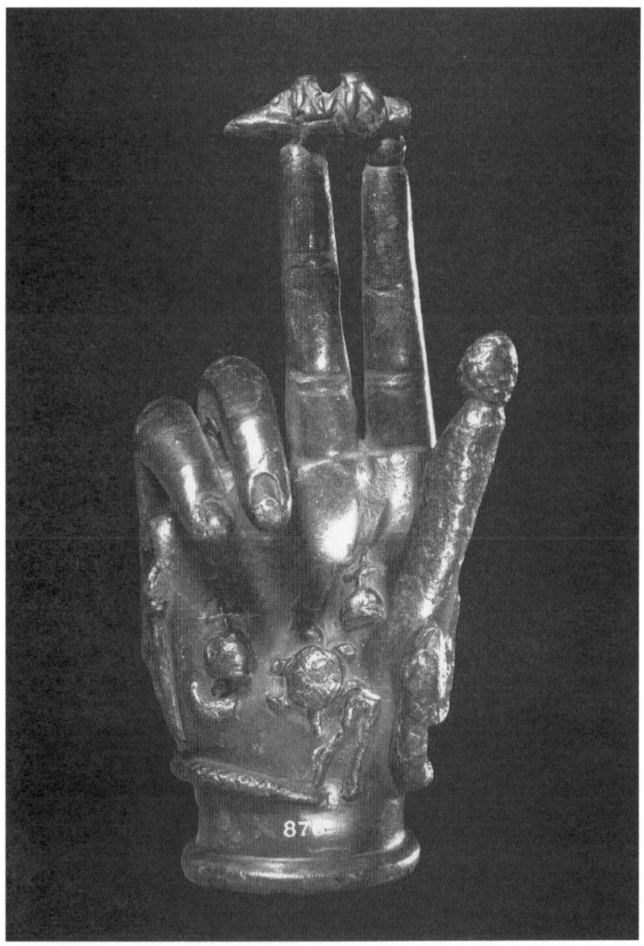

Hand of Sabazius, Roman (second or third century C.E.), found at Tournai, Belgium; such hands were associated with the cult of the god Sabazius and were carried in religious processions. (© The Trustees of the British Museum)

The Bacchanalia were festivals to honor the god Bacchus, called Dionysius in Greek. The Bacchanalia began around 200 B.C.E. as secret women-only festivals, but men quickly joined in. Because Bacchus was the god of wine, the festival included a great deal of wine drinking and could also involve wild sex and other unrestrained behavior.

The *ludi Romani*, or Roman games, were the games held every year to celebrate the festival of Jupiter Optimus Maximus on September 13. By the time of the Roman Republic (509–27 B.C.E.) the games went on for 10 days and included chariot races, boxing, wrestling, and many plays. Most of the events occurred in Rome's Circus Maximus, a giant arena.

The Lupercalia, held on February 15, honored the god Faunus and seems to have been named after a wolf god. Young men sacrificed a dog or goat at the Lupercal, a temple on the Palatine Hill, and skinned it. They then stripped naked, wrapped themselves in pieces of the fresh skin, and ran through the streets of the neighborhood hitting onlookers with strips of the skin. This treatment was said to enhance fertility, so women who wanted children made sure they were in the path of the runners.

Quirinalia happened two days after the Lupercalia, on February 17. This festival honored the Sabine god Quirinus, the patron god of Rome's Quirinal Hill and one of the gods associated with the founding of the city by Romulus. Quirinus was believed to watch over the government and citizenry of Rome, and the citizens were sometimes referred to collectively as *quirites*.

The Saturnalia, a feast honoring the god Saturn, or Saturnus, every December 17, was a major public festival. Modern scholars are not sure what exactly Saturn represented to the Roman people. Some suggest that he was responsible for the sowing of wheat and that the festival celebrated the successful completion of the autumn sowing. Romans celebrated the Saturnalia by performing a sacrifice at the temple of Saturn and then spending several days feasting. During the republic the Saturnalia lasted seven days. The emperor Augustus reduced it to three days, but most people continued to celebrate it for the full week. In addition to eating and drinking, people visited friends and relatives and gave one another gifts. The most notable aspect of the Saturnalia was the inversion of the social order. Slaves were given the day off, and their masters waited on them at meals for a change.

Several festivals celebrated the military and warfare. Festivals for the god Mars in March included sacrifices and horse races. Another festival in honor of Mars occurred on October 15. At this festival the army selected its best warhorses and ran them in pairs in chariot races on the Campus Martius, Rome's drilling ground. The right-hand horse of the winning team was killed with a spear on an altar dedicated to Mars. The priests then cut off its head, genitals, and tail. The genitals and tail were rushed to the Forum, where the horse's blood was dripped onto the altar of the Regia, one of the oldest buildings in the Forum. Meanwhile, at the altar at the Campus Martius, the priests conducted various ceremonies over the horse's head, including covering it with cakes. When they were done, they tossed the head to the crowd of onlookers. These onlookers came from two separate neighborhoods, the Subura and the Via Sacra, and they fought to take possession of the head for their own neighborhoods. Whichever team won took the head home and nailed it in a prominent place.

Romans celebrated numerous other major and minor festivals throughout the year. The Agonalia, celebrated in January and in other months, honored the god Janus. The Matronalia on March 1 honored Juno and was a day for families to give gifts to their wives and mothers. March 19 was the Quinquatria, a festival sacred to Minerva. The goddess Venus had a feast day on April 1. Mercury had his on May 15. In addition to formal festivals, many days were considered bad luck and people avoided conducting important business on them.

THE AMERICAS

BY PENNY MORRILL

Archaeological records provide knowledge and understanding of the earliest high cultures in the Americas. Large-scale ceremonial centers, such as La Venta, the Olmec site in Veracruz (ca. 900–ca. 400 B.C.E.); Chavín de Huántar, the Chavín site on the northwestern coast of Peru (ca. 900–ca. 200 B.C.E.); and those constructed by the Adena (ca. 1000 B.C.E.–ca. 200 C.E.) and Hopewell (ca. 200 B.C.E.–ca. 400 C.E.) groups in the Ohio River Valley, were settings for festival activities. These centers consisted of pyramids, platforms, altars, and open plazas, indicating societies that were hieratic, led by chieftains or shaman-lords. The festivals followed the agricultural cycle, a characterization that would have been true for early ceremonial sites throughout the Americas. Thus, religion, politics, and economics would have revolved around the ceremonial complex.

Many of the peoples of the Americas believed in a multileveled universe with an axis mundi (center of the world). For the Olmec this center was represented as a tree, a mountain-pyramid, or a dragon. For the Chavín in Peru the sacred center was marked by the sculpted Lanzón figure, a statue of the central god. The Hopewell culture adopted the circle and the cross of four directions in their architecture and artwork. Across the Americas the shaman was able to move through multiple cosmic realms by transforming himself through bloodletting or the use of hallucinogens or accompanied by an animal alter-ego. Masks worn by the shaman-leaders had symbolic features that provided new identities. In Mesoamerica a shaman could call up ancestral spirits, assume the identity of an animal, or act out myth, and the audience would have understood his masquerade as transformation.

Ritual, festival, trade, and the ball game brought dispersed people from the surrounding villages and farmlands to the centers. The farmers of the Americas looked to their shaman-leaders for critical advice on plant husbandry—when and how to plant, what seeds to store, and methods of hybridization. The ceremonial center's architecture tracked and revealed astronomical phenomena: the movements of the sun, moon, planets (especially Venus), and stars and the timing of the solar equinox, solstices, and eclipses. A metaphor for the cosmos, the carefully configured architectural setting allowed the shaman seemingly to manipulate astronomical events for the betterment of the subject peoples, especially concerning agriculture. The festival audience would have gathered to await the occurrence of the phenomenon, brought about by the costumed shaman from his platform stage or atop a pyramid. Examples of such sites include Building J at Monte Albán in Oaxaca, Mexico (after 150 B.C.E.); Structure 5 at Cerros, a Mayan site in Belize (after 100 B.C.E.); and the Nasca lines in Peru (after 100 C.E.), the latter probably considered visible only to a transcendent birdlike shaman.

Much of the artwork that has been unearthed at these sites and others indicates theater on a grand scale, appropriate to the architecture. Around the perimeter of the Sunken Court at Chavín de Huántar humans and jaguars are depicted in procession. Carvings in the Olmec heartland and at other Mesoamerican sites represent costumed shaman-leaders acting out ritual in theatrical settings. On a platform throne at La Venta a leader wearing a bird headdress is shown seated in the open jaws of the earth beneath a sky dragon and holding a rope to which are attached captives. On the upper surface is a carved jaguar pelt, a symbol of power. On this throne before his subject audience, the shaman was able to combine transcendence with military prowess to enhance and centralize his power.

In the present-day Mexican state of Morelos, a cave doorway, the opening into the underworld in the form of a monster mask at Chalcatzingo (ca. 500–ca. 300 B.C.E.), is a dramatic stage set. At La Venta and Chalcatzingo sculpted figures wear large, ornate headdresses that must have been impressive whether closely inspected or viewed from a distance. In a cave painting at Oxtotitlan, in the Mexican state of Guerrero, a shaman is seated on a throne and wears an elaborate bird costume. He raises his arms and attached wings, giving the appearance of flight. Sculptures of transformation figures depicting humans becoming jaguars or birds indicate ritual festivals that must have brought together large numbers of participants into the plazas of Chavín de Huántar, La Venta, and Monte Albán.

Stela 5 from the Late Formative (ca. 400 B.C.E.–ca. 150 C.E.) Mayan site of Izapa in the state of Chiapas, Mexico, seems to record one of these presentations acted out before an audience. Below sky symbols, a supernatural tree appears in the center of the carved scene, rising up from a platform that is elaborated with earth and water symbols. A large figure to the right creates an opening in the tree from which humans emerge. On the other side of the tree are an elderly man and woman engaged in divination, perhaps the ancestral couple.

These ceremonies inspired the production of costumes made of feathers and other fine materials, jewels, masks, and ritual objects carved of jade and other prized stones. The

Pottery dog, from Colima, West Mexico, 300 B.C.E. to 300 C.E.; dogs were believed to assist the dead in their journey to the Underworld, and the hairless type depicted here was eaten at feasts. (© The Trustees of the British Museum)

jewelry and costumes of sumptuous materials denoted high status and, at the same time, meant substantial cost for the people served by the shaman-leaders. Materials for these accessories came from distant locales. Thus, as a result of this grand ceremonial activity, production and trade moved beyond agriculture to include precious ritualistic objects for the elite.

The Olmec played a game with a rubber ball on a court at San Lorenzo in Veracruz (ca. 1500–ca. 1200 B.C.E.). From this early precedent, ball courts continued to be placed within ceremonial centers in Mesoamerica. The game was considered a metaphor for cosmic events and thus part of religious festival activity. Audiences gathered to watch for an outcome that could bring life or death to the players.

In Mesoamerica the origin of the 260-day ritual almanac and the solar festival calendar of 365 days can be traced to the activity of the shamans at the ceremonial centers. The shaman-priests joined together the two calendars to create the 52-year Calendar Round, which was both divinatory (foretelling the future or uncovering secret knowledge) and a transcription of the cycle of festivals that followed the seasonal movement of the sun and other celestial bodies. On carved stone stelae at La Mojarra in Veracruz (after 150 C.E.) and El Baúl in the Mayan region of Guatemala (Stela 1 dating to 37 C.E.), the combination of hieroglyphs with dramatically costumed shaman-lords reveals the power that came with control over the passage of time.

See also AGRICULTURE; ARCHITECTURE; ART; ASTRONOMY; CALENDARS AND CLOCKS; DEATH AND BURIAL PRACTICES; DRAMA AND THEATER; ECONOMICS; FAMILY; FOOD AND DRINK; FOREIGNERS AND BARBARIANS; GENDER STRUCTURES AND ROLES; LITERATURE; MILITARY; MUSIC AND MUSICAL INSTRUMENTS; NATURAL DISASTERS; RELIGION AND COSMOLOGY; SACRED SITES; SPORTS AND RECREATION; TRADE AND EXCHANGE; WAR AND CONQUEST.

FURTHER READING

Christopher W. Blackwell and Amy Hackney Blackwell, *Mythology for Dummies* (New York: Hungry Minds, 2002).
Michael Coe, *The Olmec World: Ritual and Rulership* (Princeton, N.J.: Art Museum, 1995).
Mark E. Cohen, *The Cultic Calendars of the Ancient Near East* (Bethesda, Md.: CDL Press, 1993).
Sherif El-Sabban, *Temple Festival Calendars of Ancient Egypt* (Liverpool, U.K.: Liverpool University Press, 2000).
Anita Ganeri, *Hindu Festivals throughout the Year* (Mankato, Minn.: Smart Apple Media, 2003).
Arthur Wallace Pickard-Cambridge, *The Dramatic Festivals of Athens*, 2nd ed. (Oxford, U.K.: Oxford University Press, 1968).
H. H. Scullard, *Festivals and Ceremonies of the Roman Republic* (Ithaca, N.Y.: Cornell University Press, 1981).
Carol Stepanchuk and Charles Wong, *Mooncakes and Hungry Ghosts: Festivals of China* (San Francisco, Calif.: China Books and Periodicals, 1991).
Robert Turcan, *The Gods of Ancient Rome: Religion in Everyday Life from Archaic to Imperial Times* (New York: Routledge, 2001).

▶ food and diet

INTRODUCTION

The earliest humans were "hunter-gatherers," meaning that their food supply came from hunting animals and gathering plant foods that grew naturally without their help. Clearly, a community's diet depended on the nature of the foodstuffs found in that part of the world. Hunters searched for large game animals, small animals (including rodents and, among some people, even bats), birds (including their eggs), seafood, and fish. Plant food included leafy vegetables and greens, nuts, roots, grains, honey, berries, and other fruits. Food supplies were affected by the season of the year, and early hunter-gatherer societies moved about in search of food as conditions in the environment changed. Famine and starvation were their principal enemies, and these enemies were never very far away. In an era of short life expectancies, the concept of a "balanced diet" would have been meaningless. Hunter-gatherers ate what they could find when they could find it, and they hoped that tomorrow they could find more.

The development of agriculture introduced some measure of security into the life of ancient peoples, and this added security enabled them to form more complex and sophisticated civilizations. Now they had at least some control over the availability of food, and with a little luck they could store food for the future and avoid starvation. One major result was a dramatic increase in the world's population. Food surpluses allowed ancient peoples to support classes of craftsmen, builders, civil servants, warriors, priests, artists, and poets, enriching the life of the community.

Still, ancient peoples were constrained by their environment, and the nature of the crops they could grow or the animals they could raise depended on such matters as temperature, rainfall, soil conditions, elevation, and the like. Ancient agriculturalists were acutely aware of changing seasons and weather conditions, and they took what steps they could to accommodate their farming practices to local conditions. The ancient Egyptians, for example, lived along the Nile River valley, a fertile region surrounded by harsh deserts. Each year the Nile flooded; when its waters receded, they left behind a layer of rich silt, where they Egyptians planted crops. The Egyptians became adept at water management, building a massive system of canals and dikes to store and distribute water for irrigation during the dry season.

Nearly every culture in the world developed a single staple crop that formed the bulk of its diet. In ancient Greece and Rome, for example, wheat was the main staple crop, so bread was an important part of the diet, supplemented by fruits and vegetables, oils (such as olive oil), legumes (that is, beans such as lentils), and fish. In Asia low-lying wetlands were ideal for rice cultivation, so rice became the staple crop, while in parts of the Americas, corn and beans were the main crops. Animal husbandry enabled some agriculturalists to maintain herds of cattle, sheep, goats, oxen, or pigs as well as birds, such as chickens, ducks, and geese. These animals supplied not only meat but also eggs, milk, and products derived from milk, such as cheese and butter. Most cultures, too, found a way to preserve beverages such as beer and wine; they could depend on these types of fermented beverages to remain wholesome and drinkable over time.

AFRICA

BY MICHAEL J. O'NEAL

The history of food and diet begins with the consumption patterns of ancient Africans, the first humans who faced the need to find sustenance in the natural world around them. As in any geographical region, the types of foods early Africans consumed tended to vary by climate and terrain. Thus, for example, coastal East Africans relied more heavily on fish and seafood than did people who inhabited the interior of the continent. Crops that flourished in the highlands of Ethiopia might not have done as well in lowland areas and vice versa. Foods that were available in lush, forested regions of the continent were not as widely available in the hot, dry savannahs of central Africa. Furthermore, climate changes over the millennia altered food and dietary habits. At one time much of the Sahara was lush and green, but in about 6000 B.C.E. the region became arid, forcing people to move and find new sources of food. Thus, over long stretches of time, the dietary habits of the ancient Africans changed.

In spite of all these variables, a number of generalizations can be made about the food and diet of ancient Africans. Until the advent of agriculture, the earliest Africans survived by hunting, gathering, and fishing. Anthropologists theorize that the earliest humans became bipedal—that is, walked upright on two legs—because natural selection favored those who could travel long distances in the search primarily for tubers, or rounded roots, such as the potato, that grew underground. While tubers were an important source of food to the very earliest Africans, Africa has few native tubers, about half a dozen species, and those that did grow were small. Other, imported varieties of tubers would later become important agricultural crops.

Meat made up a major portion of the diet of early hunter-gatherers; among many Bantu-speaking peoples, the words for "food" and "meat" are still the same as they were in ancient times. In the equatorial forests of East Africa, for example, bands of small-statured African groups (sometimes termed Pygmies) survived by using spears, snares, nets, and arrows to capture and kill a range of game, from birds and rabbits to such large animals as hippopotamuses, giraffes, antelope, buffalo, gazelles, and elephants. Women, meanwhile, gathered mushrooms, nuts, berries, fruits, some varieties of cactus, and leafy vegetables. Nutritionists believe that the diet of ancient Africans was in many respects superior to that of modern peoples. Because hunter-gatherers consumed at least 80 different types of plants and possibly many more, they had a great deal of variety in their diet and suffered no vitamin or mineral deficiencies—though starvation was an ever-present threat. Eggs were gathered as well, but in some parts of the continent eggs were a taboo item, thought to weaken men and cause women to miscarry or become sterile. In some parts of Africa eggs are still taboo.

Fineware cup decorated with frogs and lotus flowers painted in black, from Faras, Sudan, dating to the first or second century C.E. (© The Trustees of the British Museum)

In some portions of Africa termites and caterpillars were roasted and eaten, often with honey, as snacks. Most commonly, the meat from game animals was preserved by smoking and drying. When it was cooked, it was either roasted over an open fire or cooked in stews with vegetables; many of these stews were also used as sauces for meat. A common sweetener was honey, and a common beverage was made by brewing kola nuts, herbs, and berries into a drink; kola nuts contain caffeine, and the ancient Africans learned that they could energize people, especially men before a battle. Along the coasts and rivers people caught and ate fish, which they fried, boiled, pickled, or sometimes ate raw. Fish included mackerel, flounder, carp, pike, cod, and others; seafood included crab, snails, oysters, lobster, prawns, shrimp, and crayfish.

The diet of ancient Africans changed as they came to place less emphasis on hunting and gathering and more on agriculture and livestock herding. Livestock herding, which provided not only meat but also milk, cheese, butter, and yogurt, was practiced primarily by people who lived in more arid regions of the continent; in damper regions diseases spread by such pests as the tsetse fly made livestock herding more precarious. Livestock included camels, cattle, donkeys, goats, and sheep. Interestingly, modern peoples of Africa, in common with Europeans, have the world's lowest incidence of lactose intolerance, or the inability to digest the sugar in milk. It is believed that this tolerance for milk is a dietary adaptation that dates back thousands of years to ancient Africa. Historians believe that the first domesticated cattle appeared sometime between 3000 and 2000 B.C.E. The hardy Tunis sheep from North Africa had been tended for some 2,000 years when the U.S. president George Washington had some imported to help replenish his own sheep herd. While pigs could be found in North Africa, they were not domesticated. Many African tribes domesticated species of dogs as sources of food.

Crop cultivation added considerable range to the ancient African diet. The earliest African agriculturists lived in the highlands of Ethiopia, though Bantu-speaking people from East Africa and the Nilotes from northwest Africa were also among the earliest farmers. Some of the crops that formed an important part of the African diet included sorghum, millet, beans, okra, and cowpeas. In some parts of the continent pumpkins, cassava, and sweet potatoes were cultivated.

The African diet expanded again with the development of trade with other regions of the world, particularly Asia. Chief among imported foods were rice, yams, plantain, taro, and bananas. Tubers continued to be an important part of the diet. One variety of potato, for example, could weigh up to 9 pounds and was an important source of water in the diet for travelers and isolated herders. These foods, in combination with indigenous crops, enabled the African population to expand significantly. In particular, they contributed to the spread of Bantu-speaking people throughout large portions of central and southern Africa. Wheat, too, was added to the African diet, and such crops as wheat, millet, sorghum, and yams became especially important because they were not overly sensitive to intemperate weather conditions. The influence of wheat was felt particularly in North Africa, which came under the influence of the Roman Empire. The Romans introduced couscous and many bread products still common in North Africa today. Throughout the rest of Africa, grain products were used primarily to make such dishes as porridges, gruels, and pancake-like foods.

Anthropologists and archaeologists have been able to reconstruct the diet of ancient Africans, at least in part, by using modern scientific tools. They operate under the proverb that people "are what they eat." Foods that ancient people consumed leave identifiable chemical signatures in bones, teeth, and hair. By using sophisticated scientific instruments, scientists can examine, for example, carbon isotopes that remain in the skeletons of ancient people, including those of Africa. From this evidence, they can deduce what ancient peoples ate.

EGYPT

BY CHRISTINE END

Knowledge about the diet of the ancient Egyptians comes from two-dimensional depictions, three-dimensional models, and archaeological evidence such as food and animal remains. Farming was an important part of this agrarian nation, not just because it allowed individuals to feed their families. A person's crop production determined his wealth and dictated the amount of his annual tax. The Egyptians also compensated workers, paid their taxes, and bartered for other goods with food products.

In comparison with other ancient civilizations, the Egyptians ate a well-balanced diet. Forensic evidence from the examination of mummies suggests that Egyptians rarely suffered from malnutrition. The reason for Egypt's well-nourished population was the Nile River, which supplied its people with a prolific food source. The fertile soil deposited after the inundation (the annual flooding of the Nile) nourished Egypt's crops, and the river itself provided a lush habitat for many species of animals and birds.

It is common to find two-dimensional representations of food offerings as well as of hunting and food preparation on ancient Egyptian tomb walls. The Egyptians believed these images could magically materialize and perpetually be available for the deceased in the afterlife. Three-dimensional models of food and food production also offered eternal sustenance for the deceased in the tomb. Additionally, a variety of preserved foodstuffs recovered from tombs give Egyptologists information about the preferred diet of the ancient Egyptians.

The particulars of meals and the dining schedules of the ancient Egyptians are unknown. Pictorial evidence and the remains of food suggest that the Egyptians prepared their diet in a variety of ways, including stewing, frying, boiling, roasting, grilling, drying, and salting. More written and visual data survives about food-related celebrations and festivals than about customary daily meals. Elaborate banquets during which people indulged in abundant food, drink, music, and entertainment marked these events.

The two main food staples of ancient Egyptians from all social classes were bread and beer. Within the customary funerary-offering formula (texts written on funeral objects), these two items always figure prominently. Bread loaves were typically triangular or ovoid, but many shapes and sizes existed, including a variety of odd-shaped loaves specially formed for religious reasons. Stone-ground emmer or barley wheat was the principal grain used in breads. Stone grinding produced grit-laden bread that ground down people's teeth over their lifetime. Wealthy Egyptians often enjoyed sweetbreads, biscuits, and cakes, while commoners may have tasted these luxuries only on special occasions.

Egyptian beer was a thick, nutritious mixture of varying alcohol content consumed by adults and children alike. As with bread, barley and emmer were the main components in Egyptian beer. Because it was such a staple in the diet, beer brewing in the home was commonplace. Sometimes the Egyptians enjoyed flavored beers by adding fruits, honey, or spices.

Ancient Egyptians ate a variety of locally grown fruits and vegetables. Onions were the most popular vegetable, as evidenced in many offering table depictions. Other vegetables favored by the Egyptians were beets, garlic, cucumbers, celery, turnips, leeks, and lettuces. The Nile River was an additional source of other edible plants, including water-borne sedges, lotus, and tiger nut.

Fruits included dates, grapes, dom palm, pomegranates, berries, and figs. Fruit was eaten fresh but also used in cooking or preserved for future use by drying. Elite Egyptians enjoyed red and white wine produced from grapes. Ancient Egyptian wine amphorae were carefully marked with the type of wine, production year, and sometimes an indication of the quality of the wine they contained. Figs, dates, palm leaves, and possibly pomegranates were alternative ingredients used to make wine. Fruits were additionally included in recipes for sweetness, as was the carob pod, though not as frequently as honey. Although it was a luxury, honey was the primary sweetener. Bees were also kept as a source of beeswax used to create models for the casting of metal and as a waxy polish. Legumes such as beans, peas, and lentils rounded out the Egyptian diet. They supplied an easily cultivated protein source that was less expensive than meat. Of these three, lentils were the most common.

Local and imported spices seasoned the ancient Egyptian diet. Thyme, coriander, marjoram, fenugreek, dill, parsley, and cumin were all regionally grown spices. Salt improved flavor but also was used as a preserving agent for meat, fish, and fowl. Luxurious imported spices used in cooking may have included pepper and cinnamon.

The ancient Greek traveler Herodotus erroneously reported that the Egyptians did not eat fish, possibly because of a myth involving a fish eating the phallus of the god Osiris after his evil brother Seth mutilated him. Although fish do not frequently appear depicted on offering tables, many species of fish are seen in representations on tomb walls as well as in fishing scenes, indicating that the Egyptians did indeed enjoy fish as part of their diet.

Many species of birds, both domesticated and wild, were consumed by the ancient Egyptians, including most often duck and goose but also ostrich, pigeon, quail, partridge, and dove. Containers in the shape of prepared (strangled and plucked) birds from funerary contexts survive; these receptacles contain cooked or preserved fowl for the deceased to enjoy in the afterlife. Bird eggs included those from many species, even ostrich.

The ancient Egyptians both hunted mammals in the wild and bred them in captivity. With the exception of the upper classes, most individuals consumed meat only on special occasions and during religious festivals. The rich could afford meat from cows, bulls, and oxen, while the less affluent may have eaten solely sheep and goat meat. Tomb scenes depict captive animals being force-fed to produce more meat per animal. Despite rare representations and Herodotus's claim that swine were taboo to the Egyptians, archaeological evidence suggests that Egyptians domesticated pigs and consumed pork. Smaller and perhaps more abundant animal food sources may have included mice, hedgehogs, and hares. No part of a food animal was wasted; animal products and by-products included milk (from goats and cows), cheeses, fats, medicines, and oils used for fragrance and cooking.

THE MIDDLE EAST

BY KAREN RADNER

Evidence about the ancient Near Eastern diet comes from two sources. One is the analysis of the remains of foodstuffs and human skeletons discovered in archaeological excavations. The other is information found in ancient texts and, to a lesser extent, images. These materials add up to a surprisingly detailed picture, and the ancient Mesopotamian menu is one of the best known of antiquity. The basic diet of an ordinary person consisted mostly of plant products, with only about 10 percent derived from animals, usually domesticated ones. The members of the elite, because they had access to luxury foods, could have a substantially higher proportion of animal products, including milk and milk products and eggs in their diet.

The emergence of ancient Near Eastern civilization is closely connected to the development of agriculture. It is therefore not surprising to find that cereals constituted the most important part of the diet, with barley being predominant and wheat occupying a distant second place. Barley was either ground into flour to make bread or porridge or used to brew beer, which was drunk habitually by people of all ages. Although regular beer had a low alcohol content, it nevertheless had enough to kill germs in the water during fermentation. Beer was therefore the solution to the dangers of drinking contaminated water. Stronger beer, often flavored with sweet or spicy ingredients, was reserved for recreational drinking and served during festivals and in taverns. Typically beer was drunk through straws from large vessels resting on pot stands.

The palm tree was present throughout southern Mesopotamia, and its fruit, the date, played an important role in the Near Eastern diet and economy, in antiquity as today. Unprocessed dates could be stored and transported easily and, once dried, kept for a considerable time, making them ideal provisions for the road. Date syrup was widely used as a sweetener; because the climate of southern Mesopotamia was not favorable for bees, the use of honey was largely restricted to the north. Vegetable oil constituted an important element of the diet, with pronounced regional differences: Whereas olive oil was common in Anatolia and along the Mediterranean coast, where the olive tree found ideal conditions, sesame oil was used in the rest of the Near East.

From the first millennium B.C.E. Babylonian texts record the movements of the stars (hence their modern designation as "astronomical dairies"), important events, and the fluctuation of prices for key products. It is a testament to the importance of barley, dates, and sesame to find these foodstuffs among them, together with two popular spices, cardamom and mustard. Many other spices were used as well, often imported from faraway countries; together with locally grown herbs, they were used to flavor food. Salt came primarily from desert salt beds and the sea, but rock salt of a much higher quality was also imported from salt mines in the area of modern-day Iran and beyond. Salt was used as a flavoring and to preserve meat. It was a far less costly alternative to refrigeration, the method used in palaces, which imported ice at great expense from the mountain regions to stock icehouses. In the early second millennium B.C.E. icehouses enabled King Zimrilim of Mari to treat his guests to refreshing fruit sorbet.

The basic diet also included various vegetables. Most important were garlic and onions, which could be stored easily, and fruit such as figs, apples, pomegranates, and peaches, which were grown in dedicated fruit groves. Vineyards were widespread in regions with enough natural rainfall, such as along the foothills of the mountain ranges surrounding Mesopotamia and in the coastal regions of the Mediterranean Sea, but they could not be established in southern Mesopotamia. Consumption of grapes and grape products such as raisins and especially wine was always the privilege of the ruling elite; because of its exclusivity, wine, in common with all luxury foodstuffs, was also an appropriate item to sacrifice to the gods. The high prestige of wine drinking was reflected in the highly elaborate vessels, often made from precious metals, used to serve it, mix it with water, pour it, and drink it. In Assyria wine was more widely available to a wider section of society: A letter from the correspondence of King Sargon II of Assyria (r. 721–705 B.C.E.) documents the exploits of some soldiers who had enjoyed too much wine, and in the seventh century B.C.E. numerous inhabitants of the city of Assur invested in wine imports, undoubtedly destined for private consumption.

Wine was best served alongside meat, the two essential components of a festive banquet fit for kings and gods. Most common was the meat of domesticated animals. Beef, mutton, and poultry (from ducks and geese, for the chicken arrived in Mesopotamia from India only in the first millennium B.C.E.) were prepared in a variety of styles, including grilled, roasted, steamed, cooked in water, or cooked inside a pie or as part of a soup. Pork was less common, although no taboo prevented its consumption.

Recipes for various meat dishes survive in a group of texts from the city of Larsa, dating to the early second millennium B.C.E. These oldest-known recipes are extremely elaborate and give considerable insight into the haute cuisine of Babylonia, a truly international cuisine that incorporated recipes that reflected Assyrian and Elamite cooking styles. While not all ingredients, especially the many spices and herbs, can be identified with certainty, the sheer amount of effort invested in the preparation of these dishes illustrates an appreciation for rich culinary delights. As such, they counterbalance descriptions of the bland basic diet of ordinary people, who ate meat only on rare occasions, usually during festivals. Fish, however, was far more common on the menu. Fish was widely available in the rivers and, according to Greek historian Herodotus, the exclusive diet of the inhabitants of the swamps in the extreme south of Mesopotamia, who are said to have eaten cakes made from ground-up fish instead of bread.

The Near Eastern diet also included items that seem alien, such as locusts, which were either grilled on spits or ground up and processed into cakes. However, other foodstuffs that seem very ordinary were highly unusual in the ancient Near East. Eggs, for example, were almost exclusively reserved for the plates of kings and gods. When the Assyrian king Ashurnasirpal II (883–859 B.C.E.) stated in an inscription that he served, among a wealth of gastronomic highlights, 10,000 eggs at the inauguration feast of his new palace in Kalchu, many of his guests would have eaten these treats for the first time in their lives.

ASIA AND THE PACIFIC

BY CONSTANCE A. COOK

The production of food in ancient Asia and the Pacific went through the same uneven transition from hunting and gathering to farming seen in the rest of the world. Some regions were resistant to this change, while in others cultivation techniques seemed to spread rapidly. Archaeology reveals some correlation between the production and use of pottery and the rise of agricultural and sedentary communities. These communities tended also to develop ranked social patterns and reveal more material evidence for food storage and the use of food and beverages in ritual contexts.

The earliest hunter-gatherer communities occupied southern China (south of the Yangtze River) and upland Southeast Asia (modern-day Burma, Thailand, Laos, and Vietnam), possibly after having migrated from the west over one million years ago. They hunted wild pigs, deer, gaur, rhinoceros, stegodon (a type of elephant), bovids (antelope, oxen, sheep, and goats), monkeys, muntjacs (a type of deer), tapir, hyena, pandas, squirrels, rodents, bats, birds, fish, mollusks, shellfish, and other fauna. They gathered wild grains, fruits, nuts, yams, taro, legumes and other flora.

The food sources available naturally varied according to environment. Mainland Asians had access to large animals and cereals, whereas those on some of the islands of Southeast Asia and the Pacific did not. Along seacoasts and rivers, those who lived in the mangrove swamps in southern Thailand foraged for marine and river estuarine fauna. In highland areas or plains there is evidence that some early peoples began small-scale cultivation of tubers. Foraging in rainforests and forest horticulture were likely sources of food in Southeast Asia and island Southeast Asia. Wild rice was also available throughout much of south China and mainland Southeast Asia.

The transition to farming and a more sedentary lifestyle may have begun 14,000 years ago during the Paleolithic Era, although the large-scale adoption of agriculture and animal husbandry is linked to the Neolithic Revolution and occurred in different regions at different times—and some places, such as Australia, island Southeast Asia, and north and northwestern Asia not at all or not until the historical period. Because of changes in the climate, with northern areas becoming noticeably warmer, a variety of farming styles and dietary habits developed. Rice was cultivated in wetland paddies beginning in the middle Yangtze River basin possibly as early as 12,000 years ago. From there it spread southward and eventually northward.

Early peoples also cultivated yams, adzuki beans, melons, fruits, and vegetables in addition to hunting. The 8,000-year-old site of Jiahu in Henan Province in the Huai River valley shows that the people cultivated first japonica and then indica rice as well as other plants. They also had access to buffalo, alligator, fish, and other animals. In the 7,000-year-old site of Hemudu (Yuyao, Zhejiang, near the Pacific coast), where intensive rice farming occurred, archeologists have found evidence of domesticated pigs, water buffaloes, and dogs. They hunted deer, muntjac, rhinoceros, elephant, tiger, bear, and birds. As coastal dwellers, they speared fish, whales, and sharks. They also ate acorns, water chestnuts, wild jujubes (a Chinese date), water lily, gourds, and beans.

The variable climate in the north encouraged people around the Yangtze River and its tributaries to cultivate millet in dryland fields in the Yellow River basin, especially in Hebei and Henan. They cultivated foxtail and broomcorn millets and eventually soybeans, sorghum, wheat, barley, vegetables, melons, fruit, and hemp. By 6000 B.C.E. dryland farming communities were well established and extended as far west as Gansu, as far east as Shandong, and as far north as Inner Mongolia. Hunting and gathering, particularly for meat such as deer, continued to be important, though domesticated animals, such as pigs, chickens, and dogs, were also common. Horses did not become common after the third millennium B.C.E. and, then, like buffalo, were used for transportation as well as food.

By 7000 B.C.E. the spread of sedentary living, pottery making, plant cultivation, and animal husbandry had clearly spread from the river valleys of China north to the lower and middle Amur River basin in the Russian Far East, and eventually through Korea to Japan in about 1000 B.C.E. They had also spread southward through southern China into Southeast Asia and island Southeast Asia, perhaps through Taiwan around 5000 B.C.E. and the Philippines and Indonesia by 3000 B.C.E. Eventually, these practices reached the Lapita cultures of western Polynesia (1500 B.C.E.) and Polynesia to the southeast and the Ban Kao Neolithic peoples to the southwest in Thailand. By 2000 B.C.E. they had moved westward into the Late Harappan and related Indus Valley farming cultures in south Asia. Each society had its own cultural characteristics and dietary habits. This is clearly evident not only in the localized food groups, limited by the local environment, growing conditions, and habit, but also in the pottery assemblages, which reveal diversity in food preparation and serving.

The greatest evidence for elaborate food preparation and service is found in late Neolithic tombs in China. Food was processed using mortars, pestles, and rollers and then steamed, simmered, boiled, and roasted in a variety of high-footed vessels that stood over fire pits or placed on clay stoves. Food and beverages were stored in a variety of large and small jars. They could be served with ladles or poured. The elite in some areas ate off high-stemmed platters and drank out of delicately manufactured high-stemmed cups. Less prestigious ware, such as short cups with or without handles, were also used. By 2400 B.C.E. early peoples were making alcoholic beverages of rice and fruit. By this time food preparation and service, particularly in feasting environments—probably having to do with mortuary ritual and rituals involving change in the social hierarchy—had become quiet complex, as indicated by the increasingly elaborate decorations and manufacturing methods of the pottery and the range of service vessel types. By the end of the second millennium B.C.E. elite peoples controlled the large-scale production and use of ritual implements used during banquets that increasingly used bronze and jade as well as other materials.

Outside the Indus Valley and northern China this level of civilization or social complexity is not evident in the Asia-Pacific area until much later. In northern Thailand the site of Ban Chiang (2100–900 B.C.E., contemporary with the Shang and Zhou historical periods in China) reveals a sophisticated use of technology, including the production of metal vessels. The ancient Thai ate rice, taro, yams, and mangrove embryos, along with hunted animals and fish. They sweetened their foods with bananas, palm sugars, and honey. Likewise, to the northeast, the increasingly sophisticated Korean culture of the Mumun Period (1500–300 B.C.E.) produced cooking and service vessels for a diet consisting mostly of fish and millet or wheat (with soy and adzuki beans, beefsteak plants, and other vegetables), but it was not until around the eighth century B.C.E. that high-status remains with metal vessels are found. In Japan metal artifacts are not evident until the fourth century B.C.E., when the Yayoi rice farmers came over from the mainland and replaced the Jōmon culture. A combination of hunting and gathering and some cultivation of trees and roots continued in the islands. In Lapita cultural complexes in the Pacific islands at this time, archeologists have found cooking ovens, storage pits for foods, vegetable scrapers, and evidence for the use of domesticated pigs, dogs, and chickens.

EUROPE

BY JACQUI WOOD

Our understanding of prehistoric food and drink in Europe comes from a variety of sources. From the Stone Age (10,000 years ago) to the Bronze Age (3,500 years ago) information is found in archaeological data gleaned from pollen analysis. Such analysis relies on soil samples taken from excavated areas of an archaeological dig and studied to discover the sorts of plants that were growing in the local environment at the time of occupation of particular sites. Sometimes, too, the charred remains of ceramic pots leave more direct evidence of what people ate. Charring preserves the remains so that archaeologists can determine the ingredients of the last meal cooked in the pot.

Cooking fires in dwellings also can give us information as to specific types of cooking techniques used by the occupants, such as the remains of clay baking. Clay baking was a method employed to cook meat and fish slowly. The meat or fish was wrapped in grass and then smeared with silty river clay and placed at the edge of an open fire to gently cook in its clay casing. When the meat or fish was ready to eat, its casing would crack as the steam from the cooked food tried to escape. The discarded remains of this baking process are found at numerous prehistoric sites. At a site called Trethellan in Cornwall, England, dating to 3,500 years ago, a fire pit was full of these clay fragments. At this site bird bone impressions were found in the clay fragments, indicating the type of meat that had been cooked in it. Much earlier, approximately 10,000 years ago, the hunter-gatherer diet consisted of lots of meat and fish, supplemented by nuts and berries collected in the autumn. This diet was nutritious and quite adequate for thousands of years, because high-protein diets such as this would satisfy hunger for longer than a cereal-based or vegetable-based diet.

The seasonal aspect of food was very important too. Eggs, for instance, would have been taken from any bird and eaten only in the springtime. In the New Stone Age or Neolithic Period, 6,000 years ago, communities started to settle along the coastlines, owing to the abundance of wild food available in that environment. Seaweeds and shellfish were collected, and it is still true today that the tastiest wild vegetables can be found only on the shorelines of northern Europe.

From this time there is also archaeological evidence from the residues in ceramics that milk products were consumed. This evidence is confirmed by the high proportion of calf bones excavated from Neolithic camps around Europe, implying both the consumption of veal and the need for a large supply of milk. Butter making would have been an important by-product of milk consumption. Surplus butter was often placed in wooden barrels and submerged into peat bogs to keep it cool until it was needed. Archaeologists have discovered large qualities of this butter, termed *bog butter*; these discoveries range from a few pounds to as much as a hundredweight of butter at one site in Ireland.

In the later Iron Age (2,800 years ago) we have the comments of various classical historians about the food of the barbarians they encountered. It has been well documented in such texts that the barbarians of Europe loved wine and beer, and this was true for the peoples who preceded them as well. The fermenting of liquids to produce alcohol was one of the earliest culinary activities after humans started to settle in one place and grow grains. Simple beer was consumed as a regular drink, because, among its many virtues as a beverage, it contained vitamins that were often lacking in a cereal-based diet.

"Empress" pepper pot, from the Hoxne hoard in Suffolk, Roman Britain; it was buried in the fifth century C.E.*, when Britain was passing out of the control of Rome.* (© The Trustees of the British Museum)

The discovery of malt may have been the result of storing grain in underground storage pits; the dampness at the base of the pits would have caused the remaining grain to sprout in the spring. Attempts to preserve these tasty sprouts possibly led to the creation of malt, the base ingredient of our beers today. Once dried, the grain sprouts turn into sweet-smelling malt owing to the concentration of sugars in the dried sprouted grain. Malted grain ground into flour and added to hot water makes a pleasant drink. A pot of this malt drink left near a fire for a day or two would have produced a simple beer. Archaeological evidence of such malt processing was excavated in a burned-down Iron Age house in Denmark at a settlement called Osterbolle, in Jutland. Archaeologists discovered two clay pots containing sprouted barley. One was set away from the fire, presumably to ferment, and the other was next to the fire to possibly begin the drying process.

A variety of herbal teas was also consumed, not just for medical purposes but also as a refreshing drink. Herbs and flowers were put into a ceramic pot with water, and small red-hot stones the size of hen's eggs were dropped into it. Once the water was boiling, the herbs would release their flavors. The stone was then taken out and the drink set aside to cool before consuming.

The most important type of cooking equipment from the earliest times was hot stones used to heat water. Possibly one of the first skills a prehistoric child would learn was the difference between igneous stones, formed as molten rock cools and hardens, and sedimentary stones, formed by deposits of sediment in a seabed. Having been subjected to extreme heat, igneous rock can withstand the heat of a fire. Sedimentary rock, on the other hand, absorbs liquid readily; if such stones are put into a fire to heat, the water inside can expand and cause the stone to explode, possibly injuring those around the fire. Volcanic stones, however, can be heated to red hot and dropped into water pits many times before they begin to crack and become unusable.

Huge crescent-shaped mounds of these fire-cracked stones are found around Europe. In Ireland these sites are called Fulachta Fliadh, meaning "cooking places" in Gaelic. In the middle of these mounds of stones is usually found a rectangular wood-lined pit dug into the water table. In *The History of Ireland* (1908) Geoffrey Keating describes the method. Early hunters would wrap meat in moorland grasses and drop it into water pits with hot stones to cook. Cooking experiments have shown that when red-hot stones are added to water, it begins to boil within minutes. Odd stones then would be added over the course of hours to keep the water simmering until the meat was cooked. The grass was wrapped around the meat to prevent ash and grit from the stones from getting into the cooking meat.

Meat was also cooked in an earth oven. A pit was dug and lined with stone, and a fire was then lit in the pit; at the same time, another fire was started next to it to heat more stones. When the pit stones were red hot, the embers were removed, and a large piece of meat would be put directly on top of the stones; then the stones from the second fire were placed on top. This earth oven could be left for the rest of the day to slowly cook the meat for the evening meal.

The spread of the Roman Empire by 133 B.C.E. brought with it a wondrous array of exotic foods and spices to the peoples of northern Europe. Root crops began to be cultivated; in earlier days most wild root vegetables were very small and bitter to the taste. New fruits and nuts, such as figs, dates, apricots, almonds, and walnuts, were introduced, and large, sweet apples and pears began to be grown in the Roman colonies. The most prized new spice was black pepper (*Piper nigum*), which enhanced the flavor of any foods. The introduction of these delicacies and Roman wine could have been a deciding factor in the Romanization of the peoples of Europe.

GREECE

BY CHRISTOPHER BLACKWELL

The diet of the ancient Greeks was in most ways similar to that of Mediterranean peoples today, nutritious and healthy but relatively limited in its staple components. The main source of calories was bread or porridge made from grains. Einkorn (*triticum monococcum*), emmer wheat (*triticum dicoccum*), durum wheat (*triticum durum*), bread wheat (*triticum aestivum*), and spelt (*triticum spelta*) were the most common varieties. The advantage of bread wheat and emmer wheat was that the husks of the grain could be removed by threshing (striking and tossing the wheat over a hard floor), while the other varieties required more difficult processes of toasting and grinding to extract the edible grain. The other varieties, on the other hand, were the grain of choice in many communities because they tended to produce more abundant crops.

In the earliest times grain was ground into flour using simple stone grinders, or querns, but by historical time more sophisticated and productive rotary grinders, sometimes driven by oxen or donkeys, ground wheat more efficiently. Bread was leavened with yeast and could be coarse or fine, with the finer "white" bread being a luxury only the wealthy could afford. Bread was such a central part of the diet that the same Greek word *sitos* means "grain," "bread," or "food" almost interchangeably. The Greek writer Athenaeus, whose quirky book *Deipnosophistae* (Learned Men at a Dinner Party) contains much evidence for ancient Greek cookery, describes a great variety of breads and cakes, some leavened and some flat, flavored with various herbs or sweetened with honey.

The main source of fat, and an additional valuable source of calories, was oil, mainly the oil of the domesticated olive. Ripe olives were shaken from trees onto nets, collected, and pressed in mills to extract the oil. Olives were only rarely eaten. Olive oil made the bread-based diet more palatable, was easily stored and transported, and had a great number of other uses—as soap, as a lubricant for machinery, as a fuel for lamps, and as a medicinal salve. Cultivation of olive trees for oil increased steadily throughout antiquity, reaching a peak in the middle of the first millennium of the Common Era, with a devastating effect on the environment because olive trees do little to prevent topsoil erosion.

The main source of protein in the ancient Greek diet was the legume, particularly lentils, chickpeas, and field peas. These were sometimes ground into flour and incorporated into bread or boiled into soup seasoned with onions, garlic, or vinegar. For protein the ancient Greeks did eat meat and fish, but relatively rarely. The Mediterranean is too salty and too clear to support the variety of fish found in the Atlantic, and fishing was a dangerous activity yielding unpredictable results.

But the ancient Greeks liked fish, and fish provided a welcome change of taste from the regular diet of bread, olive oil, and beans. Because of its relative scarcity and the difficulties of transporting it fresh, fish was most often pickled and used as a relish to enhance the taste of bread. The ancient Greek word for "relish" is *opson* or *opsarion*, and the modern Greek word for "fish," *psari*, is derived from this word. Salted fish was popular, too, because it was easy to transport and store. It is likely that the salts and trace minerals in salted fish were as important nutritionally as the protein in the fish.

Meat was rare and expensive, and the fact that the heroes in the Homeric epics seem to eat little else suggests that a meat-rich diet was the stuff of fantasy and that meat was a food fit for the children of gods. Greeks raised pigs, sheep, goats, and a few cows, but the rocky terrain did not lend itself to animal husbandry on a large scale. Hunting also provided meat from birds, hares, or deer, but only in small amounts. For many ancient Greeks in cities, meat appeared in their diet only during public festivals, when animals killed as sacrifices to the gods were barbequed and served as a part of a public feast.

While goats and sheep provided milk, milk was used mainly for making cheeses, either salty cheeses like modern feta or sweeter ones like modern ricotta. Ancient Greeks did not drink much milk and did not use butter. In Homer's *Odyssey*, the "lawless, outrageous" Cyclops enjoys a diet that consists mostly of milk, when he is not eating human beings, which may indicate a common view that milk was barbaric.

Onions, garlic, radishes, and cabbages were the main vegetables, along with leeks, cucumbers, artichokes, and celery. The tomato was unknown before the discovery of the Americas, as was the potato. Wild herbs such as asafetida, basil, and mint served as seasonings.

Rainwater was plentiful during the winter and could be collected in barrels, pots, or underground cisterns, but wells and natural springs were more reliable during the dry summer months. Because of uncertain water supplies and their

Terra-cotta utensil with six receptacles, thought to be an egg dish or cup holder. (Alison Frantz Photographic Collection, American School of Classical Studies at Athens)

potential health hazards, the most common drink was wine, generally diluted and drunk at every meal, from morning to night, even by children. While beer was known to the Greeks because it was a common drink among their neighbors in Europe to the north and in Egypt to the south, it was considered an uncouth drink.

The science of making wine, oenology, and the science of growing grapes for wine, viticulture, were highly developed among the Greeks, who understood the complex relationship between variety of grape, climate, and condition of soil in determining the quality of a wine. Certain areas were noted for their wines. Chios, with its Chian wine, was probably the most famous, but the islands of Cos, Thasos, and Lesbos were also well known for their vintages. Coan wine, from Cos, was made by incorporating seawater into the fermenting grapes early in production, which was said to make an especially smooth drink.

Drinking undiluted wine was rare, the mark of a barbarian. The Spartan king Cleomenes was said to have learned from the Persians to drink wine "straight," and consequently he went mad. Nevertheless, at symposia, the drinking-and-discussion parties popular among aristocrats, huge amounts of wine could be consumed, resulting in drunkenness, the effects of which are often comically depicted on painted vases, particularly vases intended for use at a symposium.

ROME

BY AMY HACKNEY BLACKWELL

The ancient Roman diet was simple at its core but could rise to great heights of invention and extravagance. The staple ingredients of Roman cooking were olive oil, wine, and wheat. In many cases these components formed the entire meal, perhaps with the addition of a few fresh vegetables. Wealthy Romans, however, enjoyed dining in company and encouraged the creation of expensive and original dishes.

Numerous works by Romans on food and drink survive today. Cato the Censor (234–149 B.C.E.) wrote a great deal about food in his treatise on farm management, *De agri cultura*. He describes the best way to produce and sell oil, wine, grain, and livestock and records many recipes for preserving food made on the farm. The most elaborate source on the subject of Roman cuisine is *Apicius on Cookery*, a compilation of recipes said to have been written by the gourmet Caelius Apicius and probably completed around the fourth century C.E.

Wheat formed the foundation of most meals. In the earliest days of Rome wheat was most commonly cooked into porridge, but by the time of the Roman Republic (509–27 B.C.E.) baked bread was more common. Getting this bread to Roman tables was no small feat. During the republic most of Rome's wheat was grown in Sicily and Sardinia. To prevent famines and the peasant revolts that could accompany them, the Roman government created a system to provide wheat to all citizens. This system began under Gaius Gracchus, who in 123 B.C.E. passed a *lex frumentaria*, or grain law, that provided grain to each citizen at a subsidized price. Clodius Pulcher made grain free to all citizens in 58 B.C.E. By the time of the emperor Trajan (r. 98–117 C.E.), Rome was importing much of its wheat from Egypt and Africa and still distributing it free to citizens. Administering this enterprise required a large bureaucracy of officials to keep track of distributions.

Romans supplemented their bread with olive oil and wine. The olive grew readily in Italy and the Mediterranean, and olive oil was ubiquitous. Olive oil is packed with calories and nutrients and was the main source of fat in the ancient Roman diet. Romans also ate cured olives. Wine and water were the main Roman beverages. People typically mixed their wine with water. Women were not supposed to drink wine; one of Rome's most ancient laws made it illegal for women to drink wine, and although the law was not enforced, it was still considered improper for women to drink too much. Greek wine was popular, but Italy produced its fair share of vintages as well. Romans sometimes mixed honey and spices into wine. They did not drink beer, mead, or milk because they considered these the drinks of barbarians such as Germans. They likewise did not make distilled drinks.

Vegetables and fruits filled out most meals. The most common vegetables included onions, garlic, radishes, celery, asparagus, carrots, beets, and zucchini. Poor people gathered wild greens and boiled them. Typical fruits included figs, grapes, dates, apples, pears, mulberries, peaches, apricots, and cherries. Walnuts and almonds were popular nuts. Tomatoes and potatoes did not grow in Europe at that time; the traditional Italian tomato sauce did not arise until after the discovery of the Americas.

Many Romans were completely vegetarian, both from necessity and from inclination. Most Romans got their protein from beans and lentils eaten with bread. Fish from the Mediterranean was commonly eaten, but meat was not popular. Italy's terrain was not good for growing large livestock such as cattle, and beef was another item considered more appropriate for barbarians. People did eat chickens and their eggs, and they ate some pork and veal, but these foods were not a substantial part of the average diet. Cheese made from goat's or sheep's milk was common; some cooks mixed it with garlic.

Roman cooks loved to add sauces to food and sometimes added 10 or more spices and flavorings to a dish. The most common seasoning was *garum*, a sauce made by covering fish with salt and leaving it to ferment for several months. Other flavorings included honey, vinegar, dry or sweet wine, oregano, cumin, coriander, fennel, lovage, rue, and silphium or asafetida, the resin of a plant related to fennel. A dish of peas could be topped with a sauce of honey, vinegar, olive oil, white wine, garum, lovage, ginger, pepper, and egg yolk blended together.

Although the typical meal was simple, a Roman feast was not. Many Romans subscribed to the teaching of the Greek philosopher Epicurus (341–270 B.C.E.), who maintained that pleasure of the body achieved by satisfying physical desires was the best way to achieve a happy life. These people called themselves epicures and preferred to consume the finest of foods and wines. Epicures and other wealthy nobles seeking to impress their guests sought out the most exotic foods. Caelius Apicius describes delicacies such as flamingoes, peacocks, sea urchins, sows' wombs, camels' hoofs, and dormice. He provides a recipe for a chicken salad that involved layering pieces of bread, chicken, sweetbreads, cheese, pine nuts, cucumbers, and onions, dressed with a sauce made of celery seed, pennyroyal, mint, ginger, cilantro, raisins, honey, vinegar, oil, and wine. Gourmets in Rome itself raved about licker fish, a freshwater bass that lived in the Tiber River and fed on the outflow from the city's sewer pipes.

Breakfast was very simple and could consist merely of bread and salt. The midday meal, *prandium*, was more complicated and could include meat or eggs. The main meal of the day was *cena*, eaten in the late afternoon. Among the wealthy the *cena* could include several courses, beginning with an appetizer and honeyed wine, followed by several main dishes, and concluded with sweets and fruit. This meal was eaten in the dining room, or *triclinium*, so called because it contained three couches on which men reclined to dine. During the republic women generally sat in chairs, but it became more common for them to recline as time went on.

Roman kitchens were equipped with brick hearths that included grills and ovens. Cooks used pots and pans made of clay or metal. A pestle and mortar were essential for pureeing foods. Not all households did their own cooking. In the countryside wives did much of the cooking for their families, but wealthy families maintained elaborate kitchens and expensive slaves who did the cooking. Within Rome many poor people lived in tenement buildings and did little or no cooking because of limited facilities and the risk of fire. They purchased most of their food from the numerous street vendors who sold bread, wine, cakes, kebabs, and other snacks.

THE AMERICAS

BY MICHAEL J. O'NEAL

Archaeologists can often determine what ancient peoples ate by examining their skeletal remains, which provide clues about nutrients that were present—or absent—in their diets. They also find clues in tombs, where containers with food items were placed, as well as from traces of foods found in pots and other containers.

Like ancient peoples throughout the world, prehistoric Americans subsisted on a diet that nature provided for them until they learned to cultivate some or most of their own food. Prehistoric hunter-gatherers, depending on what was available in their area, ate wild game, fish, nuts, root vegetables, wild fruits, berries, and even insects, along with such foodstuffs as honey and occasionally eggs. Interestingly, in modern life many doctors and nutritionists recommend what is sometimes called the "Paleolithic diet," arguing that in many respects it was superior to the diets of modern people because it was low in fat and starches and high in vitamins and minerals.

Local sources of nutrition varied greatly from place to place. People who lived along the seacoasts relied on fish and seafood, and in the northernmost regions of North America, the Inuit people consumed the meat of animals such as seals and whales, along with fish. Woodlands tribes in the eastern half of the modern-day United States found in the forests they inhabited an abundance of deer and smaller game animals, game birds, and waterfowl and fish in rivers and lakes, supplemented with seasonal fruits, vegetables, and nuts. In contrast, those who lived in desert regions such as portions of Central America and the southwestern United States relied more on small game animals and such vegetable foods as the nopal cactus, which can be eaten cooked or raw (and which modern science has shown reduces cholesterol levels). They also consumed other types of cactus, as well as plants known as agaves, such as the maguey. This variety was the source of pulque, an alcoholic beverage made from the plant's fermented juices and drunk primarily on ceremonial religious occasions; pulque is still made and consumed in many rural areas of central Mexico.

With the emergence of agriculture Native American peoples found that they were able to increase dramatically the amount of food available to them. North Americans, for example, grew various types of beans, which they combined with dog meat, corn, and bear fat to make succotash. They also ate tubers, or root vegetables, which they cooked until they were the consistency of a thick soup. In the moister temperate regions of North America rice became an important staple crop. Also valued as food were organ meats, buffalo tongue, blood soup (made by mixing corn flour with animal blood), and bear meat; these items were often consumed as part of religious ceremonies. Another important food item among North American Indians was pemmican, made with preserved meat and berries. The meat came from deer, elk, rabbits, and, especially among the Plains Indians, buffalo. For beverages, maple sugar–sweetened teas that might be made from various savory twigs, roots, or leaves, such as the roots of the sassafras tree, a member of the laurel family. California Indians produced an early form of lemonade by adding citrus berries to water.

Mesoamerican Indians developed a greater variety of cultivated foodstuffs, in large part because the sparse deserts of parts of the region did not support as much wild game or as many naturally occurring plant foods, at least in the abundance needed for populations to grow. One of the most significant developments in Mesoamerican history was the cultivation of maize, or corn, a crop that was domesticated from a native plant. By about 1400 B.C.E. maize had become the most important staple food crop in Mesoamerica, used to make bread dough and porridges. Corn was especially valuable because, once dried, it can be stored indefinitely without spoiling. In addition to maize the Mesoamericans cultivated and consumed numerous grains, including millet, and beans. Uncooked beans contain natural toxins that make them resistant to pests and microorganisms and have enzyme blockers that prevent them from sprouting when dry. Thus beans, like corn, can be stored for very long periods.

Other important food crops in ancient Mesoamerica included amaranth, a coarse herb rich in proteins, amino acids, and various vitamins and minerals and still a popular food in modern Mexico. Vanilla was cultivated and widely used as a flavoring. So, too, were chili peppers, members of the nightshade family of plants that also includes potatoes, eggplant, and tomatoes. Historians believe that avocados were grown and eaten in Mesoamerica as far back as 10,000 years ago.

The ancient Mesoamericans left another food legacy for which many modern people remain grateful: chocolate. The chocolate came from seeds contained in the fruit of the cacao tree, which grew extensively in the more tropical regions of Central America and Mexico. Historians believe that cacao was first cultivated and used by the Olmec in about 1000 B.C.E. The fruit's seeds were extracted, dried, and roasted and then ground on a flat stone. The resulting powder was then usually mixed with water to make a cocoalike beverage. Because the concoction was bitter, it was commonly flavored with herbs, nuts, seeds, vanilla, honey, and even chili peppers. It was drunk primarily by the upper classes. More widely consumed was *cacao chicha,* a fermented beverage somewhat similar to beer and including the pulp that surrounds the seeds. Cacao beans (as the fruits are often called) were so highly regarded that they were sometimes used as a form of money.

It is believed that the South Americans were the first to develop squash, prized as much for its edible seeds as for its flesh. Another important food item was the potato, first cultivated in the Andes Mountains some seven thousand years ago, when people discovered that it was a highly durable crop that could grow at high elevations and in poor soil. While potatoes are eaten throughout most of the modern world, they were exclusively a South American crop until the 16th century. Yet another important food was the peanut, which is actually not a nut but a member of the bean family. Archaeologists have discovered pots in the shape of peanuts and decorated with pictures of peanuts in South America dating to roughly 1500 B.C.E. Finally, an important food crop in ancient South America was quinoa, often described as a pseudograin, for while it was handled and used like a grain, it actually consists of the seeds of a plant from the goosefoot family. This was another food plant that Andes farmers discovered to be hardy at high elevations. Quinoa is high in fiber and various nutrients, and because it is gluten free, it is easy to digest. Further, in its uncooked state, it is extremely bitter, helping offer protection from birds and other animals.

See also AGRICULTURE; CERAMICS AND POTTERY; CHILDREN; CLIMATE AND GEOGRAPHY; DEATH AND BURIAL; ECONOMY; FAMILY; FESTIVALS; GOVERNMENT ORGANIZATION; HEALTH AND DISEASE; HOUSEHOLD GOODS; HUNTING, FISHING, AND GATHERING; ILLUMINATION; RELIGION AND COSMOLOGY; SETTLEMENT PATTERNS; SOCIAL ORGANIZATION; STORAGE AND PRESERVATION; TRADE AND EXCHANGE.

FURTHER READING

Jean Bottero and Teresa Lavender Fagan, *The Oldest Cuisine in the World: Cooking in Mesopotamia* (Chicago: University of Chicago Press, 2004).

Andrew Dalby, *Siren Feasts: A History of Food and Gastronomy in Greece* (New York: Routledge, 1996).

Andrew Dalby and Sally Grainger, *The Classical Cookbook* (Los Angeles: J. Paul Getty Museum, 1996).

William J. Darby, Paul Ghalioungui, and Louis Grivetti, *Food: The Gift of Osiris* (London and New York: Academic Press, 1977).

Patrick Faas, *Around the Roman Table: Food and Feasting in Ancient Rome,* trans. Shaun Whiteside (Chicago: University of Chicago Press, 2003).

Peter Garnsey, *Famine and Food Supply in the Graeco-Roman World: Responses to Risk and Crisis* (Cambridge, U.K.: Cambridge University Press, 1988).

Ilaria Gozzinni Giacosa, *A Taste of Ancient Rome,* trans. Anna Herklotz (Chicago: University of Chicago Press, 1994).

Patrick E. McGovern, *Ancient Wine: The Search for the Origins of Viniculture* (Princeton, N.J.: Princeton University Press, 2003).

Jane Renfrew, *Food and Cooking in Prehistoric Britain: History and Recipes* (London: English Heritage Publishing, 2005).

Jacqui Wood, *Prehistoric Cooking* (Stroud, U.K.: Tempus, 2001).

► foreigners and barbarians

INTRODUCTION

In the ancient world travel for most people was difficult. In early hunter-gatherer societies people moved about in search of food supplies, and the world's relatively tiny population spread out over millennia, generally avoiding contact with one another. But as early societies turned to agriculture for their food, they lived in settled communities, and it is likely that the average person never traveled more than a day or two's distance from his or her place of birth. People tended to live in societies that were organized by family, clan, and tribal relationships, so they had little contact with people from outside their communities.

Accordingly, early peoples tended to regard "others" with suspicion. People from other communities were potential enemies, bent on conquest or thievery. Furthermore, people from other cultures were likely to have strange customs, habits, languages, modes of dress, and gods. Their very strangeness made them objects of suspicion and hostility. Almost always, they were "barbarians." Among Native Americans in North America, for example, legends and myths record contact with magical strangers who were held in fear. These myths probably originated in brief contact with other tribes.

This suspicion and hostility were not universal, however. In ancient Rome, for example, people from the outside were more or less welcome when Rome was just a small city, not an empire. The ancient Egyptians, too, absorbed foreigners who were willing to adopt Egyptian ways. In the ancient Near East people became accustomed to foreigners because this part of the world was a kind of crossroads, where people from different nations and with different religious beliefs had routine contact with one another. As time went on and nations such as these gained power and empire, they came to view foreigners with suspicion. Meanwhile, countries such as China remained closed to outsiders, who were seen as crude and barbaric. One major form of cultural contact was warfare, but during war people from other cultures were seen as potential slaves. Similarly, the development of empires, such as the Roman Empire, brought cultures into contact, but the nature of the contact was that of master and subject.

The development of trade relationships to some degree broke down these barriers between people. Ancient China, for example, developed trade relationships with people living to the west, and archaeological evidence shows that the ancient Europeans had trade contacts with one another. In Africa some similarities in the continent's many languages, primarily in the form of loan words, suggest that African tribes had trade contact with one another. And, of course, the ancient Romans maintained trade relationships throughout the Mediterranean region. The presence of traders and merchants helped introduce one culture to the customs and manners of another culture, though relationships in general continued to be conducted at arm's length, with little contact between the merchants and ordinary citizens. Religion, too, was a factor in cultural contact. In such nations as India the devoutly religious were eager to spread their beliefs, leading to contact with foreigners.

AFRICA

BY JUSTIN CORFIELD

Traders and merchants traveled throughout Africa in ancient times. Little evidence suggests that they faced any real opposition except during wars, though they were always at risk of being attacked by bandits, pirates, or brigands. It might be thought that language differences were a major obstacle, but this does not seem to have been as much of a problem as it might have been. According to the Greek historian Herodotus, some Carthaginian traders devised a system of bartering by which they would arrive at a place, spread their merchandise on the shore, and then retire to their ships, where they used smoke signals to attract attention. The locals then examined the goods and left gold. If the Carthaginians thought it was enough, they left; if not, they waited until enough was offered. As a point of honor, the locals did not take the goods nor did the Carthaginians take the gold until both sides were satisfied.

Initial contact with foreigners from outside Africa was by boat. Indeed, the Carthaginians themselves were descended from Phoenician sea traders. When she arrived on the coast of modern-day Tunisia, Queen Dido, the legendary founder of Carthage, managed to purchase land from the local ruler, Iargas. According to legend, he told Dido that she could have as much land as she could contain within a piece of leather. She then cut leather into strips and with it marked out a promontory. The city of Carthage later emerged near the site. Additionally, a large number of other cosmopolitan ports developed along the north coast of Africa. Differences in fashion seem to have been more remarkable than race in these centers. Wealth was displayed in jewelry and dress, and the Carthaginians rarely wore belts, making Roman and Greek traders all the more noticeable in the city of Carthage and other parts of Africa they controlled.

The attitude toward the Romans in North Africa changed considerably after the Punic Wars. They had been seen as enemies and invaders, but after the destruction of Carthage in 146 B.C.E. they became colonial masters. Gradually they came to be accepted throughout the ports of North Africa. Septimus Severus, born in Lepcis Magna, was emperor from 193 to 211 C.E., the only African-born emperor to rule the Roman Empire. In 212 C.E. the Edict of Caracalla, known as the Constitutio Antoniniana, or the Edict of Antoninus, was issued by the Roman emperor Caracalla (Marcus Aurelius Antoninus, r. 211–217 C.E.). According to this edict, all freeborn men in the Roman Empire became Roman citizens, thus creating a degree of equality throughout Roman North Africa.

Herodotus wrote extensive descriptions of many of the peoples of northern Africa and parts of modern-day Sudan and Ethiopia, and in these descriptions he clearly shows that travelers were able to visit these areas with few problems. Indeed, some of his descriptions are similar to those of 19th-century European anthropologists, who similarly traveled in these regions with freedom.

The trade routes from North Africa that cut through the Sahara had been traveled by merchants throughout ancient times. A number of these routes connected modern-day Morocco with the source of the Niger River, and others connected the port cities of modern-day Algeria, Tunisia, and Libya with sub-Saharan Africa. Much of this can be seen in ancient drawings of chariots, which may have been used for trade or perhaps for sport or even war. Although there are no records of hostility or friendship between the people of the Sahara and foreigners, the fact that merchants continued to venture across the desert indicates a certain mutual interest in trade.

Maritime expeditions were organized both through the Straits of Gibraltar around the west coast of Africa and from the Red Sea down the east coast to Zanzibar. Certainly the Carthaginians ventured to West Africa. Some accounts of travelers survive, usually secondhand. Some goods from the west coast of Africa did make their way into the Mediterranean and vice versa, and it seems likely that many merchants would have attempted to make contact with the source of the items wanted, mainly gold and ivory.

Pursuing this and other theories, in 1969–1970 Thor Heyerdahl, in his two *Ra* expeditions, was able to fit out a boat similar to those used by the Egyptians, made by boat builders from modern-day Chad, and sail across the Atlantic Ocean on his second attempt. With a similarly constructed boat, *Tigris*, Heyerdahl showed in 1979 it was possible for Sumerians to have sailed to Africa. Arabs certainly traded with East Africa, and the Alexandrian Greek handbook *The Peripleus of the Erythean Sea* describes people living along the Somali coast and Juba as being "men of the tallest stature." Some historians see this portrayal as suggesting that, in the absence of any description of them as blacks, they were not. That such voyages could have taken place on an ongoing basis, and possibly did, does not indicate the reactions of Africans to the arrival of foreigners. However, the existence of maritime trade routes suggests that there was extensive harmonious contact. The presence of early silk in the northeast corner of Madagascar shows that there was trade with Southeast Asia.

Archaeological work in central and southern Africa has not shown much contact throughout the African continent in ancient times, though it would seem likely that it did exist. With no written records, attitudes to foreigners are hard to extrapolate. Archaeologists have drawn conflicting conclusions about the nature of central and southern African civilizations based on pottery fragments, but linguistic analysis provides evidence of a level of contact, interaction, and use of loan words between different groups of people. For example, many words are common to 300 Bantu languages spoken from Duala in modern-day Cameroon to the East African coast and as far south as the Xhosa in modern-day South Africa. These language similarities indicate that different groups interacted; the words for "palm tree" and "fig tree," for example, are the same even in areas where these trees are not found. When combined with analysis of iron tools and some pottery designs, it is easy to see that contact over wide areas took place.

EGYPT

BY MARIE PASSANANTE

The Greek historian Herodotus, who visited Egypt in the fifth century B.C.E., was able to observe Egyptian attitudes toward foreigners at a time when the population of foreigners in Egypt was at its peak. According to Herodotus, Egyptians considered anyone who could not speak the Egyptian language a barbarian. The Egyptians defined themselves by their land and culture, not by physical characteristics. In effect, a foreigner could become Egyptian by adapting Egyptian customs, a process that was not discouraged. However, the Egyptians also viewed their neighbors in a more practical light; foreigners could be enemies. Egyptian kings affirmed their right to rule by their victories over their enemies and described themselves in the language of conquerors. For instance, the king was the one "who repels the Nine Bows" or "who protects Egypt and who curbs the foreign lands."

The Nine Bows represented the peoples conquered by Egypt, either through submission or defeat in war. These peoples were represented by bows alone or as individual prisoners labeled with their nationalities. The bow itself was a generic symbol representing the men of a tribe. As the geography of the ancient world changed, so did the names on the list; however, the number of peoples remained nine. The nations named included Nubians, Libyans, and Asiatics. Because these nations typically were named as enemies of Egypt, it is easy to believe that the Nine Bows represented the enemies of Egypt. However, Upper Egypt and Lower Egypt were also listed among the Nine Bows. In addition, the Nine Bows often were depicted alongside the *rekhyt* bird, which represents the Egyptian people. The Nine Bows defined all the peoples of the ancient world—Egyptian and non-Egyptian alike—as being equally subject to Egypt. The earliest depiction of the Nine Bows is on the ceremonial mace head of King Scorpion (Early Dynastic Period, ca. 2920–2575 B.C.E.) found at Hierakonpolis in Upper Egypt. A statue of King Djoser (r. 2630–2611 B.C.E.) portrays the bows underneath the feet of the king; the trampling of the Nine Bows by the king was a vivid representation of the king's power over the peoples of the world and was used throughout Egyptian history.

Similar to the Nine Bows are the lists recorded in the execration texts. Execration texts were written on pottery or statuettes of prisoners and list foreign kings and peoples, including the countries of Nubia—Irtjet, Wawat, Yam, Medja, and Satju—and cities throughout Palestine. The peoples listed may or may not have been current enemies; for example, the texts include both Nubia, where Egyptian military forces were constantly on alert, and Byblos, with which Egypt maintained a mainly peaceful trading relationship. Unlike the Nine Bows, the execration texts list only non-Egyptian peoples. The implication in the texts is that any non-Egyptian—any foreigner—was a potential enemy of Egypt.

Although foreigners typically were viewed as potential enemies of the Egyptian state, warriors from Nubia and Libya were recruited as mercenaries for the Egyptian army. When the Sixth Dynasty (ca. 2323–ca. 2150 B.C.E.) official Weni led the Egyptian army against Asiatics in the north and the nomadic tribes in the east, he commanded an army made up of Egyptians and Nubians from Wawat, Irtjet, Kaau, Yam, and Medja from the eastern desert. Recruits from Nubia and Medja also joined the armies of the Herakleopolitan and Theban dynasties in the First Intermediate Period (2134–2040 B.C.E.). These Nubian mercenaries fought for the Egyptians against Asiatics, but they also fought in battles meant to secure the southern border against their fellow Nubians. Middle Kingdom Egypt (2040–1640 B.C.E.) saw mercenaries recruited from the oases in the western desert. In the 19th and 20th Dynasties (1307–1070 B.C.E.) major wars with the Libyans resulted in large numbers of Libyan prisoners, who were relocated to settlements in the eastern delta. These Libyans, former enemies of Egypt, consequently were relied upon to protect Egypt's eastern border. In the Late Period the kings of the Saite Dynasty (664–525 B.C.E.) were said to have relied heavily on Greek and Carian mercenaries. The nature of foreign mercenaries and the fact that they often fought against their own people show an ambiguity on the part of the Egyptians; both the enemy of Egypt and the army protecting Egypt were of the same people.

The attitude of the Egyptians toward the Nubians in the south was increasingly one of domination and fear. In the Old Kingdom, King Merenre (2255–2246 B.C.E.) visited the southern frontier and met with the chiefs of Wawat, Irtjet, and the Medja. The Egyptian texts interpreted this as an act of homage on the part of the Nubians, but it was probably a mission geared toward promoting goodwill along the southern border. This goodwill policy was far from the normal course of action. There are records of military campaigns against Nubia from the Early Dynastic Period on. In the Middle Kingdom, Egyptian kings built two series of large fortresses along the Nile in Nubia. The largest fort had a garrison of approximately 300 soldiers and their families. In all, several thousand soldiers and supporting staff were stationed in the 13 forts. This is an immense force, given that the indigenous population of Lower Nubia has been estimated at only 10,000. The pharaohs of the New Kingdom (1550–1070 B.C.E.) built even more forts and established a branch of the Egyptian government to rule in Nubia. To assimilate the Nubians into Egyptian society, the children of the Kushite chiefs were sent to the Egyptian court to learn the language, customs, religion, and so forth of the Egyptian people. The indigenous population was subject to the viceroy of Kush, who acted on the king's behalf.

The Egyptians took less drastic measures when dealing with the lands of Palestine during the period of Egyptian domination in the New Kingdom. While warfare in this area was not unknown, the nations of Palestine were less likely to be a major threat; the Egyptians, while still cautious, did not fear them as they did Nubia. Fortified Egyptian settlements in Palestine were rare. Indigenous populations became vassal states, but in some cases were able to rule themselves as opposed to being ruled by Egyptian governors.

THE MIDDLE EAST

BY JUSTIN CORFIELD

Many of the large empires that covered the ancient Near East were multiethnic, consisting of large numbers of different and often linguistically diverse peoples. The Assyrian, Babylonian, and Persian Empires embraced much wider areas than those of the city-states of Sumer and often subjugated alien peoples through force. The Assyrians, in particular, gained a reputation for the persecution of their enemies. Their great king Ashurbanipal (r. 668–627 B.C.E.) sacked Tyre, and his subsequent suppression of the people of Elam resulted in the deportation of many leading Elamites to Samaria in Palestine. The holding of the Hebrews in exile in Babylonia from 587 to 538 B.C.E. is another well-known case, documented in the Bible.

Achaemenid Persia was a massive, multilingual empire extending over the entire Near East. The Persians used Aramaic as the written language of administration and communication between the capital and outlying areas, Elamite as the principal language of administration at the capital Persepolis, and Old Persian when erecting public monuments with royal inscriptions (which, however, were usually written in Babylonian and Elamite as well). The Persians freed the Hebrews from their Babylonian exile and began to reverse some of the deportations perpetrated by the Assyrians. As the Persian Empire grew in importance, it attracted many Greek merchants and soldiers. By the time of the invasion of Alexander the Great, large Greek communities existed throughout much of the Persian Empire, and substantial units of Greek soldiers fought in the Persian army. At Gaugamela in 331 B.C.E. these soldiers were placed around the Immortals who guarded Darius III (r. 336–330 B.C.E.), showing his trust for them on the battlefield. These Greeks were to be heavily persecuted when Alexander the Great and his successors came to power.

Alexander the Great and the "Successor States" that emerged from the Diadochi Wars after his death were also multiethnic. Although there was always a Greek-Macedonian governing class, most of the administrators were locally born. For many of the farmers in small villages and settlements throughout the Near East, the change in rule from the Persians to the Seleucids probably had little real impact. Many of the cities in the Near East most likely became increasingly multiethnic and multilingual. Although occasional racial scapegoating must have occurred, and stereotyping abounds

Detail of an Ethiopian tribute bearer, from a relief in stairway of the palace at Persepolis, Persia (modern-day Iran). (Courtesy of the Oriental Institute of the University of Chicago)

in many surviving images, ethnicity does not seem to have been a major cause for trouble except when an uprising took place. This was certainly the case in the First Jewish Revolt (66–70 C.E.), after which the Romans persecuted the Jews. This theme appeared again in the revolt led by the Jewish leader Bar Kokhba (d. 135 C.E.), after which Jews were forbidden to enter Jerusalem.

Before these two revolts the attitudes to foreigners in the Holy Land were mixed. During the period of the Old Testament the fierce battles between tribes were commonplace and ferocious, but by the time of the Roman occupation of Palestine the situation had relaxed considerably. Trade had ameliorated the previously hostile tribes in the Holy Land and presumably elsewhere in the Near East as well. Many foreigners were no doubt accepted by locals. Others were viewed with suspicion.

The proximity of areas inhabited by Jews and non-Jews meant that there were large numbers of *telones* (customs officials or, more commonly, tax collectors) around the river Galilee. There were certainly Gentiles in Tiberias, an overwhelmingly Jewish city, and Jews lived in largely Gentile cities, such as Scythopolis. Although the Jews did exclude Gentiles from their temples and had several other restrictions, relations were generally fairly harmonious. Herod the Great (r. 37–4 B.C.E.), king of Judea, helped by administering the Gentile areas in more of a Greco-Roman manner than he did the Jewish parts of his lands. The Romans respected the Jewish observance of the Sabbath and exempted Jews from conscription in Roman armies. However, there were occasional tensions, as when Pontius Pilate hung images of the Roman emperor in Jerusalem and minted coins that were seen by the Jews as bearing pagan images.

Evidence from the letters of Saint Paul clearly shows a far more harmonious Near East, whereby travelers from some parts of the region, or from outside it, were made welcome in many towns and cities. In Ephesians (2:19), Paul states, "Now therefore ye are no more strangers and foreigners." This is also borne out by the ease of travel by Romans, who were able to journey throughout the Roman Empire without any problems. In addition, a number of them established trading operations outside the empire. The emperor Valens (r. 364–378 C.E.) managed to forge a peace treaty with the Goths, allowing Roman traders to have access to parts of modern-day Romania controlled by the Goths.

ASIA AND THE PACIFIC

BY DAVID KELLY

Historically, records have not been kept of the attitudes held by individuals who were not of social prominence, as history has been written about the wealthy and powerful and not about average citizens. Still, there are some characteristics that can be noted with respect to the ways in which the ancient societies of Asia and the Pacific region viewed outsiders.

The largest and most stable culture in the region, China, has traditionally been a closed society, living in willing isolation from the rest of the world, a tradition that is only beginning to come apart in the 21st century. By far the most common connection that ancient Chinese and others in the region had with strangers from foreign lands came through trade. From the second millennium B.C.E. China was connected by trade with the Near East kingdom of Mesopotamia, centered in what is now Iran. By the first century C.E. there developed an overland trade route from the Roman Empire to China, dubbed the "Silk Road" because silk was China's most coveted export; the secret of its production was carefully hidden from foreigners until five centuries later. Although this path ran through many important cities as it wound from Damascus in the west to China's far eastern shore for nearly a thousand years, most Chinese citizens still kept their distance from the traders who traveled from Europe. Evidence suggests that westerners trading in China dealt with a limited number of merchants, while most ordinary citizens had no interaction with them. This narrow engagement of the East with foreigners was true of other countries in the area, such as Vietnam and Cambodia, which did their trading almost exclusively with China and not with foreigners.

When trade routes by sea were established between India and Asia in the second century B.C.E., there was possibly even less interaction with foreigners. For example, there was the trading polity of Funan, a kingdom at the tip of the Mekong Delta around the third century C.E. that reached as far as Malaysia and Burma. Artifacts from China, India, and Rome have been found in the remains of the Funan Empire, but foreigners were geographically limited by mountains close to the shore that inhibited travel. Unlike lands that were openly available to traders, the lands of Asia and the Pacific were not physically open to exploration. Although traders did not travel freely from India, Indian culture did have strong influences on Funan that spread across Asia. By 400 C.E. Indian writing systems, Sanskrit vocabulary, and Hindu beliefs had been adapted across China.

One social aspect that did promote positive interaction with foreigners was the spread of religion. Religious conversion generally followed routes of trade. Java and Sumatra show signs of the presence of Hinduism as early as the second century B.C.E., and from there its influence grew throughout Asia and the Pacific. Followers of Mahayana Buddhism, which also had its roots in India, made a concerted effort around 100 C.E. to spread its teachings eastward and quickly overtook the Asian continent, moving in a relatively short time through Southeast Asia to Korea, China, and Japan.

There has been speculation that the spread of Hinduism and Buddhism from India into Southeast Asia might have been related in part at least to the fact that native rulers might have welcomed missionaries from India, making them participants in their courts in order to strengthen their hold. The Hindu concept of kingship is captured in the word *devaraja*, which comes from Sanskrit and translates as "god who is a king." Rulers who welcomed the arrival of Hinduism to their lands were inviting their subjects to see them as incarnations of the Hindu gods.

In general, the countries that had means of self-sufficiency, including China, Thailand, Cambodia, Vietnam, and Korea, were naturally more insular and less open to interaction with people from other countries, while island nations, of which there are dozens scattered throughout the South Pacific, tended to be more familiar with the idea of trading with outsiders over the course of hundreds of years and were therefore more comfortable with the idea of associating with westerners when they began arriving.

Although they were more open to trading with foreigners, many cultures of the Pacific Islands retained a spiritual distance from outsiders, including those who lived in villages that were in close geographical proximity to their own. Headhunting was a common practice in many cultures throughout Southeast Asia by the second century C.E., and it was to remain an important practice for centuries to come. The practice entailed planned, unprovoked, surprise attacks against others. Victims were decapitated as they were killed, and their heads were taken by the aggressors back to their villages, where the skulls were cleaned and often painted with ceremonial designs.

There are several theories about the beliefs that compelled headhunting. Most interpretations reject the simple idea that such ritualized violence could have been motivated purely for the sake of intimidating one's neighbors for military and political gain. There was almost universally a religious motivation behind it. In many cultures beheading a stranger and keeping the head was considered a way of making them a part of one's own ancestral lineage. There were also cultures that refused to see strangers as humans and viewed them instead as demons in human form. Taking the head from such a nonhuman entity and bringing it to one's village, the headhunter could humanize the spirit that dwelled within it. In this case, the heads were often given names and spoken to in a friendly fashion. Headhunting was practiced for different reasons in different societies, and its meaning is not entirely clear; still, it is apparent that the practice was widespread and that rather than being motivated by violence, it often reflected the tribe's complex view of outsiders.

EUROPE

BY PETER S. WELLS

Human communities have always come into contact with other communities. From earliest historical times (those from which we have written texts as sources of information) literary evidence informs us about how members of one group thought about other peoples—peoples they considered to be "foreigners" or "barbarians." By the latter part of the Early Stone Age, from about 40,000 years ago, archaeological evidence shows that people were acquiring materials not available to them locally, such as high-quality flint for making tools and shells from the seashores, which they used as ornaments. To procure these items, they needed either to trade with other groups who lived near the resources or to travel to those resources, which would have brought them into contact with other groups. From these earliest prehistoric times we do not have direct evidence about what people thought about others with whom they came into contact, but ideas about "others" must have developed through these contacts. In later periods, such as the Neolithic, the Bronze Age, and the Iron Age (taken together and representing all of Europe, 7000 B.C.E.–500 C.E.), archaeological evidence for interaction between communities is increasingly abundant. People were coming into contact with others through trade, migration, war, and other kinds of travel, such as trips to visit relatives and religious pilgrimages.

In the archaeological evidence we can recognize the development of distinctive types of personal ornaments and styles of dress that probably served to mark the identities of different communities. From the distributions of such objects in different regions, we can discern "borderlands" where groups came into contact. We can gain some insight into attitudes toward foreigners and reactions to them through analysis of the patterns of display of signs of identity, such as dress pins, belt ornaments, neck rings, decoration on weapons, and other material signs.

Although we have no written sources from temperate Europe to inform us about attitudes toward the Greek world of the Mediterranean (because the Iron Age peoples of Europe did not have a system of writing), we can learn something about their attitudes from their trade for Greek objects. During the sixth and fifth centuries B.C.E. many of the larger communities north of the Alps, such as those at Mont Lassois in eastern France and at the Heuneburg in southwestern Germany, acquired Greek luxury objects, including fine painted pottery, bronze wine-serving vessels, and ornaments of coral and ivory. Such items are found in the wealthiest burials at the largest communities of the period (550–450 B.C.E.). The grave of one rich woman at Vix near Mont Lassois, with two ornate ceramic wine cups and an enormous bronze krater for mixing wine with water, all made in Greek workshops, is a good example. The presence of such objects in the graves of the elite of Early Iron Age society indicates that Greek luxury goods and the society that produced them were held in high regard by the local rulers in temperate Europe. There is even evidence to suggest that elites in Iron Age Europe adopted the wine-drinking ritual practiced in Greece as a means of expressing their status and power within their societies.

As with the attitudes toward the Greek world in the Early Iron Age, in the Late Iron Age luxury objects made in the Roman world were highly valued by the elites of society. Roman ceramic amphorae, used to bring in Mediterranean wine, as well as bronze vessels for serving it, together with fine pottery, coins, and other objects, were highly prized by wealthy and powerful individuals in Late Iron Age society. These items are found in the richest graves, frequently in association with other objects of special value and prestige. Examples of such burials are those at Welwyn Garden City in the United Kingdom and at Goeblingen-Nospelt in Luxembourg. During and after the Roman conquests many people who lived in lands north of the newly won imperial territories showed their admiration for things Roman. In graves in northern Germany, Denmark, and elsewhere beyond the frontier, Roman bronze vessels and other signs of connection with Rome were proudly displayed in the funeral ceremonies and then placed next to the deceased individuals in their graves.

GREECE

BY JOHN THORBURN

According to the Greek ideal, people from other towns or countries were to be treated in a kindly manner. In the earliest Greek literature, especially Homer's *Iliad* and *Odyssey*—probably first written down in the eighth century B.C.E.—the proper treatment of strangers and outsiders is of great significance. The most common Homeric word for an outsider is *xenos*, which usually means "foreigner," "stranger," "guest," or "guest-friend." Another Greek word, *xenia*, primarily denotes either the hospitality shown to an outsider or good relations between two towns or cities.

The Homeric epics, core texts of Greek education, provided many examples of how strangers or outsiders should be treated. In the sixth book of the *Iliad* the Greek Diomedes encounters the Trojan Glaucus on the battlefield, where they discover that their fathers had a host-guest relationship. For this reason Diomedes and Glaucus decide not to fight and even exchange gifts of hospitality with each other. In Homer's *Odyssey*, Odysseus, returning to his country after 20 years abroad, is disguised as a beggar from another land. Before Odysseus goes to his home, he encounters one of his swineherds, who despite his own lowly social and financial status offers this unknown beggar shelter, food, drink, and even clothing. In contrast to the swineherd's hospitality is the behavior of the lawless Cyclops. Although Odysseus warns the Cyclops that Zeus himself, king of the gods, protects strangers, the monster declares that he and his race are more powerful than Zeus. The Cyclops further violates the customs of hospitality by imprisoning Odysseus and several of his men and even eating six of Odysseus's companions. Odysseus eventually escapes the Cyclops's cave after blinding the monster, thus punishing him for violating the customs of hospitality.

As the Homeric epics show, those upholding the customs of hospitality could expect fair treatment, whereas those behaving in an uncivilized or barbaric manner would be punished. The English word *barbarian* comes from a Greek word, *barbaros*, which may have originated from the way the language of non-Greeks sounded to Greek speakers ("ba-ba-ba"). So, in a strict sense, the Greeks regarded non-Greek speakers as barbarians. Because the expansion of the Persian Empire in the sixth and fifth centuries B.C.E. brought increased contact with and warfare against the Greeks, they regarded the Persians in particular as *barbaroi*. Nevertheless, some Greeks, even after fighting the Persians early in the fifth century B.C.E., later associated with the Persians and other so-called barbarians either for their own benefit or the benefit of their cities.

Although non-Greek speakers were labeled barbarians, some Greeks regarded their fellow Greeks as outsiders. During the eighth and seventh centuries B.C.E. the Spartans conquered and enslaved many of their neighbors. Some of the defeated towns, called *perioikoi* ("those living round about") could keep their own governments but had to serve in the Spartan military and could not vote in the Spartan citizen assembly. Sparta's slaves, called helots, had to give their masters half of what their land produced. Because the helots outnumbered the Spartans and thus might try to overthrow them, the Spartans terrorized them with an annual practice, called the *krypteia*, in which selected Spartans assassinated suspicious helots. Sometimes, however, helots could be freed from their slavery, especially for outstanding military service when the ranks of the Spartan citizens needed supplementing.

Although the treatment of the helots is an extreme example, being an outsider in a Greek town could have disadvantages. People who were neither slaves nor citizens of the towns in which they lived were called *metics*. The laws governing *metics* differed in each town, but *metics* often had to perform some type of military service or pay additional fees to live in a town or both. In Athens *metics* could not own land. The disadvantages of being a *metic* in Athens may not have been too oppressive, however, because many outsiders resided there, such as the famous philosophers Aristotle and Theophrastus.

It was not just that Athenian *metics* faced certain restrictions; in 451 B.C.E. the Athenian statesman Pericles persuaded his fellow citizens to approve a law limiting citizenship only to those born to Athenian parents. Before Pericles' law took effect, a person with an Athenian father but a non-Athenian mother could be a citizen. Ironically, later in his life Pericles was a victim of his own law when he fathered a son by a non-Athenian woman. An exception was made for this son, however, and the law was soon repealed.

When Pericles was Athens's leading citizen, he also persuaded the Athenians to embark upon an ambitious building program. The most famous product of this program was the Parthenon, built between 447 and 432 B.C.E. Given Pericles' law on citizenship, some of the sculpture on this temple is noteworthy. The temple's southern metopes (decorated panels) show a battle between two mythical tribes, the Lapiths and the centaurs (the western end of Zeus's temple at Olympia also depicts this subject); its northern metopes have scenes from the Trojan War; the eastern and western metopes portray, respectively, the Olympian gods battling a group of giants and the Greeks battling the Amazons, a tribe of warlike women. Thus, each sculptural group portrays Greeks battling against non-Greeks (Trojans, Amazons) or beings (centaurs, giants) that threaten their civilization. According to mythology, the Greeks or their gods had triumphed over these "foreign" enemies in each case.

The Athenian ideal of triumphing over barbarians or uncivilized peoples suffered a severe blow after Pericles' death in 429 B.C.E. By 404 B.C.E. the Spartans had defeated the Athenians in the Peloponnesian War. Ironically, Greek culture experienced its widest diffusion by a people that most Greeks would have considered barbarians, even though they spoke a dialect of Greek. By 323 B.C.E. the Macedonian Philip II and his successor, his son Alexander, had conquered the whole of Greece. Alexander went on to triumph over the Persians and tribes as far away as India, and he spread Greek culture by encouraging his soldiers to intermarry with these foreigners.

After Alexander's death and the gradual breakup of his empire, both Macedonians and Greeks eventually came under the control of the Romans in the second century B.C.E. Although they were non-Greek speakers, the Romans became captivated by the culture of their captives and incorporated many Greek elements into their own society. In the first century C.E., however, Christianity began spreading through both Greek and Roman cultures, and the apostle Paul, writing in Greek, would declare to the Colossians that in the Christian way of life distinctions no longer existed between Greeks and Jews, slaves or free persons, or Scythians and barbarians.

ROME

BY KIRK H. BEETZ

During the era of Rome's first kings (ca. 753–ca. 510 B.C.E.) Romans apparently held fairly relaxed attitudes toward outsiders. Foreigners were absorbed into the city and could even achieve important positions in government. For instance, the legendary king Ancus Marcius (r. 642–617 B.C.E.) was a Sabine (a people of the Apennine Mountains) by ancestry. Perhaps this accommodating attitude reflected Rome's small size—at that time it was still a small town—as well as its not yet having achieved a view of itself as different from the other towns in its part of Italy. These circumstances changed in 510 B.C.E. when Tarquinius Superbus (r. 534–510 B.C.E.), a king who had been exiled from Rome, returned with an Etruscan army to reclaim his throne. There was no question that Tarquinius Superbus's army represented outsiders trying to impose their will on Rome.

During the early years of the Roman Republic (ca. 509–27 B.C.E.) almost everyone was a foreigner to the Romans, and nearly every foreigner was a potential enemy. Italy was populated by several cultures, with Celts in the north, Greeks in the south, and at least eight other distinct cultures, the Latin culture of the Romans being the smallest in population. Yet through conquest and diplomacy Rome managed to gain control of central Italy by 290 B.C.E. Those under its rule who were not Roman citizens were the "Italian allies." Romans regarded them with disdain, but by about 200 B.C.E. the Italian allies wished to be recognized as Roman citizens themselves.

By then the Roman government included the office of tribune, a person elected by the plebeians (lower-class Roman citizens) to represent them in government affairs. One tribune, Gaius Gracchus, was a hero to the plebeians for advocating their rights until, in 121 B.C.E., he proposed extending Roman citizenship to the Italian allies. It was a serious misjudgment of public opinion. The plebeians did not want to share the benefits of Roman citizenship with outsiders, and Gaius committed suicide just before an angry mob could kill him. In 91 B.C.E. the tribune Marius Livius Drusus was murdered because he advocated giving citizenship to everyone in Italy, all of which Rome by then controlled. His enemies insisted that other Italians were barbarians and utterly inferior to Romans. His death touched off the Social War of 91–89 B.C.E., during which the Italian allies tried to set up their own independent state. They lost the war but won Roman citizenship.

In 146 B.C.E. Rome had conquered Macedonia and most of Greece. To the Romans the Greeks were puzzling. For instance, Greeks were comfortable with homosexuality, which Romans regarded as degenerate behavior. Yet the Romans had an inferiority complex toward the Greeks, whose language, literature, and knowledge of science they considered superior to their own. Any Roman who could afford one wanted a Greek and not a Roman physician. Romans therefore made exceptions to their laws when it came to the Greeks. This policy toward the Greeks may have influenced how Rome shaped its laws for other foreigners.

To the Romans any foreigner was a barbarian, and as the Roman Empire expanded, it absorbed numerous foreign cultures, all of which had their own supposedly barbaric laws and customs. It seemed unreasonable to the Romans to apply laws to the barbarians that the barbarians would not understand. For instance, foreigners from cultures in which everyone communally co-owned the farmland would probably have trouble understanding a law against planting crops on someone else's property. The Romans were practical, and Roman magistrates based their interpretations of laws on general principles about how people should treat one another; they saw the need to make humane—rather than merely legal—decisions when a barbarian ignorant of Roman ways violated a Roman law.

Still, there were certain behaviors Romans did not tolerate from barbarians. One was rebellion. Another was disrespect to Roman gods. Romans were willing to allow worship of foreign gods, but they also expected everyone to follow the rules regarding Roman gods. When emperors became god-kings, shrines were established for them in Roman cities, and everyone was expected to pay proper respect. In regions such as North Africa this worked out well. The North Africans were content to turn whole temples over to the worship of Roman emperors because they saw themselves as being protected by those emperors.

Palestine was different. It took the Romans hundreds of years to figure out why Jews and Christians refused to offer simple, inexpensive sacrifices to the Roman emperors. After numerous very bloody revolts by Jews, Titus (r. 79–81 C.E.) the son of the emperor Vespasian (r. 69–79 C.E.), destroyed Jerusalem in 70 C.E. A sign that the Romans still failed to understand Jewish religious beliefs was the founding of the city Aelia Capitolina on the site of the ruined Jerusalem in 130 C.E., something the emperor Hadrian (r. 117–38 C.E.) expected the local people to greet with happiness. The Jews instead revolted because of the violation of their sacred city, and the rebellion lasted three years (132–35 C.E.) before the Romans put it down.

Hadrian had good reason to think Aelia Capitolina would be successful. Almost everywhere Rome built a city, people welcomed it, and it filled quickly with local people as well as Romans. This the Romans took as evidence that their way of life was better than everyone else's. Romans were sure that being Roman was the best thing any human could ever be. Romanization—the process of changing the behavior of barbarians into behavior that matched or at least closely resembled that of Romans themselves—usually succeeded, and Romans were surprised when it did not.

When Marcus Aurelius Antoninus (r. 211–17 C.E.), nicknamed Caracalla for a style of coat he supposedly designed, became emperor, the Roman Empire extended throughout North Africa, east into Mesopotamia, west through Spain, and north to the Rhine River and even into Britain. Many people in these areas came to speak like Romans, behave like Romans, and think of themselves as Romans, but Roman citizens still considered them foreigners. Then, in 212 C.E., Caracalla changed their status by declaring every free man living in the Roman Empire a Roman citizen. This sweeping decree did not, however, end Roman snobbery. Italian Romans continued to regard the accents of North Africans and northern Celts as somewhat primitive. They viewed the Parthians to the east as self-indulgent and decadent, morally inferior to "real" Romans. And they considered the Germanic peoples of northern Europe and Ukraine crude, dirty, and excessively violent. That Germanic tribes eventually overran the Western Roman Empire did not stop Romans from thinking of them as uncivilized.

THE AMERICAS

BY PENELOPE OJEDA DE HUALA

The ancient remains of the indigenous people of the Americas offer few clues about their attitudes toward strangers and foreigners. However, archaeological evidence points to a high level of interaction among the diverse groups that populated the New World, including a widespread trade network. Long-distance trade was only one component of the relationships among foreign and local communities. Along with commodities the varied societies of the New World exchanged ideas, customs, and beliefs—and sometimes forced them upon one another. These ancient cultural clashes are difficult to decipher, though scholars and scientists have gleaned valuable knowledge concerning them.

From very early times the indigenous groups of the Americas depended on local trade for survival. The diverse and sometimes harsh weather and geography of the American continents not only allowed for but indeed almost demanded interregional reciprocity. Neighboring groups often depended on one another, and over the course of time especially through migration and intermarriage, larger social and economic networks developed.

NORTH AMERICA

In the Middle Woodland Period (ca. 300 B.C.E. to 500 C.E.), Hopewell culture came to encompass a unique cultural sphere of influence. Centered in southern Ohio, the Hopewell built on the burial practices of their predecessors, the Adena culture, expanding and disseminating a mortuary ceremonialism throughout the woodland areas of the northeast and as far away as Illinois. This Hopewell interaction sphere (system of exchange) included wide-ranging interregional interactions and exchanges, where foreign and local traditions and art forms flowed freely from place to place. Mound building became especially prolific throughout this period, as did the use of copper and mica ornaments.

Hohokam culture emerged from the desert regions of the Southwest in southern Arizona around 200 B.C.E. Archaeologists trace their origin to northern Mexico. This foreign connection continued throughout Hohokam development and is evidenced in the use of ceremonial ball court, irrigation, and copper bells. Evidence also suggests a thriving trade existed between Hohokam and its neighbors, including the Mogollon (ca. 200–1400 C.E.) of southeastern Arizona and southwestern New Mexico.

Mesoamerica

In prehistoric Mesoamerica (the present-day regions of Mexico, Guatemala, Belize, El Salvador, and Honduras) attitudes toward foreigners and strangers appear in various artworks produced in the Pre-Classic Period (1500 B.C.E.–300 C.E.). Depictions of foreign captives became common beginning with the Olmec (ca. 1200–ca. 400 B.C.E.) who prospered in the Gulf coast region of Mexico. Images of defeated foreigners symbolized power and hegemony for the various civilizations that flourished in Pre-Classic Mesoamerica.

Olmec art centers on the promotion of rulership. At the archaeological site of La Venta, an early example, Altar 4 (ca. 900 B.C.E.) depicts a ruler coming out of a carved niche. In his hand he holds a rope that wraps around the base and leads to two bound captives, one on either side. This monument probably served as a throne and was a symbol of both the Olmec state (ruler) and its religion (the Olmec creation myth featured a primordial cave). However, the presence of bound captives directly tied to the seat of power also reflects the importance of warfare in Olmec power symbolism.

Similarly, in Monte Alban, capital of the Zapotec civilization (500 B.C.E.–1000 C.E.), in the Valley of Oaxaca (south-central Mexico) the so-called Temple of the Danzantes (Temple of the Dancers) contains 150 stone slabs depicting captives carved in low relief. These figures, all individually posed and all men, are incised with such an elegant line that they were at first believed to be dancers; however, they are shown with closed eyes and scroll markings indicating that they are dead and possibly mutilated. In Mesoamerica war was often waged not only for extension of territory and tribute but also for acquiring precious objects for rituals, including foreign sacrificial victims.

South America

The South American continent is a world of extremes—desert coast gives way to the majestic Andes, which give way to the mighty Amazon. This striking environment shaped the daily life and cultural development of ancient Andean cultures, creating a deeply transcendent aesthetic tradition defined by its sacred architecture, textiles, and stonework.

The archaeological site of Cerro Sechín (ca. 1000 B.C.E.) in the northern highlands of present-day Peru combines the spiritual aspects typical of Andean art with a sinister twist. A mazelike temple complex surrounded by more than 300 10-foot-tall slabs features numerous images of bodies and severed body parts. The site has been interpreted as a memorial to a horrific massacre, and there are also indications that it may refer to a shamanic initiation ritual. However, among the dismembered bodies are men with battle clubs, which suggests ritual warfare. Whatever the case may be, the gruesome nature of this depiction points to the possibility of unfriendly relations with neighboring groups. Here, as in Mesoamerica, foreigners were often depicted in scenes of war or sacrifice and seem to have been embedded in the trappings of political propaganda.

Another example, a Nazca (Peru, ca. 400 B.C.E.) ceramic in the shape of a stepped fret—an abstract form resembling a mountain and a symbol of prestige—exhibits a complicated narrative scene of a cosmic battle between bird-headed shamans and writhing opponents. Representing a victory over an enemy (whether real or supernatural), this work is testimony to the political nature of the Nazca culture and provides insight into the complicated interactions among the people of that time and place.

See also ARCHITECTURE; BORDERS AND FRONTIERS; CERAMICS AND POTTERY; CLIMATE AND GEOGRAPHY; ECONOMY; EMPIRES AND DYNASTIES; EXPLORATION; GOVERNMENT ORGANIZATION; LANGUAGE; LAWS AND LEGAL CODES; MIGRATION AND POPULATION MOVEMENTS; MILITARY; RELIGION AND COSMOLOGY; RESISTANCE AND DISSENT; SACRED SITES; SEAFARING AND NAVIGATION; SOCIAL ORGANIZATION; TRADE AND EXCHANGE; WAR AND CONQUEST; WRITING.

FURTHER READING

Rhys Carpenter, *Beyond the Pillars of Hercules: The Classical World Seen through the Eyes of Its Discoveries* (London: Universal-Tandem, 1973).

Paul Cartledge, *The Greeks: A Portrait of Self and Others* (New York: Oxford University Press, 1993).

Lionel Casson, *Travel in the Ancient World* (Baltimore. Md.: Johns Hopkins University Press, 1994).

Ernest S. Dodge, *Islands and Empires: Western Impact on the Pacific and East Asia* (Minneapolis: University of Minnesota Press, 1976).

J. D. Fage, ed., *The Cambridge History of Africa*, Vol. 2, *From c. 500 BC to AD 1050* (Cambridge, U.K.: Cambridge University Press, 1978).

Simon Goodenough, *Citizens of Rome* (New York: Crown, 1979).

Edith Hall, *Inventing the Barbarian: Greek Self-Definition through Tragedy* (New York: Oxford University Press, 1989).

Thomas Harrison, ed., *Greeks and Barbarians* (Edinburgh, U.K.: Edinburgh University Press, 2001).

Wolfram Herwig, *The Roman Empire and Its Germanic Peoples*, trans. Thomas Dunlap (Berkeley: University of California Press, 1997).

Walther Hinz, *The Lost World of Elam: Re-creation of a Vanished Civilization*, trans. Jennifer Barnes (London. Sidgwick and Jackson, 1972).

Owen Lattimore and Eleanor Lattimore, eds., *Silks, Spices, and Empire: Asia Seen through the Eyes of Its Discoverers* (New York: Delacorte Press, 1968).

Peter S. Wells, *The Barbarians Speak: How the Conquered Peoples Shaped Roman Europe* (Princeton: Princeton University Press, 1999).

Peter S. Wells, *Celts, Germans and Scythians: Archaeology and Identity in Iron Age Europe* (London: Duckworth, 2001).

David Whitehead, *The Ideology of the Athenian Metic* (Cambridge, U.K.: Cambridge Philological Society, 1977).

G

► gender structures and roles

INTRODUCTION

Much of what historians know, or think they know, about gender relationships in prehistory comes primarily from burial practices and artwork. Surviving tombs provide insight, for example, into the status of women and men, and artwork depicts men and women engaged in various activities that were likely an outgrowth of assumptions about gender in that culture. During later periods written documents survive that shed light on gender issues, at least in some parts of the world.

The concept of gender and gender roles was felt in a number of areas of ancient life, including power and rulership, religion, family structure, and occupation, and these roles were typically taught to both boys and girls early in life through initiation rituals and segregation of the sexes. With regard to power, it comes as no surprise that most ancient world cultures were dominated by men, with women playing more passive, domestic roles. This was not universally true at all times and all places, however. From time to time—in ancient Greece and Egypt, for example—a powerful woman emerged who assumed the reins of power. In doing so, though, she probably had to take on many stereotypical masculine traits, such as ruthlessness.

In religion men tended to serve as priests, shamans, and religious gurus, but again, this was not universally true. In the ancient Americas, for example, archaeological evidence suggests that women often served as shamans and priests. It was also common in many cultures for its pantheon of deities to include goddesses as well as gods. The ancient Greeks and Romans are prominent in this regard, but examples of goddess figures can be found in ancient cultures the world over. These goddess figures were thought to have ruled over various spheres of life, and this idea would have affected concepts of proper gender roles and expectations.

With regard to family structure, the status and role of women was probably determined in large part by the economic conditions of the culture. In hunter-gatherer societies it was long assumed that men did both the hunting and gathering while women tended to the home. Some scholars dispute this assumption, arguing that women took an active role in gathering food and may very well have hunted small game. As cultures turned to agriculture and became more sedentary and complex, gender specialization became the norm, with men involved in public affairs and women performing primarily domestic tasks.

Women may have taken primary responsibility for domestic tasks, but in many cultures they also held occupations, primarily crafts. In the ancient Americas, for example, women were primarily responsible for such activities as textile production and weaving. Because a great deal of craftwork took place in homes, it is reasonable to conclude that women took part as potters, wood carvers, and the like. Men generally were of higher status in patriarchal cultures and had authority over their wives and family, but some cultures, particularly in Africa, were more matriarchal, with the wife and mother ruling in the home. It was not uncommon in many cultures for men and women to spend most of their time apart, with women living in separate "women's quarters" and men taking part in separate activities. It should be noted as well that in some ancient cultures, homosexuality was more widely accepted than it is in modern life.

AFRICA

BY MICHAEL J. O'NEAL

The chief difficulty historians have with reconstructing gender roles in ancient Africa is the absence of written records. Gender is not an object, something with a tangible existence; gender is a social construct, meaning that gender roles are established by the assumptions people make about the relationship between men and women in society. Some written records touching on African gender relationships survive from the ancient Roman writers, but they tend to be unreliable, for they embody the cultural assumptions of the Romans, which may not correspond to those of the Africans they observed. Some information has been transmitted orally through the centuries, but it is difficult to determine the extent to which that information remains accurate 2,000 or more years later. Finally, a certain amount of information can be gleaned from the archaeological record. For example, tombs and artwork, and even such objects as tools and seeds, can provide insight into the relative status of men and women, but this record is spotty, so historians have to try to fill in the details.

During prehistoric times, when the primary social activity of bands of hunter-gatherers was the acquisition of food, labor was divided along gender lines. Men tended to be the hunters, particularly when they were after big game; women's hunting activities tended to be restricted to small game and birds. Otherwise, women were the primary gatherers, finding and storing nuts, grains, tubers, leafy vegetables, fruits, berries, and eggs, though men learned to gather as well when they were children at their mother's sides. In coastal regions men were the primary fishermen, but both men and women took part in the search for shallow-water seafood. Women likely chose as mates men who were adept at acquiring and sharing food.

Women were in general the primary caregivers for children and nursed them during infancy, though men, too, played an important role, particularly as children grew older. Women could not become bound to several children, for their role in gathering food was essential. Thus, women tended to space their children, typically four or five years apart, so that they could devote their attention to one at a time. Ancient African women developed slings they could use to strap infants to themselves, leaving their hands free for gathering and preparing food.

It might be assumed that ancient African women were less valued than men, especially given that most African societies were patriarchal, meaning that men were dominant, and patrilineal, meaning that descent was traced through the father's rather than the mother's bloodlines. This assumption, however, is not entirely true, for in many ancient African societies women were highly honored and, in fact, wielded a considerable amount of power. In doing so, they gained support from a worldview that placed a great deal of emphasis on collective obligations and responsibilities. Important values included group solidarity and harmony, with the group in turn integrated with nature, ancestors, and the gods. To maintain this harmony and to ensure the continued existence of the group, the interests of everyone had to be respected. Thus, women, far from being excluded, played a vital role in the affairs of many African tribes. Further, traditional gender roles did not always correspond with biological sex.

For example, kinship was important in African tribal society. Kinship networks, rather than a central government, provided a link between a person and the larger community, and kinfolk were responsible for socializing children into the community's values and folkways. But even though most African societies were patrilineal, the mother's kin were important in the lives of children. Thus, among the Sotho-Venda of South Africa, the brother of a child's mother was called the "male mother" and enjoyed a close relationship with his nephews and nieces. Similarly, the father's sister was the focus of great respect and referred to as the "female father." In family councils the father's sister was given the status of priestess and was an important link between the family and its ancestors. Ruling over the household of the tribal chief was his sister, who had great influence in tribal matters; the chief always deferred to her judgment in ruling on the tribe's affairs. In some ancient African societies, when it was necessary to name a new chief, the deceased chief's brother and sister jointly determined who the successor would be.

Among the Swazi tribe in southeastern Africa, the Queen Mother, or the chief's mother, similarly played a major role in the affairs of the community. She was referred to as the She-Elephant, and she was a joint ruler with her son. Her views were given equal weight with those of her son in such matters as legal disputes, land allocation, and community ritual. Conflict between the chief and his mother was a matter of great concern to the people because it threatened the stability of the community.

The Lovedu tribe of the Limpopo Province of South Africa provides a unique example of gender roles and relations. The Lovedu were a patrilineal society that determined descent through the male line; however, at the same time it was a matriarchal society in which women wielded the power. The governmental and religious head of the society was the Rain Queen. Among the Lovedu—and other ancient African cultures—marriages between women were common. A woman who took a wife paid to her family a bride-price to acquire her, just as men did, and then she had a male relative impregnate her. The children called the woman whose relative conceived them "father." Moreover, a daughter of every local chieftain married the queen, creating a system in which the society was integrated by the bride-price the queen paid to the chieftains. Within each district was a "mother," who could be either female or male and who served as a representative and intermediary between the chiefs and the queen.

Women also served an important function in the religious affairs of ancient African communities. Many of these communities practiced ancestor worship. This meant that dead ancestors continued to play a role in the affairs of the community. They attained mythic significance, and the link between the living and dead fostered social harmony and the transmittal of values from one generation to the next. Although men often functioned as the shamans who mediated between the living and the dead, in many tribes women fulfilled this function. And while some tribes emphasized worship of male ancestors, many accorded equal worship to both male and female ancestors, particularly a deceased mother or grandmother.

A common practice that dates back at least 4,000 years is female circumcision, or the surgical removal of the young woman's clitoris. This practiced was followed not only in ancient Egypt but also among numerous other communities, including the Nubians, the Ethiopians, and people in communities along the Sahel, or the region just to the south of the Sahara Desert. The practice had a number of purposes. One was to "mark" the girl, making her less than perfect so that the gods did not reclaim her; ear piercing had a similar function. Another was to bind the woman to the patrilineal clan into which she married by ensuring her virginity and marital faithfulness, for her circumcision was inspected by the groom's female relatives. A circumcised woman was thought to be more docile and obedient, ready to assume her place in the family. Yet another purpose was to affirm the belief that circumcision, of both men and women, purified people for the next generation.

EGYPT

BY EMILY JANE O'DELL

Any discussion of gender must first admit that categories of gender and gender expression are largely constructed by the society and culture from which they spring. Gender is usually defined in relation to biological sexual differences; however, there are many different types of intersexuality. While the numbers of genders in a society can vary across cultures, ancient Egypt recognized female and male gender, and these genders were correlated with biological sexual differences between men and women. However, before the law, men and women were equal. Both men and women could inherit and dispose of property as free agents, testify in court, initiate divorce, and participate in business contracts.

Royal women enjoyed a great deal of prestige, privilege, and power. Theoretically, the throne in ancient Egypt passed through the women of the royal family. Some of the pharaohs married members of their own family to claim a throne, and many other pharaohs married princesses in order to ally with the royal family. While a royal woman could have only one husband, a king could have multiple wives and concubines. In the Old Kingdom (2575–2134 B.C.E.) royal wives, mothers, and daughters held administrative positions as well as religious positions, such as priestesses of Thoth or Hathor. The kingship, however, was not restricted to men. While the large majority of pharaohs were men, there were also a handful of female kings, such as Sebeknefru (r. ca. 1787–1783 B.C.E.) and Hatshepsut (r. ca. 1473–1458 B.C.E.). When ruling the country, these women were seen as "kings," not queens. Many queens, however, ruled as regents for their husbands or children.

Male kings built majestic and large burial places for their prominent queens, such as the tomb of Nefertari (wife of Ramses II) in the Valley of the Queens. Many queens, such as Queen Ahhotep (of the Seventeenth Dynasty) and Queen Ahmose-Nefertari (of the Eighteenth Dynasty), were venerated long after their deaths. While women were denied many of the key positions in the state's bureaucracy, they did attempt to assert their authority through other means. For example, several conspiracies against the king were instigated by queens, and harem conspiracies arose during the reigns of Pepi I (r. ca. 2289–2255 B.C.E.), Amenemhet I (r. ca. 1991–1962 B.C.E.), and Ramses III (r. ca. 1194–1163 B.C.E.).

While men and women were equal in terms of legal rights, men held more positions in the clergy and state bureaucracy. Men and women received equal wages for their jobs. While men dominated the bureaucracy, women held many different jobs, such as selling products and food in the marketplace, harvesting crops, gathering and winnowing wheat and flax, grinding grain and baking, weaving, brewing beer, making perfume, and participating in the compulsory, temporary state labor service. Women could also serve as supervisors over these activities. Men were field laborers as well but could also be butchers or jewelers; some men made furniture, leather products, and sculpture. In many lines of work, a woman could also inherit her father's position. However, men dominated government positions because these jobs required literacy.

While there were most likely elite, literate women as well, they would have been the exception. While women in the Old Kingdom did hold administrative positions, they seem to have worked for high-ranking women, not the general state bureaucracy. During the Old Kingdom in ancient Egypt, musicians and dancers were primarily women, but after the end of the Old Kingdom men performed as musicians and dancers at private parties, festivals, and religious ceremonies. During the reign of Ramses III, women participated in the first work strike in history in support of their civil servant husbands. Women were also in charge of managing the household and the family. After the Middle Kingdom (2040–1640 B.C.E.) they had the title "mistress of the house." They were responsible for raising the children, and the royal family also employed royal wet nurses and tutors for the royal children.

In ancient Egyptian mythology there were both male gods and female goddesses. Some gods and goddesses had qualities that were peculiar to their gender, such as childbearing, but others had qualities that were uncharacteristic of their gender. For example, the goddess Neith was a goddess of war, yet women in ancient Egypt did not participate in war-related activities. Some of the goddesses were the embodiment of powerful elements of the state and universe, such as the throne, justice, and the heavens. While most priests were men, women were priestesses in the cults of Hathor, Thoth, Nut, and Neith. The cult of Hathor was restricted to women priestesses. Royal women held such titles as "great royal wife," "God's wife," and "divine adoratrice." In fact, during the New Kingdom (1550–1070 B.C.E.), the great royal wife lived separately from her husband, though the couple would still meet frequently.

Women could also be scribes, prophets, and funerary priests, jobs typically belonging to men. Musician priestesses used music to praise the gods and goddesses and to provide accompaniment to the religious rituals and recitations. Women could also be professional mourners. A woman could obtain titles through her husband if he were a priest; such titles might include "songstress of Amon" or "chief concubine of Amon Re." While the eldest male child was expected to oversee the funerary plans, women in the family or a priest could do so if necessary. Most common women participated in temple cults, even if they did not hold a religious title.

Marriage in ancient Egypt was surprisingly equitable, especially when compared with other parts of the ancient world. There was intimate and playful love poetry in ancient Egypt, and the poetry suggests that sexual intimacy occurred before marriage and that virginity was not a prerequisite to marriage. Some tomb reliefs portray naked young women at banquets and festivals, and other erotic papyri suggest that sex was not taboo. However, homosexuality was discouraged, and adultery was seen as a terrible crime. While royal men took more than one wife, common men and women were supposed to have monogamous unions.

Ancient Egyptian couples with formal marriages had marriage contracts. Men and women also practiced common-law marriage by way of cohabitation. In these marriage contracts a woman came to a marriage with some property, while the man was supposed to supply the house. A married woman could own her own property—she did not forfeit her property or her wages to her husband. She could have her own income and could sell, lease, or loan her property, land, and money without the permission of her husband or a male relative. Both men and women could sue, adopt children, or initiate a divorce. A woman could receive spousal support. If a woman's husband died, she received one-third of his estate while the children received two-thirds of the estate. A man could also "adopt" his wife to make her the sole heir of his property.

In Egyptian art and statuary, men and women are usually depicted in the ideal physique for their gender. Men are shown with reddish skin, probably as a result of their working outdoors. They are portrayed as muscular and youthful. However, older men are sometimes shown as portly to emphasize their wealth and position. Women, however, are portrayed with yellow skin and are mostly shown as young and thin, wearing tight-fitting clothes that emphasize their taut abdomens and slender hips and that accentuate the pubic area, perhaps to reflect their childbearing potential. Statues portraying common people, however, are much less idealized and represent all types, even humpbacks and dwarfs. Men and women are sometimes depicted as the same size, but men are often shown as taller and closer to the center of the scene to emphasize their dominance.

THE MIDDLE EAST

BY KAREN RADNER

From the mid-third millennium B.C.E. to the Hellenistic Period (323–31 B.C.E.) the predominant writing materials in Mesopotamia were extremely durable clay tablets inscribed in the cuneiform script. Hundreds of thousands of such texts have been unearthed in the ancient cities of modern Iraq, Syria, and Turkey, making Mesopotamia the best-documented area for gender and structure roles of the ancient Near East. Information gained from the Bible indicates a broadly similar pattern of gender structures and roles for Israel and Judah in the first millennium B.C.E., as suggested by the more limited documentation available for other parts of the Middle East, namely Anatolia, Iran, and the Levant.

While many languages of the ancient Near East distinguish grammatically between masculine and feminine, for example, the Semitic languages Akkadian, Old Hebrew, Old Aramaic, and Phoenician and the Indo-European languages Hittite and Old Persian, some do not, most prominently the Sumerian language, which was widely spoken in Babylonia during the third millennium B.C.E. and remained the dominant language of learning until the last centuries of the first millennium B.C.E. Sumerian is found in two distinct forms that use separate vocabularies and differ profoundly in pronunciation: One form was spoken by men and called the "native tongue," and the other was spoken by women and called the "high-pitched tongue." Long after Sumerian ceased to be used as a colloquial language, lamentations—songs of mourning and despair—addressed to the gods in the course of temple worship were exclusively performed in the high-pitched tongue, albeit by men, who thereby assumed the traditional female gender role of mourning and keening. This example demonstrates the difference between gender and sex, gender being a socially defined category and, hence, far more flexible than the physical characteristics of a person's sex.

Written scripts also offer some insight into gender roles and stereotypes. In the cuneiform script used to record Sumerian, Akkadian, Hurrian, and Hittite, the sign with the meaning "man, male" depicts an erect penis, while the sign with the meaning "woman, female" shows the pubic triangle. The gender stereotypes of warrior and spinstress are endorsed by another system of categories—magic. The items representing men and women in magic rituals recorded in texts from Mesopotamia and also second-millennium Anatolia are weapons and spindles and other tools for textile production, respectively. This makes it very plain that the place of a woman was considered the domestic sphere, where she gave birth and raised children; cooked, baked, and brewed; made textiles by spinning, weaving, and sewing; laundered and cleaned; and kept the household running. While women were certainly not restricted to the house and were free to go about in the city, as best illustrated by several biblical narratives in which women fetch water at the well or at the river, a woman traveling beyond the city limits was always an exception and considered in need of a male protector, as described in the relevant rules and regulations found in the Middle Assyrian Law Code (ca. 1100 B.C.E.).

In general, ancient Near Eastern gender roles are defined by a set of mutually exclusive classifications: sex (male versus female), gender (masculine versus feminine), sexuality (penetration versus receptivity), and hierarchy (domination versus subordination). Male sexuality was equaled with penetration and domination, and to be penetrated corresponded with female sexuality. Being the receiving partner in a homosexual union between men or ceding the dominant role in a sexual encounter to a woman was seen as unmanly, as is clear from a Babylonian collection of omens—or rather, as in these specific cases, moral guidelines that at least in part date back to the early second millennium B.C.E. and continued to be popular throughout the first millennium B.C.E.—"If a man has sexual relations with a male house slave, hardship will seize him"; "If a woman mounts a man, that woman will take his vigor."

With the man socially expected to be the dominant, active sexual partner, unions between older men and younger women were very common, while the reverse situation was possible but not considered ideal. This is again made clear in the already mentioned Babylonian omen collection: "If a man has sexual relations with an old woman he will quarrel daily." This attitude bears especially on the options available to widows. Married women who were fortunate to survive the birth of their children had a good chance of outliving their husbands and were theoretically able to enter a second marriage, yet ancient Near East law codes and legal documents from all periods show a clear interest in encouraging wealthy widows to remain unmarried in order to protect the family's financial assets against outsiders. The same concern lies at the root of the practice to marry one's brother's widow, as related in the Bible.

While sexuality is not exclusive to humanity, it is exactly its controlled practice—adhering to the allowed and disallowed customs defined by society—that was seen to set humankind apart from animals and to work as an instrument of civilization. This attitude is best illustrated by the Epic of Gilgamesh, popular in the entire ancient Near East from the second millennium B.C.E. onward: When the savage animal-like Enkidu consorts with a prostitute, he becomes "human" and is rejected by his previous companions, the wild beasts; he leaves the steppe for an urban and civilized life.

Mutually exclusive extremes are at the core of ancient Near Eastern gender roles, and yet one of the most important Sumerian deities transcends these polarities: Inanna, or to use her Akkadian name, Ishtar, incorporates within herself the opposites of male and female. She is androgynous and ambiguous, as is her heavenly representation, the planet Venus, which the Sumerians referred to as the masculine evening star and the feminine morning star. Inanna/Ishtar was, therefore, closely associated with all those who fell outside the binary system of male and female, including eunuchs. Far from being social outcasts, as might be expected in a culture that valued family and children over all, eunuchs had an important role in the state organization of the Neo-Assyrian Empire (ninth century B.C.E.–seventh century B.C.E.). Having been made sterile at an early age and forsaken the chance to sire children, their loyalty belonged exclusively to the royal family, and they were often chosen to act as the king's local representative as provincial governors. In contemporary art eunuchs are shown as beardless yet are otherwise dressed like men, and their legal rights were not different from men. But Inanna/Ishtar played a key role in the lives of all people, men and women alike, as the carnivalesque festivals organized in her honor offered the participants an opportunity to digress from the rigorous gender roles, thereby stabilizing what may otherwise have been a regulated and stifling society.

ASIA AND THE PACIFIC

BY AMY HACKNEY BLACKWELL

Throughout ancient Asia women were generally regarded as subservient to men, and their lives were controlled by their male relatives. Despite these circumstances, women received some honor and respect for performing their roles well, especially as they grew older and their sons married. Sexuality was considered an important part of life throughout the region, with males and females both playing a key part in relations.

In the Chinese Daoist philosophy of the first millennium B.C.E. the sexes were characterized as yin and yang. Yin, the feminine principle, was said to be soft, yielding, dark, and passive and was symbolized by water. Yang, the male principle, was considered rigid, active, and bright and was represented by fire or wind. Women were believed to possess large amounts of yin, while men were filled with yang. Chinese people thought that it was important for men and women to exchange energy types by engaging in extended sexual play with multiple female orgasms. It was believed to be especially unhealthy for men to exhaust their yang essence by ejaculating too quickly, before they absorbed the necessary yin from women. During the later Zhou Dynasty (770–256 B.C.E.) men were encouraged to visit prostitutes for the purpose of increasing their yin.

During the period between about 220 B.C.E. and 25 C.E. Confucianism became the prevailing philosophy in China. In Confucian doctrine women were considered inferior to men and were expected to be subservient to them. The Confucian writings say very little about women, which most scholars take as evidence of the insignificance of women to most men. Confucians believed that in order to maintain social harmony husbands must be superior to wives, and brothers must be superior to sisters. Thoughts on sexuality changed. Confucianism taught that sex was somewhat sinful and should be confined to the bedroom; husbands and wives were not to touch each other outside the marriage bed. Sexual acts between spouses were restricted to procreation and meant for the maintenance of family stability. Men were allowed to have concubines, but Confucianism regulated the practice with numerous rules, such as those concerning how frequently men should have sex with concubines and whether concubines could remain in the bed after the sex act was completed.

During the Eastern Han Dynasty (25–220 C.E.), Daoism once more became the prevailing philosophy, and sex was again encouraged. Scholars published sex manuals that described breathing techniques that could prolong male performance and increase female response, in an effort to transfer yin and yang energy between the man and the woman. Sex between men and women was thought to be a way to improve health and achieve a longer life. During this time the color red became associated with women and white with men.

Although they were not considered the equals of men at any time in China, women could wield a large amount of power within the household. This power came with age and the birth of sons. Young girls were valued less than boys, and female infants were more at risk of being abandoned or killed at birth. Girls were considered an expense because they were destined to leave home when they married; their parents had to furnish them with a dowry and could not count on their daughters' care in old age. When a woman married, she went to live with her husband's family and often became a virtual servant to him and his relatives. She was expected to get up early and stay up late to carry out all her domestic work and to make her home and family her only priority, living quietly and performing her spiritual duties to the family's ancestors. A wife had to please her in-laws, especially her mother-in-law, and could be punished if she protested. She gradually gained more power as she produced children and grew older. When a woman's son married and she herself became a mother-in-law, she took control of the household and was allowed to dominate a daughter-in-law. A mother-in-law's word was law to her daughter-in-law; unquestioning obedience was required at all times.

Husbands had duties toward their wives as well. Although men were considered superior to women, people believed that if men did not act properly, they lost the power to control their wives. Men and women were supposed to live in harmony. Men were not to strike their wives, and women were not to scold their husbands.

In India women married young. Men were expected to support their wives and were also responsible for their wives' behavior. They were not, however, supposed to use force to maintain discipline, aside from a small number of blows that did not inflict damage. India's caste system provided many rules for sexual behavior. Female virginity was highly prized, and violating it could bring serious punishment. A man who had sex with a virgin of the same caste as his was either heavily fined or had his hand cut off. Having sex with a virgin of a lower caste resulted in a smaller fine or the loss of the man's middle finger. If a woman had sex with a man outside marriage, she could be fined a small amount. If a man rescued a woman from some danger, such as war, fire, or flood, he was allowed to have sex with her unless she was of high caste and had children, in which case she or her family could pay him a ransom instead. The punishment for adultery depended on the castes of the partners. The higher the rank of the woman and the lower the rank of the man, the worse the punishment. A low-caste man who committed adultery with a Brahman (highest caste) woman would be burned alive, whereas a man of a higher caste would merely lose his property.

Although very little is known about gender roles in ancient Japan, there is some historical evidence that women and men were considered equals and that women served as powerful religious leaders. Ancient Australians also left little evidence about gender structures, but modern scholars believe they may have had a fair degree of equality between the sexes while also dividing work by sex.

Homosexuality existed throughout ancient Asia, with varying degrees of approval. In ancient China male masturbation and homosexuality were thought to be unhealthy because they built up an overabundance of yang energy, while the same practices were encouraged for women. In India the Vedas (the earliest sacred Hindu writings) and other ancient texts mention individuals who are neither male nor female and sometimes refer to hermaphrodites as a third gender. The Pali Canon, a set of early Buddhist scriptures in Thailand, mentions a sexual category called *pandaka*; this category is traditionally believed to include homosexual male monks. Modern Thai scholars have termed these homosexual men *kathoey*, the word used to refer to transvestites or transsexuals, on the assumption that these monks dressed and comported themselves as women or acted in some other manner that went against expected masculine behavior. Some historians are now not so sure that these *pandaka* monks were indeed transvestites in the modern sense and think that they might have acted according to the conventions of male behavior but engaged in homosexual acts with other men.

EUROPE

BY MICHAEL J. O'NEAL

The challenge historians face in studying gender structures and roles in the ancient world is the overall lack of written records. Gender has no tangible existence as a piece of pottery or a building does. Gender is a social construct, meaning that gender roles are assigned and played out in the context of social and marital relationships. Without written descriptions of these roles, historians have to rely on whatever archaeological record is available, then make inferences about what they find. This record includes tombs, remains of homes, and artwork, which can tell historians something about how men and women were regarded. Sometimes archaeologists rely on what they do *not* find to make these kinds of inferences.

Complicating the matter is that for generations, historians and archaeologists have tended to make generalizations about gender roles in ancient Europe that might be only partially true. The usual view is that men held all the power. They were the kings, priests, chieftains, warlords, shamans, craftsmen, and warriors, fulfilling functions largely outside the home. Women were thought to be peaceful; they were in charge of the domestic sphere, and their influence was limited almost entirely to this sphere. While this generalization has a great deal of truth to it, it does not tell the entire story. Some archaeological finds, along with new ways of thinking about those finds, suggest that women were not always restricted to the domestic sphere. In fact, many women held positions of power as priests, shamans, and warriors. Some took part in public activities such as trade. Others were skilled at craftwork, particularly spinning, weaving, dyeing, and textile production.

One type of written record that does exist and that has a bearing on gender relationships includes legends, myths, and tales. While these stories were not written down at the time the ancients lived, they survived because they were passed along orally throughout the generations. In many cases, these stories provide insight into the gender relationships of ancient peoples.

A good example is provided by Scandinavian mythology, much of which emerged during the Nordic Bronze Age, which extended from about 1800 to 600 B.C.E. This mythology was intimately connected with Scandinavian religious beliefs. At the center of Nordic mythology was a male sun god, depicted as traveling the heavens in a chariot. Later, this sun god evolved into a sun goddess, both in Scandinavia and among the Germanic tribes, though historians are not sure why. Also worshipped was a female mother goddess, Nerthus, who evolved into various female mother goddesses in Scandinavian and Germanic mythology. Most of the gods, such as Thor, are represented in surviving artwork as carrying swords and spears, suggesting that men were viewed as the warrior and governing class.

Female goddesses, in contrast, were associated with fertility and such events as the harvest. Nonetheless, Scandinavian mythology is rife with female giants and warrior maidens. The best example is the Valkyries. These were nine warrior maidens who served as attendants to Odin, the ruler of the gods. Their principal role was to accompany warriors to Valhalla, Odin's great hall; that is, they were to accompany slain soldiers into the afterlife. In battle they wore elaborate armor. Their leader was Brunhilda, who was the goddess not only of fertility and love but also of death and battle. Historians believe that the warrior goddess of Celtic mythology, Morrigan, was a parallel development, especially because both Morrigan and the Valkyries were able to prophesy the outcome of great battles.

Taken together, these and other mythological figures suggest that the ancient Scandinavians and the Germanic tribes of northern Europe took something of an equal view of men and women. While men were still principally responsible for war and governance, women played a prominent role as well and were not limited to the domestic sphere.

Tomb excavations also provide insight into gender relations and issues surrounding the power and influence of women. Among the ancient Celts, for example, historians know that women enjoyed a respectable amount of influence. They were able to own property and divorce their husbands, and they took part in a wide range of occupations, including those of merchant, warrior, and healer. In excavating Celtic tombs, archaeologists have discovered that many Celtic women enjoyed high social status. This can be determined by the nature of the goods that were buried with the women as well as by items of personal adornment that suggest high social status. In some instances horses and horse tack were buried with women, suggesting that these women may have played an important role in what is traditionally regarded as a male sphere. Along the same lines, archaeological sites of homes throughout ancient Europe have yielded tools used in craft production. In some cases men performed craftwork in the home, but in others it is believed that crafts production was the province of women working the home.

Archaeologists are occasionally able to make generalizations about gender relationships on the basis of what seems to be missing from the archaeological record. A good example is provided by the British Isles, where historians were long puzzled by their inability to find Bronze Age homes that contained artifacts typically considered domestic. These would include tools for food storage and preservation, cooking, and the like. Recently some archaeologists have argued that nothing is missing—that, in fact, these remains were never present. Their argument is that during the Bronze Age in Britain, no sharp distinction was made between the public and domestic spheres. Items used for domestic activity are found in many different types of sites. Their conclusion is that there was no domestic sphere presided over by women. They believe that men and women played equal or nearly equal roles in a public, community life.

Some historians have taken an interest in the nature and extent of homosexual relationships in ancient Europe. In general, it is believed that ancient Europeans were relatively tolerant of homosexuality, having absorbed this tolerance from the ancient Greeks. Among the ancient Celts, for example, poems and legends contain hints that homosexual relationships between soldiers were not uncommon. Many historians, too, point to the ambiguous sexuality of some of the region's mythological figures, suggesting that ancient Europeans were not offended by homosexuality.

GREECE

BY BRADLEY SKEEN

In the earliest period of Greek history, the Minoan civilization (ca. 2600–ca. 14,500 B.C.E.) on the island of Crete was a highly centralized culture of palaces, of which Knossos was the most important. Evidence from the material remains of this culture, including paintings on palace walls, offers grounds for speculation rather than clear evidence about gender structures and roles. Two factors are often cited to argue that the Minoan society had equality between the sexes or may even have been a matriarchy.

First, many paintings show women seemingly active in public life, especially the Minoan ritual and sport of acrobatically vaulting over the backs of dangerous bulls. But the mere presence of women does not tell us their role. There is no way to determine whether the participants (male and female) in bull jumping were aristocratic youths, trained slaves (like Roman gladiators), or even prisoners preparing to be sacrificed. (This latter fate might be suggested by the myth of Theseus and the Minotaur, in which Theseus, an Athenian prince, is sent to Crete as tribute to be sacrificed to the half-human, half-bull Minotaur but instead kills the monster and frees his city from the tyrannical rule of King Minos of Crete.)

Second, most surviving cult statues suggest that the main figures worshipped in Minoan religion were goddesses. But this fact need not imply a high status for women in society, any more than the importance of Mary (Jesus' mother) in European religion in the Middle Ages was equated with a high status of women in that culture. Interestingly, Minoan art typically depicts men as having brown skin and women as having white skin. This might suggest that aristocratic women led comparatively sheltered and inactive lives, kept away from the outside world, whereas men became suntanned from the outdoor tasks of business, war, and agriculture.

The Mycenaean civilization (ca. 1600–ca. 1100 B.C.E.) rose from the invasion of Greece and the Aegean islands by

Terra-cotta statuettes: woman holding pancake and woman kneading dough (Alison Frantz Photographic Collection, American School of Classical Studies at Athens)

Greek-speaking peoples who absorbed Minoan culture. This civilization is the background of the Homeric poems the *Iliad* and the *Odyssey* and of many Greek myths. It was dominated by a warrior aristocracy that gained status through success in battle and the collection of plunder from the conquered. Women's lives were entirely under the control of their fathers, husbands, or even sons, and as the literary tradition shows, the men were fully aware that many women felt this condition to be unjust. Nevertheless, women could often assert themselves through their personal influence over powerful male relatives.

The Mycenaean culture ended in the face of new invasions. Greece entered a dark age in which society broke down into small villages and individual farmsteads. From this primitive social organization there emerged the Greek cities of the Classical Age (ca. 480–323 B.C.E.). The amazing rebirth of Greek civilization established an ideal against which many later cultures measured themselves, but gender roles developed unequally. Greek culture had been transformed by an influx of tribal peoples who organized gender roles around bands of male warrior-hunters that lived and worked together apart from female society. In Sparta, for instance, this early pattern was reflected in a militarized state. The entire population of male youths and adult men spent all their time training for war or fighting. They lived in barracks under military discipline and visited their own families and farms only infrequently, on formal leave. This regimentation led to the unparalleled military strength of Sparta and to a male ideal famous for its fortitude, duty, and indifference to circumstance.

Spartan women lived apart from men and acted as stewards over their husbands' property, wielding a unique degree of power and independence. Greeks were very hostile to anyone who violated accepted social roles. Because Sparta's women seemed to be out from under male control, they attracted the criticism of other Greeks as being lesbians, whether or not there was any basis for the claim.

In Athens, on the other hand, aristocratic women lived secluded lives inside the women's quarters of the family house, and even in this home setting men and women ate their meals separately. The legal rights and social status of Athenian women were very restricted, but ancient dramas suggest that women could exert tremendous influence within the family through sheer force of personality. Women from the lower classes had more exposure to the outside world because they had to work in the family business or farm.

Paradoxically, some women who abandoned idealized gender roles could rise to social prominence, acting in the same cultural environment as men. These were the *hetaerae* (literally "companions," but in classical Greece a word signifying a social role somewhere between that of a mistress and a prostitute). Aspasia (469–406 B.C.E.), mistress of Pericles, leader of Athens, gained wide popularity for her wit and intelligence. Muesarete (fl. ca. 330 B.C.E.)—ironically nicknamed "Phryne" ("Toad") because of her beauty—was the mistress of the orator Hyperides and of the great sculptor Praxiteles and amassed one of the largest fortunes in Athens. However, both women had to defend themselves in court (successfully) against charges of impiety (the crime of violating religious law) occasioned by resentment over their prominence obtained apart from social expectations.

Despite the restrictions imposed on most Greek women, some reached great heights of personal achievement. Artemisia I, for instance, queen of the Greek city of Halicarnassus in modern Turkey, acted as a governor in the Persian Empire and as an admiral in the Persian force that invaded Greece in 480 B.C.E. Another exceptional woman, Sappho (ca. 630–570 B.C.E.), wrote lyric verse that sets her among the very greatest poets and can also be considered the first poet in the modern sense. Some of her poems seem to describe desire for a woman, but it is not clear whether this reflects her own feelings or those of a perhaps male character.

The male band of earlier times lived on in Athens in the typical male gathering, the symposium. Today this term usually signifies a relatively staid intellectual gathering. In ancient Greek it meant simply "drinking party." Held among male friends and relatives, the symposium was the height of fashionable life in Athens and embodied collective cultural fantasies of ideal manhood. Pederasty, one of the most striking features of the symposium, was the sexual courting of adolescent youths by adult men. (Erotic contact between adult men, however, was stigmatized in Greek society.) The men sought the sexual favors of the youths in return for education, contacts, and other forms of assistance in entering into society. This practice may have evolved from earlier initiation rites typical of tribal cultures.

The symposium properly began after dinner and involved a long night of drinking, during which the guests took turns entertaining the group by reciting poetry, composing speeches, and engaging in other elevated and not-so-elevated activities. The presence of prostitutes (of either sex) was not unusual, nor was drunkenness. In this setting the indulgence of pleasure was a more common social value than its restraint.

ROME

BY BRADLEY SKEEN

Roman social ideals were shaped during the city's early history as Romans came in contact with more sophisticated cultures. The early influence of Etruscan civilization ensured that within the household the two sexes would live in close contact, that couples would always dine together, and that women could move about more or less freely in public. Thus, there was more equality between the sexes in Roman society than in many other Mediterranean cultures. Nevertheless, gender roles in the Roman world were largely the creation of aristocratic men and are known to us through their writings.

We rarely hear women or other classes speak for themselves, though there is little reason to think that they did not embrace the social ideals of the male aristocracy.

In the early days of Rome gender roles were determined by the structure of the family. The father had absolute control (*patria potestas*) over the entire household, including his children, slaves, and other dependents; *patria potestas* gave the father even the power of life and death. This rule was less absolute with regard to the wife, who in some respects was an outsider in the family. Marriage was considered to be an alliance between two families more than an expression of romantic love. A wife was indeed under her husband's control, but she had earlier been under her father's control. Moreover, since her father would have provided her with a dowry (a substantial gift of property that was usually paid in cash in later times), she could, if the marriage became intolerable, retreat from it back to the control of her father, taking the dowry with her. (Later she could simply divorce.) In practice, however, such separations rarely occurred, and the husband generally had the use of his wife's dowry throughout her lifetime and inherited it as part of his own estate at the time of her death.

The greater mass of people had only a small farm or, especially in the Imperial Period, no property at all. For them, marriage was a more informal arrangement in which a man and a woman simply decided to live together. Many slaves (at least among those whose working conditions permitted) lived in situations amounting to marriages recognized by their masters. The social roles of lower classes were self-consciously modeled on those of aristocrats to the extent possible. The secluded lives of aristocratic women, however, could not be duplicated by poor women, who were often forced to work in family shops, as peddlers, or in other businesses.

Roman aristocratic men saw themselves as active and efficient, equally skilled in the arts of peace (civil governance) and war. They viewed business—preferably working in the law courts but perhaps managing a large agricultural or industrial concern—as a necessity that distracted them from their ideal of a retirement devoted to study and literature. The vital quality of good reputation, without which a man would be humiliated in his attempts to make his way in the world, depended not so much on his own behavior as on that of his female family members—that is, on his ability to control them.

The ideal way of life for a Roman matron consisted of domestic virtues: loyalty, obedience, affability, reasonableness, attendance to religion without superstition, sobriety of attire, modest appearance, and skill in wool working (which was praiseworthy because it was old-fashioned). Any woman who had had only a single husband throughout her life (*univira*) was considered fortunate. But Roman social ideology also had a vision of a woman who had fallen away from virtue. She began by drinking, which led to her taking a lover, with whom she would plot to murder her husband. This idea expressed male fears over the loss of control. Thus, men, especially men in the public eye as politicians, felt the need to watch their women carefully. In contrast, it was very common for a politician, such as Cicero (106–43 B.C.E.), to denounce a rival on the ground that his women were out of line, even insinuating that incest went on in his household. This accusation was made not because of factual evidence but because such activity was a direct violation of accepted gender roles and would automatically incite outrage in those who heard about it. Such political maneuvering makes it very difficult to understand whether the reports of the moral degradation of the emperors and their families have any basis in fact. Such accounts are common in writings by historical authors like Suetonius (ca. 70–130 C.E.), who claims, for example, that the emperor Caligula (r. 37–41 C.E.) slept with his sisters and that Nero (r. 54–68 C.E.) slept with his mother, Agrippina the Younger.

Although Roman women were never closeted away within the house as were women in Greece, Greek customs deeply affected Roman ideas about the interaction of gender with sexuality (especially after the second century B.C.E., when Rome conquered Greece and Greeks flooded into Italy as slaves, paradoxically more sophisticated than their masters). What the Romans borrowed from the Greeks was a very different set of social roles than we usually encounter in modern Western countries. Roman men were supposed to be active, and women were expected to be passive; other considerations were secondary.

A more ambiguous situation involved male puberty, a period of masculine life marked sharply in Roman times from around age 12, when a boy would have his first haircut (the shorn hair was dedicated at a temple in a religious ceremony) and dress in adult clothes for the first time, until the physical course of puberty was completed and the beard was growing fully. According to Roman tradition, a teenage male ought to act like a man in all respects. But the influence of Greek culture on Roman society was so great that a youth could engage in love affairs with older men, as did Julius Caesar (r. 46–44 B.C.E.), without damaging his reputation excessively. More generally, Roman men could legitimately have sexual relations with their wives, with youths, or with prostitutes or slaves of either gender, without any social judgment against them for transgressing gender roles. What mattered to the masculine image was not the physical gender of the partners but maintaining the active role. Thus, a man who became known for taking the passive role in homoerotic relations would be publicly shamed as a pervert, but so would a man who was suspected of sexual subservience to women, even to his own wife.

The image of aristocratic women demanded strict fidelity to husbands, but as society became more cosmopolitan, especially in the late republic and empire (first century B.C.E. to third century C.E.), legal reforms that resulted in a high rate of divorce liberated many women from the authority of either father or husband, granting some degree of sexual freedom. Nevertheless, the essentially passive characteristic of women's sexual lives had to be maintained. Homoerotic contact between women seems to have been extremely rare compared with such contact between men (or at least it is seldom mentioned in surviving writings); nevertheless, it is clear that in a female homosexual relationship, one of the female partners assumed an active or aggressive role that was properly seen as masculine.

THE AMERICAS

BY ARDEN DECKER

The study of gender and sexuality is key to the understanding of any culture, particularly with regard to labor practices, social status, leadership, and religion. The role of gender and sexuality differs greatly from culture to culture and across time, making it nearly impossible to identify any standard model to which all cultures adhere. Much of what is currently known about gender and sexuality in ancient America is based on archaeological evidence, particularly from burial caches and artworks. Information and evidence gathered from archaeological sites and material culture have helped scholars to begin to make deductions about the function of gender in ancient communities and provide a more complete picture of daily life.

The Paleo-Indians (ca. 13,000–ca. 8000 B.C.E.) are the earliest-known human inhabitants of the Americas. They are believed to have been hunter-gatherers. It is difficult to define any labor function or position as being conclusively identified with one gender in particular. It is generally accepted that these early societies divided labor responsibilities by sex, but these roles could shift with changes, for example, in population growth, environment, and season. Many archaeologists and anthropologists have begun to reexamine the commonly held belief that men were the hunters and women dealt only with household labor.

Women's role of childbearing often affected the amount and type of work they could perform, and individual societies would certainly have accommodated this fact. However, it would be shortsighted to assume that the activities of women in the ancient Americas were limited to the household. We must be careful not to superimpose our present-day understanding of gender roles onto civilizations that existed hundreds or thousands of years ago. In ancient cultures both men and women retained their own unique status within their respective spheres and would not have competed with each other for power or status as is done in today's society. Recent research suggests that men were not solely responsible for subsistence among the earliest cultures; women also participated in providing food by hunting small animals and birds and gathering edible plants. Both women and men would have been trained to do specialized work, such as preparing materials for clothing and making those materials into finished products. Hunter-gatherer societies throughout the ancient Americas were primarily egalitarian, and the sexes worked together and separately for the survival and improvement of the community.

Spout and bridge vessel in the shape of a woman, holding what is thought to be a spindle wrapped in cloth, from the Nasca culture (200 B.C.E. to 600 C.E.) of Peru; such figures were associated with various activities of daily life.

With the rise of agriculture, societies grew more sedentary and more complex, and they left us more information regarding the nature of gender and labor. As a society changed, so did its needs, leading to new types of specialized labor and requiring a fluid definition of gender-based labor division. Similarly, food production and the development of economy led to far more complex systems of dividing labor that were no longer based simply on sex but also on age and social status. Both men and women engaged in difficult physical labor, but craft production grew ever more important to developing economies. For example, in Mesoamerica pottery was a specialization practiced by both sexes, but textiles and weaving became associated primarily with women.

Although few monumental artworks from ancient America feature images of women, many figurines depicting both males and females (as well as some sexually neutral figures) have been recovered throughout Mesoamerica and North and South America. The greatest range occurs at the site of Tlatilco, in western Mexico, dating to the first or second century B.C.E. These ceramic figurines display the desire among early Mesoamericans to differentiate and define gender and status through costume, hairstyle, ornament, and activity.

The study of costume and ornament has greatly increased our understanding of status in the ancient Americas. Naturally, much of this information comes from later ancient cultures that were organized in a relatively stratified manner. Burial caches found throughout Mesoamerica demonstrate that ornaments buried with women and men varied according to age, sex, and social status. There are also a few exceptions to the lack of monumental images of women from the ancient period, two notable examples being the stela (a carved commemorative pillar) of a female ruler from the Olmec site of La Venta (1200–400 B.C.E.) near the central coast of Mexico and the monument of a female ruler from the central Mexican site of Chalcatzingo (900–600 B.C.E.). Although rulership and ritual may have "officially" been the purviews primarily of men, these exceptions suggest that women sometimes held positions of power. A similar example of assigning gender and status may be seen with the ceramic production of the Moche culture (1–600 C.E.) of northern Peru. A cross-section of Moche ceramic vessels demonstrates a surprising range of means for depicting gender identity and roles, particularly with regard to women. Gender is assigned not only through hairstyle, clothing, and ornament but also through social roles, as the Moches depict women as rulers, as deities, and as mothers.

All ancient American societies possessed goddesses and gods within their pantheons, and both women and men participated in ritual and ceremony. Physical evidence suggests that both sexes acted as shamans, priests, and curers and that both engaged in ritual sacrifice. Shamans were particularly important in most American cultures, serving not only as leaders but also as intermediaries between the human and spiritual realms. Thus the existence of female shamans suggests that women held at least some religious and political power. The Chavín (ca. 900–ca. 200 B.C.E.) of northern Peru were the earliest American culture known to have had women as deities and important supernatural beings, but many subsequent cultures throughout the Americas also worshipped goddesses. One extraordinary example can be seen near present-day Mexico City at the site of Teotihuacán (1–650 C.E.), where the cult of the "Great Goddess" became so prevalent that many scholars believe she was the official patron goddess of the city.

See also ADORNMENT; ART; CHILDREN; CLOTHING AND FOOTWEAR; CRAFTS; CRIME AND PUNISHMENT; DEATH AND BURIAL PRACTICES; DRAMA AND THEATER; EDUCATION; EMPIRES AND DYNASTIES; FAMILY; FESTIVALS; HOUSEHOLD GOODS; HUNTING, FISHING, AND GATHERING; LANGUAGE; LAWS AND LEGAL CODES; LITERATURE; MILITARY; MUSIC AND MUSICAL INSTRUMENTS; OCCUPATIONS; RELIGION AND COSMOLOGY; SLAVES AND SLAVERY; SOCIAL ORGANIZATION; TEXTILES AND NEEDLEWORK; WAR AND CONQUEST; WRITING.

The Middle East

Herodotus: Excerpt from The History of the Persian Wars, *ca. 430* B.C.E.

I.199: The Babylonians have one most shameful custom. Every woman born in the country must once in her life go and sit down in the precinct of Venus [Ishtar] and there consort with a stranger. Many of the wealthier sort, who are too proud to mix with the others, drive in covered carriages to the precinct, followed by a goodly train of attendants, and there take their station. But the larger number seat themselves within the holy enclosure with wreaths of string about their heads—and here there is always a great crowd, some coming and others going; lines of cord mark out paths in all directions; the women and the strangers pass along them to make their choice. A woman who has once taken her seat is not allowed to return home till one of the strangers throws a silver coin into her lap, and takes her with him beyond the holy ground. When he throws the coin, he says these words: "The goddess Mylitta prosper you." (Venus is called Mylitta by the Assyrians.) The silver coin may be of any size; it cannot be refused, for that is forbidden by the law, since once thrown it is sacred. The woman goes with the first man who throws her money and rejects no one. When she has gone with him and so satisfied the goddess, she returns home, and from that time forth no gift however great will prevail with her. Such of the women as are tall and beautiful are soon released, but others who are ugly have to stay a long time before they can fulfill the law. Some have waited three or four years in the precinct. A custom very much like this is found also in certain parts of the island of Cyprus.

From: Herodotus, *The History,*
trans. George Rawlinson
(New York: Dutton and Co., 1862).

Asia and the Pacific

Ban Zhao: Excerpt from Lessons for a Woman, *ca. 80* C.E.

The Views of a Female Confucian

I, the unworthy writer, am unsophisticated, unenlightened, and by nature unintelligent, but I am fortunate both to have received not a little favor from my scholarly Father and to have had a cultured mother and instructresses upon whom to rely for a literary education as well as for training in good manners. More than forty years have passed since at the age of fourteen I took up the dustpan and the broom in the Cao family [*the family into which she married*]. During this time with trembling heart I feared constantly that I might disgrace my parents and that I might multiply difficulties for both the women and the men of my husband's family. Day and night I was distressed in heart, but I labored without confessing weariness. Now and hereafter, however, I know how to escape from such fears.

Being careless and by nature stupid, I taught and trained my children without system. . . . I do grieve that you, my daughters, just now at the age for marriage, have not at this time had gradual training and advice, that you still have not learned the proper customs for married women. I fear that by failure in good manners in other families you will humiliate both your ancestors and your clan. I am now seriously ill, life is uncertain. As I have thought of you all in so untrained a state, I have been uneasy many a time for you. At hours of leisure I have composed . . . these instructions. . . . In order that you may have something wherewith to benefit your persons, I wish every one of you, my daughters each to write out a copy for yourself. From this time on every one of you strive to practice these lessons. . . .

Humility

On the third day after the birth of a girl the ancients observed three customs: first to place the baby below the bed, second to give her a potsherd . . . with which to play, and third to announce her birth to her ancestors by an offering. Now to lay the baby below the bed plainly indicated that she is lowly and weak and should regard it as her primary duty to humble herself before others. To give her potsherds with which to play indubitably signified that she should practice labor and consider it her primary duty to be industrious. To announce her birth before her ancestors clearly meant that she ought to esteem as her primary duty the continuation of the observance of worship in the home. . . .

Let a woman modestly yield to others; let her respect others; let her put others first, herself last. Should she do something good, let her not mention it; should she do something bad, let her not deny it. Let her bear disgrace; let her even endure when others speak or do evil to her. Always let her seem to tremble and to fear. When a woman follows such maxims as these then she may be said to humble herself before others.

Let a woman retire late to bed but rise early to duties; let her nor dread tasks by day or by night. Let her not refuse to perform domestic duties whether easy or difficult. That which must be done, let her finish completely, tidily, and systematically. When a woman follows such rules as these, then she may be said to be industrious.

Let a woman be correct in manner and upright in character in order to serve her husband. Let her live in purity and quietness of spirit, and attend to her own affairs. Let her love not gossip and silly laughter. Let her cleanse and purify and arrange in order the wine and the food for the offerings to the ancestors. When a woman observes such principles as these, then she may be said to continue ancestral worship.

No woman who observes these three fundamentals of life has ever had a bad reputation or has fallen into disgrace. If a woman fails to observe them, how can her name be honored; how can she but bring disgrace upon herself? . . .

Womanly Qualifications

A woman ought to have four qualifications: (1) womanly virtue, (2) womanly words, (3) womanly bearing, and (4) womanly work. Now what is called womanly virtue need not be brilliant ability, exceptionally different from others. Womanly words need be neither clever in debate nor keen in conversation. Womanly appearance requires neither a pretty nor a perfect face and form. Womanly work need not be work done more skillfully than that of others.

To guard carefully her chastity, to control circumspectly her behavior, in every motion to exhibit modesty, and to model each act on the best usage, this is womanly virtue.

To choose her words with care, to avoid vulgar language, to speak at appropriate times, and nor to weary others with much conversation may be called the characteristics of womanly words.

(continued)

(continues)

To wash and scrub filth away, to keep clothes and ornaments fresh and clean, to wash the head and bathe the body regularly, and to keep the person free from disgraceful filth may be called the characteristics of womanly bearing.

With whole-hearted devotion to sew and to weave, to love not gossip and silly laughter, in cleanliness and order to prepare the wine and food for serving guests may be called the characteristics of womanly work.

These four qualifications characterize the greatest virtue of a woman. No woman can afford to be without them. In fact, they are very easy to possess if a woman only treasures them in her heart.

From: Nancy Lee Swann, trans., *Pan Chao: Foremost Woman Scholar of China* (New York: Century Co., 1932), pp. 82–90.

Greece

Semonides of Amorgos: "The Types of Women," ca. 550 B.C.E.

God made the mind of woman in the beginning of different qualities; for *one he fashioned like a bristly hog*, in whose house everything tumbles about in disorder, bespattered with mud, and rolls upon the ground; she, dirty, with unwashed clothes, sits and grows fat on a dungheap. *The woman like mud* is ignorant of everything, both good and bad; her only accomplishment is eating: cold though the winters be, she is too stupid to draw near the fire. *The woman made like the sea* has two minds; when she laughs and is glad, the stranger seeing her at home will give her praise—there is nothing better than this on the earth, no, nor fairer; but another day she is unbearable, not to be looked at or approached, for she is raging mad. To friend and foe she is alike implacable and odious. Thus, as the sea is often calm and innocent, a great delight to sailors in summertime, and oftentimes again is frantic, tearing along with roaring billows, so is this woman in her temper.

The woman who resembles a mare is delicate and long-haired, unfit for drudgery or toil; she would not touch the mill, or lift the sieve, or clean the house out! She bathes twice or thrice a day and anoints herself with myrrh; then she wears her hair combed out long and wavy, dressed with flowers. It follows that this woman is a rare sight to one's guests; but to her husband she is a curse, unless he be a tyrant who prides himself on such expensive luxuries. *The ape-like wife* has Zeus given as the greatest evil to men. Her face is most hateful. Such a woman goes through the city a laughing-stock to all the men. Short of neck, with narrow hips, withered of limb, she moves about with difficulty. O! wretched man, who weds such a woman! She knows every cunning art, just like an ape, nor is ridicule a concern to her. To no one would she do a kindness, but every day she schemes to this end—how she may work someone the greatest injury.

The man who gets *the woman like a bee* is lucky; to her alone belongs no censure; one's household goods thrive and increase under her management; loving, with a loving spouse, she grows old, the mother of a fair and famous race. She is preeminent among all women, and a heavenly grace attends her. She cares not to sit among the women when they indulge in lascivious chatter. Such wives are the best and wisest mates Zeus grants to men. *Zeus made this supreme evil—woman*: even though she seem to be a blessing, when a man has wedded one she becomes a plague.

From: Mitchell Carroll, *Greek Women* (Philadelphia: Rittenhouse Press, 1908).

FURTHER READING

Ifi Amadiume, *Re-Inventing Africa: Matriarchy, Religion, and Culture*, rpt. (London: Zed Books, 1998).

Zainab Bahrani, *Women of Babylon: Gender and Representation in Mesopotamia* (New York: Routledge, 2001).

Elizabeth W. Barber, *Women's Work: The First 20,000 Years* (New York: W. W. Norton, 1994).

Maria Brosius, *Women in Ancient Persia, 559–331* BC (Oxford: Clarendon Press, 1996).

Karen Olsen Bruhns and Karen E. Stothert, *Women in Ancient America* (Norman: University of Oklahoma Press, 1999).

Cheryl Claassen and Rosemary A. Joyce, eds., *Women in Prehistory: North America and Mesoamerica* (Philadelphia: University of Pennsylvania Press, 1997).

Diotima: Materials for the Study of Women and Gender in the Ancient World. Available online. URL: http://www.stoa.org/diotima. Downloaded on February 7, 2007.

K. J. Dover, *Greek Homosexuality* (Cambridge, Mass.: Harvard University Press, 1989).

Joan M. Gero and Margaret W. Conkey, eds., *Engendering Archaeology: Women and Prehistory* (Oxford, U.K.: Blackwell, 1991).

David M. Halperin, *One Hundred Years of Homosexuality: And Other Essays on Greek Love* (London: Routledge, 1990).

Rivkah Harris, *Gender and Aging in Mesopotamia: The Gilgamesh Epic and Other Ancient Literature* (Norman: University of Oklahoma Press, 2000).

Bret Hinsch, *Women in Early Imperial China* (Lanham, Md.: Rowman and Littlefield, 2002).

Rosemary A. Joyce, *Gender and Power in Prehispanic Mesoamerica* (Austin: University of Texas Press, 2000).

Mary R. Lefkowitz and Maureen B. Fant, *Women's Life in Greece and Rome: A Source Book in Translation*, 3rd ed. (Baltimore, Md.: Johns Hopkins University Press, 2005).

Barbara Lesko, *The Great Goddesses of Egypt* (Norman: University of Oklahoma Press, 1999).

Marjorie Lightman and Benjamin Lightman, *A to Z of Ancient Greek and Roman Women, Revised Edition* (New York: Facts On File, 2007)

Sarah M. Nelson, *Gender in Archaeology: Analyzing Power and Prestige* (Walnut Creek, Calif.: AltaMira Press, 1997).

Pauline Schmitt Pantel, ed., *A History of Women in the West*, Vol. 1, *From Ancient Goddesses to Christian Saints* (Cambridge, Mass.: Belknap Press of Harvard University Press, 1992).

Simo Parpola and Robert M. Whiting, eds., *Sex and Gender in the Ancient Near East* (Helsinki: Neo-Assyrian Text Corpus Project, 2002).

Gay Robins, *Women in Ancient Egypt* (Cambridge: Harvard University Press, 1993).

Susan Treggiari, *Roman Marriage: Iusti Coniuges from the Time of Cicero to the Time of Ulpian* (Oxford: Oxford University Press, 1991).

► government organization

INTRODUCTION

The word *government* comes from the Greek word *kybernan*, meaning "to steer." Throughout history human communities have exhibited a natural tendency to create a system that steers people through chaos and prevents what the ancient Romans called *bellum omnium contra alles*, or "the war of all against all."

The earliest human communities had no real system of government as the term is understood in modern life. Early hunter-gatherers lived and traveled in small bands, and to the extent that anyone ruled, it was primarily by force. In the daily struggle for simple survival, the person in a small community who emerged as the strongest would most likely assume a leadership role. Such a person would have been able to help the community acquire valuable resources such as food, and in the event of conflict with competing tribes, the strongest, most forceful member of the community could provide valuable military leadership. This system of government continued to exist throughout the ancient world, and indeed forms of it exist in the 21st century. Sometimes called the "force theory" of government, it led to tribal leaders and warlords who seized control over a certain area and of the people who lived in that area. Such a system existed, for example, in the ancient Americas, where warlords held power in chiefdoms.

Force and strength, though, were not the only sources of power. In some cultures, such as that of ancient Japan, shamans and other religious leaders held power. Their subjects believed that shamans possessed magical influence with the gods, so they were the rightful rulers. Similarly, in some cultures, such as the Aborigines of Australia, no formal government existed, but tribal elders held power because the community believed that these elders possessed ancient wisdom.

A repeated theme in discussions of the ancient world is the profound impact of the development of agriculture. When ancient cultures turned to agriculture rather than strictly hunting and gathering, they became what historians called "sedentary." This word does not mean that they were lazy or inactive. It means that people, instead of moving around in search of food, settled in more or less permanent communities, where they could tend fields and livestock and cultivate crops.

In time, those small villages and hamlets grew, and the most prosperous among them evolved into towns and small cities. Agriculture allowed people to store food surpluses; they no longer had to survive day to day. This food surplus enabled communities to support classes of people who were not directly involved in food production, including a military, civil servants, poets and artists, craftsmen, and civic leaders. Thus, it is fair to say that without the development of agriculture, government and government organization would not exist—or that they would exist in only the most primitive forms.

In time, communities had to find a way to ensure some form of stability in their government. The alternative was repeated civil war, as a ruler would die and others would compete for his position. The solution was heredity, with power passed down usually from father to son, though the ancient world provides noteworthy instances of women assuming power. Further, many cultures' history, mythology, and religious values supported the belief that rulers ruled by divine right. That is, they were thought of as holding power that came from the hands of the gods, and the rulers themselves were often looked on as either gods themselves or as intermediaries between the gods and humans.

The result of this system of government was the emergence of dynastic families, some of which ruled for hundreds of years or longer. Good examples are the dynasties of ancient Egypt and China; in fact, historians identify periods of ancient Egyptian and Chinese history by the family dynasties that ruled. A ruling dynasty would come to an end for a number of reasons, including lack of an heir to the throne or conquest by another nation. In some civilizations, power struggles emerged when no clear heir existed, and ruling dynasties would change when, for example, a king's brother or nephew seized power.

Kingship was the dominant form of government in the ancient world, but this does not mean that the ancient world did not provide the first stirrings of democracy. While modern historians make generalizations about large nations, at the time it was difficult to extend rule over a wide geographical area. The result was the emergence of city-states. These city-states often shared a common language and culture with other nearby city-states, but they tended to be self-governing. In ancient Mesopotamia, for example, early city-states often governed themselves, and this government had some of the characteristics of a democracy, with citizens taking part in decisions that affected the community. Ancient Greece, too, consisted of a number of city-states, such as Sparta, which were often in competition and conflict with other Greek city-states. These Greek city-states, too, offered some measure of citizen government. Sometimes, for protection and trade, a handful of city-states formed a league.

Another ancient form of government organization was the oligarchy. This term refers to government by a small group, usually prominent or powerful citizens who held some interest in common. While the civilizations of ancient Europe were monarchies, they had some of the characteristics of an oligarchy, for kings remained dependent on a class of powerful land-owning nobles who supported the king with taxes and military service—but who also sometimes opposed their king when their interests demanded it.

Government and government organization necessarily became more complex as the notion of empire became more common. Ancient Rome provides a classic example. Rome began humbly as a city-state in about the ninth century B.C.E. Over the next 12 centuries, it evolved into first a monarchy ruled by a king, then into an oligarchy, and finally into a massive empire. The power of the king, and later the emperor, was restricted by various advisory and legislative bodies. The Roman Senate, for example, was a body that served in an advisory capacity to the emperor, who found it difficult to rule without the Senate's support. Over time, a large class of officials was appointed to administer the affairs of the empire. In the outlying provinces another class of officials was appointed to administer the affairs of each province.

AFRICA

BY JUSTIN CORFIELD

Ancient Africa was largely made up of kingdoms controlled by hereditary rulers. Most followed the domestication of animals, which ended the nomadic existence of many tribes and resulted in the introduction of more structured governmental systems. Although the extent of some of these entities can be ascertained from archaeological evidence, information on how most were run comes from oral sources, so there are obvious doubts about their accuracy. However, the Greek historian Herodotus, of the fifth century B.C.E., recorded a few descriptions of kingdoms in North Africa that predated the dominance of Carthage, which was, for several centuries, the major economic and military power in North Africa. Egyptian, Persian, Greek, and Roman sources also provide some information.

CARTHAGE

The city of Carthage, founded by Phoenicians from Tyre, was initially ruled by a governor appointed by the king of Tyre. This was the same as for other Phoenician settlements such as Hadrumetum (modern-day Sousse), Utica (Bordj bou Chateur), Hippo Regius (Hippone, near Annaba/Bône) and Hippo Diarrhytus (Bizerta). Similarly, the Greeks also established colonies such as Cyrene, ruled by the Theraeans since its foundation in 630 B.C.E. At Cyrene the Greek merchants seem to have established an intermediary center of trade, which may have been controlled by a business class, with the minting of their own coins to a similar standard of those produced in Athens, Corinth, and Samos.

It appears that by the seventh century B.C.E. Carthage was ruled by hereditary kings, including Mago, who may have reigned from 550 to 530 B.C.E.; his son Hastrubal, who also reigned for about 20 years; and Hamilcar, a grandson of Mago, who ruled from about 510 to 490 B.C.E. Hanno the Navigator was the ruler who extended the size of Carthage along the coast of North Africa; it already had bases on Sicily and Sardinia. The other kings recorded are Hannibal (d. 406 B.C.E.), Himilco (r. 406–396 B.C.E.), and Mago (r. 396–375 B.C.E.).

The role of the government in Carthage included taxation and the coining of money, with the revenue expended on the defense of the city of Carthage, its hinterland, and also the lands of its allies; maintaining law and order within the city of Carthage; gaining and sustaining access to reliable supplies of food; and public works projects. All of this required a relatively complicated government structure, and it seems that Carthage had a significant aristocratic and administrative class. Because important decisions were made in the city of Carthage itself, there seems to have developed a centralized form of government whereby edicts from Carthage were transmitted to the hinterland and to the Carthaginian bases in Sicily, Malta, and other locations.

By the sixth century B.C.E. Carthage had come to be dominated by a city-based aristocratic oligarchy (government controlled by a small group). Although Roman authors such as Livy (59 B.C.E.–17 C.E.) wrote extensively about the Punic Wars between Carthage and Rome, it is clear that he knew little about how Carthage was governed. As a result, many of the descriptions come from the Greek philosopher Aristotle (384–322 B.C.E.), and hence the comparisons are largely with Greek models. It is uncertain exactly when Carthage changed from a monarchy to a republic, though the date is traditionally given as 309 B.C.E. However, before then it is not clear whether all the rulers came from one family or whether they were semi-elected or indeed wholly elected by the people of Carthage or their representatives. Much of the account of the period after Aristotle comes from *The Histories* by the Greek historian Polybius (ca. 205–ca. 123 B.C.E.), who often uses the term "king" carelessly in several other contexts.

Aristotle notes in the fourth century B.C.E. that the Carthaginians operated with an unwritten constitution that was similar to that in many Greek cities. Indeed, it is clear that an oligarchy exercised total power over political decisions except in the short democratic period that followed the War of the Mercenaries in about 240–238 B.C.E. Officially Carthage was ruled through a general assembly, but it was dominated by the Senate, with several hundred members who were all elected for life, and a "Committee of Five." Members of the Senate seem to have been co-opted to form committees that advised two annually elected judges. Military generals were also elected to hold military commands when needed. For this reason even extremely powerful and successful generals like Hannibal owed their command to the Carthaginian Senate, as shown by their recall of him in 203 B.C.E.

Because Carthage relied for most of its history on mercenaries, their rebellion and subsequent blockade of the city of Carthage itself shattered the people's confidence in the government of the empire. Hanno the Great, a general put in command, was able to deploy an army but, after an initial victory, was defeated at Utica. This led to the appointment of Hamilcar. Hamilcar was not only an important general but also a keen politician. One of Hamilcar's daughters married Bomilcar, then the titular ruler (or "king") of Carthage. This gave Hamilcar not just military but also political power. According to Polybius, Hamilcar is said to have offered the troops the opportunity of choosing their general—and they elected him. This started the system by which a military monarchy could have come into existence. With the death of Bomilcar, the system of titular "king" of Carthage ended.

The uneasy relationship between the Carthaginian Senate and these generals is shown by the "Court of the Four Hundred" that tried to manage the First Punic War (264–241 B.C.E.) and was involved in ordering that four generals be crucified for their failures. As the distrust between the politicians and the generals grew, Barca (d. 229 B.C.E.) and his son Hannibal (247–183 B.C.E.) both technically held power at the behest of the Senate of Carthage. For this reason Hamilcar established a separate power base in Spain to allow him to raise money and soldiers for what would eventually lead to the Second Punic War (218–202 B.C.E.).

Hannibal's invasion of Italy may or may not have had the support of the Senate in Carthage, though when it was successful most would have rejoiced. Some, however, were clearly enemies of the Barcid family, and it showed in their attitude to him when he was unable to capture the city of Rome. The failure of the Carthaginian Senate to send reinforcements to Hannibal during his time in Italy and to recall Hannibal in 203 B.C.E. after Publius Cornelius Scipio (later "Africanus") landed an expeditionary force in North Africa, are two clear examples of the power of the Senate over the military. Livy implies this in his descriptions of Carthaginian Senate, probably based on recollections by a Roman based on what might have been said in Carthage.

Overall, the Carthaginian system of government was not dissimilar to that later adopted by the Roman Republic, by which powerful families could control the city but were not powerful enough to establish hereditary rule. However, it does not appear that the Carthaginians ever allowed a popular vote for positions, leading many historians to see the Punic Wars to a war between Roman democracy and Carthaginian dictatorship.

During the Third Punic War (149–146 B.C.E.), the Carthaginian government seemed to have a much more important role in the running of the city than was the case during the Second Punic War. In 203 B.C.E., when Carthage itself was under attack, the responsibility for the stockpiling of food seemed to have been held by the individual families themselves. With the final siege of Carthage, however, it was the task of the government to hoard much of the food to prevent the people from starving. It is also was possible that on the first occasion, in 203 B.C.E., the threat to the city was not seen as being as serious as that which led to the final siege of the city, leading to its sacking and the total overthrow of the Carthaginian government.

North Africa

Two of the major states in North Africa, Mauretania and Numidia, occupied what are now modern-day Morocco and Algeria. Both were ruled by kings who were nominally independent but who relied on strong alliances first with Carthage and then Rome, both being eventually annexed by the Romans.

In Numidia a kingdom was originally formed by former nomads, who before they established permanent settlements, were a confederation of various tribes, with leaders often linked by political marriages; some of the more powerful ones vied for control of the whole entity. Syphax (d. ca. 201 B.C.E.), the chief of the Masaesyles tribe, wore a diadem like a Hellenistic monarch, probably modeling his style of government on that of Alexander the Great, with allegiances formed in battle. He used Phoenician rather than Berber as the language of government. His system proved unsuccessful and was replaced by the formation of a dynastic government after the emergence of Masinissa (ca. 240–148 B.C.E.). The Greek writer Strabo records that Masinissa made "nomads into farmers and welded them into a state." He also turned local warlords into feudal chiefs who owed their large estates, wealth, and power to Masinissa himself, who dispensed them in return for loyalty. Masinissa also saw the role of the king in the Hellenistic mould.

The structure of government in Mauretania was probably similar, though there is clearer evidence of a hereditary aristocratic government than was the case in Numidia. However, while Numidia was being united politically, in Mauretania there seemed to have been far more regional autonomy, with different cities issuing their own coins inscribed in Neo-Punic, or Carthaginian, which seems to indicate a greater independence exercised by regional governors.

Saharan Africa

Beyond the areas which became parts of the Roman Empire, the system of government in the rest of Africa is much harder to define, owing to the lack of written records. A major source that discusses the people who lived in what is now Saharan Africa remains Herodotus, who described a number of the tribes in detail. However, Herodotus is unreliable because he has been shown to be wrong on other matters, and his detail is more about their customs than how they ruled or were ruled.

Herodotus begins his discussion of North and Saharan Africa after describing Persian rule over Cyrenaica and Libya. The first place in his account is Adyrmachidae in modern-day eastern Libya. It was ruled by a king whom Herodotus said had a right to "any girl who catches his fancy." The neighboring tribe, the Gilgamae, operated from a summer capital and a winter headquarters. Other tribes in the area included the Nasamones, the Psylli, the Garamantes, the Macae, the Gindanes, and the Machlydes. Herodotus gives no description of the government of any of them except for a reference to the Psylli's calling of a council meeting to declare war on the south wind (and whose army is alleged to have disappeared in a sandstorm), obviously an apocryphal story, but showing that some tribes had collective decision-making procedures. For most of the other tribes Herodotus describes their use of war chariots but nothing about their method of government. The Egyptians and the Romans both tried to trade in the region but tended to like to deal with other governments rather than nomadic tribes.

In the Nilotic Sudan and Ethiopia, descriptions from the ancient Egyptians, a few Roman and Greek accounts, and some archaeological work have allowed historians to gain some idea of the style of rule in that area. Certainly the governments in these regions were heavily influenced by developments in Egypt, a finding augmented by surviving inscriptions. They were based on rule by kings, in a way similar but on a less lavish scale than the Egyptian monarchy

In Kush the government centered on a king and his royal court, who lived apart from the rest of the population. There were no fixed rules on royal descent, so it was not uncommon for older brothers and people in the maternal line to ascend to the throne. This state of affairs shows that there was possibly a regency council or similar body that made the final decision on royal succession. There were certainly established roles for the Queen Mother, the Queen Sister, various other royal personages, and many other titled office bearers. One surviving image in the Indian style of a king of Kush riding an elephant indicates that the Royal Court included at least one Indian sculptor. The role of the government in Kush was clearly to defend the population from attack by outsiders, which included the construction of defensive walls as well as the raising of armies in time of war. The government also maintained supplies of food, which could be drawn upon in times of shortage. It was certainly an effective system, and it kept the kingdom together for nearly a thousand years.

In ancient Ethiopia there have been strong links between the kingdoms there and those in Egypt, with some evidence that the two areas were ruled by the same kings in about 2500 B.C.E., with the capital located at Napata, north of modern-day Sudan. This suggests that the governing structures that came to be used in Ethiopia would have been largely modeled on those of ancient Egypt, with hereditary rulers seen as divine or semidivine, a ruling class, a middle class of scribes and merchants, and the remainder of the "free" population and the slaves.

The origins of the kingdom of Axum are believed either to have come from or to have been very closely linked with developments in South Arabia. The language of government in Axum was Ge'ez, which used a modified South Arabian alphabet. The deities in Axum were also similar to those in South Arabia. Axum certainly had a number of women rulers, one of them perhaps being the legendary "Queen of Sheba." Although the names of some of the kings have survived, there is little known about the nature of government. Given the size of the kingdom, there would seem to have been a number of regional governors responsible for different parts of the kingdom. This would certainly have been necessary when Axum started to occupy the lands of the Himyarites in South Arabia. Indeed, King Ezānā of Axum (r. ca. 330–ca. 356 B.C.E.) used as a part of his title "king of Saba and Salhen, Himyar and Dhu-Raydan" and also "King of the Habshat," later adopting the title *negusa nagast* ("king of kings"). These names tend to suggest that the merger of a number of kingdoms or a merger or confederation of smaller states had taken place. As the first king in Ethiopia to accept Christianity, Ezānā was also keen to have a diplomatic alliance with Byzantium, sending a government embassy there.

Traditionally, one would expect that hereditary kings ruled African tribes, but this is largely supposition, though one based on folklore and work by early anthropologists. That the tribes had rulers and that there was wealth inequality are obvious. Archaeological work at some sites has resulted in the unearthing of the remains of large houses and also smaller ones. Objects of art with a high level of workmanship and the use of precious (and rare) metals found at some sites suggest that these were prized items of the wealthy, with the poorer people probably having wooden objects that have not survived. This has led some scholars to suggest that there might have been a small elite group that controlled the iron-making process, using it to maintain their rule over their own and even other nearby tribes.

Sub-Saharan Africa

In some parts of sub-Saharan Africa tribes operated without any predetermined rulers, with decisions reached by village elders or groups after discussions. This seems clear from linguistic evidence of non-Bantu African languages that lack many hierarchical terms used to refer to hereditary rulers. With much of the non-Bantu society operating in small villages, the decisions would be made by consensus, and the role of the government was probably fairly limited and largely confined to issues of defense and storage of grain for times of drought or famine.

Certainly, the major role of the government has long been to provide their people with protection from attack. This function is often evident in the location of villages in ancient Africa. One ancient settlement in the Hoggar region, some 1,000 miles south of Algiers, was excavated in 1926 and again in 1933. Essentially, the layout of the town was such that as many houses as possible could be protected by fortified walls. As it was in a relatively uninhabited region, it can be assumed that large bands of marauders were major potential threats. Similarly in Tichit-Walata, in the Sudan, people tended to live fortified cliff-top villages, with little access to much arable land, clearly showing that protection from attack was extremely important. Both of these examples show the origins of "government" as being essentially a way of organizing people for their own protection.

The Bantu tribes of southern Africa appear to have operated through hereditary chiefs, a form of monarchical government that developed during the first millennium C.E. The system seems to have had chiefs of tribes who ruled with the support of "headmen" of villages, who were commoners. Many of these chiefs may have had large numbers of children, and they often assimilated with commoners so that their children lost their royal status. This process left a core royal family living in the tribal headquarters, with other relatives dispersed through the population but owing their absolute loyalty, through their ancestry, to the main chief. In some ways this is similar to how many absolute monarchies existed, and some dynasties in China used this "dispersal" of members of their imperial houses as a way of controlling the empire, ensuring that the government had a level of support throughout its territory. It also served as a system that could put some constraints on unscrupulous governors and viceroys, as there were people in many villages who had direct access to rulers in periods of gubernatorial misrule.

Another aspect of the government structure of the Bantu tribes is that they often lived in large communities and that war was common between (and even probably within) tribes. This meant that there was a clear need for a hierarchical society. Most of the evidence for the Bantu tribes during this period comes from a relatively small amount of archaeological evidence, detailed linguistic studies of the differences between the tribes, and the nature of these tribes when the first Europeans arrived in southern Africa and recorded the details of their lifestyle. The developments of the early Iron Age in Africa, such as the manufacture of iron arrowheads, were as much for protection and offense as for hunting.

In the course of archaeological work the remains of large structures are often unearthed. These appear to have been storage centers for grain or other crops in anticipation of times of hardship, and the size of these stockpiles shows that the task of gathering the grain or other foodstuffs was clearly a government responsibility rather than private hoarding. In East Africa large numbers of sites of villages have been excavated by archaeologists, and they tend to have larger huts, presumably occupied by chiefs, and other buildings that would have served as stores of grain, indicating at the least a community store if not one maintained by the "government."

None of the many surviving cave paintings in southern Africa, in present-day Zimbabwe and South Africa, show any kings, rulers, governors, or other type of governmental authority, as is common in some imagery from elsewhere in the ancient world. In West Africa the finding of large numbers of statues at Nok has shown that a highly developed culture flourished in modern-day Nigeria in the mid- to late first millennium B.C.E. It was based on iron production, which was developed from about 500 B.C.E. The many ornaments and stone carvings from Nok, however, add little to the debate about the type of government that existed in the area. The legends of the Bantu tribes also show the increasing move to a hierarchical government that more and more regulated people's lives. While many scholars suggest that the Bantu people were illiterate, it is also possible that there was some system of carving onto wood or records kept in a way that has not survived.

EGYPT

BY MARIAM F. AYAD

Kingship in Egypt

At the top of the ancient Egyptian political, religious, and administrative hierarchy was an absolute ruler: the king of Upper and Lower Egypt. The king was the chief executive officer of the state, the high priest, the chief justice, and the commander in chief of the troops. There is no Egyptian word for king. Most often the king was politely referred to as "his majesty." From the time of the Nineteenth and Twentieth Dynasties (1307–1070 B.C.E.) onward the phrase *great house* (*per-aa*) referred to both the king and his residence. It is from the Greek version of this name that the title "pharaoh" comes. The king's name, enclosed in the royal cartouche (an oval figure designed for the purpose), was introduced by one of two titles: "King of Upper and Lower Egypt" or "Son of Re," referring to an Egyptian god.

As the living incarnation of Horus, the falcon god and "ruler of the living," the king was divine. In theory, the king's divinity enabled him to act as an intermediary between the gods and humankind, whose main duties were to appease the gods and gain favor with their cults. The king was responsible for maintaining the cult of the gods, and he did so by endowing the temple with land and granting temple estates special tax privileges and exemptions. But the king was also responsible for providing sustenance to the gods. The Egyptians believed that their gods needed everything that humans needed: food, drink, and clothes. Scenes preserved on temple walls show the king pouring drinks and consecrating offerings to the gods, who, in return, embraced, purified, suckled, and crowned him. Because the king was one of the gods, he was represented on the same scale as the gods. Because he was the mediator between the divine and human realms, the king's most important task was the maintenance of *maat* (order, justice, and harmony), for which he was solely responsible.

Visually, the king's divinity was expressed through the special costume he wore and the special insignia he carried: his crowns, the *nemes* (or striped headcloth), the long straight-edged false beard attached to his chin, a three-part pleated kilt called the *shendyt*, his crook and flail (which symbolized his role as the shepherd of his people), and a forked staff called a *was* scepter. At the king's brow was a rearing cobra, known as *uraeus* (a word derived from the Egyptian term for "rising goddess"). Shown in "her moment," the rearing cobra is ready for action. At the slightest threat, she would protectively spit her venom against the king's enemies. Because the cobra also protects the son god, this feature further asserts the king's solar connections.

Several types of headgear were worn by Egyptian kings. One, the double crown of Upper and Lower Egypt, comprised the red crown of Lower Egypt and the white crown of Upper Egypt. This crown was held in place by its distinctive frontal coil. Although some deities may be represented by one or the other of its two component crowns, human subjects could not wear them. Another, the blue crown, known in earlier literature as a "war crown," was worn on political occasions and was an adaptation of a close-fitting cap.

In addition, the king's titles and epithets also emphasized his divinity. Upon ascending to the throne, the king acquired a formal titulary, that is, a series of set titles. A monumental inscription of Thutmose I (r. ca. 1504–1492 B.C.E.) addressed to an official by the name of Turi, an "overseer of the southern hill country" (that is, Nubia, a region just south of Egypt), and similar inscriptions indicate that the palace sought to propagate the king's titulary in remote areas under Egyptian control. The text, which dates to the first year of Thutmose I's reign specifies, for example, that the king was Horus, He of the Two Ladies, the Golden Horus, the King of Upper and Lower Egypt, and the son of Re.

The royal titulary, such as the one for Thutmose I, was composed of five "names" or epithets and declared the king's political program. Dating to the time prior to the Dynastic Period and the earliest names, "Horus" related the king directly to the falcon god Horus—as did another name: his Golden Horus/Golden falcon name. By the middle of the First Dynasty (2920–2770 B.C.E.), two other names were in use. One, literally "he of the sedge and the bee," is more commonly translated as King of Upper and Lower Egypt. The other was "he of the two ladies," referring to the titular goddesses of Upper and Lower Egypt, Wadjit and Nekhbet, respectively. By the Fourth Dynasty (2575–2465 B.C.E.), a fifth name was added: "son of Re." Originally worshipped in Heliopolis, Re, a solar deity, was one of the earliest solar deities. In the Old Kingdom (ca. 2575–2134 B.C.E.), he became the supreme god of the Egyptian pantheon. In addition to emphasizing the king's close association with the supreme deity, this title also declared the king's solar religious affiliation.

The Son of Re name is viewed as the Egyptians' ingenious way of reconciling their realization of the king's humanity with the official dictum of his divinity. Despite all the trappings of divinity, the Egyptians were only too aware of the king's humanity and understood that his frailty and physical limitations often prevented him from acting as the immortal, omnipresent (that is, existing everywhere), omniscient (all-knowing) being that he was supposed to be. While the title relates the king to the supreme solar deity, it also implies that the king was somewhat removed from the true essence of divinity. It has been suggested that the Egyptian theologians never considered the king himself to be divine, but rather the institution of kingship. Thus a mortal became divine on ascending the throne only through the power inherent in the office of kingship itself. A deceased king was typically referred to as *netjer-nefer*, "the perfect god."

Having an accurate set of royal titles was crucial to provincial officials who oversaw multiple activities on behalf of the king, including the presentation of offerings in the temple and the construction of new monuments. Each new monument would be dated to the king's regnal year (that is, the year he ascended to the throne) and inscribed with his full titulary.

The king's divinity was also proclaimed through temple iconography, or images and symbolic representations. A series of scenes preserved on the walls of the temple of Amun at Luxor depict the divine conception and birth of King Amenhotep III (1391–1353 B.C.E.). In one scene Amun is led to the queen's chambers. Although Amun assumes the guise of her husband Thutmose IV, the god's sweet aroma betrays him, and the queen recognizes him as the supreme god and not her mortal husband. During this conjugal visit, the queen is impregnated. Attended by deities, the queen later gives birth to the future Amenhotep III. In the next scene the goddesses Mut and Hathor nurse the child while Amun looks on. Spun after the fact, the birth cycles were depicted on temple walls after the birth took place. Representations of birth cycles are portrayed in the mortuary temple of Hatshepsut at Deir el-Bahri (ca. 1450 B.C.E.) and in several Ptolemaic and Roman temples. Birth cycles were represented after a king assumed the throne and served the political purpose of further legitimating his (or her) rule. A Middle Kingdom (2040–1640 B.C.E.) literary text relates the birth of three Fifth Dynasty

(2465–2323 B.C.E.) kings. The kings are brothers born to a priest in the cult of Re at Heliopolis and his wife, Ruddjedet. The birth is assisted by the sister goddess pair Isis and Nephtys and by the god Khnum.

The Egyptians realized that the transition of power involved a certain measure of risk that could potentially lead to turmoil. To avoid potential power struggles, a ruling king might decide to share his power with his son, the crown prince. Vested with all the trappings and power of kingship, the son would rule alongside his father as his coregent. The evidence suggests that often the older king retained more authority and prestige, while the younger ruler was sent out on more physically strenuous activities, such as leading a military expedition or traveling around the country. Typically monuments built during the joint reigns of a father and his son would bear double dates, giving the regnal year and titles of the younger king alongside those of his father. Although the more common representation of a ruling king next to his predecessor, his deceased father, was initially taken by Egyptologists to signify a period of joint reign, it is now less certain that this was the case. The new king may have chosen to be represented next to his father to legitimize his claim to the throne.

Egyptian Government Organization and Bureaucracy

One the earliest and most bureaucratic administrative systems known, the Egyptian government system was highly structured and hierarchical. At the head of this complex system was an official by the title of *thaty* or *chaty*, commonly translated as "vizier" or "prime minister." For all practical purposes, the vizier was second only to the king and often served as the king's deputy. The vizier may initially have been a member of the king's immediate family, even a king's son. Several viziers of the Old Kingdom bore the title of *sa-nesou*, or "king's son." However, this title does not necessarily reflect a blood relation to the king. Officials occasionally added on such titles to indicate a certain level of achievement or their rank at court.

In later periods of Egyptian history, the title of vizier was given to individuals who were clearly not members of the royal family. Normally, the vizier was a royal appointee. However, in times of weakened royal authority, the title could become hereditary, and a certain level of nepotism existed. For example, the Thirteenth Dynasty (ca. 1783–after 1640 B.C.E.) autobiographical inscription of the vizier Ankhu suggests that not only Ankhu but also other members of his family served as viziers under several kings.

As early as the Third Dynasty (ca. 2649–2575 B.C.E.), the vizier supervised all government departments. Perhaps because the power of the vizier rivaled the king's, by the beginning of the New Kingdom (1550–1070 B.C.E.) the office was shared by two people. Residing in Memphis was the vizier of Lower gypt. The vizier of Upper Egypt had his seat in several different cities.

The installation and duties of the vizier are detailed in the 18th Dynasty (1550–1307 B.C.E.) Theban Tomb of Rekhmire. Rekhmire served as vizier under Thutmose III (ca. 1479–1425 B.C.E.). One of the best-preserved texts detailing the duties of the vizier, this text commences with a formal speech given by the king, in which the office of the vizier is described as "the support of the whole land." The king then goes on to comment on the nature of the office, asserting that "it is not sweet; it is bitter as bile." Part of a much older tradition, such statements were probably formulaic.

This text describes Rekhmire as responsible for several different departments, including the royal treasury, the bureau for land assessment and property exchange, and the court system. For tax purposes the vizier had the additional responsibility of conducting a census of cattle, produce, and land every two years. Moreover, the text refers to Rekhmire as serving as "the ears and eyes of the sovereign." Another epithet, which refers to Rekhmire as the "heart of [his] Lord," may refer to his advisory role. In ancient Egyptian the heart was the seat of thought and intellect.

In addition to providing a detailed account of the government departments supervised by the vizier, the lengthy text begins with a description of the physical layout of the office of the vizier. It describes his stool, his mat, the garb that he wore, his staff, and the placement of his assistants and scribes. The text also provides an idea of the decorum observed in the vizier's chambers. It concludes with a summation of the vizier's duties: to dispatch envoys, district councilors, and mayors and governors; to appoint officeholders such as overseers; to hear their reports and read their records; to appoint the master of the army and review the state of fortresses; to mark boundaries for districts, garden plots, and estates; and to hear legal disputes, among numerous other duties.

The vizier was thus responsible for every aspect of civil government. One of the most prominent features of the Egyptian administrative system was the royal archives. Every transaction was recorded: wills, title deeds, census lists, conscription lists, orders, memos, tax lists, letters, journals, inventories, regulations, and trial transcripts. The office of the vizier was the main repository of the archives. The vizier was *the* tax assessor of the country. As such, he was responsible for the annual budget. In ancient Egypt the main source of income was agricultural produce. In view of the generally arid climate of Egypt, the vizier needed to monitor the levels of the Nile closely. A particularly low Nile would lead to drought and was therefore disastrous, so special preparations were in order.

One of the main objectives of the treasury was to finance royal building projects. Taxes were collected in the form of grain and stored in the royal granary. The produce collected would be used to pay officials and craftsmen and may have been used to supplement the incomes of local temples and funerary cult complexes. Payment to individuals and estates was made in kind. Individual craftsmen and artisans received bread and beer as wages. Additional tax demands were regularly made whenever the need arose. Local mayors (*haty*) were responsible for the collection of these additional taxes.

Along with the treasury, other key areas of administration included the department of agriculture, the department of works, the judiciary, and the army. The title of "*imy-ra,*" or "overseer," was used by every senior or middle-ranking official in every level of the administration. Reporting directly to the vizier were the all-important overseer of the treasury (*imy-ra per hedj,* literally "overseer of the 'the house of silver'") and the overseer of the royal construction works (*imy-ra kawet nesut*). During the Fourth Dynast,, the golden age of pyramid building, several viziers also held the title of overseer of the royal construction works.

A Nineteenth Dynasty inscription found in Nuri (in Nubia, a region to the south of Egypt) instructs various government officials to observe tax exemptions granted his funerary temple at Abydos. The text, which dates to the reign of Seti I (ca. 1306–1290 B.C.E.) outlines the major officials of the realm: "the vizier, magistrates, courtiers, councils of hearers, the viceroy of Kush, the commandants, the superintendents of gold, mayors of town and controllers of camps/tribes of Upper and Lower Egypt, the charioteers, the stable-chiefs, the standard bearers, every agent belonging to the king's estate, all persons sent on mission to Kush."

Provincial Administration

Administratively, Egypt was divided into 42 discrete administrative units, or provinces, known as "nomes" (derived from the Greek *nomos,* meaning "district," which is a direct translation of the Egyptian term *spat*). To the ancient Egyptians, Egypt was known as "the Two Lands" in reference to Upper Egypt (the valley) and Lower Egypt (the delta). There were 22 Upper Egyptian nomes, with the first nome at Aswān being also the southernmost. The nomes were numbered sequentially northward. Memphis, the "Balance of the Two Lands," constituted the first Lower Egyptian nome, with the 19 other nomes of Lower Egypt lying in the delta. Despite various changes, this division of Egyptian into discrete provinces survived into the Roman period.

By the Sixth Dynasty (ca. 2323–2150 B.C.E.) the Upper Egyptian nomes were grouped together into three larger administrative units. The "northern region" comprised the 16th Oryx nome to Memphis. The "middle nomes" extended from the modern city of Akhmīm to the Hare nome (that is, nomes 9 to 15). The "southern region" included the first through the eighth Upper Egyptian nomes. Abydos and Aswān seem to have maintained their administrative separateness. Little is known about Lower Egyptian nomes in the Old Kingdom. An overseer of these administrative districts (known in Egyptian as *waret*) interacted directly with the local governors.

Each province had its own governor (or "nomarch," literally "governor of a nome"). Each nomarch was an absolute ruler in his province, running it as a miniature version of the state, with its own treasury and militia. Nomarchs were rewarded with titles and land parcels (estates) and occasionally the right to build a tomb in the royal necropolis, the greatest of all honors. The demise of central government at the end of the Old Kingdom is sometimes attributed the increased power of the local rulers, who challenged the central authority at Memphis.

Although originally a nomarch was appointed by the king (or his deputy), during the First Intermediate Period (ca. 2134–2040 B.C.E.) the office of nomarch became hereditary. Some nomarchs sought to expand their territory through the use of military force or strategic political alliances and intermarriage. Sesostris III installed several governmental reforms that curtailed the power of the nomarchs. At the local level, authority was given to capable administrators rather than to important regional families. In ancient Egypt government administration and high office were open to capable individuals from all classes. Ideally, it was a person's aptitude and hard work that brought him success, and it was that principle that propelled Egyptian society.

THE MIDDLE EAST

BY JAMES A. CORRICK

Ten thousand years ago the ancient Near East was home to small farming communities and nomadic tribes. No doubt, a variety of ways of governing these groups existed. A number of them were surely led by chiefs, with some being elected and some inheriting their position, while other bands were probably headed by priests or councils of elders. Their authority was limited to each these leader's or council's small group, numbering only a few dozen individuals on average and no more than a few hundred at the most. Over time local rule was extended to include more and more people, as first city-states, such as Uruk (beginning in the fourth century B.C.E.), Ur, and Babylon, and then larger domains, such as the Assyrian and Persian empires, rose in Mesopotamia and the rest of the ancient Near East. The cities alone had populations in the tens of thousands: Large ones like Uruk exceeded 50,000 inhabitants, and Babylon had a population of 100,000. In addition, each city controlled many thousands more in the villages surrounding it. In later periods the Assyrians and the Persians ruled over hundreds of thousands of people.

Kingship in Mesopotamia

Leadership of these states generally came to rest in the hands of a single autocratic ruler, most often a king—and occasionally a queen—who was aided by a cadre of advisers and bureaucrats. The first of these monarchs appeared in the Sumerian cities of Mesopotamia, probably sometime in the late fourth millennium B.C.E. Kings may not have originally ruled the city-states of the Sumerians. Rather, the early cities may have had a form of democratic rule exercised through an assembly. This assembly appears to have been made up of two divisions, a council of elders and a congress of all free residents, both men and women. Policy was determined through debate that eventually led to consensus; in this give-and-take the opinions of the elders carried more weight than did that of the ordinary citizen.

To carry out policy, the assembly appointed a leader known as an *en*. Originally, the *en* could be either a man or a woman. In addition to secular duties, the *en* also had religious obligations, conducting religious ceremonies and supervising temple activities as well as the working of temple lands. The power of the *en* grew with time, as did changes in the office. Women became ineligible to be the *en*; indeed, they had no place in city politics, even being banned from membership in the assembly. As the authority of the *en* grew, so did that of the assembly erode until the latter became little more than an advisory body to the *en*.

In some city-states the *en* became a king, while in others the *en* relinquished his secular duties—finding the administration of temple and city too burdensome—and turned them over to an *ensi*, or governor. The *en* thus became the high priest of the main temple. The *ensi*, meanwhile, concentrated on creating and enforcing laws, regulating commerce, maintaining city streets and buildings, collecting city taxes, and seeing to the defense of the city. Over time the powers inherent in the office may have made some of the *ensi* kings.

The kings of some city-states arrived at the throne via a third route. During the early Sumerian period a *lugal*, or "big man," was often appointed when a city-state faced a crisis, generally the threat of attack by a neighboring state. At the end of the emergency the *lugal* was supposed to step down. However, if the crisis continued for a long time or if the *lugal* was ambitious, he might retain permanent power, thus becoming a king.

Kings and Divinity in Mesopotamia

To Mesopotamians the land and everything and everyone on it belonged to the gods and goddesses. Indeed, each city had supposedly been built by a particular god or goddess, who was the city's patron deity. Thus, Uruk's patron was Inanna, later known as Ishtar, who, among her other duties, was the goddess of love, while that of Nippur was Entil, god of the wind. Since each city was the property of its patron deity, Mesopotamians came to see the king as a divinely appointed administrator. Yet despite their godly connection, most Mesopotamian kings did not actually claim to be divine. The third millennium Akkadian king Naram-Sin (r. 2254–2218 B.C.E.) and Shulgi (r. 2094–2047 B.C.E.), king of Ur, were among the few that did make such a claim, as shown by the addition of the superscript *dingir*, meaning "god," to their names.

More common was the practice of emphasizing a king's divine ties. Thus the king was spoken of as being surrounded by an aura and of being the metaphorical son of the patron deity of his city. His connection to the divine was also represented in carved reliefs by making him appear taller than other people or, as was done in a relief of Hammurabi of Babylon (r. 1792–1750 B.C.E.), by having him stand in front of the patron deity, whose light bathed the monarch. The king was also spoken of as a reflection of the divine patron and as the king of all four quarters of the earth and the heavens.

Succession in Mesopotamia

The king had three symbols of his authority vested in him by the city's patron deity: the crown, the scepter, and the throne. The crown represented the king's divine connection, the scepter stood for justice, and the throne signified his dominance over the living. A new king sat upon the throne and was given the scepter to hold and the crown to wear in a ceremony designed to underscore his power. At the time of this ceremony the king might also speak of his legitimate right to be the city's ruler. He based his claim on the fact that his ancestors had been kings before him. Still, even though a kingship was hereditary, it did not necessarily pass to a ruler's eldest son. Instead, a younger son or even a brother might be the royal heir. Cousins and nephews generally were not in the line of succession, but some sometimes did illegally seize the throne, becoming usurpers.

Indeed, such usurpation was not uncommon. Nor did a usurper have to be a member of the royal family. Strong, ambitious men made themselves king, particularly when the monarch they replaced was seen by the city populace as an ineffective or bungling leader. A king who was seen to have lost the favor of the gods—if, for example, famine ravaged the land or a war was lost—might face open rebellion and the loss of his throne to a usurper. A usurper normally claimed that the city's patron deity had ordered him to become king.

Rarely did a daughter, wife, or sister inherit the throne. The queen, the king's chief wife, generally had no real power. Even so, a strong-willed queen, or even one of the king's other wives, occasionally exerted much influence over her husband. Further, during the rule of the Akkadian dynasty (2350–2100 B.C.E.), one of the king's daughters often became the head priestess of the temple of Nanna, the moon god, in the city of Ur. Although the political function that the high priestess fulfilled is unclear, her installation was considered a major event, and clearly the post was considered important to the ruling monarch.

In the Mesopotamian Palace

The center of the kingship, and consequently of the government, was the palace. Here, the king had his and his family's living quarters. That family was often extensive and included not only his many wives, concubines, and children but also brothers, cousins, uncles, and nephews. Sometimes members of the royal family, particularly the royal heir, had their own, smaller palaces.

Also living and working in the palace, though separated from the royal living quarters, was the king's staff. Many of these people were household servants, but also present were scribes, whose ability to read and write made them the clerks, secretaries, and accountants of the king. The scribes were thus the record keepers, among whose chief duty was keeping track of tax collection. They also composed tributes promoting the king's character and achievements and made copies of myths, hymns, and epics, which often glorified the king's ancestors and their relations to the gods.

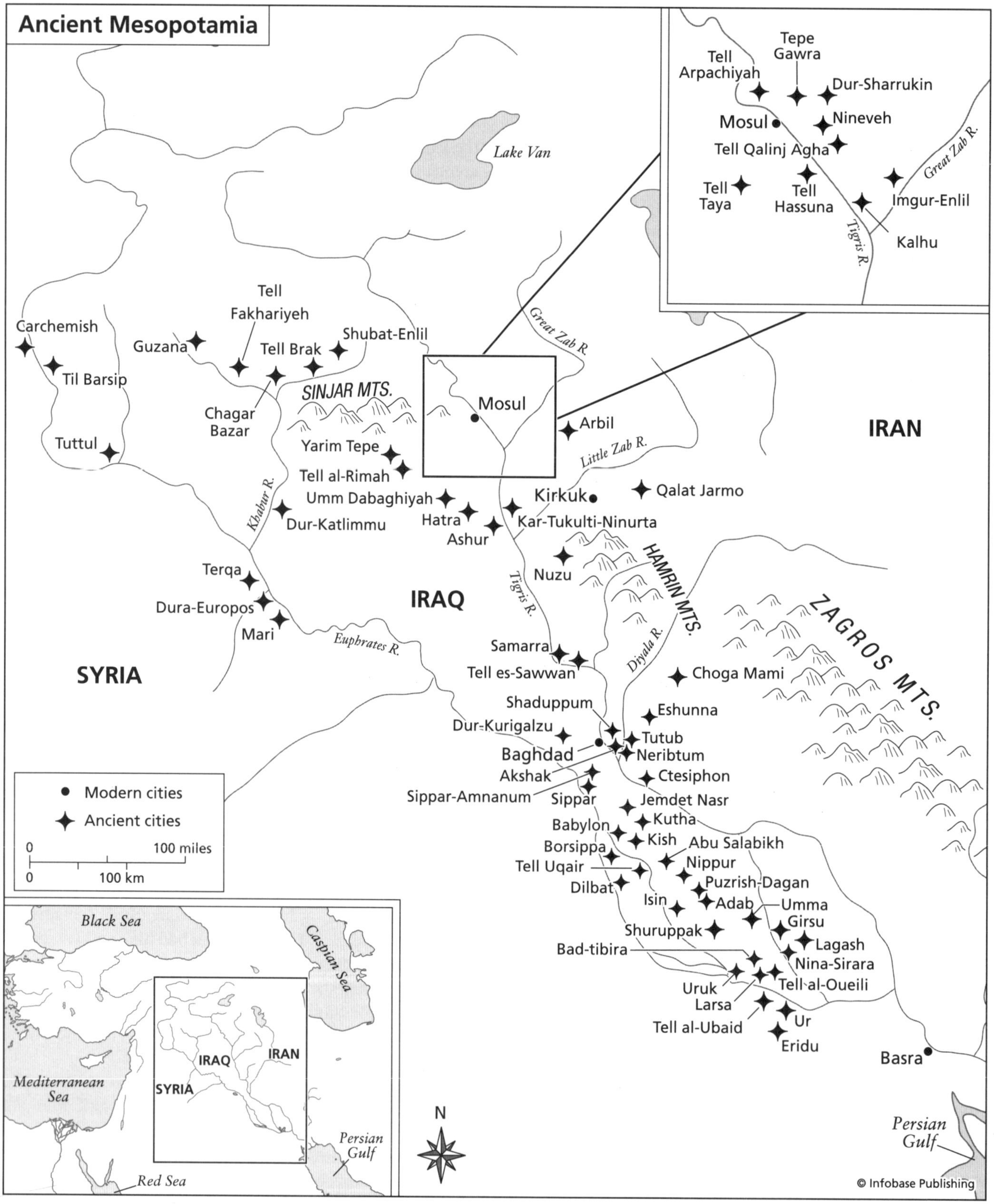

Settlements and their accompanying governmental organizations in the ancient Middle East were heavily concentrated in the basin of the Euphrates and Tigris rivers.

Being a Mesopotamian King

The king's duties were many. In times of peace he had to see to the administration of the city, the dispensation of justice, the reception of ambassadors from other states, the collection of taxes, and the construction and maintenance of public buildings and irrigation canals. In times of war he had to ensure that the army was prepared for defending the city and for campaigning against the enemy. Additionally, he had religious obligations, overseeing the main temple and participating in religious rites.

To help him, the king had a host of aides, many of whom also lived in the palace. Among the foremost officials were a chief adviser and a chamberlain, or chief of staff. The former aided the king in formulating policy and in handling diplomatic missions from other states, while the latter supervised the operations of the large palace staff. In addition to the chief adviser and the chamberlain, the king was also served by a commander in chief of the army, along with an officer corps, and the head priest and the rest of the priestly hierarchy of the city's main temple. None of these officials had any more authority than that the king chose to give him. Some kings left much of the mundane details of governing in the hands of his staff, while others did not. Hammurabi, for instance, insisted on receiving exhaustive daily reports, particularly those relating to the collection of taxes. Perhaps such intimate involvement in government affairs led some kings to be given the title of "accountant."

On the whole, however, most kings contented themselves with the larger issues of policy and to some extent the implementation of that policy. In making decisions, kings took into account practical matters, such as the need to feed their sizable urban populations, the advisability of extending the all-important irrigation system that fed water to cropland, and the state of commercial relations with neighboring cities.

One other important factor played a role in royal decision making: the reading of omens. A good omen acted as a stamp of approval of royal action. However, a bad omen, such as a mongoose running underneath the king's chariot, could cause a monarch to change his policy completely or to have to endure a purification ritual. Among the later Assyrian kings, who kept a stable of 16 astrologers to read the signs, ill omens caused the monarch to fast for several days and, then clad in a white robe, spend more days confined to a small reed hut, a typical practice for isolating the sick.

The reading of omens was also used to protect the king. Royal activities and events would be postponed and audiences with the king cancelled if the omens predicted injury to the monarch. If the omens foretold the possible death of the ruler, a temporary substitute king took his place. While the real king hid, the substitute lived in the palace, wore the king's robes, and even had an appointed queen. In this way the real king hoped that the substitute would be the one to die. If the ill-omened time passed without harm to the substitute, he was then killed.

The Akkadian State

Throughout the fourth and much of the third millennium B.C.E. Mesopotamian city-states were small enough for the entire administration to be located within or close to the palace. However, when the Sargon the Great (r. 2334–2279 B.C.E.) conquered Mesopotamia and other surrounding territories and created the first large unified state in the ancient Near East, there was no way that the Akkadian kings could directly control the affairs of all the city-states in their realm from their capital of Agade. Instead, they left local administration in the hands of the original family, which had ruled prior to conquest; if such families could not be trusted or proved disloyal, the Akkadians appointed a governor to administer the conquered city. Orders from the Akkadian king were passed by the bureaucrats in Agade to these governors. How tight the control from the Akkadian capital was is debatable, but governors, particularly those most distant from Agade, may have been free to act with a fair degree of freedom as long as the king received his annual tribute.

Outside Mesopotamia

In general, other ancient Near Eastern states had governmental organizations similar to that found in Mesopotamia. Kings, such as the Israelite monarchs David and Solomon, ruled single city-states or more extensive domains, though the latter were generally more modest than that of the Akkadians. In like manner to the Mesopotamian kings, other Near Eastern rulers were served by advisers and staffs of scribes acting as clerks, secretaries, and accountants. To what extent these other realms were influenced by Mesopotamian governmental practices and to what extent these states reinvented Mesopotamian forms are not known. Only among the Phoenicians were matters different. Although the Phoenician city-states were originally headed by kings, they eventually came to be governed by councils made up of wealthy merchants. The bureaucracy below them, however, was the same as those found in other ancient Near Eastern domains.

Assyria

All of these ancient states would eventually come under the rule of the Assyrian Empire (1000–626 B.C.E.). Twelve hundred years after the time of Sargon of Akkad, the Assyrians followed something of the same governing pattern as the Akkadian state, although with more complexity. The Assyrians ruled from a central state, located in northern Mesopotamia and made up of four cities, Ashur, Kalhu (modern-day Nimrud), Nineveh, and Arbela (modern-day Arbīl). These four cities were favored in that they were exempt from taxation and their citizens could not be drafted into the army. The remainder of the empire was divided into provinces. Each province was further split into districts, which were centered on a city or a large town.

The Assyrian capital, which at different times was Ashur, Kalhu, or Nineveh, was the home of the king. Even more than previous Mesopotamian kings, the Assyrian monarch was the absolute ruler of the state; indeed, it could be said that he *was* the state, since no one was allowed to question his decisions. His power came from Assur, the chief Assyrian god, though the king made no claims to be a god himself. Absolute the Assyrian king might be, but he still required aid in running an empire that contained much of the ancient Near East. The central Assyrian state was governed by the crown prince, and each province was administered by a governor and each district by a district chief. Both governors and district chiefs were Assyrians appointed by the king. Most governors were military men and often took part in campaigns to capture new territory or to suppress rebellions. To supervise a province in the governor's absence, there probably was a lieutenant governor.

The king also had his advisers. His chief source of advice came from a council made up of high-ranking army officers, some of whom were also provincial governors. The chief advisor was the *turtanu*, that is, the commander in chief of the army. Swift communication was essential in order for the king to maintain his control and to spread his orders throughout the empire. Consequently, he was served by a corps of mounted messengers. Riding the royal roads, the main highways of the empire, messengers changed mounts at posts every 20 to 30 miles, thus efficiently tying the empire together. Swift communication helped not only in spreading royal commands but also in stopping the occasional rebellion. Troops from the central Assyrian state or other provinces could be ordered relatively quickly to the trouble spot.

Once a rebellion was put down and its leaders tortured and executed, the Assyrian king might order some of the rebellious population's merchants, craftspeople, and aristocrats relocated as a further punishment. Such deportees found themselves far from home and surrounded by strangers. The threat of gruesome death and lifelong exile did not end rebellion, but they made such uprisings less likely.

Achaemenid Persia

Half a century after the collapse of the Assyrian state, in the middle of the sixth century B.C.E., a new empire, the Achaemenid Persian (538–331 B.C.E.), arose. For the next two centuries the Achaemenids would govern a territory considerably larger than Assyria, encompassing not only the entirety of the ancient Near East, including upper Egypt, but also the regions that are now Iran, Afghanistan, parts of Central Asia, and Pakistan as far east as the Indus River valley. The Achaemenids were hereditary kings, and like their Assyrian predecessors, they claimed absolute authority over their realm. Since the king was the representative of the Iranian god and creator of the world Ahura Mazda, the Persian monarch also claimed that he had the divine right to rule the entire world. The Achaemenids thus took the titles Great King and King of Kings to differentiate themselves from other rulers.

To emphasize the king's authority, he wore a long-sleeved purple robe embroidered in gold and much gold jewelry, including on occasion a golden crown. Four pillars supported his throne, which sat beneath a purple canopy, and he walked through his palace on purple carpets that no one else could use. Despite his claim of absolute power, the king was expected to seek the advice of important officials and members of the aristocracy, particularly since no one person could have governed a state the size of the Persian Empire without advice and help. The king, however, did not have to heed advice if it conflicted with his own desires. The chief Persian official beneath the king was the *hazarapatish* ("commander of a thousand"). This official, who belonged to the highest ranks of Persian nobility, was the supervisor of the palace staff and commander of the royal bodyguard. He arranged audiences with the monarch and personally delivered messages to the king.

The *hazarapatish*, along with other palace officials, aided the king in administering the various conquered territories of the empire. From the beginning the Achaemenid tolerated a fair amount of local rule in conquered territories. Indeed, initially, the founder of the empire, Cyrus II (r. ca. 538–ca. 529 B.C.E.), known as the Great, did not appoint Persians as governors of the empire's various conquered states. Instead, he chose those native to each region. Darius I (r. 522–486 B.C.E.), however, revamped Cyrus's system. He wanted to make the overall governing of the empire more unified and to emphasize the dominance of Persia. For this reason Darius divided the empire into 20 provinces, known as satrapies. Persia itself was not a satrapy; only conquered territories were.

Each satrapy included a number of former states and a diversity of ethnic groups. Thus the satrap of Abarnahara ("beyond the river," referring to the Euphrates) included all of Syrio-Palestine with its Phoenician cities and Jewish states along with the island of Cyprus. The capital of this satrap was probably Damascus. Except for Persia, which was under the direct rule of the king, each satrapy was administered by a governor, or satrap, who was always a Persian. This governor was rewarded for his service with rich lands and a palace in the satrapal capital. Both the satrap and his holdings were a visible reminder that the Persians had ultimate authority in the empire.

Below the satrap, government continued to be mostly in the hands of local rulers, generally, like the satraps, appointed by the Persian king. Merchant councils continued to oversee the Phoenician cities along the Mediterranean, and tyrants still ruled the Greek cities in Asia Minor. These local rulers even enjoyed some degree of autonomy. The chief duties of the satrap and of the local authorities below him were to implement royal decrees, keep order, and collect the annual tribute, which was then sent to Persia. Only Persia itself was exempt from this taxation, one of its privileges of not being a satrapy.

In order to collect the tribute and to keep order, the satrap had the help of a garrison of Persian soldiers. However, he did not have command of this military unit. Instead, it answered only to its commanding officer, who in turn was responsible only to the king. It was the king rather than the satrap who appointed this military chief. This division of power was meant to lessen the risk that an ambitious satrap would use the forces at his disposal to set himself up as an independent ruler. At least one satrap during the reign of Darius was killed by Persian soldiers on the orders of the king when he was suspected of treason.

There were further safeguards to check the ambition of satraps. First, like the chief military officer, the treasurer and secretary of each satrapy were appointees of the king and were not subject to orders from the satrap. Second, the king had a corps of inspectors, known as the king's eyes and ears, who roamed the empire examining tax records, interrogating both members of satrap staffs and the general public, and making regular reports to the king. None of these measures completely stopped rebellion, and the final safeguard was to get word to Persia as quickly as possible when trouble broke out. The Persian kings had a series of signal fires placed on the top of hills. When a fire was lit, it was visible to the next station, which would then light its own fire and so on in a string that led to a Persian military outpost.

For more detailed information and orders the Persians, like the Assyrians, had a corps of mounted messengers. By changing horses every 15 miles along the excellent road system maintained by the empire, a courier could average 250 miles a day. The 1,500-mile trip from the western Asia Minor city of Sardis in Lydia to Susa, an important administrative center in southwestern Iran, normally took three months. The king's messengers made it in seven days.

After Persia

Despite these safeguards, by the time that Alexander the Great (r. 336–323 B.C.E.) conquered the Persian Empire, many satrapies had shaken off much of the Great King's control and were operating virtually as independent states. Establishing himself if not in name at least in practice as the successor to the Achaemenid, Alexander kept most of the Persian governmental organization, particularly the satrapy divisions and much of the protocol that surrounded the Persian ruler.

After Alexander's death a series of large kingdoms—the Seleucid (311–140 B.C.E.), the Parthian (250 B.C.E.–226 C.E.), and the Sasanian (224–651 C.E.)—ruled large sections of the old Achaemenid lands, most notably the Persian heartland and Mesopotamia. These realms retained much of the Persian governmental organization, though the Seleucid added some Greek elements and eliminated the division of authority in the satrapies by giving the satrap both civil and military power. The Sassanians even revived the title of Great King. Meanwhile, Syrio-Palestine came under the rule of Rome in the last century B.C.E. Cut up into several provinces, this part of the ancient Near East would remain under Roman and later Byzantine control until the Muslim conquest in the seventh century of the Common Era.

ASIA AND THE PACIFIC

BY AMY HACKNEY BLACKWELL

China

The first government recorded in Chinese historical records was that of the Xia Dynasty, a Bronze Age kingdom that existed from approximately 2205 to 1500 B.C.E. The Xia, like the mythical kingdoms that were said to precede them, had hereditary monarchs, with members of a single family controlling the entire country. China's first legal codes were written during this time, defining crimes and creating punishments for them. The Xia Dynasty was said to have ended when the last king, the corrupt Jie, was overthrown by the Shang people.

The Shang Dynasty (1500–1045 B.C.E.) is the first dynasty for which there is historical information, though historians know little about it. During this period rulers appear to have been hereditary kings who were also considered gods and spiritual leaders. Kings performed divinations with oracle bones (bones used to determine the wishes of spirits and dead ancestors) and led rituals as part of their state duties. They believed that keeping the gods happy was an essential part of maintaining a healthy state. The rulers lived in cities that were centers of government and court life. The Shang territory encompassed a small portion of modern China's territory around the Yangtze River. Outside the capital cities the countryside was divided into territories under the control of nobles. Common people raised crops, livestock, and silkworms, which they used to pay tribute to their local nobles. The local lords maintained armies within their territories in order to render military aid to the kings. Kings controlled the armies, which were often deployed to fight neighboring kingdoms and nomadic barbarians. The Shang Dynasty ended after its army lost a war with the Zhou people, who had invaded from the west, and the king committed suicide. The survivors of the ruling family changed their name to Yin and went to work as administrators in the Zhou Dynasty.

The Zhou Dynasty (1045–256 B.C.E.) was the longest of China's dynasties. It is divided into two portions, the Western Zhou (1045–771 B.C.E.) and the Eastern Zhou (770–256 B.C.E.). It was founded by hereditary monarchs of the Ji family, who justified their power by claiming that the gods gave them the right to govern. They also claimed that if a king was dethroned, it was a sign that the gods no longer wanted him in power. The government was organized into a group of city-states that each had its own local government. Each territory was ruled by a hereditary nobleman, or duke. Within territories, each duke's land was divided into nine equal portions arranged in a square; the commoners worked all the land, but the produce of the center square belonged to the duke. This was called the well-field system. In return, the dukes were expected to pray to the gods and ancestors to ensure that the entire territory had a good harvest.

Initially, the Zhou Dynasty had no real central government. Each duke paid tribute to the king out of loyalty, but the king did not directly control dukes or their territories. As the dynasty progressed, the central government became stronger and implemented a uniform scheme of taxation on crops. The system resembled the feudal system of medieval Europe, with warlords protecting and taxing their local residents and in turn giving tribute and aid to the monarch.

In the late 700s B.C.E. western barbarians sacked the capital city, so the king moved the capital to Luoyang in Henan

Province. The first half of this period, the Eastern Zhou, is called the Spring and Autumn Period (722–481 B.C.E.). During this time the central government lost the power it had gained during the Western Zhou period. Smaller city-states led by dukes began acting on their own again, going to war with one another and annexing weaker neighbors. Dukes had the power to collect their own taxes and raise armies. Several powerful states emerged; the most important were Qin, Jin, Qi, and Chu. Eventually, the overlords of these states stopped recognizing the nominal authority of the king and instead concentrated on running their own states and local administrations. The overlords promised military aid to smaller neighboring states and gradually ended up annexing most of their smaller neighbors. These states appointed officials who handled internal administration, particularly the taxation of territories.

During the fourth and third centuries B.C.E. seven strong states emerged as major powers: Qi, Chu, Yan, Han, Zhao, Wei, and Qin. Their leaders began to call themselves kings instead of dukes, declaring themselves equal to the Zhou king. This period, called the Warring States Period, saw endless conflict between the seven major states. Rulers built walls around their kingdoms to keep out invaders. States formed alliances with one another in the hope of defeating common enemies. The overlords of this period carried out various reforms to strengthen their governments. The state of Qin did away with the older feudal system by getting rid of hereditary ranks. It abolished the well-field system and legalized private land ownership. It created counties to replace the feudal land-management practices that had accompanied the well-field systems; counties answered to the state government instead of to hereditary feudal lords. This new stronger government was able to organize large-scale agriculture and irrigation projects. By the end of this period the state of Qin had emerged as the most powerful of the states and the house of Zhou was nearly extinct From 230 to 221 B.C.E. Qin marched through the other six states, conquering them one by one. By 221 Qin was in control of all China.

The Qin Dynasty was short-lived, lasting from 221 until 207 B.C.E., but it left a lasting impression on Chinese government; for the next two millennia China followed the pattern of rule set up during this time. The ruler Qin Shi Huang turned China into a true empire. He set up a centralized government with uniform laws and procedures, specific weights and measures, standardized road widths and axle sizes, and unified coinage. He organized the empire into 36 prefectures, each of which was further divided into counties. Each prefecture had both a civil and a military governor. Counties were likewise ruled by a pair of magistrates, a civil one and a military one. County magistrates owed allegiance to their prefectural governors.

Qin Shi Huang even defined the types of philosophy that were acceptable. He embraced the school of thought known as legalism, which taught that laws must be clearly written and uniformly enforced. Legalism taught that rulers must ensure that others do not take control of the state away from them. Qin Shi Huang took this advice to heart, to the extent that many people, particularly former ruling nobles, considered him a ruthless tyrant and hated him. He had a very hands-on governing style and did not tolerate criticism or rivals. He banished critical Confucian scholars, burned Confucian books, forced his former enemies to deliver their weapons to the capital city, and destroyed most of the defensive walls that his rival states had built during the Warring States Period; the ones on the northern border he kept and connected together to fend off northern barbarians. He set up a system of national conscription to keep his own army filled with soldiers; conscripts were also forced to work as laborers on projects such as the Great Wall and his mausoleum. He made several trips around the country to inspect conditions with his own eyes. When Qin Shi Huang died, his son lost control of the kingdom, the disgruntled nobles of the other six states began fighting again for several years, and people of all social levels rose up against their rulers.

The Han Dynasty (202 B.C.E.–220 C.E.) restored order and prosperity to the empire. The dynasty's founders, the Liu family, immediately went to work to reclaim control of China and to restore the people's faith in their rulers. They renounced legalism and its harsh controls and replaced it with Confucianism as the state philosophy. Confucian scholars were allowed to return, and criticism of the government was no longer punished harshly. Confucianism taught that the king should be the calm and virtuous center of the kingdom; if the king was stable, the whole kingdom should run smoothly. Confucianism encouraged the king to do as little as possible, in contrast to the micromanagement of legalist rulers. Confucianism also encouraged promotion based on merit; an ideal king was supposed to pass down the throne to the most qualified of his sons, not the oldest.

The Han reduced taxes, got rid of the harsher Qin laws, and removed some of the restrictions the Qin had placed on individual speech and actions. The Han did not entirely end conscripted labor, but they did not require nearly as much of the people as the Qin had. They kept most of the governmental institutions implemented by Qin Shi Huang, but they gave up some central control and allowed vassal states to govern themselves to a greater extent. The emperor himself maintained control of much of China, including the region around the capital city, which continued to be governed by the Qin system of governors and magistrates.

The region directly around the capital was run by three governors, called the Three Guardians. The central government was headed by one or two chancellors, several dukes, and a board of secretaries that handled administrative matters. Law enforcement and the running of the imperial household were delegated to a chamberlain and the Nine Courts. The army was divided into several branches, each headed by a general; a single general in chief was in charge of them all. The general in chief gained increasing influence with the emperor as the Han Dynasty progressed.

Outlying states were given to the princes of the imperial family; these states were run as vassal states of the emperor.

Princes were given the power to create nobles within these territories and were allowed to pass their titles and lands to their own sons. They owed allegiance to the emperor, but the emperor did not interfere with their local operations. In order to keep track of local government activities, the emperor created regional inspectors who, along with governors, monitored magistrates and princes.

The Han returned control of property to private landowners and then taxed them based on the size of their holdings rather than on the crops they produced from year to year. Initially, many families owned their own small farms. In bad years small farmers had difficulty paying their taxes, and most of them ended up selling their land to larger landowners and working for them as virtual slaves; gradually this resulted in the growth of a separate class of wealthy landowners. This problem was exacerbated by ever-increasing taxes, as the emperor and landlords both tried to raise money from the land. Landlords were supposed to provide their peasants protection from various hazards in return for the peasants' labor in their fields. The Han government had to put down periodic rebellions by peasants frustrated with their meager existence.

The Han government is credited with creating China's civil service system. The government required many officials to run its various levels. Initially, civil service officials received their jobs through recommendations and family connections. The most famous Han emperor, Wu Ti, remembered for his efforts to make China into a true Confucian state built on education, personal talent, and loyalty, is also known for his reforms to the civil service system. To reduce the threat from nobles who wanted to keep power in their own hands, he created an administration where positions were awarded based on merit, not on family. He founded a national school system designed to identify and train intelligent boys in the Confucian classics. The graduates of this school system could then take examinations that would allow them to enter the large and complex civil service bureaucracy. Once in the government, officials could hold a variety of offices administering the government's many projects, including the several levels of government; inspections of local governments; taxation; unifying and minting of coins; producing iron, salt, and liquor; trade missions west along the Silk Road; building projects; building a state library; chronicling court events;, and maintaining relations with neighboring peoples.

The Han Dynasty began collapsing after a large peasant rebellion. The last years of the Han were marked by rivalries within the civil bureaucracy, a massacre of the court eunuchs (castrated men used as civil servants whose loyalty was supposedly assured because they would have no sons to advance), and barbarian invasions. By 220 C.E. the Han were out of power and three major states—Shu, Wu, and Wei—vied for control of China. Government during the Three Kingdoms Period (220–263 C.E.) was based on military might. The three states spent years fighting with one another, and most government institutions fell into chaos.

The emperor Wu unified China and again brought the country under control of the Jin Dynasty, which lasted from 265 C.E. until 420 C.E. Wu set up his capital in Luoyang. Although the Jin government ostensibly claimed to have renewed the Han system of government, in fact, it created a new feudal system. It kept many of the government titles of the Han and continued to run civil service examinations, but instead of exclusively awarding positions on merit, the emperor also rewarded families who helped him. Local noble families became very influential in court matters. The emperors made their relatives into kings or princes of various territories. As under the Han, the empire was divided into regions, governed by governors and overseen by inspectors, smaller commanderies, run by governors, and small districts run by magistrates. These existed alongside the territories governed by princes and other nobles. The highest officials were the Eight Dukes, who included ministers of education, works, and a general in chief.

Central Asia

Modern Mongolia, Siberia, and western Asia were home to various nomadic peoples. For the most part they lacked a central government. Most of them were organized into tribes led by chiefs and shamans. These leaders decided when the groups would move, where they would hunt, and which tribes they would fight. The leaders also enforced rules about marriages and funerals and organized religious ceremonies. Chiefs were hereditary; several families related to one another by marriage held power.

In 209 B.C.E. a group of nomads called the Xiongnu formed a confederation under the leadership of a man called Modu Shanyu. Historians do not know what prompted this move; some believe it was the influence of the neighboring Han Dynasty that inspired the Xiongnu to organize. Modu divided the Xiongnu territory into several portions. He kept the central portion to rule himself, setting up a capital in Longcheng, Mongolia. He called himself *chanyu*, or supreme leader. A few noble clans related by marriage to the *chanyu* shared authority with him. During the first century B.C.E. the Xiongnu had difficulty maintaining their administration and unity. The succession of the *chanyu* became a problem because it was not always feasible for the throne to go straight from a father to his eldest son, especially when the son was still young. The Xiongnu solved this problem by deciding that the throne should pass from elder brother to younger brother as well as from father to son.

The state government was not sophisticated, and it was at the head of a confederation, not a true kingdom. The Xiongnu people remained in their tribes and continued to operate as they always had at the tribal level. The *chanyu* kept control of them through force, using military domination and the distribution of gifts to make other tribes fight alongside him. Instead of organized taxation, groups that needed funds or goods raided their neighbors and took what they could. The leaders of the confederation regularly conquered neighboring tribes to the south and west. When they took a tribe or a city-state, they typically enslaved it. Local and regional government of these areas consisted mainly of exacting tributes of grain, fruits, and vegetables from agricultural peoples and taking horses, cattle, and sheep from nomads. The Xiongnu called the military leader in charge of such operations the "general in charge of slaves."

Japan

Little is known about the government of Japan in ancient times. Most information on the subject comes from contemporary Chinese accounts. The first highly organized societies appeared during the Yayoi Period, approximately 300 B.C.E. to 300 C.E. During this time Japanese people built villages and grew rice. They gradually adopted the use of bronze tools and weapons. From the available evidence it appears that governments were organized entirely at the local level and that there were not strong central governments anywhere. Chinese visitors to Japan (at that time they would have sailed from Korea and visited only the island of Kyushu) reported that the nation contained about 100 different states or kingdoms, though it is likely that the visitors did not know the exact number. Local governments collected taxes. Each district had a center of trade. There was social stratification, and some people clearly had higher status than others because some were buried in better graves than others. A few people owned large areas of land, and the peasants who lived in that area farmed on their behalf and gave their landlords annual tributes of rice. Villages were organized enough to store surplus food in granaries.

The main community or tribal leaders of the time were shamans (people thought to have spiritual powers) who performed sacrifices and relayed messages between humans and gods. Little is known about how these shamans worked, though it appears that many of these leaders were women. The best account comes from a Chinese description of an important Japanese ruler of the time was the woman Himiko, a female shaman who is said to have ruled in the early third century C.E.

The kingdoms near Nara developed into the Yamato kingdom, which thrived from about 250 to 710 C.E. in central Honshu. It was ruled by "great kings" who were buried in giant mounds after they died. Rulers continued to support their power by claiming that the gods wanted them to rule; as the years went by, however, they placed more emphasis on military power. These kings controlled sizable armies that allowed them to extend their power over most of Japan and into southern Korea. This brought them into contact with Chinese culture. In peacetime, Yamato kings worked to improve local conditions, building massive irrigation systems to ensure large crops of rice. Clans who belonged to the military aristocracy handled most matters of local government, including organizing the details of building irrigation systems, gathering laborers to construct massive tomb mounds for themselves, collecting tributes of grain from their local peasants, collecting any required taxes and passing them on to the kings, and organizing local military bands.

Within each clan, the oldest man was responsible for performing religious rituals to placate the family's gods and ensure prosperity for the whole locality. These clans had hereditary chiefs who cooperated with the Yamato kings in military matters. Groups of people who shared the same occupation also played an important role in government, holding duties such as guarding the palace or supplying water to the court. The Yamato kings' greatest effort of expansion came during the fifth century, but they soon began suffering from challenges to their authority and military setbacks that disrupted the monarchy.

India

The ancient empires of India were all located in the north, around the Indus and Ganges valleys. The Indus Valley was the home of the Harappan civilization, which flourished between about 2600 and 1500 B.C.E. Harappan people lived in several large urban centers. The cities were heavily fortified and the land around them was intensively farmed and irrigated, evidence of strong rulers within the cities. Historians believe that communities were led by powerful kings. The kings initially had limited power and had to consult tribal councils before making decisions, but as the Harappan civilization progressed, the kings' position became stronger.

Kings were believed to be responsible for maintaining spiritual order and ensuring the fertility of the soil. To accomplish this, kings performed a ritual called the Ashvamedha, or horse sacrifice, as a means of ensuring local prosperity and acquiring more territory. The king would release a horse to wander free for one year accompanied by 100 young men; if the horse entered foreign territory, the king was supposed to conquer it. After a year the horse was brought back and sacrificed.

The Ganges plain was home to numerous tribal kingdoms that transformed into 16 major kingdoms called *mahajanapadas* in the fifth century B.C.E. Each kingdom had one or two capital cities. The capital cities were heavily fortified with moats, ramparts, and brick walls. Rulers made coins for people to use as currency and regulated weights and measures. The kings controlled the area immediately surrounding their capitals. Affairs through the rest of the kingdoms were governed by local chiefs. These chiefs were expected to join their kings if he needed military assistance, but otherwise they had a good deal of autonomy.

Much of what historians know about government organization of this time comes from the Arthashastra, an instruction manual for kings written around 300 B.C.E. According to this book, an ideal king ruled a kingdom in the center of a circle of states; the close states were his natural enemies and the more distant ones his natural allies. A king's success depended on the quality of his advisers, his provinces, his army, his finances, his fortifications, and his allies. To improve these things, the king was instructed to build up his own fortifications, encourage trade, dig mines for metals, police the forest, improve irrigation systems to ensure regular crops, and build enclosures for elephants. Military success was a direct result of economic prosperity, so the king was to oversee all aspects of the economy, including agriculture, trade, crafts, and mining. Success also depended on a contented citizenry, so the king was to keep taxes low and burden his people as little as possible. The book describes the ideal structure of the administration, which included ministers, regional governors, priests, inspectors, and various other officers.

The king Asoka was one of the most important rulers of the Maurya Empire (ca. 321–185 B.C.E.). He ruled the central part of it himself. The rest of his territory he divided into four large provinces, each under the rule of a prince who acted as governor. The provinces themselves were subdivided into districts with their own rulers. Individual towns had local leaders, judges, and other officers. The entire system was centralized, with Asoka at the top. Rulers could be harsh, and punishments for crimes were cruel; death sentences were common. The government controlled trade and no one was allowed to travel without first registering with the government and carrying a passport.

The Gupta Dynasty ruled northern India from 240 to about 550 C.E. The structure of this empire served as a pattern for several subsequent centuries of Indian kingdoms. Gupta kings had a different philosophy from that of their predecessors. They believed that the ruler should serve his people and make their lives better. Within the kingdom, all people were classified according to caste. Most land was held by wealthy families and worked by peasants or slaves who were under their noble patrons' control; these workers were poor, but their patrons were also expected to care for them and not allow them to starve. The government provided numerous services to the people, including free hospitals that were paid for by charitable contributions from the wealthy. The government ran rest houses along highways so that travelers would have a comfortable place to stay. Punishments for crimes were reduced and people were allowed to travel freely. People were allowed to run businesses if they so chose.

The Gupta emperor lived at the center of the empire, having destroyed the governments of the kings who had lived there earlier. Royal officers administered this area directly. The edges of the empire contained several border kingdoms ruled by kings who paid tribute to the Gupta monarchs and were required to attend the imperial court. Some of these border kings had fought against the Guptas as they were establishing the empire, but they were reinstated by the emperor. Border kingdoms were not required to assist the emperor in his wars; they functioned as tributary princes but not as true vassals in the European sense. Between the border kingdoms and the central kingdom were some wilderness areas, home to tribes that were never subdued. Outside the borders of the empire lived independent kings with whom the Guptas engaged in diplomatic relations.

Southeast Asia

Several kingdoms existed in Southeast Asia in ancient times. Most of them were heavily influenced by either India or China or both. Vietnam was colonized by Chinese people from the Qin Dynasty in 208 B.C.E. The Qin general Zhao Tuo created a country on the Red River delta called Nam Viet. For the next 1,000 years Chinese people controlled Nam Viet as a subject state. Chinese rulers decided how to use the land and native Vietnamese occasionally rebelled, but they did not gain their independence from China until 939 C.E.

The Mon people of Burma built the kingdom of Suvarnabhumi around 300 B.C.E., but little is known about that kingdom. The Pyu people came to Burma two centuries later and created several city-states that never coalesced into a central government. Powerful cities demanded tribute from less powerful ones; the most powerful city was Sri Ksetra. The rulers passed laws against crimes and punished criminals by whippings or death.

Funan was a kingdom that arose around the Mekong Delta in southern Cambodia and Vietnam sometime around 1 C.E.; at its largest extent, in the third century, it encompassed parts of Malaysia and Burma. Its capital was near modern Phnom Penh. It was run as an empire headed by a royal family; the Chinese said this family came from India. Sanskrit was the official court language, and the royal family practiced Hinduism. Citizens paid taxes to the monarchs in the form of gold, silver, pearls, and perfumed wood. The rulers built up a large commercial fleet that traded with both India and China. Provinces were allowed to continue governing themselves as long as they remained loyal to the monarch.

The Malay kingdom called Srivijaya arose on the island Sumatra around 200 C.E. Some historians believe that it took over an earlier kingdom, the small Hindu kingdom called Pan Pan. Srivijaya was led by a king who functioned mainly as a military ruler. The island was divided into smaller states that were led by their own chiefs, who were organized by the king and came to his aid when needed. This kingdom was a thalassocracy, that is, one based on dominance of the local seas—a control that did not necessarily extend into the interior of the island.

The Philippines did not develop large kingdoms during the ancient period. People lived in kin groups of about 50 families led by chiefs who settled disputes and made major decisions for the community. Within the groups people were classified as nobles, freemen, or slaves.

Australia and Oceania

The ancient people of Australia, called Aborigines, did not have a formal government. They built no cities or even smaller settlements, instead living in open camps that could easily be moved from place to place. Individuals did not own anything; possessions belonged to the group as a whole. People belonged to clans that traveled together, but groups were usually small. The only leaders in the community were tribal elders, who created rules for social interactions, had the best memories for sources of food and water, and knew all the tribal mythology. Clans claimed territory based on sacred sites that were special to them, but territories could overlap; no clan claimed exclusive rights to any piece of land.

The islands of Oceania were separated from one another by huge distances, so they tended to function independently. Each one had its own chiefs and rituals considered essential to the well-being of the community. Chieftains gained their position through a combination of family position and skill. As populations grew, governments became more centralized as a way of regulating competition for land and ensuring that everyone could be fed. Chiefs implemented intensive agricultural systems, organizing groups of islanders to dig terraces and irrigation ditches and harvest crops. Priests and religious leaders also appeared; in many cases, the priests helped chiefs keep power by proclaiming them descendants of gods.

Eventually, many islands developed several layers of government bureaucracy, with intermediate chiefs to run regional and local settlements. Class stratification appeared, with people of lower status expected to give food and goods as tribute to their chiefs and priests. Warfare was common, especially on the more densely populated islands. Chiefs trained soldiers, led war parties, and built fortifications. Some groups engaged in cannibalism and headhunting as part of their war practices. Most islands were sufficient unto themselves, but some island groups developed semicentralized governments. In Micronesia, for example, individual islands began by governing themselves. The islanders gradually developed a more centralized system of government with the island of Yap at its center.

EUROPE

BY MICHAEL J. O'NEAL

Government organization was not as advanced in ancient Europe as it was in, for example, ancient Greece or Rome. Europe was slower to develop, primarily because civilization expanded outward to the north and west from Africa, the Middle East, and regions around the Mediterranean Sea. For much of prehistoric time Europe's population remained small and isolated until ice from the last ice age receded and Europe became habitable. Accordingly, through much of the ancient period Europe was populated by tribes and clans that had no central governing authority. Put simply, Europe took a while to catch up with much of the rest of the world in social, political, economic, and cultural development as successive waves of tribes migrated into Europe and created civilizations.

The principal form of political organization in ancient Europe was thus the tribe. In general, people lived in communities that remained isolated from one another because of geographical features such as mountains and rivers. The Alps, for example, were a formidable obstacle to contact between peoples in central Europe, and the tribes of Scandinavia remained isolated because of surrounding seas. While explorers and traders made contact with other communities, it was difficult for rulers to maintain authority over a wide region. Thus, kings and chieftains who held power locally ruled the communities of ancient Europe. These kings, though, were not like the pharaohs of Egypt or the emperors of Rome, who ruled vast empires with the aid of a large bureaucracy, including administrators, census takers, tax collectors, governors, and the like. Their names are largely lost to history, and to the extent that their names are remembered, they are surrounded by legends that are difficult to verify.

In reconstructing forms of ancient government, historians have to rely on a good deal of indirect and third-party evidence. The nations of ancient Europe left little in the way of written records, so historians in many cases must make educated guesses about their governmental systems. Greek and Roman writers left behind descriptions of the societies they encountered, but these descriptions were usually biased because these writers regarded the European tribes as barbaric and uncivilized enemies to be conquered. Otherwise, some archaeological evidence in the form of inscriptions, tablets, and coins has been found. Finally, historians often work backward, starting with what they know from early medieval European life. Since medieval Europeans did not spring from nowhere, it is reasonable to conclude that their governmental structures originated hundreds of years earlier.

A good example of this form of government is provided by the Scythians. These were a people who occupied the Pontic-Caspian steppes, the vast treeless grasslands north of the Black Sea and extending to the east of the Caspian Sea; the area corresponds with modern-day Ukraine and parts of Russia and Kazakhstan. The term *Scythian* is a catch-all for a number of nomadic pastoral tribes that inhabited the region over a period of many centuries. Little is known about the ancient Scythians, who first appeared sometime around 1000 B.C.E., other than what was reported by Greek historians. It is known, however, that the Scythians had little in the way of a central governing authority. The political organization was that of the tribe. There were several major tribal groups. In the modern-day Poltava region was a major tribe of agricultural Scythians. Other major tribes included the Callipidae, the Alazones, and the Aroteres.

Historians refer to the dominant tribe as the Royal Scythians, who occupied the lower region of the Dnieper River and the Crimea. This tribe established a dynasty of rulers. The region under their control was divided into four separate provinces. Each was ruled by a governor whose job it was to collect taxes, administer justice, ensure the equitable distribution of land, and collect tribute payments from city-states in the Pontic, a region on the Black Sea inhabited by Greeks. The Scythians had no system of coinage. The administration of the region was loosely conducted by tribal elders. In time, power came to be held by social elites, including kings and their military followers. These tribes maintained a loose federation for purposes of defense and trade, with herdsmen trading with agriculturalists for food.

Thrace

Other than ancient Greece, one of the oldest civilizations to form a central government in Europe was Thrace. The people were called the Thracians, though the region was home to a number of tribes, including not only the native Thracians but also the Edones, Bisaltes, Cicones, Bistones, and others. Thrace historically was a region that occupied modern-day Bulgaria, northeastern Greece, portions of Turkey and Serbia, and the eastern portion of the Republic of Macedonia.

Ancient Thrace provides a good example of the evolving nature of government in Europe. The Thracians were a collection of warlike tribes. These tribes had little connection with one another. Each occupied a fortified town and was ruled by a tribal leader. Over the centuries Thrace came under the domination of various other peoples, including the Greeks, the Macedonians, and the Romans. Until the arrival of the Romans in particular, "Thrace" as a government entity did not really exist. There was little in the way of an administrative structure, though coinage developed under the influence of the Greeks. Tribal rulers exercised power over the people in their tribes. Often these tribes went to war with one another, bringing one tribe under the sway of a stronger, more dominant neighbor. Because these tribes did not have settled systems of agriculture, they did not have to establish mechanisms for land allocation, the distribution of food, tax collection, and the like. The law was administered by the sword. Eventually, the Thracian tribes were driven out of the region by invading Celts. What they left behind was a region devoid of written records about day-to-day government activities.

Celts

The history of the ancient Celts in many respects parallels that of the Thracians. Again, the terms *Celt* and *Celtic* refer not to an empire in an organized sense of the word. The Celts were essentially an ethnic group that spread throughout much of the European continent and into the British Isles. At no point in history was there a Celtic capital, though some Celtic tribes created an *oppidum*, or fortified town that served as a central hub. Nor was there a ruling dynasty or succession of kings and emperors. The Celts, much like the Thracians, consisted of scores of largely independent tribes—at least 118 distinct tribes are known—each ruled by its own minor king or chieftain. These tribal divisions were largely an accident of geography and history. Individual tribes remained isolated from one another by geographical barriers.

As a vast conglomeration of tribes, the ancient Celts had no real governmental organization. Each of the tribes was ruled by a chieftain who gained his (or her) power by force of arms, by providing access to valuable resources, or by having been elected by members of the tribe. Beneath the chieftain was a warrior aristocracy, followed by a class of freemen farmers. The names of some of these chieftains, about whom little is known, include Orgetorix, Sinorix, Dunmorix, Cartismandua (a woman), Prasutagus, Amborix, Clondicus, Luernios, Ariamnes, and Adiatorix. The suffix *-rix* on many of these names suggests that the person was a supreme chieftain and is related to the Latin word *rex,* meaning "king." Throughout most of continental Europe there was little sense of empire or of nation-states. Small communities of people, in many cases sharing culture and language but living independently of one another, were ruled locally. There was little in the way of administration, public works, and all the other trappings of government. Leadership was exercised by force. Alliances were forged from time to time out of mutual necessity, particularly for defense. Each tribe had more or less fixed and recognized borders.

Land was held in common and consisted of forested land, wilderness, and agricultural land. Celtic societies tend to have complicated systems of land tenure. Laws governing this tenure specified the rights and responsibilities of each land holder. Sometimes the land was worked for the benefit of the particular clan that held rights to it. Sometimes it was work in common for the benefit of the clan's chief, the tribal ruler, or the priestly class. Land was also worked in common to benefit the old and sick. Foraging and grazing rights tended to be held in common rather than apportioned to individuals.

By the medieval period legal codes had developed in such Celtic countries as Ireland and Wales; in Ireland, the code was called the Brehon laws, from an ancient Celtic word for "judge." In Wales, the legal code was called the Hywel Dda. These legal codes developed from ancient law codes, usually referred to by historians as common Celtic law. These codes probably dated back to the Bronze Age, certainly to the Iron Age (from about 200 B.C.E. to 100 C.E. in that part of the world). These law codes were not written down but rather were oral. Also, no single code applied in all Celtic societies. Rather, each community developed its own code based on its own local needs, though in time these codes coalesced into a common code. In general, the code was administered by Druids, members of the ancient Celtic priestly class.

In fact, Druids and the priestly class were in many instances the chief form of government organization. This group was thought to be in possession of spiritual wisdom, so Druids were placed in charge of such matters as the calendar, the scheduling of festivals, ceremonies, and religious holidays, and other matters of concern to the tribe as a whole. Tribal business was discussed and settled at yearly meetings attended by clan leaders and directed by Druids. During these assemblies the Druids settled land disputes, conducted trials for those accused of crimes, and supervised the election of chiefs and their retainers by popular vote.

The Germanic Tribes

Historians use the term *barbarian monarchy* to refer to kingship among the ancient Germanic tribes—that is, those tribes that inhabited northern Europe, including the Scandinavian countries. They use this term to distinguish the nature of the Germanic monarchy from later monarchies under the feudal system of medieval Europe as well as the national monarchies that continue to exist in modern life.

Like the Celts, the Germans were members of a large number of tribes, some of whose names remain familiar: Angles, Saxons, Jutes, Vandals, Visigoths, Franks, Huns, and numerous others. Many of these tribes, particularly the Huns, became inveterate enemies of the Roman Empire, defeating them in battle and eventually forcing the collapse of the empire in the west. Each of these tribes was ruled by a hereditary king who had three primary functions. One was to serve as a judge during assemblies of his nobles. The second was to serve as the high priest of his tribe. The third was to serve as a commander during times of war. Outside these functions, the power of ancient Germanic kings was fairly limited. When a king died, the throne passed to his son, but when the king had more than one son, each of the sons could lay claim to the throne, often leading to co-regencies, where two sons ruled jointly. Incidentally, after the Germanic regions became Christianized, the word *kaiser* arose to refer to a king; *kaiser* is derived from the name Caesar, suggesting that later Germanic kings thought of themselves as the descendants of the Roman emperors.

The Germanic regions of ancient Europe had a more complex governmental structure than did the Celts. The foundation of the system was the clan, called the *sibbe.* Clan relationships were so important that most ancient Germans knew the names of their ancestors going back at least seven generations. A typical *sibbe* consisted of about 10 families, including members of both the father's and mother's familes, and sometimes even slaves. The English word *sibling,* referring to a brother or sister, derives from this Germanic word. Typically, *sibben* were formed by the noblest families. Not every family formed a separate *sibbe,* but rather many joined the *sibben* of more influential families.

Several *sibben,* then, composed the tribe, and each tribe had its own king. Sometimes coalition tribes formed for mutual protection and benefit, and the king of the most powerful tribe led the coalition. Each tribe exercised control over its own province, which was divided into districts called *gauen.* A *gau,* analogous to a county, was ruled by an earl, who collected taxes and raised troops. Earls who governed border provinces had the additional duty of defending the border and therefore were given more rights and privileges than ordinary earls. The word used to refer to these border provinces was *mark,* a word that survives in the name of modern Denmark, which literally means "border province of the Danes." Multiple *gauen* formed a dukedom led by a duke. These nobles did not necessarily inherit their titles from their fathers. Ancient Germanic societies were meritocracies, meaning that people achieved high positions because of merit, often success in war, rather than strictly inheritance.

At the top of the governmental system was the king, who was advised by a council. Among the Anglo-Saxons, for instance, this council was called the Witenagemot, or "Meeting of the Wise." While kingship was hereditary, kings ruled with the consent of their people and were chosen from the tribe's most important families. It was customary for the king's loyal followers to present him with gifts, including cattle, part of a harvest, or manufactured items useful in the home. Only later, during the medieval period, did this custom evolve into obligatory taxes paid to the king.

Additionally, the Germanic tribes had a *þing,* or folk assembly, which consisted of all the free people in the community, including women and often older children. (The word *þing* begins with an alphabetic symbol called the thorn, usually pronounced like the *th* in either *thick* or *though.*) Historians describe the governmental structure of the ancient Germanic tribes as a mixture of a dictatorship and a democracy. While the king during times of war and crisis was a stable ruler, endowed with far-reaching powers, he remained subject to the will of his people and the rulings of the *þing.* Vestiges of the ancient *þing* can be found in modern-day European parliaments. In Norway, for example, the parliament is called the Storting, or "Great þing," while in Denmark it is called the Folketing, or "People's þing."

The *þing* dealt primarily with judicial matters, standing in judgment when people were accused of crimes or when disputes arose between them. Additionally, the *þing* determined whether to declare war and even intervened to solve personal problems and to decide who was being truthful in a matter of importance to the tribe. The *þing* usually met on a fixed date, often shortly after a new moon or shortly before a full moon, though the body met at other times if the need arose. In the event of a dispute, the parties assembled to tell all sides of the story. Anyone, particularly influential members of the community, could speak and offer an opinion. Sometimes these assemblies became rowdy, as people who agreed with a speaker signified their agreement by stamping their feet and clanging the weapons together; the greater the noise and hubbub, the more the assembly agreed. Usually once a year larger coalitions of tribes met to discuss the state of the larger kingdom.

The Germanic tribes did not maintain standing armies. The king, with the help of his nobles, raised an army when it was necessary. This typically was not difficult. The Germanic peoples tended to be warlike, and young men were expected to be skilled in the arts of warfare and eager to join in the bloodshed. The best of these warriors became personal bodyguards for the king. The guards swore an oath that they would protect him at all costs; in turn, the king swore that he would provide for the warrior and his family. Later, the warrior was often given land in exchange for his service. Additionally, a class of warlords led military forces in battle. These warlords were elected based primarily on their bravery, giving rise to what was called the retinue system, meaning that a powerful warlord attracted around him a retinue, or gathering, of intensely loyal followers. Meanwhile, the king was always the leader of the army. A king could be deposed for not showing courage in battle. Very few Germanic kings died of natural causes; most were killed in battle.

GREECE

BY JEFFREY S. CARNES

The famous quotation from Aristotle "Man is a political animal" actually means "Man is an animal that lives in a polis"—that is, in a relatively small city that is self-governing and not subject to the control of a larger governmental entity. (*Polis* is usually translated as "city-state.") The entire history of Greek self-government from the earliest records (ca. 1200 B.C.E.) to the time of Alexander (late fourth century B.C.E.) is the history of such poleis, over 1,000 in number and ranging in size from a few thousand inhabitants to perhaps 300,000 in Athens at the height of its power in the mid-fifth century. There must have been a tremendous variety of systems of government, the details of which are mostly lost to us, but they can be broken down into three basic types. Cities were ruled by a single individual (whether a king or a *tyrannos*, a word which did not yet have the negative connotations of "tyrant"); by a small group, either a hereditary aristocracy or an economic elite (typically called an *oligarchy*, literally "rule by the few"); or by the entire citizen body, the demos (democracy, a Greek invention).

THE AGE OF KINGS

Our information about Greek political systems before about 700 B.C.E. comes primarily from the epic poetry of Homer and Hesiod. These poems show us a world in which poleis are ruled by individuals known as *basileis*, or kings. There is evidence for kingship dating back to Mycenaean times (ca. 1600–1100 B.C.E.) in the form of inscriptions in the early Greek syllabic writing system known as Linear B, and since Homer's *Iliad* (probably written down in its current form around 700 B.C.E.) was the result of a long oral tradition, we can be confident that much of the material there reflects earlier practices.

The Greek *basileus* (king) differed in many respects from the kings more familiar to us in European history. To begin with, given the relatively small size of most poleis, the area and resources controlled by even a powerful *basileus* were not large. Based on the (probably exaggerated) figures for troop strength in the *Iliad*, combined with what can be surmised about ancient population sizes, the most powerful leaders of the Homeric era ruled over kingdoms of perhaps 100,000 individuals, and most of them substantially fewer. Moreover, the power of these kings seems to have been limited both in peace and in war. The version of the Trojan War told by Homer has a Greek expeditionary force made up of several dozen *basileis*, each leading his own contingent of troops, with Agamemnon in command by virtue of having brought the largest army. He is shown using whatever force or persuasion he can to get the leaders of the coalition to follow him, but nowhere does Homer suggest that Agamemnon has absolute legal or moral authority over them. When Achilles quarrels with Agamemnon and withdraws from the war, the other Greek leaders are displeased with his action, but none questions his right to take his ships and go home.

Kings seem to have ruled with a certain degree of consent from their subjects; in both the *Iliad* and *Odyssey* they call assemblies to seek advice from other nobles. Hesiod, in his *Theogony*, explicitly values kings for their wisdom in judging and settling disputes: "In the assembly . . . wrongs are righted [by kings] with gentle persuasion"; elsewhere he speaks of bad kings as "devourers of bribes." As Greeks' conceptions of justice evolved, their views of the gods came to be influenced by their views of kingship, with Zeus serving as a representation of the ideal king. By the seventh century B.C.E., however, kingship was essentially unknown in Greece and was considered a form of government practiced by foreign peoples.

THE AGE OF TYRANTS

The word *tyrannos*, apparently of non-Greek origin, first appears in the mid-sixth century B.C.E. applied to Gyges, the ruler of Lydia, a non-Greek kingdom in Asia Minor. Unlike its modern derivative *tyrant*, the word was not necessarily pejorative: A tyrant was simply an individual who held sole power in the state. The *tyrannos* was in many ways similar to a king, the chief difference being that a tyrant generally possessed no hereditary claim to his position. Of course, most tyrants wished to pass on power to their descendants: Gyges, for example, after acquiring power by murdering the king, founded a dynasty that ruled Lydia for over 100 years, and he is usually referred to as a king himself despite his illegitimate acquisition of the throne.

Tyrants were a varied lot, with different reasons for coming to power and widely varying styles of rule. In the early days tyranny seems to have been a response to a change in social conditions that was driven largely by a change in warfare tactics, namely, the switch to hoplite warfare in the early seventh century. Hoplites were heavily armed foot soldiers who fought in tight formation, making the cohesiveness of the army of paramount importance. Hoplites came from neither the richest classes (who could afford to keep and train horses and therefore formed the cavalry) nor the poorest (who could not afford hoplite armor). This "middle class" naturally wanted a greater share of political power, and came into conflict with the established aristocracy. In this situation tyrants arose—paradoxically enough—as champions of the middle class. This theory, first put forward by Aristotle in his *Politics*, is confirmed for some poleis and quite plausible for others. In Athens the reforms of Solon in the 590s B.C.E. gave the lower property classes more power, and Solon specifically rejected taking on the role of tyrant—yet when these reforms proved insufficient to maintain harmony, a tyranny arose some 30 years later under Peisistratus. In Sparta, by contrast, the hoplite class was officially composed of equals and had a large share in ruling the state; this may be the reason there was never a tyranny in Sparta. At any rate, the Age of Tyrants can be seen as a necessary precondition for the creation of democracy, since it was an era in which political rights were being given to ever-increasing segments of the population.

The Age of Tyrants was an age of growing material prosperity, and many tyrants used their wealth to glorify themselves and their cities. Peisistratus and his sons (collectively known as the Peisistratids) were responsible for a major building program in Athens, for the promotion of great festivals such as the Panathenaea and City Dionysia, and possibly for the start of Athenian coinage. Polycrates, tyrant of Samos, was the patron of the lyric poets Anacreon and Ibycus, and the Sicilian tyrant Hiero supported such notable poets as Pindar, Bacchylides, and Aeschylus.

Tyrants could also be feared, and it is their reputation for capricious cruelty, discussed in particular by Plato and Aristotle, that eventually gave the word the entirely negative connotations it bears to this day. Tyranny was seen as the chance to exert unbridled power—tyrants lacked the traditional restraints that kings operated under and could do whatever they pleased. In the popular imagination this included various forms of sexual predation. In Athens, for example, the expulsion of the Peisistratid tyrants was popularly thought to have resulted from a murder committed by a citizen named Aristogiton to defend his lover Harmodius from the unwanted advances of the tyrant's brother. Still, opinion on tyrants varied greatly. Thucydides (who tells the story of Harmodius and Aristogiton) praises the Peisistratids for their good works for the city and the general mildness of their rule. Even more dramatic is the case of Periander of Corinth. He is said to have been ruthless in eliminating potential rivals, to have killed his own wife, and to have sent 300 Corcyraean youth to Lydia to be made eunuchs; yet he is routinely listed among the canonical Seven Sages of the Greek world.

Athenian Democracy

Athens was not only a rich and powerful state but also a center of learning and the arts. For this reason we have far more information about the Athenian democracy than about any other ancient government. But the factors that led to the development and growth of this political system were by no means unique, so that an examination of Athenian democracy will allow us to learn much about how Greek cities faced the challenges of self-governance.

Democracy was essentially an Athenian invention, with several of its key institutions put in place by Cleisthenes, who served as archon (leader) in 508–507 B.C.E. It lasted, with various changes and two brief interruptions, for nearly 200 years, until Athens was conquered by Philip of Macedon in 322. It was, however, quite different from any modern democracy in certain key respects. First, it was a direct democracy rather than a representative one: Almost all decision making was done by the citizens of Athens, who voted in popular assemblies. There were no long-term elected officials (offices were held for one year only), nor was there a bureaucracy with offices to oversee public functions (no departments of defense or the treasury and the like). Second, the Athenian democracy deliberately excluded from participation a large proportion of the population: all noncitizens, a group that would include slaves, women, and the many foreigners resident in Athens. Although the key concept of Athenian democracy was *isonomia*, meaning "equality under the law," decision making rested in the hands of perhaps a quarter of the population. (It should be noted, however, that all Greek states restricted participation to citizen males.)

The reforms of Cleisthenes were designed to promote cohesion among the citizen body and to reduce the power of older aristocratic institutions. Attica (Athens and its surrounding countryside) was divided into 139 demes, or districts, which after Cleisthenes formed the most basic units of citizenship. At age 18 a young man would be enrolled by his father into his deme register, signifying his admission to full citizen status; his full name included an indication of his deme (for example, Sophocles Labdakou Koloneus: Sophocles, son of Labdakos, of the deme Colonus). This system overrode earlier aristocratic institutions based on kinship; to diminish the geographical rivalry among city, rural, and coastal demes, Cleisthenes created ten "tribes," each composed of demes from each of the major geographic divisions.

Although the deme was the basic unit of citizenship, tribal membership lay at the heart of the most important civic institutions. The tribes were the basis for the selection of citizens for the boule, or Council, made up of 500 citizens, 50 from each tribe. Although the *ekklesia* (Assembly), composed of all men 18 or older who had been enrolled in their deme registers, was responsible for all major decisions of the city during much of the fifth century, voting on both policy matters (declarations of war, taxes, and the like) and laws, the boule had the administrative responsibility of seeing to it that these decisions were carried out. It also served as a sort of steering committee for the *ekklesia*, determining its legislative agenda: All decrees brought before the *ekklesia* had to be proposed first by the boule (though amendments could be made during the debate on the legislation). Members of the boule were male citizens over the age of 30 and served for one year (with a lifetime maximum of two terms). Each deme nominated a certain number of citizens for membership in the boule (the number varied according to the size of the deme), who were chosen by lot. Thus all citizens had not only a theoretical chance to serve in this body but also a fairly high mathematical chance of actually doing so.

During each of the 10 months of the Athenian year a different tribe supplied 50 *prytaneis*, who served as presidents or overseers of the boule during their month in office. They lived at public expense in a special building in the Agora, the city's central market and governmental area, where they were on round-the-clock duty to deal with emergencies that might arise, in which case they were empowered to call a full meeting of the boule or even the *ekklesia*. Each day a different *prytanis* was chosen by lot as chair, so that any given Athenian citizen had a reasonable chance of being, in effect, head of state for at least one day during his lifetime.

After a brief period of tyranny under the so-called Thirty Tyrants, democracy was restored to Athens in 403. In the new government the passing of laws was reserved for a smaller body known as the "lawgivers." The *ekklesia* met four times per month (at least by the mid-fourth century), with the first of these meetings being considered the most important, for it dealt with military matters, the grain supply, and the tenure of officeholders (who might be removed if charged with corruption or incompetence). Anyone who wished was entitled to speak, though the historical sources indicate that in practice most of those who addressed the *ekklesia* were accomplished politicians.

The extent of popular participation in the *ekklesia* is the subject of some debate. Certain procedures required a quorum of 6,000 citizens and were held in the Agora instead of the usual meeting place on the nearby Pnyx. From this we can infer that most meetings were smaller—one source claims that no regular meeting was ever attended by more than 5,000 citizens. Modern demographers estimate a citizen population for Athens of between 20,000 and 50,000, and given the difficulty of getting to the city from outlying districts as well as the need of most Athenians to work for a living, it seems likely that most citizens attended only occasionally. By the late fifth century there were inducements for them to do so: They were offered a modest amount of pay for attendance, and before meetings Scythian slaves (who served as the police force of Athens) used a red-dyed rope to herd stragglers from the Agora toward the Pnyx. This seems to have worked, for the Pnyx was enlarged twice during the fourth century, indicating growing attendance even in an era of reduced population.

Aristotle suggested that in an ideal polis citizens would have the opportunity to govern and be governed in turn. Athens met this criterion well: Counting the members of the boule, there were perhaps 1,000 officeholders at any one time. Thus, at any given moment 2 to 5 percent of the citizen body held public office, and most of whom would be replaced by new officeholders the subsequent year. The vast majority of offices were appointed by lot, the most notable exception being the office of general (*strategos*), of whom 10 were elected each year, one per tribe.

The generalship was also unusual in allowing those who held it to run for reelection, with the result that skilled politicians such as Pericles could remain in office for years. (In fact, he was elected for 15 years running). In the hands of an able politician the office of general was concerned with more than military matters: Pericles was responsible for the building of the Parthenon and for the revision of Athenian citizenship laws, and he was the de facto leader of Athens at the height of its empire. Nevertheless nothing could be accomplished in Athens without the will of the people: Pericles' dominance of Athenian political life depended on his ability to maintain popular approval and to persuade the *ekklesia* to do what he wanted. On one occasion, at least, he failed badly and in 430 was fined by the *ekklesia* and possibly removed from office. He did not, however, suffer the fate sometimes meted out to successful public figures, that of ostracism.

The greatest strengths of Athenian democracy—its encouragement of mass participation and its insistence on direct popular sovereignty—were in some cases also its greatest flaws. The institution of ostracism involved an annual meeting of the *ekklesia*, held in the Agora to accommodate the required number of 6,000 voters. Citizens would write on a potsherd (*ostrakon*, hence "ostracism") the name of prominent fellow citizen they wished to send into exile for 10 years. Originally designed as a check against tyranny, ostracism was used frequently in the years down to 450 and occasionally after that until 418. For critics of the democracy (and there were many, both within and outside of Athens) it stood as a symbol of the fickleness of the demos, the people.

Similarly, the emotions of the people could be easily swayed in times of crisis: Thucydides reports a vote in the *ekklesia* to put to death the citizens of Mytilene (an ally that rebelled in 427 B.C.E., during the Peloponnesian War), followed by remorse and a vote to rescind the decree on the very next day. A ship sent in pursuit of the one bearing the original order reached Mytilene just in time to prevent the mass execution. Nor was the power of the *ekklesia* subject to effective checks and balances: In 406 B.C.E. the trial of the victorious generals at the naval battle of Arginousai (for failing to rescue survivors from the water) was clearly unconstitutional, yet the generals were condemned and executed. Nevertheless, the vast majority of Athenian citizens seem to have been happy with the basics of their form of government and with the ideology of *isonomia*.

The Spartan Constitution

As the implacable enemy of Athens during its democratic era (particularly in the fifth century), Sparta is generally thought of as an oligarchy. In fact, the Spartan constitution was a mixture of oligarchic, regal, and democratic elements that together represent a unique solution to the problems faced by the polis.

The Spartans traced their form of government to the legendary lawgiver Lycurgus, who was thought to have lived in the early seventh century B.C.E. (though his historical existence is subject to debate). He is said to have authored (with advice from the oracle of Apollo at Delphi) the Great Rhetra, a set of pronouncements that set out the basic principles of Spartan law. The Spartans' favorite word to describe their system of government was *eunomia*, "good laws" (contrasted with the Athenians' *isonomia*, "equality under the law"), emphasizing the collective excellence of the Spartan citizen body as brought about by their unique way of life.

The democratic element in Sparta appears in the process by which all Spartan men became equal citizens and in their participation in the Assembly. The Spartan state maintained a precarious hold on power over its neighbors from Messenia, who had been conquered in a series of wars in the eighth and seventh centuries; their land was taken and distributed in supposedly equal shares to all Spartan citizens. (In reality, land distribution seems to have been uneven from the beginning and to have become more so over time.) In order to keep this noncitizen population (known as helots) subjugated, Spartans devoted themselves to military life to an astonishing degree. Boys were taken from their families at age seven and put under the care of a magistrate in charge of education; they spent their time engaged in military pursuits, including night raids designed to spread terror among the helot population. Boys were divided into groups of *syssitia* ("eating clubs") who ate communal meals together; as adults, each contributed food to his eating club from his allotment of land (which was worked by helots, since itizens were barred from agricultural labor). Citizens owed primary loyalty to their *syssitia* rather than to their families, and the *syssitia* (along with tribes and *obes*, units whose composition remains uncertain) formed the basis of the Assembly, which consisted of all Spartan citizens age 30 and over.

Like the Athenian *ekklesia*, the Spartan Assembly decided the major questions of state policy and could debate only questions put to it by an independent body that determined its agenda. There were two major differences, however: In Sparta the Assembly was supposed to vote yes or no on questions, with essentially no discussion (in effect, giving them something amounting to a veto power over items on the agenda), and the agenda-setting body, the *gerousia* (literally, "the old men's group"), was not representative of the citizenry as a whole. The 28 members of the *gerousia*, while elected by the Assembly, came from the leading families of the polis; all were over the age of 60 and served for life. In addition to setting the agenda for the Assembly, the *gerousia* heard criminal cases and, eventually, gained the power to overturn decisions of the Assembly.

Sparta also had two kings, who claimed direct lineal descent from two different legendary ancestors and were thought to be semidivine. Although they were exempt from the rigorous military training imposed on Sparta's citizens, the kings led Spartan troops in war. Providing a check on the kings' power was a group of five ephors, selected annually by the citizens. Each month the kings swore an oath to the ephors to uphold the city's laws; the ephors in turn swore to support the kings. Two ephors accompanied the kings on military campaigns, and their powers of oversight included the ability to prosecute the kings before the *gerousia*. They were also responsible for supervising the system of military training and for presiding over meetings of the Assembly.

Other Greek Cities

In practice, most Greek cities before the fifth century were oligarchies, which is to say that some portion of the citizen body was excluded from full political rights. The evidence suggests a wide variety of oligarchic practice: Some cities restricted political participation on the basis of birth, others on the basis of wealth. (In most poleis wealth seems to have eventually won out as the main criterion for participation.) Cities other than Sparta had ephors and a *gerousia*; it is unclear how similar these were to their Spartan counterparts.

By the middle of the fifth century the imperial ambitions of Athens led to a spreading of democracy throughout the Greek world: Athens encouraged its allies and subject states to adopt democratic constitutions (but did not always insist on it). Sparta, while having a mixed constitution that contained democratic elements, put itself forward as the champion of oligarchic states. The great alliances that led to the Peloponnesian War (431–404 B.C.E.) were based in large part on this ideological division. Ironically, the Athenians suffered their greatest military defeat in that war at the hands of Syracuse, which was itself a democracy.

Aristotle's claim that oligarchy was government of the rich and democracy the government of the poor has much merit, yet there were democratic elements in oligarchies and a tendency for the rich and well connected to dominate political life in democracies. The cases of Athens and Sparta can give us a glimpse of the complex strategies used in Greek poleis to distribute power and resources among their citizens.

ROME

BY AMY HACKNEY BLACKWELL AND CHRISTOPHER BLACKWELL

The fundamental organization of the Roman government depended on the distinction between two classes of citizens—patricians and plebeians. This distinction predated the early period of the kings. From what historians can tell of the earliest period of Roman history (before the fifth century B.C.E.), the patricians (Rome's aristocracy) alone held the offices, civil and religious, that constituted the government of Rome. Over the course of Roman history, particularly between the fourth and first centuries B.C.E., the rules limiting certain offices to the patrician class became looser, but this social distinction is nevertheless important for any understanding of the branches of Roman government and how they worked.

The Monarchy

The earliest period of Roman history is mostly the subject of myth and legend. Romans said that kings had ruled them before the Roman Republic was established in 509 B.C.E. Information about the period of kingship comes mostly from Roman writers of the first century B.C.E. and is therefore mostly traditional, but it is possible to make a few conclusions about Roman government under the monarchy.

The office of "king" (*rex*) was an elected office, not a hereditary one; the patrician Romans would choose a new king. The kings almost certainly served as supreme military commanders and acted as the final authority in matters of judgment and interpretation of laws. Otherwise, though, the king probably shared governmental duties with the various "colleges" of priests, with the patrician Senate, and with the Comitia Curiata, an assembly of all the people (not the patrician class only). The important governmental concept of imperium, the authority to lead an army and the power of life and death over citizens, was first vested in the Roman kings; later, under the republic, imperium would be the possession of elected officials and, finally, of the emperor alone. (The word *emperor* comes from the Latin word *imperium*).

The Republic

The Roman Republic lasted from 509 B.C.E. until approximately 27 B.C.E. It began with the overthrow of the monarchy and ended with a civil war that dissolved the republic and began the period modern historians call the Roman Empire. The republic took its name from its republican form of government. The word *republic* comes from the Latin words *res publica*, which mean "public thing" or "affairs belonging to the people." The Romans gave their government that name to contrast it with the earlier monarchy. The republic belonged to the people as a whole, and its government was elected by the people rather than being controlled by hereditary kings.

Only adult male Roman citizens could vote in elections. Rules of citizenship varied over time. At some periods both of a child's parents had to be citizens in order for their child to be one; at other periods it was necessary only for the child's father to be a citizen. These male citizens exercised voting power—choosing officers and approving or disapproving certain kinds of laws—through several different kinds of assemblies. The most ancient of these was the Comitia Curiata, whose job eventually was reduced to that of confirming the appointment of certain priests and witnessing adoptions and the execution of wills. The Comitia Centuriata (Centuriate Assembly) handled the election of the most senior officials and declarations of war. The Comitia Populi Tributa (Assembly of the People) oversaw the election of the lesser magistrates, and the Comitia Plebis Tributa (Assembly of the Plebs) elected the most minor magistrates and handled some of the least pressing issues of legislation.

The day-to-day governing of the city, and later the empire, of Rome was not in the hands of these assemblies, however, but in the hands of the magistrates and the Senate. The Senate was a body of 300 men, all of them wealthy but including both patricians and plebeians in their numbers. The senators were formally known as the *patres et conscripti*, the "fathers and enlisted men," with the former being the patrician senators and the latter being the plebeian ones. After 339 B.C.E. the senators were chosen by public officials called the censors, who considered the wealth, amount of property, and (supposedly) moral character of various Roman citizens; once chosen for the Senate, service was for life unless subsequent censors decided otherwise. Being removed from the Senate by the censors was a disgrace.

The Senate met in the Curia Hostilia within the Roman Forum normally, but it was authorized to meet in any public place within a mile of the city, once the proper prayers had been said. The senators debated policy, speaking in order of rank. The Senate did not pass actual laws. Its votes could result in advisory decrees that it presented to the Comitia Populi Tributa Rome's actual legislative body. The Senate did have certain powers, however. It had authority over the treasury, and no public money could be taken from the treasury for any purpose except by decree of the Senate. In the period when Rome's political power extended beyond the city to include provinces abroad, the Senate decided which officials would be sent to govern which provinces; it also decided which serving governors would have their terms of office extended and which would be recalled. Since governors were often engaged in military operations in their provinces or from their provinces to neighboring ones, this power over governorships amounted to the Senate's having considerable authority over military affairs. Furthermore, the Senate had to grant permission for a governor to raise an army before going to his province and could set limits on his efforts at recruiting.

The Senate received and ratified any treaties with foreign powers. This body was also given news of any religious portents or omens and could institute special religious rituals seemingly called for by these signs. The Senate could not actually veto laws passed by the Comitia Populi Tributa or the Comitia Centuriata, but it could declare procedural errors that would render laws invalid. In the late Republican period (the second half of the second century B.C.E. and the early first century B.C.E.) the Senate did give itself a kind of supreme veto: In times of crisis the Senate could pass a *senatus consultum de republica defendenda,* a decree that established martial law and put the Senate solely in charge of the government. This was rarely done, and each *senatus consultum* was invariably controversial. By the middle of the first century B.C.E. such decrees were likely to be ignored by certain political factions or actively opposed by serving magistrates with military force.

While the Senate dealt with the public economy, military affairs, government of the provinces, and religious portents, much of the actual legislating was in the hands of the various assemblies. These groups could vote on matters introduced by magistrates but could not introduce new measures "from the floor" or make any changes to motions brought before them. The Comitia Plebis Tributa included no patricians—patricians were not even allowed inside its meeting space. This body elected the ten Tribuni Plebis (Tribunes of the Plebs), who were important magistrates, as well as some more minor officials, the "plebeian" aediles, officials responsible for maintaining certain aspects of the city of Rome, such as roads. This assembly also conducted trials where the defendant was not at risk of capital punishment. Finally, the group could vote on measures introduced by the Tribuni Plebis, which, upon approval, became "plebiscites." Plebiscites were originally valid and binding on Roman citizens only after the Senate had approved them, but after 287 B.C.E. they had the force of laws. During the late Republican period the Comitia Plebis Tributa and its tribunes were increasingly likely to use plebiscites to confront the authority of the Senate.

The Comitia Populi Tributa was a relatively late creation, formed sometime in the early fifth century B.C.E. in imitation of the Comitia Plebis Tributa. All Roman citizens, both patricians and plebeians, could participate in this assembly. While the Comitia Plebis Tributa was called together by the ten Tribuni Plebis, the Comitia Populi Tributa was convened by the officials called consuls or praetors. This body could pass laws and elect other government officials—quaestors, curule aediles, and military tribunes. It could also conduct trials for cases less serious than treason or homicide.

The Comitia Centuriata also included all Roman citizens. This assembly could enact laws, but it met only infrequently and so rarely did any legislating. This body elected the most important magistrates: the consuls, the praetors, and the censors. It also conducted important trials, for cases of treason or murder or in cases where a Roman citizen had been sentenced to death by another court but exercised his right of appeal. Because the issues brought before the Comitia Centuriata were so important, it was required to hold several formal discussion periods before actually voting on matters.

The way the Comitia Centuriata voted explicitly favored the rich citizens. The Roman citizen body was divided into 193 "centuries" (divisions that, despite their name, had many more than 100 members), and these centuries were divided across five property classes. The top property class had the most centuries assigned to it, and each of those centuries included very few Romans citizens. Each lower property class included fewer centuries, and each century included more citizens, so most citizens were packed into a small number of centuries in the fifth property class. Voting in the Comitia Centuriata proceeded by class, with the centuries in the top class voting first. In this way, a small number of very wealthy Romans could almost always determine the outcome of voting on the important laws and offices that were the concern of this assembly.

Republican Magistrates

Every year Rome held elections to choose new officials, or magistrates. These public offices served a dual purpose; they provided Rome with people to run its affairs, and they gave ambitious men a means of ascending the political ladder. All magistrates except the Tribuni Militum (Tribunes of the Soldiers) were members of the Senate.

The lowest office was that of Tribunus Militum. This office was held by 12 young men in their late 20s. They were responsible for managing the legions of soldiers under the command of the two consuls. Next were quaestors. Between 12 and 16 men held this office every year. They handled Rome's financial matters: collecting customs or duties at ports, collecting rent for Rome's public lands, running the city's treasury, or helping a provincial governor administrate his province. Traditionally, a man tried to get elected quaestor at the age of 30, which was also the proper age for entering the Senate. Some quaestors were already senators when they were elected, and the censors usually admitted to the Senate any quaestor who did not already belong.

Aediles handled public matters. Originally, the aediles were assistants to the Tribuni Plebis and were mainly responsible for taking care of certain temples. In the fourth century B.C.E., however, the Romans added two new offices, the curule aediles, held by patricians. These were called curule because these two aediles were entitled to sit in the chair of office, the *sella curulis*. After this period all the aediles, both the curule aediles and the plebeian aediles, were responsible for taking care of the city of Rome and its inhabitants. They cared for Rome's streets, traffic, water supply, and markets and organized religious festivals and cult observances. Curule aediles were also responsible for organizing the public games called the *ludi Romani*. These games were very expensive, and aediles often had to pay many of the costs themselves. They were willing to do this because it helped them get elected to further offices. Four aediles were chosen each year, two plebeian aediles elected from the plebeian class by the Comitia Plebis Tributa and two curule aediles elected from the patricians by the Comitia Populi Tributa.

Praetors held the second-highest office in Rome (not counting censors). Six to eight praetors were elected every year. Praetors were in charge of litigation and courts of law. The urban praetor (*praetor urbanus)* handled litigation within Rome. The foreign praetor (*praetor peregrinus)* traveled around Italy performing the same role. The other praetors took care of legal matters in the provinces. The normal age for serving as praetor was 39 or 40. Praetors held imperium, which gave them the right to execute Rome's laws and to command an army. Normally, after serving a year as praetor, a man would be sent off by the Senate to govern a province.

Consuls were the highest-ranking magistrates in Rome. They also held imperium. The Comitia Centuriata elected two consuls every year, and they took their oath of office on New Year's Day. The consuls served together and alternated months in which they would run Rome, convening the Comitia Centuriata and bringing laws before it and speaking first at meetings of the Senate. Consuls could command any of Rome's armies and hold power in any part of Rome's territory. The normal age to be elected to the consulship was 42, two years after being elected quaestor. After a year as consul, Romans expected to be sent by the Senate to govern a province. The Senate generally gave consuls one of the provinces that required military authority for its governance. Former consuls were known as *consulares* and were held in high esteem, having navigated to the top of the political system.

Censors were the most senior magistrates, though they had less power than consuls because they lacked imperium. Only men who had already been consul could become censors. The Comitia Centuriata elected two censors at a time, each serving five-year terms. They conducted a census of all Roman citizens, regulated the memberships of the various bodies such as the Senate, and issued state contracts. Because censors had the right to deprive men of their citizenship and deprive Senators of their (otherwise lifetime) office, the office was both respected and feared, and candidates for the censorship were held to very high standards.

The Tribuni Plebis, those magistrates charged with calling together the Comitia Plebis Tributa, were magistrates elected by the plebeians to defend the lives and property of plebeians. During the Republic 10 such tribunes were elected each year. They did not hold the same power as other magistrates because they were not elected by all the Roman people, but they had one important right that made them very powerful: They had the right to veto any law, act of government, decree, or election.

In times of emergency the Senate could appoint a special kind of magistrate called a dictator. The dictator had almost unlimited power but was supposed to be limited to six months in office. The paradigmatic dictator was Lucius Quinctius Cincinnatus, a former consul who, in 458 B.C.E., was called from his farm by the Senate and made dictator. He then defeated Rome's enemy of the moment, the Aequi, laid down his office, and returned to his farm in the space of 15 days. In the late republic Lucius Cornelius Sulla (138–78 B.C.E.) and Julius Caesar (100–44 B.C.E.) both made themselves dictators and ignored all the official restrictions, which led the Senate to abolish the office after Caesar's death.

If a man aspired to high political office, he had to take certain steps in an order called the *cursus honorum*, or "way of honor." First he had to serve in the army as a young man. After joining the Senate at the age of 30, he had to hold each of the major offices: quaestor, praetor, and consul. He did not have to be a curule aedile, but holding that office was considered advantageous to those with political ambition. He might then become a censor. It was considered proper for a man to serve as a provincial governor at some point along the way, too. Rome had numerous provinces. To keep them in order, the government appointed Romans to serve as governors. Governors had to live in their provinces and might spend several years away from Rome while in office.

The Empire

After a period of civil war from around 44 B.C.E. to 31 B.C.E. Julius Caesar's nephew and adopted son, Gaius Julius Caesar Octavianus, assumed more or less complete power over the workings of the Roman government. He did this by winning the support of the Roman armies to such an extent that their loyalties were to him personally more than to any notion of a Roman state or the Roman people. This marked the end of the Roman Republic and the beginning of the Imperial Period.

This change was not marked by any official alteration in the constitution of the Roman government. The Senate remained the official governing body, men still pursued the offices of the *cursus honorum*, the various assemblies still met, the aediles still took care of the city, and so forth. Gaius Julius Caesar Octavianus, known simply as Octavian, simply asserted that he was the "first citizen," *princeps*. But everyone knew that with the army loyal to him alone, the Senate and assemblies legislated at the pleasure of Octavian. No law could be passed, much less enforced, without his approval, and no funds would be released from the treasury except by his permission. After the chaos of the preceding decades, the Roman Senate welcomed this new authority, which brought order to the governance of Rome. The Senate granted Octavian various honors, including the title Augustus, and passed laws giving him perpetual powers like those of a consul.

The structure of Roman government during the Imperial Period was, therefore, at once stable and unpredictable. The old republican offices remained in place for centuries, with their formal and official powers intact. But the day-to-day functioning of the government depended largely on who sat on the throne. Since no formal laws defined the office of emperor—in fact, there was no official rule, or even unofficial custom, for determining the imperial succession upon the death of an emperor—each emperor assumed different powers, for different purposes.

The focus of imperial power was always twofold: the treasury and the army. Emperors could (and did) choose to spend Rome's income, sometimes on lavish parties for the royal court and at other times for programs of road building, harbor construction, and civic architecture. Much of this work was done by the army, always at the beck and call of the emperor.

Upon assuming power over the other arms of the Roman government, Octavian focused his energies on governmental reform, to reestablish order after decades of unrest and gradual undermining of the principles of Roman government. Because the army had been instrumental in perpetuating the state of civil war, Augustus reduced its size; elevated certain units, of certain loyalty, to be his "Praetorian Guard"; and assigned them the task of keeping order in Rome and Italy. Formerly, public order was the concern of the consuls, neither of whom had the necessary authority to bring an army inside the city of Rome and who, serving two at a time, often had conflicting interests. Octavian and his ally, the general Agrippa, arranged to be appointed censors in 28 B.C.E. and used this opportunity to revise the rolls of the Senate, getting rid of any senators who did not support them. In 27 B.C.E. the Senate, now made up of senators chosen by Octavian himself, granted to the "first citizen" the title of Augustus, "Honored One."

With large amounts of public treasure freed by this reduction in the standing army and with Roman victories in Egypt, Augustus worked, through the Senate and the aediles, to reinvigorate the city of Rome through a project of public works. By exercising some control over whom the Senate chose to govern the provinces of the Roman Empire, Augustus was able to ensure that the taxes collected in those provinces made their way to Rome rather than into the pockets of the governors, further enhancing public revenues. Thus the Senate and the magistrates were better able, under Augustus's supervision, to make improvements to the city. Augustus claimed at the end of this life to have found Rome a city of bricks and to have left it a city of marble.

Subsequent emperors and their administrations made other efforts to increase revenues for the city. During the first century of the Common Era, Vespasian, for example, increased the Senate's membership from 200 to 1,000 members, and most of the new senators came from the provinces. These new senators paid the treasury for the privilege of serving Rome, and their position in Rome's governing body brought greater stability to the empire. Vespasian also increased taxes, built up a surplus in the treasury, and used the money for public works. He gave the provinces more rights and allowed the army to recruit from Gaul and Spain instead of just Italy.

During the first few centuries of the Common Era the emperor continued to hold almost total power. He was the rule maker and judge of the ultimate court. He was assisted by an advisory body, the Consilium Principis (Council of the First Citizen) drawn from Senators and nobles, and the Senate continued to meet, but ultimately the emperor retained real power. The Praetorian Guard sometimes supported the emperor but at other times worked against him. Provinces continued to have governors, assisted by officials called procurators. Very few real Romans were sent to govern, so most provinces were really governed by local bodies. Roman officials primarily concerned themselves with censuses and tax collection. Local officials handled criminal justice, public works, religious festivals, and diplomatic relations with Romans.

Between 235 and 284 C.E. Rome descended into chaos. The government had never satisfactorily decided what to do about the succession of emperors, and this failure now came home to roost. Various soldiers decided they wanted to be emperor, and so for 50 years they fought over the office. Twenty-five different soldier-emperors took control during this period; all but two of them were murdered or died in battle, defending their positions. Citizens stopped participating in government; barbarians encroached on the borders, and the military did not stop them; and inflation destroyed the economy.

To a large extent, by the second and third centuries of the Common Era the government in Rome was increasingly irrelevant except in certain very specific ways. The Senate and magistrates continued to run the city itself, and the emperor, through the army, guaranteed peace in the provinces (for failed to do so, more and more). The bureaucracy and especially public finance were handled at a very local level throughout the empire. Local magistrates in each district of each province—some of whom might have had Latin titles like aedile or quaestor and others Greek or Egyptian titles—oversaw local political affairs, and detachments of Roman soldiers kept the peace and handled recruiting for the Roman legions. By the third century C.E. the Roman Empire's army was almost entirely made up by non-Romans and even by non-Italians and non-Europeans.

Taxation under the empire was not handled by the Roman government. The Roman quaestors auctioned off contracts for taxation to private companies. Whichever company bid the most money for the right to collect taxes in a particular province won the auction and became the tax collectors for that province. In this way the state was paid a lump sum at once and was spared the expense of a large bureaucracy. The tax-collecting company, the *publicani*, then proceeded to tax the inhabitants of their territory. This taxation was supposed to be governed by laws. In theory, the *publicani* were supposed to judge how much tax they could collect, legally, given the size of a year's harvest and base their bids to the Roman treasury on that estimate. Companies of *publicani* tended, however, to bid much too high—the Roman quaestors did not complain—and then try to recoup their investment by seizing far more from the citizens of a region than was legal. Theoretically, the citizens could expect the provincial governor to protect their rights and to enforce the law by means of the soldiers at his command. But governors were easily bribed or actively in league with the tax collectors. The injustice of these practices, carried out far from the eyes of the Senate and emperor of Rome, contributed much toward the dissolution and collapse of the Roman Empire.

Corruption, more generally, undid good government, as did, ironically, efforts on the part of emperors to stem it. In the second and third centuries C.E. almost every governmental service required a bribe. As emperors and provincial governors from time to time tried to quell this corruption by punishing corrupt officials, the result was simply an increase in the amount of money demanded of each bribe—magistrates came to assume that they would eventually be caught and punished and so tried to collect as much illicit profit as possible before their careers ended. Taxation and corruption eroded government at a local level, while the emperor's efforts to manage the governance and defense of the vast empire became increasingly difficult at the highest level.

Diocletian (285–312 C.E.) tried to make the Roman government more efficient by dividing the empire into eastern and western empires, each with its own emperor. Each emperor was called Augustus, and each Augustus had an assistant emperor called Caesar, who was also his successor; this solved the perennial problem of succession. This form of government was called a tetrarchy, or rule by four.

The tetrarchy worked well at first, mainly because the first four rulers got along with one another, but it collapsed in 306 C.E. when Augustus Constantius Chlorus died. Over the next several years different men aspired to the throne, resulting in claims to places in the tetrarchy by five or six people at a time. After a brief civil war, in 313 C.E. two Augustuses divided the empire again. Constantine became Augustus of the Western Roman Empire, and Licinius became Augustus of the Eastern Roman Empire. This division lasted until 324 C.E., when Constantine defeated Licinius and became the sole emperor in the city of Constantinople (modern Istanbul, Turkey). Constantine declared Christianity to be the Roman state religion.

THE AMERICAS

BY KEITH JORDAN

Conclusions about the nature of ancient Native American governments are based for the most part on reconstructions—meaning educated guesswork—derived from archaeological data. With the exception of the Classic Maya (ca. 250–650 C.E.), these cultures either did not employ writing at all or left written records that we cannot yet decipher (as is the situation with the Olmec). Although we can now read the titles and personal names of Mayan rulers and brief descriptions of their coronation rites, military conquests, and religious duties, we lack such information for most other ancient Native American governments and must rely on other kinds of evidence.

For example, differences in grave goods, tomb construction, and other burial practices within a culture can reveal something about the nature of its government. The finding of relatively small number of burials with richer offerings or more substantial tombs than those of the majority indicates that some people were considered more important than most others. The presence of a few graves containing scarce or luxury items suggests unequal access to valued resources, indicating the presence of elite individuals or ruling classes. A burial holding the remains of human sacrifices to accompany the deceased reflects his or her importance in the community and power over life and death.

Similarly, differences in residential architecture—such as in the size, building materials (for example, stone versus wood), and location of housing structures—across a culture imply differences in social status. The existence of a few large residences in a separate or elevated area of a community points to the presence of rulers—especially if these residences are near the main structures used for civic and ceremonial purposes by the community. Large-scale public works and monumental architecture do not necessarily indicate the existence of a centralized government or a ruling class, but they do point to a high degree of social organization and cooperation. So does evidence of concentrated settlements with large populations, necessitating a system for maintaining social order.

A more direct kind of evidence comes from sculpture and paintings portraying rulers, usually in elaborate costumes, often on a massive scale, and typically engaged in actions indicating their rank, such as vanquishing captives, receiving tribute, or performing important religious rituals. The existence of monumental images of such figures also demonstrates their command of labor power and raw materials. Human remains can provide clues to social ranking. For instance, anatomical evidence of inherited illnesses or deformities can disclose familial connections among those with special access to wealth as revealed in their graves. In Mesoamerica ruling groups used artificial deformities, such as head flattening and jade-inlaid teeth, to distinguish themselves from their subjects. A riskier and more speculative approach is to interpret patterns of archaeological information from the distant past in light of accounts by European explorers and colonists after 1492 describing the Native American governments they encountered. The problem, of course, is that a lot can change in a few hundred years, let alone millennia.

Early Developments

From the available evidence it is apparent that the earliest settlers of the New World from Asia at the end of the last ice age did not possess government in the sense of centralized institutions and sharply stratified hierarchies of command. They were small migratory bands of hunter-gatherers who, like most other peoples at a similar level of social organization, were relatively egalitarian. Certain individuals may have been especially consulted in decision making because of their experience in such pursuits as hunting, and there is some evidence of ritual specialists or shamans, but there were no social classes and no formal leaders. Similar conditions seem to have prevailed for several thousand years.

The adoption of limited agriculture to supplement wild-food collection and the expansion of trade networks in eastern North America during the period from roughly 1000 B.C.E. to 500 C.E. led to greater social complexity. This change shows up in the archaeological record in the form of elaborate burials for some people and evidence of large-scale community projects, like the construction of large earthen burial mounds and ritual enclosures. However, settlements remained small and scattered, and there is little evidence of hereditary elites, suggesting that any status differences were based on individual achievements in trading or ritual activity rather than on class or a stable hierarchical structure.

Mesoamerica

Only with the expansion of population and formation of permanent villages and towns permitted by the development of intensive agriculture in Mesoamerica in the last few millennia B.C.E. did conditions emerge for the rise of centralized hierarchical governments. The earliest of these seem to have been what anthropologists call "chiefdoms." Chiefdoms are small-scale (population in the thousands) class societies ruled by individual, usually male chiefs, whose position is inherited. The chief's family constitutes the wealthiest and most powerful social class, while the majority of the population consists of agricultural laborers living on family farms. Chiefdoms lack complex bureaucracies. Permanent political offices are limited to the chief and a few subordinate positions, such as war captains or priestly authorities.

Chiefs maintain their power by public ritual, conspicuous consumption of luxury goods, and bestowing rewards on loyal followers. They control the surplus wealth of the society (such as stores of grain) and its distribution and may also control trade with outsiders. They are able to organize their subjects to labor on such public construction projects as elite residences and shrines. They often function as war leaders, but they do not have a monopoly on the use of force and usually lack absolute power over their subjects. Their influence depends to a great degree on their wealth and personal charisma. Bad fortune may lead their followers to abandon

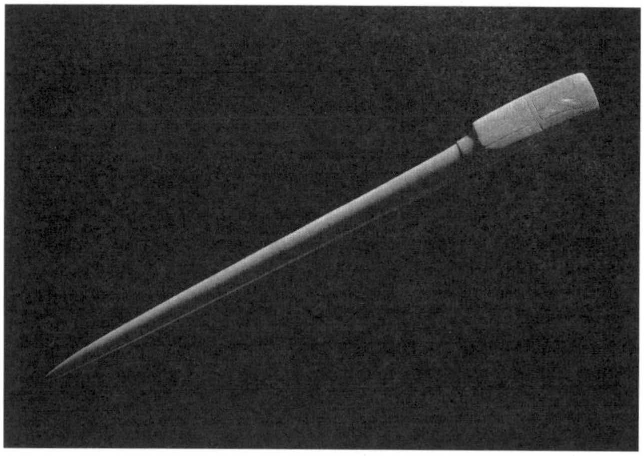

Jade perforator, Olmec, 1200–400 B.C.E., from Mexico; such instruments were used by rulers in bloodletting ceremonies to ensure the fertility of the land and the well-being of the community. (© The Trustees of the British Museum)

them. Chiefs usually govern from a large central settlement (population up to the thousands) that dominates surrounding smaller villages (populations in the hundreds or less) by military force or by co-opting local leaders through rewards and alliances. People living within an individual chiefdom are usually of the same ethnicity and speak the same language. Boundaries, however, are poorly defined and vary with the chief's influence and success.

Such institutions emerged in the present-day Mexican states of Oaxaca and Chiapas by the end of the second millennium B.C.E. At sites such as San José Mogote in Oaxaca, large settlements with public architecture such as platform mounds maintained control over surrounding small villages. Differences in grave goods and in house size show the existence of different social classes, with a chiefly elite at the top. Chiefs used force to maintain control over surrounding communities. An early stone carving from a public building at San José Mogote shows a sacrificed war captive with his heart cut out.

These early Mesoamerican chiefdoms evolved over the next millennium into archaic states or kingdoms. Anthropologists define states as systems controlled by several layers of officials and administrators serving a hereditary ruling class or, in kingdoms, a single supreme ruler. A wide range of social classes exists, and occupations become increasingly specialized. Religion takes a highly organized form, with a hierarchical priesthood, and rules of conduct may be formalized into official codes of law. The ruling class, and in kingdoms the king, has absolute power of life and death over the subjects. Government becomes concentrated in large cities, with several levels of smaller settlement types serving regional administrative needs. States usually have firm boundaries defended by a well-organized military. Trade within the state and with other areas is extensive. The territory of states expands via conquest and colonization of surrounding areas and can encompass millions of people of markedly different linguistic and ethnic backgrounds

From 1500 to 400 B.C.E. the Olmec civilization flourished on the Gulf coast of Mexico in the modern states of Veracruz and Tabasco. Whether Olmec government represents an advanced form of chiefdom or an archaic state under kings was a matter of dispute among 20th-century archaeologists. However, most scholars today consider that the huge scale of Olmec architecture and the colossal stone images of rulers reflect greater power over people and resources and a more complex organization of labor than any known historical chief ever commanded. The Olmec kings apparently ruled over small polities of some 5,000 to 20,000 people, each organized around a primary town that served as both royal residence and religious center. Kingship was already no doubt an inherited office, as in later Mesoamerican states, and rulers seem to have been exclusively male. They controlled the surplus of their simple farming economies. The kings functioned predominantly as religious and war leaders and had a trade monopoly over exotic luxury materials that could be redistributed as gifts to reward allies and followers. They commanded both small groups of specialized artists and massive public works projects to create and decorate their capitals.

In ancient Mesoamerica there was no distinction between politics and religion, no issue of sacred versus secular rule as developed in the West over the last half of the 20th century. The Olmec rulers apparently attempted to legitimize their claim to power by serving as ritual specialists. They had themselves portrayed on their monuments engaging in ritual activities and wearing elaborate costumes, suggesting that they had usurped the role played by shamans in earlier, more egalitarian societies. Like shamans, the Olmec kings mediated between the human world and the worlds of gods and ancestors and were thought to be able to travel to supernatural realms to maintain the well-being of their subjects, magically ensuring adequate rain and good harvests. Some sculptures show them transforming into powerful animals like jaguars and birds of prey, as shamans are believed to do, or emerging from caves, viewed in Mesoamerica as portals to the underworld.

At the early Olmec center of San Lorenzo (ca. 1500–900 B.C.E.) the rulers lived on the highest ground in huge palaces fitted with columns and drains of stone, in contrast to the pole-and-thatch houses of their subjects. Sculptors labored in workshops attached to these royal residences to create colossal carved portrait heads and thrones for their kings from blocks of stone brought from some sixty miles to the north—all evidence of the Olmec lords' extensive command of human labor and raw materials. At other royal workshops at the site specialized craftsmen created royal regalia and ornaments with exotic materials such as magnetic iron ore imported from faraway Oaxaca. The massive monuments were the equivalent of modern political propaganda, illustrating the ruler's power by their scale and intensive use of labor. The iron ore was ground into mirrors and worn as pendants that could be used to start fires or reflect images, no doubt underlining the king's powers as chief shaman.

Some 20th-century archaeologists claimed that the Olmec unified into an empire that conquered peoples in other parts of Mesoamerica, but there is little evidence for this claim. The spread of Olmec art objects and styles beyond the Gulf coast seems better explained by trade and imitation. Rulers at the central Mexican site of Chalcatzingo, however, seem to have enhanced their status by alliance and possibly even intermarriage with the Olmec of the site known today as La Venta, adopting La Venta's sculptural style for their monuments. Chalcatzingo's rulers are distinguished in the archaeological record by burial in stone crypts alongside precious materials like jade. Artistic representations at the site may indicate that some rulers were female.

Around 500 B.C.E. residents of Zapotec communities in the three branches of the Valley of Oaxaca joined together to create a new central capital atop an easily defended mountain. The site, known today as Monte Alban, was not on good agricultural land but nonetheless rapidly grew in population and in the scale of its temple and residential architecture. These facts suggest that it was founded with the presumption that the surrounding communities would supply it with food. The smaller chiefdoms may have merged into a larger political system to defend against enemies from outside the area or to put an end to conflicts among themselves, choosing Monte Alban as a neutral ground on which to build a regional capital. If so, this system would resemble a form of political organization in ancient Greece in which several villages joined together to create a new central city, usually for defense.

Initially, Monte Alban contained many elite residences but lacked clear-cut royal palaces or tombs. However, during the Late Formative Period (ca. 400 B.C.E.–150 C.E.) royal tombs and large palaces appeared. At the same time, the scale of collective labor on construction projects at the site increased; most impressively, the top of the mountain was leveled to build a ceremonial plaza. Carved stones from this period identify towns outside the valley that had been conquered by the rulers of Monte Alban. All of this evidence indicates that the city had evolved into the center of a state.

In the Maya area, kingdoms probably existed by about 600 B.C.E., as evidenced by the massive scale of construction at sites like Nakbe, Guatemala. The size of Mayan cities increased as more sophisticated and intensive agricultural techniques, such as elaborate irrigation systems, developed. From these beginnings the unit of political control among the Maya became the city-state, meaning an independent regional kingdom governed from a prominent city or primary center that was the seat of the royal family. Among the Maya the primary cities dominated smaller, secondary centers and sought to conquer other city-states in a pattern of ongoing warfare and shifting political alliances that persisted until the end of the Classic Period (ca. 650 C.E.).

Unlike the Olmec rulers, the first Maya kings appear not to have advertised their status in colossal portraits. Instead, they built pyramid-temples decorated with huge plaster masks of deities associated with kingship to bolster their rule through art. By the Late Formative Period the hieroglyph signifying the holy lord or king of a city-state began to be used on royal monuments depicting individual kings. Most important among these monuments are stelae, upright stones with images or inscriptions carved in relief. During the Early Classic Period these stelae became the predominant form of Mayan political art, showing portraits of individual rulers conquering enemies, performing religious rituals, and engaging in such important passages as royal marriage and accession to the throne. These stone images functioned as doubles or copies of the king and bolstered his right to rule by showing him as a shaman like the Olmec lords, able to conjure up his ancestors' spirits and bring their blessings to himself and his people. He was also seen as a divine being, equated with the Maize God.

The enormous metropolis of Teotihuacán, north of present-day Mexico City, was the center of a state that reached its height of power and influence between 1 and 650 C.E. The precise grid system of the city, the immense scale of public architecture, and the evidence for standardized systems of measurement all point to strong centralized planning and coordination of labor. One feature unique to Teotihuacán in Mesoamerica, the construction of massive, collective public housing, also points to a state bureaucracy. The exact form of rule at Teotihuacán, however, remains unclear. There are no individual portraits of rulers at the site. Teotihuacán art shows smaller humans behaving deferentially toward large deities, but there are no explicit scenes of humans dominating bound captives, as in Olmec or Maya art. Fresco paintings show elite figures in profile processions, facing a frontal deity image on an adjoining wall. They are not distinguished from one another by signs that could represent individual names until late in the city's history. However, they wear elaborate regalia, including a distinctive tasseled headdress that might signify rulership or at least high military or priestly rank. Their images are sometimes bordered by representations of the mythic deity the Feathered Serpent, associated with kingship in later Mesoamerican cultures, including the Aztec and Toltec.

The lack of images of individually named rulers in Teotihuacán has led some scholars to conclude that rather than having a single divine ruler like the Mayan city-states, Teotihuacán was governed by a collective, perhaps of warrior-priests or elite families. However, archaeological evidence gathered over the past 20 years casts doubt on this model. At the Pyramid of the Feathered Serpent, the remains of more than 100 sacrificial victims were interred as offerings. The bodies were richly ornamented, and differences in the quality of the grave goods suggest that they represented members of distinctive social ranks. These mass executions reflect a very powerful and centralized government with the power of life and death over its subjects, and the burials may have been intended to accompany an individual king in a (now looted) central tomb.

One interpretation seeks to reconcile this evidence of individual rulership with the lack of such evidence in the city's art by positing two stages in Teotihuacán's political history: An earlier despotic kingship, reflected in the Pyramid of the Feathered Serpent finds, was overthrown around 350 C.E. because of its excesses and replaced by a more collective leadership. But societies from other parts of the world show that individual ruler portraits are not a necessary feature of centralized monarchies. The Incas, for example, did not develop individual portraiture to any great degree and made few images of kings, yet they created an empire ruled by divine monarchs.

At its height Teotihuacán had a population of 125,000 to 200,000 and certainly controlled the Basin of Mexico. Whether Teotihuacán created an empire, or how far its political power extended, is another controversial topic. Imported Teotihuacán objects and local copies of the city's architecture occur across Mesoamerica, but most probably represent the attempts of local rulers to legitimize their power by emulating Teotihuacán's prestige rather than Teotihuacán conquests. Foreign rulers may have sought the endorsement of Teotihuacán's government and made pilgrimages to the city to stress their claims to power in the same way medieval European monarchs obtained the pope's blessing in Rome. Archaeological evidence indicates that Teotihuacanos did conquer and colonize part of the Pacific coast of Guatemala, 200 miles away from the city. They probably wanted to control this area in order to procure local luxury materials such as chocolate, jade, and the beautiful iridescent green tail feathers of the indigenous quetzal bird, which were used to make headdresses and other garments for ancient Mesoamerican rulers. The nature of their political relations with local Maya city-states remains unclear. At Tikal recent interpretations of hieroglyphs indicate that in 378 C.E. Teotihuacán directly intervened in the politics of this city-state, sending a military force to kill the ruler Great Jaguar Paw and install the next king, Yax Nuun Ayin. However, not all scholars accept this reconstruction, and Teotihuacán may have simply backed a faction in a local struggle for power rather than directly invading Tikal.

Peru

Although large-scale building and irrigation projects involving thousands of laborers took place in Peruvian agricultural towns as far back as 2700 B.C.E., there is not much other evidence for rulers during this time. Huge temple platforms reflect strong social organization, but there are no real differences in grave goods to suggest big differences in status among the population. Perhaps collective organizations like those still found today in indigenous Peruvian communities, based on extended family ties and reciprocal work obligations, constituted the only government. On the other hand, the presence of two types of housing suggests at least two levels of society, and the temples atop the platform mounds were small, suggesting access restricted to a few. At Kotosh in the Andean highlands as early as 2000 B.C.E. members of some families were preserved after death as mummies, indicating special positions in society, but supporting evidence for ruling classes is scanty from contemporary sites. At the coastal town of Cardal individuals buried in a shrine about 1400 B.C.E. were probably not members of noble families but religious specialists honored for their individual achievements. There is no evidence for state control in these places, despite the size of the buildings.

Between about 900 and 200 B.C.E., however, strong evidence of rulers emerges. At the religious center of Chavín de Huántar the bones of individuals living close to the main shrine during the New Temple Period (ca. 400–200 B.C.E.) show that these folks ate a more varied diet, with more meat, than people buried farther from the temple. A class with preferential access to food resources, perhaps priests, had emerged. At the contemporary site of Kuntur Wasi some burials contain gold jewelry and regalia—clearly some members of this community had higher status than others. Cemeteries from the same time near Paracas, on the south coast, provide clear evidence for powerful nobles. Some mummy bundles contain hundreds of feet of elaborately woven textiles, enclosing rich grave goods of ceramics and gold jewelry, and sometimes occupy the central position in tombs, surrounded by the smaller bundles of their subjects. Anthropologists believe that these early Peruvian elites were akin to the hereditary nobles of later Inca times, who presided over clan-based collective groups and served as religious specialists mediating between their subjects and the deities of fertility responsible for agricultural success.

North America

Little is known of the governmental organization of ancient groups in North America. During the Paleo-Indian period (ca. 13,000–ca. 8000 B.C.E.) the earliest inhabitants of North America were organized into very small, highly mobile, and presumably egalitarian hunting bands ranging over the landscape in search of prey. There is no evidence from burials of any type of social stratification or hierarchy; as with historically documented modern hunter-gatherers there was probably no centralized leadership, though older band members would have been looked to for guidance based on their experience. Archaeological traces of ritual activity hints at the possible presence of shamans among these small groups, but certainly no priestly class or caste with governing power. Through the subsequent Archaic Period (ca. 8000–ca. 1000 B.C.E.) band size grew larger, and there is archaeological evidence for longer occupation of campsites based on seasonal exploitation of natural resources, but again there is nothing to suggest the presence of elites or ruling classes. Like other hunter-gatherers, these bands seem to have been simply organized without any evidence of fixed or centralized leadership positions.

During the Early and Middle Woodland periods in the Midwest, cultures participating in the Adena (1000 B.C.E.–200 C.E.) and Hopewell (300 B.C.E.–500 C.E.) burial and ritual traditions were sufficiently well organized to bring communities together for the construction of burial mounds and ceremonial earthworks, some of them of massive size. The large quantities of luxurious grave goods accompanying some mound burials point to the emergence of status differences. However, there is still no evidence for any formal governing structure. Settlement patterns remained diffuse, with small groups, probably based on family ties, scattered into very small villages. The high-status individuals buried in the mounds probably did not represent hereditary or formal positions of leadership, but they acquired their wealth and influence by individual achievements, perhaps as traders, hunters, or shamans. There is no evidence for formal government in the form of chiefdoms in North America until the beginning of the second millennium of the Common Era.

See also AGRICULTURE; ARCHITECTURE; ART; ASTRONOMY; BORDERS AND FRONTIERS; BUILDING TECHNIQUES AND MATERIALS; CALENDARS AND CLOCKS; CITIES; CLIMATE AND GEOGRAPHY; DEATH AND BURIAL; ECONOMY; EDUCATION; EMPIRES AND DYNASTIES; FAMILIES; FESTIVALS; FOREIGNERS AND BARBARIANS; LAWS AND LEGAL CODES; METALLURGY; MIGRATION AND POPULATION MOVEMENTS; MILITARY; MONEY AND COINAGE; NOMADIC AND PASTORAL SOCIETIES; OCCUPATIONS; RELIGION AND COSMOLOGY; ROADS AND BRIDGES; SACRED SITES; SCANDAL AND CORRUPTION; SETTLEMENT PATTERNS; SOCIAL ORGANIZATION; TOWNS AND VILLAGES; TRADE AND EXCHANGE; WAR AND CONQUEST; WEAPONRY AND ARMOR; WEIGHTS AND MEASURES; WRITING.

Greece

Xenophon: "The Polity of the Spartans," ca. 375 B.C.E.

I recall the astonishment with which I first noted the unique position of Sparta among the states of Hellas, the relatively sparse population, and at the same time the extraordinary powers and prestige of the community. I was puzzled to account for the fact. It was only when I came to consider the peculiar institutions of the Spartans that my wonderment ceased.

When we turn to Lycurgos, instead of leaving it to each member of the state privately to appoint a slave to be his son's tutor, he set over the young Spartans a public guardian—the *paidonomos*—with complete authority over them. This guardian was elected from those who filled the highest magistracies. He had authority to hold musters of the boys, and as their guardian, in case of any misbehavior, to chastise severely. Lycurgos further provided the guardian with a body of youths in the prime of life and bearing whips to inflict punishment when necessary, with this happy result, that in Sparta modesty and obedience ever go hand in hand, nor is there lack of either. . . .

Again, as regards food, according to his regulation, the *eiren*, or head of the flock, must see that his messmates gather to the club meal with such moderate food as to avoid bloating and yet not remain unacquainted with the pains of starvation. His belief was that by such training in boyhood they would be better able when occasion demanded to continue toiling on an empty stomach. . . . On the other hand, to guard against a too great pinch of starvation, he did give them permission to steal this thing or that in the effort to alleviate their hunger. . . .

When Lycurgos first came to deal with the question, the Spartans, like the rest of the Hellenes, used to mess privately at home. Tracing more than half the current problems to this custom, he was determined to drag his people out of holes and corners into the broad daylight, and so he invented the public mess rooms. As to food, his ordinance allowed them only so much as should guard them from want. . . . So that from beginning to end, till the mess breaks up, the common board is never stinted for food nor yet extravagantly furnished. So also in the matter of drink. While putting a stop to all unnecessary drink, he left them free to quench thirst when nature dictated. . . . Thus there is the necessity of walking home when a meal is over, and a consequent anxiety not to be caught tripping under the influence of wine, since they all know of course that the supper table must be presently abandoned and that they must move as freely in the dark as in the day, even with the help of a torch.

It is clear that Lycurgos set himself deliberately to provide all the blessings of heaven for the good man, and a sorry and ill-starred existence for the coward. In other states the man who shows himself base and cowardly, wins to himself an evil reputation and the nickname of a coward, but that is all. For the rest he buys and sells in the same marketplace with a good man; he sits beside him at a play; he exercises with him in the same *gymnasion*, and all as suits his humor. But at Sparta there is not one man who would not feel ashamed to welcome the coward at the common messtables or to try conclusions with him in a wrestling bout; . . . . during games he is left out as the odd man; . . . . during the choric dance he is driven away. Nay, in the very streets it is he who must step aside for others to pass, or, being seated, he must rise and make room, even for a younger man. . . .

(continued)

(continues)

Lycurgos also provided for the continual cultivation of virtues even to old age, by fixing the election to the council of elders as a last ordeal at the goal of life, thus making it impossible for a high standard of virtuous living to be disregarded even in old age. . . . Moreover he laid upon them, like some irresistible necessity, the obligation to cultivate the whole virtue of a citizen. Provided they duly perform the injunctions of the law, the city belonged to them each and all, in absolute possession, and on an equal footing. . . .

I wish to explain with sufficient detail the nature of the covenant between king and state as instituted by Lycurgos; for this, I take it, is the sole type of rule which still preserves the original form in which it was first established; whereas other constitutions will be found either to have been already modified or else to be still undergoing modification at this moment. Lycurgos laid it down as law that the king shall offer on behalf of the state all public sacrifices, as being himself of divine descent, and wherever the state shall dispatch her armies the king shall take the lead. He granted him to receive honorary gifts of the things offered in sacrifice, and he appointed him choice land in many of the provincial cities, enough to satisfy moderate needs without excess of wealth. And in order that the kings might also encamp and mess in public he appointed them public quarters, and he honored them with a double portion each at the evening meal, not in order that they might actually eat twice as much as others but that the king might have the means to honor whomsoever he wished. . . .

Close by the palace a lake affords an unrestricted supply of water; and how useful that is for various purposes they best can tell who lack the luxury. Moreover, all rise from their seats to give place to the king, save only that the ephors rise not from their throne of office. Monthly they exchange oaths, the ephors on behalf of the state, the king himself on his own behalf. And this is the oath on the king's part: "I will exercise my kingship in accordance with the established laws of the state." And on the part of the state (the ephors) the oath runs: "So long as he (who exercises kingship), shall abide by his oath we will not suffer his kingdom to be shaken."

From: Fred Fling, ed., *A Source Book of Greek History* (Boston: D. C. Heath, 1907), pp. 66–75.

Greece

Plutarch: excerpt from The Life of Theseus, *ca. 110 C.E.*

Now, after the death of his father Aigeos, forming in his mind a great and wonderful design, he gathered together all the inhabitants of Attica into one town, and made them one people of one city, whereas before they lived dispersed and were not easy to assemble upon any affair for the common interest. Nay, differences and even wars often occurred between them, which he by his persuasions appeased, going from township to township and from tribe to tribe. And those of a more private and mean condition readily embracing such good advice, to those of greater power he promised a commonwealth without monarchy—a democracy, or people's government—in which he should only be continued as their commander in war and the protector of their laws, all things else being equally distributed among them; and by this means brought a part of them over to his proposal.

He then dissolved all the distinct statehouses, council halls, and magistracies, and built one common statehouse and council hall on the site of the present upper town, and gave the name of *Athens* to the whole state, ordaining a common feast and sacrifice, which he called *Pan-Athenaia*, or the sacrifice of all the united Athenians. He instituted also another sacrifice called *Metoikia*, or Feast of Migration, which is yet celebrated on the sixteenth day of Hecatombaion. Then, as he had promised, he laid down his regal power and proceeded to order a commonwealth, entering upon this great work not without advice from the gods. . . . Farther yet designing to enlarge his city, he invited all strangers to come and enjoy equal privileges with the natives. . . . Yet he did not suffer his state, by the promiscuous multitude that flowed in, to be turned into confusion and he left without any order or degree, but he was the first that divided the Athenian Commonwealth into three distinct ranks, the noblemen, the farmers, and the artisans. To the nobility he committed the care of religion, the choice of magistrates, the teaching and dispensing of the laws, and interpretation and direction in all sacred matters; the whole city being, as it were, reduced to an exact equality, the nobles excelling the rest in honor, the farmers in profit, and the artisans in number. He also coined money, and stamped it with the image of an ox, either in memory of the Marathon bull, or of the Minotaur, both of whom he vanquished; or else to put his people in mind to follow animal husbandry; and from this coin came the expression so frequent among the Hellenes, of a thing being worth ten or a hundred oxen. After this he joined Megara to Attica. . . .

About this time, Menestheos (the son of Peteos, grandson of Orneos, and great-grandson of Erechtheos), the first man that is recorded to have affected popularity and ingratiated himself with the multitude, stirred up and exasperated the most eminent men of the city, who had long borne a secret grudge to Theseos, conceiving that he had robbed them of their several little kingdoms and lordships, and having pent them all up in one city, was using them as his subjects and slaves. He put also the meaner people into commotion, telling them that, deluded with a mere dream of liberty, they were actually deprived of both that and of their proper homes and religious usages and that instead of many good and gracious kings of their own, they had given themselves up to be lorded over by a newcomer and a stranger. . . . and after Theseos death—by accident or misadventure—Menestheos ruled in Athens as king.

From: Plutarch, *Plutarch's Lives* (London: J. M. Dent and Sons, Ltd., 1910).

Rome

Polybius: "Rome at the End of the Punic Wars," ca . 200–after 118 B.C.E.

The three kinds of government, monarchy, aristocracy and democracy, were all found united in the commonwealth of Rome. And so even was the balance between them all, and so regular the administration that resulted from their union, that it was no easy thing to determine with assurance, whether the entire state was to be estimated an aristocracy, a democracy, or a monarchy. For if they turned their view upon the power of the consuls, the government appeared to be purely monarchical and regal. If, again, the authority of the senate was considered, it then seemed to wear the form of aristocracy. And, lastly, if regard was to be had to the share which the people possessed in the administration of affairs, it could then scarcely fail to be denominated a popular state. The several powers that were appropriated to each of these distinct branches of the constitution at the time of which we are speaking, and which, with very little variation, are even still preserved, are these which follow.

The consuls, when they remain in Rome, before they lead out the armies into the field, are the masters of all public affairs. For all other magistrates, the tribunes alone excepted, are subject to them, and bound to obey their commands. They introduce ambassadors into the senate. They propose also to the senate the subjects of debates and direct all forms that are observed in making the decrees. Nor is it less a part of their office likewise to attend to those affairs that are transacted by the people; to call together general assemblies; to report to them the resolutions of the senate; and to ratify whatever is determined by the greater number. In all the preparations that are made for war, as well as in the whole administration in the field, they possess an almost absolute authority. For to them it belongs to impose upon the allies whatever services they judge expedient; to appoint the military tribunes; to enroll the legions, and make the necessary levies, and to inflict punishments in the field, upon all that are subject to their command. Add to this that they have the power likewise to expend whatever sums of money they may think convenient from the public treasury; being attended for that purpose by a quaestor; who is always ready to receive and execute their orders. When any one therefore, directs his view to this part of the constitution, it is very reasonable for him to conclude that this government is no other than a simple royalty. . . .

To the senate belongs, in the first place, the sole care and management of the public money. For all returns that are brought into the treasury, as well as all the payments that are issued from it, are directed by their

(continued)

(continues)

orders. Nor is it allowed to the quaestors to apply any part of the revenue to particular occasions as they arise, without a decree of the senate; those sums alone excepted which are expended in the service of the consuls. And even those more general, as well as greatest disbursements, which are employed at the return every five years, in building and repairing the public edifices, are assigned to the censors for that purpose, by the express permission of the senate. To the senate also is referred the cognizance of all the crimes, committed in any part of Italy, that demand a public examination and inquiry: such as treasons, conspiracies, poisonings, and assassinations. Add to this, that when any controversies arise, either between private men, or any of the cities of Italy, it is the part of the senate to adjust all disputes; to censure those that are deserving of blame: and to yield assistance to those who stand in need of protection and defense. When any embassies are sent out of Italy; either to reconcile contending states; to offer exhortations and advice; or even, as it sometimes happens, to impose commands; to propose conditions of a treaty; or to make a denunciation of war; the care and conduct of all these transactions is entrusted wholly to the senate. When any ambassadors also arrive in Rome, it is the senate likewise that determines how they shall be received and treated, and what answer shall be given to their demands.

In all these things that have now been mentioned, the people has no share. To those, therefore, who come to reside in Rome during the absence of the consuls, the government appears to be purely aristocratic. Many of the Greeks, especially, and of the foreign princes, are easily led into this persuasion: when they perceive that almost all the affairs, which they are forced to negotiate with the Romans, are determined by the senate.

And now it may well be asked, what part is left to the people in this government: since the senate, on the one hand, is vested with the sovereign power, in the several instances that have been enumerated, and more especially in all things that concern the management and disposal of the public treasure; and since the consuls, on the other hand, are entrusted with the absolute direction of the preparations that are made for war, and exercise an uncontrolled authority on the field. There is, however, a part still allotted to the people; and, indeed, the most important part. For, first, the people are the sole dispensers of rewards and punishments; which are the only bands by which states and kingdoms, and, in a word, all human societies are held together. For when the difference between these is overlooked, or when they are distributed without due distinction, nothing but disorder can ensue. Nor is it possible, indeed, that the government should be maintained if the wicked stand in equal estimation with the good. The people, then, when any such offences demand such punishment, frequently condemn citizens to the payment of a fine: those especially who have been invested with the dignities of the state. To the people alone belongs the right to sentence any one to die. Upon this occasion they have a custom which deserves to be mentioned with applause. The person accused is allowed to withdraw himself in open view, and embrace a voluntary banishment, if only a single tribe remains that has not yet given judgment; and is suffered to retire in safety to Praeneste, Tibur, Naples, or any other of the confederate cities. The public magistrates are allotted also by the people to those who are esteemed worthy of them: and these are the noblest rewards that any government can bestow on virtue. To the people belongs the power of approving or rejecting laws and, which is still of greater importance, peace and war are likewise fixed by their deliberations. When any alliance is concluded, any war ended, or treaty made; to them the conditions are referred, and by them either annulled or ratified. And thus again, from a view of all these circumstances, it might with reason be imagined, that the people had engrossed the largest portion of the government, and that the state was plainly a democracy.

Such are the parts of the administration, which are distinctly assigned to each of the three forms of government that are united in the commonwealth of Rome.

From: Oliver J. Thatcher, ed., *The Library of Original Sources*. Vol. 3, *The Roman World* (Milwaukee: University Research Extension Co., 1907), pp. 166–193.

FURTHER READING

A. S. Altekar, *State and Government in Ancient India.* (New Delhi, India: Motilal Banarsidass, 2001).

Antony Andrewes, *The Greek Tyrants* (London: Hutchinson, 1956).

Stephen Bertman, *Handbook to Life in Ancient Mesopotamia* (New York: Facts On File, 2003).

Paul Cartledge, *The Spartans: The World of the Warrior-Heroes of Ancient Greece, from Utopia to Crisis and Collapse* (Woodstock, N.Y.: Overlook Press, 2003).

Gilbert Charles-Picard and Colette Charles-Picard, *The Life and Death of Carthage* (London: Sidgwick and Jackson, 1968).

John Clark, "Mesoamerica Goes Public: Early Ceremonial Centers, Leaders, and Communities." In *Mesoamerican Archaeology*, ed. Julia A. Hendon and Rosemary A. Joyce (Oxford, U.K.: Blackwell, 2004).

Philip Drucker, "On the Nature of Olmec Polity." In *The Olmec and Their Neighbors: Essays in Memory of Matthew W. Stirling*, ed. Elizabeth P. Benson (Washington, D.C.: Dumbarton Oaks, 1981).

Moses I. Finley, *Politics in the Ancient World* (Cambridge, U.K.: Cambridge University Press, 1983).

Nikolai Grube, ed., *Maya: Divine Kings of the Rain Forest* (Cologne, Germany: Konnemann, 2000).

E. H. Gwynne-Thomas, *A Political History of the Roman Empire* (Lanham, Md.: University Press of America, 1984).

Barbara Levick, *Government of the Roman Empire: A Sourcebook*, 2nd ed. (London: Routledge, 2000).

Joyce Marcus and Kent V. Flannery, *Zapotec Civilization: How Urban Society Evolved in Mexico's Oaxaca Valley* (London: Thames and Hudson, 1996).

Karen Rhea Nemet-Nejat, *Daily Life in Ancient Mesopotamia* (Westport, Conn.: Greenwood Press, 1998).

Wilfried Nippel, *Public Order in Ancient Rome* (Cambridge, U.K.: Cambridge University Press, 1995).

Josiah Ober, *Mass and Elite in Democratic Athens: Rhetoric, Ideology, and Power of the People* (Princeton, N.J.: Princeton University Press, 1989).

A. R. Radcliffe-Brown and Daryll Forde, eds., *African Systems of Kinship and Marriage* (New York: Kegan Paul, 1987).

Saburo Sugiyama, "Governance and Polity at Classic Teotihuacan." In *Mesoamerican Archaeology*, ed. Julia A. Hendon and Rosemary A. Joyce (Oxford, U.K.: Blackwell, 2004).

H

► health and disease

INTRODUCTION

Many common themes run through discussions of health and disease in the ancient world. The first is low life expectancy. Infant mortality rates were extremely high by modern standards, and many women lost their lives in giving birth. Among those who survived their first year of life, the prospects for a long life were limited. In most ancient civilizations people in their mid-thirties would have been considered old. Among the most ancient cultures death by starvation was a constant threat; even when food was somewhat plentiful, diets were often unbalanced, leading to medical conditions that result from the lack of essential vitamins or minerals.

A second common theme is a lack of sanitation, usually reflecting ignorance about the causes of infectious diseases. In many parts of the world clean drinking water was scarce. As human communities grew and became more crowded, unsanitary conditions were commonplace. Even the ancient Romans, known for their plumbing and water systems, often lived in unsanitary conditions, with latrines located in kitchens and water wells dug in the vicinity of cesspools. Further, insects and rodents frequently invaded homes and food-storage facilities, bringing waste and therefore diseases with them. These conditions gave rise to a host of infectious diseases, such as malaria, as well as parasites. Before the development of antibiotics, a person could die as a result of a simple infection from an unhealed wound.

A third theme is that ancient cultures sought cures for the diseases that afflicted them. Many of these treatments involved substances derived from plants, including herbs, thought to have medicinal value. In some cases, the ancients were correct. Chewing the bark of a willow tree relieved pain, and modern scientists discovered that willow bark contains a chemical that is closely related to the chemical in aspirin. Healers who acquired knowledge about medicinal substances occupied a high place in most ancient cultures, the ancient Chinese providing a good example. They were often thought to possess special wisdom from the gods. In some cases, these healers were sought out, giving rise to the earliest hospitals. The earliest-known hospital dates to the fourth century B.C.E. in modern-day Sri Lanka.

A fourth theme concerns the role of shamans and medicine men (and women) in ancient cultures. At a time when people believed that they were subject to mysterious forces in nature and that their afflictions were the work of the gods, shamans were often looked on as healers because it was believed that they could read the will of the gods in omens and signs. In a sense, these early healers were the world's first psychologists, for they often linked illness with the mental condition of the patient. In ancient Africa illness was seen as the result of a combination of physical, mental, and even social factors. While their cures may have lacked medicinal value, they provided patients with the will to fight their illnesses. In many instances, the patients' improved mental state helped them recover.

AFRICA

BY JULIAN M. MURCHISON

Health and disease in African prehistory has been largely understudied. As a result of historical stereotypes and misconceptions, non-Africans often think of the African continent as dark, dirty, and diseased. However, a detailed look at the prehistory of the continent and an examination of information derived from research that sheds light on the past shows that Africans have developed long-standing and flexible systems of health that have allowed them to treat and cope with a wide range of diseases and other health concerns. What we know about Africa today and about the past suggests that some of the most important concerns of the residents of Africa in ancient times included the health and welfare of infants and children, fertility, calamitous events, and their relationship to the environment in which they lived. Many healing practices undoubtedly addressed these types of concerns, along with broken bones and the specific, widespread diseases such as malaria, schistosomiasis (infection with a parasitic worm), and sleeping sickness that probably affected some inhabitants of the continent during the ancient time period.

As in modern times, diseases were closely connected to the environment in which humans lived on the African continent. Understanding the human inhabitants' natural and cultural environments is crucial to comprehending the experiences with health and disease that those humans had during the ancient era. The fact that humans and their biological ancestors have a long history of residence on the African continent probably means that the viruses, parasites, and other causes of diseases in humans have an equally long history on the continent. These diseases and their carriers have evolved in concert with the human populations that they infect. The natural environment—whether tropical forest, savanna grassland, or arid desert—shaped the nature of health and especially disease. Different conditions either did or did not lend themselves to specific diseases and other health concerns.

Water, as a direct carrier for diseases and as a breeding ground for other carriers of disease, especially mosquitoes, was a key part of the environment that directly affected Africans' ability to remain healthy. Malaria and schistosomiasis are both closely linked with the presence of bodies of water and were probably particularly prevalent in communities engaged in agriculture, especially agriculture involving irrigation. The absence of water, in the form of drought, was also a frequent health concern. In the search for a healthy balance with their environment, Africans probably used healing practices both to ensure enough water to support their lives and to treat illnesses associated with water-borne illnesses.

Africans also shaped their environments culturally in terms of their settlement patterns, their economic activities, and their beliefs and associated behaviors. These cultural environments created circumstances that helped reinforce the likelihood of health or disease. Many of the inhabitants of the African continent during this time period lived in relatively small groups that were often fairly mobile. These cultural characteristics meant that they were less subject to large-scale epidemics and other health concerns associated with bigger settlements and the domestication of plants and animals. On the other hand, their health was often a direct product of the unpredictable natural environment, which was sometimes unfriendly. Residents of the continent who depended on domesticated plants and animals may have had more protection from some of the vagaries of the natural environment, but they most likely also experienced more problems with malnutrition and the transmission of disease among humans and between animals and humans.

The study of human cultures and historical evidence suggests that African cultures tended not to compartmentalize health by separating it completely from other important activities and concerns. It seems reasonable to assume that many African cultures in ancient times had a similarly broad understanding of health and healing. Health tended to be thought of in physical, mental, and social terms. Healers who were sought out to treat diseases and physical ailments probably often provided other services, such as protection from witchcraft, magic to ensure success in hunting or agriculture, and medicines to protect infants from harm. The fact that healers frequently dealt with a wide range of issues signals the ways in which health blended together with issues of economics and politics as well as religion and spirituality. Sometimes the medicines and treatments were widely known by members of a particular society; in other cases, medicines and treatments were known only by specialist healers. Individuals with specialized healing knowledge often occupied positions of political and religious authority. Therefore, healers were important figures in many African societies during ancient times.

Healers seem to have practiced both imitative (or "sympathetic") and contagious magic, where certain magical acts are performed or formulas followed in the hope of effecting the desired end, whether it is to improve crops or heal illness. In sympathetic magic, for example, it is thought that acts performed on ritual objects (such as a doll that stands in for an actual person) will transfer to the person. Prehistoric art forms have been interpreted to indicate that art was part of the practice of imitative magic, designed to ensure the success of the hunt or other desired outcomes. In contagious magic it is thought that things or persons that have once been in contact can afterward influence each other. Along these lines, it seems likely that healing practices involved elements of imitative and contagious magic as well as detailed knowledge of the medicinal properties of locally available plants and minerals and other resources. These healing practices, supported by substantial knowledge, are indicative of the sorts of cultural responses to disease and ill health that would undoubtedly have been found on the African continent in ancient times. Humans on the continent sought to ensure their health and to treat diseases using a combination of spiritual and physical means.

In all, the physical and cultural environments shaped both health and disease for residents of the African continent during ancient times. Healing practices designed to ensure or to restore health responded to elements of nature as well as to social and cultural concerns. The diseases that afflicted human inhabitants at the time were also a product of the physical environment, which determined whether certain viruses or parasites existed to infect humans. Human activities, like agriculture or pastoralism, often altered the environment in certain ways that directly or indirectly helped spread or control certain diseases. Through cultural knowledge and cultural practices, inhabitants of the African continent in ancient times sought to maintain or restore health by focusing on a combination of balance with the environment, relationships with neighbors and ancestors, and personal illness.

EGYPT

BY CHRISTINE END

Mummies, artistic representations of human beings, and medical papyri all contribute to what Egyptologists know about the quality of health and hygiene in ancient Egypt. While examining mummies remains the most thorough means of investigating diseases and illnesses of the ancient Egyptians, protecting these irreplaceable time capsules of the ancient world is of paramount concern. Radiography, CT scanning, endoscopy, and small-scale tissue sampling are scientific methods of examining mummies with a minimal amount of damage.

Contrary to popular belief, ancient Egyptian physicians did not master the study of human anatomy. What was known of physiology was largely based on the butchery of animals. Many ancient Egyptian words for human body parts or concepts have a determinative (a hieroglyph that depicts the meaning of a word) showing animal's body parts following such words. The removal of organs by the embalmer during mummification was limited to a tiny opening in the flank of the deceased person and did not provide much visual anatomical information. Dissection of humans simply did not take place and was taboo. According to the histories of Diodorus Siculus, the man who made the mummification incision was ritually stoned after finishing his work, for defiling the body.

By modern standards ancient Egyptian life spans were relatively short. Living to the mid-30s was considered living to a good age, though some individuals (including the pharoah Ramses II of the 14th century B.C.E.) lived well into their eighties. Signs of arthritis and hardening of the arteries are apparent in mummies of older people; documented complaints relating to these conditions also survive. Infant mortality was high in ancient Egypt, and death during childbirth was common. Both pregnancy and menstruation appear to have been viewed with a certain amount of suspicion and considered unclean. Fertility problems, contraception, and pregnancy are topics discussed in the Kahun Medical Papyrus (dating to ca. 1900 B.C.E.) and the Berlin Papyrus (dating to the 1200s B.C.E.). Birth defects were common but not often depicted, aside from cases of dwarfism. Dwarfs were accepted, if not embraced by ancient Egyptian society.

Coffin with skeleton of a child, from Speos Artemidos, Egypt, Twenty-second Dynasty, around 850 B.C.E.; the skeleton shows clear signs of "brittle bone" disease. (© The Trustees of the British Museum)

According to physical and pictorial evidence, circumcision for males was common, possibly for reasons of hygiene. Circumcision appears to have taken place not in infancy but at an age just before puberty.

The Greek historian Herodotus, of the fifth century B.C.E., remarked on the general cleanliness of the ancient Egyptians. Washing the body with animal or vegetable oils and the mineral natron as "soap" was routine. Persons of the upper class would bathe in an indoor shower powered by servants who poured water over the bather's body. The commoners washed their bodies and clothing in the waters of the Nile. Perfumed oils applied to the body masked unwanted odors and was thought to promote youthful skin. The washing of clothing was also frequent; a clean, white outfit was the indication of high status. Funerary trappings portraying the deceased depict them in fine clothing of this type to perpetuate an elite appearance for all eternity.

Maladies and their causes varied. Sand brought about several physical ailments for the ancient Egyptians. The dental health of the Egyptians was enormously poor, owing to sand and not sugar. Teeth cleaning may have been done with twig "toothbrushes" or a cloth. Sand within food and particles of stone from stone-ground grains were the culprits in the wearing down of teeth. Over time, such wear would cause abscesses (a collection of pus and related inflammation) and infections. The eye makeup worn by men and women to help with the glare of the sun also had antiseptic properties to prevent infections of the eyes caused by blowing sand. Another result of sand in the air was pneumoconiosis, a disease of the lungs caused by inhalation of sand and other irritating particles.

The Egyptians suffered from skin ailments as well. Head lice found in the hair of mummies suggest that shaving the head and wearing wigs may have been an attempt to prevent this, but the Egyptians were also known to wear wigs over their natural hair. Shaving body hair may also have been practiced for hygienic reasons. Lice on the head or body would have caused rashes prone to infection from persistent scratching. Other conditions of the skin may have included the highly contagious smallpox. Smallpox may be the cause for the skin condition visible on the face of the mummy of King Ramses V (r. 1156–1151 B.C.E.).

Parasitic infection was a serious problem in ancient Egypt. The Nile's waters also harbored hookworms, guinea worms, and the schistosome worms. Ingesting these parasites or allowing them to gain entrance into the body by wading in the Nile or through contact with soil from the river, insects and animals harboring the worms, or an infected person were sources of much illness in the population of Egypt. Schistosomiasis, with symptoms ranging from fever and cough to fatigue, abdominal pain, and enlargement of the liver and spleen, is evident in the examination of ancient mummies. This disease is still a great problem to modern-day Egyptians who venture into the still areas of the Nile.

Other parasites came from the land. Feces, which was used as fertilizer, was also the source for parasitic illness in ancient Egypt. Hookworms, roundworms, and tapeworms transferred to humans via crops grown in manure. Heat can encourage the breeding of flies, thus promoting the spread of disease. The hot climate of Egypt also made a breeding ground for filarial worms, which can cause blindness in humans harboring the parasites.

Even the home could be an unsanitary environment. Overcrowded living quarters, sometimes shared with livestock, promoted the spread of such illnesses as tuberculosis. (Representations of humpbacked people may indicate sufferers of spinal tuberculosis.) Bedbugs and fleas were certainly frequent household pests, causing chronic skin irritations. Rodents invading household food storage were also responsible for spreading illness of all types, including plague.

Treatments for ill health took the form of a combination of prescribed medicines and magical rituals. Cures may have involved something as simple as wearing a magical amulet, or charm, in conjunction with taking a prescribed medicine. This dual physical and spiritual approach to health is especially apparent in the cases recorded in the London Papyrus (dating to the early 14th century B.C.E.).That both methods of treatment were contained in the one document suggests that the Egyptians did not consider either approach to be the sole cure. The occurrence of physical injury and first aid is the focus of the Edwin Smith Medical Papyrus (dating to the 1600s B.C.E.). This papyrus records the injuries of several laborers, including diagnoses of their injuries, decisions concerning whether they should be treated, and the prescribed course of treatment, if any.

THE MIDDLE EAST

BY MARKHAN J. GELLER

Our information about medicine in the ancient Middle East derives almost entirely from Babylonian sources. One of the noticeable differences between the Hippocratic medicine of Greece and Babylonian medicine is the lack of any texts dealing with diet and health regimens. While Greek medicine invested a great deal of interest in diet and exercise and ways to preserve one's good health, Babylonian medicine was primarily focused on how to treat or alleviate symptoms and distress caused by disease that had already been diagnosed. Disease, in Babylonian terms, could be either physical or psychic and could express itself through symptoms such as pain and fever and loss of appetite or through anxiety, insomnia, impotence, or other *maladies d'esprit*, or "illnesses of the soul."

One reason why Babylonian medicine did not address itself to health regimens or healthy living is that prevention was considered to be the bailiwick of magic and exorcism, rather than medicine. Incantations were essentially intended to ward off demons and misfortune that might arise in the future. Hence, Babylonian health therapy was divided between the activities of the *ashipu*, the "exorcist," and the *asû* the "physician," each operating within his own area of expertise though not in a way intuitively obvious to modern medical practitioners. The *ashipu* was responsible for magical prevention of attacks by demons, angry gods, or even witchcraft and unfavorable omens, but he also acted as the attending physician who visited the patient on his or her sickbed to give a prognosis, predicting the nature and course of the disease. The *ashipu* also had the social advantages of being a priest. The *asû*, on the other hand, was more of an apothecary who prepared the complicated recipes for healing treatments and drugs, though we have little information regarding his contacts with patients. As a layman, he had no access to the temple and presumably operated from a corner shop in the street or from his home.

The respective positions of these two health professionals affected their approach, to some extent. The *ashipu* operated primarily under the assumption that disease was ultimately caused by divine will or fate; the *asû*, while generally agreeing with this position, concentrated more on natural causes of symptoms (bites, excessive exposure to draughts or sunlight, kidney stones, and so on). In essence, magic focused on disease, while medicine concentrated on symptoms.

It is not particularly easy to classify diseases within Babylonian medicine, but they fall generally within categories similar to diseases within Hippocratic medicine. Some diseases are simply associated with parts of the body, such as head disease, tooth disease, eye disease, nose disease, and even foot disease as well as kidney disease and anus disease. Even baldness was treated as a disease. There were a variety of skin diseases, including rashes and pox, as well as leprosy-like conditions affecting the nose and mouth, but it is impossible to diagnose these conditions according to modern disease terminology.

Other diseases are listed as being "caused" by the hand of a particular god, with special attention being given to "Hand of the Ghost disease." Although the diseases may have, at one time, been thought to have originated from the actions of a particular god, ghost, or demon, by the time we see such terminology within Babylonian medical literature, these labels identify specific diseases, without much in the way of religious overtones.

Typical medical texts in the Babylonian medical literature often consist of a brief statement of the problem and a remedy. For urinary problems, one treatment stated that a man "should keep drinking one *sila*-measure of ash of the hoof of a spring lamb, one *sila* of ash of male mandrake, on an empty stomach in water for five days." This was thought to be curative. Medical literature from Babylonia always leaves the impression of being optimistic, in the sense that most medical remedies end with the positive statement that once the drugs are administered, the patient will recover from the illness. Such statements are hardly realistic, since other diagnostic texts, which list symptoms from many different types of diseases, often give a rather grim prognosis, saying that the patient will die or that the disease will persist for a time and then the patient will die. The Babylonian *Diagnostic Handbook* lists all symptoms from head to foot, in the following case also referring to symptoms associated with the urinary tract: "[If] his [urine] is red, it is the hand of his god, (his disease) will be prolonged; . . . [If] his [urine] is black, he is affected by the fatal disease, he will die; . . . [If] his urine is continually blocked up, he will die; if his urine keeps flowing, [he will die]."

The question often asked is whether any part of Babylonian medicine was actually effective. Did it work? Hundreds of drugs are cited in Babylonian medical recipes, in addition to long lists of plants and minerals used for medicinal purposes, often with descriptions of the drugs and the diseases for which they could be used. We have no idea, however, how such data was compiled, since there were no such things as clinical trials. How would ancient physicians know which plants were effective against which diseases? In the absence of any information, we can surmise that plants were identified over a very long period, perhaps going back to Neolithic times, and the use of such plants was determined by the hit-or-miss means of trying something to see what happens and then keeping careful records of the results. The crucial point was to remember, later on, if the drug seemed to work.

We have little evidence of surgery, since almost all medical texts deal with pharmacological preparations administered as potions, salves, ointments, fumigations, or suppositories or as drugs blown into the urethra or ears through bronze tubes. Surgery would have been dangerous without either proper antiseptics or anesthesia. Nor is there any evidence of bloodletting, an ancient remedy used in other cultures. For this reason, the Babylonian physician probably caused less harm to his patient than his colleagues in later medieval Europe.

ASIA AND THE PACIFIC

BY JUSTIN CORFIELD

In India the system of medicine using professional healers dates to at least 2000 B.C.E. and probably developed in China at about the same time. The earliest Indian literature, the Rig-Veda, mentions herbal and other remedies. It also accredits the divine twin gods known as the Asvins ("horsemen") with the power to heal the sick. Gradually the role of doctors came to be officially recognized.

Medical concepts appear in the Indian Vedas, dating back to the second millennium B.C.E. As early as 800 B.C.E., when many of these ideas were written down, treatments were listed for various diseases, along with "charms" that served to expel demons from the body—an early interpretation of the root of diseases. One writer attributes the origin of Indian medicine to the god Brahma, who gave the ideas to Dhanvantari, later deified as the god of medicine.

King Asoka, ruler of the Maurya Dynasty of eastern India, is reported to have founded some 18 hospitals throughout his kingdom in about 230 B.C.E. An inscription notes that Asoka "established gardens and hospitals for man and beast," suggesting that there were also veterinary clinics. Certainly, medical care in India was well advanced, and many medical treatises were published, including two attributed, respectively, to a physician called Caraka and a surgeon called Suśruta. The former treatise dates to the first century C.E. and the latter, in its present form, to the seventh century C.E., though parts of it are undoubtedly much older.

One of the major problems with Indian medicine was that Hindus were prevented by their religion from conducting surgery on dead bodies. This meant that they had a weak knowledge of internal organs, believing that bodies were made from spirit, phlegm, and bile, with health relying on the balance of the three substances. Medicines later took the form of herbal drugs, animal remedies, and even mineral concoctions. Drugs were often used to sedate patients, some of them made from such plant extracts as cardamom and cinnamon. In 2001 archaeologists found evidence from a burial ground in the Indus Valley that dentists had been at work in about 2000 B.C.E. and had managed to deal with problems in molar teeth. It is unknown exactly how they did this, but it is presumed that they used quite advanced dental hand drills.

China has had a long history of the use of medicine. Much of it was herbal, and many early treatises survive that describe the use of various herbs for curing particular diseases. The first emperor of China, Qin Shi Huang (r. 220–207 B.C.E.), ordered the "burning of the books" in 213 B.C.E. and particularly excluded works of a medical nature, showing the importance of them at that time. Indeed, he helped put together the major medical work the *Nei ching su wen* (Yellow Emperor's Classic of Internal Medicine). This treatise still forms the basis of many other Chinese medical tracts, such as the *Mo ching* (Pulse Classic), written in about 300 C.E.

Chinese medicine essentially relied on the dualist cosmic concepts of the yin and the yang—the "hot" and the "cold." The former is the female principle, represented by the earth; the latter, the male principle, is represented by the heavens. The body itself is made up of five elements, wood, fire, earth, metal, and water, which are associated with five planets. As with the Indians, most Chinese were forbidden by religious beliefs from dissecting dead bodies, and hence the knowledge of many diseases remained limited. However the *Nei ching* did refer to circulation of the blood, anticipating the discovery of the English physician and anatomist William Harvey by 13 centuries.

Chinese doctors traditionally relied heavily on herbal cures, especially using *Ephedra vulgaris* (mahuang), and *Cannabis sativa* (Indian hemp). The root ginseng has also been used in China, Korea, and Japan for many years. Early Chinese medical practices likewise included diet regimens, the use of mineral "cures," and acupuncture. Acupuncture has a history dating to 2500 B.C.E. and, it is thought, was discovered when several soldiers were hit by arrows in battle and found themselves cured of other ailments. The idea behind using needles inserted into various points in the body was essentially to free blocked energy, bringing the yin and yang back into balance. The needles would work on particular nerves or cause activity in another part of the body, which would allow the person's inbuilt defenses to cure the body naturally. Starting in about 180 B.C.E. hydrotherapy was also used, with cold baths serving as a cure for some fevers.

Mention should also be made of Chinese alchemy. The practice seems to have started at least as far back as the Warring States Period (the fifth to the third centuries B.C.E.); it was closely associated with the Daoist philosophical ideas of Laozi. One early alchemist, Ge Hong (382–343 B.C.E.), came up with a large number of potions from which to make elixirs. Some of the many mineral elixirs in ancient China were poisonous, and several emperors died from taking them in search of immortality.

The first-known hospital where patients were brought for treatment was developed by King Pandukabhaya during the fourth century B.C.E. in modern-day Sri Lanka. An ancient Sinhalese royal chronicle, the *Mahavansha*, records that the king established hospitals for ill people in parts of his lands and also at his capital, Anuradhapura. Many people believe that the Sri Lankan hospital at Mihintale may be the oldest in the world for which a site is known. Located in north-central Sri Lanka, near the city of Anuradhapura, the remains of the buildings have inscriptions on the walls showing that the institution had a bone and muscle specialist and also a leech doctor.

While Korean medical practices were similar to those in China, in Japan diagnoses were based on expelling evil spirits from the bodies of sufferers. Gradually, however, the Japanese began to follow Chinese medicine. Similarly, in Southeast Asia, many people used Chinese and Indian medicines and practices, and some doctors from China and India settled in the area. None of these practitioners were able to deal with what is thought to be the main cause of death in the region, malaria. Some Chinese and Indian medical practitioners may also have lived on various Pacific islands, but medical care in the Pacific remained well behind that on mainland Asia. Although ancient medical practices have long been dismissed by 19th-century and early-20th-century historians, archaeological work has unearthed a far more advanced state of medical treatment in India and China, as well as in other parts of Asia, than was previously thought to exist in ancient times.

EUROPE

BY MICHAEL J. O'NEAL

The health of the ancient Europeans was not especially good. Among prehistoric peoples life was precarious, a constant struggle against starvation, famine, accident, disease, and early death. And this state of affairs assumes that a person lived long enough to carry on the struggle. The rate of infant mortality was extremely high, with perhaps as many as a quarter of children either stillborn or dying shortly after birth and as many as a quarter more dying during their first year of life. Things were not much better for women, many of whom died while giving birth.

A person who survived the first year of life had a life expectancy much lower than life expectancies in the modern world. Archaeologists, for example, have discovered a burial pit in Austria that dates to the Bronze Age. The pit contains seven skeletons of people whose ages are estimated at three, six, eight, nine, 30, and 40, respectively. In Scotland an Iron Age burial chamber yielded skeletons of people estimated to have been 10, 19, 30, 35, 40, and 45, respectively; three additional skeletons were of people who were older than 45.

Throughout ancient Europe, living past age 40 would have been an unusual accomplishment.

Disease was rife among ancient Europeans, primarily as a result of poor hygiene combined with ignorance about the causes of disease and about bodily processes. Of course, infections were common, for people did not bathe or change and wash clothing very often, and they lived in close proximity to livestock and domesticated animals, along with their waste. Communicable diseases, such as smallpox and measles, were an ever-present threat, and infections from wounds could easily turn deadly. People suffered from a host of complaints, including intestinal parasites (often from unsanitary water and poor waste disposal), eye disorders, respiratory infections, and dental disease. All of these relatively simple complaints could have dire effects. Intestinal disorders, for example, could lead to diarrhea and consequent dehydration, shock, and death. Eye problems contributed to accidental injuries and death; at best, they severely limiting the sufferer's quality of life. Respiratory infections could turn into pneumonia, and tuberculosis was common. Dental disease made it difficult for older adults to chew food, with resulting consequences to their health.

Further, diets were not always well balanced, given that the availability of foodstuffs was dependent on the seasons. During the summer, fruits, vegetables (primarily roots and leafy vegetables), and berries would have been available, providing people with essential vitamins, but during the long winters people relied primarily on meat (preserved by salting or drying), dairy products from livestock, and stored grain. Some diseases were genetically based. One example is a disorder called Dupuytren's disease, a genetically transmitted deformity of the fingers. This disorder was relatively widespread among the ancient Scandinavians and later extended to the rest of Europe after the Viking invasions in the Common Era.

None of this is to say that the ancient Europeans did not make efforts to practice a form of medicine. One form of "medicine," of course, involved religious beliefs put into practice. To cure their disorders, people turned to the gods, usually enlisting the help of shamans (native healers) and priests, many of whom were thought to have magical powers. Examples of shrines, with replicas of human organs, suggest that people went to such shrines seeking cures. Another common practice was the sacrificing of an animal, such as a bull, to effect a cure. Also popular among the ancient Europeans were healing springs, including numerous springs in Gaul (modern-day France) and in Bath, England. People believed that the waters in these places had medicinal properties. In some respects, they may have been correct. The warm, soothing waters of these springs and baths undoubtedly provided at least some psychological benefits, giving the sufferer relief from pain and the will to get better.

Herbal remedies were also popular. Among the ancient Celts, for example, mistletoe was thought to have healing properties; in fact, mistletoe contains chemicals that have been shown to reduce blood pressure, and it is the basis of several modern-day homeopathic remedies. Ancient Roman historians who traveled in such places as Gaul wrote about the healing properties of various plants, including "*samolus*," "*selago*," and "*anguinum*," though modern historians have been unable to identify these plants. Celery and parsley were also thought to have medicinal properties.

In general, ancient Druid healers among the Celts were familiar with a wide range of plant substances that had beneficial health effects. Examples include the bark of the willow tree, which contains a substance that is chemically similar to the active ingredient in aspirin, though it caused a great deal of stomach pain because it was not "buffered," as modern aspirin is. They probably gathered these substances according to a strict schedule based on the phases of the moon, in the belief that all the powers of nature worked hand in hand. They were also familiar with poisons and thought that a poisonous plant was not harmful if it was picked with the left hand. In

Terra-cotta votive womb, Italy, 400–200 B.C.E.; such models of afflicted body parts were placed in healing sanctuaries throughout Italy. (© The Trustees of the British Museum)

many senses, these ancient healers functioned as experimental scientists, observing symptoms, trying herbal treatments, and assessing what seemed to help.

The ancient Europeans also practiced a form of surgery. Near Munich, Germany, archaeologists discovered the tomb of a "warrior-surgeon" that contained a number of medical and surgical implements. This tomb dates to about the third or early second century B.C.E. Among these instruments were probes, retractors, and a trepanning saw, or a saw used to cut holes in the skull. Trepanning was a widely used technique for treating head injuries and psychological disorders, and healers used both saws and drills to make their holes. A large number of skulls have been found that have neat holes drilled or cut into them. While many people died during this type of surgery, a surprising number did not, for the holes in some skulls show evidence of healing. Trepanning evolved from the notion that the health of the body was based on a balance of substances. Allowing substances that caused ill health to escape the body could, it was believed, lead to a cure. For the same reason, blood-letting (opening a vein to let blood flow out) was a common early practice.

GREECE

BY TOM STREISSGUTH

Asclepios reigned in ancient Greece as the god of health and medicine. According to Greek myth, Asclepios was the son of Apollo and was taught the arts of healing and surgery by the centaur Chiron. His daughter Hygieia was the goddess of cleanliness and good health; his daughter Panaceia was the goddess of healing. In ancient Greece the *asclepeion* was a sanctuary built to honor Asclepios and as a health retreat, to treat the sick and the injured. There were *asclepia* in Athens, Corinth, Trikkala, Pergamon, Kos, and Epidauros in the Peloponnesus, the traditional center of the cult. Asclepia were also built in distant Greek colonies and throughout the Mediterranean region. Patients arrived to receive the god's blessing through healing waters and treatment, through offerings at the temple altar, and through the interpretation of their dreams by the priests of the sanctuary. The fame of the healing god spread to the early republic of Rome, where sanctuaries were built in imitation of the Greek *asclepeion*. On the outbreak of a plague in the early third century B.C.E., the Romans appealed directly for his services. The Greeks responded by sending the god in the form of a snake; in many depictions of the god, a snake adorns the Rod of Asclepius. This symbol of the healing arts survives in medical emblems to the present day.

Traditional Greek medicine relied on the use of herbs and other natural remedies and on incantation and prayer to the gods. Greek medicine began to pass from religious belief to scientific observation at a school of medicine at Cnidus in the seventh century B.C.E. Historians believe that Egyptian medicine, which had some supernatural elements and which prescribed very strict courses of treatment for every occurrence of a disease, had an important influence on the early medical practices of the Greeks. (The skill of Egyptian healers and the power of their medicines are mentioned in the *Odyssey* of Homer.)

Alcmaeon (fl. sixth century B.C.E.), a member of the school of Cnidus, was the first Greek to set down in writing his observations of the human body. His surgical experiments led to the first rational debates over the structure and functions of the human body. On performing the first eye operations, Alcmaeon theorized that the brain was the seat of memory, thought, and emotion. Empedocles (fl. fifth century B.C.E.), a philosopher from the island of Sicily, advanced the notion of the four elements—earth, air, fire, and water—and extended this idea to the human body in the four "humors." The Greeks believed that a combination of four elements, or humors, made up an essential balance within the human body. The humors originated in the physical location of the person and the place of his or her birth, with the ideal balance being found in the civilized people of the Greek world. The humors were blood, phlegm, yellow bile, and black bile. Through their proportions, the humors shaped the human intellect and personality and also affected life's physical existence from birth to maturity and on to old age and death. A balance of the humors was needed to keep the body free of disease, and achieving or repairing that balance was the task of a physician. A patient suffering from disease could be put right by purging, by bloodletting, or by some other method of relieving the body of a humor found to be in excess.

The theory of the four humors was followed by Hippocrates (460–377 B.C.E.), the most renowned Greek physician. Hippocrates was a native of the island of Cos who founded a new school of medical practice, which for a time became the most important center of healing in the Greek world. Using case histories, Hippocrates took a scientific approach to disease, discarding religious superstitions and investigating causes, symptoms, and *physis*, or the overall state of the body, including its inner functioning as well as environmental effects. In dealing with their patients, physicians at Cos carried out observation, diagnosis, prognosis, and treatment—the basic elements of clinical medicine that survive to this day. They discarded the Egyptian notion of strictly prescribed treatment; all patients were considered individually through careful observation and treated accordingly.

Medical students at Cos served a paid apprenticeship of several years, which involved classroom teaching, study of medical texts, and observation and treatment of patients. The most enduring product of the school was the *Corpus Hippocraticum*, a collection of essays by several authors that described case histories and accounts of treatment. This work included essays on nutrition, surgery, and obstetrics, as well as the Hippocratic oath, a lengthy instruction on proper care and treatment of patients that survives as the foundation of modern medical treatment and ethics.

After the conquest of North Africa by Alexander of Macedon (r. 356–323 B.C.E.) and the founding of Alexandria

Ivory figure of a hunchback thought to show signs of Pott's disease, Hellenistic, about first century B.C.E. (© The Trustees of the British Museum)

by his general Ptolemy, the seat of medical research moved to this new city on the Mediterranean coast, which attracted scholars and physicians from all over the Greek world. Famous Alexandrian medical scholars include Herophilus, who lived in the early third century B.C.E. Herophilus investigated the eye and brain and deduced the usefulness of the pulse in the diagnosis of disease. His written work on the topic of dissection (which has not survived) described his study of human anatomy. A contemporary of Herophilus, Erasistratus, made a famous study of the brain, nerves, arteries, and veins and went further than Herophilus in understanding the structure of the brain and the nervous system.

The theory of the humors was further advanced by Galen, a physician of Pergamum (129–200 C.E.) in Asia Minor, who was renowned for his public dissection of pigs, apes, dogs, and goats. His works include *On the Elements according to Hippocrates* and a work in 17 volumes, *On the Usefulness of the Parts of the Body.* Galen explored the nervous system and the spinal cord, demonstrated the function of the veins and arteries, and showed that urine originated in the kidneys. Galen's works circulated widely in the Arab-speaking and Persian-speaking world as well as in Europe, where physicians relied on his theories and practices for the next 1,500 years.

ROME

BY BROOKE HOLMES

The Romans considered health to be both a private and a public affair. The majority of responsibility for maintaining health rested with the individual and the family, and patients had access to a range of options in their pursuit of health, depending on their location and their resources. The health of the populace also benefited from the construction and maintenance of public aqueducts, sewers, latrines, and baths. Official interest in public health, however, was largely restricted to the army.

Life was precarious in the ancient Roman world. The average life expectancy at birth was about 25 years of age, and infant mortality rates were high. The risk of death remained serious during the child's first year, although those who survived had better odds thereafter, with a life expectancy extended into their thirties and forties. The analysis of skeletal remains has shown that environmental and demographic factors determined the unique disease profiles of individual settlements. Dental health, for example, could be affected by fluoride levels in the water, and low-lying areas were prone to malaria. Poor sanitation, particularly in the overcrowded areas of Rome, fostered the spread of ailments such as diarrhea, pneumonia, jaundice, parasites (such as tapeworm), and infections of the liver, bladder, and kidney.

Malnutrition, caused by an irregular food supply, posed a serious threat everywhere, affecting poor women and children particularly hard. Childbirth, too, exacted a heavy toll on women. For Romans who survived past their twenties, degenerative diseases such as arthritis would have made later life difficult and painful, and chronic pain was a problem at any age, especially for slaves and free laborers. Roman remedies are considered largely ineffective by modern standards, though they may have had a placebo effect. Patients may have improved because of their positive expectations rather than as a result of the remedies themselves.

In the early Roman Republic, the health of the household, both free persons and slaves, was overseen by the paterfamilias, the male head of the family. The remedies recommended by Cato the Elder (234–149 B.C.E.), who wrote in this tradition, are primarily herbal and magical, drawn from Italic folk medicine. Cato saw medicine as an internal affair that did not require professional expertise. He was writing, however, at a time when Romans were becoming Hellenized, that is, more Greek, following their military conquests across the Mediterranean and the influx of Greek ideas, goods, and persons into Rome. A vocal critic of these changes, Cato's defense of traditional medicine coincided with a denunciation of professional Greek physicians as greedy and even murderous. Cato's remedies nevertheless show his familiarity with Greek medicine.

Ambivalence characterizes the Roman experience with Greek medicine. In 293 B.C.E., after three years of plague, the Roman Senate summoned the healing god Aesculapius from his shrine in Epidaurus, in the Greek Peloponnese. According to the myth, the god traveled in the form of a snake to Rome and promptly ended the plague. His cult was established on Tiber Island, where the river Tiber takes a double bend through the city of Rome, and later spread throughout the Roman world, attracting patients from all backgrounds. Romans also continued to appeal to the healing gods of their native pantheon and patronize older shrines, such as that of Diana Nemorensis at Nemi in central Italy, established perhaps as early as the eighth century B.C.E. about 16 miles from Rome.

The first mortal Greek doctor, Archagathus (later known as Caecilius of Calacte), who arrived in Rome in 219 B.C.E. on the invitation of the Roman Senate, did not assimilate as easily. He was granted citizenship, and a practice was set up with public funds. Soon, however, his harsh techniques earned him the nickname "the executioner," and he left Rome. Greek medicine found a more successful representative in Asclepiades of Bithynia (fl. ca. 120–50 B.C.E.). Asclepiades arrived in Rome toward the end of the second century B.C.E. and gained renown for his gentle therapies. His teachings were modified by his student Themison of Laodicea (fl. ca. 50 B.C.E.), who identified three causes of disease, called the commonalities: "tightness" in the body, "looseness," and a mixture of the two; the physician simply noted the state of the patient's body and prescribed the appropriate cure. His ideas were elaborated in the next century by Thessalus of Tralles, the founder of the "Methodist" school of medicine, which essentially saw disease as an imbalance of solid particles and spaces in the body. By this time Greek medicine was well established in Rome. Julius Caesar had granted citizenship to all physicians in 49 B.C.E., and the emperor Augustus exempted them from taxes in 23 B.C.E. Yet while many elite men consulted physicians, they continued to value self-sufficiency, and the care of the body was an important component in Roman practices of self-mastery.

Altar from Roman Britain (second century C.E.) dedicated to the goddess Fortuna (who set life's course), the healing god Aesculapius, and Salus, goddess of health. (© The Trustees of the British Museum)

While the Methodist school was popular at Rome, practitioners competed for patients with physicians loyal to medical doctrines developed in Hellenistic Alexandria. Empiricists believed that physicians should rely on past experiences with a disease when determining the proper response to symptoms. Others, called Dogmatists by their adversaries, argued that the physician needed knowledge of the human body and the hidden causes of disease to treat patients successfully. Galen of Pergamum (129–200 C.E.) brought the theory and practice of medicine together. He was an expert anatomist, well versed in philosophical debates about health and disease, the emperor Marcus Aurelius's personal physician, and a prodigious writer. Galen's version of medicine, which developed Hippocratic ideas about the importance of balance between humors, elemental fluids inside the body, influenced Byzantine, Arabic, and medieval Western medicine.

Imperial expansion brought physicians into contact with new medicaments and herbs. Exotic substances were in high demand as both remedies, such as mithridatium, a drug composed of thirty-seven different ingredients, and cosmetics. The most famous treatise on pharmacology, or the study of drugs, was written in Greek in 64 C.E. by Pedanius Dioscorides of Anazarbus (fl. ca. 40–90 C.E.). His five-book *De materia medica* is an attempt to provide a complete list of known medicinal substances, organized according to their effects. Dioscorides' work was consulted for the next 1,500 years.

The Roman army benefited from some of the most advanced medical care under the empire. With the establishment of a permanent military presence on the frontiers, care became more institutionalized. Production of Greco-Roman surgical instruments sharply increased in the first century C.E., and many of the new fortresses included hospitals. Civilians had no equivalent until Christians in the east began to establish shelters for the poor, the sick, and travelers, which spread under the emperor Julian in the third century C.E.

The organization of the Roman household did not observe basic principles of sanitation. Latrines were often situated in kitchens; wells were dug near cesspits. Public works projects made the city cleaner but did not always improve hygiene. Rome's sewer system, the Cloaca Maxima, was first laid out in the sixth century B.C.E. by the Etruscans and covered in the third century B.C.E. The statesman Marcus Agrippa (64–12 B.C.E.) directed extensive repairs to the system in 33 B.C.E. and had it paved and vaulted. Sewage emptying into the Tiber was, however, a source of pollution for those downstream and could back up with changes to the water level.

Although water from the aqueducts provided residents with a relatively safe water supply, opportunities for contamination remained—some as a result of the use of lead pipes. Aqueducts also supplied public latrines and baths. Across the empire, baths were popular social hubs. Physicians also prescribed them for their patients, and medical services, massages, and beauty treatments would have been available onsite. While they were unhygienic by modern standards, the baths ensured a relatively high level of cleanliness in the population.

THE AMERICAS

BY KIRK H. BEETZ

Of the many controversies involving the interpretation of ancient American history, the matter of health and disease is one of the most heatedly debated, more because of what the history may mean to modern politics and society than what it may mean in terms of the actual archaeological evidence. At present historians believe that syphilis originated in the Americas, and there is skeletal evidence that indicates that syphilis afflicted ancient Mayans by 1000 B.C.E. Still, a minority of archaeologists suggest that syphilis already existed in Europe when Columbus reached America in 1492, though documents indicate a spread of syphilis from Columbus' home port in Spain through Spain and then to the rest of Europe. What gives the debate its heat is the notion that someone is to blame for the disease, an issue that matters nothing to the facts of the disease itself.

Not as contentious an issue is the origin of tuberculosis. This disease seems to have afflicted ancient Americans as well as people in the Old World; its DNA has been found in naturally mummified corpses in Peru dating from the 900s C.E., and lesions are evident on lungs of ancient peoples. Some archaeologists argue that the disease could have started in only one place or the other and thus disagree about whether tuberculosis began in the Old World or the New World. One possibility is that tuberculosis was carried into the Americas by people during one of the ancient migrations from northeast Asia into Alaska. Another is that it was carried by an unknown contact between ancient Americans and Asians or Europeans. Perhaps the likeliest possibility is that tuberculosis first developed in rodents and eventually developed into a disease that could pass from rodents to humans in both the New World and the Old World, perhaps at different times.

Many severe diseases developed in the Old World that were unknown in the New World until the coming of Columbus, but ancient Americans were afflicted various diseases anyway. There were vitamin deficiencies, especially of vitamin C. Some North Americans of the Southwest learned to eat wild garlic cloves to treat the problem, but it seems to have afflicted Mayans without successful treatment. Other vitamin deficiencies caused poor tooth enamel growth, a problem detected by archaeologists more among ancient Mesoamericans than among other ancient Americans. By 7000 B.C.E. Chagas disease affected early settlers in the Andes. Chagas, a disease that leads to fever and swelling of the lymph glands and can progress to serious nervous system and heart damage, among other symptoms, is caused by a protozoan and carried from host to host by mosquitoes. The protozoan burrows into body tissues, eventually overwhelming the body and causing death. About 41 percent of tested mummies from about 7000 B.C.E. had the disease. Another disease was yaws, a tropical skin infection that causes infection of the skin, bones, and joints.

Some of the health problems suffered by ancient Americans were caused by their own activities. For instance, archaeologists have reported throughout the Americas that ancient Americans had trouble disposing of human waste. From large settlements in North America to South America, communities were troubled by the buildup of human waste, though after the ancient era some cultures developed sewer systems. Archaeologists debate the cause of the collapse of Mayan cities, and one theory is that disease made their cities unlivable, forcing them out of lowland cities into highland cities and then out of cities altogether. Poor disposal of human waste is often cited as a possible source of diseases of the skin that would make life in the cities unbearable. Further, poor disposal of waste may have attracted animal carriers of disease. American rodents carried, for example, viruses that could attack human hearts and cause severe fevers. Poor nutrition may have resulted from expanding human populations that put too much stress on the land's ability to provide enough food for everyone, which would have resulted in vitamin-deficiency diseases. Studies of Mayan skeletons indicate that prior to 400 B.C.E. Mayans were taller than those after 400 B.C.E., which may indicate poor nutrition caused by overpopulation after 400 B.C.E.

The ways in which ancient Americans dealt with their health problems are best known for the regions of the Andes, Central America, eastern North America, and southwestern North America. The peoples of southwestern North America may have been influenced by the cultures of Mesoamerica. The use of smoke for curative power seems to be very old in ancient American cultures. A large smokehouse dating to about 3700 B.C.E. has been found in Canada. At its center was a large hearth. Inhaling fumes thick with smoke may have been thought to cure breathing diseases and perhaps skin diseases. The Mayans seem to have been using smoke for similar purposes by 650 B.C.E. An ill person would be cloaked in smoke, which was supposed to draw the disease out of the body. Sweat houses were also used by Mayans because it was thought that the sweating caused by heat would carry poisons out of the body.

Other cures and treatments came from plants. In North America it is likely that shamans, or native healers, had practical knowledge of how to use certain plants to treat illnesses. Headaches could be treated with powdered Indian turnips and upset stomachs with a drink of boiled mint. A therapy for asthma might have been powdered skunk cabbage root. Even tuberculosis seems to have had a treatment, the eating of black nightshade. A salve from yarrow could be used to treat cuts. Energy could be recovered by eating the peyote cactus. In Mesoamerican cultures herbs were used to treat illnesses, and surgery was used to amputate diseased bones. In the Museum of the Bank of the Pacific in Ecuador is a sculpture showing a man chewing coca; it dates from about 1500 B.C.E. Coca was probably used to renew energy.

In ancient American cultures disease was not only physical but also spiritual. Some ancient Americans may have believed that diseases resulted from the loss of part of the soul. A shaman would "suck in" the missing part of the soul and blow it back into the patient. Often, diseases were thought to be spiritual poisons. In North America and Central America eggs were passed over a patient's body to suck out the spiritual poison. The egg would then contain the poison and would be disposed of. Ancient Mayans would place the egg underground.

In Central America caves were thought to be sources of illness. Breezes from the caves were believed to carry diseases to humans. Thus, placing charms at the entrances of caves might prevent the spread of disease by keeping it contained in the caves. On the other hand, a patient might have been treated in a cave, perhaps to send his or her illness back into the cave. Among the Maya, shamans engaged in "earth magic," using crystals in their healing rituals, probably as a way to draw on the power of the earth from which the crystals had come.

See also AGRICULTURE; ART; CALENDARS AND CLOCKS; CITIES; CLIMATE AND GEOGRAPHY; DEATH AND BURIAL PRACTICES; ECONOMY; EMPIRES AND DYNASTIES; FAMILY; FOOD AND DIET; NATURAL DISASTERS; NOMADIC AND PASTORAL SOCIETIES; PANDEMICS AND EPIDEMICS; RELIGION AND COSMOLOGY; SACRED SITES; SETTLEMENT PATTERNS; SOCIAL ORGANIZATION.

The Middle East

Tabu-utul-Bêl: "Ludlul Bêl Nimeqi," ca. 1700 B.C.E.

I advanced in life; I attained to the allotted span.
Wherever I turned there was evil, evil—
Oppression is increased, uprightness I see not.
I cried unto god, but he showed not his face.

I prayed to my goddess, but she raised not her head.
The seer by his oracle did not discern the future
Nor did the enchanter with a libation illuminate my case.
I consulted the necromancer, but he opened not my understanding.
The conjurer with his charms did not remove my ban.

How deeds are reversed in the world!
I look behind, oppression encloses me.
Like one who the sacrifice to god did not bring
And at meal-time did not invoke the goddess
Did not bow down his face, his offering was not seen; . . .

Into my prison my house is turned.
Into the bonds of my flesh are my hands thrown;
Into the fetters of myself my feet have stumbled.

With a whip he has beaten me; there is no protection;
With a staff he has transfixed me; the stench was terrible!
All day long the pursuer pursues me,
In the night watches he lets me breathe not a moment
Through torture my joints are torn asunder;

My limbs are destroyed, loathing covers me;
On my couch I welter like an ox
I am covered, like a sheep, with my excrement.
My sickness baffled the conjurers
And the seer left dark my omens.

The diviner has not improved the condition of my sickness—
The duration of my illness the seer could not state;
The god helped me not, my hand he took not;
The goddess pitied me not, she came not to my side
The coffin yawned; they [the heirs] took my possessions;

While I was not yet dead, the death wail was ready.
My whole land cried out: "How is he destroyed!"
My enemy heard; his face gladdened
They brought as good news the glad tidings, his heart rejoiced.
But I knew the time of all my family. . . .
This is the dream which I saw by night:

[He who made woman] and created man,
Marduk, has ordained that he be encompassed with sickness. . . .

He said: "How long will he be in such great affliction and distress?
What is it that he saw in his vision of the night?"
In the dream Ur-Bau appeared
A mighty hero wearing his crown

A conjurer, too, clad in strength,
Marduk indeed sent me;
Unto Shubshi-meshri-Nergal he brought abundance;
In his pure hands he brought abundance.
By my guardian-spirit he stopped,"

By the seer he sent a message:
"A favorable omen I show to my people." . . .

He sent a storm wind to the horizon;
To the breast of the earth it bore a blast
Into the depth of his ocean the disembodied spirit vanished;
Unnumbered spirits he sent back to the underworld. . . .

The sea-flood he spread with ice;
The roots of the disease he tore out like a plant.
The horrible slumber that settled on my rest
Like smoke filled the sky. . .
With the woe he had brought, unrepulsed and bitter, he filled the earth like a storm.

The unrelieved headache which had overwhelmed the heavens
He took away and sent down on me the evening dew.
My eyelids, which he had veiled with the veil of night
He blew upon with a rushing wind and made clear their sight.
My ears, which were stopped, were deaf as a deaf man's

He removed their deafness and restored their hearing.
My nose, whose nostril had been stopped from my mother's womb—
He eased its deformity so that I could breathe.
My lips, which were closed he had taken their strength—
He removed their trembling and loosed their bond.

My mouth which was closed so that I could not be understood—
He cleansed it like a dish ; he healed its disease.
My eyes, which had been attacked so that they rolled together—
He loosed their bond and their balls were set right.
The tongue, which had stiffened so that it could not be raised

He relieved its thickness, so its words could be understood.
The gullet which was compressed, stopped as with a plug—
He healed its contraction, it worked like a flute.
My spittle which was stopped so that it was not secreted—
He removed its fetter, he opened its lock.

From: George A. Barton, *Archaeology and the Bible*, 3rd ed. (Philadelphia: American Sunday School, 1920), pp. 392–395.

Asia and the Pacific

The Yin Fu Ching, *or Clue to the Unseen, excerpts* *ca. 1200* B.C.E.

To observe the TAO of Heaven, and grasp its method of operation, is the limit of all achievement.

The root of Heaven is in TAO; and TAO being fixed, Heaven secures it and so brings about its transmutations. Principles have their root in circumstances, or facts; and facts being determined, it is Principles by which they are modified or varied. Thus Principles have no unvarying course, and facts no essential uniformity; both belong to the region of the unlimited. It is only by observing the TAO of Heaven, and grasping that, that the limit can be reached.

Thus Heaven has Five Despoilers: and he who perceives them will flourish.

There is no benefit intended towards man when the Five Atmospheric Influences are set in motion; how, then, can there be any intentional injury to things? Observing the nourishing and beneficial results of these Influences, men call it virtue; observing the injury and ruin they cause, men call it spoliation. As soon as we see a thing produced, it is destroyed; and having witnessed its destruction, we see it come into being again. The Afflatus of the East is antagonistic to the Centre; the Afflatus of the Centre is antagonistic to the North; the

(continued)

(continues)

Afflatus of the North is antagonistic to the South; the Afflatus of the South is antagonistic to the West; the Afflatus of the West is antagonistic to the East. When these Five Afflati promote the growth of one another, they move freely; but the very ease with which they flow leads to their exhaustion. When they act in antagonism to each other, their motion is arrested; but if such arrest be counteracted, they are re-established [in their course]. Man is in the centre of Heaven [and Earth]; the heart is in the centre of man. When anything occupies a central position, it may be removed to the outside. If one wishes to control much by means of a little, it is necessary to use contrivances—or, to employ one's faculty of contrivance—in manipulating the material under one's hand. Nevertheless, let the mind be once set in motion, everything under Heaven may be accomplished; while by using antagonistic agencies, that which is complete and permanent may be produced. . . .

When Heaven sends forth its engines of destruction, the stars are moved out of their places and the constellations metamorphosed. When Earth sends forth its engines of destruction, dragons and snakes appear on the dry land. When Man puts forth his faculties of destruction, Heaven falls and Earth is overthrown. When Heaven and Man do so in concert, all the disorganised phenomena are re-established on a new basis.

The stars and constellations are the countenance of Heaven. In like manner, when a man is angry, his countenance will surely change. Dragons and serpents are the breath and blood [the hidden agencies] of earth. In like manner, when a man is sick, his breath and blood will surge up, or overflow. Man, situated in the centre of the Universe, is as it were the abdomen of Heaven and Earth. When the viscera are injured, the effects are manifest from top to toe; everything, from the head down to the feet, is thrown into disorder. When Earth is in harmony with Heaven, Man occupies the same relation towards each. For Heaven to respond to human requirements, or affairs, it is necessary to wait until such affairs be brought to a state of completion. If any one such affair be uncompleted, even the Sage will be unable to undertake its achievement; but when it is perfected—in such a forward state as to be prepared for the co-operation or assistance of Heaven—the response of Heaven will come. . . . This may be compared to the capture of Wu by the Prince of Yueh.

The Five Despoilers pertain to the Heart, but their operation is diffused all over the world. The Universe is in one's Hand; all transmutations take their rise from the body.

Thieves, or despoilers, are so called because they are unseen; if, in acting as thieves, they are perceived, their depredations are put an end to. The antagonism which exists between Water and Fire is turned to advantage when brought into contact with matter, and eventual welfare is the result. The Five Despoilers of Heaven are identical with the Five Despoilers of men. These Five Despoilers residing in the human heart, their agency is diffused far and wide; but is Heaven within the range of my—[i.e., any man's—activity]? Now cooperation implies the same object being held in view by two persons. If the other man acts, it is as though I myself acted; just, for instance, as in riding,—the rider is identified with his horse; and where the horse arrives the rider arrives too. Therefore a journey of a thousand li may be said to be held in the hollow of one's hand; for if a desire arises in the mind to go, say, from Yen in the north to Yueh in the south, you will be able to reach your destination supposing you make proper use of your intellectual faculties. . . .

The Abuse of the Nine Openings of the Body having specially to do with the Three which are most important, action and rest are both possible.

The Nine Openings are, all of them, the organs of intelligent perception; even those which have least capacity serving as passages for air. Eight of these openings are channels for the exercise of sagacity; it is only the private part behind, which is without any such faculty. The implication [in the text] that they are all liable to misuse, is simply made as applying to the majority, [the one exception] being wrongly included for the sake of convenience. But it is the Ear, the Eye, and the Mouth, which are the most liable to deception and abuse; therefore their action should be confined within certain limits, and subjected to the will of their owner. Then they may be made to act and abstain from action; by which means the body may be nourished and provision made [for any exigencies that may arise].

The diseases to which men are subject are the result of abuse. It is only the Sage who knows how to value this abuse [of the bodily organs], for, when it becomes violent, it is only the Sage who is able to hinder its operation. Then [the man's] action becomes in accord with the principle Yang, and his repose in accord with the principle Yin; [the man himself] developing mental powers of superhuman excellence.

From: Frederic Henry Balfour, *Taoist Texts: Ethical, Political, and Speculative* (London: Trubner, 1884).

Greece

Galen: Medicine, ca. mid-second century C.E.

There are in all three branches of the study of medicine, in this order. The first is the study of the result by analysis; the second is the combining of the facts found by analysis; the third is the determining of the definition, which branch we are now to consider in this work. This branch of the science may be called not only the determining of the definition but just as well the explication, as some would term it, or the resolution, as some desire, or the explanation, or according to still others, the exposition. Now some of the Herophilii, such as Heraclides of Erythrea, have attempted to teach this doctrine. These Herophilii and certain followers of Erasistratus and of Athenaeus, the Attalian, studied also the doctrine of combination. But no one before us has described the method which begins with the study of the results, from which every art must take its beginning methodically; this we have considered in a former work.

Chapter 1. Medicine is the science of the healthy, the unhealthy, and the indeterminate, or neutral. It is a matter of indifference whether one calls the second the ill, or the unhealthy. It is better to give the name of the science in common than in technical terms. But the healthy, the unhealthy, the neutral, are each of them subject to a threefold-division: first, as to the body; second, as to the cause; and third, as to the sign. The body which contains the health, the cause which affects or preserves the health, and the sign or symptom which marks the condition of the health, all these are called by the Greeks *hygienia*. In the same way they speak of the bodies susceptible to disease, of causes effecting and aiding diseases, and of signs indicating diseases, as pathological. Likewise they speak of neutral bodies, causes, and signs. And according to the first division the science of medicine is called the science of the causes of health; according to the second, of the causes of ill health; and according to the third, of the causes of neutral conditions.

Chapter 2. The healthy body is simply that which is rightly composed from its very birth in the simple and elementary parts of its structure, and is symmetrical in the organs composed of these elements. From another point of view, that is also a healthy body which is in sound condition at the time of speaking.

From: Oliver J. Thatcher, ed., *The Library of Original Sources*. Vol. 3, *The Roman World* (Milwaukee, Wis.: University Research Extension Co., 1907): pp. 286–292.

Greece

Hippocrates: Aphorisms, ca. fifth century B.C.E.

Section I.

1. Life is short, art is long, occasion sudden, experiment dangerous, judgment difficult. Neither is it sufficient that the physician do his office, unless the patient and his attendants do their duty and external conditions are well ordered.

6. In extreme diseases extreme and searching remedies are best.

13. Old men easily endure fasting, middle-aged men not so well, young men still less easily, and children worst of all, especially those who are of a more lively spirit.

14. Those bodies that grow have much natural heat, therefore they require good store of food or else the body consumes, but old men have little heat in them; therefore they require but little food, for much nourishment extinguishes that heat. And this is the reason that old men do not have very acute fevers, because their bodies are cold.

20. Those things that are or have been justly determined by nature ought not to be moved or altered, either by purging or other irritating medicine, but should be let alone.

Section II.

4. Neither satiety nor hunger nor any other thing which exceeds the natural bounds can be good or healthful.

51. It is dangerous much and suddenly either to empty, heat, fill, or cool, or by any other means to stir the body, for whatever is beyond moderation is an enemy to nature, but that is safe which is done little by little, and especially when a change is to be made from one thing to another.

Section III.

1. Changes of seasons are most effectual causes of diseases, and so are alterations of cold and heat within

(continued)

(continues)

the seasons, and other things proportionately in the same manner.

Section IV.

37. Cold sweats in acute fevers signify death, but in more mild diseases they mean the continuance of the fever.

38. In what part of the body the sweat is there is the disease.

39. And in what part of the body there is unusual heat or cold there the disease is seated.

Section VII.

65. The same meat administered to a person sick of a fever as to one in health will strengthen the healthy one but will increase the malady of the sick one.

Section VIII.

6. Where medicines will not cure incision must be made; if incisions fail, we must resort to cauterizing; but if that will not do we may judge the malady incurable.

18. The finishing stroke of death is when the vital heat ascends above the diaphragm and all the moisture is dried up. But when the lungs and heart have lost their moisture, the heat being all collected together in the most mortal places, the vital fire by which the whole structure was built up and held together is suddenly exhaled. Then the soul leaving this earthly building makes its exit partly through the flesh and partly through the openings in the head, by which we live; . . . thus it surrenders up this cold earthly statue, together with the heat, blood, tissues, and flesh.

From: Oliver J. Thatcher, ed., *The Library of Original Sources*. Vol. 3, *The Roman World* (Milwaukee, Wis.: University Research Extension Co., 1907): pp. 286–292.

FURTHER READING

Bob Brier, *Ancient Egyptian Mummies: Unraveling the Secrets of an Ancient Art* (New York: William Morrow, 1994).

Aidan Cockburn and Eve Cockburn, eds., *Mummies, Disease, and Ancient Cultures* (Cambridge, U.K.: Cambridge University Press, 1980).

Audrey Cruse, *Roman Medicine* (Stroud, U.K.: Tempus, 2004).

Rosalie David and Rick Archbold, *Conversations with Mummies* (New York: William Morrow, 2000).

Paul Ghalioungui, *The Physicians of Pharaonic Egypt* (Mainz, Germany: Zabern, 1983).

Rebecca Green, ed., *History of Medicine* (New York: Haworth Press, 1988).

Ralph Jackson, *Doctors and Diseases in the Roman Empire* (Norman: University of Oklahoma Press, 1988).

Helen King, *Greek and Roman Medicine* (Bristol. U.K.: Duckworth, 2001).

Charles Leslie, ed., *Asian Medical Systems: A Comparative Study* (Delhi, India: Motilal Banarsidass Publishers, 1998).

G. E. R Lloyd, *In the Grip of Disease: Studies in the Greek Imagination* (New York: Oxford University Press, 2003).

James Longrigg, *Greek Medicine: From the Heroic to the Hellenistic Age* (New York: Routledge, 1998).

Guido Majno, *The Healing Hand: Man and Wound in the Ancient World*, rpt. ed. (Cambridge, Mass.: Harvard University Press, 1991).

Jyotir Mitra, *History of Indian Medicine from Pre-Mauryan to Kusaṅa Period* (Varanasi, India: Jyotiralok Prakashan, 1974).

John F. Nunn, *Ancient Egyptian Medicine* (Norman: University of Oklahoma Press, 1996).

Vivian Nutton, *Ancient Medicine* (London and New York: Routledge, 2004).

Priya Vrat Sharma, *Indian Medicine in the Classical Age* (Varanasi, India: Chowkhamba Sanskrit Series Office, 1972).

► household goods

INTRODUCTION

The household goods of ancient peoples were in general made of nondurable materials, so few of these goods, other than those made of metal and, to a lesser extent, clay pottery, survive. Archaeologists know about the kinds of household goods found in typical homes primarily from surviving paintings and mosaics that depict these goods as well as from surviving household goods placed in the tombs of royalty and prominent people. In some cases, written descriptions of household goods survive.

Nothing is mysterious or unpredictable about the household goods of ancient people, for no matter where or when they lived, they had roughly the same needs that modern people do. People needed to rest, so they had beds and chairs. To keep warm, they used blankets woven from local fibers or comforters stuffed with down, and in colder climates they had tools for tending a fire. They needed to eat, so they had a table for dining as well as plates, bowls, and cups—but not always utensils like forks and spoons—for food. They needed to store and preserve food and beverages, so they had jars, pots, and flagons, sometimes kept in a pantry, sometimes in what amounted to a basement below the house. They needed to cook food, so they had pots and pans, ladles, and cook stoves and ovens, in a kitchen or outdoors, depending on the region's climate. They needed to dress, so they had not only clothes but also places to keep them, and they had mirrors to check their appearance. They needed to eliminate waste, so they had some type of privy or toilet. When it was dark, they needed lamps to provide light. Because most households had to provide many of their own goods for personal use, household goods usually included tools for carving, cutting, polishing, sewing, weaving, sharpening, butchering, gathering crops, cultivating, and any other necessary task.

The ancients constructed household goods out of the materials at hand. In some cases, furniture was made of mud brick and incorporated into the structure of the building itself. Thus, a mud brick bench might have been built into an interior wall. In many cases, though, furniture was made of wood. Early furniture was crude, consisting of branches woven together or small logs assembled into a chair, table, and the like. As time went on, though, and civilizations became more developed, many craftsmen throughout the world became expert carpenters and wood carvers and created furniture that was not only functional but also decorative. Even the most luxurious of homes did not contain a great deal of furniture. In ages before machinery and mass production, furniture and other household goods were made by hand, one piece at a time. Rich people could perhaps have afforded more household goods, but the goods often were simply not available.

Other materials were used to fashion household goods. In addition to clay and local wood were metal (including primarily copper, bronze, and iron but also silver and gold). In time, luxury goods made of such materials as ivory, glass, precious and semiprecious stones, and exotic hardwood from other regions of the world became available to the elite through trade.

AFRICA

BY KIRK H. BEETZ

It is challenging to determine the sorts of household goods used by ancient Africans, because the wood and reeds most Africans would have used to make most of their furniture and other household goods decays quickly in much of Africa. Thus, archaeologists have only rock paintings, pottery, stone, and metalwork to study to gain an understanding.

At one time all Africans were hunter-gatherers. In about 27,500 B.C.E. these ancient hunter-gatherers began painting on rocks in southern Africa and in the Sahara. The people of southern Africa were the San, also called Bushmen, while the Saharans were a mixture of ethnic groups. As the Sahara became drier, its residents changed their ways of life, shifting from hunting and gathering to herding cattle. After 3000 B.C.E. some of these herders began settling at oases and adopted agriculture. Rock paintings offer glimpses of what the Saharans owned. Herders are shown using sticks to guide their animals. Sometimes they wear robes, probably for special occasions. One painting from about 1000 B.C.E. is a diagram of two men drawing water from a well. They use what appears to be a leather bucket. This image suggests that leather was used to store water, perhaps for use in homes, though this is not known for certain.

As the Sahara dried, many of its people moved eastward. Others were probably already part of a culture that included the forests of West Africa and probably moved south to live among their own people. Among their descendants may have been the Bantu speakers. These were an agricultural people, which meant that they had homes where they lived year round. This contrasts with the San, who were mobile and ranged far over the land where they lived. The San had some household goods, mostly clay vessels for cooking. These they made themselves if clay was available, or they traded for the vessels. On the other hand, the Bantu could accumulate goods because they did not have to carry them far afield. Perhaps by the 400s B.C.E. they had pottery, woven baskets, and metalwork they could call their own. By the 100s C.E. Bantu households had iron utensils for cooking, iron spearheads for hunting, and iron hooks for fishing.

Ancient Bantu speakers apparently had little or no household furniture. People sat on the floors of their houses, which would have been dirt, perhaps covered by matting. Mats were made out of loosely woven reeds or other grasses. Bantu speakers' houses were usually circular, with hearths or ovens in their centers. Ovens were ceramic, apparently with one chamber for baking. Most cooking would have been done on top of the oven.

Cooking utensils seem to have varied from place to place, with ceramic, copper, iron, or presumably wooden spoons being used to stir, serve, or eat some foods. The Bantu speakers had a fairly wide range of foods to cook, including cereals, roots, milk, and meats, both from domesticated animals such as cattle and sheep and from wild animals such as elephants and monkeys. Stew would probably have been common, cooked in ceramic pots on ovens or in open fires. Ceramic cups found in Kenya are associated with the Bantu speakers.

Other household goods included grinding stones for making flour. In western Africa people made ceramic pots as large as human beings to store grain. These pots were elevated above the ground to keep them safe from termites. Still other household items included toys, which were small ceramic animals probably made by children, perhaps to introduce them to an important craft or because children often will make their own toys when none are available.

Somewhat more is known about the household goods of the major civilizations of eastern and northeastern Africa: Kerma (ca. 2400–ca. 1550 B.C.E.), Kush (ca. 900 B.C.E.–ca. 350 C.E.), and Axum (ca. 500 B.C.E.–ca. 900 C.E.). Kerma and Kush were Nubian nations, occupying an extensive region south

Stone chopping tools from Olduvai Gorge, Tanzania, dating to the Lower Paleolithic, almost two million years ago. (© The Trustees of the British Museum)

of Egypt, whereas Axum developed near the Red Sea in the region of modern Ethiopia. In Nubia of Kerma's era, people favored Egyptian-style jars for storage of grains and perhaps beer. For cooking and eating they used copper utensils that were either imported from Egypt or copied from Egyptian designs. Household objects included brushes, perhaps for cleaning house, and cups and bowls.

More is known about Kush's household items, partly because of Kush's long association with Egypt and also because Kush made more extensive use of metal, which is not as perishable as most other substances used in manufacturing household goods. The homes of wealthy Kushites had bowls as thin as eggshells that were made of very strong, well-fired clay. These bowls compare well with the best ceramics of China and Korea of the same era. Glass bottles, jars, and vases were common; the bottles apparently contained beer. Goblets of glass, bronze, and iron were used for drinking beer or wine. That beer was popular is shown by the numerous pots made for fermenting beer found just about everywhere in Kush. Large jars were used to store wine. Even poor households had beer pots and heavy ceramic cups for drinking beer. The bowls and pots of poor households tended to be heavy, even bulky.

Ceramic jars for containing healing ointments were common, as were spoons for dishing out the ointments. These spoons were usually decorated with small figures following the Egyptian fashion, especially swimming girls, though the Kushite swimmers are plainly Kushites in color and features. Mirrors of copper or bronze were used for grooming. These tended to be well decorated on one side and may have been more common in homes of the well-to-do than in poorer households.

Stone was often used for housewares even after Kush became Africa's most important manufacturer of iron in the 600s B.C.E. There were grinding stones for turning grain into flour and simple implements of stone such as cleavers. Lamps were made of copper in many homes, while bronze or silver lamps were rarer. Razors of copper or iron were in homes, as well as combs of metal or wood. Furniture varied according the wealth of the household. In the houses of city dwellers and the wealthy, furniture included chairs and stools. Beds were sometimes made of masonry. Boxes and chests were used for storage. In poorer households in farmlands, people might have had no furniture or only baskets or boxes for storage.

Much has yet to be discovered about everyday household goods in Axum. Axumites had chairs and chests, probably made of wood. The region was a center for trade between Africa and Asia, and it is reasonable to suppose the people had many consumer goods from around the world. They did have jewelry, especially beads, from Egypt, Asia, and of their own manufacture.

EGYPT

BY CHRISTINE END

The ancient Egyptians built their homes with sun-dried mud brick. Because of the highly degradable nature of this material, domestic architecture is scantly preserved. Tombs, however, had to last an eternity, so the Egyptians furnished them with an abundance of household goods for use in the afterlife. They produced many of these objects especially for mortuary use, while others give indications that they were well-used favorite items of the deceased. The depiction of household items of many types on tomb walls magically provided their services for the deceased as well. It is from this evidence that Egyptologists know most about the trappings of an ancient Egyptian home.

Oil lamps provided light for the home. Such a lamp may have been as simple as a wick inserted in a small, oil-filled clay bowl. Salt added to the oil would have kept the home from becoming unpleasantly smoky. Other, more elaborate, lamps decorated with patterns or the heads of household gods such as Hathor and Bes also survive. Larger "floor lamps," which provided even more light, stood on top of tall stands.

Some mud-brick furniture incorporated into the structure of the house itself eliminated the need for expensive, freestanding wooden furniture. A low dais, or platform, may have functioned as a kitchen table for dining. Ingredients and preserved foods were stored in clay jars of many sizes. A cellar near the cooking area normally served as a pantry for the largest of these storage vessels. The preparation of food took place inside another set of clay vessels. Meals were cooked outside, perhaps in a courtyard, to keep cooking fires from making the house too hot. Open fires or ovens made of clay were fueled by wood, coal, or manure. Aside from the oven, a silo for storing barley or emmer and a large stone surface for making bread were all usual "appliances" of the ancient Egyptian kitchen. Pottery plates, bowls, and cups served as tableware. Eating food from these dishes using only the hands was the norm, regardless of the social status of the diner. However, an upper-class Egyptian banquet may have included a good set of dishes and cups, possibly including fancier items made of faience (a type of glasswork), stone, or metal.

In the earliest periods of ancient Egyptian history furniture created hastily and unskillfully from local woods and plant lashing was common. Over time, however, the Egyptians became highly skilled carpenters. Although the household was never overly furnished, furnishings made from wood were highly valued possessions. In early times native woods such as acacia, tamarisk, and sycamore fig were relatively inexpensive compared with imported woods, but these trees were not large enough to produce sizable lumber, nor were they strong enough for furniture. Gypsum, gesso (a type of plaster), and paint applied to the surface of the furniture covered the imperfections of inferior woods and created a clean exterior for painting the furniture. Expensive imported woods, such as beech, elm, ash, fir, maple, juniper, oak, pine, cedar, ebony, and yew, provided better quality wood for furniture. Ivory was another luxury material craftsmen used to make furniture.

A bedroom may have had a vaulted ceiling over the bed to capture excess heat, making the sleeping area more comfortable. Examples of high, boxed beds made from mud brick survive from the workmen's homes in Deir el-Medina. A reed mat rolled out on one of these platforms provided a surface for sleeping. The height of this type of bed may have also protected the sleeper from poisonous creatures during the night. The sleeper could create the illusion of privacy as well as gain additional protection from insects by the use of a bed canopy.

The Egyptians slept in wooden beds if they could afford to own one. Wooden beds were low and slightly slanted. The wood frame contained reed matting or leather in the center to create a flexible, more comfortable sleeping surface. The mattresslike cushioning of the bed, provided by folded sheets of linen cloth or a cushion of linen casing stuffed with bird feathers, gave the sleeper additional comfort. Wooden headrests, consisting of a curved surface to support the neck atop a column upon a base, cradled the sleeper's head. Headrests discovered under the heads of mummies within their coffins mimic the sleeping postures of the ancient Egyptian. For the living, headrests wound with linen provided additional padding for the sleeper's head.

A folding wooden headrest, from Akhmin, Egypt, late Eighteenth Dynasty, around 1225 B.C.E.; the head of Bes, protector of the home, shows on the neckpiece. (© The Trustees of the British Museum)

Low, sturdy stools were the most popular piece of furniture in the Egyptian home. Many varieties of stools survive from ancient Egypt. Three- and four-legged stools were both used, though the latter were more common. The ancient Egyptians also invented convenient collapsible stools much like the modern-day folding chair. A curved seat, perhaps made of woven plant material or leather, provided a comfortable place for sitting. Cushions upon the seat of the stool created a softer seat. Stools survive in alternate materials as well, including those fashioned from limestone surviving from the site of Amarna.

Chairs were used by the Egyptians, but not as frequently as stools. Their rarity suggests that chairs were more of a luxury item. Seats of surviving rush chairs are contoured, as were the chair backs. Armless models of chairs were more common than chairs with arms. Chairs were elaborately decorated more often than stools; some chairs are embellished with legs resembling a bull's or lion's legs, intricate inlays, carvings, and gilding.

Bathrooms were part of the Amarna Period (ca. 1350 B.C.E.) Egyptian household, along with toilet seats constructed of clay, wood, or, for the wealthy, stone. A chamber pot filled with sand changed by household servants would suffice for waste removal. Indoor showers, another luxury of the elite, consisted of a low walled area where water poured on the bather could drain outside.

The ancient Egyptian home lacked closets, cupboards, or dressers. Household items such as clothing, bedding, and other items not in constant use were stored in wooden chests, boxes, or baskets. Cosmetics, worn by both men and women from the earliest periods of Egyptian history, as well as other toiletry items were often stored in elaborate wooden boxes along with a mirror for application. Many examples of exquisitely designed and embellished containers, storage chests, and cosmetic storage containers survive.

THE MIDDLE EAST

BY DAVID KELLY

The area between the eastern Mediterranean, the Taurus Mountains, the northern Arabian Desert, and the Zagros Mountains is often considered the cradle of civilization. Innovations as basic to household life as the domestication of animals, cultivation of crops, weaving, and the potter's wheel first occurred there. Exotic woods and metals that were unavailable locally came to the area from Anatolia, the Plateau of Iran, the Indus Valley, Central Asia, the Persian Gulf, and

Syria, but there were plenty of readily available materials in this region to use for the fashioning of those everyday items used by most households. Clay, reeds, bitumen, wood, horn, hides, bone, and some types of stone (limestone, basalt, obsidian, and flint) provided the raw materials necessary to make most things.

The houses and campsites of the region's earliest hunter-gatherers have yielded stone mortars and pestles for the grinding of wild grains, necessary for seeds to be turned into flour and eventually bread. In addition, stone tools for cutting and bone tools (often from the long bones of wild sheep and goats or slender, hollow bird bones) for sewing cloth and leather were often abundant. Wooden bowls and basketry were used as containers; even in cases where these materials have completely deteriorated owing to humidity and poor conditions unsuited to preservation, basket impressions frequently exist. Furthermore, textiles of both wool and linen have been found in some of the drier environments, like caves in Israel and Palestine. Horn, too, was used to fashion basic tools used around the house.

From about 8000 B.C.E. onward these sorts of materials began to be accompanied by another, more durable material, namely, fired clay. Many early houses had simple pits in the ground, lined with plaster or mud to keep out the damp and the ever-present rodents, and these were sometimes burned, accidentally or intentionally. The added heat made the interior of these pits stronger, and for this reason pits served as places of storage. But it was probably not a very great conceptual leap from a fired clay or plaster pit, set in the ground, to the idea of creating a fired clay container above the ground in which to hold seed, flour, or water; in this way the earliest pottery may have been "discovered." The earliest examples of pottery were found at Mureybet, on the Euphrates River in Syria, and at Ganj Dareh, in western Iran, in about 8000 B.C.E. Archaeological evidence indicates that the potter's wheel, which made it quicker and easier to produce pottery vessels, probably first became commonly used in Mesopotamia around 3500 B.C.E.

Houses often had built-in features, like benches along the walls; steps up to the roof, where most people would have slept in the hotter months; and bins to hold things. Niches in walls served as shelves. In Mesopotamia most houses were built of mud bricks, both sun-dried and baked, with wooden rafters, often of poplar or ash, and reed matting between the bricks above the ceiling and the rafters themselves.

Archaeologists have the clearest view of what life was like in a typical urban household from excavations and texts found in Mesopotamia. The durable objects—pottery, grinding stones, stone and metal knives, and the like—survive well in the soils of Mesopotamia. Even wood is sometimes preserved. But for many types of objects, cuneiform texts give us additional details that archaeology cannot provide. Dowries, marriage contracts, and inheritance documents, for example, from the early second millennium B.C.E., itemize all sorts of goods that were deemed necessary to a well-furnished home. These goods include items made of wood, including looms, spindles, beds, chairs, footstools, tables, trays, combs, pot racks, bowls, spoons, and chests. Some types of wood, such as poplar and ash, was available from the gallery forest—the trees growing along the Tigris and Euphrates rivers and their associated irrigation canals. More exotic woods came from the Persian highlands, Lebanon, and even India. Under the Assyrians, in the first millennium B.C.E., ivory imported from Africa and India was used for inlays in elite furniture made for royal and high-status families. Other goods included pottery and metal vessels, sets of stone weights, basalt grinding stones for herbs and spices and others for flour, leather bags, and bronze scrapers. Blankets and other textiles were included too. The kitchen was outfitted not just with equipment but also with specific ingredients, like linseed oil, scented oil, barley mash (for making beer), flour, peas, and groats.

Domestic crockery came in many sizes and shapes, and until the late first millennium B.C.E. the pottery used in Mesopotamia was almost always unglazed. Because it was fired at a high temperature, however, Mesopotamian pottery was not too porous to hold liquids. The kitchen contained large jars that were used for storage, jars for water, bitumen-lined jars and vessels for storing oils and clarified butter (ghee) or beer and sometimes wine. The ancient Mesopotamians used a wide variety of cups and bowls, sieves, and basins. Archaeologists have documented hundreds of different pottery shapes, but few can be associated with a particular activity. Occasionally, though, we see pottery being used in scenes illustrating daily life, for example, on limestone plaques mounted on the walls of temples.

These scenes show, for example, a typical large jar with a pointed bottom (therefore unable to stand by itself) being carried in a sling supported by a long wooden pole by two men, who each balance the pole on one shoulder. Such a jar probably held large quantities of beer or oil being brought to a banquet. In early partly pictographic texts from the late fourth millennium B.C.E., small drawings of pottery with straight spouts sticking up from the shoulder of the vessel are associated with different types of oils, beer, and wine. Similar, spouted vessels have been found in excavations. Finally, Assyrian reliefs portray the king and his entourage drinking from a very carefully depicted bowl with lobes emanating from a disk in the center of the base. Exactly this type of bowl has been found, in pottery, silver, and bronze, at sites dating to the first millennium B.C.E. The study of ancient Mesopotamian households is therefore an area in which written sources, images, and archaeological finds complement each other.

ASIA AND THE PACIFIC

BY JUSTIN CORFIELD

Although few household goods from Asia and the Pacific have survived from ancient times, evidence about them survives from goods found in graves, including small-scale models of houses and furniture, some drawings, and written descriptions in China and India. Generally these are the household goods of the wealthy, but it is possible to extrapolate what other people may have had, or not had, in their houses.

The earliest surviving household goods in India are from excavations in the Indus Valley from the 1920s. From 2500 to 1800 B.C.E. civilization centered on two large cities, Harappa and Mohenjo Daro, as well as some 100 nearby towns and villages. Some of the houses were large, but others were more modest. The function of the various rooms was revealed by artifacts found in them, including figurines of deities and other mythical characters, including the famous bronze "dancing girl" and other sculptures and terra-cotta figures. A large number of small personal seals have also been found, as well as remains of plates, water containers, vessels for storing grain, and pots, often decorated with geometrical designs or showing images of animals in black ink. These provide evidence of the large range of crops grown in the Indus Valley, which, in turn, would have required families to own large numbers of farm implements. The most common pieces of furniture in houses were wooden storage chests, with fasteners fashioned from bronze or copper. There were also chairs—carved chair legs have been found—and beds and benches.

Apart from the Indus civilization, the earliest descriptions of Indian furniture are of thrones, and they can be seen in Buddhist reliefs from the second century B.C.E. Many have a flat and rectangular seat with four legs and sometimes an upright back but no arms. There are even images of the Buddha sitting on a similarly designed throne. Also appearing in reliefs are beds that, in the first century C.E., had a wooden frame and a mattress. Gradually both became more elaborate, but drawings continue to show Indians sitting on chairs with crossed legs.

In China many early graves have been excavated, along with sites of houses from the Han Dynasty (202 B.C.E.–220 C.E.). These sites have revealed many details about Chinese household goods connected with cooking: pots, bowls, and plates. These items varied from the cheap clay pots of the poor to better quality terra-cotta vessels and on to elaborate and delicate porcelain. In addition, utensils, especially remains of knives, have been found. For larger items some representations of early Chinese furniture have survived, and tombs contain some of the deceased's possessions, including small models of houses and miniature models of furniture. Chinese furniture was manufactured without nails, and dowels were used only when a repair had to be made. Furniture was constructed with mortise and tenon joints largely because, especially in northern China, wide differences in temperature between summer and winter caused expansion and contraction of the wood. Other Chinese items in houses included floor coverings; storage boxes, especially for food during the winter; and personal ornaments or jewelry. These vary from simple to intricately carved items made from gold and silver, sometimes inlaid with precious stones, or from jade.

Korean furniture was similar to that in northern China, again because of the need to cope with the differences in temperature. Some potsherds have also survived, and they, once again, show the heavy cultural influence of China on the Korean peninsula. Unlike the household goods in China and Korea, those in Korea tended to be much less obtrusive. With regular earthquakes, many houses were made with light walls that could be easily moved or reassembled. Many people slept and ate on the ground, and thus many household items included armrests, pillows, and small writing desks and cabinets for valuables.

In Southeast Asia wooden artifacts generally have not survived because of the wet climate. Pottery uncovered at many sites shows Indian and Chinese cultural influences. Many early Vietnamese people had musical instruments. The excavations at Dong Son, in northern Vietnam, show a highly developed Bronze Age culture from about 300 B.C.E., where a large number bronze drums have been found indicating an early importance placed on music. Some historians have suggested that the drums were solely for burying with the dead, but this seems unlikely. Numbers of miniature drums, bowls, *situlae* (bronze vessels similar to buckets), bells, and bronze tools have also been recovered. If the Dong Don culture rested heavily on music, so also did the reputation of the empire of Funan from the first through the fifth centuries C.E. Chinese chronicles describe a Funan delegation to China in 243 C.E. that brought along expensive gifts made by musicians, whose music was highly praised. Excavations of houses at Oc-Eo (in modern-day Vietnam), believed to have been the capital of Funan, have indicated that there was room for large amounts of furniture, but because the furniture was made from wood, it has not survived.

In the Pacific household goods, except for pots and tools, were probably made from wood. Carved stools, tables, wooden drums, figurines, fly whisks, and ornaments survive from later periods, and it is highly probable that these would have existed in earlier times, with a major focus being on boats and fishing equipment. In Australia the climate is good for preserving material, but the nomadic life of the aboriginal peoples limited their possessions to hunting weapons and a few other basic necessities.

EUROPE

BY JUSTIN CORFIELD

Large numbers of household goods surviving from ancient Europe reflect changes in society and technology, starting with the forming of stone implements of the Paleolithic a million or more years ago. These items, mostly flints, were used for hunting, cutting meat and crops, and cleaning animal skins. Archaeological finds around the lakeside site of Bilzingsleben in Germany, which have been dated to the Paleolithic, have shown that the devices of the hunter-gatherers there included flints, wooden tools, and bone implements. Similar discoveries in eastern Europe have established that carved bone harpoons were used for fishing in rivers. Few cooking implements have survived.

Of the stone and bone ornaments that have survived, the figure of a woman's head with what appears to be plaited hair found at Brassempouy, France, and dating to around 20,000 B.C.E. and a female figure carved from mammoth ivory found at Lespugue, France, and dating to as early as 25,000 to 18,000 B.C.E. show people making nonessential items for the household. The numbers of surviving pots and figurines dating to 4500 B.C.E. or later increase dramatically, as does the sophistication in the design on the pots that have been found.

Changes in household goods appeared with the spread of agriculture during the Neolithic Period. Bowls from about 4000 B.C.E., such as those from Fussell's Lodge, Britain, show simple decorations, while ones from about 600 years later from a Newgrange megalithic tomb in eastern Ireland depict more complicated geometric patterns. It also seems probable that there were many wooden implements from this period that have not survived.

The advent of the Copper Age in Europe, from about 2500 B.C.E. in southeastern Europe and from circa 1900 B.C.E. in Britain, saw the increasing ease of making purely decorative items such as copper collars worn on ceremonial occasions as well as copper and pottery bowls and pots. Many artifacts have been found at a Copper Age cemetery in Tiszapolgár (also called Polgár), Hungary. With so many objects buried with the dead, it is possible to work out how many possessions people may have had, with some graves containing large numbers of artifacts. Indeed, a few of the graves of children also contain expensive items, suggesting that they might have inherited them.

Much weaponry and armor of ancient Europe, including helmets, breastplates, shin plates, spearheads, arrowheads, and swords, survive from the Bronze Age, with artifacts dating to about 1800 B.C.E. until 1200 B.C.E. Many urns, pots, cooking implements, and decorative items have been found. Although wooden furniture was used, little has survived. At Cologne, Germany, a small wooden chair and bed were uncovered in the grave of a boy, and a folding stool from the Bronze Age was discovered in a grave in Denmark.

The Bronze Age was a period of comparative affluence, during which many large communities formed. By this time there were clearly greater contacts between the various peoples of Europe, with trade needed for the acquisition of some items and commodities, especially tin. Some of these traders were Phoenicians, who brought with them items to exchange, and various statuaries from the period have a distinct eastern Mediterranean style. Although there are local variations, a greater uniformity in design and similar household items has been found across the whole of Europe as a result of widespread trade.

One of the more elaborate items of the period is from an excavation in the Trundholm bog in Zealand, Denmark, in which was found a model of a horse pulling a partially gold-plated disc—possibly a mirror—dated to about 1650 B.C.E. Another significant find is a razor from Solberg, Jutland, that has been dated to 1000 B.C.E.

Further changes in ancient European household goods occurred during the Iron Age (1000 B.C.E.–150 C.E.). Many highly stylized pieces of bronze ware and ironwork from the fifth century B.C.E. survive. The appearance of such items coincided with the introduction of wine into the diet of the Celts, and the result was the production of many elaborate flagons, a type of drinking vessel with a handle and spout and typically a lid. One discovery from an archaeological excavation at Basse-Yutz, in the east of France, dated to the late fifth century B.C.E., includes intricate flagons, involving bronze work combined with enamel and Mediterranean coral. Others follow Etruscan (characteristic of the ancient civilization in modern-day central Italy) or Greek designs, with a hydria—a vessel for water mixed with concentrated wine—found at Grächwill, near Bern, Switzerland, showing a distinct Spartan pattern.

In addition to flagons, there were many different styles of drinking containers. One style, a bronze vessel designed to look like a boot, has been found in Hungary dating to the third century B.C.E., soon after the Celts moved to that region. There have also been iron frames such as those found at Welwyn, Hertfordshire, England, which were probably used for holding amphorae (a two-handled vessel with an oval shape and slender neck) and flagons. Pottery was also developing considerably. During work on the Hallstatt Cemetery in Austria, which was discovered in 1846, many pots were found along with decorated ritual axes and sword scabbards depicting scenes of battle and everyday life.

The influence of the Etruscans is clear in many household items from the fifth century B.C.E. until the second century B.C.E. These items can be seen in the La Tène culture, which flourished at the eastern end of Lake Neuchâtel, Switzerland. A mirror, following Etruscan designs, was found at La Motte-St.-Valentin, Haute-Marne, and an Etruscan-style bronze vessel with a tripod was found in the tomb of a Celtic prince at Bad Dürkheim, in Rhineland, Germany. Gradually, however, a new style of mirror made from polished metal started to be produced in workshops in southern England from the first century B.C.E. until the first century C.E. They were particularly distinguished with an openwork handle and a pattern that has plain, smooth areas with grooved basketwork-style motifs, as seen in the Desborough Mirror, which has been dated to the first century C.E. and was found at Northamptonshire, England, in 1908.

With the rise of the Roman power in Italy, Roman artifacts started to be traded throughout the area settled by the Celts. There were also many more similarities between the goods in northern France and southern Britain. The most celebrated "find" from this period was the Aylesford Bucket, found in 1886 at the cemetery of a Belgic tribe that had settled in Kent, England. The "hinges" of the bronze bucket's handle show a human face with bulging eyes in a La Tène design. It seems likely that furniture became more ornate, but being made from wood, little has survived apart from chairs and tables in some images of the period.

GREECE

BY JEFFREY S. CARNES

The most striking feature of Greek household goods is that the Greeks had significantly fewer possessions of every sort (furniture, clothing, cooking implements, decorative objects) than those found in a typical modern house. This was partly because of the difficulty of manufacturing goods. In an era with little machinery and no mass production, virtually everything was made by hand and thus relatively expensive, limiting most people's ability to accumulate material possessions. In addition, an ideology of equality (even in many oligarchic societies, that is, those ruled by a few) discouraged ostentatious displays of wealth.

Furniture and other household objects were both functional and, when possible, decorative. Ancient furniture differed from modern furniture in size and portability: Most pieces were designed so that they could be moved easily from one room to another or, for the wealthy, from one house to another. The main items of furniture were chairs, tables, stools, couches, and beds. Greek houses usually did not have large cabinets, dressers, or armoires, nor were rooms built with closets. Clothing was folded flat and stored in small, movable chests and boxes. Since most people had few or no changes of clothing, the need for storage space was limited. Greek furniture was made primarily of wood, which does not survive well at archaeological sites, so most of the information we have comes from pictures (in particular, vase paintings) and from literary sources. Metal was used for fastenings, for locks on storage chests, and sometimes for the legs or feet of couches, chairs, and tables. Some of these items, in fact, have survived long after the wood to which they were attached decayed.

Chairs were simple. The most basic type was the *diphros,* or stool, which had no back or armrests and four straight legs. A common variation on this was the folding stool with legs that crossed in an X pattern, similar to a modern director's chair without arms or a back. Such chairs were easy to store and transport. More substantial was the *klismos,* which featured curved legs and a curved, slightly reclined back; the word *klismos* derives from the Greek verb *klino,* meaning "to lean." The examples on Greek vases often have graceful curves. At the top end of the scale was the *thronos* (the source of the word *throne*), a solidly constructed, upright chair with armrests, often highly decorated, and more likely to be found in temples or palaces than in households.

One of the most versatile pieces of furniture was the *klinē* (a word also derived from *klino*), which combined the functions of bed, couch, and dining couch. It was common for food and drink to be consumed in a reclining position, particularly on formal occasions. The *klinē* was backless and designed for reclining rather than sitting on, with one end slanted upward. Legs were either straight or with a slight curve and in some cases could be carved to look like animal legs or paws. The frame of the *klinē* was wooden and light enough to allow it to be carried easily from one room to another or outdoors or onto the roof for sleeping in the warmer months. The weight of the occupant was borne by a surface of webbing, consisting of interlaced leather or rope, which was typically covered by a thin mattress. On top of this were blankets, pillows, and coverlets or tapestries, which could be highly decorated luxury items in wealthy households. Evidence for the weaving of pictures and designs into tapestries is found as early as Homer's *Iliad,* in which Helen weaves her own story into a tapestry; skilled weavers were considered among the more valuable spoils of war. There is no evidence for the use of sheets, and mattresses were typically stuffed with straw, so an ancient bed would seem uncomfortable by modern standards.

Tables were either three-legged or four-legged (*trapezai,* the source of our word *trapezoid*), and tended to be few in number, since there simply were not that many things to put on them. Most tables were used for dining and, like all Greek furniture, were light enough to be carried away when not in use. Books were rare (and typically stored in chests), and

Stone bowl and pitcher (Alison Frantz Photographic Collection, American School of Classical Studies at Athens)

lamps were normally placed on separate stands. In wealthy houses tables were sometimes used for displays of decorative objects. These objects might include the beautifully painted vases now displayed in museums and reproduced in art history textbooks. Pottery for practical purposes—for storing oil and grains and for use as cookware—was much plainer, and Greek cookware consisted of these and simple iron pots and skillets.

Decorative objects, such as tapestries and bronze plaques, could also be hung on walls, which were themselves painted, either quite simply—plain red or white was popular—or extravagantly. The packed-earth floors of the typical Greek house could be covered with rugs or mats, which were probably highly decorative in wealthier households, though little direct evidence supports this notion. In addition, dining room floors were sometimes covered with decorative mosaics.

Indoor lighting depended on the use of oil-burning lamps, which were either placed on stands or suspended from the ceiling or walls by means of cords or chains. Some were metal, but most were made of fired clay, which survives extraordinarily well when buried in the ground, so countless thousands of oil lamps survive from antiquity. These typically contained a reservoir for fuel (usually olive oil) and a nozzle into which a wick was inserted and lit. Such lighting was by no means ideal. Lamps of this sort do not produce much light and produce heat as well, which, given the warm Greek climate, would be unwanted for much of the year. The cheaper grades of olive oil used for fuel tended to produce smoke, and in addition to the obvious fire hazards of using an open flame, the mere lighting of a lamp could pose problems. Kindling a fire was not easy, and the usual practice was to keep a flame or embers burning so that a fire could be easily rekindled. Outdoor lighting (for example, for making one's way through dark streets) was often accomplished with torches, which could produce a brighter flame through use of flammable materials such as pitch, which were not suitable for indoor lighting. Poor lighting technology was only a minor problem for the Greeks, however, since they, like most pre-industrial peoples, tended to rise at dawn and spend only a small percentage of their waking hours in the dark.

ROME

BY FRANCESCA C. TRONCHIN

A number of sources of information about Roman furniture and household goods are available. Archaeological material, especially from such sites as Pompeii and Herculaneum, includes actual remains of objects of everyday use in the Roman world. Secondary visual sources, such as paintings and mosaics, depict Roman interiors. Finally, evidence from ancient literature also provides information about the types of furniture and domestic implements used in antiquity.

Because the rooms in most Roman houses were often few, small, and designed for multiple uses, furniture needed to be relatively portable. A space that functioned as a bedroom at night might also have been used for work or study during the day, so the required furniture for these activities was brought in and out of the space at different times of the day. Folding stools, for example, were very practical because they were portable and could be stored in small spaces when not in use. An exception to this rule was the *arca*, or chest, which was most frequently found in the main hall of a Roman house, the *atrium*. These cupboards functioned as strongboxes to protect household valuables and could vary in size and material from a large wooden chest to a tall iron or bronze armoire.

By far the most prevalent pieces of furniture in the Roman house were chairs, tables, and couches. Stools and chairs made of both ordinary materials such as wood and exotic materials such as ivory were common and could be used for a great number of activities. Stools were more common than the chairs with backs derived from the Greek *klismos*. Couches with turned legs and topped with cushions were common in both the bedrooms and dining rooms of Roman homes. At dinner parties guests reclined on one of three couches placed at right angles to one another in a Roman dining room, whose name, *triclinium*, comes from the Greek words for "three couches." The most elaborate couches could be inlaid with ivory and colored glass or decorated with bronze and silver animal heads on the headboards. In describing luxurious dinner parties Roman authors note the use of beautifully embroidered silk cushions on these dining couches.

Both utilitarian and luxurious tables have survived at Roman archaeological sites. Tables came in a variety of shapes and sizes. Benchlike tables made of wood and with four legs could be used for working or for dining in more modest homes. Round tables supported by three sculptural legs in the shape of animal legs or mythological figures were popular in the dining rooms of the very wealthy. This type of table was usually cast in bronze; an example in the National Archaeological Museum in Naples, Italy, is a table with three legs in the shape of satyrs with goats' legs. A rectangular table with sculpted supports in marble seems to be a Roman invention without precedent in Greek furniture. The supports terminate on both ends with animals such as griffins or lions in an opposing stance. These marble tables were popular in Roman gardens, where they were a relatively permanent part of the landscaping and decoration of the exterior space.

Utensils, tableware, and cooking vessels in the Roman world were made from a variety of materials. Terra-cotta was most popular for cups, plates, and storage containers. These fired clay objects were fairly durable and could be produced in both utilitarian and decorated varieties. Large storage containers for wine, oil, and other foodstuffs were usually made of coarse pottery, but finer tableware could be of a very high quality. Varieties of Roman terra-cotta, such as African red slip ware, red gloss, and Arretine, were frequently ornamented with stamped or molded decorations in the shapes of floral forms, mythological figures, and even gladiatorial scenes. Many of these finely decorated terra-cottas were influenced by even more costly vessels in glass or metal.

Roman jug, two-handled cup (the handles now missing), strainer, ladle, and stirrer, dating to about 100–75 B.C.E., from Arcisate, near Como, northern Italy. (© The Trustees of the British Museum)

Glass was used in the Roman world for such household objects as drinking vessels and containers for precious commodities like perfume. Colored glass imitated gemstones, while clear, colorless glass may have been developed to imitate more costly rock crystal. Glass could be blown or cast in a mold and was frequently decorated with reliefs of floral motifs. The sumptuousness of glass vessels was second only to that of gold or silver objects. Trimalchio, a fictional character based on wealthy Romans in Petronius's *Satyricon*, states that he would prefer glass cups to gold ones, were they not so fragile.

Tableware made of luxurious materials has been found in both the archaeological and literary records of the Roman world. Diners in the homes of the very wealthy would have eaten and drunk from silver plates and cups decorated with figural scenes in relief, like the famous examples from the Boscoreale Treasure found near Pompeii. It is this type of tableware that decorated pottery was most likely reproducing.

Boiling, roasting, and techniques akin to modern grilling were the most popular cooking methods in Roman domestic kitchens; baking was typically done in one of a number of bakeries throughout a given city. Pots and pans made of bronze or iron have been found among the remains of ancient kitchens. These implements were similar to modern-day pots and pans, with flat bottoms, straight or slightly angled sides, and either one or two handles based on their size and use. Bronze braziers, sometimes finely decorated, were used in Roman homes to grill food over hot coals.

The illumination of interior spaces in the Roman world was often difficult. While architects and engineers developed features that allowed natural sunlight into their buildings, lighting spaces at night was impossible without the use of artificial light. Lamps in terra-cotta and bronze were made in all periods of Roman antiquity and could take on many forms. Olive oil was the most common fuel for the lamps that illuminated public and private spaces alike. Most terra-cotta lamps had a small ring handle; a covered, bowl-shaped container for the fuel; and a rounded nozzle to hold the wick. The majority of lamps had one wick, but some had multiple nozzles to maximize illumination. A wide variety of stamped or molded imagery decorated the covers of terra-cotta lamps. Floral designs and mythological scenes were popular, but crosses came into fashion when Rome converted to Christianity. Bronze lamps were more durable and costly than the terra-cotta versions but were made in the same general shapes. The more elaborate versions in bronze (or even gold and silver) had large handles, usually in the shape of a palmette or other kind of leaf. Lamps in metal could be hung from chains or cords on tall candelabra; all lamps could be placed on a stand.

These are by far the most common items found in a Roman household—furniture, lamps, and receptacles for cooking and eating in a variety of materials. Although they are usually not preserved in the archaeological record, baskets, tapestries, rugs, curtains, and screens made of perishable fabrics and wood had functional and decorative roles in the ancient Roman house.

THE AMERICAS

BY KIRK H. BEETZ

The ancient Americans of the far north learned how to adapt their frigid environment to their needs. For instance, they built their beds out of frozen ground, laying animals skins on the bed to provide comfort. They made cradles out of wood and hung them from sturdy wooden poles in their homes. Later Arctic peoples used a mesh of branches covered with animal skins for their floors, and some of the ancient Arctic American peoples probably did, too. Their household tools tended to be focused on what they needed to prepare food. This meant that they had scraping tools made out of bone, wood, or stone for removing fat and flesh from animal hides. Their eating utensils, such as spoons, tended to be made out of bone.

In North America south of the Arctic and north of Mexico, many cultures rose and fell, and archaeological studies of their remains have only begun to form a picture of their lives. Stone mortars and pestles have been found at many sites. Some large stone outcrops have dish-shaped impressions caused by people grinding into them, but there are also mortars and pestles small enough to be used in homes, including ones barely bigger than a hand that could have been carried by nomads. Given how small they are, they were more likely used for grinding ingredients for medicines than food.

Many ancient North Americans probably made spoons and scoops out of bone. The extent of the use of wood in making home utensils is not known but probably was extensive wherever wood was available. This can be inferred from the wide use of wood for building homes, which suggests that wood would have been used for other household purposes. Ceramics were used broadly for making pots, bowls, plates, and cups. Woven baskets were probably used to store grain and for other household purposes, but pottery would have been favored for carrying liquids and for cooking. Furniture was sparse, and most people slept on mats or blankets on dirt floors.

A multitude of cultures developed in ancient Mexico and Central America, but only a few are at all well known. The earliest Americans were hunter-gatherers who used wood and bone for tools. In Guatemala stone tools dated to 8760 B.C.E. include scrapers and blades, probably for preparing meat for cooking. The most famous of the ancient Mesoamericans are the Olmec and the Maya. Little is known of the everyday habits of the Olmec, though their household goods were probably similar to those of the Maya, whom they seem to have influenced.

The Maya did not use much furniture. They slept on mats on dirt floors unless they were of the nobility, in which case their floors may have been stone. The mats were made of woven reeds. When they were not sleeping, Mayans usually used their sleeping mats as seats. In some homes, raised earth may have been covered with sleeping mats and used as seats. Chairs were made of wood and wicker and may have had backs, but they were probably used only by nobility and royalty. The homes of important people might have contained stone benches. Archaeologists imagine that those who sat on the stone benches were family patriarchs conducting important business with family or outsiders. Baskets have been found in homes. Chests of wickerwork may have been used for storing clothing or valuables. Low wooden tables may have been used in some homes. They would have been small and portable, because the Maya might sit to eat almost anywhere.

Food preparation involved stone goods such as grinding stones. It is possible that every home had a grinding stone and a cylindrical stone grinder, used primarily to process maize. Nuts may have been cracked on small, stone hand mills. Mayans used stone tools extensively in their preparation of food, using them for chopping vegetables, cutting meat, and scraping pulp from gourds. Food would have been cooked in ceramic pots, with wooden utensils that had been made with obsidian cutting tools. Food was either boiled in ceramic pots or grilled over open fires.

The majority of household goods recovered from Mesoamerican archaeological sites have been ceramic, varying from coarse bowls for soaking maize to artfully shaped plates for holding food during meals. Bottles, jars, bowls, cups, and plates were used regularly. The bottles held liquids, usually drinks. Maize beer was often poured from bottles into plain cylindrical cups that fit easily in the hand. By about 400 B.C.E. Mayans used jugs with spouts.

The populating of South America probably occurred in waves, with perhaps the first human inhabitants being people who moved along the coast of modern Argentina in small boats. Others migrated into the Andes, and more is known about the ancient Andean peoples, partly because the climate is cold and dry, meaning that goods made of wood, reeds, and cloth decay much more slowly than they do in other parts of South America.

These peoples began as hunter-gatherers but learned to cultivate maize and many varieties of sweet potatoes. Ceramic bottles appeared first on the coast and then moved inland. By about 1200 B.C.E. bottles varied considerably in shape, from balls to cubes to ornate shapes of animals or even houses. The stirrup bottle seems to have been important as a religious object as well as popular for its design. Ancient South Americans believed the stirrup represented their connection with their ancestors. The stirrup bottle derives its name from its handle, which arches far out in the shape of a stirrup from the main part of the bottle. Sometimes the bottles had two such handles, and the stirrup-shaped handle design often shows up on jugs and bowls.

The principal drink of the ancient Andeans was probably maize beer. Their housewares include many examples of fermentation jars, bottles for pouring beer, and cups intended to be used for drinking beer in particular. Their bottles began as boxy shapes with spouts in the 1200s B.C.E. and became ever more intricately shaped and colorful. By the 200s B.C.E. the Andeans were using bottles in which the spout projected out of the stirrup, so that the liquid flowed through the handle and out the spout. Another form during the first century C.E. was the double bottle, which linked two main vessels with a tube. Cups sometimes resembled those used by the Mayans, but a long, narrow, cylindrical one was in use by the mid-400s C.E.

The furniture of the ancient South Americans is not yet well known. Beds seem to have consisted of blankets, and pillows may have been used to rest sleepers' heads. Tables were low on four legs, with raised edges as if to prevent objects from slipping off. Dates for such artifacts have yet to be firmly assigned.

See also ADORNMENT; AGRICULTURE; ARCHITECTURE; ART; BUILDING TECHNIQUES AND MATERIALS; CERAMICS AND POTTERY; CHILDREN; CLIMATE AND GEOGRAPHY; CLOTHING AND FOOTWEAR; CRAFTS; DEATH AND BURIAL PRACTICES; EMPIRES AND DYNASTIES; FOOD AND DIET; GENDER STRUCTURES AND ROLES; HUNTING, FISHING, AND GATHERING; ILLUMINATION; INVENTIONS; METALLURGY; MUSIC AND MUSICAL INSTRUMENTS; NOMADIC AND PASTORAL SOCIETIES; SACRED SITES; SETTLEMENT PATTERNS; SOCIAL COLLAPSE AND ABANDONMENT; SOCIAL ORGANIZATION; STORAGE AND PRESERVATION; TEXTILES AND NEEDLEWORK; TRADE AND EXCHANGE; WEAPONRY AND ARMOR.

FURTHER READING

Penelope M. Allison, *Pompeian Households: An Analysis of the Material Culture* (Los Angeles: Cotsen Institute of Archaeology at the University of California at Los Angeles, 2004).

Bob Brier and Hoyt Hobbs, *Daily Life of the Ancient Egyptians* (Westport, Conn.: Greenwood Press, 1999).

Robert Flacelière, *Daily Life in Greece at the Time of Pericles*, trans. Peter Green (London: Phoenix Press, 2002).

Kevin Greene, *Roman Pottery* (Berkeley: University of California Press, 1992).

Michael Loewe, *Everyday Life in Early Imperial China during the Han Period, 202 B.C.–A.D. 220* (New York: Dorset, 1988).

A. G. McDowell, *Village Life in Ancient Egypt: Laundry Lists and Love Songs* (New York: Oxford University Press, 1999).

G. M. A. Richter, *The Furniture of the Greeks, Etruscans, and Romans* (London: Phaidon Press, 1966).

H. W. F. Saggs, *Everyday Life in Babylonia and Assyria* (New York: G. P. Putnam's Sons, 1965).

D. E. Strong, *Greek and Roman Gold and Silver Plate* (Ithaca, N.Y.: Cornell University Press, 1966).

Donald Strong and David Brown, eds., *Roman Crafts* (London: Duckworth, 1976).

Malcolm Todd, *Everyday Life of the Barbarians, Goths, Franks and Vandals* (London: B.T. Batsford Ltd., 1972).

► hunting, fishing, and gathering

INTRODUCTION

In modern life, many people hunt and fish as a form of recreation, and even gathering crops from a household garden is often more of a hobby than a necessity, at least in the developed nations. By contrast, among ancient peoples, especially before the development of agriculture, hunting, fishing, and gathering were serious pursuits. People lived in small bands and tribes, moving about as the seasons changed in the constant search for food. To the extent that they foraged within a limited area, they had to be careful not to deplete the food resources in their area; otherwise, they could face starvation later. They often had to compete with other species, making sure, for example, that they harvested berries before birds ate them.

Ancient hunters, who relied on such weapons as spears, had to hunt cooperatively, and they learned how to read the signs of nature that told them where they could find game and in which direction that game might be moving. In early hunter-gatherer societies, considerable emphasis was placed on sharing. In general, the food acquired in a hunt or gathered from the ground was communal property, not the property of the individual who found it. Women played an important role in acquiring food, especially as gatherers.

Game meat was the chief source of protein among early hunter-gatherers, as was fish for those who lived in coastal regions or along the banks of freshwater rivers. Early fishermen became adept at fashioning nets and underwater traps for fish and seafood. Additionally, ancient hunter-gatherers consumed nuts, acorns, seeds, herbs and spices, roots, fruits and berries, and mushrooms—always depending on what was available in the local region at a particular time of year. The most common sweetener was honey. Many common domesticated crops, including wheat, rice, and legumes (that is, beans), originally grew wild and only later were domesticated to become staple crops.

After the development of agriculture, hunting, fishing, and gathering by no means disappeared. While people who lived in sedentary communities (that is, more or less fixed communities, where people remained in one place) derived most of their food from agriculture, including livestock production, people in remote areas continued to rely on the hunting, fishing, and gathering skills learned by their remote ancestors. Even people who lived in settled communities continued to hunt and fish as a way of introducing variety into their diets. Poor people, for example, supplemented their diets by hunting rabbits and game birds.

As civilizations became more advanced and food production became more organized and even commercialized, hunting became more of the sport that it is in modern life. The elite hunted prestige animals such as wild stags, usually on horseback and with the aid of dogs bred for the purpose. Hunting, fishing, and gathering provided ancient peoples with more than just food. Animals large and small afforded hides for clothing and blankets as well as bones, horns, and teeth from which tools and decorative items could be made. Birds supplied feathers, and many plants were valued not as food but for their medicinal properties or as the source of dyes. Even fish bones could be useful for such household items as needles.

AFRICA

BY MARK ANTHONY PHELPS

Hunting, fishing, and gathering activities are collectively known as foraging. Foraging was the only economic option for all humans prior to the Neolithic Revolution (ca. 9000 B.C.E.). Given that *Homo sapiens sapiens* appeared around 40,000 years ago, the bulk of human existence has been spent foraging. The primary sources for Africa from antiquity are sparse. Written sources, aside from the Nile Valley and its immediate cultural neighbors, are foreign and are unconcerned with recording the lives of foragers. Oral sources rarely extend back beyond the 18th century C.E. One is thus left with archaeological evidence to reconstruct this aspect of human history, along with models based upon historical foraging groups.

The advent of the Neolithic Revolution is manifested in the archaeological record in the form of domesticated plants, domesticated animals, the beginnings of a sedentary lifestyle, and the appearance of ceramics as a means of storing domesticated products. However, the African evidence does not correspond neatly with this model. In Africa there is evidence of ceramics before domestication. There is also evidence of hunting, gathering, and fishing among settled groups as well as evidence of pastoralism side by side with gathering.

The Nile Valley provides the earliest evidence for sedentarization. At the delta site of Merimda Beni Salama, by 8000 B.C.E. foragers were living in houses with hearths and had large pottery vessels for water storage. In the Faiyûm there is evidence of a settlement on a shrinking lake from the seventh millennium B.C.E. Foragers lived in this settlement, with silos built to store excess food. Farther south, around Khartoum, there is evidence from around 7000 B.C.E. of a foraging society with ceramics, silos, and net weights for fishing. Evidence of a number of hunting and fishing camps has been found in modern-day Sudan. Throughout the Nile Valley the dominant fish species harvested were the Nile perch and catfish. With the development of the harpoon around 8500 B.C.E. (appearing first in Sudan), deepwater fish were exploited as well. A wide variety of species was hunted, including aurochs, hippopotamuses, crocodiles, and a number of smaller species. Birds were also harvested. Tubers seem to have been the dominant flora food source. Domestication reached the Nile Valley in the fifth millennium B.C.E.

Ceramics had appeared throughout the Sahara by 6000 B.C.E. The Sahara supported plant life until around 4500 B.C.E., when a prolonged desertification process began; through this process the basic climatic patterning of today emerged around 2500 B.C.E. During the wetter period permanent streams as well as a number of lakes were found in the Sahara. The faunal representation was more Sahel-like, with many types of wild grasses. Herding was being practiced at Ti-n-Torha (Libya) by 7000 B.C.E. It is not confirmed in the western reaches of the Sahara until the third millennium B.C.E.

As the Sahara dried, the herders apparently moved south into western Africa. Their influence is discernible all over the region from the second millennium, as herding became a staple. They also brought domesticated millet and sorghum with them. The date of the domestication of the latter two is not known but is fixed at no later than around 1800 B.C.E., evidenced by African species that are present in India.

Along the Niger yam cultivation may have begun as early as 4000 B.C.E., based upon the presence of a new type of hoe, though paleobotanical evidence is lacking. However,

INSULTING THE MEAT

Although meat accounts for a relatively small proportion of the caloric intake of the Bushmen (estimated between 15 and 30 percent), it is still the prestige food item produced by foragers. Meat distribution is among the most important issues that occupy the attention of foragers. A !Kung woman stated that the primary gender status gap appears because men are "masters of the meat."

The anthropologist Richard Lee experienced a social leveling mechanism in the course of purchasing a bull to be slaughtered for a Christmas feast for the band of !Kung he was researching. Once word of the particular bull chosen became known to the members of the band, the men began to complain to the anthropologist of his repulsive choice of animal. Thoroughly depressed by the continuous complaining concerning his choice, Lee watched the killing of the bull and the unmistakable joy the animal brought the crowd. The animal's flesh appeared to be in perfect accord with what he had been told was the ideal. Confused, he was told by an informant that he had experienced the mechanism of "insulting the meat."

For the !Kung, there is a fear that a good hunter could become vain, begin to hoard meat, and try to assert his will upon others. Thus, when an animal is killed, those who go with the hunter to retrieve the carcass will complain about investing so much work for a useless "bag of bones." The hunter will apologize profusely. Likewise, when a hunter announces that he has had no real luck but may have injured a little animal, the rest of the band knows to get excited, as a large animal must have been hurt. Hunters engage in self-deprecation when announcing their luck. In an environment in which death is a constant threat, bands must take care that all their members freely share risks and resources. It is impossible to assert that such was the case among ancient African foragers, but the logic behind the mechanism probably was at work in these societies as well.

throughout most of the valley, to the middle of the first millennium B.C.E., data point to semisedentary foragers, existing on riverine fish, or more mobile groups of foragers. Along Lake Chad, by 2000 B.C.E. herding, fishing, and hunting occupied people dwelling in permanent wooden buildings. Shell middens (piles or refuse heaps) dating to the sixth millennium B.C.E. have been discovered in Mauritania. By the middle of the second millennium B.C.E. the oil palm may have been domesticated. By the end of the millennium millet was clearly being cultivated. The Kintampo culture of central Ghana from the second millennium B.C.E. seems to have been a point of cultural fusion between Saharan traditions and rain forest gathering cultures.

Eastern Africa was a zone of foraging until the second millennium B.C.E., as pastoralism became the dominant economic activity around the lakes and along the Rift Valley highlands. The Ethiopian highlands became a place of domesticated farming, primarily with species native to the region. Before the advent of pastoralism, the fishers on the lakes harvested a wider variety of species as the lake levels dropped. At Lake Turkana the fishers used boats. Nile perch was the dominant species, but catfish and cichlids and soft-shelled turtles were also present. Crocodiles, elephants, gazelles, giraffes, hippopotamuses, rhinoceroses, warthogs, and zebras were among the species hunted. As throughout most of Africa, foragers in the east had ceramics before the advent of agriculture, around 4000 B.C.E.

Southern Africa consisted exclusively of foraging societies throughout all but the last four centuries of the ancient period. Herding and agriculture entered the region at the beginning of the Common Era. Ceramics, domesticated plants, domesticated animals, and iron all arose in the region roughly at the same time as Bantu peoples. There is no firm evidence of the ancient foraging way of life, but we can make what are widely evidenced generalizations about historic foraging societies, which may or may not be an accurate embodiment of their ancient forbearers. Foragers live in bands for at least part of the year, often in areas of marginal climate, meaning that they must not overuse the resources at their disposal, or they might not have these resources in the future. Thus, foragers are intimately tied to nature. The !Kung of the Kalahari are aware of seven distinct seasons in an area in which climatologists distinguish two. They consume at least 80 distinct floral food sources. They are able to recognize each band member's footprint. From animal droppings, they can discern the size, gender, and health of each animal, where an animal has recently been, what time of day it passed, which direction it was heading, and the number of animals that have passed by.

Foragers have an understanding that they are but bit players in an intricately balanced world. Religion traditionally has taken the form of animism. The chief value in foraging societies is sharing. Both the risks and the resources of the group must be shared to facilitate survival in marginal areas. Hoarding is the most heinous act one can commit. Gift giving and regifting are important social mechanisms to prevent accumulation of items and to establish ties among members, as items are briefly possessed by all members of the band.

Not only are males relatively equal, but women are indeed nearly equal to men in foraging societies. Anthropologists attribute this gender equality to the role women play in food production, as gathering provides some 80 percent of the calories consumed by the band. Given that there is no property to inherit, men are not concerned with controlling women's reproduction. Thus, women are decision makers in their marriages and divorces. Women interact freely with men, including in public discussion. Men will help women gather. In some societies women can hunt larger animals, and in most, women can hunt small animals or use traps.

EGYPT

BY LINDA EVANS

The ancient Egyptians observed their surroundings closely and drew upon aspects of the natural world to form many of their religious and philosophical concepts. By using various methods and technologies, they also exploited the plentiful food sources that could be found in the fertile Nile River valley and adjoining deserts.

Petroglyphs, or rock carvings, in the cliffs that border the Nile provide clear evidence that animals were hunted extensively during the Paleolithic and Neolithic Periods. In these images, men armed with harpoons and bows and arrows pursue a variety of game, including hippopotamuses, Nile crocodiles, scimitar oryx, giraffes, and African elephants. Bones and scales recovered from prehistoric settlement sites also show that the indigenous population consumed a great deal of fish, especially Nile catfish. Later, during the Predynastic Period (before ca. 3000 B.C.E.), art objects, such as ceramic pots, knife handles, and palettes, were often decorated with images of game. By the dawn of the Egyptian state, however, many prey species had become extinct locally owing to the combined effects of climate change and human disturbance.

With the development of agriculture, the Egyptians were no longer dependent upon hunting for their survival. Nevertheless, images that were carved into and painted upon the walls of tombs reveal that the practice continued throughout the historical period, during which it achieved a ritual significance. Hunts took place in both the desert fringes and the marshes of the northern delta region. In desert scenes from the Old Kingdom (ca. 2575–ca. 2134 B.C.E.), hunting dogs are commonly used to attack prey. These slender, greyhound-like animals, with tightly curled tails and pricked ears, are shown pulling down and savagely biting a range of species, including scimitar oryx, hartebeest, dorcas gazelles, Nubian ibex, striped hyenas, red foxes, golden jackals, and Cape hares. The dogs are often accompanied by a hunter wearing a striped tunic who, while kneeling beside his pack, points out potential victims.

Other hunting practices are also depicted. In a few tomb scenes men use lassos to rope wild cattle or wrestle desert

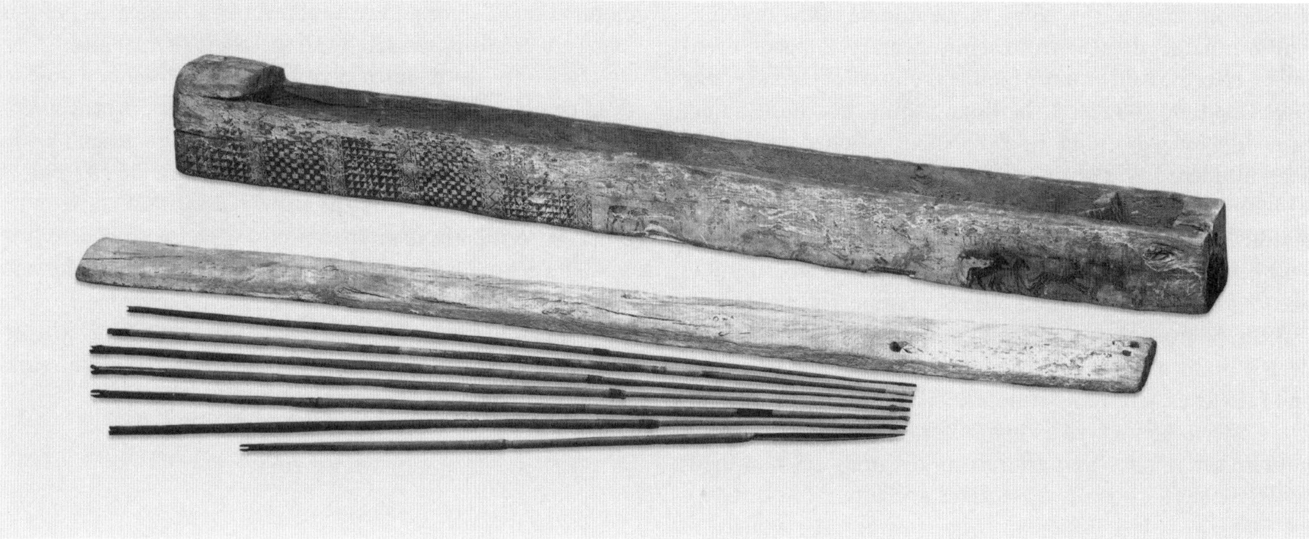

Archery case painted with a hunting scene, from Thebes, Egypt, Middle Kingdom, (2040–1640 B.C.E.). (© The Trustees of the British Museum)

ungulates by hand; it is possible that such animals were captured alive and then killed later for ritual purposes. At first only the king is shown using a bow and arrow. Scenes from the late Old Kingdom, however, show private tomb owners using this weapon to bring down various species of antelope as well as wild ass, Barbary sheep, dama deer, and ostriches. The sparsely vegetated rocky landscapes in which these depicted hunts take place are occasionally bordered by netting fences, suggesting that the animals were sometimes captured first and then released into a corral before being set upon. The necessity for such "hunting parks" may reflect a gradual decline during the Dynastic Period in the populations of some species in their natural habitats.

Tomb paintings also show men hunting in the marshes. Set within impenetrable papyrus thickets, these images usually feature an abundance of birds, such as ducks, Egyptian geese, sacred ibis, pied kingfishers, and little egrets. In a scene that was popular from the Old Kingdom until the New Kingdom (ca. 1550–1070 B.C.E.), the tomb owner, while holding "decoy birds" in one hand, hurls a throwing stick at wild fowl to knock them to the ground. In other scenes, groups of hunters employ a "clap net" to catch large numbers of waterbirds. This device consisted of netting panels laid out across the water surface. Once a sufficient number of birds had alighted upon the submerged trap, the men, while hidden from view, pulled on a rope to close the panels over the animals. Scenes from the Old Kingdom frequently show a gray heron standing prominently nearby; the heron was used as a decoy to attract birds to the trap.

Wild birds were also captured in the surrounding countryside. For example, wall scenes show that common quail attracted to harvests were flushed into weighted nets, which teams of running workmen dragged across grain fields. Similarly, golden orioles drawn to orchards were caught in nets slung over fruit trees after the shouts of waiting men caused them to fly upward.

Both pictorial and physical evidence has provided details about ancient Egyptian fishing methods. Spear and harpoon points made of bone, ivory, and copper have been recovered from archaeological sites dating from the Predynastic to the Greco-Roman Period. These objects are also represented in wall paintings that depict tomb owners using a bident (a two-pronged spear) to stab fish while canoeing in the marshes and in scenes where men hunt hippopotamuses with barbed harpoons. Wall scenes often illustrate large-scale fishing operations in which long seines (a type of large net) overflowing with tilapia, Nile perch, gray mullet, catfish, and European eels are hauled in to shore by groups of fishermen. However, small wooden models found in tombs dating to the Middle Kingdom (ca. 2040–ca. 1640 B.C.E.) show that the seine could also be dragged through the water while slung between a pair of boats. In some scenes weir traps (basket traps) are deployed in shallow canals to intercept fish swimming upstream, while in other images workers strain to lift from the water large dip nets filled to capacity with a variety of species. Hand lines were also used, and fishhooks of bone, ivory, shell, and copper have been recovered from many sites. Simple barbless hooks were common at first, but barbed examples became popular during the Middle Kingdom, a time when the first depictions of fishing rods also appear.

Once the catch was brought to land, tomb scenes show that the fish were gutted and then the flesh was dried by either hanging it from lines or laying it out on the ground, often with the heads and spines still intact. Mullet roe was especially prized; this was also removed and eaten either fresh or dried. Despite occasional religious restrictions, fish were consumed throughout Egyptian history. The remains of a fish-processing plant have been found in a Fourth Dynasty (ca. 2575–ca.

2465 B.C.E.) workers' village at Giza, and documents show that soldiers, priests, and artisans were often paid with quantities of fish. During the Roman period, dried catfish were exported from Egypt to many parts of the Mediterranean.

Although their early development of agriculture enabled the Egyptians to cultivate most vegetables, they nevertheless continued to gather important wild plants. For example, wall scenes show men carrying large bundles of papyrus back from the marshes. This aquatic plant had multiple uses, particularly in the production of paper, but the rhizomes were also eaten. The rhizomes of white and blue lotus plants were also consumed, and their petals, which have narcotic qualities, were used in medicines. The sweet fruits of the wild sycamore fig, the thornbush, and the doum palm were so relished by the Egyptians that they were frequently included among tomb offerings left for the dead to enjoy in the hereafter.

THE MIDDLE EAST

BY LYN GREEN

The Fertile Crescent of the Middle East is usually regarded as one of the areas where humans first domesticated plants and animals. However, the earliest cultures of the region relied on hunting, fishing, and gathering for their subsistence. These activities continued to be important sources for foodstuffs to supplement people's diets and for trade. Although many types of plants and trees would eventually be cultivated in some way or another, wild plant gathering continued to be the usual way to obtain various herbs for medicine and cooking and for certain types of food.

Nuts and seeds or kernels were a significant part of the subsistence diet throughout ancient Near Eastern history. Acorns could provide both animal fodder and food for the poorest classes of people. Almonds, pine nuts, pistachios, and kernels from the fruit of the terebinth tree were widely eaten throughout Mesopotamia and Persia. Greek authors such as Strabo and Plutarch, of approximately the first century C.E., mention pistachios and terebinth kernels as particular foods of the Persians. Although some varieties of trees eventually were cultivated in orchards or gardens, in areas where these trees grew plentifully on their own it was often much easier just to gather the nuts, fruits, and kernels in the forests. Some varieties of mushrooms also did not lend themselves easily to cultivation and continued to be gathered in the woods. Truffles were considered a delicacy by the Babylonians.

Even after the rise of agriculture, fishing was part of food production throughout the ancient Near East. Archaeological finds and texts recording trade or rations for workers show that both saltwater and freshwater fish were a part of the diet. It is also clear that many varieties of freshwater fish were raised in ponds for easy access. Saltwater fish, of course, would still have been caught by fisherman in boats. Once caught, fish of all types might be dried, salted, or otherwise preserved for trade. The bones of a saltwater fish called a tunny have been excavated in the ruins of the inland Sumerian city of Ur in southern Iraq, showing that preserved fish might have been traded over long distances.

There is some evidence that in Israel during the Iron Age fish were both salted and pickled. Fishing was done with hooks of bone or metal much like modern ones. Nets were also used: Individual fishermen cast nets with stone or lead sinkers, and groups of fisherman used dragnets to catch fish in rivers or in the sea. These nets were originally made of plant fibers, but eventually linen and cotton became more common. Clams and other mollusks were gathered and eaten by most of the cultures of the ancient Near East. However, seafood was often considered food for the poor. The well-off preferred to show their wealth by eating red meat, especially from large animals that were either were expensive to raise or dangerous to hunt.

Although the domestication of animals such as sheep, goats, and cows proceeded at the same time as the development and spread of agriculture, there was always a place for hunting in food production. However, as hunting is a time-consuming and unreliable method of meat production compared with the slaughter of domesticated animals, hunting tended to provide meat for two widely disparate classes of people. At one end of the social scale, hunting would still have been important in the lives of those fringe groups who lived outside the urban centers.

A group of early cuneiform tablets called the Yale Culinary Tablets (housed at Yale University in Connecticut), dating to about 1700 B.C.E., includes a number of recipes for various types of meat, including stag. The recipes on the Yale

Impressions of cylinder seals on clay, depicting hunting scenes; found in the treasury of the palace at Persepolis. (Courtesy of the Oriental Institute of the University of Chicago)

tablets were those used by the upper classes of society, and the mention of venison shows that they valued game. The Greek authors also mention venison when describing the diet of the Persians, and at Persepolis both antelope and gazelle are shown among the animals prepared for a feast. It is also likely that rabbit and other small wild animals were hunted by the poorer country dwellers—everywhere but in Israel, where religious rule prohibited people from eating them. Onagers (wild donkeys) were also hunted for their skins. Other wild game, including wild oxen and wild boar, were hunted and eaten in most of the Near East. Both wild bulls and wild boar were dangerous animals, and those who hunted them gained both prestige and protein after a successful hunt. Hunting, especially lion hunting, became a symbolic activity of kings to promote an image of bravery.

Not all hunting activities were equally prestigious. Birds and small game such as hares and rabbits were hunted or trapped, but without the fanfare that surrounded other game hunting. Among the wild birds eaten were partridges and duck. Other birds used for their meat, feathers, and eggs were sometimes raised on farms, including geese, pigeons, and chickens. The chicken was a latecomer to the Near East, arriving from the Indian subcontinent around the time of the Assyrians (1813–609 B.C.E.). Even in classical Greek times chickens were sometimes still called the Persian Bird.

Apart from obvious food sources, such as domesticated cattle, both wild and domesticated birds, and fish, the ancient Israelites also gathered and ate insects, specifically grasshoppers and locust. A taste for locusts was apparently shared by others in the Near East: Assyrian reliefs show attendants carrying long skewers of (presumably roasted) locusts or very large grasshoppers to a royal banquet. These, too, were probably gathered from the fields where cultivated crops were sown. Locusts and grasshoppers were not only a useful protein supplement to the diet but also reduced the depredations caused by these pests on other food sources.

A number of ancient Near Eastern cultures, including the Persians, ate camel. Although camels were more or less domesticated by the first millennium, their use as food undoubtedly began when these animals were still wild. They would have been hunted for their meat. Some cultures, such as the Babylonians, also caught and ate mice, jerboas, turtles and wild hare. Gazelles and similar animals (such as ibex) were hunted and eaten as delicacies. The trapping or hunting of wild animals gradually evolved from a necessary means of subsistence to a source of luxury foodstuffs.

ASIA AND THE PACIFIC

BY KIRK H. BEETZ

The Asia and Pacific region is vast, with many different climates that affect what sort of food is available from place to place. At one time all people were hunter-gatherers, people who moved around the landscape learning what to eat and what not to eat. Some of them settled in one place or chose to migrate between winter and summer homes. Others chose to follow herds of animals. Still others chose to press ever onward. This last group continued until they reached Australia. Their descendants remained primarily hunter-gatherers.

For the ancient Australians, the landscape offered vast, open lands where spears, arrows, and boomerangs were effective in bringing down game. For other peoples of Oceania, there were small islands with big mountains, vast rain forests, and much open water. One group, by far the most ancient, was ethnically similar to the Dravidians of southern Asia and to the Australian Aborigines. Another group, only beginning to colonize the Pacific islands near the end of the ancient era, was the Polynesians. Both groups had a dramatic effect on wildlife.

The migration of people through Indonesia and across the Pacific to Australia is just beginning to be studied, but one aspect of it stands out: Wherever these ancient peoples went after leaving the Asian mainland, they tended to exterminate the wildlife. They would reach an island, feed off its game animals until they were gone, and then move on to the next island. They used spears with fire-hardened tips, stone tips, or bone tips. The ecological catastrophe such habits of hunting could cause can be seen in Easter Island (settled in the 400s B.C.E.), where the people exterminated edible native land animals and plants, leaving mostly fish to eat, and even trapped themselves by destroying the trees from which they could build boats, using the trees for timber for the roofs of their homes and as logs for rolling massive stone monuments from their quarries to the edges of the island.

Among the Polynesians, special hunting skills were developing during the early Christian era. The Polynesians hunted game not only on land but also in the sea. They made harpoons tipped with stone or coral. They learned to use nets to gather in fish in shallow waters and to hunt dolphins and large fish out at sea. When foraging on land, they sought out tubers, perhaps because starchy tubers were filling and supplied energy. The people on every island in the Pacific near Asia, such as the Philippines, Indonesia, and Japan, learned to harvest shellfish. On the Japanese island of Honshū, people ate so many shellfish that they were able to pile the shells into large burial mounds.

The first fishhooks were used even before the last great ice age. The first may have been gorge hooks—double-pointed hooks with a line attached in the middle. Bone, antlers, and stone were used throughout southern Asia. Fish from freshwater streams were an important source of food. The earliest depictions of bows and arrows may be in rock paintings in North Africa from about 20,000 B.C.E., but some paleontologists believe that the bow and arrow developed much earlier. Prior to the development of the bow and arrow, hunters used spear launchers to maximize the force of their throws. These launchers were hollowed out wood, stone, or antlers in which the base of the spear would rest. With an overhand motion, the spear could be flung hard enough to pierce the flesh of elephants and rhinoceroses. The bow and arrow allowed a hunter to increase the force of an attack by using the stored energy of the bent bow and string. Among hunters of large game from at least 1500 B.C.E. the bow and arrow were the weapon of choice.

Little is known about the customs for hunting in India before 500 B.C.E., though the Aryans who migrated into India in the 1500s B.C.E. esteemed hunting prowess. Hunting and fishing became controversial in India after 500 B.C.E. By 300 B.C.E. hunting and fishing had become detestable acts that only outcastes (those people who had no caste status and were thus at the lowest end of the social order) were permitted to do, yet hunting and fishing were recognized professions under the laws of India, and the restrictions on eating meat were often ignored or explained away. For instance, Buddhist priests could eat meat so long as they did not kill the animal themselves. Fishing was excused because the fish was partly at fault for choosing to bite the fishhook. Further, hunters were expected to capture animals alive to transfer to parks owned by monarchs and nobility, who hunted the animals for sport.

Ancient Indian professional hunters lived near forests, sometimes in villages of nothing but hunters. Farmers who lived near wild lands also hunted, even though doing so was against the rules governing the castes. The primary weapon in hunting was the bow and arrow. Hunters would station themselves near trails used by deer and other animals and strike with poisoned arrows. Sometimes they incorporated traps into their hunt. A pit would be dug large enough for an elephant, and the pit would be covered to look like normal ground. Poison arrows would finish off a trapped elephant, and then its tusks would be sawed off and carried away for sale.

Other animals were also trapped. Loops of rope attached to trip wires would wrap around an animal's legs, hobbling it. An unusual method for capturing deer and antelope involved attracting deer with the scent of tasty food and then letting the animal see the hunter. This activity could go on for days until the deer had become used to the hunter and was unafraid. Then the hunter would scoop up the animal and carry it away.

In China monarchs and noblemen would go hunting with their retainers and servants. The monarchs and nobles rode on chariots during the Shang Dynasty (ca. 1500–ca. 1045 B.C.E.) and were traveling on horseback by the Han Dynasty ca. 202 B.C.E.–ca. 220 C.E.). They used dogs and servants to stir up game, which they hunted with bows and arrows. Such a hunt was intended to be a grand entertainment, during which the nobility would win honor by killing animals. Sometimes they used trained falcons to bring down game.

Even peasants could use trained hawks, usually to bring down game birds. While peasants hunted mostly to feed themselves and their families, professional hunters brought their kills to city markets to sell. They hunted birds with bows and arrows and brought ducks, geese, and pheasants to market. Fishermen salted the fish they caught to preserve it until they brought it to market. They used nets made of hemp in rivers and the sea. Under law and by custom, the ancient Chinese valued their game animals. When a Chinese hunter had the opportunity to kill two deer, he would kill only one. The Chinese believed that enough game animals should survive from year to year to keep their numbers sufficiently high to feed people indefinitely.

EUROPE

BY RICK SCHULTING

Until the arrival of domesticated plants and animals from the Near East, prehistoric populations in Europe relied upon hunting, fishing, and gathering for their subsistence. The Mesolithic Period began at the end of the last ice age, around 12,000 years ago, and ended with the arrival of farming, which began around 7000 B.C.E. in southeast Europe, around 4000 B.C.E. in northwest Europe, and even later in the more northern parts of Scandinavia.

Great changes took place at the end of the last ice age, as the large herd mammals—horse, reindeer, bison, and mammoth—became extinct or moved to the far north. With the retreat of the ice came the forests, with an entirely different set of animals, including red and roe deer, elk (the European moose), aurochs (wild cattle), and wild boar. These now formed the main prey species sought by human hunters, who by this time were well acquainted with the use of the bow and arrow. Domestic dogs were present as well and may have helped in the hunt. In some parts of Europe different animals, such as ibex and chamois in the Pyrenees and the Alps, were found and were also hunted. A great variety of smaller game was also hunted or trapped, some, including pine marten, fox, and wolf, mainly for their furs.

Where people had access to rivers, lakes, and coasts, fish and shellfish often featured in the diet. Much evidence for coastal settlement at this time has been lost to rising sea levels, but where the ancient coastlines do survive, and most particularly in southern Scandinavia, there is abundant evidence from ancient kitchen middens (accumulations of food and other debris of human occupation, such as discarded tools and ashes from hearths) of the exploitation of marine foods. The largest of these middens contain many cubic yards of oyster shells and other shellfish as well as the abundant remains of a variety of fish. Eels and flatfish appear to have been particularly important here. A relatively new technique known as stable carbon and nitrogen isotope analysis has been used to test surviving human bone from burials at these sites. These tests show that in many cases the great majority of the protein in the diet came from the sea. But the bones of terrestrial mammals in the same sites show that these animals were also hunted, as were such sea mammals as seals and porpoises. It seems that on occasion even small whales

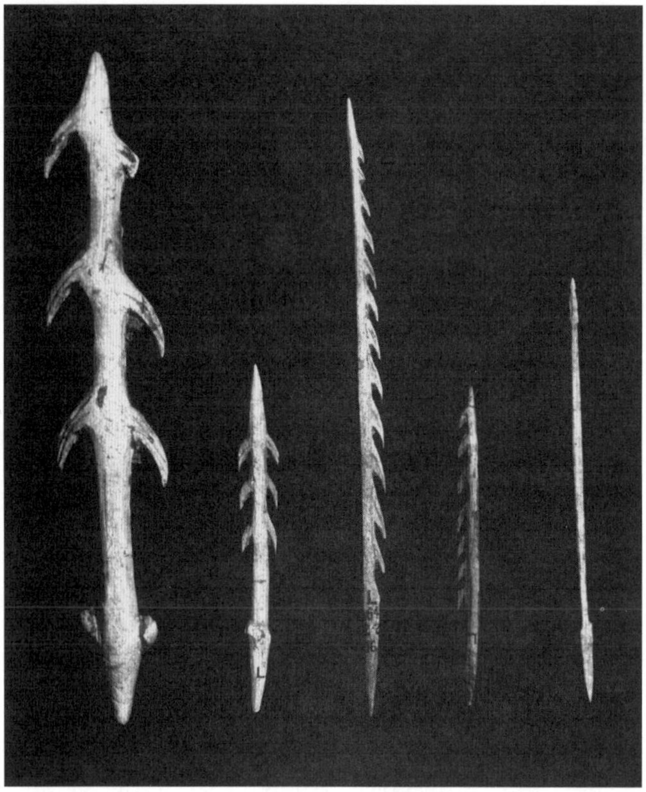

Harpoon tips made of antler from the cave of Courbet, Penne-Tarn, France, and dating to about 10,500 B.C.E. (© The Trustees of the British Museum)

were actively hunted, though more often these animals were probably found and used when they were stranded.

The waterlogged conditions of some of these coastal sites led to the preservation of wood and plant fibers only very rarely found elsewhere. This evidence shows that ancient peoples had developed a complex technology, including stationary fish traps of wooden stakes and woven withies, as well as eel baskets that differ very little from those still in use today. Dugout canoes and paddles have also been found, though mainly these items seem suited for calmer waters near the shore.

Many species of birds were also exploited, some in large numbers, taken when their migration routes brought them within reach. Others, such as the white-tailed eagle, were used less often, but their feathers may have been important for arrow fletching as well as for ornamental and ceremonial purposes. Nets, small fragments of which survive from some sites, were probably as useful for capturing birds and other small game as they were for fishing.

A great variety of plants was gathered, for a variety of purposes, including food, medicines, and raw materials for clothing, basketry, and dyes. Unfortunately, rather less is known concerning the exploitation of plants than of animal resources, partly because plant remains do not survive as well as animal bones and are more difficult to recover during excavations. An exception is the hazelnut, the charred shells of which are ubiquitous on Mesolithic sites across Europe. The stones of wild fruits, such as plum and apple, and the pips of many types of wild berries have also been found where preservation conditions were favorable. Far less well represented are herbs and other greens that would have added flavor and variety to the diet and would have been of medicinal importance as well. A greater abundance and variety of edible plants would have been available in southern than in northern Europe, including sweet foods, such as figs and honey. Indirect evidence of their use is seen in the much higher rates of caries (cavities) in the teeth of human skeletons from this period in southern Europe.

A reliance on hunting, fishing, and gathering does not mean that people wandered endlessly over the landscape. Their use of the environment was both highly knowledgeable and highly structured, often following a distinct seasonal round, with return visits to, for example, productive berry patches or animal migration routes year in and year out. In areas that were favored with especially rich and varied resources, communities were able to live in larger and more permanent villages, comparable in many ways to the earliest farming villages. There is evidence of such settlements patterns in parts of southern Scandinavia and on some stretches of the Danube River, most famously at the site of Lepenski Vir.

Based on comparisons with people practicing a hunting, fishing, and gathering economy in more recent times, we can surmise that different activities were often carried out by different age and gender groups but that there was at the same time a considerable degree of flexibility in these arrangements. Thus, in many cases, young men were probably the most active hunters, while young women may have ranged farthest in gathering plants and shellfish as well as seeking out or taking any small game that opportunistically presented itself. Young children and older men and women likely stayed closer to the camp or village, contributing in other ways. Many men probably also gathered, especially at certain times of the year, such as when the berries were ripe and would soon be lost to birds and bears if not gathered quickly. And no doubt some women enjoyed and were skilled in hunting larger game. Other activities, such as game drives, or preparing and setting nets for migratory fish or birds, would have required the participation of everyone.

GREECE

BY CHRISTOPHER BLACKWELL

Hunting figures prominently in the mythology of ancient Greece. Several of the famous Twelve Labors of Heracles (Hercules to the Romans) involved hunting: his killing of the Nemean Lion, his hunt for the Ceryneian Hind and the Erymanthean Boar, and his killing of the Stymphalian Birds. The famous Boar Hunt of Meleager, which ended in tragedy, brought together a number of mythological heroes. The hunter was a romantic figure who existed outside the normal life of the farm and town. Artemis was the goddess of the hunt and is often portrayed as an untamed spirit, exotic but dangerous.

Most hunting by real people of the ancient Greek world was for food rather than for sport. Since the main source of protein for most people came from legumes such as lentils, meat was a welcome addition to the table. Our best source for techniques of ancient hunting is the work by the fourth-century philosopher, historian, and adventurer Xenophon. Cynegeticus, literally Dog Leader but often translated as Hunter, describes techniques for hunting rabbits and hares, deer and hinds, and the most challenging prey, the wild boar. He writes of how dogs or human "beaters" were employed to drive animals out of the brush and into the open. Many of the other techniques Xenophon describes are clearly those of a practical-minded hunter rather than a sportsman. He mentions using pits and snares to trap animals, setting out clogs (blocks of wood intended to trip a running animal) and nets to impede animals until dogs could take them down, and even capturing young animals, holding them, and beating them so that their cries would draw their larger mothers to the dogs or the spear.

Boar was prized as a catch both for its meat and because of the danger and difficulty of hunting it. Even when hunting from horseback and with dogs, a human being had ultimately to face the boar and kill it with a spear. An enraged animal could move quickly, dodging the spear or even impaling itself on the weapon so deeply that its tusks could wound the hunter. An alternative was to kill the beast with thrown javelins, but this had its own risks; the historian Herodotus describes how the son of King Croesus of Lydia was killed by friendly fire during a boar hunt on Mount Olympus in Mysia.

Dogs were indispensable assets for a hunter, as the title of Xenophon's treatise indicates. The Greeks kept various breeds of hounds. The most common of these was the Laconian hound (named after the southern region of Laconia, near Sparta), which was bred into a larger breed, the Castorian hound (perhaps like a modern greyhound), and crossed with foxes to form a smaller breed called the Vulpine hound, which may have resembled a modern whippet. For hunting boar, the ancient Greeks preferred so-called Indian hounds, which may have been akin to the modern mastiff. For the most part, hunting was not conducted from horseback except among Greek communities of Asia Minor.

Xenophon's writing on hunting, as well as references in the works of Plato and those of Greek writers from later centuries, tend to support an elitist distinction between aristocrats, who could afford to hunt for sport, and the lower classes, who hunted for profit. This reflected a general bias toward land ownership and agriculture as the proper pursuit of the upper classes, while any activity aimed at financial profit was considered a base pursuit for the masses.

Fishing appears widely in the art of the Bronze Age, particularly that of the Minoan palaces on Crete dating from the second millennium B.C.E. Nonetheless, seafood was not a particularly important part of the ancient Greek diet. The water of the Mediterranean Sea is too salty and too clear to support the variety of fish found in the Atlantic Ocean. Fish populations around areas inhabited by Greeks in antiquity were migratory and variable, making them an unreliable source of food. In fact, ancient literature tends to portray fishermen as figures of excess, swinging from utter poverty to wild, temporary wealth, with comic effect.

But the ancient Greeks liked fish, which provided a welcomed change of taste from the regular diet of bread, olive oil, and beans. Because of its relative scarcity and the difficulties of transporting it fresh, fish was most often pickled and used as a relish to enhance the taste of bread. The ancient Greek word for relish is *opson* or *opsarion*, and the modern Greek word for fish, *psari*, is derived from this ancient word.

Fish were often salted and dried by laying them out in shallow lagoons of seawater, which the sun would evaporate; the increasing salinity of the evaporating water would preserve the fish, which would end up very salty, dried, and easily stored. The salts and trace minerals in this dried fish were probably as important nutritionally as the protein.

There were few rivers in the world of the ancient Greeks, and most rivers dried to mere trickles during the summer months. There is virtually no evidence for freshwater fishing of any kind. The Greeks caught fish close to shore with hand nets whose hauls included small octopuses and shellfish, from small boats offshore with cast nets, and in the deeper ocean with spears for larger fish such as tuna. Fishing in deepwater was dangerous, since the seas of the Greek world were subject to sudden violent storms. These storms were particularly dangerous for boats because of the relative shallowness of the sea

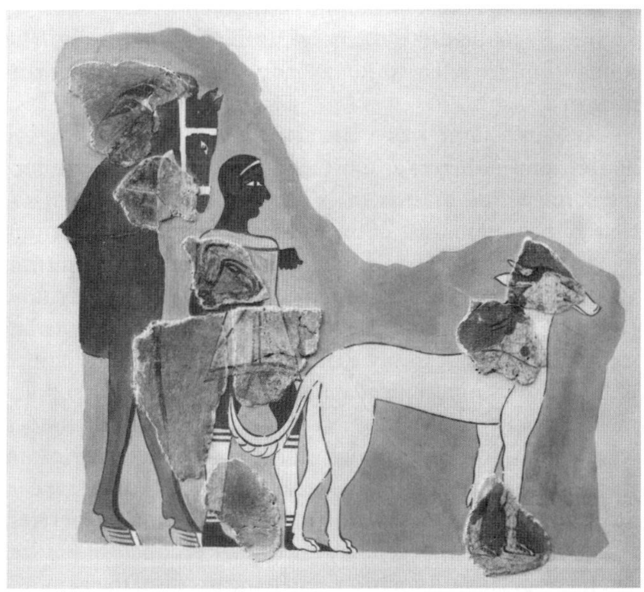

Fragments of a fresco from Tiryns, showing hunter and dog (Alison Frantz Photographic Collection, American School of Classical Studies at Athens)

and the proximity of rocky coasts. Paintings on ancient vases depict boats with lanterns hanging from prow and stern, suggesting that fishing was conducted by night.

Various straits and narrows in the seas around the Greek world were known as rich sites for fishing. The straits of Messina, the Hellespont, and the Bosporus all saw populations of fish pass by, closely packed, during their annual migrations. Certain bays and inlets along the convoluted eastern coastline of Greece were rich in populations of eels, another prized delicacy.

Most of the vegetables in the ancient Greek diet, such as onions, leeks, garlic, and turnips, were the produce of gardens or small farms, but wild greens and herbs were prized as seasoning. Fennel, particularly, grows wild all around the Aegean Sea, and it was valued for its seeds and its stalks. Other herbs that were probably gathered wild were basil (whose name comes from the Greek word *basileus*, meaning king) and the pungent, sulfurous asafetida, a plant originally from Iran but common throughout the ancient world and frequently used in cooking. Honey and some fruits, such as figs, could be gathered in the wild, but both of these sources of sweetening were domesticated by the historical period, after the seventh century.

ROME

BY MICHAEL J. O'NEAL

The civilization of the ancient Romans developed later than most ancient civilizations. The first inhabitants of the area around Rome arrived in about 1400 B.C.E. Then, by about 625 B.C.E., numerous settlers had arrived and drained the marshes around what would become the city of Rome, along the banks of the Tiber River. The Etruscans and Greeks settled portions of the Italian peninsula, but the political entity known as the Roman Republic did not emerge until about 500 B.C.E. The Roman Empire refers to Rome and its many colonies beginning in 27 B.C.E.

Because Rome was a late arrival, its people were never hunters and gatherers as most ancient peoples had been during some period of their early history. Rome was a civilization in the fullest sense of the word, so Romans quickly came to sustain themselves through manufacture, agriculture, and especially trade and military conquest. The entity now called "Rome" was never a Paleolithic, hunter-gatherer, tribal society. This is not to say that some people in rural regions did not live by hunting and gathering or, more likely, supplement their living by these activities. Rome encompassed a wide region, so people under its control in North Africa, in the Middle East, in Europe, and around the Mediterranean Sea undoubtedly hunted, fished, and gathered nuts, berries, fruits, tubers, leafy vegetables, and other products of nature. But no respectable Roman citizen living in one of the empire's cities would have survived in this way. Rather, Romans lived in large part by imported luxury foods and massive supplies of imported grain.

Fishing in ancient Rome was either a sport or a commercial activity. Roman men, particularly those from the affluent classes, often traveled to the countryside, where they hunted and fished for sport. Fly-fishing was an especially valued form of recreation. The bulk of fishing, though, was commercial in nature. The Italian peninsula thrusts deeply into the Mediterranean Sea and is surrounded by water on three sides, so it comes as no surprise that fishermen plied its waters, as had the ancient Greeks before them.

Much of the evidence for ancient Roman fishing practices comes from references in literature and from surviving artwork. These demonstrate that Rome and its colonies around the sea maintained a thriving fishing industry, both from boats and from the shore. They caught fish primarily with nets, though sometimes they used traps. Some of these nets were relatively small and could be managed by just two men. Others were quite large and required a crew of men to handle. Some nets required draw ropes to close the nets; others required the fishermen simply to gather the edges of the nets and pull. The technology of nets was advanced, and Roman writers refer to a wide range of net types, each suitable for fishing under different conditions—in shallow water or deep water, for example. Unfortunately, these nets were made from organic materials, such as flax, so none have survived the ravages of time.

Catches were sold in marketplaces in Roman cities. In comparison with modern life, transportation was relatively slow, and the Romans did not have the advantage of refrigeration, so the fish that arrived at markets was sometimes "fishy," suggesting that it was getting old and on the verge of spoiling. For this reason fish by itself was not always a major portion of the Roman diet, though wealthy people were able to get fresh fish specially delivered to their doors. Fish was consumed primarily in the form of a processed sauce called *garum*. The empire maintained numerous fish-processing plants along the coast for producing this sauce, and people who lived in these coastal regions often made their living by supplying the plants.

Hunting, like fishing, was primarily done for sport, again by affluent men who journeyed to the countryside to hunt game animals, usually with the aid of dogs. Hunting was also memorialized in the Roman pantheon of gods and goddesses, most prominently by Diana, who evolved from the Greek goddess Artemis. Diana, the virgin goddess of the hunt, is usually depicted with a bow and arrow and accompanied by a hunting dog and a stag.

Hunting as a sport was so popular that it actually became a spectator sport called the *venatio*. In ancient Rome this term had different meanings, depending on the context in which it was used. Sometimes it referred to big-game hunting in places like Africa. Sometimes it referred to spectator hunting that took place in Roman arenas. And because such "beast hunts" were often conducted in connection with gladiatorial contests, *venatio* became a general term for these spectator sports taken together.

Thus, at Rome's Circus Maximus, for example, a gladiatorial contest would be scheduled for the afternoon; the hunt, or *venatio*, would serve as a warm-up act in the morning, though sometimes the *venatio* went on for a period of days. Wild animals, such as lions and tigers that had been captured and kept in cages below the arena, were raised by ropes and pulleys and then released in the arena, where trained hunters called *venators* stalked and killed them, often as the animals were being goaded by assistants. The spectators were protected from these animals by large nets or polished metal rollers attached to the tops of the surrounding walls that separated spectators from the killing ground. Archers were positioned on balconies around the arena as a last line of defense.

These trained hunters held a position high in the public's esteem, just below that of gladiators. Sometimes expert hunters from Africa and other regions were imported; in 79 B.C.E. the Roman statesman Pompey organized games in which skilled desert nomads were brought in to kill 20 elephants. On other occasions slaves and prisoners of war with no training were forced into the arena in the expectation that they themselves would become the hunted, and their gruesome deaths would entertain the crowd. These people, called *bestiarii*, were frequently unwilling to face the wild animals in the arena. In one case, a slave managed to get his head through the spokes of a wheel in the cart carrying him and thus break his neck before the hunt began; in another, the writer Seneca tells the story of a German who killed himself in the lavatory rather than face the ferocious beasts in the arena.

THE AMERICAS

BY MICHAEL J. O'NEAL

The usual stereotype of early hunter-gatherer cultures suggests that they were primitive and unsophisticated, perhaps almost subhuman. They lived short lives that consisted of nothing but hardship as they engaged in a desperate, ongoing search for food. They had no property, no art, no government, no social organization—in short, none of the fruits of civilization that accompanied the advent of agriculture and the settled communities that agriculture produced. In the famous words of the 17th-century English philosopher Thomas Hobbes, their lives were "nasty, brutish, and short."

This stereotype, like many stereotypes, had a grain of truth to it among ancient Americans. It is true that people tended to live in smaller bands of perhaps 50 to 100 people, with 20 to 30 being the optimal size; larger communities strained the carrying capacity of the band's territory, often leading to conflict and fissures in the band, as some members broke away to form new bands. It is also true that population densities were small, on the order of just one person per 30 to 50 square miles in resource-poor environments, perhaps as many as 10 to 30 people per square mile in more resource-rich environments, such as the Pacific Northwest. Early hunter-gatherers (including those who subsisted by fishing, a form of hunting) were often on the move, so they had few possessions. Archaeological evidence such as that uncovered in the southeastern United States suggests that they also formed more permanent communities, with public buildings and burial grounds. These more permanent communities established a type of base camp to which groups returned at various points during the year. Otherwise, the band moved about according to changes in the seasons, exploiting resources as they became available.

The social organization of early foragers tended to be egalitarian, with everyone sharing in the fruits of the community's labor. The only specialization tended to be along gender lines, with men engaged in hunting and women engaged in gathering vegetables, fruits, berries, nuts, and even protein-rich insects. Both men and women gathered firewood, and both found small game and such food items as mollusks in marine settings. Artwork was a blend of craft and technology, as even ancient hunter-gatherer societies produced decorative clothing, masks, wood carvings, baskets, pottery, and other artifacts out of the materials available to them. While life expectancy was often low, primarily because of a high rate of infant mortality and high death rates among women giving birth, archaeological remains also suggest that a surprising number of people lived to a relatively advanced age, cared for by the larger community.

The earliest hunter-gatherers migrated to the Americas from Siberia to Alaska via a land bridge across what is now the Bering Sea. It is estimated that the sea level rose to cover the land bridge in about 8000 B.C.E. It is likely that the very first Americans crossed the land bridge to hunt, and after about 11,000 B.C.E. and perhaps much earlier, they hunted mammoths, mastodons, bison, and other large game. The chief archaeological evidence comes from the vicinity of Clovis, New Mexico, which gave its name to the Clovis peoples, bands of Paleo-Indian hunters who, many historians believe, were the first people to inhabit the Americas, arriving in the New Mexico region around 9500 B.C.E. and moving on from there to South America. So-called Clovis points, or stone spear points that historians believe were mounted on wooden hafts, have been discovered in this area. These points are unique in their design in that they snap off on impact, allowing the hunter to reuse the haft if the animal escapes.

In addition to hunting and foraging for food, the Clovis people exploited other natural resources, including stone (especially flint), bones, and ocher (for dye). Many historians believe that the Clovis people were the first Americans; however, many questions surround where they came from and what happened to them. Some of the richest archaeological Clovis finds have been in the southeastern United States, but no archaeological evidence has been found in Alaska. Further, while some disagreement exists about the cause of their disappearance sometime after 8500 B.C.E., when the archaeological record ends, most archaeologists believe that overhunting of big game contributed to their extinction.

Early hunter-gatherers naturally gravitated to environments that were rich in resources, including wild game, for-

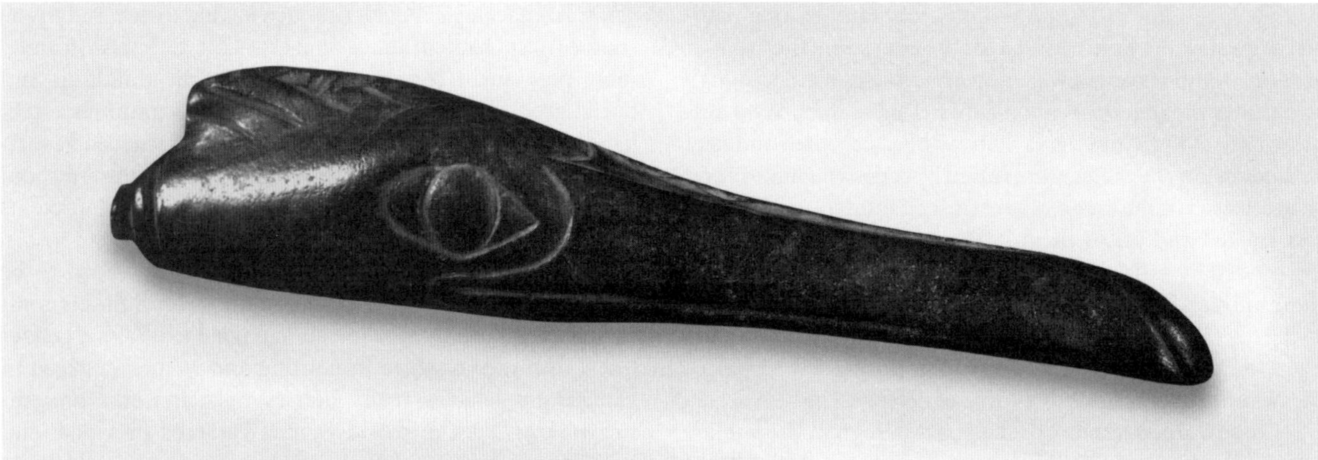

Stone weight carved in the form of the head of an aquatic bird and thought to have been used in fishing, from Orange County, Florida, dating to the Middle Woodland Period (about 400 B.C.E. to 1 C.E.) (© The Trustees of the British Museum)

ests, grasslands, and river valleys. The tribes of the American Northwest, for example, found abundant resources in the region's forests and along the coastlines. Salmon satisfied a large percentage of people's nutritional needs. In the grasslands of the North American Plains and the savannas of South America, large game animals, including prominently the bison in North America, provided not only meat but also hides for clothing, blankets, and shelters, as well as bones, hooves, and other remains that could be put to use. In regions where vegetation was sparser, evidence suggests that early hunter-gatherers burned grasslands and woodlands. This practice encouraged the growth of new, tender vegetation, which attracted game animals that could be hunted.

Hunting and gathering were done almost exclusively on foot. Muscle power was the only form of power available. The horse was not used for hunting in North and South America until much later. The primary exception was among people who lived in aquatic environments along coastlines throughout the Americas and eventually on the islands of Central America. These people relied more heavily on boats, rafts, and canoes to fish and hunt such animals as seals and whales in the far north.

These two subsistence patterns had relative advantages and disadvantages. Aquatic foragers were able to secure larger amounts of food with relatively little physical effort, so their communities became much denser with people. The disadvantage was that they tended to be dependent on a limited range of foods. A sudden change in weather patterns or a disease that wiped out an important food species could leave them vulnerable to starvation. In contrast, pedestrian foragers, because they moved about within a wide geographical region, relied on a much wider range of foods, making them less susceptible to climatic changes, changes in rainfall, and similar catastrophic events. However, they had to exert much more physical effort than did aquatic foragers, sometimes burning more calories in the quest for food than they were able to acquire. Put simply, aquatic foragers had more than pedestrian foragers had, but the food supply of pedestrian foragers tended to be more secure and reliable.

See also AGRICULTURE; ART; CERAMICS AND POTTERY; CLIMATE AND GEOGRAPHY; CRAFTS; DEATH AND BURIAL PRACTICES; FOOD AND DIET; GENDER STRUCTURES AND ROLES; HEALTH AND DISEASE; LITERATURE; MIGRATION AND POPULATION MOVEMENTS; NATURAL DISASTERS; RELIGION AND COSMOLOGY; SETTLEMENT PATTERNS; SOCIAL ORGANIZATION; SPORTS AND RECREATION; TRADE AND EXCHANGE; WEAPONRY AND ARMOR.

FURTHER READING

Jeannine Auboyer, *Daily Life in Ancient India, from 200 B.C. to 700 A.D.*, trans. Simon Watson Taylor (New York: Macmillan, 1965).

Tønnes Bekker-Nielsen, ed., *Ancient Fishing and Fish Processing in the Black Sea Region*, vol. 2 (Aarhus, Denmark: Aarhus University Press, 2005).

Robert Bettinger, *Hunter-Gatherers: Archaeological and Evolutionary Theory* (New York: Plenum Press, 1991).

David L. Bomgardner, *The Story of the Roman Amphitheatre* (London and New York: Routledge, 2000).

Douglas J. Brewer and Renée F. Friedman, *Fish and Fishing in Ancient Egypt* (Warminster, U.K.: Aris and Phillips, 1989).

Peter Garnsey, *Famine and Food Supply in the Graeco-Roman World: Responses to Risk and Crisis* (Cambridge, U.K.: Cambridge University Press, 1988).

Patrick Houlihan, *The Animal World of the Pharaohs* (London: Thames and Hudson, 1996).

Richard Lee, *The !Kung San: Men, Women, and Work in a Foraging Society* (Cambridge, U.K.: Cambridge University Press, 1979).

Lisbeth Pedersen, Anders Fischer, and Bent Aaby, eds., *The Danish Storebælt since the Ice Age: Man, Sea, and Forest* (Copenhagen, Denmark: A/S Storebælt Fixed Link, 1997).

Marek Zvelebil, *Hunters in Transition* (Cambridge, U.K.: Cambridge University Press, 1986).

I

► illumination

INTRODUCTION

Before the advent of electricity, people had to find ways to illuminate their homes at night. They also needed to light workspaces and caves and cellars where they stored food and other goods and to illumine their paths if they traveled at night. The technologies for providing illumination in the ancient world were remarkably similar from culture to culture. Fire, of course, was the source of artificial light. Among the most ancient peoples, bonfires provided light around which the community gathered, thus affording people an early form of social gathering where the events of the day could be discussed, stories and legends could be told, and successful hunts could be celebrated. But people needed more portable sources of light as well as sources of light that were relatively safe and controllable for use in their homes. This concern with safety, especially in crowded and poorly built tenements in ancient cities, led to the development of the *couvre-feu,* a cover for fires at night. The *couvre-feu* is the source of the modern word *curfew.*

Throughout the world, the oil lamp was the most common source of artificial light. These lamps were typically made of stone, clay pottery, or metal. For fuel, the earliest lamps relied on bark, wood shavings, and the like, but the preferred fuels in later lamps were oils derived either from animal fats or from plants. Typically, a wick was fashioned to soak up the oil, which then burned faster than the wick. To make such lamps less smoky, salt was added to the oil, which also had the advantage of causing the flame to burn more brightly. In addition to oil lamps, ancient people relied on torches, tapers, rushlights, and other forms of portable lighting. The ancient Chinese were the first to mine coal for burning, and they even developed natural gas wells. Both of these fuels provided light.

Ancient lighting served a variety of purposes other than just to add illumination in homes and work spaces. The ancient Romans, for example, developed lighthouses along coastal regions, using mirrors to project light that provided guidance to ships at sea. Ancient military organizations also used light to send signals in stages over long distances. Cities in ancient China used lamps as streetlights.

Among many ancient peoples, illumination from the sun had religious meaning. The sun, as the source of warmth, light, and the growth of plants and crops, was often worshiped as a god. Most ancient religious texts highlight the separation of the light from the dark in stories about Creation, and light and fire played an important role in their mythologies. The story of how Prometheus stole fire from the gods is a good example. Accordingly, fire and light were central to religious rituals throughout the ancient world, and fires were often kept lit in honor of the gods.

Fire and illumination even played a role in ancient forms of entertainment. Ancient China and Japan developed magic lanterns and used light to form puppet shows by casting shadows that created the illusion of motion. In effect, the ancient Chinese and Japanese produced the world's first cinema.

AFRICA

BY KIRK H. BEETZ

For much of ancient Africa, light had both practical and religious purposes. Practical purposes included being able to see in the dark as well as marking the edges of a path. For religion, there were many purposes, including marking sacred ground or altars and indicating places for worshipping the sun. Many Africans believed the sun to be sacred, and archaeologists have found evidence that a profound interest in the sun dates back several thousand years.

As in other parts of the world, management of light probably began with campfires. In modern times the San of southern Africa centered many of their activities on a fire that provided a central gathering place in their communities. In Saharan Africa there was a mix of ethnic groups for thousands of years, as their rock paintings make clear. For regions where different cultures mixed, the area around a campfire became a gathering place for people to share information and stories. Thus, the fire's light in the dark not only helped people to see but also drew them together.

When the Sahara was a fertile land, it was populated first by hunter-gatherers (perhaps 27,500–5095 B.C.E.) and then herders of cattle and sheep. They used torches of wood to light their way at night. The exact mechanisms of the torches have yet to be defined, but these early peoples probably just ignited sticks of wood at one end and then let them burn down. However, the ancient Saharans had at hand what they needed to make more sophisticated torches, such as sticks wrapped at one end with grass or cloth soaked in animal fat. Whether the Saharans used torches in their religious ceremonies is uncertain.

The history of ancient Africa is very incomplete, but here and there archaeology offers hints at how ancient Africans dealt with illumination. The management of light seems to have been very important for them by the time they begin to show up in ancient histories. Their homes show that sunlight was often an enemy. Whether the homes were woven huts, grass and wood huts, houses of clay, or houses of stone, throughout central and northern Africa, from west to east, houses tended not to have windows. They did not even have openings in their roofs to let out smoke from hearths. A single door was often the only source of outside light, perhaps because the sun can be harsh in Africa, and keeping cool inside one's home may have been more important than having light.

During the Meroitic Period (ca. 590 B.C.E.–ca. 350 C.E.), the Kushites (ca. 900 B.C.E.–ca. 350 C.E.) of eastern Africa south of Egypt developed a way of managing sunlight that would be duplicated in later cultures in West Africa. City dwellers built homes that consisted of a walled enclosure with rooms at its corners. A single door opened into the enclosure, giving the homeowners the privacy of a home, but the enclosure was open to the sun. The rooms had single doorways into the enclosure, and they were otherwise without openings. Those who lived in the house could have the benefits of sunlight for their daily activities but could retreat into cooler rooms when they wished to escape the heat.

The Bantu-speaking peoples of the third century C.E. seem to have used torches to light their villages at night. Some of their ancient altars consisted of a large uncut stone on which a statue or mystical symbol rested. To the sides of these altars were torches, perhaps just to frame the altar in light. The torches may also have had a ritual purpose, now unknown. The Kushites were heavily influenced by the Egyptians, and they adopted Egyptian lighting techniques for their own homes, temples, and civic buildings. As early as the 2600s B.C.E. Egyptians were using indirect sunlight to illuminate interiors of underground tombs. An aperture was cut at an angle through the roof and ceiling so that direct sunlight did not fall into the passage below but a haze of light did. This construction may have been used in Kushite temple passages, keeping some of the heat of the sun outside while enabling sunlight to play on bright, glistening interior decorations of precious metals, creating a display of sparkling art.

The Egyptians are often credited with inventing the oil lamp. This method of lighting quickly became known to the peoples in touch with Egypt, called "Libyans" to the west of Egypt and "Nubians" to the south of Egypt, where the kingdom of Kush eventually arose. Archaeology has yet to reveal how extensive the use of oil lamps was in Kush, but it was probably widespread. The simplest oil lamps, shallow bowls made of clay with impressed lips for holding wicks of cotton, could have been used by even ordinary Kushite farmers. In Kushite cities there may have been stands of metal to hold them or niches in the walls of stone buildings. They probably did not entirely supplant torches, because torches made a dramatic image when arrayed in a large assembly hall or along an otherwise dark passage leading into the depths of a large temple.

An example of Kushites' managing light is the Sun Temple outside the city of Meroë, once the capital city of Kush. The temple is in a hollow in the ground but is raised above the ground at the bottom of the hollow, perhaps to accumulate rainwater, which was used to water a grassy lawn around the temple. The floor of the temple was yellow, and its walls were blue. Its sanctuary was surrounded by columns. On the back wall, facing the entrance, was a golden circle representing the sun. It would have dazzled people, with the reflected sunlight seeming to thrust out of the earth, while the temple seemed to float on yellow light.

By the time Kush fell out of history around 350 C.E., another ancient kingdom, Axum (ca. 500 B.C.E.–ca. 950 C.E.), was on the rise. The Axumites were a cosmopolitan people who were constantly visited by traders from Europe, the Near East, and southern and eastern Asia. They built houses with columns similar to those used in India's architecture. Short awnings of stone or wood extended over the columns, and behind them were windows, often arched at their tops. These windows had latticework shutters that would allow some light into the rooms beyond but that would keep the rooms somewhat shadowy. It is possible that the shutters were carved so that decorative patterns would fall on the floor as sunlight passed through. The windows probably had panes of glass. Glass windows inspired an explosion of creativity when Axumites converted to Christianity in the mid-fourth century C.E. Techniques for making colored glass were probably known from India, Syria, and Egypt, and Axumites demonstrated a mastery of creating religious images in glass for their churches. Their colored glass windows were feasts of radiant color for the eye.

EGYPT

BY LINDA EVANS

Light had great significance for the ancient Egyptian people. The sun was considered to be the preeminent source of life and was worshipped in the form of the solar god Re. One of the many Egyptian creation myths also declares that the world began when light in the form of a benu bird pierced a dark abyss of primordial waters, causing the earth and the sky to separate. Light thus created order out of chaos, a vitally important concept in Egyptian thinking.

While we can only speculate about how the prehistoric population of the Nile Valley used fire to illuminate the darkness, archaeological evidence indicates that by the dawn of Egyptian civilization, people had found ways to perpetuate flames and make them portable. Indeed, in ancient times Egypt was credited with the invention of the oil lamp. The most common form of lamp, which was used throughout Egyptian history, consisted of a shallow dish, made of metal or pottery, that contained a small amount of oil and a floating wick. The Egyptian term for both lamps and torches was *tekah*. When written in hieroglyphic script, this word often includes the image of such a lamp, rendered as a half-circle from which projects a snakelike wick. Olive and sesame oils, as well as animal fat, were used for fuel, while wicks were produced by first twisting a narrow length of linen or natural fiber and then folding the length in two and twisting it once again.

Although the dish lamp was the most enduring form, other shapes were also developed in Egypt during different eras. In the Old Kingdom (ca. 2575–ca. 2134 B.C.E.), for example, the rim of the bowl was sometimes pinched to form a small spout, the purpose of which was to hold the lighted wick in position. In another example recovered from the Old Kingdom, the wick of a metal lamp was supported by a series of strips projecting from the rim. Lamps dating to both the Middle Kingdom (ca. 2040–ca. 1640 B.C.E.) and the New Kingdom (ca. 1550–ca. 1070 B.C.E.) occasionally feature a broadly channeled rim. The purpose of this outer gutter is unclear, but it may have held water to act as a barrier and to prevent the oil from seeping into the fabric.

During the Middle Kingdom covered lamps began to be produced in order to contain the oil and to prevent spillage. The rim of these vessels was gradually extended to enclose the top of the bowl, leaving only a small hole by which to add the oil and position the wick. Some lamps of this kind included a second aperture in the wall of the vessel into which the wick was inserted. Many lamps of a similar design were imported into Egypt during the Greco-Roman era. However, in the third and fourth centuries C.E. "frog lamps" were produced in great numbers in Upper Egypt. These popular and distinctive ceramic vessels are so named because they display the features of a frog modeled in relief on their upper surface as well as palm branches and rosettes.

Pottery and metal lamps were common in Egypt, but some lamps were rendered in stone. Indeed, hollowed stone vessels probably was the earliest lamp type. For example, a limestone lamp in the form of a papyrus bud has been recovered from a tomb dating to the First Dynasty (ca. 2920–ca. 2770 B.C.E.). Two alabaster lamps were also found in the 18th Dynasty tomb of Tutankhamen (r. ca. 1333–ca. 1323 B.C.E.). One of these delicate objects is carved in the form of a lotus plant featuring two buds and an open flower, each of which acts as an oil reservoir. The other lamp, which resembles a lotus-shaped chalice, consists of two cups nested one inside the other. When the lamp is lit, a scene painted on the inner vessel displaying the king and his wife becomes visible.

Lamps placed upon the floor, on stands, or in wall niches were used in houses and temples, but they also illumined commercial operations, such as mining. Craftsmen probably relied upon lamps when working inside underground tombs. However, as very little smoke staining or soot has been found in these structures, the precise method that was employed has yet to be determined. Since individual handheld lamps would have provided insufficient light by which to carry out the delicate artwork, it has been suggested that many were placed together in a larger vessel and that salt was added to the oil to reduce the amount of smoke. It has also been supposed that an elaborate system of polished metal mirrors captured sunlight and streamed it deep underground, but this notion is not supported by archaeological evidence.

Lamps were not the only form of lighting technology used by the ancient Egyptians. Archaeological and textual evidence reveals that torches and tapers were also employed for both practical and ritual purposes. Tapers, which were made from strips of twisted linen soaked in fat, were either held by hand or placed in holders when lit. A linen taper was found in one of four bronze lamp holders, each rendered in the shape of an ankh symbol, that were discovered in the antechamber of the tomb of Tutankhamen. Wall reliefs and inscriptions in temples reveal that tapers were lit, carried, and offered to deities during daily rituals and that spells were recited to ensure that their flames endured. Torches, consisting of a conical bolus of fat or resin-soaked linen surmounting a pole, were also introduced in the 18th Dynasty and used extensively throughout the Ramesside Period (ca. 1307–ca. 1070 B.C.E.). Both tapers and torches played an important role in religious festivals, especially those associated with the arrival of the New Year.

The harsh climate in Egypt deterred the use of large windows to admit daylight into buildings, in favor of high, narrow apertures. Sunlight was instead cast obliquely into the rooms of houses and other structures via inner open courtyards. Recent evidence has hinted that artists may also have taken advantage of the strong light in Egypt to create special effects in their work. Statues of King Khafre, builder of the second great pyramid at Giza, were originally placed in an open court of his pyramid temple, where they were exposed to the sun. Some of these royal effigies are rendered in anorthosite gneiss, a hard and rather unattractive stone. It has been revealed, however, that when placed in strong sunlight, the stone generates a deep blue glow, suggesting that it was chosen specifically for this purpose, to give the statues a mysterious, celestial quality.

THE MIDDLE EAST

BY KIRK H. BEETZ

Before the invention of the oil lamp, ancient peoples of the Near East used torches, candles, hearths, and ovens for artificial light. In many parts of the Near East sunlight was harsh and something to be escaped. Located in central Anatolia (modern-day Turkey), the city of Çatalhüyük (ca. 7000 B.C.E.) had no streets. Houses were joined together without space between them. People climbed through trapdoors onto their roofs and then walked from rooftop to rooftop. Although the roofs were flat, they were of different heights; thus, people used ladders to go from level to level. As a result, the interiors of homes were very dark and probably much cooler than the outside. Illumination probably came from hearths, with open trapdoors in roofs venting the smoke. Some buildings, such as temples or shrines, had windows. A small window high in a wall would allow sunlight to fall on an altar or on worshippers. In some cases, in large chambers, torches seem to have been used for light.

In ancient Mesopotamia houses were refuges from the sun. Brick houses with walls up to eight feet thick were usually built without windows. The thick walls were intended to keep out the heat. Usually the only opening a house had was a door, but some houses had a window. Windows were fitted with grillwork, probably wooden. Many well-to-do Mesopotamians had homes with courtyards; some such homes were in Babylon. In that city such houses varied in size from 18 feet long and 8 feet wide to 45 feet long and 17 feet wide. Palm-wood planks overlaid by rushes would cover much of the courtyard, providing shade and shielding interior doors from direct sunlight.

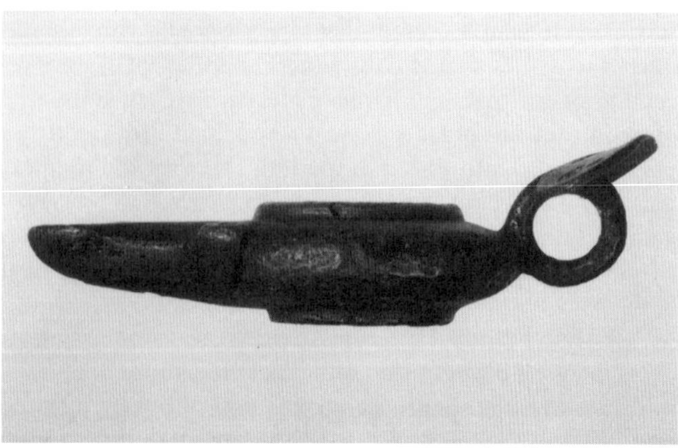

A bronze lamp found at the palace of Persepolis, Persia. (Courtesy of the Oriental Institute of the University of Chicago)

Mesopotamians made extensive use of oil lamps to illuminate the interiors of their homes. Torches were used to light fortifications, city streets, and temples at night. Interiors of temples were often kept shadowy, with torches barely illuminating the statues of gods within. This dim lighting added to the mystery of the temples. Interiors of palaces were usually lit by torchlight. Torches were typically made of bound reeds, though wood was used in parts of the Near East where trees were plentiful. One end of the torch would be bound with cloth that had been soaked in animal fat. For night travel torchlight would have been essential for seeing one's way.

Candles were made of wicks of cotton or flax dipped in tallow. Although candles were probably used in religious ceremonies, oil lamps were the preferred form of artificial light for everyday use. The first oil lamps in the Near East were very simple affairs made of fired clay. Finding oil suitable for lamps was difficult in Mesopotamia; sesame oil was usually used. In other parts of the Near East, palm oil or olive oil was used, with olive oil preferred by most people in the western regions of the Near East.

In about 2200 B.C.E. oil lamps were shallow ceramic bowls with four lips impressed on their sides. Onto the lips were laid wicks of cotton or flax. Most of the wick settled in the oil. Some archaeologists suspect that four wicks were used, one for each lip. At most, these lamps would have provided light for about an hour. For many hardworking Mesopotamians, an hour was about all they needed between quitting work for the day and going to bed. Oil lamps became more varied, with round or square shapes and only one lip. The lip began small, but over time it gradually lengthened until it became a spout. By 1200 B.C.E. oil lamps had become larger and were able to hold more fuel than before, and the spout had become pointed. The longer lip moved the flame farther away from the main body of the lamp, making the lamp somewhat easier to handle because the flame made the body of the lamp hot.

The bottoms of lamps were either flat or rounded. The rounded bottoms may have served a couple of purposes. First, rounded bottoms made the ceramic lamps easier to stack, with the rounded bottom fitting into the open bowl of the lamp underneath. Second, rounded bottoms may have fit lamps into holders. Lamps could be set atop platforms with legs, with the rounded bottom cradled in a circular band, perhaps of metal, at the apex of the platform. The lamps could be fitted into frameworks that were hung from ceilings. Lamps with either flat or round bottoms could be set into niches in walls. Lamps made of copper or bronze could be nailed to walls or hung from hooks from walls.

The development of metal lamps in the Near East is harder to trace than that of ceramic lamps because ceramic lamps were always more numerous and were in constant use from the time of their invention to long after the end of the Roman era. Some molds for metal lamps have been found. The molds were made of stone, plaster, and ceramics. Plaster and ceramic molds were easier to make than stone molds, but plaster molds decay much faster than do ceramic ones; therefore, most of the surviving molds are ceramic. Archaeologists believe that they can tell the difference between lamps made with plaster molds and those made with ceramic molds. On metal lamps, plaster would leave speckles caused by tiny bubbles in the plaster; these bubbles occurred much less often in clay. The molds show that some metal lamps were mass-produced. These lamps would have had handles, and they were made not only of copper and bronze but also of brass, iron, and silver.

There were regional variations in style. For instance, during the Achaemenid Dynasty (ca. 600s–331 B.C.E.) of the Persian Empire, Persian lamps had a long, flat pinch in the side for holding a wick and thin sides, and they were large enough to hold about three hours' worth of oil. The Samaritans of about 100 B.C.E. to about 600 C.E. may have manufactured the lamps most esteemed in the ancient Near East. Their ceramic lamps were decorated with images of plants and religious symbols. Several religions in the Near East of that era used oil lamps in religious rituals, and the Samaritan lamps were well suited to temple use as well as home use. Among their designs were lamps with more than one nozzle. Nozzles were somewhat like spouts on jugs, but wicks were placed in them. Lamps with two nozzles, decorated with images of plants, were especially popular among the Hebrews. Some lamps looked like boxes with nozzles; others looked like horseshoes attached to a bowl.

ASIA AND THE PACIFIC

BY TOM STREISSGUTH

To the ancient Chinese, fire was one of the five elements. Fire corresponded to the summer and to the south. Its color was red; it was generated by wood, another element, and was overcome by a third, water. In ancient China a new light struck during the spring festival represented renewal and purification. The evils and misfortunes of the previous year were forgotten with the extinguishing of the old flame. In addition, the time before the new flame was struck was a time of fasting, as no cooking fire burned, and the family had to eat raw or uncooked food.

According to traditional belief, demons feared the home fires as well as loud and sudden noises. To contend with these bad spirits, the Chinese lit numerous small lanterns or torches in public places and set off fireworks—the noisier and more startling the better. They also protected their homes by painting doors with the color red, symbolic of fire.

The first lamps of Asia may have been stone containers holding dry wood, bark, leaves, or other kindling. Hollow shells could also serve as fuel containers. At some point, animal fat was separated from the carcasses of animals and used as a source of lamp fuel—although one that burned with considerable smoke and smell. Torches were handheld lamps that burned bark, strands of bound and dried vegetation, or combustible cane or bamboo.

Lighting served military commanders as well as the keepers of religious ceremony. Signal fires were burned from mountaintops and walls to convey orders and messages. Commanders sent out spies to gauge the size of an enemy force by the number of camp fires it burned at night. By the same token, a commander could deceive his opponent by gradually reducing the number of evening fires, giving the false impression that he was retreating from the field.

Flammable oil from rendered animal fat served as the earliest fuel for lamps in China. The demand for lighting fuel supported a whaling industry, in which fleets of ships set out in northern waters in search of whale blubber, one of the most economical lamp fuels. These fat-based fuels were so abundant that the Chinese did not turn to oil pressed from plant sources, such as almond, sesame, and hemp oil, until around the first century B.C.E., making the use of fuel oil one of the few technologies in which imperial China lagged behind classical Greece and ancient Rome.

The Chinese were the first in the world, however, to mine and burn coal and to develop natural gaslights. The gas was collected from underground wells that were known occasionally to burn at the surface. Later the Chinese began sinking wells and building iron drill bits to extract gas as well as petroleum from underground reservoirs. They built pipelines of bamboo to transport underground brine, gas, and petroleum to nearby villages. Gas was first put to use to heat basins containing seawater, which when evaporated left a film of edible sea salt. It was also piped into sealed leather bags, which could be carried to the home and then lit for the purposes of heating, lighting, and cooking.

The basic design of Chinese homes and temples, with large eaves overhanging exterior porches and courtyards, allowed lamps to be hung from roof edges and to burn without the obstruction—and the fire danger—of nearby walls. However, these same overhanging eaves, and a lack of windows, made interior spaces dark. Each household had a few burning tapers, made from rendered animal fat, and terra-cotta lamps, but the expense of fuel and the danger of fire such lights posed made artificial lighting in private homes relatively rare.

In India one of the ancient religious texts known as the Upanishads names fire, or *agni*, as the first of the elements. This element is associated with butter, oil, and fat—three forms of basic fuel that were used in the ancient Indian lamps. Ghee, or clarified butter, was a common fuel for home lamps while torches and exterior lamps used castor or linseed oil. Natural petroleum was rare in India and too costly to use as lamp fuel.

The oldest lamps of India were found by archaeologists in Mohenjo Daro, a city of the Indus Valley that had been abandoned by 1700 B.C.E. These round or oval lamps had a small opening for placing a wick. As in all ancient lamps, the wick—

made of cotton, linen, or other dense woven fabric—absorbs the fuel at a steady rate. The fuel is distilled into carbon at the end of the wick, which burns with enough energy to give off a visible flame. In the making of lamp wicks, the Chinese took an important step forward with the invention of the asbestos wick in about the fourth century B.C.E. These wicks burned without being consumed, providing a steadier and more dependable light. They were more costly to produce, however, making the use of such permanent wicks a mark of wealthy and royal households.

The color and brightness of the lamp flame depended on the type of fuel and wick used; some ancient societies added salt to lamp oil to make it burn a brighter shade of yellow. A single lamp with a small reservoir might have burned for eight to 10 hours before its fuel ran dry. Some oils gave off pungent smells and created soot as they burned, covering the walls, ceiling, and furniture with a thin film of carbonized black dust.

Lamps were designed in various shapes and in terracotta, stone, and metal. The city of Mohenjo Daro also had street lights and lights illuminating gates and doorways. Public lighting was well advanced in China under the Han Dynasty (202 B.C.E.–220 C.E.), which was contemporary to ancient Rome. Such lighting remained a mysterious phenomenon closely associated with the otherworldly and the sacred. It was also a source of entertainment. The shadow play, in which hands or puppets are illuminated by a lantern and silhouetted against a sheet of linen, dates back more than 2,000 years. Shadow plays and "magic lanterns" were popular in ancient China and Japan. In the second century C.E. a Chinese inventor named Ting Huan created a device on which the figures of birds and animals moved, and sounds were created, in a shaft of projected light. The magic lantern, the ancestor of the modern cinema, spread in the following centuries to Southeast Asia, Malaysia, and Indonesia, giving rise to illuminated puppet theaters that remain a vital art form in many parts of Asia.

EUROPE

BY MICHAEL J. O'NEAL

The ancient world was a dark place at night. Throughout the lunar year the moon provided some illumination for a few nights each month, assuming that skies were not cloudy. But in common with modern people, ancient people had to find ways to provide artificial light to illuminate their world. Even during daytime illumination was needed in such places as caves, underground food storage facilities, and homes.

The ancient Europeans illuminated their world with fire. Archaeologists routinely find evidence of fire in the form of charred wood or smoke on the walls and ceilings of caves, such as the famous Lascaux cave in France, known for its ancient wall paintings. In the earliest human communities—in Europe and throughout the inhabited world—humans learned to harness fire to provide light. The earliest such fires were probably communal bonfires, around which an entire community gathered at night. This communal fire was the source of fires used by individual families in their homes. Fire, then, became not only a practical way to provide light but also a key part of the social life of the community. People had to work together to provide fuel for the fire, tend it throughout the night so that it did not go out, and keep it smoldering during the day so that it could be rejuvenated the next night. Fire formed the center of an early form of social organization and provided a place where people met to discuss the events of the day and to transmit stories and legends about their community.

While many fires were set outdoors, many were built in caves, up against rock formations, and even in individual huts. Many huts in ancient Europe were round, with the fire built on the floor in the center so that smoke could exit through a hole in the center of the roof. The roundness of the hut ensured that the fire's warmth and light were somewhat evenly distributed throughout.

Early on, fire acquired symbolic and religious connotations. Fire was associated with light and warmth, and creation myths inevitably focus on the separation of the light from the darkness. Accordingly, even in ancient societies, light played a major role in religious observances, and fires in some form were kept lit at shrines and places of worship. The ancient Celtic Druids, for example, used fire in religious ceremonies and kept fires lit as a way of paying homage to gods and goddesses.

Bonfires, though, were unwieldy and potentially dangerous, and communal bonfires were less useful in windy, rainy, or cold conditions, so early Europeans learned to control fire for light in other ways. The principal light management tool was the lamp, which had the advantage of portability. Early lamps were made of stone, with a hollowed-out depression into which fuel could be placed. Some of these lamps were fashioned by hand, but sometimes a person was lucky enough to find a suitable rock with a depression. Limestone was a preferred rock for at least two reasons. Because limestone is soft, it was easy to fashion into a lamp by carving out a depression. Furthermore, limestone does not conduct heat well, so the lamp remained relatively cool to the touch and could be carried about. Many ancient European lamps, though, were made of sandstone, which conducts much more heat. Accordingly, sandstone lamps were fashioned with handles.

The most common fuel, other than such materials as bark shavings, was oil. Rendered animal fat (fat that has been melted down) from game animals and livestock was a good fuel, but it had the disadvantage of being smoky. Vegetable oils were efficient and less smoky, but archaeological evidence from ancient Europe shows that vegetable oils were not widely used. A third fuel was beeswax, or the waxy substance from which bees make honeycombs. Wicks were probably made of such materials as cedar bark (cedar contains its own oils that make it useful as kindling for a fire, and the bark tears off the tree in strips) or any other material that would readily absorb

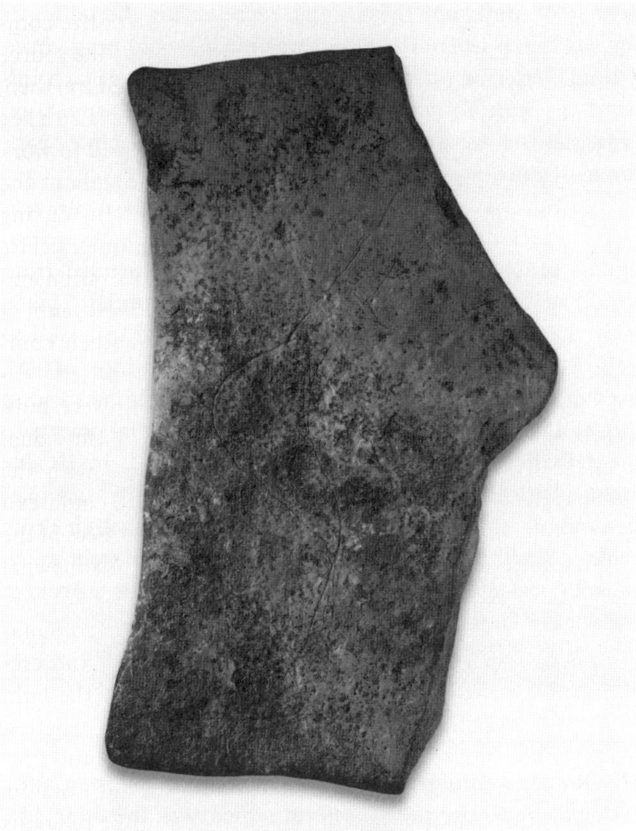

Broken limestone lamp from the cave of Courbet, Penne-Tarn, France, dating to 10,500 years ago; it shows a blackened hollow that suggests it held animal fat to burn like a candle. (© The Trustees of the British Museum)

the oil and conduct it upward so that the fuel burned faster than the wick itself.

Another form of portable lighting was the torch. Any type of hardwood stick, often soaked in pine pitch (the sticky, tarlike sap from pine trees), would have burned to provide light for some hours. Another type of torch consisted of tree bark which comes off in sheets that naturally curl into tubes, such as the bark of birch trees. These tubes were stuffed with tinder and could be carried as torches. Also, ancient Europeans probably used rushlights, a kind of candle that consisted of the pith of plants (the spongy inside of the stalk) soaked in fat. Many marsh plants worked well for this purpose. The outer part of the stalk was peeled away, leaving the soft, fragile interior. This pith was then dried and soaked in fat. A one-foot length of rush candle would probably burn for about 20 minutes. Ancient Europeans used other plants in a similar fashion, sometimes by rolling their leaves, drying them, and soaking them in oil.

The question remains as to how the ancient Europeans started a fire in the first place. The technologies for starting fire are nearly as old as humankind. One way to start a fire was with friction. Hardwoods were the most useful materials for this purpose. A pointed stick was inserted into a small hole in a block of wood and then rapidly twisted back and forth until the friction produced enough heat to ignite a small amount of tinder, such as dried grass. Later Europeans, who were especially knowledgeable about metals, learned that a piece of flint struck with steel produced sparks. Flint is a crystalline quartz often found primarily in the form of nodules of rock in limestone formations. Flint is found, for example, in the chalky White Cliffs of Dover, England, and all over the nearby beaches.

GREECE

BY LISA R. BRODY

Interior spaces in the ancient Greek world were often illuminated with natural light through windows and skylights, but various types of oil-burning lamps were also commonly used whenever artificial light was required, as for nocturnal activities. These lamps evolved from their first appearance in the Bronze Age (ca. 3000 B.C.E.) until the Roman conquest (31 B.C.E.) and beyond, into the Roman period. They could be made of terra-cotta, stone, or metal—usually bronze but in some instances also lead, silver, or gold. The simplest lamps were plain and purely functional, while more elaborate examples contained ornamental or figural relief scenes that often came from mythological or religious contexts. Even these decorated lamps were relatively inexpensive (with the exceptions of those made with precious metals) and soon were reproduced on a widespread scale by using molds.

A typical ancient Greek lamp was approximately 3–4 inches in length and 1 inch high. One of these lamps would have burned for two to three hours before running out of oil, though Greek legend spoke of a wondrous golden lamp on the Acropolis in Athens that burned for a full year. Linen was probably the most common wick material, but wicks could be also made of various plant fibers, such as flax, papyrus, and hemp. The twisted strand would be inserted into an oil-filled reservoir, with the end of the wick protruding from the nozzle so that it could be lit. The fuel of choice was generally olive oil, though animal fat or fish oil also were used.

The earliest oil lamps found in the Greek world date from the Bronze Age (ca. 3200–1200 B.C.E.); many examples of these lamps have been found at sites from Minoan Crete as well as from the Mycenaean Greek mainland. In this era and continuing through the ninth century B.C.E., common terra-cotta lamps were generally bowl shaped or saucer shaped, with the thickened rim pinched to form the nozzle spout for the wick. The earliest of these open lamps were made by hand and usually had four distinct spouts. In the Middle and Late Bronze Ages they were thrown on a potter's wheel, and their shape began to develop toward a single spout; these are sometimes known as "cocked hat lamps." Such lamps were usually unglazed and undecorated.

By the onset of the Classical Period in the fifth century B.C.E., the Greeks began to make lamps with a more rounded, closed form. This development was practical, in that it reduced the likelihood that the oil might spill. By the third century B.C.E. the lamp body was even more closed, with a small fill hole usually less than an inch in diameter. The typical classical and Hellenistic oil lamp had a globular body with a flattened base and a flat top. Centered in the top of the lamp was a pour hole or fill hole, through which oil was poured into the reservoir. The upper surface, surrounding the fill hole, is called the "discus" and was sometimes decorated with a geometric, floral, or figurative design. In some instances this design dictated an off-center placement of the fill hole.

Ancient terra-cotta oil lamps were decorated in a variety of ways. The surface could be burnished or covered with a slip or glaze. Stamped or raised patterns are often found on the shoulder of the lamp, around the fill hole. The fabric, manufacture, and decoration of these lamps reflect contemporary ceramics, and it is very possible that some potters produced lamps in their workshops along with other types of vessels. In Athens of the Classical Period, for example, lamps were made with the same reddish-orange fabric and glossy black slip seen in ancient Greek pottery. Once molds began to be used, even more elaborate lamps could be created. Often the lamp's discus would be decorated with a relief design that could be floral, geometric, or figural. One of the simplest, most common motifs is a repetitive pattern of ridges and grooves radiating from the fill hole. Greek lamps with figural scenes could draw their inspiration from a wide variety of sources, including daily life, cult, literature, and myth. The images on such lamps resemble in many ways the compositions on contemporary coins. Mold-made lamps could also be created in the form of any other object or figure, such as an animal, a human or satyr head, or a sandaled foot; such lamps are called "plastic."

Ancient lamps often had one or more elongated nozzles, through which the end of the wick could protrude for lighting. If there were many nozzles and many wicks, more fuel was consumed and more illumination provided. A lamp might or might not have had a handle; if there was one, it was generally modeled and attached to the lamp body opposite the nozzle. Some lamps had small pierced or unpierced projections, called lugs, in lieu of a handle. The pierced lug could be used to hang the lamp by a string when not in use, while the unpierced versions seem to have had no practical function. Classical Greek terra-cotta lamps were made on the same wheels that were used to make pottery, but artisans in the Hellenistic era developed the ability to fashion them by using plaster or clay molds; this became the preferred method of manufacture from the third century B.C.E. through the Roman period and allowed lamps to be even more easily mass-produced. Lamp molds are often found on archaeological sites along with lamps themselves, allowing for the identification of lamp workshops.

Another important source of information about lamp manufacture and trade in antiquity is the maker's marks and owner's signatures that were sometimes stamped on the underside of the lamp. These signs, representing the potter or the workshop where the object was made, could range from a single letter or pictograph (a symbolic drawing) to a full word or name. Votive inscriptions also sometimes appear on examples that were dedicated to a member of the Greek pantheon of gods.

Lamps were used in a variety of contexts in ancient Greece, including private homes, public buildings, and religious sanctuaries. They were sometimes suspended from a wall or ceiling and sometimes placed on specially made lamp stands. Niches could also be constructed in a wall to hold a lamp and illuminate the room or hallway. Lamps, used or unused, were also typical offerings in temples and in tombs. Like pottery, lamps not only were essential objects in the daily lives of ancient Greeks but also provide invaluable archaeological artifacts for scholars. The ubiquity and relative indestructibility of both types of artifact (though easily broken, small pieces of vases and lamps survive well on archaeological sites) help us to "illuminate" various aspects of the ancient Greek world.

ROME

BY LUCAS G. RUBIN

The Romans employed a range of methods for generating artificial light, the most basic of which was the open fire. Torches were also used, fabricated in a variety of means from the simple to the elaborate. Some were simple wooden stakes while others were fastened bundles with a crown composed of a flammable material and soaked with a chemical accelerant, a substance that speeds the development of fire.

Candles were also used, probably inherited from the Etruscans. Because of their biodegradable and fragile nature, they have not survived well in the archaeological record, but there is sufficient evidence of their use in the form of extant candlesticks and candleholders. Candle shafts were made of tallow or beeswax as well as the reed of vegetable fiber. Beeswax was readily obtainable through apiculture, or beekeeping, an agricultural enterprise in which the Romans excelled. Because the manufacturing process was rather involved, widespread use of candles was restricted primarily to the wealthy.

By far the most common device for generating artificial light was the oil lamp, which was ubiquitous throughout the Roman world. The basic oil lamp consisted of a body (*infundibulum*) with a flat top (*discus*) bordered by an ornamental rim (*margo*), an opening for a wick near the front (*ellychnium*), and a handle at the back (*ansa* or *manubrium*). In the middle of the *discus* there was usually a hole for replenishing the fuel. Lamps were most commonly fueled with olive oil, though less expensive castor oil—which was particularly smoky—may have been more common among the poor. Many different types of wicks were used, including castor, mullein, asbestos, linen, and papyrus.

Lamps were typicaly made of clay, metal (gold, silver, iron, lead, and especially bronze), and stone. The most common material was fired clay, and large factories that manufactured mass-produced terra-cotta lamps were prevalent throughout the empire. Clay lamps were usually made with molds, the top and bottom halves pressed into hollow forms and joined together. Once assembled, they were often glazed. With this simple fabrication technique, elaborate decorative elements could easily be impressed into the surface of the clay. Decoration included patterns as well as images of a religious, mythological, or quotidian nature. In addition, manufacturers often stamped their names into the bottom of the lamp, a feature that permits archaeologists to look in some detail at patterns of production and distribution.

Analysis of these distribution patterns suggests that Italian lamps dominated the provincial markets in the first century of the empire but were later superseded across the empire by locally made products. Manufactured lamps could be shipped in bulk or perhaps used as filler with (or packed within) other commodities and sometimes transported over great distances. A wooden shipping box found at Pompeii in 1881 contained 37 lamps from southern Gaul, with a range of manufacturers' stamps that suggest that they may have been shipped as a consignment.

Lamp showing a chariot race, Roman, about 175–225 C.E. (© The Trustees of the British Museum)

There were numerous and frequent variations on the basic lamp design. Lamps with multiple wicks were manufactured, and models with as many as a dozen wicks arranged in a circle around the *discus* were not unusual. Portable lamps (lanterns), with bodies made of bronze, iron, clay, or wood, were also common. These had high, protected sides and windows covered with a translucent material, such as thinly shaved animal skin, horn, or parchment. Stationary lamps were frequently placed upon purpose-built stands or suspended from chains in order best to radiate their light.

The Romans utilized artificial illumination for a range of functions. Private residences and businesses (both commercial and industrial) required some degree of lighting in the evening, though the Romans chose as much as possible to organize their activities around the daylight hours. At night public spaces were often lit by torchlight, and the city of Antioch was reported to have had an organized street lighting system by 350 C.E. For certain industrial operations, such as mining and tunneling activities, extensive artificial lighting was required. Open-flamed torches would have presented problems, so portable lanterns and lamps placed within wall niches could have been used. The author Diodorus Siculus (ca. 90–ca. 30 B.C.E.), in his *Bibliotheca historica*, mentions that lamps were also mounted on miners' heads, but there is no other evidence of this practice.

Artificial illumination also played an important role in transmitting information. The Romans built many lighthouses along the coasts, both to mark harbors and to warn against shoreline hazards. During the day large mirrors were used to alert ships while fires were ignited at night. A number of these lighthouses survive, including well-preserved structures in La Coruña, Spain, and Dover, England. Additional information is provided about other major lighthouses—such as the one at Ostia—by surviving depictions on coins and in mosaics. The most famous lighthouse of antiquity, the Pharos of Alexandria in Egypt, was actually built by the Hellenistic rulers Ptolemy I Soter and his son and successor, Ptolemy II Philadelphus, but may not have been transformed into a lighthouse until the first century C.E. by the Romans. Although it was destroyed by earthquakes in 1303 C.E. and 1323 C.E., we are well informed about its size and appearance by later Arab chroniclers.

One especially sophisticated use of artificial illumination was its application to military signaling. Signaling was important in ancient warfare, and various communication systems permitted complex messages to be relayed by torches over great distances. The Romans adapted and modified systems from the Greeks and the Carthaginians, among others, and employed them both tactically (on the battlefield) and strategically (along the frontier). These systems were akin to an early form of Morse code, in which a patterned display of torches could relay letters, phrases, or codes.

Illumination also played an important role in several aspects of religious practice. Lamps were an important feature of the household altar (*lararium*) and were used in various religious functions, including funerals. Among Jews in the Roman Empire, lamps were used in observance of the Sabbath, some even equipped with an additional oil reservoir to keep the light burning for the time required. A large candelabrum from the Great Temple in Jerusalem appears in relief on the Arch of Titus in Rome, a monument that celebrates the Roman victory over the Jewish revolt in 70 C.E. Similarly, the early Christians decorated their lamps with early symbols of their faith, such as the Chi-Rho.

Paradoxically, the widespread use of artificial lighting presented some considerable problems. The materials used as fuel (fats and oils) were also sources of food, and individuals—especially the poor—would have had to weigh the need for calories against the need for light. Further, open flames dramatically increased the risk of fire, and large, often rambling and jerry-built neighborhoods in cities like Rome would have been particularly vulnerable to accidents or negligence.

Although artificial illumination was used in a variety of contexts in the Roman world, the technologies for generating light remained fairly static. It was the Roman genius for production, distribution, and adaptation, however, that permitted the widespread and effective use of artificial illumination in various capacities among the populace.

THE AMERICAS

BY MICHAEL ALLEN HOLMES

Illumination was obtained in the ancient Americas as among the most ancient of all civilizations: with fire. With wood gathered from forests, which were especially ubiquitous in Mesoamerica, small fires could be made both for cooking purposes and for light by which to see at night. The more elaborate houses of the elite often included fireplaces. Especially at ceremonial sites, torches would be used. While incense made from copal, a tropical tree resin, was often burned at these ceremonial sites, its function was more aromatic than visual.

See also ARCHITECTURE; ART; CALENDARS AND CLOCKS; CERAMICS AND POTTERY; CRAFTS; EMPIRES AND DYNASTIES; FOOD AND DIET; INVENTIONS; METALLURGY; MILITARY; MINING, QUARRYING, AND SALT MAKING; MONEY AND COINAGE; RELIGION AND COSMOLOGY; SACRED SITES; SEAFARING AND NAVIGATION; SOCIAL ORGANIZATION; TRADE AND EXCHANGE.

FURTHER READING

Sean Anderson, *Flames of Devotion: Oil Lamps from South and Southeast Asia and the Himalayas* (Los Angeles: University of California Press, 2006).

Donald M. Bailey, *Greek and Roman Pottery Lamps* (London: Trustees of the British Museum, 1963).

Donald M. Bailey, *Greek, Hellenistic, and Early Roman Pottery Lamps* (London: British Museum Publications, 1975).

Stephen Bertman, *Handbook to Life in Ancient Mesopotamia* (New York: Facts On File, 2003).

Hella Eckardt, *Illuminating Roman Britain* (Montagnac, France: M. Mergoil, 2002).

W. V. Harris, "Roman Terracotta Lamps: The Organization of an Industry," *Journal of Roman Studies* 70 (1980): 126–145.

J. W. Hayes, *Ancient Lamps in the Royal Ontario Museum.* Vol. 1, *Greek and Roman Clay Lamps: A Catalogue* (Toronto: Royal Ontario Museum, 1980).

"Oil Lamps from the Holy Land from the Adler Collection." Available online. URL: http://www.steve-adler.com/OilLampsMain.htm. Downloaded on November 14, 2006.

Ed Semmelroth, "A History of Fire and Its Uses." Available online. URL: http://hearth.com/what/historyfire.html. Downloaded on January 30, 2007.

► inventions

INTRODUCTION

The topic of inventions among ancient peoples is a difficult one to compass, for the modern understanding of *invention* might not always be applicable to the ancient world. Throughout the Industrial Revolution in the West and the technological revolutions of the 20th and 21st centuries, inventions took the form of objects that were fundamentally new and that changed the way people thought about their world. While many of these inventions built on the scientific and technological discoveries of others, they themselves were a major leap forward as people learned to harness what they knew about the natural world.

In studying the ancient world it would be almost impossible to date the invention of a tool, process, or technique to a certain time and place. Rather, the world's ancient peoples took part in a process of discovering the principles of their world over a period of millennia, each new generation making tiny advances on the discoveries of the previous generation. Invention, then, was more of a process of uncovering the secrets of the physical world, finding ways to adapt human activities to the demands of the nature world, and discovering ways to modify that natural world to promote the comfort and security of people. Another complication in tracing ancient inventions is that the peoples of the world were exploring and innovating in isolation from one another. Thus, while the ancient Egyptians were discovering the uses of papyrus, particularly as paper, so the ancient Americans were also discovering an early form of paper. Who "invented" paper? No one can really know, especially since paper has so little durability over many centuries.

The world's earliest inventors were no doubt those anonymous hunter-gatherers who devised tools to make their hunts more successful: a type of stone that worked better as a spear point, then a way to slice or pound the stone to make it sharper, then a better way of affixing the point to the shaft of a spear, and finally a way to give the spear better balance and heft. One can imagine a group of hunters who had to encircle their quarry until someone had the idea of using cord made from tree bark to make a kind of fence around the quarry; his descendants generations later would then have learned to weave cord into nets to make the process more effective. Perhaps that weaving of nets gave someone the idea of a way to make clothing out of fibers or some other innovation that can only be imagined.

Inventiveness was fostered as people began to settle into permanent, fixed communities with the advent of agriculture. Now they were in more direct communication with one another, observing others' techniques and tools, sharing them, and adapting them. Moreover, a critical mass of people could pool their efforts to come up with an innovative solution to a problem. Throughout ancient Mesopotamia, Egypt, and Mesoamerica, for example, people carried out massive public works projects that led to innovations in architecture (columns and arches), agriculture (plant breeding), irrigation (the water wheel), road building (the crowned road), sewage and drainage systems (the lead plumbing of the Romans), and the like. People interested in medicine could observe the successes and failures of others, over time developing know-how in the use of medicinal plants and even surgical techniques. Farmers could learn new ways of harvesting, threshing, and storing grain. Others who were more interested in crafts work could learn to make use of new tools, techniques, and materials as they collaborated with others. Miners could become skilled at new ways to find ores, mine them, process them, and forge metals.

This process continued as trade and commerce developed, bringing novel tools and materials to new regions of the world, leading to further innovation. One can only imagine the excitement of a European wood carver the first time he or she acquired a piece of ivory from an African elephant tusk or a jewelry maker encountering imported glass for the first time.

AFRICA

BY MICHAEL J. O'NEAL

Ancient Africa was the cradle of human civilization, the home of the world's first people, so it is no surprise that Africans were among the world's first inventors. As the earliest Africans struggled to adapt to and control their environment, they naturally learned how to modify that environment and use the resources that surrounded them to help ensure their survival and to make their lives more comfortable.

The word *invention* suggests thinking of something entirely new, the development of a tool or process that had not existed in the past and that fundamentally changes the relationship between people and their environment. Among the ancient Africans, and probably ancient peoples generally, invention was probably more of a process of discovery and adaptation. Over millennia people inherited the knowledge of their ancestors, but whether from necessity or from simple curiosity they introduced innovations, refinements, and improvements to existing technology to make it work better.

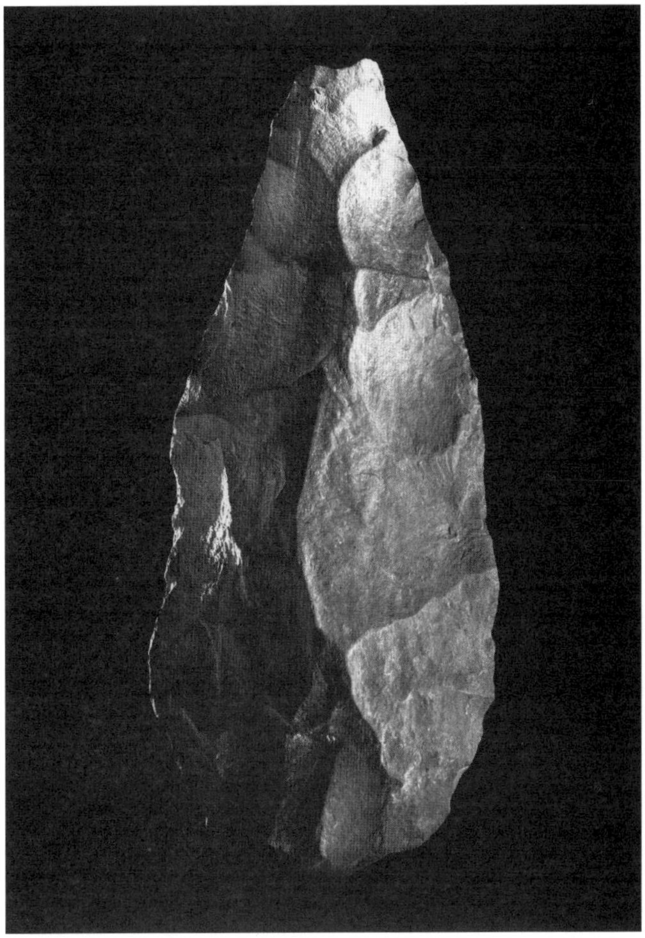

Stone hand ax (Lower Palaeolithic, about 1.2 million years ago) from Olduvai Gorge, Tanzania, representing one of the earliest technological inventions. (© The Trustees of the British Museum)

The ancient Africans did not invent fire, for example. Fire is a process of combustion that already exists in nature. Rather, they discovered that fire could be put to human uses and learned to control it to keep themselves warm, cook food, weaken rock so that it could be split into pieces for use as tools, clear fields of stubble to encourage the growth of the next season's crop, and so on. Historians and archaeologists believe that the first human use of fire occurred some 1.4 million years ago in Chesowanja, near Kenya's Lake Baringo.

Many African developments had to do with the most basic necessities: food, shelter, and clothing. Africans were the first to develop Stone Age cutting tools, and in time they learned to produce handles for those and other tools. Later they developed a great variety of tools, including fishhooks, grindstones, awls, spears, and bows and arrows. They were the first to domesticate crops, some 15,000 years ago, and to domesticate and graze cattle. This took place in what is now the Sahara Desert but at the time—around 6000–3000 B.C.E.—was covered with grasses.

Ancient African inventors, many of them women, devised methods and devices for gathering, preserving, and preparing food (including the mortar and pestle for grinding and pulverizing foods), herbs, and medicines. They created devices for carrying both food and infants (often at the same time), including slings for infants. They learned to use sticks as levers for moving rocks, tree stumps, logs, and other objects. They created hoes and similar tools for digging plants and, later, for cultivating the earth for planting, and they invented one of the world's first plowshares (the metal blade of a plow). They learned how to tan and preserve animal hides for use as clothing and blankets, which they sewed with needles made of bone and dyed with natural substances such as henna. Later they learned how to weave and spin fabrics. They created the first pottery and learned to use kilns to fire the pots, which were then used for food storage or carrying water.

One important adaptation of fire in ancient Africa took place some 2,000 years ago in the region around Lake Victoria. There archaeologists havc discovered ancient blast furnaces used in the production of carbon steel. (Carbon steel is an alloy of iron and carbon. Iron not alloyed with carbon remains relatively soft, but the introduction of carbon hardens the metal.) Carbon was introduced into the iron ore by an ingenious process. First a bowl-shaped hole was dug in the ground. The hole was then lined with soil taken from a termite mound, and a handle that rose above ground level was inserted so the steel could be removed. The chief innovation the Africans introduced to existing furnaces was to insert tubes or blowpipes through the walls of the mound into the pit. These tubes channeled air into the fire, creating a blast-furnace effect as the hot air from the fire rose, sucking air through the pipes into the fire. Grasses and reeds were then burned in the pit, and when the temperature reached a high enough level, charcoal and iron ore was added. The carbon from the burned grasses and charcoal added carbon to the iron, resulting in carbon steel. It is estimated that these furnaces could achieve a temperature of nearly 3,300 degrees Fahrenheit. Of course, the ability to produce carbon steel presupposes the existence of mining technologies, and the oldest-known iron mine in the world, dating back some 43,000 years, has been found in Swaziland.

Ancient Africans invented several systems related to calculation. The Yoruba tribe had a number system based on 20, and the so-called Ishango bone, dating to 8,000 years ago, has a system of notches that indicates a number system. In East Africa accurate calendars were developed in the first millennium B.C.E., and megaliths (vertical stone slabs) enabled ancient Africans to make accurate observations of star constellations. Ancient Africans also developed water clocks, an aerodynamic glider, and the game of chess.

In the area of health care, ancient Africans developed various medicines, including aspirin, a treatment for diarrhea, and a smallpox vaccination remarkably similar to the smallpox vaccine developed by Robert Jenner in the late 18th century. Cosmetics invented in ancient Africa included eye shadow to reduce the glare from rivers, similar to the black patches modern-day football player use to reduce glare. Other cosmetics were fingernail polish, breath fresheners, wigs, pomades, perfumes, and various dyes to enhance skin color. To apply these cosmetics, African women invented the first mirrors, made of polished copper.

The drum, probably the world's first musical instrument, was invented in Africa and used on ceremonial occasions and for communication. Africans also crafted seaworthy boats, and some archaeological evidence suggests that ancient Africans were able to reach the coasts of the Americas. Petroleum, too, was produced around 4000 to 3000 B.C.E. To this list must be added the invention of civilization itself, for the Africans were the first to live in human communities that survived, grew, and spread in large part by passing their inventions down to future generations.

EGYPT

BY WILLIAM H. PECK

The inventions of the ancient Egyptians include ideas and innovations both great and small. One important innovation that still affects us today is the observation of the 365-day solar year. The Egyptians divided the year into 360 days—three seasons of 120 days, 12 months of 30 days—and added five days dedicated to the gods to complete the cycle. They also added the rough equivalent of a leap year to make the calendar correspond more closely with their observations of the sun. They divided the day into 12 hours of daylight and 12 of darkness, giving us the 24-hour division we also still use.

The Egyptians produced the first paper, which they manufactured from the papyrus plant, in contrast to the clay tablets used by the ancient Mesopotamians. With the introduction of papyrus as a convenient writing surface that was flexible and portable, they also developed the inks necessary for writing. Papyrus made possible a giant step forward in the creation and preservation of documents of all kinds.

With the use of papyrus, one of the most important inventions sometimes credited to the ancient Egyptians was the ability to make meaningful signs that could be understood to record sounds and ideas—a written form of language. Historians debate whether the Egyptians or the Sumerians in Mesopotamia came up with the idea first. Recent discoveries at Aswan in the south have led some scholars to reassert the idea that writing was first invented in Egypt. Not everyone agrees with this. In any case, before 3000 B.C.E. a method of recording lists of foodstuffs or other objects began to be developed in Egypt.

As with many other early written languages (such as Sumerian, Chinese, and Mayan), the first stages were essentially pictographs, pictures that stood for things. When this method was extended to convey ideas as well as objects, it was necessary to use pictures as phonograms, signs that conveyed sounds. What is almost unique about Egyptian writing is that the pictures were never completely replaced by abstract signs. Throughout Egyptian history hieroglyphic writing was a combination of signs that expressed sounds with those that expressed ideas. Along with these two types of signs was a third that could be added to designate classes of related words. The ancient written language was complex and became highly developed to a level where it could be used to convey any kind of information, including poetry, prose, religious texts, and scientific, mathematical, and medical treatises. If written language was not an independent invention in Egypt, credit is due for a complex and comprehensive method of recording information.

Egypt was an agricultural country throughout its ancient history. The people were completely dependent on the annual flooding of the Nile for successful food crops. The yearly flood, or inundation, was the result of the winter rains in central Africa. When the flood waters reached Egypt, a new layer of silt was deposited, the land was thoroughly watered, and the natural buildup of salts in the earth was leached out. The Egyptians developed a system of basin irrigation that enabled them to retain the floodwater for a time and then release it into the fields. Because of the annual flooding, the river valley had gradually built up a system of natural dikes or levees made up of the fresh silt deposited by the waters each year. These were pierced to help draw water through canals to the fields and then closed, creating temporary reservoirs. When it was time to begin planting, the dikes were pierced again to allow excess water to escape.

To move water from the level of the river to higher fields, the Egyptians invented a device called a *shaduf*. This was a simple lever pole with a bucket on one end, counterbalanced with stone or mud, which made it possible to lift water 5–6 feet. This was a highly labor-intensive method, but it was the only mechanical solution to raising water known to the Egyptians until late in their history. In the Ptolemaic Period (304–30 B.C.E.) a second method was introduced. The *sakkia* was an animal-driven waterwheel that increased volume and reduced human labor. Both the *shaduf* and the *sakkia* were still being used well into the 20th century.

Although glass was not widely manufactured in ancient Egypt, the basis for its production was known. Rare examples of glass objects have been found, but the principles used in glassmaking were also those used to make Egyptian faience. Blue or green glazed objects of all kinds were produced using this technique. Egyptian faience is a ceramic-like material composed of powdered quartz and a small amount of lime, usually with a copper compound to give it color. The powdered quartz—essentially crushed sand—was made into a paste that could be modeled by hand or pressed into a mold.

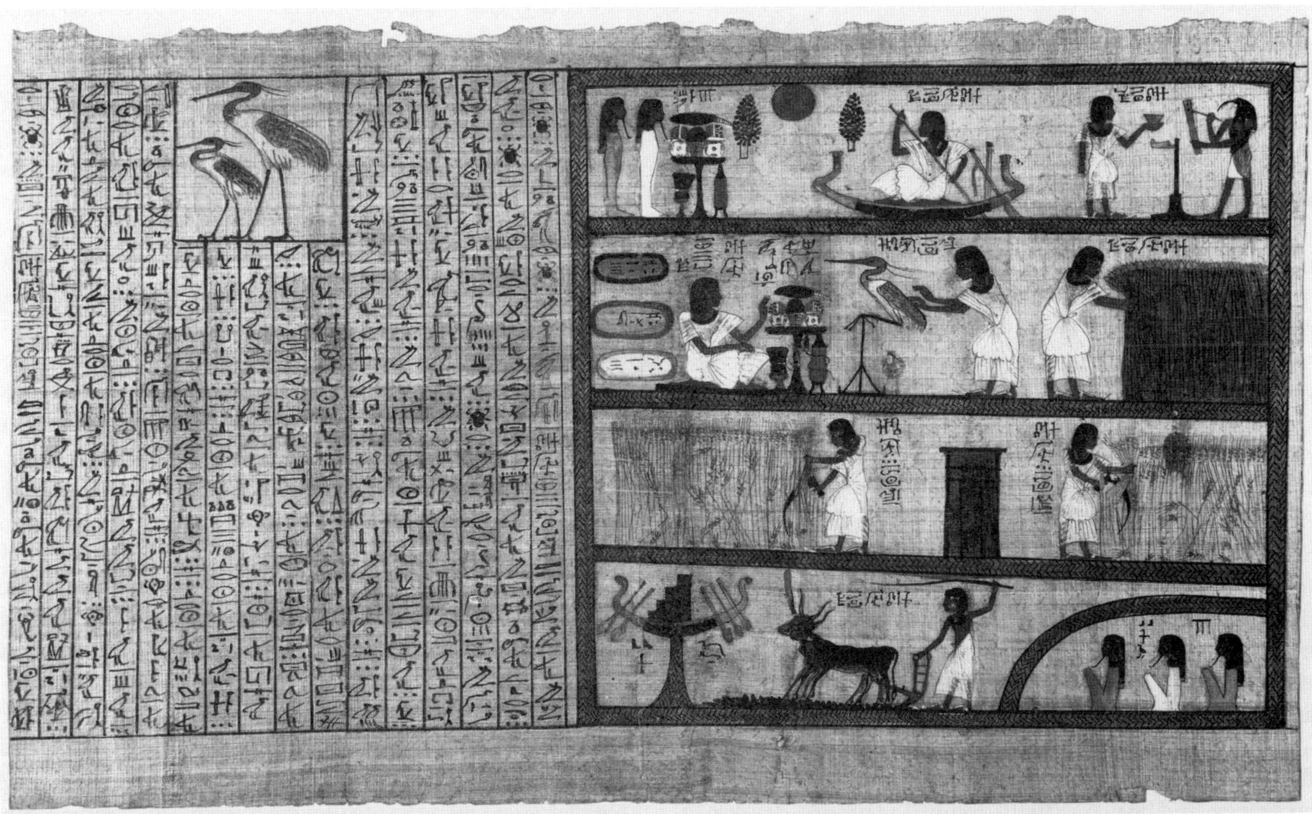

Papyrus from the Book of the Dead of Nakht with agricultural scenes, from Thebes, Egypt (1350–1300 B.C.E.); the introduction of papyrus as a convenient, flexible, and portable writing system made possible the preservation of many documents. (© The Trustees of the British Museum)

PYRAMID AND TEMPLE CONSTRUCTION

It is almost impossible to see an Egyptian pyramid or temple without wondering about the methods used in their founding and construction. Of all of the inventions ascribed to the Egyptians, some techniques have hardly been surpassed. The massive amounts of stone needed for such projects was cut from quarries, moved to the construction site, and placed with great precision. There has been a great deal of discussion and speculation about how the blocks of stone, often weighing many tons, were handled. Some of the theories have been very imaginative, but the simple answers seem to be the best. Egyptologists have used the scant information available to deduce the ancient methods. These clues consist of paintings in tombs and the remains of temporary ramps.

In a tomb in Middle Egypt there is a painting of a gigantic statue being moved. It rests on a sled being pulled with ropes by hundreds of men. Standing on the front of the sled is a workman pouring a liquid on the ground to lubricate the way. The liquid may be milk, oil, beer, or simply water. There is no written evidence to tell us, but there are also no rollers or wheels beneath the sled. In another tomb on the west bank at Luxor (ancient Thebes) is a representation of pieces of stone being moved up an inclined ramp. In the first court of the great temple of the god Amun at Karnak part of the mud-brick and rubble ramp used to construct the pylon gateway is still preserved. Taking the tomb paintings with the remains of actual ramps, it has generally been concluded that there was nothing particularly mysterious about construction techniques. It simply required careful planning, ramps that would later be dismantled, and the use of massive manpower.

The construction of a pyramid might have required long ramps that extended far into the desert or a series of shorter ramps that were placed against the four sides. This method is still debated by historians. However, scholars generally agree on the method of constructing a temple, with its gigantic walls and columns. The first course of stone for walls and columns was put into place, looking like a three-dimensional plan of the finished structure. Then the enclosed space was filled with earth and debris to the level of the tops of the stone. This made a flat platform on which the next layer of stone could be moved and placed. When that layer was finished, the filling was repeated, and this continued until the roofing blocks were in place. Then the process was reversed. The fill inside the top of the building was removed, and the decoration of carving and painting was begun. This continued downward until the building was completed, level by level. This technique was simple and slow, but it also made it unnecessary to use scarce wood for scaffolding during construction and decoration.

When heated, the material hardened, and the surface developed a colored glaze. The material is known from many examples of amulets (charms), scarabs (the figure of a beetle used as a charm), and small sculpture, as well as containers such as cups and bowls.

Probably the best-known and most characteristic invention of the ancient Egyptians was the process of mummification. The Egyptian belief in life after death required that the body of the deceased be preserved as a resting place for the spirit. Early in Egyptian history it was determined that the body had to be treated to prevent decay. This process, as it evolved, was essentially one of desiccation, or drying out. Since the internal organs were apt to decay rapidly, they had to be removed and treated separately. An incision was made in the side so the lungs, liver, intestines, and stomach could be taken out. The body was cleaned and packed in a material that would draw out any remaining fluids. When this was accomplished, it was wrapped in many layers of linen cloth and put into one or more coffins, usually with the face of the deceased on the lid. The organs were placed in a set of four containers and buried with the coffin. The process developed over the centuries of Egyptian history, generally becoming more elaborate.

THE MIDDLE EAST

BY MARK ANTHONY PHELPS

Inventions made in the ancient Near East encompassed agricultural processes, technology, and intellectual life. The Neolithic (or agricultural) Revolution occurred first in this region. The hallmarks of the Neolithic Revolution were the cultivation of plants and selective breeding of animals, which gave humans more control over the production of food.

Einkorn and emmer wheat were the first plants to be domesticated, the former by the Natufian culture of Israel and the latter at Umm Dabaghiyah in Syria, both around 9000 B.C.E. Wine appeared by 6000 B.C.E. in Iran and Mesopotamia, and by the same date lentils were prevalent throughout Southwest Asia. Goats and sheep were domesticated in Iran and Afghanistan by 9000 B.C.E., and pigs and cattle in Anatolia by 7000 B.C.E. Dogs had been domesticated in Israel and Kurdistan since around 12,000 B.C.E. The wheat domesticated by the early farmers may have included forms of the grain that were not intended as food, as one ancient source states that 40 percent of the harvest went for the production of beer, which had made its appearance by 8000 B.C.E.

The production of food begat a societal revolution, as humans would never live the same lifestyles as their foraging ancestors. Food production demanded that people stay in one place to care for fields. These fields were not interchangeable, as some plots were more productive than others. With the desire to control the more productive fields came the concept of property ownership. As the concept of private property evolved, society changed at its core. A prime example was that of the role of marriage. Concerns about the devolution of property from generation to generation spurred most agricultural societies to begin to monopolize access to women to ensure paternity. Many anthropologists believe the subjugation of women arose from this agricultural revolution.

Moreover, the ability to create surpluses meant that wealth, or surplus products, became common for certain members of society while remaining out of reach for others. Economic classes emerged that were mirrored in political structures as the economic elite created societal laws to protect their position. Another change was found in the collection, storage, and distribution of agricultural surpluses. Protecting these surpluses required city walls, which were first built in Jericho in Israel about 8000 B.C.E. Silos with lime plaster also appeared there for the first time.

It is assumed that public works demanded a centralized political system with enough power to coerce citizens into building and maintaining such works. Complex political systems tend to arise in such circumstances, and the first empire to encompass a number of ethnic groups was founded at the Mesopotamian city of Akkad by Sargon (r. 2334–2279 B.C.E.) in the 24th century B.C.E.

The need to keep track of property was clearly the motive in the development of cuneiform, the world's earliest form of writing. Fired clay tokens, as means of legal proof of ownership, first appeared in Syria in 8000 B.C.E. Seals, which by imprinting established ownership, appeared by 4000 B.C.E. The earliest clay envelopes came from Syria about 3500 B.C.E., followed by the earliest cuneiform writing, Sumerian, around 3300 B.C.E. The oldest datable preserved contract is from 2700 B.C.E. The first decipherable alphabet appeared at Ugarit in Syria approximately 1500 B.C.E. The Phoenician alphabet, the precursor to European alphabets, was developed around 1100 B.C.E. Mathematical innovations, too, were tied to the need to keep track of economic actions. Geometry, for example, was developed for the figuring of taxes. The concept of positional values for numerical expressions emerged in the Near East about 2000 B.C.E.

An administrative text in cuneiform (the world's earliest form of writing) recording food supplies, probably from southern Iraq (about 3000 B.C.E.). (© The Trustees of the British Museum)

The wheel made its first appearance at Ur in Iraq about 3500 B.C.E., at the same time that the pottery wheel was known to exist in Mesopotamia. The wheel is the prerequisite for most machines. One use of the wheel was in the creation of an astrolabe-like device, around 1250 B.C.E., for plotting items due south of the viewer from Babylon.

The Near East was the innovation center for early metalwork and glasswork. Copper was being cast by at least 6400 B.C.E. in Anatolia. Silver and gold were smelted in Sumer by 4000 B.C.E. By 3000 B.C.E. tin had appeared in Iran, and gold was being soldered at Ur. An iron dagger from Anatolia is dated to 2200 B.C.E., and large-scale iron smelting was undertaken by 1500 B.C.E. in Mitanni. The Assyrian army of the 10th century B.C.E. is the first army known to have used iron weapons. Lead glazing was being applied to bricks by 1000 B.C.E. Glass was manufactured by at least 2000 B.C.E. (though later Akkadian texts claim it was a Sumerian invention) and was manipulated while hot by 1500 B.C.E. Glassblowing was developed in Syria by 100 B.C.E. Coinage, which revolutionized economic systems, appeared first at Lydia in Anatolia around 700 B.C.E.

The need to corral the floodwaters of the Tigris, which came at harvest time, and to dissipate and store the waters of the Euphrates led to the development of irrigation by 6000 B.C.E. The Sumerians did large-scale work, with massive public works projects, including one preserved canal regulator at Girsu that required 750,000 bricks. The *shaduf,* a rotating lever for moving water from one canal to another, was developed in Mesopotamia by 2000 B.C.E.

One can make a case for Mesopotamia being the birthplace of modern science. The cosmos, according to local thought, was ordered by the gods. When an oddity occurred in nature, it implied to these cultures an indirect message that the gods could not reveal directly to humans. Thus, the practice of recording odd natural events (such as a malformed sheep liver) and associating the oddity in nature with an event in the human realm (such as the birth of a king) became a means of predicting the future by unraveling the clandestine communication of the gods. Searching for cause and effect by recording empirical observations in a universe that is understood to function regularly is the basis for Western science. All of these firsts were diffused to the rest of the world within centuries of their innovation in this region. Virtually every society can be considered the offspring of the ancient Near East on some level.

ASIA AND THE PACIFIC

BY KIRK H. BEETZ

Tracing inventions, especially when they are from illiterate cultures, can be difficult. For example, ancient Australians, Indians, and Europeans all used the boomerang to hunt small game. Who invented it? The answer is that they each did, separately from the others. How they invented the boomerang is a mystery that puzzles engineers to this day because of its complex aerodynamics. Another example is the bronze making of the Shang Dynasty of China (ca. 1500–ca. 1045 B.C.E.): Did the Shang invent bronze making independently? The answer is that they probably did not. The techniques for making bronze probably were imported from the Near East. Ancient cultures were far more connected than modern people may realize, with inventions that were useful moving across great distances over hundreds of years.

The inventions of ancient China are far better known than for the rest of ancient Asia and the Pacific because the Chinese wrote about their inventions, and archaeologists have been able to trace when certain inventions arose. For Oceania archaeologists are fairly sure that the ancients invented harpoons with teeth pointing backward so that the harpoon would stick and not be shaken loose, but when or exactly where they arose is not known. People of the Philippines probably invented the yo-yo as a device for hunting game; a hunter could hide up a tree and send a heavy yo-yo spinning down onto his prey. Still, the details for when the yo-yo was invented are so vague that it could have been invented elsewhere and been taken to the Philippines, where it survived because it remained useful.

For Korea and Japan the rarity of written records hampers historians' efforts to identify their inventions. Both were notably creative in the manufacture of ceramics, but Korea's great era of invention in ceramics came in the 1100s C.E., long after the ancient era. Japan's ceramics were among the best of the ancient world, but what archaeologists have so far found of advances in ancient Japanese technology consist of innovations developed first in China and then transferred to Japan through Korea. On the other hand, there is one well-known Japanese invention that predates 200 C.E.: the *zori*, sandals with a strap next to the big toe that attaches to the sole and a strap that arcs over the top of the foot. This invention is worn throughout the world and is often called "flip-flops."

In most of the ancient world, technology was learned by being passed down from master to student. Over several generations the knowledge would become tradition that each new student was expected to learn. This tended to discourage inventions, because innovation would seem like tampering with unwritten laws for the manufacturing of goods. This meant that changes in technology were usually minor adjustments in technique, as when Indian metalworkers of the Maurya Dynasty (321–185 B.C.E.) of India figured out how to make iron that resisted rust. Moreover, passing on knowledge by word of mouth meant that innovations could be lost, as was the case for making white ceramics during the Warring States Period (453–221 B.C.E.) of China, which was not reinvented until the 700s C.E.

The Chinese developed an appreciation of scientific research for its own sake, and inventors were often celebrated figures. In fact, the Chinese developed the practice of pure research, meaning learning about the natural world simply for the sake of acquiring knowledge. They believed that learning about the natural world contributed to a person's moral development. The impetus for research resulted in significant inventions before they even became notably useful. For instance, the Chinese knew that lodestone was magnetic and that when hung from a string the lodestone would point north and south. By the 400s C.E. they had carved lodestone into the shape of a spoon called *sinan* that was used to help miners know the direction in which they headed. It was several hundred years before the device was adapted for navigation by the Chinese, becoming a compass.

The Chinese were also good at taking an invention and reinventing it to make it more useful. For instance, the Scythians of central Asia invented the stirrup for horseback riding in the 380s B.C.E. It consisted of a loop of leather in which a foot was inserted, giving a rider stability. In about the 100s C.E. the Chinese transformed this into a metal loop with a flat bottom that allowed horseback riders to stand up in the stirrups and remain stable while firing arrows or throwing spears. Thus, in hunting and battle the Chinese stirrup gave riders an advantage they would not have had with the leather stirrup. Another Chinese innovation for horseback riding was the padded saddle in the first century C.E. Not only did it make riding more comfortable, it also enabled people to stay in the saddle for longer periods and cut down on the number of sores and injuries to the backs of riders.

Many Chinese inventions were practical, and while they may seem obvious now, they were world changing when they were introduced. For example, the Chinese invented the wheelbarrow in the first century C.E. It was basically a cart with only one wheel in front, but it was a remarkable labor-saving device that allowed farmers and construction workers to work faster and move heavier loads than they could by carrying them. It allowed a worker to quickly move loads that might have taken two men to move before. For ships the Chinese invented the sternpost rudder for steering in about 200 B.C.E. In the 400s C.E. they created transverse bulkheads. When a ship had a leak, the transverse bulkheads allowed sailors to seal off the leaking section of the ship and thus keep the ship afloat. For land transportation the Chinese invented carts with two shafts in the first century B.C.E. The shafts went outside instead of down the middle in front of the cart, making it possible to use only one horse or other draft animal to pull a cart rather than the two a single shaft would usually require.

Two of the most widely used inventions have been silk and paper. At present no one knows for sure when silk

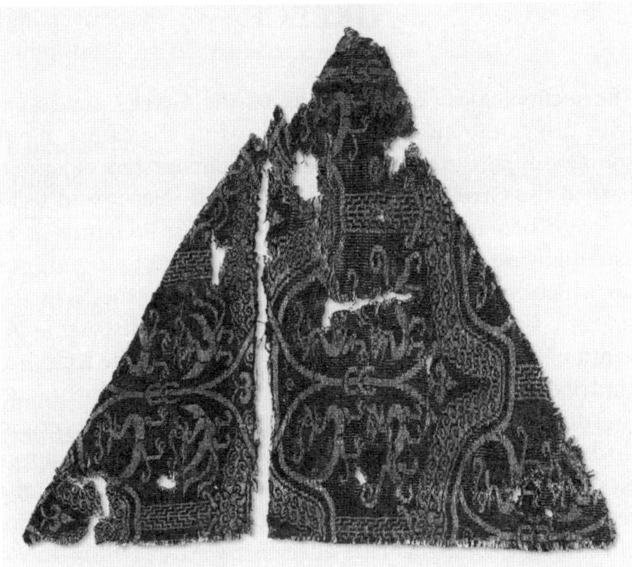

Pair of fragments of silk, from Cave 17, Mogao, near Dunhuang, Gansu Province, China (third to fifth century C.E.*); archaeologists believe that the Chinese invented silk thread.* (© The Trustees of the British Museum)

thread was invented, though archaeologists and historians are sure it was originated by the Chinese. In ancient Chinese folklore the wife of the mythical Yellow Emperor Huangdi was drinking a hot beverage in about 2700 B.C.E. when the cocoon of a silkworm dropped into it. The cocoon unraveled, revealing strong strands of silk that the queen could twist together to make thread. The queen is almost certainly a mythological figure, but the discovery of silk may not have been much different from the tale because to make silk the cocoons were boiled and the strands carefully unwound. They were then twisted together to make a tough thread. Archaeologists disagree about when silk cloth was first invented, with many believing it did not occur until the Shang Dynasty, while some believe it occurred as early as 7000 B.C.E., based on an ivory cup with a silkworm design dated to that era. In Zhejiang, silk thread that may date to 3000 B.C.E. has been found.

Before the invention of paper, silk cloth and bamboo slats were used in China for writing. In the second century C.E. a eunuch in the emperor's court, Cai Lun, explained to his emperor that bamboo was too heavy and silk too expensive for writing, so he experimented with substances that he could substitute for silk. Through experimentation he hit upon combining hemp from fishing nets, old rags, and tree bark; chopping and pulping the combination; and then spreading the wet pulp on screens to dry. He is credited with making the first paper in 105 C.E., though some older examples of rag paper have been found dating to about 49 C.E., which suggests that he was building on preliminary work already done. The Chinese used the paper not only for writing but also for painting, wrapping, and clothing.

EUROPE

BY MICHAEL J. O'NEAL

The word *invention* in modern life implies a sudden breakthrough, a moment of inspiration when a curious inventor solves a problem in the physical world by creating something that was unknown before—a tool, a process, or a material—and thereby changes the relationship between humans and their physical world. The discovery can often be attributed to a particular individual or a team of researchers. In the ancient world, however, inventions cannot be attributed to particular individuals or even groups. Instead, technology advanced gradually in response to particular environmental or economic conditions.

In ancient Europe, where written records were largely absent until the end of the first millennium B.C.E., information about inventions could not be transmitted except by word of mouth. As a result, similar inventions arose independently at different times and places in ancient Europe. A key point to consider is whether an invention was an accidental novelty or was the platform on which a new and lasting technology was based. During the Paleolithic Period in central Europe (ca. 24,000 B.C.E.), for example, people developed the ability to fire clay, but they used it for only a short while to make clay figurines and other small objects. The use of fired clay to make ceramic containers would not be invented until thousands of years later.

Metallurgy was a key area for invention in ancient Europe. In southeastern Europe around 5000 B.C.E. prehistoric people developed the ability to produce very high temperatures to fire their pottery. They realized, perhaps accidentally, that copper could be smelted from its native ores at these temperatures as well, thus yielding a material that could be hammered and eventually cast into ornaments and tools. Subsequently, around 2500 B.C.E., they discovered that mixing the copper with tin or arsenic made a much harder metal called bronze. The demand for this metal triggered further inventions in casting and alloying to make more complex items.

The appearance of iron metallurgy around 1000 B.C.E. offered further opportunities for invention. While the Europeans did not invent the metal sword, for example, they carried sword-making techniques to new heights. One good example is the so-called Kilburn sword, discovered in East Yorkshire, England, and dating to about the third century B.C.E. The sword consists of more than 70 separate parts, including those made of iron, horn, and glass, each carefully engineered and assembled to create a weapon that represented the highest degree of technical innovation in metalsmithing.

An invention of process in ancient Europe was the use of domestic animals, specifically oxen, to pull plows and wagons. The first traces of plow use appear around 3500 B.C.E. The first plows, called ards, simply scratched the soil to create furrows in which seeds could be planted. These plows worked only on light, dry soils. To deal with heavier, wetter soils that had not been cultivated previously, European farmers had to devise a heavier plow that turned over heavy clods of turf rather than merely scratching the top of the soil.

Animal power could also be applied to transportation. The earliest wheeled vehicles appeared around 3000 B.C.E. in central Europe. They were probably wagons used for hauling agricultural products and firewood from fields and forests into the settlements. Such vehicles were then improved with further inventions. The Celts of central Europe, for example, produced extremely high-quality carriages and wagons, many of which archaeologists have found in such places as Germany and Austria. An important innovation was the use of iron on wheels. Rather than relying on purely wooden wheels, which deteriorated rapidly and often broke if the driver hit a stone, the skilled metalworkers of central Europe learned to create an iron hoop that served as a kind of tire for wagon wheels. The hoop was heated and then rapidly cooled around the wooden portions of the wheel, shrinking it and thus binding it firmly to the wheel. These wheels were far more durable than anything that had been produced before.

Further inventions in transportation technology took place late in prehistoric times. One was the bearing, created by the ancient Scandinavians. By the first century B.C.E. the Vandals and Goths of northern Europe had invented a wooden roller bearing they used on wagons. This bearing was durable and provided a more reliable and comfortable ride than anything the more technically proficient Romans produced. To fill some of their wagons, the Europeans invented the wine barrel (as opposed to such containers as jars) to transport wine, a prestigious commodity, from the Mediterranean region.

To go along with their wheels and carriages, the ancient Europeans also developed engineered roads. The ancient Romans are often credited with the earliest and best road-building technology, but in fact the oldest known engineered road in the world—that is, a road that was built rather than simply cut through the forest—is the so-called Sweet Track, a causeway in Somerset, England, named after its discover, Ray Sweet. It was built in about the 3800s B.C.E. and was constructed with crossed poles of hardwood, along with lime, that were sunk in the spongy, wet soil to support a walkway. Subsequently, roads made from timbers laid side by side across the direction of the road were built across many of the wetlands of northern Europe and the British Isles, especially as trade flourished during the Iron Age.

The ancient Europeans, like people the world over, looked for ways to improve their physical conditions. In domestic architecture they developed new techniques of timber construction and joinery that enabled them to build warm and durable houses and barns. The cold northern climates of Europe created the need for heavy, durable, and warm clothing, so a precursor of knitting called *nålebinding*, or "binding with the needle," emerged from the Danes. The Danes used this technique, which involved passing a needle through a loose loop to create a chain of loops, to make what may have been the world's first true socks and mittens.

GREECE

BY JEFFREY S. CARNES

The technological contributions of the Greeks are somewhat difficult to measure, owing in part to the nature of our sources, in part to political and social circumstances, and in part to the Greeks' own attitudes toward science and technology. There is, for example, little scientific literature—and essentially no technical literature—for the first four centuries for which we have historical records. Only in the Hellenistic Period (323–31 B.C.E.) do we find scientists discussing inventions, so there is only indirect evidence for the technical contributions Greeks may have made in the eighth through fourth centuries B.C.E. To some extent this is due to a certain disdain for practical matters among members of the upper classes: Typical is the contempt shown by Plato and Aristotle for the "banausic" (mechanical) professions for their negative effect on the soul. Theorists of science were generally drawn from the elite classes (there were no "pure science" occupations at which to make a living) and therefore tended to be ignorant of or unconcerned with technological developments.

Political and social conditions played a further role in slowing the progress of Greek technology. Necessity truly is the mother of invention, and in many cases the Greeks lacked the necessity that might spur technological innovation. There was little large-scale manufacturing of the sort in which costs might be reduced and profits increased by the invention of new machinery or processes. Further, Greece was a slave-owning society on a large scale—perhaps one-third of the population of Athens was made up of slaves—and with so much forced labor there would have been little incentive for labor-saving devices. Given the lack of records for all but the Hellenistic Period, we must content ourselves with noting aspects of Greek technology that do not appear previously elsewhere and speculating that these may be inventions.

In agriculture the main improvements probably attributable to the Greeks were in the area of processing. Various minor innovations in milling technology are known, mostly designed to mill more grain at once and allow more animal power to be applied to the mill. Presses for wine and olives show steady improvement, starting with primitive lever presses using stone weights and progressing to a variety of screw and lever-and-screw presses in the Hellenistic Period. The screw itself seems to have been developed in the third century B.C.E., making it the only one of the basic machines to have been invented in the historical period. The screw was also used in devices for lifting water, which had applications in both agriculture and mining.

The remains of the Athenian silver mines at Laurium include washing devices that represent an improvement on earlier washing techniques, allowing for more efficient separation of the metal from its ore. These machines also allowed the water to be recycled, a serious consideration in the semi-arid climate of Greece. Ironworking became more efficient with the development of the shaft furnace in about 500 B.C.E.

with the air supply now controlled by bellows and blowpipes. A much earlier metallurgical invention, however, was the lost-wax process for casting bronze, which dates to the Mycenaean Period (1600–1100 B.C.E.) and is still used by artists today. The making of a wax mold of an artwork into which molten bronze is poured allows for great detail, making the Greeks renowned throughout the ancient world for the quality of their bronze sculptures. Since bronze is easily melted down and reused, few artworks have survived. Another innovation of great artistic import was the development in Athens of a black high-gloss permanent glaze for pottery, which made Athenian vases highly sought-after exports throughout the Mediterranean.

The Hippocratic Corpus, a series of writings attributed to the physician Hippocrates (ca. 460–ca. 377 B.C.E.), contains numerous references to medical instruments: In this sense it is the earliest extant scientific work to discuss technology. Of particular interest is the Hippocratic bench, a device with posts, straps, and cords designed for traction and the reduction of dislocations.

As in the modern world, compelling state interests led to a great deal of innovation in military matters, and we are also well supplied with sources on military technology. In addition to archaeological finds, there exist treatises on military technology and descriptions of such innovations in the historical accounts of battles. The Greeks were the first to develop artillery (without gunpowder) by making use of a variety of mechanical means to launch projectiles. The gastraphetes, invented in 399 B.C.E., was a device for launching arrows or stones and resembled a medieval crossbow. Torsion catapults were developed later in the fourth century B.C.E. and underwent a steady series of technical improvements throughout antiquity. The Greek mathematician and inventor Archimedes (ca. 287–212 B.C.E.) is credited with the development of various siege engines and defensive weapons, including a pivoting crane to drop stones on enemy ships and scaling ladders, a crane with a claw for grabbing the bow of an enemy ship and overturning it, and a series of parabolic mirrors that could be focused on an enemy ship to set it on fire. (A recent experiment by students at the Massachusetts Institute of Technology has suggested that this was, in fact, feasible.)

A clever but entirely low-tech military invention developed in Sparta by the fifth century B.C.E. was the scytale (also spelled skytale), a device for transmitting messages in code. The scytale consisted of a rod around which a leather strap was wrapped in a long spiral. A message would be written across the strap, which would then be unrolled and sent to the recipient, who would possess a rod of equal size. When rolled around the recipient's rod, the strap would reveal the original message; anyone intercepting it without the decoding rod would find a string of apparently random letters.

The intellectual atmosphere at Alexandria was particularly conducive to innovation, owing perhaps to the combination of royal patronage for the sciences and access to Egyptian learning. The most important of the surviving treatises are those of Hero (fl. first century C.E.), who wrote on a vast variety of subjects, giving details on the building of surveying devices, hydraulics, and pneumatics. Of these innovations, many are of practical value: the pump and the accurate water clock developed by his predecessor Ctesibius (fl. second century B.C.E.), for example, and the water organ (the world's first keyboard instrument). Others are clearly designed to be impressive rather than practical. Hero wrote an entire book devoted to automata (self-operating mechanisms), which include slot machines for dispensing water for ritual cleansing before entering a temple, pneumatically powered temple doors that would open automatically when a fire was lit on the altar, steam-powered tops, and a variety of devices for making small mechanical birds and other animals move. It is unknown how many of these devices were actually built or how widespread their use was, but the discovery of a complex, multigeared mechanism for computing the positions of the stars and planets (the Antikýthēra device, named after the island near which it was found) shows that the Greeks were capable of precise engineering, building what was in effect a mechanical computer.

ROME

BY DAVID KELLY

Many of the inventions that are credited to ancient Rome are related to construction, travel, and water management. One of the principal reasons that Romans were able to build large-scale projects was their improvement in concrete. Starting in 237 B.C.E. the Romans developed a method of mixing traditional claylike building materials with such diverse elements as volcanic ash from Pozzuoli, a village near Naples, which was found to be a strong binding agent; horsehair, which gave the concrete flexibility; and blood, which helped inhibit frost. Roman improvements in concrete enabled them to make a product that could be molded to different shapes and yet was resistant to moisture. With this basic invention they could be more imaginative with architectural design, incorporating arches and domes to raise buildings up toward the sky, freed of having to rely on stone blocks as their main building material.

The improved concrete also enabled Romans to build hundreds of miles of water-transportation tunnels, or aqueducts, which are considered one of the greatest achievements of the Roman Empire. Roman aqueducts transferred water from sparsely inhabited regions to all of the urban capitals of the empire. In the city of Rome itself, for instance, roughly 300 million gallons of water were brought in from the surrounding countryside each day, all without the use of pumps or any machinery whatsoever, relying solely on the power of gravity. Besides the flexibility that concrete gave them, the Romans also developed a precision in their understanding of hydraulic engineering that made aqueduct technology possible: They calculated the downward angle needed to move

Roman aqueduct in Tunis; Roman improvements in concrete enabled them to build hundreds of miles of water-transportation systems, considered one of the greatest achievements of the Roman Empire. (© Board of Regents of the University of Wisconsin System)

water over hundreds of miles of channels without running into the ground before it arrived at its intended destination.

In addition to the aqueducts, concrete also enabled the construction of an unprecedented series of roads and highways throughout the Roman Empire. The Romans built approximately 53,000 miles of roads; by comparison, the U.S. Interstate Highway System had a total of about 47,000 miles at the beginning of the 21st century. Romans invented the layered method of building roads, starting with large stones at the bottom to absorb moisture and prevent shifts in the ground and ending with smooth stones held together with concrete. Many of the roads constructed during the Roman Empire are still in use today, such as the Via Appia (the Appian Way), which was begun in 312 B.C.E. Roman roads are found throughout Europe, Asia, and Africa, where many of the paths laid out before the birth of Christ have been paved over with modern materials and are still used.

Inside the home Romans are credited with the invention of the hypocaust heating system, a way of moving heated air through houses to warm them. This method, which is the basic design for modern-day heating and air conditioning systems, consisted of raising houses a few feet above the ground and leaving space in the walls for air flow. Vents in the walls would pull warm air from a small fire under the house, distributing it throughout the entire building. Because a large fire would create smoke the fire had to be small, but it had to be constantly going or it would lose its effectiveness. The Romans relied on slaves to tend to the house fires throughout the day.

Many of the inventions credited to Rome are actually variations on designs developed by other civilizations, particularly the Greek culture that preceded Rome in history. Often adaptations were just the result of the natural process of improving on what works, though in some cases there were changes significant enough to consider the Roman version a new entity. This is true of the Roman version of the waterwheel, which captures the power of flowing water to move a heavy stone to grind grain into flour, credited to Marcus Vitruvius, an architect and engineer who served under Augustus in the first century B.C.E. His wheel improved on a similar concept from the Greeks: While the Greek wheel was moved horizontally as water flowed by, the Roman waterwheel stood horizontally and had water stream down onto it. Gravity gave the falling water much more force than its natural flow provided. At eight pounds per gallon, water is a fairly heavy substance; consequently, the Vetruvian waterwheel was the most powerful source of energy in the ancient world. Considering this fact, it should be expected that the vertical waterwheel would have been used widely throughout the Roman Empire, but that turns out not to have been the case. With slave labor inexpensive and abundant, the Romans simply were not interested in new energy sources.

A case where Roman invention does not appear to be a direct adaptation of another culture's design but rather a new product in itself is the Roman abacus. Modern people are perhaps more familiar with the Chinese abacus, which was in use well into the twentieth century. Records indicate that the Roman version predates the Chinese abacus by several hundred years. Interestingly, it is thought that the Babylonian abacus predates both cultures with indications that it may have been developed between 1000 B.C.E. and 500 B.C.E. Despite similarities in design, there is no conclusive evidence that any one was an influence on the development of the other. While both the Chinese and the Roman abacus used the manipulation of beads to help a person keep a running tally of whatever was being counted, the Chinese abacus held the beads on strings and the Roman version had slots in which the beads could roll loosely and quickly. Still, the Roman version is considered a significant innovation because it was portable and included spaces for fractions.

THE AMERICAS

BY LAWRENCE WALDRON

The people of the ancient Americas contributed countless inventions to the world as we know it today. They devised these technologies in response to a wide range of environments and circumstances. Some ancient American inventions were similar to those of other world cultures, such as weapons and hand tools, but other inventions, like the igloo, were uniquely suited to American needs and were found nowhere else. While it might seem surprising that ancient Native Americans had no carts, chariots, swords, or sailing ships, it is equally notable that they had the largest buildings in the ancient world, even larger than Egypt's; had invented paper in the first millennium B.C.E., more than one thousand years before the Chinese; and had developed counting systems that employed the numeral zero centuries before any other civilization. People in each ancient American culture developed technology that was influenced by the opportunities, necessities, and limitations of their lives and times.

Since the native cultures of the Americas seem to have developed with little or no contact with people from other parts of the world, the technological achievements of the ancient Americans seem all the more outstanding. Ancient Americans produced some of the earliest metalwork and sewn clothes, and they demonstrated some of the most innovative agricultural and medical techniques in the ancient world. In the first millennium B.C.E. Peruvian doctors occasionally performed brain surgery with obsidian scalpels while the patient was under herbal anesthesia.

Although Native American discoveries could be similar to those from other parts of the world, they were not always used in the same ways. Metal tools and jewelry from the Great Lakes region of the United States date back to more than 6,000 years ago. Unlike metalworkers elsewhere in the world, however, the North American metallurgists showed little interest in making weapons. Similarly, archaeological findings in Mesoamerica show that Native Americans had invented the wheel but did not use it to make wagons or coaches: With no horses, cattle, or elephants to pull such vehicles, ancient Mesoamericans had little use for the wheel except on push toys for their children and in a few minor tools.

In many instances ancient Americans were the first to come up with ideas that would be either reinvented or adopted later by Asians, Europeans, or Africans. For example, the ancient Americans developed many kinds of waterproofing for their containers and vessels, using materials and methods unknown or undeveloped in other parts of the world: The ancient Chumash of California used asphalt from the La Brea tar pits to seal their boats, and the ancient Olmec used (non-synthetic) latex for similar purposes. There were many such inventions and innovations in the fields of art, architecture, agriculture, athletics, and urban planning.

The art of the ancient Americans was varied and ingenious. Given their great antiquity, many of these ancient artworks survive only in fragments. Pottery and metalwork are among the most durable of the ancient American arts, but some textiles and other arts also survive. Native North Americans of the Great Lakes had been annealing metal—heating and changing the shape of metal objects—since around 7000 B.C.E. Other ancient Americans throughout the continents hit upon the same techniques, and by the second millennium B.C.E. they had developed them substantially. Chavín Andeans hammered semiprecious and precious metals into thin foils to be used in decorating objects made of other materials. By 200 B.C.E. other Andeans had begun to cast and alloy metals into solid tools and weapon points. Eventually they refined their casting methods into what ancient Greeks would have recognized as the lost-wax method, a complex process of casting hollow metal sculptures shared only by a few ancient cultures.

Perhaps the most amazing Andean achievement in metallurgy was an early form of electroplating used by the Moche sometime in the very early Common Era. In Moche electroplating, an anode and cathode were inserted into an acidic solution (like the negative and positive poles of a battery) to produce an electric charge. This current caused the positively charged gold particles, intentionally dissolved in the acid, to migrate to the negatively charged copper artwork connected to the cathode. In this electrical process a copper object gradually becomes plated with gold. Thus we can credit Andeans not just with the discovery of electricity but with its use in the production of consumer items.

As textile artists, ancient Americans were great innovators. Peruvians and Bolivians began using looms for weaving sometime in the second or third millennium B.C.E. and pioneered a staggering range of textile techniques, including simple warp-and-weft weaves, scaffold weaving (discontinuous warp-weft), single-needle knitting, and a host of other demanding ways of weaving and decorating cloth. These textiles of animal hair and domesticated cotton were used by ancient Americans for clothing, shelter, wrapping the dead, decoration, and furnishings, and they were even used as containers. Even tie-dyed textiles, a kind of cloth associated with southern Asia today, were produced in the Americas by the ninth century B.C.E. The use of woven containers among Amazonians may have inspired their clever invention of the hammock, a swinging bed suspended off the ground between two trees or posts.

In the later part of the Pre-Classic period (nearing the start of the Common Era) the Maya civilization developed a full-fledged calendar system. Since the second millennium B.C.E. early Maya astronomers and their Zapotec and Olmec contemporaries had followed the movements of the sun, moon and Venus and had come to mark time by the movements of these celestial bodies. They invented three separate calendars to trace and regulate the lives, agricultural activities, dynasties, and mythic sagas of their civilization. The first was a 365-day *haab*, or solar year (much like our modern calendar), made up of 18 months. There was also a 260-day *tzolk'in*, or cycle of religious ceremonies and festivals, with each day assigned its own name and ritual significance. Finally, a great era or Calendar Round was celebrated every 52 years at the coincidence of the other two calendars. The Calendar Round, functioning much like the Gregorian century, was a large period used by historians and some religious leaders to mark ages, the return of rare celestial events, dynastic changes, cultural trends, and even the fulfillment of prophecies.

Many modern sports were born of early antecedents in the ancient Americas. Most notable of these sports is basketball, which was a ceremonial game played by religious devotees in eastern Mexico from about 1000 B.C.E. The very possibility of the bouncing ball originated in another Mesoamerican invention, that of vulcanized rubber. Both the rubber and sapodilla trees of eastern Mexico produce latex. The Mesoamericans were the first to put latex to use as a sealant and sculpture material. The Olmec developed the process of vulcanizing rubber, whereby it was heated to make it more malleable so the material could be fashioned into any shape desired. Thus, the ancient Olmec civilization contributed one of the most important materials to the development of the modern world.

There is evidence that soccer and football also existed in early versions among the ancient Mesoamericans as ritual games played at religious ceremonies. Both field and ice hockey have ancient origins in early versions of shinny, a sport played in the North American Great Plains region up to European colonial times.

The early urban centers of the Andes date back as far as the third millennium B.C.E. Many early cities such as Caral and Kotosh feature centrally located plazas, sunken courtyards, and pyramidal temples. The adobe pyramids at Caral and El Aspero in Peru were built around 3000 B.C.E., several centuries before the stone ones in Egypt. The ancient Olmec employed outdoor and indoor plumbing to conduct water through their cities. They installed carved canal blocks in three- to five-foot lengths to create aqueducts centuries before the Romans or Maya employed similar concepts in their urban centers. The so-called New Temple at Chavín de Huantar in Peru also shows knowledge of aqueduct technology.

The Chavín culture of the first millennium B.C.E. employed conduits for air as well as water in a fully functioning hydraulic system that drew both substances into the New Temple. This design created a constant roar of running water and a steady circulation of air that is still functioning today. Indeed, Native American structures from ancient Chavín's temple complex to medieval-era cliff dwellings in Arizona all employ ventilation concepts pioneered sometime in the first or second millennium B.C.E.

In their use of durable, carved basalt aqueducts, the Olmec showed a mastery of stonemasonry, which they seem to have developed to a fine point by 1000 B.C.E. Later civilizations in both Mesoamerica and South America, who had little contact with the Olmec civilization, also became well known for their stonemasonry, which suggests that this inventive engineering was developed in several places independently. The Late Pre-Classic Maya (400 B.C.E.–250 C.E.) adapted earlier stonemasonry to their own needs, adding a stone and lime compound that Romans, who were inventing it at roughly the same time, would call concrete. The early Maya also developed a softer mortar, now called stucco, that they carved into beautiful designs on their palaces and temples.

Many hunting tools were invented by early Americans to support a lifestyle that was far from sedentary. Detachable harpoon points from the Northwest Coast North Americans and fluted arrow points from the Clovis culture allowed whalers and hunters to fire at their prey and then get out of the animal's way as it rampaged. The weapons were carefully recovered from the dead animal by the fisherman or hunter. By sea, river, and estuary, ancient Americans also became master fishers in their canoes, kayaks, or reed or skin boats, all invented in ancient times. Combining efficient weapons and watercraft with woven fishing nets and waterproof garments, ancient Americans invented an almost modern ensemble of fishing apparatuses.

American agriculture was apparently in progress by the seventh millennium B.C.E. By the second millennium B.C.E. a full range of farming techniques existed in the Americas, from terraced fields to desert, swamp, and jungle plantations. Some scientists believe ancient Americans may have loosely tailored certain North and South American forests to increase the density of food sources, modifying established forests. The ancient Americans exhibited some of the world's most creative methods of agriculture. Their development from around 8000 to 7000 B.C.E. of milpa, or slash-and-burn agriculture, was probably influenced by the observation of nature's own replenishing forest fires. Raised-bed agriculture, by contrast, seems to have been invented without the inspiration of a natural process.

Around the second millennium B.C.E. raised-bed agriculture was separately invented in Mesoamerica by the Maya and by several peoples in the Andes. In this process, mounds of earth (and sometimes composted, biodegradable debris) were built up in artificially drained or flooded swamps. Thus, farmers could make islands of food grow in otherwise dry areas (like the Andes) or vary an ecological system to include drier-climate plants, such as corn, in a swampy area (like some parts of the Maya territory). Guano, a fertilizer derived from bird droppings collected along the Pacific coast of Peru, had been used in the Andes since around 3000 B.C.E. to boost crop production.

Perhaps the most influential of ancient American inventions is biological. Selective breeding by Native Americans, perhaps over a period of centuries, has produced the plant we know as maize. Maize, or corn, is a plant that has no apparent wild relative, except perhaps a grass called teosinte that produces a very small grain. Maize cannot grow by itself. Hidden inside a protective husk, kernels of corn cannot germinate unless they are removed and tended by a farmer. Between 7000 B.C.E. and 2500 B.C.E. Mesoamerican farmers seemed to have biologically engineered corn from a wild variety, probably teosinte, into a high-yielding, starchy grain. Thus, Mesoamericans did far more than domesticate a preexisting species; they created a new one. This engineered food source is now a staple in Africa, Europe, and Asia, having been adopted by almost every society that can grow it.

See also ADORNMENT; AGRICULTURE; ARCHITECTURE; ART; ASTRONOMY; BUILDING TECHNIQUES AND MATERIALS; CALENDARS AND CLOCKS; CERAMICS AND POTTERY; CITIES; CLOTHING AND FOOTWEAR; CRAFTS; DEATH AND BURIAL PRACTICES; ECONOMY; EMPIRES AND DYNASTIES; FESTIVALS; FOOD AND DIET; GENDER STRUCTURES AND ROLES; GOVERNMENT ORGANIZATION; HEALTH AND DISEASE; HUNTING, FISHING, AND GATHERING; METALLURGY; MILITARY; MINING, QUARRYING, AND SALT MAKING; MONEY AND COINAGE; MUSIC AND MUSICAL INSTRUMENTS; NOMADIC AND PASTORAL SOCIETIES; NUMBERS AND COUNTING; RELIGION AND COSMOLOGY; SCIENCE; SEAFARING AND NAVIGATION; SHIPS AND SHIPBUILDING; SLAVES AND SLAVERY; SOCIAL ORGANIZATION; SPORTS AND RECREATION; STORAGE AND PRESERVATION; TEXTILES AND NEEDLEWORK; TRANSPORTATION; WEAPONRY AND ARMOR; WEIGHTS AND MEASURES; WRITING.

FURTHER READING

Susan J. Herlin, "Ancient African Civilizations to ca. 1500," 2003. Available online. URL: http://www.louisville.edu/a-s/history/herlin/textsup.htm. Downloaded on January 24, 2007.

Peter James and Nick Thorpe, *Ancient Inventions* (New York: Ballantine Books, 1994).

Emory Dean Keoke and Kay Marie Porterfield, *American Indian Contributions to the World* (New York: Checkmark Books, 2003).

Stuart Piggott, *The Earliest Wheeled Transport* (Ithaca, N.Y.: Cornell University Press, 1983).

Ivan Van Sertima, ed., *Blacks in Science: Ancient and Modern* (New Brunswick, N.J.: Transaction Books, 1983).

Silkroad Foundation, "History of Silk." Available online. URL: http://www.silk-road.com/artl/silkhistory.shtml. Downloaded on February 26, 2007.

Jack Weatherford, *Indian Givers: How the Indians of the Americas Transformed the World* (New York: Fawcett Columbine, 1988).

K. D. White, *Greek and Roman Technology* (London: Thames and Hudson, 1984).

Trevor I. Williams, *The History of Invention* (New York: Facts On File, 1987).

VIVA-FACTS ON FILE
ENCYCLOPEDIA OF SOCIETY AND CULTURE IN THE ANCIENT WORLD

Volume III • L–R

Editor in Chief
Peter Bogucki

Viva Books

New Delhi | Mumbai | Chennai | Kolkata | Bangalore | Hyderabad | Kochi | Guwahati

First Indian Edition 2010

VIVA BOOKS PRIVATE LIMITED

- 4737/23 Ansari Road, Daryaganj, New Delhi 110 002
  E-mail: vivadelhi@vivagroupindia.net, Tel. 42242200
- 76, Service Industries, Shirvane, Sector 1, Nerul, Navi Mumbai 400 706
  E-mail: vivamumbai@vivagroupindia.net, Tel. 27721273, 27721274
- Jamals Fazal Chambers, 26 Greams Road, Chennai 600 006
  E-mail: vivachennai@vivagroupindia.net, Tel. 28290304, 28294241
- B-103, Jindal Towers, 21/1A/3 Darga Road, Kolkata 700 017
  E-mail: vivakolkata@vivagroupindia.net, Tel. 22836381, 22816713
- 7, Sovereign Park Apartments, 56-58, K. R. Road, Basavanagudi, Bangalore 560 004
  E-mail: vivabangalore@vivagroupindia.net, Tel. 26607409, 26607410
- 101-102 Mughal Marc Apartments, 3-4-637 to 641, Narayanguda, Hyderabad 500 029
  E-mail: vivahyderabad@vivagroupindia.net, Tel. 27564481, 27564482
- First Floor, Beevi Towers, SRM Road, Kaloor, Kochi 682 018, Kerala
  E-mail: vivakochi@vivagroupindia.net, Tel: 0484-2403055, 2403056
- 232, GNB Road, Beside UCO Bank, Silpukhuri, Guwahati 781 003
  E-mail: vivaguwahati@vivagroupindia.net, Tel: 0361-2666386

www.vivagroupindia.com

Published by arrangement with
Facts on File, Inc.
132 West 31st Street
New York 10001
USA

ISBN : 978-81-309-0929-5 (Set of 4 Volumes)

Published by Vinod Vasishtha for Viva Books Private Limited, 4737/23, Ansari Road, Daryaganj, New Delhi-110 002. Printed and bound by Sanat Printers, Kundli-131 028, Sonepat, Haryana.

Contents

Volume IV

Advisers and Contributors

EDITOR IN CHIEF

Peter Bogucki
Associate Dean for Undergraduate Affairs,
School of Engineering and Applied Science
Princeton University

ADVISORY BOARD

Lisa R. Brody
Assistant Professor of Art
Queens College, City University of New York

R. Hunt Davis
Professor Emeritus of History and African Studies
University of Florida

Leo Depuydt
Associate Professor of Egyptology
Brown University

Paul R. Goldin
Associate Professor of East Asian Languages
and Civilizations
University of Pennsylvania

Eloise Quiñones Keber
Professor of Art History
Baruch College, City University of New York

Amelie Kuhrt
Professor of Ancient Near Eastern History
University College, London

Daniel Potts
Edwin Cuthbert Hall Professor of
Middle Eastern Archaeology
University of Sydney

CONTRIBUTORS

Saheed Aderinto is a Ph.D. student at the Department of History, University of Texas at Austin. Some of his most recent publications include "Prostitution and Urban Social Relations" and "Policing Urban Prostitution: Prostitutes, Crime, Law and Reformers in Colonial Nigeria" in *Nigeria's Urban History: Past and Present* (2006) and "Discrimination in an Urban Setting: The Experience of Ijebu Settlers in Colonial Ibadan, 1893–1960" in *Inter-group Relations in Nigeria during the 19th & 20th Centuries* (2006). His writings have also appeared in *IFRA Special Research Issue, Ethnic and Third World Review of Books, African and Asian Studies Journal,* and *The Encyclopedia of Prostitution and Sex Work* (2006).

Olutayo Charles Adesina, Ph.D., teaches at the Department of History, University of Ibadan, Nigeria. He is the author of "The Underground Foreign Exchange Market in Ibadan during Devaluation" in *Money Struggles and City Life: Devaluation in Ibadan and Other Urban Centres in Southern Nigeria, 1986–96* (2002) and "Teaching History in Twentieth Century Nigeria: The Challenges of Change" in *History in Africa: A Journal of Method*, vol. 33 (2006).

David Otieno Akombo, Ph.D., teaches music education and world music at Wabash College of Indiana. He is the author of *Music and Healing across Cultures* (2006).

Francis Allard, Ph.D., teaches in the Department of Anthropology at Indiana University of Pennsylvania. His research interests include the archaeology of early China and Mongolia. He has contributed articles to *Archaeology of Asia* (2005) and *Beyond the Steppe and the Sown: Proceedings of the 2002 University of Chicago Conference on Eurasian Archaeology* (2006).

Miguel Arisa is finishing his doctoral studies in art history at the Graduate Center, City University of New York. He teaches at Technical Career Institutes and is a regular lecturer at the

Cloisters and a docent at the Metropolitan Museum of Art, New York.

Mariam F. Ayad, Ph.D., teaches graduate-level classes on Egyptian language and literature at the University of Memphis, where she is the assistant director of its Institute of Egyptian Art and Archaeology. Her main research interests focus on the role of women in ancient Egyptian temple ritual and the selection and transmission of funerary texts in post–New Kingdom Egypt. Her book on the God's Wife of Amun is under contract with Routledge.

Heather D. Baker, D.Phil., is a researcher at the University of Vienna, Austria, specializing in Babylonian history, society, and culture. She has published widely on Babylonian and Assyrian history and is writing a book to be titled *The Urban Landscape of First Millennium BC Babylonia.*

Robin Barrow, Ph.D., FRSC, is professor of philosophy of education at Simon Fraser University, Canada. His most recent books include *Plato* (2007) and *An Introduction to Moral Philosophy and Moral Education* (2007). He is the author of *Athenian Democracy* (2001) and *Greek and Roman Education* (1996).

László Bartosiewicz, Ph.D., D.sc., teaches archaeozoology at the Loránd Eötvös University in Budapest (Hungary) and the University of Edinburgh (United Kingdom). He is the author of *Animals in the Urban Landscape in the Wake of the Middle Ages* (1995) and principal author of *Draught Cattle: Their Osteological Identification and History* (1997) and has published more than 200 scholarly articles.

Kirk H. Beetz, Ph.D., emeritus, has published over two dozen books and more than 900 articles. His books span topics from endangered mammal species to children's literature, including *Exploring C. S. Lewis' "The Chronicles of Narnia"* (2000). His recent writings have focused on the history and culture of ancient Japan.

Craig G. R. Benjamin, Ph.D., teaches world and ancient Eurasian history at Grand Valley State University. He is the coeditor of vols. 2 (1998), 4 (2000), and 6 (2002) in the Brepols Silk Roads Studies series and the author of *The Yuezhi: Origin, Migration and the Conquest of Northern Bactria* (2007).

Uffe Bergeton, Ph.D., is in the Ph.D. program in the Department of Asian Languages and Cultures at the University of Michigan. He is the author of *The Independence of Binding and Intensification* (Ph.D. dissertation, University of Southern California) and various articles on theoretical phonology and syntax.

Amy Hackney Blackwell has degrees in history from Duke University and Vanderbilt University and a J.D. from the University of Virginia. Her books include *Mythology for Dummies* (2002), *LSAT for Dummies* (2004), *The Everything Irish History and Heritage Book* (2004), and *Essential Dictionary of Law* (2004). She has contributed to the *Encyclopedia of World Nations and Cultures* (2006), *Alternative Energy* (2006), and *Chemical Compounds* (2006).

Christopher Blackwell, Ph.D., teaches classics at Furman University. He is the author of *In the Absence of Alexander: Harpalus and the Failure of Macedonian Hegemony* (1999) and various protocols and software applications for building digital libraries, and he serves as technical editor for the Center for Hellenic Studies of Harvard University.

Amy Bogaard, Ph.D., teaches prehistory and archaeobotany at the Department of Archaeology, University of Nottingham, United Kingdom. She is the author of *Neolithic Farming in Central Europe* (2004).

Peter Bogucki, Ph.D., is an archaeologist who is associate dean for undergraduate affairs of the School of Engineering and Applied Science at Princeton University. He has studied prehistoric settlements in Poland and has a particular interest in the spread of farming in Europe. He is the author of *The Origins of Human Society* (1999) and the editor (with Pam J. Crabtree) of *Ancient Europe 8000 B.C.–A.D. 1000: An Encyclopedia of the Barbarian World* (2004).

Larissa Bonfante, Ph.D., professor of classics at New York University, is the author of several books on Etruscan and early Roman culture as well as publications on ancient dress and nudity, including *The World of Roman Costume*, coedited with Judith Sebesta (1994).

Charlotte Booth is a Ph.D. student at the University of Wales, Swansea, and teaches Egyptology for Birkbeck College and other institutions in the United Kingdom. She is the author of *People of Ancient Egypt* (2007), *The Hyksos Period in Egypt* (2005), and *The Role of Foreigners in Ancient Egypt* (2005).

Lisa R. Brody, Ph.D., teaches Greek and Roman art history at Queens College, City University of New York. Her research interests include Greek iconography and cult, ancient lamps and their decoration, children in antiquity, and representation of ethnicity in Greco-Roman art. She compiled the revised edition of David Sacks's *Encyclopedia of the Ancient Greek World* (2005) and is author of *Aphrodisias III: The Aphrodite of Aphrodisias* (2007).

David Brown, Ph.D., is researching the interactions of the pre-Islamic astral sciences of Mesopotamia, Greece, India, Egypt, Iran, the western Semitic world, and China at the Free University of Berlin. He is the author of *Mesopotamian Planetary Astronomy-Astrology* (2000) and *The Interactions of Ancient Astral Science* (forthcoming).

Deborah N. Carlson, Ph.D., teaches in the Nautical Archaeology Program of the Department of Anthropology at Texas A&M University. She also directs the Institute of Nautical Archaeology's shipwreck excavation of a Roman marble carrier off the Aegean coast of Turkey at Kizilburun and is preparing the final publication of the Classical Greek ship excavated by the Institute of Nautical Archaeology at nearby Tektas Burnu.

Jeffrey S. Carnes is associate professor of classics at Syracuse University. He is the author of *The Uses of Aiakos: Pindar and the Aiginetan Imaginary* (forthcoming) as well as articles on Greek lyric poetry, gender studies, literary theory, and Plato.

Julia Marta Clapp is pursuing her doctorate in art history at the Graduate Center, City University of New York. Her research interests include modern and pre-Columbian Latin American art.

Wendy E. Closterman, Ph.D., teaches ancient history and Greek at Bryn Athyn College. Her research focuses on Athenian burial and funerary ritual. She is the author of "Family Members and Citizens: Athenian Identity and the Peribolos Tomb Setting" in *Antigone's Answer: Essays on Death and Burial, Family and State in Classical Athens*, edited by C. Patterson (forthcoming).

Leah A. J. Cohen is an independent writer and editorial consultant with a master's degree in geography from the University of Florida. She specializes in Africa area studies and food security. She was a senior author for the *Encyclopedia of African History and Culture*, volumes 4 and 5 (2005).

John Collis is professor emeritus in the Department of Archaeology, University of Sheffield, where he taught for over 30 years. He has had a major role in the development of university and professional training in archaeology in Britain, and is secretary of the European Association of Archaeologists' Committee on Training and Education. He is author of several books and excavation monographs, including *Digging Up the Past* (2004) and *The Celts: Origins, Myths and Inventions* (2004).

Constance A. Cook, Ph.D., directs the Asian Studies program and teaches Chinese language and literature courses at Lehigh University. She is the author of *Death in Ancient China: The Tale of One Man's Journey* (2006) and coeditor of *Defining Chu: Image and Reality in Ancient China* (1999).

Susan Cooksey, Ph.D., is the curator of African art, Harn Museum of Art, University of Florida.

Justin Corfield, Ph.D., teaches history and international relations at Geelong Grammar School, Australia. He is the co-author of *Historical Dictionary of Cambodia* (2003) and has written extensively on Asia, Australia, and European colonial history.

James A. Corrick, Ph.D., is a full-time editor and writer with 25 books to his credit. His most recent titles are *The Early Middle Ages* (2006), *The Byzantine Empire* (2006), and *The Renaissance* (2007).

Arden Decker is a Ph.D. candidate in the history of art at the Graduate Center, City University of New York. Her research interests include Mesoamerican art as well as modern and contemporary art of Mexico.

Leo Depuydt, Ph.D., teaches Egyptology at Brown University and is curious about everything relating to ancient Egypt in its Near Eastern and Mediterranean context, especially the area's languages and history. He wrote *Civil Calendar and Lunar Calendar in Ancient Egypt* (1997) and *The Other Mathematics: Language and Logic in Egyptian and in General* (2007).

Haig Der-Houssikian, Ph.D., is professor emeritus (2003), linguistics, at the University of Florida, Gainesville. His research and publication interests are in morphology, Creolization, and sub-Saharan Africa.

Christine End, M.A., works on the Giza Archives Project at the Museum of Fine Arts, Boston. Her main interests of research are Middle Kingdom funerary iconography, material culture, burial practices, and mummification. As a researcher and illustrator, her work has appeared in Egyptological publications and documentaries.

Linda Evans, Ph.D., specializes in ancient Egyptian art at Macquarie University, Sydney, Australia. She recently completed her doctoral dissertation on the representation of animal behavior in Egyptian tomb paintings and has published several papers on the role and depiction of animals in the ancient world. She has also contributed chapters to *Egyptian Art: Principles and Themes in Wall Scenes* (2000), *The Encyclopedia of Animal Behavior* (2004), *Egypt: The Land and Lives of the Pharaohs Revealed* (2005), and *Historica* (2006).

Stephen M. Fabian, Ph.D., is an anthropologist and currently teaches seminars on religion, myth, and ritual at Princeton University. He is the author of *Space-Time of the Bororo of Brazil* (1992), *Clearing Away Clouds: Nine Lessons for Life from the Martial Arts* (1999), and *Patterns in the Sky: An Introduction to Ethnoastronomy* (2001).

Erin Fairburn is a graduate student in the Department of Egyptology and Western Asian Studies at Brown University. She has contributed to *The City and Urban Life* (forthcoming).

Alessia Frassani is a Ph.D. candidate at the Graduate Center of the City University of New York. Her research interests in-

clude the art and civilizations of ancient Oaxaca and issues surrounding the cultural interaction between the Old and New Worlds.

Markham J. Geller is professor of Semitic languages at University College London, in the Department of Hebrew and Jewish Studies. He has recently published a text edition of cuneiform medical texts, *Renal and Rectal Disease Texts, Babylonisch-assyrische Medizin* VII (2005).

J. J. George is working on his Ph.D. at the Graduate Center, City University of New York. His research area is pre-Columbian art and architecture.

Wolfram Grajetzki, Ph.D., wrote his dissertation at the Humboldt University of Berlin and has taught Egyptology there. He has excavated in Egypt and Pakistan and was principal archaeologist and author for the online learning project Digital Egypt for Universities (University College London). He is preparing the catalogue of Egyptian coffins in the Fitzwilliam Museum, Cambridge. His publications include *Burial Customs in Ancient Egypt* (2003) and *The Middle Kingdom in Ancient Egypt* (2006).

Lyn Green, Ph.D., has taught at several Canadian universities and for the Royal Ontario Museum. She has contributed to several encyclopedias, including *The Oxford Encyclopedia of Ancient Egypt* (2000) and the *Encyclopedia of the Archaeology of Ancient Egypt* (1999) as well as *The Royal Women of Amarna* (1996). Currently she is devoting her time to her duties as president of the Society for the Study of Egyptian Antiquities, which has over 400 members and subscribers internationally, and to writing.

Angela Herren, Ph.D., teaches pre-Columbian art and architecture as an assistant professor in the Department of Art and Latin American Studies at the University of North Carolina at Charlotte. A specialist on painted manuscripts from central Mexico, she completed a 2005 dissertation entitled "Portraying the Mexica Past: A Comparative Study of Accounts of Origin in Codex Azcatitlan, Codex Boturni, and Codex Aubin."

David B. Hollander, Ph.D., teaches ancient history at Iowa State University. He is the author of *Money in the Late Roman Republic* (2007).

Brooke Holmes, Ph.D., is an assistant professor of classics at the University of North Carolina, Chapel Hill. She is at work on a book about the symptom in early Greek medicine and classical Greek literature.

Michael Allen Holmes is a freelance editor and writer who recently contributed to *Shakespeare for Students*, 2nd edition (2007). He has also written an unpublished novel.

John W. Humphrey, Ph.D., is professor of Greek and Roman studies at the University of Calgary. A veteran of many seasons of archaeological excavation in Turkey and Greece, he is the author of *Greek and Roman Technology: A Sourcebook* (1998, with J. P. Oleson and A. N. Sherwood) and *Ancient Technology* (2006).

Keith Jordan, M.Phil., is a Ph.D. candidate in pre-Columbian art history at the Graduate Center of the City University of New York. He is currently finishing his doctoral dissertation, entitled "Stone Trees Transplanted? Central Mexican Stelae of the Epiclassic and Early Postclassic and the Question of Maya 'Influence.'"

Amr Kamel is an Egyptologist in the Rare Books and Special Collections Library at the American University in Cairo, Egypt.

David Kelly is an instructor of English writing and literature at Oakton Community College in Illinois. He has written over 100 published literary analyses and wrote the instructor's manual for the *Exploring Poetry* computer program. His short fiction has been published in *The Rockford Review*, *Grub Street*, and *The Iconoclast*, among other places.

Panagiotis I. M. Kousoulis, Ph.D., is a lecturer in Egyptology at the Department of Mediterranean Studies of the University of the Aegean. He is the author of *Moving across Borders: Foreign Relations, Religion and Cultural Interactions in the Ancient Mediterranean* (2007) and *Ancient Egyptian Demonology: Studies on the Boundaries between the Demonic and the Divine in Egyptian Magic* (2007).

Philippa Lang teaches ancient science and related subjects, with research interests in ancient medicine and philosophy, in the Classics Department of Emory University, Atlanta. She is the editor of *Re-Inventions: Essays on Hellenistic and Early Roman Science*, *Apeiron* special issue vol. 37 (2004).

Russell M. Lawson, Ph.D., is associate professor of history and chair of the Division of General Studies at Bacone College in Oklahoma. He is the author of *Science in the Ancient World* (2004), *The Land between the Rivers: Thomas Nuttall's Ascent of the Arkansas, 1819* (2004), and *Passaconaway's Realm: John Evans and the Exploration of Mount Washington* (2002, 2004).

Anne Mahoney, Ph.D., teaches Greek and Latin linguistics and literature at Tufts University. She is the author of *Plautus: Amphitryo* (2004) and *Roman Sports and Spectacles: A Sourcebook* (2001). She is also the editor of revised editions of *Allen and Greenough's New Latin Grammar* (2001), *Morice's Stories in Attic Greek* (2005), and *Bennett's Essentials* (2007).

Susan Malin-Boyce, Ph.D., serves as deputy director of the Regime Crimes Liaison Office, Mass Graves Investigation

Team, in Baghdad, Iraq. She has contributed to *Ancient Europe 8000 B.C.–A.D. 1000: Encyclopedia of the Barbarian World* (2004) and to publications addressing Early and Late La Tène settlement in Bavaria, Germany.

Renee McGarry is a student in the Ph.D. program in art history at the City University of New York Graduate Center. Her research interests include Aztec sculpture of the natural world and religious manuscripts from the post-Conquest period.

Paul McKechnie, D.Phil., is a senior lecturer in classics and ancient history at the University of Auckland, New Zealand. He is the author of *First Christian Centuries: Perspectives on the Early Church* (2002) and *Outsiders in the Greek Cities in the Fourth Century B.C.* (1989).

John M. McMahon, Ph.D., teaches at Le Moyne College in Syracuse, New York, where he directs the classics program. He is author of *Cave Paralysin: Impotence, Perception and Text in the Satyrica of Petronius* (1998) and numerous articles on the intersection of ancient literature and natural history. His most recent work includes nine entries in the forthcoming *Biographical Encyclopedia of Astronomers* (2006).

Jianjun Mei, Ph.D., teaches the history of science and technology at the University of Science and Technology Beijing. He is the author of *Copper and Bronze Metallurgy in Late Prehistoric Xinjiang: Its Cultural Context and Relationship with Neighbouring Regions* (2000).

James E. Meier, Ph.D., is assistant professor in the Department of Humanities and Social Sciences at Central Florida Community College. He is a contributor to the *Encyclopedia of African History and Culture* (2005).

Francesco Menotti, Ph.D., is a lecturer in European prehistory at the Institute of Prehistory and Archaeological Science, Basel University, Switzerland. He is the author of *Living on the Lake in Prehistoric Europe* (2004).

Melissa Moore Morison is associate professor of classics and classical archaeology at Grand Valley State University. She has extensive experience in archaeological fieldwork in Greece, Turkey, and the United States. Her research interests include Roman provincial archaeology, Greek and Roman pottery, and ceramic technology.

Penny Morrill, Ph.D., teaches pre-Columbian and early colonial Mesoamerican art at Hood College, Frederick, Maryland. She has an essay, "The Queen of Heaven Reigns in New Spain: The Triumph of Eternity in the Casa del Deán Murals," in a Brill anthology, *Woman and Art in Early Modern Latin America* (2006). She has authored several books on modern Mexican silver: *Mexican Silver: 20th Century Handwrought Silver Jewelry and Metalwork* (4th ed., 2007), *Silver Masters of Mexico: Héctor Aguilar and the Taller Borda* (1996), and *Maestros de Plata: William Spratling and the Mexican Silver Renaissance*, a catalog for a traveling exhibit (2002–2004).

Julian M. Murchison, Ph.D., teaches in the Department of Sociology and Anthropology at Millsaps College. His work in cultural anthropology examines the intersections of medicine and religion in East Africa. He recently published a chapter examining stories about a cure for HIV/AIDS in *Borders and Healers* (2005).

Caryn E. Neumann, Ph.D., teaches history in Ohio Wesleyan University's Black World Studies Department. She is a former managing editor of the *Journal of Women's History.*

Emily Jane O'Dell, is a Ph.D. candidate at Brown University and has taught at Brown University in both the Department of Egyptology and Ancient Western Asian Studies and the Department of Literary Arts. She has been the chief epigrapher of the Cairo-Brown University Abu Bakr Epigraphic Survey in the western cemetery of the Great Pyramids in Giza, Egypt, for the past five years.

Simon O'Dwyer is founder and researcher for Prehistoric Music Ireland, author of *Prehistoric Music of Ireland* and prehistoricmusic.com, and contributor to *The Encyclopedia of Music in Ireland* and *The Encyclopedia of Ireland.* He has published four papers for the International Study Group on Music Archaeology.

Penelope Ojeda de Huala is a Ph.D. candidate in art history at the Graduate Center of the City University of New York, where she studies pre-Columbian to contemporary art of Latin America. Her research focus is Guatemala and Peru, particularly the enduring thoughts and practices of indigenous cultures as manifested in art.

Michael J. O'Neal, Ph.D., is a writer who lives in Moscow, Idaho. He is a frequent contributor to reference and educational books, including *Lives and Works: Young Adult Authors* (1999), *The Crusades* (2005), and *America in the 1920s* (2006).

Dianne White Oyler, Ph.D., teaches African history at Fayetteville State University. She is the author of *The History of the N'ko Alphabet and Its Role in Mande Transnational Identity: Words as Weapons* (2005) as well as articles in the refereed journals *Research in African Literature, the Mande Studies Journal*, and the *International Journal of African Historical Studies.*

Katie Parla is an art historian and archaeological speleologist working in Rome and Naples as a docent leading didactic seminars of archaeological sites. She consults for the History

Channel and will appear in their 2007 series *Cities of the Underworld* as an expert on underground Rome and Naples.

Marie Passanante is a doctoral candidate in the Department of Egyptology and Ancient Western Asian Studies at Brown University.

William H. Peck teaches at the College for Creative Studies, Detroit, and the University of Michigan, Dearborn. He was for many years the curator of ancient art at the Detroit Institute of Arts and is at present a member of the Brooklyn Museum excavations in Egypt at Karnak. He is the author of *Drawings from Ancient Egypt* (1987) and numerous contributions to reference books and encyclopedias on the ancient world.

David Petechuk is a freelance writer specializing in educational texts focusing on the sciences, literature, and history. The former director of publications for the health sciences at the University of Pittsburgh, he is the author of *The Respiratory System* (2004), *LSD* (2005), and *Health & Medical Issues Today: Organ Transplantation* (2006).

Mark Anthony Phelps is taking a leave after teaching continuously since 1994 (primarily at Drury University, in five different departments) to finish his dissertation at the University of Arkansas entitled "Sewage from the Orontes: Roman Elite Attitudes toward Ecstatic Religion in the 3rd and 4th centuries C.E." This degree in ancient Mediterranean history augments his graduate degrees from Harvard and Johns Hopkins in Hebrew Bible and ancient Near Eastern languages and cultures. His research interests reflected in his writings are widely eclectic, spanning Paleolithic to contemporary society and including the disciplines of archaeology, linguistics, cultural anthropology, physical geography, historical geography, classical history, ancient Near Eastern history, medieval history, modern history, religion, and biblical history.

Jen Piro is a Ph.D. candidate in anthropological archaeology at New York University. Her dissertation research focuses on the development of pastoral economies in Early Bronze Age Transcaucasia.

Karen Radner, Ph.D., is lecturer in ancient Near Eastern history at University College, London. She specializes in the Assyrian Empire and is the author of *Die neuassyrischen Texte aus Tall Seh Hamad* (2002), *Das mittelassyrische Tontafelarchiv von Giricano/Dunnu-sa-Uzibi* (2004) and *Die Macht des Namens: Altorientalische Strategien zur Selbsterhaltung* (2005).

Judith A. Rasson, Ph.D., teaches in the Department of Medieval Studies, Central European University, Budapest (a post-graduate American-accredited university). Her research interests lie in southeastern Europe (especially the countries of the former Yugoslavia) and focus on Neolithic and historic archaeology and ethnographic material culture.

Kelly-Anne Diamond Reed, Ph.D., teaches ancient Egyptian history and archaeology at Villanova University's Department of History. She is investigating early Egyptian funerary rituals and burial customs.

Duane W. Roller is professor of Greek and Latin at Ohio State University. Trained as an archaeologist, he has over 30 years' experience in field archaeology in numerous Mediterranean countries. He is the author of *The Building Program of Herod the Great* (1998), *The World of Juba II and Kleopatra Selene* (2003), and *Through the Pillars of Herakles* (2006) as well as many other publications in history, classics, and archaeology.

Kelley L. Ross, Ph.D., teaches philosophy at Los Angeles Valley College. He specializes in Kantian epistemology, metaphysics, and ethics, with emphasis on members of the Friesian tradition—Jakob Fries, Leonard Nelson, Rudolf Otto, Sir Karl Popper, and others. Since 1996 he has been the publisher and editor of the online philosophy journal *Proceedings of the Friesian School, Fourth Series.*

Edward M. W. A. Rowlands, M.Phil., has research interests in Mycenaean political geography, trade, and religion.

Lucas G. Rubin, Ph.D., develops master of science programs for Columbia University. He was previously administrator of the university's Center for Archaeology, where he managed multiple excavations and projects. His research and scholarship have focused on fires and firefighters in ancient Rome.

Michael M. Sage, Ph.D., teaches classics and ancient history in the Classics Department at the University of Cincinnati. His main areas of study are historiography and military history. He is the author of *Cyprian: A Biography* (1975) and *Warfare in Ancient Greece: A Sourcebook* (1996).

Rick Schulting, Ph.D., is a lecturer in scientific and prehistoric archaeology at the University of Oxford. His current research interests lie in understanding the Mesolithic-Neolithic transition in western Europe, emphasizing the use of radiometric dating and stable isotope analysis, and in skeletal evidence for interpersonal violence in earlier prehistoric Europe.

David R. Sear, a fellow of the Royal Numismatic Society in London and the American Numismatic Society in New York, has authored an extensive range of numismatic books over the past four decades, aimed at collectors and students of ancient Greek, Roman and Byzantine coinage. He has been a resident of Los Angeles for the past 25 years and operates a research service authenticating ancient coinage. His

numerous publications include *Roman Coins and Their Values* (1964; rev. ed., 2000–2005), *Byzantine Coins and Their Values* (1974, rev. ed., 1987), *Greek Coins and Their Values* (1978–1979), and *The History and Coinage of the Roman Imperators, 49–27 B.C.* (1998).

Robert Shanafelt, Ph.D., teaches courses in anthropology, religion, and Africana studies at Georgia Southern University. He has published a number of articles on different aspects of life in southern Africa, among them, "Crime, Power, and Policing in South Africa" in *Democratic Policing in Transitional and Developing Countries* (2006).

Alison Sheridan, Ph.D., is head of early prehistory in the National Museums Scotland, Edinburgh, specializing in the British and Irish Neolithic and Bronze Age. Exhibition work includes *Heaven and Hell—and Other Worlds of the Dead* (2000), for which she was lead curator and book editor. Other books include *From Sickles to Circles* (with A. M. Gibson, 2004) and *Vessels for the Ancestors* (with N. M. Sharples, 1992).

Spyros Siropoulos is senior lecturer of Greek philology and history at the Department of Mediterranean Studies, University of the Aegean, Greece. He has published various articles in three books: *Unlike a Woman: Gender and the Social Function of the Athenian Tragedy* (2003), *The Goat's Skin: The Other Side of Alexander the Great's Power* (2003; in Greek with English summary), and *The Things after Alexander: The Centrifugal Potencies of the Hellenistic Kingdoms* (2005, in Greek).

Bradley Skeen, M.A., has taught at the University of Minnesota, Webster University, and Washington University. He is a specialist in magic, religion, and philosophy in late antiquity and has contributed to research in that field in *Die Zeitschrift für Papyrologie und Epigraphik*, among other journals.

Christopher Smith, D.Phil., is professor of ancient history at the University of Saint Andrews in Scotland. He is the author of *Early Rome and Latium: Economy and Society c 100–500 B.C.* (1996) and *The Roman Clan: From Ancient Ideology to Modern Anthropology* (2006) as well as editor of several collections of essays, including *Trade, Traders and the Ancient City* (with Helen Parkins, 1998); *Sicily from Aeneas to Augustus* (with John Serrati, 2000), and *Religion in Archaic and Republican Rome and Italy: Evidence and Experience* (with Edward Bispham, 2000). He is engaged in work on Roman historiography and oratory.

Nancy Shatzman Steinhardt is professor of East Asian art and curator of Chinese art at the University of Pennsylvania. She is author of *Chinese Traditional Architecture* (1984), *Chinese Imperial City Planning* (1990), *Liao Architecture* (1997), and *Chinese Architecture* (2002) and more than 60 scholarly articles.

Tom Streissguth is a freelance author, editor, and journalist who has published more than 70 nonfiction and reference books. His most recent titles include *Clay v. United States, Genghis Khan's Mongol Empire, Library in a Book: Hate Crimes, Eyewitness History: The Roaring Twenties,* and the *Greenhaven Encyclopedia of the Middle Ages.*

Ananda Cohen Suarez is a Ph.D. student at the Graduate Center of the City University of New York, specializing in pre-Columbian and colonial Latin American art history. She is particularly interested in cross-cultural encounters, vernacular religious art, and manuscript production in the early colonial Americas.

Frank J. Swetz, D.Ed., is professor emeritus of mathematics and education, Pennsylvania State University. His research interests focus on cultural and societal impact on mathematics learning and teaching. Among his recent books are *Legacy of the Luoshu: The 4000 Year Search for the Meaning of the Magic Square of Order Three* (2002) and *Teaching Mathematics to Children* (2003).

John Thorburn, Ph.D., is associate professor of classics at Baylor University, where he teaches a variety of subjects dealing with the classical world. He has published on Greek tragedy, Greek comedy, Greek and Roman history, and a variety of ancient subjects. He is the author of *The Alcestis of Euripides* (2002) and the *Facts on File Companion to Classical Drama* (2005).

Alain Touwaide, Ph.D., is a historian of sciences in the Department of Botany of the National Museum of Natural History at the Smithsonian Institution (Washington, D.C.). He has extensively published on the history of medicine in the Mediterranean world from antiquity to the Renaissance. Recently, he coedited the volume *Visualizing Medieval Medicine and Natural History, 1200–1550* (2006).

Francesca C. Tronchin, Ph.D., teaches Greek and Roman art and archaeology at Ohio State University. Her primary area of research is Roman domestic decor and issues of eclecticism in ancient sculptural displays.

David K. Underwood, Ph.D., teaches Western humanities, art history, philosophy, and Latin American studies at the University of South Florida in Tampa and at Saint Petersburg College in Clearwater, Florida. He is the author of two books and several articles and essays on Iberian and Latin American art and architecture.

David Vallilee is an independent scholar.

Frans van Koppen, M.A., teaches Akkadian at the School of Oriental and African Studies, London. He contributed to *The*

Ancient Near East: Historical Sources in Translation (2006) and *The Babylonian World* (forthcoming).

Lawrence Waldron, M.F.A., is an associate professor and doctoral candidate at the City University of New York, specializing in non-Western fields of art history and culture. He has presented and published various articles on the art and culture of the pre-Columbian Caribbean and Southeast Asia.

Ezekiel A. Walker, Ph.D., teaches African and world history at the University of Central Florida. His forthcoming book is entitled *Growth, Crisis and Transformation in the Cocoa-Farming Economy of Southwestern Nigeria* (2007).

Peter S. Wells is professor of anthropology at the University of Minnesota. His publications include *The Barbarians Speak: How the Conquered Peoples Shaped Roman Europe* (1999), *Beyond Celts, Germans and Scythians: Archaeology and Identity in Iron Age Europe* (2001), and *The Battle That Stopped Rome: Emperor Augustus, Arminius, and the Slaughter of the Legions in the Teutoburg Forest* (2003).

Jacqui Wood is an archaeologist and authority on prehistoric cooking and the lifestyles of prehistoric Europeans. She runs her own excavation in Cornwall, England.

Ronald Young, Ph.D., teaches in the Social Sciences Department at Canterbury School in Fort Myers, Florida. His teaching and research interests are in the area of Latin American Studies. In addition to numerous reference articles, he is presently working on a general history of Colombia to be published by Greenwood Press.

Katharina Zinn, M.A., is writing her Ph.D. dissertation on ancient Egyptian libraries and archives at the University of Leipzig, Germany. She works in a project on scarabs in the Fitzwilliam Museum, Cambridge (United Kingdom) and a project on Middle Kingdom Reliefs from Lisht in the Princeton University Art Museum. She has published articles on the organization of collective wisdom as well as multilingualism in ancient Egypt.

List of Illustrations

VOLUME II

VOLUME III

VOLUME IV

List of Maps and Primary Source Documents

MAPS

VOLUME I

VOLUME II

VOLUME III

VOLUME IV

PRIMARY SOURCE DOCUMENTS

VOLUME I

VOLUME II

VOLUME III

Entries L to R

L

► language

INTRODUCTION

Most paleontologists believe that modern humans, called *Homo sapiens*, as well as their language originated in Africa. The language spoken by the San (commonly called Bushmen) is believed to be related to the first languages spoken in Africa. In ancient times the San populated most of sub-Saharan Africa, only to be pushed aside by the Bantu-speaking peoples who now populate most of Africa. Their language includes clicking sounds that are unique, and these clicks are thought to have been part of Africa's first languages. Over thousands of years some Africans lost the clicking sound from their speech; these people were the ancestors of the people who spread out from Africa to populate the rest of the world. This is why the clicks of the San are not found elsewhere in the world.

Linguists have struggled hard to trace the development of languages after people migrated out of Africa, but developments during and before the last great ice age, which ended about 9000 B.C.E., may be impossible to fully trace. Complicating the history of language is a side branch of human development, the Neanderthals, who may have been a subgroup of *Homo sapiens* or a different human species that evolved in Europe or the Near East rather than in Africa. Some paleontologists believe the Neanderthals could speak languages, but others think that the shape of the palate and throat of Neanderthals would have limited them to a small number of grunts.

Perhaps the earliest of ancient languages outside Africa were those of the Elamo-Dravidian group. Elamo refers to the Elamites who lived in the Near East and Dravidian refers to the peoples who migrated along the southern coast of Asia and across islands to Australia. In ancient times their descendants populated such places as the Indus River valley, most of India, and almost all of Southeast Asia, including South Vietnam and Indonesia. Other early language groups are harder to trace. According to technology that traces changes in human genes that have been passed on over time, the descendants of a group of people who settled in central Asia populated all the rest of the world, including the Americas. This could have happened more than 100,000 years ago, though paleontologists disagree vigorously with each other about the date.

Linguists can begin tracing most of the world's languages in about 9000 B.C.E. By then Indo-European had developed somewhere in eastern Europe or central Asia and was spreading west, east, and south. The languages of the ancestors of the Chinese and other east Asians were developing. The peoples who migrated to the Americas brought a root language from central Asia, a language that may have remained among the Ainu ethnic group of Japan, who during the last great ice age probably populated all of eastern Asia north of the Dravidians. Research into Native American languages is complicated by the problem of repeated migrations from the Old World into the Americas, perhaps as many as seven major migrations over thousands of years. Whether the Native American languages have only one root language or more is not yet known.

AFRICA

BY HAIG DER-HOUSSIKIAN

Languages on the African continent are divided into four distinct groupings: Afro-Asiatic, Niger-Congo, Nilo-Saharan,

Sandstone offering table with Meroitic cursive inscription around the edges, from Faras, Sudan (first to second centuries C.E.*)* (© The Trustees of the British Museum)

and Khoisan. Until several hundred years ago most African languages lacked a written tradition or archaeological support that would indicate time; nevertheless, it has been assumed that they have been present in Africa since ancient times. The exceptions to this assumption are the Semitic languages of the Afro-Asiatic group and Nubian, the only language in the Nilo-Saharan group with an ancient script derived from Coptic. These languages fit into the time frame of antiquity by evidence of their written traditions. The Semitic languages in question are ancient Egyptian (the language of hieroglyphs), Coptic, Amharic, and Tigrinya. Arabic is an uncertain member of this group. It made its presence with written documentation during the seventh and eighth centuries C.E. with the Muslim conquest of North Africa. It is assumed that the language may have been spoken in North Africa prior to Islamization.

Afro-Asiatic covers Somalia, Eritrea, Djibouti, Ethiopia, northern Nigeria, Niger, and the North African countries of Egypt, Libya, Tunisia, Algeria, and Morocco. Tunisia, Algeria, and Morocco are collectively called Maghreb, meaning "west" in Arabic. Some of the major languages in this division include Somali in Somalia, Amharic in Ethiopia, Tigrinya in Ethiopia and Eritrea, Hausa in northern Nigeria, Arabic in North Africa, and Berber in the Maghreb. The largest grouping within Afro-Asiatic is the Semitic subgroup that extends beyond Africa into the Middle East and the Arabian Peninsula where Arabic and Hebrew have remained current since antiquity. Semitic includes ancient Egyptian, of which Coptic is the most recent evolution, now used only in parts of the Coptic Orthodox Church mass. The word *Copt*, "*qubt*" in Arabic, is etymologically the root of the word *Egypt*. Thus, one can appreciate the term *Afro-Asiatic* for the entire group of languages under this rubric.

Niger-Congo covers the countries collectively referred to as sub-Saharan Africa. Interestingly, the next three divisions are geographically embedded within this vast area. The term Niger-Congo was first coined and the subgroupings within it were explicitly established by Joseph H. Greenberg in a series of articles and books from 1949 to 1966. There were others, of course, both before and after Greenberg who contributed to what has emerged as the widely accepted distinct division called Niger-Congo. A look at a map of sub-Saharan Africa will show that the Niger River with its diverse tributaries covers much of sub-Saharan western Africa. Similarly, the Congo River is the most extensive in subequatorial Africa; hence the name Niger-Congo.

The Niger-Congo group is itself divided into six subgroups: West Atlantic, Mande, Gur (also called Voltaic because of the Volta River), Kwa, Benue-Congo, and Adamawa-Ubangi. The most common languages under these subgroups are Wolof, Fula (also known as Fulani, Fulfulde, Pular, and Pulaar), Mandinka (also known as Mandingo, Manding, Maninka, and Madinka) under West Atlantic; Bambara (also known as Bamanankan) under Mande; Moore and Kabyle under Gur; Akan, Ewe, Yoruba, and Ibo (also spelled Igbo) under Kwa; and Efik under Benue-Congo.

The Benue-Congo subgroup is especially significant because it is through this subgroup that sub-Saharan western African and subequatorial African languages have been shown to be typologically and, to a certain extent, lexically related. The subequatorial languages within this subgroup are collectively known as Bantu. The word *Bantu* means "people," and the root *-ntu* is the most commonly, if not universally, shared lexical item in the Bantu grouping.

Efik in southeastern Nigeria is notable. Historically the languages generally spoken in the adjacent areas between southeastern Nigeria and southwestern Cameroon have been called Bantoid or semi-Bantu because of typological and lexical similarities with both Bantu and sub-Saharan western African languages. The Bantu languages, despite their sub-subgroup status, cover the largest amount of territory and probably have the largest number of speakers. The most commonly recognized languages in the Bantu grouping are Swahili in East Africa and central Africa, Kikuyu (also spelled as Gikuyu) in Kenya, Shona in Zimbabwe and central Mozambique, Zulu and Xhosa in South Africa, and Tswana (also spelled Setswana) in Botswana.

Nilo-Saharan covers southern Sudan, northern Uganda, the western side of Lake Victoria, and the central border areas of Kenya and Tanzania. Commonly known speakers within this division are the Dinka of southern Sudan, the Acholi of northern Uganda, the Luo of Kenya, and the Massai on the border of Kenya and Tanzania. Historically, the most prominent speakers of a Nilo-Saharan language are Nubians in southern Egypt and northern Sudan.

The Khoisan are spread over a large territorial space covering parts of Namibia and South Africa. They are known in popular literature as the "Bushmen." Statistics on the number of people who belong to this division are not reliable. A common number often cited is 200,000. Two small pockets of speakers from this speech community are found in central Tanzania. The presence of these two isolated pockets, known as Hatsa and Sandawe, has led many linguists and anthropologists to hypothesize that much of southern Africa was once populated in much larger numbers by the Khoisan. The same theory claims that migrations southward by speakers of Bantu languages absorbed the vast majority of this population, in other words, migrations Bantuized and otherwise marginalized them geographically.

It is popularly held that there are "thousands" of African languages; however, this widely held impression is exaggerated. Early and diverse missionaries gave the languages they came across different names. Colonial administrators repeated the diverse naming practice. The native speakers of the languages themselves had their own names for their languages. Often the differences were due to legitimate community or clan territorial imperatives. Consider the two examples given earlier: Fula, Fulani, Pular, Pulaar, and Fulfulde, on the one hand, and, on the other, Mandinka, Mandingo, Mandingo, Madinka, and Maninka. Five names are cited for one and the same language in each case, creating a 5 to 1 ratio. If we were to take a popularly exaggerated figure of 3,000 African languages and apply an admittedly unscientific ratio of 5 to 1, the result would be 600. This may well be at the low end of possible numbers; nevertheless, it is a more rational number.

EGYPT

BY LEO DEPUYDT

The language of ancient Egypt was Egyptian. That language has died out, and modern Egyptians speak Arabic. Along with related languages in western Asia and northern Africa, Egyptian forms the family of Afroasiatic languages. Other branches of this family are Semitic and Berber. Among the members of the Semitic branch are Akkadian, Arabic, and Hebrew, but Egyptian is the only language in its branch.

Egyptian was both written and spoken for over 4,000 years, from about 3000 B.C.E. to about 1500 C.E. That makes Egyptian the oldest known written language. During these four millennia Egyptian changed greatly, just as any language does. The five stages usually distinguished in Egyptian, along with approximate dates for the time periods from which written sources exist, are Old Egyptian (2500–2100 B.C.E.), Middle Egyptian (2100–1500 B.C.E.), Late Egyptian (1500–1000 B.C.E.), Demotic (650 B.C.E.–500 C.E.), and Coptic (300–1000 C.E.). The word *Coptic* (*CCpt*) is another form of the word *Egyptian* (*gCpt*). Literacy was probably always the privilege of a small group of people. Only about 1 percent (but probably less) of the Egyptian population had some degree of literacy at any given time in Egyptian history.

Egyptian evolved by countless infinitesimally small leaps. At certain intervals the language would be fixed in writing while the spoken language gradually changed. As time passed, the gap between the written language and the ever-evolving spoken language grew. After some centuries the gap was so large that the current written language was abandoned and the language spoken at the time was committed to writing. This process repeated itself more than once. In principle, there are no "stages" of Egyptian. The stages identified by historians amount to a sort of deception caused by the surviving evidence: written testimonies providing frozen snapshots of the evolving spoken language at certain moments in time. In reality, language change is a continuous process.

One typically begins a study of Egyptian by focusing on one stage. The stage traditionally chosen is Middle Egyptian, which is also called Classical Egyptian, for two main reasons. First, it is the first stage of Egyptian in which great works of literature were written. Second, when Middle Egyptian ceased being spoken, it remained in use as a literary and liturgical language by scribes in temples and schools. As a dead stage of the language, Middle Egyptian coexisted with later spoken stages. This written or artificial Middle Egyptian differs from the original spoken Middle Egyptian in that the later spoken stages influenced the written form, and Egyptians in later years lacked sufficient knowledge of Middle Egyptian to keep the written form static.

The three main types of hieroglyphic writing are hieroglyphic proper, hieratic, and Demotic. Just as handwritten English differs from printed English, hieroglyphs written with a pen on papyrus differ from those carved or painted on tomb walls. Carved or painted hieroglyphs are hieroglyphic proper. *Hieroglyph* is, in fact, Greek for "holy (*hiero*) carved character (*glyph*)." Hieroglyphs written in pen are called hieratic. In hieratic, the pictorial character of many hieroglyphs has become unrecognizable. *Hieratic* is Greek for "(script) of the priests." Saint Clement of Alexandria (ca. 150–ca. 211 C.E.) gave it this name around 200 C.E. because hieratic was used at the time for religious purposes only. Demotic, which evolved from hieratic, is evident from about 650 B.C.E. onward. *Demotic* is Greek for "(script) of the people (*demos*)." Demotic evolved from hieratic. This form is even more cursive than hieratic and is used to write the fourth stage of the language, which is also called Demotic. Demotic is therefore both a script and a stage of the language.

Hieroglyphic proper and hieratic script remained in use alongside the Demotic script, mainly for ceremonial and religious purposes. In sum, Old and Middle Egyptian were written in hieroglyphic proper and in hieratic. Late Egyptian was written mainly in hieratic. The Demotic language was written almost exclusively in the Demotic script. Finally, modern Egyptologists write hieroglyphic proper with a pen. That is something Egyptian scribes rarely did, since hieroglyphic proper was carved with a chisel or painted with a brush. To write hieratic, however, scribes typically used pens.

The last specimens of hieroglyphic writing date to about 450 C.E. The hieroglyphic tradition had been in strong decline since about 150 C.E. Between 200 and 300 C.E. the Greek alphabet was adopted to write Coptic, the final stage of Egyptian. The last person who could read hieroglyphic writing probably lived in the sixth or seventh century C.E. Long after, in 1822, the French Egyptologist Jean-François Champollion (1790–1832) began to decipher the hieroglyphic script.

The rise of Christianity had been the principal cause of the demise of the hieroglyphic tradition. In the fourth century C.E. Christianity became the official religion of Egypt. Hieroglyphics remained exclusively linked with the native pagan religion; there is no such thing as Christian hieroglyphic writings. The end of hieroglyphic writing, therefore, coincided with the end of the worship of the ancient Egyptian gods. The end came soon after 550 C.E., a century or so after the latest dated hieroglyphic inscription and about a century before the Muslim conquest of Egypt. Around 550 C.E. the Byzantine emperor Justinian (r. 527–565) ordered the last native Egyptian religious compound at Philae in the deep south of Egypt to be closed down.

After hieroglyphic writing died out, the Egyptian language lived on in its latest stage, Coptic. Around 640 C.E. Islam came to Egypt. From then on, the Coptic language was gradually replaced by Arabic as the spoken language of Egypt. Probably sometime between 1000 and 1500 C.E. Coptic ceased to be spoken. The knowledge of the Coptic language and of Coptic writing, however, did not vanish. Coptic manuscripts continued to be read, copied, and understood for liturgical purposes. Thus, while the knowledge of hieroglyphic writing became extinct, the language itself never did. Egyptian lived on in an evolved stage, as the liturgical Coptic used in the Coptic Christian church. The term *Coptic* therefore has two meanings. It denotes the last stage of the Egyptian language, and it is also a synonym for Christian Egyptian. Today, Christian Egyptians, or Copts, are a minority in Egypt.

If not for the surviving liturgical Coptic, ancient Egyptian might have remained undeciphered. It had long been assumed that hieroglyphic Egyptian was a form of early Coptic, which gave linguists some sense of the language they were trying to decipher from the hieroglyphic script.

THE MIDDLE EAST

BY JUSTIN CORFIELD

Many languages were spoken in the Near East during ancient times. The earliest to have survived in transcribed form is Sumerian. It is known only through inscribed texts, mainly on clay tablets, that show a simple pictograph system known as Archaic Sumerian. The oldest tablets date to about 3300 B.C.E. and were found at the city of Uruk. On them a pictograph represents an object or idea. Around 3000 B.C.E. the pictographs changed to become a more coherent script in which the inscription came to represent a sound. This allowed for a greater variety of new words and ideas to be expressed.

The language of Sumerian rapidly seems to have developed into Akkadian, a Semitic language to which Hebrew and Arabic both are related. Akkadian first arose in southern Mesopotamia and gradually started supplanting Sumerian. Surviving texts in Akkadian date to about 2400 B.C.E.; the language, an inflected one, in which words take different forms to reflect grammatical information, remained in use until about 75 C.E. From 1800 until 1200 B.C.E. Akkadian was clearly the major written language in western Asia for trade and diplomacy. Subsequently, it was overtaken by two variants or dialects, Babylonian and Assyrian. Babylonian, starting in southern Mesopotamia, by the ninth century B.C.E. quickly became the lingua franca, or common language, of the region. It varied from Akkadian, but Akkadian was still used by the Babylonians. At Susa, King Hammurabi (d. ca. 1750 B.C.E.) erected a stela (a monumental stone slab) on which he wrote his laws for the whole of the Babylonian Empire. The inscription was in Akkadian, with many Sumerian terms incorporated into it. Akkadian would have gained some loanwords from Hebrew when the Jews were held in exile in Babylon from 587 to 538 B.C.E. The Assyrian dialect arose in northern Mesopotamia and is often called Assyrian Neo-Aramaic.

Gradually the cuneiform script, a wedge-shaped form of writing used by the Babylonians and the Assyrians, came to be the basis of other languages of the ancient Near East, such as Eblaite, Elamite, Hittite, and Hurrian. This common descent allowed Akkadian cuneiform, in all its variations, to remain the major script used for administration and also for diplomatic correspondence and regional trade until the emergence of the use of Greek in the region in the late seventh century B.C.E.

The Achaemenid Persian Empire (538–331 B.C.E.) was polyglot, speaking different languages. Three languages were used for the administration of the empire, and surviving stelae show inscriptions in Old Persian, Elamite, and Akkadian. Persian represented the major language of the government, with a new writing system used for official proclamations. It was always the first language for any official inscriptions, followed by Elamite, showing the Persian support for the former "underclass" in Assyria. The oldest surviving inscriptions in Elamite come from 2200 B.C.E. and were found in modern-day Khūzestān and Fārs in Iran. Elamite rulers exerted significant control over much of Mesopotamia until the Babylonians and Assyrians insisted on the sole use of their own languages on stelae. By 600 B.C.E. Elamite had developed very differently from Babylonian and Assyrian. The language of the Elamites gradually fell into disuse during Assyrian rule but was revived by the Persians to harness goodwill from the surviving Elamites as well as to demonstrate that the empire extended far beyond the borders of modern-day Persia. Similarly, the Persians also used Akkadian, though only on official Achaemenian inscriptions in the empire; Akkadian was used only rarely by ordinary people outside Mesopotamia.

The Phoenician alphabet, with 22 letters, was introduced in about the 11th century B.C.E., with the oldest inscription being the epitaph at the tomb of King Ahiram at Byblos (Jubayl in modern-day Lebanon). The 22-letter alphabet gradually came to be more important than the cuneiform script. With the rise of Carthage in the sixth century B.C.E. the Phoenician language developed into what is known as Punic, the official language of Carthage. A number of Greek, Latin, and Hebrew words have Phoenician origins. In turn, the Phoenician alphabet came to be adapted by various groups to form the basis of the alphabets of Hebrew, Aramaic, and then Greek. The influence of these languages and their alphabets gradually eroded the use of cuneiform, which dwindled to recording religious ceremonies and some scientific discoveries. Cuneiform continued to be used in southern Mesopotamia until the second century C.E.

Aramaic is believed to have been spoken from about 2000 B.C.E. and was probably a written language from 950 B.C.E. It was used throughout the Persian Empire for business and in provincial administration. Only one royal inscription in Aramaic survives, on the side of a cliff at Bīsitūn, in Media, showing that its use was accepted by the Persian court. It continued to be spoken in Palestine and was the language used by Jesus. At the time of Christ, Aramaic was developing into Western Aramaic and Eastern Aramaic, the latter being influenced by the related languages of Syriac, Mandean, and Eastern Neo-Assyrian. Aramaic was also the basis of the Nabataean alphabet, which was used in the kingdom of Petra. It remained widely spoken until 650 C.E. when it was supplanted by Arabic, and it is still spoken in the town of Maaloula in modern-day Syria. Another language in that region was Moabite, closely related to Hebrew, and using an early Semitic alphabet.

Two other languages that came to be spoken in the Near East were Greek and Latin. Greek was widely spoken and indeed was effectively the lingua franca of the Near East from well before the time of Alexander the Great (r. 336–323 B.C.E.). It was the principal language that grew from the spread of Greek influence, or Hellenization, across the Near East. Over

Clay tablet with Elamite inscription found in the treasury of the palace at Persepolis, Persia (modern-day Iran) (Courtesy of the Oriental Institute of the University of Chicago)

many centuries Greek merchants had settled in ports along the coast of Anatolia and the Eastern Mediterranean. There was also a large Greek presence in the Achaemenid Persian Empire, with many Greeks serving in the Persian army.

During the brief rule of Alexander the Great, Greek became the language of administration of his empire, which incorporated the Persian Empire, and continued as such in many of the successor states. Certainly during the wars of the Diadochi (323–281 B.C.E.), the rival successors to Alexander, it is clear that Greek was extensively spoken, and the Seleucid Empire (311–ca. 140 B.C.E.), the Hellenistic successor state to Alexander's empire, also used Greek for administrative purposes, with inscriptions surviving on votive tablets of the period. Greek was also used as far east as the Kushan Empire, which covered parts of modern-day Afghanistan, northern India, Pakistan, and Tajikistan during the first through the third centuries of the Common Era. Although Latin was the language of government of the Roman Empire that covered much of the Near East, it never gained the acceptance accorded to Greek; for this reason on some official notices, such as the *titulus crucis* (the headboard above the cross upon which a person was crucified), it did not appear first. For example, the inscription on the headboard of Jesus was in Aramaic, then Latin, and Greek.

ASIA AND THE PACIFIC

BY KELLEY L. ROSS

Southern India has a language family, the Dravidian languages, that probably included the original languages on the subcontinent. One Dravidian outlier (a language that is related but geographically detached), Brahui, survives in the north of India. Linguists speculate that the Dravidian languages originally were dispersed throughout India and that the language of the ancient Indus Valley civilization (ca. 3000–1600 B.C.E.) was a Dravidian language. There is no direct evidence of this, as the Indus Valley script remains undeciphered. There are indeed no bilingual texts and most remaining inscriptions, on seals, are no more than five characters long. This is a poverty of evidence compared with what was used for the decipherment of other ancient scripts, such as Egyptian hieroglyphics or Mesopotamian cuneiform.

The other languages of the north of India are descendants of Vedic Sanskrit, the language of the ancient sacred scriptures of Hinduism, the Vedas, which date to about 1500 B.C.E. These scriptures could be committed to writing starting around 800 B.C.E., when an alphabet writing system was borrowed from the Middle East. A later script, the Karoshthi, still reflects components of an Aramaic original. Out of Vedic Sanskrit were derived Classical Sanskrit and a group of spoken languages, the Prakrits. Classical Sanskrit (from a word meaning "prepared, purified, corrected") was in part created by grammarians trying to fix the Vedic language and preserve it from phonetic and grammatical changes that were becoming evident in the Prakrits. Sanskrit then remained the principal language of religion, literature, and philosophy in India for many centuries.

Possibly the most important Prakrit language was Pali, the language of the earliest version of the Buddhist scriptures. These scriptures were first preserved in the region of modern-day Sri Lanka, where Buddhism was established by missionaries of the emperor Ashoka (r. ca. 269–232 B.C.E.). Other Prakrits, like Magadhi, are found in subsequent ancient Indian history, down to the dynasty of the Guptas (ca. 240–550 C.E.). From the early Brahmi writing system Sanskrit grammarians created the Devanagari syllabary (a list of characters representing syllables), which thenceforth was used to write Sanskrit and is still used to write modern languages such as Hindi. It is the basis of the development of many later writing systems in India and Southeast Asia.

Because of the similarities of Sanskrit to classical Greek and Latin, in 1786 the British linguist Sir William Jones proposed that the three languages had arisen from a common source. These languages are now viewed as members of the Indo-European family of languages. Jones's proposal was the beginning of what in the 19th century was called philology and is now historical linguistics, the study of the history and development of languages.

The Indo-European languages of India were closely related to ancient Persian and Avestan in Iran, and the group of Indian and Iranian languages is called "Indo-Aryan." Iranian languages also extended far into central Asia by way of the highway of grassland that stretches from Hungary to Mongolia, the Steppes. Indeed, both Iranian and Indo-Aryan languages appear to have arisen in the Steppes, perhaps earlier than 2000 B.C.E. Recent finds of well-preserved mummies in central Asia may belong to these peoples. In the Ukraine at the western end of the Steppes the Scythians spoke an Iranian language, though we know about it only from words preserved by Greek writers. At the eastern end of the Steppes lived an earlier Indo-European speaking group, called the Yuezhi by the Chinese. This was apparently the group that later left Buddhist texts in Xinjiang, whose language is now called "Tocharian." This group appears to be the one known as the Kushans, who invaded India and ruled in the north of the country from about 20 B.C.E. to the fourth century C.E.

In central Asia we find speakers of Altaic languages, but the earliest evidence of an Altaic language is Turkish from the fifth or sixth centuries C.E. Prior to that we have the conflict of the Chinese of the former Han Dynasty (202 B.C.E.–220 C.E.) with a people they called the Xiongnu. There is considerable uncertainty about the language or languages of the Xiongnu. There is at least the presumption that they were principally or entirely Altaic speakers, along with some proto-Turkish or proto-Mongolian language, but this is largely speculative. Equally speculative is whether the Xiongnu were actually the Huns who later turned up in India and Europe. Still, there is little evidence even about the language of the Huns in Europe, where their most famous leader, Attila ("Little Father"), carried a name from Gothic, a Germanic language. There is also

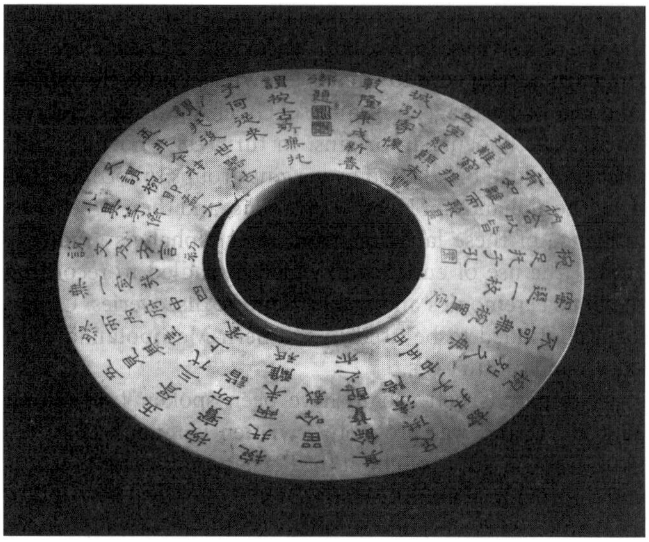

Jade disc of ancient times, later inscribed with a poem by the Qianlong emperor, from China (ca. 1500–1050 B.C.E.) (© The Trustees of the British Museum)

ground for skepticism about the identification of the Xiongnu with the Huns, since many centuries elapsed between Chinese accounts of the former and accounts from Rome or India about the latter. Either way, we are faced mostly with a mystery about these ancient peoples from central Asia.

Some linguists question whether the Altaic languages even constitute a proper family. Others not only accept the kinship of the Altaic languages but also include Korean and Japanese in the family. Otherwise, it is not obvious whether Korean and Japanese are related to any other language or even to each other. In ancient history there is no evidence of the Japanese language. The Korean states of Silla, Paekche, and Koguryo began under the cultural influence of the Chinese in the period of the Han Dynasty, but in the early days Koreans mainly wrote Chinese rather than their own language, and the use of Chinese characters tended to conceal the nature of the Korean language even when it was being written. The languages of Korea and Vietnam in the ancient period (and later Japanese) were strongly influenced by Chinese, borrowing the system of Chinese characters and much of the vocabulary that went with the characters. Phonetic systems to write those languages, as with the hangul system for Korean, would not come until long after the ancient period.

It is generally but not universally agreed that Chinese belongs to the Sino-Tibetan family of languages. The Tibeto-Burman subgroup is relatively distinct from the Sinitic, or Chinese, subgroup. Although there appears to be much common vocabulary across the family, there are otherwise few affinities that linguists normally like to see uniting language families. In this family, evidence is found only of Chinese in ancient times. We know it mainly as the written language, from the Shang Dynasty (1500–1045 B.C.E.) forward. Chinese literature (history, philosophy, and so on) reached its full flowering during the Spring and Autumn Period (722–481 B.C.E.).

Chinese characters provide only indirect evidence of pronunciation, and even today the characters in the ancient and classical language are read with the phonetic values of the modern languages. Chinese characters have been described as originally "pictographic," writing characterized by pictorial signs and symbols of objects; as "ideographic," writing that depicts concepts or ideas but not sounds; or as "logographic," writing that stands for words of the spoken language. Although the latter description is now preferred in linguistics, there is no doubt that most characters began as representative depictions, and sometimes characters take on a conceptual life of their own, independent of the spoken language. Thus, all the descriptions of the characters are appropriate in varying degrees. Ancient Chinese as a spoken language, however, is a matter of reconstruction, inference, and speculation, calling on the full skills of modern linguistic science, with the help of some ancient testimony by the Chinese themselves. The results involve great measures of uncertainty and are the subject of dispute. Thus the study of the ancient language can focus with greatest certainty on the grammar of the language and on the development of the system of writing.

In Southeast Asia there was only one literate culture in ancient times, and that was in Vietnam. Vietnamese is a member of the Austroasiatic family of languages, which is divided into the Mon-Khmer branch, whose principal representative is Cambodian, and the Vietnamese languages. Evidence of Mon-Khmer languages dates to the Middle Ages. Written Vietnamese, however, originally was expressed by writing Chinese (as was Korean) or by using Chinese characters to represent the Vietnamese language. The word *Vietnam* itself is simply the Vietnamese pronunciation of the name that would be *Yuenan* in modern Mandarin or *Yütnam* in modern Cantonese. The earliest Vietnamese state, Annam, was contemporaneous with the Chinese Qin Dynasty (221–207 B.C.E.), but by 111 B.C.E. it had been absorbed by Han China. Annam was not independent again until 544 C.E. A phonetic system, as in Korea or Japan, was never developed to write Vietnamese. The modern language is written in a form of the Latin alphabet.

There is no evidence from ancient times of the other major language family of Southeast Asia, the Thai-Lao, Kadai, or Daic languages. This family seems to have originated in southwestern China, where some members, such as Zhuang and Dai, still exist, and then moved down through Burma (where today the Shan people live) into Southeast Asia. But this dispersal did not happen until as late as the 13th century C.E.

Before European exploration the most extensively distributed language family in the world was the Austronesian family, which spread southeast from Asia and across the Pacific. None of the languages of this family was a written language in ancient times, and none would ever be written until writing systems from India, Islam, or the West were introduced in the Middle Ages or later.

EUROPE

BY AMY HACKNEY BLACKWELL

Almost all ancient European languages were part of the Indo-European language family that includes English, German and Germanic languages, Celtic languages, Greek, Latin and the Romance languages, Armenian, Iranian, and the Slavic tongues. Scholars believe that these languages all evolved from a single ancient tongue called Proto-Indo-European, which originated between 6500 and 4500 B.C.E., either in the region between the Black Sea and the Caspian Sea or in Anatolia. Proto-Indo-European gradually traveled east through India and west through Europe and evolved into distinct tongues.

The people who lived in ancient Europe north and west of Greece and Rome spoke languages from two Indo-European branches, Celtic and Germanic. People in eastern Europe spoke Thracian languages. Scholars do not know much about the languages that these ancient people actually spoke. Most ancient Europeans could not write, and so they did not record their own history or write grammars or dictionaries of their own languages. Written evidence of ancient European tongues comes from a small number of inscriptions that survive on stone, ceramics, and coins. Modern linguists have reconstructed parts of ancient European languages by comparing words that appear in many languages and by applying linguistic rules to more recent forms of a language to restore the older forms of the same language.

The Celtic languages evolved from a common Indo-European ancestor called Proto-Celtic, or Common Celtic. Proto-Celtic was closely related to Italic, which evolved into Latin. Proto-Celtic emerged in Europe around 1000 B.C.E. and seems to have been centered in central Europe in the area of the Alps. By 400 B.C.E. most people in northwest Europe and the British Isles spoke Celtic languages. As Proto-Celtic spread across Europe, it split into several subfamilies, including Gaulish, Brythonic, Goidelic, and Celtiberian. Gaulish, named by scholars for the people of Roman Gaul, was spoken from France and Belgium to Italy and as far east as Turkey. Historians have reconstructed Gaulish from inscriptions on stone and pots found throughout Roman Gaul. The earliest inscriptions date to the sixth century B.C.E. Gaulish inscription writers used both Italic and Greek letters. People were still speaking Gaulish in the area that is now France as late as the 500s C.E. Gaulish was related to the languages called Lepontic and Galatian. Speakers of Galatian settled in Asia Minor around the third century B.C.E. but gradually stopped using their Celtic language in favor of Greek. Lepontic, which was spoken in what is modern-day northern Italy, seems to have died out around 400 B.C.E.

Brythonic languages, which include Breton, Welsh, Cornish, and possibly Pictish, were spoken in Brittany, Wales, and Cornwall, and they developed in Britain around the sixth and fifth centuries B.C.E. Brythonic languages adopted numerous Latin words during the Roman occupation of Britain in the first four centuries C.E. The Brythonic language known as Breton arrived in Brittany (France) around the fifth century C.E. as British people moved to the Continent fleeing Germanic warriors who were invading Britain. Scholars believe that the residents of Scotland spoke Brythonic languages before Goidelic-speaking Irish people displaced them in the first or second century B.C.E. and brought Goidelic languages to Scotland.

People in Ireland, Scotland, and the Isle of Man spoke Goidelic languages, which include the Gaelic tongues of Irish, Scottish, and Manx. The name *Goidelic* comes from the Irish Celts' name for themselves, *Goídil*. Goidelic is not closely related to Brythonic, but it seems to be linked linguistically to the Celtic languages of Spain; this has led scholars to believe that the ancestors of the Irish Celts traveled from Spain, probably arriving in Ireland around 350 B.C.E. These people moved from Ireland north into Scotland and the Isle of Man in the early centuries C.E., bringing Goidelic languages with them. The Romans called the Irish people Scotti and named the territory north of Britain Scotia after its Irish settlers. Scotia eventually became Scotland.

People on the Iberian Peninsula, modern-day Spain and Portugal, spoke Celtiberian. Historians have found little information to help them reconstruct Celtiberian, but they know that locals were speaking it during the Roman Republic and Roman Empire. A few Celtiberian inscriptions survive; Celtiberian writers used a unique script that appears to have been a hybrid of Greek and Phoenician writing systems.

Proto-Germanic is the ancestor of the Germanic languages, which include German, English, and the Scandinavian languages. People probably began speaking Proto-Germanic around 500 B.C.E. in northern Germany and southern Scandinavia. The earliest firm evidence of Germanic languages comes from a single inscription on a helmet dated to the second century B.C.E., but besides that almost nothing is known about Germanic languages before the first century C.E. During the first five centuries C.E. Germanic tongues split into three groups: North, East, and West Germanic. Between 300 and 700 C.E. Germanic peoples migrated widely throughout Europe, spreading Germanic dialects that were probably mutually unintelligible. The earliest well-known Germanic language was Gothic, the language of the Visigoths. The best source of information on Gothic grammar and syntax is a fourth century C.E. Gothic translation of the Bible.

People north of Greece in the territory that includes modern-day Bulgaria, Serbia, Romania, Ukraine, Hungary, and Slovakia spoke Thracian languages. What little is known about Thracian languages comes from inscriptions written in Greek characters and reconstruction from modern Bulgarian and Romanian. Greeks and Romans colonized most of this territory, and the inhabitants gradually adopted Greek and Latin as their primary languages. Thracian languages had completely disappeared by about 400 C.E. Greek and Latin were the most important languages of the Classical Period (480–323 B.C.E.), and many Europeans learned one or both of them. During the Roman Empire the use of Latin in particular became widespread throughout Gaul, Spain, and Britain. Greek was more common in eastern Europe.

A few European languages did not come from the Indo-European family. Before Celts arrived in Spain, people on the Mediterranean coast spoke non-Indo-European languages

RECONSTRUCTING ANCIENT LANGUAGES

In the late 1700s scholars noticed that the languages they knew shared certain similarities. Take the word for *father*: *father* is *pater* in Greek, *pater* in Latin, *fadar* in Gothic (an early form of German), and *pita* in Sanskrit (the language of ancient India). The word for man was *wir* in Latin, *wair* in Gothic, *were* in Old English, and *virah* in Sanskrit. Clever scholars deduced that these languages must have all come from a common root. They called this root a *protolanguage* and envisioned languages taking the shape of a family tree with a protolanguage splitting into sublanguages that could become protolanguages themselves; for example, Proto-Indo-European could split into Proto-Celtic and Proto-Germanic, each of which split into several new languages.

This discovery led to the invention of a new field of study called linguistics. Linguists look for rules that show how languages evolve. They find the oldest examples they can of known languages and trace the language forward in time, analyzing the way words and grammar change. Languages change in predictable ways. For example, the *d* sound often turns into a *t* sound. A short *e* can become a short *a*. Linguists apply these rules to available information to reconstruct old languages. Jacob Grimm, better known (along with his brother, Wilhelm) for his *Grimm's Fairy Tales*, was one of the first linguists to reconstruct a language; in the early 1800s he compiled a comprehensive study of the development of German dialects from a common Germanic source.

Linguistic information allows historians to trace the paths of different peoples who moved around Europe in ancient times. Scholars of Celtic believe that Gaulish and Brythonic are more closely related to each other than are Goidelic and Celtiberian because of a sound difference. They classify Gaulish and Brythonic as P-Celtic and Goidelic and Celtiberian as Q-Celtic because sounds that are pronounced *p* in Gaulish and Brythonic languages are pronounced *q* in Goidelic and Celtiberian. This is why many scholars believe that the Celts who colonized Ireland came from Spain, not nearby Britain.

known as Iberian; these languages died out by the first century C.E. and were replaced by Latin. People in the Pyrenees spoke a language that became the ancestor of Basque; these people were isolated enough to keep their language into modern times. The Finno-Ugric languages, ancestors of modern Finnish and Hungarian, came from western Asia and may have arrived in the area between the Baltic Sea and the Ural Mountains as early as 4000 B.C.E.

GREECE

BY JEFFREY S. CARNES

Ancient Greek is one of the branches of the Indo-European language family; that is, it is one of the several dozen descendants of Proto-Indo-European, a language spoken at least 4,500 years ago in Central Asia and whose "daughter languages" (descendants) include English and almost all modern European languages. Proto-Indo-European left no written records, but its existence and much information about its vocabulary and structure have been reconstructed by historical linguists based on similarities among its daughter languages, including obvious similarities in vocabulary. We find Greek *mētēr* cognate with, or similar to, Latin *mater*, Sanskrit *mat*, Russian *mat'*, German *Mutter*, and English *mother*. Related Indo-European languages form subgroups (Germanic, Italic, and Balto-Slavic); Greek is the only surviving member of the subgroup to which it may have belonged. (Although Greek has obvious structural similarities to Latin, and there was much borrowing of vocabulary between the two, the idea that the languages belonged to the same Indo-European subgroup has been discredited.)

Greek is a heavily inflected language; that is, one in which the relation between words in a sentence is conveyed by changes in the form of the word, typically by the addition of suffixes. Greek nouns and adjectives can be inflected to form five different cases (nominative, accusative, genitive, dative, and vocative), which have different functions in syntax, or the grammatical arrangement of words in a sentence. The nominative, for instance, is used for the subject of a sentence and the accusative for the direct object of a finite verb. A practical consequence of this is that Greek word order is freer than that in English: *anthrōpos tima theon* ("a man honors a god") could equally well be written with its three elements (subject, object, and verb) in any other order (*theon tima anthrōpos* or *tima theon anthrōpos*) with almost no difference in meaning. In English, where word order determines meaning, this would be impossible. The Greek case system is inherited from Indo-European and shows the tendency of languages to simplify case systems; thus, older cases like the ablative (still found in Latin) have been lost in Greek, their functions taken over by the genitive (which expresses possession) and the dative (expressive of the indirect object of a verb). The vocative indicates the speaker's direct address to another person.

Greek nouns and adjectives exhibited gender and number. Number included not only the expected singular and plural but also a form called the dual, sometimes used for beings or items in pairs, as in a team of oxen or a pair of shoes. Grammatical gender, another Indo-European inheritance whose original function is obscure, divides nouns into three classes: masculine, feminine, and neuter. Nouns representing male humans and animals typically belonged to the

Linear A tablets, from Agia Triada, Heraklion (Alison Frantz Photographic Collection, American School of Classical Studies at Athens)

"masculine" group and females to the "feminine." Inanimate objects, however, could belong to any category, and the fact that a table is feminine or a foot masculine ultimately says little about the Greek (or Indo-European) worldview.

Verbs in Greek were also heavily inflected, with suffixes (and occasionally prefixes) used to express differences in person, number, mood, voice, and tense. (Most of these are expressed in English with auxiliary verbs: I free; I will free; I will be freed, in contrast to the Greek equivalents *luō, lusō, luthēsomai.*) Moods include not only the indicative (for statements of fact) and subjunctive (for possibilities) but also the optative (similar in use to the subjunctive, expressing a doubt or wish, and eventually abandoned in favor of it). The Greek voices were active, passive, and middle; this last category was used to emphasize the subject's participation or involvement in the action described. Tenses included not only the time of an action but also its aspect—in other words, its status as complete or incomplete. Aoristic aspect viewed an action as happening once ("Socrates spoke in the agora" on one particular occasion); imperfective aspect showed incomplete or repeated action ("Socrates was speaking/kept speaking/used to speak in the agora"). A typical Greek verb had three different stems (to be used with different tenses) and might have well over three hundred distinct forms.

The large number of verb forms made it easy for the language to create a complex syntax: For example, conditional sentences used different moods to express differing degrees of probability. A speaker wishing to say "If it snows tomorrow" would use the subjunctive to indicate there was some distinct possibility this might happen; the optative would indicate that it was far less likely (from the speaker's perspective). Syntactic constructions tended to be simpler in poetry (especially in the Homeric poems, which were composed orally), but historical, oratorical, and philosophical prose works display a great variety of subordinate clauses and long, periodic sentences.

The pronunciation of Greek is understood surprisingly well for an ancient language, thanks to the data provided by historical linguistics. Most Greek dialects had five short vowels and seven long, plus a small number of diphthongs (a double vowel sound forming one sound forming one syllable); most of these have at least rough equivalents in English. Among consonants the most surprising feature is the treatment of aspirated consonants (pronounced while breathing out) such as *phi* and *theta*. While English derivatives of Greek words containing these letters (for example, philosophy and theater) treat them as fricatives (the consonant sound in speech made by forcing breath through a narrow opening), they were in fact voiced stops—that is, the equivalent of the initial sounds of "top" and "pot." The Greek letters *pi* and *tau* represented an unvoiced version, closer to the final sounds of "top" and "pot," a distinction that is extremely difficult for native speakers of English to hear. The least understood feature of Greek pronunciation is pitch accent: the vast majority of words bore an accent that indicated not stress but instead a change in pitch, rising (acute), falling (grave), or rising-falling (circumflex). By sometime in late antiquity the pitch accent was abandoned in favor of a stress accent (which continues in Greek to this day), and scholars do not agree on precisely what Greek pitch accent sounded like. Modern tonal languages such as Chinese are thought to provide an imperfect analogy for the sound of Greek.

Our earliest historical records show that Greek was already widespread throughout the eastern Mediterranean: It was the language of the Greek mainland, the coastal areas of Asia Minor, and the islands that lay between. In addition, the language spread along with the great colonization movements of the Archaic Period—mostly to southern Italy and Sicily but also to North Africa, southern France, and the shores of the Black Sea. Different cities and regions had distinct dialects, which spread along with the settlers (colonies spoke the dialect of their mother city); despite differences in spelling and pronunciation, all Greek dialects seem to have been mutually intelligible. The Greeks themselves roughly classified their numerous local dialects into two main groups, Doric and Ionic, a classification that came to possess cultural and political significance. This was particularly true in the fifth century B.C.E. when the Athenians, who spoke Attic (a variant of Ionic), were opposed to the Spartans and their allies, who spoke Doric. In literature dialects reflected not only the author's place of origin but also the demands of the particular genre: The epics of Homer were composed in a mixed dialect with Doric features; the comedies of Aristophanes use a particularly colloquial version of Attic; and the choral odes of Athenian tragedy were written in a semi-Doric style. Eventually a form of Attic became the dominant dialect of the Greek-speaking world. Called the koine, or common dialect, it became the language of the Eastern Roman Empire, and it is from koine that Byzantine and Modern Greek are descended.

ROME

BY JUSTIN CORFIELD

The Latin language is officially classified by linguists as being one of the Italic group of Indo-European languages. It was originally spoken by small numbers of people who lived on the Latium plain near the Tiber River in central Italy. It was related to Greek, Germanic, Celtic, and many other languages in Europe at the time. As the language of the city of Rome, its importance resulted from the rise of Rome and its domination first of Italy and then of the Mediterranean region, central and southern Europe, and much of the Near East.

At the foundation of Rome, according to tradition in 753 B.C.E., several related dialects were used in central Italy. Umbrian, Samnite (or Oscan), Volscian, and Marsian, for which inscriptions survive, all appear to differ from Latin slightly in inflections and pronominal roots, that is, the roots of pronouns. There are also many loan words from Etruscan, mainly technical and religious terms, as well as a large number of personal names, such as Sulla and Casca.

The oldest surviving example of Latin is a brief inscription of four words on a cloak pin in Greek characters. This shows that the full vowels were used in unstressed syllables, a system that changed gradually as the Latin language developed. The other early surviving Latin scripts show a stress accent on the first syllable of any word, whereas by the late republic the accent fell on the second or second-from-last syllable. Indeed, one of the striking features of Latin is the importance placed on accentuation.

As the Romans expanded their rule, with Latin as the language of administration, the use of the language became common throughout the empire. Roman citizens and many others became fluent in Latin. Through the Roman system of education many Roman boys and also people all over the empire learned Latin grammar. Cato the Censor (234–149 B.C.E.) told everybody that he had taught his son to read and write, and the Roman scholar Pliny (23–79 C.E.) also believed that children should be taught by their parents. Many tutors, sometimes slaves, were employed to teach children Latin, and secondary schools taught boys both grammar and rhetoric (the study of methods of speaking and writing effectively and persuasively). When the Edict of Caracalla (212 C.E.) extended Roman citizenship to all freeborn men throughout the Roman Empire, the desire to learn Latin increased further.

Although they were certainly not the first texts, the earliest surviving extensive works in Latin were the comedies of Titus Maccius Plautus (ca. 254–184 B.C.E.) and Terence (ca. 185–159 B.C.E.). The latter was a slave born in Carthage and freed by his Roman master, a senator. There was also the poetry of Quintus Ennius (239–169 B.C.E.) and Gaius Lucilius (ca. 180–ca. 102 B.C.E.). Literature from the middle of the first century B.C.E. is dominated by the works of Marcus Tullius Cicero (106–43 B.C.E.), and this period is often known as the Age of Cicero. It was also the era of Lucretius (ca. 100–ca. 55 B.C.E.), Gaius Sallustus Crispus (86–34 B.C.E.), and the military victories of Julius Caesar (100–44 B.C.E.). The works of the latter, *The Conquest of Gaul* and *The Civil War*, are the oldest surviving accounts of a military campaign by one of its leaders. Caesar himself established the first state library in Rome, which was completed by Asinius Pollio (76 B.C.E.–4 C.E.). This had works in Greek as well as Latin, but eventually works in Latin began to overtake those in Greek. Gradually many cities throughout the Roman Empire established their own libraries, a process that coincided with the rise in *bibliopolae* (publishers). These used scriveners (professional copyists) to produce copies of books and made many works available throughout the empire, indicating that there was an extensive market for books.

During the Augustan Age (27 B.C.E.–14 C.E.) writers such as Horace (65–8 B.C.E.), Virgil (70–19 B.C.E.), Ovid (43 B.C.E.–17 C.E.), and Livy (59 B.C.E.–17 C.E.) wrote what are regarded as some of the major Latin texts. Virgil's *Aeneid*, describing the arrival in Italy of Aeneas, a Trojan prince, was one of the longest Latin epics of its period. Livy's massive *Ab urbe condita libri* (Books from the Foundation of the City) comprised 142 books, but only 35 survive. The detail in the surviving books demonstrates an extensive literary tradition wherein Livy was able to base his work on previous historians. Horace, Virgil, Ovid, and Livy were followed by Seneca the Elder (ca. 55 B.C.E.–ca. 39 C.E.), Seneca the Younger (ca. 4 B.C.E.–65 C.E.), Tacitus (ca. 56–ca. 120 C.E.), and Petroneus (d. 66 C.E.), the first writer of fiction. Suetonius (ca. 69–ca. 140 C.E.) and Juvenal (ca. 55–ca. 127 C.E.) represented the climax of the Roman Silver Age.

Literary works from the Age of Cicero showed that there were at least three different types of Latin used by the Romans. Cicero wrote in what has become known as classical oratorical Latin. This was used for oratory, senatorial and other records, legal texts, and an old form of poetry called Saturnian verse. Some other writers used classical written Latin, and evidence from references in texts and also from inscriptions and votive tablets (a tablet used for sacred or religious purposes) show that the colloquial Latin used by many citizens of the Roman Empire was quite different and also changed extensively over time, diverging from the other two and becoming known as Vulgar Latin. There are also references to these differences by Roman grammarians. By the third century C.E. books were written in this colloquial form. Both Saint Jerome and Saint Augustine, writing in the fourth and fifth centuries, continued to write in classical Latin.

In terms of grammar Latin had six cases (forms of a noun or pronoun indicating its role in a sentence) for the declensions (changes in form to designate grammatical function) of nouns and adjectives, and some nouns also had a locative case (indicating place or direction). Some of these cases survived in languages derived from Latin. In the early Christian Church, Latin played a crucial part in recording information. It was the language of the city of Rome, which became the center of western Christendom, of the Vulgate (the Roman Catholic Bible), and of administration throughout the empire. The language's extensive reach ensured that it would survive within the Christian Church and remain the language of learning and diplomacy for many centuries.

THE AMERICAS

BY MICHAEL J. O'NEAL

Unraveling the history of language development and dispersion in the ancient Americas is a daunting task for historians, linguists, and archaeologists. The first problem is the sheer number and diversity of languages. Linguists have identified some 200 distinct language families in the Americas, many with subfamilies and sub-subfamilies, but even that number is in dispute. (A language family is a group of languages that have important similarities, suggesting that they developed from a common older language. These languages can be grouped into a family "tree.") Efforts to compare languages that, in most cases, are long extinct or nearly extinct require gathering and analyzing immense amounts of information, and linguists have barely begun the process.

Further, historians dispute the origins of these languages. If the first Americans arrived in North America by crossing a land bridge between Siberia and Alaska—a theory that is not universally accepted—and then over millennia migrated and settled throughout North, Central, and South America, this would suggest that American languages originated in Asia. Comparing even one of the many Native American languages with an ancient Asian language, however, is a process fraught with difficulties. Nonetheless, some language historians have claimed to find similarities between the structure of Pacific Asian languages and that of one or more ancient American languages, particularly those of northwestern North America. Meanwhile, many historians remain convinced that the earliest people who settled in the modern-day southeastern United States were of European origin, meaning that they imported an entirely different family of languages to the Americas.

A third difficulty is assigning a language to a particular geographic locale. When archaeologists do find evidence of an ancient language, the natural tendency is to conclude that the language in question had been spoken in the place where the evidence surfaced. However, such a conclusion is not always defensible. Over time, as people moved about in the ancient Americas, they took their languages with them. The result was the blending of languages or, in the case of military conquest, the replacement of languages. Upon encountering each other through trade, people often borrowed words from one another. There is no way to "carbon-date" a language in the same way that physical objects can be dated. The ongoing swirl of peoples and languages over thousands of years makes it nearly impossible to peg a particular language to a particular place.

The final difficulty is the near-complete absence of written records. Few of the languages of the Americas had a written form until after Europeans arrived many centuries later. Archaeologists have found glyphs, or written symbols, at sites throughout the Americas, but attempting to reconstruct an extinct language from this scant evidence is nearly impossible. In many cases the best linguists can do is to make inferences on the basis of what they know about languages that survived well past ancient times and perhaps into the modern world.

It is highly likely that language families developed in the Americas by much the same process that occurred in other parts of the world. Over time communities of speakers dispersed throughout the Americas from the far northern reaches of arctic North America to the woodlands of the eastern United States, the deserts of Central America and Mexico, and eventually the southern tip of South America. These communities remained isolated from one another primarily because of natural barriers such as mountain ranges, rivers, and uninhabitable deserts. Communities themselves often fractured as competition for food and other resources increased, causing part of a community to break off and travel in search of a new home. Thus, languages can be grouped into families because at some time in the distant past, the speakers' ancestors spoke a common tongue, and many of these commonalities were preserved over time. But over hundreds of years and many generations, the language of each new community evolved and changed, creating a new language with roots in the more ancient tongue. That language would have "cousins" that developed within other breakaway groups from the common ancestral tongue.

A simple list of ancient American languages, often referred to as AmerInd languages (from *American Indian*), is extensive. In the eastern half of the United States, for example, was the Algonquian family of languages, consisting of 33 or more languages, including those of the Arapaho, Blackfoot, Ojibwe, and Shawnee. Another major family of North American languages is referred to as either the Athabaskan or the Na-Dene languages, spoken from northwestern Canada down to the Rio Grande. This family includes various languages spoken by the Inuit as well as those spoken by tribes in the Pacific Northwest, along the coast of California, and in portions of the American Southwest.

Farther south the Hokan languages were spoken by communities along the southwestern coast of the United States and into northwestern Mexico. This family included some 28 distinct languages. The ancient Aztecs gave rise to two branches of their language, northern and southern, with a total of about 31 languages. The northern group included the languages spoken by the Hopi, the Paiute, the Shoshone, and the Comanche.

The Mayan languages of Central America have attracted the particular interest of scholars, largely because Mayan continues to be spoken by some six million people, primarily in Mexico and Belize but also because of the existence of a Mayan hieroglyphic script that dates back to the first millennium B.C.E. The spoken language descended from a language referred to as Proto-Mayan, first spoken about 5,000 years ago. The language appears to have originated in the highlands of Guatemala, and it began to spread in roughly 2200 B.C.E. The family tree that descended from Proto-Mayan is complex, consisting of four main branches, some of which in turn gave rise to other branches that developed into separate tongues. Scholars know of at least 31 and perhaps 33 distinct Mayan languages.

In Central and South America at least 15 additional distinct language families have been identified. Linguists have identified at least 17 additional South American languages that they have not been able to classify. Making matters more complicated is the fact that numerous languages from the interior of South America are known to have existed and perhaps survived but have not yet been named or identified. Some of these languages, not only in South America but also in Central and North America, are known as isolates because they have no known connection with other languages and may have developed independently.

See also CLIMATE AND GEOGRAPHY; DRAMA AND THEATER; EDUCATION; EMPIRES AND DYNASTIES; GOVERNMENT ORGANIZATION; LAWS AND LEGAL CODES; LITERATURE; MIGRATION AND POPULATION MOVEMENTS; RELIGION AND COSMOLOGY;

SEAFARING AND NAVIGATION; SOCIAL COLLAPSE AND ABANDONMENT; WRITING.

FURTHER READING

Martin J. Ball and James Fife, eds., *The Celtic Languages* (New York: Routledge, 1993).

Carl Darling Buck, *The Greek Dialects: Grammar, Selected Inscriptions, Glossary* (Chicago: University of Chicago Press, 1955).

Robert S. P. Beekes, *Comparative Indo-European Linguistics: An Introduction* (Philadelphia: John Benjamins Publishing Company, 1995).

Michael D. Coe and Mark Van Stone, *Reading the Maya Glyphs* (London: Thames and Hudson, 2001).

Peter T. Daniels and William Bright, *The World's Writing Systems* (New York: Oxford University Press, 1996).

Haig Der-Houssikian, *A Bibliography of African Linguistics* (Edmonton, Canada: Linguistic Research, Inc., 1972).

A. M. Devine and Laurence D. Stephens, *The Prosody of Greek Speech* (New York: Oxford University Press, 1994).

Benjamin W. Fortson, *Indo-European Language and Culture: An Introduction* (Oxford, U.K.: Blackwell Publishing, 2004).

Joseph H. Greenberg, *The Languages of Africa* (Bloomington: Indiana University Press, 1966).

R. G. Kent, *Old Persian: Grammar, Texts, Lexicon* (New Haven, Conn.: Yale University Press, 1953).

Vivien Law, *The History of Linguistics in Europe: From Plato to 1600* (Cambridge, U.K.: Cambridge University Press, 2003).

Roy A. Miller, *Japanese and Other Altaic Languages* (Chicago: University of Chicago Press, 1971).

Leonard R. Palmer, *The Greek Language* (Norman: University of Oklahoma Press, 1996).

Laurence R. Palmer, *The Latin Language* (London: Faber and Faber, 1954).

Maurice Pope, *The Story of Decipherment: From Egyptian Hieroglyphic to Linear B* (London: Thames and Hudson, 1975).

S. Robert Ramsey, *The Languages of China* (Princeton, N.J.: Princeton University Press, 1987).

Graham Thurgood and Randy J. LaPolla, eds., *The Sino-Tibetan Languages* (London: Routledge, 2003).

Vic Webb and Kembo-Sure, eds., *African Voices: An Introduction to the Languages and Linguistics of Africa* (Cape Town, South Africa: Oxford University Press, 2000).

► laws and legal codes

INTRODUCTION

Laws and legal codes among ancient hunter-gatherers were probably primitive and administered by force. A person would have looked to a tribal leader for redress if another member of the tribe had wronged him, and justice would have been administered swiftly and according to custom and tradition rather than by reference to any formal legal code. As people settled into fixed communities after the development of agriculture, and as those fixed communities evolved into more populous towns and cities, legal obligations became more complex, and more formal legal codes were developed to define the obligations between private citizens and between citizens and the state. Thus, ancient legal systems dealt with many of the same matters that modern-day legal systems do: criminal matters, such as murder, assault, and robbery, and civil matters, such as taxes, inheritance, and land ownership.

Many codes and laws were transmitted orally and continued to be based on custom and tradition, but others were written down. Ancient Mesopotamia was home to the world's first written legal code, the Code of Hammurabi, named after the Babylonian king who formulated it. Historians continue to take an interest in the Code of Hammurabi not only for its specific laws but also for its philosophical discussion about justice and how it should be administered. In particular, the Code of Hammurabi created the legal principle often known as "an eye for an eye." This principle was not a call for revenge. It introduced the concept of equivalent retaliation, the idea that punishment should be proportional to the offense.

Many ancient legal codes were structured according to social classes. It was common for these codes to identify classes of nobles and aristocrats, property owners, free people, and slaves and peasants. Very often, the severity of an offense was determined in part by the social class of the victim. For a free landowner to assault a peasant or steal that peasant's bull, for example, was considered a much less severe offense than if the victim had been a noble, and the punishment would have been correspondingly less severe. Physical punishment in the ancient world was common, and so, too, were fines for various offenses. Physical punishment, including death, was often administered only if the offender was unable to pay the fine. With a few exceptions, there were no prisons; people considered dangerous were often simply exiled to other lands.

Just as laws and legal codes evolved to reflect the increasing complexity of society, so, too, did the administration of these laws. In early civilizations it was common for the king to act as judge in all legal disputes, rendering judgments and determining penalties. Later, civilizations such as the Roman and Chinese empires developed classes of magistrates and civil servants who were educated and trained in the law. In some civilizations, including that of ancient India, police forces existed to enforce the law. In others, the enforcement of the law was more of a private matter, requiring parties who believed that they had been wronged to lodge complaints, find witnesses, and bring cases to court.

AFRICA

BY SAHEED ADERINTO

Legal codes such as those we have today did not exist in ancient Africa. Codification of African customary laws is therefore a 20th-century development—a product of colonial rule. Laws are part of the custom and tradition of every community. Law forms an integral part of oral literature, which is transmitted from one generation to another. By and large, it is often difficult to differentiate between laws and tradition and custom. Basic aspects of the laws of a society are intertwined with the customs and values of that society. When laws are respected, custom and tradition are also respected.

The origin of law in Africa is closely connected to the origin of communities. Founders of each community laid down rules and regulations for people to follow and respect. As time unfolded in the history of states and empire building, new forms of social, political, and economic developments had far-reaching consequences on the nature of law and how society was governed and structured. In other words, as African society underwent the natural process of transformation, the need to maintain the status quo and move ahead led to the establishment of regulations and orders.

Since rulers played significant roles in determining the tranquility of each community, the law of succession seems to have been one of the most significant laws. In traditional Africa laws needed for the peaceful running of society could work only if the right person was allowed to rule. The gods and goddesses might be infuriated by any attempt at doctoring the law of succession—a situation that could lead to the collapse of the state. Each community laid down principles on how rulers were to be selected. In most cases rulers were selected from the clan or family of the founder of the community. The idea of rulers as "naturally ordained" suggested that a ruler was sanctioned by the gods and goddesses. Rulers were naturally selected if the law of the society stipulated that the first child of the reigning ruler should rule. Such was always the case in societies with one ruling house. Selection might be done rotationally if there was more than one ruling house. In these two instances, the gods would have been consulted before rulers were allowed to rule.

By and large the authority of a ruler was derived from his or her role as the intermediary between gods and goddesses and human beings. A significant part of the coronation ceremony involved initiation into several secret societies and the transformation of the ruler from an "ordinary" human being to a "supernatural" being who communed with ancestors and other apparitional entities. The perception of the king among the Yoruba of modern southwestern Nigeria was *Kabi o osi, Oba alase ekeji orisa* ("someone who cannot be questioned, king, ruler, and deputy of the gods"). This appellation indicated that the king could not be questioned or reprimanded for his or her actions and that he or she was the deputy of the gods. Kings represented the gods on earth, and their command was therefore that of the gods. Since the gods and the ancestors were considered the founders of the community who also laid down the foundation of its custom and convention, a person who disobeyed the king automatically incurred the wrath of the gods.

Laws are needed to ensure the smooth running of a society. A very old proverb among the Yoruba indicates the role of law in their society: *Ilu ti ko si ofin, ese kosi ni be*, or "There is no offense in a place where there is no law." This proverb suggests that the prime purpose of making and enforcing law is the need to avoid a breakdown of order. Moreover, every community has its own laws that must be obeyed. A Yoruba poem that sheds a considerable amount of light on the significance of law and order is as follows:

> The king whose reign is peaceful
> Will have his name remembered for life.
> The king whose reign is marred with tribulations
> Will have his name remembered for life.

Ancient African rulers were aware of the implications of the breakdown of law and order. They were capable of incurring the wrath of the gods. Their ruling house and succeeding generations might be prevented from having access to the throne in the future. It was therefore not unusual for rulers to commit suicide to avoid the humiliation associated with an inability to make or enforce laws.

The operation and scope of laws and their enforcement varied from one part of the continent to another. Centralized societies developed a larger instrument of law enforcement compared with their noncentralized counterparts. Enforcement of laws seemed to be diffused in societies that were governed by more than one administrative body. It was typical, for instance, for secret societies to have their own courts where members were tried. Secret societies were groups that drew their members from the class of priests, elders, and people whose age, position, or status was important in the day-to-day running of the community. Laws of secret societies tended to have direct impact on the larger society in part because most of their members were political elites. There seems to have been no sharp dichotomy between people who made laws and those who enforced them. Rulers had the power to enforce laws through their agents, including lesser chiefs as well as heads of lineage, clans, compounds, and servants. Associations, such as the age grades (a social category based on age) among the Igbo of modern southeastern Nigeria, also performed some law-enforcement roles.

Laws could also be enforced through sorcery and by religio-magical means. Ancestral worship, offerings, and sacrifices could be employed in enforcing laws. People naturally abided by laws to avoid incurring the wrath of the gods and goddesses. Some deities were associated with the enforcement of laws. Because they were associated with spirituality, taboos and superstitions had a strong impact on people's attitudes about laws. For instance, people naturally abided by a law ordering that no one should hunt in a sacred forest if spirits or gods lived there. Game animals from a forest where the gods resided were thought to be possessed by spirits that could kill human beings or were considered food that the gods were not expected to share with human beings.

EGYPT

BY PANAGIOTIS I. M. KOUSOULIS

In contrast to the codified legal theory and practices of the people in the ancient Near East (Sumerians, Assyrians, Hittites, and Babylonians), Greece, or Rome, the ancient Egyptians did not compose or possess an organized and strictly specified law. No formal Egyptian legal codes have been preserved, at least not until the seventh century B.C.E., when the demotic language (a simplified form of Egyptian hieroglyphic writing) developed and Egyptians began using written legal documents and contracts instead of the traditional oral agreements of the Pharaonic Period (third to first millennium B.C.E.).

That is not to say that the writing down of laws was unimportant at earlier dates in Egypt. Specific enactments were issued, published, and consulted as laws. The surviving evidence of documents, however, is scanty, preserved in a fragmentary form on stelae (monumental stone slabs), in archives on papyrus, or in funerary texts. Important information about crimes and punishment derives mainly from official records rather than private documents. Those include decrees on behalf of temples or funerary cults that describe the means by which a decree was to be enforced, records of the Great Prison from the late Middle Kingdom (2040–1640 B.C.E.), and papyri documenting actual criminal investigations of the late New Kingdom (1550–1070 B.C.E.).

Quite common in the vocabulary of these enactments is the term *hep*—like the English term *law*—which refers to the specific enactment but also to the normative custom and to the law as an abstract moral order. *Hep* belonged to *maat.* It existed from the very beginning of time as the embodiment of the order given to the organized world by the creator god. The tight relationship between these two concepts of cosmic and political order and justice was best exemplified by the appearance of the *maat* goddess symbol as an amulet (charm) motif around a judge's neck, as described by the ancient Greek historians Herodotus and Diodorus.

The ultimate authority in the settlement of disputes was the pharaoh, whose decrees were supreme. Law in Egypt, especially during the New Kingdom, was specifically "what Pharaoh had said." The king referred to himself as a "fixer of laws." The Great Edict of Horemheb (r. ca. 1319–1307 B.C.E.) and the Nauri Decree of the Seti I (r. 1306–1290 B.C.E.) provide idealized literary expressions of royal control of judging and administering, presented in the form of specific instructions to limit the independence of authority. For example, in his edict, Horemheb proclaims that he is "the one who fixes laws for the king and gives regulations to the courtiers." Because of the complex nature of legal administration, the pharaoh delegated powers to provincial governors and other officials. Most prominent among them was the vizier, who could appoint magistrates as part of his legal duties.

In modern legal systems there is a clear distinction between public or official law and private cases. Public law includes basic penal law, administrative law, and relationships between individuals and functionaries. Private law deals with relationships between individuals. In ancient Egypt, however, no basic distinction existed between administrative and judicial authority or function. "Courts," or "courts of auditors," were formed, with officers who held administrative as well as judicial duties and sat "as a court constituted to judge" (according to the Great Edict of Horemheb). All local courts were controlled by the "great court" of Thebes and the court of Heliopolis; both consisted of the most prominent civil or military officers of Upper and Lower Egypt under the vizier's command. Important lawsuits, such as those involving land or influential people, were brought directly to the great court after a written complaint had been laid before the vizier. Lesser cases were left to local courts. Specialized courts and judges sitting in permanent rooms developed only after the Twenty-sixth Dynasty (664–525 B.C.E.).

The court was responsible for keeping legal records and documents, such as depositions, and dealt with litigation and punishment. The members of the court were responsible for the preliminary investigations of a case—questioning witnesses and suspects, examining the validity and truth of their statements, hearing the depositions of litigants, and examining the written evidence. In New Kingdom texts from Thebes (southern Egypt), those agents who were responsible

The Rosetta Stone, from Fort St. Julien, el-Rashid (Rosetta), Egypt (Ptolemaic Period, 196 B.C.E.); the inscription is a decree passed by a council of priests, one of a series that affirm the contol of the royal cult of the 13-year-old Ptolemy V on the first anniversary of his coronation. (© The Trustees of the British Museum)

for investigating an accusation were sometimes identified as "officials of the Place of Examination." The only criminal hearings that are described in detail are the Great Tomb Robbery investigations of the late Twentieth Dynasty (ca. 1196–1070 B.C.E.). The robberies were a series of assaults by various gangs of thieves on the tombs and temples of western Thebes. The vizier seems personally to have been involved in most criminal investigations and probably in all cases involving individuals of the official class.

In a legal proceeding the plaintiff was required to bring suit. The tribunal then ordered the defendant to appear in court if a point of law seemed to be involved in the dispute. Usually the judge ruled on the grounds of the documents and the testimony of each party. Egyptian officials asserted that they always acted according to "what His Majesty loves" or to "what the king favors." According to an Egyptian inscription, an ideal judge is "a man of justice before the Two Lands . . . who causes two men to go out content with the utterance of his mouth."

According to the *Teachings of Ptahhotep*, an instructional text from the Old Kingdom (2575–2134 B.C.E.), whoever transgressed the laws was punished. Reporting crime and criminal behavior was every official's duty. Failure to do so was itself a crime and was punished almost as heavily as the original offense. Punishments included property restrictions, imprisonment, beatings, tortures, and even mutilation. Incarceration with hard labor is well documented, most notably in the Middle Kingdom records of the Great Prison at Thebes. This and other prisons were not only places of confinement but also workhouses or labor camps. Moreover, they served as places of detention for criminals awaiting harsher penalties.

For state officials the most serious punishments were loss of property, office, status, and even political and social identity, whereby an esteemed official was reduced to the status of a laborer in the fields. The death penalty or severe mutilation of the face, nose, and ears was reserved for crimes against political or religious authorities. Such capital offenses and rebellions lay outside the formal executive competence even of the vizier and required referral to the king himself.

THE MIDDLE EAST

BY JAMES A. CORRICK

The ancient Near East produced the first known written laws, in the form of decrees handed down by kings. Typically, they were first read to the populace and then inscribed on clay tablets. Later, all the royal edicts of a particular ruler would be engraved on a stone pillar, called a stela. The laws carved on the stelae were often organized in no particular order, with criminal and civil laws, covering a variety of legal issues, being mixed indiscriminately. Crimes such as murder, thievery, and assault were addressed, as were civil issues, including inheritance, land ownership, and divorce. Some codes also specified wages and prices and regulated the sale and treatment of slaves. Each king's legal code often superseded the laws of his predecessors. This practice did not mean, however, that older laws were necessarily discarded. Instead, laws from earlier codes were frequently brought forward and copied word for word by the new king.

In addition to these written legal codes, a large body of unwritten laws may also have existed. These unwritten laws would have been passed down orally through the centuries. Some would eventually have been incorporated into the written legal record. It is remarkable that in the thousands of legal texts—records of judgments in cases of divorce, land sales, slave sales, and so on—the law code of Hammurabi is never referred to.

From the beginning much of ancient Near Eastern law was what would later be called *lex talionis*, or the law of equivalent retaliation. Often described as a "tooth for a tooth" or an "eye for any eye," *lex talionis* required the punishment to mirror the crime. Thus a man who broke another's arm had his own arm broken. If he caused the death of someone else's child, he had to give up the life of one of his own children. However, it was not unusual for a fine to be substituted for the punishment. Ancient Near Eastern law did not apply equally to all. Aristocrats normally paid higher fines than commoners, while commoners were more likely to receive harsh punishment, such as flogging, or to be executed for capital crimes.

The earliest known legal code was that of the Mesopotamian king Urukagina (or Uruinimgina), who ruled the Sumerian city of Lagash beginning in 2351 B.C.E. Concerned with rectifying social injustice, Urukagina forbade several practices in the collection of taxes. Thus, for example, a priest or palace official could not take wood or fruit in tax payments from a poverty-stricken widow. Law codes also survive from the early second millennium B.C.E., such as the laws of Eshnunna (modern-day Tell Asmar, Iraq) and the law code of the Mesopotamian ruler Lipit-Ishtar (r. ca. 1934–ca. 1924 B.C.E.).

The most famous code from the ancient Near East was that of Hammurabi (r. 1792–1750 B.C.E.). At capital of Babylon, Hammurabi erected a polished black stela that stood 8 feet tall. In the 12th century B.C.E., Shutruk-Nahhunte, king of Elam, took the stela as booty back to his capital Susa, in southwestern Iran. On one side of the stela was a relief showing the king conferring with Shamash, the god of justice; on the other was the code. As was traditional with such legal codes, the divine inspiration of Hammurabi's laws was made clear by a prologue in which the king explained how the gods of his city required justice and order and that the laws set down below were an attempt to meet these divine needs. Like Urukagina, the Babylonian king set himself up as a protector of the weak. Thus he sought justice by preventing the exploitation and victimization of the powerless and the destruction of the lawbreaker.

The prologue was followed by the laws themselves. In 51 columns of cuneiform characters containing 282 laws, Hammurabi covered commercial and real estate dealings; personal property disputes; injuries, both accidental and intentional; and labor matters. After the body of laws came the epilogue, which urged those seeking justice to read and heed the laws of Hammurabi. Additionally, the Babylonian ruler called on all later kings to follow the laws carved on the stela. Hammurabi's appeal to future kings revealed that his code was not so much a set of laws describing what was and was not illegal as it was a model for how justice should be dispensed. Indeed, on the stela Hammurabi's legal statements were termed *decisions* rather than *laws*. In other words, the code was a list of decisions, each of which was probably based on a number of cases but not on any specific case, and each of which was meant to serve as a guide in rendering future judgments.

To what extent Hammurabi's code was used in actual judicial proceedings is unknown. Still, stelae, some with additional commentary expanding on the meaning of Hammurabi's laws, were erected throughout the ancient Near East as late as the fourth century B.C.E. The Assyrians appear to have accepted Hammurabi's code, though they imposed considerably harsher penalties than did the Babylonians for the same crimes. There were no police to enforce the laws of the ancient Near East. In general when one person accused another of wrongdoing, the accuser, along with relatives, friends, and neighbors, would see that the accused appeared at the trial. In cases of treason or other crimes against the king, soldiers would bring the suspect to trial.

Most trials were local affairs, at which the accuser would lay out his complaint before a council of elders who acted as judges. Serious crimes, such as murder, would be heard by a judge appointed by the king. Verdicts from local councils could also be appealed to these royal judges as well as to the king. For most of the ancient Near Eastern period, there were no lawyers; the accuser prosecuted, and the accused defended. In the Persian Empire, however, a group called *speakers of the law* specialized in explaining legal matters to those involved in court cases as well as helping them present their cases. At a trial witnesses would be called, some of whom had to make long journeys to be present. Documents would be produced and examined. If all else failed in reaching a verdict, the judges would order the accused to undergo a "river ordeal," in which he or she was thrown into a river. Those who survived were declared innocent, while those who drowned were deemed guilty.

ASIA AND THE PACIFIC

BY KIRK H. BEETZ

Only the ancient Indians and Chinese left extensive written legal codes; therefore, the laws of other cultures are mostly lost. The history of laws in Asia suggests that laws were regarded as a defense of civilization against barbarism. For example, by the Han Dynasty (202 B.C.E.–220 C.E.) the rulers of China regarded human sacrifice as evil, and laws were made to outlaw it, giving regional legal authorities the backing of the government in stamping out the practice.

In India the first laws were Vedic laws, which were derived from the religious epics of the Aryan invaders who migrated through most of northern and central India from 1500 to 500 B.C.E. As the Vedic peoples adapted to their environment and mixed with the original populations, much of the religious law became too vague and unrealistic for practical use; from about 500 to 200 B.C.E. the laws were revised. The laws were written down as *sastras* and sutras. The *sastras* were books of rules written in verse, and the sutras were books of prose combined with verse. The book most often cited by historians is the Code of Manu, a *sastra* dating to between 200 B.C.E. and 100 C.E.

The Code of Manu and other codes made kings ultimately responsible for justice in their kingdoms. Kings were expected to hear complaints from petitioners, to make sure that justice was served, and to prosecute cases when there were no plaintiffs. Kings delegated much of their legal authority to magistrates who were expected to know thousands of laws and were supposed to be of irreproachably high moral character. Three magistrates were responsible for 10 villages. They had scribes and police to serve them. The tradespeople of Indian society frequently belonged to guilds devoted to their professions. Sometimes entire villages were devoted to just one trade. In such cases the guild was responsible for maintaining the law in the city and could punish people convicted of crimes, usually by fining them.

In the case of some crimes, punishment was swift. If the police caught someone burglarizing a home or other property, he or she could be taken to the center of town and executed, but in most cases people accused of crimes would be tried in court. A defendant was given three days to write a defense, with the aid of a legal scribe. Up to three witnesses could speak for the defendant in court. Brahmans, criminals, women, and certain other people could not be called as witnesses. Witnesses who were caught lying could be tortured as punishment. In cases when guilt was likely but not certain, the defendant could be tortured until he or she confessed or until an appeal was granted. Each defendant was allowed to appeal to higher authorities until reaching the king, who had the final word.

Not much is known of China's laws during the Shang Dynasty (1500–1045 B.C.E.) and the Zhou Dynasty (1045–256 B.C.E.), but the laws tended to favor emperors and aristocrats. During the Warring States Period (453–221 B.C.E.) of the Zhou Dynasty, several legal philosophies arose. One of these was legalism. This philosophy was law taken to the extreme. Every action was supposed to have a law governing it, and everyone, except the king, was subject to the law. Every profession had its designated responsibilities and its social rank. Even nobles were ranked in importance. Each person was allowed a certain amount of land and a certain number of servants according to his or her status. Punishments for breaking the law were severe, to dissuade people from committing crimes; actions considered beneficial to society, such as valor in battle, were rewarded. People who did not report a crime that they knew about were executed.

Jade cicada, China (second to first century B.C.E.); jade cicadas were placed as protection on the tongue of the dead, but full burial suits of jade were restricted by sumptuary laws to royalty. (© The Trustees of the British Museum)

In the 300s B.C.E. the province of Qin adopted legalism. There its chief advocate was Shang Yang (d. 338 B.C.E.). He saw to it that even the crown prince of Qin was punished for a crime. He was known for his cruelty and political treachery. When the crown prince became king of Qin, Shang Yang had to flee the province. When Zheng of Qin reunified China and renamed himself Qin Shi Huangdi, he imposed legalism on the empire. He tried to regulate all of the business of the nation. Some of his efforts had practical value. For example, a law that standardized the width for all axles on carts meant that ruts in roads could be standardized, allowing for greater speed in transporting goods to market and putting an end to the tipping over of carts because one wheel was in a rut while the other was not. Other laws made tax collecting easier. However, the criminal laws were unbearable. It seemed that no one could go a day without violating a few laws, and the punishments for breaking those laws were cruel. Qin Shi Huangdi took advantage of people's tendency accidentally to break laws, amassing a huge force of convicted laborers who worked on building projects, such as the Great Wall. Legalism was so loathed by the Chinese that they exterminated Qin Shi Huangdi's entire family in 210 B.C.E., ensuring that the Qin Dynasty and legalism would not rise again.

The founder of the Han Dynasty, Liu Bang, instituted Confucianism as the philosophy of his government. The law retained some of the doctrines of legalism, such as those enforcing taxation and obedience to the emperor, but Confucianism replaced most of the harsh laws of legalism with the principle of compassion. It took until about 100 B.C.E. for Confucianist magistrates fully to supplant legalist magistrates.

In 145 B.C.E. Governor Wen Weng of the province of Shu, not satisfied with the number of educated people available for employment in his government, began schools that taught Confucianism to boys of all social classes. His idea was adopted by the empire as a whole, and the schools produced the magistrates and the law enforcement officers of China. A magistrate was expected to be impartial, with his court being the one place in the empire where a poor person could challenge a rich one. People could appeal to higher authorities in government if they lost their cases. The emperor was expected to right wrongly decided cases in order to maintain his divine right to rule, which the gods could take away from him if he were unjust, but by 1 C.E. a census showed that there were nearly 60 million people in China, making it impossible for the emperor to hear every appeal. The emperor's magistrates were expected to memorize the laws they enforced and to prove themselves knowledgeable before being appointed to office. These magistrates helped maintain a sense of a single nation with one legal code through the centuries of upheaval after the Han Dynasty ended, even though there were often three or more governments vying to rule the empire.

A lack of written records for ancient laws makes identifying any laws outside China and India very difficult. Many Pacific islands were not yet settled, and those that were settled were only beginning to form societies governed by laws. The islands of Java and Borneo seem to have begun forming kingdoms late in the ancient era, perhaps in the 200s or 300s C.E., but the possible existence of these kingdoms is mostly inferred from scant Chinese records of trade in southeastern Asia during the medieval era. The formation of legal systems on these islands may not have begun before the medieval era.

The major nation in Southeast Asia from the 100s to 500s C.E. was Funan, which controlled territory from the Mekong Delta into what is now Cambodia. It left behind Hindu temples, the existence of which suggests to archaeologists that Funan's laws probably resembled those of ancient India. Direct evidence of Funan's laws is scant. Korea was influenced by China, which established trade cities on the Korean peninsula during the Han Dynasty. In about 384 C.E., when the royal family of the Korean kingdom of Paekche converted to Buddhism, Chinese forms of government and Chinese laws began to be adopted by Paekche, and the Chinese legal system moved through the Korean peninsula over the next 200 years. Ancient Korea is believed by most historians to have had a strong influence on ancient Japan; through Korea, Chinese culture came to Japan. The laws of ancient Japan are not known, but sometime in the 100s or 200s C.E., the Japanese on the island Kyushu, and probably the island Honshu as well, began adopting Chinese customs. During the 300s and 400s C.E., governments on these islands began modeling themselves on Chinese governments, and they probably adapted Chinese legal practices to their own needs. Early Japanese written records from the medieval era suggest that the laws mostly applied to the upper classes of Japan and that traditional Japanese tribal customs prevailed among the rest of the Japanese.

EUROPE

BY AMY HACKNEY BLACKWELL

The people of ancient Europe did not record their laws in writing. Historians have reconstructed ancient European laws from the descriptions of Roman observers and from laws that were written slightly after the ancient period. The best evidence of Celtic legal codes comes from Ireland's Brehon laws, which were first written down in the 600s C.E. but are presumed to have come from ancient Celtic laws. Historians think that these laws may have developed among Celtic peoples in Europe during the Bronze Age, between 2300 and 900 B.C.E. Legal experts memorized the laws and transmitted them orally over the years. After many years of study, these experts became skilled at interpreting the law, advising rulers, and arbitrating disputes. (The name *Brehon* is an Anglicization of the Irish word for "judge.")

Celtic law divided people into five social classes. At the top were kings, followed by nobles. Free people who owned property formed a third class and free people without property a fourth. The fifth class consisted of slaves and other nonfree people. These ranks indicated how people had to behave with respect to other members of society. Kings and nobles owned their own property and paid no rent to anyone. Men of the third class, freemen with property, did not own land but did own cattle and other movable goods, which allowed them to function as the lowest level of chiefs. The vast majority of people fell into the bottom two classes. The fourth class rented land from nobles, to whom they owed allegiance in war. Some members of the fifth class were slaves, many of them captured from other tribes; others were not slaves but did not hold all the rights of full members of the tribe.

In addition to defining social classes, Celtic laws organized people into groups that served as the basis for distributing land. The family was the smallest group. The clan was a larger group of relatives descended from a common ancestor. A tribe consisted of several clans likewise descended from a common ancestor. Each tribe and clan was governed by its own chief, who in turn owed allegiance to higher rulers. Allegiance took the form of yearly payments of property and military assistance.

Celtic laws did away with the ancient practice of retaliation for crimes and replaced them with a scheme of compensation designed to end disputes peacefully. If a person harmed another, the victim or the victim's family would bring the case before a chief and a legal expert. The legal expert would listen to the facts and decide the appropriate punishment. Every crime merited a specific compensation; cutting off someone's hand earned a smaller fine than murdering someone would. There were several levels of court; petty disputes went to the courts of local chiefs, while major disputes might go all the way to a king. A party who brought a case to court had to bring at least two witnesses to testify on her behalf. Social rank was important in courts; a person of lower rank could not always testify against someone of higher class.

One notable aspect of ancient Celtic law is its near absence of capital punishment for crimes. The only time Celtic laws recommended death was when a murderer failed to pay the full amount of the specified fine. Celtic kings and chiefs did execute criminals, but this practice was done outside the legal setting. Methods of execution included hanging and drowning.

Germanic tribes did not begin to compile formal legal codes until the very end of the Roman Empire in the 400s. For almost all of the ancient period they governed themselves according to custom, passed orally from generation to generation. These laws specified the treatment of criminals and the settlement of disputes.

German tribes assembled periodically to hold a festival that in medieval times was called the *Thing*, which was an occasion to trade, exchange spouses, and settle disputes. People who believed they had been wronged would wait until a major gathering and then bring their grievance before the king, who acted as a judge. Both parties were allowed to speak and bring witnesses to back them. The king would then issue a judgment. If all went well, both parties would abide by the agreement, and the dispute would be ended. Sometimes people settled disputes themselves by force, but there was community pressure to follow the king's judgment and settle matters peacefully. If the king summoned a person to appear at the Thing and he failed to come, he would be fined. Any party who summoned another person to appear because of a dispute and then himself failed to appear would have to pay a fine to the person he had summoned.

German laws covered many different types of crime. Stealing cattle was a serious offense, and penalties varied depending on the value of the cattle stolen; a bull owned by the king merited a higher fine than a bull that serviced only the cows of a single herd owned by an ordinary man. Stealing an object that lay outside a house was not as serious as breaking into a house to steal something. Merely breaking into a house without stealing anything was also a crime, especially if the thief broke a lock to get in. Rape, assault, insult, and murder were all criminal offenses punishable by fines. Tribes set fines according to the value of the victim. Killing a pregnant woman merited a higher fine than killing a woman past her childbearing years. If a murderer concealed his victim in an attempt to hide his crime, the punishment was greater than if he did not. A murderer who did not have enough money to pay the fine was expected to ask his relatives and friends for help. If he still could not raise enough money, he might be executed. Germanic inheritance law favored male heirs. If a father died and left sons, they would inherit his property. If he had no sons, then his property would go to his parents, his siblings, or his relatives on his father's side. In most cases, the inheritance could not go to a woman.

During the 400s C.E., Germanic groups began compiling codes of laws. The Visigothic leaders Theodoric I, Thorismund, and Theodoric II all created bodies of law that they used to govern their people, but they did not write these laws down. The Visigothic king Euric (d. 484 C.E.) made the first compilation of Visigothic law in 471, gathering the laws of his predecessors and arranging them in a single volume. His laws regulated only disputes involving Goths or Goths and

Romans. Even after the fall of Rome, Roman law continued to apply to disputes with only Roman parties.

GREECE

BY JEFFREY S. CARNES

The earliest views of Greek legal systems come from the poems of Homer (ninth or eighth century B.C.E.) and Hesiod (ca. 800 B.C.E.). In Homer's *Iliad* a relief on the shield of Achilles displays vignettes from daily life, including a legal case involving a dispute over a homicide. Two men argue about the payment of a blood price to atone for the murder, and the case is settled by elders and arbitrators, with a prize going to the one who "speaks the straightest opinion." Similarly, Hesiod's *Theogony* praises kings primarily for their role in administering justice. Both poems reflect a world in which justice was administered on a somewhat improvised basis by social elites and in which law was a matter of custom rather than something created by a legislative body or an individual lawgiver. More important, they show the origins of legal practice in private matters: in the settling of disputes between individuals, presenting a socially agreed-upon alternative to retribution and vengeance.

By the seventh century B.C.E. the various city-states began to develop legal codes and permanent legislative bodies. These early developments were typically assigned to individual lawgivers, such as Lycurgus (ninth century B.C.E.) in Sparta or Draco (seventh century B.C.E.) and Solon (ca. 630–ca. 560 B.C.E.) in Athens; many cities held that their oldest laws had been established by their lawgivers and handed down unchanged, though this was rarely historically accurate. In fact, lawgiver traditions reflect the social realities of the Age of Tyrants (sixth century B.C.E.), in which strong individuals brought about changes to break the monopoly on legal power held by the aristocracies of their cities.

Writing is typically associated with these reforms as a way to ensure the fairness and transparency of the judicial system. Lawgivers such as Draco and Zaleucus of Locri Epizephyrii (ca. 660 B.C.E.) are said to have ensured that the laws would be written down and publicly accessible so that all citizens could read them and see that they were being applied fairly. This development implies a certain degree of literacy throughout the Greek world; there must have been enough literate citizens to make public postings of laws worthwhile.

In Athens the laws were originally written down on wooden blocks called *axones*, which seem to have been attached to wooden pillars and mounted in such a way that readers could turn them, thus allowing more laws to be displayed in a limited amount of space. By the late fifth century B.C.E. the Athenian laws were written in stone, as was the case in numerous other Greek cities. Much of the current information about Greek law codes, especially during the Archaic Era (600–480 B.C.E.), comes from inscriptions. Of particular value is the inscription from Gortyn in Crete, dating to about 450 B.C.E. but thought to reflect the laws of a somewhat earlier era. The inscription, one of the longest to survive from antiquity, deals with a wide variety of matters both civil and criminal, including rape, inheritance, gifts, mortgages, and the status of slaves.

With the exception of Gortyn, however, Athens is the only city for which we have a detailed picture of the legal system, with sources including inscriptions, speeches from law courts, theoretical treatises such as the *Constitution of the Athenians* by Aristotle (384–322 B.C.E.), and even the comedies of Aristophanes (ca. 450–ca. 388 B.C.E.), in which the Athenians' litigious nature is frequently parodied. The Athenians held that their first code of laws was given to them by Draco in 621 B.C.E.; these laws were famous for their severity (thus the English word *draconian*, meaning "cruel" or "severe"), with the death penalty prescribed for even minor offenses. The laws ascribed to Draco, with the exception of the one concerning homicide, were replaced by those of Solon in 594 B.C.E. Publicly displayed on the *axones*, the law code of Solon formed the basis of Athenian law for more than 250 years, supplemented by the numerous laws passed by other legislative bodies during Athens' era of democratic rule (508–322 B.C.E.). The laws were of two sorts: *nomoi*, laws that established a permanent rule, and *psephismata*, decrees that were designed to apply to a particular instance. Legal reforms in the late fifth century ensured that *psephismata* could not override *nomoi* and that different legislative bodies were responsible for the two types of law.

The Athenian legal system (and probably other Greek systems) retained strong vestiges of the Greek law's origins in the settling of private disputes. Until the time of Solon, all actions at law were essentially private; only the injured parties or their families could bring a case to court, even in criminal matters. After Solon, Athenian law permitted *dikai demosiai* (public actions) for offenses that were regarded as affecting the community as a whole. Categories of offense subject to *dikai demosiai* included matters related to public administration (such as bribery or misconduct while in office) and to civic life generally (including accusations of impiety, as religion was considered a state matter). There were, however, no public prosecutors: actions could be brought by magistrates holding other offices or by *ho boulomenos* ("the one who wishes"); that is, by any free adult male, usually including noncitizens. The line between public and private matters was drawn differently from the way it is in most modern legal systems: Most crimes, including murder, remained a matter for private actions, and it was up to the victim or the victim's relatives to prosecute.

Participation in the legal system was encouraged by popular sentiment. The Athenian statesman Pericles (ca. 495–429 B.C.E.), in his Funeral Oration, expressed disdain for those who take no part in government. It also was encouraged by financial incentives. Monetary fines were the most common punishments for guilty defendants, and in a private suit the money went to the prosecutor, who was either the injured party or a member of his family. In some public suits there was a monetary reward for successful prosecution; this led to a class of professional prosecutors known as *sykophantes*. Measures were taken to reduce the number of frivolous or opportunistic prosecutions: A prosecutor who failed to secure 20 percent of the votes of the jurors was liable to a hefty fine and was prohibited from bringing similar actions in the future.

Participation in jury service was also encouraged with financial incentives starting in the mid-fifth century B.C.E. As a result, law courts were extremely democratic; the poorest citizens could participate as jurors, and courtroom procedure in many ways resembled that of the popular Assembly, a meeting of the citizens to discuss affairs of state. Juries were extremely large—typically several hundred people, and in some cases as high as 6,000. As in the Assembly, decisions were reached after listening to speeches. There were no professional lawyers, and both prosecutor and defendant pleaded their own cases. Professional speechwriters, such as Demosthenes (384–322 B.C.E.), sometimes wrote speeches for their clients to deliver.

There were few rules of evidence; hearsay, popular opinion (what Pericles referred to as "unwritten law"), and appeals to the emotions of the jurors were commonly brought to court. The authority of the spoken word was still strong in the legal system. Witnesses were given precedence over written testimony at least until the mid-fourth century, and although they could be questioned by the side that called them, they could not be cross-examined. As in the Assembly, a simple majority was necessary to decide conviction or acquittal, and voting was carried out by dropping pebbles or tokens into urns. If the vote was for conviction and the offense carried no fixed penalty, a separate penalty phase of the trial would be carried out, with each side proposing a punishment; the jury then would choose one or the other but could not compromise between them.

ROME

BY JAMES A. CORRICK

The earliest Roman legal writings were the Twelve Tables. Completed in 450 B.C.E. and modeled on the Athenian legal code, the Twelve Tables, though not a comprehensive listing of Roman law, covered such matters as debt, inheritance, property questions, liability, perjury, and bribery. The tables mostly addressed what the Romans called *ius privatum*, or private law, as opposed to *ius publicum*, or public law. Public law, which included criminal law, was the body of ordinances that regulated the relationship between citizens and the Roman state. Conversely, private law dealt with legal relations between citizens, such as contracts and suits.

For much of the Roman Republic (509–27 B.C.E.) private law covered some acts that later were deemed criminal. For example, robbery began as a private affair in which the victim sought redress through a lawsuit against the thief. By the late republic, however, theft was a crime with a state-imposed penalty. Public law initially was restricted to very serious threats against the state. Therefore, treason was a matter for public law. By the end of the republic and continuing into the empire, *ius publicum* grew to include such crimes as extortion, embezzlement, murder, and forgery.

Roman law was also divided into *ius scriptum* and *ius non scriptum*. Although these terms literally mean "written law" and "unwritten law," respectively, both were in fact written down. *Ius scriptum* referred to statute laws, those passed by legislative or other official action, while *ius non scriptum* referred to laws that by tradition and custom were accepted as binding, very similar to later English and American common law.

Roman private law was controlled by male Romans. Rome never had a staff of prosecutors, and it was therefore up to each individual citizen to prosecute his own case. The first of the Twelve Tables gave each citizen the right to summon any who wronged him before a magistrate, before whom the plaintiff and the defendant would argue their sides of the case. The table also gave the plaintiff the right to use force to bring the defendant before the magistrate if he would not come voluntarily.

The body of magistrates originally included only officers known as consuls. The office carried a certain status known as imperium, which gave the bearer, among other rights, the right to interpret and execute the law, including imposing the death penalty. In 366 B.C.E. a new office, praetor, took over many of the consuls' judicial duties, particularly those involving private law. Like the consuls, the praetor's office carried imperium. Dictators also had imperium, as did the emperors of imperial times; they, too, were considered magistrates.

As Rome brought first Italy and then much of the rest of the Mediterranean region under its control, it found a need for a *praetor urbanis*, who dealt solely with legal matters involving Roman citizens, and a *praetor peregrinus*, whose responsibility was suits between citizens and foreigners. The law of the former was called the *ius civile* ("citizen law"), while that of the latter was *ius gentium* ("law of nations"). Eventually six more praetors were added to help the *praetor urbanis*. Praetors continued to act as magistrates through the first centuries of the empire. By late imperial times, however, the judicial duties of praetors were taken over by officials appointed by the emperor.

When assuming his duties, a praetor would issue an edict explaining the legal principles under which he would operate. These edicts often expanded upon or clarified existing law, and they accordingly became known as praetorian law. Along with laws passed by the plebian assemblies under the republic or issued by emperors under the empire, praetorian edicts became part of the Roman legal code. *Ius privatum* proceedings were handled solely by a praetor for as long as the office existed. Under the republic a praetor did not act as a judge. Rather, his role was to review each case brought before him, determine its legal merits, issue a formula that explained the legal points under which the case would be tried, and then appoint a judge to hear the case. For an important case a five-judge tribunal was authorized to try the case. Judges were prominent private citizens, though they were rarely trained in the law. Under the empire this procedure was modified. Private citizens no longer were asked to act as judges. Instead, a single magistrate both reviewed and tried each case.

In *ius publicum* cases any magistrate who had imperium could preside over a trial. Under the republic *ius publicum* cases were initially tried before the centuriate assembly and then, beginning in the second century B.C.E., before *quaestiones perpetuae* ("standing jury courts"), composed of juries of 50 to 75 members. Eventually, under the empire, the *quaestiones* were replaced by trials conducted solely before a single magistrate.

Since praetorian-appointed judges, as well as plaintiffs and defendants, generally had little legal knowledge, they often depended upon legal advice. Beginning in the third century B.C.E. a group of professional jurists, or lawyers, appeared. These jurists offered their services as advisers and sometimes advocates at trials and in the drafting of praetorian edicts and other legal legislation. For these services they were not paid, though they often accepted gifts in exchange for their help. Around 304 B.C.E. one of the earliest of these jurists, Gnaeus Flavius, published the rules by which trials were conducted as well as a calendar of the days that legal business could be conducted. Prior to Flavius, only the patrician-controlled priesthood had such knowledge, whose possession now allowed plebians to have greater access to the Roman legal system.

Rome's jurists also produced a large body of legal writing, much of which was detailed analysis of specific cases, often from each jurist's own career. Jurist writing began with Appius Claudius Caecus, who lived in the fourth and third centuries B.C.E. and wrote a treatise on property. One of the most notable legal writers was Quintus Mucius Scaevola (d. 82 B.C.E.), who produced the first standard Roman law work. In 18 volumes Scaevola collected together Roman law and organized it by category. To what extent Scaevola's work was a complete collection of Roman law is unknown, since it did not survive the centuries. Even if complete, however, the work would not have been a legal code because it was not an official state-produced document. Indeed, apart from the Twelve Tables, republican Rome made no attempt to codify its laws.

In imperial times the occasional effort was made to create at least a partial legal code. The emperor Hadrian (r. 117–38 C.E.) had the edicts of the praetors edited during the final years of his reign. Diocletian, who ruled from 284 to 305 C.E., issued an incomplete legal code. At the end of the fourth century C.E. the emperor Theodosius I (r. 379–95 C.E.) issued what was probably to that date the most complete code, which included the laws passed since the reign of Constantine I (r. 306–37 C.E.) as well as Diocletian's work. It was not until after the fall of the western empire that a comprehensive code was issued by the eastern emperor Justinian I (r. 527–65 C.E.) in 529 C.E. The *Codex Justinianus* was based on the study of some 2,000 texts of Roman law.

THE AMERICAS

BY KIRK H. BEETZ

Little is known of the legal codes and the practices of law in the ancient Americas. For North America north of Mexico, anthropologists rely on comparisons of ancient American cultures to similar cultures about which more is known. For ancient South American cultures, almost nothing of their laws is known; either they are little studied, or scant evidence is left for archaeologists to find. Of the great ancient civilizations of Mexico and Central America more is known, though little is known about the Olmec and other predecessors of the Maya.

Ancient North Americans formed a variety of cultures, from hunter-gatherers to city dwellers. The legal needs of those who lived in small hunter-gatherer groups and those of people who lived in large settled communities would have been very different. Legal authority usually rested with a senior member of a small group, a shaman, or a group of elders. For the large communities of eastern North America and of the Mississippi River region, laws governing social conduct almost certainly existed. For small hunter-gatherer groups, theft was probably not a problem because almost everything was owned by everyone in the community. In villages and towns, laws governing theft probably existed.

Although the ancient Maya were a literate culture who left much for archaeologists to discover, little is known about their laws. The laws of modern Mayans are of little help in understanding ancient laws because modern Mayans have long been scattered in communities that often have communicated little with others, giving rise to many different laws that may have little to do with ancient practices. Records of ancient Mayan laws are rare. Therefore, historians often draw information about ancient laws from the myths of the Mayans, a somewhat unreliable approach because the laws of the supernatural world could vary from those of actual Mayan practice. Some aspects of Mayan law are known, but only in fragments. Thus a law about marketplaces might survive from one Mayan city, another about marriage from another city, and another about theft from another city. The ancient Mayans lived in many different communities, each with its own laws and legal code. The legal codes may have varied from one place to another and from one time to another, but it is not known by how much. If one pieces all the hints at laws together, a general picture of Mayan legal life emerges that may be altered as new discoveries are made.

Ancient Mayan kings ruled over city-states. They were responsible not only for making laws but also for leading the military and their city's religious life. In legal cases the king was the last court of appeal; whatever he decided was final. Every village and town as well as the main city within a king's territory had its own courts. Small villages might have had only one judge, and for most minor problems that judge's decision would not be appealed. When a decision was appealed, the case would be taken to a judge in a large town or city.

Beyond that, a case had to be taken to the capital, where it would be heard by a higher judge. The appeal after that was to the king himself. A king probably devoted part of every day to hearing legal appeals.

A person on trial probably was not compelled to testify. Neither the accused person nor any witnesses would be tortured in order to force testimony. Everyone was subject to the law, including judges and nobility. A difference in punishment between a noble and a commoner may have been that a noble was punished in private while a commoner was publicly humiliated. Convicted thieves were required to repay their victims or became slaves to their victims. Slavery was dangerous. In some cities slaves could be freed after fulfilling their obligations to their victims or for virtuous behavior, but the Maya practiced human sacrifice, and slaves were usually the first to be sacrificed.

The marketplace was an essential part of the economic and social life of Mayan villages, towns, and cities. Crimes committed in marketplaces were taken seriously. Apparently, some Mayan cities had police forces that patrolled marketplaces, and anyone could complain to them about someone dishonestly weighing or measuring their goods, about someone selling stolen goods, or about shoplifters. Judges were available to hear such complaints almost immediately, and it was possible for a case to be tried and resolved before the day was over.

People could file lawsuits, and there may have been lawyers to help them. Adultery, criminal business dealings, and breech of contract could draw lawsuits. The same judges who heard criminal cases would hear civil cases. The loser of a lawsuit could be fined, in which case his or her family would be summoned to make payment. If the family could not make payment, the defendant and some of his or her family could be forced to become slaves.

Judges worked long hours, probably beginning to hear cases within moments after sunrise. They were expected to be examples of virtue to other people, and if they were caught committing crimes, they could be put to death. If they were found to be taking bribes or showing prejudice by favoring nobles over commoners or the reverse, they probably were executed. Being drunk while at work also brought penalties. Even the highest judge below the king was subject to punishment.

Laws may have been written down, but at present it appears that the laws of the Maya may have been transmitted verbally, perhaps by experts who memorized the laws. Scribes held a high place in Mayan society, and some of them may have been assigned to record court proceedings, especially testimony by witnesses. The highest courts in a city almost certainly had scribes. Mayan laws may have derived in part from those of previous civilizations, especially the Olmec, and their laws certainly influenced cultures even as late as the Aztecs. How far they influenced communities north or south of Mayan lands is not really known, but some archaeologist speculate that Mayan laws influenced cultures in what is now the southwestern United States.

The laws of the cultures south of the Maya are mostly unknown. Archaeologists are only just discovering some of the civilizations that existed in South America, in part because the earliest ones seem to have built their structures mostly of dirt, which has left mounds only recently recognized as remnants of structures, and in part because they existed in places in the mountains that are hard to reach and very dangerous. Given the sophistication of the arts and crafts of some of these ancient cultures as well as their evidently vigorous trade, they probably had laws governing social conduct and the means to enforce those laws. It is known that most Andeans were expected to treat strangers well and that their punishments were severe.

See also ART; CRAFTS; CRIME AND PUNISHMENT; EMPIRES AND DYNASTIES; FESTIVALS; GENDER STRUCTURES AND ROLES; GOVERNMENT ORGANIZATION; LITERATURE; OCCUPATIONS; RELIGION AND COSMOLOGY; ROADS AND BRIDGES; SLAVES AND SLAVERY; SOCIAL ORGANIZATION; TRADE AND EXCHANGE; WRITING.

Egypt

The Precepts of the Vizier Ptah-hotep, ca. 2350 B.C.E.

Precepts of the prefect, the lord Ptah-hotep, under the Majesty of the King of the South and North, Assa, living eternally forever.

The prefect, the feudal lord Ptah-hotep, says: . . . Who will cause me to have authority to speak, that I may declare to him the words of those who have heard the counsels of former days? And the counsels heard of the gods, who will give me authority to declare them? Cause that it be so and that evil be removed from those that are enlightened; send the double . . . The majesty of this god says: Instruct him in the sayings of former days. It is this which constitutes the merit of the children of the great. All that which makes the soul equal penetrates him who hears it, and that which it says produces no satiety.

(continued)

(continues)

Beginning of the arrangement of the good sayings, spoken by the noble lord, the divine father, beloved of Ptah, the son of the king, the first-born of his race, the prefect and feudal lord Ptah-hotep, so as to instruct the ignorant in the knowledge of the arguments of the good sayings. It is profitable for him who hears them, it is a loss to him who shall transgress them. He says to his son:

. . . Inspire not men with fear, else Ptah will fight against you in the same manner. If any one asserts that he lives by such means, Ptah will take away the bread from his mouth; if any one asserts that he enriches himself thereby, Ptah says: I may take those riches to myself. If any one asserts that he beats others, Ptah will end by reducing him to impotence. Let no one inspire men with fear; this is the will of Ptah. Let one provide sustenance for them in the lap of peace; it will then be that they will freely give what has been torn from them by terror. . . .

If you are one of those who bring the messages of one great man to another, conform yourself exactly to that wherewith he has charged you; perform for him the commission as he has enjoined you. Beware of altering in speaking the offensive words which one great person addresses to another; he who perverts the trustfulness of his way, in order to repeat only what produces pleasure in the words of every man, great or small, is a detestable person.

If you are a farmer, gather the crops in the field which the great Ptah has given you, do not boast in the house of your neighbors; it is better to make oneself dreaded by one's deeds. As for him who, master of his own way of acting, being all-powerful, seizes the goods of others like a crocodile in the midst even of watchment, his children are an object of malediction, of scorn, and of hatred on account of it, while his father is grievously distressed, and as for the mother who has borne him, happy is another rather than herself. But a man becomes a god when he is chief of a tribe which has confidence in following him. . . .

Do not repeat any extravagance of language; do not listen to it; it is a thing which has escaped from a hasty mouth. If it is repeated, look, without hearing it, toward the earth; say nothing in regard to it. Cause him who speaks to you to know what is just, even him who provokes to injustice; cause that which is just to be done, cause it to triumph. As for that which is hateful according to the law, condemn it by unveiling it. . . .

If you are a son of the guardians deputed to watch over the public tranquility, execute your commission without knowing its meaning, and speak with firmness. Substitute not for that which the instructor has said what you believe to be his intention; the great use words as it suits them. Your part is to transmit rather than to comment upon. . . .

Do not plunder the house of your neighbors, seize not by force the goods which are beside you. Exclaim not then against that which you hear, and do not feel humiliated. It is necessary to reflect when one is hindered by it that the pressure of authority is felt also by one's neighbor. . . .

If you hear those things which I have said to you, your wisdom will be fully advanced. Although they are the means which are suitable for arriving at the *maat*, and it is that which makes them precious, their memory would recede from the mouth of men. But thanks to the beauty of their arrangement in rhythm all their words will now be carried without alteration over this earth eternally. That will create a canvass to be embellished, whereof the great will speak, in order to instruct men in its sayings. After having listened to them the pupil will become a master, even he who shall have properly listened to the sayings because he shall have heard them. Let him win success by placing himself in the first rank; that is for him a position perfect and durable, and he has nothing further to desire forever. By knowledge his path is assured, and he is made happy by it on the earth. The wise man is satiated by knowledge; he is a great man through his own merits. His tongue is in accord with his mind; just are his lips when he speaks, his eyes when he gazes, his ears when he hears. The advantage of his son is to do that which is just without deceiving himself.

To attend therefore profits the son of him who has attended. To attend is the result of the fact that one has attended. A teachable auditor is formed, because I have attended. Good when he has attended, good when he speaks, he who has attended has profited, and it is profitable to attend to him who has attended. To attend is worth more than anything else, for it produces love, the good thing that is twice good. The son who accepts the instruction of his father will grow old on that account. What Ptah loves is that one should attend; if one attends not, it is abhorrent to Ptah. The heart makes itself its own master when it attends and when it does not attend; but if it attends, then his heart is a beneficent master to a man. In attending to instruction, a man loves what he attends to, and to do that which is prescribed is pleasant. When a son attends to his father, it is a twofold joy for both; when wise things are prescribed to him, the son is gentle toward his master. Attending to him who has attended when such things have been prescribed to him, he engraves upon his heart that which is approved by his father; and the recollection of it is preserved in the mouth of the living who exist upon this earth. . . .

A son who attends is like a follower of Horus; he is happy after having attended. He becomes great, he arrives at dignity, he gives the same lesson to his children. Let none innovate upon the precepts of his father; let the same precepts form his lessons to his children. "Verily," will his children say to him, "to accomplish what you say works marvels." Cause therefore that to flourish which is just, in order to nourish your children with it. If the teachers allow themselves to be led toward evil principles, verily the people who understand them not will speak accordingly, and that being said to those who are docile they will act accordingly. Then all the world considers them as masters and they inspire confidence in the public; but their glory endures not so long as would please them. Take not away then a word from the ancient teaching, and add not one; put not one thing in place of another; beware of uncovering the rebellious ideas which arise in you; but teach according to the words of the wise. Attend if you wish to dwell in the mouth of those who shall attend to your words, when you have entered upon the office of master, that your words may be upon our lips . . . and that there may be a chair from which to deliver your arguments. . . .

Do that which your master bids you. Twice good is the precept of his father, from whom he has issued, from his flesh. What he tells us, let it be fixed in our heart; to satisfy him greatly let us do for him more than he has prescribed. Verily a good son is one of the gifts of Ptah, a son who does even better than he has been told to do. For his master he does what is satisfactory, putting himself with all his heart on the part of right. So I shall bring it about that your body shall be healthful, that the Pharaoh shall be satisfied with you in all circumstances and that you shall obtain years of life without default. It has caused me on earth to obtain one hundred and ten years of life, along with the gift of the favor of the Pharaoh among the first of those whom their works have ennobled, satisfying the Pharaoh in a place of dignity.

It is finished, from its beginning to its end, according to that which is found in writing.

From: Charles F. Horne, *The Sacred Books and Early Literature of the East*, Vol. 2, *Egypt* (New York: Parke, Austin, and Lipscomb, 1917): pp. 62–78.

The Middle East

The Code of Hammurabi, ca. 1780 B.C.E.

Code of Laws

2. If anyone bring an accusation against a man, and the accused go to the river and leap into the river, if he sink in the river his accuser shall take possession of his house. But if the river prove that the accused is not guilty, and he escape unhurt, then he who had brought the accusation shall be put to death, while he who leaped into the river shall take possession of the house that had belonged to his accuser.

3. If anyone bring an accusation of any crime before the elders and does not prove what he has charged, he shall, if it be a capital offense charged, be put to death. . . .

6. If anyone steal the property of a temple or of the court, he shall be put to death, and also the one who receives the stolen thing from him shall be put to death.

7. If anyone buy from the son or the slave of another man, without witnesses or a contract, silver or gold, a male or female slave, an ox or a sheep, an ass or anything, or if he take it in charge, he is considered a thief and shall be put to death.

8. If anyone steal cattle or sheep, or an ass, or a pig or a goat, if it belong to a god or to the court, the thief shall pay thirtyfold therefor; if they belonged to a freed man of the king he shall pay tenfold; if the thief has nothing with which to pay he shall be put to death. . . .

14. If anyone steal the minor son of another, he shall be put to death. . . .

16. If any one receive into his house a runaway male or female slave of the court, or of a freedman, and does not bring it out at the public proclamation of the

(continued)

(continues)

major domus, the master of the house shall be put to death.

17. If any one find runaway male or female slaves in the open country and bring them to their masters, the master of the slaves shall pay him two shekels of silver.

18. If the slave will not give the name of the master, the finder shall bring him to the palace; a further investigation must follow, and the slave shall be returned to his master. . . .

21. If any one break a hole into a house (break in to steal), he shall be put to death before that hole and be buried.

22. If any one is committing a robbery and is caught, then he shall be put to death.

23. If the robber is not caught, then shall he who was robbed claim under oath the amount of his loss; then shall the community, and . . . on whose ground and territory and in whose domain it was compensate him for the goods stolen. . . .

25. If fire break out in a house, and some one who comes to put it out cast his eye upon the property of the owner of the house, and take the property of the master of the house, he shall be thrown into that self-same fire. . . .

44. If any one take over a waste-lying field to make it arable, but is lazy, and does not make it arable, he shall plow the fallow field in the fourth year, harrow it and till it, and give it back to its owner, and for each ten gan [a measure of area] ten gur of grain shall be paid.

45. If a man rent his field for tillage for a fixed rental, and receive the rent of his field, but bad weather come and destroy the harvest, the injury falls upon the tiller of the soil.

48. If any one owe a debt for a loan, and a storm prostrates the grain, or the harvest fail, or the grain does not grow for lack of water; in that year he need not give his creditor any grain, he washes his debt-tablet in water and pays no rent for this year. . . .

125. If any one place his property with another for safe keeping, and there, either through thieves or robbers, his property and the property of the other man be lost, the owner of the house, through whose neglect the loss took place, shall compensate the owner for all that was given to him in charge. But the owner of the house shall try to follow up and recover his property, and take it away from the thief. . . .

129. If a man's wife be surprised (in flagrante delicto) with another man, both shall be tied and thrown into the water, but the husband may pardon his wife and the king his slaves. . . .

135. If a man be taken prisoner in war and there be no sustenance in his house and his wife go to another house and bear children; and if later her husband return and come to his home: then this wife shall return to her husband, but the children follow their father.

136. If any one leave his house, run away, and then his wife go to another house, if then he return, and wishes to take his wife back: because he fled from his home and ran away, the wife of this runaway shall not return to her husband. . . .

138. If a man wishes to separate from his wife who has borne him no children, he shall give her the amount of her purchase money and the dowry which she brought from her father's house, and let her go. . . .

141. If a man's wife, who lives in his house, wishes to leave it, plunges into debt, tries to ruin her house, neglects her husband, and is judicially convicted: if her husband offer her release, she may go on her way, and he gives her nothing as a gift of release. If her husband does not wish to release her, and if he take another wife, she shall remain as servant in her husband's house. . . .

LAWS of justice which Hammurabi, the wise king, established. A righteous law, and pious statute did he teach the land. Hammurabi, the protecting king am I. I have not withdrawn myself from the men, whom Bel gave to me, the rule over whom Marduk gave to me, I was not negligent, but I made them a peaceful abiding-place. I expounded all great difficulties; I made the light shine upon them. With the mighty weapons which Zamama and Ishtar entrusted to me, with the keen vision with which Ea endowed me, with the wisdom that Marduk gave me, I have uprooted the enemy above and below (in north and south), subdued the earth, brought prosperity to the land, guaranteed security to the inhabitants in their homes; a disturber was not permitted. The great gods have called me, I am the salvation-bearing shepherd, whose staff is straight, the good shadow that is spread over my city; on my breast I cherish the inhabitants of the land of Sumer and Akkad; in my shelter I have let them repose in peace; in my deep wisdom have I enclosed them. That the strong might not injure the weak, in order to protect the widows and orphans, I have in Babylon the city where Anu and Bel raise high their head, in E-Sagil, the Temple, whose foundations stand firm as heaven and earth, in order to bespeak justice in the land, to settle all disputes, and heal all injuries, set up these my precious words, written upon my memorial stone, before the image of me, as king of righteousness.

From: the Internet History Sourcebooks. Available online. URL: http://www.fordham.edu/halsall/.

Greece

The Law Code of Gortyn (Crete), ca. 450 B.C.E.

I. Whoever intends to bring suit in relation to a free man or slave shall not take action by seizure before trial; but if he do seize him, let the judge fine him ten *staters* for the free man, five for the slave, and let him release him within three days. But if he do not release him, let the judge sentence him to a *stater* for a free man, a *drachma* for a slave, each day until he has released him. But if he deny that he made the seizure, the judge shall decide with oath, unless a witness testify. If one party contend that he is a free man, the other that he is a slave, those who testify that he is free shall be preferred. But if they testify either for both parties or for neither of the two, the judge shall render his decision by oath. But if the slave on account of whom the defendant was defeated take refuge in a temple, the defendant, summoning the plaintiff in the presence of two witnesses of age and free, shall point out the slave at the temple; but if he do not issue the summons or do not point him out, he shall pay what is written. And if he do not return him, even within the year, he shall pay in addition to the sums stated onefold. But if he die while the suit is progressing, he shall pay his value onefold.

II. If one commit rape on a free man or woman, he shall pay 100 *staters*, and if on the son or daughter of an *apetairos* ten, and if a slave on a free man or woman, he shall pay double, and if a free man on a male or female serf five *drachmas*, and if a serf on a male or female serf, five *staters*. If one debauch a female house slave by force, he shall pay two *staters*, but if one already debauched, in the daytime, an *obol*, but if at night, two *obols*. If one tries to seduce a free woman, he shall pay ten *staters*, if a witness testify. . . .

III. If one be taken in adultery with a free woman in her father's, brother's, or husband's house, he shall pay 100 *staters*, but if in another's house, fifty; and with the wife of an *apetairos*, ten. But if a slave with a free woman, he shall pay double, but if a slave with a slave's wife, five. . . .

IV. If a husband and wife be divorced, she shall have her own property that she came with to her husband, and the half of the income if it be from her own property, and whatever she has woven, the half, whatever it may be, and five *staters*, if her husband be the cause of her dismissal; but if the husband deny that he was the cause, the judge shall decide. . . .

V. If a man die, leaving children, if his wife wish, she may marry, taking her own property and whatever her husband may have given her, according to what is written, in the presence of three witnesses of age and free. But if she carry away anything belonging to her children she shall be answerable. And if he leaves her childless, she shall have her own property and whatever she has woven, the half, and of the produce on hand in possession of the heirs, a portion, and whatever her husband has given her as is written. If a wife shall die childless, the husband shall return to her heirs her property, and whatever she has woven the half, and of the produce, if it be from her own property, the half. If a female serf be separated from a male serf while alive or in case of his death, she shall have her own property, but if she carry away anything else she shall be answerable.

VI. If a woman bear a child while living apart from her husband after divorce, she shall have it conveyed to the husband at his house, in the presence of three witnesses; if he do not receive the child, it shall be in the power of the mother to bring up or expose. . . .

VII. The father shall have power over his children and the division of the property, and the mother over her property. As long as they live, it shall not be necessary to make a division. But if a father die, the houses in the

(continued)

(continues)

city and whatever there is in the houses in which a serf residing in the country does not live, and the sheep and the larger animals which do not belong to the serf, shall belong to the sons; but all the rest of the property shall be divided fairly, and the sons, howsoever many there be, shall receive two parts each, and the daughters one part each. The mother's property also shall be divided, in case she dies, as is written for the father's. And if there should be no property but a house, the daughters shall receive their share as is written. And if a father while living may wish to give to his married daughter, let him give according to what is written, but not more. . .

X. As long as a father lives, no one shall purchase any of his property from a son, or take it on mortgage; but whatever the son himself may have acquired or inherited, he may sell if he will; nor shall the father sell or pledge the property of his children, whatever they have themselves acquired or succeeded to, nor the husband that of his wife, nor the son that of the mother. . . . If a mother die leaving children, the father shall be trustee of the mother's property, but he shall not sell or mortgage unless the children assent, being of age; and if anyone shall otherwise purchase or take on pledge the property, it shall still belong to the children; and to the purchaser or pledgor the seller or pledgee shall pay twofold the value in damages. But if he wed another, the children shall have control of the mother's property.

XI. If a slave going to a free woman shall wed her, the children shall be free; but if the free woman to a slave, the children shall be slaves; and if from the same mother free and slave children be born, if the mother die and there be property, the free children shall have it; otherwise her free relatives shall succeed to it.

XIV. The heiress shall marry the brother of the father, the eldest of those living; and if there be more heiresses and brothers of the father, they shall marry the eldest in succession. . . . But if he do not wish to marry the heiress, the relatives of the heiress shall charge him and the judge shall order him to marry her within two months; and if he do not marry, she shall marry the next eldest. If she do not wish to marry, the heiress shall have the house and whatever is in the house, but sharing the half of the remainder, she may marry another of her tribe, and the other half shall go to the eldest. . . .

XVI. A son may give to a mother or a husband to a wife 100 *staters* or less, but not more; if he should give more, the relatives shall have the property. If anyone owing money, or under obligation for damages, or during the progress of a suit, should give away anything, unless the rest of his property be equal to the obligation, the gift shall be null and void. One shall not buy a man while mortgaged until the mortgagor release him. . . .

XVII. Adoption may take place whence one will; and the declaration shall be made in the market-place when the citizens are gathered. If there be no legitimate children, the adopted shall received all the property as for legitimates. If there be legitimate children, the adopted son shall receive with the males the adopted son shall have an equal share. If the adopted son shall die without legitimate children, the property shall return to the pertinent relatives of the adopter. A woman shall not adopt, nor a person under puberty.

XVIII. Whatever is written for the judge to decide according to witnesses or by oath of denial, he shall decide as is written, but touching other matters shall decide under oath according to matters in controversy. If a son have given property to his mother, or a husband to his wife, as was written before these writings, it shall not be illegal; but hereafter gifts shall be made as here written.

From: the Internet History Sourcebooks. Available online. URL: http://www.fordham.edu/halsall/.

Rome

The Twelve Tables, ca. 450 B.C.E.

Table I.

1. If anyone summons a man before the magistrate, he must go. If the man summoned does not go, let the one summoning him call the bystanders to witness and then take him by force.

2. If he shirks or runs away, let the summoner lay hands on him.

3. If illness or old age is the hindrance, let the summoner provide a team. He need not provide a covered carriage with a pallet unless he chooses.

4. Let the protector of a landholder be a landholder; for one of the proletariat, let anyone that cares be protector.

6-9. When the litigants settle their case by compromise, let the magistrate announce it. If they do not compromise, let them state each his own side of the case, in the *comitium* of the forum before noon. Afterwards let them talk it out together, while both are present. After noon, in case either party has failed to appear, let the magistrate pronounce judgment in favor of the one who is present. If both are present the trial may last until sunset but no later.

Table II.

2. He whose witness has failed to appear may summon him by loud calls before his house every third day.

Table III.

1. One who has confessed a debt, or against whom judgment has been pronounced, shall have thirty days to pay it in. After that forcible seizure of his person is allowed. The creditor shall bring him before the magistrate. Unless he pays the amount of the judgment or some one in the presence of the magistrate interferes in his behalf as protector the creditor so shall take him home and fasten him in stocks or fetters. He shall fasten him with not less than fifteen pounds of weight or, if he choose, with more. If the prisoner choose, he may furnish his own food. If he does not, the creditor must give him a pound of meal daily; if he choose he may give him more.

2. On the third market day let them divide his body among them. If they cut more or less than each one's share it shall be no crime.

3. Against a foreigner the right in property shall be valid forever.

Table IV.

1. A dreadfully deformed child shall be quickly killed.

2. If a father sell his son three times, the son shall be free from his father.

3. As a man has provided in his will in regard to his money and the care of his property, so let it be binding. If he has no heir and dies intestate, let the nearest agnate have the inheritance. If there is no agnate, let the members of his gens have the inheritance.

4. If one is mad but has no guardian, the power over him and his money shall belong to his agnates and the members of his gens.

5. A child born after ten months since the father's death will not be admitted into a legal inheritance.

Table V.

1. Females should remain in guardianship even when they have attained their majority.

Table VI.

1. When one makes a bond and a conveyance of property, as he has made formal declaration so let it be binding.

3. A beam that is built into a house or a vineyard trellis one may not take from its place.

5. Usucapio of movable things requires one year's possession for its completion but usucapio of an estate and buildings two years.

6. Any woman who does not wish to be subjected in this manner to the hand of her husband should be absent three nights in succession every year, and so interrupt the usucapio of each year.

Table VII.

1. Let them keep the road in order. If they have not paved it, a man may drive his team where he likes.

9. Should a tree on a neighbor's farm be bent crooked by the wind and lean over your farm, you may take legal action for removal of that tree.

10. A man might gather up fruit that was falling down onto another man's farm.

Table VIII.

2. If one has maimed a limb and does not compromise with the injured person, let there be retaliation. If one has broken a bone of a freeman with his hand or with a cudgel, let him pay a penalty of three hundred coins. If he has broken the bone of a slave, let him have one hundred and fifty coins. If one is guilty of insult, the penalty shall be twenty-five coins.

3. If one is slain while committing theft by night, he is rightly slain.

4. If a patron shall have devised any deceit against his client, let him be accursed.

(continued)

(continues)

5. If one shall permit himself to be summoned as a witness, or has been a weigher, if he does not give his testimony, let him be noted as dishonest and incapable of acting again as witness.

10. Any person who destroys by burning any building or heap of corn deposited alongside a house shall be bound, scourged, and put to death by burning at the stake, provided that he has committed the said misdeed with malice aforethought; but if he shall have committed it by accident, that is, by negligence, it is ordained that he repair the damage or, if he be too poor to be competent for such punishment, he shall receive a lighter punishment.

12. If the theft has been done by night, if the owner kills the thief, the thief shall be held to be lawfully killed.

13. It is unlawful for a thief to be killed by day . . . unless he defends himself with a weapon; even though he has come with a weapon, unless he shall use the weapon and fight back, you shall not kill him. And even if he resists, first call out so that someone may hear and come up.

23. A person who had been found guilty of giving false witness shall be hurled down from the Tarpeian Rock.

26. No person shall hold meetings by night in the city.

Table IX.

4. The penalty shall be capital for a judge or arbiter legally appointed who has been found guilty of receiving a bribe for giving a decision.

5. Treason: He who shall have roused up a public enemy or handed over a citizen to a public enemy must suffer capital punishment.

6. Putting to death of any man, whosoever he might be unconvicted is forbidden.

Table X.

1. None is to bury or burn a corpse in the city.

3. The women shall not tear their faces nor wail on account of the funeral.

5. If one obtains a crown himself, or if his chattel does so because of his honor and valor, if it is placed on his head, or the head of his parents, it shall be no crime.

Table XI.

1. Marriages should not take place between plebeians and patricians.

Table XII.

2. If a slave shall have committed theft or done damage with his master's knowledge, the action for damages is in the slave's name.

5. Whatever the people had last ordained should be held as binding by law.

From: Oliver J. Thatcher, ed., *The Library of Original Sources,* Vol. 3, *The Roman World* (Milwaukee, Wisc.: University Research Extension Co., 1901): pp. 9–11.

FURTHER READING

Shafik Allam, "Egyptian Law Courts in Pharaonic and Hellenistic Times," *Journal of Egyptian Archaeology* 77 (1991): 109–127.

The Avalon Project, "The Twelve Tables," The Avalon Project at Yale Law School. Trans. E. H. Warmington. Available online. URL: http://www.yale.edu/lawweb/avalon/medieval/twelve_tables.htm. Downloaded on February 10, 2007.

Mary Dowling Daly, *Traditional Irish Laws* (San Francisco: Chronicle Books, 1998).

Jack H. Driberg, "The African Conception of Law," *Journal of Comparative Legislation and International Law* 16 (1934): 230–246.

Taslim O. Elias, *The Nature of African Customary Law* (Manchester, U.K.: Manchester University Press, 1956).

Christopher J. Eyre, "Crime and Adultery in Ancient Egypt," *Journal of Egyptian Archaeology* 70 (1984): 92–105.

Michael Gagarin and David Cohen, eds., *The Cambridge Companion to Ancient Greek Law* (Cambridge, U.K.: Cambridge University Press, 2005).

Jean-Marie Kruchten, "Law," in *The Oxford Encyclopedia of Ancient Egypt*, vol. 2, ed. D. Redford (New York: Oxford University Press, 2001): pp. 277–282.

Douglas M. MacDowell, *The Law in Classical Athens* (Ithaca, N.Y.: Cornell University Press, 1978).

Martha T. Roth, *Law Collections from Mesopotamia and Asia Minor*, 2nd ed. (Atlanta, Ga.: Scholars Press, 1997).

Aristide Théodoridès, "The Concept of Law in Ancient Egypt," in *The Legacy of Egypt*, ed. J. R. Harris (Oxford, U.K: Clarendon Press, 1971): pp. 291–322.

J. A. C. Thomas, *Textbook of Roman Law* (Amsterdam, Netherlands: Elsevier, 1976).

R. F. Willetts, *The Law Code of Gortyn* (Berlin, Germany: de Gruyter, 1967).

literature

INTRODUCTION

Even people who have studied literature most of their lives are often unsure how to define what literature is and what it is not. Perhaps everything that has ever been written is literature. Some people would exclude such writings as laundry lists and legal documents, yet a historian might be able to see a world of information about an ancient culture in its laundry lists and legal documents. This fuzziness in definition can be maddening when one wishes to be precise, but part of the attraction of the study of literature is its tendency to transcend boundaries, changing its shape to suit the needs of a particular author or culture.

In general, literature can be divided into four categories: poetry, fiction, drama, and prose nonfiction. Poetry is expressed in verse, using rhythms and associations of sounds, as in the case of rhyme. Fiction tells a story and usually has a plot and characters whose actions make up the plot. Drama also tells a story but through actors depicting the characters of the story. Nonfiction prose is harder to define. Prose is writing that is not in verse, and nonfiction prose is a factual accounting of the subject under consideration, often taking real events and people as its starting point. Some literary scholars insist that prose is more than that; they assert that writing should be artful and graceful in order to be considered prose, meaning that laundry lists do not count. These four categories are commonly used to discuss literature because they are convenient. When looked at closely, however, they are not as well defined as they may seem, because they sometimes overlap.

Take the matter of poetry. Poetry is the oldest-known literary form, owing to its oral tradition. Long before people created written languages, they learned to tell stories. These stories were passed down orally from one generation to the next; hence the term *oral tradition*. In illiterate societies or in societies in which literacy was limited to a minority of people, the oral tradition was a way to preserve religious stories, tales of heroes, wisdom acquired through experience, and stories that were just plain fun to hear. In almost every known society certain people became professional storytellers.

Storytelling was a way for a traveler to earn food and lodging for a night. A good storyteller could barter the telling of a story for goods or exchange it for money. A professional storyteller would be expected to know certain tales, long and short, that audiences wanted to hear over and over again. This required storytellers to memorize lengthy historical and religious tales as well as numerous small stories. That ancient people were illiterate did not mean they also were stupid; an audience would often know the most important stories by heart and would know when a storyteller got something wrong. This is how poetry became important, because poetry has rhythm, and rhythm makes remembering words easier. Thus, many ancient religious works were first written down in verse, because they were originally part of the oral tradition. If one looks at pictures of ancient storytellers such as Homer, one may notice that the storytellers often hold a stringed instrument or are accompanied by a musician. The rhythmic strumming of the instrument would help the storyteller keep his or her rhythm when reciting a tale, which would assist the storyteller in remembering the words. Long epics such as Homer's *Iliad* were composed in verse and memorized and recited in verse. In fact, in the *Iliad* itself Homer refers to storytellers as singers. One can see immediately the fuzziness in the four categories of literature, because the ancient epics were both poetry and stories. The people who first heard them probably appreciated them for both their poetic use of language and their plots and characters. When studying drama, one is likely to see the same sort of blending. Many ancient dramas were written in verse, and audiences admired the poetic language as well as the plots.

Dramas may have been the next step in the development of literature. Most of what is known about ancient dramas comes from plays that were composed by writers who were self-consciously creating literary works, which means that they are imperfect representations of the dramas that preceded them, before people could write. Most anthropologists believe that drama developed out of religious rites. In dramas people portrayed religious figures, perhaps singing or dancing to show the spiritual nature of the figures. The earliest such dramas seem to have been presented during celebrations of the coming of spring. In many parts of the world, these festivities included the ritual killing of one or more of the actors, usually youngsters, whose deaths were meant to renew the fertility of the soil for the upcoming planting of crops.

Once a culture became literate, it was difficult to stamp out this practice. Even after a government managed to end the practice of sacrificing actors, a playwright might be ritually killed if his play did not satisfy his audience. This seriousness is sometimes a help to people studying ancient societies, because various literary works were intended to express the hopes, fears, dreams, and nightmares of the authors and audiences. For example, the Epic of Gilgamesh from ancient Mesopotamia reveals a concern for defining what is good and what is evil, a concern about loneliness, an interest in what makes someone a friend, bewilderment at why people suffer, and a longing for immortality. The very fact that ancient peoples wrote down this epic and preserved it for centuries shows that it touched on matters of importance to them; by reading the epic, a person can learn about them. Further, a great literary work touches on our common humanity, and Gilgamesh speaks of issues that still interest people today, allowing modern audiences to see how another group of people in circumstances different from our own viewed issues that still matter.

AFRICA

BY DIANNE WHITE OYLER

Literature in ancient Africa represents the creative thought of indigenous people in both oral and written forms of communication. In the ancient world these forms of communication most likely transmitted knowledge in the language spoken by the community. As the community expanded into kingdoms and empires, people were exposed to other languages through trade and conquest. Ancient African written literature may have used a writing system invented by the indigenous people of the region. However, this writing system probably recorded literature in the language of the upper class rather than the vernacular language spoken by the peasants. Written literature may have also used a writing system from a nearby community or trading partner that was adopted or adapted to the needs of the community.

For most of the continent literature was in an oral form that today is called *orature*. This oral literature preserved indigenous thought by committing it to memory and passing it down from one generation to the next. In many cases certain members of society were charged with the responsibility of remembering the oral literature and maintaining its accuracy. This literature included such forms as oral tradition, religious poems and songs, and myths and legends of past heroes whose actions should be emulated. Individual families also passed down similar stories that specifically involved their family members and told these stories from their own point of view. These families transmitted the accepted morals and practices of the community in stories, poems, riddles, proverbs, and songs to the children, who would become the next generation of leaders. It was the responsibility of each of the family members to communicate this type of literature.

The earliest-known written literature appeared as early as 3000 B.C.E. when Egypt began recording governmental, religious, and business documents as well as creative thought. They were transcribing indigenous thought from the canon of oral literature of the upper class into the indigenous writing system, hieroglyphics. Having an intimate relationship with Egypt, Nubia and the kingdoms of Kush and Meroë (present-day Sudan) on the upper Nile River borrowed Egypt's hieroglyphics, adopting the writing system. Later, however, it changed the hieroglyphic writing system by adapting it and thus creating the Meroitic script. Spanning the Red Sea, early Axum (present-day Ethiopia) developed its own writing system, called Ge'ez, based on the Sabean alphabet from southern Arabia. In addition to these three indigenous writing systems, the Greek language and alphabet became a dominant writing system after the conquest by Alexander the Great, and cultural diffusion brought literature from southern Europe and western Asia as the continent became more engaged in the larger Mediterranean world.

Ancient African literature can be found written on papyrus, the paper of the day used by many societies, and recorded on the walls of palaces, temples, tombs, and monuments such as obelisks and stelae, both forms of monolithic pillars. However, in these literate societies, only a small segment of each community could actually read and write. It was the duty of the scribe to keep official records and write literature. Nevertheless, all segments of the community participated in and enjoyed both oral and written literature. And while literacy remained in the northern and eastern part of the continent until the arrival of Islam, each community had its own canon of oral literature.

Oral Literature

Oral literature is creative thought delivered by word of mouth. Other than the manipulation of language to communicate in prose or verse, oral literature used performance techniques, including music, repetition, song, and phrasing. Oral literature included various genres: historical tales, folktales, legends, epics, myths, divination prose and verse, hunter's tales, as well as poetry such as praise poetry, songs, proverbs, and riddles. This literature was passed down from generation to generation until it was fixed in the written record. The storytelling activity was a form of local entertainment that could be found within the extended family compound, among the clans, or in the larger village or town setting. As the family gathered in the evening to share the events of the day, storytelling provided entertainment and an education that enabled children to participate in the intellectual life of the community. African literature was unique in that audience participation was required in all genres. Children were not passive in the storytelling process, and their inclusion began the process of the memorization that preserved this type of knowledge. However, the family's oral literature could change from one generation to the next despite efforts to preserve its accuracy. These stories continued in this way until they were written down, which fixed them so that they could no longer change.

Folktales presented scenarios of questionable human behavior. The action of the story centered on a human or animal that portrayed dubious human characteristics such as greed or jealousy. Using an animal to portray negative human characteristics allowed society to correct inappropriate behaviors without accusing any one individual, especially an individual who was highly placed in society. Regardless of the central actor in the folktale, the story had a twofold purpose; it entertained while either teaching or reinforcing an intrinsic message as to the family or community's standards of appropriate behavior. There were two types of folktales. The trickster folktale was usually about an animal that was smart but mischievous and lacked a sense of what is right and wrong. The dilemma tale posed a problem that could be solved many different ways. Those who engaged in the trickster folktales saw what could happen to someone who used poor judgment, and those who engaged in the dilemma tale participated in an open-ended discussion that provided practice in honing oral arguments and choosing appropriate solutions to problems faced by the community each day.

The historical tale included stories of genealogy and those of the community's heroic and historic past. The genealogy traced the ancestors of the family lineage who first settled in the area from whom the first community leader was chosen. The historical tale could also share the exploits of a larger-than-life person from the past. The legend was a tale of ancestors or events from the heroic historic past that the community considered memorable and instructive to be retold. It could also be a historical tale.

The myth often described a tale of the origins of the community's ancestors. These often included the environment, culture, gods, and authoritative ancestors. These myths could also be legends. In South Africa around 2000 B.C.E. two groups inhabited the region. The Khoikhoi who lived in present-day Botswana had a creation myth concerning Tsui Goab, who was a great powerful chief. Tsui Goab was the first Khoikhoi from whom all the Khoikhoi clans took their origin. At the same time, the neighbors of the Khoikhoi during this period, the Khoisan of present-day South Africa, Namibia, and Botswana, had a creation myth about Cagn, the first being, who created the world. In eastern Africa around 1000 B.C.E. the founding myth of the kingdom of Axum relates the origins of the kingdom through the birth of Menelik I, son of Axum's Queen of Sa'aba (Sheba) and King Solomon of Israel.

The divination tale came from a large body of community wisdom collected and incorporated in the decision-making process. The Yoruba of West Africa (present-day Nigeria and Benin) date back to 350 B.C.E., and they developed divination texts that were a large corpus of Yoruba wisdom reflecting the group's history, culture, moral values, and views on specific issues. The diviner was the repository of this type of specialized knowledge, which was passed down from one generation to the next. This knowledge was related in verse, "the sixteen cowries," which was recited as required by the events.

The hunter's tale was a story from the hunt of bygone days where the community's hunters regaled one another and their families with stories. They also told tales of their ancestor hunters, who were remembered and who became larger than life as their exploits were recounted.

Poetry is thought communicated in verse and an important genre found in most communities of the continent, where the people enjoyed rhyming and rhythmic composition. For many, poetry was synonymous with language, and it was an integral part of daily life. Members communicated about serious issues, such as local politics, or recreational topics, such as romantic love. Poetry included epic poems, songs, praise poetry, proverbs, and riddles. Oral poetry was composed according to a predetermined formula. It may have been composed, remembered, and performed, or it may have been composed as it was performed.

The epic poem was a historical tale told in verse form in which the accomplishments of a larger-than-life family or community figure from the heroic historic past was further embellished. Epic poems were either part of oral tradition or stand-alone stories. In any case the poem was accompanied by music and or dance and used varying performance techniques.

The song was an important form of communication used by all communities on the continent. As an example of the concept of African oral literature being participatory, songs used the call-and-response method. Work songs were call-and-response because they were sung in a specific rhythmic pattern to pace the work, where the group leader called out the lyric and the group answered.

The praise poem could be found in most communities on the continent. This elaborate poetry detailed the important qualities and accomplishments of historic family or clan members that were singled out for praise. Praise poetry was composed and sung by professional artists who performed them at public functions. While different singers could perform a praise poem, the content remained the same, as the poems were improvised by applying the techniques of suggestion and insinuation from language and imagery in the portrayal of the person or event. Praise songs were incorporated into the performance of the epic poem. Praise songs praised the gods, the deeds of the hunter or warrior, the family of a bride or groom at a wedding ceremony, or ancestors who were important for the family to remember. However, praise poetry used to extol the virtues of the community members who might be considered leaders of the group was composed for actions that were more than just praiseworthy; these acts had to be remarkable, even for them.

The proverb used language and imagery to bring into focus daily lessons for living. They were succinct and could be in prose or verse. In many communities the knowledge of proverbs demonstrated wisdom and was used to prove a point or to correct behavior. For some of these communities knowledge of proverbs was important or even required to participate in effective conversation. The riddle was much like the proverb in that the focus was on analogy; however, the riddle was a question that asked for the identification of common qualities between different objects and situations. The riddle was part of evening storytelling, and it, too, had an educational dimension as it helped to develop perception.

The oral tradition is another form of literature passed down from one generation to the next. For many societies this form of oral literature was a kind of specialized knowledge controlled by a specific group identified as such by the community. For example, many of the Mande speakers of West Africa had a socially constructed cultural caste of storytellers known as the *djelw*, who possessed this specialized knowledge. Many other groups also had this specialized job, called by the French term *griot*. Identified by families, these storytellers or local historians were charged with the responsibility of maintaining the accuracy of the tradition as it was passed down from generation to generation. Some families kept this knowledge for the king, the royal *griot*, while others kept knowledge for the local community. Each family or community had its own cultural historians with its own version of the facts that amplified its own contribution to the tale.

Nevertheless, while the emphasis of the story may have shifted from community to community or performer to performer, the facts of the story were accurately remembered and presented. The audience judged the purveyor of the oral tradition based on their own memories of these stories that had been told to them in the family setting. They also judged the performance based on their perception of how well the storytellers portrayed the contribution made by their ancestors to the events in the story. Oral tradition is performance art in which the storyteller or historian used prose, verse, song, dance, and accompaniment by instruments such as drums, harps, or xylophones. While the oral historian's performance had to be compelling, it also had to maintain a delicate balance between the facts and the portrayal of the contributions by the ancestors of the local audience. The audience or the performer may have changed, but the factual content remained the same.

Written Literature

Written literature existed in the ancient African world since the founding of the state of Egypt by King Menes around 2920 B.C.E. In fact, more is known about ancient Egyptian civilization than any other because of the extensive writings on papyri preserved in the library at Alexandria built in 283 B.C.E. by Ptolemy II Philadelphus (r. 285–246 B.C.E.). Following this invention, most written literature in indigenous writing systems occurred in the upper Nile kingdom of Kush and in the Red Sea kingdom of Axum. Other written literature was brought to the North African Maghreb by Christians using Greek written in the Greek alphabet and Latin written in the Roman alphabet to teach and copy the Bible and write important doctrines for the Christian world.

Written literature in prose along the upper Nile and the kingdoms of Kush and Meroë included literature that used adopted Egyptian hieroglyphics. This writing system was adapted from the eighth to the fourth centuries B.C.E., the Napatan period, using a form of hieroglyphic writing for texts. After Kush under the rule of Kashta and later Piye conquered Egypt, the Nubians ruled as the pharaohs of Egypt's Twenty-fifth Dynasty. Piye ruled from 750 to 712 B.C.E. "The Stele of Victory," the Piye stella, is the longest and most detailed text about ancient Egypt. Written in Egyptian hieroglyphics, the text is inscribed on a stele of pink granite with 159 lines describing Piye's military prowess and his deliberations as king. The Nubian pharaoh Shabaka, who ruled Egypt from 712 to 698 B.C.E., inscribed theological issues shared by the Egyptians and the Nubians on a black stele known as the "Memphite Theology." The tomb of Queen Shanakdakhete (r. 170–160 B.C.E.), the first female ruler of Kush's Meroitic period, is inscribed with the oldest known Meroitic hieroglyphs. Adapted from Egypt hieroglyphics, these hieroglyphs were changed to meet Nubian needs. While the writing has been deciphered, the Meroitic language has not, so understanding this document is difficult. In addition there are more than 800 funerary texts that cannot be deciphered. Under King Taniydamani (first to second century B.C.E.) two stelae of funerary texts provide the first long Meroitic texts. In the sixth century C.E. the Nubian kingdoms converted to Christianity, and written records of their Christian religion include fragments of scripture, liturgical texts, and lives of saints.

Written literature in prose from Axum includes Ge'ez inscriptions from the feudal empire as early as the fifth century B.C.E., though some of these inscriptions are also in verse similar to folk poetry. While many of these inscriptions were religious, some provided detailed accounts of battles fought and won, like those fought by King Ezana in defeating the failing kingdom of Kush at Meroë. A body of literature does not begin until King Ezana accepted Christianity and made it the state religion in the fourth century C.E. Biblical scripture and religious texts were translated into Ge'ez from the Greek language and alphabet, preserving texts that date to before the schism in the Christian Church that created Western Roman Christianity and Eastern Roman Christianity. These translations preserved entire books of biblical text, such as the book of Enoch, the book of Jubilees, and the Ascension of Isaiah. Monasteries were the repositories for the Ge'ez manuscripts and also acted as schools that educated those who became Axumite writers. Secular literature existed in the form of history and the recording of the founding myths of the kingdom.

Written literature in poetry was important in the religious world of Axum. Hymns provide the bulk of Ge'ez poetic literature, and a large book of Ge'ez hymns, *Diggua*, is a collection of songs that rhyme. The compilation of this book is credited to the sixth-century priest from Axum who later became Saint Yared. As a part of the liturgy, ceremonial singers participated by singing these religious hymns. Ge'ez hymn poetry includes *qine* hymns that were a form of praise poetry. Different from the ceremonial singers, the composer of the *qine* hymn observed rules concerning length and number of rhyming lines and the rhythm of the grammar. The composer also chose effective figures of speech to create a powerful statement. The *qine* hymns eulogized political and religious leaders or admonished them for their mistakes. The *qine* hymn was verse that could be used only once at a particular church for one particular event.

Written literature in prose in the North African Mahgreb concerned Christian religious texts. In the area previously known as Carthage, Latin written in the Roman alphabet was established as the language of the Western Roman Christian Church. In the second century C.E. Quintus Septimus Florens Tertulianus (born ca. 155–160) played an important role in the development of early Christianity. He composed works defending Christianity against corrupting beliefs, including "Against Valentinus," "Against Marcion," and "Against Hermogenes." Aurelius Augustinus of Hippo (354–430 C.E.) became Saint Augustine, the Western Christian bishop of Hippo (Algeria). Saint Augustine was an important contributor to the institutionalization of the Western Roman Christian Church. He was instrumental in clearly articulating the relationship between the concepts of predestination and free will and grace and good works. After his conversion to Christianity he wrote a spiritual biography, the *Confessions* (397 C.E.), which is a prose poem. His work *The City of God* (410–426 C.E.) is an epic that vindicates Christianity against those who claimed that it was the reason for the fall of the Western Roman Empire to the Visigoths.

Literature in ancient Africa represents oral and written indigenous creative thought. Although many documents appear to have been written during this time, few people could read them because they were either not literate or the language of the text was foreign to them, like the new Christian religious texts that began to permeate society. Preliterate and literate members of society could appreciate indigenous written literature as it was read in an oral performance. They also were exposed to the reading of and the chanting performance of liturgical literature written in foreign languages. However, all members of society could enjoy and appreciate the many forms of oral literature that eventually were later transcribed into text or incorporated into other written texts.

EGYPT

BY KELLY-ANNE DIAMOND REED

The ancient Egyptians produced many types of written texts, such as religious works (funerary texts and autobiographies, hymns, and litanies, or collections of prayers), administrative documents (inventories and payrolls), legal documents, medical texts, historical texts, letters, manuals, *onomastica* (catalogues of things arranged by kind), spells, narratives, love poems, teachings, dialogues, and lamentations. The texts are diverse, so the question arises as to which of them can be categorized as literature in the Western sense of the word. This question is difficult to answer, and not all scholars agree.

Unfortunately, there is no Egyptian word to define the different types of writings. The blanket term *writings* was used by the ancient Egyptians to describe most of their textual material. Alternatively, the terms *command* and *teaching* were also sometimes applied. Modern scholars tend to categorize the documents based on their context, content, physical form, date, or script. The majority of what was written down was written to communicate or record information. However, there are several texts that seem to conform to modern ideas of literature.

OLD KINGDOM

In the beginning writing was used to label items, such as a person, a place, or a belonging and sometimes even an event. The art of writing was said to be derived from the gods, and there was a certain mystique that went along with the written word. The first time that writing emerges on a large scale is in the Offering List that appears in the Old Kingdom (ca. 2575–ca. 2134 B.C.E.) private tombs. These tombs belonged to the wealthy nobles who generally invested everything they had in their tomb construction. This sort of list enumerates such items as materials, ointments, and food products. These were the items that the deceased wished to receive. The Offering List was a significant step toward the development of literature, and this occurred in the private realm.

Eventually the list increased in size and warranted reorganization. The Egyptians then decided to substitute for the list a "Prayer for Offerings." This prayer became the focal point for all tomb decoration. Simultaneously, with the addition of narrative, the long lists of the deceased's titles evolved into an autobiography. It was during the Fifth Dynasty (ca. 2465–ca. 2323 B.C.E.) that both the prayer and the autobiography were standard features in tomb decoration. However, the "Prayer for Offerings" had certain limitations in that it was tightly bound to the cult of the dead; the autobiography, on the other hand, became quite elaborate in the Sixth Dynasty (ca. 2323–ca. 2150 B.C.E.) and remained in use for the next two millennia.

The autobiography focused on the positive characteristics of the deceased, or the idealized characteristics created by society. Nothing negative or derogatory was ever included in these inscriptions. The purpose of the autobiography was to preserve the name of the deceased for all eternity. The deceased himself would be reborn in the hereafter, and his name would live forever on earth. An example of a Sixth Dynasty tomb autobiography is that of Weni, which consists of 51 vertical columns of hieroglyphs. It is from Abydos. A short excerpt reads as follows: "While I was senior warden of Nekhen, his majesty made me a sole companion and overseer of the royal tenants. I replaced four overseers of royal tenants who were there. I acted for his majesty's praise in guarding, escorting the king, and attending. I acted throughout so that his majesty praised me for it exceedingly." Often the tomb autobiography seems very self-laudatory to the modern reader. One of the most well-known Old Kingdom tomb autobiographies is that of Harkhuf, which also dates to the Sixth Dynasty and is found at Aswān.

Accompanying the autobiography was the more formulaic catalogue of virtues. This set of moral standards mirrors the ethical code illustrated in the second type of literature that emerged in the Old Kingdom: wisdom literature. Wisdom literature can be broken down further under the headings teachings (instructions), laments, and dialogues. Short maxims were created and then consolidated to form the instruction. The teachings, or didactic texts, take the form of instructions given by a father to his son. In some examples the characters involved are officials or royalty from the past.

The earliest surviving instruction is that of Hardjedef. This text has been compiled from nine ostraca (pieces of pottery with inscribed writing) of New Kingdom date (ca. 1550–ca. 1070 B.C.E.) and a wooden tablet of the Late Period (ca. 712–ca. 332 B.C.E.). However, it is thought that the text dates to the Fifth Dynasty; it opens, "Beginning of the Instruction made by the Hereditary Prince, Count, King's Son, Hardjedef, for his son, his nursling, whose name is Au-ib-re." One of the preserved instructions advises that one should found a household, take a wife, and have a son.

The "Instruction Addressed to Kagemni" and the "Teaching of the Vizier Ptah-hotep" also date to the Old Kingdom. The former text is preserved in the Papyrus Prisse, but

Page from the Book of the Dead of Hunefer, Thebes, Egypt (ca. 1300 B.C.E.) (© The Trustees of the British Museum)

its beginning is lost. It is followed on the papyrus by the only complete copy of the latter text. The "Teaching of the Vizier Ptah-hotep" is also preserved on two additional papyri and a wooden tablet. This work is a very long instruction and consists of 37 maxims, a prologue, and an epilogue. The main themes of this work are self-control, moderation, kindness, generosity, justice, and truthfulness. Both of these two texts are thought to date to the Sixth Dynasty. At this time the evolution of the written word had come into its own and exhibited many similarities with the work of the succeeding period, the Classical Period of Egyptian literature.

The instructions are some of the few texts that identify an author. It is generally thought that the people to whom the texts are attributed are genuine people, for example, Prince Hardjedef, the son of King Khufu of the Fourth Dynasty (ca. 2575–ca. 2465 B.C.E.), and the vizier Ptahhotep, who lived under King Isesi of the Fifth Dynasty. Some scholars, however, suggest that the names are pseudepigraphic, meaning that these were false names. These attributions do not correspond to other dating criteria, namely, the language in which the text was written. The "Instruction of Hardjedef" contains certain archaic phrases that may indicate a Fifth Dynasty date, but its structure makes a Fourth Dynasty date seem unlikely. The "Instructions Addressed to Kagemni" and the "Teaching of the Vizier Ptahhotep" are written in Middle Egyptian; therefore, they could not date to the early Old Kingdom, at least not in the form in which they are preserved. This situation in turn presents a whole new set of problems for dating because there is no parallel for an Old Egyptian text being translated into Middle Egyptian. Likewise, the mention of King Huni, the last king of the Third Dynasty (ca. 2649–ca. 2575 B.C.E.), and Snefru, the first king of the Fourth Dynasty, at the end of the "Instruction Addressed to Kagemni" confuses the matter further, in that the art form is more evolved in this text than in that of Hardjedef. These Old Kingdom examples inspired scribes to continue this genre, and it became very popular.

The situation was slightly different in the royal sphere in the Old Kingdom. Kings had no tomb inscriptions. Some scholars suggest that the lack of royal autobiographies is due to the sanctity of kingship, because a king's persona was stylized and idealized. The royalty of the Old Kingdom created three types of monumental inscriptions: the decree, the annals, and the recording of one event, none of which qualifies as literature. However, the royal religious compositions did include literary notions. The Pyramid Texts offer myriad literary devices that were written to ensure the successful transfiguration of the king's spirit into the afterlife. These texts were inscribed on the inside walls of the pyramids of some of the late Old Kingdom kings and queens. Various scholars have categorized them as poetry. As an example, Pyramid Texts "Utterance 337" reads as follows:

> Heaven shouts, earth trembles
> In dread of you, Osiris, at your coming!
> O you milch-cows here, O you nursing cows here,
> Turn about him, lament him, mourn him, bewail him,
> As he comes forth and goes to heaven
> Among his brothers, the gods!

First Intermediate Period

In the following period, the First Intermediate Period (ca. 2134–ca. 2040 B.C.E.), the tomb autobiography appeared on stelae, monumental slabs of stone or sometimes wood. The autobiography was accompanied by the offering prayer and a scene. The stela was the focal point of the private funerary cult. Since most of the tombs dating to the First Intermediate Period have been destroyed, these stelae function as an all-in-one funerary memorial. At the time, they were also handy because they were easy to transport to Abydos, the cult place of Osiris, so that the deceased could be near him.

The second type of literature that the First Intermediate Period produced was the royal instruction. This genre follows the idea of the Old Kingdom instruction, but instead the departing king educates his son and successor. Most likely such a work as the "Teaching for Merikare" was not composed by the father of Merikare but was commissioned by the reigning king. The "Teaching for Merikare" is an ambitious literary work and surpasses all previous instruction compositions. It is a treatise on kingship, and the historical context is assumed to be accurate. This type of literary genre was further developed in Hellenistic times and in the Islamic world; however, there is no direct correlation between its appearance in ancient Egypt and its later popularity. The work is preserved on three New Kingdom papyri. The topics presented in this composition consist of ways in which to defeat rebellion, deal with subjects (both rich and poor), acquire troops for battles, perform required religious duties, and be a good king.

Middle Kingdom

The works that were created up to this time were, for the most part, experimental. The Middle Kingdom (ca. 2040–ca. 1640 B.C.E.) was known as the Classical Period for both its use of language and its literary output. Vast numbers of works were composed at this time, and many new genres of literature appeared. The autobiographies of the Old Kingdom continued to be used and were now much more elaborate than before. They contain additional elements, such as hymns to deities and exultations of the king. The "Teaching of Amenemhet I" develops the themes first presented in the royal "Teaching for Merikare," in which the king cautions against fully trusting one's subjects. The themes of wisdom literature expanded in the Middle Kingdom, and two more types developed: laments and dialogues. The laments discuss the absence of truth and justice in a chaotic world. It has been postulated that the emergence of this type of literature at this time has to do with the poor state of affairs in Egypt during the First Intermediate Period. The prosperity that Egypt had previously enjoyed no longer existed. Others think that "pessimistic" literature was only a literary theme and had very little to do with the actual state of affairs when the pieces were composed.

Two examples of this type of wisdom text are the "Prophecy of Neferti" and the "Admonitions of Ipuwer." The "Prophecy of Neferti" was probably created as a form of propaganda to legitimize the rule of the reigning king Amenemhet I (r. ca. 1991–ca. 1962 B.C.E.), the same Amenemhet mentioned earlier. The "lament" takes the form of artificial despair that pervades the prophecy of the sage Neferti, who foretells the civil war and destruction that are to come. Amenemhet is the savior who will rescue Egypt from ruin. The idea of "national distress" was a societal issue that became a literary theme. This composition is preserved on Papyrus Leningrad, which dates to the Eighteenth Dynasty (ca. 1550–ca. 1295 B.C.E.), and on various ostraca that date to about 1295–1069 B.C.E.

The "Admonitions of Ipuwer" is another work that is thought to be centered on the notions of order versus chaos and social disorder—themes that did not carry over to New Kingdom literature. In this text the sage Ipuwer recounts the anarchy occurring within Egypt while he is speaking with a divinity, possibly the creator god:

> Lo, hearts are violent, storm sweeps the land,
> There's blood everywhere, no shortage of dead,
> The shroud calls out before one comes near it.
> Lo, many dead are buried in the river,
> The stream is the grave, the tomb became a stream.
> Lo, nobles lament, the poor rejoice,
> Every town says, "'Let us expel our rulers."
> This text could also be categorized as a dialogue.

The third category of instruction literature is the dialogue. Dialogues present contemplative discussions on various themes. The composition modernly entitled "Dispute between a Man and His Soul" is one example of a dialogue, or discourse. This text is very intriguing, and there is a variety of interpretations as to its exact significance. In general, the work explores the idea of death, its dreadfulness and its sacredness. One of the mainstream interpretations sees a man who is not enjoying life and is longing for death. His soul, on the other hand, wishes that he would stop complaining and enjoy life. The man is tired of living and repeatedly says so; his soul is angry at the man's complaints and threatens to leave him. According to ancient Egyptian religious belief, one cannot resurrect in the hereafter without one's soul (*ba*). This threat scares the man, and he tries to convince his soul of his opinion. In the end they rectify their differences and stay together.

"The Tale of the Eloquent Peasant" is another example of a dialogue, or discourse, of which there are four Middle Kingdom copies. In this narrative a peasant is robbed by a nobleman and appeals to the king's high steward for help. The peasant returns to the high steward nine times, each time providing the opportunity for a poetic speech, before his goods are returned. As it turns out, the high steward fervently enjoys the man's eloquence and therefore makes the man continue his speech until he can do so no longer. In this tale it is eloquent speech that is used to defend justice. In essence, this work is a serious discourse on social justice that humorously expounds the virtues of fine speech.

The second major category of Middle Kingdom literature is the fictional narrative. Examples of the fictional narrative include "The Shipwrecked Sailor," "The Tale of Sinuhe," "The Tale of King Neferkare and General Sasenet," and *Three Tales of Wonder*. These stories would be most familiar to the Western reader as examples of literature. Some suggest that these tales are derived from the educated class and were the products of the court. Thus, it would not appear that these written works evolved from oral folklore because of their content and the style in which they were written. Others believe that these narratives appear for the first time fully formed, perhaps suggesting that these same stories did exist in the oral tradition. Those pieces that belong to the late Middle Kingdom are less elaborate than those that date earlier; likewise, those appearing from the Twelfth Dynasty (ca. 1991–ca. 1783 B.C.E.) onward are written in a more colloquial language. These texts were privately owned. The Middle Kingdom stories were regarded as classics and have been discovered in private libraries from later periods. Some date to the Middle Kingdom, while a larger number of them date to the New Kingdom; examples are preserved from later periods. In the New Kingdom this corpus of texts was organized and used to instruct scribes on the classical language of Middle Egyptian.

The "Shipwrecked Sailor" survives in only one manuscript whose provenance is unknown. The story is about an official who is returning home from an unsuccessful venture and is worried about reporting to the court. He is accompanied by a subordinate who attempts to cheer him up. The subordinate tells him a wondrous tale about his own ship having once capsized, thus causing him to land on a desert island inhabited by an enormous snake. This tale is one of the simpler stories as far as Egyptian grammar is concerned and is actually a story within a story.

The "Story of Sinuhe" is considered the most advanced piece of Middle Kingdom literature. Numerous fragmentary copies of this work have been preserved, confirming its prominence within the literary sphere. This composition is a fictional autobiography of an official who takes flight from Egypt when he hears of the king's death. He lives abroad, marries a local chieftain's daughter, has a family, and achieves success. When he reaches old age, he wishes to return to Egypt. One of the major themes of this piece is the contrast between the ordered state of Egypt and the impulsive way of life abroad.

New Kingdom

The New Kingdom brought with it a continuation of all the old genres of literature. The autobiography is still represented in the "Autobiography of Ahmose, Son of Abana." Annal-style historical writing flourished in this new international age, as evidenced by the "Annals of Thutmose III" (r. 1479–1425 B.C.E.), the "Poetical Stela of Thutmose III," and the "Sphinx Stela of Amenhotep II" (r. 1427–1401 B.C.E.). Hymns to the gods were very popular in the New Kingdom, and the works from this period elaborate on those from the previous period. Two of the more significant hymns are the "Great Hymn to Osiris," recorded on the stela of Amenmose, and the "Great Hymn to the Aten," from the site of Amarna. In the realm of funerary literature the Book of the Dead continues the ideas of the Coffin Texts, which comprise a set of spells that were inscribed on coffins in the Middle Kingdom. These texts evolved from the Old Kingdom Pyramid Texts. Likewise, new books of the underworld emerged. There was also continuity from the Middle Kingdom in the narrative fiction.

Two new genres of literature appear in the New Kingdom—love poetry and the epic poem. Some suggest that the love poems are immature and simple; however, the appearance of new and rare words within this group of compositions reflects the precision with which these works were created. "The Poem" in the "Kadesh Battle Inscription" and the "Poetical Stela of Merneptah" are two examples of the latter genre. These works represent the first time that poetry had a narrative purpose. There were many relations between nations at this time, and many new ideas and concepts arrived in Egypt from its neighbors. Another interesting development was the emergence of school texts. A school text may consist of a variety of texts put together to make a "schoolbook," these texts having no relation to one another.

Late Period

In the Late Period narratives and instructions flourished. The tales at this time became longer and more complex. In the Ptolemaic Period (304–330 B.C.E), Greek themes mingle with Egyptian themes, and animal fables appear for the first time. So far, no school texts or love poems have come to light from this period. Many ancient Egyptian texts cannot be categorized under just one heading. For example, "The Tale of the Eloquent Peasant" is both a literary narrative about a man who petitions to get his goods back through dialogue and a lament that has a somewhat didactic undertone.

Most of Egyptian literature was anonymous. The emphasis was not placed on the author, and the texts were identified by their protagonists. The narratives also lacked titles; only the wisdom texts had titles. Specifically in the New Kingdom, there existed a series of literary texts that praised the scribal profession. The Egyptians held the idea that the tomb could crumble, but writing was imperishable. This idea was probably reinforced in society by the fact that ancient wisdom was clearly admired and wisdom literature was cherished. Certain preserved texts patently declare that the idea of being a scribe was a virtuous occupation. One such text states, "As for those scribes and sages from the time which came after the gods—those who would foresee what was to come, which happened—their names endure for eternity, although they are gone, although they completed their lifetimes and all their people are forgotten. . . . Be a scribe! Put it in your heart, that your name shall exist like theirs!" This text is a eulogy to dead scribes from Papyrus Chester Beatty IV. The ancient Egyptian scribes imagined writing as a means to immortality.

Ancient Egyptian literature was written in either hieroglyphic or hieratic (cursive) script. There was also an intermediary stage of cursive hieroglyphs. If hieroglyphic script corresponds to our modern printing, then hieratic script corresponds to our writing. Hieroglyphs were inscribed on stone, plaster, or wood and could be written from left to right, right to left, or top to bottom. Cursive hieroglyphs usually appear on wood or papyrus, and hieratic script usually appears on papyrus or writing boards. The Egyptians used papyrus as their main writing surface. This material came from the papyrus plant, which was grown in the marshy delta region in the north. Strips were cut from the plant and made into sheets. The papyrus rolls were used over and over again. Some papyri have various documents on them while others had the original text erased and then were reused. These are called "palimpsests." Scribes used both red and black ink. The red was used for titles and headings, corrections, insertions, and highlighting.

THE MIDDLE EAST

BY KIRK H. BEETZ

Among the world's earliest civilizations were those of the Near East, particularly those that arose in and around the modern-day countries of Iran and Iraq. The people who forged these civilizations thousands of years ago, including the Sumerians, Akkadians, Assyrians, and Babylonians, developed advanced and sophisticated cultures, with cities, libraries, scientific inquiry, legal codes, mathematical systems, trade and commerce, and religious institutions. They also gave the world some of its earliest written literature. For this reason, the ancient Near East, stretching from the eastern shore of the Mediterranean Sea to the easternmost border of modern-day Iran, has often been called the "Cradle of Civilization."

The most common literary form that survives from ancient Mesopotamia is the epic. An epic is a long narrative poem that chronicles the adventures of a heroic individual. This individual was often thought of as partly human and partly divine, so he was able to serve as a kind of mediator or link between gods and humankind. Typically, an epic has many of the characteristics of an adventure story. Historians as well as literary critics are interested in epics because they record myths and legends that are important to the culture from which they arose because of their legendary, religious, and historical significance.

Like many epics, the epics that emerged from ancient Mesopotamia were not strictly speaking "written" by one author as authorship is understood in modern life. Rather, these epics were compilations of stories and legends that had been transmitted orally for hundreds of years. Accordingly, while we sometimes have a colophon, in effect, the name of the scribe who copied a particular text and sometimes a date, at the end of a text, such names are only those of the learned scribes involved in the transmission of a given work, not its original composition. Mesopotamian literature was widely transmitted in written form wherever the tradition of cuneiform writing (a wedge-shaped script) was found. Thus, copies of well-known works also have been found at archaeological sites in Turkey, Syria, Iran, and Lebanon.

THE EPIC OF GILGAMESH

One of the world's great epic poems is the Epic of Gilgamesh, which was written sometime around 2000 B.C.E. The Epic of Gilgamesh is one of the oldest surviving works of literature, and its author, Shin-eqi-unninni, is the oldest writer of literature whose name is known. To call Shin-eqi-unninni the text's "author," though, is a little misleading, for stories and legends had been told about Gilgamesh for hundreds of years, and while the epic is the main Gilgamesh text, other poems and stories claim to record his deeds. Shin-eqi-unninni was therefore as much a compiler as he was an author, for he did not make up the stories and legends. However, he gave them a form that remains memorable, and the Epic of Gilgamesh has been translated into virtually all the world's major languages. It is also a common text read in literature courses, especially those that deal with ancient literature or the development of the epic form. Its topic is a historical king named Gilgamesh, who ruled the city of Uruk in southern Mesopotamia and is credited with building its city wall, probably around 2700 B.C.E.

The Epic of Gilgamesh was written on 12 clay tablets in Sumerian. This language has no resemblance to any other language in the world. The version of the epic that survives, though, is written in Akkadian, a Semitic language that was related to Arabic and to Hebrew. Akkadian was the language spoken by the Akkadians, Assyrians, and Babylonians. The first exemplar of the Epic of Gilgamesh known to Western scholars was found at Nineveh, near the modern-day Iraqi city of Mosul, in the ruins of a library amassed by Ashurbanipal, king of Assyria from 669 to 633 B.C.E.

The story of the Epic of Gilgamesh is a timeless one of adventure, seduction, rivalry, peril, battles, twists of fate, and floods. It influenced later epics, such as those written by the Greek poet Homer, as well as later epics written in the medieval period. The first tablet, or book, introduces Gilgamesh, the king of Uruk. He is one-third human and two-thirds god, and he is the strongest, most heroic person every created. At the opening of the epic he has become somewhat saddened and uncertain of his role as king. His subjects, however, believe his rule is too harsh; when they complain, Aruru, the goddess of creation, creates Enkidu to serve as Gilgamesh's rival, thinking that a rival will both perk up Gilgamesh and keep him in line. Enkidu is described as a wild man, but he is seduced by a priestess, Shamhat, who tames him and makes him a fitter companion for and rival to the king.

In the second book Enkidu challenges Gilgamesh. The two engage in a mighty battle, but Gilgamesh breaks off the fighting and proposes that the two adventure to the Cedar Forest to kill a demon. Cedar was a highly valuable wood in the region, for its oils make it resistant to rot from moisture; for this reason, cedar would have held great cultural significance as a symbol of some permanence in a world that could abruptly change from flooding. The third book details their preparations for the journey, and readers learn that they have gained the support of Shamash, the sun god. The fourth book narrates the events of their journey to the Cedar Forest, and then, in the fifth book, Gilgamesh and Enkidu, with help from Shamhat, kill Humbaba, a demon who guards the forest. They then fell the trees, turn them into a huge raft, and float them back to Uruk.

In the sixth book Gilgamesh is tempted by Ishtar, a goddess who is the daughter of Anu. Ishtar grows angry because Gilgamesh rejects her sexual advances, so she asks her father to send the Bull of Heaven to avenge her, but Gilgamesh and Enkidu kill the bull. Now the gods are angry, and in the seventh book they want to exact punishment on someone for killing the bull. The gods condemn Enkidu to death, but in the meantime he becomes ill. As he is dying, he describes the Netherworld, or underworld, to Gilgamesh. The eighth book consists of Gilgamesh's lament for the death of the man who has become his friend and companion.

Gilgamesh, having seen his friend die, wants to avoid death, so in the ninth book he makes a journey filled with perils to consult with Ut-napishtim and his wife. These two were the only humans to have survived the Great Flood, and the gods granted them immortality. Gilgamesh hopes that they can share with him the secret of immortality. While he is on the journey, he encounters Siduri, an alewife who tries to turn his from his quest.

In the 10th book Gilgamesh crosses the Waters of Death in the company of a ferryman, Urshanabi. In the epic's climactic 11th book Gilgamesh meets up with Ut-napishtim, who recounts for him the events surrounding the Great Flood—again, a common motif in a region susceptible to flooding. With reluctance, he agrees to offer Gilgamesh a chance at immortality by telling him that if he can remain awake for six days and seven nights, he will achieve immortality. Gilgamesh, however, has been fatigued by his travels and adventures and falls asleep. Ut-napishtim believes that Gilgamesh will deny that he has slept, so he has his wife bake one loaf of bread for each day Gilgamesh sleeps. The loaves of bread would be proof of Gilgamesh's failure.

When Gilgamesh awakens, Ut-napishtim offers his king another chance at immortality by telling him about a plant that will make him young again if he eats it, but only if he can retrieve the plant from the bottom of the sea. Gilgamesh succeeds in obtaining the plant, but he does not eat it, for he wants share it with others in Uruk. He decides to bathe, so he places the plant on the shore, where a snake steals it. Gilgamesh has lost both of his opportunities to achieve immortality. When he returns to Uruk and sees its imposing walls, he realizes that mortals can achieve a kind of immortality by building lasting cultures and civilizations. While the epic nominally consists of 12 books, the last book was written later and added to the first 11. In that book Enkidu is still alive, so the book is out of sequence. Most literary historians regard the 12th book as a separate work.

The Atrahasis Epic

In a region of the world that flooded every year, it comes as no surprise that floods and their consequences would play a major role in the fate of characters. Flooding, too, occurs in cycles, and it was this cycle of death and rebirth that people wanted to understand and, if possible, escape. In the Epic of Gilgamesh, one of the central events narrated is the Great Flood, but as noted, the epic is in a sense a compilation of stories and myths. One of these myths is the Atrahasis epic, which provides more detail about a great flood. Scholars believe that the Atrahasis epic formed the basis of the flood story in Gilgamesh and that, in fact, the Atrahasis epic was incorporated into Gilgamesh. It is also worth noting that historians and theologians believe that the Babylonian flood stories formed the basis for the story of the biblical Flood and Noah's ark in the book of Genesis. For this reason the Atrahasis epic is sometimes referred to as the "Babylonian Genesis."

Historians date the oldest copy of the Atrahasis epic to sometimes around 1646 to 1626 B.C.E., during the reign of Ammisaduqa, the great-grandson of the great Babylonian lawgiver, Hammurabi. For hundreds of years scribes continued to copy and transmit the epic, which was originally written in Akkadian. The epic outlines the cosmology of the ancient Babylonians—that is, their view of the world and or creation—who saw the heavens as ruled by the god Anu, the earth ruled by Enlil, and the oceans by Enki. The epic opens with Enlil ordering the lesser gods to work the land as farmers and to control the waters with irrigation ditches, but when the lesser gods refuse to continue work after a period of 3,600 years, Enki proposes that humans be created to do the work. Thus, a goddess named Mami creates humans out of clay mixed with spit and the blood of the god Aw-ilu, who dies in the process.

Enki, who regards humans as his creation because he proposed creating them, warns Atrahasis, whose name means "extremely wise," to tear down his reed house and build a boat to escape a great flood that Enlil is planning to send to destroy humankind—after already having sent a plague, a drought, and a famine. Throughout, Enki acts as a savior to humankind, filling the river with fish, for example, to feed the people during the famine. Atrahasis complies, builds an elaborate boat similar to Noah's ark, and boards the boat with his family and animals.

The flood rages for seven days. When it ends, Atrahasis offers sacrifices to the gods, who realize that by destroying humans, they also have destroyed their labor force and the source of food offerings to them. Enlil, who had been upset by the noise of the cities that disturbed his sleep, is angry, for he had planned to eliminate humans, but Enki stands up to him; eventually the two reach an agreement about how they will control the human population in the future. At this point the story breaks off, and readers never learn the fate of Atrahasis.

The Atrahasis epic closely parallels the story of the Great Flood narrated in the 11th book of the Epic of Gilgamesh. In comparing the two versions, scholars note many similarities in language and detail, but they also see differences that show the hand of an editor, who changed details. In particular, the Atrahasis epic depicts the gods as having human characteristics, such as the ability to experience hunger, thirst, and fear. In the Epic Gilgamesh, these particulars are changed or omitted, thereby giving the gods more divine, all-powerful qualities.

The *Enûma Elish*

So far, the focus has been on myths of destruction, with flooding as an important motif. The ancient Sumerians also had a creation myth, one that, like the flood story, has many parallels with the biblical account of Creation in the book of Genesis. This creation myth, called *Enûma Elish* from its first words, meaning "when on high," dates probably to around the eighth century B.C.E. It was written in Akkadian and, like the Gilgamesh epic, was found in fragmentary form at the ruined library of Ashurbanipal. It consists of about 1,000 lines on seven tablets. While most of the fifth tablet is lost, most of the rest of the text is relatively complete. Historians have concluded that the text was used in religious ceremonies and probably was read aloud to mark the beginning of the new year.

The *Enûma Elish* focuses on Marduk, the greatest of the gods. His greatness is attested to by the sixth and seventh tablets, which record the 50 names by which he was known. The origins of the world, at a time before the sky and the earth were separated, are described in the first tablet. Again, biblical historians note the similarly between this myth and the account in Genesis, when "the earth was without form and void, and darkness was upon the face of the deep." At that time, there were two gods, a male god named Apsu and a female goddess named Tiamat. Apsu is the god of freshwater and Tiamat the goddess of the salt ocean waters, and it was as bodies of water that these two gods existed.

These two give birth to Lahmu and Lahamu, who are depicted as snakes and represent the life-giving silt of the rivers, in much the same way that God in Genesis ordered "the dry land appear" and separated the land from the water. They give birth to Anshar and Kishar, who in turn give birth to a son named Anu, who gives birth to Ea. Although each new generation of gods has more power than the previous generation, the younger gods become unruly and ill behaved. They refuse to listen to their father, Apsu, while the matriarch, Tiamat, does nothing to restrain them.

In disgust, Apsu decides to dispose of his progeny, but Ea learns of his plans, casts a spell on him, and kills him while he sleeps. Ea then builds a temple on the body of Apsu, where he lives with his consort Damkina, who gives birth to a son, Marduk, destined to be a hero-king. For Marduk's amusement, Anu creates the four winds, which continuously disturb Tiamat, the ocean, and finally goad her into action, with the backing of the other gods. She decides to declare war on Marduk, so she gathers an army of monsters and gods to fight Marduk. This army was lead by Kingu, variously described as her son and lover.

At this point, portions of the text are missing, so scholars can only infer details, but when the story resumes, Marduk has agreed to fight Tiamat, but only if his backers name him the supreme god if he emerges victorious from the battle. Armed with a bow, one arrow, a mace, lightning, a net, and seven hurricanes and with his body filled with fire, Marduk goes off to do battle in his chariot. With his hurricanes churning up the ocean, he challenges Tiamat to a battle and then throws the net over her and her army. When she tries to swallow him, he uses the hurricanes to split open her jaw and a single arrow to rend her body. Now the supreme god, he sets about creating the world, including humankind, doomed to physical labor so that the gods can live in leisure.

ASIA AND THE PACIFIC

BY JUSTIN CORFIELD

Literature in the Asia and Pacific regions of the ancient world was well advanced, and many works survive from the period either in original form or, more often, in later copies. During the late 19th century and the early 20th centuries many of these works were translated into European languages, mainly English, and provide historians with an understanding of society in the respective areas at the time.

India

Although some writing survives from the period of the Indus Valley civilizations from between 2500 and 1800 B.C.E., it comes from seals and short inscriptions and cannot really be regarded as literature. Indian literature traces its origins to the Vedas, the main Hindu sacred writings, which were written in Sanskrit. To these have been added later prose commentaries called the Brahmanas and the Upanishads. The Vedas have been regularly updated; although some parts date to 1400 B.C.E., most come from the first to seventh centuries C.E., with other sections being added as late as 1200 C.E.

The Vedas, written in archaic Sanskrit, represent the religious thinking of the Indo-Aryan peoples who settled India in the period 1400–1200 B.C.E. Forming the basis of Hindu beliefs, the Vedas refer to the cosmic forces, such as fire, the sun, war, storms, rain, and creation. In them various gods, such as Indra and Vishnu, appear to explain these concepts. Initially these ideas were remembered orally, possibly with the help of brief manuscripts, but later were written down. As a result, there are several different versions of the work. The Upanishads build on some of the ideas in the Vedas and take their name from the term that means "sitting at the feet of a teacher." In all there are 108 surviving Upanishads, and they have a special philosophical concern with developing the idea of a supreme being and directing knowledge at a reunion between mortals and that being.

The other great epics of Sanskrit literature are the Mahabharata and Ramayana. The former is a heroic epic based on a battle for supremacy between two families of cousins, the Kauravas and the Pandavas. The story evolved considerably during the period 400 B.C.E.–200 C.E. and runs to about 100,000 couplets (or about 1.8 million words), making it the longest surviving epic of this period; it is about seven times as long as the *Iliad* and the *Odyssey* combined, making it also the longest surviving epic poem in the world. The date for its setting is said to be 1302 B.C.E., and according to legend, its authorship is attributed to the sage Vyasa. It begins with a prince who is blind and is passed over for succession to the throne by his father, the king. Rivalry starts between the prince's descendants and those of his younger brother, who takes the throne. This rivalry leads to a series of great battles that shows the balance between good and evil and, like the *Iliad* and the *Odyssey*, serves to teach people about the problems people face in life, including romance, greed, valor, and human frailties. The story does not end with the "great" battle but continues with details of bickering following the battle, further infighting among members of the successful faction, and continued troubles. It ends with the life of Krishna. There are numerous subplots, with many characters from the contending families and also gods and demons. One aim of the poem is to elucidate the four main goals in human existence: *kama* ("pleasure"), *artha* ("wealth"), *dharma* ("duty"), and *moksha* ("liberation").

The Ramayana dates to 300 B.C.E., though a few historians believe that some parts are possibly 200 years older. Altogether it consists of 24,000 couplets. It tells of the romance of Prince (later King) Rama in Ajodhya (modern-day Oudh), from his royal birth through to his falling in love with Sita. Rama manages to bend the great bow of Siva in a test of strength (showing some similarities to the end of the *Odyssey*). Rama is then banished to the forests with his new wife and also his brother. There Sita is seized by Ravana, the 10-headed king of the demons, and taken to Lanka (modern-day Sri Lanka).

Rama then allies himself with Hanuman, the monkey god, and a war ensues, with Rama seeking to rescue Sita and Ravana and calling on a collection of demons to protect him. The monkeys attack Lanka, eventually taking the island. Ravana is killed, and Sita is rescued. Although the story revolves around Rama, the loyalty of his brother, Laksamana, and the cunning of Hanuman are both major factors in the story. In addition to these main characters, numerous other Indian gods make brief appearances, and the Ramayana serves to introduce them to the reader. However, because many people of ancient times were unable to read, the literary tradition quickly lent itself to theater, with the Ramayana being relatively easy to perform and the ex-

Sculpted panel depicting Vishnu Trivikrama, eastern India (10th century C.E.); the myth of Vishnu Trivikrama appears in the earliest of Indian texts, the Rig-Veda. (© The Trustees of the British Museum)

aggerated nature of many of the characters leading to their easy recognition by the audience.

While Sanskrit was the language used for Hindu scriptures, Buddhist literary works tended to be written in Pali, and those of the Jains in Ardhamagadhi. All three, especially the first two, were to have a major influence on Indian culture and also on the Indian diaspora. Tamil, in southern India, gradually established a literature of its own, though it has incorporated some Sanskrit stories. Pali would also become important in Buddhist areas of Southeast Asia, such as modern-day Cambodia and Indonesia. Indeed, the Buddhist literary tradition also served to explain many problems of the world as experienced through the life of Lord Buddha and his subsequent teachings.

Southeast Asia

In Indian-influenced Southeast Asia the Mahabharata and especially the Ramayana became an important part of literature in modern-day Cambodia and Indonesia. In the former some early local legends survive from the ancient period, mainly involving the *nagas*—many-headed snakes—and also the founding of the Funan Empire in about 200 C.E. by Kaudinya, an Indian prince who married the daughter of a local naga.

Early literature in Indonesia also involved the Ramayana, albeit a slightly different version, adapted for Sumatran or Javanese circumstances. As in Cambodia, the story was acted rather than written down, and gradually the plot was adapted to allow for local traditions to be incorporated. Although it was still acted out as in Cambodia, in Indonesia the central part of the story was often told within the context of a *wayang kulit* performance, with shadow puppets and necessarily few characters.

China

Unlike the oral literary traditions of Southeast Asia, China has the longest continuous written literary tradition in the world, dating back to at least the 14th century B.C.E. Although there have been many changes in the Chinese language, and the characters have changed since the early scripts of the Shang Dynasty (ca. 1500–ca. 1045 B.C.E.)—and pronunciation has changed dramatically—the tradition is certainly a continuous one. Curiously, invaders often adopted the Chinese script rather than compelling the Chinese to use their own, and the Chinese script was also used in Vietnam until the French romanized the script in the 19th century. It was also used in Korea in ancient and early medieval times.

The earliest examples of Chinese script are carved on bones and tortoiseshells from the Shang Dynasty. These are often called "oracle bones" because there was a tradition by which questions were carved on the shoulder blades of oxen or on tortoiseshells, which were then heated, with the cracks that appeared determining the answer to a question posed. In 1899 a scholar, Wang Yirong, started to transcribe some of the inscriptions, and many of the early surviving ones that have been deciphered describe royal and religious activities. In all there are some 20,000 pieces in the Academia Sinica, now in Taiwan. Those on late Shang bronze vessels and also brief surviving genealogies are too brief to be regarded as literature by some scholars. However, they do show the use of 3,400 characters (of which two-thirds have been deciphered), indicating a wide vocabulary.

It was during the Zhou Dynasty (1045–256 B.C.E.) that many great works of literature were compiled. These detailed myths about the creation of the world and the founding of China seek to explain many natural and historical events. Unfortunately, the vast majority have not survived in their original form, largely because the first emperor of China, from the Qin Dynasty (221–207 B.C.E.), Qin Shi Huang, ordered the "burning of the books" in 213 B.C.E. Although he did allow some exceptions, notably medical works and some works praising him, his order resulted in the destruction of many early works of Chinese literature. The great Confucian works, however, survived the burning of the books. These works consist of the *Lun yü* (Conversations), and the *Analects,* which are collected teachings of Confucius (551–479 B.C.E.). Confucius taught extensively about philosophy and morality. His request for filial piety and for people to respect the emperor ensured that his works survived when those of many other sages were undoubtedly destroyed. In addition to having many works destroyed, Qin Shi Huang also had a large number of scholars executed. According to one account, 460 scholars were buried alive. According to Wei Hong, a second-century scholar, 1,160 scholars were buried alive. The "burial of the scholars," as the incident came to be known, ensured, at least in the short-term, that Qin Shi Huang's view of history survived.

After Qin Shi Huang's reign there were attempts by scholars to reconstruct the texts that had been lost. During the Han Dynasty (202 B.C.E.–220 C.E.) scholars tried to write down many of the old stories. Some were clearly later literary works, but many incorporated pieces of literature that may have survived or may have been remembered by people. On occasion Han historians quite clearly added new material or in some cases tried to clarify ambiguities in previous works.

Apart from the works of Confucius, another survivor from before the reign of Qin Shi Huang was the *Dao de jing* (Classic of the Way of Power) of Lao-tzu. It is the principle work of Daoism, a Chinese philosophy that venerates the "feminine" qualities that promote longevity as well as equanimity and unity with nature. There was also the book of Meng-tzu, or Mencius (ca. 371–ca.289 B.C.E.), the collected thoughts of the sage put together by his students. The other major work to survive is a series of five books from the Zhou Dynasty known as the *Wu ching* (Five Classics). These consist of the *I ching* (Classic of Changes), the *Shu ching* (History Classics), the *Shih ching* (Poetry Classics), the *Li chi* (Record of Rites), and the *Ch'un-ch'iu* (Spring and Autumn Annals).

The *I ching* describes cosmology, and the *Shu ching* is a collection of official documents. The *Shih ching* is an anthology of poetry from the time of Confucius and includes some 305 separate poems. Four of the longer ones, about 400 lines each, go over historical events. None of the poems is very long, suggesting that there was no epic poetry tradition as there was in India and elsewhere in the ancient world. The *Li chi* covers many court rites, along with anecdotes, and the last book, the *Ch'un-ch'iu*, is a history of the feudal kingdom of Lu, which included the town where Confucius was born.

During the Qin Dynasty, Qin Shi Huang ensured that his own accomplishments were recorded in detail. By this time printing was being used in a limited way; the earliest fully printed book was not produced until 868 B.C.E. Printing obviously made it easier to produce many copies of works. As the Chinese language did not suit movable type, books were produced from a carved wooden block of an entire page. Printing methods became more effective during the Han Dynasty, and the *Huai-nan-tzu* (The Master of Huai-nan) was written in about 140 B.C.E.

The next major work was the first detailed history of China. Written from about 85 B.C.E., the *Shih-chi* (Historical Records) took 18 years to complete and ran to 520,000 words, in 130 chapters, covering the 2,000 years of Chinese history. In some ways it is similar to the *Histories* of the Greek writer Herodotus (ca. 484–between 430 and 420 B.C.E.), who sought to write down everything he knew about history. However, the *Shih-chi* is a far more serious work, lacking the idiosyncrasies of Herodotus's text, though it is lively and does tell anecdotes about some of the characters. The work seems to have inspired the poet and historian Pan Piao, who put together the *Han shu* (Han Documents), which relate in 800,000 words the history of the Han Dynasty. The aim of the book is to draw from previous texts, and the *Shih-chi* includes a "catalogue" of works consulted. A large number of the texts listed in this bibliography have not survived.

In 26 B.C.E. one of the emperors of the Han Dynasty, Cheng Di (r. 32–7 B.C.E.), tried to undo some of the damage done during the destruction of the books by Qin Shi Huang, ordering that copies of all literary works be assembled in his capital, with a view to copying them and augmenting the imperial collection. He was also keen on ensuring that the "correct" manuscripts were being kept. The works were all copied onto silken scrolls, helping to preserve many works that might otherwise have been lost.

The poetry of the Qin Dynasty and especially that of the Han Dynasty often led to long poems reflecting the glory of the Chinese Empire, its wealth, and its structure, and also starting to include information about everyday life. The Yüeh Fu (Music Bureau) was reestablished in 125 B.C.E., and it started to gather earlier songs and music that were collected together centrally, possibly for the first time on an organized scale. The ballads collected include some early poems, such as *Lo-fu hsing* or *Mo-shang sang* (The Song of Lo-fu or Roadside Mulberry Tree), in which a government commissioner gives a ride in his carriage to a young lady he meets in his travels.

The collapse of the Han Dynasty and the subsequent wars resulted in the period known as the Six Dynasties (220–589 C.E.). In northern China warlike tribes invaded and gradually came to adopt Chinese ways, including literary traditions. In the south Chinese culture prevailed, with poems with a romantic theme being more popular than the military epics of the north. These differences became accentuated for several centuries, though the unity of the later Sui Dynasty and Tang Dynasty did result in a fusion of the two concepts. The relative peace of the Tang Dynasty also allowed for more literary works from earlier periods to be written down and reinterpreted.

Vietnam and Korea

In Vietnam, occupied by China for more than a thousand years, from 111 B.C.E. to 939 C.E., the Chinese literary tradition took over from the previous folk ballads, and the Vietnamese came to adopt the Chinese script. Classical Chinese was used for official proclamations as well as for inscriptions on a number of early Vietnamese stelae that survive from this period. The variations in language tended to come from the recording of legends and Vietnamese mythical heroes as well as from stories that sought to portray Vietnamese as different from Chinese, such as the early accounts of the Trung sisters, who led the Vietnamese against the Chinese for three years (39–42 C.E.). Although the main account of their lives was from a chronicle written in 1272 C.E., the amount of detail in it shows that it must have come from an ancient text.

At the same time, Chinese merchants came to settle in other parts of Asia and proved to be a major influence on early literature in Korea, which also used Chinese characters before adopting its own national alphabet. Ancient Korean poems tend to follow Chinese themes and styles, using a system known as Hyangga poetry, in which Korean and Chinese words are used, with some characters taken from one language and other concepts expressed in characters from the other. This system continued until medieval times, with the first changes coming about in the seventh century C.E. Many of these Korean poems survive, as do other early literary works that include texts on Confucian ideas, Buddhism, and also Daoism.

Japan

Japanese literature also traces its origins from Chinese literary styles, and the Japanese originally used the Chinese script to record their thoughts. The oldest-known Japanese inscription, on a sword from 440 C.E., clearly shows the use of Chinese characters to cover Japanese names and expressions. Gradually the Japanese came to use their own characters, but not until the eighth century C.E. Indeed, the term "ancient" Japanese literature often refers to the works of the eighth century C.E.

Polynesia

Although there is no written literature from the Pacific during this period, there are legends and stories that may have originated from ancient times. Many of them concern great sea epics and journeys of early Polynesian sailors, many entwined with legends of the gods and deities, often reflecting some degree of violence and cruelty. The strong oral traditions in Polynesia were noted during the 19th century by many of the early European anthropologists, who were able to compare the oral literary traditions of various islands and detail the common themes, some of which appear to date back to the original settlement of the Pacific islands by the Polynesian seafarers. There is also some linguistic evidence of seafarers from mainland Asia having arrived in some of the Pacific islands by 2500 B.C.E. If scholars are correct about this date, then some early Chinese literary traditions also survive in the Pacific. If one rejects the concept of Mu, the "submerged sea kingdom" of the Pacific, as most scholars do, the similarity in concepts around the Pacific islands can be explained only by regular contact between the various islands.

Australia

Although there was no written literature of the Aboriginal peoples of Australia, they have maintained a very strong oral tradition, with stories that seek to explain the creation of the world, the formation of land and sea, and the origins of rivers and other land features. From the oldest continuous civilization in the world, in the areas where it still flourishes, Aboriginal oral tradition has been shown to reflect stories going back thousands of years. Some early drawings illustrate many of these stories, known as the "Dreamtime," and anthropologists have worked hard to record these epics. Differences in the stories reflect the many Aboriginal tribes that exist in Australia and provide a far more philosophical outlook than many of the other stories of the Asia and Pacific region during ancient times.

EUROPE

BY RUSSELL M. LAWSON

The literature of ancient Europe includes some of the finest examples of oral and written expression in epic verse and poetry by the illiterate and literate peoples of the British Isles and western, central, and eastern Europe. Like the early poetry that the Greeks created, the Germans, Gauls, Celts, Saxons, and Norse of ancient Europe (before 500 C.E.) composed stories and poems about great heroes, past events, the divine and supernatural, nature, and human feelings. Whereas the Greeks after 700 B.C.E. put into written words their oral compositions—for example, Homer's *Iliad* and *Odyssey* and Hesiod's *Theogony* and *Works and Days*—northern Europeans of antiquity maintained their exclusive reliance on the spoken word.

Illiterate bards made their living traveling, composing, and reciting great epics and poems. Verse allowed for ease of recollection. The basic structure of the story was tailored specifically to the circumstances of each telling. Bards relied on memory as well as the creative impulse present at each performance. Repetitions in poems and stories were techniques that helped bards get their poetic bearings and helped the audience not to lose track of the story. Eventually, a literate bard recorded in writing the poem or story in its final rendering. Indeed, much of the ancient literature of Europe is known only through medieval (after 500 C.E.) versions.

Germans and Gauls

Since ancient northern European cultures were oral and illiterate, evidence of their eloquence and verse comes from external sources, especially those of the Romans and Greeks, who had much contact with the Gauls, Germans, and Celts. The Roman Cato approved of the eloquence of the Gauls, as did the first century B.C.E. Greek writer Diodorus Siculus. The Roman historian Cornelius Tacitus, who wrote *De origine et situ Germanorum*, commonly known as *Germania*, in Latin in the early second century C.E., described the oral culture of the ancient German tribes. The Germans, according to Tacitus, sang of the deeds and travels of heroes of the past and of the gods of the woodlands and streams. "In the traditional songs which form their only record of the past," he wrote in *Germania*, "the Germans celebrate an earth-born god called Tuisto. His son Mannus is supposed to be the fountain-head of their race and himself to have begotten three sons who gave their names to three groups of tribes—the Ingaevones, nearest the sea; the Herminones, in the interior; and the Istaevones, who comprise all the rest." Tacitus also recorded that the Germans lauded Hercules and sang songs in his honor.

That the Germans and Gauls worshipped Hercules, whom the ancient world pictured as a human of supernatural strength, as the god of eloquence, reveals that they considered eloquence to be as important as physical strength. The Gauls were specialists in the panegyric, a formal writing of praise for a person that was often used in the Roman Empire in the third and fourth centuries C.E. Indeed, Gauls were frequently hired as tutors to Roman students seeking to learn eloquence. The Roman orator Symmachus of the fourth century C.E. was trained in the art of rhetoric by a Gallic orator.

The northern European bards, like their counterparts in the ancient Mediterranean and Near East, were possessed of a singular, mystical gift, blessed by the gods, it was believed, above all others with the ability to perceive and sing the truth. Lords and kings retained bards at their great halls during feasts, to entertain the dinner guests with songs of old. One lord, named Lovernius, a Celt who lived in the first century B.C.E., loved his feasts and entertainments. "When at length he fixed a day for the ending of the feast," wrote the Greek observer Posidonius (ca. 135–ca. 51 B.C.E.), "a Celtic poet who arrived too late met Lovernius and composed a song magnifying his greatness and lamenting his own late arrival. Lovernius was very pleased and asked for a bag of gold and threw it to the poet who ran besides his chariot. The poet picked it up and sang another song." A century later the Roman satirist Juvenal (ca. 55 or 60–ca. 127 C.E.) joked that "eloquent Gaul has taught the Britons to plead a case."

The ancient Gauls were Celtic peoples. During the several centuries before and after the birth of Christ, the free and independent Celts who resisted conquest and incorporation into the Roman Empire became isolated in the British Isles. Julius Caesar (100–44 B.C.E.), the Roman conqueror of Gaul (France) and first Roman invader of England, wrote an account of his military conquests in the *Commentarii de bello Gallico*. Caesar's book focused mostly on military affairs, though he also provided scattered accounts of the culture of the Gauls. The ancient Celts, he wrote, held the Druids in the highest esteem. The Druids were religious leaders whose authority extended to education, criminal proceedings, and government. As the intellectual and cultural leaders of the Celts, they attracted many students. "It is said," Caesar wrote, "that these pupils have to memorize a great number of verses—so many, that some of them spend twenty years at their studies. The druids believe that their religion forbids them to commit their teachings to writing," as they do "not want their doctrine to become public property, and in order to prevent their pupils from relying on the written word and neglecting to train their memories."

With the power of the spoken word at their disposal, the Druids taught their disciples about the great mysteries of life, such as the idea of reincarnation. During his attempted conquest of Britain in 55–54 B.C.E., Caesar discovered the commonalities of the Celtic culture of Gaul and Britain, that Druidism was important in both places, that the Gauls considered Britain as the source of Druidism, and that the British people had a long oral tradition of being the original inhabitants of the island.

The Celts of the British Isles

The Celtic peoples of Britain initially repulsed the Roman invasion under Caesar, but finally succumbed to the larger, more organized attack of the emperor Claudius in 43 C.E. Under the Roman occupation of almost four centuries, the Celts resisted political and cultural Romanization, and varied Celtic kingdoms retained some independence in what is today Scotland and Wales; the Romans never attacked Ireland, which remained a Celtic stronghold. As Roman control lessened in the late fourth and early fifth centuries C.E., the Celts were forced to contend with a new invasion by the Saxons of Europe. The Celtic defense sparked heroic legends told for centuries. One story involved a Celtic king, Arthur, identified by the later Celtic historian Gildas (d. 570 C.E.) as Aurelius Ambrosianus, who made a heroic defense against the Saxons on the Welsh border. Celtic Wales was dominated by oral rather than literary tradition, and professional bards, the *cyfarwyddiaid*, passed along prose stories based on ancient tales into the European Middle Ages.

Celtic oral traditions in poetry and prose found a home in ancient and medieval Ireland. The Irish bards, the *filid*, told stories and poems with a strong emphasis on nature and the supernatural, on heroic warriors and great battles. Bards were attached to the court of a king or lord and nightly entertained the feasting revelers at the lord's hearth. Like the heroic literature of other cultures, such as the ancient Mediterranean, Irish Celtic heroic verse and prose focused on kings and warriors of extraordinary strength and courage whose martial abilities relied on a high degree of hubris and extreme individualism in the pursuit of honor and glory. Warriors bragged of their prowess on the field of battle before taking to arms. Warfare was a human's highest calling, hence only members of the aristocracy were warriors. Duration of life was less important than whether or not one acted according to a code of valor. Gods who took human form (anthropomorphic gods), spirits of nature, were capricious and jealous, and played an often-disruptive role in human affairs.

Early Irish heroic sagas include the *Táin Bó Cualnge*, which is the account of warfare among Irish nobles over a prize bull. Another, the *Fled Bricrenn*, is the story of warriors at a feast fighting over the best portions of the meat. Diodorus Siculus described such a competition among Gauls of the first century B.C.E.: "When they dine, . . . they have hearths with big fires and cauldrons, and spits loaded with big joints of meat. . . . Some of the company often fall into an altercation and challenge one another to single combat—they make nothing of death." An early Irish epic love story is the *Longas mac n-Usnig*, the tragic story of lost love, in which Deirdre, raised to marry Lord Conchobar, falls in love instead with Naisi, a warrior serving under the lord. The two lovers flee north but eventually come back under promise of safety. On returning, however, Naisi and his men are attacked and killed, and Deidre kills herself in despair.

Irish bards composed beautiful verse about nature and the mysteries of the divine. One of the earliest examples is *The Mystery*, composed (perhaps) before the Common Era by the Druid Amergin. *The Mystery* is one of a series of poems from *Lebor Gabála*, *The Book of Invasions*, which describes the settlement of Ireland as a series of military invasions by various groups of warriors. The theme of *The Mystery* is that all of nature—its beauty, power, glory—can be summarized by the "I," the poet himself. "I am the wind which breathes upon the sea, / I am the wave of the ocean, / I am the murmur of the billows."

Irish verse about the natural world is brief, descriptive, and powerful in evoking the grandeur and wonder of nature. Poetry about the supernatural involves heroic people, usually princes and princesses, who fall in and out of love, and repeatedly suffer a range of emotions—sickness, despair, longing, fulfillment. The divine is shadowy and inexact in these poems, often making its appearance by means of magic and supernatural phenomena.

Anglo-Saxons

By the end of the sixth century C.E. the Celts of Britain had scattered to remote locations (Wales and Ireland) in the face of the onslaught of Germanic invaders from Europe—the Angles, Saxons, and Jutes. The Anglo-Saxons who ruled Britain during the subsequent four centuries brought their Germanic customs, heritage, and language, including reliance upon ancient stories and songs to recall past heroes and heroic deeds. The Anglo-Saxon bards were called *scops*, and the poems they recited were *lays*. As in other cultures relying heavily upon oral tradition, the scop performed before warriors, lords, and ladies banqueting in great halls. The performance took place nightly for successive days, as the scop sang songs of the past, changing and adapting them as warranted by circumstances and the audience. The theme of the lay was the heroic code of valor and brave deeds. An example is *Widsith*, which in its current literary form dates from the seventh century, but which is mentioned here because it includes structure and verse that dates from an earlier ancient time. The poem is an account of the journey of the poet Widsith and a recollection of all the places he has visited and all the kings and warriors he has known from earlier times in Europe, before the Anglo-Saxon invasion of England.

Another example of a lay recited by a scop is *Beowulf*, the eighth-century literary version of which, like *Widsith*, was based on earlier oral traditions and stories. Indeed *Beowulf*, like Homer's *Iliad* and *Odyssey*, was meant to be sung by a bard rather than read. The story is based on a heroic code of the Germanic past, where the worth of a person is based on great deeds and courage. Beowulf, a king of the Geats, is a hero who fights monsters such as Grendel without flinching, emerging victorious in the end. Even when he dies of wounds suffered from fighting the Dragon that threatens his kingdom and people, it is an honorable death, made memorable by his courage, the stuff of which bards will sing for years to come.

Runes

The Germanic tribes of Europe and their descendants, the Saxons and the Norse, devised a script that was native to their lands and peoples and not significantly influenced by Latin or Greek. The runic script, called the *futhark*, developed during the third century c.e., was based on 24 characters. The runic script was a simple form of inscribing a single word or short phrase of identification or indication, which was done by cutting letters into wood or stone with a blade or chisel. Runic letters were composed of single-stroke lines that were vertical or diagonal but never circular or horizontal. A straight vertical line | was the letter *i*. The symbol < was the letter *k*. The symbol ↑ was the letter *t*. The symbol ◊ was the letter *n*, pronounced as an *ng* sound.

The Germanic peoples developed and used the runes at the close of the ancient world to identify personal ownership of property or to indicate the name of the rune master who carved the letters. Some ancient Germans believed that the runic letters and words themselves were magical. Runes were carved into battle implements, such as shields or swords, as a means of magic for protection or to help wage battle. The owner of a sword that had been named *Márr* inscribed on it the magic words: "May Márr spare nobody." The ancient runic script was not a literary device, though some of the earliest Anglo-Saxon poems used runes as abbreviations for phrases.

GREECE

by David K. Underwood and Michael J. O'Neal

The literature of the ancient Greek world spans more than a thousand years, from the epic poetry of Homer in the late eighth century b.c.e. to the first century of the Common Era. Turning their oral traditions and legends into written form, the Greeks created the first great body of Western literature: a vast corpus of poetry, prose, dramatic art, philosophy, history, biography, and criticism, which, through its availability to a large literate public, preserved and passed down a tradition of canonical works that defined the identity of their civilization, its ideals, and its standards. The earliest works of Greek literature reflect the impact and creativity of the roving bards, who retold the heroic stories, myths, and legends of the world of ancient Mycenae and the Heroic Age.

The Iliad and the Odyssey

Foremost among these heroic tales is the story of the Greek expedition that conquered the wealthy trading city of Troy, also known as Ilium, on the Ionian or western coast of Asia Minor, in modern-day Turkey. The oral tradition recounting this episode of Greek history served as the raw material from which a great poet, whom the Greeks called Homer, composed the two epic masterpieces in hexameter verse (consisting of six metrical feet) that became the classic texts of Greek literature: the *Iliad* and the *Odyssey*. Dating to the end of the eighth century b.c.e., Homer's works were probably among the first to make use of a new alphabetic script that developed in the Greek world at that time. These two texts were more than literature: They represented the ethical standards by which Greek men and women were to lead their lives in relation to each other and to the gods. Like the Bible, Homer's works set a standard and established a foundational tradition for subsequent Western literature.

The *Iliad* deals with the Trojan War, the wrath of the proud Greek hero Achilles, and the eventual demise of his Trojan enemy, Hector; the *Odyssey* concentrates on the character Odysseus, king of Ithaca, and his long and arduous voyage home after the end of the war. A major theme of the *Iliad*, announced in the very first line, is the destructive effects of the anger of Achilles, which is brought on initially by the loss of his slave girl to a fellow Greek and then by the death of his friend Patroclus. Achilles' prideful anger further intensifies when he temporarily withdraws from the battle against Troy, brooding in resentment because the Greeks believe they can succeed militarily without him. Restored to the battlefield, Achilles slays Hector and drags his body in front of the city gates for all to see. This brash violation of the body and honor of a great hero foreshadows the demise of Achilles himself. Homer's point seems clear: Uncontrolled rage and unbridled hubris can have only one result—the death of the hero.

The opening lines of the *Iliad* announce a second major theme, one that is explored in the *Odyssey* as well: that this "sovereign doom" of human war and strife is the will of the gods, a will that no mortal man can hope to oppose. The war, however, ends with a spark of willful human improvisation—the defeat of the Trojans by the cunning device of the Trojan horse, the brainchild of Odysseus himself. Homer continues to offer moral lessons by relating the character and motivations of his hero to their eventual outcomes. The patience and mental cunning of Odysseus eventually enable him to return home and reclaim his throne in the face of adversity from both men and gods. But in the end it could be argued that this homecoming would not have been possible without the intervention of the goddess Athena, his protectress, and Poseidon, god of the sea, who for years throws Odysseus's ship off course until his own anger at the hero finally subsides.

The *Odyssey* explores all the major elements of what the anthropologist Joseph Campbell calls the "hero's journey." Homer's poem begins with the search for Odysseus by his son Telemachus, who refuses to believe that his father has been killed in the war. The background is important. Odysseus's departure for Troy on the day his son is born is motivated by the Greek sense of honor, the oath of loyalty sworn between fellow Greek kings. Helen, the wife of the Greek king Menelaus, has been carried off by the Trojan prince Paris. Torn by the conflict between the code of honor and an equally strong Greek love for his family, Odysseus sets sail with his comrades to conquer Troy and reclaim Menelaus's wife, or so the story goes. In fact, the Greeks had imperial ambitions toward the rich trading city of Troy and longed to control its trade routes and resources. In the story, however, Athena, goddess of war and wisdom, visits Odysseus on board ship and tells him that she "wants him to go" for the glory of the ages. The war rages for 10 long years, as described in the *Iliad*. In the *Odyssey*, the episode of the Trojan horse is recounted as a distant memory, but this episode brings an end to the war and enables Odysseus to begin his journey home.

The hero's journey back to Ithaca is plagued with difficulties because of Poseidon's anger at Odysseus. Soon after leaving Troy, Odysseus's ship washes ashore on the island of the Cyclops Polyphemus, Poseidon's son. Odysseus endures many more dangers and confrontations with death in his attempt to get back home. Washed ashore on an island ruled by the witch Circe, he discovers that during their shore leave she has turned his men into pigs, and he is forced to submit to her terms (to have sex with her) in order to get his men back and find his way home. Later, Odysseus and his crew encounter the Scylla, a multiheaded, cave-dwelling monster who kills several of Odysseus's men as they try to navigate through her cave, at the far end of which lurks the Charybdis, a deadly whirlpool that sucks all save Odysseus himself down to their deaths. Left to his own devices, Odysseus is again blown off course and comes upon the island of Calypso, a sea nymph who seduces him and keeps him on her island for seven years, until Hermes, the winged messenger of the gods, interceding on behalf of Athena, arrives and insists that he be released.

After further adventures, the dramatic denouement of the story comes when the anger of Poseidon finally subsides enough to allow Odysseus, war torn and beaten, to wash ashore near Ithaca. He has an emotional reunion with his son and a faithful slave of many years. They tell him of the intruders and their plans to take over his palace, but rather than impulsively falling on the enemy, Odysseus characteristically reflects on his situation and contemplates his strategy. Impressed with his patience and wisdom, Athena appears to him and transforms him into an old beggar so that he may move about his palace unrecognized, until such time as he can safely resume his throne without being killed by the intruding suitors. The suitors have devised a plot to provoke Telemachus into a fight so that one of them can kill him, thereby removing any lingering bloodline to the throne. Odysseus advises his son to be patient, saying that "to be angry is easy." Meanwhile Penelope, unaware that Odysseus is alive and back, has prepared a test, under the advisement of the slave who knows of Odysseus's plan. The suitor who can string the bow of Odysseus and shoot an arrow clean through a series of rings will take his place as her new husband and rightful king. When none of the suitors is able to accomplish the task, the old beggar steps up, strings the bow, and fires the arrow straight through the rings, at which moment he is transformed, before the eyes of all, back into the true king of Ithaca.

Loyalty, bravery, courage, and honor; the heroic journey; the love of family and comrades; persistence and the virtue of patience; the ability to control one's anger; the importance of timing and rational contemplation; humility toward the gods; the equation of happiness and a man's world with his home, his wife, and his family—these are some of the major themes of Western literature established in their most complete and powerful form in the works of Homer.

Hesiod: *Works and Days* and *Theogony*

Homer's near contemporary Hesiod (active ca. 700 B.C.E.), another great Greek poet who wrote in hexameter verse, is considered to be the father of Greek didactic poetry (as opposed to the epic poetry of Homer). Didactic poetry was so called because it was intended to teach moral lessons or offer important instruction or factual information. The *Theogony*, for example, gives an account of the emergence of the universe from chaos and a detailed genealogy of the gods, carrying strong moral implications for humankind. *Works and Days*, Hesiod's other major work, however, is the more interesting of the two, in part because it deals with a subject—farming—that had not been given any attention by Homer and in part because it contains what little information we have on Hesiod's life. He was the son of an impoverished farmer who went to sea to make a better living. Hesiod spent most of his life farming in Boeotia, living in resentment of his brother, who had apparently cheated him out of his share of the family property. Hesiod's personal experience would thus appear to be a valuable background for understanding *Works and Days*, which consists of a series of moral maxims and precepts on farming.

Frieze of three Muses; the Muses typically are invoked at or near the beginning of a Greek epic poem. (Alison Frantz Photographic Collection, American School of Classical Studies at Athens)

The poem glorifies the solid, earthbound values of hard-working agricultural people, who at that time constituted the majority of humankind, and their never-ending, backbreaking work of plowing, sowing, reaping, threshing, and grinding. These were the peasants whose hard labor made possible the privileged lifestyles of the warrior-kings and princes of Homeric legend.

Works and Days deals first with the questions of why humans have to work so hard. Hesiod's answer places the blame on the demigod Prometheus, who defied Zeus, king of the gods, by giving humanity the forbidden gift of fire, forging thereby the arts and crafts of civilization. Enraged by this defiance, Zeus punished both Prometheus and humanity by sending down a woman, Pandora, who unleashed on the world all manner of evils—work, disease, hatred, envy, old age, and every other problem that continues to plague the human race.

As a follow-up to this troubling scenario, Hesiod describes his "Myth of the Five Ages," which is a further attempt to characterize the wretched state of humanity in his day. Before the defiance of Prometheus and the wrath of Pandora, humanity lived in a golden age, free of toil and trouble. But this idyllic situation was followed by three successive stages—the Silver Age, the Bronze Age, and the Iron Age—each one regressively worse than the last. Hesiod's sequence also makes room for a nonmetallic "Heroic Age," which drew from the collective Greek memory of the glories of the Mycenean civilization. Such heroic memories served only to intensify the sense of human wretchedness in Hesiod's own time, the Iron Age.

Archaic Lyric and Iambus: Archilochus of Paros

Archaic lyric refers to the earliest Greek poetry that expresses subjective thoughts and feelings, often in a songlike style or form. The poets who wrote after Hesiod explore a variety of poetic forms and rhythms, including the elegiac couplet (a combination of the epic hexameter and a shorter line), the pentameter (five metrical units rather than six), and iambic rhythms (metrical units consisting of an unstressed syllable followed by a stressed syllable, or a short syllable followed by a long syllable, as in the word *betray*). The earliest lyric poet, Archilochus of Paros (mid-seventh century B.C.E.), explores a wide variety of forms but never allows them to overwhelm his directness of expression and emotion.

The dithyramb is a frenzied, impassioned choric hymn and dance of ancient Greece, performed in honor of Dionysus, god of the harvest and wine. It also refers to an irregular poetic expression or an enthusiastic piece of writing, like that of Archilochus, that is suggestive of the original dithyramb. Such impassioned forms and style seem appropriate given the controversial nature of Archilochus's life. The poets Critias and Pindar considered him a scoundrel because some of his poetry speaks directly of a life of scandalous episodes and attitudes, especially toward women and family. But Archilochus also wrote passionately of military battles and heroic struggles with the enemy, in terms that offer moral guidance and urge men to overcome the whining hubris of Achilles.

Tyrtaeus and "The Spartan Creed"

Not all poetic characterizations of the glory of battle are sensitive to the emotional aspect of war. The poet Tyrtaeus (seventh century B.C.E.) was the official voice of the stern military ethic that made his native city, Sparta, famous. The Spartans are remembered today for their rigorous discipline and fighting skills, the products of a long and arduous training that created an intense spirit of community belonging and an efficiency admired by Plato and the Athenians of the Classical Age. Inspired by Homer's *Iliad*, "The Spartan Creed" of Tyrtaeus uses elegiac verse to celebrate, in even-tempered terms, the noble values of Spartan warrior-chiefs and their city: "For no man ever proves himself a good man in war / unless he can endure to face the blood and the slaughter, / go close against the enemy and fight with his hands."

Sappho and the World of Lesbos

There could hardly be a world more different from the harsh Spartan society than that of the Island of Lesbos, with its rich farmland, olive groves, wide pastures, orchards, vineyards, gardens, and, above all, atmosphere of wealth and leisure. This world was the setting for the idyllic and passionate lyric poetry of Sappho (ca. 610–ca. 580 B.C.E.). Uninterested in political matters, Sappho wrote about themes of intense concern to the young female devotees who surrounded her and together celebrated the cult and festivals of Aphrodite, goddess of love. Especially poignant is her exploration of the love of these young women for one another and the inevitable separation they would experience as they moved from girlhood to wedlock. Often nostalgic and sentimental, Sappho composed some of the most moving poetry ever written. Sappho's muse, Aphrodite, is frequently invoked as the powerful source of the emotions explored in her poetry.

Xenophanes and the Critique of the Gods

Not every Greek poet of the late sixth century and early fifth century B.C.E. gave himself or herself over to the adoration of the Greek gods so wholeheartedly as did Sappho. An exception to the rule and the first Greek writer seriously to question the idea and power of the anthropomorphic gods of Mount Olympus was Xenophanes of Colophon. His logic, leading toward a kind of monotheism, was that the obvious imperfections of the gods were based on all-too-human characteristics; therefore, humans must have created the gods in their own image and not vice versa. Xenophanes' poetry anticipates the skeptical humanism of the Classical age of Athens.

Pindar and the Olympian Ode

Some of Xenophanes' humanistic sentiments are found as well in the odes of Pindar of Thebes (ca. 522–ca. 438 B.C.E.), a prolific poet who addresses many different themes in various genres—hymns to the gods, dithyrambs to Dionysus, funeral dirges, heroic eulogies, and four books of odes, dedicated mostly to the winners of Olympic competitions throughout Greece. A particularly moving piece is his "Third Pythian Ode (for Hiero of Syracuse)," written to comfort and console a man who was mortally ill. Its ending recalls the thought of Xenophanes—the idea of a humble human thinker, a self, who confronts the power and glory of one god: "I will be small in small things, great among great. / I will work out the divinity that is busy within my mind / and tend the means that are mine."

Herodotus, Thucydides, and the Birth of History

Greek literature encompasses not only a rich variety of poetry but also historical, political, biographical, and philosophical writing. Historical writing as a serious enterprise and fine art began with Herodotus (ca. 484–between 430 and 420 B.C.E), and was further developed by Thucydides (d. ca. 401 B.C.E.). First called the father of history by the Roman writer Cicero, Herodotus was the first writer to conduct research into the events of the past and the history of foreign lands and to attempt to treat them in a rational rather than a mythical manner. Although he was often forced to rely on spurious sources, usually oral accounts that were frequently secondhand, his narratives are informative, vivid, and extensive in their treatment; his history of the Persian invasions of Greece up to 479 B.C.E. takes up nine books. Thucydides was an exiled Athenian general who wrote a remarkably objective account of the Peloponnesian war between Sparta and Athens. His account stresses painstaking reporting and a descriptive analysis of contemporary events that reveal considerable appreciation for cause and effect. The most famous passages are those dealing with Pericles' funeral oration and the plague at Athens.

The Birth of Western Drama

In the history of dramatic literature five names from ancient Greece stand out. Three dramatists—Aeschylus, Sophocles, and Euripides—were tragedians. Additionally, Aristophanes wrote comic plays that are still part of the theater repertoire around the world, and Menander was a major figure in Greek comedy.

Aeschylus (525/524–456/455 B.C.E.), probably the world's first writer of tragic drama, expanded the possibilities of stage drama. He wrote about 90 plays, 80 of which are known by name but only seven of which have survived in their entirety: *Persians, Seven against Thebes, Suppliants, Prometheus Bound*, and the three plays of the *Oresteia* trilogy—*Agamemnon, The Libation-Bearers,* and *The Furies.* Until Aeschylus, drama was largely a static affair, recited by a chorus and a single main actor. Aeschylus added a second actor, expanding the possibilities for dialogue and incorporating action into the play. Sophocles (ca. 496–406 B.C.E.) was a prolific writer, author of at least 123 plays, though only seven survive in their entirety: *Ajax, Antigone, Trachinian Women, Oedipus the King, Electra, Philoctetes*, and *Oedipus at Colonus*. It is known that at least 24 of his plays won major dramatic competitions and that he never came in lower than second place. Two of his plays, *Antigone* and *Oedipus the King*, remain perennial favorites on the stage and are widely read by students for their tragic vision of the interaction of flawed judgment and cruel fate, leading to disaster. Euripides (ca. 484–406 B.C.E.), the author of some 92 plays, 19 of which survive, wrote darker, more frenzied tragedies in which the disaster that befalls the central characters is more a result of their personal flaws and irrationality than a cruel fate. His most famous plays include *Medea, Hippolytus, Electra, Trojan Women, Ion, Iphigenia at Aulis,* and *Bacchae.* In most of his plays he used legendary and historical figures as his main characters, turning them into ordinary, contemporary people.

Among comic dramatists, two names stand out. The first is Aristophanes (ca. 450–c. 388 B.C.E.), who wrote about 40 plays, only 11 of which survive intact: *Archarnians, Clouds, Wasps, Peace, Birds, Lysistrata, Women at the Thesmorphoria, Frogs, Knights, Women at the Ecclesia*, and *Wealth.* Among these plays, perhaps *Lysistrata* is the most famous and widely performed because of its contemporary theme: The women of Athens, led by Lysistrata, seize the Athenian Acropolis and the city's treasury and declare a ban on sexual relations with their husbands until they put an end to the 20-year-old Peloponnesian War. Overall, Aristophanes' plays continued to be admired for their wit, their biting political satire, and their overall good humor.

Later, Menander (ca. 342–ca. 292 B.C.E.) wrote more refined plays in a sophisticated literary language that became a model for educated Greeks. While earlier Greek comedies, such as those of Aristophanes, were devoted largely to politics and public affairs, the comedies of Menander seem more modern in their depiction of the manners and foibles of ordinary people and their wider range of character types: the stern father, the wily slave, the misanthrope (one who dislikes other people), pairs of young lovers, and the like. Menander is known to have written about 70 plays, but, unfortunately, the complete text of only one survives. Large portions of other plays have been found, and Menander survives largely because Roman writers adapted many of his plays.

Hellenistic Literature: Theophrastus, Callimachus, and Apollonius of Rhodes

Cultural diversity and innovation characterized the Hellenistic Age that was ushered in by Alexander the Great, king of Macedonia (r. 336–323 B.C.E.), conqueror of Asia Minor, Syria, Egypt, Babylonia, and Persia. In literary terms, the new sense of variety and experimentation is reflected in the works of Theophrastus (ca. 372–ca. 287 B.C.E.), Callimachus of Cyrene (ca. 305–ca. 240 B.C.E.), and Appolonius of Rhodes (ca. 295–ca. 215 B.C.E.). Theophrastus, Aristotle's successor as the head of the School of Philosophy in Athens, wrote many scientific and philosophical studies, but his most colorful work is a book called *Characters*, which consists of a series of lively sketches of different human types: the Chatterer, the Talker, the Eager to Please, the Skinflint or Stingy Man, the Tiresome Man, the Boaster, and the Authoritarian. These multifarious types suggest a veritable gallery of Hellenistic diversity, noteworthy for their observant detail and humorous characterizations.

The fundamentally modern feeling of Theophrastus's *Characters* reflects a trend toward novelty that would give rise to the major intellectual debate of later Greek literature: tradition versus innovation. The traditional position was upheld by Apollonius of Rhodes, head librarian at the library at Alexandria and author of an epic poem in the Homeric tradition, the *Argonautica*. The search for new forms for Greek writing is promoted by the poet and scholar Callimachus, the dominant intellectual figure at Alexandria under the kings Ptolemy II (r. 285–246 B.C.E.) and Ptolemy III (r. 246–221 B.C.E.).

Callimachus criticizes Greek poets for continuing to use the lengthy form of the Homeric epic, whose day, he believes, has passed. He claims that "a big book is a big evil." His proposed alternative includes the elaboration of the epigram—a short, witty poem expressing a single thought or observation—and the *Pinakes*, a series of biographical and bibliographical tablets documenting "those who were outstanding in every phase of culture, and their writings," a sort of *Who's Who* of Greek literature and culture. Callimachus was thus the "father of bibliography," the first person known to have catalogued and classified an extensive collection of literature, according to such major categories as philosophy, poetry, oratory, history, law, medicine, and miscellany. Callimachus thus consolidates for the future the vast legacy of Greek literature. This catalogue of literature was not his only contribution, however. In the prologue to one of his major works, *Aitia* (The Causes), he closes out the ancient Greek literary tradition by creating a new one—that of the critic of the literary critic. He calls them "malignant gnomes and "tone-deaf ignoramuses" in their critiques of his work, ending by saying, "So evaporate, Green-Eyed Monsters, / or learn to judge poems by the critic's art . . . / and don't snoop around here for a poem that rumbles: / not I but Zeus owns the thunder."

Philosophy

No discussion of ancient Greek literature would be complete without mentioning some of the major Greek philosophers. While the works of numerous of these philosophers survive, those of three in particular stand out and continue to be read and studied: Socrates, Plato, and Aristotle.

Socrates (ca. 470–399 B.C.E.) is often regarded as the founder of Western philosophy. Most of what is known about him comes from later sources, including Plato. Because most of his work survives through Plato, it is difficult to distinguish the philosophical views of the two. Socrates is perhaps best remembered not for his unorthodox life as a wandering gadfly but for his death. He was executed by being forced to drink hemlock, a poison, for being perceived as a threat to the Athenian state. Whether Plato (428/427–348/347 B.C.E.) was a student of Socrates is unclear. Much of Plato's philosophy was written in the form of dialogues, the so-called Socratic dialogue, featuring Socrates as the "teacher" and various other contemporary figures as his "students," who have to explain and defend their positions through a seemingly endless series of questions, but Plato never explicitly says that he ever took part in dialogues with Socrates. Either way, it would be difficult to overstate the influence of Plato on Western thought.

Among modern philosophers, a common expression is that all Western philosophy is a "footnote to Plato," meaning that modern philosophy is an attempt to refine and explain philosophical views outlined by Plato over two millennia ago. Perhaps the best-known and most widely read of Plato's dialogues is the *Republic*, a wide-ranging discussion of the nature of justice, courage, wisdom, morals, and virtues as they pertain both to individuals and to society as a whole. Perhaps the most famous portion of the *Republic* is referred to as the Allegory of the Cave. In this passage people are imagined confined in a cave where the only reality they know is shadows cast on the wall. When they are released from the cave, they see reality as it really is.

Finally, Aristotle (384–322 B.C.E.) was one of Plato's students. He began his career as a scientist and physician, and throughout his work he explored a wide range of subjects, including science, poetry, biology, zoology, logic, ethics, politics, government, and rhetoric. It is almost impossible to give a thumbnail sketch of Aristotle's philosophical views, but he remains important for his efforts to understand the nature of the real and the universal, to categorize and systematize knowledge, and to apply reason and logic to philosophical problems. In connection with literature, his *Ars poetica* (Poetics) was an effort to define the essential nature of such literary genres as tragedy, comedy, and the epic. While Plato tended to focus on the moral qualities of literature, Aristotle was more interested in the formal structure and internal logic of such works.

Aesop and Plutarch

The works of two additional writers survive, though neither fits into any of the categories outlined. The first, Aesop, is probably a legendary figure. His name is connected with some 200 "Aesop's fables" that continue to be read for their moral lessons, usually taught through the behavior of animals. Most of these stories were traditional, and their written versions were probably the production of numerous authors. Some of these fables have become woven into the fabric of modern life. Schoolchildren are familiar, for example, with the tale of the hare and the tortoise; the swift hare should beat the slow tortoise in a race, but he keeps getting distracted while the tortoise focuses his attention on what he is doing and wins. The fable of the fox and the grapes is the source of the expression *sour grapes*, referring to the claim that a person did not really want something that he or she was unable to attain, just as the fox claims that he does not really want the grapes he is unable to reach.

Finally, Plutarch (ca. 46–ca. 119 C.E.) is best known for history, essays, and biography. Plutarch wrote an immense number of philosophical essays about a wide range of topics, but many do not survive. His most famous work is generally referred to simply as *Lives*, but more formally the English translation of the title is *Parallel Lives*. In this collection of essays, which has not survived in complete form, he paired famous Greeks and Romans, writing biographical sketches of them with emphasis on their moral strengths and failings. For some historical figures of the time, Plutarch is the only source of information or, in some cases, one of few such sources. His work has been criticized for historical inaccuracies and reliance on gossip and legend, but it survives because of his keen insight into human character.

ROME

BY JAMES A. CORRICK

Roman literature prior to the third century B.C.E. was often associated with specific events. Thus, poetry about the deceased was recited or sung at funerals; later, this poetry was replaced by an oration, a formal speech. At harvest festivals, weddings, and other celebrations, humorous poetry—generally racy and vulgar as well as improvised—was popular. Banquets were the occasion for reciting or singing the deeds of heroes. Political debate generated speeches. Although much of this early Roman literature was oral, some—how much is now uncertain—was written down. The names of these early Roman authors of both the oral and the written have been lost.

The Greeks and the Epic

Beginning in 272 B.C.E. with the capture of the Spartan colony of Tarentum in southern Italy and the subsequent conquest of other Greek colonies and finally Greece itself, Greek slaves began arriving in Rome by the thousands. Some of these slaves became tutors to Roman youths and passed on to their charges a love and reverence for much of Greek culture, particularly poetry. Indeed, Greek poetic forms would dominate Roman verse until the end of the empire in 476 C.E.

As with the Greeks, Romans considered the noblest poems to be epics. From the Greek *epos* for "word," an epic is a long narrative poem that, for the ancients, detailed the deeds of a single hero or band of heroes. This heroic story plays out among a large cast of other characters, both human and divine, with the latter often aiding or hindering the hero. It was the heroic nature of the epic that led the Romans and Greeks to hold it in such high regard. The Greek models for the Roman epics were the *Iliad* and *Odyssey* of the poet Homer (fl. ca. ninth century B.C.E.).

The common meter for the epic is dactylic hexameter. Meter is the poem's rhythm, which is determined by the pattern of its lines. Each line of classical poetry is divided into sections known as feet; in each foot a set number of syllables occurs in a specific order. In classical verse some of these syllables are long and some short, the longer taking more time to say than the shorter. Long syllables generally contain a long vowel or a short vowel followed by two consonants, while short syllables have a short vowel. For example, in English the "a" in *day* is long, while that in *hat* is short. A line of dactylic hexameter has six feet; in each foot, known as a dactyl, is a long syllable followed by two short ones. Other types of feet also exist. The iamb, for example, has a short syllable followed by a long one.

Other Greek-Inspired Roman Poetry

Also borrowed from the Greek is the elegy, a short poem that alternates a line of dactylic hexameter with one of dactylic pentameter, a line of five rather than six feet. A hexameter and pentameter line together form a two-line unit, known as an elegiac couplet, with each couplet presenting a complete thought. The subject of the Roman elegy is mainly love, detailing the passion and trials of a lover.

Lyric poetry also entered Rome from Greece. Generally short, lyric poetry expresses the poet's emotions or state of mind. A lyric poem usually has a single focus: love, sadness, or regret, for instance. Originally meant to be sung, this poetic form derives its name from the lyre, the stringed musical instrument that once accompanied the singer. For the most part, however, Roman lyric poetry was meant to be read rather than sung.

The epigram is another Roman form derived from the Greek. Typically composed of a single elegiac couplet, it presents a witty observation about love, the gods, morality, or human activities. Pastoral poetry, which idealizes country life and often focuses on the loves of shepherds and shepherdesses, is also of Greek origin.

The Roman Nature of Latin Poetry

Although Roman poetry owes much to Greek poetry, it retains features of earlier Roman verse, such as the favorite device of alliteration. In alliteration two or more words in a line have the same initial sound. In English, for instance, the words of the childhood jingle "Peter Piper picked a peck of pickled peppers" are alliterative. More important, the subject matter of Latin verse is Roman. Roman deeds, heroes, history, and values provided the subjects of Roman verse. Roman failings also became the subject of satire, the only important native Roman form of poetry after the third century B.C.E. Satire criticizes, often both humorously and harshly, the faults of Romans, particularly hypocrisy and bad behavior. In satire the author typically addresses the reader directly; sometimes the writer's tone is mocking, while at other times it is cynical or sneering, and the language can be obscene. Roman epigrams are frequently satiric.

Roman Prose

Although much satire was written in verse, it could also be in prose or a combination of poetry and prose. Roman prose was much less strongly influenced by Greek traditions than was poetry. Out of funeral orations came biographies and, later, imperial autobiographies. From Roman public speeches grew a whole body of political and judicial writing. From a desire to argue persuasively in public debate came a host of works on rhetoric, the study of principles and techniques that aid in the effective presentation and defense of a line of reasoning. Other native Roman prose works included letters, frequently meant for publication, and novels; the latter were considered mainly a low form of entertainment, however.

Despite its generally native roots, Roman prose shows Greek influence, particularly in the writing of histories and philosophy that used Greek models (some history and philosophy appeared as verse). Initially, Roman histories were written in Greek because Latin was thought to lack the vocabulary needed for historical writing. Using Greek also allowed Roman authors to propagandize Rome's right to rule the Greek city-states.

The New Literature

Greek-inspired Roman literature began with Livius Andronicus (ca. 284–ca. 204 B.C.E.), a Greek slave from Tarentum who eventually won his freedom. Although he was mostly a playwright, Livius also translated the *Odyssey* into Latin; his translation would prove to be popular for the next two centuries. Instead of the Greek dactylic hexameter, Livius used a native Roman meter known as Saturnian. Each line of Saturnian verse is divided into just two feet, separated by a caesura, that is, a break denoting a pause. The second foot is either shorter or the same length as the first. Reading Saturnian verse may have depended on a sequence of long and short syllables or on a succession of accented and unaccented syllables, the former being emphasized, or stressed, during pronunciation. Livius probably used Saturnian meter to make his work more accessible to the Romans, who were still mostly unfamiliar with Greek poetry. Gnaeus Naevius (ca. 270–ca. 201 B.C.E.) also used Saturnian meter in his epic poem on the First Punic War, *Bellum Punicum*. After Naevius, Saturnian meter disappeared from Roman poetry.

It was Quintus Ennius (239–169 B.C.E.) who first introduced Greek meter to Roman verse. Born of Greek and Italian parents in southern Italy, in 204 B.C.E. he arrived in Rome, where he became one of the foremost authors of his time. A versatile writer, Ennius wrote plays, elegies, epigrams, satires, and even a philosophical poem, *Epicharmus*, which describes the physical nature of the universe. His most lasting work was an epic poem, the *Annales*, which is a history of Rome and became the model for future Roman epics. The *Annales* begins with the story of Aeneas, who flees Troy when that city is overrun and destroyed by the Greeks. Aeneas eventually arrives in Italy, where he settles; according to Roman legend, it would be his descendants Romulus and Remus who would found Rome. Ennius's elegies appear to have made the first use of the elegiac couplet in Roman poetry, while his *Annales* first used dactylic hexameter.

The first Latin prose history was begun just before Ennius's death. In 168 B.C.E. Marcus Porcius Cato (234–149 B.C.E.), who was known as the Elder and the Censor and who was an important military and political leader of his time, wrote the *Origines*, a seven-volume history of the founding of Rome. Left unfinished on Cato's death, *Origines* was the first Roman history written in Latin and became the model for subsequent histories. Cato also wrote a treatise on agriculture, *De agri cultura*, and produced many political speeches, which he may have revised for publication and which were studied as models of the effective use of rhetoric by later Roman orators such as Cicero.

Not long after Cato's death, Gaius Lucilius (ca. 180–ca. 102 B.C.E.) wrote the first important Roman satires. Using Greek hexameter, Lucilius wrote some 30 books of verse, much of the verse attacking both the public and private behavior of his fellow citizens, particularly influential people and other writers. He remained popular until the end of the empire. The period from 70 B.C.E. to 17 C.E. is termed the golden age of Roman literature. The golden age saw the appearance of many major Roman writers, more than at any other period in Roman history. Among prose authors were Cicero and Julius Caesar, and among the poets were Virgil, Horace, and Ovid.

Cicero

The first half of the golden age is sometimes called the Ciceronian age after the Roman orator and statesman Marcus Tullius Cicero (106–43 B.C.E.). Cicero's literary reputation rests on some 60 speeches, 800 letters, and numerous books that he wrote during his successful career as lawyer and political leader. Born to a minor aristocratic family in Arpinum, a small town southeast of Rome, Cicero studied philosophy and rhetoric in both Rome and Greece before launching his legal career in 81 B.C.E. by successfully defending a client accused of murdering his father.

Cicero's earliest-known speech was given in 81 B.C.E. and was a plea in a case whose outcome is unknown. His most famous speeches were the four *In Catilinam* (Against Catiline), which he gave in 63 B.C.E. Catiline had organized an unsuccessful takeover of the Roman government. Cicero's speeches argued successfully for the execution of Catiline and his followers.

Cicero's letters covered a wide range of topics, from politics to poetry to idle gossip. His most important other writings are numerous works on rhetoric and political theory. Among his works on rhetoric was *De claris oratoribus* (On Clear Speaking) (ca. 46 B.C.E.), a study of Roman oratory and, in particular, Cicero's own style. Among his political works was *De legibus* (On Laws), which he finished in 45 B.C.E. and which describes the laws of an ideal state. Cicero's prose, particularly his speeches, came to be seen as excellent examples of the use of argumentative language and have been used from classical times to the present to teach the art of persuasion.

Julius Caesar

The other major prose writer of the Ciceronian period was Gaius Julius Caesar (100–44 B.C.E.). Caesar produced several books, including one of jokes and sayings, and a little poetry. He is best remembered for two histories, *De bello Gallico* (On the Gallic War) (ca. 51 B.C.E.) and *De bello civili* (On the Civil War), begun in 49 B.C.E. and left unfinished at his assassination.

Both of Caesar's histories are vivid accounts, told in straightforward prose, of his military career. In *De bello Gallico*, Caesar details his campaign (58–50 B.C.E.) that added much territory to the Roman province of Gaul. In his second history Caesar describes the war between himself and Pompey the Great (106–48 B.C.E.). Both histories were first and foremost propaganda to enhance Caesar's image and to help him fulfill his political ambitions. In addition, however, both accounts are filled with details of Roman military life and tactics. The commentary on the Gallic War also provides a great deal of information on the land and its people. Nevertheless, *De bello Gallico* does not reveal the brutality that often marked Caesar's war against the Gauls.

Lucretius and Catullus

The Ciceronian age also produced many poets, two of the most notable being Titus Lucretius Carus (98–ca. 55 B.C.E.) and Gaius Valerius Catullus (ca. 84–ca. 54 B.C.E.). Little is known about Lucretius except for his single long philosophical poem *De rerum natura* (On the Nature of Things). A follower of the Greek philosopher Epicurus (ca. 340–ca. 270 B.C.E.), Lucretius explains in his poem how being modest in the pursuit of pleasure combined with an understanding of the workings of the physical world leads to tranquility that in turn frees one from the fear of death. The polished hexameter meter of *De rerum natura* was studied by later poets such as Virgil.

As with Lucretius, few details of Catullus's life are known except that he came from a wealthy family. Also like Lucretius, Catullus influenced the poets who came after him and who were impressed with the polish and sophistication of his verse, which ranged in length from a mini-epic to epigrams. Using a variety of Greek meters, Catullus wrote more than 100 poems on erotic love and friendship, with some 25 addressed to a married woman whom he calls Lesbia and with whom he may have had an affair. His main theme was faithfulness in love and friendship.

Virgil

The second part of the golden age is known as the Augustan age, named for the emperor Augustus Caesar, who solidified his sole rule in 31 B.C.E. Much of the literary bloom of this part of Rome's golden age was due to Gaius Cilnius Maecenas (ca. 70–8 B.C.E.), a long-time adviser to Augustus and a patron of the arts. Maecenas supported many young poets, thus allowing them to write full time. Among Maecenas's clients was Publius Vergilius Maro (70–19 B.C.E.), better known as Virgil. Born in Andes, just south of the Alps, Virgil spent his childhood on his father's farm. Beginning at age 12, Virgil was educated first in Cremona, then in Milan, and finally in Rome, where he studied philosophy and rhetoric.

Virgil's first important work was the *Ecologues*, a collection of 10 short pastoral poems written between 42 and 37 B.C.E. The collection's title means "selections from a larger work," though the *Ecologues* is complete in itself. The poems are full of star-crossed lovers who live in an idealized rural setting. However, among the traditional pastoral concerns are more contemporary ones. Ecologues 2 and 9 deal with the policy of land confiscation that Mark Antony and Augustus (still named Octavian at the time of the *Ecologues*) enacted as a way to give land in payment to their soldiers. The desire to see the end of the strife of the decades of civil war also influences the fourth eclogue, which predicts the arrival of a new age of peace.

Virgil met Maecenas soon after the publication of the *Ecologues*. Maecenas urged the poet to take on a new project that would present country life more realistically than the conventional idealized pastoral. Both he and Augustus believed that Romans needed to return to their old traditions, which included farming. Virgil obliged his patron by writing the *Georgics* (On Farming), which he composed between 37 and 29 B.C.E. The poem's four books are filled with practical farming instructions on such matters as the cultivation of crops and the raising of livestock. It also contains many passages about the satisfactions of the farming life as well as the beauty and restfulness of being surrounded by the natural world.

The last 10 years of Virgil's life was consumed in writing his masterpiece, the 12-book *Aeneid*, which alone among Roman epic poems came to stand as an equal to Homer's *Iliad* and *Odyssey*. The hero of Virgil's epic is Aeneas, of whom Ennius wrote in his *Annales* and who gives his name to the poem. Virgil's Aeneas, son of the goddess Venus, is the first Roman and indeed a model one, devoted to duty and resolute in pursuit of his destiny, which is to seek Italy, where his descendants will found Rome.

The first six books of the *Aeneid* are a mini-*Odyssey* as Aeneas sails from Troy to Italy. The highlight of this section is his arrival in Carthage, where he falls in love with its queen, Dido. Tempted to remain, Aeneas is forcefully reminded of his destiny in Italy by the god Mercury, so he leaves Carthage. In despair at her abandonment by her lover, Dido commits suicide. In the final six books Aeneas becomes involved in a struggle between the early Latin states. In single combat, reminiscent of that between Achilles and Hector in the *Iliad*, Aeneas slays the enemy of his Latin allies and sets the stage for the eventual appearance of Rome.

Maecenas had originally hoped that Virgil would write an epic about Augustus, but the poet believed that he could serve the emperor better with an older story. Still, Virgil did not forget Ausgustus. Upon arriving in Italy, Aeneas travels to Hades, where the dead go and where he is shown a shield that contains a pictorial record of future Roman history. The last picture on the shield is of a peaceful, unified Rome under the rule of Augustus.

Horace

It was Virgil who introduced the poet Quintus Horatius Flaccus (65–8 B.C.E.), or Horace, to Maecenas. Although Horace came from a landed family, he had fought on the losing side of a civil war and had had all his property confiscated. Maecenas set Horace up with a small farm whose income allowed the poet to live comfortably. An extremely prolific writer, Horace produced a substantial body of work, beginning around 40 B.C.E. with the writing of the 17 poems that made up the *Epodes*, published in 30 B.C.E. (In verse, an epode is the third part of a three-part lyric ode.) Using a variety of lengths and meters, Horace specialized in lyric poetry and satires that his contemporaries and later generations considered unequaled in quality. He also coined a number of phrases that remain in use to this day, such as "the golden mean" and "seize the day."

The verse in the *Epodes* is minor, and Horace's first major work were the *Sermones* (Conversations), two books of satire, the first being published in 35 B.C.E. and the second in 30 B.C.E. Horace's satires are not vicious and do not attack public figures. Instead, in a colloquial, conversational style, he pokes fun at the foibles of his fellow citizens. For instance, he writes about those who wish to be in the country and, once there, desire to be back in Rome. He even includes himself in these humorous musings, ridiculing his own short temper and indecisiveness.

Next followed the four books of the *Carmina*, or *Odes*, which contain Horace's major lyric poetry. The first three books were published around 23 B.C.E. and the fourth about 13 B.C.E. In 103 poems Horace covers love, the gods, and friendship, among other subjects. Ever mindful of his patron Maecenas's loyalties, Horace takes pains to celebrate Augustus's victory over Antony at Actium in 31 B.C.E. and voices approval of the emperor's campaign to restore traditional Roman virtues. Around 20 B.C.E. Horace published his *Epistles* (Letters). These are letters written in verse that cover many of the topics found in the satires and lyric poetry. The *Ars poetica* (The Art of Poetry) (ca. 18 B.C.E.) is another verse letter that offers detailed advice on writing poetry.

Ovid

The third of the major Augustan poets was Publius Ovidius Naso (43 B.C.E.–17 C.E.), or Ovid. From an aristocratic family, Ovid studied rhetoric in Rome in preparation for a career in law, but he soon abandoned law in favor of poetry. Much of Ovid's verse is written in elegiac couplets, of which he was considered in his time and later to be the master. Two of his major subjects are seduction and erotic love, neither of which endeared Ovid to Augustus, who was attempting to reform the morals of Romans. Additionally, Ovid often wrote irreverently about the emperor and his policies. One or more of Ovid's indiscretions—exactly which remains a mystery to this day—earned him permanent exile to Tomis on the Black Sea in 8 C.E.

Ovid's first work was the five-book *Amores* (Loves), begun around 20 B.C.E. It describes, mockingly at times, Ovid's affair with a woman he named Corinna. Ovid followed with *Ars amatoria* (The Art of Love) (ca. 1 B.C.E.), a step-by-step guide to seduction, particularly of married women. In the *Heroides* (Heroines) (ca. 2 C.E.), Ovid collected 20 poems that were supposedly love letters from famous women to their husbands or lovers.

Ovid's major work was the *Metamorphoses* (Transformations), a 15-book poem completed by 8 C.E. that Ovid may have considerd an epic because he abandoned the elègiac couplet for dactylic hexameter. The *Metamorphoses* describes the creation and history of the world mostly by telling tales in which divinities or humans are transformed. The poem begins with Prometheus, who changes earth into humankind, and ends with the assassinated Julius Caesar changing into a star. Ovid's theme, as usual, is human passion, as seen in the actions of both his divine and human characters. The *Metamorphoses* is told with wit, a mature and elegant style, and a deep knowledge of Greek and Roman literature and myth.

During his exile Ovid continued to write. His collection of elegies *Tristia* (Sorrow), written between 8 and 12 C.E., and *Epistulae ex Ponto* (Letters from Pontus), written between 12 and 16 C.E., were more sober and personal than his previous work and were unsuccessful pleas for an end to his exile. His last work was the *Fasti*, a description in verse of the Roman calendar and religious festivals. It was unfinished at his death.

The Silver Age

The death of Ovid in 17 C.E. marked the end of the Roman literary golden age and the beginning of the silver age, which lasted for a little over a century. Although none of this period's writers would match in stature those of the golden age, the era did produce a number of notable poets and prose writers.

Among these poets were Martial, Juvenal, and Lucan. Marcus Valerius Martialis (ca. 40–ca. 103 C.E.), or Martial, was from Spain, and wrote mostly epigrams using the elegiac couplet. In his *Epigrams*, consisting of 12 books published between 86 and 101 C.E. and containing more than 1,500 epigrams, Martial satirized the outrageous behavior of his friends; depicted realistically life in Rome, even as he satirized it; and idealized his childhood in Spain. Decimus Junius Juvenalis (ca. 60–ca. 127 C.E.), or Juvenal, was a sharp-tongued satirist who attacked with vigor injustice and vice in Roman society. His 16 *Saturae* (Satires) (110–127 C.E.) are filled with cynicism, pessimism, and venom. In his short life Marcus Annaeus Lucanus (39–65 C.E.), or Lucan, produced a number of poems, the most famous of which was *De bello civili* (On the Civil War), sometimes also know as the *Pharsalia*, an epic about the battle between Julius Caesar and Pompey.

The silver age produced one of the foremost Roman historians, Publius (or Gaius) Cornelius Tacitus (ca. 56–ca. 117 C.E.). Tacitus's most important works were his *Historiae* (Histories) (106–107 C.E.) and *Annales* (Annals; ca. 116 C.E.). The former covers the period between the death of the emperor Nero in 68 C.E. and that of the emperor Domitian in 96 C.E., while the latter covers the time from Augustus's death in 14 C.E. to that of Nero. Complementing Tacitus's histories were the biographies of Gaius Suetonius Tranquillus (ca. 70–ca. 140 C.E.), whose *De vita Caesarum* (*Lives of the Twelve Caesars*, as it appears in English), published sometime after 122 C.E., contains biographical sketches of Julius Caesar and the first 11 emperors. Suetonius also wrote other biographies of famous orators, poets, and historians.

Among other noted prose writers were Pliny the Elder, Pliny the Younger, Seneca the Younger, and Petronius. Despite much public and military service, Pliny the Elder (Gaius Plinius Secundus) (23–79 C.E.) found time to write histories, biographies, and a work on natural history, the 37-volume *Naturalis historia* (Natural History) (77 C.E.). The latter compiled—without any attempt to separate fact from fiction—every report about the world that Pliny could discover. Pliny died while trying to obtain a closer look at the erupting Mount Vesuvius that buried the city of Pompeii. His nephew Pliny the Younger (Gaius Plinius Caecilius Secundus) (ca. 61–ca. 111 C.E.) was a noted orator and prolific letter writer, the latter of which covered many topics, such as his vivid description of the eruption of Mount Vesuvius that killed his uncle.

Seneca the Younger (Lucius Annaeus Seneca) (4 B.C.E.–65 C.E.) wrote extensively on Stoic philosophy, explaining that self-control, moderation, and detachment from pleasure and pain were necessary to find truth. Petronius (often identified as Titus or Gaius Petronius) (ca. 27–66 C.E.) wrote one of the first novels, the *Satyricon*, or more properly *Satyrica* (Tales of the Satyrs; ca. 60 C.E.), which chronicles the misadventures of two young Greeks. The highlight of the novel is a banquet thrown by a wealthy former slave, Trimalchio—an extravagant and vulgar display of the host's wealth.

Later Writers

Competent but minor poets populated Rome in its last centuries. Prose faired somewhat better. The *Meditations* of the emperor Marcus Aurelius (121–180 C.E.), published after Marcus's death, collects the emperor's private musings about life and the gods while pondering the role of Stoicism in public and private life. Marcus's contemporary Lucius Apuleius (ca. 124–ca. 170 C.E.) wrote the novel *Metamorphoses*, also known as the *Aureus asinus* (The Golden Ass), in which the protagonist Lucius's mishandling of magic turns him into an ass. Before returning to human form, Lucius has a series of humorous and lewd adventures.

Beginning in the fourth century, numerous important Christian writers appeared and dominated Roman writing. Aurelius Ambrosius (ca. 340–397 C.E.), later Saint Ambrose, wrote many hymns, sermons, letters, and treatises defending Christianity against paganism. Eusebius Hieronymous (ca. 347–420 C.E.), or Saint Jerome, wrote biblical commentaries and biographies of Christian writers; his translation of the Bible became the standard Latin text. Aurelius Augustinus (54–430 C.E.), or Saint Augustine, was a prolific writer. His most famous work is his *Confessions* (ca. 397–400 C.E.), an examination of his life that contains a vivid and forceful account of his conversion to Christianity.

THE AMERICAS

BY ALESSIA FRASSANI

Writing and recording knowledge in Native America was limited, and no texts have survived from the pre-Columbian period. Archaeologists, historians, and anthropologists who study ancient indigenous cultures agree that Native American literary traditions were essentially oral. In ancient times tools were used to support memorization of different types of texts, from tribute accounts to religious chants. These tools only partly recorded the spoken word and were meant to give clues for recitation, which was largely improvised. Although this may seem unusual to modern readers used to the support of the printed word for preserving and transmitting information, the human mind has the ability to memorize long texts provided they have a rhythmic, repetitive, and redundant formal structure. People can be specially trained from a young age to become proficient in the art of memory. Schools and tutoring provide the necessary intellectual environment to stimulate this activity, which preserves and creates at the same time. It aims at preserving a preexisting body of literature while the performers are free and even expected to elaborate further during the actual performance. All this was the case with Native American poetry, which historians have been forced to study by examining historical and contemporary cultures from the 16th century onward in order to draw inferences about the content and form of earlier literature.

The single most important element of Amerindian poetics is parallelism. Two verses are coupled by a tight repetition of the syntactic structure (that is, the structure of the sentence and its grammar), with only a slight variation in the wording. This gives the verse its basic rhythm, in a way comparable to the rhyme and metric systems of Western literature. The elementary two-verse unit can be either introduced or concluded by a third line with a different structure and wording from the other two verses. This additional feature creates variations in pitch and stress and enables the performers to pause before starting again with a new sequence of parallel verses. A good example can be found in the creation account contained in the ancient Mayan Popol Vuh, which includes the lines: "now it still ripples / now it still murmurs / ripples, it still sighs / it still hums / and it is empty / under the sky." Performers and the rhythms of their delivery over a fixed narration and story are ultimately the most remarkable features of Amerindian literature.

Archaeological remains that bear traces of what may have been a literary tradition in the Americas in the early period include carvings and paintings meant for public display. The context points to the function of some literary production and performance as a propaganda tool. Archaeologists and anthropologists tend to view the rise of complex mythology in the early ancient Americas as tied to the emergence of social complexity and the establishment of an elite class that employed literature to justify claims to power. Members of the ruling class impersonated literary and legendary figures during ceremonies and were actively involved in creating a perception of rulership's durability and legitimacy based on the mythological quality of the stories narrated. In other cases agricultural cycles and crops were the main theme, expressing an obvious concern for community sustenance and well-being. Paintings decorated rooms and plazas where fertility rituals took place, and the decoration served as a backdrop for ceremonies taking place in them.

In Mesoamerica the period of pre-Columbian history from 400 B.C.E. to 150 C.E. is known as Late Preclassic or Formative. Both terms define an early stage of Mesoamerican history in relation to later, and better-known, sociopolitical developments. Anthropologists believe that during this period states emerged, along with intensive agriculture. From relatively small and simple societies, cities and even empires came to dominate the Mesoamerican political arena. In the Maya area, including modern southern Mexico, Guatemala, Belize, and Honduras, the importance of ritual reenactment and public sacrifice of rulers during ceremonial occasions is well known. The continuation of political rulership, especially at the critical moments of dynastic succession, was metaphorically tied to the constant renewal of the maize-planting cycle. At the base of this ideology was the Popol Vuh, an epic tradition known only from a text written in the 16th century but widely represented in pre-Columbian pottery and murals. The central part of Popol Vuh deals with the myth of the Hero Twins and is considered the most ancient part of the text. Depictions of events from the Popul Vuh are, in fact, frequently found on numerous monuments from the Pacific slope region of Mexico and Guatemala, home during the Preclassic Period to the so-called Izapan style (from the archaeological site of Izapa in Chiapas, Mexico).

The creation of maize, conceived as the capture, death, and resurrection of the maize god, is narrated in the Popol Vuh through the story of Hun Hunahpu, a demigod who went to the underworld and was kidnapped and killed by Lords of Death. His sons, the Hero Twins, came to his rescue; when they revived him, he sprouted like a young corn plant. He cracked through the surface of the earth, which is represented by either a turtle shell or a serpent. The whole story takes place in the underworld, a primordial place represented as a dark and cold sea. Stelae (vertical stone slabs decorated with low-carved relief) from Izapa depict the maize god resurrection. A man wearing a godly mask is seen emerging from a large pool of water, arms outstretched, while two flanking figures help his ascension by pulling a cord he is grasping. Scholars believe that the masks the characters are wearing signal that they are performers (rulers or priests) impersonating well-known characters from the Popol Vuh.

Among the Maya of the Classic Period (150–650 C.E.) the poetic tradition of the Popol Vuh continued to flourish, and it is often found depicted on vases, found mostly in tombs, that reveal an important aspect of Maya ceremonial and courtly life. Images and text strictly interact. Although only a few inscriptions have been translated so far, episodes from the ancient epic deeds of the Hero Twins abound, including the resurrection of the maize god. The refined and private setting of the vase images point to a courtly tradition that was not concerned as much with propaganda as it was with sheer entertainment.

Teotihuacán was the most important center in Mesoamerica during the Classic Period, flourishing between 1 and 650 C.E. It was perhaps the largest city in the ancient Americas, and its domination was felt well beyond the borders of the Valley of Mexico, where its ruins can still be visited. Maya cities to the south largely borrowed from Teotihuacán art its symbols and ideology, pointing to close political, economic, and perhaps military ties between central and southern Mesoamerica. Archaeologists have not as yet discovered written historical documents from the metropolis, and it seems most likely that if written records ever existed, they were destroyed in later times. Nevertheless, mural painting, which covers the walls of many residential compounds throughout the city, bear traces of what was probably a well-developed literature, mostly revolving around fertility and agricultural themes.

Depictions include supernatural or animal figures most often depicted in profile and proceeding in procession. Richly dressed, they seem to be actively involved in sacrificial ritual activities, as indicated by the thorns and incense they often carry. Speech scrolls, indicating chanting, are often coming out of their mouth. As in later Aztec art, flowers and green jade decorations attached to the scrolls indicate poetry. The flower and jade metaphor refers to the preciousness of the words uttered during chanting and praying. Maize decorations may further allude to prayers said to spur the growth of crops.

A striking feature of Teotihuacán mural painting is its repetitiveness. Within large borders of elaborate abstract or representational designs unfold series of very similar depictions of animals, plants, or human figures, which create patterns found throughout the rooms of the same compound. Templates may vary in specific iconographic elements (that is, symbolic representation), especially garments, adornments, and colors. Some scholars suggest that the standardization of Teotihuacán representation can be linked to a writing system, one that was perhaps more fully developed in other media such as books. Repetitions and variations in painting may reflect other well-known and similar conventions of Amerindian poetry noted earlier.

Murals from the residential compound of Techinantitla, a compound in Teotihuacán, now found in fragments in museums all over the world, offer a striking example. Four feathered serpents, with long, undulating bodies, curl around a rectangular room. The bright yellow, green, and blue of the feather mantle can still be appreciated. The bodies end with elaborate jeweled rattle tails. From the mouths, streams of waters, flowers, and precious stones pour out. Below the serpents, which serve as a border, is a row of trees depicted in repeated series of nine. They all have the same basic shape and exposed roots, while variations occur in the flowers and fruits they bear.

These kinds of visual representations have been seen in relation to known incantations from the later Aztec (1250–1521) period. Plants were used for medicinal purposes, and their curative effect was sometimes translated into special qualities that were invoked during rituals. Nine was a highly significant number among Mesoamerican civilizations, especially related to the underworld. Shaman-curers were often said to enter this world in a state of trance when curing a patient. Finally, trees were important symbols of genealogy and clans. Techinantitla murals may depict a lineage song, a common form of poetry that reckoned and celebrated dynastic histories.

See also ART; CERAMICS AND POTTERY; DEATH AND BURIAL PRACTICES; DRAMA AND THEATER; EDUCATION; EMPIRES AND DYNASTIES; FESTIVALS; LANGUAGE; MUSIC AND MUSICAL INSTRUMENTS; RELIGION AND COSMOLOGY; SOCIAL ORGANIZATION; WAR AND CONQUEST; WRITING.

Africa

Saint Augustine: Excerpts from The City of God *(410–426 C.E.)*

Book 14, Chapter 28: Of the Nature of the Two Cities, the Earthly and the Heavenly

Accordingly, two cities have been formed by two loves: the earthly by the love of self, even to the contempt of God; the heavenly by the love of God, even to the contempt of self. The former, in a word, glories in itself, the latter in the Lord. For the one seeks glory from men, but the greatest glory of the other is God, the witness of conscience. The one lifts up its head in its own glory; the other says to its God, "Thou art my glory, and the lifter up of mine head." In the one, the princes and the nations it subdues are ruled by the love of ruling; in the other, the princes and the subjects serve one another in love, the latter obeying, while the former take thought for all. The one delights in its own strength, represented in the persons of its rulers; the other says to its God, "I will love Thee, O Lord, my strength." And therefore the wise men of the one city, living according to man, have sought for profit to their own bodies or souls, or both, and those who have known God "glorified Him not as God, neither were thankful, but became vain in their imaginations, and their foolish heart was darkened; professing themselves to be wise,"—that is, glorying in their own wisdom, and being possessed by pride,—"they became fools, and changed the glory of the incorruptible God into an image made like to corruptible man, and to birds, and four-footed beasts, and creeping things." For they were either leaders or followers of the people in adoring images, "and worshipped and served the creature more than the Creator, who is blessed for ever." But in the other city there is no human wisdom, but only godliness, which offers due worship to the true God, and looks for its reward in the society of the saints, of holy angels as well as holy men, "that God may be all in all."

Book 15, Chapter 4: Of the Conflict and Peace of the Earthly City

But the earthly city, which shall not be everlasting (for it will no longer be a city when it has been committed to the extreme penalty), has its good in this world and rejoices in it with such joy as such things can afford. But as this is not a good which can discharge its devotees of all distresses, this city is often divided against itself by litigations, wars, quarrels, and such victories as are either life-destroying or short-lived. For each part of it that arms against another part of it seeks to triumph over the nations through itself in bondage to vice. If, when it has conquered, it is inflated with pride, its victory is life-destroying; but if it turns its thoughts upon the common casualties of our mortal condition, and is rather anxious concerning the disasters that may befall it than elated with the successes already achieved, this victory, though of a higher kind, is still only short-lived; for it cannot abidingly rule over those whom it has victoriously subjugated. But the things which this city desires cannot justly be said to be evil, for it is itself, in its own kind, better than all other human good. For it desires earthly peace for the sake of enjoying earthly goods, and it makes war in order to attain to this peace; since, if it has conquered, and there remains no one to resist it, it enjoys a peace which it had not while there were opposing parties who contested for the enjoyment of those things which were too small to satisfy both. This peace is purchased by toilsome wars; it is obtained by what they style a glorious victory. Now, when victory remains with the party which had the juster cause, who hesitates to congratulate the victor, and style it a desirable peace? These things, then, are good things, and without doubt the gifts of God. But if they neglect the better things of the heavenly city, which are secured by eternal victory and peace never-ending, and so inordinately covet these present good things that they believe them to be the only desirable things, or love them better than those things which are believed to be better,—if this be so, then it is necessary that misery follow and ever increase.

Book 19, Chapter 17: What Produces Peace, and What Discord, between the Heavenly and Earthly Cities

But the families which do not live by faith seek their peace in the earthly advantages of this life; while the families which live by faith look for those eternal blessings which are promised, and use as pilgrims such advantages of time and of earth as do not fascinate and divert them from God, but rather aid them to endure with greater ease, and to keep down the number of

(continued)

(continues)

those burdens of the corruptible body which weigh upon the soul. Thus the things necessary for this mortal life are used by both kinds of men and families alike, but each has its own peculiar and widely different aim in using them. The earthly city, which does not live by faith, seeks an earthly peace, and the end it proposes, in the well-ordered concord of civic obedience and rule, is the combination of men's wills to attain the things which are helpful to this life. The heavenly city, or rather the part of it which sojourns on earth and lives by faith, makes use of this peace only because it must, until this mortal condition which necessitates it shall pass away. Consequently, so long as it lives like a captive and a stranger in the earthly city, though it has already received the promise of redemption, and the gift of the Spirit as the earnest of it, it makes no scruple to obey the laws of the earthly city, whereby the things necessary for the maintenance of this mortal life are administered; and thus, as this life is common to both cities, so there is a harmony between them in regard to what belongs to it. . . . This heavenly city, then, while it sojourns on earth, calls citizens out of all nations, and gathers together a society of pilgrims of all languages, not scrupling about diversities in the manners, laws, and institutions whereby earthly peace is secured and maintained, but recognizing that, however various these are, they all tend to one and the same end of earthly peace. It therefore is so far from rescinding and abolishing these diversities that it even preserves and adopts them, so long only as no hindrance to the worship of the one supreme and true God is thus introduced. Even the heavenly city, therefore, while in its state of pilgrimage, avails itself of the peace of earth, and, so far as it can without injuring faith and godliness, desires and maintains a common agreement among men regarding the acquisition of the necessaries of life, and makes this earthly peace bear upon the peace of heaven. . . . In its pilgrim state the heavenly city possesses this peace by faith; and by this faith it lives righteously when it refers to the attainment of that peace every good action towards God and man; for the life of the city is a social life.

From: The Internet History Sourcebooks. Available online. URL: http://www.fordham.edu/halsall/.

Egypt

"The Tale of The Eloquent Peasant," ca. 1800 B.C.E.

There was a man, Hunanup by name, a peasant of Sechet-hemat, and he had a wife. . . . Then said this peasant to his wife: "Behold, I am going down to Egypt to bring back bread for my children. Go in and measure the grain that we still have in our storehouse." . . . Then this peasant went down to Egypt after he had loaded his asses with all the good produce of Sechet-hemat.

This peasant set out and journeyed southward to Ehnas. He came to a point opposite Per-fefi, north of Medenit, and found there a man standing on the bank, Dehuti-necht by name, . . .

Then said this Dehuti-necht, when he saw the asses of this peasant which appealed to his covetousness: "Oh that some good god would help me to rob this peasant of his goods!"

The house of Dehuti-necht stood close to the side of the path, which was narrow, not wide. .. . Upon one side of it was the water and upon the other side was growing grain. Then said Dehitu-necht to his servant: "Hasten and bring me a shawl from the house!" . . . Then he spread this shawl upon the middle of the road, and it extended one edge to the water and the other to the grain.

The peasant came along the path which was the common highway. Then said Dehuti-necht: "Look out, peasant, do not trample on my clothes!" The peasant answered: "I will do as you wish; I will go in the right way!" As he was turning to the upper side, Dehuti-necht said: "Does my grain serve you as a road?" Then said the peasant: "I am going in the right way. The bank is steep and the path lies near the grain and you have stopped up the road ahead with your clothes. Will you, then, not let me go by?" Upon that one of the asses took a mouthful of grain. Then said Dehuti-necht: "See, I will take away your ass because it has eaten my grain."

Then the peasant said: ". . . As one side was made impassable I have led my ass along the other, and will you seize it because it has taken a mouthful of grain? But I know the lord of this property; it belongs to the chief steward, Meruitensi. It is he who punishes every robber in this whole land. Shall I, then, be robbed in his domain?"

Then said Dehuti-necht: "Is it not a proverb which the people employ: "The name of the poor is only known on account of his lord?' It is I who speak to you, but the chief steward of whom you think." Then he took a rod from a green tamarisk and beat all his limbs with it, and seized his asses and drove them into his compound.

Thereupon the peasant wept loudly on account of the pain of what had been done to him. ...

The peasant consumed four days, during which he besought Dehuti-necht, but he did not grant him his rights. Then this peasant went to the south, to Ehnas to implore the chief steward, Meruitensi. He met him as he was coming out of the canal-door of his compound to embark in his boat. Thereupon the peasant said: "Oh let me lay before you this affair. . . ." Then the steward Meruitensi, sent one of his servants to him, and he sent back by him an account of the whole affair. Then the chief steward, Meruitensi, laid the case of Dehuti-necht before his attendant officials, and they said to him: "Lord, it is presumably a case of one of your peasants who has gone against another peasant near him. Behold, it is customary with peasants to so conduct themselves toward others who are near them. Shall we beat Dehuti-necht for a little natron and a little salt? Command him to restore it and he will restore it."

The chief steward, Meruitensi, remained silent. . . . The peasant then came to entreat the chief steward Meruitensi, for the first time, and said: "Chief steward, my lord, you are greatest of the great, you are guide of all that which is not and which is. . . . Let me place your name in this land higher than all good laws: you guide without avarice, you great one free from meanness, who destroys deceit, who creates truthfulness. Throw the evil to the ground. . . . Do justice, O you praised one, whom the praised ones praise. . . ."

This peasant came to implore him for the eighth time, and said: "Chief steward, my lord, . . . Greed is absent from a good merchant. . . . Your heart is greedy, it does not become you. . . . The officers, who are set as a protection against injustice,—a curse to the shameless are these officers, who are set as a bulwark against lies. Fear of you has not deterred me from supplicating you; if you think so, you have not known my heart. . . . Your real estate is in the country, your bread is on your estate, your food is in the storehouse. Your officials give to you and you take it. Are you, then, not a robber? . . . Do the truth for the sake of the Lord of Truth.. . . ."

Then . . . the chief steward, Meruitensi . . . caused them to bring, written on a new roll, all the addresses of these days. The chief steward sent them to his majesty, the king of Upper and Lower Egypt, Neb-kau-re, the blessed, and they were more agreeable to the heart of his majesty than all that was in his land. His majesty said, "Pass sentence yourself my beloved son!" Then the chief steward, Meruitensi, caused two servants to go and bring a list of the household of Dehuti-necht from the government office, and his possessions were six persons, with a selection . . . from his barley, from his spelt, from his asses, from his swine.

[The ensuing words cannot be made out, but it appears that the goods of Dehuti-necht were given to the peasant and he was sent home rejoicing.]

From: George A. Barton, *Archaeology and the Bible*, 3rd ed. (Philadelphia: American Sunday School, 1920), pp. 418–421.

The Middle East

Enûma Elish (The Epic of Creation), excerpt (eighth century B.C.E.)

The First Tablet

When in the height heaven was not named,
And the earth beneath did not yet bear a name,
And the primeval Apsu, who begat them,
And chaos, Tiamut, the mother of them both
Their waters were mingled together,
And no field was formed, no marsh was to be seen;
When of the gods none had been called into being,
And none bore a name, and no destinies were ordained;
Then were created the gods in the midst of heaven,
Lahmu and Lahamu were called into being. . . .
Ages increased, . . .

(continued)

(continues)

Then Ansar and Kisar were created, . . .
Long were the days, then there came forth . . .
Anu, their son, . . .
Ansar and Anu . . .
And the god Anu . . .
Nudimmud, whom his fathers, his begetters . . .
Abounding in all wisdom. . . .
He was exceeding strong . . .
He had no rival—
Thus were established and were . . . the great gods.
But Tiamat and Apsu were still in confusion. . . .
They were troubled and . . .
In disorder. . . .
Apru was not diminished in might . . .
And Tiamat roared. . . .
She smote. . . .
Their way was evil. . . .
Then Apsu, the begetter of the great gods,
Cried unto Mummu, his minister, and said unto him:
"O Mummu, thou minister that rejoicest my spirit,
Come, unto Tiamut let us go!
So they went and before Tiamat they lay down,
They consulted on a plan with regard to the gods, their sons.
Apsu opened his mouth and spake,
And unto Tiamut, the glistening one, he addressed the word:
. . . By day I cannot rest, by night I can not lie down in peace.
But I will destroy their way. . . .
Let there be lamentation, and let us lie down again in peace."
When Tiamat heard these words,
She raged and cried aloud. . . .
She uttered a curse, and unto Apsu she spake:
"What then shall we do?
Let their way be made difficult, and let us lie down again in peace."
Mummu answered, and gave counsel unto Apsu, . . .

and hostile to the gods was the counsel Mummu gave:
Come, their way is strong, but thou shalt destroy it;
Then by day shalt thou have rest, by night shalt thou lie down in peace."
Apsu harkened unto him and his countenance grew bright,
Since he (Mummu) planned evil against the gods his sons. . . .
His knees became weak; they gave way beneath him,
Because of the evil which their first-born had planned. . . .
Then Ea, who knoweth all that is, went up and he beheld their muttering. . . .

[The lines become unintelligible.]

. . . he hath conquered and
. . . he weepeth and sitteth in tribulation.
. . . we shall not lie down in peace.
. . . Apsu is laid waste,
. . . and Mummu, who were taken captive
. . . let us lie down in peace. . . .
And Tiamat harkened unto the word of the bright god, and said:
. . . shalt thou entrust! let us wage war!" . . .
They banded themselves together and at the side of
Tiamat they advanced;
They were furious; they devised mischief without resting night and day.
They prepared for battle, fuming and raging;
They joined their forces and made war,
Ummu-Hubur [Tiamat] who formed all things,
Made in addition weapons invincible; she spawned monster-serpents,
Sharp of tooth, and merciless of fang;
With poison, instead of blood, she filled their bodies.
Fierce monster-vipers she clothed with terror.
With splendor she decked them, she made them of lofty stature.
Whoever beheld them, terror overcame him.
Their bodies reared up, and none could withstand their attack.
She set up vipers and dragons, and the monster Lahamu,
And hurricanes, and raging hounds, and scorpion-men,
And mighty tempests, and fish-men, and rams;
They bore cruel weapons, without fear of the fight.
Her commands were mighty, none could resist them.
After this fashion, huge of stature, she made eleven [kinds of] monsters.
Among the gods who were her sons, inasmuch as he had given her support,
She exalted Kingu; in their midst she raised him to power.
To march before the forces, to lead the host,
To give the battle-signal, to advance to the attack,
To direct the battle, to control the fight,
Unto him she entrusted; in costly raiment she made him sit, saying:
I have uttered thy spell, in the assembly of the gods I have raised thee to power.
The dominion over all the gods have I entrusted unto him.
Be thou exalted, thou my chosen spouse,

May they magnify thy name over all of them the Anunnaki."
She gave him the Tablets of Destiny, on his breast she laid them, saying:
Thy command shall not be without avail, and the word of thy mouth shall be established."
Now Kingu, thus exalted, having received the power of Anu,
Decreed the fate among the gods his sons, saying:
"Let the opening of your mouth quench the Fire-god;
Whoso is exalted in the battle, let him display his might!"

From: Leonard William King, *The Seven Tablets of Creation* (London: Luzac and Co., 1902).

Asia and the Pacific

Bhagavad Gita, excerpt from the Mahabharata, *(ca. 400 B.C.E.)*

Chapter 1

Dhritirashtra:

Ranged thus for battle on the sacred plain On Kurukshetra—say, Sanjaya! say What wrought my people, and the Pandavas?

Sanjaya:

When he beheld the host of Pandavas Raja Duryodhana to Drona drew, And spake these words: "Ah, Guru! see this line, How vast it is of Pandu fighting-men, Embattled by the son of Drupada, Thy scholar in the war! Therein stand ranked Chiefs like Arjuna, like to Bhima chiefs, Benders of bows; Virata, Yuyudhan, Drupada, eminent upon his car, Dhrishtaket, Chekitan, Kasi's stout lord, Purujit, Kuntibhoj, and Saivya, With Yudhamanyu, and Uttamauj Subhadra's child; and Drupadi's;—all famed! All mounted on their shining chariots! On our side, too,—thou best of Brahmans! see Excellent chiefs, commanders of my line, Whose names I joy to count: thyself the first, Then Bhishma, Karna, Kripa fierce in fight, Vikarna, Aswatthaman; next to these Strong Saumadatti, with full many more Valiant and tried, ready this day to die For me their king, each with his weapon grasped, Each skilful in the field. Weakest—meseems Our battle shows where Bhishma holds command, And Bhima, fronting him, something too strong! Have care our captains nigh to Bhishma's ranks Prepare what help they may! Now, blow my shell!"

Then, at the signal of the aged king, With blare to wake the blood, rolling around Like to a lion's roar, the trumpeter Blew the great Conch; and, at the noise of it, Trumpets and drums, cymbals and gongs and horns Burst into sudden clamor; as the blasts Of loosened tempest, such the tumult seemed! Then might be seen, upon their car of gold Yoked with white steeds, blowing their battle-shells, Krishna the God, Arjuna at his side: Krishna, with knotted locks, blew his great conch Carved of the "Giant's bone;" Arjuna blew Indra's loud gift; Bhima the terrible Wolf-bellied Bhima—blew a long reed-conch; And Yudhisthira, Kunti's blameless son, Winded a mighty shell, "Victory's Voice;" And Nakula blew shrill upon his conch Named the "Sweet-sounding," Sahadev on his Called "Gem-bedecked," and Kasi's Prince on his. Sikhandi on his car, Dhrishtadyumn, Virata, Satyaki the Unsubdued, Drupada, with his sons, (O Lord of Earth!) Long-armed Subhadra's children, all blew loud, So that the clangor shook their foemen's hearts, With quaking earth and thundering heav'n. Then 'twas

Beholding Dhritirashtra's battle set, Weapons unsheathing, bows drawn forth, the war Instant to break—Arjun, whose ensign-badge Was Hanuman the monkey, spake this thing To Krishna the Divine, his charioteer: "Drive, Dauntless One! to yonder open ground Betwixt the armies; I would see more nigh These who will fight with us, those we must slay To-day, in war's arbitrament; for, sure, On bloodshed all are bent who throng this plain, Obeying Dhritirashtra's sinful son."

Thus, by Arjuna prayed (O Bharata!) Between the hosts that heavenly Charioteer Drove the brightfcar, reining its milk-white steeds Where Bhishma led, and Drona, and their Lords. "See!" spake he to Arjuna,

(continued)

(continues)

"where they stand, Thy kindred of the Kurus:" and the Prince Marked on each hand the kinsmen of his house, Grandsires and sires, uncles and brothers and sons, Cousins and sons-in-law and nephews, mixed With friends and honored elders; some this side, Some that side ranged: and, seeing those opposed, Such kith grown enemies—Arjuna's heart Melted with pity, while he uttered this:

Arjuna:

Krishna! as I behold, come here to shed Their common blood, yon concourse of our kin, My members fail, my tongue dries in my mouth, A shudder thrills my body, and my hair Bristles with horror; from my weak hand slips Gandiv, the goodly bow; a fever burns My skin to parching; hardly may I stand; The life within me seems to swim and faint; Nothing do I foresee save woe and wail! It is not good, O Keshav! nought of good Can spring from mutual slaughter! Lo, I hate Triumph and domination, wealth and ease, Thus sadly won! Aho! what victory Can bring delight, Govinda! what rich spoils Could profit; what rule recompense; what span Of life itself seem sweet, bought with such blood? Seeing that these stand here, ready to die, For whose sake life was fair, and pleasure pleased, And power grew precious:—grandsires, sires, and sons. Brothers, and fathers-in-law, and sons-in-law, Elders and friends! Shall I deal death on these Even though they seek to slay us? Not one blow, O Madhusudan! will I strike to gain The rule of all Three Worlds; then, how much less To seize an earthly kingdom! Killing these Must breed but anguish, Krishna! If they be Guilty, we shall grow guilty by their deaths; Their sins will light on us, if we shall slay Those sons of Dhritirashtra, and our kin; What peace could come of that, O Madhava? For if indeed, blinded by lust and wrath, These cannot see, or will not see, the sin Of kingly lines o'erthrown and kinsmen slain, How should not we, who see, shun such a crime We who perceive the guilt and feel the shame Oh, thou Delight of Men, Janardana? By overthrow of houses perisheth Their sweet continuous household piety, And - rites neglected, piety extinct Enters impiety upon that home; Its women grow unwomaned, whence there spring Mad passions, and the mingling-up of castes, Sending a Hell-ward road that family, And whoso wrought its doom by wicked wrath. Nay, and the souls of honored ancestors Fall from their place of peace, being bereft Of funeral-cakes and the wan death-water.[1] So teach our holy hymns. Thus, if we slay Kinsfolk and friends for love of earthly power, Ahovat! what an evil fault it were! Better I deem it, if my kinsmen strike, To face them weaponless, and bare my breast To shaft and spear, than answer blow with blow. . . .

So speaking, in the face of those two hosts, Arjuna sank upon his chariot-seat, And let fall bow and arrows, sick at heart.

From: Edwin Arnold, *The Song Celestial; or, Bhagavad-Gîtâ (from the Mahâbhârata)* (Boston: Roberts Brothers, 1885).

Greece

Plato: The Allegory of the Cave, from The Republic, *ca. 360* B.C.E.

Compare our nature in respect to education with our condition. Imagine men in an underground cave with an entrance open toward the light which extends through the whole cave. Within the cave are people who from childhood have had chains on their legs and their necks so they could only look forward but not turn their heads. There is burning a fire, above and behind them, and between the fire and the chains is a road above, along which one may see a little wall built along, just as the stages of conjurers are built before the people in whose presence they show their tricks. . . . Imagine then by the side of this little wall men carrying all sorts of machines rising above the wall, and statues of men and other animals wrought in stone, wood, and other materials, some of bearers probably speaking, others proceeding in silenced. . . . [Do you think] that such as these [chained men] would have seen anything else of themselves or one another except the shadows that fall from the fire on the opposite side of the cave? How can they . . . if indeed they are forced to always keep their heads unmoved? . . . . [S]uch persons would believe that truth was nothing else but the shadows of the exhibitions. Let us inquire then, as to their liberation from captivity, and their cure for insanity. . . . [What if one of these chained persons was] let loose and obliged immediately to rise up, and turn round his neck and walk, and look upwards to the light, and doing all this still feel pained, and be disabled by the dazzling form seeing those things of which he formerly saw the shadows. What would he say if anyone were to tell him that he formerly saw mere empty visions, but now saw more correctly, as being nearer to the real thing, and turned toward what was more real. Then, what if you specially pointing out to him, and made him tell you the nature of what he saw. Do you think that he would be embarrassed? Do you think that he would think now that what he saw before was truer than what he sees now?

Even if a person could force him to look at the light itself, would he not have pain in his eyes and look away? And then, would not he turn to what he really could see [without pain] and think that these are really more clear than what had just been shown to him? But if a person was then to forcibly drag him out of the cave without stopping, until he was in the light of the sun, would he not be pained and indignant? Would not he, while in this light and having his eyes dazzled with the splendor, be able to see anything that he thought was true? No, he could not, at that moment. He would need to get some degree of practice if he would see things above him. First, he would most easily perceive the shadows, and then the images of men and other animals in the water, and after that the things themselves. And then he would more easily see the things in heaven, and heaven itself, by night, looking to the light of the stars and the moon, than after daylight to the sun and the light of the sun. How else? Finally, he might be able to perceive and contemplate the nature of the sun, not as respects its images in water or any other place, but itself by itself in its own proper place.

From: Plato, *The Republic*, George Burgess, trans. (New York: Walter Dunne, 1901).

Rome

Horace: The Secular Hymn (ca. 17 B.C.E.)

Phoebus! and Dian, you whose sway,
Mountains and woods obey!
Twin glories of the skies, forever worshiped, hear!
Accept our prayer this sacred year
When, as the Sibyl's voice ordained
For ages yet to come,
Pure maids and youths unstained
Invoke the Gods who love the sevenfold hills of Rome.

All bounteous Sun!
Forever changing, and forever one!
Who in your lustrous car bear'st forth light,
And hid'st it, setting, in the arms of Night,
Look down on worlds outspread, yet nothing see
Greater than Rome, and Rome's high sovereignty.
You Ilithyia, too, whatever name,
Goddess, you do approve,
Lucina, Genitalis, still the same
Aid destined mothers with a mother's love;

Prosper the Senate's wise decree,
Fertile of marriage faith and countless progeny!
As centuries progressive wing their flight
For you the grateful hymn shall ever sound;
Thrice by day, and thrice by night
For you the choral dance shall beat the ground.

Fates! whose unfailing word
Spoken from lips Sibylline shall abide,
Ordained, preserved and sanctified
By Destiny's eternal law, accord
To Rome new blessings that shall last
In chain unbroken from the Past.
Mother of fruits and flocks, prolific Earth!
Bind wreaths of spiked corn round Ceres's hair:
And may soft showers and Jove's benignant air
Nurture each infant birth!

Lay down your arrows, God of day!
Smile on your youths elect who singing pray.
You, Crescent Queen, bow down your star-crowned head
And on your youthful choir a kindly influence shed.
If Rome be all your work—if Troy's sad band
Safe sped by you attained the Etruscan strand,
A chosen remnant, vowed
To seek new Lares, and a changed abode—
Remnant for whom thro Ilion's blazing gate
Aeneas, orphan of a ruined State,
Opened a pathway wide and free
To happier homes and liberty:—
Ye Gods! If Rome be yours, to placid Age
Give timely rest: to docile Youth

(continued)

(continues)

Grant the rich heritage
Of morals, modesty, and truth.
On Rome herself bestow a teaming race
Wealth, Empire, Faith, and all befitting Grace.

Vouchsafe to Venus' and Anchises' heir,
Who offers at your shrine
Due sacrifice of milk-white kine,
Justly to rule, to pity and to dare,
To crush insulting hosts, the prostrate foeman spare
The haughty Mede has learned to fear
The Alban axe, the Latian spear,
And Scythians, suppliant now, await
The conqueror's doom, their coming fate.
Honor and Peace, and Pristine Shame,
And Virtue's oft dishonored name,
Have dared, long exiled, to return,
And with them Plenty lifts her golden horn.
Augur Apollo! Bearer of the bow!
Warrior and prophet! Loved one of the Nine!
Healer in sickness! Comforter in woe!
If still the templed crags of Palatine
And Latium's fruitful plains to you are dear,
Perpetuate for cycles yet to come,
Mightier in each advancing year,
The ever growing might and majesty of Rome.
You, too, Diana, from your Aventine,
And Algidus' deep woods, look down and hear
The voice of those who guard the books Divine,
And to your youthful choir incline a loving ear.

Return we home! We know that Jove
And all the Gods our song approve
To Phoebus and Diana given;
The virgin hymn is heard in Heaven.

From: William Stearns Davis, ed., *Readings in Ancient History: Illustrative Extracts from the Sources*, Vol. 2, *Rome and the West* (Boston: Allyn and Bacon, 1912–1913).

Rome

Virgil: Excerpt from the Aeneid *(30–19 B.C.E.)*

Book 6

[Anchises, in the realms of the dead, is reciting to his son, Aeneas, the future glories of the Roman race.]

Lo! Caesar and all the Julian
Line, predestined to rise to the infinite spaces of heaven.
This, yea, this is the man, so often foretold you in promise,
Caesar Augustus, descended from God, who again shall a golden
Age in Latium found, in fields once governed by Saturn
Further than India's hordes, or the Garymantian peoples
He shall extend his reign; there's a land beyond all of our planets

Yond the far track of the year and the sun, where sky-bearing Atlas
Turns on his shoulders the firmament studded with bright constellations;
Yea, even now, at his coming, foreshadowed by omens from heaven,
Shudder the Caspian realms, and the barbarous Scythian kingdoms,
While the disquieted harbors of Nile are affrighted!

[Anchises now points out the long line of worthies and conquerors who are to precede Augustus, and adds these lines.]

Others better may fashion the breathing bronze with more delicate fingers;
Doubtless they also will summon more lifelike features from marble:
They shall more cunningly plead at the bar; and the mazes of heaven
Draw to the scale and determine the march of the swift constellations.

Yours be the care, O Rome, to subdue the whole world for your empire!
These be the arts for you—the order of peace to establish,
Them that are vanquished to spare, and them that are haughty to humble!

From: William Stearns Davis, ed., *Readings in Ancient History: Illustrative Extracts from the Sources*, Vol. 2, *Rome and the West* (Boston: Allyn and Bacon, 1912–1913), pp. 174–179.

FURTHER READING

Michael Alexander, trans., *The Earliest English Poems* (London and New York: Penguin Classics, 1992).

Kenneth J. Atchity and Rosemary McKenna, eds., *The Classical Roman Reader: New Encounters with Ancient Rome* (New York: Oxford University Press, 1998).

W. H. Auden, ed., *The Portable Greek Reader* (New York: Penguin, 1977).

Kathleen Berrin, ed., *Feathered Serpents and Flowering Trees: Reconstructing the Murals of Teotihuacán* (San Francisco: Fine Arts Museums of San Francisco, 1988).

Jeremy Black, Graham Cunningham, Eleanor Robson, and Gabor Zolyomi, eds., *The Literature of Ancient Sumer* (New York: Oxford University Press, 2006).

Elaine Fantham, *Roman Literary Culture: From Cicero to Apuleius* (Baltimore, Md.: Johns Hopkins University Press, 1996).

Michael V. Fox, *The Song of Songs and the Ancient Egyptian Love Songs* (Madison: University of Wisconsin Press, 1985).

Douglas Hyde, *The Story of Early Gaelic Literature* (London: T. F. Unwin, 1905).

Bernard Knox, ed., *The Norton Book of Classical Literature* (New York: Norton, 1993).

John T. Koch, ed., *The Celtic Heroic Age: Literary Sources for Ancient Celtic Europe and Early Ireland and Wales* (Malden, Mass.: Celtic Studies Publications, 2003).

Lai Ming, *A History of Chinese Literature* (New York: John Day, 1964).

Peter H. Lee, ed., *A History of Korean Literature* (New York: Cambridge University Press, 2003).

Henrietta McCall, *Mesopotamian Myths* (Austin: University of Texas Press, 1990).

F. Max Müller, *A History of Ancient Sanskrit Literature* (New Delhi, India: South Asia Books, 1993).

R. I. Page, *Runes* (Berkeley: University of California Press, 1987).

R. B. Parkinson, *Voices from Ancient Egypt: An Anthology of Middle Kingdom Writings* (London: British Museum Press, 2004).

William Kelly Simpson, ed., *The Literature of Ancient Egypt: An Anthology of Stories, Instructions, and Poetry* (New Haven, Conn.: Yale University Press, 1973).

Karl A Taube, *The Writing System of Ancient Teotihuacán* (Barnardsville, N.C., and Washington, D.C.: Center for Ancient American Studies, 2000).

Dennis Tedlock, trans., *Popol Vuh: The Definitive Edition of the Mayan Book of the Dawn of Life and the Glories of Gods and Kings* (New York: Simon and Schuster, 1985).

M

▶ metallurgy

INTRODUCTION

Historians identify major periods in ancient history by the primary materials people used to make tools. Thus, the Stone Age, the longest period identified this way, extended back some two million years ago. It ended at various times throughout the world, perhaps about 6000 B.C.E. in the Near East and Asia, 4000 B.C.E. in Europe, and 2500 B.C.E. in the Americas. What brought the Stone Age to an end was the widespread adoption of metal rather than stone for making tools and weapons. The first "metal age" was the Copper Age, when tools made of copper began to be used along with those made of stone. While copper was malleable and easy to work and copper tools did not easily break, its usefulness was limited because it was not very hard.

A major advance in human civilization was the development of bronze, an alloy of copper and tin. The combination produced a much harder metal, allowing people to forge tools that were more durable and could do more work. So important was this development that historians refer to the period running from about the fourth or third millennium B.C.E. to roughly 1200 B.C.E. as the Bronze Age. These dates, though, are very approximate and differed widely depending on the region of the world. Bronze did not even reach the Americas, for example, until roughly 900 B.C.E. For this reason, historians often specify a region of the world in referring to the Bronze Age, such as the Nordic Bronze Age or the Central European Bronze Age.

The Bronze Age came to an end with the emergence of iron as the favored metal, primarily because iron ore was more plentiful and iron was cheaper to mine and refine. Accordingly, historians refer to the Iron Age, which followed on the heels of the Bronze Age cultures that preceded it and lasted through the remainder of ancient times. A further refinement of iron was the development of steel, which hardened iron and enabled metalsmiths to make highly durable tools. It is believed that the ancient Africans were the first to form hard carbon steel in the world's first blast furnaces, which could reach extremely high temperatures.

The discovery of these metals required ancient peoples to develop the science of metallurgy, referring to technologies for extracting metals from ores, purifying them, combining them with other metals to form alloys, and fashioning them into useful objects. To create metal objects, the ancients learned many forms of casting, or the process of pouring molten metal into molds, where it would cool and harden. The mold was removed, often by breaking it, leaving behind the metal object.

Another way of working metal, especially soft metal, was hammering it into shape; annealing was a process to reduce of the brittleness of hammered metal by heating it. Soft metals such as gold and silver were easily worked into primarily decorative objects such as jewelry; they could also be used to decorate objects made of iron and other materials, enhancing their value and aesthetic appeal. Some historians have theorized that ancient cultures discovered primitive batteries that used electric current to deposit thin layers of metals on the surface of other metals in a process called electroplating.

AFRICA

BY KIRK H. BEETZ

Almost guaranteed to set a gathering of African archaeologists to arguing is the subject of metallurgy. Where it started, how it developed, and how it spread has been disputed in many publications. It is possible that the first metal Africans worked was gold, because it often appears as nuggets that can be hammered into shapes. Other metals available to Africans were copper, tin, and iron. Ancient Africans may have found silver, too, but the archaeological evidence suggests that silver was imported from the Mediterranean world, perhaps from the Iberian Peninsula, the land where Portugal and Spain are today.

Most archaeologists and historians agree that the smelting of metals in Africa probably began in Egypt. The technology for making bronze out of copper and tin probably was imported from the Near East into Egypt. When Egypt solidified its control of Nubia, the land south of Egypt, during the reign of Pepy II (r. ca. 2246–ca. 2152 B.C.E.), Africans outside Egypt were still in the Stone Age. Is likely that the Egyptians introduced the copper to the Nubians; the Nubians used copper to make spearheads that looked like long leaves, though most of their spears were still tipped with stone. Nubian copper tools from that era were either imports from Egypt or copies of Egyptian tools.

Nubia was rich in gold, and over the years Nubia's gold mines yielded about 65 pounds of pure gold from about 9,000 tons of ore annually. This gold went to enrich Egypt, helping to make Egypt one of the wealthiest nations of the ancient world. Elsewhere in Africa gold was being made into jewelry. Whether techniques for smelting gold ore were passed from Egypt to Nubians and then to the rest of Africa or Africans figured out these techniques for themselves is unclear. That Africans loved the decorative possibilities of gold is plain. In central and western Africa people learned to sift gold nuggets out of streambeds and even how to mine gold dust from quartz.

In the 1600s B.C.E. the kingdom of Karmah stretched its dominion northward over lands to the south of Egypt nearly to the first cataract of the Nile River. The Karmahn culture was still in the Stone Age and did metalworking. Between 1504 and 1492 B.C.E. Egypt conquered Karmah and swept south to take control of Nubia. Until Egypt's withdrawal in 1070 B.C.E., Egyptian technology passed to other Africans through Nubia. By that time the secrets of making bronze were known to the peoples of northeastern Africa, but they still worked primarily in copper, perhaps because tin was hard to find locally and had to be imported from the north or from western Africa, where there were tin mines.

The kingdom of Kush arose around 900 B.C.E., encompassing most of the Blue Nile and White Nile rivers. During several military campaigns from about 728 to 702 B.C.E. Kush conquered Egypt. Although ironworking was established in the Near East in the early 1000s B.C.E., Egyptian armies still used bronze weapons, and Kushites used mostly stone weapons. The use of iron for tools and weapons came crashing in on the Kushites in about 671 B.C.E. when Assyria invaded Egypt. Although bronze held its edge better than iron, iron was easier to manufacture in large quantities and had special qualities for armor, including its ability to be case-hardened. The ancient smiths would either pour liquid iron into molds or hammer it into shape by repeatedly heating it until it was soft, beating it, heating it again, and so on. In a bed of carbon, possibly charcoal but more often the ashes of husks of grain, the hot iron would be set to rest. This might be done several times, during which the iron would absorb the carbon and harden on the outside while remaining soft and flexible on the inside. This meant that when it was struck, iron armor flexed rather than broke. Superior tactics and superior armor were the advantages of the Assyrians.

In 593 B.C.E. Kush moved its capital from Napata to Meroë, where iron from mines was plentiful. There, a large iron-making industry developed. Kushite ironworkers built furnaces out of clay. Into these furnaces were inserted clay tubes. Bellows, probably made of animal skins, were attached to the outside of the tubes. When the bellows were pumped, outside air flowed into and through the furnaces, creating the effect of a blast furnace. The superheating caused by the blasts of air allowed the smiths to reach the 2,797 degrees Fahrenheit required to make iron liquid and pourable. The smiths could therefore make almost anything they wished out of iron, and although bronze remained the preference for decoration, iron vaulted Kush out of the Stone Age. Numerous large slag heaps still exist in Meroë.

The long-standing African custom of remelting metal objects, especially gold, to be remade into whatever was currently fashionable has made it hard to trace how metallurgy spread. Sometime between 700 and 500 B.C.E. a major metalworking culture emerged in a valley along the Niger River in western Africa, almost due west of Kush. It is called Nok after the village near the tin mine where the first remnants of the culture were found in 1928. Its exceptionally well-sculpted ceramic figures have caught the imaginations of archaeologists, but little is known about the Nok. One of the greatest puzzles they present is that they were working metals when Kushites were doing so, and they may have begun smelting iron before the Kush.

Archaeologists and historians have proposed various ways this could have happened. One is that traders brought the knowledge with them from the Phoenicians or the Greeks who traded with the Noks. Another is that people fled west from Kush when nomads invaded their kingdom. They would have fled along the Sahel corridor, grassy steppes that stretch west to east along the southern edge of the Sahara. Another possibility is that the knowledge flowed from tribe to tribe along the Sahel corridor. Yet another possibility is that the Nok learned to make bronze and smelt iron on their own. In any case, as early as 500 B.C.E. the Nok were using blast furnaces of clay with ceramic tubes that may have functioned like the Kushite blast furnaces.

During the first 500 years C.E. the knowledge of how to mine, smelt, and work iron may have been spread by the Bantu-speaking peoples of Africa during their great migrations across central Africa. Among them, certain crafts became the specialties of certain clans. An entire village might have been devoted to the manufacture of iron products. People probably processed iron mostly outdoors, but they probably turned iron into tools or other items indoors in huts similar to ones used for homes. Typically, men smithed the iron, but it seems women were more likely to trade iron products to other people. Much of the spread of ironworking to the south of Africa seems traceable to the movements of the Bantu-speaking peoples.

EGYPT

BY MARIE PASSANANTE

Metallurgy is the science that deals with the procedures used in extracting metals from their ores, purifying and alloying metals, and creating useful objects from metals. These procedures include smelting, casting, and annealing. Smelting is the melting of ore to extract metal from it. Unfortunately, there are no references to smelting in Egyptian texts. All the information we have is from archaeological evidence as well as from experimentation based on recovered artifacts.

Smelting, a relatively simple process, had been developed by the Early Dynastic Period (2920–2575 B.C.E.), and it is possible that the process was used as early as 4000 B.C.E. During smelting, crushed ore is mixed with charcoal. This mixture, called the charge, is then placed in a crucible or mud brick-lined furnace and roasted.

This procedure reduces the metal to prills—small pellets—embedded in slag, or waste material. The prills are extracted by crushing the slag and then melted together to form ingots. A simple smelting furnace would consist of a hole in the ground rimmed with a wall of mud bricks. Holes in the wall would accommodate tuyeres, or nozzles through which air is delivered into the furnace. Blowpipes or bellows would introduce air into the tuyeres. Blowpipes are represented in tomb reliefs as early as the Fifth Dynasty (2465–2323 B.C.E.). Pot bellows were probably in use as early as the Middle Kingdom (2040–1640 B.C.E.), but there is no direct evidence of their use before the Eighteenth Dynasty (1550–1307 B.C.E.). Pot bellows consist of a pottery nozzle, a piece of leather covering the wide end. The leather would be squeezed either by hand or by foot, driving air into the connecting tuyere.

Casting is the process by which an object is created by pouring molten metal into a mold. Cast objects have been dated as early as the Predynastic Period (4000–3000 B.C.E.). The process is depicted in the reliefs in the tomb of the Eighteenth Dynasty vizier Rekhmire (ca. 1450 B.C.E.). In these reliefs metalworkers are creating a pair of bronze doors for the shrine of Amun in Karnak. The molten bronze is contained in a crucible (a vessel used to melt or heat metal), which is handled by two men using wooden sticks as tongs. The men pour the liquid bronze into series of funnels inserted into the mold; the multiple funnels ensure the even distribution of metal. The crucible containing the metal is bowl shaped and has a hole in the side for pouring. A mold could be carved in stone, shaped in pottery, or even formed in sand.

The lost-wax method of casting allowed the craftsman to fashion an object with greater detail, and for this reason it was a favored method for creating figurines and amulets. First the craftsman sculpted in wax a model of the desired object. He then covered the wax model in clay and fired the result. The heat hardened the clay to create the mold and melt the wax, leaving a space into which the molten metal would be poured. After the metal had cooled, the mold was broken to extract the casting. Alternatively, the craftsman could use a modified version of the lost-wax method called hollow casting. Instead of modeling a figure wholly out of wax, he would model the wax around a clay core. This model would be covered in clay and fired just as in the lost-wax method. The core would be held in place by iron struts, which were in use by the Third Intermediate Period (1070–712 B.C.E.), or possibly by pure copper struts. Hollow casting was favored in the production of larger objects because less metal was used and because the process reduced potential shrinkage and distortion in the mold.

In annealing, a piece of worked metal is heated to reduce the hardness and brittleness that result from hammering. The heat rearranges the internal structure of the metal, making it easier to shape. The earliest object showing evidence of annealing is a copper ax head from the Naqada II Period (3500–3000 B.C.E.). There are few textual references to annealing. The captions in the metalworking scenes in two Fifth Dynasty tombs mention heating sheet metal after hammering it. In the tomb of Wepemnofret, the caption states that the reason for heating the metal is to reduce chance of cracking and imperfections, the very definition of annealing.

Copper was made into a wide range of objects, from tools and weapons to statues, both as pure copper and in alloys with arsenic, tin (bronze), and lead. The earliest examples of cast copper date from the Naqada Period (3300–3000 B.C.E.), and lost-wax casting was in use by the Old Kingdom (2575–2134 B.C.E.). Copper statuary is rare before the Middle Kingdom, and production peaks only in the Third Intermediate Period.

Gold is perhaps the easiest metal to work, and it did not need to be smelted. Gold was extracted from the earth by placing gold-bearing sand or crushed rock in a vessel with water and agitating the mixture to separate the particles; gold is heavier and sinks to the bottom, while the sand and crushed rock are discarded with the water. Gold was not refined further until the Late Period (712–332 B.C.E.), despite having been in use since the Predynastic Period. Gold was worked both by casting and by cutting and shaping sheet gold (gold hammered into a thin sheet). However, because casting wasted metal, objects made from sheet gold outnumbered cast objects; most jewelry and amulets were made from sheet gold, and objects that were cast often had components made from sheet gold.

Despite the availability of iron ore, iron objects were extremely rare, mainly because the refining processes are very complex. Iron has to be worked hot, a practice for which the Egyptian handheld hammers were not suitable; hafted hammers were not introduced until the Late Period. Therefore, the few advantages of wrought iron over copper alloys did not compensate for the cost of production.

Most native silver occurred in the form of a natural alloy with gold, and true silver objects are rare before the New Kingdom (1550–1070 B.C.E.), when expanding contact with the silver-producing nations of the Near East increased the availability of silver. Silver objects were fashioned both by hammering and by casting.

THE MIDDLE EAST

BY LYN GREEN

The Near East, especially Mesopotamia, contains some of the oldest examples of metalworking in the world. From 6000 B.C.E. the peoples of the ancient Near East began exploiting a number of different metals: copper, tin, gold, silver, iron, lead, arsenic (in alloys), and to a limited extent antimony. They also used naturally occurring or artificial alloys, such as electrum and copper. Electrum is a mixture of gold and silver that often occurs in nature. Since gold alloyed with silver is much harder than pure gold, ancient metalsmiths often would not have bothered to try to refine the gold further. Silver occurs in almost all gold and also may be found in association with lead. Copper was also found with other metals, including arsenic, creating a sort of natural bronze. The term *bronze*, however, should be applied only to an alloy of copper and tin. Most of the techniques used in metalworking were standard throughout the Near East, though certain regions had advantages in terms not only of the minerals available but also of other substances useful in refining and working metals.

Although no metals can be mined in southern Iraq, where Sumer was located, the Sumerian and Akkadian languages of that area have names for numerous types of metals and metalworking techniques, and many finely worked metal artifacts have been uncovered there. One explanation for these developments may be the presence of petroleum products, such as asphalts, which could have been used in furnaces to produce temperatures high enough to melt many metals. The Dead Sea also produced bitumen. In Roman times the Nabataeans controlled this trade, though bitumen was usually used in industries other than metalworking. Other civilizations were not so fortunate, however.

One of the major difficulties for ancient metalworkers was the purification of the ore. Recent excavations and experiments have clarified how this might have been done. The first stage was smelting. Researchers who studied the production of tin at the 4,500-year-old mine of Goltepe in Turkey concluded that ancient workers first ground the ore into powder with stone grindstones. Then they put the powder between layers of charcoal in a shallow container and fired it to about 1750 degrees Fahrenheit (much lower than the temperature of over 2370 degrees Fahrenheit used in tin smelting today) so that the tin would crystallize in the melted charcoal. This procedure was repeated a number of times—perhaps with the addition of arsenic—until the tin was separated from the glassy melt.

Impurities in a metal were not always a drawback, however. Arsenic present in copper meant a harder metal, as did silver in gold. In addition, the mixture of metals in an alloy resulted in a much lower melting point than that of a pure metal, in turn making the metals easier to work. Some scholars have suggested that bronze was discovered when ancient miners and metalworkers exhausted the surface deposits of copper, which were comparatively pure, and had to go underground for ores. These underground ores were much more likely to contain a variety of other substances, especially sulfides, that would have changed the properties of the copper in different ways and inspired smiths to try different combinations of ores to get a desired result.

One of the best examples of a coppersmith's workshop dating to the Bronze Age was excavated in Iran at Tepe Ghabristan. The workshop, which seems to have been active

Copper vessel with silver wire, from Ur, southern Iraq (ca. 2600–2400 B.C.E.) (© The Trustees of the British Museum)

about 4500 B.C.E., was full of molds, crucibles, and a tuyere (a pipe or nozzle to force air into a forge or furnace) as well as many chunks of copper ore. In the ancient Near East the primary method of shaping all metals, including gold and silver, was through annealing (in the case of copper, gold, bronze, and silver) or forging (in the case of iron). Gold, silver, and bronze were also hammered into sheets, which could then be decorated with incised or raised relief. Cast iron was not made, though objects of gold, silver, copper, and bronze were occasionally made by the "lost wax" method from about 3000 B.C.E.

The earliest copper objects appeared in the Near East about 4000 B.C.E., and bronze was being worked about 500 years after that, but it was not until more than 2,000 years later that iron mining and ironworking spread throughout the Near East. There were a number of reasons for the slow development of iron metallurgy, but the most important was the difficulty of working the ore and of building furnaces (as opposed to forges) capable of the high temperatures needed to melt iron. Because ancient smiths were working with ore or iron that contained appreciable amounts of impurities, the furnaces did not need to reach 2800 degrees Fahrenheit (the melting point of pure iron), but they had to be significantly hotter than those used to work the metals in use in the Bronze Age. Such furnaces needed to allow air to circulate, to have the quantity and types of fuel necessary to create high temperatures, and to be tall so that the melted iron could drop.

When copper is smelted, the metal and the impurities become liquid and drop to the bottom of the furnace, where the impurities float on top of the pure copper. Iron ore, on the other hand, would remain more or less unmelted at the highest temperatures an ancient furnace could reach. Some of the other elements (impurities) would melt but would be caught in the spongy-textured iron. Smiths could reheat the spongy blob and hammer it until the impurities squirted out, but this process had to be repeated many times before a relatively pure metal was achieved—and that metal was actually more difficult to work. However, if small amounts of carbon were deliberately added to the iron, the result was a harder metal, something discovered by ancient Near Eastern smiths.

Another reason for the slow spread of iron metallurgy was that certain cultures or groups of people seem to have kept the techniques of ironworking a craft secret. For example, in the book of Samuel, it is mentioned that the Israelites had to take their iron tools and weapons to the Philistines for repair. The reasons for such reluctance to share knowledge are obvious. Not only did those who possessed the skills have a monopoly on the market for them, but there also were distinct military and economic advantages in having iron, rather than bronze, weapons and tools. However, smiths of all kinds were respected as skilled artisans, and their services were keenly sought after, no matter whether they worked in common metal, such as iron, or luxury metal, such as gold.

ASIA AND THE PACIFIC

BY JIANJUN MEI

Metallurgy is absent from the Pacific islands in ancient times, owing to a lack of mineral deposits in the region. The first sign of the emergence of metallurgy in southern Asia is the finding of copper beads from graves dated to the fifth millennium B.C.E. at Mehrgarh, in southern Baluchistan. Evidence from the site of Nal in Baluchistan shows the use of lead and silver as early as the fourth millennium B.C.E. Gold came into use in Punjab (modern-day India and Pakistan) slightly later. Arsenical copper was known in the Indus civilization of the third millennium B.C.E. and became prevalent among the "copper hoards" of the Ganges valley, some of which date from the second millennium B.C.E. The examination of early metals from Mohenjo Daro (Pakistan) demonstrates that tin bronze was in use from the late third millennium B.C.E. Iron first appeared in southern Asia in the second half of the second millennium B.C.E. and became more common from the beginning of the first millennium B.C.E.

Metallurgy emerged in eastern Asia and Southeast Asia later than in Mesopotamia and the Near East. The earliest metal object found in eastern Asia is a piece of copper from Banpo in Xi'an (Shaanxi Province) China, which is dated to the fourth millennium B.C.E. This piece of copper has a high zinc content and could be described as being made of brass. Such a compositional feature is distinctly different from the earliest metals known in Mesopotamia and the Near East, which were without exception made of pure copper. Curiously, two other brass objects dating to the fourth to the third millennium B.C.E. were found separately in Shaaxi and Shandong provinces.

The early third millennium B.C.E. witnessed the beginnings of the use of tin bronze in China. A bronze knife from Linjia, Dongxiang (Gansu Province) dating to about 2800 B.C.E. is the earliest bronze object known so far, not just in China but also in eastern Asia. The knife was made of bronze with 6 to 10 percent tin and cast in an open mold. Increasing metallurgical activities came into sight across northwestern and northern China from the middle of the third millennium B.C.E., as demonstrated by archaeological finds such as metals, fragments of crucible (a vessel used to heat and melt), slag, and casting molds from various sites. These finds are mostly ascribed to the Neolithic cultures of Machang, Longshan, Shijiahe, and Hongshan and date to about 2500–2000 B.C.E.

During the first half of the second millennium B.C.E. northwestern China and the central plains of China were the two major areas where remarkable innovations in metallurgy took place. In northwestern China (mainly the Gansu, Qinghai, and Xinjiang regions), new metals such as gold, silver, and arsenical copper appeared and a new range of objects such as socketed axes, spearheads, mirrors, and earrings came into use. In the central plains of China, piece-mold casting emerged and developed into a unique Chinese metallurgical technology. Thousands of magnificent bronze ritual vessels were then cast by using piece-mold technology during the following Shang and Zhou dynasties (ca. 1500–256 B.C.E.). These vessels were mainly used to hold food and drink in ancestral rites, the way that the Shang kings or elite communicated with their ancestors. The production of bronze ritual objects reached a scale that was unparalleled anywhere else in the world at the time.

Outstanding new developments in bronze metallurgy can be seen in the growth of several regional bronze-working traditions in the border areas of the Shang cultural sphere during the late second millennium B.C.E. Among these regional traditions, the bronzes found at Sanxingdui, Sichuan, Southwest China are most spectacular. With an astonishing emphasis on the human form and adoration for gold, the Sanxingdui tradition shows unique and mysterious characters, which have attracted considerable research interest worldwide. To the north of the Shang cultural sphere stretched the so-called Northern Bronze Complex, which is well known for its weapons and implements decorated in animal style. These bronzes had a close connection with bronze working in the Eurasian steppes or were even imported from the steppes. They played an important role in bridging the transmission of metallurgical technologies between the central plains of China and Eurasia. To the south of the Shang cultural sphere, along the Yangtze River valley, developed a regional tradition of bronze production that may be called "southern." The southern tradition is characterized by a prominent stress on musical instruments (bells) and vessels in the designs of animal shape. While strong connections with the Shang bronze technology can be observed, the southern tradition preserves a great variety of local tastes and preferences in bronze design and production.

The emergence and development of ironworking was the major technological advance in eastern Asia during the first millennium B.C.E. Although archaeological evidence for the use of meteoritic iron in China can be traced back to the late Shang Dynasty, from about the 13th century B.C.E., it was not until the eighth century B.C.E. that iron made from the ore came into use in the central plains of China. More than a dozen knives or swords made from the smelted iron have been excavated at various sites in Henan, Shanxi, Shaanxi, and Gansu, all dating to the eighth to sixth centuries B.C.E. Some are swords made with two kinds of metals, for example, an iron blade with a gold handle. This may indicate the rarity and high value of iron at the very early stage when it came to be used. Of great importance is the invention of cast iron, which actually defined the track of the development of Chinese iron metallurgy in the following two millennia. To use cast iron on a large scale changed the Chinese society profoundly with the introduction of iron tools in agriculture.

Under the cultural influence of China and the Eurasian steppes, Korea entered the Bronze Age in the beginning of the first millennium B.C.E. Bronze metallurgy appeared in Japan even later, in the Yoyoi Period, probably around the fifth century B.C.E. Iron technology diffused from China into Korea and Japan during the third century B.C.E.

The beginning of bronze metallurgy in Southeast Asia was a hotly debated topic in the 1980s. Some scholars believed that metallurgy began there as early as the early third millennium B.C.E. In other words, Southeast Asia could be an independent center for the beginnings of bronze metallurgy. However, an increasing number of scholars take a conservative view on the dating of early bronzes found in Thailand and Vietnam. The earliest bronzes have been redated to about 1700 B.C.E., making it possible for some scholars to suggest the possible influence from China or India in the emergence of metallurgy in Southeast Asia. Bronze metallurgy in Southeast Asia is widely known now for its small-scale production, which was most likely organized at the village level.

EUROPE

BY KIRK H. BEETZ

Metallurgy is the art of working metals. Metal is first smelted from its ore (though some metals can also be found in a pure form) and then is worked through hammering, casting, alloying, forging, annealing, riveting, and welding to produce finished products. Metalsmiths in the ancient world developed innovative ways to decorate metal products to create objects that even today are astonishing in their beauty.

The first evidence for metallurgy in Europe dates from before 5000 B.C.E. in southeastern Europe, where copper was smelted from ores such as malachite. Copper is a soft metal by itself and must be alloyed, or combined with other metals, to be hardened. The earliest copper was used for relatively simple ornaments such as beads, pendants, and bracelets, but around 4000 B.C.E. it became possible to cast it into tools such as axes. Ötzi, the famous naturally preserved human found in an Alpine glacier, was carrying an ax made from pure copper when he died around 3300 B.C.E. Copper metallurgy spread to other parts of Europe, reaching the Iberian Peninsula around 3000 B.C.E. and the British Isles late in the third millennium B.C.E.

In the Near East arsenic sometimes occurs naturally with copper ore, which may be how ancient smiths learned that copper hardens and holds its edge better when mixed with arsenic. In central Europe the copper occasionally occurs naturally with tin, which may have been how early smiths learned that mixing tin with copper created true bronze, a very durable and tough alloy that holds its edge better than copper or tin alone. The possibility that Europeans may have discovered true bronze on their own has led some archaeologists to speculate that true bronze making occurred in eastern Europe before it occurred in the Near East. In southeastern and central Europe the period known as the Bronze Age began around 2500 B.C.E., and in northern and western Europe it began around 2000 B.C.E.

The ancient smiths had two principal problems to overcome in making true bronze. One was that tin was scarce. In ancient Europe the best sources were in Iberia and Cornwall (southwestern England), far from the best sources of copper

Gold cup of the Bronze Age (ca. 1700–1500 B.C.E.), beaten out of a single lump of gold and found in Rillaton, Cornwall, England (© The Trustees of the British Museum)

in eastern Europe. Another was that mixing the proportions of tin to copper was tricky. The ancient smiths did not have modern scientific techniques for measuring and mixing copper and tin in the best proportions and therefore had to use their firsthand experiences working with the metals to decide what proportions to use. In general, they created a bronze alloy of 90 percent copper and 10 percent tin. At first they mixed copper ores with tin ores and melted the two together. This left impurities in the final product in the form of minerals that had been present in the ores. Around 1500 B.C.E. the smiths began smelting the ores separately and then blending the melted tin and melted copper.

People used molds to make bronze objects. Numerous molds for axes of various sizes and shapes have been found in eastern Europe. The molds usually included dowels that resulted in holes in the finished product for sliding it onto a wooden handle. Between 2000 and 1800 B.C.E. ancient Europeans began making rivets, nails, and pins of gold, copper, or bronze. Rivets could be used to screw an ax blade into place, and pins were used to fix clothing in place and became status symbols.

During the Bronze Age the working of gold also came into prominence in the parts of Europe where it was available. Gold was generally obtained from placer deposits in streams and hammered into sheets, which were then hammered into ornaments and vessels. Some of the most remarkable gold objects were made in Ireland between 1500 and 500 B.C.E., including bracelets, arm rings, and especially collars of sheet gold called *lunulae*. Some of these gold objects are decorated with repoussé, in which a design is made by embossing the back of the metal sheet with a hammer or a punch.

In about 1200 B.C.E. iron smelting came to Europe from the Near East. Iron ore was more common than tin, but it posed special problems for the ancient smiths. Iron requires 2,797 degrees Fahrenheit to melt enough to be poured, whereas copper requires only 1,981 degrees Fahrenheit to liquefy. A furnace hot enough to melt iron appeared first in eastern Europe and then in southern Europe. This began what is often called the Iron Age. By about 600 B.C.E. the use of iron had spread throughout Europe, though bronze continued to be used in great quantities, especially for luxury goods.

Ancient smiths usually had great lumps of iron of 55 pounds or so after smelting. These iron lumps were almost inevitably mixed with charcoal, which may be how the smiths learned that mixing carbon with iron could alter the metal's properties. If the proportion of carbon to iron is not exactly right, the resulting product can be too brittle or too soft. This meant that iron tools and weapons were rarely as good as bronze ones. Once the problem of smelting temperature was solved, however, it was easier to manufacture iron objects in larger quantities than bronze ones, because iron ore was more common than copper or tin ore and it did not require the careful mixing of two metals to create an alloy.

Iron was thus very cheap. European agriculture was revolutionized when molten iron was poured into molds for blades that could be fitted on plows in the first century B.C.E., allowing farmers to break deeper into tougher soils than before. The boom in agriculture from this resulted in a population boom that created the mass movements of people that shaped much of European history during the first millennium C.E.

A problem found in a metal object that has been cast in a mold, and especially in iron castings, is a brittleness caused by the uneven alignment of metal molecules. This meant that tools and weapons that looked fine would sometimes break prematurely. A solution to this problem, discovered in the Near East, was annealing—repeated heating and cooling of metal, which results in the alignment of molecules, making a metal object tougher. The smiths in Europe combined annealing with another method they already used: the pounding of metal to create sheets. Copper and gold lent themselves easily to this method, and beaten sheets of those metals were used to cover wooden sculptures or to make masks. Soon after 1000 B.C.E. people in central Europe were pounding sheets of bronze into new shapes, most notably for helmets and other armor. This involved hammering a lump or a casting of metal until it had a desired shape. Annealing allowed the smith to soften hard metal such as bronze or iron so it could be repeatedly beaten and shaped. The results were sharp edges that could be resharpened without breaking as well as workaday objects, such as bits for harnesses and hammers for construction work, that could endure frequent use without breaking.

For warriors, this meant not only durable armor but weapons that were less likely to break under stress.

GREECE

BY JOHN W. HUMPHREY

As early as the second half of the Neolithic Age (ca. 5000–ca. 3000 B.C.E.), people began to work soft native metals such as copper and gold, which they could form into shapes by hammering with traditional stone tools; hence this period is called the Chalcolithic, or Copper Age. But the shapes of these items were so limited and the malleability of the native metals so high that they could not be used as functioning tools or weapons. The discovery of primitive casting techniques produced more functional shapes, but the off-gassing of molten copper restricted the casting to open, one-piece molds of sandstone or clay, so this technique left one flat surface on the tool and used much precious metal.

By the Bronze Age (ca. 2800–700 B.C.E.) kilns designed originally for firing ceramics produced temperatures high enough (about 2000 degrees Fahrenheit) to smelt copper from its carbonate and oxide ores. It seems likely that copper-based pigments used to decorate ceramics were accidentally smelted in pottery kilns, leaving behind beads of pure copper. This copper was then combined with arsenic or tin to produce bronze, a metal superior to copper because of its lower melting point, ease of casting, and hardness. The invention of two-piece molds then allowed symmetrical tools to be cast, and it saved metal because a removable core could be inserted into the mold to create a hollow object. Such metal tools had several advantages over those of stone: They were thinner, sharper, and more durable; they allowed a greater variety of forms; and they could be reworked when dull or broken.

The processing of ore to extract the desired metal generally followed a common procedure, though some stages were omitted for certain metals. What follows is applicable to ores of copper, tin, and lead/silver, but not gold (which was always available naturally in its pure form) or iron.

Because most ores contain sulfur or oxygen, the first requirement is to separate these from the desired metal. This was done in a simple roasting oven, in which the ore was layered with the fuel (usually charcoal), covered with a temporary shell, and burned in a reducing atmosphere; the carbon combined with the sulfur or oxygen and gassed off, leaving the desired metal behind, though still combined with impurities.

The ore was then broken up by crushing it either in mortars with an iron pestle or in mills that resembled the large "hourglass" grain mills familiar from Pompeii and Ostia. The crumbles were then either sieved or, more commonly, washed to remove the unwanted gangue (surrounding rock), which, because it was heavier than the metal, was left behind on the washing table. This process is well known from the surviving washing tables at Laurion, Greece, which ingeniously used recirculated water.

The remaining concentrated ore was then heated in a smelting furnace with sufficient temperature to produce a molten metal that separated from the unwanted slag; the two would generally be tapped off at different heights according to their specific gravities. Three elements were required for this procedure: a furnace, suitable fuel, and a supply of forced air. Open hearths were first used as furnaces, but they proved unsatisfactory because they could not sustain the necessary temperatures. However, in classical shaft furnaces, like those used for firing pottery, the charcoal and ore could be properly layered and the heat concentrated within the restricted space.

The preferred fuel was charcoal, the only material that could generate sufficient and continuous heat for smelting. Other fuels were tried—wood (before the deforestation of the Mediterranean), lignite coal, and even dried dung—but with little success. The Greeks (like their Egyptian predecessors in the Bronze Age) used bellows to provide a constant supply of forced air to maintain the necessary temperature for smelting copper, though pipettes were used for smaller quantities of precious metals. These bellows were generally fabricated from the skins of animals, with flaps of skin serving as inlet and outlet valves and terra-cotta nozzles to protect them from the heat of the fire. These bellows were often used in pairs and operated by foot to produce a constant flow of air.

Once the metal had been tapped off, it was usually allowed to cool and solidify into ingots before being remelted and cast. Only occasionally did the casting of a final product seem to have been done directly from the smelting stage. Before being worked into its desired form, silver was subject to further refining by cupellation: The smelted ore was placed in a porous clay crucible and heated; the residual lead was

Gold mask from Mycenae (Alison Frantz Photographic Collection, American School of Classical Studies at Athens)

either absorbed into the clay or transformed by a steady blast of air into lead oxide that evaporated, leaving the purest silver obtainable.

At this stage, precious metals could be tested for their purity, a necessity for the minting of coins, when the state was guaranteeing the quality of the metal. Gold was scraped over touchstones (black siliceous schists like basalt or chert), leaving behind a streak whose color was compared with those of known pure and alloyed gold. The Greek mathematician Archimedes, of the third century B.C.E., famously discovered that his body submerged in a tub displaced not its weight but its volume in water; so by first determining the volume of a complex gold wreath made for his king, then calculating the weight of that volume of pure gold, and finally comparing it to the actual weight of the wreath, he could prove that the object was too light to have been made of unadulterated gold.

The smelting of iron was a quite different procedure, since (unlike the ancient metallurgists of central and eastern Asia) the Greeks and Romans were unable to attain the melting point of iron (over 2,700 degrees Fahrenheit) and so could not produce the pure metal in liquid form. But at the manageable temperature of about 2,000 degrees Fahrenheit, the lighter slag could be separated from the iron and tapped off, leaving at the bottom a spongy mass called the bloom. This, in turn, was repeatedly hammered to drive off the remaining impurities and then worked into usable tools and weapons by cold-forging or, more commonly, by annealing. Alternately heating, hammering, and quenching the iron, which both hardened it and combined it with carbon from the charcoal fire, created a form of steel.

Because of iron's different treatment from other metals, the objects made from it were more limited in design than tools, weapons, and decorative objects cast in bronze. The smith was metallurgist and metalworker, responsible for both smelting and working the iron in a single continuous process. His requisite tools—tongs, hammer, and anvil—were unique to his specialization. His work required considerable upper-body strength, which almost certainly created the common image of an ironworker with weak legs, a barrel chest, and powerful arms, a caricature reflected in the almost comical description of Hephaistos, mythological god of the forge.

Casting, on the other hand, was the principal ancient technique for working bronze, gold, and silver, in the Iron Age as well as earlier. Purified metal was heated to liquid form in crucibles and poured into two-piece molds made of stone, clay, or sand. The cast object could be made hollow by inserting a removable core into the mold. The final product was smoothed, polished, and perhaps further decorated. One significant advantage of this technique was that the molds were generally reusable, so multiple copies of almost identical items could be produced with ease. As an alternative to casting, the Greeks produced sheet metal by hammering out thin plates of metal, from which they would then "raise" cups with a soft hammer of bone, working in a spiral from the center and gradually thinning the metal by forcing it outward and upward to create the sides of a round vessel.

The ancient Greeks practiced various techniques of fine metalworking that took their creations beyond the functional to the highly decorative. Relief work included chasing (the hammering of a design from the outer surface) and its counterpart, repoussé work (hammering from the inside to create a raised design on the outside). Inlaying had been successfully practiced by their Mycenaean ancestors, who produced elegant ceremonial dagger blades decorated with delicate scenes of wild animals and hunters made of gold, electrum, and silver set in an adhesive bed of black niello (a black enamel-like alloy). Filigree and cloisonné enameling involved the use of thin wires to create settings for precious stones, and granulation was the application of tiny beads of gold to the surface of a vessel.

An advanced form of hollow casting is known as *cire-perdue*, or the "lost wax" process, which produced not just a hollow object but one with remarkably fine details cast on the surface. A rough core of destructible material was first fashioned, slightly smaller than the finished object would be, with one or two protruding "anchors" that kept the core in place when the next layer, the wax, was removed. A layer of liquid wax was applied that, when hardened, was carved to the exact design of the finished object. Over this was smeared a clay shell that was attached to the "anchors" of the core, with an unobtrusive hole giving access to the wax. Once the shell was set, the wax was melted out of the interior, leaving a thin cavity into which the molten bronze or silver was poured, taking on both the thickness and the fine external decoration of the lost wax.

When the metal cooled, the outer shell was broken (there was no reusing of these molds) and the inner core picked apart and removed using thin probes. The result was a hollow object with a detailed surface design that could be touched up using files and polishes. On a large scale this technique was used in the casting (in multiple parts) of large bronze sculptures such as the Zeus/Poseidon statue in Athens's National Archaeological Museum, the Charioteer of Delphi, and the sole surviving bronze equestrian statue from antiquity, the unparalleled Marcus Aurelius on Rome's Capitoline Hill. The achievements of the Greeks and Romans were not reproduced until the Renaissance, when the technique of *cire-perdue* casting was reinvented.

ROME

BY JOHN W. HUMPHREY

The basic facts of Greek metallurgy apply equally to the Romans, who introduced advances in only a few areas. First, they mined the deeper copper sulfides, which were more difficult to smelt than the superficial carbonates and oxides, requiring a preliminary roasting to drive off most of the sulfur and other impurities before they could be smelted; they did, however, increase dramatically the quantities of copper ore available for working. Second, they perfected the design of shaft furnaces to allow continuous production of the metal by making it possible to add new ore and tap off slag without shutting down the furnace. And third, they developed the technique of amalgamation, by mixing in a crucible ground, unpurified gold with mercury; the two combined to form an amalgam (gold being the only metal attracted to mercury), leaving behind the impurities. The amalgam was then forced through leather to leave the gold behind or was heated to vaporize the mercury (with its lower boiling point), which was then condensed through cooling, the only known ancient application of distilling.

The Romans practiced and sometimes improved on all the Greek techniques of casting, forging, and annealing together with the more delicate metalworking techniques. Advances in enameling and the production of gold leaf were two of their principal contributions in the latter category. According to Pliny in his *Natural History*, Roman metalworkers could beat a single ounce of gold into 750 leaves of foil, each 4 inches square: a remarkable achievement, even if gold is the most malleable of metals. Enameling they appear to have borrowed from the Celts of western Europe, who as early as the fourth century B.C.E. were applying a fine powder of ground glass and metallic oxides mixed with water to the surface of small bronze objects (brooches seem to have been the most common) that were then heated until the enamel fused. Attractive, multicolored designs were achieved by placing different oxide mixtures into separate cells on the surface of the metal object, formed in various shapes either by cutting directly into the metal (called champlevé) or by applying a mesh of wires over the surface (cloisonné).

For the hollow casting of small metal objects, the Romans used the same *cire-perdue*, "lost-wax," process as the Greeks. Metalworkers of both cultures were also capable of producing life-sized bronze statues using the same technique but by casting many parts individually and then fastening them together. To ensure that the constituent elements would fit properly, the artist started from a full-sized model of the entire piece in clay or plaster, from which he would take separate two-piece molds of the individual parts. These molds would then be coated on the inside with a layer of melted wax of the same thickness as the final bronze product, and an inner core of clay would be inserted. The two halves of each mold would be reassembled, the wax melted out, and the liquid bronze added. Once all the parts had been cast, they would be welded together by first heating the points of attachment almost to melting and then applying molten metal around the joint, causing the two pieces to bond. Once cooled, the welding on the surface was filed down to the level of the cast pieces, fine details chiseled out of the metal or engraved into it, patches added to camouflage the inevitable casting flaws, and the statue given its final polishing. With this technique, multiple copies could be made of the same original model.

Although there are documentary claims that the Romans were casting large bronze statuary as early as Romulus in the eighth century B.C.E., it seems more likely that it was the Etruscans who first borrowed from the Greeks the *cire-perdue* technique: one of the earliest surviving Italian examples is the famous Capitoline wolf (without the familiar suckling twins Romulus and Remus, who were added in the Renaissance), dated to around 600 B.C.E. But within a few centuries the Romans were producing bronze statues of a size and quality that matched their predecessors' work, an achievement in the fine casting of metal that was not reproduced until the Renaissance, when the technique of *cire-perdue* casting was reinvented.

THE SURVIVAL OF BRONZE STATUARY

From classical Greece to the Roman Empire statuary of cast bronze was as popular as sculpted stone, though proportionately less survives today because the material demands of postclassical societies made bronze artistic creations vulnerable to recasting into more practical tools. Many of the few large bronze statues that grace Athens' National Archaeological Museum or the piazza of the Capitoline Museums in Rome owe their survival to a combination of ancient accident and modern luck—the Zeus/Poseidon and Horse with Jockey now in Athens were recovered from a shipwreck off the east coast of Greece in 1928—or to misplaced reverence: in Rome the bronze Marcus Aurelius on horseback escaped medieval recasting because he was misidentified as Constantine, the first Christian emperor in the Church's view. This is our sole surviving formal equestrian statue from the ancient world, among what must have been the thousands to which Pliny alludes when he tells us in his *Natural History* that the style was almost certainly developed by the Greeks and was very popular among the Romans.

THE AMERICAS

BY PENNY MORRILL

The history of metallurgy in the Americas is based primarily on the archaeological record. Although most sites have been looted over the centuries since the arrival of the Spaniards, several tombs have been opened and excavated in modern times to reveal magnificent works in gold. In the interpretation of these mortuary caches, it is helpful to consider the cautionary note sounded by the historians Paloma Carcedo Muro and Izumi Shimada, that these works may not have been produced exclusively for burial. They have said that gold artifacts were used in public contexts—courts and temples, for example—to propagate symbolic messages. Then, on the death of a ruler the gold artifacts would have been gathered up and buried.

The earliest-known use of metals in the Americas was in the Central Andes in about 1500 B.C.E. Subsequently, metallurgy spread into southern Peru, Bolivia, and Chile and into the north to Ecuador and Colombia. In South America the mining and extraction of gold and the production of gold objects were closely related to geographical, social, and historical circumstances. The discovery of gold and copper sources led to local production among the people of Chavín de Huántar in northern Peru (900–200 B.C.E.). Such was also true of the peoples of Malagana (300 B.C.E.–300 C.E.), Calima (1000 B.C.E.–1600 C.E.), Tolima (200 B.C.E.–1000 C.E.), and Tumaco–La Tolita (200 B.C.E.–500 C.E.) in southwestern Colombia.

Gold was discovered in rivers and streams. These placer deposits came in the form of nuggets and flakes that were usually not pure gold but were mixed with silver and other metals. South Americans were not insistent on finding pure gold; rather, their metallurgy developed out of what metals were available to them. Fine metalwork appeared when there were agricultural surpluses and a stable social order with a powerful elite group, thus resulting in a demand for gold objects for ritual use and as emblems of status and the need for full-time artisans. Another important factor in providing the setting for the production of gold objects was a complementary ceramic technology. Technological sophistication was required to build refractory furnaces and create crucibles and molds that could withstand the heat of molten metals.

Gold was the metal most worked in South America. It is exceedingly malleable; the ancient Americans could hammer flakes, chunks, or ingots into flat sheets. Gold would not harden with cold hammering, and its ductility (capability of being easily fashioned) made it possible for smaller gold sheets to be hammered together to form a large sheet. Two final characteristics made gold highly valued: Gold has the color and reflective light of the sun, and it is resistant to corrosion.

Copper was used as an alloy with gold. Before the arrival of the Spaniards it was mined horizontally, not in vertical shafts. Veins of copper, usually on mountainsides, would have made their appearance on the surface as copper carbonates, malachite (green) or azurite (blue). The bright colors appealed to the ancient Americans, and the stones were excavated along the vein. The malachite or azurite was pulverized and mixed with granulated charcoal and placed in a crucible over fire. Using blowpipes to increase the intensity of the heat, the ancient Americans burned away the carbonates as gases and were left with the melted copper in the bottom of the crucible.

The Chavín produced gold sheets, and from these sheets they formed crowns, face masks, pectorals, and ornaments that were sewn onto clothing. The Chavín used soldering to create three-dimensional objects, an indication that they were using alloyed metals. The Chavín goldsmiths were remarkably adept at repoussé. This technique required the application of the design by hammering on the reverse side of the gold sheet.

Hammered gold standing figure (first century B.C.E. to first century C.E.), Colombia or Ecuador (Copyright the Metropolitan Museum of Art)

From 500 B.C.E. to 500 C.E. the peoples of southwestern Colombia developed a unique gold-working tradition in a region where gold was much more plentiful than copper. Trade among the sites of the area—Malagana, Calima, Tolima, and Tumaco—led to shared metallurgical technology. Colombian goldsmiths used sheet metal to produce cutout human figures, tweezers, face masks, and hanging plaques. They covered shells and ceremonial wooden staffs with gold foil. The goldsmiths were adept at creating three-dimensional, hollow metal figures and lime flasks by soldering together pieces of gold sheets. Goldsmiths used embossing to provide these complex figures and receptacles with distinctive curvilinear and geometric surface designs. Pectorals and masks exhibit extraordinary detail in repoussage.

Unique to Malagana is the grand variety of beads produced in gold, copper and gold alloy, rock crystal, and colored stones. Beyond the simple tubes and spheres are naturalistic and abstract renditions of birds, animals, and insects. Some of the larger beads are hollow spheres with surface decoration, possibly sewn onto clothing. The goldsmith hammered two small sheets of gold over a doming block, enhanced them with embossing, and joined them without solder.

The goldsmiths of southwestern Colombia achieved a high level of excellence with lost-wax casting. They were able to take advantage of a lower melting point with the higher copper content, much better suited for casting. Artisans began by carving a rough semblance of the image in the core, made up of a mix of clay and pulverized charcoal. This core (or several cores or molds) was filled or lined with beeswax. When there were various parts in beeswax, they were joined together with small pegs. The entire assembly was then placed in an outer mold of clay and charcoal, pierced with holes. The gold was melted in a crucible and poured into the holes in the outer mold, melting away the wax. The mold was broken open to reveal the gold object.

There are indications that Colombian goldsmiths were capable of depletion gilding, a technique that produced a seamless surface layer of gold. The object was formed of tumbaga, a gold-copper alloy, with a high (60 percent) copper content. Goldsmiths removed the surface copper by heating the piece in an open hearth until the copper oxidized. The black oxidized copper was dissolved from the surface with a plant-based acid solution, leaving behind a thin layer of almost pure gold that could be burnished to a high finish.

See also ADORNMENT; AGRICULTURE; ART; CERAMICS AND POTTERY; CRAFTS; DEATH AND BURIAL PRACTICES; ECONOMY; GENDER STRUCTURES AND ROLES; INVENTIONS; MIGRATION AND POPULATION MOVEMENTS; MINING, QUARRYING, AND SALT MAKING; MONEY AND COINAGE; SETTLEMENT PATTERNS; TRADE AND EXCHANGE; WAR AND CONQUEST; WEAPONRY AND ARMOR.

FURTHER READING

D. Brown, "Bronze and Pewter," in *Roman Crafts*, ed. D. Strong and D. Brown (New York: New York University Press, 1976).

S. A. Butcher, "Enameling," in *Roman Crafts*, ed. D. Strong and D. Brown (New York: New York University Press, 1976).

P. T. Craddock and M. J. Hughes, eds., *Furnaces and Smelting Technology in Antiquity* (London: British Museum, 1985).

B. M. Fagan, *The Seventy Great Inventions of the Ancient World* (London: Thames and Hudson, 2004).

Michele Feder-Nadoff, ed., *Ritmo del Fuego/Rhythm of Fire: The Art and Artisans of Santa Clara del Cobre, Michoacan, Mexico* (Chicago: Cuentos Foundation, 2004).

Robert J. Forbes, *Studies in Ancient Technology*, 3rd ed. (Leiden, Netherlands: Brill, 1993).

Herbert Garland, *Ancient Egyptian Metallurgy* (London: Charles Griffin, 1927).

Ian Glover, P. Suchitta, and J. Villiers, eds., *Early Metallurgy, Trade and Urban Centres in Thailand and Southeast Asia* (Bangkok, Thailand: White Lotus, 1992).

J. F. Healy, *Mining and Metallurgy in the Greek and Roman World* (Ithaca, N.Y.: Cornell University Press, 1978).

J. W. Humphrey, J. P. Oleson, and A. N. Sherwood. *Greek and Roman Technology: A Sourcebook* (London and New York: Routledge, 1998).

George Kuwayama, ed., *The Great Bronze Age of China: A Symposium* (Seattle: University of Washington Press, 1983).

H. Lechtman and A. Steinberg, "Bronze Joining: A Study in Ancient Technology," in *Art and Technology: A Symposium on Classical Bronzes*, ed. S. Doeringer, D.G. Mitten, and A. Steinberg (Cambridge, Mass.: MIT Press, 1970).

Jian Leng, *Early Paleolithic Technology in Eastern and Southern Asia* (Oxford, U.K.: J. and E. Hedges, 2001).

Alfred Lucas, *Ancient Egyptian Materials and Industries*, 4th rev. ed. (London: Edward Arnold Publishers, 1962).

C. C. Mattusch, *Classical Bronzes: The Art and Craft of Greek and Roman Statuary* (Ithaca, N.Y.: Cornell University Press, 1996).

Colin McEwan, ed., *Pre-Columbian Gold: Technology, Style, and Iconography* (London: British Museum Press, 2000).

Jean-Pierre Mohen and Christiane Eluère, *The Bronze Age in Europe*, trans. David Baker and Dorie Baker (New York: Harry N. Abrams, 2000).

Paul T. Nicholson and Ian Shaw, eds., *Ancient Egyptian Materials and Technology* (Cambridge, U.K.: Cambridge University Press, 2000).

Ray Smith, "Ray Smith's Notebook of Metalworking Origins." Available online. URL: http://www.anvilfire.com/21centbs/stories/rsmith/RSindex.htm. Downloaded on February 20, 2007.

Rebecca Stone-Miller, *Art of the Andes: From Chavín to Inca*, 2nd ed. (London: Thames and Hudson, 2002).

Trevor I. Williams, *The History of Invention: From Stone Axes to Silicon Chips* (New York: Facts On File, 1987).

► migration and population movements

INTRODUCTION

In a broad sense, the history of human migrations is the history of two profound desires: the desire to have a place that is home and the desire to live a better life. These desires have manifested themselves in settlements and movements for thousands of years. At present most anthropologists believe that the ancestors of the modern human being developed in eastern Africa, during a period when the land was dry and resources for survival were few. Some of these first human beings migrated south in Africa, others west in Africa, and others remained in eastern Africa.

What motivated human beings to leave eastern Africa is not known, but the hostility of the climate may have had something to do with it. People may have left to find better sources of game and edible plants. Some people moved northward, perhaps following game, and they may have followed game, perhaps migratory animals, out of Africa and into the Near East. They may not have realized that they were doing anything exceptional; they would just have been providing themselves and their families with food from wherever they could find it.

It is worth remembering that the people who migrated throughout the world in ancient times probably had motivations similar to those of modern people, and their reasons for moving could be every bit as personal as the reasons why modern people sometimes leave their homelands to move somewhere else. There would have been heroes leading their suffering peoples to new lands, great visionaries foreseeing prosperity just beyond the next mountainside, people wanting to give their children better lives than they had, and people who had no clue as to what they were doing. Their motivations both heroic and mundane have been reduced to enigmatic works of art—paintings on rocks and cave walls, carvings of stone and antlers, and clay sculptures. The art only hints at the complex lives of the ancient migrants.

One of the great controversies about human movements is where the Neanderthals came from and how they were related to modern humans. At present, most evidence suggests that the Neanderthals were a different species from modern humans and may have developed in Europe or the Near East, but their origins remain cloudy. Their remains have been found throughout southern and central Europe as well as in parts of western Asia and the Near East. Their spread may have been motivated by their following the migrations of herds of animals.

Modern humans may have brought something new to migration: the desire to explore. Amid the discussions of famines, wars, and other motivations for great movements of ancient people, one may take note that there are people who like to explore, to know what is beyond the horizon. One explorer or a small number of exploring companions could find a new place to live and go home and tell about it, inspiring others to move to that new place.

The ancient world was a vast place, but people seemed to move through it as rapidly as the climate would allow. Glaciers expanded, blocking people, but then retracted, opening new routes for movement. It seems remarkable from the archaeological discoveries of ancient peoples that when an opportunity for movement presented itself, somebody took that opportunity and moved on. One group of ancient peoples moved east along the southern coast of Asia. The lands of southern India would have been very different from those of the southern Near East, yet people migrated into the lands and adapted to their new environment.

A migration almost inevitably requires adaptations to new environments, and the first migrants would have been challenged by new animals and plants and would have had to figure out what was edible and what was not. Resources for tools would have varied, and the first migrants would have had to adapt their tool-making skills to the woods, fibers, and stones that they found. The first people in Southeast Asia would have found themselves in immense bamboo forests populated by wildcats and giant apes twice as tall they were. The first people in the Americas would have encountered animals unlike any they had seen before, such as giant sloths. Even so, people made their moves into new lands and figured out ways to survive in environments for which they had no natural adaptations. It seems likely that some migrations failed only to be tried again by new groups of people.

By the time written language developed in Sumer, the migrations into new territories were not yet complete. A multitude of islands in the Pacific Ocean were still unpopulated. Much of the interior of Asia was cold, dry, and unwelcoming, and people were only just beginning to find ways to live there. For some cultures, migration had become a way of daily life. For instance, the Lapps had begun following herds of reindeer in ancient prehistory; as the northern glaciers melted, the reindeer changed their routes ever more northward, and the Lapps followed. Some migratory peoples had taken charge of their migrations. These people domesticated horses, sheep, or cattle and drove their herds to summer quarters and then to winter quarters, back and forth, until outsiders forced them out of their traditional ranges or killed them or they chose to settle down.

War was a powerful motivator for migrations. Some peoples developed warrior cultures, and they migrated by invading lands occupied by farmers or pastoral peoples. These peoples sometimes succumbed to the invaders, fought the invaders off, or fled. Prosperous regions could attract migrations and war. The cultures of ancient Mesopotamia had a persistent problem with attempts by nomadic cultures to settle on their lands. Ancient Egypt drew Libyans who wanted Egypt's farmlands. The Western Roman Empire had to cope with Germanic tribes that wanted to move into Gaul and share the benefits of Roman civilization. Ancient history has many cases where entire populations of people abandoned their homes to escape war, only to displace some other group of people who in turn moved on. For example, the Chinese drove the Xiongnu out of central Asia. The Xiongnu were a violent people who had long vexed China with their raiding of Chinese settlements. Many historians believe the Xiongnu were the ancestors of the Huns, who drove ever westward, displacing the people in their way and reshaping the societies of Asia and eventually Europe.

AFRICA

BY AMY HACKNEY BLACKWELL

Ancient Africa was home to many ethnic populations, but scholars know little about their history or movements. What is known is that discrete groups of people gradually spread throughout the continent, so that by the end of the ancient period Africa's regions were home to specific ethnic and language groups. Most peoples are defined by language groups. Historians assume that groups that share similar languages must have come from a common culture. So, for example, the "Bantu" people are defined by the language they speak, a branch of the Niger-Congo language family that is spoken today in much of sub-Saharan Africa. The Berber people of North Africa spoke Afro-Asiatic languages, related to the Semitic languages of the Near East. The Khoisan of southern Africa spoke a unique language that included clicking sounds.

For most of the ancient period, the majority of Africans lived as hunter-gatherers who did not necessarily inhabit permanent homes, instead choosing to move about the countryside in search of food supplies. A major trend in ancient population movement was the displacement of hunter-gatherers by agricultural peoples. Agricultural societies tended to have better technology and larger populations, which allowed them to take land from the less organized hunter-gatherers. For example, one of the most significant population movements of the ancient period was the expansion of the Bantu peoples throughout sub-Saharan Africa between about 3000 B.C.E. and C.E. 500. The Bantu peoples were farmers who gradually claimed almost the entire continent south of the Sahara, displacing local hunter-gathering populations as they went.

Population movement did involve some warfare, and certainly some indigenous peoples were pushed out of their homelands at great personal cost. In many cases, though, the movement of populations was not as violent as it sounds. Historians track the spread of ancient populations partly by the spread of languages and technologies because it is impossible to track the movements of actual ethnic groups. The Bantu expansion and other movements almost certainly included a large amount of intermarriage with local groups, or local peoples' adoption of Bantu language and customs. In North Africa and northeastern Africa there was much blending of populations and cultural exchange as well as some wholesale warfare.

The geography of the African continent prevented the easy movement of peoples and ideas from place to place. Africa is very large and covers a vast range of latitudes. Its territory lies in both the northern and the southern hemispheres as well as on the equator. Africa also contains a variety of terrains, from extremely dry deserts to very wet rain forests. The range of latitudes and climates made it difficult for people to move agricultural plants from north to south, which impeded the movement of agricultural societies.

The main exceptions to the difficulty of free movement were the Nile, the coastal areas of North Africa and northeastern Africa and the Sahara. Traders did not begin regularly traversing the Sahara until the Islamic period, but ancient Africans had some desert trading networks. Towns that lay on the edge of the desert became important centers of cultural exchange. The Mediterranean coast was easily accessible to ancient sailors, and North Africa received many visitors and settlers from Rome, Greece, and the eastern Mediterranean. The Red Sea coast was close to Arabia and Yemen, so there was regular movement between the two areas. The Nile River also allowed free movement between Egypt and parts south, particularly Nubia. In all of these areas population movement happened more frequently than it did in the rest of Africa.

North Africa and Eastern Sahara

The Berber people lived in North Africa throughout the ancient period, despite repeated invasions by foreigners who wanted to settle there. Their population stretched from Egypt to the Atlantic coast of Morocco and gradually moved south into the Sahara. The origin of the name *Berber* is unknown. The ancient Greeks called the Berbers "Libyans," and the Romans called them "Numidians," "Moors," and other names based on the region of North Africa from which they hailed. The Berbers generally had a Semitic appearance, with lighter skin and straighter hair than Bantu and other African peoples.

Language offers some clues about the movements of people in this area. The Berber people, like the peoples of East Africa (Ethiopia and surrounding countries) spoke Afro-Asiatic languages. Afro-Asiatic languages include the Semitic languages of the Middle East. Scholars disagree about the origin of the Afro-Asiatic languages. Some believe that they originated in the Middle East and were brought to Africa by people traveling from Yemen to Ethiopia and Eritrea. Others believe they originated in Ethiopia and spread from there throughout the Middle East and North Africa.

Archaeologists have found evidence that the ancestors of the Berber were living in North Africa as early as 9500 B.C.E. The Berber people were living in North Africa by 3000 B.C.E., when the ancient Egyptians first wrote about them. The Meshwesh Berbers of Libya had extensive contact with Egypt. During the Eighteenth Dynasty (1550–1307 B.C.E.) they traded cattle with the Egyptian rulers. The Meshwesh moved into Egypt from Libya during the 12th century B.C.E. During the Nineteenth and Twentieth Egyptian Dynasties Berber rulers fought constantly with the Egyptian kings. Finally, around 945 B.C.E., the Berbers took control of Egypt and ruled it until native Egyptians reclaimed the throne around 720 B.C.E.

Between 1000 and 600 B.C.E. the Phoenician people sailed from their home in Lebanon and colonized North Africa from Libya to Morocco. They brought Near Eastern crops such as wheat to the region and used the fertile coastal plain to grow grain for export. During the fifth century B.C.E. Carthage in modern Tunisia became a cosmopolitan city with a large Phoenician population. Romans moved into North Africa during the second century B.C.E. They turned North Africa into public land and rented it to absentee landlords who continued to farm grain there. The local population remained largely Berber.

The Sahara and Northwestern Africa

Several groups of people lived in northwest Africa in ancient times. Berbers had begun moving into the Sahara long before the time of the Greek historian Herodotus, who wrote of a desert people called the Garamantes. The Garamentes lived in the Libyan Sahara between 500 B.C.E. and C.E. 500. Historians believe that the ancestors of the Garamantes probably moved into the Fezzan area of the Sahara around 1000 B.C.E. Herodotus wrote that the Garamantes herded cattle and drove chariots. They often fought with the Ethiopian people who lived in caves, and they were also known to raid Roman towns on the Libyan coast. They grew wheat to trade with the Romans, digging tunnels to retrieve underground water. Another desert center was the city of Aoudaghost, which appeared in southeast Mauritania around the fifth century B.C.E. It sat at the edge of the Sahara and became a terminus for one of the trans-Saharan trade routes.

Around 1 C.E. the Berbers of the Sahara adopted camels from Arabia. These beasts allowed them to establish trade routes across the desert. Berber traders began traveling across the desert in this period, which allowed for some exchange of peoples and goods. The major Saharan trade routes did not develop, however, until the seventh and eighth centuries C.E.

The region known as Chad was inhabited long before the ancient period. Many humans settled there during the seventh millennium B.C.E., at a time when the Sahara was quite wet. Archaeologists have found rock art dating to that period that shows people hunting and engaging in other activities indicating a fertile climate. Historians believe that most of Africa's sub-Saharan languages originated in this region and must have spread from there during the ancient period, though the details of this spread are unknown.

The Bafour people lived in modern Mauretania in the first millennium B.C.E. The Sahara of this period was wetter than it became, which made it possible for the Bafour to hunt, raise livestock, and fish. As the Sahara grew, the Berber people from North Africa moved into the Bafour region during the third and fourth centuries C.E. Some Bafour became Berber slaves. Others moved south into southern Mauretania and eventually into Ghana.

The people of western Africa spoke languages from the Mande group of the Niger-Congo language family. The Soninke people were Mande language speakers who formed the Ghana kingdom in the early first millennium C.E. This kingdom included the states of Mali, Mema, and Wagadou, in modern Mali, Senegal, and Ghana.

The major form of population migration in this region occurred through trade, which brought people of diverse cultures in contact with one another. The Soninke people traded with people from both north and south, receiving goods from Berber traders crossing the Sahara and salt and gold from the Senegal River. The Soninke also began trading in slaves, capturing local Africans and selling them to merchants who took them to other parts of Africa and abroad, which resulted in a certain amount of inadvertent population migration on the part of the slaves. The town of Djenné in Mali lay on the inland delta of the Niger River. It was built by the Bozo people. It was large town by the third century B.C.E., and by the fifth century C.E. it had became a major trading center. Traders could sail up the Niger River with their goods. Traders also came through the forests or the desert to the north.

Nubia

Ancient Nubia encompassed northern Sudan and southern Egypt along the Nile. People lived in the area during the early ancient period, but the first distinct culture to leave behind archaeological evidence arose around 3800 B.C.E. This culture was similar to that of Egypt of the same period. Around 3300 B.C.E. the Nubian people organized themselves into a kingdom, which may have helped create the earliest Egyptian dynasties. The Egyptians took over Nubia around 3000 B.C.E.

Nubia was best known during the Egyptian Dynastic Period as a trade corridor between Egypt and southwestern Africa. Traders began traveling this route starting in the fourth millennium B.C.E. Egyptian craftsmen of this period used materials such as ebony wood and ivory, which must have come from tropical African trees and animals. Egyptians and Africans would have encountered one another and local Nubians as they traveled north and south carrying goods. During the Old Kingdom (ca. 2575–ca. 2134 B.C.E.) Egyptian and African traders passed through Nubia to exchange an increasing variety of goods, including incense, gold, and wild animals. This trade made Nubia a prosperous region. A small kingdom arose there between 2240 and 2150 B.C.E. Historians are not sure whether this kingdom was inhabited by descendants of the earliest cultures in Nubia or by people who had moved there from elsewhere. It is possible that this kingdom was founded by invaders from the Sahara, who moved into Sudan as the desert became too dry for them to live there.

Between 2040 and 1640 B.C.E., Egyptians moved south into Nubia. They took control of the Nubian trade routes and built forts along the Nile to solidify their power, but they appear to have allowed the local people to live unmolested. The people of southern Nubia founded a kingdom of their own during this period, the kingdom of Kerma, which flourished from 2500 to 1520 B.C.E. Kerma was a major trading center, and archaeologists have found artifacts from southern Africa and Egypt as well as Nubian goods. During the period from 1620 to 1550 B.C.E., a period of Egyptian disarray, Egyptians moved back north from Nubia, and Kerma took control of northern Nubia as well. Egyptians returned to the area under Thutmose I (1504–1492 B.C.E.) and conquered Kerma, annexing Nubia as Egyptian territory.

During the 11th century B.C.E. Egypt suffered another period of governmental disarray and abandoned Nubia after locals rebelled. Local Nubians created a new kingdom based at the city of Napata, near modern Khartoum. This kingdom developed into the Kushite kingdom, founded around 708 B.C.E. The Kushites moved north into Egypt and conquered all of Egypt's territory under King Piye (750–712 B.C.E.). Around 690 B.C.E. Assyrians from the Near East moved southwest into Egypt, conquering the northern part of the Egyptian empire and forcing the Kushites back into Nubia. The Kushites lost control of Egypt in 656 B.C.E. when Psamtik I reunited Egypt. In 591 B.C.E. the Egyptians invaded Kush and destroyed Napata.

The Kushites moved south and built a new capital city called Meroë on the banks of the Nile. This city was an important center of government and commerce until about 350 C.E., when it was conquered by the Axumites of East Africa. The Kushite kingdom was strong during the Roman era. Kushites occasionally attacked Roman settlements in Egypt, but the kingdom also engaged in a great deal of trade with Rome and other Mediterranean powers.

East Africa

Although eastern Africa around the Horn of Africa (including Ethiopia, Eritrea, Djibouti, and southern Sudan) has been inhabited by humans for millennia, the first historical mention of human beings dates to about 2400 B.C.E. The Nilotic languages were spoken in northeast Africa, originating around the southern part of the Nile. People who spoke Nilotic languages lived in Sudan from at least 3000 B.C.E. The Nilotic people were tall and slender. They appear to have been genetically related to the ancient Khoisan of southern Africa.

The ancient Egyptians called the region Punt, or "God's Land." Punt appears to have encompassed coastal Sudan and Eritrea and perhaps some of Ethiopia and Somalia. It definitely had a coastline on the Red Sea and was south of the region known as Nubia. Egyptian pharaohs sent several expeditions to Punt during the second millennium B.C.E. The people of Punt sold exotic goods such as ebony, ivory, wild animals, and incense.

East Africa is very close to the Middle East, and Middle Eastern people have been traveling to Africa for several thousand years. Some historians believe that Semitic peoples from Yemen and Arabia began settling in Ethiopia around 2000 B.C.E. During the first millennium B.C.E. Ethiopia and Eritrea were inhabited by a Semitic people called the Sabaeans. The Sabaeans came to Africa from Yemen. During this period they dominated the Red Sea region. The Sabaeans did not, however, rule all of East Africa. In the eighth century B.C.E. an indigenous African kingdom called D'mt arose in northern Ethiopia and Eritrea. This kingdom thrived until the fifth century B.C.E. Historians are not sure about D'mt's cultural composition. Some believe that D'mt was entirely African, whereas others argue that it was heavily influenced by the Semitic Sabaeans.

In the fourth century B.C.E. the Axumite kingdom appeared in northeast Africa. This kingdom encompassed the Red Sea coast of Sudan, southern Egypt, Ethiopia, Yemen, Djibouti, and part of Saudi Arabia. Historians believe the Axumites were indigenous Africans, not Semitic Sabaeans from Yemen; the current theory is that they were a mix of Semitic and Kushitic peoples. Axum was a major power by the first century C.E. For the rest of the ancient period it engaged in international trade with Arabia, Persia, Rome, India, and China. It also controlled the government of Saudi Arabia during the third century. In 350 C.E. Axumites conquered the kingdom of Kush, just to the north of Axum. Because of Axum's international contacts, the Axumite people spread through the region and people from other places came to Axum as emissaries or slaves. Foreign visitors and inhabitants included Indians, Arabs, Jews, Romans, Egyptians, and Sudanese people, as well as people who had traveled there from southern and western Africa.

Sub-Saharan Africa and the Bantu Expansion

Between 40,000 and 8000 B.C.E., southern Africa was occupied by people known as Sangoan. By the beginning of the ancient period these people had developed into the culture known as Khoisan, or Bushmen. They spoke a distinctive language that included many clicking sounds. Archaeologists believe that the Khoisan were one of the oldest distinct groups of humans. Studies of modern Khoisan genes show that the Khoisan people were isolated from other genetic groups up to 100,000 years ago. The Khoisan people had a distinctive appearance, with copper-colored skin, high cheekbones, long legs, and an overall short stature. Their eyes had distinctive folds of skin, similar to those of Asian peoples. Khoisan women had a tendency to accumulate fat in their buttocks, possibly an adaptation to life in a harsh climate with an unpredictable food supply. The Khoisan lived throughout the southern half of the continent, in modern-day Angola, Namibia, Botswana, and South Africa. They were adapted to life in dry desert conditions and lived as hunter-gatherers, hunting wild animals and gathering wild plant foods.

During most of the ancient period the jungles of central Africa in the modern Congo nations—Cameroon, Central African Republic, and Gabon—were home to groups of small-statured people most commonly known as today as Pygmies, though this term is considered derogatory. Pygmies also lived further east. For example, the Twa people were the earliest inhabitants of Rwanda. Adult males were less than five feet tall, and many adults were smaller than that. The Pygmies had muscular bodies, short legs, long arms, and large heads. They lived as hunter-gatherers. Historians do not know when Pygmy groups appeared in the jungles. The earliest references to them are in ancient Egyptian writings dating to about 2500 B.C.E. The Greek historian Herodotus also wrote about the small jungle people. The Pygmies did not develop cities or large governments. They instead roamed through the forests, erecting temporary homes and moving when an area's food supply ran out.

Much of the rest of sub-Saharan Africa was inhabited by small groups of hunter-gatherers. Very little is known about these people. The ones living in East Africa had some contact with traders from Nubia and surrounding regions, but for the most part they were isolated for centuries. This gradually changed during the Bantu expansion. The Bantu people originated in the region that is now Cameroon, Nigeria, and Niger, particularly in the Benue-Cross river region of Nigeria. Sometime during the third, second, and first millennia B.C.E. the Bantu people spread throughout central, eastern, and southern Africa. This spread is known as the "Bantu migration." The Bantu languages, part of the Niger-Congo language family, are identified by a shared word for "person," which is *ntu*. The Bantu people had dark skin and curly black hair.

Modern scholars do not agree about the details of this migration. Historians once thought that the Bantu people in

Nigeria developed both agriculture and ironworking during the first millennium B.C.E. The Nigerian Bantu were believed to have somehow learned ironwork in the Middle East and brought it back to Nigeria with them; Nigeria's Nok people were believed to be some of the first expert metal workers. According to this scenario, by about 500 B.C.E. the Bantu were skilled enough at working metal that they were able to quickly conquer the hunter-gatherers of southern Africa.

Historians today believe that the Bantu migration happened over a much longer period of time and was probably a process of gradual cultural transmission instead of a sudden burst of ethnic conquerors. According to the present interpretation of the data, starting around 3000 B.C.E. the Bantu people of Cameroon, Nigeria, and Niger started moving slowing south and east. The reasons for this move are unknown. The Sahara became very dry during the second millennium B.C.E., and Berber inhabitants of the desert may have pushed the Bantu south as they moved into wetter regions. This would have forced the Bantu into the rainforests of central Africa.

The Bantu migration was not necessarily a journey of conquest. As the Bantu moved south and east, local peoples adopted Bantu languages and intermarried with the migrants. Over the generations the Bantu language slowly spread southward, and Bantu physical traits appeared in populations where intermarriage occurred. Modern historians also believe that the Bantu-speaking peoples did not bring ironworking to Nigeria from the Middle East but instead discovered it when they arrived in eastern Africa. The non-Bantu people of Tanzania and Rwanda may have started working with iron around 800 B.C.E., without any influence from the Middle East or Europe, and the Bantu may have learned the craft from them.

However the Bantu learned to work with iron, by the fourth century C.E. they were quite skilled at it and could make good metal farming tools. These tools made it much easier for Bantu farmers to cut grain from tough sorghum and millet stalks, which gave them an advantage over peoples who did not have metal tools. Even if they did not kill native peoples to take their land, the Bantu were much better equipped to raise food, which helped them become the dominant culture. However it happened, the Bantu languages spread down the coast of east Africa by 400 C.E.

The Pygmy groups came into early contact with the Bantu, who lived near them. Pygmy hunters traded with Bantu farmers, exchanging meat and hides for vegetables, pottery, baskets, and metal items. In areas where the Bantu population grew rapidly, the Pygmies were sometimes forced to move, and this could have resulted in decreased Pygmy populations. For example, the Twa of Rwanda gradually disappeared when the Bantu Hutu arrived in the second half of the first millennium C.E.

Around 1000 B.C.E. the Bantu moved into the southern Africa, bringing agriculture and herding techniques with them. Their progress was slow; Africa's terrain does not allow for rapid transmission of crops and livestock, and diseases spread by tsetse flies killed large numbers of people and animals. As the Bantu population grew in Khoisan territory, the Khoisan Bushmen split into two groups. The Khoisan remained hunter-gatherers, but they moved into more marginal habitats, such as the Kalahari Desert. The Khoi, or Khoikhoi, became pastoralists. They acquired livestock, brought to their region by the Bantu, and lived by herding. The Khoi lived throughout the pastureland of South Africa. As the Bantu spread through the region, they adopted some Khoisan practices. The southern Bantu language, for example, acquired some click sounds and Khoisan words.

Around 1 C.E. Bantu culture had moved into Uganda, bringing along agriculture and metalworking. Nilotic peoples also moved into Uganda from the north during the first century C.E. These people included the Luo and Ateker groups. They herded cattle and practiced subsistence farming. Although there were some conflicts, the Luo soon intermarried with the Bantu and adopted Bantu customs. Some Luo continued moving south into Tanzania and Kenya. The Bantu arrived in northern South Africa around 450 C.E. This event corresponds with a period in which local animals such as wildebeest and white rhino began to disappear from the area, presumably displaced by Bantu cattle.

The Bantu included many groups that emerged as separate tribes during the ancient and subsequent periods. The Nguni people spoke the Nguni group of Bantu languages. They lived throughout southeast Africa, inching their way south over the centuries. The Nguni included peoples that developed into the Zulu, Swati, Phithi, and Ndbele. The Xhosa were Nguni people who appear to have arrived in South Africa sometime in the fifth century C.E.

EGYPT

BY KATHARINA ZINN AND MICHAEL J. O'NEAL

One way to know of migration (both emigration and exile) is to study the archaeological evidence of prehistoric societies. The material culture found in excavations tells the story of the links between different cultures. Thus, for example, archaeologists have found tombs that contain luxury goods that were clearly manufactured elsewhere, using processes and materials that were not available at the time in the area of the tomb. It is often difficult to decide whether these links developed from intensive trade exchanges, invasions, or migration movements. Concerning ancient Egypt, another important source used to explain migration movements—and sometimes the only fruitful one—is Egyptian texts, along with the artwork in tombs. While surviving texts do not provide a complete, continuous record, those that do survive give hints about the movement of people throughout ancient Egypt.

Egyptians sometimes migrated to other countries. Such migration movements were recorded in ancient texts, but the number of people who went to other countries was not high, and many wanted to return to Egypt to have an Egyptian burial with all the attendant funerary rituals. Further,

Egypt fostered a mind-set of superiority to other cultures and nations. Put simply, Egyptians looked down their noses at other countries and their people, so few had any real incentive to intermingle with them on their own territory. With the exception of a small number of texts, only a few hints help identify Egyptians outside Egypt. During the Nineteenth and early Twentieth Dynasties (1307–1070 B.C.E.), Egyptian and Egyptian-styled pottery is to be found in Canaan (Palestine) and shows cross-cultural relations between Egypt and its northwestern neighbors. At the same time, fortified towns in Nubia had a fairly uniform design, for example, Amara West and Sesebi. It can be assumed that Egyptians were living in such settlements.

Ancient Egypt was very much a crossroads. Positioned as it was in the northeast sector of the African continent, it became a central hub, engaging in trade relations with the Near East, countries surrounding the Mediterranean Sea, and nations to the south. Egypt became a beehive of activity, with builders, traders, farmers, diplomats, nomads, travelers, and others passing across its borders and moving about within the country. Archaeological evidence suggests that late in the Predynastic Period (ca. 3000 B.C.E.) many of these people came from such regions as Mesopotamia, bringing their science, literature, art, mathematics, and other cultural attributes with them. Many of these people from other lands became the earliest Egyptians; later arrivals chose to remain in Egypt, primarily because it was the most advanced civilization of its time, providing opportunities for wealth, education, and social relationships. In general, Egypt tended to welcome people from other lands, thinking of them as Egyptian as long as they made a point of acting like Egyptians. The result was a swirl of population movement within Egypt, though this population movement was, in general, not organized, nor did it occur among masses of people.

Colonization

At all periods of Egyptian history transplantations of population, or inner colonization, apparently occurred. The central government divided the Egyptian countryside into organized agricultural parts centered on larger settlements, the beginning of the organized nomes, or provinces, of later periods. Some of these settlements were in sparsely populated regions. The land was cultivated by peasants recruited from more populous regions. During the Fourth Dynasty (ca. 2575–2465 B.C.E.) a kind of colony program existed. King Snefru, the first king of the Fourth Dynasty, brought captives from different campaigns in Nubia and possibly Libya to Egypt and settled them in newly founded manors in the eastern delta and in Upper Egypt. In this period administration increased, and the great pyramid-building projects required a large number of new cultivated agricultural areas as economic support.

King Sesostris III (r. 1878–1841? B.C.E.), the fifth king of the Twelfth Dynasty of the Middle Kingdom, constructed a full-scale model town called Wah-sut in connection with a cenotaph and the cult of the death god Osiris near Abydos

Granite statue of Sesotris III, from Deir el-Bahri, Thebes, Egypt (ca. 1850 B.C.E.); Sesostris constructed a town in northern Upper Egypt for the purpose of internal colonization. (© The Trustees of the British Museum)

in northern Upper Egypt. Earlier model towns that suggest internal colonization included the modern Tell el-Dab'a in the eastern part of the Nile delta, known as Auaris at the beginning of the Twelfth Dynasty, and Kahun in the vicinity of modern El-Lahun from the reign of Sesostris II (r. 1897–1878 B.C.E.).

Inner colonization also took the form of resettlement projects during the creation of new capitals like Akhetaten (present-day Tell el-'Amârna) by Akhenaton (r. 1353–1335 B.C.E.) in the Eighteenth Dynasty or Pi-Ramses by Ramses II (r. 1290–1224 B.C.E.) during the Nineteenth Dynasty. Often foreigners were involved in this effort. A land register from the fourth regnal year of Ramses V (r. 1156–1151 B.C.E.) lists Sherden men who were cultivating farmland that they probably obtained under lease, turning them from enemies into loyal peaceful foreigners. Other examples of colonization are to be found outside Egypt. In Nubia forts with citadels were built, including Buhen or Semna, and Egyptians were settled there, mainly during the Middle Kingdom (2040–1640 B.C.E.).

The ancient Egyptians were able administrators. While Egypt's power and wealth declined during certain periods, in general Egypt's pharaohs recruited a capable bureaucracy for administering the affairs of the nation, including tax collection, land surveying, construction supervision, water management, and the like. These activities required small armies of trained and educated functionaries to move about the country, establishing settlements, organizing the administrative affairs of the nomes, overseeing activities in village and settlements, importing labor forces (including slaves), and similar activities.

Migration in the Predynastic Period

The development of Egypt cannot be adequately comprehended without a view to its changing position within several existing networks, especially communication and trade with large areas of the ancient world, including northeast Africa, southwest Asia, and the eastern Mediterranean. At all times—especially during periods when Egypt's power was at its height and the state was highly organized, Egypt acted like a magnet on its neighbors. The direction of this effect varied, but the pull was strong.

Contacts with other areas began in the fifth millennium B.C.E. At that time Egypt was not unified into the states of Upper and Lower Egypt. Upper Egypt toward Middle Egypt formed a unit around modern-day Khartoum, while Lower Egypt had a different social and cultural structure. The distinction between the Nile Valley and Lower Egypt was more salient than that between the Nile Valley and Sudan. Whether there were large-scale migrations between the Nile Valley and the eastern and western desert is not certain, but large amounts of products and resources from the desert areas found in the valley suggest regular networks of exchange, possibly combined with migration movements.

Such intensive contacts through trade and cultural exchange provided advantages to nomads, who continued to populate the region. The clearest evidence for these contacts derives from Neolithic burials rather than settlements. Such findings provided the earliest clear images of art that can be dated as well as ritual treatments of human and animal bodies. Around 3500 B.C.E. close trade contacts existed between South Canaan and the Lower Egyptian culture of Maadi-Buto, followed by settlements of these people in each other's cultural area. Locally produced Egyptian pottery has been found in South Canaan, while Canaan houses have been found in Egypt.

With the start of the age of pyramid building beginning with Djoser in the Third Dynasty (2630–2611 B.C.E.), the number of men recruited to build visible signs of dramatically improved knowledge, better organization, and centralization of the state increased enormously. The influx of more and more foreigners after the end of the Third Dynasty brought cheap manpower. Settlements of Nubians during the Fourth Dynasty can be demonstrated. There is less information available for the Old Kingdom (2575–2134 B.C.E.) than for later periods.

Climate change played a marked role in the movement of ancient Egyptian peoples. For the past 5,000 years the Sahara has been a harsh, forbidding desert, unsuitable for farming and supporting only a very small population of nomads and herders. Running through this desert is the Nile River, a thin but fertile lifeline. The Sahara, though, has not always been this way. Until about 3000 B.C.E. large portions of the Sahara were savanna grassland. This grassland supported a relatively large population of herders and farmers. As the land became dryer, perhaps in part the result of overgrazing and too much cultivation, the desert began to expand. Large numbers of people could no longer make a living in the relentlessly expanding desert. While many of these people moved south or relocated to the northern coast of Africa, many others moved into the Nile River valley, which provided them with fertile alluvial soil that supported agriculture. In this way, the population of ancient Egypt became more concentrated in a narrow strip of land bordering the river.

This early movement of peoples raises a larger question: Who, really, could claim to be "Egyptian" at that time? Being Egyptian was not a matter of race. The people who inhabited the Nile Valley during the Dynastic Period were for the most part not indigenous people who had lived in the area from time immemorial. Rather, ancient Egypt was a melting pot of peoples from around the larger region: nomadic herders and traders from the desert, people from the countries of the Near East and Mesopotamia, and Africans from other parts of the continent.

Egypt and Nubia

Any discussion of population movements of Egyptians has to include Egypt's relations with Nubia to Egypt's south. While the Nubians technically were not Egyptian, the close contact that developed over time "Egyptianized" the Nubians to the extent that it would have been difficult to distinguish a Nubian from an Egyptian. During one portion of its history, Egypt was ruled by pharaohs from Nubia, and many of Nubia's cultural institutions, including government, art, pyramids, and funerary practices, were virtually indistinguishable from those of Egypt. In time, the cultural contacts between Egypt and Nubia became so extensive that Nubia and Egypt became essentially one. That process, though, took time.

Throughout much of its early history Egypt existed in relative isolation from its neighbors. The Nile Valley was bordered on the north by the Mediterranean Sea, and marshland imposed an obstacle to access to the sea. On the east and west the fertile valley was bordered by desert. The only direction in which Egyptians showed any inclination to move was to the south, into the interior of the African continent.

The region to the south of ancient Egypt is still referred to as Nubia. This region was home to people the later Greek historians would refer to as *Aethiopians* (or Ethiopians), a word that means "burnt faces." This was the name the Greeks gave to all black Africans. The Egyptians themselves referred to the Nubian people as the Kush—usually prefacing the word with a descriptor such as "miserable." As the Egyptian empire grew in power, wealth, and sophistication, Egyptians looked on the "miserable Kush" to the south with disdain. They had little desire to explore the area, but that lack of desire may have had as much to do with geographical factors as anything else.

Along the Nile River are a series of numbered cataracts, or rapids, where the river falls dramatically and passage by boat is difficult. Near the modern-day Aswān Dam was the first cataract, which formed a natural barrier between Egypt and the kingdom of the Kush. To the north, Egyptians were content to remain in their wide, fertile valley, which provided them with the land they needed to support a thriving agricultural industry. But to the south of the first cataract, the landscape changed dramatically. Because the Egyptians were stretched out along the river, they did most of their travel by boat; they could get to nearly everywhere they wanted to go by river or canals that connected with the river, and there was little incentive to follow overland routes through the desert. But above the first cataract, the river narrowed and featured massive, irregular rock outcroppings. (The Nile River flows north to south, so "above" extends southward and "below" extends northward; "Upper" Egypt is to the south, while "Lower" Egypt is to the north.) There was little in the way of arable land, only small, patchwork areas that provided the kind of soil conditions that made Egypt's land so productive. In short, the river was not very navigable, so the Egyptians did not try.

That was to change. In time, the Egyptians came to realize that Nubia had an immense number of valuable resources. The most important of these were gold, ivory, and slaves, but these three resources merely stood at the head of a long list of items that Egyptians coveted, including various other stones, precious metals, and minerals. Animal products such as ivory can be obtained through trade and slaves through warfare, but metals and mineral products are best procured through colonization, for colonization enabled Egyptians to be on the spot to oversee the immense amount of labor necessary to extract these materials. Eventually, that is what happened.

The earliest Egyptians to move into Nubia were isolated and unorganized traders, adventurers, and plunderers during the Predynastic and Early Dynastic Periods (ca. 3000–2575 B.C.E.). These people were not acting under the authority of the state, which indeed at this point had not consolidated its power. However, they served an important function for the state, for they returned to Egypt with accounts of Nubia's great natural wealth. At this point there was no significant movement of Egyptians into Nubia. The first expedition of Egyptians was led by the pharaoh Djer in the First Dynasty, prior to 3000 B.C.E. It was during the Old Kingdom, though, that Egypt began to covet Nubia's mineral resources. These were necessary primarily for the construction projects taking place throughout Egypt. During the Fourth and Fifth Dynasties (2575–2323 B.C.E.), Egyptians moved into Nubia, in the region between the first and second cataracts, and ran a diorite mine and a copper-smelting operation. These operations were overseen and conducted by towns established for the purpose and populated by Egyptians. The power of the pharaohs waxed and waned during the Old Kingdom, so trade and the movement of Egyptians into Nubia was intermittent and unorganized.

It was during the Middle Kingdom that relations between Egypt and Nubia became more frequent and complex. During the Eleventh Dynasty (2040–1991 B.C.E.) the pharaohs once again consolidated their power. They began to colonize Nubia, backed by the weight of their armed forces. Between the first and second cataracts they established forts, at least 10 of them over a distance of about 40 miles. The result was a significant movement of Egyptians to the forts themselves, though little evidence suggests that the troops garrisoned there made any effort to subdue the Nubians, other than to engage in occasional raids to capture slaves.

In fact, it is likely that the forts existed not for offensive or defensive purposes but as a kind of coast guard that oversaw traffic on the river and offloaded and reloaded goods as boats navigated the treacherous second cataract. The positioning of these forts, all but one on the west bank of the river or on islands facing the west bank, suggests that such was their purpose. Meanwhile, Egyptians moved into Nubia to establish trade and diplomatic relations with tribal chieftains, content to allow production of local goods to remain in the hands of locals. As colonists, the Egyptians were primarily concerned with protecting the Nile River and keeping trade relations open. Over a period of centuries Egyptians who were garrisoned at the forts or were involved in trade relations intermarried with Nubians, and they and their descendants were simply absorbed into the Nubian population.

The New Kingdom and Nubia

For hundred of years Egypt's colonial enterprise in Nubia was interrupted. Egypt was weakened and divided; the Hyksos ruled northern Egypt, an Egyptian ruled southern Egypt from its capital in Thebes, and the Nubians reasserted control over trade between the two nations. But beginning in the Eighteenth and Nineteenth Dynasties this state of affairs changed dramatically. The Egyptians were able to expel the Hyksos and reunite their country. With their power reestablished, they turned their attention again to the south. Ahmose (r. 1525–1504 B.C.E.), the first pharaoh of the Eighteenth Dynasty, reoccupied lower Nubia and refurbished Egypt's forts. Over a period of a hundred years his successors pushed the frontier between Egypt and Nubia southward some 350 miles to a point below the fourth cataract. In the reign of Thutmose II (r. 1492–1479 B.C.E.) Nubia was entirely subdued; in

Thutmose's words, "Then this army of His Majesty arrived at wretched Kush. . . . This army of His Majesty overthrew those barbarians. . . . They were placed under the feet of the Good God. . . . The land was made a subject of His Majesty."

At this point, "wretched Kush" became a full-fledged Egyptian colony. Large numbers of Egyptians moved to Nubia, occupying the forts and building walled towns, residences, temples, and workshops. Egyptians in Nubia included not only soldiers but also artisans, priests, settlers, and a small army of overseers, mayors, and other civic officials. Archaeologists have discovered hundreds of ordinary tombs (as opposed to the lavish tombs of pharaohs and other high officials), suggesting that there was a mass movement of settlers into Nubia. At this point, too, the old forts below the second cataract became of less importance. They continued to be occupied but largely for the purpose of assisting trade.

Over hundreds of miles above the second cataract large administrative centers grew around new fortifications that had been built. Quickly, these administrative centers outgrew the forts that protected them. Spilling out around them were towns and residential areas inhabited by Egyptians who had migrated to Nubia. Egypt undertook a massive building program, constructing temples as symbols of its imperial power, including one temple built on a site sacred to Nubians at the Nubian capital of Napata, the southernmost extent of Egyptian colonization. Ramses II (r. 1194–1163 B.C.E.), in particular, littered Nubia with temples built for his own glorification. Ruling over Nubia and the southernmost nome of Upper Egypt was a viceroy who was given the title "King's Son of Kush." This viceroy was responsible for collecting taxes and tribute and overseeing the activities of the thousands of Egyptians who had moved to Nubia.

Egyptian migration into Nubia changed the economic life of the Kush. Previously, the country had been inhabited primarily by herders and farmers; many of the people were nomadic. The presence of large numbers of Egyptians, though, turned Nubia into a productive colony. Land ownership was in the hands of Egyptian officials and, particularly, the Egyptian temples. Tribute paid from working the land was used to supports a large class of Egyptian priests and their servants, artisans, miners, farmers, administrators, shipbuilders, and craftsmen. Prospectors from Egypt scoured the desert areas to the east of the Nile in search of gold, and their success led to the construction of numerous mines and mining settlements, all populated by Egyptians looking for gold to finance Egypt's military campaigns.

The colonization of Nubia was complete. Nubia was essentially absorbed into Egypt, annexed to it and part of the state. Under the influence of massive Egyptian immigration, the Nubians became almost entirely Egyptian in their religion, economy, and general outlook. No longer were they the "miserable" or "wretched" Kush. Although the highest governmental positions remained closed to them, many achieved relatively high positions in the bureaucracy. They adopted Egyptian customs and ways, and even their tombs were virtually indistinguishable from those of the Egyptians—no minor matter given the Egyptian emphasis on the afterlife and the importance of tombs and funerary goods in easing passage into the afterlife.

Third Intermediate, Late, and Ptolemaic Period

The first millennium B.C.E. was affected by foreign kings and dynasties. The Twenty-second Dynasty was of Libyan origin, and the Twenty-fifth Dynasty was Nubian. Shortly before the Twenty-sixth Dynasty the Assyrians ruled much of Egypt. The Persian army overwhelmed Egypt twice: during the Twenty-seventh and Thirty-first Dynasties. Alexander the Great came to Egypt, and one of his officers became Ptolemy I and established the Ptolemaic Dynasty (304–30 B.C.E.) before the Romans ruled the land. All these events are barely recorded in Egyptian records or texts but were described by Greek historians. Egypt was Egypt again with a strong Egyptian society, temple-building projects, literature, administration, trade, and foreigners in the role of pharaoh, but all with a more multicultural influence. One example of Egypt's multiculturalism was the island Elephantine near Aswān in Upper Egypt. Elephantine was settled from Early Dynastic times on and had a Jewish colony during the fifth century B.C.E. These Jewish soldiers and their families rapidly abandoned their own cultural markers and were no longer recognizable from archaeological material but only from Aramaic documents. Aramaic was the universal language of the Near East at this time. This community intermarried but retained its distinctiveness. Greek settlements from this time also have been found; the most famous was Naukratis in the western delta.

Again, the difficulty is defining an "Egyptian." While these movements of people had more to do with migration *into* the country rather than *within* the country, the ability of Egypt to absorb foreign cultures and peoples suggests that populations could become Egyptian, thus blurring the lines between movement of Egyptians and movement of foreign communities within the country that became largely Egyptianized.

Exile

The other side of migration—going into exile—is described in the "Tale of Sinuhe." Sinuhe, who flees in panic after the death of the king (which he hears about during a campaign in Libya), details his long journey from southern Libya, across the Nile, and past the fortresses to Asia, where he remains in temporary exile in the vicinity of Coele-Syria or the north Jordan valley, in Egypt called Retjenu. It has been suggested that he fleees because he is implicated in a court conspiracy, but this has not been established. Living there, he is befriended by Palestinians and marries a daughter of the chief of Upper Retjenu—the area of his exile. He settles in the territory belonging to the tribe in the manner of a Bedouin sheikh. Only homesickness and the desire for an Egyptian burial give him the desire to go back to Egypt and praise the new king,

Sesostris I. After his return and an audience with the king, Sinuhe is reinstated, bathed, and given a house and tomb with a funerary endowment and a statue. Thus, his life comes to a good end after a long period in the foreign countries. Sinuhe moves from the periphery of the world back to its center, the better world. The readership of this well-known poem, written in about 1950 B.C.E., was the literate class. It emphasizes the beliefs that Egypt was home for all Egyptians and that loyalty to the king brings prosperity. This text was still being copied seven centuries later as a school exercise.

Other hints that people went into exile come from other types of sources. A memorial slab stele from the beginning of the Twelfth Dynasty describes a kind of police action. Kay, overseer of the desert hunters, is sent to the western oasis to bring back fugitives. From the context of the text it seems clear that these escapees must be people who went into exile and were not banished people.

An example of an unintended exile is given by the "Tale of Woe" from the Third Intermediate Period, possibly the late Twenty-first or Twenty-second Dynasty The first-person narrator Wermai, a resident perhaps of Heliopolis in Lower Egypt, has to flee from his hometown as a victim of slander, charged with misdeeds against the god. He goes into exile in different regions of Egypt, and he is lonely and hungry. It is interesting that his exile is within his country but outside his beloved hometown, a kind of internal exile. He hopes for a saver, maybe Atum—the solar deity of Heliopolis.

In the "Report of Wenamun," written in the Twenty-first Dynasty at the beginning of the Third Intermediate Period, the protagonist Wenamun, an Egyptian diplomat, goes into unintended foreign exile along the Syro-Palestinian coast. He undertakes a mission to the Phoenician coast to bring back wood for the bark of Amun-Re, one of the most important gods in the Egyptian pantheon and the main god of the main temple in Wenamun's hometown, Karnak. This routine trip turns into an odyssey because of the loss of Egyptian power and influence during this time. Wenamun cannot go back for a long time and has to stay in Syria.

THE MIDDLE EAST

BY AMY HACKNEY BLACKWELL

Climate, water supply, and war were the factors that controlled migration and population movements in the ancient Near East. These three factors often were tied closely to one another. Water supply was frequently low, and droughts appeared with dismaying regularity. When droughts occurred, people moved. In many cases, they moved into cities, which were the best places to find food. When droughts were too extreme, people moved out of cities into the countryside once more in search of food.

City-states were the predominant form of settlement in much of the region, and they often vied with one another for control of precious water resources. Many cities fell to the armies of other city-states or to wandering nomadic tribes. Whenever this happened, populations often moved. Frequently, ancient rulers would force conquered peoples to leave their homelands to work as slaves in other places. Conquered peoples also simply fled their native lands, seeking refuge in the lands of other nations.

Tracking the movements of ancient peoples is difficult for many reasons. There are few historical records, and the records that do exist are sometimes contradictory or do not correspond with archaeological evidence. For example, it is impossible to reconcile the events recorded in the Hebrew Bible with contemporary Egyptian records and modern archaeological finds. It is also hard to identify specific populations. Ethnic identities were fluid, and ethnic groups did not always travel as a people. One of the best ways to track population movements is through the dispersion of languages; the path of a language as it moves through a region can be evidence of the movement of a population.

Most of the peoples of the ancient Near East were Semitic, meaning that they spoke Semitic languages. These languages include Akkadian, Assyrian, Babylonian, Hebrew, Phoenician, Nabataean, and Arabic. Semitic languages first appeared in the Arabian Peninsula during the fourth millennium B.C.E., perhaps from a point of origin in Africa. Other peoples in the region spoke Indo-European languages, including the Iranian and Anatolian languages. These people are believed to have traveled into the Middle East from the Caucasus, central Asia, and the Indus Valley. Still other languages in the region have no known linguistic relations. Sumerian, for example, is neither Semitic nor Indo-European, which makes it difficult to determine where the Sumerian people originated.

EARLY HUNTER-GATHERERS

The Middle Eastern climate following the last ice age was mild and allowed people to spread throughout the region between 12,000 and 5000 B.C.E. They congregated in wet areas with adequate rainfall or access to rivers, because these areas had the best fruits and vegetables for foraging and the largest populations of animals to hunt. They avoided the arid deserts.

These prehistoric people lived as hunter-gatherers throughout the Fertile Crescent, a region encompassing Israel, Lebanon, and the floodplains of the Tigris and Euphrates rivers from the mountains of Anatolia to the Persian Gulf. Early hunter-gatherers did not live in permanent homes but instead wandered from place to place following food sources. Starting in about 10,000 B.C.E., however, people living in areas with particularly rich sources of food began to occupy the same sites throughout the year and build permanent homes. Over the next 2,000 to 3,000 years they developed agriculture and learned to breed and raise livestock. Agriculture tied people to their farmlands and made it difficult for them to move. After the advent of agriculture, people moved only if they absolutely had to as the result of some catastrophe or natural disaster, such as sudden climate change or war.

Mesopotamia

The civilizations of ancient Mesopotamia ebbed and flowed with the water supply and periodic droughts. When the rivers flowed reliably, the people of the region built large cities that allowed them to share the water supply. Some people continued to live in the countryside as nomads. When the weather turned arid, as it did several times during the ancient period, the populations of the cities grew as people crowded into urban areas in search of food. When droughts became too extreme for the cities to continue to function, the city residents flowed back into the countryside and resumed nomadic living habits.

The first peoples to build cities on these river banks of the Tigris and Euphrates were the Sumerians. They spoke a language that is unrelated to any other known language. The geographic origins of the Sumerians are unknown, but their ancestors probably migrated down the rivers from Anatolia or northwestern Iran. The Sumerians built cities near the combined mouth of the two rivers sometime between the sixth and fourth millennia B.C.E. Eridu may have been their first city, though Ur and Uruk are also very ancient.

Around 3800 B.C.E. the climate grew drier, changing the timing of the annual river floods. It became much harder to produce or find food. Many people had lived in the countryside surrounding the Sumerian cities, either in smaller towns or in the open as nomads. These people now moved into the cities, which had stores of grains and offered them some hope of finding food. Between 3200 and 2800 B.C.E. huge numbers of people lived in cities; historians estimate that some 80 percent of the Sumerian population lived in southern Mesopotamian cities at this time.

The Akkadian civilization arose in northern Mesopotamia during the 24th century B.C.E. As was the case with Sumerian cities, people flocked to cities on the banks of the upper Tigris and Euphrates when drought made it impossible for them to survive in the countryside. Around 2200 B.C.E. Mesopotamia suffered a major drought. The cities were no longer able to feed their populations, and people dispersed into the countryside to live as they might.

The Akkadian Empire fell around 2100 after its territory was invaded by a nomadic people called the Gutians who came from the Zagros Mountains in Iran. The Gutians also traveled south into Sumerian territory and attacked Sumer's cities. This period was something of a dark age for Mesopotamia. The presence of Gutian raiders throughout the region made travel and farming dangerous. Even after the Gutians had turned civilized and been absorbed into cultured Mesopotamian society over a century or two, the term *Gutian* was still used to refer to hostile barbarians from Iran.

Another group ventured into Mesopotamia during this period, the Amorites, called Martu by the Sumerians. The Amorites lived in Syria and Canaan from the late third through the early first millennia B.C.E. and had a great deal of contact with the Sumerians. Sumerian historians described them as nomads who roamed the landscape without permanent homes or agriculture, though this appears not to have been entirely true. During the Third Dynasty of Ur (2112–2004? B.C.E.), many Amorites lived in and around Ur and other Mesopotamian cities and served in Ur's armies.

Around 2000 B.C.E. ample rainfall returned to Mesopotamia. People again populated the riverbanks and built new cities along the rivers' new courses. The Amorites used this opportunity to seize power in the region. Between about 2000 and 1600 B.C.E. Amorites ruled Mesopotamia as the Old Babylonian regime. They conquered the city of Ashur and moved into the Khābūr River delta area around 1800 B.C.E. The Amorite's capital was the city of Babylon, located on the Euphrates River some distance from the mouth; cities of this period were not located as far south on the river as older Sumerian ones. Babylon attracted large numbers of immigrants from the surrounding countryside, and during the 17th century B.C.E. it was the largest city in the world.

The Assyrians first appeared in the upper Tigris region after 2000 B.C.E. The Assyrian people spoke a Semitic language that was closely related to Akkadian. Assyrians spread through Anatolia, establishing trade colonies in Cappadocia. Their empire reached its peak during the early first millennium B.C.E. The Assyrians were responsible for a great deal of population movement. Their empire covered much of Anatolia, Mesopotamia, and the Levant, including the city of Babylon. Assyrian kings made a practice of deporting conquered peoples to destroy their national identities and make it harder for them to revolt. During the eighth century the populations of Israel, Judah, and Syria were all deported elsewhere. Their new homes included the cities of Nineveh and Gozan and the territory of the Medes far to the east, in modern-day Iran. The Assyrian rulers moved their own nobles into the vacated territories, hoping to create a permanent ruling class in the conquered lands.

The Levant

Several civilizations came from the land called Canaan, which was located in present-day Lebanon and Syria. The Canaanites were the first Semitic peoples to occupy Canaan. Canaanites appear in the Hebrew Bible (the Old Testament in the Christian Bible) as the nation founded by Canaan, the son of Ham and grandson of Noah. Canaanites thought of themselves as a distinct political unit by the 18th century B.C.E.

The Israelites appeared in Canaan during the time recorded in the book of Genesis, which is impossible to pinpoint historically. The Old Testament patriarch Abraham was said to have lived in the city of Ur, in Mesopotamia, and to have moved his family to the land of Canaan. The book of Genesis tells of Abraham's pact with his god, in which his descendants were given the land of Canaan. Abraham's descendant Jacob, also called Israel, was the father of 12 sons with whom originated the 12 tribes of Israel. All of his family is said to have immigrated to Egypt during a famine. According to the Old Testament, the Israelites spent some 500 years in Egypt. At the end of this time the patriarch Moses led them out of Egypt and back to Canaan after 40 years of wandering the desert in the Sinai region. At the beginning of this journey the Red Sea is said to have parted to allow the Israelites to pass through it and then closed upon the Egyptian army.

Historians are not at all sure that any of these events really happened. It is known that some Canaanite tribes lived in Egypt during the first half of the second millennium B.C.E. Some scholars have suggested that the Exodus from Egypt under Moses happened during the 13th century B.C.E. under Ramses II. Still, Egyptian archaeologists have announced that there is no physical evidence suggesting that the Red Sea parted.

If the Exodus did occur during the 13th century, the so-called Sea Peoples may have played a part in the events of the time. The Sea Peoples were a group of seafarers who wandered the eastern Mediterranean during the second millennium B.C.E. Their identities and origins are unknown. They may have come from Crete, the Aegean, southern Anatolia, or the coast of Lebanon and Israel. What is known is that there were numerous marauding seafarers roaming the eastern Mediterranean, especially during the late Bronze Age. Many of them ended up in Egypt after attempting to attack it and being captured during the reign of Ramses III (ca. 1194–ca. 1163 B.C.E.).

The Philistines may have belonged to the Sea Peoples. They moved into Canaan during the 12th century B.C.E. In about 1180 B.C.E. they took the southern Canaanite cities Gaza, Gath, Ashqelon, Ashdod, and Ekron. They appear not to have been Semitic peoples; in the Old Testament they are often described as "uncircumcised," which differentiated them from Israelites. What little is known of their language seems to indicate that it was an Indo-European and not a Semitic language. Their culture seems to have shared some similarities with Mycenaean Greek culture, and Philistine pottery resembles Mycenaean work of that period. They may have belonged to the Sea Peoples. Some historians believe that the Egyptian pharaoh Ramses III imprisoned the Sea Peoples in Egypt and then settled the Philistines in southern Canaan, where he could tax them.

According to the biblical account, when the Israelites arrived back in Canaan, they found the land inhabited by Canaanites. They attacked and conquered several cities, including Jericho, Ai, and Hazor. Historians are unsure of what happened; if these events occurred in about 1200 B.C.E., they took place in a setting of general chaos and destruction at the end of the Bronze Age. The Sea Peoples and Philistines were active in the region and may have participated in the overthrow of the Canaanite cities.

In any case, the Israelites did move back into Canaan at some point, perhaps around 1200 B.C.E. They divided the land among the ancestral tribes. Around 920 B.C.E. the Hebrews divided into two kingdoms, Israel to the north and Judah to the south. The Babylonian captivity or the first diaspora, as it was called, came when Mesopotamian armies conquered Israel in 722 B.C.E. and Judah in 586 B.C.E. When Israel fell to Assyria, the Assyrians attempted to move the Israelites en masse to Media. Many Israelites instead fled south into Judah, settling in the capital city of Jerusalem. The Assyrians moved their own people into Israel in an attempt to create a new noble class there.

In 586 B.C.E. Judah fell to Babylon. Much of the nobility was deported to the city of Babylon. Other Jews were enslaved and taken to Assyrian cities to work. Still others fled to Egypt, Persia, or Syria. In 539 B.C.E. the Persian emperor Cyrus conquered Babylon. He allowed the Jews in Babylon to go back to Jerusalem and surrounding areas. There they remained for the next six centuries. In 70 C.E., at the end of the first Jewish-Roman War, the emperor Titus destroyed the temple at Jerusalem and deported some 100,000 Jews to Rome as slaves. Many thousands of others fled the Levant to Mesopotamia and other nations in the Mediterranean region. In 135 C.E. Rome put down a revolt by some of the Jews remaining in Judea. Thereafter, Judea ceased to exist as a political entity, the province was renamed Syria-Palestine, and the Jewish people were dispersed from the region they considered their homeland. This is known as the second diaspora of the Jews.

Phoenicians

The Phoenicians occupied the coast of Lebanon between 1200 and 800 B.C.E. Historians have debated the origin of the Phoenician people for millennia. Some modern archaeologists believe that they were simply the descendants of previous Canaanite peoples who lived in the area. Other historians, including the Greek historian Herodotus, argue that the Phoenician people came to Lebanon from some other place, bringing with them their knowledge of the sea. Suggested places of origin include Minoan Crete, eastern Africa, or the land of the Philistines. Some historians believe that the Phoenicians learned their sailing skill from the Sea Peoples.

Wherever they came from, the Phoenician people spread their culture quite a distance. The Phoenician people were skilled traders and seamen. They sailed throughout the Mediterranean on galleys to sell their major products, chief of which was a deep purple dye known as Tyrian purple made from the murex snail. They built settlements along the entire southern coast of the Mediterranean as well as in Sicily, Sardinia, Cyprus, Crete, and Spain. Their most important settlement was Carthage in modern Tunisia, founded in 814 B.C.E. Other major cities included Tyre, Sidon, Tripoli, Hippo (in present-day Algeria) and Abdera (in modern-day Spain). They took with them an alphabet, which the Greeks adopted and later turned into the Greek alphabet, and the worship of a god called Baal.

The heyday of the Phoenicians ended with the rise of the Assyrians. The city of Tyre remained strong, and the Lebanese Phoenician population was concentrated there until 539 B.C.E. when Cyrus the Great conquered the city. Historians believe that many of the Phoenician people migrated to Carthage and the other Mediterranean colonies around that time.

Anatolia

Anatolia, modern-day Turkey, was fertile and heavily forested. During the seventh and sixth millennia B.C.E. many people settled on the banks of the Black Sea, then the Euxine Sea (or lake). People flocked to the coasts from surrounding areas, attracted by the rich soil. Around 5800 B.C.E. it appears that the lake flooded. This forced the inhabitants to flee to higher ground, either within Anatolia or in eastern Europe.

During the third millennium B.C.E. northern Anatolia was inhabited by a people called the Hattians, who spoke a non-Indo-European language. They were displaced by the Hittites, who appeared in Anatolia sometime around 2000 or 1900 B.C.E. Historians do not know where the Hittites came from, but it appears that their ancestors may have lived in the Ukraine during the previous two millennia. They were not a Semitic people, and they spoke an Indo-European language. They were excellent charioteers and skilled horsemen.

They created a capital at the city Hattusa, named after the earlier Hattian inhabitants. From there they spread throughout western Anatolia and the Levant. The Hittites arrived in Mesopotamia around 1600 B.C.E. Their arrival ended the Old Babylonian regime of the Amorites. At the height of the Hittite empire (1430–1180 B.C.E.) the Hittites encroached on Egyptian territory in Canaan. The Hittites traded with people throughout Mesopotamia. They depended particularly on Mesopotamian metal for their weapons and chariots and thus needed to keep control of Syria, which gave them access to the Euphrates and Tigris rivers. The Hittite empire collapsed in the 12th century B.C.E. amid the general chaos of the time. It may have fallen victim to assaults by the Sea Peoples.

The ancestors of the Lycians moved into southwestern Anatolia in prehistoric times. They spoke an Indo-European language called Lycian, which appears to have developed from an earlier Anatolian language called Luwian. The Lycians were allies of the Hittites and may have been related to them. The Lydian people also were related to the Hittites; Lydian was another Indo-European language of the Anatolian branch. They inhabited western Anatolia in the area of modern Izmir. The Phrygians are believed to have been part of the Sea Peoples. They moved into central Anatolia around 1200 B.C.E. and may have participated in the fighting that toppled the Hittite capital Hattusa. They inhabited this area through the rest of the ancient period.

Hurrians and Hyksos

The Hurrians were a group of people who migrated into northern Mesopotamia from the Caucasus region around 2500 B.C.E. Their language was neither Semitic nor Indo-European but may have been related to other languages of the Caucasus. They established several small nations in southeastern Turkey and Syria and migrated far to the south, east, and west. During the second millennium B.C.E. there were Hurrians throughout Turkey, Mesopotamia, and the Levant. By about 1000 B.C.E., however, Hurrians had been assimilated into other ethnic groups and ceased to exist as a people.

The people known as the Hyksos rode south through the Levant and entered Egypt in the 17th century B.C.E. The traditional story has been that they invaded Egypt, but new interpretations of the evidence suggest that the Hyksos may simply have migrated to Egypt from Canaan without violence. Historians have long debated who the Hyksos were. They drove chariots and rode horses, like the Indo-European people from the Caucasus and Central Asia. They had Semitic names, like the Canaanites and Hebrews. Some historians think they were a mixture of Indo-Iranian peoples. They may have been Hurrians. Whoever they were, the ruled Egypt for about 100 years before being driven out. Many historians have tried to equate the departure of the Hyksos from Egypt into Canaan with the exodus of the Hebrews from Egypt under Moses, but there is no historical evidence for this.

Desert Nomads

The deserts of modern-day Arabia and Jordan were home to a number of nomads who moved freely throughout the Middle East. They often did not have permanent homes. Instead, they regularly migrated from place to place along standard trade routes. The Edomites were Semitic nomads who lived in the Negev Desert in Jordan and southern Israel. They certainly existed during the eighth century B.C.E. and may have been in the area as long as three centuries earlier than that. They supported themselves by running caravans to carry goods between Arabia, the Levant, Egypt, and Mesopotamia.

The Nabataeans lived in Jordan and Arabia. They were Semitic nomads who moved throughout the desert on trade routes between the Euphrates and the Red Sea. Some historians have suggested that the ancestors of the Nabataeans may have been in the desert during the time of the events in the biblical book of Genesis, but the first real documents mentioning them date to the fourth century B.C.E. The people called Arabs lived in Arabia and Sinai. The earliest mention of Arabs dates to 853 B.C.E. Assyrian records describe Arab queens who led tribes of caravan traders.

Persia

The Elamites created one of the earliest civilizations in Persia. They moved into western Persia around 3200 B.C.E. Their civilization was centered on the city Susa, which had been built around 4000 B.C.E. by even earlier inhabitants. The Elamites spoke a language that was not related to any of the surrounding languages, including Sumerian and the Semitic and Indo-European languages. Historians believe that the Elamite language may have been related to the Dravidian languages spoken by the earliest inhabitants of southern India. This could suggest that the Elamite people were descended from the people of the Indus Valley and migrated to Persia from what is now Pakistan, but there is no good evidence to prove this hypothesis.

The Persians were an Indo-Iranian (Aryan) people who migrated into Persia from central Asia during the second millennium B.C.E. These people split into two groups with separate languages, the Persians and the Medes. Some of them intermarried with the Elamites. Around the ninth century B.C.E. the Persians occupied the land in southern Iran, southeast of the territory of the Elamites. The Medes took the land to the north, along the southern coast of the Caspian Sea. The Scythians, a nomadic people from Pontus, moved into Media in the seventh century B.C.E. The Scythians also spoke an Iranian language.

The Persians began to spread through Mesopotamia under Cyrus the Great, who unified Persia in 559 B.C.E. Under his leadership Persians moved into Media, Lydia in Asia Minor, parts of central Asia, and Babylon. Under his son Cambyses (r. 529–522 B.C.E.), Persians took over Egypt. Darius I (r. 522–486 B.C.E.) led Persian armies into the Indus River valley, Thrace, and all the way to Greece. Xerxes I (r. 486–465 B.C.E.) also led a Persian army into Greece. These Persian expeditions were populations of their own; Xerxes' forces may have numbered 60,000, which was a large number of people to move across the countryside.

Although the Persians usually allowed the inhabitants of their conquered lands to keep living in their homes, they also deported many of them to other places. Many Greek slaves ended up living in Persia. Persians themselves made new homes in conquered territories. Both of these phenomena facilitated the spread of cultures from place to place.

To the east of Media was the land of the Parthians. This land was occupied by horse-riding nomads from the Caucasus and Iran. They spoke an Indo-European language of the Iranian family. During the third century B.C.E. the Parthians used their cavalry to occupy most of northern Persia, Assyria, Babylonia, and Elam and moved east into Bactria.

ASIA AND THE PACIFIC

BY CRAIG G. R. BENJAMIN

The history of ancient Asia and the Pacific is characterized by migrations on an often vast scale, and in Asia by the interaction of those migrants with the sedentary agrarian settlements, kingdoms, and civilizations already established in the region. Ever since the evolution of *Homo erectus* some 1.6 million years ago (the first hominid to migrate out of Africa and into Asia) and certainly since the migration of groups of *Homo sapiens* out of Africa perhaps 100,000 years ago, the valleys, steppes, and desert tracks of Asia have acted as conduits along which successive waves of migrants have passed. In inner Asia the emphasis really was on passing through, at least until comparatively recently, because even in the more benign environments of the region the generally harsh climate and forbidding terrain often made permanent settlement difficult. The sporadic evidence available indicates that before approximately 50,000 years ago there were only occasional attempts to settle even the more hospitable regions around the fringes of the Inner Asian heartland.

However, by the Upper Paleolithic Era (about 40,000 to 50,000 years ago) more reliable archaeological evidence from a large number of sites ranging from the Ukraine to eastern Siberia and southern Mongolia indicates the presence of substantial numbers of hunter-gatherers who had migrated into Inner Asia. In the millennia that followed, these communities gradually adopted a seminomadic, semisedentary way of life, so that by the middle of the fourth millennium B.C.E., subsequent waves of migrating pastoralists from the southern Russian steppes were confronted by semiagrarian communities already in occupation of the more fertile niches. Confrontations between aggressive, often militarized migrants and sedentary farmers generally progressed from invasion to occupation to cultural assimilation.

This tension between residents and invaders remained the fundamental dynamic of much of inner and eastern Asia during the pre- and protohistoric eras. There is evidence of periodic aggressive migrant activity right across the southern Siberian and Mongolian steppes from the first millennium B.C.E. until the Mongol invasions of the sedentary kingdoms of Eurasia during the 12th and 13th centuries. But it would be incorrect to suggest that all interactions between migrating pastoralists and farmers were necessarily confrontational, as there is also evidence of long periods of relatively stable, mutually cooperative relationships between the two.

The geography of Asia remained a crucial determinant. With the available routes for large-scale movement often limited by impassable deserts and high mountain ranges, it was inevitable that the migration of a group or tribe into any given area would affect other communities already occupying sites along those routes. Because of this, a second characteristic of ancient Asian migration was a domino effect whereby any substantial migration from one region to another would often result in the disruption of a whole series of other groups ahead of the invading tribes. It hardly mattered what the cause was of the original migration. Once a group had chosen (or been forced) to uproot and relocate, they had few options other than to follow a very limited range of possible routes, and this inevitably brought them into conflict with other communities already settled along the selected path. If the invading party was strong enough, the occupants were expelled, and they in turn moved ahead along the same route, disrupting and expelling other communities until each had found a new location in which to resettle, or achieved some compromise with the invaders.

PASTORALIST MIGRATION AND COLONIZATION IN THE BRONZE AGE

The most significant migrations in ancient Asian history were those undertaken by nomadic pastoralists speaking Indo-European and Indo-Iranian languages. These migrations were an indirect result of the appearance of agriculture in southwestern Asia from about 9000 B.C.E. A range of at least three alternative lifeways subsequently emerged over the following millennia. Certain communities embraced farming and became solely dependent on agricultural produce for their livelihood. Others remained nomadic hunter-gatherers by migrating into areas outside of the sedentary zones, often following conflict over resources with the farmers. And yet others adopted elements of both lifeways, opting for the semisedentary, seminomadic lifeway of nomadic pastoralism.

Pastoralists (people who are dependent chiefly on their herds of domestic stock for subsistence) went on to play a major role in the history of ancient Asia. While sheep, goats, and cattle had all been domesticated from at least 6000 B.C.E., it was only when humans had learned to exploit the traction power of animals as well as their secondary products (including blood, milk, and hair), that they were able to extend their range by colonizing large areas of grassland otherwise unsuitable for sedentary agriculture.

The impact of migrating pastoralists on the Eurasian landscape was immediate and profound because of their military virtuosity and their capacity for rapid mobilization. Archaeological evidence indicates periods of considerable disruption in the steppes from at least the middle of the fourth millennium B.C.E., which can be explained only by the influx of migrating pastoral nomads into the region. Three waves of migration (ca. 3400–ca. 3200 B.C.E.; ca. 2600–ca. 2400 B.C.E.; and ca. 2000–ca. 1800 B.C.E.) can be detected, representing the invasion of Inner Asia by various groups of Indo-European and Indo-Iranian-speaking pastoral nomads.

Groups of nomads began to appear in western, central, southern, and eastern Asia from the mid-fourth millennium B.C.E. The speed of migration of the earliest pastoralist communities, whose horse-riding skills and equipment were probably rudimentary, was slow and gradual. There is evidence of widespread migratory episodes through the region by pastoralists with ox-drawn carts and powerful tribal leaders. The substantial number of ornamental metal objects discovered at steppe-land burial sites dating from the late fourth millennium B.C.E. is evidence of the arrival of powerful chiefs and aristocracies. If the region was indeed one of low population densities, the invading nomads would have occupied sparsely populated lands and easily expelled the residents.

But the impact of the Indo-European migrations varied considerably across ancient Asia, depending on the level of social and technological development already achieved in the occupied regions. Although the invaders were able to establish themselves as ruling aristocracies in Mesopotamia and across the Fertile Crescent in general, they were rapidly assimilated into the prevailing more advanced cultures. In the less-developed regions of inner Asia, however, it was the invaders who imposed their languages, culture, and social organization on the geopolitical landscape.

The nomadic invasions of Mesopotamia and Asia Minor between about 2500 and 1600 B.C.E. have been well documented. Groups such as the Kassites, the rulers of Mitanni, the Hurrians, the Luwians, and the Hittites all made a significant impact upon the sedentary urban-based states of the Fertile Crescent. The progress and effects of Indo-European migrations into central and eastern Asia are less well understood. Chronological disagreement between western and Russian archaeologists over the dating of Indo-European migrations is just one of the problems associated with the subject. But there is no disputing Russian archaeological evidence of nomadic invasions from the western steppes through southern Siberia and the former Soviet Republics of central Asia, extending progressively further east with each wave of migration.

These waves of pastoralist expansion can be followed by tracing the incidence and variety of barrows (called *kurgans* in Turkic) that mark the burial sites of the different nomadic migrant cultures. The so-called Kurgan theory argues that the earliest Indo-Europeans emerged in about 5000 B.C.E. in southern Russia (north of the Black and Caspian Seas), when hunter-gatherer populations gradually adopted both semisedentary agriculture and mobile stock herding. From here the Indo-Europeans migrated out to the west, south, and east in the three waves of Bronze Age migrations noted earlier.

Much of the archaeological evidence for the Early Bronze Age comes from the western steppes, particularly the pit-grave *yamnaya* pastoralist culture that flourished from between the Bug and Dniester rivers in the west to the Ural River. The pit-grave culture provides evidence of horse riding and the use of wheeled vehicles on the steppe that might have been vital in the logistics of mass migration, including both two-wheeled and four-wheeled wagons that were probably pulled by oxen. Many of the metal goods discovered in *yamnaya* sites, including daggers, axes, and maces, had been imported from agricultural metal-working zones, indicating that pastoralists, farmers, and artisans of the western steppes were already linked into a single regional system of exchanges as early as the mid-fourth millennium B.C.E.

By the Middle Bronze Age pastoral nomads had migrated farther to the east, occupying parts of southern Siberia and the central Asiatic steppes, driven perhaps by overpopulation in the western steppes or by climate change. The most significant pastoralist culture of the central and southern steppes is that of the Afanasevo (named after the site of Afanasyeva Gora excavated in 1920). Their cultural artifacts excavated from a number of burial sites show many similarities to those of the pit-grave cultures, suggesting that the Afanasevo culture was a product of pastoral nomadic migrants from the west combined with the assimilation of indigenous hunter-gatherer populations. The Afanasevo culture perhaps represents the most easterly extension of Asian steppe cultural migration. However, the movement may not have halted at the Altai but perhaps extended southward at some later date into the Gansu and Tarim Basin (present-day Xinjiang Province) of western China.

Linguistic and archaeological evidence also exists for an overlay of Indo-Iranian-speaking cultures upon the earlier Indo-European strata as well as the physical displacement of the Indo-European invaders. That there were two major Indo-European branch language groups spoken by the different groups of nomads is indisputable. By the Late Bronze Age (ca. 2000–ca. 1500 B.C.E.) there is evidence of further widespread disruption across the steppes, indicating a third wave of large-scale migration, this time most probably by pastoral nomads speaking an Indo-Iranian branch. These later migrants occupied regions as far east as the western and southern regions of the Tarim Basin, wedging the earlier Indo-European migrants into eastern Xinjiang.

The steppe-bronze culture that emerged in the wake of this invasion is known as the Andronovo. The Andronovans lived in small, fortified villages and towns in large houses that were at least partly subterranean. Their economy was based on stockbreeding (cattle, sheep, goats, pigs and horses), and their way of life was one of mobile pastoralism with occasional periods of semisedentary agriculturalism. The immediate predecessor to the Andronovans was the Sintashta culture (ca. 2300–1900 B.C.E.), which was based in the southeastern Urals, particularly near modern Magnitogorsk. Associated with the emergence of both the Sintashta and subsequent Andronovo cultures was the appearance of many fortified settlements and royal burials with chariots, indicative perhaps of the troubled nature of this period.

However, the chariot did not make any significant military impact on ancient inner Asia. Although the introduction of the chariot transformed warfare in Southwest Asia and India, it was less practical in the steppes of central and East Asia and was replaced from about 1500 B.C.E. by more effective horse-riding archer warriors using compound bows. It was pastoral nomadic forces of this type that the Chinese Zhou and Han chroniclers later described when discussing the "barbarians" to China's north, including the Wusun, Xiongnu, and Yuezhi.

The Andronovan culture continued to spread eastward through present-day Kazakhstan and into eastern central Asia. Archaeological evidence indicates the eventual existence of a dividing line that developed in Mongolia between both the Indo-European Afanasevan and Indo-Iranian Andronovan migrants from the west and the ethnic Proto-Mongolians in the east, representing the most easterly expansion of the migrants through northern Inner Asia by about 1800–1500 B.C.E. To the south, beyond the reach of Soviet and Russian archaeologists, the evidence is less plentiful, but both Indo-European and Indo-Iranian pastoral nomads must also have spread into the eastern steppes, particularly along already well-trodden routes through the Tarim Basin, until they were brought to a halt perhaps by the indigenous peoples who dwelt in eastern Mongolia and along China's northwestern borders.

Colonization of the Border Regions of Ancient China

From early in the 20th century explorers began finding mummified remains at a number of sites in the Tarim Basin. More recently several hundred such "mummies" (actually the remains of dried-out bodies) have been discovered in the region. The oldest of these corpses dates from about 2000 B.C.E. and the earliest Indo-European corpses from perhaps 1750 B.C.E., which suggests at the very least that from the Late Bronze Age a significant and increasing proportion of the population of Xinjiang began to be of Indo-European/Caucasoid ethnicity. Many of the bodies have been subjected to DNA and textile analysis, but the results have been inconclusive.

Archaeological research into the prehistoric cultures of the Tarim Basin has provided evidence of a number of cultures, the earliest of which appears to be the Qawrighul (early second millennium B.C.E.), whose remains have been found about 50 miles west of Lop Nur. Mummies of the Yanbulaq culture (located near Hami and dated to about 1750–700 B.C.E.) were mainly of Mongoloid stock, though also found were eight Caucasoid types, which represent perhaps the oldest Europoid human remains so far discovered in the Tarim. The presence of three different grave types has led some researchers to suggest that this is evidence of the movement of Caucasoid migrants into a region in which Mongoloid populations had already established themselves from the east.

One possibility is that Afanasevo groups migrated south from their homeland in the Altai-Yenisei region. One branch headed toward the Huanghe River, where they may have interacted with the ethnic Chinese Qijia culture, and another moved southwest into the Gansu and Tarim areas. As noted earlier, subsequent migrations of Indo-Iranian-speaking nomads also entered the Tarim and established their languages on top of the earlier Indo-European dialects, but they were never able to achieve linguistic supremacy in the north and east, where Indo-European variants remained dominant. The obvious route for both the Indo-Europeans and Indo-Iranians was south through a mountainous funnel that opens up near Urumqi and which then offers passes to both the Dunhuang region of the Gansu or southwest into the Turpan Basin and the eastern Tarim.

At the same time that Indo-European groups were migrating south to take up residencies in the Gansu and Xinjiang sometime between the 18th and 17th centuries B.C.E., farther to the east and to the north of the main zones of irrigated agricultural communities along the valley of the Huanghe, large communities of Mongoloid nomads also began to emerge between the 18th and 12th centuries. These and other pastoral nomadic communities are listed in the chronicles of the Chinese Zhou Dynasty. Farther north again, in northern inner Asia and southern Siberia, the Karasuk culture replaced the Andronovo between the 13th and 10th centuries.

Evidence of the importance of livestock to the Karasuk indicates that they followed more mobile lifeways than did the Andronovans, though the discovery of large dugout dwellings in the Minusinsk basin also indicates the retention of a semisedentary way of life. The basin of Minusinsk is made up of undulating land on either side of the Yenisey River. It is one of the largest prehistoric graveyards in all of Eurasia, with numerous barrows having yielded vessels, amulets, and weapons. Archaeological evidence clearly shows that from the middle of the second millennium B.C.E. a succession of cultures and ethnicities occupied the region, each of which gradually adapted to a sedentary, agricultural way of life.

Migration of the Yuezhi (Tocharians) and Saka (Scythians)

The most significant Indo-European-speaking group that may have migrated into Xinjiang and the Gansu late in the Bronze Ages was the Yuezhi (also known as the Tocharians), who were destined to play a significant role in the history of ancient Asia. The ancestors of the Yuezhi were pastoral nomads who probably migrated to the eastern steppes during the Middle Bronze Age. They eventually found themselves sometime in the second millennium B.C.E. occupying a strategic part of the Gansu corridor, where they exercised some sort of commercial control over extensive areas of the Tarim Basin. Adopting a seminomadic, semisedentary lifestyle, they prospered through trade and achieved a considerable reputation amongst the Zhou and Han Chinese because of their wealth, prestige, and force of arms.

In the second century B.C.E., however, the Yuezhi were forced to move away from the borders of Han China by their rivals the Xiongnu (who may have been the ancestors of the Huns, militarized nomadic people whose fifth century C.E. migration to the west would play a critical role in the downfall of the Western Roman Empire). Leaving the Gansu in 162 B.C.E. and heading north into the Ili valley, they moved into a region already occupied by Saka peoples (also known as the Sai to the Chinese or the Scythians to Greco-Roman historians). As a result, these Ili basin Sakas were themselves displaced and forced to migrate to the south along the western edge of the Tarim Basin, before finally crossing into Kashmir. Here at least one group of Scythians would rule for up to 180 years, almost without interruption, until the reign of the last Indo-Scythian satrap of Kashmir, Zeionises.

The Indo-Scythians were eventually defeated by Kujula Kadphises, the first king of the Kushans, sometime soon after about 45–50 C.E. The Sakas then fragmented into a number of smaller statelike divisions and spilled out into the Punjab and northern India, establishing the significant Saka kingdoms, whose era in Indian history dates from 78 C.E. In this way events that unfolded along the borders of Han China early in the second century B.C.E. were directly responsible for significant developments in the history of ancient Central Asia and India well beyond the area of their immediate impact. The migration of the Ili basin Sakas that led eventually to the establishment of Saka kingdoms in northern India some 250 years later is a good example of the domino effect of migration in inner Asian geopolitics and of the critical role of migration in the history of ancient Asia.

Eventually, after passing through Ferghana and Sogdia, the Yuezhi defeated and evicted another resident group of Sakas, who may have been responsible for the conquest of the disintegrating Greek kingdom of Bactria. These displaced Saka tribes were forced south of the Hindu Kush, where they eventually resettled in Sacastan (present-day Sistān) sometime after 123 B.C.E. Some decades later (ca. 80 B.C.E.) the Yuezhi crossed the Amu Dar'-ya en masse and occupied Bactria, where they went on to establish the Kushan Empire (ca. 1–450 C.E.) which became major player in the Silk Roads trade during the first two centuries of the Common Era.

Impact of the Aryan Migrations on Ancient India

The earliest evidence of human activity in India or Pakistan so far discovered goes back to the Second Interglacial Period between 400,000 and 200,000 B.C.E. The spectacular Indus Valley civilization was the most extensive prehistoric civilization of the region and dates from about 3000 B.C.E. It was preceded by an agrarian village culture in the Baluchistan hills and the Makran coast. The Harappan civilization was an urban-based state structure (similar to that which developed in the late fourth millennium in southern Mesopotamia), and its two principal cities of Mohenjo Daro and Harappa displayed an advanced sense of civic planning and organization. By the early second millennium B.C.E. the Indus civilization had declined, to be replaced from about 1500 by (probably) an invasion of migrating Indo-Iranians (sometimes called Aryans) from the north, part of the third wave of Bronze Age nomadic migrations noted previously. The Aryan (meaning "noble ones") tribes were led by aggressive warrior aristocrats on horse-drawn chariots armed with good-quality copper and bronze weapons.

These Indo-Iranian invaders probably set out from their southern Russian homeland late in the third millennium but may have settled for some centuries in Bactria and the Iranian plateau before resuming their migration south through where the Hindu Kush passes into northern India. Our knowledge of Aryan culture is largely derived from the Rig-Veda and it is possible to trace, through geographical references in the Rig-Veda, the slow but certain progression of the Aryans from the Indus Valley down the western portions of the Ganges and its tributaries. After possibly playing a limited role in the decline of the Indus Valley civilization, the Aryans took up residence in the Punjab before eventually entering the Deccan and the Ganges Valley, home of the so-called Painted-Grey Ware culture (ca. 1100 to 500 B.C.E.)—agrarian communities based on the domestication of crops and animals.

The archaeological and literary record indicates that by the first half of the first millennium B.C.E. there are unmistakable signs of a superior technology arriving in both the Deccan and the Ganges Valley, evidence of the invasion of India proper by the Indo-Iranians, who soon abandoned pastoralism and also adopted an agrarian lifeway. By the sixth century B.C.E. monarchical states (like Kosala and Magadha) began to dominate the Ganges Valley, absorbing or establishing dominance over the smaller republican states of northern India and shifting the focus of Indian culture eastward, away from the valley of the Indus. The immediate aftermath of the Aryan invasions of the Deccan and Ganges Valley was a heroic age. It is to this age that the great Indian epic, the Mahabharata, refers in its description of a war between two rival coalitions of noble charioteers.

Migration and Colonization of the Ancient Pacific

Turning from the Asian continent to the Pacific Ocean, the occupation of the islands of Hawaii is perhaps the most striking example of the extraordinary achievements of the Polynesian peoples, who are responsible for the colonization of a large number of isolated islands in the central Pacific. Over a period of approximately 2,500 years (from ca. 1500 B.C.E. to ca. 1000 C.E.) voyagers from Fiji, Tonga, and Samoa migrated to and colonized islands across an ocean area of millions of square miles. By the 16th century, when European navigators began to explore the Pacific, virtually all the habitable islands were already settled.

These maritime migrations were made in outrigger and double-hulled canoes built with stone, bone, and coral tools. By alternately paddling or sailing (using sails woven from coconut or pandanus leaves) Polynesian migrants regularly completed voyages of more than 2,000 miles across the Pacific. Navigation was done by skilled mariners using observations based on ocean currents, winds, and the setting points of stars. Navigators also employed a system of dead reckoning, memorizing the distance and direction being traveled until the destination was reached.

When European explorers first arrived in the islands of Polynesia, it was immediately obvious that the Polynesian inhabitants must have shared a common ancestry. Island residents were similar in appearance, and their language, technologies, domesticated species, and cultures varied very little across thousands of miles of ocean area. It is now believed that all Polynesian peoples came from common an-

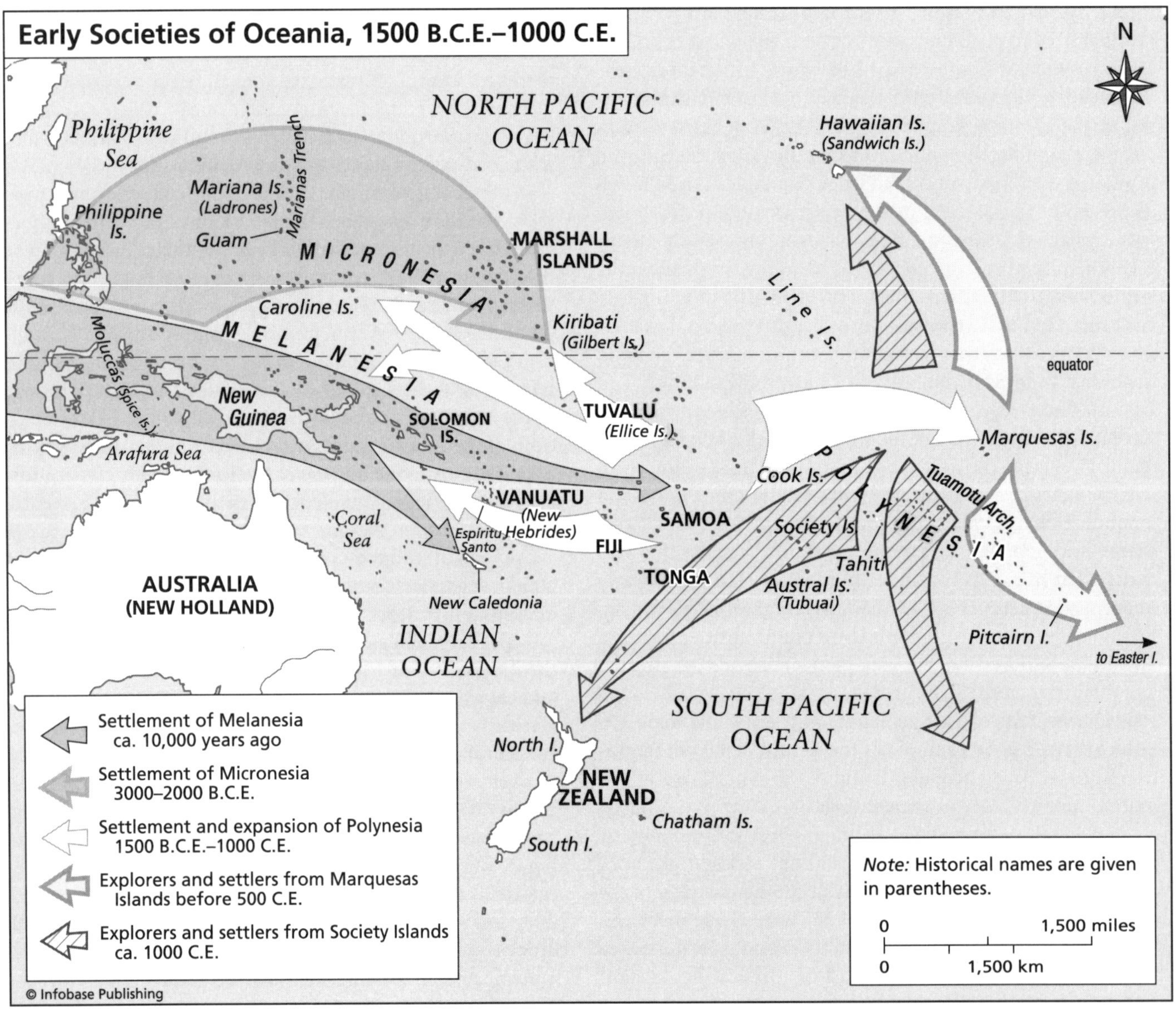

Among the peoples of ancient Oceania were the Polynesians, who colonized a large number of isolated islands in the central Pacific after 1500 B.C.E.

cestors who had developed a distinctive fishing and agrarian culture in the islands of Tonga and Samoa. There is also general agreement on a chronological sequence for the migration of the Polynesian peoples.

Archaeological evidence and DNA analysis suggest that early humans had migrated (by land and sea) to New Guinea and Australia by at least 60,000 years ago. In Australia these migrants maintained a hunter-gatherer way of life until the arrival of Europeans in the 17th and 18th centuries, but in New Guinea several groups adopted an agrarian lifestyle. From about 1600 B.C.E. members of the so-called Lapita culture began to migrate from New Guinea in Melanesia farther east to Fiji, Samoa, and Tonga, and it was at the eastern edge of this region (that is, in Samoa and Tonga) that a distinctive Polynesian culture emerged.

By about 300 B.C.E. migrants from Samoa and Tonga had discovered and colonized several island groups farther to the east, including the Cook Islands, Tahiti-nui, and Hiva (or the Marquesas). Some 600 years later (by 300 C.E.) migrants from (probably) the Marquesas discovered and settled Easter Island, and sometime within the next century (by ca. 400 C.E.) voyagers from the Cook Islands, Tahiti-nui, and the Marquesas discovered and colonized Hawaii. The final wave of Polynesian migration and colonization took place sometime between 800 and 1000, when groups of migrants from the Society Islands or the Cook Islands settled Aotearoa (New Zealand).

The pattern of migration outlined here is supported by ethnobotanical evidence, particularly through the incidence and spread of different plants (taro, breadfruit, banana, coconut, and sweet potato) and animals (pig, dog, chicken) from the western Pacific through central Polynesia and on to Hawaii. Linguistic evidence also supports the direction and dates of the migratory pattern, with the Hawaiian language being closely related to the Marquesan language (proto–Central Eastern Polynesian). Both languages also share similar phonological changes from Proto–Central Eastern Polynesian (the hypothetical original language). Computer simulations likewise support the idea that Hawaii was settled by migrants from the Marquesas, as does archaeology; artifacts found at early Hawaiian sites are very similar to those found in the Marquesas. The colonization of the islands of the Pacific by Polynesian maritime peoples remains one of the most extraordinary examples of long-distance migration in human history.

EUROPE

BY SUSAN MALIN-BOYCE

Human migration is the term used for both voluntary and involuntary population movements. Throughout prehistory and into the modern era people have chosen to relocate, have left their land and homes under duress, or have been traded as slaves. For prehistoric migrations it is generally impossible to ascertain whether movement was elected or forced. Reconstructing the timing of migrations and numbers of migrants is also largely unachievable. Even a massive movement of peoples leaves almost no trace for archaeologists to recover. Therefore, migration is generally inferred from patterns of resettlement, the appearance of new subsistence regimes, and the widespread distributions of new technologies. The bulk of the evidence for change is interpreted from the analysis of material remains. For prehistoric Europe early migratory expansion populated regions that had never been occupied by people. These colonization episodes are frequently identified by such data as the first appearance of tools or settlement traces and in rare cases by burials. Later events are marked by dramatic changes in material culture, and debate is frequently focused on the mechanism of these apparent material and social transformations. Analogy is used to infer the scale and form of ideological conquest or social emulation. Historical migrations provide ample material for explanations that rely on analogy.

Causes that contributed to prehistoric migrations are various and sometimes appear contradictory. They included environmental factors such as climate changes caused by glacial advance and retreat or by drought. Warfare was another primary vector of change, forcing the abandonment of whole regions in advance of warring armies, such as the Huns by 395 C.E. Wars also attracted mercenaries, and eligible members of populations frequently went to war for the potential rewards—the plunder used to compensate armed volunteers. Mercenaries may have left an area in large numbers, as in the Marne region during the first historical migration of the Celts around 400 B.C.E.

Trade is an equally attractive draw for people who have had access to certain commodities. When a trade infrastructure is disrupted and the flow of goods stops, large groups of people may go in search of resupply. The sack of Rome around 390 B.C.E. may be attributable to such motivations. During the protohistoric period—the period during which firsthand and secondhand accounts were written by literate peoples about events involving preliterate populations—there is evidence that groups sometimes migrated seasonally, probably to alleviate subsistence pressure on their home territories. In these cases warring parties crossed into regions controlled by other groups and pillaged or extorted provisions on a temporary basis. Harassment of the resident population ceased when the interlopers were routed in combat or bought off. For mass movements such as the spread of agriculture or early migrations from Africa, combinations of factors both pushed and pulled people into and across Europe. In the examples provided here these factors are explored based on the archaeological record and accompanying anthropological theory.

Several major migration events are presented using a somewhat arbitrary two-part classification scheme: first, migrations that colonized Europe, and second, migrations that transformed preexisting social organizations via the introduction of new technologies or ideologies. Even within this simple bi-partite scheme there is overlap. The movement of *Homo sapiens neanderthalensis* into Europe and the replacement of that population by modern *Homo sapiens sapiens*, along with the encroachment on hunter-gatherers and herder-horticulturalists by agriculturalists, were colonizing episodes. These population movements extended across vast territories and occurred over many thousands of years. The social reorganization of the metal ages and corresponding Urnfield/Celtic migrations were part of a process during which societies ruled by chiefs developed an increasingly centralized authority. Finally, the migrations of Germans and Huns that precipitated the eventual decline of the Roman Empire were part of a series of strategically directed migration events targeting people and places with more wealth and resources than the migrating forces controlled. It is significant that migration in prehistory frequently served very different purposes than it does today. Many populations prided themselves on their mobility, and movement over vast distances was not necessarily perceived as a hardship. For the brief historic period from about 400 B.C.E. until 400 C.E., this model of migration as a socioeconomic opportunity is well illustrated.

Several models have been developed to account for the successive episodes of population increase following glacial maximums (times of maximum extent of ice sheets), during which people and other animals were restricted to areas with microclimates that allowed survival. Human populations appear to have increased during these episodes, as can be seen in the example provided by the Dordogne region in western France. Cave sites and rock shelters there attest to the presence of concentrated populations in the deeply eroded river valleys that provided a refuge from the glacial advance. During the warmer interstadials (a short period of relatively warmer climate within an ice age) people left the area, again following the grazing ungulates (mammals with hooves). The success of these groups frequently depended on their ability to anticipate and plan ahead, using tool-making technologies and food-storage facilities that ensured group survival. Throughout the period that hunter-gatherers occupied Europe they continued to migrate. Even in areas where settlement first appears—typically coastal settings with abundant resources—transhumance, or the seasonal movement of people between grazing lands) is evident. Regular movement occurred between summer and winter camps, where access to different resources promoted dietary variability and intergroup dependence.

The Domestication of Europe

The spread of agriculture and animal domestication is a colonizing process that established largely sedentary communities across temperate Europe beginning as early as 7000 B.C.E. This expansionist movement emerged out of the Levant and migrated north and east into western, central, and eastern Europe. According to one theory, the diffusion of farming communities—whose subsistence economy was based on wheat and barley, along with sheep, goats, cattle, and pigs—spread like a wave geographically and over time. Farming communities were established from Hungary to Scandinavia in less than 2,000 years, beginning around 5600 B.C.E. Another model used to explain this distribution relies on the division of communities, with steady movement into optimal farming and grazing territories away from other farmers.

The Linear Pottery culture (also called Linearbandkeramik, or LBK), named for its distinctive pottery, is the culture associated with the beginning of the Neolithic and the spread of farming and animal husbandry into areas formerly occupied by hunter-gatherers and herder-horticulturalists (ca. 5500–4500 B.C.E.). Chemical analyses of teeth and bones confirm a relatively high rate of immigration for the Rhineland in Germany well into the Middle LBK Period, and the demography and numbers of immigrants diminished by the Late LBK Period. Evidence from this research project also suggests a high degree of mobility within the region.

People who occupied environmental zones that attracted farmers, such as the loess belt (an area of fine-grained soil suitable for cultivation), were eventually forced to change their course of seasonal migration or were incorporated into the new subsistence system. While the coexistence between groups with differing lifestyles was probably beneficial at a time when regions were sparsely populated, the practice of land clearance for farming may eventually have threatened wild populations of animals upon whom the nomads depended. Evidence from coastal Scandinavia demonstrates not only a shift to the domesticated economy but also a subsequent rejection of wild sea species that had previously dominated local diets. In these areas of settlement continuity, from the Mesolithic to the Neolithic, migration probably played a less determinative role in subsistence strategies. Dependence on domesticated species became pervasive, however, and human migration was the mechanism by which plant and animal domestication initially transformed European populations.

The Indo-European Expansion

The Indo-Iranian, Indo-Aryan, and Indo-European migrations describe the movement of language groups, technologies, and ideas that have been interpreted as a sign of massive population shifts. Competing hypotheses outline the mechanisms for this transformation of European cultures. One model suggests that the expansion developed at around 2000 B.C.E. during the terminal Neolithic Period. In this model warrior societies, whose technologies included horsemanship and bronze metallurgy, diffused in waves from the steppes that crossed Europe and Asia to dominate agriculturalists. Community subsistence in the affected areas continued to be based on agriculture and animal management, but economic strategies were supplemented with metallurgy and a form of petty warfare that was maintained through an elaborate social hierarchy by an increasingly elite warrior class. Linguistic evidence links this expansion with agricultural subsistence technologies from an origin in Anatolia.

The impact of peoples from the steppes was felt across Europe as they made forays into neighboring regions to conduct petty warfare. The transmission of steppe material culture and ideals was partly a result of conquest and partly from peaceful trade, adoption, and emulation. Steppe cultures were mobile, engaged in a nomadic lifestyle in which they raised horses, cows, sheep, and goats and depended on raiding and trading to acquire grain and other staples not produced within their own communities. Technologies that included the composite bow and mounted-horse warfare made the steppe raiders nearly impossible to subdue. As theirs was an extremely successful way of life, the duration of their impact and influence was thousands of years. The replacement of these groups from the steppes by subsequent migrants from the south and east continued from an initial cultural development in the Ukraine well into the historic period. Mediterranean cultures and Celtic cultures were profoundly influenced by Scythians by about 500 B.C.E., and Scythians and Sarmatians, both Indo-Aryan–descended cultures, are described by the Greek historian Herodotus at about 440 B.C.E. in his firsthand accounts.

The Bronze Age Reorganization and Historic Celtic Migrations

As it was with the initial spread of agriculture, all of Europe was eventually transformed by the horse riders. The difficulty for archaeologists is in determining the roles to ascribe to conquest and to emulation. Evidence for the adoption and adaptation of materials and ideas does not necessarily mean that force was the primary mechanism of change. The elite transmission of ideas and technologies is sufficiently top down in its influence that only a very few individuals need to be impressed by the efficacy of a weapon or material, such as bronze, to ensure its adoption within the community and eventually throughout the region.

The proto-Celtic expansion seems to have occurred during the Urnfield Period (ca. 1300–ca. 750 B.C.E.) of the Late Bronze Age and to have changed the landscape of central and western Europe by about 1100 B.C.E. An increase in the number of small settlements across Europe suggests a rapid influx of people who brought with them the technological and ideological elements first seen on the Eurasian steppes. From areas such as the Rhineland and Switzerland into France, the pattern of technological and cultural dissemination appears to have expanded almost like a pulse. The development of Celtic culture is now thought to have taken place within the areas of the Rhineland and the Marne as an indigenous expression of sociopolitical change. Artistic styles from the La Tène region, which are the hallmark of Celtic culture, demonstrate an association with Scythians and Mediterranean peoples.

Relations between Celts and their neighbors probably promoted migrations such as the first historical migration that began sometime around 400 B.C.E. This movement reached Rome to terrorize its urban population nearly a decade later, following the battle of Allia in 387 B.C.E. The impact of the Celts' looting of the city lingered with the Romans long after the Celts had been supplicated with a ransom and had returned to Gaul. At issue for this multicomponent movement of people are its causes. Whole regions seem to have emptied of those who were suitably equipped and fit to fight. In the Champagne region there was a dramatic decrease in warrior burials, suggesting that the warrior class left their communities and migrated south for plunder. Depopulation is also evident from settlements in Burgundy and throughout southern Germany. Classical sources, such as those of the Roman historian Livy (59 B.C.E.–17 C.E.), recorded events surrounding the invasion of the Italian peninsula and the sack of Rome several centuries after they had occurred. In Livy's account, along with that of the Greek scholar Dionysius of Halicarnassus (fl. ca. 20 B.C.E.) and the Greek geographer Strabo (ca. 64 B.C.E.–after 23 C.E.), the Celts were drawn south in search of plunder that included exotic produce. Olive oil, figs, and wine had been traded up the Rhône corridor for several hundred years. Access to these riches ranked highly as a motivator for migration.

An example of a well-documented historic migration appears in Julius Caesar's *Commentarii de bello Gallico* (Commentaries on the Gallic War), his self-serving account of his campaigns in France. Caesar fought the Helvetii in 58 B.C.E., and in his commentaries he describes the process and objective of that group's migration. According to Caesar, their motive for migration was to acquire territory through the conquest of Gaul. Once the decision to migrate had been made, three years was allocated as the time for preparation, and an individual named Orgetorix (fl. first century C.E.) was given the responsibility of organizing the movement. Orgetorix developed an alliance with members of the Sequani and Aedui in an effort to further his own cause; the conspiracy backfired, resulting in his demise.

The Helvetii chose to carry out the migration anyway and established a date to gather for the proposed move. They were joined in their journey by members of other Celtic groups, including the Boii, all of whom had set fire to their own villages and towns to discourage anyone from staying behind. At issue was the path of migration into Gaul; there were only two options, and one led south through a Roman province that was protected by Caesar. Eventually Caesar turned the migrants back to their formerly held territory. Caesar makes it clear in his account that he wished the Helvetii to remain in their own lands lest the empty area become occupied by Germans, who would readily have moved into the fertile vacated zone between the Alps and the Roman province.

Germanic Migrations and the Huns, Goths, and Visigoths

Like the Celts before them, German tribes placed tremendous pressure on Roman provincial administrators in Gaul and northern Italy. Roman commentary on the Germans appears in Caesar's works and in the descriptions of the Roman historian Cornelius Tacitus (ca. 56 C.E.–ca. 120 C.E.) in *Germania*, written 150 years later, in 98 C.E. Tacitus provides information on German social organization, primarily with respect to the attitudes and behaviors of warriors. According to Tacitus, Germans held land based on social status, councils met regularly, leaders may have been elected for life, and landless warriors attached themselves to particularly effective chiefs in anticipation of the glory and spoils of battle. A pithy quote tells how spiritless it is to toil over a plow when one's needs could be met by the loss of a little blood.

In Caesar's time land was not held privately, and agriculture was deemphasized in favor of pastoralism. Animals were often acquired through raiding, and warfare was endemic. Roman coinage provides clues to the pressures that warfare placed upon the empire. Coins were a widely distributed medium of communication that leave little doubt that the Romans felt a continual need to reinforce the image of victory over German peoples in commemorative issues for individual Roman leaders and, in some cases, for specific conflicts. Most images of Germans depicted on coinage were of bound and subjugated Germans, both male and female. Often when the images of German people were absent, they were represented by their distinctive weaponry.

In the account of Caesar's meeting with the German chief Ariovistus (fl. ca. 71–58 B.C.E.), who was spending the summer in lands held by the Celtic Sequani near the Seine, Caesar indicates that the Germans had been joined by a number of other groups, all of them eager to take advantage of the seasonal fruits extracted from the harassed Sequani. Ariovistus had led his people into the region to reduce stress on the valuable resources of his home territory across the Rhine River. He boasted that his undefeated people were superior to Caesar's own soldiers in courage and pointed out that their skill with weapons had enabled them to avoid living under a roof for 14 years. Caesar ultimately interceded with force, defeating Ariovistus and his multitribal army and pushing them back across the Rhine, but the account promotes an understanding of the Germans' esteem for independence and for the role of mobility in maintaining it.

The movement of waves of Germans marks the beginning of a period of migration that started around 300 C.E. and continued well past the collapse of the Roman Empire. Extraordinary disruption, both internal to the imperial Roman provinces and external among various Germanic groups competing for resources, may have favored the most aggressive or persuasive warriors, and tribal or group affiliation appears relatively fluid, depending upon the motivations and objectives of the group members. Entry into temporary alliances between otherwise competitive groups was facilitated by common cultural referents that promoted petty warfare as an economic strategy and by the Germanic warrior-class ideology. This type of economic base differed dramatically from the Roman system of agrarian estates and town markets that immediately preceded it.

Breaches of the frontier by migrating peoples cut swaths into imperial territory, further decimating the Roman system of distribution and communication. The initial phases of German resettlement, the mechanism by which one group successfully replaced another on the landscape, can be said to follow models proposed for Britain: that is, a complex combination of internal uprisings against a crumbling Roman regime coupled with continual external assaults by groups of people attempting to be incorporated into the various systems, whether for trade, general access to goods, relative stability and security, or access to land. There seem to have been many reasons for migrating people to try to get into Roman-held regions.

Germanic peoples who migrated into Roman-controlled territories included groups such as the Friedenhain-Prestovice from Bohemia, the present-day Czech Republic and Slovakia, who had been on the Roman payroll in defense of towns on the Danube and were settled before the withdrawal of Roman forces from Raetia. Moving westward, the Alamanni or Swabians occupied the area of present-day Switzerland, the German state of Baden-Württemberg, and the Bavarian administrative district of Swabia. The Bavarii, also identified as Boioarians (again from Bohemia), occupied southeastern Bavaria and Austria, having moved into territory vacated by the Ostrogoths. These peoples were associated with the Marcomanni and with the Celtic Boii from Bohemia. They appear to have been forced west into Raetia under pressure from Czechs in Bohemia, who were being pressed by Serbs and Slavs. All of these groups were moving westward in advance of the Huns, who had reached the Danube in 376 C.E.

The period of stress and resettlement lasted for several centuries. Changes apparent from the archaeological record indicate a pattern of settlement, conquest, and consolidation and the development of tribal coalitions that, in some ways, are differentiated between central and western Europe. In the first place, the degree of Romanization in eastern-central Europe appears to have been less tenacious than farther west in Gaul and East Anglia. In the second, the demographic structure of the resettled populations is more varied. The collapse of the Roman estates happened relatively quickly. This can be seen in examples such as that provided by the Gutshof (a private farmstead or estate) at Nördlingen, a site of Alamanni conquest in Schwaben, where the Roman-style estate was gutted and a large German wooden house was constructed in the middle of the complex between the ruined Roman structures. In addition to the relative weakness of institutionalized Roman systems in place by the mid-fourth century C.E., the demographic breakdown for Austria, Germany, Switzerland, and France differs from that of Anglo-Saxon Britain if models are accurate that assert that invading forces in Britain were predominantly male. Burial evidence for other parts of Europe demonstrates an inclusive population.

GREECE

BY JEFFREY S. CARNES

What is now mainland Greece was settled during the early Neolithic Era (ca. 7000 B.C.E.) by peoples about whom little is known. The arrival of Greek speakers came considerably later, during the Bronze Age (ca. 4000–1100 B.C.E.), as part of the great expansion of Indo-European language speakers from their original homeland. The location of this homeland has been the object of much speculation, but most linguists would now locate it in central Asia, in the vicinity of the Caspian Sea.

The process of migration and diffusion must have been a gradual one, with the original Proto-Indo-European language changing into its various daughter languages along the way, so that the settlers arriving in Greece will have spoken some early form of Greek. Their arrival came most probably via Anatolia (modern-day Turkey), though it does not seem to have had an immediate effect on the culture or political organization of the region. Rather, the Minoan civilization on Crete, which comprised non-Greek speakers, continued to dominate the Aegean until the rise of the Mycenaean civilization on the Greek mainland starting about 1600 B.C.E. The downfall of Mycenaean civilization (ca. 1100 B.C.E.) was the last in a series of Bronze Age dislocations, causing a cycle of expansion and contraction of populations, with larger states alternating with smaller village settlements and more primitive economies. It was after the collapse of the Mycenaean civilization that Greek speakers (evidently fleeing chaos in Attica on the mainland) first settled Ionia, the region consisting of the islands and coastal areas of the eastern Aegean.

The Greeks' own views of this process were rather different; while they were historically inaccurate, they are well worth examining for the light they shed on how they perceived later population shifts in the historical period (particularly colonization). Thucydides lays out a standard narrative in the opening chapters of his *History of the Peloponnesian War*: that the population of Achaeans (in the northwestern part of the Peloponnese) were conquered by Dorian invaders coming in from the north. This Dorian invasion was dated to sometime shortly after the end of the Trojan War (ca. 1200 B.C.E.) and was said to be the origin of the dominance of Doric-speaking Greeks (such as the Argives and Spartans) in the Peloponnese. The invaders were said to be the sons of the hero Hercules (Heracles), whose persecutor Eurystheus kept them from returning; after a failed attempt and a lapse of a hundred years, their descendants succeeded. During their time of exile they were given aid by the Athenians, which became a commonplace in Athenian mythic propaganda during the time of greatest hostility to Sparta in the fifth century B.C.E. The archaeological record for the region does suggest a shift in population but in about 900 B.C.E., considerably too late to match the chronology handed down in the literary sources.

A similar mythologizing of the historical record may be found in the case of the Ionian migration. The settlement of Ionia after the apparent chaos following the collapse of Mycenaean power was also considered the result of the Dorian invasion. The Athenians, however, claimed that they were the ancestors of all Ionians, who were descended from an Athenian named Ion. For modern historians there is clearly some connection between Athens and the Ionians: Their dialects are closely related, and they share certain social structures and religious customs. Yet the story in fifth-century Athenian sources is clearly designed to assert the primacy of Athens over Ionian Greeks at a time when the Ionians were the allies (or subject states) in the Athenian naval empire known as the Delian League. The Athenians, by contrast, portrayed themselves as autochthonous: that is, as never having come from anywhere else and in fact being literally sprung from the soil of Athens. (The word *autochthon* means "of the land itself" and could literally refer to origin from the soil, or to a claim to have been in a particular place since time immemorial.) Migration was viewed as a strong negative in mythic terms: To have always been in the same location not only gave a particular people an inalienable claim to their native land but also allowed them to claim inherent superior to "latecomers." There was a tendency for Greek cities to invent myths of origin tying them to the land: The name Pelasgian, used to refer to the pre-Greek inhabitants of Greece, came in some places to be synonymous with *autochthon*, and a hero Pelasgus was invented accordingly.

Colonization in the Archaic Age

From approximately 734 to 580 B.C.E. the Greek world underwent a tremendous expansion, with the foundation of dozens of new Greek-speaking cities along the shores of the Mediterranean and the Black Sea. In understanding this process of colonization, the lens of modern colonialism and the ideological biases of the ancient sources themselves must be avoided. Greek colonization in the Archaic Age was not generally an attempt to expand political influence or a means of conquering a distant territory with a view to exploiting its labor and natural resources for the benefit of the mother country. Rather, it consisted of a series of independently motivated decisions to found cities elsewhere, caused by a desire for advantages in overseas trade, by the desire for more and better land, or as the result of population pressures or political strife at home. And just as "Greece" is largely an abstract concept, a way of describing the cultural identity of a vast number of independent poleis (city-states), so, too, is "Greek colonization" an abstraction, one which suggests unity in what was actually a diverse set of phenomena.

There were two basic types of Greek colony: the *emporion* and the *apoikia*. *Emporion* is the Greek word for "market," and such colonies were in essence trading outposts, with no claim to polis status and relatively loose ties to the cities that founded them. *Emporia* were often jointly established by more than one polis. By contrast, an *apoikia* was an entirely new and independent polis, laid out according to certain specific rules. Settlers in *emporia* presumably remained citizens of their home cities; in an *apoikia* the settlers became citizens of the new settlement.

Greek long-distance trade throughout the Mediterranean dates from the Mycenaean era, but the first evidence of trading outposts dates to about 800 B.C.E., on the island of

Pithecusae (modern-day Ischia, in the Bay of Naples). Historical sources say that it was settled by traders from Chalcis and Eretria, from the island of Euboea just off the coast of mainland Greece. Its population was probably several thousand. Substantial archaeological remains reveal not only a settled city core but also outlying industrial districts devoted to metalworking and pottery production (both of which were Euboean specialties). Its location gave excellent access to Italy, Sicily, and the western Mediterranean, and given its size and degree of organization, it has been suggested that Pithecusae served as a sort of "protocolony," a model for the settlements founded under more formal auspices a quarter century later. It is presumably no coincidence that Chalcis and Eretria were among the leading cities in the establishment of such *apoikiai*.

Other *emporia* were more clearly limited to trade. The most important of these was Naucratis, on the banks of the Nile some 50 miles inland from the coast. Founded in about 630 B.C.E. by Miletus (an Ionian city on the coast of Asia Minor), it welcomed traders from all Greek cities, as evidenced by the foundation of a Hellenion (pan-Greek temple) in the mid-sixth century B.C.E. Any ambitions it may have had of attaining polis status were kept in check by the pharaoh, and in fact it seems to have become a polis after Alexander's conquest of Egypt. Similarly, the *emporion* at El Minya (the ancient name is unknown) existed for many years without becoming a polis, despite being an apparently important rival to nearby Phoenician trading centers along the Levantine coast. More remote settlements, such as the Black Sea *emporion* described by Herodotus as a center for trade with the Scythians, also failed to attain polis status.

Colonies in the more formal sense, *apoikiai*, start to show up in the late eighth century. The earliest known colonies are Corcyra (modern-day Corfu, off the western coast of mainland Greece), founded sometime before 734 B.C.E., and Cumae, on the Bay of Naples, founded by the Chalcidians apparently before 725 B.C.E. Corcyra, an Eritrean foundation, lay on the sea route between Greece and southern Italy; Cumae's location was due to the success of nearby Pithecusae. Thus the earliest known colonies were founded by cities that had already participated heavily in *emporia* and in locations particularly advantageous for trade. Still, trade itself is not enough to explain the foundation of *apoikiai*. The traditional explanation for the wave of colonization is that a surge in population put too great a strain on the resources of mainland Greece and that colonists fled in search of land that was not only more abundant but also more fertile. In fact, both trade and population pressure played a part in motivating colonization, as did other factors, such as the political interests of the cities involved, the desire of some individuals to earn the glory accorded to *oikistai* (founders of colonies), and the commercial and military value of controlling strategic locations such as the Bosporus and the Straits of Messina.

The course of Greek geographical expansion is easy to trace. Chalcis took the lead in colonizing Sicily, with foundations at Naxos (not to be confused with the island of the same name), Leontini, and Catana, all on the southeastern part of the island; colonies at Zancle and Rhegium gave them control of the Straits of Messina. These were just the first of many foundations on the Italian peninsula: Sybaris, Croton, Paestum, and Tarentum are particularly worthy of mention. The Greek presence in southern Italy was so significant that the region later came to be known as Magna Graecia ("Large Greece"; the name sometimes included Sicily as well).

Other colonies of Chalcis and Eretria were closer to home. The large peninsula on the north shore of the Aegean became known as Chalcidice because of its numerous Chalcidian foundations, including Methone, formed for the refugees from Corcyra, who had been expelled in 733 B.C.E. when Corinth founded a colony there. Thus, even in the earliest days of colonization, rivalries and competition for land could be fierce. Corinth and its neighbor Megara continued their rivalry overseas. In 733 B.C.E. Corinth founded Syracuse, which became the most powerful of the Greek colonies thanks in part to its excellent natural harbor. Five years later Megara founded Megara Hyblaea some 15 miles to the north, a distance very nearly equal to that separating the two mother cities. (The rivalry ended 250 years later when Syracuse destroyed Megara Hyblaea.) Expansion westward into Sicily led to the foundation of Acragas and Selinus, whose prosperity is shown by the magnificent Doric temples that still remain. Both of these were "daughter-foundations"; that is, they were founded by cities that were themselves colonies. (The practice went back to the earliest days of colonization: Zancle was founded in part by Cumae.)

The Megarians also had success in the east, establishing colonies at Chalcedon and Byzantium, which gave them control of access to the Black Sea. Miletus, on the coast of Asia Minor, is said to have founded cities along the coast and along the shores of the Black Sea as far north as the Danube. Farther west, the Phocaeans founded colonies in France and Spain, including Massilia, Nicaea, and Antipolis (present-day Marseille, Nice, and Antibes), while Thera established Cyrene on the North African coast (in modern-day Libya).

The great age of colonization ended by 580 B.C.E., by which time most of the easily colonizable areas had been taken. (Some areas were too remote, while others were inconveniently dominated by Etruscans, Carthaginians, Egyptians, or Persians. The fact that Rome was in its infancy allowed the formation of Magna Graecia.) The major players in the colonization process were not then the great powers of the fifth century B.C.E.: Athens and Thebes had no overseas colonies, Sparta only one (Tarentum, in the arch of the Italian boot).

The procedures for setting up an *apoikia* were well defined, probably dating back to the earliest years of colonization. The first step was the appointment of an *oikistes* (city founder), who would lead the expedition and was responsible for establishing temples to the gods, for naming the city, and for distributing the land. (Equal shares of land seem to have been the norm, even in colonies founded by oligarchic states.)

Typically the *oikistes* was revered by future generations and received heroic honors (that is, he attained a semidivine status and was the object of civic worship).

City foundation was steeped in ritual. There was first of all the necessity of consulting the oracle of Apollo at Delphi, which might give advice on the proper location for the city (though many of the oracles that have come down to us in the literary sources are forgeries). Delphi was also charged with settling disputes that might have arisen, including deciding who the *oikistes* should be. In many cases Apollo himself was considered an *oikistes* and was worshipped in the Sicilian colony of Naxos under the cult title Archegetes (city founder). According to Thucydides, this shrine was much revered by colonists of all cities. There is perhaps a sense in which the colonization movement, by bringing the citizens of various Greek-speaking cities into proximity with other cultures (who were, not surprisingly, often hostile to new settlers), helped establish a sense of common Greek identity. In addition, the age of colonization coincides with the development of the polis, and the foundation of colonies may be seen as a series of experiments in how to govern a state.

A colony was expected to maintain close relations with its metropolis (literally, "mother city"), symbolized in the first instance by the sending of the sacred hearth fire from the metropolis along on the founding expedition. The foundation document of Cyrene specifies the oaths to be sworn by both sides, which oblige the settlers not to return home (this colony was founded because of population pressures) and which commit the metropolis, Thíra, to come to the aid of its colony. Such obligations could be of extremely long duration: Thucydides shows the city of Epidamnus in 431 B.C.E. appealing for help to its metropolis of Corcyra; when rebuffed, they carried the appeal to Corinth, which had founded Corcyra 300 years earlier. Thucydides lists a number of instances where colonies fought against their metropoleis. His point is that such instances were rare and noteworthy. Syracuse thus found itself opposed to Athens in the Peloponnesian War because of its ancestral tie to Corinth, despite the fact that it shared with Athens a democratic constitution. The colonial relation outweighed political ideology.

The motives for individuals to join colonial expeditions must have varied greatly. In addition to the obvious financial and personal motives (grants of land, adventure, and the chance for a fresh start), in some cases political strife at home provided an impetus. Colonies could be a place of refuge for those with political (or legal) difficulties, and in some cases daughter cities took in subsequent waves of exiles from their metropoleis. (Modern parallels would include the colonization of Australia and much of the eastern United States.) In Xenophon's *Anabasis* a group of Greek mercenaries, abandoned far from home by the death of their patron, seriously consider founding a colony (as did the Athenian army when stranded in Sicily, in Thucydides' account). This shows that founding a city could be born of desperation and also raises indirectly the question of gender. Presumably, city foundations included both men and women but perhaps not in equal numbers, given the rigors of founding a city in hostile territory and the Greeks' views that most such activities were better done by men. In this case intermarriage with native peoples may have been common, yet the Greek sources are silent on this issue.

The narratives Greek cities developed about their own colonial enterprises are worth looking at. There is a strong tendency to portray the foundation of a colony in what we would think of as mythic terms. (For the Greeks myth and history were not always separate categories.) The impulse to found the city is expressed in terms of crisis, often of a personal nature: strife between brothers, exile as a result of a crime, the physical deformity of the future *oikistes*. Even an impersonal force such as population pressure can be personalized: Thíra's foundation of Cyrene (in a version reported by Herodotus) is said to be the result of a drought sent by Apollo when the Therans ignored his first command to found a colony. The consultation at Delphi involves not merely approval for the colony but the granting of a sign (particularly a command to follow an animal guide to the site of the new city), and in some cases a riddle to be figured out by the *oikistes* (correctly interpreting, for example, "an attack of the earthborn" to refer to an infestation of mice). Further, colonization can be viewed through the metaphorical lens of marriage: Colonists establish a new city as a married couple establishes a new household. It has been suggested that the metaphor expresses the Greeks' ambivalence about their relations with native peoples. Rather than being expelled, they and their land welcome the newcomers, perhaps with rights of intermarriage.

Whatever its origins, colonization in the Archaic Age had a tremendous impact on Greek civilization, particularly in regard to the settlements in the west. Sicily and Magna Graecia were the Greek version of the New World. The abundance of fertile land created prosperity, reflected in the region's still magnificent architecture and other material remains, and the region served as a constant source of cultural innovation, giving birth to such important figures as Parmenides, Empedocles, and Archimedes.

The Second Phase of Colonization

Colonization in the sixth and fifth centuries B.C.E. tended to become more overtly imperial and designed to promote the overseas interests of the metropolis; this was especially true with the rise of the Athenian empire in the years after the Persian Wars. Corinth was a pioneer in this regard even in the late seventh century B.C.E.: There it became common practice to choose as *oikistai* the sons of the city's tyrant (sole ruler of a polis, who differed from a king chiefly in the lack of a hereditary claim to power), establishing an overseas dynastic link. Similarly, the Athenian tyrant Peisistratus sent family members to be in charge of colonies at Sigeum and Lemnos. In the fifth century B.C.E., after the tyrannies had died out, it was necessary to secure the interests of the metropolis by other means. There exists a foundation decree for an Athenian colony at Brea, dateable to about 445 B.C.E., which specifies that "the cities" (that is, Athens's imperial subjects and allies) are obligated to come to the defense of Brea. Further, the *oikistes* has limited powers: It is the city of Athens that determines the details of the expedition and appoints officials to divide the land. The *oikistes* in this instance seems to have been an official who later returned to Athens; this is certainly the case for the later foundations of Thurii and Amphipolis. The strategic importance of Amphipolis (in the region near Thrace) was great, and after the city was lost to the Spartans in the Peloponnesian War the city changed its *oikistes*, honoring as its founder the Spartan general Brasidas, who had died in capturing it. The Spartans also sent out colonies for imperial purposes, being the dominant participants in the mixed settlement at Heraclea, a strategic location near Euboea.

Athens developed a new type of colony in the fifth century B.C.E.: the cleruchy, a settlement, typically on land seized from a rival state, in which the settlers maintained their Athenian citizenship. (In this respect, the cleruchy comes closer to modern systems of colonialism than does the standard Greek model.) The cleruchs (in Greek, "allotment holder"), drawn primarily from the poorer classes, received an allotment of land (*kleros* in Greek) and had the normal citizen obligations regarding military service and taxes. It seems likely that most cleruchs lived in their appointed cities rather than staying in Athens and receiving income from their *kleroi*. Cleruchies often were established when the native population had been expelled: this is the case for Greek lands such as Melos and Aigina and also for lands with non-Greek populations such as Lemnos and Scyros. In other cases a cleruchy could be established on top of a native population. While some cleruchies seem to have served as military outposts, most of them served Athenian military interests less directly, by effectively expanding the Athenian empire. The cleruchies of the fifth century B.C.E. were all lost after Athens' defeat in the Peloponnesian War in 404 B.C.E., but several others were established in the fourth century B.C.E. and at the beginning of the Hellenistic Age. Ironically, Athens's first cleruchy was in Chalcis, which had been one of the pioneers of the colonization movement during its heyday 200 years earlier.

Colonization in the Hellenistic World

The final wave of Greek colonization came as a result of the conquests of Alexander the Great. Unlike the Archaic colonizations, which were haphazard and the product of many individual decisions in rival cities, the settlements established by Alexander were centrally planned, the product of a single individual's will. Moreover, they were established with a specific goal in mind: to spread Greek civilization throughout the vast realm he had conquered. Evaluation of Alexander's colonization program is hampered, however, by the biases of the sources. He was revered as a hero by many later Greeks, who tended to exaggerate his accomplishments. The Greek biographer Plutarch, for example, claims that colonization was Alexander's highest achievement and credits him with establishing 70 cities. This is presumably an exaggeration, though there are some 20 known foundations (many named Alexandria, modesty not being a common trait among conquerors). It seems that many of these were originally set up as military garrisons; others were renamed or resettled with new populations.

After the death of Alexander, the Seleucids (who inherited the eastern part of his kingdom) maintained his policy of colonization, with many settlements relatively close to home (in Syria and Asia Minor) but with some in central Asia as far as what is now northern Afghanistan. The Seleucids took over many administrative practices from the Persian Empire, but the cities they settled were indisputably Greek, with Greek-style temples, houses, and public spaces. Inscriptional evidence shows that even the more remote locations stayed in regular contact with Greeks in the Mediterranean. It seems that local peoples kept their traditions as well: Examples from Babylon and Caria show a process of Hellenization, which was more a matter of cultural fusion than of imperialism. Nowhere is this more evident than in Alexandria in Egypt, the most successful of Alexander's foundations. It became, thanks to institutions like the library (which aimed to have a collection of every book written in Greek), a cultural center for all of Greece, which until Alexander had been culturally as well as politically disunited. But it also welcomed other peoples and their traditions, Egyptians, Jews, and Romans in particular, and was the most complex and interesting city in the ancient world. Alexander's policy of Hellenization, though founded in brutal conquest, succeeded on a cultural level long after his empire fell apart: The eastern half of the Roman Empire, including Egypt, Syria, and Asia Minor, remained Greek in language and outlook for another millennium or more.

Other Population Movements

The warfare endemic to the Greek world led to population shifts not related to colonization. There were resettlements of populations displaced by war: the Ionians in the early years of the fifth century B.C.E., after their failed revolt against the Persian Empire, and the Aiginetans in 431 B.C.E. after their defeat by Athens. In these cases the refugees presumably settled in cities in which they had friends or that were sympathetic to their plight. The fate of Melos provides a grimmer example. Defeated by Athens in 416 B.C.E. despite its attempt to maintain neutrality, its adult male population was killed, and its women and children sold as slaves. Slavery was a fact of Greek life, and mass enslavements of prisoners of war was common.

Large groups of individuals also moved for economic reasons: Cities such as Athens and Alexandria had many resident foreigners (called *metics* in Athens), both Greek and non-Greek. Groups of mercenaries, such as the 10,000 soldiers whose expedition under Cyrus the Younger (424?–401 B.C.E.) is described in Xenophon's *Anabasis*, also had the potential to become permanent residents elsewhere; this sort of settlement, in fact, was encouraged under Alexander. Finally, there were a small number of nomadic peoples on the fringes of the Greek world and minor pastoral nomadism within it. That is, some shepherds and goatherds practiced transhumance, moving seasonally in search of better pastures—typically to higher ground in winter. This practice was limited in scope, however, by the political fragmentation of the Greek world: A move of any great distance involved crossing from the territory of one polis to another and was therefore more difficult than in places (such as Persia) where a large amount of territory was under the authority of a central government.

ROME

BY MICHAEL J. O'NEAL

The history of migration and population movements in ancient Rome corresponds in many respects to the history of the Roman Republic and the Roman Empire. For a period of nearly a millennium, Rome and its influence on culture, politics, religion, art, engineering, commerce, and government spread outward throughout the Mediterranean region into western and eastern Europe, Asia Minor, the Middle East, and North Africa. In the wake of Rome's spread—and sometimes in advance of it—the peoples of these regions, principally their Roman overlords, were often on the move.

Archaeological evidence shows that the first inhabitants of the area around Rome arrived around 1400 B.C.E. By around 625 B.C.E. numerous settlers had moved into the region and had drained the marshes in the low-lying areas around Rome, laying the foundations for the largest and most civilized city of ancient Europe. There they created a marketplace, the Forum, which was destined to become the center of the Roman Empire.

At about the same time, an ancient people called the Etruscans, from the region of Italy called Etruria, north of the Tiber River, moved into the region and contributed to the development of Roman civilization by ruling the area around Rome. Further, by about 750 B.C.E. the Greeks had moved into the southern portions of the Italian peninsula and into Sicily, a large island just off the "toe" of Italy. They, too, influenced the development of Roman civilization to the extent that historians often refer to "Greco-Roman" culture rather than just Roman culture.

ROMAN EXPANSION

The first major historical event that had a bearing on Roman expansion was the establishment of the Roman Republic in about 500 B.C.E. A popular uprising against the Etruscan king led to the formation of a republican form of government, and Rome, with its own constitution, popular assemblies, and Senate, was formed. At this point in its history, though, expansion and population movements were difficult, in large part because of the geography of the Italian peninsula. Mountains, in particular the Apennines, extend across the top of Italy and then down the "boot." They divide the peninsula into regions, and the Po River to the north was a formidable obstacle to the movement of peoples in that direction. What is called "Italy" in modern times did not exist; rather, the peninsula consisted of a number of discrete regions, including not only Etruria but also Umbria, Latium, Samnium, Campania, Puglia, and Magna Graecia (or "Greater Greece," the southern region inhabited by Greeks).

The process of uniting these regions into a single political entity was long, beginning in the fourth century B.C.E. Sometimes the early Romans defended and expanded their frontiers through negotiation and treaty, including a treaty with Latium, the region that surrounded Rome, leading to the outward migration of the early Romans. Sometimes they did it through conquest, such as Rome's victory over the Etruscans in 396 B.C.E., which allowed the Romans to migrate farther throughout the peninsula. Sometimes, though, there were setbacks, such as the successful invasion of Rome by the Gauls, the Celtic people from north of the Po River, in 390 B.C.E. A century later the Greeks in Magna Graecia recruited King Pyrrhus of Epirus to lead an invasion of Rome; the invasion was successful but at the cost of many casualties (giving rise to the modern expression "Pyrrhic victory," or a victory that comes at a great price). In both cases Rome was able to rebound and continue its expansion.

The great age of Roman expansion around the Mediterranean began in 264 B.C.E. with the first of three so-called Punic Wars. These wars were launched against the Phoenicians (whom the Romans called the Phoeni, the source of the word *Punic*). The Phoenicians ruled an empire from Carthage, a city they had founded in northern Africa, so they are usually referred to as the Carthaginians. In the First Punic War, Rome seized the island of Sicily from the Carthaginians in 241 B.C.E. Then in 238 B.C.E. it seized the islands of Sardinia and Corsica, which had both been ruled from Carthage. The Second Punic War erupted in 219 B.C.E., when the Carthaginians, under the leadership of the general Hannibal, expanded their empire into Spain and then invaded Italy. (Hannibal is most famous for his use of elephants in crossing the mountains into Italy.) But while Hannibal won a victory over the Romans, he was unable to break up the alliance of states in the Roman Republic, and he had to withdraw when Roman troops invaded Spain and, in 204 B.C.E., Carthage itself. The Third Punic War began in 149 B.C.E and ended when Rome captured and destroyed Carthage in 146 B.C.E. With its victory over the Carthaginians complete, Rome ruled a strip of North Africa. In the aftermath of these wars the Roman people spread steadily outward from their capital.

To the east Rome continued its expansion, first into Macedonia (in modern times a portion of Yugoslavia but at the time part of the Greek Empire) in 190 B.C.E. A major event took place in 146 B.C.E., when Rome annexed Greece, ending the Greek Empire. Thus, by 146 B.C.E. Rome was the undisputed power in the region surrounding the Mediterranean Sea.

During the first and second centuries B.C.E. Rome expanded into the region known as Gaul, which corresponds roughly with modern-day France and a portion of northern Italy. Gaul, like Italy, was a collection of smaller regions. Rome subdued the region called Narbonensis, along the southern coast of Gaul, in about 120 B.C.E. Later conquests included Cisalpine Gaul (in today's northern Italy) in 81 B.C.E., Aquitania (a large region along the western coast) from 56 to 51 B.C.E., Lugdunensis (also a large region extending from the northwest coast into central Gaul) from 58 to 51 B.C.E., Belgica (corresponding to modern-day Belgium) from 57 to 51 B.C.E., and regions of Germania (Germany) in 17 C.E. Also, in 29 B.C.E. the Roman emperor Octavian conquered Egypt. Again, these conquests led to the migration of Roman people throughout the Mediterranean region.

The Roman Empire

Although these conquests and expansions suggest an "empire," historians refer to the period up to 27 B.C.E. as the Roman Republic. They use the term *Roman Empire* to refer to the period from 27 B.C.E., when the emperor Octavian imposed his vision of government on the Roman Senate, to 476 C.E., the end of the empire in western Europe.

Further expansion of the Roman Empire took place into the second century C.E.; the most important event was the conquest of Britain in 43 C.E. Thus, by the second century of the Common Era the Roman Empire essentially encircled the area around the Mediterranean Sea and extended as far north as the British Isles. To the west and north it encompassed Britain, Spain, portions of modern-day Germany, and all of Gaul; the northern border of the empire was marked by the Rhine and Danube rivers, where such northern European tribes as the Huns, the Vandals, and the Visigoths massed until they spilled southward and eventually defeated the Romans. Until then, though, these rivers were major barriers to the movement of populations. The empire extended eastward from Italy into Greece, Asia Minor, and such areas as Cappadocia, Armenia, Assyria, and Mesopotamia, then south through Palestine into Egypt. To the south the empire included a wide strip of northern Africa.

Rome's most difficult province was probably Britain. Over three centuries of rule the Romans met with frequent resistance, not only in modern-day England but in Scotland and especially in Wales. During these centuries numerous bodies of troops had to be dispatched to Britain to quell uprisings led by local leaders. The result was a two-tiered administration, with peaceful areas under the control of the Roman Senate but areas of resistance under the emperor and his troops. The areas were controlled by resident governors whose role was primarily military but included keeping up diplomatic relationships with local kings, building roads, supervising cities and their surrounding areas, recruiting troops, collecting taxes, and administering the law. The governor also supervised a large number of managers whose job was to gather intelligence about the activities of local kings and their followers, communicate with Rome, order and store military supplies, take charge of prisoners, and perform similar administrative functions.

Determining the population of the Roman Empire is almost impossible, given the lack of accurate records. Also, what records do exist remain unclear about who precisely was counted. The best historians can do is offer a range of likely estimates and arrive at a consensus. It is estimated that in 1 C.E. the Roman Empire comprised about 45 million people, out of a world population of 200 to 300 million. Other historians use a figure of about 55 to 60 million. Conservative estimates put the number at about 65 million by the second century C.E., but some historians argue that the number was much greater, perhaps as many as 130 million, or some 40 percent of the world's total population.

Using the lower estimate, historians have concluded that among the population were 600 senators, the top tier of Roman society. Below the senators were some 30,000 equestrians, or knights. The military consisted of some half a million soldiers, many of whom were stationed along the empire's frontiers and included not only Romans but locally conscripted mercenaries. Between 10 percent and 30 percent of the population, or six to nine million people, occupied cities, including one million in Rome. (By the sixth century wars and plague had reduced the population of Rome to just 30,000 to 100,000 people, and it would take 1,500 years for a European city again to reach a population of one million). Finally, historians estimate that the slave population of the empire, imported from throughout the empire typically as a consequence of military conquest, totaled anywhere from two to 10 million, with half a million living in and around Rome itself.

The Role of Roads

Roads and road-building technology played a major role in the expansion of the Roman Empire and the movement of peoples. Such a vast empire required means of travel to accommodate military troops, trade, and communications and to allow large numbers of administrators, civil servants, and other officials to move freely about the empire. The colloquial expression "all roads lead to Rome" was in fact true. At the center of the road system was the Forum, the earliest site in ancient Rome. From that central point a traveler could get to virtually any place in the empire on 50,000 miles of paved roads, some of which are still in use in the 21st century. In large part because of the road system, large numbers of Romans could move from the empire's capital to the most far-flung areas of the empire, taking with them all the elements of their culture: the monetary system, art, administration, military tactics and technology, engineering, roads, water and waste management systems, government, and so on.

Roman roads were more than just tracks through the woods. The roads were built in much the same way as modern roads are, with firm underlays capped by paving stones. One innovation the Romans developed was that of the crowned road; that is, the roads were slightly higher in the center and sloped off to the sides, allowing rain to flow off. Many Roman roads also had gutters at the side to aid in keeping the roads relatively dry and passable. For centuries these roads enabled people to move freely about the empire.

The Migration Movement

With each outward expansion of the Roman Republic and the later empire, substantial numbers of Roman people, primarily military troops and civil servants but also colonists and settlers, moved into newly conquered regions. Thus, in about 400 B.C.E. Roman colonies were established along the Po River valley. After the Romans conquered Sicily, Sardinia, and Corsica, Roman settlers established colonies on these islands. Similarly, after the capture of Gaul, colonies of Romans were established throughout the region, and eventually these colonists crossed the English Channel and settled in parts of England. In Germania the Romans drove out the Huns, who moved eastward and settled in the south of modern-day Russia. To the east the Romans established colonies in such regions as Pannonia and Illyria (in modern-day Hungary) and Thrace (part of the defunct Greek Empire).

Additionally, considerable population movement came about as a result of slavery. Slavery led to the movement of populations because of the ongoing need to replenish the supply of slaves. During this time period the average life expectancy of any person was much lower than it is in the 21st century. A person who reached the age of 30 would have been considered old. Archaeologists have deduced this information by examining inscriptions on surviving tombstones. Further, it is estimated that at birth the life expectancy of a slave was no more than about 20 years, only a portion of which would be spent as a slave. Thus, it is estimated that the Romans needed about half a million new slaves each year to maintain the slave population. While many of these slaves were held in the outlying areas of the empire, many were carried to Rome and surrounding areas; it has been estimated that up to a third of the population of Rome was enslaved.

During the period of the Roman Republic, most slaves were prisoners of war captured during any of Rome's military conquests during the period. This source of slaves diminished after the establishment of the Roman Empire, for the number of wars diminished as the empire became more stable. Nonetheless, Roman troops took part in a number of local wars. For example, the Romans crushed the Jewish rebellion in Palestine in 66–70 C.E., and it is estimated that some 97,000 Jews were enslaved. A later Jewish revolt in 132–135 C.E. resulted in the capture of more than 100,000 slaves. As a result of other border skirmishes, Roman soldiers captured slaves and either kept them for their own use or sold them to masters closer to Rome. Other sources of slaves included those seized by kidnappers and pirates, those who became slaves because they were in debt, and those who actually sold themselves into slavery in hopes of later being freed and becoming Roman citizens. A major source of slaves was children who were abandoned by their parents because they had too many mouths to feed. All of these sources of slaves could have come from anywhere in the empire.

Another source of population movement was religious persecution, particularly in the Common Era, when Christianity began to spread. The religion of the Romans was polytheistic, meaning that they believed in many gods and goddesses. In contrast, the religion of both Jews and Christians was monotheistic, meaning that they worshipped a single supreme being. During the early decades of the Common Era, many Jews in Rome converted to Christianity. They

THE TOWN OF NUMANTIA

As Roman troops spread throughout the Mediterranean region, they typically met with little resistance, for local, disorganized tribes were no match for the Romans' superior numbers and organization. One major exception was the town of Numantia in modern-day Spain. In what is called the Numantine War, the Numantians successfully resisted the Romans for a long period of time.

Numantia was populated by the Arevaci people, a tribe formed by the mingling of Iberians (the natives of the Iberian Peninsula, encompassing Spain and Portugal) and Celtic migrants from the sixth century B.C.E. In 137 B.C.E., after Rome had invaded the Iberian Peninsula, the Numantians fought the Roman invaders, and in fact some 20,000 Roman troops surrendered to them, even though the Numantian population amounted to no more than about 8,000 people.

The siege of Numantia began in 134 B.C.E. under the leadership of Scipio Aemilianus, the local Roman consul who commanded some 30,000 Roman troops. The Roman army built fortifications around the city, cut off its connections with other towns, and settled in for a long siege. In time the Numantians, who refused to surrender, were starving, and many historians believe that, in desperation, they practiced cannibalism. They attempted to lure Scipio into open battle, but Scipio refused to take the bait. At one point Scipio caught wind of an effort by a party of Numantians to escape to the nearby town of Lutia to seek help. Scipio responded by occupying Lutia and cutting off the hands of all men of fighting age. After eight months nearly all of the residents of the town, rather than surrendering to the Romans and becoming slaves, committed suicide. Only a small handful of the town's citizens survived. With the fall of Numantia, the conquest of Iberia was complete.

practiced their religion in secret, however, and suffered relatively little persecution.

The situation changed in 64 C.E., when, under the Roman emperor Nero, Rome burned. Nero, generally regarded as mentally unbalanced, wanted to build a magnificent palace to himself, and many Romans believed that he set the fire deliberately as an excuse to rebuild. To deflect suspicions away from himself, Nero blamed the fire on the Christians, who were widely perceived as a subversive cult. The result was widespread persecution of Christians, many of whom fled Rome for other parts of the empire.

These persecutions continued well into the second century, and they extended to other parts of the empire. In 177 C.E., for example, the emperor Marcus Aurelius persecuted Christians in Lyons, in Gaul, driving them out of the city, and Christians in Italy were persecuted as well. Many of these Christians left for Britain and other areas of Gaul, where the persecutions were not as widespread. In 303 C.E. the emperor Diocletian and his successor, Galerius, began an eight-year purge of Christians in the east, particularly in such places as Syria, Egypt, and Asia Minor, driving them out of the empire or to other places in the empire where the fires of persecution did not burn as hotly. The persecution and consequent movement of Christians came to an abrupt halt when the emperor Constantine converted to Christianity in 313 C.E. and declared Christianity the official religion of the empire.

Consequences of Migration

In general, the formation and spread of the Roman Empire did not lead to massive movements of people. For the most part, peasants and farmers—those who lived in rural areas and very small towns and villages—lived their lives much as they had before the Romans came. They provided food and craft items, and they did not attract much attention from their Roman rulers. Most of the consequences of Roman immigration were felt in the larger towns and cities, particularly in Europe. There people began to use the various products that the Romans brought with them. A good example is wine, which had been unknown in many of these areas prior to the spread of the empire, when beer was the favored beverage. Particularly among the upper classes, many people began to dress like the Romans and otherwise adopt their ways, including elements of their religion. Many towns began to feature buildings—temples, bathhouses, and theaters—that strongly resembled those in Rome. Many of these buildings, as well as military fortifications and roads, still exist and can be seen in Europe.

Similarly, the migration of Romans led to the spread of the Latin language. Latin, which used elements of the Greek and Etruscan alphabets, was the language of the people in the province of Latium, which surrounded Rome. As the empire expanded, first throughout Italy and then throughout the Mediterranean regions, soldiers, administrators, and civil servants took the language with them. In time Latin became the official language of the entire empire. Official documents, for example, were written in Latin, and Latin became the language of educated people, as well as of the Christian Church. In contrast, local languages were preserved in the Eastern Roman Empire.

By about the eighth or ninth century C.E. communities of Latin speakers, isolated from one another, began to develop their own versions of the language, and these versions evolved into the Romance languages of Europe, including Spanish, Italian, Portuguese, French, and, to a lesser extent, Bulgarian. These languages are called "Romance" languages not because they have anything to do with affairs of the heart but because they evolved from the language of Rome. While English is a Germanic language rather than a Romance language, fully 60 percent of English words derive from Latin through the Romance languages as a result of the much later invasion of the British Isles by the French Normans. (Simple, everyday words in English tend to be Germanic while longer, more formal words tend to come from Latin. Thus, *house* is a Germanic word; *domicile* is a Latin-based word.) Had it not been for the migration of the Romans during the empire, the map of European languages would probably be very different than it is.

It should be noted that the Roman Empire comprised two distinct parts, the western empire and the eastern empire. The western empire included primarily Europe; the eastern empire included such areas as Asia Minor, Greece, and the Middle East. These two regions were markedly different. While the population of the eastern empire was dense, that of the western empire was sparse. Easterners were more urban, and they tended to be more literate and to engage in commerce using a fixed monetary system; westerners were more rural and tribal, and they tended to be illiterate and to pursue agriculture using a system of barter. In the east laws were written; in the west law was based on local custom. While easterners tended to be wealthy, or at least comfortable, westerners were poor.

The spread of the Roman Empire, with its movement of Romans outward, united these two very different regions, often through the use of force. Taxation was heavier in the east as a way of transferring wealth to the poorer regions of Europe. Because all the parts of the empire were within easy reach of Rome (with the possible exception of Britain), it was relatively easy for the Roman emperor to impose a common language, a common currency, a system of weights and measures, a standing army, canals and roads, and, in particular, a class of civil servants. Trade established contact between the regions of the empire, and a well-developed system of laws, a trained bureaucracy, a standing military, and a uniform system of government gave rise to what has been called the Pax Romana, an era of peace when tribes that would likely have warred with one another lived under Roman rule.

In addition to conquest, the military put an end to piracy and artificial barriers to the movement of peoples, such as tolls collected by local warlords that were essentially protection money. When the military was not fighting, troops constructed dams, aqueducts, canals, bridges, and roads, and by maintaining permanent outposts, they "romanized" the people under their sway. The military and civil servants created what was called Romanitas, or a feeling of belonging to a great empire, and for many people achieving Roman citizenship was a major goal. By spreading the culture of Rome and Greece, the Roman migrants gave Europe, in particular, a common cultural heritage that is still felt.

THE AMERICAS

BY LAWRENCE WALDRON

The people who first set foot in the Americas have long been a favorite topic of speculation. Native Americans have been worked into Western myths in an attempt to explain their origins. The various Native Americans, for their part, have always had their own myths, with which they not only explained their origins but also gave themselves a sense of purpose, morality, and hope. Over the past two centuries the geographic origin of America's most ancient settlers has also been a research interest for scientists. In that time some aspects of myth have given way to scientific theories based on empirical evidence. The science of archaeology was one of the first disciplines to propose theories and possible time frames for the peopling of ancient America. Archaeologists and anthropologists were eventually followed by many other scientists on the trail of the very first Americans.

Many different kinds of evidence of ancient American people have been uncovered, and some of the evidence has been difficult to interpret. Scientists have therefore developed a variety of theories and have disagreed about the time of first arrival. In the 20th century alone, professional and amateur anthropologists proposed dates ranging from 200,000 to 12,000 years ago. However, the vast majority of the evidence dates back to a time somewhere between 14,000 and 12,000 years ago.

FROM SIBERIA TO ALASKA

From about 18,000 years ago the last ice age began to wane. Glaciers slowly melted and sometimes refroze in centuries-long cold snaps. This general warming trend continued for more than 8,000 years, and ocean levels began to swell with glacial meltwater. Even as they were fed by the melting glaciers, the oceans at that time were still well below their

Albert Bierstadt (1830–1902), The Rocky Mountains, Lander's Peak, *1863; Paleo-Indians seemed to have migrated along the base of the North American Rockies and then the Mexican Sierras and the Andes, hunting on the plains in sight of the sheltering mountains.* (Copyright the Metropolitan Museum of Art)

present levels, so landmasses we would not recognize today remained above water. One of these was the sprawling landscape of Beringia, an area encompassing parts of modern-day Alaska and easternmost Siberia. This landmass provided an inhospitable yet solid land bridge between Russia and North America. Siberian hunter-gatherers on the trail of large prey, such as mammoth, musk ox, and saiga antelope, could have crossed some 60 miles of open tundra into Alaska. There, they gradually would have become stranded by rising sea levels. They might have settled near Beringia's rivers for an easy supply of fresh water but would eventually have moved on in search of territories more fertile than this dry scrub land. As the ice age ended, much of Beringia became submerged beneath the icy waves of today's Bering Sea. Ocean levels continued to rise.

The submergence of the Bering Strait (the narrow passage between modern-day Alaska and Siberia) took many generations, so the new settlers would have had an opportunity to return to the Siberia of their forbears. It is possible that some did rejoin their countrymen on the Russian side of Beringia, but today's Native Americans are descendants of the ones who attempted to push farther and farther into the new territory.

Once they were in North America, their path to the rest of the continent was not yet clear. Glaciers still covered much of Alaska and Canada so that these early Americans may have lived for centuries trapped between their submerged land bridge to the north and Canada's glacial ice sheets to the south. In the unstable climate the ice sheets sometimes convulsed violently, occasionally advancing toward the settlers. As they did so, the glaciers slowly crushed and enveloped entire forests, diminishing vital habitat and destroying food and shelter. Often the ice would suddenly retreat again, leaving a flattened landscape in its wake. Even in times of retreat, glacial meltwaters could inundate grazing land and woodlands and cause massive flash flooding as millions of cubic tons of water came bursting out from behind dams of half-melted glacial ice. Enormous boulders and jagged chunks of ice tumbled within these floods, smashing everything in their path.

It was a millennium or more before the two major Canadian ice sheets, the Cordilleran in the west and the Laurentide in the east, parted and permitted the new settlers to enter the rest of the Americas. From there the migrants diversified into more than 2,000 societies with more than 1,000 languages and produced some of the greatest civilizations in human history.

It is apparent from studies of Native American languages and DNA that American settlement began with migrants from Siberia. The linguist Joseph Greenberg and other scientists have proved that ancient America was settled not by just one but by several separate waves of eastward migration from Asia. Greenberg had been suggesting since the 1950s that Native American languages fell into three distinct families. By the 1980s, after many years of collaboration and comparison among several disciplines, scientists were able to demonstrate that North America had been settled in three separate waves: Paleo-Indians had arrived near the end of the last ice age and spawned the majority of native languages, a second group consisting of Na-Dene speakers (the Athabascan family from whom the Apache and Navajo descend) arrived some 9,000 years ago, and just 4,000 years ago a final group arrived speaking a language from which modern Inuit (Eskimo) and Aleut have developed. Discovering the exact means by which these later migrants arrived, whether by land or sea, has become a new quest of archaeologists.

From Beringia to Clovis

By the time they were cut off from their Siberian heartland the ancient Alaskan settlers had already begun to adapt to their new home. Different bands of settlers quickly diversified into distinct hunting, fishing, and foraging cultures in reaction to their maritime, tundra, valley, or highland environments. As they began to differ from each other, they also differed considerably from their Siberian relatives in culture, technology, and language. Anthropologists call these distinct people Paleo-Indians ("ancient Indians") to distinguish them clearly from their Asian antecedents. For some 2,000 years they may have lived confined to northwestern Canada, but as the ice age ended and the Cordilleran and Laurentide ice sheets finally melted, the new settlers were free to issue forth into the vast American landscape.

The oldest sites in North America south of the ice sheets are located in the western United States. The sites of Folsom and Clovis in New Mexico date back as far as 11,000 and 11,500 years ago, respectively. At both of these sites stone projectile points from spears and arrows were found among the bones of extinct ice age mammals, indicating that people had been in America at least 10,000 years ago. In fact, the finely wrought projectile points had been found between the ribs of a bison skeleton at Folsom and between the ribs of several mammoths at Clovis. Thus these ancient "kill sites" contained different prey and slightly different kinds of projectiles but illustrated similar hunting techniques. The Clovis and Folsom people appeared to be hunter-gatherers who stalked large prey that would supply them with large amounts of food at a time, which they could eat on the spot or preserve until the next hunt.

When radiocarbon dating was introduced in the 1950s, almost two decades after the first excavations at Folsom, it was determined that Clovis was the older site. All biological organisms absorb carbon isotopes while they are alive. Some of these isotopes decay at a steady rate after an organism's death. Radiocarbon (or carbon 14) testing measures the degree of isotopic decay to approximate the year or period of death of an organism. Radiocarbon dating is commonly used to fix the age of artifacts in conjunction with other contextual information, such as location, materials, and methods of manufacture. Although varying designs of projectile points had by then been found in Texas and as far east as the Mississippi, these roughly 11,000-year-old hunting artifacts were attributed to a general "Clovis culture," suggesting the primacy of Clovis as the oldest site.

From the Rockies to the Andes

It is unlikely that the Clovis culture was a "mother culture" to all the Americas. The first settlers who came through the break in the Canadian ice barrier may not all have settled first in New Mexico or even in the western part of North America. Some may have immediately started migrating southeast, going all the way to the Gulf of Mexico. Some may have gone directly south, right past New Mexico, to settle in Central America. Others may have followed opportunity or comfortable weather all the way to present-day Colombia and Venezuela or to Peru and Bolivia. This would explain the apparent antiquity of some South American sites, many of which seem to have arisen at the same time as the Clovis culture or even before. While controversy surrounds many of the Paleo-Indian sites in Latin America (for excavations there have often been done by Europeans and Latin Americans using techniques not always accepted by North American scientists), the site at Monte Verde in Chile seems to be older than Clovis.

Several layers, or strata, of artifacts at Monte Verde contain wood and stone tools; the remains of hutlike dwellings; and the fruits, plants, and meat that were eaten in them. In the archaeological practice of stratigraphy, excavation proceeds from the upper strata, or layers, of soil to the lower, with the assumption that objects buried deeper in the soil are older. Radiocarbon testing often bears this assumption out, but sometimes earth movements and water or wind erosion can jumble the contents of the soil deposits. These shifts can complicate the stratigraphic record and corrupt the carbon content of the site, rendering radiocarbon dating unreliable or useless. Monte Verde's location near both a river and a damp bog casts doubts on the carbon test results, which state that the upper level of artifacts is 12,500 years old and that an even lower stratum of artifacts is some 33,000 years old.

While the age of the lower strata (which may have been corrupted by water action or other agents) is in doubt, the artifacts dated to 12,500 years ago are probably that old. If this theory is correct, then Monte Verde is 1,000 years older than Clovis. Sites such as Pikimachay in Peru and Taima-taima in Venezuela and many other South American sites have also yielded stone tools and butchered animal bones. From their technology and materials these sites seem to be of the same approximate age as Clovis and Monte Verde, but like the latter site, they suffer from dubious stratigraphic evidence whereby doubt is cast on their radiocarbon dates. It is noteworthy that a great many South American sites, excavated by unaffiliated archaeologists in the past 30 years, tend to yield radiocarbon dates between 13,400 and 14,200 years ago. If the age of any of these sites proves to be incontestable, then South America will have the oldest proven Paleo-Indian site. Older South American dates could establish that Paleo-Indians emerging from Canada's ice-free corridor headed straight for the south. If this were the case, communities in South America could have emerged virtually simultaneously with their Clovis counterparts up north, or even earlier.

Far from the controversy of South America's radiocarbon dates are archaeologists who see that hunter-gatherers from just south of the Canadian ice sheets could indeed have settled the entire length of the Americas in a single millennium. Computer models and comparisons to the movements of historic marooned populations indicate that with opportunistic migration (say, in the pursuit of food sources) and even conservative population growth, Indians could have expanded from Canada to Chile within 100 generations. It seems that once ancient Siberians crossed into the Americas, their settlement of the new landmasses, even with any delay caused by the gradually receding Canadian ice sheets, was remarkably fast.

From the Amazon to the Caribbean

The vast majority of early Paleo-Indian sites are concentrated along the Pacific side of the Americas. This may be more than circumstantial evidence. Paleo-Indians seemed to have migrated along the base of the North American Rockies and then the Mexican Sierras and the Andes, hunting on the wide-open plains but within sight of the sheltering mountains. Their eastward expansion into the North American Woodlands and the South American Amazon may be obscured by the environment itself, tangling the stratigraphic evidence in vegetal undergrowth. However, it may simply be that Paleo-Indians spent much of their early prehistory nearer the western longitudes and open spaces to which they had grown accustomed in their early migration. Either way, most Paleo-Indians seem to have kept the rising sun to their left during their early expansion.

In South America a change in the overall southward migration pattern also marked a change in lifestyle from almost exclusively hunting and gathering to partial and then full agricultural settlement. This agrarian phase, which commenced in different regions between 5,000 and 10,000 years ago, was an important shift in Native American culture. Some anthropologists cease referring to these agrarians as Paleo-Indians, choosing instead to describe them as archaic cultures. Three patterns of migration signal the archaic shift: the exploration of the coastlines in search of diversified food sources (for example, the addition of fish and shellfish to the regular diet), the absolute cessation of migration after phased adaptations to agriculture, and finally a movement into the Amazon forests after developing a certain familiarity with its environment.

Prearchaic Paleo-Indians would have had little incentive to settle in the Amazon forests, since their quarries as hunters were large, migratory animals that favored open landscapes.

However, between 7,000 and 9,000 years ago people in the forested river drainages of Brazil, Uruguay, northern Argentina, and Paraguay began to use a greatly diversified tool kit. At sites along the Paraná River, the familiar projectile points and scrapers are joined by an increased number of woodworking tools, knives, choppers, bolas, anvils, and grinders. All of these are tools adapted to building, subsisting, and preparing food in a wooded environment. The varied vegetable sources within the forest would have provided food, shelter, and clothing to settlers, and they may also have been the inspiration to manipulate the growth of certain desirable vegetation. Bottle gourds, pumpkins, beans, peppers, and avocados were among the crops purposefully grown by 5,000 to 10,000 years ago. By 4,000 years ago archaic Indians had begun to cultivate the staple food manioc, or cassava root, a starchy crop that would transform many societies, chiefly by supporting population explosions.

In the last 2,000 years before the Common Era, many archaic groups settled down and developed into agricultural societies with far-reaching trade relationships. This is the period in which the civilizations of Caral, Paracas, Chavín, and Chinchorro emerged in Peru and Bolivia with agriculture and fishing as the basis of their economies; the Olmec and early Pre-Classic Maya organized in Mesoamerica, having cleverly doctored a wild grass into the high-yield staple known today as maize; and the egalitarian Adena culture emerged in the eastern Woodlands of North America, based on a combination of agriculture, forest gathering, fishing, and the hunting of woodland fauna and migrating ducks. All of these civilizations illustrate the archaic transition to forest life, which in turn contributed to the domestication of plants and the development of agriculture. With the archaic expansion throughout the continents, albeit by small groups, the settlement of the Americas seemed complete. But there was one great Indian migration yet to commence.

The movement of Amazonian peoples to the Caribbean islands represents the last migratory expansion in the pre-Columbian Americas. The first Caribbean settlements appear to have taken place quite early, as Paleo-Indians preceded archaic Indians. Excavations in the 1970s at Banwari Trace in Trinidad yielded the oldest-known human artifacts in the Caribbean archipelago. These 8,000-year-old remains include stone tools, human bones, and a large midden of discarded shells. The human artifacts at Angostura in Puerto Rico date from just 1,000 years after those at Banwari Trace. With habitations at opposite ends of the Caribbean archipelago showing such close dates, it appears that the Caribbean islands were settled very quickly. This maritime expansion of Paleo-Indians testifies to their intelligence, skill, and determination.

Successive groups of Paleo-Indians followed by later settlers appear to have come in canoes from the delta of the Orinoco River. Some may have traveled down the Orinoco from as far away as the foothills of the Andes. Others may have migrated along the coast of Guiana from the Amazon. With seafaring skills developed on the great and often perilous rivers of South America, they struck out for Trinidad, an island visible from some parts of Venezuela. From there they settled Tobago and Grenada. Within a single millennium they island-hopped all the way to the Bahamas and Cuba, islands located in the far northwest. Given the northern Caribbean's proximity to the Yucatán and the Florida peninsulas, archaeologists have not entirely dismissed the possibility of migrations from North and Central America.

While the earliest hunter-gatherers left mostly simple stone tools as evidence of their habitation, later Indians began arriving in the Caribbean some 4,000 years ago with elaborately decorated pottery, complex weaving techniques, and sculpture made of wood, stone, shell, and bone. It is mostly by their pottery that archaeologists have classified their distinct cultures. Anthropologists and linguists also have identified at least a dozen distinct groups of settlers from at least two major South American language families.

The transition to island life was not always as difficult as might be expected, since many of the local species had originated on the mainland, blown or carried by hurricanes, marine currents, and prevailing winds. The settlers had also brought stalks of manioc and other reproducible food sources, and intermittent contacts with the South American mainland were maintained. In the Caribbean islands, however, these settlers developed insular cultures with unique dialects, arts, and religions. They relied heavily on agriculture and fishing and did only part-time hunting and gathering in the limited island interiors. Since the terrain of some islands was radically different from that of others (ranging from volcanic to sedimentary to coral soil), a vital trading system among the islands developed by the beginning of the Common Era. Eventually, the brave explorers who had arrived with only bare necessities in the second millennium B.C.E. would evolve into the Taíno kingdoms that greeted Columbus in 1492.

See also ADORNMENT; AGRICULTURE; ART; ASTRONOMY; BORDERS AND FRONTIERS; BUILDING TECHNIQUES AND MATERIALS; CERAMICS AND POTTERY; CITIES; CLIMATE AND GEOGRAPHY; CRIME AND PUNISHMENT; DEATH AND BURIAL PRACTICES; ECONOMY; EMPIRES AND DYNASTIES; EXPLORATION; FOREIGNERS AND BARBARIANS; FOOD AND DIET; GOVERNMENT ORGANIZATION; HUNTING, FISHING, AND GATHERING; INVENTIONS; LANGUAGE; LAWS AND LEGAL CODES; LITERATURE; METALLURGY; MILITARY; MONEY AND COINAGE; NATURAL DISASTERS; NOMADIC AND PASTORAL SOCIETIES; PANDEMICS AND EPIDEMICS; RELIGION AND COSMOLOGY; ROADS AND BRIDGES; SEAFARING AND NAVIGATION; SETTLEMENT PATTERNS; SHIPS AND SHIPBUILDING; SLAVES AND SLAVERY; SOCIAL COLLAPSE AND ABANDONMENT; SOCIAL ORGANIZATION; TOWNS AND VILLAGES; TRADE AND EXCHANGE; TRANSPORTATION; WAR AND CONQUEST; WEAPONRY AND ARMOR.

Europe

Tacitus: Excerpt from Germania *(98 C.E.)*

I shall now deduce the institutions and usages of the several people, as far as they vary one from another; as also an account of what nations from thence removed, to settle themselves in Gaul.

That the Gauls were in times past more puissant and formidable is related by the Prince of authors, the deified Julius [Julius Caesar], and hence it is probable that they too have passed into Germany. For what a small obstacle must be a river, to restrain any nation, as each grew more potent, from seizing or changing habitations; when as yet all habitations were common, and not parted or appropriated by the founding and terror of Monarchies? The region therefore between the Hercynian Forest and the rivers Moenus [Main] and Rhine, was occupied by the Helvetians; as was that beyond it by the Boians, both nations of Gaul. There still remains a place called Boiemum, which denotes the primitive name and antiquity of the country, although the inhabitants have been changed. But whether the Araviscans are derived from the Osians, a nation of Germans passing into Pannonia, or the Osians from the Araviscans removing from thence into Germany, is a matter undecided; since they both still use the language, the same customs and the same laws. For as of old they lived alike poor and alike free, equal proved the evils and advantages on each side the river, and common to both people. The Treverians and Nervians aspire passionately to the reputation of being descended from the Germans; since by the glory of this original, they would escape all imputation of resembling the Gauls in person and effeminacy. Such as dwell upon the bank of the Rhine, the Vangiones, the Tribocians, and the Nemetes, are without doubt all Germans. The Ubians are ashamed of their original; though they have a particular honor to boast, that of having merited an establishment as a Roman Colony, and still delight to be called Agrippinensians, after the name of their founder: they indeed formerly came from beyond the Rhine, and, for the many proofs of their fidelity, were settled upon the very bank of the river; not to be there confined or guarded themselves, but to guard and defend that boundary against the rest of the Germans.

From: *Voyages and Travels: Ancient and Modern*, ed. by Charles W. Eliot (New York: P. F. Collier and Son, 1910).

Greece

Herodotus: Excerpt on the founding of Cyrene (ca. 630 B.C.E.), from The Histories *(ca. 430 B.C.E.)*

Book 4

Grinus (they say), the son of Aesanius, a descendant of Theras, and king of the island of Thera, went to Delphi to offer a hecatomb on behalf of his native city. On Grinus consulting the oracle about sundry matters, the Pythoness gave him for answer "that he should found a city in Libya." When the embassy returned to Thera, small account was taken of the oracle, as the Therans were quite ignorant where Libya was.

Seven years passed from the utterance of the oracle, and not a drop of rain fell in Thera: all the trees in the island, except one, were killed with the drought. After a while, everything began to go wrong. Ignorant of the cause of their sufferings, they again sent to Delphi to inquire for what reason they were afflicted. The Pythoness in reply reminded them reproachfully "that if they and Battus would make a settlement at Cyrene in Libya, things would go better with them." So, as there was no help for it, they sent messengers to Crete, to inquire whether any of the Cretans, or of the strangers living amongst them, had ever traveled as far as Libya: and these messengers fell in with a man named Corobius, a dealer in purple dye. In answer to their inquiries, he told them that contrary winds had once carried him to Libya, where he had gone ashore on a certain island which was named Platea. So they hired this man's services, and took him back with them to Thera. A few persons then sailed from Thera to reconnoiter. Guided by Corobius to the island of Platea, they left him there with provisions for a certain

(continued)

(continues)

number of months and returned home with all speed to give their countrymen an account of the island.

The Therans who had left Corobius at Platea, when they reached Thera, told their countrymen that they had colonized an island on the coast of Libya. They of Thera, upon this, resolved that men should be sent to join the colony from each of their seven districts and that the brothers in every family should draw lots to determine who were to go. Upon this the Therans sent out Battus with two penteconters, and with these he proceeded to Libya; but within a little time, not knowing what else to do, the men returned and arrived back off Thera. The Therans, when they saw the vessels approaching, received them with showers of missiles, would not allow them to come near the shore, and ordered the men to sail back from whence they came. Thus compelled, they settled on Platea.

In this place they continued two years, but at the end of that time, as their ill luck still followed them, they went in a body to Delphi, where they made complaint at the shrine to the effect that they prospered as poorly as before. Hereon the Pythoness made them the following answer: "Know you better than I, fair Libya abounding in fleeces? Better the stranger than he who has trod it? Oh! Clever Therans!" Battus and his friends, when they heard this, sailed back to Platea: it was plain the god would not hold them acquitted of the colony till they were absolutely in Libya. So they made a settlement on the mainland directly opposite Platea, fixing themselves at a place called Aziris.

Here they remained six years, at the end of which time the Libyans induced them to move, promising that they would lead them to a better situation. So the Greeks left Aziris and were conducted by the Libyans toward the west, their journey being so arranged, by the calculation of their guides, that they passed in the night the most beautiful district of that whole country, which is the region called Irasa. The Libyans brought them to a spring, which goes by the name of Apollo's Fountain, and told them, "Here, Hellenes, is the proper place for you to settle; for here the sky leaks."

During the lifetime of Battus, the founder of the colony, who reigned forty years, and during that of his son Arcesilaus, who reigned sixteen, the Cyreneans continued at the same level, neither more nor fewer in number than they were at the first. But in the reign of the third king, Battus, surnamed the Happy, the advice of the Pythoness brought Greeks from every quarter into Libya to join the settlement. Thus a great multitude were collected together to Cyrene, and the Libyans of the neighborhood found themselves stripped of large portions of their lands.

From Herodotus, *The History*, trans. George Rawlinson (New York: Dutton and Co., 1862).

FURTHER READING

William Y. Adams, "The First Colonial Empire: Egypt in Nubia, 3200–1200 B.C.," *Comparative Studies in Society and History* 26 (1984): 36–71.

Thomas Barfield, *The Nomadic Alternative* (Englewood Cliffs, N.J.: Prentice-Hall, 1993).

Jerry Bentley, *Old World Encounters: Cross-Cultural Contacts and Exchanges in Pre-Modern Times* (New York: Oxford University Press, 1993).

Manfred Bietak, *Avaris: The Capital of the Hyksos* (London: British Museum, 1996).

John Boardman, *The Greeks Overseas: Their Early Colonies and Trade* (London: Thames and Hudson, 1980).

John Boardman and N. G. L. Hammond, eds., *The Cambridge Ancient History*, 2nd ed., Vol. 3, *The Expansion of the Greek World Eighth to Sixth Centuries B.C.* (Cambridge, U.K.: Cambridge University Press, 1982).

John Chapman and Helena Hamerow, eds., *Migrations and Invasions in Archaeological Explanation* (Oxford, U.K.: Archaeopress, 1997).

Roger Cribb, *Nomads in Archaeology* (Cambridge, U.K.: Cambridge University Press, 1991).

Moshe Dothan and Trude Dothan, *People of the Sea: The Search for the Philistines* (New York: Macmillan, 1992).

Carol Dougherty, *The Poetics of Colonization: From City to Text in Archaic Greece* (New York: Oxford University Press, 1993).

Brian M. Fagan, *The Great Journey: The Peopling of Ancient America* (Gainesville: University Press of Florida, 2003).

Clive Gamble, *The Palaeolithic Settlement of Europe* (Cambridge, U.K.: Cambridge University Press, 1986).

A. J. Graham, *Colony and Mother City in Ancient Greece* (Manchester, U.K.: Manchester University Press, 1964).

János Harmatta, ed., *History of Civilizations of Central Asia.* Vol. 2, *The Development of Sedentary and Nomadic Civilizations: 700 B.C. to A.D. 250* (Paris: UNESCO Publishing, 1994).

Herodotus, *The Histories*, trans. Aubrey de Sélincourt (Harmondsworth, U.K.: Penguin Books, 1954).

John Iliffe, *Africans: The History of a Continent* (Cambridge: Cambridge University Press, 1995).

Geoffrey Irwin, *The Prehistoric Exploration and Colonisation of the Pacific* (Cambridge, U.K.: Cambridge University Press, 1992).

Steven J. Mithen, *After the Ice: A Global Human History* (London: Weidenfeld and Nicolson, 2003).

David O'Connor and Stephen Quirke, eds. *Mysterious Lands* (London: UCL Press. 2003).
John Reader, *Africa: A Biography of the Continent* (New York: Vintage, 1999).
Thucydides, *The Peloponnesian War*, trans. Rex Warner (Harmondsworth, U.K.: Penguin Books, 1954).
David Wengrow, *The Archaeology of Early Egypt: Social Transformations in North-East Africa* (Cambridge, U.K.: Cambridge University Press, 2006).

► Military

INTRODUCTION

Murderous conflict among people dates back to ancient times. Rock and cave paintings from the last great ice age show people armed with spears and shields, sometimes trying to kill one another. This does not mean that those ancient warriors had military outlooks on what they were doing; it is possible that anyone in a community would be expected to take arms to protect it or to attack others.

Military thinking may have developed among people who had something special to protect, such as an oasis in a dry land, a crossing for a trade route over a river, especially fertile farmlands, or accumulated wealth, as in a prosperous city. Fortifications to protect a community are very old. In many lands, villages were surrounded by wooden palisades (a strong fence made of stakes) or defensive ditches. The first large-scale fortifications may have been earthen walls. These could be very extensive, surrounding even large cities and requiring thousands of workers to construct. Clay bricks were popular in the Near East and Egypt, where walls more than a dozen feet thick were built around fortresses or cites. Both earth and brick had significant problems. One was that they were subject to erosion by water. Another problem came with the development of siege weapons, which could knock down bricks. Thus, stone eventually became favored. For instance, the Great Wall of China began as mostly earthworks, slowly replaced over hundreds of years with stone.

Some historians have argued that all great empires have been built by warfare, and many ancient peoples believed that a strong military was essential to survival. Of the various kinds of writings that show up in ancient cultures, military ones are among the most common. Theories of warfare and rules for warfare abounded, but the successful military commander was often someone who surprised his enemy by breaking the rules. An advance in technology was often the secret to breaking the rules. For instance, chariots created more mobility on the battlefield for elite warriors, playing key roles in wars and sometimes changing the course of an entire culture, as in the Aryan invasion of northern India. Still, the stirrup made the chariot obsolete by providing a horseback rider with the stability to fire arrows into the enemy or hack with a sword and remain in the saddle.

Militaries became complex organizations as military technology advanced. A government needed to create a chain of command and policies for when and how military forces were to be used. Some cultures organized their armies around heroes, elite warriors who fought for individual glory. Those cultures that learned to organize their armies so that all their troops worked together usually overcame the armies that emphasized individualism. Thus military discipline became a matter of great importance. Governments learned to train their officers and troops.

The military was often the most expensive part of government. If a government wanted a successful army, it had to be sure its army was fed. The soldiers needed proper quarters in which to live, and they required armaments and training in how to use the armaments. This expense meant that standing armies were usually small, with professionals being supplemented by militias or untrained people in times of war.

AFRICA

BY KIRK H. BEETZ

Only three ancient African nations outside Egypt had militaries: Karmah, Cush, and Axum. Not much is known about Karmah, and much of its territory is now under Lake Nasser, the reservoir behind the Aswān Dam, which hampers archaeological research into the kingdom of Karmah and the ancient Nubians. The Karmahns were a mix of Nubians and people from farther south, and the Karmahn kingdom existed from about 1900 to 1492 B.C.E. Sometime before 1650 B.C.E. Karmah extended its dominion to just south of the first cataract on the Nile river, beyond where the Aswān Dam is now.

The Karmahn military still used stone spears. Its organization is not known, but it seems to have been influenced by the nomadic cultures to the west, which would mean that it favored individual heroism rather than group cooperation in combat. Between 1504 and 1492 B.C.E. Egypt conquered Karmah, sacked the capital, and seized land far to the south of Karmah, bringing nearly all of Nubia under Egyptian rule.

Most of what is known about Kush comes from the Egyptians. The Kushites created their own alphabet, but their language has yet to be deciphered. They regarded themselves as the true inheritors of the ancient Egyptian culture and often wrote in Egyptian hieroglyphics, which have been interpreted and provide some light on Kush's military. Kush arose in Nubia in about 900 B.C.E., filling a power vacuum left when Egypt withdrew after about 500 years of ruling Nubia. Kush organized its military along Egyptian lines. One aspect of its military not shared by Egypt was the use of elephants in parades and as elevated platforms for archers.

By the time Kush took over northern Nubia after the Egyptians withdrew, the Egyptian fortifications in Nubia had become showpieces rather than serious military installations. The fortifications tended to be inside a Nubian city, impressively decorated but not of much value for protecting the city.

Archaeologists think that this means the Egyptians had become very secure in Nubia and had nothing to fear from the local people.

The military's function in Kush was to keep the kingdom's trade routes open and to protect the kingdom from nomadic raiders who would steal crops and loot villages and towns. For this, Kush maintained a standing army, perhaps a few thousand troops at first and possibly as many as 40,000 at the kingdom's height of power. Kush may have had a military academy for training its officers. It is not clear who was and was not eligible to become an officer, but it is known that women sometimes led the army into battle. A queen was called *candace*, and ancient Greeks recorded an attack in 7 C.E. led by such a woman, Candace Amanirenas, against the Romans in Egypt.

There exist some impressive stone structures that may once have been part of Kushite fortresses, but archaeologists disagree over the purposes of the edifices. For maintaining garrisons in its territories, particularly on its frontiers, Kush seems to have followed Egyptian patterns of constructing clay brick fortresses. These had outer walls with towers at their corners and an interior keep also made of brick. Defensive ditches lay outside the walls. Siege engines were rarely used in Egypt and Kush, so an attacking force would have to overcome defenders in the ditches while archers on the walls rained arrows on them. The typical way to lay siege to a fortress was to surround it and wait to starve out the defenders, which could take a few years. The nomads who raided Kush did not have this staying power, and the Kushite army could relieve a fortress long before the raiders could overcome it.

The Kushite general Piye, who invaded Egypt in about eighth century B.C.E., had as the core of his army veteran troops who were highly disciplined. Army units tended to be divided into archers, spearmen, and swordsmen. The spearmen undertook the heaviest fighting. The archers fought behind the spearmen, and the swordsmen protected the archers. Even ordinary Kushites tended to be good warriors, and they were often hired as mercenaries by Near Eastern kingdoms and Egypt. Kush could therefore field an army of fierce fighters, all of whom had some understanding of military discipline.

As he advanced north through Egypt, Piye renovated Egypt's fortresses and city defenses. He eventually took on the duties of pharaoh (r. ca. 750–ca. 712 B.C.E.). His successors continued to rebuild Egypt's defenses. Although they organized Egypt's military intelligently, their weapons and thinking were still in the Bronze Age, whereas the Near East was in the Iron Age. When the Kushite pharaoh Tantamani (r. ca. 664–ca. 657 B.C.E.) tried to reestablish Egyptian influence in Palestine, the Assyrians attacked. Plague helped to destroy the first Assyrian strike force, but superior armor, weapons, and tactics enabled the Assyrians to drive the Cushites out of Egypt around 656 B.C.E.

The Kush government took note of how Assyria had defeated Tantamani's armies and took firm measures to advance into the Iron Age. Although Kush's soldiers appear to have continued to use shields made of hide, their weapons and tactics advanced to a level unmatched elsewhere among Africans. The military became focused on protecting the southern reaches of Kush as well as protecting its northern and western territories. Commerce in eastern Africa seems to have flourished in part because Kush's army kept the peace among the region's southern tribes.

When Kush's military power faded is not known. It seems to have still been formidable in the 200s C.E., but little else is known of the region during the early years of the Common Era. By 330 C.E. the Kushites had fled their country, and it was occupied by nomadic tribes. By then a new power had risen in eastern Africa, in present-day Ethiopia. This was the kingdom of Axum. It had begun as a trading city that was visited by Arabs and Indians from the east. By the 200s C.E. it controlled much of eastern Africa.

Not much is known about Axum's military. Axum seems to have had a small coastal navy. Imposing forts made of stone and masonry sat atop coastal hills and controlled access to the interior of Axum. In 330 C.E. the nomads who had invaded Kush violated a treaty they had with Axum, and Ezānā, king of Axum, led an invasion of Kush that found only the nomadic tribes Red Noba and Black Noba, who were soundly defeated. Overall, Axum seems to have preferred diplomacy to taking military action, and it emphasized commerce over war, using its military mostly to keep pirates and bandits at bay. Its hilltop fortresses suggest that it had a standing army to man them and that the army was expected to defend Axum from invasion. Perhaps Axum's military played a role in protecting the country from Arab invasions from the seventh century C.E. onward, but this is not yet known.

EGYPT

BY AMR KAMEL

Egypt had no standing professional army before the New Kingdom (ca. 1550–ca. 1070 B.C.E.). When the need arose, provincial governors, temples, and estates provided units under the command of local officials, as in the case of Unas (r. 2356–2323 B.C.E) in the Fifth Dynasty. The official related in his autobiography that the army under his command, who fought the "Asiatic Sand Dwellers," was originally composed of men from Upper Egypt, Lower Egypt, and Nubia and that he did not have strong military background or a previous military title. Evidence does exist of a permanent royal army led by professional officers during the Middle Kingdom (ca. 2040–ca. 1640 B.C.E.) in lower Nubia, which became a heavily militarized zone, and references to a variety of military titles increased toward the end of that period. During the New Kingdom a large professional army with a fully developed hierarchy fulfilled the pharaohs' plans to form a great empire, including territories in Nubia and Palestine and areas of present-day Lebanon, Syria, and northern Iraq.

The Egyptian military was composed primarily of infantry, which was organized into four divisions named, under Ramses III (r. 1194–1163 B.C.E.), after the gods Amun, Ptah, Re, and Seth. Each division was divided into about 20 companies of 250 men and each of these into five platoons of 50, in addition to 20 administrative supervisers and military scribes for managing provisions and other logistics. By the middle of the Eighteenth Dynasty (ca. 1550–ca. 1307 B.C.E.) the Egyptian army had an organized chariot division, which functioned mainly as a mobile platform for archers. The cavalry division was, until the campaign of Sheshonk I (r. ca. 945–924 B.C.E.) of the Twenty-second Dynasty, limited mainly to scouting parties.

The navy was not a separate division of the Egyptian army, and for most of Egyptian history sailors appear to have been regular soldiers who used boats simply as waterborne platforms. These troops were normally stationed in barracks at Thebes, Heliopolis, Memphis, and Piramesse, the royal residence during the Nineteenth Dynasty (ca. 1307–ca. 1196 B.C.E.). For one military campaign abroad the 20,000 soldiers mobilized immediately, and large Egyptian warships, such as *Star of Egypt*, *Soul of the Gods*, *Wild Bull*, *Beloved of Amun*, or *Thutmose Appears in Memphis*, transported troops and supplies via the Pelusiac Branch of the Nile to Byblos (later called Jubayl) on the coast of what is now Lebanon.

Like any modern army, the Egyptian forces were organized along strictly hierarchical lines. They were under the command of the king, who had an advisory council made up of a vizier (sometimes called the "overseer" of the troops), generals, and senior functionaries. Divisions, companies, and platoons had supervisers equivalent to modern officers and noncommissioned officers. As in every other sphere of the Egyptian bureaucracy, sons were able to follow their fathers' military profession for the sake of a career and a secure livelihood.

During the Old Kingdom (ca. 2575–ca. 2134 B.C.E.) the Egyptian army was largely considered a national one, with the exception of Nubian archers, who joined the army in the Sixth Dynasty. From then on, notably in the New Kingdom, foreign units began to form with the gradual subjugation of neighboring people in Asia, the Mediterranean, and the region of modern-day Libya. From the time of King Seti I (r. 1306–1290 B.C.E.) the army included a contingent of Sherdan mercenaries, originally from the Mediterranean islands, who were distinct from the Egyptian forces with their swords, spiked helmets, and shields. It was not unusual for foreign mercenaries to reach the senior ranks in the Egyptian army or even to join the king's elite bodyguard. For instance, the guard of Amenhotep III (r. 1391–1353 B.C.E.) was composed of Nubians and Canaanites. Beginning in the Second Intermediate Period (ca. 1640–ca. 1532 B.C.E.) the Egyptians employed the Medjay, a pastoral people who lived in the Arabian Desert, as police within Egypt and along its southern frontier. By the New Kingdom the term *Medjay* had become virtually synonymous with *police*, which, like the military, were organized hierarchically and headed by the chief of the Medjay.

Many kings during the New Kingdom campaigned in western Asia on a nearly annual basis. As might be expected from a temporarily mustered force, the troops left Egypt after the harvest was gathered and returned in time for the planting season. Textual evidence refers to the transportation of food and fodder by ships to the large port centers in the eastern Mediterranean region. There is no evidence that the soldiers' families accompanied the troops during any campaign. Instead, they prayed to the deity Amun in temples or in domestic shrines to return their sons and relatives home safely. The family members of the scribe Dhutmose in the Twentieth Dynasty (ca. 1196–1070 B.C.E.), for example, are recorded "calling upon Amun, Mut, Khonsu, Re-Horakhti in his rising and in his setting and all gods of Thebes" to return their son Dhutmose, who was sent in military mission in Nubia, "back alive from the next war."

In early times a young man's military service began at the age of 20, and in later periods the recruits were much younger. A recruit faced a hard school of discipline and toughening up. His uniform was a short kilt or merely a penis sheath, and he wore a feather in his hair as an ornament. Physical exercise and wrestling alternated with training in weaponry. For breaches of discipline the commander would order a thrashing; one text refers to an offender being beaten by his fellow recruits "like papyrus." Military reviews were held on state holidays or after the return of a victorious army in presence of the kings, to the accompaniment of trumpets, fifes, and drums.

During such festivals officers and soldiers could receive gold awards for bravery and other awards, including decorated axes, daggers, or swords, for other military virtues. Trinkets such as little golden lions, representing bravery, and gold flies, symbolizing perseverance in the attack, could be considered the world's oldest medals. Esteemed officers could be granted numbers of prisoners, male or female, to be kept as slaves, and sometimes plots of land.

Military strategy was usually adapted according to the natural conditions and situations the Egyptians encountered. Textual and pictorial sources describe, for example, the tactics of the battle of Kadesh, which took place around 1274 B.C.E. during the reign of Ramses II (r. 1290–1224 B.C.E.). Ramses II apparently believed the story of two Hittite spies who presented themselves as Bedouins and reported to the king that the Hittite army had retreated. Ramses II therefore rapidly moved through enemy territory without scouting the area ahead, ignoring one of the most basic military principles. Having crossed the Orontes River without sending troops ahead, he was attacked by the Hittites, and the river lay between him and his supporting troops. Egyptian forces traveling by warship managed to save the Egyptian army from destruction.

Several series of forts, watchtowers, and way stations facilitated the Egyptian army's march and served as part of a signaling system adjacent to the cliffs along the Nile in Nubia and along the northeastern border with the ancient Near East. The system of military stations in this frontier region was known during the New Kingdom as the Ways of Horus. Recent excavations in the western Nile delta have identified a parallel chain of forts that were presumably constructed to protect the Egypt's northwestern frontier, which began at Zawyet Umm el-Rakham, about 200 miles west of Alexandria, where Ramses II built his substantial citadel. These forts were surrounded by massive enclosure walls and sometimes ditches. Fortified gateways, watchtowers, loopholed ramparts on the inside, and covered glacis on the outside made them almost impregnable. Granaries and cisterns were attached to the forts. Probably 50 to 300 soldiers were stationed in one fort at a time, depending on its size, which implies that small military units were able to hold their positions.

THE MIDDLE EAST

BY CARYN E. NEUMANN

Throughout the ancient Near East, war made and unmade political and cultural worlds. The social orders of the time were formed and maintained by brute force and compulsion. Long royal reigns produced and were reproduced by military stability. Short reigns reflected weakness in war. As a result, the military played a crucial role in the lives of the ancients.

The first literate civilizations and the first organized armies appear almost simultaneously in the river valleys of the Tigris and the Euphrates. The Sumerians invaded southern Mesopotamia in about 3100 B.C.E. and subjugated the inhabitants, the Subarians. As the Epic of Gilgamesh, an epic poem recounting the deeds of the mythical hero-king Gilgamesh, indicates, rulers were chosen by the army from a hereditary and divinely approved list. The ruler represented a god, and his job was to ensure that the god was satisfied. Rulers fielded armies of 5,000 to 10,000 men who fought in a phalanx, shoulder to shoulder. The Sumerians used copper weapons, spear, and ax. Phalanx tried to break phalanx by shoving, jabbing with the spear, and hacking with the ax. At first, the Sumerians dominated Mesopotamia because their opponents had ill-disciplined, stone-armed forces. In time, however, the Akkadians, Gutians, and Elamites adopted copper weapons and organized tactics. About 1950 B.C.E. a coalition of Subarians, Gutians, and Elamites ravaged Sumer and led the last ruler off as a prisoner.

At the beginning of the second millennium Indo-Europeans tribes invaded the Near East. These tribes had developed the chariot and combined it with the composite bow to produce a highly mobile platform from which they could deliver accurate, rapid fire. The Hittites, the first of these invaders, used the mountains by the Halys River to protect themselves from their enemies before they fanned out to conquer the rest of Anatolia. They viewed war as the only honorable calling for a man. The Aryans formed the military into a separate class, led by the nobility. They organized their army by tribe, clan, and family in units of 180 men. Chariots led the charge and guarded the rear. The chariots did not rush into battle but organized to give each other protection, with the least experienced charioteer encouraged to learn from the more seasoned soldiers.

The Assyrians dominated Mesopotamia in the ninth, eighth, and seventh centuries. They possessed the largest army in the Near East with perhaps 200,000 Assyrians and another 800,000 men drafted from conquered territory. The Assyrians hired mercenaries, replaced the annual call up of militia with a standing army, and organized their kingdom to ensure a sufficient agricultural base to support the chariot and cavalry units on a permanent basis. They were the first to organize regular cavalry units and to use transportation as a tactic. The Persian army was organized, like the Assyrian army, into regiments of 1,000 men further divided into hundreds and 10s. The 10 would form in file, the leader armed with a lance while the other men had bows or swords. The shields were placed in front as wall behind which all could fire their arrows.

The balance of evidence suggests that in premodern warfare the mobilization of manpower mattered more than any other factor in the long run. To get enough men to win combat that was often hand-to-hand fighting, nations recruited

Detail of a Persian soldier from the stairway of the palace of Darius, king of Persia, at Persopolis (modern-day Iran) (Courtesy of the Oriental Institute of the University of Chicago)

THE HORSE

Few battles in Mesopotamia and the Near East were won without the assistance of horses, yet while kings and men are celebrated, horses receive little credit for their military contributions. Domesticated horses were initially believed to be natives of the Zagros Mountains in present-day Iran that spread throughout the Near East while pulling chariots. The currently accepted thinking favors a gradual spread of horse from the Russian steppe, so that the inhabitants of Mesopotamia were familiar with these equines from the third millennium B.C.E. onward.

The horse did not immediately replace the mule or the ass, the common beasts of burden in the ancient Near East. Adoption was slow because of the qualities of the animal. Of all domesticated animals, the horse remains the most temperamental and nervous. An animal of flight rather than fight, the first reaction of a horse to danger is to gallop to a safer place. This tendency presents a problem in battle or when hauling men and materials to a battlefield.

Horses also proved more difficult to train, partly because more is expected from them. Horses pulled wagons, carts, and chariots while holding bone and metal devices in their mouths and tolerating a number of straps and weights on their heads and bodies. When four horses were used for a chariot or wagon, only the two closest horses were yoked, with the two outsiders controlled by reins alone. As herd animals, horses were easier to manage in teams than alone. They were also competitive at speed. The outside horses, feeling less pressure against their throats and less yoke pressure on their necks than the inner animals, would have set the pace for the whole team. During the journey the inner horses would periodically exchange places with those on the outside. The ease of training horses to work together explains the initial popularity of chariots over cavalry. Ridden horses did not become a regular feature of armies in the Near East until the first millennium B.C.E.

from outside their borders. The Sassanian state (224–651 C.E.) in Persia is typical. When Shapur II led his expedition into Mesopotamia in 359 C.E., his army included Armenians, Arabs, Albani, Chionitai, Gelani, Segestani, and others. Some of the armed forces consisted of slaves. There is also a tradition of slave-soldiers in the Arabian peninsula, with such soldiers regularly serving in the armies of the Near East.

Still, actual fighting typically turned on individual set battles. Despite the large size of their empire, the Sassanians fielded small combat units. The small operational units and the need to deal with armed threats in geographically limited zones of confrontations resulted in strategies and plans that were often ad hoc decisions made either by the commander in the field or, given the political dangers of such autonomy, after consultation with the king. The close connection between war and political power put constant pressure on rulers to direct war in person on the field of battle and to prove their worth as monarchs by showing success in war.

Much of the success of a leader rested on the fighting ability of the men under his command. Battle madness of elite warriors is known from the myths of many Near East nations. Berserk warriors, mad for fighting, scorned armor and were among the most feared soldiers. Chiefly swordsmen, they were first identified as fighting in the army of Tukulti-Ninurta, king of Assyria when he defeated the Babylonians in 1228 B.C.E. Tukulti-Ninurta's berserks had armor but threw it off along with their garments in sight of the enemy. The effect on the Babylonians undoubtedly contributed to the victory of the Assyrians.

Fortifications also led to specific types of combat, notably the siege. Siege warfare arose when there was a clearly defined frontier between relatively balanced opposing forces and when large and heavily fortified urban centers were present in the frontier zone. These cities were expensive to attack, limiting the use of siege only to those nations wealthy enough to finance it. When the Roman and Sasanian empires met each other in the great plain between the upper Tigris and Euphrates rivers, both sides wanted the wealth stored in the treasuries of heavily fortified cities controlled by the opposition. Both the Romans and the Sassanians resorted to sieges in the fourth century C.E.

The conflicts followed a close routine for both the besieged and the besiegers. Usually the attacking forces first made a tremendous display of power with the hope of frightening the besieged into surrendering. If this tactic failed, it was usually followed by a parlay in which the besiegers attempted to negotiate the surrender of the city on equitable terms by a mixture of threats and offers of security and safe conduct. If these moves failed, the besiegers then moved to the next step of simultaneous attacks directed at the full circuit of the city's walls. The attackers looked for a weak spot or to induce surrender by demonstrating the seriousness of the besieger's intentions. If this tactic failed, the attackers finally brought in heavy siege equipment and began large-scale mining operations. Throughout this sequence, activity stopped at darkness and resumed at daybreak.

As did the availability of light, weather dictated military tactics. In winter armies retreated from war only to advance when spring returned. Sometimes these responses to natural conditions were translated into traditional cultural prohibitions, such as the time around the spring equinox when Saracens entered a two-month-long sacred period during which they refused to undertake raids against their enemies. The history of warfare in the Near East is one of extreme stability.

There were long periods of peace and a style of combat that remained constant over the centuries.

ASIA AND THE PACIFIC

BY KIRK H. BEETZ

The first Chinese dynasty that historians and archaeologists can confirm was the Shang (c. 1550–1045 B.C.E.). The Shang were a warlike people, constantly trying to expand their territories through conquest and frequently defending their territories against barbarian raiders. The head of the Shang military was the king, and below him were nobles who were expected to be officers. Governors of Shang provinces led military campaigns on their own. Most of the soldiers in a Shang army were peasants, usually poorly equipped and poorly trained. They did most of the dying.

In the Zhou Dynasty (1045–256 B.C.E.) peasants still made up most of a Chinese army, but the elite status of the aristocratic warriors was emphasized. These warriors fought while on horseback. A battle could be very stylized, with nobles showing off their skills in front of assembled armies. In matters of conquest, however, battles could be very serious affairs, with tens of thousands of troops perishing. The Zhou favored fighting one huge, decisive battle rather than several small ones, and a war was often decided in one engagement. The Qin Dynasty (221–207 B.C.E.) changed the way officers were selected, choosing to promote military leaders on the basis of their performance in battle rather than on the basis of noble birth. It was replaced by the Han Dynasty (206 B.C.E.–220 C.E.), which brought order and discipline to its military policies by establishing a clear chain of command that limited the ability of individual commanders to establish their own armies and wage their own wars in pursuit of political power.

For the rest of the ancient era Chinese governments imposed a draft. Every district of China had an official responsible for finding people to serve in the military. The age requirements varied from time to time, but in general any man between the ages of 23 and 56 was expected to serve two years in the army or the small navy. Weapons and armor were usually provided once the new soldiers had marched to where they were expected to serve. They lived in small forts made of brick or stone.

The Great Wall was one long fortress with numerous towers. Each tower had a way to signal that it was under attack, usually by raising flags. Soldiers were expected to help maintain the wall. They lived in barracks behind the wall where armories and food stores were placed near them, also behind the wall. When an emergency arose, soldiers rushed to defend the wall. At other times they were drilled in how to fight in formation and in how to use their armaments. In this way the government ensured that it always had well-disciplined soldiers available for defense and conquest.

In ancient India wars were fought frequently, and the military was an important institution in its kingdoms. Nothing is as yet known about how the Harappan culture (2600–1500 B.C.E.) of the Indus River valley conducted its military affairs. In the 1500s B.C.E. it was overcome by Aryan tribes invading from the north. These tribes had a heroic culture, which means that they celebrated warriors and military heroism over all else. Their elite warriors used chariots.

By the 400s B.C.E. most kingdoms followed a pattern required by tradition and religious law. Any monarch who wished to remain a monarch needed to retain a standing army, because kings were expected to increase their status through war on other kings. They were members of the Kshatriya caste. This caste encompassed warriors and rulers. It was the king's calling to aspire to become a *maharajadhiraja*, a king of kings. He achieved this by forcing other kings to become his vassals. If he became a king of kings, his son would sacrifice a horse in an ancient Vedic ritual, making his father's status official. The king could then aspire to be a *cakravartin*, a king of the world, by expanding his kingdom's frontiers to encompass almost all of the territories of India that he knew to exist.

Every capital city was heavily fortified, because attacks on capitals were often the most direct way for a king to force another monarch to become his vassal. Defensive works could be impressive. A tall earthen wall, sometimes several miles in circumference, would encircle the city. The wall would be patrolled day and night by soldiers, and its gateways would have squads of soldiers stationed at them. Some cities had ditches and wooden barricades outside their walls. Within the city was a fortress that served as the king's residence. He would make his last stand in that fortress if he had to do so.

An Indian army originally was divided into four parts. One was the infantry. The infantry included guild militias. Each guild of tradesmen, members of the Sudra caste, was expected to maintain a militia that could be called to arms to fight bandits, preserve public order, or fight in a war. Another part of the army was the cavalry. This consisted of horsemen mostly from the Kshatriya caste, but it could include members from other castes. A third part of the army consisted of elephants and their handlers. The elephants were covered in armor and ridden by a driver and two or three soldiers, who were armed with arrows or spears. The fourth part of the army consisted of chariots with their drivers and soldiers. A chariot driver sat on the shaft, while as many as three soldiers rode inside the chariot. Maneuvering a chariot on India's frequently muddy battlefields was difficult, and the chariots could not keep up with men on horseback. After the 600s B.C.E. chariots were supplanted by the cavalry.

According to the Chinese, the people of Japan, called the Wa, were very warlike. Archaeologists have found a settlement on the island of Honshu with two ditches dug around it, as if for defense. A Chinese ambassador to the court of Queen Himiko, during the 200s C.E., noted that Himiko's palace was surrounded by a wooden palisade, with fearsome guards at its gates, which suggests that she had at least a small standing army. The Wa were mostly illiterate and apparently left no military records.

In 108 B.C.E. the Chinese established their first Korean colony, the city of Lolang. From Lolang, Chinese customs filtered through Korea, and it may be from the influence of the Chinese that Koreans developed disciplined armies, notable for their courage and their quick maneuverability. The most advanced militaries in Southeast Asia before the medieval era were probably those of Nam Viet and Funan. The Viets came from the area of the Yangtze River, from which some migrated to what is now northern Vietnam and southern China in 333 B.C.E. In 207 B.C.E. they were conquered by a Chinese general who created Nam Viet, meaning "Southern Viet." It is possible its military was organized like the Chinese military. Funan stretched from the Mekong Delta in South Vietnam to central Cambodia, from the 100s to mid 500s C.E. It fought often with tribes in South Vietnam. It had strong ties to India and probably followed Indian military customs. Little is known about military affairs in Oceania before the emergence of a kingdom in Tonga in the medieval era.

EUROPE

BY CARYN E. NEUMANN

In all societies of the ancient world the military played a critical role as the protector and shaper of political and cultural life. While the importance of the military in ancient Europe is well known, little evidence of the military's actual operation has survived the passage of time. The preliterate societies of Europe did not leave written sources, and while the archaeological record provides evidence for warfare in the form of weapons and violent death, it does not reveal much about fighting organizations until relatively late in prehistory.

What is known is that prehistoric societies in Europe generally fought to dominate other groups and to compel their surrender of various forms of wealth. Territorial control was probably not a basic issue, since beyond the level of the farmstead and village there was little sense of fixed political or ethnic boundaries. Most military actions probably involved raiding parties that were composed of individuals who were taking a leave from farming or craft production. After doing their damage and carrying off their booty, they then returned to their normal pursuits.

During the late Neolithic and Early Bronze Age in northern and western Europe, around 2000 B.C.E., there is evidence of the emergence of a warrior aristocracy, an elite group of individuals who shared common values of fighting and ritual feasting and drinking. The archer found buried at Amesbury near Stonehenge with his drinking cup and arrowheads may have been a member of this group, whose burials have been found throughout northwestern Europe. Archaeologists are only beginning to understand the nature of this elite group and its role in Bronze Age society, and at this point it is unclear whether it controlled any significant numbers of specialist fighters.

There is more and more evidence during the Iron Age of the activity of organized raiding parties. In coastal areas these parties moved by boat, and the Hjortspring boat found loaded with shields and swords in Denmark is probably the remains of one such vessel. In fact, it may have belonged to the losers in a confrontation that took place around 350 B.C.E., since the circumstances of this find suggest that it was a victory sacrifice. Many bogs and lakes in northern Europe have yielded large numbers of weapons, some deliberately broken, that were deposited as offerings by victorious fighting groups.

When the Romans entered northern and western Europe, they encountered native armies whose organization and fighting styles were very different from theirs. While the Greeks and Romans embraced a disciplined style of warfare, the ancient peoples of Europe continued to cling to fighting styles that had changed little since the Bronze Age. Styles arose from beliefs and states of mind. These styles became evident in the choice of dress, weaponry, and fighting technique. One style involved berserk warriors. These men, especially common among the Celts, threw off their clothing when entering a trance of recklessness that goaded them to awesome efforts.

Another style of fighting involved the imitation of ferocious animals. European warriors, especially those from the Germanic nations, were entranced by the idea of changing into animals. They sought to have the qualities of animals, such as ferocity, speed, stealth, and the ability to frighten an enemy. Wolves were the most popular warrior model throughout Europe, though boars, bucks, martens, and horses were also common choices. Bear warriors seem to be mostly Germanic, for few are known among the Celtic tribes.

Warriors who imitated animals were useful because, in ancient times, combat was often reduced to brutal hand-to-hand fighting. Warriors dressed as animals believed that they possessed the fighting abilities of those animals, whether wolves or tigers. As a result of such fighting, there was constant pressure to recruit beyond the bounds of one's own ethnic group or state in order to acquire the manpower needed to meet or exceed the enemy's ranks of fighters. The Goths are typical, in that the Goth army that crossed the lower Danube in 376 C.E. consisted of several subethnic groups of Goths (including the Tervingi and Greuthungi) along with Huns and Alans. When Romans fought civil wars, they often recruited so-called barbarians from along the frontier to attack rivals. Alans, Goths, Huns, Iberians, and Isaurians were all recruited on a large scale by the Romans.

The fighting in ancient Europe did not spare civilian populations. Many of the military attacks were simply massacres of people in villages and rural farmsteads for the purpose of terrorizing civilian populations. Rape was part of these attacks. In an era when soldiers did not receive regular pay, soldiers were often recruited with the promise of plunder—including sexual plunder—as their reward. This form of payment was nonetheless regulated because uncontrolled pillage meant, in effect, that the control of the army had been lost. Rape had military value because it wounded the honor of the enemy. Enemy soldiers unable to protect their women suffered a loss of masculinity that affected morale. Conversely, the rapists experienced an elevation of masculinity.

A potential form of overwhelming superior force lay in the use of the chariot, but the genesis of the chariot is still disputed. The invention of key components, such as the wheel, took place in Europe, while various peoples in eastern Europe experimented with light, bentwood, fast, horse-drawn carts. The horse itself originated in the Russian steppes and was first trained in this region. The absence of the horseshoe, however, meant that mounted troops were at a disadvantage when compared with charioteers. Shooting arrows while riding and controlling a galloping horse remained far harder than firing a bow from a speeding chariot until the invention of the stirrup during the first millennium C.E. Only the mounted bowmen from the steppes, notably the Parthians, were to succeed in mastering this difficult skill in the West.

The European style of battle involving both infantry and chariots initially showed little organization. The objective was to reach a suitable place of battle in order to overwhelm the enemy before he could prevail. Essentially, a campaign differed little from a large raid. Maneuver in battle was largely accidental. Sometimes the initial charge of chariots and horsemen would strike terror into the opposite side, in which case battle quickly became a chase, with only the fleetest men escaping the slaughter. More often, the two masses simply converged to carry on the butchery. The Roman style of disciplined warfare spread gradually throughout Europe.

Styles of warfare among the European people did not include sieges. While the Romans had the money to finance such expensive conflicts, the smaller European kingdoms did not have the resources to do so. For the same reason, they generally did not engage in naval warfare. Ethnic groups such as the Goths in the mid-third century C.E. did sometimes seize ships to use for raiding or, more often, simply for transportation. The practice of fortifying settlements and other important locations dates back to Neolithic times. Fortified sites, called *oppida*, were often built in easily defended locations such as hilltops and peninsulas. Earthen ramparts and ditches were supplemented during the Bronze and Iron Ages by timber and stone walls. A common construction technique used by the Celts to build their *oppida* was called the *murus gallicus*, in which heavy timber beams were used to construct a framework between which stone walls were built.

In ancient Europe climate controlled war. Weather imposed seasonal rhythms that dictated periodic campaigning seasons. In Gaul and on the Rhine frontier the war season was signaled by the beginning of summer. In other regions war began with spring. In autumn and winter roads were slippery with ice, and no grass grew that could be used as fodder for horses and mules. These temporal patterns were so well known that they were regularly presented as part of normal tactical advice. But emergencies could alter tactics. The people along the northern frontier of the Roman Empire sometimes found themselves facing midwinter subsistence crises that drove them to enter the developed regions of the empire. In 366 C.E. the Alamanni crossed the Rhine. The Lentienses crossed the same river in 378 C.E. They attacked agricultural settlements to fend off famine. By attacking these settlements, the Lentienses could steal and eat the crops grown by the farmers and avoid starvation.

GREECE

BY MICHAEL M. SAGE

The Mycenaean Period (ca. 1600–ca. 1100 B.C.E.) is the earliest for which there is any evidence for Greek military forces. Greece appears to have been divided into a number of small kingdoms that had their own armies. There is evidence that these kingdoms had central military stores, at least for their chariot forces, and that a class of chariot warriors existed. It is not known whether these men were professional soldiers, nor is it known how they were selected. Equally lacking is any information on how armies of this period fought. Archaeological finds indicate that the heavy thrusting spear was the most common weapon, so it is likely that fighting was done in some sort of close formation. Toward the close of this period there is some evidence for standardization of equipment.

At the end of the Mycenaean Period these kingdoms disappeared, and there was a decline in population. The communities of this time appear to have been small and isolated. Most of the evidence for warfare, apart from weapons finds, is concentrated after 800 B.C.E. and consists of portrayals of combat on pottery and descriptions in the Homeric poems, which probably reflect warfare in the period from 750 to 650 B.C.E.

The fighting forces were led by local chiefs and princes for whom success in warfare was crucial to their standing as leaders. Their war bands were held together by the promise of the rewards they could offer. These bands appear to have been made up of two types of warriors: the nobles, who were relatively well equipped and played a leading part in the fighting, and the mass of poorly armed and poorly protected fighters who followed them. There was mass combat of a relatively open type dominated by missile weapons and the sword, which allowed for individual demonstrations of prowess by the nobles.

A series of important changes marked the end of this so-called dark age around 700 B.C.E. Militarily the most important was the growth of a new kind of community, the city-state, in central and southern Greece. The city-state consisted of an urban core, which served as the political, religious, and economic center, and a dependent countryside of towns and villages. Along with the city-state came the idea of citizenship as a collection of rights and duties, one of which was military service. The strong connection between citizenship and military service is evident in the prohibition of military service for slaves, while in some states full citizenship was reserved only for those who did military service. Given the limited revenues of the communities, citizens were required to serve

The fortifications of Eleutherae, a city in the northern part of Attica, bordering the country of Boeotia (Alison Frantz Photographic Collection, American School of Classical Studies at Athens)

at their own expense, and this restricted military service to those who possessed a minimum amount of property.

The nucleus of this army was a heavy infantry made up of soldiers called hoplites, who were well protected by armor consisting of a bronze helmet, a cuirass that covered the body from waist to neck, and a set of greaves for the shins. A hoplite's main offensive weapon was a heavy thrusting spear. This was used in a rectangular phalanx formation in which the soldiers fighting close together mutually reinforced one another, protecting one another with their large circular shields. Their attacks were launched frontally against other armies that were armed and deployed in the same fashion. The key to victory was to break apart the enemy phalanx. These engagements tended to be sharp and short, and, since there was little in the way of well-thought-out logistics, most campaigns were undertaken either to defend against a neighboring state or to take control of some nearby territory.

There appears to have been no organized cavalry force until the middle of the fifth century B.C.E. After that time the cavalry was drawn from those wealthier citizens who could afford to maintain horses. The poorer citizens served as light-armed troops who used missile weapons, especially javelins. These troops were used to open the battle and to cover the movements of the hoplites, who, as the heavy infantry, were the decisive force. In areas of Greece that did not form city-states, older styles of open fighting continued.

Outside Sparta there is little evidence for training methods before the end of the fourth century. There must have been some instruction in marching in formation, but it seems that training in the use of weapons was left to the individual. The Spartans were an exception to this part-time soldiering. All full male citizens were trained and served as full-time soldiers. A rigorous course of physical hardening lasted from the age of six to 18 in groups that segregated the boys from normal family life. Weapons training and marching training were included and repeated when on campaign. In some other city-states there were special formations of hoplites that seem to have received special training, but Sparta remained unique in fielding a professional army. That advantage allowed it to become the preeminent land power and to create a military alliance in the Peloponnese that further strengthened its dominance.

Greeks serving as mercenaries are known as early as the seventh century B.C.E. For the most part that service was performed in the Near East. There are occasional references to small groups of mercenaries serving in the homeland, but it is not until the Peloponnesian War (431–404 B.C.E.), fought between Athens and the Peloponnesian League (led by Sparta), that there is evidence for large numbers. Mercenaries were predominantly drawn from the poor regions of Greece, such as Arcadia and Achaea; specialist troops, especially from Thrace, were also used. The fourth century saw a rise in the demand for mercenaries as a result of the increased use of light-armed troops whose style of fighting required long training to be effective. In the Hellenistic Period (323–31 B.C.E.) the armies of all the major Greek kingdoms except for Macedonia consisted of mercenaries who served for life, and attempts were made to retain their loyalty by granting them areas for settlement and right to land.

Before the Peloponnesian War the tactics of hoplite battle had been relatively simple. Dense arrays of soldiers in rectangular phalanx formation each attempted to break the order of the opposing phalanx to achieve victory. The simple nature of such encounters was marked by the absence of reserves—since massing men added to the impact of the charge—and by the participation in the fighting of the commander who, once he arrayed his men, had nothing do to but serve as an example to them. But by the last phase of the Peloponnesian War more complicated tactics had been developed by the Spartans. They attempted to use their right wing to encircle the enemy's left and to roll up their phalanx.

By the 370s the Thebans had developed a tactic to counter the Spartan outflanking maneuver by massing their left wing very deeply, up to 50 men in contrast to the normal depth of eight. These changes in tactics were accompanied by the first use of reserves. The Peloponnesian War also saw a further development in the use of combined arms, a strategy that was to develop extensively in the fourth century in smaller encounters. Normally a phalanx of hoplites was used to hold the enemy heavy infantry while it was worn down by repeated attacks of light-armed troops and cavalry. The effective use of combined arms in set-piece battles came with the Macedonians and Alexander the Great. Alexander used the oblique advance first developed by the Thebans to thin the enemy line and, while holding it with his phalanx, delivered the crucial blow on a weak point with his cavalry. In the period after Alexander there was a shift back to the heavy infantry as the decisive arm, given the expense of maintaining cavalry.

Hoplite armies were poorly adapted for siege warfare, and so city fortification remained relatively simple through the fourth century B.C.E. with some exceptions. Often the fortification consisted of a simple vertical wall made of sun-dried brick on a stone foundation with square towers placed at varying intervals. In the fifth century there was an expansion of fortification from the acropolis to cover the entire urban area. Another major innovation of the mid-fifth century were the Long Walls at Athens (which was dependent on the sea for much of its grain supply), which ran from the city to its harbor at Piraeus and provided a secure connection to the sea. In the next century and continuing into the Hellenistic Period, border forts and fortifications appear and become increasingly complex. The same period also saw an increase in the height of towers and the use of tower platforms for artillery, an innovation that had begun in the course of the fourth century. Ditches also appear with increasing frequency as a means to keep the attackers' siege equipment as far from the walls as possible.

ROME

BY MICHAEL M. SAGE

The earliest Roman army consisted of 3,000 infantry and 300 cavalry with each of the three Roman tribes supplying 1,000 infantry and 100 cavalry. Nothing is known about how this army was gathered or in what manner it fought. It was a militia of citizen-soldiers, as were all later Roman armies until the end of the Republic in 27 B.C.E.

Around 550 B.C.E. a census of property was instituted for all male citizens, and those above a certain minimum level of wealth were obliged to serve while they were between the ages of 17 and 46. The size and amount of a man's property also determined whether he would serve as a heavy-armed or light-armed infantryman or in the cavalry. All service was at the individual's own expense until the beginning of the fifth century, when the state instituted a tax to defray expenses. Each citizen had to complete 16 campaigns in the infantry or 10 in the cavalry. This system remained in force until the end of the first century B.C.E., though requirements changed over time. The introduction of the census was related to the adoption of the phalanx, a densely packed array of soldiers composed of citizens wealthy enough to equip themselves fully. These heavily armed infantry soldiers were protected by metal helmets, breastplates, and large round shields and armed with heavy thrusting spears as their main offensive weapon.

The army was assembled and led by the consuls, the chief executive officers of the Roman state, who were popularly elected. Lesser magistrates with imperium, or the power to command, and proconsuls—those magistrates whose imperium had been extended after their year in office—held independent commands. These generals were assisted by a junior elected official, the quaestor, whose job it was to provide supplies for the army, and by military tribunes who acted as general assistants to the commander. The army was organized in units called *legions*, which in the mid-second century B.C.E. consisted of 3,000 heavy armed infantry, 1,200 light-armed infantry, and 300 cavalry. The number of legions increased over time. In the civil wars of the mid-first century B.C.E. as many as 60 legions were in service. A consul normally commanded an army of two legions and a praetor a single legion. Later armies commanded by proconsuls could be much larger. Caesar in Gaul from 58 to 49 B.C.E. eventually had an army of 14 legions. In addition to Roman citizens, each Roman force included allied Italian cavalry and infantry organized in their own formations and serving under Roman commanders. Normally the number of allied infantry equaled the citizen infantry; the number of allied cavalry was considerably larger.

In the course of the fourth century Roman tactics underwent a major change. In place of the phalanx the army was now organized in three separate lines. In front were the *hastati*, then the *principes*, and finally the *triarii*. Men were assigned to each of these lines on the basis of age, with the youngest men assigned to the front line. Each line consisted of 10 units called *maniples*, which were small phalanx-like formations. In the front two lines the maniples were 120 men strong, divided into two parts called *centuries*, while the maniples of the rear line were half that size at 60 men. Each century was commanded by an appointed officer, the centurion, and the entire maniple was under the orders of the senior of the two centurions. The centurions were the backbone of the army, and its performance in the field depended on them. The main offensive weapons were the javelin and the short stabbing and thrusting sword. (The third line retained the heavy thrusting spear.) The light-armed troops, numbering 1,200, supplemented the 3,000 heavy infantry of the legion.

On the battlefield the maniples of the legion were arranged in checkerboard fashion. The maniples of the first line were separated by gaps from one another. The maniples of the second line covered the gaps in the first line, and the maniples of third line covered the gaps in the second. These gaps permitted the maniples to operate independently and allowed those in front to withdraw to the rear, so that the enemy was faced with fresh troops. Allied troops who gradually adopted Roman equipment and tactics were normally placed on each wing of the legions with the cavalry covering the right and left ends of the battle line.

Several important changes had taken place before the end of the first century in the equipment and structure of the army. By about 100 B.C.E. the *triarii* were armed in the same fashion as the other lines. Next, the basic tactical unit on the battlefield changed from the maniple to the cohort, a unit of between 500 and 600 men. The size of the legion also increased to 6,000 men.

After 88 B.C.E. the Italians became Roman citizens and served in the legions or in the Roman cavalry. Roman cavalry and light infantry disappeared after 100 B.C.E. and were replaced by units from Rome's empire or allied states. As the empire grew, Roman soldiers began serving for prolonged periods far from home. These extended absences were incompatible with a civilian militia system, and the army gradually became professionalized. Finally, the loyalty of the legions became detached from the state and focused on the various army commanders. This resulted in a period of intense civil war lasting for about 20 years (49–31 B.C.E.) and led to the establishment of a military monarchy.

Under the first emperor Augustus (r. 27 B.C.E.–14 C.E.) the army became completely professionalized, with service standing at 25 years. This professional army was stationed along the distant frontiers of the empire. There were now two types of troops: the legionaries, who were Roman citizens, and the auxiliaries, who were noncitizens but who could gain citizenship at the end of their service. In addition to heavy infantry that fought along with the legions, the auxiliaries provided specialist troops such as archers and most of the cavalry. By 14 C.E. the army totaled 300,000 men divided among 25 legions and an equal number of auxiliaries. The number of legions increased until by 200 C.E. there were 33. Under the empire for the first time troops were stationed in the city of Rome, of which the best known were the nine cohorts of the Praetorian Guard, whose main tasks were to guard the emperor and to keep the peace in the city. The emperor was closely tied to the army, and its loyalty to him provided the basis of his power.

Marble statue of a youth on horseback and wearing a military cloak, Roman, made in Italy (ca. 1–50 C.E.) (© The Trustees of the British Museum)

With the professionalization of the army came the professionalization of training. During the Republic there was no formal system of training either before entry or during campaigns. A commander decided whether to train his troops, and most soldiers seemed to have learned their weapons skills on their own initiative. Under the empire a formal training system was instituted within the army. Specialists with military rank were employed to teach basic skills. These remained the same as they had been earlier; physical toughening, marching in formation, care of equipment, and weapons drill. This training was one of the keys to Roman military success, as it instilled a level of discipline and expertise that Rome's enemies normally could not match.

The earliest Roman military fortification was the marching camp, which was constructed daily while the army was en route. The basic fortification consisted of three parts: a ditch, an earthen wall inside of the ditch constructed of the dirt removed from the ditch, and a wooden palisade built on top of the wall from stakes carried by the legionaries. This was not meant as a permanent fort but as temporary protection and was destroyed as the army marched. Toward the end of the first century C.E. permanent stone fortresses replaced the earlier earth and wood structures but kept their basic plan. This reflected the now-static positioning of the legions. Also in this period separate stone forts for housing units of auxiliaries appeared. At the same time much larger fortifications, such as Hadrian's Wall that separated the Roman province of Britain from unconquered Scotland, were built. In the third and fourth centuries C.E. forts and other fortifications became more elaborate in response to increased military threats. Stone was standard, and towers and elaborate gate defenses were constructed.

THE AMERICAS

BY J. J. GEORGE

An organized military, like other developed social institutions, implies a sophisticated authority structure often attributed to advanced societies and is thus linked to the origin of civilization. Nonstate entities typically show less military organization than formal states and rely more on a warrior culture in which every male in society is a serviceable militia member. Arguably, military institutions may be necessary for the transition to state organization and civilized life. Whatever their causal role, military institutions lie very close to the core of civilizations as they have developed. In the Americas fully developed militaries recognizable to modern eyes—state-supported institutions operating in an occurrence of violence to pursue political goals—emerged only toward the end of the ancient period, while earlier military practice took rudimentary but recognizable forms.

The earliest American military institutions probably developed around 1000 B.C.E. among the Olmec in Mexico's Gulf Coast region. The Olmec, an early state or semistate, introduced specialized weaponry, such as maces, exclusive to warring as they pursued expansion. Taking prisoners was tied to political rulership, and kingly responsibilities assumed a military quotient, as indicated by depictions of Olmec kings with bound captives. Defensive tactics are evidenced by a site called La Oaxaqueña, south of the major Olmec settlement of San Lorenzo, which was encircled by a ditch about 30 feet deep by 50 feet wide, probably made for fortification purposes.

Easily defensible and further fortified, the Zapotec mountaintop site of Monte Albán, above what is contemporary Oaxaca, Mexico, was a naturally defensive position, which made it an obvious choice of stronghold. Its central location also helped to unify three converging valleys. Conquest bas-relief monuments at the site, often referred as *los danzantes*, testify to military activity. Similarly, there is evidence of the burning of villages and sacrifice of prisoners cut in stone by 600 B.C.E.—evidence, again, of military progressiveness tied to military expansion. Further evidence of military activity can be found in architectural constructions at Zapotec-affiliated sites called Quiotepec and La Coyatera, where garrisons were built expressly for housing military units with the singular intention of ensuring control over more distant territory. Evidence suggests, however, that the Zapotec military was later based on nobles and lacked standardized weaponry, indicating a lack of command structure and organized units that could fight in formation.

By 500 C.E. at Teotihuacán, often considered the earliest true city and empire in the Americas, a broad military architecture was well in place that indicated a highly organized state bureaucracy. Fortified walls within the city acted both as a partition defining social boundaries within the city and as a defensive mechanism protecting the city limits. The artistic record also provides insight into the nature of Teotihuacán's military. Warriors are depicted wielding atlatls and rectangular shields or thrusting spears and bucklers. The depictions suggest the use of standardized weaponry, which typically indicates state control, formations, and complementary arms use. For example, the atlatlists would engage the enemy with projectile fire, and then the spearmen would close in hand-to-hand combat.

Murals depict gaily clad warriors as eagle and jaguar deities bearing elaborate knives on the ends of which are stuck bleeding hearts, which is suggestive both of a growing war cult and of sacrificial practices meant to indulge the gods, a ritual especially common later in Mesoamerica among the 15th- and 16th-century Aztec. Military recruitment apparently extended to all classes of society, and with military service came the possibility of upward class mobility. Mass recruitment is reflected in standardized weapons and suggests that training must have been standardized and carried out by military societies, formal schools, or a combination of both.

At the peak of Teotihuacán's power, its military armaments underwent profound and standardized changes. Spun-cotton body armor and helmets were introduced to protect the head, body, and limbs. Some scholars have tied the sudden increase in the use of cotton to acceleration in the downfall of Teotihuacán because the state could not afford to provide armor to everyone. After 500 C.E. Teotihuacán began to decline, and in the ensuing power vacuum regional centers emerged, all on hilltops and fortified, including Xochicalco, Cacaxtla, and Teotenango.

Among the ancient Maya the military was largely an enterprise of the nobility with small forces, no apparent chain of command, no standardized weaponry, and no drill-formation combat. Raids rather than battles occurred first to legitimate kings and their right to rule and, second, to gain tributaries and labor rather than to conquer and control foreign centers or cities. Scholars suggest that raiding included burning enemy villages and killing their defenders but rarely annexing land. Similarly, prior to broad agricultural-related settlement, early hunter-gatherers probably limited warfare to occasional raids in which men used stone tools as weapons and sought booty and glory rather than territorial conquest.

Scholars suggest that technological innovation of almost every kind has historically answered more to military purpose than commonly allowed, and that this is not simply a matter of technological change fostered by wartime demands. The impact and demands of a specific war or war in general, especially as it outgrows simpler warrior societies, is a powerful and persistent social force. Similarly, changing technologies, whether or not they are explicitly military, exert profound institutional effects. What archaeological data there are for North America provide only a glimpse of the most rudimentary technology in the form of projectile points dating from approximately 10,000 B.C.E. Because they were too large to be arrow points, they must have been spear points used to hunt mammoth and possibly for primitive warfare. A hunter-gatherer paradigm of isolated raiding probably best describes military action for much of the ancient period, with changes occurring in areas where agricultural settlement took hold and prompted reorganization of a basic defensive nature. Although evidence exists that suggests primitive warfare, little evidence has been found to indicate the presence of organized military institutions in North America in ancient times.

In South America some of the clearest evidence of military activity in the first few centuries C.E. comes in the form of Moche and Nazca painted vessels showing warriors and war-related scenarios. The two civilizations were contemporaneous but centered in different parts of Peru. Stylistic similarities between the two in later painted vessels are still being decoded in terms of the relationship between their respective iconographies, though it is safe to say that military and conquest activity is portrayed in the narratives of some vessels and thus was an active part of society.

See also AGRICULTURE; ARCHITECTURE; ART; BORDERS AND FRONTIERS; CLIMATE AND GEOGRAPHY; EMPIRES AND DYNASTIES; FESTIVALS; FOREIGNERS AND BARBARIANS; HUNTING, FISHING, AND GATHERING; PANDEMICS AND EPIDEMICS; RELIGION AND COSMOLOGY; RESISTANCE AND DISSENT; SEAFARING AND NAVIGATION; SHIPS AND SHIPBUILDING; TRADE AND EXCHANGE; WAR AND CONQUEST; WEAPONRY AND ARMOR.

Asia and the Pacific

Sun Tzu: Excerpt from "The Art of War" (sixth century B.C.E.)

IX. The Army on the March

1. Sun Tzu said: We come now to the question of encamping the army, and observing signs of the enemy. Pass quickly over mountains, and keep in the neighborhood of valleys.

2. Camp in high places, facing the sun. Do not climb heights in order to fight. So much for mountain warfare.

3. After crossing a river, you should get far away from it.

4. When an invading force crosses a river in its onward march, do not advance to meet it in midstream. It will be best to let half the army get across and then deliver your attack.

5. If you are anxious to fight, you should not go to meet the invader near a river which he has to cross.

6. Moor your craft higher up than the enemy and facing the sun. Do not move upstream to meet the enemy. So much for river warfare.

7. In crossing salt-marshes, your sole concern should be to get over them quickly, without any delay.

8. If forced to fight in a salt marsh, you should have water and grass near you and get your back to a clump of trees. So much for operations in salt marshes.

9. In dry, level country, take up an easily accessible position with rising ground to your right and on your rear, so that the danger may be in front, and safety lie behind. So much for campaigning in flat country.

10. These are the four useful branches of military knowledge which enabled the Yellow Emperor to vanquish four several sovereigns.

11. All armies prefer high ground to low and sunny places to dark.

12. If you are careful of your men and camp on hard ground, the army will be free from disease of every kind, and this will spell victory.

13. When you come to a hill or a bank, occupy the sunny side, with the slope on your right rear. Thus you will at once act for the benefit of your soldiers and utilize the natural advantages of the ground.

14. When, in consequence of heavy rains up-country, a river which you wish to ford is swollen and flecked with foam, you must wait until it subsides.

15. Country in which there are precipitous cliffs with torrents running between, deep natural hollows, confined places, tangled thickets, quagmires and crevasses should be left with all possible speed and not approached.

16. While we keep away from such places, we should get the enemy to approach them; while we face them, we should let the enemy have them on his rear.

17. If in the neighborhood of your camp there should be any hilly country, ponds surrounded by aquatic grass, hollow basins filled with reeds, or woods with thick undergrowth, they must be carefully routed out and searched; for these are places where men in ambush or insidious spies are likely to be lurking.

18. When the enemy is close at hand and remains quiet, he is relying on the natural strength of his position.

19. When he keeps aloof and tries to provoke a battle, he is anxious for the other side to advance.

20. If his place of encampment is easy of access, he is tendering bait.

21. Movement amongst the trees of a forest shows that the enemy is advancing. The appearance of a number of screens in the midst of thick grass means that the enemy wants to make us suspicious.

22. The rising of birds in their flight is the sign of an ambuscade. Startled beasts indicate that a sudden attack is coming.

23. When there is dust rising in a high column, it is the sign of chariots advancing; when the dust is low but spread over a wide area, it betokens the approach of infantry. When it branches out in different directions, it shows that parties have been sent to collect firewood. A few clouds of dust moving to and fro signify that the army is encamping.

24. Humble words and increased preparations are signs that the enemy is about to advance. Violent language and driving forward as if to the attack are signs that he will retreat.

25. When the light chariots come out first and take up a position on the wings, it is a sign that the enemy is forming for battle.

26. Peace proposals unaccompanied by a sworn covenant indicate a plot.

(continued)

(continues)

27. When there is much running about and the soldiers fall into rank, it means that the critical moment has come.

28. When some are seen advancing and some retreating, it is a lure.

29. When the soldiers stand leaning on their spears, they are faint from want of food.

30. If those who are sent to draw water begin by drinking themselves, the army is suffering from thirst.

31. If the enemy sees an advantage to be gained and makes no effort to secure it, the soldiers are exhausted.

32. If birds gather on any spot, it is unoccupied. Clamor by night betokens nervousness.

33. If there is disturbance in the camp, the general's authority is weak. If the banners and flags are shifted about, sedition is afoot. If the officers are angry, it means that the men are weary.

34. When an army feeds its horses with grain and kills its cattle for food, and when the men do not hang their cooking pots over the campfires, showing that they will not return to their tents, you may know that they are determined to fight to the death.

From: Lionel Giles, trans., *Sun Tzŭ on the Art of War, the Oldest Military Treatise in the World* (London: Luzac and Co., 1910).

Greece

Xenophon: "The Spartan War Machine" (ca. 375 B.C.E.)

In the first instance, the ephors announce in proclamation the limit of age to which the service applies for cavalry and heavy infantry; and, in the next place, for the various artisans. So that, even on campaign, the Spartans are well supplied with all the conveniences enjoyed by people living as citizens at Sparta. All the implements and instruments whatsoever which an army may need in common are ordered to be in readiness, some on wagons and others on baggage animals. In this way anything omitted can hardly escape detection.

For the actual encounter under arms, the following inventions are attributed to Lycurgos: the soldier has a crimson-colored uniform and a heavy shield of bronze, his theory being that such equipment has no sort of feminine association and is altogether most warrior-like. It is most quickly burnished; it is least readily soiled. He further permitted those who were about the age of early manhood to wear their hair long. For so, he conceived, they would appear of larger stature, more free and indomitable, and of a more terrible aspect. So furnished and accoutered, he divided his hoplites into six *morai* [regiments] of cavalry and heavy infantry. Each of these hoplite *morai* has one *polemarchos* [colonel], four *lochagoi* [captains], eight *penteconters* [lieutenants], and sixteen *enomotarchs* [sergeants]. At a word of command any such *morai* can be formed readily into either *enomoties* [single file], or into threes [three files of men abreast] or sixes [six files of men abreast].

As to the idea, commonly entertained, that the tactical arrangement of the Spartan heavy infantry is highly complicated, no conception could be more opposed to facts. For in the Spartan order the front-rank men are all leaders, so that each file has everything necessary to play its part efficiently. In fact, this disposition is so easy to understand that no one who can distinguish one human being from another can fail to follow it. One set have the privilege of leaders, the other the duty of followers. The evolutional orders by which greater depth or shallowness is given to the battle line are given by word of mouth, by the *enomotarch*, and they cannot be mistaken. None of these maneuvers presents any difficulty whatsoever to the understanding.

I will now speak of the mode of encampment, sanctioned by the regulation of Lycurgos. To avoid the waste incidental to the angles of the square, the encampment, according to him, should be circular, except where there was the security of a hill or fortification or where they had a river in the rear. He had sentinels posted during the day along the place of arms and facing inwards; since they are appointed not so much for the sake of the enemy as to keep an eye on friends. The enemy is sufficiently watched by mounted troopers perched on various points commanding the widest prospects. To guard against hostile approach by night, sentinel duty according to the ordinance was performed by the *sciritai* outside the main body. At the present time the rule is so far modified that the duty is entrusted to foreigners, if there be a foreign contingent present, with a leaven of Spartans to keep them company. The custom of always taking their spears with them when they go their rounds must certainly be attributed to the same cause which makes them exclude their slaves from a place of arms. . . . The need of precaution is the whole explanation. The frequency with which they change their encampment is another point. It is done quite as much for the sake of benefiting their friends as annoying their enemies.

Further, the law enjoins upon all Spartans, during the whole period of the campaign, the constant practice of gymnastic exercises, whereby their pride in themselves is increased, and they appear freer and of a more liberal aspect than the rest of the world. The walk and the running grounds must not exceed in length the space covered by a *morai*, so that one may not find himself far from his own stand of arms. After the gymnastic exercises, the senior *polemarchos* gives the order by herald to be seated. This serves all the purposes of inspection. After this the order is given "To get breakfast," and for "The outpost to be relieved." After this, again, come pastimes and relaxations before the evening exercises, after which the herald's cry is heard "To take the evening meal." When they have sung a hymn to the gods to whom the offerings of happy omen have been performed, the final order, "Retire to rest at the place of arms," is given.

From: Fred Fling, ed., *A Source Book of Greek History* (Boston: D. C. Heath, 1907).

Rome

Josephus, "The Roman Army in the First Century C.E." (ca. 75 C.E.)

Book 3, Chapter 5 Description of the Roman Armies and Roman Camps

. . . 2. As for what is within the camp, it is set apart for tents, but the outward circumference hath the resemblance to a wall and is adorned with towers at equal distances, where between the towers stand the engines for throwing arrows and darts, and for slinging stones, and where they lay all other engines that can annoy the enemy, all ready for their several operations. They also erect four gates, one at every side of the circumference, and those large enough for the entrance of the beasts, and wide enough for making excursions, if occasion should require. They divide the camp within into streets, very conveniently, and place the tents of the commanders in the middle; but in the very midst of all is the general's own tent, in the nature of a temple, insomuch, that it appears to be a city built on the sudden, with its marketplace, and place for handicraft trades, and with seats for the officers superior and inferior, where, if any differences arise, their causes are heard and determined. The camp, and all that is in it, is encompassed with a wall round about, and that sooner than one would imagine, and this by the multitude and the skill of the laborers; and, if occasion require, a trench is drawn round the whole, whose depth is four cubits, and its breadth equal.

3. When they have thus secured themselves, they live together by companies, with quietness and decency, as are all their other affairs managed with good order and security. Each company hath also their wood, and their corn, and their water brought them, when they stand in need of them; for they neither sup nor dine as they please themselves singly, but all together. Their times also for sleeping, and watching, and rising are notified beforehand by the sound of trumpets, nor is any thing done without such a signal; and in the morning the soldiery go every one to their centurions, and these centurions to their tribunes, to salute them; with whom all the superior officers go to the general of the whole army, who then gives them of course the watchword and other orders, to be by them cared to all that are under

(continued)

(continues)

their command; which is also observed when they go to fight, and thereby they turn themselves about on the sudden, when there is occasion for making sallies, as they come back when they are recalled in crowds also.

4. Now when they are to go out of their camp, the trumpet gives a sound, at which time nobody lies still, but at the first intimation they take down their tents, and all is made ready for their going out; then do the trumpets sound again, to order them to get ready for the march; then do they lay their baggage suddenly upon their mules, and other beasts of burden, and stand, as at the place of starting, ready to march; when also they set fire to their camp, and this they do because it will be easy for them to erect another camp, and that it may not ever be of use to their enemies. Then do the trumpets give a sound the third time that they are to go out, in order to excite those that on any account are a little tardy, that so no one may be out of his rank when the army marches. Then does the crier stand at the general's right hand, and asks them thrice, in their own tongue, whether they be now ready to go out to war or not? To which they reply as often, with a loud and cheerful voice, saying, "We are ready." And this they do almost before the question is asked them: they do this as filled with a kind of martial fury, and at the same time that they so cry out, they lift up their right hands also. . . .

8. This account I have given the reader, not so much with the intention of commending the Romans, as of comforting those that have been conquered by them, and for the deterring others from attempting innovations under their government. This discourse of the Roman military conduct may also perhaps be of use to such of the curious as are ignorant of it, and yet have a mind to know it. I return now from this digression.

From: Flavius Josephus, *The Complete Works of the Learned and Authentic Jewish Historian, Flavius Josephus,* Vol. 3, *The Jewish War,* trans. William Whiston (London: J. G. Murdoch, 1870?).

FURTHER READING

Alfred S. Bradford, *With Arrow, Sword, and Spear: A History of Warfare in the Ancient World* (Westport, Conn.: Praeger, 2001).

John Carman and Anthony Harding, eds., *Ancient Warfare: Archaeological Perspectives* (Stroud, U.K.: Sutton, 1999).

Peter Connolly, *Greece and Rome at War* (Hong Kong: Prentice-Hall, 1981).

Arthur Cotterell, *Chariot: From Chariot to Tank, the Astounding Rise and Fall of the World's First War Machine* (Woodstock, N.Y.: Overlook Press, 2004).

Robert Cowley and Geoffrey Parker, eds., *The Reader's Companion to Military History* (New York: Houghton Mifflin, 1996).

Pierre Ducrey, *Warfare in Ancient Greece*, trans. Janet Lloyd (New York: Schocken Books, 1986).

Dave Eggenberger, *An Encyclopedia of Battles: Accounts of over 1,560 Battles from 1579 B.C. to the Present* (New York: Dover Publications, 1985).

Katie Emblem et al., eds., *Dictionary of Ancient and Medieval Warfare* (Mechanicsburg, Pa.: Stackpole Books, 1998).

Clive Foss and David Winfield, *Byzantine Fortifications: An Introduction* (Pretoria: University of South Africa Press, 1986).

Yvon Garlan, *War in the Ancient World* (London: Chatto and Windus, 1975).

Adrian Goldsworthy, *Roman Warfare* (London: Cassell and Co., 2002).

Andrea Gnirs, "Ancient Egypt," in *War and Society in the Ancient and Medieval Worlds: Asia, the Mediterranean, Europe, and Mesoamerica*, ed. Kurt Raaflaub and Nathan Rosenstein (Cambridge, Mass.: Harvard University Press, 1999).

Victor D. Hanson, *The Western Way of War: Infantry Battle in Classical Greece*, 2nd ed. (Berkeley: University of California Press, 2000).

Ross Hassig, *War and Society in Ancient Mesoamerica* (Berkeley: University of California Press, 1992).

John Keegan, *A History of Warfare* (New York: Random House, 1993).

Lawrence H. Keeley, *War before Civilization* (New York: Oxford University Press, 1996).

Lawrence Keppie, *The Making of the Roman Army* (New York: Barnes and Noble, 1984).

John F. Lazenby, *The Spartan Army* (Warminster, U.K.: Aris and Phillips, 1985).

Daithi O'Hogain, *Celtic Warriors: The Armies of One of the First Great Peoples in Europe* (New York: St. Martin's Press, 1999).

Daniel Pipes, *Slave Soldiers and Islam: The Genesis of a Military System* (New Haven, Conn.: Yale University Press, 1981).

John Rich and Graham Shipley, eds., *War and Society in the Roman World* (London and New York: Routledge, 1993).

Michael M. Sage, *Warfare in Ancient Greece: A Sourcebook* (London and New York: Routledge, 1996).

Alan R. Schulman, "Military Organization in Pharaonic Egypt," in *Civilizations of the Ancient Near East*, ed. J. M. Sasson (New York: Scribner's, 1995).

Ian Shaw, "Battle in Ancient Egypt: The Triumph of Horus or the Cutting Edge of the Temple Economy?" in *Battle in Antiquity*, ed. Alan Lloyd (London: Duckworth in association with the Classical Press of Wales, 1996).

Hans Van Wees, *Greek Warfare: Myth and Reality* (London: Duckworth, 2004).

Graham Webster, *The Roman Imperial Army*, 3rd ed. (Totowa, N.J.: Barnes and Noble, 1985).

▶ mining, quarrying, and salt making

INTRODUCTION

Throughout the ancient world people engaged in an endless quest for resources to make their lives a little more comfortable and secure. Food, of course, was at the top of the list, followed by fuel. But once these material needs had been met, the ancients turned their attention to extracting resources out of the earth. They used the materials they found there, including stone, minerals, and metal ores, to make tools, buildings, weapons, and decorative objects. The result was the development of civilizations that were far advanced over those of primitive hunter-gatherer bands.

The Stone Age was defined by ancient peoples' ability to make tools and weapons from stone. The earliest humans used whatever stones lay at hand on the earth's surface, but in time they learned to quarry stone. Historians, archaeologists, and tourists continue to be amazed at the massive stone construction projects carried out in the ancient Americas, Egypt, Mesopotamia, Asia, Greece, and Rome. Using such stone as limestone, basalt, obsidian, marble, and sandstone, the ancients were able to quarry massive blocks of stone, transport them, and raise them into position to create some of the world's most breathtaking monuments, such as the pyramids of Egypt. Meanwhile, they used these and other stones to make tools, weapons, and artwork. Various minerals, too, were used in the production of artwork, jewelry, and religious artifacts, primarily because these minerals were soft and workable and because their colors were aesthetically pleasing.

The emergence of metal and metalworking, however, changed the nature of ancient toolmaking. The earliest metal used extensively was copper. Later, bronze, an alloy of copper and tin, became the favored metal because it was harder than copper. While copper and tin are relatively abundant, iron ore is much more abundant, so following the Bronze Age was the Iron Age, when iron—and, in time, hardened steel—were used in toolmaking. Particularly in Europe, where iron ore was extremely abundant, iron dominated mining in such areas as modern-day Austria and Switzerland. Precious metals such as gold and silver were mined to make jewelry and similar goods. Extracting these metals from the earth required backbreaking labor, carried out with stone hammers, chisels, shovels, picks, levers, and other simple tools. Because the nature of the work was so difficult, it is likely that slaves, criminals, and prisoners of war were often used.

In addition to stone and metal the ancients needed salt. Salt is necessary in the diet, but it was also was used in food preservation. So important was salt that the ancient Romans often paid soldiers with salt—the origin of the modern word *salary*—and salt trading was such a profitable business that some trade routes around the Mediterranean Sea were built primarily to transport salt. In some cultures, small amounts of salt could be extracted from ocean water through evaporation. More valuable were salt mines, where large amounts of salt could be extracted. Salt mining differs from rock mining and stone quarrying primarily because salt dissolves in water. It could therefore be allowed to dissolve to create a brine, which was then pumped out of the mine into shallow cisterns, where the water would evaporate, leaving behind the salt.

AFRICA

BY JUSTIN CORFIELD

In ancient times peoples all over Africa were involved in mining for precious metals, such as gold and silver, and also for copper and iron. The great trading empire of the Carthaginians, based in modern-day Tunisia, was heavily involved in mining ventures along the North African coastline, and its expeditions in Africa may have been in search of more minerals. Certainly some of the Carthaginians' naval expeditions to the west coast of Africa had this in mind, and it is known that they secured gold from mines in modern-day Senegal, though much of the wealth of Carthage came from silver mines in what is now Spain. Gold was also mined at an early date in Sofala, in modern-day Mozambique, and Kilwa, in modern-day Tanzania, but the massive gold and copper deposits in southern Africa in modern-day Democratic Republic of Congo, Zambia, and Zimbabwe were not used until between 800 and 1000 C.E.

The first excavations of both copper and iron in Saharan Africa took place at similar times, according to archaeological evidence. This is somewhat contradictory, because there is a relative abundance of ironworkings throughout the continent while copper deposits are scarce in many parts. Across the continent, however, the transfer of technology was very gradual. That transfer clearly started in North Africa with the Egyptians and the Carthaginians, who used minerals before other African peoples. The Egyptians seem to have begun using iron after the Assyrians manufactured it and used it in battle against them. The Carthaginians developed iron from Phoenician settlers, who regularly used and traded metals. Gradually the use of iron spread into Nubia, where there were large deposits of iron ore that was then turned into iron to satisfy the demand for the metal in Egypt.

The technique of smelting iron ore seems to have spread gradually from Egypt and Nubia. People at two locations, the southwestern and the central part of the Sahara, were involved in mining copper from the first half of the first millennium B.C.E., with iron being smelted in the Sudan at about the same time. Certainly in the kingdom of Meroë in modern-day Sudan, from 650 until 350 B.C.E., the local people were familiar with working iron. This indicates that technology was being transferred by land contact, but the next area that seems to have worked iron was in modern-day Zimbabwe, where some of the settlements show stones cut with the help of iron tools. It therefore seems likely that the methods of mining iron ore and smelting it may have come from traders working their way down the East African coast. Seeming to confirm this, some ironworkings from the same period have been found at Hydrax Hill, near Nakuru in Kenya.

Some scholars believe that both the technologies of mining minerals and producing metals from them were used by tribal chiefs and ruling oligarchies to establish control over regions and to dominate trade. For these reasons some tribes in Africa kept their methods of smelting secret, giving them a trade or military advantage over their neighbors.

In West Africa, by about 500 B.C.E., the Nok culture in what is now northern Nigeria was also involved in the use of metals. The Nok tended to use iron for weapons and agricultural tools, with copper preferred for making ornaments or decorative and symbolic items. It is possible that the techniques of mining for minerals came by land to the Nok's inland civilization across the Sahara, along the trade routes of caravans that, among other things, took ornaments from North Africa to western Africa and returned with salt.

The development of the use of metals in southern Africa has been heavily researched, and it appears that the people who used metals came to the region in small numbers, possibly from the coast. They made contact with the Khoikhoi and other peoples, bringing with them some metal tools and the knowledge of how to make more from smelting ore. These appear to have been either traders working their way down the east coast of Africa or Berber ship merchants bringing goods down the west coast. Either way, iron must have been rare, and its use was limited to weapons and essential tools. There is some evidence of its use by 200 C.E., but the absence of many iron tools from archaeological sites, some archaeologists have suggested, might be largely owing to the way the metal rusts rather than its absence from the society. It is also possible that iron tools were too valuable to bury and were passed on to children and others at the death of their owner. Certainly it was the Bantu who brought iron with them in abundance when they arrived.

If the spread of metalworking can only be surmised because of a lack of evidence for the technology's presence in some regions, the spread of quarrying stones is even more speculative. Certainly ideas of quarrying came from ancient Egypt and northern Africa, with the use of stone tools in Africa being common in many places until the seventeenth century C.E. Some stone quarries were run by the Carthaginians outside the city of Carthage, largely kept going by slave labor.

Routes of communication have long crisscrossed the Sahara, used by caravans bringing salt to remote places in the desert and also to the relatively heavily populated parts of northern Africa. In eastern and southern Africa so many of the settlements were small enough and close enough to the coast that the acquiring of sufficient salt was never a major problem.

EGYPT

BY AMR KAMEL

Egypt has been favored with rich and abundant stone and mineral sources that extend over the deserts surrounding the Nile River and into the Sinai Peninsula. The ancient Egyptians quarried and mined these sources, seeking out stone as permanent material for their pyramids, temples, shrines, and monumental tombs, which were furnished with sarcophagi, statues, stelae, and obelisks that were also made of stone.

From the earliest periods of recorded history in Egypt, kings sent major expeditions to various places in the Western and Arabian deserts as well as to Sinai and Wadi Allaqi in Nubia, to gather stones, minerals, and other materials. One expedition dating to the Old Kingdom (ca. 2575–ca. 2134 B.C.E.) that went to the alabaster quarries at Hatnub in the hills of the Eastern Desert consisted of 1,600 artisans, while New Kingdom (ca. 1550–ca. 1070 B.C.E.) expeditions, which were sometimes supervised by the vizier himself or the high priest of Aton, were even larger. During the reign of Ramses IV (r. 1163–1156 B.C.E.), an expedition was sent to Wadi al-Hamam (in Palestine) for building blocks. It included, among others, 170 administrative staff, 130 skilled stonemasons, 2,000 bondsmen for transporting the blocks, 5,000 soldiers, and 50 guards.

In general, after the required materials were quarried or mined, they were transported by donkeys, which were able to move easily along steep and stony mountain paths, to the river Nile bank, where boats and barges would carry them to the building sites.

The ancient Egyptians found the ideal materials for their eternal architecture and sculpture in the great varieties of stone available in the surrounding hills. In the Predynastic Period (ca. 3000 B.C.E.) stone for vases and plates, such as limestone, sandstone, gypsum, and calcite (Egyptian alabaster), were taken from these hills as well as from the Arabian Desert. Also from the Arabian Desert came volcanic porphyry, marble, graywacke, quartz, schist, serpentine, and talc. Slate was quarried in Wadi Hammamat near the Red Sea and used for sleeping and ceremonial palettes. The soft stone gypsum was obtained from Umm el-Sawwan, at the northern edge of the El Faiyûm region of Upper Egypt. Egyptian alabaster (calcite or travertine) was obtained from the Wadi Gerrawi, south of Helwan and opposite Memphis on the western side of the Nile, but the most important quarries were at Hatnub, southeast of Tell el-ʿAmârna.

Quartzite, a naturally cemented sandstone, was available near Cairo, at Al-Gebel Al-Ahmmar, and found in association with the Nubian sandstones south of Idfu. Another variety of quartzite was quarried in Gebel Abu Dokhān and Gebel Fatira in the Arabian Desert. In the Greco-Roman Period (ca. 332 B.C.E.–ca. 395 C.E.) a variety of porphyritic rocks, including the so-called imperial porphyry, was obtained from Gebel Abu Harba, and Gebel Gattar, from west of Al Ghurdaqah in the Red Sea hills. Basalt, which was used as a special building material because of its black color, occurred in many parts of Egypt; sources close to the Nile and to building sites include Abu Rawash and Gebel Qatrani, north of the Faiyûm Depression. The Faiyûm was the main source of the basalt used in ancient Egypt.

Linen bag of salt for mummification, from Deir el-Bahri, Egypt, New Kingdom, 1550-1070 B.C.E.*; salt was used to dry bodies before wrapping and entombing.* (© The Trustees of the British Museum)

Graywacke, a dark, varicolored, attractive stone, was obtained from Wadi Hammamat between Luxor and Quseir. Chephren diorite was quarried from Gebel el-Asr, an area in the Western Desert, about 40 miles northwest of Abu Simbel. The pink granite was one of the favorite building and ornamental stones and is widespread in various spots around Aswān and in the Arabian Desert. As pictorial evidence from the causeway of King Unas (d. 2345 B.C.E.) indicates, in ancient Egypt granite was quarried, shaped into objects, and polished before being transported by boats down the Nile.

Sandstone was the principal element in any construction in Upper Egypt and Nubia, while limestone was widely used in Middle Egypt and Nile Delta buildings. The limestone varied in quality. The harder and less brittle white limestone was located on the eastern side of the Nile, opposite Memphis, and along the Mokkatam Hills, near modern-day Tura el-Asman and Masara, and the outcrops continue from there to far beyond Luxor (Thebes). The Egyptians used blocks of limestone from nearby quarries in constructing pyramid complexes and mustabas (tombs) in the Memphite necropolis (city of the dead), but the outer casings and wall facings of these monuments required the superior Tura limestone. Although sandstone became the predominant stone in the cliffs running from Isna to Aswān, it was not widely used until the New Kingdom. It could be obtained at Qertassi in lower Nubia, but the most important quarry was at Gebel es-Silsila, located between Kom Ombo and Idfu, where the vertical walls are still crisscrossed by the outline of various sized blocks.

There are many surviving records, both archaeological and textual, concerning mining expeditions to obtain copper, gold, and tin within the ancient Egyptian territory. (Other minerals, such as silver, lead, and iron, were obtained through trade or pillaging.) The oldest indication of such mining expeditions can be traced back to prehistoric times, when the preserved jewelry from that time was made of Arabian Desert carnelian and sard. Copper ores came from both the Arabian Desert and from the southern Sinai at Bir Nasib. There is archaeological evidence indicating that Wadi Dara, in Upper Egypt, was one of the earliest-known copper mines, and remains of a copper-working settlement were unearthed at Buhen, on the western bank of the Nile, near the second cataract. Nonetheless, the Nile Valley copper ores for productions of copper metal were relatively limited compared with that of Wadi ʿArabah region, about 19 miles north of Elat, which apparently was in use as early as the fifth millennium B.C.E. There is no evidence that the Egyptians themselves mined copper at that site; they seem to have employed local inhabitants instead. Iron ores are known in various locations in Egypt, notably in the Arabian and Western deserts, and in Sinai. Even as late as the New Kingdom the technology of iron smelting seems not to have been developed there.

In ancient Egypt gold was obtained from at least 90 gold mines in the Arabian Desert (both Egyptian and Nubian), which possibly were in use as early as the Old Kingdom. The Egyptians recorded in detail their work in the gold mines of Wadi Hammamat and Wadi Allaqi, which were used continually up to the Ramesside Period (ca. 1307–ca. 1070 B.C.E.). There even survives a unique map of a Twentieth Dynasty (ca. 1196–ca. 1070 B.C.E.) gold mine at Bir Umm el-Fawakhir in the Wadi Hammamat.

Turquoise and malachite as well as red agate and red-brown carnelian were highly desired and were obtained from a variety of sources. The main sources of turquoise, mined by the Egyptians from the Third Dynasty (ca. 2649–ca. 2575 B.C.E.) to the end of the New Kingdom, were located in western Sinai at Wadi Mughara and Serabit el Khadim, where at times there was a semipermanent Egyptian settlement.

Galena, which was used for kohl eyeliner, was obtained, from the earliest times, from Gebel el-Zeit mines, located on the Gulf of Suez to the south of Ras Ghārib. Talc and serpentine, softer and easier to work than granite, were used for a variety of objects, including weights, spinning wheels, and beads. Both were common in the Arabian Desert region east of Idfu.

Amethyst was primarily obtained from the Wadi el-Hudi, southeast of Aswān, and it was greatly prized during the Middle Kingdom (ca. 2040–ca. 1640 B.C.E.). In the Greco-Roman Period emeralds were mined from Zabara, Um Kabo, and Sekkait and from Hugrus in the Arabian Desert; peridot was obtained from Zabargad Island (Saint John's Island) in the Red Sea, southeast of the port of Berenice. Apparently, lapis lazuli, the deep blue gemstone that was frequently used in Egyptian jewelry as early as the Predynastic Period, was imported from the modern-day Badakhshan region in northeastern Afghanistan.

For common use, salt was obtained from the shores of the Mediterranean and from Red Sea lagoons. There is only textual evidence suggesting Khārga Oasis as another possible location of salt extraction, especially during the New Kingdom, but archaeological evidence is lacking. Natron, which was used with other substances for dyes and for mummification, was obtained from Wadi an-Natrūn, Beheira Governorate, and the Elkab region in Upper Egypt.

THE MIDDLE EAST

BY LYN GREEN

Salt was one of the most ubiquitous substances used by ancient peoples, but relatively little is known about how they extracted it. The Phoenicians were famous traders and producers of salt, which they probably got by evaporating seawater. In fact, all the cultures of the ancient Near East would have relied on surface salt left in salt pans by the evaporation of ancient seas rather than on labor-intensive mining. Many of the earliest minerals and metals to be used and exploited were also those that could be found literally lying around. For example, some of the earliest copper was obtained from malachite or other copper-rich rocks that lay on the surface. The green color of these rocks (which comes from the oxidized copper in them) would make them easy to spot.

Similarly, red or yellow stains on rocks show the presence of iron oxide and would have signaled to ancient prospectors that iron was at hand. Iron, however, was far harder to find on the surface than copper, and some scholars have speculated that early peoples first made use of the iron that they found in meteorites. Occasionally, lead could be found on the surface. For example, beads of lead dating to around 6000 B.C.E. have been found at a Neolithic site in Turkey. There were also places where bitumen and other petroleum products rose naturally to the surface of the earth. Ancient Sumerians used bitumen in place of mortar between bricks, made boats watertight with it, and even inlaid it in jewelry and furniture as decoration. Bitumen sealing was found on the oldest-known boat in the world, discovered in Kuwait and dating back 7,000 years. The Sumerians apparently also made use of the petroleum products they found on the surface as fuels in the crucibles and furnaces they used to extract metals from ore.

Once surface deposits of such metals as gold, copper, iron, and lead were exhausted, ancient Near Easterners had

Stone panel from the palace of Sennacherib, Nineveh, northern Iraq (Neo-Assyrian, ca. 704–681 B.C.E.); together with a companion panel, it shows the transport of a winged bull from quarry to palace, part of Sennacherib's construction work.

to work extremely hard to extract the ore—or at least their slaves and criminals did. The conditions of mining in the ancient world were so horrific that only the most despised criminals were sent to the mines. The ore-bearing rock had to be extracted from the surrounding stone without the use of hard metal tools. Instead, the workers pounded at the stone with hammers made from the hardest rock they could find, usually dolorite or basalt. Picks and levers of antler or bone were used to work the larger pieces loose. At Timna Valley in Israel, miners laboriously dug vertical shafts linked by galleries. They brought the chunks of ore to the surface for processing and then to higher ground for smelting.

The pounding of stone on stone produced huge quantities of rock dust that would have been inhaled by the miners. In addition, the ores themselves often contained toxic materials. Lead, for example, is poisonous on its own. The copper found in the Near East often contains large quantities of arsenic. It has been estimated that an ancient copper mine in Jordan produced more pollution (in the form of toxins entering the environment via water, land, and air) than many 19th-century industrial operations. This polluting Jordanian mine at Wadi Faynan was in use from about 4500 B.C.E. and continued to supply copper to civilizations throughout the Near East until Islamic times.

Throughout the first few millennia of its existence, techniques for extracting and refining copper ore would have changed little. Researchers who have studied the production of metals from mines in Turkey and Jordan concluded that the ancient workers first ground the ore into powder with stone grindstones. Then they put the powder in a shallow container and fired it to as high a temperature as they could. Ancient miners could rarely achieve temperatures as high as those used in the 21st century, even when they had fuels such as asphalt or bitumen. Thus they often relied on repeated firing and sometimes the addition of minerals, which would lower the firing temperature.

Although copper containing natural arsenic was harder than pure copper, it was still relatively soft. Ancient miners also sought tin to add to the copper in order to make bronze. At one time scholars believed that the peoples of the ancient Near East had to trade over great distances to get their tin. However, in 1989 an archaeologist claimed to have discovered a source of tin ore in the mountains of Turkey, and radiocarbon dating revealed a mine that had been worked as early as 2500 B.C.E. This discovery has led historians and scholars to conclude that early peoples may have relied much more heavily on small local deposits of minerals, including stone.

For example, unlike the Romans, the peoples of the Neolithic and Bronze Age ancient Near East would not have bothered trading for luxury building stones like marble and granite. Instead, they would make use of local stone wherever possible, even when the stone was extremely hard (and therefore difficult to work) and not particularly attractive. For example, the sculptors of Sumer, where stone was scarce, may have relied on boulders and even reused fragments of other statues. The types of stone that were most often used in art and architecture were limestone, calcite, gypsum, and shale as well as harder stones such as marble, granite, schist, serpentine, steatite, diorite, and basalt. These were obtained from the Nur, Zagros, and Taurus mountain ranges and from modern-day Azerbaijan, Saudi Arabia, Oman, and southern Iran.

The techniques of stone quarrying and hard rock mining were extremely similar. Before the Iron Age, quarrymen had to rely on stone hammers, bone or wooden picks, and mallets and saws of bronze or hardened copper (which would constantly need resharpening). By the Neo-Assyrian Period (ca. 1050–ca. 609 B.C.E.) kings recorded that they sent men with iron axes and pickaxes to extract stone from quarries. Images of quarrying show men with saws and shovels as well as pickaxes of two different types. The stone they extracted was moved out of the quarry on wooden sledges, which were pulled along over log rollers. There were rarely any roads to the quarries and it would not have been until the stone was loaded onto boats that transporting it became relatively easy. To save time and weight, the stone was often roughly shaped before being transported. Much the same processes would have been used throughout the ancient Near East to obtain and quarry stone for statues, reliefs, and buildings.

ASIA AND THE PACIFIC

BY TOM STREISSGUTH

Prehistoric inhabitants of Asia used a great variety of objects and material produced by the earth. Some of this material was gathered at the surface. Erupting volcanoes, for example, sometimes ejected a shiny, glasslike rock known as obsidian, an extremely hard material that could be formed into tools and arrowheads. Along the Caspian Sea and the Dead Sea, salt collected at the shoreline, and pitch-black asphalt occasionally rose to the surface. These materials had important household uses: salt as a preservative for food and asphalt for burning in cooking fires.

Near Hong Kong archaeologists discovered a stone quarry on a steep hillside facing the South China Sea. Thousands of carefully shaped rocks, some dating to the Paleolithic Era (ca. 30,000–ca. 40,000 B.C.E.), litter the hill and the beach lying at its base. The stones were used as axes, grinders, scrapers, picks, awls, and arrowheads. Many other ancient quarry sites have been unearthed in central Asia, where a dry climate preserves traces of ancient human habitation and industry.

People in China and throughout Asia also put stone and metal ores to work, creating basic tools and weapons that allowed them to gather and hunt their food, build shelter, and decorate their bodies. As settled cities and urban civilization developed, artisans began specializing in the use and handling of metal ores. Through trial, error, and observation, the earliest miners and smiths learned how to find, extract, and use copper, iron ore, and tin. They hammered these ores to separate them from the surrounding rock and then smelted the ores over charcoal fires, heating them to temperatures that would draw out useful metals in a pure and usable form. Mining technology and the knowledge of smelting techniques arose independently in China, India, central Asia, and southeastern Asia.

Much of the ancient Chinese knowledge of mining and metallurgy is contained in *Shan hai jing* (The Classic of Mountains and Seas), a set of books of mythology and natural science that was produced sometime between the third century B.C.E. and the second century C.E. This classic summarizes millennia of experimentation and observation, classifying minerals and grouping surface rocks with the ores that were likely to be found within and beneath them. By the time it was written the Chinese had long been mining copper, silver, gold, tin, and zinc. The authors carefully catalogued properties of minerals known to them and listed the best methods of finding and working mineral ores and stone. Mining for iron ore eventually led to the discovery of magnetite, a rock that was attracted to iron ore and was used in the first navigational compasses. The Chinese also learned to drill for petroleum, or "weak water," a sticky black substance that, in certain regions, seeped from the ground surface. The Chinese used petroleum for axle grease and burned it for light.

The Chinese were the first in the world to develop deep-drilling technologies. They first carried out underground drilling for the briny water present in deep aquifers, an underground rock bed yielding groundwater. They raised tall derricks—platforms constructed from wood and bamboo—and used iron-tipped bits to drill deep boreholes. The drills were operated by hand and suspended from the derricks by cables made of long bamboo strips (bamboo was strengthened by contact with water and was much more durable than rope made of hemp). Miners raised and then dropped the bits onto the rock at different angles to chip away at it. The underground water was raised by buckets or, under high pressure, was forced to the surface and then directed to huge iron evaporation pans set up near the boring site. The pans were used to boil off the water, which left a thin film of salt—a valuable commodity that was used to flavor and preserve meat.

Some boreholes, which reached as deep as 5,000 feet, produced natural gas, which could be used as a fuel for light and heat. The wells that produced only natural gas and not water were known as fire wells. Drilling for natural gas at these sites dates to the second century C.E. The gas either was piped directly from the wellhead or, if present in sufficient amounts, was stored in underground tanks made of wood. Ventilators in these tanks allowed the gas pressure to be controlled and the gas to be released and collected when needed. The gas was distributed by bamboo pipelines that led away from the borehole; gas also could be transported using leather pouches.

Ancient mines have been discovered in Mesopotamia, Anatolia, Iran, Afghanistan, and central Asia, where copper and gold mines were being worked around 1500 B.C.E. Central Asia was renowned for silver mining during this period, while Anatolia was home to the world's earliest ironmaking industry. Afghanistan was famous as the source of lapis lazuli, a blue gemstone in high demand throughout the Middle East and Egypt for use in statuary, jewelry, and clothing. The Harappan civilization in India, which lasted from about 2600 to 1500 B.C.E., mined copper, gold, silver, alabaster, marble, granite, basalt, and sandstone. The Harappans were skilled in the smelting of copper and tin to make the alloy bronze; their weapons were traded in Mesopotamia, India, and as far west as Greece and central Europe. Harappan artisans used marble and alabaster stone for use in making pottery, and they also worked gold and silver mines for jewelry. After the decline of the Harappan civilization, the Indus Valley in what is now Pakistan continued as an important center of iron and steel production.

Diamonds were mined in ancient India, and rubies, sapphires, and amethyst were mined in what are now Myanmar, Thailand, and Vietnam. Mogok in Myanmar has been a center of gem mining since the Bronze Age. Northern Myanmar also yielded jadeite, the rock from which the highest-quality jade was and is still produced. (The Chinese have mined and worshipped jade since Neolithic times and still use this translucent green stone for decorative sculpture, jewelry, and talismans.) The gem industry in Sri Lanka dates to about 500 B.C.E., when the island's many high-quality gemstones were set into portable jewelry that was traded throughout southern Asia by Buddhist monks.

EUROPE

BY MICHAEL J. O'NEAL

The extraction of stone, ores, and minerals was an important complement to the farming economy of ancient European peoples. Early farmers mined flint for their tools at sites like Grimes Graves in England, Spiennes in Belgium, and Kremenets in what is now Ukraine, where the high quality flint was extracted from veins several feet below the surface. They also quarried outcrops of stone like amphibolite to grind into stone axes. The best-quality flint and stone would be traded over long distances. When the early farmers of northern and western Europe began to build large stone tombs and monuments called *megaliths*, either they used stones that were lying about the landscape, or they quarried stones and transported them over substantial distances. The bluestones that form the innermost circles of standing stones at Stonehenge came from the Preseli Mountains in Wales, 155 miles away.

Beginning around 5000 B.C.E. metals began to be used first for the manufacture of ornaments and then for tools. The earliest metal to be mined and used extensively in the production of tools, household implements, and other goods was copper. Early copper mines from the fifth and fourth millennia B.C.E. are found at places such as Aibunar in Bulgaria and Rudna Glava in the Federal Republic of Yugoslavia. Subsequently, copper sources were located in other parts of Europe, such as in Liguria in northwestern Italy and at Mount Gabriel in southwestern Ireland.

Copper tools were better than the stone tools of the earlier Stone Age because copper can be hammered and molded into many different shapes. Copper, however, is a relatively soft metal with limited usefulness. Early in the fourth millennium B.C.E. metalworkers discovered that they could toughen copper by mixing it with tin. The resulting alloy, bronze, gave its name to the Bronze Age, which extended roughly between 2500 and 800 B.C.E. Settlements where bronze played a prominent role in the culture and technology of the community have been found in islands of the Aegean Sea, home to the earliest European civilizations, the Minoans and Mycenaeans, as well as in central Europe, Spain, Britain, and Scandinavia.

While bronze was an advance on copper, it still was less durable and more expensive to make than the metal that supplanted it, iron. While iron came to be used extensively in the Near East, it was not until about 1100 B.C.E. that it found its way to Europe. In discussing European Iron Age cultures, historians and archaeologists refer to two primary periods. The first was the Halstatt Period, named after a town near Salzburg, Austria, where extensive salt-mining operations were conducted beginning about 1000 B.C.E. About 500 years later the La Tène culture developed in modern-day Switzerland. This culture produced an enormous amount of iron, and archaeologists have discovered numerous Iron Age artifacts from this region.

Mining for metals was a backbreaking business. While some metals such as gold could be found in nuggets in sandy soil or in water, the mining of copper and iron was more difficult, because the ore had to be dug out of the earth. First, a deposit had to be found. Ancient mining engineers were often able to locate a vein of metal by looking for stains in rock formations, riverbeds, and even in the water itself. Copper oxidizes (combines with oxygen) to form a greenish hue, while iron oxidizes to form brownish-red rust. Once a site had been located, workers dug shafts with picks and shovels. The shafts were generally not very deep, perhaps about 30 feet, but deeper mines—some as deep as 300 feet—have been found.

Bronze Age miners then used stone hammers to break up the rock, but they also used picks and levers made from hardwood or antler. Archaeologists have discovered many hundreds of broken stone hammers at ancient mining sites, and the large number of such tools suggests that a separate group of men were on hand to make and repair tools; otherwise, the miners would not have been able to carry on their work. Another technique that ancient miners used was to heat the rock by building large fires against it. The heating and cooling cracked the rock, often to a thickness of a foot, making it easier to break it into pieces and haul it to the surface.

Iron Age mining was not radically different. Again, shafts were dug using picks and shovels. The ore was broken up with hammers and then carried in sacks up ladders to the surface, where it was further broken down, washed (that is, the ore separated from smaller bits of rock and sand), and made ready for smelting. Large cisterns of water were kept on hand for the washing process.

An important activity in ancient Europe was the mining of salt. Salt was a valuable commodity, for it was used in the preservation of food; it was so valuable that ancient Roman soldiers were often paid with salt, the origin of the modern word *salary*, and the ancient Greeks readily traded slaves for salt (giving rise to the modern expression that people "are not worth their salt"). A major center of salt production in ancient Europe was the area around Salzburg, Austria and the lakes to the east in a region called Salzkammergut (note the syllable *Salz-*, the German word for "salt"). Also, many German and Austrian place names contain the syllable *hall*, the ancient Celtic word for "salt." This salt was left behind by ancient seawaters that covered the continent before they receded.

When salt occurs in large concentrations and is easily accessible, it can be mined just like any other mineral and carried out of the mine in large blocks, as at Hallstatt, where the miners had special leather backpacks for bringing out the salt. Where it is less concentrated or where groundwater flows through the salt deposits, it can be extracted by an evaporation process. Salt is highly soluble in water, so it can be extracted easily from the ground by dissolving it. Some ancient European salt mines consist of deep shafts dug into the earth, often into mountainsides. After the shafts were dug, ancient salt miners let groundwater do much of the work. Large chambers were opened and then allowed to slowly fill with water, a process that could take up to 15 years. When the chamber was filled with brine, or salty water, it would be pumped out of the mine. At that point, the salty water was placed in large, shallow containers so that the water could evaporate. The salt left behind was fashioned into cakes for transporting. Over the centuries, numerous road systems were built principally for the transportation of salt. The Via Salaria in Italy is a good example.

GREECE

BY JOHN W. HUMPHREY

Mining was first practiced in the lands bordering the Mediterranean long before the Mycenaean Greeks of the late Bronze Age excavated shallow pits at Laurium, southeast of Athens, where silver reserves were later to become the engine that drove the golden age of the fifth century B.C.E. As early as the upper Paleolithic (after ca. 30,000 B.C.E.), nomadic hunters were digging vertical shafts to recover flint, their principal material for flaked tools and weapons, while others in southern France and northern Spain excavated ochres, those natural earths that they used to paint the walls of deep caves with images of their hunting culture. Some metals were available in a pure and native state—gold and copper are two—and could simply be gathered from the surface or sluiced from rivers and worked by Neolithic farmers (8000–3000 B.C.E.) into decorative shapes without the invention of special techniques. Later, the new empires of the Bronze Age (3000–1000 B.C.E.), like Egypt, Mesopotamia, and Mycenaean Greece, sank deep vertical shafts and extended narrow horizontal galleries in their pursuit not just of precious metals but also of ores that contained copper, tin, and arsenic, which they learned to combine into the first truly useful metal, the alloy bronze.

Mainland Greece, its islands, and the colonized lands of the eastern Mediterranean supplied the Greeks of the Classical and Hellenistic periods (480–31 B.C.E.) with a rich variety of metals and ores. The difficulty was not in supply but in discovering the ore-bearing veins, since the principal prospecting technique available to the Greeks was to search for surface indications of what might lie beneath, a particularly unreliable method, as the ancients themselves knew well. Despite the haphazard nature of their discoveries, they had productive mines throughout the eastern Mediterranean: gold mines are known of in the northern regions of Macedonia and Thrace; gold and silver were both mined on the Aegean islands of Thásos and Sífnos; and silver, which might have been imported for some time from Asia Minor (the coasts and high central plateau of Turkey), became available locally when the Athenians reopened and expanded the shallow Mycenaean workings at Laurium, where the precious metal was actually an impurity in galena, a lead sulfide.

Copper was mined on Cyprus and at the town of Khalkís on Euboea, both places whose names derive from the Greek words for copper and bronze. Oxides and carbonates were found in deposits close to the surface, though when these were exhausted the Greeks dug deeper to recover copper sulfides, all of which would be combined with tin extracted from its ore, cassiterite, which soon began to be imported from the distant mines of Cornwall in Britain. And, finally, the metal that defines the period—iron—was found in quantity in ores from the Aegean islands, Anatolia, and Cyprus.

Knowledge of Greek mining operations comes from both the workings of the Laurium silver mines, which have been cleared and closely studied, and from ancient writers (more often Roman than Greek) who described the extraction techniques that changed little from the Bronze Age to the end of antiquity. While any miner would prefer horizontal shafts dug into the sides of hills and mountains, through which the movement of laborers and material was much easier and safer, necessity forced the Greeks to dig vertical shafts, about 7 feet square in section, to depths sometimes exceeding 328 feet, from which cramped galleries as low as roughly 3 feet high were driven horizontally to follow the veins of ore, their roofs supported by pillars of unexcavated stone and only rarely by shoring with wooden timbers. In this confined environment miners (who were almost always slaves, since no free person would choose to expose himself to such life-threatening dangers) lay for hours on their backs, sides, or stomachs and chipped away at the rock face with a tool kit of iron picks, chisels, and hammers, without even primitive safety equipment and with only the most basic illumination from torches and oil lamps.

Fire, poor ventilation, and absence of drainage all presented hazards. Documentary sources reveal that the ore-bearing rock face was often heated by an open fire and then doused with water (or vinegar), the sudden change of temperature causing the rock to fracture: one can hardly imagine the cumulative effect of the heat, the scalding steam, and the flying shards of ore. Fires were also set to create a downdraft in the shafts to draw in air for ventilation, when natural convection or surface fans made of linen sheets were insufficient. The Greeks appear not to have introduced artificial drainage to their mines, which (as at Laurium) were sunk only to the water table. Generally speaking, mines in the Greek world were controlled by the state (Athens, in the case of Laurium), which issued concession leases to private companies for terms of three to seven years, some of which survive to give detailed information about the administration of these operations.

During the regressive dark ages that followed the collapse of the Mycenaean Bronze Age (ca. 1100 B.C.E.), the Greeks' skill at monumental construction was temporarily abandoned, until the city-states recovered in the eighth century B.C.E. and began to replace with stone structures those temples and public buildings that had, for several centuries, been modestly constructed of wood, clay, and terra-cotta. The building stone was, ideally, quarried near the city, to mitigate the labor and expense of transportation; for this reason, Athens made use of the fine marble from nearby Mount Pendelikón, both for buildings (including most of those on the Acropolis) and stone sculpture.

Sources like the Greek historian and geographer Pausanias of the second century C.E. give information about the location of important quarries and supplement the archaeological evidence from known sites. The quarries were almost always open pits, so the workers avoided most of the life-threatening dangers experienced by miners. The rectangular blocks were first defined by shallow outlines cut with iron chisels; wooden wedges were then inserted in deep sockets cut along the grooves and hammered down, to fracture the stone along its natural lines of cleavage. The blocks were removed with levers, leaving steps that made continuing access to the rock faces easier. They were roughly finished on site using hammers, chisels, and hard balls of dolomite (a kind of limestone or marble) to smooth out rough patches and then transported to the building site for final finishing and erection.

Despite the importance of salt in Greek antiquity, when—together with curing—it was one of the essential means of preserving food (there being no artificial means of cooling in the ancient world), surprisingly little is known about where and how it was generally obtained. Jewish law had required salt to be added to all sacrifices. Homer (ninth to eighth century B.C.E.) records the use of salt for seasoning and gives it the epithet "holy." Later Greeks saw the serving of salt as an important token of friendship. In Egypt salt pans were constructed for the evaporation of seawater. There was a flourishing trade in salt from the desert oases well into the Hellenistic Period. Salt, like drinking water, was considered such a necessity for life that public access was guaranteed: A story was told about Lysimachus, a Macedonian general under Alexander the Great and later king of Thrace (306–281 C.E.), who decided to levy a tax on the freely available salt from a spring at Tragasae near coastal Hamaxitos in the southwestern Troad. The salt springs immediately dried up, Lysimachus revoked his edict, and the salt miraculously reappeared.

ROME

BY JOHN W. HUMPHREY

As with Greek mining, understanding of Roman practices depends on a combined study of excavated sites (in this case, especially Rio Tinto and other Spanish mines) and documentary sources (the ancient scholars Diodorus Siculus, Strabo, and the Elder Pliny). But the Romans, unlike their Greek predecessors, often attached to mining a moral interpretation: the violation of earth for unnecessary human desires, an attitude that pervades Pliny's *Natural History*.

The Romans depended for their mineral resources on mines generally located in the western Mediterranean. Gold was mined in Gaul and Spain; silver in Spanish sites like New Carthage and Rio Tinto (though the Romans also reworked and reprocessed, with some success, the old deposits and dumps near Mount Laurium in Attica); lead in Britain; copper in Spain and Britain (also the source for the tin used in bronze making); and iron in Gaul (near Lyon) and Spain, though the most abundant sources were found closer to hand on the island of Elba (which is estimated to have yielded 11 million tons of iron ore in antiquity), and in the early empire at extraordinarily large workings in Noricum (central Austria).

The Romans made no important advances in the design of tools—the typical iron hammers and picks and wooden wedges for fracturing rock faces—or in the techniques of prospecting, which remained surprisingly basic. A comment by Pliny in his *Natural History* reveals that visible surface sightings were the principal means of detection: "Silver is found only in shafts and, because it does not have a shining sparkle like gold, gives no easy indication of its presence."

In mining processes, however, the Romans made significant improvements to Greek practices. In the search for gold, for example, they developed sophisticated sluicing techniques using aqueducts constructed specifically for bringing sufficient quantities of water to provide forced jets to separate the gold from the alluvium (lose material deposited by running water), best seen at the workings of Las Médulas in northwestern Spain. They also lined the sluices with gorse branches, to trap the particles of gold. Safety was somewhat improved, though not necessarily intentionally. The use of open-pit iron mines on Elba must have reduced the mortality rate of miners, though their environmental impact was huge. Wooden timbering to support the roofs and walls of galleries became more common (as, for example, at New Carthage), though it was still not standard practice. There seems to have been a greater understanding of the effects of poisonous

Lead pig (ingot), Roman Britain (76 C.E.), from Hints Common, Staffordshire; lead was obtained as a by-product of silver mining. (© The Trustees of the British Museum)

fumes, but detection techniques were primitive. And, typical of the Romans' interest in hydraulic engineering, deep mines were equipped with mechanical drainage devices to allow mining below the water table and lessen the risk of drowning; these included Archimedean screws and waterwheels with compartmented rims, of which four pairs in Rio Tinto, operated by treadmills, raised the water about 100 feet out of the shafts.

As in Greece, most miners were slaves and criminals, an indication that safety practices had not improved enough to attract free labor. Almost all mines were state property but were leased to corporations of capitalists (the *publicani*) for their administration, though with strict regulations known from surviving contracts.

The Romans throughout their history relied on plentiful native Italian rock like volcanic tufa and limestone travertine, which they quarried for the building blocks of their monumental structures. Marble, which became desirable in the middle Republic as Greek cultural influences began to permeate Roman society, at first had to be imported from the established quarries of the eastern Mediterranean; this was true until late in the first century B.C.E., when extensive marble deposits were discovered in the Carrara Mountains near Luna (modern-day Luni) in northwestern Italy; the quarries begun there by the Roman stonemasons produced excellent white and blue-gray marble and are still in use in the 21st century.

Basic quarrying techniques mirrored those of the Greeks: hammers and iron chisels were used for the initial cutting of rectangular blocks, which were then split from the parent rock by inserting wooden wedges that, when soaked with water, expanded with sufficient force to fracture the stone. The Romans introduced saws for cutting the blocks, and one late-imperial example of a river-powered waterwheel is known, which provided the necessary reciprocal motion to operate the saws. These saws also gave the Romans a significant advantage in producing remarkably thin marble veneers, which they applied with mortar to the surface of brick-faced walls of poured concrete, producing an elegant appearance that mimicked worked blocks of marble, but at greater speed and considerably less expense. Despite this economy of stone, there seems to have been a fear that the supply would eventually be exhausted, which probably prompted the fantastic stories in Pliny and others about marble quarries in which the stone was magically regenerated.

Salt played the same important role as a preserver of food for the Romans as it did for the Greeks. The city of Rome itself was blessed almost from its foundation with control of the natural salt beds at the mouth of the Tiber River near Ostia, which gave it an economic advantage over its Latin neighbors. The Latin adjective *salarius* ("pertaining to salt") was applied not only to the road that led from these salt beds to Rome but also to part of the payment to soldiers for their subsistence (our word *salary*). Rock salt was mined for export in some locations (like Cappadocia in central Turkey), but evaporated sea salt was the most important source: terra-cotta salt pots and lead saltpans, in which the brine was heated to drive off the seawater, have been found throughout the Roman Empire, from Egypt and the eastern port cities of Caesarea and Ephesus to towns in remote Britain. The most useful description of techniques used to extract salt is given by Pliny, who notes in his *Natural History* that fresh water (from rain or rivers) was often added to seawater before evaporation, to "make the salt sweet."

THE AMERICAS

BY KEITH JORDAN

Stone quarrying in the New World dates back to the time of the first human inhabitants during the last ice age, 12,000 or more years ago. Since stone was the primary material used to make tools and weapons throughout the Americas right up to the 16th century C.E., numerous quarry sites have survived to be excavated by modern archaeologists. In most cases stone hammers were used to extract flint, chert, and other useful stones from surface outcrops. In southern New England, for example, Native Americans during the Terminal Archaic into the Early Woodland periods (ca. 1500–700 B.C.E.) extensively worked deposits of steatite (soapstone), from which they carved cooking vessels. They broke up the surrounding rock with handheld hammer stones and used pointed stones to further reduce detached pieces of stone. Stone spades were employed to clear away the fragments.

The oldest-known and longest-lasting large-scale mining operations in the ancient New World were the copper mines of the Keweenaw Peninsula and Isle Royale, Michigan, which were worked from the Late Archaic Period (ca. 3000 B.C.E.) to the time of European invasion in the 17th century C.E. Although Native North Americans did not smelt or cast copper, they produced implements and ornaments by cold hammering nuggets of pure copper or by hand working heated material (a process called annealing). The copper extracted from these Lake Superior mines was traded across the eastern half of North America and was the source for most of the copper ornaments and ritual objects found in the Adena and Hopewell burial mounds. While local sources in the Appalachian Mountains may account for some of the copper found in southeastern archaeological sites, no evidence of prehistoric mining has yet turned up in this region.

Native American miners in Michigan dug trenches and pits to reach deposits of copper. They used five- to 40-pound stone hammers, or mauls, to break up the surrounding rock and smaller hammers to extract lumps of copper from detached chunks of stone. Some of these hammers were attached to wooden hafts or swung on thongs, while others were probably held in the miner's hand. The diggers also may have employed a process of alternatively setting fires over bedrock and then dousing the area with water to shatter the stone for easier digging; they then used wooden spades or scoops to dig out the loosened pieces of copper. Stone or copper wedges may have been inserted to pry chunks of metal away from the surrounding rock. In some locales the miners needed to sink their shafts as deep as 50 feet to reach the ore. They presumably removed the usable metal in baskets or skin bags, and baskets and wooden buckets served to bail out the frequently flooded pits. Some excavations were lined with wood or stone blocks to prevent cave-ins.

By 1500 B.C.E. Olmec workers were quarrying basalt, a volcanic stone, in the Tuxtla Mountains of the modern Mexican state of Veracruz and transporting huge blocks to political and religious centers some 60 miles south to be worked into monuments for royalty. The stone was detached by bashing it with smaller stones—a laborious effort in itself. Tons of basalt were then transported to the Olmec sites through 60 miles of jungle, perhaps by floating the material on log rafts down local rivers and then rolling it on logs once on land—a truly astonishing achievement for this ancient workforce.

In addition to material for monumental construction, the Olmec and their contemporaries quarried and traded many other minerals. Obsidian, a volcanic glass used for making extremely sharp blades and spear points, came from surface outcrops in the Basin of Mexico and in southern Guatemala. The source of the blue-green jade favored by the Olmec for ornaments and ceremonial objects was once a mystery, but accidental discoveries now indicate that it is found as easily removed cobbles or boulders along the Motagua River in Guatemala.

The Maya used the local limestone underlying the forests of Yucatán and Guatemala for construction at least as far back as 600 B.C.E. Limestone bedrock was broken up using stone hammers and chisels and by setting fires. Fire was also used to reduce limestone to powder useful in the manufacture of stucco and plaster to decorate building facades and serve as mortar.

In the early centuries C.E. demands generated by the central Mexican metropolis of Teotihuacán and partners in its far-flung trading network seem to have catalyzed the development of extensive mineral mining to the north, in the cultural area of the Chalchihuites in modern Zacatecas and Durango. Red hematite and cinnabar and blue turquoise were mined in the north and traded south across Mesoamerica. To reach the deposits of conglomerate rock containing these precious materials, Chalchihuites miners sunk shallow open pits and deep shafts into hills and gouged horizontal excavations along hillsides and canyon walls. Both horizontal and vertical shafts were dug, splitting off into multiple branches connected by tunnels and running up to 3,000 feet underground.

Pillars of rock left untouched by the quarrying held up the roofs of these galleries, which were reinforced as well by wooden cribbing, and blocks of stone not useful for mineral extraction were used to reinforce the walls of the tunnels. The spoils were piled up around the mine entrances, creating mounds as high as 40 feet. Like the Michigan miners thousands of miles to the north, the Mesoamerican miners employed simple stone tools—heavy stone hammers to break the surface and excavate the shafts, small hammers to extract minerals from the surrounding rock. The dry conditions of northern Mexico preserved many wooden artifacts left by the miners, including torches, the handles attached to some of the stone hammers, and buckets to carry water and rock fragments. The bulk of this mining took place between 400 and 600 C.E., the time of Teotihuacán's fall from political power.

Andean cultures created gold jewelry and other objects from the second millennium B.C.E. onward. Gold mining must have been quite extensive, but few traces of it survive in the archaeological record, since the Spanish conquistadors set to work immediately exploiting the same gold deposits and destroying evidence of earlier efforts. What have survived are the remains of some copper mines that were used to extract metal for casting objects and for alloying with tin to create bronze. At Atacama in northern Chile copper salts preserved not only the tools used by miners 1,500 years ago but also the body of one of the miners, killed in a cave-in. The tools found near his naturally mummified remains indicate that the ancient Andean miners, like those elsewhere in the Americas, used large stone hammers as their primary tools, along with baskets to transport the quarried materials.

See also ADORNMENT; ARCHITECTURE; ART; BUILDING TECHNIQUES AND MATERIALS; DEATH AND BURIAL PRACTICES; FOOD AND DIET; HEALTH AND DISEASE; HOUSEHOLD GOODS; ILLUMINATION; INVENTIONS; METALLURGY; ROADS AND BRIDGES; SACRED SITES; SEAFARING AND NAVIGATION; SETTLEMENT PATTERNS; SHIPS AND SHIPBUILDING; SLAVES AND SLAVERY; STORAGE AND PRESERVATION; TRADE AND EXCHANGE; WEAPONRY AND ARMOR.

FURTHER READING

T. K. Derry and T. I. Williams, *A Short History of Technology: From the Earliest Times to A.D. 1900*, rpt. ed. (New York: Dover, 1993).

J. C. Fant, ed., *Roman Marble Quarrying and Trade* (Oxford, U.K.: British Archaeological Reports, 1988).

Robert James Forbes, *Studies in Ancient Technology*, Vol. 7, *Ancient Geology; Ancient Mining and Quarrying; Ancient Mining Techniques* (Leiden, The Netherlands: E. J. Brill, 1997).

J. F. Healy, *Mining and Metallurgy in the Greek and Roman World* (Ithaca, N.Y.: Cornell University Press, 1978).

J. W. Humphrey, J. P. Oleson, and A. N. Sherwood, *Greek and Roman Technology: A Sourcebook* (London and New York: Routledge, 1998).

M. Korres, *The Stones of the Parthenon* (Los Angeles: J. Paul Getty Museum, 2000).

Alfred Lucas, *Ancient Egyptian Materials and Industries*, rev. ed. (Mineola, N.Y.: Dover, 1999).

Susan R. Martin, *Wonderful Power: The Story of Ancient Copper Working in the Lake Superior Basin* (Detroit, Mich.: Wayne State University Press, 1999).

James Muhly, "Metallurgy." In *Encyclopedia of the Archaeology of Ancient Egypt*, ed. Kathryn A. Bard (London and New York: Routledge, 1999).

William H. Peck, "Quarrying." In *Encyclopedia of the Archaeology of Ancient Egypt*, ed. Kathryn A. Bard (London and New York: Routledge, 1999).

Ian Shaw, "Minerals." In *The Oxford Encyclopedia of Ancient Egypt*, ed. Donald Redford (Cairo: American University Press, 2001).

Ian Shaw, "Quarries and Mines." In *The Oxford Encyclopedia of Ancient Egypt*, ed. Donald Redford (Cairo: American University Press, 2001).

R. Shepherd, *Ancient Mining* (London: Chapman and Hall, 1993).

R. F. H. Summers, *Ancient Mining in Rhodesia and Adjacent Areas* (Salisbury, Rhodesia: Trustees for the National Museums of Rhodesia, 1969).

Robert K. G. Temple, *The Genius of China: 3,000 Years of Science, Discovery, and Invention* (New York: Simon and Schuster, 1986).

Dick Teresi, *Lost Discoveries: The Ancient Roots of Modern Science* (New York: Simon and Schuster, 2002).

Amelia M. Trevelyan, *Miskwabik, Metal of Ritual: Metallurgy in Precontact Eastern North America* (Lexington: University Press of Kentucky, 2004).

R. E. Wycherly, *The Stones of Athens* (Princeton, N.J.: Princeton University Press, 1978).

► money and coinage

INTRODUCTION

The concept that forms the basis of money is that there is something of value that can be used to measure how much goods are worth. In many cultures of the ancient world, at first cattle were used to measure what goods were worth. A house, a farm, a cart, or some other good could be measured in how many cattle it would take to purchase it. This did not mean that cattle were always exchanged whenever someone bought something, though cattle often were exchanged for a purchase. A bushel of wheat might be worth one half a head of cattle, but a horse might be worth four head of cattle. If a person wanted to purchase a horse with wheat, for example, he would have to pay eight bushels.

Bartering goods seems to have been the beginning of all trade. Merchants would have to carry with them items they thought people elsewhere would want, and then the merchants would have to find goods they wanted and dicker with other merchants until they could work out a trade. Such dickering could take weeks, and the merchant night not find anyone who had what he wanted who also wanted what the merchant had. Produce could spoil. Workers could quit if they were not paid. The trade goods could end up being dumped.

In many parts of the world, people hit upon the idea of using as a medium of exchange something everyone liked but could carry on their persons. It had to be available in enough quantity that many people could use it; otherwise, it would be useless because not enough people would know what it was worth, but it could not be too numerous, or it would cause inflation, which would make it worthless because it would take too many make even a small purchase. It is not known what became the first money, but in much of the world, sea shells, especially cowry shells, served as cash. This may seem strange, but a fisherman mining for cowry shells is not much different from someone digging for gold. In some places metal became valuable once people learned how to use metal to make useful tools. For instance, in ancient China, bronze shovels and knives were used like money, and when the Chinese started minting coins, the coins often looked like small shovels or knives. The Chinese had an agricultural economy, and bronze tools such as shovels and knives would have had universal value in their culture.

Archaeologists seem to agree that coins as they are now thought of were invented in Anatolia, probably by the Hittites but perhaps by the Lydians in about 600 B.C.E. The idea caught on quickly in other parts of the world. The basic idea was that certain metals had agreed-upon value; if coins containing a certain amount of valuable metal were available, people could trade them for goods without worrying about trying to persuade someone with sheepskins to take ceramic vessels in exchange. Purchasers could exchange the coins for the sheepskins and leave sellers of the sheepskins to worry about what they wanted to buy.

AFRICA

BY OLUTAYO CHARLES ADESINA

The concept of money, which can be defined as commodities or tokens that serve as measures or media of exchange in economic transactions, has been well established in Africa since ancient times. The continent had some of the most varied forms of money currencies in the preindustrial world. Early on, Africans developed dynamic commercial relationships that required the adoption of money. The particular type of money was dictated by the type and scale of commercial activities. The money in use ranged from coins to copper ingots, raffia cloth, beads, cattle, and cowrie shells. Other objects used and accepted as means of payment included symbolic tools like daggers, representations of valuable objects, and precious metals.

In different parts of Africa, market and trading transactions were accomplished by means of currencies, though few societies possessed the market or exchange systems that required a universally acceptable form of currency. In other societies barter arrangements appear to have characterized the daily economic life. Historical records in Africa have affirmed the existence of several forms of exchange within a particular system of markets. One early form was the simple exchange mechanism known variously as the barter or the silent trade. This took the form of the exchange of goods for goods or the exchange of goods for services. In the exchange of goods and services, diviners and priests, drummers and singers were paid with goats, oil palm, and roosters. These transactions were carried on by people who might or might not have known each other. There was the common account of the Carthaginians' silent trade for West African gold. The system involved a lot of uncertainty in the value of goods. It also required that a person locate someone who wanted the particular good being offered. Barter was quite limited compared with trade with money.

The earliest evidence of the cultural use of money occurs in Egypt with the adoption of cowrie shells as currency. The trans-Saharan trade that began between North and West Africa, around 1000 B.C.E. spread the use of cowrie shells as currency. The trade expanded significantly with the influence of the Carthaginians from about the fifth century B.C.E. Carthage, the great trading nation established by the Phoenicians in 814 B.C.E., began to issue minted coins in the fourth century B.C.E. The circulation of money received greater impetus from the Romans, following their expansion into North Africa three centuries later. Gold and cowries were the major currencies, and this trans-Saharan trade might have been responsible for the diffusion of cowries into the interior of Africa as far afield as the Niger Bend.

Ancient African monies took other forms in addition to cowrie shells. Livestock and plant products were utilized as money in different societies at different epochs. Cattle became a vital form of money, most especially in pastoral societies. Pastoral communities especially in East and southern Africa interacted with and exchanged some goods with hunter-gatherer communities.

Many groups in Africa also used metallic currencies such as gold and silver coins. This use owed much to Roman and Greek influences. The earliest coins in Africa can be traced to the sixth century B.C.E. in Cyrenaica on the northern coast of Africa (modern-day Libya). Silver and electrum (an alloy of gold and silver) coins were in use here. One of the coins was the Valentine coin in circulation between 500 and 480 B.C.E. Embossed in the coin was the image of silphium, a plant used as a spice and contraceptive that was quite important to the Cyrenaic economy. About 25 B.C.E. in Mauretania a bronze coin depicted Cleopatra Selene, the queen of Mauretania who was the daughter of Cleopatra VII by Marcus Antonius. One side of the coin featured an embossed crocodile, which symbolized Egypt, a land she had the hereditary right to rule..

Around 270 C.E. the kingdom of Axum (in modern Ethiopia), which emerged about the time of the birth of Jesus, began minting its own coins. It became the only currency issued by Africans without outside influence. The coin facilitated the Red Sea trade and had the tendency to promote the nation's religion and prestige.

Human society in Africa in the ancient period adopted several materials that could be exchanged for other articles. Both special purpose currencies and general purpose currencies developed in prehistoric Africa. The cowrie shell and gold and silver currencies were general purpose currencies. They served as a means of exchange, an acceptable tender in making payments or settling debts, a standard of value, and a store of wealth. The value of money depended on supply and demand, measured by the goods for which it was exchanged and by other forms of money. Highly organized societies often possessed currency that had a greater number of general purposes than simpler societies. In other words, the more complex a society, the more likely it was to possess some form of general purpose currency.

Special purpose currency may be an artifact useful for other things, such as a tool or ornament. It may also include rare items, art, and jewelry. Such materials can be collected for the sheer pleasure of collecting them. They are better prized the rarer and the less forgeable the articles are. Special purpose currency is restricted to specific spheres of the economy, such as hunter-gatherer communities and serves only some of the functions of money. (This form of money is also referred to as an *intermediate commodity.*) It is more secure from loss or theft, harder to forge, and its value is more accurately judged by observation and measurements.

EGYPT

BY PANAGIOTIS I. M. KOUSOULIS

The ancient Egyptian economy was based on three principles: barter and market exchange, redistribution, and reciprocity and tributes. The underlying connection between these three principles that aided the evolution and wealth of the Egyptian society was that of a centralized state authority (the pharaoh) and the temple institutes. Daily economic transactions and storage were based on the exchange of goods and commodities rather than on the use of money. That held true at least for the Pharaonic Period (ca. 3050–712 B.C.E.). The import and use of money and coinage were inaugurated toward the first millennium B.C.E. with the advent of foreign mercenaries in the armies of the pharaoh. Even at that time, though, ancient Egyptians did not appraise the value of coined money. They regarded them as artistic objects in gold or silver appreciated only by metalworkers.

The Egyptians used four units of value to price and trade commodities, including the deben, senyu, hen, and kher. These units coincided with quantities of certain commodities: weights of silver and copper/bronze and units of capacity of grain and sesame oil. More specifically, the deben was a measure of weight used mostly for copper but also for precious materials such as gold and silver. One deben of copper weighed about 3.3 ounces. Silver and gold deben are not mentioned in ostraca (pottery shards that contain inscriptions) but only in papyri, since the former were used and distributed only among the low-class populace. On the contrary, papyri generally recorded greatly valued transactions among the high officials and the palace.

The senyu was a weight in silver equal to one-half deben or about a quarter ounce. Its use was inaugurated during the Nineteenth and early Twentieth Dynasties (ca. 1307–ca. 1155 B.C.E.). The senyu could be used to express a value in the same column of figures with deben. One could find in an ostracon the value of certain objects in senyu but the total of the column in deben of copper. The hen was a measure of volume equal to about a half quart. Its value could vary according to the substance or liquid to be measured, but generally it was regarded as equal to one deben. Finally, the kher was a measure of the volume of grain, either emmer or barley, equal to about 20 gallons, and it was valued at two deben. The kher was most commonly found as a unit of value for baskets, both because the volume of a basket was equal to its value and because baskets were inexpensive.

The ratios among the four units as well as their exact values are not fixed in the sources. For example, one document values a basket at one-quarter senyu for a volume of one-half kher. As mentioned earlier, one kher is equal to two deben, which means that one senyu equals four copper of deben in value. In another document, though, one senyu of garment was equal to five copper of deben. Weight and price, both expressed in deben, were hardly distinguishable from each other. In the Egyptian mind there was no difference at all, for the deben was not money. Cases of inflation and price fluctuation have been recorded. Quite often one deben of silver was valued as 100 deben of copper. This uncertainty in the value system was a strong indication that the Egyptians were not looking for money profit in their transactions; it was the objects themselves that they tried to obtain.

The picture changed during the Late Period (712–332 B.C.E.) with the advent of foreign mercenaries from Greece, Syria, Israel, Persia, and other areas in the ancient Near East in the Egyptian army. The first reference for the import and use of foreign coins for payment is found in the writing of the ancient Greek historian Diodorus Siculus. He mentions that the king Achoris (r. 393–380 B.C.E.) offered to pay Athenian and Spartan mercenaries in coins. Later in the fourth century B.C.E. two series of coins were introduced. The first was based on the Athenian gold unit and struck on the Persian standard with Egyptian motifs. The second consisted of tetradrachms, struck by the Persian king Artaxerxes III (r. 359 or 358–338 B.C.E.) shortly after his conquest of Egypt in 342 B.C.E.

Alexander the Great and his successors, the Ptolemies, introduced coins that were purely Greek in style and

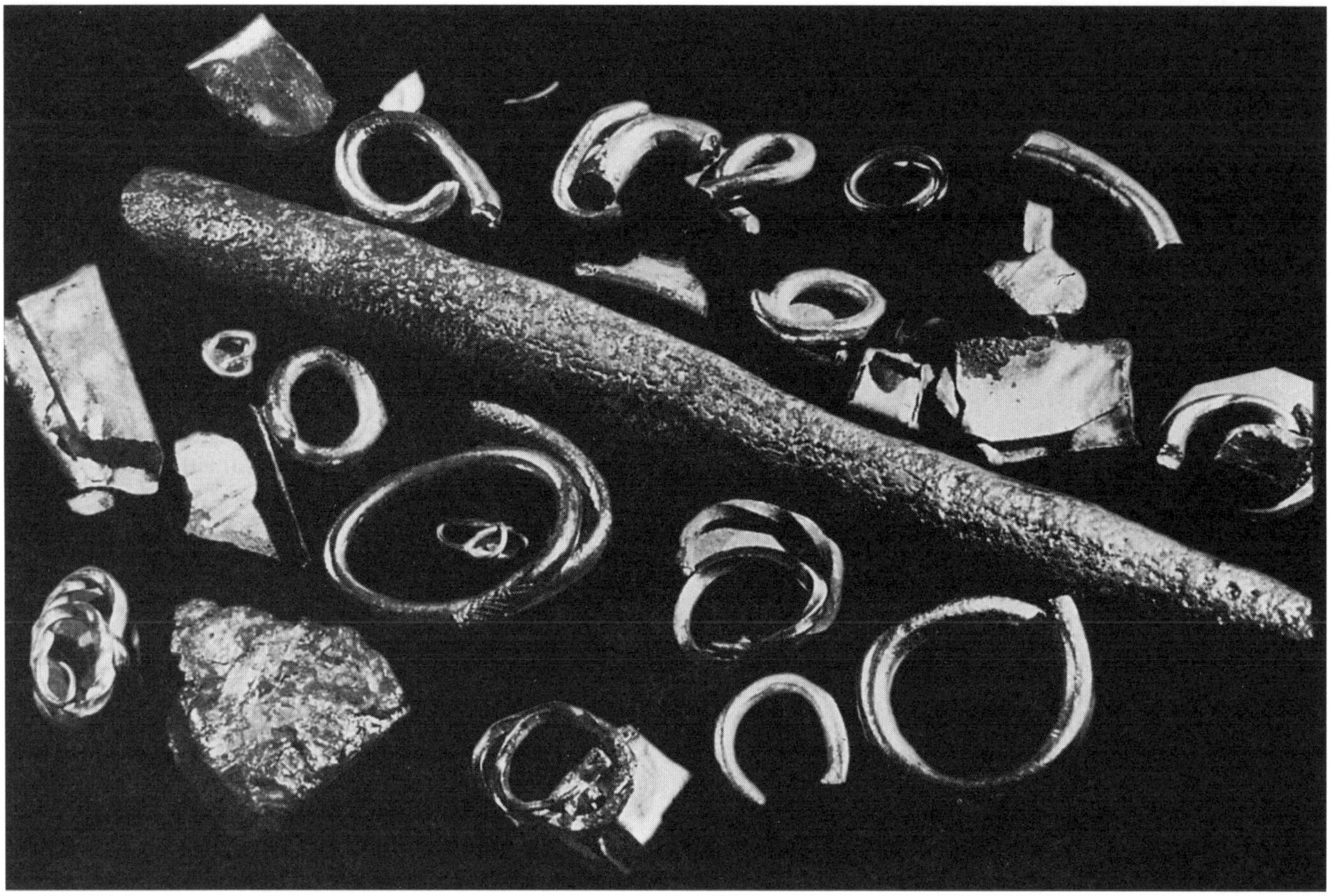

The el-Amarna Hoard, from el-Amarna, Egypt (14th century B.C.E.); these ingots and metal rings represent Egypt's earliest money. (© The Trustees of the British Museum)

inscription. They were struck in gold and silver and were based on the denominations of the Greek drachm, approximately one-eighth ounce in weight. Still, the standard silver coin of the Ptolemaic Dynasty (304–30 B.C.E.) was the tetradrachm, which became an international currency of the Mediterranean world in the fourth century B.C.E. Gold and silver coins bore an image of the ruler under whom they were minted or of a distinguished ancestor. The distinctive feature of Ptolemaic Dynasty coinage is the repeated use of the bust of Ptolemy I on the obverse, or "heads" side of the coin, throughout the period. Bronze coins bore similar motifs and portraits, though very little is known about the dates and means of their manufacture.

The establishment of coined currency in Egypt by the Ptolemies did not progress without difficulties. One major problem encountered was the silver standard used in the Greek world, which was based on a 10-to-1 ratio of silver to gold. In Egypt silver was imported, which meant that its value was high and thus inexpedient for coin production. Also, commodities value in dynastic Egypt was based solely on weights in copper. To solve this problem, the Ptolemies introduced bronze coins in multiple weight groups, some featuring very large coins that corresponded exactly to the deben (a little more than 3 ounces). Thus, it seems that a dual currency was in use throughout the Ptolemaic Dynasty: a silver-based currency used for foreign trade and a copper standard for internal trade and economic transactions.

The Roman occupation of Egypt did not alter the coinage form and production. Coins were by then of much inferior quality and value, incorporating similar Pharaonic and Ptolemaic stylistic motifs and images on the obverse. In addition to the use of coinage for the transactions, contemporary documents recorded the much more frequent use of trading in kind (wine, oil, beer, for example) outside Alexandria before the economic reforms of the emperor Diocletian (r. 284–305 B.C.E.).

THE MIDDLE EAST

BY AMY HACKNEY BLACKWELL

For most of the ancient period people living in the Near East did not use money. Instead, they conducted business by bartering, exchanging goods or services for other goods and services presumed to be of equal value. A bartered transaction could involve nearly any item or service, including land, livestock, grain, silver, copper, farm labor, or anything else essential to ancient life.

Long before coinage or paper currency was invented, people began trading commodities in standard measurements. The most common precurrency gauges of value were units of grain measured by volume and silver measured by weight. The standard units of weight were the shekel, which weighed about 0.3 ounces, and the biltu, or talent, which was the largest measure of weight-based value. One talent of gold weighed between 50 and 100 pounds, depending on the time and place. People were conducting exchanges in shekels and talents during Old Testament times, well before the advent of coinage in the sixth century B.C.E.

All metals were valuable, even in the days before they were made into coins. Metals were measured in terms of their weight in silver; even gold was valued by its equivalent in silver. Gold was considered the most precious metal and was valued at eight to 15 times its weight in silver. Next came silver, lead, copper, and iron after its introduction around 1200 B.C.E.

Coins were not invented until about 600 B.C.E. when the earliest electrum (an alloy of gold and silver found in nature) coins appeared in a hoard found in the temple of Artemis at Ephesus on the coast of Asia Minor, dating to the mid-sixth century B.C.E. But the first silver and gold coins known in the Near East date to the reign of Croesus, king of Lydia (r. ca. 561–547 B.C.E.), whose fabulous wealth sparked the phrase "rich as Croesus," used to this day. Croesus's capital was Sardis, and his Croesids, with their opposed lion and bull heads on one side and deeply impressed square shapes on the reverse, were staters varying in weight between 1 and 8 grams; there were also smaller denominations representing one-third, one-sixth, and one-twelth of a stater.

Soon the practice of minting and using coinage spread throughout Greece and, with Greek colonists, to Sicily, southern Italy, southern France and Spain. But coinage also spread eastward. In 546 B.C.E. the Persian emperor Cyrus captured Sardis and took over its mints to produce Persian coins. Darius I became emperor in 521 B.C.E. and began issuing gold coins known as Darics. These archer coins depicted an image of Darius running with a bow and spear. The Persian emperor Xerxes the Great (r. 486–465 B.C.E.) continued to issue Darics. Darics were famous and desirable in the ancient world because of their high value; pure gold coins were rare.

Currency became more widely accepted during the Hellenistic Period (323–31 B.C.E.). Seleucid, Attalid, Ptolemaic, Parthian, and other monarchs established national systems of coinage, creating single sets of coins that could be used throughout their kingdoms. They build national mints to produce all those coins to ensure consistency of weight and composition. After Alexander the Great conquered the Persian emperor Darius III in 330 B.C.E., Persia and most of the Mesopotamian region adopted Greek coins or made local, imitative issues based on the Attic weight standard. These coins were predominantly silver. The main coins were the drachma and the tetradrachm. Kingdoms throughout the region, including Pontus and Parthia, minted their own silver coins. Parthian coins of the Hellenistic Period were produced at the mints in Seleucia. They typically depicted the king's portrait on one side and the goddess Tyche or some other deity on the other, usually in some pose in which the goddess presented the king his crown. The images on coins are an extremely useful source of information on the ancient world. Persian satraps, or governors, often had their portraits stamped onto coins. Coins are the only source of portraits of some rulers, such as the kings of Bactria in modern Pakistan. Other coins contain religious imagery, such as depictions of gods.

THE RICHES OF CROESUS

All the kingdoms of Asia Minor seemed fabulously wealthy to their European neighbors to the west, particularly to the Greeks, who turned this reputation into several legends that remain well known. The biographer Plutarch and the poet Virgil describe King Midas of Phrygia and the famous blessing and curse that made everything he touched turn to gold. The historian Herodotus, however, is the main source for the story of Croesus, whose wealth was an entirely historical fact, real and visible to the Greeks of the fifth and fourth centuries.

Croesus was king of Lydia around 560 B.C.E., ruling his kingdom between the Halys River and the Aegean Sea in Asia Minor. Croesus was believed to be the wealthiest man ever to live; he was the origin of the expression "as rich as Croesus." Before making major decisions, Croesus liked to consult the oracle at Delphi so that he could get advice from the god Apollo. He also liked to send gifts to the temple before asking questions, perhaps thereby assuring himself of a positive reply. Herodotus, writing a century after Croesus' reign, provides this list of Croesus' gifts to the temple: 117 ingots of gold, totaling 240 talents (18,000 pounds) in weight, a lion made of gold weighing 10 talents (750 pounds), a large bowl of gold and another of silver, each approximately 500 pounds, and various other gifts. Finally, "along with these Croesus sent, besides many other offerings of no great distinction, certain round basins of silver, and a female figure five feet high, which the Delphians assert to be the statue of the woman who was Croesus' baker. Moreover, he dedicated his own wife's necklaces and girdles."

Croesus came to a bad end; his kingdom was taken over by the Persians, and he threw himself (or someone threw him) onto a pyre to burn alive. His treasures remained in the temples at Delphi until the middle of the fourth century, when they were melted down to pay for a vicious civil war over possession of the god's shrine.

Silver coins of various cultures found at Persepolis, Persia (modern-day Iran) (Courtesy of the Oriental Institute of the University of Chicago)

Coins offered several advantages over barter. They were easier to move than grain and livestock. The state guaranteed the quality and amount of metals in coins. Coinage allowed the state to take more control of commercial transactions, which served to increase the power of nations. Despite these advantages, coins were still not perfect. They were not standardized from state to state. Most early series of coins did not include small denominations, so they were useless for small transactions. Historians believe that the first coins were used mainly for large payments by states to armies or other states.

Early coin making was a laborious process. Mints first made blanks—blank coins of the correct size and weight but with no marks on them—by pouring molten metal into a clay mold. Most of the earliest coins were made of electrum, but the gold component of the alloy soon became too expensive, and most cities and states switched to silver coins. Minters took great care to ensure that their molds were the right size and that the molten metal contained the correct combination of ores. The mint would then make the blanks into actual coins by imprinting it with dies made of iron or bronze; they would place the blank in the die and strike it with a hammer. The die would leave an image on the coin, such an eagle or a king's head. The minters would then engrave the back side by hand. Sometimes mints remade old coins with new dies, stamping the old coins with new images instead of making fresh blanks. Most ancient coins were rather rough; they were usually not perfectly round, and the edges of the die used to mark them could be clearly seen within their borders. During the 200s C.E. Middle Eastern minting techniques improved, and coins became much thinner and flatter.

During Roman times Roman coins were legal tender in much of the Mediterranean world. By the first century B.C.E. Roman coins were accepted throughout Greece, western Turkey, and the Levant and in many places farther east as well. During the Roman Republic (509-27 B.C.E.) the main Roman coins were called the sestertius and the denarius. During the Roman Empire, lasting until 476 C.E., the common coins were the aureus and the denarius. Romans also minted coins customized to individual localities. For example, in Asia Minor Romans minted coins called cistopori. In Syria they made local coins called tetradrachms. Individual provinces continued to mint their own coins as well; most of these coins were made of bronze, and people knew how much they were worth in relation to Roman coins.

ASIA AND THE PACIFIC

BY KIRK H. BEETZ

Barter never entirely disappeared in ancient Asia and Oceania because many people lived outside the countries that developed cash economies. Furthermore, in hard economic times, people often ventured outside cash economies to trade on their own through barter. The desire to attach an objective value to goods developed in Asia sometime before 1500 B.C.E. By that time the Vedic culture that was moving into northern India was valuing goods on the basis of how many cattle they were worth. Farther east in central Asia, nomads valued goods by how many horses they were worth. The first medium of exchange that functioned like money was the cowrie shell. Through most of Oceania, the region in and around China, and India cowrie shells were used as early as 1000 B.C.E. in the way coins would later be used: to buy goods without having to trade other goods.

The first coins made of metal probably originated in Anatolia, a region that is inside modern Turkey. Archaeologists tend to credit either the Lydians or the Hittites with minting coins that were intended to be used as money in about 600 B.C.E. Fairly quickly, the practice of minting coins made its way to India, with coins appearing in the 500s B.C.E. At first, the Indian coins were silver bars, weighing about half an ounce to an ounce and a half. By then, Indians had formed the custom of wearing armlets of metal and of using these armlets to purchase goods in their marketplaces; thus the concept of money was already familiar to them. This helps to explain why coins for purchasing goods and services were quickly accepted throughout most of India. The major exception to their use was among Stone Age tribes still living in jungles scattered through India.

The first Indian coins were probably produced by guilds, called *srenis*. Run by the fourth-level caste, the Sudras, guilds were responsible for regulating their trades. They may have introduced coins from a desire to standardize prices within their individual guilds. By the 400s B.C.E. minted coins had appeared in a variety of shapes and sizes, some bulky and good only for large purchases and others round, square, or in a variety of other shapes. The multitude of organizations that minted coins through the end of the ancient era created chaos. Not only *srenis* but also rich merchants, temples, towns, and kingdoms all made their own coins.

During the Maurya Dynasty (321–185 B.C.E.), the pana became the most common denomination of coin. It weighed about an ounce and was 70 percent silver, 25 percent copper, and 5 percent base metals such as lead. It was joined by the masa, worth one-sixteenth of a pana, and the kakini, one-sixty-fourth of a pana, as well as the cowrie shell, which was one-eightieth of a pana. After the reign of Asoka (r. ca. 268–ca. 233 B.C.E.) these coins were adulterated (that is, made inferior by replacing valuable metal with less valuable metal, such as replacing copper with lead) and lost their value for trade. During the 100s C.E. a new golden coin called a *dinara* was introduced; it was named for Roman coins that were popular in India. The dinara was supposedly worth 48 panas, but given the chaos in Indian coinage at the time, its actual value in the marketplace probably varied from place to place.

Indian coins were typically punched. A blank coin was made in a mold. It was placed on a carved die, and a punch with a carving on one end then was placed over the blank coin and struck with a mallet. The result was a coin with images on both sides, often a portrait of a monarch with his name on one side and marks identifying the mint on the other. Some Indian kings are known to archaeologists only because their portraits and names are on coins.

Prior to the minting of coins in China, cowrie shells, bronze knives, and bronze shovels were used as money. Minted coins made of metal appeared in China before 450 B.C.E. Early ones were made of bronze and resembled in their shapes the knives and shovels that had been previously used for money. Coins were slow to catch on as money, but as urban areas grew and demand for goods increased, coins came to be used more and more, probably because they cut past the inconveniences of trading goods for goods. By about 250 B.C.E. coins were generally accepted throughout China, though a barter economy continued among peasants, especially in the outer provinces. Early Chinese coins were bulky and heavy, primarily useful for making large purchases. Military officers were still frequently paid in goods, even after the end of the Han Dynasty (202 B.C.E.–220 C.E.). Rolls of silk, rather than coins, were often used to pay people for their services.

The government of the Qin Dynasty (221–207 B.C.E.) tried to standardize China's coins. In 112 B.C.E. it introduced a five shu coin. This coin was circular, with a square punched in its middle, which allowed it to be strung with other coins. Typically, five shu coins would be strung together in units of

Fragments of a stone mould and bronze knife money, from northeastern China (ca. 350 B.C.E.); the inscription indicates that it was the "legal tender" of the Chinese state of Qi. (© The Trustees of the British Museum)

100. The coins were 80 percent copper and 20 percent other metals, usually lead. They were punched after the manner of Indian coins, with the blank coins being heated to soften them before punching.

Copper coins remained the fundamental coinage of ancient China, but the government did not always have control over their size and contents. Mine owners minted their own coins. Their shapes varied, with oval becoming common by the first century C.E. They tended to have symbols representing their value where Indian coins would have portraits, and on their other sides they would have the name of the minter and the approximate date the coin had been struck. The dates were not precise because the punch with the date would be used until it wore out, probably within a few months of use.

In 9 C.E. the Chinese government introduced 28 new denominations of coins, made of gold, silver, copper, tin, iron, lead, cowrie shells, and tortoiseshell. They came in many patterns, including circular, spoon-shaped, and shaped like a person standing. Apparently, the new coins did not catch on. In 25 C.E. the Chinese government again exerted control over coinage, reestablishing the five shu coin as the basic denomination. Gold ingots were sometimes used as money, but only for large purchases, because an ingot was worth about 10,000 five shu coins.

In the Japanese islands Chinese copper coins were used as money starting perhaps in the first century C.E. When Queen Himiko (flourished in the 200s C.E.) sent tribute to the Chinese emperor, she would receive gifts in return. Among these gifts would be sacks of copper coins, which would then be circulated among the Japanese.

EUROPE

BY KIRK H. BEETZ

Until the early 200s B.C.E. Europe outside Italy and Greece probably did not mint coins. At that time, the favorite coins among Europeans were Macedonian coins from the 300s and 200s B.C.E. Eastern Europeans were particularly fond of Macedonian coins featuring chariots, from the era of Phillip II (r. 359–336 B.C.E.) and Alexander the Great (r. 336–324 B.C.E.) and preferred them to Roman coins. Until the Roman Empire imposed silver coinage on most of Europe, eastern and southern Europeans preferred silver coins, but western and northern Europeans preferred gold coins. The problem with silver coins was that their silver content could be adulterated (corrupted or debased) without the visible loss of silver. Among western and northern Celts, gold was thought to be more trustworthy because when it was mixed with less valuable metals, the loss of gold would be visible.

For most of its history before the coming of the Roman Empire, Europe relied on barter for buying and selling goods. Among the Celts, cattle were the most valuable asset for most people, and goods were often valued by how many heads of cattle they were worth. This continued to be the case in Ireland and parts of Britain even at the fall of the Western Roman Empire in 476 C.E., even though southern Britain was the closest region in northern and western Europe to having a true cash economy at the time Julius Caesar conquered Gaul in 58–50 B.C.E.

As early as 1500 B.C.E. Europeans used copper ingots, gold ingots, and torques of gold, silver, copper, or bronze as mediums of exchange. A torque was a thick neck ring worn as decoration and as a sign of social status; torques were often exchanged with merchants for goods. The Germanic peoples of northern Europe and Scandinavia wore armlets that they could remove to exchange for goods. The armlets were sometimes gifts from kings to their followers. A king could improve his reputation and secure the loyalty of his followers by distributing armlets, known as *rings*, among them.

The first coins minted in Europe outside Rome and Greece were meant to be used like the Germanic armlets. A chief or king would have coins minted with his or her likeness and a mark that showed where the mint was located. The numbers and words on the coins would be copied from Greek coins. It was unlikely that what the numbers or words meant was important, because until the Roman conquest most Europeans were illiterate. It was the resemblance to the coinage of Macedonia that was important.

Celtic chiefs manufactured coins to display their power and to give to followers as symbols of the followers' indebtedness to their chief. When diners left the chief's house, the chief would present them with a gift as they were leaving. These gifts were often coins, and the more coins the chief gave, the more indebted the recipient was. In about 100 B.C.E. the Greek historian Posidonius observed Louernius, a chief of the Celtic Arverni tribe, stage a great feast lasting several days to display his wealth. He then rode his chariot through the countryside while tossing "pieces of gold and silver" to the crowd that followed him. These "pieces" were probably coins, and their distribution among the people was intended to bind those people to Louernius.

The coins were not necessarily for spending. The portrait of the chief or king on one side reminded the coin's holder of the power of that chief or king, and possessing the coin showed that its owner shared in that power. It was important that a coin have the amount of gold or silver in it that the minter claimed was in it, because some of the chief or king's reputation, and therefore some of his or her power, lay in the actual value of the coin, even if it was not meant to be spent. Thus, the Celts manufactured coins, but the coins were not inevitably part of a cash economy. In most of Europe north of southern France, even where there was an abundance of coins, barter remained the basis of trading until Roman times. Among many Gauls and the Germanic peoples, coins were hoarded, probably valued more for the gold or silver in them than as cash.

During the late 200s B.C.E. carving dies became a specialized craft. Dies were the stamps used to impress designs on blank coins. First, minters would weigh the metal for the coins. Then they would melt the metal, usually using ingots of metal smelted by metalsmiths. The minters had ceramic rectangles with rows of holes in the shape, usually circular, of the coins to be minted, and the minters would pour the liquid metal into the carved holes. After the metal had cooled, they would have blanks, which were coins that had yet to be stamped. Their dies had two parts, one engraved with the image for one side of the coin and another with the image for the other side of the coin. A blank would be placed on one of the engravings, and the other engraving would be placed over it. The die was held together by hand while the minter struck the top of the die hard enough to impress both images into it. It is likely that a wooden mallet was used.

By about 70 B.C.E. southern Europe was developing a cash economy in which coins were the primary medium of exchange. There are indications that some tribes were becoming sophisticated in their use of money. For instance, Julius Caesar noted that when Gauls married, the wife was expected to contribute a dowry. The husband was expected to contribute the equivalent of the wife's dowry and invest the total money. If the husband died, the wife would receive the total value of the investment. This indicates that banking existed in parts of Europe by Caesar's time and that banking was safe enough to entrust with a woman's future prosperity. Further, it indicates that money as wealth had become part of the thinking of many Europeans.

Even after Caesar's conquest of Gaul, Europeans never stopped minting their own coins, even though they may have minted fewer of them during the Roman era. Local peoples who wanted to show their independence from Rome sometimes minted their own coins to display their independence. In other cases, wealthy people minted their own coins because local business depended on reliable coins and their local economies did not trust Roman owing to the fact that the Roman government often adulterated the silver in coins to counteract inflation, which in the long term just fueled inflation. By 400 C.E. almost all of Gaul had slipped back to the barter system. As different Germanic tribes moved through Europe during the 400s C.E., their leaders tried to display their legitimacy as rulers by issuing coins.

GREECE

BY PAUL MCKECHNIE

Even before coins were invented in the ancient Greek world, the Greeks had a conception of relative value. In Homer's *Iliad* and *Odyssey* value is sometimes expressed in terms of the number of oxen an item is worth. For example, in the *Iliad* Achilles holds a wrestling competition in which the first prize is a bronze tripod worth 12 oxen, and the runner-up gets a slave woman worth four oxen. In the *Odyssey*, when the suitors attempt to apologize for their misbehavior at Odysseus's house, their leader offers compensation, saying, "Each of us shall pay you a fine worth twenty oxen, and we will keep giving you gold and bronze till your heart is softened."

Oxen, however, were not exactly "money." Sometimes they were used in payments—as when Lycaon was ransomed for 100 oxen when he was captured by Achilles. More often they were a conventional measure—as when Glaucus and Diomedes, discovering that their fathers were friends, agree to exchange armor: Diomedes' bronze suit of armor was worth nine oxen, but (according to Homer) Zeus made Glaucus lose his mind and exchange his gold suit of armor, worth 100 oxen, for it.

In the seventh century B.C.E. in Asia Minor (particularly Lydia) to the east of Greece, stamped precious metal coins began to be produced. Before then, precious metals had been used as a means of exchange, and sometimes they had been made into unmarked disks of a set weight. Coinage hastened economic change. One of the consequences of the widespread use of money was that people could save and accumulate their spending power.

In the sixth century B.C.E. Greeks began minting coins, usually in silver. Cities stamped coins with their individual marks. Some of the earliest Greek coins are from Aegina, marked with a turtle, and from Corinth, marked with Pegasus, Bellerophon's mythical winged horse. Peisistratus (d. 527 B.C.E.), a contender for power at Athens, began minting coins marked with an owl (symbolizing Athena, goddess of Athens) and an olive branch. "Owls" were minted at Athens and widely recognized and trusted for centuries.

There were hundreds of city-states in Greece, and many had mints and coins that were not necessarily acceptable outside their own cities but were made of precious metal and could be exchanged for local currency by bankers or melted down and reminted. Some Greek coins in museums today are overstruck with marks showing that they were once weighed and passed for use somewhere other than where they were minted. Different cities used different weight standards, so a drachma in one place did not necessarily have the same value as a drachma elsewhere. The two most widespread weight standards were the Attic standard (used at Athens) and the Aeginetan standard.

According to the Attic standard, money was measured in the obol, drachma, mina, and talent. The obol was the smallest denomination, and the drachma was worth six obols. The larger units (minas, talents) were not single coins: a talent, for example, would represent a heavy chest full of coins. Back in the sixth century B.C.E. the most widespread kind of coin was a didrachm, also known as a stater, but by the fifth and fourth centuries B.C.E. Greek cities minted mostly tetradrachms, which were worth four drachmas. Smaller coins, including fractions of an obol, were minted in silver, but not until the fourth and third centuries B.C.E. did bronze coins begin to be regularly minted in Greece.

For centuries the conventional daily pay for ordinary work in the eastern Mediterranean was unchanged. Rowers on Athenian warships in the fifth century B.C.E. were paid one drachma a day, and in the first century C.E. vineyard laborers were to receive one denarius a day, which was equivalent.

Skilled and specialized work, as in building the temple at Epidaurus in the fourth century B.C.E., might attract higher pay.

Credit, banking, and insurance were rudimentary. A financially sound borrower, when times were not difficult, might hope to borrow at 1 percent per month simple interest. Profiteering or scarcity of money might drive interest rates up two to four times as high. Bankers would accept deposits and pay interest to depositors, but checks were unknown. Insurance was likewise unknown, except that under Athenian law a loan to finance a trading voyage need not be repaid if the ship was lost at sea: The interest rate, when a trading venture succeeded, was correspondingly high, recognizing the share of the risk that the lender had accepted.

Gold coins were uncommon in Greece until the time of Alexander the Great (r. 336–323 B.C.E.). When Alexander captured the treasury of the Persian Empire at Persepolis in 330 B.C.E., however, he and his men claimed 120,000 talents when, according to the ancient Greek historian Diodorus Siculus, "the gold was estimated in terms of silver." Most of the Persian treasure was in gold, which the Greeks assumed to be worth 12 times as much, weight for weight, as silver. They thought silver was 120 times as valuable as bronze. When this gold came to the Mediterranean area, the price of gold fell. Alexander's treasurer, Harpalus (ca. 355–323 B.C.E.), worsened the shock by absconding with 5,000 talents of Alexander's money and traveling back to Greece, where he spent freely.

In the Hellenistic Period (323–31 B.C.E.) the rulers of the empires that took over Alexander's conquests minted coins picturing themselves; previously it had been almost unprecedented for a human being to be pictured (though gods and goddesses might be shown). In these centuries Greek coins were minted and used far into Asia. Indeed, the Greek kingdoms of Bactria and India, for which there is scant surviving literature, are almost best known from the coins they minted. Soon after the time of Alexander in the western Mediterranean, Greek moneyers began to mint Romano-Campanian coins—essentially Greek coins produced for Rome.

ROME

BY LUCAS G. RUBIN

The Romans adopted coinage fairly late, around 300 B.C.E. The earliest Roman currency was based upon the use of lumps of bronze called *aes rude*. These bronze pieces were difficult to use because they had to be weighed in order to determine their value. These inefficient tokens were later replaced by cast bars known as *aes signatum*, which were in turn replaced by bronze pieces of various denominations, one of which was known as an *as* (two or more were *asses*). The Romans also experimented with early types of silver coins based upon the Greek drachma, but they failed to obtain widespread use. During the Second Punic War, the Romans introduced a silver coin, the denarius, which was to form the basic unit of Roman currency for the next four centuries. The first denarius was valued at 10 asses and went through periods of reassessment and revaluing. Gold was not regularly coined until the later Republic (which spanned 509–27 B.C.E.).

By the time of the emperor Augustus (r. 27 B.C.E.–14 C.E.), the Roman system of coinage was firmly established around the denarius, which became the dominant currency of the Mediterranean basin and the lands controlled by Rome. Along with the denarius, a gold coin (*aureus*) was produced, worth 25 denarii, and also a range of fractional bronze denominations of various amounts. This system remained more or less static until the introduction of an important new denomination, the *antonianus*, in the reign of Caracalla (r. 211–217 C.E.). The antonianus was minted as a "double denarius," though its silver content was actually less than two denarii. This was, in fact, one step in a steady progression of reducing the silver content (called *debasement*) of coins that were about 94 percent pure in the first century C.E. to less than 1 percent by 270 C.E. Significant reforms were undertaken by the emperor Aurelian in 274 C.E. to correct this trend, but the problem of debasement and inflationary currency was not fully addressed until the reforms of Diocletian.

Diocletian (r. 284–305 C.E.) radically overhauled the economy, establishing a new coinage system shaped around a silver argenteus and instituting an edict on maximum prices in 301 C.E., both radical attempts to control the vagaries of pricing fluctuation. This eventually failed as well, and different systems of bronze and gold coinage became the norm over the course of the next few centuries until the final collapse of the Roman Empire in the west.

Facilities for the production of coinage were established in Rome with the institution of the first Roman coined money. During the Republic, the primary mint was believed to be located in or near the Temple of Juno Moneta on the Capitoline Hill. By the Imperial Period (14–180 C.E.) there were also several provincial mints, including a major facility at Lugdunum (modern-day Lyon, France). By the first century C.E. the mint in Rome had been relocated, and it is possible that its remains are partially preserved within the church known as the Basilica San Clemente. By the end of the third century C.E., in response to the increased disunity, discord, and distress within the empire, there were several major centers of imperial production scattered throughout the empire.

In the Republic the administrative board most commonly associated with the minting of coins was the *IIIviri aere argento auro flando feriundo* (*tresviri monetales* for short). This was a college of lower magistrates who oversaw the striking of bronze, silver, and gold coinage and whose establishment probably coincided with the institution of the denarius. During the empire the officials and personnel involved in minting activities became sufficiently more complex, with a range of different workshops, skilled laborers, and technical support staff reporting to a senior administration responsible for the production of coinage.

Ancient coins were minted by striking heat-softened blanks, usually cast or cut from a specially prepared bar. The

Cast ingots of bronze (early third century B.C.E.), used as money in Rome before the invention of silver coinage (© The Trustees of the British Museum)

coins were then laid on an anvil that held the obverse die and struck with a hammer by a punch that contained the reverse die. By the nature of this process, the obverse die lasted three to four times longer than the reverse die and was considered the more important side, the side upon which the most important images and inscriptions were incised. In general, the obverse side of a coin would contain a portrait head, most commonly of a deity in the Republic and of the emperor during the empire, while the reverse contained a range of images—individuals, structures, gods, and events. Emperors were usually presented with a range of standard and honorific titles. Julius Caesar was the first living Roman to have his portrait on a coin.

The various designs that appear on both the obverse and reverse of a coin can provide valuable material for the historian. Coins were a useful vehicle for the dissemination of information and offer an important resource for evaluating official communication and propaganda. The Roman government, for instance, could advertise its military success to the whole empire by minting and distributing a commemorative issue. The emperor Vespasian, for instance, minted a coinage series commemorating the end of the first Jewish revolt (70 C.E.) that portrayed a personification of the province of Judaea mourning beneath a Roman soldier. Conversely, the government could attempt to mask national problems by minting coins that celebrated nonexistent virtues or military successes. For example, an emperor might choose to mint a coin series celebrating national unity ("Concordia") at times of civil war. Such propagandistic issues were particularly popular during the crisis-plagued period of civil wars and instability of the third century C.E. In rare instances, coins provide the only known evidence for some would-be emperors and usurpers. Similarly, some coins contain representations of buildings and famous statues that no longer, or only partially, remain. These images, though highly stylized, can provide a wealth of information about the basic form and decorative schema of a wide range of public structures. One example of this is the Temple of Neptune in Rome, whose representation survives only on a coin and whose location even within the city is unknown.

Other forms of studying coins can provide information about economics (through analysis of metal content in coins), the numbers of coins in circulation, circulation and movement of coins (through analysis of wear patterns), and patterns of economic exchange (by mapping the distribution of coin finds). The content of metals (especially silver) can reflect economic difficulties. The pattern of debasement is interesting, as it demonstrates a naive approach to managing decreasing access to silver. The resulting inflationary crises were significant and ultimately devastating to the Roman economy and its stability.

One particularly interesting area of inquiry is the pattern of coin hoards in the Roman world. A coin hoard exists when more than two coins are found together. Three major types of hoard can be identified: purse, emergency, and savings. The purse hoard is a small collection of coins, usually of fractional denominations. Such an assemblage is similar to the money carried in one's wallet for everyday purposes. At Pompeii, for instance, a tremendous number of purse hoards were found in association with human remains. The purse hoard can be valuable in demonstrating certain aspects of a cash-based economy, by suggesting the types of coins that people regularly carried. The emergency hoard consists of coins collected and hidden hastily, sometimes buried alone or under the floor of a residence to prevent it from being discovered. Such hoards are usually distinguished by their haphazard collection of coins and frequent inclusion of precious metal in other forms, as well as jewelry and gems. In contrast, the savings hoard is distinguished by its often-striking regularity in the types and quality of the coins gathered together. Like an emergency hoard, these coins were usually placed in a ceramic vessel or strongbox; in this regard, they are similar to a piggy bank (and have been found in such containers). Savings hoards of Roman coins have been found as far away as India.

The prevalence of Roman coins throughout the empire suggests that there was a strong degree of popular acceptance for their use. Although it can be assumed that some form of barter also existed within the economy, the overwhelming amount of evidence—from coins and hoards, price lists, and the frequent mention of economic interchange in Roman literature—illustrates the widespread use of money and coins.

THE AMERICAS

BY PENNY MORRILL

In Mesoamerica from the 10th century B.C.E. and up to about 200 C.E., the Olmec on the Gulf Coast, the early Maya, people in the Oaxaca region, and the peoples of Tlatilco, Teopantecuanitlan, and Chalcatzingo in central Mexico lived in villages surrounding ceremonial centers. Village life was dedicated to subsistence farming. There was always a need for utilitarian stone tools, ceramics, and clothing as well as ritual objects. The development of the ceremonial centers and an elite class requiring luxury and ritual goods created a demand for a greater variety of products; thus, a growth in specialty production and regional exchange networks developed. These same changes in the social hierarchy and in production specialization were taking place among the Chavín at Chavín de Huántar in central Peru.

Archaeological research has verified that jade and obsidian in Mesoamerica acquired a high value, as did gold and textiles in Peru. However, there is no archaeological evidence for a specific value given an object, whether for use by villagers or for the elite shaman-lords. It is not possible to ascertain what was bartered or exchanged for gold or jade. For these early cultures in the Americas and others in North America there is no archaeological proof to date for the use of currency in exchange for goods.

See also AGRICULTURE; ART; CERAMICS AND POTTERY; CITIES; CLOTHING AND FOOTWEAR; ECONOMY; EMPIRES AND DYNASTIES; EMPLOYMENT AND LABOR; GOVERNMENT ORGANIZATION; LITERATURE; METALLURGY; MIGRATION AND POPULATION MOVEMENTS; MINING, QUARRYING, AND SALT MAKING; NUMBERS AND COUNTING; RELIGION AND COSMOLOGY; RESISTANCE AND DISSENT; SACRED SITES; TOWNS AND VILLAGES; TRADE AND EXCHANGE; WEIGHTS AND MEASURES; WRITING.

FURTHER READING

Edward Bleiberg, "The Economy of Ancient Egypt." In *Civilizations of the Ancient Near East*, ed. Jack M. Sasson (New York: Scribner, 1995).

Edward Bleiberg, "Prices and Payments." In *The Oxford Encyclopedia of Ancient Egypt*, ed. Donald B. Redford (Oxford, U.K.: Oxford University Press, 2001).

P. J. Case, *Understanding Ancient Coins: An Introduction for Archaeologists and Historians* (London: B. T. Batsford, 1986).

Glyn Davies, *A History of Money, from Ancient Times to the Present Day* (Cardiff: University of Wales Press, 1994).

Toyin Falola and Akanmu Adebayo, *Culture, Politics and Money among the Yoruba* (New Brunswick, N.J., and London: Transaction, 2000).

Kenneth W. Harl, *Coinage in the Roman Economy, 300 B.C. to A.D. 700* (Baltimore: Johns Hopkins University Press, 1996).

Phillip Hill, *The Monuments of Ancient Rome as Coin Types* (London: Seaby, 1989).

A. G. Hopkins, *An Economic History of West Africa* (London: Longman, 1973).

Christopher Howgego, *Ancient History from Coins* (London: Routledge, 1995).

Colin M. Kraay, *Archaic and Classical Greek Coins* (Berkeley: University of California Press, 1976).

Paul F. O'Rourke, "Coinage." In *The Oxford Encyclopedia of Ancient Egypt*, ed. Donald B. Redford (Oxford, U.K.: Oxford University Press, 2001).

David L. Vagi, *Coinage and History of the Roman Empire, c. 82 B.C.–A.D. 480* (Chicago: Fitzroy Dearborn, 2000).

David Warburton, *State and Economy in Ancient Egypt: Fiscal Vocabulary of the New Kingdom* (Göttingen, Germany: Vandenhoeck and Ruprecht, 1997).

► music and musical instruments

INTRODUCTION

Music is produced by making something vibrate. A singer makes the vocal cords vibrate, but the principle is the same for instrumental music. Sometimes music is created by making a membrane vibrate, such as the animal skin of a drum, or by making a string or a column of air vibrate. All such music was made in the ancient world. The ancients, though, left behind no written scores, so historians of music can only speculate about how ancient music sounded.

The desire to make music runs deep through human history and into the human psyche. The most ancient hunter-gatherers no doubt learned that they could make music with their voices. The earliest musical instruments were probably drums and rattles used in religious observances, celebrations, and perhaps as a form of communication. In time, percussion instruments evolved into hand bells to produce music in ancient churches and temples. Sometimes glass crystals served the same purpose.

Among ancient stringed instruments were various forms of lyres, harps, and zithers. Paintings depicting harps, for example, are found on the walls of ancient Egyptian tombs, and an early form of the guitar was used in such places as ancient Persia and India. Generally, these instruments were played by plucking, either with the fingers or with a pick.

Ancient wind instruments date back to the dawn of history and include flutes of bone found in ancient Europe and horns of metal—yet another legacy of the later development of mining and metallurgy. These early horns are the ancestors of modern-day trumpets, trombones, and the like. In Asia bamboo was perfectly suited for making flutes, for bamboo is already hollow; with the addition of a row of holes, bamboo flutes are little different from modern metal flutes. In the Americas flutes were often fashioned of cedar and are still used by Native American tribes to play haunting melodies. Also used in some parts of the world were instruments made of reeds and similar materials. These instruments evolved into modern-day clarinets, oboes, and other reed instruments.

Music in the ancient world had purposes that are little different from its purposes in modern life. Farmers—and probably slaves as well—chanted songs to make their labor lighter and to make the time pass. Soldiers used music in marching as well as to celebrate military victories. Music was used during festivals, parades, and celebrations and to accompany theatrical presentations, such as mimes. In the ancient world, epic poems, legends, and tales were often sung or chanted to make them more memorable not only for the audience but for the poet or storyteller as well. Music also played a key role in religious rituals. Like modern people, the ancients believed that music was a way to honor or appease the gods and to take part in the divine spark that gave people life. Music has no tangible existence; it disappears as soon as it is produced.

AFRICA

BY DAVID OTIENO AKOMBO

Throughout Africa vocal music has been sung for millennia. All cultures in Africa have used vocal music, believing that vocalization of thought through some musical medium such as song and chant is effective in reaching out to the supernatural deities ruling the land. These ancient beliefs are supported by contemporary production of vocal music in various cultural settings.

Even though vocal music is a distinctively older genre in the African musical repertory, compared with other genres of instrumental music and declamatory dirges (songs of mourning) such as those performed by griots (oral historians who recount cultural tradition through song), a systematic study of the variety of its forms has lagged for two reasons. One is that the use of vocal music among Africans is still an area of esoteric knowledge. Another is that the ownership of vocal music is communal rather than individual. For example, when a work song is composed, the composer delegates the work to the community, and the community owns it as they sing it within the context of their social events. When an individual musician composes a puberty song to be sung at ritual ceremonies such as Orunyege, a tribal courtship dance of the Nyoro (also called Banyoro, Bunyoro, or Kitara) people of western Uganda, the community and the new initiates will eventually claim ownership of both the song and the dance. This sense of collective ownership of song and dance artifacts makes it difficult for the work of art to remain purely a solo piece, for it is transformed into a group performance intended as a collective social phenomenon.

Classification of African musical instruments is generally fraught with difficulty. According to one widely accepted classification of musical instruments, there are four broad categories of instruments: membranophones, which produce sound by a vibrating membrane; idiophones, which produce sound by vibrating themselves; chordophones, which produce sound by vibrating strings; and aerophones, which produce sound by vibrating columns of air.

It has been theorized that the possible sequence of instrumental evolution in Africa can be traced from drums to pipes to strings. Since rhythm antedates melody, Africa's oldest instruments are hypothesized to have been percussive—specifically, hands and feet used to create rhythm. Other percussion instruments included pieces of wood or even skulls of animals. The drum has been the instrument of religious ritual among many African peoples from prehistoric to present times. Later ancient Africans added pipes, such as bamboo woods and horns that easily transformed into the aerophones. The chordophones, similar to lyres, were also created from various artifacts, such as the hunting bows of the Kamba people of Kenya.

Geography influenced the origins of ancient African musical instruments. For instance, people living in sub-Saharan Africa migrated slowly, with strong and weak tribes scrambling for richer valleys. These migratory patterns reshaped the musical instruments found in sub-Saharan Africa in three ways: Vegetation from swamps and forested areas gave rise to large membranophones and idiophones, aerophones such as reeds were found mainly in the semiarid regions, and unaccompanied choral singing was established mainly in open grassland.

The African scales (series of notes differing in pitch, varying with the frequency of vibration) and modes (set patterns of notes played over an octave using the white keys of a keyboard) took centuries to develop. It is difficult to determine how many modes actually exist, since the music is functional as opposed to contemplative, like that of Western forms. The musical scales and modes of African music are based mainly on impassioned speech and as such have never been fully conventionalized. In essence, musical melody is subordinated to some form of meaningful tone by following the natural inflection of speech within the language. This is because most African languages are tonal; hence, the base meaning of the words will change according to the intonation, the rise and fall of the voice's pitch. As such, these idiosyncratic attributes have influenced the way Africans view their scales and modes and have made it difficult to point to the exact tonal and modal characteristics of African music.

These African modes can also be heard when a drummer plays in the speech mode by reproducing the tonal and rhythmic patterns of speech on the drums. This type of transfer is drawn from ritual, work, or play, and so the modes are externally motivated. This is, in a sense, contrary to the conventional Western staff transcriptions, because the African scales differ in microtones and the pitch classifications are completely dissimilar.

For much of the history of the people of Africa, vocal music has been a universal experience. Such beliefs in the power of music are found throughout the world. Sound is used to reach outward toward the deities. In turn, it is through the vibratory matrix that sound provides that the deities themselves, it was thought, descend from the spiritual abode to participate in the human world. Vocal music is the vortex of religious ritual. The main purpose of vocalization was to appease the supernatural powers, solicit divine protection, and give thanks to the guardian spirits of the community. For millennia Africans have tended to approach their cultural activities, such as healing, through vocal music. In addition to these roles, Africans also relay these songs as entertainment. When the community likes the songs, they all join in and develop other tones to create naturally blended harmonies.

African musical instruments have a complex sociocultural significance. In keeping with their intricate musical system, Africans have used every known type of portable instrument; thus, it is important to examine African society in the cultural contexts in which instruments are played. While they may be used to produce a human experience, they are also used to teach societal norms, including respect for the aged and a continuing relationship between dead ancestors and the living. Instruments were used as media for communication and for imitating animals and birds to create the symbiotic relationship between animals and people. This coexistence is an ancient African tradition. The belief that the highest gods were part animal and part human led Africans to look upon animals with great reverence and love; accordingly, instruments were sometimes played to imitate the sounds of the animals.

Since ancient times African instruments have been used in the cycle of human life, including daily, social, political, and religious life. African musical instruments also serve as artistic works and as cultural symbols. They may represent specific social hierarchies, such as the *atsimevu* drum of the Ewe people of Ghana that symbolizes the commander. The *sabar* master drummer of the Wolof tribe of Senegal is conferred status through the performance of his drum and is, therefore, a leader in the community. His repetitive drum patterns symbolize stability in the community.

EGYPT

BY EMILY JANE O'DELL

While we have many depictions of musical instruments and musicians from the tombs of ancient Egypt, we know very little about the actual nature of the music itself. The frequent portrayal of musicians and musical events suggest that music was an integral part of both religious and secular gatherings, but without any notation it is virtually impossible for Egyptologists at this point to know what the music sounded like and how it was composed, written, and disseminated.

Musicians in tomb representations usually are shown playing in an ensemble and frequently are accompanied by singers, hand clappers, and dancers in palaces and temples and at funerary events. Musicians in ancient Egypt were both male and female, though female musicians did not appear until after the end of the Old Kingdom (ca. 2575–ca. 2134 B.C.E.). Men and women played together in ensembles, especially in the Middle Kingdom (ca. 2040–ca. 1640 B.C.E.), but in the New Kingdom (ca. 1550–ca. 1070 B.C.E.) women played in groups without men. These ensembles ranged in size, but some were composed of as many as 10 sistrum players and 10 hand clappers. Women wore light dresses and braided their hair with small balls hanging from the ends of their tresses, whereas men wore kilts. Both men and women could be overseers of these ensembles. There were titles for musicians (most meaning "temple singer"), and the abundance of designations suggests that musicians could function in many different capacities. Women singers were usually referred to as songstresses or chantresses.

Music was used to accompany ancient Egyptian religious rituals, such as the recitation of religious and funerary texts. Some gods and goddesses were associated with music. One of Hathor's incarnations was as the goddess of festivity and mistress of music. Priestesses of Hathor used sistrums to produce percussive rattling. Blind Horus was a god of the harp. Interestingly, many musicians in ancient Egypt are portrayed as blind or wearing a blindfold. The goddess Meret was appealed to in order to bring sacred texts to life. Thus, Meret could be said to be a goddess of sacred chanting. The male deity Bes is shown in ancient Egyptian art playing instruments, in depictions in Egypt as well as abroad. Music also was used to praise Osiris and Isis and Amun-Ra, among other gods and goddesses.

Music was used in both religious and royal contexts for rituals and festivals, and it was also used in daily life in the secular sphere. Family members would dance and sing for their deceased ancestors at their tombs. In the New Kingdom there are even examples of laborers who sang in the fields. During the New Kingdom a genre of harper's songs emerged, so called because a harper was illustrated alongside the text of these poems. These texts, which would have been sung at a banquet at the tomb in honor of the tomb owner, are quite rare when compared with the rest of the Egyptian corpus, owing to their insistence on the celebration and appreciation of earthly life over the afterlife.

The ancient Egyptians used a variety of instruments that would have produced a range of sounds, scales, tones, and tunes. There were a number of percussive instruments. Sistrums, as noted previously, were used to produce a rattling sound, especially in praise of Hathor and Isis. Sistrums were metal rattles held with a handle that would often be in the shape of the goddesses Hathor. On top of the hand was an oval-shaped frame that held metal horizontal rods on which beads were placed to shake and make noise when rattled. In fact, some large stone columns in the Hathor chapel of Queen Hatshepsut's mortuary temple at Deir el-Bahri and in the temple of Queen Nefertari in Abu Sir resemble Hathor sistrums. Hand clappers produced sound with their hands, but they could also use "clappers," which were a set of boomerang-shaped instruments that could be struck together to create sound. These clappers eventually became decorated with hands to serve as a visual pun on the act of clapping. Clappers, like sistrums, also could be decorated with the face of Hathor. Wooden drums appeared in Egypt in the Middle Kingdom and seemed to have been introduced from Palestine. There were barrel-shaped drums as well as tambourines.

Ancient Egyptian musicians also played string instruments, especially the lyre and lute, which were similar to those found in other Middle Eastern areas. The harps, however, were distinctly Egyptian in shape and first appeared around 2500 B.C.E. in Egypt.

Harps were made of ebony but could be elaborately decorated with gold, silver, lapis lazuli, and malachite. One style of harp was arched, while the other was angular. Arched harps would have had between three and 10 strings, whereas angular harps would have had 21 to 29 strings. Angular harps appeared in Mesopotamia around 1900 B.C.E. and eventually usurped the arched harps that were there. However, the arched harp was the most popular kind in Egypt, and it took much longer for the angular harp to prevail over the arched harp than it had in Mesopotamia. Ancient Egyptians played three types of lyres. The thin lyres hailed from Syria, whereas the thick lyres, larger and with more strings, came from Anatolia. Giant lyres came to prominence and popularity in the Amarna Period (ca. 1353–ca. 1307 B.C.E.), and some could even be played by two musicians at a time. While lutes arrived in Egypt in the New Kingdom from the Middle East to much popularity, they became virtually nonexistent when Egypt became a member of the Hellenistic world.

Ancient Egyptians also played a variety of wind instruments—including flutes, divergent double pipes, and parallel double pipes—all of which were constructed from reed pipes. The tomb of King Tutankhamen (r. 1333–1323 B.C.E.) also contained trumpets that were made of silver and bronze fitted with gold and silver mouthpieces. Trumpets seemed to have been reserved for military occasions. We do not know the notation of ancient Egyptian music, so it is uncertain how the music would have been sung and arranged. It seems apparent from some textual evidence that there were antiphonal songs, containing verses to be sung in alternation, similar to call-and-response songs, and perhaps also a rondo form, in which a principal theme is repeated between contrasting musical sections. While music was an integral part of ancient Egyptian religious and secular life, we may never know how the music sounded and how exactly it would have added to the atmosphere of sacred and daily life gatherings.

THE MIDDLE EAST

BY LYN GREEN

In the ancient Near East music was an essential part of the daily life of both gods and mortals. Human beings could bridge the gap between the ordinary world and the divine through music and song. Music was also a sort of international language, as ancient texts tell of musicians and musical instruments being sent from country to country. In the 14th century B.C.E., for example, the Egyptian king recorded the visit of a foreign princess accompanied by a retinue that included many entertainers.

A great variety of musical instruments are mentioned in texts or represented in art: stringed instruments, wind instruments, and rhythm instruments. Defining ancient musical instruments, especially stringed instruments, can be a challenge, since their shapes often are not only different from those of today but also changed over time and from region to region. We do know, however, that the peoples of the ancient Near East had what we would classify as drums, cymbals, tambourines, pipes, lyres, harps, and lutes. Musical instruments seem to have been highly prized, and some were elaborately crafted and decorated.

A cuneiform tablet from the 26th century B.C.E. is the oldest-known record of musical theory and records names of musical instruments. It cites 23 types of musical instruments as well as musical terms, such as the names of notes. By the Old Babylonian Period (2004–1595 B.C.E.) examples of musical notation appear, as do more tablets of musical terms. In addition, we have the lyrics of numerous hymns, which would have been chanted or sung by trained choirs. Other types of vocal performance are believed to have resembled modern Arabic and Asian singing.

Drums made of bull hide and wood appear in sizes from small hand-held drums to giant, shoulder-high instruments. Pipes were made of all kinds of materials, including reed, bone, wood, and metal, and came in many shapes. There is so little information about wind instruments, however, that we cannot say whether ancient Near Eastern musicians had flutes, trumpets, or other wind instruments familiar to us in their modern forms. We do know that the hollowed horns of animals, such as ibexes and bulls, were blown in the temples.

Although drums and tambourines are undoubtedly very ancient, some of the oldest pictures of musicians depict stringed instruments such as harps and lyres, and these are also some of the oldest instruments ever found. In the Third Dynasty of Ur (ca. 2112–ca. 2004 B.C.E.), in modern-day Iraq, rulers were buried with their servants, animals, and a great quantity of treasures, including beautifully made harps and lyres. These instruments were crafted of wood inlaid with lapis lazuli, shell, and bitumen and lavishly covered in gold foil and ornamented with sculptures of bulls' heads. Over the millennia the weight of earth entering the tombs crushed them flat, and the organic parts, such as the strings and sound box, decomposed, so that what we see in museums today are reconstructions based on photographs and records of the excavation and on ancient images of music making. (One of the lyres conveniently featured an image of a lyre being played on its sound box.)

Relief plaque of harpist from the Old Babylonian Period (ca. 2000–1600 B.C.E.) (Courtesy of the Oriental Institute of the University of Chicago)

Impressions on clay seals reveal that the harp was known in ancient Persia from about 3000 B.C.E. onward. The earliest harps had an arched shape, but after about 1900 B.C.E. angular versions replaced them. In some angular harps the sound box was horizontal, in others vertical. The instruments had between 15 and 25 strings probably made of animal sinew. (The early arched harps had far fewer strings.) Some Persian angular harps were large enough to rest on the ground, and others were small enough to be carried. There are many depictions of the smaller versions from the rest of the Near East as well.

Like the harp, the ancient Near Eastern lyre came in two sizes: small and portable and large and stationary. In some cuneiform texts the small lyres are called *zinar* and the large ones *hunzinar.* The lyre differs from the harp in that the lyre's sound box is on the bottom and the strings are suspended from a horizontal bar that passes between the instrument's two upright arms. Three different lyres were found at Ur, all on the large side. However, they pale in comparison with the giant lyres of the Late Bronze Age, which stood taller than the musicians. Images of these instruments show that they were played by two people, one at either end or side of the lyre.

Lutes arrived relatively late in the Near East—the first mention of them comes from around 2000 B.C.E. Having only a couple of strings, they did not look much like the medieval European lutes familiar to us, and the instrument remained a novelty in many areas. For unknown reasons lute players are often shown dancing and even depicted naked, unlike other musicians in ancient Near Eastern art.

Given the close association between music and religion in the ancient Near East, it is not surprising that many of the most important positions held by singers or musicians were connected with religion. In Sumer the highest-ranking position in some cities was that of precentor, the leader of singing or chanting in religious worship. Musicians and singers in Mesopotamia formed guilds and sometimes lived in the temple colleges, though many of these performers were not full-time temple employees. Over time some musicians began playing or singing for funerals and magic rites and became private, rather than public, servants.

Several Mesopotamian gods and goddesses were associated with music. Ea, god of wisdom and freshwater, was the patron god of all music, and Ishtar/Inanna (goddess of love and war), her husband Tammuz/Dumuzi, and the storm god Ramman were the patrons of singing and pipe playing. Even the many divinities with no direct links to music all apparently loved it, for most of the important religious rituals required singing, music, or both.

ASIA AND THE PACIFIC

BY AMY HACKNEY BLACKWELL

Music was an important art form throughout ancient Asia and the Pacific. People sang, chanted, and played instruments of various types. In China people were making music long before recorded history. In Henan Province archaeologists have found a flute made of a bird bone that dates to 7000 B.C.E.; other prehistoric instruments may be even older. Music was a well-developed art form in China during the Zhou Dynasty (1045–256 B.C.E.). The imperial court had its own musicians and styles of music, while the ordinary people played and sang folk music. During the Qin Dynasty (221–207 B.C.E.) the emperor created a bureau of imperial music to regulate the music played throughout China; this bureau established rules for court music, military music, and folk music. Although musicians played for emperors, they had low social status. Ancient Chinese musicians invented a number of instruments to play music on the Chinese five-note scale. The flute was one of the earliest instruments. In the first three millennia B.C.E. flutes were usually made of bamboo, which was readily available and easily worked, allowing common people to make flutes.

Stringed instruments were widely played in ancient China. One of the most common was a seven-stringed instrument called the *qin*, or *guqin*, which resembled a modern zither and was played by plucking. The *qin* is still played in modern China. Ancient *qin* were only about one-third the size of modern ones and were played with open strings. The modern form of the *qin* is believed to have been invented during the Han Dynasty. According to myth, the *qin* was invented around 3000 B.C.E. by the legendary kings Huang Di, Fu Xi, and Shennong; the tale says that the first *qin* had only five strings and that two more were added later. Actual historical mentions of the *qin* date to about 1000 B.C.E., and archaeologists have found *qin* in tombs that date to about 500 B.C.E. Other ancient stringed instruments included the *pipa*, a four-stringed fretted lute; the *ruan*, a four-stringed lute with a round body resembling a banjo; and the *konghou*, or harp, invented around 600 B.C.E.

Bowed fiddles (stringed instruments played with a bow instead of by plucking) were invented in Persia around 1000 B.C.E., and travelers in central Asia carried them east along the Silk Road. The Mongols developed this design into several types of bowed instruments called *huqin*, a name meaning "barbarian instrument" in Chinese. During the Han Dynasty, Chinese music was heavily influenced by the music of the Mongols and other peoples of central Asia, and Chinese musicians adopted some central Asian instruments, such as the *morin khuur*, a fiddle played with a bow of horsehair by Mongol horse herders. During the Song Dynasty (420–479 C.E.) Chinese musicians began playing the *erhu*, a two-stringed bowed fiddle that was played sitting down as the musician held the base of the instrument on his knee.

Music was widely performed and sung in India by the time people began writing down the Vedas, the oldest Hindu texts, starting between 2000 and 1500 B.C.E. Much of Indian music had a religious purpose. The Vedas were transmitted orally through chanting. Priests intoned sacred hymns in a musical style with notes associated with particular syllables and a prescribed rhythm. Often groups of priests and believers would chant mantras (sacred words or phrases) together; a leader would call out the words and tune, and the group would repeat the mantra after him. According to Hindu doctrine, singing the correct musical notes was essential to summoning the spiritual power of the words. This style of vocal music was called *Carnatic music* and was the predominant musical form in all of India from about 2000 B.C.E. until the end of the ancient period. Indian people also played instruments to accompany vocal chants. The main instruments were the flute, temple bells, and several stringed instruments, such as the sarod, which resembled the guitar.

Ancient Japanese people developed a complex musical tradition. To the Japanese, poetry and songs were closely linked and in some cases indistinguishable. Japanese musicians recited or chanted poems to a musical accompaniment on a stringed instrument, a flute, or a drum. The Japanese divided their music into categories, such as court music, military music, and popular music. Listening to a particular style of music evoked for them the culture from which that music originated.

Much of what historians know about Japanese music comes from songs and poems from the later Nara Period (645–710 C.E.), which scholars have used to reconstruct some ancient Japanese musical principles. Archaeologists have found statues of musicians dating to the ancient Jōmon (ca. 13,000–ca. 300 B.C.E.) and Yayoi (ca. 300 B.C.E.–ca. 300 C.E.) periods, but Japanese musicians of these periods did not write down any of their musical pieces. The Nara Period texts *Kojiki* (Records of Ancient Matters) and *Nihon shoki* (The Chronicles of Japan) were the first recorded archives of Japanese history; these documents contain many songs of ancient origin. By the time scholars started writing about music, they had a well-established body of work to describe, which means that modern historians can surmise a fair amount about ancient Japanese music that predated the sixth century C.E.

The evidence for ancient Korean music is fragmentary and comes mostly from Chinese sources. Korean had both formal court music, performed at seasonal festivals and ceremonies, and more casual folk music, played and

Red sandstone railing pillar in the form of a flute player (second century C.E.), Mathura, northern India

sung by common people. Historians know that a seven-stringed zither of Chinese design was played in Korea during the third, fourth, and fifth centuries C.E. Koreans also played a uniquely Korean stringed instrument called the *komun'go* starting in the fourth century; numerous tomb paintings from that period depict the instrument. This instrument was placed in a horizontal position and played by striking the strings and pressing them against frets. People in central Korea played a vertical harp that may have been influenced by central Asian instruments.

Southeast Asian music was influenced by that of India and China. Burmese music most resembled ancient Indian music; Burmese musicians adopted the Indian harp as a favorite instrument. In Java during the second and third centuries B.C.E. smiths used bronze to create gonglike instruments that were carried into battle by soldiers. By the fourth century C.E. these gongs had evolved into the gamelan, a collection of bronze gongs played by a group of musicians. People believed that the gamelan had supernatural powers over the weather and human emotions; they were often played in ceremonies to bring rain or at weddings.

Pacific islanders composed many hymns and chants that they sang a cappella, or without the accompaniment of instruments. The people of Tahiti sang chants in a microtonal scale, a scale that contains more notes within an octave than the traditional 12 notes of the Western scale. Islanders also used drums to accompany vocal music. In Australia traditional music was part of ritual and entertainment. Songs commemorated the history of clans and heroic deeds, mourned the dead, and told of religious traditions. The most common instrument was the didgeridoo, a pipe made of wood; although the earliest historical record of the instrument comes from cave paintings from the fifth century C.E., historians believe that the didgeridoo may be the oldest wind instrument in the world, which means Aborigines could have been playing it in 7000 B.C.E. or earlier.

EUROPE

BY SIMON O'DWYER

Music in Europe has its origins some 40,000 years ago with the arrival of the modern human being. A number of bone flutes have been recovered from caves in France and Germany, including a swan-bone flute found in the Geissenklösterle Cave, Germany, dated to about 37,000 B.C.E. and generally considered to be the oldest surviving musical instrument in the world. Many of these early flutes were recovered in proximity to cave paintings, and audio experiments in caves in France suggest that the paintings occur in areas of caves with good acoustics and not in those with bad acoustics. Thus it would appear that music and visual art were associated from the very origins of both.

Musical instruments that survive from the European Stone Age tend to be animal- or bird-bone whistles and flutes, simple stone flutes, and rock gongs (rocks that produce a resonant tone when struck). One notable exception is the remarkable set of wooden tubes known as the Wicklow Pipes, recovered from an ancient cooking place in County Wicklow, Ireland. These six cylindrical pipes of varying lengths are finely carved from yew wood and presented together in a panpipe arrangement. Carbon-dated to about 2135 B.C.E., the pipes each have a socket carved at one end to accept a mouth-blown tone generator that was not present with the find. The sockets would allow a player to fine-tune the pipes by moving the tone-generator extension inward or outward. Such a facility is highly unusual in the Late Stone Age and clearly demonstrates that the musicians then were achieving accurate and complex music.

In the Middle to Late Bronze Age (ca. 1500–600 B.C.E.) two distinct types of metal wind instruments emerged. Some 60 cast-bronze trumpets known as *lurs* have been found in northern Germany, Denmark, and Scandinavia. They are made in a double opposing conical curve over 6 feet in length with a circular decorated plate at the bell. Thus the instrument, when played, curves around the upper body of the player, and the plate is presented over the head facing forward. The *lurs* were made in pairs with opposing curves so that two paired players would make a balanced right and left presentation. Many of the instruments have chains attached, believed to have made sounds that contributed to the performance. It is generally thought that *lurs* were played as part of religious or royal ceremonies.

The second great family of metal wind instruments emerged in Ireland and perhaps Britain around 1100 B.C.E. In Ireland no fewer than 104 horns are known to exist, while a fragment of one and a drawing of another survive from Scotland and England, respectively. This number represents about 40 percent of the entire world collection of prehistoric metal wind instruments. A single find, known as the Dowris Hoard, from County Offaly, Ireland, contains 26 bronze horns—the largest such group ever found anywhere—accompanied by 39 bells or rattles.

The Bronze Age horns of Ireland and Britain were all cast from a two-part clay mold with a central core held in place by bronze pins. The Irish examples, found throughout the island, occur as two distinctive types. About half had a mouthpiece or mouth hole fitted into the side of the horn, while the rest employed a more conventional end-blown arrangement. The way in which both kinds of horns were found together suggests that they were played in pairs or multiples of pairs of end-blown and side-blown instruments. Recent research and reproduction have revealed surprisingly rich and complex musical properties for the horns. By employing tone variation and circular breathing techniques, a good player can produce a variety of sound and rhythm. It is particularly noteworthy that the horns can be used to play an overtone series over the fundamental note. This is a playing technique whereby a series of higher notes are produced above a continuous drone. Normally it can be achieved only by specialized singing, which is practiced in Nepal, Tuva, and Tibet. It is now generally accepted that these Bronze Age horns were played throughout the islands as entertainment and in ceremonies such as religious rituals and celebrations of the inauguration of kings.

The 39 bells or rattles found as part of the Dowris Hoard are known as *crotals*. The name *crotal* is a Gaelic word derived from the Latin *crotalum* meaning "rattle." Each is roughly the size and shape of an avocado, hollow, with a loose pebble inside and a ring fitted at the top. Sounded by hand or perhaps attached to a belt around the waist of a dancer, they can produce a light, tinkling rhythm. Oddly, with a single exception (from County Antrim, in what is now Northern Ireland), these 39 *crotals* found together are the only ones of their kind known to exist. Perhaps a distinctive musical subculture was thriving in the area of County Offaly in the Late Bronze Age.

The European Iron Age (ca. 500 B.C.E.–300 C.E.) saw the emergence of long trumpets and horns made of sheet bronze (bronze beaten or compressed into thin sheets that can then be formed into tubular or other shapes). The most common of these was the carnyx, a great war or ceremonial conical trumpet presented vertically over the player's head and having a stylized bronze head of a boar, dragon, or snake at the top. Fragments of these trumpets have been found across northern Europe. The most important find, near Bordeaux, France, included five complete instruments in company with other plundered artifacts of war. A small number of more conventional sheet-bronze horns survive from northwestern Europe. Of these, the two most famous examples are the Ard Brinn (ca. 200 B.C.E.) from a place of that name in modern-day County Down, Northern Ireland, a two-part, conical, S-shaped instrument almost 10 feet in length, and the Loughnashade ("Lake of the Treasures") from County Armagh, Northern Ireland (ca. 100 B.C.E.). Accurate reproductions have been made of each, and surprising discoveries have come to light as to how they were made and to what uses they may have been put.

The more notable is the Loughnashade, which was probably assembled in the S position. Today the two quarter-circle parts of the trumpet are displayed assembled in the National Museum of Ireland in a semicircular, or C, position. Studies of the first reconstruction have established, however, that the circular tubes were probably originally connected in an opposing, or S, position and then played while being held up vertically over the player's head. The distinctive circular plate is positioned at the end and faces forward. Thus, these war trumpets would have functioned in a similar manner to the carnyx.

There is a tendency among scholars of ancient musical instruments to ignore the achievements of prehistoric northern Europe in favor of the great civilizations of Egypt, Greece, and Rome. However, the great antiquity of the bone flutes and the very fine design, manufacturing, and musical qualities of the metal horns and trumpets from the northern European Bronze and Iron Ages clearly point to a rich and inclusive musical tradition spanning many thousands of years. A region that the Romans labeled as savage or barbaric produced some of the most beautiful instruments, both in appearance and in sound, that have ever been made and played.

GREECE

BY JEFFREY S. CARNES

The Greeks considered a life without music the grimmest sort of existence. Music permeated ancient Greek culture at every level, from officially sponsored public festivals to the daily lives of working-class men and women. Already in the Homeric era it was everywhere: In the *Iliad* Achilles strums his lyre and sings heroic songs while sitting out from the fighting; boys and girls sing harvest songs later in the poem; the *Odyssey* gives examples of singers at banquets and women singing at the loom. In a real-life context the historian Thucydides reports that Athenian prisoners of war working in the quarries of Syracuse were forced to entertain their captors by singing choral odes of the tragic poet Euripides.

Greek instruments were surprisingly few in number. Lyres of various descriptions and a pipe instrument called the *aulos* were far and away the most common. Lyres have either box-shaped or bowl-shaped sound boxes. The latter type was called a *lyra* or sometimes a *chelus*—literally "tortoise," since a tortoiseshell typically formed the sound box. The face of the instrument was composed of ox hide; this supported the bridge, while curving arms made of horn or wood extended above the sound box. A horizontal bar connected the arms, and the strings (made of gut or sinew and usually seven in number) were fastened to this. The *lyra*, like all Greek stringed instruments, was plucked (the bow was a later invention); the pick, or plectrum, usually made of bone or ivory, was considerably larger than a modern guitar pick.

The *lyra* was small and not capable of producing much volume; sources suggest that it was played mostly in home and classroom settings. For public performances musicians preferred various types of box lyres. Pictorial evidence for these goes back as far as Mycenaean painting (ca. 1200 B.C.E.); the instruments look to be heavily built. The most evolved form was the kithara, in use from approximately 600 B.C.E. Other stringed instruments, such as harps, were of secondary importance. On all of these it seems the strings were normally played open rather than stopped.

The most important wind instrument was the *aulos*, consisting of two cylindrical tubes, each equipped with finger holes, and sounded with a double reed, like the modern oboe. It could produce not only strong volume but also moving dramatic effects. The *aulos* was the instrument of choice to accompany choral poetry (including tragedy) and provided music at large public events as well as smaller private gatherings. Other wind instruments included panpipes (a wind instrument composed of a series of pipes bound together), flutes, and the *hydraulis*, a water-powered organ invented in the third century B.C.E., which was the world's first keyboard instrument. Brass instruments served primarily to give signals in military

The Greek god Apollo with a kithara, a stringed instrument similar to a lyre (Alison Frantz Photographic Collection, American School of Classical Studies at Athens)

contexts; percussion instruments (which included cymbals, castanets, and hand-held drums) were used in entertainment and in ecstatic religious worship.

Our knowledge of how Greek music actually sounded comes largely from numerous ancient works on music theory, based on the tuning of stringed instruments. The fundamental unit of the Greek scale was the tetrachord: four tones, with the top and bottom forming an interval of a fourth and the other two varying. An octave scale or mode could be built up of two tetrachords, with varying combinations possible, named after their alleged national origin (for example, Dorian, Lydian, or Phrygian). The sequence of intervals in most was different from our major and minor scales. The Dorian, for example, roughly corresponded to a scale played entirely on the white keys of a piano starting on E. The modes, however, had varying tonal centers: In a modern scale, the lowest note is the tonic, with the function of other notes determined in relation to it; for a Greek mode the tonal center might lie elsewhere. Tuning of instruments was also different: Octaves were not necessarily divided into equal parts as in modern equal-temperament systems. Furthermore, the size of intervals could vary: Modern systems use only the whole tone and the semitone, but the Greeks made frequent use of quarter tones and other small intervals (non-Western musical traditions and some innovative jazz and modern composers make use of such intervals).

Greek music was almost entirely melodic rather than harmonic; that is, in most cases only one note was played or sung at a time. Choruses sang in unison or in octaves; although the musical accompaniment may have played a different note from the sung one, there was no counterpoint or complex harmony. The rhythm of Greek music was complex and tied closely to the rhythms of Greek poetry, which it frequently accompanied. There exist nearly 50 examples of Greek musical notation; recreations of Greek music based on these examples tend to sound exotic to Western ears, sometimes reminding listeners of Indian or Middle Eastern music.

Audiences for musical performances ranged from a few guests at a symposium (a drinking party in someone's home) to 30,000 or so spectators in a theater. Most musical genres were also poetic genres. Epic poetry was accompanied by the *phorminx* (a type of kithara), lyric by a lyre or kithara. Perhaps the most significant and certainly the most spectacular genre was choral poetry, in which a group of performers sang and danced (the word *chorus* means "dance") to the accompaniment of an *aulos*. This was a diverse genre, ranging from the victory odes of the poet Pindar to the choral sections of tragedy (a dramatic form that developed when individual performers were added to engage in dialogue with the chorus). In typical Greek fashion both choral poetry and solo performances of songs with kithara accompaniment became objects of competition at major festivals: Musicians as well as athletes could be Olympic victors. Literary sources describe (not always with approval) the virtuosity and innovation of composers and musicians in this highly competitive environment.

Music was an important part of education, and to be an accomplished lyre player was a valued sign of upper-class status. Moreover, music was thought to have important effects on moral character. Plato, drawing on the work of earlier theorists, rejected musical modes that supposedly promoted excessive emotion and approved of only those believed to engender courage and moderation (the Dorian and Phrygian). Similarly he condemned the *aulos* for its overly expressive nature. Aristotle's *Politics* contains an extended discussion of the effects of music on the souls of citizens. For the mathematician-philosopher Pythagoras the harmonies present in music, based on mathematics, were a sign of the harmony of the world as a whole—a mystical line of thought followed by many other ancient Greek philosophers.

ROME

BY AMY HACKNEY BLACKWELL

Ancient Romans loved music. Music was a part of most social gatherings, from dinner parties to parades. Farmers sang folk songs as they worked in the fields, women sang as they went about their daily chores, and admired performers were treated as celebrities. Despite music's popularity, ancient Romans left behind little information on their music and musical practices. The Greeks wrote a great deal about music and considered musical training an essential component of a gentleman's education, but it appears that Romans did not feel the same way about music as a subject. They considered it a necessary component of religious ceremonies and public celebrations and thought it entirely appropriate for young people to learn the basics of music, but they did not dwell on its philosophical implications the way the Greeks did.

For many Romans music was trivial entertainment, nothing more. Roman poetry, unlike Greek poetry, was designed to be recited without music. Romans who did write about music preferred to dwell on the musical artistry of Greek music, not on Roman compositions or performances. Aristocratic Romans considered professional musicians somewhat disreputable and often bewailed the lax morals of musicians and actors. With the exception of a few celebrated professionals, most musicians were of the lower or middle classes and did not associate socially with the upper classes.

Young nobles of both sexes studied music as part of their education, but respectable Romans did not encourage their children of either sex to aspire to be professional performers paid for their work. Music teachers were generally slaves, often Greek. Girls were expected to learn enough music to perform at home for their families. Noble children occasionally performed publicly, such as on one occasion when the Roman poet Horace trained a choir of children to sing at the Secular Games in 17 B.C.E.

Music was essential to numerous public events. Sacrificial rituals were not complete without pipe players. Practitioners of foreign cults brought their music with them to Rome; the worshippers of Isis, for example, played daily hymns to their goddess. Parades usually included singers and dancers who performed to the music of drums, tambourines, pipes, and lyres. Musicians played trumpets and pipes during funeral processions. In the theater comic plays were accompanied by musicians playing pipes, brass, and percussion instruments; actors often sang and danced to this accompaniment. Pantomime, a popular dramatic form, consisted mainly of silent actors moving to music created by pipes and singers. Wealthy people often hired musicians and dancers to entertain their guests at parties. The most popular musicians achieved fame throughout Rome; for example, the writers Cicero and Horace both mention the famed piper and singer Tigellius.

Romans did not leave behind any musical scores, so historians have never been able to reconstruct Roman musical styles or melodies. Historians do, however, know something about the musical instruments Romans played. They used stringed, wind, and percussion instruments. Singing was also common.

Ancient stringed instruments were all plucked with the fingers or with a pick called a plectrum; no instruments of this time were played with a bow. The lyre was one of the most ancient stringed instruments, supposedly invented by the Greek god Apollo, who made the first lyre out of a tortoiseshell strung with cow intestines. The lyre consisted of two arms and a crossbar affixed to a sound box, with strings strung from the crossbar to the base of the instrument. Some lyres used a tortoiseshell as a sound box; others were made of wood and hide painted to resemble a tortoiseshell. Lyres had between four and seven strings made of gut, sinew, or flax.

CARMINA: MAGIC SONGS

Although Romans did not leave behind much evidence of their musical compositions, there are numerous examples of a type of song called a *carmen*, the plural of which is *carmina*. *Carmen* was a generic Latin term for a song; the word derived from the verb *cano*, meaning "to sing." It originally referred to anything chanted, particularly religious incantations or magic spells. To perform magic spells, people would sing or chant verses in a specified order and perhaps perform other ritual actions such as spitting. Repetition of the verses was necessary to make the magic work; three or nine were common numbers for required repetitions. Spells could be used for anything, from winning love to cursing an enemy. Carmina were considered serious business in Rome's early days; the Twelve Tables, Rome's most ancient laws, forbade the casting of a *malum carmen*, or an evil spell.

Although by the time of the Roman Republic (509–27 B.C.E.) the term *carmen* generally meant just a song, the word continued to have a sense of enchantment. Priests sang several types of *carmen* at festivals. The historian Livy (59 B.C.E.–17 C.E.) describes priests dancing and leaping through the streets as they chanted their hymns. The *carmen arvale* was a song to the Roman god Mars and the Lares, Roman household gods, performed during the sacrifice to the Dea Dia, a goddess whose festival occurred in May. The *carmen saliare* was a hymn sung by the Salii, priests of Mars, during the parade to celebrate their annual festival. For this parade the priests dressed up in ancient armor, carried ancient weapons, and performed an ancient dance that involved leaping and jumping; the name *Salii* refers to their leaping performance. Historians believe that these songs were slow and solemn.

Not all *carmina* were religious. When Roman soldiers paraded through the city during a triumph, a parade celebrating a major victory over an enemy of Rome, they sang the *carmina triumphalia*, a collection of ancient songs that either praised their general or mocked him satirically in order to ward off the evil eye.

The player plucked the strings with a large plectrum made of wood, bone, or horn.

Roman musicians often played the kithara, a stringed instrument that produced a more piercing sound than the lyre. (The word *kithara* evolved into the English word *guitar*.) Kithara could be much larger than lyres, though there were also small ones that were often played by women. The kithara could be tuned more precisely than the lyre. Some Roman sculptures depict kithara with triangular tuning pegs that look as though they were turned with a key to adjust the tension of the strings.

Lutes, which had round sound boxes, long necks, and three strings, were also popular. Ancient lutes were very similar to lutes played in Europe in the medieval period. People also played several different kinds of harp. Both harps and lutes were plucked with the fingers, usually of the right hand; the player used the other hand to damp strings that he did not want to sound.

Romans played several types of wind instruments. One of the most common was a pipe called a *tibia*, played throughout the Mediterranean region. The tibia took several forms. One was a flute made of a single pipe held sideways to the player's head and played by blowing across the mouthpiece and covering combinations of holes with fingers. Another version had two reeds and two pipes fastened side by side. Players fingered one pipe with each hand. A player might wrap a cloth band around his head to support his cheeks while playing.

The panpipe consisted of several tubes attached to one another side by side. The player blew across the ends of the tubes to create different notes. The Roman version of the panpipe had tubes of different lengths, unlike the Greek version, which used tubes of the same length plugged with wax to achieve different pitches. Panpipes were considered a rustic instrument most appropriate for rural settings.

Both Greeks and Romans played bagpipes. Romans loved a type of pipe organ called a *hydraulis*. The earliest form used a hydraulic mechanism to blow air across the pipes. Operators used levers to pump air into a vessel of water; this compressed the air and forced it over the ends of the pipes, making noise. By the second century of the Common Era the hydraulic mechanism had been replaced by a bag inflated by bellows. The *hydraulis* was large and loud. It was commonly used at the Colosseum to enliven gladiatorial events. Romans also used several types of trumpet, both straight ones called *tuba* and curved types called *cornu*. The army used trumpets to deliver military orders and in parades. Civilians used them whenever they needed to signal the start of some event, such as a theatrical performance or the beginning of a festival.

Musicians used several kinds of percussion instruments to keep the beat of musical performance. The simplest form of percussion was snapping, clapping, or stomping in time to the music. Musicians also used drums, castanets, wooden clappers, and cymbals. Tambourines called *tympani* were a very common instrument used in parades and at parties; dancing girls often played them as they danced.

THE AMERICAS

BY LAWRENCE WALDRON

It is difficult to imagine the sound of ancient American music from the scant evidence available today. Early musical instruments were often made of biodegradable materials, such as wood, hides, and horn, and few of them have survived to inform the theories of anthropologists and ethnomusicologists, those who study music in its sociocultural context.

Ceramic instruments outlast those made of organic matter, and various ceramic drums, wind instruments, and noisemakers have been found in Central and South America. Anthropologists working in those regions have also uncovered ceramic eating and drinking vessels on which are painted scenes of musical rituals and celebrations. Scholars also can compare the remains of ancient instruments with later, similar versions to extrapolate the sounds and uses of ancient music. Still, most of what is known about ancient American music is inferred from a very imperfect archaeological record, many artifacts being made of materials that may not have been the most typical in their time.

Music in ancient America was produced using three major classes of instrumentation. Wind and percussion instruments seem to have played the most important role in rituals and festivals. A variety of idiophones—devices that make specific, unusual, and often atonal noises—constituted the third class of musical instruments. Wind instruments were made of wood, reeds, ceramic clay, or bone; as the name suggests, they were blown like flutes or trumpets. A vast range of percussion instruments were beaten for rhythm, most of them resembling drums from other parts of the world. Idiophones were the most widely varied instruments. Some were struck like percussion instruments, but many were shaken, turned, twirled, spun, or even worn in dance to produce a plethora of sounds. Stringed instruments rarely played a part in ancient American music.

If later Native American music can give any clue to earlier forms, ancient musical instruments may have been used to accompany singing, chanting, and speech during rituals and sacred spectacles. Here the voice would have been the chief source of tone and melody, while rhythms and sounds from musical instrumentation may have functioned theatrically: to draw or fix the audience's attention, to mark important passages in sung or spoken performance, or perhaps to aid in memorization of myths and legends. Fully instrumental music was seldom part of ancient American performances.

It is easy to assume that drums were universal, but some groups in South America evidently had no use of them even at the time of European contact. Nevertheless, percussion instruments were very widespread in the ancient Americas, and their design ranged widely as well. The most rudimentary may simply have been wooden planks beaten with sticks, sometimes over a chamber dug out of the ground, a method customary among some Pacific Northwest Coast Indians. Cultures in both North and South America, however, developed a variety of skin drums. These were essentially wooden tubes or barrels across the mouths of which were stretched membranes of animal skin. They could be played either with sticks or with the hands. Some Mesoamericans made slit drums, hollow lengths of logs into which slits were cut to vary the sound of the instrument.

From Costa Rica to Bolivia ancient Indians developed ceramic variations on the more common wooden skin drum. By the beginning of the Common Era, Indians of the wooded regions of the American Northwest Coast were already expert at joining and bending wood with heat, making it possible to give skin drums almost any desired shape, thereby producing a variety of sound qualities as well. Many drums may have been carved or dyed with symbolic or decorative motifs.

Southwest Indians of what is today the United States played double-headed drums, while Indians of the Northeast used wooden kettledrums to accompany their cane flutes and singing. From paintings on ceramic vessels anthropologists know that Andean peoples such as the Moche and their ancestors made tambourines and gongs, instruments easily carried in royal and religious processions.

With their airy, sometimes shrill tones, ancient flutes, whistles, and trumpets produced sounds that resembled those found in nature. The human voice, the stirring wind, and various species of birds could all be imitated by Native American wind instruments. Among North American and Amazonian Indians, with their rich shamanic traditions, wind instruments could also be used to represent spirits of the natural world and the hereafter. In their ritual performances the ancient Plains Indians of North America played flutes fashioned out of cedar and perhaps other woods. They also made eagle-bone whistles whose exact use remains unclear, though it may have been connected to mystical practices.

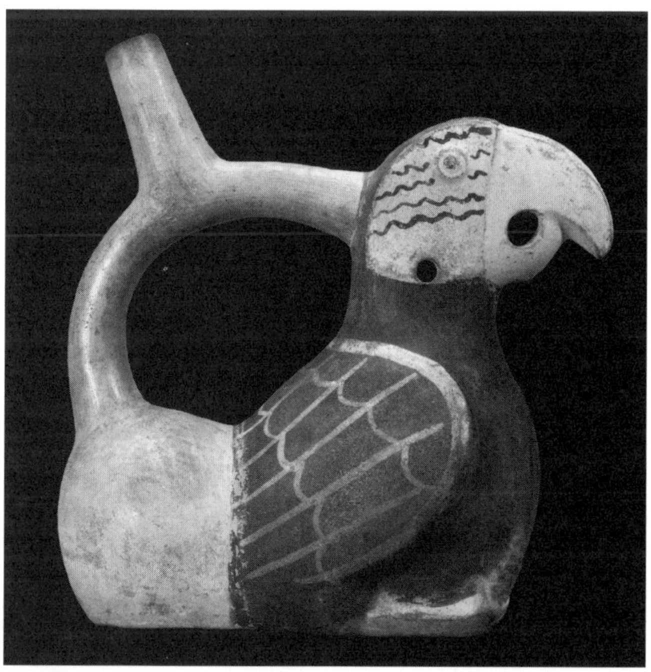

Whistling vessel in the form of a macaw, Peru, Moche culture (ca. 100–700 C.E.) (© The Trustees of the British Museum)

Northwest Coast Indians played reed instruments whose tones could be varied by the force of the player's breath. Indians living in coastal regions throughout the Americas often adapted marine materials to make idiophones, such as clamshell clappers. They also acquired wind instruments ready-made from the sea: conch shells blown at religious and military ceremonies.

Using wooden panpipes or ceramic ocarinas (sculpted clay vessels blown like woodwinds), Andean Indians developed richly melodious and harmonic music. This was probably one of the few ancient American musical forms enjoyed for its own sake rather than in a supporting ritual role. In fact, the Andeans produced several whimsical devices that served to delight the listener. Potters excelled at creating utilitarian ceramic vessels that whistled when the water inside them was agitated. They also made pots that contained closed chambers filled with ceramic beads, which made rainlike noises when the vessels were shaken.

Mesoamericans seem to have used music both for religious ritual and for the entertainment of royals. The early Maya developed clay, wood, and cane trumpets, to which they sometimes added a gourd on the end as a resonator. Some of these wind instruments may have been inspired by even earlier Olmec prototypes.

Some instruments were used to produce singular, peculiar noises that may not have had any clear tones like, say, those of sweetly blown ocarinas or flutes; others may have supplemented the powerful beats of drums with more tonal, delicate, or rapid percussions. In the North American coastal Northwest rattles of animal skin filled with pebbles were shaken at shamanic rituals and possibly during pronouncements from tribal leaders. Northwest coastal Indians also made rattles from gourds, turtle shells, and insect cocoons, any of which could be filled with seeds or stones and attached to a handle. Clappers, to be played on their own or to accompany drums, were made by splitting sticks to create two separate tongues that slapped against each other when the instrument was shaken.

Plains Indians made rattles of rawhide, while Southwest Indians used hollowed horns. Employing their wide trade contacts, southwestern peoples imported metallic bells from the Late Pre-Classic Maya far to the south. The bells, attached to cords or bands and either shaken by hand or worn by dancers, produced a constant rhythmic ringing at sacred dances. The Maya themselves probably learned metal casting through their indirect contacts with South America, where there may have been similar instruments employing metallic resonance.

Some Indians of the North American West are known to have played music on their hunting bows, strumming the string as they held it between their teeth. A change in the shape or position of the player's mouth changed the sound of the plucked string. Interestingly, this musical weapon seems to have been the only string instrument used in ancient America.

See also ADORNMENT; ART; CHILDREN; CLIMATE AND GEOGRAPHY; CLOTHING AND FOOTWEAR; CRAFTS; DEATH AND BURIAL PRACTICES; DRAMA AND THEATER; EDUCATION; EMPIRES AND DYNASTIES; FAMILY; FESTIVALS; GENDER STRUCTURES AND ROLES; INVENTIONS; LANGUAGE; LITERATURE; METALLURGY; MILITARY; OCCUPATIONS; RELIGION AND COSMOLOGY; SACRED SITES; SLAVES AND SLAVERY; SOCIAL ORGANIZATION; SPORTS AND RECREATION.

FURTHER READING

Robert D. Anderson, "Music and Dance in Pharaonic Egypt." In *Civilizations of the Ancient Near East,* ed. Jack M. Sasson (New York: Scribner, 1995).

John Miller Chernoff, *African Rhythm and African Sensibility: Aesthetics and Social Action in African Musical Idioms* (Chicago: University of Chicago Press, 1979).

Giovanni Comotti, *Music in Greek and Roman Culture,* trans. Rosaria V. Munson (Baltimore: Johns Hopkins University Press, 1989).

Emory Dean Keoke and Kay Marie Porterfield, *American Indian Contributions to the World: 15,000 Years of Inventions and Innovations* (New York: Checkmark, 2003).

Gerhard Kubik, *Theory of African Music* (Wilhelmshaven, Germany: Florian Noetzel Press, 1994).

John G. Landels, *Music in Ancient Greece and Rome* (London: Routledge, 1999).

Andy Lowings, "Lyre of Ur." Available online. URL: http://www.lyre-of-ur.com/intro.htm Downloaded on March 2, 2007.

Martha Maas and Jane McIntosh Snyder, *Stringed Instruments of Ancient Greece* (New Haven: Yale University Press, 1989).

Lise Manniche, *Music and Musicians in Ancient Egypt* (London: British Museum Press, 1991).

J. H. Kwabana Nketia, *Drumming in Akan Communities of Ghana* (Edinburgh, U.K.: Thomas Nelson and Sons, 1963).

Simon O'Dwyer, *Prehistoric Music of Ireland* (Stroud, U.K.: Tempus, 2004).

Dale A. Olsen, *Music of El Dorado: The Ethnomusicology of Ancient South American Cultures* (Gainesville: University Press of Florida, 2002).

Prehistoric Music Ireland. URL: www.prehistoricmusic.com. Downloaded on April 5, 2007.

Curt Sachs, *The History of Musical Instruments*, rpt. ed. (New York: W. W. Norton, 1968).

Jenny F. So, *Music in the Age of Confucius* (Washington, D.C.: Smithsonian Institution, 2000).

Emily Teeter, "Female Musicians in Pharaonic Egypt." In *Rediscovering the Muses: Women's Musical Traditions,* ed. Kimberly Marshall (Boston: Northeastern University Press, 1993).

M. L. West, *Ancient Greek Music* (Oxford, U.K.: Clarendon Press, 1992).

Akin P. Harper, "Dance In Nigeria," *Ethnomusicology* 9, no. 1 (1969): 280–295.

N

► natural disasters

INTRODUCTION

Natural disasters are a fixture of life on earth. From the dawn of history to the 21st century, people have had to contend with floods, fires, earthquakes, volcanic eruptions, storms, plagues of destructive insects, and other deadly visitations of nature. These and other natural occurrences wreaked havoc on farms, cities, and coastal communities and disrupted patterns of farming, fishing, and other activities. In the ancient world these events often led to the loss of entire communities, as people were often unable to flee natural disasters. They also destroyed ancient monuments that represented some of the high achievements of ancient cultures.

Few written records of these natural disasters exist. Once major exception is the Roman Empire, which left behind written records of major volcanic eruptions, such as the eruption of Mount Vesuvius in 79 C.E. that buried Pompeii and other nearby cities. The archaeological ruins of Pompeii have provided historians with a unique look at the region's culture, for the city was covered in volcanic ash and lava so quickly that people were "frozen" in their homes going about their daily tasks. Ancient Mexico was also devastated by volcanic eruptions, and ancient Japan was the frequent site of volcanic eruptions as well as tsunamis.

In the absence of written records, historians have had to rely on archaeological evidence for natural disasters. Using sophisticated tools, as well as old-fashioned digging, they have uncovered the effects of natural disasters throughout the world. Around the Mediterranean Sea, for example, countries such as Greece and the many islands in the region were susceptible to earthquakes. It is believed that a major earthquake devastated the island of Crete, home of the Bronze Age Minoan culture, in about 1700 B.C.E. Lost in this earthquake was the magnificent palace of King Minos. While written records from the Minoan culture survive, historians have not been able to decipher them. These records could very well contain records of the earthquake, but archaeologists know that the palace was destroyed because excavations have shown that a new palace was built on the ruins of the destroyed palace. Earthquakes were also responsible for obliterating four of the ancient Seven Wonders of the World: the Hanging Gardens of Babylon, the Lighthouse of Alexandria, the Colossus of Rhodes, and the Mausoleum of Maussollos at Halicarnassus.

Sometimes the effects of natural disasters were less visible but no less disruptive. Along the coast of South America, for example, people had to contend with changes in ocean weather patterns that killed off the fish and seafood populations on which the people depended. Throughout the history of the ancient world famine was a constant threat, as prolonged periods of drought or higher-than-normal temperatures could lead to shortages of food and widespread death from starvation over long periods of time.

Ancient peoples tended to attach religious significance to natural disasters. The ancient Chinese, for example, thought drought and extreme high temperatures were signs that demons were loose in the land. They often saw such disasters as a form of punishment, a sign that the gods were displeased with humans. In ancient China a series of major disasters over the centuries actually led to the fall of emperors, who, the people believed, were being punished for brutality or for living in luxury.

AFRICA

BY LEAH A. J. COHEN

Research on historic and prehistoric natural disasters in Africa is still a new field and continues to result in major new findings. One of the oldest Holocene natural disasters to be uncovered in archaeological and geologic research in Africa is the eruption of Mount Menengai around 8,000 years ago. This eruption occurred in the East Africa Rift Valley in present-day Kenya and produced a 5- by 7.5-mile caldera, or volcanic crater. Another eruption took place about the same time in Madagascar (a very large island off the southeastern coast of Africa), creating a number of crater lakes and hot springs. There are little data on how these eruptions affected the local population of humans or animals or the surrounding vegetation.

A volcanic eruption at Mount Jebel Marra (in present-day Sudan) has been dated to around 3,500 years ago. The blast formed a 3-mile-diameter caldera and sent lava flows more than 18 miles. Again, little is known about this natural disaster's effects on local human and other populations. A Carthaginian navigator in the fifth century B.C.E. reported witnessing an eruption of what was probably Mount Cameroon, a large volcano in West Africa. There has been no modern research on the impact of this event on the local area, nor has it been dated using modern dating methods.

About 4,000 years ago people in northern Africa were responding to an extreme 300-year drought. This drought created barren, inhospitable sand dunes in areas of the Sahara that had previously been occupied since the end of the last ice age. Mass migration resulted in increases in population in places near water, such as the Nile River valley. Historical records suggest that this population growth may have been a factor in mounting conflict in the Egyptian empire.

"Plagues" of locusts are a particular area of new research on natural disasters in Africa. Locusts are a species of grasshopper. Hatching from eggs in the ground at specific periods (in some cases there are years between outbreaks), they grow into adults and swarm en masse across the landscape, devouring most of the vegetation, including crops, in their path. There is evidence of the presence of such locusts in western Africa from three to five million years ago, but little is known about these ancient outbreaks.

The record on natural disasters in Africa is far from complete. Numerous events undoubtedly remain to be uncovered and investigated. Some of what is suspected about past natural disasters in Africa comes from modern anthropological accounts of local myths. For example, people who currently occupy the area around Lake Nyos in Cameroon (on the western coast of central Africa) have a legend that the lake causes numerous deaths from time to time. Although little is known about the historical basis for this myth, a disaster in the 1980s resulted in the sudden death of over 1,800 people near the lake. Scientists have since discovered that the water was releasing large amounts of carbon dioxide into the air, but much remains unknown about this occurrence and whether earlier events of the same kind might have given rise to the myth.

EGYPT

BY PANAGIOTIS I. M. KOUSOULIS

According to ancient Egyptian conceptions, the creator god fashioned the cosmos out of chaos, a dark, watery abyss that surrounded the universe and the created world. He then established *maat*, the divine and political order. *Maat* (also personified as a goddess of the same name) was the cornerstone of the Egyptian belief system and Egyptian ethical values. Harmony in nature, as well as in social and private life, was the result of the establishment and perpetuation of *maat*. By contrast, natural disasters or political and social decline occurred when chaotic forces prevailed over *maat*.

Despite the often dire consequences of earthquakes, floods, storms, and fires, Egyptians do not seem to have been interested in keeping historical records of such events. Evidence of natural disasters is limited to religious and magical texts, which often allude to them mainly in terms of various mythological concepts and traditions. The Pyramid Texts, engraved on the walls of the funerary chambers of a succession of pharaohs, form the oldest funerary and religious corpus of the ancient world. The first of these texts, in the pyramid of the last ruler of the Fifth Dynasty, Unas (r. ca. 2356–2323 B.C.E.), describes the return of the pharaoh to life in the appearance of a new god, violent and powerful: "The sky flies cloudy, the stars darken, the [celestial] bows move, the bones of the Akeru tremble, the Moving-ones, as for them, become silent after they have seen Unas apparent and provided with *ba*, as a god who lives of his Fathers and feeds of his Mothers." The Akeru were a group of subterranean genies, leonine watchers of the netherworld. Their bones could well have been interpreted as the stronger parts of the earth's body, the rocks. Some scholars view this passage as the first historical reference to the Egyptian explanation of earthquakes.

Another passage from the Pyramid Texts, this one from the tomb of the pharaoh Pepi Neferkare, whose reign (ca. 2246–2152 B.C.E.) remains the longest in human history, clearly describes heavy rain and floods, seismic events, and some sort of conflagration: "The water of life which is in the sky comes! The water of life which is in the earth comes! The sky burns for you, the earth quakes for you, before the god's birth."

Evidence of seismic phenomena also appears in a famous tale from the Middle Kingdom known as "The Shipwrecked Sailor." A man reaches a mysterious and beautiful island unharmed after having survived a storm at sea. He discovers plenty of food there and makes a burnt offering to the gods to thank them. The description is particularly precise and without doubt refers to a seismic event. As in the Pyramid Texts, however, such an event is closely interrelated with symbolical

Rock inscription at Seheil, Egypt, recording a seven-year famine (Courtesy of the Oriental Institute of the University of Chicago)

connotations: The earth's motion on the island of the shipwrecked is a sign of divine manifestation or epiphany.

All of these texts place disastrous natural phenomena in a positive framework. The dark and negative effects of natural disasters on people's lives are found more often in Egyptian magical texts, such as the *Calendars of Lucky and Unlucky Days.* Dating to the reign (ca. 1290–1224 B.C.E.) of Ramses II, the *Calendars* cast the fortunes of each day of the year in terms relating to a mythical event or, at least, a mythical depiction of a natural event, an archetype. For example: "Third month of the Inundation-season; fourth day: Uncertain! Uncertain! Uncertain! To move by this earth under the forepart of Nun. As for anyone who sails in this day: destruction in his house." (Nun was a god personifying the primeval waters out of which the creator god emerged.)

Similarly, a literary work of the late 13th century B.C.E., the "Dialogue of Ipuwer and the Lord of All," blames natural disasters for the downfall of the Egyptian political authority and society of the First Intermediate Period (ca. 2134–2040 B.C.E.) and Second Intermediate Period (ca. 1640–1532 B.C.E.). The protagonist of this lament, Ipuwer, describes Egypt as afflicted by natural catastrophes and in a state of social collapse. The poor have become rich and the rich poor; servants are leaving their masters and acting rebelliously; and warfare, famine, and death are everywhere.

An inscription on the so-called Famine Stele from the time of Ptolemy V Epiphanes (r. 205–180 B.C.E.) records a disastrous famine that took place during the reign of the Third Dynasty king Djoser (r. ca. 2630–2611 B.C.E.). The text states that Djoser was worried because Egypt had been gripped by a drought for seven years, during which time the Nile did not flood. Djoser asked for aid from the priests of Imhotep (a historical high official and architect who had been deified as a god). The priests investigated in the archives of the temple of the moon god Thoth (who also presided over scribes and knowledge) in Hermopolis and informed the king that the god was angry and for this reason did not allow the Nile to flow properly. Djoser ordered offerings sent to try to placate the god. The following night the king had a dream in which the ram god Khnum, who had created life on a potter's wheel, promised an end to the famine. The king issued a decree settling vast riches and resources on Khnum's temple in Elephantine.

The ancient Egyptians seem to have had relatively limited interest in disastrous natural phenomena and, except for the oldest funerary conceptions in the Pyramid Texts, rarely mentioned them even in metaphorical terms. The most frequently described phenomenon, the earthquake, is understood as a marker of epiphany and as a model for the movement of life.

THE MIDDLE EAST

BY LYN GREEN

Natural disasters such as floods and earthquakes afflicted parts of the ancient Near East with relative frequency. Anatolia (modern-day Turkey) and Persia (modern-day Iran) are still the sites of frequent earthquakes, which in ancient times were perhaps even more disruptive than they are today: Not only did they bring death, disease, widespread destruction of property, and loss of livelihood on their own, but they also could open up a society to outside attack. One geologist has used an attack on Jerusalem in 31 B.C.E. as an example of how the weakening of city fortifications caused by a quake could result in military disaster. Other scientists have tried to link the end of the Bronze Age cultures of the Near East with earthquakes and their aftermath.

Among the many disasters that nature could visit on humankind in the ancient Near East there were also the oft-cited examples of plagues of locusts. The biblical story of Exodus tells of the various plagues that swept through Egypt, the eighth of which was a plague of locusts. Swarming locusts easily cut a path of destruction through cultivated fields, denuding them of their crops. Another Old Testament book, Joel, also speaks of a locust plague and more: "That which the palmerworm hath left hath the locust eaten; and that which the locust hath left hath the cankerworm eaten; and that which the cankerworm hath left hath the caterpillar eaten."

Many seismically active areas of the world, including those in the Near East, exhibit volcanic activity as well.

Volcanic eruptions can have disastrous effects far beyond their immediate vicinity. Ash or other debris in the atmosphere reduces the amount of sunlight reaching the earth, thus lowering the temperature in the affected area. Less sunlight means smaller crops, and lower temperatures can produce shifts in patterns of precipitation, leading to either flooding or drought. Soil debris from Mesopotamia suggests that some sort of catastrophic event—perhaps a volcanic eruption or even a meteorite impact—occurred in the Near East around 2350 B.C.E. Some scientists have speculated that this event caused an abrupt climatic change in the area, in turn leading to a change of dynasties in southern Mesopotamia. However, the climate change appears to have occurred over the course of some 100 years following the mysterious catastrophe, making it unlikely that this single event caused the shift in weather patterns.

Seismic disturbances are not the only catastrophes linked with shifts in cultures. Probably as a result of the renewed interest in comets in the 1990s, some scientists have attempted to explain cultural changes in the Near East as the long-term consequences of comet impacts. For example, there is a great deal of evidence for sudden climate changes (leading to widespread drought) and changes in water levels of seas and lakes, disastrous floods, earthquakes, and volcanic eruptions in the third millennium B.C.E. Scientists have suggested various explanations, including a comet or asteroid exploding in the earth's atmosphere, as is believed to have happened near Tunguska, Siberia, in 1908. The power of such an explosion or impact, equivalent to thousands of atomic bombs, could have produced huge fires, seismic tremors, tsunamis, and gargantuan clouds of debris. Such an event would have been universally seen as a message from the gods, would doubtless have been recorded as a notable event in any king's reign, and probably also would have been transformed into myth, but clear written evidence is lacking.

Despite the frequency of earthquakes, not to mention windstorms and sandstorms, drought, and (in some areas) wildfires, the one type of natural disaster that had the most impact on all the cultures of the ancient Near East is floods, or rather the story of the Flood, which appears in the literature of ancient Mesopotamia as well as the Bible. Swirling floodwaters are an integral part of every ancient story of creation from Egypt to Babylonia. Symbolically they represent the chaos from which order can emerge and which the creator deity tames and transforms into something beneficial. However, many scholars see these stories as reflections of real events.

The earliest-known stories of a flood that covered all the earth are told in several ancient Mesopotamian epics. In one version a man called Ut-napishtim is warned by Ea, god of wisdom and of freshwaters, that the gods are angry with humans and that the chief god, Enlil, is about to flood the earth in order to get some peace and quiet. Ea gives Ut-napishtim interesting directions on how to build a boat (for example, it is to be in the form of a cube) and tells him to go into the vessel with his family and a few animals. Enlil, assisted by the storm god and the god of the Underworld, floods the earth from both above and below, effectively killing all those irritating human beings and forcing even the gods themselves to flee. Ut-napishtim and his family and livestock float off into the Zagros Mountains, where after seven days they eventually come aground on the sides of a high peak.

Although this story was lost for thousands of years, when it was rediscovered it was immediately familiar to anyone who had read the biblical book of Genesis. In both cases a man who is wiser and godlier than others is chosen to survive the destruction of humankind by an angry deity. Like Ut-napishtim, Noah is divinely warned of the impending disaster. He, too, builds a huge boat according to divine direction and fills it with animals. The flood described in the Bible, however, lasts 40 days and 40 nights rather than just one week, and Noah brings with him pairs of living creatures. Noah's Ark also ends up in a slightly different set of mountains, those of Ararat.

Modern scholars have made many attempts to relate the ancient flood stories to scientifically documented phenomena such as the era of rainy weather that followed the last ice age, but without any conclusive result. This uncertainty is unsurprising, given that the story is about 5,000 years old and the events it chronicles are probably much older—typical of the problems that face those historians and scientists known as catastrophists, who try to connect ancient natural disasters with specific historical events.

ASIA AND THE PACIFIC

BY KIRK H. BEETZ

The ancient people of Australia offer a good example of how hunter-gatherer cultures learned to cope with natural disasters. Australia is a vast territory with a variety of habitats such as rain forest, grassland, and desert. Its weather cycles can last for years at a time, which means that its droughts can persist for several years. Australia is also prone to wildfires that can burn hundreds of square miles of territory at a time. Still, the ancient Australians learned to live with both drought and fire.

The ancient Australians were mobile and lived in small groups. During good times they had more than they could eat available to them because of their minimal population; during droughts their low population density allowed them to find enough to at least survive. Droughts meant not only a decrease in the amount of food that would otherwise be available but also dry forests and grasslands. Lightning could easily start fires. The ancient Australians sometimes ventured near fires rather than running away, because a fire drove game out into the open, which they would kill or capture for food. After fires burned out, what might look desolate to outsiders was for the Australians a potential bounty because among the earliest plants to appear would be edible ones—especially those that had evolved to cope with drought by retaining water, which meant the ancient Australians would eventually have moist food to eat. Thus, because they lived in small groups that allowed them to move quickly and they did not have towns or farms to defend, the ancient Australians survived what could be catastrophic disasters for other cultures.

Natural disasters can be swift, catastrophic events, or they can be slow occurrences—at times aggravated by human technology—that over centuries destroy what humans build. The Harappan civilization of ancient India (ca. 2600–1500 B.C.E.) offers examples of both. Its largest settlements were built near rivers. The Harappans irrigated their lands with water that flowed from the north, carrying with it silt that built up in the rivers, raising the beds of the rivers until they changed their courses, sometimes flooding settlements. Further, watercourses deposited salts in the soil that were not washed away because rainfall was insufficient to do so. Over hundreds of years the Harappans began to go hungry because their poisoned land could not grow as much food as it once had.

Their cities were increasingly subject to floods as the rivers jumped their banks, but the Harappans either repaired their damaged cities or built on top of the silt deposited in them. Even so, there was one flood that may have been too much for them. The Indus River valley is subject to frequent earthquakes. Sometime after 2000 B.C.E. an earthquake reshaped the territory near the delta, blocking the river's way to the sea and causing it to flow backward and cover Harappan cities in the Indus River valley. The Harappans built huts on top of where their cities had been; however, they were easy to overcome by nomads from the north who swept into India on chariots.

Of all the natural disasters to which India was subject, flooding attracted the most community effort, probably because it was the most likely to respond to human action. Accounts of floods are a part of Indian mythology, and various gods were believed to intervene to help human beings or to harm them. Thus, one way Indians coped with floods and storms was to pray to gods to spare human beings from the wrath of nature. India's peoples also took practical steps to tame water and make it useful. They built levees to contain rivers in their banks, dams to create reservoirs, and irrigation canals to take water to where farmers could use it. One such irrigation system, dam, and reservoir that created a fertile valley was built in Gujarat. In 150 C.E. the dam was destroyed by a storm, but it was rebuilt. In about 500 C.E., after the dam was again destroyed, they did what people often did when natural disasters overtook them too many times; they moved away.

The Silk Road stretched through central Asia from northwestern China to the ancient Near East. Along this road were impressive cities that were full of life with thriving economies and arts, yet they were doomed by a creeping natural disaster. The world's climate was changing, and the regions north of China and in central Asia were becoming colder and drier. This process of drying out is called *desiccation*, and along the Silk Road the land was drying out. Archaeologists are beginning to piece together the lives of the ancient peoples in the cities of the Silk Road, aided by the dryness and cold, which has preserved corpses thousands of years old. The cities of the Silk Road were abandoned when there was no longer enough water to drink.

Although droughts and floods were concerns throughout Chinese history, from the time of the Shang Dynasty (ca. 1500–ca. 1045 B.C.E.) to the end of the Six Dynasties era (220–589 C.E.) they were of special concern to the rulers of China. Droughts brought famines, and famines brought rebellions. Floods could kill people by the millions and destroy crops and cities. In each case, an emperor could pay with his life because it was the duty of emperors to remind the gods to provide good weather and prevent natural disasters. An emperor ruled by divine right, and natural disasters showed that the gods were not listening to him, meaning he had lost his divine right to rule and could be killed and replaced.

Thus, the Chinese government devoted much time, wealth, and manpower to finding ways to control water in times of flood and drought. About 80 percent of China's rainfall is in the summer, and its rivers fill with silt; the Yellow River can look like thick, flowing mud. A buildup of silt can raise riverbeds, which can result in their changed courses. Therefore, the Chinese dredged their rivers to keep the riverbed low. They also made levees ever higher, but this sometimes resulted in floods when a levee gave way to the pressure of flowing water. To relieve the water pressure, the directional flow of a river was controlled.

Possibly the greatest example of this is the work directed by architect Li Bing on the Min River in the 200s B.C.E. He had a man-made island built in the middle of the river to divide its flow into two directions. One direction was the old course of the river; the other direction sent the river east into a channel that carried water to irrigate about 2,000 square miles of farmland. A spillway sent excess water away from the channel to the main river; meanwhile the channel relieved the river of pressure against its banks, reducing the chance of flooding.

Little is known about disasters in Japan and Korea in ancient times. Japan certainly had earthquakes, but how the Japanese coped with them is not known. The work of archaeologists indicates that Honshu's northeast coast was struck by tsunamis, but dates for these events have yet to be established. Korea probably had floods, but as is the case for Japan, there is an absence of documentary evidence for the ancient era.

EUROPE

BY CARYN E. NEUMANN

Natural disasters frequently struck the ancient world. Without knowledge of science, the ancients struggled to make sense of earthquakes, tsunamis, floods, and volcanic eruptions. Additionally, such celestial events as eclipses and meteor showers, though they had little direct catastrophic impact on human life, were regarded as natural disasters by prehistoric people because they were such a deviation from the normal appearance of the sky. Stunned by the evident power behind such events, they could explain them only as the work of the gods. Detailed accounts of natural disasters in Europe, outside Rome and Greece, are rare. Archaeological evidence and the theories of astronomers fill in some of the gaps in the historical record.

The Stone Age hunters and gatherers had to cope with changing environments during the ice age. While these changes lacked the suddenness that is normally associated with natural disasters, the new conditions often caused people to modify their lifestyle and occasionally to retreat into warmer parts of southern Europe when the cold became too intense. After the ice age, the climate warmed up, but rising sea levels in many parts of northern Europe caused coastal settlements to become inundated. In 5900 B.C.E. a tsunami in the North Sea was caused by a massive submarine landslide off the coast of Norway that affected the entire North Atlantic basin.

Although the evidence is the subject of controversy, some scholars have argued that the Black Sea basin was flooded around 5000 B.C.E. by a breakthrough of a geological formation at the Bosporus that allowed Mediterranean water to flow through in a torrent. If this indeed happened, then this flood would have rapidly displaced the farmers and hunter-gatherers who lived around the Black Sea, forcing them to move quickly inland to avoid being drowned.

It is difficult to minimize the risk associated with volcanoes. A major group of volcanoes, both active and inactive, stretches across the Mediterranean through Anatolia and into the Caucasus. Besides the damage caused by lava and falling ash, volcanic eruptions can trigger landslides and giant waves. Prehistoric volcanic eruptions in 4700 B.C.E. prompted the sides of submerged hills in Lake Lucerne in present-day Switzerland to slump. The sliding sides of the hills displaced water and resulted in tsunami-like effects. Waves almost 10 feet high struck the lakeshore opposite the submerged hills within a minute of the slide of earth. The waves had lengths greater than half a mile, which is entirely different from the situation with ordinary wind-induced surface waves; they resembled mountains of water rising in the center of the lake and undoubtedly terrified witnesses. Any structures around the lake and any watercraft on it would have been destroyed by the waves. Sardinia apparently suffered a similar event. In Sos Furrighesos, Sardinia, a wide landslide in about 3000 B.C.E. smothered a settlement that had lasted for about 100 years. The survivors rebuilt in the same area, devising a new style of decoration for tombs that had survived undamaged. The tombs severely damaged by the landslide were abandoned.

The response of the Sardinians is typical of ancient people. In preindustrial societies people recovered from a disaster by harmonizing their responses to nature rather than employing technological solutions to manage and control nature. Individuals and small groups, rather than governments, took actions that were flexible and easily abandoned if they proved unsuccessful. Deaths and other losses from natural disasters were perceived as inevitable. Gods, not humans, were in charge. The mind-set of the ancients was dominated by notions of supernatural punishment or vengeance. Lacking scientific knowledge, ancient Europeans believed that the course of a volcanic eruption could be affected, if at all, only through divine appeasement.

GREECE

BY JOHN THORBURN

Although the ancient Greeks did not face threats from tornadoes, hurricanes, or typhoons, a tradition of dangerous winds does exist in their culture. Whereas the modern definition of "typhoon" restricts this type of storm to the western Pacific Ocean and the oceans around India, the English word is related to a Greek word, *typhos*, which means "whirlwind." According to Greek mythology, Typhon was a hundred-headed monster that tried to overthrow Zeus and the other gods. Ultimately, Zeus blasted Typhon with a lightning bolt and pinned the monster beneath Mount Etna on Sicily, where his fiery breath causes that volcano to erupt. Another well-known myth connected with wind is the story of Boreas, the god of the north wind, who abducted Oreithyia, the daughter of the Athenian king Erechtheus, and whisked her away to Thrace and impregnated her. She gave birth to twin sons, Zetes and Calais. Like their winged father, the twins could fly and assisted the hero Jason in his quest for the Golden Fleece.

Besides stories about powerful winds, Greek mythology also preserved tales of a major flood, which share similarities with the Sumerian Epic of Gilgamesh and the Flood story in the Old Testament. According to the Greek tradition, Zeus decided to destroy the human race because of their wicked behavior and thus prepared to send a flood. Deucalion, the son of Prometheus, and his wife Pyrrha, the daughter of Prometheus's brother Epimetheus—thanks to a warning from Prometheus—built a boat and managed to survive the high waters, which drove them from their home in northeastern Greece. After traveling in their boat for nine days and nights, Deucalion and Pyrrha landed on Mount Parnassus in central Greece.

Like Noah in the book of Genesis, Deucalion is said to have released a dove to determine if the weather would be favorable. After landing on Parnassus, Deucalion and Pyrrha went to the shrine of the goddess Themis and consulted her oracle about what they should do next. The oracle told them to throw the bones of their mother behind them. Initially, the couple thought this oracle meant they would have to dig up the bones of their dead mothers. Eventually, though, they realized that stones were the "bones" of Mother Earth. Accordingly, Deucalion and Pyrrha picked up stones and threw them over their shoulders. The stones Deucalion threw turned into men, whereas those Pyrrha threw became women. In this way, the couple repopulated the earth.

Although Greek mythology preserves stories of threats from wind and flood, the most dangerous natural disasters faced by the Greeks were connected with earthquakes, whose causes the Greeks traced to the god Poseidon, whom they nicknamed the "Earthshaker." In 373 B.C.E. an earthquake destroyed Apollo's temple at Delphi. Between 228 and 226 B.C.E. an earthquake toppled the giant statue of the sun god Helios, known as the Colossus of Rhodes. The island of Rhodes also suffered a serious earthquake again around 142 C.E. Ancient sources tell us that earthquakes severely damaged cities, such as both Myrina and Philadelphia in 17 C.E., and they destroyed others, such as Boura (also Bura and Bira) and Helice in 373 B.C.E. An earthquake may have disrupted the Minoan culture on Crete around 1700 B.C.E. and eventually caused the abandonment of the Cretan city Knossos about 2,100 years later.

One of the most significant earthquakes in Greek history occurred in 464 B.C.E. in the area around Sparta. So many Spartans died as a result of the earthquake that their slaves, called helots, revolted against their masters. The revolt continued for many months and became so serious that in 462 B.C.E. the Spartans called upon their rivals, the people of Athens, for military assistance. The Athenians agreed to help, but when their forces arrived the Spartans changed their minds about wanting assistance from Athens. This rejection angered the Athenians and further strained relations between the two cities.

As is common in areas frequented by earthquakes, the Greeks were also familiar with volcanoes. Like with other natural disasters, mythological traditions were connected with volcanoes. The monster Typhon, trapped beneath Mount Etna, was said to cause that mountain's eruptions. Signs resembling volcanic activity on the island of Lemnos were attributed to the workshop of Hephaestus, the craftsman of the gods.

Beyond the realm of mythology, we know that on mainland Greece, near the southeastern coast, the Methana volcano sent a flow of lava over 500 yards into the nearby Saronic Gulf in the third century B.C.E. Several Greek islands in the southern part of the Aegean Sea have volcanoes. The island of Melos (modern-day Mílos) has experienced volcanic activity and was, along with some other nearby islands, formed by such activity. Off the coast of southwestern Turkey the Greek islands of Kos, Gyali (also spelled Yali), and Nísiros (also Nísyros) were all formed by volcanic activity.

The most famous volcanic eruption in Greek history took place on the central Aegean island of Thíra (modern Santorini) around 1600 B.C.E. This eruption, also one of the most powerful known in the history of the world, completely blew apart the western half of the island and led to the abandonment of the island for the next four centuries. Fortunately, some of the inhabitants seem to have evacuated the island before the eruption. As in the case of Roman Pompeii, volcanic ash from the eruption buried a city; in this case Akrotiri, a town on the island of Thíra, was covered. Excavations of the site have revealed a vibrant civilization that shared much in common with that on the island of Crete to the south. In fact, the eruption on Thíra may have disrupted civilization on Crete. In the early second century B.C.E. further eruptions and lava flows from Thíra's volcano formed two small islands in the volcano's caldera, or crater. Some modern scholars have suggested that Thíra was the mysterious island of Atlantis, which Plato describes in both the *Timaeus* and the *Critias* and says suddenly vanished into the Atlantic Ocean because of earthquakes and flooding. Plato's description of the island's immense size, its location west of Africa, and his time frame for the destruction of Atlantis make it an unlikely equivalent for the tiny Aegean island of Thíra.

ROME

BY DAVID R. SEAR

Rome dominated the Mediterranean world for more than 600 years, from the time of the pivotal victories over the Carthaginian Hannibal in 202 B.C.E., Philip V of Macedon in 197 B.C.E., and Antiochus the Great of Syria in 190 B.C.E. to the collapse of Roman power in the West in the fifth century C.E. Inevitably, over such a long period of time and in a region so extensive and geographically diverse the occurrence of natural disasters was of some frequency.

With population levels generally much lower than in modern times many of these disasters, especially those in remoter regions, went unrecorded, or at least no knowledge of them has come down to us. Others, however, were fully documented, most famously the eruption of Mount Vesuvius on the Bay of Naples on August 24, 79 C.E., just two months after the accession of the emperor Titus (r. 79–81 C.E.). The writer Pliny the Younger (61 or 62–ca. 113 C.E.) was an eyewitness to this catastrophe, which buried the towns of Pompeii, Herculaneum, and Stabiae (modern Castellammare di Stabia) in ashes and took the life of Pliny's own uncle and adoptive father, Pliny the Elder (23–79 C.E.). Pliny's account is contained in letters to his friend, the historian Tacitus (ca. 56–ca. 120 C.E.). Later eruptions of Vesuvius took place in 203 C.E., 472 C.E., and 512 C.E., but less is known of these events.

A valuable source of information on many of the important historical events of the Roman Empire is provided by the reverse types and inscriptions of the imperial coinage. The currency was used extensively by the Roman government as a vehicle for official propaganda and frequent reference was made to contemporary events, especially when the emperor and his advisers considered that by so doing the popularity of the regime could be enhanced. An excellent early example of this is to be found on the coinage of the emperor Tiberius (r. 14–37 C.E.), stepson and successor of the Roman Empire's founder, Augustus (r. 27 B.C.E.–14 C.E.). The Roman historian Tacitus records that a great earthquake had shaken the Roman province of Asia Minor (western Turkey) in 17 C.E., causing extensive damage to at least a dozen

Roman wall painting showing a coastal landscape (early first century C.E.*), from Boscoreale, Campania, Italy; Boscoreale was only one of many sites on the Bay of Naples that were overwhelmed by the catastrophic eruption of Mount Vesuvius in 79* C.E. (© The Trustees of the British Museum)

famous cities. The worst affected was Sardis (also Sardes), the old Lydian royal capital, and Tiberius made a grant of 10 million sesterces toward its restoration as well as remitting all taxation for a period of five years. This magnanimous gesture was recorded on a handsome sestertius type showing a seated figure of the emperor accompanied by the inscription *CIVITATIBVS ASIAE RESTITVTIS* ("the restoration of the cities of Asia").

Earthquakes in the Mediterranean basin were of quite frequent occurrence in Roman times, as they are today. The empire's eastern provinces were especially affected, and in the winter of 114 and 115 C.E. the Syrian capital of Antioch (modern-day Antakya) was badly damaged by a major seismic event. The emperor Trajan (r. 98–117 C.E.) happened to be wintering in the city while on campaign in the ancient Near East and had a lucky escape when, reputedly through divine intervention, he was led from a building just prior to its collapse. This miraculous deliverance was recorded on the coinage of 115 C.E. by a type bearing the inscription *CONSERVATORI PATRIS PATRIAE* ("to the preserver of the Father of his People") and showing a colossal figure of Jupiter protecting a much smaller image of the emperor.

Fire posed a constant threat to the populations of large cities in the Roman world. Our knowledge of these events tends to be focused on Rome itself, though similar events were certainly taking place in the empire's other great urban centers. The most famous conflagration is that which occurred in the capital in July 64 C.E. during the reign of Nero (r. 54–68 C.E.). Whether it was deliberately set by the eccentric emperor (as charged by the historian Suetonius) we cannot be sure, but the devastation of central Rome on this occasion allowed Nero to launch an ambitious rebuilding program, much of which was personally beneficial to him; for example, he had built the Domus Aurea, or Golden House, an extravagant new imperial residence. Contemporary coin types again make reference to these events. An extensive series in gold, silver, and brass was issued throughout Nero's final years (64–68 C.E.) showing a handsome seated figure of the goddess Roma symbolizing the restoration of the city after the disaster of the fire. Another type, appearing on gold aurei and silver denarii only, depicts the restored Temple of Vesta in the Roman Forum. It is a testament to the frequency of fires in central Rome that Nero's restored structure was the sixth temple to occupy this site and was itself to be destroyed in yet another conflagration late in the reign of the emperor Commodus (r. 180–92 C.E.).

THE AMERICAS

BY KEITH JORDAN

The cultures of the ancient Americas have not left us any written records of natural disasters and their impact, either because those cultures did not possess writing (as in North America and Peru) or because (as in the case of the Maya) they used their hieroglyphic scripts to record the military and political prowess of kings rather than the adversities presented by nature. We have no New World Pliny the Younger to bear literary witness to volcanic eruptions (as he did for that which destroyed Pompeii in 79 C.E.) or even the counterpart of the vague and flimsy allusions to the Thíra eruption discerned in Egyptian texts, the Old Testament, and the writings of Plato.

In the absence of written records, we have very little evidence for the cultural impact of natural disasters on the indigenous peoples of North America for this period. The most significant and widespread environmental change affecting ancient North American culture history was certainly the end of the last ice age 10,000–12,000 years ago and the subsequent extinction of many species of large mammals, such as mammoths, mastodons, giant sloths, and wild horses. Since these animals provided food sources for the earliest Native American hunters, their demise forced a shift in lifestyle away from highly mobile big-game hunting to a less nomadic hunting and gathering way of life.

What we do have in Mesoamerica is the archaeological and geological evidence of massive volcanic eruptions that buried settlements, adversely affected agriculture, and occasioned migration and population shifts. While polities in the immediate vicinity of the disasters collapsed and were abandoned because of these events, other political centers may have benefited by the influx of migrants and a gain in religious prestige. In Peru climate change and catastrophic weather events on the coast, related to the phenomenon of El Niño, may have led to the collapse of ritual centers and their associated ideology, paving the way for the spread of a new religious cult originating at Chavín de Huántar in the highlands.

In the basin of Mexico the eruption of the volcano Xitli devastated the city of Cuicuilco during the Late Formative to Early Classic phases of cultural development. Precise dating of this geological event is still a matter of dispute, but it occurred over about a decade sometime between 400 B.C.E. and 400 C.E., perhaps close to 50 B.C.E. Cuicuilco, situated in what is now the southern outskirts of Mexico City, was first blanketed with ash and then buried under up to 33 feet of lava. The resultant volcanic layer covers a 30-square-mile area and has made excavation of the site difficult, forcing early-20th-century diggers to resort to explosives to clear buried structures. It is possible that because of earlier volcanic episodes, the site had been wholly or partly abandoned prior to the main eruption. Some scholars speculate that both the displaced population and the city's possible loss of religious prestige in the face of what would have been interpreted as the wrath of the gods contributed to the growth and influence of the city of Teotihuacán in the northern part of the basin. Ironically—or perhaps appropriately—stone sculptures retrieved from beneath the lava flow indicate that a deity in the form of an old man, corresponding to the later Aztec fire god, was among the chief gods of Cuicuilco.

In present-day El Salvador extensive ashfall from an eruption of the volcano Ilopango around the turn of the fourth century C.E. seems to have rendered local agricultural land unusable and precipitated an exodus from the area. As in the case of Cuicuilco, a rising city may have benefited from this calamity. In this instance it was the Maya city-state of Copán, north and east of Ilopango in western Honduras. Refugees from Ilopango's eruption, drawn by the rich lands of the Copán region, may have increased the city's population, which in turn contributed to the city's rising influence over the next several centuries.

In Peru the recurrent phenomenon of El Niño seems to have massively and negatively affected the cultural history at several junctures in the last three millennia. Named in historic times for the Christ child because of its appearance around Christmas, El Niño is a warm-water current that reaches the coast of Peru every year, usually for only a few weeks. The cause of this eastward-moving current is a decrease in easterly trade winds, which leads to the flow of warm water from the western Pacific to Peru. Every three to seven years a major El Niño event occurs in which the warm current affects the Peruvian coast for longer than usual—up to months—creating havoc with the coastal environment. Cool-water marine life dies off in the warmer temperatures, and torrential rains create extensive flooding onshore.

Some of these events are of truly catastrophic magnitude. Some evidence suggests that major events of this kind beset the coast of Peru around 500 B.C.E., killing the cold-water fish that were a staple of the local economy and destroying desert irrigation systems through flooding. These disasters may have led to the decline of coastal ceremonial centers (though some archaeologists think they were already in decline owing to other factors) and with them the prestige of the cults they supported. This change may have left the area receptive to new religious ideologies emanating from the highland site of Chavín de Huántar. The new beliefs are reflected in the adoption of highland deity images and other motifs in coastal ceramics and textiles.

Interestingly, an increase in social stratification and centralized political power may have occurred in the Chavín area sometime around 400–200 B.C.E. as a consequence not of floods but of drought, leading to increased competition for resources, a situation frequently conducive to the rise of strong leaders and growing differentiation of social classes.

See also AGRICULTURE; ARCHITECTURE; ASTRONOMY; BUILDING TECHNIQUES AND MATERIALS; CERAMICS AND POTTERY; CITIES; CLIMATE AND GEOGRAPHY; ECONOMY; EMPIRES AND DYNASTIES; FOREIGNERS AND BARBARIANS; HEALTH AND DISEASE; HUNTING, FISHING, AND GATHERING; INVENTIONS; LITERATURE; NOMADIC AND PASTORAL SOCIETIES; MIGRATION AND POPULATION MOVEMENTS; MONEY AND COINAGE; PANDEMICS AND EPIDEMICS; RELIGION AND COSMOLOGY; RESISTANCE AND DISSENT; SACRED SITES; SETTLEMENT PATTERNS; SLAVES AND SLAVERY; SOCIAL COLLAPSE AND ABANDONMENT; TOWNS AND VILLAGES; WAR AND CONQUEST.

Egypt

"The Shipwrecked Sailor," ca. 2200 B.C.E.

. . . THE wise servant said, "Let thy heart be satisfied, O my lord, for that we have come back to the country; after we have been long on board, and rowed much, the prow has at last touched land. All the people rejoice and embrace us one after another.

The sailor then answered, "Now I shall tell that which has happened to me, to my very self. I was going to the mines of Pharaoh, and I went down on the sea in a ship of one hundred and fifty cubits long and forty cubits wide, with one hundred and fifty sailors of the best of Egypt who had seen heaven and earth, and whose hearts were stronger than lions. They had said that the wind would not be contrary, or that there would be none. But as we approached the land, the wind arose, and threw up waves eight cubits high. As for me, I seized a piece of wood; but those who were in the vessel perished, without one remaining. A wave threw me on an island, after that I had been three days alone, without a companion beside my own heart. I laid me in a thicket, and the shadow covered me. Then stretched I my limbs to try to find something for my mouth. I found there figs and grain, melons of all kinds, fishes, and birds. Nothing was lacking. And I satisfied myself; and left on the ground that which was over, of what my arms had been filled withal. I dug a pit, I lighted a fire, and I made a burnt offering unto the gods.

"Suddenly I heard a noise as of thunder, which I thought to be that of a wave of the sea. The trees shook, and the earth was moved. I uncovered my face, and I saw that a serpent drew near. He was thirty cubits long, and his beard greater than two cubits; his body was as overlaid with gold, and his color as that of true lazuli. He coiled himself before me. "Then he opened his mouth, while that I lay on my face before him, and he said to me, "What has brought you, what has brought you, little one, what has brought you? If you say not speedily what has brought you to this isle, I will make you know yourself; as a flame you shall vanish, if you tell me not something I have not heard, or which I knew not, before you.'

"Then he took me in his mouth and carried me to his resting-place, and laid me down without any hurt. I was whole and sound, and nothing was gone from me. . . .

"Then said he to me, "Fear not, fear not, little one, and make not your face sad. If you have come to me, it is God who has let you live. For it is He who has brought you to this isle of the blest, where nothing is lacking, and which is filled with all good things. See now, you shall pass one month after another, until you shall be four months in this isle. Then a ship shall come from your land with sailors, and you shall leave with them and go to your country, and you shall die in your town.' . . .

"Then I bowed in my obeisance, and I touched the ground before him. "Behold now that which I have told you before. I shall tell of your presence unto Pharaoh, I shall make him to know of your greatness, and I will bring to you of the sacred oils and perfumes, and of incense of the temples with which all gods are honored. I shall tell, moreover, of that which I do now see (thanks to him), and there shall be rendered to you praises before the fullness of all the land. I shall slay asses for you in sacrifice, I shall pluck for you the birds, and I shall bring for you ships full of all kinds of the treasures of Egypt, as is comely to do unto a god, a friend of men in a far country, of which men know not.'

"Then he smiled at my speech, because of that which was in his heart, for he said to me: "You are not rich in perfumes, for all that you have is but common incense. As for me, I am prince of the land of Punt, and I have perfumes. Only the oil which you say you would bring is not common in this isle. But, when you shall depart from this place, you shall never more see this isle; it shall be changed into waves.'

"And behold, when the ship drew near, according to all that he had told me before, I got up into an high tree, to strive to see those who were within it. Then I came and told to him this matter, but it was already known unto him before. Then he said to me, "Farewell, farewell, go to your house, little one, see again your children, and let your name be good in your town; these are my wishes for you.' . . ."

From: Eva March Tappan, ed., *The World's Story: A History of the World in Story, Song and Art*, Vol. 3, *Egypt, Africa, and Arabia*, trans. W. K. Flinders Petrie (Boston: Houghton Mifflin, 1914).

The Middle East

The Bible, excerpt from Exodus (fifth to seventh centuries B.C.E.*)*

Chapter 10

1 Then the LORD said to Moses, "Go in to Pharaoh; for I have hardened his heart and the heart of his servants, that I may show these signs of mine among them, 2 and that you may tell in the hearing of your son and of your son's son how I have made sport of the Egyptians and what signs I have done among them; that you may know that I am the LORD."

3 So Moses and Aaron went in to Pharaoh, and said to him, "Thus says the LORD, the God of the Hebrews, 'How long will you refuse to humble yourself before me? Let my people go, that they may serve me. 4 For if you refuse to let my people go, behold, tomorrow I will bring locusts into your country, 5 and they shall cover the face of the land, so that no one can see the land; and they shall eat what is left to you after the hail, and they shall eat every tree of yours which grows in the field, 6 and they shall fill your houses, and the houses of all your servants and of all the Egyptians; as neither your fathers nor your grandfathers have seen, from the day they came on earth to this day.'" Then he turned and went out from Pharaoh.

7 And Pharaoh's servants said to him, "How long shall this man be a snare to us? Let the men go, that they may serve the LORD their God; do you not yet understand that Egypt is ruined?" 8 So Moses and Aaron were brought back to Pharaoh; and he said to them, "Go, serve the LORD your God; but who are to go?" 9 And Moses said, "We will go with our young and our old; we will go with our sons and daughters and with our flocks and herds, for we must hold a feast to the LORD." 10 And he said to them, "The LORD be with you, if ever I let you and your little ones go! Look, you have some evil purpose in mind. 11 No! Go, the men among you, and serve the LORD, for that is what you desire." And they were driven out from Pharaoh's presence.

12 Then the LORD said to Moses, "Stretch out your hand over the land of Egypt for the locusts, that they may come upon the land of Egypt, and eat every plant in the land, all that the hail has left." 13 So Moses stretched forth his rod over the land of Egypt, and the LORD brought an east wind upon the land all that day and all that night; and when it was morning the east wind had brought the locusts. 14 And the locusts came up over all the land of Egypt, and settled on the whole country of Egypt, such a dense swarm of locusts as had never been before, nor ever shall be again. 15 For they covered the face of the whole land, so that the land was darkened, and they ate all the plants in the land and all the fruit of the trees which the hail had left; not a green thing remained, neither tree nor plant of the field, through all the land of Egypt. 16 Then Pharaoh called Moses and Aaron in haste, and said, "I have sinned against the LORD your God, and against you. 17 Now therefore, forgive my sin, I pray you, only this once, and entreat the LORD your God only to remove this death from me." 18 So he went out from Pharaoh, and entreated the LORD. 19 And the LORD turned a very strong west wind, which lifted the locusts and drove them into the Red Sea; not a single locust was left in all the country of Egypt. 20 But the LORD hardened Pharaoh's heart, and he did not let the children of Israel go.

From: The Internet History Sourcebooks. Available online. URL: http://www.fordham.edu/halsall/.

FURTHER READING

Miriam S. Balmuth, David K. Chester, and Patricia A. Johnston, eds., *Cultural Responses to the Volcanic Landscape: The Mediterranean and Beyond* (Boston: Archaeological Institute of America, 2005).

Christos G. Doumas, *Thera, Pompeii of the Ancient Aegean: Excavations at Akrotiri, 1967–79* (New York: Thames and Hudson, 1983).

Walter L. Friedrich, *Fire in the Sea: The Santorini Volcano: Natural History and the Legend of Atlantis*, trans. Alexander R. McBirney (Cambridge, U.K.: Cambridge University Press, 2000).

Michael Grant, *Cities of Vesuvius: Pompeii and Herculaneum* (London: Weidenfeld and Nicolson Ltd., 1971).

Benny J. Peiser, Trevor Palmer, and Mark E. Bailey, eds., *Natural Catastrophes during Bronze Age Civilizations* (Oxford, U.K.: Archaeopress, 1998).

Michael Schnellmann, Flavio S. Anselmetti, Domenico Giardini, Judith A. McKenzie, and Steven N. Ward, "Ancient Earthquakes at Lake Lucerne," *American Scientist* 92 (January–February 2004): 46–53.

Nomadic and Pastoral Societies

INTRODUCTION

Historians and archaeologists take a keen interest in the ways in which ancient societies were organized and how they scratched a living out of the resources available to them. The earliest Stone Age peoples were largely hunter-gatherers, meaning that they lived in small bands and survived by moving from place to place, usually following seasonal patterns, to find game, fruits, berries, roots, nuts, and leafy vegetables. Most Native American tribes and the aboriginal people of Australia provide good examples of nomadic communities. These early people were called *nomads,* meaning that they lived in temporary settlements.

As early human communities made the transition from hunting and gathering to agriculture, many came to depend on herds of animals, including cattle, sheep, goats, llamas, camels, and yaks. They already knew about the behavior of the animals they hunted, especially those that ran in herds, so herding was a way to ensure a steady and reliable source of food using similar knowledge and skills. These animals provided people with meat, milk, cream, and butter. They also supplied hides for leather, horns and bones for tools and other objects, and dung to burn for fuel or use as fertilizer. Ancient herders even discovered that enzymes from the stomachs of these animals are useful in coagulating milk to make cheese. In the ancient world, where people struggled to survive, virtually every part of the animal was used in some way.

Communities that relied on herding for their livelihood are said to be *pastoral,* a word derived from the Latin word *pastor,* meaning simply "herdsman." Ancient herders needed to find grazing land for their herds, so many maintained a nomadic life, moving from place to place to find vegetation for their herds. These nomads not only provided food for large numbers of people but also played a role in the diffusion of ideas. In moving about, they made contact with other communities, lessening the isolation of these communities and sharing knowledge, technologies, medical practices, and the like. They were also traders, bringing their products to communities of agriculturalists and exchanging them for crops and other goods that they could not provide for themselves.

Some, however, settled into relatively fixed communities; historians use the word *sedentary* to refer to ancient communities that were more or less permanent and fixed. These pastoral communities, like agricultural communities, played a major role in human development. By tying people to the land and a defined community, they allowed people to form towns and eventually cities that gave rise to the major achievements of the ancient world.

It should be noted that historians disagree about the sequence of developments that led to pastoralism. Some see it as a natural outgrowth of hunting and gathering. Thus, they believe that pastoralism was the second step in a sequence that began with hunting-gathering and led to agriculture. Others, however, believe that pastoralism was the third step in this sequence, so that farming predated pastoralism. These historians argue that as human populations became denser and more pressure was placed on farms to be productive, people turned to pastoralism as a way to exploit land farther away from towns and cities.

AFRICA

BY KIRK H. BEETZ

The history of ancient African nomads and pastoralists is one of people trying to adapt to climate and geography. It is a story with many twists and turns. For instance, the Fulani in central Niger have a history stretching back perhaps 6,000 years; during that time, they have been nomadic pastoralists, herders who migrated from highlands to lowlands and back according to the seasons, herders with fixed homes, and farmers of grain, and they have shifted from one way of life to another more than once as they adjusted to changes in rainfall.

The Fulani are often cited by people studying the ancient Saharan pastoralists, because some of their religious rituals duplicate ones found depicted in Saharan rock paintings dating back to 3000 B.C.E. For instance, in one rock painting dating back 5,000 years a cow is depicted being herded through a doorway of palm fronds shaped like a large letter U, with people dancing nearby and others tending to the cow. This ritual is still performed by the Fulani; it is intended to protect people from illness. One should take care in making inferences about an ancient culture that has had several thousand years to develop and change, but archaeologists nonetheless infer from modern Fulani customs that their ancient Saharan society was patriarchal and one in which individual people developed their places in society through complex family relationships, making those relationships more important than any fixed territory. As the nomadic Fulani moved across the grasslands of the Sahara, family relationships would be the social constants of their lives, rather than villages.

Another people thought to have a lineage as ancient as that of the Fulani are the modern Beja people of Nubia, who were called "Blemmye" in ancient times. Like the Fulani, they had a nomadic pastoralist culture that changed over thousands of years as the climate of North Africa changed. They, the Fulani, and other herders are thought by archaeologists to have been nomads when they began herding cattle; they wandered with their herds across vast grassy plains, moving according where they found food for their cattle. Wars would have been fought over possession of cattle, not territory. Some pastoralists used their cattle for food, but others kept them as signs of wealth. The development of territorial conflicts would have come after the Sahara began to dry up around 3000 B.C.E. As rivers dried, wells would have been needed to water the herds, and those wells would have been protected from outsiders. The response of the Blemmye to the drying of the Sahara was to move to sources of water to the east of the Sahara and settle in villages near water, seldom moving their herds far from their villages.

Most archaeologists believe that the desert of the Sahara is a combination of natural climate change and the activities of humans. Archaeologists infer from the conduct of modern pastoralists at the southern border of the Sahara that ancient herders took little care to preserve their environment, allowing their herds to overgraze land to the point that even seasonal rains were not enough for plants to be able to renew themselves. Except for a brief period of increased rainfall in about 500 B.C.E., the Saharan desert has steadily expanded. The cutting back of forests at the southern edge of the Sahara by pastoralists and grain farmers is thought to have increased the pace of climate change by reducing the moist updraft of air generated by the dense African forest south of the Sarah. The moisture released into the air would have been blown northward, where it would have fallen as rain.

The nomadic pastoralists eventually became transhumant populations, meaning that they migrated to different grazing areas according to the seasons. For instance, some Berbers, perhaps including the Imazighen, known as the Meshwesh to the Egyptians, would drive their herds into the Atlas Mountains in spring, when rain caused new growth of grasses, and then into the flat lands in fall, where they could water their herds at oases and wells. This practice continued until modern times, when the seasonal rainfall became too little to sustain the cattle, sheep, and goats of the local people.

It is not known exactly when people in southern Africa began herding animals, though it was probably after people began herding cattle in North Africa, because the cattle of the people of southern Africa seem to have derived from the cattle of the north. The first animals to be herded were sheep. The practice of herding sheep probably passed into North Africa from the Near East and then through western Africa south through the Kalahari and into the grasslands of southern Africa. It is possible that herders from the Sahara fled south to escape the desert, bringing their animals and customs with them. One theory holds that several thousand years ago southern Europe, North Africa, and western parts of southern Africa were all one cultural group in which knowledge of herding animals spread quickly. Archaeologists cite similar painting styles in North Africa and Spain and similar depictions of humans in paintings to link them with western regions of southern Africa.

Herding cattle could have been transmitted in at least three ways. One was through the western forests and the

Petroglyph showing herders and cows, from Sahara Desert at Tassili, Algeria, North Africa (© Board of Regents of the University of Wisconsin System. Photographer: Jeanne Tabachnick)

Kalahari of Africa, and another was along the east coast from the Blemmye to herders south of the kingdom of Kush through grasslands until reaching southern Africa. One other possibility is a complex route due south through the center of Africa. The latter view is based on linguistic studies of the Khoikhoi, also known as Hottentots. The Khoikhoi lived from the southern coast of Africa to the central African forests, and linguists have established that the Khoikhoi language was spoken by people in central Africa near the Sahel steppes that spread west to east south of the Sahara. The northernmost Khoikhoi may have acquired cattle from the Sahara and transmitted them south until they reached the Khoikhoi of the southern African plains. These Khoikhoi were nomads who adapted cattle to their wandering lives, moving their herds to new pastures whenever the latest pasture ran short of food for the cattle. The Khoikhoi who lived near the southern coast of Africa were transhumant, migrating north to take advantage of the winter rains on the plains and then migrating back south for the summer.

Complications for the theories of transmission of herding through western and central Africa are twofold. One is that there were large rain forests without suitable pasture, thus discouraging adoption of pastoralism as a way of life. The other was the presence of the Baka, who lived in areas stretching from Cameroon to eastern Africa. They had a culture well adapted to the rain forest. They were fully nomadic, moving through the forest to follow game. To this day some Baka continue to be fully nomadic. They built no villages, using plants and perhaps elephant skins to create shelters that they would abandon when they needed to find more game. Their lives may have focused on elephants, which provided them with large amounts of food. Reliance on following game for survival meant that the Baka could not support large, dense populations, making their population sparse. The Baka were often hostile to intrusions into their forests by other cultures, and their poisoned arrows and spears would have made moving cattle through their forest very difficult.

There was probably no part of Africa that was untouched by nomads, but pastoralists were somewhat restricted to open territories, though some cut down forest to create more pastures. Their adaptations to the Sahara were long-term failures, partly because their overgrazing probably increased the speed of the Sahara's drying as well as helping make the desert larger. The Khoikhoi apparently did not have a similar problem; their effort to expand into new pastures was motivated not so much by degradation of the land but by population growth.

EGYPT

BY MARK ANTHONY PHELPS

Pastoralism predated agriculture in the Nile Valley. Domesticated cattle imported from southwestern Asia were unquestionably in the Delta by the middle of the sixth millennium. Some scholars argue that two cow bones found in Nabta Playa in the Western Desert and dating to 9300 B.C.E. are domesticated, but the theory has not found many proponents. Early pastoralists continued to engage in foraging activities in the Nile Valley and western oases. Agriculture was imported from southwestern Asia in the fifth millennium. The advent of agriculture necessitated moving the animals between the times of planting and harvesting. As the Nile Valley became more intensively farmed, herders in Lower Egypt began to seasonally migrate to the Delta with their herds.

Another factor in the presence of nomadism in the region is the drying of the Sahara. The eastern Sahara (comprising Chad, Libya, Sudan, and Egypt) experienced a wet period from about 8500 B.C.E. to 4000 B.C.E. The subsequent drying period, which continues to the present day, corresponded with a dramatic rise in Nile Valley agricultural settlements. Cattle were the first animals that were herded on a large scale, but as the Sahara was becoming drier during the fifth millennium and native grasses were dwindling, sheep and goats came to replace cattle in many areas. Evidences of both are found in the El Faiyûm region and at Merimda by about 5000 B.C.E.

Settlements have been discovered from the Neolithic Period in the Western Desert. These seasonal settlements are spotted by the presence of hearths. Cattle were the predominant species herded, though sheep and goat remains also have been found. Burial sites show a particular ceramic style, known as tulip beakers, which seem to have been produced solely as grave goods. Pigment and palettes also are found, as is jewelry. These goods indicate a broad trade network, extending to the Red Sea and the Sinai Peninsula.

With the advent of the pharaonic period of Egyptian history (ca. 3000 B.C.E.), the role that pastoralism played in society can be studied through texts and artwork. Branding scenes are found, as are scenes of the process of milking and of aiding cows in the process of calving. Artwork also shows differing breeds of sheep and goats. Before the Middle Kingdom (2040–1640 B.C.E.) sheep were hairy and thin tailed and had twisted horns. During the Middle Kingdom they became woollier with a thicker tail. The fat-tailed sheep common to the Mediterranean basin entered the Nile Valley during Roman times. Goats also changed in artistic depiction, as the breed that had been common throughout the Old Kingdom (2575–2134 B.C.E.) gave way during the reign of the Hyksos of the Second Intermediate Period (1640–1532 B.C.E.), evidenced by horn structure (going from a scimitar-shaped horn to a twisted shape). Egyptians did not eat pork until the Eighteenth Dynasty (1550–1307 B.C.E.). Large herds of pigs are mentioned in written sources from this time, and evidence from middens (refuse heaps) indicates that craftspeople consumed pork frequently during this era. The use of pork increased with the advent of Roman rule.

Distinguishing pastoralist societies, in which a portion of the population is engaged in herding during certain seasons, from mixed farming societies is difficult. Typically, seasonal camps provide evidence of some sort of herding (animal dung and animal remains). The more distant the sites are from the floodplain and agricultural villages, the more likely that they are those of pastoral nomads. Sites that date to the dawn of the pharaonic era and are probably the remains of nomads are found in peripheral Upper Egypt south of Aswān. One is the Kiseiba Plateau in the Western Desert, which contains a number of seasonal sites. The presence of Red Sea shells in the Nile Valley points to trade with groups operating in the Arabian Desert, presumably as pastoralists.

With the advent of writing in Egypt, the presence of pastoral groups gains concreteness. The best known of these groups is the Medjay. They may have originally come Lower Nubia. Precisely how they became displaced and settled in the Arabian Desert is not clear. The Semna Dispatches of the Twelfth Dynasty (ca. 2000 B.C.E.), a collection of military reports from an Arabian Desert outpost, mentions the Medjay. They were compelled by drought to sneak into the Nile Valley, a survival mechanism common to nomads throughout Egyptian history. Tomb paintings from the Twelfth Dynasty represent Medjay herding cattle. Nomads appear in tomb paintings as lean, with short hair and beards. They carry long sticks with a roll of matting attached, which they used for bedding as well as for shade. They also are depicted with bundles of pots and food.

The presence of the Medjay in Egyptian society is underscored by their use during the Second Intermediate Period as mercenaries, especially by Kamose against the Hyksos (ca. 1550 B.C.E.). Eventually the term *Medjay* came to denote a corps within the Egyptian army. After Ahmose I's ousting of the Hyksos, the Medjay were the primary component of the police force of the Nineteenth Dynasty (1307–1196 B.C.E.). In the Merneptah stela (ca. 1209 B.C.E.) the Medjay are depicted as being at rest thanks to the warring prowess of the pharaoh, who has pacified Palestine. Curiously, a few lines below this is a reference to pastoralists, demonstrating that there has been a shift in what the audience understands as the prime occupation of the Medjay. During the New Kingdom (ca. 1550–1070 B.C.E.) the Medjay probably served as a source of labor for the Egyptians in Arabian Desert gold mines. Given that there are references to the military operations against the Medjay in monuments of Akhenaton and Thutmose IV of the Eighteenth Dynasty, it seems the Medjay had returned to life beyond the fringe of Egyptian control, probably again as pastoralists.

Increasingly, fields belonged to large-estate owners, who employed herdsmen to take care of their flocks and herds. These herdsmen specialized in particular animals. Nomads typically herded several species. This diversity cut the economic risk of disease and broadened their economic options with regard to trade. Evidence provided by roadside forts skirting the Western Desert points to the need to police nomads to allow for overland trade. As Roman influence waned in Upper Egypt and Lower Nubia, with forts being abandoned, the political and economic voids left were filled by nomadic groups. These groups took over gold mining and overland trade.

THE MIDDLE EAST

BY JEN PIRO

The term *pastoralism* in its most basic sense means the herding of domestic animals such as cattle, sheep, goats, or (in the Near East) camels as a main, or even the only, source of livelihood for a given group of people. However, that definition covers a very broad range of activities. Anthropologists generally further categorize pastoralist societies according to two criteria: how settled (or how mobile) the society is, and how much (or how little) it engages in agriculture in addition to herding. The result is a spectrum of pastoralist societies.

At one end of this spectrum are *sedentary* pastoralists, who live in permanent settlements (typically villages) and feed their herds year-round on pastures relatively nearby. If, as often happens, these people also engage in agriculture, they may be classed as *agropastoralists*. At the other end of the spectrum is *nomadic* pastoralism. In a purely nomadic pastoralist society all or almost all of the population moves with the herds from place to place and from one elevation to another in search of pasture throughout the cycle of seasons, living in temporary encampments and often traveling hundreds or even thousands of miles over the course of a year.

Because of their continual movement, pure nomadic pastoralists have little opportunity to practice agriculture. However, another form of pastoralism, *transhumant* pastoralism, offers that opportunity. In transhumant pastoralist societies some of the people range with the herds as nomads, while most remain in a permanent "home" settlement as agriculturists. It is important to note that both groups regard themselves as part of the same society; they merely perform different tasks. Obviously no clear lines separate the various kinds of pastoralism. They blend together at the edges as more or fewer people live in permanent settlements, engage in agriculture, and so on. Moreover, a given society may adopt different forms of pastoralism over time.

In Near Eastern prehistory the emergence of nomadic pastoralism, centered on herding sheep and goats, was a pivotal development. It played an integral role in transforming the economy and society of the region and influencing the course of ancient Near Eastern civilization. But while scholars agree that the rise of nomadic pastoralism was a critical turning point, they disagree on exactly when it took place. Some archaeologists claim that nomadic pastoralism could have emerged as early as the seventh millennium B.C.E. Others suggest that the mid-fourth or third millennium B.C.E. is a better estimate. Still others argue that although different forms of pastoralism existed before the second millennium B.C.E., pure nomadic pastoralism arose only in historical times on the borders of ancient empires. Part of the problem is that early forms of pastoralism are not always clearly identifiable in the archaeological record. Also, nomadic pastoralism appeared in different parts of the Near East at different times and under different environmental, social, and economic conditions.

Some of the earliest evidence for nomadic pastoralism in the region comes from the central Zagros Mountains (in modern-day Iran). Archaeological finds of temporary campsites in marginal ecological zones unsuitable for agriculture and of isolated cemeteries along seasonal migratory routes far from permanent settlements are examples of such evidence. Moreover, historical texts from early urban centers in the general vicinity attest to social, economic, and political relations—and sometimes battle—with nomadic groups in the Zagros by the mid-fourth millennium B.C.E.

Much research has focused on explaining how nomadic pastoralism emerged as a new way of living out of village-based herding in the Zagros region. Traditional views on this subject theorized a direct transition from agropastoralism to highly mobile nomadic pastoralism. However, recent investigations have demonstrated that the shift occurred in several intermediate stages before arriving at an economy emphasizing nomadic pastoralism by the fourth millennium B.C.E. Besides the spread of seasonal camps and isolated cemeteries like those already mentioned, the archaeological evidence includes a reduction in the number of permanent settlements and the broad distribution of small quantities of distinctive pottery at sites throughout the west-central Zagros, perhaps reflecting far-flung trade associated with increasing mobility.

The archaeological evidence also indicates growing interaction between the west-central Zagros and the lowlands to the west and southwest in the late fifth and fourth millennia B.C.E. As pastoral groups moved down to the lowlands in the winter months, they would have come into contact with settled farming communities and formed trading relationships. Archaeologists believe that economic exchange was a significant and mutually beneficial aspect of nomad-villager relations. Villagers received animal products and raw materials from the mountains in exchange for agricultural goods that the nomads lacked owing to their highly specialized economy. Manufactured items, especially pottery, also would have been exchanged—as would ideas, styles, and other cultural information. Nomadic pastoralists may have served as intermediaries in longer-distance trade connecting different regions.

The economic ties forged between highland pastoralists and settled villagers may have contributed to the development of social complexity on a regional scale. During the late fifth and fourth millennia B.C.E. a number of sites in southern Mesopotamia and southwestern Iran began to exhibit signs of increasing socioeconomic and political complexity (for example, monumental architecture, urban planning, and the use of seals to regulate certain economic activities) that eventually led to the rise of early states. Mobile pastoralist populations in the Zagros may have helped to urbanize their neighbors to the southwest by, among other things, stimulating local economies through surplus production and trade. The rising urban demand for animal products and raw materials would have encouraged pastoralists to intensify production and exchange, strengthening economic ties between both groups. The growing economic interdependence between nomadic pastoral societies and early towns may have influenced such sociopolitical developments of the following millennia as the control of production and distribution of goods by centralized institutions, the emergence of inequalities in wealth and status, and the formation of a shared social identity among nomadic groups. Meanwhile, the construction of forts along the foothills of the Zagros by early Mesopotamian state societies indicates that relations with the nomads were not always amicable.

Far southwest of the Zagros, nomadic pastoralism may have also appeared in the "marginal" environments of the Negev and Sinai and nearby desert/steppe zones of what are today Jordan, Syria, western Iraq, and northwestern Saudi Arabia. However, scholars disagree as to whether prehistoric nomadic pastoralism could have existed in this region, and if so, when it began. Some argue that nomadic pastoralism arose in the mid-seventh millennium B.C.E.; they point to the spread of new forms of material culture beyond areas favorable for intensive agriculture and into marginal zones during this time. Archaeological evidence of this migration includes distinctive stone tools, architectural remains such as stone circles and circle complexes, rock art, and a rise in sheep and goat herding, possibly in response to the declining numbers of wild gazelles. Moreover, the growing numbers and size of sites in desert/steppe areas appear to reflect close symbiotic relations between nomadic groups and their settled neighbors in the agricultural zone. After their first incursions into these marginal lands the nomadic pastoralists spread rapidly throughout the region over the next few millennia, culminating in the conquest of southern Mesopotamia by the Akkadians in the late third millennium B.C.E.

Other researchers doubt that pure nomadic pastoralism in this region dates to the mid-seventh millennium B.C.E. Some argue that a nomadic pastoral economy could have arisen only after milk and wool began to be systematically exploited in the fourth millennium B.C.E. Some suggest that earlier systems could have been cases of transhumant, rather than purely nomadic, pastoralism. (However, archaeologists also diverge in their estimates of when transhumant pastoralism began.) Finally, some scholars question whether these marginal lands could have sustained a pastoral nomadic system in prehistory. In historical times nomadic groups who migrated into the region from other areas usually shifted to other forms of pastoralism to diversify their economy. According to this viewpoint, pure nomadic pastoralism was possible only after dromedaries were domesticated in Arabia in the late third millennium B.C.E. and spread across the desert environments of the Near East by the early first millennium B.C.E.

Historical texts and archaeological materials from ancient Near Eastern empires attest to the presence of nomadic groups both within and on their borders. When the Romans began their conquest of the Near East, they faced a long-established network of interaction and interdependence among settled and nomad populations. These nomadic groups practiced different types of mobile pastoralism, ranging from fully nomadic camel breeding to seminomadic sheep and goat herding mixed with farming. Some of these societies, such as the Nabataean Kingdom in Arabia, became wealthy and powerful through merchant activities, transporting goods from all over the ancient world in their camel caravans. Both Rome and Persia, who were dueling for power in the ancient Near East, often developed alliances with nomad tribal chiefs, sometimes granting them official governmental titles in exchange for their loyalty. Such attempts to enlist the services of nomadic tribes increased the power and standing of their leaders and strengthened their military capability, which they sometimes used against their patrons. From the fourth century B.C.E. onward the ascending power and influence of nomadic groups began to undermine the Roman and Persian Empires and ultimately contributed to their collapse.

ASIA AND THE PACIFIC

BY KIRK H. BEETZ

The ancient Australians were mostly nomadic. One of their skills for survival was mobility: When fires or floods came, they moved out of the way. They even learned to turn fire to their advantage by setting fires that would drive game to them and would clear grassland or forest so that edible plants could grow. Thus, the ancient Australians shaped their environment to suit their needs.

Hunter-gatherer populations in the islands of the Philippines may have been seminomadic, moving within a set tribal range from place to place, relocating when game or edible plants ran short. It is possible that the island of Honshu in Japan had people on its eastern coast who lived by the sea in summer and moved inland in winter, eating seafood when on the shore and perhaps venison when the deer moved down from the mountains in winter.

The earliest nomads of eastern Asia probably followed wild game on their migrations. Some took to following reindeer; as the glaciers of the north melted and the reindeer shifted their own migrations northward in response, those people following the reindeer learned to endure bitter cold. Some of them migrated from northeastern Siberia to Alaska during what may have been as many as seven separate migrations from Asia to the Americas.

Most of what may have happened among the nomadic peoples of eastern Asia beyond the reach of the knowledge of the Chinese is unknown. In the northern reaches of China, perhaps as recently as 1500 B.C.E., nomadic peoples hunted elephants and rhinoceroses. These scattered, thin populations of people posed little threat to the young civilization of the Yellow River region until they learned to herd cattle, sheep, and Bactrian camels. Herding helped their populations grow, and they often bumped into China when they wanted to expand their pastures.

There were hundreds of nomadic tribes, but the names of only a few are known. The Xiongnu were a federation of cattle-herding tribes, very warlike. They harassed China until about 106 B.C.E., when a Chinese army drove them away from the Silk Road and into central Asia. Most historians believe their descendants became the Huns, invaders of Europe in the 400s C.E. The Yuezhi were shepherds who were driven out of their lands by the Xiongnu, but in 130 B.C.E. they settled in what is now Afghanistan. The Fergana in what is now Turkestan bred superb horses, which they supplied, sometimes unwillingly, to China in the 400s B.C.E.

In the 300s C.E. five nomadic groups, the Five Hu, invaded northern China and ruled it for about 150 years. They formed 16 states in northern China. In 383 C.E. they united under one leader and formed an army of 900,000 men that tried to conquer the rest of China. The cavalry was made up almost entirely of nomads, but the infantry was composed of Chinese conscripts, many of whom deserted during the Battle of Fei River, when the nomads were decisively defeated by the Chinese army. In 398 C.E. the Toba tribe led a confederation of 119 tribes and formed the Northern Wei state (ended ca. 534 B.C.E.).

Little is known about the nomads of western Asia, and archaeology is only just beginning to uncover their past. The principal nomadic peoples of Asia north of the Near East and east of Europe were the Cimmerians and the Scythians. Both lived in the steppes of Asia. So little is known about the Cimmerians that they were long thought to be mythical. The Cimmerians and Scythians raided the Near East and southeastern Europe, carrying away booty and slaves. The Scythians sometimes kidnapped Greek artists, who created sculptures for the Scythians. Many historians credit the Scythians with inventing the first stirrup, a leather loop. In 529 B.C.E. Persia's Cyrus the Great (r. 559–529 B.C.E.) died in battle against the Scythians.

Little is known for certain about activities in central Asia, between the Near East and northwestern China, but there must have been a lively mix of nomadic tribes. Nearly all of them spoke Indo-European languages, though some spoke languages from the Far East. The Aryans are probably the most famous of these Indo-European-speaking groups. The word *Aryan* is often used as if the Aryans were a single tribe, but the ancient Indian writers who wrote down the oral history of the Aryans about 500 B.C.E. used the word *arya* to describe the languages spoken by the nomads, not their tribe. The word *Aryan* comes from the word *arya*. The Aryans were probably several different tribes.

The nomads of central Asia had probably had trading relations with the Harappan civilization of the Indus River region for hundreds of years before moving into Harappan territory. At the height of their civilization the Harappans had built city walls over 13 feet thick and perhaps as high. Had they been healthy, it is unlikely that the Aryans could have overcome them, but a series of natural disasters had ruined the Harappans' cities, and they were probably easy targets for the warlike Aryans.

The Aryans were cattle herders, and they measured the value of goods by how many cattle the goods were worth.

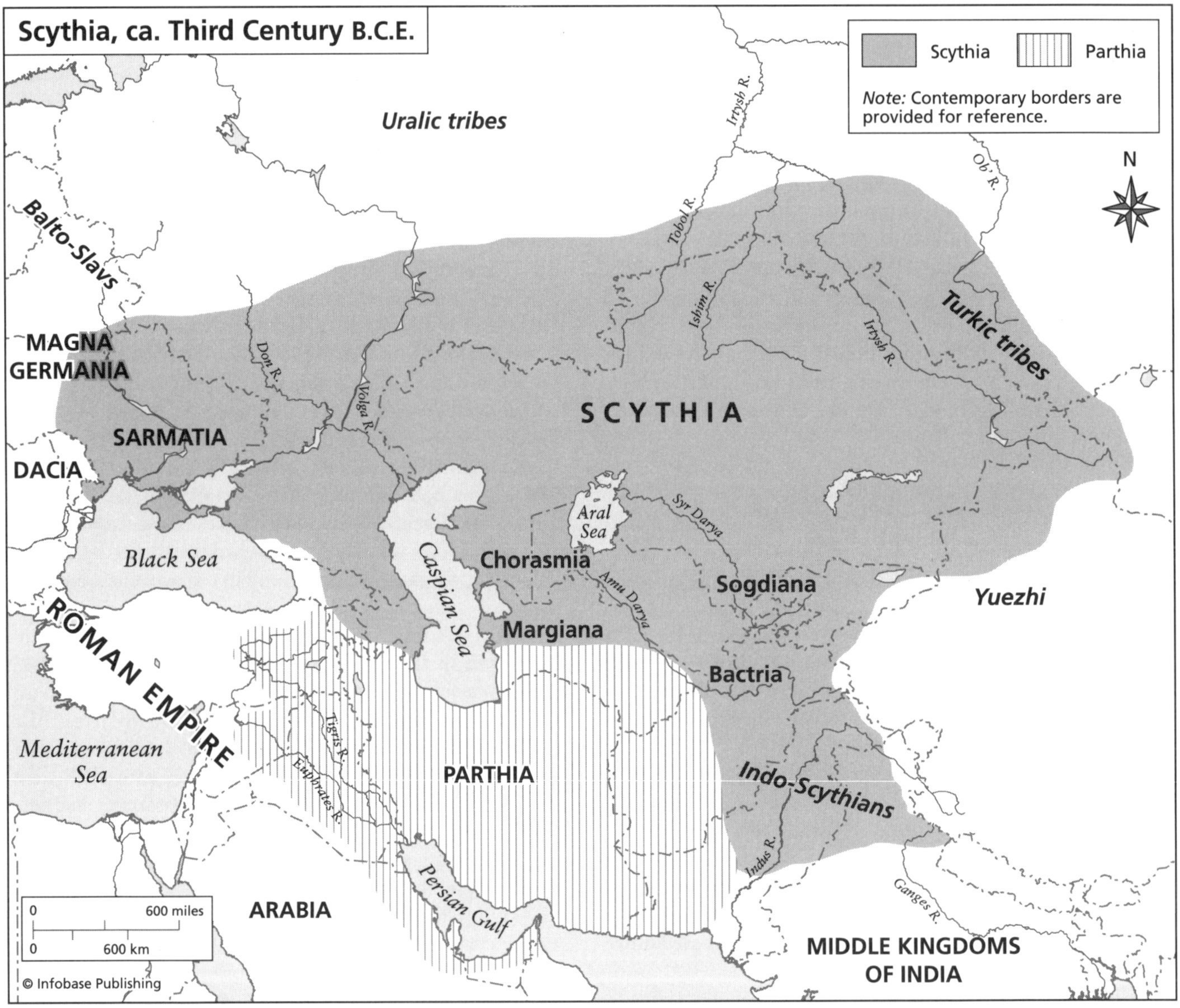

The Scythians were one of the principal nomadic peoples in ancient Asia. Their domain was situated east of Europe and north of ancient Mesopotamia.

They probably moved into Harappan territory looking for pasture for their cattle about 1500 B.C.E. They esteemed warriors over all others. When they found no outsiders to fight, they fought with one another. Their oral history hints that they fought many battles.

From 1500 to 900 B.C.E. the Aryans raided and eventually invaded throughout northern India. Their elite warriors rode into battle in chariots pulled by two horses apiece. Each chariot had a driver who road on the chariot's shaft. The elite warrior was an archer who had two assistants who supplied him with arrows or the weapons he needed if he chose to dismount and fight hand to hand. The other peoples of India had nothing to match the chariots for speed and maneuverability, because they lacked strong horses like those that had been bred in central Asia. About 900 B.C.E. the Aryans began settling along the Ganges River in northern India. By about 500 B.C.E. they had become part of the settled peoples of northern India, fending off attacks by nomads from the northeast of India, who may have been driven out of their homes by the Chinese. Still, some of the Aryans remained nomadic cattle herders in remote parts of northern India into the 21st century.

EUROPE

BY LÁSZLÓ BARTOSIEWICZ

Archaeologists and anthropologists who study ancient societies use the term *nomadic* to refer to societies that do not have permanent settlements but rather relocate them, usually in response to the availability of key resources such as game and grazing land. The hunter-gatherers who inhabited Europe until the appearance of agriculture between 9,000 and 6,000 years ago could be called *nomads* in the sense that they relocated their settlements periodically. Archaeologists try to figure out how often campsites were moved and for what reason. For example, the hunter-gatherers who recolonized northern Europe after the retreat of the ice sheets migrated in pursuit of herds of reindeer, which were abundant in the territory of modern-day Germany, Poland, Denmark, and Sweden.

After the introduction of agriculture based on the cultivation of crops, the sort of nomadism that characterized the ice age inhabitants of Europe generally disappeared. Farmsteads, and eventually villages and towns, were built in fixed locations near fields, streams, and communication routes. Initially, domestic animals such as cattle, sheep, and goats were used only for their meat, which they could provide only once, when they were killed. Eventually, however, these animals became valued for the products that they could supply while they were living, such as milk and wool. Such products can be collected from the animal over and over, making the living animal valuable. People began to amass large numbers of livestock, and with their animals they began to accumulate wealth.

In some areas domestic animals became the foundation of the farming economy. Instead of fertile soil, herders sought rich pasture for their livestock. Grazing animals deplete grass, so it is necessary to relocate from exhausted grazing land to fresh pasture periodically. Such societies returned to a nomadic way of life, but one much different from that of the ice age. Such mobile people who move their herds in search of pasture and water are known to archaeologists and anthropologists as *mobile pastoralists.* Mobile pastoralism is a complex way of life, determined by the relationships among agriculture and animal husbandry in society, by natural geography and the kinds of livestock, and by the ownership of herds. These factors combined in different ways to create a wide range of adaptations in livestock management in ancient Europe. While hardly ever manifested in their pure form, several basic types of mobile pastoralism can be distinguished on the basis of known historical and ethnographic examples.

Nomadic pastoralism is the traditional form of land use in the Old World, from deserts to savannas, mainly practiced in the ecozone of the tropical and subtropical arid regions. In the classic sense, it is practiced by entirely mobile human populations, who often follow seasonal routes, generally along a north-south axis, in search of pasture for their herds. These paths are not necessarily followed repeatedly, but they tend to be bound to vegetation along the courses of rivers or near other sources of freshwater. Aside from this technical definition, the term *nomadic* also refers to sophisticated civilizations, such as the Scythians and the Xiongnu, both flourishing before the Christian era. The Eurasian steppes saw a succession of nomadic empires that largely relied on nomadic pastoralist communities.

Transhumance is a more specialized form of mobile pastoralism in which part of the livestock is moved to seasonal pastures over the course of the year, usually from a permanent home settlement. Ethnographic examples show, for example, that large herds of sheep may be thus moved with only a few goats or cows that supply daily milk for the herders. Many of them, however, as well as pigs and chicken, remain in the main settlement. Transhumance thus involves a degree of specialization both in terms of the animal species herded and the part of the population, usually families of herdsmen, who are assigned to this task. Transhumant pastoralists tend to cover shorter distances and follow routes used by many generations. The most common form, vertical transhumance, moves herds to summer pastures at high altitudes. Today this system remains best known in the Alps in Europe. Ancient references to it in peninsular Italy are found in the Roman scholar Varro's *Rerum rusticarum libri III* (Agricultural Topics in Three Books)

Inverse transhumance means that inhabitants in mountain areas take their flocks to low-lying winter grazing areas in better-protected valleys, a form of animal husbandry that was documented not only for Vlach shepherds living in the Carpathians in the Middle Ages but indeed during the time of Augustus in the early Common Era. The Roman poet Horace, in his *Epodes*, mentions flocks exchanging Calabrian fields for Lucanian ones while it is cool.

Horizontal transhumance refers to the cyclical movement of herds in plains, largely dependent on the seasonal extremes of water conditions. This makes its archaeological evidence especially elusive. The hypthosis has been put forward that the first farming communities of the Starčevo/Körös cultures, who inhabited the low-lying section of the Carpathian Basin, practiced seasonal exploitation of floodplains and must have herded their sheep between seasonally inundated areas. According to recent ethnographic documents, large stock (cattle and horses) were seasonally grazed between shoals and river bars in the inland delta of the Danube River between modern-day Slovakia and Hungary. At the other extreme, examples of aridity's imposing seasonal limitation on grazing have been identified since the Chalcolithic (fifth to fourth millennium B.C.E.) in the Middle East.

Because they are mobile, these types of pastoralism share many traits and are often confused with each other. Identifying them in the archaeological record is difficult because these mobile lifestyles leave little evidence behind. The presence of nomads is indicated primarily when archaeologists find a single layer of settlements, temporary in appearance, and the remains of mobile domesticated animals, such as horses, cattle, or sheep (as opposed to pigs, which are considered a more sedentary animal). Identifying transhumant pastoralism is difficult because excavations usually recover architectural remains of centralized settlements, while the lightweight, transient structures in temporary summer pastures leave much less of a trace and might also occur outside intensively excavated areas altogether.

Earlier research suggested that nomadism developed directly from the hunting of wild herd animals that eventually became domesticated, as might have been the case with reindeer. Most nomadic animal keeping, however, seems to have come from the need to exploit marginal areas so that the animals would pose the least threat to the cultivated fields of sedentary agriculture. Although friction and even warfare sometimes took place between farmers and nomadic pastoralist groups, intensified by ethnic differences, the two could also coexist in mutually beneficial relationships.

In Europe their influence is represented by cultural contact or direct incursions, apparent in the archaeological record. It is thought that there were pre-Scythian waves of immigration from the southeast around the seventh century B.C.E., on the basis of the finding of luxury artifacts in the Thraco-Cimmerian style—a style that refers to the Thracians and Cimmerians who lived in east-central Europe and north of the Black Sea. These artifacts include weapons, horse tacks, and jewelry, recovered from a small number of burials. The work of the Greek historian Herodotus from the fifth century B.C.E. is probably the best-known classical source treating ancient Eurasian nomads, especially the Scythians who ruled the eastern European steppe north of the Black Sea at the time. His work also created negative stereotypes of strange and savage nomads that play a role in present-day perceptions.

Arts and crafts that traveled with the nomads, such as weapons and jewelry, as well as the remains of special mortuary practices, including horse burials, are most commonly used to identify nomads in the archaeological record. "Nomadic" influx in Europe culminated in the Great Migration roughly between 300 and 700 C.E., representing a transition from antiquity to the Middle Ages. It included, among other Germanic tribes, the Franks, Goths, and Vandals, as well as Bulgars and Slavic tribes. Equestrian peoples on the northern and eastern fringes of the Roman Empire contributed eventually to its transformation and demise. This is best illustrated by the short-lived rule of the Hunnish Empire, another nomadic society, in the Carpathian Basin during the middle of the fifth century C.E. It is therefore the warlike advance guard of these people that is known from both archaeological and historical sources of the Great Migration. Although their equestrian military tactics must have relied on traditional skills developed during a nomadic life, in fact, very little is known of their animal husbandry practices and of the ownership of their herds. It is known, however, that many of these warriors were the most visible members of complex societies with organized power centers that had a segment of the population that was sedentary.

GREECE

BY SPYROS SIROPOULOS

The term *nomad* refers to a small social unit better known as a "band" without a specific, permanent area of residence or settlement. Bands usually number less than a hundred members; the next largest kind of community is the tribe, with people inhabiting permanent settlements, such as villages. In the ancient world people were dependent upon the land; landscape determined much of their way of life. Greece is a small country, with many beaches, without many fertile areas, and with only a few valleys surrounded by mountains. Traveling from one area to another in ancient times was not extremely time-consuming or arduous because there are no difficult passages through the Greek mountains. Many people moved around with the seasons, leaving their marks behind on the landscape. Archaeologists cooperate with geologists and others to study remains of ancient pollen traces to read these marks. Their common efforts can determine the locations of ancient communities and whether they changed the environment, by deforestation, by planting domesticated trees, and by other types of cultivation.

From the beginning of the Neolithic Period in about 7000 B.C.E. domesticated animals, such as sheep, goats, oxen, and swine, appeared. The dates of the domestication of certain animals vary with the regions. Scientists have dated finds of domesticated sheep at 9000 B.C.E. in northern Iraq, cattle in the sixth millennium B.C.E. in northeastern Iran, goats at 8000 B.C.E. in central Iran, pigs at 8000 B.C.E. in Thailand and 7000 B.C.E. in Thessaly, donkeys at 7000 B.C.E. in Iraq, and horses around 4000 B.C.E. in central Asia. Goats and sheep soon became very popular. Swineherds and shepherds are often mentioned by Homer in the *Odyssey*, from the one-eyed giant Polyphemus, who was a shepherd, to the swineherd Eumaius, who played a major role in Odysseus's reestablishment on the throne of Ithaca.

The Balkan region was always a good place for grazing oxen, since the mild climate favors pastures. Animals were kept mostly to provide a supply of meat. Pigs, too, were favored. Goats and sheep mainly provided milk; dairy products were a substantial part of the ancient Mediterranean diet. The wool and hides of these animals were valuable commodities, too, since they not only served the practical needs of the community but were also used as trading materials. As for oxen, they were useful not only for meat and milk but also often served as draft animals, pulling carts and plows of farmers, as late as Hellenistic times.

The needs of animals dictated, to a great extent, the way of living in pastoral society. Seasonal migration in search of pastures was essential. Of course, animal products alone were not enough to sustain the pastoral communities. Small-scale farming was practiced, and exchange of goods with farming communities was common.

The social scale of the pastoral communities was usually simple. The family was the principle social module, with the elder person being the leader. Status was immediately related to the number and the quality of the animals owned. Formation of larger bands was common when the weather was good and the land was fertile. Antagonism toward neighboring bands was set aside, and smaller teams came together for migration in order to ensure the protection and safety of all.

Daily life in these societies revolved around animal husbandry and the fulfillment of basic needs, such as the preservation of food, which was vital for the sustenance of the community. Food, such as grain, was stored in holes in the ground, covered with a simple rock. Milk was drained through cloth and turned into cheese that could be preserved for a longer time. Meat was cut and smoked over fire or cured and smoked. Spinning of wool and making clothes was the task of women. Only wars with other tribes disrupted this life; such wars were not uncommon. Disputes over grazing sites and thefts of animals were the most usual reasons for fights.

Since the nomadic way of life is characterized by mobility, monuments and other permanent signs of culture are absent. This is very far from the traditional view of Greek society seen in the Archaic and the Classical periods (600–323 B.C.E.). This is not to say that there were no cultural aspects to the life of these communities. Myths and rituals abounded. Also, it seems that singing, accompanied by the flute, was part of the culture of pastoral societies. Homer gives such information in the *Iliad*, and the historian Diodorus Siculus describes a celebrated bucolic hero, the shepherd Daphnis.

The nomadic and pastoral way of life adapted itself to harsh environments, where it was difficult to maintain permanent settlements. Climatic conditions in Greece were never that harsh, however, and the few fertile areas were big enough to sustain main bands. Seasonal migration from more mountainous areas in summer to the plains in winter was always part of life, but the ancient Greeks soon passed from the nomadic stage to a more sedentary agricultural way of life. Animal husbandry remained important, but it became part of a less mobile life organized around permanent settlements in villages and towns. As early as 6000 B.C.E. Greeks had become farmers. Archaeologists have discovered agricultural tools, such as flint sickles and clay slabs, in the fertile areas of Thessaly and the Peloponnese, Thrace, and Macedonia.

ROME

BY MARK ANTHONY PHELPS

Pastoralist traditions were an integral part of ancient Roman society. Many concepts were tied to a pastoral lifestyle. For example, *pecunia*, the Latin noun translated as "money," finds its root in the older meaning of "wealth in flocks or herds." Prehistoric rituals preserved in Roman society include the Parilia, a ritual for fertility for the flocks, and the Fordicidia, in which pregnant cows were killed and their fetal calves were burned in the spring and pregnant sows and their fetuses were sacrificed in the winter. A festival for ensuring the harvest of crops, the Ambarvalia, involved the killing of a pig, a sheep, and a bull, followed by an examination of the victims for omens. Historians of religion see the offering of animal sacrifice as evidence of a pastoral economic component in a society. Rituals involving sacrifice are also tied to the cults of Juno, Mars, and Jupiter (all originally gods of agriculture, transformed by Rome's emerging political power). The Romans later considered sacrifice as a mark of barbarianism but still continued these rituals.

The geography of the immediate environs of Rome, however, could not support a large population of animals, at least not before those environs began to be expanded by conquest. Some historians thus see legendary struggles, such as the conquest of the Sabines, as an attempt at securing access to mountain pastures. The Sabines in Roman legend were a group of pastoralists living near the site of Rome. According to legend, the founding generation of Romans was made up entirely of males who were without kinship ties. This group of men attacked the Sabines, carrying off their women and livestock. Though it is speculative, this legend may have some basis in fact.

The transhumance that was practiced in prehistory in the Apennines continues in the 21st century. (Transhumance dictated that some people live in villages while others go out with the flocks and herds.) Sheep, goats, and pigs have always predominated. During Roman history the southern third of the Apennines was more intensely grazed. The typical transhumance cycle in this region has the flocks going higher into the mountains as the heat and dryness of the Mediterranean summer increases. The herders return after harvest, as the animals feed upon the stubble of the harvested fields and then on fodder crops once the stubble has been exhausted.

The rise of the villa does not seem to have interfered with the traditional pastoral interaction with village life. Villas focused on the cultivation of vines, fruits, and grains and tended to be near the coast or in river valleys, areas not traditionally devoted to animal husbandry. It is clear that larger operations (with herds numbering in the hundreds or thousands) were concerned with the production of wool. Among the ways this is evidenced is by the presence of a higher percentage of rams. These operations were often run by large estates, though arrangements typically were made to graze the flocks on distant pasturage. Lower percentages of rams in small herds indicate that herders were engaging in either subsistence or small-scale production of milk. The Romans considered sheep's milk more easily digestible than cow's milk, though they preferred the taste of cow's milk. Goat's milk was more common than either of the others, but it was considered least digestible of all.

Despite the advice offered in the works of the classical authors known as agronomists (among them, Varro, Cato, and Virgil), there was no streamlined system employed by the Romans either in Italy or elsewhere in the empire. Further, the Romans did not interfere in the methods employed by local pastoralists. Roman presence did alter demand for animal products, in the form of taxes and requisitions for military needs. Roman improvement of roads and development of aqueducts and new trade networks often expanded local production as well. Wool and woolen garments for export have been noted at some sites, such as Timgad in modern-day Tunisia, but surveys done throughout the empire show no dramatic change in lifestyle practiced by pastoralists anywhere after the advent of Roman political domination. The lone exception is found in the areas in which former troops were settled. Some of those settled engaged in pastoral pursuits. Beef consumption dropped noticeably with the demise of the empire. The breakdown of trade networks and the lack of military consumption played roles in this shift. The move to raising sheep and goats cut down on expenses as well as risk for farmers in a world that was making the transition to a more localized economy.

Pastoralism left its mark upon the Roman psyche. The pastoral lifestyle became the idyllic antidote to the rancor and chaos of city life (as characterized by the Roman poet Horace in his *Epodes*, written in 30 B.C.E.). Beginning with Virgil's *Eclogues* (42–37 B.C.E.), the Latin genre of pastoralism emerges. The genre emphasizes rustic purity and innocence. Virgil used his work to underscore political and social events occurring in the Roman world as well.

THE AMERICAS

BY DAVID VALLILEE

The term *nomadism* derives from the Greek word *nomás*, meaning "feed" or "pasture." Generally, it has been defined as a circumstance in which people have no permanent home and wander in search of food for themselves and pasture for their animals. It also applies to peoples whose subsistence is based largely on hunting migrating mammals, with the result that the location of their temporary shelters is determined by herd movements and a need to avoid excessive hunting in one place. Nomadic pastoralism is a life that is based on herding domesticated animals and often requires moving the animals to the best pastures. For example, pastures in arid regions may not be useful outside of the rainy season, while pastures in mountainous and colder regions may not be accessible in winter. These conditions require that livestock be moved between different regions seasonally. Nomadic pastoralists may travel to a wide variety of places according to the availability of pastureland, whereas transhumant pastoralists move between fixed locations each season, typically between lowlands and mountains.

In a general sense, all the early inhabitants of the American continent during the Paleo-Indian Period (ca. 13,000–8000 B.C.E.) can be described as nomadic, with no fixed year-round settlements and with livelihoods based on hunting and gathering that required frequent movement. While scholarship of the Paleo-Indian Period previously focused on the hunting of now-extinct big game or megafauna, such as mastodons, mammoths, ground sloths, and saber-tooth tigers, scholars now agree that the Paleo-Indian hunters relied more heavily upon species of mammals that did not become extinct: bison, caribou, moose, elk, and ox.

The Archaic Period (ca. 8000–1000 B.C.E.) in the Americas generally is viewed as a gradual period of transition from nomadic hunting and gathering societies to sedentary, agriculturally based societies. Despite the introduction of agriculture, many cultures retained a hunting-and-gathering component in their diet. For some a seminomadic existence based on seasonal movements that followed animal migrations continued throughout the period. Toward the end of the Archaic Period small year-round settlements—and in rare cases large settlements, such as Poverty Point in Louisiana (ca. 1600–1300 B.C.E.)—began to appear, and nomadism became less common.

In many of the mountainous regions of South America, parts of northern Mexico, and the Great Plains and Great Basin regions of North America, however, nomadic existence and reliance upon hunting remained central throughout the Archaic Period and later (until 500 C.E.). The Paleo-Indian Period in central Mexico was characterized by small nomadic families, or microbands, who moved their camps three or four times a year, hunting horses, antelope, and, occasionally, mammoths and other now-extinct species of megafauna. They also hunted smaller game: rabbits, turtles, birds, gophers, rats, and other small mammals. Extensive archaeological study of the Tehuacán Valley (in the state of Puebla, Mexico) has led to a number of conclusions about the Archaic Period in central Mexico. One conclusion is that in the Tehuacán Valley (ca. 8000–5000 B.C.E.) subsistence depended upon plant collecting, trapping of small mammals, and hunting of a variety of animals and birds. The cultivation of maize (corn) first appeared in the region around 5000 B.C.E. Beans, amaranth (a grain), chili peppers, plums, avocados, squashes, and gourds were also cultivated. Between about 5000 and 2300 B.C.E. agriculture gained an increasingly larger proportion of the Tehuacán Valley diet (25 percent), but hunting of mammals also continued. Year-round occupation of hamlets began approximately between 3400 and 2300 B.C.E., after which nomadism for the Tehuacán Valley can be said to have ceased.

With the extinction of mammoths, prehistoric horses, and camelids in the Great Plains region during the early Archaic Period, a shift to bison hunting became ever more central to survival. The tools of this period, particularly finely carved, razor-sharp spear points, were essential components for increasing the success of bison hunting. Hunting parties drove herds of bison over cliffs, such as at the Head-Smashed-In bison jump in southern Alberta, Canada, and into canyons, ravines, and corrals (bowl-shaped rock formations), where large numbers of bison could be slaughtered quickly.

The settlement systems of the Archaic Plains Indians adhered to a flexible and mobile pattern with an emphasis on hunting bison augmented by hunting smaller animals (deer, raccoons, beavers, rabbits, squirrels, muskrats). Shelter typical of the period included open-air and rock-shelter field camps, and post-in-ground structures, while portable perishable shelter—presumably hide-covered tepees—were probably the most prominent. After the Archaic Period, these patterns of subsistence continued.

The Archaic Period Desert culture (ca. 9000–1000 B.C.E.) located in the Great Basin area was primarily a foraging society. At one site, Danger Cave in Utah, millstones used for grinding grain, seeds, and nuts, along with some of the earliest basketry in North America, have been excavated. The Cochise culture (ca. 7000–200 B.C.E.), which evolved out of the Desert culture, hunted and trapped small mammals (deer, antelope, and rabbits) as well as small reptiles (snakes and lizards). The people migrated with the seasons, inhabiting the desert floor in the winter and higher elevations (mesas) in the summer. They also gathered wild plants, such as yuccas, prickly pears, junipers, and piñons. Some archaeologists believe that the first evidence of the cultivation of maize (corn) north of Mexico occurred in this region around 3500 B.C.E. This may have been a result of contact with Mesoamerican cultures to the south.

In the early part of the Archaic Period in South America the mastodon, prehistoric horse, and ground sloth species died out, and hunters shifted to deer, camelids (such as llamas and alpacas), guanacos, guinea pigs, and other small mammals. Coastal sites began to exploit marine resources (fish and shellfish), especially after 5000 B.C.E. Maize was first cultivated in the Peruvian highlands around 3500 B.C.E. and a shift to agricultural and agropastoral subsistence became widespread in South America by 2000 B.C.E. The emergence of ceramics, another indicator of sedentary non-nomadic existence, occurred at roughly the same time, around 1800 B.C.E.

It is likely that the llama and alpaca were domesticated around 3000 B.C.E. In the late Archaic Period and afterward, hunting on the high plains of mountain regions in South America combined with domestication of camelids resulted in a system of regular migration (transhumant nomadism) between different altitudes, from the valleys in the wet, summer season to higher elevations in the dry, winter season.

See also AGRICULTURE; ART, CITIES; CLIMATE AND GEOGRAPHY; CLOTHING AND FOOTWEAR; ECONOMY; EMPLOYMENT AND LABOR; FAMILY; FESTIVALS; FOOD AND DIET; GENDER STRUCTURES AND ROLES; HUNTING, FISHING, AND GATHERING; LANGUAGE; LITERATURE; MIGRATION AND POPULATION MOVEMENTS; MILITARY; MINING, QUARRYING, AND SALT MAKING; NATURAL DISASTERS; RELIGION AND COSMOLOGY; ROADS AND BRIDGES; SETTLEMENT PATTERNS; SOCIAL ORGANIZATION; STORAGE AND PRESERVATION; TOWNS AND VILLAGES; TRADE AND EXCHANGE; WAR AND CONQUEST.

FURTHER READING

L. Bartosiewicz and H. Greenfield, eds., *Transhumant Pastoralism in Southern Europe* (Budapest, Hungary: Archaeolingua, 1999).

Ofer Bar-Yosef and Anatoly Khazanov, eds., *Pastoralism in the Levant: Archaeological Materials in Anthropological Perspectives* (Madison, Wisc.: Prehistory Press, 1992).

Barbara Bender, *Farming in Prehistory: From Hunter-gatherer to Food-producer* (London: J. Baker, 1975).

J. L. Bintliff, *Natural Environment and Human Settlement in Prehistoric Greece* (Oxford, U.K.: British Archaeological Reports, 1977).

Juliet Clutton-Brock, ed., *The Walking Larder: Patterns of Domestication, Pastoralism, and Predation* (London: Unwin-Hyman, 1989).

Roger Cribb, *Nomads in Archaeology* (Cambridge, U.K.: Cambridge University Press, 1991).

Rada Dyson-Hudson and Neville Dyson-Hudson, "Nomadic Pastoralism," *Annual Review of Anthropology* 9 (1980): 15–61.

George C. Frison, *Prehistoric Hunters of the High Plains* (New York: Academic Press, 1978).

Daniel H. Garrison, ed., *Horace: Epodes and Odes*, vol. 10 (Norman: University of Oklahoma Press, 1991).

Anatoly M. Khazanov, *Nomads and the Outside World*, trans. Julia Crookenden, 2nd ed. (Madison: University of Wisconsin Press, 1994).

Henri Lhote, "When the Sahara Was Green." In *The World's Last Mysteries* (Pleasantville, N.Y.: Reader's Digest Association, 1978).

Richard MacNeish, "Food-Gathering and Incipient Agriculture Stage in Prehistoric Middle America." In *Handbook of Middle American Indians: Archaeology of Northern Mesoamerica*, vol. 1, eds. Gordon F. Eckholm and Ignacio Bernal (Austin, Tex.: University of Austin Press, 1971).

James L. Newman, *The Peopling of Africa: A Geographic Interpretation* (New Haven, Conn.: Yale University Press, 1995).

Karim Sadr, *The Development of Nomadism in Ancient Northeast Africa* (Philadelphia: University of Pennsylvania Press, 1991).

C. R. Whittaker, ed., *Pastoral Economies in Classical Antiquity* (Cambridge, U.K.: Cambridge University Press, 1988).

► numbers and counting

INTRODUCTION

Systems of numbers and counting emerged and developed at different times throughout the ancient world. The earliest, most advanced systems came from Mesopotamia and the Indus Valley of India. In contrast, numbers and counting were much slower to develop in ancient Europe. In most cases, the ancients were not interested in developing complex systems of mathematics to solve abstract problems. Counting and numbers arose as a way to help people solve practical, day-to-day problems.

Thus, counting was typically synonymous with measurement. The ancients needed to take accurate measurements of, for example, fields and tillable ground in order to assign land to farmers, particularly in areas of the world where boundaries could change because of flooding, as in ancient Egypt and Mesopotamia. They also needed to calculate the volume of crops or the number of bricks needed for a construction project. Linear measurements were needed for such activities as constructing buildings, and some cultures, such as the Mesoamericans and the Mesopotamians, developed fairly sophisticated forms of geometry for this purpose.

The ancients lacked sophisticated tools for making these kinds of measurements and for fixing consistent units of measurement. Accordingly, they often turned to the physical world, including their own bodies, to devise units of measurement. A good example is the cubit, a unit of length from a person's elbow and the tip of the middle finger. Sometimes, these units varied depending on what was being measured. The common cubit was used for everyday purposes, but the "royal cubit" was used for public construction projects. For counting purposes, the fingers and toes proved useful, giving rise to systems of counting that were based on the number 20, as in ancient Mesoamerica. Still today, many people in the British Isles use "stone" as a measure of weight.

Counting was used for other purposes as well. The ancients devised systems of counting to create calendars, which in turn required mathematical calculations of the movements of heavenly bodies. As trade and commerce began to emerge, systems of counting were needed to keep track of accounts. Also required were primitive monetary systems, which began as objects such as clay tokens used to keep track of quantities and transactions and later evolved into true money.

The development of systems of numbers and counting was bound up with the development of writing. For this reason, the ancient Europeans fell far behind other regions of the world; lacking systems of writing until much later, they had no means of recording measurements. Some historians believe that ancient scripts found in eastern Europe may have included numbers, but so far they have been unable to decipher these scripts, so historians remain uncertain. In contrast, the ancient Asians and Mesopotamians had systems of writing that record mathematical measurements, and historians have been able to reconstruct these systems with some completeness.

AFRICA

BY OLUTAYO CHARLES ADESINA

The development of a sense of quantification was basic to the construction of number and counting systems in Africa. The concept of numbers and counting represented a certain apprehension of reality and became the foundations of mathematics, which in turn provided the key to existence. Despite this awareness, however, ancient Africans never formulated uniform numerals and systems of counting. Neither did they devise a set nomenclature for native methods of counting. Various cultures and ethnic groupings ultimately worked out different ways of thinking about mathematics and numerals. The sense of quantification, however, had universal application to reality.

These diverse groups had numeral systems that ranged from the simple to the complex. The Yoruba of West Africa, for instance, adopted an intricate system woven around addition, subtraction, and multiplication. They formulated different terms for numbers from 1 to 10 as well as for 20, 30, 200, and 400; the rest were multiples or compounds. Thus 11, 12, 13, and 14 were reckoned as 10 plus 1 or plus 2 up to 14, while 15 to 20 were reckoned as 20 less 1 to 5. But as there were such groups as the Yoruba, the Galla, the Danakil, and the Shiko whose numerical scale extended to 1,000, there also existed those such as the San (Bushmen) of South Africa, who possessed numerals not greater than 10. Among such groups, and even among those with more highly developed civilizations, higher numbers were represented by the use of words equivalent to "much" and "many."

Evidence suggests that base 10 and base 20 counting systems were popular among Africans, probably originating from the number of human fingers and toes. As in other ancient cultures, standards of length, numbers, and measures existed with reference to parts of the human body. To several groups, fingers became an important instrument of calculation. Ancient Africans developed the quinary and denary scale of numeration, or counting by the fingers of one or both hands. Toes and fingers and their multiples were used at different stages of enumeration. Part of the culture of counting that ancient Africans transmitted to their offspring was the capacity to handle the various kinds of currency in use. Similarly, games and puzzles formed part of the prehistoric system of numeration.

With the adoption of a numeral system, ancient Africans were able to develop a concept of mathematics. Ancient astronomy became a significant tool in this regard. Conversely, numbers and counting also became major tools for understanding nature. Thus, the celestial order helped in the creation of an earthly order. This philosophy led to a number of complex number symbolisms. The seconds, minutes, days, and months derived from the celestial arrangement became an integral part of a numeral system. Early humans divided the day into temporal hours with length conditioned by the time of the year, the summer having a longer period of daylight than the winter.

In various parts of Africa wood, bone, and stone were adopted as instruments of counting. The bone was a counting tool for simple arithmetical procedures. There existed tally sticks, bones with orderly notches that represented the number of days in a moon cycle or days spent by a group in one geographic location. A piece of baboon fibula with 29 notches, dating to around 35,000 B.C.E. and found between South Africa and Swaziland, is the oldest-known mathematical artifact. Several groups in Africa adopted such bones as calendar sticks. Other examples include the Ishango bone found on the border of Zaire and Uganda. This small animal bone, which has been dated to around 20,000 B.C.E., is inscribed with markings thought to represent numbers. It is assumed to have been used as a counting tool for mathematical purposes. Commodities also were used in this regard. Such products as salt and slaves were used more often as accounting units or standards against which goods were valued. In the western Sudan cowries (shells) adopted as currency were strung together and used in counting.

Among ancient Africans, mathematics was concerned with numbers and their operations, with which calculations could be achieved. This belief translated into the "multitude" and the "magnitude." It encapsulated arithmetic, philosophy, geometry, and stereometry (the measurement of volume). Rather than being an abstract concept, mathematics became a major tool for understanding nature and existence. Ancient Africans used the reality of mathematics to make inferences from general truths to particular truths and constructed an order that enabled them to understand life. Mathematics became a tool for achieving perfection, truth, and stability. The entire universe, it was believed, is an arrangement of numbers. There are an infinite number of proofs for the harmony of mathematics and human existence in ancient Africa.

EGYPT

BY BRADLEY SKEEN

From the early Predynastic Period (ca. 6500–3500 B.C.E.) to the Greco-Roman Period (332–30 B.C.E.), native Egyptian civilization made extensive use of practical mathematics in architecture, astronomy, calendar making, and above all geometry (the measurement of agricultural fields). However, Egyptians showed little interest in pure mathematics in any abstract sense. The rope stretchers or surveyors who retraced the boundaries of fields after the Nile flood commonly used the Pythagorean theorem in their work, but they could not have stated it in an abstract form or given it a formal mathematical proof.

Aside from the incidental representations of numbers in numerous texts, our knowledge of Egyptian mathematics comes from two main sources: the Ahmes Papyrus and Moscow Papyrus. Both are small textbooks that would have been used in scribal schools. They demonstrate techniques to solve simple mathematical and algebraic equations, but only by representing specific examples from which the student must infer general rules and procedures, exactly the opposite of the modern approach to mathematics. Ordinary people would have been illiterate and also unable to perform any but the simplest mathematical operations "in their heads."

Egyptians used a decimal, or base 10, number system just as we still do today. While this system ultimately derives from the fact that human beings have 10 fingers, Egyptians may have been the originators of this formal mathematical system distinct from the older Babylonian mathematical system that was partially base 10 and partially base 6 (for five fingers and one hand). In hieroglyphs, the oldest form of Egyptian writing, only the number 1 (a straight upright line representing a finger) and multiples of 10 could be directly shown. The number 10 was indicated by a heel bone, 100 by a snare, 1,000 by a lotus flower; 10,000 by a more detailed sketch of a finger, 100,000 by a tadpole, and 1,000,000 by a man holding his hands stretched widely apart, still an innate gesture to indicate a large size. There was no conception of zero as a number. Other numbers could be written only by giving combinations of these signs that added up to the number in question, as if

The Rhind Mathematical Papyrus, showing mathematical problems and solutions, from Thebes, Egypt (1550 B.C.E.) (© The Trustees of the British Museum)

in modern writing we showed the number 149 by this combination of symbols: 1 1 1 1 1 1 1 1 1 10 10 10 10 100. Moreover, the individual components of the number could be shown in any order that the scribe found pleasing or best suited to the space available in the text. Thus, even reading a simple number would require performing a series of additions (though no doubt this would have become more or less automatic for experienced scribes).

Similarly, fractions could, in general, be represented only by unit fractions; that is, 1 over the divisor. Thus, a more complex fraction would have to be represented by a series of unit fractions equal to it. For example, $2/15$ would have been written as $1/10 + 1/30$. Fractions were denoted by drawing the sign for *mouth* (an oval) over the numeral. There were, however, special signs for $2/3$ and $3/4$.

Operations like multiplication also were carried out as a series of additions. For instance, if a scribe wanted to square 13 (that is, 13 × 13), he might start by making a table like this, doubling each row and also keeping track of how many 13s were in each row:

13	1
26	2
52	4
104	8

Then, knowing that 8 + 4 +1 = 13, he would add 104 + 52 + 13 to produce the answer of 169. With practice, much of this work could be done automatically without writing out the whole process.

Hieratic (or cursive) script was used for everyday writing and supplemented the formal hieroglyphic script found in inscriptions and official documents. In this style of writing, the numbers from 2 to 9 came to be represented by an abbreviated sketch of what the group of upright strokes in hieroglyphic form typically resembled. In this way something like our individual numerals existed.

Egyptian mathematical notation and procedures were at once highly practical and terribly cumbersome and inelegant. Counting and mathematical problems recorded in Egyptian sources were intended to provide solutions to the practical problems of everyday life, including the distribution of provisions, the valuations of commodities against precious metals (because Egyptian civilization lacked coinage), and various forms of farm accounting. It is easy to see that the reverent awe in which the ancient Greeks and many later people held Egyptian mathematical thought was quite undeserved. It was based on the inherent difficulty of reading the hieroglyphic script and the glamour of the antiquity of Egyptian civilization rather than any sophisticated or mysterious Egyptian mathematical science.

In the Hellenistic and Roman periods (after 330 B.C.E.), Greek scholars working in Egypt, especially at the Museum in Alexandria, made tremendous advances in both theoretical and applied mathematics. For the most part, they drew on Greek and Babylonian mathematical science, not that of native Egyptian civilization. Euclid (fl. 300 B.C.E) perfected the concept of the formal mathematical proof. Claudius Ptolemy (ca. 90–168 C.E.) created a system of mathematical astronomy that is both ancestral to modern astronomy and remained unchanged until the time of Copernicus in the 16th century. However, Eratosthenes (ca. 276–ca. 194 B.C.E.) drew upon the Egyptian tradition of geometry as land surveying in his calculation of the circumference of the earth. He relied on the skills of native surveyors to determine the distance between the cities of Alexandria and Syene (modern-day Aswān); since he also knew the number of degrees of arc that separated them on the earth's surface, he used that information to calculate the total size of the whole earth.

THE MIDDLE EAST

BY JUSTIN CORFIELD

Various numbering systems were used in Mesopotamia during ancient times. The earliest was that of the Sumerians and is known to have been used from at least 2800 to 2600 B.C.E. It involved lines of signs listing numbers from left to right. This system was developed by the Elamites, who occupied what is now Iran, and at the same time by the Akkadians, whose numeral notation system provided a basis for that developed by the Babylonians. It is known that the Babylonian numerals had appeared between 1900 and 1800 B.C.E., though some scholars think they may have been introduced in Akkad 500 years earlier. The Babylonian system was the first that used a place-value numeral, in which the value of a particular digit depends not just on the character but also on where it appears in a number, as in the difference between 82 and 28. Curiously, neither the Sumerians nor the Akkadians (from whom the Babylonians drew their numerical system) used place-value numerals.

The Babylonians had a sexagesimal system, that is, with a base of 60. They wrote numbers by making marks on soft clay using a wedge-tipped stylus. A symbol similar to a letter *Y* denoted the units. One of these symbols indicated 1, two for 2, and so on up to 9. To denote the "10s," a symbol similar to a left angle was used. Thus "<<<YY" meant 32. This system allowed the Babylonians to compute complicated mathematical sums, including linear equations, though they did not have a digit for zero, which was denoted by its absence.

The reason for the algebraic achievements of the Babylonians is unknown, because it is commonly believed that all pre-Hellenic mathematics, including theirs, was largely used for practical matters rather than for pure mathematics, or mathematics engaged in for its own sake. One tablet in the Plimpton Collection at Columbia University, New York, dating to 1600 to 1900 B.C.E., was initially thought to have been a set of business accounts, but some scholars have suggested that it was part of a much larger tablet. The numbers on it are not listed in a haphazard order but follow a pure mathematics inquiry.

Because of the Babylonian interest in mathematics and astronomy, the base of 60 survives in the number of minutes in an hour and partially in the number of degrees for an equilateral triangle and in the 360 degrees in a circle. The Babylonians were able to use their system for reciprocal numbers, square roots, cubes, and cube roots of numbers. There is evidence that mathematics was taught in schools, and some tablets survive with mathematical problems and with the working out of pure mathematical theories.

The Assyrians followed the same system as the Babylonians; indeed, they seem to have added nothing to the Babylonian advances in mathematics. They used the numbers for purely applied purposes, such as for building temples and palaces, for computing taxation owed to their rulers, and for military reasons. As a result, when the Achaemenid Persian Empire (538–331 B.C.E.) was established, it was from Babylonian science and numbering that it drew its inspiration. Although the Persians did embark on a number of premathematical inquiries, their primary focus was applied mathematics.

There were many other numeral systems that operated in the Near East at the time, including that used by the Jews. The Hebraic numeral system uses the additive principle, in which the numeric values of the individual letters are added together to form the whole. Different numerals denote each number from 1 through 10 and then 20, 30, 40, and so on until 100; different numbers are used for 200, 300, 400, 500, and so forth. There are 27 Hebrew numerals in all. The Hittites also had their own numbering system, as did the Phoenicians.

By the time Alexander the Great conquered the Achaemenid Persian Empire in the 330s B.C.E., Greek numerals tended to dominate notation in the ancient world. In many ways it had come about as Greek learning permeated much of the Near East, even before Alexander's conquest. This remained the case throughout the rest of the ancient world, so much so that Greek mathematicians dominated the field during the Roman Empire.

ASIA AND THE PACIFIC

BY FRANK J. SWETZ

The development of Asian counting systems and mathematics was greatly influenced by two pervasive civilizations: the Hindu empires of the Indian subcontinent and the dynastic empires of imperial China. Through conquest, trade, and religious evangelization these civilizations spread their customs, beliefs, and rituals over much of the Asian region. In particular, Korea, Annam (northern Vietnam), and Japan became the intellectual heirs of China. Contacts resulted in the adoption of Chinese mathematical practices.

From the Shang Dynasty (ca. 1500–ca. 1045 B.C.E.) onward the Chinese had been using a decimal system of counting and recording numbers. The earliest evidence of such numbers has been found on Shang oracle shells and bones used for fortune-telling. More formal systems of numeration appear in bronze inscriptions of the following Zhou Dynasty (ca. 1045–ca. 256 B.C.E.). Finally, during the Han Dynasty (ca. 202–ca. 220 B.C.E.), this decimal numeration system was standardized. By the early centuries of the Common Era, Chinese use of number symbols had evolved into four distinct systems: a form for common use, a more elaborate form for legal and administrative documents, a commercial form that allowed for quick recording, and a scientific, counting-rod, or rod-numeral, form that lent itself to calculations on a computing board. It was the latter set, the rod numerals, that was most influential in terms of mathematical facility and cultural transmission and eventual adoption in the territories influenced by China.

Rod numerals actually represented configurations of a set of wooden computing rods employed on a counting board. They were basically tally symbols representing numbers; thus 3 would be represented by three vertical rods, recorded as a numeral by three vertical strokes. In designating digits, this process continued up to recording 5 by using five vertical strokes; for numbers above 5 a horizontal stroke would be added, serving as a cap over the vertical strokes. This horizontal stroke represented a count of 5. The vertical strokes added below it would then represent units to be added to the 5. So a horizontal stroke covering one vertical stroke would represent the number 6 and a horizontal stroke with four vertical strokes would stand for the number 9. These symbols were used to designate collections of units—100s, 10,000s, and so on (alternating powers of 10). For the remaining alternating powers of 10—10s, 1,000s, 100,000s, and so on—the orientation of the strokes was changed; vertical strokes were replaced by horizontal strokes and horizontal by vertical. Thus, alternating 10's positions in a decimal-based numeral would be symbolized by contrasting sets of strokes.

In this system numerals would be written from left to right, with the highest power of 10 occupying the left-most position in the numeral. An empty space in the numeral indicated an empty position on a counting board (a "zero"). A detailed description of Chinese counting rods and their computational procedures is given in *Sun zi suan jing* (The Mathematical Classic of Master Sun), written about the year 400 C.E. This rod counting and numeration system was most efficient and was used throughout Asia for many years until it was replaced by the abacus.

Common Chinese numerals were (and still are) written in a vertical column with the highest place value at the top. These columns of characters are unique in that they serve as numerals, counting symbols, and number words or phrases. There are separate characters for each grouping of 10s—10, 100s, 1,000s—and, in a numeral, each 10's grouping would be preceded by a counting character; thus a reader would note two characters (words), such as *three hundreds* or *five tens*. In such a numeration system there is no need for a "zero" symbol as a placeholder, the name of the particular 10's place is just missing from the designation.

The positional value scheme of the Chinese numerals was very efficient and flexible, allowing for the recording of large numbers, up to 10^7; it could even, conceptually, express numbers up to powers of 10^{80}, but such numbers were limited to ritual use. The Chinese common or standard numeral system and the computational rod system were adopted and readily used in Japan, Korea, and Annam. Chinese mathematical techniques were also adopted by these cultures, as were the Chinese classical manuals describing applications of mathematics. The most famous and influential of these manuals was the *Jiu zhang suan shu* (Nine Chapters on the Mathematical Art), written in about 100 B.C.E.; this was a bureaucratic handbook of the mathematics needed to run an empire.

The earliest epigraphic evidence of a counting system in India can be traced back to the Maurya Empire (321–185 B.C.E.) and to the activities of its greatest ruler, Asoka (r. ca. 286–231 B.C.E.), who constructed cast-iron pillars listing the precepts of his rule. On these structures is found evidence of a decimal system of numeration, the Kharosthi numerals. These numerals are basically tally symbols but conceived around the use of base 10. The tally symbols eventually evolved into a cursive form that could be written down easily. Like the rod numerals of China, this system also left an empty space to indicate the lack of an enumerator for a power of 10 (a "zero"). Numerals were written horizontally from left to right with the digit representing the highest power of 10 occupying the position farthest to the left. This later Brahmi form spread throughout the Hindu sphere of influence.

Indian scholars also devised a collection of computational algorithms to accompany these numerals. These algorithms could be undertaken using the writing materials at hand and did not require an auxiliary computing device. Early Hindu traders and missionaries, brought this knowledge and these techniques to their clients and converts throughout Asia, specifically into the Malay Archipelago, including the present-day Philippines, Sri Lanka, the Srivijaya maritime empire of present-day Sumatra, the Khmer kingdom of Angkor (Cambodia), the Champa kingdom (central Vietnam), Majapahit (Java), and among the Mon people (Thailand). This decimal system of enumeration and its variants became very popular along the trade routes of the East Indies, where it was also adopted and perpetuated by traveling Arab merchants who would eventually introduce it into Europe.

Before the Common Era an extensive trade system was established among the peoples of the Pacific region both between themselves and with foreigners. It is most likely that these contacts promoted various systems of counting and enumeration. Language similarities within the traditional counting systems of the Chamorro people of the Mariana Islands, the Ilocano and Kapampangans of the Philippines, the Napu and Batak of Indonesia, and the inhabitants of Fiji and Samoa all support this conclusion. For example, all their ancient, traditional languages share the same word for the number 5, *lima*, a proto-Malay word for *hand*, referring to the origin of finger counting. Similarly, Tongans and Tahitians employed a decimal system of counting, one that could accommodate enumeration into the millions. The Hawaiians, descendants of these people, also employed a base 10 counting system, one in which groupings of four—4, 40, 400, and so on—bore special significance in counting specific items such as taro and coconuts.

This early prevalence of decimal notation, in many cases, depended upon exposure to foreign, external influences imparted by traders and missionaries. Thus, coastal peoples and inhabitants of administrative urban centers may have used decimal counting, but their isolated hinterland peers employed other systems. For most of these remote peoples there is little historical evidence in existence as to their ancient counting practices, but anthropological research among traditional peoples of the Pacific region, especially those of Papua New Guinea, supplies insights into their ancestors' mathematical systems. Findings indicate that probably these isolated peoples had limited number vocabularies and employed a variety of counting bases, among which the base 5 was popular in emulating the number of digits on the human hand. Many of their number terms would have been more qualitative than quantitative, comparable to words such as "couple," "herd," and "flock" that not only designate a general number but also convey further information about the objects under consideration. These people also might have employed several counting systems, that is, using different number words for counting special items, such as yams, pigs, and canoes, and for doing time reckoning. Some of these societies were known to have used four or five such different systems for their counting purposes.

EUROPE

BY AMY HACKNEY BLACKWELL

Ancient Europeans did not develop mathematics and counting to nearly the degree that the peoples of the Mediterranean region did. Most ancient European peoples outside Greece and the Roman Empire did not write at all, so almost no written records remain that could show the level of mathematical knowledge in Europe. People in Mesopotamia and the Mediterranean used mathematics to trade and build objects, but the Celts, Germans, and other European peoples did not leave traces of numerical systems for accounts, records, or architectural calculations. One of the earliest uses of numbers was to keep track of days and seasons. Bones dating from as early as 11,000 B.C.E. contain regular scratches that may have corresponded to the phases of the moon. People early gained a sense of the numbers that were important for keeping track of time, such as 28 to 30 days per month and 12 months per year.

Prehistoric European peoples were good enough at astronomical calculations to build stone structures precisely engineered to catch the sun at a particular time on a certain day. For example, the tomb at Newgrange in Ireland, built around 3500 B.C.E., is designed so that the rising sun on the winter solstice (approximately December 21) falls on a design deep within a grave chamber. Stonehenge and other giant stone sites also are placed in such a way as to catch the sunlight on particular days of the year.

The Druids, Celtic spiritual leaders, became quite adept at the mathematical computations required to keep the calendar in order. The Celts considered several numbers to be sacred or spiritually significant. The number 3 was extremely important. Celts saw the world as composed of three components: earth, sea, and sky. The human soul also was thought to have three components. Celtic deities often appeared as triads, such as the three Irish goddesses of war. The number 9 was important as well, because it was three times three and possibly because it was the length of a lunar week. The number 5 symbolized the family and, in Ireland, the kingdom. The number 27 was the number of warriors in a Celtic king's royal court and in his war band; it contained the combined spiritual power of 3 and 9, which when multiplied equals 27. The number 33 was also important, representing the total number of gods in the divine court.

The Celtic peoples used mathematics to create their elaborate knotted decorative patterns, which appeared in Celtic metalwork and stone carving. The earliest patterns used parallel lines and carefully drawn circles, but by the first century C.E. Celtic patterns were quite complicated and required a solid understanding of geometry. Celtic artists designed their patterns on a square grid. The number of lines on the grid determined the number of strings or lines in the pattern. A two-by-two grid would produce an image from two pieces of string or lines. A four-by-four grid required four pieces of string or lines. By using a solid geometrical plan, a Celtic artist could create a complex design that was entirely complete within itself, with all lines woven together and no strings left untied. Almost all Celtic knot patterns were made on even-numbered grids; it was impossible to tie all ends on patterns made from odd-numbered grids, so they were rarely used. Historians believe that knot patterns may have evolved from basket weaving, which also required a practical knowledge of geometry.

Ancient Celtic and Germanic languages had their own counting words. Counting words in the different Celtic languages were similar to one another because of their common origin in Proto-Celtic. They also resemble the counting words in other Indo-European languages, including modern languages such as English or French. (This is easiest to hear when reading them aloud.) In Proto-Celtic, the numbers from 1 to 10 were as follows: *oinos, dwossu, treis, kwetwar, kwenkwe, sweks, sektn, okto, nauin, dekn.* In Brythonic, spoken in Wales, Brittany, and Cornwall, the numbers were *oino, dau, tri, petuar, pempe, hweh, seht, oht, nau, dek.* In Goidelic, spoken in Ireland, Scotland, and the Isle of Man, these numbers were *oino, dassu, triss, keuur, kwessik, swe, sehtn, oht, nowin, dehn.* And in Gaulish, spoken by the Gauls in France, the numbers ran *oino, do, tri, petor, pempe, suekos, sextam, oxtu, nau, decam.*

Numbers in Germanic dialects resembled those in Celtic dialects. In Proto-Germanic, 1 through 10 ran *ainaz, twai, orijiz, fidwor, fimfi, sehs, sibum, ahto, niwun, tehun.* In Proto-German, the numbers were *eins, tswass, drioss, fiossr, fimf, sehs, sibun, ahto, niwun, tsehun.* In Gothic, spoken by the Visigoths during the early centuries C.E., the sequence was *ains, twai, dries, fidwor, fimf, saiehs, sibun, ahtau, niun, taiehun.*

During the classical Greek and Roman periods European peoples began using Greek and Roman number systems. Greek numbers were more common in eastern Europe and Roman numbers in the west. The most widespread use of numbers was in commerce and in wills and testaments. Both Greek and Roman numbers had some deficiencies; neither of them was well suited for computations with very large numbers, and expressing fractions was difficult with both. Nevertheless these were the best mathematical systems available at the time and they were certainly an improvement on the existing unwritten European numerical systems.

GREECE

BY JEFFREY S. CARNES

The Greeks had two number systems in common use: the acrophonic and the alphabetic. The acrophonic system used the straight line for the number 1, but the initial letters of the numeral words for higher numbers. Thus they had Π (pi for *pente*, or 5), Δ (delta for *deka*, or 10), H (eta for *hekaton*, or 100), X (chi for *chilioi*, or 1,000); and M (mu for *myrioi*, 10,000). *Myrioi* was the biggest numerical unit—all higher numbers were expressed as multiples of *myrioi*. Multiples of 5 could be expressed by combining pi with another symbol: thus pi with a delta hanging from it would be 50 and pi with a mu hanging from it, 50,000. Other multiples were expressed by repeating the sign: 42,324, for example, would be MMMMXXHHHΔΔ||||. This system was used in public inscriptions in Athens until about 100 B.C.E., and until about 200 B.C.E. in other cities.

The alphabetic system is the older of the two, but it was refined and came into widespread use in the fifth century B.C.E. It probably originated in Ionia (the area on and around the coast of Asia Minor) and consists simply of the letters of the Ionian alphabet, with the addition of three obsolete letters left over from the Phoenician alphabet: ς (stigma), ϙ (koppa), and ϡ (sampi). This brings the total up to 27, making it usable as a quasi-decimal system: the first nine letters (alpha through theta) represent 1 through 9; the next nine, 10 through 90; and the final nine, 100 through 900. The lack of a zero as placeholder kept it from being a true decimal system, and, in fact, the order of numbers might vary. For this reason it was useful to distinguish numbers from letters: in inscriptions this could be done with a space or a raised dot; in print the convention came to be that numbers were written with a following superscript prime mark: thus ψοα′, 771. A preceding subscript prime indicated multiplication by 1,000: ͵ψοα, 771,000. There was no zero in common use, though astronomical treatises sometimes used one consisting of an omicron with a line over it: ō. (This, along with the base 60 system for measuring minutes and seconds of angles, was borrowed from the Babylonians.) There existed as well the use of letters to list items in order (the *Iliad* was divided into 24 books, which were given consecutive letters of the alphabet), but this is not a true counting system.

Neither of the number systems was very easy to use for calculation, but they were designed for recording numbers, not manipulating them. Calculation was done with devices such as the abacus: The word comes from the Greek word *abax*, meaning a "board" or "slab," which would be divided into columns (sometimes covered with sand); numbers were marked in writing or represented by pebbles.

Although the Greeks acquired mathematical knowledge from the Babylonians (and to a lesser extent the Egyptians), their original contributions to the field were immense. The work of the mathematical pioneers Pythagoras and Thales (both from the sixth century B.C.E.) is shrouded in legend: the first mathematician whose work is directly known is Hippocrates of Chios, active at Athens in the late fifth century. He is said to have compiled an "Elements of Geometry," which anticipated the work of Euclid by more than 200 years, and to have worked on the problem of squaring the circle (that is, the construction of a square with area equal to that of a given circle). The greatest significance of his work is that it exhibits the concept of formal proof, which remains the single greatest contribution of the Greeks to the development of mathematics.

The existence of irrational numbers was a problem for early geometers. (Colorful stories are told about Pythagoras's reaction to the discovery of the square root of 2, geometrically the most obvious irrational number.) Infinitesimals (infinitely small numbers) also caused concern and may be the source of Zeno's famous paradoxes about the impossibility of motion (Zeno "proved" that an arrow could not travel through the air and that the famously swift-footed Achilles could not catch up to a tortoise in a footrace). Logic and geometry developed greatly in the fourth century, as seen in the works of Eudoxus and Aristotle. A culmination of these trends is the work of Euclid, whose *Elements* provides a summary of the geometric knowledge of his day and is perhaps the single most influential textbook of all time, especially for its use of the axiomatic method, in which all conclusions are derived from a small set of simple, apparently self-evident statements ("axioms"). Euclid exhibits knowledge of algebraic geometry (showing further Babylonian influence) and devotes part of the *Elements* to number theory, including a proof that the number of primes is infinite. His other surviving works include the *Phaenomena* (an application of the geometry of spheres to astronomy) and the *Optics*, a treatise on perspective; that is, Euclid worked in what is known as both applied and pure mathematics, as did most Greek mathematicians.

An even more noteworthy example is provided by the career of Archimedes, whose work included systematic treatments of statics and hydrostatics (branches of mathematics dealing with the equilibrium of weights, in and out of water) but who also put this knowledge of mechanics to use as a designer of siege engines. (He was killed when Roman troops sacked his native city of Syracuse in 212 B.C.E.) His work exhibits an originality far beyond that of any other ancient mathematician. In describing mechanical theorems, he uses a procedure of dividing figures into infinitely thin strips, which is quite similar to the procedure that led to the development of the calculus in the 17th century C.E. In his book *The Sand Reckoner* he describe a numerical system capable of dealing with extremely large numbers far superior to any system used in antiquity. Paradoxically, his influence on subsequent mathematics was relatively small: few ancient mathematicians were capable of understanding the implications of his work.

Painted Greek stele with metrical inscription (Alison Frantz Photographic Collection, American School of Classical Studies at Athens)

While the greatest achievements of the Greeks were in geometry, there was also important work in arithmetic and something approaching algebra. The work of Heron and Diophantus (in the first and second centuries C.E.) shows the Greek attitude toward these branches of math: their works present specific number problems (for example, "find three numbers such for which the product of any two of them plus their sum is a square"), but their solutions lack general application or formal proof.

Mathematics came to hold tremendous symbolic importance in Greek culture. Pythagoras saw in numbers a model for the underlying harmony of the universe, and the mysticism of his worldview influenced many later philosophers, including Plato. The famous story that the entrance to Plato's Academy bore the inscription "Let no one who is ignorant of geometry enter" may be of doubtful authenticity; nevertheless, it reflects well the Platonic attitude toward the centrality of mathematics in the education of the ideal citizen or philosopher.

ROME

BY JUSTIN CORFIELD

The system of numbers and counting used in Rome and the Roman Empire was developed from Etruscan numerals. These numerals, in turn, were adapted from the Greek Attic numerals. Although there are only a few archaeological finds that have Etruscan numerals, there are enough to show that the letter *I* represented 1, an inverted *V* represented 5, and *X* represented 10. The first two of these figures can be seen on surviving Etruscan six-sided dice, on which the opposite sides add up to seven, as in the dice of today. Several Roman dice also have survived, again with the opposite sides adding up to seven. Six small ivory dice were found at Pompeii, all the numbers denoted with small dots; the Romans often played with two dice as opposed to the Greek system, in which three dice were used.

It has been suggested that the original use of numbers possibly came from notches on a tally stick, with the Romans using a *V* for 5. Apart from the ordinary people who needed to count out money and commodities as well as tell time and work out the calendar, the Romans also had tax collectors and mathematicians who needed to use larger numbers. The Romans used the letters *I* for 1, *V* for 5, *X* for 10, *L* for 50, *C* for 100, *D* for 500, and *M* for 1,000; they also indicated large numbers by placing a bar over a numeral to indicate a numeral in the thousands. Above one million there was no standard format, with five million denoted either by placing a double bar over a letter *V* or by underlining, as in $\underline{V}$.

There is conflicting evidence regarding the use of some Roman numerals, especially subtractive ones, whereby IV represents one less than 5 (that is, 4). Older Roman material tends to have IIII for 4, making mathematics easier. However, gradually the subtractive notion tended to be used more and more, eventually becoming the accepted form despite the fact that IV was also similar to initials representing the god Jupiter (the name in Latin being IVPITER).

It was also from Roman numerals that the number 666 became known as the devil's number. In Roman numerals 666 was represented by the letters *DCLXVI*, using every basic numeral except the letter *M*. Those familiar with this phenomenon must have seen a bad omen when the Great Fire of London broke out in 1666 (MDCLXVI).

Interestingly, the Romans did not have a concept of a zero. Indeed the first Roman mathematician who is known to have used the concept was Dionysius Exiguus in 525 C.E., though it seems probable that the concept of zero was in use before then. Later the letter *N* for *nullus* (nothing) was used to denote zero.

While many Greek mathematicians are household names, there are no details about Roman mathematicians, and it seems likely that the Romans had little interest in pure mathematics. Indeed, it was said to have been a Roman soldier who killed the Greek mathematician Archimedes of Syracuse in 212 B.C.E., and most mathematicians in the Roman Empire, such as Diophantus of Alexandria, were actually Greek. However, the Romans must certainly have had people who studied applied mathematics to work out architectural plans, load bearings, astronomy, and the supervision of the raising of revenue. The poor notation of the Roman numbers did, however, handicap any major advances in mathematics. For counting, the Romans used small bronze counters on occasions, these having on them pictures of hands with a particular number of fingers raised. Cicero refers to these counters, which effectively were early "counting boards." Gradually the Romans started using the abacus for more complicated sums, the abacus also often being called a "counting board." Many mathematical instruments have been found in the excavations at Pompeii.

Surviving surveying manuals show the combination of arithmetic, geometry, and optics for the Romans' work. Weights and measures followed what now appear to have been arbitrary calculations but must have had some meaning at the time. For example, the *pes*, a Roman foot (in measurement), was just over 11.5 inches, making their pace 4 feet, 10.25 inches. With a thousand of these feet making a Roman mile, the mile was 1,618 yards. Roman numerals have been used many times since the ancient world; they are regularly found in Christian ecclesiastical documents and in European accounts and are still used in calendars, clocks, and watches.

THE AMERICAS

BY PENELOPE OJEDA DE HUALA

Very little information exists regarding the function of numbers and counting in the ancient Americas. We know that the inhabitants of the Americas probably used the lunar and solar cycles to track the change of seasons, as these changes were vital to their survival. Archaeological remains show evidence of early engineering, which required forms of mathematics. However, by the time of European contact, numbering systems existed throughout the Americas.

The Archaic Period (7000–1800 B.C.E.) in North America saw a near extinction of big-game animals, forcing native groups to rely on local resources to supplement their diets. While full-scale agriculture would not be introduced until about 800 C.E., around 3000 B.C.E. some forms of early cultivation occurred throughout North America. Agricultural developments, in turn, forced indigenous groups to pay attention to the passage of seasons and to develop systems of keeping track of those changes to procure food. Tracking change required mathematics and some form of calendrical system, but archaeological evidence for such practices does not appear until around 900 C.E.

Early architectural engineering suggests the creation of a form of mathematical measurement system. For example, in Shabik'eschee Village in New Mexico, as many as 18 pit houses were discovered. These small, sunken structures were probably household compounds. Usually round or square in floor plan and made with mud and clay, these structures were often a foot or more deep. The entryways of some of these structures have been found to be oriented toward the north-south axis, suggesting some form of astronomical observation. Pit houses were discovered throughout the Southwest and were one of the earliest permanent structures in North America.

Oral traditions of many indigenous groups indicated that certain numbers were revered. For example, among the Ojibway, an Algonquian-speaking people centered in the Lake Superior region, including the present-day areas of Michigan, Wisconsin, Minnesota, and parts of Canada, the number 4 appears in several versions of their creation and migration myths that date back to ancient times. In one version of their creation myth the Good Spirit creates four beings who will become the first people. Another version tells of the Maker, who sends four men to create the world. There are also four grandfathers and four colors of man (red, yellow, black, and white). This reverence for the number 4 is also seen in Ojibway birch bark scrollwork.

In ancient Mesoamerica the earliest evidence of a numbering system appeared in the Preclassic Period (ca. 1800 B.C.E.–150 C.E.), carved on upright stone monuments called stelae. In the present-day region of Veracruz, Mexico, at an Olmec (1200–400 C.E.) site called Tres Zapotes, a series of bars and dots appear on the back of one such monument, Stela C. These bars and dots also appear on later Maya (1000 B.C.E.–1521 C.E.) monuments. The bar-and-dot counting system was based on a vigesimal system, or a base 20 system, which corresponds to the number of digits on the hands and feet. A dot corresponds to one unit, and a bar corresponds to five units. On Stela C, the dot and bar correspond to the numbers 7.16.6.16.18, which archaeologists and epigraphists (scholars who study inscriptions) have determined to be a specific date, the third day of September in the year 32 B.C.E. Using similar numbering systems on many later Mayan monuments, it has been determined that this counting system relates to a Mesoamerican calendrical system called the Long Count; along with a ritual and solar calendar, this system was used throughout Mesoamerica.

The Long Count calendar, unlike the ritual and solar calendar, which was cyclical, was a linear count from a specific origin point. Each number corresponds to a multiple of 20, except for the last. For example, in the Long Count date on Stela C, the 7 corresponds to the number of Bak'tuns, or the cycle of 144,000 days that have passed. In this way, the Maya and other Mesoamerican groups could configure large numbers. The Maya also invented the concept of zero, which was represented by a shell or Maltese cross. Certain numbers had specific significance in Mesoamerica, such as the number 13, which is the common number for the layers of the heavens and also important in the ritual calendar. The numbers 18 and 20 also have calendrical significance, as they are the common configuration of the solar calendar. Finally, the numbers 9 and 7 are both associated with the underworld in myth.

See also AGRICULTURE; ARCHITECTURE; ART; ASTRONOMY; CALENDARS AND CLOCKS; CLIMATE AND GEOGRAPHY; CRAFTS; ECONOMY; EDUCATION; LANGUAGE; RELIGION AND COSMOLOGY; SACRED SITES; TRADE AND EXCHANGE; WEIGHTS AND MEASURES; WRITING.

FURTHER READING

Carl B. Boyer, *A History of Mathematics* (Princeton, N.J.: Princeton University Press, 1985).

Michael P. Closs, ed., *Native American Mathematics* (Austin: University of Texas Press, 1986).

Toyin Falola and Akanmu Adebayo, *Culture, Politics, and Money among the Yoruba* (New Brunswick, N.J.: Transaction Publishers, 2000).

John Fauvel, *Mathematics in the Ancient World* (Milton Keynes, U.K.: Open University Press, 1987).

Richard J. Gillings, *Mathematics in the Time of the Pharaohs* (New York: Dover, 1982).

Thomas Heath, *The Thirteen Books of Euclid's "Elements"* (Mineola, N.Y.: Dover, 1956).

Thomas Heath, *A History of Greek Mathematics*, vol. 1 (Mineola, N.Y.: Dover, 1981).

Jacob Klein, *Greek Mathematical Thought and the Origin of Algebra* (Mineola, N.Y.: Dover, 1992).

David Matz, *Ancient World Lists and Numbers: Numerical Phrases and Rosters in Greco-Roman Civilizations* (Jefferson, N.C.: McFarland, 1995).

Aidan Meehan, *Celtic Knots* (London: Thames and Hudson, 2003).

Karl W. Menninger, *Number Words and Number Symbols: A Cultural History of Numbers*, trans. Paul Broneer (Cambridge, Mass.: M.I.T. Press, 1969).

O. Neugebauer and A. Sachs, *Mathematical Cuneiform Texts* (New Haven, Conn.: Yale University Press, 1945).

Gay Robins and Charles Shute, *The Rhind Mathematical Papyrus: An Ancient Egyptian Text* (New York: Dover, 1990).

Peter Strom Rudman, *How Mathematics Happened: The First 50,000 Years* (Buffalo, NY: Prometheus Books, 2006).

G. J. Toomer, "Mathematics and Astronomy." In *The Legacy of Egypt*, 2nd ed., ed. John R. Harris (Oxford. U.K.: Clarendon Press, 1971).

B. L. Van der Waerden, *Science Awakening* (New York: John Wiley, 1963).

Claudia Zaslavsky, *Africa Counts: Number and Pattern in African Cultures*, 3rd ed. (Chicago: Lawrence Hill Books, 1999).

O

► occupations

INTRODUCTION

The earliest modern humans probably had only one occupation: survival. In most of the world they would have traveled and lived in groups of a dozen or so people. Even when they settled in villages, there would be only a small number of villagers. Each member of a group of people would have had to learn everything about survival: how to tell dangerous animals from safe ones; how to track animals to hunt them; how to identify edible plants; how to prepare food; how to make pottery, baskets, tools, and so on. Many anthropologists believe that early modern humans divided some occupations by gender. They base this idea mostly on observations of hunter-gathering peoples who have survived into modern times as well as on archaeological evidence that tells something about the creatures ancient people had to deal with and about the physical makeup of ancient humans. These anthropologists believe that men were probably the hunters of game, especially in areas where the game was large and dangerous. Bison, elephants, and rhinoceroses would be the kinds of animals that might require men, presumed to be physically stronger than women, to hunt.

According to many archaeologists and historians, a division of labor into occupations would not have occurred until agriculture was invented. The reasoning is that ancient hunter-gathers had to be mobile; even when they lived in small villages they had to range far over the countryside and be able to move quickly out of the way of such dangers as floods and wildfires. Their need for mobility would have made it difficult for them to develop any settled occupations; given the dangers of their lives, everyone had to be a generalist, not a specialist in a particular craft.

With the coming of agriculture people settled in areas where crops could be planted. The work required to nurture crops would have necessitated larger groups of people than were needed for hunting and gathering. Further, a steady supply of food probably began a population boom. These may have been the two requirements for the development of occupation: cooperative work to raise crops and enough food on a steady basis to allow people to stay in one place. As people became more skilled in raising food and developed better, more nourishing varieties of crops, food surpluses would have allowed some people to spend their time on projects other than raising food. Where archaeologists find evidence of artisans, especially in the making of luxury items, they tend to assume that they have found evidence of a culture that produced surpluses of food.

It is tempting to assume that the first occupations were those that focused on products needed for survival, but ancient people were still people, and like people throughout the modern world, they seem to have wanted beauty in their lives and spiritual fulfillment. Thus, early occupations included making pottery and baskets and also making decorative ornaments for the body and artistic expressions of spiritual beliefs, such items as totems and charms. Thus, when one studies the occupations of ancient peoples, one may learn not only what they required for survival but also what they valued in their lives beyond just surviving.

AFRICA

BY LEAH A. J. COHEN

In very early times all human groups in Africa lived primarily by hunting, gathering, or fishing or a combination of these occupations. Based on studies of modern hunter-gatherer groups, it is thought that in ancient times women probably were responsible for the daily tasks of child care and gathering wild roots and seeds, while men hunted, but on a more periodic basis than gathering was done. These same studies reveal that women's gathering efforts produced most of the food consumed on a daily basis and that in general the hunter-gatherer lifestyle was less grueling than that of the early agriculturalists. These livelihoods were practiced throughout Africa from the Berbers in the far north to the San and Khoikhoi in the far south.

Domestication of plants and animals (and the birth of farming and herding) occurred gradually, no doubt starting with hunter-gatherers' experimenting with planting while still depending on wild food sources for survival. Such experimentation may have begun as early as 6,000 to 10,000 years ago in central and northern Africa. Climatic conditions changed in northern Africa around 4,500 years ago, resulting in an environment that was less able to support the growing human population through hunting and gathering alone and providing a strong incentive for human groups to become better at farming and herding. Initially, humans broadened their livelihood activities to include hunting, gathering, herding, and agriculture. Eventually, some groups became principally farmers and others principally herders, while still others remained hunter-gatherers. In general, adoption of farming and herding moved from north to south. It is thought that herding did not become common in the southern Africa Cape until about 2,000 years ago. Specialization into farming and herding was possible only with trade among these different groups, which initiated localized trade networks throughout in ancient Africa.

Over time, better agricultural techniques throughout Africa allowed for surplus crops, which, in turn, spawned further labor specialization. Individuals and families who had skills other than farming could trade their products for food. As local trade increased, new occupations continued to emerge in the more densely populated areas, such as Nubia (eastern Africa), Axum (eastern Africa), and Jenne-Jeno (western Africa). There grew a demand for builders, woodworkers, masons, ironworkers and metalsmiths, jewelry makers, religious experts, and government officials. Some people made their living as scribes in literate societies, such as ancient Ethiopia after the fourth century B.C.E. It is thought that prior to the development of grand empires in ancient Africa, aside from hunting, gathering, farming, and fishing, people also engaged in the "part-time" occupations of healing; storytelling, from which the griot (a musician-entertainer who specialized in tribal histories) traditions emerged; and artwork.

Pottery making became desirable with the adoption of farming and more sedentary lifestyles. Many of the more rural farming human groups and villages acquired the technology to make pottery. Some of the earliest examples of pottery (though it was not necessarily made by full-time potters) are from the central Sahara (dating to about 9,500 years ago) and in Nabta Playa, just west of the Nile (dating to about 8,000 years ago). Most of the civilizations in ancient Africa employed skilled potters. Two notable examples are the Nok and the inhabitants of Jenne-jeno. The Nok, who lived in present-day Nigeria around 500 B.C.E., are known for their terra-cottas. The potters of Jenne-jeno (ca. 200 B.C.E.) also were highly skilled and left mounds of pottery fragments from various types of vessels.

Some people made their living as masons. Nubian masons made homes out of brick and also created pyramids similar to those in Egypt in the 11th century B.C.E. The most impressive stone sculptures are the tomb markers from Axum: The tallest is 79 feet high and intricately carved to resemble a multistory building, showcasing the skill of these early craftspeople and the extent of the stone-carving industry. It would have taken a team of mason months or years to create these sculptures.

The weaving industry of ancient Africa has been dated to at least as early as 3200 B.C.E. in Nubia with the Kush, a civilization that flourished from about 300 B.C.E. to 500 C.E. Weaving tools that have been uncovered in these areas include spindles and loom weights. Although evidence dates many of Africa's weaving modern weaving traditions to medieval times, they certainly have their roots in a long history of weaving in Africa. Sculptures from the ancient Nok civilization depict cloth and indicate that a weaving industry was present at the time there as well. Archaeologists have uncovered the remains of loom weights and spindle whorls at Jenne-Jeno.

The jewelry-making tradition has long been a part of culture and economic life in many places in Africa. Jewelry makers in Jenne-jeno used imported iron and Roman beads in their craft. At the very end of the ancient period (400 C.E.) copper and bronze were also used in Jenne-Jeno to create ornaments. Many of the other civilization centers, among them, Axum and Nubia, had a jewelry-making industry.

Trade flourished and local trade networks became vital during this period. By around 800 to 600 B.C.E. the trading settlement of Carthage (on the Mediterranean in northern Africa) began to bustle with the activity of importing and exporting goods to and from the Middle East, Europe, and northern Africa. Carthage's merchants were supported by farms worked either by slaves or by independent Berber farmers who sold their produce in the city. Nomadic pastoralists also came to urban areas to trade their goods. In general, trade in Africa during ancient times was based on barter and there were very few professional merchants. Later, as coinage systems developed, a merchant class emerged.

The Iron Age is often cited as beginning in Africa around the sixth to seventh centuries B.C.E., first in Nubia with the

Kush as well as Meroë and Axum. There is evidence that ironworking was present in the Nok civilization by 1200 B.C.E. Many scholars believe that this technology moved with the Bantu groups into southeastern and southern Africa. Iron ore mining followed in the footsteps of copper and bronze mining in many areas of Africa. Iron ore or other metal ores were removed from the earth either from areas already exposed (opencast mines) or from holes (shafts) dug down (sometimes as deep as 40 to 60 feet) below the surface, into which miners were lowered to chip away at the rock and send pieces of rock and ore up in baskets. In present-day Swaziland, iron ore shaft mines date to approximately 400 C.E. There is evidence that the task of mining was often done by native African slaves and by men, women, and children. Iron was forged into tools for use in farming and mining and for weapons.

With the growth of human populations and civilization centers and the adoption of sedentary lifestyles came a demand for military professionals. Ancient empires such as those of Axum and Nubia had strong armies. There were many titles within the military hierarchy, and the king or queen frequently was the leader of military conquests. Ancient Nubia, particularly after 300 B.C.E., is known for its tradition of strong queen warriors who led troops into battle. The army of Carthage (northern Africa) in the first millennium B.C.E. consisted mainly of Berbers (who themselves had become successful traders, manufacturers, and farmers); these men either were recruited or enslaved into military service from the surrounding area as a result of the expansion of the empire of Carthage.

EGYPT

BY CHARLOTTE BOOTH

Like people in all civilizations, the ancient Egyptians worked hard, and many titles have survived indicating positions held by the elite. Some titles, however, were honorary and did not have any responsibilities attached to them. Other titles described the individual responsibilities within a broader blanket title. There were three categories of occupations available to men: administration, the priesthood, and the military. One occupation that crossed all categories was the scribe. About one in 100 people in ancient Egypt could read and write, so the services of scribes were needed. Scribes were proficient in hieratic script, the cursive form of hieroglyphs that was used for administrative purposes; only temple scribes were able to read the hieroglyphic script.

A talented scribe could rise to the position of vizier, which was often a stepping-stone to the throne. The vizier was very powerful and in close daily contact with the king. The entire palace and its internal operations were under his control. The vizier also was involved in the safety of the king. In addition, the greater security of Egypt and the police force were under his control. He presided over the legal court, dealing with the daily petitions of the ordinary people, which were normally concerned with petty crimes or offenses. He acted as judge, sentencing and administering punishments on behalf of the king.

The priesthood was open to all, men and women, whether they were literate or not, and the priestly positions reflected their skills. The temple scribes often entered the House of Life, an institution where all the religious texts were written, restored, and archived. The House of Life is reputed to have stored knowledge of medicine, geography, geometry, and astronomy, and it also produced physicians who were trained in medicine and religious incantations.

There were many priestly titles, among them, the *sem* priest, who carried out all funeral rites and prayers, including the "opening of the mouth" ceremony—a ritual in which the mummified body of the deceased was symbolically animated through the opening of the mouth so that the person could breathe in the afterlife. This priest was normally the deceased's heir and eldest son, though from the First Dynasty (ca. 2920–ca. 2770 B.C.E.) professional *sem* priests were employed. *Ka* priests were responsible for supplying sustenance for the deceased, and they would have worked in the mortuary temples of the king and the chapels of the wealthy.

Many part-time priests worked one month in four and would return to their villages when they were not required. The lower clergy, known as *wab* priests ("pure ones"), played a supporting role by carrying the sacred bark, or boat, in which the statue of the god traveled; cleaning the temple; supervising painters and draftsmen; and engaging in other general tasks around the temple. There were also a number of subsidiary temple workers—caretakers, janitors, workmen, bakers, butchers, and florists—among them, so-called sacrificers who slaughtered sacrificial animals; all were essential to the successful running of the temple.

The third occupational avenue for men was the military, which became available at the start of the Eighteenth Dynasty (ca. 1550–ca. 1307 B.C.E.) when the permanent army was introduced. There were many specialist units that required different abilities, including charioteers, spearmen, and infantry soldiers. Training would have started in childhood. Scribes were also an essential part of the army entourage. They accompanied the military to chronicle the events of the campaign, and they were responsible for counting the enemy dead and recording the collected booty and prisoners.

The opportunities available for women were different, though many women were housewives and remained in the home. The poorer women married to farmers would be expected to help during the busy harvest period. Winnowing grain was often carried out by women, and young girls were sent to glean. In the home women were responsible for grinding grain for bread and for baking it. The loaves could then be sold at the market along with other household produce, such as baskets, pots, beer, and linen. Even the royal women were instrumental in the manufacture of linen, and evidence suggests that the harem at Gurob was a large producer of royal linen.

Granite statue of Ankhwa, the shipbuilder, possibly from Saqqara, Egypt (ca. 2650 B.C.E.); Ankhwa holds an adze, a woodworking tool indicative of his trade. (© The Trustees of the British Museum)

Women were unable to hold bureaucratic positions except in private houses, and titles such as steward of the storehouse, steward of the food supplies, steward of cloth, and seal bearer, who would have held the official seal of the homeowner, exist from the Old Kingdom (ca. 2575–ca. 2134 B.C.E.). The titles of treasurer, major domo ("mayor of the palace"), and superintendent of the dining room have also been discovered from the Middle Kingdom (ca. 2040–ca. 1640 B.C.E.). Women generally worked in the service of other women and were not allowed to oversee the work of men, though there is a rare example of a female vizier in the Sixth Dynasty (ca. 2323–ca. 2150 B.C.E.). In the palace women held many titles, including overseer of the singers, overseer of amusements, and mistress of the royal harem. Titles of retail careers have also been discovered, such as overseer of the house of weavers and overseer of the wig shop, and evidence also suggests that women sold their own products at market.

The most prestigious profession for women, however, was the priesthood. Women normally functioned in the cult of Neith, the patron goddess of the city of Saïs, protector of women, and goddess of weaving and of war and hunting, and the cult of Hathor, the cow-headed goddess of childbirth, sexual love, music, and dancing. Women had lesser roles in the cults of all gods. They functioned as impersonators of the goddess and as musicians or dancers during temple rituals. Priestesses also worked one in four months on a rotation system. Some priestesses would have undergone training as midwives in the Temple of Neith at Saïs. Most midwives, however, would have learned their skills at the hands of the village women and would have received no formal training. Midwives would have been in great demand, as most women had at least five children.

Other women became wet nurses for the elite. Royal wet nurses were held in very high esteem, and children of a royal wet nurse were considered "milk siblings" to the king. It was normal for children to be nursed for three years as a safeguard against pregnancy and also a way of ensuring that they were not exposed to contaminated food.

The role of professional mourner—hired for funerals to wail, throw dust over their heads, tear their clothes, and scratch their cheeks in grief—was also available for the unskilled woman. In paintings of tomb mourning scenes, young girls can be seen standing among the women, indicating that they were taught the skill from an early age.

THE MIDDLE EAST

BY HEATHER D. BAKER

The sources for information about occupations in the ancient Near East are cuneiform tablets inscribed in a variety of languages, especially Sumerian, Akkadian, Hittite, and Old Persian. Among the earliest intelligible tablets are some bearing lists of professions. These tablets come from the site of Uruk in southern Mesopotamia, from archaeological levels dated to about 3200 B.C.E. They show that the specialization of labor was already highly developed in Sumerian cities at this early period. Not only are many different occupations listed, but there are also clear signs of hierarchical organization, with terms for various kinds of officials and administrators and also for supervisors and overseers responsible for groups of craftsmen and workers.

In addition to the lists of professions, which were kept in scholarly libraries, a no less important source of information is provided by the vast amount of archival material. This consists primarily of legal and administrative documents recorded and kept by the major economic institutions (palaces and temples) as well as by private individuals and families. These archives of cuneiform tablets shed a great deal of light on the range of craftsmen and professionals and on their social backgrounds, the conditions under which they worked, and the way in which they were organized. Lists of rations allotted to workers are particularly informative. Occasionally, archaeological evidence for specialist workshops has been found, such as the remains of potters' kilns.

The range of occupations established in the course of over 3,000 years of written history in the region is vast. Some are familiar—baker, brewer, potter—but others arose as a response to the specific needs and material conditions of the day and have no close parallel in the 21st century. Many essential crafts were passed down from father to son, but some skills were taught to apprentices by experts. Cuneiform tablets recording apprenticeship contracts have survived, and they set out the penalty to be paid by the master if he failed to teach the apprentice properly. (The possibility that the apprentice might be a poor learner does not seem to have been considered.)

The palaces and temples employed large numbers of specialized craftsmen and skilled workers. Food preparation was one of the most important areas of activity. Bakers, cooks, butchers, and brewers were needed, and setting out the tables for the meals of the gods was a skilled occupation. The grinding of flour was an onerous task often performed by prisoners. Oil pressers produced the oil (from sesame seed) needed in food preparation and for other purposes, such as treating wooden objects, making perfume, and filling oil lamps.

The production of textiles and finished garments was another important craft activity. Weavers worked in wool and linen, and a variety of garments had to be made up by specialist tailors, not just for human use but also to clothe the divine statues in the temples. The cloth that they used could be dyed by the dyers in a variety of shades made from minerals and plants. Evidence for washermen and washerwomen is also found, especially in the temple archives, since caring for the precious divine garments was vital. Leather workers had to treat the skins of dead animals and manufacture items out of them, such as sandals and various kinds of containers. Metalworkers manufactured the tools and utensils used in the everyday activities of agriculture and canal digging. Goldsmiths, silversmiths, and jewelers produced finery for members of the elite and for adorning the statues of the gods in the temples. Raw materials that were not available locally would be procured by merchants specializing in overland trade with distant regions.

Construction involved a variety of skilled occupations. The design and layout of the great monumental structures, such as the ziggurats, palaces, and temples, not to mention the defensive walls surrounding the cities, required highly skilled architects, surveyors, and site managers. The ancient terms for these kinds of professions can be identified in the cuneiform tablets, though it is not always easy to determine the exact range of duties that went with each particular job. In much of the region mud brick was used for building, though kiln-fired bricks were preferred for the more prestigious structures of palaces and temples. Brick making was a skilled activity, but usually a seasonal one. Carpenters and joiners were needed to manufacture the doors and other fittings and to prepare the beams used in making the roof. Furniture is written about in the cuneiform tablets, and occasionally the remains of intricately made pieces have been found in excavation. Usually, however, wooden items do not survive, with the result that much information about craftsmanship has been lost.

In southern Mesopotamia, where reeds grew in abundance, they were widely used in construction and in the manufacturing of such household items as baskets and mats. Specialist reed workers had to prepare the reeds by soaking, peeling, and bleaching them before they could be used. Some structures were made from reed rather than brick, a building tradition that survived into modern times in the marshes of southern Iraq.

A great many people would have been employed in agriculture and animal husbandry. In southern Mesopotamia orchard keepers were required to look after the date palm groves. Throughout the region the cultivation of grain fields needed teams of plowmen to work with the ox-driven plows; these teams often operated in family groups, including children as young as five years old.

The occupations practiced by women are less well documented. At certain periods women are known to have figured prominently in the textile industry. Occasionally, women were employed to serve as wet nurses for children who had lost their mothers. Women from wealthier families could own property and conduct business. Priestesses are also known.

The army was vital in defending the land and conquering new territories; among the troops many specialized roles are known. Finally, there were a number of professions open only to very learned individuals. These men would have undergone lengthy training in the scribal schools before completing further, specialized training in a particular field. Scholars at the royal court, such as astronomers, exorcists, physicians, and diviners, played an important role in advising the king. This is especially well illustrated by a large group of letters from scholars to the Assyrian king Esarhaddon (r. 680–669 B.C.E.), which have been found in excavations at the city of Nineveh alongside many other documents and literary works from the royal libraries.

ASIA AND THE PACIFIC

BY KIRK H. BEETZ

The number of ancient Indian occupations can seem bewildering, with occupations often having numerous subcategories of specialists. Certain occupations were common almost everywhere in ancient India. Carpenters practiced religious rituals, perhaps the most important of which was asking the spirit in a tree to forgive him before the tree was cut down. Usually another group of workers, foresters, would chop down the tree, but when foresters were unavailable, the carpenter would do it himself. Carpenters carefully measured the fallen tree and then cut it into the number and size of planks and beams they needed for a project. The planks and beams then were loaded onto carts and taken to the workplace, either a construction site or a workshop. In addition to working on buildings, carpenters made toys, wooden sandals, chests, and furniture.

Basket makers could be men or women. They gathered their grasses themselves, mostly from the sides of lakes, ponds, and waterways. They wove matting used for walls, fences, roofs, and floor coverings. They also wove watertight umbrellas as well as watertight baskets. Some of their baskets were fashioned into strainers, allowing water to pass through while retaining solids. Every Indian home had brooms, and most had woven hampers and chests.

Blacksmiths worked long hours beside a furnace. Using pincers, they worked hot metal so that they could hammer it into shape. They made nails, hammers, axes, saws, spades, sickles, plowshares, sewing needles, razors, and knives. Copper, tin, bronze, and iron were used to make cooking pans for the home and armor for warriors. The blacksmith's work was so important to the success of other occupations that even tiny villages usually had at least one blacksmith.

A potter mixed wet clay with cow dung and ashes. He placed this mixture on a potter's wheel. After shaping the clay with his hands while the wheel spun, he set it aside to dry. Later he would put it and other shaped items into a trench piled with wood. The wood was ignited to fire the pottery. The ancient Indian potter's work was rarely highly refined because the potter made items for basic uses, such as hauling water or boiling food. A potter either owned a shop or carried his wares through the streets of his village, town, or city, while calling for people to buy his pots.

The *malakaras* were garland makers. *Malakaras* kept their own gardens, where they grew the flowers they wove. Cutting the flowers was a family affair, with sons and daughters joining in the work. To give a garland stiffness to support the flowers, *malakaras* used reeds and cotton stalks. Garlands were expected to be colorful, and *malakaras* wove into the garlands leaves, berries, feathers, shells, and ornaments carved from horn. They employed people who were out of work to hawk their wares in the streets of cities.

In China peasants were the foundation of ancient society. The Chinese themselves recognized the importance of peasants, and the work of peasants was considered more important than any occupation except warfare. Taking good care of the land he farmed was the peasant's principal duty. Peasants were expected to devote their days to laboring in fields, except when the lord conscripted them into his army for waging a war. Husband, wife, and children were expected to spend their waking hours toiling in their fields, except when performing other tasks related to farming, such as milling grain. During the Shang Dynasty (ca. 1500–ca 1045 B.C.E.) and most of the Zhou Dynasty (ca. 1045–ca. 256 B.C.E.), peasants worked with wooden hoes and hand plows. Sometimes the hand plows would be edged with bronze. The lords, kings, and emperors of China often took trouble to ensure the welfare of peasants, on whom their prosperity rested; during the fifth century B.C.E. some landowners provided their tenant farmers with iron plows and teams of oxen to pull the plows.

Although farming was not considered an honorable profession, it was placed higher than most occupations. Ancient Chinese writers slighted most trades and jobs, and for this reason it is not fully known what those occupations were, who performed them, and how many there were. Archaeological evidence is only just beginning to fill in bits of the large gaps in present knowledge of ancient China's workaday world.

During the Han Dynasty (202 B.C.E.–220 C.E.) the government established 20 levels of rank. The top 12 could be attained only by people of high birth, but the bottom eight were open to anyone. This system gave peasants and other laborers a chance to improve their lot and may have inspired some specialization. For instance, some peasants specialized in keeping mulberry orchards, the leaves of which fed silkworms. Women in peasant families prepared the silk from the silkworms' cocoons as part of their cycle of work. An ambitious peasant could take out a loan and purchase equipment for milling the harvested grain. This venture could result in the hiring of farmhands who ran the equipment that removed hulls from the grain and produced flour.

There was a demand for metal. The government set up factories in which ore was mined, smelted, and poured into ingots. These ingots, in turn, were sent to factories where metal objects were made. This demand seems to have created specialists in metallurgy, but their skill levels are unknown. If only one person was in charge of arranging the molds, melting the metal, pouring it into the molds, and applying finishing touches to the objects, then that person would have been highly skilled; if the tasks were divided, it is possible that unskilled labor could have been used for the tasks of melting and pouring.

Weavers often worked out of homes and were probably peasant women. They worked mostly with hemp, which provided the cloth for most garments. Silk was highly prized but also was woven in homes in the countryside. The mechanisms of the looms as yet unknown, but surviving fabrics show that during the Han Dynasty very thin to very thick fabrics were woven.

Carpentry became specialized during the last years of the Zhou Dynasty, when the tropical forests to the south were opened through conquest. Logging required teams of workers, needed more for their muscle than their skills. Using ropes, they hauled felled trees to a stream, where the trees would be loaded onto boats for transport to a city. In the city

FISHING

Many of the islands of the Pacific Ocean are small and hard, and as such offered the people who settled them little opportunity to cultivate agriculture or livestock. They do, however, offer excellent access to the ocean and to the thousands of types of fish there. As soon as humans spread out from Papua New Guinea to the smaller islands to the northeast, beginning in approximately 28,000 B.C.E., fishing became the principal source of sustenance, marking them as some of the earliest people on the planet to pursue fish. Fossils show a huge range of fish and shellfish consumed on the islands, from crab, lobster, and turtle to three species of sharks. Since there are no signs of fishhooks from the Pleistocene, the general assumption is that fishing was done either by spearing or by catching fish in motion in nets or traps.

Fishing was practiced throughout the Pacific Islands, though different islands had different species of fish, from cod in the temperate Chatham Islands to the parrotfish that were overwhelmingly common in more tropical waters. While abundance certainly had much to do with the kind of fish that were sought, there also developed over the centuries cultural traditions that imparted social preferences for some species over others. For instance, among the people of Kapingamarangi Atoll of Pohnpei, it is common to hear stories about the various methods of pursuit of the rainbow runner, even though that fish is small and its population is certainly much less significant to the islanders' eating habits than the grouper.

Of course, centuries of fishing have led to the evolution of different methods of catching fish. In lagoons and inland freshwaters, spearing and bow-and-arrow fishing eventually gave way to baited hooks. Since fishing was such a significant part of the oceanic life, it is only natural that some cultures carved ornate hooks that resemble works of sculpture. For ocean fishing, nets were the preferred method, manipulated by crews in large canoes. There is evidence that as far back as 2,000 years ago, individuals in small canoes braved the ocean to fish individually, with hooks, for larger, big-game fish, like marlin.

carpenters used saws to cut planks from the tree. From these they built furniture, beams for buildings, or coffins.

Most people in Japan, the Philippines, Indonesia, and Australia followed one occupation: survival. Each person needed to know many crafts in order to make what was needed to stay alive. It is likely that the peoples of the Japanese islands began to develop specialized occupations after about 200 B.C.E.. The numerous works of pottery and the building of wooden palisades and wooden palaces by the third century C.E. suggest that potting and carpentry may have become specialized occupations by then.

EUROPE

BY JUSTIN CORFIELD

Throughout Europe during ancient times most people were involved in farming, with the vast majority of families living in their farmhouses, which often incorporated protective walls encompassing the house as well as the shelters for livestock. In some areas a wider expanse of land was surrounded by protective walls against outsiders and invaders, incorporating some farming or grazing land and gardens.

One of the main considerations for European farmers was (and still is) the difference in climate from north to south. In the north farmers enjoyed short summers with abundant water and very fertile soil. In the south, on the other hand, long, hot summers, some water shortages, and poorer soil resulted in the need for more intensive cultivation.

On ancient farms the whole variety of agricultural pursuits would have been followed: plowing fields; planting, nurturing, and then harvesting crops; maintaining the farm; using organic fertilizers; tending the animals; and slaughtering them for eating. In addition, milking cows, churning milk, baking bread, preparing food, and maintaining herb gardens were tasks often done by women, with the children, even small children, used for scaring away birds, watching over grazing animals, or generally helping their parents and family. In addition, women were often involved in spinning, with both men and women operating weaving looms. Members of the farming household made and decorated ceramic vessels, baskets, tools, and weapons. The collection of firewood was a very time-consuming task.

Around 2000 B.C.E. we see the first evidence for craft specialization in ancient Europe; certain people minimized their role in farming or gave it up completely to specialize in making particular types of artifacts. The earliest specialists were probably metalworkers. In each village there would also have been blacksmiths and metalworkers who were capable of dealing with copper and subsequently bronze and then iron. Many of these men would have been involved in simple tasks, such as making agricultural tools or simple weapons. Especially in towns, a number, such as the mirror makers in southern Britain, became quite skilled at decorative work. Because of the need for horses for transport and war, there were many horse breeders as well as people involved in "breaking in" and then looking after the animals. There were also leather merchants who engaged in treating leather products, including saddles, reins, harnesses, and household items. Coopers, who made barrels, and wheelwrights, who made carts, were also important.

There were also tribal chiefs, their families, administrators, and people in charge of collecting taxes. Their roles

Spinning and weaving tools, Iron Age England (800 B.C.E. to 50 C.E.)
(© The Trustees of the British Museum)

varied throughout Europe, with small tribes operating in Scandinavia and larger tribal confederations being formed in Gaul and Britain, especially to withstand the Romans. In both places the tribal chiefs Vercingetorix (d. 46 B.C.E.) and Caratacus (fl. first century C.E.), respectively, were able to rely on large war machines to try to stop the Romans invading their lands. There was only a small middle class at the time, consisting of merchants and traders, a few doctors or medical practitioners, and also those connected with religious worship—for the Celts, these included the Druids, who led the people in religious observations. The merchants varied considerably, from those who sailed long distances to those who sold goods from one village to the next. It is quite clear from the near uniformity of some of the Celtic designs that trading must have been extensive. Wine was a major commodity, with craftsmen turning out elaborate wine flagons. There was also a demand for tattoo artists, with Celts often wearing bright tattoos.

In some parts of Europe, such as around the silver mines of Spain or the tin mines of Cornwall, England, there were many who earned their pay as miners. In other parts of Europe, hunters, fishermen, or sailors predominated, depending on the locality and opportunities.

With many wars, a significant number of men were soldiers. A large number fought as or when needed and spent the rest of their time as farmers, but in some parts of Europe there were professional soldiers. The best-known examples of professional soldiers are the Balearic slingers of the Punic Wars. These were men who were trained from youth to use slings in battle. Similarly, there were professional fighters in other parts of Europe, such as the many Spanish men who served in the Carthaginian army or the many others who served as legionnaires in the Roman army or in the auxiliary units.

The advent of Roman rule over much of Europe led to a significant change in the nature of everyday life. The large armies that the Romans maintained throughout their empire, especially on the borders, such as on the Danube River or in northern England, resulted in livelihoods for many people in supplying the soldiers with their needs. Local people built and maintained Roman military bases, provisioning them with food and water and then providing services for the soldiers. Initially, these soldiers had to be Roman citizens or men capable of becoming citizens upon their retirement after 25 years' service; with the Edict of Caracalla in 212 C.E. the army was opened up to all, and the previously established distinction between legionnaires and auxiliaries ended.

More towns were established, with a higher number of people constituting the middle class and thus becoming involved in the production of luxury goods. The Roman Empire also brought about the need for gladiators, charioteers, and other "sportsmen," and created a demand for musicians and writers. The Roman Empire was to change the nature of slavery. In Celtic Europe slaves constituted such a small part of the population as to have no real importance. By contrast, the Romans had vast numbers of slaves, many working on farms and in mines, manning galleys, looking after houses, training children, and cooking for families.

The Dacians, the Thracians, the Germans, the Goths, and the Vandals all had large numbers of warriors in their population, similar to those of the warring Celtic tribes of the Bronze Age and Iron Age. The numbers of weapons used in wars against the Romans must have led to the mass manufacture on a scale previously unknown beyond the Roman Empire. The same mass-production techniques also would have been applied to footwear, uniforms, camp equipment, and materials needed for transportation.

GREECE

BY JEFFREY S. CARNES

Farming is the most basic occupation, and the development of other occupations depends on the ability of farmers to generate surplus food, that is, the economic capital to fund the acquisition of other goods. Throughout Greek antiquity (as in most preindustrial societies) farming remained the most common occupation, and farmers were well represented in all social and economic classes. At one end of the scale were small landholders engaged in subsistence farming. Given the arid climate and poor soil of most of Greece, it was not uncommon for agricultural crises to turn landholders into sharecroppers or even slaves. By contrast, the wealthiest citizens of most Greek city-states were farmers, at least nominally. Farming was generally considered a suitable occupation for wellborn people, who tended to share a disdain for crafts and business.

The world depicted in Homer's *Odyssey* gives us insights into the development of occupations. There the *oikos*, or household, is the basic economic unit and strives insofar as possible for self-sufficiency. Agricultural labor and domestic chores are performed by family members and by slaves, with clothing production and food preparation in the hands of the female members of the *oikos*. Necessary crafts, such as carpentry, are performed by the head of the *oikos*. (Odysseus builds his own house and is capable of shipbuilding when necessary.) In ancient Greece the chief exceptions were metals (for which specialized workshops, often linked to major shrines, such as Delphi, existed from an early date) and luxury goods, which were obtained from itinerant traders. Settlement in cities led to specialization, but for nonurban dwellers of sufficient means most work was done in-house throughout the historical era. Related food-production occupations (sheepherding, goat herding, and fishing) were common in some areas, though notoriously difficult to make a living at.

In cities there was a variety of manufacturing industries, but of limited size. The largest we know of is a 120-person operation to manufacture shields; workshops of 10 or so people were much more common. Given its size and wealth, Athens gives us the most complete picture of the variety of manufacturing trades: stonemasons, carpenters, shipbuilders, shoemakers, potters, and blacksmiths. Surviving goods show that some of the work was of the highest quality. Athens was a magnet for talent, and many workers were foreigners, often slaves. Citizens were involved in the crafts as well—Socrates' father was a stonemason—but the presence of slave labor presumably drove down the profitability of most crafts, and even skilled artisans did not enjoy great prestige. Among practitioners of the other arts, poets and musicians sometimes enjoyed high status.

Given the frequency of war in the Greek world, most city-states were in a more or less permanent wartime economy, which provided many career opportunities. Armies were made up of citizen soldiers—unpaid part-timers expected to supply their own equipment, so that military service, far from being a career, was a detriment to having one. There were exceptions, however. In Athens during the fifth century B.C.E. the development of a naval empire led to increased demand for sailors and ships, and paid service in the navy became an economic cornerstone of the Athenian democracy. (The number of jobs for shipbuilders must also have been significant.) Greeks could serve as mercenaries, often in the armies of non-Greek rulers, such as the king of Persia. The historian Xenophon (ca. 431–ca. 352 B.C.E.) was one such mercenary, and Greeks were highly sought after for their discipline and their specialized fighting skills.

Trade grew in importance, along with Greek prosperity, and provided a variety of employment opportunities. Banking and insurance were of particular importance for long-distance trade. Some cities, such as Aegina, became wealthy on account of long-distance trade (especially with Egypt and Italy), and successful merchants became the new elite. Piracy flourished alongside trade, as did robbery on land. Groups of individuals, or even whole communities, could earn their livelihoods in this way, especially given the possibility of selling captured travelers as slaves.

Retail sales of food were a common way of earning a living among the poorer classes. Vegetable and fish merchants plied their trade in the market, and purveyors of hot foods were to be found at festivals and other public gatherings. Cities also would have had hot food for sale in small shops (large, sit-down restaurants being a modern invention), and there were many bakeries as well. Most houses had cooking facilities, but ovens were rare.

Healing professions provided employment for some. Doctors were probably in short supply and often were itinerant. The surviving works of the Hippocratic corpus show a remarkable degree of sophistication but depict the status of only a small segment of the medical professions. Most doctors were probably ill trained. Surgery was performed by specialists (who often were not doctors). Midwives usually were responsible for childbirth and probably for other gynecological issues as well. Healing also came from drug specialists (sometimes called *rhizotomoi*, or "root cutters," in reference to the source of their medicines) and from magicians. Although magic is rarely mentioned in literary sources, nonliterary evidence shows that it was always popular and must have been a vocation or an avocation for many.

Education was limited to the upper classes, and the number of teachers must have been small. They included many household slaves, but at the far end of the scale were the Sophists, the great teachers of rhetoric who came to Athens in the fifth century B.C.E. Athens's status as a center of

Frieze of hydriaphoroi (water carriers) from the Parthenon (Alison Frantz Photographic Collection, American School of Classical Studies at Athens)

learning allowed teachers and rhetoricians of all stripes to flourish there throughout antiquity. Athletic trainers were also sought after, but not in large numbers.

Upper-class women were expected not to work outside the confines of the *oikos* and were kept out of public view as much as possible. Women in other classes worked from economic necessity. Certain fields, such as textile production, washing, domestic service, and midwifery, were traditionally female. Prostitution was common and legal, and the profession ranged from low-status *pornai* (prostitutes) to *hetairai* (literally, "female companions"), who served well-to-do men and often were valued for their wit, education, and musical talent. Young men also worked as prostitutes, though Greek sexual mores made male prostitution a short-term career option. Fully mature men were not considered desirable by other men.

There were relatively few lawyers in the Greek world, despite the large amount of legal activity in such cities as Athens. Citizens represented themselves in court, but they did hire speechwriters, who might have given advice about the law. Civil servants were few. Despite being the seat of an empire, Athens had no permanent bureaucracy, and most magistracies were filled on a year-by-year basis by citizens selected by lot. There were likewise few managers. Industries and commercial concerns, such as banks, were on a small scale. Nor were there many jobs in sales. Greeks had few material possessions compared with modern Western societies, and what they had was typically bought from producers.

ROME

BY KIRK H. BEETZ

Bakeries could be found in every Roman town and city as well as in almost any village. In even a modest-sized town of 12,000 or so people, there would have been a few dozen bakeries because bread was the basic food of Romans from about 200 B.C.E. onward, replacing porridge. A small bakery would have had at least two rooms, one for grinding grain and for baking and the other for displaying baked goods for purchase. A large bakery could have had several rooms, with as many as five grinding mills and with ovens that could hold more than 80 loaves of bread at a time. Bakers ground their own flour using mills shaped like hourglasses. A donkey was hitched to a mill with a simple harness. The donkey would pace in a circle, turning the hourglass stone, which ground grain on a circular stone beneath it. Flour would spill out onto a wide, circular base of stone from which the baker would gather it.

Bread and sugared pastries were prepared in the same room as the flour. The most popular shape of bread seems to have been circular with eight divisions or slices. The baker took care that his baked goods were in attractive, usually geometric, shapes. The baker did not grow his own grain but purchased it from peasants who hauled the grain to market in sacks on oxen. His workday began before sunrise so that he could be sure to have fresh bread ready for the breakfasts of his customers. Some bakeries were busy enough for baking to continue all night after the baker's shop closed. When open for business, the baker's counter, which would have been even with the street or sidewalk, was watched by a clerk, usually the wife or child of the baker. Customers were not allowed into the bakery but had to wait outside while their purchases were fetched by the clerk or the clerk's assistant. The clerk or assistant kept track of purchases on a waxed tablet.

Butchers did a thriving business in Roman villages, towns, and cities as well. Butchers prepared different kinds of meat, but Romans favored beef over all others. The Roman government regulated weights and measures, and a butcher with faulty scales could be fined. A hunk of meat was fixed on a hook that dangled from a rod. The rod had a weight that could slide back along the rod until it balanced. Like the baker, the butcher often had to work at night because farmers were allowed to bring in animals for slaughter only at night. A butcher shop was arranged like that of the baker, with the butchering taking place in a back room behind the shop.

A butcher worked while standing up, with an assortment of cleavers of copper or iron. He set meat on a masonry table, where he hacked or sliced it. The butcher hung his roasts, chops, ribs, and steaks from hooks attached to boards on the walls. Some of these meats would have been taken to the street-side shop and hung on hooks for display. The clerk was usually the butcher's wife, who had an assistant to go into the back to fetch meats for customers. Customers were not allowed inside.

Blacksmiths worked in almost every village as well as in towns and cities. In a village the blacksmith worked with several different metals. He would not have been expected to smelt metals or to mix alloys, such as bronze. Instead, he worked from ingots either imported from abroad or made locally by a smelter. His principal products were nails, pieces for bridles and harnesses, and tools. In a town or city blacksmiths often specialized. For instance, cutlers specialized in making knives. A cutler produced several different shapes and sizes of cleavers and knives for household use or for professional use by butchers. Other smiths specialized in tools for carpenters and construction workers, such as pliers and hammers. Still others made medical instruments. In towns and cities blacksmiths would have had shops that looked much like those of bakers and butchers, but the smith himself probably would have dealt directly with customers. Against one of his walls would have been shelves that displayed the different products he could make.

Barbers were among the cutler's customers. Roman men preferred carefully trimmed hair and shaved faces, and they patronized barbers often. Barbers were either men or women, and their shops were called *tonstrinas*. They used iron scissors and razors, and they often are depicted in Roman writings as dangerous people who carelessly cut the skin of their customers. Barbers were expected to be gossips, and a visit to a barber included listening to the barber recount all the rumors he had heard. Women went to hairdressers, who were men or women. Hairdressers worked with oils and perfumes to create the latest in hairstyle fashions. A visit to a hairdresser was a woman's chance to relax.

Important to any Roman community was the fuller, who had one of the most miserable occupations. A fuller cleaned and mended clothing and fabrics. A clothes maker sent new fabric to a fuller, who prepared it for cutting and sewing not only by cleaning it but also by softening it, shrinking it, and bleaching it. Very few people cleaned their own clothes, preferring to have a fuller do the job. For cleaning, the fuller used soda or potash. Bleaching was done by burning sulfur under cloth spread over wooden frames. To thicken cloth, the fuller treated it with urine he had collected from public lavatories. He would spend hours stamping on urine-soaked cloth. When fabric or a garment was ready, the fuller would spit a fine spray of water on it. He would also patch or stitch tears. A fuller always smelled foul, and his presence was rarely tolerated by others outside his shop, unless there was a local fuller's guild house he could visit. He suffered from skin diseases caused by the urine and chemicals he used, and his lungs were damaged by the sulfur fumes he breathed during bleaching.

The Romans often tore down buildings in order to rebuild them, and they had numerous ongoing construction projects throughout their empire. Many construction workers were unskilled laborers who were given the dangerous jobs of hoisting stone with cranes or carrying stones and bricks to where they would be used. On the other hand, stonemasons were skilled with many tools, such as drills, chisels, hammers, and saws. They not only shaped and fit together stones for building but also were expected to be able to carve images to decorate buildings and to carve tombstones. Carpenters were also skilled workers who mastered several different kinds of tools, such as planes, saws, and levels. In cities carpenters could specialize, with some working in building construction and others making furniture. Outside of cities carpenters would have been expected to be able to do both.

THE AMERICAS

BY PENELOPE OJEDA DE HUALA

Ancient American occupations revolved around subsistence. The people of the Americas varied in the jobs they performed, from primarily hunting and gathering in North America to engaging in agriculture in Mesoamerica and South America. The development of native societies can be traced through the various ways in which people labored. Archaic culture is defined by its adaptation to the environment. By 8000 B.C.E. the glacial ice that had once covered the North American continent had completely receded. As a result, the Archaic Period (ca. 8000–ca. 1000 B.C.E.) saw a spreading out of indigenous groups throughout the North American continent. At the same time, big-game animals, such as ground sloths, mammoths, giant beavers (as large as modern bears), mastodons, camels, musk oxen, and horses became extinct. The changed environment necessitated adaptation on the part of the North American inhabitants. Because of the lack of big game, local resources had to be exploited by hunting of smaller game, gathering of wild plants, fishing, foraging, and early cultivation. The most prestigious position during the Archaic Period was that of a local ruler, who fostered such activities as intertribal ties, marriage alliances, and trade. Religious specialists were undoubtedly also honored positions.

The people of the Great Plains, an area that lies east of the Rocky Mountains and includes parts of the present-day states of Colorado, Kansas, Montana, Nebraska, New Mexico, North Dakota, Oklahoma, South Dakota, Texas, and Wyoming as well as parts of southern Canada, were predominantly occupied by hunting. People hunted rabbits, beavers, and some of the surviving big-game animals, such as bison, elk, black bear, grizzly bear, and deer. They supplemented their diet by foraging for berries and nuts. The Archaic desert people of the present-day states of Utah, Nevada, and Arizona also hunted small game and foraged for seasonal wild plants, nuts, and seeds.

For the people of the northwest coast, who resided in the present-day states of Washington, Oregon, and parts of Alaska, fishing became a major occupation. The migratory fish runs, such as the salmon spawning season, provided a livelihood that allowed for more established settlements. Hunting of big game, such as moose, elk, and deer, along with foraging of various local plants, supplemented food obtained by fishing.

The movement from large mobile resources to small fixed resources throughout North America led to fixed settlements and more sophisticated group structures. The appearance of mound building in the eastern part of North America as early as 2500 B.C.E. indicates that societies had become more stratified and that ritual specialists, probably priest-rulers, held the highest social positions. Artists also became prominent, as ritual objects for burials became highly prized. Merchants, who worked in concert with community elites, became increasingly important in the long-distance trade for luxury materials and items.

The successive cultures that prospered in Mesoamerica shared a unique set of cultural traits, including the use of a 260-day ritual calendar, a dependence on maize agriculture, the development of pictorial or hieroglyphic writing systems, and certain rituals such as the ball game. The first great agriculturally based society in Mesoamerica, the Olmec civilization, flourished in the Gulf Coast area of Mexico from around 1500 to 400 B.C.E. The success of maize-based farming led to more complex social structures. Archaeological evidence points to a cult centered on a ruler-shaman. The use of a 260-day ritual calendar and the development of hieroglyphic writing entailed the use of scribes, diviners, and specialized priests. Finely worked jade objects and ceramics found at various Olmec sites, along with the stone monumental sculptures, point to the presence of artistic specialists. Warrior imagery suggests the importance of this occupation, and evidence of extensive trade routes indicates the existence of local and long-distance merchants.

Preclassic Period (ca. 1500 B.C.E.–ca. 150 C.E.) occupations centered on farming and craft specialization for the creation of ritual objects, monumental architecture, and historical stone monuments. In Maya culture, beginning about 600 B.C.E., the nobility were often scribes, since writing was an elite occupation. In addition to functioning as scribes, Maya elites were also artists. Rulers commissioned historical and mythological sculptural programs in the form of stelae (standing stone slabs). Specialized carvers, builders, and plaster workers were needed to create structures and their associated decoration. Like the Olmec, the Maya also employed skilled jade workers to create ritual objects as well as painters to produce elaborate murals and painted ceramics.

The rise of the first sites with monumental architectural, such as the platform mound of the Huaca de los Idolos (3000 B.C.E.), a late Preceramic Period (ca. 3000–ca. 1800 B.C.E.) site situated on the coast of present-day Peru, signals a shift from small, simple groups to more complex types of social organization. The construction of monumental architecture reflects a substantial investment of human labor along with the social structure and leadership to oversee such construction. The lack of sumptuous burials, however, also points to collective labor and communal societies. Coastal sites such as these depended on marine resources, such as fish and shellfish; agriculture; and long-distance trade. Dependence on marine resources also required textile workers to produce nets and fishing lines. This early specialization was connected to the development of a Peruvian textile tradition whose achievements would become almost unparalleled in human history.

The development of large agriculturally based societies did not begin until much later, in the Early Horizon Period (ca. 800–ca. 200 B.C.E.). The Chavín culture, the first of the great Andean civilizations, was established in the Peruvian highlands. Centered at the site of Chavín de Huántar, its distinctive style was disseminated throughout the Andean region. Chavín art drew upon various sacred sites for its religious iconography, which synthesized earlier traditions. Artistic specialists, including textile artists, gold workers (metallurgists), and ceramic artists, were employed to create Chavín's unique cultural program. Its ritual iconography indicates the importance of the shaman, an occupation that would continue to be prominent in Andean society. Burial caches provide evidence of distinct elite burials that indicate the stratification of society and give evidence of craft specialists to provide funerary offerings.

During the Early Intermediate Period (ca. 200 B.C.E.–ca. 500 C.E.) further specialization in ceramics, textiles, and gold work is apparent in the artistic production of such southern coastal cultures as Paracas (ca. 600–ca.200 B.C.E.) and Nazca (ca. 1–ca.700 C.E.). These coastal farmers and fishermen produced time-consuming works for burials. These exquisite funerary goods reflect their high value and an increased level of skill from fiber artists, potters, and metallurgists. The items were deposited in elaborate burials that included mummies wrapped in dozens of textiles and accompanied by numerous ceramics and gold objects. The variety of these burial caches reflects the social hierarchy of the Early Intermediate Period. The image of the shaman (a religious practitioner and healer), which becomes more prominent in Paracas and early Nazca art, probably reflects the high social status of this occupation.

See also AGRICULTURE; ARCHITECTURE; ART; ASTRONOMY; BUILDING TECHNIQUES AND MATERIALS; CERAMICS AND POTTERY; CHILDREN; CLIMATE AND GEOGRAPHY; CLOTHING AND FOOTWEAR; CRAFTS; ECONOMY; EDUCATION; EMPLOYMENT AND LABOR; FOOD AND DIET; FOREIGNERS AND BARBARIANS; GENDER STRUCTURES AND ROLES; GOVERNMENT ORGANIZATION; HEALTH AND DISEASE; HOUSEHOLD GOODS; HUNTING, FISHING, AND GATHERING; LITERATURE; METALLURGY; MILITARY; MINING, QUARRYING, AND SALT MAKING; MUSIC AND MUSICAL INSTRUMENTS; NOMADIC AND PASTORAL SOCIETIES; RELIGION AND COSMOLOGY; SHIPS AND SHIPBUILDING; SLAVES AND SLAVERY; SOCIAL ORGANIZATION; TEXTILES AND NEEDLEWORK; TRADE AND EXCHANGE; WEIGHTS AND MEASURES; WRITING.

FURTHER READING

James N. Davidson, *Courtesans and Fishcakes: The Consuming Passions of Classical Athens* (New York: St. Martin's Press, 1997).

Gay Robins, *Women in Ancient Egypt* (London: British Museum Press, 1993).

Serge Sauneron, *The Priests of Ancient Egypt* (London: Cornell University Press, 2000).

Malcolm Todd, *Everyday Life of the Barbarians: Goths, Franks, and Vandals* (London: B. T. Batsford, 1972).

Ruth Tringham, *Hunters, Fishers, and Farmers of Eastern Europe 6000–3000 B.C.* (London: Hutchinson, 1971).

G. P. F. Van den Boorn, *The Duties of the Vizier: Civil Administration in the Early New Kingdom* (London: Kegan Paul, 1988).

Barbara Watterson, *Women in Ancient Egypt* (Stroud, U.K.: Sutton, 1998).

P

pandemics and epidemics

INTRODUCTION

Archaeologists and historians of medicine face difficulties in studying ancient pandemics and epidemics. (The words *pandemic* and *epidemic* differ in scope. An epidemic occurs when an illness occurs suddenly and spreads throughout a community, affecting many people; a pandemic spreads through a much wider geographical region.) The chief difficulty is that diseases that spread rapidly and strike down large numbers of people affect various tissues and organs and the blood, which rapidly decay and disappear, leaving behind little evidence of the diseases. Further, in prehistoric times no one produced written records of disease. Even in historical times contemporary written accounts were often inaccurate, for ancient observers may not have even known which disease was ravaging their communities.

Thus, historians often have to make inferences on the basis of whatever records exist, along with physical evidence, such as a large number of burials during a short period of time. But historians often disagree. For example, one of the most famous plagues in history, the plague of Athens, killed the Athenian statesman Pericles during the Peloponnesian Wars of the fifth century B.C.E. Some historians believe that the disease was bubonic plague, but others disagree. Similarly, in 700 B.C.E. the Assyrian army ended a siege of Jerusalem. Some historians believe that the cause was a cholera outbreak, but others think that the Assyrians were paid off. These examples show that studying ancient plagues can be fraught with uncertainty.

The diseases that afflicted ancient civilizations were often the same ones that afflicted communities in later eras. Smallpox, malaria, typhoid, typhus, cholera, bubonic plague, and perhaps polio were common epidemic illnesses. Some were more obscure, such as schistosomiasis, a disease caused by blood parasites. In the absence of effective treatments, these diseases frequently were fatal. Worse, most were highly communicable, meaning that they could rapidly spread from one person to another, decimating entire communities. These diseases took hold principally because ancient people did not know that the source of disease was poor hygiene. Poor hygiene could be compounded during times of social upheaval and war, when people packed into towns and cities for protection. Similarly, famine could weaken a population, leaving people with little strength to survive a disease.

Ancient people were not always against epidemics. Although inoculations against disease are thought of as a relatively modern development, ancient peoples observed that they could inoculate themselves against some diseases, such as smallpox, by giving themselves a slight case of the disease. Evidence suggests that people fought smallpox in this way as early as the second or third century of the Common Era. Smallpox was such a scourge in ancient China that the Chinese had a goddess of smallpox.

Trade and travel increased the chances that epidemics would turn into pandemics. The fleas on rats, for example, carried bubonic plague, the so-called Black Death of medieval times. But evidence indicates that outbreaks of the disease occurred much earlier, before the start of the Common Era. Rats were common stowaways on ships that transported goods around the known world, carrying disease and death with them. After arriving at a port, the rats or an ill crewman could easily infect local people who had no immunity to the disease.

AFRICA

BY JULIAN M. MURCHISON

The long history of human evolution in Africa carries with it a long history of pathogens (disease-causing agents) that evolved alongside the human populations, especially in the tropical environments that characterize most of the continent. Humans evolved both biologically and culturally in response to the presence of different diseases, in ways that allowed resident populations to survive and even to flourish.

Many of the diseases that would later emerge as the cause of major epidemics and pandemics in Africa and the rest of the world seem to have existed and developed as endemic—that is, more or less permanently established in a place or among a population—during African prehistory. The presence of endemic diseases almost certainly helped determine where groups of people came to reside in different parts of ancient Africa and played an important role in shaping their lifestyles. Changes in culture and in the environment, especially associated with the domestication of plants and animals, probably contributed to the development of diseases and the likelihood that these diseases would cause debilitating epidemics.

As in other parts of the world, epidemics and pandemics in Africa have been associated most often with the relatively high population densities supported by agriculture and domesticated animals. In much of ancient Africa population densities were low and not conducive to the development of large-scale epidemics among humans. Nevertheless, historical and archaeological evidence indicates that in those areas of the continent where agriculture and the accompanying larger and denser human settlements arose in ancient times, epidemics began to occur among the residents. For instance, there is evidence that the kingdom of Axum (in the highlands of what is today Ethiopia), which had dense urban settlements two millennia ago, suffered sporadic but serious epidemics of various diseases, including smallpox.

Archaeologists and historians have identified several diseases that probably existed in Africa during the ancient period, including smallpox, trypanosomiasis (any of several blood-borne illnesses caused by infection with a certain microorganism), malaria, and schistosomiasis (a set of diseases caused by parasitic infection with a particular worm). The primary evidence for smallpox on the continent comes from Egypt, where mummified human remains have skin marks that may indicate smallpox infection. Some written records from Egypt also suggest possible smallpox outbreaks during ancient times. While these pieces of evidence are subject to interpretation and are not definitive, they are highly suggestive of smallpox's presence. If smallpox existed in Egypt, there was almost certainly enough human contact to diffuse the disease to other parts of the continent. During subsequent periods smallpox appears to have spread from Africa to neighboring areas of the world, such as the Arabian Peninsula. At the time of European contact residents of southern Africa utilized a form of traditional smallpox prevention involving inoculation with the smallpox virus. We do not know how long this prevention was practiced or its origins, but it is suggestive of the creative and effective ways that ancient Africans might have responded to endemic diseases and to the threat of epidemics.

Traditional healer in anti-smallpox costume, Nigeria, West Africa; smallpox epidemics arose sporadically in ancient times in Africa. (© Board of Regents of the University of Wisconsin System)

One form of trypanosomiasis, often referred to as "sleeping sickness," also seems to have a long history in Africa. The disease is transmitted by the tsetse fly, and a variety of environments on the African continent supported this fly. These environments changed as humans cleared land for agriculture and other endeavors. In humans sleeping sickness can be fatal, and a closely related form of the disease can be fatal for cattle and other animals. Therefore the presence or absence of the disease almost certainly helped determine the primary sources of food and other materials that residents of the continent could rely on in any given region. Today the herding of animals exists as a traditional lifestyle in those areas where the environment was not historically conducive to tsetse flies and trypanosomiasis.

Malaria has caused suffering and death on the African continent for a long time. Transmitted by a certain type of mosquito, malaria thrives in locations where these mosquitoes breed in shallow pools of standing water and is frequently associated with human populations that are engaged in agriculture. Malaria may very well have originated in Africa and spread to other places on the globe. It is basically a chronic, endemic disease, but it can reach epidemic proportions when environmental conditions produce large numbers of the disease-bearing mosquitoes. Written references from the Classical Period provide evidence for malaria's long history in Africa, as does modern biological research. Scientists have found that individuals who can trace their ancestry back to western Africa are more likely to have the sickle-cell trait, which carries inherited resistance to the malaria parasite. This finding suggests that over the long course of human history environmental conditions in this region helped to select for these connected traits. This sort of selection generally occurs over the course of many generations.

Like malaria, schistosomiasis, a disease caused by a parasite that lives in water, probably also has a long history on the African continent. The disease may originally have occurred in tropical forests but spread with the advent of irrigation for agricultural purposes. Thus, human cultural adaptations probably contributed to its dispersal. As with smallpox, evidence for schistosomiasis in ancient Africa comes primarily from mummified human remains that show strong indications of infection with the disease.

On the whole, large-scale epidemics and pandemics appear to have been relatively rare in ancient Africa, mainly because the demographic characteristics did not lend themselves to these sorts of outbreaks. However, there is good evidence for a number of endemic diseases with the potential for epidemic or pandemic spread under the right conditions. As domestication of plants and animals became increasingly important, the circumstances for epidemic-type outbreaks grew more common. Future archaeological research and other sources may help us to understand better the specific ways in which these diseases spread and affected the lives of people in different parts of the continent.

EGYPT

BY PANAGIOTIS I. M. KOUSOULIS

Until the 19th century, modern knowledge of ancient Egyptian medicine depended mainly on the reports of the Greek authors Herodotus (ca. 484–ca. 425 B.C.E.), Strabo (ca. 64 B.C.E.–after 23 C.E.), Diodorus Siculus (first century B.C.E.), and Clement of Alexandria (ca. 150–ca. 211 C.E.). With the decipherment of hieroglyphs, Egyptian medical documents could be translated from the second half of the nineteenth century onward. Such documents were written on papyri in hieratic (cursive) hieroglyphs, and they are concerned mainly with the identification of diseases and their treatments, which often were a combination of rational and "irrational" (magical) methods. The medical papyri tell us nothing of the prevalence or the epidemiology of the diseases.

Other sources for the study of pandemics and epidemics in pharaonic times are artistic portrayals and scientific research on mummies and human remains. The process of mummification, dry weather conditions, and the location of tombs and burial grounds favored excellent preservation of human remains. Modern scientific paleopathologic research, including the use of such modern techniques as fiber-optic endoscopy, electron microscopy, and the recovery and replication of DNA, can shed light on various pandemics and epidemic deceases. Moreover, artistic representation, such as the famous statues and other images of the king Akhenaton (r. ca. 1353–ca. 1335 B.C.E.) and his family from the Eighteenth Dynasty offers clues to the causes and results of certain diseases and body deformities.

Most common epidemic diseases in ancient Egypt were caused by parasitic and bacterial or viral infections. Schistosomiasis was one such parasitic disease. According to the World Health Organization, it affects more than 12 percent of the Egyptian population today; it is acquired by infection with a certain species of worm. It can result in fever, fatigue, serious anemia, and even liver damage. Schistosomiasis has been detected in bodily remains from predynastic times up to the Roman period, though it cannot be recognized in the medical terminology of the relevant papyri.

By contrast, bacterial infections, such as leprosy, cannot be detected on mummies or skeletal remains. A few clues in medical papyri or tomb illustrations shed light on chronic progressive infections. The earliest case of nodular leprosy comes from a Christian burial in Nubia, south of Egypt in modern Ethiopia, of the sixth century C.E. The absence of material evidence on earlier mummies might have been the result of refusal to mummify victims of a disease if it was known to be infectious and required isolation from the community during life.

Evidence for leprosy in the medical papyri is tenuous because of the difficult terminology used. One helpful papyrus is the Ebers papyrus, which is said to have been found between the legs of a mummy in Thebes on the west bank of the Nile, opposite Luxor, in southern Egypt. Two cases (numbers 874 and 877) from the Ebers papyrus refer to the tumor of a certain Khonsu, which has been translated as tubercular (or nodular) leprosy: "Instructions for a tumour of Khosnu. If you examine a large tumour of Khonsu in any part of a man and it is terrible and it has made many swellings. Something has appeared in it like that in which there is air. . . . Then you shall say concerning it: it is swelling of Khonsu. You should not do anything against it." This passage, however, could equally well relate to cancer or bubonic plague. Case 813 of the Ebers papyrus refers to an "eating" of the uterus, which might also be construed as cancer. Still, both cancer and bubonic plague are extremely rare in both mummies and skeletons of pharaonic times. In part, this may be due to relatively early deaths, but an additional factor might be low levels of carcinogens.

Another epidemic disease, malaria, must have existed in ancient Egypt, when conditions for the mosquito carrier were probably more favorable than today. No traces on mummies and no mention of relevant symptoms (such as the characteristic recurrent fever at three- to four-day intervals) in the medical papyri occur. The application of a particular test on embalmed mummies from different periods of pharaonic history has suggested that certain afflictions might have been caused by malaria.

Similarly, osteomyelitis and poliomyelitis, two well-known infections, are rare in skeletal remains. On a funerary stela from the Eighteenth or Nineteenth Dynasty (ca. 1550–ca. 1196 B.C.E.), the owner is depicted with a grossly wasted and shortened leg and deformity of the foot. He is accompanied by his wife and son. Some favor the view that this is a case of poliomyelitis contracted in childhood. It is interesting that the deformed man appears to be holding a stick, which could be used as a crutch, and that his disability had not prevented his attaining high office, marrying, and having at least one child.

Even for seriously affected patients medical treatment in an isolated environment, such as a sanatorium or healers' camp, was not done only for rational reasons. The sanatorium was a precinct where patients could be totally or partially immersed in healing holy water or practice incubation (temple sleep) in the hope of having a dream in which a deity would indicate a cure. Such practices are known mainly from the middle of the first millennium B.C.E. onward, and the only archaeologically attested example is within the temple enclosure of the Great Temple of Hathor at Dendera, a sacred site in southern Egypt. The structural remains show a number of cells around a sunken corridor. These cells are presumed to have been for incubation, and the corridor leads to a series of basins that were filled with water from the sacred lake nearby.

Healing statues with inscribed magical and medical incantations were used as mediums for the healing process. The sacred water was poured over the statue and collected in a basin, which then was used for the immersion of parts or all of the body. The influence of the inscriptions would be absorbed into the water and their effects obtained by drinking the water. Magic played a very important role in treatment of the sick. Malign influences were thought to be the cause of many diseases, and it was common to invoke the help of a benign deity to counteract the malign influence. Sometimes a spell was recited in isolation and at other times in conjunction with conventional medical therapy.

THE MIDDLE EAST

BY MARKHAM J. GELLER

Epidemics are not well documented in the ancient Near East, nor do we have any text even remotely comparable to the Greek historian Thucydides' detailed firsthand account of the great plague of Athens in 430 B.C.E. Hardly any of the scattered references that exist to ancient Near Eastern plagues and epidemics can be related to any dated historical event; most merely express a general fear of epidemics or make ominous predictions of plagues. Literary accounts dealing with plague, such as the biblical 10 plagues in Egypt, are not supported by historical data that can substantiate when, or even whether, such plagues actually occurred.

The strongest evidence for epidemics in ancient Mesopotamia comes from the epistolary archives of the city of Mari on the Euphrates. Dating from about 1700 B.C.E., these texts refer to epidemics affecting various towns and cities in the vicinity. For example, they tell of a serious plague in the city of Terqa, though no remedy (such as quarantine) is mentioned. On a personal level one letter records that every member of the Bahlu-Gawum family or clan had died from a plague. We can safely suppose that plagues were considered to be manifestations of divine anger, since an epidemic is referred to as *ukulti ili*, "the devouring of a god." The only specific symptom associated with plague is fever, but we can only assume that these reports refer to a contagious pestilence. Some reports of "plague" refer to animals as well as humans being affected. Two letters from Mari refer to attacks by rabid dogs.

Terra-cotta figure of an animal thought to be a dog (ca. 700–500 B.C.E.), from Mesopotamia; figures of dogs were considered magically protective, especially against rabies, which was becoming widespread in Mesopotamia at this time. (© The Trustees of the British Museum)

The next epistolary archive containing references to epidemics is from Amarna in Egypt, though the letters were sent to Egypt from Mesopotamia and the Levant and report on events in those regions. One writer asks whether a disease affecting donkeys, which prevents them from walking, also affects people. Armies and cities were often attacked by plague during times of war, as exemplified by an Amarna letter sent from Megiddo in Palestine referring to a plague in the city as a result of its being under siege.

In later periods such contemporary reports of epidemics are rare. One Babylonian chronicle refers to an epidemic in Assyria during the reign of Merodach-baladan II (ca. 715 B.C.E.), but otherwise historical sources from the first millennium B.C.E. reveal very little about epidemics. One possible reason for this lack of information is that there was no ancient bureaucratic structure dedicated to dealing with public health, and no officials were permanently assigned to this task. Illness was treated on an ad hoc basis whenever it occurred.

The usual word for plague in the Akkadian language widely used in ancient Mesopotamia, *mutanu*, which literally means "deaths," occurs mainly in contexts of omens and divination. Plague was often predicted based on examinations of the livers of sacrificial sheep or on omens drawn from the movements of stars and planets, but such reports provide few clues to the nature of epidemics or pandemics in the region. The information is usually general, such as "There will be constant epidemics in the land" or "An epidemic will occur in a city" or "There will be an epidemic every day."

One clue to the nature of such epidemics, however, occurs in lists mentioning specific diseases that will affect the land following particular unfavorable omens. Babylonian planetary omens taken from sightings of Jupiter, for instance, predict plague in the land but also foretell that a type of joint disease, known as *rapadu*, will "seize" the land. Although we cannot diagnose this specific disease with any accuracy, the omen occurs with other health-related predictions, such as that a cattle epidemic will take place or that "pregnant women will die with the child in their womb." Such phenomena, of course, were probably unrelated to each other, but these omens were intended to refer to widespread conditions affecting the entire country, not to individual cases of affliction. Another unfavorable planetary omen, associated with sightings of Venus, warns that dogs will become rabid, biting men, cattle, sheep, and donkeys, and that whatever is bitten will not recover. It is likely that many diseases besides rabies were thought to be caused by dog bites. As we learn more about the nature of the diseases mentioned in omens such as these, we will have a better chance of identifying diseases that were considered epidemics as well as illnesses attacking individual patients.

Diseases and pestilence were often considered to be the work of Nergal, the Babylonian god of pestilence and cattle disease, who was associated with the planet Mars. Diseases were considered to originate from the "evil dew of the gods" or were associated with divine spittle or even divine semen raining down from heaven. These are all religious metaphors for the cosmic origins of disease, which was thought to have been created when the rest of creation took place; disease was often regarded as the handiwork of demons emanating from the netherworld. The technical literature of diagnosis and medicine often refers to diseases as the "hand of a god," with the god or demon mentioned by name, but many of these labels eventually came to serve as proper names of particular diseases, without much theological importance.

ASIA AND THE PACIFIC

BY KIRK H. BEETZ

Much is mysterious about the nature and frequency of epidemics in ancient Asia and the Pacific. In general, anthropologists believe that epidemics were rare or nonexistent among many peoples of the Pacific before the coming of Europeans, whose diseases killed numerous Australians and Pacific islanders. During ancient times there were migrations from the Asian mainland to Japan, the Philippines, New Guinea, and some of the islands of Indonesia, and the migrants brought their diseases—and their developed immunities—with them, which may explain why peoples of these places did not suffer from diseases later imported from Europe as severely as others did. The most prevalent ancient scourge among these islands was leprosy. Another that was common among the Indonesian islands was malaria.

Malaria, caused by a single-celled parasitic organism transmitted to humans by one particular type of mosquito, occurred throughout southern Asia. The disease—but not its cause—was well known to ancient Asian writers. Malaria was responsible for much suffering and countless deaths among both dense and sparse populations wherever pools of quiet water abounded during warm weather—conditions in which the disease-bearing mosquitoes bred prolifically. Ancient Indian physicians, in particular, tried to find treatments for malaria but in the end could do little more than attempt to reduce the fever it entailed.

In China an epidemic was taken as a sign that a ruler had lost the mandate of heaven and could be lawfully deposed. Thus it is not surprising that government officials were reluctant to record epidemics. Surviving Chinese medical writings from the Han Dynasty (202 B.C.E.–220 C.E.) indicate that epidemics occurred in various parts of the empire so frequently that they could be discussed in broad general statements rather than in descriptions of specific outbreaks.

Influenza was a common disease among pigs and ducks in Asia, and it mutated frequently into forms that could be transmitted to human beings. Archaeologists suspect that influenza began in China because early in Chinese culture pigs became an important part of everyday life. Although a new strain of influenza might begin in a rural area, it was easily carried by pigs or infected humans into towns and cities, where it took on epidemic proportions. Like modern strains of influenza, those of ancient China probably varied in severity, but the worst strains killed thousands. Chinese physicians apparently deduced that influenza could be transmitted through the air, though this knowledge had little practical use in ancient times. Along with magic spells and potions, however, doctors devised treatments that included sensible measures, such as having patients rest and drink water.

The smallpox virus developed somewhere in Asia. Related to the cowpox virus, it seems to be a mutation of cowpox that became capable of infecting human beings. Thus some archaeologists suspect that it developed either in central Asia among nomadic cattle herders or in India, where cattle often roamed freely among people. Traders along the ancient land route known as the Silk Road may have carried smallpox eastward. In 162 C.E. a disease that was probably smallpox killed over 30 percent of the population of northwestern China.

During epidemics the Chinese often left people unburied, fearing that handling the dead could transmit the disease. Sometimes government authorities ordered the burying of the dead, but some physicians argued that burning the corpses would destroy the disease that killed them, preventing its transmission. During severe epidemics bodies lay where they had died, in fields and on roads. In 162 C.E. they would have lain everywhere in the northwest China, unmistakable evidence that the emperor had lost his mandate from heaven.

A faith healer named Zhang Jiao formed a Daoist sect popularly known as the Yellow Turbans because of their headdress. In 162 C.E. Zhang advocated the overthrow of the imperial government. By 184 C.E., when the Yellow River flooded and killed many people, followed by deaths from epidemic disease, the Yellow Turbans had followers in most of China, and they rebelled, seizing control of much of northern and eastern China. Zhang and other leaders were killed, and their armies were eventually defeated, but the Han government never fully recovered; the revolt led to the political chaos that eventually ended the Han Dynasty in 220 C.E.

In India physicians tried to learn when epidemics were most likely to occur and searched for ways to prevent them. For smallpox Indians took dried scabs of the disease from people who were recovering from it and scraped them into the skins of uninfected people—an early effort at inoculation. About 1 percent of inoculated people caught the disease, but since smallpox could virtually wipe out entire towns and rural areas, the rate of infection from inoculations seemed small.

Cholera, a deadly water-borne bacterial disease, was a common affliction in ancient India. Cities were customarily surrounded by moats into which human waste was dumped. City dwellers took their drinking water and cooking water from these moats as well as from nearby rivers or streams that were often quite polluted. Although Indian physicians believed that cholera was caused by pollution, it was apparently beyond their abilities to persuade people to find their water elsewhere, stop dumping human waste into the water supply, or discontinue building moats to help protect their cities from attack.

Annual flooding caused by monsoons was known to precede epidemics of cholera. Even so, the month of harvests, Margali, was considered to be the month that ruled epidemics. Shiva was the god of the month of Margali, and Indians prayed and made offerings to him in the hope that he would prevent epidemics. When epidemics occurred, Indians usually recited magical incantations and used charms to aid the sick and asked magicians to cast spells and mix magical potions for the afflicted.

Indians, however, had also long exhibited a practical streak in their treatment of epidemics, with medicine becoming an important profession before 500 B.C.E. There were several classifications of physicians. Two of them, general practitioners and a group that would in modern times be described as toxicologists (doctors who study and treat the effects of poisons) and epidemiologists (doctors who study the spread and control of epidemic diseases), often dealt with epidemics. Some epidemic diseases, such as tuberculosis, were considered incurable, and the physicians tried to ease patients' suffering with mixtures that included opiates similar to morphine. Cholera was classified as a "fever" disease, and the "epidemiologists" linked it to pollution of air and water. They treated it with opiates to ease the terrible pain but also with the root of a plant known today as serpentwood or Indian snakeroot. Nowadays the root is used to treat high blood pressure, but it also reduces fever; ancient Indian physicians used it to lower the fever of cholera. It was hardly a perfect treatment, but it gave patients a chance to survive the worst stages of the disease.

EUROPE

BY CARYN E. NEUMANN

Infectious diseases devastated human populations in ancient Europe, especially in later times as people began to cluster together in settlements and then towns. Epidemics and pandemics of such diseases claimed more lives than all wars and natural disasters taken together. Infectious diseases have probably been the primary agent of natural selection over the past centuries, eliminating human hosts who were more susceptible to them and sparing those who were more resistant.

Prehistoric Europeans who lived in hunter-gatherer societies were probably relatively free from the effects of epidemic diseases. The small size of these groups, their remoteness from one another, and their frequent movement would have made it difficult for airborne or crowd diseases, such as tuberculosis, influenza, and diphtheria, to become established. Diseases of the digestive tract may not have spread as rapidly as in more concentrated populations either, even though sanitation was not particularly good. When an infectious disease struck, it probably worked its way through the population and then vanished. Certain diseases, however, can flourish and be transmitted readily even among small and scattered hunter-gatherer populations. Measles and smallpox, for example, could occur in lethal epidemic outbreaks. In general, however, people in prehistoric Europe were more likely to die of degenerative conditions or to be killed in accidents or violence than to succumb to epidemic diseases.

When humans embraced agriculture and herding, they also embraced cattle, horses, sheep, and other domesticated or semidomesticated animals that were chronic bearers of infection. In the wild, herd animals constituted large, concentrated populations of a single species—a condition that allowed numerous bacterial and viral infections to become endemic. (An endemic disease is one that is more or less permanently established in a population or an environment.) The chain of infection would never have stopped. Over time these animal populations, though they still carried the pathogens (disease-causing agents), had developed resistance to them. Thus, even though viral and bacterial infections were probably rife among wild herds of cattle, sheep, and horses, many of them provoked only mild symptoms or none at all.

The domestication of herd animals brought them and their endemic infections into close, regular contact with human populations. Many of the infectious agents, of course, did not transfer to humans, and some that did transfer caused only minor effects. Others, however, became virulent. One such disease, brucellosis (also known as contagious abortion), attacks cattle and swine. In humans, it is known as undulant fever. Brucellosis is commonly transmitted by direct contact with infected animals or with an environment that has been contaminated with discharges from infected animals. The initial symptoms in humans are fatigue and headaches, followed by high fever, chills, drenching sweats, joint pains, backache, and loss of weight and appetite.

Europeans initially lacked any acquired immunities to the new invaders and, as a result, suffered a high number of deaths from these animal-to-human diseases until human populations developed immunities. Early farming communities were also sedentary, meaning that the inhabitants lived in one place year-round, where they were in close contact with one another. As a result, a communicable disease was likely to spread quickly and with devastating effect—an effect that became even more pronounced as more and more people lived in villages and towns.

Europeans who came into close contact with the Roman Empire and large Mediterranean populations suffered exposure to parasitic disease. Until medieval times the Germanic and Slavic peoples of Europe did not suffer from these diseases. Leprosy, also known as Hansen's disease, first appeared in ancient Egypt, Africa, China, and India. It traveled to Greece from Egypt and spread throughout Europe through military movements. An infectious disease caused by a bacterium, leprosy spread easily through direct contact, by inhalation of sputum or nasal discharges, or by indirect contact with recently contaminated objects. All victims have nerve damage, and these injuries are responsible for the severe deformities that can result from leprosy.

Malaria, a disease prevalent in tropical and subtropical climates and transmitted by a particular species of mosquito, has long been one of the most widely distributed and most severe illnesses to strike humans. The pressure of malaria on natural selection has made a much greater impact than any other pathogen on recent human evolution. Natural selection has favored the spread in many human populations of hundreds of genetic mutations that appear to give varying degrees of resistance to malaria. Ancient Europeans who lived in the warm, swampy areas that malaria-bearing mosquitoes prefer developed these mutations. They also adopted certain ways of living that helped them avoid these mosquitoes. For example, the combination of small settlements and movement to high elevations in summer served to reduce exposure to malaria. Even diet played a role. For instance, some European peoples regularly ate fava beans, which have antimalarial effects. These lifestyle adaptations were largely coincidental, since the cause of malaria was unknown until modern times, but they were nevertheless useful.

One form of response to epidemic diseases in late ancient times may have helped Christianity become established in Europe. When a serious infectious disease strikes a population, normal services often break down; some people are too sick to function, while others are too frightened of becoming infected to perform their usual tasks. In an epidemic, elementary nursing, such as cleaning and the provision of water and food, can usually greatly reduce mortality rates. Pagans had no religious duty to provide nursing to the sick. In contrast, Christians considered nursing to be a religious obligation. Moreover, those who survived with the help of such nursing were likely to feel gratitude and a sense of solidarity with those who had saved their lives. The effect of a disastrous epidemic in Europe after the advent of Christianity, therefore, was to strengthen Christian churches at a time when other institutions were being discredited. Another advantage that Christians enjoyed was that the teachings of their faith made life meaningful even amid sudden and surprising death. Moreover, even the survivors of a deadly epidemic could find comfort in the notion that their deceased loved ones were in heaven. Pagans did not receive the same sense of consolation from an afterlife. As a result, pagan survivors may have struggled with depression as an aftereffect of epidemic disease. Such emotional upset would have complicated recovery for individuals and communities.

GREECE

BY ALAIN TOUWAIDE

The concepts of pandemics (disease affecting an entire area or group of persons) and epidemics (disease affecting at the same time a large number of persons and spreading from one person to another, as a disease not normally prevalent among this group) were not theoretically formulated in Greece before the fifth century B.C.E. and the development of medical thinking, mainly (but not only) among Hippocratic physicians. Nevertheless, the existence of diseases affecting a large group of individuals was recognized as early as the development of Greek mythical and epic literature. In the mythical cycle of

Greek marble block from the frieze of the Temple of Apollo Epikourio, meaning "Apollo the Helper" (420–400 B.C.E.), from Bassae, Arcadia; the name Helper was given to Apollo by citizens of nearby Phigaleia, as thanks for their deliverance from the plague. (© The Trustees of the British Museum)

Thebes (in Boeotia, central Greece), a pestilence affects the city at the beginning of the play *Oedipus tyrannos* (Oedipus the King) by Sophocles. In the epic literature a similar affliction decimates the Greek troops besieging Troy at the beginning of the *Iliad*. The term used for such disease is *loimos*, usually improperly translated as "plague." The cause was seen to be of a religious nature: An individual transgresses a law of the group. As a punishment, a disease affecting the group is sent by a god. Significantly, in the *Iliad* this disease takes the form of arrows falling on the warriors and killing them. The cure involves offering sacrifices to the god who provoked the disease (including a scapegoat) and compensating for the transgression by reestablishing the natural order of the group, which has been broken.

In historical times the existence of diseases affecting a large number of people is affirmed in the didactic poem *Works and Days* by Hesiod (fl. ca. 800 B.C.E.). Such disease is sent by a god (Zeus), though without reference to a transgression. It is rather the result of the human condition, submitted to work, pain, and suffering. Three major outbreaks of epidemic diseases were described in the sixth and fifth centuries B.C.E. The first is mentioned in the pseudo-Hippocratic *Embassy*. The text reveals that during the First Sacred War (ca. 590 B.C.E.), troops besieging the sacred site of Delphi suffer a *loimos*. For the first time in preserved literature a physician is called. However, he does not use any medicine: The god involved in the outbreak of the disease stops it.

The second epidemic is known through the pseudo-Hippocratic *Letters*. The troops of the Persian king Artaxerxes I (r. 465–425 B.C.E.) are suffering such a disease. Although the letter is of doubtful authenticity, it contains an interesting statement on the origin and treatment of epidemics: Such diseases are not considered to be natural and, contrary to natural disease that nature cures, need to be treated by the art of physicians. For this reason Artaxerxes calls Hippocrates (ca. 460–ca. 377 B.C.E.).

The third major outbreak of an epidemic disease is the famous so-called plague of Athens (430 B.C.E.) described by the historian Thucydides (d. ca. 401 B.C.E.). Again, such disease affected a population during a war (the Peloponnesian War, 431–404 B.C.E.). It appeared among the besieged population of Athens. According to Thucydides' report, the disease came from Ethiopia, passed through Libya and Egypt, and from there spread to Persia. It suddenly appeared in Athens, through the harbor of Piraeus. In the city the death toll was higher than anywhere else. Physicians were of no help, as they did not know the nature of the disease and died themselves because they were in close contact with sick patients. No therapeutic method was efficacious. The disease stopped spontaneously. The nature of the disease has been disputed for a long time. (Smallpox is among the hypotheses.) Recent archaeological and laboratory research has led to the conclusion that it might have been typhoid fever. In the late fifth century and early fourth century B.C.E. another epidemic disease was the so-called cough of Perinth described in the Hippocratic work *Epidemics 6*. It affected the city of Perinthus, on the shore of the Propontis (Sea of Marmara) sometime around 400 B.C.E. and probably was several different medical conditions, the most important of which has since been diagnosed as diphtheria.

At the time of these major outbreaks of epidemic diseases the concept of general disease was gradually formulated among Hippocratic physicians. A distinction was made between individual and general disease, including a notion of cause and, as a consequence, of treatment. These physicians concluded that individual diseases, affecting a single patient, result from the alimentary habits of the patient (even though several individuals using the same diet can suffer of the same disease). Such diseases could be cured by changing the diet and compensating for the insufficiencies or rectifying the improper diet. General diseases, affecting an entire group, are provoked, it was thought, by a corruption of the air (the so-called miasmas, that is, impurities floating in the air and resulting from any kind of pollution). They could be cured by applying a proper pharmaceutical therapy that rectified the damages caused by the disease.

There was no notion of a treatment that could eliminate the cause of the disease. The concept of the impact of the environment on the health conditions of a population is further refined in the famous Hippocratic treatise *Airs, Waters, Places*, traditionally dated to the second half of the fifth century B.C.E. and attributed to a physician from the school of Kos. A distinction was made between the constant conditions of a place (provoking the endemic diseases, that is, those peculiar to a particular population or place) and the occasional conditions, independent from the place itself, but coming from external factors and causing a general disease. The word *epidêmios* was applied to diseases affecting a large number of patients, without implying any notion of contagion. The word constitutes the title of seven books in the so-called Hippocratic collection describing the diseases present in a specific place at a moment of the year and affecting a certain number of patients.

ROME

BY ALAIN TOUWAIDE

Historical sources, including those of the Roman historian Livy (64 or 57 B.C.E.–12 or 17 C.E.), the Greek philosopher Dionysius of Halicarnassus (born ca. 60 B.C.E.), and the Greek historian Polybius (ca. 200–ca. 118 B.C.E.), report outbreaks of epidemic diseases in the Roman world shortly after the foundation of the Roman Republic (509 B.C.E.) at a higher frequency than those in the Greek world. This apparently higher frequency might be the result of better record keeping; Roman historians relied on the tradition of *annales*, which recorded the notable events of each year. According to the descriptions by the historians who recorded the *annales*, epidemics often were linked with military expeditions, wars, food shortages, famines, and natural calamities affecting crops. In some cases epidemic diseases also were described as coming from cattle. While some of these epidemics arose from local conditions, others were introduced into the Roman world from the west or the south. The Athenian epidemic in 430 B.C.E. might have been carried westward; Rome was struck in 428 B.C.E., according to Livy. In Sicily epidemics were said to have been introduced repeatedly by troops from the Athenian expedition of 413 B.C.E. through the outbreak in 212 B.C.E. among Roman and Carthaginian troops

The best-known epidemic in the Roman world was the so-called Antonine plague. This was a series of epidemics, including two major outbreaks, in 165 C.E. and in 180 C.E., respectively, that struck the Roman population under the Antonine emperors (138–192 C.E.). The disease was introduced into the Roman world from Mesopotamia by the troops from the expedition against the Parthians, which began in 162 C.E. and was led by Lucius Aurelius Verus (r. 161–169 C.E.). In 165 C.E. the Roman troops were affected by the disease and retreated. They spread the disease westward to Italy and Rome. The epidemic progressed to Gaul and into Germany as far as the Rhine. The emperors Lucius Verus and Marcus Aurelius (r. 161–180 C.E.) died of the epidemic. The Greek physician Galen (129–ca. 199 C.E.), who stayed in Rome at that time, escaped from the city and did not return until 169, when he was summoned by the emperor. The death toll is thought to have been extremely high throughout the empire. Thrace, for example, supposedly lost half of its population. Such a mortality rate has been attributed to the high level of urbanization of the Roman Empire, as opposed to the fragmentation of the Greek world in smaller cities.

The nature of epidemic diseases in Rome has been addressed frequently in medical and historical literature. Because the epidemics of 428 B.C.E. in Rome supposedly came from the East, and since the so-called plague of Athens of 430 B.C.E. has been identified as smallpox, one conclusion is that the Roman epidemic represented the introduction of smallpox to the West. A similar hypothesis has been made for the Antonine plague. According to this view, this was the second attack of smallpox in the West, which proceeded according to a pattern of diffusion east to west from Mesopotamia. Another identification of the plague of Athens as typhoid fever, however, contradicts the traditional history of the diffusion of smallpox.

The categorization of diseases according to their geographical diffusion, chronological frequency, and statistical importance was initiated by Galen. He developed a threefold categorization: First, sporadic diseases are those of a single individual at a certain moment. Second, epidemic diseases affect a high number of individuals at the same time in a single place. Third, endemic diseases are those that are perpetually common in a single place. A few more general notions, probably of popular wisdom, can be found in the *Historia naturalis* (Natural History), by the Roman scholar Pliny (23–79 C.E.). They include the observation that diseases followed certain patterns; for example, epidemics moved from south to north and almost never in the opposite direction, they did not start during the winter, and they never lasted more than three months.

As in the Greek world, the cause of epidemic disease was considered to be miasmas, or particles of a corrupted nature floating in the air that people inhaled. Therapeutic methods among the Romans reproduced those of Greek medicine but were augmented with a new pharmaceutical strategy: compound medicines associating many ingredients. This strategy, which supposedly started with the experiments of the king of Pontus, Mithridates VI Eupator (r. 120–63 B.C.E.), took root in Rome during the first century C.E., mainly with Andromachos, the chief physician of the emperor Nero (r. 54–68 C.E.).

The most significant medicine resulting from this strategy was the so-called theriac. First created as a medicine against venoms and poisons, it also was used as a broad-spectrum medicine thanks to its wide range of ingredients (among them, opium and the flesh of the viper). Many of those ingredients were credited with the properties of producing heat. The preparation resulting from their mixing purportedly had the property of burning the matter that provoked the disease (whatever the nature of the disease or the matter). Thanks to this supposed property, the use of theriac was expanded to prevention. In the case of epidemics the compound was taken to protect against contagion. The principle underlying such use led to other preventive measures, such as spreading perfumed plants and substances credited with a warming property to burn the miasmas believed to be responsible for epidemic diseases and their diffusion.

THE AMERICAS

BY CARYN E. NEUMANN

Infectious disease is one of the greatest killers in human history. But while ancient civilizations in the Americas created works that paid tribute to other aspects of life, few reports of disease have survived the passage of the centuries. Meanwhile, much of the modern literature about the Americas depicts the pre-European contact world as a disease-free paradise. It was not. Pandemic disease killed ancient Americans as it killed other ancient people.

Ancient hunter-gatherers in the Americas were relatively free from the acute, epidemic infectious diseases that later took a toll on more advanced agrarian societies. Many acute infectious diseases require large numbers of susceptible individuals to support their chains of transmission, which are characterized by brief and rapid stages of infection. In ancient food-foraging groups, populations of no more than 200 to 300 persons would not have been large enough to sustain such a chain of transmission. If introduced, these acute infections would have run their courses and then died out. From the perspective of natural selection, pathogens (disease-causing agents) that live inside the body of a host for an extended period of time (such as those that cause typhoid and amoebic dysentery) would have been favored. Infections (like measles) that spread rapidly and immunize a majority of the population in one epidemic would have been rare or absent. As populations became more sedentary, they were felled by devastating epidemics of smallpox and measles.

It is not clear whether malaria, another of the great ancient killers, was present in the New World. Malaria historically has been one of the greatest plagues of human societies. When it does not kill, it leaves a victim weakened. Malaria is found in the present-day Americas, but it is still uncertain whether the disease existed in the Americas before the arrival of Columbus. No Native American population of the present day has elevated frequencies of any of the genetic mutations that confer degrees of resistance to malaria in so many Old World populations.

Other plagues can be clearly identified. Paleopathologists, scientists who study disease in prehistoric populations, have filled in gaps in the knowledge of the history of pandemic disease in the Americas by using various types of evidence to describe disease patterns of ancient populations. By looking at pottery, these scientists have determined that epidemic leishmaniasis (a skin disorder caused by a protozoan carried by sand flies) was present in ancient Latin America. Pottery from Peru and Ecuador, dating to about 100 B.C.E., indicates the presence of facial ulceration, scarring, and malformation of the mucous membranes among the pre-Inca. Such signs are an indication of epidemic leishmaniasis. In more severe forms the disease strikes the liver, lymphatic system, and spleen, causing lesions, anemia, and death.

Much of the evidence for the presence of disease in the New World is based on data obtained from research on archaeological human skeletal remains. One of the limitations in studying infectious disease in such samples is that acute diseases are rarely expressed in the skeleton. Almost all infectious diseases are chronic diseases, meaning that most of the great epidemics which have punctuated human history will leave, at best, nonspecific and indirect evidence in a skeletal sample. The infectious diseases that do affect the skeleton are those caused primarily by bacteria, but even these infectious organisms rarely affect the skeleton unless there is long-term survival with the disease.

Paleopathologists have examined skeletal evidence to conclude that tuberculosis, venereal syphilis, yaws (a bacterial skin infection marked by red skin eruptions and joint pain), and bejel (endemic syphilis) were present in the ancient Americas. Tuberculosis has been identified in several prehistoric Andean populations. The earliest evidence for tuberculosis in the Americas comes from Chile and dates to about 290 B.C.E. It has not been found in ancient peoples of North America. Tuberculosis is a chronic disease caused by the microorganism *Mycobacterium tuberculosis.* In cases from defined geographical areas, most people in each generation are initially infected in early childhood, typically from inhaling pathogen-laden droplets expelled by sick individuals. If general levels of health are good, more than half of those infected will never show any clinical symptoms of disease. Individuals with weakened immune systems will become visibly ill and may die. If death does not occur, the bacteria may become walled up within fibrous capsules in the body and can remain viable for decades. Severe stress in later life may prompt a recurrence of tuberculosis.

Yaws and bejel are usually acquired as childhood diseases, with transmission typically occurring in play groups. Syphilis is acquired from the mother or through sexual transmission, with an onset that usually begins after childhood.

Yaws leaves lesions on the skin and bone. Bejel affects the skin, bone, and cardiovascular system. Venereal syphilis involves skin, bone, the cardiovascular system, and the nervous system. It may severely dampen human fertility through miscarriages and stillbirths of infected fetuses. Congenital cases of yaws and nonvenereal syphilis are rare. Bones lying close underneath the skin may have lesions through spread of infection from adjacent skin lesions. Joint destruction is seen in yaws but not in syphilis. Paleopathologists have concluded that venereal disease originated in the Americas, because skeletal evidence of syphilis in the New World predates the same sort of evidence in Europe.

See also ASTRONOMY; CITIES; DEATH AND BURIAL PRACTICES; FOOD AND DIET; HEALTH AND DISEASE; INVENTIONS; LITERATURE; NATURAL DISASTERS; RELIGION AND COSMOLOGY; SETTLEMENT PATTERNS; SOCIAL ORGANIZATION; TOWNS AND VILLAGES; TRADE AND EXCHANGE; WAR AND CONQUEST.

FURTHER READING

Jared Diamond, *Guns, Germs, and Steel: The Fates of Human Societies* (New York: W. W. Norton, 1999).

Mirko D. Grmek, *Diseases in the Ancient Greek World*, trans. Mireille Muellner and Leonard Muellner (Baltimore, Md.: Johns Hopkins University Press, 1989).

Jacques Jouanna, *Hippocrates*, trans. M. B. DeBevoise (Baltimore. Md.: Johns Hopkins University Press, 1999).

Kenneth F. Kiple, ed., *The Cambridge World History of Human Disease* (New York: Cambridge University Press, 1993).

William H. McNeill, *Plagues and Peoples* (New York: Doubleday, 1976).

John F. Nunn, *Ancient Egyptian Medicine* (Norman: University of Oklahoma Press, 1996).

John F. Nunn, "Disease." In *The Oxford Encyclopedia of Ancient Egypt*, vol. 1, ed. Donald. B. Redford (Oxford, U.K.: Oxford University Press, 2001).

John F. Nunn, "Medicine." In *The Oxford Encyclopedia of Ancient Egypt*, vol. 1, ed. Donald. B. Redford (Oxford, U.K.: Oxford University Press, 2001).

Robert Sallares, *The Ecology of the Ancient Greek World* (Ithaca, N.Y.: Cornell University Press, 1991).

Mary Ellen Snodgrass, *World Epidemics: A Cultural Chronology of Disease from Prehistory to the Era of SARS* (Jefferson, N.C.: McFarland, 2003).

John W. Verano and Douglas H. Ubelaker, eds., *Disease and Demography in the Americas* (Washington, D.C.: Smithsonian Institution Press, 1992).

R

▸ religion and cosmology

INTRODUCTION

When religion began is not known, but archaeologists, paleontologists, and historians often speculate about it. Some point to early graves containing goods such pots and jewelry as signs of a belief in an afterlife and therefore signs of religion. A significant problem with this idea is that some ancient peoples believed in gods and the supernatural but did not believe that human beings had any life after death. For them, a human being had only one life, and once it was ended the human being was gone forever.

Other researchers point to artworks as signs of religious belief. All over the world ancient peoples painted on and carved into large rocks. Some sculpted images of animals and people. For some people works of art were magical; when the works were created, reality itself changed to conform to the painting or carving. One of the problems the earliest rock art and carvings present modern observers is that they can indicate that religious belief existed but cannot show when that belief began. Early religious objects may have been made of perishable substances such as wood and leather, and early people may not have chosen to express their religious beliefs in art. For many religions the substance of religious belief and practice was not in scripture, in art, or in altars but was in everyday behavior, passed on by spoken word and examples of behavior from one generation to the next.

Some anthropologists see religion as a part of culture that developed through stages. For these researchers religious ideas would have begun in Africa before modern humans left Africa to colonize the world. Their religion would have been a form of animism, a belief that almost everything had spiritual significance, including bodies of water, large geological formations, and any living thing.

Religions have been an expression of a fundamental aspect of being human, and it has long been thought that religion separates human beings from all other creatures. Religion is an expression of a feeling or sensation in people that there is something more to the world than can be readily observed by their senses, something that underlies the cosmos. This something is conveyed to people spiritually. It does not necessarily mean that human beings have souls, though in almost all religions people believe that they sense the supernatural nature of the universe because they have souls that are related to the supernatural. In some religions this has meant the loss of individuality, which was submerged in a universal spirit; in other cases, it has meant liberation of a person because his or her individual spirit is able to be an active participant in the great enterprises of the supernatural world.

In general, religions have required rituals on the part of people. To get in touch with the supernatural may have required waiting in a particular spot known to be a way station for traveling spirits or speaking in certain ways to invoke spirits or gods. Clapping hands could be a way to attract the attention of spirits. Kneeling could be a way to show a god that one was sincere. In the context of many religions being able to invoke the immediate presence of a god or gods was important, because their presence signified their interest in the local community. Many sculptures of gods were intended to function as places where gods could make themselves part of the living world. In ancient Egypt priestesses would bring food to statues of gods and then dance, sing, and tumble to entertain the gods, who were present in their statues, observing all. In ancient Mesopotamia statues of gods were paraded through cities and taken to watch entertainments. Although the statues were stone, the gods could inhabit them to observe and enjoy the spectacles.

Giving spiritual life to inanimate objects may seem primitive, but most ancient peoples saw it as a sign of civilized behavior. For instance, many ancient cultures substituted inanimate objects for living ones in the confidence that in the otherworld of spirits or gods, the power of art and spoken word would make the inanimate objects real. It is an uncomfortable fact that many ancient religions practiced human sacrifice. If one studies ancient sculptures and paintings of people being sacrificed, they look miserable and frightened. In fact, for some religions, the fear and suffering of victims were important assurances of the effectiveness of the sacrifice, whether the victims were girls in the Andes or children in Burma. The Druidic cult involved bloodily torturing people to death to foretell the future or please a god. Wars sometimes were waged just to acquire prisoners for sacrifices, and those prisoners knew only terror as they were killed. The substitution of statues for people as sacrifices was for some ancient societies a sign that they had matured in their religions, that they realized spirits made their own reality and would accept symbols instead of living people because in their aspect of the universe, symbol and reality were the same.

Another aspect of ancient religion that can make modern observers uncomfortable is the seeming lack of logic. The modern world has been shaped and is constantly being reshaped by the scientific method, but in the ancient world few people approached learning via empirical research, that is, actually observing how the natural world functioned. The modern scientific method developed in the 1500s. On the basis of the logic of the scientific method, aspects of religion do not make sense. An example cited frequently is the presentation of two stories of the creation of human beings in the Bible. If a person of today were to say to someone of the ancient world—even one who was not Hebrew or Christian—that the two stories in the Bible cannot both be true, the ancient might consider such a person to be crazy. Did the authors of the Old Testament sabotage their own work by including contradictory stories? No. They believed both stories to be part of the truth. Thus it was that in ancient Egypt the gods Horus and Seth were both brothers and uncle and nephew at the same time, revealing part of the truth of their relationship and of the supernatural world. In the complexities of contradictions ancient people hoped to glimpse a little of what made the universe what it was in its wholeness.

AFRICA

BY ROBERT SHANAFELT

Religion can be difficult to define. One definition is that religion is belief and practices concerning supernatural phenomena of all sorts, from those about God to those relating to various deities, spirit beings, and magical forces. A problem with this definition is that not everyone agrees about what is supernatural. Another approach is to emphasize special behavior in the form of prayer or other types of worship. This definition works well enough for situations where worship is clearly separated from other activities, such as in cases where people go into a special building like a mosque, a temple, or a church to pray and listen to religious leaders. But not everything that might be called religious is separated out that way from ordinary life. Is someone being religious if they attend a wedding? Visit a grave site? Paint a picture? Hope for a prosperous future? In these cases, the answer can depend on the context and details. This is true of much that is called traditional religion in Africa. What is religious is determined by the context of the case because, in much of Africa, religious life is a pervasive part of the everyday world.

Another point to keep in mind when studying religions with deep traditional roots, such as those in Africa, is that ideas do not have to be written down to be part of a complex system of religious thought. For example, Africa has a rich set of traditions about cosmology, or the nature of the universe. That is, there are rich oral accounts in various African religions of how the universe, the world, human beings, and other living things have been created and have developed through time. These sacred stories, commonly called myths but better understood as oral scriptures, often run to hundreds of pages when written down.

Examples of myths that can be traced to specific time periods in the ancient past are difficult to come by, but some hints of ancient western African images of the world are given in epic songs. Especially relevant are those described in the 19th century as being sung among the Soninke and Fula peoples. Fragments of these songs seem to be traceable to the fourth century C.E. These songs tell of heroic contests and mythic battles in ancient cities, with the legendary city of Wagadu, most prominent. The heroes in these epics are worthy of attention not only for their legendary deeds but also because they are the ancestors of great lineages of peoples.

In the epics it is also significant that Wagadu is presented as a woman with extraordinary qualities. As such, she symbolizes an ideal to be praised and honored. Wagadu, it is said, "is not of stone, not of wood, not of earth. Wagadu is the strength that lives in the hearts of men." Epic accounts also talk of a mythic serpent to whom the people of this city made sacrifices. Some scholars have suggested that there are connections to this story and archaeological findings at the ancient city of Jenne-jeno, near Djenné, Mali. In particular, they point to serpent motifs on ceramics discovered there by archaeologists. However, as with most things where evidence is incomplete, much remains open to speculation.

The special acts of a religion are called its rituals. Rituals are like habits in that they occur regularly, but they are more than habits because they are imbued with special meaning. Common rituals in Africa as in other parts of the world include those connected to birth and naming, coming of age, marriage, agriculture, change of seasons, and death. In many parts of Africa there are also special ceremonies held to honor one's ancestors. These traditions run very deep, but it is often difficult to tell exactly how old they are.

At least one anthropologist has argued that the widespread African ritual of divination has roots traceable to Neolithic times. Divination refers to techniques used to tell the future. As practiced in contemporary times, it generally involves the casting of shells, nuts, or bones and the recitation of special phrases or poems that are associated with each particular pattern that can possibly appear. Such divination requires a prodigious memory and implies a special period of training between a master and an apprentice.

No matter what definition is used, there are many different African religions. Most of these are fully indigenous systems, developed completely in Africa. However, Africa has also long been the home of Judaism, Christianity, and Islam. In fact, one could find communities of Jews, Christians, or Muslims in Africa quite soon after these religions first began to be practiced. Islam, however, did not begin as a religion until the time of Muhammad in the seventh century after the beginning of the Christian era. Obviously, Islam could not have influenced Africa before this time.

Early Religion

One of the earliest forms of evidence about religious belief is the demonstration that the dead were intentionally buried and that valuable objects were placed into the graves of the deceased. This type of discovery suggests both that the living maintained an emotional connection with the dead and also that they may have thought there was something beyond death. Archaeologists have shown that human beings were using colorful dyes for funeral purposes tens of thousands of years ago in Africa. This is supported by excavations at Twin Rivers, Zambia, where red, yellow, and other shades of ocher have been found in abundance. Ocher is a naturally occurring, powdery compound that can be smeared onto the body directly or mixed with water or grease to form paint. The practice of using ocher and other natural pigments to paint the body for ritual and aesthetic purposes is one that continues in many parts of Africa up to contemporary times.

Art and decoration are associated with religious behavior because they help in making powerful symbolic connections. It is through such symbolic connections that feelings of the divine are linked with everyday activities. Scholars of comparative religion have shown that ocher, in its red form, was widely used throughout the ancient world as a symbol of blood and life. Other examples of apparently symbolic connections are found in much of the ancient rock art that is widely distributed throughout the continent. Many of the rock paintings have to do with the connections humans made with animals. During the days when hunting and gathering was the way of life, people all over the world developed a spiritual connection particularly with the largest and most dramatic of the animals around them. African rock art can be divided into different phases depending on the animals that are most often represented. In one phase, for example, representations of a gigantic buffalo called *Bubalus* were commonly featured. This period extended from about 6,000 to 11,0000 years ago.

There are a few cases in which connections have been established between ancient forms of art and the religions of contemporary people. For example, a hexagonally shaped jewel stone found in a prehistoric site called Tin Felki in West Africa has been shown to be identical to precious stones used by Fula women today as fertility charms. Even stronger evidence links the practices of the ancient rock artists of South Africa and the religion of the people commonly referred to as Bushmen. Most observers believe that the rock art and engravings of southern Africa were made by the ancestors of the Bushmen.

The Bushmen, or Khoisan, were hunters and gatherers who made their living off the land. A number of paintings found widely in the South African region show scenes suggestive of the trance-dances that are still practiced by some contemporary Bushmen. In these dances the dancers enter into an altered state of consciousness by evoking the spirit of powerful animals. Dancers are thus spiritually energized and often feel they have the power of healing touch in their hands. Based on his observations of such rituals, the South African rock art specialist David Lewis-Williams has developed a theory that all the early rock art in the world involved some elements of trance. Other analysts have shown how particular rock paintings reflect concerns about fertility or were expressions of hunting magic.

Two of the most important figures in the religion of the contemporary Khoisan are Mantis and Eland. Mantis is a trickster god who is capable of transforming himself into other life forms. Eland, a favorite of Mantis, is also thought to have special spiritual potency. It is the spirit of the eland antelope, in particular, that contemporary trance-dancers seek to encounter in their altered states of consciousness. Significantly, eland paintings are commonly featured in ancient South African rock art.

Polytheistic Religions

Civilizations with kings, queens, and other ranks of nobility often have a religion that is also divided into different ranks of gods and spirit beings. Religions with a hierarchy of gods and an elaborate mythology about their activities are called polytheistic religions. The complete list of the gods of a polytheistic religion is called its pantheon. The ancient Egyptians practiced a polytheistic religion with a very elaborate pantheon. Many other African peoples were also pantheistic, though their pantheons varied. In reference to contemporary times, it has been observed that those African religions that are pantheistic also have a supreme being who is all powerful, but distant from human affairs. The lesser divinities are merely manifestations of the absolute powers of the supreme being. Not enough is known to say for sure how long this has been a general African belief.

Complex early civilization, such as that of Egypt, necessarily depended on rich agricultural production, but farming was not the only way to develop social complexity. In the African Sahel, on the southern fringe of the Sahara, at about the same time that Egyptian civilization was developing, a way of life called pastoralism began. Pastoralism is based on the herding of cattle and other livestock, and it has survived through the centuries into modern times. Cattle, because they are the key source of life, necessarily play a prominent role in the religions of pastoralists. For example, they may be sacrificed as a ritual offering or gift to the gods or to the ancestors. There is evidence of animal sacrifice from the very earliest period of pastoralism. Early pastoralists left small stone and earthen monuments in various locations across the Sahel and the Sahara, some of them associated with animal bones. (In earlier times, the Sahara was wetter and thus could support this pastoralist way of life.) In Niger and Chad archaeologists have discovered evidence of cattle sacrifices that are approximately 7,000 years old.

Not all the monuments associated with the pastoralists of this region and time period had to do simply with cattle; some clearly had other functions. One of the most notable sites of African prehistory is Nabta Playa, a ceremonial center located in southern Egypt near the border with Sudan and Libya. Among its monuments stands a small circle of stones that was aligned to face the north and south on one axis and the axis traversed by the sun as it rose across the sky on the longest day of the year, the summer solstice. This is said to be one of the world's earliest circular astronomical monuments, predating Stonehenge by many centuries.

Limestone stela with images of the goddess Tanit (first century C.E.), from Carthage (modern-day Tunisia); such stelae were set up over burial urns containing the cremated bodies of babies, small children, and animals sacrificed to the goddess. (© The Trustees of the British Museum)

Burials have been found in Sudan that date from the Neolithic period, from around 7,000 years to 4,000 years before our era. The dead were buried wearing adornments such as ostrich eggshell beads, with their bodies painted with red or yellow ocher. During their lifetimes, people from this era also commonly had their teeth filed, probably as a marker of adult status or for some other ritual purpose. This custom was practiced widely in North Africa and was also known to have been practiced in Kenya.

The religion of the ancient Nubians of southern Egypt and northern Sudan appears to have some association with the religion of Sahelian peoples, as well as that of the Egyptians to their north. At Karmah, the first Nubian center and the oldest urban site yet found in Africa, there are round tumuli with cattle sacrifices that appear similar to those constructed by the pastoralists. But the people of the kingdom of Karmah elaborated upon these practices and took them in their own direction. During the height of its power (ca. 1700–1550 B.C.E.), a massive mud-brick temple with an area of some 1,700 square yards dominated the city skyline. Nearby, powerful kings were buried in huge mounds. One of the largest of these measures nearly 300 feet around. The king was accompanied in death by nearly 400 of his subjects. They appear to have been sacrificed and buried in the king's grave in order to serve him in the next world. They were not simply ordinary people, but archers interred with their bows and valuables such as semiprecious stones, bronze mirrors, and jewelry.

At the end of Egypt's New Kingdom (ca. 1550–ca. 1070 B.C.E.), in the first millennium B.C.E., the Nubian kingdom of Kush came to power. Its rulers would become the pharaohs of all Egypt, forming the Twenty-fifth Dynasty (ca. 712–ca. 657 B.C.E.). During this time their most important shrines were located in Upper Nubia in and around Napata, a town situated along the Nile to the south of old Karmah. For centuries Napata had been the southernmost outpost of Egyptian rule, and the New Kingdom pharaoh Thutmose III had constructed on the nearby sacred mountain of Jebel Barkal a temple to the mystical god Amon. This was a crucial event in Nubian religious history because it led to the spread of Egyptian religion among the Nubian people.

The Nubian pharaohs of the Twenty-fifth Dynasty looked to both Egypt and to their own traditions. To show their connection to ancient Egypt, for example, they revived the practice of pyramid building, but on a smaller scale and in a different style than had been seen during the Old Kingdom (ca. 2575–ca. 2134 B.C.E.). Still, the continued loyalty of these pharaohs to Nubia is demonstrated by the fact that all of their pyramids and the burial sites associated with them were located in their homeland, not far away in Lower Egypt, where their kingdom had also to be administered. Nubians also interpreted the god Amon in their own way, particularly emphasizing his form as a powerful ram. Similarly, the Nubian lion god was emphasized as their protector. Indeed, despite the cultural influences of Egypt, Nubians retained their own distinct cultural identity and practices throughout the centuries.

After the Nubians lost control of Egypt as a result of their military defeat in the first decade of the sixth century B.C.E., their capital shifted farther to the south of Napata, to the city of Meroë. Here their beliefs and customs would survive and be transformed. Temples near Meroë that are dedicated to the Nubian lion god Apedemak still stand. It is here in the period between the fourth century B.C.E. and the first century C.E. that the brick pyramids of the Nubian kings were constructed. Archaeologists have also found large statues of rams there. Some scholars have suggested that in this period a Nubian-inspired veneration of the sacred ram spread widely across the continent, influencing religious worship among such diverse people as the Libyan Berbers, the Fon of Benin, and the Yoruba of Nigeria.

Much still remains to be learned about the early religious practices of western Africa. Undoubtedly, one important center of Iron Age culture was that around the Nigerian town of Nok. Here terra-cotta sculpture and iron goods have been found ranging across a 700-year time span starting approximately from 500 B.C.E. The most famous of the sculptures are human heads and faces that were originally part of entire bodies. While their religious or ritual meaning and use are not known, it has been suggested that they are connected to the religious practices of later peoples, possibly the Yoruba. The Yoruba people say that their city of Ife was the center of creation. Here the supreme being Oludumare (Owner of Endless Space) sent an assistant down from heaven to create land from a watery chaos. The first dry land to emerge was called Ife.

The religion of the Akan people of Ghana is also known to have very deep roots, with possible connections to a more regional pantheism. For example, there are similarities between the mother goddess Tanit of the North African city of Carthage and the Akan goddess, Mother of the High God Nyame, both of whom are said to have given birth to the universe. The Yoruba, too, have a goddess who brought order to the world through the release of *ase*, her spiritual power that activated the world's creative energy.

As mentioned previously, it is quite common for African religious traditions to depict a supreme being who is somewhat remote from everyday human affairs. While this view of God can be found prominently in kingdoms, it is also found among pastoralists such as the East African pastoralists, the Nuer and Dinka. The fact that it also typifies much of the traditional religions of southern African societies, whether kingdoms or not, also suggests that this perspective is one of considerable antiquity.

There are varieties of accounts of how the remoteness of God came to be. In one version told by the Akan of Ghana it is said that God and humans once lived so very close together that people could stretch out their hands to touch him. This changed one day after an old woman began to pound her grain vigorously to make porridge, using a mortar and a long pestle. The problem was that, with God being so close, she hit him every time she pounded. Consequently, God was forced to move farther and farther away until he was high in the sky and no longer in reach of her pounding. While details vary, it is a common theme in African traditional religion that God was once close but was driven away by human actions.

Monotheism

Archaeological evidence from the Middle East and Africa indicates that polytheistic forms of religion are associated with the most ancient civilizations. Monotheism, particularly when it means the worship of a single god to the exclusion of other gods that also exist, appears to be a more recent development. The conflicts between monotheism and polytheism are described in the Hebrew Bible. As the Bible relates it, even the faithful Jews often turned away from God to worship one or another of the gods of their neighbors.

The story that most stands out about Egypt in biblical narrative is the story given in Exodus about Moses and the liberation of Egypt's Jewish slaves. In contrast to the Bible's version of events, Egyptians circulated a different story of a rebellious man they called Moses. Although it is known only in fragmentary form, in the Egyptian account Moses is described as a heretic against the Egyptian faith and a rebel who led a revolt of outcaste lepers against the state. No mention is made of Judaism.

In Ethiopia the biblical narrative of the ancient Jewish king Solomon and the queen of Sheba (also called Makeda) has taken on great significance. According to legend, the king of Ethiopia's Amhara people is said to be the direct descendant of Menelik, a child from a liaison between the Egyptian queen and the Jewish king. Written accounts of this story date back at least to the 13th century B.C.E., but it is not known how long it may have existed in oral tradition.

Ethiopia also has been home to more ordinary people who claim deep Jewish roots; among them are the Beta Israel, most of whom emigrated from Ethiopia to Israel in the late 1980s and early 1990s of the 20th century C.E. Although there are different accounts of the details, their oral traditions suggest their ancestors were of the House of Dan, one of the Lost Tribes of Israel. Africans with Jewish links are found in other parts of Africa, as far away from the Middle East as South Africa. In South Africa claims of Jewish ancestry by the Lemba people have recently been confirmed by DNA tests.

Christianity in North Africa and Ethiopia goes back nearly to the beginning of the religion. According to traditional accounts, Egypt's first church was founded by one of the 12 disciples of Jesus—Mark. The Ethiopian kingdom of Axum adopted Christianity as a state religion in the early fourth century, and the religion continues to be Ethiopia's main religion. The city of Axum's fourth-century church,

Saint Mary of Zion, is said to house the chest that contains the original Ten Commandments, the sacred Ark of the Covenant. This city is also known for having some of the tallest and most beautiful obelisks of the ancient world.

EGYPT

BY KELLY-ANNE DIAMOND REED

Religion permeated all aspects of ancient Egyptian society, and there was no separation between church and state. The disciplines of science, magic, and what the Western world terms *religion* all functioned as one. There was no canon, nor was there any form of revelation. Because there was no set doctrine for the ancient Egyptians, there were many contrasting and contradictory ideas and concepts. This did not seem to trouble the Egyptians, who never took the time to systematize all of their beliefs. Instead, it was perceived as quite normal to consider, for example, Horus and Seth as both nephew and uncle and brothers at the same time. It seems that logic did not play a role in Egyptian religious practices.

EGYPTIAN GODS

The ancient Egyptians had a pantheon of gods. These gods could be conceived of separately or in dyads (two deities), triads (three deities), ogdoads (eight gods), or enneads (nine gods). Horus and Seth, Osiris and Isis, and Isis and Nephthys are three examples of a dyad. These pairs of divinities regularly complemented each other and are innately connected. Likewise, sometimes a god or goddess was created to form a balanced, sexually paired couple, such as Sesha and Seshat.

Triads often take the form of a family, including father, mother, and child: for example, Ptah, Sakhmet, and Nefertum; Amun, Mut, and Khonsu; and Osiris, Isis, and Horus. Additionally, one god could have a variety of forms. For instance, the sun god manifests in the following three forms: Khepri, Ra, and Atum. Khepri is the form of the sun god when he is the sun disk rising in the eastern sky, the dawning sun. Ra is the form of the sun god in the middle of the day. Atum is the aspect of the solar deity that appears as the evening sun.

Ra may be considered Egypt's most important deity. He was a universal god, and most of Egypt's major divinities were associated with him at one point or another. Ra played five major roles in Egyptian theology: on earth, in heaven, in the underworld, in creation myths, and as divine father and protector of the king. The cult of Ra is first seen in the Second Dynasty (ca. 2770–ca. 2649 B.C.E.), where his name is included in personal names. Likewise, in the Fourth Dynasty (ca. 2575–ca. 2465 B.C.E.) the kings took the epithet "Son of Ra." By the Fifth Dynasty (ca. 2465–ca. 2323 B.C.E.) Ra was firmly established as the state god, and Heliopolis was his cult center.

The number 8 was seen as potent in Egyptian theology. Sometimes the eight deities were not named, which demonstrates that the number was of more importance than the deity. Often the eight divinities consisted of four pairs and at other times as two sets of four. The so-called Hermopolis Ogdoad was one of the most important ogdoads, consisting of eight primeval gods: Nun and Nunet (water), Heh and Hehet (infinity), Keku and Kekut (darkness), and Tenem and Tanemet (invisibility or wind). In the New Kingdom (ca. 1550–ca. 1070 B.C.E.) Amun and Amenet replaced the last pair.

The Egyptian ennead refers to nine gods. The Egyptians had numerous enneads, including the Great Ennead, the Lesser Ennead, and the Dual Ennead. The number 9 represented a large amount of something. The Ennead of Heliopolis was one of the more significant enneads, which consisted of Atum, Shu, Tefnut, Geb, Nut, Osiris, Isis, Seth, and Nephthys. Atum was envisaged as the father, while the rest were seen as the subsequent generations. In addition to the groupings, some gods, such as Amun and Ra, were combined to be one god, Amun-Ra, through a process of syncretism.

Each of the gods' names can be translated by either a word or a phrase. For example, Hathor means "mansion of Horus," Isis means "the seat/throne," Amun is "the hidden one," and Atum is "the complete one." The meaning of some divine names is clear, but the meaning of others remains a mystery. There were also local gods who had been connected with specific villages from time immemorial. These early associations can be seen in the examples of personal names that include the names of a divinity.

CREATION MYTHS

Different creation myths in Egypt account for the existence of the world. Unfortunately, the funerary texts do not give detailed accounts of the myths but were used to help the deceased ascend to the afterlife. Certain excerpts from the Pyramid Texts, Coffin Texts, and Book of the Dead, among other sources, reveal some of the ideas the Egyptians held about the creation of the world.

The Pyramid Texts were first inscribed on the inside walls of the pyramids of some late Old Kingdom (ca. 2575–2134 B.C.E.) kings and queens. With the democratization of religion beginning at the end of the Old Kingdom, this corpus of utterances was transferred to the private sphere. In the Middle Kingdom (ca. 2040–1640 B.C.E.) the Coffin Texts emerged, consisting of a series of spells inscribed on coffins. The Coffin Texts are directly related to the earlier Pyramid Texts. During the New Kingdom the evolution of this group of texts appears in the form of the Book of the Dead. This book was written on papyri and was included among the grave goods in private burials; there are also some royal examples. Likewise appearing during the New Kingdom are various other books concerning the afterlife, such as the Amduat, the Book of Gates, and the Book of Caverns. These funerary texts are laden with mythological allusions, indicating that mythic stories were culturally important and demonstrating that both royal and private persons were familiar with the mythic traditions, possibly through oral means.

Different creation myths were formed at different theological centers. For example, the ennead was the focus of the creation myth that developed at the cult center of Heliopolis during the Old Kingdom. Atum, the "complete one," was first created alone in the Nun, or the watery abyss. There are a variety of ways in which his progeny were spawned, including masturbation, coughing, spitting, or sweating. Atum's successive generations make up the air (Shu), moisture (Tefnut), earth (Geb), and sky (Nut).

During the Middle Kingdom the ogdoad was the focus of the Hermopolis creation myth. The Hermopolis Ogdoad was made up of four frog-headed gods and four snake-headed goddesses. These were the primeval deities and were symbolic of the chaotic waters in which the world was created. Together they formed the original mound, lotus flower, or egg that existed prior to the sun god's birth. In a different version of the creation myth from the New Kingdom, Ptah (the creator god) was said to have fashioned the gods and human beings on his potter's wheel. Thebes, which was the cult center for the god Amun during the New Kingdom, embraced yet a different idea about how the world was created.

The Egyptians viewed the world as consisting of the earth and the sky. The earth was said to be the god Geb, while the sky was the goddess Nut. Funerary contexts often display the goddess Nut arching her body in imitation of the sky. Her rear was in the east and her head in the west. She would swallow the sun every evening, it would pass through her body, and she would give birth to the sun every morning. Shu was thought to hold up the sky. He also created the eight Heh gods to hold up Nut in her bovine form. Additionally, the earth was seen as masculine, while the sky was perceived as feminine. Anything that was not the earth or sky was considered the Duat, or netherworld. Many myths surround the original creator god. One version suggests that he was a great falcon who came forth from an egg; another proposes that he emerged from the great lotus flower that was in the Nun. Yet another version posits the existence of a primeval mound that appeared out of the Nun.

The Coffin Texts and the Book of Gates, among others, explain that humankind came from tears (from different gods, depending on the source). One Hymn to Amun states that Atum was responsible for the creation of everything that exists—"from whose eyes men came forth and from whose mouth gods came about." Likewise, he distinguished them by their character, created their life, and differentiated them from one another by the color of their skin. The Hymn to Aten states that this god "created the earth according to (his) wish, when (he) was alone, consisting of mankind, cattle, and all flocks." A document called the Instructions to Merikare explains that humankind was made in the image of god.

Other Religious Myths

Numerous popular myths recount interactions between the gods. *The Contendings of Horus and Seth*, for example, tells of the struggle between the gods Horus and Seth for the vacant position of king of Egypt that was left by the passing of Osiris, the god of death, resurrection, and fertility. In the end, Horus is victorious and assumes the office of his father. This story replicates the fashion in which a son would succeed his father as king of Egypt. Likewise, the living king was seen as the incarnation of Horus, while the dead king was imagined as Osiris. This story takes place entirely in the world of the gods.

Another example of a popular myth is *The Destruction of Mankind*, which also forms a portion of the *Book of the Heavenly Cow* inscribed in some New Kingdom tombs. In this myth the sun god Ra is angry with humankind for plotting rebellion against him. The major theme presented here is similar to that found in the biblical story of Noah's Ark and the flood: human wickedness and god's wrath. Further examples of popular myth consist of the *Secret Name of Ra*, the *Myth of Isis and Osiris*, and the *Myth of Horus at Edfu*.

Priests

The ancient Egyptian priest was not at all similar to the Christian idea of a priest. He did not preach to the masses and was not responsible for the spiritual well-being of the populace. He had a very specific job, and that was to maintain the cult of the god. This was, in fact, the job of the king; however, the king delegated this duty to the priesthood. The king was the one who needed to maintain the world as the gods had defined it; this also meant keeping the gods active through the maintenance of their cults. If the gods were happy, then Egypt would flourish. The priests were responsible for clothing the god, feeding the god, anointing the god, and other physical jobs that served the deity. This is why they were called the servants of the gods. Greek authors mistakenly called them prophets.

The physical presence of the gods existed only in the temples, which were not available to the masses as places of worship. They were the homes of the gods and allowed only limited access. The ancient Egyptian temple was made up of various pylons and courts that led to the holy of holies where the cult statue stood. A well-preserved example of an ancient Egyptian temple stands at Idfu and dates to the Ptolemaic Period (ca. 304–30 B.C.E.). A large pylon stands at the front. Next one walks into the forecourt; then the pronaos, or outer entrance hall; the great pillared hall, which is flanked by auxiliary rooms; the hall of offerings; the central hall; and finally the sanctuary, or the holy of holies. Outer rooms surround the last three halls. These rooms have names like the Mansion of the Prince, Throne of the Gods, Mansion of Linen, and Chapel of Hathor. The entire temple complex was surrounded by a great wall. In general, the scenes on temple walls progress from public scenes, such as the king in battle, to scenes of the king's private relationship with the gods and the performance of cult rituals. The priests' job was to protect the deity who was located in the holy of holies. As one penetrated the inner rooms of the temple, the floors rose and the ceiling lowered so the focus was on the cult statue alone.

A priest had to undergo certain rites prior to being considered pure. Purifications in the form of a bath took place in the sacred lake belonging to the temple. Certain texts suggest that this was performed twice each day and twice each night while a priest was on duty. If there was no sacred lake, then another water source was used. Additionally, priests were required to rinse their mouths with a salt solution consisting of natron (a form of salts from dried lake beds) and water. Likewise, priests had to shave their bodily hair. There is also evidence to support the shaving of eyebrows and eyelashes.

Another ritual performed for the sake of cleanliness was circumcision, but this does not seem to have been a universal practice among Egyptian men. Once a priest began his work, however, he had to undergo the procedure. In the later periods this was a characteristic mark of a priest. Ancient Egyptian priests did not have to be celibate; however, they could not copulate in the temple and had to abstain from sex for a few days prior to beginning work in the temple. Priests did take wives and have families. Some priests even took more than one wife, though this was uncommon.

According to Greek and Roman sources, there were many dietary restrictions for priests. In actuality, the prohibited foods were not quite as numerous as the later sources would have one believe. Dietary rules depended on which deity the priest served. For example, if one worked in the hare nome, or province, and the hare was the sacred animal of that area, then one would not consume that sacred animal. Ancient sources reveal that some would eat the sacred animal of the neighboring nome in order to be unpleasant.

Finally, priests could not wear wool. Since this material came from living animals it would pollute the sacred areas within the temple. This, however, was not the case with panther skin, which was the characteristic garb for the high priests. Other distinguishing outfits worn by the priests consist of a sash for the lector priests (those who spoke the ritual texts in the temples), a "skin spangled with stars" for the priests of Heliopolis, and a special collar for the priests of Memphis, who would also wear their hair in a side lock. All priests wore palm sandals. This proved to be an item of prestige in a society where people walked barefoot.

There were four ways for one to become a priest: hereditary right, royal appointment, co-optation, and purchase. It was the tradition for a son to take over his father's post. In ancient Egypt there were priestly dynasties consisting of numerous generations of priests who served the same deity. These families grew close to their god and gained significant local power. Since all priests were theoretically supposed to be royally appointed, a particular royal appointment could always trump a hereditary rite. Usually the king had far greater matters to worry about than who would fill the vacant office within a temple, especially within the smaller temples. The king would intervene in only two scenarios: when he wanted to reward a particular person with a special post or when he needed to curb the power of a particular priestly dynasty by importing an outsider to a high-ranking post. In general, the organization of the smaller temples was performed on the local level. If there was a vacant position, the committee of clergy would nominate someone to fill it. This committee probably approved the appointing of any new priest, even when the post was passed from father to son. The last way that one could become a priest was by purchasing the office. There is much evidence for this practice in the later periods, though it is known to exist as early as the Middle Kingdom.

There were different classes of priests, but it is difficult for the modern scholar to understand the hierarchy of the priestly class. Certain types of priests were more or less important in different temples. There was probably also a variation over time. Some of the largest temples, such as the temple of Amun at Karnak, had a separate staff of administrators. In the smaller temples the administrative jobs, like counting and recording the agricultural products, were done by the same people who performed the purely ritual activities. It was possible for a temple to possess fields, gardens, and animals, all of which contributed to its wealth. The temple staff was paid through these agricultural yields. The amount of property owned by a particular temple was directly related to its income level and therefore the number of staff it could support. For example, the temple of Amun at Karnak had 81,322 personnel, the temple in Heliopolis had 12,963, and the temple of Ptah at Memphis had 3,079. These were three of the largest and most important temples in Egypt. It is thought that a modest temple would have anywhere from 10 to 25 personnel. Some temples, however, lacked a financial source of their own and had only one or two clergy members.

There were high clergy and low clergy. The high clergy, or priestly elite, consisted of four levels of "prophets" (mistranslated by the Greeks). There was also a fifth level of prophet, but these priests did not seem to have been included in the ranks of the high clergy. The first four levels of prophets were strictly servants of the god and acted in the same manner as a personal servant would act, taking care of the owner of the house—in this case, the god. The office of first prophet was the highest priestly title, especially in the case of the wealthiest temples. The first prophet was also called the high priest and had many political duties as well as religious ones. The second prophet was the second in command and often took the place of the high priest in the temple when other duties interfered. There was only one first prophet and only one second prophet in each temple. In the case of the temple of Amun, the second prophet had many workers underneath him. It was his job to manage his subordinates and oversee such tasks as making sure the administration ran smoothly, receiving tribute, and overseeing the workshops. Royal favor played a major role in advancement within the priesthood. It was possible for one to work his way up, but other factors came into play as well.

The low clergy were essentially assistants. They were called pure ones and helped the other clergy members with the cult rituals. These priests performed such functions as slaughtering animals for sacrifice, interpreting dreams, carrying sacred objects, and supervising secular workers. In addition to the clergy members, numerous lay people helped the temple function properly.

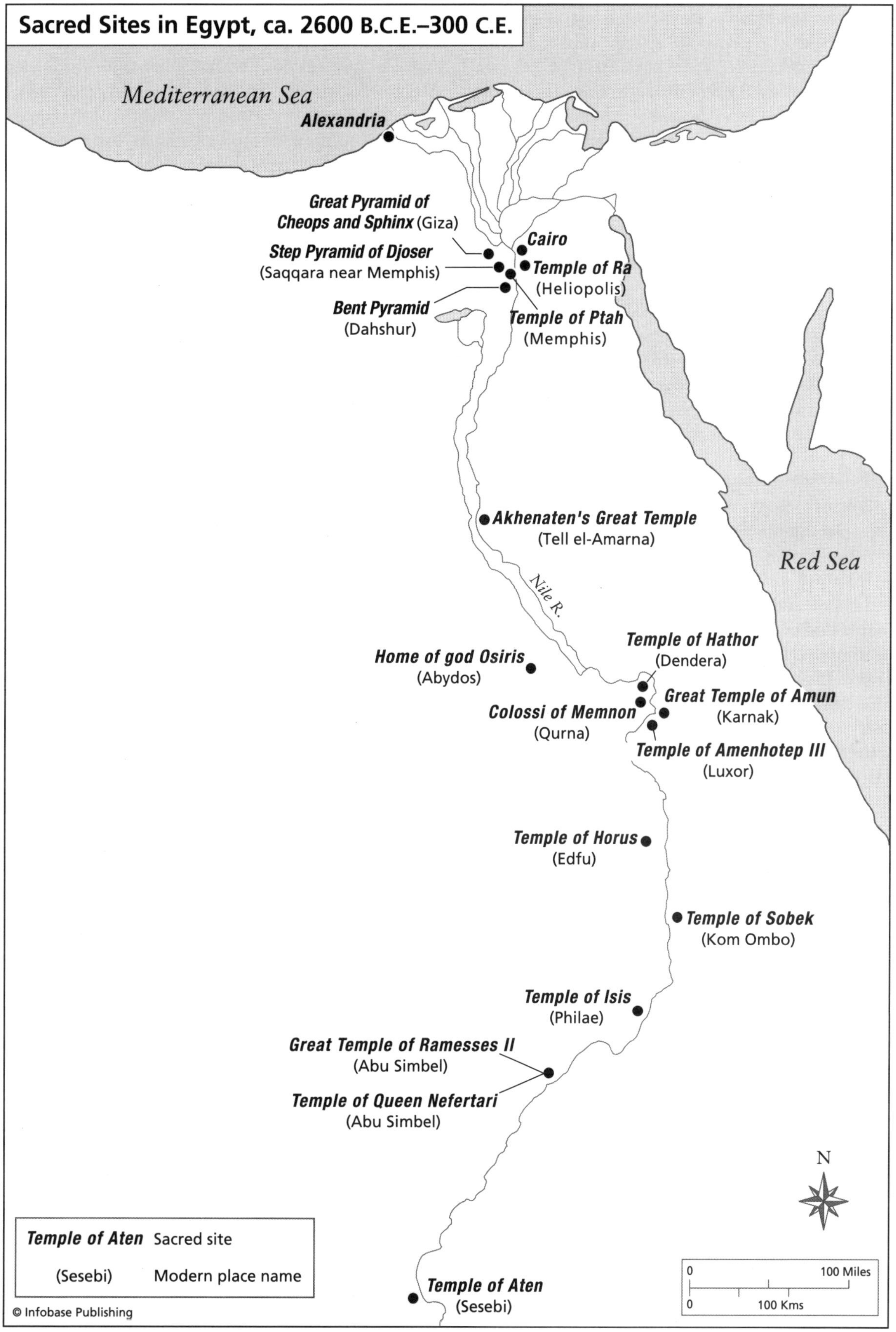

The idea of religion permeated all aspects of ancient Egyptian society.

Fitting somewhere between the high and low clergy were the specialists, those who performed specific functions with the cult. Some temples ranked their specialists in the higher class, while others ranked them in the lower class. These specialists include the stolist, who dressed the divine statue; the academics of the House of Life, who prepared the religious works necessary to the functioning of the cult; the lectors, who were not always priests but could function as funerary ritualists, learned scribes, popular magicians, or scientists; the hour priests who serve as astronomers; the horoscope priests who were calendrical specialists; and musicians and singers of both sexes.

Among the priests were permanent priests and priests who alternated in groups. The groups were called *phyles*. There were four *phyles*, each of which consisted of the same number of priests who performed the same functions in the temple. Each *phyle* worked three months a year; each month of work was separated by two months of freedom.

Religious Rituals

A variety of events took place in conjunction with the ancient Egyptian temple: foundation rituals, daily rituals, festivals, and oracles. Foundation rituals were performed by the king as early as the third millennium B.C.E. The scenes from the late temples at Isna and Kom Ombo show the king performing these same foundation rites. The scenes appear to depict the following events. The king leaves his palace and arrives at the temple site. The king and a goddess hammer in two posts to determine the orientation of the temple. Next a hole is dug to water level to make the structure sturdy. Then bricks are molded at the four corners of the temple, and the foundation is filled with sand. There is a presentation of plaques made of a variety of materials such as gold, silver, copper, and stone. Finally the temple is ready to be built, and chalk is sprinkled on a model temple for purification purposes. At the end there is a symbolic delivering of the temple to the god it will house.

Included in the daily rituals were the morning ritual, which comprised the morning song, the opening of the shrine, and the care of the god (divine repast and toilette). The midday ritual was shorter: The priests sprinkled water and burned incense for the other gods worshipped in the temple. The evening service was a repetition of the morning service except that the sanctuary remained closed. This service took place simultaneously in all temples in Egypt.

Numerous festivals and processions were associated with the temple. Ancient calendars indicate that the god would be taken on procession from five to 10 times each month. Sometimes the god would be in the sacred bark (a small boat), but other times it would not. Examples of some of the festivals are the Festival of the Valley, the Festival of the Nile, and the Festival of Drunkenness. Some festivals involved the public, and others were conducted in secrecy.

In the New Kingdom the consultation of oracles became popular. The priests acted as intermediaries in these matters. Oracles by statues, divine barques, prophetic voices, dreams, and animals were some of the many ways that people accessed the divine. Divine oracles were also supposed to decide legal matters. This was done at the temple gate. The ancient texts state that the gate was the place to hear petitions and tell truth from falsehood. Unfortunately, there is not enough documentation to allow the modern scholar to understand the fine workings of this religious justice system.

THE MIDDLE EAST

BY BRADLEY SKEEN

The religions of the ancient Near East bound together their societies, creating a religious culture and patterns of thought quite unlike those of modern Western civilization. The sacred writings of the Near Eastern religions are among the oldest and greatest classics of world literature. Their interactions gave rise to Judaism and thereby also to the other two modern monotheistic faiths of Christianity and Islam.

Prehistory

By the end of the last ice age hunter-gatherer communities of the so-called Natufian culture (ca. 12,000–ca. 10,000 B.C.E.) in what is today Palestine and Israel already buried their dead with considerable care, accompanied by grave offerings (weaponry and personal adornments), suggesting some level of concern with an afterlife. In the Neolithic (ca. 8000 B.C.E.) the inhabitants of Near Eastern villages, such as Çatalhüyük in eastern Turkey or Jericho in Palestine, further developed a cult of the dead and the veneration of animals that were believed to embody magical or supernatural powers, such as wild aurochs, gazelles, and mountain goats. Horned headdresses, indicating the possibility of shamanistic behavior, are illustrated in early symbolic images on painted pottery and seals.

Mesopotamia

The first cities were founded in Mesopotamia. A place like Uruk was not just many times larger than a village but also had a different social organization. The agricultural surplus created by farming the land watered by the great rivers of Mesopotamia, the Tigris and Euphrates, allowed some people to stop working merely for their own food and survival and become specialists: kings and aristocrats in governance, soldiers in warfare, artisans in building, and priests in religion. Large building complexes, often called *temples* in Western literature, were, in fact, the households of individual deities, managed by stewards whom we usually denote by the term *priest* or *priestess*. Large landholdings; workshops for pottery manufacture, metallurgy, weaving, and other crafts; and enormous agricultural enterprises supported the household of each deity. The king was both the human master of the society and the intercessor with the divine on the part of its human subjects. Although ancient Mesopotamian societies were polytheistic, each city had a major god or goddess, who was worshipped alongside a host of minor ones.

Mesopotamians had no hope of any kind of reward of eternal life or paradise. During life each person was under the protection of a kind of guardian angel (personal god). It was generally believed that after death the ghost of a person journeyed to a dark place under the earth, the Land of No Return, and continued forever in a fitful slumber. There were no exceptions. Even the great king of Sumer, Gilgamesh (r. ca. 2600 B.C.E), according to the mythological epic named after him, spent much of life in quest of eternal life but discovered that all of his hopes were vain and that human beings received no reward other than the brief pleasures of life on earth. The afterlife was no paradise, but the deceased needed to be provided with various grave goods to ease the journey into the netherworld, and periodic rituals had to be performed at the grave of the deceased long after his death. The form of burial mattered little—kings received large, elaborate tombs, while commoners might be buried in a simple pit covered with a reed mat—but the proper funerary rites were necessary in all cases. If the rites were neglected, the shade of the deceased might come back to haunt the living, wandering restlessly for all eternity.

A Mesopotamian temple or "house of a god" was often grander than a royal palace. The images of the gods in the temples were dressed in the finest clothes and adorned with gold and jewels. Each day the gods went through the same kind of schedule as the king, being dressed and undressed for various activities, eating (sacrifices), enjoying entertainments (hymns), and hearing petitions (prayers). Periodic festivals saw the gods (in the form of their statues) moved around the city or even between cities, attending entertainments such as athletic competitions and festivals. One of the greatest calamities that could befall a conquered city was the removal of the cult statue of the city's chief deity. Numerous cases are documented in ancient Near Eastern sources. Moreover, such an occurrence carried a double penalty. The fact that a deity had abandoned his or her city showed that the city and its inhabitants had fallen out of favor with the god or goddess. The absence of the deity brought ruination and desolation to the populace. The return of the cult statue—examples include the statue of Marduk, chief deity of Babylon, taken to Susa in southwestern Iran by the Elamites—offered the king responsible for such an act the opportunity to proclaim his righteousness, piety, and paternal pride in delivering is people from such a scourge.

Animal sacrifice was common. The animals offered in sacrifice had to be pure or perfect, meaning young and healthy. Typically, bulls, goats, or sheep were used, the same animals commonly eaten by people. The animals would be decorated with ribbons and ornaments and led to the god's temple in a joyous procession, with the people singing hymns and dancing. A lock of the animal's hair would be cut off and burned. Then the animal would be led outside to a place of sacrifice and slaughtered. The most divine organs in Mesopotamian estimation, such as the liver and gallbladder, would be returned to the god wrapped in fat, sliced, and served on bread like a human meal. These organs would be completely burned for the enjoyment of the god. The bulk of the meat would be served as a stew to the participants in the sacrifice. Especially at a festival, when as many as a thousand animals were sacrificed, this could amount to quite an abundance of food, and its distribution would become a type of charity to the poor, who might obtain meat in no other way. The hide of the animal was given to the butcher and cooks who had performed the sacrifice on behalf of the king and other priests. In unusual circumstances, when there was a special reason to solicit the god or for great thanksgiving, the entire animal might be burned and in this way offered directly to the god.

Mesopotamians believed that nature was to be understood on the model of language. Metaphor is a figure of speech by which we say that one thing resembles another. One might say that a thunderstorm is like the raging of an angry king or that the feeling of love is like a beautiful woman. For ancient people that kind of explanation seemed a reasonable way to describe reality. So a thunderstorm is the raging of a storm god like the Babylonian Marduk, and love is a goddess like Ishtar (Semitic equivalent to the Sumerian goddess Innana). The ancients saw divinity everywhere: in the statues of the gods in the temples, in the planets in the night sky, in the signs found by examining the livers of sheep sacrificed to the gods, or wherever one sees majesty or love in the world. It did not occur to them to think of the name of a thing as arbitrary; rather they thought it was the thing itself. Hence the world and its representation in language were equivalents, and manipulating one could manipulate the other. Therefore, they believed, prayers and spells could change the way things are or what might happen in the future.

In this worldview, writing and language ought to be able to control the world; it certainly did so for the tiny literate elite who used writing to monopolize wealth and political power through access to the law courts and government denied the illiterate masses. But language, especially written language, also controlled the world in another way in Mesopotamian myth. Everything the gods accomplished was done through spells. In myths their speech creates reality. When the Israelite god creates the universe in the biblical book of Genesis, he does so through the power of language, speaking commands that become instantly real: "Let there be light! And there was light."

Mesopotamian myth both mirrored contemporary culture on a higher plane and explained the existence of that culture. It had a tremendous impact on the beliefs of younger civilizations such as Greece or Israel. The *Enûma Elish*, or *Epic of Creation*, was sung at the New Year's festival in Babylon. It extols the Babylonian god Marduk at the highest level of divinity. Its account of Creation as moving from an undifferentiated primal cosmos to the final order of the world we see around us populated by human beings is thought by many scholars to be the basis for the account of Creation in the first chapter of Genesis. Its description of the generations of gods fighting among themselves and against monsters for cosmic supremacy is generally thought to have been the inspiration for the Greek creation myth in Hesiod's *Theogony*.

The epic is essentially the history of a family or royal dynasty. The preexisting universe within which the gods act is the *apsu*, or cosmic water. Nothing else exists, but when names are assigned, Creation begins to assume order. The first divinity, Tiamat (or saltwater), gives birth to the other gods, whose king is Enlil. Annoyed by her offspring, Tiamat decides to wipe them out and start again with a new race of gods. Enlil feels impotent to oppose his mother, but the young god Marduk comes forward to champion the divinities. After Marduk defeats Tiamat, he splits her body in two and uses half of it to build the vault of heaven over the waters, in which he creates the stars and orderes the constellations and the zodiac, fixing the ordered progression of time. From the other half he makes the surface of the world floating above the *apsu*.

The Akkadian myth of Atrahasis, which dates to about 1750 B.C.E., describes the formation of humankind. At the beginning of the myth the great gods are served by lesser gods, who give them food and drink and dress and house them (doing for the great gods precisely what priests did for the cult statues of the gods in temples). But the lesser gods come to resent their subservient role and refuse to continue. As a result, the gods actually suffer hunger and thirst. Enki, the "wise man" among the gods, solves the problem. He produces human beings as a new race to serve the gods. Humans are made from clay (as in Genesis) and so can never hope to be divine, and yet they have a divine intelligence, because Enki sacrifices one of the lesser gods and infuses his blood into human beings.

In a passage closely echoed by the flood myth in Genesis, the gods descend to earth to found the Mesopotamian cities and to establish their own temples: to order human life by teaching all the arts of civilization. This works for a time. Because humans are so long-lived, the world soon becomes crowded with them, and their noise prevents Enlil, the king of the gods, from sleeping. So Enlil sends a great flood intended to wipe out humankind. Enki sees that the gods would suffer if humanity's service to them were ended and so instructs one, Atrahasis, to build an ark in which he and his family and pairs of all the animals would be saved from the flood. Because the gods suffer during the flood, Enlil permits humanity to exist but forces Enki to limit their numbers by creating demons to spread disease among them to shorten their lives and to kill infants. (About half of all children born in antiquity died before their fifth birthday.)

Atrahasis explains and justifies the relation between the powerful elites that ruled the ancient Near Eastern world and its masses of dependent farmers and laborers; it was like that of the gods' to humankind. It shows how myth was used to think about and solve problems in the ancient world.

The rule of the Mesopotamian gods over the world was by the power of a mythical book called the Tablets of Destiny. Because the destinies had been written down (preordained) by the gods all at once, it was possible to foretell events in the future. Signs and traces of what the gods had written could be read in nature (through divination) by a priest wise in the ways of the gods, called the *baru* or diviner. Everything in the world was studied by the diviner, especially anything unusual that called attention to itself (an omen): Gods communicated important matters to mortals through omens.

Sacrificial animals, typically sheep, were of special concern to the gods. The main art of the *baru* was to examine the internal organs of sheep at the time of sacrifice, especially the liver. They produced clay models of livers in which something like lines and columns of script were laid out over the organ as though it were a tablet; marks in any given area were interpreted as if they were a specific word with a meaning relevant to the future. In particular, one could ask of the gods through sacrifice whether some contemplated action was favorable or unfavorable and receive guidance about what could not be found out through mere reason. This kind of divination, while it seems unlikely to modern thinking, was impressive enough that it was enthusiastically taken up by the Greeks, Romans, and Persians.

One of the places where the gods were most manifest was in the sky, their home, in the form of stars and planets. So the motions of the planets were studied carefully to see what they might reveal about the divine will. By the first millennium B.C.E., when many traditions changed because Mesopotamia was conquered by foreign peoples—the Persians (539 B.C.E.) and then the Greeks under Alexander the Great (336 B.C.E)— the discovery that it was possible to predict the regular motions of the planets led to the belief that other kinds of prediction should be possible from observing the planets.

Since the gods were in charge of the universe, they were responsible for evil (reasonless human suffering). Disease and infant mortality were inflicted on humanity by the gods simply to keep the population down. In general, though, royal rule was used as a metaphor to explain misfortune. If someone violated the laws of a city, the king would punish him for his crime. In the same way, if someone violated any of the many divine laws that governed the universe and humanity, the gods would punish that person. The punishment was left in the hands of lesser spirits, who might well be called demons and who would inflict disease, defeat, or misfortune on human beings who had offended (sinned against) the gods. Naturally, these questions were always considered after the fact: In the midst of suffering, people would question why and would be conscious of having committed some sin or would remember the sin of a father or grandfather.

One could seek the cause of divine punishment and relief from it with the help of a special kind of priest, an exorcist. The exorcist would take something like a medical case history, ascertaining the nature of the "illness" from which the patient was suffering and what might have happened to have caused it. He would then consult manuals of exorcism (approximately 30,000 tablets of these documents survive, indicating how vast the literature and how widespread the practice of exorcism was) and find the right ritual to pay for the particular offense.

Sometimes the immediate cause of evil was thought to be a curse put on a person by a witch. The exorcists believed that a witch might be a person the patient had met in his daily life; at the same time, a witch was more like a demon than a human being. Witches lived either in the lifeless desert or among the dead in cemeteries. They could fly across the world in the space of a single night and had supernatural bodies that allowed them to enter a house through a locked door. This image of the witch as human and not human at the same time, a member of the community and a supernatural monster, was influential not only in Greece and Rome but also among later Christian societies. Witchcraft was outlawed in Mesopotamian law codes, but there is no certain instance of anyone known to have practiced witchcraft or of the prosecution of anyone for the crime of witchcraft; it served rather as an explanation for misfortune after the fact.

The Levant

The Levant (including parts of modern-day Syria, Lebanon, Jordan, and Israel-Palestine), received many cultural influences from Mesopotamia and Egypt. Libraries from cities on the border of the Levant and Mesopotamia, such as Ebla (destroyed ca. 2225 B.C.E.) and Mari (destroyed 1759 B.C.E.), tell us something about communication between the two areas. But the peoples of the Levant nevertheless made some of their own contributions as well. The Levantine storm god was a model for the Babylonian Marduk. The Levant was especially important for transmitting Near Eastern ideas and practices to Greece and to modern religions such as Judaism, Christianity, and Islam.

One distinctive feature of the religion of the Levant was the role of the storm god. While the fertility of the land in Mesopotamian came from the two great rivers, the Mediterranean coast was dependent on rain from thunderstorms coming in off the sea during the winter. Crops could then be planted and harvested in the spring. Summer was a dead time of the year when crops would not grow. As a consequence, the storm god was the most important figure in the Levantine pantheon, whether called, Hadad (Syrian), Yahweh (Israelite), by any other local name, or simply Lord (Baal).

Baal/Hadad's myth must have varied tremendously from city to city and tribe to tribe. We are fortunate to know it in detail from the version current in Ugarit, a city on the northern coast of present-day Syria. The city was destroyed about 1200 B.C.E., preserving the library of Ilimiku, the chief priest. The myth's three parts concern Baal's struggle for cosmic supremacy in succession to his grandfather El, who created the universe but no longer took a very active role in its governance. In the first part Baal defeats Yam, the god of the sea, together with his sea monsters Leviathan and Behemoth. Compare this to the winter thunderstorms to be seen at night over the Mediterranean from the Syrian coast.

The second part of the myth concerns the building of Baal's house. First, Baal must obtain permission from Asherah, El's wife. Then the house is built in the sky by the craftsman god Kothar-wa-Hasis. This "house" corresponds both to Baal's temple in Ugarit and to his dwelling place on Mount Saphon just outside the city.

In the third part of the myth Baal is dragged down to the land of the dead by its ruler Mot, but he is rescued by his sister, the virgin warrior Anat. She defeats Mot by a process identical to harvesting grain: she reaps him, winnows him, grinds him, and sows him back into the ground. Baal then returns triumphantly to heaven. It is not hard to see this episode in relation to the agriculturally dead Mediterranean summers, whose drought is defeated by the return of the winter thunderstorms.

In later times the traditional gods were worshipped under Greek and Roman names at prominent temples in the Levant, and their cults also spread throughout the Roman Empire. Local Levantine gods continued to thrive until the time of the Islamic conquest of the Near East in the seventh century C.E..

Persia

Persia (modern-day Iran), a country of Indo-European culture and language like Greece or Rome, conquered the Near East in the sixth century B.C.E. and, in particular, acted as the sponsor of Judaism in the return from the Babylonian captivity. The Persian religion was based on a text called the Avesta, written by the prophet Zoroaster (sometimes rendered as Zarathustra) and his disciples. The date span of Zoroaster's lifetime is unknown; while some scholars believe he lived around 1400 B.C.E., this remains speculative. Zoroastrianism is a "dualistic" religion. The prophet Zoroaster taught that the world was the scene of warfare between God (Ahura Mazda) and an evil power (Ahriman or Angra Mainyu) that wished to destroy the cosmic order. In the end god would triumph, and all the people who had ever lived would be resurrected (brought back to life) and judged with reward or punishment according to whether they had followed god or his enemy. Zoroaster also thought that the gods worshipped by other peoples were the demonic agents of Ahriman. It was believed that Zoroaster would be reborn at the end of time to play a vital role in the final triumph of good over evil.

Ahura Mazda was symbolized by light, so the main form of worship in Zoroastrianism was the maintenance of fire altars whose flames might be kept continuously burning for centuries. The priests who tended these fires and carried out other religious functions were called magi. They also kept Zoroastrian religious texts alive through memorization—these texts were written down only in later times when the very existence of the religion was threatened by the Islamic conquest of Persia in the seventh century c.e. The word magician comes from their name, because Greeks and Romans saw them as the embodiment of everything foreign and improper in religious terms. A small portion of Zoroastrians refused to convert to Islam, and their descendents continue to live in present-day Iran; others fled to India (particularly Mumbai, formerly called Bombay). These groups (about 250,000 in number) are called Parsis.

Israelite Religion and Judaism

The Hebrew Bible is the religious scripture of Judaism, which has survived continuously from its origins in the Bronze Age (before 1000 B.C.E.) into the modern world. It is also the foundation document of Christianity and Islam, the two most widespread religions in the modern world. As a literary text it is an incomparable world classic with vast influence.

Judaism began within the matrix of Levantine religion but made a radical new interpretation of tradition. The Hebrew Bible has a great deal of mythology related to other Near Eastern myths, for example, Yahweh as a storm god living on a mountaintop, his slaying of Leviathan and Behemoth, and his creation of humankind from clay (the name *Adam* means "clay"). There is also nothing exceptional in terms of cult. Yahweh had a temple on one of his home mountains—Zion in Jerusalem—and received there the sacrifice of animals according to a fixed cultic calendar. But while Baal/Hadad had been the chief god worshipped in the Levant (polytheism) and Marduk had transcended his fellow deities to become a national god in Babylon (henotheism), the Bible introduces something quite new to Semitic religion—monotheism, the belief that there is only one god. The cult of other deities was characterized as idolatry, the worship of statues devoid of life and a terrible affront to Yahweh.

In the ancient Near East a common explanation for misfortune was that something had been done wrong in the worship of the gods: In order to counteract the misfortune, the gods must be worshipped again in the proper manner. Many scholars believe that this is how Jewish monotheism, the belief that Yahweh is the only god, developed, in reaction to the national catastrophe of the Babylonian captivity (587–537 B.C.E.), when the Israelite state was conquered by the Babylonians and its ruling elite transported to Babylon. Another factor may be the essentially monotheistic beliefs of the Persian patrons of the restoration (when the Jews were allowed to return to Israel). In any case, monotheism became the principal feature of all later Judaism and eventually of Christianity and Islam.

Part of what is new in Judaism is its moral dimension. A very clear example of this is the flood myth. In Atrahasis the gods want to destroy humankind because human beings are too loud and disturb the divine sleep, but humanity is spared because its service to the gods through cult is deemed useful. But in Genesis god destroys the human race because it has become wicked and promises not to do it again as a spontaneous act of mercy. These are concerns of a later era and can be paralleled with the development of ethical thought in Greek philosophy that was going on at the same time the Bible was being compiled during and after the Babylonian captivity.

Another new element in Judaism is eschatology. As we saw, there is almost no concern in Semitic religion about the survival of human beings in a life after death or of the end of the world as the completion of any kind of cosmic cycle. These eschatological ideas are, however, characteristic of the Zoroastrian religion of Persia. Later, Judaism and Christianity were happy to read eschatological ideas into the Hebrew Bible by allegorical interpretation (reading something manifest in the text as a symbolic representation to something that is not referred to). But eschatological themes do not become dominant in Jewish writings until the book of Daniel, the youngest biblical book (ca. 167 B.C.E.). Thereafter these topics become dominant in postbiblical Jewish religious writings, such as the Dead Sea Scrolls and the books of Enoch, and in Christian texts.

In 70 C.E. Jerusalem and its temple were again destroyed, this time by the Romans, and the Jews exiled from the land. Thereafter the cult of Yahweh ceased in its traditional form. Judaism became something new, Rabbinic Judaism, a religion of the book, whose main purpose was to read and interpret scripture. The traditional priesthood ended also, to be replaced by rabbis who led synagogues in reading and prayer.

ASIA AND THE PACIFIC

BY KIRK H. BEETZ

Animism was the root religious belief in most of Asia and the Pacific during ancient times. In general animists believe that the universe has a multitude of spirits. Human beings are only a small and insignificant part of the cosmos. Some spirits are gods of various things on the earth. It is possible for animists to believe that everything has a spirit—every tree, blade of grass, animal, mountain, lake, stream, and stone—but most animistic religions do not go to this extreme.

Certain places on the earth serve as spots on paths commonly traveled by spirits. At such places a person may be able to summon a spirit or at least talk to one. Doing so is dangerous, because a human being can be driven insane or killed by a spirit passing through on business of its own. For such spirits, to kill a human who gets in the way is comparable to accidentally stepping on an ant.

Oceania

In what is today Oceania various versions of animism developed in ancient times. In Australia and Indonesia sacred places tended to center on large stones or rocky outcrops. People sometimes asked spiritual beings to help with hunting or to provide beneficial weather. Although individual animals had their own spirits, many animal species were represented by greater spirits. Although these spirits were usually far away and invisible, they sometimes took the form of their special animal on earth to communicate with earthly beings. Animals as diverse as kangaroos, wolves, and whales could have such spirits.

Japan

The ancient Japanese had a complex set of animistic religious beliefs. Many historians and archaeologists have argued that the ancient Japanese had no religion because they had no church authorities and no theology. However, the Japanese were a very spiritual people, and the fact that they had no central authorities or scriptures was actually part of their religious view, because they believed that no one person had a monopoly on spirituality. To them every human being had the potential to communicate with the numerous spirits that made up their world.

This is not to say that they did not have people with special spiritual talent. The legendary Queen Himiko (fl. 200s B.C.E) was reputedly a sorceress whose powers helped her maintain control of her fractious, warlike people. The second monarch after her rule was a 12-year-old girl who was also a sorceress. This suggests that ancient Japanese beliefs allowed for magic and for people who were specialists in it.

The Japanese developed a concept now called *kami*. The word *kami* implies both an individual spirit and a spirituality that stems from great power or force. Thus not every tree had its own *kami*, but very big trees, by virtue of the spiritual force their size gave them, had their own individual spirits. Mountains likewise had spirits because of the power their size imparted, as did lakes, rivers, and other features of the landscape. Animals could have their own *kami*, but animal spirits often manifested themselves as much larger than the ordinary animal, showing that they had spiritual power. These special spirits could be huge wolves, pigs, or deer and were often guardians of forests. People could talk to these special animals and the animals could talk back.

The exact language spoken by the ancient Japanese is debated by archaeologists. Their names for their gods may have been different from those recorded when the Japanese became a literate people. Since each area could have its own special spirits, spiritual beliefs probably varied somewhat from place to place. In essence, the Japanese believed that the earth was special only to those who lived on it. Their gods were spirits with powers much greater than those of human beings, but they were mortal and subject to many of the inconveniences and miseries that human beings endure.

The world had an earth god and a sky goddess who were married to each other but could not embrace. The islands of Japan were created in the ocean by a husband-and-wife team later known as Izanagi no Mikoto and Izanami no Mikoto. Izanami no Mikoto died while giving birth to the god of fire, and she went to the land of the dead. Early references to the sun god indicate that he was male, though it is possible that some Japanese thought of this god as female.

Other gods represented the principal concerns of the Japanese. For example, there was a food goddess, Uke-Mochi, who was murdered and whose corpse gave rise to rice, millet, wheat, and red beans. There was a god for hunting and a god for fishing. There were also demons that could be evil or good.

The massive burial mounds of the 300s B.C.E.–200s C.E. in Japan suggest that people believed in an afterlife and may have practiced ancestor worship. Local warlords and Japanese monarchs were entombed under these mounds, atop each of which was a shrine, probably for people asking the help of the spirit of the person in the tomb. Near the end of the period during which the tombs were built, some had passages into the crypt, perhaps for people to go inside to communicate with the dead. Tombs were typically surrounded by small ceramic figures placed upright and facing outward, perhaps to ward off evil spirits.

Korea

Two factors have hindered research into ancient Korea's religions. First, several military invasions since ancient times have resulted in the looting and destruction of ancient religious sites. Second, many of the best religious sites are in North Korea, whose government allows foreign archaeologists little access to them. The existence in Korea of burial mounds that seem to be duplicates of the massive burial mounds of Japan suggests to many archaeologists that some ancient Koreans were of the same ethnic group as the ancient Japanese and shared their religious beliefs and customs. It is possible that three distinct religious traditions held sway in ancient Korea, each animistic. One was that which was shared with the Japanese. The other two were derived from northern and central Asia.

Buddhism probably first reached Korea in 372 C.E. In 384 C.E. an Indian monk named Marananda converted the royal family of the kingdom of Paekche, which formed the western part of Korea. Paekche swiftly became a Buddhist nation, but little of the process of converting its people is known because most of Paekche's ancient sites have been destroyed. The kingdom of Silla in the southeast of Korea was introduced to Buddhism in 424 C.E., but the religion did not take hold until the 500s C.E., when the royal family converted to the new faith. Throughout the era of Buddhism's ascendancy Koreans' animistic beliefs survived, mostly in the form of magical rituals performed by shamans.

India

Not much is known about the religion of the Harappan civilization (2600–1500 B.C.E.) of the Indus River area. Among the remains of that civilization are images of a man with antlers on his head, who may represent a god, and small statues of a large-breasted woman, who may have been a fertility goddess. Bulls are prominent in Harappan art and may represent a reverence for cattle that would later be continued in Hindu religious beliefs. In the rest of India animism underlay the numerous religions of peoples across the land. Animism never disappeared in ancient India, and it lay behind some of the magic and mysticism of country people. In the jungles of India were Stone Age peoples, clad only in leaves around their hips and who hunted with poisoned arrows and were said to kidnap travelers to sacrifice to their gods.

The Vedic Period lasted from about 1500 to 600 B.C.E. The Vedic culture emphasized sacrificing to its gods, but it may not have included human sacrifice. The word *Vedic* comes from the Vedas, which were stories, poems, and proverbs transmitted orally for a thousand or more years before being written down in the 300s B.C.E. They reflect the religious beliefs of the Aryans, cattle-herding nomads who spoke closely related languages and invaded the Harappan area starting in about 1500 B.C.E. The Aryans shared a belief, probably derived from animism, that all things of the world have a divine nature.

Before the Aryan migration into India, the chief god was Dyaus, god of the sky. He and Prithivi, goddess of the earth, had a son, Indra. During the Vedic Period, Indra was the most celebrated of all the gods. He was the god of storms and a great warrior. The demon Vritra had caused a worldwide drought by corralling the world's clouds; when he was born, Indra drank the mystical drink soma and then led the spirits of thunder into battle against Vritra. He released the clouds, which spread across the sky and brought rain to the earth. In a couple of accounts, after his victory over Vritra he killed his father, symbolizing his ascendancy as the most important Vedic god.

Limestone relief panel depicting the departure of Prince Siddhartha from his palace, to start on the spiritual journey that brings him to Buddhahood; this panel is from the dome of the Great Stupa at Amaravati, India (second century C.E.). (© The Trustees of the British Museum)

The Vedic religion mixed with the religions of the areas the Aryans conquered, mostly in northern India, though their religious beliefs continuously moved southward to include ever more people. It is not known exactly when the Vedic religion became Brahmanism, which became Hinduism. Hinduism represented a significant break from animism, because instead of there being many spirits or gods, there was only one God and all the many gods of Hinduism were just different manifestations of the one God. The Aryans brought with them a social structure of four castes: the top caste was made up of the Brahmans, who were priests and teachers; then came the Kshatriyas, who were warriors and political leaders; after them were Vaishyas, who were farmers and tradespeople; then came the Shudras, who were laborers. Beneath them all were the Untouchables, for whom the worst jobs were reserved. Some historians believe that the Sudras and Untouchables were the native peoples of the lands the Aryans conquered.

These castes became part of Brahmanism. Brahmanism taught that there was an eternal law, Sanatana Dharma, which had always existed. The word *dharma* is often interpreted as "fate," but it is not exactly fate. Instead it is *the way things are*, a statement asserting that there are facts about the universe that cannot be changed. When in the spring of 326 B.C.E. Alexander the Great's Macedonians defeated an Indian army led by Porus, the monarch of the Indian kingdom of Chenab, Porus was asked how he expected to be treated. He was recorded as saying, "As befits a king." He was not expressing pride or bravado but simply his dharma, the unchangeable fact that he was a king. Thus members of the castes were living their dharmas. Each person was born into a caste because of the divine law of the universe. Each person was expected to strive to be the best he or she could be according to the rules of his or her caste.

Dharma was in part determined by karma—a form of divine energy that people acquired during their lives. It was believed that every human soul goes through cycles of death and rebirth, or reincarnation, in a new earthly body. How well a person fulfills his or her duties as a member of a caste in one life builds karma that will determine into which caste he or she will be reborn in the next life. By the 300s C.E. some Hindus believed this process included every single action a person ever took. Moment by moment what people did created positive or negative karma. In some parts of India people believed that the souls of people with too much negative karma could be reborn in animals, including insects. For some people this belief made vegetarianism a religious necessity. For others it was simply the animal's dharma if people killed and ate it.

The foremost deities of Brahmanism were Brahma, Vishnu, and Shiva. In the beginning of the universe a divine force created life-giving waters in which an egg arose. In that egg was Brahma. After a year floating on the waters of the cosmos, Brahma broke out of his shell, using half of the shell to make the sky and the other half to make the earth. He then created the deities and the plants and animals of the world. Eventually he looked within himself and found the divine source of his being.

Vishnu originated during the Vedic era as a minor deity who was an ally or servant of Indra. During the first and second centuries C.E. he became a major object of veneration, deemed the protector of the earth. Whenever the earth was threatened with destruction, he would take a physical form called an "avatar." Among his many avatars was the fish Matsya, who saved Manu, the first man, from a flood. Another was a boar that, when a demon threw the earth to bottom of the cosmic ocean, killed the demon and returned the earth to its proper place. Another two of Vishnu's avatars were Ramacandra and Krishna, who developed their own worshippers.

Ramacandra, or simply Rama, was the son of a king who exiled him when he married Sita, a princess from another land. Ravana, the demon-king of Sri Lanka, kidnapped Sita. With the help of his brother Lakshmana and the monkey Hanuman, son of a deity and a monkey, Rama defeated Ravana and rescued Sita. Rama represented the ideal man: virtuous, courageous, a good husband, and a good leader. Krishna was the son of the sister of a wicked king in northern India. The king tried to have Krishna killed, but Krishna's mother sneaked him to safety in the country. As a baby he killed a demon. He grew up to be entrancingly handsome, and many young women yearned for his company. Later he killed the wicked king and taught people how to live good spiritual lives.

Shiva was both creator and destroyer. His meditating generated the spiritual energy that sustained the entire universe. When his female companion, Parvati, covered his eyes for fun, the universe was almost plunged into darkness, but Shiva manifested a third eye on his forehead; as long as he could see, the universe would have light. He later turned his third eye to look inward to meditate. Shiva was also a fertility figure, as well as the deity of medicine and of dance. His worshippers used dancing as a way to express joy but also to express the chaos that could destroy the universe.

In the 500s B.C.E. a member of the Kshatriya caste, Vardhamana (ca. 599–527 B.C.E.), established Jainism. Jainism took its name from *jina,* meaning "conqueror." Jainists were expected to swear that they would not kill, lie, have sexual relations for any purpose other than to procreate, or be greedy. Jains were supposed to be nonviolent and very strict vegetarians. They were forbidden to take any animal's life and would place strips of gauze over their nostrils and mouths to avoid breathing in any tiny creatures. Brahmanists regarded them as heretics because they did not accept the Vedas as religious scriptures and ignored the caste system.

Siddhartha Gautama (ca. 563–ca. 483 B.C.E.) was a member of the Kshatriya caste. Through meditation he had a divine revelation that made him the Buddha, a person who achieved true enlightenment. After his revelation he spent most of his life teaching across northeastern India. The Buddha believed that to live is to suffer, and that suffering is caused by desire. To escape suffering, a person should eliminate desire through meditation and should do what is morally right. If someone did this, his or her soul would skip reincarnation and go to Nirvana, where it would join with the universal spirit.

When Asoka (r. 265–238 or ca. 273–232 B.C.E.), king of the Maurya Empire (321–185 B.C.E.), converted, Buddhism became the state religion. Asoka followed the Buddhist doctrine of tolerance and allowed other religions to be practiced in peace. He tried to make his subjects more moral through public proclamations explaining why he was a Buddhist. During his reign Buddhism spread through most of India. It eventually reached the island of Sri Lanka, where it became the dominant religion. Buddhism began to wane in India in the 100s C.E. By then it had spread into China.

China

During his reign (221–210 B.C.E.) China's emperor Qin Shi Huangdi tried to have all documents about the past destroyed. He wanted to eliminate the possibility of imitating the errors of past governments, and he wanted world history to begin with him. He had over 40,000 Confucian scholars buried alive to eliminate their knowledge, but a few managed to survive and, in the welcoming Han Dynasty (ca. 202 B.C.E.–ca. 220 C.E.), recited what they remembered of the ancient texts. Almost everything about China's religion before Qin Shi Huangdi's reign was lost. What is currently thought about Chinese religion before that time comes from archaeological discoveries and inferences about past beliefs drawn from writings of the 100s B.C.E.

There were many cultures in ancient China, and each probably had its own special gods and spirits. The earliest religious beliefs were probably animistic. Animism never entirely left ancient China, and it was a source of magic among peasants. Human sacrifices were common. For instance, in the 400s B.C.E. a governor of the upper Yellow River discovered that people were still sacrificing girls to be brides of the river in springtime; he put a stop to it, but especially in the areas south of China human sacrifices to fertility goddesses continued into modern times.

Animal sacrifices were also common. In 30 B.C.E. the Yellow River was close to flooding. The local governor walked to the riverbank and offered the sacrifice of a gray horse to the river. The governor used his magical jade ornaments to cast spells to protect his people. As the river rose, all his aides fled; only he and one assistant stayed. After the waters stopped just short of breaking free to flood the land, the governor was rewarded with gold and a promotion. Such mystical practices deriving from animism continued for thousands of years.

By the time of the Shang Dynasty (ca. 1500–ca. 1045 B.C.E.) ancestor worship had become prevalent not only in the Yellow River area but also in surrounding regions that would one day fall under the rule of China. People would leave offerings to their ancestors at tombs of their ancestors. Kings were expected to consult their ancestors in times of crisis and to ask their ancestors to speak with gods to help ensure weather appropriate to each of the seasons, for good harvests, and to prevent floods. During the Shang Dynasty and most of the Zhou Dynasty (ca. 1045–ca. 256 B.C.E.) servants were sacrificed to be buried with their masters. Their heads were chopped off with special axes and buried separately from their bodies. Why they were buried separately is not known, but the practice was common enough to occur even in the burials of some ordinary peasants and soldiers. The servants were expected to serve their masters in the next life. By the end of the Zhou Dynasty human sacrifices at the burials of nobles and monarchs were rare, though they still sometimes occurred. The sacrificing of servants was replaced by the burying of ceramic sculptures of people. It is likely that the ceramic figures were magically endowed with spirits that would serve their masters and mistresses after death. The human sacrifices may have been one of the ancient practices that Qin Shi Huangdi hoped to end with his rule. His tomb has China's most spectacular collection of ceramic sculptures—thousands of life-size figures.

Most archaeologists believe that women took subordinate roles in ancient Chinese religion. Little mention is known of women divinities, although belief in a great witch whose body was carved into the lands of the earth seems to have been widespread. The most important female supernatural being was said to live in the Kunlun Mountains, a range near modern Tibet. Ancient Shang records on bamboo found in tombs mention a mother goddess to the west. By the 900s B.C.E. this goddess had become the focus of a cult. She was said to live in a mystical land that existed apart from the ordinary world, but people could find their way to it through the Kunlun. She was called Xi Wang Mu, "Queen Mother of the West," and was said to have the secret to immortality. In about 113 B.C.E., during the Han Dynasty, an army was dispatched to northwestern China to secure the safety of the Silk Road. Another purpose of the expedition may have been to find the way to the land of the Queen Mother of the West.

During an era when the Zhou Dynasty was divided among several states the philosopher Confucius (551–479 B.C.E.) taught his belief that government should be benign. Although he insisted that he himself had no original ideas but was only reminding people of wisdom learned by ancient leaders, he and his followers tried to replace what they regarded as irrational religious views with rational ones. This did not mean that Confucianism opposed religion; Confucius insisted on following religious rituals, arguing that in them people could find ways to communicate properly with gods and their ancestors. What Confucians opposed were the practices of folk magic, including witchcraft and human sacrifice. In religious rituals was rationality; in magic spells and the invocation of demons was nonsense. Although the Han Dynasty adopted Confucianism as its philosophy of government and Confucius became a venerated figure, Confucianism itself was never a religion.

Another teacher of the same era, Laozi (ca. 604–521 B.C.E.), did found a religion, called Daoism. Credited with writing *Dao de jing* (The Way and Its Virtue), he advocated self-control as a way to preserve the body and live long. His followers created rituals that were supposed to bring the body under control and subdue the forces within it that made it grow old. The chief god of Daoism was Yu Huang, the Jade Emperor. The Queen Mother of the West was his wife. He was assisted by many gods. Each year he summoned them to his palace and gave each god new duties based on how well the god had performed his work during the previous year. When there were troubles such as droughts, floods, or plagues, Daoist priests told the god in charge that he was performing poorly, and Yu Huang took note. The offending god could be dismissed from his post during the annual review of his work.

The parallel between Yu Huang and the Chinese emperor was intentional. The emperor ruled because he was appointed by the gods, and he had to maintain a good relationship with them if he was to remain in their favor. Should he fall out of favor, religious doctrine dating all the way back to the Shang Dynasty said he should be replaced by someone the gods had blessed. It thus was the custom for usurpers of the throne to declare that they were only acting on behalf of the gods. During the second half of the Zhou Dynasty emperors had little political power but were treated with respect by the rulers of the various Chinese provinces, because without the emperors they would have little to justify their own rule. The emperor maintained the fiction that he appointed the rulers of the Chinese states on the basis of divine authority: He was emperor because of divine favor, and divine favor passed through him to the various warlords, chiefs, and kings of China's provinces.

During the 300s B.C.E. the concept of yin and yang developed. Yin and yang represented the universe as a duality of opposing forces. Yin was dark, soft, receptive, and "female," while yang was hard, bright, active, and "male." Without yin and yang in constant opposition, the world would not be possible. Much folk magic depended on mediating between yin and yang to find the proper balance between them, and much that was wrong in the world was attributed to an imbalance of the two.

During the Han Dynasty an entire department of government was devoted to religious matters. There was much for the officials to keep track of. For instance, the emperor had to wear particular kinds of clothing at particular times of year because his clothes were a reminder to the gods to change seasons at the appropriate times. If he wore the wrong clothing, disaster could follow, with the seasons becoming mixed up. There were rituals for him to perform—probably more than any one person could remember—which meant the government needed priests who could keep track of what was needed.

During the second half of the Han Dynasty two things occurred that would shape Chinese religion for centuries. First, in about 142 C.E. the mystic Zhang Daoling declared that he had had a revelation from Laozi telling him to start a new religion. By then Daoism had fragmented into different sects. Zhang Daoling created the Way of the Heavenly Masters, which provided a model for earthly as well as heavenly rule. He established a religious government in the province of Sichuan, with himself and his heirs ruling a bureaucracy intended to imitate that of Yu Huang. Thus renewed, Daoism became a central feature of Chinese religion.

The second important religious occurrence was the spread, beginning about 50 C.E., of Buddhism into China. By about 65 C.E. it was known to the emperor's court. During the 100s C.E. it became the most prominent religion in the capital city, Luoyang. In 166 C.E. Chinese emperors began holding rituals in which they sacrificed to both Laozi and the Buddha. For common people in China, Buddhism held the promise of salvation, of a chance to go to heaven. Early Buddhist translators of scriptures into Chinese often used images from Daoism to explain their faith to people, and the way of Daoism and the pious way to Nirvana of Buddhism often blended. For centuries most Chinese saw little difference between the two and venerated both religions even while continuing to worship their ancestors and believe in magic.

EUROPE

BY KIRK H. BEETZ

Some of the earliest artworks from Europe may also be the earliest signs of religion there: cave paintings from France and Spain dating to about 32,000–30,000 B.C.E. and small stone carvings of large-breasted women, such as the so-called Venus of Willendorf found in Austria, dating from roughly 28,000 to 23,000 B.C.E. The principal subjects of the paintings are animals, richly detailed by the prehistoric artists. Also found in caves are sculptures, mostly relief carvings, of animals and of women. Archaeologists have long debated the significance of the ancient cave art, but most speculate that the depictions of animals were intended to give people power over them in order to make hunts successful. Human figures often are portrayed hunting the animals, and perhaps by painting or sculpting these scenes the artists believed they were making the animals and the hunts real.

Statuettes like the Venus of Willendorf may represent a fertility cult or an earth-mother cult. Whether the carvings were intended to be worshipped or were totems representing a goddess is not known. Some archaeologists suspect that they represent a matriarchal religion or society, meaning that women were the dominant priests or social leaders. However, there is considerable debate over the purpose of these figurines.

Ancient religion often is connected with death and burial. Burying the dead goes back at least to the last great ice age, and many archaeologists believe that the practice is a sign of belief in an afterlife. On the other hand, burying the dead might be merely a sanitary measure—corpses bring disease and attract predators, and burying them covers both decay and odor.

By 3500 B.C.E. Europeans were building monuments of huge stones, or megaliths (from the Greek *mega*, meaning "large," and *lithos*, meaning "stone"). Usually these people placed corpses within the stone chambers and then covered the structures with large earthen mounds, termed *tumuli* by archaeologists. In a few places the megalith builders took more elaborate measures, such as building stairs down into chambers and constructing several niches for the dead, making it clear that more than one person was interred inside a single tumulus.

Even such large and laboriously built burial structures as these, however, are not necessarily evidence of belief in an afterlife. The imposing megaliths might, for example, have been intended to announce that a particular village or clan owned the surrounding land. The tumuli, some of them visible for miles, might have carried the same message. On the other hand, there are indications that mourners left burial goods in the stony chambers of some tumuli, which would suggest a belief that the dead needed supplies for an afterlife.

In Ireland, England, and western Europe many megalithic complexes took centuries to build. Some are merely enigmatic rows of upright stones weighing tons each, their purpose unknown. Others provide hints to their ritual significance. The most famous of these is Stonehenge in England. Stonehenge was erected in an on-and-off fashion over hundreds of years, and periodically people, presumably individuals with high social status, were buried among the stones. This and many similar monuments were situated so as to line up with astronomical events. At Stonehenge the sunrise on the summer solstice aligns with the axis of the main passage between the exterior of the circle and the interior. The significance of this arrangement is unclear, but it must have had some symbolic or ceremonial meaning.

CELTIC RELIGION

The Celts appear to have developed in east-central Europe, perhaps in the area of today's southern Germany and Czech Republic, though they may have migrated there from central Asia. They begin appearing in the historical record about 500 B.C.E., at which time their culture was flourishing. Greek and Roman writers tried to fit Celtic religious beliefs into their own understanding of religion, sometimes doing as Julius Caesar did and giving Celtic gods and goddesses the names of their Greek or Roman counterparts to make things easier for their reading audiences.

However, Celtic beliefs were too complicated to fit comfortably with the sorts of gods and goddesses the Greeks and Romans worshipped. Some archaeologists believe that ancient European religions sprang from a core religion (perhaps belonging to the megalith builders) that once existed in central Europe. In Greece and Rome the gods and goddesses of this core religion each gained preeminence over some special realm, such as war, agriculture, or the sea. When the Greeks and Romans ventured into the rest of Europe, they brought their specialized gods with them. But the people they met, the

Celts, had taken another direction in their religion. The Celts believed there were gods and goddesses everywhere. Bodies of water, even small ones, had their own individual spirits, as did particular pieces of land. Dark parts of forests could harbor spirits of great power.

By the first century B.C.E. the Celts inhabited almost all of northern Europe, and they had become a diverse group of peoples with diverse religious beliefs. For instance, the Celts of the Iberian Peninsula (present-day Portugal and Spain) held somewhat different beliefs from Celts in Britain, Gaul, and the Balkans. Ideas about life after death, an afterworld, and the human soul had variations depending on which group of Celts one studies. These differences defied Greek and Roman efforts to describe a single set of Celtic beliefs.

For example, one aspect of Celtic belief mentioned by Caesar involved the transmigration of souls. The word *transmigration* is here chosen with care, because it is not the same as *reincarnation*. Celts did not believe in reincarnation—the rebirth of the soul into a new human being—but some believed that the soul of a dead person could migrate to the body of another living person. Thus the souls of the dead were dangerous. One way of dealing with the danger was to decapitate an enemy and carry the head home to be placed in a chest or in a shrine. Because the head was believed to be the seat of life, control of it imparted control of the dead person's spirit, which could be used for protection from other spirits.

Other Celts, however, believed that the souls of the dead went to an afterlife. They envisioned a special land where no one ever lied, where good fruit abounded, and where hunting was always successful. It seems to have been universal among the Celts that they did not believe in sin or in good deeds as having effects after death. Everyone, good and evil, went to the afterlife and shared in it. For those who believed in this afterworld, it was ruled by the first man who ever lived, who when he died became the first person in the afterlife and made the land of the dead his own.

The land of the afterlife was not a well-defined place, partly because the living could visit it and even live there. In parts of western Europe, Britain, and Ireland a person could walk through a supernatural mist and emerge in a strange land with amazingly beautiful and imposing fortresses inhabited by people who were courteous and kind. Elsewhere people believed that crossing a lake or spring or walking through a sacred grove or among old stone megaliths could bring a person into the otherworld, which could have been the land of the dead or a mystical alternate dimension to the earth. The Celts themselves seem to have been vague about the nature of the otherworld, regarding it as something removed from the laws of the ordinary world and therefore something that ordinary people could not fully comprehend. During the festivals of Beltane (May 1) and Samhain (November 1) the borders between the everyday world and the otherworld disappeared, and both humans and supernatural beings could cross from one to the other without trouble.

The roles of the priests, shamans, seers, and magicians of the Celts are almost as unclear to scholars today as they were to ancient observers. The Druids are the best known of these figures, but they did not have influence much beyond the British Isles and western Europe. When Caesar wrote of them, he noted that they had probably originated in Britain, because those who studied to be Druids usually went there for their education. Archaeologists and historians have speculated that what Caesar actually saw was a dying cult, with the Druids already disappearing from the Continent but holding out in parts of Britain. This notion implies that the Druids flourished for only a few hundred years. Whatever the period of their existence, they were certainly among the best organized of Celtic religious groups. They met annually in the land of the Carnutes (the area around modern-day French cities of Chartres, Orléans, and Blois), where they discussed political, theological, and legal business. They had a leader who was elected at this assembly, when necessary, and who served for life.

Druids seem to have been exclusively male. A woman could be executed for witnessing any part of certain sacred rites. The Druids resisted the use of a written language. Each priest was expected to spend 20 years memorizing laws and rituals, and no outsider was allowed to learn them. Druids served as judges in legal matters, as priests in worship, and as seers who through ritual could foretell the future. The Greeks and Romans depicted the Druids and Celtic priests in general as very murderous and bloody, and the archaeological record supports their claims. For instance, the Druids foretold the future by cutting out a living human being's intestines and studying their configuration. Another approach to telling the future was to stab a person in the diaphragm and observe where the blood spurted and how the victim writhed in agony. Torturing, maiming, and mangling human sacrifices occurred at festivals and during efforts to win the favor of certain gods. Sometimes horses were sacrificed. Wars may sometimes have been waged for the purpose of taking prisoners to be used in ritual sacrifices.

Although the Druids tried to make themselves the exclusive intermediaries between human beings and the supernatural, most Celts believed that anyone could have contact with the supernatural. One way to achieve this kind of individual contact was by making sacrifices during public rituals. This practice was taken very seriously, as evidenced by the very rich sacrifices given to spirits of rivers and lakes. The river Thames in England has yielded numerous artifacts, such as finely cast bronze armor and gold jewelry. Some armor, shields, and swords are extraordinarily ornate, as if made specifically for sacrifice to the river god, perhaps in the hope of future military victories. (When a Celtic war party led by Brennus looted the temple at Delphi in Greece in 279 B.C.E., much of the booty seems to have been deposited in a lake in eastern Europe.) Sometimes the sacrifices were deposited on sacred sites on land, and people did not touch the gold and other valuables for fear of retribution from gods and other Celts.

Iron Age horned helmet (150–50 B.C.E.), from the river Thames at Waterloo Bridge, London, England; horns were often a symbol of the gods in different parts of the ancient world, suggesting that this was a ceremonial helmet made for a god. (© The Trustees of the British Museum)

Magicians had a strong hold on many Celts. Even long after being absorbed into the Roman Empire, Celtic peasants practiced the old magic of their ancestors. The Romans regarded magical practices as dangerous because a magician might develop a cult following that could cause trouble. The rebellion of 53 B.C.E. may have been sparked in part by shamans or magicians stirring up notions of freedom among the Celts. In (probably) 60 C.E. a Roman army attacked the island of Anglesey, off the coast of Wales, and annihilated the Druids living there. The island was perhaps the last remaining center for Druidic education and had been the scene of numerous human sacrifices; the Druids seem to have made themselves troublesome by encouraging revolt against the Romans. At that moment Queen Boudicca of the Icenians of Britain led a revolt that nearly drove the Romans out of England. The source of her power among the Britons seems to have been her status as a sorceress.

Over 200 names of Celtic gods have been discovered, and historians are far from sorting them out. Some gods seem to have had several names, while other names seem to belong to individual local gods. For the Celts religion was a matter of locality, because each area had its own gods of the land and water. These gods sometimes reappear in medieval tales—for example, the Lady of the Lake and Lancelot du Lac (Lancelot of the Lake) in the legends of King Arthur—revealing their powerful long-term hold on people's imaginations.

It is likely that sun gods and earth goddesses were worshipped throughout the lands of the Celts. The sun god was often represented by wheels, and carts in eastern Europe seem to have become symbols of the sun's movement through the sky. Spoked wheels appear to have been included in sacrifices to the gods. Domestic goods were sacrificed to the earth goddess, who seems to have been in charge of the fertility of the soil. She was sometimes celebrated in spring festivals. Sky gods were common and tended to be represented by a hammer, which was associated with thunder.

Associating other gods with specific aspects of the world is difficult, because Celtic gods and goddesses tended to be good at doing everything. For instance, the god Lenus of northern Gaul was associated with the Roman war god Mars by Caesar, but Lenus was a healing god as well as a warrior. Lugos of Gaul and Ireland was associated with the Roman messenger god Mercury by Caesar, but Lugos was also a good warrior. His mate, Rosmeta, represented abundance and was symbolized by buckets of wine. Danu was celebrated by many Celts as a fertility goddess. A goddess known throughout Gaul and among southern European Celts was Badhbh, perhaps the most terrifying of Celtic gods. Many Celtic gods were shape-shifters—that is, they could change into animals or even human beings—and Badhbh could change into a crow. In that form she flew over battlefields, waiting to feast on the souls of the dead; she could carry souls from life to the otherworld. Celtic warriors were mindful of her and took care not to offend her. She waited at river crossings for warriors to pass by and knew which ones would die that day.

Regional gods and goddesses of note include Sequana, the goddess of the Seine River. At the headwaters of the Seine, her water could heal people. Sulis was a goddess at the site of present-day Bath, England. Another deity who was good at almost everything, she offered healing and retribution.

Germanic and Scandinavian Religions

Even less is known of the religions of the Germanic and Scandinavian peoples before the era of the Vikings than is known of Celtic religion, mostly because literate observers such as Greeks and Romans had far fewer contacts with them than with the Celts. The early Scandinavians may have had an earth goddess or a fertility goddess at the center of their religious beliefs. She granted her followers prosperity that was represented by displays of wealth. The peoples of northern Europe may have had a war god at the center of their beliefs. When they and the Scandinavians mixed, creating the Germanic peoples known to history, they may have had a fundamental conflict between their religious views, with the worshippers of the war god regarding the lavish wealth of the earth goddess as immoral and wasteful.

Over time the diverse Germanic peoples evolved a compromise religion that became the foundation for the Norse beliefs known from Viking sagas. The gods of the worshippers of the earth goddess became known as the Vanir, whereas the gods of the worshippers of the war god became known as the Aesir. Their compromise manifested itself in a myth about a war among the gods. The war god and his followers tried to kill a giantess who could not die, and she endured terrible tortures because of their efforts. Perhaps taking pity on her, the Vanir came to her rescue and fought the Aesir. The Vanir possibly represented healing and mercy. The gods reached a stalemate in their battle and then made a treaty.

They exchanged hostages, with one of the hostages being the earth goddess herself, who went to live with the war god. If she was the basis for the Norse goddess Freyja, it would explain Freyja's sexual promiscuity, which would represent her exceptionally fruitful powers. It may be significant that the earth goddess ended up as a hostage to the forces of the war god, making him the chief of all gods.

This war god would have become Odin, perhaps by the 400s C.E. It worth noting that an early Christian writer, known as the Venerable Bede (673–735 C.E.), wrote that Odin had been a great Germanic king who was deified. Although Bede was biased against the pagan religion of the Germans, he may have touched on a truth, because sometimes historical figures become gods or goddesses in their cultures. For instance, two of the avatars of Vishnu—Rama and Krishna—in the Hindu faith may have been important leaders during the preliterate era of the Vedic religion.

If in fact a core European religion once existed that was transformed into the pantheons of Greece and Rome and into the elaborate and contradictory beliefs of the Celts, then it took another interesting turn among the Germanic peoples. Where the Celts had gods all over the landscape, the Germanic peoples developed supernatural beings that were usually mortal. They had dragons, dwarfs, light elves, dark elves, trolls, and giants. Dragons were frightful creatures who loved wealth and hoarded treasure that they fiercely guarded. The dwarfs lived in the ground. If exposed to light, they turned to stone. Light elves were beautiful and airy. They may have inhabited the sky. Dark elves lived underground and were sullen and unfriendly. Trolls were monsters, perhaps associated with specific spots of land. They served the giants, who inhabited mountains and lands of frigid cold. (All these different beings seem to have been part of a creation-of-the-world myth in which all appeared at about the same time, with human beings inhabiting a realm between the sky and the ground. Thus the ancient Germanic religion had a world of three parts, with humanity in the middle.)

The mortality of these and other supernatural beings is perhaps the most unusual aspect of the Germanic belief system. Only rarely does any being have immunity from being killed. Even the gods can die. This mortality even for gods is part of a dark view of existence that all the Germanic peoples seem to have shared by the first century B.C.E. Everything was temporary in their faith. The gods would perish, and the world would end. Even those who had gone into the afterlife would eventually be snuffed out. The later Vikings viewed the end as a great battle between good and evil, full of betrayal and futile heroism. The war god himself would perish. The earth would be destroyed, taking the earth goddess with it.

It is not known for sure when runes began to be used in Germanic rituals. A form of writing made up of straight lines set at various angles, ideal for engraving into stone, runes may have been a late development, but they may have predated the onset of Christianity in the 100s C.E. They were considered sacred, and most people were not allowed to know their meaning. It seems that just as Druids wanted to keep their supernatural knowledge to themselves, the priests of the Germanic peoples wanted exclusive knowledge of how to write. Part of the importance they attached to writing was that it could reshape reality. To them the written word had a supernatural creative power. A written word could kill, could create an animal, could change the weather, or could change much else.

The Germans may have shared with the Celts a belief that the spoken word had the power to alter reality. This belief was wrapped in mysticism. Common in the German culture were women seers and sorceresses. The Germans did not have temples, so their ceremonies often took place in homes. Female seers traveled the countryside, perhaps making annual rounds, and they held ceremonies in people's houses. They could tell women whether they would become pregnant in the near future and tell farmers whether they would have good or bad crops. During early medieval times the female seers wore cloaks made of many different animal skins, and they probably did so in ancient times too. Archaeologists have found bronze caps, dating to the last few centuries B.C.E., that were attached to staffs the female seers carried with them. Perhaps they served as signs of a woman's status as a magician. The staffs themselves may have served to focus their owners' supernatural powers.

It is possible that these female seers sacrificed animals on occasion to help them foretell the future. They may have claimed certain powers over the dead, such as being able to bring them back to life for a short time to speak with the living and even take action. The female seers' powers were to be used only by women. Men who practiced the magic of the female seers were put to death; apparently they represented a danger to the community because the magic could get out of their control.

The ancient Germanic peoples practiced human sacrifice extensively, but this does not seem to have been associated with the female seers. Animals were often sacrificed by chiefs or kings. The blood of the animal could consecrate a building or meeting place. The animals were cooked and eaten by the chief and his guests, symbolically uniting them in mutual obligation. Those assembled were expected to aid the chief in his rule, and the chief was expected to guide his followers to prosperity. In Sweden and Denmark special gathering places existed where tribes made sacrifices to mark the seasons. Human beings were killed on such occasions, probably nine or 99 at a time, as was the practice of the Norse. Hanging, strangling, cutting the throat, and drowning were among the methods employed. The corpses were hung from trees in a sacred part of a wood or sometimes dumped in bogs. Even in Denmark's sacred groves of Nerthus, the goddess of peace, prisoners were drowned as sacrifices to her in the first century C.E.

Some ceremonies were practiced by all Germanic people. For example, they made sure to leave food as offerings to the elves, took care not to offend the easily insulted dwarfs, and used charms to ward off evil spirits. That they buried their dead with goods such as food suggests that they believed in an afterlife in which the dead would need or want the goods. They seem to have believed that deceased family members could be good influences for their living kin. Historians and archaeologists disagree about exactly where the Germanic peoples thought people went after death. Many argue that the notion of Valhalla, the home in the afterlife for those slain in battle, came late to the Germanic peoples, the ancient peoples believing only in a dark place in the earth governed by a goddess of the dead.

Early European Christianity

Christianity was making itself felt in Europe by the end of the first century C.E. It was one of several religions circulating at the time, especially in central Europe. One competing faith was Mithraism, an exclusively male religion especially popular among soldiers. Mithras was a warrior god, and dead soldiers could hope to join him after death in a battle against evil. Perhaps the key to the growth of Christianity in Europe in these early years was that it welcomed women in its religious rites. Roman men often served decades in the army, leaving women at home to raise the children. It is a tiny logical step to imagine many women taking their sons and daughters to a church that treated women with greater respect than did other European religions. By the time the Roman emperor Constantine the Great converted to Christianity (ca. 312 C.E.), the faith already had a strong European following. Thereafter, Christian priests often became secular as well as spiritual leaders—for example, as bishops who governed towns and regions around towns.

During this same period, however, Christians themselves were embroiled in bitter theological disputes with one another. The main issues concerned the divinity of Christ and particularly whether, if divine, he was of the same substance as God. Conflict over such questions, resulting often in executions and sometimes in wholesale massacres of "heretics," continued in Europe long after the fall of the Western Roman Empire in 476 C.E.

GREECE

BY BRADLEY SKEEN

Religion was the main binding force in ancient Greek culture. Greek religion gave birth to philosophical speculation that in time not only led to the development of science but also provided the theological language of Rabbinic Judaism, Christianity, and Islam. It formed the basis for the creation of the first modern literature, which is still among the most important ever produced. Greek religion has remained a source of inspiration for artists, writers, and composers as well as theologians and philosophers down to the present day.

Minoan Religion

The Minoan civilization on the island of Crete (ca. 2000–ca. 1400 B.C.E.) was the beginning of Greek civilization, though its people did not speak Greek. Minoan culture centered on a number of palace complexes; the most important was Knossos. The agricultural produce of the surrounding countryside was dedicated to various gods in the palace storehouses; obviously religion was very important.

We know about the religion of Minoan Greeks from their art and from myths that were written down centuries later. For example, frescoes in the palace at Knossos make it clear that one of the most important activities of Minoan culture was an athletic festival in which young male and female athletes leaped over bulls. Meanwhile, the classical myth of Theseus (a legendary king of Athens) tells that each year every city in Greece had to send young men and women to Knossos, where they were sacrificed by being killed by the Minotaur—a monster with a human body and the head of a bull. No definite connection between the historical evidence and the myth can be made, however. The Minoans left extensive records written in an alphabet known as Linear A, but these texts have never been deciphered.

Minoans did not build temples like later Greeks but instead worshipped the gods on hilltops and in caves. Perhaps they thought these locations were nearest the gods of the sky and the gods below the earth, respectively. These shrines were generally located near palaces, and their service was one of the chief duties of the kings. The most important form of worship was animal sacrifice, especially of bulls. Cave shrines sometimes contained a statue of the goddess honored in them, but shrines also held many offerings of double-headed axes and swords that suggest important male deities. Private houses generally had small shrines. Many statuettes of a woman have been found, wearing the clothing of a Minoan aristocrat and holding her arms above her head with a writhing snake in each hand. Undoubtedly, the statuettes depict goddesses.

Invaders from the north—the first people we know of who spoke the historical Greek language—eventually overwhelmed the Minoan civilization. They founded many new cities, especially on mainland Greece; the most important was Mycenae, so their culture is called Mycenaean (1400–1100 B.C.E.). They wrote a form of Greek in a Minoan alphabet later than Linear A and known as Linear B, generally inventories of the royal palaces of the cities. Many of the listed items were dedicated to various gods, the same as those worshipped by later Greeks, such as Zeus, Poseidon, Athena, and Dionysus.

The Homeric epics of the *Iliad* and the *Odyssey* are another source of information about the Mycenaeans. The most important works of Greek literature, they were written down around the sixth century B.C.E. but are both set in Mycenaean times (as was the narrative of much Greek myth) and were based on oral traditions that went back to that era. These texts suggest that many institutions of historical Greek religion, such as priesthood and sacrifice, were already formed in the Mycenaean culture. But as in the case of the Minoans, the sparse evidence provides more questions than answers.

Between 1200 and 1000 B.C.E. the whole eastern Mediterranean world, including Greece, underwent a terrible collapse.

Larger governmental structures and the economy failed. Several waves of barbarians raided at will throughout the area. Every major Greek city was destroyed. Greece entered a dark age lasting many centuries, with no social organization above the level of the village and no contact with the outside world. The ability to read and write was completely lost.

The Religion of the Greek Cities

During the Archaic Period (600–480 B.C.E.), Greece recovered politically and economically and once again had extensive overseas contacts with the Near East, not only through merchants but also through the many Greek mercenaries who served foreign kings. Greeks reacquired literacy and developed their own alphabet, modified from Phoenician writing, which was also the ultimate basis for the Latin, Hebrew, and Arabic alphabets still used today. They borrowed many religious ideas and forms from the Near East, such as the idea of the temple as a house of a god, the ritual of animal sacrifice, and myths that were incorporated into literary works like the poet Hesiod's *Theogony* (Generation of the Gods). The Archaic Period established the conditions for the flourishing of Greek culture and religion in the Classical Age (480–323 B.C.E.), a period admired as an ideal by many later cultures.

By the eighth century B.C.E. Greek cities (or city-states, since each city in Greece was an independent country) began to be established or reestablished, often by bringing together all the villages in a given locale under one government and even relocating the population to a central point. New religious institutions had to be created for the benefit of the cities. Each city established temples for its particular gods—places where people gathered to pray and sacrifice to a god and where property dedicated as offerings to the god was stored. The temples were controlled by the city and administered by priests chosen from among the aristocratic classes. The city also fixed a calendar of festivals and sacrifices for the gods it honored. The official religion, with all of its public rituals carried out by the citizens all together in great public ceremonies, was the most important factor in unifying the city and providing it with a national identity. By the same token the religion of the city was the chief form of religious experience of the Greeks.

Frieze of the gods Poseidon and Apollo and the goddess Artemis from the Parthenon (Alison Frantz Photographic Collection, American School of Classical Studies at Athens)

The private religion of the family continued as earlier at household shrines. Cemeteries became centers of family religion also. Traditionally the dead were believed to sleep peacefully, and families brought wine and food to graves to keep their dead ancestors content and prevent troublesome ghosts from returning.

The principal form of worship in civic religion was animal sacrifice, nearly identical to the practice of the Near East and certainly imported into Greece from the older civilization. Descriptions of sacrificial practice in Homer indicate that Eastern rituals were adopted by Greeks of the Mycenaean era and remained almost unchanged through classical and later times. The purposes of sacrifice were to honor the god who received it, to give a gift in exchange for the many gifts the god had bestowed on humanity (such as rain, peace, or justice), and to ask for more benefactions. Since everyone who attended a sacrifice shared equally in the following meal, the ritual was often also a gift from the wealthy to the poor (who might otherwise rarely have meat in their diets).

Sacrifice usually took place after a procession through the city with hymn singing and dancing, leading the animals to the temple. A Greek temple was meant for housing the cult statue of a god, but its dark interior was rarely entered. The outside of the building was the important part, ringed by a row of columns to act as a backdrop, its facade topped by a frieze illustrating a well-known myth of the god. The ritual centered on an altar in front of the temple. The sacrificial animal, preferably a bull, had to be perfect, free from illness or deformity. A girl carrying a basket of grain on her head led the procession. When it reached the altar, the priest and the professional butchers who would actually kill the animal purified their hands by washing them with water. The animal was asked if it was willing to be sacrificed; it could be induced to nod its head by giving it water or food in a bowl on the ground.

The participants in the sacrifice threw the grain from the basket over the animal and the altar. The priest used a knife hidden in the grain to cut off three hairs from the animal's back and threw them onto a fire built on the altar; this was the sacrifice in symbolic form. A single blow from an ax then cut the bull's spine. At the moment this deadly blow fell, the women present made a shrill cry. Two attendants held up the animal's limp head, while a third used the knife to slit its throat. The blood was caught in a basin and splashed on the altar to purify it. Then the animal was butchered. If the sacrifice was made in order to perform divination—that is, to learn whether the will of the gods was favorable or unfavorable to a particular action—the diviners examined the animal's liver for special indications. The liver, certain other organs, and the thighbones were wrapped in a sheet of fat cut from the carcass and burned on the altar. The remaining meat was usually cut into chunks, roasted on sticks over fires, and eaten. The hide became the property of the temple or priests. If the person who initiated the sacrifice had a special reason to do great honor to the god, all the meat was burned.

Panhellenic Shrines and Games

All Greeks recognized themselves as a people bound together by common culture and language. Organization above the level of the city-state was of a religious rather than a political character. When the city-states were established in the Archaic Period, national religious institutions also came into existence at what modern scholars call Panhellenic shrines. Available to all Greeks (*pan* means "all," and *Hellenes* was the Greeks' name for themselves), these shrines helped form a Greek identity and dealt with issues whose importance went beyond individual cities.

The most important shrine was Delphi, founded in the ninth century B.C.E., where a priestess known as the Pythia gave oracles from the god Apollo. Delphi, as the most prestigious source of divination in Greece, was especially important, and its oracle often adjudicated disputes between cities where no ordinary legal recourse was possible. The Delphic Amphictyony, a league of Greek states organized to administer and protect Delphi, could also act as an embryonic federal body for Greece. For example, in 334 B.C.E. the league declared war on Persia in retaliation for the Persian sacking of Delphi in 480 B.C.E.; this was the legal pretext for Alexander the Great's conquest of Persia.

Other Panhellenic shrines also pointed toward ideas of national unity. At the temples of Zeus at Olympia and Nemea and that of Poseidon at Corinth as well as at Delphi, athletic and artistic contests were held in an annual rotation, with competitors from all of Greece. These games had a political dimension, since during them a general truce was enforced on all Greek cities at war with each other (as many often were). Other temples of Panhellenic importance included the temple of Demeter at Eleusis (near Athens), where initiates into the goddess's mysteries received a kind of personal salvation, and that of the hero Asklepios at Epidaurus, famed for healing the sick and disabled through the interpretation of dreams.

Magic

Many rituals that had existed in early Greece were not suited to the religion of the new cities because they served private rather than public interests. These were mostly of two kinds: purifications meant to cure disease or remove guilt from personal or ancestral sin, or initiations into secret mysteries that were supposed to bring salvation of the soul after death. These ceremonies were performed by ritualists, especially priests of the god Dionysus or the hero Orpheus, who wandered from city to city and thus were not part of the religious hierarchy of any city. Since these initiates stood apart from the city in some way, they were thought of as alien and hostile and their rituals characterized as foreign. After the Persian invasion of Greece in 480 B.C.E they began to be called "magicians" and their practices denounced as magic. A magician, or *magus*, was, properly speaking, a priest of the Persian national religion, but the term came to be used in condemnation of Greek religious figures whom the city found subversive or threatening. Many of the practices denounced as magic and therefore foreign were, in fact, based on old Greek traditions, while many elements of civic religion—such as the temple and animal sacrifice—had been borrowed from the Near East. The point of using a loaded term like *magic* was ideological, not historical. For all these same reasons Christians were also later accused of magic.

The attack on these old-fashioned Greek practices as magic was led by such philosophers as Heracleitus (ca. 540–ca. 480 B.C.E.) and Plato (ca. 428–348 or 347 B.C.E.) and by the Hippocratic physicians, who, beginning in the fifth century B.C.E., wished to establish a new sort of medical practice based on reason. These groups were most hostile to magic precisely because they were themselves trying to make the betterment of the soul and the healing of the body a respectable part of civic culture and felt they had to distinguish themselves from what the city rejected. Other philosophers, however, like Pythagoras (ca. 580–ca. 500 B.C.E.) and Empedocles (ca. 490–430 B.C.E.), embraced the image of the magician because of its aura of mystery and subversive power.

Magic was a sort of phantom of religion, one that worked for the individual against the city. Even members of the elites who ruled cities found certain situations in which their own interest conflicted with the interest of the city as a whole. By the mid-fifth century, the very period that is often considered the golden age of Greece and the high point of Greek rationalism, some people saw an advantage in fulfilling the role of a magician who could use the mysterious powers of secret rituals to advance private interests against that of the city—in return for a fee. They began to practice new rituals, especially those involving so-called curse tablets. Such a tablet consisted of a letter written on a sheet of lead under the name of a god to the ghost of a dead man. The tablet, deposited in the man's grave or in a cave or well, commanded the ghost to carry out certain orders. For example, it might tell the ghost to change the outcome of a lawsuit (and so prevent the working of justice in the city). Another common command was to make a woman want to commit adultery with a certain man (which also attacked the city because citizenship was tied to membership in certain clans and thus the whole fabric of the city would be undermined by uncertainty about the paternity of children). Other tablets sought to damage the business of some businessmen in favor of a rival (which would subvert the economic structure of the city). Still other tablets tried to "fix" the outcome of sporting events (which in Greece were religious festivals and part of civic religion).

While we might think of this kind of "magic" as naive, the archaeological discovery of thousands of curse tablets from all over the Greek world (and later the whole Roman Empire, which readily accepted this kind of ritual) shows that it was very common. The formation of the Greek cities had many benefits for their citizens, but at the price of limits on individual freedom and subordination to the collective. Individuals trying to maintain a balance between duty to the city and their personal desires released the emotional pressure through agencies like magic and secret initiations, attacking the city in a symbolic way, as they would not do in more direct action. Magic was a protest against the city.

Myth

A myth is an attempt to explain something that is not understood, using linguistic models such as metaphor or analogy. Myths interpret the world in the way the mind most easily understands, through the structure of language itself. An example is to say that the world is like a human being with its many interconnected parts ruled by a mind or that a storm is like the anger of a great king. This might seem simplistic compared with modern scientific explanations, but it is not intended to be the same kind of answer to questions about the world. Myth begins in oral tradition and ritual, but in Greece it became the basis of one of the greatest world literatures, especially in the Homeric epics and in the first plays in the modern sense, the dramas of Aeschylus (525–456 B.C.E.), Sophocles (ca. 496–406 B.C.E.), and Euripides (ca. 484–406 B.C.E.) and the comedies of Aristophanes (448–385 B.C.E.), and the first poems in the modern sense, by Sappho (fl. ca. 610–580 B.C.E.), Pindar (ca. 522–ca. 438 B.C.E.), and others. These authors are among our best sources for understanding Greek religion.

Perhaps the most important Greek myth is told by Hesiod in his *Theogony*. Drawing on older Near Eastern mythology, Hesiod describes the creation of the world through successive generations of the divine family. The Greek word for world is *cosmos,* which means "order." The universe moves from an undifferentiated state toward the order we see around us today. Hesiod imagines first an emptiness or gap (*chaos*). Creation begins when love (*Eros*) binds together whatever is separated by chaos. This calls into being the first two gods, Gaia (the earth) and Uranus (the sky). They give birth to the Titans, a race of wild and cruel gods. The chief of these is Kronos, who is incited by his mother to castrate and dethrone his father and become the ruler of the universe. He then marries his sister Rhea but devours their children as they are born so that he will not suffer the same fate as his father. Finally, Rhea hides one of her children, Zeus, from Kronos. Once he reaches adulthood, Zeus indeed attacks his father and frees his brothers and sisters from their father's belly. These siblings are the first Olympian gods. They defeat the Titans and bind them under the earth. Zeus and the Olympians go on to finish the process of creation, giving the world its final form, destroying various monsters, and creating humankind. This myth explains the creation of the world in terms that anyone can understand, as the genealogy of a family. With each generation the gods (and therefore the world) become less abstract, less terrible, and more human. At the same time, we see that Greek gods were free to do the very things that were most forbidden in Greek society, such as attacking their parents or committing incest.

The 12 Olympian gods were honored as a distinct group in Greek religion and figure prominently in Greek literature. The original children of Kronos and Rhea were Zeus, Poseidon, and Hades and their sisters Hera, Demeter, and Hestia. The three brothers cast lots to see which part of the world each would control: Zeus receives the sky, Poseidon the sea, and Hades the underworld, where he rules over the dead. Hera takes charge of marriage, Demeter of agriculture, and Hestia of the hearth, the life of individual homes. Aphrodite, the goddess of love and desire, comes into existence from the foam generated when Uranus's castrated genitals fell into the sea. The other Olympians are the offspring of Zeus. Zeus fathers the twins Apollo and Artemis (the sun and the moon) with the Titan Leto. Zeus engenders a son by Metis ("thought"), who is prophesied to supplant him just as Zeus did his own father. So Zeus swallows up the pregnant mother and, in due course, gives birth himself to the child, miraculously changed in gender: Athena, the mistress of warfare, who becomes his most powerful and most loyal ally.

Zeus marries his sister Hera and fathers Hephaestus, the craftsman of the gods, and Ares, the god of battle. Hermes is another son of Zeus and his messenger in charge of conveying the dead to the underworld and of everything in human life that concerns mediation (such as speech) as well as of merchants and thieves (who each transfer goods from one to another). Finally, Dionysus usually is considered an Olympian (though he exceeds the number 12, he is counted in alternation with Hestia). He is the god of wine and the offspring of Zeus and the mortal woman Semele. When her body is destroyed on beholding Zeus's true divine form (jealous Hera tricks her into asking for this), Zeus carries Dionysus in his thigh and gives birth to his son.

Cosmology

The Homeric poems imagined the earth as a flat disc like a warrior's shield, because if one stands in an open place and surveys the horizon in all directions, it appears to be a circle. Delphi, the sacred center of Greece, was thought to be at the center of this circle. The sky appears to be a solid dome arching over this disc, making it also easy to imagine a corresponding hemisphere under the earth, the underworld. This worldview is inherent in all Greek myth and probably goes back to the earliest times.

In the sixth century B.C.E. the first philosophers—called the "pre-Socratics" because they wrote before the great flowering of Greek philosophy with Socrates (ca. 470–399 B.C.E) and his successors—began to question the mythic conception of the world. Their questions led to the new idea that the nature of the world could be investigated through reason rather than through the creation of myth. Philosophers did not deny the presence of divinity in the world—they affirmed it—but it was a divinity deduced from the observation of the world rather than the traditional anthropomorphic gods of Homer. Philosophical investigations eventually led to a geocentric model of the solar system, in which the earth was at the center and orbited by the sun, moon, and planets. Some speculations by philosophers, however, anticipated important discoveries of modern science: Aristarchus (ca. 310–ca. 220 B.C.E.) suggested a heliocentric solar system (with the sun orbited by the planets, including the earth), and Democritus (ca. 460–ca. 370 B.C.E.) posited the atomic nature of matter—although neither idea gained wide acceptance in antiquity. The achievement of philosophy was to replace tradition with reason as a way of knowing the truth, if only for a small elite group.

At the same time, the abstraction of their conceptions about the heavenly bodies (as opposed to the older anthropomorphic gods) led Greeks to invent the pseudoscience of astrology (based on older Mesopotamian ideas). Its essential idea is that the stars and planets influence events on earth and that astronomical calculation can therefore predict people's personalities and future events. The view became very widespread, though it was countered to an extent both by traditional philosophical ideas about the freedom of the individual and by skepticism that such detailed knowledge of the future was possible.

The Late Classical and Hellenistic Periods

Alexander the Great of Macedon (356–323 B.C.E.) conquered first Greece and then the whole of the Persian Empire from Egypt to India and central Asia. This brought Greek culture into an entirely new world, exposing Greeks to new influences as they colonized this vast area. Religion underwent many changes. One result of this extraordinary achievement was that Alexander became worshipped as a god in his own lifetime. The spirits of the exceptional men of past ages had always been worshipped as heroes, but Alexander demanded and received this worship for himself (a legend circulated that Alexander was actually the son of Zeus, who had mated with his mother in the form of a serpent). Thereafter, during the Hellenistic Period (323–31 B.C.E.), his successors in the various Greek kingdoms carved out of Alexander's empire were routinely worshipped as saviors and protectors by their subjects.

Another feature of Hellenistic religion was the re-creation of native religions as Greek mystery cults. The worship of the goddess Isis in Egypt was only the most prominent of many foreign religions that were given a Greek interpretation and exported to cities throughout the Greek and later the Roman world. Greek philosophers like Pythagoras and Plato interpreted the belief that the dead were reborn like new plants from harvested seed to mean that they were reincarnated into new life determined by the moral judgments of the gods. These phenomena helped pave the way for Christianity, which eventually replaced Greek religion and incorporated many of its features. The Greek world was gradually conquered by Rome, and the Roman emperor Constantine announced toleration of Christianity within the empire in the Edict of Milan (313 C.E.). The emperor Justinian finally outlawed traditional Greek and Roman religion in 529 C.E.

ROME

BY MICHAEL J. O'NEAL

The complex religious beliefs of the ancient Romans are difficult to describe for at least three reasons. First, they changed over time, often radically so. Second, the Romans incorporated the beliefs of numerous cultures that lived within their vast empire. Finally, the Romans tended to be tolerant of divergent religious beliefs within their borders as long as these religions did not disrupt the social order.

The chief generalization that can be made is that Romans were pagans, meaning they practiced a polytheistic religion. The word *paganism* comes from the Latin *paganus*, meaning "country dweller," and was a term Roman city dwellers often used as something of an insult directed against less-sophisticated people in the countryside. *Polytheism* means belief in more than one god. Even people who are not students of Roman life are likely to be familiar with the names of some of the many Roman gods, if only because planets in the solar system are named after them, including Mercury, Venus, Mars, Jupiter, Saturn, and Neptune. The term *pantheon*, which originated in Greece, is used to refer to a set of officially recognized gods such as these. The makeup of the Roman pantheon, particularly as it was recognized by the state, changed over time.

The polytheism of the Roman Empire did not endure until the empire's end. In the early years of the Common Era, Christianity was spreading throughout many parts of the Roman Empire, particularly in the east. In the fourth century C.E. Christianity became the official religion of the empire, and pagan beliefs and practices were officially outlawed.

EARLY ROMAN RELIGION

Rome borrowed a number of its gods from the ancient Greeks, often simply giving a Greek god a Roman name. Thus, the Greek god Zeus became the Roman god Jupiter; the Greek Hermes became the Roman Mercury. However, historians of religion note a peculiar difference between the Greek and Roman pantheons of gods. The Greeks developed an elaborate mythology, or set of narratives, surrounding the activities of their gods. Many of these narratives remain foundational narratives in Western life. For example, the Greeks originated the story of Narcissus, a handsome youth who fell in love with his own reflection in the water. His name is still used to refer to narcissistic people, or those who are vain and overly concerned with their appearance. The story of Icarus, who plunged to his death when he flew too close to the sun and caused his wax wings to melt, survives as a warning against arrogantly setting aspirations that are too high.

The Romans, in contrast, attached little in the way of narrative to their early gods, identifying them by name and function only. The earliest Romans saw their gods in animistic terms, which meant they believed in gods who ruled over or influenced places and aspects of their daily lives, but they did not create stories about them or their relationships with other gods. In time, genealogies and a complex system of mythology grew up around these gods. The earliest Romans, however, saw these gods in simple terms, referring to them as *numina*; this word that is difficult to translate, though "presence" or "power" comes close. Early Romans believed that these gods were present everywhere in life. Many were adopted from the Etruscans, who predated the Romans on the Italian peninsula. Roman theologians referred to these gods and goddesses as *di indigetes*, from which the modern word *indigenous* comes. These were the native Roman deities, in contrast to the *di novensides*, or "newcomer gods" imported from other cultures, especially in later centuries. A list of *di indigetes* runs to at least 180 names.

An important early Roman goddess was Ceres, the goddess of growing plants, especially grains, and motherly love (and the source of the modern word *cereal*). Ceres is an example of the way Roman communities adopted gods and goddesses as patrons, particularly in times of crisis. Ceres was the patron of the Mediterranean island of Sicily, but in 496 B.C.E. the Italian peninsula suffered a famine, so Ceres was absorbed as part of the Roman pantheon as a way to overcome crop failure.

Additionally, Ceres is a good example of how sets of minor gods and goddesses served as assistants to look over particular human affairs. Thus, Ceres was attended by numerous other minor gods and goddesses who oversaw various aspects of agriculture. A few examples include Insitor, the sower; Obarator, the plower; Occator, the harrower; and Sarritor, who weeded. Thus, when a farmer was about to sow his crop, he invoked the name of Ceres and her attendant Insitor. But Ceres and her attendants were only a few of the many gods and goddesses of archaic Rome. January, for example, is named after Janus, the god depicted with two faces facing in opposite directions. Janus was the god of doors, gates, and beginnings and endings. Again, in the early Roman cosmology these spirits, or presences, were considered part of the fabric of the world and human endeavor, to be honored and appeased in response to circumstances.

In the ancient Roman home the senior male, often called the paterfamilias, was regarded as the chief priest of his family, perhaps of his larger clan. He supervised worship in his family and headed his family's cult, which included its ancestors. With regard to public religious activity, the king was the nation's religious leader, but religion was very much a local affair, conducted primarily within the family. Each family worshipped its own cult, or favored gods.

Over time, though, a system of public observances and practices evolved. A class of priests, called flamens, ensured that proper observances and sacrifices were made to the gods. Just as the gods were ranked in order of importance, so too were the priests. The highest rank included those responsible for the most important gods. These were Jupiter (the chief god, equivalent to the Greek Zeus and responsible for rainfall, thunder, and the sky), Mars (originally the god of agriculture but later the god of war), and Quirinus (the god of the state, or the people, and of the army during times of peace). These gods were called the Capitoline Triad because they were worshipped in a temple on Capitoline Hill in Rome. Historian call this particular group of gods the Archaic Triad because a later Capitoline Triad emerged, consisting of Jupiter, Juno (the queen of the gods), and Minerva (the goddess of wisdom).

Just below these more prestigious flamens were those associated with less important gods and goddesses, such as Janus and Vesta. Vesta was the goddess of the hearth, and in the ancient Roman Forum a fire, the "hearth" of the state, was kept perpetually burning. It was attended by a group of women called the vestal virgins, who were obligated to maintain the site for a period of 30 years and whose chief duty was to keep the fire burning. In the home, wives and mothers honored Vesta, prayers to Vesta were offered before and after meals, and every town had a perpetual fire in honor of her. When the Romans established a new colony, coals from the "mother fire" in Rome were carried to the vestal hearth in the new location.

Some of the other major gods and goddesses of the Roman pantheon included Apollo, the god of the sun, festivities, music, and dancing; Bacchus, the god of orgies and drinking; Cupid, the god of romance and love; Diana, the goddess of the moon and hunting; Mercury, the messenger god; Neptune, the god of the sea; Venus, the goddess of sex and beauty; Pluto, the king of the underworld; Saturn, the god of agriculture; and Vulcan, the god of smithing.

Religion in the Roman Republic

Religion during the early monarchial period of Rome (the period from the founding of Rome up to 509 B.C.E., when the Roman Republic was created) was therefore fairly simple. It was based on a belief in animistic spirits that influenced human activities, particularly those associated with the home and the farm. While public worship was conducted under the auspices of the king, religious belief was centered in the home. A small class of priests was responsible for ensuring that the major gods were honored, but in rural Rome a family's senior male was responsible for maintaining religious observances in the home. Much of early Rome's religion was inherited from other nations, blending native Etruscan religious beliefs with those of the Greeks.

Religious matters became remarkably more complex during the period of the Roman Republic and beyond. The early founders of the republic were the first to give thought to the modern doctrine of the separation of church and state. During the earlier monarchial period the king was Rome's chief religious figure. Under the republic religious duties were separated from political duties, though religion continued to affect political decisions. The founders of the republic created a priesthood called *rex sacrorum,* meaning "king of rites." Priests carried out the duties of the earlier kings, but, to prevent them from abusing their authority, they could not hold public office or become members of the Senate.

Several classes of priests existed to carry out various duties. The most important of these classes was the College of Pontiffs, led by the pontifex maximus, the chief religious figure in Rome. Until the third century B.C.E. the pontifex maximus was chosen by members of the college. Later the position became a publicly elected one. The pontifex maximus supervised the *rex sacrorum,* the vestal virgins, and the major flamens. As noted earlier, each flamen was associated with an individual god and carried out the rituals performed to honor that god.

Throughout the late Roman Republic the requirements for becoming a pontiff changed. At first only members of the patrician class could become pontiffs. In about 300 B.C.E., however, membership was opened to the lower class of plebeians. Although the office of pontifex maximus came to be publicly elected, not anyone could be a candidate. A candidate had to be a member of the College of Pontiffs and be nominated by members of the college. Members were appointed to the college by existing members, so the entire process remained somewhat closed. Not until 104 B.C.E. were pontiffs elected by the public.

Despite this opening of the process, most members of the College of Pontiffs were members of the social elite. Many were also prominent ambassadors, politicians, and generals. Perhaps the best example is Julius Caesar (100–44 B.C.E.), one of Rome's most famous emperors, who served as pontifex maximus early in his career. Evidence suggests, however, that these prominent people did not abuse their religious authority. For example, no single prominent family ever had more than one member in the College of Pontiffs.

The College of Pontiffs had a number of duties. In many respects, the college could be said to have assumed any duties that were not fulfilled by other colleges. Thus, members of the College of Pontiffs were experts in Roman law. They knew, for example, the exact wording of legal documents that had to be used to gain access to courts of law. The college also maintained the calendar and records of public events. Members supervised such legal matters as burials, wills, adoptions, and inheritances. It also supervised the vestal virgins, public rituals, and rituals having to do with sacrifices and vows. Finally, the College of Pontiffs supervised the *ludi Romani,* or Roman Games, held annually in September in honor of the god Jupiter beginning in 366 B.C.E.

While the College of Pontiffs was the principal administrative arm of Roman religion, the College of Augurs represented the efforts of Romans to communicate with their gods. The chief duty of the augurs was to interpret the will of the gods through various rituals and omens. The word *augur* survives in modern English in such expressions as "that augurs well," meaning that something promises to turn out well.

To understand the position of the augur, it is necessary to understand how Romans conceived their relationship with their gods. In modern life religious devotion generally suggests that believers submit themselves to God's will and that the deity is a loving one who cares for the welfare of the people he created. The ancient Romans saw their relationship with the gods in somewhat different terms. A god was to be honored, but the relationship was often one of bargaining. Public vows, for example, were made to form a legal contract with a god, in which the person making the vow promised to perform an act to honor the god in exchange for the god's favor. Thus, for example, armies vowed publicly to build a temple to a god in exchange for a victory in war. The god might or might not choose to grant the person's wish, but the person still owed a duty of loyalty to the god.

The notion of bargaining required a way for people to communicate wishes to the gods and for the gods to communicate their intentions to humans. The ancient Romans believed that the gods communicated their wishes through omens that had to be read by a class of priests. This was the role of the College of Augurs. To carry out their function the augurs took part in two types of activities; the activities were supervised by civil magistrates, but the augur was present to interpret the results and report his conclusions.

One activity was to read the intention of the gods by interpreting patterns in the flights of birds in a *templum,* or sacred space. The magistrate and augur marked out the sacred space and then waited for birds to fly overhead. Alternatively, augurs interpreted the behavior of specially selected sacred chickens. For example, grain would be fed to the chickens by a *pullarius,* or "chicken man," and whether they ate the grain or how enthusiastically they did so was taken as an omen. These kinds of omens were read in connection with virtually any sort of political activity: an election, a war, the passage of a statute, and so on. The rules for conducting these rituals were extremely detailed and complex. If even the smallest detail was overlooked or conducted improperly, the ritual was deemed invalid and had to be redone. Often the Roman Senate reviewed the conclusions of the augurs and, if they determined that the ritual was improperly conducted, ruled that it had to be conducted again.

The other ritual activity the augurs supervised was divination through animal sacrifice. An animal such as a goat was ritually sacrificed and its *exta,* or entrails, especially the gallbladder and liver, were examined. The augurs who conducted this ritual were a suborder of the augurs called haruspices—literally, "men who look at guts." There were 60 official haruspices, though others practiced this type of divination unofficially. It is believed that this type of divination was an Etruscan practice that the Romans absorbed. Again, the requirements were very specific. A particular animal had to be selected, including size, gender, age, and color, depending on the god whose will was being questioned. The animal was blessed, carried to an altar in procession, and killed with a single blow. If the animal struggled or if the haruspex tripped or slipped, it boded ill. The haruspex then examined the entrails. If there was anything wrong with them, such as gallstones or spots, it was a sign that the gods had rejected the sacrifice and a new animal had to be slaughtered. If the entrails were flawless, that was a sign that the gods approved the course of action being proposed.

The Romans believed that they could read the will of the gods in at least three additional ways. One consisted of *monstra,* or prodigies, from which the modern word *monster* comes. *Monstra* could consist of any natural but strange occurrence, such as the birth of a calf with two heads or severe lightning. When such an event occurred, the Senate called in haruspices to inquire into the prodigy and interpret the gods' will. The *monstra* were not necessarily punishments or prophecies of doom; rather, they were warnings that the gods felt neglected, giving the Romans a chance to respond and perhaps mend their ways.

A second additional way the Romans read the will of the gods was through the Sibylline Books. These books date back to the monarchial period in Rome and the reign of Lucius Tarquinius Superbus (r. 534–510 B.C.E.), or Tarquin the Elder. This was a period in Roman history that remains shrouded in legend. It is known that the Sibyls were priestesses and prophets in ancient Greece. One of these, who lived in Cumae, a Greek colony northwest of Naples, Italy, was the most famous and has been known to history as *the* Sibyl. According to the legend, she arrived in Rome to sell Tarquin nine books that, she claimed, foretold the history of Rome. Initially Tarquin rejected her offer, so she burned three of the books and renewed her offer. Again Tarquin refused, so she burned three more. Tarquin relented and purchased the remaining three.

The Sibylline books were not prophetic, but they did include advice on what Romans should do when signs from the gods were inauspicious, or unfavorable. The books were housed in the Temple of Jupiter on Capitoline Hill in Rome until the temple and its contents were destroyed by fire in 83 B.C.E. In charge of the books were the *duoviri sacris faciundis,* or "the two men for sacred actions," yet another order of priests, albeit a small one. Later the number of priests in charge of the books increased to 10 and then to 15. Normally the Senate ordered the *duoviri* or haruspices to consult the books in cases of crisis or emergency or when they had observed *monstra.* The usual recommendation that came from consulting the books was for Rome to import a new god or cult, often from Greece. The *duoviri* played some role in establishing the new cult, at which point their role ended.

A final additional way the Romans believed they could learn the will of the gods was in the interpretation of dreams. According to the Roman historian Livy (59 B.C.E.–17 C.E.), in 293 B.C.E. an epidemic broke out on the Italian peninsula. After the Sibylline Books were consulted, it was concluded that they directed the Romans to build a cult site and temple for the Greek god of medicine, Aesculapius, on an island in the Tiber River. This temple became a hospital of sorts, where ill or troubled Romans went to recover by making sacrifices to Aesculapius. Patients slept in the temple and asked the god to explain what was wrong with them in a dream. The temple priests then interpreted the dream.

The priests in the College of Fetiales had a single job: to ensure that when Rome declared war, it did so properly. The procedure for declaring war was complex. Four of the 20 members of the College of Fetiales were dispatched to the foreign nation with demands for restitution and threats of war. If a month passed with no response, the *fetiales* declared war. The *fetiales* then sacrificed a pig, returned to the border of the country's land, and hurled a spear over the border into the land. It was believed that in this way, Rome's wars would be just. Beginning in 280 B.C.E. Rome thought it was impractical for the *fetiales* to hurl a spear into a far-flung foreign land, so the ritual was conducted at the temple of Bellona, a goddess of war, which the Romans thought of as "enemy" territory.

Religion in the Roman Empire

The period modern historians refer to as the Roman Empire began in the first century B.C.E. In the early centuries of the empire a number of changes took place in Roman religion. One was the greater popularity of foreign cults from such countries as Iran and Egypt. The second was the growth of the Imperial Cult. The third was a growing trend toward monotheism (belief in one supreme God) and the eventual conversion of the Roman Empire to Christianity.

The Romans ruled a vast empire that contained many different cultures and traditions. Accordingly, Romans were exposed to a variety of religious beliefs. Many of these were absorbed into the Roman belief system. In particular, cults from such places as Iran, India, the Iberian Peninsula (Spain and Portugal), Britain, and Egypt became popular.

Several examples could be cited. One was the cult of Cybele, referring to a Phrygian goddess regarded as an earth mother and the goddess of fertility, caves, mountains, wild animals, and nature in general. (Phrygia was an ancient country in Asia Minor.) In Rome she became Magna Mater, or "great mother." Many of Cybele's followers took part in ecstatic ceremonies that included dancing, drumming, and drinking. She was officially adopted by Rome in 203 B.C.E. A second major cult was that of Isis, a goddess from Egyptian mythology. Throughout Egypt and in many places outside Egypt, Isis was the center of a mystery cult—that is, a cult that believed it had secret, mystic knowledge and wisdom that could be known only impartially and intuitively. Many Romans regarded Isis as an aspect of Cybele. The emperor Caligula (r. 37–41 C.E.) was an enthusiastic follower of the Isis cult and established a festival in her honor. Another foreign mystery cult that gained popularity in Rome was the cult of Mithras, a Persian god associated with the practice of astrology. Finally, Sol Invictus, meaning "the undefeated sun," was a pagan nature cult adopted by a succession of Roman emperors to emphasize their relationship with the sun god.

One of the most important cults during the Roman Empire, however, was native. It is generally referred to as the Imperial Cult and refers to the belief that the emperor was divine. The purpose of this cult was to strengthen the loyalty of the Roman people and Rome's many colonies to their emperor. Among the emperors who were deified in this way were Augustus (r. 27 B.C.E.–14 C.E.), Claudius I (r. 41–54 C.E.), Vespasian (r. 69–79 C.E.), and Titus (r. 79–81 C.E.). The deification of these emperors was declared by the Roman Senate after the emperor's death. Although the practice seems strange in modern life, ancient peoples, particularly those in the eastern half of the Roman Empire, had a long tradition of regarding their kings and emperors as having a special relationship with the gods, and many prominent Romans during the empire began to claim descent from the gods. Many Roman public buildings, including temples, baths, theaters, and arenas, were built as monuments to the Imperial Cult.

Christianity in the Roman Empire

For a period of some three centuries Christians were cruelly persecuted by the Roman Empire. Rome regarded the new religion as a threat to its power. Emperor Nero (r. 54–68 C.E.) claimed that the Great Fire of Rome in July 64 C.E. was the work of Christians, though some historians believe that he started the fire because he wanted to rebuild Rome in his own image. Under the emperor Diocletian (r. 284–305 C.E.) the persecution of Christians was particularly severe.

Despite this persecution, Christian missionaries won converts and created Christian communities throughout the empire. The persecution of Christians ended abruptly in 313 C.E. when the emperor Constantine I (r. 306–337 C.E.) converted to Christianity. Some historians believe that his conversion was sincere; others argue that he converted only because he could see the growing influence of Christianity and wanted to preserve his power. In any event, he established religious freedom in the empire in 313 C.E. with the Edict of Milan. In 325 C.E. he called the Council of Nicea, the Catholic Church's first ecumenical council, which established some of the bedrock doctrines of the church. Then in 380 C.E. the emperor Theodosius I (r. 379–395 C.E.) issued an edict that made Christianity the official religion of the empire. In 391 C.E. Theodosius outlawed all other religious cults, and many ancient Roman temples were either destroyed or rededicated to Christian saints. The Pantheon, for example, had been a temple dedicated to all the Roman gods but became a Christian church dedicated to all the Christian saints. In the fifth century the Roman Empire fractured, the western portion coming to an end with the abdication of the emperor Romulus Augustulus (r. 475–476 C.E.) in 476 C.E. Although the empire came to an end, Christianity survived. The most dominant Christian figure in Europe was the bishop of Rome, which remained the seat of the Catholic Church.

THE AMERICAS

BY KEITH JORDAN

Reconstructing the religious beliefs, cosmologies, and ritual practices of the ancient peoples of the New World is a difficult and uncertain task because of the nature of the surviving evidence. The majority of early Native American cultures did not develop systems of writing, so they left no religious texts or mythic epics. In Mesoamerica several ancient civilizations employed hieroglyphic scripts to record information. However, in some cases, like the early Olmec culture (ca. 1500–ca. 400 B.C.E.), we are not yet able to decipher these writing systems. Advances in the decipherment of Maya glyphs (symbolic characters used in writing) have opened new windows into the mythic cosmology and royal religious rituals of this culture. However, Maya inscriptions do not become plentiful until the Early Classic Period (ca. 150–ca. 550 C.E.), and earlier examples are more difficult to read and interpret.

For other Mesoamerican groups and for all of the peoples of ancient North and South America, scholars must make inferences about their beliefs from archaeological evidence. Finding objects buried with the dead, for example, allows archaeologists to infer belief in an afterlife where the deceased would have need of such items. Excavated artifacts or arrangements of objects that appear to have served no practical purpose may yield information on religious rituals—or such an interpretation might simply reflect our own lack of knowledge of ancient behavior. Large, elaborate, or specialized buildings lacking traces of domestic activities often are best interpreted as shrines or temples. Human and animal images carved in stone, modeled in clay, or painted on rock faces, ceramics, or architecture provide glimpses of gods, spirits, and ritual practitioners, though in the absence of written texts, interpretation of these works of art necessarily involves speculation.

All of these archaeological finds require considerable interpretation. In some areas and cases, archaeologists use the religious beliefs of much later historical Native American peoples from the same geographic region as a framework to understand the ancient material. This practice can be risky guesswork—we rarely can be sure whether later peoples were truly related to ancient cultures in the same areas or represent relative newcomers. In any case, religion and cosmological ideas can change drastically over millennia, as the documented history of Old World religions clearly show. A more cautious approach uses the behavior of later Native Americans as well as other peoples at similar levels of social organization as possible analogies for understanding ancient religion, without suggesting direct historical connections.

Beginnings

We possess very little information to help us understand the religious beliefs of the first settlers of the Americas from Asia at the end of the last ice age 10,000 to 12,000 or more years ago. Their deliberate burial of the dead, accompanied by tools and weapons, and evidence of funerary rituals, like cremation, indicate a belief in an afterlife. Some scholars attempt to reconstruct the basic ideas of the religion of the earliest Native Americans by comparing the beliefs and practices of much later Native American groups across the Americas. Certain ideas about the universe and patterns of ritual behavior are shared by many indigenous peoples throughout North, South, and Central America, suggesting that these concepts were introduced by the ancient common ancestors of all of these diverse cultures. For example, many Native American cosmologies view the earth as the middle level of a multilayered universe, with a watery underworld beneath and the sky realm of sun, moon, and other celestial spirits above. Often a mythical central axis or pathway, seen as a giant tree, unites all three levels and passes through the center of the earth, allowing spirits and humans to cross from the earth to other levels of the universe. Frequently, the four cardinal directions—north, south, east, and west—are also sacred and determine the plan of the universe, and each is equated with a symbolic color.

Closely related to these widespread beliefs among Native Americans is a common type of religious specialist, the shaman. Modern shamans are ritual practitioners who are believed to be able to travel to the spirit worlds above and below the earth, often along the central axis of the cosmos, while in trance states induced by fasting, repeatedly drumming and dancing, using hallucinogens, or employing other means. They use their abilities to contact and control nature spirits, spirits of the dead, or deities in order to cure illnesses, predict the future, and obtain good hunting results or harvests for their clients. Shamans throughout the Americas are believed to ally themselves with guardian spirits, often in animal form, who help them perform magic. In a trance state the shaman may experience being transformed into an animal and may do battle against evil spirits and other shamans in this form. Because shamanism is common along the Pacific coast of Asia from Vietnam north to Siberia as well as in the Americas and because the ice age ancestors of Native Americans came from northeast Asia, some anthropologists see shamanism as part of the cultural "baggage" brought into the New World by the first settlers.

We also have little evidence for religion among the archaic hunting and collecting peoples who succeeded the first Native Americans (ca. 7000–ca. 1800 B.C.E.). Burial practices in some areas, like eastern North America, grew more elaborate, suggesting more complex ideas of a hereafter. Rock paintings across the New World show human and animal figures. Some rock art in the American West shows strangely costumed figures, who may be shamans, and geometric patterns that some anthropologists equate with visual patterns experienced in hallucinatory trances. In Oaxaca in southern Mexico, remains of dismembered bodies at a cave site hint at the beginnings of human sacrifice some 7,000 years ago.

Eastern North America

A striking increase in the complexity of burial and other rituals took place in the North American Midwest and Southeast during the Early and Middle Woodland Periods (ca. 1000 B.C.E.–ca. 500 C.E.). The Adena culture of southern Ohio erected large burial mounds over burials with elaborate grave goods. Among these objects are stone tubes used as pipes for smoking wild tobacco, a plant still used by native South

American shamans as a hallucinogen. Comparing these pipes to similar objects produced by recent Native North American groups suggests that the pipes might also have been "sucking tubes" employed by shamans to suck spirits of disease out of a patient's body. One pipe was sculpted into a figure of a man whose strange body shape suggests dwarfism or a goiter. In historic Native American groups deformed individuals were sometimes viewed as having special connections to the spirit world. One man buried in an Ohio Adena mound had his upper front teeth removed so that he could insert the upper jaw and fangs of a wolf into the space. Was he a shaman thought to transform into a wolf during his trances?

The Hopewell cultures of Ohio and Illinois (ca. 200 B.C.E.–ca. 400 C.E.) created massive square and circular enclosures bounded by earthen mounds and ditches. These sites are free from domestic trash and objects associated with daily life, suggesting that they had a ceremonial use. They are frequently located near springs, caves, mountains, and other landscape features regarded as sacred by later Native Americans, and some are aligned to permit observation of the solstices and equinoxes as well as other astronomical events. Small wooden buildings associated with these earthworks may have been shrines or lodging for pilgrims visiting the sacred site from distant regions.

We do not know what sorts of spirits were worshipped in these enclosures. Human forms do not show up frequently in Hopewell sculpture, but animals are shown in a realistic fashion on carved stone effigy pipes. These sculptures face the smoker when the pipe is in use and could represent the animal spirit allies of shamans. Stone and clay sculptures of men with single horns protruding from their foreheads hint that such ritual specialists were present in this culture. Ancient West Mexican and 19th-century C.E. Plains Indian shamans wore their hair in a similar fashion. In one Hopewell sculpture a possible shaman is shown wearing a bearskin. Among many later Native North American groups, bears are strongly associated with healing. Hopewell burials yield bone tubes that may have been sucking tubes and copper headdresses in the form of deer antlers, possibly used by shamans in hunting magic. At one Ohio Hopewell site, a face mask made out of a human skull could have been part of the costume of a shaman, perhaps for burial rites.

The Hopewell peoples buried their dead under mounds, frequently after keeping the bodies above ground in a shrine or charnel (a building or chamber in which the dead are kept) that was then ritually destroyed and buried. They may have envisioned such events as releasing the spirits of the dead into the afterlife and renewing the world and the community in symbolic parallel to cycles of life and death in nature.

MESOAMERICA

During the Early Formative (ca. 1800–ca. 1200 B.C.E.) in Mexico, village farmers produced and buried thousands of small clay figurines. Most of these images represent women, sometimes with exaggerated breasts and hips. Religious specialists might have used such objects as part of curing rituals, perhaps aimed at correcting infertility in both land and humans. Other figures from central Mexico show masked and costumed males—perhaps the religious specialists themselves.

On the Gulf Coast of Mexico in the modern states of Tabasco and Veracruz, the Olmec civilization (ca. 1500–ca. 400 B.C.E.) constructed large sites with monumental architecture that served as both political capitals and religious centers. Many archaeologists interpret Olmec religion as a kind of shamanism, but with the Olmec kings taking on the duties and traits of shamans as a way of justifying their claims to power. Some small Olmec stone carvings show male figures apparently transforming into jaguars, the most common guardians or alter egos for Mesoamerican shamans. Figures showing varying mixtures of human and feline features may represent different stages of the transformation. The hallucinogenic "fuel" for this process might be indicated on one

Jade votive ax of a figure combining human and animal traits and thought to represent a supernatural being, Olmec, from Mexico (1200–400 B.C.E.); the flaming eyebrows mimic the crest of an eagle, and the cleft in the head compares with the groove in the head of a jaguar. (© The Trustees of the British Museum)

of these images where an engraving of a toad appears on its head. The venom of the toad species *Bufo marinus* has hallucinogenic properties, and toad bones discarded in trash heaps at the Olmec ceremonial site of San Lorenzo support its religious use by the Olmec. Some small stone and ceramic Olmec figures also portray individuals in strangely contorted positions resembling yoga and other postures that some scholars interpret as facilitating altered states of consciousness by comparison to spiritual practices from other cultures. Other images seem to show the king identified with the World Tree, the center of the shamanic universe, representing his ability to mediate between this world and the supernatural realms above and below.

Colossal Olmec stone sculptures and a cave painting show rulers emerging from the mouths of fanged reptilian or jaguarlike monsters. Some wear bird costumes, perhaps representing "flying" in a hallucinatory trance. Based on the beliefs of the later Maya, many archaeologists interpret these monster mouths as symbolizing caves, seen by many Mesoamerican peoples as entrances to the underworld. These sculptures may represent Olmec kings journeying to the world of ancestral spirits magically to assist their subjects. Since raindrops and corn plants are also shown in these scenes, their goal was probably to bring rain and maintain agricultural fertility.

The architecture of the Olmec ritual centers seems to symbolize a multitiered concept of the cosmos similar to later Native American cosmologies. At La Venta (ca. 900–ca. 400 B.C.E.) a colossal clay pyramid may represent the central axis of the world. It may also symbolize the first mountain of later Maya and Aztec myth, which emerged from watery chaos at the beginning of time. Huge mosaic pavements of serpentine, a mottled green stone, deliberately buried under a plaza at the site could signify the waters of the underworld upon which the earth floats in later Mesoamerican cosmologies. Another mosaic and a stone sarcophagus in the form of a crocodile-like dragon buried at higher levels might symbolize the reptilian earth monster of later Aztec myth, representing the earth floating on the underworld sea. The court itself, bounded on the north end by tombs, may have been intended to represent the world of ancestors. The Olmec may have designed the site as a model of the cosmos that, with the proper performance of rituals, not only represented but also magically sustained the universe. We must be cautious and skeptical, of course, in assessing models of what the Olmec thought or intended based on the beliefs of other Mesoamerican cultures documented up to more than 2,000 years after these sites were constructed.

Similar problems make it difficult to identify which deities the Olmec conceived as inhabiting their universe. Olmec sculpture shows a range of strange mythical beings that combine the features of humans with animals, including jaguars, crocodiles, and eagles. Interpretations of what these creatures might have represented range from nature spirits to a pantheon of distinct deities. For those scholars who believe in the second model, several theories attempt to distinguish different gods in Olmec art by their distinctive features. Some art historians agree that the crocodilian monster depicted on the La Venta sarcophagus was an important mythic being, now referred to as the Olmec Dragon. The creature combines reptilian with toad, jaguar, and bird features, like harpy eagle feathers above its eyes. It represented the earth—plants are shown growing from its back on the sarcophagus—and its mouth formed the entrance to the underworld. The same or another dragonlike deity may have symbolized the sky and might also be the earliest version of the famous Feathered Serpent of later Mexican mythology. According to an alternative theory, an eaglelike bird deity was the Olmec god of the sky and sun. A sharklike monster may represent an underworld god. The most common figure in Olmec art, the "werejaguar," is a strange, childlike creature with a cleft forehead and a snarling, downturned mouth and seems to have portrayed a rain god. A similar being with vegetation growing out of his head is commonly interpreted as a corn god.

Olmec ritual included human sacrifice. The bones of infants are among the offerings deposited in a sacred spring at El Manati near San Lorenzo, and images of rulers carrying baby rain gods in their arms may also represent child sacrifice. Dwarfs and fetuses appear in Olmec sculpture, and it is possible the Olmec equated deformities in children with their deities. Olmec rulers apparently used stingray spines and jade awls to let their own blood as offerings and perhaps to help induce trance, like the later Maya. Not surprisingly for a farming society, many of their rituals centered on water. They tossed offerings into springs and at San Lorenzo built an elaborate system of drains, pools, and fountains, apparently for religious purposes. Artistic images and actual rubber balls indicate that the Mesoamerican ritual ball game had been developed by Olmec times.

Mayan kings followed in the path of their Olmec predecessors, taking on the role of chief ritual specialists for their subjects. Despite older theories about Mayan theocracies, there is no evidence for priests outside the ruling family among the ancient Maya. Mayan gods known from much later inscriptions and sources, like the maize god, Itzamna, and Chaak, appear as giant plaster masks adorning royal pyramid temples from the Late Formative (ca. 400 B.C.E.–ca. 150 C.E.). The maize god figures in an ancient version of the epic Popol Vuh, dating to the 16th century C.E. In this saga he is defeated in the ritual ball game and killed by the gods of death, rulers of the underworld. His sons, the Hero Twins, later defeat and destroy the underworld gods in turn and resurrect their father, who then creates the world in its present form by erecting the World Tree, the axis of the universe. The story reflects the life cycle of corn and the hoped-for rebirth of the king as a god after death. By the Late Formative, the Mayan rulers were already identified with the maize god, and recently discovered murals at San Bartolo, Guatemala, show a king enacting the rebirth of this deity. Itzamna, a sky and creator deity, was closely associated with the king's shamanic role. A related entity, the so-called Principal Bird Deity, also makes his appearance on

Late Formative monuments. He can be understood as both the shamanic alter ego of Itzamna and as the false sun, the monster Vucub-Caquix, defeated by the Hero Twins. Chaak, a long-nosed god, presided over rain and thunder.

The Mayan version of the multilevel universe also seems to have been established by the Late Formative. Buried offerings of jade and pottery at Cival, Guatemala, were laid out in the shape of a cross with jade axes and a wooden post at the center, representing the four cardinal directions and central axis. Pyramid temples at Uaxaktún and Calakmul, Guatemala, represent the sacred mountain, rising out of the water at creation and bridging the levels of the universe. Masks on the Calakmul pyramid represent the earth and sun, while the entrance depicts a monster mouth, the cave entrance into the underworld.

At Teotihuacán near modern Mexico City, a number of deities were worshipped during the city's heyday (ca. 1 B.C.E.–ca. 650 C.E.). As is the case with the Olmec, our ideas about the nature and number of these gods are based only on artistic evidence and represent points of disagreement among anthropologists and art historians. A male deity with goggle-like rings around his eyes, a moustache, and fangs resembles the later Aztec storm god Tlaloc and probably had the same function, presiding over rain, storms, and perhaps warfare. At least one major goddess, also associated with the earth, water, and fertility, is known from mural paintings and stone sculpture. Recent work suggests that this "Great Goddess" may be in fact several deities confused with each other by earlier interpreters. The Feathered Serpent appears as a border in paintings of elite figures and may have been a patron of royalty here, as he was later among the Aztecs. At the Temple of the Feathered Serpent, stone images of this deity alternate with heads of another reptilian creature, who may be the War Serpent, associated with war and fire, or Cipactli, the later Aztec crocodilian earth monster.

Water and symbols of life and preciousness emanate from the storm god and goddess's hands and the Feathered Serpent's mouth, but if these gods brought plenty, they demanded blood in return. Over 100 victims were sacrificed and buried in the Temple of the Feathered Serpent. While Teotihuacán art is not explicit in its depiction of human sacrifice, warriors or priests in frescos carry impaled human hearts, and the symbolism of a painted image of coyotes tearing a deer to shreds is obvious. Rulers or priests are also shown drawing their own blood as penance with spines of the maguey cactus and inserting the spines into balls of fiber as offerings. Butterfly and owl gods may be associated with conquest and sacrifice, and a fertility god who looks like the later Aztec Xipe Totec, dressed in the flayed skin of a sacrificial victim, makes his first appearance in the city's art.

Peru

Evidence of organized religion and large temple construction in Peru dates back to the Late Preceramic Period (ca. 2700 B.C.E.). On the coast Preceramic peoples built huge adobe ritual platforms arranged in U-shaped configurations, perhaps symbolizing a balance of opposing forces in the cosmos. They deposited groups of unbaked clay sculptures of humans, textiles, and shell and stone jewelry in these structures, presumably as gifts to the gods. At the same time, the inhabitants of the Peruvian highlands built small chambers for use as shrines, where they burned foodstuffs and textiles in sacrifice to unknown deities. These respective styles of temple and cult persisted in both areas through the second millennium B.C.E. Shamanism may have played an important part in these early religions. At Garagay in the central highlands, modeled adobe building decorations show strange beings that combine jaguar and spider features. Forms hanging from their mouths may be fangs or a mucous discharge—a known side effect of using hallucinogenic snuff. At Mina Perdida on the coast a clay effigy of a creature with jaguar fangs and vulture features was buried wrapped in cloth. Did it represent a shaman in transformation, a god, or an ancestral spirit? At another highland religious center there is evidence of human sacrifice in the form of reliefs of dismembered prisoners—or are these also images of experiences in trance states?

The great ritual center of Chavín de Huántar flourished in the Andean highlands between 900 and 200 B.C.E. The site was constructed near a confluence of rivers and may embody an idea like the later Inca *tinkuy*—a sacred juncture or transition point between parts of the cosmos. By analogy between the finds here and those of later Peruvian cultures, Chavín may have been the home of an oracle, visited and consulted by pilgrims from distant regions. Its central temple was riddled with dark galleries and unusual acoustic properties that priests could manipulate to create dramatic "supernatural" effects for the faithful. Attendants left offerings of food and the remains of human sacrifices in its labyrinthine corridors.

The decoration of the main shrine during its first, or Old Temple, phase (ca. 900–ca. 500 B.C.E.) shows themes probably related to shamanism. Stone heads attached to the walls of the temple seem to show humans transforming into jaguars, with mucous from snuffing hallucinogenic plants pouring from their noses. Other reliefs portray jaguars with harpy eagle claws and fanged humans carrying hallucinogenic cacti. Like the Olmec, the builders of Chavín viewed powerful predators as sacred animals. The principal deity seems to be represented by a human figure with jaguar mouth and fangs, the so-called snarling or "smiling" god. During the New Temple Period (ca. 400–ca. 200 B.C.E.) sculpture at the temple depicts mythic beings, combining human features with those of birds of prey and caimans bearing plants. Perhaps the caiman was thought to have taught the builders about agriculture in their mythology. The snarling god now carried a rod or wand in each hand, and archaeologists call this image the staff god.

The influence of Chavín spread from the highlands to the Pacific coast, as evidenced by the distribution of images of supernatural beings in Chavín style. Based on comparison with later Peruvian oracles, the Chavín cult might have been adopted by local peoples as a kind of "franchise," with local versions of the original shrine built and staffed by priests from Chavín in return for gifts and tribute paid to the main center. Textiles from the coastal site of Karwa show a figure like the Chavín staff god, but female—perhaps related to the understanding of later Peruvian local versions of oracle centers as "daughters" or "wives" of the original.

At Paracas (ca. 600–ca. 175 B.C.E.) on the south coast, painted ceramics and embroidered textiles show a creature with large, round eyes, called the Oculate Being, apparently an important deity. The textile designs also depict flying humans with bird wings and dancing humans in contorted positions, with their heads thrown back. Some scholars interpret these figures as shamans transforming into birds or dancing themselves into a trance. Perhaps the most important aspect of religious life for the Paracas culture was the cult of ancestors. The textiles came from large tombs holding hundreds of mummies.

See also ADORNMENT; ARCHITECTURE; ART; ASTRONOMY; CALENDARS AND CLOCKS; CITIES; DEATH AND BURIAL PRACTICES; EMPIRES AND DYNASTIES; FESTIVALS; FOOD AND DIET; FOREIGNERS AND BARBARIANS; GOVERNMENT ORGANIZATION; LANGUAGE; LAWS AND LEGAL CODES; LITERATURE; OCCUPATIONS; SACRED SITES; SOCIAL ORGANIZATION; SPORTS AND RECREATION; WAR AND CONQUEST; WRITING.

Egypt

The Egyptian Legend of the Creation, excerpt, ca. 311 B.C.E.

The Book of Knowing the Evolutions of Ra, and of Overthrowing Apep

[These are] the words which the god Neb-er-tcher spake after he had, come into being:—"I am he who came into being in the form of the god Khepera, and I am the creator of that which came into being, that is to say, I am the creator of everything which came into being: now the things which I created, and which came forth out of my month after that I had come into being myself were exceedingly many. The sky (or heaven) had not come into being, the earth did not exist, and the children of the earth, and the creeping, things, had not been made at that time. I myself raised them up from out of Nu, from a state of helpless inertness. I found no place whereon I could stand. I worked a charm upon my own heart (or, will), I laid the foundation [of things] by Maat, and I made everything which had form. I was [then] one by myself, for I had not emitted from myself the god Shu, and I had not spit out from myself the goddess Tefnut; and there existed no other who could work with me. I laid the foundations [of things] in my own heart, and there came into being multitudes of created things, which came into being from the created things which were born from the created things which arose from what they brought forth. I had union with my closed hand, and I embraced my shadow as a wife, and I poured seed into my own mouth, and I sent forth from myself issue in the form of the gods Shu and Tefnut. Saith my father Nu:—My Eye was covered up behind them [i.e., Shu. and Tefnut], but after two *hen* periods had passed from the time when they departed from me, from being one god I became three gods, and I came into being in the earth. Then Shu and Tefnut rejoiced from out of the inert watery mass wherein they were, and they brought to me my Eye [i.e., the Sun]. Now after these things I gathered together my members, and I wept over them, and men and women sprang into being from the tears which came forth from my Eye. And when my Eye came to me, and found that I had made another [Eye] in place where it was [i.e., the Moon], it was wroth with me, whereupon I endowed it [i.e., the second Eye] with [some of] the splendour which I had made for the first [Eye], and I made it to occupy its place in my Face, and henceforth it ruled throughout all this earth.

When there fell on them their moment through plant-like clouds, I restored what had been taken away from them, and I appeared from out of the plant-like clouds. I created creeping things of every kind, and everything which came into being from them. Shu and Tefnut brought forth [Seb and] Nut; and Seb and Nut brought forth Osiris, and Heru-khent-an-maati, and Set, and Isis, and Nephthys at one birth, one after the other, and they produced their multitudinous offspring in this earth.

From: E. A. Wallis Budge, *The Egyptian Texts, Edited with Translations* (London: Kegan Paul, Trench and Trübner & Co. Ltd., 1912).

The Middle East

The Enûma Elish (Babylonian Creation Myth), excerpt, ca. 12th century B.C.E.

1. The holy house, the house of the gods, in the holy place had not yet been made;

2. No reed had sprung up, no tree had been created.

3. No brick had been laid, no building had been set up;

4. No house had been erected, no city had been built;

5. No city had been made, no creature had been created.

6. Nippur had not been made, E-kur had not been built;

7. Erech had not been created, E-ana had not been built;

8. The Deep had not been created, Eridu had not been built;

9. Of the holy house, the house of the gods, the habitation had not been made.

10. All lands were sea.

11. At that time there was a movement in the sea;

12 . Then was Eridu made, and E-sagil was built,

13. E-sagil, where in the midst of the Deep the god Lugal-dul-azaga dwelleth;

14. The city of Babylon was built, and E-sagil was finished.

15. The gods, the Anunnaki, he created at one time;

16. The holy city, the dwelling, of their hearts' desire, they proclaimed supreme.

17. Marduk laid a reed upon the face of the waters,

18. He formed dust and poured it out beside the reed.

19. That he might cause the gods to dwell in the habitation of their hearts' desire,

20. He formed mankind.

21. The goddess Aruru together with him created the seed of mankind.

22. The beasts of the field and living creatures in the field he formed.

23. He created the Tigris and the Euphrates, and he set them in their place;

24. Their names he declared in goodly fashion.

25. The grass, the rush of the marsh, the reed, and the forest he created,

26. The green herb of the field he created,

27. The lands, the marshes, and the swamps;

28. The wild cow and her young, the wild calf; the ewe and her young, the lamb of the fold;

29. Plantations and forests;

30. The he-goat and the mountain-goat . . . him.

31. The Lord Marduk laid in a dam by the side of the sea,

32. [He . . .] a swamp, he made a marsh,

33. [. . .] he brought into existence.

34. [Reeds he form]ed, trees he created;

35. [. . .] he made in their place.

36. [Bricks he laid], buildings he set up;

37. [Houses he made], cities he built;

38. [Cities he made], creatures he created.

39. [Nippur he made], E-kur he built;

40. [Erech he made, E-an]a he built.

. . .

3f. Thy exalted minister is Papsukal, the wise counselor of the gods.

5. May Nin-aha-kudû, the daughter of Ea,

6. Purify thee with the pure censer,

7. And may she cleanse thee with cleansing fire!

8f. With a cup of pure water from the Deep shalt thou purify thy way!

10. By the incantation of Marduk, the king of the hosts of heaven and earth,

11. May the abundance of the land enter into thee,

12. And may thy decree be accomplished for ever!

13f. O E-zida, thou glorious dwelling, thou art dear unto the hearts of Anu and Ishtar!

15. May [Ezida] shine like the heavens, may it be bright like the earth, may it [be glorious] like the heart of heaven,

From: Leonard William King, *The Seven Tablets of Creation* (London: Luzac and Co., 1902).

Asia and the Pacific

The Rig-Veda, excerpt (ca. 1700–1100 B.C.E.)

HYMN CXXIX: Creation

1. THEN was not non-existent nor existent: there was no realm of air, no sky beyond it.

What covered in, and where? and what gave shelter? Was water there, unfathomed depth of water?

2 Death was not then, nor was there aught immortal: no sign was there, the day's and night's divider.

That One Thing, breathless, breathed by its own nature: apart from it was nothing whatsoever.

3 Darkness there was: at first concealed in darkness this All was indiscriminated chaos.

All that existed then was void and formless: by the great power of Warmth was born that Unit.

4 Thereafter rose Desire in the beginning, Desire, the primal seed and germ of Spirit.

Sages who searched with their heart's thought discovered the existent's kinship in the non-existent.

5 Transversely was their severing line extended: what was above it then, and what below it?

There were begetters, there were mighty forces, free action here and energy up yonder

6 Who verily knows and who can here declare it, whence it was born and whence comes this creation?

The Gods are later than this world's production. Who knows then whence it first came into being?

7 He, the first origin of this creation, whether he formed it all or did not form it,

Whose eye controls this world in highest heaven, he verily knows it, or perhaps he knows not. . . .

HYMN CXXX: Creation

1. THE sacrifice drawn out with threads on every side, stretched by a hundred sacred ministers and one,—

This do these Fathers weave who hitherward are come: they sit beside the warp and cry, Weave forth, weave back.

2 The Man extends it and the Man unbinds it: even to this vault of heaven hath he outspun, it.

These pegs are fastened to the seat of worship: they made the Sama-hymns their weaving shuttles.

3 What were the rule, the order and the model? What were the wooden fender and the butter?

What were the hymn, the chant, the recitation, when to the God all Deities paid worship?

4 Closely was Gayatri conjoined with Agni, and closely Savitar combined with Usnih.

Brilliant with Ukthas, Soma joined Anustup: Brhaspati's voice by Brhati was aided.

5 Viraj adhered to Varuna and Mitra: here Tristup day by day was Indra's portion.

Jagati entered all the Gods together: so by this knowledge men were raised to Rsis.

6 So by this knowledge men were raised to Rsis, when ancient sacrifice sprang up, our Fathers.

With the mind's eye I think that I behold them who first performed this sacrificial worship.

7 They who were versed in ritual and metre, in hymns and rules, were the Seven Godlike Rsis.

Viewing the path of those of old, the sages have taken up the reins like chariot-drivers. . . .

HYMN CXC: Creation

1. FROM Fervour kindled to its height Eternal Law and Truth were born:

Thence was the Night produced, and thence the billowy flood of sea arose.

2 From that same billowy flood of sea the Year was afterwards produced,

Ordainer of the days, nights, Lord over all who close the eye.

3 Dhatar, the great Creator, then formed in due order Sun and Moon.

He formed in order Heaven and Earth, the regions of the air, and light.

From: Ralph T. H. Griffith, trans., *The Hymns of the Rigveda* (Benares, India: E. J. Lazarus, 1889).

FURTHER READING

Mary Beard, John North, and Simon Price, *Religions of Rome*, Vol. 1, *A History* (Cambridge, U.K.: Cambridge University Press, 1998).

Gideon Bohak, "Traditions of Magic in Late Antiquity." Available online. URL: http://www.lib.umich.edu/pap/magic/. Downloaded on April 16, 2007.

Jean Bottéro, *Religion in Ancient Mesopotamia*, trans. Teresa Lavender Fagan (Chicago: University of Chicago Press, 2001).

Mary Boyce, *Zoroastrians: Their Religious Beliefs and Practices* (London: Routledge, 1988).

James H. Breasted, *Development of Religion and Thought in Ancient Egypt* (Philadelphia: University of Pennsylvania Press, 1972).

Jan N. Bremmer, *Greek Religion* (Oxford, U.K.: Oxford University Press, 1994).

Anthony Bullock, "Ancient Greek Religion." Available online. URL: http://www.greekreligion.org/. Downloaded on April 17, 2007.

Walter Burkert, *Greek Religion: Archaic and Classical*, trans. John Raffan (Oxford, U.K.: Basil Blackwell, 1985).

Michael Coe, ed., *The Olmec World: Ritual and Rulership* (Princeton: Princeton University Press, 1995).

Stephanie Dalley, *Myths from Mesopotamia: Creation, the Flood, Gilgamesh and Others* (Oxford, U.K.: Oxford University Press, 1989).

Mircea Eliade, *Shamanism: Archaic Techniques of Ecstasy* (Princeton, N.J.: Bollingen/Princeton University Press, 1970).

Israel Finkelstein and Asher Silberman, *The Bible Unearthed: Archaeology's New Vision of Ancient Israel and the Origin of Its Sacred Texts* (New York: Free Press, 2001).

Benjamin R. Foster, *The Epic Of Gilgamesh: A New Translation* (New York: Norton, 2001).

John G. Gager, ed., *Curse Tablets and Binding Spells from the Ancient World* (Oxford, U.K.: Oxford University Press, 1992).

Harry A. Hoffner, *Hittite Myths*, ed. Gary M. Beckman (Atlanta, Ga.: Scholars Press, 1998).

Erik Hornung, *Conceptions of God in Ancient Egypt: The One and the Many* (Ithaca, N.Y.: Cornell University Press, 1996).

Erik Hornung, *Akhenaten and the Religion of Light* (Ithaca, N.Y.: Cornell University Press, 1999).

Norman Bancroft Hunt, *Shamanism in North America* (Toronto, Canada: Key Porter Books, 2002).

Sarah Iles Johnston, *Religions of the Ancient World: A Guide* (Cambridge, Mass.: Harvard University Press, 2004).

Peter David Joralemon, "In Search of the Olmec Cosmos: Reconstructing the World View of America's First Civilization." In *Olmec Art of Ancient Mexico*, ed. Elizabeth Benson (New York: Abrams, 1996).

Gwendolyn Leick, *A Dictionary of Ancient Near Eastern Mythology* (London: Routledge, 1991).

Jon D. Mikalson, *Ancient Greek Religion* (Oxford, U.K.: Blackwell, 2005).

Mary Ellen Miller and Karl Taube, *The Gods and Symbols of Ancient Mexico and the Maya* (New York: Thames and Hudson, 1993).

Robert Parker, *Athenian Religion: A History* (Oxford, U.K.: Clarendon, 1996).

James Rives, *Religion in the Roman Empire* (Malden, Mass.: Blackwell, 2007).

Serge Sauneron, *The Priests of Ancient Egypt* (Ithaca, N.Y.: Cornell University Press, 2000).

Byron E. Schafer, ed., *Religion in Ancient Egypt: Gods, Myths, and Personal Practice* (Ithaca, N.Y.: Cornell University Press, 1991).

John Scheid, *An Introduction to Roman Religion*, trans. Janet Lloyd (Bloomington: Indiana University Press, 2003).

Robert Turcan, *The Gods of Ancient Rome* (New York: Routledge, 2001).

Greg Woolf, ed., *Ancient Civilizations: The Illustrated Guide to Belief, Mythology, and Art* (San Diego: Thunder Bay Press, 2005).

► resistance and dissent

INTRODUCTION

People can resist and dissent from government, religion, or society. The degree to which a culture tolerates dissent tells about what was important to the culture's people. Studying what resistance and dissent means can be a tricky business. For example, India's Emperor Asoka (r. 268–233 B.C.E.) was tolerant of religious faiths other than his own, even building places of worship for them, but this did not mean he cared little about his religion. To the contrary, he was a very devout Buddhist, but his faith included the principal of tolerance of others. Thus, when trying to learn about a culture, both the motives for resistance and dissent and the motives for repressing resistance and dissent need to be examined carefully.

In general, ancient governments reacted to dissent brutally. Dissenters were seen as enemies just as foreign armies were, and both dissenters and prisoners of war were primary candidates for torture, humiliation, and sacrifice to gods. Often, governments did not need to react forcefully to dissent because society would take care of the problem for them. In cultures, there is a strong impulse among ordinary people to see to it that everyone conforms to the rules. It may seem to them to be just a matter of fairness—no one should be allowed special privileges—or it may be out of fear of government or religion. Many an ancient government reacted to dissent or rebellion by killing not only the dissenters but also the entire families of dissenters and even complete villages, towns, or cities. Few people would wish to risk their families' lives by dissenting, and both family and community would put pressure on dissenters to shut up and conform to the rules. Indeed, the community might take it upon itself to kill or exile a dissenter.

Many mythologies have accounts of dissenters. In mythologies in general, the fates of dissenters are horrible. People who dissent from religious customs bring down the wrath of capricious gods or make a mess of the natural world. Floods, droughts, seasons that fail to come or to leave, earthquakes, wildfires, and other afflictions of the natural world are blamed on dissenters. Thus, dissenters are afflicted with boils and diseases or die in horrible ways. The end of their dissent can bring the world back to an orderly existence, or the mythology may say that an entire nation or city disappeared because of a permanent disruption of the way life had been.

It was for these reasons that resistance and dissent were serious matters in ancient cultures. Dissenters who rebelled for only their own desire for power tended to be resented by most people, unless they actually won political or religious power, in which case they would style themselves saviors or as divinely favored. Sometimes by example, dissenters could change society. Dissenters could inspire new religions or political movements, as did the Buddha and Confucius. People who bore persecution with dignity could attract sympathy and converts to their point of view. Occasionally, society was changed for the better. On the other hand, many dissenters won by killing those who opposed their point of view, and the history of resistance and dissent has many cases in which the dissenters became the rulers and were themselves opposed by dissenters.

AFRICA

BY MICHAEL J. O'NEAL

It is difficult for modern historians to re-create patterns of resistance and dissent in ancient Africa, primarily because of the absence of written records and the nomadic nature of many early African communities. The social organization of most ancient African societies was based on the tribe, with the clan and the family being other vital components of the community. This social structure was combined with an ethic that bound people to the community, including its community of ancestor spirits. This ethic, which was instilled from an early age through legends, fables, and social training, discouraged the kind of power struggles, factionalism, and dissent characteristic of more complex, but less integrated societies. In general, ancient African communities found ways to quell dissent and achieve social harmony.

One way in which this goal was achieved was through orature. *Orature* means roughly the same thing as *oratory*, or "making speeches," but *orature* generally refers more specifically to the rhetoric employed by indigenous African peoples in sermons and, particularly, for social protest. Again, no instances of orature from ancient Africa were recorded, so there were none to survive. However, the tradition of orature has been passed down through many generations, and historians are confident in their belief that the roots of more modern traditions of orature extend deep into the African past.

The purpose of orature was to bind people to the community. It was a way for prominent people in the community, usually those with the best speaking skills, to raise issues that were of concern to the community, protest matters that were causing dissent and divisions in the community, and find a way to quell dissent and reforge the bonds that held the community together. The basic structure of orature consisted, first, of a "caller," the person who invoked the ancestral and creator spirits and raised the issue of concern for the community. The caller had to be a person of high moral character who could stir the spiritual forces of the community. Because there was very little distinction between the spiritual realm and the secular (or nonspiritual) realm, the caller drew on the spiritual beliefs of the people to create a sense of harmony and inclusiveness. In response, the community functioned as a "chorus," commenting on and validating the caller's words. In the traditions of orature the community did not sit and listen politely and quietly; rather, the community interjected its own commentary, thus forming a community with the speaker. In some cases these responders were people specifically assigned to that role. In many cases, though, the responders included the larger community.

Rebellion and dissent may have been a marked feature of life in the ancient Nubian kingdom of Kush. (Nubia was the name of the region, roughly modern-day Sudan; Kush was the name of the civilization.) Again, the historical record is sparse, and historians have had to piece it together from fragments of evidence, including surviving records from the Egyptian Empire to the north. Further, historians are not always in agreement about the meaning of the available evidence.

Egypt had long had its eye on Kush territory. As the Egyptian Empire spread, it expanded southward into the region occupied by the Kush people. In about 1500 B.C.E. Egypt began a major push southward, but it encountered stiff resistance from the Kush, though whether from their own organized kingdom or from a confederation of city-states is unclear. The reason that Kush opposition can be considered a form of rebellion rather than simply war between two states is that for over three millennia the ever-changing and constantly shifting relationship between Egypt and Kush had been close. During some periods Kush was an Egyptian colony. During others Kush was powerful in its own right, and Kush rulers actually ruled Egypt as that nation's Twenty-fifth Dynasty in the eighth century B.C.E. The shifting power relationship between Kush and Egypt continued, and the Kushite state survived into the Common Era. But about 350 C.E. Kush collapsed. In large part the state disappeared because it was taken over by the kingdom of Axum. However, the Kush state had been weakened by internal politics and skirmishes with tribal factions on its borders. Few details are known about these events.

The empire of Carthage, on Africa's northern coast, also faced rebellion and dissent. Throughout its history, Carthage and Rome were major rivals in the Mediterranean Sea. Carthage had a large navy, which it used to protect its merchant fleet. Because of its trading prowess, Carthage was a threat to Rome's interests on the African continent. Their rivalry erupted into three wars, called the Punic Wars, which extended from 264 to 146 B.C.E. It was during the interlude between the First and Second Punic Wars that Carthage faced dissent from its army. The outcome of the First Punic War, from 264 to 241 B.C.E., was indecisive. However, to put an end to the war, Carthage had had to pay a great deal of tribute to Rome. These payments exhausted Carthage's treasury, with the result that it was unable to pay its army, particularly the mercenary soldiers it had hired to fight in the war. (Carthage relied for its power almost entirely on its navy, hiring mercenaries to fight its land battles.) Some unpaid mercenary rebels seized control of one of Carthage's main assets in the Mediterranean, the island of Sardinia. Armed conflict between the rebels and the main force of Carthage's mercenary army erupted in 240 B.C.E. Carthage won, and the conflict ended in 237 B.C.E. after brutal fighting. The so-called Mercenary Revolt further weakened Carthage, laying the groundwork for its eventual defeat at the hands of the Romans.

Although Carthage as a major military and trading empire was crushed by the Romans in 146 B.C.E., Carthage continued to exist as a political unit into the Christian era. As the Christian church grew and spread, it expanded into Africa, and Carthage became the home of a major diocese of the church. In 397 C.E., for example, a church council met at Carthage, and it was there that the accepted canon of books of the Bible was established. However, many African Christians were disaffected. Not only did they disagree with one another over church doctrine but they also rebelled from the authority of Rome, which was still under the control of the Roman Empire. In the eyes of some historians this religious dissent weakened the region, making it ripe for conquest by the Vandals from the north in the fifth century.

EGYPT

BY EDWARD M. W. A. ROWLANDS

Ancient Egypt was a very centralized and conservative state, where the ability to influence the direction of the government was restricted to a privileged few. Even so, throughout ancient Egyptian history dynasties of pharaohs could rise and fall owing to the impact of political factions. The priesthood, high officials of the kingdom, members of the royal family, and army generals all at various times achieved and exercised significant influence on the pharaoh.

The political history of Egypt before its unification is unclear, but the success of the first ruling families probably came from a combination of war and dynastic marriage. Early regional monarchs in the Naqâda III Period (ca. 3300–ca. 3100 B.C.E.), such as the ruler known only as "King Scorpion" of Hierakonpolis, would undoubtedly have been driven by their own desire for glory and craving for power. As the number of kingdoms in Egypt decreased, the successful ruling families grew powerful enough to be taken very seriously by any king. Evidence of this power appears in the concentrated wealth of small groups of people in burials found at Buto, Abydos, and Hierakonpolis. The ability to distribute luxury items to the aristocracy was important, and as kings came to dominate commercial routes and ever-increasing territory, they were able to meet these leading families' demands.

After the unification of the country around 3100 B.C.E., Egypt was dominated from Memphis in Lower Egypt. The pharaoh, considered divine and omnipotent, held absolute power, as can be seen especially in the Old Kingdom (ca. 2575–2134 B.C.E.). Snefru (r. ca. 2575–2551 B.C.E.) was able to build three pyramids. His successor, Khufu (r. ca. 2551–2528 B.C.E.) built the Great Pyramid, a structure so enormous that it was the tallest man-made object on earth for several millennia. Any sort of political protest to a regime this strong and centralized could have come only from the very top of society. Public expressions of defiance would have been crushed.

The vizier, the official who headed the pharaoh's administration, was essentially second in command in the kingdom. Imhotep, vizier to the pharaoh Djoser (r. ca. 2630–2611 B.C.E.), was the genius who designed the Step Pyramid at Saqqara. He was showered with titles by the pharaoh and is likely to have wielded considerable influence at court. The holder of the viziership had a variety of important roles, from collecting taxes to leading military campaigns, and this power sometimes led a vizier to challenge the authority of the pharaoh. Amenemhet I (r. ca. 1991–1962 B.C.E.), for example, is thought to have been the vizier of a previous monarch and used his position to gain the throne. In the New Kingdom (ca. 1550–1070 B.C.E.) the power of the viziership was split, with one vizier for Lower Egypt and another for Upper Egypt.

In the transition from the Old to the Middle Kingdom (ca. 2140–1640 B.C.E.) the power of the pharaoh crumbled. Egypt was administered by nomarchs, officials who controlled the nomes (provincial administrative centers) of the kingdom. In the Old Kingdom the pharaoh appointed the nomarchs, usually choosing members of his own family. By the end of the Old Kingdom these officials had become a power to rival his own. Their positions became hereditary as the pharaoh gradually lost his control over them. During the Old Kingdom the nomarchs had raised armed forces when the pharaoh demanded it. By the end of this era and into the First Intermediate Period (2134–2040 B.C.E.) nomarchs had caused strife and decentralization by their control of local forces and taxation. Their independence from the pharaoh can be seen by the growth of their statuary and the size of their tombs. The country was united again in the Middle Kingdom by Amenemhet I, but the nomarchs' threat to the pharaoh did not end until Sesostris III (r. ca. 1878–1841? B.C.E.) established a royal army that was no longer levied by the nomarchs.

The successful military campaigns of the Eighteenth Dynasty (1550–1307 B.C.E.) and long-running wars in Syria-Palestine, first against the Hurrians and then against the Hittites, brought the army into a very powerful position. Before the New Kingdom the military had not been as powerful as the priesthood or the bureaucracy, but this changed after the Hyksos invasion of Egypt that ended the Middle Kingdom. After the Hyksos occupation ended, Egyptian pharaohs attacked areas outside Egypt's traditional boundaries in an attempt to make sure that there would be no repeat foreign invasion. These foreign campaigns started to bring in vast wealth and gradually moved to the acquisition of an empire. The army was now needed not only to defend Egypt's borders but also to maintain an empire that kept Egypt prosperous and strong. As a result, over time certain elements of the military were able to threaten the power of the pharaoh, and army officers such as Horemheb (r. ca. 1319–1307 B.C.E.), and Ramses I (r. ca. 1307–1306 B.C.E.) became pharaohs themselves.

Priests of the great temples gained enormous power and influence on the back of successful military campaigns into Nubia and Asia Minor. Pharaohs proudly embellished the main cult center of the god Amon at Karnak with successive extensions. Temples employed large numbers of workers and possessed vast estates. By the reign of Amenhotep III (r. ca. 1391–1353 B.C.E.) the priests of Amon had such power and wealth that they may even have begun rivaling the pharaoh himself. The monotheistic pharaoh Akhenaton (r. ca. 1353–1335 B.C.E.), with his cult of the sun god Aton, attempted to curtail the threat from the priests, even ordering the name of Amon obliterated from temples. However, after Akhenaton's death the cult of Amon regained its original position, its priests a powerful political faction whom pharaohs had to heed and respect.

Pharaohs throughout ancient Egyptian history had large families. Ramses II (r. ca. 1290–1224 B.C.E.), for example, is said to have had more than 50 sons. Political factions developed within these large families and strove to influence the pharaoh and his succession. Some members of the royal family were involved in the attempt to assassinate the last great pharaoh of the New Kingdom, Ramses III (r. ca. 1194–1163 B.C.E.). The conspiracy was led by one his principal wives, Queen Tey, in an attempt to change the line of succession and place her son Pentawere on the throne. It is clear that the coup failed, as it was Ramses IV (r. ca. 1163–1156 B.C.E.), his father's chosen successor, who ascended.

After the New Kingdom declined, Egypt would never be as powerful again. The Twenty-first Dynasty (1070–945 B.C.E.) saw the high priests of Amon come to rule Middle and Upper Egypt at the expense of the pharaoh. The last ruler of the Twentieth Dynasty, Ramses XI (r. ca. 1100–1070 B.C.E.), had to tolerate an army officer and self-anointed high priest named Herihor taking the royal title and ruling beside him. Foreigners—from Libya, Nubia, Assyria, Persia, and Greece—then came to dominate the country. From 30 B.C.E. the Romans held Egypt as a province with a Roman governor. Even then, however, the priesthood remained a powerful faction. Foreign rulers wanted to maintain the idea that the pharaoh had divine sanction, and with this goal in mind temples such as those at Luxor and Karnak were restored and even expanded.

THE MIDDLE EAST

BY FRANS VAN KOPPEN

Royal monuments are omnipresent in the archaeological heritage of Mesopotamia, Persia, and other ancient Near Eastern cultures. The first modern explorations of these monuments reinforced the concept of the local monarchy as an unopposed hierarchical system where the welfare of the nation depended on the whims of brutal kings, a notion that was inspired by classical and Old Testament writings and was fueled by 19th-century political concerns. The understanding of ancient Near Eastern rulership changed considerably once indigenous sources, in particular cuneiform records from ancient Mesopotamia, were taken into account. These sources shed light on the ideological underpinning of the royal office and illustrate how kings could at times apply decisive power but often were limited in the exercise of their authority. Royal power was founded on the force of tradition, but long-established values also prescribed how this authority should be put into effect. In practice kings were able, with varying success, to impose their will on the top levels of government but had limited direct control over lower tiers of the system. Ancient states therefore knew more autonomy at the bottom of the hierarchy than the rhetoric from the top would lead one to believe.

The literature of the ancient Near East embodies the views of the ruling elite, expressed in royal inscriptions and poetic compositions that were disseminated outside the court as part of the educational curriculum familiar to all who had learned how to read. This literature celebrates the magnificence of kingship, including the victorious confrontation with foreign enemies, but internal opposition against the king was here obviously out of place. Tendentious works criticizing affairs of state are rare, and most of them cannot be dated exactly, precluding the opportunity to confirm whether they circulated at the time of the events they condemn or afterward and in support of a different regime. The search for protest and dissent thus requires one to read between the lines of the official propaganda or depends on the availability of incidental explicit sources. One textual genre reveals how ancient scholars thought about the topic: Mesopotamian handbooks of divination dealing with the significance of ominous signs include among their predictions scenarios of doom for the king and his dynasty.

Royal ideology is culturally embedded, and no single profile can do justice to the long history and vast areas of the ancient Near Eastern world. All societies, however, seem to have agreed on one thing: Kingship was established by the gods, originally "descended from heaven," according to the Sumerian King List, and was therefore an essential requisite for the proper working of society. (The Sumerian King List is an ancient text listing the kings of Sumer, including foreign dynasties.) Whereas the institution of kingship was thus never questioned, the human occupant of the throne certainly was if he failed to adhere to the traditional values of his culture: being of proper descent, enjoying the approval of the gods, taking the leading role in the cult, and promoting the economic well-being and security of his subjects.

Historical writings frequently condemn past kings for failure in these domains, and public support of a ruler waned if his performance was considered inadequate. A case in point is the Babylonian king Nabonidus (r. 556–539 B.C.E.), who promoted the moon god Sin at the expense of other gods. He stayed in Arabia for a number of years, and this resulted in an interruption of the annual festival in honor of Marduk, the head of the Babylonian pantheon, for which the king had to lead the ceremonies in person. This resulted in popular disaffection, particularly in the circles of the Marduk clergy, and Nabonidus himself refers to the animosity of the residents of Babylon as one of his reasons for leaving the capital. Open criticism of his religious politics, however, first appears under his successor, the Persian king Cyrus II (r. 539–ca. 529 B.C.E.), and it is possible that the extent of popular discontent was deliberately exaggerated to defend the legitimacy of the new dynasty.

While good rulership was thought to promote the well-being of society, national setbacks cast a shadow over the suitability of the king. Public dissatisfaction could even culminate in his disposal, as is suggested by such omen predictions of the diviners as "his own city will rebel against the king" and "the eldest of his city will dismiss the king"—though incidents of this kind did not often come to pass. Most dynasties, however, were stable because the king could rely on the continuous support of powerful servants whose fortunes were tied closely to their lord. They owed him absolute obedience, backed by oaths of loyalty, and in return enjoyed the king's favors and the material benefits that derived from it. Given the very personal nature of this relationship, members of the top tiers of the administrative hierarchy were at risk of losing their positions and having their rewards revoked if a rival king ascended the throne, and it was their collective intent to support their ruler through periods of adversity.

Paradoxically, the most dangerous forms of internal opposition arose from the same class of royal servants. Essential functions at the court and the provincial administrative centers were fulfilled by powerful dignitaries who were eager to increase their share of royal favors, influence, and wealth at the expense of other members of the elite. They typically allied together to attain these goals. Now and then dignitaries were able to build up sufficient support to assassinate the king and claim the throne, but normally they chose to promote their preferred candidate among the king's potential heirs. Some political systems, such that of the Neo-Assyrian Dynasty (ca. 1000–626 B.C.E.), did not adhere to the principle of succession by the firstborn son but allowed the king to select his heir or even change his mind more than once during the course of his reign. Court factions threw in their lot with a particular candidate in expectation of future rewards, and the presence of more than one contender with sufficient support led to internal struggle or even civil war.

A particularly fierce episode started toward the end of the reign of the Assyrian king Shalmaneser III (r. 858–824 B.C.E.), when prince Assur-da'in-aplu, who had been passed over for succession, led the heartland of the Assyrian state in a rebellion against the designated crown price, Shamshi-Adad V (r. 824–811 B.C.E.). After five years of civil war the crown prince managed, with the support of the outer provinces, to defeat his rival and reunite the realm. That both contenders depended on separate domains indicates that members of the old aristocracy supported their respective candidates for the throne.

Given the potentially devastating consequences of factional struggle, kings dealt carefully with powerful clans among their servants. They tried to break up interest groups by cautionary punishments of disloyal servants and rewards to those who reported the culpable acts of others; some kings did not hesitate to have large numbers of their highest servants executed. Powerful kings were in this way able to enforce the personal dependence of their direct entourage, and they depended on the top of the state apparatus to enforce loyalty at the lower tiers of the system.

ASIA AND THE PACIFIC

BY UFFE BERGETON AND MICHAEL J. O'NEAL

Just as political power and state control are inextricably intertwined with ideology, so also are the ways in which resistance and dissent can be conceived and expressed. From the earliest period of Chinese history for which we have extensive written documents, that is, the Western Zhou (1045–771 B.C.E.), the world was thought of as a hierarchical pyramid with the highest deity, Heaven (*Tian*), at the top, followed by his human counterpart, the king as the son of Heaven (*Tian Zi*); the royal vassals; and the lower ranks of nobility down to the common people. Some of the earliest expressions of social protest are found in the *Shi jing* (Book of Songs), a collection of anonymous poems from the Western Zhou and Spring and Autumn Periods (722–481 B.C.E.).

At the time of Confucius (551–479 B.C.E.) rulers were still born into power, but whether they retained it depended on whether they could keep the mandate of Heaven, which was bestowed or taken away by Heaven based on their moral virtue (*de*). In the Spring and Autumn Periods increasingly large state administrations demanding specialized administrative skills gave rise to a relatively independent class of scholar-officials (*shi*). Before Confucius, moral authority and charismatic power (*de*) had been concentrated in the hands of the son of Heaven, who had the most direct access to divine powers. Confucius's most important innovation was to shift the locus of moral and religious authority from being an exclusive royal prerogative to being accessible to any individual, regardless of birth, who was able to purify his charismatic virtue through self-cultivation.

Thus, in the emerging *shi* class, engaging in self-cultivation, the ground was laid for a class of political "dissenters," of which Confucius and his follower Mencius (ca. 371–ca. 289 B.C.E.) were themselves prime examples. While still adhering to a hierarchical aristocratic worldview, the *shi* often remonstrated with rulers whose misguided policies and moral behavior put them in danger of losing the mandate of Heaven. When remonstration failed, they would sometimes leave their home states in search of a more virtuous ruler elsewhere. In a sense, by thus "hiding" from a ruler through self-imposed exile to avoid moral pollution through forced collaboration, such traveling *shi* can be classified as moral-political recluses, demonstrating their dissent by resigning from office.

A more desperate form of protest is exemplified in the person and legend of Qu Yuan (ca. 340–278 B.C.E.), a government official of noble birth who committed suicide to make a political statement and to vent his frustration over the destruction of his home state of Chu through the slander and pernicious influence of sycophants. Before drowning himself in the Mi Luo River, Qu Yuan wrote the *Li Sao* (On Encountering Trouble), a long, allegorical poem in which he casts himself as a beautiful concubine neglected by the king. Ever since, Chinese statesmen have often used similar metaphorical poetry—involving frustrated women, symbolically referring to the ignored voices of wise ministers—as veiled political statements of dissent.

While different in other respects, the Warring States philosophies of Laozi and Zhuangzi (fourth century B.C.E.) agreed that their age was so chaotic that whole-scale rejection of contemporary forms of government and social values through reclusive withdrawal was the only meaningful course of action. In contrast, being firmly rooted in social philosophy, Confucius and his followers were unable to accept these radical forms of political protest, which to them amounted to "living with the birds and beasts."

In legalism, a Machiavellian political philosophy associated with the late Warring States thinker Han Fei (d. 233 B.C.E.), dissent was no longer an option, and anyone showing resistance to the government would be ruthlessly suppressed. The *Han feizi*, a philosophical work attributed to Han Fei, mentions a case of two sagelike retired recluses who were executed simply for wanting to live independently of the state. By placing themselves outside the jurisdiction of the government and by being immune to the lure of monetary compensation and the fear of punishment, they were seen as subverting the authority of the ruler and thereby endangering the foundation of state control. Legalist-inspired policies were adopted by the ruthless Qin Dynasty (221–207 B.C.E.), which consequently strove to discourage all forms of resistance, as exemplified in the infamous incidents of the burning of books and the killing of scholars to preempt dissension.

These examples of resistance illustrate how politically engaged individuals expressed dissent in isolation, through remonstration, reclusion, suicide, or allegorical poetry. In other cases individuals grouped together to voice political disagreement. Two such cases from the late Han Dynasty (202 B.C.E.–220 C.E.) have often been linked to the fall of the empire: the party proscription and the Yellow Turban Rebellion.

The party proscriptions arose in the bitter feuds between the palace and the reformist officials of the imperial administration. In his successful coup d'état in 159 C.E., the emperor Huan relied on eunuch (castrated) officials, whom he subsequently awarded with noble titles and political influence. As the wealth and political clout of the eunuchs grew, the local elites and powerful officials came to view them as inefficient parasites sucking the lifeblood out of the empire through lavish spending. University students joined the reformists in turning public opinion against the eunuchs through the use (one of the first in historical records) of critical essays, pamphlets, rhymed political slogans, and student demonstrations.

In 167 C.E., when the eunuchs responded by accusing the reformist movement of forming a faction and conspiring against the emperor, the reformist leaders were imprisoned and barred from office. However, the death of the emperor Huan dealt a heavy blow to the eunuchs, and by 168 C.E. some of the formerly imprisoned reformists were again occupying important government offices. In 168 C.E. the tide turned in favor of the eunuch who in 169 C.E. launched the second great proscription, which lasted until the Yellow Turban Rebellion in 184 C.E. and during which the accusation of factionalism was repeatedly used to discredit, imprison, proscribe, and even execute the enemies of the eunuchs. Since in the Han Dynasty the classics were part of the repertoire of the educated, political elite, the discussion of factions in the *Analects* of Confucius greatly influenced Han conceptions of dissent: "The gentleman . . . is sociable, but does not form factions." The eunuch thus could shrewdly exploit the terminology of Confucius, one of the cultural heroes of the reformist tradition, against the reformist officials themselves.

The reformist movement used the pen to express opposition to the Han government, and the Daoist-inspired Yellow Turban peasant uprising resorted to armed revolt. Together they contributed to the destabilization of the Han Dynasty, eventually leading to the disintegration of the empire under various warlords and many short-lived simultaneous courts during the Six Dynasties Period (220–589 C.E.).

While the historical record for ancient China is relatively complete, the corresponding record for most of the rest of Asia is not. Much of this history is shrouded in myth, legend, and conflicting accounts, usually by Chinese writers, including both contemporaries and those who wrote in later centuries.

A good example is provided by Japan. The history of ancient Japan is conventionally divided into three major periods. The earliest was the Jōmon Period, which extended from about 13,000 B.C.E. to about 300 B.C.E. During this period Japan was not a unified nation but a tribal society. Following the Jōmon Period was the Yayoi Period, which extended from 300 B.C.E. to about 300 C.E., though some historians believe that the Yayoi culture may have begun as early as 900 or 800 B.C.E. A main distinction between the two cultures is that the population increased dramatically, and social organization became more complex. Following the Yayoi Period was the Kofun Period, which extended to 539.

Japan, though, continued to remain largely a tribal society. One major effort to unite the tribes was the work of a woman named Himiko, who lived from about 175 to 248 C.E. Himiko was a shaman, or a priestess, who organized a number of Japanese tribes into a state called Yamataikoku, located in either the Yamato or the Kyushu region of present-day Japan (the archaeological evidence is ambiguous). The historical record about Himiko is thin. She is mentioned in an ancient Chinese text titled *Sanguo zhi* (Records of Three Kingdoms), written in about 297 C.E. She is also mentioned in an ancient Japanese history titled *Nihon shoki* (Chronicles of Japan) and a later Korean text called *Samguk sagi* (Chronicles of the Three Kingdoms). According to these accounts, Himiko unified up to 100 tribes primarily through sorcery and shamanism. She lived in a palace, attended by a thousand women and one man. She never married or appeared in public, and her younger brother served as her political adviser.

According to historical accounts, after Himiko's death, her position was assumed by a female relative, perhaps a niece. Rebellion broke out, however, when a tribal king named Shujin (a name that means "Lord-person") led a military force against Himiko's successor. He and his force overthrew the ruling house. He then proclaimed himself emperor of that part of Japan, establishing the tradition of male rule. Few details are known about this rebellion.

Japan, though, was on its way to becoming a unified state. Beginning in about 300 C.E., tribes and clans began to coalesce. A strong, military aristocracy began to emerge. The rulers that replaced Himiko are referred to as the Yamato rulers, and sometimes the period itself is called the Yamato Period. Rivalry and dissent, though, by no means disappeared. As the Yamato Dynasty tried to expand its domains, it met with resistance from nearby rival tribal confederations. One figure at the center of the effort to subdue these rebellious provinces was Yamato Takeru, a half-historical, half-legendary prince who was said to have been dispatched in the fourth century to crush a rebellion in eastern Honshu, where rebels were judged guilty of refusing to submit to the Yamato emperor's authority.

The history of ancient India followed a similar arc. Through much of the subcontinent's prehistory, shifting portions were ruled by separate kings; no unified Indian state existed. That state of affairs changed, however, in the third century B.C.E. under the Maurya Dynasty, and particularly under the rule of Asoka the Great (304–232 B.C.E.). Historians regard Asoka as one of the greatest kings who has ever lived. Early in life he subdued portions of India through military conquest. Later in life he renounced violence and ruled over a vast kingdom that corresponded with modern-day India.

Asoka was the son of the emperor Bindusara and a low-ranking member of Bindusara's harem. Thus, he had numerous half-brothers who shared a father but had different mothers. By all historical accounts the brothers were extremely competitive, and they began to look with suspicion on Asoka because he excelled at military arts and at his studies. The oldest of these brothers, Prince Susima, would in the normal course of events have inherited the throne, but he saw Asoka as a rival, so he persuaded their father to send Asoka to quell a rebellion in Takshashila in northwest India. Susima's belief was that Asoka would be killed, especially since Takshashila was an extremely warlike region, where the population was bullied by militias and military clans that wreaked havoc. Asoka ended the rebellion without a fight. Later, Susima tried the same tactic when a rebellion erupted in Ujjain in central India. Again, Bindusara dispatched Asoka, except that this time fighting took place between Asoka's forces and the rebels. Asoka was injured, but his generals quelled the rebellion. Later, after he ascended the throne in 273 B.C.E., Asoka led the largest army in Indian history up to that time to quell rebellion in the Kalinga Province, whose rulers refused to submit and who, in fact, gave refuge to one of Asoka's rebellious half-brothers.

Political unrest continued after Asoka's death. The Sunga Dynasty assumed control in 185 B.C.E. when the last of the Mauryan rulers, Brihadratha, was assassinated by the commander in chief of his armed forces. The Sunga Dynasty was overthrown in 73 B.C.E. by Vasudeva, who established the Kanva Dynasty in 71 B.C.E. Even during the so-called middle period, which extended to about the middle of the first millennium C.E. and has been described as India's "golden age," this type of power struggle and rebellion remained commonplace. The nation again fragmented into warring kingdoms and states, with feudal lords establishing power over various regions of the country. Further destabilizing the country were invasions from various tribes from the north and west, which themselves established dominance over the regions they conquered. The Gupta Dynasty of the fourth and fifth centuries reasserted control over large portions of India, particularly in the north. Like their predecessors, the Gupta emperors had to unify their realm by quelling rebellious provinces and feudal states by armed force.

Korea, like China and India, consisted of city-states. During the first millennium B.C.E. the three city-states that dominated were Koguryo, Paekche, and Silla, though other minor city-states existed as well. Within each of these city-states were many tribes. Historically, these city-states have been called the Three Kingdoms, and the Three Kingdoms Period, when they reached the height of their influence, extended from the first century B.C.E. to 668, when Silla defeated Koguryo.

Militarily, the most powerful and dominant of the kingdoms was the Koguryo (the name from which "Korea" evolved). Beginning in 37 B.C.E. and into the first centuries of the Common Era, a succession of monarchs overcame resistance to unite the kingdom's tribes and extend the kingdom's boundaries. Resistance, though, often focused on Chinese invaders. During the reign of Taejo (53–146 C.E.), for example, the Koreans mounted a number of attacks on the Chinese garrisons at Lolang, Xiantu, and Liaodong. Their efforts were successful, and Koguryo became entirely independent. The regime also launched attacks against smaller states to absorb them. Later, under King Gwanggaeto the Great, who reigned from 391 to 412 C.E., the kingdom further expanded its territories through military conquest, overcoming resistance from the feudal lords who controlled various regions of the peninsula. His army conquered at least 64 walled cities and 1,400 villages against a tribe called the Buyeo. He subdued additional tribes, annexed portions of the peninsula, conquered Silla, and waged war against Japan. The result of his efforts and those of his son was to turn Korea into a unified country for some 50 years.

EUROPE

BY BRADLEY SKEEN

The ancient Mediterranean civilizations of Greece, Macedonia, and Rome approached the rest of Europe with a desire to control events there for their own advantage. The response to this imperialistic interference was violence: among different tribes fighting each other on behalf of or against the outsiders, in devastating raids on the homelands of the great powers themselves, and finally in the conquest of the Western Roman Empire once political and economic circumstances had radically changed.

The ancient Greeks and Romans built upon older cultures (Etruscan, Minoan, Egyptian, and Assyrian) around the Mediterranean to establish cities and develop the sophisticated economic and political structures that mark civilization. But their neighbors in Europe—Gauls or Celts in present-day Spain, France, the British Isles, and northern Italy; Germans in modern-day Germany and Czech Republic; and Iranian peoples around the Black Sea—maintained a more traditional way of life as farmers or nomadic herdsmen. The primary units of social organization were the household and clan, while chiefs exerted loose control over limited areas. Larger political structures that the Romans called "tribes" theoretically united larger areas populated by speakers of a common dialect, but in practice kings and chiefs had little way to enforce their rule, precisely because they lacked such tools of more complex societies as taxation and standing armies.

An extensive commercial trade conditioned relations between northern and Mediterranean Europe. The northerners had access to raw materials, including furs, amber, tin, and gold, which they were eager to exchange for luxury goods, especially wine, from the southern societies. Because of the prestige they would gain from possessing the trappings of those societies, northern rulers were keenly interested in obtaining items such as sets of ornamental gold and silver dinnerware and dies to strike their own coins. Greeks and Romans attempted to exert control over leaders in the north by granting or denying them access to such goods. Alternatively, Greeks and Romans occasionally launched military expeditions against groups who were hostile to their interests.

Resistance to imperial control could take only a military form. Although leaders in northern Europe had little actual power through their office, they were sometimes able to attract a large following through a personal charisma that made them seem destined for victory, a quality called *rede* in the Germanic languages. Endorsement by religious authorities—for example, the pagan priesthood of the Druids—certainly helped build such a reputation. Favored leaders could attract large war bands not only from their own tribes but also from more diverse groups. Sometimes bands of as many as 50,000 warriors raided Greek or Roman territories with devastating effect. About 390 B.C.E. a band of Gauls sacked Rome itself. In 281 B.C.E. another band of Gauls attacked Greece, getting as far as the shrine of Delphi (279 B.C.E.). Turned away, they crossed over into Asia and were defeated in 277 B.C.E. by the Macedonian king of Syria, Antiochus I, though he could not prevent them from settling in what is now Turkey and founding the new kingdom of Galatia, named after them. After 113 B.C.E. a force composed of two German tribes and many Celts ravaged Italy and Spain until it was defeated by the Romans in 101 B.C.E.

As Rome consolidated its political organization and military power in the Mediterranean, however, the situation changed. Roman leaders increasingly had to develop a charismatic reputation through military victory and build up a military apparatus personally loyal to them as civil war became common at the end of the republic. At the beginning of the empire prestige was still an important concern of the emperors, as was the assurance of security for the empire by acquiring defensible borders. Accordingly, Roman generals undertook the conquest of much of northern Europe around the turn of the era.

Julius Caesar conquered Gaul (modern-day France and the Low Countries) between 58 and 51 B.C.E. Although local peoples tended to ignore invaders of this kind unless they were directly threatened, once the scope of Caesar's ambitions became clear, the Gallic chieftain Vercingetorix (d. 46 B.C.E.) managed in 52 B.C.E. to attract a large war band of various tribal groups to make a concerted defense of the fortified hill town of Alesia (in present-day France). His efforts were ultimately unsuccessful.

Once his position was secure at the beginning of the empire, the emperor Augustus (r. 27 B.C.E.–14 C.E.) decided to conquer Germany. In 9 C.E., after initial campaigns by his stepsons, Augustus sent an army of three legions (30,000 men) to pacify the area. Under the command of Varus, a bureaucrat rather than a military specialist, this force was opposed by a large band of Germans led by Arminius (also known as "Armin" or "Hermann," 18 B.C.E.–19 C.E.), who had led German warriors as auxiliaries fighting for the Romans in pervious campaigns. He caught the Roman force in an ambush in the Teutoburg Forest (near modern-day Bremen) and annihilated it; the victors dedicated the slaughtered legions' battle standards to the Germanic gods in sacred groves. This stunning victory effectively ended Roman ambitions in Germany, though renewed Roman military actions and diplomacy among Germanic rulers eventually broke up Arminius's alliance, which depended on nothing more than the magic of his name. The emperor Claudius (r. 41–54 C.E.) conquered Britain (43 C.E.). After years of occupation a local queen, Boudicca (d. 60 C.E.), managed to stage a revolt against Roman rule, but her efforts were quickly suppressed. Thereafter the Romans reverted to the traditional policy of controlling events in Europe through diplomacy and bribery of local leaders, with only occasional limited military interventions.

In late antiquity (third to fifth centuries C.E.) the situation in Europe changed dramatically. Because of the richer economic prospects available in Roman territory and because of pressure from new migrations from the east of such peoples as the Huns and Slavs, Germanic tribes, who had been partially romanized through centuries of contact, wanted into the empire, not to plunder but to live. Now huge war bands of Goths, Vandals, and Franks penetrated especially into the western part of the empire, ranging as far as North Africa, establishing independent kingdoms.

Because of population changes brought about by the migrations themselves, as well as the inability of central governments based in Rome and Constantinople to provide security despite an ever-increasing burden of taxation, local people in its western provinces ceased to support the empire as a unified political entity, and it collapsed. The last western emperor, Romulus Augustulus (b. 463 C.E.), was deposed by the Goths in 476 C.E. The Eastern Roman Empire (now called by historians the Byzantine Empire), secure for the time being, no longer had reason to intervene to try and impose its authority in the West.

GREECE

BY JEFFREY S. CARNES

The Greeks thought of themselves as a free people, particularly in contrast to the Persian Empire. This encompassed not only freedom from political domination but also the positive freedom to engage in open debate about political matters and to live as one pleased with a minimum of interference from the state. This was particularly true in democratic states, but oligarchies as well valued freedom, albeit for a much more restricted class of citizens. This attitude is evident in two works of the Greek poet Homer (eighth or ninth century B.C.E.), the *Iliad* and the *Odyssey*, where kings regularly hold councils to receive advice from other nobles. The limits on this sort of speech are evident as well: There is an open acknowledgment at the start of the *Iliad* that angering a great king is dangerous; when a common soldier named Thersites speaks out against Agamemnon, he is publicly humiliated by Odysseus, with the approval of the entire army.

Although many *tyrannoi* were good rulers, the Greeks made the figure of the *tyrannos*—a term that describes a sole ruler without hereditary claim to the throne—a sort of bogeyman, emblematic of the ways in which a sole ruler might exercise power capriciously and quash dissent. The Greek historian Herodotus (ca. 484–ca. 425 B.C.E.) tells the story of Periander (r. ca. 627–586 B.C.E.), tyrant of Corinth, taking to heart the metaphoric advice of a fellow tyrant to cut down the stalks of wheat that stood higher than the others, that is, to kill the most powerful people in the state, who might pose a threat to his rule. The king of Persia was seen in a similar light, and all Greek cities, even the most repressive, viewed themselves as bastions of liberty and were proud of their ability to be self-governing and open to debate, whether the deliberative body was a small council of elders or an assembly of the entire people. "Slaves to none, nor are they subject" marvels the chorus of Persian elders in *Persai*, a drama by the Greek dramatist Aeschylus (525–456 B.C.E.).

Political factions existed everywhere and at all times in the Greek world, a culture in which dozens of independent and frequently warring states existed in an area the size of Iowa, less than 60,000 square miles. The word *stasis* (literally, "standing") was used for a faction that took a stand in a political dispute and also for the political unrest caused by such groups. Sometimes these stands were based on class or regional antagonisms. Sixth-century Athens, for example, experienced civil strife between those who lived in city, seaside, and hillside districts. By the sixth century it was common for a faction to present itself as the champion of an economic or social class (such as landowners, debtors, or the poor) even where the connection was tenuous. Larger states also were ready to offer aid to factions elsewhere as a way of extending their spheres of influence: By the time of the Peloponnesian War between Athens and Sparta, virtually every polis (or city-state) in Greece had oligarchic and democratic factions. The extremely bloody *stasis* on Corfu in 427 B.C.E. was the first of many. The Greek historian Thucydides (d. ca. 410 B.C.E.) paints a grim picture of the extent to which factionalism led to revenge, paranoia, and the utter breakdown of Greek civic life.

Apart from the more violent forms of *stasis*, political disagreement and dissent were tolerated to varying degrees throughout the Greek world. As is often the case, the best evidence comes from Athens. This is not only because of the relative abundance of Athenian sources compared with those from other cities but also because Athens was the freest and most open of the cities now known; if Athens failed to tolerate certain types of dissent, it is therefore likely that other cities also failed to do so.

The Athenian democracy was based on the principle of *isonomia* (equal protection of the laws); closely related to this was the principle of *isegoria* (equal right to speak, such as in the Assembly and other political fora). Later in the fifth century B.C.E. the term *parrhesia* (frankness or freedom of speech) appears as a quality in which the Athenians prided

Head of Greek philosopher Socrates (Alison Frantz Photographic Collection, American School of Classical Studies at Athens)

themselves, as was their ability to be "free and tolerant in their private lives," according to the funeral oration by the Athenian stateman Pericles (r. ca. 460–429 B.C.E.) as recorded by Thucydides. There was a striking degree of frank speech, particularly in the theater.

The comedies of the Athenian playwright Aristophanes (ca. 450–ca. 388 B.C.E.) are full of scurrilous attacks on politicians; their competence, honesty, physical characteristics, and sexual proclivities are all fair game. Further, Aristophanes mercilessly criticizes state policy even in wartime. In his *Lysistrate*, produced in 411 B.C.E., he shows the women of Greece taking power (by means of a sex strike) to end the unpopular war the men had created. The play is unstinting in assigning blame to politicians, military leaders, and the people of Athens, and it jokes about the pro-Spartan factions within the city. Yet Athens was in serious danger at the time: The disastrous Sicilian expedition four years earlier had cost the lives of thousands of its citizens, and the oligarchic conspirators Aristophanes mocks overthrew the democracy within a matter of months. It is hard to imagine a modern democracy under similar circumstances tolerating this degree of dissent.

Alongside this openness were times in which citizens were punished for exceeding the limits of tolerance. Despite the extreme freedom of speech usually granted to the theater, the tragic poet Phrynichus (fl. ca. 500 B.C.E.) was fined 1,000 drachmas for "reminding the audience of their own troubles" by putting on a play about the Persian sack of Miletus at a time when the Athenians themselves feared the Persian threat. Aristophanes, too, was prosecuted (apparently unsuccessfully) in the 420s B.C.E. by the Athenian politician Cleon (d. 422 B.C.E.) for making fun of the city's magistrates.

For religious issues there was a similar alternation between freedom and intolerance. Athens in the fifth century B.C.E. included several philosophers who challenged traditional notions of morality and religion; in addition, cults such as Orphism and Pythagoreanism were popular. At the same time there were several high-profile prosecutions for impiety. In 437 B.C.E. the philosopher Anaxagoras (ca. 500–ca. 428 B.C.E.) fled the city in the wake of such a charge; in 415 B.C.E. Alcibiades (ca. 450–404 B.C.E.) and others were charged with mutilating statues of the god Hermes and holding mock versions of the Eleusinian Mysteries (initiation ceremonies in the cult of the goddesses Demeter and Persephone); and in 399 B.C.E. the charge of "believing in strange new gods" was one of the accusations against the philosopher Socrates (ca. 470–399 B.C.E.), for which he was sentenced to death. In a sense these prosecutions actually were about religion: Religion was a state matter, and to offend religious sensibilities was to threaten the state. For the most part, however, the religious prosecutions were motivated by politics: Anaxagoras and Alcibiades had powerful enemies, and Socrates was associated with many notoriously antidemocratic characters (including Alcibiades), some of whom had played a role in the brutal dictatorship of the Thirty Tyrants in the aftermath of Athens's defeat in the Peloponnesian War.

Some conclusions may be drawn from this information. First, the Athenians tolerated a great deal of free speech as long as it did not seem immediately threatening to their physical safety or to their sense of well-being. The comedies of Aristophanes probably did not normally pose such a threat but were instead a type of contained dissent: He poses revolutionary ideas in a circumscribed, well-defined space but does not argue for revolution or even serious change. (It is noteworthy that *Lysistrate*, like many of his other comedies, ends with a return to a kinder, gentler version of the status quo.)

Second, the principle of *parrhesia* was a tradition, not a constitutionally guaranteed right. Pericles speaks of the unwritten laws that govern conduct; Socrates recognized at his trial that the unwritten accusations against him were more damaging than the actual charges. Popular opinion and prejudice could be worth more than the force of law; Pericles' idealized vision of the city notwithstanding, Athens was full of petty jealousies. The law was extremely flexible: Irrelevant charges could be used to punish political enemies, and courtroom procedure was ill defined and very much subject to the immediate will of the people. Cleon's prosecution of Aristophanes may have been technically without merit, yet it may well have stood a chance of success.

Third, freedom of speech did not protect the speaker from retaliation at the hands of his enemies. Greek culture honored the values of competitiveness and aggression, and Athens, in particular, was known for being wordy and litigious. One should perhaps be surprised that the punishment of dissenters by their enemies was apparently so rare.

ROME

BY KIRK H. BEETZ

Perhaps the most successful dissenter in Rome was one of the first, Lucius Junius Brutus (sixth century B.C.E.). King Tarquinius Superbus (r. 534–510 B.C.E.), meaning "Tarquin the Proud," apparently murdered Brutus's brother. This event motivated Brutus to conspire against Tarquinius Superbus. Brutus had help in this conspiracy from members of the social elite who belonged to the Senate. They had been accustomed to being consulted by Rome's kings on matters of public policy, but King Tarquinius Superbus ruled by edict, without consulting the Senate, a practice that probably angered senators. In addition, Brutus's brother had been a senator, making it clear that the king was a threat even to members of the Senate.

Brutus's opportunity came in about 510 B.C.E. Tarquinius Superbus was expanding Rome's dominance of its area through wars against local cities, and that year the Romans were laying siege to the city of Ardea. While her husband, Lucius Tarquinius Collatinus, was at the siege, Lucretia was raped by Tarquinius Superbus's son, Sextus. She wrote to her husband about what had happened. When he and his fellow officers rushed back to Rome, she told them what had happened and then stabbed herself to death. Brutus seized the moment and persuaded his companions to rebel against the king. According to tradition, he became one of Rome's first two consuls, Lucretia's husband being the other, but he fell in battle soon thereafter when Etruscans tried to reinstate Tarquinius Superbus as Rome's king.

As the Roman Republic expanded its territories though warfare, the difference in wealth between the aristocrats, called patricians, and the commoners, called plebeians, widened, creating broad discontent among plebeians. Three important champions for their cause arose: Tiberius Gracchus (163–133 B.C.E.), his brother Gaius Gracchus (153–121 B.C.E.), and Gaius Marius (ca. 157–86 B.C.E.). Tiberius Gracchus came from a wealthy family but was not an aristocrat. He saw that common soldiers, who were required to come from landed families, were losing their farms to wealthy patricians, and he tried to reform the laws by requiring that retired soldiers be given public lands. The Senate opposed this action, but Tiberius Gracchus persuaded the Plebeian Council, the assembly that represented the plebeians, to pass the reform. He then urged other reforms, including one that would give Roman citizenship to Rome's Italian allies—something even some plebeians opposed because they feared it would dilute their own privileges as Roman citizens. Tiberius Gracchus ran for reelection as tribune, and on election day he and hundreds of his supporters were attacked by a mob led by senators and were slaughtered.

Gaius Gracchus emerged as the new leader of the reform movement. Like his brother, he served in the army. In spite of his brother's murder, he chose to advocate some of the same reforms his brother had advocated. He was elected to two terms as tribune (123–122 B.C.E.) During his terms he managed to have laws passed that took public lands out of the hands of the wealthy and redistributed them among the poor. He advocated Roman citizenship for Italian allies, and he undertook a more comprehensive reform of Roman government than had his brother. He lost his race for a third term as tribune when rival candidates pretended to favor his reforms, and thereafter the new tribunes dismantled his work. Gracchus's supporters began carrying weapons for protection, and their enemies pretended that Gracchus's supporters were in rebellion. As a consequence, the Roman army slaughtered over 3,000 of the supporters, and Gracchus was stabbed to death by one of his slaves. One of the enduring legacies of the Gracchus brothers was the development of two opposing political views: the popular, called Populares, and the elite, called Optimates.

Gaius Marius served as consul seven times between 107 and 86 B.C.E. He was a highly successful general with a large following of active and retired soldiers. He eliminated the requirement that soldiers be landowners, allowing tens of thousands of poor and out-of-work Romans to join the army—something that alarmed some senators because such men had little to lose and everything to gain from political reform. In 91 B.C.E. the tribune Marcus Livius Drusus was assassinated for advocating the Gracchus brothers' reforms. Rome's Italian allies rebelled, demanding citizenship. This conflict became the Social War (90–89 B.C.E.). During that war the Roman general Lucius Cornelius Sulla (138–78 B.C.E.) attacked Rome with his army and forced Marius to flee. Sulla belonged to the Optimates faction, but his actions were viewed as illegal. Marius himself led troops into Rome in 87 B.C.E. and ordered the murders of members of the Optimates faction, including patricians. About a month after becoming consul for the seventh time, he died unexpectedly.

In 49 B.C.E. Julius Caesar became dictator of Rome. He was a populist reformer and was despised by the Optimates faction. A prominent member of the Optimates was Marcus Junius Brutus (85–42 B.C.E.). During the civil war between Caesar and Pompey, Brutus joined Pompey's army because Pompey represented the Optimates faction. After the war Brutus wrote to Caesar, asking to be forgiven, and in 48 B.C.E. Caesar pardoned him. He and other Optimates members conspired to assassinate Caesar, on the ground that they would be protecting the republic and civil liberties. They murdered Caesar in 44 B.C.E. but were defeated by Octavian in the war that followed. Brutus committed suicide.

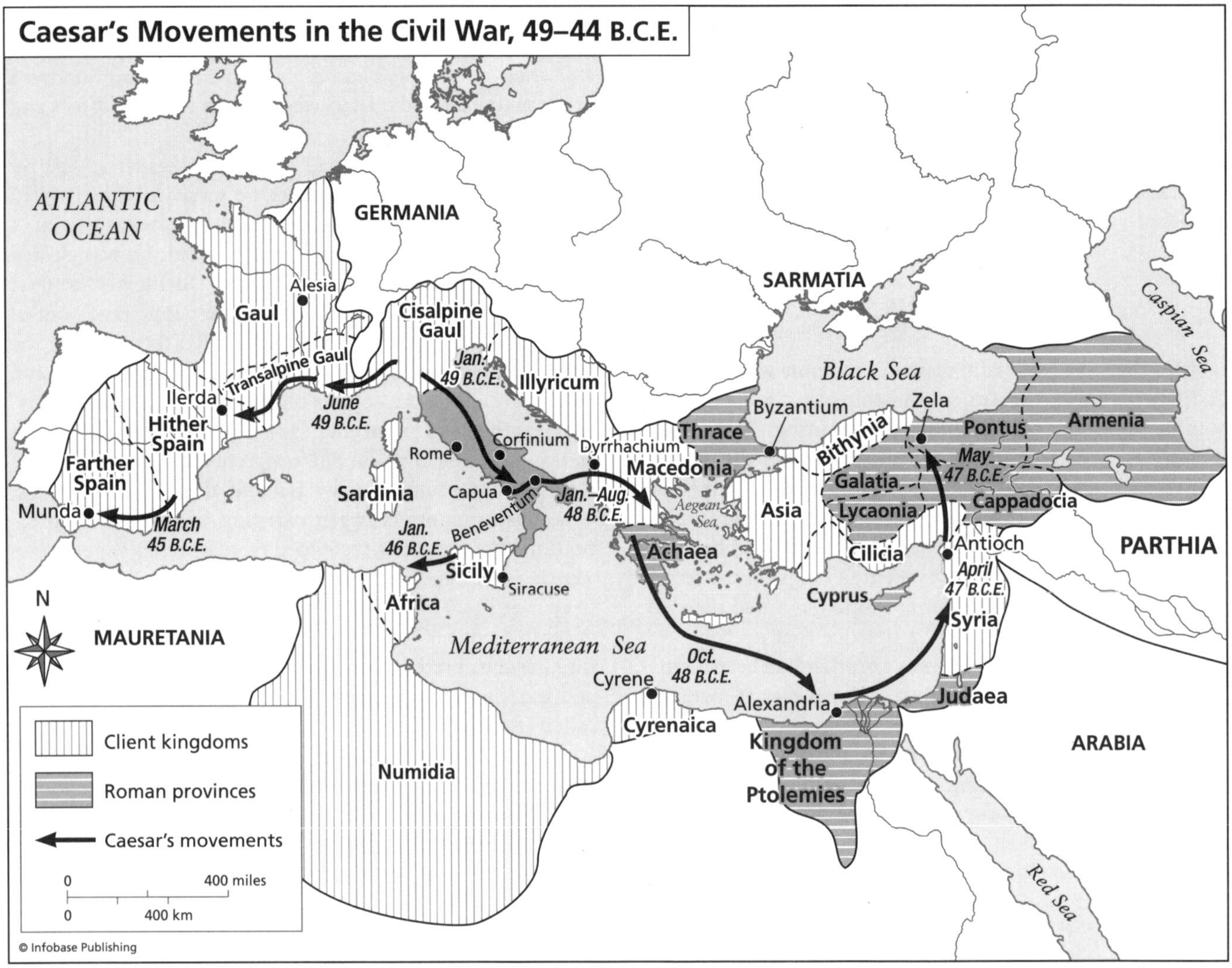

During the Roman Civil War of the first century B.C.E. Marcus Junius Brutus and others conspired to assassinate the dictator Julius Caesar, which they accomplished in 44 B.C.E.

The competition between the Optimates and the Populares continued, with Tullius Cicero (106–43 B.C.E.) championing the Optimates against Octavian. As a consequence, he was murdered.

After the transformation of the republic into the Roman Empire, there were many conspiracies to assassinate emperors and other political leaders, but the most notorious faction of dissent was a religious organization. Eastern religions had made their way into Rome and Roman Europe. One of these religions was Christianity. The Christians came to political prominence in 64 C.E., when most of Rome was consumed by fire. Rumors circulated that the emperor Nero (r. 54–68 C.E.) had started the fire to clear land for a palace and gardens he wished to build. He made scapegoats of the pacifistic Christians, who were regarded as anti-Roman. The cruelty of torture and murder to which Christians were subjected won for them sympathy among many Romans. The emperor Diocletian (r. 284–305 C.E.) renewed the persecution of Christians with vigor, but in some Roman provinces the local governments did not press the persecutions. In 312 C.E. there was a dramatic reversal in fortune because the emperor Constantine I (r. 306–337 C.E.) converted to Christianity.

With Constantine's conversion, pagans became the dissenters. Prominent among them was Quintus Aurelius Symmachus (ca. 345–ca. 402 C.E.). In 382 C.E. he protested the removal of the Altar of Victory from the Senate, and the emperor Gratian (r. 367–383 C.E.) sent him into exile. Gratian was assassinated in 383 C.E., and Symmachus was allowed to return to Rome. In 391 C.E. he became a consul. In 391 C.E. Emperor Theodosius I (r. 379–395) issued edicts suppressing Rome's traditional religion, and Symmachus protested. His written arguments for tolerance of differing religions survive, as does a large collection of his letters. He was one of the last supporters of the traditional Roman religion to engage Christians in debates about religion and its place in Roman culture.

Ivory panel commemorating Quintus Aurelius Symmachus, an orator and figure in Roman government and a prominent pagan; he was banished by the emperor, a Christian. (© The Trustees of the British Museum)

THE AMERICAS

BY KIRK H. BEETZ

In the ancient Americas people who openly disagreed with or resisted those in power tended to be treated harshly. Dissent was seen as a threat to the entire community for its risk of upsetting the social structure or incurring the wrath of the supernatural world. The mythology of North Americans suggests that dissenters were ejected from their tribes or villages. Sometimes these outcasts founded a new home and became celebrated as persecuted people who began a new and glorious village or culture. Behind the mythology is the implication that people needed to be in groups to survive, and outcasts usually did not survive expulsion.

More is known about the effects of resistance and dissent in the societies of ancient Mesoamerica than in those from lands farther north. Perhaps the greatest city of the ancient Americas was Teotihuacán, which reached its peak from before 100 C.E. to about the mid-500s C.E. It had a highly regimented society. Its commoners lived in apartments that were organized into gridlike blocks. Each apartment housed three families, with sleeping, cooking, and working areas for each family. Archaeologists speculate that the housing was intended to keep commoners well organized. One effect would be that an individual family would have little privacy in which to conspire against the government. For those people who did resist the rulers of Teotihuacán, appalling fates awaited. They would be tortured and executed, perhaps sacrificed to a god.

Despite the government's efforts to keep its people in line, dissent seems to have become a problem. During the 400s C.E. the commoners may have become restive, perhaps even rebelling on occasion. Their grievances may have included the conspicuous and ever-widening gap between their welfare and that of the social elite. Eventually, much of the center of the city was burned during either an attack from outside or a revolt of the residents of the city. Because there seems to have been no one outside the city powerful enough to challenge it, archaeologists are inclined to believe that the destruction was caused by residents fighting against their rulers. The revolts marked the decline of Teotihuacán. Most of the people of the city moved away to join Mayan city-states or to found agricultural communities in Mexico.

When the Olmec flourished is debated among archaeologists, but the culture seems to have lasted about a thousand years, from about 1500 to 500 B.C.E. The Olmec developed a complex culture and built some large monuments. They are now best known for their huge carvings of stone heads. They did not develop large cities and presumably did not have city cultures. Dissent among the Olmec may have taken the form of religious protest, and one reason they did not build big cities may have been resistance by commoners to being organized in large groups separated from the life of the land—agriculture, hunting, and gathering.

The Maya drew some of their culture from the Olmec, though many archaeologists believe that the Maya were not necessarily descendants of the Olmec. Near the end of their era the Olmec developed writing, something the Maya used to organize their society. Writing allowed rulers to extend the reach of their laws and traditions through written documents, much as other literate cultures have done in other parts of the world.

The Maya worked at creating a society in which every person knew his or her role in the community. Each person was supposed to have a place and a duty within society from birth and was expected to focus on that place and duty throughout his or her life. This became a social contract between commoners and their lords in which the elite had obligations to the commoners just as binding as those the commoners had to the elite. The Maya may have escaped some of the problems experienced by Teotihuacán by having even their kings endure the same privations as the poor. Kings and nobles wore better clothes, had better housing, and had their pick of the best food, but they lived among their people and starved when their community starved and suffered from war when their people suffered from war. Indeed, kings and nobles were expected to be among the first to risk their lives when they waged war.

Even so, people sometimes became angry with their government. Mayan culture provided an outlet for this: Groups of people could shift their allegiance to another city or just pick up their belongings and move away. When they shifted allegiance to another city, they did so as groups. Probably under the leadership of local elders or a local governor, they would reallocate whole villages or community farmlands to a neighboring city-state, making its king their king and sending their taxes to their new government. This would have made them subject to raiding for slaves and human sacrifices by their old government, so they would have needed to join a city-state that was willing and able to protect them. In the absence of such a government, entire villages or groups of villages would sometimes abandon their homes and carry what they could to a new place out of reach of their former government. Such movements may explain why certain styles of pottery would mix with another style from a region far away, resulting in the creation of a new style or the loss of one style as the other became dominant.

Violence arose when cities tried to throw off the dominance of another city. Both Tikal and Calakmul experienced repeated revolts as the nobility of smaller cities tried to end the paying of tribute to those cities. Such revolts were very risky; if the rebels were captured, they would be tortured for days and then ritually sacrificed. If the commoners of the rebel cities believed they endured too much misery because of the revolt, they could shift allegiances or pick up and leave, which they sometimes did. Further, when a city's monarch was replaced by force, people might resist his orders. In 378 C.E. a noble from Teotihuacán, Siyaj K'ak', killed the king of Tikal and made himself king of the city. Depictions of Siyaj K'ak' show him in Teotihuacán clothing and armor, but his successors are pointedly in Tikal garb; in one depiction a later king's Mayan clothing contrasts with Siyaj K'ak's Teotihuacán clothing, a public effort to distance the monarch from his ancestor by showing that he was committed to Tikal's traditions.

For South America little is known about dissent and resistance of the ancient era, except that resistance could bring terrifying consequences. The Moche (ca. 100–ca. 600 C.E.) of Peru left murals that show the cost of resisting its rulers. Whether rebels or prisoners of war, the fate was torture and then mass bloodlettings, during which a priest sliced open the throats one at a time of hundreds of prisoners, all in a public display during which the prisoners had to watch what was happening. To risk such a fate, people had to be highly motivated and prepared to die rather than be captured. Perhaps dissidents among the Moche did as the Maya sometimes did and, if they could, moved away.

See also AGRICULTURE; ARCHITECTURE; ART; BORDERS AND FRONTIERS; CERAMICS AND POTTERY; CITIES; CRIME AND PUNISHMENT; EMPIRES AND DYNASTIES; FOREIGNERS AND BARBARIANS; GOVERNMENT ORGANIZATION; HUNTING, FISHING, AND GATHERING; LAWS AND LEGAL CODES; LITERATURE; MIGRATION AND POPULATION MOVEMENTS; MILITARY; RELIGION AND COSMOLOGY; SCANDALS AND CORRUPTION; SETTLEMENT PATTERNS; SOCIAL ORGANIZATION; TOWNS AND VILLAGES; TRADE AND EXCHANGE; WAR AND CONQUEST; WRITING.

FURTHER READING

Julius Caesar, *The Gallic War*, trans. H. J. Edwards (Cambridge, Mass.: Harvard University Press, 1917).

Hans Delbrück, *History of the Art of War within the Framework of Political History*, Vol. 2, *The Germans*, trans. Walter J. Renfroe (Westport, Conn.: Greenwood, 1980).

Nikolai Grube, ed., *Maya: Divine Kings of the Rain Forest* (Cologne, Germany: Könemann, 2001).

Peter Gwin, "Peruvian Temple of Doom," *National Geographic* 206 (July 2004): 102–117.

Adetokundbo F. Knowles-Borishade, "Paradigm for Classical African Orature," *Journal of Black Studies* 21 (1991): 488–500.

Andrew W. Lintott, *Violence, Civil Strife, and Revolution in the Classical City, 750–330 B.C.* (Baltimore, Md.: Johns Hopkins University Press, 1982).

Josiah Ober, *Political Dissent in Democratic Athens: Intellectual Critics of Popular Rule* (Princeton, N.J.: Princeton University Press, 1998).

J. N. Postgate, "Royal Ideology and State Administration in Sumer and Akkad." In *Civilizations of the Ancient Near East*, ed. Jack M. Sasson (New York: Scribner, 1995).

Donald B. Redford, *Akhenaten: The Heretic King*, repr. ed. (Princeton, N.J.: Princeton University Press, 1987).

John. F. Robertson, "Social Tensions in the Ancient Near East." In *A Companion to the Ancient Near East*, ed. Daniel C. Snell (Malden, Mass.: Blackwell, 2005).

Isidor F. Stone, *The Trial of Socrates* (Boston: Little, Brown, 1988).

Tacitus, *The Agricola and The Germania*, trans. S. A. Handford and H. Mattingly (New York: Penguin, 1971).

Peter S. Wells, *The Barbarians Speak: How the Conquered Peoples Shaped Roman Europe* (Princeton, N.J.: Princeton University Press, 1999).

Peter S. Wells, *The Battle That Stopped Rome: Emperor Augustus, Arminius, and the Slaughter of the Legions in the Teutoburg Forest* (New York: W. W. Norton, 2003).

► roads and bridges

INTRODUCTION

The earliest roads in the ancient world consisted of tracks made by game animals and migrating herds. Ancient hunter-gatherers followed these tracks in pursuit of game and used them to travel from one place to another. In time, however, more sophisticated roadways were built, and the extent and quality of some of these roads might come as a surprise to modern people accustomed to traveling at high speeds on interstate highways. The first paved streets were built probably in about 4000 B.C.E. in the Indus Valley of India. The first engineered road was built in England in about 3800 B.C.E., primarily to span marshland. In about 3000 B.C.E. the ancient Egyptians constructed a road paved with stones to aid in the construction of the Great Pyramid. Between about 1100 and 20 B.C.E. the Chinese constructed a road network of some 25,000 miles, and the Silk Road from China through central Asia to the Mediterranean Seas became a major trade route. Couriers through the Andes Mountains in South America relied on roads for travel, and Darius the Great's Royal Road in Persia, built around 500 B.C.E., was of such high quality that postal couriers could travel almost 250 miles per day on it. The Greeks and Mesoamericans also built extensive road systems, along with bridges to span rivers and marshes.

The most sophisticated ancient road system, however, was built by the ancient Romans, attested to in part by the word *pavement,* from the Latin word *pavimentum,* referring to the layer of concrete at the base of Roman roads. Many Roman roads were so well constructed that they survive in modern times to be seen by tourists in France (Gaul), Italy, England, and other parts of the old Roman Empire. Roman road building began in about the sixth through the fourth centuries B.C.E., but it was not until the Roman Republic, from the fourth through the first centuries B.C.E., that major engineered roads were constructed. In time, these roads would link every part of the Roman Empire. A person could travel from the far reaches of the empire to the center of ancient Rome, the Forum, using constructed roads nearly the entire way. Perhaps the most famous of these roads is the Via Appia, or Appian Way, which extended over 300 miles. Some of the earlier roads followed the natural contours of the land, but later roads represented massive excavation projects, because the builders modified those contours. To match the sophistication of their roads, the Romans also built bridges, some of which extended for hundreds of yards.

Ancient roads and bridges were often constructed primarily for the purpose of military conquest and the movement of troops and provisions. Later, they facilitated the administration of an empire, as officials, inspectors, couriers, tax collectors, and the like could travel relatively rapidly and safely. In time, roads and bridges also came to facilitate trade and commerce. While boats and ships were used extensively in the movement of goods, many communities were inaccessible by water, so roads had to be constructed to enable goods to be transported. Some of these roads were even named for their trade purposes. Perhaps the best example is the Via Salaria, a Roman road built primarily for the transportation of salt.

AFRICA

BY MICHAEL J. O'NEAL

A system of roads and bridges was crucial to the development of ancient civilizations, including those of Africa. Roads served a number of key purposes: They enabled central authorities to communicate with far-flung regions; they allowed people from the countryside to engage in trade and exchange with people in the larger towns and cities, putting them on a more equal footing socially and economically; they enabled nations to trade with other nations, expanding the range of products available to their people; and perhaps most important, they allowed people to overcome the limitations of geography and come in contact with one another, trading ideas, information, and beliefs. A strong, vibrant empire or state was almost impossible without a system of roads.

The earliest roads in Africa probably were game trails people used to travel from place to place as they searched for food and water. Of course, none of these trails survives, but little imagination is needed to envision people following paths through the forest or over the savanna that animals had beaten down in their movements. While game trails were probably the earliest roads the world over, in Africa the wide, packed-down trails made by elephants no doubt were of particular use. Like these ancient trails, no prehistoric bridges survive for the simple reason that such bridges would have been crudely constructed of logs, though evidence exists of later suspension bridges built with vines.

The first true roads probably developed with the advent of agriculture. As ancient farmers and herders moved about with their livestock, they beat down more permanent paths over the terrain linking parts of their community with others nearby. In some instances these paths, hardened by centuries of use, can still be found in Africa. They are observable because grasses and other vegetation still have difficulty taking root in the densely compacted soil. Further, these ancient roadways probably were forged on higher ground; low-lying ground was more likely to be boggy or thick with vegetation. On higher ground the action of human and animal feet, and later carts and wagons, wore down the ground into the bedrock over a period of thousands of years.

As far as archaeologists know, none of these ancient roads was improved or engineered in any way; primitive peoples lacked the tools and time for making such improvements. Further, trying to improve roads in the shifting sands of the Sahara would have been fruitless. Nonetheless, trade routes between western Africa and the Middle East took at least four clearly defined routes. Caravan leaders led traders over the routes, which required about 40 days of travel between Arabia and such West African nations as Mali and Ghana. These routes were not established until about the third century C.E., when the camel was domesticated. Camels were necessary in the Sahara because they can go without food or water for long stretches of time. Some of these caravans consisted of as many as 12,000 camels, though 1,000 was a more common number. The route was marked by a sequence of oases that provided water.

Among the earliest improved roads of Africa were those built in the kingdom of Nubia, the region to the south of Egypt. Archaeologists discovered some of these roads in the 1960s during salvage operations in connection with the construction of the Aswān Dam on the Nile River. Archaeologists discovered two types of roads. One type consisted of stretches where all of the rock was removed and placed in low mounds at the edge of the roadway to form a border. The sand was smoothed after the rocks were removed. The width of the roads varied depending on the terrain, but generally these roads were about 30 feet wide. In some places, such as a 4-mile stretch of road that ran west from the Nile River at the city of Denduz, this type of road was built on sandstone bedrock. It is clear that the rock borders were deliberately placed to mark the route, for they are found in places where there is no loose rock, so they had to have been carried into position over some distance.

The other type of road, an example of which was found running from the city of Dakkah to Kalabsha, is marked not by lines or piles of loose rock but by pairs of stone markers. These markers are roughly 1 foot in diameter and up to 3 feet tall, but in nearly every instance one of the markers is taller than its pair. Pairs of markers occur at roughly even intervals of a mile.

These roads, however, were not constructed in the modern sense of the word. Rather, they were more in the nature of clearings, with loose rock and other obstacles moved away. The first engineered roads in Africa were built by the Roman Empire, which required a complex system of roads and bridges for trade, administration, and military transport. These roads were built using methods that were surprisingly modern, with packed underlayments and crowning to allow water to run off. One of the most important Roman roads in Africa was the coastal highway that ran from Alexandria in Egypt all the way west to the coast off Gibraltar in Spain. While the road no longer exists, its existence is documented in itineraries from the time. Stretches of the highway were constructed in the centuries prior to the Common Era; the road was completed at about the end of the first century C.E. Although these roads were built by the Romans, they were used by Africans, even after the Romans withdrew, for trade and travel.

One of the signal achievements of the Roman Empire was bridge construction. While many of Rome's bridges in North Africa and elsewhere were constructed of timber (and thus do not survive), others were constructed with stone and concrete. With the exception of crude log bridges and perhaps suspension-type bridges made with vines, the bridge did not arrive in Africa until the Romans expanded into the continent.

EGYPT

BY MARK ANTHONY PHELPS

Roads, in the sense of paths that have been cleared by humans to facilitate travel and transport, arrive with of urban living. Footpaths existed from the moment that humans discovered other humans. With the advent of agriculture and the rise of urban areas, larger paths were needed to transport larger loads of goods longer distances. These early paths would follow the terrain that offered the least difficulty for travel. Often these ancient paths have become modern roads. The function of roads has remained constant throughout history. Goods are transported, salesmen carry their wares, people visit family members and others, pilgrimages are made, diplomatic embassies travel, official messengers bear royal documents and goods, and armies move from place to place. The bulk of transport in the Nile Valley was naturally done by means of the river. Given the annual inundations, or periods of flooding, the paths were generally buried every year. Dried canals served as pathways and roadways. There are a number of roads outside the valley that have been preserved.

The best-explored road system in Egypt is that which connects the oases of the Western Desert. This road was the subject of intense study from 1992 to 1997, under the auspices of the Luxor-Farshut Desert Road Survey. This road system connects a number of oasis sites, which in turn connect to more distant oases and to the Nile Valley. Human activity along these roads is known from Paleolithic times (up to 7000 B.C.E.). Given that there were no wheeled vehicles until the Twelfth Dynasty (ca. 1991–ca. 1783 B.C.E.), the traffic for most of the history of this road was by foot or by donkey. Later inscriptions and artwork point to the use of horses on the route, probably as part of a royal courier service.

Like any road of its nature, this road had a number of forts. The forts served two purposes. First, they were there to collect taxes for the royal treasury, presumably at nome, or province, boundaries. Second, they were there to provide security, both for individuals and for the kingdom. The presence of soldiers would discourage travelers from avoiding the tolls. Also, soldiers could keep some sense of order in the region by protecting against desert raiders and by guarding access to the oasis wells. Further, they could serve as watchmen on the alert for the movement of rebels and other hostile groups. Towers became employed more frequently by later Hellenistic and Roman armies.

Likewise like any road of its nature, this route preserves both the graffiti of the literate segment of the population and stelae and inscriptions that date from the advent of writing to modern scribbles. Among these writings is a significant inscription from the time of the unification of Upper and Lower Egypt. It is written on behalf of the ruler known as the Scorpion (end of the fourth millennium B.C.E.). The inscription seems to record the use of the road to outflank the armies of Naqâda by the Scorpion's army from Abydene.

The Wadi Hammamat forms a natural pathway from the Nile to the Red Sea and has long served as a way for trade between Upper Egypt and points south in the Nile Valley. A road dating to the Predynastic Period (ca. 5300–ca. 3000 B.C.E.) connected the port of Sawaw to the Nile at Coptos (present-day Qift). The presence of quarries and gold mines created a demand for the roadway as well. Road systems grew up around Nile cataracts, generally consisting of roads at least 16 feet wide. These roads enabled cargoes of any size to be

GRAFFITI

The graffiti along the Luxor-Farshut Road in the Western Desert is typical of what is found along ancient roadways. What follows are samples of what individuals wanted to proclaim to the world. Some of these proclamations are more than 5,000 years old. One can find a traveler at leisure, writing, "Regnal Year 17, first month of the Shemu season, day 17: Spending the day by the scribe Monthuhotep beneath this mountain on holiday." Another traveler was not feeling so relaxed. He inscribes a letter on a rock wall requesting that the priest pray to a number of gods for his safety on the journey.

Pilgrimages are a common reason to travel, and pilgrims often left graffiti behind them that served as reminders to the god and proclamations to fellow travelers in the mundane world that this pious act was being performed. One example: "He has made [it] as his monument at the time of his coming from the Abydene nome in order to perform rites for king Mentuhotep." Priests also reminded both divine and mundane observers that they were present: "Made by the second prophet of Amun, Roma." It so happens that Roma was already well known before this graffito was discovered. He became the high priest of Amon (the most significant and most powerful priest in the empire) under the pharaoh Ramses II (r. ca. 1290–ca. 1224 B.C.E.). Roma was by no means the only official to leave his mark, nor was he the most significant one. That would have been "the son of the king of Upper and Lower Egypt, Mentuhotep." He would later become pharaoh himself.

The first five lines of an otherwise lost literary work were inscribed along this roadside. It was in praise of an unnamed Theban ruler of the Second Intermediate Period (ca. 1640–ca. 1532 B.C.E.). It begins, "Oh people great and small, and the army in its entirety—behold, a man is in the City [Thebes], whose like has not been known!" Finally, a happy text greets the literate traveler, "As for the one who will read these writings, he will arrive [home] in peace."

moved from ship to ship on the river. In urban areas, processional ways to temples were often paved. The stones were laid directly upon the soil. Typically the processional way would be from a river quay to the entrance of a temple.

The Ways of Horus, the royal road that led from the Nile Valley northeast through the Sinai to Palestine was the main overland route connecting Egypt to most of the significant commercial centers of the ancient world. The route brought in goods from Anatolia, the Arabian Peninsula, Mesopotamia, and all points east. Networks grew up connecting the main road to cities and villages throughout the inhabitable regions of the area. The roadway had forts, which in addition to the normal duties also protected wells for travelers. Way stations also dotted the route.

Open roads were basically areas that were cleared of rocks, which were then piled along the edges. Roads to quarries were often hewn out of solid rock for some portion of the trip to the river. The Egyptians had the technology to level rock surfaces, which they often used for building roads. Quarry roads were typically at least 16 feet wide and occasionally were paved. The need for paving was determined by the soil, which often was too sandy to haul blocks weighing multiple tons. The longest quarry road was located in Lower Nubia and was some 50 miles long. The oldest surviving quarry road with paving stones terminated on a quay in what used to be Lake Moeris. The construction of this road consisted of virtually no leveling prior to the laying of the stones, which were placed in the soil with the largest slabs laid on the outside of the road, while smaller stones were used in the center. This road was uniformly four cubits wide (ca. 7.3 feet). In addition to clearing surfaces or laying paving stones on the ground, Egyptians also would make log roads, which they lubricated with mud so that sledges could be dragged along them. There were officials with the titles "master of the roads" and "overseer of the masters of the roads." An important task for these officials was the creation and maintenance of quarry roads.

There is virtually no mention of bridges prior to Roman domination. Seti I (ca. 1306–ca. 1290 B.C.E.) is depicted as crossing a bridge on his way back from a Syrian campaign. The Greek historian Diodorus Siculus (first century B.C.E.) writes that there was a fort at each mouth of the Nile. These forts were situated on both sides of the river with a bridge that had defensive installations straddling the river, but it is a claim found nowhere else.

THE MIDDLE EAST

BY MARK ANTHONY PHELPS

Routes followed by ancient peoples to traverse the land—whether for hunting or herding or some other purpose—began as simple footpaths. Roads smoothed or otherwise specially prepared for transport and transit came later, typically with settled living in villages, towns, and cities. No paved open roads have been discovered in the ancient Near East from the period prior to Roman domination. They are described as being "dusty" in a number of sources. The Gutians, invaders of Mesopotamia from modern Iran during the 22nd century B.C.E., were accused of allowing roads to be covered with weeds. The Egyptian work known as the "Satirical Letter" describes roads in coastal Syria-Palestine as being covered with pebbles, weeds, and briars. In the Bible roads are a place where one can hide snares, ropes, and traps. Old Assyrian texts mention that trade resumes in the spring after the "opening of roads" in Anatolia, a process necessary after winter rains would have washed boulders and other debris into pathways. This event is also mentioned in the Jewish text the Talmud. The Greek historian Xenophon (ca. 431–ca. 352 B.C.E.) also refers to the necessity of clearing the Persian Royal Road and the problem of mud in the spring.

Thanks to the Assyrians, the Iron Age was a period of expansion in road construction throughout the region. Paved processional routes cropped up in cities. Campaign accounts recount the frustration of Assyrian kings in encountering narrow roads in mountainous terrain. Many accounts describe engineers with picks widening routes through stone so that the army could pass. Mention is also made of roads being so narrow that the king's horse could not fit on the path and of terrain that was too treacherous for horses to pass. The widened roads were still of use to the Persians, who seem to have followed the Assyrian roads through the area. The Persian army was employed in road building. According to Xenophon, Persian spearmen carried axes, bowmen carried mattocks, and slingers carried shovels.

Evidence of urban paved roads has been found on occasion. Cobbled streets appeared in towns in the Halaf Period in Mesopotamia (ca. 5500–ca. 4500 B.C.E.). An Early Bronze Age (ca. 3800–ca. 2000 B.C.E.) paved street has been discovered at Beth Yerah in Israel, and a Middle Bronze Age (ca. 2000–ca. 1500 B.C.E.) street has been found at Nābulus in Israel. Typically, urban paving was restricted to processional ways to temples, areas around gates, and occasionally other major streets. Few have been preserved. During the Neo-Assyrian Period (ca. 1000–ca. 626 B.C.E.) a number of paved roads were built in Assyrian cities. The royal road ran through Nineveh on its way to points west. The best-known paved road in Mesopotamia was Aiburshabum, the processional street of Marduk in Babylon, built in the Neo-Babylonia Period (625–539 B.C.E.). It has been unearthed. For the bulk of its length, the street is approximately 22 yards wide, narrowing to under 7 yards as it approaches the temple.

The method of construction of paved streets varied. A number of different styles are evidenced in Iron Age Israel. These methods included paving consisting of reeds and clay, shards and pebbles, rubble and plaster, and wedge-shaped cobbles, with the point of the wedge inserted in plaster. In Mesopotamia the preferred method of construction consisted of setting bricks in a layer of asphalt and then topping the roads with limestone slabs, which were sealed with asphalt. Maintenance of the roads was a function of governments. Local governments were responsible for roads in their territory, while the overall road network was the product of the central government.

The width of roads naturally was determined by their function and usage. Roads were at their widest in cities, evidenced by Aiburshabum street in Babylon. Other recovered streets in Babylon were from 2 to 11 yards wide, usually in the range of 3 to 6 yards. The royal road through Nineveh widened by Sennacherib (r. 704– 681 B.C.E.) was 33 yards wide. Archaeologists assert that a road needed to be at least 2.6 yards wide for two small two-wheeled carts to pass. Mountain roads often were narrower.

There is evidence of way stations beginning with the reign of Shulgi (ca. 2094–ca. 2047 B.C.E.) throughout the ancient Near East. Some of them may have been private capitalist ventures, especially those closer to urban centers. In open areas these stations provided protection from raiders, gathered intelligence on both traveling parties and locals, and helped the government collect duties and tolls. They also provided lodging, food, drink, and prostitutes for travelers.

Bridges in the ancient Near East were rare prior to Roman rule. A number are mentioned in the Neo-Assyrian Period. Sennacherib built one of bricks and limestone in Nineveh. Bridges are mentioned in a number of places in Neo-Assyrian texts. The remains of a bridge in the city of Babylon have been uncovered, presumably built by Nebuchadnezzar II (r. 605–562 B.C.E.), consisting of five to seven piers. It is cited by the Greek historian Herodotus (ca. 484–between 430 and 420 B.C.E.). Nebuchadnezzar claimed to have built a bridge of wood over the East Canal in Babylon, in turn covered with bricks supporting Aiburshabum street.

Most bridges in the ancient Near East were pontoons rather than permanent structures. Ownership of a bridge was the source of serious income, as tolls would be charged for access. There are Neo-Babylonian contracts preserved concerning bridge ownership. The surface of these bridges often consisted of logs or dirt, occasionally having guide ropes. The pontoon bridge built across the Hellespont (the strait that separates Anatolia from Greece) by the Persian king Xerxes (r. 486–465 B.C.E.) had not only dirt over logs and guide ropes but also a fence.

With the coming of the Romans and then the Byzantines, bridges became a more common sight. Syria and Palestine were fully integrated into these societies, as is evidenced by the wide network of roads. Roads further had a symbolic value, as Roman engineering conquered nature, evidenced in paving and bridge building. They demonstrated that Roman rule brought tangible benefits, a key hurdle in trying to maintain control over a conquered region.

ASIA AND THE PACIFIC

BY KIRK H. BEETZ

In looking at the history of roads and bridges in Asia and the Pacific it is important to understand the distinction some archaeologists make between paths and roads. Paths are ways that are worn by foot traffic, but roads are the products of construction. They may follow an old path, or they may, through human effort, create new avenues for traffic. They may even be intended to send traffic in new directions. The Silk Road, contradicting its name, consisted of several interconnected paths that led in a general east-to-west direction from northwestern China through central Asia to northern India or through the Persian Empire to the Mediterranean world, followed for the purposes of trade. Trade along the Silk Road was a significant factor in the development of many ancient civilizations. When the paths became eroded from use, travelers created new paths by walking, riding, or hauling carts over untrodden terrain. Thus, archaeologists tend to prefer to call the Silk Road a "route" or a collection of "routes," rather than a road.

Rivers have functioned as highways for the Chinese ever since the Shang Dynasty (1500–1045 B.C.E.), when the Chinese culture was focused on the Huang River. During the Zhou Dynasty (1045–256 B.C.E.) the capitals Xi'an and Luoyang were far away from the most productive farms of the empire, which were on the eastern reaches of the Huang River and the Yangtze River. The rivers and their tributaries meandered in loops and turns, making shipping on them slow. Food from the east could spoil by the time it reached the capital. The response to this problem was to build roads that were as straight as possible from the lower rivers to the capital.

Often, soldiers were given the task of building roads, but peasants were frequently drafted also. They were unpaid. Convicted criminals might be sentenced to hard labor working on roads. Sometimes rich convicts paid poor people to serve their sentences. Many road-building tasks required tens of thousands of workers. The workers were expected to carry all that they would need, including their own food.

Some roads were constructed following old trails. Others were built to be as straight as possible, especially if they were to connect with the capital city. There were roads built for use by the military to move troops and supplies. Others were built for commerce, especially the transport of grain from rural areas to city markets. There were even roads built for postal carriers. During the Han Dynasty (202 B.C.E.–220 C.E.) roads were built for the use of the emperor and his officials. Many roads had three lanes. The two outer lanes were for the carts and carriages of commoners, allowing them to pass oncoming traffic without having to leave the roads. The middle lane was higher and flatter than the outer lanes and was reserved for use by the emperor.

Among the most remarkable roads of China are those built in the western mountains, beginning about 500 B.C.E. Roads were often carved out of mountainsides and were often very narrow and dangerous to use. On some cliff sides, wooden roads several miles long were built. Workers would carve out deep holes in the rock and then fit a large log into each hole. Exactly how this was done is not known. Ancient Chinese records tell of messengers and government officials riding horses at a gallop across these wooden roadways, often cantilevered out thousands of feet above a sheer drop.

Ancient Chinese bridges tended to be made of wood. Although records occasionally mention stone bridges, it seems that only a few from the Han and the Six Dynasties (220–589 C.E.) survive. For the ancient Chinese, bridges served two purposes. One was practical, with bridges allowing traffic to move over a river or gorge without trouble. The other was decorative. Practical bridges included ones made of stone over the Wei and other rivers. Posts were sunk into riverbeds, and long, heavy stones were laid across them to form roadways. These stones often weighed several tons. Some wooden bridges, which were built much the same way as stone bridges, had roofs. Decorative bridges were often placed in gardens or ponds. One popular form was the cross bridge. It was shaped like a cross, with four bridges converging on a central point. These bridges were designed to give people good views of gardens or ponds. Another form of bridge was the moon bridge, which was a semicircle over a stream or moat. Its very high arch made it difficult to use in a practical way, but it was usually intended for ceremonial use.

The ancient Indians built few bridges. They reserved their bridge construction for spanning the moats of cities and perhaps they built rope bridges high in mountain ranges. Whenever travelers met a stream they could either cross it at a shallow ford, fell trees that spanned the water, or build rafts from nearby trees.

By the time of the Maurya Empire (ca. 321–ca. 185 B.C.E.) road building had become complex. A road was laid out by an architect and, to help the road's designers decide which materials to use during construction, the soil was studied along which the road would pass. Trees and bushes would be cleared from the path of the road. The surface of the road would be raised higher than the surrounding land and would be flat and level. Ditches were dug along each side of the road to carry the runoff from rain. Local towns were often given the responsibility of maintaining nearby roads. Some roads were very important to the economy of India, and central governments would take charge of maintaining those roads. To pay for maintenance, the governments charged merchants about 1/20th of their goods when they used a road.

Rest stops were built alongside roads, providing travelers with protection from sun and rain. They were maintained by workers who kept them clean. Artificial ponds were built near rest stops so that travelers could replenish their water supplies and bathe. Wide-spreading banyan trees were planted about every mile to provide shade.

Most historians date road building in Japan from about 576 C.E., because medieval records mention roads being built on the island of Honshū at that time. Many archaeologists do not look past that date. One of the problems archaeologists have is that Japan is densely populated and roads have been built over or reconstructed many times as the nation's population has grown. Archaeologists have found evidence for some ancient road building on Honshū, perhaps before the 100s C.E. These were roads running straight north-south; they were imposed on the land to create straight lines in eastern Honshū. Their north-south orientation was probably influenced by the Chinese custom of orienting structures according to the points of the compass. Japanese of later generations built palaces and even cities next to or between these roads, indicating that they were spiritually important. The purposes the ancient Japanese had for building the roads was to make trade easier, to allow for the government to stay in touch easily with its provinces, and to allow its armies to move quickly.

EUROPE

BY JUSTIN CORFIELD AND MICHAEL J. O'NEAL

During the Mesolithic (ca. 10,000–ca. 4,000 B.C.E.) and Neolithic (ca. 7000–ca. 2000 B.C.E.), the emergence of sedentary settlements led to their connection by trails and pathways through the forested landscape and along major rivers. The earliest-known constructed pathway is the wooden causeway across marshy terrain in southwestern England called the Sweet Track. The wood used in the construction of the Sweet Track has been determined by tree-ring dating to have been cut in the spring of 3806 B.C.E. Throughout Europe in the Bronze Age (ca. 2800–ca. 700 B.C.E.) and Iron Age (ca. 1000 B.C.E.–ca. 500 C.E.), increased trade led to the establishment of well-traveled routes between settlements, and wheeled vehicles and draft animals came into use. An increasing number of trackways and causeways were built across marshy ground and shallow water, where the damp conditions have led to their preservation. Open bodies of deep water, such as rivers and straits, still posed obstacles, however, and crossing them required watercraft, since true bridge-building techniques had not yet been developed.

The Celts formalized the process of building roads in many areas, especially around larger settlements. Groups of people were involved in building specific roads, which often were covered with timber, brushwood, or stones so they would not turn into quagmires when it rained. This was especially important in marshy areas such as The Fens in England. Many Celts in Gaul and Britain traveled long distances by chariot, and pathways that were wide enough for a horseman or person on foot eventually were widened for ox-pulled wagons or horse-drawn chariots. The Roman general Julius Caesar (100–44 B.C.E.), in his *Gallic Wars*, refers to this use, noting that his main opponent during the second invasion of Britain in 54 B.C.E. was planning to wait for the Romans to send out their cavalry before using the chariots to attack "out of the woods by well-known lanes and pathways."

Section of the Sweet Track, the oldest prehistoric timber trackway in Britain (Neolithic, 3807/3806 B.C.E.), from Somerset, England (© The Trustees of the British Museum)

Some of the Celts' most heavily used roads were extensive. One coastal road began in modern-day Genoa, Italy, and traveled along the Mediterranean coast through Marseilles and Narbonne in France to Cadiz in southern Spain. Another important road in England was the Ridgeway, which followed the crest of the Wessex Downs and had operated as a trade route beginning in Neolithic times. A number of important paths and passes crossed mountains, especially the Pyrenees and the Alps. They were eventually expanded and used by large armed convoys, perhaps the most famous being that of the Carthaginian general Hannibal (247–183 B.C.E.), along with his elephants, in 218 B.C.E.

Many of the Bronze Age and Iron Age roads and pathways became major roads used by the Romans and subsequent civilizations. In addition, many roads that fell into disuse have been unearthed or can be seen by aerial archaeology. Entrances to Iron Age forts were particularly important, and the roads were often lined with flint, giving an impression similar to that of cobblestones, which allowed carts and chariots to cross the ground easily.

One road that existed before the Romans but that was later used by the Romans is the so-called Amber Road. No one knows when the Amber Road was constructed—although "constructed" is the wrong word, for the Amber Road was essentially a network of paths or routes that were carved out over time primarily for the transport of amber. The roads were not developed in the sense of having been constructed using principles of road technology. However, generations of foot travelers, beasts of burden, and carts created the roadways. In this respect, it was like the Silk Road that ran through Asia or the Salt Road of southern Europe, especially Italy. Amber, a fossil resin, was a valued resource in ancient Europe and around the Mediterranean region, used in many ornamental objects, such as beads and even in coins, primarily because it could be brought to a high polish. Long before the Romans arrived, Europeans had conducted an active trade in amber, transporting it over these routes.

The Amber Road comprised a number of stretches that connected various portions of Europe. Much of the Amber Road consisted of overland routes, but to the extent that it was a trade route, it also included stretches of rivers. One main route extended east-west and connected Europe with

Asia. The other main routes ran north-south and connected northern Europe and the Baltic region with southern Europe and the Mediterranean region. Perhaps the oldest of these stretches ran from the Baltic coastline down through present-day Poland, the Czech Republic, and Austria to the Adriatic Sea. Another ran from the North Sea through the Brenner Pass through the Alps into Italy and Greece. A number of routes ran through portions of modern-day Switzerland, the Netherlands, Belgium, France, and as far south as Spain. Later, another north-south route ran from northern Prussia through Bohemia to the Adriatic Sea.

The Amber Road contributed significantly to the development of European culture. The Egyptian pharaohs traded for amber with people from the north, as did the later Romans. The Amber Road was an important link between the cultural centers of the Mediterranean and northern Europe during the Nordic Bronze Age, roughly from 1800 to 600 B.C.E. In modern times archaeologists and historians have devoted considerable resources to locating these ancient routes. In particular, the Old World Trade Route Project has traced an entire network of such routes throughout Europe (and Asia), such that a map shows a thicket of them that differs little from a modern road map. They note that these routes were not used exclusively for trade. They were also used as postal routes, routes for pilgrims, administrative links, routes for the movement of troops, and even routes followed by nomadic peoples.

The Celts built many bridges over rivers they could not ford easily. These would have been made of wood, and their ability to build them quickly before sieges and battles indicates that such bridges would have existed throughout Europe for everyday trade and communication. It also seems likely that the Celts specifically did not build bridges in some places to make a settlement harder to attack or to make an invading army less likely to use a particular route. When Hannibal crossed through southern France, he encountered fewer bridges than one might expect. Perhaps the Celts, for strategic purposes, had refrained from building bridges there, or perhaps they had destroyed existing bridges to delay Hannibal's passage.

GREECE

BY SPYROS SIROPOULOS

Roads became a necessary aspect of social life from the moment human communities became organized and exchanging goods and traveling became common. Travel was not always easy or safe in antiquity. The myth of Theseus, who journeyed from Troezen to Athens, killing a number of thieves and murderers on the way, indicates the difficulty of journeying in the ancient world and the need for establishing safe passage for travelers and tradesmen alike.

Since walking was the usual means of transportation in antiquity, the first roads were nothing but clear-cut paths in the countryside. Religious and commercial purposes led to the construction of more carefully designed routes. Opposite the strategically located island of Salamis and on the crossroad between Athens, northern Greece, and the Peloponnese lay the city of Eleusis. During the time of the Athenian statesman Solon (ca. 630–560 B.C.E.), Salamis and Eleusis were attached to Athens. A biennial celebration in honor of the goddesses Artemis and Persephone was established. A road leading from Athens to Eleusis was constructed, called Ierá Hodós (Sacred Way). Some stretches of this road survive. On the roadbed, paving was undertaken. Traces of retaining walls and the roadbed cut in limestone rock survive in some areas. This road is perhaps the most impressive finding of ancient country or interstate roads from antiquity.

Another impressive discovery is the 3-yard-wide road from the Peloponnese to central Greece. Since it was mainly a road used by merchants, provision for places where carts could pull and pass one another is visible today. A different kind of road was the Diolkos, constructed along the Isthmus of Corinth. Beginning in the eighth century B.C.E. the Greeks' colonization of the West made the transportation of goods imperative. The Greeks tried to avoid the dangerous circumnavigation of the Peloponnese. The Corinthians pulled the smaller ships traveling from east to west over the isthmus, earning money from payments of toll. Later, in the sixth century B.C.E., the Corinthian tyrant Periander (d. 586 B.C.E.) constructed over the narrowest part of the isthmus (3.7 miles long) a paved road, with two parallel channels cut for the wheels of specially designed transporters, on which ships were loaded.

Ancient sources do not give details of the Diolkos's function. Systematic excavations from 1956 until 1962 brought to light many parts of the road, allowing archaeologists to determine its route and the starting point at the Corinthian gulf. Although it was initially thought that the road was wooden, excavations have proved that it was 3.2 to 6 yards wide, paved with limestone cubes. The parallel channels for the transporters, about 1.6 yards apart, were curved alongside the road, but specially designed gutters were constructed around curves for added security. The ships were pulled by slaves who walked along the sides of the road in wide paths. Letters of the Corinthian alphabet were carved on various points of the Diolkos; these, with some fragments of broken pottery found there, help to date the road, which was used until at least 833 C.E.

Road planning in cities was not always easy, especially for great centers such as Athens or Piraeus, where community life from years ago had already formed small, narrow roads before the civic way of life's explosion in the Archaic and Classical Periods (600–323 B.C.E.). To an extent, natural topology determined the planning of roads. Consequently, two kinds of street layouts developed: the regular, with straight, parallel, and rectilinear streets, and the irregular, where roads did not follow straight lines but sometimes led in a radial fashion to the same spot. Aristotle suggested that the second style of street layout was better for the defense of the city. According to the second-century C.E. writer Philostratus, it seems that this irregular style was named Attic because of its establishment in various demes (small political divisions) of Attica, though it is found in other cities, too.

The main road in the city of Athens was the road of the Panathenaia, named after a festival for all Athenian citizens. This road originated from the central place of Agorá ("marketplace") or Kerameikós (the area where potters, called *kerameis* in Greek, lived). This road not only ran through Athens; it also connected Athens with all the demes of Attica and the rest of Greece.

Hippodamus from Miletus (fifth century B.C.E.) is often falsely considered the inventor of a street planning that bears his name. Hippodamus did not come up with the specific way of town planning, but he adapted elements of the Greek city to fit roughly the following ideal: rectangular divisions of town areas, with roads that were 6.2 yards wide and blocks of 94.26 by 39.04 yards, divided in 10 square building sites of 18.81 yards—that is, five properties on each side divided by a narrow street 1.31 yards wide. Excavations at the town of Olynthus, built in 432 B.C.E. according to this Hippodameian plan, brought to light a part of it that fits this description.

Even since the Bronze Age bridges have been constructed out of wood for passage over streams and rivers. Stone bridges were common in the fifth century B.C.E. The style is usually the same: Pillars with lintels, or horizontal beams, on top support the bridge. The space between the pillars serves as water passage, in order to lessen the impact of water on the bridge and ease the construction process. A wooden passage with planks was constructed on top of the stones. We have examples of arched water passages on solid bridges, too, from the Classical Period, although it is uncertain whether any bridges with true arches date from before the Roman Period.

A famous bridge of the Classical Period was that over the river Cephissus at Athens. On the way to Eleusis people would stand on the bridge, singing rude or befooling limericks to passersby, thus giving a new meaning to the verb *gefyrizein* (from the Greek word *gefyra*, meaning "bridge"), which meant to mock someone from a bridge.

In war, too, bridge making was essential for the carriage of troops over water. During his invasion of Greece in 480 B.C.E., the Persian king Xerxes I (r. 486–465 B.C.E.) is said to have crossed the Hellespont by a bridge of boats tied side by side for nearly a mile in length. According to the tragedian Aeschylus (525–456 B.C.E.), this event was an act of *hybris* (an act that went beyond established moral codes), partly responsible for Xerxes' defeat by the Greeks. Alexander the Great had specialized mechanics in his army, one of their tasks being the construction of bridges. During the Hellenistic Period many bridges were built, some of them over 325 yards long.

ROME

BY KATIE PARLA

The maxim "all roads lead to Rome" describes Rome as the nucleus from which major routes for conquest, trade, and communication originated. The adage, while accurate, does not adequately describe the complexity and organization of the Roman road system, which stretched far beyond the capital city and the Italian peninsula for a total of more than 50,000 miles of paved roadways across Europe, Asia, and Africa.

During the earliest periods of Rome's urban development, in the seventh and eighth centuries B.C.E., the necessity for road construction was minimal, as Rome had limited contact with its neighboring regions. Many routes were unpaved paths in the countryside created by foot and wagon traffic over short distances linking minor settlements.

During the early to middle Roman Republic, of the sixth through fourth centuries B.C.E., preexisting roads from the Bronze and Iron ages, as well as conquest and trade routes established by Etruscan and Sabine tribes, were adapted and extended. The Via Latina began as a series of dirt trails that the Etruscans transformed into fixed routes for their conquest of Campania in Italy. Later the Romans paved and extended the Via Latina. The Via Salaria was another pre-Roman road that was later transformed by the Romans. The Sabines established this unpaved road to reach the salt marshes along the Tiber River. These and other pre-Roman roads typically followed the natural topography of the land, winding around mountains and avoiding valleys and other natural obstacles.

During the middle to late Roman Republic, in the fourth through first centuries B.C.E., the Romans began building major paved highways known as consular roads. These courses were built by censors, elected officials of the Roman government who were responsible for building and maintaining roads and aqueducts, and they began in Rome and radiated outward to other parts of the Italian peninsula. Rather than avoiding natural obstacles like their archaic predecessors, the Roman roads often took the most direct routes, which required the manipulation of topographical elements by cutting through mountains, leveling out elevation irregularities, and building bridges over valleys, rivers, and swamps.

The first major consular highway was begun in 312 B.C.E. by the censors Appius Claudius and Caius Plautius and was called the Via Appia after Appius Claudius. The first-century poet Statius (ca. 45–96 C.E.) praised the Via Appia as the *Regina viarum*, queen of all roads, for the vital role it played in Rome's conquest, communication, trade, and travel. The road was built in stages over the course of more than a century, and the first segment reached Capua, 132 miles southeast of Rome. It was later extended as Rome conquered more territory approaching the Adriatic Sea, and it eventually reached the Italian cities of Benevento, Taranto, and ultimately the port city of Brindisi, for a total length of 364 miles.

Most of Rome's roads were originally built for purpose of conquests. Roads were built to move troops and conquer territories as well as to transport slaves and war booty back to Rome from these areas. The roads later took on other

Iron hipposandal from Roman Britain (first to second century C.E.), found in London; hipposandals were a form of temporary shoe that could be fastened to the horse's hoof for use on metal roads. (© The Trustees of the British Museum)

functions, serving as administrative and commercial links between the capital city and its distant territories and connecting other cities and ports.

To help the Roman republican or imperial government control conquered lands, provincial governments were established to communicate and enforce the Roman laws. Roads linked the capital city of Rome to the distant provinces, thereby allowing the central government to communicate with its bureaucrats abroad. Provincial governors could carry out the decrees of the Roman government based on messages delivered along the routes.

Roman roads were a critical component of the infrastructure that allowed the economy to grow rapidly from the middle republic to the high empire. Raw materials, manufactured goods, building materials, and commodities could be imported and exported along these routes, fueling economic growth. The provincial governments in Roman territories were also responsible for protecting Roman business interests abroad, which was possible due to the communication facilitated by the road network.

Roads were built by soldiers, slaves, and local workers under the direction of engineers. Local materials and conditions determined the depth of a road's foundations, its width, and the technique used to build it. Road foundations were not flat but featured an *agger*, a ridge in the center sloping downward toward the edges of the roadway to facilitate drainage.

The construction process was begun by clearing the land of trees and other major obstacles along a straight route. Then a trench was dug, the earth at its bottom was packed down, and a layer of concrete, or *pavimentum*, was poured. The next stratum was the *statumen*, a mixture of stones, followed by the *rudus*, a mixture of sand or soil with clay or concrete. Durable, flat paving stones were cut to fit together to create a smooth road surface. Sidewalks for pedestrian traffic flanked many roads, and milestones on the roadside reported the distance from the road's origin.

For routes over marshy land the approach was different. Pavements were laid over wooden rather than concrete foundations. Steep inclines and natural obstacles also required the builders to deviate from standard building practices. Roads sometimes followed a zigzag course to minimize the human effort in climbing an incline once the roadway was paved. While tunnels could be cut through mountains and bridges could be constructed over rivers, valleys, and marshy land, sometimes it was necessary to avoid these obstacles altogether, causing the road to curve or change its straight course.

The materials and techniques used to construct Roman bridges developed over time. Some of the first bridges were made with wood and rope to connect commercial and residential areas on opposite sides of the Tiber River. Rome's first stone bridge, the Pons Aemilius, was constructed from 181 to 179 B.C.E. to connect the city's cattle market to the opposite side of the Tiber.

By using the arch, the Romans were able to build stone and concrete bridges with one or more spans across valleys and rivers. Local materials determined the method of construction. In one common method, concrete piers were built on riverbanks or through ravines to serve as the supporting columns for the arches. A wooden framework was built and concrete arches poured onto it, linking the piers. Stone veneer was then used to cover the bridge's concrete core. A pulley system, operated by slaves or animals and possibly driven by a treadmill, was used to lower huge pieces of stone into place. When concrete was not readily available, stone was used to build both the piers and the spans. Bridges that had to be built quickly or were temporary were made out of wood that was harvested locally. During military campaigns troops carried small boats for making pontoon bridges to allow speedy transportation across bodies of water.

The legacy of Rome's network of roads and bridges can be witnessed to this day from Great Britain to the Middle East. The permanence of the materials and expert engineering employed in their construction makes these wonders as impressive today as they must have been in antiquity.

THE AMERICAS

BY PENNY MORRILL

It is helpful to start by defining the different types of roadways in the Americas. A path or trail normally follows the most efficient route between two points. Paths avoid major geographic obstacles and usually do not follow a straight line. Paths are the result of the wear of traffic and are maintained by tradition.

Roads are constructed by a labor force. They are intentionally prepared surfaces of the landscape that attempt to provide the most direct route, usually between two points. Formal road systems have a definable width and can incorporate bridges, roadbeds and pavement, curbs, side walls, drainage culverts, and other architectural elements. Causeways are raised roadbeds. In many cases, formal roads are ceremonial. Over time, a road can be abandoned as a formal route but possibly be retained as a path. North American roads dating to the ancient period have not been uncovered by archaeologists.

Before the Spanish conquest in Mesoamerica in 1521 there were no pack animals or wheeled vehicles. All movement of agricultural products and trade goods was by human carriers across land or by canoe. For this reason, finding physical evidence of early roadways is difficult and, in some cases, impossible. This is particularly true at the center of Olmec civilization (1500–400 B.C.E.) in Tabasco and Veracruz, a low-lying coastal area of bogs, marshes, and rivers.

The Olmec ceremonial and political centers at San Lorenzo (1200–900 B.C.E.) and later at La Venta (900–400 B.C.E.) provide evidence that there were local routes, probably paths, for transportation from subordinate villages to the center of each of these chiefdoms. In addition, regional trade routes existed for the large-scale export of materials that were produced in the extensive workshops discovered in the Olmec heartland. The Olmec also imported from great distances. For example, the major sources of the highly prized greenstone were in Guerrero and the Montagua valley of Guatemala. For the large portrait heads and other major sculpted works found at San Lorenzo and later Olmec sites, huge basalt boulders were brought by land and water routes from the Tuxtla Mountains, 60 miles from San Lorenzo. In this early trade and exchange network, human carriers walked across land or used canoes along the river systems, leaving behind very little physical evidence, even though their routes were later used by other chiefdoms.

Farther afield there is evidence of interaction among the Olmec and the peoples of central Mexico, Oaxaca, and the Maya region. While this points to the possibility of formal roadways extending from the Olmec center, other trade relationships existed beyond the Olmec sphere, for example among elite families in the Tehuacán and Oaxaca valleys. Archaeological investigations have provided evidence that elite families of the Tehuacán and Oaxaca valleys were importing goods from other regions. The pottery styles of these two areas were similar, also an indicator of contact. The relationship between these valleys gained importance because of the obsidian trade through the Cuicatlan Cañada. Obsidian, used to make tools and weapons, was being brought from Otumba, at a great distance from this region. Archaeologists now believe that Cuicatlan Cañada, a long river canyon running north-south between the valleys of Tehuacán and Oaxaca, remained a critical trade route into the Spanish colonial period. After the end of Olmec domination, widespread dispersion of Zapotec pottery in the Tehuacán and Nochistlán valleys and in the Cuicatlan Cañada reflect trade expansion by the Zapotec (600 B.C.E.–900 C.E.) into these regions, probably using the roads that were already in existence.

In many regions of the Americas archaeological evidence of trade is all that remains to prove the existence of ancient roads and bridges. The Chavín people (after 1000 B.C.E.) on Peru's northern coast traded actively. At Chavín de Huántar ceramics of various stylistic traditions came from areas far away. Chavín-style gold work has been found at Chongoyape, far up the northern coast. Chavín textiles were used in a southern coast burial at Karwa, some 300 miles from Chavín de Huántar. As in early cultures of Mesoamerica, stylistic elements become the markers for trade and indicators of the existence of roadways. Also on the southern coast the burials of the Paracas people (after 600 B.C.E.) indicate that the members of the elite were trading over long distances for luxury goods.

A survey of the Virú, Moche and Chicama valleys along the northern coast of Peru has brought to light more than 150 ancient roads. The identity and dating of both formal and informal routes were verified by analyzing cross-cutting through older roadbeds and by taking note of related ancient structures, canals, and walls. Over the span of 2,500 years roads in the Moche valley were cleared and graded, with roads cut through small hills and with stone-faced ramps. For certain distances the roads were curbed with debris from road construction, or they were walled. Early in the history of this area the Cuspisnique (500 B.C.E.) built roads exclusively with walls.

The most intriguing of all the roadways throughout the Americas are the Nazca Lines. The Nazca people occupied the Ica and Nazca valleys on the southern coast, and their civilization reached its height in the centuries after the birth of Christ. The Nazca built a pilgrimage center at Cahuachi on the southern bank of the Nazca River facing the Pampas, where the lines were inscribed. It also can be surmised that the Nazca people approached Cahuachi along ceremonial roads. The Pampas cover a large area (130 square miles) that is unique geologically. Light-colored stone is covered by a thin layer of dark stone, allowing for subtractive drawing onto the landscape. The Nazca Lines were created by removing the dark stones to reveal the light ones.

Archaeological investigations at Cahuachi indicate that perishable houses were constructed, perhaps tents. From this it can be surmised that Cahuachi was not a permanent community but a place where ceremonial roads intersected. Archaeologists believe that entire communities of Nasca people walked in processions along these sacred roads. The sacred roads seem to have served ritual purposes and were not always thought of in a utilitarian sense.

See also AGRICULTURE; BORDERS AND FRONTIERS; BUILDING TECHNIQUES AND MATERIALS; CERAMICS AND POTTERY; CITIES; DEATH AND BURIAL PRACTICES; ECONOMY; FESTIVALS; INVENTIONS; MIGRATION AND POPULATION MOVEMENTS; MILITARY; MINING, QUARRYING, AND SALT MAKING; NOMADIC AND PASTORAL SOCIETIES; SACRED SITES; SEAFARING AND NAVIGATION; SETTLEMENT PATTERNS; TOWNS AND VILLAGES; TRADE AND EXCHANGE; TRANSPORTATION; WAR AND CONQUEST.

FURTHER READING

Jean-Pierre Adam, *Roman Building: Materials and Techniques* (London: Batsford, 1994).

Lionel Casson, *Travel in the Ancient World* (Baltimore, Md.: Johns Hopkins University Press, 1994).

Raymond Chevallier, *Roman Roads* (Berkeley: California University Press, 1976).

Tim Cornell and John Matthews, *Atlas of the Roman World* (New York: Facts On File, 1982).

Sir Gavin de Beer, *Hannibal's March* (London: Sidgwick and Jackson, 1967).

Ivana Della Portella, *The Appian Way: From Its Foundation to the Middle Ages* (Los Angeles: J. Paul Getty Museum, 2004).

David A. Dorsey, *The Roads and Highways of Ancient Israel* (Baltimore, Md.: Johns Hopkins University Press, 1991).

James J. Hester, Philip M. Hobler, and James Russell, "New Evidence of Early Roads in Nubia," *American Journal of Archaeology* 74, no. 4 (1970): 385–389.

Romolo Augusto Staccioli, *The Roads of the Romans* (Los Angeles: J. Paul Getty Museum, 2004).

Charles D. Trombold, ed., *Ancient Road Networks and Settlement Hierarchies in the New World* (Cambridge, U.K.: Cambridge University Press, 1991).

Steve Vinson, "Transportation." In *The Oxford Encyclopedia of Ancient Egypt*, vol. 3, ed. Donald Redford (Oxford, U.K.: Oxford University Press, 2001).

VIVA-FACTS ON FILE

ENCYCLOPEDIA OF SOCIETY AND CULTURE IN THE ANCIENT WORLD

Volume IV • S–Z

Editor in Chief
Peter Bogucki

Viva Books

New Delhi | Mumbai | Chennai | Kolkata | Bangalore | Hyderabad | Kochi | Guwahati

First Indian Edition 2010

VIVA BOOKS PRIVATE LIMITED

- 4737/23 Ansari Road, Daryaganj, New Delhi 110 002
  E-mail: vivadelhi@vivagroupindia.net, Tel. 42242200
- 76, Service Industries, Shirvane, Sector 1, Nerul, Navi Mumbai 400 706
  E-mail: vivamumbai@vivagroupindia.net, Tel. 27721273, 27721274
- Jamals Fazal Chambers, 26 Greams Road, Chennai 600 006
  E-mail: vivachennai@vivagroupindia.net, Tel. 28290304, 28294241
- B-103, Jindal Towers, 21/1A/3 Darga Road, Kolkata 700 017
  E-mail: vivakolkata@vivagroupindia.net, Tel. 22836381, 22816713
- 7, Sovereign Park Apartments, 56-58, K. R. Road, Basavanagudi, Bangalore 560 004
  E-mail: vivabangalore@vivagroupindia.net, Tel. 26607409, 26607410
- 101-102 Mughal Marc Apartments, 3-4-637 to 641, Narayanguda, Hyderabad 500 029
  E-mail: vivahyderabad@vivagroupindia.net, Tel. 27564481, 27564482
- First Floor, Beevi Towers, SRM Road, Kaloor, Kochi 682 018, Kerala
  E-mail: vivakochi@vivagroupindia.net, Tel: 0484-2403055, 2403056
- 232, GNB Road, Beside UCO Bank, Silpukhuri, Guwahati 781 003
  E-mail: vivaguwahati@vivagroupindia.net, Tel: 0361-2666386

www.vivagroupindia.com

Published by arrangement with
Facts on File, Inc.
132 West 31st Street
New York 10001
USA

ISBN : 978-81-309-0929-5 (Set of 4 Volumes)

Published by Vinod Vasishtha for Viva Books Private Limited, 4737/23, Ansari Road, Daryaganj, New Delhi-110 002. Printed and bound by Sanat Printers, Kundli-131 028, Sonepat, Haryana.

Contents

Volume IV

Advisers and Contributors

EDITOR IN CHIEF

Peter Bogucki
Associate Dean for Undergraduate Affairs,
School of Engineering and Applied Science
Princeton University

ADVISORY BOARD

Lisa R. Brody
Assistant Professor of Art
Queens College, City University of New York

R. Hunt Davis
Professor Emeritus of History and African Studies
University of Florida

Leo Depuydt
Associate Professor of Egyptology
Brown University

Paul R. Goldin
Associate Professor of East Asian Languages
and Civilizations
University of Pennsylvania

Eloise Quiñones Keber
Professor of Art History
Baruch College, City University of New York

Amelie Kuhrt
Professor of Ancient Near Eastern History
University College, London

Daniel Potts
Edwin Cuthbert Hall Professor of
Middle Eastern Archaeology
University of Sydney

CONTRIBUTORS

Saheed Aderinto is a Ph.D. student at the Department of History, University of Texas at Austin. Some of his most recent publications include "Prostitution and Urban Social Relations" and "Policing Urban Prostitution: Prostitutes, Crime, Law and Reformers in Colonial Nigeria" in *Nigeria's Urban History: Past and Present* (2006) and "Discrimination in an Urban Setting: The Experience of Ijebu Settlers in Colonial Ibadan, 1893–1960" in *Inter-group Relations in Nigeria during the 19th & 20th Centuries* (2006). His writings have also appeared in *IFRA Special Research Issue, Ethnic and Third World Review of Books, African and Asian Studies Journal,* and *The Encyclopedia of Prostitution and Sex Work* (2006).

Olutayo Charles Adesina, Ph.D., teaches at the Department of History, University of Ibadan, Nigeria. He is the author of "The Underground Foreign Exchange Market in Ibadan during Devaluation" in *Money Struggles and City Life: Devaluation in Ibadan and Other Urban Centres in Southern Nigeria, 1986–96* (2002) and "Teaching History in Twentieth Century Nigeria: The Challenges of Change" in *History in Africa: A Journal of Method*, vol. 33 (2006).

David Otieno Akombo, Ph.D., teaches music education and world music at Wabash College of Indiana. He is the author of *Music and Healing across Cultures* (2006).

Francis Allard, Ph.D., teaches in the Department of Anthropology at Indiana University of Pennsylvania. His research interests include the archaeology of early China and Mongolia. He has contributed articles to *Archaeology of Asia* (2005) and *Beyond the Steppe and the Sown: Proceedings of the 2002 University of Chicago Conference on Eurasian Archaeology* (2006).

Miguel Arisa is finishing his doctoral studies in art history at the Graduate Center, City University of New York. He teaches at Technical Career Institutes and is a regular lecturer at the

Cloisters and a docent at the Metropolitan Museum of Art, New York.

Mariam F. Ayad, Ph.D., teaches graduate-level classes on Egyptian language and literature at the University of Memphis, where she is the assistant director of its Institute of Egyptian Art and Archaeology. Her main research interests focus on the role of women in ancient Egyptian temple ritual and the selection and transmission of funerary texts in post–New Kingdom Egypt. Her book on the God's Wife of Amun is under contract with Routledge.

Heather D. Baker, D.Phil., is a researcher at the University of Vienna, Austria, specializing in Babylonian history, society, and culture. She has published widely on Babylonian and Assyrian history and is writing a book to be titled *The Urban Landscape of First Millennium BC Babylonia.*

Robin Barrow, Ph.D., FRSC, is professor of philosophy of education at Simon Fraser University, Canada. His most recent books include *Plato* (2007) and *An Introduction to Moral Philosophy and Moral Education* (2007). He is the author of *Athenian Democracy* (2001) and *Greek and Roman Education* (1996).

László Bartosiewicz, Ph.D., D.sc., teaches archaeozoology at the Loránd Eötvös University in Budapest (Hungary) and the University of Edinburgh (United Kingdom). He is the author of *Animals in the Urban Landscape in the Wake of the Middle Ages* (1995) and principal author of *Draught Cattle: Their Osteological Identification and History* (1997) and has published more than 200 scholarly articles.

Kirk H. Beetz, Ph.D., emeritus, has published over two dozen books and more than 900 articles. His books span topics from endangered mammal species to children's literature, including *Exploring C. S. Lewis' "The Chronicles of Narnia"* (2000). His recent writings have focused on the history and culture of ancient Japan.

Craig G. R. Benjamin, Ph.D., teaches world and ancient Eurasian history at Grand Valley State University. He is the coeditor of vols. 2 (1998), 4 (2000), and 6 (2002) in the Brepols Silk Roads Studies series and the author of *The Yuezhi: Origin, Migration and the Conquest of Northern Bactria* (2007).

Uffe Bergeton, Ph.D., is in the Ph.D. program in the Department of Asian Languages and Cultures at the University of Michigan. He is the author of *The Independence of Binding and Intensification* (Ph.D. dissertation, University of Southern California) and various articles on theoretical phonology and syntax.

Amy Hackney Blackwell has degrees in history from Duke University and Vanderbilt University and a J.D. from the University of Virginia. Her books include *Mythology for Dummies* (2002), *LSAT for Dummies* (2004), *The Everything Irish History and Heritage Book* (2004), and *Essential Dictionary of Law* (2004). She has contributed to the *Encyclopedia of World Nations and Cultures* (2006), *Alternative Energy* (2006), and *Chemical Compounds* (2006).

Christopher Blackwell, Ph.D., teaches classics at Furman University. He is the author of *In the Absence of Alexander: Harpalus and the Failure of Macedonian Hegemony* (1999) and various protocols and software applications for building digital libraries, and he serves as technical editor for the Center for Hellenic Studies of Harvard University.

Amy Bogaard, Ph.D., teaches prehistory and archaeobotany at the Department of Archaeology, University of Nottingham, United Kingdom. She is the author of *Neolithic Farming in Central Europe* (2004).

Peter Bogucki, Ph.D., is an archaeologist who is associate dean for undergraduate affairs of the School of Engineering and Applied Science at Princeton University. He has studied prehistoric settlements in Poland and has a particular interest in the spread of farming in Europe. He is the author of *The Origins of Human Society* (1999) and the editor (with Pam J. Crabtree) of *Ancient Europe 8000 B.C.–A.D. 1000: An Encyclopedia of the Barbarian World* (2004).

Larissa Bonfante, Ph.D., professor of classics at New York University, is the author of several books on Etruscan and early Roman culture as well as publications on ancient dress and nudity, including *The World of Roman Costume*, coedited with Judith Sebesta (1994).

Charlotte Booth is a Ph.D. student at the University of Wales, Swansea, and teaches Egyptology for Birkbeck College and other institutions in the United Kingdom. She is the author of *People of Ancient Egypt* (2007), *The Hyksos Period in Egypt* (2005), and *The Role of Foreigners in Ancient Egypt* (2005).

Lisa R. Brody, Ph.D., teaches Greek and Roman art history at Queens College, City University of New York. Her research interests include Greek iconography and cult, ancient lamps and their decoration, children in antiquity, and representation of ethnicity in Greco-Roman art. She compiled the revised edition of David Sacks's *Encyclopedia of the Ancient Greek World* (2005) and is author of *Aphrodisias III: The Aphrodite of Aphrodisias* (2007).

David Brown, Ph.D., is researching the interactions of the pre-Islamic astral sciences of Mesopotamia, Greece, India, Egypt, Iran, the western Semitic world, and China at the Free University of Berlin. He is the author of *Mesopotamian Planetary Astronomy-Astrology* (2000) and *The Interactions of Ancient Astral Science* (forthcoming).

Deborah N. Carlson, Ph.D., teaches in the Nautical Archaeology Program of the Department of Anthropology at Texas A&M University. She also directs the Institute of Nautical Archaeology's shipwreck excavation of a Roman marble carrier off the Aegean coast of Turkey at Kizilburun and is preparing the final publication of the Classical Greek ship excavated by the Institute of Nautical Archaeology at nearby Tektas Burnu.

Jeffrey S. Carnes is associate professor of classics at Syracuse University. He is the author of *The Uses of Aiakos: Pindar and the Aiginetan Imaginary* (forthcoming) as well as articles on Greek lyric poetry, gender studies, literary theory, and Plato.

Julia Marta Clapp is pursuing her doctorate in art history at the Graduate Center, City University of New York. Her research interests include modern and pre-Columbian Latin American art.

Wendy E. Closterman, Ph.D., teaches ancient history and Greek at Bryn Athyn College. Her research focuses on Athenian burial and funerary ritual. She is the author of "Family Members and Citizens: Athenian Identity and the Peribolos Tomb Setting" in *Antigone's Answer: Essays on Death and Burial, Family and State in Classical Athens*, edited by C. Patterson (forthcoming).

Leah A. J. Cohen is an independent writer and editorial consultant with a master's degree in geography from the University of Florida. She specializes in Africa area studies and food security. She was a senior author for the *Encyclopedia of African History and Culture*, volumes 4 and 5 (2005).

John Collis is professor emeritus in the Department of Archaeology, University of Sheffield, where he taught for over 30 years. He has had a major role in the development of university and professional training in archaeology in Britain, and is secretary of the European Association of Archaeologists' Committee on Training and Education. He is author of several books and excavation monographs, including *Digging Up the Past* (2004) and *The Celts: Origins, Myths and Inventions* (2004).

Constance A. Cook, Ph.D., directs the Asian Studies program and teaches Chinese language and literature courses at Lehigh University. She is the author of *Death in Ancient China: The Tale of One Man's Journey* (2006) and coeditor of *Defining Chu: Image and Reality in Ancient China* (1999).

Susan Cooksey, Ph.D., is the curator of African art, Harn Museum of Art, University of Florida.

Justin Corfield, Ph.D., teaches history and international relations at Geelong Grammar School, Australia. He is the co-author of *Historical Dictionary of Cambodia* (2003) and has written extensively on Asia, Australia, and European colonial history.

James A. Corrick, Ph.D., is a full-time editor and writer with 25 books to his credit. His most recent titles are *The Early Middle Ages* (2006), *The Byzantine Empire* (2006), and *The Renaissance* (2007).

Arden Decker is a Ph.D. candidate in the history of art at the Graduate Center, City University of New York. Her research interests include Mesoamerican art as well as modern and contemporary art of Mexico.

Leo Depuydt, Ph.D., teaches Egyptology at Brown University and is curious about everything relating to ancient Egypt in its Near Eastern and Mediterranean context, especially the area's languages and history. He wrote *Civil Calendar and Lunar Calendar in Ancient Egypt* (1997) and *The Other Mathematics: Language and Logic in Egyptian and in General* (2007).

Haig Der-Houssikian, Ph.D., is professor emeritus (2003), linguistics, at the University of Florida, Gainesville. His research and publication interests are in morphology, Creolization, and sub-Saharan Africa.

Christine End, M.A., works on the Giza Archives Project at the Museum of Fine Arts, Boston. Her main interests of research are Middle Kingdom funerary iconography, material culture, burial practices, and mummification. As a researcher and illustrator, her work has appeared in Egyptological publications and documentaries.

Linda Evans, Ph.D., specializes in ancient Egyptian art at Macquarie University, Sydney, Australia. She recently completed her doctoral dissertation on the representation of animal behavior in Egyptian tomb paintings and has published several papers on the role and depiction of animals in the ancient world. She has also contributed chapters to *Egyptian Art: Principles and Themes in Wall Scenes* (2000), *The Encyclopedia of Animal Behavior* (2004), *Egypt: The Land and Lives of the Pharaohs Revealed* (2005), and *Historica* (2006).

Stephen M. Fabian, Ph.D., is an anthropologist and currently teaches seminars on religion, myth, and ritual at Princeton University. He is the author of *Space-Time of the Bororo of Brazil* (1992), *Clearing Away Clouds: Nine Lessons for Life from the Martial Arts* (1999), and *Patterns in the Sky: An Introduction to Ethnoastronomy* (2001).

Erin Fairburn is a graduate student in the Department of Egyptology and Western Asian Studies at Brown University. She has contributed to *The City and Urban Life* (forthcoming).

Alessia Frassani is a Ph.D. candidate at the Graduate Center of the City University of New York. Her research interests in-

clude the art and civilizations of ancient Oaxaca and issues surrounding the cultural interaction between the Old and New Worlds.

Markham J. Geller is professor of Semitic languages at University College London, in the Department of Hebrew and Jewish Studies. He has recently published a text edition of cuneiform medical texts, *Renal and Rectal Disease Texts, Babylonisch-assyrische Medizin* VII (2005).

J. J. George is working on his Ph.D. at the Graduate Center, City University of New York. His research area is pre-Columbian art and architecture.

Wolfram Grajetzki, Ph.D., wrote his dissertation at the Humboldt University of Berlin and has taught Egyptology there. He has excavated in Egypt and Pakistan and was principal archaeologist and author for the online learning project Digital Egypt for Universities (University College London). He is preparing the catalogue of Egyptian coffins in the Fitzwilliam Museum, Cambridge. His publications include *Burial Customs in Ancient Egypt* (2003) and *The Middle Kingdom in Ancient Egypt* (2006).

Lyn Green, Ph.D., has taught at several Canadian universities and for the Royal Ontario Museum. She has contributed to several encyclopedias, including *The Oxford Encyclopedia of Ancient Egypt* (2000) and the *Encyclopedia of the Archaeology of Ancient Egypt* (1999) as well as *The Royal Women of Amarna* (1996). Currently she is devoting her time to her duties as president of the Society for the Study of Egyptian Antiquities, which has over 400 members and subscribers internationally, and to writing.

Angela Herren, Ph.D., teaches pre-Columbian art and architecture as an assistant professor in the Department of Art and Latin American Studies at the University of North Carolina at Charlotte. A specialist on painted manuscripts from central Mexico, she completed a 2005 dissertation entitled "Portraying the Mexica Past: A Comparative Study of Accounts of Origin in Codex Azcatitlan, Codex Boturni, and Codex Aubin."

David B. Hollander, Ph.D., teaches ancient history at Iowa State University. He is the author of *Money in the Late Roman Republic* (2007).

Brooke Holmes, Ph.D., is an assistant professor of classics at the University of North Carolina, Chapel Hill. She is at work on a book about the symptom in early Greek medicine and classical Greek literature.

Michael Allen Holmes is a freelance editor and writer who recently contributed to *Shakespeare for Students*, 2nd edition (2007). He has also written an unpublished novel.

John W. Humphrey, Ph.D., is professor of Greek and Roman studies at the University of Calgary. A veteran of many seasons of archaeological excavation in Turkey and Greece, he is the author of *Greek and Roman Technology: A Sourcebook* (1998, with J. P. Oleson and A. N. Sherwood) and *Ancient Technology* (2006).

Keith Jordan, M.Phil., is a Ph.D. candidate in pre-Columbian art history at the Graduate Center of the City University of New York. He is currently finishing his doctoral dissertation, entitled "Stone Trees Transplanted? Central Mexican Stelae of the Epiclassic and Early Postclassic and the Question of Maya 'Influence.'"

Amr Kamel is an Egyptologist in the Rare Books and Special Collections Library at the American University in Cairo, Egypt.

David Kelly is an instructor of English writing and literature at Oakton Community College in Illinois. He has written over 100 published literary analyses and wrote the instructor's manual for the *Exploring Poetry* computer program. His short fiction has been published in *The Rockford Review*, *Grub Street*, and *The Iconoclast*, among other places.

Panagiotis I. M. Kousoulis, Ph.D., is a lecturer in Egyptology at the Department of Mediterranean Studies of the University of the Aegean. He is the author of *Moving across Borders: Foreign Relations, Religion and Cultural Interactions in the Ancient Mediterranean* (2007) and *Ancient Egyptian Demonology: Studies on the Boundaries between the Demonic and the Divine in Egyptian Magic* (2007).

Philippa Lang teaches ancient science and related subjects, with research interests in ancient medicine and philosophy, in the Classics Department of Emory University, Atlanta. She is the editor of *Re-Inventions: Essays on Hellenistic and Early Roman Science*, *Apeiron* special issue vol. 37 (2004).

Russell M. Lawson, Ph.D., is associate professor of history and chair of the Division of General Studies at Bacone College in Oklahoma. He is the author of *Science in the Ancient World* (2004), *The Land between the Rivers: Thomas Nuttall's Ascent of the Arkansas, 1819* (2004), and *Passaconaway's Realm: John Evans and the Exploration of Mount Washington* (2002, 2004).

Anne Mahoney, Ph.D., teaches Greek and Latin linguistics and literature at Tufts University. She is the author of *Plautus: Amphitryo* (2004) and *Roman Sports and Spectacles: A Sourcebook* (2001). She is also the editor of revised editions of *Allen and Greenough's New Latin Grammar* (2001), *Morice's Stories in Attic Greek* (2005), and *Bennett's Essentials* (2007).

Susan Malin-Boyce, Ph.D., serves as deputy director of the Regime Crimes Liaison Office, Mass Graves Investigation

Team, in Baghdad, Iraq. She has contributed to *Ancient Europe 8000 B.C.–A.D. 1000: Encyclopedia of the Barbarian World* (2004) and to publications addressing Early and Late La Tène settlement in Bavaria, Germany.

Renee McGarry is a student in the Ph.D. program in art history at the City University of New York Graduate Center. Her research interests include Aztec sculpture of the natural world and religious manuscripts from the post-Conquest period.

Paul McKechnie, D.Phil., is a senior lecturer in classics and ancient history at the University of Auckland, New Zealand. He is the author of *First Christian Centuries: Perspectives on the Early Church* (2002) and *Outsiders in the Greek Cities in the Fourth Century B.C.* (1989).

John M. McMahon, Ph.D., teaches at Le Moyne College in Syracuse, New York, where he directs the classics program. He is author of *Cave Paralysin: Impotence, Perception and Text in the Satyrica of Petronius* (1998) and numerous articles on the intersection of ancient literature and natural history. His most recent work includes nine entries in the forthcoming *Biographical Encyclopedia of Astronomers* (2006).

Jianjun Mei, Ph.D., teaches the history of science and technology at the University of Science and Technology Beijing. He is the author of *Copper and Bronze Metallurgy in Late Prehistoric Xinjiang: Its Cultural Context and Relationship with Neighbouring Regions* (2000).

James E. Meier, Ph.D., is assistant professor in the Department of Humanities and Social Sciences at Central Florida Community College. He is a contributor to the *Encyclopedia of African History and Culture* (2005).

Francesco Menotti, Ph.D., is a lecturer in European prehistory at the Institute of Prehistory and Archaeological Science, Basel University, Switzerland. He is the author of *Living on the Lake in Prehistoric Europe* (2004).

Melissa Moore Morison is associate professor of classics and classical archaeology at Grand Valley State University. She has extensive experience in archaeological fieldwork in Greece, Turkey, and the United States. Her research interests include Roman provincial archaeology, Greek and Roman pottery, and ceramic technology.

Penny Morrill, Ph.D., teaches pre-Columbian and early colonial Mesoamerican art at Hood College, Frederick, Maryland. She has an essay, "The Queen of Heaven Reigns in New Spain: The Triumph of Eternity in the Casa del Deán Murals," in a Brill anthology, *Woman and Art in Early Modern Latin America* (2006). She has authored several books on modern Mexican silver: *Mexican Silver: 20th Century Handwrought Silver Jewelry and Metalwork* (4th ed., 2007), *Silver Masters of Mexico: Héctor Aguilar and the Taller Borda* (1996), and *Maestros de Plata: William Spratling and the Mexican Silver Renaissance*, a catalog for a traveling exhibit (2002–2004).

Julian M. Murchison, Ph.D., teaches in the Department of Sociology and Anthropology at Millsaps College. His work in cultural anthropology examines the intersections of medicine and religion in East Africa. He recently published a chapter examining stories about a cure for HIV/AIDS in *Borders and Healers* (2005).

Caryn E. Neumann, Ph.D., teaches history in Ohio Wesleyan University's Black World Studies Department. She is a former managing editor of the *Journal of Women's History.*

Emily Jane O'Dell, is a Ph.D. candidate at Brown University and has taught at Brown University in both the Department of Egyptology and Ancient Western Asian Studies and the Department of Literary Arts. She has been the chief epigrapher of the Cairo-Brown University Abu Bakr Epigraphic Survey in the western cemetery of the Great Pyramids in Giza, Egypt, for the past five years.

Simon O'Dwyer is founder and researcher for Prehistoric Music Ireland, author of *Prehistoric Music of Ireland* and prehistoricmusic.com, and contributor to *The Encyclopedia of Music in Ireland* and *The Encyclopedia of Ireland.* He has published four papers for the International Study Group on Music Archaeology.

Penelope Ojeda de Huala is a Ph.D. candidate in art history at the Graduate Center of the City University of New York, where she studies pre-Columbian to contemporary art of Latin America. Her research focus is Guatemala and Peru, particularly the enduring thoughts and practices of indigenous cultures as manifested in art.

Michael J. O'Neal, Ph.D., is a writer who lives in Moscow, Idaho. He is a frequent contributor to reference and educational books, including *Lives and Works: Young Adult Authors* (1999), *The Crusades* (2005), and *America in the 1920s* (2006).

Dianne White Oyler, Ph.D., teaches African history at Fayetteville State University. She is the author of *The History of the N'ko Alphabet and Its Role in Mande Transnational Identity: Words as Weapons* (2005) as well as articles in the refereed journals *Research in African Literature, the Mande Studies Journal*, and the *International Journal of African Historical Studies.*

Katie Parla is an art historian and archaeological speleologist working in Rome and Naples as a docent leading didactic seminars of archaeological sites. She consults for the History

Channel and will appear in their 2007 series *Cities of the Underworld* as an expert on underground Rome and Naples.

Marie Passanante is a doctoral candidate in the Department of Egyptology and Ancient Western Asian Studies at Brown University.

William H. Peck teaches at the College for Creative Studies, Detroit, and the University of Michigan, Dearborn. He was for many years the curator of ancient art at the Detroit Institute of Arts and is at present a member of the Brooklyn Museum excavations in Egypt at Karnak. He is the author of *Drawings from Ancient Egypt* (1987) and numerous contributions to reference books and encyclopedias on the ancient world.

David Petechuk is a freelance writer specializing in educational texts focusing on the sciences, literature, and history. The former director of publications for the health sciences at the University of Pittsburgh, he is the author of *The Respiratory System* (2004), *LSD* (2005), and *Health & Medical Issues Today: Organ Transplantation* (2006).

Mark Anthony Phelps is taking a leave after teaching continuously since 1994 (primarily at Drury University, in five different departments) to finish his dissertation at the University of Arkansas entitled "Sewage from the Orontes: Roman Elite Attitudes toward Ecstatic Religion in the 3rd and 4th centuries C.E." This degree in ancient Mediterranean history augments his graduate degrees from Harvard and Johns Hopkins in Hebrew Bible and ancient Near Eastern languages and cultures. His research interests reflected in his writings are widely eclectic, spanning Paleolithic to contemporary society and including the disciplines of archaeology, linguistics, cultural anthropology, physical geography, historical geography, classical history, ancient Near Eastern history, medieval history, modern history, religion, and biblical history.

Jen Piro is a Ph.D. candidate in anthropological archaeology at New York University. Her dissertation research focuses on the development of pastoral economies in Early Bronze Age Transcaucasia.

Karen Radner, Ph.D., is lecturer in ancient Near Eastern history at University College, London. She specializes in the Assyrian Empire and is the author of *Die neuassyrischen Texte aus Tall Seh Hamad* (2002), *Das mittelassyrische Tontafelarchiv von Giricano/Dunnu-sa-Uzibi* (2004) and *Die Macht des Namens: Altorientalische Strategien zur Selbsterhaltung* (2005).

Judith A. Rasson, Ph.D., teaches in the Department of Medieval Studies, Central European University, Budapest (a post-graduate American-accredited university). Her research interests lie in southeastern Europe (especially the countries of the former Yugoslavia) and focus on Neolithic and historic archaeology and ethnographic material culture.

Kelly-Anne Diamond Reed, Ph.D., teaches ancient Egyptian history and archaeology at Villanova University's Department of History. She is investigating early Egyptian funerary rituals and burial customs.

Duane W. Roller is professor of Greek and Latin at Ohio State University. Trained as an archaeologist, he has over 30 years' experience in field archaeology in numerous Mediterranean countries. He is the author of *The Building Program of Herod the Great* (1998), *The World of Juba II and Kleopatra Selene* (2003), and *Through the Pillars of Herakles* (2006) as well as many other publications in history, classics, and archaeology.

Kelley L. Ross, Ph.D., teaches philosophy at Los Angeles Valley College. He specializes in Kantian epistemology, metaphysics, and ethics, with emphasis on members of the Friesian tradition—Jakob Fries, Leonard Nelson, Rudolf Otto, Sir Karl Popper, and others. Since 1996 he has been the publisher and editor of the online philosophy journal *Proceedings of the Friesian School, Fourth Series.*

Edward M. W. A. Rowlands, M.Phil., has research interests in Mycenaean political geography, trade, and religion.

Lucas G. Rubin, Ph.D., develops master of science programs for Columbia University. He was previously administrator of the university's Center for Archaeology, where he managed multiple excavations and projects. His research and scholarship have focused on fires and firefighters in ancient Rome.

Michael M. Sage, Ph.D., teaches classics and ancient history in the Classics Department at the University of Cincinnati. His main areas of study are historiography and military history. He is the author of *Cyprian: A Biography* (1975) and *Warfare in Ancient Greece: A Sourcebook* (1996).

Rick Schulting, Ph.D., is a lecturer in scientific and prehistoric archaeology at the University of Oxford. His current research interests lie in understanding the Mesolithic-Neolithic transition in western Europe, emphasizing the use of radiometric dating and stable isotope analysis, and in skeletal evidence for interpersonal violence in earlier prehistoric Europe.

David R. Sear, a fellow of the Royal Numismatic Society in London and the American Numismatic Society in New York, has authored an extensive range of numismatic books over the past four decades, aimed at collectors and students of ancient Greek, Roman and Byzantine coinage. He has been a resident of Los Angeles for the past 25 years and operates a research service authenticating ancient coinage. His

numerous publications include *Roman Coins and Their Values* (1964; rev. ed., 2000–2005), *Byzantine Coins and Their Values* (1974, rev. ed., 1987), *Greek Coins and Their Values* (1978–1979), and *The History and Coinage of the Roman Imperators, 49–27 B.C.* (1998).

Robert Shanafelt, Ph.D., teaches courses in anthropology, religion, and Africana studies at Georgia Southern University. He has published a number of articles on different aspects of life in southern Africa, among them, "Crime, Power, and Policing in South Africa" in *Democratic Policing in Transitional and Developing Countries* (2006).

Alison Sheridan, Ph.D., is head of early prehistory in the National Museums Scotland, Edinburgh, specializing in the British and Irish Neolithic and Bronze Age. Exhibition work includes *Heaven and Hell—and Other Worlds of the Dead* (2000), for which she was lead curator and book editor. Other books include *From Sickles to Circles* (with A. M. Gibson, 2004) and *Vessels for the Ancestors* (with N. M. Sharples, 1992).

Spyros Siropoulos is senior lecturer of Greek philology and history at the Department of Mediterranean Studies, University of the Aegean, Greece. He has published various articles in three books: *Unlike a Woman: Gender and the Social Function of the Athenian Tragedy* (2003), *The Goat's Skin: The Other Side of Alexander the Great's Power* (2003; in Greek with English summary), and *The Things after Alexander: The Centrifugal Potencies of the Hellenistic Kingdoms* (2005, in Greek).

Bradley Skeen, M.A., has taught at the University of Minnesota, Webster University, and Washington University. He is a specialist in magic, religion, and philosophy in late antiquity and has contributed to research in that field in *Die Zeitschrift für Papyrologie und Epigraphik*, among other journals.

Christopher Smith, D.Phil., is professor of ancient history at the University of Saint Andrews in Scotland. He is the author of *Early Rome and Latium: Economy and Society c 100–500 B.C.* (1996) and *The Roman Clan: From Ancient Ideology to Modern Anthropology* (2006) as well as editor of several collections of essays, including *Trade, Traders and the Ancient City* (with Helen Parkins, 1998); *Sicily from Aeneas to Augustus* (with John Serrati, 2000), and *Religion in Archaic and Republican Rome and Italy: Evidence and Experience* (with Edward Bispham, 2000). He is engaged in work on Roman historiography and oratory.

Nancy Shatzman Steinhardt is professor of East Asian art and curator of Chinese art at the University of Pennsylvania. She is author of *Chinese Traditional Architecture* (1984), *Chinese Imperial City Planning* (1990), *Liao Architecture* (1997), and *Chinese Architecture* (2002) and more than 60 scholarly articles.

Tom Streissguth is a freelance author, editor, and journalist who has published more than 70 nonfiction and reference books. His most recent titles include *Clay v. United States, Genghis Khan's Mongol Empire, Library in a Book: Hate Crimes, Eyewitness History: The Roaring Twenties,* and the *Greenhaven Encyclopedia of the Middle Ages.*

Ananda Cohen Suarez is a Ph.D. student at the Graduate Center of the City University of New York, specializing in pre-Columbian and colonial Latin American art history. She is particularly interested in cross-cultural encounters, vernacular religious art, and manuscript production in the early colonial Americas.

Frank J. Swetz, D.Ed., is professor emeritus of mathematics and education, Pennsylvania State University. His research interests focus on cultural and societal impact on mathematics learning and teaching. Among his recent books are *Legacy of the Luoshu: The 4000 Year Search for the Meaning of the Magic Square of Order Three* (2002) and *Teaching Mathematics to Children* (2003).

John Thorburn, Ph.D., is associate professor of classics at Baylor University, where he teaches a variety of subjects dealing with the classical world. He has published on Greek tragedy, Greek comedy, Greek and Roman history, and a variety of ancient subjects. He is the author of *The Alcestis of Euripides* (2002) and the *Facts on File Companion to Classical Drama* (2005).

Alain Touwaide, Ph.D., is a historian of sciences in the Department of Botany of the National Museum of Natural History at the Smithsonian Institution (Washington, D.C.). He has extensively published on the history of medicine in the Mediterranean world from antiquity to the Renaissance. Recently, he coedited the volume *Visualizing Medieval Medicine and Natural History, 1200–1550* (2006).

Francesca C. Tronchin, Ph.D., teaches Greek and Roman art and archaeology at Ohio State University. Her primary area of research is Roman domestic decor and issues of eclecticism in ancient sculptural displays.

David K. Underwood, Ph.D., teaches Western humanities, art history, philosophy, and Latin American studies at the University of South Florida in Tampa and at Saint Petersburg College in Clearwater, Florida. He is the author of two books and several articles and essays on Iberian and Latin American art and architecture.

David Vallilee is an independent scholar.

Frans van Koppen, M.A., teaches Akkadian at the School of Oriental and African Studies, London. He contributed to *The*

Ancient Near East: Historical Sources in Translation (2006) and *The Babylonian World* (forthcoming).

Lawrence Waldron, M.F.A., is an associate professor and doctoral candidate at the City University of New York, specializing in non-Western fields of art history and culture. He has presented and published various articles on the art and culture of the pre-Columbian Caribbean and Southeast Asia.

Ezekiel A. Walker, Ph.D., teaches African and world history at the University of Central Florida. His forthcoming book is entitled *Growth, Crisis and Transformation in the Cocoa-Farming Economy of Southwestern Nigeria* (2007).

Peter S. Wells is professor of anthropology at the University of Minnesota. His publications include *The Barbarians Speak: How the Conquered Peoples Shaped Roman Europe* (1999), *Beyond Celts, Germans and Scythians: Archaeology and Identity in Iron Age Europe* (2001), and *The Battle That Stopped Rome: Emperor Augustus, Arminius, and the Slaughter of the Legions in the Teutoburg Forest* (2003).

Jacqui Wood is an archaeologist and authority on prehistoric cooking and the lifestyles of prehistoric Europeans. She runs her own excavation in Cornwall, England.

Ronald Young, Ph.D., teaches in the Social Sciences Department at Canterbury School in Fort Myers, Florida. His teaching and research interests are in the area of Latin American Studies. In addition to numerous reference articles, he is presently working on a general history of Colombia to be published by Greenwood Press.

Katharina Zinn, M.A., is writing her Ph.D. dissertation on ancient Egyptian libraries and archives at the University of Leipzig, Germany. She works in a project on scarabs in the Fitzwilliam Museum, Cambridge (United Kingdom) and a project on Middle Kingdom Reliefs from Lisht in the Princeton University Art Museum. She has published articles on the organization of collective wisdom as well as multilingualism in ancient Egypt.

List of Illustrations

VOLUME I

VOLUME III

List of Maps and Primary Source Documents

MAPS

VOLUME I

VOLUME II

VOLUME III

VOLUME IV

PRIMARY SOURCE DOCUMENTS

VOLUME I

VOLUME II

VOLUME III

Entries S to Z

S

sacred sites

INTRODUCTION

Probably the first sacred sites were aspects of the natural world that people identified with the supernatural. Large formations, such as big rock outcrops, mountains, lakes, and rivers, all could serve as impressive sources of spiritual power. Mountains are imposing not only because of their size but also because they seem closer to the sky. Many cultures have placed shrines or altars atop mountains in the belief that people could be better heard by gods when they were nearer the sky than when they were at the bases of mountains. Rock outcrops often have the advantage of having faces on which sacred images could be painted or carved, allowing people to show in their images what is special about the sacred place. Lakes and rivers frequently are associated with the life force, because water is believed to be part of the life force; after all, people quickly die without water. Lakes and rivers were thought to have gods dwelling in them, and many ancient peoples made sacrifices to lakes and rivers in the hope of making the gods there happy or to persuade the gods to help with crops or wars.

A place in a dense forest where light cannot penetrate past the branches and leaves of trees could be construed as a place where forest spirits would gather or dwell. Shrines in such places might not have survived if they were wooden or consisted of no more than the space among the trees, but historical records suggest that ancient cultures in Europe, Africa, Asia, and America had such places, where good and evil spirits were thought to dwell.

Sacred places can be associated with historical events or important people. Where a special person received enlightenment about the supernatural or spoke with spirits can become a holy place to which the faithful will make pilgrimages. Shrines could be built to mark locations where a single religious leader received or proclaimed divine knowledge over his or her lifetime, with the shrines marking stations for religious pilgrimages of the followers of the religious leader or of the religion of which the religious leader's revelations became a part. The locations of great battles that were important sites in mythology sometimes were commemorated with altars, shrines, temples, or tombs. There were so many such places that some ancient people wrote tour guides to the sacred sites.

Otherwise ordinary places could be made sacred by people. One way was to deposit a sacred relic, such as a fragment of hair, bones, fingernail clippings, or a personal item worn or used by a sacred or holy person. Great mounds could be built over the relics, or temples could be erected to house them. Another way to make a place sacred was through ritual. Sometimes ancient cities were made sacred and even objects of worship by depositing icons of gods in central temples or through ritual blessings of the cities. Sometimes the ground on which a city was to be built was consecrated through rituals, making the new city a sacred place that was set apart from the ordinary world.

AFRICA

BY ROBERT SHANAFELT

Sacred sites in ancient Africa include special areas of the natural landscape such as mountains, caves, forests, and springs and human constructions such as mounds, tombs, and pyramids. The continent contains some of the oldest sites in the world that seem to have had ritual significance for human beings. By 10,000 years ago religious symbolism was well established in art, body decoration, burial, and monument building. One substance very widely associated with burial was the red pigment ocher. Ocher is further connected with the land and with sacred sites in that it was painted or smeared on rock surfaces or onto artifacts left in the ground. Studies of ancient religions from around the world suggest that this pigment was a common symbol for blood and life.

A substantial number of ancient engravings on stone and paintings on rock walls have been discovered in many regions of Africa, including the region that is now the Sahara. In very early times graphic images of animals and abstract geometric forms made on rock faces probably were meant to establish supernatural connections among people, animals, spirit beings, and the landscape. Southern Africa provides some of the very earliest examples of rock art with undoubted religious connections, dating back to perhaps 30,000 years ago but continuing into the time of European colonialism.

There appears to be a direct relationship between the religion of the so-called Bushmen (the San) and the ancient rock art sites found in southern Africa. For example, some paintings depict ritual dances similar to those still practiced by Bushmen today. The modern-day Tswana also claim an ancient religious connection. According to one oral tradition a set of engraved footprints in southeastern Botswana marks the spot where the first Tswana man emerged from the underworld. In North Africa the Atlas Mountains of Morocco were favored locations for ritual activities. Here rock engravings made between 5,000 and 7,000 years ago depict otherworldly images such as horned women and men with animal heads.

Deep gorge in the Atlas Mountains; these mountains were a favored site for ritual activities in ancient times. (© Board of Regents of the University of Wisconsin System)

The impressive megaliths (large standing stones) and pyramids that often mark the sacred sites of the ancient world are usually associated with civilizations that had substantial populations and productive farming. While this is also true for the sites in Africa with the largest monuments and pyramids, in some cases pastoralists (groups who herd animals as their principal occupation) or other societies with relatively small populations constructed megaliths. Herders and early farmers in what are today Niger, the Central African Republic, and Chad built stone monuments to cover the graves of their revered leaders. Ritual cattle sacrifices also occurred in many of these locations. Stone circles and other megalithic monuments are especially pronounced in the region around the present-day town of Bouar in the Central African Republic.

Nabta Playa, a site bordering on what is today Libya, Sudan, and Egypt, served as a ceremonial center for pastoral nomads between 6,000 and 7,000 years ago. In addition numerous tombs, the site has five rows of megaliths that radiate out from a center point. It also has an important stone circle. This stone circle is particularly significant because it is one of the earliest examples of an astronomical observatory in the world, predating England's Stonehenge by some 1,000 years. Although it is quite small compared with Stonehenge, being only about 12 feet in diameter, it is still impressive given its early date. It consists of four sets of upright slabs, with one set aligned in a north-south direction and the second set aligned eastward to face the sun as it arises during the summer solstice.

The Egypt-Sudanese border area that in ancient times was known as Upper Nubia is also the location of a mountain called Jebel Barkal that was sacred for both Egyptians and Nubians. This site became especially important during the Twenty-fifth Dynasty (ca. 712–ca. 657 B.C.E.), when Nubian pharaohs ruled all Egypt. Later Nubian pharaohs built pyramids for themselves and their queens and were laid to rest at nearby Meroë. Another example of a sacred mountain in Africa is Makade Egzi in Ethiopia, near the ancient city-state of Axum. Axum itself is famous for impressive stone gravesites and obelisks. In a much earlier time, around 3000 B.C.E., many stone dolmens (upright stones across which lies a stone slab) were erected in what is now the eastern region of the country.

As mentioned earlier, features of the land and the landscape are sacred in many traditional African religions.

Among the hunting-and-gathering peoples who inhabit the forests of central Africa—so-called Pygmy peoples such as the Mbuti of Congo and the Aka of the Central African Republic—the forest is thought to be a divine being or spiritual force. Many peoples of West Africa also consider portions of the forest sacred, while other groups, like the Tswana, consider the homeland of their ancestors to be the most sacred ground. The elders and keepers of traditional knowledge among the Mijikenda of Kenya also work to protect special areas of forests that they associate with their ancestors. Here it is difficult to tease apart today's spiritual inspiration and imagination from the realities of the past. For example, while oral tradition suggests the Mijikenda sacred forests were inhabited by their ancestors for at least the past 10 generations, some archaeologists think they were occupied more recently. On the other hand, other experts think the occupation goes back to antiquity, much further than oral tradition suggests. Similarly, while it is known that people have inhabited the forests of central Africa for thousands of years, it is not known at what point people began to consider the forest itself as sacred.

Finally, it should not be forgotten that both Christianity and Judaism established early roots in North Africa and in Ethiopia. Today a special treasure house near the Church of Saint Mary at Axum is said by many followers of the Ethiopian Orthodox Church to house the Ark of the Covenant, the chest that contains the original Ten Commandments.

EGYPT

BY CHRISTINE END

The ancient Egyptian worldview was embodied in the concept of *maat*, or divine order. Under *maat*, Egypt was at the center of the universe; night, day, and the seasons were perfectly governed, and the cosmos was harmoniously balanced. Appeasing the gods who presided over every aspect of the Egyptian world was necessary to perpetuate *maat*. A goddess, also named Maat, personified the concept. Kings frequently included "beloved of Maat" in their titles to show their devotion, and surviving reliefs show kings offering small Maat figures to a variety of gods. By giving a figure of Maat, the king was ensuring that the deity would uphold *maat* and therefore Egypt's position in the universe.

The king was not the only one to appeal to the gods; offerings were a part of life for the ancient Egyptians. Excavations revealing abundant offerings indicate an especially sacred site. Individuals left gifts at specific locations to venerate a particular god, to ask for help, or to mark a pilgrimage to a revered place. These offerings could have been amulets, statues, mummified animals, notes or spells written on pottery, foodstuffs, offering tables, or poured unguents or pure sand. Some offerings were much larger, such as shrines, stelae, or even temples. These places were considered sacred because of mythological or religious connotations, the presence of exploitable resources (such as water or metal) in the area, or symbolic natural or man-made landforms. There are many overlaps within these categories. For example, sometimes a temple was built on a natural sacred mound, or a building's design might have imitated a natural sacred land formation.

The Egyptian perception of the sacred often combined the mythological and tangible worlds. Some myths include descriptions of the beginning of the universe. One popular Egyptian creation story begins with chaotic primordial waters, called *nun* (sometimes represented by a god of the same name). *Nun* was the first thing in the universe out of which the primeval mound, or *benben*, emerged. This mound was the first thing the sun's rays fell upon. Bodies or sources of water were sacred because water symbolized mythological creation and also, in the tangible world, was an essential resource, particularly in the desert. The Nile River was the most important body of water; it was the source of agriculture, transportation, and sustenance for Egypt's people and wildlife. This river was so sacred and boat travel was so engrained in the ancient Egyptian consciousness that some royal burials included boats so that the deceased could navigate the waters of the afterlife.

Sacred bodies of water could also be man-made. Artificial lakes were frequently created at temples if a natural water source was not available. The temples of Amon and Mut at Karnak, Hathor at Dendera, Osiris at Abydos, and other temples and temple complexes at Medinet Habu, Armant, and Tanis all incorporated man-made lakes into their environment. These lakes were used for daily washing, ritual libations, watering sacred animals, and sailing sacred barks during festivals. Wells, a natural water source accessed in a man-made fashion, were another way to exploit water. On desert roads or in towns far from lakes or the Nile, wells were of life-sustaining importance.

Water was not the only exploitable natural resource for the Egyptians. Mines and quarries were considered sacred places where the riches of the earth were accessible. Certain gods were associated with particular types of metal or stone. For example, Hathor was deemed the lady of turquoise, and Ra, the sun god, was said to possess bones of silver, skin of gold, and hair of lapis lazuli. Shrines and stelae dedicated to gods were frequently erected at their mine sites.

Man-made mound structures were sometimes incorporated into sacred sites such as tombs, symbolically associating them with creation myths. In ancient Egyptian creation mythology, the primeval mound was the first thing to emerge out of the turbulent waters. Papyrus was the first thing to grow on the newly emerged mound. This mimicked the agricultural cycle of the emergence of fertile silt-covered land after the Nile flood. Therefore, including a mound at a site would connect it with both the tangible and mythological worlds.

A different type of man-made mound is found at Abydos on the west bank of the Nile. Abydos was considered the mythical burial place of Osiris, god of the dead and the afterlife. Pilgrimages to Abydos honoring Osiris began in early dynastic times. A mound created from the accumulation of centuries of small offerings brought to this sacred site is still visible today. Offerings at Abydos also included structures such as temples and cenotaphs.

Temples were extremely sacred places to the Egyptians. Commoners were not permitted inside the boundaries of the temple. Interaction between the common person and the gods occurred only when shrines were carried out of the temple precincts. Important precincts included the temple of Amon and Mut at Karnak, Luxor Temple in the south, the temple of Ptah at Memphis, and the sun temple of Heliopolis in the north. Architectural elements of the Egyptian temple appear to refer back to the primeval mound and the waters of *nun*. The hall that led into the temple contained columns topped with papyrus (representing its growth on the mound) and sometimes lotus, thus creating an artificial marshland. Papyrus and lotus plants additionally symbolized Lower and Upper Egypt, respectively. In the most sacred area at the back of the temple, the ground rose and the star-painted ceiling became lower, leading into the highest, darkest area representing the primeval mound. The temple therefore stood as a mythological microcosm within which the priests ritually duplicated the creation of the universe.

Limestone stela of Heqaib, from Abydos, Egypt (1990–1750 B.C.E.); Abydos was the principal cult center of Osiris and a place of pilgrimage for Egyptians. (© The Trustees of the British Museum)

Natural land formations may have been the sign of a sacred area. Some scholars believe that the choice of the Valley of the Kings for New Kingdom (ca. 1550–1070 B.C.E.) royal burials was made because of a pyramid-shaped hill at the site, echoing the shape of pyramids used for Old Kingdom (2575–2134 B.C.E.) royal burials. If true, this is an example of a natural site chosen for a sacred purpose because it resembled a man-made structure. Further, there is some argument as to whether the pyramid shape itself derives from a natural mound formation or is a logical progression in the evolution of man-made structures. Areas surrounding pyramids were considered sacred places in which to be buried. In the Old Kingdom it appears that the king was thought to be the only one with the ability to rise from the dead, but individuals buried around his tomb might have a chance at the afterlife because of their location near him.

The sun was also revered, inspiring the building of many sacred structures. The Egyptians identified several solar deities, each representing the sun at various times of the day. Solar worship, especially of the sun god Ra, was an important part of Egyptian religious belief from the time of the Old Kingdom. Obelisks and *benben* stones (the predecessor of the obelisk that represented the primeval mound) were erected at several sites sacred to Ra. Additionally, kings deemed themselves *sa Ra*, or "son of the sun."

THE MIDDLE EAST

BY AMY HACKNEY BLACKWELL

The people of Mesopotamia believed that temples functioned as physical homes for their gods and goddesses. Accordingly, Mesopotamians built their temples specifically to accommodate deities and not as a place for worshippers to gather. A temple would contain a statue of the resident god and a repository to store votive offerings given by the faithful. Priests and priestesses lived next to the sanctuary and performed daily rituals, including furnishing large meals for the gods. Workshops for the manufacture of everything from tools to till the deity's fields to pottery to hold the deity's beer were associated with each temple.

Each city had numerous temples dedicated to different gods and goddesses, but typically one deity would function as the city's patron and inhabit the city's largest and richest temple. The city of Babylon was considered sacred to the god Marduk and his son Nabu. Nabu also had a shrine in the neighboring city of Borsippa. Nippur, another Babylonian city, was sacred to the god Enlil. Assur, the capital of Assyria, was the home of the god Assur, the chief god of the Assyrian pantheon and a counterpart of the Babylonian god Marduk. Nineveh was another important Assyrian city; its most important temple was that of the goddess Ishtar. The city of Ur, near the mouth of the Tigris and the Euphrates, was the sacred city of the god Nanna. In some cities a pair of temples housed a divine husband and wife; for example, in Babylon, the temple to Marduk was next to the temple dedicated to his wife, Sarpanitum.

Israel was home to several sacred sites important to Jews and Christians. Jerusalem has been the holy city of the Jews since about 1000 B.C.E. and has been a destination for religious pilgrimages since that time. The Temple Mount was the site of the Jewish temple, the center of organized worship, and the holiest place in Judaism. Two temples succeeded each other there in ancient times. The first one, Solomon's Temple, was built in the 10th century B.C.E. and was destroyed by the Babylonians around 587 B.C.E. The second temple was built in 515 B.C.E. and was destroyed by the Romans in 70 C.E. The Western Wall, or Wailing Wall, is the retaining wall that supports the western side of the Temple Mount. It was built along with the second temple and survived when the Romans destroyed the temple. According to Jewish tradition, the emperor Titus (r. 79–81 C.E.) left it standing to remind the Jews that Rome had conquered them, but the Jews regarded it as a sign of God's promise that they were his chosen people. The wall has been a popular site for prayer since ancient times.

The tomb of the biblical Jewish woman Rachel (wife of Jacob) was traditionally believed to be on the outskirts of Bethlehem. The town of Bethlehem also contained a grotto where the Roman Church father Jerome (ca. 347–419 or 420 C.E.) translated the Bible into Latin—a translation known as the Vulgate—around 400 C.E. Bethlehem's Church of the Nativity was built by the emperor Constantine the Great (r. 306–337 C.E.) in 330 C.E. over a holy cave where Jesus was believed to have been born. Constantine also built the Church of the Holy Sepulchre over the spot in Jerusalem where Jesus was said to have been crucified.

Ancient Persian worshippers of Zarathustra, or Zoroaster, centered their worship on fires. Each home had its own sacred fire at which family members worshipped daily. In the fourth century B.C.E. Persians began building fire temples that became centers of community worship. Cities and towns had their own temples; famous temples were located in the cities of Shiz, Baku, and Kabulistan. Zoroastrians disposed of dead bodies by leaving them on mountaintops inside stone-walled enclosures called towers of silence, where the bodies were eaten by vultures and dried by the sun. This was considered the cleanest way of dealing with the dead because it prevented decaying flesh from polluting the ground.

Many sacred sites were located in Asia Minor. Mount Ararat, in the mountains of Armenia, was a sacred site for millennia. The Asklepion in Pergamum was a hospital built in honor of the god of health, Asklepios; it was famed for a sleeping cure in which the god was supposed to visit patients in their dreams. The Temple of Artemis at Ephesus was one of the Seven Wonders of the Ancient World. Christian sites included the Cave of the Seven Sleepers in Ephesus, a cave in which seven Christian boys pursued by persecuting Romans hid themselves; the soldiers walled them up inside, and they were said to have fallen asleep until the fifth century C.E., when they were released by an earthquake and learned that Christianity was now prevalent.

ASIA AND THE PACIFIC

BY KIRK H. BEETZ

For many in the ancient Asia and Pacific region, unusual or impressive geological features carried spiritual power. For example, in ancient Japan a mountain would have *kami*, a spiritual power, just because it was massive. Mount Fuji, which stands tall over eastern Honshū, was especially sacred not only for its size but also for its individuality, standing separate, as it does, from the main mountain chain of the island.

Ayers Rock in Australia is another example. Called Uluru by the ancient Australians, it fell from the sky during the dreaming time, the era of the Creation. It was also the site of a great battle between the lizard men and the snake men, before human beings appeared. Uluru is impressive: made of sandstone, it stands 1,143 feet high and is a mile and a half long. It seems to glow red as the sun sets. The rock was said to be "owned" by a single person at a time. This person controlled who visited the rock. Many ancient sacred sites in Australia were "owned" by someone. The owner also owned all the stories associated with the sacred place. He or she could tell others the stories, but they were not supposed to repeat the stories unless they themselves became "owners" of the sacred place. This custom continued through the 20th century for Uluru, with owners taking people into special meeting areas, usually just outside caves, to tell them the stories about the sacred site. As is the case with many ancient sacred rocks, Uluru was painted with symbols. Some of them tell the story of Creation. They were painted with ocher shades and blood drawn from the arm of the painter, which emphasized the artist's spiritual connection to the rock and what he was depicting. Caves that were painted often served as places for initiation rites for children moving toward adulthood, where they would learn some of the sacred lore of their people.

The Chinese had many sacred places. During the Shang Dynasty (ca. 1500–1045 B.C.E.) there were many cultures outside the Shang Empire, and they had numerous different beliefs about their sacred places. Most of these beliefs have been lost. One site that was sacred throughout ancient times was Mount Tai Shan. It is about 5,000 feet high, and its summit is a huge crag of rock that seems to thrust out into the sky, giving those who stand on it a breathtaking view of the rocky, lumpy countryside in Shandong Province. The route up to the summit is marked by shrines. A pilgrim in ancient times was expected to leave offerings at each shrine, and even today people leave gifts of fruit and flowers as they scale the mountain. Confucius climbed the mountain and was recorded as saying, "I feel the world is much smaller," as he gazed at the world from the summit. The emperor Liu Ch'e (r. 141–87 B.C.E.) of the Han Dynasty (202 B.C.E.–220 C.E.), climbed Mount Tai Shan to speak with the gods. He made his climb a proper pilgrimage by stopping at every shrine to pray and leave offerings. By his era Mount Tai Shan had become a symbol of Chinese culture, and Liu Ch'e's climbing the mountain displayed his commitment to Chinese civilization as well as his own important place in Chinese religion. He was expected to speak with the gods on behalf of the Chinese.

In addition to building shrines on already-sacred sites, people made some sites sacred through rituals and the building of religious structures. In India people built stupas, originally tombs of dirt piled in the shape of hemispheres. Stupas took on great importance after the death of Siddhartha Gautama (ca. 563–ca. 483 B.C.E.), who was the Buddha. Parts of his body were entombed in several stupas. Emperor Asoka (r. 268–233 B.C.E.) of India had seven of these stupas opened and their contents divided among 84,000 stupas scattered through India. The most important was the Great Stupa in Sanchi, north of the Narmada River in Madhya Pradesh in central India. Over hundreds of years, people added to it, coating it in brick, surrounding it with a wall, and building ornate gates alive with sculptures of gods and goddesses.

A stupa typically had a circular crown projecting around its top. The one for the Great Stupa looks like many fingers thrusting out horizontal to the ground. The crown was called *chatra*, meaning "umbrella." The dome of the stupa was the *garbha*, meaning "womb." *Garbha* referred not to a physical birth but to the Buddha's passing out of the cycle of birth and rebirth into nirvana, a blissful spiritual state in which the soul escapes the pain of life in the physical world. The dome was also sometimes called an *anda*, meaning "egg," because it symbolized the first egg from which the universe emerged.

Hindus used the concept of the *garbha* to create the *garbhagriha*, a shrine where a person might be seen by a god. Hindu shrines and temples often had images of gods inside them, but the Hindus did not believe that the statues were gods, and they did not believe that gods ever actually entered the statues. The statues frequently were placed in a shadowy part of a shrine, because it was intended to set an observer's mind to thinking about the mysteries of spirituality. It was this train of thought that could bring a person into touch with a supernatural being. This encounter with a supernatural being was *darshana*, meaning "viewing."

Sacred sites were also built with the intention of inspiring awe in visitors. In India, during Asoka's reign, people began carving sacred sites into large stones. At first these were just caves where a monk could sit by himself and meditate. Eventually, they became huge temples that are amazing even today. The best may be at Ajanta in western India. From the 100s B.C.E. to the 600s C.E. temples were carved into immense rocky cliffs. Some temples began in natural caves, but others were carved either from the side of a cliff or from the top down into a cliff. Cracks were hammered into the rocks and filled with wood that was then doused with water, which slowly widened the cracks as the wood swelled. Rock masons carved openings into spaces that became rooms and corridors, with columns and statues. The detail work was done by artisans using tools as fine as those of jewelers. Walls were then painted with religious scenes. The central shrines were often in shadows, with openings allowing light to highlight statues representing the Buddha or gods. Both Hindus and Buddhists carved such temples.

EUROPE

BY AMY HACKNEY BLACKWELL

Long before the Celtic peoples arrived, prehistoric Europeans created sacred sites by arranging giant stones, or megaliths, in ways that were to them spiritually significant. These stones remained standing during Celtic times, and the Celts adopted some of them as their own sacred sites. Celts and Germans also found spiritual power in many natural formations, such as groves of trees, mountains, caves, and islands.

Hundreds of megalithic sites remain throughout Europe, from Ireland to the eastern Baltic area, containing stone structures and graves erected between 4500 and 2000 B.C.E. Many megalithic sites were tombs, and human remains have been found in some of them. Others reveal no obvious purpose, consisting only of upright stones arranged in a pattern but without burials. The most accepted explanation is that megaliths had religious or ceremonial significance. Many of them are aligned in such a way that they catch the sun on specific days of the year, which may be evidence that prehistoric peoples used them in sun worship.

There are several common types of megalithic structures. A menhir is a single standing stone. Some standing stones are arranged in circles or rows, called alignments. A dolmen is a tomb made of several large upright stones supporting a flat stone roof, while a passage grave consists of a corridor lined and roofed with large stones leading to a stone burial chamber. Many megalithic tombs were once covered with mounds either of earth or of small stones. The earthen mounds are known as tumuli; the stone mounds are called cairns.

Most surviving megalithic sites are in northwestern France, Britain, and Ireland. The largest known menhir, the so-called *grand menhir brisé* ("great broken stone") in Brittany, France, stood about 67 feet high before it was broken in an earthquake in 1722. Carnac, another site in Brittany, contains over 3,000 standing stones arranged in straight lines, all erected between 4500 and 3300 B.C.E. Carnac also has several tumuli and several dolmens. Gavrinis Island off the coast of Brittany holds a huge megalithic cairn that dates to about 3500 B.C.E. Inside the cairn a passage leads to a grave chamber constructed of large granite stones. The walls of the passage and chamber are elaborately carved with spiral decorations. Ireland is home to several similar tombs, the most famous of which is Newgrange, built about 3200 B.C.E. Newgrange is especially notable for the way the rising sun of the winter solstice shines directly on a design in the main chamber.

Perhaps the most famous sacred site in prehistoric Europe is Stonehenge in England, which was built in several stages between 3100 and 1600 B.C.E. Stonehenge is a complex monument, and the standing stones that are visible today are only the most recent version of it. Moreover, it was at the center of a landscape of monuments that all had some sort of symbolic or sacred purpose. Barrows dot the surrounding countryside, while a roadway lined with ditches and banks leads the way to the nearby river Avon. Debate rages as to Stonehenge's purpose, but it may have had a calendrical or ceremonial function.

Bronze Age rock art chiseled on rocky outcrops in many parts of Scandinavia as well as in the Alps includes images of animals, people, and boats, as well as abstract spirals and suns. These carvings clearly conveyed some sort of spiritual significance. Some of the scenes found in Sweden show rituals and processions.

Celts adopted ancient megalithic sites as their own; historians believe that the Celts created legends of fairies and other supernatural beings to explain the existence of these mysterious structures. The Hill of Tara in County Meath, Ireland, was a particularly sacred site in Celtic times. The Celts believed that the hill had been the capital of the mythical people who lived in Ireland before them. On top of the hill was a fort built during the Iron Age, perhaps around 1000 B.C.E.; this fort contained a standing stone called the Lia Fáil, or Stone of Destiny. Celtic kings were crowned next to the Lia Fáil, which was supposed to shriek out loud if the feet of the rightful king rested on it.

Most ancient Europeans believed that trees had spiritual significance. The Roman historian Tacitus observed that ancient Germanic peoples worshipped sacred groves of trees, especially oak trees. He described a ritual in which Germans performed annual human sacrifices in the sacred groves. In Denmark and Scandinavia people selected particular ash trees as sacred objects. Oddly shaped trees often gained particular spiritual significance and were believed to be the homes of spirits.

Celtic people throughout Europe believed that certain groves of trees were sacred. Forests sacred to the Celts of France included the Forest of Paimpont near Rennes, the grove in the Greek colony of Massilia (modern-day Marseilles), the Augustonemeton in the Auvergne region of central France, the Memetacum in the Artois region of northern France, and the Forest of Huelgoat in Brittany. The Roman historian Pliny mentioned a Spanish people called the Nemetatae, named after a sacred grove in northern Spain. (One Celtic word for a "sacred grove" was *nemeton.*) A Celtic group in Germany called themselves the Nemetes, or "people of the sacred grove." Sacred groves left their mark on some modern place names, such as Nemetostatio in Devon and Vernemetum in Nottinghamshire, England.

Many rivers, wells, springs, bogs, and hot springs were sacred to ancient European peoples. Archaeologists have found religious artifacts at many watery locations, such as the river Shannon in Ireland and the Seine in France. At Flag Fen in England, Bronze Age and Iron Age people deposited hundreds of bronze objects, as well as animal sacrifices, in the bog. Across northern Europe bogs and marshes have yielded thousands of objects that could only have been thrown in deliberately as offerings. The famous Iron Age bog bodies,

Lindow Man (Iron Age, mid-first century C.E.*), found in Lindow Moss, Cheshire, England, and thought to have been ritually murdered; Germanic and Celtic human sacrifice took place at the site of peat bogs, where the bodies were then thrown.* (© The Trustees of the British Museum)

of which Tollund Man and Grauballe Man in Denmark and Lindow Man in England are but three examples, were probably individuals who were sacrificed ritually (or perhaps executed for crimes) and then cast into the bogs, where the soil's unusual chemistry preserved the bodies remarkably well.

Hot springs were especially attractive to ancient peoples. The natural hot mineral springs at Bath, in southwestern England, were first frequented by hunter-gatherers around 8000 B.C.E. Celts built a shrine to the water goddess Sulis there around 700 B.C.E. This shrine became a major religious center for Celts in the area. Romans took over the shrine around 65 C.E. Although their name for the town was Aquae Sulis (Waters of Sulis), they replaced Sulis with the Roman goddess Minerva as the focus of worship. Among her many other roles, Minerva was the goddess of medicine, and the shrine became a destination for people hoping to regain their health. Over the next four centuries the townspeople improved the facilities, constructing temples and bathhouses. Other well-known sacred hot springs existed (and still exist) at Baden-Baden in Germany, Perrier in France, and Evian-les-Bains on Lake Geneva.

Ancient Europeans often considered mountains sacred. Celts believed that their gods lived on top of high mountains. Islands were also sacred. The island of Anglesey in northern Wales was believed to be the home and power base of Druids. In about 60 C.E. Romans attacked the island, slaughtered the defenders, and burned the Druids' sacred oak groves in an effort to end their power and influence.

GREECE

BY BRADLEY SKEEN

Pausanius, a Greek of the second century C.E., wrote a tourist guide to his homeland. A modern book of this kind might concentrate on art galleries and battlefields, but Pausanius's main interest was in religious practices and religious places. For the Greeks the sacred was the most important part of life and found its expression in the hearts of cities, in villages, in the wild places of the countryside, and beside the hearth of every Greek home.

The earliest Greeks, the Minoan civilization of Crete (2000–1400 B.C.E.), carried out religious rituals in rural places whose nature seemed connected to the divine. Mountaintops were the closest places to the gods of the sky, while caves seemed connected to the deities of the dead who lived under the earth. Other gods were worshipped within sacred enclosures set off around large trees.

Household shrines also existed in Minoan times and continued throughout Greek history. Each house had its own altar dedicated to the family's ancestors and to whatever gods protected the home according to family tradition. Frequently, such shrines had small statues of divine figures. A ceramic tube usually hung on the wall above the shrine; the tube contained a live snake, the *agathos daimon* ("good spirit") that represented the powers watching over the family.

Greece experienced a cultural collapse or dark age (1100–800 B.C.E.) during which many religious traditions were lost. When Greek cities were established or reestablished in the Archaic Age (after 600 B.C.E.), the sacred had to be brought into them (though many rural shrines had kept their sacred character and maintained their rituals even through the time of collapse). The idea of the temple was imported from the older civilization of the Near East. Because of the central importance of religion to the creation and existence of cities, the temples were built in the very hearts of the cities—either on the agora (business district) or the acropolis (fortress), the places that in modern society would be reserved for government or commercial buildings as the most important public structures.

When a temple was built, its sacred precinct was cut off from ordinary space, usually by a wall, and purified through ritual. The space was further sanctified by a foundation deposit of holy objects buried under the floor of the new temple. A sacred zone such as this was created so that sacrifices could be performed within it. This ritual was performed at an altar that stood in the open air and used the facade of the temple as a backdrop. The interior of the temple usually housed a statue of the god but was rarely entered, since the rituals were conducted outside.

When the temple of Athena Pronoia (Athena of Forethought) was begun at Delphi in the eighth century B.C.E., the foundation deposit included not only the bones of sacrificed animals but also a cache of Mycenaean religious statuettes (dating to about 1600–1000 B.C.E.) that had been hoarded and preserved for centuries, ever since the collapse of Mycenaean civilization. In this way the sacredness of the past was used to create a new sacred institution, which was different from what had gone before yet could not be separated from tradition. This is emblematic of what happened all over Greece in the Archaic Age as Greek civilization renewed itself.

A Greek god was always the god of a particular place. Athena, for example, was not simply one goddess but had a different aspect in each cult place. In Athens alone there were temples of Athena Parthenos (Virgin Athena), Athena Nike (Victorious Athena), and Athena Polias (Civic Athena)—to name only the most important—each with its own form of worship, sacred calendar of festivals and sacrifices, and myths.

The Greeks recognized themselves as a people bound together by common culture and language, and especially by common religion, above the level of the city. When the city-states were established in the Archaic Period, national religious institutions also came into existence, what modern scholars call "Panhellenic" shrines. These sacred sites were available to all Greeks (*pan* meaning "all" and *Hellenes* being what the Greeks called themselves) and helped form a Greek identity.

The most important such shrine was Delphi, where a priestess known as the Pythia gave oracles from the god Apollo. In legend Delphi had originally housed a temple of the earth goddess Gaia, but Apollo had slain the dragon (*python*) that guarded it and took the temple for himself. A stone stood near the temple of Apollo, as raised stones did in many Greek sanctuaries. This one was called the *omphalos* ("navel") of the earth because Zeus had released two eagles from the edges of the world at the same time, and this was the spot where they met: the exact center not only of the earth but of the universe. Each Greek city maintained its own treasury at Delphi, which housed the lavish gifts of artworks or precious materials that the city or its citizens might dedicate in thanks to Pythian Apollo.

Greeks had used athletic contests as a form of worshipping the gods since Minoan times. The most famous games were held at another Panhellenic shrine, the temple of Zeus at Olympia (the same Olympic Games that were revived in 1896 C.E. and continue today). These games (beginning in 776 B.C.E., according to tradition) were held once every four years in alternation with others held at Delphi, Nemea, and Corinth. The contests included artistic as well as athletic competitions. Although no cash or prizes other than honor were given, the contestants were not amateurs. Winners usually received valuable rewards from their home cities, and many other contests existed that did award cash prizes, so there was a large corps of professional athletes and performers, some wealthy from this kind of work. The temple at Olympia used a very ancient kind of altar, a simple pile of the ashes of the sacrificed animals that was allowed to build up into a vast mound year after year through the centuries.

View of Mount Olympus, in Attica (*Alison Frantz Photographic Collection, American School of Classical Studies at Athens*)

Other Panhellenic sites dealt with purely personal concerns that were beyond the scope of civic religion, such as healing and salvation. Epidaurus in the Peloponnesus was the home of the main temple of Asklepios. As a son of Apollo by a mortal woman, Asklepios was technically only a semidivine "hero," but Greeks soon began to worship him as a god. His priests provided the healing of illness, a subject obviously removed from the collective religion of the city. Patients came to the shrine and slept in the courtyard of the temple overnight. The next morning the priests interpreted any dream a patient might have had and devised a treatment for him or her accordingly. Like many temples, this one had a sacred tree nearby from which offerings were hung—in this case figurines of the patients' body parts that the god had healed. The temple of the grain goddess Demeter at Eleusis (outside Athens) offered initiation into mysteries that would secure for the participants a kind of personal salvation that would let them partake of the same kind of blessed existence as heroes after death, rather than the near nonexistence Greek believed to be the common end of humankind.

ROME

BY KATIE PARLA

Defining sacred space in ancient Rome was the responsibility of high authorities—first of kings and then later of priests. Both used ritual interpretations of occurrences in the natural world when creating sacred sites. The myth of the founding of Rome itself by the twins Romulus and Remus describes such an event. Romulus, by interpreting the flight of birds more masterfully than his brother, was able to define the ritual boundary that divided the sacred space of the city from the world beyond. Supposedly he passed this skill and this privilege on to the kings who followed him. Over time, however, the right of establishing sacred areas became the province of priests called augurs (*augures*).

The augurs were one of the main priestly colleges in the augurs Roman state religion. Originally these authorities divined the will of the gods just as Romulus had done, by interpreting the flight of birds. Later in Rome's history they also interpreted a variety of other natural phenomena: thunder, lightning, and different kinds of animal behavior. By reading these signs—or "taking auspices," as it was known—the augurs could determine the boundaries of sacred space. Occasionally the signs came unsolicited—for example, the sudden appearance of an eagle over the Capitoline Hill—but more often they were the result of deliberate ritualistic attempts to communicate with the divine world.

In Rome—and later in the territories Rome controlled—the augurs could define several types of sacred sites. One type was the *templum*, a consecrated space or site where the augurs would take auspices. For the Romans a *templum* could be a building, but it could also be plot of ground or even a fixed place in the heavens where signs from the gods might be read. Hence the word *templum* does not correspond to the modern concept of a temple, though it does have a religious connotation.

The concept of the *templum* was very broad. It covered areas where magistrates could exercise power and therefore included a wide range of government buildings, such as the Curia (Senate house), as well as open spaces of official public assembly on the Roman Forum. The *templum* could also refer to the city as a whole. In this case it was defined by the *pomerium*, a ritual boundary that divided Roman cities from the world beyond. Since the area within the *pomerium* was consecrated space, cremations, burials, military exercises, and other activities deemed inappropriate for a sacred site had to take place beyond it. The authority of a magistrate was no longer valid once he left the sacred space within the *pomerium*, emphasizing the strong bond between Rome's state religion and its political authority.

Another type of sacred site was an *aedes*. This word was applied to any place where a god was believed to dwell, whether an enclosed space or an outdoor area such as a forest, spring, mountain, or lake. An *aedes* did not have to be large or the god a major one. Many Romans kept small altars in their homes to venerate household divinities, and these altars were considered *aedes*. Minor deities, such as the female nature divinities known as nymphs, were believed to inhabit countless outdoor settings. For instance, the nymph Albunea was worshipped at a sulfurous spring near Tivoli. The legendary she-wolf that suckled Romulus and Remus as babies was worshipped at a cave on the Palatine Hill. During Rome's republican era (ca. 509–27 B.C.E.) and through much of the existence of the Western Roman Empire (27 B.C.E.–476 C.E.), temples and altars were erected to divinities throughout Roman territory, often replacing the outdoor settings of archaic traditions.

Roman gold ring bought by a pilgrim and showing the Temple of Aphrodite at Palaepaphos (ca. 150–250 C.E.), made in Cyprus and found near Koskieni, Rhodes (© The Trustees of the British Museum)

The layout of major religious and ritual sites evolved during the course of Rome's history. The earliest evidence for sacred sites on the Roman Forum and the Palatine and Capitoline Hills are terra-cotta votive offerings left at a sacred place. A dearth of archaeological evidence makes it difficult to determine the precise layout of these places. During the republican and imperial eras proper temples begin to populate cities, frequently replacing older sacred areas. Contacts with Greece, Etruria, and Carthage influenced Roman temple architecture.

The development of religious structures in Rome began in the sixth century B.C.E. with the Temple of Jupiter Optimus Maximus on the Capitoline Hill. According to legend the king Tarquinius Priscus (r. 616–578 B.C.E.) located it on a site deemed appropriate by the augurs. Its style and decoration were heavily influenced by Etruscan architecture, and it in turn influenced early republican temple design. During the mid- to late republic Rome increased its contact with Greece through alliances and conquest and began to assimilate Greek gods into the state religion. Consequently Roman temples emulated Greek architecture.

During the republic private individuals such as victorious generals or politicians commissioned temples. Accordingly, these structures were less majestic in scale than the imperial structures that followed them. During the empire the Roman state and the imperial family commissioned sacred sites in monumental dimensions. The *aedes* of the empire served not just as holy places but also as symbols of Rome's power and the relationship between the gods and the state.

With the growth of Christianity in Rome and its empire new ideas about sacred places and sites emerged. In the fourth century C.E. the importance of Rome's traditional sacred sites diminished as Christianity spread and ultimately replaced the older state religion. To Christians pagan temples were not sacred areas, and with the end of the old religion the *pomerium* was no longer respected, and *templum* and *aedes* were pillaged, turned to other uses, and neglected. For Christians sacred areas included sites of martyrdom and pilgrimage, the locations of holy relics such as saints' bones, and the burial sites of saints and martyrs. During the first to fourth centuries worship, catechism, and baptism took place in small community centers, often apartment buildings or converted villas, rather than in large churches. Even in such rudimentary sanctuaries as these, however, some delineation of sacred and nonsacred space existed. For example, since unbaptized individuals could not enter the places of worship, baptisteries had to be built beyond the consecrated space. During the reign of the emperor Constantine (r. 306–37 C.E.), Christians began erecting the first large sacred buildings of their own, including several on the sites of martyr cults and burials.

THE AMERICAS

BY ALESSIA FRASSANI

Sacred sites in the ancient Americas were connected with the natural world and deeply rooted in the surrounding landscape. Either man-made or natural, sacred sites reflected AmerIndian cosmology that considered natural forces a manifestation of the divine. The ecological and cultural diversity of the American continent created cultural and subsistence systems that were highly integrated and interdependent. Sacred sites reflected this feature of AmerIndian life and usually attracted visitors from vast areas over periods of hundreds or even thousands of years. Sacred sites, from the northern woodlands to the southern Peruvian desert, share similar characteristics, which include orientation to cardinal points of the compass or landscape, giant effigy constructions, nearness to water resources, and economic importance as trade centers of valued and symbolic items. Religion was a pervasive aspect of AmerIndian daily life and could not be separated from economic activities. Religion and ritual, including pilgrimage to distant places, was an important part of the increasing social complexity that was developing during the rise of intensive agriculture in the ancient period.

In North America the earliest sacred sites recovered are related to the cult of the dead. The so-called Mound Builders left impressive man-made constructions throughout the eastern and midwestern woodland region of the present-day United States. These mounds, large and low, sometimes conical in shape, are most commonly found along the meanders of the Ohio, Illinois, and Mississippi river drainages, from the Gulf Coast to the Great Lakes region. These places were used and visited for generations before being eventually abandoned. People made special travels to these places to bury their dead. (No evidence of residential settlements has been found close to these mounds.) Once there, the pilgrims engaged in elaborate funerary rituals that probably lasted for several days. The mounds' closeness to the transportation system of the rivers and their visibility from afar, in an otherwise featureless landscape, made them significant and helped spread the cult of the ancestors over wide areas.

The mounds take different shapes. The Hopewell of south-central Ohio (ca. 200 B.C.E.–400 C.E.) created earthworks in the shape of connected rectangular and circular enclosures. They served as plazas for large public gatherings that were probably ceremonial. The Hopewell followed a tradition and geography of sacred places that had been previously established in the region. Serpent Mound, in Ohio, was long thought to be an Adena culture (1000 B.C.E.–200 C.E.) site because of ancient burials found nearby. Recent excavations, however, proved that the mound was built at least by the end of the Hopewell culture. The mound takes its name from the serpentine shape that mimics the flow of the nearby river. Burials and other signs of occupation were found close to the mound, but not on it, indicating that Serpent Mound was visited only occasionally. Among the vast quantities of exotic materials found in the burials, a testament to the wide-reaching wealth accumulated by the deceased, are effigy pipes carved in the shape of birds, fish, and mammals. They were used to smoke tobacco, a ceremonial activity that linked the mundane world to the spiritual one. The animals represented may be mythical founders of clans, and the pipes may have been used in rituals to the ancestors during family burial rituals.

In Mesoamerica the earliest sacred sites either mimic or decorate natural features of the landscape, such as mountaintops or caves, where water supply is generated. Concerns for the crops and general well-being were primary motivations for the visit and care of sacred places. The cave of Chalcatzingo in the modern state of Morelos in central Mexico, dates to the Middle Formative Period of Mesoamerica from between 700 and 500 B.C.E. Chalacatzingo carvings are in an Olmec style, the major civilization of early ancient America settled in the Gulf Coast. Whether or not the site was actually built by foreigners, Olmec-related style and symbols at Chalcatzingo reveals cultural interaction between the different areas of Mesoamerica in a period of economic and religious change. The site is located on and around a mountain peak of the same name. The most famous carving depicts in low relief an enthroned character wearing elaborate attire. His headdress is tall, and he is holding a horizontal bar, symbol of authority, in his arms. He is shown in profile inside a cave, from which large volutes, or scroll-shaped forms, are emanating. The cave itself is an animal creature, as the oval eye on top indicates, while the scrolls can be interpreted as signs of water or of speaking. The enthroned character is perhaps an oracle or ruler in charge of bringing water to the region.

Teotihuacán, the most important urban center in Mesoamerica between 50 and 650 C.E., is dominated by the impressive Pyramid of the Sun. Located along the main axis of the city, the pyramid was both a symbolic and material manifestation of the power of the city throughout Middle America. The pyramid duplicates a mountain looming in back of it, called Cerro Gordo. In this way the gigantic monument is connected to its natural surrounding. In 1971 a man-made tunnel leading to a multichambered cave was discovered under the pyramid. Although it is natural, this cave has been remodeled by humans and was visited centuries before the pyramid was built. Water-related rituals took place inside this cave and contributed to making the place sacred enough that eventually the monumental pyramid was built there.

In South America sacred sites played a major role in the cultural, political, and religious unification of the Andean, coastal, and tropical regions. The earliest sacred place of interregional importance is Chavín de Huántar in the northern Andes, Peru. Set between two mountain ranges where two rivers come together, Chavín is strategically located at the gathering point of natural forces and was visited and celebrated in an effort to maintain a prosperous balance of these forces. It was at the center of a pilgrimage network that extended for over 200 miles in every direction. The most sacred and secret place at Chavín is an inner chamber where hides the so-called Lanzón, a vertical stone in the shape of a knife depicting a mythical fanged creature. Archaeologists have found that openings inside the temple were carefully designed to create sound and light effects produced by water and wind.

In the southern desert coast of Peru hundreds of earth drawings, or geoglyphs, have been found, created between 200 B.C.E. and 600 C.E. by the Nazca people. These geoglyphs were created by removing the upper layer of pebbles and revealing the underlying darker stones. Their designs range from straight lines and geometric shapes to animal representations. The giant drawings can been seen only from the air and are located away from residential dwellings. Contemporary inheritors of the Nazca region still walk in processions along straight lines in the desert. Their pilgrimage is meant to symbolically connect water resources from the sea and mountains in this harsh environment, one of the driest places in the world. Drawings of monkeys, fish, and other exotic animals from the ocean and the Amazon forest lead scholars to believe that the Nazca Lines were sacred enclosures celebrating the economic and natural interdependence of the Andean area.

See also ARCHITECTURE; ART; ASTRONOMY; CALENDARS AND CLOCKS; CLIMATE AND GEOGRAPHY; DEATH AND BURIAL PRACTICES; EDUCATION; FESTIVALS; HEALTH AND DISEASE; LANGUAGE; MINING, QUARRYING, AND SALT MAKING; RELIGION AND COSMOLOGY; ROADS AND BRIDGES; SPORTS AND RECREATION; WAR AND CONQUEST.

FURTHER READING

Mary Beard, John North, and Simon Price, *Religions of Rome*, Vol. 1, *A History* (Cambridge, U.K.: Cambridge University Press, 1998).

Jeremy Black and Anthony Green, *Gods, Demons, and Symbols of Ancient Mesopotamia* (Austin: University of Texas Press, 1992).

Jean Bottero, *Religion in Ancient Mesopotamia*, trans. Teresa Lavender Fagan (Chicago: University of Chicago Press, 2001).

Walter Burkert, *Greek Religion: Archaic and Classical*, trans. John Raffan (Oxford, U.K.: Basil Blackwell, 1985).

David Coulson and Alec Campbell, *African Rock Art: Paintings and Engravings on Stone* (New York: Harry N. Abrams, 2001).

Matthew Dillon, *Pilgrims and Pilgrimage in Ancient Greece* (London: Routledge, 1997).

Henri Frankfort, *Ancient Egyptian Religion: An Interpretation* (New York: Dover, 2000).

Manfred Lurker, *The Gods and Symbols of Ancient Egypt* (London: Thames and Hudson, 1995).

Siegfried Morenz, *Egyptian Religion* (Ithaca, N.Y.: Cornell University Press, 1973).

John Pedley, *Sanctuaries and the Sacred in the Ancient Greek World* (Cambridge, U.K.: Cambridge University Press, 2005).

Simon Price and Emily Kearns, eds., *The Oxford Dictionary of Classical Myth and Religion,* 3rd ed. (New York: Oxford University Press, 2003).

Stephen Quirke, *Ancient Egyptian Religion* (London: British Museum Press, 1993).

Chris Scarre, *Exploring Prehistoric Europe* (Oxford, U.K.: Oxford University Press, 1999).

John W. Stamper, *The Architecture of Roman Temples: The Republic to the Middle Empire* (Cambridge, U.K.: Cambridge University Press, 2005).

Lawrence E. Sullivan, ed., *Native Religions and Cultures of Central and South America* (New York: Continuum, 2002).

Richard Townsend, ed., *The Ancient Americas: Art from Sacred Landscapes* (Chicago: Art Institute of Chicago, 1992).

Richard Townsend, ed., *Hero, Hawk, and Open Hand: American Indian Art of the Ancient Midwest and South* (Chicago: Art Institute of Chicago, 2004).

Panos Valavanis, *Games and Sanctuaries in Ancient Greece: Olympia, Delphi, Isthmia, Nemea, Athens,* trans. David Hardy (Los Angeles: Getty, 2004).

Greg Woolf, ed., *Ancient Civilizations: The Illustrated Guide to Belief, Mythology, and Art* (San Diego, Calif.: Thunder Bay Press, 2005).

► scandals and corruption

INTRODUCTION

Bribery, corruption, and scandal were as much the part of the ancient world as they are of the 21st century—and of the centuries between. One problem historians have in reconstructing the nature and effects of corruption and scandal is that written records from the ancient world are often incomplete or nonexistent. Without a free press serving as watchdog over the activities of kings and queens, nobles, civil servants, and institutions such as churches, no one chronicled these events objectively. The written record in many cases is limited to royal decrees, letters, legal judgments, and similar documents—all written from the viewpoint of those in power or from the viewpoint of their political opponents. Court historians and similar figures in the employ of rulers were paid to enhance the reputation of their masters, not to expose scandal and corruption. Accounts provided by outsiders and later historians may have been colored by prejudices, oral legend, and incomplete information.

Bribery was undoubtedly commonplace in the ancient world. People struggled to survive and accumulate some measure of wealth that would secure their old age and give them something to leave to their heirs. In empires throughout the world, legions of inspectors, civil servants, tax collectors, surveyors, and other public officials were in positions to accept bribes to allow an illegal activity to go unnoticed, to modify records in someone's favor, to alleviate a tax burden, to extend the boundaries of a person's property, and so on.

Corruption in the ancient world often centered on the ruling classes. A common feature of government in the ancient world was the dynasty, where rulers inherited the position of king, queen, or emperor. Conflict arose, however, when the line of succession was unclear (for example, when a king died without a male heir), when the inheritor of a throne was mentally unbalanced or a minor, or simply when an individual or group wanted to seize the throne and the power that went with it. Sometimes the corruption resulted from power struggles among groups. The ancient Chinese Han Dynasty (202 B.C.E.–220 C.E.), for instance, fell because of corruption and infighting among powerful groups, including the clan to which the Han empress belonged and Confucian scholar-officials at court.

Finally, some ancient rulers themselves were simply corrupt and ruled entirely with a view to enhancing their own power and wealth rather than the welfare of their people. The ancient Roman emperor Nero (37–68 C.E.) is a good example—though much of what is known about Nero's life was written by his political rivals, who characterized him as a tyrant and even as insane. Nonetheless, many historians believe that in the year 64 Nero deliberately set the great fire of Rome that burned on the nights of July 18 and 19, destroying much of the city, because he wanted to rebuild Rome as a monument to his personal greatness. At a time when rulers held absolute power over their subjects, the potential for corruption and tyranny was enormous.

AFRICA

BY KIRK H. BEETZ

Most of ancient Africa was preliterate, and such matters as scandals and corruption are usually transmitted from the past via written records, leaving much of Africa a blank for the subject. Further, most of the writings of the major civilizations of Kush and Axum are in languages that have yet to be translated, leaving just the Kushite texts that were written in ancient Egyptian and the writings of outsiders, mostly Greeks, for records that modern readers consult.

A scandal that is still renowned involved Queen Makeda (r. ca. 1005–ca. 955 B.C.E.) of Axum, a kingdom of Africans and Sabeans, a people who populated the southern Arabian Peninsula. The name Sheba is derived from Sabean, and Makeda was probably the queen of Sheba mentioned in the Old Testament. The details of her meeting with King Solomon have been distorted over the centuries by writers seeking to modify the tale to support their particular social, political, or religious prejudices. In essence, the story says that a merchant named Tamrin from Axum ventured to King Solomon's court in search of trading opportunities and was very impressed by the king's display of wealth. He reported what he saw to Makeda, who chose to see for herself the wonders of Solomon's court. Solomon was enamored of her beauty and tried to seduce her. She refused his advances. Solomon made a bargain with her: They would sleep in separate beds in the same room, and if Makeda took nothing without his permission, he would leave her alone, but if she did take something, she would have sex with him. He served her very spicy foods that evening, and she awoke very thirsty that night. Finding a glass of water on a table in the middle of the room, she drank from it; in an instant, Solomon was up, pointing out that she had no permission to drink. Her protests that water was common and surely not part of their bargain were to no avail. Makeda returned home and gave birth to Solomon's son.

The scandal endured during the life of Makeda and Solomon's son. When he was grown, the son visited Solomon, bringing a ring that Solomon had given Makeda. Solomon celebrated the arrival of his son and gave the young man the name Menelik. Solomon asked Menelik to stay with him and, as his eldest son, to become the next king. Menelik refused, insisting that he return to his mother to become the next monarch of Axum. Solomon declared that the eldest sons of his ministers were to go with Menelik and serve as his chief advisers. These eldest sons resented this order very much. For revenge, they sneaked into the temple room where the Ark of the Covenant was stored and replaced it with a copy, taking the original with them. It was not until Menelik and his companions reached Egypt that the theft was discovered. Solomon sent an army in pursuit of Menelik, but by the time the army reached Egypt, Menelik and the Ark had left Egypt. The army returned home, saddened by its failure, and Menelik was delighted when he learned of the theft. According to Axumite tradition, the ark has resided in or near Axum ever since.

How much of this entire story is true is open to debate. For instance, Axum's territory included the Sabean region of the southwestern Arabian Peninsula as well as much of eastern Africa, and Solomon's army could have reached the Sabean region without much trouble and could have waged war on the Axumites there, but it did not. Nevertheless, even if only the barest part of the story is true, it would likely have been a big scandal in Axum, where the queen was expected to remain a virgin until marriage. Further, it gave Axumite Christians a national tradition to cling to during the years in which they were cut off from other Christian nations by the pagans and Muslims of the medieval era.

The ancient African civilization of Kush had its own scandal of corruption that reshaped its national traditions: Egypt had long taken children of Kushite nobility and raised them according to Egyptian customs, especially Egyptian religious beliefs, hoping to make the kingdom of Kush a friendly ally. The children were treated like nobility, and they did indeed return home as practitioners of Egyptian religion when they were adults. As a result, when Egypt fell apart in the ninth century B.C.E., the kings and queens of Kush regarded themselves as the saviors of the Egyptian way of life and eventually invaded Egypt, founding the Twenty-fifth Dynasty of Egypt (770–657 B.C.E.).

At that time Napata was the capital of Kush. Jebel Barkal was a sacred hill or bluff on the other side of the Nile from

Napata, where a great religious complex had been built. The chief temple was dedicated to Egypt's chief god, Amun, who was also at that time Kush's chief god. The queens of Kush would go into the depths of the temple of Amun to give birth, implying that Amun was the father of their children, linking themselves with a tradition of Egyptian religion that Amun recognized his children in their wombs. An oracle also resided in the temple. A statue of Amun spoke to people, telling them the god's will. Priests conveyed Amun's words to the outside world. Thus, the priests had great power. Their temples and dwellings at Jebel Barkal were covered in gold, silver, and gems. Hallways were dazzling with their glittering walls and many statues of Egyptian gods. The statue of Amun even foretold when kings were to die. In fact, the priests actually ordered a king to commit suicide, on Amun's orders, and he obeyed.

Then came King Aspelta (r. 593–568 B.C.E.). The outset of his reign must have been very challenging because a revitalized Egypt had sent an army into Kush, and it had sacked Napata in about 593 B.C.E. Then the priests of Amun declared that the god had said Aspelta was to die. Perhaps not as gullible as his predecessors, or perhaps not as faithful, Aspelta not only refused to commit suicide but also conspired with one of his generals to have the buildings and caves of Jebel Barkal seized and the priests killed. Apparently, nearly every priest was killed, helping to end the importance of Jebel Barkal. Perhaps the invasion by Egypt had soured public sentiment against all things Egyptian enough for Aspelta to get away with such sacrilege. He moved his court to Meroë, farther south along the Nile, formerly an Egyptian military outpost but by then a thriving trading center. He and his successors promoted a lion god as their new chief god.

EGYPT

BY AMR KAMEL

Ancient Egypt, like any other place ancient or modern, was not an ideal society. People who engaged in bribery and all manner of crime and corruption existed alongside people who were humble, law-abiding, and religious. The Egyptians attempted to hold their society together using a group of fundamental principles called *maat*, which eventually came to represent the cosmic order as well, since Egyptians believed their land to be the center of the world. Maintaining *maat* was the major duty of Egyptian kings, and it was the subject of many ancient Egyptian teachings. Any abuse of power by an official could be controlled only if there was ethical awareness and a sense of loyalty in the community. When these faltered, officials increasingly took advantage of their positions, especially when the purchase of offices and the abuse of oracles were concerned. These abuses become apparent notably from the Nineteenth Dynasty (ca. 1307–ca. 1196 B.C.E.) forward.

Desiring reform, Horemheb, the last king of the Eighteenth Dynasty (ca. 1550–ca. 1307 B.C.E.), conscientiously enforced *maat*, issuing a royal decree against bribery and corruption that can still be read on the 10th pylon at Karnak. In the decree Horemheb states that corrupt behavior on the part of the authorities represents an offense and warns that these offenses "from today onward" will be punished by such penalties as flogging and cutting off of noses and, in some cases, will require the redress of any damage inflicted on an individual. He advises his newly appointed officers: "Do not compromise yourselves with people! Do not accept rewards from others!"

Nonetheless, such instructions did not guarantee a peaceful life. Ancient Egyptian literature refers from time to time to scandals, corrupt people, and other illegal behavior. The earliest example was mentioned in the biography of Weni, an important Sixth Dynasty (ca. 2323–ca. 2150 B.C.E.) officer. There appears to have been an unsuccessful conspiracy against Pepi I plotted by one of his numerous wives. Weni seems to have been singled out to hear about that confidential matter when he was in the royal women's quarters. From the same Sixth Dynasty period, a scene in the Saqqara mustaba of the vizier Khentika depicts the judgment and corporal punishment of five district governors brought before the vizier and charged with corruption in collecting taxes. All were punished swiftly and harshly.

Egyptian texts do not mention other cases of immoral behavior until late in the New Kingdom, when abundant evidence of corruption appears, possibly because of a deficiency in the administration. The inscription of Mes, engraved in his tomb at Saqqara from the Nineteenth Dynasty, describes a lawsuit about the ownership of some fields inherited by various members of the family to which Mes belonged. The text refers to a certain Khay, who originally was not a family member but who claimed his right based on forged documents that he submitted to the highest law court in Egypt, presided over by the vizier who pronounced his judgment in favor of Khay.

A literary document dating from the late Nineteenth Dynasty describes the career of a corrupt man named Paneb—the foreman of a group of workers at Deir el-Medina—who, with his son Aapehti, committed several crimes. Paneb is accused of having obtained his position by bribing the vizier. Paneb stole some statues from the temple of King Seti I, with the intention of decorating his own tomb. He then went on to murder his adoptive father, Neferhotep. He was arrested and sent for trial before the vizier Amenope. Nonetheless, by the exercise of some influence or chicanery, he was able to secure his acquittal and not only obtained the murdered Neferhotep's position but also eventually had himself buried in a handsome tomb. He and his son made love with five of his colleagues' wives and their daughters. He was also accused failing to pay for clothes that had been made for him and of drunkenness.

In the reign of Ramses III legal documents describe a trial of persons who planned the murder of the king. The principal defendant was the secondary queen Tiy, who apparently wanted the throne for her son Pentewere. The jury was composed of 14 officials, four of whom were convicted of having sexual intercourse with the wives of some of the defendants and were accordingly deprived of their titles and punished with mutilation. In year 17 of the reign of Ramses III a gang was being shortchanged by a greedy official who used undersized measures to distribute rations and then presumably kept the difference for himself. The matter was brought to the attention of Akh-pet, another scribe of the vizier, who checked the grain measure and found that it held 38 *hin* instead of the standard 40 (ca. one-half bushel). Thus the workmen had been receiving 5 percent less than their due.

The famous Tomb Robbery Papyri also describe the looting of graves and temples during the reigns of Ramses IX and XI, sometimes with the complicity of officials who took bribes to keep silent and release those who were under arrest. Another mid-Twentieth Dynasty (1196–1070 B.C.E.) papyrus records charges of large-scale embezzlement and misconduct against personnel of the temple of Khnum at Elephantine, including an unnamed priest. Another papyrus describes the crimes of a certain Djehutihotep, the chief guard of the Karnak temple. Since this was arguably the most sacred public place in Egypt, his crimes provide evidence of the extent of negligence and corruption at the highest levels of the Theban administration.

In the prayers of ordinary Egyptians, preserved in letters and documents from the village housing the workers at Deir el-Medina, there are pleas to the gods for justice after all other doors were closed to them, pleas to hear their petitions, and pleas to ease their suffering from the rapidly increasing corruption in their society. In one prayer, Amun is "the vizier of the poor; he does not accept bribes from the guilty, he does not speak to the one who witnesses, he does not look to (favor) the one who makes promises." In another source, a lady invokes Amun to protect her from gossip and rumors. Although these documents portray the dark side of ancient Egyptian society, there were nonetheless ordinary good people who attempted to bring up their offspring with ethics and good principles.

THE MIDDLE EAST

BY HEATHER D. BAKER

In Mesopotamia political power was concentrated in the hands of the ruler. The surviving sources for the exercise of royal power therefore have to be treated with caution because they almost always originate with the king and his court; independent testimony is rare indeed. The written documentation available about political scandal at the highest level tends to concern episodes when the transition from one ruler to the next was contested or when a king saw fit to condemn the actions of his predecessor or both. In such cases as these the king whose account survives may have been motivated by a desire to enhance his own reputation at the expense of a previous ruler by seeking to question the legitimacy of his reign or his actions while in office.

The circumstances surrounding the death of the Assyrian king Sennacherib (704–681 B.C.E.) reflect one such instance of a troubled succession from one ruler to the next. Many details of what happened are still unclear, because the cuneiform sources are fragmentary and difficult to interpret. Still, it is clear that there was a plot to murder Sennacherib, who had taken the unusual step of naming his younger son, Esarhaddon, as his successor. Esarhaddon's case may well have been promoted by his mother, Naqia, a powerful woman well versed in palace intrigue. Following the death of his father, while Esarhaddon was in hiding for safety, his older brothers fought among themselves for the throne, but on his return Esarhaddon defeated them in battle. He took the throne and ruled for 11 years (680–669 B.C.E.).

Another political scandal, of a rather curious nature, involves the Babylonian king Nabonidus (r. 556–539 B.C.E.), who left his country to live in apparently self-imposed exile in Taymā' (in Saudi Arabia) for 10 years. Although he went to Arabia in the role of military conqueror, this does not explain why he remained there for so many years, leaving his son Belshazzar to rule in Babylonia in his stead. A conventional view holds that the Babylonian priesthood opposed his unorthodox religious beliefs, especially his attempts to promote the moon god Sin at the expense of the head of the Babylonian pantheon, Marduk. Nabonidus's own inscriptions hint at such a background to these events. His successor, Cyrus the Great, the Persian conqueror of Babylonia, certainly portrayed Nabonidus as an oppressive ruler who did not worship Marduk. Cyrus claimed to have been chosen by Marduk and to have restored Babylonian religious life to the peaceful state it had enjoyed before Nabonidus disrupted it.

A more informal insight into the affairs of state can be found in the correspondence kept in the royal archives. Of course, it has to be borne in mind that letters written to the king were intended to promote the cause of the sender by casting him in a favorable light, sometimes at the expense of his rivals. Sometimes the letters contain reports of alleged injustice; one scholar, for instance, writes to the king complaining that a local governor had taken away a field of his. It seems to be expected that the king will intervene personally in cases such as this where officials abused their power.

The sources for information about economic scandal and corruption are of a rather different nature. Some of the Laws of Hammurabi are concerned with the misappropriation of property, both private and institutional, and with fraud. They include, for example, the case of a (female) innkeeper who gives out short measures of beer. They also set out regulations governing the conduct of trading ventures so as to protect the merchants from fraud.

The great palace and temple institutions of the ancient Near East were extremely bureaucratic, and much effort was expended on controlling and recording the movement of goods between different establishments and their responsible officials. Precious items could be stored in sealed containers or rooms. Sealing was the ancient equivalent of a locking mechanism. The official in charge would impress his seal upon a lump of clay applied to the door bolt. When the room needed to be opened, the sealing would be broken

Stone panel from the palace of Sennacherib, Nineveh, northern Iraq, Neo-Assyrian, about 700–695 B.C.E.; this panel shows soldiers of the royal guard; the king's death was thought to have been the result of a plot within the palace to murder him. (© The Trustees of the British Museum)

in front of witnesses. In this way it would be immediately clear if someone had gained unauthorized access. Livestock could be branded in such a way that marked them as temple property, and even the temple dependents who formed part of its workforce could be marked to make it difficult for them to escape.

Thus the institutional administration contained inbuilt deterrents against fraud and theft, but they could not be entirely eliminated. Normally it is difficult to extract information on these subjects from the cuneiform tablets that made up the institutional archives. To shed light on them, documents that tell a story rather than simply recording the transfer of commodities are needed. In records of accounts there are many cases where the figures do not add up, but it is impossible to prove that these represent a deliberate attempt to defraud rather than simply errors on the part of the scribe.

Suitable sources include records of lawsuits and letters containing anecdotal evidence of corruption. Fortunately, some of the surviving archives contain material of this kind. The Eanna temple archive from Neo-Babylonian Uruk is one; it contains many documents recording cases brought before the temple authorities. Most involve relatively minor episodes of theft and embezzlement. There was one particularly persistent offender, a man named Gimillu. His career is documented over a period of around 20 years; at first he was in charge of the livestock owed to the temple, and later he was responsible for the income from the temple's agricultural land. Gimillu misappropriated temple property on a large scale; even after being convicted and fined heavily and then trying to abscond, he continued to work for the temple in a responsible position. There does seem to have been a high degree of tolerance toward convicted thieves and fraudsters. From the private sphere in the Neo-Babylonian Period (625–539 B.C.E.) there is a court record concerning attempted extortion by a man who tried to pass off a forged cuneiform tablet. When challenged by the intended victim, he snatched the clay tablet from his victim's hands and tried to destroy it by chewing it. Other records reveal that even though he was found guilty, the villain continued to conduct business. The scribe who wrote the fake tablet was also liable to be punished when caught.

ASIA AND THE PACIFIC

BY KIRK H. BEETZ

Although Confucius (551–479 B.C.E.) believed that China had an ancient past that featured good and just governments, it seems that no ancient Chinese government at any time was free of corruption. Written records for the Shang (1500–1045 B.C.E.) and early Zhou (1045–256 B.C.E.) dynasties are scant, but those that exist suggest that corruption among military leaders and government officials was constant throughout the history of ancient China. One corrupt practice involved the trading of women by powerful men. During the Six Dynasties (220–589 C.E.) women were used as bribes, and if the bribes persuaded generals to switch sides during a war, the fates of millions of people changed based on a man's lust for women. Many military leaders were not susceptible to being bribed with women but could be bribed with gifts of horses or money. Thus, the corruption of some Chinese leaders reduced women to the level of horses, and for the sake of their bribes they betrayed their province or country, their lord or king, and broke their oaths of loyalty. Sometimes tens of thousands of people died when the man who was supposed to protect them changed sides for a bribe and killed them.

Many historians consider the era of Confucius to have been notably corrupt. Most of the people of China were peasants who were forced to work every day in their fields. From the Zhou Dynasty through the end of the ancient era kings occasionally tried to redistribute land to peasants, but members of the nobility would confiscate land or loan peasants money at interest rates that were impossible to repay. They would then take the peasants' lands and force the former owners to work the lands for the profit of the nobles, making the peasants slaves in all but name.

A government that had intended to end corruption became one of the most corrupt of all. This was the government of the Qin Dynasty (221–207 B.C.E.), which imposed the legalist philosophy of government. Under legalism, every action was either sanctioned or forbidden by law. The idea was to regulate life so that everybody did what they were supposed to do and never did what they were not supposed to do. The laws were so strict and so numerous that people could not help but break a few every day, and punishments were harsh. Even slight offenses could result in a sentence of mutilation and several years of hard labor on the government's construction projects. Emperor Qin Shi Huangdi used the laws to force hundreds of thousands of people to work on the Great Wall and elsewhere, where many died from the harsh conditions.

When the emperor died, his advisers Li Si (ca. 280–208 B.C.E.) and Han Fei Zi (d. 233 B.C.E.) pretended that he was still alive and sent his eldest son a phony message ordering him to commit suicide. Prince Fusu ignored the pleadings of his father's chief general to make sure the order was real before he killed himself, but he committed suicide anyway. Prince Huhai became emperor, controlled by Li Si and Han Fei Zi. The corruption of this period was so severe that the Qin Dynasty was already crumbling when rebels toppled it.

During the Han Dynasty (202 B.C.E.–220 C.E.), Confucian scholars were allowed to try to impose a more benevolent form of government. It proved impossible to stamp out bribery, especially in remote provinces. The court system was corrupted by wealthy criminals who paid poor people to serve their sentences for them. In cities young people sometimes formed gangs and beat, killed, and robbed people. The government tried to eliminate the gangs with diligent police work and informants, but the police were too often bribed. Tax collectors frequently took more than the law allowed and kept it for themselves. The punishment for this practice was death, but it was common enough to help inspire a peasant revolt in 14 C.E.

Throughout the recorded history of India corruption was a problem. Indian literature, folktales, and historical writings from about the first century C.E. onward feature many tales of corrupt practices, and historians have found accounts in records from as early as the 300s C.E. In the court system witnesses often slanted their testimony in court to favor whichever side was paying them. This meant that innocent people were often convicted and punished for crimes. To make matters worse, the convicted criminal's spouse and children were imprisoned as well. They all were bound by the ankles amid filth and beaten and tortured two or three times a day.

Gambling and prostitution were common. Gambling was forbidden by Hindu religious rules of conduct, but it was usually sanctioned and regulated by the government. Gamblers often lost their family's fortune, forcing them to become slaves or to spend their lives trying to pay their debts. Sometimes a gambler made a fortune, which was known as "black" money, as opposed to money earned honestly through government service or a trade.

Prostitutes almost always associated with such criminals as con artists, burglars, and extortionists, so the government often used them as spies on criminals. A prostitute could earn a good name this way because she worked for the secret police, making her work in the public interest. Prostitutes varied from sickly streetwalkers just trying to earn enough for food to women who were well trained from childhood to seduce rich men. The latter group were well educated, had excellent taste, knew what to say on every occasion, and were gifted in all the various sexual acts that would ensnare men. The education of prostitutes was regulated by the national government, and their teachers were often paid by the government because the work of prostitutes was considered a contributing factor in the health of the nation. When beginning their careers in brothels, they were taught to be without pity; their object was to seduce men, discard them, and move on to the next rich man. Occasionally a prostitute became a man's wife, and typically she worked extra hard to be a good wife.

Sex scandals sometimes shaped India's history. For example, there is the legendary account of Amrapali, a famous courtesan in the Licchavi Republic in northern India around 400 B.C.E. She was so successful that she had become the land's leading lady. King Bimbisāra of Magadha, an enemy of the Licchavis, sneaked into their capital of Vaisali and spent a week undetected enjoying the company of Amrapali. Their pride injured, the knights of Licchavi attacked Magadha with great vigor and sparked a war that Magadha won, which helped to propel Magadha toward building an empire that eventually ruled most of India.

Perhaps equally scandalous was the death of Bimbisāra, who was starved by his son Ajatashatru (fl. 300s B.C.E.). This seems to have been common among the monarchs of ancient India. The king was alleged to have chosen to starve himself to death, but usually a scheming son was responsible. When Ajatashatru's old enemy Prasenajit, king of Koshala, was overthrown in his turn by his son, Prasenajit fled to Ajatashatru and then died of exhaustion. This gave Ajatashatru an excuse to avenge Prasenajit, and he attacked Koshala, ending its existence.

Very little is known of scandals and corruption in ancient Japan, but there are hints from Chinese observers. One such was an ambassador, Zhang Zheng, to Queen Himiko's court in the 200s B.C.E. Himiko lived to a great age but apparently died without a successor. Her kingdom was called Yamatai and was composed of about 50 states, each with its own chief. After her death the chiefs selected a man to replace her. According to Zhang Zheng, the king's rule was marred by constant murders and inept government administration. Zhang Zheng claims that after two years he helped engineer the ouster of the king and his replacement by a 12-year-old girl whose name may have been Inoye.

The rest of Asia and the Pacific's cultures probably had their own forms of corruption and scandal, but archaeologists and historians are making slow progress in uncovering evidence for such practices in central Asia, Southeast Asia,

Korea, Australia, and the Pacific Islands, with most records appearing as inscriptions on public monuments such as megaliths and temples—places where the people who erected them were unlikely to confess their misdeeds.

EUROPE

BY BRADLEY SKEEN

The peoples of Europe living outside the Greek and Roman worlds in a region that scholars often call temperate Europe did not leave behind any significant written records. What is known about their public affairs, including what they considered scandalous, comes only from Roman historians. Of these historians, Tacitus (56–117 C.E.) is the most important. Although he wrote during the Pax Romana, the height of the Roman Empire's power and prosperity, he was deeply dissatisfied with the political and social life of the empire. Much of his criticism is indirect, made in connection with Roman policies in temperate Europe. He denounces the decadent and politically and morally ineffectual life of Roman aristocrats by implicitly contrasting that life with his exaggerated account of the virtues of the Germans in his *Germania* (Germany), a work devoted to the national character of the Germanic peoples. In his *Annales* Tacitus openly criticizes the cruelty deemed necessary for maintaining imperial power in his famous aphorism, "They make a deserted land and call it peace!" referring to the Romans' tactic of slaughtering civilians and warriors alike in their campaigns in Europe.

Along with his praise of the Germans, Tacitus regularly describes German kings and chiefs as betraying the cause of German nationalism, which he considers they should have taken up in order to resist the decadent influence of Rome. He presents the local leaders as bribed and bullied by Roman officials and at the same time greedy for Roman luxuries. He sees these weaknesses on the part of German leaders as scandalous. Tacitus develops the scandalous weakness of German leaders as a literary theme to be used in the criticism of his own culture. What he writes cannot be accepted at face value as objective fact or even as a representation of how things might have seemed to the Germans themselves. He never considers alternative interpretations: for example, that the people outside the Roman Empire might have wanted the peace and prosperity that existed inside the empire in order to make their lives better lives. This very desire was certainly present in temperate Europe, as is seen from the works of a later Roman historian, Ammianus Marcellinus (ca. 325–391 C.E.). Ammianus makes it clear that when the German tribes invaded the Roman Empire beginning in the fourth century C.E. (eventually leading to the collapse of the Western Roman Empire), their initial goal was simply to be allowed to live inside the empire to gain protection from Huns and other tribes pressuring them from the East.

Julius Caesar (100–44 B.C.E.), in his account of his conquest of Gaul, establishes the stereotype of the tribal peoples of temperate Europe when he writes that they possess some kind of innate virtue—characterized as manliness—because they live simple lives devoted to subsistence agriculture and warfare. This way of life could be corrupted through luxury by contact with Roman civilization into a morally inferior condition characterized as effeminacy. Tacitus takes up this theme. He treats as a social scandal the fact that the virtuous barbarian Germans should become corrupted like the effeminate civilized Romans, treating both Germans and Romans as stereotypes. For example, while the simple German people in the interior knew nothing of gold and silver, those living along the borders of the Roman Empire had been corrupted by the greed and luxury associated with these metals in the so-called civilized world, and this he considers scandalous.

Similarly Tacitus admires the Germans' idea of the sanctity of marriage, making a contrast with the adultery that he finds distasteful in his own society. On the other hand, Tacitus considers the Germans' love of gambling scandalous. He says that it is not uncommon for a German to become a slave by gambling away his own freedom after he has lost all his possessions. There is no way to verify this, but given the criticism of the Roman love of gambling by contemporary Roman authors, this was probably meant to make the Roman reader think of his own culture. Tacitus seems to move into fantasy at the end of the *Germania*, where he claims that the Germans farthest removed from the Roman world are even worse than Romans and are actually ruled by women, a condition that he says is worse than slavery. This must be a reference to the vast influence and great freedom of aristocratic Roman women in Tacitus's own society and not necessarily a true statement about ancient Europe.

Tacitus lived during an era in which the imperial government had curtailed the political power and even the property and freedom of his own senatorial class. Therefore he considered the greatest good for humanity to be freedom, the very thing that he and those like him had lost. Accordingly, he considered the greatest scandal among the Germans to be their trading of freedom to the Roman government for what

Base-silver radiate of Carausius, with the emperors Diocletian and Maximian, Roman Britain, late third century C.E.; in the years 287–296 C.E. Britain had its own emperor, Carausius, who had been accused of corruption and assumed power to save himself from punishment.

he thought to be luxury, which he considered trivial, since he and his class had it in abundance.

The last great chance for German freedom came with Armin (18? B.C.E–19 C.E.). He was a chief of the German tribe of the Cherusci and served in the Roman army as an auxiliary. He became an important Roman ally and was given the wealth and status of a Roman knight, the second-highest position in Roman society. But he rejected all of this to turn on his Roman overlords and used his position to destroy the Roman army occupying Germany by ambushing them in the Teutoburg Forest (near modern Bremen). He fought other successful campaigns against the Romans also, until they abandoned all hope of conquering Germany as a province. According to Tacitus, Arminius boasted of fighting for the freedom of the German nation rather than for his own fame and power.

Tacitus contrasts Armin with Armin's father-in-law, Segestes, another German prince, who remained loyal to the Romans, claiming that this loyalty was in the Germans' interest since it brought peace and prosperity, if not freedom. Tacitus defames Segestes by pointing out that, acting as a coward, he handed over Armin's wife and son—his own daughter and grandson—to the Romans as hostages. Tacitus also relates how Armin fought against other German chieftains who were attempting to establish a united monarchy over all of Germany for the purpose of becoming a satellite of the Roman Empire and how still others offered to assassinate Armin out of servility to the Romans. Finally, Tacitus gives an account of Armin's death in a battle with other Germans who opposed his plans to become king of a free Germany.

While much of Tacitus's information may be factually correct, his interpretation of those facts served his purpose of criticizing his own culture. His writing tells more about what he considered scandalous in Rome than how the Germans themselves thought about the excesses of their political leaders.

GREECE

BY PAUL MCKECHNIE

The national myth of Greece began with scandal—namely, the corruption behind the Trojan War. Three goddesses, quarrelling over an apple labeled "for the prettiest" that Eris, goddess of discord, had rolled into a party where she was not invited, decided to parade for a beauty contest. Zeus wisely refused to judge, and Hera, Athena, and Aphrodite were forced to select a mortal judge. They chose Troy's king Priam's son Paris, a foolish young man who was alone in the hills keeping his father's flocks.

When they appeared before him, each goddess proposed a bribe. Hera offered to make Paris a great king, Athena promised to make him a celebrated hero, and Aphrodite, goddess of love, pledged to reward him with the most beautiful woman in the world as his wife. Paris accepted the last offer and judged in Aphrodite's favor. The most beautiful woman in the world, Helen, however, was already married to Menelaus, king of Sparta. When Paris visited Sparta on his father's business, Menelaus was out of town; Paris, captivated by Helen, whispered, "Run away with me," in her ear, and she did not hesitate.

Homer's *Iliad*, written in (probably) the eighth century B.C.E., is the tale of the 10-year war fought by Menelaus, his brother Agamemnon, and their Greek army against Troy to get Helen back. There, the personal is the political with no dividing line between politics and war. But Hesiod, another Greek poet, perhaps after 700 B.C.E., refers to a more recognizably "political" scandal in *Works and Days*, his long poem about how to succeed as a farmer. He and his brother, Perses, were supposed to divide the land that their father left them, but (Hesiod claims) Perses took it all—and Hesiod's court case against him went nowhere because of the "bribe-devouring *basileis*" judging it. They expect presents from both sides, he says, but giving a present is no guarantee of a favorable result—though failing to give a present guarantees that you will lose. Reading *Works and Days*, we can hear only Hesiod's side of the story. If Perses could give us his version, we might look at the matter differently.

In his *Histories* the Greek historian Herodotus of the fifth century B.C.E. wrote about many stories of bribery and corruption, both successful and unsuccessful. He insists that the Alcmaeonidae, a noble Athenian family exiled from their home, caused the Spartans to march to Athens in 510 B.C.E. and expel Peisistratus, an Athenian tyrant. The Alcmaeonidae accomplished this by bribing the priestess of Delphi to give oracular answers to the Spartans in which the supposed voice of the god advised them to liberate Athens. The Delphic oracle was so deeply respected that any advice it gave had a good chance of being accepted: It was a matter (the Alcmaeonidae found) of ensuring that the right advice was dispensed.

Less successfully, in 499 B.C.E. Aristagoras of Miletus went to the Spartan king Cleomenes (r. ca. 521–490 B.C.E.) and tried to talk him into supporting the Ionians in their revolt against Darius I (r. 522–486 B.C.E.), king of Persia and their overlord. He showed Cleomenes a map and explained the campaign to him, but foolishly admitted that he was asking the Spartans to travel three months' march away from the sea. Cleomenes told him that this was an unrealistic request; but Aristagoras came back and tried to change his mind with cash, eventually offering 50 talents, which would have been a large sum of money. According to Herodotus, when Cleomenes hesitated, his eight-year-old daughter, Gorgo, said, "Get up and go, father, or the stranger will certainly corrupt you." He took her advice, and the Ionians had to fight without Spartan help.

In other scandalous stories, Herodotus links the political with the personal. Periander, tyrant of Corinth from 627 to 586 B.C.E., once lost something he had borrowed. Hoping to find it, he sent to the oracle of the dead in Thesprotia to ask the ghost of his wife, Melissa, where it was. The ghost told Periander's messengers that she refused to answer because she was cold—clothes had been buried with her at her funeral but not burned. (The idea seems to be that unless they were burned, the clothes could not go to the world of the dead.) The ghost added that Periander would know that she was really Melissa because he had put his loaves in a cold oven. When he heard this, Periander remembered that he had had sex with Melissa's corpse after she was dead. He announced to all the women of Corinth that they should come to the temple of the goddess Hera. They dressed as if it were a festival and turned out, but then Periander's guards stripped them naked, and all their clothes were heaped in a pit and burned. Afterward, Melissa's ghost revealed the information Periander wanted. In Book 5 of Herodotus's *History*, Socles, a Corinthian, tells this story and concludes by saying, "This, then, is the nature of tyranny, and such are its deeds." Corrupt governments treat people the way Periander treated the women of Corinth.

At Athens under the democratic government of the fifth and fourth centuries B.C.E. officials had to report to the boule, or legislative council, at the end of their year in office and have their accounts examined. In general, transparency was expected, but the Greek biographer Plutarch (ca. 46–after 119 C.E.), in his *Life of Pericles*, records how in the early 440s B.C.E. the Athenian statesman Pericles bribed King Pleistoanax (r. 459–409 B.C.E.) of Sparta and his assistant Cleandridas to lead their Spartan army home instead of fighting. When Pericles presented his accounts for the campaign, he listed 10 talents mysteriously as "necessary expenses," and the council passed the accounts without inquiring closely.

In the fourth century B.C.E. the growing power of Macedon placed a strain on Athenian standards of conduct. Demosthenes (384–322 B.C.E.), the leading anti-Macedonian politician at Athens, prosecuted Aeschines in 343 B.C.E. over events in 347 B.C.E., when Aeschines had been part of an embassy sent to King Philip II (r. 359–336 B.C.E.) to administer oaths confirming a peace treaty. Philip cunningly made important gains between when the peace was agreed and when oaths were taken. Demosthenes alleged in his speech "On the False Embassy," in effect, that Aeschines (and other ambassadors) had been bribed to be complicit. Aeschines delivered a counter oration, and the jury acquitted him by a narrow majority. But in 324 B.C.E., when Alexander the Great's treasurer, Harpalus, had run away with 5,000 talents of Alexander's money and come to Athens for protection, Demosthenes was accused by the Athenian orator Hypereides (ca. 390–322 B.C.E.) in his speech "Against Demosthenes" of accepting a 20-talent bribe from Harpalus: Demosthenes was found guilty.

ROME

BY KIRK H. BEETZ

When looking at the great depravity of some Romans, it is worth remembering that Rome did not survive as a culture for over a thousand years because of fools such as Nero (r. 54–68 C.E.); it survived because for hundreds of years it had midlevel civil servants who were dedicated to the welfare of their nation. A multitude of hardworking government employees kept the empire running in spite of the greed, lust, and cruelty of some of its leaders.

The Roman Republic began with a scandal, the rape of Lucretia by Sextus, the son of King Tarquinius Superbus (r. 535–510 B.C.E.). At the time, the Roman army was laying siege to the city of Ardea, and as a game some Roman officers decided they would discover whose wives were the more faithful by paying them a surprise visit in Rome. Of all the wives only Lucretia was doing exactly what she told her husband she had been doing in her letters to him. The officers returned to the siege, but Sextus remained behind and forced himself on Lucretia, who wrote to her husband to tell him. Her husband, Lucius Tarquinius Collatinus, and some of his friends rushed back to Rome where Lucretia explained what had happened, then killed herself. This triggered the rebellion that threw King Tarquinius Superbus out of Rome and began the Roman Republic.

During the centuries after the founding of the Republic, the upper class of Rome, the patricians, who controlled the Senate and were expected to take leadership roles in government, worked hard to maintain their elite status. In the process, some of them engaged in extreme corruption. Magistrates of Italian cities and governors of provinces looted the public treasury. They stole taxes and property and sold free families into slavery for profit. This rapacious corruption reached its peak during the dictatorship of Lucius Cornelius Sulla (r. 81–79 B.C.E.). He was a Roman general who committed a grave breach of public trust by invading the city of Rome with his army.

Sulla had his political opponents murdered and then went on to murder anyone he disliked. He tried to undo reforms that had given power to common people. Among his laws was one that allowed only juries of senators to hear cases of senators accused of crimes. Senators found they could get away with murder, literally, because their fellow senators on the juries were easy to bribe. Among those who profited illegally was the governor of Sicily, Gaius Verres. He and his henchmen stole almost everything that could be moved. It took almost 10 years to bring the Roman legal system back to a condition where a rich criminal such as Verres could be brought to justice. The lawyer and orator Cicero prosecuted him and used the forum of the court to describe the corruption that had infected the Roman government.

The First Triumvirate (r. 60–53 B.C.E.)—Marcus Licinius Crassus, Gnaeus Pompeius Magnus (Pompey), and Gaius Julius Caesar—was formed in part as a way of ending corruption and conflict in government. Crassus died in an eastern military campaign, and Pompey was closely associated with Sulla and some of the corrupt officials who had profited from Sulla's laws. This left Julius Caesar the only leader common people looked to for help. Caesar became dictator in 49 B.C.E. Although he was a tough and sometimes brutal military

THE VILE VERRES

Gaius Verres (ca. 120–43 B.C.E.) belonged to Rome's social elite. He was a political opportunist who supported whatever person had power, first the reformer Gaius Marius and then Marius's enemy Lucius Cornelius Sulla when Sulla invaded the city of Rome. Already Verres was accused of embezzlement, but Sulla protected him. Verres became an assistant to the corrupt governor of Cilicia, Gnaeus Cornelius Dolabella, in 80 B.C.E. In 78 B.C.E. Dolabella was tried and convicted of numerous crimes, but Verres won a pardon for himself, despite having been Dolabella's partner in the crimes, by testifying against Dolabella. He became a government official in the city of Rome, where he used his office to promote the interests of Sulla, who appointed him governor of Sicily in about 73 B.C.E.

During Verres's time in Sicily he made himself not only one of the most corrupt but also one of the most loathed people in Roman history. He organized his administration like a gang of criminals, and there was no limit to his greed and cruelty. He and his henchmen stripped Sicily's temples of their art, especially their statues. Using government authority his gangs broke into private homes and looted them of everything that was valuable. The loss to Sicily was greater than the loss it had experienced in war. Its once-thriving tourist industry collapsed. When people protested, Verres accused them of being traitors and prevented their cases from being sent on to the city of Rome, which was their right under Roman law. He had them tortured and then crucified.

When Verres returned to the city of Rome in 70 B.C.E., Sicilians asked Cicero to prosecute him for his crimes. Cicero chose to use Verres as an example of corruption throughout government, detailing how Verres used his status as a high government official to brutalize and murder hundreds, perhaps thousands, of people. The lawyers for Verres tried to delay the trial, but Cicero pressed forward. In court he delivered a devastating case, and Verres fled into exile even before he was found guilty. In the south of Gaul he led a comfortable life, having kept much of the wealth he had stolen, until Marcus Antonius had him killed in 43 B.C.E.

leader, he tried to rule with compassion, pardoning many of his enemies. Some of these pardoned enemies murdered him in 44 B.C.E. Among the murderers was Cassius Longinus, who became a symbol of cruel selfishness. During his war against Marcus Antonius and Octavian, he sold four Judaean towns and many Judaean officials into slavery to finance his army, and he looted Rome's ally Rhodes of almost all its wealth.

Octavian, renamed the emperor Augustus, ruled Rome from 27 B.C.E. to 14 C.E. Augustus's successor, Tiberius (r. 14–37 C.E.), was an outstanding general with a sober temperament. Yet his sober temperament became very dark. He neglected his civic duties and eventually retreated to the island of Capri in 26 C.E., where he indulged in a taste for sex with children. His absence from Rome allowed the leader of the Praetorian Guard, Lucius Aelius Sejanus, to take over much of the Roman government. Sejanus was greedy and ruthless, using the charge of treason as an excuse for murdering anyone who seemed to be between him and something he wanted. Tiberius was told by his sister-in-law Antonia about Sejanus's corruption, and Sejanus and his supporters were executed.

For sheer depravity historians tend to single out two Roman emperors, Caligula (r. 37–41 C.E.) and Nero (r. 54–68 C.E.). Both started out with a great deal of public goodwill. Nero, in particular, had experienced and talented advisers to help him. But Caligula seems to have been criminally insane. His behavior was bizarre, violent, and cruel. He had sex with all three of his sisters, raped a bride on her wedding day, and tortured people. His public acts were weird; he even nominated a horse, Incitatus, for a consulship. He was murdered and quickly replaced by Claudius (r. 41–54 C.E.). The greatest scandal of Claudius's reign was the marriage of his wife, Messalina, to consul-designate Silius while Claudius was away. She and Silius were executed. Claudius himself may have been poisoned by his last wife, Agrippina the Younger, apparently in the hope that she would rule through her son Nero, who instead had her murdered.

Nero castrated a boy and then married him. He fancied himself a singer and stage actor and forced people to watch him for hours as he performed. Pregnant women gave birth in the audience because they were not permitted to leave. After most of Rome went up in flames, Nero began the construction of a large and very expensive palace in Rome, and rumors circulated that he had started the fire and sang and danced while it burned. This story seems to have been untrue; Nero actually seems to have tried to put out the fire. To direct blame away from himself, he blamed the Christians. He took delight in torturing them and had many tied to stakes and ignited to serve as torches during celebrations at his palace or in the amphitheater. Eventually, when Nero was away from Rome, the Senate sentenced him to death, and he committed suicide.

During the 200s and 300s C.E. corruption was most often found in the collection of taxes. Wealthy men would buy a high public office in a province and then divert government funds into their own pockets. Courts were subject to bribery, and serving on juries and taking bribes proved to be very profitable. Emperors tried to put a stop to the corruption of the courts, and Diocletian (r. 284–305 C.E.), in particular, seems to have struck fear into the hearts of many a corrupt court official as well as provincial leaders who were enriching themselves at the public's expense. Even so, even after the general public had lost faith in government leaders, there were still the midlevel public servants, organizing tax collecting, maintaining roads, and seeing to it that the poor received food. After the Western Roman Empire collapsed, these public servants continued to work, serving the Germanic tribes that established kingdoms in Europe and North Africa.

THE AMERICAS

BY KIRK H. BEETZ

When people gather to live in groups, there tends to be scandal, and where they have governments, they tend to have corruption. Still, the nature of scandal and corruption in the ancient Americas north of Mexico is a mystery because there are no written records. In general, written records are the best and often the only way to learn the specifics of scandals and corruption. It is likely that well before 5000 B.C.E. North Americans had diversified enough that what constituted scandal in one tribe did not necessarily constitute scandal in another. For example, in some societies a man could have as many wives as he wished. Scandal would attach to him only if he had more wives than he could support. In another society, however, having more than one wife would in itself be scandalous. The ancient civilizations of South America also left virtually no records related to particular scandals or corruption.

When one looks at Mesoamerican cultures (those ancient societies of Central America and Mexico) that did have written records, another problem appears. Modern people may have very different views of what constitutes scandal or corruption than what might have been held by people living in ancient Mesoamerica. For instance, the torture and slaughter of people in religious rituals would horrify many modern people, but to most Maya torture and execution ennobled victims, turning them into honored offerings to the gods that satisfied the gods' needs for human blood for nourishment and thus staved off disasters the gods could cause if they were hungry. A chink in this confidence might be found in the sacrifice of powerless children. Children without families to protect them were commonly made slaves and sacrificed, mostly because they had no one to protest their murders.

A prominent Mesoamerican center was Teotihuacán, a city in Mexico that was not Mayan but through its military power forced many Maya cities to pay tribute to it. Rumors of scandals probably traveled quickly through the city, because most people lived in apartments that each housed three families and the apartments were tightly packed together in a grid pattern. Any scandal would have passed by word of mouth rapidly in such a place where people had little privacy and could be easily overheard. Of scandals and corruption in Teotihuacán there are few details, though an ever-increasing gap between the prosperity of the ruling elite and the common people probably was viewed as a sign of corruption by some commoners.

In Mayan culture every person was supposed to know his or her place and duty in society. Those who did not have places became slaves. The social contract of the Maya meant that even the *k'uhul ajaw*, or "divine king," had duties that he had to perform or risk losing his mandate to rule. He was expected to speak to the gods on behalf of his people. Members of his family were expected to join him in tormenting themselves with thorns. His wife would pull a rope with thorns through a hole in her tongue. She and others would pierce their ears and tongues to spill their blood, and the king and his first son would pierce their penises and draw their blood, all because the Maya believed that royal blood was the most nourishing blood for the gods. Giddy from blood loss and delirious from taking drugs, the king and his family might cross the divide between physical life and the spirit world and seem to speak directly with supernatural beings. If such communicating with the gods failed to alleviate a natural disaster, for instance, a drought that lasted for a few years, people might believe the king no longer had divine authority.

Knowing this can help one understand how scandalized the ancient Maya probably were by events in the late 300s C.E. In cities such as Tikal and Uaxactún, an increase in trade was generating wealth, but the wealth was going primarily to the nobility; this was creating social instability because commoners no longer perceived their leaders as sharing the risks of Mayan life in the way they were supposed to do. To hang on to their authority, the *ahauob*, or "nobility," tried to enhance their prestige by raiding their neighbors and bringing home goods that could be used for the city as a whole. Most important, they brought home captives for sacrifice, with captured nobles being particularly important because their blood was especially desired by hungry gods. Raiding for people to sacrifice had been a part of Mayan life for centuries, but Chak Toh Ich'ak I, known as King Great Jaguar Paw (fl. 376 C.E.), of Tikal changed the rules of warfare. Instead of trying to capture just enemies, he chose all-out killing; he chose conquest.

His brother Siyah K'ak', known as Smoking Frog, led an army to attack Uaxactún. This was no ordinary raiding party: It was a force drawn from Tikal's many communities; it may have been the largest Mayan army up to that time. One problem the Maya may have had with this event was that the king himself apparently stayed home. For the Maya, there could have been few excuses for this. Thus, his position at home would have been weakened. Meanwhile, Smoking Frog led his forces to victory, capturing the city of Uaxactún and seizing the king of the city. The sacrifice of a king was a special event because a king's blood was sacred and therefore most desired by gods. Kings were occasionally captured in battle, but they ruled their cities as divine monarchs; someone from their line was expected to replace them, perhaps paying tribute to the victors. In the case of Tikal and Uaxactún, Smoking Frog's forces exterminated the nobility and the royal line of Uaxactún, leaving the people of Uaxactún with no one to speak to the gods for them. This would have been reprehensible; it would have been the murder of the spirits of an entire people.

The scandal thereafter became even more intense. Smoking Frog made himself king of Uaxactún, without the divine right to do so. When Great Jaguar Paw died, Smoking Frog put someone of his own choosing on Tikal's throne. This was Nun Yax Ayin, known as Curl Snout, who may have been the son of an as yet unidentified brother of Smoking Frog and Great Jaguar Paw. Although Tikal was supposed to be the preeminent city, it was controlled by Smoking Frog from Uaxactún. These events would have created anxiety among the people of Tikal and the lands Tikal controlled because the world order, which was a divine order, had been twisted and overturned by ambitious leaders. It brought forth a new age of Mayan warfare in which total destruction of a rival society was the object.

See also BORDERS AND FRONTIERS; CHILDREN; CRIME AND PUNISHMENT; DEATH AND BURIAL PRACTICES; EMPIRES AND DYNASTIES; FAMILY; FESTIVALS; FOREIGNERS AND BARBARIANS; GENDER STRUCTURES AND ROLES; GOVERNMENT ORGANIZATION; LAWS AND LEGAL CODES; LITERATURE; MIGRATION AND POPULATION MOVEMENTS; NATURAL DISASTERS; RELIGION AND COSMOLOGY; RESISTANCE AND DISSENT; SACRED SITES; SLAVES AND SLAVERY; SOCIAL COLLAPSE AND ABANDONMENT; SOCIAL ORGANIZATION; TRADE AND EXCHANGE; WAR AND CONQUEST; WEIGHTS AND MEASURES.

Greece

Aeschines, excerpt from "On the Embassy" (343 B.C.E.)

[2.1] I beg you, fellow citizens, to hear me with willing and friendly mind, remembering how great is my peril, and how many the charges against which I have to defend myself; remembering also the arts and devices of my accuser, and the cruelty of the man who, speaking to men who are under oath to give equal hearing to both parties, had the effrontery to urge you not to listen to the voice of the defendant and it was not anger that made him say it; for no man who is lying is angry with the victim of his calumny, nor do men who are speaking the truth try to prevent the defendant from obtaining a hearing; for the prosecution does not find justification in the minds of the hearers until the defendant has had opportunity to plead for himself and has proved unable to refute the charges that have been preferred.

[2.3] But Demosthenes, I think, is not fond of fair argument, nor is that the sort of preparation he has made. No, it is your anger that he is determined to call forth. And he has accused me of receiving bribes—he who would be the last man to make such suspicion credible! For the man who seeks to arouse the anger of his hearers over bribery must himself refrain from such conduct.

[2.4] But, fellow citizens, as I have listened to Demosthenes' accusation, the effect upon my own mind has been this: never have I been so apprehensive as on this day, nor ever more angry than now, nor so exceedingly rejoiced. I was frightened, and am still disturbed, lest some of you form a mistaken judgment of me, beguiled by those antitheses of his, conceived in deliberate malice. And I was indignant—fairly beside myself at the charge, when he accused me of insolence and drunken violence towards a free woman of Olynthus. But I was rejoiced when, as he was dwelling on this charge, you refused to listen to him. This I consider to be the reward that you bestow upon me for a chaste and temperate life.

[2.5] To you I do, indeed, give praise and high esteem for putting your faith in the life of those who are on trial, rather than in the accusations of their enemies; however, I would not myself shrink from defending myself against this charge. For if there is any man among those who are standing outside the bar—and almost the whole city is in the court—or if there is any man of you, the jurors, who is convinced that I have ever perpetrated such an act, not to say towards a free person, but towards any creature, I hold my life as no longer worth the living. And if as my defense proceeds I fail to prove that the accusation is false, and that the man who dared to utter it is an impious slanderer, then, even though it be clear that I am innocent of all the other charges, I declare myself worthy of death. . . .

[2.181] And all the rest of you, toward whom I have conducted myself without offence, in fortune a plain citizen, a decent man like any one of you, and the only man who in the strife of politics has refused to join in conspiracy against you, upon you I call to save me. With all loyalty I have served the city as her ambassador, alone subjected to the clamor of the slanderers, which before now many a man conspicuously brave in war has not had the courage to face; for it is not death that men dread, but a dishonored end. . . .

(continued)

(continues)

[2.183] A word more and I have done. One thing was in my power, fellow citizens: to do you no wrong. But to be free from accusation, that was a thing which depended upon fortune, and fortune cast my lot with a slanderer, a barbarian, who cared not for sacrifices nor libations nor the breaking of bread together; nay, to frighten all who in time to come might oppose him, he has fabricated a false charge against us and come in here. If, therefore, you are willing to save those who have labored together with you for peace and for your security, the common good will find champions in abundance, ready to face danger in your behalf.

[2.184] To endorse my plea I now call Eubulus as a representative of the statesmen and all honorable citizens, and Phocion as a representative of the generals, preeminent also among us all as a man of upright character. From among my friends and associates I call Nausicles, and all the others with whom I have associated and whose pursuits I have shared. My speech is finished. This my body I, and the law, now commit to your hands.

From: Charles Darwin Adams, trans., *Speeches of Aeschines* (Cambridge, Mass.: Harvard University Press, 1919).

Rome

Appian, "The Civil Wars—On the Gracchi" (from Roman History, *before 162* C.E.*)*

Gaius Gracchus, who had made himself popular as a triumvir, stood for the tribuneship. He was the younger brother of Tiberius Gracchus, the originator of the law. He had kept silent concerning the killing of his brother for some time, but as some of the senate treated him disdainfully, he offered himself as a candidate for the tribuneship, and as soon as he was elected to this high office began to intrigue against the senate. He proposed that a monthly distribution of grain should be made to each citizen at the expense of the state. This had not been the custom prior to this. Thus he put himself at the head of the populace at a bound by one stroke of politics, in which he had the assistance of Fulvius Flaccus. Right after this he was elected tribune for the next year also, for in cases where there were not enough candidates the law permitted the people to fill out the list from those in office.

In this way Gaius Gracchus became tribune a second time. After, so to say, buying the plebs, he began to court the *equites*, who hold the rank midway between the senate and the plebs, by another similar stroke of politics. He handed over the courts of justice, which had become distrusted on account of bribery, from the senators to the equites, upbraiding the senators particularly for the recent instances of Aurelius Cotta, Salinator, and, thirdly, Manius Aquilius (the one that conquered Asia), all shameless bribe-takers, who had been set free by the judges, even though envoys sent to denounce them were still present, going about making disgraceful charges against them. The senate was very much ashamed of such things and agreed to the law and the people passed it. Thus the courts of justice were handed over from the senate to the knights. It is reported that soon after the enactment of this law Gracchus made the remark that he had destroyed the supremacy of the senate once for all, and this remark of his has been corroborated by experience throughout the course of history. The privilege of judging all Romans and Italians, even the senators themselves, in all affairs of property, civil rights and exile, raised the *equites* like governors over them, and placed the senators on the same plane as subjects. As the *equites* also voted to support the power of the tribunes in the *comitia* and received whatever they asked from them in return, they became more and more dangerous opponents to the senators. Thus it soon resulted that the supremacy in the state was reversed, the real mastery going into the hands of the *equites* and only the honor to the senate. The *equites* went so far in using their power over the senators as to openly mock them beyond all reason. They, too, imbibed the habit of bribe-taking and, after once tasting such immense acquisitions, they drained the draft even more shamefully and recklessly than the senators had done. They hired informers against the rich and put an end to prosecutions for bribe-taking entirely, partly by united action and partly by actual violence, so that the pursuit of such investigations was done away with entirely. Thus the judiciary law started another factional contest that lasted for a long time and was fully as harmful as the previous ones.

Gracchus constructed long highways over Italy and thus made an army of contractors and workmen dependent on his favor and rendered them subject to his every wish. He proposed the establishment of a number of colonies. He prompted the Latin allies to clamor for all the privileges of Roman citizenship, for the senate could not becomingly deny them to the kinsmen of the Romans. He attempted to give the right to vote to those allies that were not permitted to take part in Roman elections, so as to have their assistance in the passing of measures that he had in mind. The senate was greatly perturbed at this and commanded the consuls to set forth the following proclamation, "No one that does not have the right to vote shall remain in the city or come within forty stadia of it during the time that the voting is taking place upon these laws." The senate also got Livius Drusus—another tribune—to intercede his veto against the measures brought forward by Gracchus without telling the plebs his reasons for so doing; for a tribune did not have to give his reasons for a veto. In order to curry favor with the plebs they gave Drusus permission to found twelve colonies, and the people were so much taken with this that they began to jeer at the measures that Gracchus proposed.

From: Appian, "Civil Wars," in Oliver J. Thatcher, ed., *The Library of Original Sources*, Vol. 3, *The Roman World* (Milwaukee, Wisc.: University Research Extension Co., 1907).

FURTHER READING

Anthony T. Edwards, *Hesiod's Ascra* (Berkeley and Los Angeles: University of California Press, 2004).

Bettany Hughes, *Helen of Troy: Goddess, Princess, Whore* (New York: Knopf, 2005).

Andrea G. McDowell, *Jurisdiction in the Workmen's Community of Deir el-Medina* (Leiden, Netherlands: NINO, 1991).

Raphael Sealey, *Demosthenes and His Time: A Study in Defeat* (New York: Oxford University Press, 1993).

Pascal Vernus, *Affairs and Scandals in Ancient Egypt*, trans. David Lorton (Ithaca, N.Y., and London: Cornell University Press, 2003).

► science

INTRODUCTION

In the modern world scientists adhere to the scientific method in pursuing their work. They make hypotheses about problems, test those hypotheses by gathering data under controlled conditions, and then arrive at generalizations that might in time gain the status of scientific laws, such as the law of gravity. Ancient scientists did not approach science in this systematic way and in fact might not have regarded themselves as "scientists" at all. Among ancient peoples, science was associated with magic and religion, two areas of thought that often overlapped. People saw themselves as subject to the will of the gods and to mysterious natural forces. Their only hope for survival was discovering ways of controlling those forces. Knowledge consisted primarily of knowing the will of the gods and possibly making predictions about future events.

Ancient science, then, often overlapped with what the modern world sees as superstition. In many ancient cultures the scientists were often the seers, the diviners, the shamans and priests, who acquired insight into the properties of nature, the movements of heavenly bodies, the functioning of the human system, and the like. Ancient astronomers and healers provide good examples. Both of these classes of scientists were believed to have divine, supernatural knowledge, which they could use for the benefit of people in their communities.

Another distinction between ancient and modern science is that ancient science was almost never theoretical. Ancient people did not have time to pursue purely theoretical knowledge, or scientific knowledge for its own sake. They were too busy with the practical concerns of day-to-day survival. Thus, science tended to be more in the nature of technology, of finding solutions to practical problems. In attacking those problems, they looked around and saw four fundamental elements that affected their lives: earth, fire, air, and water. Science represented an effort to control these four elements. Thus, perhaps the best way to categorize and summarize ancient science is to focus on how they learned to tame these four elements.

The earth was the most stable, tangible reality, so ancient peoples made efforts to achieve some understanding of it and of ways to use it. Stone Age peoples, for example, learned to make weapons, cutting tools, and the like out of the stones on the ground that surrounded them. Their Bronze Age and Iron Age descendants learned to make these weapons and tools out of metal. To do that, they needed to develop ways to find metal ore, mine it, smelt it, purify it, and cast it into the objects they needed. As ancient chemists, they learned ways to harden metals. Copper workers discovered that by combining copper with tin, they could create bronze, a much harder and more useful metal that defined a historical period, the Bronze Age. Later scientists discovered that they could convert iron, an abundant but somewhat soft metal, into hard and durable steel by the addition of carbon.

The earth also provided abundant building materials. The earliest structures were built with logs, reeds, and mud bricks, but in time people learned to quarry stone such as marble, limestone, and sandstone to make buildings. Along the way they discovered principles for engineering these buildings and in some cases developed sophisticated mathematics to help them.

Early farmers became chemists and botanists by learning how to domesticate crops, cultivate them, store them, and convert them into food. Chemistry, for example, enabled them to convert milk from livestock into cheese. Perhaps one of the most successful plant-breeding programs in history was carried out by the ancient Mesoamericans, who domesticated maize (corn) from a wild plant. Other farmers became chemists when they learned that the dung from their domesticated animals or from animals such as bats promoted crop growth or that burning the stubble from last year's crop provided the soil with nutrients that encouraged this year's crop.

This leads to fire, the second element. Ancient civilizations learned to use fire not only for warmth and light but for other purposes as well. Ancient miners, for example, learned to crack stone during the quarrying process by building a fire next to the rock to heat it and then dousing the rock with cold water. The rapid temperature changes cracked the rock, making it easier to mine. They also learned to create blast furnaces that achieved the high temperatures they needed to refine and melt metal ores. Meanwhile, ancient pottery makers were making detailed scientific observations about materials that would work best for clay pots, substances that could be used as dyes for coloring the pots, and ways to fire and glaze the pots to make them more durable. They also learned to make such materials as glass, using silica (sand) and fire, and to use minerals mined from the earth to make decorative objects.

With regard to air, ancient civilizations observed the power in a gust of wind and decided that they could put the air to work. This led to at least two primary developments. One was to attach sails to boats, giving these boats far greater range for purposes of exploring, trading, and conquest. The other was the development of the windmill, allowing ancient farmers to pump water, irrigate land, and thresh grain in far greater amounts and with much greater efficiency. Meanwhile, ancient astronomers were looking into the heavens and observing regularities in the movements of the sun, moon, and stars.

Water posed a particular problem for ancient civilizations, particularly those that settled near rivers. The ancient Egyptians, for example, found their livelihoods tied to the Nile River and the thin strip of fertile soil along its banks. The problem they faced was that the river flooded each year. When the floodwaters receded, they left behind a great deal of fertile silt. In ensuing dry months, however, the ground dried out, threatening the survival of the crops. Out of necessity, the ancient Egyptians developed skills as hydrologists and engineers. They learned to build systems of dikes, canals, dams, and storage grounds for water, which could then be released when necessary to irrigate crops. In order to become engineers and build these facilities, they had to acquire knowledge in materials science, construction techniques, and the like, all of which required some ability in mathematics and measurement.

The modern world takes for granted an extensive base of information about the physical world and how it works. Ancient civilizations had to discover this information out of nothing. Without their scientific achievements it is unlikely that they would have survived in any appreciable numbers. Had that happened, the world might still be a frightening place of pure mystery and magic.

AFRICA

BY TOM STREISSGUTH

Ancient Africans viewed the natural world and all that occurred within it as expressions of the unseen realm of spirits. Events on earth were predetermined, the result of malevolent or benign forces that acted at whim. Humans could never hope to control the fertility of the soil, the coming of the rains, the occurrence of drought or illness, or the seasonal flood of rivers and lakes. They could only propitiate the spirits of the natural world, look for guidance in signs appearing on the earth and in the heavens, and seek out the environments that were best suited to their own survival. They did not pursue science for its own sake or by the modern method of testing theories in controlled experiments. Ancient chemistry, botany, metallurgy, physics, medicine, astronomy, and so on came in the form of practical knowledge applied to everyday needs: growing food, fighting wars, curing the sick, or relieving the pain of giving birth. Further, there was no sharp line between religious and scientific practices, since a spiritual outlook governed virtually all aspects of life. Generally speaking, any activities that ancient Africans carried out for the purpose of enhancing their livelihood and manipulating their environment should be considered science.

TOOLMAKING: THE FIRST APPLIED SCIENCE

Early human beings needed to master the environment in order to find food, protect themselves from hostile strangers, and hide from dangerous animals. A vital ingredient in these endeavors was the use of tools. The shaping of stone implements, according to archaeologists, first occurred in Africa. At Olduvai Gorge (in present-day Tanzania) primate species probably ancestral to modern humans were using sharp rocks as tools some 2.6 million years ago. They may have created these rudimentary tools simply by cracking brittle stones to produce a sharp edge. Later ancestral species and modern humans found ways to work harder stone into tools through abrasion or flaking. Drilling and incision allowed a still greater variety of tools as well as a means of fashioning decorative necklaces, pendants, bracelets, and rings. Stone axes and spear points were useful for killing game, stone adzes for hollowing out tree trunks to make canoes, and simple stone hoes for turning the soil and clearing brush.

The control of fire brought a revolution in useful technologies, allowing ancient Africans to harden earth for pottery and, later, to fashion metal tools and weapons. Pottery making developed along with settled agricultural societies, which needed storage for food, water, and seed. The first clay pots were made from river mud heated in a fire and decorated with simple geometric forms. Potters experimented with different soils, with controlled heating for firing and curing their vessels, and with various paints and dyes. Without understanding basic chemical principles or the complex effects of heat and light, they found better methods and ingredients through centuries of trial and error.

Agriculture

Ancient Africa grew imported as well as native crops. Archaeologists believe that wheat and barley arrived in Africa from the Near East and were first cultivated in the Ethiopian highlands as well as father north. These crops required intensive labor and close attention to weather, soil, irrigation, and general growing conditions. Seeking to enhance the soil, African farmers mixed it with the ashes of trees cleared and burned to make room for cultivating plants. They turned the soil with hoes to make it easier for roots and stalks to penetrate and found that cattle dung improved its fertility. In hilly regions they terraced land to control drainage and provide a greater area of cultivation. They rotated crops or allowed land to lie fallow in order to renew exhausted soil. All of these innovations came from centuries of observation and experiment.

In the northern half of Africa native crops such as millet, sorghum, and yams were cultivated and propagated. Instead of simply gathering edible plants, African farmers began working in a systematic manner, controlling the environment as best they could and reading the sky for signs of coming weather and for favorable or unfavorable omens. They shared their knowledge and passed it down to younger generations.

Animal husbandry developed as societies living in the Sahara region captured and raised wild cattle, a development that began around the fifth millennium B.C.E. Sheep and goats also flourished in what is now the Sahara, at the time a well-watered region with a moderate climate. Cattle herding spread southward across the Sahara. Cattle were useful as beasts of burden, for their meat and milk, for fertilization of the soil, and as a store of wealth. Herders bred their animals selectively to increase and improve them. They learned to avoid environments where disease-carrying insects such as the tsetse fly threatened deadly epidemics.

Metallurgy

The techniques of working and shaping stone were most useful for hunters in perpetual search of game. As land came under cultivation, African artisans began exploring the more complex science of metallurgy. Iron production in Africa dates to at least the second millennium B.C.E. For example, in what is now Nigeria the Nok civilization began making iron tools and other objects sometime around 500 B.C.E. The new iron implements allowed people to hunt more effectively, cultivate larger areas for crops, protect themselves from animals, and make war on their neighbors.

The craft of metallurgy gave rise to a new class of skilled artisans. Making and working iron were complex, difficult processes that could be mastered only through years of practice. The first step was to smelt the iron—that is, to separate the metal from the rocky ore in which it occurs in nature. This was done by heating the ore in a furnace, where the temperature could be controlled by the introduction of air through vents. Shaft furnaces were developed, which drew air through holes in the base. These furnaces were easier to use than bellows furnaces, in which air is blown over the fire, but they burned more wood fuel (a demand at first easily met in most regions of Africa, but one that often caused serious problems as local iron industries expanded). Metalsmiths learned to separate usable metal from impurities in order to produce a stronger material. The molten iron was consolidated in heavy crucibles and then poured into molds to cool. Once the iron solidified, the smith could craft tools and weapons by forging it—that is, by shaping it with heavy hammers while it was still hot enough to be relatively soft or after reheating it. The secrets of this craft were held closely by the few who could practice it, and who passed on its mysteries to their heirs and apprentices.

Metalworking encouraged long-distance trade, as iron tools and weapons were in high demand throughout the continent. The industry also supported permanent settlement, as groups with knowledge of the process located themselves near useful ore deposits. In many places the hunter-gatherer existence faded into memory, and life became more settled, with larger communities divided into distinct classes defined by their skills and employment. The need to adjust to the environment led to the development of more sophisticated tools. The iron implements used in the tropical parts of Africa, for example, tended to be stronger than the ones developed by people who lived in the desert.

From about 500 B.C.E. iron and copper metallurgy spread throughout sub-Saharan Africa. Copper deposits were discovered and worked in Mauritania and Niger, in the western Sahara region, and in central and southern Africa. Ancient ironworking sites have been found from about 500 B.C.E. in Nigeria as well as in the eastern Lake District, in what are now Rwanda and Tanzania, in Doulo (in modern-day Cameroon), and in the Termit Mountains region of Niger. In African societies the practice of metallurgy required cooperative effort and expertise that was the privileged knowledge of certain clans, who knew the techniques of locating ore, building smelters, producing charcoal, and maintaining a constant high temperature in a closed furnace. Metal craftsmen trained in the art of iron making eventually mastered other media, such as jewelry making. Some historians believe that in ancient Africa, iron, copper, and bronze were most important in the production of ornaments, and not in the making of tools or weapons.

Historians have noted that Africa did not experience the usual transition from copper and bronze to iron. Copper making usually preceded the iron making in ancient cultures because copper has a lower melting point, making it easier to produce. Iron smelters had to mix burning charcoal and crushed ore in a closed furnace or crucible, steadily raise the temperature of the mixture, separate the metal from the ore, and then hammer their products into shape. As it was harder than copper, bronze, or tin, iron took greater strength and skill to forge into anything useful. Apparently, however, African smiths started working with these two very different materials more or less at the same time.

Further, there is no evidence in Africa for the usual first step in developing metalsmithing techniques—by experimentation in pottery kilns. Finally, no African metalworking sites date from earlier than similar sites in the Near East and Asia Minor, where ironworking technology originated. Together these facts suggest that metal technology probably arrived in Africa over a short period of time from outside the continent. African iron smelters may have learned metalworking from contact with the Near East, which spread new implements and the methods for making them into Africa via Egypt.

The first African iron kingdom was Kush, lying on the southern frontier of Egypt in what is now northern Sudan. This civilization was based on ironworking technology that was spreading from the Nile Valley and the Sahara to West Africa, the Sahel region south of the Sahara, and then to the Bantu populations of southern and southeastern Africa. The effect of the new technology in Kush and elsewhere was profound. Iron tools were better at clearing forests and cultivating the soil. Iron axes, machetes, and hoes increased the food supply, allowing communities to stay in one place longer and grow in population. Iron also made larger areas of the continent habitable, as people moving into a new region could cultivate more land and more effectively hunt. Iron weapons were important catalysts of urbanization; they also strengthened armies in wartime. Iron, copper, and gold produced in surplus were traded over long distances, allowing societies that mastered metallurgy to enrich themselves and, as a result, develop a merchant class and a wealthy aristocracy.

The iron industry of the capital city of Meroë allowed the Kushite civilization to flourish—and it may also have led to its downfall. To fire the charcoal furnaces, iron makers had to cut a tremendous amount of wood. The resulting loss of forests led to severe soil erosion and loss of soil fertility in the lands around Meroë, reducing the supply of locally grown food and requiring more and more food to be imported. The cost impoverished the city and affected other forms of trade. In about 350 B.C.E. Meroë collapsed, its industries shutting down and its people scattering.

Medicine and Spiritual Healing

In ancient Africa there was no sharp separation of religion, custom, and science. This can be clearly seen in the field of medicine. Although there is very little written evidence of ancient medical practices in sub-Saharan Africa, historians can surmise some general aspects of ancient doctoring through time-honored traditions that have survived into modern times.

Ancient Africans believed (and many people in present-day Africa still believe) in three different worlds: the worlds of the living, the dead, and the generation unborn. Ancestors, gods, goddesses, and other invisible entities resided in the world of the dead. Also in the world of the dead were spirits that brought bad omens, disease, and misfortune. In order to avoid such problems, the ancestors or gods who brought them had to be consulted to discover the underlying cause, which could be man-made or supernatural.

Man-made medical problems, for example, are those arising from such causes as poor hygiene or a lackadaisical attitude toward one's physical well-being. Some medical conditions, however, such as madness, infertility, or protracted sickness, demand more serious metaphysical understanding. They may result, it is thought, from malevolent humans who are capable of transforming themselves into a different spiritual realm for the purpose of doing mischief. Witches, for example, are human beings with the power of entering the spiritual realm. To counter this kind of problem, the doctor consults a deity that is associated with beneficial and restorative outcomes. In all instances remedies for spiritual anomalies and medical problems involve communication with the spirits by the doctor, who may also be a diviner (a person who has supernatural powers to discover hidden knowledge). Sacrifices are usually needed to appease the entities, return the sick to normal health, and beg for forgiveness.

A spiritual or medical problem can often result from disrespect to the deity. One of the numerous methods of enforcing laws in Africa is through oracular intervention. For example, a person who kills game in a sacred forest might develop a swollen belly until he or she confesses the offense. Remedies are procured through appeasements to the gods or through banishment from the community. In ancient times offenders might even be sacrificed to the affronted deity.

In sum, scientific understanding in traditional Africa is closely tied to spiritual insight and is the concern of doctors, shamans, and priests who are trained in an esoteric body of knowledge. The African priest was, and still is, responsible for conducting the spiritual affairs of the community in accordance with long-established customs. Most important, the priest ensures that the gods do not get angry with the people of the community. The best means of avoiding the wrath of the gods is by making sure that all the rules and regulations of the community are adhered to. Whenever there are problems that might lead to a serious crisis, the gods communicate with the priest, who in turn works with the rulers and the entire community to ensure that the danger—a poor harvest, famine, or a short rainy season—is averted. Spiritual cleaning is needed to appease the gods and put things on the desired track.

Astronomy and Divination

Astronomy was the most esoteric science known in ancient Africa. The appearance and movements of the stars, planets, and moon posed a difficult question to ancient observers. In attempting to explain their observations, African astronomers relied on religious traditions and their knowledge of the spirit world. They also devised pragmatic systems in order to make something useful of the mysterious celestial events. In some ancient societies the time and position of sunrise and sunset were gauged to plan journeys and decide the activities required for each day. The appearance of certain stars, particularly Sirius, the brightest star in the night sky, delineated the annual calendar of river flood and proper dates for planting and harvesting. The moon, the Milky Way, the constellation Orion, and the bright planet Venus also played important roles in astronomical science.

Archaeologists have excavated several sites in Africa that may have served as observatories or celestial calendars. Stones placed artificially in a row or circular arrangement may have marked the position of heavenly bodies at certain times of year. Such arrangements have been discovered in Zimbabwe, the Central African Republic, Sudan, Kenya, and the western African nations of Togo and Benin. For example, in what is now Kenya a stone circle known to archaeologists as Namoratunga II was laid out by ancestors of the Borana people. This site is an early calendar that fixed the dates of the year by measuring the positions of seven different stars and the moon.

One of the most famous ancient objects possibly relating to astronomy is the Ishango bone, found in what is today Zaire and dated to about 20,000 B.C.E. The bone (a baboon's femur) has markings that may indicate the 28-day cycle of the moon. Some experts have seen in the pattern of marks a counting system or some kind of mathematical table. Without a written record, however, the specific uses and purposes of this object and of such astronomical sites as Namoratunga II remain unknown.

Ancient societies commonly took celestial phenomena into consideration for important undertakings, such as wedding ceremonies, going into battle, migration to a new region, and building their homes. In Togo and Benin the people known as Tamalimba built their houses so that they were aligned with the sun at the time of the equinoxes. The pyramids of Meroë, the capital of the Kushite kingdom, are aligned to face Sirius as it rises on the eastern horizon. Contemporary Africans still hold to many of these traditions. Sirius, Orion, and the star cluster known as the Pleiades guide coastal navigators in eastern and western Africa. The Dogon of Mali consider Sirius and a small companion star, known to them as Po Tolo, as celestial anchors, keeping all other heavenly bodies in their proper courses and guiding events and important decisions on earth.

The appearance of heavenly bodies was interpreted both as a guide to present events and as a portent of the future. Like medicine, divination was a skill reserved to those with specialized knowledge, whose secrets were carefully kept. The purpose of this craft was to access information not available through empirical means. Divination allowed people to understand problems or prepare for imminent danger. Diviners were, and are, consulted before naming a baby, before undertaking a journey, in preparation for war, and to judge the worth of a potential spouse.

The origin of African divination systems is shrouded in mystery. In modern times they fall into two broad categories: the tool system and the medium system. In the latter a human being serves as a medium who interprets coded information accessed through an earthly entity—typically, messages from dead ancestors who communicate through selected individuals. This type of divination is popular among the Shona of modern Zimbabwe. In the tool system a diviner makes use of tools such as palm-nut shells, stones, or animals. The Banen and Mambila of modern Cameroon use spiders and land crabs as tools of divination.

The Ifa system, as one example, is a well-studied system that survives among the Yoruba of Nigeria. The priest of Ifa divination is called *babalawo* (father of secrets). To become a *babalawo*, an apprentice required several years of training and the study of an enormous body of literature, the *odu*, which consists of 256 parts further subdivided into verses called *ese*. There are about 800 *ese* in each *odu*. A person becomes a *babalawo* after going through all the initiation ceremonies and mastering enough verses needed for communication with Orunmila, the deity associated with divination.

Among the Yoruba and other African cultures evidence of ancient divination science exists only in the form of modern practices that echo those of the past. In a continent where archaeological evidence is often scanty, this is the best resource historians have for reconstructing the knowledge systems of societies that have long been extinct.

EGYPT

BY LEO DEPUYDT AND TOM STREISSGUTH

Among the ancient societies of the Mediterranean region, Egypt was home to esoteric and practical knowledge that placed it in a realm apart from all others. Egypt was the center of advanced medicine, mathematics, and astronomy. Moreover, Egyptian engineering technology—embodied by towering monuments, pyramids, palaces, and public works—had no rival in the ancient world. The ancient knowledge of Egypt, however, was hidden in hieroglyphics, a system of picture writing that fell into disuse in the time of the Roman Empire. Until the 19th century the tablets, papyri, and inscriptions of ancient Egypt were undeciphered, and Egypt's medicine, astronomy, and technology were lost to the world.

By the time of the pharaohs the Egyptians were making various household utensils, building clay vessels on a wheel, forging bronze weapons, weaving cotton, and controlling the flood of the Nile to the fields that bordered the river. Most importantly for scientific knowledge, the predynastic Egyptians developed a system of writing and record keeping.

Absent, however, was a tradition of experimentation, theory, and proof by empirical observation. Egyptian science was hidden knowledge, revealed to a select few among the priestly caste, who placed their skill and research at the service of the pharaohs. Their patron god was Thoth, the deity of knowledge and wisdom, represented by the figure of a human bearing the head of an ibis. The knowledge of Thoth was set down by scribes on papyrus rolls that were privileged reading for the few. In a broad sense, nearly every ancient Egyptian text exhibits some aspect, however minimal, of scientific thought. There were mathematical texts and medical texts, as well as astronomical texts and texts related to the reckoning of time and the calendar. Other genres include classifications of reality (as in *onomastika,* or name books) and explanations of dreams as well as texts on geography, botany, chemistry, metrology, mineralogy, pharmacology, philosophy, physics, and technology.

Medicine

Works of medicine and mathematics show that these were the most advanced scientific endeavors in ancient Egypt. Only one cluster of sources rivals mathematical texts in size, the medical texts. These include the Edwin Smith Papyrus, the Ebers Papyrus, and the Kahun Papyrus. Within these documents are spells and incantations, diagnoses of various diseases, and anatomy. The Kahun Papyrus focuses on the reproductive system, the mechanisms of conception and pregnancy, and the complications of birth.

The various papyri reveal that medical science in ancient Egypt was bound closely to religious belief and ritual. All in all, Egyptian medicine is perhaps better known as systematic observation of disease and anatomy rather than medicine. For the Egyptians, disease was the manifestation of evil and malevolent spirits, and curing disease was the work of priests skilled in the use of incantation, ritual, talismans, and spells. Along with this magical approach came practical knowledge closer to the modern conception of medical science.

Without the benefits of sanitation and the knowledge of bacteria, viruses, and the nature of contagious illness, the Egyptian physician had a limited arsenal with which to treat a host of mysterious ailments. Egypt was home to endemic malaria, tuberculosis, measles, smallpox, cholera, and bubonic plague; waterborne illnesses included schistosomiasis (an infection of the blood caused by a parasite). Eye diseases, including trachoma, were common, as were malnutrition; neural diseases like epilepsy; hazards of the natural world such as snakebite, insect stings, and poisonous fish and vegetation; and digestive ailments caused by poor food preservation.

Ancient Egyptians classified afflictions and had an intimate knowledge of organs and their function. The practice of mummification contributed greatly to that knowledge. The first mummies were created naturally, by preservation of the human body by the dry heat of the Egyptian desert. The preservation of natural mummies led the ancient Egyptians to the conclusion that artificial mummification could render a body impervious to the forces of time and decay. The process of mummifying a body took as long as 70 days, with each step a ritual presided over by priests trained and expert in the art. The brain, lungs, pancreas, liver, spleen, heart, and intestines were removed with various instruments, and the body was placed on a bed of natron, a mineral salt that dried the skin and tissue. Once the body was dried, the priests

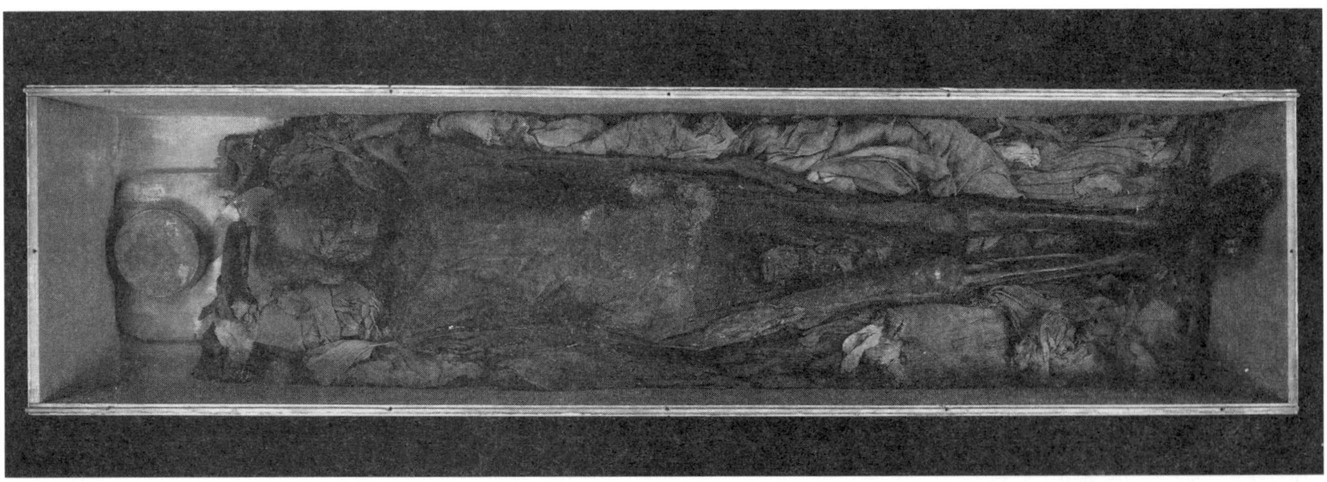

Unwrapped mummy of a woman, perhaps from Thebes, Egypt, Late Period, after 600 B.C.E.*; the process of mummification contributed to the Egyptians' knowledge of anatomy and disease.*

anointed it with oil and spices and then wrapped it in linen bandages. Amulets, talismans, precious stones, and other objects were placed within the bandages as they were wound about the body.

Mummification was not the sole privilege of Egyptian royalty. Members of the wealthy aristocracy also were afforded this practice, as were favored pets and sacred animals, such as cats. Some historians consider mummification as forming the ancient origins of medical science, because the elaborate process allowed Egyptian priests to make a careful study of the symptoms of disease and the causes of physical death.

Egyptian physicians developed skills in surgery, setting broken bones, treating burns and wounds, dentistry, and preparing medications from vegetable plants, herbs, and minerals. Treatments included honey to dress wounds and soothe pain; aloe vera for burns and headache; and frankincense, dill, camphor, mustard seed, onions, garlic, sandalwood, sesame, thyme, and poppy seeds for various ailments and symptoms. An ancient Egyptian prescription could comprise several of these ingredients as well as much more repulsive substances meant to drive away evil spirits: the blood or fat of lizards and snakes, ground pig's teeth, rotten meat or other food, and boiled beetles or rhinoceros horn.

Medical science in ancient Egypt was also preventive in nature. Ritual bathing and purification played a key role in the prevention of disease, and dream interpretation was used to diagnose the causes of illness. The ancient Greeks considered Egypt the home of the medical arts. It was common for Greek scholars and physicians to make pilgrimages to the Nile Valley to study and learn from Egyptian priests and shamans.

Metallurgy and Chemistry

The Greeks and the people of the Near East took much of their knowledge of metallurgy and chemistry from the Egyptians, who were already systematically mining copper in the Predynastic Period, which ended in the late fourth millennium B.C.E. In the Eastern Desert between the Nile Valley and the Red Sea, copper ores were dug from the earth, refined into base metal, and formed into tools and weapons—a business carried on exclusively under the control of the state. Later the Egyptians learned to combine copper and tin to make bronze and developed uses for lead, cobalt, and galena.

Around 800 B.C.E. Egyptian smiths learned methods of smelting iron, which may have first been mined from meteorites. The "metal of heaven," as it was known, was rare and valuable, and its handling was restricted to the priestly caste and privileged artisans working for the state. By the middle of the seventh century B.C.E. these smiths had learned new ways of hardening iron to make tools more durable and to lend weapons a sharper edge.

Gold mining was another monopoly of the state. Gold (*nub*) gave its name to an entire region, Nubia, which was renowned for its valuable deposits. The precious metal was extracted from gold-bearing ore as well as river sands. The Egyptians developed an efficient method of washing this "gold of the river" by placing the ore in bags of fleece and running water through it, thereby removing the soil and dross and leaving behind small gold fragments and nuggets.

The Egyptians also developed an early glassmaking technology in which glass threads were wound around a core of hardened clay. When the clay was burned away, glass jars and bottles were left behind. Glassmaking employed soda, lime, and lead in various combinations and was the subject of constant experimentation and refinement, with the goal to create larger and more transparent pieces. The Egyptians developed an extensive industry around the use of various paints and dyes to create imitation pearls and precious gems from glass. Egypt's glassmaking technology was exported to the Near East and later to ancient Greece and Rome.

Mathematics

Of the two kinds of ancient scientific texts, mathematical texts are more compatible with modern standards of science. (Accomplishments in medicine possible before the discovery of bacteria were, after all, very limited.) The earliest evidence of hieroglyphic mathematics dates to the first half of the second millennium BC.E. A similar but more sophisticated development in mathematics occurred around the same time in cuneiform sources from Mesopotamia. Near Eastern mathematics then stagnated until the Greek miracle of the later first millennium B.C.E. Two factors put Egypt at the forefront of this resumed growth. First, Alexander's conquest in the fourth century B.C.E. made Greek into an Egyptian language, Egypt's preferred vehicle of intellectual discourse. Second, royal philanthropy transformed Alexandria into the world center for the study of mathematics for several centuries.

Much knowledge of Egyptian mathematics is contained in the Rhind Mathematical Papyrus, a document dating from around 1600 B.C.E. and which contains tables of fractions; formulas for addition, subtraction, multiplication, and division; a table of prime numbers; and a method for solving linear equations. In ancient Egypt mathematics was a practical and not a "pure" theoretical science. Egyptian numbers and calculation developed with the need for precise measurement in construction; surveying land boundaries; building canals and roads; and performing government functions such as calculating taxes and measuring inventories of grain, gold, and other public goods. The numbering systems allowed merchants to trade and exchange goods of various weights and volumes and enabled the state to calculate the size of granaries used for storing corn. The Egyptians developed an advanced system of geometry, a key element in positioning and constructing pyramids and royal tombs and in building various public structures: monuments, sphinxes, obelisks, lighthouses, and gardens.

Egyptian mathematics attained great precision and sophistication. Its number system was decimal, without a zero or a place value system, such as the one in which the first 5 in 55 means 50 and the second 5 means just 5. The Egyptians were the first to develop a base-10 numbering system, which allowed the use of unit fractions and binary fractions. Square roots were in use by about 2000 B.C.E., at which time the Egyptians were also calculating and using the value of pi, the ratio of the diameter of a circle to its circumference. Egyptian mathematicians created tables of addition and subtraction, solved algebraic problems, and developed a precise system of weights and measures.

The Egyptians also studied the aerodynamics of sails and the phenomenon of draft employed by a curving sail. Some historians speculate that the Egyptians used kites and sails to raise obelisks and other monuments.

Astronomy

The gods of ancient Egypt were present in all creation and in visible form. They were present in the stars and the prominent constellations, a fact that bound astronomical knowledge with the practices and rituals of religion. Osiris was visible in the constellation Orion, for example, and the goddess Nut could be seen in the Milky Way. To the Egyptians, the sky was a great roof, supported by immense pillars at the four corners of the world, which corresponded to the four cardinal points of the compass. The sun made a daily course around the earth in a celestial boat, doing constant battle with Set, the god of darkness and night. This striving forced the sun to move from north to south in the course of the year; at the time of the summer solstice, the sun reached its furthest point north. The earth itself was a flat rectangle, extending north to south and having its center in the valley of the Nile, which arose in a great river that lay at the southern boundary of the world.

Egyptian astronomers were priests as well as scholars, for whom a close knowledge of the heavens was most useful in its application to agriculture. The annual rising of Sirius before the sun at the summer solstice, for example, presaged the flooding of the Nile, the event that renewed the fertility of the Nile Valley. The prediction of this event every year lent the priestly caste its aura of mysterious power and esoteric knowledge. It also provided a natural starting point for the annual calendar of days, weeks, and months.

The Egyptian methods of mapping and measuring the heavens gave the world one important basis for its advanced time measurement systems. Egyptian astronomers divided the heavens into 36 decans, with each group of stars covering 10 degrees of the sky. Each of these groups rose at dawn for a period of 10 days, which formed a basis for the Egyptian calendar of 12 months of 30 days, each composed of three 10-day weeks. Egyptian astronomers further divided the year into three seasons—the season of the flood, the season of planting, and the season of harvest—with each season four months in length. The system of months left an extra five days each year that were set aside for feasting and a rest from labor. These intercalary days (inserted between others) were associated with a legend of the god Thoth, who allowed the goddess Nut an extra five days to give birth to her children.

The actual solar year, being slightly longer than 365 days, caused the months and seasons to gradually go out of phase. The result was a long period known as the sothic cycle, in which the seasons returned to their original positions in the calendar every 1,460 years. Later astronomers of Alexandria created a new calendar in which an extra day was added every fourth year, a system adopted by the Romans and which gave rise to the modern leap year. The system of decans and constellations also led to the division of night and day into 12 equal parts, which in turn led to the 24-hour day now used throughout the world. The Egyptians also considered the position of the stars and constellations in raising the pyramids. The faces of these monuments are very carefully aligned. Most face the rising sun at the summer solstice; others are aligned with important stars or the points of the compass. The north face of the Great Pyramid at Giza, for example, lies almost precisely at a right angle to true north. Some have seen in the arrangement of the three pyramids at Giza an imitation of the stars in the belt of the constellation of Orion. The alignment of foundations and walls with the cardinal points of the compass was done with the help of an instrument known as a *merkhet*, a sighting tool made from the central rib of a palm leaf, a string, and a weight, which gives a precise vertical line and allows the user to make a determination of true north and set the north–south axis.

Technology

The Egyptians invented several devices to aid construction of their palaces, monuments, and pyramids. The ramp, an inclined plane that allows large blocks to be raised using less force, and the lever, which uses a fulcrum point to multiply lifting force, were both applied to moving and positioning heavy objects, such as the immense blocks of stone laid for the pyramids. The Egyptians invented papyrus as a writing medium, developed long-distance ships, and adopted the wheel and chariot—originally inventions of the Mesopotamians. Egyptian farmers developed sophisticated irrigation systems, including canals, dikes, and reservoirs to bring water to their fields in times of drought or low rainfall.

Weaving and dyeing technology also made important advances in ancient Egypt. The Egyptians developed new methods of weaving and dyeing cotton and invented the royal purple dye adopted by ancient Greece and Rome. They learned to manufacture pigments and dyes from minerals like cobalt (for blue), iron oxide (for red), azurite or copper carbonate (light blue), malachite (green), and charcoal or charred bone (black).

The perception is widespread that Egyptian science was less sophisticated than its Babylonian and Greek equivalents. Hieroglyphic mathematics and astronomy never reached the level of sophistication of Babylonian or Greek astronomy. But this fact needs to be put in a proper historical perspective. It would be false to conclude that Egypt somehow disappointed or did not perform to expectation. Historically, thinking progressed more or less along parallel lines in Egypt and other advanced early civilizations. A significant increase in sophistication occurred sometime after 500 B.C.E. By then, however, the great epochs of hieroglyphic Egyptian civilization had ended.

Around 525 B.C.E. Persia conquered Egypt. The Persian Empire's intellectual capital, Babylon, lay outside Egypt. In 332 B.C.E. Alexander of Macedonia followed the Persians into Egypt and put a permanent end to the pharaonic dynasties. A Greek presence had been in Egypt since the seventh century B.C.E., but with the coming of Alexander began the Greek Ptolemaic Dynasty, which ruled Egypt until the Romans arrived in the first century B.C.E. Alexander's general Ptolemy made his capital at Alexandria, a city founded by Alexander, who kept a company of philosophers and scientists with him for the purpose of spreading Greek learning and civilization to the barbarous parts of the world he conquered. Ptolemy built the greatest library of the ancient world at Alexandria, which flourished as a center of learning. The Museum, or Temple of the Muses, which housed the library, was a precursor to the modern university, with lecture halls, laboratories, experimental gardens for the study of botany, a zoological collection, and departments of medicine, astronomy, literature, and mathematics. For several centuries Alexandria and its Museum attracted the most brilliant astronomers and mathematicians of the ancient world. The work of the Alexandrian scientists remained dominant even after the fall of the Roman Empire in the fifth century and until new systems of thought were developed in the 17th century by Galileo, Copernicus, and Isaac Newton.

The activity at Alexandria is Egyptian, even if research was conducted in Greek. Claudius Ptolemy, antiquity's greatest astronomer (second century C.E.), was an Egyptian who wrote in Greek and had a Latin-Macedonian name. Egyptian developments in science and medicine, therefore, were not minor but were made obscure by the medium of hieroglyphic writing. For much of the period in which the hieroglyphic script was dominant, Egyptian learning did not significantly lag behind that of any other nation.

THE MIDDLE EAST

BY MICHAEL J. O'NEAL

The Sumerians, Akkadians, Assyrians, and Babylonians did not think in terms of scientific laws, and nothing like the modern scientific method of inquiry existed, with its emphasis on formulating hypotheses and testing them to arrive at general principles about the physical world. They did, however, develop mathematical reasoning to a high level of sophistication, enabling them to calculate everything from the area of a field to the amount of seed required to be sown in order to achieve a predicted yield. Mathematics in turn fed into architectural design, astronomical reckoning, time keeping, and all manner of economic control over seed, yields, rations, and productivity. There was no self-conscious discussion of science per se, but it is clear that the ancient Mesopotamians were fully capable of thinking and calculating in a rigorous, predictable, and, above all, accurate manner.

MATHEMATICS

The ancient Mesopotamians developed a sophisticated system of mathematics. Early on they learned that they needed a precise system of measurement. Arable land had to be measured accurately so that the requisite amount of seed and irrigation water could be calculated to make the land deliver a high yield. Irregularly shaped plots of land were divided into triangles and rectangles, and area was calculated by summing the areas of the parts. Volumetric calculations were also necessary. In constructing a wall or digging a pit, the need to calculate volumes of earth, the numbers of bricks required, and the amount of labor to be hired and for how long were all important to the planning of a project. The amount of food rations (barley, beer, salt, oil, fish, and so forth) had to be calculated as well. The best surviving records come from what historians call the Old Babylonian Period, dating roughly from about 2000 to 1600 B.C.E.

The mathematical system of the Babylonians (and the Sumerians before them) was a sexagesimal system, meaning that it was based on the number 60 rather than on the number 10. Any metrological system contains within it units of measure with fixed conversion factors. Thus, for example, a foot consists of 12 inches, a mile of 5,280 feet, and so on. The sexagesimal system of the Sumerians and Babylonians evolved out of their conversion factors. In the late third millennium B.C.E. a final step took place, that of place holding. In the modern numerical system, the value of the digit 3 varies depending on its place. By itself it stands for 3, but in the numeral 30 it represents three 10s, in 300 it represents three 100, and so on. The Babylonians developed a similar system. Now they needed only two symbols, one for the digit and one for its place. A vertical wedge was the "base unit." A corner wedge, derived from the small circle, had a value of 10 vertical wedges. A further vertical wedge was worth six corner wedges, and so on. These symbols could be repeated as often as necessary to arrive at such figures as 1, 60, 360, 3,600, and the like. From there it is easy to see the roots of many peculiarities of modern measurement systems. There are 360 degrees in a circle, 12 inches in a foot (for 12 is a factor of 60), three feet in a yard (for three is also a factor of 60), and the like.

Several hundred clay tablets exist in two forms: table tablets and problem texts. The table tablets could be considered an extension of the interest in listing discussed earlier. The tablets have a simple structure and show the two-symbol system of counting, along with the place-holding system. There are no subtraction or addition tables, but there are numerous tables for multiplication. These tables list multiples of one number, called the principal number (p). Thus, there were calculations for $1p$, $2p$, and so on. The tables calculate up to $20p$ and then skip to $30p$, $40p$, and $50p$. For a number such as 53, for example, the results for $50p$ and $3p$ were added. Some of these tables also provide the square of the principal number.

The Babylonians had no division tables, but they did make extensive use of reciprocal tables. (A reciprocal is simply 1 divided by the number in question, so that the reciprocal of 60 is 1/60.) Thus, instead of dividing, they multiplied by a reciprocal. To aid them in this task, they created extensive reciprocal tables. There are hundreds of these tables, along with tables for squares, square roots, and cubes, many of them compiled by students. Finally, there are coefficient lists, which list conversion factors used in geometry (for example, the ratio of a diagonal to a square's side) and weights and measures problems.

In addition to these tables are so-called problem texts, that is, exercises used in schools. Some of the tablets that record these texts contain a number of problems on a single topic; others contain problems related to different topics. They have given historians insight into the kinds of problems examined in schools. Nearly all of the problems ask students to come up with a number, never with any kind of proof. Thus, they are "algebraic" problems, in contrast to the "geometric" problems that ancient Greek students studied. (In algebra the goal is to arrive at a correct answer, expressed as a number; in geometry the goal is often to prove, for example, that the angles of a triangle add up to 360 degrees). Interestingly, modern mathematicians have taken a more extensive interest in Babylonian mathematics because of its emphasis on algorithms, or following a process to arrive at an answer.

Most such problems were what modern students know as "story problems," that is, problems couched in everyday terms by calling for calculations of things in the real world: the length of a canal or broken reeds, the weight of a quantity of stones, or the number of bricks used in a building. Many of the problems are complex, requiring students to use not just single equations but more complex linear and quadratic equations. Some of the texts record the procedures students would follow to solve the problem, but none state general principles. Instead, the emphasis seems to have been on working problems as examples often enough so that the student could then work a new problem with different values. In many cases, all the problems in a group have the same answer, suggesting that the group of exercises was designed to teach a process of computation rather than to arrive at a correct answer.

Although the Babylonians did not have an organized system of geometry—they did not compute angles, for instance—many of the problems have geometric implications, and many contain drawings of squares, rectangles, circles, and triangles. Some problems required the student to compute such quantities as lengths of diagonals or sides or to calculate volume or area. Bricks and calculating a quantity of bricks seem to have been a preoccupation with Babylonian math teachers.

For reasons that historians do not fully understand, the mathematical record of the Old Babylonians comes to an abrupt halt after about 1600 B.C.E. What follows is a thousand-year gap in the record. After this millennium the record resumes, and historians have records of continued interest in mathematics in the Mesopotamian region.

Astronomy

During the first millennium B.C.E. the Babylonians compiled columnar lists of stars, with the columns listing the stars and their positions in relation to the positions of other stars. So great became the interest in observation of the stars that temples became astronomical observatories. It should be noted that at the same time, the Assyrians of the Near East also gave great importance to astronomy, and Assyria's capital, Kalhu (modern Nimrud), was a center of astronomical observation and study. In both Babylon and Assyria, lists of such events as eclipses were meticulously kept after about 800 B.C.E.—so accurately that future eclipses could be and were predicted.

Again, the Babylonians lacked a system, an underlying theory to explain and systematize the phenomena they observed in the heavens. Only after about the sixth century B.C.E. did they begin to organize their knowledge into a system. They did so only because they began working alongside Greek astronomers, who seemed, in common with the ancient Greeks, generally to have been better equipped to think systematically. Many of the famous Babylonian astronomers from this period even took Greek names. Naburimanni, who lived around 500 B.C.E., became called Naburianos, and the later astronomers Kidinnu and Belussur became, respectively, Cidenas and Berossus.

Babylonian astronomical observation was not, however, a "scientific" endeavor in the sense of an activity intended to develop an understanding of the atmosphere or the planets and the stars. Rather, the purpose of astronomical observation was completely different than it is today. It was employed in divination, akin to modern and medieval astrology. Celestial divination was used to foretell the fate not of individuals but of kings and the state. The decision to launch a military campaign, like almost all major decisions, was almost always preceded by celestial or some other form of divination.

Medicine

Much of the interest in the natural sciences among the ancient Mesopotamians focused on medicine and healing, an early effort to exert some human control over inexplicable forces. In the ancient Akkadian language, the word for *doctor* is literally translated as "fluids expert." Over millennia doctors in the region accumulated a vast store of information having to do with drugs, salves, and other medicines either taken orally or applied to the body. Most of these drugs consisted either of minerals or plant extracts, including spices.

The practice of medicine was closely interwoven with magic and the science of omens. The application of drugs was typically accompanied by prayers and incantations. The goal was to strengthen the patient's will to recover. Interestingly, modern medicine has come to recognize that a patient's frame of mind can play an important role in recovery; modern scientists have begun investigating the power of prayer and religious faith in the healing process, believing that they can boost the patient's morale and promote healing. The ancient Mesopotamians, too, were interested in the psychosomatic properties of the healing arts—that is, the relationship between psychology and medicine.

From a modern standpoint, the fundamental flaw in Mesopotamian medicine was that practitioners were unable to formulate laws based on some overall theory of how the human body worked, in contrast to, for example, the ancient Greeks. Most of the medical literature that survives consists of what modern researchers would call case studies. That is, the texts record the particular cases of individual doctors, without any attempt made to impose some systematic organization on them. Other medical texts consist of letters, those written by both doctors and patients, along with questions that patients put to the doctors. From these texts, historians have even learned the names of some ancient doctors, such as Urad-Nanâ, the court physician at the city of Nineveh sometime around 680 B.C.E.

Most of these early texts contain only minimal efforts at diagnosis, with only cursory descriptions of patients' symptoms. Much of the emphasis is on diagnostic omens, along with indications of whether a particular illness can be healed or whether it is likely to result in death. If a disease was diagnosed as fatal, the texts often note that "the hand of" a particular demon was on the patient. Because some demons were more powerful than others, the demon specified represented a kind of prognosis for how long the patient might hope to survive. Similarly, when the prognosis was good, "the hand of" a particular god was on the patient. These kinds of statements, then, indicate the nature of the rituals that were to be carried out in connection with a patient's treatment. Somewhat later texts contain more exhaustive lists of symptoms and possible treatments, including lengthy courses of medicinal treatments with plants or minerals. Some of these later medical texts also include efforts by practitioners to summarize findings contained in earlier texts, allowing them to follow treatment plans from previous generations.

Again, this process of preserving records represents a form of scientific thinking. Scientists are members of a community of other scientists. They publish and share their findings, and other scientists can replicate their work and either confirm or deny the conclusions. That the Babylonians preserved medical records suggests an effort to forge a community of physicians who could draw on one another's work.

Persian Science

Science in ancient Persia owed a great deal to Mesopotamia, and during the first millennium B.C.E., following the Persian conquest of Mesopotamia, much Babylonian mathematical, astronomical, astrological, and calendric lore certainly passed into Persian awareness and diffused, via the Persian Empire, as far east as India. Much scientific activity took place during the Sasanian Period beginning in 224 C.E. In 271 the Sasanian king Shāpūr I (r. 241–272 C.E.) founded a learned academy at Gundeshapur, in what is today Khūzestān, the southwestern province of Iran. Gundeshapur became the empire's intellectual center. The academy was home to the world's first teaching hospital and included a library and a university. Two important contributions of Persian science include the discovery of alcohol and the development of a more sophisticated windmill than the Babylonians had developed.

One intriguing aspect of Persian science was the discovery of the principles of electromagnetism and possibly the world's first electric battery. Housed in a museum in Iraq is a 5-inch-tall clay jar that was discovered outside Baghdad, Iraq's capital city, in 1938. The jar contains a copper cylinder encased in an iron rod. Further, the jar itself shows evidence of corrosion, possibly by an acidic agent such as vinegar or wine. Since then, about a dozen similar jars have been found. While it is unlikely that the Persians understood the principles of electromagnetism, it is a common occurrence in science for something to be invented before scientists understand the underlying principles. What is known is that modern attempts to reproduce these ancient batteries have been successful in creating a current of 0.8 to 2 volts; batteries like these arranged in a series could have produced more voltage.

The basic principle that the Persians seem to have stumbled on is that an electric current is produced from two metals with different electric potentials, with some sort of an agent—an electrolyte—that carries electrons from one to the other, producing current. Wine and even grape juice can function as an electrolyte. It is quite possible that the discovery was made as a result of experiments by ancient alchemists, in both Mesopotamia and Persia. These alchemists, the forerunners of modern chemists, often worked with base metals such as lead, trying to turn them into gold. Alchemists, in their efforts to discover the chemical principles of the natural world, can be thought of as the world's first experimental scientists.

Historians have offered a number of explanations about the purpose of these batteries. One purpose may have been medicinal. Low-voltage electric currents can sometimes ease pain, a principle the Chinese use in the ancient art of acupuncture for healing. Another purpose might have been electroplating. To cover a base metal, such as lead, with a precious metal, such as gold or silver, ancient craftsmen typically had to pound the precious metal into a thin layer and then mix it with mercury to paste it onto the base metal. Electroplating is a much more efficient method for depositing a thin and even layer of one metal onto another.

Other historians have suggested that the batteries may have been used for religious purposes. The battery could have been held inside a metal idol so that a person who touched the idol received a slight electric shock and could see a blue spark. It has been speculated that ancient priests could have asked followers questions; if the follower gave the "wrong" answer, he or she would receive a slight shock from the idol, convincing the person of the idol's power.

ASIA AND THE PACIFIC

BY TOM STREISSGUTH

The earliest scientists in Asia, as elsewhere, were farmers, miners, and smiths. The need to supply large communities with food gave rise to settled agriculture as well as the science of botany. Early Asian farmers cultivated rice, wheat, and barley, experimenting with those strains that could be easily grown, managed, and harvested. They domesticated fruit trees and collected wild plants they knew to have useful medicinal properties. Botanical knowledge came about through long periods of questioning, observing, and experimenting. In ancient China farmers developed new techniques of agriculture using the same methods. They learned to plant in rows, irrigate their fields, and build crop terraces on hillsides. Observation of the skies and measurement of the year and the seasons—the earliest scientific astronomy—gave them a method of timing their planting and harvesting.

The Chinese also undertook the world's first geological research. They collected and classified various kinds of rocks and came up with theories as to how the rocks were made. They investigated the properties of soil and climate that allowed crops to flourish in certain regions. They speculated that the earth and the mountains were in constant motion and that the weathering of rock and soil erosion lay at the origins of natural features such as valleys and mountains.

Throughout Asia the growth of farming allowed settlements to gather and store surplus food. This gave rise to a class of artisans who made weapons, tools, utensils, jewelry, and furniture. Mining and smelting metal ores that came from underneath the ground began the science of metallurgy. By observing the properties of ores and heating them in combination, metalsmiths created bronze, an alloy of copper and tin, as well as iron and steel. Bronze making arose independently in China and Southeast Asia, where hunter-gatherers in what is now Thailand were smelting copper and tin and making bronze goods as early as 2000 B.C.E.

ASIAN COSMOLOGIES

Pure science, or theoretical science, arose from observation of the natural world. Scientific understanding varied with the language, religion, and culture of the observers. During the Vedic Period (1500–600 B.C.E.) of India, for example, powerful deities were understood to reign over the earth, the heavens, and all manifestations of life. Brahma was the creator god who dreamed the world into being. Agni was the god of fire and Varuna the god of the sky. Surya was the sun and Mitra the moon. The ancient religious text known as the Rig-Veda, which dates to at least 1000 B.C.E., laid the groundwork for Indian science and mathematics through their ideas about the origin and nature of the universe and of all matter.

In China the philosophy of Dao ("the Way") came to dominant the thinking of sages and scientists. Dao was the basic working principle of the universe, expressed through the concept of yin and yang, the balance of opposites. Yang was the expression of action, dominance, creativity, light, and the sun; yin was the moon and night, the completion of action, and the female characteristics of reticence and submission. Imbalance of yin and yang brought about sickness, poverty, and war; when the two forces were in harmony, peace and health reigned, with yin and yang in an uneasy and always temporary agreement.

In the Chinese view, the yin-yang balance was but one aspect of energy and matter (*qi*), which also manifested in *wuxing*, or the five elements of metal, wood, water, earth, and fire. The *wuxing* acted on one another in many ways: water overcame fire, for example, while wood restrained earth and generated fire. Fire symbolized upward movement, while water always ran downhill. Together these properties and their interactions gave the Chinese a comprehensive explanation of the infinitely varied phenomena of the natural world.

SCIENCE IN ANCIENT CHINA

During China's Han Dynasty, which began in 202 B.C.E., these various ideas and the schools of thought they had engendered, were melded into a single philosophical doctrine, known to historians as the Han synthesis. Chinese scientists of this period attempted to explain all natural phenomena—observations of astronomy, the human body, geology, botany, chemistry and alchemy, physics, biological processes, the weather, mathematics—in terms of the balance of opposing and complementary elements.

The Chinese had already been actively observing the natural world for millennia. Prehistoric Chinese accurately recorded the length of the year, at 365.25 days, as is recorded on inscribed bones. They also estimated the length of the lunar month to 29.53 days; this calculation gave rise to an accurate lunar calendar beginning at the winter solstice. (By order of the emperor's astronomers, a month was inserted at the appropriate time to keep this calendar aligned with the seasons.) A lunar calendar is still in use in determining festival days in China and throughout Asia.

Under the Chinese emperors, astronomers and all other scientists were part of the imperial household. They worked at the behest of the emperor to lend the ruler greater knowledge and glory and to strengthen his claim as the link between the earth and the unseen world. Astronomical observatories, first built during the Neolithic Age, were common structures in China by 1000 B.C.E. They were used to record the motion of the moon, planets, and comets against the apparently fixed stars and constellations. Chinese astronomers also observed sunspots, which are sometimes large enough to be visible to the naked eye, and began recording them in detail in the "imperial histories." They recorded the appearance of comets (including the appearance of Halley's comet in 240 B.C.E.). In the fourth century B.C.E. the astronomer Gan De created a comprehensive star catalogue, plotting the position of more than 1,000 stars. A tradition also records that Gan De made the first observation of Ganymede, a moon of Jupiter, without a telescope or artificial optics of any kind.

Earth Science

Geology and metallurgy made important advances in the early Chinese dynasties. Geologists carefully recorded their discoveries while keeping the practical application of their knowledge foremost. For example, they constantly compared rocks and soils above the ground with those found beneath it. The Chinese discovered, for example, that the presence of hematite, or metallic stones, above ground indicates the existence of underground veins of iron ore and that the reddish mineral cinnabar is a good indicator of gold or mercury deposits. These observations led to classification systems for minerals, one of which is found in the *Shan hai jing* (The Book of Mountains), a work of the fifth century B.C.E. This book classified rocks according to their hardness, color, and shape, and guided metalsmiths in collecting mineral ores and smelting them into useful finished metals.

Ancient Chinese iron miners discovered magnetite, a rock with magnetic properties. This discovery led to the navigational compass, one of the most important technological breakthroughs in history. The Chinese built south-pointing compasses to guide themselves over land and sea. The pointers on these devices were commonly spoons or representations of animals such as frogs. Later the spoons were replaced by needles, which allowed the compass or pointer much greater accuracy.

The Chinese were also expert in the science of meteorology. They were setting down weather records by the second millennium B.C.E. and making daily calculations of temperature, rainfall amounts, and wind speed and direction. This diligent record keeping brought them knowledge of the earth's hydrologic cycle of precipitation and evaporation, which manifests in wind, clouds, and storms to keep the earth watered and fertile.

Applied Science

In all scientific endeavors of ancient China, theory and observation had practical uses. While observing the sun, an unknown Chinese inventor realized that the sun's position can be measured by the length of its shadow. He then created the gnomon, a simple vertical pole placed upright to cast the sun's shadow. The shadow shrinks to its smallest length at the summer solstice and to its greatest length at the winter solstice. Thus, using the gnomon, the Chinese measured the length of the year and marked the beginning of the seasons. The taller the gnomon, the more accurate the measurement; to raise large gnomons, the Chinese constructed massive brick structures, many of which still stand. The scientist Zu Gengzhi took the gnomon a step further by adding a horizontal measuring scale and making the device small and light enough to be carried.

Other Chinese breakthroughs include the making of cast iron and the forging of harder, more durable steel by blowing oxygen onto the cast iron and causing its carbon content to drop. This process relies on another ancient Chinese invention, the double-action piston bellows, which forces air continuously into a forge or oven. Chinese inventors also came up with gimbals—small iron rings that support an object and allow that object to remain upright no matter how the rings around it are turned. The gimbal became an important component of marine compasses, which must function accurately aboard ships in constant motion, and the gyroscope, which was invented by the second century B.C.E. The Chinese also invented, in the ancient period, umbrellas, stirrups, porcelain, hot-air balloons, iron plows, kites, and paper. Chain pumps, which allow users to raise water from a canal or ditch into a field of crops, are still in use in rural China. The south-pointing carriage was used for navigation on land. The device supported the figure of a man, pointing toward the horizon; no matter which way the carriage was turned, the figure always pointed south. A complex series of gears governed the transfer of motion from the wheels to the figure.

One of the marvels of early Chinese science and engineering was the curious object known as the spouting bowl. This large, precisely cast bronze bowl was filled with water. When the bowl was carefully rubbed at the handles, the water within the bowl began to spout and the entire bowl began to hum. The steady rubbing created a certain wavelength and frequency in the water's motion that caused a standing wave—one that moves up and down, not sideways.

One of the most important scientific quests of ancient China was the search for an elixir of life. Chinese alchemists sought to create gold and silver from baser elements and experimented with the properties of semiprecious stones such as jade. One could be made immortal, it was believed, if one ingested an eternal substance, such as gold, which does not rust or burn.

Chinese alchemists undertook long and complex experiments, always basing their work on the five elements and the concept of yin and yang. They heated and mixed chemicals derived from rocks, soil, and earth, as well as bones, teeth, and hair. They dissolved them in water, vinegar, mercury, and saltpeter. They studied the changes in the color and appearance of the elements, noting that different metals have different melting points and give off different colors when put in the fire. Alchemists also studied the effect of these substances on the body when applied to the skin or when taken in through drinking or eating them. Early chemical experimentation was held to be a great secret in ancient China and forbidden to common workers and peasants. Chemists, astronomers, geologists, and other scientists worked diligently for the emperor and were kept within the palace quarters and the imperial capital, where they were closely watched.

One of the most important scientists of ancient China was Zhang Heng, a scholar of the Han dynasty, who was born in 78 C.E. He served the dynasty as imperial historian and studied astronomy, geography, and the physics of earthquakes. A brilliant mapmaker, he created detailed renderings of the empire while relying on the magnetic compass, which had allowed greater accuracy in maps and navigational charts. As tools for military campaigns, these maps were of vital importance to the emperor, who kept them a closely guarded state secret.

By recording the locations and dates of earthquakes, Zhang also took a scientific approach to understanding this dangerous natural phenomenon. His ingenious seismograph, known as the earth motion instrument, was a large bronze bowl that held thin copper rods placed horizontally across its mouth. The rods were attached to dragon's heads, positioned at the edge of the bowl at the eight major points of the compass. The dragon's heads held small copper balls and lay directly above small bronze frogs, cast with their mouths open and directed upward. A tremor or earthquake caused the ball to fall from the mouth of the dragon closest to the tremor into the frog's mouth, causing a small warning bell to ring. The device was activated by the wave motion of earth tremors, which move at great speed through the earth's crust. In 138 C.E. the instrument successfully recorded an earthquake 310 miles west of the Han capital.

As an astronomer, Zhang correctly surmised that eclipses were caused by the shadow of the moon passing over the earth. The ability to predict eclipses was sought after by the emperors, who thus gave themselves the aura of seers and prophets who lived closer to the gods. Zhang also constructed a model of the universe, showing the changing positions of the stars. In the field of mathematics he calculated the value of pi (the ratio of the circumference of a circle to its diameter) to 3.162, the most precise calculation of this number up to that time.

Mathematics in Ancient China

Many historians also claim China as birthplace of the decimal system, in which place values are used to express single digits, 10s, 100s, and so on. The earliest Chinese counting systems used a system of rods placed in small boxes; the rods represented certain values depending on their position. No rods meant a value of zero, a concept that was vital to mathematical calculations and which originated in China (though its representation by a symbol came later and may have actually been invented in Southeast Asia.) Later this physical system of representing numbers developed into the abacus—a small, portable counting device that is still in use throughout China and the rest of Asia.

The Chinese also invented the concept of negative numbers, which in their counting system were represented by black rods (as opposed to red, used for positive numbers). The Chinese were the first to use decimal fractions and algebraic calculations for geometrical relationships. By the fifth century C.E. Chinese mathematicians had calculated the value of pi to 10 decimal places, putting them far ahead of Greek mathematicians working out the same value at that time.

The philosopher Mo Zi, who lived in the fifth century, applied himself to important questions in mathematics as well as physics, including the nature of light and matter. His followers, known as Mohists, lived in small communities and devoted themselves to scientific experiment and theorizing. They studied the force of gravity, the laws of motion, the nature of space and time, the use of fulcrums, and the equilibrium of objects floating in water. One of their inventions was a room-sized camera that projected an image through a small hole bored into a wall facing the sun. Mohists also carefully studied shadows cast by animals and natural objects, and the reflections in convex and concave mirrors. They were the first in the world to use experiments to draw conclusions about the nature of light waves. Their ideas were compiled in a book known as the *Mo jing* (The Mohist Canon), a work that has been closely studied by Chinese scientists since the 18th century.

Science in India

The civilization of the Indus River valley, in what is now northwestern India and Pakistan, developed while the first large cities were also growing in Mesopotamia (along the Tigris and Euphrates rivers in what is now Iraq) and the Yellow River valley of China. The early cities of India developed a precise system of measurement and made several breakthroughs in technology and engineering. Indus Valley cities, including Harappa and Mohenjo Daro, had drainage and sewer systems, indoor toilets, and paved roads. Chemists applied their knowledge to the craft of smelting molten metal ores to create steel and other useful products. Indus Valley steel was in wide use throughout Asia, the Middle East, and Europe by the first millennium B.C.E.

In later Vedic (or classical) times, Indian philosophers divided the natural world into five elements: earth, fire, air, water, and ether (or space). According to this philosophy, the first four elements are made of invisible small particles, the smallest of which was called *parmanu*. Each element has a corresponding sense in the human being: touch, sight, sound, taste, and smell. Everything on earth was created by chance combinations of the five elements, while the earth itself is a large round object under the control of the sun. The sun, in fact, controls all the planets that wander through the sky against the background of the fixed stars. The earth is divided into seven large islands, all surrounded by oceans of water.

The ancient texts known as the Upanishads delve into the essential nature, or *svabhāva*, of the elements and all objects in nature. These objects are subject to the workings of chance, or random occurrence, known as *yadrccha*. The philosopher Kaṭāda, writing in the sixth century B.C.E., is given credit by some historians as the first creator of the atomic theory—the idea that all matter is composed of invisible, and indivisible, atoms—in his work known as the *Vaiśe Ṣikasūtra of Kaṇāda* (which precedes a similar theory of the Greek philosopher Democritus). Kaṇāda claimed that matter can never be created or destroyed; atoms combine to form particles, which in turn make up all objects in the universe.

The school known as the Jainists came up with some startling ideas about the nature of matter. They theorized that atoms might have a positive and negative charge, a phenomenon that has been proved by modern particle physics. The Jainists also believed that atomic particles had a property of "spin," or intrinsic motion. This is a central idea in quantum mechanics that was further developed by Western scientists in the 20th century.

Indian Astronomy and Mathematics

The ancient Indians were skilled observers of the skies. Texts known as the *Siddhāntas* covered mathematics and astronomy. The authors tackled the problems of planetary motion, the force of gravity, and the position of the sun relative to the earth and planets. Indian mathematics was the most advanced of the ancient world. India developed the set of numerals that now prevail in calculations all over the world, including the Western world. These numbers date back to the earliest civilizations of the Indus River valley. They were employed in a system of weights and measures used by farmers and builders. The Vedic literature of ancient India contains calculations of the proper placement of sacred fires and the sizes and dimensions of sacrificial altars. The writers of these texts worked out the nature of square roots and the concept that became known as the Pythagorean theorem on the area of a right triangle, long before the Greek mathematician Pythagoras existed.

The ancient Indians used and understood addition, subtraction, multiplication, division, algebra, trigonometry, and logarithms. They worked out a basic form of calculus—the science of measuring and representing variable quantities in the natural world. The leading astronomer and mathematician of ancient India, Āryabhaṭa, collected all this knowledge in the *Āryabhaṭa*, a text explaining how to calculate square and cube roots as well as volume and area. Attempting to come up with unified mathematical models of planetary motion, Āryabhaṭa concluded that the apparent motion of the stars and planets is caused by the rotation of the earth and its movement around the sun. Āryabhaṭa understood that the other planets orbit the sun, they orbit in elliptical rather than circular paths, and lunar eclipses are caused by the shadow of the moon. He came closest of all ancient astronomers to understanding the true nature of the earth, sun, moon, and solar system.

Another important field of research in ancient India was the science of linguistics—the study of languages, vocabulary, and grammar. The religious texts of the Vedic Period advanced the idea of tenses, verbs, and noun cases and the concept of the two basic meanings of words: that expressed by the speaker and that perceived by the listener. The linguist Pāṇini, who lived in the early fifth century B.C.E., analyzed the elements of Sanskrit, the language used in religious texts of the Indian subcontinent, and detailed its working in 3,959 rules, which are still studied in modern times. His theories were further developed by Bhartrihari, a linguist of the fifth century C.E. These two experts laid an important foundation for modern linguistics, which originated with studies in Sanskrit in the 18th century.

EUROPE

BY MICHAEL J. O'NEAL

The concept of *science* as a field of formal scholarly inquiry and organized thought has arisen only in recent centuries, so to speak of science in ancient Europe is not entirely accurate. Modern scientists pursue their research using the scientific method. They assume cause-and-effect relationships between natural occurrences. They make hypotheses about problems, test them by gathering data under controlled conditions, and then make generalizations about cause and effect that might in time gain the status of scientific laws. When the topic of science in the ancient world is discussed, what is generally meant is evidence for a system of observation of the physical world and the evidence for some forms of calculations. The challenge in ancient Europe is that there are no texts, so scholars have relatively few primary sources they can study to learn about ancient European science. In large part they have had to rely on the writings of Greek and Roman historians, who recorded what they observed about scientific practices in their northern colonies and client regions. Their observations, though, were made in late antiquity, so little is known about European scientific practice in earlier ages, such as the Bronze Age.

Ancient Europeans lived in a world in which they were subject to mysterious natural forces: the weather, disease, earthquakes, floods, and the like. Thus, one motivation for making observations about the physical world was to discover ways of controlling those forces, control that could be accomplished by trying to know the gods' will and make predictions about the future. Diviners, seers, shamans, and priests studied the attributes of nature—the movement of heavenly bodies, or the magical properties of plants—to learn how to exert some control over the natural world. These people were believed to have divine, supernatural knowledge, which they could use for the benefit of their communities.

Another way of considering ancient European science is to see it as the sort of science employed in engineering and medicine, where observations about the physical world are used to develop skills in various technologies, including, for example, agriculture, metalworking, and medicine. In the 21st century this is called *applied science*. Agriculture arrived in Europe about 9,000 years ago from the Near East, and over the next 4,000 years agricultural communities were established throughout the Continent. Early European farming communities planted wheat and barley as their main crops and raised cattle, sheep, goats, and pigs.

Clearly, these agriculturalists needed to make observations about the physical world and to develop innovative ways of raising crops that had been brought from the Near East into the European environment. They made observations about the weather and soil conditions. They experimented with fertilizers and various types of crops, primarily grains such as barley and wheat. Early European farmers understood the differing properties of flint and other types of stone and used the ones that best suited their needs. They developed methods for storing their crops. Techniques for making pottery were continually refined using higher and higher firing temperatures. They learned that allowing fields to remain fallow for a period of time increased future yields. Herders learned to breed varieties of cattle that originated in the Near East but had to adapt to the colder climate of Europe. Animals like cattle that had previously been used primarily for their meat were harnessed for power to pull wagons and plows. Early Europeans learned that enzymes mixed with milk produce cheese and that reducing the moisture content of meat, fish, fruits, and vegetables by drying them is a way to preserve them. They also learned to make underground grain silos that kept grain from rotting and succumbing to pests by denying oxygen to the grain. All these activities presume some basic scientific knowledge about how the world works, about the properties of matter, about measurement and engineering, and the like. All of them presume, too, a process of trial and error over time, as agriculturalists tried crops and farming methods, passing along what they learned to their descendants.

Aiding the development of agriculture was the development of metalworking. Like most of the world's cultures, ancient European culture evolved from the Stone Age, when tools were crafted of stone, to the discovery of metals. The first metal widely used in tool making was copper. The Bronze Age began at different times in different regions when it was discovered that mixing tin with copper resulted in bronze, a much more durable metal than copper. At some point during the fifth millennium B.C.E. it was observed that certain ores contained copper, which could be smelted and collected and then pounded into simple forms. Over time, the technology for working copper improved to the point where it could be cast into more complicated shapes. Around 3000 B.C.E. in southeastern Europe, ancient chemists discovered that adding about 10 percent tin to a mixture of copper would produce an entirely new metal, bronze, which revolutionized metallurgy. Again these discoveries and innovations were the product of systematic observations that bordered on what might be considered science.

By about 1100 B.C.E. ancient Europeans entered the Iron Age, having discovered both that the ground in much of Europe was rich in iron ore and how to use that ore. Among the ancient Celts two primary cultures emerged around ironworking. The first was the Hallstatt culture, named after a town near Salzburg, Austria, where extensive mining operations were conducted beginning in about 1000 B.C.E. About 500 years later, the La Tène culture developed in modern-day Switzerland. These cultures produced an enormous amount of iron, and archaeologists have discovered numerous Iron Age artifacts from this region. These developments indicate that there were scientific advances in mining, separating metal from ore, controlling temperatures in furnaces, and turning iron into useful products. Eventually ironworkers became chemists of sorts when they discovered that mixing carbon with iron produced much harder steel.

The development of iron led not only to better weapons—the Europeans carried the art of sword making to new heights—but also to better farming tools such as plows and harrows. Similarly, the Europeans were adept at building carriages and wagons and learned to cover wooden wheels with a metal band, or tire, that made the wheels more durable.

Medicine and healing were other forms of applied science. These activities were often associated with magic and with the ability of some people to understand the will of the gods. The Druids, the priestly class of the ancient Celts, gained wisdom about the healing power of plants. This wisdom was accumulated over long stretches of time by trial and error, as well as by making detailed observations about the effects of substances on the human body. Examples include willow tree bark, which contains a substance that is chemically similar to the active ingredient in aspirin. Celery and parsley were also thought to have healing powers. These substances were probably gathered according to a strict schedule based on the phases of the moon, in the belief that all the powers of nature worked hand in hand. In many senses ancient healers worked like experimental scientists, observing symptoms, trying herbal treatments, and seeing what seemed to help.

The ancient Europeans showed some skill in surgery. Near Munich, Germany, for instance, archaeologists discovered the tomb of a so-called warrior-surgeon that dates to about the third or second century B.C.E. and contained a number of medical and surgical implements: probes, retractors, and a trepanation saw, used for cutting holes in the skull. Trepanation was widely used to treat head injuries and psychological disorders, and healers used both saws and drills to make their holes. A large number of skulls have been found with neat holes drilled or cut into them. While many people died during this type of surgery, many others did not, for the holes in some skulls show evidence of healing. Earlier skeletal remains of two people found in Moravia, a region in the modern-day Czech Republic, show that surgeons operated successfully on them. In one case they removed a portion of bone, and in the other case they amputated a limb. In both cases the surgery took place sometime around 5500 B.C.E. The skeletal remains show that the patients healed and survived for several years following the surgery.

Little is known about the mathematical inquiries of the ancient Europeans. What is known has been discovered from practical applications. For instance, the circular stone megalithic monuments of the British Isles, including not only Stonehenge but also the megaliths at Avebury and other sites, suggest that their builders may have had some understanding of pi, the Greek letter that represents the relationship between the radius of a circle and its circumference. The geometric layout of these sites also suggests that their builders may have grasped the principle of the Pythagorean theorem before Pythagoras, the Greek mathematician usually credited with discovering the relationship between the squares of a triangle's sides and that of its hypotenuse. Clearly, the ancient megalith builders understood principles of measurement and engineering. Measurement was also vital to European farmers, who had to devise ways to measure agricultural output and fields.

Extending back to the Neolithic Period the ancient Europeans were keen observers of the skies. A bronze disk with gold inlays found at Nebra in central Germany and dated to about 1600 B.C.E. is a controversial find owing to the circumstances of its discovery, but it is interpreted as bearing a depiction of the star cluster known as the Pleiades. By the time of the Roman Empire, Roman historians were praising the Celts for their astronomical skill. The writer Martial (ca. 40–103 C.E.), for example, noted that the Celts believed that the world was round, not flat. The Celts devised an astronomical calendar as far back as 1100 B.C.E., and for many years the ancient Greeks debated the question of whether the Celts borrowed their astronomical skills from the Greeks or the Greeks borrowed them from the Celts. In either case the Celts kept meticulous records of astronomical events and were even able to predict many regularly recurring events. A good example is provided by the tides and their relationship with the phases of the moon. A primary motivation was not simple human curiosity but the desire to understand the will of the gods, including the later Christian God, and to exert some measure of control over natural forces.

GREECE

BY PHILIPPA LANG

In ancient Greece before the sixth century B.C.E. people could roughly predict the movements of the stars and constellations throughout the year, relate the movements to seasonal change, and use the stars to navigate their boats and ships. They had the technology to make metals and other materials, such as pottery, both for practical use and pure decoration. They used plants and foodstuffs for medicine, and they had stories that explained the world around them and its origins, usually in terms of gods. The sea god Poseidon was the cause of earthquakes, and thunder came from Zeus. None of this is what is now called science. No word for science existed in ancient Greece, and the category of science, its methods, aims, and content, is a modern construction that does not transfer back to the distant past.

From the sixth century B.C.E. onward, however, some Greeks developed ways of thinking about the world and efforts at controlling it that were similar enough to the modern concept of science that the term can be used. Ancient science can be defined as attempts to explain, understand, predict, and sometimes control the natural world. But it is important to realize that the ancient Greeks did not think of themselves as doing science, and they had no agreed-upon scientific method.

In the sixth century B.C.E. a small group of people now known as the pre-Socratics developed several theories about the origins of the universe and its fundamental components. These theories survive only as fragmentary summaries and quotations in later writers, so not very much is known about them. They did not agree with one another, but what they had in common was the belief that the universe had a consistent and ordered nature that could be understood and explained by human reason. The Greek word for nature is *physis*, which is where the modern word *physics* comes from. The theories explain natural phenomena without involving traditional gods or other supernatural forces, though they may describe natural forces in terms of the gods or they may view the whole of ordered nature as itself divine. This new approach is now often called *naturalistic* or *natural philosophy*. Thales, the earliest pre-Socratic, suggested that the world floated on water and that earthquakes were caused by waves, not by Poseidon. Xenophanes looked at fossils of fish and argued that they showed parts of the earth had long ago been under water.

Most pre-Socratics also argued that the world and everything in it was made out of the combination of a very few elements, or sometimes that it was only one element in many different forms. Such basic elements were usually earth, air, fire, and water, but there were also other views. Democritus theorized that the basic units of matter were tiny unbreakable shapes called *atoms* that fell through a void. When they collided and stuck together, they made larger objects of many different kinds.

Another common pre-Socratic theme was a concern with what counts as truth and what kinds of evidence are reliable. This concern is called *epistemology*, the study of theories about knowledge, truth, and reliability, and it is closely related to science. But pre-Socratics were not scientists. Later Greek thought called them *philosophers*, which means "those who love knowledge." Pre-Socratic inquiries made little to no use of experiment and appealed selectively to everyday observations. They agreed neither on most theories nor on how to evaluate them and decide which is better, or more nearly true. They were often as interested in ethics and politics as in scientific topics. Most pre-Socratics were charismatic individualists with radical and highly speculative views, rather than scientists in any modern sense. For example, Empedocles was a wonder-worker who claimed to be able to control the weather and cure the sick.

ARISTOTLE

The philosopher Aristotle (fourth century B.C.E.) was the first person to do something very similar to science as it is understood now. He argued that the causes of things were within the natural world and could be explained by a careful investigation of nature. He systematically collected information on living creatures and classified them by types and characteristics, trying to grasp how things worked and why. He dissected many animals; made first-hand observations of insects, fish, mammals, and birds; and asked experts and specialists such as fishermen and beekeepers for information. His books *History of Animals* and *Parts of Animals* describe more than 500 species of living creatures, and his account of the dogfish was not equaled until the 19th century.

Aristotle's aim was not just to record details for their own sake but also to gather and use reliable data to arrive at theories about how and why things worked. An important guiding principle for him was the concept of teleology, which assumes that everything in nature is the way it is for a reason, except for unavoidable side effects. Aristotle said that "nature did nothing in vain." So when Aristotle looked, for example, at a heart, he assumed that the heart did something useful for the organism and did it well, and he tried to work out what that purpose might be and how the heart accomplished it. This can be a useful principle of discovery in biology, but it also meant that Aristotle and his followers rarely accepted that anything could happen just by chance, without a final purpose.

Aristotelian physics, though incorrect, was extremely influential. While Aristotle did a lot of sustained and organized investigation into nature, like most other Greek thinkers he rarely carried out experiments. Experiment was rare in the ancient world and did not usually have much authority, and the notion of test by falsification of a predicted hypothesis (the modern scientific method) was never suggested. After the ancient period a later thinker John Philoponus (sixth century C.E.) is said to have done experiments disproving Aristotle's claim that heavier objects fall faster than lighter ones, but no one took much notice until Galileo finally disproved Aristotle some 2,000 years later, in the 16th century.

Despite the lack of experiment, the concept of proof was very important in ancient science and philosophy. Aristotle developed the first explicit system of logic, in which, if the starting points are true, the proof is so constructed and worked out that the conclusion must also be correct. It is an important idea and works well in mathematics, but it is much more difficult, as Aristotle recognized, to apply to biology and other real-world situations that have many complicated variables.

The Lyceum

Aristotle set up a like-minded group of thinkers and learners, a school (the Lyceum or the Peripatetic), and many of his followers did similar research. Theophrastus (371–287 B.C.E.), the head of the Lyceum after Aristotle's death, investigated and collected data on plants and stones and wrote books about fire and weather. Strato (d. 269 B.C.E.), who was the leader of the Lyceum after Theophrastus, was interested in basic matter and problems such as how people could hear through solid walls. Little of Strato's work survives, but he seems to have argued that there were tiny pockets of void (empty space) within matter that explained how sound traveled through solids. Strato's theories had practical applications in the work of the mechanists.

The kind of science done by the ancient philosophers and other thinkers was an intellectual project largely restricted to the social and literate elite. Philosophers often justified what they did as the highest form of human endeavor, the acquisition of knowledge for its own sake and not for gain or use, practiced by people who did not need to work. But there were tensions. A comedy of the fifth century B.C.E., *The Clouds*, by Aristophanes, satirizes this kind of thought as ivory tower navel-gazing.

Specialist Thinkers

For Aristotle, scientific understanding of the natural world, natural philosophy, or natural history was part of a broader project to understand and thus to be able to manage human life and ethics in its entirety, from poetry to theology and from politics (Aristotle defined humans as political animals) to the nature of friendship, and he was as interested in rhetoric as in logic. Thus philosophy is not the same as science, even for Aristotle, the most scientific philosopher of the ancient world.

But there were contemporaries of Aristotle who specialized in certain areas of intellectual and scientific enquiry. Mathematics was a developing field. Greek mathematics is primarily geometrical rather than arithmetical (algebra had not been invented). Although many theorems were known to other older civilizations, such as the Babylonian and Egyptian, a distinctive Greek addition, perhaps influenced by philosophy's concern with standards for truth and certainty, was a concern to prove a general theorem would be true for all possible values.

Well-known mathematicians of this era include Theodorus and Theaetetus, both of whom have roles in one of Plato's fictional philosophical dialogues on the nature of knowledge. The Pythagorean philosopher and mathematician Archytas, in the early fifth century B.C.E., viewed mathematics as essential to understanding reality. Archytas developed many solutions and proofs, including the solution to the problem of doubling the cube, and provided a mathematical account of musical scales. There was increasing agreement on methodology, terminology, and what counted as a proof. By around 300 B.C.E., the mathematician Euclid could write a book called *Elements* (of Mathematics) that laid out all known mathematics as a set of demonstrated proofs from which, beginning at the most basic hypotheses and definitions, increasingly complex theorems could be reliably derived. Mathematics had become an ideal of intellectual inquiry, the successful pursuit and discovery of knowledge for the sake of knowledge. It was also vital in several other kinds of investigation, especially astronomy and mechanics.

Astronomy

Naturalistic theories about the universe and its origins, called *cosmology* and *cosmogony*, respectively, had been a major theme of pre-Socratic thought. Anaximander, for example, said that the world was a cylinder, with humans living on one of the flat ends, surrounded by a thick mist that obscured the spheres of fire that enclosed the mist. People could glimpse the enclosing fire through pinpoint holes in the mist, holes that were perceived as the sun, moon, and stars.

Astronomical observations of the movement of the stars and their relationship to seasons were much older, because they were crucial to a largely agricultural society. Official calendars followed the phases of the moon, but over many years such calendars become out of phase with the solar year, until an event originally placed in the spring took place when the leaves were falling.

In the fifth century B.C.E. Meton, probably working partly from Babylonian written observations of the movements of the heavens (going back much further than those of the Greeks), worked out a 19-year lunisolar calendar that would have kept the moon and the sun in step over a 19-year period to a precise degree of accuracy. The Athenian state did not adopt this as the official calendar. The results of specialist intellectual inquiry were not always viewed as socially useful or as an improvement on tradition.

In astronomy itself, however, observations were becoming fuller and more detailed, including Callippus's work (fourth century B.C.E.) on the exact dates of the summer and winter solstices and the realization that the year's four seasons are not of equal length. These observations were incorporated into attempts to produce models of the cosmos that would account for such phenomena as the movements of the sun, the lunar cycle, and the movements of the so-called wandering stars—the planets. (*Planet* is Greek for "wanderer.")

The traditional story is that Plato challenged astronomers and mathematicians to come up with such a model and that in response Eudoxus developed his theory of concentric spheres. In this theory the sun, moon, and five planets are fixed to 27 spheres around the common center of the stationary earth, and these spheres revolve on different axes of rotation and at different speeds. The theory was elaborated by Callippus, mechanized by Aristotle (by which time it had 76 spheres), and eventually abandoned in the second century B.C.E. when the mathematician-astronomers Apollonius of Perga and Hipparchus invented models of epicyclic and eccentric rotation. Their model was further refined into the Ptolemaic universe worked out by the astronomer Claudius Ptolemaeus (Ptolemy) in the second century C.E., a system that survived until Copernicus.

The aim of all such models seems at least partly to have been "to save the phenomena"—that is, to discover a working mathematical model of the heavens that allowed observations to be accepted and not explained away as optical illusions or untrue in some other way. Some of these models may have been largely exercises in mathematical ingenuity, but many astronomers were certainly interested in trying to discover how the universe actually worked. In the third century B.C.E. Aristarchus of Samos proposed a heliocentric cosmos, but only one person supported the idea, and later astronomers such as Claudius Ptolemaeus attacked it on the grounds that it was not supported by observation or by current (Aristotelian) theories of physics.

Astronomy was an enterprise that required considerable mathematical knowledge, beyond that even of most philosophers, although most people probably had a very basic form of astronomical knowledge. Specialized and difficult though mathematics was, it did have practical applications in the everyday world in meteorology, geography, and especially astrology.

Meteorology

The Greeks traditionally associated changes in the weather with changes in the sky. Storms, for example, were more frequent around the time of the equinoxes. The sun, moon, stars, and planets were thought to be much closer to the earth than they actually are, and so their movements were thought to affect the air around the earth and thus the weather. As astronomy's observations and models became increasingly detailed and precise, predictions of the weather also grew much more elaborate. In the third century B.C.E. the poet Aratus of Soli recast a famous astronomical book by Eudoxus about the movements of the stars and related weather patterns into poetry. It was extremely popular among the literate population of the ancient Greek and Roman world.

Geography

The early Greeks believed that the lands around the Mediterranean Sea were surrounded by a huge ocean. Going far enough east, west, north, or south would take a person to the edge of the world. Slowly, traders and other travelers brought back information about foreign lands, and the world the Greeks knew about got bigger.

By the fourth century B.C.E. many intellectuals had realized the world must be a sphere. Aristotle pointed out that someone watching a ship sailing away sees the front end of it disappear first. In the third century B.C.E. Eratosthenes calculated the circumference of the earth, possibly to within about 311 miles. (The exact length of the unit of measurement he used is not known.) Although only a few experts and, to a smaller extent, educated laymen, traders, and the military needed to know much about astronomical geography, those who did were slowly building up a three-dimensional picture of the Northern Hemisphere.

Astrology

Before the Greeks, Babylonian priests watched the sky for omens, and their long-term observations provided vital astronomical data for the Greeks. The data enabled astronomers to predict the future movements of the stars based on past patterns. Although the details are unclear, sometime between the third and first centuries B.C.E. this ability to predict movements developed among the Greek population of Egypt into an astrological system, a synthesis of Greek thought with Babylonian omen-based astronomy and some small Egyptian influence. An important part of this astrological system was the notion of a horoscope, in which the positions of the heavenly bodies at the moment of a person's birth determined that person's future; thus astronomy was crucial. There are surviving Greek horoscopes from the first century B.C.E. Astrology quickly became extremely popular, though not everyone was convinced and those who were held many different views as to how it worked. Astrology relied on the astronomical and mathematical knowledge of a very small group of experts, and thus made mathematics relevant to the lives of many people in society other than the literate, intellectual elite.

Mechanics

Mathematics, with an understanding of certain physical principles, was also crucial to the emerging discipline of mechanics. From very early times in Greek society there had been craftsmen and engineers who could build a ship, a fountain, or a defensive wall. This kind of specialist expertise, which could be written down but was usually passed on in oral and practical lessons from teacher to apprentice, is called a *techne*, usually translated as "art" or "craft." The word *technology* is derived from it.

Some arts, such as architecture, required mathematical knowledge. The physics of motion, materials, and machines was also a topic of interest to some philosophers and other intellectuals. Aristotle's school, the Lyceum, produced a treatise called *Mechanical Problems* that discussed the workings of common machines such as pulleys and windlasses, not to mention the physics of the knee joint.

Theories were developed about the behavior of air and liquids under pressure, or pneumatics and hydraulics. Pneumatics, hydraulics, and other applications of physics resulted in the production of machines made by a specialized group of intellectual inventors, the mechanists. Many of the mechanists' devices involved steam power. Ctesibius of Alexandria, working in the third century B.C.E. invented, among other things, a water organ and statues and doors that moved automatically. These kinds of toys and spectacular set pieces did not usually have any practical purpose. The ancient world had very little industry in the modern sense. They were perhaps made to display cleverness and to surprise and entertain a client base, an audience of the social elite, or anyone else who saw the mechanists' products.

But there were important practical roles for mechanists as developers of improved military technology, defensive structures, and civic buildings. The mechanist Philon of Byzantium, in the second century B.C.E., described how the Greek kings of Egypt, the Ptolemies, funded engineer-mechanists to conduct a series of experiments that would result in building the most effective kind of catapult. The lighthouse of Alexandria was also an example of the mechanists' practical technology.

Mechanics was heavily utilized by governments and had considerable social importance. Many relatively well-off individuals used architects and engineers to construct private buildings and machines for them. But the fact that mechanics and engineering were largely practical and that practitioners were professionals who got funding and payment—and probably also because manual labor was involved—meant that many of the elite regarded the discipline of mechanics as inferior to mathematics and natural philosophy. The ancient Greek intellectual ideal was to study the nature of the universe for the sake of knowledge alone.

Many mechanists argued against this downgrading of their expertise, and some experts managed to become famous both for their mathematical ability and their useful machines. Archimedes (287–212/211 B.C.E.), known for having allegedly shouted "Eureka" (I've found it!) in the bath on discovering the law of buoyancy, was well known both as a highly theoretical mathematician and the inventor of many practical machines. The Archimedean screw, named after and probably invented by him, made it much easier to lift water from the ground and was widely used for centuries in agriculture. During the siege of his city, Syracuse, by the Romans, Archimedes is said to have constructed many innovative war machines, such as a claw that pulled ships out of the water. It is unclear how reliable these reports are in their details, but certainly Archimedes was believed to have been important to the defense of Syracuse.

Medicine

Traditional healing in Greece consisted of a combination of the use of plants and foodstuffs as drugs, surgical procedures that were traumatic in themselves, and the use of incantations. This combined approach to medicine became a *techne*, an art, though people might also take care of themselves by self-medicating, appealing to the gods and participating in healing cults, or going to experts such as drug collectors (root cutters), purifiers, and magicians.

In the fifth and fourth centuries B.C.E. many practitioners of medicine adopted a more exclusively naturalistic approach, which both influenced and was influenced by contemporary developments in philosophy. In this naturalistic concept of medicine, physicians developed theories about the nature of the human body as a biological animal and treated illness on the basis of this understanding. The texts of the so-called Hippocratic Corpus were written by an unknown number of anonymous authors during this period. They were later collected together under the name of the famous physician Hippocrates of Cos (fifth century B.C.E.), though it is not known whether Hippocrates actually wrote any of them.

Some of these Hippocratic texts explicitly assert a naturalistic approach and describe theories of physiology and pathology; others are more practically oriented but assume a naturalistic view. The theories described in these works differ, but they often involve one or more substances in the body called *humors*, such as phlegm, bile, and blood, which need to be in balance for health. Physicians demonstrated their authority and expertise by being able to predict the course of a disease and, if it did not seem likely to be fatal, by intervening with advice on diet and activity and sometimes with more drastic remedies such as purgative drugs or bloodletting, all with the aim of rebalancing the humors. They also practiced traumatic surgery and cauterization of wounds. Diet and exercise (together known as *regimen*) were also widely prescribed as preventive measures.

Anatomy in the Hippocratic corpus is very speculative and often inaccurate. Aristotle carried out animal dissections in the fourth century B.C.E. In Alexandria during the third century the physicians Herophilus and Erasistratus performed human dissection and even, according to a later but almost certainly reliable report, human vivisection, or operation on living beings. This greatly improved anatomical knowledge, including discovery of the heart valves, the ovaries and Fallopian tubes, the structure of the eye, the difference between motor and sensory nerves, and many other findings. But physicians still disagreed widely on how to interpret their findings. Herophilus seems to have held a largely traditional theory of humoral imbalance. Erasistratus developed a radical new theory, influenced by contemporary developments in mechanics, of the heart as a pump and the mechanical movement of fluids around the body according to pressure and vacuum. He argued that the arteries contained only air, while veins contained only blood.

Possibly because even systematic investigation of human anatomy had produced neither agreement on theory nor improvements in clinical treatment, some doctors rejected theory altogether as useless. They called themselves *empiricists* and said that doctors should merely remember that certain remedies had in the past been associated with recovery from certain symptoms, without speculating about causes and effects.

Medicine consisted of a specialized and practical expertise carried out by professionals, usually for a fee. As such, some philosophers criticized it as being limited in scope and as having less intellectual status than philosophy. In response, some physicians claimed that medicine was an exemplary form of knowledge and very difficult to master. Other doctors argued that medicine should not be too theoretical but should be based on practical experience and paying attention to the individual case.

Some contemporary dramas and epitaphs for the dead attacked doctors as incompetent. Certainly their rate of success was not high, though probably not noticeably worse than other kinds of healers. The Hippocratic text *Epidemics* seems to imply that physicians treated all social classes, including the very poor, but it is difficult to assess whether doctors were called in for routine illness or only when the situation became obviously serious.

Medicine, in the sense of a naturalistic or scientific medicine exclusive of other forms of healing such as religion or magic, had several roles in society. First, as a practical system of knowledge like that of a craft, it was widely used but perhaps little trusted. Second, as an intellectual enterprise, it tried to investigate and understand the human being as a biological animal, using methods of observation, dissection, and occasionally experiment and reasoning from the data thus produced. This role was strongly associated with literacy, high social status, and natural philosophy, and there was some conflict between philosophy and medicine over their relative intellectual merits.

ROME

BY PHILIPPA LANG

The word *science* is derived from the Latin verb *scio*, which means "to know" and in particular "to know by finding out," though it is not simply equivalent to what we mean by science today. We can roughly define science in ancient Roman as any investigation or understanding of the material and natural world that proceeds by carefully reasoned argument on the basis of empirical data and assumes that the world will be consistent and ordered. If a stone always rises for a little way and then falls back to earth, the presumption of natural philosophy, or science, is that the stone will always behave in the same way and for the same reasons and that we can work out why it does so.

Science in Roman society and culture was derived to a large extent from science and philosophy in Greek culture. Many of the Roman aristocratic elite during the late Republic (second to first centuries B.C.E.) and then in the Roman Empire of the following centuries translated and discussed Greek philosophy and science, while many Greeks in the Roman Empire also continued to investigate and argue about the way in which things worked. In fact, many leading figures in the fields of science during the Roman Empire were of Greek descent and culture, but they resided in places under Roman control and worked for Roman emperors.

These kinds of investigations were strongly associated with the upper classes, who had the education, time, and inclination to pursue scientific and philosophical knowledge either for its own sake or as part of a general understanding of the world. At this time the major Greek philosophies of the Hellenistic Period (323–31 B.C.E.) each offered a comprehensive understanding of the world and humankind's place in it, though none of them agreed with each other. Many Roman aristocrats and intellectuals aligned themselves with one of these philosophies and contributed to them, and their ethics and theology were interdependent with their natural philosophy—their theories of biology, physiology, psychology, and what we would call physics and chemistry.

At the same time, areas of science with important technological and practical applications were used by both Roman individuals and the Roman government. These included civil, personal, and military engineering and surveying, from architecture to ballistics. Medicine was also very important. Roman and Italian culture incorporated a large amount of traditional medicine in which foods and plants were administered for illness, often accompanied by incantations, magical rituals, and appeals to the gods and other supernatural powers. Contacts with Greek culture, however, introduced the professional phy-

Bust of Pseudo-Seneca, before 1626, by Peter Paul Rubens; this drawing is of a Roman portrait bust thought to be the Roman Stoic philosopher Seneca, who wrote several scientific treatises. (Copyright the Metropolitan Museum of Art)

sician and methods of surgery, cauterization, and sometimes strong drugs. The first Greek doctor in Rome was nicknamed "the butcher" because of his use of such methods, and some Romans, like Pliny the Elder (23–79 C.E.), criticized medicine as un-Roman. Nonetheless, Greek medicine became popular, and doctors in Rome and throughout the empire were usually Greek.

In general, Roman reactions to Greek ideas, including much of Greek science, were complicated. Many traditional Romans thought that the influence of Greek culture might weaken Roman society through its focus on inessential speculation and ways of life, unlike the conventional Roman emphasis on farming, the army, and the duties of political office. Many elite Romans, however, could speak Greek and were interested in such ideas, and they adapted or developed them, writing epic poetry, history, and drama of their own—all forms of literature that the Greeks had invented. Similarly, Greek works on science and philosophy found an elite Roman audience and some Roman practitioners. The Roman politician and philosopher Seneca (4? B.C.E.–65 C.E.), tutor to the future emperor Nero (r. 54–68 C.E.), wrote many works related to his Stoic philosophy, including *Natural Questions*, which explains and discusses such scientific problems as the causes of rainbows and comets.

Social and Intellectual Status

There was to some extent, as in Greek society, a social divide between those working on science and philosophy as a matter of intellectual interest and personal development and those who practiced scientific specialties as a profession, for which they received payment. This was closely related to a common attitude, at least among the first kind of intellectuals, that scientific inquiries were greater if they did not involve actual physical materials or things. "Pure" mathematics, for example, was thought to be superior to applied math. This idea was held partly because the notion of the general proof—one that applies to a class of objects and can be logically proved in the abstract rather than having been tested only for specific, concrete examples—was central to the development of Greek geometry and became an ideal for all intellectual enterprises. Thus, Pythagoras's theorem is expressed thus: "The square of the hypotenuse is equal to the sum of the squares on the other two sides." It is not stated as the numerical formula $5^2 = 3^2 + 4^2$, and so on for every actual set of triangle lengths actually tested.

There was also a common assumption that abstract reasoning was more reliable than sense perception and observable data, even though the former obviously must rely to some extent on the latter. The result is that "practical" or productive forms of knowledge, including some applied science, were seen as less true and certain than more abstract inquiries, as well as being usually practiced by people of less wealth and social status.

However, many people actually working in such fields as engineering and medicine strongly resisted that their subjects were evaluated at this lower status. The Roman Empire Greek mechanist Hero of Alexandria claimed—possibly as a joke—that mechanics was actually better at producing the philosophical ideal of a tranquil life lived without fear or worry than philosophy was because a city with good mechanists and ballistics engineers would never be attacked. The Greek physician Galen (129–ca. 99 C.E.), who was the personal physician of the Roman emperor Marcus Aurelius (r. 161–80 C.E.), tried to work out a set of logical and mathematical rules for medicine, such as a theorem for the length of time it took for a wound to heal based on its size and shape.

Many such practitioners, certainly those at the top of their fields, were literate and well-educated men who argued that their discipline was just as reliable and worthwhile as philosophy or pure mathematics. The dividing line was far from absolute. Many elite lay Romans read works on medicine and mechanics, even if they did not regard them as suitable subjects for a gentleman to practice.

Philosophy Schools

Scientific theories formed an extensive and integral part of several philosophical schools of the Roman age. In this context, a school was a group of like-minded people who learned from each other, sometimes at a shared physical location. No qualifications or formal educational process was implied by the term. These groups had formed in Greece in the third century B.C.E., though their arguments continued to develop. Two important schools were the Stoics and the Epicureans. They had systematic—though completely different—theories about such things as the basic materials of the universe, the physiology of sense perception, and the workings of body and mind. They offered a naturalistic understanding of every kind of phenomenon, from lightning to the way mirrors work to the development of human society. These theories were compatible with, and used to supply evidence for, the Stoics' and Epicureans' theories on ethics, epistemology (the study of nature and the grounds of knowledge), and theology. The Stoics, for instance, considered God to be a material substance present throughout the actual world. Everything that happened was according to God's plan via a mechanistic, completely determined, causal chain. The Epicureans, on the other hand, maintained that the gods were perfect beings made like everything else of constituent particles and void, and they were completely irrelevant to human affairs. For both groups, science was not separable from other areas of human understanding.

A third group, the Skeptics, was not committed to any theory at all because their epistemological position was that there was no definite, clear instance of incontrovertible knowledge about anything and there was no definite proof that any theory was more true than any other. These radical Skeptics in philosophy, and their medical equivalent, the empiricist physicians, criticized the theories and beliefs of everyone else. This meant that people who believed that some theories were true had to improve their arguments against the Skeptics' attacks. It can be argued that skepticism was overall not helpful to philosophy and science because it focused attention away from the actual content of scientific theories and instead highlighted underlying epistemological positions. All theories, whether they were well supported by the evidence or not, were equally vulnerable to skeptical attack because 100 percent certainty was the only standard for truth they would allow.

The scientific theories of the philosophical schools were not often updated. This is primarily because their main aim was to offer the best understanding of the world as a means of achieving what they called *ataraxia*, or a life without disturbance, fear, and worry. They competed with each other as to which of them offered the most convincing way of achieving this state of being, so the philosophical schools had no incentive to revise their basic principles or their scientific theories and tended to be conservative.

Medical Sects

Professional physicians in ancient Roman society—most of them Greeks—were divided into three broad methodological categories: the Empiricists; the so-called Rationalists or Dogmatists; and, from about the first century C.E., the Methodists. These groups were called the medical schools or sects.

The Empiricists emerged in the third century B.C.E. as a group of doctors who shared a common epistemology and methodology. They seem to have been popular among patients, including high-status ones such as kings. Their position was in many ways similar to that of the skeptical philosophers. The Empiricists said that there was no point in investigating the body with the aim of deducing theories about physiology or illness because no such theory could be proved true beyond any doubt and so might be false. They also said that this kind of theoretical knowledge was unnecessary for good medical practice. Empiricist doctors relied on their own experience of treating diseases (*autopsia*) and the recorded or reported experience of other people (*historia*). They associated certain symptoms with particular successful treatments and when they saw the symptoms again, they were reminded to use the same treatments. But they did not draw any conclusions from this about the nature of the disease or why the treatment seemed to work. Empiricists rejected dissection as useless and maintained that observation of internal organs exposed by accident when someone was wounded was enough to learn basic anatomy for the purposes of surgery.

Methodism may go back to the physiological theory and treatments of Asclepiades, a famous Greek doctor who lived in the Roman province of Bithynia in the first century B.C.E. and taught himself medicine as a second career after having been an orator. Asclepiades developed a theory in which he determined that pores in the body are sometimes blocked by some kind of corpuscle (thought of as a minute particle) and that this is what makes people ill. But Methodists themselves did not think that this information was relevant to being a good doctor. According to the Methodists, all diseases shared one of three common features: the patient was too constricted, too lax, or a mixture of the two. They believed that treatment should be based on that alone and that patients should be treated "by opposites"; thus, patients who were too constricted should be treated with relaxants. This was the method (*methodos*). Other knowledge acquired through experience, deduction, or dissection may have been possible but was unnecessary for medical practice. Medicine was, therefore, easy to learn—the Methodist founder Thessalus is reported to have said it took only six months. Methodists did not think that dissection was useful, though they may have thought it was interesting. One famous Methodist, Soranus, a Greek physician of second century C.E. who practiced in Rome, is remembered for his work on gynecology, which has survived largely intact.

All physicians who were neither Empiricists nor Methodists contended that reliable knowledge about physiology and illness could be rationally deduced to at least some extent. For this reason they became collectively known as "Rationalists" or "Dogmatists." This very general agreement, however, was their only common factor. There were many subgroups and even individuals within the rationalists who disagreed with each other about theories, methods, and treatments. Most of them would have agreed that dissection was useful, but few physicians seemed to have done any themselves in the Roman period, even on animals. A notable example of a rationalist who performed dissections is Galen, who carried out dissections and vivisections (operations performed on the living) on many animals, including dogs, goats, Barbary apes, and once an elephant. Galen's dissections were often carried out in public settings, where anyone could watch as a kind of popular theater that Galen used to lend dramatic visual support for his claims about physiology.

Medical Training and Treatments

The usual way to learn medicine was by apprenticeship to a practicing physician. Sons of physicians probably often became doctors themselves as part of a family business. Many elite doctors studied in several places famous as centers of intellectual medicine, such as Pergamum and Alexandria. They may also have been educated in philosophy more generally, as Galen was. It was possible to teach oneself by reading works on medicine, as Asclepiades is said to have done. There were no examinations or legal qualifications to take, so anyone who wanted to set up as a doctor could do so. However, whether people came to a particular doctor depended on his reputation and what they knew about him, and in the early stages of a practice it would have helped to have learned from a locally known doctor or a famous physician elsewhere. Doctors were usually men, though it is possible that female midwives, some of whom were literate and trained in medical methods, treated female patients for a broader range of problems than those associated with childbirth.

In ancient Rome a very common medical treatment was the prescription of a combination of diet and lifestyle recommendations, such as exercise and baths, known as a *regimen.* For illness, drugs could be prescribed. In the Roman period these became increasingly complicated. Drugs that contained only one or two ingredients were called simples, but many drugs were made of numerous ingredients, sometimes more than 100, and such a medicine was called a *polypharmacy.* Women might use contraceptives, abortifacients (a drug that causes abortion), and drugs to bring on menstruation. There were many kinds of surgical operations, both for trauma and internal conditions, including an operation to remove cataracts from the eye. Since there were no anesthetics, several assistants were needed to hold conscious patients still for operations.

The combination of mathematics and astrology produced *iatromathematics* (medical astrology). The movements of the stars were thought to affect the course of a disease and the times and ways in which a physician could most effectively intervene. Medical astrology was popular and accepted by many physicians, but not all.

Mathematics

The administration of the Roman Empire required a great deal of organization, much of which depended upon some degree of mathematical knowledge. Arithmetical expertise was needed by the government and army officials and secretaries who dealt with taxes on land, trade, and goods; public expenditure and accounting; army provisions and the payment of soldiers; the regular census of the population; and many other aspects of a large empire. Many traders and other businessmen also needed to be able to manage numbers quickly and reliably or to employ people who could. Bronze abaci were widely used in this period.

Geometry was also vital for the taxation and management of land. Architects and engineers used geometrical theorems in major civic projects like Rome's sophisticated water supply of aqueducts, fountains, sewers, public baths, and private houses; in private enterprise such as the building of luxury villas; and in the military. The Roman architect Vitruvius of the first century B.C.E. describes how to build a water system for a city, as well as many other machines.

The Roman army employed surveyors for mapping military terrain as well as for constructing and attacking siege defenses and fortifications. One example of such a fortification is Hadrian's Wall in Great Britain, a stone-and-turf wall that ran for 73 miles across the width of the country at a height of almost 20 feet and with regular forts. Roman roads tended to be very straight, and roads within the empire might be tunneled straight through a mountain. Surveyors used mathematical techniques and simple instruments like the *dioptra,* or sighting rod, to keep the construction on track.

Astronomy and Calendars

By the Roman period the movements of the stars were well understood. The traditional Roman calendar had 12 months and a year consisted of 355 days. To keep the calendar year in approximate agreement with the solar year, which is longer than 355 days, the state priests in charge of the calendar had to add a month every other year. In the first century B.C.E. the calendar was not properly managed, so in 45 B.C.E. Julius Caesar replaced the old system with a solar calendar on the advice of a Greek astronomer, Sosigenes of Alexandria. This system was slightly altered again by Pope Gregory XIII in 1582, and the Gregorian calendar is the one we still use today.

The Julian calendar reform shows that technical expertise in astronomy belonged largely to the Greek tradition of mathematical astronomy. Although many elite Romans took a lay interest in the stars, they were not concerned with exactitude. The main source for astronomical theory was the Hellenistic Period poem of Aratus of Soli (ca. 315–ca. 240 B.C.E.) on stars and weather titled *Phaenomena* (Appearances). This work had been adapted into verse from a much older astronomical text, which by the time of the Roman Empire was, in fact, rather out of date.

Caesar consulted foreign experts and then used the results to organize the way in which the Roman Empire counted time. (Local cities and regions would have simultaneously often used older methods as well.) Mathematical astronomy thus had an enormous impact on the Roman world because

Roman government perceived it as reliable and useful. It remained, however, the specialty of a few experts, usually those of Greek descent and culture, often from the Greek populations and settlements of Asia Minor, Syria, and Egypt.

The ancient Romans also used armillary spheres, an astronomical device that had moving parts and modeled the movements of the heavenly bodies. Some scholars have suggested that Nero's Golden House contained one. An armillary sphere is depicted in a wall painting of a luxury villa from the Stabiae (modern-day Castellammare di Stabia) region of Italy. The Roman elite liked to own gadgets and to demonstrate an awareness of contemporary intellectual endeavor, but they did not build their own.

Geography and Astronomy

Ptolemy, a Greek astronomer of the second century C.E. who worked in Alexandria, is known for his theory on the motions of the stars and planets, which built upon earlier Greek astronomy and became the accepted model of how the cosmos worked until the discoveries of Nicolaus Copernicus and Johannes Kepler in the 16th and 17th centuries, respectively. Ptolemy's *Geography* gives the latitudes and longitudes of over 8,000 places on the earth, just as astronomers located the stars in the heavens through their celestial coordinates, though not all of his information was accurate. He also developed a mathematical way to project the three-dimensional world onto a two-dimensional surface such as a map.

Maps existed in ancient Rome but were probably not often used by ordinary individuals for the purpose of finding their way about. More common were "itineraries," which listed the times it would take to travel between two places. Geographical knowledge of the Northern Hemisphere in the Roman period was quite detailed and extensive, especially of the lands of the empire and, to a lesser extent, of the trade routes to India and China. There was a strong link between geographical knowledge and imperial power, both ideological and practical. To know a terrain well was to have some control over it, especially from a military point of view. To be able to display maps, such as the map of the empire that the Roman general Agrippa (63?–12 B.C.E.) had carved in marble, showed the general population the size and importance of the empire and demonstrated the competence of the empire's leaders. Individuals may have known much less about the world beyond the places that concerned them directly.

Astronomy and Astrology

Astrology was almost indistinguishable from astronomy in the ancient world since its development in Ptolemaic Egypt over the third to first centuries B.C.E. Many astronomers believed that the stars and planets influenced human lives. The astronomer Ptolemy wrote *Tetrabiblos* (Four Books) as a scientific account of astrology. He thought that the heavenly bodies shaped earthly environments and so affected the character of people according to what time of the year they were born. Although not every event in a person's life was entirely determined in this way, a good astrologer could estimate the probability of certain events. For instance, a very confident, adventurous person was more likely to die at sea. Other astrologers and intellectuals had different accounts of how astrology worked or how rigidly deterministic it was. Some viewed it as a matter of theology, contending that the movements of the stars were messages from the gods.

There were also skeptics, especially among intellectuals such as the philosopher Favorinus (fl. second century C.E.), who attacked inconsistencies in astrological theories, asking why twins did not always have the same fate and pointing out that many astrological predictions did not come true. The Roman philosopher and statesmen Cicero (106–43 B.C.E.) gave similar arguments in his dialogue *De divinatione* (On Divination), which discusses methods of predicting the future through the observation of signs. It was, however, always possible to explain a false prediction by saying that the astrologer was incompetent or that astrology, like medicine, is difficult and that using it cannot always be done with perfect success. Some astrological predictions could be self-fulfilling, or identified in retrospect. The horoscope of the emperor Augustus (r. 27 B.C.E.–14 C.E.), drawn up after he had become ruler of Rome, unsurprisingly predicted a remarkable career. Augustus put his sign of Capricorn on some of his coinage.

Astrology could also be politically dangerous. Predictions that the emperor would die could easily be connected to assassination attempts. In 11 C.E. Augustus made it illegal to make a prediction about anyone's death. Astrology was also seen as in origin a foreign expertise, connected to Greece, Egypt, and Babylonia. Astrologers were usually called Chaldeans, which was the name of the Babylonian order of priests who watched the sky for omens. Both astrology and magic were at times banned in Rome.

Nonetheless, astrology rapidly became extremely popular in Roman society. In his poems the Roman satirist Juvenal (ca. 55–ca. 127 C.E.) mocks many of its adherents, especially women and the lower classes. Most astrologers were not, in fact, astronomers. By the early second century C.E., however, there was sufficient data to compose planetary tables in which the relevant information could simply be read off for any year and time.

Astronomy and astrology had a close relationship. Astronomy remained a demanding and specialized form of mathematics. Astrology, on the other hand, was widespread and practiced both by professionals and by individuals who wanted to predict their own future. Astrology was, however, ultimately dependent on astronomy and using astronomy's reputation for precise mathematical certainty for its own advantage. Astronomy, meanwhile, could explain its relevance to human life through the predictions of astrology.

Science in the Late Empire

The late empire included many notable mathematicians, such as Pappus of Alexandria, Theon of Alexandria, and Eutocius, as well as medical writers, such as Oribasius and Paul of Aegina. However, intellectual activity in such subjects increasingly centered on the explication of earlier works, and little new research was done. Philosophy flourished for a while in the form of the Neoplatonism and also as Christian theology, but neither of these doctrines emphasized the investigation of the natural world. Non-Christian philosophy was increasingly linked to magic and to evil, and Christian understanding of the world located authority in sacred texts rather than in inquiry and experiment and the pagan works of the past. Saint Augustine, considered a brilliant theologian of the fourth and fifth centuries C.E., did not believe that the world was round, a fact well known to Greek and Roman intellectuals since the fourth century B.C.E. Many pagan works of science and philosophy were translated into Arabic and survived in the Islamic tradition. The Western world became reacquainted with them after the Middle Ages.

THE AMERICAS

BY MICHAEL J. O'NEAL

Although the chronology and routes by which the Americas were populated are still debated, one version envisions people spilling over the Bering land bridge into Alaska beginning some 30,000 years ago. Migrating steadily southward to form communities throughout North, Central, and South America, they had to become astute observers of nature. For thousands of years they had to adapt to new and sometimes changing climates, new flora and fauna, new food supplies, and new landscapes and terrains. Some settled in the wet regions of the Pacific Northwest, some in the dry regions of Central America, some in the flat plains of the American Midwest, some in the mountainous regions of South America. Some coped with tropical heat and others with arctic cold. In time they adapted so successfully that they were able to build some of the greatest civilizations of the ancient world.

COSMOLOGY AND SCIENCE

The way the aboriginal peoples of the Americas looked at their universe can be difficult for the modern world to understand. In modern life a sharp distinction is made between the natural and supernatural worlds. Some people do not believe in a world of the supernatural, but among those who do, the two realms tend to be thought of as separate; the very word *supernatural* suggests that the world of the gods and the spirit exists above ("super") or outside the physical world. This separation, however, would have been unthinkable to ancient Americans. Every aspect of their lives had religious significance. They saw the universe as composed of spiritual and divine forces that affected them every moment of their lives.

At the center of this view of the world was a cosmos that ancient Americans saw as a hierarchy of spheres or planes. Some of them were superior to the world of the earth; others were inferior. One example is provided by the Nahua people of central Mexico, precursors to the Aztec, also a Nahua people. The Nahua believed that above the earthly level were numerous other spheres, variously nine, 11, 12, or 13, with 13 being the most common. This belief influenced the calendar, which was composed of 13 periods, somewhat inaccurately called "months," each in honor of the divinity that ruled each sphere. The highest divinity was referred to as Ometeotl, which translates roughly as the "god of duality." Ometeotl was responsible for what the Nahua saw as the duality of the universe: positive and negative, male and female, the spirit and the physical worlds. Artworks depicting Ometeotl are few. Modern researchers working in sophisticated laboratories with the most advanced equipment might regard this duality as myth, not science. To the Nahua, however, it was science. Their belief was based on observations of the world they lived in and explained the origins and development of their universe and humankind.

Because they were keen observers and experimenters, like many other ancient civilizations, the ancient Americans can be regarded as scientists in fields like agriculture, architecture, engineering, construction, metallurgy, and mathematics. Ancient American peoples, for example, made early observations in the fields of astronomy, biology, chemistry, geology, and physics. As astronomers they learned about the movements of heavenly objects and used those observations to create calendars and to predict changes in the seasons. They observed the "hole" in the Big Dipper long before European astronomers did. In fact, so keen was the interest of the ancient Americans in astronomy that priests and astronomers were often one and the same. Because science throughout much of the ancient world was associated with magic and with understanding the power and will of the gods, the earliest scientists were shamans, priests, and others who claimed knowledge of the divine and could read it in the heavens.

As geologists, early Americans knew long before the Europeans did that the world was round. This knowledge was reflected in their myths about the origins and creation of the world. (In this context, a myth is not something that is untrue; rather, it is a narrative that conveys a fundamental truth about the nature of the universe and humans' place in it.) For example, the ancient Lakota nation of North America saw the world's four original beings—Inyan (rock), Maka (the earth), Taku Skan Skan (the sky), and Wi (the sun)—as round, because in the cosmology of the Lakota roundness was the most sacred shape.

As chemists, early Americans often turned their attention to their food supply. They learned, for example, how to deal with stored corn that had become lignified, or hardened. They learned that if they applied alkaline substances (that is, substances that are bases rather than acids) to the corn, they could break down the hardened outer layer and soften the kernel inside. In this way they could return dried corn to an edible state, and the alkaline substance, usually lime water, added valuable calcium to their diet. Sometimes they left the corn in its hardened state to make popcorn.

Even in physics the early Americans made astute observations. During lightning storms, for example, they learned to throw pieces of cedarwood onto a bonfire to ward off the lightning. Even though they could not have fully understood the physical laws that explained why this was successful, successful it was. When cedar burns, it emits a negative electrical charge that repels the negative electrical charge in the atmosphere that produces lightning.

As biologists, the ancient Americans also recognized the principle modern scientists refer to as biodiversity—the notion that there is value in maintaining diverse genetic strains of plants and animals. Doing so allows species to adapt more successfully to changes in conditions. Thus, for example, they developed a bean that sprouted in underground storage chambers; their purpose was to develop a plant they could use in winter religious ceremonies. The bean, it turned out, was resistant to a common pest that attacked bean crops. Thus the new bean became a reliable source of food when pest outbreaks occurred. In cultivating various crops, the ancient Americans appear to have valued diversity in strains of the crop and did not try to breed that diversity out.

Maize

The ancient Mesoamericans (that is, the people who inhabited modern-day Mexico and parts of Central America; from the prefix *meso-*, meaning "middle") carried out one of the most successful plant-breeding programs in the history of the world with the development of maize, known to most North Americans as corn. Maize became an important staple crop among early Americans, contributing to immense population growth and cultural development in regions throughout North and South America

Maize, however, does not reproduce wildly and could not grow without human cultivation. Early Americans bred maize out of a wild plant called teosinte over a period of many years, though whether their success was an event or a process cannot really be known. Teosinte can be found in small patches at higher elevations west of the Sierra Madre in western Mexico. Historians estimate that it was domesticated into maize sometime between 4000 and 3000 B.C.E. Using sophisticated tools they can even locate where it was domesticated: in the drainage areas of the Balsas River in Michoacan, in western Mexico. Its origins lay with small hunter-gatherer bands that had migrated throughout the region, following the changes in the seasons to find deer, antelope, rabbits, and plant foods like nuts and berries. Archaeological evidence, found primarily in excavated caves in Puebla, shows that these early Mesoamericans were experimenting with meals and grains.

Maize was not the first cereal grain the early Mesoamericans domesticated. The first was a grain related to modern-day millet. But by about 2700 B.C.E., historians believe, people in the region were subsisting in part on a type of maize with very small ears and just six to nine kernels per ear. The process of domesticating maize continued over the next 2,000 years, and by about 1400 B.C.E. maize cultivation had spread throughout Mexico, along with methods for grinding and cooking the dough in the form of round, flat cakes. By that time maize had become the staple crop of the Mesoamericans, and the development of Mesoamerican culture, including the invention of irrigation and the emergence of pottery and weaving, corresponded with the spread of maize as a reliable food source.

The development of maize is intimately bound up with Mesoamerican cosmology and creation myths. (Cosmology is the branch of philosophy that deals with the origins, structure, and purpose of the universe.) In these myths the world originated at a time when maize was trapped inside mountains and boulders, where it was inaccessible to humans. Small animals such as foxes could get to the maize, but humans were able to get to it only as a result of divine intervention. Both the Maya and the Aztec envisioned the process of creation as one of the gods progressively providing humans with better and better food. In the earliest stages of humankind, humans ate only fruits and acorns. In the next stage pine nuts were a primary food, followed by a third stage dominated by millet. In the fourth stage of human development, people ate the grains of the teosinte. The Mayan version of the story relates that they were attracted to the teosinte plant because they had observed grains in the dung of wildcats that had eaten the plant. Finally, in the fifth stage the gods gave Mesoamericans maize, the perfect food. Even early Mesoamerican mythology incorporated a kind of anthropology and recognized that over time the conditions of their lives improved.

Maize, put differently, was divinity itself. It meant life, so it was closely associated with fertility and regeneration. The rain that nourished it, which came from the heavens, enabled people to share in the fundamental life spark of the divine. So important to the ancient Americans was maize and maize cultivation that the plant was central to their everyday thought and activity.

Mayan Mathematics

The ancient Maya occupied the Yucatán Peninsula in modern-day Mexico, Belize, Guatemala, and sections of Honduras and El Salvador. The Maya began to inhabit the region in roughly 2000 B.C.E., reached the peak of their influence in the early centuries of the Common Era, and began to decline in the ninth century C.E. In studying Mayan history and culture, historians refer to the classic period, extending from about 250 to 900 C.E., as the period of the Maya's greatest achievements. While much of what historians know about them dates to that period, they also know that classic Mayan culture was built on the achievements of their ancestors dating back many hundreds of years before then.

In the 16th century Spanish explorers landed on the Yucatán Peninsula and eventually overran the regions inhabited by the Maya and the Aztec. Unfortunately, the early Spanish explorers and missionaries regarded all manifestations of Mayan religious beliefs as the work of the devil and had them destroyed. These included not only religious artifacts but also written texts on many subjects. Only a handful of these texts survived and are housed in museums in Paris, France; Dresden, Germany; and Madrid, Spain. While these texts, called codexes (or codices), date to the centuries just preceding European contact, they were based on texts originally written in earlier periods, which in turn were based on knowledge that had been acquired for hundreds of years before that.

Historians of science are especially intrigued by the ancient Mayan system of mathematics, which they applied to fields like astronomy and architecture. Much of this system has been preserved in the codices. Mayan mathematics was a vigesimal system, meaning that it was based on the number 20. Such a system probably evolved because ancient people probably first counted with their fingers and toes, and when they reached the number 20 they had to start over with a new set of 20 in much the same way that modern systems of mathematics are based on the number 10 and its multiples.

Thus in Mayan texts the numeral 1 was represented by a thick dot, 2 by two dots, and so on. The numeral 5 was represented by a straight horizontal line, 6 by one dot above a line, 7 by two dots above a line, and so on. The numeral 10 was then represented by two horizontal lines, 11 by a dot above two lines, and so on up to 15, represented by three lines, and so on up to 20, represented by a single dot above a shell representing zero.

The Mayan system, though, had some irregularities that historians of mathematics believe related to the Mayan calendar—or rather, the two Mayan calendars. One was a ritual calendar that consisted of 13 periods, each with 20 days. Historians are unsure why this calendar was structured in this way, but they speculate that each of the 13 periods represented a god and the 20 days represented humans (because of their base 20 system of math). The other calendar was a solar calendar consisting of 360 days, with 18 periods each consisting of 20 days (and the extra five days regarded as unlucky). The two calendars coincided with each other after 18,980 days, equivalent to 52 years or 73 ritual years. The Maya also observed that the planet Venus returned to its original spot after two 52-year cycles, and in fact they held a great celebration after 104 years—that is, after two 52-year solar cycles or one 104-year cycle of Venus.

But how does this explain the irregularity in the counting system? To answer that, it is necessary to recognize that the Maya also counted time as a linear sequence of days. They calculated, for example, that the world was created on a date that coincides with August 12, 3113 B.C.E., and they dated many of their historical monuments in terms of the number of days that had passed since this creation. In the city of Tikal, for example, is a historical marker dating construction of the structure as occurring 1,253,912 days after the world was created. Put differently, rather than counting determining the structure of the calendar, the structure of the calendar determined counting, enabling the Maya to incorporate into their mathematical system their conception of the gods, creation, the movement of heavenly bodies, and the like.

Geometry, Architecture, and Astronomy

Ancient Americans had a sophisticated grasp of geometry, and geometric patterns can be found in a wide range of Native American structures, from major temples to small ceremonial structures. Geometry and architecture intertwined with astronomy as well, with many of these structures mirroring the movement of heavenly bodies, particularly the sun as it changes position in the sky throughout the year. The geometric regularity of these buildings reflects geometric and astronomic understandings that date back at least 2,000 years.

Ancient American geometry in many respects reflected the geometry of the natural world. It included not only simple squares and circles but also arcs, hexagons (six-sided figures), octagons (eight-sided figures), and dodecagons (12-sided figures, as in a clocks). Thus, geometric understanding among the ancient Americans was a process of discovering and unfolding the geometry found in nature, rather than an artificially constructed system of thought. Ancient Americans began with the simple notion that two points could define a line that extended infinitely in either direction. Additionally, either or both of those two points could become the center of a circle, and the line connecting the two points could serve as the radius of a circle. If circles were drawn using each of the two points as the center, the two circles would intersect at two points. In turn, each of those points could serve as the center of yet another circle. If the process is continued, the result is a six-petaled "flower," known among some ancient American cultures as the Flower of Life.

More important, this system of intersecting points can be used to make many other geometric shapes, including perfect triangles, pentagons (five-sided figures) hexagons, octagons, decagons (10-sided figures), dodecagons, and even polygons with 24 and 48 sides. (The word *polygon* refers to any of these enclosed, flat shapes with angles; *poly-*, means "many.") Once these shapes and how to derive them were understood, architects could apply them to the construction of buildings, including temples, homes, and ceremonial structures, with simple tools like string. Each of the points in an octagon, for example, would become the position for a vertical post, which then evolved into more complex architectural designs.

What role, though, did astronomy play in all this? Historians and archaeologists have long noted that many of the structures of ancient America were oriented along north–south and east–west axes. In recent decades, however, many scholars have turned their attention to a subfield called archaeoastronomy—the study of the relationships between building practices and astronomical knowledge. In connection with ancient American structures they have found that many are built with an understanding of the concept of azimuths, particularly the azimuth of the sun at the points of the winter and summer solstice.

An azimuth is an angle measured from a reference point. Perhaps the best way to understand azimuths is to think about satellites in the sky that beam down television signals. When the customer's dish is mounted, it has to be pointed at the satellite; otherwise, it fails to pick up the signal. But satellite dish installers do not have a single, fixed angle at which they mount the dish. This is because while the satellite is in a fixed place relative to the horizon, usually over the equator, homes are located at various points north or south of the equator. For a home near the equator, the satellite dish would have to point upward at a severe angle; for homes in Alaska, the dish would point at a much lower, flatter angle. This angle is the azimuth. Like the azimuths used to point to satellites, the azimuths of the sun at the summer and winter solstices—that is, the dates when the sun is highest in the sky in summer and lowest in the sky in winter—differ depending on latitude.

Evidence shows that many ancient American structures were positioned with their angles lined up with the point in the sky that marked the azimuths of the summer and winter solstices. The purpose in doing so was probably part religious, part practical. From a religious perspective, it reflected the ancient Americans' view that all of creation is unified. From a practical perspective, it enabled ancient Americans to take maximum advantage of light and warmth from the sun.

South America: The Search for Resources

The ancient South Americans, particularly the people of Peruvian Andes, made remarkable technical advances in metalwork, agriculture, and energy production, all based on early understanding of science. In the field of metallurgy, archaeologists have discovered that the Peruvians began to exploit deposits of copper beginning sometime around 1400–1100 B.C.E. They created an alloy called tumbaga, which was a mixture of gold and copper, though the ratio of these elements varied widely, from 97 percent copper to 97 percent gold. A chief technical innovation was adding the element mercury, which hardened the metal and made it more durable.

Additionally, the Peruvians found gold and silver resources and developed complex technologies for mining, purifying, smelting, and crafting them into useful and decorative objects. Along the way they found uses for other minerals they mined, including hematite (an iron oxide), limonite (a mineral with various combinations of other minerals, including hematite), and manganese oxide. The many varieties of hematite, including rainbow hematite, kidney ore, martite, bloodstone, iron rose, and paint ore, suggest that depending on the mineral's composition, it had different appearances, making it a versatile mineral for objects with differing aesthetic properties.

With regard to energy, the ancient Americans, like people throughout the world, burned wood, along with dried dung and charcoal. In time, however, they also discovered and mined coal, particularly as some of the forests became depleted. Archaeologists disagree about whether the Peruvians used coal in the metal-smelting process. Some argue that little evidence suggests that they did, but others claim to have found coal ash in ancient Peruvian smelting sites. The Peruvians also found uses for bitumen, a substance that is similar to asphalt or tar and can occur naturally or as a byproduct of a refining process. The Peruvians used this sticky material as a sealant in coffins and as caulking for ships. The effectiveness of that sealant, along with the Peruvians' skill in mummifying bodies, has given modern scientists unique insight into the physical condition of the ancient Peruvians.

The Peruvians learned to make use of guano, or bat dung, on nearby islands as fertilizer. Guano is still used as a fertilizer because it is high in nitrogen, phosphate, and potassium, all substances essential to healthy plant growth and abundant crops. It is believed that the Peruvians used small reed boats to travel to the islands and transport the guano back to the mainland for use on fields. In some places the guano is believed to have been as much as 65 feet thick.

Medicine

An important part of the scientific achievements of any civilization is its ability to find treatments for illness and disease. Again, much of what might have been known about medical lore in ancient Mesoamerica has been lost because the invading Spaniards destroyed the manuscripts that recorded their various branches of knowledge. Some of this ancient knowledge was later reconstructed, and modern paleopathologists—those who study disease and illness by examining preserved tissues from ancient times—have been able to add to that knowledge. Generally, medical practitioners in the ancient Americas were shamans. Like the astronomer-shamans discussed earlier, shamans who practiced medicine were believed to have had access to supernatural power and wisdom.

In common with ancient civilizations the world over, the ancient Americans made wide use of herbs and other medicinal plants. One early colonial manuscript catalogues 204 medicinal plants from a wide variety of climate zones. While this manuscript was copied much later, it doubtless reflects insights into medicinal cures that were hundreds, if not thousands, of years old. Modern people who think of themselves as addicted to chocolate might take heart in knowing that ancient healers of Mesoamerica recognized the therapeutic benefits of chocolate and cacao. They used it not only to deliver other medicines but as a medicine in its own right. It was thought to help people gain weight, stimulate the nervous system, and improve digestion and elimination. Ancient Americans also used cacao to treat anemia, poor appetite, gout, kidney stones, fevers, and, in paste form, burns. Interestingly, modern medical researchers have confirmed what the ancient Americans knew. Chocolate has been shown to be an effective cough medicine. More important, consumed in moderation, it is a good source of polyphenols—chemicals that protect the heart.

See also AGRICULTURE; ARCHITECTURE; ASTRONOMY; BUILDING TECHNIQUES AND MATERIALS; CALENDARS AND CLOCKS; CERAMICS AND POTTERY; CITIES; CLIMATE AND GEOGRAPHY; CRAFTS; DEATH AND BURIAL PRACTICES; EDUCATION; EMPIRES AND DYNASTIES; EXPLORATION; GENDER STRUCTURES

AND ROLES; HEALTH AND DISEASE; INVENTIONS; LANGUAGE; LITERATURE; METALLURGY; MIGRATION AND POPULATION MOVEMENTS; MILITARY; MINING, QUARRYING, AND SALT MAKING; NATURAL DISASTERS; NUMBERS AND COUNTING; OCCUPATIONS; RELIGION AND COSMOLOGY; ROADS AND BRIDGES; SACRED SITES; SEAFARING AND NAVIGATION; SETTLEMENT PATTERNS; SHIPS AND SHIPBUILDING; SOCIAL ORGANIZATION; STORAGE AND PRESERVATION; TEXTILES AND NEEDLEWORK; TRADE AND EXCHANGE; WAR AND CONQUEST; WEIGHTS AND MEASURES; WRITING.

Egypt

Herodotus, "Mummification," from The Histories *(ca. 440 B.C.E.)*

The mode of embalming, according to the most perfect process, is the following: They take first a crooked piece of iron, and with it draw out the brain through the nostrils, thus getting rid of a portion, while the skull is cleared of the rest by rinsing with drugs; next they make a cut along the flank with a sharp Ethiopian stone, and take out the whole contents of the abdomen, which they then cleanse, washing it thoroughly with palm wine, and again frequently with an infusion of pounded aromatics. After this they fill the cavity with the purest bruised myrrh, with cassia, and every other sort of spicery except frankincense, and sew up the opening. Then the body is placed in natrum for seventy days, and covered entirely over. After the expiration of that space of time, which must not be exceeded, the body is washed, and wrapped round, from head to foot, with bandages of fine linen cloth, smeared over with gum, which is used generally by the Egyptians in the place of glue, and in this state it is given back to the relations, who enclose it in a wooden case which they have had made for the purpose, shaped into the figure of a man. Then fastening the case, they place it in a sepulchral chamber, upright against the wall. Such is the most costly way of embalming the dead.

If persons wish to avoid expense, and choose the second process, the following is the method pursued: Syringes are filled with oil made from the cedar-tree, which is then, without any incision or disemboweling, injected into the abdomen. The passage by which it might be likely to return is stopped, and the body laid in natrum the prescribed number of days. At the end of the time the cedar-oil is allowed to make its escape; and such is its power that it brings with it the whole stomach and intestines in a liquid state. The natrum meanwhile has dissolved the flesh, and so nothing is left of the dead body but the skin and the bones. It is returned in this condition to the relatives, without any further trouble being bestowed upon it.

The third method of embalming, which is practiced in the case of the poorer classes, is to clear out the intestines with a clyster, and let the body lie in natrum the seventy days, after which it is at once given to those who come to fetch it away.

From: Internet History Sourcebooks. Available online. URL: http://www.fordham.edu/halsall/.

Greece

Archimedes, Letter to Dositheus (ca. 220 B.C.E.)

Archimedes to Dositheus, greeting: Formerly I sent to you the studies which I had finished up to that time together with the demonstrations, which were to show that a segment bounded by a straight line and a conic section is four-thirds of the triangle on the same base as the segment and of the same height. Since that time certain propositions as yet undemonstrated have come to my mind, and I have undertaken to work them out. These are: 1. The surface of any sphere is four times the surface of its greatest circle; 2. The surface of any segment of a sphere is equal to the surface of that circle the radius of which equals the straight line drawn from the vertex of the segment to the circumference of the circle which serves as the base of the segment; 3. That a cylinder with a base equal to the great circle of a given sphere, and a height equal to the diameter of the sphere contains half the volume of that sphere and its surface is equal to half the surface of that sphere.

These propositions, of course, were always true of these figures, but they were hidden to the men who studied geometry before my time. Therefore, since I have discovered that these things hold true of these figures I do not fear to place them alongside my own previous results and the most thoroughly established theorems of Eudoxus, such as: any pyramid is equal to one-third of the prism of the same base and height, and any cone is equal to one-third of the cylinder of the same base and height.

First Postulate. Supposed that a fluid is of such a character that when its component parts are undisturbed and in immediate contact the part which is subject to the less pressure is moved by the part which is subject to the greater pressure; and that each part is forced in a perpendicular direction by the part above, if the fluid is compressed.

Proposition 1. If a surface is always cut by a plane passing through a given point, and if the section thus formed is always a circle whose center is the given point, the surface is that of a sphere.

Proposition 2. The surface of any still fluid is always the surface of a sphere whose center is the center of the earth.

Proposition 3. Those solids which are of the same weight as a fluid in proportion to their size, when sunk in that fluid will be submerged in such a way that they neither extend above that fluid nor sink below it.

Proposition 4. A solid which is lighter than a given fluid will not sink below the surface when placed in that fluid, but part of it will extend above the surface.

Proposition 5. A solid lighter than a given fluid will, when placed in that fluid, be so far submerged that the weight of the solid will be equal to the weight of the fluid displaced.

Proposition 6. If a solid lighter than a given fluid be forced into that fluid the solid will be driven upwards again by a force which is equal to the difference between the weight of the fluid and the weight of the amount of fluid displaced.

Second Postulate: If a solid lighter than a given fluid rest in that fluid the weight of the solid to the weight of an equal volume of the fluid will be as the part of the solid which is submerged is to the whole solid.

From: Oliver J. Thatcher, ed., *The Library of Original Sources*, Vol. 3, *The Roman World* (Milwaukee, Wisc.: University Research Extension Co., 1907).

FURTHER READING

Andis Caulins, *Stars, Stones and Scholars: The Decipherment of the Megaliths as an Ancient Survey of the Earth by Astronomy* (Victoria, B.C., Canada: Trafford, 2003).

Marshall Clagett, *Ancient Egyptian Science: A Source Book*, vol. 3, *Ancient Egyptian Mathematics* (Philadelphia: American Philosophical Society, 1999).

Clifford D. Conner, *A People's History of Science: Miners, Midwives, and "Low Mechanicks"* (New York: Nation Books, 2005).

Alan Cromer, *Uncommon Sense: The Heretical Nature of Science* (New York: Oxford University Press, 1993).

Moustafa Gadalla, *Egyptian Cosmology: The Animated Universe* (Greensboro, N.C.: Tehuti Research Foundation, 2001).

D. C. Heggie, *Megalithic Science: Ancient Mathematics and Astronomy in North-West Europe* (London: Thames and Hudson, 1981).

Constance B. Hilliard, ed., *Intellectual Traditions of Pre-Colonial Africa* (Boston: McGraw-Hill, 1998).

Narendra Kumar, *Science in Ancient India* (New Delhi: Anmol Pulications, 2004).

James E. McClellan and Harold Dorn, *Science and Technology in World History: An Introduction*, 2nd ed. (Baltimore: Johns Hopkins University Press, 2006).

Joseph Needham, *Science and Civilisation in China* (New York: Cambridge University Press, 1996–2004).

T. E. Rihll, *Greek Science* (Oxford and New York: Oxford University Press, 1999).

Peter Schmidt, *Iron Technology in East Africa: Symbolism, Science, and Archaeology* (Bloomington: Indiana University Press, 1997).

John Staller, Robert Tykot, and Bruce Benz, *Histories of Maize* (Burlington, Mass.: Academic Press, 2006).

Robert Temple, *The Genius of China: 3,000 Years of Science, Discovery and Invention* (London: Prion Books, 1998).

Dick Teresi, *Lost Discoveries: The Ancient Roots of Modern Science—from the Babylonians to the Maya* (New York: Simon and Schuster, 2002).

Gloria Thomas-Emeagwali, ed., *Science and Technology in African History: With Case Studies from Nigeria, Sierra Leone, Zimbabwe, and Zambia* (Lewiston, N.Y.: Edwin Mellen Press, 1992).

Ivan Van Sertima, ed., *Blacks in Science: Ancient and Modern* (London: Transaction, 1983).

Wolfram von Soden, *The Ancient Orient: An Introduction to the Study of the Ancient Near East*, trans. Donald G. Schley (Grand Rapids, Mich.: Eerdmans, 1994).

Anthony Kennedy Warder, *A Course in Indian Philosophy* (Delhi, India: Motilal Banarsidass Press, 1998).

seafaring and navigation

INTRODUCTION

Seafaring has always been a dangerous business, and it was no less so in the ancient world. The fact that ancient civilizations took to the sea despite the dangers of storm, shipwreck, and piracy is testimony to their courage and unquenchable desire to explore the world that surrounded them. Ancient seafarers faced a number of obstacles. One was a lack of navigational tools. More modern seafarers had sextants, compasses, chronometers, and other implements that enabled them to fix their position at sea and determine their direction and speed. Ancient civilizations did not have these tools, though one tool, which was found off the coast of a Greek island and dated from about the first century B.C.E., may have been used for navigational purposes. Otherwise, seafarers learned to navigate using the sun and star constellations, water currents, and the movements of birds and marine animals, and they passed their knowledge along orally.

Few ancient seafarers, however, took to the open sea, although ancient whalers and fishermen sometimes traveled far from land in search of their prey. For the most part, ancient seafarers tended to follow coastlines. They could use mountains visible from sea to maintain their course, and by staying close to the land they could find refuge during storms as well as put in for fresh water and provisions. The ancient Greeks and Romans navigated the coastlines of the Mediterranean Sea; seafarers from the Near East and Middle East navigated the Red Sea, the Persian Gulf, and other bodies of water in the region; and the ancient Chinese, with their large fleet of massive ships, explored the coastline of China and the areas around Japan and Korea. Ancient Americans and Asians of the South Pacific, much like the ancient Greeks, took to the sea to hop from island to island.

Another constant danger was storms and shipwrecks. In general, ancient seafarers kept to the land during the spring and autumn, when storms were more prevalent. Nonetheless, many ancient ships were caught in storms at sea and went down, often carrying valuable cargo with them. Because most of these shipwrecks occurred in deep water, and because water is not kind to the wood from which ships were made, relatively few ancient shipwrecks have been located. The lack of harbors was also a problem, but ancient seafarers learned to make use of natural harbors to escape storms when possible.

Ancient ships lacked artificial sources of power, so seafarers relied on river currents, the power of the wind, or the backs and arms of rowers. Sails were typically square, making them useful when the wind was at the ship's back but of little use when a ship was sailing into the wind. Most ancient ships made use of rowers. The so-called triremes, used by the ancient Romans, were ships that were powered by three rows of rowers. Some ships had up to 10 such rows. Rowers were able to power ships when the wind was not favorable or when the ship needed a burst of speed and maneuverability, as during naval battles.

AFRICA

BY MARK ANTHONY PHELPS

People from the western Mediterranean and Atlantic regions were engaged in trade with the Phoenicians, based in modern Syria and Lebanon, since at least the ninth century, despite the claim of classical authors who placed colonization of the Atlantic coast in the 12th century. On or near the Atlantic coast from Morocco to Senegal lie 13 Phoenician or Carthaginian sites. It is generally not possible to attribute colonies to either, as the distinction between the two centers of Semitic seafaring civilization was blurred by ancient authors. Likewise, technology bearing the label "Phoenician" by ancient authors could have denoted Carthaginian developments as well. One will recall that the wars with Carthage are known to the Romans as the Punic Wars, as *Punic* is derived from the Greek word for the Phoenicians. (The English term is likewise derived from the Greek root.)

Colonies served a variety of economic purposes. Primarily they served to protect Phoenician and Carthaginian (the latter are also known as Punic) vessels. This was accomplished by using their own navies as defense against pirates and other potential enemies and providing safe haven for endangered ships. This ensured that Phoenician and Carthaginian ships would have access to the resources of the western Mediterranean and Atlantic to themselves. These ports also were outlets for their own economic production, both from the cities and the hinterlands. The ports provided repairs for ships and resupplied provisions for ships continuing on their circuits.

Navigation in the Mediterranean was a skill acquired by experience. An intimate knowledge of nature was a requisite for sailing in antiquity. Navigation at night, which tended to be rare, was done by fixing points in relation to stars. Ursa Major was known as the "Phoenician star" because it served as their prime orientation point. The sun, by contrast, is a relative guide, moving as the seasons progress.

Understanding winds was important to navigation. The Phoenicians or Carthaginians invented the wind rose, a device to discern the direction of winds. Winds possessed discernable features to the trained observer. By the first century C.E. Greek sailors were aware of eight distinct winds. Winds were valuable for determining direction and predicting coming danger in the form of storms. Storms and unpredictable winds limited most commercial sailing in the Mediterranean to the months between March and October. Warships patrolled all year long.

Birds were of value in determining distance and direction of land. Land-based birds released from a ship would elevate to locate land and head directly toward it. Likewise, an awareness of the flight patterns of flocks of birds could help one discern direction or nearby landfall.

Naturally, the easiest way to navigate distance was to be in sight of land. This was probably the method employed by the Phoenicians and Carthaginians along the Atlantic coast of Africa and nearby islands. For Greek and Roman sailors, handbooks known as *periploi* described landmarks to guide one along a coast. The *periploi* also gave information about the lands, peoples, and resources the sailors might encounter.

The Phoenicians are credited with circumnavigating Africa on an expedition funded by the Egyptian pharaoh Necho II (r. 610–595 B.C.E.), a feat that took three years. Having no ports, the crews had to plant and harvest wheat twice to provide provisions. The report describes the sun changing sides of the ship, confirming that the crew had entered the southern hemisphere. Based on the account of the Carthaginian navigator Hanno (fifth century B.C.E.), some scholars hold that the Carthaginians may have explored the Atlantic coast of Africa as far south as Mount Cameroon, though a majority assume they never ventured south of Senegal.

During the period of Greek colonization from the eighth to the sixth centuries B.C.E. the region known as Libya to the Greeks (northern Africa outside of Egypt) was an ideal place for establishing new centers. The hinterland of the coast in this region possessed a plain useful for agriculture. In addition, the southern Mediterranean shipping route passed close by as ships looking for the African coast after passing Crete would typically sight landfall in this region. Likewise, eastbound ships would head north from this landmark.

Trade on the Indian Ocean is dictated by the monsoons. The northeastern monsoons occur during winter in the northern hemisphere. These winds abate in March and reverse (become southwesterly) in April. The period from mid-May to mid-August is typically too rough for sailing. The equatorial current flows southward after striking the Somali coast, facilitating vessels heading west from the Arabian Peninsula. With the coming of the southwest monsoon, the current strikes farther south, near Cape Delgado in Mozambique. This produces a strong northern current, facilitating the return from the east.

The kingdom of Axum was located in northern Ethiopia and Eritrea. Its port at Adulis, founded in the mid-second century B.C.E. by the Egyptian king Ptolemy III (r. 246–221 B.C.E.), became a major center for exchange of goods between the Roman, Red Sea, South Asian, and sub-Saharan African worlds. Few of its coins are found in the homeland, while most appear in Yemen and in India.

The kings of the Ptolemaic Dynasty sought to circumvent the Seleucid stranglehold on overland trade by exploiting water routes to India. By the end of the era, Ptolemaic weakness and political anarchy had reduced the trips to some 20 a year. Under the Roman emperor Augustus (r. 27 B.C.E.–14 C.E.) that number was elevated to 120 a year. After destroying Carthage in 146 B.C.E. the Romans had assumed control of shipping throughout the entirety of the Mediterranean, including all African ports.

EGYPT

BY AMR KAMEL

Although ancient Egypt was considered a riverine civilization, where everything was associated with the Nile, it was thought also to be a nation of sailors, navigators, and explorers, who were able to navigate and sail up and down the Mediterranean and the Red Sea as early as the Old Kingdom (ca. 2575–ca. 2134 B.C.E.) and perhaps even before. Although no seagoing ship has survived, numerous pieces of textual and pictorial evidence have fortunately been preserved from most of Egyptian history and particularly from the New Kingdom (ca. 1550–ca. 1070 B.C.E.) onward, referring to the activation of an Egyptian maritime network on both seas.

The earliest evidence for Mediterranean seafaring is a short text from the reign of Snefru (r. ca. 2613–2589 B.C.E.), which mentions 40 ships that sailed to the land now known as Lebanon to obtain cedar and other woods. An Egyptian crew on such a voyage almost 50 years later left its name on an inscribed ax head at Byblos (modern Jubayl). However, the earliest detailed portraits of seagoing ships come from decorated blocks in the mortuary temple of the Fifth Dynasty ruler Sahure (r. ca. 2487–2475 B.C.E.) at Abusir, which illustrates 12 ships, with careful attention to construction, rigging, and passengers, including a mixture of Egyptian and Syrian crewmen. In a relief from the time of Unas (r. ?–2345 B.C.E.), two slightly later ships are shown returning from Syria. Such scenes could help modern archaeologists to estimate the actual sizes of these ships; for instance, a cedar ship built in the Fourth Dynasty (ca. 2575–ca. 2465 B.C.E.) was 100 cubits, or 50 yards, long.

As early as the reign of Sahure ships sailed on the Red Sea for Punt, famed for its incense, precious woods, gold, and other raw materials. Punt is most likely located on the Somali coast of East Africa. In the Sixth Dynasty (ca. 2323–ca. 2150 B.C.E.) a helmsman named Khnumhotep left an inscription describing his 11 round-trips to that land. Although no textual or representational evidence exists for seagoing ships in the Middle Kingdom (ca. 2040–ca.1640 B.C.E.), recent excavations have revealed a Red Sea harbor used by Middle Kingdom ships that sailed to Punt and to the turquoise mines of the Sinai Peninsula, at Marsa Gawasis, about 15 miles south of modern-day Safaga and 31 miles north of Quseir. At this site archaeologists have unearthed 12 large stone anchors, fragments of cedar wood imported from Lebanon, and a man-made cave in which ancient Egyptian sailors stored their gear.

In the New Kingdom seafaring seems to have been more common, with refinements in rigging and steering gear traceable through images and models of ships. No physical remains of New Kingdom hulls have been found as yet. The most remarkable report is preserved in both text and images on the walls of the mortuary temple of Hatshepsut (r. 1503–1482 B.C.E.) at Deir el-Bahri. These scenes show five ships with upright bows and curved papyriform sterns, hogging trusses (thick ropes to keep the bow and stern from sagging), and single masts with broad sails, entering and leaving the anchorage at Punt. Only one includes an illustration of beam ends; otherwise, artistic attention was lavished on the rigging. Fifteen oarsmen shown as well on the side facing the viewer would have required about a yard of room each, suggesting that the ships were at least 24 yards long and perhaps three times longer than broad. Apparently, Hatshepsut reactivated Egypt's Red Sea route to Punt, and this extraordinary series of illustrations suggests that she invested heavily this expedition.

Records from the reign of Hatshepsut's successor, Thutmose III (r. 1504–1450 B.C.E.), document the movements of ships in an expedition to Syria-Palestine, and further records describe cedar acquired and goods stored at harbors for Egyptian use. An Amarna tablet refers to a royal ship moored at Tyre (modern-day Sūr), in southern Lebanon. According to cuneiform texts, Egyptian products, notably grain, were transported to Palestine and Anatolia in vessels, but whether Egyptian or local ships were used is still obscure. In the first two years of Ramses II's reign (1304–1237 B.C.E.), Ramses had to conduct a military campaign against sea pirates, known as Shirdana. Several Egyptian seagoing ships participated in the war of Ramses III (r. 1198–1166 B.C.E.) against the Sea Peoples, as is illustrated on the walls of his temple at Medinet Habu.

In the Late Period (ca. 712–332 B.C.E.) as well as in Greco-Roman times, the Egyptians apparently continued investment in seafaring, and they sometimes built special cargo ships. For instance, they transported obelisks from Alexandria to Rome, and textual evidence refers to a seagoing ship built for Caligula (r. 37–41 C.E.). Unfortunately, ancient Egyptian sources do not say much about the life of the sailors, the length of the sailing season, the durability of ships, and their costs. Nonetheless, these sources refer to numerous titles associated with seafaring occupations and activities, held by ancient Egyptians and sometimes by foreigners, especially Syrians, notably in the construction and operation of maritime ships. Among these titles were navigator, sailor, man at the prow, man at the poop, manager of the crew, captain, and commander of the ship. These titles suggest that their holders had a sufficient knowledge of navigational techniques required to make a voyage possible.

These techniques, theoretically at least, developed over years in the form of oral tradition, with no trace in any written records. A few glimpses can be obtained from Egyptian tomb paintings reflecting these skills. To ancient Egyptians, navigation apparently was an art rather than a science, and it was based mainly on determining position and location. They had several methods for determining direction, among them the winds. The ancient Egyptian language reflects the Egyptians' knowledge of the four winds, from north, east, south, and west, and includes terms for favorable winds and headwinds as well. A scene from an early Old Kingdom tomb shows a ship commander teaching the crew how to steer the ship with the wind. The Egyptians sometimes called upon various gods associated with creation of these different winds to aid in the journey, notably Amun, who was believed to drive back the adverse wind. In daytime a gnomon (the pointer of a sundial) also could be used as a tool to indicate northerly direction in navigation, as shown on a ship model in an Egyptian museum, where it was mounted on the ship's axis.

A scene from a tomb at Thebes suggests that the Egyptians were familiar with using birds in navigation. It shows a Syrian fleet moored at an Egyptian quay (a wharf built parallel to the shoreline) and a bird flying toward the city. In the ancient Near East, land birds that were unable to land on water, such as ravens, crows, doves, and swallows, were carried on board and released when the crew needed to know how to reach the shore. This scene and a few others show that river and seagoing ships had crow's nests with lookouts, who played a role in determining the direction of land lying beyond the horizon.

THE MIDDLE EAST

BY EDWARD M. W. A. ROWLANDS

In ancient times the sailors from the Near East were famous for their seafaring skills. Written evidence suggests that sailors from Mesopotamia were able to navigate great distances, but there is a lack of archaeological evidence available to support their navigation capabilities. Sailors established successful sea routes by following the coastline. They learned the best times for sailing and discovered ways to counter harsh weather conditions. Navigation was improved by the observation of the sun and stars; seafaring was further enhanced with the addition of several rows of oars to increase speed.

There was a great abundance of cedar trees in what is now Lebanon. These trees supplied the local inhabitants with a valuable supply of wood, which was used in the construction of ships. The port of Byblos, close to modern-day Beirut, is thought to have traded considerable amounts of wood to Egypt (under the reign of the pharaoh Sahure) as early as around 2487–2475 B.C.E. The availability of wood to the inhabitants of Byblos, Sidon, and Tyre meant that they had the resources to attempt seafaring very early in their histories. It is from those locations that the Phoenician civilization, well known for its highly developed seamanship, began.

It is difficult to go into great detail about Mesopotamian seafaring owing to a lack of shipwrecks available for study and the poor quality of the surviving representations of ancient ships in the area. Depictions of ships have been found on seals and reliefs, but this evidence is inadequate to paint a complete picture of seafaring. Sumerian texts, however, do refer to Mesopotamian trade with Magan (Oman or Egypt) and Meluhha (a civilization in the Indus River valley or Africa) in the Akkadian Period, the Third Dynasty of Ur, and the Isin-Larsa Period. This activity spans a period from around 2350 B.C.E. to around 1800 B.C.E. It thus appears that from a very early time in Mesopotamian history, seamen from this area were able to navigate their way down the Persian Gulf to locations as distant as Africa and India, implying a considerable degree of navigational skill.

In ancient sea travel following the coast was essential. Staying near the coast made shelter, fresh food, and water supplies available on a daily basis. Following the coastline and keeping in sight of land also helped with navigation. For example, ships trying to find the right direction in the Mediterranean were helped by the many high mountains that are visible from the sea. The Uluburun (late 14th century B.C.E.) and Cape Gelidonya (late 12th century B.C.E.) shipwrecks are both thought to be ships that were following the eastern Mediterranean trade circuits, through which ships would travel from the Levant to Cyprus and on to Rhodes and Crete. These ships would have stayed close to land as much as possible and traveled from port to port.

Before Artabanus's attack on Greece in the early fifth century B.C.E., the Greek historian Herodotus (ca. 484–between 430 and 420 B.C.E.) quotes Artabanus (younger brother of King Darius I) as saying to the king of the Persians that harbors would be needed all along the coast to receive his fleet "and give it protection in the event of storms." The weather plays an important role in seafaring, and ancient sailors tried to avoid sailing in the autumn and winter. By sailing in the spring and summer, sailors hoped to avoid the worst storms. Protection could be achieved by taking cover behind islands or high points of land. In the eastern Mediterranean many such harbors could be found and were exploited, giving ships the best access to land as well as the best shelter from weather conditions.

It was crucial for any ancient vessel to have experienced sailors who could observe changes in the wind, tides, and current. They would have had the expertise to navigate by monitoring changes in the sky. Navigational instruments, such as the compass, would not have been available to them. By day, Near Eastern sailors would have used the direction of the sun to distinguish between east (Asu) and west (Ereb). By night they would have navigated by following star constellations, such as Ursa Major and Ursa Minor. The Phoenicians developed a reputation as excellent celestial navigators, with the North Star, for example, being known to the Greeks as the "Phoenician Star." Such navigational skills allowed the Phoenicians and their successors, the Carthaginians, to travel considerable distances. Herodotus wrote that the pharaoh Necho II (r. 610–595 B.C.E.) manned ships with Phoenicians, and the ships were then able to circumnavigate the whole African continent.

The use of oars gave ships speed and flexibility. Ships could adjust their position using steering oars. Ancient ships used a square sail that was very effective in helping the ship through heavy seas. When there was a lack of wind to move the sails, the oars were used to move a vessel. From the seventh century B.C.E. there was a gradual increase in the number of oars and the manpower used to propel a ship. Warships developed several rows of oars in the aim of outmaneuvering the enemy, which required extensive manpower and coordination. The Hellenistic Period (323–31 B.C.E.) saw an explosion in the number of the rows of oars. This development was seen in the Wars of the Diodochi (322–281 B.C.E.). For example, in the Battle of Salamis in 306 B.C.E., next to the island of Cyprus, ships were in battle with as many as seven rows of oars.

The ancient Near East and Mesopotamia was to be dominated by such peoples as the Assyrians, the Babylonians, the Hittites, the Persians, the Greeks, and the Romans. Nevertheless, the necessity to maneuver a ship with precision and accuracy remained the same. Sailors needed to focus their attention, to maintain the safe navigation of the ship, and to watch out for any possible dangers. Examining changes in the weather and the sea, keeping a close eye for land, and observing the stars and the sun required an understanding and an awareness that were essential throughout the whole of this period.

ASIA AND THE PACIFIC

BY KIRK H. BEETZ

Among the great seafaring feats of ancient times was the migration of people from southeastern Asia to Australia during the last great ice age in about 30,000 B.C.E. At that time the ocean was lower than it is now, and much more land around Australia was exposed. Australia, Tasmania, and New Guinea were all connected by land. The areas where seafarers would have landed are now underwater; consequently, archaeologists have little evidence for how ancient sailors crossed the open sea. Even though there would have been less sea to cross, those sailors still had to cross hundreds of miles of ocean. Archaeologists disagree about whether the sailors used rafts or dugout canoes, with some saying canoes had not yet been invented.

It is possible that people had learned to fish in the ocean and had gained knowledge of the currents for their particular fishing areas, so when winds blew them away, they were able to return home by finding the currents they knew. Some of these fishermen may even have landed on Australia and then returned home and brought their families with them to live in the new land they had discovered. At that time Australia would have been much wetter than it is now, with forests filled with inviting life. These people would have rowed, used currents, and possibly used sails to cross not only to Australia but also to islands between Australia and the Asian mainland.

The most accomplished seafarers of ancient Asia and the Pacific that are presently known about were the Polynesians. Archaeologists disagree considerably over the dates for Polynesian exploration, but by the end of the ancient era they had probably reached Easter Island but had not yet reached many islands such as those of Hawaii in the Pacific. There were about 20,000 unpopulated islands scattered across an enormous expanse of ocean when the Polynesians began their push to explore and settle them beginning in about the third century C.E.

Their process of exploration seems to have been very risky, but it had a high rate of success. They would have outfitted outrigger canoes—boats with floats extended by wooden spars, or poles, from the sides of the craft to prevent the craft from capsizing. Carrying men, women, and probably children, as well as pigs, seeds for planting, and other foods, they would have set sail into open ocean beyond the last island they knew. This practice probably caused many people to be lost at sea, but the Polynesians had great navigational skills to aid them.

Even today, some Polynesians still can read wave patterns to navigate across large expanses of water with no land in sight. Where most people would just see a chaos of waves, Polynesian navigators would recognize patterns in the directions of the waves, their heights, and their speed. They would be able to tell where a boat was by how waves of different types bumped into each other. This knowledge made navigating between known islands mostly science, not luck. Polynesians also used the sun, moon, and stars to help them find their way. The sun and moon told them whether they were going west or east. For these ancient seafarers, this method alone was valuable for exploring because they knew they wanted to go eastward. The stars gave them an idea of how far they had gone in their journeys. To determine their latitudes—how far north or south they were—they chose what they called "on top stars." By keeping under a particular star, they could sail east or west and know how far north or south they were. For example, the star Sirius was over the latitude for Tahiti, and if one were west of Tahiti, then sailing east under Sirius would enable one to find Tahiti. For exploration, knowing the latitudes of the stars enabled sailors to avoid retracing unsuccessful routes and to find home if they had to do so.

For the mainland cultures of ancient Asia, navigators tended to stick close the coastlines. The Chinese tended to emphasize sailing on China's great rivers, and China's navy was intended primarily for warfare inland on rivers. Piracy was a problem along China's eastern coast, which provided many coves and inlets in which pirates could hide, and the navy was expected to patrol the coastline. It is possible that one reason the Chinese sought out the Japanese as allies in the third century C.E. is that they hoped the Japanese would aid them in curbing the activities of pirates in the ocean near Korea and northeastern China. In about the fourth century C.E. Chinese merchants began to venture farther from the coastline, following routes used by Indian traders. Although the Chinese long knew of the tendency of lodestones (magnetite) and magnetized iron to point north and south, they did not employ them in navigation until the medieval era, perhaps the 12th century C.E.

The feats of Indian seafarers were justifiably legendary because these sailors overcame many great hazards as well as their own fears of giant fish, dragons, and other monsters of the deep that could swallow them up. Under Hindu religious law, people were not supposed to sail across the sea. A Brahman who did so could lose his status, becoming an outcast without home or sanctuary. Others could suffer the loss of funeral rites. This practice left Buddhists, outcasts, and those willing to risk the loss of their status in their communities to be sailors.

The most important person on a ship was the pilot, and no ship left port without one. The pilot knew how to read currents, winds, stars, and birds for directing the course of a ship over open water. A pilot actually trained birds to fly in the direction of land but to return to the ship if they did not see land midway in their flight, and several of the birds would be kept in cages on deck for this purpose. Pilots had their own guilds, through which captains could find pilots for their ships and which regulated the work of pilots. Ordinary sailors were expected to show their inferior status at all times, to pilot, captain, and passengers. Living quarters on ships were always cramped and uncomfortable, with the rocking of the ship causing misery for passengers, but apparently those ships that sailed west toward the Near East, Africa, and the Mediterranean were filled with people willing to take the risks of a sea voyage to visit foreign lands. If they made some good trades, they could return home as rich people.

It seems that most Indian ships reached their destinations despite the dangers. When a ship was in trouble, its crew and passengers would pray to the goddess Manimekhala, who drowned sinners but would save others. When a ship sank, those on board had little hope of survival. If they did not drown, sharks and other predators would eat them, sometimes turning the sea red with blood. If a ship were becalmed for days, those on board would draw lots to see who would be put out of the ship on a raft to be abandoned as a sacrifice to bring wind.

EUROPE

BY MICHAEL J. O'NEAL

The oldest-known European boat, hollowed out from a single log, was discovered at Pesse in the Netherlands and dates to about 7000 B.C.E. Many other such prehistoric boats have been found at submerged and waterlogged sites across northern Europe in which wood was preserved. For example, the Hasholme boat, in Yorkshire, England, dates from about 300 B.C.E. It was crafted from the trunk of a single oak tree that was probably more than 800 years old when it was felled. In inland areas such boats were used along streams and across lakes, but in coastal areas people rowed them a short distance out to sea to catch fish and also used them for transportation along the coast and to nearby islands. Scholars have traditionally believed that during this period navigation relied primarily on the observation of landmarks along coasts and that people usually did not venture far out of sight of land. Supporting this assumption is the large number of ancient boats that have been discovered in shallow coastal waters.

In recent years some archaeologists have been rethinking this long-held belief. In 2005, for example, archaeologists discovered flints and other objects on the Mediterranean island of Cyprus that date from about 10,000 B.C.E. Cyprus, however, was not inhabited until about 9000 B.C.E., so the objects had to have been left there by seafarers from the mainland who had ventured out of sight of the Turkish or Syrian coast at least 30 miles away. This find provides evidence of the earliest seafaring in the Mediterranean Sea. Evidence for adventurous seafaring has also been found in northern waters. The first Stone Age settlers to reach Ireland would have required watercraft to cross the Irish Sea, for example; except for the very narrow northern part where Ireland is visible from Scotland under ideal conditions, they would have been out of sight of land for some part of this trip.

In any case, the sea may not have been the obstacle that historians long thought it was. They note that the archaeological record shows remarkable similarity among cultures up and down the Atlantic seaboard and around through the Strait of Gibraltar into the Mediterranean Sea during the Mesolithic Period, or the Middle Stone Age, ranging roughly from 12,000 or 10,000 B.C.E. to at least 7000 B.C.E. and perhaps as late as 3200 B.C.E. (Dates for these broadly defined periods can differ for different geographical regions.) Some believe that these similarities could have come about only if people along the Atlantic coast traveled by sea, carrying artifacts and practices of their culture with them. The cultural connections seen around the coasts of the North Sea and the Baltic Sea could have been possible only thanks to the ability to navigate across open seas.

An increasing number of finds have offered considerable insight into prehistoric European seafaring. By the Bronze Age people in northern Europe were building boats out of planks that were propelled by more than a dozen rowers. The earliest-known plank-built ships date from about 1900 B.C.E., and others have been found dating from perhaps 800 B.C.E. An important recent example is the Dover Boat, found in 1992, which appears to have been used for crossing the English Channel. In addition, a large collection of bronze axes found at the bottom of Langdon Bay, also near Dover, appears to be a cargo load that did not make it all the way across. The chief advantage of these plank boats was that the freeboard, the distance between the waterline and the top of the hull, was higher than those of other boats, making them more stable in ocean swells. Meanwhile, the Iberians (in modern-day Spain and Portugal) and the Irish were building lightly framed boats covered with hides. These types of vessels were probably used for trade, particularly to carry tin to Gaul and Rome.

The ancient Celts, in particular, were seafaring peoples and developed sophisticated boat-building and navigational skills. The Celts were an ethnic group that spread across large portions of Europe and into the British Isles. One Celtic group was the Veneti, who, along with several other nations, inhabited the region of Gaul the Romans called Aremonica. This region included Brittany, a peninsula that juts westward and is surrounded by the English Channel and the Bay of Biscay. Largely surrounded by water, the Veneti developed sophisticated seafaring technology.

The Roman emperor Julius Caesar (r. 49–44 B.C.E.) fought his greatest naval battle against the Veneti in 55 B.C.E. In his account of the battle in his work *Commentarii de bello Gallico,* he described the Celtic fleet as consisting of 220 ships. The ships were tall and graceful—Caesar called them "swan ships"—and each was able to carry 200 men. The ships were powered by leather sails rather than rowed with oars; because the hulls did not need openings for oars, the hulls were far stronger than those of the Romans' ships. These ships were able to navigate the open seas during storms, but because of their broad beams and shallow draft, they were also able to sail in shallow waters and estuaries. Their timbers were made of oak and fastened with iron nails rather than the wooden pegs the Romans used in constructing ships. Adding to the Veneti's advantage was the rocky and tempestuous coastline, which they could navigate better than the Romans could in their oar-powered galleys. Caesar eventually was able to defeat the Veneti by having his sailors use long grappling hooks to shred the ships' sails, leaving the ships dead in the water.

GREECE

BY EDWARD M. W. A. ROWLANDS

Ancient Greek sailors were first able to sail to the islands around them and then later used those islands as stepping-stones to other locations in the Mediterranean and into the Black Sea. They learned how to use the sun and the stars as a means of direction and determined the best times of the year to sail. Seafaring could be tough, but the experience that sailors would acquire, along with the technological improvements to ships, meant that speed and flexibility would increase over time.

In the Late Bronze Age (ca. 1600–1100 B.C.E.) people from Greece were able to travel from island to island in the Aegean. The Minoan and Mycenaean civilizations spread throughout the Aegean from Crete and Greece, respectively. Depictions of ships, for example, have been found on fresco fragments from the island of Thera (now Thíra) that date from around 1600 B.C.E. Islands were used as landing stages and could be accessed in a day's journey. Shelter, fresh water, and food supplies could then be found on land. Navigation was accomplished by keeping in sight of land and following the coast.

Greek ships were constructed so that they could be moved onto dry land upon arrival. This design was to prevent the destruction of the boat by any sea storm. Homer describes boats as being fast and hollow, suggesting that these boats would have been light and easy to move ashore. This practice continued for many centuries. Ships were also moved overland so that sailors could gain access to other branches of the sea. The port of Corinth became very famous for its Diolkos. The Diolkos was a paved road that was used for the transportation of boats on a platform from the Saronic Gulf to the Corinthian bay, which are on either side of the Peloponnese in Greece. This route proved very successful and was used from the seventh century B.C.E. up to the ninth century C.E.

Ancient Greek navigation was based on observation, and it was important for every ship to have experienced sailors.

Early Greek sailors were able to travel throughout the Aegean Sea and from there eventually to other locations in the Mediterranean and the Black seas.

Having an understanding of wind, currents, and tide was vital to maintain the correct course. For long-distance voyages, the Greeks made use of the sun and the stars. Since no compass, chronometers, sextants, or octants existed, and as it could be difficult to observe landmarks, using the North Star (known to the Greeks as the Phoenician Star) and following the sun were vital in gaining direction. By 600 B.C.E. a philosopher named Thales (ca. 625–ca. 547 B.C.E.) was able to teach sailors how to get to Miletus (on the Aegean coast of modern-day Turkey) by following the Ursa Minor constellation of stars. However, a mechanism found on a wreck off the Greek island of Antikýthēra, dating to the end of the first century B.C.E., may have been used to calculate astronomical positions and could have been used in seafaring.

The weather and the season of the year in which the voyage was to take place were very important factors. Large cargoes were carried by Greek ships all across the Mediterranean, and it would have been wise to avoid the autumn and winter rains and storms. Goods could be lost and crews of men killed, and ship owners would have been well aware of the financial risks. In the spring and summer, as the Greek writer Hesiod (ca. 800 B.C.E.) says, "You are not likely to smash your ship, nor the sea to destroy your crew. . . . At that time the breezes are well defined and the sea harmless."

Seafaring could be a harsh experience for sailors. For hundreds of years little accommodation was given to living space or preparation of food on ancient Greek ships. There was a threat from being attacked by pirates, and iron spearheads found rooted into the hull may suggest that a ship had been attacked. The use of oars provided speed and flexibility. Single steering oars are seen depicted on the frescoes from Thera as early as the 16th century B.C.E. and double steering oars from the sixth century B.C.E. The oars were important to ships in helping them maneuver around islands, keeping close to the coast. Oars were used to propel a ship when there was not enough wind. For vessels such as warships, oars could also provide a valuable means of gaining speed during battle with an enemy. Several rows of oars could be used to give the ship additional pace. According to the Greek historian Thucydides (d. ca. 401 B.C.E.), triremes (ships with three rows of oars) were the invention of boat builders from Corinth around 700 B.C.E. Later the kingdoms of the Hellenistic Period (323–31 B.C.E.) would have tens of rows of oarsmen. These ships required extensive manpower and coordination.

The ancient Greeks would have used a square sail when traveling by sea. A single square sail could be effective in heavy seas. However, it was not very adaptable when the wind was blowing against the course of a ship. The settlement of Troy was situated on the Dardanelles. As it was a protected harbor, it became prosperous, since ships would often stay there while they waited for the direction of the wind to change so that they could move through the Dardanelles and into the Black Sea. Numerous images of square sails on ships have been found. For example, Attic black-figure pottery dating to the mid-sixth century B.C.E. depicts ships with square sails.

Only small amounts of evidence for nautical guides have survived; it may be that sailors passed on their expertise orally. Even as the Roman Empire came to dominate Greece and the Mediterranean, ships still needed to be maneuvered with precision and accuracy. Watching out for changes in the weather and the sea, keeping a close eye for land, and observing the stars and the sun required an understanding and familiarity that were essential throughout the whole of this period. Sailors needed to maintain total concentration to navigate their ships safely and to watch out for any possible dangers.

ROME

BY JAMES A. CORRICK

The fastest method of transporting freight and passengers during the Roman Republic and the Roman Empire was by sea. With the exception of some swift naval vessels, Roman ships averaged 6 knots, a knot being 6,076 feet per hour, and thus they moved along at about 7 miles per hour. A ship, for example, took one to two days to travel from the Roman port of Ostia, at the mouth of the Tiber River, to Massalia (present-day Marseilles in southern France). By land the same journey took weeks. Business travelers, government officials, tourists, and others journeying long distances consequently sought passage via ship.

Despite a healthy passenger trade, no passenger ships existed in the Roman world. Instead, voyagers had to travel on merchant vessels. Nothing except drinking water was provided to passengers, who had to bring their own food, cooking utensils, beds, and servants. Travelers slept on deck with the crew. The crew was generally foreign born, its members most commonly being Greeks or Egyptians because few Romans became sailors. Even on military ships, except for officers, the crew was not Roman. Additionally, it was not unusual for merchant ships to be crewed entirely by slaves, one of whom was the captain.

Without any method of weather prediction, a ship could easily be caught in a sudden storm, and if it could not quickly reach a safe harbor, it might well be sunk or run aground. Because of numerous storms, few ships sailed in the winter months, the summer being considered the best sailing time. Another danger that Roman ships faced was attack by pirates. After seizing a vessel, the attackers either killed the crew and

Altar to the sea god Neptune, an offering from the Roman admiral of the British fleet, second century C.E., from Lympne, Kent, England
(© The Trustees of the British Museum)

passengers or, as was more common, sold them into slavery. Indeed, until the middle of the first century B.C.E., pirates were one of the chief sources of slaves for the Roman world. Important captives, particularly high-ranking Roman citizens, were held for ransom. Even Julius Caesar was a captive of pirates. The pirate menace was ended in 67 B.C.E., when the Roman general Pompey swept the Mediterranean free of them. Pirates would not again be a threat until the empire began to lose control of the seaways in the third century C.E.

Navigating a Roman ship was more art than science, since the Romans had no navigational instruments. As a consequence, whenever possible, a ship of the period kept the shore in sight, its crew watching for landmarks to tell them their position. An important aid to navigation was the lighthouse. Most major Mediterranean ports had such structures, the Pharos at Alexandria being the most famous. Lighthouses ranged in height from four to 12 stories and used a mirror of polished bronze to reflect light from a fire. The beacon would warn night-traveling ships of hidden rocks and shallow water or act as a guide into port.

In addition to landmarks and lighthouses, Roman crews often depended on changing water depths to tell them where they were, since specific locations along a coast had known depths. To measure the depth of water, mariners used a lead line. This line was a rope that had a series of knots at spaced intervals and that had a lead or stone weight tied to it. The weighted end of the line was tossed overboard, and when it hit bottom, the number of knots were counted to determine the depth.

Another piece of knowledge useful in Roman navigation was the composition of the sea bottom across which a ship was sailing. That composition could often provide a clue as to a ship's location because certain types of material—gravel, sand, or mud, for instance—were known to be present off certain coastlines. Roman mariners sampled the sea bottom with the lead line, whose weight had a depression filled with tallow, or animal fat, to which sea floor material stuck then to be drawn up to the surface.

The Romans probably had charts and certainly had *periploi*, books containing the distances between various seaports, along with the locations of rivers and freshwater sources. A ship's navigator could calculate his ship's position along its route using the distances given by a *periplus* if he knew how far his vessel had traveled during a day. He made this calculation using dead reckoning. He first had to determine how fast his ship was traveling. The navigator estimated this speed by observing seaweed or driftwood passing by the ship. This observation gave him an approximation of how much distance the ship covered in an hour. Then, at the end of a day's sail, based on his observed speed, the navigator calculated how far the vessel had traveled. He now had a rough idea of where along its route the ship was. The method was imprecise, and often the calculation was far off the mark.

Determining position by dead reckoning also required that the navigator know in which direction his vessel was headed; otherwise, the craft might be sailing away from its destination. During the day the navigators determined direction by observing the sun. Sailing into it was going west; sailing away from it was going east. Additionally, the navigator knew the ship was going north or south depending on the sun's height above the horizon at noon. The sun would be higher or lower in the sky depending on whether a ship was headed north or south. The height of the sun also depends on the time of year, the sun rising higher in the summer than in the winter, but an experienced navigator took this fact into account. To measure the sun's height, the navigator would hold out a hand and determine how many fingers were needed to span the gap between the sun and the horizon.

At night the navigator established direction using the stars. One star—the polestar, or Polaris—was particularly useful since it marks the position of the North Pole and remains fixed throughout the night. (Other stars appear to revolve around the sky due to the rotation of the earth.) A ship traveling east would have the polestar on its right, and a ship traveling west would have the polestar on its left. A navigator could also obtain a rough idea of a ship's north-south position using the polestar by counting how many fingers were needed to span the gap between Polaris and the northern horizon. The fewer the fingers, the farther south the ship was since in moving south, Polaris drops toward the northern horizon.

THE AMERICAS

BY LAWRENCE WALDRON

Native American hunters have long been credited with possessing the most acute tracking skills. Their ability to observe signs on the earth, in the air, and in the movements of animals and birds has astounded many observers. There is no reason to assume that Native American seafarers were any different. Just as earthbound hunters would observe the movement of celestial bodies to predict changes in weather, animal behavior, and crop growth, so too would Native Americans living on coasts, along rivers, and on arctic ice navigate by observing and predicting their environment.

Native Americans in ancient times were intimately familiar with the courses of key celestial bodies; the different kinds of cloud cover; the varieties of terrestrial, riverine, and marine species; and the flight patterns of birds. They also would have possessed some knowledge of geology, though they would have employed taxonomic classifications and nomenclature very much unlike our own. All these skills would have constituted the Native American navigation kit, necessary knowledge not only for achieving intended destinations and predictable travels but also for preserving self, family, and culture along the course of those travels.

Both on foot and by boat, Native Americans displayed great maneuverability and speed, due largely to their success as navigators, trackers, and aquatic farers. The American continents from Alaska to Argentina appear to have been settled within a thousand years of the first arrival of

Asiatic migrants, testimony to the Native Americans' ability to navigate and negotiate even unknown territories. Once in America, Native Americans greatly diversified their means of water travel and their techniques of navigation as well. From predominantly coastal seafaring, they developed great prowess in the negotiation of rivers, rapids, lakes, and various inland waters unlike anything that would have existed in their Paleolithic Siberian homeland.

Ancient Native Americans took to the water for many reasons, including trade, whaling, and fishing. Ancient whaling could be quite dangerous. Boatmen harpooned the massive animals and attached animal-skin flotation devices to the prey to fatigue it, mark its location, and float its carcass. North American whaling traditions, among Alaskan peoples especially, included journeys in open water far beyond the sight of land. Thus, northern whalers, among the most proficient seamen of all Native Americans, illustrate that Native Americans did not always follow coastlines in their maritime expeditions.

Circum-Caribbean groups such as the Maya and the Arawaks of the Caribbean also made long journeys across open water, culminating in discoveries of the island territories of today's Caribbean. Arawak explorers in the Caribbean some 3,000 to 4,000 years ago encountered Paleo-Indian hunter-gatherers who had arrived thousands of years even before they arrived, bearing out the theory that even the most ancient Native Americans were expert seafarers. In the case of the Maya mariners, the impetus for their travels was largely trade, and Maya objects have been found from the North American Southwest to the Mississippi to the Caribbean islands.

The ancient Americans are known to have exhibited a highly developed directional sense in the building of their monuments and architecture. Palaces, pyramids, and other tombs often opened facing one of the cardinal directions or were aligned to the solstices. Likewise, the celebrated Nazca Lines in Peru demonstrate that ancient Andeans possessed advanced surveying techniques, which they would have also used in their fishing and military expeditions up and down the Peruvian, Ecuadorian, and Bolivian coasts. Both the Nazca and Moche civilizations maintained their empires through the movement of troops, goods, and ultimately their cultural influence by sea.

Their orientation to cardinal points and navigation through the unpredictable marine conditions induced by mist, glacial cycles, and the occasional El Niño effect show a great familiarity with the movement of heavenly bodies and marine currents. There was knowledge of true north and perhaps even magnetic north. The discovery of what is believed to be a 3,000-year-old Olmec compass may confirm that ancient Americans also possessed some tools that helped them approximate the location of cardinal points when celestial bodies could not be seen.

The ancient Americans are not known to have ventured far upon the high seas. They never devised the large ocean-going sailing vessels of their contemporaries in Europe, Africa, Arabia, or Asia. Rather, with their development of a variety of quick-moving and highly maneuverable vessels, from one-man kayaks to massive canoes, they were able to feed communities, stimulate economies, and even build empires.

See also ASTRONOMY; BUILDING TECHNIQUES AND MATERIALS; CLIMATE AND GEOGRAPHY; ECONOMY; EXPLORATION; FOREIGNERS AND BARBARIANS; HUNTING, FISHING, AND GATHERING; INVENTIONS; MONEY AND COINAGE; OCCUPATIONS; RELIGION AND COSMOLOGY; SHIPS AND SHIPBUILDING; SLAVES AND SLAVERY; TRADE AND EXCHANGE; TRANSPORTATION; WAR AND CONQUEST.

FURTHER READING

George Bass, ed., *A History of Seafaring Based on Underwater Archaeology* (London: Thames and Hudson, 1972).

Philip Brooks, Will Fowler, and Simon Adams, *The Illustrated History Encyclopedia: Civilizations, Explorations, and Conquest* (London: Hermes House, 2003).

Lionel Casson, *Ships and Seamanship in the Ancient World* (Princeton, N.J.: Princeton University Press, 1971).

Lionel Casson, *The Ancient Mariners: Seafarers and Sea Fighters of the Mediterranean in Ancient Times*, 2nd ed. (Princeton N.J.: Princeton University Press, 1991).

Barry Cunliffe, *Facing the Ocean: The Atlantic and Its Peoples, 8000 B.C.–A.D. 1500* (London: Oxford University Press, 2001).

Barry Cunliffe, "People of the Sea." *British Archaeology* 63 (February 2002). Available online. URL: http://www.britarch.ac.uk/BA/ba63/feat2.shtml. Downloaded on May 7, 2007.

David Fabre, *Seafaring in Ancient Egypt* (London: Periplus, 2005).

Robert Gardiner, ed., *The Age of the Galley: Mediterranean Oared Vessels since Pre-Classical Times* (London: Conway Maritime Press, 1995).

Emory Dean Keoke and Kay Marie Porterfield, *American Indian Contributions to the World: Trade, Transportation, and Warfare* (New York: Facts On File, 2005).

Fik Meijer, *A History of Seafaring in the Classical World* (New York: St. Martin's Press, 1986).

John S. Morrison and J. F. Coates, *Greek and Roman Oared Warships* (Oxford, U.K.: Oxbow Books, 1996).

Shelley Wachsmann, "Seafaring." In *The Oxford Encyclopedia of Archaeology in the Near East*, vol. 4, ed. Eric M. Meyers (New York: Oxford University, 1997).

► settlement patterns

INTRODUCTION

Before the advent of agriculture, people did not settle in one place for very long. They survived as hunter-gatherers, moving about in search of game animals and edible plants. The basic unit of settlement was the camp, which small numbers of people, usually related by clan ties, used as a base of operations for hunting and gathering. As the seasons changed and food supplies diminished, they moved on to a new camp. Archaeologists learn about prehistoric ways of life by studying stone tools, artifacts, and middens (trash piles) that survive from these ancient settlements.

After the advent of agriculture in roughly 8000 B.C.E. people began to form more permanent settlements. Generally, they favored areas that provided fertile soil, a moderate climate, and water for irrigating crops. Accordingly, settlements in the ancient world were most often formed on the banks of lakes and rivers and along ocean coastlines. Major civilizations such as those of the ancient Mesopotamians and Egyptians grew up along rivers, where fertile soil was left behind after annual flooding. By this time the basic unit of settlement was the village and hamlet, where clusters of houses were built by farmers who tended the land and their herds of livestock. In time, some of these villages grew into towns, which served as administrative centers and places where farmers could sell their crops. Some of these towns evolved into cities, becoming the seats of kings and emperors.

Patterns of settlement could change as a result of changing climatic conditions. As glacial ice receded at the end of the ice age in about 11,000 B.C.E., people moved northward into such regions as Europe, including Scandinavia. Sometimes, though, climatic conditions took a turn for the worse. Parts of ancient Egypt that were (and are) desert were once fertile and green, but climate changes forced people to abandon their settlements to cluster in the fertile Nile River Valley. A similar fate awaited some of the peoples of Mesoamerica, whose fertile land turned into desert, forcing many of them into cities.

Settlement could be influenced by changes in the face of the earth. A good example is provided by Japan, which consists of about 3,000 islands, about 600 of them inhabited. Throughout most of its history, Japan was cut off from Asia and thus remained home to a Stone Age culture long after the rest of Asia had progressed. But Japan was not always an island nation. Sometimes around 30,000 B.C.E. people moved from the Korean Peninsula across a land bridge that connected Japan to Asia; at the same time, many of Japan's islands were connected until rising ocean levels separated them. For thousands of years the Neolithic Jomon culture dominated Japan, but this domination came to an end in about the third century B.C.E. when northern China experienced an extended drought that turned the region into desert. The northern Chinese, in search of more hospitable ground, streamed into Korea, in turn forcing Koreans into Japan. These types of migration patterns, brought about by changing conditions, were commonplace in the ancient world.

AFRICA

BY MICHAEL J. O'NEAL

Settlement patterns in ancient Africa were largely a function of geography and climate. Because Africa is a large continent—about 4,600 miles from east to west and approximately 5,000 miles from north to south—and is bisected by the equator, it contains a wide range of terrains and climate zones. Much of the continent is covered either by savanna (broad, open plains covered with grasses) or desert. Additionally, the continent includes forested lowlands as well as high mountain peaks, such as Mount Kilimanjaro (in Tanzania) and Mount Kenya. The continent also features five major river systems, including the Nile, the Congo, the Zambezi (where Victoria Falls, the world's largest waterfall, is found), the Volta, and the Niger.

Human history began on the plains of east Africa. During the Stone Age people migrated from these plains to other regions of the continent. They were able to do so because the human species became more intelligent and thus able to develop tools that enabled them to survive in new environments. Central to this history was the search for resources. Among the earliest Africans, the chief resource was food sought by nomadic bands of hunters and gatherers. In time, Africans searched for fertile land where there was sufficient water and a temperate climate for growing crops. Others settled along lakes, rivers, and the coasts, where bodies of water provided fish and seafood. Additionally, this search for resources included materials for building shelters and making household goods and, in time, resources that could be traded for other, scarcer resources provided by people in the ancient Near East, around the Mediterranean Sea, and from other regions within Africa.

The climate zones of Africa had a profound impact on settlement patterns. These climate zones differed by temperature and rainfall. In the lowlands along the equator, rainfall was frequent in lush forests. The heavy forests made farming difficult, and herding was not practicable because of the prevalence of disease in livestock. For this reason, the people who settled in the equatorial regions of Africa relied on hunting and gathering, fishing, and trade and exchange for their livelihood.

Farther from the equator the forests thinned out, and the climate was somewhat dryer. To the north and south were the savannas with seasonal rains (rather than the nearly daily rains of the tropical forests), longer dry seasons, and warm days but cool nights. Although the quality of the soil was poorer than in the forest regions, the open land, combined with sufficient rainfall and moderate temperatures, made these regions attractive to farmers and herders. Historically, the savannas were home of Africa's breadbaskets, where people settled to grow fruits, palm oil, peas, yams, sorghum, millet, and other crops. Incidentally, much of the modern Sahara was savanna until about 3000 B.C.E. Climate change at this time forced people to adopt new settlement patterns.

It was in the savannas and the border regions between the savannas and the forests that the major civilizations of ancient Africa emerged—for the simple reason that these regions provided the most resources combined with the most hospitable climate. Historians have identified at least eight such civilizations in a band from east to west. To the east were the ancestral lands of the Bantu-speaking peoples. Next was

Aerial view of the Niger River and surrounding savanna during the rainy season; savanna farming communities were the most common form of settlement in ancient Africa. (© Board of Regents of the University of Wisconsin System)

the region surrounding Lake Chad, the ancestral lands of the modern Kanuri. The lower Niger River region was home to the Nok, a metalworking culture. The middle Niger River region and Volta River valley were the ancestral homelands of the later Akan, Mossi, and Songhai peoples. The upper Niger River provided a home for one branch of the Mande, while the area surrounding Tichît (in modern Mauritania, the likely site of Africa's oldest city) was home to another branch of Mande. The Wolof and Serer (also spelled Sérère and Sereer) settled in the Senegal River valley and along the African coast. Finally, the ancestors of the later Fulani, Taureg, and Berber peoples occupied semiarid regions on the border of the desert. This band of civilizations formed a major east–west trading route.

Farther away from the equator are deserts, including the vast Sahara of northern Africa. Here, people settled primarily around rivers such as the Nile. The Nile River valley was home not only to the ancient Egyptians but also, farther south, to the Nubians and the Kushites. Water was provided entirely by the rivers, which flooded during rainy seasons at their source and then carried silt and water for irrigation to the desert regions. This fertile silt was the lifeblood of agriculture for these cultures. Nomadic herders lived in the deserts, where they could move their livestock about in search of scarce brush.

Finally, the northernmost and southernmost portions of the continent became temperate, with seasonal climates and rainfall similar to those of agricultural regions in the United States and Europe. Here people settled to grow such crops as grapes, olives, and wheat, and to raise livestock, such as cattle and goats. The emergence of agriculture produced major changes in settlement patterns. People had to gather and strike down more or less permanent roots to tend their fields and herds, and they lived their lives according to the rhythm of planting, tending, and harvesting crops. The result was the formation of villages and the allocation of the land that surrounded them. As people gathered in villages, more formal lines of authority had to be developed, typically those surrounding the rights and duties of the lineage or clan. In general, these communities did not form "states." Rather, they remained autonomous (independent), forming alliances and networks as necessary.

Resources had to be managed so that people had equal access to them. Practices surrounding marriage and the raising of children became more formalized. Social and economic patterns changed as people developed new specialties, such as pottery making. Religious practices became more formalized as people worshipped ancestors and gods associated with land, crops, the weather, and so on. African society became more "female" as the emphasis shifted from hunting, the preserve of males, to social and family relationships combined with sedentary gardening and crop raising. New roles developed as people took the lead as heads of clans, as storytellers and historians, as healers and diviners, and the like. Meanwhile, nomadic herders developed their own settlement patterns. While they did not stay in one place, they had to return regularly to places where they could provide shelter and pasturage for their herds. As people produced surpluses of food and other goods, commerce and exchange became more common, with people settling along trade routes and providing services to traders and their caravans. Finally, as communities formed and competed with other populations for resources, conflict and ways of managing it developed. The result of this conflict was often warfare.

EGYPT

BY WOLFRAM GRAJETZKI

In order to understand the location of Egyptian towns and villages, knowledge of the special landscape of Egypt is important. As was true in ancient times, Egypt is dominated by the Nile River and the desert. The Nile, flowing from south to north, was the only regular water source. Fertile land, only a narrow strip along the river, was less than 2 miles wide. There were some oases in the western desert, and in the north the Nile divided into several branches, forming the Nile delta, a broad and highly fertile region. In the west there was also Lake Moeris, connected to the Nile via a branch of the river. The Faiyûm Depression, a region area around this lake, was low and marshy and needed human intervention to convert it into arable land. It was only in the Middle Kingdom (ca. 2040–ca. 1640 B.C.E.) and in the Ptolemaic and Roman periods (304 B.C.E.–395 C.E.) that there were substantial towns and villages in this part of the country. In late summer the Nile rose and flooded most of the fertile land, making transport here only possible by boat. An important point, at least for bigger towns, was the connection to the Nile, either directly or via a canal. In ancient times transport over land was very expensive while water freight was easier to handle.

All settlement types in Egypt adapted to this special environment and the Nile flood. The settlements had to be placed close to the Nile to secure a regular drinking water supply and proper transport, and they had to be built on a place that remained dry throughout the year and was not flooded by the Nile. In general, these are natural "islands" of higher ground within the flood plain. (These hills in the Nile delta are often called after their general appearance "turtlebacks.") The mounds are sometimes not very big, and thus the space for settlements was restricted. If a town grew larger, people might move to another island. In the Nile delta there arose several double cities where the population lived on two or even more of these hills, which were treated in inscriptions as separate towns but were indeed single-population centers.

Desert areas were settled more often in the Greek and Roman periods, when towns and villages were built into the desert around Lake Moeris. Other settlements built at the desert edge often had specific functions, such as workmen villages for quarries or building projects like the tombs in the Valley of the Kings in Thebes. When these building projects were finished, the settlements were abandoned. The biggest building projects in Egypt were the pyramids in the Old Kingdom (ca. 2575–ca. 2134 B.C.E.). For these projects special towns for the workmen and the administration of the building project were erected. While the workmen's places were no longer used after the pyramids were finished, other parts of the settlements could develop into regular towns. Here the cult for the dead king buried in the pyramid was performed, and from this starting point these places became local centers. This is most clearly seen at El-Lahun, the pyramid town of Sesostris II (r. 1897–1878 B.C.E.). El-Lahun flourished as an administrative center for the whole region for the next two centuries. The mortuary temple of Ramses III (12th century B.C.E.), called today Medinet Habu, also became a center that functioned as an important town for 1,500 years. The temple had strong walls, and after the death of the king the local population moved there, perhaps for security reasons.

It is hard to identify the pattern of settlement types in the Nile Valley and the Nile delta, as only a few have been surveyed and a small percentage of the sites have been excavated. In addition, the excavated examples are often exceptional rather than the norm. One such place is the well-researched island of Elephantine. The southernmost settlement of Egypt, Elephantine had special significance as a trading post for Africa and also functioned as a frontier and fortress town.

In Middle Egypt near the modern villages of Qau and El Badâri, a chain of cemeteries was excavated. These cemeteries were placed close to the ancient settlements, and at least for this region it is possible to gain a picture of the distribution of settlements in pharaonic times. The center of this region was the town called in ancient times Tjebu (modern-day Qau el-Qebir). Here was found the biggest cemetery of the region, including the monumental tombs of the local rulers. Tjebu was the center of the local governor with the palace of the local government. It was also the location of an important temple. The temple was closely connected with the administration of local government. Here the taxes of the province were stored and given back to the people when needed.

From ancient texts we know that each province had a main town with a temple of the most important deity of the province. These temples in the local centers not only functioned as religious capitals of a region but were also the contact place between the royal capital of the country and local

(opposite page) Most settlements in ancient Egypt were placed close to the Nile. A high proportion of the population of towns probably lived from agricultural work, taking advantage of the yearly rise and fall of the Nile that left deposits of rich black silt along the riverbanks.

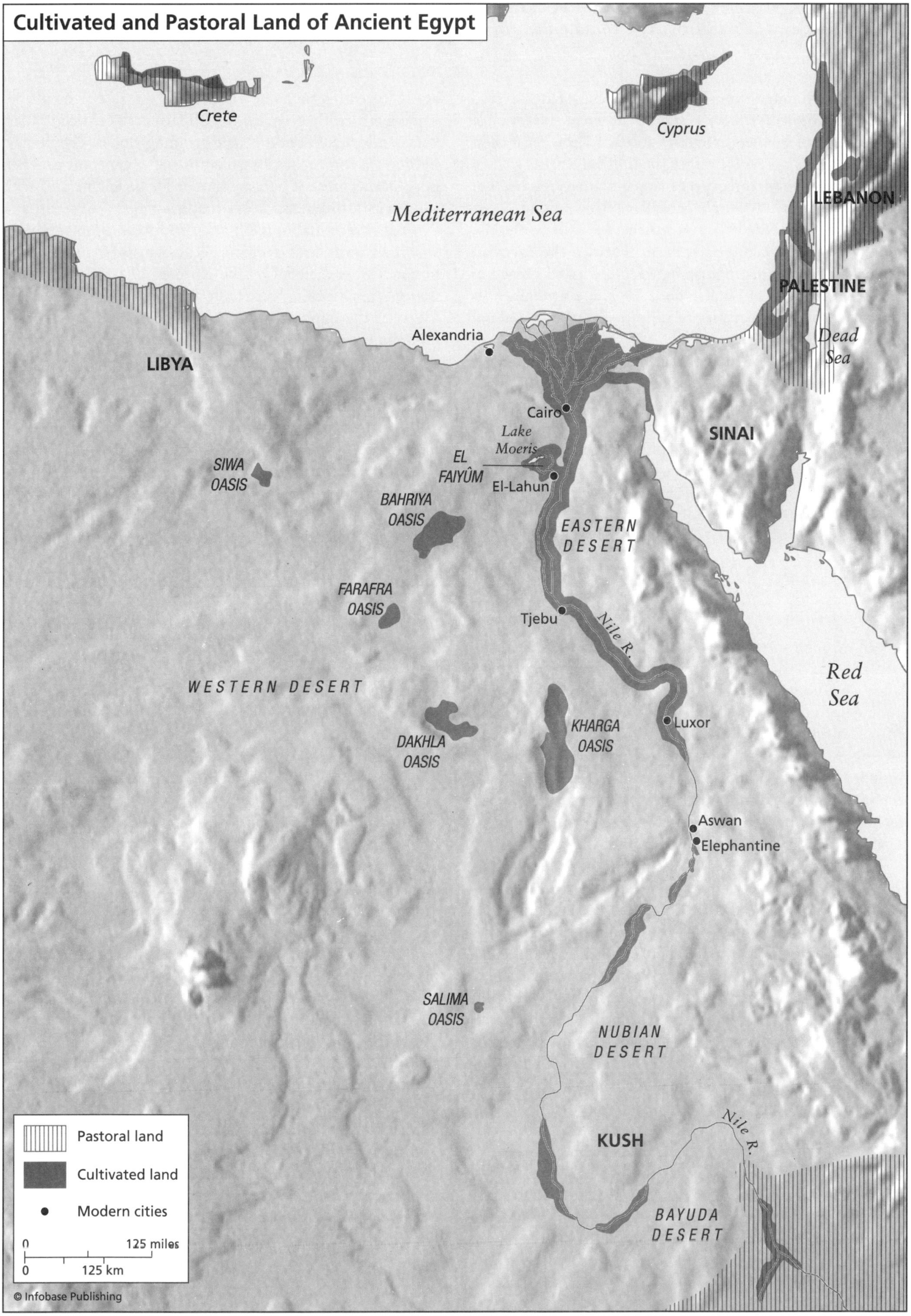
Cultivated and Pastoral Land of Ancient Egypt
Crete
Cyprus
Mediterranean Sea
LEBANON
PALESTINE
Dead Sea
Alexandria
LIBYA
Cairo
Lake Moeris
SINAI
SIWA OASIS
EL FAIYÛM
El-Lahun
BAHRIYA OASIS
EASTERN DESERT
FARAFRA OASIS
Tjebu
Nile R.
Red Sea
WESTERN DESERT
KHARGA OASIS
Luxor
DAKHLA OASIS
Aswan
Elephantine
SALIMA OASIS
NUBIAN DESERT
KUSH
Nile R.
BAYUDA DESERT
Pastoral land
Cultivated land
Modern cities
0 125 miles
0 125 km
© Infobase Publishing

government. Around these centers, which must have covered the whole Nile Valley, were villages of different sizes, visible from a chain of smaller cemeteries north of Tjebu. In ancient Egyptian times they were rather small; from what is known of the cemeteries we can expect that populations reached not much more than 100 people per village. However, in Greek and Roman times Nile Valley settlements were often quite big, and many of them had the size of small towns. The Egyptian language does not distinguish between town and village in precisely the way that English does. There are several words for settlements, but they may relate to their function and not necessarily to their size.

Not much is known about farmhouses and small agricultural units. In general, we can assume that even in towns and local centers a high proportion of the population lived from agricultural work. From written sources we know that houses or estates existed in the countryside and were involved in food production. Only farmhouses of the Ptolemaic Period (ca. 304–30 B.C.E.) have been excavated showing that they at least were sometimes big buildings.

THE MIDDLE EAST

BY AMY HACKNEY BLACKWELL

When the last ice age ended about 11,000 B.C.E., humans spread through the Middle East. The climate was good, and rainfall was relatively high for the region. As a result, grasslands and forests expanded and provided more food for humans, who quickly inhabited the entire Fertile Crescent, an area stretching from Israel and Lebanon to the Zagros Mountains. These hunter-gatherers sought out regions that included more than one ecological zone so that they could exploit a variety of food sources. They lived in small, highly mobile bands, sheltering in temporary camps that they could easily dismantle when conditions deteriorated.

Starting around 10,000 B.C.E. people began settling in locations for longer periods as they grew dependent on certain types of plant foods. For example, the Natufian people of modern-day Israel lived on acorns and pistachio nuts that grew in a belt in the central part of the region. They built permanent villages with underground storage pits and occupied these settlements for many generations. The people of Abu Hureyra on the Euphrates River in Syria also built a permanent village, hunting and fishing and gathering plant foods from the nearby forests. By about 9500 B.C.E. permanent settlements were common throughout the region.

The first farming settlements appeared around 8000 B.C.E. in the Levantine corridor, a narrow strip about 15 miles wide along the Jordan River from the Damascus Basin to Jericho. This corridor had ample water supplies with a naturally high water table, a rarity in the region. The readily available water meant that people could farm without irrigation. The area also had plentiful sources of wild food, including legumes, nuts, and game. These settlers built villages of mud-brick huts that housed perhaps 100 to 200 residents. As the products of agriculture furnished more of peoples' diets, settlements became more nearly permanent with farmers were tied to their fields and women tied to their grinding stones. People now lived in the same place for generation after generation. When populations grew, it became harder for people to deal with sudden catastrophes such as droughts.

Because rainfall was low and rivers were the only reliable source of water in the region, settlement patterns in Mesopotamia were dictated by the presence of rivers. All major Mesopotamian cities were built near the banks of either the Tigris or the Euphrates. Some of the earliest-known Mesopotamian cities were Ur, Uruk, and Eridu, built by the Sumerians near the mouth of the combined Tigris and Euphrates sometime between the sixth and the fourth millennia B.C.E. Some archaeologists believe that Eridu was the first city ever built; Sumerian tradition held that Eridu was the first city before the Great Flood to have a king. Southern Mesopotamia was wetter than it is now, and it was conveniently located on trade routes, which made it an attractive location for settlement.

The population of the Mesopotamian river settlements grew quickly. At first the cities were fairly small and surrounded by farming villages, but the climate changed this pattern. Around 3800 B.C.E. the climate grew drier, and the floods that the farmers relied on began arriving later, after harvest. People who had lived in the countryside were unable to farm anymore and abandoned their homes. Some became nomadic herders, wandering with their animals in search of pasture. Others left the outlying villages and moved into the cities in search of food. By 3200 B.C.E. Sumerian civilization had become highly urbanized. Historians estimate that by 2800 B.C.E. some 80 percent of the Sumerian population lived in cities clustered in southern Mesopotamia.

Ur, Eridu, and a group of several other cities within sight of one another were home to thousands of Sumerian farmers who used the rivers' annual floods to irrigate their fields. Small villages extended out from the cities along networks of canals that carried water away from the rivers. Different communities specialized in different products, such as pottery, fishing, or metalwork. Each city had a government that organized irrigation and food distribution and conducted the rituals considered necessary to propitiate the gods. Several land and sea trade routes converged on the area. The cities in the region constantly fought over scarce water and land resources.

People had begun colonizing the upper part of the river during the fifth millennium B.C.E. These cities grew larger during the third millennium B.C.E. and came under the leadership of warlords who competed with one another for water and land. When water was plentiful the settlement pattern resembled that of the early fourth millennium in southern Mesopotamia, with towns spread out from cities, but urbanization proved inevitable there as well. The Akkadian civilization (2350–2100 B.C.E.), for example, arose in the fertile Habur plain south of the Anatolian plateau when, as had happened around 3800 B.C.E., a drought drove people from the countryside into the cities.

While cities were a viable solution to minor drought, major droughts were too much for them. Around 2200 B.C.E. a major drought afflicted all of Mesopotamia. The cities could no longer feed their residents, and the people dispersed, leaving their former homes to sink into ruin. When the rains returned about 1900 B.C.E., the people returned as well, though to different sites; the rivers had changed course, and some of the former city sites were no longer habitable. Cities continued to be the dominant settlement form in the region.

Throughout the Middle East people followed similar patterns, gathering around rare water sources. In the Levant people settled near rivers, lakes, and other sources of water. The Jordan River and the Sea of Galilee were major population centers from early times. The coastline was also valuable to fishermen and sea traders. In Arabia there was so little water that very few people lived there. The ones who did manage to settle there permanently built towns on the coasts of the Persian Gulf and the Red Sea.

In Anatolia most people lived along the Black Sea and Aegean coastlines, which had fertile land and a healthy climate. People had settled the coast of the Black Sea (at that time called the Euxine Sea) by the seventh century B.C.E. When the weather grew warm and wet around 5800 B.C.E. the population on the shores of the sea increased as more farmers took advantage of the fertile soil. Also around 5800 B.C.E. the waters of the sea began rising, and the entire area flooded, forcing residents to abandon their homes and flee to higher ground. Many of them moved into eastern Europe. The central part of the Anatolian peninsula was mountainous and heavily forested, which made living conditions difficult, though some hardy souls lived in caves in the rocks. By the time of the Greek and Roman empires, the western and northern coasts of Anatolia were heavily populated with towns, large cities, and farmsteads.

In Persia the most fertile area was the coastline of the Caspian Sea, which received more rain than any other part of the country. Human settlements were concentrated in this region. Settlements also clustered along the trade route that led between India to the east and Mesopotamia to the west. Persian rulers built cities throughout their realm; major cities were Susa, near Babylon, and the Seleucid capital of Persepolis.

Relief fragment showing Assyrian soldiers towing a boat through shallow water (Courtesy of the Oriental Institute of the University of Chicago)

ASIA AND THE PACIFIC

BY KIRK H. BEETZ

Most paleontologists believe that early humans spread eastward from Africa along the southern coast of Asia. Many of their settlements would now be underwater. They would have chosen to settle where the fishing was good, spreading inland only where the hunting and gathering were easy and probably not establishing villages inland until population pressures forced them to move. Their villages would have been far apart and their overall population would have been thinly spread over the landscape.

Humans reached the southeastern edge of Asia long before the beginning of the last ice age. From Southeast Asia people moved slowly to outlying islands. In about 30,000 B.C.E. people began to settle Australia, probably inhabiting its northwestern coast, where they could establish fishing villages. They spread slowly through what was then a mostly wet continent, arriving at Tasmania in about 29,000 B.C.E. and reaching the far southern edge of Australia in about 22,000 B.C.E. By 10,000 B.C.E. they were a thinly spread population of about 300,000 people whose villages tended to be near sheltering rocks and forests, where they could escape direct sunlight in what was becoming a mostly dry, hot land.

The earliest-known Indian culture is the Harappan civilization (ca. 2600–ca. 1500 B.C.E.) of the Indus River valley in northwestern India and Pakistan. The first major cities discovered by archaeologists were Harappa and Mohenjo Daro. Both of these cities were near the Indus River, which for a long time had archaeologists believing that the Indus River was the focus of Harappan settlements. Yet the Vedas tell of a major river, the Sarasvati, that was the focus of important events. The Vedas are sacred works of Hindus that were the oral tradition of the Vedic peoples who invaded India in about 1500 B.C.E. and which were written down sometime between the 500s and 300s B.C.E.

It turns out that the Sarasvati had existed but dried up between 2000 and 1000 B.C.E. It was east of the Indus River, and it appears to have had far more Harappan settlements along it than did the Indus. The Harappans were farmers and traders. Most of their population lived near rivers, and they used irrigation canals to water their farmlands. In general, they used every bit of arable land for growing crops and built their homes on land that was more rocky than the land they farmed. Although most of their settlements were along the Indus and Sarasvati rivers, every river in the valley had at least one village along it. They also had many villages in wet lowlands near the Gulf of Kachchh and the Gulf of Khambhat on the coast of the Arabian Sea and at least a few villages well to the east on the Narmada and Tāpi rivers. To further their trade with other cultures, the Harappans established towns far from their river valley: Shortughai in the Hindu Kush mountains to the north and Mundikak, Shahr-e Sokhte, and Bampūr far to the west. Shortughai was in a place to take advantage of trade in lapis lazuli, and the far western settlements may have been for trade with Mesopotamia. The oldest settlement appears to be Mehrgarh near the Bolan Pass west of the Indus River, which was first settled in about 6000 B.C.E.

By about 1500 B.C.E. the Harappan civilization had collapsed, probably because of a combination of natural disasters and invasion by nomadic Aryan groups from central Asia. These groups became the Vedic peoples, and over hundreds of years they migrated through the Indus River valley and southeastward through northern India. They did not immediately settle down into permanent homes but migrated with their cattle. In about 1000 B.C.E. they began to adopt agriculture, and during the 800s B.C.E. small Vedic kingdoms arose, mostly along the Ganges and Yamuna rivers that ran southeastward across northern India. Much of the Ganges flowed through plains that were good for both growing crops and herding cattle.

While the Vedic peoples were slowly expanding southward, they encountered other peoples, often called Dravidians by archaeologists. Many of these people belonged to Stone Age cultures, living in forests as hunter-gatherers. They resisted efforts to settle their territories and continued their ways of life all through the ancient era. Others became farmers. Like the Harappans, they tended to settle along rivers, but in central and southern India rains were so frequent that communities could settle in wet, open lands away from rivers and reasonably hope to receive enough rain to water their crops. When India formed kingdoms, governments tried to take advantage of rains by building dams to create reservoirs, particularly in mountainous highlands. Public works such as dams and irrigation canals allowed people to spread their villages into areas previously unsuited for farming.

Although the Harappans are still mysterious to modern archaeologists, societies in China during the same era are even more perplexing. In much of what is now China, people did not create settlements until modern times, and many in the north still remain nomads, pitching their tents in different places every day. In about 6500 B.C.E. people began farming. By about 5000 B.C.E. there was a fairly cohesive culture farming millet along the lower reaches of the Yellow River, also known as the Huang River. Around the Yellow River and its tributaries was a belt of loess soil, silt blown into layers over many years, and the Yangshao culture of about 5000 B.C.E. spread villages away from rivers into regions where the soil allowed for easy digging. Rice farming was introduced from the south, and the Longshan culture of about 3200 B.C.E. developed to organize people to take advantage of rice's superior yields and nutrition, because rain was less frequent in the Yellow River area and irrigation requiring community cooperation was needed to provide rice with the moisture it needed.

South of the Yellow River was the Yangtze River, where farmers settled along the riverside to grow mostly rice. From about 4500 B.C.E. on the region around the mouth of the Yangtze and a region upstream around the lake Dongting Hu became heavily populated by farmers. The Shang Dynasty (ca. 1500–ca. 1045 B.C.E.) tried to absorb the people of the Yangtze, but it took until the Zhou Dynasty (ca. 1045–256 B.C.E.) for China to conquer the Yangtze settlements, and thereafter the Yangtze farmlands became vital to feeding the empire.

The Zhou, Qin (221–207 B.C.E.), and Han (202 B.C.E.–220 C.E.) dynasties each made the establishment of settlements part of government policy. They made special efforts to settle peasants from central China in the north near the Great Wall to act as deterrents to nomadic raiders, and during the Han Dynasty to help make the Silk Road secure. To absorb conquered lands into the empire, Chinese governments often moved large groups of peasants south or west, going as far south as North Vietnam.

For almost all of the ancient era the majority of people in Korea and Japan settled near ocean shores. Those people who moved inland tended to settle beside lakes or streams. In Japan the mountains were sparsely populated. In Korea invasions and wars influenced some people to move into highlands, where travel was difficult and water sometimes scarce but where the rough territory helped them defend themselves. During the Yayoi Period (300 B.C.E.–300 C.E.) of Japan people often settled near marshes or swamps because they would scatter rice seed in the marshes or swamps and later harvest the new rice. This unsophisticated approach to growing rice was sufficient for Japan's population of about two million people.

Extensive rain forests grew in southeastern Asia. That these lands were populated is known from the records of Chinese and Indian explorers, but little is known of their settlement patterns. The Mekong River attracted many settlements, probably at first because of good fishing and later because rice could be cultivated along it. By about 100 B.C.E. the Mekong Delta in modern southeastern Vietnam was heavily populated, mostly by farmers.

EUROPE

BY JUDITH A. RASSON

The Paleolithic cultural period dates to the geological Pleistocene (the ice ages). Although the climate all over Europe was affected, there were many large ice-free areas. People lived in small groups that moved around throughout the year to hunt and gather wild animals and plants, resulting in a settlement pattern made up of campsites used by different groups at different times. A good campsite needed not only a safe place to set up tents or other shelters but also access to water and food. Some campsites were near sources of stone for tools. People returned to favorable locations year after year, such as Dolní Věstonice in the modern-day Czech Republic, which was on a nonglaciated route between eastern and western Europe.

The shelters that people constructed were only temporary; they took their tents with them when they traveled or built new shelters from brush and tree branches. A conveniently located cave also made a good temporary home that might be revisited every year.

During the Paleolithic everyone lived in groups based on families, and their settlements were similar, though the groups varied in size depending on how much food they had available and what tasks they were carrying out. These tasks and activities mainly had to do with everyday living, such as preparing and cooking food and making tools and clothing. While no group stayed long in any particular place, perhaps once a year different groups gathered for a day or two to renew friendships, find marriage partners, and share information. A few special sites, like the Lascaux Cave complex in France, were not just for the activities of everyday life. At Lascaux and a handful of other places the cave walls were decorated with pictures of animals and other designs. They had social and religious significance.

At the end of the Pleistocene the climate changed, although people remained gatherers and hunters for hundreds more years, adapting to the supply of plants and animals brought by the new warmer climate. Eventually people found out how to domesticate plants and animals to supply their needs for food and other materials, and they developed ceramics, though they still relied on stone for sharp-edged cutting tools. This was the beginning of agriculture, called the Neolithic Period, which began in about 7000 B.C.E. in Greece but not until 2000 B.C.E. in England.

Houses built by Neolithic settlers were made of timber and mud plaster (or the equivalent), more substantial and usually larger than in the Paleolithic. They were occupied for long periods, probably because groups now maintained their own food supplies. Settlements functioned as hubs from which many activities were carried out, such as cultivating fields and herding animals. It is hard to generalize about the locations of Neolithic settlements because their locations were always compromises that made it possible to meet a number of needs, such as access to water, arable land for crops, and grazing land. More people lived in Europe than before, and because their lifeways left more remains than earlier, hundreds of Neolithic settlements are known throughout Europe, for example, Cuiry-lés-Chaudardes in France, Brześć Kujawski in Poland, and Selevac in Serbia. In general, each settlement fulfilled the same social and economic functions as every other settlement, but Neolithic people in many parts of western Europe built special-purpose monuments interpreted as expressions of their supernatural beliefs. Arrangements of large stones called *megaliths* can be seen at Carnac in Brittany (France). Passage graves were made with stones grouped in various ways with or without soil coverings; the most famous is New Grange in Ireland.

Although settlements were similar, the length of time each was occupied differed. Some settlements were used for long periods throughout the Neolithic, resulting in the accumulation of cultural debris in a large mound (or tell), like Karanovo in Bulgaria. These are more common in eastern and southeastern Europe than in western Europe. Sometimes smaller settlements, occupied for less time, were located surrounding a tell, as at Polgár-Csőszhalom in Hungary. This suggests that the older (tell) settlement had some economic or social function beyond that of the smaller younger settlements.

During the Bronze Age, when metalworking became widespread, some earlier patterns persisted. The basic economic activities of cultivating fields and grazing livestock continued; thus settlement sites were still placed to provide access to the necessary resources. But settlements began to be distinguishable from one another by the number or variety of their differing functions. In western Germany and the Low Countries, for example, there were both single farmsteads and larger villages. As can be seen by their size and internal complexity, some settlements began to benefit from increased trade activity.

In the social system of the Bronze Age (starting as early as 2800 B.C.E., in southeastern Europe) some people earned elite status and political power. Trade intensified, even with far-distant areas, including trade in valuable bronze objects. It was during this period that many settlements throughout Europe began to show signs of defensive fortifications, such as being located on hilltops (sometimes called hill forts) or being surrounded by ditches and wooden palisades. A Bronze Age tell in Hungary has a double ditch and palisade system surrounding it; in Spain, a Bronze Age site with stone walls stands on a high promontory. In Sardinia, in addition to village settlements, Bronze Age people built stone towers called *nuraghi*.

Later still, iron objects began to be made and used in different parts of Europe—albeit at different times. By the Iron Age (starting around 1000 B.C.E.) iron objects and tools became widely available to most members of society for all aspects of daily life. New technology, such as iron-tipped plows, enabled people to occupy new areas. The Iron Age is associated with increasing social and economic complexity, which was reflected in a hierarchical settlement pattern. Territoriality was evident when some groups began to control important locales, such as river fords or mountain passes. Some villages or farmsteads remained strongly connected to farming and stock raising, whereas others added functions, such as being the residence of a socially elite group. In the Halland area of Sweden agricultural villages are located on well-drained soil, and smaller sites are located adjacent to wet areas, perhaps for special purposes such as hunting. The large site of Slöinge was probably the residence of elite people because the artifacts found there include such unusual items as garnets, amber, gold, silver, and imported glass.

Important settlements were usually protected in some way, often by a ditch, palisade, or rampart, sometimes even by a water barrier such as the crannogs, or artificial islands, constructed in Ireland. In Poland the site of Biskupin is fortified and located on a peninsula in a lake for protection. The Iron

Age settlement of Százhalombatta Földvár in Hungary was protected by both a ditch and an earthen rampart, construction of which was a huge earth-moving project that probably required direction by a respected person of higher social status than most people. Another manifestation of the existence of a social elite was the use of distinctive burial practices. In many areas the elite were buried in specially constructed mounds (sometimes called tumuli). The Iron Age is the first time in European prehistory that something is known about the group names people called themselves. The most famous are the Celts, who were spread from southeastern Europe to the British Isles. Their elite lived in hill forts (often called *oppida*). The settlement of Bibracte, now called Mont Beuvray, in France was surrounded by a wall of timber, stone, and earth, 3 miles long.

GREECE

BY MARK ANTHONY PHELPS

Two geographic factors are paramount in understanding Greece from either a social or an economic context. First, this is an extraordinarily hilly and mountainous land, as over 40 percent of the land is more than 1,600 feet in elevation. The Pindus Mountains extend the length of the region until they submerge into the Aegean Sea, creating most of the islands found there as well as a jagged coast that provides a vast number of protected harbors. Settled life focuses on valleys and a handful of plains scattered throughout the country. Second, no point of the peninsula is more than 38 miles from the sea.

The soil of the region is rocky and often of marginal fertility. Adding to the fragility of the soil is the climate, known as dry summer subtropical. Summer dryness, wind, and heat contribute to crop failure, while winter rains demand modifications of the farmland to enhance drainage and to stop soil erosion. Natural springs and man-made cisterns, necessities for rural life, influence where cities can grow. In ancient times the marginal land that could not lend itself to intensive agriculture was used for pastoralism. After the collapse of the Mycenaean civilization (ca. 1100 B.C.E.), the depopulation of cities may reflect a period of nomadic pastoralism. For the rest of the ancient history of Greece, transhumant pastoralism was the norm.

The hills and mountains of Greece contributed to the political fragmentation that characterizes Greek history. Isolation fosters ethnocentrism, which contributes to the history of independent city-states and continual rivalries. The majority of ancient Greeks were farmers. Wheat was the dominant crop in the plains and valley bottoms, while olives and grapes were typically grown on terraced hillsides.

The model traditionally espoused for ancient farmers is taken from the pattern of farming found in medieval and modern Greece. Historians theorized that farmers lived in villages, leaving in the morning to tend to scattered plots. The distribution of plots was the product of equal devolution of property among sons and the usage of land in dowries. This dispersion was ultimately advantageous, as land in plots that have some ecological differentiation serves as insurance in the face of droughts, because one piece of land may fare better than others. Further, the village provided protection from raiders. Given the scarcity of water, it was assumed that farmhouses in the countryside would have been impossible to maintain.

However, this model has been successfully challenged by the recent attention to rural archaeology and a closer reading of certain classical texts. The rise of villages and the increase in trade at the beginning of the Iron Age points to a rise in agricultural production. The need for land for intensive farming was a contributing factor to the phenomenon of colonization as Greeks established colonies throughout the Aegean coasts, the Black Sea, Libya, and other scattered centers in Asia Minor and the rest of the eastern Mediterranean.

The image of Odysseus's father Laertes in Homer's *Odyssey* serves as antithetical evidence to the traditional model of ancient Greek farming. In contrast to the notion of living in a village, Laertes resides in a house on his farm with outbuildings constructed on it for storage and drying. He works his farm daily, which must be done if one is growing vines and maintaining orchards. He has a fence and dogs for protection. He labors alongside his slaves, sharing equally in toil. He rarely enters the town, where he owns a lavish house, and he has a profound disdain for urban dwellers. He has a reputation as a warrior.

Archaeological evidence indicates that small-scale irrigation emerged at the time of Homer and Hesiod in the late eighth century B.C.E., providing another argument for the need to have farmers on farms for continual maintenance. In his writings Aristotle (384–322 B.C.E.) asserts that in early days the population of the polis was small, as most were working farms. Surveys in Attica, Boeotia, the Argolis, the Peloponnese, Aegean Islands, Magna Graecia, and the Crimea all support these images where a number of rural structures from these areas have been located.

Ancient Greek farmers would have needed to both protect their land from raiders and hide from invaders. Given that most farms were small, neighbors were not terribly distant. Protection from farming neighbors seems to have been a greater concern than raiders given the attention that Plato assigns to legal codes regulating the relationship between farming neighbors in his work *Laws*. Clearly, settlement in rural areas was dense enough to cause troubles. The largest estates were by no means enormous. The politician and general Alcibiades (fifth century B.C.E.), nephew of Pericles, was fabulously wealthy with an estate of some 80 acres.

The choice for urban settlement was based primarily on access to water, generally springs or (less often) rivers. Sites needed to have an agricultural hinterland to support the urban population that did not farm. This hinterland would have needed a population base to trade its surplus for certain manufactured and imported goods. The two most powerful states during the bulk of the ancient Greek period were the two city-states with the largest agricultural hinterlands, namely, Sparta and Athens. Access to the sea was beneficial for trade but by no means a requisite for cities in classical Greece. These factors account for the resettlement of former urban areas (usually with the same Mycenaean name) during the Iron Age, as Greece has always been a land of limited water and limited agricultural land.

The abundance of harbors and ease of access to the sea for most of the interior fostered a culture of seamanship. This orientation was further driven by the poor mobility between Greek regions and cities owning to the mountainous and hilly terrain. In turn, the period of colonization of distant shores from the eighth through sixth centuries B.C.E. was facilitated by the experience of the Greeks in managing the geographic circumstances of their homeland.

The hills contributed to the isolation and fragmentation of the city-states that emerged in the Iron Age. The rare plains lent themselves to the formation of leagues among the cities and villages ringing them. The members of these leagues would fight among themselves over access to resources, but they formed a united front against outside invaders.

The origin of the institutions of classical Greece can be traced and attributed to the values and experiences of farmers living on this land. The sense of individual worth, egalitarianism, and independence all followed from attitudes expressed by and attributed to farmers. Greek writers took pride in the difficulty of their climate and soil in regard to agricultural production. Such characteristics as courageousness, fierceness, physical strength, and intelligence all sprang from life on farms, according to classical authors.

ROME

BY DAVID B. HOLLANDER

In the Roman world agriculture was the foundation of the economy, and owning land was the basis of social status. Thus both the settlement and use of land were of considerable importance in the development of the empire. Political and military factors influenced where colonies were established, while economic, cultural, climatic, and geographic factors determined the location of farms, villages, and towns and whether they flourished or failed.

A number of different kinds of sources shed light on Roman settlement patterns, each with its drawbacks. Literary sources, such as agricultural manuals and the writings of elite Romans including Cicero and Pliny the Younger, provide some information about the size and location of farms and villas, but these authors rarely discuss the situations and concerns of any but the wealthiest Romans. Survey archaeology, in which a team of archaeologists examines land for surface traces of ancient activity by walking over it, can provide a much fuller picture of settlement patterns. In many parts of the empire one still finds traces of the boundaries established by centuriation, the process Roman surveyors used to mark out land allotments for new settlers. Surveys reveal the remains of ancient farmhouses and villages as well as those of larger villas. They can also indicate how settlement patterns changed over time. Nevertheless, survey archaeology cannot determine who owned a given structure or how much land was associated with it. Furthermore, it is likely that the dwellings of the poorest farmers left few traces for archaeologists to find. The excavation of the remains of rural structures can suggest how the surrounding land was exploited and the nature of a villa or farm's interaction with the local environment and market. Inscriptions and papyrus manuscripts also sometimes provide information concerning the ownership and use of land.

Several Roman agricultural manuals have survived from antiquity. The earliest, written by Cato the Elder, dates to the second century B.C.E.; Varro wrote another about a century later, and a third was composed in the first century C.E. by Columella. Pliny the Elder, author of 37 volumes on natural history, provides additional information. These writers discuss not only estate management and the cultivation of crops but also the question of where to build a farm. Many factors had to be considered when buying agricultural land. According to Cato, ideally, the climate should be good, and the property should be at the base of a mountain facing south, having access to water and a supply of labor as well as roads, navigable waterways, or a nearby town. Good neighbors and land capable of growing a variety of crops also were considered desirable features. Varro discusses two other important factors related to the establishment of rural estates: health and safety. Proximity to swamps and marshes is undesirable, while, in certain regions, a farmer might have to contend with brigands. Varro stresses the advantages of having property near a town or village, where one could sell produce and purchase necessities.

Small estates on the outskirts of Rome could prove immensely profitable if their production was geared toward the city's insatiable demand for game, fish, and flowers. Wealthy Romans frequently built luxury villas where they might relax or entertain guests. Prior to the eruption of Vesuvius in 79 C.E., the land around the Bay of Naples was a particularly popular location.

Little can be said with certainty about the earliest phase of Roman settlement during the regal period. Tradition held that shepherds and outlaws formed the bulk of the followers of Romulus, Rome's legendary founder. It is likely that pastoral agriculture played a more important role in Rome's first centuries than it did later. Romans of the late Republic believed that their ancestors had worked small plots of land on the outskirts of the city. As the Roman Empire expanded, three important trends emerged: colonization, the designation of conquered land as *ager publicus* (public land), and growth in the size of upper-class estates. Colonies served several functions. The Romans founded some small colonies, such as Antium and Ostia, on the coast to protect against seaborne attacks. Other colonies were essentially garrisons in newly conquered territory.

Colonists, who might be Roman citizens, veterans, or allies, received small plots of land to farm in their new communities. Vast tracts of land were confiscated from Rome's defeated enemies and designated *ager publicus*. Despite the efforts of some Roman lawmakers to limit individual holdings, wealthy Romans came to control much of this land. The rich landowners used slave labor to operate their large estates, which were called *latifundia*. In the 130s and 120s B.C.E. the plebeian tribunes Gaius and Tiberius Gracchus attempted to enforce the limits on holdings of *ager publicus* and distribute the recovered land to less fortunate Romans. They encountered stiff resistance from the Senate; even though both men were ultimately murdered in riots, they did manage to settle thousands of Romans on small plots of Italian land. Such conflicts over land possession and ownership continued into the first century B.C.E. The proscriptions instituted by Sulla in the 80s led to the confiscation of tremendous amounts of land. A number of the Roman general Sulla's associates gained wealth by purchasing confiscated estates. Many landowners continued to rely heavily on slaves to work their estates, as the great slave revolt led by Spartacus suggests. Civil war, debt crises, and the need to find land to reward Roman veterans made the Italian real estate market especially volatile in the final decades of the Republic.

Given the size and varied nature of the Roman Empire, it is difficult to make generalizations about settlement patterns in the Imperial period. Farms of varying sizes, villages, towns, and rural sanctuaries as well as seasonal shelters for farmers and shepherds could be found dotting the landscape. While some individuals amassed large landholdings and debt frequently forced peasants to sell their land, the practices of dividing inherited land among heirs and colonizing conquered regions tended to create new smallholders. Many provinces received groups of Roman colonists, especially in the early empire. Some provincial cities grew substantially under Roman rule due to their status as provincial capitals, their role in the transportation of foodstuffs to Rome, the presence of military units, or the patronage of the emperor. Alexandria, Carthage, and Antioch became particularly important. Other cities and regions suffered from natural disasters, revolts, or proximity to volatile border areas. The relative peace of the first two centuries of the Common Era saw an increase in population and rural settlement in many regions. But beginning in the late second century C.E. plague, civil wars, and Germanic invasions caused a decline in population and rural settlement in some places.

THE AMERICAS

BY J. J. GEORGE

Settlement patterns in the ancient Americas overlap with traditional migration theories on the origin of the first peoples. The traditional theory held that the first Americans crossed Berengia, the Bering Sea land bridge from Siberia to Alaska, around 11,500 years ago. The term *bridge* is somewhat misleading because some models suggest that open land was in excess of 1,000 miles wide, affording ample territory for multiple bands of persons traveling on foot to make their way into the New World. Why did they come? In brief, they came because they were following megafauna, or large animals hunted for food, such as mammoths, mastodons, bison, and giant sloths—the latter as large as 20 feet tall. While Berengia is now under water, save for a scattering of islands, during the period of initial settlement much of the earth's water was locked up in ice sheets that covered much of Canada, dramatically lowering the earth's sea levels and exposing greater expanses of land.

The appearance of the first Americans coincided neatly with evidence indicating that an ice-free corridor had opened between two large Canadian ice sheets referred to as the Laurentide and Cordilleran, allowing these early migrants access to nonglaciated lands in mid-latitude America. These original inhabitants are now called Clovis people, named after the town in New Mexico where their fluted spear points used for hunting mammoth were first found in 1932. Clovis and Clovis-like points are recorded from the late Pleistocene in Alaska to Panama and in California and Nova Scotia. Following this model, the first settlements spread slowly southward, eventually reaching the edge of North America to the east and the southern tip of South America.

However, a well-studied site called Monte Verde in southern Chile, dated to around 12,500 years ago, calls into question the traditional model of a slow and orderly procession southward. The site contains the buried remnants of simple residential structures, stone tools including bifacial projectile points—a stone tool with two sides or faces worked to form an edge for scraping or cutting—and preserved edible and medicinal plants. The question, then, is how did these peoples reach so far south so fast? A competing settlement theory posits a much more rapid southern advance via open coastal routes along the Pacific Coast into Alaska and northwestern Canada and eventually south to Peru and Chile by approximately 12,500 years ago. Any remnant archaeological data that might pinpoint and date coastal settlements are unfortunately lost; as the last ice age receded, rising sea levels worldwide advanced inland, burying the previous coastline and along with it any markers of coastal inhabitation. To date, then, there is agreement only in that the first Americans were *Homo sapiens sapiens*, who were in North and South America by Clovis times, about 11,500 years ago.

Viewed archaeologically, settlement patterns are, like any prehistoric residue, the incomplete and fragmentary markings of something that was once vital and whole, essentially a reconstruction of the physical and material presence of long-disappeared persons. A settlement might be thought of as an archaeologically discernible site, a unit of space that was characterized during some culturally definable period of time by the presence of one or more dwellings or structures. The arrangement of structures on a site with respect to one another forms unit patterns. The arrangement of these patterns, in turn, through a wider segment of space, might be termed a complex pattern. These complex patterns relate to the adjustments of human beings and culture to environment and to organization of society in a broad sense.

Over time a range of settlement types developed, some coalescing into complex settled social units based on agricultural production and others maintaining hunter-gatherer economies. Classifying the variety of settlements presents its own difficulties, with definitions differing by scholar and discipline. In general, however, much of the literature includes the following settlement types: camps, villages, towns, ceremonial centers, village clusters, and, eventually, cities. Generally speaking, these classifications represent advancing complexity based on differing social, economic, and political determinants, and it should be further noted that characteristics are often complementary and overlapping.

The simplest archaeological discernible site, or *camp,* would cover sites with areas between a few hundred square feet and perhaps an acre, where midden (refuse) deposits are thin and impermanent, lightly built shelters were erected without any definite community plan. Camps are most closely affiliated with hunter-gatherer and semisedentary units. Camps persisted in areas such as the eastern United States, Brazil, Central America, Mexico, and the Caribbean from the time of the first human being until at least the historic period, or the period when Europeans first arrived and began recording written history.

A *village* occupies an area of several acres. The number of dwellings might run as high as 30 to 40. The appearance of sturdier structures, which remained in place and were occupied for extended periods of time; deeper refuse deposits; and some level of village planning are in evidence. The spatial and temporal distribution of villages is similar to that of camps, which they began to replace or at least to supplement. It would be common for a village to be politically dominated by a chief with extended kin or clan affiliations. Examples of this type of settlement range from the Tehuacán Valley of Mexico, with pit houses and domesticated plant use in evidence by 3400 B.C.E.; to Hopewell Indian sites in the American Midwest by roughly 200 B.C.E.; to coastal villages in British Columbia and Southeastern Alaska, with evidence of plank houses by 200 B.C.E.; to the burial mounds and earthworks of the Adena people in Ohio, Kentucky, and West Virginia between 1000 B.C.E. and 200 C.E..

Village clusters and *ceremonial centers* are closely related and particularly common, representing a number of neighboring villages so closely related culturally that it is assumed constant contact was common and sociopolitical organization overlapped. It was not uncommon for these affiliated villages to share a ceremonial center. Unlike camps, which lacked complex patterns and seemed not to cluster, religious sites often became linked by larger social and ceremonial considerations and thus could be called a village cluster. Hopewell and Adena temple mound complexes between 1000 B.C.E. and 200 C.E.; Mayan centers in the Central America, including Cuello in Belize (possibly as early as 2400 B.C.E. until 500 C.E.) and Tikal (250–850 C.E.) in Petén; Guatemala in the second through ninth centuries C.E.; Chavín between 900 and 200 B.C.E.; and Moche from perhaps 1 to 600 C.E. in Peru are all examples of villages or village clusters with a ceremonial center in common.

The key relation in settlement is between settled life, domestication, and population. Greater population density becomes possible with advanced domestication, where people tend to favor plants and produce food in surplus, which is necessary to support larger populations as well as nonagricultural members of society, such the elite, craftsmen, and soldiers. In one sense, towns and cities are simply greater agglomerations of persons gathered in a single area with refined abilities to domesticate and store foodstuffs, such that by the second through eighth centuries of the Common Era a city like Mexico's Teotihuacán, it became possible to support a population estimated at around 125,000.

See also AGRICULTURE; BORDERS AND FRONTIERS; BUILDING TECHNIQUES AND MATERIALS; CITIES; CLIMATE AND GEOGRAPHY; DEATH AND BURIAL PRACTICES; EMPIRES AND DYNASTIES; EXPLORATION; FOREIGNERS AND BARBARIANS; GENDER STRUCTURES AND ROLES; GOVERNMENT ORGANIZATION; HUNTING, FISHING, AND GATHERING; LAWS AND LEGAL CODES; LITERATURE; MIGRATION AND POPULATION MOVEMENTS; NATURAL DISASTERS; NOMADIC AND PASTORAL SOCIETIES; SACRED SITES; SEAFARING AND NAVIGATION; SLAVES AND SLAVERY; SOCIAL COLLAPSE AND ABANDONMENT; SOCIAL ORGANIZATION; TOWNS AND VILLAGES; TRADE AND EXCHANGE; WAR AND CONQUEST.

FURTHER READING

Tim Cornell and John Matthews, *Atlas of the Roman World* (New York: Facts On File, 1982).

Tom Dillehay, *The Settlement of the Americas: A New Prehistory* (New York: Basic Books, 2000).

Gary Feinman, ed., *Settlement Pattern Studies in the Americas: Fifty Years since Virú* (Washington D.C.: Smithsonian Institution Press, 1999).

Daniel J. Gargola, *Lands, Laws, and Gods: Magistrates and Ceremony in the Regulation of Public Lands in Republican Rome* (Chapel Hill and London: University of North Carolina Press, 1995).

Victor Davis Hanson, *The Other Greeks: The Family Farm and the Agrarian Roots of Western Civilization* (Berkeley: University of California Press, 1999).

Oswyn Murray and Simon Price, eds. *The Greek City: From Homer to Alexander* (New York: Oxford University Press, 1990).

David O'Connor, "Urbanism in Bronze Age Egypt and Northeast Afrcia." In *The Archaeology of Africa: Food, Metals, and Towns,* eds. Thurstan Shaw, Paul Sinclair, Bassey Andah, et al. (London: Routledge, 1993).

Evon Z. Vogt and Richard M. Leventhal, eds., *Prehistoric Settlement Patterns: Essays in Honor of Gordon R. Willey* (Albuquerque: University of New Mexico Press, 1983).

Gordon Randolph Willey, *Prehistoric Settlement Patterns in the New World* (Westport. Conn.: Greenwood Publishing Group, Inc., 1981).

► ships and shipbuilding

INTRODUCTION

The archaeological record concerning ships and shipbuilding is thin. Few watercraft from the ancient world have survived, because generally they were made of perishable materials. Some of the earliest were made with such materials as reeds, and ancient kayaks, canoes, and similar small craft were typically covered with animal skins. Later, lumber was used in boat construction, resulting in larger, more durable craft, but over the centuries the wreckages of these ships have largely deteriorated. Still, marine archaeologists have located portions of the wreckages of ships in such areas as the Mediterranean Sea, giving them insight into ancient shipbuilding techniques. The archaeological record also includes artwork that depicts boats and ships, watercraft that were entombed with ancient rulers, and in some cases written descriptions.

Ancient civilizations constructed ships and other types of watercraft to serve a variety of purposes. One, of course, was exploration. As ancient peoples migrated into new regions of the world, they used watercraft to navigate rivers and coastlines, often in search of new food supplies or new places to settle. These craft were powered by oars or, in the case of river barges and rafts, poles. In some parts of the world, this impulse to explore led to the development of larger, more ocean-worthy vessels, along with sails to harness the power of the wind. However, other ancient cultures, such as those of the Americas, were less interested in exploring the world than they were in exploring the region that surrounded them.

Fishing required the use of watercraft. People who lived in coastal communities or along rivers developed a range of watercraft that allowed them to harvest fish, seafood, and in time even whales. These types of watercraft had to be highly maneuverable and able to operate in shallow water. Rafts, canoes, barges, and small boats and ships were used for this purpose.

Trade in the ancient world was often conducted with the help of watercraft. Because large volumes of goods had to be transported and because land routes were both dangerous and difficult, transport by water was often the preferred method. The wreckage of one ship found off the coast of Turkey yielded 20 tons of cargo, an amount of cargo that would have been nearly impossible to transport by land. Similarly, watercraft often were used to transport materials for construction. Many of the stone monuments that survive from the ancient world were built with massive stones quarried in one location and then transported by barges closer to the construction site. In some case, barges were used to ferry goods between islands, such as the many islands of Greece.

Finally, watercraft were used for military conquest. As shipbuilding methods became more advanced and ships became larger, they could be used to transport troops, weapons, and provisions. Additionally, some of the world's great naval battles took place during ancient times. The Chinese, with their immense coastline, led the world in shipbuilding technology during the Qin (221–207 B.C.E.) and Han (202 B.C.E.–220 C.E.) dynasties and built a large fleet of huge warships that came to symbolize China's power and prestige.

AFRICA

BY JUSTIN CORFIELD

Although many ships—Roman, Greek, Persian, and Phoenician—in the ancient world sailed to Africa, the only African state besides Egypt that maintained a large fleet of its own was Carthage. It had not only a massive navy, located in a secret inner harbor at Carthage, but also a sizable merchant navy.

The Carthaginians inherited their naval traditions from the Phoenicians, from whom they trace their civilization. At the height of their power during the First Punic Wars (264–241 B.C.E.), the Carthaginian navy was very large. The Greek historian Appianos (second century C.E.) wrote that the naval harbor at Carthage had the capacity to take 200 ships, and archaeological work at the site confirms this possibility. Because the Carthaginians had bases throughout North Africa and also Sicily, they probably had many more ships. The Greek historian Polybius (ca. 200–ca. 118 B.C.E.) stated that in 256 B.C.E. Carthage was able to put to sea some 350 ships, which would involve a crew of about 150,000: 300 oarsmen and 120 marines on each vessel. Given the number of people used to make the ships, it is evident that Carthage placed a great deal of emphasis on its navy.

The major fighting ship used by the Carthaginians was a quinquereme. There are no archaeological remains of such vessels, but historians believe that they had a large central sail and three rows of oars, with two men pulling each of the top two oars. The Carthaginians also had quadremes and triremes. The trireme had three banks of oars, but the quadreme is thought to have had one row of oars with four men pulling each oar, two rows of oars with two men pulling each oar, or three rows of oars with two men pulling the top oars. All three types of designs might have been used. The ability of the Carthaginians to produce such large numbers of ships was confirmed in 1971 when the hull of a Carthaginian galley was found near the port of Marsala in Sicily. Some of the wood had the marks of shipwrights, proving that they were mass-produced, which would be the only way they could have had such a large fleet.

Many of the Carthaginian sea battles of the First Punic Wars took place around Sicily. The Romans initially copied the design of a Carthaginian ship for their vessels. It must have been an old design because later in the war they captured a faster vessel, which enabled them to build better ships. At the first encounter, at Milazzo in 259 B.C.E., a Carthaginian admiral called Hannibal (not to be confused with the general of the same name who invaded Italy during the Second Punic Wars) attacked the Romans but lost 50 ships.

The admiral narrowly escaped being captured himself and lost his flagship. After they were defeated by the Romans off the coast of Sardinia, the Carthaginians crucified Hannibal as a punishment.

In addition to their navy, Carthaginians also had a large merchant fleet. Their vessels sailed the Mediterranean before the First Punic War and through the wars until just before the outbreak of the Third Punic War in 149 B.C.E. These were the ships involved in trade with Spain and Cornwall, where the Carthaginians and the Phoenicians bought tin. The Roman poet Avienus (fourth century C.E.) makes a reference to a visit of the Carthaginian navigator Himilco (fl. ca. 450 B.C.E.) to Cornwall. Carthaginian ships also sailed down the western coast of Africa. They are believed to have traded with West Africa, although whether they did this directly or through middlemen is not known. According to one theory, the Carthaginian navigator Hanno (fifth century B.C.E.) sailed to modern-day Cameroon.

Apart from the Carthaginians, the Numidians had small trading vessels, but as a client state first of Carthage and then of Rome they had no need for their own fleet. Trading vessels were certainly being built on the western coast of Africa, but most traveled short distances and kept close to the coastline. However, the Norwegian explorer Thor Heyerdahl (1914–2002), in his *Ra* voyages in 1969 and 1970, managed to prove to his skeptics that it was possible to build a vessel that could cross the Atlantic Ocean. Archaeologists have not found the remains of any of the Carthaginian trading vessels, but from descriptions of the goods they carried it would seem that they were similar to the Phoenician merchant ships. These ships relied far more on the use of sails, as the costs of maintaining large numbers of oarsmen, even slaves, would have been too high to justify the gains in speed and the loss of large storage areas for merchandise.

Many small vessels undoubtedly traveled the eastern coast of Africa, including Egyptian ships sailing to Punt, the Egyptian name for a coastal region probably in modern-day Eritrea and Djibouti. Merchants from these and other ships were probably the transmitters of knowledge of metallurgy from Nubia to southern Africa. The dates of the iron objects found in Africa seem to show that the technical advances occurred in coastal areas before permeating inland, which may explain why the Buganda people of modern Uganda learned to utilize iron in comparatively recent times. It is also possible that this trade was carried out not by African ships but by ships from India or elsewhere whose owners plied their wares along the African coast. Items designed by the Chinese and Indians have been found in Madagascar, indicating that this trade did exist from ancient times. In addition, beginning in the second century B.C.E. the use of dhows—sailing vessels with triangular sails—for trade between Africa and southern Arabia started to become important as the exchange of goods between Axum and Arabia significantly increased.

Besides the ships used for navigating in seas and oceans, there was also a need for vessels for crossing rivers and trading along rivers. Rafts would have been used to cover the shorter distances, along with boats made from hollowed logs and small watercraft. Being made entirely of wood, none of these have survived, although some archaeologists have suggested hints of their existence in some of the rock carvings found in the Sahel.

THE *RA* EXPEDITIONS OF THOR HEYERDAHL

The *Ra* expeditions of the Norwegian explorer Thor Heyerdahl, which took place in 1969 and 1970, followed the Norwegian adventurer's success with the *Kon-Tiki* crossing of the Pacific. Heyerdahl intended to demonstrate that it was also possible for people to cross the Atlantic Ocean. He had been interested in connections between the ancient civilizations, and he believed it might have been possible for seacraft to have made the long and hazardous voyages.

For that reason Heyerdahl hired boat builders from Lake Chad, and the boat was constructed out of reeds in Egypt based on designs shown in ancient Egyptian drawings, and then taken to Safi, Morocco. It was accepted that the Egyptians could have sailed along the coastline of North Africa and through the Strait of Gibraltar. Here they might have taken on extra crew or replenished supplies on the boat. Although Heyerdahl's intent was to show that ancient Egyptians could have reached the Americas, the fact that the boat departed from the Atlantic Coast of Morocco also showed that people before even the Carthaginians could have made the journey.

With a seven-man crew, *Ra* sailed on May 25, 1969, but foundered in July after traveling 2,700 miles. It was abandoned after being waterlogged and in danger of sinking. It was a great disappointment for Heyerdahl and the multinational crew, but, undeterred, the team started work on another boat. The second boat, *Ra II*, with almost the same crew, was built by Aymara Indians from Lake Titicaca on the border of Peru and Bolivia. It was then taken to Safi, from where it managed to cross the Atlantic and arrive at Bridgetown, Barbados, in the West Indies in 1970, having completed the crossing in 57 days.

EGYPT

BY ERIN FAIRBURN

Because ancient Egyptian civilization developed in the valley and the delta of the Nile River, it is only natural that watercraft appeared early in Egyptian history. Developed technology in the creation of river craft appeared in the Predynastic

Period (before ca. 3000 B.C.E.), and clear evidence of seacraft is known by the Old Kingdom (ca. 2575–ca. 2134 B.C.E.). Egyptian traditions in boat construction were unique in the ancient world until late in the Dynastic Period, and some techniques have persisted into modern times.

The earliest Egyptian watercraft were developed in response to the need for transport along the Nile and the marshes of the delta, especially during the inundation season, when settlements along the Nile Valley would effectively be turned into islands. These were simple rafts, constructed by tightly binding bundles of papyrus reeds. They were easy to construct, made of readily available material, and required little technology. Longitudinally binding the bundles as tightly as possible made the craft more watertight and reduced the rate at which the reeds would become waterlogged. The binding gave the resultant raft a crescent shape, the front and rear curving upward, with the ends of the bundles splaying outward in the shape of a lotus flower. The appearance of these river craft would be imitated in later Egyptian wooden vessels.

These rafts are probably the types of boats that are depicted on Naqada II (ca. 3500–ca. 3200 B.C.E.) pottery from the late Predynastic Period. Such images show cabin structures and standards on these vessels and seem to indicate that they could carry a fair contingent of rowers. One representation on a Naqada III (ca. 3200–ca. 3000 B.C.E.) jar seems to indicate that sails had been developed by this time and were used on such craft. These simple vessels were used throughout the history of ancient Egypt.

Construction of boats in wood is not known in Egypt prior to the Early Dynastic Period. Native Egyptian woods are of very poor quality and produce only short lengths of timber. However, longer lengths could be produced from timbers imported from the eastern Mediterranean, and it is of note that the apparent advent of wooden boat construction in Egypt coincides with the earliest evidence of imported woods in Egypt. It does seem that Egyptian craftsmen frequently used native and imported woods in combination within a single vessel.

Wooden craft from their inception until the Middle Kingdom (ca. 2040–ca. 1640 B.C.E.) are evidenced archaeologically only from royal funerary contexts, where special pits were excavated in order to inter the boats alongside a king's tomb. This practice began in the First Dynasty (ca. 2920–ca. 2770 B.C.E.), and more than 30 such pits from this time have been identified, at a handful of sites throughout Egypt. Most of the pits' contents were no longer recognizable, but 12 brick structures from the funerary enclosure of the king Khasekhemui (d. ca. 2686 B.C.E.) were discovered in 1991 with their planked boats intact.

Most other known boat pits from the Old and Middle Kingdoms were found at Giza and Dahshûr. From these pits came eight vessels: the famous reconstructed boat of Khufu housed today beside the Great Pyramid in Giza; a second, unexcavated boat from the same pyramid complex; and six boats from the pyramid of Sesostris III (r. 1878–1841? B.C.E.) at Dahshûr. These vessels give vast insight into the construction of planked vessels in Dynastic Egypt.

Egyptian wooden vessels were created hull first, any framing being installed afterward. Egyptian vessels did not have a keel proper, but they were sometimes built up from a long plank (or a connected series of planks) that was somewhat thicker than the surrounding planks and that may have served as a rudimentary keel. More planks would be placed around this central piece, building up the bottom and sides. These planks were initially attached through a series of mortise-and-tenon joints and then fastened by lashings made through a number of V-shaped cuttings within the thicknesses of the planks. This "sewn" technique persisted through the Ptolemaic Period (304–30 B.C.E.).

Once the hull was complete, crossbeams and other framing elements would be installed, and decking would be laid. Cabin structures could be built on the deck planking. The stem and stern posts were often large and decorative affairs, curving upward to a vertical or bent post with a lotiform (like a lotus petal) finial; as noted earlier, such features mimicked the appearance of reed rafts. The boats would be fitted out with a number of oars and one or two rudder paddles at the stern.

When ships were fitted with sails, they were hung from a bipod (forked) or post mast that was set well forward of the middle of the ship. At first the sails, probably made of linen, appear to have been taller than they were broad, but by the Sixth Dynasty (ca. 2323–ca. 2150 B.C.E.) they were consistently broader than they were tall. The use of a bipod mast was soon abandoned, and the mast itself moved closer to the middle of the ship through time.

Seagoing vessels had additional adaptations. One important addition was the hogging hawser, a rope extending from stem to stern that could be twisted to maintain tension. This line helped maintain hull tension and kept the bow and stern from sagging. Before the New Kingdom (ca. 1550–ca. 1070 B.C.E.) sailing vessels also seem to have had rope netting fitted around the hull above the waterline, which probably served to maintain hull integrity. New Kingdom vessels, however, do not seem to have included this feature. Some of these later vessels do seem to have had a different internal layout that allowed rowers to sit below the hull line.

These seagoing vessels were used by Egyptian kings to conduct trading and military expeditions in the Mediterranean and Red Seas. Egypt is known to have had contacts with the eastern Mediterranean by the First Dynasty and with the Aegean by the late Middle Kingdom and into the Second Intermediate Period (ca. 1640–ca. 1532 B.C.E.). Military campaigns were launched against kingdoms of the Levant as early as the Sixth Dynasty and sporadically throughout the rest of the Dynastic Period. Beginning in the Old Kingdom, trading expeditions were also sent to Punt, a kingdom located on the eastern coast of Africa in the Red Sea region. Hatshepsut (r. 1473–1458 B.C.E.) famously recorded an expedition during her reign on the walls of her mortuary temple at Deir el-Bahri, including wonderful depictions of her ships.

Painted wooden model of a boat, from Meir, Middle Egypt, Twelfth Dynasty, around 1900 B.C.E. (© The Trustees of the British Museum)

One other type of vessel had a vitally important purpose in ancient Egypt and was used throughout the Dynastic Period: the barge. These vessels were similar in construction to seagoing vessels but had no sails and were of potentially massive size. They were used from the earliest times to transport stone for monumental sculpture and construction from quarry sites between modern Cairo and Aswān. These boats had to be tugged upstream or downstream by up to 30 smaller vessels.

Once Egypt fell under foreign rule, first by the Persians and then by the Greeks, Egyptian methods of seagoing vessel construction shifted to those of the greater Mediterranean region. However, river craft design remained essentially the same, as recorded by the Greek historian Herodotus (ca. 484–between 430 and 420 B.C.E.).and the famous Palestrina mosaic of Roman date.

THE MIDDLE EAST

BY EDWARD M. W. A. ROWLANDS

In the ancient world people began to designs ships specifically to carry goods on long journeys. They left the eastern Mediterranean and Persian Gulf to travel great distances. Warship designs were constantly modified to keep up to date with any changes in naval warfare tactics. Various weapons, such as the ram, were developed to fight the enemy, and boats were continually enhanced to increase their speed and defensibility.

In the second millennium B.C.E. merchant ships were broad-beamed craft, which enabled them to have a large cargo space. Square sails were used, and oars were utilized in the absence of wind. Early evidence of these ships comes from the tomb of Kenamun, a mayor of Thebes, in Egypt (ca. 1400 B.C.E.). Ships that are thought to have come from modern-day Syria had dense beams at the front and back ends of the ship. At the front of the ship was a large clay amphora that was probably used to store potable water. On the back end of the boat were two stern oars that would have been used for steering. A wicker fence also stretched across the ship to protect the deck cargo.

By the first millennium B.C.E. merchant ships had adapted to react to any possible enemy attack by placing iron on the bow (front) of the ship. The bodies of these ships were low in height and less rounded than their predecessors. The ships are depicted on pottery beginning in the eighth century B.C.E. For short distances, there is evidence of a small craft that was rowed by one or two men. This ship is represented in the reliefs of the Assyrian king Sargon II (r. 721–705 B.C.E.). The front of the ship, which carried a cargo of timber, is in the shape of a horse's head. The ship's oars would have been used to steer the ship.

There is little archaeological evidence of Mesopotamian ships, owing to the poor quality of surviving representations and a lack of shipwrecks. They certainly once existed, however, as Sumerian texts refer to ships sailing down the Persian Gulf to locations as far away as Africa and India. These texts date from around 2350 to 1800 B.C.E. and suggest that from an early period the Mesopotamians were able to construct ships that traveled great distances. The Persians did not have a standing fleet, since most of their military campaigns were on land in Asia Minor. They relied instead upon their conquered coastal territories to supply them with the ships they needed. They also used sailing ships from the Levant to import wine, oil, metals, and other products into their empire.

In the 11th century B.C.E. a group known as the Sea Peoples caused havoc along the eastern Mediterranean. Areas of the Hittite Empire, Cyprus, and important cities in the Near East such as Ugarit (in modern-day Syria) were laid waste. The Sea Peoples seem to have been defeated by the Egyptians under the reign of Ramses III (r. 1198–1166 B.C.E.). Representations from Medinet Habu in Egypt show the naval battle between the Egyptians and the Sea Peoples. They suggest that naval warfare at first involved mainly hand-to-hand combat, with troops boarding each other's vessels.

Beginning in the late eighth century B.C.E. naval warfare changed with the invention of the ram. Representations of the ram have been found dating from this period in the sculptures of Sennacherib (ca. 681 B.C.E.), who followed Sargon II as king of the Assyrian Empire. This new weapon could cause considerable damage to opposing vessels. The oldest ram that has been discovered was found off the coast of Israel at 'Atlit and dates from the second century B.C.E. The ram was found without any other ship wreckage around it.

Besides the right weaponry, speed was an important factor in naval warfare. The ability to outmaneuver a rival was vital. Large steering oars on the back of the boat meant that the ship could change direction quickly. Ships were also built very long to counter the effects of a bow wave. This wave was created when ships attempted to sail at high speed. Vessels needed to use a great deal of energy to climb the wave created, which would slow down the ship. Longer, narrower ships could better cut through this wave and so travel more quickly.

On the reliefs of Sennacherib there is early evidence of vessels with a second row of oars, called biremes. This increase in the number of oarsman helped to propel ships at ever-increasing speeds. To maintain the stability of the ship, the platforms where the oarsmen sat were lowered. As a defensive measure, warships often had a balustrade on the top deck that was covered with shields. By the late sixth century B.C.E. ships called triremes had developed a third row of oars. Such ships were used in large numbers at, for example, the battle of Salamis between the Persian and victorious Greek navy in 480 B.C.E.

Beginning in the fourth century B.C.E. changes in design were needed to adapt ships to new changes in battle tactics. Vessels became increasingly used as stages to fire artillery at the enemy. In naval warfare the frequency of troops boarding other ships increased. To counter this, larger and larger ships were constructed. During the period of wars between the rival successors to Alexander the Great (r. 336–323 B.C.E.), called the Diodochi (322–281 B.C.E.), sexiremes, vessels with six sets of oars, were used in the battle of Salamis in 306 B.C.E. After the political unification of the Mediterranean by the Romans the demand decreased for such large war vessels. Triremes were used again, for example, in the Battle of the Hellespont in 324 B.C.E. when Constantine's son Crispus (d. 326 C.E.) defeated the Roman emperor Licinius (r. 308–324 C.E.).

Terra-cotta model of a merchant ship, Amathus, Cyprus, about 600–500 B.C.E. (© The Trustees of the British Museum)

ASIA AND THE PACIFIC

BY JUSTIN CORFIELD

Nautical technology in China was highly developed in the ancient world. The Chinese had vessels for traveling along rivers and navigating the seas. Asians took a number of sea voyages around the Pacific, although details on many of them rely on legends or remain conjecture. With few images surviving of the ships used and no archaeological confirmation, much of the evidence for ships and shipbuilding techniques come from descriptions in chronicles.

It seems probable that vessels were used during the Shang (1500–1045 B.C.E.) and the Zhou (1045–256 B.C.E.) dynasties, but most of the historical records were destroyed during the famous burning of the books by the order of the emperor Zheng (r. 221–210 B.C.E.) in 213 B.C.E., so little information about them survives. The kingdoms of Wu and Yue were known to be important naval powers with significant coastlines, and they often used river-based fleets to attack the inland kingdom of Chu. Their boats would have been constructed entirely from wood, using sails and a rudder for navigation and rowers for military vessels. Given their developed use of siege machinery, it is highly probable that they would have used rams on the front of their ships as was common in Europe during this period. One surviving fifth-century vessel shows the scenes of several battles, including one of a naval battle with oarsmen rowing barges that have mounted platforms with marines engaged in combat. These were made from wood lashed together with rope and, instead of sails, relied entirely on large numbers of oarsmen. While they were easy to maneuver in battle or as river ferries, this design was impractical for ships at sea.

There are many written records from the Han Dynasty; one of them, the *Han shu* (the history of the Han Dynasty), includes detailed accounts of sea voyages to "Tu-yüan" and "I-lu-mo." It took five months to travel from China to the first and another four months to reach the second. It is believed that the first refers to a settlement on the northern coast of Sumatra and the second to Arramaniya, in southern Burma. There are also references to sailing to a place called "Huang-chih," which some scholars surmise is Kanchipuram in southeastern India. Although no images of the boats survive, they were clearly reliant on the use of sails and rudders. The boats were designed with a hull that was large enough to transport goods and supplies and to shelter the crew in bad weather or at night. Surviving descriptions of voyages at the time make it clear that pirates could be a problem. This would have necessitated building the boats with relatively high sides, not only to protect the merchandise from the sea but also to prevent surprise attacks by people using canoes. Although the story survives only in legend, the attack on the ship carrying Prince Kaudinya of India, the legendary founder of the empire of Funan, when he arrived in coastal Cambodia presents the possibility of surprise attacks.

Ships may indeed have gone farther, judging by the existence of Chinese and Indian goods—or at least Chinese and Indian styles—in Madagascar. Silk from the Han Dynasty was sold to the Romans, though it may have gone by land or through middlemen. There are records of a man who claimed to be a Roman envoy arriving at the Han court in 166 C.E., and two Roman coins have been found in Oc-Eo, a Funanese port in what is now southern Vietnam. That Roman merchants might have sailed to eastern Asia is also surmised from the name the Han used for Rome: "Country West of the Sea." In addition to trade, it seems probable that the Han also used ships for war. Officials had government barges that were rowed along rivers and canals. It is recorded that the general Han Xin was able to cross the Yellow River with rafts that were made from wood and empty, closed pottery vessels used as floats.

Throughout Southeast Asia there would also have been many merchant ships and river vessels. The Funan Empire (first through sixth centuries C.E.) constructed large canals, and they probably used vessels to navigate them, though none have been found. They could have used rafts or simple barges. For their missions to China beginning in 243 C.E. they would have needed vessels capable of navigating the South China Sea, but it is possible that the embassies used Chinese vessels. Mention should also be made of a delegation from the embassy of the Roman emperor Marcus Aurelius (r. 161–180 C.E.) in 166 C.E., which is said to have visited southern China.

In northern Vietnam there are images of ships on the side of several drums that date to 300 B.C.E.; similar drums from the early first century C.E., found in the Sunda Islands, show images of vessels with somebody clearly working a rudder. Carvings on the temple of Borobodur in Java (eighth century C.E.) show the type of vessel that existed at that time.

Canoes with outriggers were used in the Pacific to travel from one island to another, and larger vessels would have been used for making more significant journeys. The presence of people in most of the Pacific Islands, in Australia, and on islands off the coast of Australia during this period is clear evidence of substantial seafaring skills, and the Norwegian explorer Thor Heyerdahl (1914–2002) in the *Kon-Tiki* expedition of 1947 proved that it would have been possible for groups of people to navigate the Pacific. Although there are no historical records detailing these ancient voyages, the aboriginal people of Australia and those of many of the Pacific Islands have preserved legends of sea voyages.

EUROPE

BY MICHAEL J. O'NEAL

The oldest-known European boat, made from a single log, was discovered at Pesse in the Netherlands and dates to about 7000 B.C.E. Numerous other Mesolithic and Neolithic dugout canoes have been found in many parts of Europe, such as the ones at Noyen-sur-Seine in France and Tybrind Vig in Denmark. Dugout canoes were used for fishing in lakes and streams and for transportation on slow-moving rivers and in coastal waters. Paddles found at Tybrind Vig were carved with geometrical designs. Dugout canoes continued to be used in ancient Europe throughout the remainder of prehistoric times. Other early European boats were made of animal hides stretched over frames made of flexible saplings called withies. They were waterproofed with pitch and possibly even butter. Eventually this early form of boat-building technology was overtaken by more sophisticated methods, yet ancient seafarers continued to use skin-covered boats until well into the Common Era. Because these types of boats were made of organic materials, they survive in the archaeological record only when conditions permit their preservation.

During the Bronze Age the inhabitants of northern Europe developed greater skills in shipbuilding, including the construction of boats from planks. Among the first boats that show evidence of advanced shipbuilding technology are the three so-called Ferriby boats, which archaeologists found buried in clay in northeastern England. These boats, built of oak, date to about 1600 B.C.E. While still relatively crude, they show evidence of woodworking skill. The keel was built in two sections joined by a scarf joint, or a joint made by notching the wood so that the pieces overlap, where they can be joined together. Additionally, the keels were grooved to accept vertical planks, and crossbeams were used to strengthen the boat's bottom. The result was a broad, flat-bottomed boat, the largest of which is 5.33 feet wide and 43.5 feet long. This boat illustrates the convergence of two European shipbuilding traditions: One was the "skeleton" structure of hide-covered boats; the other was a tradition of heavy timbered boats. Similar to the Ferriby boats is the boat found at Dover in 1992, a large craft that is estimated to have been rowed by as many as 18 oarsmen during its crossings of the English Channel.

Archaeologists have discovered other wooden boats that date from the second and first millennia B.C.E. Many of these were constructed from a single tree trunk, in effect making them dugout canoes, though they also included transoms (cross pieces, or beams), decks, joinery, and fastenings made with iron and, in some cases, wooden dowels. One of these, called the Brigg raft, was found in Brigg, Lincolnshire, England, and dates to about 600 B.C.E. It is called a raft because only the flat bottom survives. Another, called the Hasholme boat, was discovered in Yorkshire, England, and dates to about 300 B.C.E. This boat and others like it show that their builders lived in a wood-rich environment where trees were cut down to build boats and a good deal of the wood was likely wasted.

The importance of boats in Scandinavia is reflected by their frequent appearance in the rock carvings that cover exposed outcrops in many parts of Sweden and Norway. Long boats constructed by planks carried goods and people across the Baltic Sea and North Sea and among the numerous small islands that line their coasts. The Hjortspring boat, built around 350 B.C.E., was found in a bog in Denmark in 1921. It had probably been used to carry a raiding party, which was then defeated. The victors then dragged the boat to the bog and sank it there as a war sacrifice, along with the weapons and shields of the raiding party. Like the Ferriby and Dover boats from the previous millennium, the Hjortspring boat was built from planks, but its framing system is very sophisticated.

The ancient Celts exhibited relatively advanced shipbuilding capabilities by the first century B.C.E. While the Celts were spread out over large regions of Europe, many groups lived in marine environments, particularly along the Atlantic coast. These ancient mariners faced problems that were much different from those faced by the Romans. While the Romans navigated primarily in the Mediterranean Sea, the northwestern Celts navigated in the more open waters of the eastern Atlantic and Baltic seas. Heavy swells and rocky coastlines required the development of heavy, stable craft that could survive this environment. And unlike the ships of the Romans, these ships could not be powered usefully by rowers.

One group that met the challenges was the Veneti, who lived in Brittany, a peninsula that juts westward into the Atlantic. The Veneti built a large fleet of massive, heavy-bottomed ships with tall masts, sails made of animal hides, and heavy metal cleats to hold the ships together. These ships were highly maneuverable in the ocean. While broad and flat-bottomed, reflecting the tradition of log shipbuilding that was more than 1,000 years old in northwestern Europe, they were also tall and graceful, with high sides that enabled sailors to keep their feet relatively dry. These ships were far more advanced than anything the Romans could throw against them. When the Veneti refused to submit to Roman authority, Julius Caesar (r. 49–44 B.C.E.), before he became the Roman emperor, led a fleet of Roman ships against the Veneti, whose ships he referred to as "swan ships." Caesar initially met with frustration, for his ships were powered by rowers and could not match the nimbler Veneti ships or navigate in the rough waters of the Atlantic. He finally defeated the Veneti in 55 B.C.E. by outfitting his soldiers with long, sharpened grappling hooks, which they used to shred the masts on the Veneti ships. Once the ships were still in the water, Roman soldiers could board them and fight.

In the centuries following Rome's conquest of Europe, Celtic shipbuilding began to show evidence of Roman design. The New Guy's Hospital ship, dating from about the second century C.E., was built with a keel that was similar to Roman keels. The County Hall ship, dating to about the third century C.E., used the mortise-and-tenon joinery common on Roman ships. It had to have been built in the north, though, because it was made of northern oak. The Blackfriars ship, also from the second century, continued the tradition of Celtic shipbuilding but used Roman wood-joinery techniques.

Shipbuilding was not restricted to the seas. River and inland lake societies also built and used ships. Small ships have been discovered in Swiss lakes, and barges were built for transport on the Rhine River. The Romans actually copied certain Celtic shipbuilding methods to design ships with shallow drafts that could navigate the Rhine and other rivers.

GREECE

BY DEBORAH N. CARLSON

The evidence for early seafaring in Greece is indirect and consists of tools of obsidian (a black volcanic glass) and large fish bones excavated in the Franchthi Cave on the Greek mainland and dated to about 9000 B.C.E. Chemical analysis of the obsidian indicates that it can have come only from the Cycladic island of Melos, meaning that it had to have traveled by boat with the earliest seafarers, who were apparently also skilled fishermen, though we have no idea what their vessels looked like. Farther east on the island of Cyprus, stone tools appear suddenly about 8000 B.C.E. in association with the bones of pygmy hippos, pointing again to the presence of ancient mariners.

Travel by sea was a logical development of prehistoric life in the Aegean, which has at its heart a network of small islands known as the Cyclades. In the Early Bronze Age (3000–2000 B.C.E.), a dynamic and artistic culture of stone carvers inhabited several Cycladic islands, including Melos and Syros. The importance of seafaring to the Cycladic way of life is immortalized in miniature model boats of lead and painted depictions of what seem to be long, open galleys. Evidence for the ships themselves has not survived in the archaeological record, but they may have resembled skin boats or dugout canoes.

A Late Bronze Age trading vessel wrecked off the southern coast of Turkey at Uluburun ranks among the most significant finds in the history of archaeology. When it sank around 1300 B.C.E. to a depth of between 140 and 200 feet, the Uluburun ship was carrying a mixed cargo of copper, tin, and glass ingots as well as finished materials, such as glass beads, faience (glazed earthenware) drinking cups, Cypriot pottery, gold and bronze jewelry, and ivory cosmetic boxes. These 20 tons of cargo were sufficiently heavy, and the seabed conditions sufficiently favorable, to preserve intact a small portion of the ship itself, which currently represents the only substantial section of a ship's hull from the Bronze Age Mediterranean.

Study of the hull remains from Uluburun has shown that the ship was constructed in the "shell-first" technique, which was to become the conventional method of Greco-Roman shipbuilding across the Mediterranean for the next two millennia. Unlike the modern approach to building a wooden boat, the ancient shipwright conceived of his vessel from the outside in, first building up a shell of planks connected to one another at their edges with mortises (cavities) and tenons (pieces of wood used to join planks), which were locked in place with wooden pegs. Once the shell was complete, the shipwright made it stronger and stiffer by nailing wooden frames to the planking at regular intervals along the bottom and sides of the hull. The excavation at Uluburun uncovered no indication of a framing system, perhaps suggesting that the Bronze Age shipwright did not feel the need to incorporate frames or that the surviving hull section is simply not large enough for evidence of these timbers to have been preserved.

Roughly a millennium after the Uluburun shipwreck, another small merchant vessel sank in the eastern Mediterranean, this time off the northern coast of Cyprus at Kyrenia. More than 60 percent of the Kyrenia ship's hull was preserved on the seabed, giving archaeologists an opportunity to excavate, raise, conserve, and reassemble over 6,000 pieces of this ancient Greek merchantman. An in-depth study of the Kyrenia ship has made it possible to recreate the construction process: First the keel and posts were erected, and then the hull planking was built up. The floor timbers were fastened to the hull by driving copper nails through wooden treenails, helping to make the vessel watertight. Finally, to protect the wood from the destructive effects of timber-boring worms, the ship's 47-foot-long hull was smeared with gooey, black pitch.

The Kyrenia ship carried a cargo of oil and wine stored in amphoras—two-handled clay jars used for shipping commodities like wine, oil, nuts, fruit, meat, and pine tar. Because many Greek city-states tried to manufacture unique amphora shapes and because these shapes change over time, amphoras are among the most diagnostic and ubiquitous artifacts found on the seafloor. Two other important amphora wrecks from the Greek world illustrate the range in scale of ancient shipping: The modest merchantman excavated at Tektaş Burnu, Turkey, was laden with 213 amphoras, while the shipwreck explored at Alónnisos, Greece, is estimated to have been carrying as many as 4,000 jars.

Pegged mortise-and-tenon joinery was the benchmark of ancient Greek ship construction, but it was not the only method utilized. Excavations of several Archaic (600–480 B.C.E.) wrecks off the coasts of France, Italy, and Turkey reveal the existence of an alternate tradition of sewn or lashed construction. In this method, the planks are still edge-joined according to the shell-first philosophy, but in the place of mortises and tenons the shipwright stitches planks together with plant fibers pulled through angled holes drilled in the plank edges. In one ship from the late fifth century B.C.E., excavated at Ma'agan Mikhael, Israel, both construction techniques (pegged mortise-and-tenon joinery and lashing) were utilized in different parts of the same vessel.

Any study of Greek warships must rely heavily on iconographic and written sources, since the archaeological evidence is effectively nonexistent in that most galleys were likely towed away by the victors or, if badly damaged, floated away in pieces at the surface. The most significant development in Greek naval warfare was the invention of the ram, which probably occurred in the Iron Age (ca. 900 B.C.E.) as suggested by images painted on vases. The ram became the primary offensive weapon of the Greek fleet, and for the next five centuries galleys underwent a rather linear progression, increasing in size and speed with the addition of more and more rowers.

In 480 B.C.E. an allied Greek navy under Athenian leadership won a stunning victory over the Persian king Xerxes at Salamis. The ships taking part in the battle included some older-style pentecontors (50-oared ships), but the majority consisted of larger, faster triremes (warships with three banks of oars), the classic Greek ship of the line. Scholars have long debated how the oarsmen aboard a trireme were arranged—did they sit on three superimposed benches, or were there three men to a bench? The visual evidence, which consists mostly of vase paintings and sculptural reliefs, is plentiful and varied, while the textual evidence includes historical and theatrical works as well as naval inventories from the Athenian port at Piraeus.

Debate about the trireme question, as it is known, will likely continue in earnest until nautical archaeologists can provide more conclusive physical evidence (if it survives) for Greek warships. Until this happens, scholars and naval historians continue to test their hypotheses on full-scale working models, such as the trireme *Olympias*, launched in 1987. The replication of the ancient merchant ship lost at Kyrenia, too, has proved to be an effective tool for understanding the characteristics and capabilities of an ancient sailing ship.

ROME

BY DEBORAH N. CARLSON

During the last three centuries B.C.E. the monarchs of several Greek kingdoms embarked upon a kind of naval arms race dedicated to the construction of enormous oared warships, or galleys, descended from the famed Athenian trireme (a warship with three banks of oars). Various ancient authors describe the thousands of oarsmen required to row these enormous vessels, called polyremes. If the numbers are to be trusted, then these ships must have been outfitted with multiple-rower sweeps, or several rowers pulling each oar on one or two levels. The growth in vessel size brought with it an increase in the number of marines as well as a tactical shift away from ramming and toward the deployment of artillery, such as arrows, grapnel, and missiles, fired from catapults.

According to the historian Polybius (ca. 200– ca. 118 B.C.E.), Rome's entrance into the world of naval warfare occurred rather suddenly, with the emergency construction of a fleet against the Carthaginians in the First Punic War (264–241 B.C.E.). The warships built and employed by the Romans during the Punic Wars were quinqueremes, or "fives," powered by 300 oarsmen and equipped with 120 marines and 50 crewmen. The Romans' early success at sea was due in no small part to their efforts to turn a naval confrontation into a land battle at sea, as exemplified by the *corvus* (Latin for "raven"), a boarding plank outfitted with a large metal tooth, which, when deployed onto the deck of an enemy ship, held fast, locking the two vessels together and allowing Roman marines to board and fight at sea as they did on land.

The large polyremes that had dominated the fleets of Hellenistic Greece gradually became less and less common among Roman commanders, who favored instead a smaller, more maneuverable vessel called a *liburna*. The *liburna* was probably the creation of piratical groups living along the Dalmatian coast of Illyria (modern-day Croatia), for whom speed at sea was a professional necessity. Piracy remained a persistent threat to commercial shipping in the Mediterranean until the campaign of Pompey the Great in 67 B.C.E. The *liburna* played a key role in Octavian's (r. 27 B.C.E.–14 C.E.) historic defeat of the allied fleet of Marc Antony and Cleopatra at Actium, Greece, in September 31 B.C.E. Following his victory at Actium, Octavian erected a commemorative stone monument that had as its centerpiece about 30 bronze rams taken from the captured ships of Antony and Cleopatra.

Although none of the rams has survived, comparison of the sockets in this image with the bronze ram found in isolation off the coast of Israel at 'Atlit suggests that the latter belonged to a vessel about the size of a quinquereme. The Actium monument continued a tradition that dates back to at least the fourth century B.C.E., when the Romans, fighting the Italian Volsci at Antium, captured some enemy ships and displayed the prows along the facade of a low platform in the center of the forum. This speaker's platform, called the rostrum, takes its name from the Latin word for "prow."

Nautical archaeologists have virtually no detailed information about the construction of Roman seagoing warships, since none has yet been found, but they are markedly better informed about the size and construction of Roman merchant vessels, owing to the thorough and meticulous excavation of dozens of ancient shipwrecks. The Roman shipwright followed the same general principles of "shell-first" construction as did his Greek predecessor, first creating a shell of wooden planks fastened together using pegged mortise-and-tenon joinery. Next he nailed large frames (often called floor timbers) inside the hull over the keel and shorter timbers (often called half-frames) along the sides of the hull's interior. Atop the frames the shipwright nailed thin ceiling planking to protect the frames from the weight of the cargo, and outside he coated the ship's planks with pitch or thin sheets of lead to protect the hull from the destructive effects of wood-boring worms. Depictions of sailing ships indicate that most were rigged with a single square sail and occasionally a second smaller sail at the bow and were maneuvered by a pair of steering oars slung on the stern quarters.

Other, less conventional but no less interesting construction techniques existed in various regions of the empire, including the Adriatic, where some shipwrights produced what may be the vessels that the Romans called *naves sutiles*, or "sewn ships." Farther north, archaeological excavations have shown a distinct tradition of assembly characterized by large iron nails, represented in part by the shipwrecks at Blackfriars (England), Zwammerdam (Netherlands), and Mainz (Germany).

The shipwright himself was called either a *faber navalis* or an *architectus navalis*, to judge from various surviving epitaphs and dedicatory inscriptions. In some Roman cities, like Portus at the mouth of the Tiber River, shipwrights organized themselves into *collegia*, or guilds, and excavations at nearby Ostia have uncovered the remains of that local guild's headquarters building. The excavation of Roman harbors on occasion also has yielded the remains of boats and ships abandoned and covered with riverine silt (as at Pisa) or deliberately incorporated into the various concrete structures that constitute the quays and breakwaters (as at Ostia). Careful study of the harbor at Caesarea, Israel, suggests that shipwrights were directly involved with the construction of several concrete-filled wooden caissons (large water-tight chambers) that formed part of a massive breakwater.

Archaeological evidence indicates that most Roman merchant ships transported a wide range of commodities, including wine, oil, garum (fish sauce), fish, nuts, and fruit, in two-handled clay storage jars called amphoras. To date, the largest amphora carriers are represented by the shipwrecks at Madrague de Giens, France, and Albenga, Italy, with thousands of jars amounting to some 400 to 600 tons. The Romans would have classed these vessels as *naves onerariae* (ships of burden), but there also existed a number of specialized ship

Wall painting of Ulysses and the Sirens, Roman, mid-first century C.E.*, from Pompeii, Italy; the ship, a war galley, is shown in considerable detail.* (© The Trustees of the British Museum)

types, such as *naves lapidariae*, or the stone carriers, which transported hundreds of tons of marble and granite from virtually every quarry in the ancient world, to be sculpted into architectural elements (columns, friezes, and monuments), sarcophagi, statuary, and furniture. To gain a better sense of the wide range of vessels that existed in the Roman world, one need only examine the late Roman ship mosaic from Althiburus, Tunisia, or consult the lexicon of ship types assembled by the grammarian and lexicographer Nonius Marcellus in the early fourth century C.E.

By the early seventh century C.E. the shell-first ship construction technique of the Greeks and Romans had changed drastically, as evidenced by the shipwreck excavated at Yassi Ada, Turkey, in the early 1960s. The shallow, widely spaced mortises and loosely fitting, unpegged tenons of this Byzantine cargo vessel no longer contributed the primary source of hull strength; they probably served only to keep the planks aligned long enough for them to be nailed to the ship's frames.

THE AMERICAS

BY LAWRENCE WALDRON

The history of watercraft in the Americas harks back to the very first arrival of people in those continents. As scholars continue to debate whether people during the ice age first arrived from Asia on foot or by boat, it is evident that the original settlers already possessed some knowledge of seafaring. Watercraft and maritime navigation in and around the Bering Strait in the late ice age would have been used mostly for fishing in coastal waters. Any seafaring skills would have had to adjust to many new environments once people had arrived in the Americas.

Varied American coastal conditions as well as reefs, rivers, rapids, lakes, swamps, and estuaries all presented unique restrictions and opportunities to early American boatmen. Despite the numerous local innovations, ancient American watercraft can be grouped into four major types: skin boats (including kayaks, umiaks, and other bullboats), canoes, rafts, and reed boats. Such watercraft served either as transportation between one seasonal habitat and another or as fishing or whaling vessels. Watercraft were also used in trade expeditions between neighboring groups and between civilizations as far apart as Mexico and Peru.

Coastal and riverine voyages of exploration were made in search of new food sources and trading partners, but it appears that once in the Americas, ancient Indians were never again moved to cross to another continent and so never developed large oceangoing vessels. Many ancient natives turned their attention not to developing sailing ships that might carry seamen beyond the horizon but to pioneering a wide variety of small, highly maneuverable watercraft.

The ancient Indians along the northwestern coast of Canada and the United States developed an unusual kind of boat. In the absence of a steady supply of timber, the obvious choice of wooden boats was not available to far-northern and Arctic Indians. These groups were already adept at making a series of aquatic devices out of sealskin and whale skin, including inflatable flotation devices and wetsuits that remained relatively warm and buoyant in the icy northern waters. Before the Common Era, therefore, the idea of a skin boat had already occurred to them. Made of skin stretched across a frame of wood, these boats proved to be lightweight and easily manageable in water that could sometimes be an obstacle course of floating ice chunks. The Inuit, Aleuts, and other groups call these craft umiaks or kayaks depending on their design.

Seasonal movements enabled ancient northern Indians to maximize their food sources. When it was time to move, they gathered their possessions and piled into large, round skin boats called umiaks. These boats were probably paddled mostly by women, as they were in later times. The male hunters would have traveled alongside the umiaks in smaller boats also made of skin. These smaller, one-person craft were the kind later known as kayaks and were used in both fishing and the hunting of large marine mammals.

Made in a sleek, elongated shape that seemingly sliced through water, kayaks were made of skin stretched over even the top of the boat. Only a small opening was left topside into which the rider could slip his lower body and sit comfortably. In this way the kayak acted like an extension of the boater's body, with only his upper torso visible as he whisked through the water, arms moving the paddle in a circular motion. An ingenious aspect of the craft's design was that it could easily be righted if it was capsized by rough water or large prey. With a skillful turn of his body, the paddler could quickly roll his kayak back into an upright position without even getting his feet wet. The single opening in the top trapped air inside and would not permit water to enter.

While the kayak and umiak are the best known of American Indian skin boats, several other varieties of this technology were used by western Indians as far south as California. The Indian group later called the Gabrielino by European colonists may have used their skin bullboats (a circular vessel much like an umiak) since ancient times. Groups as far inland as Wyoming and the Great Plains also used skin boats, although these were made of the hides of buffalo and other land mammals. The Crow, Omaha, Assiniboin, and Arikara are all known to have used skin boats for inland travel on rivers and lakes.

In wooded areas many of the ancient Americans employed wooden rafts of various kinds for the short transportation of people and heavy goods, often within a single territory. They would have been common in river systems throughout North and South America. The high and often frigid Andes may not have seemed a likely place for residents to develop a strong tradition of rafting, much less boating, but the Andean peoples were daring seafarers and creative builders of rafts and boats.

Some 2,000 years ago early seafarers from the Nazca civilizations employed a kind of inflatable sealskin raft in a number of ways. These inflatable rafts were used not only as vehicles and flotation devices for the fishermen but also as water transports for heavy loads. Nazca and later Moche farmers are known to have acquired tons of guano (bird and bat droppings they used as crop fertilizer) from caves and rocks on the islands off the coast of Peru. Loads of this guano were put in containers and floated back to the mainland on the inflatable sealskin rafts.

Additionally, the Lake Titicaca region between Bolivia and Peru has been inhabited for millennia by groups of natives who employed the use of reed and grass rafts. The Aymara Indians devised a raft, more like a temporary boat in its shape, made entirely of the fibers of *totora* and other kinds of bulrush that grew in the region. The raft of tightly bound reeds was used until it became waterlogged, after which it was discarded. Many centuries later the Inca and various descendants of the Aymara were still making and using the same kind of raft.

The canoe, a boat with two pointed ends, is by far the most common and varied of ancient American watercraft. The majority of canoes, from the northwest coasts of Canada to the islands of the Caribbean, were made of local trees. These canoes varied in design from the plank canoes of California's Channel Islands to the dugout canoes of ancient British Columbia, Florida, Nicaragua, and Venezuela. All canoes, like their kayak counterparts, were propelled by paddles rather than oars so that the boatmen faced the direction they were headed rather than rowing backward as in some Old World boats.

Ancient Indians living in California, such as the Chumash or their ancestors, developed a canoe that at first glance might have resembled a European rowboat in its carvel-planked construction, in which long strips of wood are joined at their edges. Upon closer inspection, however, an ancient observer would notice that the planks were not nailed to the underlying boat frame but rather were cleverly strapped to that frame and to each other with vegetable fibers or strips of leather. To waterproof all the joinery and stitches in this unusual craft, the ancient Californians took advantage of a unique resource: pitch from the La Brea tar pits.

Except for those along the U.S. West Coast, almost all canoes were one variety of dugout or another. The dugout canoe was made by felling a tree of a suitably buoyant species, carving out its shape from the wooden matrix, then hollowing out the hull. The "digging out" from which the design derives it name was usually done with simple stone or bone axes and awls. The shaping of a canoe could take weeks and perhaps even two or three months, especially if any other work was required, such as decorative carving or special treatments of the wood. The types of wood varied with the local habitat, and these different woods might have exerted some influence on the shape of the canoe.

Some canoes, such as the small cedar, poplar, and cypress ones used by the ancient Seminoles, Caddo, and Creek, had a shallow design for skimming across the meniscus of vine-choked swamp or river water. The large, elaborately decorated canoes of early Haida, Kwakiutl, and other Northwest Coast Indians could hold as many as 50 people and were hewn from a variety of large trees, including red cedar, spruce, and birch. These canoes were designed to displace water with their heavy hulls and pointed bows and were used for both river transport and whale hunting. Delaware Indians were known to have used pine for their streamlined dugout canoes, which also glided across the water in the manner of their Seminole counterparts.

Amazonian and Caribbean Indians from the Mesoamerican Maya to the Antillean Taino, like their northern neighbors, fashioned large dugout canoes out of single lengths of trees. Slightly earlier Olmec dugouts were used for inland river travel and for journeys along the coastal waters and swamps of the Olmec heartland in eastern Mexico. Olmec boatmen may have caulked their damaged dugouts with the latex from their Veracruz rubber trees. The Maya of the first millennium B.C.E. diversified into greater coastal travel once they settled the Yucatán. They also built much larger canoes than the earlier Olmec to supply their extended trade expeditions throughout Central America.

Ancient Americans used various different kinds of heat-expansion techniques to alter the shape of their dugout canoes. Amazonian groups expanded the width of their canoes using heat expansion to twice the width of the original tree trunk. They achieved this pot-bellied shape by filling the dugout portion of the canoe with water and heated rocks. The heated water slowly softened the fibers along the grain of the trunk, expanding the hollowed hull. Heat-expansion technology was also used by North American Indians along the Northwest Coast to alter the shape of their canoes. Many Central and North American groups were likewise aware of the use of steam to render wood pliant in the construction of boat frames and hulls. The rounded hull of the vessel not only increased the capacity of the vessel but also added to its stability in rough water.

See also ART; BUILDING TECHNIQUES AND MATERIALS; CLIMATE AND GEOGRAPHY; EMPIRES AND DYNASTIES; EXPLORATION; GENDER STRUCTURES AND ROLES; HUNTING, FISHING, AND GATHERING; INVENTIONS; METALLURGY; MIGRATION AND POPULATION MOVEMENTS; MILITARY; OCCUPATIONS; SEAFARING AND NAVIGATION; TRADE AND EXCHANGE; TRANSPORTATION; WAR AND CONQUEST.

FURTHER READING

George F. Bass, ed., *History of Seafaring: Based on Underwater Archaeology* (New York: Walker, 1972).

Lionel Casson, *Ships and Seamanship in the Ancient World*, 2nd ed. (Baltimore. Md.: Johns Hopkins University Press, 1995).

Basil Greenhill, *Archaeology of the Boat* (Middletown, Conn.: Wesleyan University Press, 1976).

Herodotus, *The Histories*, trans. Robin Waterfield (Oxford, U.K.: Oxford University Press, 1998).

Thor Heyerdahl, *The Ra Expeditions* (London: George Allen and Unwin, 1971).

G. Adrian Horridge, *The Design of Planked Boats of the Moluccas* (Greenwich, U.K.: National Maritime Museum, 1978).

Emory Dean Keoke and Kay Marie Porterfield, *American Indian Contributions to the World* (New York: Checkmark Books, 2003).

Sean McGrail, *Boats of the World: From the Stone Age to Medieval Times* (New York: Oxford University Press, 2002).

Fik Meijer, *A History of Seafaring in the Classical World* (New York: St. Martin's Press, 1986).

John S. Morrison, John F. Coates, and N. Boris Rankov, *The Athenian Trireme*, 2nd ed. (Cambridge, U.K.: Cambridge University Press, 2000).

R. B. Nelson, *Warfleets of Antiquity* (Sussex, U.K.: War Games Research Group, 1973).

J. Richard Steffy, *Wooden Ship Building and the Interpretation of Shipwrecks* (College Station: Texas A&M University Press, 1994).

Jack Weatherford, *Indian Givers: How the Indians of the Americas Transformed the World* (New York: Fawcett Columbine, 1988).

► slaves and slavery

INTRODUCTION

Slavery was a nearly universal practice throughout the ancient world, and some of the world's great civilizations, such as that of ancient Rome, were built on the backs of slaves. Slaves served a variety of functions. Some were domestic slaves, working in homes, while other worked in fields. Many did the most backbreaking work, including mining, stone quarrying, digging, and construction, though some who were relatively privileged did work that was more administrative.

Slavery took on differing complexions in different parts of the ancient world. In some cases, slaves were pure chattel. They had no rights and could own no property, and their masters had absolute power of life and death over them. A master could arbitrarily kill a slave with no legal consequences in some parts of the world. Sometimes slaves were ritually killed and sacrificed in religious observances, and in ancient Rome they were even trained as gladiators to provide amusement for the upper classes. In other cases, slavery was at least a little bit more bearable. Sometimes people lacked freedom because of the social class—the caste—into which they were born. They might enjoy some legal rights and protections and might even have been able to lift themselves out of servitude. Their masters could not legally abuse them and in fact were sometimes required by law to teach them a trade. Many such slaves, especially those who were literate and showed aptitude, were promoted to responsible positions on estates, in municipalities, and the like. In some cases, child slaves could not legally be required to do adult work.

Slavery was the only option for survival for some people. A person with no prospects in life or who was heavily in debt might have found servitude, with food and a place to live, preferable to imprisonment or a slow death from starvation. Indeed, some people became voluntary slaves as a way of working off debt. In parts of the ancient world slaves were able to own their own property, have their own money, and even themselves own slaves. They could participate in economic activities on their own account, enabling them in time to buy their freedom and attain the rights of full citizenship.

The sources of slaves varied, and slavery was rarely based on racial categories; slaves in ancient Rome, for example, came from all over the known world. Again, some slaves volunteered to become slaves as a way to pay off debt. Others became slaves because they had been convicted of a crime, and slavery was a common form of punishment at a time when there were few prisons. The most common source of slaves was warfare. Wars or raiding parties were launched with the purpose of acquiring slaves, and slaves were part of the normal booty of conquest, seized in the hope that someone would pay a ransom for their return. In many cases, women and children became slaves as a result of conquest. Because conquerors did not want to have to deal with captured soldiers, who might pose a danger to slave owners, they seized family members instead.

AFRICA

BY SAHEED ADERINTO

Slavery was prevalent in ancient Africa. Its history can be traced roughly to the time Africans began to develop villages and towns. The development of a sedentary lifestyle, which paved the way for the emergence of large settlements, has been attributed to the agricultural revolution that took place on the continent some 200,000 years ago. Slavery in ancient Africa is akin to that in other parts of the world: It involved physical, emotional, and psychological containment. By and large, the master of a slave had the power of life and death over the slave. A slave, like chattel, could be sold and bought by someone who occupied a privileged position in the prevailing power configuration.

It is important to differentiate between slavery and other forms of servitude. In Africa pawnship was a form of subordination that differed from slavery. A person could be pawn as a collateral security for debt. People could surrender themselves to pawnship because of the need to raise money for marriage, a funeral, or another purpose that required a lot of money. A pawn was most likely a member of the community where he or she served, but a slave in most cases was brought from another community. While slaves were not likely to be free throughout their lifetime and their masters could enslave their children, a pawn was automatically free after rendering the services equivalent to the debt owned. A master could not exercise any form of control over the relatives of a pawn. A master did not have the power of life and death over a pawn but could kill a slave at will.

The condition of a slave was degrading; a slave could be asked to perform any type of labor, and the most unpalatable works were reserved for slaves. A Yoruba proverb from West Africa that highlights the difference between slavery and pawnship is *Ohun t'o ni oun o so ni d'eru, bio ba so, ni d' iwofa, ki a dupe*, meaning, "If what threatens to make us a slave makes us a pawn, we should be thankful." Only in rare instances did slaves manage to remove the yoke of domination and rise to important positions. Royal slaves in some communities, such as the western Sudanese region of West Africa, were said to have been able to gain freedom, inherit the property of their dead masters, and emerge as prominent members of the place were they had previously served as nonentities. Aside from this exceptional situation, former slaves could not remove the stigma of being formally enslaved.

There were many sources for slaves in ancient Africa. People accused of antisocial behavior, such as murder, thievery, and witchcraft, were sold into slavery. Wars, kidnapping, and raids also produced slaves as part of the booty. There is limited evidence, however, to suggest that wars were fought for the sole purpose of acquiring slaves. Although a trans-Saharan slave trade had already existed, the act of waging wars primarily for the purpose of enslavement came largely through the advent of the trans-Atlantic slave trade, which did not begin until the second decade of the 16th century.

Ancient Africa was predominantly agrarian, and the use of slaves for agricultural purposes was important. Slaves could also be part of tributes that a subordinate state paid to an overlord. Aristocratic families had slaves, and slaves in some palaces were eunuchs (castrated men) who watched over the large harem of royal wives. Others performed domestic functions associated with royalty. A master had control over a slave's sexual relations and reproduction. This implies that a slave could not get married without the knowledge of his or her master. Unsanctioned copulation among slaves carried a serious degree of punishment. A male slave master could use his slaves as concubines, which partly explains why female slaves were more expensive or highly priced than their male counterparts. The offspring produced from such a union became free upon birth, and the status of the mother improved considerably compared with others who did not have children for their masters.

Slaves could serve religious functions. There is much evidence that slaves were killed and used as offerings during periodic sacrifices to the gods. In fact, in most parts of Africa slaves of different ethnic groups were traditionally used to appease the gods and goddess. There is an important connection between this aspect of the religious use of slaves and African belief in life after death. The oral history of people of Africa is replete with references to how slaves were killed and buried with kings and important rulers. According to one belief, dead kings entered another realm, where they lived and communed with the gods and ancestors. In this realm or world they would need the services of domestic servants.

EGYPT

BY MARIAM F. AYAD

In its most basic definition, slavery implies a loss of freedom, regardless of the degree or nature of this loss. There is little doubt that in ancient Egypt certain groups of people enjoyed less freedom than others. Egyptian slavery, however, was very different from forms of slavery experienced centuries later in Europe and North America. In Egyptian there are no words for *slave* or *slavery*. The word sometimes translated as "slave," *hem*, was also used to indicate "servant." Thus, the Egyptian word for "priest," *hem-netjer* can be translated as either a "god's servant" or a "god's slave." Inherently, the word *hem* did not necessarily indicate servitude. It was used, for example, to refer to the king of Egypt. *Hem-ef*, traditionally translated as "his majesty," may also be rendered as "his incarnation" or "his body."

Meret, a collective noun, is another term that may refer to a group of people without complete freedom, in particular, agricultural workers who could be owned by individuals or temple estates. Mostly found in legal and administrative documents, the term *meret* is closely linked with the transfer of property, especially land and cattle, from one owner to another. Like other kinds of property, people who were considered *meret* could be passed down from father to son as part of an individual's inheritance. *Meret* may have referred to serfs, a special kind of conscripted workforce.

There were several different sources of slaves in ancient Egypt. War and conquest was the principal and oldest way to acquire slaves. Some information about enslaved prisoners of war comes from the tomb biography of Ahmose, son of Ibana, a military officer whose career spanned the reigns of three different kings of the early Eighteenth Dynasty: Ahmose I (r. ca. 1550–1525 B.C.E.), Amenhotep I (r. 1525–1504 B.C.E.), and Thutmose I (r. ca. 1504–ca. 1492 B.C.E.). The inscription indicates that not only were slaves captured at war, but they also were often granted to individuals who exhibited exceptional military prowess. Detailing the conquest of the Hyksos cities of Avaris and Sharuhen, Ahmose indicates that from the former he brought "one man, three women; total, four persons," and "His majesty gave them to [Ahmose] as slaves." Ahmose also was allowed to keep the two women he had captured at Also Sharuhen. Ahmose's valor was recognized by the king and duly rewarded with gold.

While occasionally military officers retained their captives as slaves, such was not always the case. While fighting in Nubia, Ahmose, son of Ibana, captured "two living men" but was rewarded with "two female slaves." On another occasion he brought "two young warriors as captives" but was given "five persons" as a reward. In all four accounts Ahmose's receipt of slaves was part of a greater package that showed the king's appreciation of his military prowess. In addition to slaves, Ahmose was rewarded with gold, parcels of land in his hometown, and a promotion. This and similar texts indicate that prisoners of war were not limited to soldiers from the rival army but also included the inhabitants of the captured towns. The process outlined in Ahmose's biography indicates that Egyptian military personnel were obliged to present their captives to the king, who became the primary owner of these newly acquired slaves. It was the king's prerogative to assign captured prisoners to his officers, the temples, or his own royal household. Occasionally Near Eastern slaves were imported into Egypt.

Certain legal documents dating to the sixth century B.C.E. indicate another source of slavery in ancient Egypt: self-enslavement. To satisfy a debt, not only would a debtor offer all the property he owned, but he also could offer himself, his family, and his children as slaves if the value of his property was insufficient to repay his loan. Legal documents suggest that debts and the inability to repay loans were the primary motives for this type of enslavement. Another source of slaves were the children born to a slave woman. Children inherited their mothers' freedom status and could not become free men or women regardless of the status of the father.

Very little information survives regarding slave trading in ancient Egypt. According to a document dating to the eighth century B.C.E., a special tax was levied on the sale of 32 slaves. In another document 35 slaves were part of a sale involving of some fields. This transaction took place before the council of magistrates (the *qenbet*) and seems to imply that special registers recorded transactions involving the sale of slaves. Royalty and private individuals alike often handed over slaves to the religious establishment to serve at a temple. Bequest, reassignment, acquisition, and the sale of slaves had to be registered with the *qenbet*. The small community of workmen at Deir el-Medina included several state-owned and a few privately owned slaves.

Egyptian slave owners had several obligations toward their charges, foremost among which was to legally record the acquisition or relinquishment of slaves at the *qenbet*. As soon as a slave was purchased, the owner gave the slave a name and taught him or her a trade. A literate slave could be promoted to the position of estate manager. The owners were also responsible for the slaves' health, making sure they were adequately nourished and well cared for. A letter from the Eighteenth Dynasty indicates that enslaved children could not be given hard labor.

Egyptian slaves could enjoy a measure of freedom and dignity. They could negotiate transactions and own personal property. For example, the Wilbour Papyrus, a document dating to the New Kingdom (ca. 1550–ca. 1070 B.C.E.) on which is recorded the sale of some agricultural land, lists at least 11 slaves (*hem*) as holders of agricultural land. Slaves could also testify at court. Several appear as witnesses in the legal account of the great tomb robberies at the end of the Twentieth Dynasty (ca. 1196–ca. 1070 B.C.E.). In fact, it was the testimony of these slaves that later implicated their master as the main culprit in these tomb robberies. The slaves were not treated any worse than any of the other individuals named in the document: All were made to swear to the truth, and some were beaten to extract confessions.

Although no extant documents record marriage agreements among enslaved men and women, in the New Kingdom freed slaves could marry into high society. In one instance a king's barber gave his niece in marriage to his former slave, indicating that freed slaves could marry members of their former masters' immediate families.

THE MIDDLE EAST

BY FRANS VAN KOPPEN

Slavery in the sense of legal ownership of persons in the manner of chattel was universally accepted in cultures of the ancient Near East, with slaves being extracted from foreign soil but also legally drawn from among the slave owner's fellow citizens. Notions of race or skin color were immaterial for enslavement, and slavery was in effect the most radical form of control over humans alongside other servile conditions that did not constitute full ownership. Slave labor was in demand at wealthy urban households but was economically less important in the ancient Near East than in the Mediterranean world of classical antiquity.

Ancient slavery and the livelihood of slaves have been studied on the basis of literary texts and law codes, including the legal parts of the Old Testament and numerous archival sources in cuneiform script. The terms for slaves in many of the region's languages primarily connote social status and could be used for any socially inferior individual. This ambiguity means that it is sometimes difficult to distinguish slaves from other people who endured exploitation within the framework of social and economic dependency relationships and whose conditions share characteristics with slavery. Some servile conditions could be temporary; for instance, debt bondsmen labored for their creditors as long as the debt was unsettled, or famine refugees voluntarily accepted a servile status in exchange for food and shelter. Other forms of servitude were permanent, such as those of oblates and serfs. Oblates and serfs are modern terms for categories of dependent people who were attached to the temples of the gods and the soil they tilled, respectively. Their status of property was immutable (oblates were actually branded with the god's symbol) and heritable, but their standing also gave them rights that were denied to chattel slaves, such as protection against separation from their families through sale. The distinctive characteristic of slaves is hence their legal status of chattel, which included the owner's right to sell, donate, or devolve them to his heirs but also to liberate them at will.

Slavery was typically a permanent condition; only few people experienced a transition into or out of slavery. The status of slave was heritable, and most slaves were born to unfree mothers whose offspring belonged to their master unless special provisions had been made. Sources for slaves other than biological reproduction were threefold. The first was the capture of foreigners and the purchase of foreign slaves. Second, fellow countrymen could be obtained as slaves as a result of economic failure, with people being sold into slavery by the head of their household or by themselves. Finally, people could be enslaved for their crimes, a punishment that could be imposed by the head of the household (for example, by fathers punishing disobedient adoptive sons) or by the public authorities.

Foreigners were an important component of the slave population since early times: the cuneiform signs for male and female slave, first recorded around 3000 B.C.E., are pictographs combining the sign "foreign land" with the signs "man" and "woman," respectively. Severed from their remote homelands, foreign slaves were considered loyal and more devoted to their masters than domestically created slaves. Many of them had been captured during foreign military campaigns and were brought into the country as the soldiers' share in the booty, where they could, if not redeemed by their families, be sold profitably on the slave market. Supply for these markets was also in the hands of traders, some of whom are known to have specialized in long-distance trade in people. Not every foreigner, however, was prey to slave agents, as subjects of allied sovereigns partook in the state's protection of its citizens against kidnap for the purpose of enslavement.

The state's care at safeguarding its subjects against involuntary enslavement did not mitigate the fall of insolvent people into slavery. Nonpayment of debts brought the human pledge or the defaulting debtor into a servile condition in the household of the creditor. Their condition was, at least in theory, temporal and would be remedied once the debt had been settled; in practice, however, this was often impossible. The transition of debt servitude into slavery can be represented in legal texts as a voluntary act of sale, with debtors selling their children or themselves to their creditor with the original debt functioning as their purchase price. This way into slavery was often considered a social abuse, and different solutions were proposed to repair this disorder; for example, there existed the biblical rule of releasing debt slaves in the seventh year and the Mesopotamian "clean-slate acts" that canceled consumptive debts and stipulated the repair of their negative consequences, including the release of debt slaves. These measures were largely ideologically motivated and their implementation usually failed to halt a trend of the rural underprivileged toward economic dependency on the rich and powerful.

Although slaves were owned by temples and the palace, most of them were found in urban residences, where many of them, females in particular, were occupied in household tasks. Some slaves had received training in specialist skills and practiced their trade within the master's household or as hired hands for others, but workshops that employed large numbers of slaves seem to have been uncommon, as was the use of slaves in agriculture. Slaves who were particularly trustworthy could be employed as their owners' agents, take up managerial tasks, and have documents drawn up in their own name on behalf of the family business.

Slaves were sometimes distinguished from free citizens by certain marks, such as a distinct hairstyle or a brand with their owner's name or symbol. The risk of slaves absconding was real; their freedom of movement was often controlled with chains and shackles, and they were mostly not allowed to leave the city unattended. Masters could punish their slaves physically, but they usually did not have the legal power to take a slave's life.

As lifelong members of a household, slaves often developed close ties with their owners, although they were never regarded as part of the family. Slaves could be married, even to freeborn persons, and female slaves could become concubines of the master of the house. This relationship could be legally recognized in a polygamous marriage, where the second wife was regarded as a slave of the main wife but a spouse of the man, and her children were considered the free, legitimate issue of their father. Slaves could also be adopted, most often in combination with their emancipation, with a duty to support their former owner in old age. Termination of slavery was an uncommon phenomenon; however, when freedom was granted, it was most frequently bestowed by the owner.

ASIA AND THE PACIFIC

BY KIRK H. BEETZ

When slavery began or whether the practice always existed in Asia is not known. Many anthropologists assume there were slaves of one sort or another throughout Asia and the Pacific, mostly in the form of people belonging to a particular person or to a particular family. So little is known, however, of the ancient cultures south of China and east of India, as well as of Japan, the Philippines, and other island cultures, that it is possible that there were places where slaves were unknown.

In China the earliest details for slavery come late in its history, from the Han Dynasty (202 B.C.E.–220 C.E.). During the Han Dynasty slaves, tradespeople, and merchants were legally nonpersons, ranking lower in importance to peasants, government officials, professional warriors, nobility, and royalty. Writers during the Han Dynasty often noted, however, that slaves lived better than peasants. The generally cruel conditions for peasants during the Shang Dynasty (ca. 1500–ca. 1045 B.C.E.) and the Zhou Dynasty (ca. 1045–256 B.C.E.) have led some historians to refer to ancient China having a "slave economy" similar to that of ancient Rome, but the actual status of peasants probably put them outside the realm of slavery.

Peasants would sometimes borrow money they could not repay, and the lender could take over their land and require that they work it. Nobles and rich merchants could gather land to themselves this way, and the peasants would work for them with little hope of ever owning land again. Emperors occasionally tried redistribute land to the peasants, but the nobility would just start reacquiring the land. Nonetheless, in times of crisis peasants ranked higher in China's priorities than anyone except the nobility and royalty. It seems that the Chinese government, from the era of the Shang on, recognized that peasants were essential to the nation's survival, and governments usually tried to see to it that peasants were cared for.

Slaves primarily served in households. Rarely did slaves work on farms. The proportion of slaves to the general population was always small, perhaps less than 1 percent of the people. The proportion may have seemed higher to people living in cities because most slaves lived in cities or towns, where they served in the households of nobles and wealthy people.

Relatives of convicted criminals were often enslaved by the government. Government-owned slaves worked to haul barges up and down rivers. They cared for the emperor's horses and dogs and worked as gamekeepers in government parks, especially those used by royalty. In the emperor's court they kept track of water clocks and banged drums to mark the hours of the day, they waited on guests and the royal family, and they opened and closed doors for people walking through the palaces. These duties were fulfilled by both men and women.

During hard times peasants sometimes killed their children because they could not feed them, and they sometimes sold their children into slavery in exchange for money. Others sold themselves into slavery to have food to eat or a place to live. Some merchants traded in slaves even though the government disapproved of the practice. A few emperors tried to abolish the slave trade but failed.

Privately owned slaves were house cleaners, cooks, and kitchen staff. Some were used as bodyguards or to guard ancestral cemeteries. Others waited on their masters or mistresses, helping with hairdressing and other cosmetic tasks. Skilled slaves made ceramics and fabrics for sale. Some owners used slaves to form gangs to batter or even kill their enemies, terrorizing a town or city. Both government-owned and privately owned slaves were sometimes given confidential tasks such as bookkeeping and carrying messages.

It was possible for slaves to earn their own money, but in general a slave was a slave for life, without being able to buy freedom. Slaves typically were regarded as lazy and greedy, and many free people resented that slaves were able to earn their own money, especially when ordinary people had to work to survive while slaves had food and housing even when they did no work.

A similar resentment prevailed in India, where slaves were often regarded as lazy and insolent. As sometimes happened in China, people without financial resources would sell themselves into slavery to have food or a place to live. They often received cash from their new owners, and they were allowed to live freely until the money ran out, at which time they had to work for their owners. They lived much like members of the Sudra caste, as laborers and servants. They were rarely Brahmans (members of the highest Hindu caste) because people were expected to give food and other goods to Brahmans without getting anything in return.

Hindu religious law forbade the mistreatment of slaves. An owner was expected to feed slaves well, to provide them with good clothing, and to give them good quarters in which to live. A slave could be beaten in certain cases, but only on the back. A pious owner would treat his or her slaves well. Under law, slaves were allowed to try to escape once; if they were successful, they were allowed to rejoin their caste. The reality of slave life was often very different from what was required by religious law. Slaves were beaten, maimed, and killed. Any slight to their owners could occasion their torture or death, and their lives were constantly beset by terror.

The royal governments often imported slaves. Both men and women imported from Greece served as palace guards. Women often protected the king's harem of concubines, and sometimes the imported female slaves were themselves made concubines. People could become slaves when they were prisoners of war, but they served only one year of involuntary servitude and were then freed. People convicted of crimes could be sentenced to serve as slaves for a certain time, but they were freed when the time ended. Others who lost lawsuits or bets could become slaves, but they were freed if they paid the fine or bet. Still others became slaves to their creditors when they failed to pay their debts, and they were freed if they managed to pay what they owed. Those who sold themselves into slavery had to buy their freedom. In many cases people remained slaves for life, and children born to them were also slaves.

For many slaves life was one of hard labor. They were expected to haul water from a nearby stream or lake regardless of the weather, to carry loads of goods, and to maintain the homes of their owners. Owners often complained of their slaves' laziness, noting that their slaves tended to watch for sundown, when their labors for the day were supposed to end, rather than attending to their chores. Others complained that slaves in cities were not only lazy but arrogant, using much of their time to earn money of their own while having none of the expenses of feeding, housing, or clothing themselves. Even so, household slaves were often treated like part of their owner's family, and when they became too old to work, they were cared for by their owners.

EUROPE

BY AMY HACKNEY BLACKWELL

Slavery was a fact of life throughout the ancient world. Almost every society had some form of servitude in which people exploited the labor of others. Among ancient Europeans slavery existed but not nearly to the extent that it did in the Mediterranean region. European society was not heavily agricultural or urban, so there was not as much need for labor as there was in the Greek and Roman economies. Many thousands of Celts and Germans became the slaves of Greeks and Romans, who used them in a variety of ways.

The Celts, like many ancient peoples, often enslaved the people they conquered when they moved into a new territory. For example, this may have happened in ancient Ireland when the Celts arrived; some historians believe that the Celts enslaved the prehistoric people to build tombs such as Newgrange. The favored slaves were usually women and children, who were more docile than men and better suited for the domestic tasks the Celts needed performed. Celts would use slaves to gather wood, carry water, cook, weave, and perform sexual favors.

It appears that the Gauls, the Celts who lived in France, were using slaves during the eighth and seventh centuries B.C.E. Slaves came from conquered nations in the region. Well-to-do Gauls used women and children as domestic slaves to do basic household chores. Noble families would exchange gifts of slaves as a way of solidifying friendships. Historians believe that Gauls of this period engaged in trade of slaves with the Etruscans in Italy, and some further contend that the Gauls were still engaging in the slave trade with Italy during later Roman times. During the late second and first centuries B.C.E. Gauls are said to have sold their brethren as slaves in exchange for wine. Some 15,000 Gauls may have been enslaved in this way. It is not known whether these slaves were family members of the traders or if they were already slaves of the Gauls.

The Celtic peoples had clear laws about slavery. They divided themselves into several social classes, including nobles, free property owners, and freemen who did not own property. The bottom of the Celtic social ladder was occupied by people who were not free. Some nonfree people were not slaves at all; these individuals did not hold the full rights of the group, but they were still allowed to support themselves by farming on tribal lands. In Ireland, for example, there was a class of nonfree farmers called *fudirs*. These people were not exactly slaves in the modern sense, in that their master could not buy and sell them, but they had almost no legal rights. They worked the land for their master and were forced to pay rent or tribute every year. This rent supposedly obligated the master to feed and house them. However, their master could throw them off the land at any time and for any reason. When a *fudir* died, the land he occupied did not pass to his children unless the master chose to allow them to stay.

Other individuals were genuine slaves, that is, owned by other people and forced to work without wages. Celtic law set values for slaves; male slaves were considered more valuable than female ones. Celtic slaves were usually Celtic peoples who had lost their liberty through a variety of causes, such as financial misfortune or losing in battle. Sometimes Celts imported slaves from other areas, but usually slaves were local. Occasionally parents sold their children into slavery if they felt they needed the money. Slave traders often raided farms at night to steal children and sell them for slaves. These raiders typically attacked houses on the coast of Roman Britain (modern-day Wales) and carried their slaves over to Ireland. The Irish Saint Patrick (fifth century C.E.) was himself stolen as a boy from his family's estate in Britain and spent several years working as a slave shepherd in Ireland before escaping and taking on a religious vocation. Some sources say that it was a law in Ireland that slaves were freed every seventh year and suggest that Patrick may have been freed under this law instead of escaping.

Both categories of slave were at a severe disadvantage under the Celtic legal system. A person's rank determined the value of his evidence and whether he would be allowed to testify at all. A freeman could testify against a *fudir*, but a

SLAVERY AND DIVINE VISIONS

A youth spent in slavery produced what many consider to be Ireland's greatest saint. Born in Roman Britain (modern-day Wales), Saint Patrick was a teenager when he was stolen from his home and sent to Ireland to work as the slave of a pig farmer. He ate the pigs' food and dressed in whatever rags he could scrounge up. He was always hungry and cold.

In his misery, Patrick prayed to God 100 times a day and 100 times a night. After a few years he began to see visions telling him that he should escape. These visions instructed him to walk to the sea, where he would find a ship waiting to take him away. The visions were persuasive and certainly more attractive than his current life as a slave, so Patrick walked away from his pigs and continued walking to the ocean. Sure enough, there was a ship waiting to take him to Europe. He sailed away and became a priest, but Ireland was deeply ingrained in his soul. He devoted the rest of his life to converting Ireland's people to Christianity.

fudir was not allowed to testify in response. Punishments for slaves who committed crimes were harsher than those meted out to freemen.

The Roman historian Tacitus (ca. 56–ca. 120 C.E.) observed that the Germans kept and used slaves. According to Tacitus, when Germans defeated enemies in battle the losers would go into voluntary slavery, allowing the victors to bind them and sell them. The victors always sold or traded away such slaves because they would have been ashamed to keep them around. German slaves lived in their own households, and their masters treated them as tenants; each slave was required to pay his master a yearly tribute of grain, cattle, or cloth, but otherwise the slaves were free to live as they liked. Slaves did not perform the master's household duties, as Roman slaves did. Tacitus remarked that Germans did not chain or beat their slaves or work them to death. Masters occasionally did kill their slaves in anger; this was apparently acceptable behavior and not considered worthy of punishment.

During the Roman Empire, German society adopted many Roman laws concerning slavery. German slave owners of this time treated their slaves much as Romans did, sometimes paying them and offering them opportunities for social advancement. Slaves were allowed to marry free people, though this meant that the free partner would become a slave. A woman slave owner was not allowed to marry her own slave, and sexual contact with slaves was discouraged. German men, however, had ample sexual contact with their female slaves.

Many ancient Europeans experienced slavery under the more powerful and better organized Greeks and Romans. Some 40,000 Gauls, for example, became slaves of the Romans after Julius Caesar's army won the battle of Alesia in 52 B.C.E. Historians estimate that Caesar may have enslaved half a million Gauls throughout his career. During the early Roman Empire huge numbers of European slaves passed into Roman territory. Romans and Greeks appreciated the exotic appearance of slaves from northern Europe and admired the strength of large German men, who made excellent soldiers and gladiators.

GREECE

BY JEFFREY S. CARNES

For the Greeks, as for most human societies until quite recent times, slavery was an accepted fact of life and, with rare exceptions, it was not subject to analysis or moral criticism. Greece, however, stands out for the degree to which slavery was central to the economy, and every Greek polis had a significant number of slaves, both agricultural and urban.

There existed in Greece both chattel slavery, in which the slave was the legal property of another person, and a number of intermediate forms of servitude, in which a person was forced to labor for another while still remaining technically free; in other words, an individual was not subject to sale. One such form was debt bondage, in which a free person who was unable to pay off a debt came under the power of another until such time as the debt was paid. In practice, interest on a debt could turn this into a form of long-term or permanent servitude, and the creation of a "sharecropper" class in many Greek cities was a key factor in the rise of tyrants and other political reformers. For example, in Athens the lawmaker Solon (ca. 630–ca. 560 B.C.E.) canceled debts to eliminate debt bondage. In Sparta nonchattel slavery took a political form: A permanent noncitizen class—the Helots, literally "the captured ones"—was created as a result of Sparta's conquest of Messene in the 10th through seventh centuries B.C.E. Helots were forced to perform agricultural labor for their Spartan masters (who were themselves forbidden from engaging in such labor), and they were subject to terror at the hands of the Spartans. Helots were not, however, subject to sale or removal; on the contrary, they were bound to the land, and their status was akin to that of serfs.

Chattel slavery dates back to the earliest historical records. Indeed, the initial written records of most societies reveal slavery as an already existing institution. Documents from Mycenae, dating to before 1200 B.C.E., refer to slaves, and Homer's *Iliad*, the earliest work in the Greek literary tradition, begins with a dispute over a slave. The Homeric world shows the Greek attitude toward slavery both explicitly and through its silences: no one questions the morality of slavery, and the lot of slaves is pitied. One of the distinguishing factors of Greek slavery (as opposed to the more familiar model from the pre–Civil War United States) was that anyone could become a slave.

Wars were frequent, and those captured in war were typically ransomed (if their families could afford to pay), kept as slaves by their captors, or sold on the open market. Piracy and brigandage were also common throughout antiquity, and anyone whose fortune was sufficiently bad could wind up a slave. There was some sentiment (particularly from the fourth century B.C.E. onward) that Greeks should not enslave their fellow Greeks, but this was by no means a hard-and-fast rule. By the fourth century B.C.E. it seems that most slaves in Athens were non-Greek, coming instead from a variety of areas, particularly those to the north and east of mainland Greece, including Thrace, Scythia, and Asia Minor. Slaves were not normally permitted to have families, so most of the slave population was purchased rather than homebred, and the slave trade was a thriving one throughout antiquity.

Slaves worked in every sector of the economy, and only a few occupations (such as mining, which was harsh and dangerous work) were viewed as exclusively servile. In Athens state-owned slaves formed the police force and served as clerks in certain courts, but there was no large slave-dominated civil service bureaucracy as there was in Rome. Since Greece was an agricultural society, most slaves worked on farms, but in cities they formed part of the industrial labor force. The largest factory we know of produced shields and employed a labor force of 120 slaves, but many enterprises employed a mix of slave and free labor. Inscriptions for public

Apollo (left), a Scythian slave (middle), and the satyr Marsyas (Alison Frantz Photographic Collection, American School of Classical Studies at Athens)

works projects, which list the status of the laborers, provide ample evidence for this. Household slaves were generally better off than those who worked in the fields, and their duties could include child care and education. The loyal household servant became a common character on the dramatic stage.

Buying a living human being was not very expensive: inscriptional evidence from the late fifth century B.C.E. shows prices below 100 drachmas (perhaps three months' wages for a semiskilled worker), so slave owning was widespread. The slave population in Athens is estimated to have been at a third of the total inhabitants of the city, perhaps 100,000 in the late fifth century B.C.E.; even states with less developed industry must still have had a large percentage of slaves. The absence of large-scale slave revolts is perhaps a consequence of the ethnic diversity of the slave population. Revolts were more likely when large numbers of slaves shared a common language and culture, as the major slave revolts in the Roman world and the Helot rebellions in Sparta made clear. While organized resistance was rare, running away was not: some 20,000 Athenian slaves escaped during the chaos caused by the Spartan capture of Dhekélia. Many of those who escaped were said to have been skilled craftsmen who would presumably have sought employment elsewhere as freemen. Professional slave catchers were as much a part of the slave economy as were slave traders.

It was possible for Greek slaves to obtain their freedom, though this was not nearly as common as in the Roman world. In some cases slaves were freed in their owners' wills, and in others they were able to purchase their freedom; typically they were denied citizenship and would have a status equivalent to that of other free noncitizens. The case of Pasion, an extremely wealthy freed slave and banker of the fourth century B.C.E. who was granted Athenian citizenship because of his generosity to the city, was exceptional, as was the granting of freedom to slaves who fought on behalf of Athens in the battle of Arginusae.

The intellectual revolution of the late fifth century B.C.E. brought the institution of slavery into question for the first time. Aristotle's defense of slavery can be seen as a response to these issues: He refers to slaves as "animate tools" and argues that some people are by nature suited to slavery, which runs counter to the usual Greek perception that anyone could become a slave. In political theory and popular discourse the concept of slavery was an important one for the definition of citizenship, since the slave was everything the citizen was not: unfree, forced to labor for another, and lacking enforceable rights.

ROME

BY PAUL MCKECHNIE

Most slaves in Rome were foreign in origin, captured in war or bought in slave markets. In the early days it was also possible for a Roman citizen to become a slave; the Twelve Tables (a code of laws of the early Roman Republic, established around 450 B.C.E.) allowed a creditor who was not paid to sell the debtor "beyond the Tiber" as a slave. Within Roman territory it was possible for loan agreements to involve a kind of voluntary mortgage on the debtor's person (*nexum*). A borrower who failed to pay became a debt bondsman but was still a Roman citizen of a sort and not exactly the property of the creditor. The historian Livy (59 B.C.E.–17 C.E.) tells of the abolition of *nexum* in his *Annals of the Roman People*. Livy's account describes public outrage at the sexual abuse of a debt bondsman, whereas the sexual abuse of a slave would not have provoked such outrage. An important disadvantage of the system was that it made Roman debt bondsmen ineligible to fight in the Roman army. The *lex Poetilia Papiria*, a law passed in 326 B.C.E., ended the system of *nexum*.

Slaves, as distinct from debt bondsmen, were the property of their masters and could be bought and sold. In principle, they had no rights at all and could be punished or abused exactly as their masters chose. The emperor Antoninus Pius (r. 138–161 C.E.) changed the law that had given masters the power of life and death over their slaves and introduced the principle that if a master killed his slave without good reason, he would be subject to the same penalty as if he had killed another person's slave; in effect, he could be fined up to the value of the slave.

Slaves were a source of unpaid labor anywhere for the Romans: in homes, in agriculture, and in supporting the army. They were not expected or trusted to fight for Rome. Slaves who survived being captured in war were usually women and children because it was normal for men captured in war to be put to death if there was no one to pay a ransom for them; keeping them alive was a risk their captors would not usually take.

In the third and (especially) the second centuries B.C.E. the Romans' successes in expanding their conquests across the Mediterranean resulted in a great influx of slaves to Italy. The Roman upper classes were able to buy larger estates and work them with slave gangs. The disadvantage was that one had to be a landowner to serve in the army, and as Roman and Italian peasants sold their property to the rich their absence from the military ranks threatened to weaken Rome. Gaius Marius (ca. 157–86 B.C.E.), who was consul seven times between 107 and 86, solved this problem by making it possible for unpropertied Romans to join the army.

Although they could not fight for the army, slaves could be made to fight for sport. Gladiators, who fought in the amphitheaters, were usually either slaves or condemned criminals. Along with his law discouraging killing slaves, Antoninus Pius legislated against sending a slave to the gladiator school without a good reason; making a slave into a gladiator was a punishment virtually equivalent to death.

Life for most slaves was difficult most of the time, but the Roman system of slavery had features that presented opportunities for some slaves. A slave could own no property, but Roman law recognized something called a *peculium*, which was in effect a slave's own money. In a case where, for example, a master went into business with his slave, the fact that some of the capital behind the business was the slave's *peculium* might prevent the master from being liable for all legal claims that might arise against the slave in the course of business. Even though the idea behind a *peculium* was perhaps to protect masters from liability for their slaves' mistakes, in practice a successful slave might manage to use his *peculium* to buy his freedom from his master.

During the Imperial Period (after 31 B.C.E.) the Romans seem to have freed many of their slaves. The emperor Augustus (r. 27 B.C.E.–14 C.E.) was behind the *lex Fufia Caninia* of 2 C.E., a law that limited the number of slaves a master could manumit in his lifetime, and the *lex Aelia Sentia* of 4 C.E., which made 30 the minimum age at which a slave could be manumitted. When the slave of a Roman citizen was manumitted, he became a Roman citizen himself. Slaves had one name, while characteristically Roman citizens had three names: *praenomen* (first name), *nomen gentilicium* (family name), and *cognomen* (last name). A freedman (*libertus* or *libertinus*) had his original name as his *cognomen*, and he took his first two citizen names from his former master. Freedmen had most of the rights of freeborn Roman citizens—for example, the right to vote, to make wills, to marry Roman citizens, and to produce legitimate-citizen children—but they could not hold political office.

Slaves were important at the very heart of the Roman Empire. When the first emperor, Augustus, took over, he used his own slaves and the resources of his own household to administer the empire by, for example, making appointments, keeping accounts, directing the army, keeping records, and managing relations with the Senate and political officeholders.

He and later emperors based bureaus that were virtually government ministries in the palace under the direction of their own freedmen: The *ab epistulis* (minister of the provinces) managed correspondence with Roman governors across the empire; the *a rationibus* (minister of finance) kept the emperor's accounts; and the *a libellis* (minister of justice) processed the petitions that came to the emperor from across the world. As the first and second centuries C.E. went forward, emperors brought in Roman knights instead of freedmen to hold many important posts in the palace, but they were cautious enough to keep the money in the hands of someone they could rely on—one of their own freedmen.

Image of Psyche on a lead coffin lid, Roman; made in Lebanon during the second to third centuries C.E.*, said to be from Sidon, Lebanon; the lead is thought to be an import from Spain or Sardinia, where there were extensive mines worked by Roman slaves.* (© The Trustees of the British Museum)

THE AMERICAS

BY KIRK H. BEETZ

It is not known when slavery began in the Americas. It is possible that the first migrants to the New World already practiced slavery. How ancient Americans north of Mexico practiced slavery is something that anthropologists infer from archaeological information and the practices of Americans when first recorded by Europeans. The earliest peoples to populate the forests and grasslands of North America were nomadic. Their slaves probably would have been people taken captive from other groups during raids that may have been staged for the very purpose of taking slaves. Because there were no beasts of burden native to North America, the captives would have been responsible for carrying goods during migrations.

Some early nomadic people settled and built one village to inhabit during warm months and another for cold months. Others settled year round into permanent villages. Slaves in such villages might have been responsible for mundane chores such as cleaning and cooking. The ancient villagers may have raided other villages or preyed on nomads, taking captives, possibly children. When a village had a shortage of women, girls and young women would sometimes be taken to provide men with mates and to bring in children to repopulate a village that had been decimated by natural disasters or warfare. It is possible that both nomadic peoples and settled peoples had rituals in which slaves could become free members of the nations that held them.

The region for which there is the most information about slavery is Mesoamerica, made up of parts of modern Mexico and Central America. Perhaps the greatest ancient Mesoamerican city was Teotihuacán, in Mexico. Its peak of power was from the first to the seventh century C.E. It was the greatest military power in Mesoamerica during that period, and it forced distant Mayan communities to pay tribute. It seems that the government of Teotihuacán preferred goods such as jade, obsidian, and brightly colored feathers, but sometimes a city did not have enough goods for tribute and sent instead human beings. These slaves were probably used as human sacrifices. The other aspects of slavery in Teotihuacán are unclear, but it is probable that through debt or conviction of a crime, a person could become a slave, and that such a slave might have had the opportunity to earn his or her freedom. In the case of people enslaved because of crimes, their slavery might have been limited to a specified period of service.

The Maya had a long-lived culture, and their practice of slavery almost certainly varied as customs changed over time and from one Mayan city-state to another, but Mayan writings and archaeological evidence allow for some generalizations about how the Maya practiced slavery. Slaves were at the bottom of the social structure. Commoners caught in battle and then enslaved were possibly regarded as almost nonhuman, ranking no higher than animals and perhaps lower than jaguars and other animals associated with Mayan mythology. They existed only to serve their owners, such as the individual warriors who had captured them. During festivals they were often sacrificed. To the Maya these sacrifices, which involved torture, elevated the victims from the status of commoners to temporary gods. If slaves survived long enough, they could earn freedom either through clemency or through good service to their owners.

Nobles captured in battle might also be enslaved. After being tortured, they were usually sacrificed, because their deaths brought prestige to those who captured them, to their cities, and to their kings. Much Mayan warfare was conducted for the purpose of capturing enemy nobility, and warriors who captured nobles often added the nobles' names to their own, enhancing their standing in their community. A captured noble or member of a royal family rarely served long as a slave because sacrificing him or her to a god was valuable in winning the god's favor.

The Maya had an elaborate social structure with a multitude of customs that governed behavior and specified the duties of each member of society. Slavery involved many such customs as well as laws. Children without parents almost always became slaves. People convicted of crimes could become slaves of the people they had victimized. It is possible that people could voluntarily become slaves, perhaps because of burdensome debts or the loss of place in a community. For instance, tradespersons who lost the ability to practice their craft would no longer have a niche to fill in Mayan society.

There is disagreement among archaeologists about how slaves who were not prisoners of war were regarded and treated. These disagreements may stem from variations in Maya culture over hundreds of years. One view is that these slaves were cruelly abused and counted as nothing in Mayan society. They were worked to death, tormented, and sacrificed. They could be killed any time or for any reason by their owners. If someone other than the owner killed a slave, that killer took the place of the slave.

Another view holds that slaves were protected by laws that prohibited an owner from killing a slave anytime the owner wanted to do so. The slaves could hold important positions in households, even becoming the directors of the estates of wealthy people. They could earn their own money, save it, and spend it as they wished. Indeed, the law seems to have specified that a person was a slave only until he paid off a debt he owed someone. Slaves could be as well dressed and well fed as their owners. An owner who did not properly care for a slave could lose the slave, who might be freed, and in extreme cases might find himself the property of his former slave. Thus, slaves were not beaten or otherwise abused. In some cases, if slaves died before their debts were paid, their families would be expected to provide a substitute. How long the substitutes served is unclear; the substitute either served until the debt was paid or was replaced periodically by another member of the family until the debt was paid.

Slavery was practiced in South America, but to what extent has yet to be established. For many South American groups the customs regarding slaves would be much like those of the nomads and villagers of North America. Girls especially were valued, becoming sexual partners of their captors or possibly serving as a sacrifice to the gods. The Moche culture of about 100 to 600 C.E. seems to have practiced slavery. They may have raided other cultures to obtain captives who would be ritually sacrificed. Otherwise, slaves probably became servants in prosperous households.

See also AGRICULTURE; CALENDARS AND CLOCKS; CHILDREN; CRIME AND PUNISHMENT; DEATH AND BURIAL PRACTICES; DRAMA AND THEATER; ECONOMY; EMPLOYMENT AND LABOR; FAMILY; FOREIGNERS AND BARBARIANS; GENDER STRUCTURES AND ROLES; GOVERNMENT ORGANIZATION; LAWS AND LEGAL CODES; LITERATURE; MIGRATION AND POPULATION MOVEMENTS; MILITARY; NOMADIC AND PASTORAL SOCIETIES; OCCUPATIONS; RELIGION AND COSMOLOGY; SETTLEMENT PATTERNS; SOCIAL ORGANIZATION; SPORTS AND RECREATION; TOWNS AND VILLAGES; TRADE AND EXCHANGE; WAR AND CONQUEST.

The Middle East

The Code of the Nesilim, excerpt (Hittite, 1650–1500 B.C.E.)

1. If anyone slay a man or woman in a quarrel, he shall bring this one. He shall also give four persons, either men or women, he shall let them go to his home.

2. If anyone slay a male or female slave in a quarrel, he shall bring this one and give two persons, either men or women, he shall let them go to his home.

3. If anyone smite a free man or woman and this one die, he shall bring this one and give two persons, he shall let them go to his home.

4. If anyone smite a male or female slave, he shall bring this one also and give one person, he shall let him or her go to his home.

5. If anyone slay a merchant of Hatti, he shall give one and a half pounds of silver, he shall let it go to his home.

6. If anyone blind a free man or knock out his teeth, formerly they would give one pound of silver, now he shall give twenty half-shekels of silver. . . .

8. If anyone blind a male or female slave or knock out their teeth, he shall give ten half-shekels of silver, he shall let it go to his home. . . .

10. If anyone injure a man so that he cause him suffering, he shall take care of him. Yet he shall give him a man in his place, who shall work for him in his house until he recovers. But if he recover, he shall give him six half-shekels of silver. And to the physician this one shall also give the fee. . . .

17. If anyone cause a free woman to miscarry, if it be the tenth month, he shall give ten half-shekels of silver, if it be the fifth month, he shall give five half-shekels of silver.

(continued)

(continues)

18. If anyone cause a female slave to miscarry, if it be the tenth month, he shall give five half-shekels of silver. . . .

20. If any man of Hatti steal a Nesian slave and lead him here to the land of Hatti, and his master discover him, he shall give him twelve half-shekels of silver, he shall let it go to his home.

21. If anyone steal a slave of a Luwian from the land of Luwia, and lead him here to the land of Hatti, and his master discover him, he shall take his slave only. . . .

24. If a male or female slave run away, he at whose hearth his master finds him or her, shall give fifty half-shekels of silver a year. . . .

31. If a free man and a female slave be fond of each other and come together and he take her for his wife and they set up house and get children, and afterward they either become hostile or come to close quarters, and they divide the house between them, the man shall take the children, only one child shall the woman take.

32. If a slave take a woman as his wife, their case is the same. The majority of the children to the wife and one child to the slave.

33. If a slave take a female slave their case is the same. The majority of children to the female slave and one child to the slave.

34. If a slave convey the bride price to a free son and take him as husband for his daughter, nobody dare surrender him to slavery. . . .

36. If a slave convey the bride price to a free son and take him as husband for his daughter, nobody dare surrender him to slavery. . . .

98. If a free man set a house ablaze, he shall build the house, again. And whatever is inside the house, be it a man, an ox, or a sheep that perishes, nothing of these he need compensate.

99. If a slave set a house ablaze, his master shall compensate for him. The nose of the slave and his ears they shall cut off, and give him back to his master. But if he do not compensate, then he shall give up this one. . . .

170. If a free man kill a serpent and speak the name of another, he shall give one pound of silver; if a slave, this one shall die. . . .

173. If anyone oppose the judgment of the king, his house shall become a ruin. If anyone oppose the judgment of a lord, his head shall be cut off. If a slave rise against his master, he shall go into the pit. . . .

191. If a free man picks up now this woman, now that one, now in this country, then in that country, there shall be no punishment if they came together sexually willingly. . . .

194. If a free man pick up female slaves, now one, now another, there is no punishment for intercourse. If brothers sleep with a free woman, together, or one after the other, there is no punishment. If father and son sleep with a female slave or harlot, together, or one after the other, there is no punishment. . . .

From: Oliver J. Thatcher, ed., *The Library of Original Sources*, Vol. 3, *The Roman World* (Milwaukee, Wisc.: University Research Extension Co., 1901).

Asia and the Pacific

Kautilya: excerpt from the Arthashastra (ca. 250 B.C.E.)

Book III, Chapter 13, Rules Regarding Slaves and Laborers

The selling or mortgaging by kinsmen of the life of a Shudra who is not a born slave, and has not attained majority, but is an Arya in birth shall be punished with a fine of twelve panas; of a Vaisya, twenty-four panas; of a Kshatriya, thirty-six panas; and of a Brahman, forty-eight panas. . . . Any person who has voluntarily enslaved himself shall, if he runs away, be a slave for life. Similarly any person whose life has been mortgaged by others shall, if he runs away twice, be a slave for life. . . . Deceiving a slave of his money or depriving him of the privileges he can exercise as an Arya, shall be punished with half the fine levied for enslaving the life of an Arya. . . . Employing a slave to carry the dead or to sweep ordure, urine, or the leavings of food; or a female slave to attend on her master while he is bathing naked; or hurting or abusing him or her, or violating the chastity of a female slave shall cause the forfeiture of the value paid for him or her. Violation of the chastity of nurses, female cooks, or female servants of the class of joint cultivators shall at once earn their liberty for them. Violence towards an attendant of high birth shall entitle him to run away. . . . When a man commits or helps another to commit rape with a girl or a female slave pledged to him, he shall not only forfeit the purchase-value, but also pay a certain amount of money to her and a fine of twice the amount of sulka to the government. . . .

From: Kautilya, *Kautilya's Arthashastra*, 2nd ed., trans. R. Shamasastry (Mysore, India: Wesleyan Mission Press, 1923).

Greece

Aristotle, excerpt from "On Slavery" (from **The Politics**, *ca. 330* B.C.E.*)*

Let us first speak of master and slave, looking to the needs of practical life and also seeking to attain some better theory of their relation than exists at present. . . . Property is a part of the household, and the art of acquiring property is a part of the art of managing the household; for no man can live well, or indeed live at all, unless he be provided with necessaries. And so, in the arrangement of the family, a slave is a living possession, and property a number of such instruments; and the slave is himself an instrument which takes precedence of all other instruments. . . . The master is only the master of the slave; he does not belong to him, whereas the slave is not only the slave of his master, but wholly belongs to him. Hence we see what is the nature and office of a slave; he who is by nature not his own but another's man, is by nature a slave; and he may be said to be another's man who, being a human being, is also a possession. And a possession may be defined as an instrument of action, separable from the possessor.

But is there anyone thus intended by nature to be a slave, and for whom such a condition is expedient and right, or rather is not all slavery a violation of nature? There is no difficulty in answering this question, on grounds both of reason and of fact. For that some should rule and others be ruled is a thing not only necessary, but expedient; from the hour of their birth, some are marked out for subjection, others for rule. . . . Again, the male is by nature superior, and the female inferior; and the one rules, and the other is ruled; this principle, of necessity, extends to all mankind.

Where then there is such a difference as that between soul and body, or between men and animals (as in the case of those whose business is to use their body, and who can do nothing better), the lower sort are by nature slaves, and it is better for them as for all inferiors that they should be under the rule of a master. For he who can be, and therefore is, another's and he who participates in rational principle enough to apprehend, but not to have, such a principle, is a slave by nature. Whereas the lower animals cannot even apprehend a principle; they obey their instincts. And indeed the use made of slaves and of tame animals is not very different; for both with their bodies minister to the needs of life. Nature would like to distinguish between the bodies of freemen and slaves, making the one strong for servile labor, the other upright, and although useless for such services, useful for political life in the arts both of war and peace. But the opposite often happens—that some have the souls and others have the bodies of free men. And doubtless if men differed from one another in the mere forms of their bodies as much as the statues of the gods do from men, all would acknowledge that the inferior class should be slaves of the superior. It is clear, then, that some men are by nature free, and others slaves, and that for these latter slavery is both expedient and right.

There is a slave or slavery by law as well as by nature. The law of which I speak is a sort of convention—the law by which whatever is taken in war is supposed to belong to the victors. But this right many jurists impeach, as they would an orator who brought forward an unconstitutional measure: they detest the notion that, because one man has the power of doing violence and is superior in brute strength, another shall be his slave and subject. Even among philosophers there is a difference of opinion. The origin of the dispute, and what makes the views invade each other's territory, is as follows: in some sense virtue, when furnished with means, has actually the greatest power of exercising force; and as superior power is only found where there

(continued)

(continues)

is superior excellence of some kind, power seems to imply virtue, and the dispute to be simply one about justice (for it is due to one party identifying justice with goodwill while the other identifies it with the mere rule of the stronger). If these views are thus set out separately, the other views have no force or plausibility against the view that the superior in virtue ought to rule, or be master.

Others, clinging, as they think, simply to a principle of justice (for law and custom are a sort of justice), assume that slavery in accordance with the custom of war is justified by law, but at the same moment they deny this. For what if the cause of the war be unjust? And again, no one would ever say he is a slave who is unworthy to be a slave. Were this the case, men of the highest rank would be slaves and the children of slaves if they or their parents chance to have been taken captive and sold. Wherefore Hellenes do not like to call Hellenes slaves, but confine the term to barbarians. Yet, in using this language, they really mean the natural slave of whom we spoke at first; for it must be admitted that some are slaves everywhere, others nowhere. The same principle applies to nobility. Hellenes regard themselves as noble everywhere, and not only in their own country, but they deem the barbarians noble only when at home, thereby implying that there are two sorts of nobility and freedom, the one absolute, the other relative.

From: Aristotle, *The Politics of Aristotle*, trans. Benjamin Jowett (New York: Colonial Press, 1900).

FURTHER READING

H. D. Baker, "Degrees of Freedom: Slavery in Mid-First Millennium B.C. Mesopotamia," *World Archaeology* 33 (2001): 18–26.

Keith R. Bradley, *Slavery and Society at Rome* (New York: Cambridge University Press, 1994).

Daphne Nash Briggs, "Metals, Salt, and Slaves: Economic Links between Gaul and Italy from the Eighth to the Late Sixth Centuries B.C.," *Oxford Journal of Archaeology* 22, no. 3 (2003): 243–259.

Muhammad A. Dandamaev, *Slavery in Babylonia: From Nabopolassar to Alexander the Great (626–331 B.C.)*, (DeKalb: Northern Illinois University Press, 1984).

M. I. Finley, ed., *Classical Slavery* (London and Totowa, N.J.: Frank Cass, 1987).

N.R.E. Fisher, *Slavery in Classical Greece* (London: Duckworth, 1993).

Yvon Garlan, *Slavery in Ancient Greece*, trans. Janet Lloyd (Ithaca, N.Y.: Cornell University Press, 1988).

Paul E. Lovejoy, *The Transformations in Slavery: A History of Slavery in Africa* (Cambridge, U.K.: Cambridge University Press, 1983).

R. Westbrook, "Slave and Master in Ancient Near Eastern Law," *Chicago-Kent Law Review* 70 (1995): 1631–1676.

► social collapse and abandonment

INTRODUCTION

Throughout the world archaeologists discover the remains of human settlements that were abandoned at some point in ancient history. These remains include homes, artifacts, middens (that is, trash piles), piles of shells, figurines, household objects, tombs, and public buildings. After studying their discoveries, archaeologists and historians conclude that the people who lived there either abandoned the settlement or died. Even great empires such as the Roman Empire at some point collapsed. While the Romans themselves continued to exist on the Italian peninsula, their empire around the Mediterranean Sea shattered, and the civilizations they had conquered gained their independence from Rome.

Social collapse and the abandonment occurred for various reasons. A common cause was a catastrophic natural disaster, such as an earthquake, volcanic eruption, flood, fire, or tsunami (in coastal regions). Perhaps the most famous example is the eruption of Mount Vesuvius in 79 C.E., a volcano whose ash and lava buried the Roman cities of Pompeii and Herculaneum, entombing people almost literally in their tracks. Natural disasters also include plagues, which often took hold during times of warfare and social unrest. In response, people from the surrounding countryside fled their villages and hamlets to take refuge in nearby cities. The cities, however, were not equipped to handle a large influx of people. Hunger became commonplace, since rural people were no longer producing food. Conditions often became crowded and unsanitary so that disease was easily spread. A plague of this nature killed a quarter of the population of ancient Athens, severely weakening the Greek empire.

Sometimes social collapse and abandonment was a gradual process, often brought about by climatic change. As a region became colder or warmer, rainfall amounts changed dramatically, affecting the flora and fauna of the region. Good examples are provided by parts of Egypt and Mesoamerica, where lush, green areas turned into harsh desert over relatively short periods of time, forcing people to move. Even comparatively minor cooling or warming could play havoc with agriculture, leading to crop failures that forced people to abandon their settlements in search of new farmland. When such changes occurred over a wide region, entire peoples could disappear. Some of these changes were caused by human activity. When farmland was overworked or forests were cleared, the result was soil erosion, flooding, and other disruptions that wiped out communities. Of course, these changes worked in the other direction; as land formerly covered by glaciers warmed and the glaciers receded, new communities of people moved in.

Warfare, too, often led to the collapse of societies. For nearly 3,000 years, Egypt stood at the summit of human civilization. But beginning in the Late Dynastic period Egypt could no longer defend its empire. Successive wars and occupations by the Assyrians, Persians, and finally Greeks led to the end of dynastic rule and the collapse of Egypt as a major world power. The Romans suffered a similar fate when their empire split under the weight of its own sheer size and finally collapsed when it could no longer fend off Germanic peoples from the north.

AFRICA

BY MICHAEL J. O'NEAL

The peoples of ancient sub-Saharan Africa lived primarily as hunter-gatherers until about the second century B.C.E. Accordingly, they did not form cities or permanent settlements that expanded into empires or dominant civilizations. Housing and other structures were built with temporary material, such as mud and wattle, rather than the stone and brick used by some other cultures. Thus, little can be known in detail about the collapse and abandonment of settlements in the ancient sub-Sahara, although social scientists can make inferences about the processes that led them.

One such process was probably environmental degradation. Although the sub-Sahara was rich in resources that allowed people to subsist and even thrive as hunters and gatherers, it was inevitable that as the population of a given area increased, resources were strained, particularly the food supply. As game animals became scarcer and native plants were exhausted for their food value, communities would simply pick up, abandon the region they inhabited, and move on to a new region, where the process began again.

Similar processes affected the ironworking cultures of the sub-Sahara. This region was unique in that it seems to have skipped the Bronze Age that was so important to the development of other world cultures and passed directly from the Stone Age to the Iron Age. Iron smelting, however, requires high heat in furnaces. The most common fuel used to fire these furnaces was wood—and wood in massive amounts. The result was deforestation in the area immediately surrounding an ironworking community. As time went on, firewood had to be brought to the site from farther and farther away. This deforestation led to soil erosion and the disappearance of game, making it increasingly difficult for surrounding populations to feed themselves.

Another process that led to social collapse and abandonment was climate change. The most noteworthy example in ancient Africa had to do with the Sahara. For thousands of years this vast region has been a harsh, forbidding desert. It was not always this way. Until about 3000 B.C.E. much of the Sahara was fertile grassland that supported populations of people. In the area that is modern-day Mauritania, for example, an early Berber culture called the Bafour survived by farming and grazing herds. Then the climate began to change, the rains disappeared, and the desert grew relentlessly southward (overcultivation and overgrazing of the land may have contributed to its decline). The Bafour had to abandon the region. Many people simply moved to urban centers, including those of Egypt, where they and their descendants forged a new kind of life. Historians believe that the descendants of the Bafour include the Imraguen, who became fishermen on the African coasts; the Toucouleur, who moved to Senegal; and the Wolof peoples, who settled in Gambia, Senegal, and Mauritania. All three of these ethnic groups survive in the 21st century. The process was intensified as the Berber people from the north, themselves facing environmental degradation and political turmoil, expanded southward in the third and fourth centuries C.E., driving out surviving members of the indigenous groups. This example illustrates the complex movement of peoples as they faced crisis, abandoned their communities, and were absorbed into other cultures.

Disease and famine, too, contributed to the collapse of ancient African civilizations. A noteworthy example is the Nok civilization, which emerged in modern-day Nigeria in about 500 B.C.E., survived into the Common Era, and then mysteriously disappeared. The Nok were an advanced civilization best known for ironworking and, especially, terra-cotta sculptures. Historians do not know with any certainty why the Nok simply disappeared, but they speculate that famine or disease led to a sharp decline of the population and the merger of the Nok with the Yoruba people. Famine and disease are mutually reinforcing; food shortages make hungry people more susceptible to disease, and as people die, less and less food can be produced. A civilization weakened in this way could not survive.

Finally, warfare and the desire for empire led to the collapse of African civilizations. A good example is provided by Kush, a region just south of the Egyptian Empire. The Kushites developed a flourishing culture between about 1700 and 1500 B.C.E., primarily because Egypt was under the control of the Hyksos, a Semitic people from Asia. However, when the Egyptians expelled the Hyksos, they set their sights on Kush, wanting control of the region not only as a buffer to protect their southern border but also as a trading colony. Then, in about 1000 B.C.E., the Kushites again asserted their independence, unified their kingdom, moved their capital city upriver (that is, to the south, since the Nile River flows south to north) to Napata, and became a major power in the region. They had access to rich gold mines and grew so strong that they attacked and conquered Egypt for a time.

However, this power was not destined to survive. Kush came under attack from the Assyrians and later the Persians.

When Napata finally fell in the fourth century B.C.E., the Kushites abandoned it and moved their capital farther south, to Meroë. They survived for the next several hundred years as traders. Meanwhile, a new power in the region emerged, the kingdom of Axum, which lay to the Kushites' east. In the second century C.E. Axum conquered Kush, and the Kushite civilization for all intents and purposes disappeared.

Warfare also contributed to the decline and disappearance of the Carthaginian culture along Africa's northern coast. Carthage had been founded in the ninth century B.C.E., and over time it developed into a major trading power, supported by a sophisticated agricultural system. Protecting its large mercantile fleet in the Mediterranean Sea was a massive navy. However, Carthage was a threat to the Roman Empire, and Rome concluded that Carthage had to be subdued. A series of three wars began in 264 B.C.E. Although the outcome of the first war was indecisive, the treaty the two powers signed forced Carthage to pay huge indemnities to Rome, depleting its treasury and beginning the process of collapse. At the end of the third war, in 146 B.C.E., Rome decisively defeated the Carthaginians; sacked the capital city, Carthage; and effectively wiped out Carthaginian culture and society.

EGYPT

BY MARIAM F. AYAD

The Egypt of the pharaohs lasted more than 3,000 years. The wonderful monuments preserved at Luxor, Saqqara, and other archaeological sites testify to the greatness this civilization enjoyed. Except for those magnificent ruins, however, little remains of this ancient culture.

Egypt's long history is divided into Old, Middle, and New Kingdoms, spanning the period from about 2575 to 1070 B.C.E. These periods of prosperity, expansion, and massive construction projects are interrupted or followed by times of weakened royal authority and even chaos known as the First, Second, and Third Intermediate Periods, respectively. The Second (ca. 1640–ca. 1532 B.C.E.) and Third (ca. 1070–ca. 712 B.C.E.) Intermediate Periods witnessed foreign domination over parts of Egypt; the First Intermediate Period (ca. 2134–ca. 2040 B.C.E.) is unique in that internal rather than external factors seem to have caused the collapse.

The First Intermediate Period survived in literary works long after stability was restored to the land. More than any other period of Egyptian history, it affected the Egyptian collective psyche. For centuries after its end Egyptians viewed it as a time of social collapse in which fundamental notions of justice and social order were overturned. Several literary works, including *The Complaints of Khakheperre-sonb* and *The Admonitions of Ipuwer*, vividly describe the social conditions prevalent during the First Intermediate Period.

In *The Complaints of Khakheperre-sonb* we read of a land destroyed and broken up, where "order is cast out," chaos rules, and the temples are deprived of their regular rations. This text describes a general state of mourning, distress, inequity, and crime. It paints a picture of reversed social norms wherein the rulers become ruled. *The Admonitions of Ipuwer* describes similar conditions. The author imparts a sense of overarching futility and infertility: "Lo, . . . the women are barren, none conceive." Several passages explicitly refer to bloodshed: "There's blood everywhere. . . . Lo, the river is blood." Others mention that there was "no shortage of dead," that "many dead are buried in the river," and that "the stream [became] the grave, the tomb became stream." *The Admonitions of Ipuwer* has been cited as evidence of an Egyptian civil war.

Another text, known as *Instructions to Merikare*, written sometime in the Middle Kingdom, may also contain references to a civil war, such as in a warning that "troops will fight troops." Traces of the name "Khety" preserved in *Merikare* and written within the royal cartouche (the oval that typically encircles the king's name in ancient Egyptian writings) may indicate that the events referred to took place in the First Intermediate Period, as "Khety" could conceivably be another way to write Akhtoy, a name held by several rulers during that difficult time. Yet another text, known as the *Prophecy of Neferti*, suggests that Egypt's rulers were "many" during this period and that the land was in "turmoil" and "uproar." People "seize[d] weapons of warfare," the son becoming as enemy, "the brother as foe," and "a man slaying his father."

Scattered references in *The Admonitions of Ipuwer* and in the *Prophecy of Neferti* as well as in other texts suggest an extended severe drought. In the *Prophecy of Neferti*, "Dry is the river of Egypt. One crosses the water on foot; . . . The land is bowed down in distress." This text also describes the land as "ruined" and "shrunk," "bare" and "deprived of produce" and "lacking in crops." Indeed, it has been suggested that toward the end of the Sixth Dynasty (ca. 2323–ca. 2150 B.C.E.) a series of low Niles and the ensuing economic decline may have directly contributed to the collapse of centralized power so characteristic of the First Intermediate Period.

Literary and autobiographical texts as well as archaeological evidence indicate that the Second Intermediate Period witnessed a massive wave of Asiatic infiltration into the Nile delta. Whereas early scholars have assumed that an outright invasion resulted in the Hyksos rule in Egypt (*Hyksos* being a Greek version of the Egyptian *heqa khasut*, "rulers of foreign lands"), it is now believed that the Hyksos infiltrated the delta gradually but massively at the end of the Middle Kingdom. What exactly caused this mass immigration is not known, but possibly it resulted from a period of drought in western Asia. The Second Intermediate Period ended with the military expulsion of the Hyksos through campaigns initiated by a series of Theban rulers of the Seventeenth Dynasty (ca. 1640–ca. 1550 B.C.E.), leading eventually to the establishment of the Eighteenth Dynasty (ca. 1550–ca. 1307 B.C.E.) and the New Kingdom.

The Third Intermediate Period shares some similarities with the first two. Like them, it was characterized by much

Sarcophagus of Nectanebo II, the last native ruler of Egypt, from Alexandria, Thirtieth Dynasty, around 343 B.C.E.; Nectanebo's reign was ended by the second Persian occupation of Egypt, and it is said that he fled to Ethiopia. (© The Trustees of the British Museum)

internal conflict and long periods of foreign domination. Competing claims over the Egyptian throne at the beginning of the Twentieth Dynasty (ca. 1196–ca. 1070 B.C.E.) undermined the royal authority, and toward the end of the dynasty a series of weak kings ruled, often only briefly. Inevitably, weakened royal authority led to a drastic rise in the influence and power of prominent figures of the priesthood, who added military titles with civic duties to their priestly roles. One such figure was Herihor, a high priest of the god Amun who assumed royal titles and enclosed his name in the royal cartouche even while Ramses XI, the last pharaoh of the Twentieth Dynasty, still ruled.

With the death of Ramses XI the New Kingdom ended, and an era of "foreign" dominion began. Because of its rulers' foreign names, the Twenty-first Dynasty (ca. 1070–ca. 945 B.C.E.) is often characterized as Libyan. Although Libyan by origin, these rulers had been assimilated into Egyptian society. Some had been members of the Egyptian court or army and had used their positions to gain power. The Twenty-second through Twenty-fourth Dynasties (945–712 B.C.E.) were also Libyan in origin and often contentious, with various dynasts claiming royal titles even though they controlled only small areas. The resulting competition divided Egypt into warring fiefdoms. It may be that the Libyans' decentralized approach to rule was their cultural heritage as people who had led a tribal, nomadic existence. Texts from earlier periods of Egyptian history often mention wars with the "Libyan tribes" along Egypt's western border.

The Libyan period ended in the second half of the eighth century B.C.E. when invaders from Nubia to the south of Egypt took power in Memphis. The Nubians claimed to be restorers of order who wanted to reunify Egypt and purify it of sacrilegious Libyans. In 664 B.C.E. Necho, a ruler from the western delta city of Sais, formed a military alliance with the Assyrians and with their help drove the Nubians out of Egypt. Necho's son Psamtik I (r. 664–610 B.C.E.) became the first ruler of the Egyptian Twenty-sixth Dynasty, which lasted until the Persian invasion of Egypt in 525 B.C.E.

During the Twenty-sixth Dynasty contacts with other Mediterranean and Near Eastern countries strengthened, and Egypt became increasingly involved in the politics of the region. Egypt was invaded twice by the Persians, in 525 B.C.E. and 343 B.C.E., and then by Alexander the Great's Macedonian troops in 332 B.C.E. After Alexander's death in 323 B.C.E. one of his generals, Ptolemy, declared himself ruler of Egypt. His descendants reigned for almost 300 years, during which Egyptian culture became increasingly Hellenized. After Cleopatra VII's defeat at the battle of Actium in 30 B.C.E., Egypt was annexed to the Roman Empire, and its distinctive pharaonic culture gradually disappeared.

THE MIDDLE EAST

BY FRANS VAN KOPPEN

The ancient Near East offers a historical record of unparalleled length, continuity, and complexity for the development of human society over time. From the beginning of urban culture in late prehistory up to the Middle Ages, this record is replete with evidence for episodes of social collapse after periods of relative stability. These episodes typically involved settlement desertion on a regional scale, changes of subsistence strategies, and political fragmentation. Evidence for these events comes primarily from archaeological surveys using landscape investigation to determine the growth and decline of regional settlement systems. Excavations, climatic data, and ancient texts shed further light on social collapse and help reveal the complex interplay of socioeconomic and environmental factors that lay at the root of it.

Differences in landscape, rainfall, and temperature divide the Near East into distinct environmental zones, each of which accommodated specific forms of human subsistence: sheep and goat herding in the semiarid and mountainous regions, trade and crafts along the interregional routes, dry farming and small-scale cattle herding in the low-rainfall zones, and intensive cereal cultivation in the floodplains, again in combination with herding away from the rivers and fields. Maximum population density occurred near the rivers, and the Mesopotamian floodplains, in particular, exhibited the greatest size and number of settlements throughout the millennia.

Ancient agriculture was, however, always a dangerously fragile system operating under critical social and environmental constraints and therefore susceptible to abrupt fluctuations. Strong central control coincided with agricultural expansion and an increase in settlement, while disruptions of the political order were typically characterized by a reversion to local self-sufficiency and the abandonment of villages and smaller rural towns. In the face of such fluctuations the rural population maintained a spectrum of subsistence options and moved back and forth between village-based farming and other economic strategies such as herding, relocating if necessary to neighboring environmental zones.

A typical cycle of rural settlement and abandonment includes some or all of the following elements: Expansion is instigated by the urban centers, the seats of elite governments and their trappings of symbolic identifications on which regional states are founded. Growing demand in the center stimulates agriculture and settlement of the countryside, including ecologically marginal areas. Maximal growth is contained in order not to cross the threshold of the environmental carrying capacity, but the system at its greatest expansion is vulnerable when this threshold drops—for example, if yields diminish because of minor shifts in rainfall or river levels. Political demands for surplus remain constant, and pressure on the rural producers therefore increases, leaving them no alternative but to grow more on their land, which compounds the problem of diminishing returns by increasing soil poverty and salinity. Once producers start fleeing the oppression of their urban landlords, the agricultural infrastructure can no longer be maintained, and the downward spiral accelerates, ending with the desertion of rural settlements and the decline of the urban political center, usually resulting in dynastic collapse.

Ancient Mesopotamian texts show that sequences of political growth and waning and the associated expansion and contraction of settlement were thought to obey universal cyclical patterns. The Mesopotamian word for "dynasty" designates any temporary term of public duty, and dynastic collapse was considered an inevitable shift in office. Political discontinuity sometimes occurred well before expansion endangered the resilience of the rural economy—for example, when the last indigenous Mesopotamian dynasty fell and the land was integrated in the Persian Empire (535 B.C.E.)—but more often dynastic change took place when the fragility of the rural social and ecological systems had already eroded the state's economic foundations. Under these circumstances even relatively minor external pressure, such as an attack by rival powers, could topple dynasties.

Basalt relief of a gazelle, Neo-Hittite, ninth century B.C.E., from Carchemish, southeastern Anatolia (modern-day Turkey); after the collapse of the Hittite Empire around 1200 B.C.E., Hittite culture survived in places such as Carchemish that had once been under Hittite control.

Major cities suffered during phases of settlement reduction and agricultural decline but usually survived. Cities were the custodians of divine worship, high culture, and learning, institutions that were quickly revitalized by new contenders to power who sought to be recognized and took up the traditional seats of rule. Nevertheless the archaeological record contains ample evidence for crises that disrupted a region's urban centers over and beyond its rural settlements. In many cases large cities were permanently abandoned, often with telltale signs of destruction in their final moments. Extreme instances reveal widespread breakdown—for example, the great collapse that occurred around 1200 B.C.E. when the Hittite capital, Hattusha, and the Syrian cities Emar and Ugarit (as well as many centers of Mycenaean Greece and Cyprus) were abandoned, never to be reoccupied. This and similar episodes clearly represent major disruptions in the development of human society. A comparable cycle of urban decay occurred at the transition from the Early to the Middle Bronze Age (ca. 2200–2000 B.C.E.).

Many of the theories proposed to account for collapses of this scale attribute them to external forces. Two factors, in particular, are often brought into the debate: abrupt climatic deterioration, leading to droughts and famines; and foreign invasion. Current consensus is that no single factor was decisive and that combinations of a variety of causes—external as well as internal—could lead to societal breakdown. Economic interdependency through trade networks explains how episodes of collapse could simultaneously affect large areas of the Near East and beyond.

Despite the fragility of the Near Eastern environment, agriculture, and settlement, ancient societies were remarkably successful in preserving their civilizations over time, an endurance that can be credited to the cities and their palace and temple resources. Only when the collapse of a state involved the total destruction of its urban centers—for example, during the fall of Assyria in 614–612 B.C.E.—was it possible to fully eradicate an ancient Near Eastern civilization.

ASIA AND THE PACIFIC

BY FRANCIS ALLARD

Asia and the Pacific region make up a large and culturally diverse area with a history marked by the rise of numerous states and empires, some of which display continuity with present-day nations. Less well known are the many archaeological cultures and polities that emerged as culturally and politically distinct entities but eventually collapsed or underwent transformation. Early instances of social collapse in Asia are evident in various areas and periods and exemplify some of the reasons scholars have proposed for collapsed societies, including environmental disturbances, social upheaval, military defeat, and even peaceful contact with other regions. It is important to note that the nature of the evidence—solely archaeological in the case of prehistoric cultures and archaeological and textual for the more historical polities—affects the type of interpretation proposed, with military conflict more likely to be advanced as the trigger to collapse for polities discussed in written sources. Also worth noting is the likelihood that the various names given by archaeologists to successive periods and cultures may not necessarily reflect dramatic instances of social collapse, concealing instead more gradual, but nevertheless significant social and political transformations.

The prehistory of the Korean peninsula and Japanese archipelago provides evidence of the long-term impact of external forces on local cultures, transformations that witnessed the abandonment of sites and undoubtedly challenged their social and political structures, although the details of such strains are difficult to identify in the archaeological record. In Korea the 6,000 years of the Chulmun (ca. 6000–ca. 1500 B.C.E.) and Mumun (ca. 1500–ca. 300 B.C.E.) periods were characterized by the presence of village life, the use of pottery, and a reliance on the products of fishing, hunting, and gathering. By the third millennium B.C.E. millet cultivation had been introduced from northeast China. Further reflecting the diffusion of ideas, skills, and even materials (for example, bronze daggers, and mirrors) from China, the Mumun Period is marked by intensification of agriculture, megalithic tombs, and greater social and political differentiation.

In Japan the Jōmon Period (13,000–300 B.C.E.) is similarly characterized by villages, pottery, a reliance on wild (nonagricultural) resources, and incipient agriculture. The succeeding Yayoi Period (300 B.C.E.–300 C.E.) points to a significant transformation of Jōmon society as the arrival of immigrants, styles, and ideas from the Korean peninsula was associated with the intensification of wet-rice agriculture, metallurgy, defensible sites, objects imported from the mainland (like mirrors), and an increasingly hierarchical society.

The Neolithic Period of mainland China, typified by the highly distinctive archaeological cultures known as Hongshan (ca. 4500–ca. 3000 B.C.E.) and Liangzhu (ca. 3200–ca. 2100 B.C.E.), provides clearer instances of apparent social and political collapse, though the absence of texts renders interpretations of the archaeological data highly tentative. Centered in northeast China, the Hongshan culture is characterized by what are believed to have been ceremonial centers (including so-called temples and altars), female figurines and statues, and large complex tombs. The grave goods include finely crafted jades (representing birds, clouds, turtles, and "pig dragons") that suggest the presence of elites. It is significant that by the middle of the third millennium B.C.E. these features had disappeared, and the number and size of residential sites had decreased.

Located along the coastal regions of central China, the Liangzhu culture shares with the Hongshan culture the presence of ceremonial centers and wealthy tombs whose exquisite jades (tubes, discs, bracelets, and pendants) point to control of production by an elite. At the end of the period Liangzhu residential sites, which were concentrated on riverbanks, were abandoned. The succeeding Maqiao culture (ca. 2100–ca. 1300 B.C.E.) is marked by a dramatic reduction in the number of sites and an almost complete disappearance of Liangzhu traits.

Explanations proposed to account for the collapse of Hongshan and Liangzhu include climatic change (associated with flooding in the case of Liangzhu) and an inability to manage economic resources efficiently. In addition, the elite of both cultures may have lost the support of their respective populations when workers felt they were not adequately rewarded for their efforts at producing the elite's symbols of power.

Instances of social growth and collapse become easier to chart over the course of the first millennium B.C.E., when increasingly detailed texts become available. This is especially true of the region encompassed by present-day China. During that region's Warring States Period (453–221 B.C.E.) numerous small states (Zhao, Shu, Chu, Yue, Han, Wei, Qi, Song, Lu, Yan, and Qin) emerged and suffered subsequent defeat through military conquest. The Qin Dynasty (221–207 B.C.E.), the eventual victor of this period of instability, was led by China's famous "First Emperor," an autocratic and firm ruler whose harsh treatment of detractors and forced conscription of laborers (used, for example, in the building of the Great Wall) led to popular uprisings and the downfall of the dynasty. The succeeding Han Dynasty (202 B.C.E.–220 C.E.) proved highly successful at expanding China's territory to reach close to its present-day borders, an increase in territory that, like the contemporaneous Roman Empire, led to contact with sometimes powerful foreign cultures. In the end the Han Dynasty would fall victim to internal rebellions and the problem of maintaining control over distant regions of its empire.

Not surprisingly, the territorial expansion of the Han Dynasty in eastern Asia was associated with the collapse of a number of preliterate and culturally distinctive polities, events that the Chinese recorded in their historical texts. Two examples pertaining to the Han's southern periphery illustrate this. First, the Dian culture (third century B.C.E. to first century C.E.), centered in southwestern China's Yunnan Province, is known for its highly distinctive and elaborate material culture, which includes bronze drums and cowry shell containers. Although the Chinese texts relate the defeat of the Dian by Han forces in 109 B.C.E., burial evidence points to the survival of Dian cultural traits for another century following its incorporation into the Han Dynasty. The second example is the Dongson culture, located in present-day North Vietnam and noted for its large bronze drums. The Dongson culture survived through much of the first millennium B.C.E., finally succumbing to the Han in 43 C.E. after an earlier defeat in 111 B.C.E. It is significant that Chinese cultural traits had already infiltrated Dongson culture by the second century B.C.E. The histories of the Dian and Dongson cultures signal the need to distinguish between military defeat and cultural decline in reference to "collapse."

Centered on the Indus Valley of Pakistan and northwestern India and represented by the large sites of Harappa and Mohenjo Daro, the Indus civilization (3000–1600 B.C.E.) provides a dramatic example of a flourishing South Asian culture as well as a fitting illustration of the complexities of societal collapse and transformation. Although the absence of clear textual references to the Indus civilization limits an understanding of its political structure and religious life, it nevertheless displays a range of features common to other civilizations of the ancient world, including urbanism (centers with streets, specialized quarters, amenities, public structures, and populations numbering in the tens of thousands), a writing system (as yet undeciphered), a system of weights and measures, long-distance trade (with Mesopotamia, among other regions), and craft specialization (bead making, metallurgy, shell working, weaving, and the like).

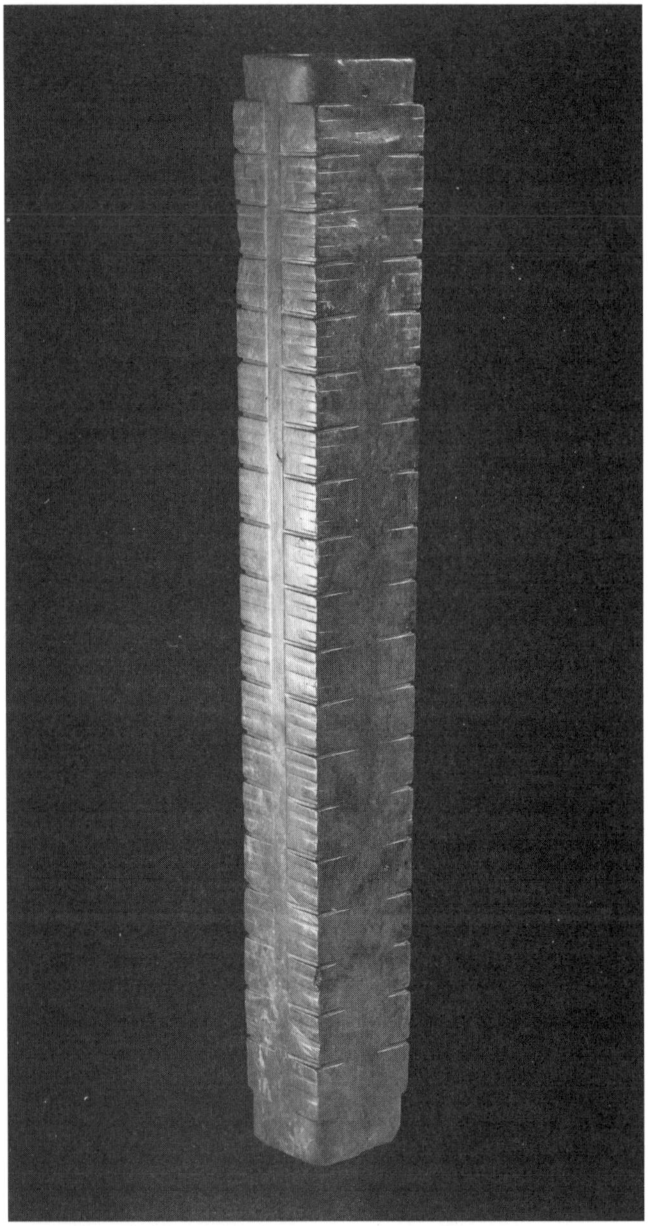

A burial jade carved with faces, from southern China, Neolithic Period, Liangzhu culture, around 2500 B.C.E.; tombs rich with jade objects were characteristic of this culture, whose sites were abandoned in the mid-third millennium B.C.E. (© The Trustees of the British Museum)

By the beginning of the second millennium B.C.E. it appears that both Harappa and Mohenjo Daro had stopped functioning as urban centers, a change paralleled by a reduction in the number of sites in a large sector of the region encompassed by the mature phase of the Indus civilization. This transition might represent a migration out of this area or a restructuring of the settlement pattern or both. The possible forces behind this change remain open to debate. They include the destruction of the civilization by invading Aryan peoples (mostly rejected, owing to an absence of clear evidence for such destruction at the sites themselves), the drying of the large Ghaggar-Hakra River, the decline of the trade system, and the flooding of a large area resulting from the formation of a natural dam.

Population and urban decline apparently characterized only a portion of the area encompassed by the Indus civilization, with some sectors experiencing continued growth during the second millennium B.C.E. Moreover, certain features of the Indus civilization appear to have been maintained throughout later periods. For example, Hinduism has retained some of the civilization's customs, such as ceremonial bathing, the importance of bulls and elephants, and Yogic positions. This illustration of the maintenance and transformation of cultural features over long periods underscores the need to disentangle the many strands subsumed under the term *societal collapse*.

EUROPE

BY JUSTIN CORFIELD

Throughout Europe traces exist of ancient settlements long ago abandoned. Sometimes the reason for this abandonment is known, but often it is not. Mobile hunter-gatherers lived in a spot for several weeks or months and then moved on, but they often returned to the same locations. Neolithic farmers lived in farmsteads and hamlets for decades. Sometimes they needed to shift their settlement locations owing to changes in their agricultural systems. Some archaeologists have speculated that settlements were abandoned when a lineage died out and no longer had an attachment to a particular location. Resource depletion of the surrounding countryside is another possible reason for abandoning ancient farming settlements. Occasionally warfare and raiding may have driven out the inhabitants of local settlements. Given the relatively simple organization, based on households and hamlets, of societies in Europe before about 2000 B.C.E., it is not really possible to speak of true social collapse on any large scale.

Rural farmsteads were the prevailing settlement form during the Bronze Age (ca. 2800–ca. 700 B.C.E.) and Iron Age (ca. 1000 B.C.E.–ca. 500 C.E.) in most of Europe, though some larger sites arose that could be considered villages. The settlement at Biskupin in Poland, built between 750 and 720 B.C.E., was inhabited by several hundred people but abandoned after several decades. The two major theories have been advanced for the abandonment of Biskupin and similar sites nearby. One is that rising water levels in the lakes that surrounded the peninsulas on which these sites were built forced the residents to leave. The other is that the local population was driven out by marauders, possibly Scythians from lands to the east, since some of the sites show traces of fire and Scythian-type arrowheads have been found in the archaeological deposits.

Farther north there have been studies of Iron Age settlements in Denmark. Some of these settlements may well have been more densely populated in ancient times than today. Many other sites appear to have been abandoned when the food supplies ran out or when the population increased to such a level that a new settlement had to be established.

Inhabitants of Bronze Age and Iron Age Britain and France built numerous hill forts. Very many of them are located in the southeast of England at sites that have never been populated since and that were clearly abandoned in ancient times. Because these settlements had low population densities and good agricultural land, it seems unlikely that they suffered from a lack of food crops. A more probable reason for their abandonment is social collapse following the emergence of a more powerful local group or federation. For example, the Celtic hill fort at Danebury, on the South Downs, England, near the river Test, was built from the sixth century B.C.E. and abandoned around 100 B.C.E. after what appears to have been an enemy attack—there is archaeological evidence that the east gate was burned down, and the remains of bodies were found in charnel pits.

On a much larger scale the Roman invasion of Gaul (which consisted essentially of present-day France, Belgium, and Germany and the Netherlands west of the Rhine River) under Julius Caesar in 58–51 B.C.E. brought widespread destruction of villages and towns. Many communities were wiped out. As a large number of those killed were men, many groups lacked the ability to collect the harvests, leading to collapse of their societies, with the result that Gaul remained the most quiescent of Roman provinces until the fall of Rome itself in the fifth century C.E. Similarly, military campaigns in Spain as part of a Roman civil war despoiled some of the country in 46–45 B.C.E. The civil war, which pitted Caesar against other powerful Romans and their armies, led to the destruction, temporarily, of many other cities across Roman-held territory, such as Massilia (modern-day Marseilles, France).

In Germany the Romans managed to seize the lands west of the Rhine, but even in the areas they did not control the Roman legions destroyed much of the infrastructure. In 9 C.E. the campaigns of the Germanic tribal leader Armin ("Arminius" to the Romans) and the Roman commander Varus spread mass destruction, though Armin and his forces all but annihilated three Roman legions at the battle of the Teutoburg Forest. Fighting continued for the next four years and then recurred sporadically from 17 until about 200 C.E.

In eastern Europe fighting between the Romans and such peoples as the Dacians and the Goths and later wars with the Bulgars led to the abandonment of many inland settlements, but a number of coastal ones remained, suggesting that the more isolated places were perhaps harder to defend and the coastal ones more easily reinforced or rebuilt. Certainly in Roman Britain, when the cities of Camulodunum (Colchester), Londinium (London), and Verulamium (Saint Albans) were destroyed during the revolt of the Iceni under Queen Boudicca in 60 C.E., the three cities were easily rebuilt on the same foundations; archaeologists have found a layer of ash in many places representing the destruction. Other cities flourished under the Romans but after the fall of the Western Roman Empire in 476 C.E. never regained their former wealth and size. Although most Roman cities have been built over and massively enlarged in the last 2,000 years, there are still some, such as Cirencester (Roman Corinium) in England, where the old city walls extend well beyond the current size of the town.

GREECE

BY SPYROS S. SIROPOULOS

Greece had never been a rich country. Small-scale agriculture, including the cultivation of olive trees, along with animal keeping and fishing were the basis of its population's nutrition. The scarce natural resources were balanced by a favorable climate that allowed the Greeks to remain outdoors for most of the year to cultivate the earth and to engage in trade and seafaring. To make most of the natural resources, large parts of the country's population did not inhabit the famous civic centers of antiquity but instead lived permanently in the countryside. In a typical city-state the polis, or city, was the decision-making center; a relatively small agricultural area called the *chóra* lay outside the polis and included a number of smaller settlements called *kómai*. A fine balance was formed between the city and the *kómai*: The civic way of life and the stability and growth of the civic community were sustained and secured by the provisions from the agricultural settlements.

This delicate balance could easily be upset in the ancient world. The mass desertion of rural settlements, with all the catastrophic repercussions for neighboring cities, could occur for various reasons, including natural causes, economic or political causes, and war.

Because people depended upon the climate to produce the maximum of the land's potential, any unpredicted natural catastrophe, such as a flood, prolonged draught, fire, or earthquake, could drive the people to abandon the countryside and move to cities to earn a living. Civic communities were not always prepared to handle such events. It was easy for agricultural problems to become social problems if the city could not compensate the devastated farmers or provide alternative ways to incorporate them into the broader social mechanism. In some cases extreme situations called for extreme solutions. The Greek historian Herodotus (ca. 484–ca. 425 B.C.E.) describes the case of the small island of Thíra in the fourth century B.C.E. Unable to provide for the needy farmers or to handle the political and social tension created by the dissatisfied citizens, the state of Thíra sent a large population to colonize another territory. The state released a decree that prohibited the colonists from returning to Thíra before five years had elapsed. In this case the successful colony of Cyrene was founded in northern Africa. Between 750 and 550 B.C.E. colonization became a common way to diffuse internal social tension and to divert the surplus of a city's male population outside the society.

The economic and social organization of the city-states were closely connected to the way a given city handled the economic and political crises that manifested toward the end of the Homeric Period (ca. 1600–ca. 1100 B.C.E.). Rapid population growth and the inability of city governments to redistribute land satisfactorily led to social unrest. Sparta tried to solve this problem by waging war on other regions to gain more land, the Athenians encouraged trade, and most cities turned to colonization. The demand for greater amounts of raw materials or agricultural products and the heavy taxation of farmers often drove farming communities to desperation. In the Hellenistic Period (323–31 B.C.E.) the abandonment of the countryside (a phenomenon the Greeks called *anahorisis*) became an economic and political problem for the Ptolemaic Dynasty of Egypt. The first rulers of this dynasty tried to expand their power by rapidly developing their naval economy; for this they demanded heavy taxes from farmers. Consequently, the farmers deserted the countryside and sought guidance and protection at the local temples, thereby upsetting both the local Greek economy and the intentions of the Ptolemaic kingdom.

War is an obvious reason for the abandonment of rural settlements. Farmers, woodsmen, goatherds, and inhabitants of small fishing villages often were forced to seek protection behind the walls of a nearby city with the advent of war. This was bad for the city in two ways. First, the city was deprived of the replenishment of natural goods upon which the civic population depended for sustenance. This was the intended result of a prolonged siege on a strong, fortified city: to exhaust the resources and compel the citizens to surrender.

Second, other practical problems arose from an unpredicted overpopulation. The Greek historian Thucydides (d. ca. 401 B.C.E.) describes how a plague was added to the problems of the Athenians during the Peloponnesian War (431–404 B.C.E.). Pericles (ca. 495–425 B.C.E.), the leader of the democratic party in Athens at the time, had thought that the famous "long walls," the fortification that connected Athens with Piraeus, would secure the country's population. He also thought that the walls would enable the city to communicate undisturbed with the vital harbor of Piraeus during the siege, thereby replenishing its products and withstanding the Spartans' siege. But Pericles had not provided for proper housing for all of these refugees. In 430 B.C.E. the inevitable pestilence, caused by a lack of elementary hygiene and the concentration of thousands of people, wiped out more than a quarter of the population of Athens. Among the victims of the pestilence were Thucydides' family and Pericles himself.

War puts a stop to the development of a society in more than one way. In the western plain of Boeotia there was a marshy lake called Copais that was a source of illnesses. The Minyae, a native people of the 13th and 14th centuries B.C.E., had tried to drain the lake to provide arable land for the local farmers. This ambitious plan was stopped because of a war with Orchomenus.

Some historians see a definite connection between the collapse of the Mycenaean society around 1100 B.C.E. and the formation of cities. When the Mycenaean civilization, also known as the Palace civilization, collapsed and the Dorians colonized Greece, many important social changes took place. People ceased being dependent upon the prosperity of palaces and stopped living in small settlements around them. This and the repopulation of the countryside led to the formation of the first cities, marking the beginning of a new social and political era for Greece. The interdependence between social order and the agricultural economy of Greece was a defining factor in the development of Greek cities throughout antiquity.

ROME

BY CHRISTOPHER BLACKWELL

The third century C.E. was a time of social crisis for the Roman Empire even as the emperors completed some of the most striking and enduring monuments to Roman greatness. From 193 to 312 C.E. the Column of Marcus Aurelius, the Arch of Septimius Severus, the Baths of Caracella, the Aurelian Walls, and the Basilica of Maxentius were added to the splendor of the city of Rome. Also during this period the death of the emperor Commodus (r. 180–192 C.E.) led to the chaotic "Year of Four Emperors" (193 C.E.), the emperor Severus (r. 193–211 C.E.) died campaigning in Britain, Ardashīr I (r. 224–241 C.E.) took the throne of Iran and began a war with Rome that would continue for 400 years, and Rome and its provinces suffered invasions from Goths, Heruli, and other Germanic groups. The entire Mediterranean world suffered from a recession in trade, and prices soared. Despite the Constitutio Antoniniana, or Constitution of Antoninus (r. 211–217 C.E.), issued in 212 C.E.—a law that granted universal citizenship to all free men living under Roman rule—the population of Rome was neither growing nor harmonious;

birthrates declined, and communities were wracked by official and unofficial persecutions of the Christians, a new but growing religious minority.

By 280 C.E. these pressures came close to destroying Rome, but a new and strong emperor, Diocletian (r. 284–305 C.E.), took office in 284. For the 23 years of his reign and the 31 years of his successor, the emperor Constantine (r. 306–337 C.E.), imperial policies both averted immediate collapse and perhaps ensured that it would eventually occur.

Diocletian attempted to take control of the economic crisis by putting strict control on the prices of certain goods, which prompted farmers, artisans, and merchants simply to stop dealing in those goods. When Constantine tried to increase trade and commerce by distributing gold from the Roman temples, inflation increased even more dramatically. Under Diocletian the bureaucracy of the Roman Empire was split in two, east and west, and Constantine reacted to the pressures of foreign invasion by virtually eliminating the authority of the Senate, thereby putting all power into the emperor's hands, and by building up the army. These changes did allow Rome to ward off invasion, but they also had immediate consequences for Roman society.

Diocletian's splitting of the empire doubled the weight of bureaucracy. Always prone to corruption, the now more numerous civil officials became generally more rapacious. Citizens found themselves subject to extortion or required to pay bribes to secure basic services such as protection under the law. In succeeding years, the emperors' various efforts to crack down on corruption only made matters worse. Officials came to realize that they could lose their jobs at any time, and they reacted by trying to amass as much illicit profit from their positions as they could before being caught.

New laws against usury, which began during Constantine's reign, had a similarly paradoxical effect. These laws forbade lending money at exorbitant interest, and they were passed as the result of influence from Roman Christians. But citizens still needed to lend money, and bankers continued to make loans. Under the new laws, however, a lender could not expect the courts to support claims against debtors who defaulted on loans. This increased the risk to the lender, which led creditors to charge ever-higher rates of interest. The common citizens suffered accordingly.

Constantine's efforts to consolidate military power under the emperor and to defeat the invasions of groups from northern Europe, while largely successful, held long-term consequences for Roman society. In Constantine's army increasingly more legions, and eventually all of the most effective legions, were composed of soldiers from the very Germanic peoples that Rome was resisting. These soldiers served and became Roman citizens, some of them reaching high military and civil office, and introduced new cultural elements into Roman society.

The rise of Christianity had other effects on Roman culture. For example, in the middle of the fourth century C.E. the Greek prelate Gregory of Nyssa (ca. 335–ca. 394 C.E.) published tracts arguing, from a Christian perspective, against the institution of slavery. While enslaved people revolted numerous times and earlier philosophers had argued against the cruel treatment of slaves, Gregory is the earliest example of any writer from the Greco-Roman world suggesting that slavery was, in itself, an evil institution. The economic consequences of a rejection of slavery, by the late Roman Empire, may not have been great, but such a radical rethinking of a universal social institution was destabilizing. Similar Christian arguments against capital punishment and aggressive wars drove wedges between the Christian and non-Christian populations.

Coins from the Hoxne hoard, Roman Britain, buried in the fifth century C.E. and found in Hoxne, Suffolk; the hoard is thought to have been buried for safekeeping during difficult times for the Roman British, who were left without any help from the Roman Empire to defend themselves from the attacks of the barbarians. (© The Trustees of the British Museum)

As the official institutions of Rome became dominated by Christians and, after Constantine, officially Christian, divisions within the faith continued to disrupt society at all levels. Starting in the fourth century C.E. a series of schisms between Orthodox Christianity (whose definition changed decade by decade) and various alternative sects, branded heretical by defenders of orthodoxy, often brought legislation to a standstill and repeatedly sparked riots in all the major cities of the Roman world. Nestorians, Monophysites, Donatists, Monothelites, and Arians all differed in theology (sometimes only by exceedingly fine points of doctrine), but each claimed to represent true Christianity. Each sect argued, legislated, and fought against the others whenever and wherever they could.

During the fourth and fifth centuries imperial power grew weak and dispersed. The city of Rome itself became less hospitable as the mouth of the river Tiber silted up and became a malarial marsh. The center of political activity in Italy moved to Ravenna and Milan. Constantinople, the splendid new capital, became less involved in affairs to the west and increasingly Greek in its language and customs. New generations of

THE DEATH AND REBIRTH OF THE LATIN LANGUAGE

Augustine of Hippo (354–430 C.E.) and Jerome (ca. 347–419 or 420 C.E.) were the last two masters of the classical Roman literary tradition. Both of these writers, while writing on Christian topics, were steeped in the Latin of Cicero (106–43 B.C.E.), Virgil (70–19 B.C.E.), and other writers of classical Latin. As early as the fifth century C.E., however, the Latin language had begun to split apart. In some quarters people tried to preserve the classical language by continuing to write in an elaborate style; works such as those of Martianus Capella (fourth to fifth century C.E.), a Vandal writing in Carthage around 470, are full of allusions to classical literature. In other quarters, local dialects became more pronounced, beginning as early as the fourth century C.E. Egeria, a woman who made a pilgrimage from Spain to Jerusalem in 384 C.E., left a diary that shows a version of Latin that would have been hard for a classical Roman to understand.

The elaborate system of Latin grammar became simplified, and its verbs became more regular. By the seventh century the language of Italy resembled medieval Italian more than classical Latin. In the eighth century in formerly Roman parts of France, the definite article (*the*) first appears as *lo, la, lis*, moving toward modern French's *le, la, les*.

In the western part of the former empire Latin survived as a tool that allowed scholars and church officials to communicate with each other. As a means for communicating with the common people, it died by the ninth century when, in 813 C.E., a decree from the bishop of Tours forbade sermons in Latin, which the common people could no longer understand.

rulers, while considering themselves Roman, were more likely to be Gothic or Germanic in ethnicity and culture. For ordinary people, the Roman Empire was no longer the organizing institution, upholder of laws, or guarantor of security. Ecclesiastical institutions (churches and monasteries) and ecclesiastical officers (priests, monks, abbots, and bishops) were more likely to take over local government and play central roles in local economies.

So, for example, Apollinaris Sidonius (ca. 430–487 or 488 C.E.), from Lugdunum in Gaul, grew up in an aristocratic Roman family and married a Roman woman whose father, Avitus (r. 455–456 C.E.), would eventually become a Roman emperor. But his political career ended when Avitus was killed and Apollinaris Sidonius became bishop of Auvergne. There he dedicated his life to writing histories of Roman emperors. His numerous letters reveal, however, that he was not, in fact, preserving a corner of Rome (as he believed) but governing a small, independent fragment of a collapsed empire.

THE AMERICAS

BY KEITH JORDAN

Several episodes of cultural and political change in the ancient Americas fit modern definitions of social collapse—the breaking down of a complex (by modern Western standards) sociopolitical arrangement into what look like simpler or more chaotic systems. We must be careful, however. *Collapse* carries a negative connotation, but ancient peoples may not necessarily have experienced these changes as negative or as forced upon them. Nor can we cling to discredited theories of cultural evolution, claiming that societies develop toward greater complexity (often defined in Western terms) and that a change in the opposite direction constitutes disaster. Finally, since we lack written records for any of these developments in the ancient Americas, our reconstructions from archaeological data are always speculative and tentative and may be invalidated when the next major find is unearthed.

In the North American Midwest the Hopewell culture (200 B.C.E.–400 C.E.)—more accurately described as a ritual and burial complex linked by trade networks—seems to have vanished by 400 C.E. No more Hopewell burial mounds or ceremonial centers were constructed, and the trade networks linking areas as distant as the Rocky Mountains and the Gulf Coast ceased to bring exotic materials to Ohio and Illinois sites. Pottery decoration became less elaborate and objects included in graves simpler and scantier. Societies seem to have become more egalitarian: No longer do burials include a very few with especially rich items, suggesting the existence of an elite.

Some archaeologists once believed that a shift toward cooler weather in the Midwest around 300 C.E. spurred the decline of the Hopewell phenomenon by making it difficult to grow the corn on which the culture supposedly relied for food. However, we now know that Native Americans in the Hopewell areas did not start growing corn on a large scale until five centuries after Hopewell culture disappeared, and there is no firm evidence for the alleged climate shift. On the contrary, in the centuries following the Hopewell "collapse" the peoples of eastern North America became more dependent on corn agriculture, leading to growing populations, bigger settlements, and ultimately the rise of the complex Mississippian cultures (900–1600 C.E.) with their huge towns, massive mounds, and powerful chiefs.

Other proposed reasons for the disappearance of the Hopewell include economic factors. In one theory trade networks collapsed because Native Americans in the southeast started to work local copper deposits instead of relying on copper mined in the Lake Superior region. But the archaeological evidence indicates that Lake Superior copper was mined and widely traded up to the European invasion in the

17th century. Another factor implicated in the Hopewell decline is increased warfare. War does seem to have become more common after roughly 500 C.E., but this may be the result of the increase in population and rise of chiefs with the adoption of corn farming after Hopewell's demise, rather than being the cause of that demise. Some late Hopewell structures once thought to be forts are now regarded as ritual centers. Similarly, although use of the bow and arrow became more common after 500 C.E., we cannot say that its introduction increased warfare and led to the Hopewell decline—the weapon may have been used for centuries before this time. Ultimately the disappearance of the Hopewell culture remains a mystery.

Another mystery confronts us near the Gulf Coast of southern Mexico, where the Olmec political and religious center of San Lorenzo flourished between 1500 and 1200 B.C.E. Its rulers erected monumental images of themselves and conducted trade in exotic materials with other ruling groups across Mesoamerica. Around 1200 B.C.E. the creation of monumental sculpture seems to have ceased, and the palaces of the rulers were abandoned. Although San Lorenzo itself was not abandoned at that time, its influence over the Gulf Coast and other parts of Mesoamerica ended. When the site was excavated in the 1960s, finds of broken statues seemed to suggest destruction by foreign invaders or by a revolution of local farmers against their kings, whose statues they purposely smashed. However, more recent excavations reveal that the broken statues simply represent the recycling of the monuments of previous kings into new ones by artists working for their successors. Recent geological evidence indicates shifts in the courses of the rivers surrounding the site, possibly as a result of silt buildup from erosion after the Olmec cut down forests to clear land for agriculture. These changes may have damaged the local environment and interfered with trade and travel.

Whatever the reason for San Lorenzo's decline, La Venta, to the east, succeeded it as the dominant Olmec center. La Venta flourished from 1200 B.C.E. to around 400 B.C.E.—after which it, too, collapsed and was abandoned. At this same time Olmec civilization itself began to fade, developing into the so-called Epi-Olmec culture (ca. 400 B.C.E.–250 C.E.). Like San Lorenzo's demise, La Venta's may have been related to the silting of adjacent rivers, whether due to natural factors (even a volcanic eruption) or to the effects of agriculture. But that would not explain why the culture itself disappeared or why the population of the eastern half of the Olmec Gulf Coast dropped drastically around the same time. Nor can we say that the Epi-Olmec culture represents a decline. This culture created sophisticated art and played an important role in the development of hieroglyphic writing and the calendar in Mesoamerica, influencing the Maya. It was hardly decadent, as some archaeologists have described it.

A third mystery of social collapse and abandonment exists in South America. Sometime around 2700 B.C.E. inhabitants of the Peruvian coast began building huge ceremonial structures in U-shaped arrangements. They continued this practice for more than 2,000 years. Then, in the early first millennium B.C.E., it came to an end. Few new large coastal cities were built between about 900 B.C.E. and 600 B.C.E., and construction at many existing sites ground to a halt. Large settlements were abandoned, sometimes reoccupied by small groups of squatters who left their rubbish in the deserted temples. Where new construction took place, as on the north-central coast, the old U-shaped pyramid groups were replaced by labyrinthine arrangements of smaller structures, and fortifications became increasingly common. Meanwhile, religious influences from the highland site of Chavín de Huántar made their appearance, supplanting the long-dominant coastal traditions.

The mechanism for these changes remains poorly understood. The religious system that led to the creation of the U-shaped enclosures suddenly lost its influence and prestige, but why is unclear. Invasions from the highlands have been suggested as a cause, but there is no solid evidence for this. Conflict might have broken out between priestly leaders and their followers in the relatively egalitarian coastal cultures—especially if those leaders tried to emulate the new class of hereditary nobles that seems to have arisen in highland cultures at the same time. Finally, there is evidence that an El Niño climatic event in the middle of the first millennium B.C.E. created catastrophic flooding and killed off much of the cool-water marine life on which coastal folk depended for much of their food supply.

See also AGRICULTURE; BORDERS AND FRONTIERS; CITIES; CLIMATE AND GEOGRAPHY; ECONOMY; EMPIRES AND DYNASTIES; EMPLOYMENT AND LABOR; FAMILY; FOOD AND DIET; FOREIGNERS AND BARBARIANS; GOVERNMENT ORGANIZATION; HEALTH AND DISEASE; LANGUAGE; LAWS AND LEGAL CODES; LITERATURE; MIGRATION AND POPULATION MOVEMENTS; MILITARY; MINING, QUARRYING, AND SALT MAKING; NATURAL DISASTERS; NOMADIC AND PASTORAL SOCIETIES; RELIGION AND COSMOLOGY; SETTLEMENT PATTERNS; SLAVES AND SLAVERY; SOCIAL ORGANIZATION; TOWNS AND VILLAGES; TRADE AND EXCHANGE; WAR AND CONQUEST.

FURTHER READING

Robert McC. Adams, "Strategies of Maximization, Stability, and Resilience in Mesopotamian Society, Settlement, and Agriculture," *Proceedings of the American Philosophical Society* 122, no. 5 (1978): 329–335.

Gina Barnes, *China, Korea, and Japan: The Rise of Civilization in East Asia* (New York: Thames and Hudson, 1993).

Carlos E. Cordova, "The Degradation of the Ancient Near Eastern Environment." In *A Companion to the Ancient Near East*, ed. Daniel C. Snell (Oxford, U.K.: Blackwell, 2005).

Roland Enmarch, *The Dialogue of Ipuwer and the Lord of All* (Oxford, U.K.: Griffith Institute/Alden Press, 2005).

K. A. Kitchen, *The Third Intermediate Period in Egypt (1100–650 B.C.)*, 2nd ed. (Warminster, U.K.: Aris and Phillips, 1986).

social organization

INTRODUCTION

The topic of social organization speaks in many ways of why people study ancient history. It speaks of the vast possibilities of the human imagination, revealing that there have been and still are many solutions to the problems human beings have faced over their existence. Some solutions have been successful, helping cultures survive for hundreds or thousands of years, while other solutions have been unsuccessful, resulting in the decline and extinctions of some cultures.

The sheer variety of social organizations is in itself an attraction to modern readers, but there are practical reason for looking at ancient ways societies organized themselves. One reason is highly personal, belonging to each individual student of ancient life: Ancient social organizations can help tell people why they are here and why they are living as they are. Many problems the individual person faces in modern society are not new. For instance, when a modern Western woman wonders why she faces social barriers in the business world, she may wonder about the truth of the common notion that her biology has fated her to a difficult career. She need only study the ways of ancient Sumer to see that a society in which women could have equal opportunities with men is possible, because it has existed. Further, she can discover how civilizations evolved to restrict her opportunities. Knowing why she is where she is can be spiritually liberating—reason enough to study ancient social organizations. Beyond that, there may be clues to why the culture of Mesopotamia changed from one where women were social equals with or even superior to men to one in which women were treated as less than human, as in the Neo-Assyrian culture. From that understanding can come ideas for solutions to her modern difficulties, because she will have learned that society changes and that creative minds can be the agents of change.

When human societies began to form, they were almost certainly kinship groups, composed of parents, their children, siblings, and cousins. Even within such close groups, there had to be rules of conduct. For instance, the young had to learn to be respectful of their elders for the very good reason that they would die without their parents' knowledge of how to survive. The larger social organizations that emerged with larger groups of people probably had that imperative: survival. In ever-larger social groups there are greater opportunities for the young to learn from their elders and a better chance of being cared for if sick or injured. Still, larger social groups mean more chances for conflict among people. Many ancient social organizations were created in part to find ways in which people could conduct their lives without harming or being harmed by others in their groups.

With the development of agriculture, the need for social rules that were organized in a manner that most people could understand became more important. Agriculture gave human beings an enormously greater opportunity to survive childhood by making the food supply more reliable and regular than it had been previously. The chances for survival increased even more if people found ways to manage their harvests so that they could eat well during seasons when food would normally be scarce, and those chances could increase further if they found a way to manage their harvests so that they did not starve during years of drought or other disasters that caused poor harvests. Such management of harvests required progressively more complex rules for storage and distribution of food. Some societies became very successful at management of food supplies. For instance, Egypt's granaries kept its people fed through lean times as well as fat times for thousands of years. Cultures that mismanaged food or kept food supplies to a small minority of elites faced uprisings, as China did, or collapse of their economies, as the ancient Maya did.

It is perhaps part of human nature that people, whatever their stations in their societies, wish to share in the benefits of their cultures. Good clothes, good food, and good schooling seem to be desired in almost any culture, yet rarely are there enough supplies of anything that everyone can share in. To deal with the problem, cultures have devised various solutions. In many cultures outright repression holds society together, with those in charge of the armies controlling the benefits of society. In others, it is religion. In ancient India religious doctrine developed in such detail that every person could know what he of she was supposed to do throughout life. Who shared in which benefits was determined by birth and explained by a doctrine that held that people were born into certain social groups because of the good and evil they had done in previous lives. The hope for a better life lay in fulfilling one's duties in the present life, providing motivation for one to contribute to society in the role allotted. The notion of being able to improve one's life has been a safety valve for many cultures.

When reading about social organization, look for how rigid the organization was as well as for the ways in which it was flexible. This requires thought, because a culture might, in theory, have very strict rules for organization but, like ancient India, be somewhat flexible in how the rules were actually applied. Then, too, look at how much a society allowed for social mobility. Even for someone who had no realistic chance of improving his or her life, just having the possibility for improvement could be a powerful motivator, one that could encourage people to be industrious and faithful to the organization of their society because the organization gave them hope. It can be enlightening to see how cultures with long histories, such as ancient Egypt and China, organized and reorganized themselves to cope with changes in environment, technology, and their neighbors. Perhaps some of what they did still has value for the modern age.

AFRICA

BY LEAH A. J. COHEN

Many factors contributed to the forms of social organization in ancient Africa, including environmental and climatic conditions that affected animal and plant resources as well as social, political, and livelihood characteristics. Common social structures during this ancient period in history grouped people by family, lineage, kinship, clan, and tribe. Later there were social structures based on caste or trade (occupation). The political systems that existed in ancient Africa are often categorized into three distinct forms: stateless societies, centralized city-states, and centralized kingdoms or empires (although not all human groups fit so neatly in these three categories). People in early ancient Africa lived primarily by hunting and gathering or fishing and harvesting of aquatic resources. Changes in the climatic conditions over time led to mass migrations and changes in ways of surviving that resulted in the widespread development of societies based on pastoralism, agriculture, and eventually skilled trades.

Nomadic Hunter-Gatherer Groups

Around 10,000 years ago (at the start of the Holocene), the climate was becoming increasingly moist as much of Africa entered a humid period that would last until around 4,000 years ago. At least during the early part of this humid phase most human groups in Africa were engaged in nomadic hunting and gathering activities in which they occupied no single location permanently. This ancient wetter African landscape, which included the Sahara, provided ample resources to support this lifestyle. Furthermore, population densities were low, meaning that there was relatively little competition for animal and plant resources.

While the specific characteristics of social structure for hunter-gatherer groups certainly varied based on culture and location, the archaeological record indicates some common structures. Hunter-gatherers were generally organized into small bands. Given the existing archaeological evidence, it is difficult to know the size of these ancient groups; modern hunter-gatherer groups range from 20 to 60 people. Although there was a richer natural resource base, which might have affected the size of these groups, ancient groups would nevertheless have been relatively small because of their need to move from place to place, at least seasonally, to follow the water, plant, and animal resources that sustained them. Physical evidence from burial sites shows a lack of material objects, since the nomadic lifestyle left little time for the accumulation of material wealth. This evidence is interpreted as indicating that there was little social or political stratification within ancient hunter-gatherer groups compared with later, more settled or sedentary agricultural and pastoral groups.

In contrast, burial sites of the elite class in more hierarchical societies, such as ancient Egypt, are bigger, more elaborate, and filled with more nonessential items compared with those of non-elite members of society. Archaeological records also show few differences in size and condition of individual homes in ancient hunter-gatherer sites (unlike more socially hierarchical societies), and this lack of difference indicates little social stratification.

One problem with archaeological evidence is that while it can speak about the material characteristics of ancient hunter-gatherers, material wealth might not be the only basis for social stratification. There might have been ancient hunter-gatherer societies in which social hierarchy was based on hunting skill or the ability to communicate with deceased ancestors rather than on material objects, but these bases for status are more difficult to detect in the archaeological record.

To supplement archaeological evidence, travel records of European, Arab, or Mediterranean explorers and traders have been used to shed light on ancient human groups. However, these records describe the social situations of African groups only after foreigners entered Africa (around the fifth century C.E. for Arabs and the 15th century C.E. for Portuguese), and they were certainly colored by the worldview of the writers. In addition, many assumptions made about social organization of ancient hunter-gatherer groups are based on the study of modern hunter-gatherer groups. If modern groups can be used as a window into the life of ancient hunter-gatherers, a much more complete picture of social organization can be painted. One criticism of this commonly accepted technique of exploring the lives of ancient hunter-gatherers is that many aspects of life for ancient hunter-gatherers—for example, climate and available resources—were too different to make accurate assumptions.

Ethnographic studies of modern hunter-gatherers indicate that labor is divided according to gender and age, a feasible division for ancient hunter-gatherers as well. Based on these studies of modern groups it is thought that women were primarily responsible for gathering the wild roots, tubers, berries, and plants that made up the majority of the daily diet, and men were responsible for hunting to provide meat on a periodic basis. Because women carried young children long distances and breast-fed them for long periods (which often served to limit population growth), there were probably long periods of time between the birth of each child that allowed the women to do the gathering.

Hunter-gatherer bands were composed of several families often related by lineage (descendants of one common ancestor). Lineage systems are a more specific type of kinship group in which individuals and families are organized by bloodlines, often traced back to the group's founding ancestor. Today these lineages are most commonly patrilineal (familial connections and lines of descent recognized through the father's bloodline) or matrilineal (familial connections and lines of descent recognized through the mother's bloodline), although there are rare cases today where social systems recognize both lines of descent. In more hierarchical lineage systems, individuals with closer links to the founding ancestor are often granted more decision-making power. In a lineage system a council of elders is often responsible (to varying degrees) for the group decisions. It is difficult to know what importance lineage had for early hunter-gatherers and how strongly it influenced the system of hierarchy they lived within.

Lineages have often been the basis by which individuals have access to resources and groups. In traditional hunter-gathering bands, lineage determines whether individuals remain with their birth group or migrate to another group. When young men leave their parents' group to find their mates, the culture is called matrilocal; when young women leave their parents' group to live with their mates' band, the culture is referred to as patrilocal. This kind of social organization serves to diversify the gene pool and keep bands small. Bands also might have split in ancient Africa once a critical threshold for population was reached, a threshold possibly created by whether resources were available.

Although lineage is a type of kinship system, not all kinship systems are necessarily based on genetic descent. Hunter-gatherer and later agro-pastoral groups could have also been organized based on more generalized kinship relations not necessarily rooted in blood relations. In some kinship systems, subgroups have differential degrees of influence over the entire society. All societies have underlying kinship groups, but the degree to which they are the basis of organization and structure varies considerably.

Early hunter-gatherer groups often are referred to as acephalous societies, meaning they had no centralized, specialized political leader, such as a chief or a king. Informal leaders might have emerged based on skill and accomplishment, but these leaders are thought to have had little absolute control and to have led more by group support than coercion, force, or intimidation. Decisions might have been made on a consensus basis by all group members or with heads of families having a stronger vote. Consensus-based decision making was possible because of the small size of the groups.

Emergence of Sedentary Societies

At some point in the ancient period human groups began to experiment with domestication of animals and plants in northern Africa. The exact dates for the origins of farming and herding are not certain, since many of the early steps toward domestication of animals and plants are not detected in the archaeological record. What is detectable in the record is that increased reliance on agriculture led to more sedentary lifestyles, since agriculture requires farmers to remain in one location for at least one crop season. Once humans started manipulating the land, they realized the benefits of staying in one spot and were able to improve their ability to grow the food they needed where they needed it.

One of the earliest examples of sedentary villages is the site of Nabta Playa (western deserts of southern Egypt), some 62 miles west of the Nile River. Nabta Playa is the site of a village with permanent houses from as early as 8,000 years ago that were formally organized around a "street." This village had wells and granaries to store food; although in the beginning the majority of their diet still came from wild animals and plants, evidence of domestic animals appears as early as 7,000 years ago, and agriculture may have been adopted as early as 6,500 years ago. There are some who believe that human groups may have experimented with agro-pastoral activities in the Nile Valley prior to the Holocene.

Although many (but not all) human groups would eventually rely mostly or only on farming or herding, the transition from hunting and gathering to farming and herding was gradual, and there were long periods during which human groups continued to rely on all of these activities simultaneously. Changes in climatic conditions were instrumental in the spread and eventual dominance of herding and farming activities. Around 4,000 years ago the African continent began to dry out, which forced human groups to migrate out of the increasingly dry Sahara region into the Sahel and the oases around rivers and lakes. When people moved out of the desert areas, more and more people were compressed into smaller and smaller areas, which further encouraged development of herding and farming activities as the climate change brought a decrease in wild animals and plants. Adoption of herding and farming moved south and east, eventually reaching southern Africa around 2,000 years ago with the mass migration of the Bantu farmers across the continent that started around 1000 B.C.E. In general, in the densely forested areas of central Africa, hunting and gathering persisted much longer.

This change in livelihood strategies had profound effects on the population and organization of human groups. When human groups became more sedentary and skilled in herding and farming, populations grew even more, and people had the opportunity to accumulate material objects and build permanent structures. The increased importance of a specific area of land led to ownership of property, which in turn led to the development of rules and laws to enforce ownership rights. Over time, increases in population densities and accumulation of material possessions led to labor specialization and more and more complex social organization. Competition for resources, wealth, and social status started to increase in importance and affect social organization through the dictation of alliances based on a variety of relationships, not just family, lineage, and kinship.

Anthropologists, using more modern human groups to draw conclusions about ancient cultures, often apply E. E. Evans-Pritchard's term *segmentary societies* (coined in 1940 for his study of groups in southern Sudan) to ancient agricultural human groups. This term is commonly used to describe societies that are subdivided into groups based on kinship that are relatively equal in status. Segmentary societies are often led by elders, and participation in the collective decisions and activities is accomplished through relationships with these elders.

Another ancient system of governance and stratification was based on the power an individual was granted as a result of the size of the group loyal to him or her (that is, patron-client relationships). Kinship-based societies might have had this type of organization, which brought more (but not necessarily absolute) power over decisions affecting the entire society to individuals who had larger families or more "clients" that pledged loyalty to them.

Centrally Organized Hierarchical Societies

The ancient civilization of Nubia in present-day Sudan and part of southern Egypt (also known as Kush during certain periods) formed around 3100 B.C.E. This area came under Egyptian rule between 2000 and 1000 B.C.E. and as such is outside the terms of this discussion, but for much of its history it was autonomous from Egypt. (Nubia even governed Egypt from around 800 to 700 B.C.E.) From about 900 B.C.E. this civilization was based on a divine kingship, which developed from a loosely related collective of locally governed human groups. This might have been partly due to the nature of their livelihoods as nomadic pastoralists and the low population density of the region. Women appear to have had an important role in Nubian culture. Nubian queens were depicted in art as defending the nation's interests, and in religion the cult of the goddess Isis was widespread. The Nubians developed a system of writing and were also known for their skilled warrior bowmen.

The great African kingdom of Axum (present-day Ethiopia, northeastern Africa) emerged as a city-state during the first century C.E. and dominated trade in the Red Sea by around the third century C.E. This state was another centrally organized, hierarchical, sociopolitical system. The king was the leader of the political, military, and religious systems. Axum was founded in the Ethiopian highlands, which at the time was fertile ground where agricultural innovations such as terracing and the ox-drawn plow increased productivity. This civilization developed an indigenous written script, engaged in extensive trade with Arabia, and issued its own coinage. Axum gained control over other lands (including ancient Nubia) and, at the height of the empire, there was a firmly established elite class whose members surrounded themselves with luxury goods from Axum and beyond.

Less Centrally Organized and Less Hierarchical Societies

Urban societies that appear from archaeological evidence to have been less centrally governed also existed in Africa. One example is the settlement of Jenne-jeno, which appeared sometime in the third century B.C.E. in Mali (West Africa) near the modern town of Djenné. (It reached its height around 900 C.E. in the medieval period.) Despite the apparent lack of centralized governance and rigid hierarchy, the city grew to be very densely populated with houses situated very close together, and there may have been a centralized marketplace. Households were often organized based on trade (farming, metallurgy, fishing, and ceramics). Other than the location of housing, dedication to a specific craft did not seem to indicate any hierarchical status.

It is thought that many of the pastoralists, agriculturalists, and fishermen in the region around Jenne-jeno had moved from the drying-out Sahara. West African rice became an important agricultural product. Houses were made of mud bricks. Despite numerous human groups in the region and different ethnic backgrounds, centralized, rigid hierarchical political systems did not prevail in the Niger delta. Archaeologists typically look for evidence of monumental architecture as one of the main signs of a political system ruled by one person or a relatively small group of wealthy individuals. Sites in the Niger delta offer no such evidence (with the exception of the wall surrounding the city of Jenne-jeno, which has been interpreted somewhat tentatively as a defensive structure to protect the city from floods).

In other areas of ancient Africa many nomadic and seminomadic pastoral groups (for example, some of the Berber—also known as Amazigh—groups) in northern Africa near the Nile delta during the first millennium B.C.E. were organized into segmentary societies characterized by social and political systems that often did not have a specified leader but that placed individuals within a series of progressively larger networks such as family, lineage, clan, and tribe. These networks played a primary governing role only when it was necessary to settle disputes with opposing networks.

The archaeological record is not as complete yet for social organization in ancient southern Africa, but it is known that around 300 to 400 C.E. sedentary groups that relied on agriculture and herding lived in villages. Many of these villages engaged in trade for goods from at least as far away as the eastern Africa coast.

Ancient Social Organization in Light of Modern Systems

The term *chiefdom* is applied to societies in which one individual holds the decision-making power and in which his or her authority is related to his or her relationship to an important ancestor of the group (often the founder); ability to communicate with the ancestors; success in wielding the power and maintaining or improving living standards; or obtaining loyalty in a patron-client relationship through a large following. There were African chiefdoms in western Africa that were connected by a council of chiefs who shared power among many leaders representing their respective chiefdoms. Many of the southern African Bantu societies that were observed by the first European travelers (after 1400 C.E.) were organized into chiefdoms where successive chiefs inherited their position based on their lineage back to previous chiefs. Another feature of these societies was the categorization of clans in which some were less definitively associated with the royal lineage but were recognized as related enough to allow clan members to be part of the higher leadership community. In this way a system of hierarchy was established based on clan membership. However, there is little evidence from ancient times that tells when human groups developed into chiefdoms, what their social and political organization had been prior to that development, or if they had always been organized into chiefdoms.

Colonialists may have created the concept of tribe, which has been applied to African societies from the ancient past (as well as today). A tribe has been defined as a society larger in number than a band (hundreds of individuals) that is composed of subgroups united by associations or social constructs, such as councils of elders who are members of the same age set, secret societies, warrior societies, and religious cults. Tribes often have a lead headman or less commonly headwoman, although this person may not be occupied with the task of leadership full time. The application of *tribe* and other terms to describe the social organization of human groups has often served as the focus of strife and conflict and may not be useful. These terms can hide unifying characteristics between groups and overly accentuate irrelevant differences. So although the perception of Africa as a multitude of competing tribes seems to be one that has stuck to the concept of Africa's ancient history, it is difficult to assess the accuracy of this picture.

The age-set system (known as *gerontocracy*) draws lines of distinction based on gender and age. It is a social, political, and economic system in which elders hold power. Among the modern Masai in East Africa, one age set is responsible for cattle and community safety. The individuals that carry out this service are supervised by the elders, who are male. Individuals move from one age set to another as a group, often in a very ceremonious fashion known to anthropologists as a rite of passage. For many ethnic groups in African history circumcision has been a manifestation of movement from one age set to another. Most commonly, the consensus of the entire age set determined those individuals who would emerge as leaders to act on behalf of the age set. In this system, which was and is widespread in sub-Saharan Africa, age is highly respected. This system balanced a system in which family lineage might concentrate power in a way unrelated to individual skills recognized by the group. Despite the fact that upon European contact with Africa there were many examples of age-set social systems, which may indicate a long history of this type of social organization, it is not known whether this system dominated the social organization of ancient sub-Saharan African human groups or how far back it dates.

EGYPT

BY WILLIAM H. PECK

The social structure in ancient Egypt, like almost every other aspect of Egyptian life, underwent changes over 3,000 years of history. However, the general structure of the society can be visualized as a pyramid, with the ruler at the top supported by progressively larger groups underneath. Directly below the ruler were the royal family and kin and then, in progressively larger groups, the high-level administrators, middle-level functionaries, supervisors of labor and crafts, specialized craftspeople, and finally the peasant class, made up mainly of agricultural workers, who were the base of the pyramid. This multilevel society reflected the complex bureaucracy that had begun to develop in the country as early as the emergence of a unified Egypt and was well established by the beginning of the Old Kingdom (ca. 2575–ca. 2134 B.C.E.)

KING, GOVERNMENT, AND EXTENDED FAMILY TIES

The concept of kingship is central to any discussion of Egyptian society and Egyptian civilization. The king was the absolute monarch, supreme ruler, considered a personification of a god on earth and inheritor of his position by divine right. He was not only chief executive, head of state, and commander of the military but also the chief priest and main intermediary between humankind and the gods. The king was considered responsible for guaranteeing the cosmic order of the universe by his continued attention to the gods. He ensured that the gods were pleased by the uninterrupted sacrifices and offerings made to them and the rites carried out for them in all the temples of the land. In theory, the king led all of the activities in the country, both civil and religious. In actual fact, a large bureaucracy and well-organized civil service shouldered these responsibilities as his appointed representatives. The social structure of the country was dependent on the complexities of the bureaucracy and cannot be examined without reference to the levels of governance.

In the Old Kingdom the upper level of the administration was largely based on close family relationships such that most important posts were occupied by the ruler's closest relatives. As an example, the person responsible for overseeing the construction of the Great Pyramid, King Khufu's burial monument at Giza, was Hemiunu, a cousin or nephew of Khufu. This tradition of family ties was somewhat modified and gradually relaxed as history progressed, but the king's family continued to be appointed to important posts. In the Nineteenth Dynasty (ca. 1307–ca. 1196 B.C.E.), as a further example, sons of Ramses II filled a number of key positions. One was commander in chief of the army, another was high priest of the god Ra at Heliopolis, a third was the overseer of the royal vineyards at Memphis, and a fourth was the administrator of the entire Nile delta region.

On other levels many posts and positions were hereditary, evidenced by fathers and sons who had the same titles and ranks of office. This allowed for considerable continuity and probably increased overall efficiency. The training received by a son who learned his job as an apprentice and assistant to his father was more personalized and specialized than an organized education along academic lines could be. Although family relationships played an important part in the rule and administration of the country, ambition and talent could also be rewarded. From the biographies found on the walls of tombs it is possible to trace the careers of functionaries as they rose through the various levels of the bureaucracy. While these biographies were more in the nature of a tribute or eulogy than a real life story, they did detail important accomplishments and virtually every title that the deceased might have held during his lifetime. They give a good idea of the key events in a person's career and also illustrate how mobile the society might have been.

Although the upper classes were originally created from the family and relatives of the ruler, it was still possible for talent and ambition to be recognized. A prime example of social mobility is illustrated in the career of Senenmut, an official in the reign of Queen Hatshepsut of the Eighteenth Dynasty (ca. 1550–ca. 1307 B.C.E.). His family origins were undistinguished, but Senenmut rose through the ranks from a relatively low position, when he may have been Overseer of the Royal Seals or Overseer of the Audience Chamber, to an appointment as tutor to the queen's only daughter. During the period when Hatshepsut reigned alone, he became the chief Steward of the Temple of the god Amun at Karnak and thus one of the most powerful and influential men of his time. He was also chief adviser to the queen and is credited as being the chief architect of Hatshepsut's mortuary temple at Deir el-Bahri. On the other hand, a reversal of fortune was also possible. In the Middle Kingdom (ca. 2040–ca. 1640 B.C.E.), when the office of nomarch (semi-autonomous provincial ruler) was abolished, those officeholders were demoted and striped of their rank by royal decree.

Class Structure

Within the pyramidal structure of Egyptian society there were essentially two clearly delineated classes for which designations in the Egyptian language have survived. The wealthy and privileged (usually termed "nobility" or "elite" in the modern literature) were the leaders in every aspect of life; the lower class included workers, farm laborers, and servants. From the few examples of communities that have been preserved, it is possible to study the evidence of this division in the arrangement of villages and towns. These arrangements generally reflect the stratification of Egyptian society into two main parts. The archaeological excavation of sites clearly shows class difference, as at el-Lahun, a village built for those constructing a pyramid in the Middle Kingdom, and at Deir el-Medina, the settlement inhabited by the artisans who excavated and decorated the tombs in the Valley of the Kings. At el-Lahun the class distinction is unmistakable because the town was divided in two by a wall that separated the district with the large and lavish villas of the administrators from the much smaller row houses of the workers.

At Tell el-Amarna in Middle Egypt, the capital built by Akhenaton during his religious revolution, about 10 percent of the dwellings are large, many-roomed structures, while the workers' houses are much smaller and simpler. But that does not necessarily mean that all the family activities took place in limited, cramped quarters. In the climate of Egypt it was possible to cook out of doors and sleep on the roof for relief from the heat as well as to sit and congregate in the narrow streets. Although the family was the basic unit of society, interaction with neighbors and community was obviously necessary for day-to-day activities and for the mutual support provided by a community.

The two basic classes, the elite or nobility and the workers or commoners, were sharply divided not only in privileges but also in responsibilities. The nobles were the administrators and governors, the members of the priesthoods, and the officers of the military. These duties brought the usual rewards of material goods, social position, and community respect. The workers were for the most part free laborers, but there is some indication of a serflike arrangement where the workers were tied to the land they cultivated. The class of individuals who were actual slaves generally consisted of enemies captured in battle, convicted criminals, and debtors. Slavery was not so common in Egypt until the New Kingdom (ca. 1550–ca. 1070 B.C.E.) when more foreign conquests made it practical to employ the growing number of captives as slaves. These defeated foreigners were used at the will of the king. Slaves captured in battle could be employed on state projects or awarded to outstanding members of the military as reward for service. The old fiction that the pyramids were built by slave labor generally has been discounted. The workers on the pyramids were essentially field hands employed generally during the period of the annual flooding of the Nile, when they were not needed to sow and reap the crops.

Organization of Work and Economy

A system of corvée (or drafting) of workmen for state projects was used throughout Egyptian history. Members of the general population were called to duty for service in the military, for work in mines and quarries, and on state construction projects, such as the building of temples or pyramids. Drafted crews were also used to work on roads, canals, and the complex irrigation systems. This draft was so much a part of Egyptian life that a tradition of substitute figures to be buried with a workman developed for use of the spirit in the afterlife. The *shabiti*, mummy-shaped statuettes equipped with symbolic tools and baskets, were intended to magically answer for the deceased if he was called on to do any kind of draft labor in the next life.

The economy of Egypt was essentially based on agriculture. The largest landholders were the state and the temples, and a system of taxation on these lands, worked by tenants, provided the means to pay the employees of the governmental and religious institutions. All of the land of Egypt was in theory the domain and possession of the king. The system of tenant farming, where free individuals were allowed by contract to work the fields of royal or religious (temple) establishments, was vital to the national economy. In the New Kingdom, as the powers of the temple priesthoods became stronger and the temple holdings larger, tenant farming was one obvious solution to the management of temple estates. Since most of the economy was organized and controlled by the government, the workers in state institutions were dependent on rations provided for them. Many of these employees were also able to supplement their incomes by other activities carried on privately. Members of the upper class enjoyed the privilege at the pleasure of the king of owning property and estates and profiting from the produce of them. It was also possible for free men who were not members of the elite to own land and cultivate crops that could be used to sustain their families or traded for other goods. These landowners had the possibility of moving up in the administrative ranks to offices of responsibility. This was one of the avenues of upward mobility for those not born to rank.

Coinage as it is known today did not exist in ancient Egypt until very late in its history. Weights and measures were standardized, and some metals, such as gold and silver in bars and rings, were used as one medium of exchange. Far more common was a system of barter. The basis of this trade was generally wheat so that workmen who were paid in wheat could make bread from part of it and exchange the rest for other needs. Therefore the chief measure of wealth was land and other possessions rather than some bankable instrument of exchange.

Much of the information about the material display of wealth comes from the tombs. This evidence is either in the form of the actual objects preserved for the use of the spirit in the next life or represented in wall paintings, relief carvings, or models. Lists of estates owned by the deceased with their locations occur as part of the offerings depicted in the tomb. Models of activities to benefit the spirit suggest the wealth necessary to provide the services of the craftspeople depicted in the models. In one case, the grave of a mayor of Thebes, 15 model boats were included, giving some indication that a person of his rank would be well equipped for travel on the Nile. One additional measure of wealth, in life and in the tomb, was the possession of large quantities of cloth. This could be in the form of garments or simple sheets. In the Old Kingdom there are a small number of offering reliefs that include a "linen list" detailing great quantities of linen cloth of different types and quality. In some tombs piles of folded linen have been found, giving added evidence of the use of cloth as an indication of affluence.

Craftsmen—sculptors, painters, and furniture and jewelry makers—were generally in the service of the state or the religious establishment. They enjoyed regular employment and income and were able to pass their craft occupations on to their sons. Where it was possible or desirable, they lived together in a community of others who were similarly employed. Deir el-Medina on the West Bank at Luxor was inhabited by the workers who made and decorated the tombs in the Valley of the Kings. It is the best example of a village especially intended for workers and craftsmen. As such, excavations there have produced a great deal of information about the organization of this specialized labor, the worker's family relationships, and their day-to-day activities.

Nuclear Family, Women, and Marriage

The basic nuclear family was the most important societal unit in ancient Egypt. The ancient Egyptians were especially proud of family and lineage. The family was a close-knit group of father, mother, and children not usually extended to a larger organization such as a clan. Inscriptions on statues of individuals often give parentage and sometimes grandparentage with details about the rank and title of these forebears. However, a modern understanding of the relationship within the family is complicated because the same words in the Egyptian language were used to designate different members of the family. The word for *brother* could also be used to identify the husband, just as *sister* could also designate a wife. *Father* could easily mean a grandfather or an ancestor. Teachers were also sometimes called "father" and coworkers might be termed "brother," not signifying an actual relationship but another close affiliation or other bond. This somewhat ambiguous use of language caused earlier scholars to believe that there was a general tradition of brother-sister marriage in Egypt, but this was not the case and can rarely be proved. This confusion of language still occasionally leads to difficulties in clearly understanding of family structure.

There were exceptions to the general rules against brother-sister marriage, however. Kings sometimes did marry their sisters, and marriage with their daughters is also attested, but this was rare and had to do with providing an heir of royal blood. Likewise, only royalty enjoyed the custom of multiple wives, though commoners could have concubines as well as a wife.

Adulthood was considered to begin for women at the start of menses and for men with circumcision, performed in adolescence. For the most part, daughters lived with the family until marriage, but it was possible for sons to join others of their age group and live outside the family home. Newlywed couples might live for a time with either partner's parents, but generally this was not considered an ideal arrangement. Marriage usually took place when the man had the means to establish his own separate household. Unmarried, divorced, or otherwise single female members of the family, such as widowed mothers, divorced sisters, or maiden aunts, might live with their sons, nephews, or other close male relatives. For reasons not completely clear, two households could be joined so that two families shared living arrangements. This kind of extended family, though it was not the norm, was not unusual.

Since the family was a close-knit group, its members might be held responsible for the actions of one another. This meant that punishment might be applied for a crime committed by one to others or that family members could be held hostage to ensure the loyalty of others. It also meant that heirs could be forced to make good the debts of deceased family members. The obligations of family membership extended not only to resolving the matters of inheritance but also to securing the proper burial rites for the dead. One of the most important obligations an Egyptian had was to provide parents with the guarantees of continued life after death. This included not only the traditional preparation of the corpse (mummification) and the tomb or burial place but also the maintenance of continued rites and offerings for the spirit of the deceased.

Even though the importance of the family in Egyptian society is clear, no evidence for a formal marriage ceremony is known, and there is also no evidence that government records were registered or kept. Marriage can be characterized as a social contract, not a legal one. It is also not clear how matches were arranged or how partners were chosen. Some marriages were arranged by parents, but there is no strong indication that the arrangement could be forced on the participants. Marriage was essentially a private affair, to which the husband and wife both agreed. Both members brought property to the union, and it was possible for the wife to maintain title to her portion. Divorce was possible, and the penalties were carefully spelled out, at least there is evidence that this was regularized in the later centuries of Egyptian history. Even though society in Egypt was clearly male dominated, women held a position unequaled in any other ancient culture. Women could own property and slaves, could manage their own affairs to a certain extent, and were even able to institute legal suits. They could also conduct businesses and engage in trade. The weaving of cloth was just one example of a home-based industry carried out by women for profit. Women also had a part in the temple cults, but those responsibilities were generally limited. There are some records of women with the title "priestess" in the service of a god, but generally the title found is "chantress" or ritual singer, attached to a particular temple.

Vocations, Education, and Social Mobility

Craftspeople in Egypt enjoyed occupations that were relatively secure and respected. Since coinage did not exist until late in Egyptian history, they were paid in grain and sometimes cloth or other products that could be used for barter for other necessities. On the level of the trades and crafts there is a clear gender division. Women are seen in representations of spinning and weaving, in the textile crafts. Occasionally they were also employed as potters, but sculptors, painters, carpenters, boatwrights, chariot makers, metalworkers, and jewelers are almost exclusively male.

The priesthood in Egypt was not an exclusive vocation as it is in many other cultures and in modern religious institutions. The position of priest was a rotating one, where an individual would serve for a prescribed length of time, continue to occupy his secular positions, or return to his other duties after his service was finished. Priests could also serve in several different capacities, devoted to different deities, at the same time. It was only with the growth of the power of the priesthoods in the New Kingdom that the temples became important economic powers, owning vast tracts of farmland and collecting the income from estates. With this added influence the higher levels of the clergy became managers similar to the executives of large corporations. The career of Nebwenenef, high priest of the god Amun in the early years of the reign of Ramses illustrates both service in multiple cults and concurrent civil duties. He served as high priest in the cult of the god Anhur and the goddess Hathor, Lady of Dendera, before being appointed to the priesthood of Amun. His several secular titles included "overseer of the Double House of gold and silver" (the treasury) and "chief of all the craftsmen of Thebes." He exemplified the ability of individuals to occupy the top levels of power and influence in Egyptian society in both the religious and governmental spheres.

In a society that had an estimated literacy rate of 1 to 5 percent, the training to acquire the ability to read and write was very important, especially where a premium was put on record keeping. Scribes were vital to every aspect of life, from the simplest duties of letter writing and keeping accounts to the greater responsibilities of serving as administrator, emissary, or ambassador. Scribes were held in high esteem, and the initial training was sought after by bright and able young people. It was mainly the children of the elite who were able to study to be scribes, but there are examples of students from the lower classes finding access to scribal schools. The subject matter was essentially designed to prepare students for practical applications and consisted of the basics of reading, writing, and applied mathematics. The scribes' education took place in the palace or temple precincts, and its method consisted essentially of repetition and rote learning, which included the copying of classic texts. Many of the important literary texts that have been preserved, often in several versions, were copied by apprentice scribes.

There is a preserved document called "The Satire on the Trades," a glorification of the occupation of the scribe, which is written in the form of a father's advice to his son. In it the father describes many of the other occupations, with their obvious drawbacks, in contrast to the life of the scribe. He tells his son that other jobs are dirty or smelly or otherwise undesirable but not the life of the scribe. "You never see a sculptor sent as an emissary, but scribes are always chosen for such tasks"—a typical observation intended to make the young person devote himself to his studies. It is clear that the person with scribal training enjoyed a privileged position.

Most scribes were attached to governmental or temple service, but there is some indication that there was also a class of independent literate individuals whose services were available for hire. However, the importance of keeping accurate state records and managing the system of taxation required large numbers of specialists who were well trained. Tomb paintings and funerary models attest to the varied activities of the scribes, mainly keeping accounts of the produce of the fields for tax purposes. They are almost always depicted in twos and threes at the same work, suggesting a system of careful accounting.

The Social Organization of Death

The stratification within Egyptian society can be illustrated with a variety of examples. A simple and obvious illustration is the size (or even the existence) of a tomb. Certainly only the well-to-do had the resources to construct or carve out tombs for burial. The very fact that an individual was buried in a tomb automatically demonstrates that he or she had wealth and influence. The ability to plan, commission, and carry out the preparation and decoration of a tomb of any size implies considerable wealth. The quality of the tomb furniture, including the mummy cases and ritual vessels, gives a good indication of disposable capital. Even the differing sizes of private tombs imply differences in rank and status. This evidence serves to correct the notion that everyone in ancient Egypt was mummified at death and accorded a lavish burial. The truth of the matter is quite different. The remains of ordinary people were treated simply. A grave furnished with a few personal possessions was all that the lower classes could expect. The relatively small number of tombs preserved from all periods in proportion to population estimates offers yet another example of the separation between the small upper class and the much larger lower classes.

When the unlimited expenditure used for a royal burial is compared with the simple preparation for a common grave, the disparity between the two major classes in ancient Egypt becomes even clearer. The often-cited example of the material from Tutankhamen's tomb includes one coffin of solid gold that weighed 300 pounds. In contrast, the grave of a workman might have contained a bronze razor or a mirror. It is hardly necessary to add that Tutankhamen was a minor ruler who died young and was buried in a tomb prepared for someone else. It is difficult to imagine what would have accompanied such great kings as Amenhotep III or Ramses II in their burials, a reminder of the pyramidal structure of society in ancient Egypt with the supreme ruler at the apex and a gradual lessening of responsibility and wealth at each wider level below.

THE MIDDLE EAST

BY KIRK H. BEETZ

There are large gaps in modern knowledge of the ancient societies of the Near East, partly because many did not leave relics in durable materials such as stone, partly because on occasion entire peoples were wiped out with few traces of their having existed and partly because much of the modern Near East has been and still is very dangerous for archaeologists, with many important sites having been out of their reach for decades at a time.

ÇATALHÜYÜK

One ancient people whose existence was forgotten for thousands of years lived at Çatalhüyük, in south-central Turkey. The ruins of this large village or small town—its population was perhaps 5,000 to 8,000—lay undiscovered until 1958. The earliest structures so far excavated date to before 7200 B.C.E., predating sites in Mesopotamia that were long thought to be the oldest urban areas in the world. The people at Çatalhüyük seem to have left no written language, so their social organization has to be deduced from physical remains.

Çatalhüyük consisted of mud-brick houses built side by side with no streets or passageways between them, making it look somewhat like a beehive. It had no defensive walls, but attackers would have had to fight house by house to get into and through it. In effect, the houses themselves were walls. They had no doorways and rarely had windows. People moved about by climbing through trapdoors in their ceilings and walking from roof to roof, sometimes using ladders when the roofs were uneven.

Many, perhaps even most houses had shrines in them, suggesting that religious ritual was an important part of everyday life. Some houses were much bigger than others, and the burials that are richest in goods tend to be under the floors of the larger houses, suggesting that some members of society ranked higher than others, perhaps forming a social elite group. The people of Çatalhüyük often buried their dead in their homes, under large platforms on which people could sit. Paintings on walls of headless people being picked at by vultures suggests a custom of leaving corpses out to be cleaned by scavenging birds, but many burials were of completely intact bodies, which seems to contradict the idea that corpses were picked clean before burial. Perhaps there were divergent burial customs; perhaps the paintings have another meaning. The dead were segregated by gender into separate graves, with women typically having the larger coverings and the better burial goods, suggesting that Çatalhüyük had a matriarchal society, meaning a society in which women were dominant over men. Many archaeologists believe that early societies in the region of Turkey were matriarchal.

The dwellings of Çatalhüyük are rich in manufactured products such as ceramic vessels. Excavations have revealed that these objects were created in homes. A section of each house seems to have been designated for craft work. At present, archaeologists suspect that every member of society was expected to know basic crafts such as basket weaving and home building. Çatalhüyük was abandoned sometime around 5600 B.C.E. The cause for its desertion is unknown. Some of the skeletons that have been recovered show signs of a mosquito-carried disease that may have killed many people, but this evidence does not necessarily mean that the settlement was afflicted with an epidemic. Instead, some residents may simply have come from marshlands to the south, where the disease and mosquitoes were more likely to be found.

JERICHO

Among very ancient remains are those of Jericho, in what was later known as Palestine. In about 8000 B.C.E. people built a large stone wall and a 30-foot-tall tower at this location. Archaeologists disagree over what the tower was for, with some insisting it was a watchtower, others supposing it was used for astronomical observations, and still others believing it was a defensive structure intended to protect either stored grain or a spring, or both. The tower has a sophisticated design and is not just a pile of rocks. It had an interior stairway, and its stones were fitted carefully together. The skill shown in the construction suggests that even earlier stone walls and towers must have existed somewhere in the area, since the builders at Jericho clearly were sure of their techniques.

The wall and tower are associated with human skulls that were apparently cleaned and then covered with clay sculptures of human faces, with seashells for their eyes. This treat-

Servants carrying food for the king's tables, palace of Xerxes, Persepolis, Persia (modern-day Iran) (Courtesy of the Oriental Institute of the University of Chicago)

ment may indicate that the builders of the wall and tower worshipped their ancestors and that the skulls represented dead leaders or priests who could be consulted by the living. An alternative possibility is that people thought they could capture and hold prisoner the spirits of the dead, forcing the spirits to do as they were ordered. Some art historians think that the tradition of realistic depictions of human beings found in such places as Egypt and ancient Greece derives from a similar ancient tradition begun in Jericho.

Eridu

Most archaeologists point to ancient Sumer, in what is now southern Iraq, as the first broadly influential culture of the Near East, starting in the 4000s B.C.E., when city-states arose. The ancient Mesopotamians believed the city of Eridu was the oldest in the world and that it stood on the very spot where the world was created. Ancient Mesopotamian writers claimed that Eridu was founded before 72,000 B.C.E. Although it is not nearly that old, the city does seem to be the oldest yet discovered in the region of the Tigris and Euphrates rivers. At the bottommost layer of Eridu is a small shrine, which may mean that the city was built on a site already considered sacred as well as that the builders were very religious. Eridu was part of a region archaeologists designate as southern Mesopotamia, the lands approximately south of the Diyala River, a tributary of the Tigris. Northern Mesopotamia, encompassing lands mostly near the north of the Tigris, did not come into cultural prominence until about 1900 B.C.E.

Many archaeologists dispute whether Eridu should be considered a real city, because its population probably did not exceed 9,000. To them Uruk just to the north, which at its peak in about 2700 B.C.E. had a population of at least 50,000, was the first true city. In the 4000s B.C.E., however, Eridu was the by far the largest settlement in a region in which villages of 250 or so people were regarded as notable, and it must have seemed crowded and metropolitan to the people of its era. It also represented a more complex social organization than would have been found in the villages of Mesopotamia. It did not become a capital of an empire or kingdom, and it was not even a great economic power, but it was the focus of religion for the Sumerian culture, and it therefore remained an example for the Sumerian cities that followed.

Many archaeologists have assumed that cities could not have been built without centralized leadership—for example, a king—because of the large public works projects required for building and maintaining an urban center. For the ancient cities of Sumer these projects included streets, irrigation canals, and walls to guard against invading armies, but Eridu and other Sumerian cities until about 3000 B.C.E. probably did not have monarchs. Instead, they developed an institution that was called the *lugal*, which translates as "great man." In a crisis such as a great flood or a war, an assembly of free citizens chose a leading fellow citizen to take charge until the crisis was over. It is possible that at some point crises came so frequently that a *lugal* was able to stay in power permanently.

Some historians call the earliest Sumerian city-states simple democracies because people in them supposedly had equal civil rights. Individual cities varied in how they organized themselves around the concept of free, socially equal citizens, but in general no one person was supposed to be born superior to another. These societies may have been matriarchal in outlook, with female ancestry being more important in identifying a person's heritage than male ancestry and with priestesses dominating religious rituals, but gender rights seem to have been equal in matters of social standing, control of land, marriage, and divorce. Much about the social organization of Eridu's era, about 5000 to 4000 B.C.E., is vague because of the absence of written records.

The Uruk Period

The Uruk Period (ca. 4000–ca. 2900 B.C.E.) is somewhat clearer because written documents exist both from that time and from soon afterward. The period is named for the dominant city of the age, Uruk, known as Erech in the Bible. During this period men and women shared civic duties, with a man called *en* and a woman called *nin* holding chief administrative powers over a bureaucracy, each serving a term of one year. Divisions of labor seem to have been developing between the genders, with women in charge of the textiles industry, which was important to a city's wealth through trade. Wool was the primary material.

Although some archaeologists believe that there was no social differentiation in Uruk, with all free people being equal, there is evidence of an elite group of government workers who organized and directed group activities. Governments combined civil administration and religious practices, making public service an act of faith. Although the *en* and the *nin* supposedly controlled both government activities and religious rites on behalf of the general population, the existence of a permanent bureaucracy indicates that those who knew procedures and rituals well could manipulate the short-term administrators.

Archaeologists sometimes point to physical evidence that Uruk had an egalitarian society, meaning a society in which no one had special privileges by right of birth. They note that the temples and government buildings were open, airy places with numerous large doorways that were open to the outside, so that anyone passing by could see what was taking place inside. This free access implies that the government was open to public scrutiny. Citizens could know all they wanted about government and religious business merely by observing from a doorway or simply strolling in among the government and religious officials. From this point of view, the *en*, the *nin*, the bureaucrats, and the priests and priestesses were all accessible to any citizen and were accountable to the public for what they did.

The institution of the assembly, even though it lingered for hundreds of years after kings and dynasties appeared, is another indication of egalitarianism. The assembly originally consisted of all free people, probably including women (but excluding slaves). At some point women lost their right to vote in the assembly; exactly when this happened is unknown, and possibly they retained their right to vote in some cities long after they lost it in others. By 3200 B.C.E., however, the egalitarian aspects of Sumerian society had begun to fade. Cities had not only *ens* and *nins* as well as the occasional *lugal* but also governing boards composed of wealthy landowners. Previously burials had shown no difference in status between rich and poor, but this began to change as landowners asserted their economic power to influence society. Even so, an assembly of citizens could overrule the governing board if someone, perhaps an *en* or a *nin*, brought a board decision to a public vote, which was typically held outside in a courtyard or other large, open public space.

Dynastic Period

During the Early Dynastic Period (ca. 2900–ca. 2340 B.C.E.) in southern Mesopotamia, permanent kingship developed, but the kings had an uneasy relationship with their subjects, who retained many of the rights they had held during the Uruk Period. Perhaps the most interesting and most unaccountable change during this period was the loss of civil rights for women. They still had some legal protections, but by and large they were owned by the men in their lives, with their wealth always controlled by a male family member.

Social organization was dominated by the *oikos*. Archaeologists use this Greek word, which means "household," to refer to an extended family of close relatives who jointly own land and perhaps workshops. An *oikos* always had a male as its head, whose responsibilities included using family funds to support infirm family members, provide dowries, and pay fines for criminal convictions of relatives; possibly it was also his responsibility to carry out court orders for punishments of family members. One of his most important duties was to find mates for the unmarried men and women of his *oikos*. Marriages were arranged on the basis of wealth, although discrimination based on social class seems to have been rare.

By the time of Babylon's King Hammurabi (r. 1792–1750 B.C.E.) society had divided itself into three groups: the *awilum*, the *mushkenum*, and the *wardum*. The *awilum* were landowners. They had the most political power, and as the centuries passed they came to possess most of a city-state's wealth. They tended to hold the highest posts in government and religion, and they expected the best government jobs to go to their family members. The *mushkenum* were free people but did not own land. They retained the right to assemble in public places, and they could vote during assembly meetings. In most places women were now excluded from these rights. The *wardum* were slaves. They consisted mostly of prisoners of war who were forced to work for the government in public works projects or were sold to private citizens. Sometimes free people were sold into slavery. The head of an *oikos* could sell family members for money; a father could sell his children or his wife or even himself to escape poverty or debts. Slaves had few rights, and everything they made belonged to their owners. In a social practice that continued at least through the Old Babylonian Empire of about 2000 to 1600 B.C.E., members of one of these classes could move to another. A member of the *awilum* could join the *mushkenum* by selling all his land, and a member of the *mushkenum* could become part of the *awilum* by purchasing land. Slaves had to be freed first but then could join either of the classes of free people.

Women held on to one principal source of power, religion. In what was probably a relic tradition of the past, certain rituals had to be performed by women. In a practice that lasted at least through the Old Babylonian Empire, women could join a *gagum*. A *gagum* was a cloister for women whose lives were devoted to the priesthood. In the Uruk Period, if these women gave birth to children it probably would have been seen as a blessing, a sign of their fertility in service to the gods and therefore a good omen for the city. After women had lost most of their civil rights, however, members of a *gagum* were forbidden to have children. In a patriarchal culture, denying them the right to bear children was a means of symbolically taking away their creative power in religious life. A member of a *gagum* who even visited a tavern was put to death because taverns were where people often met to find partners for sexual relations. The women of the cloisters may have had a small victory over their oppressors, however: They were avid writers and many, possibly most, of the writings surviving from the Old Babylonian Empire are theirs and reflect their view of their society.

Sexuality was an important part of civic life in southern Mesopotamia. Every city was believed to be sacred, and the cities themselves were worshipped. One way to increase the health of a city was to have sexual relations in it. This was considered to be a joyful activity, and people were discouraged from having sexual relations in private. Indeed, some ancient writers bemoaned the antisocial behavior of young lovers who had sex in private rather than out in the street as proper people did. On the other hand, childbirth was an occasion for anxiety because only about one in two babies lived long after birth. Women giving birth were subjects for artists, probably because giving birth was an affirmation of life in the city and among its people.

The Hittites

Archaeologists disagree greatly about when the Hittites migrated from southern Europe into Anatolia (modern Turkey), dating it to between 2750 B.C.E. and 1700 B.C.E. In any event, by the 1600s B.C.E. the Hittites were expanding their domain, attacking their neighbors and raiding deep into the lands of Babylon. Their kings were remote and usually inaccessible to ordinary people, with a large bureaucracy between them and commoners. The king's palace was its own community within the broad community of the empire, with its own priests, physicians, craftspeople, and animal tenders. Princes lived within the palace's compound but in a house separate from the king's residence.

The apex of society was the king and queen. If the king died, the queen became the ruling monarch. Even while he lived, she exercised considerable control over the government bureaucracy and public ceremonies. Possibly this queenly power was a legacy of earlier matriarchal cultures in the Anatolian region, adopted by the Hittites in order to provide stability for their government: If a king died prematurely, he was succeeded by someone who already had experience of rule. Beneath the monarchs in social standing were nobles and beneath them government officials. Next in line came craftspeople and tradespeople: manufacturers of ceramics, blacksmiths, weavers, carpenters, sculptors, and the like. Farmers ranked below the craftspeople and tradespeople, and below them were slaves.

Arabia and Israel

While the Hittites were building their empire in the northwestern Near East, another culture was making itself felt in the south. These were the people of the Arabian Peninsula. By 1154 B.C.E. the Arabs had become a significant distraction to the Kassite Dynasty (ca. 1530–ca. 1155 B.C.E.) of Babylon. The Kassite kings devoted so many resources to coping with the Arabs that the kingdom of Elam was able to invade Babylon and overthrow the Kassites.

The peoples of Arabia were nomads, herders of sheep. They raided their neighbors for food and wealth. Sometime before 1000 B.C.E. one of these groups, known as the Sabeans, settled in the region of modern-day Yemen. (The biblical place-name Sheba is derived from *Sabea*.) The Sabeans were a mercantile people, specializing in being go-betweens for the shipping of goods from Africa and the Near East to southern Asia, especially India, as well as for the return trade. They formed part of the kingdom of Axum, named for its capital city in eastern Africa.

Little is known about the social organization of the Sabeans, partly because their written language has yet to be translated and partly because during the 20th century their buildings and canals in Yemen were dismantled, the stones and bricks being used for modern house building. They had a long tradition of rule by queens and seem to have been a fairly open society for women, allowing them to become merchants as well as members of the ruling elite. Ethiopian oral tradition says that around 955 B.C.E. this legacy was abandoned when Queen Makeda was succeeded by Menelik, her son by King Solomon. Thereafter, so the oral tradition says, only men could rule. Women seem to have been limited to officiating in the worship of female gods.

King Solomon of Israel was probably viewed as something of an upstart at that time. Israel had been a backwater dominated by the Sumerian culture. Israel had a social organization similar to that of southern Mesopotamia. Women were severely limited in what they could do and were probably excluded from most religious rituals. Although Solomon's kingdom had a strong military force, merchants tended to dominate social life. Government officials seem to have been preoccupied by tasks intended to smooth trade within Israel and with other nations. The many wives of Solomon were part of the effort to gain protection for Israeli traders; the wives tended to be political brides, the marriages intended to cement goodwill between Israel and the kings and queens who were their parents. This was a common practice among Near Eastern rulers of the time. Among Israel's commoners polygamy tended to be reserved for political leaders and the rich. Enslaved women were often kept as concubines.

Neo-Assyrian Empire

The culture of the Near East suffered a significant upheaval with the rise of the Neo-Assyrian Empire of 934–612 B.C.E. in northern Mesopotamia. Assyria of the Old Assyrian Period (ca. 1813–ca. 1365 B.C.E.) had been primarily a trading empire with customs derived from Sumer, but the new empire was a military state in which warriors were the elite of society. Women were reduced to the status of nonhumans. They were forced to wear garments that covered them entirely, not for the sake of modesty but to symbolize their utter lack of worth. Further, the garments made clear that the women belonged to certain men, who were the only ones allowed to see them without their coverings. Female babies were often killed at birth because only male babies were valued. A woman's duties consisted of bearing male babies to supply the army and obeying her husband, father, or brothers in all matters. The Neo-Assyrian social practices toward women influenced all of the Near East and much of central Asia, even pervading some Hindu sects in India. The Neo-Assyrians created such loathing among their subject peoples that after their overthrow they were hunted down and killed for another 10 years, until they were exterminated, but the status of women in the Near East never recovered from their suppression under the Neo-Assyrian regime.

Persia

During the reign of Cyrus the Great from 559 to 529 B.C.E., Persia (modern-day Iran) conquered much of the Near East. The Persian government typically allowed conquered peoples to continue to live their lives as they had before, provided they paid their taxes and supplied soldiers for the Persian army. Thus, even at this late date, Sumerian customs continued to be practiced in much of the Near East. Most of what is known about Persian social customs comes from Greek writers, who tended to be very biased in their accounts because Greece and Persia were bitter enemies. From these Greek authors comes the image of the decadent oriental potentate, based on their depictions of Persian courts as places of idle luxury and lazy nobility. One Greek historian who provided an alternative view was Herodotus, in the 400s B.C.E. According to him, the Persians were courageous fighters and intelligent statesmen.

The Persian monarch kept himself remote from his subjects, surrounding himself with impressive buildings and elaborate rituals intended to awe outsiders. He employed many artists and craftspeople who decorated his public works. The Persian social order is not clear to modern historians, but it seems that after the king came nobles, who were born to their high status. After them came governors of conquered territories and then officials who ran the day-to-day operations of the government. Among the latter were probably the generals of Persia's large armies. Persian rulers were much occupied with enhancing communications and trade within their empire, which suggests that merchants were important members of society. There were many slaves, mostly prisoners of war.

Greeks already had settled in parts of the Near East near the Mediterranean Sea, and they had made themselves nuisances to the Persians, sparking wars that made Persians and Greeks long-term enemies. From 336 to 323 B.C.E. the Macedonian king Alexander the Great conquered and occupied most of the Near East, bringing Greek culture all the way into India. Out of Alexander's conquests arose the Seleucid Kingdom (ca. 311–ca. 140 B.C.E.). Although they were Greek in outlook, the Seleucid monarchs imitated the trappings of a Persian court.

Parthians

The Parthian Empire began in about 250 B.C.E. in northeastern Iran, and under Mithridates I (r. 174–136 B.C.E.) the Parthians supplanted the Seleucids through most of Mesopotamia. Although the Parthians had migrated into Iran from central Asia and had used Iran as their base for conquering much of the Near East, they made their capital city of Ctesiphon in Mesopotamia, near modern-day Baghdad, and they ruled their empire as if it were a Mesopotamian one. The first Parthian dynasty, the Arsacids, ruled from about 250 B.C.E. until they were overthrown in 226 C.E. by people from western Iran. The newcomers founded the Sassanid Dynasty, which lasted until an invasion by Arabs in the 600s C.E. Although it is sometimes confusingly called the Persian Empire, the Sassanid Dynasty had little in common with the original Persian Empire. Like the Arsacids, the Sassanids ruled as a Mesopotamian culture from Ctesiphon.

The official language of the Parthians was Greek. They derived their laws and social customs from the Near Eastern peoples they conquered, and little is known of their native customs, which had been replaced by those of Mesopotamia. Women had few rights, children were expected to follow the professions of their parents, and local cultures were compelled to provide the Parthian military with troops. The preoccupation of Parthian monarchs was war, and they often fought Greeks and Romans in the west and nomads from central Asia in the east. Despite the emphasis on military conquest, trade was essential to life of the empire, with numerous trade routes extending as far as China and Africa. This activity brought the rise of a merchant class whose members used their wealth to climb the social ladder by buying their way into government. Government officials, like nobles, ranked higher than ordinary members of society.

ASIA AND THE PACIFIC

BY KIRK H. BEETZ

INDIA

The earliest-known civilization in India was that of the Harappans, named by modern archaeologists for a place near one of their major cities. Although the Harappans had a written language, it survives mostly on seals, meaning that it is in fragments, and it has not yet been translated. The ancient Sumerians made only a few written references to the Harappans. Therefore, the social organization of the Harappans must be deduced from their physical remains, which consist of two or three cities and numerous towns and villages scattered throughout the valley of the Indus River, with some farther south and others farther west or north.

Mohenjo Daro seems to be the best preserved of the cities. The city was well planned, with a grid pattern for streets, a well-maintained sewer system, and separate areas for public gatherings and residences. The residential areas are divided distinctly into sections with big houses with brick walls that were laid in decorative, abstract patterns and sections with small houses with little or no fancy brickwork. To some archaeologists, these divisions mean that the Harappans had class distinctions between rich and poor. Archaeologists infer that those with small houses were oppressed by those with big houses. Nevertheless, all residential areas had the same sort of narrow streets and the same high-quality sewers, with manholes giving access to sewer repair workers in all areas. This evidence suggests that while there may have been a difference in wealth among the Harappans, the poorer Harappans had access to civic services equal to richer Harappans. Further, public areas seem to have been accessible to all.

There was a large public swimming pool, perhaps for ritual bathing. There were large buildings that may have been used for worship. Archaeologists have also discovered foundations to a long building, with air ducts to keep its interior dry, which was a huge facility for storing grain. The existence of this structure implies that food was collectively owned by the community, in turn implying that the land on which the grain was grown was collectively owned by the community. From this information, some archaeologists surmise that the Harappans had a social elite who owned all the means of production and that most people were slaves or serfs who worked the land for the benefit of the elite. Other archaeologists think the evidence indicates that the grain was kept in public trust and belonged to all.

Exactly when the Harappan culture began is not known, but it was thriving by 2600 B.C.E. and began to decline between 1900 and 1700 B.C.E.; it was eclipsed by Aryan invaders by 1500 B.C.E. These Aryans were nomadic cattle herders from central Asia who overwhelmed the Harappans, who had already been weakened by natural disasters. The era from about 1500 to about 600 B.C.E. is known as the Vedic because of the Vedas, sacred works of the Hindus that began as an oral tradition telling of the events of the Aryans' migration into northern India.

The Vedic peoples were slow to settle, preferring for hundreds of years to move their herds across the land, especially the grassy plains near the Ganges River, which ran northwest to southeast across northern India. Their culture mingled with the local cultures to become the Brahmanic social order, the basis of Hinduism. Much of the history of India is the story of the Vedic culture spreading ever southward over thousands of years. The Vedic people brought with them the caste system of social organization. A caste was a class based on birth that restricted the professions, civil rights, and marriage possibilities of people born into it. How many castes the Vedic peoples originally had is not known, but by the fourth century B.C.E., when the Vedas were written down, there were four. The top caste was that of the Brahmans, followed by Kshatriyas, Vaishyas, and Shudras. After these came the people without caste.

People born into the Brahman caste were priests and were expected to be spiritual leaders. They could not be punished for many crimes and could not be put to death or physically harmed. Even to annoy a Brahman was a crime. Sometimes, however, even a Brahman could commit a crime so vile that it had to be punished, in which case the knot of hair on the head—which in Brahman tradition was tied at the age of three years old—was cut off. This act made a Brahman a nonperson. It cut off a Brahman from all family and friends and denied a Brahman any social rights.

Many Brahmans lived off donations from members of other castes. It was considered a social obligation for members of lower castes to make gifts to Brahmans. Social customs and religious laws forbade someone to give his family's entire wealth to a Brahman, but Brahmans often received houses, even whole villages, as gifts. Giving gifts to Brahmans was thought to improve a person's karma, the spiritual energy that governed how many times a person would have to be reincarnated before becoming one with the universal spirit. Many Brahmans worked at professions that were supposed to be outside their caste. Brahmanic laws allowed them to take such jobs if they were in distress, a rule that applied to members of other castes as well.

The Kshatriyas were the caste of high government officials and warriors. Kings and nobles belonged to this caste. Such was the power of India's social organization that even at the end of the ancient era, kings were bound by the rules of their caste and usually followed the rules. Not to do so could invalidate their right to rule, but if they followed the rules carefully, no one had the right to depose them. In actual practice, however, kings were often deposed, sometimes by their own sons.

Kshatriyas were supposed to devote themselves to the good of the nation. As warriors, they were expected to serve their king and to strive to increase the power of their king. As government officials, they were supposed to be honest and impartial when making decisions. As court officials, they were expected to be above bribery and other inappropriate influences. Brahmans did not have to pay taxes because they were expected to improve the welfare of the public through their piety, but the Kshatriyas were expected to pay taxes. Their taxes were lower than those of the lower castes, a circumstance that inspired resentment among members of lower castes. Even so, members of the lower castes were expected to be respectful toward Kshatriyas.

The Vaishyas were merchants, moneylenders, and farmers. They were expected to pay extra high taxes because under Brahmanic law it was their duty to support the Brahmans and the Kshatriyas. Even so, some Vaishyas managed to become wealthy. The Vaishyas, Kshatriyas, and Brahmans were all allowed to learn the holy writings of the Vedas, and they were twice-born, meaning that as children they underwent rituals that resulted in a spiritual birth. Shudras were barred from reading most religious works and were not allowed to be spiritually reborn. They could not participate in public religious rituals, only private ones.

Craftspeople, servants, laborers, wage earners, and minor government officials were Shudras. Some historians believe that when the Aryan nomads invaded India, they made the local peoples members of this fourth caste. The Shudras tended to be paid poorly and usually worked for the same employer from one generation to the next. The Shudras were subdivided into three groups: pure, unexcluded, or excluded. The pure Shudras could hope to read minor religious works. The unexcluded and excluded Shudras were treated with disdain. Beneath them were outcastes. Outcastes were expected to do the work that would defile members of the four castes, such as hunting, fishing, butchering live animals, executing human beings, and carrying the dead. They were not allowed to walk on roads but had to walk to the sides of roads. A Brahman could kill an outcaste with little or no penalty.

There were two kinds of outcastes that were treated better. One included people who had detached themselves from society to live as hermits, forsaking most of the pleasures of life. Such people could be respected and could even become considered holy and were often treated well. The other kind consisted of foreigners. Foreigners could be treated well, though their lack of caste meant that they could not be accepted to meals; Brahmans often could not let foreigners into their homes. There was a feast day on which foreigners and Indians were allowed to dine together, and sometimes foreigners were absorbed into castes, with foreign dignitaries joining a high caste.

Women were protected by laws, but those of lower castes could be abused by those of higher castes. A woman's word could not be taken over that of a man of her caste or higher. In matters of law, women were not to be subjected to the same severity of tortures and punishments as men. On the other hand, if they were wives or daughters of a man sent to prison, they were sent to prison as well and suffered as he suffered. A woman's testimony was usually unacceptable in court proceedings. Women often earned their own money, but those who belonged to the Brahman or Kshatriya castes were not supposed to work at menial jobs. Sometimes they had to, and they then usually worked at home weaving cloth, which they could sell to a factory. The workers at the factory were not allowed to look at the women while the transactions took place.

Rebellion against Brahmanic laws came in the form of new, rival religions. One such religion was Buddhism, which began as just a sect within the Brahmanic tradition. Buddhists rejected the caste system, holding as a tenet of their faith that any person could attain enlightenment through good deeds, religious rituals, and prayers. Some parts of India became primarily Buddhist. In those places even Brahmans had to have jobs to support themselves, and they took jobs under the rule of duress that allowed people to work outside their caste if they had to do so.

Although the rules of ancient Indian social organization sound very strict, the Brahmanic rules were not followed as scrupulously as they are now followed by many Hindus. For instance, in the ancient world marriages between castes were common, and a stigma was attached to the marriage for two generations but no more. It was possible to find Brahmans doing jobs of any of the other castes, and they were sometimes important government officials. Clever Shudras could become rich and influential.

China

Knowledge of the social organization of China before the Han Dynasty (202 B.C.E.–220 C.E.) is sketchy at present. Emperor Qin Shi Huangdi (r. 221–210 B.C.E.) tried to have the records of previous governments destroyed and even had Confucian scholars executed so that they could not transmit their knowledge to later generations. He did so because he wanted history to begin with him. He wanted to eradicate bad influences from the past, and he wanted the system of legalism to replace all previous systems of government. Legalism advocated laws to govern every action a person took, even trivial actions.

For a long time the Shang Dynasty (ca. 1500–1045 B.C.E.) was thought to be a myth, the primary records of existence being the transcription of histories from the memory of a 90-year-old scholar who survived Qin Shi Huangdi's purges. Archaeological discoveries have revealed the existence of the Shang, including their written language, but most of their known writings come from bamboo sticks that were used for magical records. Much about their society must be deduced from their physical remains.

Peasants made up the vast majority of Shang society. They lived primarily in the region of the Yellow River, and the food they produced kept the empire fed. When there were public works projects, such as building roads or city walls, peasants were conscripted to do the work. They formed the bulk of Shang armies and were often forced into war. Those who marched to a part of the empire far from home rarely returned. It seems that the Shang rulers learned that they were dependent on the peasants and may have made some efforts to care for the peasants, at least well enough to keep the peasants healthy and working. A peasant was expected to devote his or her life to work, laboring every moment possible.

Like the Shang, the Zhou were warlike. Much of society during their dynasty (1045– 256 B.C.E.) is still a mystery. As with the Shang, nearly everyone was a peasant. The Zhou placed nobles in charge of provinces, creating a feudal system in which the nobles had principal authority within their provinces. The lives of peasants were very hard. Nobles often took their land away from them, forcing them to pay rent for the land or to work the land as sharecroppers—people who have to give a share of their harvest to the landowner in order to be allowed to farm the land. Occasionally, a Zhou emperor would redistribute the land to the peasants, but the nobles would retake the land, often by making loans to peasants that the peasants could not repay, forcing them to forfeit their lands. During the second half of the Zhou Dynasty, the emperors had little military power and could not enforce their edicts, ending their ability to care for the peasants. The lives of peasants became so dire that some archaeologists and historians refer to their being slaves, but for all their miseries, peasants were not considered slaves. In fact, they were far higher on the social scale than were slaves.

During the Zhou Dynasty much of the pattern for Chinese social organization was set. At the top of society was the royal family, with the emperor ruling because he had been blessed by the gods. Below him were the nobles, who held their stations from the authority granted to them by the emperor. This situation meant that the nobles needed to keep the emperor even after the emperor had lost almost all his power because the nobles were accepted by the rest of the Chinese only as a result of the authority supposedly derived from a divinely appointed emperor. After the nobles came warriors, most of whom were minor nobility. After them came the peasants. During the Han Dynasty these would be the only true people of the nation. Everyone else, wealthy or not, was not socially recognized, including traders, craftspeople, servants, and slaves.

Perhaps the most socially significant change during the end of the Zhou Dynasty was the elevation of government officials in social standing. The period from 453 to 221 B.C.E. is known as the Warring States Period. During that time China's provinces had been combined into several large provinces, each competing with the others to rule all of China. The governors of these provinces took to calling themselves kings. One of these rulers was King Zheng of the Qin province in the western part of China. Qin had already adopted legalism as its philosophy of government. In its harsh organization of life, legalism had become the tool of scholars, men educated in the intricacies of running a government with complex rules. Some of these scholars traveled through China looking for sponsors; in Qin they had attained a standing below only that of King Zheng himself.

King Zheng became Qin Shi Huangdi, and his enforcement of legalism throughout China made him hated by nearly everyone. His government officials were loathed. Legalism sought to reorganize society so that no one except the emperor was exempt from the law. People would be persuaded to behave according to legalist principles by severe punishments for violating the rules and by rewards for obeying the rules. In theory, anyone could climb the social ladder by obeying the rules. In practice, legalism was corrupt, with people unable to avoid breaking at least a few laws every day, giving the emperor an excuse to send millions of unfortunate people into slave labor camps working on the Great Wall or other construction projects as punishment for their crimes. The legalist government officials became devoted to betrayal and political scheming.

When rebellion finally came, rebels slaughtered the entire royal family, even after the emperor surrendered. It is to Liu Bang's credit that when he finally emerged as emperor in 202 B.C.E., he did not continue the bloodbath, and he did not slaughter government scholars. He was a rough man with little respect for scholars, but he did see the good sense of having educated people run government. He chose Confucians. He often made fun of them, but he allowed them to reform the laws of the empire.

Liu Bang (r. 202–195 B.C.E.) founded the Han Dynasty, and the basic social organization of the Han remained the organization of Chinese society through civil wars and new dynasties throughout the rest of the ancient era. The basic social order was the emperor, then the nobles, then government officials, and then peasants. When disasters struck, these were the people who were to be saved because they were deemed essential to the survival of the nation. Although being a peasant was still usually miserable, the Han instituted new opportunities for social mobility. One of these was the institution of 20 ranks within society. Peasants had access to the first eight, while the others were reserved for members of higher social standing. Through contributions to community welfare, hard work, and acquisition of wealth, a peasant could ascend the first eight ranks, gaining prestige and rights with each rank. Whether the government officials who devised the 20 steps intended this result or not, the system was a powerful motivational tool because it gave hope to people in a culture where respect mattered greatly. A peasant at the eighth level was a significant member of his community. Further, the ranks allowed for downward mobility. A person in the highest ranks could lose so many ranks as punishment for a crime that he fell below the eighth level and could end up beneath the peasants he had once dominated.

Another opportunity for social advancement was through education. Schools open to boys from many walks of life began in 145 B.C.E. in the province of Shu, where modern Sichuan is, when Governor Wen Weng (ca. 1231–ca. 1135 B.C.E.) opened schools to boys from throughout the province because he needed a pool of educated people from which to hire government officials. The schools of China were Confucian, and students were expected to learn the principles of the philosopher Confucius (551–479 B.C.E.) and become skilled in the sciences and the law. If a student passed tests given by the government, he could gain a government job and rise through the ranks of government, acquiring higher social rank as he did.

Girls could become educated, too, but they had to be educated in private, usually by other women. This practice limited the opportunities for education to daughters of the wealthy, nobles, and government officials. Some women were marvelously gifted and even became influential advisers to emperors. Even so, they complained about restrictions placed on them because of their gender. The women of ancient China were notable for their industriousness and contributed greatly to the economy, but they were expected to submit to the authority of men. When they rose in rank, they did so usually because their husbands rose in rank. They may have found their greatest opportunities in trades and crafts because tradespeople and craftspeople were outside official recognition, but even a woman who made herself wealthy might find that her money was not her own if she married.

Japan

In Japan people did not begin building an agricultural economy until about 300 B.C.E. Even in the third century C.E. they had not yet learned to irrigate their farms; they did not plant rice as seedlings and, in fact, just scattered rice seed in wet areas, such as marshes. When they first formed governments is not known, but the earliest ruler for whom there are written records, mostly Chinese, is Queen Himiko (fl. third century C.E.), who ruled a nation called Yamatai, whose people the Chinese called Wa. This culture existed in the late second century and third century C.E. The Wa lived in more than 50 small chiefdoms. It is possible that Himiko ruled by the consent of the chiefs. That she was a sorceress suggests that women held high rank in religion. Although her being the monarch implies a matriarchal society, the effort to replace her with a man after her death suggests that male chiefs wanted a male leader.

Ceramic sculptures left by the Wa indicate that they had a society with many crafts because the sculptures portray many people in everyday work. It is easy to suppose that ceramics makers were highly respected because the people of Japan had produced magnificent pottery for thousands of years.

Jōmon Period pottery, Japan (about 13,000–300 B.C.E.); the development of production techniques and decoration of this style of pottery over such a long period suggests that the country was stable and enjoyed a continuity of social organization. (© The Trustees of the British Museum)

Central and Northern Asia

Most of what has been recorded about the peoples of central and northern Asia was written by people who hated them. Historical records are of raids by central and northern Asians on farms and towns, of rampant slaughter of civilians and theft of a year's harvest as well as of valuable goods. However, the people of those parts of Asia were among the world's greatest explorers. Several times they crossed from Asia to North America, and their descendants populated two unfamiliar continents. Many in the far north of Asia followed nomadic animal herds, as some still follow reindeer. There is little record of these far northern Asians being warlike or raiding others. They seem to have had their societies organized around the herds they followed, which were regarded as owned by everyone in the society.

Those who raided the settled peoples of Asia had ethics so different from those of the settled areas that their points of view seemed almost incomprehensible to the settled peoples. In general, such groups as the Xiongnu, who lived north and northwest of China, regarded other peoples as prey. Their societies were organized around taking what they needed to survive, either from herds of sheep or cattle or from people who grew crops and manufactured goods they wanted. Efforts to reason with them by the Chinese and Indians failed for lack of a common ground of understanding.

The Xiongnu had kings, men selected from among many tribal chiefs. Their authority was limited because chiefs would sometimes choose to disobey them. Both men and women were trained from birth to be expert horsemen, and both genders held responsibility for carrying and raising tents, providing food, and defending their camps. Within a traveling group, there seems to have been social ranking, with some people owning more cattle or horses than other people. One way for someone to raise his or her social standing was to steal horses or cattle from another tribe.

Some nomads of central Asia moved into settled territories in order to find pasture for their herds. Central Asia had been drying out for centuries when Aryans moved into India and Iran to find new grazing areas. A growth in population may have provided additional pressure to move south into new lands. The best records of their societies known to exist are the Hindu religious works the Vedas, based on the ancient oral history of the Aryan invasion of India.

Oceania

Very little is known of the social organization of ancient Oceania. Thus, archaeologists and historians study the customs of people of Oceania of recorded history, from the 18th century C.E. to the present, and make inferences about social behavior. Sometimes they make assumptions about social organization that lack scientific foundation, based on what they know of similar societies in other parts of the world. Thus, much that is thought to be true of ancient Oceania is subject to sometimes radical change when new evidence is discovered. In general, the peoples of the ancient Pacific probably organized themselves by family relationships, with immediate relatives being the smallest social unit, followed by membership in a clan. The peoples of Tonga may have been organizing themselves into a larger social unit, a nation, during the last couple of centuries of the ancient era, when they were likely moving toward creating a monarchy and a kingdom. In Australia people probably moved across the landscape in family groups, forming larger groups only for religious observances. Elsewhere the social dynamics are murky. For instance, Indonesia almost certainly had cultures in which loyalty to one's clan was being replaced by loyalty to a monarch, but what form this change took is unknown. During the medieval era powerful kingdoms emerged on Java, suggesting that society was already organized and developing as distinct groups or nations earlier, during the ancient era.

EUROPE

BY AMY HACKNEY BLACKWELL

Although social organization is very difficult to determine from nonwritten sources, archaeologists use information from settlements and burials to infer how the ancient people of Europe structured their social relationships. The ice age hunter-gatherers before 10,000 B.C.E. were organized into bands that had only a loose connection to kinship and were based more on friendship and trust. Such groups may have coalesced at some times of the year and split apart at other times to take advantage of seasonal conditions for hunting and collecting. It is difficult to tell whether the family was a central element of social life at this time. The establishment of farming communities across Europe between 7000 B.C.E. and 3000 B.C.E. brought the emergence of distinct households, residential groups related by kinship and probably organized in a family structure. Such households were the basic building blocks of Neolithic society. Differences in status, power, and wealth were transient, and no lasting hierarchies appear to have formed.

Social structure changed in the late Neolithic and the Bronze Age, when we see for the first time clear differences in status, power, and wealth that persisted across generations. Farming households were still the fundamental basis for social structure, but starting in about 3000 B.C.E. in southeastern Europe and 2000 B.C.E. in northwestern Europe, there began to be rich burials and the accumulation of goods that marked social differences. Many archaeologists believe that the societies at this time took the form of what anthropologists call "chiefdoms," in which a small group of elite individuals and families were in control of a larger population of commoners. On the other hand, it is also possible that the lines of authority and status were not so hierarchical at first, and while some individuals may have been leaders in some spheres of activity (such as trade), others may have had leading roles in other activities (such as warfare and ritual). It is clear, however, that the complex social organization of Celtic and Germanic Europe that is known to us from written records emerged from these formative periods centuries and millennia earlier.

Most of what is known in written sources about ancient European social organization comes from the Celtic and Germanic peoples. The Celts, or more precisely the Celtic languages, spread through Europe during the first millennium B.C.E., radiating out from the Alps of Central Europe. By 400 B.C.E. most of the people in northwestern Europe and the British Isles spoke Celtic languages. The Germanic-speaking peoples appeared in northern Germany and southern Scandinavia around 500 B.C.E. and migrated throughout Central Europe over the next 1,000 years. Although there were other language groups and accompanying cultures, Celtic and Germanic peoples predominated in non-Mediterranean Europe.

Almost every ancient European culture was organized around a tribal structure. Both Celts and Germans organized their societies around two principles: family and war. Kinship determined tribal membership and battle companions. Family relationships and skill in battle also determined an individual's position in the social hierarchy. Social institutions were designed to help people behave within the hierarchy and to maintain the peace within a warlike society.

Ancient European social organization was also largely determined by the fact that Celtic and Germanic peoples moved around frequently. The Romans observed that the Celts and Germans sometimes wandered for generations at a time, loading their wagons with their worldly goods and traveling from place to place in the forests of Central Europe. They occasionally settled in small villages and farmed the surrounding land, but they often abandoned these settlements and wandered around. Social mores facilitated this frequent movement. For example, both Celtic and Germanic people would kill old people or newborn infants if keeping them around would slow down the group too much. By the time of the Roman Empire, Celtic and Germanic societies had become fairly civilized. People lived in cities and traded with people from several nations. In this period social organization was influenced by Roman and Greek practices.

Celts

The Celtic peoples who occupied most of Europe by the fifth century B.C.E. had a loose social structure that revolved around family and warfare. Tribes, clans, and families were the primary social groupings. The largest grouping was the tribe, or *tuath* in Irish. This group provided people with their ethnic identity. Within the tribe, people belonged to a clan, an extended family that was the real source of social organization. Nuclear families formed the smallest social group but were less significant than clans.

Celts seem to have thought of themselves first as soldiers. The chiefs of Celtic tribes were expected to be extremely brave in battle to show an example to their soldiers. Soldiers grew very close to their comrades in arms and were expected to sacrifice their lives for one another or to avenge their fallen companions. It went without saying that clan members would rally to the aid of their fellow clansmen. If a Celtic man was insulted or murdered by someone from another clan, his kinsmen would all assume the responsibility of avenging him. This practice resulted in extended feuds between families throughout the Celtic world.

Because feuds were so common, Celtic societies created a class of men who arbitrated disputes. These men were experts in the complex body of laws (called Brehon laws in Ireland) used throughout Europe in Celtic communities. Historians believe that these laws originated among European Celtic peoples during the Bronze Age, between 2300 and 900 B.C.E. For centuries Celtic legal experts memorized the body of laws so that they could interpret them and resolve disputes. One of the main purposes of Celtic laws was to prevent the frequent blood feuds from resulting in a never-ending string of murders by forcing murderers to compensate the families of their victims. This compensation would effectively end a feud, allowing the rival clans to resume peaceful relations.

Celtic society was organized into a number of different classes. Kings and noblemen sat at the top. These men were wealthy and counted in their clans large groups of powerful kinsmen who could support them in battle. Nobles often functioned as chiefs of their tribes. The people in the clan of a nobleman's tribe owed him allegiance. The nobleman himself might owe allegiance to a higher nobleman or a king. In Ireland a number of lesser kings would owe allegiance to a single high king. Anyone who owed allegiance to someone else was required to pay that nobleman tribute every year, in the form of grain, livestock, and military assistance.

Below the noble classes there were two classes of free people (as opposed to slaves). Members of the higher class owned some movable property, such as cattle, but they did not own land. Below them were free people who owned nothing. These freemen rented land from nobles, paying rent in the form of crops and fighting for their landlords during wartime. Below the free classes were slaves captured from other tribes and free clansmen who had somehow lost their tribal rights.

Celts also ranked themselves within classes, according to age, birth, and skill and courage in battle. This social ranking helped Celtic people know how to relate to one another. They knew who owed what to whom, who could own land and who could not, and who could testify in court. Social rank determined which crimes were prosecuted and how they were punished. It even determined the sort of funeral a person would receive; chiefs were often buried with chariots and weapons as well as gold jewelry.

Two categories of Celts operated somewhat outside the usual system of rankings. Priests, called Druids, maintained the calendar and determined the dates of festivals. Druids also memorized the body of mythology and taught it to people. They served as advisers to the kings and officiated at rituals. Professional poets, or bards, composed and memorized long poems describing mythical or historical events. Nobles and kings kept bards at their courts to serve as official historians and entertainers. Bards were allowed to travel more freely than other people and were often welcomed as visitors because they offered entertainment. Although Celtic society was patriarchal and kinship was traced through male lines, women had a fairly high position in society. They could own property, and they fought alongside men in battles.

During the first millennium B.C.E., settlement patterns varied from place to place. Many early Celts lived in small settlements that might house several extended families who farmed and hunted in the surrounding area. In the British Isles people lived in and around hilltop forts. Others lived in larger groups in towns. The people of the Hallstatt culture (1200–500 B.C.E.) lived in towns and in hill forts. Some Gallic tribes were large, amorphous groups of migrating warriors and families. They seem not to have believed that they had a homeland of their own and were willing to move long distances.

Several kings appear to have taken advantage of Celtic military skill and lack of national ties by buying their services as mercenary soldiers. In the days of the early Roman Republic (509–27 B.C.E.) the Gauls encroached on the Mediterranean world several times. Gauls of the Senones tribe, led by the chief Brennus (fourth century B.C.E.), attacked Rome in 387 B.C.E. and then immediately left; some historians believe that Brennus was hired by Dionysius of Syracuse (r. 405–367 B.C.E.) to attack Rome. In the late third century B.C.E. several thousand Gauls wandered through Thrace and were invited into Asia Minor by King Nicomedes I (r. 278–250 B.C.E.) of Bithynia, who wanted them to help him fight his brother. These Gauls settled in central Anatolia, where they became known as the Galatians.

Celtic people seem to have been trading with one another and with other Europeans long before the Romans arrived. Archaeologists have found prehistoric roads in Ireland and Germany that might have been used to transport goods from place to place. Celtic smiths used a variety of metals that had to come from other places. Celtic goods made their way throughout the Mediterranean region. Most trade among Celtic peoples was done by barter and exchange, and its primary purpose was the cementing of kinship ties and military alliances. Cattle were a particularly important form of wealth, and attempting to steal the cattle of enemies was apparently a fairly common enterprise among Celtic nobles.

The Celts did make some coins during the Roman Period, but these were of limited use, and most people preferred to hold their wealth in more tangible forms, such as gold jewelry, weapons, chariots, cloth, slaves, and livestock. As time went on and the Roman Empire grew, however, Celts became increasingly Romanized in their behavior and trading practices.

Gauls

By the time of the Roman Republic, the Celts in France and Belgium, known as the Gauls, had developed a complex society with defined territories and military alliances. Julius Caesar (r. 49–44 B.C.E.) wrote a lengthy description of Gallic life in his account of the Gallic Wars. Caesar describes three main groups of Gauls: the Aquitani, the Galli or Celtae, and the Belgae. The Belgae appear to have been at least part Germanic, though historians do not know much about them. They were particularly warlike because they lived far from the Mediterranean world.

According to Caesar, the Gauls of his time organized themselves into tribes, which were subdivided into *pagi*. Each *pagus* was a subdivision of the tribe's overall territory; the Romans also used the term to refer to the individuals who lived in a given *pagus*. Every tribe was led by a council of elders and a single leader, either a hereditary king or an elected official. The Aeduii tribe called their king Vergobret. These kings ruled together with the councils, preventing the kings from taking complete control of their tribes.

Tribes were also organized into larger groups that contained several tribes. Although these organizations, called "*civitates*" by the Romans, encompassed large amounts of territory and had large populations, they were not equivalent to nations. The Gallic tribes occasionally united to fight a common enemy, but generally they did not get along well enough to stay together for long. The chief Vercingetorix (d. 46 B.C.E.) of the Averni led a union of Gallic tribes in battle against the Romans in 52 B.C.E. Vercingetorix had enough authority to make alliances with other Gallic tribes and to hold supreme command of all the Gallic armies. He engineered an overarching defense strategy that would have been impossible with a looser arrangement. However, he was captured by Caesar, and the union of the tribes dissolved.

The Romans knew of numerous tribes. Gallic tribes included the Allobroges of the region near Geneva; the Aquitani of southwestern France; the Carnutes from modern Chartres, France; the Helvetii of Switzerland and southwestern Germany; the Nervii, a Belgic tribe from northern France; the Parisii, who lived on the site of modern Paris; and many others. Many of these tribes were "half-civilized," according to Roman estimations. They lived in well-organized towns and traded with their neighbors, but they did not value education as Romans did, and their governments were disorganized by Roman standards.

The Gauls who lived near the Mediterranean lived in cities, many of them elaborately fortified to serve as safe havens in battle. Gallic towns were often built on top of hills, the better to defend themselves. These cities were home to large numbers of people. Caesar calls these towns *oppida*. Each tribe might have several cities, but one would be more important than the others and serve as a capital of the tribe's territory. The Averni were centered in a city called Gergovia. The tribe known as the Mandubii called their capital Alesia. Alesia, in particular, left behind good archaeological remains, where historians have found evidence of a thriving town that traded with outsiders, including Romans. There were many large buildings, including a number of public buildings constructed during the Roman period. Contemporary writers mention the fine metalwork produced by smiths from Alesia, and archaeologists have found artifacts confirming this account.

Germans

The best source on Germanic social organization is the Roman historian Tacitus (ca. 56–120 C.E.), who describes the people in his work *Germania*. Tacitus observes that family and kinship formed the strongest ties among German people. Clans and families organized themselves into tribes. Male relatives fought together. Military squadrons were composed of clans and families instead of random groups of strangers, a bond that Tacitus claims gave the Germans great courage in battle. To add to the power of family, German women and children came to watch their men fight in battle, cheering on the brave and tending the wounds of the injured. Germans were said to have dreaded being taken captive and especially to have feared having to give noble women to enemies who beat them in battle.

German government was very loose, and the Germans had nothing that could be called a state. The only time they organized into large groups was during wartime, when large numbers of Germans might fight together under a single leader. This arrangement was very flexible, allowing them to adapt to threats as necessary; some historians believe it was this flexibility that helped the Germans avoid being conquered by the Romans.

According to Tacitus, the Germans had three types of leaders: chiefs or kings, generals, and priests. Kings were hereditary; the sons of a king could hope to become kings themselves. Kings were expected to provide a good example for their people, especially in battle, but their power was quite limited. They could make certain minor decisions on their own, but for major matters the entire tribe had to participate and make a group decision. Chiefs were required to be excellent soldiers and to lead the charge in battle. Their followers, who were also their male kinsmen, were expected to defend the chiefs with their lives. It was considered a disgrace for a chief to show cowardice or for a follower to walk away alive from a battle in which his chief had fallen.

Generals were chosen based on their ability. Soldiers who proved themselves in battle and who combined courage with intelligence and energy could win the admiration of their peers and thus become military leaders. Generals, like kings, lacked arbitrary power over their soldiers and civilians.

Tacitus wrote that German priests had the most real power. Priests alone were allowed to punish people by reprimand or flogging, typically for cowardice or other error in battle. Religion was the foundation of much of German social activity. Priests organized numerous festivals. Divination was a primary method of making decisions. Priests would perform various rituals to see what the future was likely to bring, and the Germans would base their decisions on the results.

German society was hierarchical, organized roughly according to birth, age, and military might. The various chiefs were ranked by birth and military prowess, so there was a chief of the chiefs. The highest-ranking chief was the man with the most followers. The followers themselves knew their respective ranks, determined by the nobility of their lord, their age, and their skill in battle. Young men vied to fight at the side of a chief because doing so was one of the best ways for them to advance. These young men would also walk around with a chief during peacetime because it was considered an honor for a chief to be surrounded by a large group of faithful soldiers. Chiefs solidified their power by giving large feasts for their followers. They also gave presents to their soldiers and to fellow chiefs.

Chiefs made minor decisions by themselves. For major matters, the entire tribe would consider the matter and make final decisions that the chiefs would respect. Tacitus notes that German tribal meetings were somewhat disorganized. The Germans did not have an accurate means of accounting for days and nights, so it was difficult for them all to assemble at once. Instead, they would take two or three days to assemble in one place. Then they would sit down, still wearing their weapons, and the priests would order everyone to be silent. The tribe members were then allowed to speak in order of rank, starting with the king or chief. The other participants ranked themselves by age, family, prowess in battle, or speaking ability, all of which were considered important and worthy of distinction.

According to Tacitus, German men had little to occupy themselves when they were not fighting. He wrote that they spent most of their free time either hunting or lying around sleeping. The women and old men were responsible for the daily care of the home and the production of food. Each German family had a nominal male head, usually the father, who could make decisions about family members, deciding who should marry whom and who would live where. German families lived in close quarters. Children had the run of the local clan area, whether they lived in a village or were in the midst of travels. Uncles, aunts, and other relatives were expected to help care for children. The relationship between men and the sons of their sisters was especially close; these men considered their nephews as important as their own sons. Germans also solidified family ties through the practice of fosterage, in which children went to live with relatives for a time.

The Germans had no cities. They did not even really have towns. Their villages sprung up with no plan, arising simply because groups of people all chose to build houses around the same site. Their homes were roughly built of timber, though the Germans were known to live in caves if they were convenient.

The Germans did not use actual currency, but they did have forms of wealth that allowed them to distinguish rich from poor. Germans loved gold and silver, which they wore as jewelry. Chiefs wore the best jewelry. Chiefs also used jewelry as a form of reward for faithful followers. Fine weapons were also appreciated. When couples married, they exchanged gifts of oxen, weapons, and horses.

Like the Celts, the Germans kept slaves. Slaves were typically prisoners taken in war. German slaves were allowed to live in their own homes and have families. They functioned more as tenants of their masters than as household servants.

By the end of the ancient period, the Germanic peoples had divided into numerous groups, including the Franks, the

Goths (who split into the Visigoths and the Ostrogoths), the Alamanni, the Vandals, the Suebi, and the Burgundians. The Visigoths and the Ostrogoths organized themselves into actual kingdoms in the third century C.E. Their social organization was heavily influenced by Roman culture over the next century. The two groups of Goths had kings and genuine governments and adopted Christianity, which added a church hierarchy to their society.

Thracians

The region north of Greece was home to various peoples who spoke Thracian languages. This area encompassed modern Bulgaria, Serbia, Romania, Ukraine, Hungary, and Slovakia. Homer wrote about the Tracians in the *Iliad*, describing Thrace as including the region bordered by the Black Sea and Hellespont to the east and the Vardar River to the west. According to the ancient Greeks, the people who lived in Thrace organized themselves into tribes led by kings or chiefs. These tribes were defined by kinship, military power, and geography.

Most people in Thrace lived in small villages and did not venture far from home. Thrace had no cities or large social groups. The region is mountainous, and travel was very difficult during ancient times. Therefore, groups of people were isolated from one another. The Greeks thought that the mountain tribes were the most warlike and uncivilized of the Thracian peoples. Tracians who lived in lower, flatter areas close to Greece were more peaceful and better informed about the larger world than those who lived in the mountains.

The only organized Thracian nation was the Odrysian Kingdom, which existed in Bulgaria, Romania, northern Greece, and the European portion of Turkey between the fifth century B.C.E. and the third century B.C.E. Its first capital was located in Edirne, Turkey. This kingdom was formed by King Teres (r. 480–440 B.C.E.), who gathered several tribes together in a rough union. Not all Thracian tribes joined the union, and though contemporary Greeks occasionally mentioned kings of Thrace, these kings did not control all tribes living in the region. Kings tried to unify the tribes, to increase both their own power within the kingdom and the power of the Thracians against kingdoms to the south, such as the Macedonians, but they had little success. In the fourth century B.C.E. the Thracian Kingdom divided into three smaller kingdoms. These smaller kingdoms proved easier for rulers to run. One of them moved its capital to Seuthopolis, Bulgaria, where its rulers kept it together for the century. The Greeks and Romans gradually colonized the area, influencing social structures. By 400 C.E. Thracian languages had disappeared, and the tribal structure had been replaced by Greek and Roman customs and styles of administration.

GREECE

BY JEFFREY S. CARNES

Greek societies were hierarchical, with clearly marked social classes and kinship groups. The place of an individual within society was defined by birth and family connections, property or other wealth, and status, particularly with respect to citizenship. Social structures varied from one polis (city-state) to the next but tended to fall into certain basic categories; they were, moreover, subject to manipulation and change over time; as always, ideology (of class, equality, or freedom) could cover over the actual social conditions under which people lived.

Freedom and Slavery

The most basic social distinction at all times in ancient Greece was between the free person and the slave. Greeks prided themselves on freedom, and this freedom was defined by contrast with those who lacked it: slaves in Greek cities and the inhabitants of other, non-Greek nations. Slaves made up a large percentage of the population during the Classical Period (fifth and fourth centuries B.C.E.), perhaps as high as one-third in Athens and somewhat lower elsewhere. Inscriptions show the categories of liberty that the slave was denied: freedom to live where one chooses (including the possibility of migrating to another polis), freedom to act on one's own behalf in legal matters, freedom from arbitrary capture or seizure, and freedom of action. Greeks believed that other peoples, in particular, the Persians, also lacked such freedoms. It was common to portray the inhabitants of the vast Persian Empire as slaves to the Great King while the Greeks were their own masters.

As is always the case with ideological constructs, the simple free-slave, Greek-barbarian dichotomies masked a more nuanced reality. *Eleutheria* (freedom) became the rallying cry of Sparta in its imperialist struggles with Athens, despite the fact that citizens of Athens enjoyed far greater personal liberty than did Spartans. Nor was the distinction between slave and free always hard and fast. In addition to chattel slavery, a variety of types of limited servitude existed (such as debt bondage and serfdom). As Aristotle points out, the Greek ideal of freedom also included not having to work for the benefit of another person; however, a relatively small percentage of the population could make this claim, and many free laborers must have led lives more difficult and more constrained than those of some slaves (and in some instances may even have enjoyed lesser social status). In addition, the freedoms denied slaves were also denied women, and women of higher status were more subject to male scrutiny and control and thus enjoyed less freedom than did lower-class women.

Society in the Homeric Age

The poems of Homer (ca. ninth to eighth centuries B.C.E.) present a vivid, if idealized picture of early Greek society as it existed in the years prior to the eighth century B.C.E., told from the viewpoint of the upper classes (though with a great deal of sympathy for others). The *Odyssey* shows a world in which the self-sufficient household (*oikos*) is the basic social and economic unit. Landholders with relatively large estates dominate the political and social landscape; Odysseus, as the largest of these landholders, is the king (*basileus*) of Ithaca. Other noble landholders compete for honor and power within Ithaca, but there exists as well the ethos of *xenia* (guest friendship), which governs relations between members of different households and different communities. *Xenia* demands that strangers be treated with respect and provides them protection, since it is viewed as a sacred bond protected by Zeus Xenios, the god of strangers. Moreover, *xenia* forges reciprocal bonds of friendship and obligation that last from one generation to the next. When a man of high status travels to a distant land, he will call upon other noblemen to provide him with shelter; the exchange of guest presents, often quite lavish ones, is customary. His descendants will be governed by the same obligations of *xenia*. The most striking example of this practice is in the *Iliad*, in which Glaukos and Diomedes meet on the battlefield. Upon learning that their grandfathers had entertained each other as *xenoi*, the two warriors refuse to fight each other and exchange armor in a gesture of mutual friendship. (Homer remarks that Diomedes gets the better of the exchange, receiving gold armor in return for bronze; this observation is perhaps a commentary on the rivalry and craftiness that might lurk behind the practice of gift giving).

The actual practice of *xenia* was perhaps less important than its ideological significance. For the upper classes it marked a way of life that set them apart from those below them. Contempt for merchants and those who make their living by trade is evident in the *Odyssey* and shows up in pro-aristocratic sources centuries later. Nevertheless, the Homeric worldview also exhibits sympathy for those of lower status. Those who overstep the limits of their class (the common soldier Thersites in the *Iliad* and the beggar Iros in the *Odyssey*) are treated harshly, but in general slaves and beggars are accorded sympathy. Being a wanderer or an exile is considered one of the worst possible fates (thus the poignancy of Odysseus's plight), especially for those who lack the safety supplied to the upper classes by the practice of *xenia*. Slavery was a condition to which anyone might be subject (piracy and warfare being common), and Homer expresses compassion for those who were subject to it. (The poems' dominant ruling-class ideology is reflected, however, in the expectation that slaves be loyal to their masters' interests.)

The Archaic Period

In the eighth century through the sixth century B.C.E. the poems of Homer became the central texts for the Greeks' conception of themselves as a people (or group of peoples). During this time interest in genealogy grew, with oral or written genealogies becoming a way for noble families to trace their descent from the great heroes of the past as well as a foundation for the kinship systems that formed the basic social structures of archaic Greece. The poems of Hesiod (fl. ca. 800 B.C.E.) reflect the importance of heroic genealogies: Descent from a heroic or divine ancestor guaranteed the prestige of a particular group, whether a city or a family, and intercity alliances were made and unmade on the basis of such genealogies. It was during this time that the distinction between Dorians and Ionians solidified. Greeks had always spoken a variety of dialects (Doric and Ionic among them), but it was during the early Archaic Period that these dialects took on an ethnic and political dimension. Thenceforward states could claim solidarity based on ethnicity and distant kinship, so that the fifth century B.C.E. conflict between the Spartan and Athenian Empires could be portrayed as a Dorian versus Ionian struggle.

The structure of Greek society was permanently altered by the events of the Archaic Period. A combination of factors led to material prosperity and expansion, in both colonization and trade. The influx of new wealth challenged the older aristocratic order, and colonization allowed more Greeks to possess more land, which remained the main source of wealth throughout antiquity. In many cities tyrants arose to champion the newly prosperous classes against the aristocracy; in others reforms kept the cities free from one-man rule. Material culture reveals a tendency toward equality. The rich tended to avoid ostentatious displays of wealth, and taste in art and handicrafts became relatively uniform throughout society. Literary sources reveal a flourishing debate on the nature of citizenship, wealth, and power. Some poets, such as Archilochus (seventh century B.C.E.), claim to represent the voice of the common soldier or citizen, while others, such as Theognis (sixth to fifth century B.C.E.), take a reactionary viewpoint, expressing disdain for poorer citizens' claims to social and political equality. This point of view was represented even into the fifth century B.C.E., with the odes of Pindar (ca. 522–ca. 438 B.C.E.) expressing a preference for inherited excellence over acquired skill and using the language of older aristocratic institutions such as *xenia* in an era in which they had long since lost their original significance.

The reforms of the statesman Solon (ca. 630–ca. 560 B.C.E.) in Athens illustrate the social developments of the Archaic Period. A rapidly changing economy led to a situation in which many small farmers had become heavily indebted to their landlords or even enslaved for debt. Solon abolished debt slavery, gave the tenant farmers ownership of their land, and divided the citizen body into four property classifications, with varying degrees of citizen rights. The top two classes, for example, could hold the major elected offices. The third could hold minor offices and the fourth none. All four classes could participate in the Assembly. Solon thus reestablished land ownership as the basis for citizenship, a tendency that continued throughout antiquity in many Greek states and was removed in Athens only with the advent of the democracy in 508 B.C.E. Land, however, remained the main source of wealth for citizens even in Athens, and various measures were enacted to prevent the concentration of land in too few hands.

Phratries

The most significant kinship groups were the phyle (tribe) and the phratry. Membership in a phratry was determined by heredity and was normally linked to a particular place. Its members were *phrateres*, a word derived from the Indo-European root meaning "brother." The names of phratries normally used the patronymic (name derived from the father's name) ending *-idai* (thus Demotionidai, "sons of Demotion"), and while membership was inherited, the phratry was thought of as a larger unit than the family; "clan" is sometimes used to translate the term. Phratries were probably in existence in Mycenaean times (ca. 1600–1100 B.C.E.) but are first mentioned in the *Iliad* and existed in many Greek cities, both Dorian and Ionian. For citizens of the Ionian cities (including Athens), phratry membership was an essential component of their Ionian identity. The creation of the phratries was traced to Ion, the hero for whom the Ionians are named, and virtually all Ionian cities celebrated a festival known as the Apatouria, which was devoted mainly to enrolling new phratry members. In some instances, phratries seem to have been subdivisions of phylae, though in most cities it seems that the two institutions were separate and overlapped.

Membership in a phratry was a necessary condition of citizenship in Athens, even after the reforms of Cleisthenes (ca. 570–after 508 B.C.E.); this practice seems to be true for other Ionian cities as well. Their functions generally reflect the notion of phratry as brotherhood or extended family. They were responsible for enrolling citizens (usually young men coming of age and occasionally naturalized citizens) and oversaw questions of legitimate descent and inheritance. The Draconian law on homicide, which dated from the 620s B.C.E. and was the only one of Draco's (seventh century B.C.E.) laws reenacted in the fifth century B.C.E., provided that in a case of homicide, the victim's fellow *phrateres* were responsible for supporting his family and were to take on the responsibilities of his family (including prosecuting the alleged killer) if he had no family.

Phratry membership evolved with the changing needs of the polis. In the early days phratries may have been strongholds of aristocratic privilege (though the link of phratry membership to citizenship makes this theory somewhat less likely). Phratries could split up into smaller phratries or merge (whereas the number of demes, or local communities, and phylae were fixed). In democratic Athens phratries were themselves democratic: All members voted by secret ballot, and an official called a phratriarch was elected to a one-year term. There were perhaps 30 phratries in Athens, subdivided into *genē*, whose function is less clear. Not all citizens belonged to *genē*. They seem to be self-identified groups, claiming descent from a common ancestor. In some cases priesthoods were reserved for members of a particular *genos*.

Phylae

Later to develop than the phratry but ultimately more important was the phyle, or tribe. Unknown in the Homeric poems, phylae were in place by the eighth century B.C.E. in most but not all Greek cities. There were two main sets of phylae in the Archaic Period: the Dorian, consisting of the Hylleis, the Dymanes, and the Pamphyloi, and the Ionian, consisting of the Geleontes, the Hopletes, the Argadeis, and the Aigikoreis in Athens and including the Oinopes and the Boreis in other Ionian cities. The names common to various cities most likely owe to the development of Dorian and Ionian ethnic identity, thus establishing the relatively late origin of the phylae.

Phylae often served as military units or as voting constituencies. Each tribe would be responsible for providing a certain number of soldiers or entitled to elect a certain number of magistrates. Like the phratries, phylae often had subdivisions—in some cases phratries themselves, or *genē*, but more often numerical subdivisions, such as thirds, hundreds, or thousands. Phylae were less stable than phratries, perhaps because they were viewed as more strictly political divisions, lacking some of the phratries' religious aura. Almost all cities for which we have evidence had altered their basic tribe structure by the start of the fifth century B.C.E. In some cases new tribes were added to accommodate an increase in population or an influx of immigrants; in others a political upheaval or a consolidation of several smaller communities (a process known as synoecism) provided the impetus for realignment. The Greek historian Herodotus (ca. 484–between 430 and 420 B.C.E.) tells the story of Cleisthenes (r. ca. 600–ca. 570 B.C.E.), who became tyrant of Sicyon and gave the local Dorian tribes insulting names (such as Hyatai, "pig-men") while naming his own tribe Archelaoi ("rulers of the people").

The best-known tribal reform is that of the Athenian Cleisthenes (grandson of the Sicyonian tyrant), which was effected in the years immediately following the establishment of the democracy in 508 B.C.E. The system was both complex and central to civic life. Attica (Athens and its surrounding territory) is one of the larger areas controlled by a polis, some 930 square miles. There existed within Attica a number of formerly independent cities (such as Marathon) that had been brought together via synoecism during the early Archaic Period. As a result, there were many local communities known as *demoi* (demes), representing villages or neighborhoods within the city. The demes were grouped into three main divisions: city demes, coastal demes, and hill demes (the inland parts of Attica), which had developed rivalries based on their perceived differences in economic interests. Cleisthenes made 30 groups (known as *trittyes*) out of contiguous demes (10 in each division), then formed 10 phylae by taking one *trittys* from each of the three divisions. The phylae were named after local heroes—Erechtheis for Erechtheus, Kekropis for Kekrops, and so on—thus distinguishing them from the older Ionian tribes (whose use was kept only for certain limited religious contexts) and marking them as a uniquely Athenian institution. The distribution of demes irrespective of geographic location had the effect of breaking down rivalries within the city so that any Athenian citizen would find himself sharing civic duties with citizens from far-flung parts of Attica.

A citizen in Athens, then, would find himself a member not only of a phratry but also of a deme, a *trittys*, and a phyle. The deme as a small-scale political unit had a substantial degree of autonomy; more important for social organization was its status as the basic unit of citizenship. Young men were enrolled at age 18 in their deme registers, thus becoming citizens; thereafter they would be known in formal contexts by name, father's, name, and deme affiliation. Thus, the statesman Pericles (ca. 495–429 B.C.E.) was known as *Perikles Xanthippou Cholargeus*, "Pericles, son of Xanthippus, of the deme Cholargos." Although it was geographic in origin, deme affiliation was inherited and did not change if a citizen moved from one locality to another. In practice, few did move unless compelled by circumstance. The Greek historian Thucydides (d. ca. 401 B.C.E.) speaks of the forced evacuation of the countryside during the Peloponnesian War (431–404 B.C.E.) as a time when citizens felt they were leaving their own native cities to move into Athens.

The *trittys* was by far the least important of the social units. It does not seem to have had an elected governing body or officials, although *trittyes* seem to have played some part in the organization of the navy and perhaps the army. The phylae, however, were central to civic life, and most state institutions were organized along tribal lines. The Boule, or Council, was composed of 500 citizens, selected by lot, 50 from each tribe; the 6,000 jurors for the law courts were selected in a similar way. The tribes became the basis for military organization, and the *strategoi* (generals) who led the army and became the de facto leaders of the city, were elected annually, one from each tribe. Civic competitions (in athletics, dancing, or singing) were contested according to tribal divisions; even the great tragic festivals chose their judges with equal representation from each tribe.

Status and Ideology

There existed throughout the democratic era in Athens a strong ideology of equality, which emphasized that all citizens had an equal share in the government, enjoyed equal protection of its laws, and possessed an equal right to speak freely. The typical Athenian citizen believed himself to be *metrios*, "in the middle," neither extremely rich and powerful nor extremely poor or cut off from the governance of the city. The word does not exactly describe an economic middle class. Even well-off Athenians could be *metrioi* if they lived without extravagance or obvious arrogance. Rather, the term suggests a habit of equality and civic competence. The vast majority of Athenians were deemed capable of running the state (and, in fact, did so in turns, thanks to the large numbers of offices that were filled by lot). The free and equal status of the citizen was taken very seriously indeed. *Hubris* was the term used for the deliberate and gratuitous personal insult to a citizen's dignity, and such an insult was punishable by law. Those who committed certain crimes could be punished with *atimia* (loss of citizen rights), while those who were found guilty of making a false claim of citizen status could be taken and sold into slavery.

Officially, wealth brought obligation (higher taxes, usually in the form of expensive public services known as liturgies) rather than privilege; officially, noble birth likewise counted for little. Nevertheless, the rich and well-connected were, even in Athens, overrepresented in public life and enjoyed more comfortable lives. It is an open question as to what extent the rich were really in control of the state; certainly the ideology of equality guaranteed high status for middling Athenians, and most scholars believe that the common people really did have a large share in the running of the polis.

The ideology of equality among citizens was found in most other cities as well, though its practice varied greatly from one location to the next. In particular, cities with oligarchic constitutions (government in which a small number of people were in control) might restrict full citizenship to those who met certain property qualifications (often tied to their ability to undertake and pay for their own military service); in other instances, descent from some particular ancestral group was a requirement. In Sparta there was a radical social and economic equality among citizens, who were known as *homoioi* (equals). Together they owned the best land in Sparta, which could not be transferred to outsiders and which was worked by a subservient group known as helots ("the captured ones"). Spartan men devoted their lives to military training and service. After a rigorous and austere upbringing, they became members of *syssitia* (eating groups), to which each contributed produce from his ancestral land. Power was by no means equally shared. Two hereditary kingships, a body of elders, and a small group of annually elected officials essentially ruled the city, with the Assembly of Citizens having little more than veto power. Nevertheless, the Spartans viewed themselves as having an equal share in the state and remained a relatively harmonious political unit for several hundred years.

Sparta shows with particular clarity the ways in which citizenship and social status were defined in opposition to those on the outside. For Sparta to have its military society, a nonfree class of helots was necessary; in addition, there was a group called *perioikoi* ("surrounding inhabitants"), who, while free, lacked a voice in the governance of the polis. Indeed, every Greek city had in its midst a large number of noncitizens—slaves, women, local but disenfranchised freemen, and Greek and non-Greek foreigners. In the modern world, citizenship is a matter of birth or naturalization, and virtually every inhabitant of the planet is a citizen of one country or another (and sometimes more than one). For the Greeks, to be a citizen was a special and privileged status, one that entitled its possessor to a share in his government (a frequent turn of phrase in the ancient texts) and that guaranteed four basic abilities: to vote, to hold office, to fight for the polis, and to own land.

Greek cities marked out resident noncitizens in a variety of ways, often using the term *metic* (Greek *metoikos*, "dweller among"); the status of metics varied from place to place, and, as usual, Athens provides the best evidence. Any foreign residents in Athens who stayed longer than a month were required to register as metics—as such they had to pay a special tax of one drachma per month and needed to be sponsored by an Athenian citizen. The metic enjoyed the privileges of residence at Athens—admission to theaters and festivals as well as economic opportunity—but was also liable for military service or (if wealthy enough) for expensive liturgies, without the opportunity to have a voice in making the policies that might send him to war. Most metics were of modest means—traders and craftspeople, both male and female, Greek and non-Greek—who had come to Athens to make a better living. A few were wealthy and prominent, including the orator Lysias (ca. 445–after 380 B.C.E.), whose father had come to the city to set up a large shield factory. The literary sources show wealthy metics moving easily among the upper crust of Athenian society.

The status of women in Greek society presents several paradoxes. Women were excluded from citizenship and were thus automatically of lower political status than men, yet upper-class women enjoyed not only a comfortable standard of living but also privileges appropriate to their class. The chorus of women in Aristophanes' (ca. 450–ca. 388 B.C.E.) *Lysistrata* provides an example of the privileges enjoyed by wellborn women, mainly holding certain religious offices and fulfilling specific roles in the city's religious festivals. They go on to make a further point: Women contribute sons to the city and therefore have a share in the city's well-being. The language used is similar to that for citizenship and is designed to counter the argument (found in a variety of sources dating from the time of Hesiod) that women are an economic burden to the men who are responsible for them.

Indeed, women in Athens were treated as perpetual minors, unable to own property or exercise basic legal rights and in need of a legal guardian if not under the control of a husband or a father. However, while women could not be citizens, it makes sense to speak of women of citizen class, particularly in light of Pericles' citizenship law of 451 B.C.E. Under this law citizenship was restricted to those born of two freeborn Athenian parents; thus, women were capable of passing on citizenship to their sons but could not possess it themselves. Needless to say, one effect of this law was to give all metic women—who ranged in wealth and status from the poorest vegetable seller to the most celebrated entertainer or courtesan—the same permanent outsider status as male metics. And, as noted, both women and slaves were characterized by a lack of the basic freedoms that even the lowest freeborn male took for granted.

ROME

BY MICHAEL J. O'NEAL

Rome began its existence as a small settlement on the banks of the Tiber River. The possibility that it would rule a territory that stretched across the Mediterranean Sea and northward into Europe was remote. Still, over a period of a millennium, Rome would come to shape the culture, politics, and social organization of a vast empire.

THE LEGENDARY PERIOD OF KINGS (753–509 B.C.E.)

Historians often refer to the time from 753 B.C.E., the fabled year of the founding of Rome, to 509 B.C.E., the beginning of the Roman Republic, as Rome's "legendary period." This period of Roman history is not very well documented. Most of what is known about the kings who ruled during this period comes from the later writings of the Greek historian Herodotus (ca. 484–ca. 430 B.C.E.). While much of the history of this period is based on legend, including the story of the founding of Rome by the twin brothers Romulus and Remus, archaeological evidence suggests that at least some of what Herodotus and others wrote was true.

The social organization of the earliest Romans was strongly influenced by the Etruscans, who occupied a large portion of the western coast of the Italian peninsula and swatches of territory extending northward. Not much is known about the origins of the Etruscans, but they interacted with the earliest Romans and exerted considerable social influence on them. The Etruscans were ruled by kings, and cities were controlled by nobles. Etruscan women occupied a place of equality relative to men. In the fifth century B.C.E., as Rome was extending its reach throughout the peninsula, it defeated the Etruscans in a major sea battle, and the distinct Etruscan culture began a slow decline as it was assimilated into Rome.

During this early period Rome was principally an agrarian society. The pillars of its society were family and religion. Just as an absolute monarch ruled the state, so too the early Roman family was ruled by the senior male, the *paterfamilias*, who wielded absolute power (*patria potestas*) for life. Children and the fruits of their labor on a farm were regarded as belonging to the father. A father had the legal right to kill a son or sell him into slavery if he was guilty of disloyal behavior, and fathers frequently practiced infanticide when children were born with deformities or illnesses. The father was, in effect, the chief priest of his clan, and one of his major roles was to foster worship of the gods. Romans during this period tended to be conservative, frugal people who lived simple lives.

Despite the absolute power of the *paterfamilias*, evidence suggests that families in early Rome were bound by strong ties of loyalty and warm feelings. The family and clan were the basic units of social organization. Divorce was uncommon, and women enjoyed privileges that were denied to women in Greece, Rome's rival but also its role model at the time. Daughters inherited property equally with sons, and after they married, they managed the household with a level of authority that rivaled that of their husbands. Households of the affluent were likely to include slaves, usually people who were captured in war or who were in severe debt. Slaves were relatively well treated. They could save their own money and in many cases buy their freedom. Slaves who were freed were granted citizenship, and many stayed with the family that had owned them to work for pay in the fields or in the household.

The Roman Republic (509–27 B.C.E.)

Historians refer to the period after 509 B.C.E. as the Roman Republic because in that year the monarchy came to an end and families of leading citizens ruled Rome. According to the Roman historian Titus Livius (ca. 59 B.C.E.–17 C.E.), better known to modern readers as Livy, the last of the Roman kings was Lucius Tarquinius Superbus ("Tarquin the Proud"). His son, Sextus Tarquinius, raped a Roman noblewoman named Lucretia (an event memorialized in William Shakespeare's long poem *The Rape of Lucrece*). She told her kinsmen what had happened and demanded justice before she committed suicide. Her husband and brother led a popular uprising that expelled the ruling house and established a republican form of government with elected magistrates.

The end of the Roman Republic and the beginning of the Roman Empire is a modern distinction that the Romans themselves did not make. Modern historians variously date the beginning of the empire at 44 B.C.E., when Julius Caesar was granted complete authority as emperor; 31 B.C.E., when Octavian defeated Marcus Antonius in the Battle of Actium; or 27 B.C.E., when Octavian was granted the title *Augustus*. The precise date is not important. What is important is that over a 500-year period, Rome grew in size and influence, primarily through military conquest.

The growth in the power and military prowess of Rome is relevant to its social organization. Repeated military victories lent a great deal of prestige to Rome's most important families and to its senators. Booty seized during military campaigns gave many Roman ambassadors and generals, who all served in the Senate, a great deal of wealth. With this wealth came a major shift in values and growing divisions and antagonisms in the social structure of the republic.

During the legendary period Romans valued frugality, modesty, public service, family, and worship of the gods. Among women, the ideal was the Roman "matron" who ruled her household and labored at crafts such as weaving. As the Roman Republic grew wealthier from conquest, a large class of nobility and statesmen became more arrogant and ostentatious. Many had traveled in the East, where they came into contact with the Greeks. They tried to imitate the Greeks by building large, elaborately decorated homes and massive public buildings. They seemed to compete with one another over who could hold the most lavish banquets or otherwise display their wealth. Women, too, began to imitate the Greeks by creating lavish lifestyles, often using inheritances from husbands or fathers who had died in warfare. This kind of ostentation got so out of hand that laws were passed allowing the state to confiscate excessive jewelry and gold.

During the Roman Republic considerable friction grew between the wealthy elites in the cities and the nation's rural population. Many men from the countryside were recruited into the military, meaning that they were not able to tend their fields. Then the republic embarked on a series of wars, called the Punic Wars, with the Carthaginians. During the Second Punic War, the Carthaginians' leading general, Hannibal (247–182 B.C.E.), led an army over the Alps from Spain into the Italian peninsula, laying waste to the countryside as he went. Meanwhile, Rome was cutting down the peninsula's forests to build ships for its navy. The result was that rural Rome was devastated. Its farms became far less productive, forcing the Romans to rely more heavily on imported grain from such places as Sicily. Many people tried to convert their farms into vineyards and olive orchards, but these types of operations required a large financial investment and years of work before they paid off.

With farm prices plummeting, many members of the Roman elite purchased land in the countryside. They used this land in part for recreational pursuits such as hunting and fishing. The also took over tracts of land that had been seized when Rome subdued other areas of the peninsula. In many cases they farmed this land, adding to their wealth, using thousands of slaves they had captured in war. Because of the greed of these landlords, the slaves were treated cruelly. The result was a series of slave revolts beginning in 135 B.C.E. The most famous of these revolts was the one led by Spartacus in 73 B.C.E.

Many rural Romans were unable to complete with the absentee Roman landlords whose land was worked by slaves. Many were forced off their land into the cities, where they could get jobs. Because of the immense amount of building taking place, jobs were plentiful, at least for a while. Most jobs were in the construction trades, as wealthy Romans built large homes and the government funded the construction of public buildings, aqueducts, and the like.

This new class of workers enjoyed the attractions that city life offered, but their relocation caused another problem for the republic: increasing difficulty finding military recruits. During the time of the Roman Republic a man had to own property to serve in the military, in part because he had to provide his own weapons and horses. As men left the countryside for the cities, they were no longer property owners, so the pool of potential military recruits was shrinking, and, given the farm crisis, those who remained on the land were reluctant to leave it for military service. The quandary for Rome was that this difficulty in manning the army came when Rome was essentially living off tribute (money paid by foreign rulers for protection and as a sign of submission) and booty seized in war. Making matters worse, Rome had to maintain armies of occupation in conquered territories. The result was a strain on the economy—Rome essentially spent its entire yearly revenue—and growing friction between social classes.

This friction between social classes not only affected the relationship between city elites and people in the countryside. It also affected social classes within the cities, especially the city of Rome itself. Two major social classes existed, the patricians and the plebeians. The patrician class included those who could trace their ancestry back to the first Roman Senate at the beginning of the republic. They were the aristocrats, the people who enjoyed wealth, status, and political influence. The plebeians consisted of everyone else (excluding slaves). During the early centuries of the republic, only patricians could hold public office. Intermarriage between patricians and plebeians was against the law. In general, patricians thought of plebeians as a mob, as the dregs of society who in many respects were barely human. In fact, however, many plebeians were themselves landowners, and some were fairly wealthy in their own right.

Over a period of some 200 years, conflict often erupted between the patricians and the plebeians (often called plebs). According to some historical accounts, this conflict led to a number of developments, including repeal of the laws barring plebs from holding public office and intermarrying with patricians. Further, the plebs frequently threatened, in effect, to go on strike and secede from Rome. Their interests were represented by the Plebeian Council (or Plebeian Assembly), which claimed the power to pass laws, giving rise to the modern word *plebiscite*, referring to a measure voted on by the population as a whole rather than its legislature. Collectively, these developments and threats are referred to as the Conflict of the Orders; the primary source of information about this conflict is Livy and his history of Rome, *Ab urbe condita* (From the Founding of the City).

Over time, the patrician class met many of the plebs' demands so that by the early third century B.C.E., the distinction between the two classes was eroding. In fact, many members of the patrician class were falling on hard times and petitioned the government to be reclassified as plebeians so they could reduce their tax bill. (Patricians, because of their alleged wealth, paid far higher taxes.) They also tried to reclaim their fortunes by marrying into plebeian families that had become affluent through trade and commerce. The political distinctions between the two classes diminished in the later years of the republic, though the social distinction between the two survived as a matter of prestige rather than law.

It should be noted that some historians dispute Livy's account of the Conflict of the Orders. While they agree that changes took place in the republic's social order, they maintain that nothing like an organized "conflict" took place and that the plebs never threatened to secede from the republic. Historians continue to dispute the exact nature of the events that took place.

The Roman Empire (27 B.C.E.–476 C.E.)

During the period referred to as the Roman Empire, Roman society remained exceptionally hierarchical, though historians know more about the lives of upper-class Romans than they do about the lower classes. It is known that "Rome" was a diverse entity difficult to define. It included not only descendants of Rome's founders and earliest citizens but also large numbers of people from conquered territories who were granted citizenship, slaves and former slaves who had been able to buy their freedom and gain citizenship, rural immigrants who came to the cities for economic opportunity, people in conquered territories who were granted some citizenship rights, and large numbers of "easterners" from Greece and elsewhere who made Rome a cosmopolitan city. While aristocratic Romans looked down their noses at foreigners, former slaves, and rural immigrants, many Romans welcomed the mix of people, seeing it as a source of strength and vitality. Many of the legal distinctions between patricians and plebeians had been eliminated, but this did not mean that social distinctions ceased to exist.

The imperial court was the center of power and influence during the empire. Senators and knights were among the most important people at court. Historians estimate that at any given time there were about 600 senators and perhaps 30,000 knights, often referred to as equestrians, or *equites*. Numerous other people, including actors and astrologers, hung around the court seeking patronage and influence. The result was a kind of feudal system, where senators and knights rewarded the loyalty of their followers and retainers with offices and money, while the followers themselves often had a train of dependents who relied on them for their living.

So rigid was this sense of hierarchy that the Roman census actually divided people into six classes based on the amount of property they owned. The senatorial class (which did not necessarily mean that a person was a member of the Senate) required ownership of at least a million sestertii, referring to a silver or bronze coin. (A sesterti was equal in value to one-fourth of a denarius. It is difficult to attach a modern value to a sesterti, but using the price of bread as a standard of value, it was equal roughly to $5.00.) Membership in this class was based on estate ownership, and a person in this class was not allowed to engage in trade or commercial activity. The next class included the *equites*, who could engage in business and had to be worth at least 400,000 sestertii. These two were the most influential classes. Below them were three additional classes of property owners, followed by the *proletarii*, who owned no property. These census classes were important because they determined voting rights, with more voting power, of course, going to the higher classes than to the lower ones. Further, voting took place from the top down, and as soon as a majority was attained, the result was announced. Therefore, the *proletarii* rarely got to vote.

Social relationships were often based on the concept of patron and client. A patron (*patronus*) was typically a person of higher wealth, rank, status, or talent. In return for special attention and services from people of lower status, he provided them with benefits, which could include jobs or loans at low rates of interest. These patron-client relationships did not involve a single patron and a single client. These relationships formed a network, so the same patron would have numerous clients—a large retinue of clients was a sign of social status—and an individual client could have more than one patron. This social system emerged rooted in the belief that a network of mutual obligations based on status created a stable social order, one in which everyone knew their place.

The elite in Rome did not have to work. Because many owned large estates in the countryside, their source of income was secure, so they turned to public service. When they could, they lived in large villas on these estates. The elite received preferential treatment in many ways. They were able to eat fresh game meat and fish from the Mediterranean or specially stocked fishponds at lavish banquets and at everyday meals, while the diet of commoners consisted largely of beer, bread, lentils, processed fish sauce, and occasionally vegetables and bits of fruit. The elite often got away with criminal offenses and, unlike commoners, could not be tortured by the authorities if they were arrested. Even those convicted of a capital crime such as murder received preferential treatment. Commoners were thrown to beasts, crucified, or burned alive, but aristocrats were put to death relatively humanely with swords—assuming they were convicted. Among the top of the elite, the emperor heard cases and would probably have been reluctant to pronounce a death sentence on a member of his imperial court.

It has been estimated that the population of the city of Rome was about 500,000, but many scholars believe that the number was closer to a million, including a large population of slaves. An elite family lived in a single-story dwelling called a *domus*. Such a house typically had several rooms and a central courtyard. But as much as a quarter of the city of Rome was taken up with public buildings, so masses of commoners had to live in apartment buildings called *insula*. These buildings were a constant danger. The upper stories were supported by wooden beams that sometimes collapsed, and the threat of fire was ever present. Additionally, the streets were dark at night, making them dangerous and not just because of criminals. Commoners frequently discarded objects or emptied chamber pots through windows onto the street, often to the dismay of people walking below. Conditions were similar in other Roman cities, where aristocratic elites held power and commoners lived in less comfortable conditions.

Privilege among the upper classes extended to the education of children, especially boys. Early in the Roman Republic there was no system of education. Children learned what they needed to learn, usually farming, at home. But during the Macedonian Wars with Greece (215–148 B.C.E.), many Romans gained exposure to Greece and the system of education it had for its sons. Because many Romans wanted to imitate the lifestyle of the Greeks, they began to believe that Rome needed a similar education system as a means to a successful public career as an administrator or even a senator.

Wealthy Romans hired tutors for their children. For the less wealthy, private schools provided instruction in reading, writing, and arithmetic; the teachers in these schools were often Greek or Greek-speaking slaves. At the age of 12 or 13, talented students went on to attended a *grammaticus*, where they continued their studies in rhetoric, philosophy, history, literature, music, astronomy, geometry, and the Greek language. The very best students completed their studies in Athens, studying Greek oratory. In the wealthiest homes, books were highly valued and slaves were often employed as copyists to produce a copy of a book for the home.

The lower classes of the Roman Empire consisted of a diverse set of people. They included, of course, poor citizens, but also noncitizens, slaves, and freedmen, or people who had formerly been slaves. Manual laborers were regarded as lower class, but so too were large classes of people who in modern life would be regarded as professionals. These people included craftspeople, actors, musicians, and philosophers. Many people even scorned doctors as members of the lower classes. Doctors were often hated because they did not pay taxes.

To represent their interests, members of the lower classes joined *collegia*. These were similar to modern-day fraternal lodges. They gave poor people a place where they could find social relationships. They also functioned as burial societies to ensure that poor people received proper burials. They were often under the patronage of a wealthy citizen, who provided money for banquets and other activities. Patrons also gave members of a *collegium* some measure of legal protection. In return, the *collegium* honored the patron with prayers and respect. *Collegia* were open to slaves and freedmen as well as poor citizens.

Slaves were the lowest class of Romans. Estimating the number of slaves is difficult, but historians put the number between two million and 10 million, with as many as a half million living in and around the city of Rome. Slavery was an odd institution in ancient Rome. Slavery was never based on race or ethnicity. Slaves were prisoners of war, people in debt, or people who voluntarily sold themselves into slavery as a way of escaping debt or crushing poverty to a way of life that at least provided them with shelter and food. Many people treated their slaves with great kindness; others, especially in the countryside, were cruel. A slave had no legal status and was regarded as property. A male slave was responsible for his master's welfare to the extent that if the master was murdered, the slave was put to death for failing to protect him. Yet slaves could testify in court. Many were able to save their own money and eventually buy their freedom. Perhaps the oddest thing of all was that some Roman slaves themselves owned slaves.

Slaves served their masters in many capacities. The largest class included agricultural laborers. Many slaves worked on construction projects in and around cities. Still others worked in Roman households. Many slaves were relatively well educated and had talents that led to work as barbers, schoolteachers and tutors, accountants, secretaries, hairdressers, carpenters, messengers, goldsmiths, and even doctors. The most talented and educated slaves served as architects, business managers, and civil servants in the empire's bureaucracy. Owning slaves was a mark of status. While many Romans owned just one or two slaves, with 10 or fewer being a common number for middle-class people, others owned huge numbers; the historian Pliny claimed that one slave owner he knew owned 4,000 slaves.

Freedmen were slaves who had gained their freedom. In some cases, slave owners freed slaves for meritorious service. Some earned their freedom through service in the military. Still others were able to buy their freedom. Many freedmen continued to work for their former masters. The political rights of freedmen were limited in the early years of the empire, but their children were often able to enjoy all the rights of Roman citizenship, and the political rights of freedmen expanded later during the empire period. In some cases, the transformation from slave to prominent citizen took only one generation. Publius Helvius Pertinax, who became Rome's emperor in 193 C.E., was the son of a former slave. Many freedmen became quite wealthy through commerce, often wealthier than many members of the patrician class. Still others became wealthy through bribery and fraud in civil service jobs.

The experiences of women in ancient Rome were mixed. They did not have direct political power. While other nations in the region were at one time or another ruled by women, Rome never had a woman emperor. In some cases, such as that of Augustus and his wife, Livia, women served as advisers and could exert a great deal of indirect influence over public matters. Additionally, women could own property, including estates and commercial enterprises, giving them some measure of economic power. Otherwise, women were expected to serve primarily as managers of the home and family, which often included not only their own children but also the children's spouses and children. Women were highly visible in public; in contrast to Greece, they were never sequestered from life in public. Overall, upper-class women were expected to live up to the ideal of the virtuous, dignified Roman matron. In upper-class families, girls were given some measure of education, but they did not take part in advanced studies alongside men. Little is known about the lives of lower-class women, though archaeological evidence strongly suggests that many worked as midwives, food sellers, and nurses and in crafts production, including jewelry, leatherwork, and textiles.

THE AMERICAS

BY MICHAEL J. O'NEAL

Archaeologists and historians generally agree that the first human inhabitants of the Americas arrived about 30,000 years ago, possibly earlier. At that time the earth was much colder than it is today. Large glaciers, often a mile thick, had pushed southward as far as present-day Ohio and Indiana. Because so much of the world's water had turned to ice, sea levels were much lower than they are now. As the seas fell, a large bridge of dry land opened between the eastern tip of Asia and the western tip of Alaska in North America. That bridge is now submerged under the Bering Sea.

Historians speculate that the first Americans were Siberian hunters who were simply following game across the land bridge—entirely unaware that they were the first humans to set foot on a new continent. (Because the land bridge was roughly 1,000 miles wide from north to south, they would not have thought of it as a "bridge" at all, but as a vast stretch of open country.) In time other hunters followed, and by about 8000 B.C.E. humans had migrated as far as the southern tip of South America. Clearly, when Christopher Columbus "discovered" America, he was only establishing contact between Europe and the Americas, which had been inhabited for thousands of years.

When the first migrants arrived, the Americas were entirely uninhabited. Groups of people were able to spread out and live in nearly total isolation from one another, although occasionally trade and barter took place between nearby groups. The result was the existence of a large number of distinct cultures and language groups, including the many tribes of Native Americans in what are now Canada and the United States and similar bands in present-day Mexico and Central America and South America. (In contemporary usage *Native American* refers to the tribes that inhabited, and still inhabit, the United States, such as the Apache, Sioux, and other familiar groups. In a larger historical context, though, the term refers to any of the many groups of people who occupied North, Central, or South America before the European contact—including, for example, the Maya and the Toltec.) Historians estimate that northern Mexico alone was home to between 300 and 350 distinct language groups. Because of the immense diversity of social groups any general statement about their social organization has to be supplemented with more specific statements about the organization of any particular group.

THE AMERICAS IN PREHISTORY

Unfortunately for historians, the archaeological record for the vast majority of early Native American groups is either sparse or nonexistent. Before about 12,000 B.C.E. most of the social groups of the Americas were hunter-gatherers. They moved from place to place following sources of food and left behind only the sparest evidence of their presence—for example, burial sites, bones, and a few stone tools. Almost everything they made with nondurable materials has long since decayed and disappeared. They had no writing systems.

From 12,000 to about 5000 B.C.E. the record holds a little more detail, giving historians a somewhat better picture of how people lived and enabling them to offer a few generalizations about social organization among ancient Americans. They believe that Americans in these years lived in hunter-gatherer bands of perhaps up to 100 members. The bands were based on kinship, and their members assumed that they all had a common ancestor. Occasionally, when they felt threatened by natural conditions or by aggression from other groups, several bands would forge alliances with one another, forming a loose community of perhaps 1,000 people. Neighboring bands sometimes traded with each other, and they also cemented alliances through intermarriage, primarily because each band wanted to maintain a rough equivalence in the number of men and women. Only in this way could they ensure the bearing of children to sustain the population and continuity of the band. For the most part, however, individual bands were self-sufficient.

The social organization of these bands was essentially egalitarian, meaning that no person or group of persons held a higher status or social position than others because of birth, though, of course, a person could achieve status through greater skill as a hunter. Because the groups were constantly on the move, following food supplies and seasonal changes, opportunities to accumulate possessions were few. People lived in caves or built temporary shelters out of perishable materials, and for the most part they owned only what they could carry.

Accordingly there was little sense of caste or social class within these bands. Men typically hunted, often leaving the settlement for days at a time (but carefully avoiding encroachment on the territory of other bands). Women stayed near the settlement to rear children and to gather plant foods. In coastal communities or those near major bodies of fresh water fishing and the collection of shellfish were important sources of food. (Parts of ancient Mexico and the southwestern United States were much cooler and wetter than they are in modern times, so the region contained larger and deeper inland bodies of water.)

To say that a culture is egalitarian does not mean that status differences do not exist. In what is today the southwestern United States along the Rio Grande there lived numerous Pueblo peoples. One of these groups made up the ancestors of a culture that came to be called the Tewa. The ancestral Tewa were an egalitarian society, and yet status differences were part of their culture. The Tewa identified levels of earthly beings, as well as levels of inhabitants of the spirit world. The top rung of earthly people, for example, included the *patowa,*

HOW DO ARCHAEOLOGISTS KNOW?

How can archaeologists detect something as abstract as an "egalitarian ethic" in a society with no written historical records and only a sparse and incomplete archaeological record? How can they look at bones or tools or pieces of pottery and make statements about the social relationships and organization of people who lived thousands of years ago?

In the case of a hunter tribe one specific technique that archaeologists use is to examine such objects as arrowheads and spear points. These points, made of stone, have survived through the millennia, while the wooden spear shafts, arrows, and the like have long since decayed and disappeared. These stone objects may not be writing, but they can tell a story about the people who made them in much the same way that a written account can.

In examining points used on hunting weapons, archaeologists are interested in at least three different things. First they examine the style of each point they find, looking for points that were probably made by the same person. An arrowhead or spear point is like a small sculpture, with a style unique to the person who made it. Such matters as size, shape, and the way the sharp edge was formed come into play. Archaeologists can sort the points found in an area according to the individual styles in which they were made.

Second, archaeologists try to determine how many people in a community made points for hunting weapons. Sometimes they find a number of points, but all seem to have been made by the same person or perhaps by just two people. In other cases they find a variety of styles, suggesting that numerous people made points and perhaps even that each hunter was responsible for making his own.

Finally, archaeologists are interested in where the points are located. If they find points made by a particular hunter in a narrow geographical zone, they can infer that use of those points was restricted to the hunter who made them, along with perhaps a limited number of others in his band. If the points are found over a wider geographic zone, they can infer that the points were used by a wider range of people in the band and perhaps even in other bands.

In Mexico's Oaxaca Valley, for example, archaeologists have discovered that the same small band of hunters made use of six or seven distinguishable styles of points. This tells them that each hunter in the band was responsible for making his own points; a smaller number, perhaps one or two, would suggest that one or two people had responsibility for making points for all the members of the hunting group.

In other societies the existence of unique points, each made by an individual hunter, suggests that a point could be used to identify the hunter who made the kill; this in turn could determine who got the meat. Among the people of the Oaxaca Valley, however, the existence of six or seven unique points found over a relatively wide geographic area strongly suggests that points were exchanged with friends and relatives. Points, then, could not have been used to identify the successful hunter, since several hunters may have been using the same point. For the same reason, the points could not have been used to determine who could lay claim to the meat. The effect was to diffuse meat distribution. Put simply, it did not matter who made the kill; the meat was equally distributed to everyone. Archaeologists can infer that the social organization of the band was egalitarian, with no one person seen as deserving more game meat than any other because of higher social status.

or "Made People." These were ritual leaders who earned their position through their skills and service to the community. They served as intermediaries between the earthly and spiritual realms. These people achieved their position by climbing through ranks or orders, starting with the "scalp" society and continuing through the "hunt," "warm clown," and "bear medicine" societies. These "societies" were in the nature of fraternal orders. At the bottom of the social order were the Dry Food People. These were ordinary citizens who had no official position. The Made People could choose to select ritual assistants from among the Dry Food People. While serving as assistants these people acted as mediators between the Dry Food People and the Made People. The key point is that rank and prestige were earned by service and skill, not birthright.

Mesoamerican Society

The most extensive archaeological record in the Americas exists for the people of Mesoamerica (Mexico and parts of Central America) beginning about 2500 B.C.E., although the roots of these civilizations extended even farther back in time. Some Mesoamerican civilizations were highly advanced. They built immense cities—cities larger than were, for example, Paris or London at the time the first Europeans arrived in the Americas—and had many of the characteristics usually thought of as belonging to modern societies, including government bureaucracies, systems of writing, calendars, sophisticated art and architecture. Because of the depth and detail of the historical and archaeological record, historians know more about the social organization of the Mesoamerican cultures than they do about those of other ancient American civilizations.

Between roughly 5000 and 2500 B.C.E. life in Mesoamerica began to change dramatically. The major change was a shift from hunter-gatherer societies to societies whose major source of food was cultivated plants. Plant cultivation required an entirely new way of life, for agriculture demands that people remain in one place for all or much of the year, rather than roaming from one place to another in search of game.

When people settle to grow food and tend plots of land, they form communities, and some of these communities eventually grow into cities. The cities, however, cannot provide their own food, so they come to rely on the surplus grown by surrounding rural areas. This surplus supports a larger and growing class of priests, artists, engineers, civil servants, and others who are not directly involved in the production of food. Further, it supports the existence of an elite that holds power, making decisions for the community as a whole. The result in the ancient Americas was the development among these cultures of a social order that differed from that of their hunter-gatherer ancestors, a social order that included a high-level class or ruling elites, a middle class of artisans and craftsmen, and a lower class of farmers and peasants.

Historians are not certain why this change took place. One theory emphasizes population growth: A larger number of people rendered hunting and gathering no longer practical, for

Double-spout-and-bridge vessel with pelican and fish, Nasca culture of Peru (ca. 200 B.C.E.-ca. 600 C.E.); birds played an important role for Nasca people, and bird feathers were used as ornaments for people of high social rank. (© The Trustees of the British Museum)

hunter-gatherer bands would be stumbling across one another, leading to competition and to the depletion of game. Others attribute the shift to ecological change. Much of the Mesoamerican region became more arid at this time, requiring people to find ways to produce and store their own food supply and to domesticate plants that could survive in the more desertlike climate. The best example is corn, which was developed from a wild plant (though botanists are not sure which plant). Over time people experimented with seeds from corn plants, developed varieties that could grow in the area's unique conditions, and turned corn into a major subsistence crop.

In discussing ancient Mesoamerica, historians conventionally identify three major periods. The first, the Preclassic, extended from about 1800 B.C.E. to about 150 C.E. (The Classic and Postclassic Periods came later and gave rise to the great civilizations of the Aztec and the Maya.) The Preclassic Period itself is typically divided into three subperiods: the Early Preclassic, from 1800 to about 1200 B.C.E.; the Middle Preclassic, from 1200 to 400 B.C.E.; and the Late Preclassic, from 400 B.C.E. to 150 C.E. These dates are approximate, and each Mesoamerican culture underwent changes at its own pace. The divisions, though, enable historians to make meaningful generalizations about the social organization and other characteristics of Mesoamerican culture.

During the Early Preclassic Period social organization remained much as it was during the region's prehistory. Cultures tended to be egalitarian, without any rigid social order or inherited social power. People lived in tribal communities consisting of hamlets of perhaps 20 or so huts built near the fields the inhabitants tended. No one's hut was much better or worse than anyone else's. Much of the society's activity centered on agriculture and seasonal changes in the weather. Most communities were entirely independent, but some contact and trade occurred as one community, because of ecological factors, was able to produce a commodity useful to a neighboring community that was unable to produce it for itself.

It was during the Middle Preclassic Period that a social order began to develop. Throughout Mesoamerica important changes took place, particularly in agriculture. People began to control the environment by building bridges, dams, and canals to store and channel water. They began not only to grow and harvest larger crops but also to grow a greater variety of crops. Further, they began to specialize. Each microregion increasingly focused on the crops that were best suited to the local conditions and then traded with other communities for crops that were better suited to those communities' environments. Ultimately, a greater abundance of food enabled some people to specialize in nonagricultural activities, such as pottery making.

Along with this increased prosperity and technical innovation came social stratification, meaning that a social hierarchy began to develop. (The word *stratification* comes from the Latin *strata,* meaning "layers.") For example, archaeologists studying the Olmec civilization of the Gulf Coast of Mexico have discovered that this society was the first in Mesoamerica to bury some people in more elaborate tombs, filled with richer funerary offerings, than they buried most of the population. Surviving art depicts people wearing sumptuous clothing, and it appears that the elite came to place high value on clothes made from exotic materials, often imported from far-flung locations. Further, archaeologists have discovered a considerable number of artifacts that could have been owned only by higher-class, wealthier people. These artifacts include ceramics made with rich and various colors, mirrors made with exotic minerals, figurines made of greenstone, cinnabar powder (used as a pigment), and jewelry made of semiprecious stones, shells, and bones.

Historians have offered many theories about why social stratification took place. Most of the theories have to do with the control of precious resources. Some people may have achieved a higher status because they had better access to valued resources. Others may have acquired special skills that had value as populations became larger and denser. Others may have possessed particular knowledge about agriculture or waterworks or some such useful subject. Still others may have acquired control over networks for trade and exchange with other communities, becoming the Americas' first entrepreneurs and business moguls. Finally, some belonging to a priestly class may have been thought to have special divine or supernatural powers.

No matter what the cause, it is likely that kinship groups played a role, as families acquired resources or means of social control that were passed down through the generations. Thus power and social status were now inherited rather than earned, as they had been in earlier societies. Another important factor was the development of writing systems. The ability to write—and therefore to record history, myth, and political information—placed power and prestige in the hands of an educated few.

The Zapotec

The shift toward stratified societies is illustrated by the Zapotec people of the Oaxaca Valley of Mexico, whose civilization began to flourish in about 600 C.E. and who built a number of large cities. The Zapotec believed that there was a genealogical connection between people and the spirit world. In other words, they believed that certain people had divine origins. This belief was rooted in the Zapotec cosmology—the branch of thought that deals with the history and origins of the universe.

The Zapotec believed that there were two realms, that of the earth and that of the sky. The earth was generally kind, but it occasionally expressed anger, primarily through earthquakes. The celestial realm, too, was generally kind, but it expressed anger through bolts of lightning and thunder—a thunder roll was called "lightning's earthquake." Highly stylized images depicting earthquakes and lightning began to appear on the earliest Zapotec pottery. These images appear on burial pottery, but only for males—suggesting to archaeologists that the Zapotec believed that the earth and sky were the ancestors of some male descent groups.

Other evidence supports the notion that Zapotec civilization was marked by status differences. One is called the "mat" motif. It is believed that the civilization's rulers showed their status by not allowing their feet to touch the ground. Unlike ordinary people, the elite wore sandals rather than going barefoot; they sat on benches, thrones, or stools, and they placed reed mats on the floors when they held an audience with others. Pottery illustrates all of these behaviors.

Burial position also can provide clues about social status. Archaeologists have excavated a number of Zapotec cemeteries, and their findings shed light on the status of the people buried there. In one cemetery most of the people were buried in a prone position with a jade bead in the mouth and a modest collection of pottery in the tomb. Their arms were at their sides. However, six people, all men, were buried in a kneeling position. Archaeologists believe that these men, as well as people in other cemeteries who were buried in a sitting position or with their knees drawn up (perhaps seated on stools that have since decayed), were of higher status and probably rulers. Those buried prone were in a subordinate position. Similar differences in burial practices have been found in other parts of Mesoamerica. In Panama, for instance, the bodies of chiefs were first dried out in a smokehouse and then buried in common graves.

Cranial deformation, or reshaping of the head, is another mark of social status. In human infants the cranium (skull) is pliable and flexible. Among the Zapotec, cranial deformation was regarded as a sign of nobility. Typically, a few days after being born a noble infant was placed on a bed and its head was tightly compressed with boards. This gave the head an elongated appearance. The key point about this practice is that it shows hereditary rank. Clearly, an infant is not able to achieve high status through skills or service, so cranial deformation was practiced only on highborn children. Cranial deformation is easily spotted in skeletons found in tombs.

Differences in housing also suggest differences in status. Excavations of Zapotec hamlets have uncovered different types of houses. Some of the houses were modest; they were not very well made, the poles supporting them were slender, and walls were not covered with whitewash. Artifacts found in these structures suggest a simple life and include sewing needles, a few modest ornaments, and little in the way of minerals, pottery, and so on that would indicate affluence. Some other houses were larger, more elaborate, and more solidly constructed and had whitewashed walls. Some had lean-to roofs similar to the roof covering a deck or porch on a modern house. More important, artifacts found in these houses suggest a more affluent life. These artifacts include articles for use in crafts, such as minerals, basket-weaving tools, imported pottery, mother-of-pearl, jewelry, ceramic masks, shells, jade beads, and so on. Through their skill in crafts, the people who lived here occupied a higher status and thus had more comfortable and elaborate houses.

The Maya

One of the best-known ancient American civilizations is that of the Maya, whose roots extended back into the first millennium B.C.E. but who flourished from the fourth through about the tenth centuries C.E. For a long time archaeologists and historians believed that the Maya lived in an egalitarian society. They thought that Mayan rulers assumed positions of leadership on a rotating basis and that heredity was not a source of power. That view, however, changed after excavation of a major Maya site at Tikal, in modern-day Guatemala. The archaeological evidence strongly suggests that Mayan society was rigidly organized, with an elite class of rulers, a servant class, middle classes of artisans and civil servants, and a lower class of laborers and peasants.

Archaeologists discovered, for example, marked differences in housing, with elites commanding more space and privacy provided by stairways, screens, and gates. They also discovered elaborate royal residences. Burial practices, too, were stratified, with the elites buried in larger tombs, often engineered to keep earth from seeping in, and the tombs containing a larger number of decorative artifacts.

The skeletons of people buried in these tombs also reveal indications of class differences. Working much like the scientists who examine evidence at crime scenes, archaeologists have found differences in wear and tear on joints, differences in bone length, and cranial deformation, all suggesting an elite royal class that enjoyed a better diet, less physical labor, and longer life. Evidence of certain inherited diseases and other physical conditions suggests that certain families intermarried, indicating, in turn, that these were elite families who used intermarriage as a way of preserving power and status.

See also AGRICULTURE; ART; CHILDREN; CITIES; CLIMATE AND GEOGRAPHY; CLOTHING AND FOOTWEAR; CRAFTS; CRIME AND PUNISHMENT; DEATH AND BURIAL PRACTICES; ECONOMY; EDUCATION; EMPIRES AND DYNASTIES; EMPLOYMENT AND LABOR; FAMILY; FOREIGNERS AND BARBARIANS; GENDER STRUCTURES AND ROLES; GOVERNMENT ORGANIZATION; HUNTING, FISHING, AND GATHERING; LANGUAGE; LAWS AND LEGAL CODES; MIGRATION AND POPULATION MOVEMENTS; MILITARY; MONEY AND COINAGE; NOMADIC AND PASTORAL SOCIETIES; OCCUPATIONS; RELIGION AND COSMOLOGY; SETTLEMENT PATTERNS; SLAVES AND SLAVERY; SOCIAL COLLAPSE AND ABANDONMENT; TOWNS AND VILLAGES; TRADE AND EXCHANGE; WAR AND CONQUEST; WRITING.

Africa

Herodotus, excerpt from **The Histories** *(ca. 430 B.C.E.)*

Book IV

The Libyans dwell in the order which I will now describe. Beginning on the side of Egypt, the first Libyans are the Adyrmachidae. These people have, in most points, the same customs as the Egyptians, but use the costume of the Libyans. Their women wear on each leg a ring made of bronze; they let their hair grow long, and when they catch any vermin on their persons, bite it and throw it away. In this they differ from all the other Libyans. They are also the only tribe with whom the custom obtains of bringing all women about to become brides before the king, that he may choose such as are agreeable to him. The Adyrmachidae extend from the borders of Egypt to the harbor called Port Plynus. Next to the Adyrmachidae are the Gilligammae, who inhabit the country westward as far as the island of Aphrodisias. . . . The customs

(continued)

(continues)

of the Gilligammae are like those of the rest of their countrymen.

The Asbystae adjoin the Gilligammae upon the west. They inhabit the regions above Cyrene, but do not reach to the coast, which belongs to the Cyrenaeans. Four-horse chariots are in more common use among them than among any other Libyans. In most of their customs they ape the manners of the Cyrenaeans. Westward of the Asbystae dwell the Auschisae, who possess the country above Barca, reaching, however, to the sea at the place called Euesperides. In the middle of their territory is the little tribe of the Cabalians, which touches the coast near Tauchira, a city of the Barcaeans. Their customs are like those of the Libyans above Cyrene.

The Nasamonians, a numerous people, are the western neighbors of the Auschisae. In summer they leave their flocks and herds upon the sea-shore, and go up the country to a place called Augila, where they gather the dates from the palms, which in those parts grow thickly, and are of great size, all of them being of the fruit-bearing kind. They also chase the locusts, and, when caught, dry them in the sun, after which they grind them to powder, and, sprinkling this upon their milk, so drink it. Each man among them has several wives, in their intercourse with whom they resemble the Massagetae. The following are their customs in the swearing of oaths and the practice of augury. The man, as he swears, lays his hand upon the tomb of some one considered to have been preeminently just and good, and so doing swears by his name. For divination they betake themselves to the sepulchers of their own ancestors, and, after praying, lie down to sleep upon their graves; by the dreams which then come to them they guide their conduct. When they pledge their faith to one another, each gives the other to drink out of his hand; if there be no liquid to be had, they take up dust from the ground, and put their tongues to it. . . .

Above the Nasamonians, towards the south, in the district where the wild beasts abound, dwell the Garamantians, who avoid all society or intercourse with their fellow-men, have no weapon of war, and do not know how to defend themselves. These border the Nasamonians on the south: westward along the sea-shore their neighbors are the Macea, who, by letting the locks about the crown of their head grow long, while they clip them close everywhere else, make their hair resemble a crest. In war these people use the skins of ostriches for shields. . . . Adjoining the Macae are the Gindanes, whose women wear on their legs anklets of leather. Each lover that a woman has gives her one; and she who can show the most is the best esteemed, as she appears to have been loved by the greatest number of men.

A promontory jutting out into the sea from the country of the Gindanes is inhabited by the Lotophagi, who live entirely on the fruit of the lotus-tree. The lotus fruit is about the size of the lentisk berry, and in sweetness resembles the date. The Lotophagi even succeed in obtaining from it a sort of wine. The sea-coast beyond the Lotophagi is occupied by the Machlyans, who use the lotus to some extent, though not so much as the people of whom we last spoke. . . .

The next tribe beyond the Machlyans is the tribe of the Auseans. Both these nations inhabit the borders of Lake Tritonis, being separated from one another by the river Triton. Both also wear their hair long, but the Machlyans let it grow at the back of the head, while the Auseans have it long in front. The Ausean maidens keep year by year a feast in honor of Minerva, whereat their custom is to draw up in two bodies, and fight with stones and clubs. They say that these are rites which have come down to them from their fathers, and that they honor with them their native goddess, who is the same as the Minerva (Athena) of the Grecians. If any of the maidens die of the wounds they receive, the Auseans declare that such are false maidens. Before the fight is suffered to begin, they have another ceremony. One of the virgins, the loveliest of the number, is selected from the rest; a Corinthian helmet and a complete suit of Greek armor are publicly put upon her; and, thus adorned, she is made to mount into a chariot, and led around the whole lake in a procession. . . . These people do not marry or live in families, but dwell together like the gregarious beasts. When their children are full-grown, they are brought before the assembly of the men, which is held every third month, and assigned to those whom they most resemble.

Such are the tribes of wandering Libyans dwelling upon the sea-coast.

From: Herodotus, *The History*, trans. George Rawlinson (New York: Dutton and Co., 1862).

Asia and the Pacific

Arrian, excerpt from Anabasis Alexandri *(Campaigns of Alexander, second century* C.E.*)*

Book VIII (Indica)

XI. The Indians generally are divided into seven castes. Those called the wise men are less in number than the rest, but chiefest in honour and regard. For they are under no necessity to do any bodily labour; nor to contribute from the results of their work to the common store; in fact, no sort of constraint whatever rests upon these wise men, save to offer the sacrifices to the gods on behalf of the people of India. Then whenever anyone sacrifices privately, one of these wise men acts as instructor of the sacrifice, since otherwise the sacrifice would not have proved acceptable to the gods. These Indians also are alone expert in prophecy, and none, save one of the wise men, is allowed to prophesy. And they prophesy about the seasons of the year, or of any impending public calamity: but they do not trouble to prophesy on private matters to individuals, either because their prophecy does not condescend to smaller things, or because it is undignified for them to trouble about such things. And when one has thrice made an error in his prophecy, he does not suffer any harm, except that he must for ever hold his peace; and no one will ever persuade such a one to prophesy on whom this silence has been enjoined. These wise men spend their time naked, during the winter in the open air and sunshine, but in summer, when the sun is strong, in the meadows and the marsh lands under great trees; their shade Nearchus computes to reach five plethra all round, and ten thousand men could take shade under one tree; so great are these trees. They eat fruits in their season, and the bark of the trees; this is sweet and nutritious as much as are the dates of the palm. Then next to these come the farmers, these being the most numerous class of Indians; they have no use for warlike arms or warlike deeds, but they till the land; and they pay the taxes to the kings and to the cities, such as are self-governing; and if there is internal war among the Indians, they may not touch these workers, and not even devastate the land itself; but some are making war and slaying all comers, and others close by are peacefully ploughing or gathering the fruits or shaking down apples or harvesting. The third class of Indians are the herdsmen, pasturers of sheep and cattle, and these dwell neither by cities nor in the villages. They are nomads and get their living on the hillsides, and they pay taxes from their animals; they hunt also birds and wild game in the country.

XII The fourth class is of artisans and shopkeepers; these are workers, and pay tribute from their works, save such as make weapons of war; these are paid by the community. In this class are the shipwrights and sailors, who navigate the rivers. The fifth class of Indians is the soldiers' class, next after the farmers in number; these have the greatest freedom and the most spirit. They practise military pursuits only. Their weapons others forge for them, and again others provide horses; others too serve in the camps, those who groom their horses and polish their weapons, guide the elephants, and keep in order and drive the chariots. They themselves, when there is need of war, go to war, but in time of peace they make merry; and they receive so much pay from the community that they can easily from their pay support others. The sixth class of Indians are those called overlookers. They oversee everything that goes on in the country or in the cities; and this they report to the King, where the Indians are governed by kings, or to the authorities, where they are independent. To these it is illegal to make any false report; nor was any Indian ever accused of such falsification. The seventh class is those who deliberate about the community together with the King, or, in such cities as are self-governing, with the authorities. In number this class is small, but in wisdom and uprightness it bears the palm from all others; from this class are selected their governors, district governors, and deputies, custodians of the treasures, officers of army and navy, financial officers, and overseers of agricultural works. To marry out of any class is unlawful—as, for instance, into the farmer class from the artisans, or the other way; nor must the same man practise two pursuits; nor change from one class into another, as to turn farmer from shepherd, or shepherd from artisan. It is only permitted to join the wise men out of any class; for their business is not an easy one, but of all most laborious.

From: E. Iliff Robson, trans., *Arrian, with an English Translation* (London: W. Heinemann, 1929–1933).

Europe

Julius Caesar, "The Germans," excerpt from De bello Gallico (The Gallic Wars, ca. 51 B.C.E.)

21. The customs of the Germans differ widely from those of the Gauls; for neither have they Druids to preside over religious services, nor do they give much attention to sacrifices. They count in the number of their gods those only whom they can see, and by whose favors they are clearly aided; that is to say, the Sun, Vulcan, and the Moon. Of other deities they have never even heard. Their whole life is spent in hunting and in war. From childhood they are trained in labor and hardship.

22. They are not devoted to agriculture, and the greater portion of their food consists of milk, cheese, and flesh. No one owns a particular piece of land, with fixed limits, but each year the magistrates and the chiefs assign to the clans and the bands of kinsmen who have assembled together as much land as they think proper, and in whatever place they desire, and the next year compel them to move to some other place. They give many reasons for this custom—that the people may not lose their zeal for war through habits established by prolonged attention to the cultivation of the soil; that they may not be eager to acquire large possessions, and that the stronger may not drive the weaker from their property; that they may not build too carefully, in order to avoid cold and heat; that the love of money may not spring up, from which arise quarrels and dissensions; and, finally, that the common people may live in contentment, since each person sees that his wealth is kept equal to that of the most powerful.

23. It is a matter of the greatest glory to the tribes to lay waste, as widely as possible, the lands bordering their territory, thus making them uninhabitable. They regard it as the best proof of their valor that their neighbors are forced to withdraw from those lands and hardly any one dares set foot there; at the same time they think that they will thus be more secure, since the fear of a sudden invasion is removed. When a tribe is either repelling an invasion or attacking an outside people, magistrates are chosen to lead in the war, and these are given the power of life and death. In times of peace there is no general magistrate, but the chiefs of the districts and cantons render justice among their own people and settle disputes. Robbery, if committed beyond the borders of the tribe, is not regarded as disgraceful, and they say that it is practiced for the sake of training the youth and preventing idleness. When any one of the chiefs has declared in an assembly that he is going to be the leader of an expedition, and that those who wish to follow him should give in their names, they who approve of the undertaking, and of the man, stand up and promise their assistance, and are applauded by the people. Such of these as do not then follow him are looked upon as deserters and traitors, and from that day no one has any faith in them.

To mistreat a guest they consider to be a crime. They protect from injury those who have come among them for any purpose whatever, and regard them as sacred. To them the houses of all are open and food is freely supplied.

From: Frederic Austin Ogg, ed., *A Source Book of Mediaeval History: Documents Illustrative of European Life and Institutions from the German Invasions to the Renaissance* (New York, American Book Company, 1908).

FURTHER READING

Géza Alföldy, *The Social History of Rome*, trans. David Braund and Frank Polluck (Baltimore, Md.: Johns Hopkins University Press, 1988).

Alfredo López Austin and Leonardo López Luján, *Mexico's Indigenous Past*, trans. Bernard R. Ortiz de Montellano (Norman: University of Oklahoma Press, 2001).

K. R. Bradley, *Slaves and Masters in the Roman Empire: A Study in Social Control* (New York: Oxford University Press, 1987).

Lionel Casson, *The Horizon Book of Daily Life in Ancient Egypt* (New York: American Heritage, 1975).

Barry Cunliffe, *The Ancient Celts* (New York: Penguin Books, 2000).

Geoffrey E. M. de Ste. Croix, *The Class Struggle in the Ancient Greek World: From the Archaic Age to the Arab Conquests* (Ithaca, N.Y.: Cornell University Press, 1989).

Ian Hodder, *The Leopard's Tale: Revevealing the Mysteries at Catalhoyuk* (London: Thames and Hudson, 2006).

Simon James, *The World of the Celts* (London: Thames and Hudson, 2005).

T. G. H. James, *Pharaoh's People: Scenes from Life in Imperial Egypt* (London: Bodley Head, 1984).

Nicholas F. Jones, *Public Organization in Ancient Greece* (Philadelphia: American Philosophical Society, 1987).

A. G. McDowell, *Village Life in Ancient Egypt: Laundry Lists and Love Songs* (New York: Oxford University Press, 1999).

Sarah B. Pomeroy, *Goddesses, Whores, Wives, and Slaves: Women in Classical Antiquity* (New York: Schocken Books, 1995).

Michael E. Smith and Marilyn A. Masson, eds., *The Ancient Civilizations of Mesoamerica: A Reader* (Malden, Mass.: Blackwell, 2000).

Miriam Stead, *Egyptian Life* (London: British Museum, 1986).

▶ sports and recreation

INTRODUCTION

The word *recreation* suggests the idea of "re-creating," or "creating again." In turn, this suggests that recreation serves to reinvigorate and strengthen people so that they can face life's trials. Sports and recreation in the ancient world were in many senses forms of "re-creation." Sports, for example, often served ceremonial purposes. Sporting events were frequently held in conjunction with religious festivals. Sometimes these events were staged to symbolize the creative powers of the gods. In other cases they reaffirmed the power and authority of a ruler and reinvigorated him to continue his rule. In some cultures, sporting events were held in connection with funerals as a way of honoring the dead. In the ancient Americas a ball game that bore characteristics of soccer and basketball held a ceremonial purpose. The participating teams were engaged in a literal life-and-death struggle, for the losing team might be ritually sacrificed to the gods.

While cultures throughout the world used balls for games, the ancient Americans, having discovered rubber, were the only ones to use rubber balls. In other parts of the world, balls were typically either stone or made by wrapping an animal skin around straw or a similar material. The ancient Chinese developed a game in which balls were hit with sticks into holes in the ground, a precursor of golf.

Sports and recreation were also regarded as a way of training a person for such activities as hunting and military service. The ancients knew what modern people know: that running, rowing, and other strenuous activities build muscle and increase endurance. Running, for example, was a necessary part of the training of couriers, who carried news of the progress of battles to commanders. Indeed, the modern 26.2-mile marathon recreates the legend (which is probably untrue) that an Athenian ran 26 miles to carry the news from Marathon to Athens that the Greeks had defeated the Persians in the Battle of Marathon in 490 B.C.E. In many cultures young men being initiated into the adult community had to prove their mettle by taking part in long races and similar challenging activities.

Some ancient cultures developed the concept of the spectator sport—that is, a sporting event people watched but in which they did not participate. In this regard the Romans led the way. In the Roman Empire people gathered in arenas that closely resemble modern football stadiums to watch mock hunts, contests between gladiators, chariot racing, animal exhibitions, and even brutal executions of criminals (suggested by the common phrase "throwing him to the lions"). For private recreation ancient Roman and Egyptian men went to gyms, often with the chief purpose of associating with other men.

Common sports in the ancient world included horse racing, boat racing, wrestling, track-and-field events (such as foot races and discus and javelin throwing), boxing, and archery. People who lived near bodies of water swam for sport and recreation. Other forms of entertainment included board games, dice, gambling, dancing, and bathing at public baths, where people could relax in the company of others.

AFRICA

BY KIRK H. BEETZ

In ancient Africa sports and games seem to have been important. What is known about African sports in earlier centuries, however, can be gleaned only from tenuous hints, some of which linger in the customs of modern Africans. For example, wrestling seems to have been a favorite pastime for some ancient Africans, because old wrestling traditions survive into modern times among some Bantu-speaking peoples. How prevalent wrestling was in ancient Africa and how important it was to society probably cannot be known. Still, it is apparent that young men in some places tried to prove their strength and social worthiness by grappling with others. Like ancient African warfare, wrestling matches could be very stylized events, with opponents moving as if choreographed by a set of rules designed to display their skills. Blood probably was rarely shed, and pinning an opponent's shoulders to the ground was enough for victory. It is possible that some groups—particularly those in which women chose their mates—used ritualized wrestling to show off marriageable men to marriageable women.

Racing was possibly a sport in ancient Africa; in North Africa especially, racing horses, camels, and elephants might have been popular. Among the ruins of ancient Kush, a kingdom along the Nile River south of Egypt, there is a large complex of buildings that may have housed elephants. The elephants would have been a type more easily trained than the African elephants from farther south. Near the ruined buildings is an area where these elephants may have been raced.

Most ancient African games involved numbers. Traders and nomads of North Africa, in the Sahara and along the steppes south of the desert, seem to have had games involving guesses at how long it would take to reach a certain place and word games involving the counting of words, perhaps to form a particular phrase. Number systems and number patterns were sometimes used in rituals for foretelling the future, and number and word games may have been played for the amusement of seeing what sort of predictions could be made with them.

Most ancient African games that modern people know anything about involved mathematics. There seems to have been a general cross-cultural fascination with mathematics that attracted people from all sorts of walks of life in almost all parts of Africa. Other sorts of games probably existed, but of those only game boards without rules remain, and it is possible that even boards that do not imply mathematical contests nonetheless involved mathematics. Boards from Kush and Axum are sometimes beautifully inlaid with ivory and variously colored woods. An interesting aspect of these boards is that even though their rules are long forgotten, the tradition of gaming with boards is so deep within modern cultures that a person seeing a relic from ancient Africa could easily recognize it as something people played games with.

Some African mathematical games were very simple, so lacking in complexity that whoever started first was the probable winner. Such games may have been used to teach children how to count and how to do simple addition and subtraction. Other games may have been intended to teach multiplication and division. Others involved such complex reasoning that they may have kept adult minds sharp for the complicated business of trading with outsiders, which could require people to keep in mind several different quantities of different goods along with how much they were asking or offering for the goods. Successful bargaining often depended on all the involved traders understanding and agreeing on numbers derived from hours of negotiations.

One of the oldest games is now called morabaraba. Its origins are obscure, but it spread through herding communities in northern, eastern, and southern Africa. It may be the ancestor of the European game called nine-man Morris. According to tradition, it was a way for African elders to teach young people how to steal livestock, especially cattle. The basic idea is to capture an opponent's cattle while moving one's own cattle toward the opponent's edge of the board. A cow is captured by lining up in a straight line three of one's own cattle in front of a cow of the opponent.

An interesting aspect of morabaraba and other ancient African games is that a game board could be drawn on the ground. All the players needed was a fairly flat, open area of sufficient size for both them and the board. Even when boards were fashioned from stone, clay, or wood, these materials were readily available, so play could begin at almost any time—an indication of how much some ancient Africans loved their games. Some boards were made to fold up to hold game pieces and be easily carried.

One of the most popular types of games in Africa is the sowing game, so named because its premise is planting seeds for crops. The general name for all such games is mancala. Although sometimes a game is sold in the Western world as mancala, the word actually was meant to refer to all sowing games. The name derives from *naqala*, which is Arabic for "to move." Sowing games probably originated in eastern Africa, perhaps in the ancient kingdom of Axum. They spread through most of Africa, along southern Asia to Indochina, and along the Mediterranean coast to southern Europe. In ancient Africa both men and women played these games avidly.

The games were probably originally played on the ground, with holes dug in rows and stones, seashells, or seeds used for playing pieces. Ancient boards made of stone and clay indicate that there were several variations of play, because holes would be arranged in different patterns on different boards. In general, the objective of the game was to force an opponent into a position in which no move was possible or to have more game pieces than one's opponent at the end of play.

Numerous variations evolved over many centuries, but a sowing game was usually played by two people, each controlling one side or end of a game board. Game pieces, called seeds, were usually gathered in a starting hole. A player could move seeds from his hole into neighboring holes, which usually meant that he controlled those holes and could, during a later turn, move seeds from them into other holes. Often a player was allowed to move to capture a hole controlled by her opponent, with the rules for how to capture a hole varying greatly depending on the variation of the game. A player's turn often ended when he ran out of moves, which could happen when he reached a hole he could not take. Moving seeds, choosing how many to move and where to move them, often involved complex thinking, requiring a player to have the ability to foresee an opponent's reactions to her moves, as well as the ability to thwart her opponent's strategy.

EGYPT

BY EMILY JANE O'DELL

Ancient Egypt was not all work and no play. In fact, there are many examples of sports and games from ancient Egypt. We know of the recreational habits of ancient Egyptians from surviving game pieces, written texts, and temple and tomb carvings. Although the ancient Egyptians had nothing like the Olympics of the ancient Greeks, they did participate in athletic and recreational activities that included throwing, running, wrestling, archery, boating, and board games.

We do not know very much about organized sports activity in ancient Egypt, but we do know that the pharaoh had a recurring athletic event that symbolically and magically rejuvenated him for the kingship. During the sed festival, a jubilee that traditionally occurred after 30 years of rule and thereafter every three years, the king was required to run around a special courtyard in front of his courtiers and the public. Such a court can still be seen at the step pyramid of the pharaoh Djoser (r. ca. 2630–ca. 2611 B.C.E.) at Saqqara. Relief carvings show royal guards running alongside kings' chariots, and some soldiers held the title "swift runner." However, we do not have evidence of competitive running until the time of King Taharqa (r. ca. 690–664 B.C.E.), when a stela (a carved standing stone) at Dashur records a government-sponsored footrace by units of the army, with prizes awarded to the best runners.

Many people associate horses and chariotry with ancient Egypt, but neither existed there until the Hyksos, a western Asian people who ruled much of Egypt during the Fifteenth and Sixteenth Dynasties (ca. 1674–ca. 1567 B.C.E.), introduced them, along with powerful new composite bows. These new elements of sport and war were quickly assimilated into ancient Egyptian culture. While target archery had been around since the Fourth Dynasty (ca. 2575–ca. 2465 B.C.E.), the addition of the composite bow and moving chariots made the sport that much more difficult and exciting. King Thutmose III (r. ca. 1479–ca. 1425 B.C.E.) claims on his stela in Armant to have pierced copper with his arrows, but the most famous example of such archery boasts comes from his son Amenhotep II (r. ca. 1427–ca. 1401 B.C.E.): Known as the most athletic of the kings, having been trained since childhood in many athletic pursuits, Amenhotep II claimed not only to have pierced four copper targets "as thick as a man's palm" while riding full-speed in a chariot but to have cleaved each target in two.

Wrestling appears in Egyptian art from the First Dynasty (ca. 2920–ca. 2770 B.C.E.) onward. During the Old Kingdom (ca. 2575–ca. 2134 B.C.E.) servant statues—statues buried with the dead to serve and entertain them in the afterlife—often depicted wrestlers. Naked boys who are wrestling are carved in relief in the tomb of Ptahhotep (a philosopher and high government official in the 24th century B.C.E.) at Saqqara. The most famous scenes of ancient Egyptian wrestling come from the Twelfth Dynasty (ca. 1991–ca. 1783 B.C.E.) tombs at Beni Hasan, which house more than 100 depictions of wrestlers. There is debate as to whether these figures are of recreational wrestlers or simply Egyptians fighting each other in one of the many civil conflicts of that time. However, at nearby Bersheh similar art clearly depicts sports wrestlers, as they are shown with a referee. During the New Kingdom (1550–1070 B.C.E.) wrestling became incorporated into royal ceremonies in which Egyptians wrestled foreign opponents. Art at Medinet Habu portrays stick fighting as another part of these competitions, with the fighters wearing shields on their forearms and padding on their faces.

Ancient Egyptians also played ball sports, and original balls from some of these games have survived. They were generally made by sewing a leather cover around a filling of clay or tightly packed straw, hair, papyrus, palm leaves, or yarn. In Twelfth Dynasty tombs women are shown juggling balls and throwing them back and forth, sometimes while sitting on the shoulders of other people. Some Egyptologists have read mythological meaning into the juggling games, but this explanation is speculative and not universally accepted. There are a few examples, however, of balls being used ceremonially and magically to stave off chaos. For example, during the Late Period (ca. 712–332 B.C.E.) the king would hit a ball with a stick as if he were striking the eye of Apophis (the god of evil and darkness), and in the edifice of Taharqa at Karnak the king is shown throwing four balls, each toward one of the four cardinal points of the compass. Apart from royal sports activity tomb art at Beni Hasan shows ancient Egyptians using a ball and long sticks in a manner that resembles field hockey.

In addition to juggling, ancient Egyptian art portrays women dancing and contorting in many different poses in gymnastic activity. For example, a painting from 2000 B.C.E. shows one woman doing a full backbend and another doing a front handspring or front walkover. Further, at Beni Hassan there are examples of ancient Egyptians holding certain yogic positions, including one in a headstand. Ancient Egyptians also had a unique form of weightlifting: They used bags full of sand that could be raised with one hand, much like dumbbells, to work their arm muscles.

Because most ancient Egyptians lived near water—along the Nile and its tributaries, as well as the Red Sea and Mediterranean—it seems probable that many people knew how to swim. The *Biography of Khety,* from the Eleventh Dynasty (ca. 2040–1991 B.C.E.), mentions swimming lessons given to the royal children. Both the Old Kingdom and the Middle Kingdom (ca. 2040–1640 B.C.E.) provide many carved depictions of men, women, and children fishing and hunting birds with throw sticks along rivers, and in some of these scenes men on papyrus rafts on the water are trying to push each other overboard with poles. Although there is no direct evidence of boat races, they must have occurred, as boating was part of daily life for people living on the Nile. Further, in the Late Egyptian text *The Contendings of Horus and Seth* the gods Horus and Seth compete against each other in a boat race, indicating that there must have been real-life precedents for such events.

Game pieces from ancient Egypt survive to this day. Egyptologists have identified four board games, but it is likely that more existed. The most popular was *senet,* played from the very earliest times all the way down to the Roman conquest. Besides recreational value, it had magical and religious significance: A person had to play a game of *senet* in the afterlife in order to proceed toward eternal happiness and peace. Thus, in effect, one played *senet* for one's life. The game appears in the Egyptian Book of the Dead, and a scene of the queen playing it for her life is beautifully painted in vibrant colors in the Tomb of Nefertari in the Valley of the Queens at Luxor. *Senet* was played by two players on a rectangular board of 30 squares (10 by 3). Each player had seven pieces, and flat two-sided dice sticks determined the moves that could be made. Much as in checkers, a player could jump the opponent's pieces to remove them and reach the opposite end of the board.

Another game, *men* (from the word for "endurance"), was contested by two players on a long narrow board divided into 13 or more sections. Not much is known about this game, but it seems that each player controlled five pieces and moved them according to throws of stick dice as in *senet.* After *men* disappeared at the start of the Old Kingdom, a somewhat similar game played with pegs became popular and lasted for 2,000 years. Players moved carved pegs on boards that had two tracks of 30 holes each. It is not known whether the peg game developed from *men* or was something new, perhaps imported from the Near East.

In the Old Kingdom tomb of the physician and scribe Hesy-Ra there is a depiction of a game called *mehen,* "serpent," named for the serpent god Mehen, who protects the sun as it sails across the sky. The board for the game is in the shape of a coiled snake and divided into six compartments, each holding six marbles of one color and a lion-shaped piece. In the tomb of King Reshepses at Saqqara four people are shown playing. The game, however, disappeared sometime around 2000 B.C.E., possibly because worship of the serpent god Mehen died out. A game called "20 squares" (for the number of squares on the board) became popular in the Seventeenth Dynasty (ca. 1640–1550 B.C.E.) and may have been introduced by the Hyksos. It was played by two people, each using five pieces.

In addition to board games children in ancient Egypt played with assortment of tiny figurines carved from wood and clay. Many such figurines and toys are found in the Cairo Museum. Children also played with hoops and sticks, engaged in jumping and whirling contests, and competed in tug-of-war.

THE MIDDLE EAST

BY MARK ANTHONY PHELPS

Defining what constitutes sports in the context of leisure activities in the ancient Near East is difficult before the advent of Greek colonization in Asia Minor and the later Hellenization of the region. What passes for sport by modern definition generally constituted three classes in the ancient Near East: children's games, military training, and professional acrobatics. All this changed after the conquest of the Greek king Alexander the Great (r. 336–323 B.C.E.), as sports and theater became a major component of social life.

Wrestling is the most widely depicted sport in Mesopotamian texts and artwork. The wrestlers are shown naked except for a type of belt. It seems that the belt was a necessity, owing to its ubiquitous artistic representation and its appearance in texts. It is not clear whether this equipment functioned as a grip for wrestling moves or served something in the capacity of a modern athletic supporter. The most famous literary image of the wrestler in Mesopotamia actually occurs as a simile in one of the earliest-known epic poems, wherein Gilgamesh, the legendary king of Uruk, and his foe Enkidu fight "like wrestlers." A copper vase from the third and fourth millennia B.C.E. shows the sculpted image of two wrestlers grasping each other's belts while balancing large vases on their heads.

Boxing is the next most commonly presented sport in iconography and textual evidence. A votive tablet from around 3000 B.C.E., found at Khafaje (in modern-day Iraq), shows a pair of boxers along with two pairs of wrestlers. Boxers almost universally wear the same belt as wrestlers, leading one to wonder if there was indeed always a strong division between the activities. Other representations show boxers wearing typical skirts with some sort of binding on their wrists, probably functioning in the same fashion as modern taping for strengthening the joint.

Life-and-death duels served as a spectator sport, if the Egyptian story of Sinuhe is to be believed. Sinuhe, stranded in Palestine, becomes adopted into a kin group and manages to become chief. He then is forced to encounter a "strong man from Retenu" (referring to Syria-Palestine), doubtless for the political control of a kin group. Challenged to single combat, he fights with his challenger before spectators, including women. The crowd initially roots for the man they thought was the underdog, the Egyptian, who soon proves his worth by killing the challenger.

This practice is in line with a scene depicted in the Hebrew Bible (2 Samuel 2:12–17). In this event, 12 representatives each of the armies of David and Ishbaal, Saul's son and successor, meet near the pool at Gibeon to determine which army is favored by Yahweh, the Israelite deity, to rule Israel. These two dozen pair off, grab each other by the hair, and kill each other with the flint knives all were carrying. Divine favor unrevealed, open warfare begins. The story of David and Goliath, told in 1 Samuel 17, is also one of representational combat to the death through the use of weapons.

Sinuhe and the biblical examples are certainly not sport by modern definition, but the need for witnesses to validate the outcome of these life-and-death struggles for political supremacy finds some parallel in the "death for entertainment" context of gladiatorial shows. The fact that all ancient Near Eastern competition was a reflection of military training might suggest that these episodes may well be understood as sports writ large.

A Phoenician vase depicting runners, a Hittite tablet making reference to races at a New Year's festival, and references to the New Year's festival in Babylon call attention to another sport in the ancient Near East. The Bible (Ecclesiastes 9:11) states that "the race goes not to the swift," a reference in all probability to distance running. It is hard to fathom that there were no horse or chariot competitions, especially given the Hurrian manu-

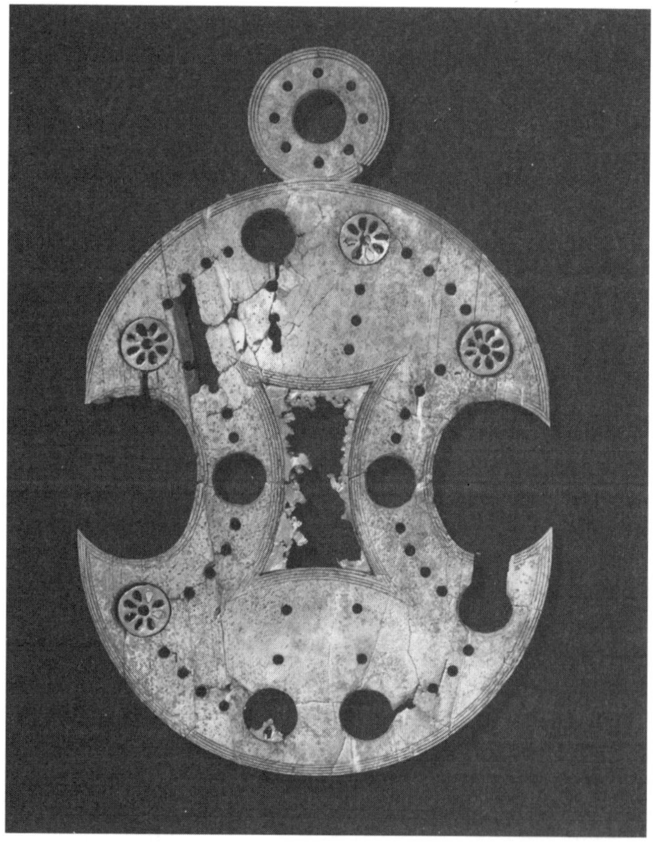

Game of 58 Holes, made of ivory inlaid with gold and blue paste, from Megiddo, Palestine, Late Bronze Age, 13th century B.C.E. (Courtesy of the Oriental Institute of the University of Chicago)

als translated into Hittite for horse training from the 13th and 14th centuries B.C.E. Likewise, there probably existed competition that involved lifting or throwing objects.

The king engaged in leisure pursuits that were calculated to increase his majesty. Domination over wild predators spoke well of his ability to deal with human adversaries. For example, Assyrian palaces were covered with scenes of the king killing lions for the benefit of the vassal delivering tribute. The ritualization of actual hunts by the king would involve animals that were typically captured or raised and then placed, perhaps bound, in a context that would present no actual danger to the ruler. A relief depicting a hunt by the Assyrian king Ashurnasirpal II (r. 883–859 B.C.E.) shows a lion being released from a cage. The depictions of hunting scenes on vessels used by individuals points to the hunt as being the activity of the elite as well. It is impossible to determine whether there was any influence of Egypt upon such activities as boxing, wrestling, or hunting. Although these activities doubtless developed independently of each other, the rules, social contexts, and individual moves could have been influenced from either cultural realm to the other.

Astragali, animal knucklebones, were an integral part of gaming. They functioned as four-sided dice, as each edge was distinct. These bones were also used in divination. Imitation astragali were made of stone, metal, or glass. Game boards, some with holes or depressions, have been discovered as well. One Babylonian game board included the signs of the zodiac. Among the best-known influences of Egypt upon leisure time is the presence of the board game *senet*, found throughout Syria and Palestine beginning in the Neolithic Period (ending ca. 3800 B.C.E.). The game board has been found from Cyprus to Iran and most points in between.

Musicians, dancers, jugglers, and acrobats are depicted in literature and artwork. Music was ubiquitous at work (as work songs), at festivals (as religious or wedding songs), and in daily life (as perhaps lullabies or taunts). Dancing accompanied many festivals. Watching acrobats and jugglers perform is probably as close to viewing spectator sports as the bulk of the population could come.

With the coming of the Hellenistic world, the face of ancient Near Eastern sports and leisure changed dramatically. Athletic competitions and theatrical performances became an integral part of the social life of at least some strata of the cities of the region. Hippodromes, gymnasiums, palaestrae (facilities for sports practice), and amphitheaters appear throughout the ancient Near East. Athletic competitions were spectator sports in this era, a big business that in turn spawned other affiliated businesses, such as concessions and prostitution. Fans of chariot racing arose in the provinces as well as the Roman heartland, evidenced by graffiti extolling both green and blue factions at Alexandria.

In addition to spectator sports and theater, the coming of the Greeks and Romans also provided for new types of games, new music, and other novel entertainment staples. Along with sports, the presence of public baths presented a cultural challenge throughout the ancient Near East as public nudity was nearly a universal mark of shame in the region.

ASIA AND THE PACIFIC

BY KIRK H. BEETZ

In ancient Asia and the Pacific sports and games served not only as entertainment but also to train players in physical and intellectual skills they needed to survive. Two sports, wrestling and archery, were common in most cultures. In China wrestling matches could attract large audiences in cities and were often part of celebrations staged by the rich and powerful. By the time of the Han Dynasty (ca. 202 B.C.E.–ca. 220 C.E.) the sport had become ritualized, taking a form similar to modern Japanese sumo wrestling. In India victors in even one tournament sponsored by a king not only became famous but indeed made their fortunes for the rest of their lives. These contests took place outside the gate to the king's palace, and individual wrestlers often were sponsored by nobles. The opponents began the contest by grasping each other around the waist, with their chins resting on each other's shoulder. Each then tried to force the other down or to break his hold, either of which brought victory.

Archery was a popular sport. In China nobles took excursions into the countryside to hunt game, usually birds, with their bows. These hunting parties could be extremely elaborate, with the nobles or kings accompanied by professional hunters and large retinues of servants. It was long the rule in Chinese society that no hunter take more than one of every two animals he killed, but during the Han Dynasty many of the rich or the nobility slaughtered every game animal they could find, ruining once-healthy forests. Hunting as a sport was open to people of every walk of life in China, with even poor peasants being able to show off their prowess occasionally with a bow. Archery contests, by contrast, were usually formal affairs, sponsored by a king or a provincial ruler, in which aristocratic participants shot at targets.

In India archery as a sport was reserved for the nobility. Only kings and nobles actually hunted for sport. By the Gupta Empire (ca. 320–ca. 600 C.E.) kings had hunting parks stocked with animals captured by professional hunters in the wild. A king's hunt was an elaborate undertaking, with the king riding a chariot, a horse, or an elephant, surrounded by dancing girls and assisted by servants and game wardens. Archery contests were open to nobles. A target was placed atop a tall pole. The winning archer received a prize, sometimes even marriage to a daughter of the king.

Spectator sports in China included horse racing, dog racing, and cockfighting. All involved gambling, with people wagering on the outcomes. The Chinese officially regarded gambling as a vice because it meant that people were gaining money without contributing anything worthwhile to society. High-stakes betting was particularly scandalous and sometimes resulted in even nobles being punished by the king or

Ceramic Liubo players, from China, Eastern Han Dynasty, first to second century C.E.*; the board is marked with divination symbols, and the game pieces show the animals of the four directions.* (© The Trustees of the British Museum)

emperor. Nevertheless, gambling was prevalent. One very popular betting game was *liupo*, which may have meant "six dice." It was a board game played by two or four people who shook six marked bamboo sticks in a cup and then spilled them out. Players moved pieces on the board according to what the sticks displayed. The pieces consisted of five pawns and one general, the objective of the game being to capture the opposing general. The board's design was meant to represent the universe. The game was played with much shouting and gesturing.

India had numerous games of chance, all condemned by the predominant religion, Brahmanism, because money changed hands without producing anything of social value. Governments regulated gambling, and players were forbidden to use their own dice. Gambling dens paid 5 percent of the value of their property in taxes, and both dice and stakes were taxed. Dice were sometimes made from seashells or the five-sided nut of the *vibhitaka* fruit or were sometimes cubes of ivory or wood. The game of *vibhitaka*, named for the dice that were used, called for a player to grab a handful of dice from a heap of them and declare how many he had grabbed while throwing them onto the ground. The number declared had to be a multiple of four. The player won when the number he or she shouted matched the total number of dice thrown. If more than one player guessed correctly during a round, play continued until only one correct guesser was left. Another popular game was *pasaka*, which used four-sided oblong dice. Gamblers agreed beforehand on a number, as well as on their bets, and winners were those whose throws resulted in the dice matching the agreed-upon number.

Board games in India dated from Harappan times (ca. 2600–ca. 1500 B.C.E.). Harappan boards were made of stone with grids etched on them. Playing pieces looked like mushrooms and towers. The most famous game of ancient India was *caturanga*, the ancestor of chess. Intended to teach people to think like military strategists, it was played by four people who sat around a board or a tabletop marked with a grid. Each player had four pawns and four other pieces representing a king, a horse, an elephant, and either a ship or a chariot. These last four pieces represented the traditional divisions of four corps in an army. Two dice were rolled to determine which moves could be made. *Caturanga* called for strategy and deception, with each player contending against three others, which required alertness and an ability to keep track of movements from multiple directions. Other ancient Indian board games include ones similar to modern backgammon and Parcheesi.

China had an ancient military strategy game of its own, called *yi* during the Han Dynasty but later called *weiqi*, ancestor of Chinese checkers and Go. Its first mention in surviving documents is from 559–548 B.C.E., but its origins probably extend back to the Shang Dynasty (ca. 1500–ca. 1045 B.C.E.), and it was played avidly throughout ancient times. Ancient Chinese tradition held that the game was invented in the 2300s B.C.E., during the legendary Xia Dynasty by the emperor Yao, as a way to teach his son how to think. The game was typically played on a wooden board etched or painted with a grid of black lines. Playing pieces were usually circular bits of stone or wood. The object of the game was to surround an opponent's playing pieces with one's own. It was easy to learn but could involve very complex strategy. A game between masters of *yi* could last several hours. In China emperors or nobles sometimes commissioned tournaments in which almost anyone, whether peasant or emperor, could participate. By the end of the ancient era the popularity of the game was spreading to Japan and Southeast Asia.

Little can be said with certainty about sports and recreation in the rest of Asia and Oceania during the ancient era. During the medieval era, counting games like those found in Africa became popular in Southeast Asia, but it is unlikely these games had as yet made their way along the southern coast of Asia to Southeast Asia before the ancient period ended. It is possible that Indian games made their way into Funan and that Chinese games made their way into Vietnam, but evidence for this is scant. The game of Go and sumo wrestling both had their origins in China, but documentary evidence for their existence in Japan before the medieval era is lacking. That the ancient Japanese played games is probable. Given the nearly universal popularity of wrestling, it probably existed in various forms throughout Asia and the Pacific. Surfing, the best known Polynesian sport, probably was not invented until after the ancient era, because the Polynesians had yet to colonize those islands where it seems to have emerged.

EUROPE

BY JUSTIN CORFIELD

The archaeological record of prehistoric Europe tells us very little about recreation and sport, and indeed these concepts as they are familiar to us in the modern Western world may not have existed. People probably found small amusements frequently in the course of their everyday life, but they may have involved telling stories, making music, or joking. Sports as competition in games and recreation as involving sport seem to have been relatively late developments in the human story; until modern times they seem to have been unknown in many parts of the world. At the Neolithic settlement at Skara Brae in the Orkney Islands of Scotland, a number of small well-carved stone balls have been found. Were they used in a game possibly similar to marbles, or did they play some ceremonial function? We can only guess.

Throughout Europe during the Bronze Age and the Iron Age many sports may have been connected with training boys and men for battle. Although there is little direct evidence for them, competitions in archery, javelin throwing, horse riding, and swordplay would have been natural accompaniments to training in these activities. It also seems probable that the Celts in Gaul and Britain engaged in chariot racing. Certainly their agility in battle, which Julius Caesar commented upon, meant that they had much practice, and it is reasonable to surmise that the development of these skills might have had a recreational aspect to it prior to their employment in combat.

A number of games and sports were limited to specific peoples or areas. Many Celts, for example, took part in games such as shinty, which seems to have been popular from the start of the Iron Age. Players on two opposing teams used sticks to hit a hard ball into a goal, much as in field hockey. A modern version of *shinty* is still played in Scotland, and hurling, a related sport resembling lacrosse, is still popular in Ireland. The ancient Celts seem to have believed that such sports provided good training for men and boys who were going to serve in battle.

Bronze group of a bull and acrobat, Minoan, about 1700–1450 B.C.E., from Crete; bull jumping is frequently shown in Minoan art and was thought to be a sport associated with ritual activity. (© The Trustees of the British Museum)

In Scotland many men engaged in weight sports such as tossing the caber, which was popular among the Picts and remains a feature of present-day Highland games, as a test of strength. The sport, highlighting accuracy and skill rather than distance, consisted in throwing a long, tapered length of wood such that it turned over in the air and landed pointing at the thrower. In the Balearic Islands boys were trained intensively from a young age to use the sling.

As to indoor games and recreations, it seems likely that dice were used—certainly many dice have survived in Roman settlements, and it seems likely that enterprising traders would have sold dice to the Celts. Celts also played games with knucklebones as well as a form of chess.

In the area of music Europeans had been playing instruments such as flutes, drums, lyres, and cymbals for many centuries, and by around 1000 B.C.E. they were making bronze trumpets, as indicated by numerous finds in northern Germany, Denmark, Scandinavia, and especially Ireland. In addition to music there was spoken entertainment. Celtic bards, in particular, had a reputation for being able to recite stories of ancient times, former kings, and valorous deeds. During Roman times poetry reading and oratory became more important in cities throughout the Roman Empire.

Eating and drinking at large communal feasts was a popular recreation both in the Celtic world and after the Romans took control of Gaul and Britain, with some references in Roman works to similar events taking place in Germany, and archaeological evidence in Denmark also pointing to the use of large halls for eating. Feasts of this kind often provided a venue for dancing, music, and the telling of old stories. Women and girls danced for their own pleasure and also for the entertainment of others.

Large-scale spectator sports seem not to have existed in most of Europe before the Romans brought their gladiatorial shows, which became popular in larger cities throughout the conquered lands. Ancient Europeans attended these events as onlookers, and many who had been captured in war and enslaved fought in them as gladiators, with particular dress codes for those who were Germans, Celts, Thracians, and so on. A glass cup found at Colchester, England, clearly shows two gladiators fighting.

Other blood sports of the period included badger-baiting, bull-baiting, cockfights, and hunting. While much of the hunting was to provide food, there was also an element of sporting prowess, with trophies such as horns or the heads of the animals being displayed after the hunt. There are also descriptions of bullfighting taking place in Spain, with men in Baetica, Andalusia, in about 220 B.C.E. attacking bulls with a lance or an ax in an arena, after using a cloak or skins to confuse the bull.

GREECE

BY JOHN THORBURN

The Greeks were one of the few ancient cultures to engage in athletic activity for purposes other than religious ritual or training for either war or hunting. With few exceptions athletic competitions were limited to men, but some women (especially those from Sparta) did exercise for recreation or physical fitness. Although Greek athletics may originally have been connected with war, hunting, or worship, eventually people began to engage in sports for the joy of competition and the desire to display their *aretê* ("goodness" or "excellence").

The earliest evidence for athletic activity in the region near Greece comes from wall paintings found on the islands of Thíra (modern-day Santorini) and Crete. The fresco from Thíra (ca. 1650–1500 B.C.E.) shows two children boxing; the Cretan fresco (ca. 1500 B.C.E.) shows a person leaping over a bull, an activity that may have had some religious significance.

The next significant evidence for athletic activity among the Greeks comes from two epic poems attributed to Homer, the *Iliad* and *Odyssey*. First written down during the eighth century B.C.E., these poems contain several descriptions of athletic events. The competitions described in the *Odyssey* occur in Phaeacia, which cannot be identified with certainty as a Greek land, but the events—running, wrestling, jumping, discus throwing, and boxing—are comparable to those described in the *Iliad* where the hero Achilles honors a dead companion with athletic competitions: chariot racing, boxing, wrestling, running, sparring in battle gear, throwing the quoit (similar to a discus), and archery.

Although the historical accuracy of the *Iliad* and *Odyssey* is uncertain, about the same time they were written down the first athletic games took place at Olympia, in southwestern Greece (in 776 B.C.E.). By 500 B.C.E. several other athletic festivals were being held regularly: the Pythian Games at Delphi, the Isthmian Games near Corinth, the Nemean Games at Nemea, and the Greater Panathenaea at Athens. In each case these games honored a divinity, and except at the Panathenaea the victors received crowns of vegetation (for example, the olive crown at Olympia).

For the first five decades of the games at Olympia a footrace, the *stadion*, was the only event. The name (the source of the modern word *stadium*) referred both to the setting in which the race occurred and to the distance it covered (a stade). The length of the *stadion* varied somewhat from site to site, but at Olympia it was about 210 yards. As with most Greek athletic events, the athletes competed in the nude.

At Olympia and at the newer festivals other events were gradually added. A second running event, the *diaulos*, was named after a Greek musical instrument with a double pipe because the race covered two lengths of the *stadion*. The course was straight, not oval or circular, and it is uncertain how the runners turned at the race's midpoint. Apparently they started out in individual lanes and then turned around a single post at the opposite end of the *stadion*.

The *dolichos* and the *hoplitodromos* were grueling events. As the name *dolichos* ("long") indicates, this was a distance race. Its length differed at the various festivals; at Olympia it was 24 stades, or just under 3 miles. In the *hoplitodromos* ("running in armor") the athletes competed in military gear.

Hockey game, found in the Themistoclean wall, Athens (Alison Frantz Photographic Collection, American School of Classical Studies at Athens)

Ancient vase paintings show runners carrying shields and wearing helmets and other armor. The *hoplitodromos* appears to have been from 2 to 4 stades in length.

The Greeks also engaged in boxing, wrestling, and the *pankration* ("all fighting"), which combined boxing and wrestling. The opponents neither fought in a ring nor had rounds lasting for any specific time. Unlike their modern counterparts, Greek boxers, wrestlers, and pankratiasts, though divided into different age classifications, could be matched against opponents much heavier than themselves. Greek boxers and pankratiasts did not wear gloves but wrapped their hands in leather thongs. They won by either knocking out the opponent or having him give up. Wrestlers won when the opponent gave up or when a certain number of falls, probably three, occurred. What determined a fall is not completely clear, but causing an opponent's back or shoulders to touch the ground seems to have counted as one.

The Greeks also competed in a pentathlon (javelin, discus, jumping, *stadion*, and wrestling). An athlete who won three of the five events obviously would claim the prize, but otherwise the pentathlon's scoring system is debated. The javelins used in athletic competition seem to have been about 6 feet long. Unlike in the modern event, Greek athletes wrapped the shafts of their javelins with a strap that they looped around one of their fingers. The strap apparently caused a rifling effect that made the throws more accurate and possibly longer than they would have been without it.

Other events in the pentathlon also differed somewhat from their modern counterparts. Whereas the men's discus in the modern Olympics weighs 4.4 pounds, the Greeks threw disks whose weight probably varied from location to location. Modern competitors in the event whirl around two and three-quarters times before releasing the discus, but the Greek discus throwers apparently made only a single three-quarters turn. Meanwhile, Greek jumpers seem to have engaged in a standing broad jump rather than taking a running start. The most unusual feature of this event was that the jumpers held weights in their hands. Apparently swinging the weights forward and then dropping them after takeoff increased the distance of the jump.

Besides track-and-field events various equestrian competitions occurred. Greek riders, who had neither saddles nor stirrups, made six laps around an oval track about three-quarters of a mile long. The competition was divided into races involving horses either less or more than a year old. Chariot racing made the same age division but also had races for chariots drawn by two or four horses. Chariot races were twice as long as the horse races.

ROME

BY ANNE MAHONEY

In ancient Rome spectator sports and individual exercises were distinct: The games people played on their own were not the same ones they watched other people playing. Spectator sports included gladiator combat, wild-animal shows, and chariot races. Few Roman citizens participated in these events except as onlookers.

Gladiator combats began at least as early as the third century B.C.E. The Latin word for such a combat was *munus*, "duty," because at first they were held only at funerals, as an offering for the dead person. In about 50 B.C.E. Julius Caesar held a memorial service for his daughter Julia that featured gladiators, even though this was not her actual funeral. From then on gladiator shows were no longer necessarily connected with funerals. Most gladiator fights were between two combatants. A showy, expensive *munus* would involve several pairs fighting one after another. There were several styles of fighting, each with its special weapons and equipment. For example, a *hoplomachus* used the heavy armor and weapons of a Greek infantry soldier or "hoplite." A *retiarius* used a net (from Latin *rete*).

Gladiators were almost always slaves. The person putting on a *munus* hired the troop of gladiators from its owner. Fights might or might not end with the death of the loser. Sometimes the audience was asked whether the winner should kill the loser, and the spectators would shout and gesture their opinions. We know that they could give thumbs-up or thumbs-down, but the ancient evidence does not tell us clearly what these gestures meant.

Wild-animal shows included exhibitions, combats, and public executions. There were no permanent zoos in Rome, but travelers sometimes brought back exotic animals and showed them off. For example, Pompey the Great (Gaius Pompeius Magnus, 106–48 B.C.E.) showed elephants in his games of 55 B.C.E. celebrating the dedication of a theater he had paid for. More exciting were animal fights and staged hunts. In the hunts armed slaves called *venatores* ("hunters)" chased down and fought various dangerous animals. *Venatores* were not as skilled as gladiators, and theirs was a less prestigious kind of combat.

Gladiator shows and animal shows took place in an amphitheater or arena much like a modern football stadium. The Colosseum in Rome is one such amphitheater, and others still exist in several former cities of the Roman Empire. A day at the arena might start with a staged hunt in the morning and finish with gladiators in the afternoon. In between there might be public executions. Criminals were often executed by wild animals in a spectacle much like the staged hunts except that the humans were not armed. Another form of execution was to perform a story from mythology with the condemned criminal in the role of a character who dies brutally. For example, the Roman historian Suetonius (ca. 69–ca. 130 C.E.) tells us that someone was made to act out the story of Icarus, the boy who in myth flew too close to the sun, which melted his artificial wings. Suetonius adds that the condemned man playing Icarus splashed the emperor with his blood when he fell.

Chariot races were the other major spectator sport. In these events chariots, usually pulled by two or four horses, raced around a track. The stadium was called a *circus*, "circle," although the track was an oval; the Circus Maximus ("biggest

DYRRHACHIUM

The Roman amphitheater in the port city of Dyrrhachium (Durrës), in Albania, is the largest in the Balkans, the city being a Roman stronghold in their wars with the kings of Macedon. During the Roman civil war between Julius Caesar and the Roman Republic, Caesar's rival general Pompey used Dyrrhachium as his base, with a series of engagements fought there in 49–48 B.C.E. The famed orator and statesman Cicero had lived in the city 10 years earlier when he was exiled from Rome. However, it was not until the reign of the emperor Hadrian (r. 117–38 C.E.) that construction of the amphitheater began on the side of the rocky hill that overlooks the city. Although the city was formerly Greek, there is little trace of Greek design in the architecture of the building, which was primarily for gladiators, and the showing and killing of wild animals—a popular Roman pastime.

The amphitheater could hold some 15,000 to 20,000 spectators and was no doubt popular with the many landless, discharged Roman soldiers settled in the region. The whole of the structure has not yet been excavated, with some later buildings occupying the east and west sides of the arena, where many of the people would have sat during the gladiatorial performances. The amphitheater was used until 1081, when the town was attacked by the Normans, and then the stones became a source for building elsewhere in the city. Work did not begin on the excavation of the amphitheater until 1966, when Albania made great play of the Roman use of slaves and prisoners as gladiators. They opened up the underground tunnels where gladiators and wild animals had been held. The animal chambers were found to have neatly rounded corners to prevent the animals from injuring themselves when they charged out into the arena to be killed.

circle") in Rome was the most famous example. The charioteers belonged to four different teams or "factions"—Blue, Green, White, and Red—which were part of an organization that covered the entire Roman world. (The emperor Domitian created Gold and Purple "expansion teams" in the late first century C.E., but they did not last.) A race might involve one chariot of each color, or there might be two or four of each color, which allowed for team tactics in the race. Charioteers were generally free or freedmen, not slaves; they got a share of the purse for races they won, and the best became fairly wealthy. Chariot races took place at the civic or religious festivals called *ludi* ("games") along with theatrical performances and other entertainments. They were a standard part of the major annual *ludi* and were also typically included in games given in celebration of military victories or other special occasions.

At Roman sporting events, unlike most Greek ones, the audience included both men and women. Elaborate rules dictated who could sit where, with the best seats reserved for senators and the wealthiest equestrians (also known as *equites*, just below patricians in the Roman social order). Most cities in the provinces had amphitheaters and chariot racetracks: Gladiator combats and chariot races were popular throughout the Roman world. Although some intellectuals found the games boring or unsophisticated, most Romans seem to have enjoyed them. The emperor Augustus (r. 27 B.C.E.–14 C.E.) included the games he sponsored in his list of major achievements, and Suetonius in his biographies of the first 12 Caesars always tells us what kinds of spectacles they staged.

The sports and games that Romans played on their own were far less dramatic. Upper-class men might go to a Greek-style gymnasium or a palaestra (wrestling school) to exercise and socialize. The public baths were another place for recreation, open to Romans of all classes and both sexes. In all these places people would talk, have snacks, and play games. Mosaics from Ostia, Sicily, and Pompeii show people playing with balls ranging in size from softballs to large exercise balls. Although we do not know the rules of the games, the pictures and literary references indicate that there were throwing games and kicking games. Adults and children, men and women all played ball games.

The Romans also played games much like modern board games. There were gambling games with dice and games

Roman terra-cotta sculpture of two gladiators fighting, first to second century C.E. (© The Trustees of the British Museum)

similar to backgammon and checkers. The dice were typically made from the small bones of animals' knuckles but also could be blocks of wood or ivory like present-day dice. Game pieces varied from simple pebbles to elaborately carved figures. Romans played these games almost anywhere, in the baths, in taverns, and at home.

THE AMERICAS

BY RENEE MCGARRY

People in the ancient Americas played a variety of sports and games. Many of these larger-scale sports, such as the ball game and the popular foot races, served ritual purposes. Other, smaller games often served the purpose of diversion and were leisure activities. Many games were played universally across the Americas, although the rules and practices of each varied greatly from civilization to civilization and group to group.

The ancient ball game is the oldest game known in the Americas. It originated about 1200 B.C.E. with the Olmec civilization and spread throughout Mesoamerica and even into the Caribbean islands. By about the year 1290 B.C.E. it was common for artists to dress figurines of Olmec rulers in ball-court costume, demonstrating the importance of the sport in society. Many ancient ball courts are still in existence, and scholars have used these courts and ancient figurines to determine the purposes, rules, and play of the ball game. While these remaining ball courts are principally located in areas where people played the game most frequently and extravagantly, archaeological evidence indicates that civilizations as far north as Arizona played less elaborate versions of the ancient ball game.

The Maya story of creation, the Popol Vuh, dates to the sixth century B.C.E. and illustrates the divine beginnings of the ancient ball game. In the story the gods known as the Hero Twins prove themselves to be extraordinary ball players, defeating even the Lords of the Underworld in a ball game. This early story establishes the game as more than simply a sport but indeed a contest of life and death, with the losing team ultimately suffering sacrifice to the gods.

The purpose of the ball game has been difficult to decipher. Many scholars believe that it was a fertility ritual that began as a simple game and evolved into a ceremony. This correlates with the blood sacrifice of the game, as many Mesoamericans believed that to perpetuate human life societies must take lives as offerings to their gods. These sacrifices could serve as a representation of a keeping of cosmic order, the victory of the sun over darkness, or an agricultural ritual.

The rules of the game varied by location, but many elements remained consistent across distance. Remarkably, each game was played with a rubber ball, a material entirely unique to the Americas in this period of history. Mesoamericans began harvesting and using rubber in approximately 1600 B.C.E., thousands of years before Europeans were familiar with the material. This rubber ball weighed 5 to 8 pounds and was bounced rapidly up and down the ball court during the game.

Stone hacha, Classic Veracruz, possibly as early as 300 C.E.; hachas were ax heads related to the Mesoamerican ball game and thought by some to be used as ball court markers. (© The Trustees of the British Museum)

In each culture the ball game was played with formalized teams and protective gear. From both depictions of the game and Spanish accounts, it is clear that neither the hands nor the feet were allowed contact with the ball. The body parts used to transport the ball varied across civilizations, though the manner of scoring points was rather consistent. A team scored a point with the use of two central hoops, or goals, midfield. Ball courts were generally large structures, complete with seating and a central field. Walls were decorated with depictions of the civilization's gods and often contained depictions of the ritual sacrifice at the end of the game.

The ball game was not the only sport played in the ancient Americas, but it is the one with the most remaining evidence. Foot races were perhaps the most popular and exciting sports for Native Americans. These races evolved out of a long tradition of running for transportation, but because little archaeological evidence exists there is no way to date the origin of the races. Much like the ball game, foot races have mythological origins. Several groups believed that races between their gods and the animals shaped the world, providing an explanation for constellations and the differentiation between species.

In advance of foot races participants took care to train and prepare themselves accordingly, which included such extreme measures as tying weights to their ankles for the weeks before the race. Runners also painted their bodies to identify themselves in the race and for ritual purposes. In many races wagering also became an important element, piquing interest in the sport.

Indigenous inhabitants of the southwestern United States and northern Mexico often participated in kick-ball races, long-distance races that involved kicking a ball for more than 25 miles at a stretch. Both men and women participated in these races, although women used a stick to toss a hoop ahead of them as they ran. Children began training for the kick-ball race when they were young, as it was seen as a religious ritual as well as a sporting event. Ceremonies were held the night before and the morning of the race, and there was a strong belief in supernatural intervention in these races. Many groups even believed that they were able to run faster while kicking the ball than without, as if a supernatural force were pulling each member of the team forward.

In Peru foot races were often included in the initiation of a boy reaching puberty. With other rituals, these foot races established each boy as a member of the adult community by showing his mental and physical fortitude. Foot races in North America were also run as part of growing up. Nations living in the Great Plains and along the Mississippi often viewed these races as preparation for future warfare.

For North American Indians in snowy climates, such as the ancestors of the Iroquois and Seneca nations (who can be traced to these regions to 4000 B.C.E.), the snow-snake game used the weather to its advantage. The object of the game was to toss an object called a snake (most commonly a pole) the farthest on ice or in snow. The lanes intended for the snow-snake were long and free from obstruction, but there were no specific rules about the paths or the snake itself. Snow-snake was generally an individual sport, although it could be played in teams, with each member tossing a snake and each team accumulating points for the longest throws. The game did not attract the attention of either the ball game or the races, nor did it have a supernatural or spiritual component. This game, then, seems to have been played simply for diversion and leisure activity.

Sports and games, then, did serve a purpose outside of a ritual one, particularly games of chance that originated in prehistoric times. In fact, the ancient dice playing of North American Indians can be traced back nearly 2,000 years using archaeological remnants of dice found in the southwestern United States. This prehistoric game did not use skill or calculation. Rather, each player relied on chance to win the game. As was the tradition with such games of chance, Indians often placed wagers on who would win. Some players were certainly luckier than others, and it was believed that those players had a special relationship with the gods or themselves had supernatural powers.

The dice that have been uncovered in Arizona, Utah, and Colorado are referred to as two-sided dice and are very unlike the six-sided dice of modern times. These dice resembled sticks and were decorated on each side, using light colors on one and dark colors on the other. As with most games of chance, the goal was to guess a number or a series of numbers involving the dice. The dice game has been found in more than 100 distinct groups in North America and is generally considered universal to nations in North America. As with the kick-ball race and the ball game, the rules and means of playing the game varied from nation to nation. Both men and women played the game in all nations, but they generally did so separately. Score was kept either with another set of sticks or using an abacus.

Ancient games were also played among children, and one of the best known is the skin or blanket tossing game of the Eskimo. In this game a large animal hide was spread, and a child climbed on it. When the hide was pulled taut, the child was thrown into the air. The object of this game was for each boy to land on his feet. Oftentimes the children were doing so after having been thrown more than 20 feet in the air.

Children all over the Americas also played with dolls, which were most frequently made using the most convenient materials. Those living in the region now occupied by the Chippewa used cattails in making their dolls, and clay figures were used in other parts of the Americas. Children often made their own dolls out of cornhusks where corn was most prevalent. Children played with dolls in much the same way as they do today, and these dolls were used by boys and girls alike.

See also ADORNMENT; AGRICULTURE; ARCHITECTURE; ART; CHILDREN; CRAFTS; CRIME AND PUNISHMENT; DRAMA AND THEATER; FESTIVALS; GENDER STRUCTURES AND ROLES; INVENTIONS; LITERATURE; MILITARY; MUSIC AND MUSICAL INSTRUMENTS; NUMBERS AND COUNTING; RELIGION AND COSMOLOGY; SOCIAL ORGANIZATION; TRADE AND EXCHANGE; WEAPONRY AND ARMOR.

Greece

Pindar, Olympian Odes (ca. 470 B.C.E.)

No. 9

Fit speech may I find for my journey in the Muses' car; and let me therewith have daring and powers of ample scope. To back the prowess of a friend I came, when Lampromachos won his Isthmian crown, when on the same day both he and his brother overcame. And afterwards at the gates of Corinth two triumphs again befell Epharmostos and more in the valleys of Nemea. At Argos he triumphed over men, as over boys at Athens. And I might tell how at Marathon he stole from among the beardless and confronted the full-grown for the prize of silver vessels, how without a fall he threw his men with swift and coming shock, and how loud the shouting pealed when round the ring he ran, in the beauty of his youth and fair form and fresh from fairest deeds.

No. 10

Ample is the glory stored for Olympian winners; thereof my shepherd tongue is fain to keep some part in fold. But only by the help of Zeus is wisdom kept ever blooming in the soul. Son of Archestratos, Agesidamos, know certainly that for your boxing I will lay a glory of sweet strains upon your crown of golden olive and will have in remembrance the race of the Locrians in the west.

No. 11

Who then won to their lot the new-appointed crown by hands or feet or chariot, setting before them the prize of glory in the games, and winning it by their act? In the foot-race down the straight course of the stadion was Likymnios' son Oionos first, from Nodea had he led his host: in the wrestling was Tegea glorified by Echemos: Doryklos won the prize of boxing, a dweller in the city of Tiryns, and with the four-horse chariot, Samos of Mantinea, Halirrhotios' son: with the javelin Phrastor hit the mark: in distance Enikeus beyond all others hurled the stone with a circling sweep, and all the warrior company thundered a great applause. Then on the evening the lovely shining of the fair-faced moon beamed forth, and all the precinct sounded with songs of festal glee, after the manner which is to this day for triumph.

No. 13

Also two parsley-wreaths shadowed his head before the people at the games of *Isthmus*, nor does *Nemea* tell a different tale. And of his father Thessalos' lightning feet is recorded by the streams of Alpheos, and at *Pytho* he has renown for the single and for the double *stadion* gained both in a single day, and in the same month at rocky *Pan-Athenaios* a day of swiftness crowned his hair for three illustrious deeds, and the *Hellotia* seven times, and at the games of *Poseidon* between seas longer hymns followed his father Ptoiodoros with Terpsias and Eritimos. And how often you were first at *Delphi* or in the *Pastures of the Lion*, though with full many do I match your crowd of honors, yet can I no more surely tell than the tale of pebbles on the sea-shore.

From: Fred Morrow Fling, ed., *A Source Book of Greek History* (Boston: D. C. Heath, 1907).

Rome

Suetonius, excerpt from The Divine Augustus *(ca. 120 C.E.)*

43. In the number, variety, and magnificence of his public spectacles, he surpassed all former examples. Four-and-twenty times, he says, he treated the people with games upon his own account, and three-and-twenty times for such magistrates as were either absent or not able to afford the expense. The performances took place sometimes in the different streets of the city, and upon several stages, by players in all languages. The same he did not only in the forum and amphitheatre, but in the circus likewise, and in the Saepta and sometimes he exhibited only the hunting of wild beasts. He entertained the people with wrestlers in the Campus Martius, where wooden seats were erected for the purpose; and also with a naval fight, for which he excavated the ground near the Tiber, where there is now the grove of the Caesars. During these two entertainments he stationed guards in the city lest, by robbers taking advantage of the small number of people left at home, it might be exposed to depredations. In the circus he exhibited chariot and foot races, and combats with wild beasts, in which the performers were often youths of the highest rank. His favorite spectacle was the Trojan game, acted by a select number of boys, in parties differing in age and station; thinking that it was a practice both excellent in itself, and sanctioned by ancient usage, that the spirit of the young nobles should be displayed in such exercises. Gaius Nonius Asprenas, who was lamed by a fall in this diversion, he presented

(continued)

(continues)

with a gold collar, and allowed him and his posterity to bear the surname of Torquati. But soon afterwards he gave up the exhibition of this game, in consequence of a severe and bitter speech made in the senate by Asinius Pollio, the orator, in which he complained bitterly of the misfortune of Aeserninus, his grandson, who likewise broke his leg in the same diversion.

Sometimes he engaged Roman knights to act upon the stage, or to fight as gladiators; but only before the practice was prohibited by a decree of the senate. Thenceforth, the only exhibition he made of that kind, was that of a young man named Lucius, of a good family, who was not quite two feet in height, and weighed only seventeen pounds, but had a stentorian voice. In one of his public spectacles, he brought the hostages of the Parthians, the first ever sent to Rome from that nation, through the middle of the amphitheatre, and placed them in the second tier of seats above him. He used likewise, at times when there were no public entertainments, if any thing was brought to Rome which was uncommon, and might gratify curiosity, to expose it to public view, in any place whatever; as he did a rhinoceros in the Saepta, a tiger upon a stage, and a snake fifty cubits long in the Comitium. It happened in the Circensian games, which he performed in consequence of a vow, that he was taken ill, and obliged to attend the Thensae [procession] reclining on a litter. Another time, in the games celebrated for the opening of the theatre of Marcellus, the joints of his curule chair happening to give way, he fell on his back. And in the games exhibited by his grandsons, when the people were in such consternation, by an alarm raised that the theatre was falling, that all his efforts to reassure them and keep them quiet, failed, he moved from his place, and seated himself in that part of the theatre which was thought to be exposed to most danger.

From: Suetonius, *The Lives of the Twelve Caesars*, trans. Alexander Thomson (New York: G. Bell and Sons, 1893).

The Americas

Excerpt from the Popol Vuh (oral tradition, unknown date)

II. Chapter 2

THE messengers of Hun-Camé and Vucub-Camé arrived immediately.

"Go, Ahpop Achih!" they were told. "Go and call Hun-Hunahpú and Vucub-Hunahpú. Say to them, 'Come with us. The lords say that you must come.' They must come here to play ball with us so that they shall make us happy, for really they amaze us. So, then, they must come," said the lords. "And have them bring their playing gear, their rings, their gloves, and have them bring their rubber balls, too," said the lords. "Tell them to come quickly," they told the messengers.

And these messengers were owls: Chabi-Tucur, Huracán-Tucur, Caquix-Tucur and Holom-Tucur. These were the names of the messengers of Xibalba.

Chabi-Tucur was swift as an arrow; Huracán-Tucur had only one leg; Caquix-Tucur had a red back, and Holom-Tucur had only a head, no legs, but he had wings.

The four messengers had the rank of Ahpop-Achih. Leaving Xibalba, they arrived quickly, bringing their message to the court where Hun-Hunahpú and Vucub-Hunahpú were playing ball, at the ball-court which was called Nim-Xob-Carchah. The owl messengers went directly to the ball-court and delivered their message exactly as it was given to them by Hun-Camé, Vucub-Camé, Ahalpuh, Ahalganá, Chamiabac, Chamiaholom, Xiquiripat, Cuchumaquic, Ahalmez, Ahaltocob, Xic, and Patán, as the lords were called who sent the message by the owls.

"Did the Lords Hun-Camé and Vucub-Camé really say that we must go with you?"

"They certainly said so, and 'Let them bring all their playing gear,' the lords said."

"Very well," said the youths. "Wait for us, we are only going to say good-bye to our mother."

And having gone straight home, they said to their mother, for their father was dead: "We are going, our mother, but our going is only for a while. The messengers of the lord have come to take us. 'They must come,' they said, according to the messengers."

"We shall leave our ball here in pledge," they added. They went immediately to hang it in the space under the rooftree. "We will return to play," they said.

And going to Hunbatz and Hunchouén they said to them: "Keep on playing the flute and singing, painting, and carving; warm our house and warm the heart of your grandmother."

From: Delia Goetz and Sylvanus Griswold Morley, trans., *Popol Vuh* (Los Angeles: Plantin Press, 1954).

FURTHER READING

Carlin A. Barton, *The Sorrows of the Ancient Romans: The Gladiator and the Monster* (Princeton, N.J.: Princeton University Press, 1992).

Alan Cameron, *Circus Factions: Blues and Greens at Rome and Byzantium* (Oxford, U.K.: Oxford University Press, 1976).

Stewart Culin, *Games of the North American Indian* (New York: Dover Publications, 1975).

Wolfgang Decker, *Sports and Games of Ancient Egypt*, trans. Allen Guttmann (New Haven. Conn.: Yale University Press, 1992).

Irving Finkel, ed., *Ancient Board Games in Perspective* (London: British Museum Press, 2007).

Alison Futrell, *A Sourcebook on the Roman Games* (Oxford, U.K.: Blackwell, 2006).

H. A. Harris, *Greek Athletes and Athletics* (Westport, Conn.: Greenwood Press, 1964).

"History of Weiqi." Available online. URL: http://www.yutopian.com/go/misc/gohistory.html. Downloaded January 30, 2007.

Ulrich Hubner, "Games." In *The Oxford Encyclopedia of Archaeology in the Near East*, vol. 2, ed. Eric M. Meyers (New York: Oxford University Press, 1997).

George Jennison, *Animals for Show and Pleasure in Ancient Rome*, 2nd ed. (Philadelphia: University of Pennsylvania Press, 2005).

Anne Mahoney, *Roman Sports and Spectacles: A Sourcebook* (Newburyport, Mass.: Focus, 2001).

"Mancala." Available online. URL: http://www.search.com/reference/Mancala. Downloaded on November 29, 2006.

Stephen G. Miller, *Ancient Greek Athletics* (New Haven: Yale University Press, 2004).

Peter Nabokov, *Indian Running: Native American History and Tradition* (Santa Fe, N.M.: Ancient City Press, 1987).

Věra Olivová, *Sports and Games in the Ancient World*, trans. D. Orpington (London: Orbis, 1984).

Joseph B. Oxendine, *American Indian Sports Heritage*, 2nd ed. (Lincoln: University of Nebraska Press, 1995).

Michael B. Poliakoff, *Combat Sports in the Ancient World: Competition, Violence, and Culture* (New Haven, Conn.: Yale University Press, 1987).

D. S. Potter and D. J. Mattingly, eds., *Life, Death, and Entertainment in the Roman Empire* (Ann Arbor: University of Michigan Press, 1999).

Larry Russ, *The Complete Mancala Games Book: How to Play the World's Oldest Board Games* (New York: Marlowe, 2000).

David Sansone, *Greek Athletics and the Genesis of Sport* (Berkeley: University of California Press, 1988).

Judith Swaddling, *The Ancient Olympic Games*, 2nd ed. (Austin: University of Texas Press, 1999).

Malcolm Todd, *Everyday Life of the Barbarians, Goths, Franks, and Vandals* (London: Batsford, 1972).

E. Michael Whittington, ed., *The Sport of Life and Death: The Mesoamerican Ballgame* (New York: Thames and Hudson, 2001).

storage and preservation

INTRODUCTION

Hunter-gatherers in prehistoric times paid minimal attention to long-term food storage and preservation. Their way of life dictated that they move about in search of food supplies and then consume what they found as they found it. Food typically would not have been preserved for more than a few days or perhaps weeks, depending on how long it would keep. Meat and fish, of course, had to be consumed within days, while plant foods could be kept on hand for a period of weeks.

It was with the advent of agriculture that ancient peoples turned more attention to longer-term food storage and preservation. Agriculture offered the possibility of making a community's food supply more consistent and predictable over time. By storing and preserving food, people could measure out their food consumption over the year and eliminate the need to pick up and move when food supplies ran out. Accordingly, they developed a number of techniques for storing and preserving food.

At the household level, food was stored primarily in such containers as woven baskets and clay pots; pots were also used for storing beverages. Grains (often ground into meal and flour), beans, and rice could be stored in this way for long periods of time. Foods more susceptible to spoilage were preserved principally by drying. The food was spread out on the ground or on racks and placed in the sun or over a fire. When its moisture content was low enough, it would be suitable for storage because microorganisms would not grow in it. In this way ancient peoples preserved fruits, berries, corn, vegetables, and especially meat and fish.

Smoking was another common method for preserving meats and fish. The smoke coated the food's cells with substances that inhibit the growth of microorganisms. Similarly, freezing was a good way to preserve food in cold-weather climates. North Americans, for example, killed game late in the fall and then allowed the meat to freeze, often grinding it up and mixing it with other foods such as berries. Another major way of preserving meat and fish was by salting them. Salt, inexpensive and taken for granted in the modern world, was a highly valued commodity in the ancient world, necessary not only for nutrition but for food preservation. In addition to salt, certain herbs and other plants were found to have preservative properties, particularly in discouraging insects and rodents. Enzymes from cow stomachs and some plants enabled people to preserve dairy products in the form of cheese. Pickling, too, used acids to preserve vegetable crops.

Larger, more advanced communities needed to find ways to preserve and store large quantities of food. The ancient Egyptians, for example, developed highly sophisticated techniques for growing grain in the silt left behind by the floodwaters of the Nile River. After the waters receded, millions of acres of grain crops were planted and then irrigated with water stored in a complex system of fields, dikes, dams, and sluices. Annual crop yields amounted to millions of tons, most of which was stored in community granaries for later distribution. On a smaller scale, some ancient peoples developed underground storage silos for grain, sealing the silos off from the air to prevent rotting, molds, and pest infestations.

AFRICA

BY KIRK H. BEETZ

Archaeological evidence for ancient African storage and preservation is patchy, known only from a smattering of sites scattered across the continent. Archaeologists have used physical evidence, records from ancient historians such as Herodotus (ca. 484–ca. 425 B.C.E.), and the practices in historical times of ancient ethnic groups to reconstruct a little of how ancient Africans stored food and valuables. There are hazards in using the practices of people in the present day to reconstruct what their ancestors may have done, because even a very traditional culture may change some of its practices over a period of thousands of years.

Even so, what little is known about storage and preservation in ancient Africa offers clues to the matters of ancient relationships among cultures and the diffusion of knowledge in ancient times. Grass-lined pits have been discovered in West Africa and in the central Sahara in which food, probably millet, would have been stored, and the peoples around ancient Lake Chad had silos made of mud bricks, possibly for storing grain. The pits of West Africa may date from about the early 4000s B.C.E., around the same time as similar ones found in Egypt, whereas the pits and silos of Chad date from about 1800 to 400 B.C.E. Some archaeologists take these finds as evidence of a shared culture that predated the ancient Egyptian culture and probably developed in the Sahara, then spread into the region of the Nile. Others suggest it is evidence that storage practices spread either from the newly agricultural peoples of the lower Nile region to the west or from central or western Africa to the region that became central Egypt.

Archaeological work in Chad is especially interesting because it is one of the few places in Africa where archaeologists have been able to begin constructing a record of continuous cultural development. Very early, people built villages near the shores of Lake Chad, which was much bigger before the Sahara dried. As the shores of the lake receded, people moved their homes to remain near the vital source of water. This has allowed archaeologists to go from one site to another, progressing ever more recently in history as they move ever closer to the modern lake. Thus there is evidence for the development of storage practices from about 1800 to 400 B.C.E.

The most significant finds have been pits. Some pits were dug to remove clay for building homes. Others were dug to provide clay for building defensive walls around villages. Still others are of a more mysterious purpose. Some probably stored valuables such as pottery and metal objects. Some of the pits may have stored food, especially cowpeas. Not yet securely dated are the silos, which were probably built after 1800 B.C.E. They were for grain, probably pearl millet, a type of grain that was durable when stored. The silos are taken as an indication that the ancient villagers were able to have surpluses of crops from their harvests and had the social organization to store the surpluses for periods of poor harvests. Given that pearl millet was a summer crop and that winters could be very dry, the silos and pits at least may have provided storage of food for use during the winter. People in the region still use storage pits, and archaeologists draw some of their conclusions about pits being used for storing food from the similarity of the ancient pits to the modern ones.

As the Sahara and much of northeastern Africa dried in ancient times, storing and preserving water became more and more important. Evidence for how this was done in the Sahara comes mostly from ancient rock paintings dating to about 8000 B.C.E. onward. Many of the paintings depict ordinary life, which has allowed archaeologists to trace some of the developments in Saharan culture as the climate changed. During the period from 2780 to 600 B.C.E. residents of the Sahara drew water from wells. One painting shows what appears to be a leather bucket being hoisted from a well. The belief that it is leather is based on the artist's depiction, which makes it look like animal hide, and the fact that the Saharans were longtime herders of cattle. From this it may be inferred that leather bottles were used to store and transport water much as the peoples of the Sahara have done in historical times.

In the kingdom of Kush (ca. 900 B.C.E.–ca. 300 C.E.), south of ancient Egypt, water management seems to have been more sophisticated. Cisterns made of stone have been found in Kush's towns and cities. Archaeologists debate about the use of the cisterns, suggesting that they were swimming pools, baths, or storage for drinking and cooking water. They tend to be located in or near homes, and the ancient Kushites boiled food extensively, both of which suggest that the cisterns were intended to store water for consumption.

South of Kush, along the coast of East Africa, lived people who seemed to put water to another use. According to the Greek geographer Strabo (64 or 63 B.C.E.–after 23 C.E.), fishermen of the region stored shellfish and fish in pools of water near the shore to keep for eating later, perhaps when catches were poor. This is a logical practice, and Strabo took greater pains than most ancient geographers to make his accounts accurate. A later development was the use of baskets to catch fish and keep them in water. This use of baskets was also found among Bantu-speaking peoples of West Africa.

The Bantu speakers were farmers, and by 200 C.E. they were advancing east and south out of West Africa, using their iron tools to carve out farms from forests. How they stored their harvests is not entirely clear, but inferences can be made from the recorded practices of their descendants. One is that their granaries were elevated above the ground on posts made of tree branches. This helped protect the grain not only from pests such as rats but also from flooding, a common problem in central Africa and parts of eastern Africa south of Kush. Another practice was that of making granaries out of walls of woven mats and conical roofs of long rushes that ran lengthwise from the peaks down to the edges, thus making rainwater flow out and away from the granary. Much of this inference is speculative because archaeologists have not made much progress in researching in Africa's forests; the central regions are remote and therefore hard to reach, and the region has been very dangerous for scientists because of bandits and warfare.

EGYPT

BY KATHARINA ZINN

Most food in ancient Egypt was not produced or consumed daily, and to be kept longer it had to be preserved. Methods of storage and preservation were designed to solve this problem and to accommodate the growing population of the region. Stored or preserved food could include grain, fruits, vegetables, meat, fish, poultry, and wine. The storage facilities in ancient Egypt showed a wide range of types and extended from single storage jars or basketwork containers for domestic use to large storeroom complexes. Meat, fish, and poultry were stored in pottery vessels. Plates or bowls were used to hold offerings (it was necessary to offer food to the deceased daily), and tightly closed jars were used for long-term storage. Oil, fat, and suet were stored in stoneware jars. Grain was stored in small domestic pits or jars as well as large-scale granaries controlled by the state or a temple, such as the Ramesseum (a mortuary temple in Thebes dedicated to the Egyptian king Ramses II [r. 1290–1224 B.C.E.]) and Medinet Habu (dedicated to Ramses III [r. 1194–1163 B.C.E.]). Storerooms for grain and other agricultural products were named *shenut* ("barns") and had a specific administrative structure devoted to their maintenance. Precious goods, such as herbs, spices, and salt, were kept in small leather or linen bags. Of further importance was the form of rations for food supply. In a society without money, rations had a special significance; food had to be stored within the food circle from harvest or slaughtering to ration distribution.

Grain was stored in large quantities at the local, provincial, and state level in granary silos whose maximum capacity was calculated by scribes. Some silos are partly excavated, while others have been depicted in artwork or as model granaries in tombs. Depictions of stored grain or models placed in tombs were meant to guarantee a supply of food for the dead. Scenes portray people sacking up and carrying the grain from fields to the granaries, sometimes using donkeys. Grain was put directly into storage facilities after winnowing, sieving, recording, and measuring by scribes. At the granary porters carried the baskets up the stairs to the charging hole, where the grain was poured in. The process was supervised by a scribe or administrator who recorded intakes, storage, and removal. All harvested goods belonged not to the farmer but to the king or to the temples or nobles who had received the land as a gift from the king.

The first small-scale granaries were pits with basketry linens and a total yield of about 7.5 pounds. In El Faiyûm, a large oasis, Egyptologists have found well-preserved wheat and barley from the Neolithic Period (dating to about 5200 B.C.E.). This shows the long tradition of storage that preceded dynastic times. Other early examples are in El Badâri in northern Upper Egypt about 4500 B.C.E., where postholes, pits, and storage jars were found. The oldest large granaries were cones with round bases and domed tops that were made of mud brick or seasoned wood and sometimes plastered. The larger ones had steps or a ladder leading to a hole at the top

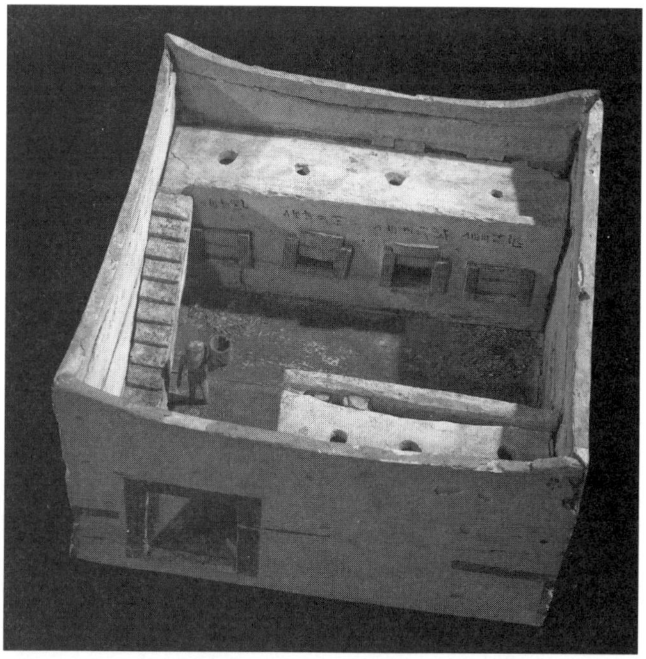

Painted wooden model of a granary, from Aswān, Egypt, Sixth Dynasty, around 2200 B.C.E. (© The Trustees of the British Museum)

where the grain was poured in. Another opening at the bottom was used to remove the grain. This structural form existed until the beginning of the Greco-Roman Period in 332 B.C.E. and was supplemented by trapezoidal structures used for storing cereals to be used for sowing in the next season. Quadrangular chambers, filled through small holes on the ceiling, also are evidenced by models and drawings. Sometimes terms for the contents were written on the models.

The Egyptian temples were given estates and royal endowments as offerings to the gods. The priesthood, in turn, received food and other offerings through an elaborate allocation formula called the Reversion of Offerings. Holding and redistributing the offerings required the use of large storage facilities, which belonged to the temples. The best-preserved set of large storage facilities is attached to the Ramesseum, which could support about 3,400 families (about 17,000 to 20,000 people) for a year with grain. The temple storehouses consisted of long mud-brick, barrel-vaulted halls of varying size with filling holes at the top, erected in groups with a shared vestibule. The temples built up substantial reserves for grain and other goods. From these or state granaries each farmer got his grain for sowing, again recorded by scribes. The granaries housed the food that was used as payment for the army, workers on building projects, and other citizens.

Egyptian houses, including palaces, also contained storerooms and granaries. Some of the houses of the planned towns in El-Lahun, Tell El-'Amârna, and Medina had a row of storerooms. El-Lahun shows evidence of several locations within the town rather than a central granary. Large estates had large private storerooms, while those who lived in the country had smaller, mostly conical ones that stored nearly everything in the Egyptians' diet.

As a form of preservation, most food was dried in air and sunlight. There is little evidence for smoking, probably for lack of wood. Pickling with brine, oil, or salt was common as salt draws out liquid. The use of vinegar is assumed but not evidenced. Meat and poultry were preserved through the use of fat, honey, or beer.

If meat was not consumed immediately after hanging, it was cut, wet- or dry-salted, dried in sun and air, possibly smoked, and cured in jars. As the food cooled inside the jars, a sort of vacuum was created that kept the food from spoiling. Some of these jars were made of marl clay, which kept their contents cool. The food was later cooked before it was eaten, which killed most bacteria in the process.

Another perishable food was fish. Much of the catch was cleaned, gutted, and dried in the sun on wooden frames. It sometimes was salted or pickled in oil. Roe was dried or pickled in salt and then pressed and dried. Drying, salting, and pickling were methods of preservation for small birds, too. Dairy products such as cheese were salted and sometimes preserved in oil, dried, and hardened. Dates, figs, olives, or grapes could be dried, ground, pickled, or pressed. Storing grain in spikelet form, rather than threshed, helped to protect it from attacks by insects or other pests. Herbs such as coriander, black cumin, and fenugreek were added as insecticides, as evidenced in a model granary of the Egyptian king Tutankhamen (r. 1333–1323 B.C.E.) containing emmer with other seeds.

THE MIDDLE EAST

BY LYN GREEN

The first permanent settlements appeared in the ancient Near East during the Neolithic Period. They were small and usually clustered around sources of water, as all later towns would be. These most ancient farmers tended to settle particularly along rivers, where alluvial soil carried by the water spread out and made fertile, easily cultivated agricultural land. Their houses and probably storage buildings were made of the same unbaked river mud. The crops grown by these earliest farmers did not have a high yield, since they were still essentially wild forms of the plants. The farmers, therefore, would not have been able to put aside large quantities of food between growing seasons. To supplement the grains and pulses such as barley, einkorn, emmer, lentils, peas, chick peas, and bitter vetch, they also ate wild fruits and nuts, fish, birds, and game. Because storage facilities did not need to be large or to keep food for extended periods of time, the earliest-known storage facilities (from the Pre-Pottery Neolithic A Period, perhaps as early as 8500 B.C.E.) were small bins and silos and probably baskets or sacks. The latter have not survived because they would have been made of rushes, reeds, or hide.

Later civilizations of the area, such as the Halaf culture (dating to as long ago as the sixth millennium B.C.E.), practiced agriculture and stored grain in beehive-shaped communal granaries. Many centuries later, granaries of the same shape were built at the sites of Arad and Beth Yerah. The Halaf storage facilities were small and shared only among a few dwellings. By contrast, the Bronze Age (ca. 3500–ca. 1200 B.C.E.) granaries of Arad and Beth Yerah were much larger and served whole communities. They rested on stone foundations and were usually from 13 to 30 feet in diameter. All of these storage buildings were built above the ground, but farmers of the fifth millennium B.C.E. in the Negev desert stored their food in below-ground chambers linked to each other and to the living quarters by a serious of subterranean tunnels. Within the underground storerooms were pits where grain, lentils, and other foodstuffs were stored. Underground storage in the desert was both cool and dry and proved so effective that these farmers continued to store grain underground even after they began to build their houses on the surface.

The earliest storage containers of the ancient Near East, dating to the early Neolithic Period, differ markedly from all later forms of storage because they appear before pottery was made. All later civilizations depended heavily on pottery storage jars in all sizes and shapes. These pottery pieces were almost always of undecorated fired clay, though they could be covered with a thin clay coating called a slip. Slip makes the surface of the pot less permeable to air and moisture and helps prevent the contents from spoiling. By the Chalcolithic Period (also known as the Copper Age, ca. 4500–ca. 3300 B.C.E.) pottery was becoming a specialized craft, and pots could be made in a variety of sizes and shapes. These new shapes became necessary because Near Eastern farmers from the Chalcolithic Period onward were experimenting with new ways of preserving foodstuffs. Around this time they began to crush grapes and olives for wine and oil, which obviously required quite different storage containers from whole olives or dried grapes (raisins). Scholars believe that around this time the farmers also began to dry figs and dates, though it is possible that in a hot, dry climate this sort of preservation would have been happening all along.

After the Chalcolithic Period centralized government arose in the Fertile Crescent, first in the form of city-states and later as kingdoms and even empires. It is often said that developments in food technology, including storage, are inseparable from this change. The evidence of texts and of archaeology makes it clear that the structures of the ruling elite were economic centers as well as residences or temples. In early Sumer, for example, where the priesthood often ruled the cities, storehouses were often located close to the temples. These government storehouses served multiple purposes: They provided long-term storage for grain and other foodstuffs for seed and as a guard against famine, and they were used as shorter-term storage for goods to be traded or redistributed as rations or wages.

Many different types of food were now being kept for a longer term, and this necessitated new preservation techniques. For example, while yogurt may have been made in the Chalcolithic Period, by Sumerian times the milk of sheep, goats, and cattle was preserved by being made into cheese and ghee (clarified butter). Grapes and dates were dried or pressed for their juice, which could be left to ferment into either wine or vinegar. The grape and date juice itself could also be boiled down until it became a synthetic form of honey. (Real honey was expensive and probably mostly imported.) The concentration of sugars caused by boiling down the juice inhibited the growth of bacteria, so the syrup would keep without spoiling. Pomegranates, another widely grown fruit, would keep without processing if stored carefully.

Pulses, legumes, and similar vegetables were dried for storage. Some other vegetables, such as mushrooms, could also have been dried. Drying, salting, and possibly smoking were used in various parts of the ancient Near East to keep meat and especially fish. The bones of saltwater fish found at inland sites in Sumer show that some sort of preservation of fish for shipment was taking place by the third millennium B.C.E. Sumerian texts show that they were making a kind of fermented fish sauce as well. Although most meat was eaten right away, the types that would have been available for processing included goat, beef, mutton, venison, and pork. Poultry such as ducks and geese were also raised and their meat dried or smoked.

As urban centers and the centralized control of commodities grew, larger storage facilities were needed. Grain, which was made into bread and (since the fourth millennium B.C.E.) beer, was stored in great quantities. The Middle Bronze Age (ca. 2000–ca. 1500 B.C.E.) silos at Beth Yerah are estimated to have held as much as 40 tons of grain. Other contemporary cities in this area, however, had a different solution to the problem of grain storage. They excavated downward rather than building upward to make their granaries. By the Iron Age (ca. 1200–ca. 586 B.C.E.) cities like Jericho and Megiddo were building rectangular storehouses and storerooms with thick walls to keep the grain and foodstuffs cool and dry. Archaeologists in Israel have uncovered storehouses in which the stored items were kept in pottery bins or jars. Occasionally, commodities such as grain were stored loose in these rooms. The remains of barley and wheat show that these were the main cereals grown and stored in the granaries.

ASIA AND THE PACIFIC

BY KIRK H. BEETZ

The need to provide food during lean times was met in many different ways in Asia and the Pacific, depending on the food that was available, the climate, and people's cultures. The first people in Australia found a fairly wet climate and big forests, but the continent gradually dried out, leaving only small forests in areas that remained wet. The Australians coped by spreading out in a thin population over the continent. By living in small, family-oriented groups with a great deal of space for hunting and gathering food, the ancient Australians were able to thrive when food was plentiful and still find enough food to survive when times were lean. Rather than store large caches of food, they made sure there were not too many people to use what food was available to them throughout the year.

In tropical climates storing food was difficult because the regions tended to be wet, and moisture helped to decay food. One way to preserve fish was to smoke it. This involved suspending fish over a low-burning, smoky fire that would rapidly dry the fish. Fish devoid of moisture could remain edible for weeks or even months. Cultures throughout the South Pacific and the Indian Ocean used this technique. In areas where tapirs or other sources of meat were available, meat was smoked. Techniques for storing smoked meat varied but usually involved hanging the dried meat either inside the home or underground in a chamber dug for the purpose of storing smoked meats, keeping the food away from scavenging animals.

Nomads in central and northern Asia hung meat from poles or skewers to allow the wind to dry it. It was important to allow the meat to dangle and to cut it thinly enough for the wind to dry it thoroughly. The climate of central Asia was drying out during the ancient era, creating excellent conditions for drying meat rapidly. It was difficult for the nomads to store bulky foods such as the grains most often grown in their regions: millet, wheat, and barley. Thus they sometimes took to raiding farming communities to steal the harvests when they wanted the food rather than producing and storing the food themselves.

Keeping grains dry was very important. The Harappan civilization of about 2600 to 1500 B.C.E. made the preservation of grain a science in which they engineered sometimes spectacular granaries for storing grain against hard times. The cities of Harappa and Mohenjo Daro had granaries that may have represented the apex of grain-storage technology. The granary in Mohenjo Daro was about 150 feet in length and about 75 feet wide, and it rested on a base of bricks about 20 feet high. Atop the base was a wooden, roofed structure perhaps 12 feet high. Although the city had mostly narrow streets, a large open space around the granary allowed easy access for carts bringing in grain or unloading grain for distribution. There was a loading platform along one side of the building where grain could be hoisted up or lowered down. Inside were wooden silos that held the grain. Under the floor were air ducts, channels that circulated air to keep the grain dry to prevent rotting. The granary looked like a fortress, which has inspired some archaeologists to speculate that the granary was like a bank that held the nation's wealth. The huge structure probably ensured that Harappans would have food to eat during poor harvests.

Insects and rodents were threats to stored grain. In ancient China their feasting in granaries sometimes resulted in a shortage of food. Keeping grain sealed helped keep out insects, and large ceramic jars with tight lids were used in China, India, and Japan to protect grain. Although the ancient Japanese typically built their structures with pits in the ground, they raised their granaries on posts to help keep the stored grain out of reach of mice and other pests. The shape of a granary was rectangular. Four holes in the ground were pounded until their bottoms were rock hard, then circular wooden posts were set in them. A wooden floor a few feet above the ground was installed, followed by walls attached to the posts and a roof that was probably peaked and covered with dried grass, although archaeologists disagree greatly among themselves about this detail. It seems that by 100 C.E. nearly every village in the Japanese islands had such a granary.

Another way to preserve food was to pack it in salt. The salt would keep meat from going rancid for a time, usually long enough to carry it through a season when food was scarce. Meat preserved with salt had something in common with dry grain: It needed water to make it edible. Rice is almost not chewable unless moistened. Salted meat needed to be soaked in water to wash out enough salt to make it digestible. In much of central and northern Asia water became increasingly harder to find throughout ancient times. For nomads, this left them their wind-dried meats. For farmers, this meant digging pits in which to store their foods, though this practice seems to have come late to northern China. The soldiers of the Great Wall had storage depots for food and other supplies, but the farmers of the region still needed to be taught about granaries and storage pits as late as the 100s C.E.

In India the need for water to make dry grain and salted meat edible created a dangerous problem. People from cities went to nearby rivers or to moats to fetch their water for cooking, and the rivers and moats were dreadfully polluted by 300 B.C.E. Diseases transmitted by human waste, garbage, and rodents lurked in the water, and underheated cooking water could result in outbreaks of disease that could kill thousands in crowded residential districts. The usually wet climate of most of India also made it difficult to keep foods dry. Indians got around some of their food preservation problems by tending gardens for fresh food. Even a small household usually had a garden from which fruits and herbs could be picked daily. Except for the cold and sometimes dry far north of India, it was possible to have something ripe and edible in a garden year-round. Both men and women were often master gardeners, and men who were professional gardeners took care to teach their daughters what they knew, because the girls would ultimately be responsible for caring for the food in their household gardens. It also was a good trade for a woman to know, to make money for herself and her family in the marketplace.

EUROPE

BY MICHAEL J. O'NEAL

The ancient Europeans faced the same storage and preservation problems that ancient peoples the world over faced. The enemies of food stored over a period of time include moisture, temperature, microbes (including molds), and pests. Without effective systems of food storage and preservation, the ancient Europeans would have found it difficult to fend off famine and starvation during the long, cold winters of the North. Moreover, without methods of storage and preservation, it is not possible to accumulate perishable goods, transport them, and trade them, activities that were a necessary means to the accumulation of wealth and status.

Many of the technologies that the ancient Europeans used to store and preserve food are still in use today. The only fundamental difference is that ancient Europeans did not have electricity to power the tools they used for the task. Accordingly, they relied on the tools that nature provided. One method of preserving such food as meat, fish, vegetables, and fruits was to dry them. With a low moisture content, food was not as susceptible to spoilage. To dry food, the ancient Europeans placed it in the sun and allowed warm air to circulate around it. A variant of drying is cheese making. The ancient Europeans were able to preserve milk in cheese form by coagulating it and draining out the watery whey, leaving behind the milk solids that had a much lower water content than the original milk. In cool temperatures, cheese would keep for many months. In Neolithic Britain residues of milk fats have been found on fragments of pottery that date from 4500 B.C.E.

The problem the ancient Europeans faced, though, was that for food to dry effectively, three to five days of high temperatures, bright sunshine, and low humidity were needed, so drying was not always possible. Accordingly, the ancient Europeans turned to a related technique, smoking, particularly for meat and fish. Smoke contains a number of substances that bind to the surface of the cells of meat products, allowing them to resist the action of bacteria. While meat and fish would normally spoil after perhaps a week, smoked meat and fish could be consumed safely for three months or more.

Similarly, storing meat, fish, and vegetables in brine—that is, a concentrated solution of water and salt—provided similar protection against microbes. Salt was a highly valued commodity in ancient Europe, and the salt-producing region of Austria near the modern-day city of Salzburg (*salz* means "salt" in German) enjoyed a great deal of wealth by mining it. The ancient Gauls sold salted pork to the Romans. Salt was especially valuable to the Scandinavian cultures of northern Europe, whose diet included a great deal of fish that had to be stored during winter months, when bodies of water were frozen over or too stormy to allow fishing. A related technique was the use of spices to preserve food; modern scientists have shown that some spices effectively fight the formation of harmful bacteria. In ancient Europe, however, spices were extremely valuable commodities, available only from Arab traders. The average person probably would not have had access to spices, although the elite would have.

The ancient Europeans, again in common with the rest of the world, needed reliable sources of wholesome beverages that would not become stale and brackish in storage. Fermented beverages, such as beer and wine, provided them with drinkable liquids throughout the year. Of course, the Europeans by no means invented fermented beverages, but they did introduce the wooden barrel as a way of storing and transporting wine and beer.

The ancient Europeans devoted considerable resources to the storing of food. In common with other cultures of the world, they used caves where they could. Caves have the advantage of being at a constant cool temperature, with reliable humidity levels. Caves were the earliest form of root cellars and were particularly useful for the storing of root vegetables as well as fruits.

Where caves were not available, the Europeans constructed granaries and other facilities for the storage of food, particularly for grain. Throughout the Celtic lands of western Europe and the British Isles, for example, archaeologists have uncovered a large number of hill forts and, in Scotland, brochs (circular stone fortifications) that date from the Iron Age. These hill forts were settlements that housed up to several hundred people, though sometimes they were occupied seasonally or provided a place of refuge for people and their livestock in times of war. These hill forts were administrative centers for the surrounding region, and one of the major functions they served was that of food storage and preservation.

In England, for example, hill forts such as Danebury have been found with massive grain-storage capacity. Many of these hill forts were built on chalk subsoil, and in their interiors were pits used for food storage, as underground grain silos. Normally, the moisture of an underground pit would cause any grain stored in them to rot. However, the Europeans may have found a solution to the problem. The grain was poured into the pit, and then the pit was covered with an airtight clay seal. The seal was then covered with dirt to keep the seal from drying and cracking. The grain in contact with the moist earth of the pit germinated, consuming all the oxygen in the pit and releasing carbon dioxide. Because the seal was airtight, no further oxygen could enter. The remainder of the grain, then, was preserved in a state of "suspended animation." In this way it could have been preserved for months, as long as the seal remained intact.

GREECE

BY LYN GREEN

From the Minoans and Mycenaeans (2600–1100 B.C.E.) of the Bronze Age to the Hellenistic Greek world more than a thousand years later there were many similarities in food storage and preservation. No matter what the time period, the storage needs of the people did not change. For the short term, food had to be stored before eating or before it was redistributed through rations. An example of medium-term storage was putting aside an amount of food to last through the gaps between growing seasons or before it was exported or otherwise used in trade. Farmers also had to put aside enough seed each year to plant the next season's crop, and prudent householders and city rulers put aside food in case of famine or war. These were examples of long-term storage in large volumes. Although both seed for planting and food put aside against famine were both problems in long-term and large-volume storage, there was one significant difference. When it was time for crop planting, the storage areas for seeds would be emptied until the end of season. There was no need to worry about contamination or spoilage of food that was now open to air. This may have affected the choice of container or structure for storage.

Tablets from the palaces of Crete and Greece in the Bronze Age show that palatial structures served as warehouses for goods and food items from the surrounding countryside. Olives, olive oil, grain, honey, fruit, and meat all were stored there. Grains such as wheat and barley were sometimes kept in palace courtyards in huge pottery vessels called *pithoi*. There were also other means of storing grain. The earliest forms of storage were probably pits lined with clay or stone. They would have been kept tightly sealed to keep out air and vermin, such as rats and mice. There is much disagreement among scholars about the purpose of some of the large pits excavated at places like Knossos and whether they would have been an efficient way to store grain, because it might have been difficult to keep out pests and mold-causing moisture. It is generally agreed, however, that these large pits would have been most suitable for long-term storage. Clay bins were also used for keeping grain. Sometimes, however,

Amphora, a ceramic vessel used for storing and carrying oil and wine and other commodities, from Athens (Alison Frantz Photographic Collection, American School of Classical Studies at Athens)

the grain was stored loose in a granary or in one room of a larger storage building.

Some of the earliest buildings solely dedicated to storage of grain were round, with dome-shaped roofs. These would have looked very similar to the images of granaries from Egyptian tombs from the same time period. Granaries from the later Geometric Period in Greece have an almost identical shape. Grain was poured into the granary through a window near the top of the dome and removed at the base through another gap. Thus, the older grain at the bottom of the pile would always be used first.

During the fourth and fifth centuries B.C.E. people actually made less use of large-scale and long-term storage facilities. During the Bronze Age goods had been taken to the palaces for redistribution, but in the Classical Period (480–323 B.C.E.) the system of storage and distribution was based on individuals and their farmsteads. However, even though the local farmers could not grow enough grain to feed the nearby cities, archaeologists have not been able to identify the storage places of the imported grain in urban centers or their ports. This has led some scholars to suggest that the grain was stored in the countryside.

At Knossos a building called the Unexplored Mansion contained a number of storage jars of untouched food, including legumes, figs, and several kinds of grain. Some of the grain in these jars was hulled, but a similar find of stored Bronze Age grain in Macedonia had spikelets of wheat. Centuries later, ancient authors would recommend storing grain without threshing it (removing the chaff or straw) so that if weevils did get in, they would be confined to the outer layers of the grain. In the eighth century B.C.E. the Greek writer Hesiod (fl. ca. 800 B.C.E.) stated that threshed grain should be kept in storage jars within the house.

The available methods of storing food meant that food had to be preserved by other means before being put into storage. Unfortunately, most of the ancient descriptions of food processing come from the Roman Period, and the archaeological evidence is often not of much help. The evidence seems to point to the fact that meat, which was expensive and therefore rarely eaten, was consumed right away. Fish, on the other hand, was eaten in larger quantities, both fresh and preserved. Based on the information available, it seems likely that the Greeks usually salted or smoked both meat and fish. There are, in fact, many terms for preserved fish, but all seem to describe the species of fish and the shape of the preserved pieces rather than the process. Milk from goats, sheep, or cows was preserved for short-term use by being made into butter and for longer periods by being made into cheese. Milk solids could be formed into small bricks, dried in the sun, and later rehydrated for use in cooking.

Lentils, peas, and beans of all kinds were dried for storage and were easily reconstituted with water in stews or ground up into flour. Other vegetables could have been dried or pickled in brine or vinegar. Olives and cucumbers were certainly pickled in these ways. Greens such as lettuce and cresses were difficult to keep for long periods and probably were eaten only fresh. However, it is known that the leaves of fig trees were pickled and were used by almost every cook. Fruits that had an outer rind (such as pomegranates) or were hard (like quinces) could be kept fresh by careful storage. If the fruits were placed in containers in such a way that they did not touch the sides of the container or especially each other, they would stay fresh for a longer time. Juicier, softer fruits such as figs, plums, cherries, and grapes could be dried or preserved in honey. Grapes, of course, were also preserved by being made into wine. Most fruits, in fact, could be pressed for their juice and the juice allowed to ferment and become cider or wine or to sour and become vinegar. Not only did this process preserve the fruit itself, but the alcohol in the fermented drinks (or the acid in the vinegar) could be used to preserve other foods.

ROME

BY LYN GREEN

Throughout the history of Rome, as capital of both a republic and an empire, the city faced the daunting task of keeping its growing population fed and supplied. However, unlike some other urban centers of the ancient world, the local countryside around Rome was inadequate to feed its massive population. To complicate matters further, as Rome grew in size and wealth, so did the demand for luxuries of all kinds. The growth of the Roman Empire and the spread of the Roman bureaucracy also increased demand for the same sorts of products throughout the vast territories as officials tried to maintain the lifestyle they had enjoyed in Italy. This demand necessitated a complex web of shipping routes and the facilities and techniques necessary to store goods of all kinds.

Although Roman writers liked to recall the good old days when their ancestors lived on *pulmentarium* (stew or porridge made of grains or beans), bread was the most important item in the Roman diet. Although spelt, barley, or rye could be used to make bread, wheat made the best loaves. Unfortunately, wheat was not a crop that grew well in Italy. North Africa and especially Egypt were the major exporters of wheat throughout the ancient Mediterranean, and trade routes from the ports of the African coast to Ostia were vital to the survival of Rome. However, as the wheat would first be stored, then shipped to Rome by boat, and then stored at Rome, some method of processing grain for storage was essential.

In order to avoid spoilage, grain must be kept in a cool, dry, and dark place. These places must also be designed to keep out such vermin as mice or rats, which would eat or contaminate the food. In the drier areas of the Mediterranean, such as Spain, the grain could be stored in underground pits that were lined with straw and tightly sealed. The Roman author Varro (116–27 B.C.E.) also mentions that the farmers of Thrace stored their grain in caves. In northern Spain and southern Gaul, the grain was stored in huge terra-cotta jars called *pithoi* or in silos. Varro also suggests using above-ground granaries that were ventilated by windows and raised up on wooden supports to allow air circulation. Another ancient description of these granaries mentions that they had brick walls 3 feet thick and were accessed from above. The author of that description also states that *amurca*, the dregs of pressed olives, should be incorporated into all the tiles and plaster used to seal the granaries in order to discourage vermin.

Wherever Roman legions went, they built large granaries, sometimes intended to hold enough food to last through a yearlong siege. These were originally built of timber, but after Trajan's (r. 98–117 C.E.) time stone granaries became more common. In either case, the grain was probably stored in sacks or baskets rather than piled loosely in chambers. The containers would have made the job of measuring out rations much easier and would have served as barrier to vermin. The biggest civil granaries were undoubtedly those at Ostia, where the grain from Africa was delivered. Two types of granaries have been excavated at Ostia: a building consisting of long, narrow rooms facing a courtyard and two rows of rooms opening off a central corridor. Some granaries show evidence of stairs leading to an upper floor. Archaeologists are confident that grain was stored on the lower floors, but grain was of course only one of the items that could be stored in these buildings.

A number of methods of preserving food were known to the ancient Romans, and the choice of which one to use depended on the local climate and the type of food being stored. Drying, salting, smoking, and pickling were the most common ways of preserving food. Some fruits, like grapes, figs and dates, naturally lent themselves to drying without loss of flavor. They could also be packed in honey or in a mixture or honey and boiled wine. Beans, peas, lentils, and pulses were also dried, while cucumbers and olives were pickled in brine. Fish and meat were often salted by being immersed in brine, although in the hot, dry areas of the empire they could also have been wind-dehydrated. Pickling food could be done using beer vinegar, fig vinegar, wine vinegar, wine, and sour milk. The increased acidity of the food discourages the growth of bacteria, as does alcohol. As the Romans did not use distilled alcohol, wine or even beer could be used to preserve foods.

Pork was the most popular meat for upper-class Romans, but it did not keep well and care had to be taken to preserve it soon after slaughtering. To salt the meat, ancient authors recommend rubbing it with coarse salt each day for 12 days. For the first three days, between rubbings, it was kept pressed under weights to squeeze out excess moisture. Sometimes this step could be followed by further drying or smoking. Pork could also be salted in jars. The deboned pieces of meat were jammed into the jars and layered with salt until the container was crammed full. Then it was sealed tightly. The same methods were used to prepare salt fish. In the 1990s some archaeologists experimented with using spices to preserve food. They discovered that cinnamon, cumin, onion, and especially garlic slowed or even stopped the growth of microorganisms that would cause food to spoil. Black pepper, on the other hand, was not very effective in stopping bacterial growth.

Although there were ice houses in the ancient world, they were not always available. Therefore, the Romans developed other methods of keeping the color, scent, and shape of preserved foods: They prevented any air from reaching the food and starting the process of decay. There are a number of different techniques described by the ancient writer Columella (first century C.E.). For example, he states that if grapes are picked with their stems on, the ends of the stems should be sealed with pitch to keep out the air. This method is also recommended by other ancient authors for apples, quinces, cherries, plums, and pears. Quinces and pomegranates could be completely coated in a thick layer of potter's clay and left to dry. A quick wash would remove the clay from the fruits later. The Romans also understood the importance of keeping the fruits from touching one another, and fruits might also be stored in containers divided with wood into little compartments and filled with sawdust. However, all of these methods were very labor intensive and were probably most often used on the great estates that had hundreds of slave workers.

THE AMERICAS

BY AMY HACKNEY BLACKWELL

Ancient American peoples needed to store several things: wild food items that they had gathered, seeds for the next planting season, and water for daily use and in case of drought. They also needed to preserve food, both plant foods and meats, so that they would have a steady food supply throughout the year.

Drying was the most common method of food preservation throughout the Americas. People dried such grains as corn and other vegetables either by spreading them out in the sun or by placing them in a fire. How long grains would remain edible depended on local humidity; corn would last three years in the dry climate of the North American Southwest, but it lasted only one year in the humidity of the Yucatán peninsula. People preserved meat and fish by drying them as well. Women would cut meat into strips and lay it across open racks to dry in the sun. Meat and fish could be smoked by placing them in the smoke of a slow fire for several days. Dried and smoked meats would keep for many months, depending on humidity and temperature. Native Americans sometimes embellished their basic dried meats with different ingredients. For example, sometimes they would dip the meat in ground corn before drying it and then roll up the dried strips for ease of transport during travel. Pemmican was made by cutting fresh meat into chunks, mixing it with dried berries and rendered fat, and spreading it out to dry into bars.

Native Americans who lived in cold climates took advantage of natural freezing temperatures to preserve meat. They would kill animals early in the winter, cut them into pieces of meat, and allow the meat to freeze. They could then defrost it in a fire when they were ready to eat it. The people who lived in the Arctic commonly employed this technique with seal meat. People who lived in the Andes used freeze-drying to preserve some of their food, particularly potatoes. They would lay out their potatoes on the mountainside, where the potatoes would freeze; the water would then gradually sublimate out of them, resulting in very lightweight potatoes that lasted a long time. Although people ate dried foods as they were, they might also reconstitute them by soaking or cooking them in water.

Throughout the Americas people stored food in woven baskets. People throughout the two continents began making baskets about 6000 B.C.E. Both sexes wove baskets. People would sometimes weave baskets very quickly on the spot if they suddenly found a trove of food and wanted to carry it home. Basket styles and materials varied by region. People in the north made baskets of birch bark, ash, or sweetgrass. Native Americans in California used yucca, willow, or sumac. On the northwest coast weavers used spruce root, cedar bark, and swamp grass. People in the southeastern regions used pine needles. Basketry became more highly developed when people adopted the sedentary agricultural lifestyle, around 1 C.E. in North America and perhaps around 4000 B.C.E. in Central America.

Native Americans used baskets for a variety of purposes. They attached shoulder straps to conical baskets to make carrying baskets. Some baskets had an open weave; these baskets were lighter, good for carrying loads of firewood or large food items. Open-weave baskets were useful for catching and carrying fish or clams because they allowed the water to drain out of the basket. More tightly woven baskets could carry small items, such as seeds. When people harvested crops, they sometimes carried small baskets on their hips to hold the grain they picked, periodically emptying these small baskets into larger baskets on their backs. Different shapes of baskets were used for different food items. Baskets intended to hold fresh berries, for example, were shaped like cones to prevent the weight of the topmost berries from crushing the ones on the bottom. Baskets could be waterproofed with such substances as pine resin to make them suitable for carrying or storing water.

Native Americans throughout North America stored food in clay pots. Archaeologists have found pots throughout the continent, dating to the time when humans first lived in the area; numerous ancient pots date to between 25,000 and 8000 B.C.E. Plain mud can be formed into vessels that will dry hard, but unless they are fired, they will dissolve in water and crumble easily when dry. Baking clay in a hot fire makes it hard and more water resistant, though without some sort of glaze to seal the surface even fired clay will leak water. Archaeologists have found many unfired pots used by ancient Americans; these could have been used to store dry items, such as nuts and seeds.

Historians believe that the practice of firing clay pots was an outgrowth of basketry and food drying. One technique Native Americans developed to dry such food as corn was to place the grain in a basket lined with clay and then put it in or over a fire. The basket would burn, leaving behind a baked clay shell. As evidence for this practice, historians cite the many ancient pots with exterior textures that look as if they were formed in baskets.

Although Native Americans had used pots to store food for millennia before the advent of farming, it was when they settled down in agricultural settlements that potters gained real expertise with their art and different nations developed different designs for their vessels based on their storage needs. Women (who made most pottery) made water jars with bases designed to rest comfortably on the top of a human head in order to carry water from streams to homes. They built large pots with tight-fitting lids that could hold grain and protect it from insects, rodents, and moisture. They constructed large water pots with glazed interiors that would not leak. They also invented pots to store seeds for planting, using different designs to identify different types of seeds.

The Maya of the southern Yucatán peninsula in Mexico stored water in reservoirs in the ground. They dug holes in the ground and then plastered the bottoms to prevent water from running out the porous limestone bottoms. These reservoirs could hold enough water to last about 18 months with no rain.

See also AGRICULTURE; ARCHITECTURE; BORDERS AND FRONTIERS; BUILDING TECHNIQUES AND MATERIALS; CERAMICS AND POTTERY; CLIMATE AND GEOGRAPHY; CRAFTS; DEATH AND BURIAL PRACTICES; ECONOMY; FAMILY; FOOD AND DIET; GENDER STRUCTURES AND ROLES; HEALTH AND DISEASE; HUNTING, FISHING, AND GATHERING; INVENTIONS; MINING, QUARRYING, AND SALT MAKING; NOMADIC AND PASTORAL SOCIETIES; RELIGION AND COSMOLOGY; SETTLEMENT PATTERNS; TOWNS AND VILLAGES; TRADE AND EXCHANGE.

FURTHER READING

Daphne L. Derven, "Preserving." In *Encyclopedia of Food and Culture*, ed. Solomon H. Katz (New York: Scribner, 2003).

Salima Ikram, *Choice Cuts: Meat Production in Ancient Egypt* (Louvain, Belgium: Departement Oosterse Studies, 1995).

Hilary Wilson, *Egyptian Food and Drink* (Princes Risborough, U.K.: Shire Publications, 1995).

T

textiles and needlework

INTRODUCTION

Archaeologists assume that the earliest clothing worn by humans were animal skins. With textiles, people were able to make clothing from hair such as wool and plants such as flax, the source of linen. Silk, which is made from cocoons of the silk worm, was an almost miraculous discovery made by people near the Yellow River in China in about 1900 B.C.E. One disadvantage all textiles had was that they each needed to be produced in the appropriate climate. Sheep, the source of most wool, needed open grasslands for their herds. Cotton required long hot seasons. Thus, the most common textiles of early times were those that traveled well—that is, ones that prospered in a wider variety of climates than most. This meant that hemp, in particular, was the common source of fabric used by the poor, because it was durable and would grow even in nutrient-poor soils.

Textiles did not pop up everywhere at once. Indeed, a newly appointed Chinese governor to far northern China in the 100s C.E. was dismayed to find that the people of the region wore few textiles and tried to keep warm by wearing grasses. Flax, which produced one of the most durable and comfortable of textiles, spread only slowly across the Old World, probably still not having reached Japan by the 300s C.E.

For ancient people in cold climates or places with cold winters, textiles were valued for their ability to hold in warmth. Thus, among the nomadic peoples of Asia, wool was especially valued. It might be itchier than cotton or linen, but where warmth mattered most, wool was preferred. In warm climates, and even some with harsh winters but warm summers, people often did without textiles, because staying warm was not their highest priority for survival. In Sumer people often wore only wool skirts; in southeastern Asia and Japan, many people wore only loincloths, typically made of animal skin. In India the notion of wearing clothing for modesty did not arrive until the Muslim invasion. Still, in these places where textiles were not a necessity, they were valued for their decorative possibilities. Someone in India who might wear little in everyday life would nonetheless wish to wear colorful fabrics when attending a wedding or other important social event.

The earliest colors for textiles were paint and dyes. Painted textiles appeared in dry areas, such as the lands northwest of China. More common than painted textiles were dyed textiles, probably because dyes were preferred over paint. Whether dyeing textiles was an idea that originated in one place and then spread or was an idea that began in many different places is not clear, although the use of dyes by ancient Americans suggests that dyeing was an idea with different origins in different places.

The use of dyes says much about human beings and their needs. Although ancient textiles are hard to find, those that are extant are rarely plain brown or white. Usually the textiles are colored. Whether worn by the rich or the poor, they almost always have decoration, indicating that people wanted beauty in their lives even with simple textiles. Even embroidery, often associated with richly decorated robes for special occasions, would be used to brighten hems or add attractive images to textiles for everyday use.

AFRICA

BY SUSAN COOKSEY

Textiles produced on the continent of Africa in the period between 10,000 B.C.E. and 400 C.E. were made from both plant and animal fibers, including bark, reed, grass, cotton, and wool. Among textiles' many purposes were as clothing, sheets, blankets, bags, carpets, tents, and burial shrouds. Moreover, textiles were important items for trade, adornment, and markers of social, political, and economic status. Textile production in Africa and elsewhere indicates a sedentary society with skills in agriculture and husbandry; technologies used for dyeing, spinning, and various types of construction, such as weaving; and artistic ability to produce cloth that is both functional and aesthetically pleasing. Simply woven cloth probably served for everyday use, while more elaborately woven and patterned cloth was reserved for leaders and elite members of society.

In North Africa textile production was greatly affected by the influx of technologies and materials developed and distributed throughout the Mediterranean. The Phoenicians were some of the greatest purveyors of textiles, materials for textile productions, and textile technologies. After settling along the Tunisian coast, the Phoenicians introduced the eastern vertical loom to the urban Berbers, the indigenous people, around the 12th century B.C.E. In Carthage and other Phoenician towns local craftsmen wove linen and woolen rugs. In the rural areas of Tunisia textiles made of rush, reed, and alfa were produced and used for constructing tentlike dwellings for local inhabitants. Important people in rural societies may have owned woven wool textiles.

The Phoenicians are known to have traded in dyed wool by 1700 B.C.E. A purple dye derived from extracts from the murex, a shellfish, became increasingly popular in the Mediterranean world during the first millennium B.C.E. As the Phoenicians expanded trade in murex dye and murex-dyed textiles, they sought the shellfish from as far away as Africa's Atlantic coast. Evidence of textiles with murex-dyed fabric has been found in excavations of ancient Meroitic sites in Sudan, dating from 332 to 30 B.C.E. The Romans razed Carthage in 146 B.C.E. and, in the course of their occupation, taught the urban Berbers how to use a Latin loom to produce various textiles.

Cotton threads found in Dhuweila, in present-day Jordan, dated to 4450–3000 B.C.E. may have been imported across the Red Sea from India or from the area that is now the states of Sudan and Ethiopia, where a different variety of cotton was known at the time. Evidence of cotton cultivation and cotton fabrics dates back to the early fifth century B.C.E. in Meroë, located in the Nile Valley in the present-day state of Sudan.

Many Nile Valley textiles have been found in tombs. One collection from the areas of Ballana and Qustul includes burial cloths from three Nubian eras, beginning in 332 B.C.E. Textiles found in the tombs were made of various fibers, including wool from sheep, camels, and perhaps goats as well as silk, linen, and cotton. The silk samples were imported and from a later era. A few burial cloths were made of horsehair or coarse grass or reed. However, most of the textiles were made of animal fibers. Both animal fibers and cotton were available in the area much earlier than the fourth century B.C.E. It is estimated that sheep were in the Nile Valley for thousands of years before that and were among the first domesticated animals in the region. The sheep brought to Nubia were probably a breed domesticated in Egypt. Goats and camels were imported to Egypt later and eventually brought to Nubia.

Cotton was introduced into Nubia later than animal fibers, though a type of cotton may have grown locally as early as 3100 B.C.E. The earliest samples of cotton cloth date from the fourth century B.C.E., but it is possible that cotton cloth was produced at an earlier time in Nubia. Early accounts of cotton—such as that of the Roman historian Pliny the Elder (ca. 23–79 C.E.), who referred to the "wool-bearing

Ugandan woman wearing a bark cloth dress; bark cloth began to be produced in Africa before 4000 B.C.E.

trees" of Upper Egypt and Ethiopia, and that of the ruler Ezana of Axum, who spoke of destroying crops of corn and cotton in the Nile Valley in 350 C.E.—prove the existence of cotton plants at this time. Linen textiles found in the tombs may have come from Egypt, where the flax plant was cultivated; linen weaving had been known much earlier; and, by the fourth century C.E., the trade in linen cloth was thriving. Egyptian texts of the New Kingdom (1550–1070 B.C.E.) refer to flax fields in Nubia, suggesting that at least flax may have been produced in Nubia, and perhaps linen was made there as well.

Many of the cloths used as burial shrouds were adapted for this use but were originally made for other purposes, such as clothing or sheets. Textile bags and carpets were also found in the tombs. Among them the plain-weave fabrics were locally made, whereas others were imported. It is also clear that in the earlier periods, plant fibers were used before animal fibers became prevalent. Later, in the Common Era, the use of plant fibers returned. Many of the textiles were decorated or dyed. Dyeing was done before the fibers were woven. Locally made textiles were dyed with local dyestuffs, yielding colors of brown, yellow, blue, and red. Yellow and blue were combined to produce green. The imported textiles, including carpets, were more elaborately colored with purple, yellow, and orange dyes.

Fibers were spun into yarn using various spindles and techniques. Three types of spindle were used for cotton and one for wool. Most yarn was spun so that the fibers twisted together in an *S* configuration. The art of weaving was well developed by the Meroitic period. Looms had been in use in Egypt since at least the Middle Kingdom (2040–1640 B.C.E). The earliest representations of looms in Egyptian art show women using horizontal types. The more complex vertical looms used by men were introduced later. Textiles found in Nubia show evidence of both simple and complex looms. Several types of techniques of weaving were used, including plain weave, twill, and pile weave. In some cases, textiles were woven into specific shapes of garments on the loom. Finely woven mats of reed and grass may have been made on a loom as well. The Nubian textiles were decorated with geometric motifs, foliate motifs (patterns representing trees or grain, for example), and stripes rendered in various colors. One surviving cloth has purple murex-dyed stripes and was obviously imported. Some textiles had tasseled edges. Decorative elements were created using various weaving techniques or needlework. Stitching was used to decorate the cloth and to bind cloth strips on the selvedges.

Bark cloth production began before 4000 B.C.E. and is still produced in Africa in the Ituri rain forest. Bark cloth is typically made of the inner bark of mulberry or ficus, which has been stripped and retted. The glutinous sludge resulting from the retting is beaten into large, thin sheets that could be colored by pigments such as ocherous earths and tannins. The finished sheets could then be fashioned into garments, coverings, or other items.

EGYPT

BY ERIN FAIRBURN

Egypt is unique among ancient cultures in that the desert location of funerary sites has preserved many objects of perishable nature that are infrequently, if ever, to be found at other ancient sites. Textiles are especially important among these rare artifacts. They shed light on how ancient peoples adapted to and utilized their environs, and their analysis can provide interesting insights into ancient technology. Egyptian textiles were used for garments, bedding, animal equipment, and lamp wicks, among other things, and were often recycled as mummy wrappings.

Almost all ancient Egyptian textiles were made of flax (*Linum usitatissimum*). Depending on when the flax was cut, the resulting threads and cloth would be a light or a golden brown color; however, the linen could be whitened by using a substance, such as natron, or by sun bleaching, as was often done to "royal" linen. The flax fibers were obtained through a process of beating and soaking the stalks until the soft interior was separated out. The fibers were then combed and dried.

Once the fibers had been thus prepared, they were ready to be spun. The spinning process began by roving, or rolling, the fibers on the thigh until they were loosely twisted. This rove would be rolled around a reel and placed in ceramic vessel or basket with a hole on the top. The fibers would be drawn from these vessels during the spinning process. They were spun onto a spindle of wood with a whorl (pulley) on top made of wood, stone, or ceramic.

Three types of spinning were used in ancient Egypt. The first technique produced thread by feeding the fibers onto the spindle with the fingers and rolling the spindle on the thigh to twist them. The second required a forked stick or ring through which to draw the thread while twisting the spindle between both hands. The third technique, the suspended spindle method, involved grasping the fibers with one hand while letting the rotating spindle swing free, thereby twisting the fibers. Counterclockwise spinning was the most common type in ancient Egypt; that is, the fibers were *S*-spun.

At this point, the spun fibers could be dyed. Dying does not appear to have been prevalent in ancient Egypt, but textile producers clearly knew how to produce a range of colors. Egyptian textiles contained threads dyed red, blue, yellow, brown, green, and purple. These colors were all created with vegetal (plant-based) colorants; brown, green, and purple were produced by overdying. While weavers did on occasion dye an entire piece of completed weaving, it was more common for them to embellish an undyed linen garment with colored threads.

Once the threads were prepared, they could be woven. Egyptians used two kinds of looms for textile weaving: a horizontal loom that was used throughout the Dynastic Period and a vertical loom that was used beginning in the New Kingdom (ca. 1550–ca. 1070 B.C.E.). Horizontal looms lay parallel to the ground with the beams pegged into place. Vertical looms

Tapestry made of multicolored wool on linen, from Egypt, fourth century C.E., *showing Artemis and Actaeon* (© The Trustees of the British Museum)

were perpendicular to the ground, with the warp strung onto beams attached to a frame.

Longitudinal threads, or warp threads, were attached directly to the loom. Every other thread was separated, forming two separate groups. Another thread, the weft, was strung between the two groups, or shed. Lifting a rod called the heddle switched the group to the fore, creating a counter-shed. Running the weft thread successively between the shed and counter-shed created an interlocking weave around the warp.

Several different weaving techniques were used to create textiles in ancient Egypt. The most common weave, and the simplest, was the tabby weave, where a single weft thread passes over and under individual warp threads. A variation on this is the basket weave, where the warp and weft threads are paired. Both of these methods were fairly easy to achieve on a horizontal loom. Warp- and weft-faced weaves, which produced a two-to-one pattern that nearly hid the single threads, were also used in Egypt. Two tapestry weaves are also known, one that used the weft for the pattern and another that used the warp.

Weavers accommodated for broken or short threads by interweaving threads with either a long or a short splice. Short splices twisted together the ends of two threads and then twisted this back onto the main thread. Long splices were simply several inches of the two threads twisted together. Many preserved textiles have splices in them; finer linens seem to have mainly short splices, and coarser textiles often exhibit long splices.

A number of decorative and functional features were woven into Egyptian textiles. The most common was a fringe on the left selvedge (edge) of a textile. This was accomplished by extending the weft thread several inches beyond the last warp and seems to have been performed only on horizontal loom-made textiles. It may have served to prevent the weft from gathering in the warp, reducing the overall width of the textile. Decorative fringes were often added to the edges of a textile as well. These were usually created by letting the ends of the warp threads hang beyond the edge of the weft. These ends were loose or tied off. Occasionally, additional thread was woven into the edges and selvedges to increase the amount of fringe on the piece. Weft looping was also occasionally practiced. This process of letting the weft extend above the fabric surface at intervals created a sort of pile that probably increased the warmth of the resulting garment.

Weaving colors into textiles was a decorative technique commonly practiced. This usually extended only to weaving stripes into the edges of the textile. These stripes were usually in some combination of red, blue, and buff. Occasionally, what seem to be maker's marks were also woven into the textile at some point. Evidence for embroidery is slight in Dynastic Egypt, and most of what has been called embroidery by researchers was actually woven into the cloth. Tapestry weaving appears in the Eighteenth Dynasty (ca. 1550–ca. 1307 B.C.E.), beginning with pieces found in the tomb of Thutmose IV (r. 1401–1391 B.C.E). In this technique the weaver used different color wefts in just the part of the design that demanded the particular color. These textiles were packed down to reduce the visibility of the warp.

Sewing was used to a minimal extent in Egypt, mostly for crafting garments. Seams and hems were usually rolled and stitched into place. However, textiles of all types were frequently mended, indicating their worth. Mending is found on common textiles as well as on the finer pieces found in royal contexts. The mending was accomplished by working new warp threads into the damaged area and then stitching across them. Patches were uncommon. As mentioned, embroidery was rarely used, and it was most commonly used to outline woven-in decoration.

THE MIDDLE EAST

BY AMY HACKNEY BLACKWELL

Few examples of ancient Near Eastern textiles exist. Because cloth decays quickly, most do not remain in the archaeological record. Likewise, few positively identified weaving and spinning implements survive, but archaeologists have found numerous drawings and paintings depicting spindles and looms and women working with them. Some ancient Mesopotamian sculptures convey the texture of the cloth worn by the subjects, but it is impossible to reconstruct colors or patterns. To guess what ancient cloth must have looked like, historians can only read contemporary descriptions of textiles and view examples of textiles from slightly later periods. Weaving and spinning techniques have not changed greatly over the centuries, so anthropologists can gain insight into ancient textile manufacturer by studying the weaving techniques of less developed societies.

Near Eastern people began making textiles as early as 25,000 B.C.E., braiding, twisting, spinning, and weaving strips of bark and plant fibers to make primitive cloth. When people domesticated sheep and goats around 8000 B.C.E., they began making cloth out of wool and goat hair. Wool was the most common fiber in the region. People started growing flax for linen about 8,000 years ago; linen was a luxury cloth used for expensive garments. In Mesopotamia textile manufacturing became a major business. Most cloth production was done in individual homes as a cottage industry rather than in large factories, but many households participated in the trade. Weaving factories at Ur and Lagash around 2100 B.C.E. employed thousands of women and children, producing cloth in five grades of quality. Most of the cloth was given out as rations to dependents of the great temple households, and only a small amount was ever traded abroad. In ancient Anatolia groups of women ran cloth-making businesses. After 1500 B.C.E. commercial weaving operations throughout the region employed men, but women continued to do most of the spinning and weaving for their homes and families.

The Assyrians brought cotton plants to the Near East from Egypt around 700 B.C.E., although Near Eastern people apparently were importing cotton cloth from other lands as early as 1000 B.C.E., as cotton fragments from Bahrain, in the Persian Gulf (ancient Dilmun), attest. Silk appeared in Mesopotamia and the Near East during Roman times, brought from China through Persia via the Silk Road.

Making fibers into cloth was a labor-intensive process. After the fiber was collected from the field or the animals, it had to be cleaned and untangled by combs. The fibers were then spun into thread on spindles—wooden spikes weighted on the bottom and used to twist and wind the fibers. Women throughout the Middle East used a kind of spindle called a drop spindle.

Archaeologists can tell where some textiles were made based on spinning patterns. Cotton fibers naturally wind to the right, and flax fibers naturally wind to the left. Spinners usually wound their threads according to the fiber's natural pattern. Wool, on the other hand, does not naturally twist in either direction, so it can be spun either to the left or to the right. In an area in which linen was common, spinners often spun wool thread to the left, using the same techniques on wool as they used on linen. In an area where cotton was common, wool thread was often spun to the right. Archaeologists who find wool thread spun in a direction opposite that most common in the area can assume the thread was made elsewhere. Archaeologists can also use microscopes to examine wool fibers to determine the type of sheep the wool came from and the textile's likely place of origin.

After spinning, thread was sometimes dyed. Archaeologists have found evidence that Middle Eastern people were dyeing cloth by 3000 B.C.E. and perhaps earlier. Dyers used roots, tree bark, leaves, nuts, lichens, and berries to achieve various colors. The indigo plant was used to dye cloth blue. The most expensive dye in the region was a purple color made from the

Wool textile fragment from Persepolis, Persia (modern-day Iran) (Courtesy of the Oriental Institute of the University of Chicago)

murex shell, found off the coasts of Lebanon and Syria. This region became known as Phoenicia, or "purple land," and its towns grew rich selling murex dye to Greeks, Romans, and other wealthy individuals; the town of Tyre was especially known for this color, which was often called Tyrian purple. To create the dye, fishermen collected thousands of the snails, cracked their shells, and dug out the veins that contained a purple mucus. It took nearly 9,000 snails to create one ounce of Tyrian purple dye, which cost more than its weight in gold.

After dyeing, the next step was to weave the thread into cloth on a loom. Early Middle Eastern looms were vertical frames on which weavers would stretch parallel threads to form the warp of the cloth. The weavers would then weave other threads through the warp, creating the horizontal fibers called the weft. The first looms had no mechanism for separating individual warp threads to create a space for the weaver to place the weft, but very quickly people discovered that it was easier to weave cloth if they used a rod to lift half the fibers at a time. Weavers wrapped the weft threads around a wooden block called the shuttle, which they could pass from hand to hand through the warp, and they used another rod to push the weft firmly together after each pass. By varying thread colors, weavers could create elaborate patterns in their cloth.

Ancient people throughout the Middle East decorated their cloth with embroidery. Persia, Babylonia, Phoenicia, Syria, and Israel were especially known for their embroidery. Embroiderers adorned cloth with traditional motifs; Persian decorations were known for being particularly ornate. Groups developed their own unique embroidery patterns, many of which had ritual significance such as warding off evil or bringing good luck to a bride.

Carpet weaving is believed to have originated as early as 7000 B.C.E. in central Asia, where nomads wove carpets to create warm, soft, easily portable floors for their tents. Carpet making spread from central Asia into Anatolia and Persia. Anatolians were among the first Near Eastern people to weave carpets. They invented a double-knotted style of carpet weaving between the fourth and first centuries B.C.E. Village women carded and dyed their own wool and invented patterns that told stories as well as being decorative. Each group had distinctive designs. Mothers taught daughters how to weave carpets so that the young women could include them in their dowries and then produce more as married women. Carpet weaving was also important in Persia. People living on the Iranian plateau were knotting wool carpets by 500 B.C.E., though the art may have begun much earlier. Persian carpets depicted mythical events, objects from nature, or geometric patterns.

ASIA AND THE PACIFIC

BY JUSTIN CORFIELD AND MICHAEL J. O'NEAL

A wide range of textiles was used throughout ancient Asia and the Pacific, from elaborate silk and brocade (fabric with raised patterns) to coarse hemp. Very little material from this period survives, but much of it that does survive is silk and other more expensive cloths found in tombs dating from the Han Dynasty (202 B.C.E.–220 C.E.) and also outside China. However, much can be surmised from drawings, carvings, and statues of the period as well as from the small fragments of other materials that have been found by archaeologists.

The material used in China and nearby places for clothes was associated with three traditional styles of dress: the *pien-fu*, the *ch'ang-p'ao*, and the *shen-i*. The *pien-fu* was a two-piece ceremonial costume with a tunic, and underneath a skirt or trousers. The *ch'ang-p'ao* was a garment made up from one piece that covered the body from head to toe, and the *shen-i* essentially was a blend of the other two styles, usually with a *pien-fu* sewed together.

In China the most prized material was silk, which seems to have been used from about 3000 B.C.E. It was produced not only for use within China but also for export to other places, giving rise to the "Silk Road," as the major land trade route from China to Europe became known in ancient times. Silk served as a medium of exchange for the Chinese, and it appears that a large silk industry emerged in Persia and Syria, where dyeing and weaving took place. Some silk fabrics from the Han Dynasty have been found in tombs in Palmyra, Syria, dating from 83 to 273 C.E., where they were known as "damasks in Han weave." Similar material has been found in parts of central Asia, the Crimea, and other places along the Silk Road, indicating a flourishing trade. Besides being traded, silk was also given as presents to tribal chiefs loyal to China and was often taken by traders to cover their expenses. Indeed, in the later Han Dynasty it is known that some people paid their fines in silk.

The production of silk was heavily protected in China, and the export of silkworms was an offense punishable by death. Therefore, it was not until the sixth century C.E. that some silkworms were smuggled to Byzantium. This restriction on silk production kept the price of silk high, and as a result, many garments, even for wealthy people in China, were made with silk and also linings in other material, such as nettle cloth.

Poorer people in China and the areas around China used not only nettle cloth but also hemp and wool; many Chinese did not like wearing woolen garments although they were favored by many of the local tribal peoples. For patterns, traditionally cloth was dyed a particular color, such as blue, red, green or yellow, but by the Zhou Dynasty (ca. 1045–256 B.C.E.), some checked patterns began to be favored. All the "terra-cotta figures" from the tomb of Qin Shi Huang (r. 221–210 B.C.E.) were originally painted, with many fragments of different colored paints being found. By the Han Dynasty wealthier Chinese preferred geometric shapes, such as checks or diamonds, with the pattern repeated continuously; poorer people tended to have their garments made from cloth of a single color. Cotton does not appear to have been used in China until the 10th and 11th centuries C.E.

In addition to their use for clothes, many textiles were also used for drapes and awnings as well as for tents. Elaborate embroideries existed in the houses of the wealthy, with many other buildings having areas "curtained off," or separated using "silk screens," although these screens were not always made of silk.

Outside China and the surrounding areas very little cloth has survived. In Southeast Asia in the Funan Empire, located in southern Cambodia and the Mekong Delta, there are a few descriptions related to clothing. A Chinese embassy from 245 C.E. recorded that the people wore nothing but eventually were persuaded to wear clothing for reasons of modesty, beginning with small loincloths. However, by the 480s and 490s C.E. many people were wearing sarongs (long pieces of cloth wrapped around the body) made from brocade, showing an important Chinese influence. It is probable that this pattern was followed in other parts of Southeast Asia.

In central Asia many of the clothes included wool from sheep and goats, with more expensive materials imported from China. The major indigenous textile industries in the region were involved in the manufacture of tents and of carpets. The former involved the use of heavy material, such as wool. The latter varied between the hard-wearing carpets used by everybody, especially the nomadic peoples, and those for decorating houses, especially for the export trade. Prior to the arrival of Islam in central Asia, many carpets showed scenes of people, hunting, and festivities, although others had geometric patterns, which became very common after the sixth century C.E. Throughout the region needles were made from bone or horn, and few have survived, though several have been found in China, dating back to 2000 B.C.E., with some estimated to be much older.

Like China, ancient India also had a rich tradition of weaving and textile production. Archaeological excavations from the Indus Valley civilizations (ca. 3000–ca. 1600 B.C.E.) have found spindles and needles that suggest that cotton fabric was woven in homes. Mention is made in numerous ancient Indian texts, such as the Rig-Veda and the epics Ramayana and Mahabharata, of weaving, textiles, and fabrics, and ancient sculpture and murals also attest to the wide variety of textiles produced in ancient India. The ancient Indians also traded their fabrics; cotton from India has been found in ancient Egyptian tombs, and in the first centuries of the Common Era, India exported silk fabric to Rome.

The ancient Indians were particularly adept at brocade work. *Brocade* refers to any kind of fabric made with silk or silk-cotton blends with raised needlework in gold or silver (or both). The designs made with this gold or silver needlework were called *nakshas.* These fabrics were dyed with vegetable dyes, and historically color has played an important role in Indian fabrics. Thus, for example, red was regarded as the color of love, yellow the color of spring, indigo (a shade of blue) the color of Lord Krishna, and saffron (a shade of orange to orange-yellow) the color of the earth.

Because textiles and fabrics do not survive through the centuries in the same way that artifacts made of stone or metal do, less is known about textiles in ancient Japan, where traditions developed later than they did in China and were strongly influenced by those of the Chinese. It is known that by the late ancient period and into the early medieval period, the Japanese had developed a number of textile traditions. One was the use of bast fiber, which was common before the introduction of cotton. Bast was a fiber that came primarily from the gampi tree and was used principally in papermaking. It was, however, also used to produce textiles.

Another type of textile work was called *rozome,* commonly referred to as "batik" in the West. *Rozome* was a process of dyeing fabric. Wax was used to create the designs by covering those portions of the fabric that were not to be dyed. A similar technique, called *kasuri,* created designs from dyed threads. *Sashiko* was a form of decorative embroidery used primarily for functional purposes to reinforce points of stress in a piece of fabric. Also common in Japan were various methods of tie-dyeing, called *shibori,* which created designs in fabrics by folding, stitching, twisting, or binding them. While the earliest examples that have been found date to the eighth century, the traditions and techniques developed over a period of hundreds of years prior to that.

EUROPE

BY JUDITH A. RASSON

In ancient Europe cordage (thread, string, or yarn) was made by twisting fibers collected from plants or animals, most simply by rolling the fibers between one's palm and upper leg. Twisting fibers around a short rod or stick was the simplest way of spinning. The stick used to control the twisted thread was called a spindle. Cordage was used to tie things together. It was also interwoven in various ways to create cloth. Cloth was embellished by adding patterns while weaving or with embroidery. Floor and wall coverings were also made of mats, a basketry technique.

The first cordage was made in Europe during the Paleolithic Period, which coincided with the Pleistocene (up to 10,000 years ago). A piece of cordage was found in the Lascaux caves in France, famous for their Paleolithic wall paintings. The fibers were identified as bast—from a plant. No woven textiles have been found in Europe from this early period. As the climate changed at the end of the Pleistocene, people continued their nomadic lifestyles. Archaeologists call this cultural period the Mesolithic (up to 4000 B.C.E.). There is continued evidence for the use of cordage in this period. Fragments of nets made from tree bark bast have been found in waterlogged sites in Finland, Estonia, and Lithuania; the nets might have been used for fishing, but they might equally have been bags or hair coverings. No other Mesolithic textiles have been found.

As time passed, people began to rely on domesticated animals and plants, and they settled in villages. This period is called the Neolithic (up to 2000 B.C.E.). People increased their use of cordage, and this period seems to have been the time when cloth weaving was invented. People continued to use bast fibers; one example is a fishnet made of bast found in the waterlogged lake dwelling site of Zürich-Kleiner Hafner, dated from 1000 B.C.E. to 1000 C.E.

Weaving became more common during the Neolithic, and there is more evidence for both the weaving itself and the tools used. Most of the evidence for what was woven comes from impressions left in clay on pottery and elsewhere rather than the cloth itself (though a few cloth fragments have been recovered). The main fiber used was bast from flax or nettles. Plant stems, where the fibers are, had to be soaked in water and then pounded to release the fibers and combed to align them. Wool was probably not used during the Neolithic because sheep did not have fluffy coats but had many long hairs and short bristles mixed in the wool that made it difficult to spin.

Both flax and (later) wool were spun by hand on spindles. The person held the fibers in one hand or on a distaff (rod) and twisted them onto the spindle with the other hand. Spindles could be held by the thread and made to spin around to twist the fibers better. A small weight (often made of ceramic) on the spindle, called a spindle whorl, made it easier for the spindle to rotate. This method of spinning persisted into the 20th century C.E. in many parts of eastern Europe.

Weaving may have begun in Europe with belt weaving—weaving narrow bands—by fastening the end of a group of long threads (the warp) to a stable object, like a post or a tree, and maintaining the tension by fastening the other ends of the threads to the weaver's waist. Weaving would have been done by working another thread (the weft) crosswise over and under the long threads. This method is a small version of a loom.

Neolithic looms were upright, rectangular frameworks, with two legs and a horizontal bar across the top. Warp threads were attached at the top of the bar and hung down lengthwise. A stick called a shed rod separated the warp threads. Another rod, a heddle, moved alternate warp threads forward and back so that the weaver could slide the weft thread through. This process was faster than weaving each individual thread over and under. To help hold the warp threads taut, ceramic weights were attached to groups of warp threads. This process gives its name to the warp-weighted loom. It was used throughout Europe in prehistoric times and persisted in use until the 20th century C.E. in Norway, adding to our understanding of how the loom worked. Clay loom weights are found regularly at most Neolithic sites in eastern Europe.

Cloth could be woven in different patterns, depending on the over-and-under pattern of the weft and warp. A simple interlacing of the weft over and under the warp threads is called the plain weave. A patterned weave could be created by varying the number and order of warp threads skipped in each over and under. A pattern of over-and-under alternating pairs of wefts produces a twill pattern; these patterns have names like herringbone or bird's eye. Striped and plaid cloth and also embroidery began to be used in the Neolithic. Sometimes these variations were done while the cloth was on the loom by introducing extra threads in different patterns and colors. Excellent examples come from waterlogged sites like Pfäffikon-Irgenhausen in Switzerland.

Weaving plain and complex weaves continued in the Bronze Age (ca. 2800–ca. 700 B.C.E.), after the Neolithic, when there were some innovations. Wool came into use, collected by shearing or perhaps just by pulling it out when it became long and shaggy.

The technique of sprang first appears in the Bronze Age. Sprang is a type of weaving with the warp on a square frame, without weft thread. The warp threads are attached to the crossbars at the ends of the frame and twisted around each other, starting at both ends and working toward the middle. To keep the weave from springing apart, another thread is woven across the pattern when the weaving reaches the middle. Sprang fabric is stretchy, and the technique was used where stretch was important, as in socks and sleeves. It looks like knitting, which was not invented until later. Examples of sprang caps or hairnets have been found at the Danish Bronze Age sites of Skyrdstrup and Borum Eshøj. Sprang continued to be used in the Iron Age (ca. 1000 B.C.E.–ca. 500 C.E.), and knowledge of it has survived in Scandinavia until the present.

In the Iron Age, weavers added hemp to flax and wool for their textile needs. Loom weights abound on Iron Age sites in eastern and central Europe; they are also found in Scandinavia and in England. Weavers definitely used card weaving (or tablet weaving) to form narrow edges of large pieces of cloth

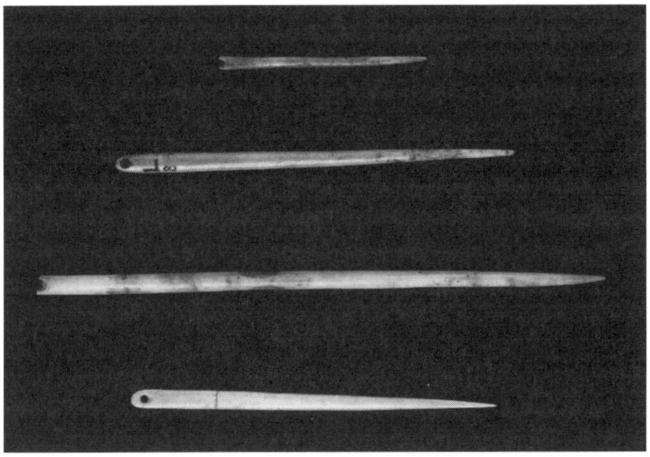

Bone needles from the cave of Courbet, Penne-Tarn, France, dating to about 10,500 B.C.E. (© The Trustees of the British Museum)

to be finished on a larger loom. In card weaving a number of cards (of wood, bone, or ivory), a bit larger than standard playing cards, had a hole drilled in each corner. The warp threads each passed through one hole. The warps were moved by flipping the cards from side to side and running the weft between them. This technique might have been used earlier, but the first unequivocal use was in the Iron Age. Iron Age skills were continued into the Classical Period, when writing and the increased use of figural depictions on ceramics provide evidence beyond archaeological deposits.

GREECE

BY SPYROS SIROPOULOS

Evidence confirms that textiles were used as far back as the Neolithic Period, although no findings of actual textiles have been preserved. Bone pins (as well as copper pins from the late Neolithic period) testify to the extended use of textiles in the area of Greece. The processing of wool and linen and the manufacture of tapestries and rugs appear to have been a major part of the Minoan economy. During the acme of the Minoan society (2200–1800 B.C.E.)—also known as the palace society because the palace was the central economic and political unit—many women offered their weaving services to the palace. Preserved on clay tablets from Pylos is information about 15 specialties of weavers. This specialization is equivalent to industry by modern standards. One tablet records 10,572 animals (goats and sheep), while others describe palace weavers also working with vegetable fibers, such as linen. Linen reached the palace by annual contributions twice a year: at the end of winter and at the beginning of spring. A series of clay tablets from Cnossus relates that 10 tons of wool were distributed to 30 workshops, where 600 to 900 female weavers labored. Other tablets from Cnossus mention the processing of 45 tons of wool, which would have required an estimated 2,700 to 4,000 workers.

Raw materials were not difficult to obtain. Out of the 3,000 tablets found at Cnossus, almost 1,000 are about goats and sheep, the number of which is estimated at 100,000. The average annual production of wool from these herds, which probably belonged to the palace, is an estimated 50 tons. A bolt of textile weighed roughly 22 pounds, so 50 tons should produce about 5,000 bolts. The L-series tablets, referring to the previous year's wool process, number about 5,000 bolts, the weight of which varies between 11 and 132 kilos, whereas their total weight reaches up to 45 tons. We are also certain that the textiles were dyed both at Pylos and Cnossus, though no traces of dying essences have been recognized by archaeologists today.

Herodotus (fifth century B.C.E.) reported in his *Histories* that in India a wild plant produced "fleece," obviously referring to cotton. It was Alexander the Great who introduced the cotton plant to Greece and made it part of the Greek economy. The two kinds of fibers—animal and vegetable—required different processing techniques. In the case of cotton and linen, the process went through the stages of opening the fruit, extracting the fibers, carding, combing, dyeing, and twisting them for the spinning frame. Women did most of the weaving at home, although specialized factories existed for processing wool. First the wool was washed with hot water. Then the yarns were combed and stretched. Workers stretched the wool over either their bare calves or a specialized tool called an *onos* or *epinetron*. The cylindrical clay tool covered the worker's knee and lower thigh.

Before the invention of the spinning wheel (around 500 B.C.E. in India), spinning was done by hand. Wool was bound loosely around a stick called a distaff. Many Grecian vase paintings depict women holding a distaff in one hand and using the other hand to draw the material onto a spindle—another stick with a weight at the bottom. Made to spin quickly,

Utensil used for unwinding balls of wool, called Ariadne's Clew Box (Alison Frantz Photographic Collection, American School of Classical Studies at Athens)

the spindle increased the pull on the fibers, turning them into workable threads.

The use of the loom is a topic of Homeric epics. The wise Penelope used a loom to trick her potential suitors by weaving a death robe for Odysseus's father, Laertes. She had promised to choose one of the suitors when the shroud was ready, but she undid each day's work during the night. The loom is a frame on which threads are passed over and under stable threads. With the help of a stem, a simple handheld device, women pulled the filling threads over and under the stable threads. Then, from the top of the loom, a kind of closely spaced comb was drawn, thus pressing the fibers together to form solid textiles. Of course, some techniques, such as knitting, were simpler.

In his *Republic*, Plato describes the work of the dyer. The first task was the lengthy and delicate process of preparing the dyeing materials, which were primarily barks, fruits, vegetables, animal products, or minerals. Before dipping threads into the dye, the dyer cleaned them by soaking them in potash and clay. Perhaps one of the best pictorial descriptions of the wool-working process is a painted vase dating from around 560 B.C.E. In five groups, women are shown combing wool, spinning thread, filling a basket with yarn, weighing balls of yarn, working on a vertical loom, and folding finished cloth.

Silk was also used in Greece. Through trade and colonization the Greeks had contact with people in the East who knew of the silkworm. The legislator Solon (ca. 638–559 B.C.E.) established sericulture—the farming of silkworms—to boost the economy of Athens. More than 5,000 cocoons of a silkworm are needed to produce about 2 pounds of raw silk. First the cocoons are boiled, and then their filaments are removed and twisted together into very long threads that are wound on reels.

ROME

BY LYN GREEN

Many of the surviving textiles of the Roman period are from the time of the empire and from the provinces, where, compared with Italy, the climate was often more conducive to the preservation of textiles. All the major fabrics used—cotton, linen, wool, and silk—have been found at sites in Egypt and the Near East. Of these, probably cotton was the rarest and silk the most valuable. Wool was the preeminent fabric of Roman culture. It was used for tunics, blankets, and of course, togas. It could be woven into various forms, including plain (tabby), twill, damask, and tapestry. Twill weave produced a hard-wearing fabric popular in the northern provinces. Damask weave is believed to have been developed in Egypt before the first century C.E. Tapestry weave was also used in Egypt, but often for fabrics of mixed fibers. The tapestry technique allowed wool decorations to be woven into the surrounding linen. These decorations were often colored.

One reason for the popularity of wool was that it was widely available, easily dyed, and relatively easy to prepare for weaving, even though much of the fleece was 50 percent dirt and grease. That problem was solved to some extent by washing the sheep before shearing. The next steps, probably performed by professional wool combers, were combing and teasing the wool to prepare it for spinning. Ancient Roman wool combs have survived, but teasing the wool to separate the fibers was done with the fingers.

To spin wool into thread, the Romans used a distaff and spindle; they appear not to have had spinning wheels. One technique for making thread easier to spin was wetting it and then spinning it in the direction that the fibers have a natural tendency to twist. Thus, cotton fibers were usually spun to the right (producing a *Z* twist), and linen fibers were usually spun to the left (producing an *S* twist). Wool, however, does not have a natural twisting direction and could be spun either clockwise or counterclockwise, though spinners in some areas seem to have preferred one direction to another. For example, the threads in many samples of wool excavated in Egypt were spun to the left, reflecting the Egyptians' preference for working with linen, which has a natural *S* twist.

The resulting wool thread was used for sewing, weaving, or knitting, depending on the thickness of the yarn. The number of knitted socks that have survived from various parts of the Roman Empire attest to the popularity of that method of producing clothing. However, Roman knitting was different from the modern technique of looping yarn around needles. An alternate method of working wool that did not involve spinning or weaving was felting. Felt was used primarily in army gear, however.

According to the Roman historian Pliny the Elder, flax was prepared for weaving into linen by being soaked in water to remove the bark of plants. Then the inner fibers of the plant were dried and beaten successively with a wooden mallet and a flat wooden blade. The beaten fibers were drawn through a wooden combing board with teeth. Egypt was one of the major linen producers of the empire. In Greco-Roman times cotton (*gossypium*) was also introduced into Egypt to counteract the expense of importing it from India, but most of the cotton used in the empire was probably still brought from southern Asia. Silk was also brought overland from China at great expense. Once silk thread arrived in the Mediterranean, it might be rewoven with another thread, such as linen. That kind of silk was called *subserica*.

Several types of looms were in use in the vast Roman Empire: the warp-weighted loom, the two-beam vertical loom, and the horizontal loom. The warp-weighted loom was most common in Italy and the northern and western provinces of the empire. The two-beam vertical loom was used widely in the empire by the end of the first century C.E. The horizontal loom may have originated in Syria about the middle of the third century C.E.

The woven cloth was finished by fullers. In a large vat or tub filled with water, fuller's earth, urine (bought or collected from public urinals), and soapwort or other cleanser, the cloth was treaded or otherwise agitated to remove dirt.

LOOMS

A warp-weighted loom consists of two upright beams connected at the top by a bar, called the cloth bar, from which the warp threads are hung. Another beam one-third of the height of the uprights from the ground and parallel to the cloth beam is called the shed rod and helps to keep the threads separate. The warp threads are gathered and tied at the bottom to a cord strung through a warp weight. The two-beam vertical loom is very similar to the warp-weighted loom, except the warp threads are not weighted but anchored to a beam at the bottom of the loom. The horizontal loom is known to have existed only because of the types of weaving, such as damask, that were being done. No archaeological remains, pictures, or textual references to them seem to have survived. This is a complex loom suitable for professionals.

Wool was then brushed with a spiked brush to raise the nap, which was then sheared to produce a smooth cloth.

Different parts of the empire produced or imported cloth suitable to local tastes and climates. In northern provinces like Britain cloth was woven in checked patterns. Other areas, such as Egypt and Syria, favored plain garments decorated with bands or medallions of tapestry or embroidery dyed in various colors. In Italy braid was used to decorate clothing. Pliny the Elder credited the Phrygians with inventing embroidery, although it seems all they did was master the use of metallic thread.

The two most expensive dyes of the ancient world were saffron and Tyrian purple. Saffron was made from the stigmas of the saffron crocus. Tyrian purple was made from the secretions of the murex, a shellfish. Thousands of murex went into producing just a few drops of the dye; fortunately, only a drop was needed to dye a whole tunic. Also known as imperial purple, Tyrian purple has a dark reddish quality. Although the Phoenicians also produced a bluish purple from shellfish secretions, it was the redder shade that was more popular, especially in Roman times. Orchil was a kind of lichen that produced a bluish purple. Madder, woad, indigo, and safflower produced red, blue, and yellow dyes. In later Roman times the Egyptians used a technique for created multicolored scenes by repeatedly dyeing a fabric. Each time a different color was applied, the rest of the cloth was covered in clay or wax to prevent it from absorbing color.

Tapestry hangings were a specialty of the Alexandrian weavers and often depicted landscapes or mythological scenes. Embroidery, which the Romans called "painting with the needle," was also used to create the multicolored and often elaborate scenes. One of the masterpieces of ancient embroidery dates to the fourth century C.E. and is part of a series depicting the seasons of the year. Its resemblance to the scenes on mosaics in other parts of the empire proves that artists of all types used pattern books, whether working in paint, stone, or thread.

THE AMERICAS

BY JULIA MARTA CLAPP

It is difficult to paint a broad picture about textile and needlework production in the ancient Americas. The inherently delicate and vulnerable construction of such materials has caused ancient textiles to disintegrate over time, leaving archaeologists with little to study. The conclusions at which they arrive can often be based upon a combination of two factors. First, archaeologists can make hypotheses based on any remaining textile artifacts that have been preserved from the ancient era. Such items are rare, much more so in certain areas than others. (For example, civilizations that existed in particularly damp climates are less likely to have preserved textiles than are civilizations in dry regions.) Second, archaeologists may examine evidence from more recent centuries and look at enduring traditions that may provide clues about the past. Any conclusions based on such observations must, however, be considered nothing more than speculation.

Among the Americas, South America arguably has the richest history of textile production. No other part of the hemisphere has left such ample or rich artifacts in this field. In general, the area that has yielded the most abundant artifacts is the northwest coast, or modern-day Peru.

The oldest textiles have been found in Huaca Prieta and are over 4,000 years old. As in North America, the majority of textiles have been excavated from gravesites that contain bodies and artifacts that are at times astonishingly well preserved. Also, similarly to the native North Americans, ancient South Americans wrapped their dead in layers of fabric, of which the inner layers have survived the best.

It is important to remember that as with some other ancient cultures, the ancient Peruvians did not have a system of writing. However, the absence of a writing system does not mean that they were unable to record thoughts or ideas. Although today we think of literacy in terms of reading and writing, some ancient cultures used other means to express themselves. In fact, weaving is an extraordinarily complex process that requires the ability to carry out intricate, advanced planning and to work with a mathematical sensibility.

We often think of textiles as being created by weaving pieces of dyed yarn together. The weaver devises in advance a color scheme, which eventually becomes a pattern. In the ancient Americas yarn was spun from either plant (for example, cotton) or animal (for example, wool) fibers. The warp consists of the strands over and under which the weft is woven. In the Chavín culture (ca. 900–ca. 200 B.C.E.), however, there is also evidence of textiles that did not have a pattern woven

Mantle border fragment made of cotton and camelid hair, first to second century C.E., *Peru* (Copyright the Metropolitan Museum of Art)

into them; instead, the pattern was painted on the surface. During this period ornamentation was an important part of textile production. Pieces of cloth with colorful, decorative borders and with embroidery have been found at burial sites from this era.

Stylistic developments can first be discerned in the Chavín culture. The weaving from this era represents not only abstract, geometric patterns but images of animals as well: jaguars, snakes, alligators, and birds. Many of the Chavín pieces depict the feline god, who appeared in textiles as early as 1200–700 B.C.E. The feline god was prominent in this civilization, and its presence remained throughout subsequent cultures in Peruvian history. The presence of this god indicates the strong religious significance of these pieces.

During this period the god was often represented in profile, but with its body depicted frontally. Later pieces, such as a burial cloth from around 300–100 B.C.E., represent animals in what we would consider a much more realistic or recognizable manner. This technique should not be mistaken for a development related only to the passage of time. In other words, stylistic representation did not become more realistic as time passed; later periods also occasionally used very schematic or abstract modes of representation.

In the Paracas Period (ca. 900 B.C.E.–ca. 300 C.E.) extraordinary and colorful textiles were still buried in gravesites. Both the quantity and the quality of the textiles of this period are a testament to the apparent value of this kind of production in the Paracas Period. In addition, new mythical and religious beings were introduced. As in other pantheistic societies, gods were designated to control various aspects of human life, such as agriculture or fertility. Such gods were represented on textiles, perhaps as offerings of appeasement. Such representations help us to understand the culture of this period as well; for example, the presence of an agriculture god in textiles indicates that agriculture was being practiced by ancient South Americans in Peru, and it was probably a significant part of their diet (relative to hunting and fishing, for example).

Certain prehistoric Native North American groups, particularly in the East and the Southeast, made for their elites elaborate burials, which are where most ancient textile remains have been excavated. Many of these sites have been excavated and might offer clues regarding ancient textile production. Conclusions about tapestries and other forms of textiles must be made based on evidence available from garments. While such hypotheses may be less precise, such a study can at least provide information about what methods of textile production these civilizations used.

Artifacts from Late Archaic (ca. 3000 B.C.E.–ca. 1000 B.C.E.) excavations in what we now consider the southeastern United States have yielded small pieces of fabric. Through examination of these pieces, we have learned that early North Americans made both interlaced and woven cloth. Unfortunately, it is not possible to know what purposes these samples may have served outside of the burial context.

From the Adena culture (ca. 1000 B.C.E.–ca. 200 B.C.E.) archaeologists have found more woven textiles. These fabrics in particular have revealed that during that era the Adena people employed several different methods of weaving. Although many of these samples are items of adornment, such as headdresses, sandals, and skirts, woven cloth was also used to wrap other buried objects. These examples disprove any speculations that such early endeavors would have resulted in crude or unskilled production. On the contrary, archaeologists working in Adena sites have discovered cloth of very fine and delicate construction.

There is a disappointing lack of information from Mesoamerica during the ancient era. The earliest civilization that has been studied by archaeologists, historians, and art historians is the Olmec (ca. 1500 B.C.E.–ca. 400 B.C.E.). They inhabited the Gulf Coast region in Mexico, a particularly damp and swampy environment. Even generally durable stone artworks and architecture are rare, compared with that of other, later cultures. The Olmec civilization remains relatively unknown and has left us with more questions than answers.

However, before the Olmec, other traces of human life have been found, though information is sketchy at best. In the arid Tehuacán valley in central Mexico, archaeologists have found burial sites containing cloth samples made from cotton as well as human remains wrapped in woven blankets. Aside from burials, no one can be sure what use these items had in everyday life.

See also ADORNMENT; AGRICULTURE; ART; CLOTHING AND FOOTWEAR; CRAFTS; DEATH AND BURIAL PRACTICES; ECONOMY; EMPLOYMENT AND LABOR; GENDER STRUCTURES AND ROLES; HOUSEHOLD GOODS; OCCUPATIONS; RELIGION AND COSMOLOGY; TRADE AND EXCHANGE.

FURTHER READING

Ferdinand Anton, *Ancient Peruvian Textiles*, trans. Michael Heron (London: Thames and Hudson, 1987).

Alison Austin, "Spinning in Ancient Rome." Available online. URL: http://www.unc.edu/courses/rometech/public/content/survival/Alison_Austin/spinning.html. Downloaded on April 20, 2007.

Elizabeth Barber, *Prehistoric Textiles: The Development of Cloth in the Neolithic and Bronze Ages with Special Reference to the Aegean* (Princeton, N.J.: Princeton University Press, 1991).

Elizabeth Wayland Barber, *Women's Work: The First 20,000 Years: Women, Cloth, and Society in Early Times* (New York: W. W. Norton, 1994).

Margaret DeRamus, "Fibers and Fiber Preparation." Available online. URL: http://www.unc.edu/courses/rometech/public/content/survival/DeRamus_Durham_Laxton/margaret.html. Downloaded on April 20, 2007.

Margaret DeRamus, "Preparation of Finished Cloth." Available online. URL: http://www.unc.edu/courses/rometech/public/content/survival/DeRamus_Durham_Laxton/margaretfin.html. Downloaded on April 20, 2007.

Brian Durham, "Ancient Textiles as Evidence for Textile Production." Available online. URL: http://www.unc.edu/courses/rometech/public/content/survival/DeRamus_Durham_Laxton/brian.html. Downloaded on April 20, 2007.

Lallanji Gopal, "Textiles in Ancient India," *Journal of the Economic and Social History of the Orient* 4, no. 1 (1961): 53–69.

Jennifer Harris, ed. *5000 Years of Textiles* (Washington, D.C.: Smithsonian Books, 2004).

Kathy Laxton, "Looms and Weaving Tools." Available online. URL: http://www.unc.edu/courses/rometech/public/content/survival/DeRamus_Durham_Laxton/kathy.html. Downloaded on April 20, 2007.

John Mack and John Picton, *African Textiles: Looms Weaving and Design* (London: British Museum Publications, 1979).

Christa C. Mayer-Thurman and Bruce Williams, *Ancient Textiles from Nubia: Meroitic, X-Group, and Christian Fabrics from Ballana and Qustul; An Exhibition Organized by the Art Institute of Chicago* (Chicago: University of Chicago, 1979).

William Jay Rathbun, ed., *Beyond the Tanabata Bridge: Traditional Japanese Textiles* (London: Thames and Hudson, 1993).

Irmtraud Reswick, *Traditional Textiles of Tunisia and Related North African Weavings* (Los Angeles: Craft and Folk Art Museum, 1985).

Mary Schoeser, *World Textiles: A Concise History* (London: Thames and Hudson, 2003).

Gillian Vogelsang-Eastwood, *The Production of Linen in Pharaonic Egypt* (Leiden, Netherlands: Textile Research Centre, 1992).

Chen Weiji, comp., *History of Textile Technology of Ancient China* (New York: Science Press, 1992).

► towns and villages

INTRODUCTION

In general, archaeologists have specific qualities in mind for defining *villages, towns,* and *cities.* They tend to disagree with one another about what makes a city. Some insist that a city must have a certain minimum population to make it a city; otherwise it is a town. For these archaeologists, the Sumerian city of Uruk was the world's first true city because by 2700 B.C.E. it had a population of 50,000 people. Others believe the size of a settlement compared with others of its time matters most. Thus Çatalhüyük in Turkey, with several thousand people, would be the first true city in 7200 B.C.E., because at that time nearly everyone lived in settlements of 250 people or fewer. This means that defining towns is difficult, because it is unclear when a town is large enough to be a city.

Archaeologists usually see distinct differences between towns and villages. A town, like a city, needs to have a municipal government that organizes public works projects. It is expected to have leadership positions that form a hierarchy such as the *en* and *nin*, council of elders, assembly of citizens, and public employees of Sumerian towns. The *en* and *nin* were the male and female coleaders elected by the assembly. Archaeologists and historians devote much study to the organization of leadership in towns, because they believe the organization will tell them about how ancient peoples experimented with organizing their lives.

Where towns might have paved streets, areas for carrying on the business of civic government, and neighborhoods of homes, villages did not have those traits. They had human-made structures, even if those structures were just huts of mud or grass, and the structures would be intended to be used over a period of years rather than just a few days or a season. From this view, people who lived in caves did not live in villages, and therefore the development of the village itself was an important step for human societies.

A village almost certainly had a form of leadership, but it would not be as formal as that of a town. Very often villages were composed of members of one family or clan, with leadership belonging to family elders and with many decisions about village life being made with the involvement of all adults in the community. Villages did not have to be inhabited all year. Some ancient peoples had two places to live—one for the summer and the other for winter. In these cases, their villages were defined by the permanence of the homes, which would be sturdy enough to survive until the villagers returned.

After developing national governments, some cultures tried to regulate the organization of towns and villages. For instance, Romans insisted on ritually sanctifying the land before building. In ancient India villages and towns were intended to imitate the structure of the capital city, only smaller. In addition to villages organized around clans, they had villages and towns that were organized around crafts. For example, a village population could be all blacksmiths, who would be governed by their guild. Such villages were suburbs, because they usually existed to service a nearby city with their goods. Such details show villages and towns responding to developments of their cultures.

AFRICA

BY MICHAEL J. O'NEAL

The emergence of towns and villages in ancient Africa writes in miniature the history of human development and civilization. The earliest hominids emerged in Africa some three million years ago and evolved into humans during the period historians call the Stone Age. During the earliest phase of the Stone Age, about one to three million years before the Common Era, the human population was small and scattered across the savannas of tropical Africa. People in small bands lived entirely by hunting and gathering, crafting primitive tools out of stone. The only thing approaching a town or village was a temporary encampment.

Later, up to 200,000 B.C.E., tools became more sophisticated, and populations increased. Greater intelligence enabled people to begin living in communities where they could share knowledge and pass that knowledge down to their offspring. As tools for digging, cutting, and carving became more specialized, and as these stone tools were attached to hafts to form spears and axes, ancient Africans were able to move off the savannas and into other regions, including forests, highlands, and more arid desertlike areas. After about 20,000 B.C.E. yet more specialized tools emerged, including fishhooks, awls, and bows and arrows, along with boats and pottery. These developments enabled people to live longer and contributed to population increases; therefore, they were crucial for the emergence of towns and villages.

Historians and archaeologists use the term *sedentary* to refer to this new, settled way of life, because people no longer lived in nomadic hunter-gatherer bands and formed relatively permanent communities. This change required the emergence of agriculture, which occurred in northern Africa beginning in roughly 16,000 B.C.E. The center of these new, more sedentary communities was the Upper Nile River. (The Nile flows from south to north, so the Upper Nile is to the south.) Throughout the following millennia the region was far wetter than it was after about 3000 B.C.E., so numerous lakes formed. Historians believe that it was in the region around these lakes, along the southern borderland of the modern-day Sahara Desert, that the first African settlements were formed. The region is called the Sahel, an Arabic word that means "shore," suggesting that the region formed the shore of the Sahara Desert, likened to a sea. The development of agriculture, including both herding and the planting of crops, paralleled the development of towns and villages because people gathered to pool their efforts in feeding themselves. Further, agriculture provided surplus food that enabled communities to support people who were not involved directly in food production, including artists, crafts workers, and the like.

In 2002 archaeologists discovered what may be the oldest agricultural settlement in the Horn of Africa, and perhaps Africa as a whole, near Asmara, the capital of Eritrea. The village is believed to be about 3,000 years old. Excavations of the site reveal that the people lived in stone houses. To conserve heat on the cool highland plateau, walls were shared, and the typical house did not have doors but was entered through a hole on the roof. Other evidence shows that the people herded and ate cattle and goats and brewed their own beer. For clothing they wore animal skins. Throughout Africa archaeologists have discovered similar villages, though buildings were more commonly constructed of mud and mud brick.

Numerous historical developments contributed to town and village life in ancient Africa. Agriculture was one. A second, which went hand in hand with agriculture, was climate change. Again the Sahel provides examples. In the 1970s archaeologists began to excavate the ancient town of Jenne-jeno, located in Sudan in the upper Niger River delta. Until about 300 B.C.E. the area was uninhabitable because of the high seasonal floodwaters of the Niger. Eventually the area began to dry out, and the floodwaters were lower and shorter lived. The result was the emergence of a fertile alluvial plain, where floodwaters left behind silt well suited to agriculture. The settlement of Jenne-jeno began in about 200 B.C.E. The original village was on a patch of high ground. People lived in circular huts made of straw covered with mud. By about 450 C.E. the village had grown to about 60 acres. The village continued to be a vital settlement until about 1200.

Jenne-jeno is a good example of two further developments that influenced the emergence of towns and villages in ancient Africa. One was an increasing amount of trade. Based on archaeological finds, Jenne-jeno appears to have actively engaged in trade. Artifacts found in the area demonstrate that Jenne-jeno imported goods from Greece and Rome. In fact, the entire Sahel, which stretches in an east–west band across the middle of the African continent, constituted a trade route. Goods from the east and from the Mediterranean area passed through the Sahel on the way to points south, where they were traded for African goods such as ivory, precious metals, and the like. The ancient Carthaginians established numerous trading posts along the northern and western African coasts. These posts were points of contact between the Carthaginians and their neighbors to the south. Along any trading route, towns and villages supported caravans of traders, providing them with food and water, forage for horses (and later, camels), markets, and resting places. Goods probably changed hands at numerous points along these trade routes, giving rise to villages.

A second development that contributed to the emergence of towns and villages was metalworking. Once again, Jenne-jeno was a site where a considerable amount of metalworking took place. Most of this work consisted of goldsmithing and jewelry. Archaeological evidence shows the presence of ironworking as well, yet the area itself holds no iron ore, suggesting that trade also took place for metals. One of the

Site of ancient walled town, Cameroon, Central Africa (© Board of Regents of the University of Wisconsin System)

peculiarities of the historical development of Africa was that the continent seems to have skipped the Bronze Age, passing from stone technologies directly to the production of iron. Good examples are provided by the Nok people of West Africa and the Soninke people of ancient Ghana. Both of these cultures developed sophisticated ironworking technologies, including blast furnaces. They also learned that the addition of carbon to iron produces the much harder steel. Just as in modern life, where towns and communities grow up around an industry, in ancient Africa towns and villages grew up as people gathered to take part in the mining, smelting, forging, and molding operations surrounding metalworking.

EGYPT

BY WOLFRAM GRAJETZKI

Over the centuries, forms and types of settlement in ancient Egypt changed considerably. An Old Kingdom town around 2500 B.C.E. must have looked radically different from one in the New Kingdom (ca. 1550–ca. 1070 B.C.E.) or from one in Roman times. At the beginning of the Naqada Period (ca. 4000–ca. 3000 B.C.E.) towns and villages were quite loosely arranged around certain areas, though always close to the Nile. Houses were built of light materials, such as straw, and featured spaces designated for economic purposes such as keeping animals, storing food, and producing handicrafts like pottery. In the north of Egypt houses were often built deep into the ground. Little evidence suggests that fortifications or town walls were constructed. These ancient settlements had a variety of functions. Bigger towns, such as Naqada or Hieraconpolis, were local centers where, in the Naqada Period, local rulers had their residences and where at least one important temple could be found. Smaller villages, meanwhile, served as residential centers for farmers. Whether these ancient villages also had temples or small shrines for local gods is not known, but in later villages, at least, such features are present.

At the end of the Naqada Period towns began to feature walls and became smaller, probably not because of a reduction in population but because the population density was higher within the town walls. Houses were now built of mud bricks, with certain parts made in wood, and were situated quite closely together, with little indication of broader planning and very narrow streets. Houses are assumed to have quite often been two stories high. Regarding the expansion of such settlements, at Elephantine and Abydos, for example, next to the original walled town a new area was attached to the existing walls and enclosed by a new wall, and land lots were given to certain individuals and families.

With the advent of the Old Kingdom (ca. 2575–ca. 2134 B.C.E.), some towns remained centers of local administration. Such a center would have at least one temple, ancestor shrines for the local governors, and workshops supplying the populace with nonagricultural products. Local centers also featured marketplaces, which are as yet known to archaeologists only from depictions in tomb chapels. These markets were most likely located close to the Nile and to the town harbors, where incoming goods arrived. Despite such ready means of trade, scholars assume that even provincial capitals and larger towns had high proportions of the population directly involved in farming and producing food. Very close to the settlements, most often just beyond the town walls, were the town cemeteries.

Almost nothing is known about farming villages in ancient Egypt. The architecture and structure of houses and their arrangements within the villages might have been similar to those in the towns; villages may or may not have been enclosed by walls or other fortifications.

In the Middle Kingdom (ca. 2040–ca. 1640 B.C.E.) planned towns and settlements were built throughout Egypt. These towns follow rigid layouts, with the poorer populations living in small standardized houses in one section and the wealthier classes in larger houses in another section. The houses were arranged in rectangular blocks. In the larger houses the ruling elite used granaries to store grain and food, allowing them to supply the working population when needed. Many of these planned towns were erected around or next to temples; almost no other public buildings were constructed. However, in Elephantine, at least, an administrative building complex with many seal impressions could be found. Here, seemingly, food was collected and given to the populace, perhaps exclusively to those involved in locally organized state projects. In general, the settlements of the Middle Kingdom provide the impression of a highly organized and regulated society. Among the known pyramid towns from the Middle Kingdom, Lahun, located next to the pyramid of Sesostris II (r. ca. 1897–ca. 1878 B.C.E.), was quite expansive, with several thousand people living there. Lahun flourished under that king and then became a regional center.

From the New Kingdom not many towns have been excavated, and these few examples seem to be exceptional cases rather than regular settlements. Akhet-Aton, better known as Tell el-ʿAmârna, was built by Akhenaten (r. ca. 1353–ca. 1335 B.C.E.) to be the capital city. Deir el-Medineh was a workmen's village, built near the desert on the way to the royal tombs at Thebes, where the people of this village worked. These settlements do not show the tight planning of the Middle Kingdom towns. In Deir el-Medina, houses were arranged side by side along two narrow streets, with the village surrounded by a wall. Directly outside were the tombs of the workmen and several chapels and small temples. On Elephantine, a New Kingdom town featured tightly packed houses and several temples within the settlement, with no real planning in evidence. At Tell el-ʿAmârna, on the other hand, another workmen's village featuring rectangular blocks of houses was found, similar to the Middle Kingdom towns.

The New Kingdom town of Sesebi, in the Nubian province, is another example of a planned Egyptian town, with rows of house arranged in a checkerboard pattern, a town wall, and large temples. Next to the temple were large storage installations, indicating that the temples had strong economic functions. At the sites of several New Kingdom towns, no town walls are in evidence; in this period, perhaps, people simply felt safe. The situation changed in the Third Intermediate (ca. 1070–ca. 712 B.C.E.), during which time town walls are well known to have existed from both the archaeological record and from descriptions in texts. With the population rising, towns became densely populated places. During the Roman period, Hermopolis, in Middle Egypt, had houses seven stories high.

Especially in the Ptolemaic and Roman periods, the general picture of provincial towns changed drastically, with the appearances of new types of public buildings such as bathhouses, theaters, and other Greco-Roman-style public institutions. These buildings were in fair evidence in several provincial capitals but were less common in villages such as Karanis and other well-known villages in El Faiyûm. Many Egyptian villages from the Roman period were on the scale of medium-sized towns from other parts of the Roman Empire, by virtue of the high population density of the region.

THE MIDDLE EAST

BY AMY HACKNEY BLACKWELL

Towns and villages arose in the ancient Near East when people built homes near permanent sources of water and food. People kept living in towns and villages because agriculture required large amounts of communal labor and water supplies were limited, forcing people to share the same sources. The earliest towns appeared in the ancient Near East around 12,000 to 10,000 B.C.E., as people settled near reliable sources of wild foods such as natural stands of wild wheat and barley. These first settlements were small communities of about 100 to 200 people living in simple huts.

One of the first towns was Abu Hureyra in modern-day Syria. Abu Hureyra was established around 11,500 B.C.E. by hunter-gatherers who settled there to take advantage of edible plants growing near the banks of the Euphrates River. At the time the area had forests of oak, pistachio, and plum trees and was close to grasslands that provided edible seeds. Gazelles migrated through the area regularly, providing a reliable source of meat. The people who settled in the area built houses by digging shallow depressions into the ground and then sheltering them with branches and reeds placed atop wooden posts. They built additional shelters to store extra plant foods, keeping the surplus in reserve in case of drought or a poor year for nut cultivation. The women of the community used stone mills to grind grain into meal, a labor-intensive task that forced the entire group to stay in one place year after year.

By 9000 B.C.E. the town of Abu Hureyra contained several hundred inhabitants living in houses made of mud bricks. The people grew their own grain in fields surrounding the town, and the women continued to grind wheat in their houses day after day. The villagers also herded sheep and goats for milk, meat, and wool used to make cloth. The entire community existed to grow crops and raise children, generation after generation.

Over the next several millennia people continued to build towns and live according to the same pattern. By 6000 B.C.E. most residents of the Fertile Crescent lived in small villages near ready supplies of water. They were all located on or near sources of water that could be used to irrigate crops; most settlements rose along the Jordan, Tigris, Karkheh, and Euphrates rivers.

Mud was the main building material because both stone and wood were scarce. The agricultural seasons and daily necessities determined the activities of the residents. People experimented with and mastered irrigation techniques, such as canals, that allowed them to plant fields farther and farther from the rivers. When a town became too crowded to support itself, people simply moved into a free space and built new settlements.

Towns were occupied by family groups that helped one another with the labor of farming and other communal tasks, such as building. It would have been impossible for anyone to live alone; towns and villages made it possible to raise food and channel water in the harsh landscape. Living communally also made it easier to arrange marriages and raise children. Because they lived among relatives, village dwellers could always turn to someone for help. Living in towns fostered the beginnings of spiritual thought. Most towns remained in the same place for centuries, and many generations of dead were buried there. The inhabitants came to believe that dead ancestors continued to watch over the living.

Beginning around 3800 B.C.E. the towns at the mouth of the Tigris and Euphrates began to grow into cities such as Eridu, Ur, and Uruk. The climate was drier than it had been, and populations were too large for people to support themselves on family or village farms because there was not enough water or cultivable land for everyone in the area to farm for themselves. The people living in the cities developed governments to organize agriculture and distribute grain as well as to worship their gods. For the next 800 years or so, however, many people continued to live in towns and villages. Mesopotamian cities were surrounded by towns connected to the rivers by long canals extending in every direction from the cities. These towns specialized in various products, including metalwork, pottery, and fishing. They traded with merchants in the cities to get grain, and they relied on the cities for defense and religious ritual. By 3000 B.C.E., however, most of these villages had been swallowed up by the larger cities, and the residents were coopted to work for the city's irrigation canals and farms.

By the first millennium B.C.E. towns and villages had been established throughout the Levant, Persia, and Anatolia as well as in Mesopotamia. Towns continued to be located near water sources and cultivable land. Most towns had a central area for people to meet and trade, and most contained a communal place of worship. Towns often sprang up along trade routes, such as the Persian Royal Road that ran across the Persian Empire. Some towns were quite small and simply organized, but as time went on they acquired more local government.

During the fifth and fourth centuries B.C.E. the Greek model of town organization spread into Asia Minor. Towns of this period were carefully planned, and the land was divided in a regular pattern. Each town contained an agora—an open space where people could gather to exchange goods or conduct business. The agora might contain a stoa—a building used for various purposes, including conducting courts of law and other civic activities. Later towns often had several stoas surrounding the agora, marking the space as an official public area. This type of town design spread throughout the Near East and Persia during the Hellenistic period, as Alexander the Great traveled through the region and founded numerous cities.

The Romans imposed their own form of order on Near Eastern towns during the empire. Towns were built on a rectangular grid pattern and included a forum—an open square used for business and politics. The local government organized the building of streets, sewers, and public water supplies. Many towns had fortifications to protect the residents from enemy attacks. The government also handled matters of taxation, grain distribution, and legal administration. During the late empire Rome's central administration deteriorated, and local people throughout the Near East took on more responsibility for their local government. In Asia Minor and the Levant local religious rulers gained power over towns and took on the financial responsibility of maintaining them.

ASIA AND THE PACIFIC

BY KIRK H. BEETZ

The region of Asia and the Pacific encompasses vastly varying climates, and the towns and villages built in ancient times varied according to people's needs for shelter from the weather, for protection, and for cooperative living. As early as 9000 B.C.E., and probably much earlier, people in Siberia and central Asia were using bones and skins from animals such as mammoths to build shelters. These people were cooperative hunters who probably gathered in small villages in order to easily form hunting packs for pursuing large game. The villages also would have allowed for greater numbers of people to deal with injuries and to gather together to keep warm in the often frigid environment.

Far to the south, in Southeast Asia, people were dealing with a very different environment: one that was warm and wet and becoming wetter. The coast offered opportunities for fishing, and people clustered together in villages to work together to harvest food from the sea. Not much is known of these ancient villages, partly because the rising ocean covered many of them with water and partly because the humid air quickly rotted the wood and leaves that were probably used for building homes.

Farther inland, in the rain forests, villages likely consisted of little more than lean-tos, shelters of branches raised on poles on one side and leaned against trees or large rocks. These villages would be found in forest clearings, perhaps beside rivers or streams. Living quarters such as lean-tos were favored in the construction of villages on the islands of the South Pacific, where warm weather made more sheltering structures unnecessary for most of the year.

Estimates for when agriculture began in the region of Asia and the Pacific vary widely among archaeologists, with some citing about 7000 B.C.E. in what is today far northern China, while others cite the more recent figure of about 4000 B.C.E. in both the Indus River valley and in far northern China. Early agricultural villages seem to have evolved out of villages constructed by hunter-gatherers who had assembled together as family groups. Along the Yellow River people who cultivated millet while still relying heavily on hunting and gathering formed villages of fewer than 40 people, probably constituting an extended family or clan. The land on both sides of the Yellow River was well suited to incipient agriculture, being easy to dig and rich in nutrients.

Who the villagers were in 4000 B.C.E. in the Indus River valley is not known, but their culture may have given rise to the Harappan civilization of 2600–1500 B.C.E. These early villagers almost certainly had contact with Sumerian cultures in the Near East, and the designs of their villages may have been influenced by those cultures. By 2600 B.C.E. these people were building numerous towns and villages, almost all along the several rivers that flowed through the Indus River valley at that time, as well as cities for up to 50,000 inhabitants. Towns and villages were usually well planned, with grids of streets and buildings made of fired brick. Granaries, for storing grain, seem to have been found in most towns and villages.

Although the Harappan civilization faded by 1500 B.C.E., the established methods of planning towns and villages did not. As Aryan invaders from central Asia spread southward into the heart of India, they imposed many of their customs on local peoples, but they were nomads without much skill in building settlements, and they seem to have adopted some of what they found among the Harappans and cultures farther south.

By about 500 B.C.E. the forms of Indian villages were generally set, with changes occurring only slowly during the rest of the ancient era. Both towns and villages were expected to be organized in the same manner as the capital cities in India's various nations. Towns and villages were often raided by bandits or other groups still living in forests, making defensive considerations important. Thus, settlements tended to have earthen walls and main gates through which people had to pass to enter. In the case of a town, the gates would usually have buildings attached where local officials worked; these officials would collect taxes from people bringing goods into town. In the case of a village, such work was more likely performed by the village chief or his relatives. Towns would feature bigger houses than would villages, with houses in towns reaching two stories in height, whereas houses in villages consisted of one story only.

Indian villages were usually self-sufficient, as help from cities was generally slow to arrive because of the distances between locales and because the weather often made roads difficult to travel. Thus, villages were usually located near reliable sources of water and would typically have agriculture as their most important industry. Sometimes, a village consisted almost entirely of members of one profession, such as with metalworking or ceramics manufacture; children tended to enter the professions practiced by their parents, which meant that some small villages that had formed around extended families or clans became focused on a single industry. Such villages were dependent on the economies of cities for selling their products. Occasionally, a village was placed under royal protection, meaning that the villagers were not to be bothered by outside government officials.

In China living conditions in villages were poor during most of the ancient era. Villagers in the Yellow River region lived in circular homes, often wood and dried mud surrounding a pit. The roofs were probably made of thatch, with a peak in the center. The houses formed irregular patterns in villages. The villages themselves tended to be built wherever high ground could be found near a river. Although the villagers were farmers, so much of what they produced was taken from them in the forms of fees, taxes, and loan payments that they needed to hunt and fish to supplement their diet.

By the beginning of the Han Dynasty (202 B.C.E.–220 C.E.), towns featured houses that were significantly different from those in villages, which were usually one-room hovels; advanced Chinese construction methods were applied to town buildings, which were usually wooden with heavy posts on which walls were hung. Crucial to a town was its marketplace, where peasants brought their harvests and merchants sold their goods. A marketplace was usually located on a town's main road, where visitors were sure to pass after entering the town.

In Japan archaeologists have discovered numerous remains of circular houses, with the walls encircling pits. While the largest settlement yet discovered had about 1,500 homes, most settlements were much smaller. The larger towns were probably founded on agriculture, which allowed more people to live in one place than did hunting and gathering, but even at the end of the ancient era many Japanese were still hunter-gatherers living in villages in the vast forests that covered most of the islands of Honshu and Kyushu. Villages sometimes had protective ditches around them, and some may have had wooden walls, as warfare was common by 200 C.E.

EUROPE

BY KIRK H. BEETZ

The earliest Stone Age populations of Europe were mobile hunter-gatherers who lived in camps for short periods and then moved in search of game. Not until agriculture began in southeastern Europe around 7000 B.C.E. were settlements established with the permanence and character of farming villages. Archaeologists refer to people who live in permanent settlements throughout the year as sedentary. The practice of agriculture demands that people stay in one place to tend their crops and have a place to store the foodstuffs after the harvest. Eventually some hunter-gatherers who lived in rich environments displayed a few sedentary characteristics. An example from Europe is the communities of the Ertebølle culture that occupied the coasts of Denmark and Sweden between 6000 and 4000 B.C.E.

By 5000 B.C.E. farming had spread across central and southern Europe, and by 4000 B.C.E. it had reached the British Isles and Scandinavia. The earliest European farmers lived in various types of settlements. In the Balkans the houses made from mud were generally clustered into settlements that suggest true villages, whereas in central Europe the earliest farmers lived in farmsteads with timber houses that formed loose groupings along small streams. It is unclear whether these settlements had the organization of villages or whether each farming household functioned relatively independently. Whatever the structure of the settlement, its inhabitants were linked to other similar settlements through a network of trails and streams. Fields and pastures surrounded the houses.

By 3000 B.C.E. ancient Europeans managed to build villages even in the extreme climates of the far north. Perhaps the most famous of these villages is Skara Brae in the Orkney Islands, northeast of Scotland, where it is very cold and very windy. Skara Brae was one of many small villages made of stone near the northern seas. It was not the oldest stone village, because an older, well-developed village was found underneath it. However, Skara Brae was well preserved, allowing its remains to tell much about ancient village life. It was deliberately built in a midden, an ancient trash heap. Its walls were made of stone slabs, and there were passageways with stone walls between the village's houses, allowing people to walk from house to house without being exposed to the wind. The roofs of the houses were dirt with grass cultivated on them to hold them firmly together. Building the houses in the midden and covering both roofs and midden with soil in which grass was grown helped keep the village warm. Each house had a room set aside for a toilet, and beneath that room ran a channel that carried away the waste.

Skara Brae comprised only six houses. The climate was not good for most crops, but judging by the numerous bones found among the remnants of the village, grass grew well enough for the inhabitants to raise sheep and cattle. Villagers were likely related to one another. Some archaeologists believe that each house was closely associated with a particular family. Bodies of elderly women were found within the walls of houses, possibly an indication of villagers' belief that by revering their ancestors they could protect their houses. The village was occupied from about 3100 to 2480 B.C.E. and may have been abandoned slowly and voluntarily. Each house seems to have been ritually filled in with varying layers of debris. A common item found in the abandoned houses was antlers, which may have marked a house so closely associated with the family that no one else would have been allowed to live in it.

Other famous settlements of the early European farmers are the lake villages in central Europe, built in the foothills of the Alps between 4000 and 1200 B.C.E. At one time archaeologists thought these villages were constructed over lake waters, but it is now known that they were actually built over marshes near lakes. The levels of the lakes had risen to and sometimes over the dwellings after the villages were built, misleading early archaeologists. Piles were driven deep into the lakeside marshes until they hit a solid subsurface. Set on these piles were wooden houses with sharply peaked roofs to shed rain and snow.

Settlements that unequivocally have the character of towns began to appear during the final millennium B.C.E. One of the best known of these settlements is Biskupin in Poland, located about 143 miles to the west of Warsaw on a marshy peninsula along a lake. The town was a planned community from the start. Instead of the irregular arrangement of houses commonly seen in earlier villages, Biskupin had houses in several neat rows. They were built end to end as one long house divided by walls into many one-room dwellings. Because of the marshy character of the peninsula, the streets had to be paved with wood. In Biskupin the wooden streets stretched under the houses from one side of the town to the other, leaving no open spaces.

Around Biskupin was a wall of wood and dirt 20 feet high and 6 feet wide. Its sides and top were wooden, and the inside was filled with dirt. Within the wall were about 100 dwellings, housing roughly 700 people by about 720 B.C.E. Within the village all the crafts work took place, including metalworking. Fires either from blacksmiths or hearths burned part of Biskupin seven times. Whom the lake villagers feared is not known, though archaeologists in general speculate that raiders from the Baltic region or from the East pressed people into fortified villages like Biskupin.

By 600 B.C.E. the Celts were spreading through Europe. Along the Atlantic seaboard their villages tended to be made of stone, but inland they favored wood. Some Celtic towns were set on top of hills and were surrounded by wooden fences, but many villages were small and scattered through lowlands, usually near water but nearly always where farming was possible. Industrial centers with population densities and probably structures similar to towns were established in central Europe, where it was possible to carry out activities like ironworking and salt mining. Two of the most important centers of industry were Hallstatt in Austria, where salt was mined, and Stična in Slovenia, where iron was smelted and forged. To the west, wealthy and powerful chiefs and their retainers lived in hilltop settlements known as hill forts, such as those at Maiden Castle in England, Mont Lassois in France, and the Heuneburg in Germany.

By the time of the Roman invasion in the first century B.C.E. the inhabitants of western Europe were beginning to expand some settlements into fortified cities called *oppida*. Described by Julius Caesar in his account of his campaigns, *oppida* combined residential, industrial, commercial, and administrative functions. Some of the most famous *oppida* are found in France at sites like Alesia and Gergovia, while others in Britain eventually became the Roman towns of Camulodunum (modern Colchester) and Verulamium (modern St. Albans). The Roman towns were laid out in a grid pattern, with wooden shops and houses lining the streets. The Roman style of towns and villages dominated until the Germanic invasions of the 300s C.E. For protection nearly every village had a small fortress, and during the Common Era churches became standard in villages and towns.

GREECE

BY SPYROS SIROPOULOS

Greece is a mountainous country. Its irregular topography makes communication and trade difficult and led to the formation of many small, independent political units. Driven by social and economic necessity, some of these small communities united, which led to the formation of larger villages and towns. In *Politics* Aristotle argued that the city was the natural culmination of a series of associations and is the only environment in which the human being can reach completion. The first union, he argued, was between man and woman and then between master and slave; the result of these unions was the household or family (*oikia*). Households came to realize that to fulfill all their needs, they needed to consolidate into a village (*kome*). Eventually various villages joined together to form a city (*polis*), which ideally were self-sustaining, independent, and dedicated to meeting people's need to live the best possible life.

Thucydides was also aware that long ago the Greeks lived in wretched villages and the union of several of them led to the formation of cities. This process, known as synoicism, also occurred in Attica, when the people from the area confined by the Parnetha, Penteli, and Hymettus mountains were united in roughly 700 B.C.E. under the leadership of Theseus. The result was Athens, whose origins may explain its plural name.

A deme was the smallest political division of a city-state. Athenian demoi are the best documented, but demoi are also found in other city-states, like Eretria, Cos, and Rhodes. The Athenian politician Cleisthenes turned about 150 demoi into the basis for the arrangement of citizenry into 10 *phylai* (tribes). Archaeological excavations have shown that smaller-sized townships and secluded cottages and farms existed all over Attica, but residence there was seasonal. Possibly small unions of villages or farms were formed, but it is unlikely that the modern equivalent of a big village, secluded in the countryside, could be found in antiquity. The deme was the ancient equivalent of the modern village or small town.

The economic character of Greece remained essentially agricultural throughout the ancient period, which means that the civic centers, irrespective of their size, depended on the farming produce of the countryside. Many Athenians had their summerhouses outside the walls of Athens, in the country or the popular suburbs of Agryle. The countryside of the Attic Peninsula abounded with disparate cottages. For a long time the noblemen of Athens had large cottages and farms in the country, which gave them the right to excel in politics because the amount of crop a man had determined his political status. The statesman Pericles, of the fifth century B.C.E., had lands and houses in Attica, too, and he had promised to bequeath them to the state unless the invading Laconians burned them. In his *Oeconomicus* Xenophon describes vividly the life of country noblemen and praises agriculture as the source of all virtue, but he also hints at the sprawl of these cottages, with people building them anywhere they fancied.

Most farmers in classical times would have lived in the urban centers for protection and easy participation in politics. Fish was never the main course of the Athenian diet; therefore, small fishing villages around Attica never grew to considerable size, unless they turned into important trade and military centers. One example is Piraeus, which grew from a modest village to the largest port city in Greece.

Many people preferred to live outside the urban centers. For instance, in his comedy *The Clouds* Aristophanes describes the play's hero, Strepsiades, as a farmer from the deme of Acharnae who curses the fact that political obligations force him to leave his village at the break of dawn. Aristophanes makes clear the distinction between the *asty* (urban center), which Strepsiades hates, and the deme, which he longs for. In Boeotia it seems that people preferred to live permanently in the countryside. According to Thucydides, before Brasidas was received at Amphipolis he "had conquered the fortunes of Amphipolis' citizens who lived scattered all over the vicinity"—a clear description of people who resided in disparate farms and cottages rather than in organized towns and villages.

Like Strepsiades, most villagers and townsfolk had to commute to Athens if they wished to actively participate in the affairs of the state. Nevertheless, each deme maintained some form of independent local administration. A *demarchos* was elected as the head official and presided over a local council. The deme possessed land and had local cults. Most important, the deme maintained a list of its members, who were officially registered after being on the list 18 years. Like cities of the classical period, smaller communities pursued the ideal of self-sufficiency. However, to sell or buy products, the villagers had to go to Athens. In Argolis (in the area of the Peloponnese) scholars have observed that two of the area's small townships evolved into great cities from the beginning of the fourth to the beginning of the third century B.C.E. The distinctive sign of this evolution is the establishment of an agora, or marketplace. The agora was such a distinctive trademark of a city that Athens allowed only two other marketplaces to operate in all its vast territory.

ROME

BY KATIE PARLA

The first towns and villages in central Italy were Iron Age settlements later expanded by various groups such as the Villanovans, Etruscans, Latins, and, ultimately, the Romans. As Rome's territory began to grow, existing buildings in acquired towns were replaced with Roman models. Accordingly, certain common features emerged in towns and cities throughout the Roman world. These similarities were the product of town planning that combined Greek, Etruscan, and Roman elements.

During the Republican and Imperial ages, Rome expanded to include territories as far as Great Britain and the Near East. By imposing town planning on old and new settlements, the Romans were able to provide a common, unifying urban experience for all. By constructing public buildings that served as communal social and commercial spaces and by providing amenities to the people living in these territories, Rome was able to offer an unparalleled quality of life even in the smallest towns and villages.

Roman towns were typically laid out in grids; the organization of a town's streets into a grid system is called orthogonal planning. This model was borrowed from Greek town planning, but the Romans used square rather than rectangular city blocks. The streets running from east to west in such a design are called *decumani*, while those running from north to south are *cardines*. Where the principal *decumanus* axis (*decumanus maximus*) intersected the principal *cardo* axis (*cardo maximus*) is where the town forum would be located.

Romans built forums in towns and villages throughout their territory to provide a communal area to be used for political, economic, religious, and legal activities. Buildings and speaker's platforms would be constructed for meetings of the town or provincial government. Warehouses, banks, and shops would provide space for commercial exchanges. Temples dedicated to gods and emperors would reinforce the town's connection to Rome and its other settlements. Law courts, called basilicae, would be where Roman law was enforced and punishments doled out. Forums in Roman towns were public places where visitors would absorb the messages of unity and Roman primacy that were communicated through architecture.

Another important aspect of Roman towns and villages was their constant water supply. Aqueducts were built to bring water from lakes, springs, and rivers to settlements. These aqueducts were aboveground or belowground channels that delivered water over a distance at a low-grade angle using gravity. Some water sources were more than 50 miles away from the towns they supplied. This constant flow of water allowed for amenities like public fountains, public bath complexes, public latrines, and even running water in some residential complexes.

Waste management was another feature of Roman towns and villages. Sewers were built below street level to channel waste away from residential, commercial, and industrial sites. Also, groups of slaves would collect trash in the streets and rinse the streets regularly to keep public areas sanitary. This would help prevent the spread of disease.

Places for pubic spectacles were a major social component of Roman town planning. Theaters for cultural performances, as well as stadia and arenas for gladiator fights, chariot races, wild beast hunts, and public executions, could be constructed from wood or stone. Typically, these buildings were erected on the outskirts of towns, where more space was available. During the Roman Republic (509–27 B.C.E.) private individuals commissioned the buildings and the events held there. In the empire, the state financed such projects and produced structures of great scale and permanence. The sites for public spectacle found in ancient Roman towns were places where the masses, citizens and noncitizens alike, could reap the benefits of the government's generosity, since the events were free to the public.

Another Roman structure found in all towns and villages was the bathing complex. Public baths provided a common space where all members of society could relax, wash, exercise, and interact; the baths were social areas that guests would visit most afternoons for a minimal price. Like arenas and theaters, bathing structures were usually built by politicians during the republic and commissioned by emperors and the government during the empire.

One of the fundamental functions of Roman towns and villages was to provide secure areas for residential life. Since Roman towns were surrounded by defensive walls guarded by soldiers, residents would be protected from invaders. Police also patrolled the streets to protect private property within the town limits. The two main types of residential buildings were the *insula* and the *domus*. An *insula* was an apartment block with commercial spaces for lease on the ground floor and apartments on upper stories. A *domus* was a single-family home or villa that had reception and dining areas in addition to the private bedrooms and slaves' quarters. Sometimes the rooms of a *domus* facing onto a street would be used as commercial spaces. Many examples of this practice can be found in both Ostia and Pompeii.

Towns and village were located in all areas of Roman territory. Sometimes the Romans would reorganize existing settlements, adapting standing structures into the Roman layout that they would impose on conquered towns. This could result in established towns not adhering precisely to the orthogonal plan. Pompeii offers an example in which the original Oscan street plan, with its only occasional right angles, was incorporated into first the Greek, then the Roman grid system.

In other instances towns and villages were built in the absence of preexisting settlements. In such cases, religious authorities would be consulted in order to ascertain if the gods found a site acceptable. If so, the boundaries of the town would be officially established, including the *pomerium*, a ritual boundary within which magistrates could exercise power and outside of which burials, cremations, and military exercises could take place.

Aside from social and commercial functions, Roman towns and villages served certain military functions. The towns would protect Roman territory against invaders and offer bases from which military campaigns would be launched; these were the primary functions of Rome's first colonial settlements. Another military function of towns and villages was to provide a Roman presence in a distant part of Roman territory. Since many towns were conquered during military campaigns, the Romans would seek to maintain territory by populating areas with Romans. Members of the military might receive land as part of their war booty after conquest in or near newly conquered towns and villages.

As Rome grew during the late republic and the empire, a greater need for natural resources developed. By establishing settlements in a given area, local resources could be exploited, managed, and exported from the towns. This was an especially common practice in North Africa, where the majority of Rome's grain supply was grown. Commercial and agricultural development was managed and expanded from the towns and villages established throughout Roman territory.

THE AMERICAS

BY J. J. GEORGE

The establishment of village and town settlements, allowing people to live sedentary lives, is often but not always brought about by agricultural development. More than 100 species of edible plants were originally cultivated by Native Americans, the most familiar and widespread of which were maize, which came from Mexico, and potatoes, which were originally grown in the highlands of Peru. Other cultigens that were staples for many early communities included sweet potatoes, manioc, several kinds of beans, squash, tomatoes, and chili peppers. As farmers settled beside their crops, permanent villages were established. Surplus crops could be stored and traded with other communities; surpluses could also allow for certain community members to move beyond subsistence tasks and develop as craftsmen, merchants, priests, or ruling elite. Thus, many scholars argue that agriculture paved the way for social and economic stratification and for urban advances that laid the foundation for later complex cities and empires.

However, not all permanent villages developed as agriculture-based entities. For example, early large villages in regions as diverse as California, the Northwest Coast, and coastal Peru illustrate that sedentary civilization can develop in the absence of agriculture. In localities where resource-rich environments offered dependable food supplies, such as the salmon available seasonally along the Northwest Coast and the sardines and anchovies found in coastal Peru, villages developed and thrived according to nonagrarian initiatives. Generally, then, no single pattern defined or predicted the likelihood that a settlement would develop or succeed; each case was unique and subject to a variety of local factors. Changes in climate, for instance, could have dramatic effects on local populations, forcing massive resettlements or even causing the collapse of complex urban or semi-urban environments, as is thought to have happened when an extended drought struck the Moche towns in the Moche valley of northern Peru around the sixth century C.E. Similarly, climate change and associated decreasing yields of wild resources have been suggested as the causes of the collapse of the Hopewell in North America in the first centuries of the Common Era.

In the context of ancient civilizations, a *village* can be categorized as a settlement of as many as 30 or 40 dwellings occupying an area of several acres. A village would typically feature sturdy structures that remained in place and were occupied for extended periods of time; deep deposits of refuse, called middens; and some level of community planning. Early villages often had basic social hierarchies ruled by chiefs, as with similarly defined chiefdoms. *Towns*, by comparison, include many of the largest prehistoric communities, which covered hundreds of acres and featured housing structures numbering into the hundreds. Characteristic of towns were deep middens; heavy structures that were rebuilt or strengthened over time; dwelling units arranged in definite patterns, often in relation to ceremonial units or structures; and fortifications. All of these characteristics indicate long-term occupation of single sites.

In North America the ancestors of many peoples who would later settle into villages and towns were present as early as 7,000 years ago. While the archaeology suggests that town-level organization did not happen until after 500 C.E., examples of early North American village settlements are extensive. Such settlements include Hopewell Indian sites formed in the American Midwest by roughly 300 B.C.E.; coastal villages formed in British Columbia and southeastern Alaska, with evidence of plank houses, by 200 B.C.E.; and the villages of the Adena people, as affiliated with burial mounds and earthwork, which were formed in Ohio, Kentucky, and West Virginia between 1000 B.C.E. and 200 C.E.

Village life based on agriculture featuring intensive irrigation appeared quite suddenly in the southwestern United States around 300 B.C.E., as immigrants from Mexico established a Hohokam culture settlement in the Gila River valley at Snaketown, in southern Arizona. These people grew maize, beans, and squash and watered their crops by means of extensive canals. Early Hohokam houses were almost square, measuring 10 to 15 feet per side, and were loosely grouped together. The population of Snaketown is thought to have been about 100.

Neighboring Anasazi and Mogollon cultures also seem to have shifted from hunting and gathering to more sedentary modes of living. The establishment of pit-house villages and the production of pottery marked the transition of the Cochise in southeastern Arizona to the initial phase of the Mogollon tradition around 250 C.E. Early Mogollon villages were usually established at the ends of mesa tops, sometimes as high as 600 feet above the valley floor, at least in part for defensive reasons. One early Mogollon village referred to as the SU site had 28 houses; maize and squash were being cultivated, and some of the dwellings were of a significant size. The Anasazi of the region where New Mexico, Colorado, Arizona, and Utah meet represent a long-lived cultural tradition still extant today.

Many different settlement patterns occurred throughout Mesoamerica. Numerous villages featuring thatched-roof houses, as founded on improved maize productivity, rose during the Preclassic (ca. 1800 B.C.E.–ca. 150 C.E.) in the humid Pacific littoral of Guatemala and western El Salvador. Along the coast of the Gulf of Mexico the Olmec civilization (ca. 1500–ca. 400 B.C.E.) consisted of a series of towns and affiliated villages scattered across Mesoamerica as far as Honduras. Debate continues over the demographic identification of the primary Olmec sites of Tres Zapotes, San Lorenzo, and La Venta, all of which bear evidence of both ceremonial priorities and more advanced urban characteristics; some scholars claim these settlements as early cities. The Maya territory at this point in time comprised numerous towns and villages. The region around contemporary Guatemala City was characterized by a distribution of villages in relation to a large central town called Kaminaljuyú, which was believed to feature a core of several hundred temple mounds at its apex.

In South America evidence of maize cultivation and sedentism in Colombia and Ecuador occurs as early as 3200 B.C.E., and in Peru there is evidence of permanent village occupation at least as far back as 5000 B.C.E. at a site near the valley of the Chilca River. Analyses there have confirmed the existence of a permanent village of oval pit-houses apparently not founded on agriculture but on the efficient harvesting of the wild resources of the coast. By about 3000 B.C.E. Huaca Prieta, a modest fishing village on the north coast of Peru, had taken hold, with evidence there showing extraordinarily complex development of fiber arts. By about 2000 B.C.E. at least 100 villages like Huaca Prieta had been established along the Peruvian coast. Peruvian settlements with monumental architecture and more substantial population centers, indicating town-level development, include Caral, Asia, Salinas de Chao, El Paraíso, La Galgada, and Kotosh.

See also AGRICULTURE; ARCHITECTURE; BORDERS AND FRONTIERS; BUILDING TECHNIQUES AND MATERIALS; CITIES; CLIMATE AND GEOGRAPHY; CRAFTS; DEATH AND BURIAL PRACTICES; ECONOMY; FAMILY; GOVERNMENT ORGANIZATION; HEALTH AND DISEASE; HUNTING, FISHING, AND GATHERING; INVENTIONS; METALLURGY; MIGRATION AND POPULATION MOVEMENTS; MINING, QUARRYING, AND SALT MAKING; NOMADIC AND PASTORAL SOCIETIES; SACRED SITES; SETTLEMENT PATTERNS; SOCIAL ORGANIZATION; STORAGE AND PRESERVATION; TRADE AND EXCHANGE; TRANSPORTATION.

FURTHER READING

James C. Anderson, *Roman Architecture and Society* (Baltimore, Md.: Johns Hopkins University Press, 2002).
Norman Bancroft-Hunt, *Historical Atlas of Ancient America* (New York: Checkmark Books, 2001).
Gwendolyn Leick, *Mesopotamia: The Invention of the City* (London: Penguin, 2003).
Susan Keech McIntosh and Roderick J. McIntosh, "Jenne-jeno, an Ancient African City." Available online. URL: http://www.ruf.rice.edu/~anth/arch/brochure/. Downloaded on August 7, 2007.
Oswyn Murray and Simon Price, eds., *The Greek City from Homer to Alexander* (Oxford, U.K.: Oxford University Press, 1990).
Marc Van de Mieroop, *The Ancient Mesopotamian City* (Oxford: Clarendon Press, 1997).
J. B. Ward-Perkins, *Cities of Ancient Greek and Italy: Planning in Classical Antiquity* (New York: George Braziller, 1974).

► trade and exchange

INTRODUCTION

Systems of trade and exchange in the ancient world required first that civilizations had desirable goods to trade, goods that were otherwise unavailable to the trading partner. With the advent of agriculture and the rapid shift from nomadic hunting and gathering to more settled, permanent communities, most trade involved agricultural goods. Thus, as towns and cities emerged, those communities traded with outlying agricultural areas for food and other agricultural products like wool. In exchange, they provided desirable goods produced by craftspeople, including tools, leatherwork, pottery, rope, and numerous other items that would be useful in a rural agricultural community.

Later, other types of goods were commonly traded, particularly after the discovery of metals. First copper, then bronze (a copper-tin alloy), and finally iron became the basis of trade and exchange in many parts of the world. Economic activity was by no means limited to farm products and metalwork. In time, a wide range of commodities were traded, including glass and glasswork, jewelry, gold and silver objects, minerals, perfumes, dyes, silks, amber, oils such as olive oil, salt, herbs and spices, lumber, furniture, decorative objects, and many other types of goods.

Usually, the basis for trade was little different from its basis in modern life. One civilization discovered that it had resources that other civilizations wanted or that its craftsmen had developed a particular genius for producing certain types of goods. Thus, for example, Lebanon discovered that its cedar trees were in great demand because the lumber is easily worked and cedar's natural oils made the wood resistant to insects and decay. This natural resource became the foundation of Lebanese trade with other nations around the Mediterranean Sea. Ancient India had the resources and skills necessary for textile production, so its textiles were highly prized.

In addition to desirable goods, trade and exchange required trade routes and modes of transportation. The two choices, of course, were land routes and sea routes. Trade and exchange by land became more extensive after the domestication of pack animals. Caravans carried goods long distances, particularly in regions with broad grasslands, where transport was relatively easy and there was plenty of grass for pack animals to eat. In time, the ancient Romans constructed a vast network of roads connecting the imperial capital with its colonies, and the Chinese created a road network, often referred to as the Silk Road, connecting China with India, the Near East, and eventually Rome. As shipbuilding technologies became more advanced, nations that bordered the sea were able to maintain vigorous trade relationships both with their colonies and with other nations. In this respect, the ancient Greeks led the way, followed by the Romans and Chinese.

Trade and exchange involved more than just the exchange of goods. Trade and exchange played a major role in the diffusion of knowledge and ideas, as cultures made contact with one another through their business relationships and road networks enabled people to travel. Moreover, the wealth provided by trade and exchange led directly to some of the world's great civilizations, as bustling cities developed to support economic activity from all over the known world.

AFRICA

BY MICHAEL J. O'NEAL

Many ancient African societies engaged in trade, and some thrived on it. This was particularly the case in the northern sectors of the continent, where large settled communities developed earlier than they did in the southern half of the continent, where many groups still lived as wandering hunter-gatherers or herders. As settled communities grew, the people in them produced goods—food, metalwork, leather, glasswork, and numerous other things—they could trade with other communities far and near, and a number of kingdoms became crossroads for trade and exchange. These trading networks were a source not only of goods that were unavailable locally but also of tax revenues for kingdoms and their rulers.

One of the most vigorous trading communities was the region known as Nubia, just south of the Egyptian Empire. Nubia acted as a major crossroad for people from Egypt, the Near East, southern Africa, and later Rome, India, and the Byzantine Empire. The first civilization that developed in Nubia was the kingdom of Kush, which became a major center for trade. Goods from the southern part of Africa, including gold, ebony, ivory, exotic animals, and slaves, passed through Kush on the way to points north.

Throughout its history, though, Kush was unstable; the Kushites had to move their capital city on two occasions. Eventually an invasion by the Assyrians severely weakened Kush, and in about 350 B.C.E. the kingdom of Kush came to an end, giving way to the kingdom of Axum to the east. The Axumites occupied the highlands of Ethiopia near the Red Sea, along with parts of modern-day northern Ethiopia, Eritrea, Yemen, southern Saudi Arabia, northern Somalia, Djibouti, and northern Sudan. Axum was a mixture of indigenous Kushite people and immigrants from the southern Arabian Peninsula who had migrated to the region in about 500 B.C.E.

Like Kush, Axum derived its power from trade, primarily in such commodities as silk, spices, ivory, tortoiseshell, rhinoceros horn, hippopotamus hides, monkeys, gold, silver, cloaks and other garments, obsidian, spices, agricultural products, sugarcane, emeralds, salt, and slaves. The kingdom became immensely wealthy, and with a powerful navy on the Nile River and the Red Sea was able to extend its imperial power by establishing trading colonies throughout the region in the early decades of the Common Era. To foster trade, the Axumites developed a system of roads maintained and protected by the state. Also used for transportation and trade were riverbeds during the dry seasons and reed boats for carrying goods on lakes. Axum remained a major trading power until the rise of Islam in the seventh and eighth centuries C.E.

Among imported goods, both those from other nations and those that circulated within Axum itself, were iron, bronze, glasswork, ceramics, wood, leather, and livestock. While the bulk of Axumite trade was internal, with city centers trading manufactured goods for agricultural products from the countryside, much also was international. Most imported goods appear to have been luxury items for the elite. These goods had to pass through customs posts, where taxes were paid. Sometimes these taxes were in the form of coinage, but usually they were paid in kind—that is, a portion of the goods themselves were paid as taxes. These taxes were an important source of Axumite wealth.

One of the most important trade routes of ancient Africa ran in an east-west direction just south of the Sahara. This band, called the Sahel, was home to numerous cities and settlements that made their living primarily through trade. Goods from the east and from the Mediterranean area passed through the Sahel on the way to points south, where they were traded for African goods such as ivory and precious metals. One of these settlements was Jenne-jeno in Sudan in the upper Niger River delta. Beginning in about 200 B.C.E. Jenne-jeno actively engaged in trade. Artifacts found in the area show that the city imported goods from Greece and Rome. Along any trading route, including that of the Sahel, towns and villages supported caravans of traders, providing them with food and water, forage for horses (and later camels), markets, and resting places. Goods probably changed hands at numerous points along these trade routes.

Carthage, founded on the northern coast of Africa (in modern-day Libya) in 814 B.C.E. by Phoenician traders from the city of Tyre in Lebanon, became one of the great trading civilizations of its time. The basis of Carthaginian power was its navy, which included as many as 350 warships that continuously patrolled the Mediterranean, primarily to keep trade routes open and to drive off competitors. Carthage also maintained a large fleet of merchant ships, each capable of carrying 100 tons of goods. Much of the empire's trade was based on the Iberian Peninsula (present-day Spain and Portugal), which had rich deposits of lead, silver, and tin ore. Tin was especially important because it was mixed with copper to make bronze, the key material for weapons, armor, and other vital implements. The Carthaginians also traded for tin with Britain and possibly the Canary Islands, giving Carthage a monopoly on the tin trade and therefore on bronze.

Besides Iberian silver, Carthage had access to silver mines in North Africa, providing a solid foundation for Carthaginian wealth. But perhaps the single most-valued commodity carried in Carthaginian ships was a dye called Tyrian purple. Painstakingly made in tiny amounts from the secretions of certain marine snails, this dye was so esteemed in the ancient world that a pound of it sometimes brought a price equal in value to 20 pounds of gold. Other important commodities included textiles (silk, wool, cotton), spices, perfumes, pottery, incense, glasswork, wood, bronze, alabaster, precious stones, plows, mirrors, cabinetry, household items (pillows and bedding, for example), slaves, horses, and weapons. Food commodities included fish and a range of agricultural products, such as wine, olives and olive oil, grapes, dates, nuts, and fruits. Much of Carthage's wealth came from brokering trade in these goods. Carthage's influence also spread southward with caravans sent deep into the continent to trade for ebony, ivory, salt, timber, gold, hides, and such animals as apes and peacocks. To the north they obtained amber from the Scandinavian countries. The Carthaginians' skills in storage, transportation, and buying and selling (they invented the auction) brought their empire wealth and power.

EGYPT

BY PANAGIOTIS I. M. KOUSOULIS

The broader Mediterranean region, which includes 25 nations today, witnessed the development of some of the most important and magnificent cultures of the past: ancient Egypt, Greece, and Rome. The Mediterranean Sea facilitated this development through cross-cultural exchanges, which took the form of diplomatic affairs, wars and treaties, social, religious, and artistic imports and exports, and, of course, trade.

Even in very early times Egypt had an extensive network of direct and indirect commercial and cultural contacts with foreign populations. Egyptian ships sailed across the Mediterranean probably as early as the Second Dynasty (ca. 2770–ca. 2649 B.C.E.), mainly to obtain raw materials. We can only estimate the size of such ships, although a cedar ship built in the Fourth Dynasty (ca. 2575–ca. 2465 B.C.E.) was said to have been 100 cubits, or 172 feet, long. Excellent representations of ships from the royal expedition of Queen Hatshepsut (r. 1473–1458 B.C.E.) to the mysterious land of Punt (perhaps in modern-day Somalia) are recorded in wall carvings at Deir el-Bahri in southern Egypt.

The main Mediterranean shipping routes follow sea currents and winds that go northward and westward along the Levantine and Anatolian coasts to the Aegean and those that go southward and eastward from Crete to Libya and Egypt. Ancient navigators considered May to September the best time for sailing the Mediterranean and might put out to sea as early as March or as late as November, but in winter the risk of storms made seafaring too dangerous, and captains kept their ships in port. Trade goods included amphorae (large clay jars used in ancient times for storage and transport) and other containers, jugs, bowls, and vases in ceramic, stone, and glass, and figurines of various materials, especially including scarabs, the carved stone beetles that Egyptians regarded as talismans. Besides ordinary trade there was considerable exchange of precious materials and other valuable items as gifts between royal authorities and foreign parties for diplomatic purposes. Many clay tablets excavated at Amarna in southern Egypt preserve lists of goods sent by Near Eastern rulers to the pharaoh as gifts.

Numerous other official writings, inscriptions, and carvings testify to an extensive trade network both within Egypt and externally. Some record expeditions to desert mines and quarries; others describe journeys to barter for goods with foreigners. The Egyptian sources report all royally authorized expeditions in standardized accounts that are all more or less alike. They record the date, the mission that the king set for the leader, and the destination. The accounts usually end with a happy and successful homecoming.

For modern readers perhaps the most striking thing in these accounts is the lack of interest in trade for the sake of profit. The aim of the expedition leaders seems to have been solely to carry out the orders of their superiors or to follow the divine will of whichever deity protected their missions. Thus the description of Hatshepsut's expedition to Punt emphasizes the god Amon's desire for the products of that land. Similarly, the Twentieth Dynasty (ca. 1196–ca. 1070 B.C.E.) *Report of Wenamun* tells the story of an official who went abroad to obtain wood for building a boat to carry the sacred image of Amon. He had no interest in buying wood for any other purpose, and he had no means of making a profit through the expedition, since he had sent from Egypt only enough commodities to obtain what he needed for the boat.

Royal control over the trade economy, especially during periods of powerful pharaohs and strong central government, left no place for private merchants. Private traders appeared only in times of weak or nonexistent central government, such as during the First Intermediate Period (ca. 2134–ca. 2040 B.C.E.) and the Second Intermediate Period (ca. 1640–ca. 1532 B.C.E.) or after the New Kingdom (ca. 1550–ca. 1070 B.C.E.).

But evidence from tombs indicates that even in times of strong central control, semiorganized barter did exist, particularly along the banks of the Nile. The most commonly exchanged items in the tomb depictions are vegetables, fish, figs, drinks, and metal containers. It appears that people engaged in this kind of trade for the purpose of enriching their diet or their home furnishings, not for profit.

Another characteristic aspect of the trade economy in ancient Egypt was gift exchange. It existed in two forms: gifts from the king to the people or vice versa and diplomatic gifts or tributes from allies and other foreign parties to the pharaoh and the Egyptian state, especially during the Middle Kingdom (ca. 2040–ca. 1640 B.C.E.) and New Kingdom. Gifts from the Egyptian populace to the pharaoh were conceived as a tribute to both the divine and the political attributes of the king. The Egyptians offered the king precious objects and commodities in order to receive from him internal peace and stability. Thus, in the step pyramid of King Djoser (r. ca. 2630–ca. 2611 B.C.E.) at Saqqara—the first monumental structure constructed exclusively from stone—a large number of inscribed jars were found, attesting to the continued practice of giving gifts to the king. Similar cases of gift giving are recorded in account papyri from the mortuary temple of the king Sesostris II (r. ca. 1897–ca. 1878 B.C.E.) at el-Lahun and in historical texts from the New Kingdom.

Tomb paintings, especially from Thebes (in southern Egypt), show porters bearing tribute to the pharaoh from almost all points of the compass. Elephant tusks, logs of ebony, and leopard skins arrived from tropical Africa. Copper ingots, amphorae filled with incense and other goods, flasks, and elephant tusks were among the items of tribute brought by Syrians and sometimes by Cretans. The gift exchange was reciprocal. The king honored the offerings and repaid the donors with equally valuable items.

A diplomatic gift carried social and cultural connotations more than it did mere economic value. Foreign rulers offered diplomatic gifts to the pharaoh as proof of the continuation of existing alliances or to offer the prospect of new ones. The custom of the diplomatic gift reached its peak during the New Kingdom, when the foreign expeditions of the pharaohs led to a greater intensity of contact with foreign lands, from Libya in the west to Nubia (modern-day Ethiopia) in the south to the countries of the Near East. Foreign tribute often included precious items and commodities that could not be found in Egyptian territory, but, again, these were not economic transactions. They were diplomatic expressions that acclaimed the pharaoh as the major delineator of action on behalf of the Egyptian society and in a superior position to the foreign emissaries.

THE MIDDLE EAST

BY FRANS VAN KOPPEN

One view of the exchange of goods and services is as a primary function of a social group, but from another perspective trade is the voluntary exchange of commodities between two parties for no reason beyond the acquisition of those goods. The two basic forms of trade are regional or domestic trade and foreign or long-distance trade. Regional trade is the exchange of raw materials and finished products inside a community or within the same region, whereas foreign trade is the movement of goods between different ecological regions that is motivated by the uneven distribution of raw materials in the natural world. The mechanisms by which commodities were distributed in ancient societies depended on particular social customs, and not all modes of exchange can be described as trade. Foreign trade focuses on the material aspect of long-distance exchange and is often considered the extraction of necessities from the periphery for the benefit of the center. In the ancient world, however, foreign trade was a function of intense interregional contacts and an essential factor in the diffusion of cultural and technological innovations, without which civilization would not have been attained.

Written sources and archaeological finds shed light on the conduct of trade. Archaeology indicates that trade predates the invention of writing by many millennia, revealing, for example, that in the Neolithic Period (ca. 8000 B.C.E.) obsidian, a volcanic glass suitable for sharp tools, was used many hundreds of miles away from its Anatolian source. Not all commodities of trade, however, are accessible in the archaeological record, and the interpretation of what has survived is often ambiguous because factors other than long-distance trade (for example, booty or tribute) also can explain the presence of artifacts of foreign material or manufacture. Ancient texts offer more conclusive evidence—in particular, cuneiform records from Mesopotamia, an area that depended on foreign imports for many essential resources, such as metals, stone, or wood, and where innumerable archival records pertaining to trade and commerce have been preserved. The existence of these records places Mesopotamia at the center of the study of ancient trade.

Ancient Mesopotamia, Persia, and other ancient Near Eastern regions were characterized by high levels of functional diversification among the population and clearly defined urban and rural sectors. These complex societies required efficient exchange mechanisms to link producers with consumers. Movements of food, craft products, and raw materials in early societies can be classified as reciprocal, redistributive, and commercial forms of exchange. Reciprocal exchange typically occurred between producers and consumers within a community and was based on long-term relationships and patterns of reciprocal obligations. Redistribution describes the collection of goods by a central authority and their disbursal to others on the basis of social status or kinship. Redistributive patterns occurred within the household and lay behind the functioning of Mesopotamian institutions that amassed agricultural produce to allocate them in the form of rations to dependents. The collection of vital resources as tribute in the Assyrian and Persian empires of the

Gold bracelet or diadem, Phoenician, seventh to sixth century B.C.E., *from the Phoenician trading center of Tharros, Sardinia; such jewelery, with its mixture of influences, demonstrates Phoenician connections across the Mediterranean.* (© The Trustees of the British Museum)

first millennium B.C.E. also has redistributive features and had a negative effect on commercial long-distance trade.

Finally, domestic trade conformed to a commercial type of exchange, with strangers trading goods or services on a market in accordance with freely varying prices. Economic value was expressed in quantities of certain goods, particularly silver, a commodity that fulfilled in antiquity many of the functions of our money. Pairs of scales and stone weights to weigh silver accurately, as well as the skill of converting into foreign weight systems, belonged to the toolkit of every ancient trader. Buying and selling, however, were often done by barter, with several items agreed on as the countervalue in a transaction, an ensemble that may include amounts of silver. Prices and commodity values fluctuated and were subject to supply and demand, but they usually adhered to customary rates attributable to social norms rather than government interference or market price fixing. Commercial, redistributive, and reciprocal modes of exchange existed alongside one another, depending on social context or transaction type, but their relative importance varied from place to place and through time.

Sellers on the domestic market were the producers themselves. Potters, for example, produced for clients but also sold their stock in marketplaces or from their workshops. Another example is people who made their living from retail. This group includes shopkeepers and vendors, occasionally specializing in products like salt or victuals. On a different scale, a class of wealthy merchants organized bulk transports of goods and relied on commercial networks for acquisition and distribution of merchandise. Those enterprises usually were undertaken on behalf of the state, with merchants collecting and selling agricultural taxes due to the state and repaying the state in silver or other commodities. Merchants held various positions; often they were entrepreneurs who entered into contractual agreements to undertake these tasks, but at other times and places they were more like government employees.

Some of these merchants also participated in long-distance commerce, but others dedicated themselves exclusively to trade expeditions to faraway destinations, exporting products of Mesopotamian manufacture, like textiles, vegetable oils, and foodstuffs, and importing resources, such as metals, stone, wood, aromatics, and slaves. City-states like Old Assyrian Assur (ca. 1900 B.C.E.) prospered as a result of long-distance trade, and merchants typically yielded much more political influence than did merchants in territorial states. Foreign commerce was based on family firms, with the younger male members traveling abroad or residing in foreign trade colonies like Kanesh, the central Anatolian settlement of Old Assyrian traders who sold Iranian tin and Babylonian textiles against Anatolian silver. Foreign trade depended on favorable political relations, and arrangements for merchants often were included in diplomatic treaties. Substantial volumes of wares also traveled abroad as diplomatic gifts between allied rulers—for instance during the Amarna Age (14th century B.C.E.)—but this exchange cannot be defined as trade as such, given that upholding social relations was its main purpose. Nevertheless, commerce and diplomacy often worked well together because diplomatic envoys took care of their trade interests during missions abroad.

The natural landscape dictates how long-distance communications and trade are conducted. Rivers are easy arteries of transport, and the Euphrates has throughout the millennia been the main pathway between the Persian Gulf and the Mediterranean coast, carrying large volumes of commerce that enrich ports of trade centers along its banks. Maritime trade over the Persian Gulf was particularly important in the late third millennium B.C.E., when traders from Mesopotamia met their colleagues from the Indus Valley on the island of Bahrain (ancient Dilmun). The Syrian and Phoenician cities of the Mediterranean coast were renowned trading centers from which the famous ship found at Uluburun (off the Turkish coast) sailed in the 14th century B.C.E. and where colonies were founded, such as Carthage in the ninth century B.C.E. An important overland trade connected Mesopotamia through the Zagros Mountains with the Iranian highlands; the same route became known as the Silk Road once trade contacts with China had been established during the Roman period.

ASIA AND THE PACIFIC

BY KIRK H. BEETZ

Trade helped build nations in ancient Asia and the Pacific, carrying with it ideas and inventions and encouraging people to learn about distant lands. Among the Pacific islands, trade was carried out using wooden boats. Near the Asian mainland, manufactured goods from China, Japan, and Korea went to islands like Sumatra, Java, and Tonga in exchange for spices, exotic woods, and rare seashells.

On the Asian mainland the economic giants were China and India. For most of ancient times China tended to look inward for trade. During the Shang Dynasty (ca. 1500 to 1045 B.C.E.) the Chinese believed that the world did not extend much beyond their borders in any direction. They focused on agriculture around the Yellow River. Important factors in the expansion of the Shang view of the world were attacks from outside and the discovery and then importation of goods from areas beyond China's borders. The most significant imported goods were wood and rice from the south. Instead of striving just to build good relations with their trading partners, the Shang adopted a policy that would remain typical of China's foreign trading for thousands of years: They tried to conquer the people who had the goods the Shang desired, making those goods part of the Shang Dynasty and thus goods at the command of the Shang king.

The Shang Dynasty and the Zhou Dynasty that followed (1045 to 256 B.C.E.) absorbed through warfare the Yangtze River region and its rich rice fields. During the Zhou Dynasty, transporting the South's agricultural products to the north, where the national capitals were to be found, became a severe problem. The great rivers of China were not entirely satisfactory for shipping food; their winding and occasional shifting courses made transportation slow and unreliable. The government started building canals by the 400s B.C.E. to aid the movement of goods across the nation, but the almost ceaseless warfare among the provinces of China disrupted those public works.

Steatite seals from the Indus Valley, dating to 2600 to 1900 B.C.E. and thought to have been used in trading with other nations and cultures (© The Trustees of the British Museum)

The western province of Qin gained an advantage when it built a canal connecting its major rivers. This had begun as a scam: An eloquent civil engineer had been dispatched by Qin's rivals to persuade the ruler of Qin to build the expensive canal, drawing resources from Qin's military. Even after he learned of the scam, the ruler was so convinced of the value of the canal that he continued its construction. As a result, Qin was able to transport goods faster than it could earlier, thus strengthening its economy so much that it became China's foremost economic and military power.

The Han Dynasty (202 B.C.E. to 220 C.E.) was aggressive in building up trade within its borders, and it continued the practice of invading nations that had goods it wanted, such as horses from the west. More than had previous dynasties, the Han Dynasty looked outward for trading opportunities. Most of its efforts focused on overland trade. At the cost of the lives of hundreds of thousands of Chinese soldiers, the Han pushed nomadic raiders out of the northwest and extended the Great Wall westward to protect the Silk Road—a network of routes that led to Persia and through Persia to the Mediterranean world. China exported silks, ceramics, and metals to Rome, which paid in gold. Further, the Chinese pioneered trade routes into India. Some of the Chinese explorers left written records of their travels through India. Silk made its way from China to India in exchange for gems such as diamonds as well as fragrant woods.

Not until roughly the 300s C.E. did China began trading in earnest by sea. Before then it had traded mostly with Japan, which exported its own high grade of silk and probably animal skins and ceramics to China in exchange for Chinese metals—especially copper coins, which became Japan's medium of exchange. Otherwise, Malaysian seafarers had conducted most of the sea trade between China and other southeastern lands. The Malaysians were heavily influenced by the Indians.

The first great Indian civilization, the Harappan (2600–1500 B.C.E.), was a trading empire. Although it was focused on the rivers of the Indus River valley, it established trading posts hundreds of miles away in central Asia and Iran to import lapis lazuli, tin, and bronze, sending out copper, gems, and grain. The Sumerians dealt extensively with the Harappans, and archaeologists have found numerous Harappan artifacts at Mesopotamian sites. How much the trade influenced Harappans is a matter of much disagreement among archaeologists, but it is possible that the political organization of Harappan cities imitated that of the Sumerians.

Much of later Indian history focuses on the spread of Aryan nomads and their Vedic culture southward through India. These nomads were a warrior people who put great store in military honor and the conquest of rival nations, yet much of southern India developed nations because of trade, not war. The peoples of southern India conducted a lively trade with each other before, during, and after the rise and fall of the Maurya Empire of about 321–185 B.C.E. and the Gupta Empire of 320–499 C.E.

The Indians of the interior formed caravans of wagons carrying goods not only produced in their own regions but also imported from other lands, thus bearing Chinese silks westward and Roman pottery eastward. The wagons transported muslin, saffron, ivory, agate, diamonds, pearls, ebony, and teak across roads to seaports. Governments arose to regulate the trade and maintain the roads. Leaders called Shatavahanas, whom historians consider somewhat mysterious figures, arose to foster trade and lead disparate peoples who organized themselves into trading nations.

India became a great generator of wealth for the Old World, trading with Africa, Rome, Persia, China, southeastern Asia, and the Indonesian islands. They established trading centers on the Malaysian peninsula, bringing their culture with them. In Indochina, the kingdom of Funan emerged as a trading nation that may have been similar to those of India. According to Chinese records, Funan was cofounded by an Indian trader.

Along India's western and eastern coasts arose trading cities. The ancient Romans sailed through the Indian Ocean to establish trading centers on the western coast, and these centers thrived for hundreds of years. In about 170 C.E. the Roman Empire suffered a recession so severe that Indians suffered economically and the Shatavahanas withdrew their trade from the west coast. To the east trade continued to thrive, with Indians opening trade with the regions of present-day Thailand and Burma, overland and by sea.

Sri Lanka, a large island in Mare Erythraeum (the present-day Indian Ocean) off the southeastern tip of India, was a way station for explorers, travels, and traders from Europe, Africa, the Near East, India, Malaysia, Indochina, Sumatra, Java, and China. From the 200s B.C.E. to the 1200s C.E. Sri Lanka was ruled by the Sinhalese kingdom.

The Sinhalese kingdom became rich from charging fees to the traders whose ships stopped in its ports. Government officials managed port facilities and docks efficiently. Ports teemed with trading fleets from Rome, Axum, Arabia, Persia, India, and Malaysia. The docks and city streets were a colorful mix of the national garb of dozens of different lands. The visitors mixed with pious monks and local people selling their wares. Especially popular were the bountiful agricultural products of Sri Lanka, such as coconuts, bananas, mangos, passion fruit, papayas, oranges, and tamarinds. The exotic flavors of those fruits would have been welcomed by travelers after weeks at sea. In addition to fruits, the Sinhalese sold rice, sugarcane, and cotton. Thanks to an irrigation system of 200 miles of canals, they had three harvests of rice per year. The Sinhalese were skilled water engineers who could build irrigation canals with only 6-inch rises per mile, and they knew the world was spherical and offered expert navigation skills to trading vessels.

EUROPE

BY FRANCESCO MENOTTI

Trade and exchange systems of the past have always been an important focus of research in archaeology. Studying trade and exchange can be difficult, however, especially within preliterate societies. In fact, scholars have available only what those societies left behind and time has preserved, such as archaeological artifacts. But useful information can be extrapolated from those seemingly useless remains. For instance, the materials from which artifacts are made can play a crucial role in identifying the movement of goods and reconstructing ancient exchange networks. Numerous methods of analysis have been developed to recognize and determine the origins of specific materials (stones, shells, metals, and so on) and to reconstruct production and distribution as well as the exchange system organization. Such analysis focuses on the various mechanisms of distribution that characterized ancient trade networks, from direct access to goods to down-the-line trade and eventually to a fully developed port of trade.

Beyond the simple economic value of traded goods, the meaning of exchange systems is also important. For example, in some instances symbolic elements might be predominant over other, more logical aspects. Circulation of ideas and communication of information imbedded in people's social behavior are therefore vital in understanding social contacts. To understand trade and exchange systems in prehistoric Europe, first it is necessary to divide the geographical area into conventional archaeological periods: Mesolithic (ca. 8000–4000 B.C.E.), Neolithic (ca. 7000–ca. 2000 B.C.E.), Bronze Age (ca. 2800–ca. 700 B.C.E.), Iron Age (ca. 1000–ca. 500 B.C.E.), and Roman times (ca. 400 B.C.E.–476 C.E.). Note that the dates provided apply to only the European continent as a whole and vary according to latitude and longitude.

Although it is flimsy and localized, evidence of trade and exchange in Europe does exist from the Mesolithic. The Mesolithic is an important transitional period in Europe, during which hunter-gatherer communities underwent significant changes in technology, economy, and social organization. The constantly changing environment triggered a steady development in tool technology, passing from bone and antler tools and the microlith (blade) industry common in the early Mesolithic to the various kinds of axes (first unpolished and then polished) in the later part of the period. In fact, the scarce availability of primary sources of raw materials in some areas was the primary factor initiating mobility, social interaction, and exchange systems. Despite evidence of material circulation on vast territories (obsidian in southeastern Europe and

Luxury imports from Italy, Rome, and the Near East, found at Hertfordshire, England, and dating to the Iron Age (20 B.C.E.–50 C.E.) (© The Trustees of the British Museum)

flint in northern areas), the exchange system was probably based on simple down-the-line trade involving balanced reciprocity. An event that changed Europe forever was the beginning of agriculture toward the end of the Mesolithic.

The first phase of agriculture diffusion occurred in a southwest–northwest direction, following the core–periphery model. Agriculture certainly brought changes in subsistence and the economy, but most significant was the social transformation. Another important event that took place in the late Neolithic was the discovery of copper. All this undoubtedly influenced social interaction and exchange systems. The quantity of traded goods increased, and some of them were seen as a way to gain social status. Significant movements of goods took place in the Mediterranean (obsidian); as far north as the Balkans (*Spondylus* shell); and in central, northern, and western Europe (axes, such as the Langdale ax in Britain and the Plussulien ax in France). Although organized long-distance trade was yet to develop, goods (especially nonperishable items) were circulated over vast distances through a system referred to as down-the-line trade. Food and other perishable materials were exchanged within much smaller areas.

Toward the end of the Neolithic, prehistoric Europe once again underwent a revolution brought about by a technological advance: metal alloying. At the beginning of the Bronze Age most artifacts, tools, and weaponry were made of bronze, a copper and tin alloy. Consequently, exchange systems became linked to the desirability and accessibility of that metal (one of the main centers of bronze production and distribution was the Carpathian Basin). Further developments in transportation, on both water and land facilitated the consolidation of established long-distance trade networks. Although trade links over long distances were already present in the Neolithic Period, it is only in the Bronze Age that archaeological records show the presence of long-distance trade routes linking north to south and east to west. All sorts of goods—including axes, swords, and pottery—were traded over these networks, but some of the longest and oldest long-distance trade routes were the amber routes in the Baltic and Mediterranean regions.

Trade routes rarely stayed the same but changed directions through space and time. Thorough analyses of archaeological records show the kinds of events (socioeconomic and political instability, migrations, wars, and so on) that caused them. Exchange mechanisms improved considerably in the Neolithic. The down-the-line system still prevailed, but the first ports of trade started to appear, especially in the Mediterranean (for example, Gadir in Spain). Coinage was not yet in use, but certain categories of artifacts definitely operated as barter tokens. The later part of the Bronze Age was characterized by a new change in social context. The appearance of hill forts, flat cemeteries, and field systems suggest a more unstable and less ordered society, a social framework that would typify the next archaeological period: the Iron Age.

The parallel expansions of the Phoenicians and Greeks in the Mediterranean and that of the Romans in continental Europe later, undoubtedly played a crucial role in the formation of important trade networks in Iron Age Europe. Barbarian societies at the edge of the advancing powers reacted in different ways to the Mediterranean expansion, but all were fascinated by the new and exotic traded goods (wine, olive oil, and luxury items). At the same time, however, Mediterranean societies were interested in continental goods, such as metals (of which iron was becoming more and more widespread), amber, and salt. The unstable equilibrium that characterized the European Iron Age, with hill forts and competition for social status in the north and fighting for supremacy in the Mediterranean, did not hinder the trade systems. In fact, more and more ports of trade were established throughout the continent as far as Scandinavia (among them, the various amber ports of trade located in northeastern Poland and Lithuania). It is well known that the Romans conquered Europe economically well before it did so politically. Paradoxically, it was the existing pre-empire trade that facilitated the Roman conquest of Iberia (present-day Spain) and Gaul (present-day France) in the first century B.C.E.

Trade and exchange between Rome and the barbarian world continued throughout the empire. A trade buffer zone had even developed just beyond the empire's borders. That area was of great economic and political importance to both the Romans and the barbarians, with ports of trade between the two worlds located there. The barbarians would obtain prestigious and valuable items from the Romans and in return would acquire everything the empire needed, including cheap labor in the form of slaves (especially from eastern and northeastern Europe). Sadly, slaves became the "items" the barbarians most often exported to the Roman world during the empire's heyday.

The fall of Rome and the subsequent Nordic southward migrations created a period of serious instability within Europe's trading networks, but trade experienced no regression. In fact, some trade centers experienced further development and would become important emporia in early medieval times; examples are Lundeborg and Gudme in Denmark. Despite sociopolitical insecurity and massive migrations of peoples, goods continued to be moved all over Europe and beyond, linking even the most remote regions of the northeast in increasingly solid and sophisticated trade networks.

GREECE

BY EDWARD M. W. A. ROWLANDS

From prehistoric times the Greeks were able to gain access to markets beyond their shores. By the sixth century B.C.E. Greek city-states had established colonies throughout the Mediterranean and into the Black Sea; this protected access to important goods such as grain, wood, and silver. Concurrently, coins developed into a popular means of exchange. In sharp contrast was the city of Sparta, which disapproved of trade and lived on the produce of its occupied territories. By 323 B.C.E. Alexander the Great from Macedon had conquered the Persian Empire, and on his death Greece became part of one of several Hellenistic kingdoms. The Hellenistic Period, and the later Roman dominance of the Mediterranean, opened up larger markets to the Greeks, but the economic power and influence of the Greek city-states were lost forever.

At Grave Circle A—a circle of six graves in Mycenae dating to the beginning of the Late Bronze Age—finds show that by 1600 B.C.E. people in the Peloponnese could import not only golden jewelry from Crete and the Aegean but also amber from as far as the Baltic Sea. At that time Greece and the surrounding islands were tied into European and Mediterranean trade networks. As a result, the powerful militaristic peoples known as the Mycenaeans were able to establish kingdoms throughout Greece, Crete, and the Aegean Islands. By controlling access to the items traded and through patronage of traded goods, the Mycenaean leadership could keep control over the elite of the kingdom.

Over the coming centuries the Greeks were to sail far and wide across the Mediterranean and into the Black Sea. Colonies were founded from the island of Sicily in the west to Crimea, in modern-day Ukraine, to the east. Through their colonies, trade centers like Athens, Thebes, Corinth, and Argos gained access to markets previously out of their reach. The Greeks imported goods such as wood, slaves, gold, silver, copper, and tin in exchange for products like wine, pottery, and olive oil. This trade increased the power of the trading centers, enabling them to monopolize production from their colonies and establishing them as powerful metropolises within their regions.

Most of the written evidence about trade and exchange that is available to modern classicists is from Athens. The city of Athens rose to serious power during the fifth century B.C.E. Western civilization has benefited from the art, drama, philosophy, and democracy developed at the height of the Athenian empire. Those developments were possible only because Athens, as a great sea power, could protect trade routes and colonies from attack. By the fifth century B.C.E. Athens had grown into a large city, and its surrounding territory of Attica could not supply enough grain to keep all Athenians alive. It was therefore imperative to maintain a route through the Bosporus and into the Black Sea, where large amounts of grain could be accessed. According to the Athenian statesman Demosthenes, in the fourth century from the Crimea alone Athens was importing 400,000 medimnoi a year, which in modern terms is equivalent to millions of gallons of grain. Athenian legislation was also written to make sure that grain produced in Attica could not be exported and that all grain coming into the port of Piraeus had to be sold in Attica.

Coinage came to Greece in the sixth century B.C.E. from cities situated on the coast of modern-day Turkey. It

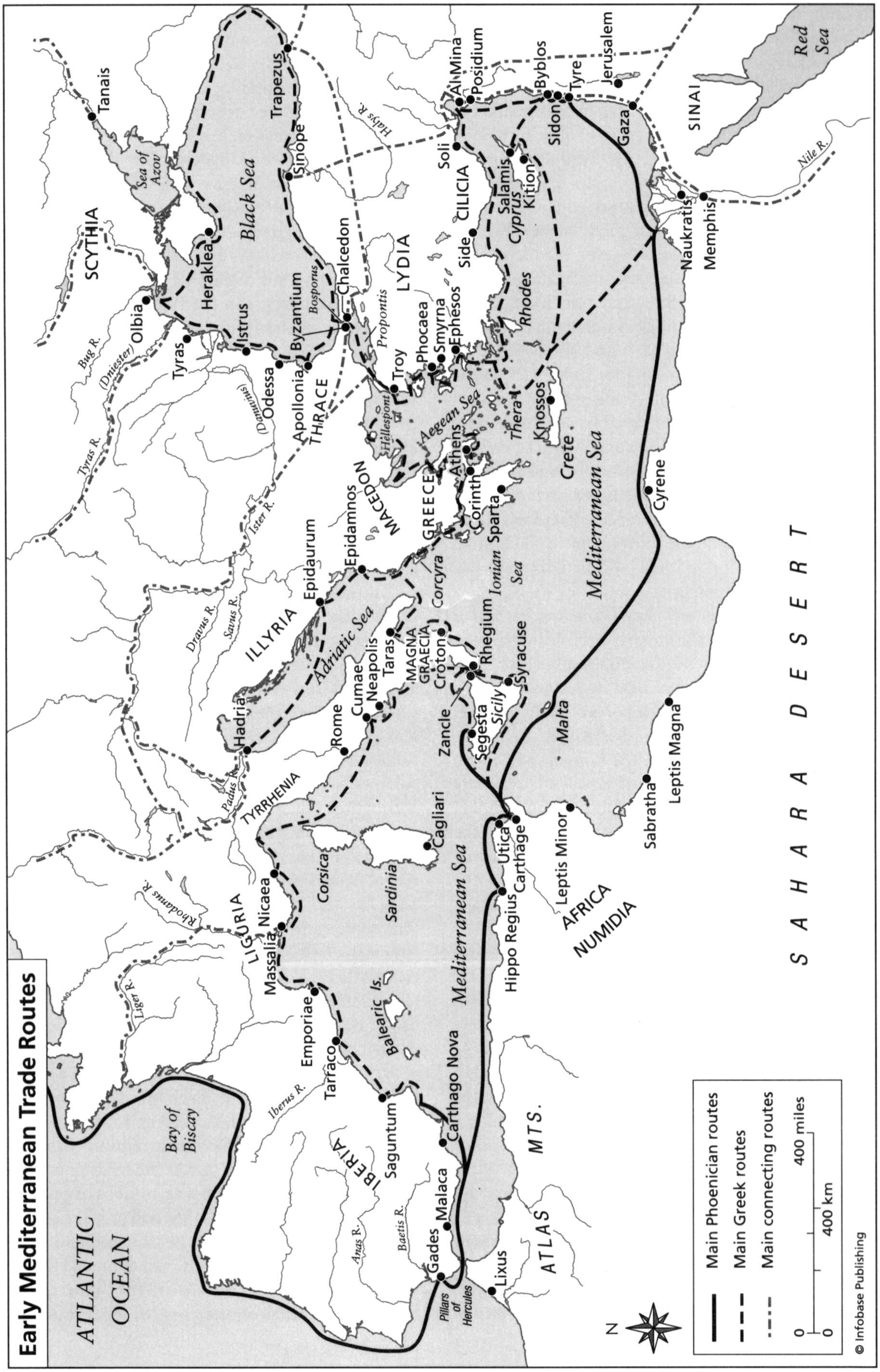

Ancient Greek trading routes extended throughout the Mediterranean.

became common for coins to be made of silver and for Greek city-states to monopolize their formation. The Athenian historian Xenophon wrote in the fourth century B.C.E. that his city was assured of trade because of its good supply of silver coins, the result of the Athenian-controlled silver mines at Laurium in Attica. Coins gave city-states a valuable way to exchange goods within Greece and for great distances beyond its shores.

Port markets (*emporia*) and marketplaces (*agora*) served as locations for trade with people from other cities. The prosperity of some of these markets, especially in Athens and Corinth, increased significantly as trade between Greek cities and overseas nations increased. In the marketplace foreigners often had to pay a tax just for purchasing goods. City-states could also collect a duty on the cargo of ships with access to their ports. Written evidence at Athens shows that it taxed the value of vessels going through the Piraeus. Although trade between short distances was possible over land, the mountainous topography of Greece usually necessitated long-distance travel by ship. Toward the end of the Peloponnesian War in 413 B.C.E., Athens further exploited trade being carried out in the Aegean by imposing a 5 percent duty on all the ports within the empire.

A noticeable contrast to Athens is apparent in the city of Sparta. In the seventh century B.C.E. Sparta conquered the territory of Messenia and enslaved the entire population, turning them into what were called helots. Messenia was a fertile territory that provided Sparta with food supplies and a workforce of helots. A deeply militaristic society, Sparta was against the accumulation of personal wealth. Its military domination of Messenia meant that it was not forced into trading with cities for grain and was able to pass laws forbidding its citizens to trade.

The activities of Alexander the Great (336–323 B.C.E.) were to have a major effect on Greek economic activity. After his death the empire he created, which stretched from Macedon to India, was split into several Hellenistic kingdoms. The Macedonian generals of Alexander then ruled territories from Egypt, Syria, Anatolia (modern-day Turkey), and Macedonia. Greece benefited because Greek became the international language of business. The use of common currencies and the production of roads fostered economic expansion not just in Greece but throughout what became known as the Greek world. Yet Greece would not become the most important part of the greater Greek-speaking world because cities like Alexandria in Egypt were to be the main centers of manufacturing and imports.

The Roman Empire came to control Greece after the battle of Pydna in 168 B.C.E. Rome became the unquestionable trading and economic power, placing Greece in a politically united Mediterranean. In the second century C.E. the Roman author Lucian describes how he saw, in the Greek port of Piraeus, a Roman grain ship that was 180 feet long and 45 feet across, and "the crew was like an army." Greek culture and technology influenced the beginnings of Roman society, but its ports remained important for trading throughout Roman times.

ROME

BY CHRISTOPHER SMITH

Rome was superbly positioned from its beginnings to take advantage of regional trade and exchange. The city of Rome is situated on the banks of the Tiber River; as one sailed up from the Mediterranean, from the first crossing point and alongside the river ran one of the oldest roads in Italy, the Via Salaria, or "salt road," which linked the salt pans of the coast with the interior. Salt was a vital commodity in antiquity, owing to its preservative function.

Some of the earliest archaeological evidence for the urban development of the city comes from an area adjacent to Rome's earliest port, called the Forum Boarium, which was primarily a cattle market. As of the eighth century B.C.E. imported pottery is in evidence at this site, signifying cults that originated in the east. The most apparent is the cult of Hercules, from the Greek Herakles, which also shows Phoenician features. These artifacts demonstrate the early growth of trade links, with key connections being formed with the East. Indeed, Greek and Phoenician traders moved westward from the eighth century B.C.E. onward, bringing such unfamiliar and exotic materials as gold, silver, and ivory, which became indicators of high social status. The Romans also learned from the Greeks the formal customs of banqueting. The Etruscans, who occupied areas both north and south of Rome, were a crucial intermediary in this process of social development.

Alongside the development of such long-distance trade, vigorous and important regional trade was conducted. The hinterland of Rome, the region called Latium, was populated

The Crawford Cup, Roman, dating to the first to second century C.E. and found on the border between Syria and Turkey; this goblet was made of fluorspar, a relatively rare mineral that in the Roman period could be found only in the kingdom of Parthia (modern-day Iran). (© The Trustees of the British Museum)

by a number of settlements scattered across a moderately fertile plain. Exchange among these settlements and Rome was frequent and enshrined in the legal concept of *commercium*: the right of any Latin or inhabitant of Latium to own Roman land and to enter into a contract with a Roman. Every ninth day in Rome was designated as a market day (*nundina*), and these days were inscribed on the formal calendars listing the annual festivals and events, which were found distributed throughout central Italy. Other calendars simply indicate the market days and their locations. The existence of these calendars demonstrates the importance of regular local markets in the economy of central Italy.

Agriculture was at the core of most of the commercial activity in the ancient world, in terms of the short-range movement of produce; long-range transhumance—or the movement of animals, typically sheep, from summer upland pastures to winter lowland pastures—and the exploitation of animals as resources, especially in terms of meat and wool; and the long-range movement of some staples, notably grain, wine, and olive oil, across the Mediterranean. As the Roman Empire grew, Rome became involved in existing trade patterns and began to influence their development. To the east, the long-established Greek cities and the Hellenistic empires already boasted sophisticated networks of trade and exchange. To the west and north, key centers such as Marseilles, in modern-day France, and Carthage, in modern-day Tunis, were already present, but the Romans may have had a similar impact on Spain, Gaul, and Britain in the first century B.C.E. as the Greeks and Phoenicians had on Rome in the eighth century B.C.E., stimulating social and economic development. One characteristic feature of this development was urbanization, which altered economic relationships by creating centers of consumption that drew from hinterlands.

With regard to modes of transport, the sea was a crucial conduit, and Rome expended significant effort, most notably through the campaigns of Pompey in 67 B.C.E., to clear the sea of pirates. The physical evidence for maritime trade consists most notably of shipwrecks, which give important information about cargoes. Also, Rome constructed roads to facilitate the movement of armies and of goods across the empire, sometimes utilizing preexisting structures and at other times applying their engineering skills to construct new roads, such as in Britain.

In time, Rome became the greatest center of consumption of all. Rome's population rose to a million by the end of the first century B.C.E., and a substantial number expected a stable supply of food, some of which was provided by the state and subsequently by the emperor. The demand for food was increasingly satisfied by the Roman provinces; huge grain ships plied the route from Egypt to Rome, and at Ostia and Portus (first created by Claudius in 46 C.E., with substantial redevelopment by Trajan in 103 C.E.) new facilities were constructed to cope with disembarkation, storage, and distribution. Another physical sign of the relatively enormous level of consumption in Rome is Monte Testaccio, a hill close to the Tiber some 160 feet high, entirely composed of broken oil amphorae, or containers. (Unlike wine amphorae, oil amphorae could not be reused.) Most of these amphorae came from the province of Baetica, in southwestern Spain, in the second and third centuries C.E., and the hill comprises more than 50 million amphorae, in which over 1.5 billion gallons of oil were imported into the city.

Other items in demand included building materials and metals. Quarrying was a major enterprise, and like many such enterprises was increasingly an imperial monopoly. At Mons Claudianus, in Egypt, marble was quarried for use in imperial palaces from Rome to Split, in modern-day Croatia. In addition to the masses of workers, the quarrying required an entire support network, such as to provide security over the transport route. Once imperial authority broke down at the end of the empire, quarrying ceased. The level of extraction of metal resources achieved during the empire was not matched again until the Industrial Age; the opencast Roman gold mine at Las Médulas, in Spain, was about 1.8 miles in diameter, and lead and copper pollution from the Imperial Period is detectable in the Greenland ice cap.

Metal was in demand, largely for coinage. After the introduction of coinage in Rome around 300 B.C.E. money became the dominant means of exchange with respect to taxation, wages, rent, and credit, although agricultural products also remained significant. Coinage was important at every level of the economy and grew increasingly centralized, with local mints disappearing and local currencies being phased out in favor of a central Roman currency. That currency was therefore vulnerable to debasement and consequent inflation, which became a problem in the third century C.E.

One commodity without which much of the rest of trading activity would have been impossible was human beings. Slaves were bought and sold across the empire—the Greek island of Delos had a notable slave market—and they contributed enormously through their labor to the productivity of the empire. A ratio of one slave to every three free persons has been suggested for Italy during this era. Owing to the Roman custom of freeing slaves, some could achieve substantial commercial standing themselves; this phenomenon is vividly portrayed in Petronius's fictional account, from the first century C.E., of the freedman Trimalchio, who was a substantial landowner, had diverse trading interests, and lent money to others, on the basis of which he sustained a comically excessive lifestyle. Roughly contemporary documents from Puteoli depict a family descended from a slave who for three generations engaged in loans and banking in a wide variety of enterprises, including ones run by other freedmen.

Regarding the overall nature of the Roman economy, scholars have long debated the extent of the impact of trade on the society and economy of the Roman Empire. In general, wealth derived from land carried more positive overtones than wealth derived from commerce. Some senators were engaged in trade, and a substantial wealthy elite across the empire had a diversity of commercial interests. In relation to growth, Rome's demand for taxes from the provinces may have meant that provincial economies were obligated to grow or suffer. Regardless, growth remained gentle and regionally distinctive in the first two centuries C.E.

Toward the end of the empire, both change and continuity were represented. Inflation led to attempts at price control by the Roman emperor Diocletian, and changes were made to the taxation system, but the volume of trade remained strong. After the fall of the Western Roman Empire, goods were exchanged and peoples were transported at much lower rates, with lesser degrees of sophistication, and without the levels of central control that had characterized the Imperial Period. In the sixth century C.E. some 5,000 cargo ships sailed in the eastern Mediterranean, indicating both the continued significance of trade and exchange and the considerably greater activity during the Roman Empire across the Mediterranean.

THE AMERICAS

BY J. J. GEORGE

Trade is typically defined as a two-way exchange—the business of buying, selling, or bartering commodities—motivated by profit or need. In a true market system, trade would be at least partially divorced from social or political entanglements, and the value of the commodities would follow laws of supply and demand, unencumbered by legislation. Trading activities in the Americas, however, were varied and complex, sometimes encumbered with political and social obligations and sometimes more freewheeling.

Generally, archaeologists consider the presence of nonlocal objects at a site to be evidence of trade, although other systems of exchange existed, including reciprocity and tribute. Reciprocity implies a mutual exchange of privileges or goods, often with socially acceptable gifts exchanged on a roughly equal basis with the aim of establishing or solidifying social or political relationships. Tribute, on the other hand, was often a one-way exchange between a dominant overlord and a subject polity. The later Aztec Empire (15th and 16th centuries) provides the primary Mesoamerican model of tribute exchange: Conquered territories were forced to contribute substantial amounts of prized goods in return for assurance that they would not be decimated. Exchange in its broadest sense also included the flow of art styles, religion, ritual, ideas, and technology as part of cultural diffusion. Although this form of exchange was often unidirectional and flowed from the impulses of empire, expansion, and diffusion, it also could be a shared enterprise and a means by which disparate political and social entities were united.

Mesoamerican cultures relied almost entirely on human carriers to transport goods, limiting the range for perishable commodities and resulting in high transportation costs. The wheel was a known concept, but there is no evidence yet of its use in transportation. Transport of items such as foodstuffs was limited geographically and reinforced localized trade in those items. Longer-distance trade emphasized high-value, low-weight luxury goods often classified as elite items. In turn, the people who controlled trade and trade routes often solidified elite status or rulership roles for themselves.

Common Mesoamerican trade items included ceramics, lithic material such as obsidian and chert, textiles, perishable tropical goods, precious stones, metals, and foodstuffs. During Mesoamerica's Formative or Preclassic Period (ca. 1800 B.C.E.–ca. 150 C.E.) chiefdoms at several sites—such as Olmec sites on the Gulf Coast, sites in the Valley of Oaxaca and Chalcatzingo in Morelos, and several sites in Chiapas—exchanged items like jadeite, obsidian tools, ceramic vessels, shell ornaments, and animal products. Obsidian is a particularly useful material to document trade systems because the absence of metal tools meant it was used extensively in toolmaking and thus was highly valued. Additionally, obsidian has few sources, and its trace element composition is distinct, making chemical sourcing possible and allowing researchers to track its distribution. Major obsidian sources include Pachuca in central Mexico and El Chayal and Ixtepeque in highland Guatemala. Obsidian from these sources was found throughout Mesoamerica.

Other examples of trade items include high-quality chert from Belize, used to make tools throughout the Mayan lowlands of northern Guatemala and Mexico's Yucatán Peninsula. Basalt, andesite, and granite were used to make grinding tools such as mortars and pestles; such volcanic material was unavailable locally to people in the Mayan lowlands and was transported in from the highlands. Textiles, a highly valued but perishable item, were also traded. Although few survive, especially from the dense, tropical lowlands, the tools from which they were made, such as spindle whorls, first show up along the Gulf Coast and later throughout Mesoamerica, suggesting some system of diffusion through trade. Perishable goods like precious feathers from the quetzal bird of Guatemala and jaguar pelts—both symbols of royalty—were distributed throughout Mesoamerica. Precious stones, whose value in part derives from limited natural distribution, rarity, and symbolic importance, were used to make fine jewelry. Jadeite from Costa Rica and Guatemala and turquoise from the southwestern North America found wide distribution throughout Mesoamerica, as evidenced in various grave caches. Foodstuffs were limited locally in most periods, although empires such as Teotihuacán (ca. 100–700 C.E.), had infrastructures substantial enough to obtain grains, maize, beans, and amaranth as tribute from greater distances.

Many North American societies up to and beyond 500 C.E. were of the hunter-gatherer type, which makes data difficult to obtain. Various forms of trade were known. One example is from the first millennium C.E., which was a kind of golden age for the Arctic Eskimo, an era that saw brilliant creativity in both arts and manufacturing, and the perfection of skills and equipment required to hunt diverse northern animals. These developments originated along the shores of the Bering Sea and the Bering Strait and spread eastward, suggesting both population diffusion and exchange systems. Because distances were often great and contact infrequent between societal territories, trade probably happened spontaneously. In other northern locations, however, trade occurred regularly between coastal and inland groups to obtain staples that their own environments did not offer. For example, during the Mesoamerican Classic Period (150–650 C.E.) sea mammal oil and blubber were traded by coastal peoples to interior peoples in exchange for furs of the caribou, fox, and wolverine. A basic form of this exchange tradition probably dates back several thousand years. A similar geographic exchange principle between interior and coast also was thought to exist in the southeastern region of North America.

In the Adena-Hopewell interaction sphere, centered in present-day Ohio with satellites spread throughout the greater Midwest, mound builders gathered periodically for funeral ceremonies and construction. Evidence suggests that some form of exchange occurred, even if it was only labor. Craft specialization, including pipes and polished stone artifacts, all highly transportable, offered prime opportunities for trade. Researchers have found a surprising concentration of Adena-style artifacts, such as stone tubes, Adena points, birdstones, gorgets, and shell and copper beads as far east as the Chesapeake Bay. Materials for Hopewell grave goods were brought in from great distances. Other traded items include obsidian from what is today Yellowstone Park in Wyoming, conch and turtle shell, shark and alligator teeth from Florida, mica and chlorite from North Carolina and Tennessee, bluish flint from Indiana, and chalcedony from North Dakota. While down-the-line, or intervillage, exchange systems may have accounted for some of the imports, long-range trading or mining expeditions also seem to have been involved.

Evidence throughout the Andes region supports a tradition of long-distance trade. In the period of 2000–1500 B.C.E. trade between coastal Ecuador and Amazonia is supported by ceramic developments, figurine traditions, and the presence in coastal Ecuador of a type of coca indigenous to the Amazon regions. In Peru evidence of long-distance trade is found in a medicine man's outfit discovered near Lake Titicaca and dated to the fourth century B.C.E. The outfit is attributed to a type of traveling herbalist called a *callahuayas*, whose business was the long-distance transfer of goods and ideas. Remains of food, arts, and crafts at Chavín de Huántar, the center of the northern Peruvian Chavín culture (ca. 900–ca. 200 B.C.E.), indicate extensive outside relations, including a far-flung trade network presumably facilitated by llama trains. In one example, obsidian from Huancavelica, some 290 miles south, was found at Chavín de Huántar.

See also AGRICULTURE; BORDERS AND FRONTIERS; BUILDING TECHNIQUES AND MATERIALS; CALENDARS AND CLOCKS; CERAMICS AND POTTERY; CITIES; CRAFTS; ECONOMY; EMPIRES AND DYNASTIES; EMPLOYMENT AND LABOR; EXPLORATION; FOOD AND DIET; FOREIGNERS AND BARBARIANS; INVENTIONS; LANGUAGE; METALLURGY; MILITARY; MINING, QUARRYING, AND SALT MAKING; MONEY AND COINAGE; ROADS AND BRIDGES; SEAFARING AND NAVIGATION; SHIPS AND SHIPBUILDING; SLAVES AND SLAVERY; SOCIAL ORGANIZATION; STORAGE AND PRESERVATION; TEXTILES AND NEEDLEWORK; TRANSPORTATION; WEIGHTS AND MEASURES; WAR AND CONQUEST; WRITING.

Greece

The Periplus of the Erythraean Sea: Travel and Trade in the Indian Ocean by a Merchant of the First Century, *excerpt (ca. first to third centuries C.E.)*

1. Of the designated ports on the Erythraean Sea, and the market-towns around it, the first is the Egyptian port of Mussel Harbor. To those sailing down from that place, on the right hand, after eighteen hundred stadia, there is Berenice. The harbors of both are at the boundary of Egypt, and are bays opening from the Erythraean Sea.

2. On the right-hand coast next below Berenice is the country of the Berbers. Along the shore are the Fish-Eaters, living in scattered caves in the narrow valleys. Further inland are the Berbers, and beyond them the Wild-flesh-Eaters and Calf-Eaters, each tribe governed by its chief; and behind them, further inland, in the country towards the west, there lies a city called Meroe.

3. Below the Calf-Eaters there is a little market-town on the shore after sailing about four thousand stadia from Berenice, called Ptolemais of the Hunts, from which the hunters started for the interior under the dynasty of the Ptolemies. This market-town has the true land-tortoise in small quantity; it is white and smaller in the shells. And here also is found a little ivory like that of Adulis. But the place has no harbor and is reached only by small boats.

4. Below Ptolemais of the Hunts, at a distance of about three thousand stadia, there is Adulis, a port

established by law, lying at the inner end of a bay that runs in toward the south. Before the harbor lies the so-called Mountain Island, about two hundred stadia seaward from the very head of the bay, with the shores of the mainland close to it on both sides. Ships bound for this port now anchor here because of attacks from the land. They used formerly to anchor at the very head of the bay, by an island called Diodorus, close to the shore, which could be reached on foot from the land; by which means the barbarous natives attacked the island. Opposite Mountain Island, on the mainland twenty stadia from shore, lies Adulis, a fair-sized village, from which there is a three-days' journey to Coloe, an inland town and the first market for ivory. From that place to the city of the people called Auxumites there is a five days' journey more; to that place all the ivory is brought from the country beyond the Nile through the district called Cyeneum, and thence to Adulis. Practically the whole number of elephants and rhinoceros that are killed live in the places inland, although at rare intervals they are hunted on the seacoast even near Adulis. Before the harbor of that market-town, out at sea on the right hand, there lie a great many little sandy islands called Alalaei, yielding tortoise-shell, which is brought to market there by the Fish-Eaters.

5. And about eight hundred stadia beyond there is another very deep bay, with a great mound of sand piled up at the right of the entrance; at the bottom of which the opsian stone is found, and this is the only place where it is produced. These places, from the Calf-Eaters to the other Berber country, are governed by Zoscales; who is miserly in his ways and always striving for more, but otherwise upright, and acquainted with Greek literature.

6. There are imported into these places, undressed cloth made in Egypt for the Berbers; robes from Arsinoe; cloaks of poor quality dyed in colors; double-fringed linen mantles; many articles of flint glass, and others of murrhine, made in Diospolis; and brass, which is used for ornament and in cut pieces instead of coin; sheets of soft copper, used for cooking-utensils and cut up for bracelets and anklets for the women; iron, which is made into spears used against the elephants and other wild beasts, and in their wars. Besides these, small axes are imported, and adzes and swords; copper drinking-cups, round and large; a little coin for those coming to the market; wine of Laodicea and Italy, not much; olive oil, not much; for the king, gold and silver plate made after the fashion of the country, and for clothing, military cloaks, and thin coats of skin, of no great value. Likewise from the district of Ariaca across this sea, there are imported Indian iron, and steel, and Indian cotton cloth; the broad cloth called monache and that called sagmatogene, and girdles, and coats of skin and mallow-colored cloth, and a few muslins, and colored lac. There are exported from these places ivory, and tortoiseshell and rhinoceros-horn. The most from Egypt is brought to this market from the month of January to September, that is, from Tybi to Thoth; but seasonably they put to sea about the month of September.

From: Wilfred H. Schoff, ed. and trans., *The Periplus of the Erythraean Sea: Travel and Trade in the Indian Ocean by a Merchant of the First Century* (London: Longmans, Green, and Co., 1912).

Rome

Petronius Arbiter (ca. 27–66 C.E.), "The Banquet of Trimalchio," excerpt from the Satyricon

"When I came here first [as a slave] from Asia, I was only as high as yonder candlestick, and I'd be measuring my height on it every day, and greasing my lips with lamp oil to bring out a bit of hair on my snout. Well, at last, to make a long story short, as it pleased the gods, I became master in the house, and as you see, I'm a chip off the same block. He [my master] made me coheir with Caesar, and I came into a royal fortune, but no one ever thinks he has enough. I was mad for trading, and to put it all in a nutshell, bought five ships, freighted them with wine—and wine was as good as coined money at that time—and sent them to Rome. You wouldn't believe it, every one of those ships was wrecked. In one day Neptune swallowed up 30,000,000 sesterces on me. D'ye think I lost heart? Not much! I took no notice of it, by Hercules! I got more ships

(continued)

(continues)

made, larger, better, and luckier; that no one might say I wasn't a plucky fellow. A big ship has big strength—that's plain! Well I freighted them with wine, bacon, beans, perfumes, and slaves. Here Fortuna (my consort) showed her devotion. She sold her jewelry and all her dresses, and gave me a hundred gold pieces—that's what my fortune grew from. What the gods ordain happens quickly. For on just one voyage I scooped in 10,000,000 sesterces and immediately started to redeem all the lands that used to be my master's. I built a house, bought some cattle to sell again—whatever I laid my hand to grew like a honeycomb. When I found myself richer than all the country round about was worth, in less than no time I gave up trading, and commenced lending money at interest to the freedmen. Upon my word, I was very near giving up business altogether, only an astrologer, who happened to come into our colony, dissuaded me. And now I may as well tell you it all—I have thirty years, four months and two days to live, moreover I'm to fall in for an estate—that's prophecy anyway. If I'm so lucky as to be able to join my domains to Apulia, I'll say I've got on pretty well. Meanwhile under Mercury's fostering, I've built this house. Just a hut once, you know—now a regular temple! It has four dining rooms, twenty bedrooms, two marble porticoes, a set of cells upstairs, my own bedroom, a sitting room for this viper (my wife!) here, a very fine porter's room, and it holds guests to any amount. There are a lot of other things too that I'll show you by and by. Take my word for it, if you have a penny you're worth a penny, you are valued for just what you have. Yesterday your friend was a frog, he's a king today—that's the way it goes."

From: William Stearns Davis, ed., *Readings in Ancient History: Illustrative Extracts from the Sources*. Vol. 2: *Rome and the West* (Boston: Allyn and Bacon, 1912–1913).

FURTHER READING

Edward Bleiberg, "The Economy of Ancient Egypt," in *Civilizations of the Ancient Near East*, ed. Jack M. Sasson et al., vol. 3 (New York: Scribner, 1995): 1373–1385.

Erik H. Cline, *Sailing the Wine-Dark Sea: International Trade and the Late Bronze Age Aegean*, British Archaeological Reports 591 (Oxford, U.K.: Tempus Reparatum, 1994).

Barry W. Cunliffe, *Facing the Ocean: The Atlantic and Its Peoples* (Oxford, U.K.: Oxford University Press, 2001).

W. Vivian Davies and Louise Schofield, eds., *Egypt, the Aegean, and the Levant: Interconnections in the Second Millennium B.C.* (London: British Museum Press, 1995).

J. G. Dercksen, ed., *Trade and Finance in Ancient Mesopotamia: Proceedings of the First MOS Symposium, Leiden, the Netherlands, 1997* (Leiden, Netherlands: Nederland Instituut voor het Nabije Oosten, 1999).

Francis Healy and Chris Scarre, eds., *Trade and Exchange in Prehistoric Europe* (Oxford, U.K.: Oxbow Books, 1993).

Panagiotis Kousoulis and Magliveras Konstantinos, eds., *Moving across Borders: Foreign Relations, Religion, and Cultural Interactions in the Ancient Mediterranean*, Orientalia Lovaniensia Analecta 159 (Leuven, Belgium: Peeters, 2007).

W. F. Leemans, *Foreign Trade in the Old Babylonian Period as Revealed by Texts from Southern Mesopotamia* (Leiden, Netherlands: E. J. Brill, 1960).

David Mattingly and John Salmon, eds., *Economies beyond Agriculture in the Classical World* (London: Routledge, 2001).

Michael McCormick, *Origins of the European Economy: Communications and Commerce, A.D. 300–900* (Cambridge, U.K.: Cambridge University Press, 2001).

Helen Parkins and Christopher Smith, eds., *Trade, Traders, and the Ancient City* (London: Routledge, 1998).

J. N. Postgate, *Early Mesopotamia: Society and Economy at the Dawn of History* (London: Routledge, 1992).

Nicholas K. Rauh, *Merchants, Sailors, and Pirates in the Roman World* (Stroud, U.K.: Tempus Publishing, 2003).

Andrew Sherratt, *Economy and Society in Prehistoric Europe: Changing Perspectives* (Princeton, N.J.: University Press, 1997).

► transportation

INTRODUCTION

Means of transportation limited empires in what they could do or expanded their horizons. The first significant empire, the Akkadian Empire (ca. 2350–ca. 2100 B.C.E.) fell apart partly because it was too large for efficient communications among its far-flung parts using the roads and transportation of its time. Good, safe transportation became a matter of importance for many civilizations.

The invention of the wheel was a crucial innovation for transportation. The earliest record for a wheeled vehicle comes from Uruk in the Near East, from about 3500 B.C.E. The wheel probably was derived from the potter's wheel and, like a potter's wheel, was originally solid. The wheel was improved and modified over centuries, with each change making the wheel capable of surviving ever-longer distances and moving faster. Speed and durability enhanced long-distance trade, enriching many cultures, and allowed ideas and technology to travel farther faster.

The first known indication of the domestication of the horse comes from Ukraine and dates to about 3000 B.C.E. The domestication of the horse presented problems that ancient peoples did not fully overcome. Although oxen have big, prominent shoulders to press against heavy yokes, horses do not. The best solution to harnessing a horse probably came from China, where a breast strap was invented. This strip of leather stretched around the horse's chest. It restricted the horse's breathing and could compress arteries that brought blood to the horse's brain, which meant the horse was limited in the loads it could haul. This meant that while horses were great for speed, oxen remained in use, as they are still, for hauling heavy loads.

The movement of people and goods were important to ancient governments, and they often tried to regulate transportation. Some tried to do it all at once, as did the Qin Dynasty of China of (221–207 B.C.E.), regulating even the lengths of axles so that the ruts in roads would be evenly spaced and could be used by all carts. Others built up their regulations through many years of traditions, as in ancient India. Still others, like the Romans, imitated the regulations of other peoples. Each culture reflected its customs in its transportation. For instance, the Romans regarded pedestrian traffic to be essential to their way of life, and they therefore forbad produce carts in their cities during the day and built sidewalks of raised stone that forced wheeled vehicles to slow down, protecting pedestrians.

When thinking of pedestrians, it would be well to remember that although the developments in ancient transportation were exciting and sometimes led to dramatic change in the fortunes of civilizations, most people continued to walk. The ancient world was one in which people mostly carried their needs themselves. Even in the advanced culture of China's Han Dynasty (202–220 B.C.E.) road workers were expected to carry all their tools and food themselves, even to remote parts of the empire. Many people were too poor to afford to ride or even to have an animal pull their goods. In some parts of the world, the use of the wheel and beasts of burden came very late or not at all, as in much of the Americas and Pacific islands.

AFRICA

BY JUSTIN CORFIELD

Inland travel in Africa was regarded as particularly hazardous, and most early traders seem to have preferred traveling by boat. Many of the large settlements in North Africa (excluding those in Egypt) were consequently close to the coast. In sub-Saharan Africa there were also large settlements along rivers and around lakes, so it seems probable that vessels were constructed primarily for navigating rivers. Goods were clearly traded along the river Niger from an early date.

Horses were domesticated in the European steppes around 4000 B.C.E. and in Egypt by 3000 B.C.E., so it seems likely that the use of horses for transportation would have come to the rest of Africa through Egypt. The horses people initially used were much smaller than the modern domesticated horse and were better for pulling carts or chariots than carrying riders. The use of the larger cavalry horses came later, and their use quickly spread throughout North Africa where the Carthaginians, Numidians, and others made extensive use of them for relaying messages. Horses or donkeys could be used as pack animals to carry people and important messages or to pull carriages or carts, which were made with solid wheels in Egypt and neighboring areas from at least 3000 B.C.E. Bullocks and oxen were also used for this purpose. The carts they pulled were large wooden ones; some had solid wooden wheels, while others had spoked wheels.

For long-distance travel across deserts and inhospitable terrain (as opposed to forest travel) caravan routes were fairly clearly defined. Camels were the principal beasts of burden in these conditions, and because their feet are sensitive, their escorts cleared paths through the stones that normally litter a desert. In this way routes were established. On shorter journeys where feed was available, horses and donkeys would be used. Oases, wells, and trading posts lay along these defined routes; for reasons of safety and security, these would be no more than one day's journey apart.

Crossing rivers was a task often solved by rafts guided by ropes. The Greek historian Polybius (ca. 200–ca. 118 B.C.E.) refers to the Carthaginians making rafts for their elephants to cross the river Rhône in Europe, and it seems likely that similar rafts would have been used to carry elephants, horses, wagons, people, and goods across rivers in North Africa.

Because the empires of Carthage and Rome were supported largely by slave labor, the used of manual labor for loading and unloading goods from ships would have been commonplace. For some vessels at small ports, it might also have been necessary to load things onto barges for transportation between the ship and its final destination or from the quay to the ship. Many items were transported in barrels, making it comparatively easy to roll them to their destination. Large numbers of slaves would have worked at the docks and in the mines and quarries around Carthage, and they would have carried tools, stones, and other materials by hand. The Carthaginians were well known for their use of elephants,

Petroglyph of camel and horse, from the Sahara Desert at Tassili, Algeria, North Africa (© Board of Regents of the University of Wisconsin System. Photographer: Jeanne Tabachnick)

and some could have been used for moving large amounts of stones or other items. Elephants also could have been used to help pull rafts across rivers.

An early method of transportation in the Sahara region was the chariot. Many pictures of chariots appear on wall paintings and on pots. They tend to indicate the prevalence of chariots along several established trade routes. One runs from Essaouira in Morocco through the deserts of modern-day Mauritania to Timbuktu. Another from the region around Edjele in southeastern Algeria also goes through to Mauritania and, halfway through, connects with another route that comes from the Al-Kufrah group of oases in southeastern Libya. Although these chariots are similar in all places—with horses pulling a chariot, often with semicircular sides, on which a person is standing—there have been doubts cast by historians about whether a chariot was a common method of transportation or merely a military vehicle or something for public entertainment, as in chariot racing.

Many people traveling together had to travel by foot. From the description of many North African towns of the period, it appears that people heading from one town to another would gather in the morning at a particular gate or market so they could cross the farmland or desert in a large company to inhibit assault or robbery. Bandits, violent peoples, and other problems often made traveling by foot hazardous, and it appears that there was little land contact between many of the sub-Saharan civilizations in the ancient world. This can be clearly seen through the transmission of technology such as the use of iron. The use of iron outside Egypt started in Nubia and progressed over many centuries down the east coast of Africa, missing many of the powerful inland kingdoms such as that of the Buganda in modern-day Uganda. As a result, knowledge of the technology traveled from Nubia to the coast of southern Africa far more quickly than the comparatively shorter distance to the kingdom of Buganda.

EGYPT

BY AMR KAMEL

Written and pictorial sources from as early as the Predynastic Period (ca. 5500–3100 B.C.E.) of Egypt record land and water transportation. Besides its obvious importance in everyday activities, transportation was deeply rooted in Egyptian religious ritual and beliefs, notably the solar cycle: The sun god, Ra, who was born in the east, sailed during the day across the "celestial wasters" (the sky) in his "day boat" before descending at sunset in the west into the hereafter and the womb of his mother, Nut. Then he sailed from west to east in his "night boat," to be reborn again at dawn.

Approaching the hereafter was a favorite theme of the Egyptians, who in their tomb art often represented this final journey as a boat ride that took the mummy from the Nile's east bank (the living world) to the west bank (the realm of the dead—the "Beautiful West," as Egyptian texts called it), where the gate to the hereafter waited to be entered.

Three factors especially affected the development of transportation throughout the history of ancient Egypt: trade, warfare, and mining and quarrying activities. The creation of an extensive network of routes and highways spanning the whole country facilitated not only the transportation of goods but also the movement of military forces, specifically along Egypt's southern frontier with Nubia and its northeastern one with the Near East. These routes included fortifications and way stations, which also formed part of a communications system. As for mining and quarrying, a government office established as early as the Third Dynasty (ca. 2649–ca. 2575 B.C.E.) and known as Masters of the Roads was responsible for coordinating and maintaining the land routes through the desert to quarries and mines. These roads required water stations and wells at regular intervals.

Besides these overland routes Egypt maintained a sea road into the eastern Mediterranean. From the inland port of Memphis large cargo ships descended a branch of the Nile to the sea, carrying trade goods or, in wartime, military supplies to Syria and Palestine. Because of the dominant influence of the Nile, water transportation played a much greater role in Egypt than in some other ancient civilizations. The Nile was the principal communication artery and provided the easiest and cheapest means of transportation. When population centers or other important areas lay distant from the Nile, the Egyptians linked them to the river by digging canals. Weni, a Sixth Dynasty (ca. 2323–ca. 2150 B.C.E.) administrator of the southern province (modern-day Aswān), mentioned a canal he built at the first cataract of the Nile to ease the movement of boats past these rapids. Presumably this was the same canal later cleaned by Sesostris III (r. ca. 1878–ca. 1841? B.C.E.) to facilitate his military campaign into Nubia. Necho II (r. 610–595 B.C.E.) dug a canal to connect the Nile with the Red Sea. This waterway was later maintained and deepened by the Persians and by the Ptolemaic pharaohs of the Greco-Roman Period (323 B.C.E.–395 C.E.). The Greek historian Herodotus remarked that two large ships could navigate the canal side by side.

The ancient Egyptians used boats and barges to carry people all along the Nile (or simply to ferry them across it) and to transport grain, cattle, and many other kinds of cargo. Water transportation linked the royal capital with all other cities and villages along length of the river. It aided in collecting grain or taxes from these places and transporting them to the central storehouses. River transport also figured prominently in religious festivals. During the famous Valley Feast, for example, statues of the god Amon; his consort, Mut; and their son, Knonsu, were carried in an elaborate boat procession from the Karnak temple down the river to Deir el-Bahri on the west bank to visit their ancestors. Art from private tombs at Thebes as well as textual evidence show that this festival was also an occasion for the public to cross the Nile and visit their relatives' tombs on the west bank. An echo of this custom still exists in present-day Egypt, where people celebrate certain feast days in cemeteries in which their relatives are buried.

Although many boats on the Nile were conducting official government business, apparently there were other craft operating for private profit. Texts from the New Kingdom (ca. 1550–1070 C.E.) mention lump-sum payments given to captains of these vessels as freight fees, part of which were portioned out among the crew at the captain's discretion. Literary sources regularly portray ferrymen as greedy and their fees as exorbitant. Even the goddess Isis had to give the ferryman Nemty a golden ring to see her son Horus in his competitions with his uncle Seth. In the Book of the Dead ferrymen make all sorts of excuses to the deceased about the unreadiness of their boats to cross the celestial river, presumably to extort higher pay. The New Kingdom writer Amenemope described the character of the evil person in a telling comparison: "He acts like the ferryman in knitting words: He goes forth and comes back arguing." Most of the mummies found in Egypt from the Greco-Roman Period gripped golden coins in their hands to pay the ferrymen in the hereafter.

The primary mode of land travel throughout ancient Egypt was by foot; even high government officials and armies normally traveled that way, as a set of model figures from the tomb of Mesheti at Assiut from the Eleventh Dynasty (ca. 2040–ca. 1991 B.C.E.) reveals. Art from temples and tombs shows ancient Egyptians walking in funerals, in holy processions during festivals, and the like, in which the distance involved was relatively short, but for many centuries there was no alternative to walking for long land journeys as well.

Donkeys have been the principal beasts of burden in Egypt from prehistory to the present. Art at Deir el-Medina shows donkeys carrying water, wood, grain, straw, hay, dung, and in one case an offering to a goddess up steep paths from the riverbank. No depictions survive from ancient Egypt of people riding donkeys as their descendants do in modern-day Egypt, although one scene preserved on an Old Kingdom (ca. 2575–2134 B.C.E.) tomb at Saqqara shows the tomb's owner supervising his farm activities while riding in a litter borne by donkeys.

Several texts describe caravans of donkeys used for long-distance overland transport. The biography of Harkhuf, a Sixth Dynasty caravan leader, reports that he returned from one of his many trips to Nubia with 300 donkeys laden with all sorts of trade goods. Sabni, Harkhuf's contemporary, mentions using 100 donkeys in his mission to the south to recover the body of his father, who had been murdered there.

Wheeled vehicles apparently originated in Sumer during the early fourth millennium B.C.E. and were later adopted by the Egyptians. The earliest example, from the New Kingdom, is a gold model of a four-wheeled wagon carrying a boat. Although it is unclear whether the model is realistic or merely symbolic, heavy wagons must obviously have existed in order for it to be made at all. Scenes of Ramses II (r. ca. 1290–ca. 1224 B.C.E.) at the battle of Kadesh show an ox-drawn wagon, presumably being used to transport supplies needed on the battlefield.

Horses and the light horse-drawn chariots were introduced to Egypt from the ancient Near East around 1700 B.C.E. as a means of transportation and quickly became invaluable military resources. New Kingdom texts and pictures indicate that kings and nobles used horses for riding and to draw chariots for travel and in hunting expeditions in the desert. However, horseback riding apparently was not greatly favored by the Egyptians.

The animal that many people automatically associate with desert transportation, the camel, was a relative latecomer to Egypt. Domesticated centuries earlier in the Near East, the single-humped camel or dromedary came into widespread use in Egypt during the Greco-Roman Period. Able to carry about five times as much as a donkey and to travel for extended periods without water, camels became invaluable for the long-distance transport of both riders and trade goods across the Egyptian deserts.

THE MIDDLE EAST

BY KIRK H. BEETZ

In the ancient Near East early roads consisted of trails pounded flat by the feet of travelers over the course of centuries. Here, as elsewhere in the prehistoric world, for many thousands of years transportation simply meant people walking, carrying on their backs such loads as they could bear. The first pack animal (meaning an animal used to carry loads on its back) in the region was the donkey, which was domesticated in Africa or the Near East sometime before 3500 B.C.E. Oxen, domesticated in the same general timeframe as donkeys, were used mainly as draft animals, pulling plows and towing carts in farm fields. Although they were very strong, oxen were too slow to be of much use for long-distance hauling. The first Near Eastern vehicles for carrying cargo were probably sledges. A sledge is essentially a framework of wood on which loads are dragged across the ground. Early sledges were soon improved by adding runners, which significantly reduced the resistance met in pulling them. It is likely that the first wheeled vehicle was a modified sledge.

The peoples of Mesopotamia were not the only inventors of wheels: Wheeled toys have been found at ancient sites in the Americas. The Mesopotamian insight was to use wheels for transportation. The old notion that the idea for the wheel came from using logs as rollers for moving heavy objects, with the logs eventually wearing thin in the middle where the weight rolled over them, leaving wider "wheels" at the sides, is probably mistaken, because wheels cut horizontally out of tree trunks quickly fall apart. Solid wheels needed to be made from planks cut vertically from tree trunks. The actual inspiration for the wheel as transportation may have been the potter's wheel.

The first known depiction of a wheeled vehicle comes from the Sumerian city of Uruk (in what is now southern Iraq) and dates to around 3500 B.C.E. It shows a sledgelike body fitted with solid wheels. The wheels were made of three boards laid side by side and held together by two boards that crossed them on the inside of the wheel. They were fixed to axles, and the axle and wheels rotated as one unit. This made maneuvering difficult, but it still allowed two or more animals to pull together as a team and thus to haul much heavier loads than ever before. Wheeled vehicles quickly became vital to the growth of cities, to which supplies had to be carried from the countryside. By 3000 B.C.E. wheeled carts had become common.

Also around 3000 B.C.E. wheelwrights added rims to their wheels to reduce wear. At first they simply studded the outer edges of the wooden wheels with nails. This made the solid wheels more durable, but even heavier. In about 2000 B.C.E. rims made of bands of copper were introduced. At about the same time, people discovered that heated wood could be bent. This discovery led to the spoked wheel. The rim became a circle of bent wood protected by a band of copper and connected to the hub by spokes. The first spoked wheels had two wide spokes. Wheelwrights experimented with different numbers of narrow spokes, with four- and six-spoked wheels becoming common. Spoked wheels were much lighter than solid ones and thus allowed greater speed.

Transportation technology advanced still further with the making of wheels that turned independently of each other and of the axle. This innovation greatly increased maneuverability (although many simple wagons and farm carts continued to use the cruder construction of fixed wheels and axles). Among other things, the combination of light spoked wheels and independent rotation led to the development, sometime around 2500 B.C.E., of the chariot. This most famous of ancient vehicles had two wheels and eventually took a wide variety of forms. At one extreme were light, swift models used for racing or for delivering messages. At the other were heavy, armored war chariots that carried, in addition to the driver, archers and lancers.

Neither the improvements to the wheel nor the invention of the chariot would have meant much without a fast, strong animal to pull the new vehicles. That animal was the horse. Horses may have been domesticated in Ukraine in the fourth millennium B.C.E. Although the nomadic peoples of central Asia rode horses, the animals may not have appeared in the Near East until about 2500 B.C.E., when Sumerians hitched them four abreast to pull four-wheeled battlewagons. The value of horses must have been obvious throughout the region after about the 1700s B.C.E., when the Hyksos, a southwest Asian people who migrated as far as Egypt, used them to great effect in both war and peace. At about the same time, the Hittites swept down from what is now north-central Turkey aboard horse-drawn battle chariots and conquered much of northern Mesopotamia and modern-day Syria. Their enemies soon adopted this same lethal combination. When the Egyptian pharaoh Ramses II finally dealt the Hittite Empire a crushing defeat, at Kadesh, in Syria, about 1275 B.C.E., it was in one of the greatest horse-and-chariot battles of all time.

Of all the people of the ancient Near East the Persians may have made best peacetime use of the horse's potential. Persian rulers created a large network of roads to connect their empire, including the Royal Road, which spanned the Near East from the city of Susa near the Persian Gulf to the

Achaemenid Persian gold model chariot dating to the fifth to fourth century B.C.E. from the region of Takht-i Kuwad, Tadjikistan (© The Trustees of the British Museum)

city of Sardis near the Aegean, covering 1,600 miles. The Persians developed a system of way stations where horses could be cared for and exchanged, allowing messengers to cover about 180 miles a day, riding from Susa to Sardis in nine days—a rate of travel unheard of at the time. Although it was not as fast as the horse, the mule—a cross between a female horse and a male donkey—contributed greatly to transportation as both a pack animal and a draft animal. Mules tolerated heat and cold well, had tough hides, and could carry heavier loads than donkeys could. The Sumerians were using mules by the third millennium B.C.E.

For long-distance travel in the desert, however, neither horses nor mules could compete with a later arrival in the Near East, the camel, which was far better adapted to hot, dry conditions. The one-humped dromedary was probably domesticated in Arabia around 1200–1100 B.C.E., quickly revolutionizing long-distance trade. Camel caravans made it possible to transport aromatics like frankincense and myrrh from the southern Arabian kingdoms northward to Mesopotamia, Syria, and the Levant. In Iran two-humped Bactrian camels were used for similar purposes. These animals originated in the Mongolian area, but by the third millennium B.C.E. they had reached the Iranian plateau. In addition, dromedary-Bactrian hybrids were being bred by the early second millennium B.C.E. These animals became the heavy-duty trucks of antiquity, capable of carrying loads of half a ton and with far greater tolerance of extremes of heat and cold than either purebred dromedaries or Bactrians.

Inland water travel was rare in the Near East except on the Tigris and Euphrates rivers. Both rivers posed problems for people who traveled on them, because they tended to fill with silt as well as to jump their banks periodically to forge new courses to the sea. By the Early Dynastic Period (ca. 2900–ca. 2340 B.C.E.) barges moved up and down these rivers, carrying goods and people. Sometimes oceangoing ships sailed up the rivers, transporting goods from the east. Smaller boats made of animal skins stretched over wooden frames were commonly used on the rivers to transport only a few people or for fishing.

ASIA AND THE PACIFIC

BY KIRK H. BEETZ

Most ancient peoples of Asia traveled on foot. Even after the domestication of draft animals and the introduction of the wheel, transportation usually meant people walking, carrying loads on their shoulders and backs. One of the remarkable things about ancient peoples was the large amounts of goods they transported in this manner, trekking through dangerous, frequently very dry or very cold environments. The paths they wore in the earth on these journeys often became the roads of empires.

On the many large Asian islands between the Indian and Pacific oceans dense tropical forests often impeded land transportation. On such islands as Sumatra and Java water transportation was the better choice for moving goods over any but the shortest distances. People poled or paddled boats such as dugout canoes and bamboo rafts over the sinuous waters of rivers, streams, and swamps. Even on the mainland, in Indochina and much of southern Asia, dense forests inhibited travel. People walked the trails of tapirs and elephants to make their way to streams where they could use boats. On many Pacific islands, forests were thick enough to inhibit travel. The islanders often found it easier to travel by boat in the ocean around their islands than to try to travel great distances inland. For large islands, such as New Guinea, islanders made their ways to streams and used dugout canoes to carry themselves and goods. In open areas such as those in Australia, people of the Pacific continued to rely on transportation on foot through the ancient era.

The amount of goods a walker could carry was obviously limited by his or her strength. In many parts of Asia poles were set across the shoulders of two people, enabling them to carry weights greater than one person could bear. From very early times people also used sledges for heavy loads. The early sledges, little more than rough wooden frames on which goods were dragged across the ground, were soon improved by the addition of sledlike runners. This innovation may have occurred in the far north of Asia. Even after the introduction of the wheel, sledges remained the preferred mode of transportation over mud, marshes, snow, and ice. For the nomadic peoples of Siberia sledges became essential to their way of life because they frequently had to pack up and move their heavy animal-skin-and-wood tents and other goods to new places.

When the domestication of draft animals reached Asia is not known, but by 3500 B.C.E. farmers near the mouth of the Yangtze River were using oxen to pull plows. The wheel as a means of transportation was first used in Sumer, in the Near East, before 3500 B.C.E. and spread from there. The original wheels consisted of three boards held together by two boards fitted crosswise on the inside of the wheel. These solid wheels were very heavy. The Harappans of the Indus River valley (2600–1500 B.C.E.) probably used four-wheeled wagons pulled by two oxen apiece. These heavy vehicles enabled them to transport enough grain to fill the huge granaries in their cities, providing a food reserve against hard times.

For many centuries in ancient India oxen remained the favored animals for hauling carts and wagons. They were so valuable that in some places in India it was punishable by death to kill one. Even long after the domesticated horse was introduced to India, oxen were preferred for pulling wagons. By 300 B.C.E. Indian traders formed long caravans of hundreds of wagons pulled by oxen. Ox-drawn carts of supplies followed Indian armies to war. Oxen were slower than horses but tolerated India's climate better. Thus horses served mainly to carry riders or to pull light chariots.

Two-wheeled chariots had the advantage of being faster than four-wheeled wagons. They transported elite warriors to battle and the rich through cities. Sometime after 2000 B.C.E. spoked wheels—lighter and therefore faster than solid wheels—were introduced to India. Another innovation improved maneuverability: Originally, axles and wheels formed one unit, rotating together, which made chariots, carts, and wagons difficult to turn. Eventually, wheelwrights found ways to allow wheels to turn independently of each other. The wheels could thus rotate at different speeds, allowing fast, tight turns without skidding.

By 2600 B.C.E. wheeled vehicles had appeared in China, probably introduced by nomads from central Asia who had learned this technology from Mesopotamians. Solid wheels and wheels fixed to axles presented the same problems to the Chinese as they did to the Indians, but the use of solid-wheeled carts persisted in southern China and southern Asia as they did in India, probably because of their durability and ease of construction. Although China had two great river systems, the Yangtze and Yellow River, the rivers wound through the landscape so much that the Chinese found it took longer to move on the rivers than to travel by land, which led to many road building projects to improve land transportation.

It was probably also nomads of central Asia who introduced war chariots to China. By 2000 B.C.E. people in what is now northern China were using wheels with 18 spokes. Chariots with spoked wheels, pulled by horses, were of great value to the Shang Dynasty (ca. 1500–ca. 1045 B.C.E.). The chariot, even a heavy, lumbering one, gave Shang armies a big advantage in battle and in the transportation of military supplies against enemies who often were limited to being on foot. The advantage became even greater when Chinese wheelwrights, like those in India, discovered how to let wheels turn independently. Meanwhile, Shang four-wheeled wagons appear to have remained clumsy vehicles because the forward axle was fixed in place and could not easily shift to follow a winding road, but they were nevertheless important for transporting heavy cargoes.

The Scythians of central Asia introduced the stirrup to the Chinese. A Scythian stirrup was just a leather loop, but it gave a rider greater stability and greater control of his mount. In about 380 B.C.E. the Chinese made a stirrup of metal rather than leather. It allowed a rider to stand up in his or her stirrups and provided enough stability that an archer could shoot accurately while riding. Until this innovation chariots had been the best mobile platform for archers. The Scythians also introduced the use of a blanket for padding under a saddle; the Chinese modified this idea by padding the saddle itself.

The Chinese were probably the inventors of the double shaft for vehicles, introducing two-wheeled carts with double shafts and one horse. The shaft of a cart or wagon is a pole extending forward, to which animals are hitched so that they can pull the vehicle. Before the introduction of the double shaft, carts had one shaft. A single shaft, however, required two draft animals, one on each side of the shaft, because a single animal would naturally pull the shaft toward the side to which it was attached. The double shaft had poles to each side of one draft animal, allowing it to pull a cart and keep it in a straight line. After 100 B.C.E. double-shafted carts became common in China.

Despite the great advances in technology, much transportation of goods was still a matter of humans carrying loads. China had many regions where the only roads were merely footpaths. Sometime around the first century C.E. an unknown Chinese inventor introduced the wheelbarrow. Essentially a small human-powered cart, this humble vehicle soon became an invaluable tool for transportation, carrying goods not only along country lanes but through the narrow streets of big cities as well, hauling tools and produce between fields and homes and moving countless tons of supplies and raw materials for the building of roads, dams, and other public projects.

EUROPE

BY MICHAEL J. O'NEAL

During the Palaeolithic, Mesolithic, and most of the Neolithic periods people in Europe traveled mainly by foot. In most cases they did not travel great distances, but sometimes they went on long treks. The frozen so-called Iceman found in the Alps in 1991 was traveling north from Italy, perhaps to escape pursuers, and was crossing the Alps when he died around 3300 B.C.E. Rivers and large lakes posed obstacles, and dugout canoes were the best means of crossing these bodies of standing water. Wetlands were crossed with wooden trackways.

In northern Europe skis were used by travelers at a very early date. They were probably invented in many different places once people began to adapt to modern climatic conditions after the ice age. Skis were found preserved in a bog in Hoting, Sweden, dating back some 4,500 years, and hundreds of others have been found throughout Scandinavia. Further, a 4,500-year-old rock carving depicting a man skiing with a hunting weapon in his hands has been found on the island of Rodoy in northern Norway, and numerous other rock carvings illustrate groups of people on skis. Russian researchers found skis in the Altay region of central Asia that are at least 6,000 years old. The word for *ski* is similar in language communities as distant as Finland and Siberia, suggesting that skis were developed across most of Eurasia very long ago.

During the fourth millennium B.C.E. two developments had a profound effect on transportation in prehistoric Europe: the domestication of the horse and the invention of the wheel. Around 3500 B.C.E. the inhabitants of the steppes (vast, open grasslands) of eastern Europe and western Asia began to keep horses as livestock, initially just for food. They subsequently discovered that horses could be ridden. Archaeological evidence includes bit marks on teeth found in horse skeletons from the third millennium B.C.E., though saddles were not used until after the fall of the Roman Empire and the stirrup was a still later innovation. The domestication of the horse and the invention of horse riding had an enormous impact on the mobility of the peoples of Eurasia. It enabled them to migrate over immense distances. It transformed warfare. In particular, it contributed to the spread of the Indo-European language, the ancient common tongue from which numerous languages in Europe and parts of the Middle East and Asia descended.

Skis and the horse can transport one person, but they are of little use in transporting goods or agricultural produce. To that end, Europeans discovered that they could use animals to pull wagons, carriages, and carts. The earliest European wagons, which date to the end of the fourth millennium B.C.E., were clumsy, lumbering vehicles. They were probably first pulled

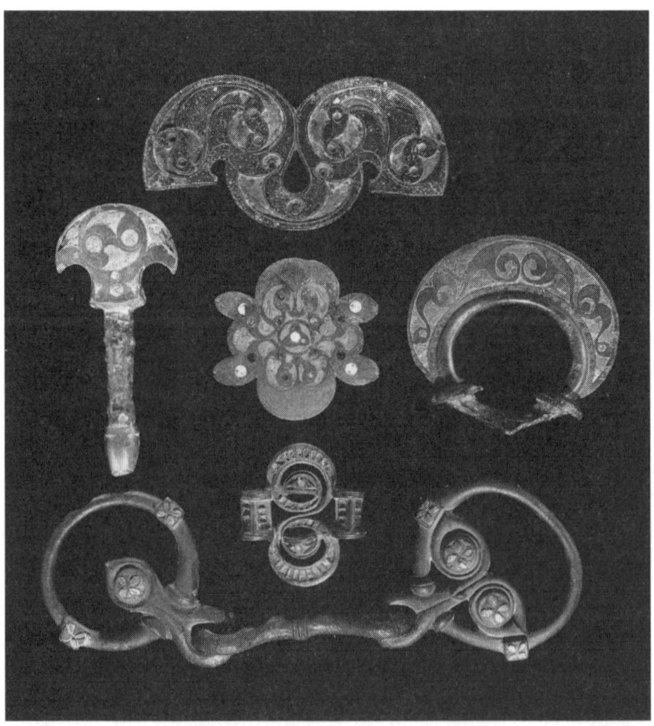

Horse harness fittings from Iron Age Britian (1–100 C.E.) (© The Trustees of the British Museum)

by oxen and only later by horses. The wheels were solid and heavy, typically constructed out of three joined pieces of wood. The axle was fixed so that only the wheels turned. In time the Europeans discovered ways to make wagons and carts more maneuverable. One chief innovation, dating from the second millennium B.C.E., was the use of spoked wheels rather than solid wheels. The earliest wheels were made entirely of wood, but Celtic metalworkers in central Europe learned to attach a metal band around wheels, making them far more durable on rough roads. Another innovation was the development of axles that turned, making wagons and carriages much more nimble.

Wagons pulled by oxen were used primarily by farmers in their fields and around their settlements during the Bronze Age. The archaeological record provides enough evidence for archaeologists to make good guesses as to what such carriages looked like. Among the most important finds are portions of wagons discovered in Holland. These wagons were constructed with solid wheels (that is, wheels without spokes), a forked undercarriage, a forked shaft, axles, and a large wickerwork "basket" on top for passengers or materials. Wagon technology improved during the Iron Age. The tomb at Hochdorf in Germany that dates to approximately 530 B.C.E. contained a four-wheeled wagon about 6.5 feet long, with a pole for attaching it to a team of oxen or horses extending over 6.5 more feet. Each wheel had 10 spokes. A similar wagon was found in a tomb at Vix in France.

Horses and particularly lightweight carriages were used primarily by the social elites. Among the most important carriage finds are six carriages called the Dejbjerg carriages, named for the bog in western Denmark where they were found. These carriages might have been built by the Celts in central Europe, who developed a tradition of expert carriage making. These wagons were probably used by headmen, and probably on ceremonial occasions primarily. They were much lighter than agricultural wagons and featured spoked and iron-banded wheels and bronze ornamentation. They were constructed of ash and beech, both of which are especially durable woods.

In addition to carriages and wagons the Europeans developed a type of chariot. The ancient Celts in Ireland drove a vehicle called a *carpat*, a word similar to the Latin word *carpentum* used by the ancient Romans, to refer to these vehicles. Historians long believed that these words and the vehicles they named were unrelated, but more recent research suggests that they are in fact related. The chariot was a light, two-wheeled, horse-drawn vehicle mounted on a flexible suspension. Above the suspension was a platform on which the rider stood and a seat—all protected by a fabric covering called a tent. Examples of these chariots, dating from as far back as 500 B.C.E., have also been found both in Yorkshire in England and on the Continent.

The chariot was used for purposes of warfare, but that was not its primary purpose. As a military vehicle, it served to transport soldiers and their gear, but actual fighting was done on foot. The chariot, rather like a modern-day sports car, was a mark of status. Members of the elite class used chariots to travel about or visit their neighbors in stately fashion. They were also used by young men who wanted to display their style and daring, for the chariot was used in races and, in particular, for such feats as riding pell-mell over creeks or ditches; the flexible suspension enabled the rider, at least most of the time, to make a relatively soft landing.

The use of wheeled vehicles for long-distance transportation required the improvement of the road system of ancient Europe, which had existed for millennia as beaten tracks through the forest. Roads connected the Celtic *oppida*, or towns, which greatly facilitated trade and movement of military groups. The invading Romans made use of this road structure as well as improving it further. The Roman Empire relied on efficient transportation for administration and trade, so in addition to building roads, the Romans built some canals in Europe. In the first century of the Common Era, the Roman general Drusus built a canal that connected the Rhine River with the IJssel River in Holland. In England the Romans built the 11-mile-long Fossdyke canal near Lincoln, connecting the river Witham with the river Trent, and the 40-mile-long Caerdyke canal in the same area. Otherwise, the Romans found canal building to be impracticable in their northern colonies.

GREECE

BY CHRISTOPHER BLACKWELL

Transportation in the ancient Greek world was dominated by the sea. Overland travel was arduous and often unnecessary. The Greek mainland is mountainous and rugged, and the Greek population was concentrated in the coastal areas to the east and west of the northern Balkan Peninsula, around the edges of the southern peninsula of the Peloponnese, and scattered across the islands of the Aegean Sea and along the coast of Asia Minor.

The many separate population centers of Greece were not politically unified in any sense of the word until the late fourth century B.C.E., and even then only into a relatively loose structure of military dominance by Macedonia. Greek communities, isolated by geography and largely self-sufficient, had no need for swift overland commerce—in contrast, for example, to the Persian Empire, whose bureaucracy required and provided a network of "Royal Roads" with well-maintained stations set at intervals and supplying food, rest, and fresh animals for official travelers.

Land transportation among the ancient Greeks was largely a matter of walking. Horses were not common outside the plains of Thessaly in the northeast of Greece and were not prized as draft animals. Along the few main roads mules or oxen were the preferred beasts of burden. Oxen (cattle trained to the harness) were stronger than mules or horses but very slow. Mules (the offspring of a female horse and a male donkey) afforded the best combination of strength and speed.

Overland travel was made perilous by bandits, especially in places where roads passed far from centers of population. The myth of the Athenian king Theseus emphasizes the heroism

TURNING SEA INTO LAND AND LAND INTO SEA

When Xerxes, the great king of Persia, was planning to invade Greece in the early decades of the fifth century B.C.E., he faced a number of challenges of transport. His army numbered at least 100,000—the numbers are not known precisely, and ancient sources are notoriously unreliable in these matters—and it was supported by a vast naval fleet. Xerxes had to get his army across the Hellespont, the channel of water connecting the Black Sea with the Aegean. He also had to get his fleet safely along the coast of Thrace, the territory to the north of the Aegean, and particularly past the Chersonese, an area of peninsulas extending into the sea, regularly wracked by storms.

Xerxes' famous solution was to "turn sea into land and land into sea," as the Greek historian Herodotus reports. He built a bridge over the Hellespont, a line of barges secured by cables woven from papyrus. His first attempt succumbed to the currents of the Hellespont, whereupon he had his servants flog the body of water with whips. His second attempt succeeded. To avoid the storms around the capes of the Chersonese, he had his engineers dig a canal across the promontory of Mount Athos (today the site of a famous monastery), allowing his fleet to make the Thracian crossing without entering the Aegean proper. To Herodotus and evidently many of the Greeks, these feats of engineering represented excessive pride, an affront to the gods, and Xerxes' eventual defeat, on sea and on land, seemed only fitting.

of his choice to travel overland between Troezen in the Peloponnese and Athens (a relatively short journey). In historical times, when cargoes of any value were transported overland they tended to go in well-armed caravans, following river valleys. But there were few cargoes that needed carrying long distances by land, and so mule- or ox-drawn wagons were mainly limited to local transport, bearing produce from the countryside to urban markets or cargoes from harbors into cities. The chariot appears in poetry as a vehicle of war but was not used, in war or peace, to any significant extent by the Greeks during the historical period. Most warfare among the ancient Greeks was between neighbors and was dominated by soldiers on foot, who marched to their battles and back home again.

Trade was by sea, with bulky cargoes (most often grain) or valuable cargoes (luxury goods such as particular vintages of wine or fine pottery or textiles) moving from one end of the Mediterranean to the other and beyond. Ancient Greek trade goods have been found in England and Sweden, perhaps brought that far north by merchants looking for tin, a metal alloyed with copper to make bronze. (Copper was common in the Greek world, but tin was not.)

Ironically, given the relative unimportance of land transport, there were occasions when ancient travelers preferred to carry their ships overland rather than sail them on the sea. Ships traveling between east and west in the Mediterranean could choose to round the southern end of the Peloponnese, risking bad weather from the open sea to the south, or to cross the Isthmus of Corinth by land. The Corinthians had constructed a dragway across the isthmus and would (for a fee) carry merchant ships across that narrow strip of land on rollers (today there is a canal).

ROME

BY KIRK H. BEETZ

The earliest remains archaeologists have found at the city of Rome are graves dating from the 800s B.C.E., but Roman tradition held that the city was founded in 753 B.C.E. By this time many of the ancient world's most important innovations in transportation had already been made, primarily in the Near East, and much of this Near Eastern technology had found its way into Italy. At the same time, Celts in Europe were making marvelous carts and chariots, experimenting and innovating in their design and uses. Still, even though the Romans acquired all the advanced transportation technology, the favored Roman method for hauling even heavy goods was humans trudging along under their burdens. Slaves were abundant, and it was easier to load them up with whatever needed to be transported, whether it was bricks or wheat, than to invest money in beasts of burden and their maintenance. Even the Roman army was apt to carry what it needed on foot. Most of its soldiers were farmers used to long hours on their feet, and the army tended to favor infantry over cavalry. Walking remained the most common mode of transport for the poor throughout the history of ancient Rome

Transporting goods by water was usually much less expensive than hauling them over land. In the time of Diocletian (r. 284–305 C.E.), it was less expensive to transport goods across the Mediterranean from Spain to Syria than to transport them over 75 miles of land. But when it came to personal travel, Romans preferred to go overland rather than travel by ship. Many did travel by ship, especially if they were in a hurry, but dry land seemed more secure to most Romans. They were also avid tourists who liked to see the sights wherever they went.

Oxen were the primary beasts of burden for pulling carts. For small farmers, oxen and a cart were essential for bringing produce to markets in towns or cities. The carts were heavy affairs, made of thick planks of wood with either two or four solid wheels. On most big Roman carts the axles were fixed to the carriage body, making turns very difficult. It required the strength of oxen to maneuver them. When taking produce to a city, the farmer walked beside the oxen rather than riding on the cart. He traveled at night, because carts carrying farm products were forbidden to be in cities during the day.

Cities were designed to favor pedestrians. There were sidewalks, and cities often had laws requiring people who owned property next to a sidewalk to provide awnings that protected pedestrians from the sun and rain. Crosswalks consisted of large flat stones laid a step apart across streets. Cart and carriage drivers had to guide the wheels of their vehicles slowly between the stones. Streets were often full of people, further slowing wheeled traffic. Wealthy people rode in palanquins, using them like battering rams to force their way through streets. The palanquin was adopted from the Near East and consisted of an enclosed carriage body on two poles. The poles were carried on the shoulders of four or more slaves or servants. In large cities it was common to see these palanquins and their bearers marching through crowds, their passengers hidden behind drawn curtains. Palanquins were often marked with the symbols of their owners and would be followed by clients of the owners, hoping for a handout whenever the palanquins stopped.

The Romans were probably the greatest road builders of the ancient world. Not only were their city streets paved and well maintained but so were the roads and highways that connected the regions of the empire. Such roads had advantages for commerce, and entrepreneurs established carriage services for transporting passengers in cities and around the countryside. A common sight was the *raeda*, a four-wheeled cart that was large enough to hold several passengers. It was heavy, slow, and difficult to maneuver, but Roman engineers tried to lay out roads as straight as possible, which minimized the number of turns a vehicle would need to make if it stayed on a main road without making detours. There were lighter carts that also carried passengers. Lighter carriage bodies and light, spoked wheels meant that every bump in the road was felt, but with spoked wheels and teams of four horses drawing them, light carriages could cover as much as a hundred miles a day on Roman-built roads. Sometimes Romans chose to ride in a light, two-wheeled carriage called a *cisium*, which could function like a taxicab. Many Romans chose to ride horseback when traveling. Inns and even whole villages arose along major thoroughfares to provide services for all kinds of freight and passengers, with cartwrights and stables available.

Chariot with horse and rider, from a sarcophagus at Heraklion (Alison Frantz Photographic Collection, American School of Classical Studies at Athens)

The lightest cart, the *birota*, could carry about 150 pounds, and the heaviest, the *angaria*, could carry about 1,100 pounds. Neither was well suited for carrying the monumental stones that the Romans used for building. Such stones were often fitted with posts in their sides on which wheels were placed, and the whole was towed as if it were a huge cart. Liquids were transported in wooden barrels seated in wheeled frames. For pulling their carts, Romans used oxen, mules, and horses. They lacked an efficient towing harness for horses, which limited horses to light carts and chariots. Oxen were common throughout the empire, although mules seem to have been favored in dry areas because they could better tolerate hot, dry conditions. Pack mules were extensively used for carrying goods in bad weather and on narrow paths.

For moving heavy goods, Romans preferred watercraft whenever they could avail themselves of them. Although they occasionally built canals in Europe, by and large they relied on existing waterways. For instance, the city of Rome itself depended on the Tiber River. Ships laden with grain and other goods from North Africa would dock at the nearby port city of Ostia at the mouth of the Tiber, where cargo would be transferred either to barges or to land transportation. The barges were hauled upstream by slaves pulling thick, heavy ropes along the riverbank.

Horses were favored by Romans for pulling chariots and other light vehicles. Horses often worked in teams of four not only in chariot races but also in pulling transport vehicles outside cities. Individual riders rode horses for hunting as well as for travel. Romans began using spurs and riding boots in the 300s B.C.E. They also invented horseshoes. The first was the *hipposandal*, which consisted of an iron plate tied to the hoof with leather strips. They eventually developed a horseshoe made of iron that was nailed to the underside of the hoof, much like that used today. The padded saddle was introduced only late in the empire, in the 300s C.E., and was marketed to riders by Roman merchants as a way to reduce the possibility of getting hemorrhoids.

THE AMERICAS

by Michael J. O'Neal

Horses, donkeys, and oxen were not introduced to the Americas until the time of European contact. Meanwhile, the large native animals, such as buffalo, were poorly suited to domestication either for riding or for pulling loads. Some smaller animals, such as the llamas of South America, could be trained to carry modest burdens on their backs but were too small to ride or to use as draft animals. Wheeled vehicles existed only in the form of a few toys, since there were no animals to pull the real thing. Thus, for thousands of years, when ancient Americans traveled by land, they went on foot, carrying whatever they needed with them.

Prehistoric Americans traveled along routes that were determined primarily by two factors. One was the movement of wild game, which they followed in search of food. Migratory animals such as mastodons, deer, elk, and bison created trails through forests and over plains, and ancient Americans followed these trails in search of food. They became adept at reading the signs that nature provided, including hoofprints and the droppings the animals left behind. From these signs they could tell when animals had passed and what they were eating, which provided hunters with clues about where to look for them.

The other factor that determined the footways of ancient Americans was the terrain. Throughout the Americas people were confronted with different types of terrain, from the Rocky Mountains of the American West and the Andes Mountains of South America to the tropical forests of Central America and the woodlands of the eastern half of what is today the United States. When the first Americans crossed the land bridge between Siberia and Alaska and then moved southward, their movements were channeled by a path between two glaciers. They faced changes in elevation, marshes and swamps, ravines, rivers and streams, mountains, and other natural obstacles. Naturally they sought to avoid these obstacles in their travels or, if that was not possible, at least to find the easiest way over them. Many modern roadways, as well as hiking trails in national parks, follow the same tracks left behind by ancient Americans.

During prehistoric times, when people survived by hunting and gathering, they moved about in search of food, often following similar routes each year as the seasons passed. The advent of agriculture required those who adopted this way of life to settle in more or less permanent communities, remaining in one place year-round or at least for much of the year. But circumstances often caused even settled farmers to pack up their belongings and travel, sometimes for great distances. In some cases they were motivated by the basic human need to explore. In other cases changes in climate conditions forced them to seek new farmland, or perhaps a natural disaster such as a flood, earthquake, fire, or volcanic eruption forced them to move.

In time the roadways that people had worn into the ground over generations became used for trade and cultural contact. Roads led to the diffusion of languages and ideas and to the construction of cities that served as administrative centers and hubs for the movement of goods and people. Roads enabled rural people to transport their goods to the cities. Empires such as those of Central America needed roads for communication and in some cases military conquest. In many cases roads were needed to transport raw materials used for building cities. They also led to ceremonial centers, where people gathered for religious purposes.

As time passed, some early Americans traveled by water. Those who settled along waterways or in coastal areas used canoes and small boats, usually for hunting purposes but sometimes to transport goods for trade as well. Most of these early boats were dugout canoes; that is, they were carved out of a single log. Numerous examples of dugout canoes dating to ancient times have been found in the southeast of what is now the United States, with its long coastline and numerous rivers and lakes. Archaeologists have discovered 400 such canoes, and although some date from the later medieval period, others are thousands of years old. In Mesoamerica water became important for the transportation of goods late in the ancient period, and the peoples of the Caribbean islands relied on seacraft to travel from island to island trading goods. By about 300 C.E. the Moche of Peru in South America were using canoes to hunt mammals at sea. This growing reliance on waterways for transportation, however, was a late development in the ancient period. Transportation by foot remained the norm for many millennia.

See also AGRICULTURE; ART; ECONOMY; FESTIVALS; INVENTIONS; METALLURGY; MIGRATION AND POPULATION MOVEMENTS; MILITARY; RELIGION AND COSMOLOGY; ROADS AND BRIDGES; SEAFARING AND NAVIGATION; SHIPS AND SHIPBUILDING; SLAVES AND SLAVERY; TRADE AND EXCHANGE.

FURTHER READING

Lionel Casson, *Travel in the Ancient World* (Baltimore, Md.: Johns Hopkins University Press, 1994).

Jac J. Janssen, *Donkeys at Deir el-Medina* (Leiden, Netherlands: Nederlands Instituut voor het Nabije Oosten, 2005).

M. A. Littauer and J. H. Crouwel, *Wheeled Vehicles and Ridden Animals in the Ancient Near East* (Leiden, Netherlands: E. J. Brill, 1979).

Robert Partridge, *Transport in Ancient Egypt* (London: Rubicon Press, 1996)

Stuart Piggott, *The Earliest Wheeled Transport* (Ithaca, N.Y.: Cornell University Press, 1983).

Stuart Piggott, *Wagon, Chariot and Carriage* (London: Thames and Hudson, 1992).

D. T. Potts, "Camel Hybridization and the Role of *Camelus bactrianus* in the Ancient Near East," *Journal of the Economic and Social History of the Orient* 47, no. 2 (2004): 143–165.

Steve Vinson, "Transportation." In *The Oxford Encyclopedia of Ancient Egypt*, ed. Donald B. Redford, vol. 2 (Cairo: American University Press, 2001): 450–453.

W

war and conquest

INTRODUCTION

In general, historians writing about the ancient world tend to define war as a military enterprise that required long-term preparation and planning and was carried out by one state or national government against another state or government. For the purposes of the definition, nomadic peoples united under a single leader or governing council count as a nation, which is why some historians will refer to nomadic peoples as "nations" even though they did not live in one place with defined borders.

Most anthropologists believe that people have been killing people from the beginning of modern humans. Those very ancient disputes may have begun over offended honor, a mistreated daughter, or the claiming of rights to a fertile territory. Rock paintings dating to tens of thousands of years ago, from Europe, Africa, and Asia, show people killing one another with bows and spears. Some of the combat looks organized, with figures wearing special clothes or body decorations specifically meant for battle.

Exactly when small conflicts became large ones is unknown. For a time the rise of cities in Sumer was thought to have brought about the beginning of war. As the cities grew, they needed more lands to feed their people, and they became envious of each other; for this reason they started killing each other to acquire land and to steal one another's wealth. This would not have begun before 3500 B.C.E. Yet Çatalhüyük in modern-day Turkey dates from about 7200 B.C.E. and was built for defense against large-scale attacks. Between 10,000 and 8000 B.C.E. the residents of Jericho built massive walls and an extraordinarily well-designed tower. Those battlements would seem to have been pointless wastes of valuable time and labor unless they were meant as defense against a large and dangerous threat, such as an army with leadership that would devote time to planning how to defeat such a stronghold. It is possible that someday the exact place and time the first war was fought will be discovered, but at present archaeologists and historians can study only the wars they know about.

War was expensive. It required a large investment of time, people, and goods to wage war. For a society to invest its energy in war, it needed to see value come from war. People had to believe that they were either gaining something valuable through aggression or keeping something valuable through defense. War had objectives that were perceived as valuable, and those objectives could be met only by sacrificing other valuables, such as human lives, money, and labor for public works. In societies in which people had to spend almost every waking moment working just to feed themselves, taking time for war was a great sacrifice. Some societies solved the problem by giving up making their own food and goods and devoting themselves to taking food and goods from other people. In northern China and northern Mesopotamia, for instance, there were nomadic peoples whose lives focused on war and whose societies' efforts centered on annual raids for looting farming communities to the south. In China hundreds or thousands of lives, much labor, and a great deal of wealth was spent on such defenses as tall, wide walls around every city.

The constant warfare that marred much of the ancient world generated an arms race in almost every culture. The classic example comes from ancient Sumer, where warriors used stone clubs to bash in heads, so people made metal helmets to absorb the blows, so weapons makers created metal axes to cut through metal helmets, so armorers styled larger, thicker, and more resilient metal helmets, so weapons makers developed new casting techniques that allowed them to make stronger, larger axes with curved blades that could smash through metal helmets, and so on. Many of the technological advances of ancient peoples were put to use in war, and many advances came from people trying to find better ways to fight wars.

This race in technology was paralleled by changes in military organization and strategy. Whereas the technology of the composite bow made Sargon I ruler of most of the Near East, the strategy of the phalanx helped make the Hittites the military masters of their era. The Neo-Assyrian Empire (1050–609 B.C.E.) combined its weapons and armor technologies with sophisticated deployment of highly trained units devoted to one kind of warfare, such as sappers for bringing down enemy walls, archers for long-range attacks, light infantry for responding quickly to events on the battlefield, heavy infantry to push massed enemy troops out of the way, and chariots for shock attacks to break up enemy formations.

Some historians argue that every great empire of ancient times was built through war. This may be too much of a generalization. For instance, there are the trade empires of ancient southern India to consider, but even those required some military power to keep trade routes free of bandits. What may be noteworthy is that war had its limits. Ancient Rome prospered while its armies looted newly conquered territories, but it declined when it did not continue to do so. During the Han Dynasty (202 B.C.E.–220 C.E.) of China, there was a period in the 100s B.C.E. when its army crushed opponents to the south, the west, and the north but at such a high cost of lives and wealth that its economy nearly collapsed. Even the Neo-Assyrians ended up fighting wars mostly using mercenaries and vassals because it was running out of its own men to fill its armed forces.

Perhaps it is most important in studying the wars of ancient peoples to note how people struggled to meet each day, to feed themselves and their families, and to endure the pain and sorrow that war inflicted on them. For most people most of the time war was something to be survived. Some cultures developed strict rules of warfare that minimized bloodshed, allowing for glory for the leaders and for victories while also allowing most warriors or soldiers to return home unharmed. Still, such cultures eventually either adopted the waging of war as massive bloodshed or were overwhelmed by the armies of cultures that made war a matter of slaughtering enemy troops. Those who failed to learn the lessons of advancing technology and improving military strategy tended to perish. Survival seems to have depended on vigilance, sacrifice, discipline, and sound military doctrine.

AFRICA

BY KIRK H. BEETZ

Rock paintings in southern Africa and in the Sahara show people fighting with bows and spears. The identification of these early people is not clear, but the depictions of conflict continue for thousands of years. By 9000 B.C.E. the people in southern Africa were probably the San, often known as Bushmen. It is not clear what the Bushmen fought over. As hunter-gatherers, they probably did not have much property to defend or covet, but they may have had territories they considered their own. In the often dry plains that many Bushmen inhabited, even a small family group of hunter-gatherers would have needed a wide territory in which to find food. Raids for marriageable women might have been another purpose for conflict. The combat probably involved no more than a dozen fighters at a time. At no time did the Bushmen number as many as 300,000 people, which meant they were so thinly spread over their lands that it would have been very unlikely that they could have gathered together enough people to form anything resembling an army. The same would be true for the small-statured peoples often referred to as Pygmies, who inhabited most of central Africa and much of the east and south.

For the ancient peoples of the Sahara the issue of war and conquest is more complex than for southern Africa. Their rock paintings hint at an evolution of warfare not found elsewhere in Africa. Most depictions of conflict prior to the Herdsmen Period (ca. 5095–ca. 2780 B.C.E.) show naked men in small skirmishes. During the Herdsmen Period some men in battle seem to wear robes, and there may even have been a hierarchy, indicated by a single figure wearing robes that were colored or tailored differently from those of others in his command. It seems that for the cultures depicted, the wearing of clothes may have been reserved for war or other official functions.

During the Herdsmen Period the rock paintings show a diverse ethnic population, with pale figures mixing with dark ones. The primary occupation of people seems to have been herding cattle. It is probable that conflicts focused on stealing cattle. Prestige could be won in a village or group by successfully stealing cattle from another village or group. Wars in which cattle were considered important booty continued into the medieval era. In any case, as time passed, the paintings of battles became increasingly common.

What happened to the ancient warriors of the Sahara grasslands is not entirely known. Some of the pale people and the dark people seem to have mixed, perhaps becoming the Berbers. Others retreated to Egypt. Some retreated to oases as the Sahara slowly dried and created farming communities. Around them developed nomadic groups who created their own culture of war in which they mastered horses and the use of weapons. These groups preyed on the farmers at the oases, forcing them to pay tribute or die. Sometime late during the Horse Period (ca. 2780–ca. 600 B.C.E.) the attacks on the farmers became too much. Apparently, raiders using chariots swept out of the northern Sahara and drove the farmers out. The Greek historian Herodotus (ca. 484–between 430 and 420 B.C.E.) suggested the attackers were the Garamantes, a Berber group from the northern coastal area of North Africa. The fighting was probably very one-sided, with the attackers using not only chariots but also javelins and shields against farmers who had only bows. The farmers were probably part of an ethnic group that already occupied much of West Africa. Their descendants may have been the Bantu-speaking people who eventually spread over most of the continent.

Warfare as modern people think of it, with large numbers of warriors or soldiers united in a single cause, may have taken place in Africa in many places, but this is not known because of the lack of archaeological or written evidence. The earliest records of war tend to come from the earliest literate peoples of Africa, the Egyptians, Kushites, and Axumites of northeastern Africa.

Nubia

Egyptian culture may have begun around 5000 B.C.E. in farming communities in Upper Egypt—the southern half of what became ancient Egypt. By 3500 B.C.E. the culture was spreading north. At the same time, a strong local culture was developing in Nubia, which was south of Egypt. The Nubians of this time were several different groups, some farmers and others pastoralists. By about 2250 B.C.E. a Nubian confederation had formed under one chief just south of Egypt in an area called Wawat. This confederation and Egypt traded with each other. Nubian warriors were noted for their ferocity, and for most of their history after 2250 B.C.E. they were in demand as mercenaries in armies as far away as Mesopotamia. Nonetheless, Wawat and much of the region around it were rich in gold, and for this prized commodity Egypt sent an army to occupy Nubia.

This was not easily done, even though the Nubians' military technology was inferior to that of the Egyptians. The Egyptians had composite bows, an import from the Near East. A composite bow had an inner lining of bone, a middle lining of wood, and an outer lining of animal skin. It sometimes was made of more than one kind of wood, each kind intended to provide strength or springiness. The composite bow was powerful, and the arrows it launched could penetrate the animal-skin shields of the Nubians. Some of the nomads among the Nubians continued to fight for decades by raiding the Egyptians, but the Egyptians built several forts in the region that eventually enabled them to defeat efforts to drive them away.

Kush

There seems to have been much activity south of the Egyptian conquests in Nubia. A kingdom called Karmah, after one of its most important cities, became an important trading center for eastern Africa. Whatever Karmah's military problems, they were significant enough for the kingdom to fortify its cities with walls. By 1650 B.C.E. Karmah had extended its territory almost as far north as the first cataract on the Nile. Karmah had taken advantage of a period of political chaos in Egypt, the Second Intermediate Period (ca. 1640–ca. 1532 B.C.E.). The Egyptian king Thutmose I (r. ca. 1504–ca. 1492 B.C.E.) invaded Karmah. His army sacked the city and extended Egyptian influence south of the fifth cataract of the Nile. Over the next 400 years Egypt tried to make the land it called Kush into a cultural disciple of Egypt. The children of the political elite of Kush were raised in Egypt, where they were taught to worship Egyptian gods, to follow Egyptian customs, and to speak, read, and write Egyptian. By 950 B.C.E. the Kushites had developed a strong kingdom, and its leaders regarded themselves as the true inheritors of ancient Egyptian culture.

Egypt had fallen again into chaos, having become divided among many petty kings who contended for power. The Nile Delta had several independent city-states. A strong dynasty had been founded in Kush by King Alura (r. ca. 780–ca. 760 B.C.E.). The wars in Egypt had cut the Kushites off from worship at important sites of their religion. Thus, Alura's successor, Kashta (r. ca. 760–ca. 747 B.C.E.), sent his son Piankhi (r. 751–716 B.C.E.) in 748 B.C.E. to secure Thebes.

The exact details about the army Piankhi took with him are not known, but it probably numbered more than 10,000 troops. Its principal soldiers were spearmen, still mostly equipped with spears with stone tips. They had chariots but not in great numbers. The Kush had war elephants of a species now probably extinct that was easier to train than the notoriously irritable African elephants from farther south. Piankhi himself probably rode an elephant; at least, Kushite kings are depicted in Kushite art as riding elephants. Their bows were probably still not composite. The organization of the army probably was into infantry, chariots, and elephants. Women could be military leaders in Kush, and it is likely that some of Piankhi's officers, including generals, were women. This suggests that women played other roles in the army, but evidence is scant for their participation in infantry or other units.

Regional Egyptian governors and chieftains usually submitted to Piankhi on his way to Thebes. His object was not to destroy but to preserve, so he did not loot and sack. Instead, he secured access to Thebes, where he worshipped. When he assumed the throne of Kush, he made his capital in Napata, far to the south of Egypt, along the Nile. Napata was a major site for the worship of the Egyptian god Amun, who at the time was the principal deity in Kush.

In the early 720s B.C.E. the Egyptian chief of the city of Saïs in the Nile Delta, Tefnakhte (r. ca. 724–717 B.C.E.), raised an army and navy and marched and sailed south along the Nile. King Nimlot of the city of Hermopolis surrendered to Tefnakhte. Tefnakhte then sent his fleet toward Thebes. How Piankhi actually regarded these events is unclear, but he may have viewed Tefnakhte's aggression toward Thebes as a threat to Kush's influence in Upper Egypt, of which Thebes was the capital. Piankhi sent an army into Egypt. He divided it into two parts, one to intercept Tefnakhte's fleet before it reached Thebes and the other to take Hermopolis from Tefnakhte.

While he had managed to take Hermopolis, Tefnakhte had problems to his rear, because the city of Heracleopolis, south of the river delta, was holding out against a siege by Tefnakhte's forces. Piankhi's army met Tefnakhte's fleet north of Thebes. A little of the battle that followed can be reconstructed. The Kushites were accomplished sailors on the Nile, and they could transport infantry quickly on their boats. The Egyptians' principal weapon was the bow and arrow. Their other weapons, which were bronze, were mostly superior to those of the Kushites. Overall, in a fight on a river, the Egyptians should have had the upper hand. The Kushites were daring fighters, however, noted for their ferocity in combat. If their spearmen could press the Egyptians into close-quarters fighting, they could overwhelm their enemy. Even at this late date, neither side's troops wore much armor. That the Egyptian fleet was decisively defeated suggests that the Kushites managed to board the Egyptian boats and force both sailors and archers into a confrontation best suited to Kush's infantry.

Piankhi then journeyed to Thebes, where he celebrated the Festival of Opet. It may have been at this time that he proclaimed himself pharaoh, thereby establishing the Twenty-fifth Dynasty of Egypt. He then joined his army at Hermopolis, where he directed the siege that resulted in the city's surrender. The wife of Nimlot asked one of Piankhi's wives to persuade him to spare Nimlot's life, which he did. Thereafter Piankhi's army sped to Heracleopolis, which was near surrender. The advantages of Tefnakhte's forces were their superior knowledge of the terrain and their bronze technology. Piankhi's forces had elephants, some warriors equipped with bronze or copper weapons, and a clear chain of command. Tefnakhte had allies and petty princes to supervise, whereas Piankhi was the undisputed commander of his troops, with a clear hierarchy of officers.

Tefnakhte's forces were driven from the field, and Heracleopolis was saved. Its people were starving. Piankhi was said to have been furious at what he saw. The starving of the city's horses especially galled him, perhaps because the horse was his emblem. Tefnakhte and his allies made a stand at the city of Memphis. For the battle Piankhi brought both his fleet and his army to the city. Instead of laying siege, which would have been the accepted military practice for Egyptians, Piankhi led an assault on the city's defenses. Apparently, attacks from both land and river overwhelmed the defenders. Again, Piankhi arrived as a savior of Egyptian culture, not as a conqueror, and it seems that civilians were not harmed.

Piankhi continued first to Heliopolis and then to Athribis, where he defeated allies of Tefnakhte. The chiefs of the cities of the Nile Delta, including Tefnakhte, then paid him homage. Piankhi was content to allow the chiefs to continue to rule their cities as long as they paid him tribute, and he returned to Napata. This made Piankhi the ruler of one of the largest empires of the ancient world, extending more than 1,400 miles north to south, eastward to the Red Sea, and westward to oases in the desert.

What happened militarily over the next several years is unclear. It seems that Nimlot rebelled against Piankhi. Tefnakhte declared himself ruler of Lower Egypt; he died in 717 B.C.E., but his son Bekenrenef succeeded him. Piankhi died in 712 B.C.E. and was succeeded by his brother Shabaka (r. 712–698 B.C.E.), who was a less forgiving conqueror. His army of spearmen, chariots, and elephants ruthlessly crushed the enemy army, and Bekenrenef was burned alive. Shabaka brought a shift in attitude to his rule of Egypt; whereas Piankhi viewed himself as a savior of Egypt, Shabaka viewed himself as the one and only rightful ruler of Egypt. Thus, he took power away from Egypt's chiefs and established a central government bureaucracy led by Kushites to run the empire, and he moved his seat of government about 500 miles north of Napata, to Thebes.

The pharaohs of the Twenty-fifth Dynasty seem to have seen it as their duty to return Egypt to the power and glory it had held during the New Kingdom (ca. 1550–ca. 1070 B.C.E.), a period marked by great public works and Egyptian control of much of Palestine. They rebuilt decaying monuments and temples and built many new ones, and Egypt returned to some of the prosperity it had once known, but Palestine was to be their undoing.

Shabaka and his successor, Shabatka (r. 698–690 B.C.E.), had maintained an alliance with Assyria, but in about 701 B.C.E. the kingdom of Judah, led by Hezekiah (r. ca. 715–ca. 686 B.C.E.), rebelled against Assyrian rule and asked Shabaka for aid. Shabaka responded as a New Kingdom pharaoh might have; he sent assistance. The Kushite-Egyptian army met the Assyrian army at Eltekeh in Judah. The Assyrians lived for war; their society was geared toward waging war. Their army was better equipped with armor and weapons than the Kushite-Egyptian army, and it was better organized into combat units. It was more mobile and more experienced. Even so, the Kushite-Egyptian army inflicted heavy losses on the Assyrian army before having to withdraw. Some Assyrian vassals took this as a good sign, and they rebelled. The Assyrian army became afflicted with a disease that killed more than 15,000 troops, and it was unable to finish the war.

The Assyrian rulers regarded the Kushite pharaohs as irritating upstarts, but they had their hands full quelling rebellions in Palestine, delaying their eventual attack on Egypt. In 674 B.C.E. an Assyrian army met a Kushite-Egyptian army in northern Palestine and was decisively defeated. In 671 B.C.E. King Esarhaddon (r. 680–669 B.C.E.) of Assyria led an army to Egypt using camels as pack animals to transport goods through the hot, dry Sinai. His army inflicted a series of defeats on Kushite-Egyptian forces. The decisive factor may have been Assyrian armor, which was made of resilient iron and was mass-produced so that every soldier had armor and iron weapons. The Kushite-Egyptians could not supply all their troops with metal weaponry and armor, and they were still living in a Bronze Age military world, whereas the Assyrians had the superior military organization of troops on the battlefield that was necessary for victory in the Iron Age world, as well as much superior discipline among their troops.

Pharaoh Taharqa (r. 690–664 B.C.E.) retreated to Thebes and then to Napata. His family in Thebes was murdered by the Assyrians. The Assyrians made the cities of Egypt north of Thebes their vassals. Taharqa was succeeded by Tantamani (r. 664–657 B.C.E.), who believed himself to be the only true ruler of Egypt. In 664 B.C.E. he led a Kushite force against an alliance of Egyptian vassals and Assyrians. The key to his success seems to have been mastery of the waters of the Nile; boats may have moved his forces swiftly into position.

By this time the Kushites had probably noted the value of the iron technology of the Assyrians, and Kush had already begun to establish an iron industry. In 664 B.C.E., however, the Kushites had to rely on their ferocity to overcome their enemies, which they did in a battle at Memphis. Tantamani regained control all the way to the Mediterranean Sea, but too much had changed in the Near East. His allies in Palestine had been defeated by the Assyrians, and combat had depleted his military's resources. Despite waging a stubborn defense, his army was driven ever southward by a determined counterattack of Assyrian forces commanded by Ashurbanipal (r. 668–627 B.C.E.). Thebes was sacked, its women raped, its children slaughtered, and its men enslaved.

Although Tantamani's line would survive until about 300 C.E. and its monarchs would call themselves the rulers of both Upper and Lower Egypt, they would not again rule Egypt. There is some indication that they tried again in about 601 B.C.E., when Babylon attacked Egypt. The Kushite army fought an army composed of Greek and other mercenaries near Abu Simbel, about 250 miles south of Thebes. The battle was ferocious, but the Kushites were forced to withdraw. Although the rule of Kush over Egypt was short, it had a long-lasting effect on Egyptian society: It reinvigorated Egypt's religion, arts, and economy for hundreds of years.

This was not the end for the Kushite military. Most Kushite kings and queens proved to be capable rulers who incorporated what had been learned from the Assyrians into their army. The Kushite iron industry focused on the city of Meroë, south of Napata, just south of where the Atbara River flows into the Nile. After an Egyptian army sacked Napata, the capital of Kush was moved to Meroë. The principal duties of the army became protecting Kush's trade routes that ran deep into southern Africa, west along the Sahel steppes south of the Sahara, and east to the Red Sea. Kushite inscriptions depict numerous battles, mostly against nomadic peoples. Kush assumed the role of protector from raiders for small tribal lands to its south. Elephants seem to have faded out of use in the army, as did chariots. They were replaced by horseback-riding cavalry armed with lances and bows. Spearmen remained the core of the army.

Specific military actions for Kush reappear in the historical record in 24 B.C.E. By then Rome controlled Egypt, and the Romans had built a series of forts south of Egypt, possibly infringing on territory that Kush regarded as its own. At that time Kush was ruled by a queen, called a *candace*, which Greek writers mistook for a given name rather than a title. This was probably Queen Amanirenas, a big woman with an imposing personality. The Roman governor responsible for the forts left with most of his troops to aid in fighting in the Near East. Although Amanirenas was probably present for the attack on the fort at Aswān, her army was led by a general, perhaps a Prince Akinadad, who is linked with her in inscriptions found in Meroë. Using boats and infantry the Kushite army assaulted and seized forts at Aswān and Philae. In the marketplaces there the Romans had installed statues of the emperor Augustus (r. 27 B.C.E.–14 C.E.), which the Kushites took home. A head that may have been from one of these statues was found by archaeologists hidden in clean sand under the entrance to a building in Meroë.

When the Roman governor, Gaius Petronius, returned, he counterattacked. Although the Kushite army dominated regional African groups, it was no match for the Romans, and despite stubborn fighting the army was driven south by the Romans. Amanirenas tried to negotiate with the Romans, but the Romans persisted until they captured and sacked Meroë. Several Kushite towns were left in ruins.

How Kush fell is not known. A rival kingdom, Axum, left some hints, and archaeologists have found additional clues. In about 300 C.E. Kush lost its constant war against nomads. Among the nomads were the Red Noba, who were in control of Kush when Axum invaded in 350 C.E. The key to the nomads' victory may have been camels, which enabled them to travel farther more quickly in dry climates than could horses, and Kush was drying up as the desert of the Sahara continued its spread. Where the Kushites went is a subject historians and archaeologists like to debate, but at present what happened to the Kushites is unknown.

Axum

Axum was located where Ethiopia is today. At its height it was one of the great powers of the Indian Ocean, where its navy transported its army to fight in distant lands. Although Axum had a distinct culture of its own by 1500 B.C.E. and developed a written language, less is known about it than about Kush.

Axum's focus was on trade, and throughout its history it was a mercantile nation. Thus its military's primary duty was to protect trade. By about 400 B.C.E. Axum's navy was large, and it sailed along the coast of eastern Africa and as far east as Sri Lanka. In the Red Sea and along Africa's east coast it protected merchant ships from pirates. By maintaining safe waters Axum attracted the sea trade to its ports. Visitors to the ports saw imposing stone forts on hilltops along Axum's coast. These forts apparently represented a military class that held much political power in Axum society.

The king of Axum was the commander in chief of the military, and he sometimes led his army into battle. The army was run by nobles who based their operations in the hill forts. Beneath them were trained officers who oversaw a well-disciplined infantry and cavalry. It is possible that Axum's army included elephants. Part of Axum's ability to protect its people from harm was its ability to project its power overseas. Its navy could transport divisions of the army throughout the Red Sea and along the southern coast of Arabia and the Near East, and Axum used this ability to effect wars and rebellions in areas it considered important to its well-being. Often when a rebellion or war of conquest disrupted Arabia, Axum would send its army to restore order and place its friends as rulers.

On the continent of Africa, Axum shared power with Egypt, Kush, and various small groups. Beginning around the 1470s B.C.E. it maintained trade relations with Egypt, which were sometimes interrupted by wars and civil wars in Egypt. Whether it meant to or not, Kush contributed to Axum's security by protecting African trade routes from bandits and nomadic marauders. Perhaps Axum's greatest king, 'Ezānā, was in power when the kingdom of Kush expired under the effects of farmland lost to desertification and attacks from nomads of the Sahara. 'Ezānā forged peace treaties with the nomads that were meant to protect Axum's borders and its trade, but the nomads who gave up their nomadic ways to settle in the remains of Kush persisted in attacking trade caravans. The breaking point seems to have come when the Red Noba mistreated ambassadors of Axum in 350 C.E. 'Ezānā led a punitive expedition into Kush, destroying villages along the way. At Meroë his army defeated the Nobu. Losses on his side seem to have been light, but his army may have killed as many as 15,000 enemy warriors. He took home with him several thousand head of cattle, many horses, and slaves.

The Bantu Speakers

Although Axum persisted as an important power for another thousand years, a people who would reshape Africa to the present day were on the move to the west by 200 C.E. These were the Zande-speaking and Bantu-speaking peoples of West Africa, probably the descendants of the farmers of the Sahara who had fled south 1,000 or more years earlier. They had iron technologies, and their blacksmiths had learned how to carbonize iron with charcoal to make steel. This was tricky, because too much or too little carbon could result in metal that was too soft or too brittle to be of good use. They were an agricultural people, and as they pushed the Pygmies and the Bushmen out of their ancient territories, the Bantu speakers, in particular, made the land permanently their own by settling and farming it. Even though it is unlikely that the Bantu speakers could summon huge armies, they could call upon more warriors on short notice than could either the Pygmies or the Bushmen.

Among themselves, the Bantu speakers at the end of the ancient era fought wars that had well-understood rules. Warriors, rarely more than 100 on each side, would gather on open land. They carried shields made of animal skins, and their weapons were usually spears. They painted their faces and their bodies to make themselves look frightening. Actual combat seldom took more than a few lives before one side fled. In the event that neither side fled, the side that was winning would refrain from wholesale slaughter by leaving an opening for the losers to use for running away. It was against the rules for one side to surround the other because it was understood that trapped warriors would fight to the death, increasing casualties for the winners as well as the losers. It was from these warriors that the important military powers of medieval central and southern Africa would evolve.

EGYPT

BY MARIAM F. AYAD

Perhaps no other civilization survived as long as that of the ancient Egyptians. In its long history Egypt not only invaded and annexed foreign territories but also was occasionally the subject of military conquest by invading armies. In discussing the development and organization of Egypt's armed forces and Egypt's imperialistic role in history, it is important to clarify terminology. The Egyptian word *mesha*, traditionally translated as "army," is used in reference not only to a body of soldiers but also to any kind of expeditionary force, such as a mining expedition or similar peaceful endeavor. Thus the meaning of the word is not inherently militaristic but much broader, perhaps even referring to any organized group of individuals who undertake state-sponsored excursions to achieve a state-sponsored objective, militaristic or peaceful. Avoiding use of the word *army* when describing Egypt's military force might be prudent, because the term would imply the existence of a national body of soldiers from the beginning of Egyptian history until the demise of pharaonic civilization, which was not the case.

Old Kingdom (ca. 2575–ca. 2134 B.C.E.)

The earliest reference to a war in ancient Egyptian evidence appears on the Narmer Pallet. On one side of the pallet is a highly stylized pictorial representation of a king grasping the hair of an enemy in one hand and holding a mace in the other upraised hand. The king is shown in the process of hitting the fallen enemy, a pose that became associated with smiting enemies throughout Egyptian history. The other side of the pallet depicts the king marching in a victory procession. The representation preserved on the pallet has been interpreted as a record of a single militaristic action that led to the forceful unification of Egypt by a king of Upper Egypt. Although most scholars subscribe to a theory of a more gradual unification process, this scene, one of the earliest preserved, records some kind of a militaristic internal struggle.

As early as the Old Kingdom, Egypt wanted to acquire the natural resources of the region immediately south of its border, Nubia. To expand their kingdom's boarders southward, Egyptian forces occasionally mounted campaigns into the southern region. Egypt's southern expansion came as a

Frieze in the temple of Ramses II, listing captured cities in Nubia (Courtesy of the Oriental Institute of the University of Chicago)

natural consequence of its unique geography. Running the entire length of Egypt from its southern border to the Mediterranean shore, the Nile River was Egypt's highway. The strong river current carried the ships effortlessly north, while winds blowing from the Mediterranean enabled boats to sail south. Moreover, originating in the Ugandan mountains, the Nile facilitated easy access to the African heartland.

Evidence suggests, however, that Egypt did not have a standing army during this period. Instead, various local governors were called on not only to join military expeditions but also to recruit troops from among their local constituents. The autobiography of Weni, an official under the Sixth Dynasty king Pepi I (ca. 2289–2255 B.C.E.), details an expedition to Nubia, Egypt's southern neighbor. Preserved in his tomb at Abydos, the autobiography lists Weni's many titles, including several hereditary positions (Weni had the social rank of an *iry-paet*, a title often translated as "hereditary nobleman" or "count.") In addition, Weni held several high-ranking administrative positions: He was both a governor and a chamberlain of Upper Egypt, the warden of Nekhen (a cultic center in Upper Egypt), and the mayor of Nekheb (an equally important cultic center).

Much like Weni, the officers under his command were hereditary noblemen and members of the civil administration of Egypt; among those Weni listed in his autobiography are "counts, royal seal bearers, sole companions, chieftains and mayors of towns of Upper and Lower Egypt" as well as chief priests and chief district officials. Remarkably, neither Weni nor his officers bore any specifically militaristic titles. The high-ranking administrators among them were required to recruit their own troops from the villages and districts they governed or administered. Farmers comprised the bulk of the Egyptian military force.

Indeed, Weni's autobiography recounts the marshaling of "tens of thousands" of troops against the "Asiatic Sand-dwellers," which was the Egyptian way of referring to Bedouins who subsisted along Egypt's eastern border. Troops were recruited from all the districts of Upper and Lower Egypt as well as from Nubia, the area immediately to the south of Egyptian border, and even included some Libyans. As the leader of this very diverse force, Weni was proud of the discipline of his forces, which he attributed to his own rectitude. In his autobiography he boasts that while he led the troops, "no one attached his fellow, . . . no one seized a loaf or sandals from a traveler, . . . no one stole a cloth from any town, . . . no one took a goat from anyone."

Weni roughly sketched the route of the campaign, but his autobiography focuses primarily on the victorious outcome of the campaign, ending in a poetic refrain that recounts the safe return of the troops, "having slain thousands. . . [and] having carried off many troops as captives." The successful outcome of the campaign ensured that Weni would head the military force sent to fight against the Bedouins five more times. At least once Weni traveled to the battleground aboard a ship, while half of his troops proceeded on land.

Middle Kingdom (ca. 2040–ca. 1640 B.C.E.)

Soon after the long reign of Pepi II, a period of political turmoil ensued in Egypt. Known as the First Intermediate Period (ca. 2134–ca. 2040 B.C.E.), the tumultuous period following the collapse of the Old Kingdom lasted from the Seventh Dynasty through the middle of the Eleventh Dynasty. Egyptian literature describing this period implies that it may have witnessed some form of civil war. In particular, the "Instructions to King Merikare," a text written in Middle Egyptian and surviving in three Eighteenth Dynasty copies, describes the following conditions: "Troops will fight troops. . . Egypt fought in the graveyard." Traces of hieroglyphs preserved in this document suggest that the text refers to King Khety, a possible conflation of Akhtoy, a name commonly held by rulers of the Ninth and Tenth dynasties.

This text belongs to a larger corpus known collectively as pessimistic literature and comprising literary works dating to the Middle Kingdom. Works belonging to this genre describe how Egypt went through a period of turmoil until order was finally restored by a savior king. The "Instructions of King Amenemhat," founder of the Twelfth Dynasty, belong to this genre. After a lengthy account of the chaos in which he found the land, Amenemhat describes how he was able not only to restore order in the land but also to vanquish Egypt's southern neighbors in Wawat and Medajj (two districts in Nubia). Amenemhat also claimed that he "made the Asiatics do the dog walk."

However, even in the Middle Kingdom and despite many campaigns into Nubia, the Egyptian military force lacked the many ranks and titles characteristic of a regular standing army. Similarly absent was a formal division of the military into units and subunits. Egypt's strategic location in northeastern Africa, lack of a formal standing army, weakened governmental authority, and lax control of the northeastern border eventually led to the occupation of the delta region by nomadic groups of western Asiatic descent, known as the Hyksos (the name is a Hellenized version of the Egyptian term *heqa khasut*, meaning "rulers of foreign countries"). The Hyksos are credited with the introduction of several technologies and inventions, not the least important of which were the wheel and its use in the military chariot.

New Kingdom (ca. 1550–ca. 1070 B.C.E.)

As founder of the Eighteenth Dynasty (ca. 1550–ca. 1307 B.C.E.), King Ahmose is famous for the successful campaign he launched against the Hyksos strongholds in the delta. Among the several texts recording the events leading to the expulsion of the Hyksos from Egypt is the autobiography of an officer in the Egyptian military, also named Ahmose, who started his military career as a crew commander under King Ahmose and later served in the Nubian and Syrian campaigns of Amenhotep I and Thutmose I. The autobiography, inscribed in the officer's tomb at El-Kab, records his early career and provides a vivid account of his involvement in the battle against the Hyksos. Ahmose portrays himself as a courageous "crew commander" who climbed the ranks of the military and was rewarded for his bravery and prowess with gold (seven times) as well with tracts of arable land. As part of his reward Ahmose the officer also received male and female slaves, some of whom he had captured himself in battle and some whom others captured.

It is clear from his autobiography that Ahmose was an infantryman who "followed the sovereign on foot when he rode in his chariot." In one episode the soldier records going to the battlefield aboard a ship called the *Wild Bull* while he was still an unmarried young man. As an infantryman Ahmose actively participated in the siege of the town of Avaris, the delta stronghold of the Hyksos. He was then appointed to serve aboard a ship named *Rising in Memphis* and took part in some "fighting on the water." This episode, however, should not be taken to indicate that a naval battle took place. Rather, the fighting occurred on a lake or perhaps a tributary of the Nile near Avaris. The ship merely served as a platform from which archers could aim their arrows. During the battle Ahmose captured a prisoner of war, and when the captive tried to escape, Ahmose waded into the waters and recaptured him.

It is clear from his autobiography that although Ahmose was aboard ship to reach western Asia, he was an infantryman who fought on land. Thus he could be considered a marine who mainly engaged in infantry warfare. The text also suggests that Ahmose fought using primarily short-range weapons, such as the club or mace for clubbing; the spear, straight sword, or dagger for stabbing; and the battle-ax or broadsword for slashing and cutting.

Ahmose's vivid descriptions of the fall of the cities of Avaris and Sharuhen indicate that he also engaged in siege warfare. Whenever forces could not infiltrate a fortified city or fortress by tunneling under, climbing over, or smashing into its walls, they would launch a siege that would continue until the inhabitants began to starve and surrendered to the attacking forces. Ahmose describes how Sharuhen was besieged for three years.

Two other types of warfare, not mentioned by Ahmose but attested to elsewhere are naval warfare, in which battles took place on water, and chariotry warfare, in which combat occurred from horse-drawn chariots. These two types of warfare, though not as well documented in the archaeological and pictorial records, are depicted on the walls of a few temples.

Although it is emblematic of ancient Egyptian warfare in popular culture and art, the chariot was rarely used in Egyptian battles. Appearing soon after the expulsion of the Hyksos, the chariot enabled a soldier to fight aboard a wheeled vehicle. A unit of mounted troops, or chariotry, was limited in size and thus considered elite. The main function of the two-wheeled, horse-drawn chariot was to provide military intelligence and reconnaissance. Protected by its mobility, a chariot would travel along the front lines of the enemy, learning the organization of its infantry forces and bombarding them with arrows. However, the chariot's use as a mobile platform from which archers could shoot their targets was only secondary. Chariots were expensive to maintain. Each vehicle required at least four horses, which needed fodder, tending, and specialized care. Eventually, the chariot became "a status symbol, and in the case of the king . . . a surrogate throne."

A mid-Eighteenth-Dynasty title, commander of horsemen, suggests the existence of a sort of cavalry or mounted troops. This is further corroborated by scenes from the tomb of Horemhet from Saqqara, which clearly depict the cavalry as an arm of the chariotry. Further evidence suggests that the cavalry unit was used extensively in Sheshonq I's Palestinian campaign of around 925 B.C.E.

Egypt's location on the Mediterranean subjected it to repeated attacks from the Sea Peoples, first during the reign of King Merneptah (ca. 1224–ca. 1214 B.C.E.) and later under Ramses III (ca. 1194–ca. 1163 B.C.E.). These invaders were groups of migrants who swept through the Mediterranean world in the 11th century B.C.E. Although the exact reason for this massive population movement remains elusive, possible reasons include severe climatic changes in the northern and western Mediterranean.

Pictorial evidence of Ramses III's naval battle against the invading Sea Peoples survives on the walls of his mortuary temple at Medinet Habu. The evidence preserved there constitutes the only known example of an active naval engagement. The scenes indicate that during the Twentieth Dynasty of the New Kingdom the Egyptians commanded large seafaring vessels. The evidence also suggests the existence of naval ranks and titles, and military ships had specific designations. Earlier in the struggle against the Hyksos and later during Piye's 25th march into Egypt, ships were used to transport troops north. But the reliefs of Medinet Habu clearly depict troops fighting from onboard ships, although the specifics of conducting naval battles cannot be reconstructed.

Along with distinct naval ranks and titles, the evidence suggests that during the New Kingdom the Egyptian forces were finally divided into distinct units, each exhibiting a clear hierarchy of ranked officials. The units were organized according to their modes of transportation. Foot soldiers, or infantry troops, made up by far the largest units. Indeed, the evidence suggests that this was the only type of unit up to the beginning of the New Kingdom.

The accounts of two major battles (Megiddo and Kadesh) shed light on New Kingdom warfare. The two accounts are propagandistic in nature, concerned primarily with the exultation of the king and expounding on his role as the great warrior-savior in great detail. Although their propagandistic tone makes the reliability of the numbers (of troops as well as booty) mentioned there quite unreliable, they remain our only primary source on warfare, strategy, and battle moves in ancient Egypt.

Prompted by rumors of a coalition of western Asiatic rulers, Thutmose III launched a preemptive campaign into Syria-Palestine in his first year of sole reign (ca. 1458 B.C.E.). The confrontation between the two armies took place on the plains of Jezreel across from the Canaanite city of Megiddo. Written in literary form, numerous accounts of the battle of Megiddo were engraved on Egyptian temple walls, the most extensive preserved on the walls of the Amun temple at Karnak. As in similar works of this literary genre, the author goes to great lengths to demonstrate the king's military prowess and strategic brilliance. The propagandistic tenor of the text is clear in its introductory lines, which give the complete titles of the king: "Mighty Bull, Shining in Thebes; King of Upper and Lower Egypt, Lord of the Two Lands; Menkheperre; Son of Re." The text then relates how all the victories he enjoyed in battle were granted him by "his father Re [the sun god]."

Under the pretext of quenching perceived rebellion, Thutmose III decided to march against the Asiatics at a time when they seemed to have "fallen into disagreement," when their infighting would have made them an easy target. The account engraved at the Amun temple details the events of the battle: the troops marched "out of Egypt to Gaza, then along the coast of Canaan to the entrance of the Aruna Pass" (probably the Wadi Ara near modern Hadera). Giving this account its particular historical appeal is the seemingly accurate date provided at the beginning of the narrative. The troops set out in Thutmose III's 22nd regnal year, on the 25th day of the fourth month of *Peret* (the winter season). The text also records the date that the king arrived at his destination at the city of Yehem in western Asia: year 23, first month of *Shemu* (the summer season), on the 16th day.

On his arrival, however, Thutmose III convened a council of war and received bad advice: to take "a safer route toward Megiddo." The king ignored the advice of his courtiers, deciding instead to take the dangerous crossing of "the Carmel ridge via the Aruna Pass" and enter the Jezreel Valley just outside of the city of Megiddo. He "commanded his entire army to march on that road, which threatened to be narrow. His majesty swore, saying, "None shall go forth in the way before my majesty. . . . He went forth at the head of his army himself, showing the way by his own footsteps; horse behind horse, his majesty being at the head of his army."

At seeing the king, considered a divine being, the enemy troops fled into disarray. According to the inscription preserved on a stela in Napata (a city in Nubia, in modern Sudan), the Egyptian forces then laid siege to the city of Megiddo until its leaders surrendered. The text gives a vivid description of the surrender and details the booty carried off by the Egyptian troops, giving exact numbers for prisoners of war captured (340), enemy troops killed (83), mares taken (2,041), and stallions seized (6). The text further details the finery of a gold chariots seized and records that 200 suits of armor were taken. Significantly, it does not mention the number of Egyptian troops deployed for battle, and there is no mention of how long the march (or the battle) lasted.

The battle of Qadesh, fought in the fourth year of the reign of the pharaoh Ramses II (ca. 1274 B.C.E.) at Tell Nebi

Mend on the Orontes River, was widely publicized, with many scenes of the battle engraved on the walls of several temples in Egypt and Nubia. The scenes, which proclaim the military prowess of Ramses II, propagate a version of events that claim Egyptian victory in the battle. Like Thutmose III at the battle of Megiddo, Ramses II was misled by false intelligence. The Egyptian forces were ambushed, and although both sides fought ferociously, the Hittites did not yield the land. In fact, extant Hittite records of the battle indicate that the Egyptian troops suffered a severe defeat and fled in chaos. The ensuing peace treaty between Ramses II and the Hittite king Mutewalis preserved the status quo, with both sides suffering considerable losses.

The Egyptian account of the battle of Qadesh is most significant because it indicates that the Egyptian military was subdivided into four battalions, each named after one of the major Egyptian deities. Indeed, the Egyptian versions focus on the bravery of Ramses II who, having been deserted by his infantry and chariotry, continued to fight gallantly. The poetic version of the battle surprisingly preserves a passage in which Ramses II complains that the god Amun-Re had deserted him in battle. Despite the lack of divine support, however, Ramses II is able to single-handedly defeat thousands of enemy troops. Indeed, this seems to be the sole purpose of the numerous inscribed versions of the battle: the glorification of the reigning king and the further establishment of his bravery and divinity.

Egyptian military forces were not always on the offensive. In its long history Egypt also experienced several invasions by the armies of other Near Eastern nations: the Nubians, Assyrians, and Persians, and later the Greeks and Romans, all invaded Egypt. At the end of the New Kingdom, Egypt witnessed a period of political fragmentation known as the Third Intermediate Period (ca. 1070–ca. 712 B.C.E.). During this period several rulers simultaneously claimed the kingship of Egypt. Occasionally these rivaling dynasts fought over territorial hegemony. Sometime in the early to mid-seventh century B.C.E. Egypt's southern neighbor in Sudan, the kingdom of Napata, rose to power. One of its earliest rulers, Kashta, marched north and may have controlled all the area to the south of Egypt up to Aswān. Located at the first cataract, Aswān was Egypt's traditional southern border. Kashta's sons, Piye and Shabaka, invaded Egypt several times: Piye twice in his fourth and 20th regnal year and Shabaka in his second year. The Nubians eventually succeeded in having a firm grip on Egypt; from 715 to 671 B.C.E. they fully controlled Egypt as its Twenty-fifth Dynasty. The penultimate ruler of that dynasty, Taharqa, was a military man who had spent the early part of his career leading his predecessor's armies. Taharqa tried to expand Egypt's northeastern frontiers.

Assyria was the main military force in the ancient Near East at the time, with a strong presence in Palestine. Taharqa's ambitious military intervention in western Asia may have prompted several subsequent Assyrian invasions into Egypt (in 674, 671, and 667–666 B.C.E.). The Assyrians' invasion of Egypt was a natural consequence of its need to secure Palestine's southern boundary. They left Egypt only after installing their Egyptian ally, Psammetichus I (664–610 B.C.E.), as a vassal king. Psammetichus I succeeded in driving Tantamani, the last Nubian ruler of Egypt, from Egypt, having chased his armies all the way to Nubia in the Sudan. Psammetichus I and his successors of the Twenty-sixth Dynasty relied heavily on the use of mercenaries. Cretans, Greeks, and Jews were among the many nationalities employed in the Egyptian military at the time.

But perhaps the most devastating of all invasions was the Persian invasion of Egypt in the spring of 525 B.C.E. Having swept through the Near East, the Persians conquered Egypt and ruled it for more than a century. An Egyptian revolt in 401 to 399 B.C.E. led to the expulsion of the Persians from Egypt. Shortly thereafter, in 343 B.C.E., the Persians reconquered Egypt. This time their rule of Egypt was short lived. After a brief decade Alexander the Great invaded Egypt in 332 B.C.E.

After Alexander's sudden death his generals divided the territories he had conquered. Egypt fell into the hands of General Ptolemy, who declared himself king of Egypt. His decedents constitute the Ptolemaic Dynasty, and the period from 305 to 30 B.C.E. is known as the Ptolemaic Period. The last Ptolemaic ruler was none other than the famous Queen Cleopatra VII. Egypt was finally annexed to the Roman Empire after Cleopatra and Marc Anthony's defeat at the naval battle of Actium in 30 B.C.E.

THE MIDDLE EAST

BY KIRK H. BEETZ

In the ancient Near East the objective of warfare was the capture or defense of a capital city. The original cities of Mesopotamia were sacred, the homes of specific gods in the religions of the peoples of the area. When a city became the urban center of a state consisting of towns and villages, it retained its central place in the hearts of its populace. To capture a capital was to capture the hearts of its people and usually to bring the end of resistance.

Until about the era of the Neo-Assyrian Empire (1050–609 B.C.E.) another objective of war was to slaughter the enemy, and prisoners of war were typically executed. Even though the Neo-Assyrians were especially bloodthirsty, they changed the practice of routinely killing prisoners, because they valued their prisoners as potential slaves and tended to ship them off to parts of their empire where labor was wanted.

The archaeology of Near Eastern warfare before about 1200 B.C.E. is sketchy, but the scant physical evidence is often all that speaks of wars. Even after writing became common, war records usually contained the statistics of victory—such as how many of the enemy were killed, how many were captured, and what sort of loot was found—rather than descriptions of tactics, military organization, or even the reasons for the wars.

Before 3500 B.C.E.

Warfare seems to have been a constant preoccupation for Near Easterners, even as far back as the end of the last great ice age. One archaeological site that indicates this is Jericho. Sometime between 10,000 and 8000 B.C.E. a giant stone wall was erected around a settlement at Jericho. It seems to have been intended to protect a small population and a spring. Of special interest to military historians is a stone tower attached to the wall. The tower was about 35 feet high and built solidly, with a stone staircase up the middle. The great antiquity of the tower is significant because of the tower's sophisticated design, which suggests that its builders drew on a tradition of erecting similar towers. The reason Jericho was fortified at such an early time is unknown, as is the identity of the enemy. Speculation has tended to focus on the spring and the likelihood that Jericho was a farming community. Nomads may have coveted the harvests of Jericho, and traders traveling the ancient trade route that passed through Jericho may have coveted the water flowing from the spring.

The physical remains at Jericho offer some idea of what warfare may have been like. An important point to consider is the significant expense of fortifications. Instead of farming more land or producing more goods, valuable time and thought were devoted to building walls and at least one large tower. It is logical to suppose that if the massiveness of the walls and tower were unnecessary, the society of Jericho would have built a less imposing fortification. Thus the structures' heavy-stone construction, great height, and massiveness indicate that the enemy could bring down or penetrate walls built of wood or small stones. This suggests that at that early date, attackers already knew about using sappers to undermine walls and fire to burn walls and may have even used battering rams. The tower's height may have been for guards to watch for enemies, which would mean that attacks could come unexpectedly. On the other hand, the tower was situated so that people on it could fire arrows or hurl stones at anyone attempting to scale the walls. Altogether, the evidence indicates that people were already thinking carefully about how to wage war.

Farther north, in present-day Turkey, another city offers hints about war. Çatalhüyük, established before 7200 B.C.E., was built to resemble a beehive. The city had no roads or footpaths, and its interlocking buildings had few, if any windows and no conventional doors. People moved from place to place by climbing ladders through openings in their ceilings and walking across roofs, occasionally climbing or descending where buildings were of different heights. The dominant theory about why the city was built as it was focuses on military defense. An enemy, whether bandits or a full army, would have had no clear entrance to attack. Attacking and entering an outer building would have left the enemy with nowhere to go but up a ladder, and defenders could heap stones, arrows, and burning oil on them. Seizing the city would have required fighting to take each building. Archaeologists believe that the lack of evidence that Çatalhüyük was ever taken by force indicates that its defensive layout was successful.

Early Dynastic Period (ca. 3000–ca. 2350 B.C.E.)

By 3000 B.C.E. the numerous Sumerian cities established in southern Mesopotamia were already warring against each other. For several reasons the waging of war was not a simple matter of a king deciding to take his army to battle. First, there were no standing armies. Early Sumerian armies consisted of militias of free male citizens. Second, kings were not absolute rulers and had to gain consent from a council of elders or an assembly of citizens. For instance, during the rule of Gilgamesh (r. ca. 2700 B.C.E.) the city of Uruk received a demand to surrender itself to the dominance of another city-state. Gilgamesh wished to fight for his city's freedom, but Uruk's council of elders voted to surrender. Gilgamesh called for an assembly of Uruk's free citizens, and the assembly overruled the council of elders and voted to fight to remain free.

Another difficulty was that typically citizens were expected to provide their own weapons: spears, daggers, stone maces, bows and arrows, and slingshots. Although shields were available, a warrior usually carried his weapon in both hands and had a dagger strapped to his side. Protective armor was typically no more than a hat of cloth or leather. Battles in open land consisted of barrages of arrows when armies were less than 300 feet apart, because the bow of the time was accurate only up to that distance. The barrage could be followed by a charge. The enemy would meet the charging warriors with spears and rocks hurled from slingshots. A battle between big city-states could result in 10,000 dead.

Gilgamesh was famous as a city builder. Songs and poems lauded him for the great wall he directed to be built around Uruk. It was constructed from fired clay bricks, which were expensive but durable for the time; good stone for building was hard to find in southern Mesopotamia. The wall was wide enough for two chariots to pass side by side, and it had many towers. Such defenses were necessary because military leaders were learning how to organize their troops for coordinated attacks that could overwhelm lesser defenses with the sheer number of warriors scaling the walls.

By the end of the Early Dynastic Period, an arms race had developed. Bigger walls meant bigger weapons for knocking walls down. Skulls crushed by maces led to the development of metal helmets, which in turn resulted in the invention of a battle-ax that could crash through metal. This, in turn, created the need for sturdier helmets, leading to the development of new casting techniques and then sturdier ax blades that curved, making cutting through helmets easier.

Old Akkadian Empire (ca. 2350–ca. 2100 B.C.E.)

The king who founded the Old Akkadian Empire may have been history's first military genius. Sargon I (r. 2334–2279 B.C.E.) established what is thought to have been the first

Clay prism of King Sennacherib, ca. 689 B.C.E., upon which are recorded eight successful military campaigns against various peoples who refused to submit to Assyrian domination (Courtesy of the Oriental Institute of the University of Chicago)

standing army, consisting of 5,400 men, with whom he ate daily. The Sumerian battlewagon was a clumsy vehicle, with four heavy wheels and pulled by onagers—wild asses from central Asia. In battle Sargon and his commanders would ride the wagons more for transportation around the battlefield than for use in combat, but from the battlewagons archers could fire on the enemy while staying out of the way of counterattacks.

The use of formations in battle and one great advance in weaponry may have been behind Sargon's ability to crush his enemies and build the world's first great empire. The advance was the composite bow. It consisted of an inner layer of bone, a middle layer of wood, and an outer layer of leather. Sometimes more than one kind of wood was used, all to give the bow more power. The result was that Sargon's archers had a range almost 200 feet greater than that of enemy archers. By having his army fire on the enemy long before the enemy could return fire, he forced opponents into disastrous charges against well-organized formations of warriors with spears at the ready, or opponents fled because they could not come to grips with his warriors.

Sargon's successors continued to innovate. Perhaps their most significant contribution to military history was the development of specialized units within the army. Rather than having every warrior fight with every weapon, they developed units of archers, spearmen, slingshot specialists who backed up the spearmen, and charioteers.

Neo-Assyrian Empire (ca. 1000–ca. 626 B.C.E.)

The foremost practitioners of war of the ancient Near East were the Assyrians. They did not begin that way. Originally they settled in a mountainous region through which several trade routes passed, making their living as traders and farmers. Both trading and farming would remain vital to the economy that funded the Assyrian military. During the Old Assyrian Period (ca. 1813–ca.1365 B.C.E.) Assyria's wars tended to be reactions to aggression. Their mountains did not afford them much protection, and their harvests attracted the greed of nomads to the north and city-states to the south.

The archer was the most important weapon in the Assyrian army. The Assyrians developed a pairing of an archer with a shield bearer. The shield was composed of reeds with an outer covering of animal skin or metal. It rose higher than the heads of the shield bearer and archer, curving up over the bearer's head. It was intended to allow the archer to focus on his job of shooting the enemy while someone else worried about keeping him alive. Both bearer and archer were usually armed with daggers for hand-to-hand fighting, but it was the Assyrian commander's intention to keep his archers away from direct contact with the enemy.

During this period the Hittite Empire (ca. 1650–ca. 1200 B.C.E.) had developed to the west, in present-day Turkey. The Hittites introduced the phalanx to warfare in the Near East. The Hittite phalanx consisted of a block of soldiers who marched toward the enemy in lockstep with spears evenly spaced. The soldiers were heavy infantry, wearing weighty uniforms draped with iron plates. The Hittites' tactics involved trapping enemies into direct encounters with the heavy infantry, whose skills and armor surpassed those of others in the Near East. Further, the Hittites used chariots as true offensive weapons. Their units of chariots moved swiftly across battlefields, pulled by horses and using spoked wheels.

In about 1200 B.C.E. the Hittite Empire collapsed. Raiders whom modern historians call the Sea Peoples cut off some of the Hittites' trade routes to the south, and the Assyrians cut off their trade routes to the east. Their capital was sacked. This left openings for lesser kingdoms to expand, and it left much of the territory to the west of Assyria open for conquest.

In 1595 B.C.E. Assyria had become a vassal of the Mittani Kingdom, but that kingdom was absorbed by the Hittites during the 1300s B.C.E., giving Assyria a chance to assert its independence, which it did under King Ashu-uballit I (r. ca. 1365–ca. 1330 B.C.E.). Thereafter, the Assyrians embarked on centuries of military adventures, not all successful. King Shalmaneser I (r. ca. 1273–ca. 1244 B.C.E.) secured Assyria's northern frontier with wars in central Asia. King Tikulti-ninurta I (r. ca. 1244–ca. 1208 B.C.E.) attacked Babylonia in 1220 B.C.E., occupying the city of Babylon until 1213 B.C.E., and he spread his conquests into the Zagros Mountains to the east before he was assassinated by one of his sons.

The Assyrian Empire thereafter fell apart, pulled itself together, and fell apart again. As the Neo-Assyrian Empire it reached its zenith and gained the military reputation that it now has. The Neo-Assyrian society was geared toward making war. Its people came to rely on war as a source of luxury goods. Their boys were trained almost all their lives to be warriors, and military service was not only expected of all young men but also considered the best thing a man could do. At the same time women were repressed. They were required to wear robes that totally covered them when they were out in public, and their principal purpose was to bear boys for the military. Newborn girls were often killed because they were considered valueless.

The Neo-Assyrian military machine was a master of propaganda. It advertised its victories, spreading accounts of the horrors it had visited on its opponents. Before attacking a major stronghold such as Jerusalem, it would attack surrounding villages and towns, slaughtering the inhabitants as a display of power to discourage the defenders of the stronghold. Typically, an Assyrian envoy would stand outside the stronghold to ask in the Assyrian language that the defenders yield to the greater might of Assyria. This would involve detailing some of the horrors visited on those who resisted Assyria. Sometimes the authorities of the stronghold would agree to surrender, and usually the Assyrians would let the residents live, though they would require a very heavy tribute and force some of the men to join their army.

Often the authorities of the stronghold refused to surrender. Then the Assyrians would speak to the defenders in their native language, telling them of how they would suffer once the Assyrians won the battle. The hope was that the common people would rebel rather than endure the misery of an Assyrian victory. Thereafter tall stakes would be driven into the ground within view of the defenders, and captured soldiers and civilians would be impaled on the stakes. This was intended to demoralize the defenders. Then prisoners would be taken in view of the defenders and tortured in ways that Assyrian scribes recorded in agonizing detail. Sometimes the victims would be put in cages on carts that were pulled in circles around a besieged city to display to as many people as possible the torture being inflicted. Such events were recorded on stone walls and monuments throughout the empire to frighten anyone who might wish to rebel.

By about 722 B.C.E. the Assyrian government had adopted a policy of avoiding fighting as many of the enemy as possible. The extraordinary cruelties inflicted on people were intended to inspire others to surrender rather than fight. Typically, in a city that did not surrender, the Assyrians raped every woman or girl they found and killed the military-age men. Boys would be made slaves. Captive populations would be shipped to parts of the empire where the Assyrian government could watch them and where they were wanted as forced labor, because the Assyrian government was depleting its lands of workers through its relentless warfare.

The Assyrians established storehouses throughout their empire, where their army could find supplies when it moved. At the core of the army was the *qurbuti*, the royal guard. This consisted of elite troops from Assyrian nobility. Assyrian kings often led their troops in battle, and the *qurbuti* accompanied them. When the king was not present, the commanding officer was the *tartanu*, who was to be obeyed as if he were the king. The army also had cavalry, called *pethallu*. However, the principal fighting units were the infantry and the chariot regiments. The most important fighters in the infantry remained the archers, who carried 50 arrows in their quivers. Most of the rest of the infantry was supposed to protect the archers. Sometimes the Assyrians fielded an army whose infantry consisted only of archers and their shield bearers. Of greatest importance were the chariots.

The Assyrian chariot was a swift vehicle, with a metal undercarriage making it tough and durable. Its spoked wheels had metal-studded rims and blades projecting from their hubs. Assyrian chariots moved as units and were used to break up enemy infantry lines. With two horses pulling each, the chariots would charge not as a line parallel to the enemy line but as a column perpendicular to the enemy line. One after another the chariots would smash into the line and then disperse as they spread the enemy line apart, their bladed wheels chewing through enemy infantry. Assyrian tactics were intended to terrify an enemy, and the chariots were truly frightful.

The driver of an Assyrian war chariot had to press forward against the front screen of the chariot to hold himself steady. On a light chariot the only other passenger was an archer or a lancer. On a heavy chariot the car would be rectangular to hold one or two shield bearers or a warrior to defend the rear of the chariot. The lancer would be armed with spears or javelins, usually tipped with iron. Sometimes lancers were used as infantrymen.

Eventually Assyria faced a shortage of men of any age; for this reason, boys younger than military age and retired soldiers often were pressed into service. The vassal troops, rarely happy about serving far from home in wars not of their own making, were unreliable. Rebellions broke out on the fringes of the empire, the Medes to the east invaded Assyria, and the army was spread too thinly to cope with all the demands at the same time. The Babylonians and Medes raced each other to the capital of Assyria, with the Medes getting there first. Over a period of about 10 years, the surviving Assyrians were hunted down and exterminated.

Persian Empire (ca. 538–ca. 331 B.C.E.)

The Persian Empire is also known as the Achaemenid Empire, named for its founder Achaemenes (r. ca. 600s B.C.E.). The first great Persian military leader was Cyrus the Great (r. ca. 559–ca. 529 B.C.E.). Persian soldiers were especially skilled in the use of slings and bows and arrows, perhaps a result of their origin in mountains in Iran, where hunting with such weapons would have been important. Although the Persians borrowed much of their military organization from that of the Assyrians, horses were rarely used by them in Cyrus the Great's era, relegating chariots to minor roles, whereas the infantry was of primary importance.

As was the case with the Assyrians, archers were very important to the Persian Empire. The Persians imitated the combining of shield bearers with archers, but they massed their archers behind a line of shield bearers. The shields were made of rectangles of leather stretched over rodlike willow twigs called osiers, and then the leather was allowed to harden, creating a tough but easily lifted shield. The shield bearers would form a line, one next to the other, allowing their shields to create a long, tall wall, behind which archers, also arrayed in lines, fired their arrows in volleys. Unfortunately, the shield bearers lacked weapons other than daggers for close-quarters fighting, a problem the Persian army continually tried to solve by experimenting with different kinds of weapons such as spears and curved swords.

The core of the army was the king's spearmen, the *arstibara*. After them came the *amrtaka* ("immortals"), a division of troops that gained its name from its never being allowed to be short of troops; its strength was always at 10,000. The major unit of the army was the *hazarabam*, the regiment, which had 1,000 troops. Its commanding officer was the *hazarapatis*. The *hazarabam* was divided into 10 units of 100 troops. Each unit was a *satabam*, commanded by a *satapatis*. Each *satabam* was divided into 10 companies of 10 men each. A company was a *dathabam*. On the battlefield each *dathabam* would be lined up in a column perpendicular to the front line, with its leader, the *dathapatis*, in front. The *dathapatis* carried a 6-foot spear or a large protective shield. The other nine soldiers in his company carried either bows or falchions, which were curved swords. When all the men behind the company leaders had bows and arrows, the company leaders would form a protective line of shields.

All Persian men were expected to serve in the army. A boy lived with his mother, apart from his father, until age five and then with his father, apart from his mother, until age 20, during which time he learned skills important to combat. From 20 to 24 years of age a man served in the army. His period of enlistment could be extended, and he was subject to recall to military service until he was 50 years old.

As he conquered much of the Near East, Cyrus the Great relied on vassal troops to supplement his core of Persian infantry, especially vassal cavalry. Cyrus the Great decided that his army should have a cavalry composed of Persians. Thus he established a new unit of the army composed of horseback riders. When horses and their supplies were captured in his campaigns, he distributed them among his nobility. Then he declared that it would be considered a disgrace for any noble to be seen walking rather than riding. The cavalry would be considered an elite unit. The most prestigious unit of all would be the 1,000 horsemen drawn from the nobility and called the *huvaka* ("king's kinsmen").

Not much is known about the organization of the Persian navy. It was developed during the reign of Cambyses (r. ca. 529–ca. 522 B.C.E.) as a response to the Egyptian navy, which had helped thwart Persian efforts to invade Egypt. It apparently borrowed ideas from the Corinthian navy, dividing its ships into units of 30 as the Corinthians did. When it was sent into battle against the Greeks in the 400s B.C.E., the Persian navy was decisively defeated. Military historians debate why this happened, but it appears that the Greek navy was more ably led and its sailors more skilled at the techniques required to disable enemy ships.

The failure of the Persian army to defeat the Greeks, first at Marathon in 490 B.C.E. and later with a massive army of between 700,000 and 1,500,000 troops, seems to have been a shock to the Near East. The perplexing methods of combat of the Scythians had been only an annoyance. The Scythians used archers on horseback, who attacked and then rode away, attacked again and rode away, and so on until the Persians stopped chasing them. In the case of the Greeks the Persians fought an enemy willing to engage in large battles of massed infantry and horsemen.

The Persian soldiers were courageous and determined fighters, but their commanders had no answer for the Greek soldier called a hoplite. The hoplites were members of heavy infantry, armed with spears and protected by shields that strapped to their forearms, allowing for a wide range of motion. Holding their shields high for protection from the Persian archers and covered by the fire of Greek archers, the hoplites were swiftly able to take advantage of changing conditions on the battlefield to close in on Persian units of archers. When the Greek style of fighting combined with the genius of Alexander the Great, the Persians often found their units outmaneuvered. From 336 to 328 B.C.E. Alexander the Great fought Persia, conquering the country just five years before his death in 323 B.C.E.

Iranian Empires

One of Alexander the Great's generals, Seleucus I (r. ca. 311–ca. 281 B.C.E.), founded the Seleucid Kingdom (ca. 311–ca. 140 B.C.E.). The Seleucid army was most notable for its cavalry, which was probably the best in the Near East in the 100s B.C.E., but they were overcome by the Parthians, who were also famous for their cavalry. The Parthians had migrated into Iran from central Asia. The Arsacid Dynasty of Parthia was founded by Arsaces I (r. ca. 250–ca. 248 B.C.E.) and lasted from about 250 B.C.E. to 226 C.E. It was King Mithridates I (r. ca. 174–ca. 136 B.C.E.) who toppled the Seleucid Kingdom.

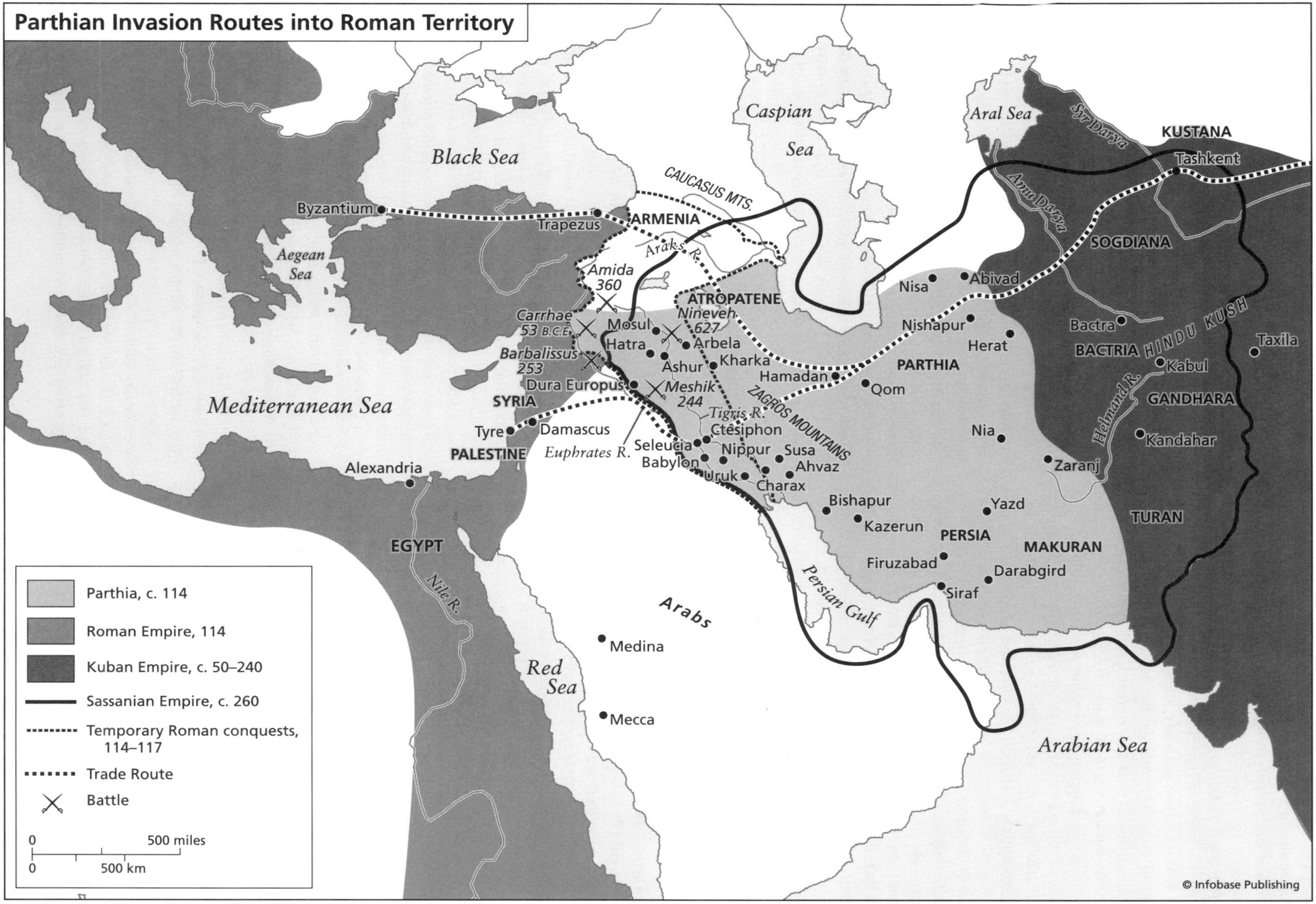

The Parthian and Roman armies battled each other for nearly 300 years, from the first century B.C.E. to the third century C.E.

The Parthians organized their army into 1,000-man units called dragons. The most important part of the army was its cavalry. The Parthians were master horsemen who developed the Parthian shot. A Parthian shot occurred when a horseman pretended to be fleeing and then twisted in his saddle to shoot backward at his enemy. The army combined unarmored horse archers with cataphracts—cavalry with heavy armor and arms. The light cavalry harassed the enemy while the cataphracts hammered enemy lines. Cataphracts were recruited from the retainers of Parthian nobility. Sometimes mercenaries were employed for other units.

The effectiveness of Parthian tactics and troops was shown in the Battle of Carrhae in 53 B.C.E., in present-day Turkey. A Roman army invaded Parthia, led by Marcus Licinius Crassus (115–53 B.C.E.). When he learned where the Parthian army awaited him, he had a choice of two routes. He took the route that crossed open land. The Parthians had anticipated his taking the other route, and their main army was waiting there for him. Mostly light cavalry was all the Parthian army had to fight Crassus's army in the open route. The Parthians gamely attacked, harassing the Romans with arrows. Crassus pulled his army into a square, open in the middle. The Parthian cavalry circled the Romans and fired without taking care to aim; the Roman formation was dense, and its troops were easy targets. After losing 20,000 men without ever coming to grips with the enemy, the Roman army retreated.

The Parthian Empire eventually fell to an insider rather than from invasion from the outside. Ardashir I (r. 224–241 C.E.) overthrew the last Arsacid king, founding the Sassanian Empire (226–641 C.E.). The Sassanian army had infantry, horse cavalry, and war elephants. The infantry mostly comprised spearmen who were ordered to hold their positions against attack. The cavalry were well armored and responsible for breaking up enemy formations. The elephants carried towers containing archers. Before battle the army arrayed itself into three parts. In the center, typically the largest part, were archers and the elephants. Although horses were armored, the elephants were not; they were protected instead by an escort of infantry.

ASIA AND THE PACIFIC

BY MICHAEL J. O'NEAL

Warfare in the modern world is typically waged between nation-states. For various reasons one of these states, with its own clearly defined borders, chooses to go to war with another. While civil wars continue to plague some countries, modern warfare has most often been between nations rather than within nations.

Warfare in the ancient world, including Asia, often had a different purpose. Modern nations such as China, India, Korea, and Japan did not always exist as clearly defined nation-states, with fixed borders and a central government accepted by the entire population. These regions tended to be more in the nature of collections of smaller kingdoms. Sometimes these kingdoms united to form larger states. Just as often, though, they fought with one another as one tried to extend the reach of its authority and influence. While external enemies remained a threat, internal enemies often were the target of warfare and conquest. The result was a long, bloody process of uniting regions into larger nations.

CHINA

The dominant military power of ancient Asia was China. In the absence of any records, little is known about war and conquest—or any other topic—in prehistoric China. China as a nation began to emerge during the era called the Three Sovereigns and Five Emperors, followed by the Xia Dynasty. Most of what is known about these eras is legendary, even mythical, although archaeological finds have confirmed that at least some of what was written about them by later Chinese writers is probably based in fact. The known history of China begins with the Shang Dynasty (sometimes referred to as the Yin Dynasty), which ruled from about 1500 to about 1045 B.C.E. Much of the history of the Shang and the dynasties that followed into the Common Era is a history of internal warfare and rebellion.

The Shang Dynasty itself began in war, for historians believe that the dynasty's founder was a rebel who overthrew the earlier Xia Dynasty. Over the next several hundred years the Shang emperors fought a series of wars to defend their realm, which encompassed primarily northern China, from invaders from the steppes (vast, open grasslands) of inner Asia. At this point China as a nation was by no means fully formed. The region consisted of numerous settlements and city-states that did not coalesce into a unified nation until much later. Thus, warfare was typically a matter of conflict between neighboring city-states as they jockeyed for power and tried to extend their authority over a broader region.

The Shang Dynasty was overthrown by the Zhou Dynasty in about 1045 B.C.E. The Zhou were a people who had settled to the west of the territories ruled by the Shang, and for a long period they submitted to Shang authority. But as the Zhou population grew, its region became more powerful than that controlled by the Shang, particularly since the Shang were continually waging war with northern invaders. Thus, the Zhou defeated the Shang and established a dynasty that ruled 200 to 250 city-states until 256 B.C.E.

Their reign was not without complications, however. Barbarians from the north, particularly the Xiongnu, a nomadic people who controlled a large central Asian empire, continued to invade Chinese lands. (The Xiongnu are frequently referred to in the literature as Huns, but they are not to be confused with the Teutonic Huns of Europe.) In 771 B.C.E. they successfully overran the western portion of the Zhou lands, including its capital city. The king was killed, and his son fled to the east. Thus, the Zhou Dynasty is divided into two periods, the Western Zhou (1045–771 B.C.E.) and the Eastern Zhou (770–256 B.C.E.) The Eastern Zhou is further divided into two periods. The first, called the Spring and Autumn Period, was a time of great instability. Among the large number of Chinese city-states, no single state had much power. Thus, they joined into a series of continuously shifting alliances as a way of defending themselves from the northern barbarians.

The name of the second phase of the Eastern Zhou, the Warring States Period, gives a clear indication of the nature of Chinese life during this time. Many of the military and political alliances that had been forged during the Spring and Autumn Period fell apart. China descended into considerable chaos as various states tried to fill the power vacuum and absorb other states, and the Zhou emperor ruled in name only. Warfare between states was nearly constant. By the end of the period, instead of hundreds of city-states, the number was eight or nine, with each vying to gain control of all of China. The nature of warfare changed dramatically during this period. Earlier, war had been conducted in feudal fashion, with aristocratic nobles each leading his own small army. During the Warring States Period armies became much larger and were made up of professional warriors.

It was during the brief, but ruthless Qin Dynasty that China's kingdoms merged for the first time into an imperial nation. The Qin emperors, who ruled from 221 to 207 B.C.E., confiscated all weapons, including those of the nobles who had fought during the Warring States Period. This step was taken to prevent uprisings. The Qin rulers also expanded China's borders by going to war against the northern barbarians. During the Warring States Period nobles had built walls and fortifications to defend their realms. The Qin emperors ordered that all these walls be linked to form China's first great wall to keep out foreign invaders. (The Great Wall of China familiar to tourists was built much later, under the Ming Dynasty.)

Despite the efforts of the Qin rulers to quell dissent and rebellion, they were unsuccessful. Near the end of the dynasty the nobles began to reassert their power. Peasants, prisoners, and soldiers rebelled. The result was the overthrow of the Qin Dynasty and the creation of the Han Dynasty, which ruled until 220 C.E. The Han Dynasty, however, began with an interregnum period from 206 to 202 B.C.E. called the period of Chu-Han Contention. During this period, in the vacuum created by the overthrow of the Qin Dynasty, two factions emerged that went to war to determine which would lead the kingdom. One faction was the Han people; the other was the Chu. These factions were led by the nobles who had been stripped of their power during the Qin Dynasty. The numerous battles these two sides fought—the battles of Julu, Pengcheng, Lingbi, and Xi River, for example—became part of the cultural identity of the Chinese and are still depicted in Chinese movies, television shows, and even board games. The power struggle was fierce; at times the warring armies were as large as half a million men. After the tide shifted back and forth several times, the Han, led by Liu Pang (r. 206–195 B.C.E.), emerged victorious and created the Han Dynasty.

The Han Dynasty tried to scale back the level of warfare. To the north the rulers paid tribute to the Xiongnu and tried to buy peace through intermarriage. The dynasty also tried to appease other neighboring nomads, which continued to be a threat. At the same time, the Han Dynasty used its superior military force to extend its borders into the regions of present-day Vietnam and Korea. The military also functioned to keep open the Silk Road, the trading route that eventually extended westward all the way to Rome. In 154 B.C.E. the military had to put down the Rebellion of the Seven States, led by several minor princes who objected to the Han Dynasty's efforts to centralize the government. The rebellion was marked by initial ferocious fighting, but in the end it lasted only three months.

Less than three decades later the Han Dynasty concluded that its treaties with the Xiongnu were ineffective and costly. In 129 B.C.E. a force of 40,000 Chinese cavalry attacked. Warfare persisted intermittently until 119 B.C.E., when a Chinese force of 100,000 cavalry and 200,000 foot soldiers drove the Xiongnu into the Gobi Desert. The campaign, while successful, was costly; the Chinese took 140,000 horses into the desert, but fewer than 30,000 returned. The Xiongnu, however, just would not go away. In the first century of the Common Era, China dispatched one of its most famous generals, Pan Ch'ao (31–101 C.E.), to subdue them and drive them out of the Tarim Basin to China's west. In 97 C.E. he commanded an army of 70,000 men to drive them even farther west; he went as far as the Caspian Sea, where he struck an alliance with the Parthian Empire. Despite all of China's successes against the Xiongnu, in 311 C.E., 100 years after the end of the Han Dynasty, the Xiongnu sacked Luoyang, the capital of the Han.

One of the last military actions of the Han Dynasty was the suppression of the Yellow Turban Rebellion, sometimes called the Yellow Scarves Rebellion. The rebellion took place in 184 and was led by Daoist peasants who objected to the regime's decision to make China a Confucian rather than a Daoist state. Despite fielding an army of 360,000, the rebels were unsuccessful and were put down in 185. Fighting erupted again in 186, 188, and 192, when the rebellion was finally ended.

For many historians, the Yellow Turban Rebellion, so called because of the yellow headscarves the rebels wore, was the unofficial start of the Three Kingdoms Period (220–263 B.C.E.) that followed the Han Dynasty. Again, China was wracked by instability. The "three kingdoms" were those of Wei, Shu, and Wu, though they were not really kingdoms but regions whose emperors each claimed to be the legitimate heir to the Han Dynasty. The period was marked by a great deal of infighting, which eventually led to the defeat of the Shu by the Wei. The Wei, in turn, were then defeated by an alliance of the Wu and the Jin Dynasty (265–420 C.E.). The period was extremely bloody, with a large percentage of the population killed during the wars that raged from about 190 to 280. On the heels of these civil wars came the War of the Eight Princes (also called the Rebellion of the Eight Kings or Rebellion of the Eight Princes), another period of civil war from 291 to 306 C.E. The rebellion was centered in northern China. Again, it led to huge population losses, which greatly reduced the power of the Jin Dynasty. The dynasty itself was rent by divisions, leading to the creation of the Western Jin Dynasty (265–316 C.E.) and the Eastern Jin Dynasty (317–420

C.E.). One of the most important battles in ancient Chinese history was the Battle of Fei in 383 C.E., when the numerically inferior eastern Jin army defeated the surviving western Jin to claim control over the throne.

One of the results of this long history of warfare was the production of texts about military strategy. One is referred to as the "Thirty-Six Strategies." The origin of the book is shrouded in mystery. Historians generally believe that it was compiled by a General Wang during the Warring States Period. It consists of a number of proverbs about warfare, many of which were probably traditional by that time. The number 36 is a figure of speech used to refer to "numerous" strategies, divided into six sections. To cite one example, the text advises military commanders to "deceive the sky to cross the ocean." The text explains this precept by saying that the clever commander hides his true intentions by going about daily activities in full view of the enemy; hiding or moving about in the darkness only attracts suspicion.

The other great military text from ancient China is *The Art of War*, written, it is thought, in the sixth century by Suntzu. The book has 13 chapters and is still regarded by military planners as the definitive treatise on military strategy—particularly on how to win a battle or war without actually fighting but rather by outsmarting the enemy. The book continues to be required reading for officers in Asian militaries. Many of the book's statements have become proverbial, such as the famous quote "All warfare is based on deception." The book was rediscovered in the West in the 1980s when corporations and political candidates began using its precepts to plot business or campaign strategies and outsmart their rivals. The book has also entered the popular culture in the West, with numerous references to it in movies, plays, sports, music, board games, and television shows.

Based on these and other texts, as well as on the archaeological record, historians and archaeologists have been able to reconstruct the nature of warfare in ancient China. They know, for example, that weapons during much of ancient China's history were made of bronze. Examples include the spear, whose point was made of bronze, and the dagger-ax, which was primary weapon of foot soldiers. A dagger-ax consisted of a dagger-shaped blade mounted perpendicularly on a wooden haft, or handle. Often the blade consisted of a dagger on one side and a scythe-shaped blade on the other. Other weapons included the sword, many quite elaborate and ornate, and the crossbow. Chinese soldiers also wore armor, which tended to be light and flexible rather than heavy and thick, trading the stopping power for speed and maneuverability. The Chinese invented gunpowder, probably in the third century C.E., but gunpowder was not used as a component of military weapons until much later.

The horse-drawn chariot was a primary instrument of war. Ancient China was a feudal society, and there emerged a warrior class that emphasized the skills of horsemanship and the handling of the chariot. Horseback riding tended to be difficult for Chinese men, who wore robes rather than trousers, but skills in military horsemanship were highly developed among members of the aristocratic warrior class, and many troops stormed into battle on horseback. In about the fifth century C.E. the stirrup was introduced, allowing mounted warriors to retain stability and balance and so fight on horseback with swords and lances.

Early warfare tended to be ceremonial and ritualized. As time went on it became more brutal and bloody. Much emphasis was placed on deception and tricking the enemy. Also common was siege warfare, where an attacking army surrounded a city, bombarded it with missiles launched by catapults, and wore down the residents over time. In more conventional battles the norm was not to arrange regiments of troops in a fixed order of battle but rather to rely on firepower using crossbows. Large numbers of archers loaded their weapons, took aim on the order of their commander, and then fired simultaneously, in this way overwhelming the enemy by the sheer number of arrows that had to be ducked.

Naval warfare played a major part in the history of ancient China. During the Qin Dynasty, for example, China had a fleet of ships capable of transporting close to one million pounds of grain to feed troops during war. The Qin also had a fleet of *lou chuan*, or "castle ships," with large, elevated decks. The Han continued to build warships, and its fleet reached 2,000 castle ships able to carry 200,000 seamen.

India

The history of warfare and conquest in ancient India in many ways parallels that of China. Rather than being a unified nation-state, India was a collection of numerous smaller kingdoms. At times the number of kingdoms was as few as 16. Such was the case during the Iron Age in about 500 B.C.E., when the 16 kingdoms were collectively called the Mahajanadapas. At other times the number of kingdoms and principalities was much larger, as many as 100 or more. As in China, these kingdoms often competed with one another for territory and resources, so they often went to war. Warfare, though, was conducted on a smaller scale than it was in China and consisted primarily of border skirmishes.

India, however, faced more external threats than did the Chinese. Like China, India was subject to invasion by barbarians from the north. One of the greatest civilizations of the ancient world, the Indus Valley civilization, was destroyed by northern Aryan invaders in about 1600 B.C.E. Additionally, in the fifth century B.C.E. India was invaded by the Persians under the king Darius the Great (r. 522–486 B.C.E.) and was ruled by the Persian Empire for nearly 200 years until Macedonia, under the leadership of Alexander the Great (r. 336–323 B.C.E.), conquered the Persian Empire, including its holdings in India. One of the key events in this conquest was the Battle of the Hydaspes River (now called the Jhelum River) in 326 B.C.E. Alexander invaded to subdue the various Indian kings, but one, Porus (d. between 321 and 315 B.C.E.), who ruled the area around Punjab, resisted. Alexander sent a large army against him. Porus and his army put up fierce resistance, but eventually Alexander won and made the area the eastern border of his empire.

India as a unified empire did not flex its military might until the Maurya Dynasty, which maintained a standing army of three-quarters of a million troops, most belonging to a warrior caste. The empire, founded about 321 B.C.E. by Chandragupta, was based in eastern India but in time stretched across western, central, and portions of southern India. One of the greatest achievements of the Maurya was the liberation of those parts of the country that were occupied by the Macedonians. One of Chandragupta's ministers, Kautilya (fl. 300 B.C.E.), wrote a text called the *Arthashastra*, a book that examined the military arts along with politics, economics, and other subjects.

One of the most important rulers of the Maurya was Chandragupta's grandson, Asoka (r. ca. 265–238 B.C.E. or ca. 273–232 B.C.E.). Early in his reign Asoka was a talented military commander. His major achievement was to lead a large army against the Kalinga, one of the kingdoms of southern India. Although he triumphed, he lost an estimated 10,000 troops, and when he saw the devastation the war had caused both to the armies and to the civilian population, he renounced war and accepted the teachings of Buddhism. However, as many historians note, he had no further reason to go to war, for he had successfully united most of what is modern-day India.

Stone figure of the war god Skanda, from eastern India, eighth to ninth century C.E.; Skanda was a poular deity in ancient India. (© The Trustees of the British Museum)

In the centuries that followed the end of Maurya rule, India again fragmented. The invading Kushans established an empire that stretched across the center of India. The later Gupta Empire, which ruled from C.E. 240 to 550, again united India, primarily because of its strong military organization.

One of the most important military weapons of the Gupta Empire, as well as the empires of its predecessors, was the chariot. Indian chariots were more like troop-transport vehicles, in contrast to the light Roman and Egyptian chariots that normally come to mind. They carried at least two men—the driver and an archer—but many carried up to seven and were so heavy that four and even six horses were needed to pull them. Sometimes the chariots were simply driven at high speed into the middle of a fight, where their large wheels crushed enemy infantrymen. Meanwhile, the archers were as high as six feet off the ground, giving them a tactical advantage over enemy troops on the ground.

Another important tool used by Indian armies, which came into use in about 1500 B.C.E., was the elephant, which Indians continued to use in war until the 19th century. Elephants were a measure of wealth and prestige; Candragutpa's army had more than 21,000. Elephants were analogous to modern-day tanks. They were covered with armor and often had long daggers, sometimes poisoned, attached to their tusks. Each elephant provided protection for as many as six infantrymen, who fought with bows and arrows, lances, and javelins and then retreated behind the elephant when necessary. Elephants were also used to break down walls and enemy fortifications. One battle tactic, used by Porus at the Battle of Hydaspes, was to range the elephants in a line, providing a kind of moving fortress or wall. Like chariots, they were often driven directly into the battle, crushing enemy troops underfoot as archers mounted on the elephant's back shot at men below. Some elephants were even trained to swing weapons such as balls and chains back and forth.

Unlike China, which made extensive use of horse-mounted cavalry, Indians did not in general fight with cavalry. One exception was the Rajput Kingdom, which had an extremely skilled cavalry. Otherwise, the main force of an Indian army was its infantry, which fought primarily with bows and arrows and hundreds of different types of swords. The armies of India tended to be huge, much larger than the armies fielded by other empires at the time. Even though the kingdoms at war might have been small, it was not unusual for their armies to number in the hundreds of thousands. India maintained a navy for military purposes; during Maurya rule the navy became quite extensive. Although the navy was used to subdue islands and provinces along the coast, naval warfare was not a prominent feature of India's military history.

India was particularly noteworthy for its use of planned battle tactics and formations. Some of these battle formations were complex and included the *chakra* (wheel), *suchi* (needle), *chayana* (hawk), *mala* (garland), *garuda* (eagle), and *padma* (lotus). These terms reflected the shape of the formations. Thus, for example, in the *padma* formation archers (as well as the commanding general) were on the inside, surrounded by cavalry and infantry in the shape of a lotus flower, protecting the archers. If enemy troops managed to force their way into the area between the "petals" of the flower, the two petals would swing together, crushing the troops between them. The *garuda* formation featured elephants and the most skilled archers at the "beak," archers who were almost as good at the "head," "wings" of swift cavalry and infantry troops, and a "body" of reserves behind.

Korea

Like China and India, Korea consisted of a number of city-states, except that the number was much smaller, reflecting the small size of the Korean peninsula. During the first millennium B.C.E., the three city-states that dominated were Koguryo Paekche, and Silla, though other minor city-states existed as well. Within each of these city-states were several groups. Historically, these city-states have been called the Three Kingdoms, and the Three Kingdoms Period extended from the first century B.C.E. to 668 C.E., when Silla defeated Koguryo.

Militarily, the most powerful and dominant of the kingdoms was the Koguryo (the name from which *Korea* evolved). Beginning in 37 B.C.E. and into the first centuries of the Common Era a succession of monarchs united the kingdom, extended the kingdom's boundaries and, in particular, resisted the Chinese. During the reign of Taejo (53–146 C.E.) the Koreans mounted a number of well-conceived attacks on the Chinese garrisons at Lolang, Xiantu, and Liaodong. Their efforts were successful, and Koguryo became entirely independent. The regime also launched attacks against smaller states to absorb them. Later, under King Gwanggaeto the Great, who reigned from 391 to 412 C.E., the kingdom further expanded its territories through military conquest; in fact, the king's name means "great expander of territory." His army conquered at least 64 walled cities and 1,400 villages against a group called the Buyeo. He subdued additional peoples, annexed portions of the peninsula, conquered Silla, and waged war against Japan. The result of his efforts and those of his son was to turn Korea into a unified country for some 50 years.

Less is known about the tactics and organization of ancient Korean armies. Although there was a measure of internal warfare, Korea did not engage in extensive armed conflict with neighbors, and weapons technology was not as highly advanced as it was among the Chinese. In general, Koreans fought using farm implements and other common objects. Among them were the *ji pang e*, a cane; the *jang bond*, or long staff; the *jung bong*, a staff of middle length; the *tahn bong*, or short stick; the *jang tan-do*, or long dagger; and the *nat*, or sickle. Koreans, though, did not carry these simple weapons into battle without training. Martial-arts training provided warriors with the skills the needed, including the *hyungs*, or patterns, to turn these objects into lethal weapons. Accompanying this was training in hand-to-hand combat. Many of these Korean martial arts continue to be taught in the modern world.

The ancient Koreans, especially those in the kingdom of Silla, maintained a strong warrior class. Boys and young men were sent to schools that emphasized training in military tactics and the use of weapons, and the most promising ones were given further training and became members of the warrior class.

Japan

Warfare was infrequent during the Jōmon Period, the earliest period of Japanese history, which began about 13,000 B.C.E. and extended to about 300 B.C.E. During the fourth and third centuries B.C.E. waves of immigrants from Korea and China changed the fundamental makeup of Japan. From about 300 B.C.E. to 300 C.E. the Yayoi Period of Japanese history (named after the modern Tokyo suburb in which archaeological remains of the culture were found in the 19th century) was marked by the introduction of metal weapons and the rise of an aristocratic warrior class. Most of the warfare in which Japan took part was internal. Japan at the time was not a unified nation-state but a collection of villages and small cities. Japan was an agricultural society, and imbalances in the productivity of its numerous communities led to conflict. The basic unit of society was the clan (*uji*), and each clan, led by a noble, fielded an army to defend its interests. This emphasis on an aristocratic warrior class continued into the Yamato Period that followed the Yayoi. The Yamato emperors continued the process of subduing groups and even attacked part of Korea in 391 C.E. The pattern, then, was similar to those of China, India, and Korea, as small kingdoms warred with each other over resources and in the attempt to forge a larger kingdom.

Little is known about ancient Japanese battle tactics or military organization. It is known that some warriors fought on horseback, but most were foot soldiers. The archaeological record shows arrow points, swords, knives, and axes made of iron. Bronze weapons included halberds, swords, and spears. Because ancient Japanese society was feudal and clan based, no nation-state mounted a centralized army; rather, military forces were small, and their members consisted of the men that the feudal overlord could press into service.

Oceania

Social organization throughout Oceania, including Micronesia, New Guinea, and Australia, was highly fragmented in ancient times. None of these peoples built an empire or even a nation. The basic unit of organization was the tribe. Tribes were typically run by a "big man," the tribal leader. Geographically, the unit of organization was the island or, on larger islands, the village. Sometimes primitive warfare broke out as populations grew and tribes competed for resources; at times they resorted to cannibalism. Also, population pressures often forced islanders to leave to find new lands.

EUROPE

BY KIRK H. BEETZ

Violence was a large part of life in ancient Europe. Evidence of interpersonal violence first appears in the Mesolithic Period (ca. 8000–ca. 4000 B.C.E.), and mass burials such as those found at the Neolithic (ca. 7000–ca. 2000 B.C.E.) sites of Asparn in Austria and Talheim in Germany contain skeletons that bear signs of blows from stone axes. Traumatic injuries on bones are common features of Neolithic skeletons throughout Europe. The nature of this violence is difficult to determine, but from about 5500 B.C.E. onward banks and ditches around Neolithic settlements are common. Sites like Darion in Belgium were very clearly fortified with palisades and ditches, and movement into the sites was channeled through gates that could be defended. Since Darion was located on the frontier of Neolithic settlement at the time, it could be speculated that the site was defended against the hunter-gatherers on whose territory the farmers were encroaching.

Warfare in prehistoric Europe did not involve the conquest and control of territory because this would entail organized political units that did not yet exist. Instead, warfare primarily took the form of raids to obtain livestock or other resources, or they were factional struggles between the adherents of one chief or leader and those of another that turned violent. They probably involved techniques such as ambushes in the forest and the terrorization of the inhabitants of isolated settlements and farmsteads rather than large, organized groups of warriors. Violence may also have been directed at individuals rather than groups, as the wounds on the frozen, 5,300-year-old "Iceman" found in the Alps in 1991 suggest.

During the Bronze Age (ca. 2800–ca. 700 B.C.E.) and Iron Age (ca. 1000 B.C.E.–ca. 500 C.E.) the increased effort expended in the fortification of settlements as well as the many types of weapons that could be manufactured from bronze and iron indicate that conflict and warfare may have increased. Sites without much evidence of permanent settlement but with elaborate fortifications may have served as refuges in times of threat. The emergence of chiefs who could command their retainers to take up arms against communities loyal to their enemies shifted warfare to a new level of organization, and the chiefs themselves may have owed much of their status to their accomplishments in battle. Such values may have resulted in further escalation of warfare throughout the Bronze Age and Iron Age as individuals sought prestige and wealth.

Soon after 2000 B.C.E. the bow and arrow almost disappeared from European warfare. This was an odd development because the bow and arrow remained very important instruments of war in and near Asia. Throughout much of Europe, however, small projectile points that could have served as arrowheads almost disappeared from the archaeological record. There may be two reasons for this, one cultural and the other technological. By 2000 B.C.E. Europeans were adopting what archaeologists and historians call a heroic culture. They usually point to the epic poem the *Iliad* by the Greek poet Homer (eighth or ninth century B.C.E.) as an example of what a heroic culture was like. In a heroic culture warriors dominate. The apex of society is the individual leader who has distinguished himself or herself in combat. For Europe this may have encouraged the use of hand-to-hand weapons that were suited to contests between two easily identifiable warriors rather than long-range weapons in which death and victory came anonymously.

The key technological development was the sword. In southern Europe and the Near East small swords and daggers were favored for combat, but in the rest of Europe swords grew increasingly longer. By 900 B.C.E. the Celtic peoples were conquering Europe, and their weapon of choice was a slashing sword. Celtic masters of metalworking found ways to make long swords tough and durable. In the Near East swords remained short partly because metalworkers could not keep a sword strong and durable after it reached the length of about 2 feet; their swords would snap when they became too long. Short swords were intended more for stabbing than slashing, and they were used only for fighting in very close quarters, as in the combat favored by the Romans.

The Celts

By the time the Romans and Celts came into direct conflict in the late 400s B.C.E. the Celts had developed a style of warfare that favored the long sword. When they met and slaughtered a Roman army near the city of Rome in 390 B.C.E., they were using long swords with blunted points that were intended entirely for slashing. They also used spears, which they made in three lengths. The longest spear was designed for thrusting, the medium-length spear was made for throwing, and the short one was used for close combat. There seems to have been no loss of prestige for using spears, but the sword was the weapon of preference for most Celtic warriors.

The Celts of that era had fully developed their warrior culture. The best way for someone to advance in Celtic society was through heroic victories in combat. Also prestigious was the taking of the heads of fallen heroes and bringing home loot. An interesting aspect of Celtic looting was that they often gave their best loot to gods or goddesses, frequently dumping what they brought home into lakes and rivers as gifts to the gods who had aided them in battle.

Headhunting by the Celts appalled many of the Greeks and Romans who explored Celtic Europe before Rome's invasions of central Europe in the middle of the first century B.C.E. The heads of cowards were not taken. There was no glory in killing someone who ran away or froze in fear. Instead, Celtic warriors cut off the heads of people they had killed face to face. Although these heads were usually those of men in the male-dominated Celtic society, some were probably of women who had earned reputations as fearsome sorceresses or masters of combat. Celtic oral tradition has many tales of warriors being taught the skills of combat by women who were masters of battle, and killing them in armed combat was considered just as glorious as killing a great male warrior. The greater the warrior, the more prestige would come from having his head. The heads were hung on the walls of Celtic homes, and the family in the home would recite the many glorious achievements of the former owners of the heads, just as they would of the ancestors or living family members who had slain them.

In battle Celtic horsemen hung the heads from the necks of their horses as part of the intimidation of opponents that was always a part of Celtic warfare.

Celtic homes offer some indication of what Celtic wars were usually like. Most Celts lived in homesteads, which were houses on farms. The ground around the houses was fortified with a wooden wall. Although the defenses of a homestead would not protect residents from large armies, they were adequate for keeping out raiders. Most Celtic warfare consisted of raids, mostly for stealing cattle. Cattle were a form of booty that successful raiders could show off to others. Young men in small groups often wandered Celtic Europe looking for adventure, gaining experience in combat skills while fighting warriors at homesteads. This activity was treated more as a sport than serious warfare.

More serious were disputes over land, insults, or large numbers of stolen cattle. Protecting one's land and defending one's honor or the honor of one's group were considered imperative. Stealing a few dozen cattle was seen as excessively greedy. To settle these disputes, sometimes hundreds of warriors met for combat. The two sides would agree to meet at a place with sufficient open ground for everyone to see and to fight. Honor came from being seen to overcome a foe.

Until about the time of the Roman general Julius Caesar (100–44 B.C.E.), chariots figured prominently in Celtic warfare in continental Europe, and they lingered in Britain and Ireland for about 100 years after Caesar's era. The chariot had a driver who was a follower of the warrior who owned the chariot. He would stand out on the shaft that thrust out between the two horses from the car, maneuvering the chariot quickly to take his warrior through battle. In doing so, he won merit for his skill and for the great courage that it took for him to be vulnerable to the enemy. In the 200s B.C.E. the Celts invented the four-pommel saddle, which had two pommels in front of the thighs to hold them in place and two at the rear of the saddle. This gave the Celtic cavalryman the stability that allowed him to become a fighting machine, protected by chain-mail armor and shield while wielding an assortment of weapons that would be given to him by two mounted followers. The team was called a *trimarcisia*, which meant "three horses" in Celtic.

Sometimes these battles ended without bloodshed. A warrior might take charge of his chariot and put on a display of acrobatic daring—handstands, leaps, and tumbles—while racing in front of the enemy. Often, the warrior rode out on horseback and performed a variety of impressive stunts. Sometimes the skill of such a warrior was so great that both sides agreed to settle the dispute in favor of the side of the outstanding performer. Roman soldiers were amazed at the skill of such warriors before combat, but they had no idea the demonstrations were intended to substitute for actually killing people. On the other hand, the Romans well understood the idea of duels between champions to settle battles without additional bloodshed.

Before battle the champions would step forward from the ranks of their sides. The champions would proclaim their heroic deeds and the deeds of the warriors they had killed. The objective was to overawe the other side. The Celts believed that the spoken word was as powerful as the might of a well-armed warrior, and they took boasting seriously. Sometimes no one would emerge to answer the boasting of the opposing champion, and the battle was settled without bloodshed. If the boasting was answered by a champion, then each would compete in oratory, trying to make the other back down. If neither backed down, then they would fight.

During the duel the other warriors of both sides would shout and blow their *carnyxes*, which were horns with the heads of animals on one end. They made a great din of harsh sounds. Many of the warriors would have drunk alcohol before battle to make themselves reckless. Once one champion or the other won, the battle could be settled, and everyone could go home. Sometimes a new challenger emerged. One oral account tells of a warrior who killed more than 100 challengers before everyone agreed to stop fighting. Sometimes after a duel was over, the warriors of both sides would charge at each other in a frenzy of bloodlust, each hoping to be seen to be heroically felling enemies. This charge was intended to settle the battle; the Celts had no backup strategy if the charge failed. Thus, the losers in a charge often ran away. The Romans learned to take advantage of this: If they could withstand the first charge of the Celts, they could win, because the Celts had no idea what to do next.

There was another kind of war for the Celts, and this was the war of conquest. When a tribe grew too big for its territory or was driven from its lands by an invader, the members sometimes abandoned their homes and carried their property on carts. If attacked while carting across country, the men would engage the enemy in combat. If they were overcome, the women would fight next. To actually seize the carts meant having to defeat the children, who would guard them. A Greek explorer, Posidonius (ca. 135–51 B.C.E.), was awed by the size and strength of Celtic women. He and others noted that if a Celtic man fell in combat, the fighting was not always over, because his wife was skilled in hand-to-hand combat and could deliver tremendously powerful blows with her feet and her fists as well as with weapons. Children were trained in fighting almost from birth.

When Caesar invaded central Europe in 58 B.C.E. he introduced a form of warfare that was unfamiliar to the Celts. The Roman troops fought as tightly structured units. Like the Celts, their objective was usually to fight hand to hand, using their superior skill, armor, and weapons to overcome their adversaries. Further, the Roman objective was to annihilate the enemy. Over hundreds of years the Celts had developed a structure for combat that usually allowed them to avoid much bloodshed. The objective was to make one's point, dazzling friends and foes, and then go home and feast, exaggerating one's heroism while telling about the battle. The Romans rarely quit, but just kept coming. Celts often panicked and ran after their initial charge if this failed to put the Romans to flight.

When the Celts had competent leadership and worked together, they were almost more than the Romans could handle.

During the Roman conquest of Europe the Romans lost an entire legion near Belgium when a group of Celtic tribes under unified leadership fought them. The charismatic Celtic leader Vercingetorix (d. 46 B.C.E.), who had recently become chief of the Averni tribe, persuaded tribes from all over Europe to join into one army under his command. He lost battles to the Romans but kept his alliance intact, and he switched to guerilla warfare, which the Romans were ill equipped to handle.

The Celts burned their farms so the Romans would not find food, and they killed Roman units that were sent away from their main army to forage. Vercingetorix's crucial mistake was to take his army to Alesia, a fortified city in central Europe. It is likely that he did not know enough about Roman tactics to grasp that Roman engineers would build a fortification to surround Alesia to starve him out. He probably hoped that the Romans would be caught between relief forces from the north and his army in Alesia. The fractiousness of the Celts contributed to their downfall. Some refused to help and were later overwhelmed by the Romans. Others refused to send all their warriors. Three times the Celts attacked the Roman fortifications simultaneously from inside and out, twice nearly penetrating Roman lines and overwhelming the Romans. More warriors might have been enough for success, but the Celts were forced to surrender. Vercingetorix was imprisoned and later executed in 46 B.C.E.

Another able leader undone by Celtic customs of war was Queen Boudicca (d. 60/61 C.E.). She was the widow of a king of the Iceni, a tribe in eastern Britain. The Romans governed the Britons harshly, but her tribe had managed to keep the peace. The spark that touched off a firestorm was the rape of two Iceni girls by Roman soldiers. How old Boudicca was is unclear. She was old enough to have had a 12-year-old daughter, but she could still have been in her late 20s. She is usually imagined as middle-aged. She was described as big, but Celtic women in general looked big to the Romans. Nonetheless, she was either imposingly tall or heavy or both. Her blazing red hair hung down to her waist. In battle she painted half her body green and wore a large robe. She was said to be a sorceress.

In western Britain 10,000 Roman troops were slaughtering Druid priests. Perhaps as many as 10,000 marched to suppress Boudicca's rebellion. She had drawn to her about 100,000 warriors from homesteads across Britain. Instead of their usual frontal charge, the Celts quietly surrounded the Romans in a forest and then attacked from all sides at once. They killed nearly every Roman soldier. Their attacks on Roman towns and fortifications were similarly disciplined. They seemed unconcerned with taking trophies but fought the Roman way, totally destroying the enemy. The Roman governor fled London with his troops, leaving it to Boudicca's army.

By the time Boudicca brought her army to bear on the 10,000 Roman soldiers marching from the west, having exterminated the Druids, she had more than 200,000 warriors, along with supply wagons and fierce Celtic women to defend them. The Romans were holed up in a small valley. Boudicca arrayed her forces in a line to face them. Charioteers put on traditional Celtic shows of skill and bravery. The Romans stepped forward in a jagged line of *V* formations designed to break up the Celts' solid line, allowing Roman soldiers to hack at their foes from the front and the sides. The Celtic mistake was to allow themselves to be provoked. They charged as a mass, making a din so frightening that the Romans nearly panicked. Then the Celts pressed in on each other, trying to get at the Romans. Chariots overturned. Warriors suffocated. The Roman line held, and the Celts panicked. Following a longstanding tradition for Celtic war leaders, Boudicca committed suicide when it was clear the battle was lost.

The Germans

By Caesar's era the Celts were beleaguered not only by the Romans from the south but also by the Germans from the north and east. In fact, Caesar began his campaign to conquer Gaul by first driving away Germanic invaders. These Germans came primarily from the north but were conquering their way through northeastern Europe and would eventually threaten Roman Europe from both north and east. Their motivations for conquest varied. Sometimes a tribe's population grew so much that the tribe chose to expand its territory to accommodate its growth. Sometimes a natural disaster or an invasion of its territory drove a tribe from its homes and into territory claimed by someone else. Often the conquest was inspired by a desire for loot. At other times a leader wanted glory.

War chiefs tended to serve only while a war lasted. Customs varied among Germanic tribes, with some choosing one leader while others chose two. One reason for choosing two might have been to prevent either one from using his power to make himself the permanent king. In early campaigns against Germanic armies the Romans noted that the Germans seemed wild and ill equipped. A German warrior was expected to supply his own weapons and armor. This meant that German armies of the first century B.C.E. often featured warriors wearing only breechcloths (loincloths), without even protection for their heads. Often they had no shields. They just carried spears and rarely axes or swords. In the close hand-to-hand combat that both Romans and Germans favored, the Romans cut the Germans to pieces.

The Germanic fighters differed from the Celtic warriors in an important way: They knew how to fight as units and were accustomed to having a long-term strategy. Like the Celts, they liked to show off their courage, toughness, and prowess. In the dead of winter men would ride naked and bareback on horses to display their contempt for discomfort. They were used to being cold, tired, and uncomfortable, and in the long run they would prove to be formidable opponents for other Europeans.

The basic Germanic fighting unit was the family. Family members stayed together during marches and battles and were responsible for each other's well-being. If a war chief failed to satisfy his troops with his leadership, families could desert, choosing to return to protect their homes rather than serve someone they did not trust. An army could disintegrate this way. Family groups were organized into clans composed of their relatives. The clans were organized into tribes. The tribes often had their own chiefs, and a war chief needed to address their worries and their ambitions, keeping those factors in check while trying to keep everyone focused on the military campaign.

Summoning warriors family by family was a slow process, and it depended on the mutual obligations between family members and their chief. Germanic armies tended to bunch together, which made them difficult to maneuver on the battlefield and hard to organize into efficient marching. Poor scouting and a focus on internal discipline among the troops meant that German armies were often taken by surprise. When surprised, they might not flee, but they were slow to respond and poorly organized at such times; they might stubbornly fight where they stood until they were cut down. Even so, when they were assembled and units were properly sorted out by family, clan, and tribe, the Germans could form large, formidable armies.

Generals were usually men from well-known warrior families. During the first century C.E. the leaders of these families became nobles, and their status and political power continually increased as their tribes forged national identities over the next several centuries. These nobles were usually dedicated full time to preparing for and waging war. Around them grew the *comites*, full-time warriors who served a noble. During the ancient era Germanic warriors were primarily infantry. They did not have the exceptionally sophisticated cavalry gear that the Celts had, making it hard to use horses as mobile battle platforms the way the Celtic cavalry did, although those few who fought from horseback were extraordinarily skilled and not to be taken lightly.

The waging of war was the preoccupation of most Germanic peoples. Their sons were taught throughout childhood how to kill their enemies, and if the family could afford it, a son's coming-of-age ceremony included a gift of weapons, helmet, and shield. Even poor families could give a son a *framea*, a light spear. Leadership in a tribe was often determined by who was the most successful warrior. In some tribes the chiefs were elected by the warriors of the tribe, but in others a notion of kingship was developing that would evolve into the system of mutual obligations that became the feudal system of the medieval era.

After Caesar's time many German tribes became *foederati*, or tribes that were federated with Rome and helped protect Roman borders. By the year 9 C.E. the Romans were making good progress advancing their borders east and north into German lands. The Germans in Roman-held territory were beginning to speak Latin as their primary language, were wearing Roman-style clothing, and were adopting Roman customs. A Roman governor, however, abused and overtaxed the Germans in Roman territory, making it easy for German nationalists to recall days when their ancestors roamed the land, terrifying their enemies. In 9 C.E. the Germans rose in revolt.

The Romans had many Germans in their armies. One was Arminius, a member of the Cherusci tribe. He had proved so valiant in battle that he had been awarded Roman citizenship, but he was still German at heart. He hoped that through warfare he would win enough glory to become chief of the Cherusci. The Roman emperor Augustus (r. 27 B.C.E.–14 C.E.) appointed a successful diplomat, Publius Quintilius Varus (d. 9 C.E.), as commanding officer of the Roman army in Germany. In September 9 C.E. he led three Roman legions, composed of 15,000 troops, toward their winter quarters through lands that were unfamiliar to him. Although other Germans with him warned that Arminius was untrustworthy, Varus followed the guidance of Arminius.

In what followed can be seen the strengths of German tactical thinking. Arminius led the Romans through muddy grounds, weakening the soldiers' legs and making them weary. Ahead of them was a large German army. As the Romans marched between a large bog to their right and a 300-foot-tall hill to their left, about 10 miles north of the modern German town of Osnabrück, they confronted a wall of mostly sand, about 4 feet in height and several feet deep. Behind it were German warriors, coordinating their defenses through cooperation. The site was discovered in 1987. The area in front of the wall shows that the Romans tried to storm it several times. The wall was a zigzag shape that broke up the Roman line and allowed defenders to stand on the wall and use their spears to strike Romans from their sides as well as their front. The absence of debris on the German side of the wall suggests that the Romans never made it over the top.

Behind the Roman column Germans who had hidden in the woodlands to the left of the Romans tried to block a Roman retreat. Others waited to storm the column from the woods. What resulted was a well-timed, carefully coordinated ambush in which an experienced army of 15,000 troops was trapped. Varus fell on his sword to avoid being captured, as did several of his officers. This left junior officers and regular soldiers to fight without a center of authority to coordinate their actions as they faced an enemy that fought with discipline. Many Roman soldiers fought as Romans often did, determinedly holding their ground when the Germans finally charged into them. The German strategy had broken up the Roman column so the German warriors could penetrate it and take on individual soldiers. Romans were very good at one-on-one combat, and this strategy by the Germans probably resulted in unnecessary deaths for many of them. But Arminius was leading Germans, not Romans, and to keep German warriors satisfied with his leadership, he probably had to let them have their battlefield glory.

Some Romans made their way into the woods and slowly went back home. Others were captured, tortured, and taken to altars set up in the woods. When Romans visited the site six years later, they found Roman heads dangling from trees and blood-drenched altars as well as the bones of Romans piled across the battlefield. Almost all died, about 15,000. Romanization of much of Germany was halted, and the Romans eventually withdrew back into Gaul. Arminius became chief of his tribe and a war leader of several tribes. He was assassinated by relatives in 21 C.E.

GREECE

BY MICHAEL M. SAGE

Warfare in ancient Greece, though it changed over time, always spanned the full range of possibilities from small-scale raiding to full-scale pitched battles. As the most dangerous of activities, it was marked by formal declarations, special religious rites, and a number of symbolic acts whose character changed over time, such as the erection of battlefield trophies, thanksgiving and victory sacrifices, and the use of special burial rites for the fallen.

Early Greek warfare tended to pursue restricted goals. City-state governments remained relatively simple and lacked the means to control large blocks of territory. Hoplite warfare focused on gaining control of the enemy's agricultural land, and normally that was enough to bring victory. Greek arms and tactics were not well suited to siege warfare, which was the only way to achieve complete victory. For the most part, warfare centered on boundary disputes, raids, and in certain cases, hereditary feuds.

It is difficult to gauge the frequency of organized warfare. The absence of sources makes any estimate impossible from the Mycenaean Period (ca. 1600–ca. 1150 B.C.E.) until the fifth century B.C.E. For the period from 500 to 338 B.C.E. Athens was at war two out of every three years. However, no comparable figures exist for other Greek states, and Athens was a special case. In all periods warfare on any scale is the most costly of activities, and Athens during this period had resources not available to most Greek states. Sources give the impression that warfare was common until the imposition of Roman domination in the mid-second century B.C.E. For the period after 400 B.C.E. there is scattered evidence in the form of inscriptions for frequent warfare among smaller communities in Crete and elsewhere.

Bust of a warrior known as Leonidas (Alison Frantz Photographic Collection, American School of Classical Studies at Athens)

ATTITUDES ABOUT WAR

The attitude of the Greeks toward warfare was, as is the case for most societies, ambivalent. On one hand, war was recognized as an evil. The historian Herodotus (ca. 484–between 430 and 420 B.C.E.) blames war for overturning the natural order of things: "In peace, sons bury their fathers. In war, fathers bury their sons." In his *Laws*, Plato (ca. 428–348 or 347 B.C.E.) asserts that that we should pray to be spared from war and civil strife and that no man can be a true statesman unless he prepares for war only as a means to peace. Despite the misery it brought, war could also be viewed as desirable. The earliest Greek literature that we possess, the *Iliad* and the *Odyssey*, composed by Homer (ninth–eighth? century B.C.E.), suggests that excellence as a warrior is a man's most important quality. The growth of the city-state, which consisted of an urban core with its dependent towns and village, and the associated stress on the importance of the community, altered this "heroic code." The emphasis shifted to a warrior's contribution to his city in battle, but the significance attached to an individual's prowess in battle remained the same. Warfare also had more tangible attractions. The normal Greek view was that the conquered and their possessions passed into the hands of the victor and were his to dispose of as he pleased. Slaves brought the highest profit, but other items, such as personal valuables or temple treasures, also brought wealth. It was the capture of cities and temples that gave the greatest returns.

In politics war always remained an option and was pursued when it offered some advantage, especially among the more powerful states. There was a change in the fourth century B.C.E., first visible in 371 B.C.E., when the notion of a common peace among Greek states developed; however, the idea had little practical effect and never excluded warfare against non-Greeks. Peace among the Greeks was achieved only by Roman control.

The Mycenaean Period

There is little available evidence for the earliest period of Greek warfare, the Mycenaean Period. It is generally assumed that the Greek mainland and islands were divided into a number of small kingdoms centered on heavily fortified citadels. Given the absence of any contemporary description of warfare, inferences have to be made on the basis of archaeological finds of weapons and contemporary pictorial representations of fighting in frescoes and reliefs. An additional source of information is provided by the Linear B tablets. These tablets are accounting documents produced by the palaces and written on clay. They highlight the importance of chariots in this period. Large numbers of tablets as well as replacement parts for them were maintained. In addition, a set of tablets from the kingdom of Pylos in the southwestern Peloponnese details the organization of a coastal watch in response to an unknown threat. It is clear that there was technological development in the period, especially in producing more effective swords, but we do not have the data to trace the interaction between changes in technology and the development of new forms of war making.

The importance of chariots in the tablets poses a problem. Mainland Greece, with its rugged topography, is not well suited to the use of the chariot, especially in the mass formations found in the contemporary Near East. It may be, given some later parallels, that chariots served as elite transport to the battlefield and that their primary function was to display the high status and importance of their owners. The weapons finds and portrayals of fighting indicate the importance of the heavy thrusting spear. Although the sword is found in all periods, the thrusting spear is found most frequently. The use of such a weapon implies some type of compact formation, though its organization eludes us.

The Dark Ages

The end of the Mycenaean Period in about the middle of the 12th century B.C.E. witnessed profound changes on the Greek mainland and islands. The palaces were destroyed and with them the writing system used to keep their accounts. The archaeological finds paint a picture of a depopulated and fragmented society based primarily on small villages with a much reduced economy during the dark ages (ca. 1100–ca. 750 B.C.E.). Most political units centered on a local chief, who functioned with the support of local nobles. The amount of surplus wealth that such a society could devote to warfare was small, and it is probable that most of the fighting centered on raiding and small-scale conflict.

The same difficulties in reconstructing warfare in this period arise as for the previous one. We have to rely on weapons finds, and from about 850 B.C.E. there are vases that show fighting. Evidence points to the importance of missile warfare, with javelins and an open and fluid manner of fighting. Chariots are pictured, and there have been occasional finds of chariots in graves dated to after 1000 B.C.E. These must have belonged to the elite, but their function remains unknown. Based on evidence from the Homeric poems, these armies must have consisted of relatively small war bands operating under the leadership of a local chief or prince whose primary adversaries were small armies of a similar nature. These formations were too small and lacked the organization to achieve permanent conquest. Warfare for the most part must have consisted of raiding and border warfare.

The Archaic Period

The warfare of the *Iliad* and the *Odyssey* has been a particular focus of discussion. There has been debate about realism and the period in which the works are set. It seems that they reflect the period towards the end of the dark ages and the beginning of the following period, the Archaic (ca. 600–ca. 480 B.C.E.). They portray a world of small-scale states controlled by kings and the nobility, where war is the primary means of enhancing one's prestige and status. The kings and nobles, such as Achilles and Hector, dominate the combat and display superhuman strength.

Despite the presence of gods and other fantastic elements, Homer's works do present a comprehensible picture of warfare. The poems reveal a style of warfare close to that of the dark ages. The elite lead individual war bands that often function independently. Combat is normally in loose formation and mostly involves the exchange of missiles. This formation responds to circumstances. Under pressure from the enemy or in pursuit, it can compact, and battles between closely formed groups of warriors occur. These masses are important in determining the course of combat despite the focus on the actions of the elite. The elite function primarily as front fighters and often fight before the masses of their men, challenging enemy leaders. The poems portray their successes as the key to victory.

The use of chariots in Homer has evoked further controversy. They are used singly and often serve as transport for warriors who drive into battle, fight dismounted, and then use the chariots as transport to the rear. The movement of these vehicles in and out of the battle has no parallel elsewhere. Chariots were normally used elsewhere in massed formations as missile platforms or as transport to the battle but were not used to fight along with the infantry. Although the use of intermingled chariots and infantry is not impossible, it seems likely that the poet's use of chariots for his heroes is the product of an attempt to emphasize his heroes' superhuman nature.

From the second half of the eighth century B.C.E. Greece underwent a profound change. Population increased dramatically, there was extensive colonization around the Mediterranean, external trade resumed, and writing was reintroduced. Accompanying these developments was the formation of a new political organization: the city-state. In essence, the city-state consisted of an urban core based on a defensible citadel surrounded by public and religious spaces. It served as the political, social, and economic center for the surrounding countryside and its dependent towns and villages. In conjunction with these changes, royal government disappeared and was replaced by aristocratic rule and a political structure consisting of magistrates, council, and assembly. The higher population of these communities as well as their greater wealth allowed them to mobilize far more resources for war than had been possible earlier.

These profound developments in Greek society provided the context for a momentous change in warfare. The decisive arm on Greek battlefields over the next four centuries was to become the heavily armored infantryman (hoplite) using the heavy thrusting spear as his main offensive weapon and fighting in a dense, rectangular phalanx formation. This transition was accompanied by changes in equipment. Metal helmets, corselets (armor covering the torso), and a new type of shield appear. Hoplites were drawn from the better-off farmers and landowners and served at their own expense. Mass, weight, depth, and cooperation among the members of the phalanx became the decisive elements in this simple type of warfare in which masses of heavily armed men engaged each other on flat, level plains. It was a form of warfare developed to protect a city's agricultural land on which it depended for its food supply. The short, sharp engagements and the ample defensive equipment were designed to limit warfare's destructive effects.

These developments were limited to central and southern Greece. Elsewhere older forms of warfare persisted. Whatever the connection between these developments and political change, it was only in areas where the city-state was common that hoplite warfare came to dominate. The evidence does not permit a firm date to be assigned to the development and spread of this type of warfare. Elements of the equipment that later became typical appear around 700 B.C.E. and the first portrayals on pottery of warriors in a phalanx-like formation occur in the middle of the seventh century B.C.E. A date around and after 600 B.C.E. is reasonable, though some hold that its full form emerged only around 500 B.C.E. How quickly it spread is unknown.

The Fifth Century B.C.E.

The dominance of this form of fighting led to changes in other arms. Light-armed troops whose main offensive arm was missile weapons lost their importance, and their main functions were now to act as a screen for the deployment of the phalanx and to aid in pursuit. Contemporary with these developments in infantry fighting, the cavalry also experienced significant changes. From the seventh century B.C.E. there are portrayals of warriors on horseback, but they appear to be mounted hoplites rather than true cavalry. The transition to true cavalry, that is, troopers who fight from horseback, may be as late as the first half of the fifth century B.C.E. under the impact of the Persian invasion of Greece in 480 B.C.E. The first organized cavalry appear in Athens in the 450s B.C.E., while Sparta had none until the 420s B.C.E., and few major states remained without such formations. This cavalry was useful for flank and rear attacks on organized infantry and for protection from enemy cavalry forces. In addition, it was employed in pursuing broken infantry and in protecting foraging parties.

The Persian War of 480 B.C.E. marked a watershed. For the first time a substantial number of Greek states served under the unified command of a single state, Sparta. Athens, building on an earlier decision to expand its navy, became the most important maritime power. The Greek victory had momentous consequences. Sparta remained focused on its supremacy in the Peloponnese, but Athens was able to create an alliance against the Persians that within a generation would develop into a naval empire of subject states. Unlike the Spartans, who demanded only military service, the Athenians demanded tribute, and the empire became a substantial contributor to the maintenance of its fleet and its citizens.

At Athens all Athenians who were between the ages of 18 and 60 and who possessed a certain level of wealth were entered in a list of those eligible for military service, with the wealthiest serving as cavalry. Athens was unique in providing pay for military service from 456 B.C.E. on. Army organization was based on units of 1,000 and 300. The larger units had their own officers, but nothing is known of the organization of the smaller ones. The cavalry had its own commander and subordinate officers, and the same must have been true of the light-armed troops, though they are not mentioned. Overall command was vested in an annually elected board of 10 generals. Normally, two or three generals exercised command on a campaign. The historian Thucydides (d. ca. 401 B.C.E.) informs us that in 431 B.C.E. the hoplite army totaled 29,000 men out of a population of about 180,000, with 13,000 serving in the field army and the youngest and the oldest defending the city.

There was no parallel to the Spartan army elsewhere in Greece. All other armies were citizen militias; only Sparta possessed a professional army. As a result of a unique social and economic system, all full Spartan citizens were freed to devote themselves to full-time military training. This was an extraordinarily rigorous training that began in childhood and continued until the end of adolescence. The army was organized on the basis of age groups and geographical districts within Sparta. This army was far better articulated than any other Greek force. The largest units of 600 men were composed of four successively larger units, each with its officers. Normally, overall command was vested in one of the two Spartan kings, though occasionally detached forces could be commanded by other officers.

Sparta's unique military system fueled a policy of expansion that resulted in the acquisition of extensive lands on the western flank. Sparta's attempt to expand its control to the north was checked by the mid-sixth century B.C.E., and a new policy of alliance in the Peloponnese was adopted. Sparta was clearly the controlling member, and the allies were bound to follow where Sparta might lead. Despite Sparta's military superiority, several large and important states in the Peloponnese, such as Argos, remained out of the league and were at times openly hostile. After its initial expansion Sparta's main military preoccupation was to ensure its local dominance.

In Boeotia and a few other areas where federalism had emerged, there were federal armies with member states contributing troops according to population, and command was held by federally elected officers. Elite units are mentioned at Thebes in Boeotia and at Argos in the fifth and fourth centuries B.C.E., but we know almost nothing of their organization. Given that most Greek armies were militias, it is probable that they were commanded by each city's magistrates.

The Peloponnesian War (431–404 B.C.E.) between Athens and Sparta and its allies precipitated a number of changes. For the first time mercenary troops from the poorer regions of Greece were employed on a large scale as well as specialist troops drawn from non-Greek sources. The dominance of the hoplite outside of decisive battles was reduced. Combined forces of light-armed troops, cavalry, and hoplites were shown to be effective in small-scale actions. The length of the war and the employment of mercenaries led to a growing professionalism, visible both at the level of the individual soldier and in positions of command. The greater professionalism and frequent warfare in the fourth century B.C.E. led to the development of new tactics and changes in hoplite equipment.

In these years Greek politics had essentially become bipolar, with most Greek states aligned with either Sparta or Athens. In addition to the war's effect on the nature of warfare, this conflict also had profound political consequences. It destabilized a number of states, leading to internal factional fighting, which was often bloody. A number of cities were destroyed and the population enslaved. It led to the Spartans' realization that the older strategy of laying waste to an opponent's agricultural land as the key to victory no longer held in Athens's case, since as long as Athens dominated the sea, it could supply itself from overseas. This realization led the Spartans to solicit Persian money to subsidize their navy and so involved them in the affairs of the Greeks of Asia Minor.

By the end of the war Sparta stood supreme. Athens was subordinated but not destroyed so that it could serve as a counterweight to the ambitions of Thebes. However, Spartan blunders created a number of coalitions of major Greek states to oppose Sparta. Sparta's supremacy lasted until 371 B.C.E. and Sparta's defeat in battle by Thebes, which now assumed Sparta's role. By 362 B.C.E. Sparta's ascendancy had ended, and no state emerged as dominant; rather, there was a series of combinations in an attempt to limit the power of any one state.

The Fourth Century B.C.E.

The rise of Macedonia radically changed the situation. The most crucial development of the fourth century B.C.E. was the rise of a powerful and expansive monarchy in Macedonia. Its creation was the work of Philip II (r. 359–336 B.C.E.). Philip consolidated a weak state rent by faction and in the process created an army superior to any the Greek world had yet seen. Macedonia had always had effective cavalry, but it was Philip's achievement to develop a superb infantry. Its organization must be inferred from Alexander's army, whose structure is far better known. The cavalry was organized into eight units, one being the royal cavalry of 300, which also served as a bodyguard. The other seven units were each 200 to 300 men strong. The infantry phalanx was levied by geographical areas and by the end of Philip's reign was 24,000 strong and divided into sections of 1,500. Two other infantry units are known, one of 250 and one of 16. There were also substantial numbers of light-armed troops of all types drawn from Macedonian and subject populations, who also provided specialized units. The king was normally in command and had a number of senior commanders drawn from the Macedonian nobility, who commanded units on the battlefield and in independent expeditions. The Macedonian army represented a departure from traditional Greek forces. For the first time a force was created that effectively used different modes of fighting in combination in large-scale battle.

The army that Philip's son, Alexander the Great (r. 336–323 B.C.E.), led against Persia in the spring of 334 B.C.E. was essentially the force his father had created except for a substantial presence of allied Greek contingents. It probably differed only in having a higher proportion of cavalry, since the main Persian strength was concentrated in that arm. One innovation Alexander may have made was the creation of an elite infantry guard, the hypaspists of 3,000 men who were armed in the same manner as other heavy infantry and under the direct command of the king. Attrition, distance, and Alexander's own vision led to an attempt to incorporate Oriental troops into his army. Oriental cavalry were added to the army as Alexander advanced eastward, but they were kept separate from Macedonian troops. Orientals were denied positions of command except in special circumstances.

Alexander's conquests of the Persian Empire and northwestern India created the initial conditions for a massive movement of population from Greece and Macedonia to the Near East. This movement, over by about 250 B.C.E., led to the spread of Greek culture and the extensive urbanization in the Near East. The kingdoms of Alexander's successors were controlled by Greeks and adopted Greek political practices. The military forces continued and completed a military revolution. The use of professional soldiers culminated in the professional standing armies of the Ptolemies and the Seleucids. Militia-based armies continued to exist on mainland Greece and in Macedonia, but even there professional soldiers were employed on a substantial scale. These were much more heterogeneous armies than those of the Classical Period (480–323 B.C.E.), consisting of Greeks, Macedonians, and mercenaries drawn from all over the Mediterranean as well as levies of subject peoples. War and conquest had created Greek states on a far vaster scale than earlier. Despite these advantages, none of the monarchies created in the wake of Alexander's death was capable of resisting the advance of a Roman army based on the militia system.

Alexander's death in 323 B.C.E. led to a half century of struggle, which ended in the establishment of three large successor kingdoms: the Ptolemaic based in Egypt, the Seleucid, whose territory stretched from the seacoast of Asia Minor to northwestern India at its greatest extent, and the

Antigonid, centered in the Macedonian heartland. Their armies were direct descendants of Philip's and Alexander's. There were changes in scale; armies were now much larger, and cavalry declined in importance. An innovation of the period was the institution of an elephant corps. Europeans had first met the elephant in battle in northwestern India and were quick to adopt it for their own use. Elephants were used to screen against cavalry, to attack infantry, and to break into fortifications. After 300 B.C.E. they were equipped with towers manned by troops armed with missile weapons. Little is known of how these elephants were organized. Difficulties in breeding as well as the general ineffectiveness of elephants in European warfare led to their disappearance from Western battlefields by the middle of the second century B.C.E.

The major Hellenistic armies, except for the Macedonian, which relied on its own population for its main military forces, used mercenaries. Greeks serving as mercenaries in the Near East are known as early as the seventh century B.C.E. However, in Greece the use of a militia as the main military force meant that mercenaries appear infrequently. The first large-scale use of such forces dates from the Peloponnesian War and continues into the fourth century C.E. Economic troubles caused by the war and by the growing need for specialist troops whose fighting techniques required extensive training spurred their use. Philip and Alexander employed them as well. The Hellenistic monarchies had an enormous need for manpower, and although the core of their armies consisted of Greek and Macedonian settlers, they hired large numbers of mercenaries from all over the Mediterranean. A parallel development can be seen in naval forces, where professional rowers had to be hired.

ROME

BY JAMES A. CORRICK

By tradition the doors to the temple of Janus in the Roman Forum were closed in times of peace and open during times of conflict. During the centuries of the Roman Kingdom and Roman Republic, these doors were shut only twice, and after the formation of the empire they were open far more often than they were closed. War was indeed a constant throughout Rome's history, for Rome was built on war and conquest. Its dominance of the Mediterranean world was through force of arms. Its treasury and many of its prominent citizens and leaders were periodically enriched through the loot of conquest and the governance of conquered provinces, whose inhabitants were forced to pay tribute under the threat of Roman military reprisal.

ROMAN ATTITUDES TOWARD WAR

The Romans were a militaristic people who saw war as a natural—indeed a proper—way of establishing their dominance over others. Thus for much of its history Rome spent half of its revenues on maintaining its military and on waging war. It gave its top officials—consuls, praetors, proconsuls, propraetors, and the occasional dictator—the imperium that gave them the authority, among other things, to command troops in battle. It demanded that its elected officials not only serve in the military but also have combat experience. Further, it elevated Mars, who had been a minor agricultural god, to the second most powerful deity in the Roman pantheon, just after Jupiter, by making him the god of war.

The Roman character itself was shaped by war and the demands of war. The Romans were a people who valued discipline, endurance, and courage and who saw duty to the state as among the highest goals to be achieved. They praised those who rejected luxury for austere living and who took no notice of physical hardship. They admired the pragmatic. All of these characteristics made for good, reliable soldiers.

Yet despite their belief in the rightness of combat and battle, Romans did not take war lightly. They knew, as the Roman poet Virgil (70–19 B.C.E.) wrote in the *Aeneid*, that war was horrible. Accordingly, the centuriate assembly was to debate the justness and necessity of any proposed military action, which its delegates then had to approve through majority vote. Nor were Romans reluctant to use other means of gaining their ends. Roman officials, for instance, often negotiated with states to avoid war; sometimes they brought these states under Rome's influence through treaties, sometimes through large bribes to foreign rulers.

Still, Rome was mostly at war somewhere in the Mediterranean, the Middle East, or along its northern European border. The deliberations of the centuriate assembly were often short-circuited by aristocratic influence over delegates who voted as their patrons desired; patricians could enrich themselves only through agriculture or war and were thus often inclined to go to war. Occasionally, Roman leaders simply ignored the assembly altogether. Diplomatic efforts were often feeble or filled with demands the Romans knew would be rejected.

In the end, successful wars of conquest led Romans to see themselves and their culture as superior to others. They were convinced that Rome's destiny was to be ruler of the world. They had no hesitation in pursuing that destiny through warfare and military occupation of other lands, nor did the Romans question that they had a right to plunder and loot their fallen enemies for the enrichment of Rome.

EARLY ROME

Nothing is known about Roman warfare prior to the eighth century B.C.E. Beginning in the eighth century, according to Roman historians such as Livy (ca. 59 B.C.E.–17 C.E.), the Roman Kingdom fought a number of wars with neighboring peoples, among them the Albans, the Fidenae, and the Sabines. The latter were defeated in several battles after they attacked in response to Romans supposedly seizing Sabine women for wives. To what extent these accounts of early war are factual is difficult to know because no actual records survive from this early period. For the most part, Rome's early wars were probably minor affairs, in general being no more than skirmishes with neighbors that consisted of border disputes or raids to seize livestock, slaves, and plunder.

Little is known about the Roman army of the early kingdom. Probably small, the army was led by the king and consisted of the royal bodyguard and a few hundred citizens of the city. By the end of the seventh century B.C.E. the army, a militia of citizen soldiers, had grown, with its organization deriving from the supposed three tribes that inhabited the Roman kingdom: the Ramnes, the Tities, and the Luceres. Each tribe contributed 1,000 soldiers, who supplied their own weapons and armor and who were under the command of a tribune, or tribal officer. Further, each tribal subdivision provided 100 men to form a unit known as a century. The total 3,000-strong body was called the *legio*, or levy, better known as a legion. Attached to the legion was the cavalry, numbering some 300.

The infantry would remain the core of all Roman armies. Infantry units could move more quickly and readily than cavalry through the often mountainous Italian terrain and in later centuries were more easily transported by sea to distant conflicts. Chariots, popular in other parts of the ancient world, were impractical and rarely employed by the Romans in war because of their legacy of fighting in rugged Italy. Because of their reliance on infantry, the Romans would always favor close-quarter, or hand-to-hand, fighting. Roman cavalry would act primarily as scouts and as protection from enemy cavalry as well as for rear attacks against opposing troops.

War for early Rome was a seasonal business, with the summer being the traditional battle season for the city. Winter conditions were generally too poor for combat, and the Roman soldiers, being mostly farmers, had to plant in the spring and harvest in the fall. At the end of summer campaigning, the legion was disbanded to be reformed the following year.

A Change in Strategy

Beginning in the fifth century B.C.E., the first years of the republic, Rome used its army to conquer and dominate its Etruscan neighbors north of the Tiber. This initial series of conquests culminated with Rome's victory over its archrival Veii in 396 B.C.E.

This series of conquests marked a change in Roman strategy that would dictate the course of all Rome's wars until the time of the later empire. Prior to the fifth century B.C.E. Rome's strategy was primarily defensive, countering specific threats posed by neighboring peoples. However, in the fifth century B.C.E. Roman warfare became almost exclusively offensive with the Romans coming to view war as a means of subjugating others and thus expanding their territory. From the fifth century onward the Romans engaged in wars of conquest that in the end would give them control first of Italy and then of much of the Mediterranean. This expansion would offer Rome increased protection from attack by pushing its enemies farther from the city itself. Expansion in Italy also brought more farm land under Roman control. An important consequence of this larger food supply was the growth of the city of Rome.

Gaining dominance over other states required a battlefield strategy of not just defeating an enemy army on the field but also destroying the enemy force by killing as many opposing warriors as possible. Without the protection of its own army, many enemy states surrendered to the Romans. Any that continued to resist through use of their remaining soldiers or by arming noncombatants suffered bloody reprisals from the Romans, who often killed many of the surviving adults and sold the rest along with children into slavery.

Rome sometimes resorted to other means of winning a war that did not involve direct combat. Roman soldiers might burn enemy fields and thus force surrender through the threat of starvation. They might wait until an enemy army disbanded, either because the soldiers had to return to tend their fields or because they ran out of money to pay mercenary troops. On the whole, however, Romans preferred meeting and besting their enemies on the battlefield.

Phalanxes and Sieges

The Roman army of the early republic had grown to a legion of 6,000 infantry, to which 18 centuries of cavalry were attached. The legion was still divided into centuries, but the number of soldiers in each century varied. (Exact numbers are not now known.) Soldiers were recruited from five social classes of citizens, with those of the top class being able to afford to equip themselves with the best weapons and armor and with those of the lowest class lacking armor and armed only with slings and stones. Additionally, the Roman army was now modeled on the Greek hoplite forces, in which warriors carrying long thrusting spears and with shields overlapping marched in a succession of rows, varying in number from eight to 16, toward the enemy. These massed lines were called a phalanx, Greek for "roller," and allowed fallen soldiers in the front line quickly to be replaced from the lines behind.

Although they continued to prefer close-quarter infantry engagement during this early period of expansion, Romans learned siege craft when they attacked the Veian city of Fidenae. Unable to breach the city's defenses, the Romans laid siege. The purpose of a Roman siege, like any siege, was to cut the enemy off from supplies—food, weapons, and sometimes water—and then through repeated attacks to wear down resistance until Roman soldiers could gain entry to the besieged city. In later centuries the Romans would employ siege engines such as battering rams to bash in gates or to knock holes in defensive walls and ballista and onagers capable of hurling large rocks against enemy walls (the latter could also throw flaming pitch into an enemy city). The use of these engines helped bring a siege to a quicker end. At Fidenae the lack of such engines led to a siege lasting six or seven years.

Defeat and Reorganization

By the fourth century B.C.E. Rome was the strongest military power in central Italy. In terms of weapons and armor, Romans were generally no better equipped than their enemies. Rather, they owed their success in war to a stress on teamwork and esprit de corps over individual heroics. Additionally, the hard—sometimes brutal—training of Roman soldiers led to proficiency in the use of arms and to disciplined obedience. At all times on the battlefield, Roman soldiers were expected to maintain their formation and to stay sheltered behind their body-length shields, from behind which they delivered quick stabbing blows with their short swords.

Nonetheless, Romans were not invincible. Indeed, in 390 B.C.E., six years after its final victory over the Veii, Rome suffered one of its most humiliating defeats at the hands of Celts from Gaul. These Gauls first destroyed a Roman army and then went on to capture Rome and to demand an exorbitant tribute before retreating back north. The weakness that the Gauls exploited was the phalanx formation. Roman training and teamwork made the phalanx effective against other massed enemy infantry. Nevertheless, it did not allow Roman soldiers much flexibility of movement on the battlefield, while the Gauls who fought as individuals or in small groups were more mobile and thus were able to outflank the Romans.

Bronze statuette of Mars, god of war, Roman Britain, second century C.E., from Earith, Cambridgeshire; Mars wears the armor of a general, including an elaborate helmet, sheet metal leg guards decorated with thunderbolts, and an embossed chest plate moulded to the form of the body. (© The Trustees of the British Museum)

The Romans quickly abandoned the phalanx and adopted a new battlefield formation that divided the legion into units called maniples. A maniple, from a Latin word meaning "handful," consisted of 160 soldiers, or two centuries of 80 each. Each maniple acted semi-independently and was arranged in three lines. The front line would engage the enemy and then, after about 15minutes, would fall back and be replaced by the second line, which in turn would be replaced by the third. This maneuver gave the soldiers a period of rest before rejoining the fight. The single legion of the army was also replaced by first two, then three, and finally four legions. Each legion had 60 centuries or 30 maniples.

Pyrrhus and War Elephants

Although the defeat by the Gauls left Rome weakened, it soon grew militarily powerful again and, with its restructured army, brought the Italian peninsula under its control over the next century. In doing so, Rome had to fight three wars with the Samnites, beginning in 343 B.C.E. It was in 312 B.C.E., during the second of these wars (326–304 B.C.E.) that the Romans, realizing that they needed a method of moving troops and supplies rapidly, built the first of their roads, the Via Appia, or Appian Way, Roman roads would be one of the keys to Rome's success in waging successful war in the centuries to come, as they were able to rush troops relatively quickly to trouble spots in their holdings.

In 280 B.C.E. Roman expansion in Italy brought war with the Greek colony of Tarentum, to whose aid Pyrrhus, ruler of the Greek city-state Epirus, came. This war was the first time that Rome faced one of the Mediterranean superpowers and the first time that its soldiers encountered war elephants. It was these latter that gave Pyrrhus a victory in his first two battles with the Romans.

The Romans may have lost the first battles, but as would be their practice in the centuries to come they refused to concede defeat. Instead, they regrouped and continued the war. They allied themselves with the other major Mediterranean power, the Carthaginians, and they adapted their battlefield tactics to deal with enemy elephants. In 275 B.C.E. the Romans met Pyrrhus for the final time and defeated him by routing his elephant corps through the use of javelins and fire and perhaps at times by hitting the animals on the head.

The First Punic War

The defeat of Pyrrhus left the Greek colonies open to Roman conquest, and Rome quickly defeated each in battle. As the Romans were finalizing their control of Italy, they became embroiled in a war with Carthage over Sicily. Rome and Carthage would fight three wars, the first from 264 to 241 B.C.E. Known as the Punic Wars, these conflicts would leave Rome with the beginnings of its overseas empire and as the strongest state in the Mediterranean world. Carthage would be destroyed.

The outcome of this conflict was by no means assured, particularly since Carthage was the great naval power of the period and Rome had no navy at all because the city's wars had to date been conducted on the Italian mainland, generally inland. When water transport was necessary to carry troops along the Italian coast, Rome turned to its allies on the Bay of Naples for ships and crews. In order to win the First Punic War, Rome built its first fleet, modeling its ships on captured Carthaginian vessels. The Romans developed a new device to aid them in this new type of warfare. The corvus was a large gangplank that could be dropped onto an enemy ship. A large spike at its end drove deep into the enemy's deck. Army legionnaires then crossed over the corvus to take the other vessel. The device worked very well, allowing the Romans to use their greatest battle strength, close-quarter infantry fighting. With the aid of the corvus the Romans defeated two Carthaginian fleets and won the First Punic War.

Despite two more wars with Carthage and other sea engagements, the republic never maintained a permanent navy. When a fleet was needed, it was built, as for Pompey's expedition in 64 B.C.E. against the pirates of the Mediterranean. Even when they existed, republican fleets often came to grief. Led by commanders with no nautical experience, entire fleets were lost to storm and shipwreck. It would not be until the empire that Rome would maintain a permanent navy, and even then the seafaring service would remain secondary to the army.

The Second and Third Punic Wars

During the Second Punic War (218–202 B.C.E.) the Carthaginian general Hannibal (247–183 B.C.E.) crossed the Alps; after inflicting a series of devastating defeats on the Romans, most notably at Cannae, he and his army ravaged the Italian countryside. Hannibal made no attempt to attack the city of Rome, perhaps because its walls, built after the Gauls' capture of the city in 390 B.C.E., made Rome a difficult target. Instead of continuing in its attempt to defeat Hannibal's army, Rome tried a new tactic: It launched an attack on the city of Carthage. Hannibal was recalled to defend his home, where he was overcome by the Roman general Scipio Africanus Major (236–184 or 183 B.C.E.).

Carthage was destroyed in the Third Punic War (149–146 B.C.E.). Following their strategy of annihilating their enemies, the Romans captured the city of Carthage after a brief siege, sold into slavery those Carthaginians not killed, and razed the city to the ground. When the Romans finished, nothing remained of the Carthaginians or their culture, and Rome was the most powerful state in the Mediterranean.

The Punic Wars left Rome in control of Sicily, North Africa, and parts of the Iberian Peninsula. Over the next century they conquered and occupied the southern part of Gaul, Macedonia, Greece, and much of the Middle East. Although Rome was still technically a republic, it was by the first century B.C.E. an empire in all but name.

Social Change

Roman war and the conquest brought power and wealth to Rome, but they did even more. They changed what was a small farming community, more town than city, into one of the largest and most cosmopolitan cities of the ancient world. Rome became a place where people from all over the Mediterranean lived, worked, and traded. Roman society itself was, if not softened, altered by exposure to other peoples, most notably the Greeks, whose literature, art, and philosophy were embraced by many Romans.

War also brought to Rome millions of slaves, whose cheap labor led to economic dislocation for many Roman citizens. By the first century B.C.E. the small farms of early Rome had mostly given way to large farming estates owned by wealthy individuals and worked by slaves. The small Roman farmers were left landless and without a livelihood. Occasionally, one of these estates was broken up and its land distributed to soldiers, such as those who served Pompey and Julius Caesar. However, such redistributions were not given to Roman peasants, many of whom made their way to Rome, where they lived in tenements and depended on food from the state grain supply. There was little but poverty for these Roman citizens, for as in the countryside, most work in the city was done by slaves.

Political Change

War and conquest also led to political change. The political organization of the republic, designed to rule a single city, was not capable of handling the administration of such a large realm. The Roman Republic lacked any true central authority and had virtually no state employees with which to handle the day-to-day details of government. Its ruling officials, two consuls, served for only one year, a period that was often insufficient to study and then handle problems in Rome's far-flung provinces. Additionally, the consuls could overrule each other and be overruled by other elected officials, so important matters frequently were left unattended for years at a time. Although they had fewer checks on their power, Rome's provincial governors, the proconsuls and propraetors, also rarely had more than a yearlong appointment, sometimes a goodly amount of that time being eaten up preparing for the job and then traveling to the assigned region. The strain of governance was one of the contributing factors leading to the eventual disintegration of the Roman Republic and the emergence of the Roman Empire, with its single source of authority, the emperor, and its elaborate bureaucracy.

This political change was also aided by the rise at the end of the second century B.C.E. of generals whose troops were more loyal to them than to the state. These generals, among them Marius (ca. 157–86 B.C.E.), Sulla (138–78 B.C.E.), Pompey (106–48 B.C.E.), and Julius Caesar (100–44 B.C.E.), became rich from the plunder of successful campaigns and used this money to buy the favor of many Roman citizens. Caesar, for instance, for one year paid the rent of everyone living in

Rome. These generals also vied with one another for power. They fought pitched battles until in 31 B.C.E. Octavian, later Augustus Caesar (ca. 27 B.C.E.–14 C.E.), emerged victorious, soon becoming the first emperor.

Military Change

The army also underwent changes during the growth of Rome as an imperial power. The Punic Wars and those fought elsewhere required an increase in the number of legions to 20, along with the creation of several urban legions made up of the old and underaged, whose duty it was to protect the city of Rome. Over the final three centuries of the republic, the number of legions would fluctuate according to military demands; the number appears not to have dropped below six.

At the end of the second century B.C.E. further changes were made to the structure of the legion. These changes would remain in place until the late empire. According to tradition, under Gaius Marius each legion was divided into 10 cohorts rather than 30 maniples. A cohort was made up of 480 soldiers divided among six centuries, thus giving each legion a complement of 4,800. When combined with a new weapon, a long spear called a *pilus*, the cohort was felt to retain flexibility in combat while increasing the strength of the Roman force. At the beginning of battle each legionnaire threw his *pilus*, the point of which was designed to bend so that it could not be used against the Romans. A *pilus* was capable of piercing light armor, and if it stuck in an enemy soldier's shield, its weight would make the shield too cumbersome to carry.

Over time, each legion was also augmented by a body of troops that came from various Latium and other Italian communities. Generally, some 500 soldiers and cavalry were drafted from each town until each legion was accompanied by an auxiliary, known as an *ala sociorum* (wing of allies), which was of equivalent size to the legion itself. Attached to each legion was also an elite group of allied fighters, the *extraordinarii*. Mercenaries, particularly archers from Crete, also fought with each legion. When on campaign, then, each legion fielded a total of between 8,000 and 10,000 troops along with 750 to 1,250 cavalry.

The Nature of Roman War

Over the centuries the nature of Roman warfare itself changed. The skirmishes and raids of the kingdom and the early republic—brief affairs at best—turned into long offensive campaigns of conquest that required extended marches or sea voyages just to reach the enemy. Once engaged, Roman soldiers might have to fight several battles in succession. Sometimes campaigns lasted years and involved not only battle but lengthy sieges of enemy cities and strongholds. Once a region was conquered, it had to be occupied by permanent garrisons. These extended campaigns and occupations also changed the character of the Roman army. By the end of the first century C.E., what had started as a seasonal, volunteer militia made up of part-time soldiers had transformed into a standing army with a core of career professionals.

When in the second century C.E. the empire reached its farthest extent, the nature of Roman war once more changed. Instead of large offensive campaigns, the army was engaged mostly in consolidating the frontier areas that were still in the process of becoming Roman—indeed, many never really did— and in patrolling and defending the imperial borders.

THE AMERICAS

BY MICHAEL J. O'NEAL

As communities of people migrated and spread throughout the Americas in ancient times, they inevitably came in conflict with one another. The usual source of the conflict would have been territory and resources. As one nation encroached on another's territorial hunting grounds, the earlier inhabitants very likely would have resisted, and conflict would have erupted. The problem for historians, as is often the case with the ancient world, is the lack of any kind of documentation for warfare. Accordingly, historians have to rely on other tools. One such tool consists of oral legends about warfare that were transmitted over many generations. Sometimes, archaeological findings can shed light on ancient conflict. In South America, for example, tombs have been found with inscriptions, weapons, and battle dress that shed some light on ancient warfare.

North America

Among the many nations of North America, conflict was inevitable and probably frequent. Numerous examples could be cited, but one that dates back to at least 1000 B.C.E. is the conflict between the ancient ancestors of the Lenape and the Allegewi (the source of the name given to the Allegheny Mountains and the Allegheny River in the eastern United States)—though again, historians have to rely on oral tradition and archaeological finds. The Lenape, also known as the Lenni Lenape, migrated eastward until they came to the Mississippi River, which they called Namesi Sipu ("River of Fish"), the source of the word *Mississippi*. Here they met up with and formed a peaceful alliance with the Mengwe, who had migrated from the north in the region around the source of the river.

On the other side of the River of Fish were the Allegewi. The Lenape sent scouts across the river to reconnoiter, and the scouts came back with tales of giants who lived in walled cities and appeared to be warlike. The Lenape had no wish to do battle with the Allegewi, so they sent emissaries requesting permission to travel through Allegewi territory to points farther east. The Allegewi granted permission, so the Lenape began to cross the river in great numbers. The Allegewi, not knowing that so many people would be crossing their land, felt threatened, and they attacked, killing a large number of Lenape. The Lenape, in turn, fought back and, according to oral legend, routed the Allegewi and drove them southward. The Lenape then occupied the region around the Ohio River valley, while the Mengwe returned to the north. In time the

Lenape continued their eastward trek into the forested regions of the eastern United States, giving rise to at least 40 nations, including the Delaware, which found homes in New York and along the eastern seaboard. The Mengwe in time evolved into the Iroquois. Ironically, the two nations that had formed an alliance during war and lived in harmony for many centuries after defeating the Allegewi themselves became bitter enemies.

Native North Americans did not mount "armies" as the term is conventionally understood. Rather, the war party generally constituted the fighting forces of Native Americans. Generally, the leader of a war party was a chief or another member of the nation who had shown courage in battle on a former occasion. Usually, such a person was said to have "medicine," meaning a kind of spiritual power that would make him and his force victorious. Individual warriors also had medicine, and this medicine was typically symbolized by an object, such as an amulet, that the warrior carried into battle. Interestingly, it is believed that among some nations, women as warriors were as fierce as men. Warfare among ancient Native Americans was not always intended to vanquish the enemy and seize his territory and resources. Rather, warfare was often regarded as a kind of ritual activity with spiritual implications. The number of casualties in these types of conflicts was often quite low, and in some cases, the goal of a warrior was merely to touch an enemy soldier and perhaps seize his weapon.

The most common battle tactic of Native Americans was stealth. Because large bodies of soldiers did not take part in battles, smaller bands of warriors moved swiftly and silently over the landscape, finding ways to sneak up on or ambush the enemy. Retreat was not considered a form of dishonor; rather, retreat was often a strategic move designed to lure the enemy to a place where he could be confronted and defeated. Related to strategic retreat was the principle of force concentration. Rather than allowing the line of battle to be spread out, it was common to lure enemy forces into a ravine, a small valley, a narrow mountain pass, or some other similar place where the attacking force could focus its attack. In many respects ancient Native American warfare was similar to guerrilla warfare. The goal was usually not to overwhelm the enemy with a large, superior force but to harass the enemy and pick off enemy soldiers one at a time or in small groups.

Weapons differed depending on the types of tools and materials that were available to a given tribe. Thus, for example, the groups of the Arctic North used spears—the same spears they used for fishing and hunting for sea mammals—often tipped with points made of bone. Other groups used spears that were otherwise used for big-game hunting, though they were likely tipped with stone. Other weapons included the bow and arrow, the club, the sling, and the tomahawk—any hatchetlike implement with a stone head, used primarily by eastern North American nations, whose soldiers threw it at enemy soldiers. Sticks and knives were also common weapons.

Also important was hand-to-hand combat, and Native American warriors were skilled at forms of martial arts that enabled them to overcome enemy soldiers in close quarters. Some Native American nations adopted forms of armor and helmets. A form of psychological warfare that was implemented involved throwing weapons that were elaborately decorated with feathers and other objects; masks with fierce grimaces were often worn. Native American war paint on the face, arms, and upper body was also common. It should be noted that ancient Native Americans did not fight on horseback. Horses did exist in ancient North America prior to at least 6000 B.C.E., when they became extinct on the continent, but they were not domesticated, meaning that ancient peoples probably used them only as a food source. The horse became a weapon of war only after the arrival of the Europeans and their domesticated horses in the 16th century C.E.

MESOAMERICA

Archaeologists for many decades believed that the societies of ancient Mesoamerica were relatively peaceful. More recent findings, however, suggest otherwise—that warfare was a way of life for some Mesoamerican cultures, at least during portions of their history. Among the Maya, the most dominant culture of ancient Mesoamerica, warfare was conducted to capture victims for ritual sacrifices and to control trade routes and resources. Additionally, warfare was a source of slaves for building temples and other monuments.

The Maya defended their cities with earthworks and walls—often systems of double walls, where enemy invaders were trapped and slaughtered after breaching the outer wall. In common with other warriors in North and South America, they fought primarily with weapons they could hurl. The atlatl was a device that gave greater impetus and range to spears; it consisted of a shaft in which the spear rested, enabling the warrior to hurl the spear by propelling the atlatl, giving the spear much more energy. The *macahuitl* was a wooden weapon that was used like a club or a sword; sharp blades made of obsidian were inserted into the wood, making the weapon lethal. Blowguns were also used, and while bows and arrows were sometimes employed, they were not common weapons. Ordinary warriors wore no helmets, but they carried shields made of wood, animal skins, or woven mats. Leaders, on the other hand, dressed themselves for battle in padded armor and elaborate headdresses, all decorated with religious symbols designed to inspire fear in the enemy.

At the head of Maya military forces was the ruler of each city. Each city had a small group of soldiers who captured sacrificial victims; this group was supplemented by a militia during times of war. Commoners were often recruited to fight, but since they had no military-style weapons, they used hunting tools and rocks. On some occasions, women took part in battles. A chief strategy was to use the forests as cover, luring in enemies and then ambushing them. Sometimes canoes were used to approach enemy cities located on rivers and lakes.

Among the Mesoamericans, warfare was very much a religious ritual activity. Warfare was sanctioned by the gods, and leaders were men of religious authority. Warriors called on help from the gods by singing, blowing horns and whistles, and beating drums as battles began. Religious items were carried into battle. Death in battle was regarded as a far more desired fate than capture by the enemy, for it was common for captured soldiers, especially their leaders, to be degraded with cruel treatment and for their religious symbols to be desecrated.

Mesoamerican warfare was much more sophisticated than warfare among more northerly Native Americans. Very often Mesoamericans fielded large armies, perhaps as many as 20,000 troops and often more. The Mesoamericans conducted warfare in a way that seems more modern. Armies sacked cities, but very often, too, they conducted field operations in open areas; in other words, while northern Native Americans conducted more guerrilla-type warfare, Mesoamericans conducted war based on superiority of forces. Further, Mesoamericans trained for war. Many young boys went to schools that emphasized not only academic subjects but the arts of warfare as well, particularly the use of weapons, such as the spear, the shield, and the others discussed earlier. When they turned 17, they were assigned to military regiments. Armies were highly organized, with trained generals, units, couriers, porters, flag bearers, bodies of foot soldiers, bodies of archers, and the like. Like modern armies, Mesoamerican armies had ranks of soldiers; a person moved up through the ranks by showing courage and skill, and a soldier's rank was indicated by an elaborate flag on his back that identified his clan, family, or city.

South America

Historians and archaeologists long believed that warfare in ancient South America was not common. They pointed to the fact that South American societies tended to be small and decentralized. Thus, dominant societies did not mount armies of conquest. However, much of the archaeological record shows defensive remains, such as walls, moats, ditches, and parapets, though some archaeologists question whether these "defenses" could possibly have been effective and suggest that they served more ritualistic purposes. For example, they note that "forts" had no source of water, suggesting that they could not have been used as refuges for armies for more than brief periods of time. Further, the forts had numerous points of entry and even gaps, making them inadequate for defense.

However, more recent archaeological thinking suggests that warfare may have been more common than was previously thought. These scholars emphasize, though, that South American warfare tended to be prosecuted not by large armies in open fields of battle. Rather, it was conducted more like the wars of Native North Americans, with emphasis on guerrilla tactics. Further, warfare tended to be ritualistic and even relatively bloodless—more a form of social negotiation rather than an effort to destroy an enemy. The word used to convey this idea is *tinku,* which means something like "ritual battle." Scholars draw these conclusions by looking at the archaeological remains, which include many pictures of ritualized war and in particular ritualized conflict between people who are not adult males. This record shows that the most common weapons in ritualized warfare were clubs, slingshots, and even whips.

The practice of capturing enemy soldiers for ritual sacrifice was common in South America. Among the Moche, for example, the purpose of warfare was not to conquer enemies so much as it was to obtain captives for ritual sacrifices conducted by warrior-priests. Surviving decorations on pottery, for example, show these sacrifices being conducted, with enemy soldiers having their throats slit and warrior-priests drinking goblets of the soldiers' blood. In conducting war South Americans used weapons that were in most respects similar to those used in North America and Mesoamerica: knives, lances, and particularly clubs. Bows and arrows do not seem to have been as widely used.

South America also provides a clear example of the relationship between warfare, resources, and climatic conditions among the Andean people of Peru. Recent archaeological findings show that the Andeans developed a complex, thriving civilization beginning in about 3000 B.C.E. They built cities, including the city of Caral, pyramids, monuments, and plazas that have only begun to be explored fully. For about 1,200 years the Andeans lived peaceably with their neighbors. Very early on ocean currents provided rich marine life along the coast as well as a climate for growing fruits and vegetables. But at some point the climate turned much drier, so the Andeans built canals to irrigate what was becoming desert. Their problem was that over time the soil became progressively less productive, leading to a decline in their civilization. By about 1800 B.C.E. the region had been conquered by neighboring states.

See also ADORNMENT; AGRICULTURE; ARCHITECTURE; BORDERS AND FRONTIERS; BUILDING TECHNIQUES AND MATERIALS; CHILDREN; CITIES; DEATH AND BURIAL PRACTICES; ECONOMY; EDUCATION; EMPIRES AND DYNASTIES; FAMILY; FESTIVALS; FOREIGNERS AND BARBARIANS; GENDER STRUCTURES AND ROLES; GOVERNMENT ORGANIZATION; HUNTING, FISHING, AND GATHERING; INVENTIONS; LITERATURE; METALLURGY; MIGRATION AND POPULATION MOVEMENTS; MILITARY; NOMADIC AND PASTORAL SOCIETIES; RELIGION AND COSMOLOGY; ROADS AND BRIDGES; SEAFARING AND NAVIGATION; SETTLEMENT PATTERNS; SHIPS AND SHIPBUILDING; SLAVES AND SLAVERY; SOCIAL ORGANIZATION; TOWNS AND VILLAGES; TRADE AND EXCHANGE; TRANSPORTATION; WEAPONRY AND ARMOR.

Africa

Herodotus: "The Carthaginian Attack on Sicily," excerpt (The Histories, fifth century B.C.E.)

VII.165: They, however, who dwell in Sicily, say that Gelo, though he knew that he must serve under the Lacedaemonians, would nevertheless have come to the aid of the Hellenes, had not it been for Terillos, the son of Crinippos, king of Himera; who, driven from his city by Thero, the son of Ainesidemos, king of Agrigentum, brought into Sicily at this very time an army of three hundred thousand men—Phoenicians, Libyans, Iberians, Ligurians, Helisykians, Sardinians, and Corsicans, under the command of Hamilcar the son of Hanno, king of the Carthaginians. Terillos prevailed upon Hamilcar, partly as his sworn friend, but more through the zealous aid of Anaxilaos the son of Cretines, king of Rhegium; who, by giving his own sons to Hamilcar as hostages, induced him to make the expedition. Anaxilaos herein served his own father-in-law; for he was married to a daughter of Terillos, by name Kydippe. So, as Gelo could not give the Hellenes any aid, he sent (they say) the sum of money to Delphi.

VII.166: They say too, that the victory of Gelo and Thero in Sicily over Hamilcar the Carthaginian fell out upon the very day that the Hellenes defeated the Persians at Salamis. Hamilcar, who was a Carthaginian on his father's side only, but on his mother's a Syracusan, and who had been raised by his merit to the throne of Carthage, after the battle and the defeat, as I am informed, disappeared from sight: Gelo made the strictest search for him, but he could not be found anywhere, either dead or alive.

VII.167: The Carthaginians, who take probability for their guide, give the following account of this matter: Hamilcar, they say, during all the time that the battle raged between the Hellenes and the barbarians, which was from early dawn till evening, remained in the camp, sacrificing and seeking favorable omens, while he burned on a huge pyre the entire bodies of the victims which he offered. Here, as he poured libations upon the sacrifices, he saw the rout of his army; whereupon he cast himself headlong into the flames, and so was consumed and disappeared. But whether Hamilcar's disappearance happened, as the Phoenicians tell us, in this way, or, as the Syracusans maintain, in some other, certain it is that the Carthaginians offer him sacrifice, and in all their colonies have monuments erected to his honor, as well as one, which is the grandest of all, at Carthage. Thus much concerning the affairs of Sicily.

From: Herodotus, *The History*, George Rawlinson, trans. (New York: Dutton and Co., 1862).

Egypt

Pen-ta-ur: "The Victory of Ramses II over the Khita," inscription on the wall of five temples, one at Karnak (ca. 1326 B.C.E.)

THEN the king of Khita-land,
With his warriors made a stand,
But he durst not risk his hand
In battle with our Pharaoh;
So his chariots drew away,
Unnumbered as the sand,
And they stood, three men of war
On each car;
And gathered all in force
Was the flower of his army,
for the fight in full array,
But advance, he did not dare,
Foot or horse.

So in ambush there they lay,
Northwest of Kadesh town;
And while these were in their lair,
Others went forth south of Kadesh,
on our midst, their charge was thrown
With such weight, our men went down,
For they took us unaware,
And the legion of Pra-Hormakhu gave way.

But at the western side
Of Arunatha's tide,
Near the city's northern wall,
our Pharaoh had his place.
And they came unto the king,

And they told him our disgrace;
Then Rameses uprose,
like his father, Montu in might,
All his weapons took in hand,
And his armor did he don,
Just like Baal, fit for fight;
And the noble pair of horses that carried Pharaoh on,
Lo! "Victory of Thebes" was their name,
And from out the royal stables of great Miamun they came.

Then the king he lashed each horse,
And they quickened up their course,
And he dashed into the middle of the hostile, Hittite host,
All alone, none other with him, for he counted not the cost.
Then he looked behind, and found
That the foe were all around,
Two thousand and five hundred of their chariots of war;
And the flower of the Hittites, and their helpers, in a ring—
Men of Masu, Keshkesh, Pidasa, Malunna, Arathu,
Qazauadana, Kadesh, Akerith, Leka and Khilibu—
Cut off the way behind,
Retreat he could not find;
There were three men on each car,
And they gathered all together, and closed upon the king.
"Yea, and not one of my princes, of my chief men and my great,
Was with me, not a captain, not a knight;
For my warriors and chariots had left me to my fate,
Not one was there to take his part in fight."

Then spake Pharaoh, and he cried:
"Father Ammon, where are you?
Shall a sire forget his son?
Is there anything without your knowledge I have done?
From the judgments of your mouth when have I gone?
Have I e'er transgressed your word?
Disobeyed, or broke a vow?
Is it right, who rules in Egypt, Egypt's lord,
Should e'er before the foreign peoples bow,
Or own their rod? . . .
Let the wretch be put to shame
Who refuses your commands,
But honor to his name
Who to Ammon lifts his hands.
To the full of my endeavor,
With a willing heart forever,
I have acted unto you,
And to you, great God, I call;
For behold! now, Ammon, I,
In the midst of many peoples, all unknown,
Unnumbered as the sand,
Here I stand,
All alone;
There is no one at my side,
My warriors and chariots afeared,
Have deserted me, none heard
My voice, when to the cravens I, their king, for succor, cried.
But I find that Ammon's grace
Is better far to me
Than a million fighting men and ten thousand chariots be. . . .
To you my cry I send,
Unto earth's extremest end,
Saying, 'Help me, father Ammon, against the Hittite horde.'"

Then my voice it found an echo in Hermonthis' temple-hall,
Ammon heard it, and he came unto my call. . . .

Then all this came to pass, I was changed in my heart
Like Monthu, god of war, was I made,
With my left hand hurled the dart,
With my right I swung the blade,
Fierce as Baal in his time, before their sight.
Two thousand and five hundred pairs of horses were around,
And I flew into the middle of their ring,
By my horse-hoofs they were dashed all in pieces to the ground, . . .

Then the wretched king of Khita, he stood still,
With his warriors and his chariots all about him in a ring,
Just to gaze upon the valor of our king
In the fray.
And the king was all alone,
Of his men and chariots none
To help him; but the Hittite of his gazing soon had fill,
For he turned his face in flight, and sped away. . . .
Then his princes forth he sent,
To battle with our lord,
Well equipped with bow and sword
And all goodly armament, . . .

(continued)

(continues)

Then, like Monthu in his might,
I rushed on them apace,
And I let them taste my hand
In a twinkling moment's space.
Then cried one unto his mate,
"This is no man, this is he,
This is Sutek, god of hate,
With Baal in his blood;
Let us hasten, let us flee,
Let us save our souls from death,
Let us take to heel and try our lungs and breath."
And before the king's attack,
Lands fell, and limbs were slack,
They could neither aim the bow, nor thrust the spear,
But just looked at him who came
Charging on them, like a flame,
And the King was as a griffin in the rear.
Behold thus speaks the Pharaoh, let all know,
I struck them down, and there escaped me none
Then I lifted up my voice, and I spake,
Ho! my warriors, charioteers,
Away with craven fears,
Halt, stand, and courage take,
Behold I am alone,
Yet Ammon is my helper, and his hand is with me now."
. . .

When my Menna, charioteer, beheld in his dismay,
How the horses swarmed around us, lo! his courage fled away,
And terror and affright
Took possession of him quite;
And straightway he cried out to me, and said,

"Gracious lord and bravest king, savior-guard
Of Egypt in the battle, be our ward;
Behold we stand alone, in the hostile Hittite ring,
Save for us the breath of life,
Give deliverance from the strife,
Oh! protect us, Ramses Miamun!
Oh! save us, mighty King!" . . .

Then the king, he hurried forward, on the Hittite host he flew,
"For the sixth time that I charged them," says the king—and listen well,
"Like Baal in his strength, on their rearward, lo! I fell,
And I killed them, none escaped me, and I slew, and slew, and slew."

From: Eva March Tappan, ed., *The World's Story: A History of the World in Story, Song and Art.* Vol. 3, *Egypt, Africa, and Arabia*, trans. W. K. Flinders Petrie (Boston: Houghton Mifflin, 1914).

The Middle East

Excerpts from Accounts of the Campaign of Sennacherib

From The Sennacherib Prism (ca. 701 B.C.E.)

In my third campaign I marched against Hatti. Luli, king of Sidon, whom the terror-inspiring glamour of my lordship had overwhelmed, fled far overseas and perished. . . . As to Hezekiah, the Jew, he did not submit to my yoke, I laid siege to his strong cities, walled forts, and countless small villages, and conquered them by means of well-stamped earth-ramps and battering-rams brought near the walls with an attack by foot soldiers, using mines, breeches as well as trenches. I drove out 200,150 people, young and old, male and female, horses, mules, donkeys, camels, big and small cattle beyond counting, and considered them slaves. Himself I made a prisoner in Jerusalem, his royal residence, like a bird in a cage. I surrounded him with earthwork in order to molest those who were his city's gate. Thus I reduced his country, but I still increased the tribute and the presents to me as overlord which I imposed upon him beyond the former tribute, to be delivered annually. Hezekiah himself, did send me, later, to Nineveh, my lordly city, together with 30 talents of gold, 800 talents of silver, precious stones, antimony, large cuts of red stone, couches inlaid with ivory, nimedu-chairs inlaid with ivory, elephant-hides, ebony-wood, boxwood and all kinds of valuable treasures, his own daughters and concubines.

From: Oliver J. Thatcher, ed., *The Library of Original Sources.* Vol. 1, *The Ancient World* (Milwaukee, Wis.: University Research Extension Co., 1907).

From The Hebrew Bible, 2 Kings 18:13–15, 19:35–37

In the fourteenth year of King Hezekiah, Sennacherib, king of Assyria, went on an expedition against all the fortified cities of Judah and captured them. Hezekiah, king of Judah, sent this message to the king of Assyria at Lachish: "I have done wrong. Leave me, and I will pay whatever tribute you impose on me." The king of Assyria exacted three hundred talents of silver and thirty talents of gold from Hezekiah, king of Judah. Hezekiah paid him all the funds there were in the temple of the Lord and in the palace treasuries. . . . That night the angel of the Lord went forth and struck down 185,000 men in the Assyrian camp. Early the next morning, there they were, all the corpses of the dead. So Sennacherib, the king of Assyria, broke camp and went back home to Nineveh. When he was worshiping in the temple of his god Nisroch, his sons Adram-melech and Sharezer slew him with the sword and fled into the land of Ararat.

From: The Bible (Douai-Rheims Version) (Baltimore: John Murphy Co., 1914).

Rome

Polybius: "The Roman Maniple vs. The Macedonian Phalanx," excerpt (The Histories, ca. second century B.C.E.*)*

In my sixth book I made a promise, still unfulfilled, of taking a fitting opportunity of drawing a comparison between the arms of the Romans and Macedonians, and their respective system of tactics, and pointing out how they differ for better or worse from each other. I will now endeavor by a reference to actual facts to fulfil that promise. For since in former times the Macedonian tactics proved themselves by experience capable of conquering those of Asia and Greece; while the Roman tactics sufficed to conquer the nations of Africa and all those of Western Europe; and since in our own day there have been numerous opportunities of comparing the men as well as their tactics, it will be, I think, a useful and worthy task to investigate their differences, and discover why it is that the Romans conquer and carry off the palm from their enemies in the operations of war. . . .

Many considerations may easily convince us that, if only the phalanx has its proper formation and strength, nothing can resist it face to face or withstand its charge. . . .

It is clear that in front of each man of the front rank there will be five sarissae projecting to distances varying by a descending scale of two cubits.

With this point in our minds, it will not be difficult to imagine what the appearance and strength of the whole phalanx is likely to be, when, with lowered sarissae, it advances to the charge sixteen deep. Of these sixteen ranks, all above the fifth are unable to reach with their sarissae far enough to take actual part in the fighting. They, therefore, do not lower them, but hold them with the points inclined upwards over the shoulders of the ranks in front of them, to shield the heads of the whole phalanx; for the sarissae are so closely serried, that they repel missiles which have carried over the front ranks and might fall upon the heads of those in the rear. These rear ranks, however, during an advance, press forward those in front by the weight of their bodies; and thus make the charge very forcible, and at the same time render it impossible for the front ranks to face about.

Such is the arrangement, general and detailed of the phalanx. It remains now to compare with it the peculiarities and distinctive features of the Roman arms and tactics. Now, a Roman soldier in full armor also requires a space of three square feet. But as their method of fighting admits of individual motion for each man—because he defends his body with a shield, which he moves about to any point from which a blow is coming, and because he uses his sword both for cutting and stabbing—it is evident that each man must have a clear space, and an interval of at least three feet both on flank and rear if he is to do his duty with any effect. The result of this will be that each Roman soldier will face two of the front rank of a phalanx, so that he has to encounter and fight against ten spears, which one man cannot find time even to cut away, when once the two lines are engaged, nor force his way through easily—

(continued)

(continues)

seeing that the Roman front ranks are not supported by the rear ranks, either by way of adding weight to their charge, or vigor to the use of their swords. Therefore, it may readily be understood that, as I said before, it is impossible to confront a charge of the phalanx, so long as it retains its proper formation and strength.

Why is it then that the Romans conquer? And what is it that brings disaster on those who employ the phalanx? Why, just because war is full of uncertainties both as to time and place; whereas there is but one time and one kind of ground in which a phalanx can fully work. If, then, there were anything to compel the enemy to accommodate himself to the time and place of the phalanx, when about to fight a general engagement, it would be but natural to expect that those who employed the phalanx would always carry off the victory. But if the enemy finds it possible, and even easy, to avoid its attack, what becomes of its formidable character? Again, no one denies that for its employment it is indispensable to have a country flat, bare, and without such impediments as ditches, cavities, depressions, steep banks, or beds of rivers: for all such obstacles are sufficient to hinder and dislocate this particular formation. . . . If the enemy decline to come down into it, but traverse the country sacking the towns and territories of the allies, what use will the phalanx be? For if it remains on the ground suited to itself, it will not only fail to benefit its friends, but will be incapable even of preserving itself. . . .

For no speculation is any longer required to test the accuracy of what I am now saying: that can be done by referring to accomplished facts. The Romans do not, then, attempt to extend their front to equal that of a phalanx, and then charge directly upon it with their whole force: but some of their divisions are kept in reserve, while others join battle with the enemy at close quarters. Now, whether the phalanx in its charge drives its opponents from their ground, or is itself driven back, in either case its peculiar order is dislocated; for whether in following the retiring, or flying from the advancing enemy, they quit the rest of their forces: and when this takes place, the enemy's reserves can occupy the space thus left, and the ground which the phalanx had just before been holding, and so no longer charge them face to face, but fall upon them on their flank and rear. If, then, it is easy to take precautions against the opportunities and peculiar advantages of the phalanx, but impossible to do so in the case of its disadvantages, must it not follow that in practice the difference between these two systems is enormous? Of course, those generals who employ the phalanx must march over ground of every description, must pitch camps, occupy points of advantage, besiege, and be besieged, and meet with unexpected appearances of the enemy: for all these are part and parcel of war, and have an important and sometimes decisive influence on the ultimate victory. And in all these cases the Macedonian phalanx is difficult, and sometimes impossible, to handle, because the men cannot act either in squads or separately.

The Roman order on the other hand is flexible: for every Roman, once armed and on the field, is equally well-equipped for every place, time, or appearance of the enemy. He is, moreover, quite ready and needs to make no change, whether he is required to fight in the main body, or in a detachment, or in a single maniple, or even by himself. Therefore, as the individual members of the Roman force are so much more serviceable, their plans are also much more often attended by success than those of others.

From: Polybius, *The Histories of Polybius*, 2 vols., trans. Evelyn S. Shuckburgh (London: Macmillan, 1889).

FURTHER READING

Elizabeth Arkush and Charles Stanish, "Interpreting Conflict in the Ancient Andes," *Current Anthropology* 46, no. 1 (2005): 3–28. Available online. URL: http://www.ioa.ucla.edu/stanish/pubs/arkush_stanish.pdf. Downloaded on May 1, 2007.

Matthew Bennett, *Dictionary of Ancient and Medieval Warfare* (Mechanicsburg, Penn.: Stackpole Books, 2001).

Fergus M. Bordewich, "The Ambush That Changed History," *Smithsonian* 36 (September 2005): 74–81.

Alfred S. Bradford, *With Arrow, Sword, and Spear: A History of Warfare in the Ancient World* (Westport, Conn.: Praeger, 2000).

M. Kathryn Brown and Travis W. Stanton, eds., *Ancient Mesoamerican Warfare* (Walnut Creek, Calif.: AltaMira Press, 2003).

Prithwis Chandra Chakravarti, *The Art of War in Ancient India* (Delhi, India: Oriental Publishers, 1972).

Pierre Ducrey, *Warfare in Ancient Greece*, trans. Janet Lloyd (New York: Shocken Books, 1986).

John Hackett, ed., *Warfare in the Ancient World* (New York: Facts On File, 1989).

William V. Harris, *War and Imperialism in Republican Rome, 327–70 B.C.* (Oxford, U.K.: Clarendon, 1979).

Lawrence H. Keeley, *War before Civilization* (New York: Oxford University Press, 1996).

Steven A. LeBlanc and Katherine E. Register, *Constant Battles: The Myth of the Peaceful, Noble Savage* (New York: St. Martin's Press, 2003).

Stuart C. Munro-Hay, "Warfare." In *Aksum: An African Civilisation of Late Antiquity* (Edinburgh: Edinburgh University Press, 1991). Available online. URL: http://users.vnet.net/alight/aksum/mhak4.html#c11. Downloaded on May 13, 2007.

John Rich and Graham Shipley, *War and Society in the Roman World* (London: Routledge, 1993).

Michael M. Sage, *Warfare in Ancient Greece: A Sourcebook* (New York: Routledge, 1996).

Pat Southern, *The Roman Army: A Social and Institutional History* (Santa Barbara, Calif.: ABC-CLIO, 2006).

Hans Van Wees, *Greek Warfare: Myths and Realities* (London: Duckworth, 2004).

► weaponry and armor

INTRODUCTION

Warfare has been a constant element of life since ancient times, yet relatively few ancient weapons and armor have survived to be studied. Iron decays easily, as does the wood and other organic materials that early people used for weapons. Bronze has a better rate of survival, but this material was not used in southern Africa, the Americas, and Oceania. The study of ancient weaponry is further complicated by confusion over how weapons were used. While surviving art and literature from Europe, the Near East, and Asia contains descriptions of weaponry and armor, the same sources are not available for other regions of the world.

In Europe weapons were used almost exclusively to kill enemies and prey. A few daggers and swords, highly decorated and in the possession of high-status men, had ceremonial purposes. Daggers, swords, and spears were typically used for combat, with only daggers intended strictly for attacks upon humans. Slings were the first missile weapon, followed by the enormously popular bows and arrows. The Greeks invented chemical warfare in the form of Greek fire and sulfur gas. Metal, wood, skins, and leather were employed to construct head and body coverings as well as shields. The users of weaponry and armor in Europe were almost exclusively male.

In the Near East warriors used the same sorts of weaponry and armor that were found in Europe. The Assyrians are the earliest warriors of history of whom we have detailed knowledge. They were armed with spears, battle-axes, maces, swords, and shields as well as bows and arrows. Assyrians show liquid fire on bas-relief artwork. Along with other people of the region, they employed simple incendiary materials such as blazing arrows, pots of boiling oil, and naphtha. Babylonian spearmen protected themselves with square shields held edge to edge, as did the Greek phalanxes and Roman legions 3,000 years later. The Assyrians were the first to develop scale armor that consisted of many small metal plates sewn on a leather jacket so that the rows overlapped.

In the Americas some of the aboriginal people used copper and bronze, but they never developed wrought iron or steel for weapons. Stone arrowheads and spearheads continued to be used century after century, as they were in Oceania. In Asia the Hindus became renowned as the best temperers of steel in the ancient world. Few clues to the weaponry of ancient Africa remain. The Africans passed from the Stone Age directly into the Iron Age, missing the Bronze Age entirely. In the context of ancient Africa a weapon has to be viewed as part of a highly complex system of interdependent actions and beliefs. Some weapons were empowered by the application of magical substances. No matter how thick the hide of a shield or well tempered the blade of a sword, both were considered incomplete without the symbolic designs applied to them. Even accessories such as sword sheaths seem also to have had great importance.

AFRICA

BY CARYN E. NEUMANN

Western understandings of weaponry have limited application to Africa. In ancient Africa the separation between military and civilian life was not as distinct as in the West. While European weapons were made to kill, ancient African weaponry came in a wide variety of forms developed for use in political, religious, or other ritual or ceremonial contexts; not all were designed to kill.

Weaponry in Africa began with rock. The oldest surviving weapons in the world are pebbles chipped into blades that were found in Africa. These weapons also could double as tools or perhaps were an adaptation from tools; their use as tools no doubt preceded their use as weapons. These rough weapons advanced into knives made of sharpened rock, spears with stone tips, and hand axes shaped like almonds. One type of hand ax, the cleaver, has been found only in Africa. It had a hefty blade used for hacking, slashing, and cutting.

A wide variety of raw materials, including quartzite, hornfels, mudstone, and chert, was used in southern Africa for stone point production. Herodotus reported that Africans used spears with heads constructed from the sharpened horns of antelope. The points, with distinctive tangs, were bound to spears with plant twine, bark, leather thongs, and sinew. The binding materials would have been moistened before application. Moistened bindings expand and become more pliable before contracting to their original size upon drying. This shrinkage, and the fact that individual strands on drying tend to adhere to one another, leaves the point firmly secured on the haft.

The first long-range missile weapon was probably a sling, although no ancient African slings have survived. Slings were originally used by ancient shepherds to scare predatory animals that were attacking their herds. They gradually became weapons of warfare, used by light-armed troops against similarly defenseless warriors. The sling consisted of two leather or sinew straps. Each strap was attached at one end to the sides of a small piece of leather or cloth. The other end of one

Stone ball, Lower Palaeolithic, about 1.2 million years old, found in Olduvai Gorge, Tanzania; such stone balls might have been tied to a leather thong and used in hunting to bring down game. (© The Trustees of the British Museum)

strap, held by the slinger, was looped securely around a finger or wrist, while the other strap, usually knotted to provide a grip, was held freely between the thumb and forefinger of the throwing hand. The missile, a stone, was placed on a piece of leather, and the straps were pulled taut, creating a pocket for the stone. A rotary motion of the wrist, usually three or four rotations, gave the stone momentum when the unlooped, held strap was released. A skilled thrower could be very accurate, and the high-speed missile could kill.

Copper technology indicates that ancient Africans mastered a considerable degree of the pyrotechnology needed for copper smelting. Evidence of early copper metallurgy has been radiocarbon dated from 4140 B.C.E. to 2700 B.C.E. in western Africa. Copper products included thin arrowheads. There is evidence of iron production in East Africa from about 1400 B.C.E. The date suggests that iron production might not have been introduced from elsewhere but instead developed in the region. Iron ore is distributed widely across Africa. Stone artifacts were always present at early Iron Age sites in the form of arrow points and axes, with metal weapons used as status objects. Africans employed iron to make tools, weapons, and points for weapons. Many central African people believed that, except on a few designated occasions, women should not come into contact with iron. To do so could render a woman barren and destroy the power of the ~~iron~~ products with which she came into contact. However, other parts of Africa accepted women warriors, and the Teda of the Tibesti region developed weaponry specifically for women.

The Iron Age brought the use of throwing knives as missiles. Throwing knives, additionally used as long-distance currency, were more popular than javelins. The sharp spikes of these weapons could inflict severe wounds on practically nude enemies. The classic form of the northern variety of throwing knife consists of a narrow piece of iron, up to 2½ feet in length, with a projecting spur a little over halfway up. Below this spur are a straight shaft and a grip, which, if not made of bare iron, is usually made of hide or reptile skin. Above the spur is the blade, often broader than the shaft and curving forward in the same direction as the spur. Weapons of this type were distributed across a wide area of Sudanic Africa from northern Nigeria to the Blue Nile province of Sudan and deep into the Tibesti region of the Sahara.

The typical southern variety of throwing knife is generally smaller than the northern variety. It usually has a number of blades radiating from the central shaft and a grip of plaited vegetal material or, occasionally, of wire or hide. It is found in a small area of northern Gabon and in a broad belt from eastern Cameroon almost to the White Nile. The Zande *kpinga*, a southern type of throwing knife, is one of the few varieties whose aerodynamic qualities and consistent use as a missile have been well documented. The heavier northern throwing knife was used more often than the lighter southern variety for ceremonial purposes.

Not every weapon was intended for war. Weapons of various types were widely used in dance and masquerade throughout Africa. The *musele*, a Kota throwing knife conceived as a bird in profile with a long bill, was not designed to be thrown. The Kota, of the eastern Ogooué River region, saw the *musele* as a prestigious weapon of chiefs to be used in dances. Throwing knives of the Wadai region were also ornithologically inspired and designed for ceremonial purposes. Among the Kota and the Fang spears, knives, and swords were considered to be emblems of the owner's status and were left on tombs of chiefs after death.

To protect against weapons, Africans used light armor that befitted their hot climate. The protective armor of the Benin warrior was a large wooden shield with a curved top and straight bottom. It was designed to be set on the ground to cover a kneeling man. The shields in the Sudan were made of hippopotamus or elephant hide. The shields of the Dinka were oval in outline and reinforced by a staff threaded through loops cut into the hide. The staff served as a handgrip. The Shuli had shields of a more nearly rectangular form, while the Shilluk and Nuer both had shields that could serve as clubs. The club shields were reinforced with a log with a cutout for the grip. The skin cover of ox hide was applied tightly in order to keep the wood from splitting when delivering blows with this shield club. Chiefs and other distinguished warriors throughout Africa wore helmets of padded basketwork or crocodile skin. For body armor they had quilted ponchos covered with leopard skins.

EGYPT

BY AMR KAMEL

Ancient Egyptian weapons apparently were manufactured in the workshops attached to royal palaces, great temples, and military headquarters. There are a few scenes from the Old and Middle Kingdom (ca. 2575–ca. 1640 B.C.E.) that depict bows and spear shafts being smoothed and others that show arrows. From the New Kingdom (ca. 1550–ca. 1070 B.C.E.) there is much pictorial evidence showing various techniques used in weapons manufacture. Scenes include a craftsman straightening the shaft of a spear over a fire after wetting it from a cup of water beside him, a bow being tested for resilience, arrows being made, metal helmets being weighted, bow cases being sewn up with an awl (a pointed tool for punching holes), and an arrow being checked for straightness by one workman while a second uses an adze (a bladed tool) to plane out another arrow resting on his knees.

A letter sent by Dhutmose, a scribe who was on a military mission in Nubia, to his son, Butehamun, the scribe of the Necropolis at Deir el-Medina, requests "fresh supplies of copper spear-heads" made by the local coppersmiths as well as spare parts for war chariots, new material for clothing, and old material "for bandages," a rare sign of concern for the wounded. Several New Kingdom tombs include representations of carpenters, joiners, and leather workers, all working on a chariot together. In addition to wood, they required large amounts of leather for fastening parts together, covering the body, tiring the wheels, and making reins, blinkers, and bits.

During the New Kingdom the Egyptians imported highly developed weapons from the Near East and adopted Near Eastern military technology. There is perhaps some evidence that non-Egyptian craftsmen participated in weapons manufacture. Bows and arrows, the most important long-range weapons, can be dated to the Late Paleolithic Period (ca. 12,000–10,000 B.C.E.). During the Second Intermediate Period (1640–1532 B.C.E.) the composite bow was introduced from the Near East. It was made from laminated wood, horn, and sinew and had a much improved range and power. It had an effective range of 500 to 600 feet, and an exceptional shot could attain a distance of 1,500 feet. Because of the laminate construction of composite bows, they were sensitive to heat and moisture and thus were usually stored in cases. Two types of cases have been discovered from New Kingdom Egypt: One was carried, and the other was attached to the body of a war chariot. They could be made of leather or wood and were sometimes ornamented.

Handheld stabbing weapons can be traced to Paleolithic times. The earliest artistic representation of a spear is on the Hunters Palette. Spears were regularly used in military contexts in later times as well. For example, the Egyptian soldiers on Hatshepsut's (r. 1473–1458 B.C.E.) mission to Punt are shown carrying spears and shields on the Deir el-Bahri reliefs, as are troops following Tutankhamun (r. 1333–1323 B.C.E.) as he drives his chariot on the "painted box." Some of the Near Eastern men in the Beni Hasan tomb painting carry spears, and the Shasu Bedouin in the Seti I (r. 1306–1290 B.C.E.) reliefs at Karnak brandish spears and axes against Egyptian forces. Spears were ideal defensive weapons in siege warfare.

A spear with much longer shaft, known as a lance, is illustrated in siege scenes from the Middle Kingdom Beni Hasan tombs. In these scenes a portable defensive structure covers a group of soldiers who attack a fortified city with a large lance, in the manner of a battering ram. Maces with mace heads of varying form were the most powerful weapons of close combat in the Predynastic Period (before roughly 3000 B.C.E.). In the Late Period (712–332 B.C.E.) and into Greco-Roman times (332 B.C.E.–395 C.E.) kings are shown brandishing maces in the head-smiting motif on temple walls. Disc- and oval-shaped mace heads are found in the Naqada I and II periods of the Predynastic Period. These shapes continued to be used through pharaonic history and beyond. The mace (and club) probably had a more ceremonial function after the Old Kingdom, despite Thutmose III's (r. 1479–1425 B.C.E.) boast on the Gebel Barkal stela regarding his victories in the Near East: "It was my mace which overthrew the Asiatics, my club which smote the Nine Bows."

The earliest form of ax was the handheld implement from Paleolithic times. When the stone blade was first affixed to a handle is not known, but at that point of development the ax became a deadly weapon. During the Old Kingdom copper blades were introduced. The ax blades were long and rounded and continued to be used during the Middle Kingdom. The duck-bill blade is the ax shown in the tomb of Khnumhotep at Beni Hasan. In two Old Kingdom battle scenes the ax is used by Egyptian soldiers to repel their enemies and to hack up the city wall. In the New Kingdom the blade is much more narrowly shaped.

Swords and daggers were of great military importance throughout Egypt's history. These weapons are similar in construction but different in length and usage. A sword is generally defined as longer than 16 inches, and a dagger is shorter. The Third Dynasty relief of King Sekhemkhet (r. ca. 2611–ca. 2603 B.C.E.) at Wadi Maghara (Sinai) shows a dagger tucked in the monarch's belt. These early daggers were made of copper and had no midrib (thickening down the middle for added strength). The dagger's usefulness as a weapon would have been in hand-to-hand combat. As copper gave way to bronze in the third millennium B.C.E., daggers in Egypt evolved into swords. Preserved examples from the Middle Kingdom resemble the daggers of earlier periods. However, swords were not commonly used in Egypt until the New Kingdom, when longer, double-edged swords were introduced from Anatolia.

Shields were the oldest means of defense and were made of wood covered with leather. They were used first by infantry. In the New Kingdom they were held by drivers of war chariots, to protect the archers standing beside them. The tomb of Tutankhamun contained wooden shields, some of which had leather or animal skins over them. Combining wood and leather made the shield a more effective defensive tool, and a metal protective surface was especially useful against arrows fired from composite bows. Helmets appeared in the Eighteenth Dynasty (ca. 1550–ca. 1307 B.C.E.), when some troops acquired helmets of bronze or leather in imitation of the Asiatic model. Other troops wore shirts made of leather strips sewn together in rows. Armor made of iron lamellae (thin plates) appeared in the reign of Sheshonk I (r. ca. 945–ca. 924 B.C.E.).

The two-wheeled, horse-drawn chariot was introduced to Egypt from Asia in the Second Intermediate Period. From that time onward the chariot significantly contributed to the art of Egyptian warfare, useful for its mobility and the element of surprise. It was constructed of wood with some leather and metal elements, making it a light vehicle on the battlefield. It was manned by two soldiers: the charioteer, who held a shield, and the chariot-warrior, who was armed with a bow and a spear. The chariot was not armored in any way and therefore was not suitable for a direct attack. Once the enemy lines were broken, the chariot was ideally suited for pursuing and harassing the scattered infantry.

THE MIDDLE EAST

BY JAMES A. CORRICK

Through the sixth millennium B.C.E. weapons in the ancient Near East were made from stone and wood. Spears with long wooden shafts and arrows made from reeds or wood were tipped with chipped-flint heads. Some crude spears and arrows lacked heads, with one end being nothing more than a fire-hardened point. Axes with stone blades were also used. During the fifth millennium B.C.E. the flint and stone heads of these weapons were often replaced by copper, and by 3500 B.C.E. bronze was in use for weapons. Around 1200 B.C.E. the Hittites were among the first to use iron for armaments. However, the quality of this iron was not good, and bronze weapons were still stronger and better made. Good-quality iron weapons did not become common until after 1000 B.C.E., with steel—iron hardened by the addition of carbon—appearing in arms manufacturing after 500 B.C.E.

Many of the weapons that became common throughout the ancient Near East were first used by the armies of Sumer. By 2500 B.C.E. infantry troops were armed with 5- to 6-foot-long thrusting spears and lightweight throwing spears, or javelins. Others carried bows with an effective range of between 150 and 300 feet. Many also carried daggers, ranging in length from 6 to 12 inches. Some weapons carried by Sumerian soldiers were everyday tools. Hunters brought slings for throwing stones that could down either game or enemy warriors in battle. Fishermen brought their nets, using them to entangle their opponents, whom they then either speared or stabbed. Nets did not long remain a part of the Near Eastern battle equipment, but slings would be used by most Near Eastern armies through the early centuries C.E., although the ammunition would sometimes be clay or lead pellets rather than small stones.

Another important Sumerian weapon was the socket ax. The bronze head of this battle-ax was narrow for better cutting and had a socket that slipped down over the end of the ax's wooden handle. A rivet driven through the socket into the handle held the head in place and allowed the wielder to deliver a strong blow without dislodging the head, as often happened to axes with heads tied to the haft. Able to cut through most forms of armor, the socket ax, its head made of iron during the last centuries B.C.E., would remain one of the most deadly ancient Near Eastern weapons.

The composite bow was the next important advance in personal weaponry, appearing sometime after 2300 B.C.E. during the Akkadian reign. Until this time bows had been carved from a single piece of wood. The composite, however, was built by gluing together different types of wood, along with bone and sinew. The resulting bow was stronger and capable of shooting an arrow twice as far as the older bows. The composite eventually became the bow of choice throughout the ancient Near East and was still being used by the Persians of the Sassanian Dynasty (224–651 C.E.).

Both Sumerians and Akkadians carried the sickle-sword, which had a curved blade much like the sickle used in harvesting crops. The straight-bladed sword eventually developed from the dagger, and Assyrians began carrying straight-bladed swords during the first millennium B.C.E., as later did Persian and other Near Eastern armies. The sickle-sword, however, continued to be used in the ancient Near East into the early centuries C.E. Its curved blade was designed for slashing at an enemy and was sharpened only on its outer edge. The straight-bladed sword might have either one edge sharpened for slashing or both edges for thrusting and stabbing as well as slashing. Long swords, measuring more than a yard, were found in the arsenals of many Near Eastern armies, but short swords, normally ranging in length from 2 to 2.5 feet, were more common. The Persian infantry of the Achaemenid Dynasty (550–330 B.C.E.) carried a very short, straight-bladed sword called an *akinakes*, which was made of iron and measured between 14 and 18 inches in length, making it not much longer than a dagger; indeed, the difference between a long dagger and a short sword was vague. Sword blades were often leaf-shaped, swelling in the middle and then tapering at the end. Bronze and iron blades were formed from a single piece of metal, while steel blades had a core of iron over which was layered a coat of steel.

The primary defenses against all weapons were armor, helmets, and shields. Sumerian armor was a linen or leather cloak to which copper or bronze disks were sewn. The most common form of armor in the ancient Near East was that worn by the Assyrians and later the Achaemenid Persians. Known as scale armor because it resembled the scales of a fish, this protective gear was made by sewing overlapping small oblongs of bronze or iron to a shirt of linen or felt. Originally, among the Assyrians, an armor shirt reached to the knees or lower, but later it was shortened so that it reached only to the waist. This short armor was also preferred by the Persians, probably because it allowed for more maneuverability. The sleeves, even on the longest armor shirts, ended well above the elbow. Sometimes Near Eastern armor was nothing more than quilted linen, as was the case with some Achaemenid Persian troops.

The first helmets were worn by the Sumerians and were either cloth or leather caps. The Sumerians eventually began using headgear made from copper that looked like metal caps. Bronze helmets appeared later. The Assyrians were among the first to wear iron helmets, although both copper and bronze helmets would remain in use in the ancient Near East throughout the last millennium B.C.E. The Assyrian helmets were noteworthy for their conical shape. They were designed so that a blow by a sword or ax, unless aimed directly, would slide down the side of the helmet. A curtain of scale mail also hung from these helmets. Modifications of this design would be adopted later by the Parthians (250 B.C.E.–226 C.E.) and the Sassanian Persians, among others.

Achaemenid Persian troops generally wore tight-fitting helmets, when they wore any headgear at all. Indeed, it was not unusual for ancient Near Eastern warriors to fight without helmets or armor. This was particularly true of archers, who might be hampered by the weight of protective gear. Instead of armor worn on the body, these troops were protected by shields, often carried for them by others known as shield-bearers. But armored and helmeted troops also generally carried shields. The earliest shield, and one that would be used as late as Sassanian times, was the wickerwork shield. It was made of woven reeds or twigs, supported by a wooden frame and sometimes lined with leather for extra protection and given additional strength by bands of metal. Even the Assyrians, with their iron scale armor and helmets, used these wickerwork shields because they were lightweight. Metal shields, made first of bronze and then of iron, also existed during this period. Shields were rectangular, circular, or oval and could be small (no more than 2 feet across) or large enough to tower above a warrior's head. The smallest shields were normally made of metal, but large metal shields were too heavy to carry into battle.

ASIA AND THE PACIFIC

BY AMY HACKNEY BLACKWELL

The basic weapons in ancient Asia were spears, swords of various designs, and bows and arrows. In prehistoric times weapons were made of wood, bone, horn, stone, and hide; bones and stones can be fashioned into very sharp points. As people learned how to work metals, they started making weapons out of them. Bronze weapons appeared during the early second millennium B.C.E. Iron weapons gradually replaced them in the next millennium, although people continued to make bronze weapons until the early years of the Common Era. Chinese weapons makers became experts at metallurgy; weapons produced during the Qin Dynasty (221–207 B.C.E.), for example, are made of carefully composed alloys of copper, nickel, chrome, iron, and several other metals. Some arrowheads contain lead, presumably for its poisonous effect. Chinese weapons makers of this period coated their blades with a thin layer of chromic salt oxide to prevent rust; this coating has preserved many weapons in good condition for more than 2,000 years.

Most ancient weapons were meant for hand-to-hand combat. Projectile weapons were harder to use and supply because they needed a stream of ammunition in battle. The sling was the most basic projectile weapon; throughout ancient Asia people used slings made of leather or some other flexible material to fling rocks or other projectiles. Bows and arrows were more effective and could propel weapons farther than slings, but the simplicity of the sling kept it in use throughout the ancient period, especially in the more remote islands of the Pacific.

The spear, or *qiang*, is one of the oldest Chinese weapons. Spears were simple to make; affixing a small, sharp tip to a long shaft did not require technological expertise. Chinese warriors began using spears in prehistoric times. Spears with bronze tips became popular starting in the 17th century B.C.E. Weapons makers started using steel instead of bronze for spear tips during the Eastern Zhou Dynasty (770–256 B.C.E.). The *qiang* spear was the most important long weapon of the Western Han Dynasty (202 B.C.E.–9 C.E.).

One of the classic Chinese weapons was the saber, or *dao*. These early *dao* were more like knives, with a straight or slightly curved blade. The oldest *dao* were made of bronze. Smiths began to make them of iron and steel between the sixth and third centuries B.C.E. As the *dao* evolved, its blade became curved, and it was often attached to a long handle, though many types of *dao* existed. The *dao* was especially popular during the late Qin Dynasty and early Han Dynasty. During the Han Dynasty cavalry became more important, and warriors took to carrying long *dao* that had single-sided blades attached to long shafts, which they could wield on horseback. Infantrymen of this time often carried short *dao* or broadswords.

Short sword of steel, bronze, and gold from east-central Asia, ca. fourth to first century B.C.E. (Copyright the Metropolitan Museum of Art)

The *jian* was a straight sword. The earliest *jian* date to the sixth century B.C.E. This weapon was most popular during the Zhou Dynasty and the Western Han Dynasty, when famous sword makers developed their craft to an art form. After the first century C.E. the warrior's *jian* grew less popular than the *dao*, which became the preferred combat weapon, especially of the cavalry. Men still wore *jian* as part of their ensembles and as a status symbol, and some warriors continued to use *jian* in combat. Martial artists of this time adopted the *jian* as a weapon to use in symbolic martial arts.

The *ji*, or halberd, was a sort of combination spear and sword; it consisted of a long shaft with a bronze point at its tip and a curved blade parallel to the shaft close to the spear tip. Sometimes a *ji* had two blades affixed opposite each other. The *ji* could be used for slashing and stabbing, and it could be wielded by men on foot or in chariots. It was popular during the Shang Dynasty (ca. 1500–ca. 1045 B.C.E.) and Zhou Dynasty. During the Han Dynasty the *qiang* spear gradually replaced the *ji* as the long weapon of choice, relegating the *ji* to martial artists.

Crossbows with bronze mechanisms are common in the archaeological record in China beginning in about 600 B.C.E. Chinese historians started mentioning crossbows in the fifth century B.C.E. Soldiers used crossbows at the battle of Maling in 341 B.C.E. During the Han Dynasty the crossbow was commonly used in infantry battles and also was occasionally deployed during fighting on horseback. Early crossbows were made of cast bronze parts attached to a wooden frame.

In India the people who lived in the Indus Valley between 2500 and 1500 B.C.E. made numerous weapons that they used for war, war games, and hunting. The Vedic sacred texts of this period describe warfare and the weapons that soldiers were expected to master. These weapons included the bow and arrow, the discus (the god Krishna was said to be an expert with the discus), the javelin, the ax, the mace, and the dagger. Archery, in particular, was highly esteemed as a soldierly skill. Indian weapons makers were among the first to build bows out of steel. Indian peoples also used swords in battle. The chariot played an important role in Indian warfare. Indian chariots were large, heavy, four-wheeled devices made of iron and wood and pulled by several horses. They could carry several soldiers, including a driver, an archer, and up to five foot soldiers. The chariots themselves were heavy enough to crush enemy soldiers, and the soldiers who rode on them used the chariots' height and speed to overpower their enemies. Indian armies also used elephants in battle starting in about 1500 B.C.E. The elephants could carry several soldiers on their backs and were themselves armed with long blades attached to their tusks.

In Japan during the Jōmon Period (ca. 13,000–ca. 300 B.C.E.) people made simple weapons from chipped and polished stone, but it was not until the Yayoi Period (ca. 300 B.C.E.–300 C.E.) that people engaged in large-scale organized warfare. During this time Japanese people began using swords and spears made of bronze and iron. Japanese weapons of this period are similar to contemporary Chinese weapons, and historians believe that Japanese weapons makers might have borrowed bronze- and iron-smelting techniques from China. The basic weapons of spears, slings, clubs, bows and arrows, and blades were used throughout the Pacific region. Australian aborigines used boomerangs, curved wooden blades that could be thrown, both for hunting and in warfare. Pacific islanders made weapons out of locally available materials. In Hawaii, for example, soldiers used slings to fling volcanic rocks. They made daggers out of swordfish spears, hammers out of stone, and spears with points made of shark teeth.

EUROPE

BY CARYN E. NEUMANN

War shaped the ancient world, with weaponry and armor determining the success of the combatants. The sheer number and wide range of military artifacts that have been unearthed speak of large-scale production and large-scale deposition of arms and armor in Europe. During the Paleolithic, Mesolithic, and Neolithic periods weapons generally included whatever blunt object was close at hand as well as any sharp object that could be thrown. Skeletons in the Neolithic mass grave at Talheim in Germany bear the traces of blows from stone axes on their skulls, and many other skulls in Neolithic burials also have evidence of blows from hard objects. Sometimes the victim survived to fight another day, but often these blows were fatal. The bow and arrow was invented during the Mesolithic, but it was some time before bows were strong and accurate enough to deliver a lethal shot to a vital organ. More often, a lucky shot would wound the victim, who then would have to be finished off by spear or ax if he had not escaped. The so-called Iceman found frozen in the Alps in 1991 had an arrowhead lodged in his shoulder, either a fatal wound or a debilitating injury that contributed to his eventual demise. He was also carrying a bow (but it was unfinished, so of no use to him) and a quiver of arrows as well as a flint dagger.

During the Copper Age, between about 3500 and 2000 B.C.E., depictions on rock carvings and finds of arrowheads indicate that the bow and arrow had increased in accuracy and killing power to become apparently the most popular weapon throughout western and central Europe. Yew and elm were the favored woods for making bows, while arrow shafts were generally made from the straight twigs of hazel. Bowstrings could have been made from animal sinew, but the Iceman's bow had a flax string. Arrowheads were often made of flint, bone, or bronze and were attached to their shafts with resin and pitch. Thus, many different raw materials had to be procured and integrated to make an effective bow and arrow. Some of the metal arrowheads were barbed to inflict more substantial wounds. Curiously, arrowheads become less common after about 2000 B.C.E., suggesting that the bow and arrow declined in popularity.

Daggers were one of the most popular weapons of the Bronze Age (2800–700 B.C.E.) and were still in common use

Spear thrower carved in the shape of a mammoth, Late Magdalenian (about 12,500 years old), from the rock shelter of Montastruc, Tarn-et-Garonne, France (© The Trustees of the British Museum)

in the Early Iron Age (beginning in 1000 B.C.E.). While some elaborately decorated daggers were apparently intended only for ceremonial use, most daggers were employed for fighting at close quarters. Unlike the bow and arrow, daggers probably were meant only for human fighting rather than hunting. It is possible, however, that they were used to deliver a coup de grace to wounded animals and people and, in the absence of other implements identifiable as knives, daggers also might have been used to butcher prey. Daggers typically had rounded pommels.

Two types of weapons emerged early in the Bronze Age that would have a substantial impact on warfare for many centuries. The sword and the spear were critical elements in combat. The spear developed out of a daggerlike blade with a long tang (attaching the blade to the handle) that might have been mounted on a long shaft rather than held close to the body. By 1800 B.C.E. the socketed version, fitting over the shaft, was in use in central Europe. With only small differences, this is the form that existed throughout the ancient era. Depictions of spears do not clearly indicate whether they were typically held or thrown. In Europe small and large spearheads were used, as were those of intermediate sizes. It is most likely that small spearheads were intended for light javelins that could be thrown over long distances. Large spearheads were probably used for heavy spears that were held firm by a warrior or group of warriors under close-quarters thrust at an opponent. Collective finds of spears in Scandinavia indicate that spear owners acted and fought in collaboration, with some throwing their spears and then taking cover behind others, who advanced holding their spears. At the moment of encounter the throwers could then have emerged to use cutting or thrusting weapons (daggers, rapiers, swords) in hand-to-hand combat.

While spears were obviously important, they were not usually decorated or given the appearance of prestige weapons, unlike swords. Early versions of the sword were in existence by 1800 B.C.E. The cut-and-thrust sword developed several centuries later. In combat, swords were usually accompanied by daggers or knives and sometimes by spears. Not everyone relied on a sword—a few relied on spears or daggers. Still, swords were the commonest weapon.

To fend off arrowheads and the blows of blades, ancient Europeans devised various types of armor. Most of the earliest examples of body armor in Europe date to the 13th century B.C.E. Leather and wood were the most popular materials for protection. Wooden shields were produced in Ireland around 1800 B.C.E. Leather, always in use, had more flexibility than bronze, and it was considerably cheaper and easier to produce. Few warriors were protected entirely by bronze, but hammered sheet bronze is so thin that it would have been relatively useless as protection against a spear or sword.

Pelts were also used as a sort of armor that offered not only the physical protection of the animal's fur and hide but also the psychological reinforcement brought about by taking on the animal's fighting skills. Warriors wore the pelts of wolves, bears, and other fierce animals when going into battle. The head of the animal sat on the warrior's head like a helmet. The animal's front legs ran down the warrior's arms, protecting them from sword blows, while its hind legs were attached to the warrior's legs. In this way the warrior inhabited the animal and took on its spirit, often in an intensely ecstatic state that made him relatively impervious to wounds and to fear and, consequently, very hard to stop.

There was another kind of ecstatic warrior that fought wearing no armor—indeed, no clothes at all. A representation of such a naked warrior has been found carved into a stone slab left by the Kemi-Oba culture at Kernosovka in Ukraine. It is the oldest-known image of a European warrior and dates from 4000 to 3000 B.C.E. The warrior is dressed in nothing but a belt, but he is heavily armed with a club, a knife or spear, and three axes. His hair is long, his arms are held tightly to his chest with his shoulders pulled up, and his penis is erect, all indicating a heightened state of passion and alertness. The same representations of tightly held arms, tense shoulders, and erect penis are also found on a Celtic statue of a "berserk" warrior. The Celts adorned their nakedness with golden neckbands, which served the double purpose of accenting their white skins and taunting their enemies to come and take the bands off their necks if they dared. They wore their naked paleness with similar bravado, as a kind of psychological armor that showed off the red blood of their wounds. Without the burden of armor, they were also faster than ordinary soldiers. At the battle of Cannae in 216 B.C.E. the Romans ran in terror from the troops of bare-chested Gauls that Hannibal had assembled. In these cases, the most effective armor was no armor. Berserks scared their opponents into fleeing the field of battle. When men did fight, wooden shields and leather coverings offered little protection against arrowheads and swords. In ancient Europe weaponry advanced more quickly than personal defenses against it.

GREECE

BY CHRISTOPHER BLACKWELL

The wall and vase paintings from the Minoan and Mycenaean Bronze Age, during the second millennium B.C.E., are the earliest evidence of the existence of weaponry and armor in the ancient Greek world. These paintings show warriors carrying shields in the shape of a figure eight, an oval with semicircles cut out on either side of the middle; these warriors wear helmets and carry long, narrow swords.

The Homeric epics, composed in their present form around the seventh century B.C.E., present a backward-looking view of warfare from an earlier age. They describe warriors armed with bronze helmets—although Odysseus, in book 10 of the *Iliad*, goes on a nighttime raid wearing a leather helmet studded with boars' tusks, bronze breastplates, and greaves (metal armor covering the shins) and carrying one or two spears and a sword. These Homeric warriors would throw their shields, either from chariots or while standing, and then engage the enemy, one on one, with their swords.

The Archaic Period (ca. 600–ca. 480 B.C.E.) saw the so-called hoplite revolution. The term comes from the Greek word *hoplon*, or "weapon; a *hoplitēs* was a soldier outfitted with heavy bronze armor and trained in the tactics of the phalanx. The phalanx was a line of infantry in close formation, each man's shield covering half of his own body and half of his neighbor's, trained to present a theoretically impregnable mass of spear points and shields. Victory depended on numbers and on the discipline of the individual soldiers.

The hoplite's armor consisted of a breastplate, or *thorax*, made of bronze; a bronze helmet, *kranos* or *korus*, closely fitted and covering the whole head and with a T-shaped slit exposing the eyes and mouth (and often a noseguard descending from the brow); bronze greaves, *knēmides*, for covering the shins; and the bronze and leather shield, *aspis* or generically *hoplon*. The hoplite's weapons were the sword (or *xiphos*), a short-bladed stabbing weapon for close combat, and the spear (*doru*), a longer thrusting weapon. Hoplites typically did not fight with the thrown spear, *akontion*, although mounted cavalry and some more lightly armed units did.

Vase from Mycenae depicting warriors in battle gear (Alison Frantz Photographic Collection, American School of Classical Studies at Athens)

Because each soldier was responsible for providing his own armor, at his own expense, there must have been a certain amount of diversity in the style and quality of arms. The historian Thucydides, in recounting how the Athenians prepared for their invasion of Sicily in 415 B.C.E., describes a certain competition among soldiers to show off by acquiring the best armor, saying that "the land forces had been picked from the best muster-rolls, and vied with each other in paying great attention to their arms and personal accoutrements."

The cost of this armor limited participation in land combat to those who could afford to arm themselves; these were generally men who owned land and who therefore had the most at stake in any conflict between neighboring states. But in contrast to the Bronze Age "heroic" warfare described by Homer, which was a series of acts of single combat between champions, hoplite warfare was communal, requiring cooperation and mutual trust. Historians see connections between the rise of this form of fighting and the increasing broadening of political participation in the Archaic Period, as power moved out of the hands of individual kings and into the hands of aristocracies or oligarchies, with governance being shared by those who were in a position to fight on behalf of the state.

The weight of metal that provided protection presented its own problems, and vase paintings of soldiers from the sixth, fifth, and fourth centuries show them, more often than not, with their heavy helmets perched back on the top of their heads, leaning on their shields, or standing by their unworn armor. Historical accounts, particularly those of Xenophon, a historian and mercenary commander of the fourth century B.C.E., contain many anecdotes of soldiers waiting to put on their armor until literally the last minute before engaging the enemy.

Cavalry did not have a large role in land warfare among Greek states until the period of Macedonian supremacy in the fourth century B.C.E. Likewise archery played a limited role, except when Greeks fought as mercenary units in the larger armies of Asia Minor. Archers, *toxitai*, do appear in accounts of siege warfare, as well as in the Homeric epics, where the Trojan Alexandros (Paris) is shown using a bow, as is the Greek Odysseus.

During the fourth century B.C.E. some Greek armies experimented with units of more lightly armed foot soldiers, called *peltasts*, some armed mainly with throwing javelins or slings. But the most significant improvements to arms came through innovations among the armies of Philip of Macedon, who arrayed his phalanxes several rows deep and armed each row with the Macedonian spear, the *sarisa*, using different

ARMING SCENES

A common feature of ancient Greek heroic poetry was the "arming scene," a description of the hero putting on his armor and gathering his weapons before entering battle. The Homeric *Iliad* has many such scenes. Book 3 of the poem describes the Trojan Paris arming for single combat with the Greek Menelaus. According to this description, Paris first "covered his legs with greave of good make and fitted with ankle-clasps of silver; after this he donned the breastplate of his brother Lykaon, and fitted it to his own body." Then "he hung his silver-studded sword of bronze about his shoulders, and then his mighty shield. On his comely head he set his helmet, well-wrought, with a crest of horse-hair that nodded menacingly above it, and he grasped a redoubtable spear that suited his hands."

The poet's vivid descriptions of the opulence of the metal and often of the history of the various pieces indicate a hero of elevated status—these heroes are rich and from illustrious families. The descriptions serve to build tension in the narrative as well: The weapons hold potential for death and destruction, but only battle itself would reveal the outcome. In the *Iliad* the arms of a hero hold talismanic powers, and fierce battles rage over the bodies of fallen warriors, with each side trying to strip the dead hero of his weapons.

The narrative technique of including an arming scene before battle, used to such good effect by Homer, is not unique to Greek poetry but appears throughout literature and art, from antiquity to the present. They range from the somewhat comic scene of King Saul arming David before his battle with Goliath (I Samuel 17: 38–40 in the Bible) through medieval epics such as *Sir Gawain and the Green Knight* to modern depictions of historical battles in literature and film.

lengths for the different ranks. The longest of these spears measured 17 feet and had a leaf-shaped iron tip, a change from the straight-sided tips of earlier hoplite spears. To offset the weight of these long spears, and reflecting the added unlikelihood of enemies penetrating the bristling hedge of iron points that the phalanx presented, the shield was reduced from a large, full-body-size rectangle to a smaller, more maneuverable disk. The supremacy of Macedonian tactics, which combined this newly re-formed phalanx with *peltasts* and cavalry, appeared most dramatically at the battle of Chaeronea in 338 B.C.E., when Philip's army defeated the forces of Athens and Thebes, and even more dramatically during Alexander the Great's campaigns against the Persian Empire in the last years of the 330s B.C.E.

By the Hellenistic Period, the period after the death of Alexander in 323 B.C.E., Greek armor had become light and tactics more fluid. Soldiers abandoned greaves and increasingly adopted a helmet with a more open face, the so-called *pylos* helmet instead of the older, more closed Corinthian style. The new helmets increased the soldier's field of vision, made breathing easier, and weighed less, and these advantages seem to have outweighed the reduced protection afforded by the open face. The old Corinthian style continued to appear on vase paintings, however, and seems to have been an iconic symbol of the warrior tradition extending back through the Classical Period to Homeric times.

ROME

BY MICHAEL M. SAGE

Little can be said about Roman arms, armor, and other military equipment before the middle of the sixth century B.C.E. Literary sources offer scant evidence, and the site of Rome has provided few archaeological finds of a military nature. There are a few fragmentary pieces of metal protective equipment and a number of spearheads, which point to the importance of the javelin.

The middle of the seventh century B.C.E. saw a profound change in military equipment in central Italy, especially to the north of Rome in Etruria. Again, there is little evidence at Rome, but given the close cultural ties of Rome and Etruria, there is every reason to suppose that the same developments took place at Rome. Greek heavy infantry equipment of the hoplite type appears in Etruria, probably under the influence of the Greek colonies of southern Italy. This hoplite equipment consisted of a metal helmet, a metal cuirass (body armor) made up of back and front plates, and the hoplite shield. The hoplite shield was usually a convex circular device, 3 feet in diameter, made of a wooden core with metal facing, usually of bronze. The arm was inserted through a curved metal band, and the hand gripped a strap on the rim of the shield. This holding mechanism distributed the weight of the heavy shield along the length of the arm, allowing the shield to be held for long periods. The usual offensive weapon of the hoplite was a heavy thrusting spear with a short slashing sword as a secondary weapon.

By 550 B.C.E. the literary sources show that the hoplite style of fighting had been adopted at Rome. Despite the artificial character of the descriptions that survive, it is clear that at Rome, as elsewhere in central Italy, there was a greater variety of equipment than in Greece. Especially important is the reference to a type of shield later known as the scutum. The construction of this shield is described in detail by the Greek historian Polybius (ca. 200–ca. 118 B.C.E.). It was 4 feet long and 2.5 feet wide, made of two wooden boards glued to each other. Its convex outer surface was covered in linen topped by leather. It was rimmed with iron and had a central iron spine to strengthen the shield and to aid in warding off blows. This type of shield first appeared in Italy in the mid-eighth century B.C.E. and eventually became the standard Roman heavy infantry shield with some modifications until the end of the ancient world.

The early Roman army fought in the manner of the Greek phalanx as a dense rectangular formation that relied on its weight and the points of its heavy thrusting spears to achieve victory on the battlefield. During the fourth or perhaps as late as the early third century B.C.E. the Roman army underwent a tactical revolution. In place of the phalanx it adopted a three-line formation, which depended not on the heavy thrusting spear but on a combination of javelin and sword for its offensive power. The front two lines carried two javelins, called *pila*, one heavy and one light. The heavy *pilum* weighed about 10 pounds, and the lighter one was about half that weight; both were about 6 feet long. The barbed spearhead and its metal tang were made as a single piece, and the head was attached to its wooden shaft by driving the tang into it. The sword that eventually became standard was a short sword with a blade, approximately 2 feet long, with two cutting edges and a long, sharp point. It was well adapted for both slashing and stabbing strokes. The third line retained the heavy thrusting spear.

The legionnaire was protected by a bowl-shaped metal helmet of bronze with a short neck guard at the rear and attached cheek pieces. His chest was protected by a small square metal pale held on by straps and worn over a leather tunic. Wealthier legionnaires provided themselves with a mail shirt. A greave (shin armor) was worn on the left leg, which was thrust forward in combat.

Each legion also contained light-armed troops. They were equipped with a light wicker shield 3 feet in diameter and a leather helmet; they carried the legionary sword and a number of light javelins. Little is known about Roman cavalry equipment during the republic. The cavalry probably carried a round shield, wore some form of chest protection, and carried a lance and a sword. Although there was some variation in equipment down to the end of the first century B.C.E., the only major change was the standardization of offensive weaponry for all legionnaires.

For the first two centuries of the empire until 200 C.E., changes in legionary equipment were evolutionary. From the middle of the first century C.E. the sword point was shortened to make it more effective in stabbing, and helmets evolved to provide increased protection for the nape of the neck and the forehead. Toward the end of the second century C.E. a longer sword with a blade of between 32 and 40 inches appeared and eventually replaced the traditional legionary sword. The most striking change was visible in chest protection. Several types appeared. The mail shirt was now standard for legionnaires, with scale armor also found. A new type of body armor was developed, consisting of metal strips attached to leather straps for both the chest and the back; this new armor was more flexible and provided greater protection against blows. The scutum, though constructed in the same way, now became rectangular instead of oval to increase the protection it offered.

Sixteenth-century shield depicting Roman battle scene; the scene shows accurate armor and clothing of the time, as drawn from antique coins and sculpture. (Copyright the Metropolitan Museum of Art)

There appears to have been a tremendous variety in the body armor of the Roman cavalry of this period. Mail shirts frequently appear in pictorial representations, but other types of cuirasses are also found. Helmets display a similar diversity. Offensive weapons also varied greatly, as many units were highly specialized, such as archers from the eastern provinces. One striking development beginning in the mid-second century C.E. was the appearance of a new type of cavalry patterned on eastern models. These were the Clibanarii, who wore a tight-fitting conical iron cap and a coat of either mail or scale armor, which covered the upper body and the thighs; the lower body was protected by metal bands. This cavalryman's main offensive weapon was a heavy lance.

Artillery was used in siege and naval warfare and on the battlefield. Roman artillery evolved from Greek models. Its propulsive force was supplied by torsion, that is, the building up of energy in some elastic material, such as braided ropes of hair or animal sinew, by twisting them and then suddenly releasing them. These devices were generally constructed of wood, though in the Imperial Period there was a greater use of metal for increased strength and durability. These machines varied in size and were used to propel either arrow-shaped projectiles or large stone balls. The larger catapults were could hurl stones of up to 60 pounds with devastating results.

THE AMERICAS

BY J. J. GEORGE

The principal weapons used by ancient indigenous North Americans were the spear-thrower, or atlatl; the sling; the spear; and the club, all of which were used in both warfare and hunting. Instruments used only for hunting included the harpoon, the bola, the blowgun, the rodent skewer, and the reptile hook. Shields and rudimentary body armor were used defensively in warfare. Weapons were normally made of stone, bone, horn, and wood. Often they were composite, the point, head, or blade being made of stone or bone and the handle or shaft of wood. Metal was rarely used for weapons because metallurgy was limited to softer metals, such as gold and silver, and largely only for decorative rather than utilitarian purposes. In Mexico, where metallurgy was most highly developed, there was an abundance of obsidian and other igneous stone, which was superior to copper and copper alloys for weapon points and blades. Iron and steel tools and weapons arrived with the Europeans in the 15th and 16th centuries C.E.

The earliest projectile points discovered in North America date from about 11,000 B.C.E.; they are attributed to the Clovis culture and were probably spear points because they are too large for arrows. The blade's unique design, a narrow, tapering profile with sharpened side edges and a technically challenging "flute" at the base for hafting, was intended to maximize the lance's ability to pierce hide or skin. The lance would have been used in close proximity to the intended target. In several instances, recovered Clovis points were found hundreds of miles from where they had been quarried, sometimes in burial caches, leading to continued speculation about who made them, how the technology was transferred, and what it meant when they were ceremonially buried. It is not until about 500 C.E. that chipped stone points, comparable in size and workmanship to modern arrowheads, first became known.

The atlatl, a device that supplies leverage by adding length to the user's arm and increases the range, force, and accuracy of the spear, seems to have been distributed throughout the world by migration or diffusion. It was used by the polar Eskimo in the Arctic, the Tlingit of the Northwest Coast, groups in Baja California and northwestern New Mexico, and Native Americans at the mouth of the Mississippi; it was also used throughout Mesoamerica and by many people of the circum-Caribbean area. The spear-thrower has existed in Europe for at least 20,000 years, but the oldest-known examples from the Americas date to about 5000 B.C.E. The spear probably preceded the bow by many thousands of years; indisputable evidence of the bow is not known until about 500 C.E.

The decline of Hopewell sites in the Illinois Valley around 400 C.E. coincides with the disappearance of finely made atlatl weights from the archaeological record, which seems to reflect the replacement of the atlatl by the new weapon system of the bow and arrow; small points, probably from arrows, occur at Illinois sites at this time. The greater range and accuracy of the bow and arrow may have affected hunting practices and probably altered the way warriors engaged. Also, an increased incidence of warfare in the Ohio Valley has been inferred from the seemingly defensive location and layout of some hilltop enclosures, a change in site planning possibly necessitated in part by changes in weapons technology.

Handheld spears varied greatly in length, diameter, and type of point. They were employed more in hunting than in warfare and appear to have been in use by at least 8000 B.C.E. in the Pleistocene to kill bison in North America. In areas where atlatls and the bow and arrow were present, it appears that the spear was not used javelin style and tended to be reserved for heavy duty at close range. Recent excavations at New Haven Harbor in Connecticut have uncovered more than 5,000 stone artifacts dated to before 1000 B.C.E., including unfinished points and dart points made of fashioned quartzite that could have been used to form the lethal end of an atlatl dart. Used primarily in hunting, the projectiles would have proved lethal against enemies.

In Mesoamerica early examples of defensive armor include quilted or rolled cotton. At Teotihuacán (ca. 1–650 C.E.) spun cotton body armor, called *escupil*, and helmets were introduced to protect the head, body, and limbs. Some scholars have tied the sudden increase in the need for and use of cotton to acceleration in the downfall of Teotihuacán. One argument suggests that because the military was essentially a state enterprise, the state's decline was facilitated by its inability to provide armor to everyone due to its cost. The art historical record also provides insight into the nature of Teotihuacán weaponry. Warriors are depicted wielding atlatls and rectangular shields or thrusting spears and bucklers. The depictions suggest standardized weaponry, which typically indicates state control, formations, and complimentary arms use. One likely scenario inferred from the depictions of warriors and weaponry suggests that the atlatlists would first engage the enemy with projectile fire, and then the spearmen would close and engage the enemy in hand-to-hand combat.

For a long time scholars believed the Mayan civilization to be peaceful and idyllic. A brief inventory of their weaponry dispels that notion: Spears, atlatls, darts, and arrow points used as weapons were common in Mayan civilization of the Classic Period (ca. 150–ca. 650 C.E.). The art historical record shows that the Maya were clearly equipped to fight. Stela 31 from Tikal records Stormy Sky, the name of a ruler in the mid-fifth century C.E., flanked by two guardians dressed in Teotihuacán-style military garb, carrying shields, spear-throwers, and feathered darts. Spear and dart points found at the rapidly abandoned fortified city of Aguateca, Guatemala, suggests that both the royal family and elite scribes and artists used them for intergroup warfare as well as for artistic and craft production under enemy threat. An important implication is that the ruler and elite scribes and artists were also warriors. In another example, an unusually high concentration of identifiable weaponry at the hilltop center of

Cerro de las Mesas indicates that warfare was critical in the development and downfall of classic Mayan civilization.

Weaponry prevalent throughout South America, including the Chaco region, which comprises territories in northeastern Argentina, eastern Bolivia, and western Paraguay, shows that warfare was a main concern, and weapons like bows and arrows, spears, and clubs, mostly made of wood, were quite common. Bolas, stones connected by cords, thrown to entangle and fell prey or an enemy, were a typical weapon. In northern Peru's Moche culture painted pottery dated to the sixth century C.E. provides a stylized glimpse of the Moche warrior and his weaponry and armor. Two animated warriors, their faces covered with fox face masks, wearing decorated helmets and belted tunics, carry round shields and war clubs. Celebrating warriors on painted pottery shows clear veneration of the warrior culture.

See also ART; BORDERS AND FRONTIERS; CERAMICS AND POTTERY; DEATH AND BURIAL PRACTICES; EMPIRES AND DYNASTIES; FOREIGNERS AND BARBARIANS; HUNTING, FISHING, AND GATHERING; METALLURGY; MILITARY; WAR AND CONQUEST.

FURTHER READING

Simon Anglin, Rob S. Rice, Phyllis Jestice, et al., *Fighting Techniques of the Ancient World (3000 BCE to 500 AD): Equipment, Combat Skills, and Tactics* (New York: St. Martin's Press, 2002).

M. C. Bishop and J. C. N. Coulston, *Roman Military Equipment from the Punic Wars to the Fall of Rome*, 2nd ed. (Oxford. U.K.: Oxbow Press, 2006).

John Carman and Anthony Harding, eds., *Ancient Warfare: Archaeological Perspectives* (Stroud, U.K.: Sutton, 1999).

James T. Chambers and Spencer C. Tucker, *Ancient Weapons: An Illustrated History of Their Impact* (Santa Barbara, Calif.: ABC-CLIO, 2007).

Arthur Cotterell, *Chariot: From Chariot to Tank, the Astounding Rise and Fall of the World's First War Machine* (Woodstock, N.Y.: Overlook Press, 2004).

Will Fowler, *Ancient Weapons: The Story of Weaponry and Warfare through the Ages* (Darby, Penn.: Diane Publishing Company, 1999).

Sir John Winthrop Hackett, ed., *Warfare in the Ancient World* (London: Sidgwick and Jackson, 1989).

Victor Davis Hansen, *The Western Way of War* (Berkeley: University of California Press, 2000).

Lawrence H. Keeley, *War before Civilization* (New York: Oxford University Press, 1996).

Eric W. Marsden, *Greek and Roman Artillery: Historical Development* (Oxford, U.K.: Clarendon Press, 1969).

John R. Mixter, "Man's First Long-Range Missile Weapon, the Sling Was a Deadly Military Asset in Skilled Hands," *Military History* 18, no. 3 (August 2001): 12–13.

Helmut Nickel, *Arms and Armor in Africa* (New York: Atheneum, 1971).

Daithi O'Hogain, *Celtic Warriors: The Armies of One of the First Great Peoples in Europe* (New York: St. Martin's Press, 1999)

Robert B. Partridge, *Fighting Pharaohs: Weapons and Warfare in Ancient Egypt* (Manchester, U.K.: Peartree Publishing, 2002).

H. Russell Robinson, *The Armour of Imperial Rome* (New York: Scribner, 1975).

Ian Shaw, *Egyptian Warfare and Weapons* (Princess Risborough, U.K.: Shire Publications, 1991).

Anthony Snodgrass, *Arms and Armor of the Greeks* (Baltimore: Johns Hopkins University Press, 1997).

Christopher Spring, *African Arms and Armor* (Washington, D.C.: Smithsonian Institution Press, 1993).

Jwing-Ming Yang, *Ancient Chinese Weapons* (Jamaica Plains, Mass.: YMAA Publication Center, 1999).

▶ weights and measures

INTRODUCTION

For a prehistoric hunter-gatherer a system of weights and measurements would likely not have been very useful. It was enough to know that an object was so heavy that it required two people to move it or that it would take a day to move to an encampment on the other side of a distant hill. The development of systems of weights and measures coincided with the development of civilization itself. As people settled into permanent communities that evolved into towns and cities and as they developed trade relationships with other communities, they needed agreed-on systems for measuring and weighing food and other goods. While these systems differed from culture to culture, they all had common elements and served common needs.

The earliest units of measurement were often based on the human anatomy. Thus, hand spans, forearms, fingers, feet, and other parts of the body were used to specify length. By extension, distance could be measured by, for example, how far a person could walk in a day, while area could be measure by the amount of land a worker could plow in a day. Similarly, ancient cultures used natural objects as the basis for specifying weights and measures. A reed, for example, could have been used to measure length. The people of ancient India used such natural objects as louse eggs and dust particles to measure very small units of length. Other cultures used such objects as mustard seeds as units of measure.

The problem with these units of measurement, of course, is that they varied from person to person and place to place. Accordingly, ancient civilizations made efforts to standardize their weights and measures. Often, this was a task assigned to the king or other ruler. The king had a vital interest in accurate weights and measures. Taxes, for example, were collected on volumes of grain or, in the case of ancient India, bolts of cloth. Similarly, agriculture required some agreement on land boundaries. Ancient builders had to have a common basis for measuring building materials. If a building was to be made of bricks, then calculating the number of bricks needed to construct a building of a given size required agreement on the dimensions of a brick.

Usually, systems of weights and measures developed in connection with systems of counting and numbers. Indeed, counting emerged because people had to weigh and measure. Systems of mathematics provided people with common units of measurement, which could then be divided by common factors to produce smaller units or multiplied by common factors to produce larger units. In this way, for example, the modern yard consists of 3 feet, a foot consists of 12 inches, and so on.

Trade and exchange, too, required systems of weights and measurements. If one country was trading wine for lumber, the merchants making the trade needed some way of measuring and agreeing on the volume of wine and lumber to determine prices. The result was that systems of weights and measures were often imported and exported along with the goods they measured. When the value of commodities came to be measured by money as a medium of exchange, it was vitally important for merchants to be able to weigh accurately coins and the gold and silver with which they were made.

AFRICA

BY MICHAEL J. O'NEAL

Historians, archaeologists, and scientists use the term *metrology* to refer to the study of weights and measures, particularly as it applies to the premodern world, when weights and measures were not universally standardized. Metrology, though, does more than simply seek to discover which specific units of measurement and weight the ancients used. It also seeks to understand the underlying system that gave rise to weights and measurements.

Thus, the types of questions metrologists ask include: Were units of weight and measure arbitrary values, or were they based on some phenomenon from the natural world? How was one unit divisible into, or a multiple of, some other unit? How did ancient traders and others convert units of weight and measure into those of another people in the process of striking trading bargains? To what extent were units of measure and weight standardized in a kingdom or region? Did royalty have one unit of measurement or weight and common people another? What can ancient artifacts, such as buildings and their dimensions, reveal about systems of measurement? What was the relationship between systems of weights and measurements and mathematical, astronomical, calendrical, timekeeping, and other systems?

The grandest question of all, however, is this: Did ancient systems of measuring weight, volume, distance, and the like derive from some common system that was spread throughout much of the ancient world, including parts of Africa? Many metrologists have devoted careers to finding common units of measurement that underlay the construction of artifacts as widely dispersed as the pyramids of Egypt and Stonehenge in England. Some claim to have found commonalities, in various cases based on common astronomical observations from which the circumference of the earth at the equator may have been deduced. Many of these conclusions, though, are highly speculative.

Few of these questions can be answered with any certainty about ancient Africa (other than Egypt). The absence of written records inhibits the work of metrologists who focus on the continent. Further casting a veil over the subject is the fact that ancient African kingdoms, cities, and settlements rose and fell with great frequency. People migrated throughout the continent, often in response to climatic change, taking with them their culture and knowledge systems and mingling them with the culture and knowledge they found in their new homes. Warfare wiped out some African cultures—the kingdom of Kush, for example, fell to the kingdom of Axum, and the Carthaginian kingdom was totally destroyed by the Romans—contributing to the lack of records and artifacts.

At the same time, more powerful empires, including that of Egypt and later the Roman Empire, would have imposed their systems on tributary people in Africa; in particular, Egyptian units of measurement probably became the norm throughout much of northern Africa. Later, Roman units probably became accepted. These units were derived from Greek measurements, which the Greeks in turn had adopted from numerous cultures in the Near East, who in turn had adopted them from such places as Mesopotamia. Furthermore, because much of Africa, particularly the northern stretches of the continent (as opposed to the nomadic southern portions), engaged in trade and other activities with a large set of other civilizations who routinely passed through the region known as the Sahel, a strip of settlements that spanned the continent below the Sahara Desert, the notion of any kind of standardized, "African" system of weights and measures remains elusive.

Despite these problems, historians and archaeologists can make some inferences. It is highly likely that ancient Africans, in common with numerous other ancient peoples, measured distances using, at least as a starting point, the human body. Thus, for example, hand spans, knuckles, arm length, feet, and forearms were probably used as units of distance. Indeed, the cubit is a unit of measurement used throughout the entire region of Africa, Rome, the Near East, and eventually Europe. The cubit was a unit of length that originally measured the distance from a man's elbow to the tip of his longest finger, although eventually the cubit settled into a measurement of about 18 inches. Such a unit of measurement, of course, would necessarily be imprecise, since the unit would be longer for a taller man than for a shorter one. In the case of royalty, the "royal cubit"—a slightly larger unit of measure—would have been longer than that used by others, in an effort to suggest that royals were larger than common mortals. Similarly, it is little accident that in the modern world, the foot continues to be a common unit of measurement. The foot was used throughout the ancient world to measure a unit of distance that was, in fact, just about a foot, or 12 modern inches. The knuckle of the thumb could be used to measure relatively small distances, and thus corresponded to a modern inch.

Longer distances were probably measured by human activities. Thus, for example, distances corresponding to modern miles were probably measured in a way that gauged the amount of ground a person could walk in a certain period of time. Similarly, a unit of area probably was measured by the amount of ground, for instance, that a farmer could plow in a given period of time.

Ancient Africans undoubtedly used natural objects in the calculation of weights. Indeed, the modern word *grain,* still used in weighing precious metals, reflects this ancient heritage. Thus, any African culture probably would have developed a system that used small stones or quantities of seed, such as wheat seed, as a unit of weight. Other objects included items such as bird claws, feathers, and, for large weights, elephants. The ancient Egyptians used a system of weights called beqa weights to measure quantities of gold. Examples have been found of beqa stones, which standardized weights, and some of these bear royal insignia. Given Egypt's dominance over much of northern Africa, this system for weighing precious metals and perhaps other commodities probably was imposed on trading kingdoms to Egypt's south and west. Such a system would have governed coinage, which ancient Africans would necessarily have had to accept.

Another natural object that played a role in ancient weights and measurements was water. Thus, for example, a cubic foot of water represented a unit of weight called the talent, divisible into various units. The Romans divided the talent into 60 minas, and various Mediterranean cultures that accepted the talent and the mina subdivided the mina into varying numbers of shekels. These units were used by Syrians, Phoenicians (the ancestors of the African Carthaginians), and others, who carried them into Africa for purposes of trade and exchange.

EGYPT

BY AMR KAMEL

With the emergence of the centralized government in the Nile Valley as early as the Third Dynasty (ca. 2649–ca. 2575 B.C.E.), Egyptians formed accurate systems of weights and measures. They developed methods for weighing grain, counting cattle, drawing up building projects, and sizing huge slabs of stone as well as issuing rations and materials to workmen and, above all, measuring the level of the annual Nile flood, on which the levying of taxes depended. This system was valid throughout the whole country and remained active until the Greco-Roman Period (332 B.C.E.–395 C.E.), without real significant changes. In general, the system that the Egyptians set up included three main subsystems that measured capacity, length, and weight.

In their literary texts ancient Egyptians frequently express quantities of products counted either by the piece or by a usual grouping of pieces, such as bunches of flowers, jars of wine, baskets of grapes, pots of honey, bundles of vegetables or flax, handfuls of reeds, and even pairs of geese. Nonetheless, ancient Egyptians used many other measures that are still obscure, such as the gsr, which was used only for milk, the g3t, which was used for cream, and the thab, which was used for salt.

Several pieces of textual evidence suggest that the measures used for official purposes, such as tax payments, were checked on a regular basis. In conducting personal business Egyptians apparently preferred to use their own measures. For example, Hekanakhte, a farmer of the Eleventh Dynasty (ca. 2040–ca. 1991), sent a messenger to his family in the delta to bring to him his own corn measure to use in measuring his grain in Thebes (modern-day Luxor) rather than using other local measures, which might not be wholly accurate.

The Egyptian capacity system was apparently grounded on the hnw for measuring fluids, now reckoned conventionally at around 1 pint. The Egyptians used multiples of 10 hnw to describe greater units: 40 hnw, 50 hnw, 100 hnw, 160 hnw, and 200 hnw. The basic unit for cereals and other dry goods was the hekat, or bushel, of 4.3 quarts. In the Old and Middle Kingdoms (ca. 2575–ca. 1640 B.C.E.) 10 ghar made the larger unit khar, or sack, of 11 gallons. With the beginning of the New Kingdom (ca. 1550–ca. 1070 B.C.E.), the value of the khar was increased to equal 16 hekat, or 17.5 gallons. This increase reflected not an economic crisis but rather the change of a decimal system to a new binary system, which made accounting easier. These 16 hekat were later subdivided into units of 4 hekat, 4.36 gallons each.

Smaller quantities were expressed as fractions of oipe, more precisely as one of the fractions of the geometric progression ½, ¼ (the former hekat), ⅛, 1/16, 1/32, and 1/64. The last quantity equaled 0.2 quarts and was divisible into 5 ro, or parts, of 0.05 quarts each, reflecting the ancient division of the hekat into 80 and of the 4-hekat into 320 ro. In the Greco-Roman Period the artabe, a Persian unit, played a major role, varying in size from 29 to 40 of the Greek choinix, a capacity unit of about 0.9 quarts.

For general length measurement the standard unit was the royal cubit. The cubit represented the length of the forearm, from the elbow to the tip of the fingers, estimated conventionally at 18 inches. The measure was composed of 7 palms, (the hand's width without the thumb), each consisting of 4 fingers, ¾ inch each. Apart from the cubit of 7 palms, there were the small cubit of 6 palms (about 17.64 inches), the remen of 5 palms (14.7 inches), the djser of 4 palms (11.76 inches), the great span of 3.5 palms (10.29 inches), the small span of 3 palms (8.82 inches), the dopple or double palm (5.88 inches), and the fist of 1.5 palms or 6 fingers (4.4 inches). Furthermore, Egyptians of the New Kingdom sometimes used a larger unit, called a nebi ("pole"); its length has been estimated at 1.25 cubits.

Land surveying required a longer unit than the cubit; thus, the ancient Egyptians seem to have used the khet, or "rod," of 100 cubits (160 feet) as the base, since a land-measuring rope was 100 cubits long, stretched between two rods driven in the ground. A larger unit, itrw, or "river," measured

20,000 cubits (6.5 miles) and was used to measure land distances, originally representing the length of a day's towing of a boat along the Nile. Textual evidence from the Twelfth Dynasty (ca. 1991–ca. 1783 B.C.E.) refers to an official estimation of the Egyptian land, from Elephantine in the south to Tell el-Balamun in the delta, at 106 itrw (670 miles), divided into 86 itrw for Upper Egypt and 20 itrw for Lower Egypt.

The basic measure of area was the stat, which represented a square of land of 100 by 100 cubits, or 1 khet by 1 khet (3,271.38 square yards). Multiples and submultiples were not defined by squaring multiples or submultiples but rather by multiplying or dividing the width while retaining the length as 100 cubits.

Volume measures were based on the denit, which was a cubic cubit (0.187 cubic yards). In the Ptolemaic Period (304–30 B.C.E.) volume and capacity measures seem to have been linked, but the absolute norms on which this relationship was based are still uncertain. This measure was used exclusively for calculating the progress made by workers in the excavation of a tomb.

The saqed expressed the slope of a masonry massive, such as a pyramid, by giving the length in palms of the horizontal base of a right triangle of 1 cubit high, whose hypotenuse was a section of the expected or measured slope. In Old Kingdom construction, for instance, there is clear evidence for the use of a saqed of 5.5 palms or 5.25 palms, corresponding to slopes of 51°51′ and 53°7′, respectively, as notably illustrated in the Giza pyramids.

Ancient Egyptians' basic unit of weight was called a deben. From the Old Kingdom the deben seems to have been around 0.48 ounces; it increased during the Middle Kingdom to 3.2 ounces. In the New Kingdom it was divided into 10 qite of 0.32 ounces each, with lesser weights expressed as fractions of qite.

As early as 1300 B.C.E. the Egyptians had developed accurate balance-beam scales that could weigh small quantities or materials with an accuracy of plus or minus 1 percent. The scales were simple in concept and consisted of a horizontal beam centered on a vertical post. Suspended from the ends of the beam were the platforms. One platform held the object or material to be weighed. The other held an object of known weight.

THE MIDDLE EAST

BY AMY HACKNEY BLACKWELL

People living in the ancient Near East standardized weights and measures so that they could accurately measure quantities—by weight and volume—of commodities important in their lives. These included seed, precious metals like silver and gold, base metals like copper and lead, and liquids like oils, beer, and wine. In conducting transactions with other peoples, traders used their own systems of weights and measures and calculated conversions to other systems developed by their trading partners, such as Egypt and the Indus Valley, referring to such alien systems in their economic texts with a phrase like "according to the standard of Land X."

Archaeologists and Assyriologists have been able to reconstruct the weights and measures of Mesopotamian civilizations because of the survival of both the weights themselves (and occasionally balance mechanisms as well) and written sources that give detailed calculations of commodities, everything from gold to grain. In some cases, annotations were inscribed on the rims or shoulders of storage jars, indicating a vessel's capacity in volumetric terms.

The shiklu, or shekel, was the basic unit of weight. One shekel weighed about 0.3 ounces. Small items were measured in she, which was 1⁄600 ounce and originally represented the weight of a single grain of barley. Larger items were measured in manu, usually called minas in English, which was a unit of 60 shekels, or in biltu, which was a unit of 60 minas. Although these terms were used widely throughout the ancient Near East, the absolute value of these weights varied so that the mina of Ur around 2000 B.C.E. is not necessarily the same as the mina of Ugarit 500 years later. Most weights were made of stone, many in the shape of a duck with its head and neck lying on its back, as though the bird were asleep. Fine, barrel-shaped weights of hematite were also common.

The Old Testament mentions seven different kinds of weights, which were equivalent to coins. In biblical times people used units of weight to barter goods for silver, long before silver was minted into actual coins. One Mesopotamian biltu was equivalent to 1 talent, the largest measure of weight in biblical and ancient times. One talent of gold was somewhere between 50 and 100 pounds of gold; it represented either a man's weight in gold or the amount of gold one man could carry, depending on who was defining it. The biblical

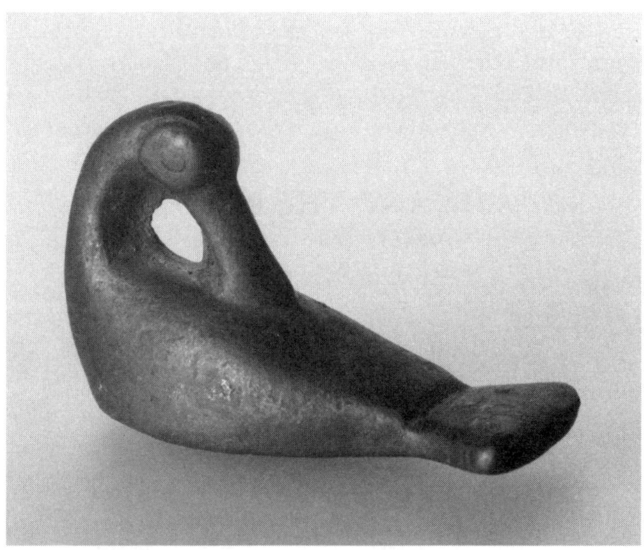

Bronze duck weight, found in the treasury at Persepolis, Persia (modern-day Iran) (Courtesy of the Oriental Institute of the University of Chicago)

talent was equal to 3,000 shekels instead of the 2,600 shekels of the Mesopotamian talent.

Ancient Mesopotamians measured volume in sila or qa; 1 sila was equivalent to about 1.5 pints. A sila was made up of 60 gin, each equal to about ⅖ ounce. Sixty sila made 1 massiktu or pi, which was about 11 gallons or 1.3 bushels. One hundred sila made 1 imeru, which was about 18.3 gallons or 2.25 bushels and was the amount one donkey was expected to be able to carry. A qurru or gur was 180 sila, about 33 gallons or 4 bushels.

The basic Mesopotamian measurement of length was the ammatu, or cubit, which was about 15 inches long. It originally was the length of a man's arm from elbow to fingertip, a convenient measuring device for merchants anywhere. An ubanu was about ⅔ inch, the length of a finger joint; 24 or 30 ubanu made up 1 ammatu, depending on the time and place. A kanu was 6 ammatu (around 8 feet), and a gar was 12 ammatu. One ashlu consisted of 10 gar. A beru was 1800 gar, about 5.25 miles.

Fields and land were measured in iku, which consisted of about ⅚ acre. One musaru was equal to 1 square gar, about 27.5 square yards; this was the standard measurement of a garden plot. One buru was equal to 18 iku, or 15 acres. One shar was equal to 1,080 iku, or 25.3 square miles.

During the Hellenistic Period (323–31 B.C.E.) Greek units of weights and measures spread throughout Mesopotamia and the Near East. During the Roman Republic and Empire (509 B.C.E.–476 C.E.) many people in the Near East and Mesopotamia used the Roman system of weights and measures. Throughout the ancient world there was much flexibility of weights and measures. For example, archaeologists have found objects in Greece and Rome that appear to have been made according to Persian weights and measures. Although these objects could have come from Persia, historians believe it is more likely that people in Greece and Rome occasionally used foreign measurement schemes to make certain objects. Even within the well-regulated Greek and Roman systems, there was a great deal of local variation, as individual towns customized weights and measurements to fit their needs.

ASIA AND THE PACIFIC

BY AMY HACKNEY BLACKWELL

The earliest documented systems of precise measurements were created in the fourth and third millennia B.C.E. in the Indus Valley, Mesopotamia, and Egypt. Chinese people are known to have developed precise weights and measures by the late second millennium B.C.E., though they may have done so several centuries earlier. Chinese systems of measurement spread throughout the rest of eastern Asia toward the end of the ancient period.

The peoples who lived in the Indus Valley between 3300 and 1500 B.C.E. developed precise systems of measurement. They divided weights and measures into units of 10. The basic unit of weight was about 10 ounces. Weights were multiples of this unit; the standard weights were 1, 2, 5, 10, 20, 50, 100, 200, and 500 units. Smaller weights were measured as fractions of the basic unit; the main fractional weights were 0.5, 0.2, 0.1, and 0.05 units. The Harappan people who lived in the Indus Valley at this time built cities and houses according to precise plans, which required them to measure bricks, boards, streets, and other units carefully. Bricks were made according to a ratio of 4 to 2 to 1; that is, a brick was twice as wide and four times as long as it was tall.

By the late first millennium B.C.E. in India, overseeing weights and measures was considered the government's responsibility. The *Manusmriti*, a book of Hindu laws written around the first or second century B.C.E., observes that one of a ruler's duties was to ensure that weights and measures remained constant. During the Maurya Dynasty (321–185 B.C.E.) the government established a system of measurements that was used throughout the realm. Despite standardization, all measurements were somewhat flexible; it is impossible to know exactly how long any of these measurements really were because they varied somewhat from place to place. Many of them were determined by body proportions and so would naturally vary from person to person.

The smallest unit of length under the Indian system was a parmanu, which was microscopically small and could not be subdivided; the parmanu was a strictly theoretical unit because no one had the technology to work with such small items. From there, units were generally defined by groups of four or eight. Eight parmanu equaled 1 rajahkan, the length of a dust particle. Eight rajahkan equaled 1 liksha, the length of a louse egg. Eight liksha equaled 1 yookamadhya. Eight yookamadhya equaled 1 yavamadhya.

Eight yavamadhya equaled 1 angul, the width of a finger, or about ¾ inch. Eight angul equaled 1 dhanurmushti, the length of a fist with the thumb sticking out, or about 6 inches. Four angul were the width of a bow grip, called dharnugrah. Twelve angul made 1 vitastaa, about 9 inches, or the distance between a stretched-out little finger and thumb. Four vitastaa equaled 1 aratni or hast, about 18 inches, or the distance from an elbow to an outstretched middle finger, a unit known as the cubit in European systems. Four aratni made 1 dand or dhanush, about 6 feet, or the length of a bow. Ten dand made 1 rajju, which was about 60 feet. Two rajju equaled one paridesh, about 120 feet. Two thousand dand equaled 1 krosh, which was about 2 or 2.25 miles. Four krosh made 1 yojan, which was about 9 miles.

The system of weight measurement in India was closely tied with ayurveda, the main type of medicine. Ayurvedic medicine used many herbs and oils as treatments, and ayurvedic practitioners developed a precise system of weights and measures to ensure accuracy in their preparations. Doctors typically needed to weigh very small amounts of substances, and they used natural seeds as standards. Mustard seeds, sesame seeds, and madatiya seeds were all common weights. Texts on ayurveda list tables describing numerous weights and measures to be used in making drug preparations.

China may have developed systems of weights and measures around the same time as the Indus Valley civilizations. According to Chinese tradition, the Yellow Emperor (ca. 2697–ca. 2598 B.C.E.) was the first ruler to issue guidelines for weights and measures, but little is known about this system. The first well-known official units of Chinese weights and measures were invented and standardized between the 13th and 10th centuries B.C.E.; these units became the basis for measurement in China for the next three millennia. The actual lengths and weights that went with the standardized measurements varied over the centuries. Governments would occasionally step in and define units; for example, during the Qin Dynasty (221–207 B.C.E.) the Chinese government standardized weights and measures.

The basic Chinese unit of length was the chi, which is about 9 or 10 inches long and served as an equivalent to the English foot. It was determined by the distance between the thumb and middle finger of an outstretched hand. One cun was equivalent to about an inch. Ten chi made up one zhang. One li was equivalent to about ⅓ mile. Long distances were generally expressed in li. One important measure was the length of one bolt of cloth, or one pi, which was about 40 feet long; most households had to pay some of their taxes in cloth, which was measured in pi. The most common unit of land area was the mu, equivalent to about 733 square yards. One qing was 100 mu.

The standard units of weight in China were the qian and the liang. The liang was a small amount, ½ ounce in the ancient period. The qian weighed between 7.7 and 9.2 ounces. These weights were based on the actual weight of coins used as cash; the minting of coins was not done according to a uniform weight standard, so weights fluctuated. The Chinese people did not use coins as currency very much, preferring to keep their gold as valuable property. Weights were more important in trade, for buying and selling specified amounts of goods. Chinese medicine, like ayurvedic medicine in India, required precise measurements of herbs and other medicinal items.

During the centuries between about 500 B.C.E. and the fifth century C.E., the Chinese system of measurement gradually spread through Southeast Asia, Korea, and Japan. The people of these nations adapted the Chinese measurements into their own languages. For example, in Japan the main unit of length was 1 shaku, equivalent to the Chinese chi. It was broken into 10 sun and 100 bu. Six shaku made up 1 ken, slightly less than 6 feet. Three hundred sixty shaku equaled 1 cho; 36 cho made up 1 ri, which was about 2.6 miles. The most common measurement of land area was the tan, which was about ¼ acre.

EUROPE

BY MICHAEL J. O'NEAL

Systems of weights and measures throughout the ancient world were highly complex, and historians have been able to decipher them only in part. In many cases they have to rely on archaeological evidence; for example, they can make inferences about systems of weights and measures from regularities they find in the measurements of surviving buildings or the volumes of containers. An essential requirement for any system of weights and measures is the ability for a community or a society to come to common agreement about their values. At the boundaries between systems of weights and measures, some understanding must be established about how these values will be converted from one system to another.

Understanding systems of weights and measures before the advent of writing is nearly impossible. The Scottish engineer Alexander Thom (1894–1985) claimed the existence of a "megalithic yard" of about 2.72 feet that served as a unit of measurement in laying out monuments such as Stonehenge, although this is impossible to document conclusively and also does not seem to be supported by evidence outside Britain. With the emergence of metallurgy, prehistoric European people appear to have developed some common understanding about units of weight. For example, copper and tin ingots of standard sizes are often found in Bronze Age shipwrecks in the Mediterranean Sea. In northern Europe bronze and gold artifacts such as axes and neck rings may have served as standard units of exchange, a sort of primitive currency. Although it is likely that there were rules for measuring and weighing commodities, we simply cannot do more than speculate about their nature.

Some ancient civilizations, including the Greeks, Romans, Egyptians, and Mesopotamians, were able to develop fairly regular, stable systems of measurement largely because they ruled over extensive empires. Because so many people from diverse areas were under their control, particularly in the extensive Roman Empire, they adhered to standards of weights and measures imposed on them from a central authority, usually by royal decree. Because of the importance of trade to these empires, both between countries within the empire and between the empire and other regions, merchants and public officials needed accurate ways of measuring volumes of goods and determining their price. They also needed accurate ways to measure the weight of gold and silver coins minted by other nations and used to pay for goods.

While the Romans were expanding their empire in western Europe, northern and eastern Europe were peopled by largely autonomous extended tribes: the Scandinavians, an assortment of Germanic tribes, the Celts, various Slavic peoples, and others. Without a central authority, each of these communities developed its own standards for weights and measures, and these standards often changed gradually over time. In time the Romans, who adopted many features of the Greek system, imposed their system of weights and measure on portions of Europe, particularly Italy, Gaul (France), and the British Isles. Many of these standards survived and were imported eventually to the New World, where such measurements as the inch and foot continue to be used. In other respects the standards shifted and have presented a challenge to historians.

Bronze steelyard with lead weights from Roman Britain, first to second century C.E.*; such weights were used by shopkeepers and traders.* (© The Trustees of the British Museum)

Some historians argue that the standards of weights and measures used in ancient Europe, as well as around the Mediterranean Sea and among the Slavic peoples of eastern Europe and Russia, all descended from a common root system, probably that of the ancient Babylonians. Thus, as people spread northward and westward throughout Europe, they based their system of weights and measures on an earlier one. Historians base their argument on sophisticated mathematical analysis that shows that these systems often had common arithmetical factors. Mathematicians refer to the science of weights and measures as metrology, and an important component of metrology is the notion that a particular unit of measurement is divisible into smaller units or can be multiplied into larger units. Ancient Europeans may have developed different standards of measurement, but those standards were convertible into the standards used by other cultures in much the same way that, for example, American dollars can be converted into Japanese yen according to an agreed-on exchange rate. Without common arithmetical factors, it would have been nearly impossible for far-flung communities to engage in trade or determine the value of gold and silver coins.

Many of the measurement units known to us from historical accounts in medieval Europe probably had their roots deep in antiquity. In Europe, as elsewhere in the ancient world, early units of measurement typically had some relationship with the physical world. The ancient Europeans started with the human body, using such standards as hand spans, the width of a finger, the length from the elbow to the tips of the fingers, and the length of a foot to measure linear distance. In this regard, their units of length were little different from those of the ancient Egyptians and Babylonians. Thus, for example, the ancient Irish had a unit of measure called the troigid, which was the length of a man's foot, so a troigid was a "foot." A troigid was made up of 12 ordlochs, or inches, with 1 ordloch being the width of a man's thumb. Sometimes objects were used. The Germans measured length by the ell, which was the length of a bolt of cloth.

Also commonly used to measure distance was the stride. The Romans, for example, used the pace of a marching soldier, based on two consecutive positions where the right foot landed, to measure a Roman mile, which consisted of a thousand paces. This measurement was imposed throughout the empire, and it remains fairly close to the British mile that survives in modern life. Evidence also suggests that ancient peoples had a fairly accurate understanding of such large measurements as the circumference of the earth and the distance between the poles. These measures were then broken down to provide smaller units of measurement that were used, for example, in determining the length and width of monumental buildings. Again, the ancient Europeans inherited some of these systems by a process that historians do not fully understand.

To measure weight, the ancient Europeans used the materials that surrounded them. In the British Isles, for example, the stone, or 14 pounds, is still commonly used to measure a person's weight, though in the past the stone was probably more like 16 pounds. Further, agricultural commodities, often the basis of trade, were used to determine weights. Throughout the ancient world people were able to develop growing, stable civilizations because of a major staple crop. In Asia the crop was rice. In the Americas it was maize, or corn. In Europe and around the Mediterranean wheat was the staple crop, so grains of wheat were often used to form a common standard of weight. Thus, for example, the weight of a certain number of grains of wheat equaled a certain measure of silver; in turn, these measures were used to determine such measures as the ounce, from the Latin word *uncia*. This system is preserved in modern medicine, where pharmaceuticals are still often measured in grains, as well as in modern measurements of precious metals. The carob seed was often used to measure silver and gold, giving rise to the modern word *carat*.

Grains of wheat were also used to measure length. Again, in ancient Ireland measurements based on wheat ran as follows: The length of three grains of wheat equaled 1 ordloch, or an inch; 4 inches were regarded as 1 bas, or hand palm; 3 palms were a troigid, or foot; 12 troigids were a fertach, or rod; 12 fertachs were a forrach; and an area 12 forrachs in length and 6 in width was a tír-cumaile. The last of these measures was significant because it represented an area sufficient to graze a cumal, or three cows. Property was often measured according to the amount of work that could be performed on it. The acre, for example, developed as an amount of land that a worker could plow in a day.

GREECE

BY SPYROS SIROPOULOS

The ability to measure and compare physical objects and to express their attributes in symbols easily understood by everyone constitutes a standard of communication and provides a way to relate abstract thought to reality. To define a measurement, it is necessary to establish a *metron*, a unit with which to count objects and various subunits or multiples. Various metrical systems have developed to measure elemental dimensions such as length, area, capacity, and weight.

From an early stage of their communal life, people realized the need for specific measurements. Representations of simple forms of balances or scales have been discovered at Knossos in Crete. The Egyptians had used scales since 2500 B.C.E., and it is possible that the use of such mechanisms passed from Crete to Greece. In any case, the first units of measurement were inspired by the human anatomy. The finger, palm, and foot were the first natural measures. Needless to say, the degree of standardization varied from place to place. Furthermore, there were situations in which these measures were inadequate; for example, in the case of measuring longer distances, the cast of a stone or spear or the distance covered by a walker in one day were used as basic units. The Greek poet Homer (eighth or ninth century B.C.E.) uses phrases like these to describe long distances.

People also needed to measure the fields they plowed, the liquids they stored or exchanged in trade, and the amount of grain they produced. Various metrical systems developed, all of them based on local conditions, habits, and needs, yet all of them interdependent and volatile because of international trade and the contact of people with their neighbors. In classical Athens the prototype measures of capacity used for market inspection were kept in the dome of the Athenian Agora (market).

The principal unit for measuring length was inspired by the foot, or pous, but its length was not standard and varied greatly from place to place. The foot of Olympia was 1.050 modern feet, the foot of Pergamon was 1.083 modern feet, and the foot of Aegina (which was used more frequently) was 1.093 modern feet. The subdivision of the pous is called daktylos, or a finger breadth, which is equivalent to 1⁄16 of the pous, or 0.063 modern feet (0.76 inch). Further subdivisions are taken by the fingers. Thus, 4 daktyloi = 1 palaesté (palm); 8 daktyloi = 1 dichas or hemipódion (half foot); 11 daktyloi = 1 orthódoron; 12 daktyloi = 1 spithamé (span of all fingers); 16 daktyloi = 1 pous (foot). Measures for higher dimensions are taken from the arm: 18 daktyloi = 1 pygmé (the length between the elbow and the beginning of the fingers); 20 daktyloi = 1 pygón (the length between the elbow and the knuckles of the fist, used by the Greek writers Homer and Herodotus); 24 daktyloi = 1 péches (the length between the elbow and the fingertips).

From farming life the Greeks developed the measure of a stádion, the distance covered by the plow in a single draft. Originally the stádion contained 600 feet, irrespective of the foot's size. The Attic stádion was therefore 606.889 modern feet; the Olympic stádion was 630.807 modern feet; and the odoiporikón (pacer's stadium) was 516.732 modern feet. The stádion produces further units, such as these: 2 stádia = 1 diaulos; 4 stádia = 1 hippikón; 12 stádia = 1 dólichos; 30 odoiporiká stádia = 1 persian paraságes; 40 odoiporiká stádia = 1 Egyptian schoinos.

The minimum measure for area was the amount that a pair of oxen could plow in the course of one day. This was called pléthron, a square of 101 by 101 modern feet. Divisions of the pléthron were the árura (¼ of the pléthron) and the

Red porphyry 1-talent weight, from Knossos (Alison Frantz Photographic Collection, American School of Classical Studies at Athens)

héktos (1/6 of the pléthron). A different measure introduced to Athens from Sicily and Cyrenaica was called médimnos, and it represented the amount of land that could be sown by a certain quantity (a médimnos) of wheat.

Since corn and wine were two of the main agricultural products, two different measuring units were established for measuring dry or wet products. The measuring unit for dry products was called kýathos. According to different local systems, it varied from 0.048 to 0.075 gallons (or 0.191 to 0.300 quarts), although it most usually was 0.055 gallons (0.218 quarts). The following units are derived from the kýathos: 6 kyathoi = 1 kotýle; 3 kotýlai = 1 kséstes; 2 ksestai = 1 choinix; 4 choinikai = 1 hemiekton; 8 choinikai = 1 hekteus; 6 hekteis = 1 medimnos (88.19 pounds).

The Athenian statesman Solon (ca. 630–ca. 560 B.C.E.) used the medimnos to calculate the citizens' wealth and to classify citizens according to their economic position. The social classes of the Athenian citizens were ordered thus: The *pentakosiomedimnoi* were those with 500 medimnoi of annual produce; the *triakosiomedimnoi* or *hippeis* were those with 300 medimnoi of annual produce; the *diakosiomedimnoi* or *zeugitai* were those with 200 medimnoi of annual produce; and the *thetai* were the poorest citizens, without land of their own.

During the Archaic and the Classical periods (ca. 600–ca. 323 B.C.E.) Greeks used the kotýle for measuring both wet and dry products. The measuring units for liquids are formed thus: 1.5 kyathoi = 1 oxýbaphon; 2 oxýbapha = 1 hemikótylon; 2 hemikótyla = 1 kotýle; 2 kotýlai = 1 ksestes; 16 ksestai = 1 chous; 12 choai = 1 metretés (10.41 gallons).

Various measures were used for weight in Greece. Clay tablets from Knossos, Mycenae, and Pylos present a weighing system in which the largest unit was about 66 pounds. The typical weight of historic Greece was a lead plaque, sometimes with the name of the issuing city or badge. Solon introduced to the Attica region the weighing measure of the Greek island of Euboea, called obolós. Initially the obolós was in the shape of a spit, or the sharp end of a lance (*obelos* in Greek), and it was 1/6 of a drachma (0.159 to 0.212 ounces of silver coin in Attica). A drachma indicates the amount that can be held in the palm of the hand, equivalent to six such spits, or oboloi. The weight of the obolós either in silver or gold depended on the local value of the coin. Thus, in Athens and Euboea the obolós was 0.026 ounces, while in Aegina (the second most established measure) it weighed 0.037 ounces. Various values of the obolós are formed thus: 1 dióbolos = 2 oboloi = 1/3 drachma; 1 dekábolon = 10 oboloi; 1 hemiobólion = ½ obolos; 1 tritemórion = 2/3 obolos; 1 tetartemórion = ¼ obolos; 1 chalkens = 1/8 obolos (copper).

There was also the mina, equivalent to 100 drachmae, and the talent, equivalent to 100 minae. A talent represented a man's load, and it would be relevant to the local standard used. An Attic-Euboic talent would weigh approximately 57 pounds, while the Aeginitic talent would weigh approximately 83.33 pounds.

ROME

BY KATIE PARLA

The use of a sophisticated system of weights and measures was born in the Middle East. As far back as the third millennium B.C.E., the Mesopotamians used common units for calculating weight, area, volume, and distance. The development of such a system was due to a growing territory and economy as a result of increased conquest and commerce. A standardized system of weights and measures was needed to ensure smooth trade across vast distances. Persians, Egyptians, and Phoenicians also implemented standardized weights and measures that would later be adapted by Greeks and Romans.

As a city-state or empire grows, it is necessary that all people in that territory have a common vocabulary in order to facilitate commerce. This vocabulary applies not only to the quantity of commercial goods but also to the monetary system, provided it is based on the gold or silver standard. For this reason the Romans, like so many civilizations before them, instituted a system of weights and measures that was used throughout their territory. While Rome's many standards of measurement were influenced primarily by Egypt and Greece, the Romans also developed their own native units.

The Romans were the first to employ the mile to measure long distances. The word *mile* comes from the Latin mille passum, or 1,000 paces. Each mile was equivalent to 1,000 double paces (2,000 individual steps) for a total of 5,000 Roman feet. The Roman mile was standardized in the first century B.C.E. by the emperor Augustus (r. 27 B.C.E.–14 C.E.) as part of his legendary administrative reform. He erected a pillar in the Roman Forum known as the Milliarium Aureum. This "Golden Milestone" listed the distances in miles from that point in Rome to important cities in the empire.

The Romans borrowed the concept of short-length measurements from the Egyptians. In Egypt finger digits, palms, feet, and arms were all used to measure short distances. These body parts were convenient rulers that could be used in daily life and casual commerce. However, for building and trade, the units were rigidly standardized, so these units would be uniform all across the Egyptian sphere of influence. The Romans used digits, palms, feet, and cubits (the distance from the elbow to the tip of the middle finger) for measuring lengths, although their values were slightly different from the Egyptian standards and also varied across Roman territory, particularly during the republic (509–27 B.C.E.). There was also a slight difference between the length of feet and their units during the republic and the length of feet and their units during the empire.

A Roman foot, or pes was divided into 12 equal units called unciae. During the republic the Roman foot measured 11.65 inches, and during the empire it measured 11.5 inches. A cubit was equal to 1.5 Roman feet, and a passus, or a double step, measured 5 feet. A stadium was another unit of measurement for greater lengths derived from the distance

Roman cup or bowl depicting a man carving the number 7 on a nilometer, a device used to measure the water level of the Nile's annual flood (© The Trustees of the British Museum)

around a Greek racing stadium. It was equal to 625 Roman feet, ⅛ of a Roman mile.

Romans measured weight in a unit called a libra, which was divided into 12 base units of equal weight, also called unciae. A libra weighed 11.5 ounces, just short of a modern pound. Accordingly, each uncia weighed just a bit less than an ounce. Another term for libra was as. Asses or librae were not just units of measurement for weighing commercial goods; they were also used to establish the value of Roman currency, emphasizing just how critical a standard of weights and measures was to the Roman economic system.

Liquid volume was measured in a unit called an amphora. Borrowed from Greece, this unit was equivalent to 6.8 gallons of liquid. In the ancient Mediterranean terra-cotta vessels called amphorae were used to transport liquids like oil and wine. The volume of the amphora is equivalent to 1 cubic foot of liquid and is thought to be derived from the amount of liquid a human being can comfortably carry. The Romans also employed smaller volume units. For example, 1 amphora was equal to 8 congii, each of which had a volume of 0.85 gallons. One congius contained 12 heminae, each of which had a volume of 0.57 pints. A sextarius consisted of 2 heminae. For measuring either dry or liquid volume, the Romans used the modius (pl. modii). This volume was equivalent to 2.4 gallons of liquid. The modius was further subdivided into 16 units for liquid measure called sextarii; each had a volume of 1.1 pints.

Romans used four main units to measure land area. They were used in land division and distribution for colonial, agricultural, and military endeavors. The basis for these calculations was the actus, a unit of length equal to 120 feet. A square actus, actus quadratus, was equivalent to 14,400 square Roman feet, or about ⅓ acre. Next was the jugerum, possibly derived from the average area two oxen could plow in a single day. One jugerum equaled 2 actus quadrati. Two jugera made a heredium, which measured approximately 1.25 acres. The largest denomination of land area was the centuria, which was equivalent to 100 heredia, approximately 125 acres during the republic but up to 200 heredia in the empire. The origin of the centuria was the approximate area occupied by an encamped century of the Roman military.

The Roman system of weights and measures was partially standardized during the late republic. Although there were slight regional variations in units, the basic units of distance, length, weight, volume, and area were uniform throughout republican and imperial territory. Elected officials called aediles were responsible for regulating the system of weights of measures in towns and cities throughout Roman territory. In Rome the standards for weights and measures were kept at the Roman Forum in the Temple of Castor and Pollux. Employing a uniform system of weights and measures, Rome was able to divide its land, mint money, and exchange commercial goods over a vast territory while using a common vocabulary from Britain to the Persian Gulf.

THE AMERICAS

BY KIRK H. BEETZ

Exactly what the weights and measures were for ancient Americans is among the mysteries of ancient American life. For most ancient cultures archaeologists rely heavily on written records for identifying weights and measures, and most ancient Americans left no such records. Some ancient American cultures did have written languages, but it seems that they did not deem their weights and measures worthy of recording. For instance, merchant transactions among the ancient Maya were written on the ground, in dirt, with stones, seeds, or other small objects serving to mark numbers, presumably including those that stood for weight, volume, and length; the transactions were then memorized and the dirt and markers reused for other transactions. A lack of physical evidence adds to the mystery. For instance, in other parts of the world metal scales for weighing objects have been found and their uses identified, but Americans made little use of metal in the ancient era. They may have used wooden measuring devices or devices that combined wood, bone, and stone. If both the wood and the bone decayed, archaeologists would have only the stones, and the stones may look like nothing special.

Researchers expect weights and measures to appear in cultures that trade extensively among themselves and with outsiders and that have a central government which can impose standards for weights and measures on people. This assumption would seem to leave the cultures of the Innuits and the people of the plains of North America out of the picture.

They may have formed weights and measures of their own, but it seems unlikely that they did.

Cultures that might have had weights and measures existed in northeastern North America, along the Mississippi River, in Mesoamerica, and in northern South America. In each case, between 1000 B.C.E. and the end of the ancient era, cultures created urban areas, the most sophisticated of which were in Mesoamerica. Towns of as many as 30,000 people may have been built in North America in the northeast and along the Mississippi River, and they seem to have had extensive trade networks, implying a need for weights and measures, as well as the opportunity for the formation of central governments that could establish weights and measures; however, evidence for these is absent at present.

One way for archaeologists to gain hints about ancient customs is to study modern descendants of the ancient cultures in the hope of finding practices that can be dated back to ancient times. In northeastern North America the cultures of the ancient towns were long gone by the time people who could read and write arrived. Along the Mississippi disease wiped out the town dwellers, who may or may not have been descended from the ancient town builders, before they could be studied. In northern South America the ancient builders of impressive monuments and towns were gone before the coming of Spanish record keepers. Nevertheless, in Mesoamerica the Mayan culture still exists. However, by the time anyone wrote about Mayan weights and measures, the Maya had adopted Spanish weights and measures. Only something to measure distance overland has survived, called a "pace."

The Aztecs known to the Spanish seem to have adopted many practices from the Maya, probably including some weights and measures. Some of their records for payments of taxes and tribute have survived, indicating a few of their measures. Gold was made into disks about 2 inches in diameter and 1 finger thick. Cotton was traded in bales, although the size of a bale is as yet unknown. Maize and other grains may have been measured by baskets, although again the exact size is not known. In each of these instances, it is possible to visualize ancient Maya making similar measurements.

There are good reasons to believe that the ancient Maya had systems of weights and measures. Their cities levied taxes on their subjects, and they exacted tribute from conquered lands. In each case, being able to weigh and measure goods would be necessary for making sure the correct amounts of taxes and tribute were paid. Further, the ancient Maya had complex legal systems that included the ability of people to file lawsuits against merchants they believed had cheated them. Weights and measures would be useful for determining whether someone was overcharged or shortchanged. In addition, kings were expected to ensure that resources were properly distributed among their people; managing the distribution of food, cloth, and other goods would be made simpler if a system of weights and measures were employed. Complicating matters is the possibility that every city or perhaps every king may have had a unique set of weights and measures.

With all those possibilities in mind, archaeologists use generalized words to represent weights and measures they hope to identify someday. For example, the word *load* may be used to represent the weight or size of goods. This term does not represent a random weight or size; instead, it represents what archaeologists believe was always a fixed amount. The term *loads* would apply to large weights or sizes, such as harvests being brought to the city from farms. Smaller sizes would be packets, articles, and bundles, which would be traded in marketplaces to families. The word *length* applies to cloth. For the Aztecs, 20 lengths would be equal to 1 load, although such may not have been the case for the ancient Maya. Such terms allow archaeologists to discuss the use of weights and measures without knowing their exact amounts.

Cotton was traded extensively among the Maya and neighboring cultures. Cotton was almost certainly baled for ease of transport, and it may be assumed that the bale was a standardized unit of measure. Of all Mayan goods, the likeliest to have been weighed or measured was cacao. The cacao bean was treasured because it could be made into a variety of drinks that were valued for their taste, either bitter or sweetened with sugar or honey, as well as incorporated as flavoring into foods. The beans were probably traded by how many there were, but they may have been traded by weight. Ground cacao would have been either weighed or measured by volume. So highly valued was cacao that it was almost certainly measured down to tiny grains. It is with cacao that archaeologists have their best hope of discovering a Mayan weight or measure because the consumption of cacao was something the Maya deemed worthy of recording, even on their monuments.

See also AGRICULTURE; ARCHITECTURE; ASTRONOMY; BUILDING TECHNIQUES AND MATERIALS; CLIMATE AND GEOGRAPHY; ECONOMY; EMPIRES AND DYNASTIES; HEALTH AND DISEASE; METALLURGY; MILITARY; MONEY AND COINAGE; NOMADIC AND PASTORAL SOCIETIES; NUMBERS AND COUNTING; SCIENCE; SOCIAL ORGANIZATION; TRADE AND EXCHANGE; WAR AND CONQUEST.

FURTHER READING

"Ancient Weights and Measure." ArchaeologyExpert.co.uk. Available online. URL: http://www.archaeologyexpert.co.uk/AncientWeightsAndMeasures.html. Downloaded on May 12, 2007.

François Cardarelli, *Encyclopedia of Scientific Units, Weights, and Measures: Their SI Equivalences and Origins*, trans. M. J. Shields (New York: Springer, 2003).

Paul Cartledge, Edward E. Cohen, and Lin Foxhall, eds., *Money, Labour, and Land: Approaches to the Economies of Ancient Greece* (London: Routledge, 2002).

Anita Ganeri, *The Story of Weights and Measures* (New York: Oxford University Press, 1996).

Pierre Grandet, "Weights and Measures." In *The Oxford Encyclopedia of Ancient Egypt*, vol. 3, ed. Donald B. Redford (Oxford: Oxford University Press, 2001).

Mabel Lang and Margaret Crosby, *Weights, Measures, and Tokens* (Princeton, N.J.: American School of Classical Studies at Athens, 1964).

Andy Meadows and Kirsty Shipton, eds., *Money and Its Uses in the Ancient Greek World* (Oxford, U.K.: Oxford University Press, 2001).

Helen Parkins and Christopher Smith, eds., *Trade, Traders and the Ancient City* (London: Routledge, 1998).

Karl M. Petruso, "Early Weights and Weighing in Egypt and the Indus Valley," *Bulletin of the Museum of Fine Arts, Boston* 79 (1981): 44–51.

► writing

INTRODUCTION

The earliest writing systems, often referred to as proto-writing, emerged during the Neolithic Period, probably in about the seventh millennium B.C.E. Archaeologists have found this type of writing, which consisted of symbols that stood for objects or ideas, inscribed on tablets or such objects as tortoise shells. Not much information, however, could be recorded by this type of writing. Writing proper is believed to have originated in ancient Sumer in the Near East during the Bronze Age, in about the fourth millennium B.C.E. At roughly the same time, a form of writing called Proto-Elamite developed in Persia (modern-day Iran), and by 3200 B.C.E. the ancient Egyptians had a form of writing. By 1900 B.C.E. writing had developed in India. The Chinese, meanwhile, produced proto-writing as far back as 6000 B.C.E. and had formed a script by 1600 B.C.E. Other early writing systems that historians have discovered (and in some cases have been unable to decipher) include Anatolian hieroglyphs and writing from the island of Crete, both from around the second millennium B.C.E., and various Semetic languages that emerged in the Near East in roughly 1800 B.C.E. With only very few exceptions, such as the writing system of the ancient Maya in the Americas, all writing scripts throughout the world descended from the writing systems of the Near East or China.

Writing in the ancient world took various forms. The earliest is called *logographic,* from the Greek word *logos,* meaning "word." Logographic writing consisted either of pictographs (symbols that were essentially pictures of the thing represented) or ideographs (symbolic representations of concepts). Later, more flexible writing systems consisted of syllabaries, or lists of symbols that stood for syllables.

These types of writing systems, however, were cumbersome and difficult to learn, for they required the use of hundreds, if not thousands of symbols. A major step forward was the development of alphabetic writing during the Iron Age. Now a small number of symbols could be used to represent the sounds contained in a word. The earliest-known alphabetic systems of writing were those of the Semitic languages, and the written languages of ancient Greece and Rome were alphabetic. Some ancient writing systems were a mixture or two or even all three of these types of writing.

Two other terms are often used in connection with ancient writing systems: *cuneiform* and *hieroglyphs.* The writing of the Sumerians was cuneiform, a word that derives from a word meaning "wedge." Cuneiform writing consists of wedge-shaped symbols that took this shape because they were pressed with a stylus into wet clay. The word *hieroglyphs* is commonly used to refer to the writing of ancient Egypt as well as the Anatolian script mentioned earlier. While the word is widely used, specialists in Egyptian archaeology and history discourage it, primarily because the word is of Greek origin and does not have a precise meaning. Generally, though, hieroglyphs refers to the complex artistic writing of the ancient Egyptians, typically practiced by trained scribes and the priestly class. This system consisted of three classes of symbols: phonetic symbols that functioned like an alphabet, logographs, and a third set of symbols called determinatives that narrowed the meaning of a logograph.

AFRICA

BY DIANNE WHITE OYLER

Writing in the African society and culture of the ancient world dates back to 3000 B.C.E. in the Nile River valley after the political unification of Upper and Lower Egypt by King Menes. *Hieroglyphics*, a Greek word meaning "sacred text," is the first indigenous African writing system.

Along the upper Nile River, south of Egypt, Nubia had been influenced by Egypt in the use of the Egyptian language and writing system through trade and conquest. Although hieroglyphics were known by people living along the upper Nile, the region was not receptive to adopting a writing system. The more rural part of the river lacked the urban, centralized government that required detailed record keeping. Both Nubia and the kingdom of Kush adopted the hieroglyphic writing system from Egypt. However, although the kingdom of Kush and the kingdom of Kush at Meroë possessed literate societies, not everyone was able to read and to write. Members of the royal and upper classes, priests, and scribes enjoyed an education through which they controlled society by possessing written knowledge. Everyone else lived in a preliterate world that coexisted in a symbiotic relationship with the literate one.

The Egyptian hieroglyphic writing system was adapted between the eighth and fourth centuries B.C.E., during the Napatan Period, when a form of hieroglyphic writing was used in texts. The Kushite rulers of Egypt's Twenty-fifth Dynasty—Kashta, Piye, and Shabaka—used hieroglyphics to write about their conquests on steles placed throughout the combined kingdoms. In 170 B.C.E. Queen Shanakdakhete became the first female ruler of the Meroitic Period. During her 10-year reign she used Meroitic hieroglyphs to inscribe texts on stone and brick walls. These texts represent the oldest-known Meroitic hieroglyphs, which were adapted from Egyptian hieroglyphics and changed to meet Nubian needs. Although the two forms of hieroglyphs appear similar, they do not represent the same meanings. Based on their connection to Egyptian hieroglyphics, the written Meroitic marks can be deciphered; however, the Meroitic language has not been translated, so it is impossible to understand what has been written.

The kingdom of Axum created its own indigenous alphabet and imported other alphabets through trade and migration. Axum's indigenous Ge'ez language and alphabet were based on the language and script of migrants from southern Arabia; the Sabaen alphabet dates from about sixth century B.C.E. The Hebraic alphabet also may have been migratory. According to one origin myth, Menelik I, son of the Queen of Sheba and Solomon of Israel, brought the alphabet from Israel in the 10th century B.C.E. Another myth proposes that the Hebraic alphabet was brought in the ninth century B.C.E. by the Hebrew tribe of Dan living in the Ethiopian highlands. In the 12th century Jewish clerics dated to antiquity the Torah used by the descendants of the tribe of Dan. The Egyptian Coptic missionaries brought the their alphabet to Axum during the fourth century C.E., and the Greek language and alphabet and Latin language and Roman alphabet came through the Port of Adulis through the Red Sea trade.

Present-day Ethiopia's Ethiopic script reportedly originated in Axum in the second century C.E. and is based on the ancient writing system of Ge'ez. This writing system was used in religious and secular inscriptions on stone and metal objects. During the fourth century C.E. King Ezana adopted Christianity as the religion of the state, and biblical texts were translated from the Coptic language and script to the Ge'ez language and Ethiopic script.

In the North African region of Maghreb inscriptions in an indigenous Berber writing called Tafineq date from as early as 500 B.C.E. This writing system was used to communicate messages, for funerary inscriptions, and to mark property lines. Tafineq may have been influenced by the Punic writing system based on the Phoenician alphabet used in the colony of Carthage. In addition, the Greek language and alphabet and Latin language and Roman alphabet were imported first through trade and later through Roman conquest in the Punic Wars (264–146 B.C.E.). From 155 to 160 C.E. the Latin language and Roman alphabet were used by the Roman Catholic Church to spread Christianity in North Africa.

Ancient African writing is the second oldest in the world. Written hieroglyphics changed as the need arose to streamline complex writing system. Egypt's gift to the world was its writing system, which was adapted by other civilizations to meet their unique needs, and papyrus, on which texts covering various subjects and in various languages and scripts are preserved for posterity. Other writing systems were imported through cultural diffusion as various groups traded with, migrated to, or conquered civilizations on the continent.

EGYPT

BY LEO DEPUYDT

Egyptians wrote their language in the pictorial hieroglyphic script. *Hieroglyphic* is a Greek word meaning "pertaining to holy carving." The unit of the writing system is the hieroglyph. Hieroglyphs are stylized but realistic pictures of beings and objects. The earliest hieroglyphic writing dates to about 3000 B.C.E. Early attempts are imperfect and difficult to decipher. Full-fledged hieroglyphic writing emerged around 2500 B.C.E. The hieroglyphic tradition steeply declined in the second century C.E., and the latest surviving texts date to the fourth and fifth centuries C.E. The last scribe presumably died sometime in the sixth or seventh century C.E. In 1822 the French Egyptologist Jean François Champollion deciphered hieroglyphic writing.

Because writing represents language, any description of a writing system must be preceded by a description of the language system. Language is composed entirely of signs. Signs have two sides, the signified and the signifier. An example of the signified is a person's image of a dog. The signifier attached to this signified is the sound pattern consisting of the three sounds written $d + o + g$. In other words, the signifier is the code in the brain that prompts the speech organs to produce the sounds. Signified and signifier are independent. The proof is a comparison of languages. French speakers also know the signified of a dog but use different sounds as the signifier, namely *chien*. In English and French the image of a dog is about the same, but the sound pattern changes. Language is neither signifieds nor signifiers but rather the links between the two. English speakers tacitly agree to link the image of a dog always to the sound pattern written *dog*. The biochemical configurations of signifiers, signifieds, and the links between them in the brain are unknown, but their existence seems certain.

Hieroglyphs can refer to either signifieds or signifiers. The hieroglyphic script is one of the few scripts that does both. A hieroglyph denoting a signified is an ideogram—that is, an "idea character." A stroke included in a hieroglyph indicates that the hieroglyphs meet two conditions: They are ideograms, and they denote a whole word by themselves. A hieroglyph denoting a signifier (one or more sounds linked to a signified) is a phonogram—that is, a "sound character." Phonograms represent one, two, or three consonants. They are therefore uniliteral, biliteral, or triliteral. Vowels are not written. Phonograms also function as phonetic complements.

Pictures come to denote sounds through the rebus principle. *Rebus* is Latin for "representing sounds by depicting objects." In English the sound made by the letter *I* might be represented by a picture of an eye. It is in this way that phonograms are derived from pictures. In rebus derivation a hieroglyph that denotes a signified as an ideogram—and that secondarily denotes the signifier attached to that signified—is cut loose from the signified and left to express only the signifier as a phonogram. Like any language, Egyptian consists of a limited set of distinctive sounds, about 25. Each sound can

Abu Simbel—hymn in praise of King Ramses II (Courtesy of the Oriental Institute of the University of Chicago)

be represented by its own phonogram. The group of phonograms in the language is called the alphabet. But hieroglyphic writing is not purely alphabetic. It uses other signs besides the alphabet. Still, about half of the signs in any hieroglyphic text are those of the alphabet.

Ideograms always denote both sound and meaning. Phonograms always denote sound but only sometimes denote meaning. The result is asymmetry. An ideogram denotes the signifier of a word. The signifier is linked to the signified in the sign. That is why an ideogram indirectly denotes a sound. In referring to both sides of a word—that is, a whole word—an ideogram is always a logogram, or a "word character." Only a full sound pattern as signifier is linked to a signified. Therefore, only a phonogram denoting a full sound pattern is also a logogram.

A third type of hieroglyph is the determinative. It appears at the ends of words and determines the meaning class to which a word belongs. Hieroglyphs often function in more than one capacity. Ideogram, phonogram, and determinative are therefore functions rather than types of hieroglyphs. A word can be written in many combinations of one or more of the three types—ideogram, phonogram, and determinative—and contains from one to five or six hieroglyphs, sometimes more.

Hieroglyphs normally exhibit their full pictorial quality only when chiseled or painted. This is hieroglyphic writing proper. When writing with a pen on papyrus, scribes used cursive variants. Pen-written hieroglyphs are called hieratic, which is derived from the Greek word for "priestly." The distinction between hieroglyphic and hieratic appears first in the religious writings of Clement of Alexandria (ca. 250–210 C.E.). Hieratic was by that time used mainly in religious texts inscribed by priest-scribes on papyri. Earlier, hieratic had been used for all pen-written texts composed in the first three stages of the language: Old, Middle, and Late Egyptian.

From about 650 B.C.E. onward an extremely cursive variant of hieroglyphic writing called demotic was used for more than a millennium. It denotes the fourth stage of the language, also called demotic. Demotic means "of the people." The name first appears in the writing of Herodotus (fl. fifth century B.C.E.). Hieroglyphic proper and hieratic had by then become limited mainly to monumental and religious texts. In demotic the hieroglyphs of a word often merge into a single composite sign taking on a life of its own. Therefore a demotic word was often written with its own signs. Demotic therefore makes great demands on a reader's paleographic memory.

Hieroglyphic writing as a rule runs from right to left, with people and animals facing right. Texts were mostly written in lines. Columns of hieroglyphs were commonly used in monuments and were the norm in hieratic in the third millennium B.C.E. The sign list in A. H. Gardiner's *Egyptian Grammar* contains fewer than 800 signs. The number of signs used frequently is less than that.

THE MIDDLE EAST

BY BRADLEY SKEEN

The cuneiform script is the oldest form of writing in the world. Its earliest form was semipictographic, devised around 3400 B.C.E. to record the language used by the ancient inhabitants of Uruk in southern Mesopotamia. This so-called protocuneiform may have been developed to write the Sumerian language (which is related to no other known language), but early cuneiform writing was not used for Sumerian until the middle of the third millennium B.C.E. After 2500 B.C.E. it was quickly adapted to record the east Semitic Akkadian language of people living in the same area. Eventually many other linguistically unrelated languages used cuneiform, including Elamite, Hittitte, Ugaritic, Canaanite, Hurrian, Urartian, and Old Persian.

Writing was invented at Uruk in the context of a complex society that produced a large agricultural surplus and needed to record the incomings and outgoings of that produce and other commodities. The invention of writing at Uruk by administrators managing the large agricultural estates and workshops of Eanna, the household of the goddess Inanna, was thus a very specific, pragmatic development driven by the need to record estate activities. Because of its difficulty, the cuneiform writing was used only by professional scribes, educated bureaucrats, and other elites whose positions in society were bolstered by their access to writing, especially in the form of legal and religious documents.

The precursors of cuneiform writing began to develop as early as 8000 B.C.E. The first step was the use of tokens—small clay objects marked with simple symbols—to record business transactions, such as the transfer of livestock from a shepherd to a temple estate. Eventually traders documented transactions by sealing tokens inside a large hollow clay ball known as a bulla. Seeing the specifics of what was recorded, however, required breaking the bulla, thus making it useless. The solution was to impress another symbol on the outside of the bulla for each token it contained. In time the documentation system was simplified by writing transactions on flat clay tablets of various sizes. Once this became common practice, the set of signs expanded, enabling people to write longer texts.

Cuneiform is a Greek word meaning "made of wedges" and is used by modern scholars to describe the Sumerian script and its offshoots. Although the writing system began as schematic drawings of things named, the images, called logograms, were quickly abstracted and reduced to a set of a few hundred signs, each composed of a unique group of wedge shapes impressed in the wet clay with the tip of a stylus made from a reed. Typically a sign had a syllabic value, and a series of signs strung together formed a word. Much cuneiform literature has survived because the clay tablets on which it was written were very durable. Even when ancient cities were burned by enemy armies, tablets survived because the fire of the burning libraries actually hardened and preserved the clay. Thus, large collections of tablets are preserved from Nineveh, Assur, Ur, Uruk, Mari, Ebla, Ugarit, and many other cities that were destroyed by fire.

Egyptians learned of cuneiform through trade contacts with Mesopotamia and, after 3000 B.C.E., created their own hieroglyphic script that shared many features with cuneiform. When Indo-European Hittites and Persians conquered Mesopotamia, they adopted cuneiform for writing their languages, which previously had been without any form of script. Because of the prestige of the Mesopotamian empires, even the Egyptian court had to maintain an office of scribes trained in the cuneiform languages to handle diplomatic correspondence. In the Iron Age (1000–550 B.C.E.) languages written in alphabetic scripts became predominant, but Akkadian and Sumerian survived as scholarly, religious, and literary languages until the first century C.E., in much the same way Latin did in western Europe after the fall of the Roman Empire.

Clay tablet with Babylonian inscription, found in the treasury of Persepolis, Persia (modern-day Iran) (Courtesy of the Oriental Institute of the University of Chicago)

As early as 1900 B.C.E. many people who spoke northwest Semitic languages developed the first alphabetic writing. This ancestor of the alphabetic scripts used in the modern world is known as the Proto-Sinaitic script because it was first discovered in graffiti and other inscriptions left by copper miners in the Sinai Peninsula. It has since been found in inscriptions from all over Egypt. Rather than a simple transliteration of words into hieroglyphs, the Proto-Sinaitic script comprises roughly 30 hieroglyphs that began with the sound of the consonants in Semitic languages; systems of adding vowels in Semitic languages were not developed until the Middle Ages (ca. 1000 C.E.).

The city of Ugarit on the Mediterranean coast of modern Syria was destroyed by invaders about 1200 B.C.E. Several surviving clay writing tablets show that many languages were spoken and written in that cosmopolitan trading city, but texts in the native language, a northwest Semitic dialectic called Ugaritic, were written in an alphabetic script that was adapted from cuneiform and inscribed on clay tablets. The influence of the cuneiform script among northwest Semitic speakers was so great that every city would have had scribes and scribal schools trained in cuneiform. The new form of writing, therefore, must have been developed in an appeal to the prestige of cuneiform writing while maintaining the relative ease of an alphabetic script. Ugaritic also reveals the first use of alphabetic letter order.

By 1000 B.C.E. the Phoenician cities developed their own form of alphabetic writing based on both the Proto-Sinaitic script and the Ugaritic script. This was important because all later alphabetic writing was derived from the Phoenician script. It was from the Phoenicians that Greeks learned the alphabet for trading purposes (before 900 B.C.E.), after which they devised their own version of the alphabet to write the Greek language (no examples of Greek texts survive from much before 700 B.C.E.). In fact, the term *alphabet* comes from the names of the first two letters of the Greek alphabet, *alpha* and *beta*. Needing fewer signs to write their consonants than did the Phoenicians, the Greeks used the spare signs to represent vowels, thus completing the development of the elements associated with the alphabet. The Greek alphabet was passed on to the Etruscans and then the Romans, who modified it into the Latin alphabet that is still used for many Western languages.

The Phoenician alphabet was adapted by people all over the Near East and turned into a different alphabet by the speakers of each Semitic language. The most important language in the Iron Age was Aramaic. People in Mesopotamia and many other areas spoke Aramaic, and its alphabetic script was written on sheets of papyrus or vellum in ink with reed pens. Because it was more convenient than writing cuneiform on clay tablets, most written pieces, such as personal letters, were probably composed in this way. Because papyrus and vellum are highly perishable materials, however, very few manuscripts of any northwest Semitic language remain from before the Common Era (although inscriptions in stone survived). Hebrew developed its own version of the alphabetic script and used it to write the Hebrew Bible (the Old Testament). The Hebrew language, script, and biblical texts became important factors in forming and maintaining Jewish identity.

ASIA AND THE PACIFIC

BY KIRK H. BEETZ

Writing in Asia and the Pacific seems to have developed and evolved to answer specific needs of societies. For example, the ancient Australians did not develop a writing system but painted rocks with images of their history and religious beliefs. Similarly, the Chinese of the Shang Dynasty (ca. 1500–ca. 1045 B.C.E.) used pictures to represent words. Although the pictorial lexicon of the ancient Australians could be interpreted only by people specially acquainted with them, it seems to have been enough to satisfy the religious needs of the ancient Australians. It was not enough for the Shang, however, because their religious beliefs included the ability to contact dead ancestors and ask them questions. These questions had to be written down on animal bones or the shells of turtles, which seers would transmit to the dead for their answers. A seer would drill a hole in the bone or shell and then touch a red-hot bronze pin to the hole, making the bone or shell crack. These cracks were the replies of the ancestors, which the seer would read and then record in writing.

Religion was not the only motivation for developing a written language. In the Harappan civilization (ca. 2600–ca. 1500 B.C.E.) of the Indus River valley, the creation of writing seems to have followed a path similar to that of the first written words of the Near East. Harappan writing is almost universally associated with commerce, with most of it being found on seals used to mark goods. As was probably the case for the Near East, writing appears to have begun as symbols representing goods and ownership of goods for trade. As time passed, those symbols may have evolved into symbols for words, which may have separated into symbols for syllables and then symbols for spoken sounds. Harappan seals were carved in tiny stones, usually soapstone, and they were impressed into clay. Although about 2,000 seals have been found, almost all in or near marketplaces, the words written on them have yet to be translated.

About 5,000 characters for the Shang written language have been found, with about 2,500 having so far been translated. Each Shang character represents a single word. Linguists call the characters logographs. They were not only written on bones and turtle shells but also on bamboo and wood. The writing implement was probably made of metal, with a sharp edge used to incise the logographs.

During the Zhou Dynasty (ca. 1045–ca. 256 B.C.E.) the Chinese written language became more complicated and versatile. Characters represented things or ideas, and when new things or ideas were to be expressed, the Chinese writers combined two or more characters to form a new image. Characters that represent things or ideas are called ideograms. The Zhou favored writing on wood, bamboo, and silk. For writing on wood and bamboo they used sharp writing implements. Silk required new tools: brushes and ink. Silk was expensive, but it was possible to write something long on silk and be able to roll it up and store it. The oldest silk scroll found dates from about 500 B.C.E.

It was during the brief Qin Dynasty (221–207 B.C.E.) that Chinese writing took on its modern form. During the Zhou Dynasty many languages were spoken in the empire, and in various parts of the empire new ideograms were added to Chinese writing to express words from the local languages. Had this process been allowed to continue, written Chinese probably would have split into several distinct and mutually incompatible written languages. The Qin Dynasty pulled together all the diverse strands of writing that had developed during the Zhou Dynasty, eliminated about 25 percent of the ideograms, and created a standard script that the law required to be used for all official business. This script has undergone little modification since.

As a matter of political policy during the Han Dynasty (202 B.C.E.–220 C.E.), government officials had to be scholars. To assume a position in government, a person had to read and write Chinese fluently; it took about 10 years for a student to learn enough ideograms to be fluent. Every scholar carried a writing toolkit—a wooden box containing a brush, a knife, sticks of solid ink, and a mortar and pestle. Ink was usually carbon made from soot, with pine soot being the most common. Ink makers made sticks of ink that were often works of art designed to remind the writer to do his best because he was destroying a beautiful object to create a written work. At the start of the Han Dynasty most brushes were tipped with horsehair, but rabbit hair came to be favored during the middle of the era. When the writer wished to erase writing on wood or bamboo, he used a knife to peel away a layer from the wood. The wood or bamboo would be prepared for writing by being dried and then cut into slats, which were then stitched together by string or thongs so that the slats could be wrapped around each other into a tube for carrying. Calligraphy was considered an art as well as an important skill; the written work, even a simple one, was supposed to be beautiful.

Less is known about the development and evolution of writing in India than about the Chinese writing system. The Indians did not have a single written language that remained intact or changed slowly. They had many. Until the 1830s scholars thought that the history of India began at about 1200 C.E., because no readable government or historical records survived from before the Muslim invasion. In 1837 a British civil servant in India released a translation of writings found on pillars. The written script is called Asoka Brahmi, after the emperor who had the pillars erected. Since then archaeologists have searched for more such inscriptions.

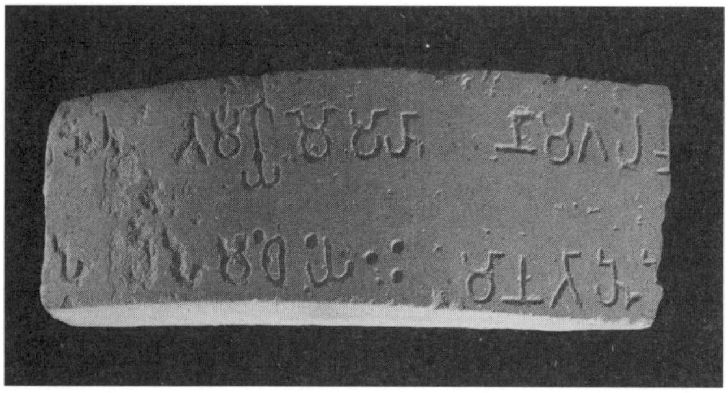

Pillar edict of Emperor Asoka dating to 238 B.C.E., from Uttar Pradesh, India: an example of the earliest readable Indian script (© The Trustees of the British Museum)

Scribes were a standard part of ancient Indian governments. Every court of law was required to have one. Kings had them for recording government business. Professional scribes attended births to record the predictions for the infant made by the attending astrologer. That Asoka had his edicts placed all over his kingdom in prominent places suggests that Indians were mostly literate. Some writings on stone, copper, and gold have survived, while those committed to bamboo and leaves have disintegrated.

The Harappan script seems to have died sometime after the Aryan invasion of the 1000s B.C.E. In about 500 B.C.E. Brahmi script emerged, becoming a robust written language by the era of Asoka (r. ca. 268–ca. 233 B.C.E.). The letters are beautifully graceful. From the end of the Maurya Empire in 185 B.C.E. to the start of the Gupta Empire in 320 C.E., Brahmi split into two or three written scripts. By the end of the ancient era the scripts derived from Brahmi were being split into new scripts to suit the languages of southern India.

EUROPE

BY BRADLEY SKEEN

Writing was invented about 3000 B.C.E. in Mesopotamia and spread from there through contacts between cultures. Writing that uses the alphabet—a small number of signs representing the various distinct sounds of speech—was developed by Semitic-speaking peoples living in Egypt after 2000 B.C.E. This system spread through the Near East and then to Greece. From there it was adopted after 800 B.C.E. by the Etruscans and Romans. Writing came to northern Europe from the Roman Empire.

By the end of the Roman Empire (476 C.E) most societies in northwestern Europe had some familiarity with the Latin alphabet and language. The Latin alphabet is the system of writing still used for English and other modern European languages. Literacy was not very widespread and was limited primarily to churchmen and government officials. Literacy in northern and eastern Europe came with the spread of Christianity into those areas.

Before writing, ancient European peoples expressed their ideas visually through a variety of media. Their modification of the landscape and the size and positions of monuments and tombs provided signals of group identity and territorial ownership. In Scandinavia and the Alps, beginning around 5000 B.C.E. but especially during the Bronze Age after 2000 B.C.E., people inscribed figures on boulders and rock outcrops to depict people, animals, and objects that had symbolic and ritual significance. Pottery designs were another important medium of communication about group identity. Other claims for writing in prehistoric Europe, such as the Tărtăria tablets from Romania, do not stand up to scholarly scrutiny.

Paper made from cotton fiber was a Chinese invention that did not become widely used in Europe before 1100 C.E. The main writing material used in classical antiquity, papyrus, was made from reeds grown in Egypt and was not widely available outside the Roman Empire. The most common writing material used in northern Europe, therefore, was parchment. This was made from animal skins. The skins were not tanned as for making leather but were stretched and scraped while held tightly in a frame. The parchment was typically cut into single sheets or bound into a book, or codex. More permanent documents, called inscriptions, were made by carving letters into stone or metal plaques. Inscriptions were sometimes made on wood, but because wood is highly perishable, they have not survived in large numbers.

Runes are the earliest system of writing the Germanic languages. They exist only as inscriptions. The runic characters appear for the first time on artifacts such as combs and jewelry dating to the middle of the second century C.E. The runic letters are clearly a variation of the Latin alphabet, but they bear a close similarity to older forms of the alphabet that were used in northern Italy as early as the fifth century B.C.E., suggesting that runes might have been invented and used

Painted pebbles from cave of Mas d'Azil, Ariége, France, dating to 8,000–10,000 B.C.E.; the decorations, which include dots and bands, are thought to represent a kind of writing. (© The Trustees of the British Museum)

for some time before the oldest surviving examples of runic script were written. Early runic inscriptions consist for the most part only of names, perhaps of the person who made the object bearing the inscription or the object's owner. In the Middle Ages some longer inscriptions were made to record, for example, the lives of important people. Once a particular German tribe was converted to Christianity, the people generally ceased to use runes and began to use the standard Latin alphabet of the new Christian writings.

A major effort was made in the ancient period to equip a language from northern Europe with its own alphabet. It was carried out by Christian missionaries in connection with translating the Bible into the target language. This was the Gothic alphabet, created to accommodate the language spoken by the Germanic tribe of the Visigoths. They originated in southern Sweden and migrated as far as the Crimean Peninsula in the southern Ukraine before turning to the Roman Empire and eventually conquering and settling in Spain. This language is not ancestral to modern German and died out not long after 700 C.E. This was because Gothic speakers gradually adopted the Latin language that was spoken by their Spanish subjects. However, in the mid-fourth century C.E. Bishop Ulfilas (ca. 311–ca. 382 C.E.) translated the Greek text of the Bible into the Gothic language for the benefit of Visigoths then living in Moesia (modern-day Bulgaria). Most of the Bibles transcribed in Gothic were eventually destroyed because Ulfilas was later denounced as an Arian heretic (that is, as holding disapproved ideas about the Christian Trinity), but a few hundred pages have survived from various handwritten manuscripts of the Gothic Bible. These texts are extremely important for the study of the history of languages (philology), since they are by many centuries the oldest substantial texts written in any Germanic language.

Ulfias invented a new alphabet for writing the Gothic language, which before had never been written. (A very small number of runic inscriptions, however, are possibly Gothic.) In general he used contemporary Greek letters. In some case the pronunciation of a letter was changed to fit the needs of the Gothic languages. A small number of other letters were borrowed from Latin, such as the *F*, whose sound did not precisely exist in Greek. Some scholars suspect, however, that these letters may instead have been borrowed from the runic alphabet since the runes were themselves derived from Latin. The names of the Gothic letters, in any case, are derived from those of a runic alphabet. Furthermore, these Gothic letters are different from the style of handwriting in the Latin alphabet commonly called Gothic in the sense of belonging to the medieval period.

GREECE

BY MICHAEL J. O'NEAL

Among the nations of Europe the Greeks were the first to write using an alphabet rather than such writing systems as pictographs used in other ancient cultures. The Greek alphabet formed the basis of the Roman alphabet, which in turn spread throughout Europe and much of the world. Thus the ancient Greek alphabet was the foundation on which western writing systems were built.

The genealogy of the Greek alphabet begins with the Proto-Sinaitic script, sometimes called Proto-Canaanite, which emerged from Egypt and spread throughout the western regions of the Middle East that Egypt controlled. Beginning in about 1100 B.C.E. an important trunk of this family tree of languages was developed by the Phoenicians, who wrote using a 22-letter alphabet with no vowels. The Greeks adopted the Phoenician alphabet and later adapted some of its letters to form vowels. Interestingly, many of these letters had pictographic meanings of their own, meanings that, with a little imagination, can still be seen in the Greek and Roman alphabets. Thus the letter *M* (Greek *mu*) originated in the Phoenician script as the letter *mem*, which means "water" and was formed to suggest the peaks and troughs of a wave. Similarly, the Phoenician letter *heth*, which means "fence," evolved into the *H*, which bears some resemblance to two fence posts with a cross rail. The ancient Phoenician letter *O* also meant "eye." These similarities are not accidental.

In about 800–750 B.C.E. numerous dialects of Greek began emerging, each using a variant of the ancient script, though the dialect called Ionic and its script became the standard in the fifth century B.C.E. Another important dialect was the Eurobean, which the Greeks carried to their colonies on the Italian Peninsula, where it was adopted by the Etruscans and eventually evolved into the Roman alphabet. A third important dialect of Greek that predated these, called Mycenaean, was spoken on the island of Crete and parts of the southern Greek mainland. The only record of this dialect is a written script called Linear B, which was written from about 1500 to 1200 B.C.E. This script consists of many symbols that represent variously letters and syllables. Historians regard it as a kind of "proto" Greek, and deciphering it was a lengthy and laborious process. (Linear A is the name given to the written script that predated Linear B on Crete.)

Writing, along with art and architecture, was one of the highest achievements of ancient Greek civilization. Originally, Greek was written right to left. Sometimes written texts "snaked" their way down the page, with the text going from right to left, continuing on the next line from left to right, and so on. The ancient Greeks used writing materials common among ancient civilizations, including the Romans. One was a metal stylus, similar to a pen, for inscribing letters on tablets covered with wax. The letters could be rubbed out with the flat end of the stylus, making the wax tablet reusable.

The ancient Greeks also wrote on papyrus, a type of early paper that came from the papyrus plant. To make papyrus, first long slits were made along the length of the plant, and then the material was unrolled. Material from the pith, or center, of the plant worked particularly well. The unrolled strips were placed side by side vertically, and then additional strips were affixed horizontally to hold the materials together.

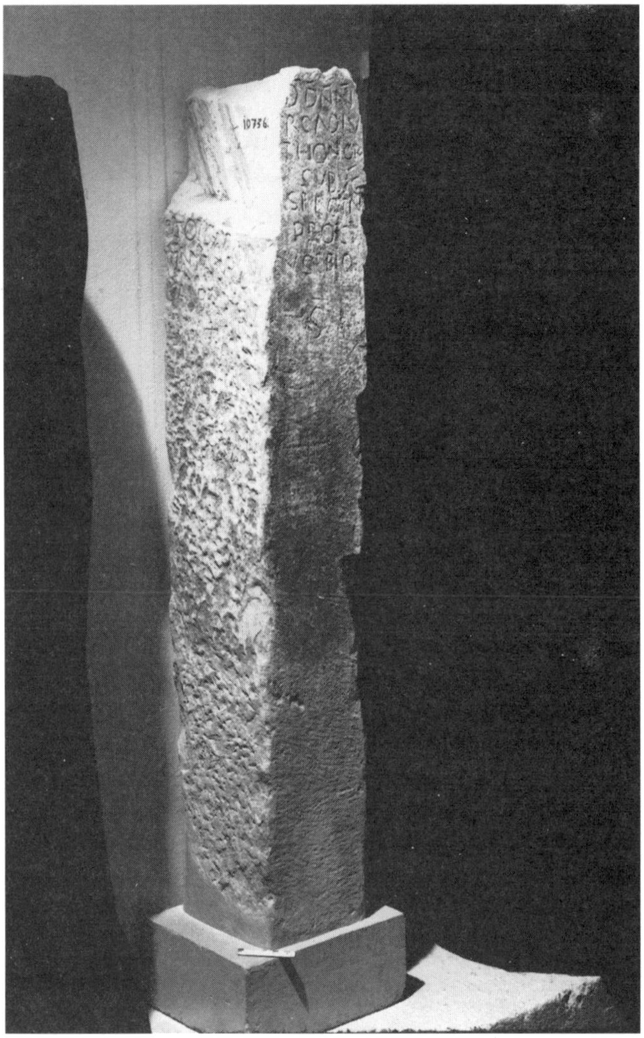

Bilingual milestone marker (Alison Frantz Photographic Collection, American School of Classical Studies at Athens)

Generally, the writing was done on the horizontal strips. Sheets made in this way were joined into scrolls about 5 or 6 yards in length, though longer scrolls were not uncommon. Sometimes single sheets were used for business documents, letters, and writing instruction. Papyrus was typically purchased from Egypt and sold by vendors.

Papyrus, though, was stiff; it could not be folded, and writing on it with pen and ink could be difficult because the writer had to fight the grain of the material. Thus parchment was often used because it was easy to write on and its light color formed a readable contrast with dark ink. The disadvantage of parchment was that it was even more difficult to make than papyrus, so it was more expensive. Parchment was made from the hides of domesticated animals, preferably very young or even unborn animals. The hide was washed to remove hair, soaked in lime, and then stretched on a frame. The stretched hide was scraped, wetted, coated with chalk, rubbed with pumice, and then allowed to dry. Another disadvantage of parchment was that the ink was easily erased. Historians believe that many important Greek documents have been lost simply because the parchment on which they were written was recycled.

Ink was often made of soot, charcoal, or resin. Examinations of many ancient Greek manuscripts reveal that their inks contained a high concentration of iron. Of course, Greek writing techniques were not limited to using a stylus on wax tablets and pen and ink on papyrus or parchment. Carving inscriptions in stone on buildings and tombs was also common.

Additionally, in roughly 440 B.C.E. the Greeks invented a form of writing called steganography, which means "covered or hidden writing." Steganography differs from modern cryptography in that the latter encodes messages that can still be seen but cannot be deciphered unless the reader has a key to the code. Steganography, in contrast, is the writing of messages that literally cannot be seen. The ancient Greeks used it for military communications, when the sender was concerned that the message could fall into the enemy's hands. The simplest form of steganography was scratching a written message on a board and then covering it with wax. The board looked like nothing other than an unused wax tablet. Some military commanders were more inventive. The Greek historian Herodotus records the story of a military commander who shaved the head of one of his slaves and tattooed his message on the slave's head. The message was hidden as the slave's hair grew out and then retrieved when the recipient reshaved the slave's head.

ROME

BY MICHAEL J. O'NEAL

The Roman alphabet has had an enormous influence on writing systems worldwide. In the modern world, languages from Afrikaans to Zulu, with scores of others in between, are written using the Roman alphabet. For ancient Romans the alphabet made the task of writing simpler compared with earlier pictographic writing systems used by other cultures. Because of this relative ease of writing, combined with fairly high literacy rates among upper-class Roman citizens, large numbers of written texts survive from Rome, though the ones that survive are only a fraction of the number produced. These texts survive not only as written documents but also in such forms as inscriptions on buildings, monuments, and even coins.

No examples of writing on the Italian Peninsula existed before the Greeks established colonies there in about the eighth century B.C.E. The native Etruscans then adopted and modified the Greek alphabet during the seventh century B.C.E. The Roman alphabet in turn developed out of the Etruscan alphabet. (Note that the word *alphabet* is composed of the first two letters of the Greek alphabet, *alpha* and *beta*.) In time the Roman alphabet spread through the earliest Roman settlements and from there throughout the Roman Empire.

Writing was important for official and military communication throughout the vast empire. One of the most important archaeological finds pertaining to ancient Rome's written communications with its colonies are the so-called Vindolanda tablets, found at the site of the Vindolanda fortress near Hadrian's Wall in ancient Britain and now housed at the London Museum. When Christianity, based in Rome, spread in the vacuum left by the collapse of the Roman Empire, it continued to use the Roman alphabet, making the alphabet a fixture of Western life.

The alphabet the ancient Romans used to write Latin consisted of 23 letters. The letters *J*, *U*, and *W* were added later, *J* as a variant of *I*; *U* as a variant of *V*; and *W*, or double *V*, added to distinguish the sounds of *W* and *V*. Also, the ancient Romans used the letters *K*, *Y*, and *Z* only in transcribing Greek words. The ancient Roman alphabet comprised only capital letters. Most look similar to modern-day letters, although because of the nature of ancient writing tools many, such as *B*, *D*, and *P*, had an angular rather than rounded look.

In ancient Rome children learned to write using boards covered with wax. They wrote in the wax using a stylus—a pointed metal tool similar to a pen—and could rub out what they had written with the flat end of the stylus. In this respect tools for teaching writing were similar to the modern blackboard or ink board. Otherwise, documents were written on wax tablets or very thin pieces of wood. The wax was poured into hollowed-out slabs of wood or sometimes into bronze frames. People who wrote letters often used wax tablets made of wood or ivory, which were then tied together and sent in a box called a seal box. More important documents, such as legal contracts, government proclamations, and such, were written with pen and ink on papyrus, a kind of paper extracted from the pith of the papyrus plant and then pressed into a flat material to write on. Because this stiff material could not be folded, documents were stored and transmitted in the form of rolled-up scrolls. Parchment—made from the skins of domesticated animals like sheep and goats—was also used as an early form of paper. Ink was made from various substances, including charcoal, soot, and gum. It is unclear what was used to bind these materials together, though vinegar may have been used. Other ink ingredients included copper, burnt resin, various minerals, and glues made from remains of animals such as oxen.

Ancient Roman books were nearly always preserved in the form of scrolls, formed by attaching single pieces of papyrus into long, continuous texts. A reader moved on to a new page by rolling it out and then rolling up the part that had already been read. The chief disadvantage of scrolls was that it was difficult for the reader to browse or go back to an earlier page; the entire scroll had to be unrolled and rolled up. In about the first century of the Common Era the Romans invented the book, using flat sheets that were sewn together. This type of book, called a codex, made storage much easier. Scrolls had to be stored in boxes or baskets, whereas flat books could be arranged on shelves.

Ancient Rome produced a large number of writers, many of whose works continue to be read for their insights into art, philosophy, history, politics, religion, and other areas of thought. These works were some of the highest cultural achievements of the Roman Empire. But much writing, too, survives in the form of tomb inscriptions, inscriptions on the walls or capitals of monumental buildings, and even in the form of *graffiti*, a word that comes from the Italian for "scratch," as in scratching an inscription on a wall or other surface. The ancient Romans were lovers of graffiti, even on the walls of their homes. Many poets enjoyed writing epigrams, or short, pithy sayings, on walls.

The ancient Romans carried the writing of personal letters to great heights. Roman letters were highly stylized, with a system of abbreviations used in the salutation and closing, initials similar to the kind of abbreviations used in modern e-mail communications. Thus, for example, *S.P.D.* stood for *salutem pluriman dicit*, or "sends very fond greeting." Because Rome had no postal system, wealthy letter writers hired messengers to deliver letters, often at great distances. One concern was that a letter intended as a personal communication might go astray and be revealed to a larger public. For this reason, Roman letter writers devoted considerable attention to the literary style of their letters in an attempt to avoid embarrassment if someone other than the addressee read them. Sometimes recipients of letters replied by writing notes in the margins of letters they received. Also, because of the danger that letters and other documents might be lost or missent, copies were generally made and kept. In the case of official documents a class of scribes and copyists did the work. It

Pottery inkwell from Roman Britain, inscribed with its owner's name, Iucundus (dating to first to third centuries C.E.) (© The Trustees of the British Museum)

could be said that ancient Romans lived in a culture of letter writing, often using daily letters and replies as a way of keeping in touch with friends, loved ones, and business colleagues throughout the empire.

THE AMERICAS

BY MIGUEL ARISA

The indigenous languages of the North and South American populations produced a diversity of writing systems, the most important of which were the hieroglyphic writings that evolved in the Mesoamerican zone. In the region of modern Canada and the United States, Native American writing systems did not develop fully until the advent of the Europeans, when syllabaries became the norm. These were symbols representing syllables, but they did not become widespread until the 19th century C.E.

Mesoamerican writing is believed to have developed with religious and political ends in sight. Writing was cunningly used for political advantage in identifying rulers and deities and driving the propaganda machine of the powerful. The calendar and a number system may have been the earliest examples. Bar-and-dot numerals made an early appearance and spread quickly. With time the ideographic signs became logographic, representing whole morphemes (collections of speech sounds) or words; finally, by the time of the Spanish conquest, logophonetic systems had developed, representing speech.

Some of these writing systems date to as early as 1500 B.C.E. At a very early stage in the Formative Period (as early as 1800 B.C.E.), elaborately carved icons in stone served the purpose of representing concepts, and they seem to have been sufficiently conventionalized to have been understood in a widespread area. This area includes a number of cultures, such as the Olmec, the Aztec, the Maya, the Zapotec, the Mixtec, and others whose writing systems evolved in tandem with reciprocal influences at different times over a millennium.

The major systems of the so-called Late Formative Period, from 400 B.C.E. to 150 C.E., were the Zapotec, the Epi-Olmec, and the Mayan. The earliest forms of writing were highly pictorial, and their most important function was to record dates and the names of government officials and rulers. The illustration of myths, liturgical instructions, and mnemonic devices cannot be ruled out in the more developed stages.

The Olmec, a culture that flourished in the Gulf not far from the Yucatán peninsula, are generally considered to have developed the first system of writing. Hieroglyphs carved in basalt columns at La Venta have led scholars to conjecture that they represent the name of a person, since the image of a bearded man is also present. Notwithstanding, glyphs in a cylinder seal and on carved greenstone discovered in San Andrés, an Olmec site in the vicinity of La Venta, have been dated to about 650 B.C.E. and are now regarded as the earliest artifacts reflecting a system that combines pictures and glyphs and that may represent oral speech patterns. The glyphs show lines coming from the mouth of a bird, in fact rendering the act of speaking. One of the symbols is *ajaw*, which means "king" or "lord," and the other is *three ajaw*, a day in the calendar.

A stone discovered in Veracruz has revealed a new system heretofore unknown, predating the Olmec but with obvious references to that neighboring culture. The 62 signs inscribed on a stone slab, called the Cascajal stone, have been dated to around 900 B.C.E., the earliest yet for such a complex set of symbols. An insect, an ear of corn (representing perhaps both deity and ruler), inverted fish, and various other pictographs displayed in repeated patterns show a distinct language system whose arrangement seems analogous to sentences. These signs show patterns that can be deduced to be syntactical (that is, making up an orderly and connected arrangement or structure) and whose repetition can even be construed as representing poetical forms, as in a couplet.

The Zapotec seem to have followed the example of the Olmec and developed a system of writing around Monte Albán, their capital, from 600 to 200 B.C.E. Carved images of dancing men now thought to be captives ready for sacrifice appear next to what some scholars deem is their names; others interpret the images as calendrical signs. Other pictographs found in tablets in a Late Formative building at Monte Albán have been considered a record of conquest and the submission of nearby towns. Not conducive to phonetic writing like the Mayan system, Zapotec inscriptions are more logographic, like Chinese, in which a symbol represents a word.

Another early form of writing is called the Isthmian script, a precursor of the Mayan. A stela found at La Mojarra, near Veracruz, contains 465 glyphs in 21 columns with the image of a ruler. It is structurally similar to the Mayan because it is logophonic and uses morphemes for meaning. Mayan writing is thought by some to predate even the Olmec system. New research from Guatemala on fragments inside a pyramid at the Mayan site of San Bartolo reveal that one hieroglyph sign may be an early version of *ajaw*. Carbon dating demonstrates that the paintings and the glyph were made around 300 B.C.E. The script next to an image of the maize god evidences the relationship between writing, kingship, and religion.

Even though Mesoamerican writing systems had undergone a long process of evolution by the time the Spaniards arrived in the New World, the conqueror's zeal in eradicating the cultures they considered heathen resulted in widespread burning and destruction of their records. Anthropologists, linguists, and art historians continue to decipher the inscriptions in temples and tombs and the few extant manuscripts from before and after the Conquest.

See also ADORNMENT; ARCHITECTURE; CALENDARS AND CLOCKS; CERAMICS AND POTTERY; EDUCATION; GOVERNMENT ORGANIZATION; INVENTIONS; LANGUAGE; LITERATURE; MIGRATION AND POPULATION MOVEMENTS; MILITARY; MONEY AND COINAGE; NUMBERS AND COUNTING; OCCUPATIONS; RELIGION AND COSMOLOGY; SLAVES AND SLAVERY; SOCIAL ORGANIZATION; TRADE AND EXCHANGE; WAR AND CONQUEST.

FURTHER READING

David N. Carvalho, "Forty Centuries of Ink." World Wide School. Available online. URL: http://www.worldwideschool.org/library/books/tech/printing/FortyCenturiesofInk/toc.html. Downloaded on May 14, 2007.

Michael Coe and Mark Van Stone, *Reading the Maya Glyphs*, 2nd ed. (London: Thames and Hudson, 2005).

Florian Coulmas, *The Blackwell Encyclopedia of Writing Systems* (Oxford, U.K.: Blackwell, 1999).

"The Development of Old Germanic Alphabets." Available online. URL: http://titus.uni-frankfurt.de/didact/idg/germ/runealph.htm. Downloaded on May 11, 2007.

A. H. Gardiner, *Egyptian Grammar: Being an Introduction to the Study of Hieroglyphs*, 3rd rev. ed. (Oxford, U.K.: Griffith Institute, Ashmolean Museum, 1988).

Jean-Jacques Glassner, *The Invention of Cuneiform: Writing in Sumer*, trans. and eds. Zainab Bahrani and Marc Van de Mieroop (Baltimore, Md.: Johns Hopkins University, 2003).

Jack Kilmon, "The Scriptorium." Available online. URL: http://www.historian.net/target.html. Downloaded on November 22, 2006.

Lawrence Lo, "Greek." Ancientscripts.com. Available online. URL: http://www.ancientscripts.com/greek.html. Downloaded on May 14, 2007.

John Man, *Alpha Beta: How 26 Letters Shaped the Western World* (New York: Wiley, 2000).

Joyce Marcus, *Mesoamerican Writing Systems: Propaganda, Myth, and History in Four Ancient Civilizations* (Princeton, N.J.: Princeton University Press, 1992).

Anna Giacalone Ramat and Paolo Ramat, eds., *The Indo-European Languages* (New York: Routledge, 1998).

Michael Trapp, ed., *Greek and Latin Letters* (Cambridge, U.K.: Cambridge University Press, 2003). Available online. URL: http://assets.cambridge.org/052149/5970/sample/0521495970ws.pdf. Downloaded on May 14, 2007.

Vindolanda Tablets Online. Available online. URL: http://vindolanda.csad.ox.ac.uk/. Downloaded on May 14, 2007.

Glossary

abacus A device used for making calculations by sliding beads or counters along rods attached to a board.

abax A flat board with vertical columns, used for calculation; the Greek version of the abacus.

ablution vessel A vessel filled with alcoholic, herb-infused, or other liquids for physical purification before encounters with spirits.

acephalous society Human group in which there is no designated political leader.

acrophonic notation A Greek system of numbering using letters to represent the initial sounds of numbers.

acropolis Literally, "high city," which was in many Greek cities the central, elevated, and fortified part of the town.

acupuncture A Chinese medical practice in which needles are inserted into various points in the body to free blocked energy, bringing the yin (the female principle) and the yang (the male principle) back into balance in the attempt to cure injury or illness.

adobe Bricks made of sun-dried mud and used for constructing buildings.

adze A bladed tool that is used to smooth wood.

aedes To ancient Romans, any site where a deity dwelled.

aedile In ancient Rome, a plebeian official in charge of various of Rome's public works and functions, among them, streets, traffic, water supply, and markets and the organization of religious festivals and cult observances.

aerarium The Roman treasury.

ager publicus Public land confiscated from Rome's enemies that could be leased by Roman citizens for farming, grazing herds, or performing other activities.

agger Rampart or embankment; the sloping of a Roman road from a high point in the center to a lower point at the roadsides to facilitate drainage.

agni Indian word for "fire," one of the three basic elements described in the early Upanishads, or religious texts of Hinduism.

agora An open space in a Greek town or city, serving as a marketplace and a political forum; typically the main business district.

agrarian Characterized by farming.

agropastoral subsistence A livelihood based on a combination of farming and herding, often involving migration of herds among pasturelands.

aguada Small water reservoir lined with clay in the ancient Americas.

ahauob Mayan term for nobility.

ahaw Mayan word meaning "lord" or "king."

aivan A type of veranda, or open-air entrance hall that leads into a reception hall.

akhet The inundation, or flooding of the Nile River, which ran roughly from July to December.

***ala* (pl. *alae*)** Open rooms off the atrium of a Roman house, used for storage or work.

alchemy The quest to create sought-after substances, such as artificial gold or an elixir of eternal life, by experimentally combining chemicals or minerals or both.

alfa A wild grass (*Stipa tenacissima*) used for weaving.

alliteration The repetition of the initial sound of one or more words in a line of verse.

alloy A combination of two or more pure metals.

altiplano A high plateau or plain.

ambergris A waxy material originating from the innards of sperm whales.

amelu A class of patricians in Babylonia that also included skilled artisans.

amphitheater A large, oval-shaped, freestanding Roman structure designed for the staging of gladiatorial contests and other spectacles.

amphora A ceramic vase with two handles used in the ancient world to transport and store wine, oil, olives, and other goods.

amulet A charm, typically carved or engraved with a magical incantation to ward off evil.

amurca The dregs of pressed olives.

ancestor worship The spiritual veneration of one's deceased parents, grandparents, and so on, practiced widely in many ancient cultures.

andrôn Living quarters for men in ancient Greek homes.

animal husbandry Breeding, feeding, and management of animals, or livestock, for the production of food, fiber, work, and pleasure.

animism A religious belief that many (or even all) places, objects, and living things have their own spirits.

ankh symbol The Egyptian hieroglyphic sign for *life*, consisting of a loop-topped cross.

annealing A process in which metal is heated to reduce the hardness and brittleness that result from hammering, making the metal easier to shape.

antediluvian Dating to the period before the Flood, described in the Bible.

anthropomorphic Having human attributes or a human-like form.

Antikýthēra device An ancient instrument that used numerous interconnected gears to calculate the motions of the planets and stars.

antiphonal Containing musical verses to be sung in alternation.

apiculture The cultivation of honeybee hives in order to collect honey and beeswax.

***apoikia* (pl. *apoikiai*)** The standard term for an official Greek colonial settlement, laid out according to specific procedures, which became an independent polis.

apotropaic wands Wands having the power to ward off evil or bad luck.

appliqué A decorative ornament made in a material such as needlework applied to another fabric surface.

apron moldings Joint stones that slightly hang over the bottom stonework of a wall.

aqueduct A man-made channel or pipeline designed to transport water across long distances; often raised above the ground, moving water by gravity.

aquifer An underground rock bed yielding groundwater.

archaeoastronomy The field of archaeology that focuses on sites with astronomical importance.

archaeological culture An assemblage of artifacts (and their stylistic attributes) that tend to be found together in a particular region at a certain time.

archaic lyric The earliest Greek poetry that expresses subjective thoughts and feelings, often in a songlike style or form.

Archimedian screw An irrigation device that uses a screw in a pipe to raise water from a river or pool to a field or container.

archipelago A group of islands.

architrave In architectural design, a beam that extends across a row of columns.

archon A chief magistrate of the Greek city-states.

ard A simple form of plow used to cut a furrow though the soil without turning it over.

aristocracy A political system under which a few prominent extended families share power and pass power from generation to generation.

armillary sphere An astronomical device that mirrors the positions and movements of the heavenly bodies.

armlet Band worn around the arm but not around the wrist, which would be a bracelet.

Arretine ware Ceramic wares from the region of Arezzo, Italy, made of fine red clay.

artifact An object created by human beings, especially one of interest to archaeologists.

artisan A skilled worker who performs a specific trade or craft.

asafetida The resin of a plant related to fennel, used to flavor Roman dishes.

asbestos A nonflammable substance, made from fiber extracted from certain rocks, that was used in the ancient world for lighting as well as fireproof clothing.

ascetic A person who forsakes comforts to live a life of severe self-discipline.

asclepeion A Greek sanctuary built to honor the god Asclepios and as a health retreat where the sick and injured were treated.

ashlar A style of building walls in which shaped stones are laid out in regular rows, one on top of another (as opposed to the more complex, but often stronger, techniques using irregular stones).

aspect Feature of a verb that describes the duration or completeness of an action.

assimilate To absorb into a culture.

asterism A small grouping of stars.

astrolabe An early astronomical instrument used in navigation.

ataraxia In ancient Greece, considered to be a life without disturbance, fear, and worry

atimia Loss of citizen rights, used as a punishment in ancient Athens and other city-states.

atlatl A hand-held stick used as an arm extension for throwing a spear or dart.

atrium The open interior area of a Roman house that was the center of domestic life.

augur A member of ancient Rome's College of Pontiffs; a priest whose role was to interpret the will of the gods through signs and omens.

aulos A reed instrument with two pipes, capable of a great range of dynamic effects; used in many contexts in ancient Greece but particularly to accompany choral poetry.

auroch A type of prehistoric giant cattle that is now extinct.

autochthony Belief in origin from the earth or in having inhabited the same place since time immemorial.

automata Devices that use hidden mechanical forces (steam, water, pulleys) to move objects in such a way that they appear to be moving of their own accord.
auxilia Mercenaries hired by Rome to serve in its legions and protect its frontiers.
avatar A physical form, human or otherwise, taken on by a deity.
axis mundi Center of the world.
axone A wooden table or roller used to record ancient Greek writings
ayurveda A system of medicine used in India that emphasizes diet as a means of correcting imbalances within the body.
azimuth The angle measured from north, eastward along the horizon to the point where a vertical circle through a celestial object intersects the horizon.
ba For Egyptians, the soul.
band The simplest form of political and social group, consisting of members (from eight to 100, though typically less than 30).
bandolier A flat band worn over the shoulder and across the chest, often as official or ceremonial dress.
***barbaros* (pl. *barbaroi*)** A word used by the ancient Greeeks to describe a foreigner—specifically one who did not understand the Greek language; often used with reference to someone rude or rough.
bard A tribal poet-singer who gave recitation performances of ancient tales and epics.
barrel vault Solid, semicircular ceiling supported and framed by horizontal arches that rise from piers along the walls.
barter economy Trading goods for each other without the use of money.
basalt Gray-black volcanic rock.
***basileus* (pl. *basileis*)** A king in ancient Greece, though one who typically enjoyed limited powers.
basilica A large Roman meeting hall for commerce.
bas-relief A technique of decorative sculpture in which the artist carves away unwanted material and allows the elements of a scene to emerge from a flat background.
bast fibers The outer stems of certain types of plants, including jute and flax, that can be extracted and used in textile production.
beasts of burden Animals that transport burdens such as goods or people.
benben In Egyptian cosmology, the first place the sun fell on earth when it emerged from the primordial waters and possibly the name of the mound itself.
benu bird A heronlike bird associated with the sun in Egyptian mythology.
berm A mound of earth.
berserk A warrior who fought, often naked, in an ecstatic state.
beveled Cut at a slant such that two surfaces do not form a right angle.
bident A two-pronged spear.
bipod mast A mast that is forked into two projections at the base.
bireme A ship with two banks of oars.
birrus A woolen hood.
bitumen A substance derived from oil deposits that was used in the waterproofing of porous material.
black-figure pottery Pottery painting in which black figures are placed on a red background.
blank A coin-shaped piece of metal without a stamp indicating its value and place of origin.
bodhisattva A person who can ascend to oneness with God but who chooses to put off salvation in order to help other human beings reach nirvana.
bolas Stones connected by cords, thrown to entangle and fell prey or an enemy.
boule A Greek city council elected by the citizens to serve as a lawmaking or advisory body.
breechcloth Sometimes called a "breechclout," a strip of cloth that hangs between the legs from a waistband.
bride-price Money or property given to a bride's family by the prospective groom.
brine Seawater that was commonly heated and evaporated, leaving behind salt for seasoning and preserving food.
broad-cella A central hall or room designed to be accessed through a maze of halls.
brocade Fabric with raised patterns.
brochs Circular stone fortifications in ancient Scotland.
bronze An alloy of copper and tin, with tin added to strengthen copper.
brooch A large, decorative pin or clasp.
buckler A small, round shield held by a handle at arm's length.
bucolic Relating to the countryside.
bulla (pl. bullae) In the ancient Near East, a spherical clay container into which were placed tokens to record quantity of goods held in storage.
burial goods Objects that are placed in or around a grave to either protect or serve the dead person.
burnishing The rubbing of the walls of a vessel with a smooth stone or similar implement, creating a smooth finish and making the vessel less permeable to liquids.
burnoose A one-piece hooded cloak.
butt joint The ends of two pieces of wood placed at a 90-degree angle and held together with pegs or tied together with leather threaded through drilled holes.
buttress A projection from a wall that prevents a wall's collapse, either under its own weight or under the weight of a roof.
byre A stable for cattle.
caber A pole or a young tree trunk used for tossing as a test of strength.
cacao Beans used to make chocolate, cocoa, and cocoa butter; in the Americas in ancient times, they were used as currency.

cadastral Relating to a register recording property ownership boundaries, typically used to apportion taxes.

caementum A mixture of sand, lime, and crushed volcanic stone known as pozzolana that provided the basic construction material for public and private buildings in ancient Rome.

caesura A break or pause in the middle of a line of verse.

caiman A small crocodile native to Central and South America.

cairn A mound of stones, often piled on top of a burial chamber.

calcei Formal laced shoes worn with the Roman toga outside the house.

caldera A crater formed by the collapse or explosion of the central part of a volcano.

camelid Any mammal from the camel and llama family Camelidae.

cameo A material, such as gem, shell, or glass, carved in relief, where the design and the background are of layers of contrasting colors.

canon of human proportions A technique used by Egyptian artists to guide them in maintaining the proportions of human figures, using a square grid and allocating a specified number of grid squares to the parts of the figure.

canopic jar In ancient Egypt, one of four jars holding the liver, stomach, lungs, and intestines of an embalmed person for entombment with that person.

capital The top of a column.

caravan A group of people, vehicles, or supervised animals that are traveling together for safety.

carbon steel An alloy of iron and carbon that is harder than pure iron.

cardo A north-to-south road that formed part of the central axis of a Roman city, crossing the *decumanus* (east-to-west road) at the city's center.

carnyx A European war or ceremonial trumpet with a stylized animal head at the bell end, usually made of beaten sheet bronze; played while being held vertically over the musician's head.

cartouche In ancient Egypt, an oval figure that enclosed the pharaoh's name.

cash economy An economy in which money rather than barter is used for buying and selling goods.

cassava A starchy root used in baking breads or cakes.

caste In ancient India, a social class based on birth that restricted the professions, civil rights, and marriage possibilities of people born into it

casting A process in which molten metal is poured into a mold and allowed to cool, taking the shape of the interior of the mold.

castros Ancient fortified towns inhabited by the Celtiberians.

cataract A rocky outcrop that produces rapids when water runs over it; there are six major cataracts along the Nile south of modern Aswān.

catasterism The transformation of a mortal into a star, constellation, or other celestial object.

cauterization Burning tissue with a very hot metal instrument in order to stop infection.

cavetto cornice A concave molding shaped like a quarter circle.

cella The inner chamber, or sanctuary, of a temple.

celt A prehistoric ax of stone or metal.

cenotaph A symbolic place of burial not containing the remains of the owner; these false tombs were erected to perpetuate the mortuary cult of the deceased or simply to have an additional tomb in a sacred place.

cenote Freshwater-filled limestone sinkhole.

censor The most senior magistrates in ancient Rome, with less power than consuls because they lacked imperium, the authority to lead an army and the power of life and death over citizens.

centaur A mythical creature that is part human and part horse.

centuriation The process ancient Roman surveyors used for marking out plots of land for Roman settlers.

centurion In the Roman army, the officer in charge of a century, a group of foot soldiers.

century In the Roman army, a group of foot soldiers, originally set at 100.

chadar A heavy strip of cloth worn by ancient Indians to protect the upper body.

chaff The husks of grain removed during threshing.

chaitya In Indian architecture, a building consisting of a set of halls that people could use when an outdoor stupa, or shrine, could not be used because of inclement weather.

chamber pot Small tublike pot specially made to be kept in the bedroom for use at night as a toilet.

champlevé An enameling technique where colored enamels fill channels cut directly into metal.

chantress A female singer engaged in religious rites.

chappal A type of sandal worn in ancient India.

characters The symbols representing concepts or words used to write ancient and modern Chinese (and some other languages) and borrowed to write Korean, Vietnamese, and Japanese.

charnel A building in which human remains are deposited.

chasing A way of working silver by hammering in a design from the outer surface.

chassis Framework attached to the axles of a cart.

chattel In law, personal portable property; in the context of slavery, a condition of ownership of slaves that included the owner's right to sell, donate, or devolve them to his heirs but also to liberate them at will.

cheng Chinese word for "city" or "wall."

chi Usually translated as "energy," the Chinese concept of the most basic physical element in the world.

Chi-Rho A symbol formed by the first two letters of Christ's Greek name (*Christos*), consisting of the letter *Rho* superimposed onto the letter *Chi*.

chiton A belted, knee-length tunic of seamless cloth worn by the ancient Greeks.

chlamys A short cloak worn by the ancient Greeks.

chóra The countryside surrounding a city.

chorobates A device resembling a long wooden bench, which allowed ancient builders to ensure that floors and other horizontal elements were correctly aligned and level.

chorus A group of performers who sang and danced in Greek dramas.

chronometer An accurate clock, particularly one used in seafaring and navigation.

chultune An underground chamber that ancient Americans used to collect water.

chun A Chinese skirt with pleats.

cinerary urn Containers used to hold the ashes of the dead.

cinnabar Red pigment derive from mercury.

cist A burial chamber formed from stone slabs set on edge.

cistern Rain collection device, usually cut out of rock and sealed with lime plaster.

citadel A city's fortress or stronghold.

civic calendar A calendar based on the sun and recognized for use in ordinary affairs.

clan A group of related lineages or kin groups tied together to a distant ancestor; often several lineage groups are contained within one clan.

clepsydra "Water thief," a term for water clocks of ancient Greece.

cleruchy A type of Greek colony in which settlers received shares of land (*kleroi*) but maintained citizenship in their native polis.

clibanus In ancient Rome, a portable oven for baking bread.

clientage A social system in ancient Europe whereby a member of the nobility provided a person or community protection in exchange for services.

clogs Blocks of wood used in hunting, intended to trip a running animal.

cloisonné An enameling process that uses thin wires to create settings for precious stones.

cob A mixture of wet clay and straw used as a building material.

codex A book in the modern sense of several groups (called quires) of pages stitched together between a stiff cover.

cohort The basic tactical unit that replaced the maniple around 100 B.C.E. and consisted of 400 to 600 heavy infantry.

coil-build To lay rolled lengths of clay, shaped into rings, on top of each other to form pottery.

cold cutting Carving a piece of glass with hammer and chisel in the same fashion as one would carve stone.

collegium (pl. collegia) A Roman society whose members paid into a common fund to cover the expenses of their funerals.

colonnade An outdoor walkway or gathering place, lined with columns and generally roofed, at least partially, to provide shade.

colonus (pl. coloni) A Roman peasant who was tied to the land despite being legally free.

colophon An inscription at the end of a text, citing the facts of its production.

columbarium An underground chamber housing the remains of the Roman dead within small niches, which held funerary urns marked by plaques and inscriptions.

combined arms The use of differently equipped soldiers in a single fighting force.

commercium The right of any Latin or inhabitant of Latium to own Roman land and to enter into a contract with a Roman.

compluvium A rectangular opening in the roof of the atrium that admitted light and rainwater into a Roman home.

composite bow A bow made by gluing together bone, sinew, and different bones for added strength, with a consequently longer range than a bow carved from a single piece of wood.

concentric Having a common axis or center point.

conciliar calendar A political calendar, in which the number of *prytaneis*, or months, varies with the number of phylai, or groups of citizens.

concubine A woman who is acknowledged as the sexual partner of a particular man; the man typically supports her and acknowledges her children as his own.

confarreatio The ancient form of marriage practiced by the Roman nobility.

confinement pavilion An ancient Egyptian structure made of plant materials and used to seclude a mother after the birth of a child and possibly for the birth itself.

conscript In Egypt, free people forced into government service for a week to a few months; their labor would substitute for paying taxes, or they would be paid.

conscripted Forced into public service.

consul The highest-ranking Roman official; this magistrate held imperium, the power to command Rome's armies anywhere and the power of life and death over citizens.

contagious magic Magic that looks to achieve its ends by using an object that has come into contact with the person or thing that a person is trying to influence.

contour rivalry Technique in which one set of lines creates two different images, as perceived by the viewer.

controversia In Roman rhetoric, an argument for or against a particular legal case.

copal A resin obtained from certain tropical trees.

corbel vaulting A method for building rough arches or domes; for a dome stones are laid in circles of successively smaller diameter until the stones meet at the apex and can lean against one another for support.

cordage Twisted fibers that form thread, string, or yarn.

cordillera Parallel chains of mountains.

core forming Forming of glass by placing vegetal matter or animal dung mixed with clay and sand at the end of a wooden handle and either dipping it into molten glass or drizzling molten glass onto it, after which the core is rolled on flat stone or metal to even and smooth the surface.

core tools Tools that are shaped by striking off flakes from the central portion of a large pebble or cobble.

core–periphery model Economic and political relationship between well-developed centers and less-advanced ones that are in contact with them.

Corinthian One of the three orders, or styles, of Greek architecture, distinguished by long, slim columns and elaborate and detailed carvings on the capital.

cornice A molding at the corner between the ceiling and the top of a wall.

corroboree Australian Aboriginal festivity with singing and dancing, usually at night, to celebrate important occasions.

corvée Unpaid labor exacted in place of taxes by a governmental authority, usually for public works.

cosmogony The study of the origin of the cosmos or universe.

cosmology A system of beliefs used to describe the origin of the universe.

cosmopolitan At home with many different cultures of the world; having a worldwide scope or composed of influences or peoples from many parts of the world.

coulter A blade placed in front of the plowshare in order to cut a vertical slice through the soil.

course A horizontal layer of brick or stone; courses are laid on top of one another in building walls.

courtesan A prostitute who associates with socially elite people.

cowrie shells The shells of a sea mollusk from the family Cypraeidae, having shiny, colorful shells that are still used as money in parts of the South Pacific.

cranial deformation The practice of using boards, mats, or vices to shape the cranium or skull of an infant before the bone has fused together and hardened.

crannog Found in prehistoric Ireland and Scotland, a fortified island in inland waters or marshes built to protect a settlement.

crucible A heat-resistant container in which ores or metals are melted or heated.

cruciform Shaped like a cross.

cubicula Bedrooms opening from the atrium of a Roman house.

cubit A unit of length that is equal to the distance between a person's elbow and his outstretched middle finger.

cuirass Body armor that covers the neck and chest.

cult statue A statue of a god, believed to contain the god's essence and housed in a temple or sacred site to be used as the focus of worship and ritual actions.

cultic calendar The schedule of interaction between a community and its deity.

cultigen A cultivated or domestic organism which has diverged enough from its closest wild relatives to be classified as a species, subspecies, or major variety.

cuneiform A form of writing invented in Mesopotamia around 3400 B.C.E. that used a reed pen called a stylus to make triangular marks on clay tablets.

cupellation A process used to purify silver by heating it to remove lead and other impurities.

curia A building where the Roman Senate met.

cursive A form of writing Chinese characters in which brushstrokes for one character flow into the brushstrokes for the next character.

curule aedile In ancient Rome, patrician officials in charge of various of Rome's public works and functions, among them, streets, traffic, water supply, and markets and the organization of religious festivals and cult observances and also for public games.

cyfarwyddiaid Professional bards of ancient Wales.

cylinder seal A small object made of stone or other hard material in which a scene or symbol is carved away from the surrounding material; the seal is rolled across wet clay or papyrus to leave a permanent impression.

dactyl A poetic foot that has one long syllable followed by two short ones.

dais A raised platform that may be used for a table.

damask Thick, heavy cloth with a pattern woven into it; the weave is named after the city of Damascus, where silks were woven in this pattern after the first century C.E.

daub Mud or clay mixed with water as a kind of plaster.

daughter language Descendent languages from a protolanguage, or "original language."

dead reckoning A method for estimating a ship's position through its speed, the distance that it has covered, and the direction of its travel.

deben Egyptian unit of weight for measuring metals, mostly copper, the equivalent to about 3.5 ounces.

debt bondage A condition in which one who owes another money or goods is forced to work until the obligation is paid off.

decimal A system of representing numbers by assigning values to different places, such as 10s, 100s, 1,000s, and so on in the base-10 system.

declamatio In Roman rhetoric, practice speeches given to fellow students.

declension An inflection of a noun or an adjective—a change in its form to indicate a change in its grammatical function.

decumanus An east-to-west road that formed part of the central axis of a Roman city, crossing the *cardo* (a road running north to south) at the city's center.

deferent A hypothetical circle along which moves the epicycle, a theoretical orbit of the earth, sun, moon, and planets.

Delphi The most sacred and famous oracle of ancient Greece, dedicated to Apollo, god of prophecy.

deluge A flood; often used to refer to the Flood mentioned in the Bible in the story of Noah and his ark.

demagogue A leader who rises to power through playing on people's prejudices or one who champions the cause of the people.

deme Basic geographic unit of Athens, equivalent to a neighborhood or ward.

democracy A political system in which governing power rests broadly on the population generally.

demography The study of a population's characteristics, such as birth and death rates, density, growth, distribution, and breeding patterns.

demos The citizen body of Athens.

demotic A simplified form of Egyptian hieroglyphic writing.

denarius (pl. denarii) A Roman silver coin.

denomination A specific class of coin with a specific value.

derrick A tall platform over an underground well that is used to raise and lower drills and containers.

desertification Process that causes fertile land to become desert.

deshret "Red land" in the Egyptian language, referring to desert, in contrast to *kemet* (cultivatable land), or "black land."

desiccation The process of drying something out thoroughly.

determinative A hieroglyph placed after the phonetic spelling of an ancient Egyptian word relating to the meaning of that word, like an ear placed after the verb meaning "to hear."

deterministic A theory or belief that any event or set of events is the inevitable consequence of what precedes and causes it and cannot be avoided.

devaraja The Hindu concept of the divinity of secular rulers.

devolution of property The transfer of land from one generation to the next.

dharma In Hindu and Buddhist philosophy, divine law as associated with the moral duty of individuals.

dhoti A wrapped Indian garment resembling loose, short trousers.

dhow A sailing vessel with triangular sails that was heavily used beginning in ancient times in the Indian Ocean, especially for trade between Africans and Arabs.

di indigetes Ancient Rome's native gods.

di novensides In ancient Rome, "newcomer gods" imported from foreign cultures.

diadem A headband, like a crown, worn as an adornment by the royalty.

dialect A subgroup of a language usually (but not always) comprehensible to speakers of the parent language.

diaspora Dispersal of a people from its homeland.

diaulos A running event in ancient Greece covering roughly a quarter mile.

dictator In ancient Rome, a special kind of magistrate appointed by the Senate to act in times of emergency and who had almost unlimited power but whose term was limited, usually to about six months.

didactic poetry Poetry that teaches a lesson.

die An engraved metal device for stamping a design into a softer metal such as a coin.

dikai demosiai In Athens, public lawsuits in which prosecution could be initiated either by magistrates or by private individuals not directly connected to the case.

dioptra In ancient Greece, a sighting rod used in mapping and surveying.

diorite A hard, grayish stone that was commonly used in ancient Mesopotamia for freestanding obelisks and commemorative slabs. Diorite could be polished to a glossy sheen.

diphros A simple stool or low chair in ancient Greece, without arms or a back.

diploidion A piece of material left long in front and folded at the shoulders worn by the ancient Greeks.

distaff Any tool used to hold fibers for spinning; in the Roman period it was a stick of wood, bone, metal, or even ivory.

distributive economy An economy in which a central authority collects food and other goods, stores the collections, and then redistributes them according to the people's social positions or needs.

dithyramb An impassioned choric hymn and dance of ancient Greece, performed in honor of Dionysus.

divination A ritual observation of nature for signs that the will of the gods is favorable or unfavorable to a specific action, as a way to determine whether a contemplated action should be taken.

dolichos In ancient Greece, a race of about 2.5 to 3 miles.

dolmen A type of stone monument in which a horizontal stone slab lies atop a set of upright stones.

domestication A process by which plants and animals are altered by human selection, resulting in loss of the ability to survive in the wild.

domus An ancient Roman home, especially in the cities.

Doric One of the three orders, or styles, of Greek architecture, distinguished by thick, sturdy columns and plain capitals.

dowel A pin fitted with holes to hold two pieces in place together.

downcutting Stream erosion that deepens a valley.

down-the-line trade A pattern of exchange whereby goods are passed from one person (or group) to another.

dowry Payment of property accompanying a bride to her new house, available for the husband's use but repaid to the wife's family should the marriage dissolve.

drachm Ancient Greek silver coin equal to the weight of a drachma, or approximately one-eighth ounce.
drachma A weight of metal in ancient Greece; a drachma of silver represented a reasonable day's wage in fifth-century Athens.
draconian Unusually harsh or severe
draft animal An animal used to pull plows, wagons, or other heavy loads.
draft The depth of a vessel's keel below the surface of the water.
dressing stone Carving stone into a desired shape and smoothness.
Druid An ancient Celtic priest or religious leader.
drystone Stones fitted together, as in a wall, without mortar.
Duat The netherworld in ancient Egyptian religion.
dux bellorum A military governor of the Roman Empire.
dynasty A succession of rulers from the same family.
earspool Circular ear ornaments that are hollow at their centers and worn by being placed within a hole in the earlobe.
eaves Roof edges that project beyond the walls of a building.
eccentric Rotation around a point that is not the center of the cosmos.
ecliptic The circle representing the apparent annual path of the sun.
edge species A species of plant or animal that lives at the edge of an environment, where it can take advantage of two different environments.
effigy An image or representation especially of a person.
efflorescence The process of developing and unfolding.
egalitarian Offering equal social and political rights, with no special privileges or status conferred by birth.
einkorn A kind of wheat (*Triticum monococcum*).
ekklesia The Assembly in Athens, responsible for all major state decisions and made up of all citizens who wished to attend.
ekphora The funeral procession from the deceased's house to the gravesite.
El Niño A recurrent warming of waters in the Pacific Ocean.
electrum an alloy made by combining gold and silver.
elegiac couplet A line of dactylic hexameter followed by one of dactylic pentameter and forming a complete thought.
elegy A short poem generally concerned with the passion of a lover and employing the elegiac couplet.
elite A group with higher status in a society that is differentiated by status, power, or wealth.
embedded economy An economic system in ancient Celtic Europe in which the aristocracy laid claim to a portion of a farmer's produce or a craftsman's goods in exchange for providing the worker with protection.
embroidery Threads added to cloth after it is woven, often in decorative patterns or colors.
emmer A kind of wheat (*Triticum dicoccum*).
empire Sometimes limited to government by a ruler known as an emperor but more generally rule over a wide area by a single political entity, such as a single nation ruling over many other nations.
empiricists Doctors in ancient Greece who relied upon observation and experience only, not on theory.
emporion The Greek word for a "market," also used to describe overseas settlements devoted to trade but lacking the status of formally established *apoikiai*.
en An official who oversaw the administration of a Mesopotamian city-state and who sometimes became a king.
enceinte The inner ring of fortifications enclosing a town.
endemic Belonging to a particular region or people.
endogamous Pertaining to the custom of marrying only within a tribe or clan.
ensi A governor who took over from an *en* the secular duties of running a Mesopotamian city-state; the office may have evolved into a kingship.
entablature The horizontal row of stone blocks under the roof of a building between the tops of the columns that support the building, often carved with friezes.
ephebeia A compulsory program of public education during the years of adolescence, designed to train young male citizens of the Greek democracy, especially in military arts.
ephors Board of overseers, five in number, who exercised control over the kings and Assembly in Sparta.
epic A long narrative poem that tells the story of the deeds of a single hero or a band of heroes and that can involve intervention by and conflict with the gods.
epicyclic Rotation around a point that is itself rotating around a different center.
epigram A short poem expressing a single thought or observation.
epistemology Theory about knowledge.
epode The third part of a three-part lyric ode.
equinox One of the two days in the year when the sun crosses the celestial equator. On these days, there are approximately equal amounts of sunlight and darkness.
equites The equestrian, or knightly class, of ancient Rome.
eschatology The usual modern scholarly designation for such religious themes as the fate of the human being after death, the end of the world, warfare between the powers of good and evil, the resurrection and judgment of the dead, the end of the world and related ideas.
escupil Spun cotton body armor used in ancient Mesoamerica.
eskers Long, narrow ridges of sand and coarse gravel deposited by glacial meltwaters.
estuarine Relating to an estuary, the section of a river that meets the sea and where freshwater mixes with saltwater.
Etesian winds The dry, relatively cool winds that regularly blow from north to south in the Mediterranean during the summer months.

ethnocentrism The concept that one's group, however defined, is superior to all other groups.
ethnography The study and systematic recording of human cultures.
ethnologist Someone who studies cultural and biological relationships among large groups of people.
etymology The structural and semantic history of words.
eunomia "Good laws," the Spartans' favorite phrase to describe their system of government.
eunuch A castrated man typically employed in a palace, often taking charge of a harem.
eustasy The phenomenon of rising and falling sea levels.
excarnation The practice of allowing a body to decay before burial.
execration text List of foreign kings and peoples written on Egyptian pottery and statuettes of prisoners of war.
exomis A short, sleeveless tunic with the right side open worn by the ancient Greeks.
exorcist A "magician" skilled in warding off disease and the other effects of evil demons.
faience Earthenware decorated with glazes.
fauces The hall leading into a Roman house.
felt Cloth made from wool treated with water, heat, and an alkaline.
fenestration Cutting out sections of a vessel wall in decorative patterns.
feng shui An ancient Chinese worldview that sought harmony and balance between the opposing forces of nature and between the physical environment and humans; its principles were applied to the siting, design, and construction of buildings.
***feria* (pl. *feriae*)** The Latin word for "festival."
fetch The distance wind travels over water unimpeded.
fetiale In ancient Rome, a member of a priestly order whose job was to ensure that war was declared properly.
feudal system A social and economic system in which land is held on condition of loyalty to a higher authority, as in nobles holding land on the condition of their loyalty to their king.
fibula A clasp or brooch used to fasten clothing in the ancient world.
fief An estate ruled by a lesser lord within a greater feudal kingdom.
filial piety In Confucian philosophy, the unquestioning devotion to and respect for one's parents.
filid Ancient Irish bards.
fillet A ribbon used for binding the hair or as a headband.
finial An ornamental projection from the top of a wall or column or at the peak or corner of a roof.
fired brick Clay bricks that have been hardened in fires or ovens, making them much more water resistant than clay bricks dried in sunshine.
firing The practice of cooking clay vessels in a fire in order to make them harder.
fishtail point A ancient projectile point that takes the form of a fish.
fjord An inlet to the sea with high cliff walls, created by the retreat of a glacier.
flagon A type of drinking vessel with a handle and spout and typically a lid.
flake tools Tools that are made from the flattish pieces that are knocked off in the formation of core tools.
flamen In ancient Rome, a member of a class of priests who ensured that proper observances and sacrifices were made to the gods.
flax A plant material that is the basis for linen.
fletching The feathers on an arrow.
fluting Concave, semicircular grooves carved into an architectural column.
fodder crops Plants grown specifically for animal consumption.
foot A division of a line of verse that contains a specific number of long and short syllables.
forging Shaping metal by hammering, often when heated to white hot or red hot.
forum An open plaza at the center of a Roman town, used for commercial, legal, political, and religious activity.
frame A timber oriented perpendicular to a ship's keel, to which a ship's hull planking was fastened.
fresco Decorative wall painting on plaster with water-based paint applied when the plaster is wet, allowing the color to permeate the plaster and become permanent.
frieze A horizontal band of carved stone, typically depicting a progression of events and procession of figures.
frontality The convention of always having a statue of a human facing to the front.
fundamental note The lowest or most dominant note that an instrument is designed to play.
funerary cult Provisions a person makes before death to provide everything the deceased would need in the afterlife, such as food offerings.
funerary priests Religious officials who oversaw burial rituals and other offerings and sacrifices in honor of the deceased.
futhark Runic script of the ancient Germans.
gables Triangular sections fastened to the top of end walls in houses with double-pitched roofs.
game drives Hunting practices that involved preparing and setting nets for migratory fish and birds.
gangue The surrounding rock in a metal ore.
garum A condiment popular in the Roman world and produced mostly in Spain, made by allowing salted fish intestines to ferment in the sun for days or weeks.
genos A Greek family or clan that shared a common ancestor and family name.
geocentric Having the earth at the center of the universe, orbited by the sun, moon, planets, and stars.
geoglyph Large-scale earth drawing created using simple geometric principles and surveying techniques.

gerontocracy A form of social organization in which the oldest men and women in a society are expected to guide and lead the community because of their wisdom.

gerousia A council of elders in Sparta, made up of 28 prominent citizens over the age of 60.

ghee Clarified butter, created by boiling unsalted butter and drawing off excess water; used as lamp fuel in ancient India.

glacial maximum The time of maximum extent of ice sheets during an ice age.

glacier A river of ice flowing slowly downhill.

gladiator A slave who fought as a professional soldier in combats staged for entertainment.

glaze A glasslike coating that seals the surface of a ceramic object and decorates it.

glyph A symbol, such as a hieroglyph, carved into stone.

gnomon "Indicator," the vertical bar that casts the shadow of the sun on the face of a sundial.

gorget An ornamental collar or throat covering.

gourd Dried and hollowed out shell of a fruit from the squash or pumpkin family that is converted into a vessel.

grafting The practice of attaching the stalk of one plant to the root stock of another to provide strong roots to a plant that would naturally have weak roots.

grammaticus In ancient Rome, a public secondary-school teacher.

grammatistēs A teacher of reading, writing, arithmetic, and poetry in ancient Greece.

granary A storehouse for harvested crops.

granulation A method of decorating metal with patterns made up of small balls of the same metal, usually gold.

gravitas A dignified bearing, one of the Roman virtues.

greave Armor that protects the legs below the knees.

griot In ancient Africa, an oral historian who recounted cultural tradition through song.

groin vault A ceiling formed by the intersection of two barrel vaults, which are in turn supported by piers that are either freestanding or set into a wall.

groma A device that allowed Roman builders to ensure that vertical elements, such as columns and piers, were set at right angles to the horizontal.

grotto A cave enclosing a body of water.

guano Bat dung; used as fertilizer.

gur In the ancient Near East, a measure of the value of an item that was approximately equal to 43 gallons of barley.

guru A teacher in the Hindu tradition, seen as a god in human form and as the sole source of knowledge for his students.

gurukula A school in the Hindu tradition.

gymnasium An area devoted to intellectual and athletic pursuits.

gymnastics In ancient Greece, any athletic training.

gynaikeion Living quarters for women in ancient Greek homes.

haft The handle of a knife, an ax, or another weapon or tool.

halberd A battle-ax mounted on a long handle.

handfasting Engagement to marry.

hangul The system instituted in 1446 to write Korean phonetically; originally used along with Chinese characters but now generally used exclusively.

haniwa Small ceramic figures, usually depicting people, made by the ancient Japanese to surround tombs, protecting the tombs from evil spirits.

harmika A finial, or ornamental projection from the top of a wall or column, found in the architecture of India.

harpy eagle A large bird of prey native to Central and South America.

haruspex (pl. haruspices) Literally, "men who look at guts": Roman diviners who read the will of the gods by examining the entrails of sacrificed animals.

heddle A rod on a loom used to guide threads.

heliacal rise The first appearance of a star near the eastern horizon just preceding sunrise, following a period of nighttime invisibility due to proximity to the sun.

heliocentric Having the sun at the center of the solar system, orbited by Earth and other planets.

Hellenization The process of "becoming Greek."

helot In ancient Greece, a slave of the Spartans.

hemp A tall herb with tough fibers used to make durable cloth and ropes.

hen In ancient Egypt, the measure of a volume equal to half a quart or less, with a value that could vary according to the substance or liquid to be measured; generally regarded as equal in value to one deben.

henotheism The worship of a single most important deity without denying the existence of others.

hep Egyptian term for law, abstract moral order, normative custom, and every kind of rule, either natural or juridical, general or specific, public or private, literary or oral.

herm A statuette of the god Hermes, usually placed at house gates or as a marker on roads.

hero In ancient Greece, a great mythical or legendary human being who was usually considered the offspring of a god and a mortal and whose spirit was worshipped much like a god.

hestia A Greek cooking stove.

hetairai (or hetaerae) In ancient Greece, courtesans, often valued for wit and education as well as beauty; these women occupied a social space between that of a prostitute and a mistress.

hexameter A poetic meter that has six feet per line.

hierarchical society A society characterized by multiple levels of authority and status.

hieratic Sacred; associated with priests; also a cursive form of Egyptian hieroglyphs used for all domestic texts and records.

hieroglyph The Greek word for "sacred carving," describing the Egyptian writing system, which consisted of pictorial signs, used phonetically and pictorially.

himation A rectangular outer mantle draped in various ways and worn by the ancient Greeks.

Hippocratic bench A bench with moveable posts and straps, used for reducing dislocations and for traction.

Hippocratic oath A statement of basic principles followed by students and physicians at the ancient school of medicine on the island of Cos and which survives to this day as a foundation of modern medical ethics.

historical linguistics The study of the derivation, changes, and relationships of languages over time.

ho boulomenos A Greek term literally meaning, "the one who wishes," a definition of who could initiate a public lawsuit.

hogging trusses On a ship, thick ropes that could be tightened to keep the bow and stern from sagging.

homoioi Literally "equals," a term applied to the citizen body in ancient Sparta.

honestiores* and *humiliores Two broad classes into which Roman citizens were divided during the empire. The *honestiores* were aristocrats, soldiers, and public officeholders; they suffered lighter punishments than *humiliores*, who made up the rest of the population.

hoplite A heavily armed Greek foot soldier, protected by a metal helmet, breastplate, and large round shield.

hoplitodromos A race in ancient Greece that the athletes ran while wearing armor.

hoplomachus Gladiator armed with Greek heavy-infantry weapons.

***horos* (pl. *horoi*)** Stones used to mark boundaries for various types of spaces: temple precincts, public spaces, and the edges of poleis, or city-states.

hubris In ancient Greece, an outrage or a deliberate affront to the dignity of another, particularly a citizen.

humor One of the elemental fluids of the body in Hippocratic, Galenic, and medieval medicine; the four canonical humors after Galen were blood, black bile, yellow bile, and phlegm.

hunter-gatherers People who survive by hunting wild animals and gathering wild plants, without agriculture.

hybris Any act that went beyond the established moral codes or surpassed human capacities, usually followed by *nemesis*, or divine punishment.

hydraulics The study of the mechanics of fluids, especially with respect to engineering.

hydraulis A water-powered pipe organ developed in ancient Greece; the world's first keyboard instrument, it used bellows or a hydraulic pump to force air through pipes.

hydria A vessel to hold water mixed with concentrated wine.

hydrostatics The branch of mechanics dealing with the equilibrium of weights in water.

hypaspists Members of an elite infantry guard in the army of Alexander the Great.

hypocaust The space underneath the floor of a building from which heat rose to warm the floors above it.

hypostyle hall A hall with a flat ceiling supported by columns.

iamb A poetic foot that has one short syllable followed by a long.

ibw Tent in which bodies underwent ritual purification before embalming in ancient Egypt.

ice core a sample of the various layers in large ice sheets taken by drilling a long, hollow tube down into the ice sheet and used for research purposes, such as the study of past climate change or ecological conditions.

iconography Symbolic representation, especially the conventional meanings attached to an image or images.

ideogram A written character that represents an object, image, or idea.

ideographic In a writing system, having symbols that denote ideas rather than words.

idiophone An instrument producing a specific, unusual, often atonal sound.

idolatry The worship of images or statues of gods instead of the gods themselves.

igneous rock A type of rock that has been subjected to extremely hot temperatures, to the point of becoming molten, and then cooled to a hardened form.

imagines Images of the Roman dead carried by the living in the form of masks during a funeral procession.

Imperial Cult During the Roman Empire, the belief that the emperor was divine, usually declared after his death.

imperium The power of military and civilian command belonging to certain magistrates and promagistrates such as consuls and proconsuls.

impiety The crime of violating religious law in a way that was viewed as injurious to the nation.

impluvium The shallow pool in the floor of an atrium that collected rainwater directed through an opening in the roof of a Roman house.

incertum An early technique of Roman masonry in which blocks of tufa were inserted randomly into drying concrete blocks.

incised or raised relief Symbols, images, or writing cut or hammered into metal surfaces to distinguish them from the plane surface.

infinitesimal A number smaller in absolute value than any positive real number.

inflected language A language in which words take different forms to reflect grammatical information such as gender, tense, and singular and plural.

inflection Change in the form of a verb, noun, or adjective (for example, the adding of *s* in English to form a plural).

ingot A metal casting that is shaped for easy working or for recasting, typically oblong in shape.

initiation Any ritual, ceremony, or cultural practice that marks the transition from childhood to adulthood.

inscription Writing carved into a solid substance such as stone or bronze.

insula A Roman apartment building, usually multistoried.

interaction sphere In prehistoric cultures, groups that had social interaction and exchanged material goods.

intercalation The addition of an extra day in the month, or an extra month in the year, to ensure that the months remain synchronized with the seasons.

interstadial A short period of relatively warmer climate within an ice age.

inundation Predictable annual flooding events that renew the soil and sustain ecosystems; often used to refer to the flooding of the Nile.

Ionic One of the three orders, or styles, of Greek architecture, distinguished by slender columns and capitals ornamented with spiral scrollwork called volutes.

isegoria The principle in Athenian democracy under which all citizens had an equal right to speak in the Assembly and other public gatherings.

isolate An ancient language that has no similarities with other languages and thus may have developed independently.

isonomia "Equality under the law," the basic idea of Athenian democracy.

isostasy The rebounding of the earth's mantle after it has been depressed.

ius privatum Private law that was concerned with the legal dealings between individual Roman citizens or groups of citizens, as well as between citizens and noncitizens.

ius publicum Public law that regulated the relationship between the Roman state and its citizens.

jamb One of two uprights in a door frame that together supports a crosspiece, or lintel, and that transfers the weight of the wall above the door to the ground.

jaundice A yellowish discoloration of the skin symptomatic of diseases affecting the processing of bile.

javelin A lightweight spear designed to be thrown.

joinery Techniques or processes used to join pieces of wood, usually referring to ways of cutting the wood so that nails or screws are not required.

ju A Chinese shirt with a stiff, upright collar.

Julian calendar A solar calendar purportedly created by the Greek astronomer Sosigenes of Alexandria and instituted by Julius Caesar in 45 BCE.

k'uhul ajaw Mayan term for divine king.

kalasiris* or *calasiris A thin linen tunic.

karma In Indian spirituality, the positive or negative energy created by people during their lifetimes, determining the states they will take in future lives.

kataginu A Japanese vest with broad, stiff shoulders.

keel A large timber running longitudinally at the bottom of a ship from which the hull is built up and that provides stabilization.

keep A fortress within a fortress.

kemet "Black land" in the Egyptian language, referring to land that could be cultivated, in contrast to *deshret* (desert), or "red land."

khapusa A heavy, knee-high boot that was worn in northern India.

kinship Ties (either biological or cultural) that determine human groups.

kitchen middens Accumulations of food and other debris of human occupation, such as discarded tools and ashes from hearths.

kithara An ancient stringed instrument used by the Greeks and Romans, similar to the modern guitar.

kitharistēs A music teacher in ancient Greece, who taught singing and playing the lyre, a stringed instrument like a harp.

klinē A bed or couch in ancient Greece, consisting of a wooden frame across which a webbing of leather or rope would be woven to support the occupant.

klismos A chair in ancient Greece, with curved legs, no armrests, and a curved, reclined back.

knight A member of the second-highest Roman social class, rated by the value of property according to the census. Knights were required to serve in the cavalry since they could afford to buy their own horse and equipment.

knot A measurement of speed at sea equal to 6,076 feet per hour.

kohl An eye cosmetic often composed of ground galena (a black mineral), sulfur, frankincense, and powdered antimony, which contains lead.

koine The "common" dialect based on Attic that developed starting in the third century B.C.E. and became the basis for Byzantine and Modern Greek.

***kore* (pl. *korai*)** Representations of standing female nudes from the Archaic Period of Greek art.

***kouros* (pl. *kouroi*)** A figure of a standing male nude from the archaic period of Greek art.

krypteia An annual secret campaign of assassination conducted by the Spartans in ancient Greece against their slaves, the helots.

ku Loose Chinese trousers.

kudurrus A boundary stone, which carried emblems and symbols of the gods.

kurios The legal lord of a Greek household, with power over and responsibility for all its members.

lacquer A coating used to made an object glossy; in China, lacquer at first came from the resin of the lacquer tree, *Rhus verniciflua*.

lamassus Large-scale architectural sculptures of human-headed winged bulls that abutted the entrance walls of Assyrian palaces.

lamellae Thin iron plates that were used in the construction of armor.

lapis lazuli Semiprecious blue stone used in creating jewelry and other objects.

latifundium Originally, in ancient Rome, a large estate relying largely on slave labor.

latitudinal Having to do with latitude, the geographic distance of any point on the earth north or south of the equator.

laudatio The Roman ceremony of displaying and eulogizing a dead person before cremation or burial.

lay Song of the Anglo-Saxon bard.

lead line A rope to which was tied a lead or stone weight and that was used to measure water depth; often the weight had a depression filled with tallow so that a sample of the sea bottom could be brought to the surface.

lector priest A ritual specialist who carried out ceremonies according to the secret books in ancient Egypt.

lee shore A shore toward which the wind blows, constituting a danger to a ship in a storm.

legion The largest independent formation in the Roman army, consisting of heavy infantry, light infantry, and cavalry and varying between 4,200 and 6,000 men.

legionary sword A short sword, used in ancient Rome, with a blade about 30 inches long with two parallel cutting edges and a long, sharp point.

legionnaires Members of a legion, or the basic unit of the Roman army.

legume A plant related to the pea family, notable for its protein content.

léine A long linen tunic worn in Ireland.

leishmaniasis A protozoan skin disorder carried by female sand flies.

***lekythos* (pl. *lekythoi*)** A Greek vessel used to store olive oil for the anointing of the dead in preparation for burial or as a burial offering

leprosy Chronic progressive bacterial infection affecting the skin and nerves, acquired by close personal contact over a long period, often among members of the same family.

levee An embankment or barrier meant to prevent flooding.

lex frumentaria In ancient Rome, a grain law, which provided grain to each citizen at a subsidized price.

lex talionis A legal concept of punishment based on equal and direct retribution, often popularly expressed as "an eye for an eye."

lexicology A branch of linguistics concerned with the study of words and their application.

libation The act of pouring liquid as a sacrificial offering, typically to the gods but also to one's ancestors.

lignified Hardened; used in reference to the hardening of the outer husk of corn.

limes A border defensive system of the ancient Romans.

limestone Stone formed from sediments laid down over eons; usually easier to carve than granite.

limitanei Light troops of the late Roman Empire who guarded the borders and frontiers to hold off invaders until heavier troops could arrive.

lineage burials Burials in grounds set aside for a single family lineage.

lineage Family ancestry traced through a line of parenthood, either fathers or mothers but not both.

linen A flexible, durable, and usually soft cloth made from flax.

lintel A beam that rests on the uprights, or jambs, of a doorway and that transfers the weight of the wall above the door to the uprights and from them to the ground.

lithic Of, relating to, or being a stone tool.

litter A chair or similar vehicle suspended from poles carried by either humans or animals to transport one or more riders.

litterator In ancient Rome, a teacher of basic literacy and numbers.

littoral A region near a shore, especially of the sea.

liturgy An institution whereby private citizens in ancient Athens were obliged to pay for public works from their own resources.

loan word A word that one culture borrows from another, either as is or with modifications, suggesting contact between the two cultures.

lodestone A piece of magnetite, having magnetic properties.

loess Chalky clay or silt created by layers of wind-blown dust over a long period of time.

logic A system or principles of reasoning.

logographic In a writing system, having symbols that denote a whole word or a morpheme, a minimal language unit.

logophonetic In a writing system, having symbols that denote the actual sounds of speech.

loincloth A strip of cloth wound about the waist and between the legs.

long barrows Elongated burial mounds.

lost-wax casting A method of creating metal objects by use of a wax cast set within a clay mold; the wax is heated and runs out of the mold to be replaced by molten metal.

***ludus* (pl. *ludi*)** A show or performance; from the Latin for "play, game."

lugal Literally, "great man"; in ancient Sumer, a leading citizen chosen to take charge in times of crisis.

lunar calendar A calendar that is based on the cycles of the moon, defining one month as the time it takes the moon to complete one revolution around the earth.

lunation The interval from new moon to new moon.

lungi An Indian skirt that resembles a loincloth.

lunisolar calendar A calendar that combines aspects of lunar and solar calendars, basing units of time on the earth's movements relative to both the sun and the moon.

lur Cast bronze horns from northern Europe, made in distinctive pairs and thought to have been used for ceremonial purposes.

lustratio A purification ceremony performed for a Roman male infant at the age of eight days.

lute A stringed instrument with a long neck, rounded body, and flat front.

lyra A small type of Greek lyre, often with a sound box made out of a tortoiseshell.

lyre A stringed instrument like a U-shaped harp with strings fixed to a crossbar at the top of the U.

lyric poetry Short, very personal poetry that deals with the poet's feelings or state of mind.

maat In ancient Egyptian cosmology, cosmic harmony (personified as a goddess) as established by the creator god at the beginning of time, including truth, justice, moral ethics, and social and political order.

mace A ceremonial staff.

madder A plant used to make red dye.

magic lantern A device used to illuminate and project images and silhouettes onto a screen.

maguey A plant from the cactus family indigenous to Mexico, used for a variety of purposes, particularly for its fibers to create cloth.

mail shirt A body covering composed of interlaced rings or chain work and normally extending below the waist.

major lunar standstill(s) The moon's farthest rising and setting points north and south on the horizon over an 18.6-year cycle.

malakaras Garland makers in ancient India.

malaria Epidemic infection caused by a parasite transmitted through the bite of a mosquito and causing recurring chills and fever.

mammoth Any large, elephantlike mammal of the extinct genus *Mammuthus*.

mangroves Woody trees that live in coastal habitats.

maniple The basic unit of the Roman army, consisting of either 120 or 60 men.

mantle A large, rectangular cloth arranged around the neck and over the shoulders.

mantra A sacred word or phrase that a person chants over and over to achieve spiritual effects.

manumit To free a slave.

manus The power that a husband held over his wife in ancient Rome.

manuscript Writing on a sheet of papyrus or vellum.

mastaba Underground tomb carved down into rock and topped aboveground with a square masonry platform.

material culture The material remains (artifacts, dwellings, and other constructions) of past societies.

matriarchal society A society in which women hold dominant positions or in which inheritance follows the maternal rather than the paternal line.

matrilineal Descriptive of a culture in which lines of descent are traced through the mother and her ancestors rather than through the father.

matron A woman in the most legitimate and respected form of Roman marriage.

mattocks Digging tools or picks.

maul A heavy stone hammer used to break up rock.

mead An alcoholic beverage made by fermenting honey and water.

meander An ornamental pattern resembling a labyrinth.

mechane In ancient Greece, a cranelike device used to lift a performer above the ground.

mechanics The expertise of making and designing machines.

medicine wheel Large patterns of linear stone alignments, many of which have the appearance of a spoked wheel.

medium of exchange Any class of objects used by people as if it were money.

megalith Literally "great stone," referring to the use of large stones in the construction of Neolithic tombs and other features (for example, geometric figures, such as circles, as well as lines or avenues for which the massive stones served as markers), especially in central and western Europe.

menhir A single tall megalith, often posited as part of a sightline for astronomical observation.

meridian A great circle on the surface of a sphere that passes through both poles.

meter The rhythmic pattern of a poem.

metics Resident "aliens," or foreigners, with no rights of citizenship in a Greek city-state; this group was made up largely of immigrants and former slaves and was concentrated largely in Athens.

Metonic cycle A lunar calendar devised by the Greek astronomer Meton, using 19-year cycles totaling 235 months.

metope A pictorial panel, part of the frieze on the entablature of a building.

metrological A system of counting that separates the unit of measurement from the thing being counted.

metropolis A large and densely populated urban area.

miasmas Impurities floating in the air and resulting from any kind of pollution.

microliths Small retouched blades or blade segments usually made of flints and commonly used in composite tools or weapons such as knives, arrows and harpoons.

microtonal scale A musical scale that contains more notes within an octave than the traditional 12 notes of the Western scale.

middens Heaps of refuse, especially kitchen waste.

midrib A thickening down the middle of a dagger for added strength.

midwife A woman who helps other women give birth.

millet A small-seeded grass that is used for food.

milpa A form of agriculture in which a clearing is cropped for one or more seasons, then abandoned.

mime In ancient Rome, a popular form of theater that featured skits, songs, dances, magic acts, and acrobatics while emphasizing sexual jokes and parodies.

mina A weight of metal in ancient Greece, equivalent to 100 drachmas.

miter joint The ends of two pieces of wood cut at complementary angles and fitted together to create a 90-degree angle.

mode A set pattern of notes played over an octave using the white keys of a keyboard.

model A small-scale reproduction of an object that could magically be animated.

moiety One of two units into which a tribe or community is divided on the basis of unilineal descent.

mold making Producing glass objects by pouring molten glass into a hollow form, in order to make a certain shape or decoration.

molding A decorative recessed or relieved surface on an edge; a decorative strip used for ornamentation or finishing.

monarchy A political system under which a single king or queen holds supreme power, which is passed through the family line by hereditary descent.

monotheism The belief in the existence of only a single divinity.

monsoon A wind pattern that follows the same course every year, bringing predictable weather, such as rain, with it; also the intense rainfall or the season o rainfall associated with this wind.

monstra "Prodigies," or a natural but strange occurrences, such as the birth of a calf with two heads, regarded by Romans as a warning from the gods.

moraine An accumulation of stones and debris carried and deposited by glaciers.

morpheme A collection of speech sounds considered to be the smallest language unit.

mortar A substance used as an adhesive to fasten courses of bricks or stones together or as a plaster to protect the surface of a wall.

mortarium A heavy Roman bowl with sharp stone fragments embedded in its interior surface, used to grind food.

mortise and tenon A method for joining two planks of wood by means of a series of projecting tongues cut into the edge of one piece and slots cut into in the other.

mos maiorum A sense of tradition, one of the Roman virtues.

mosaic A design made with small pieces of colored glass or tile.

mud brick Bricks made from mud and straw and then dried in the sun.

mummification The Egyptian process of preserving the body by the removal of internal organs, drying out the corpse, and protecting it with linen wrappings.

mummy portrait Painting on a wooden panel made to cover the face of an Egyptian mummy, usually done in encaustic (wax) technique.

mundus A hole in the ground near the center of a Roman city that was usually covered but when uncovered allowed earth spirits to communicate with the city.

munus Gladiator show; from the Latin for "duty."

murex An aquatic snail that lived in the Mediterranean near Lebanon and was used as a source of purple dye.

murus gallicus "Gallic wall," a type of rampart found at many defended sites in ancient Gaul, consisting of timbers, filled with earth and stone, backed by stone walling, and often fronted by a ditch.

music In ancient Greece, any of the arts associated with the Muses: music, poetry, dancing, and drama.

musk A perfume originating from a sac inside the male musk deer.

nadir The point on the celestial sphere directly below the place on which the observer stands and opposite the zenith.

natron A mineral form of hydrated sodium salts found in dried lake beds.

necromancy Conjuring of the spirits of the dead in order to communicate with them.

necrophilia Sexual attraction or contact with a dead body.

necropolis A cemetery, especially one of large size and usually of an ancient city.

nexum Debt bondage.

niche A setback or indented enclosure; a small concavity.

Nilometer A series of steps that were used to mark the height of the Nile inundation as well as regular water levels

nirvana In Hinduism, the union of the human spirit with Brahma (the god of creation) and in Buddhism the state of blessedness in which the human spirit is released from the cycle of reincarnation.

nomad A member of a people who move seasonally from place to place to search for food and water or pasture for their livestock.

nomadic pastoralism A form of pastoralism in which all or most of the people move with their herds year-round to find pasture, living in temporary encampments and often traveling great distances.

nomarch The ruler of a nome, a political and geographical division of territory in ancient Egypt similar to a state in the United States.

nome A Greek term for an ancient Egyptian province, of which there were 42.

nomoi In Greek, "laws; the word could denote formally enacted laws as well as to established customs ("unwritten laws").

noncultic Nonreligious.

nopal A type of cactus eaten cooked or raw by ancient Mesoamericans.

numerology The study of the occult, or mystical, influence of numbers on everyday life.

numina A term early Romans used to refer to their gods, usually translated as "presence" or "power."

numismatics The study of coins and coinage.

nun The waters of primordial chaos in Egyptian cosmology.

nundina A market day in Rome.

obelisk A tall, tapered, four-sided monument with a pyramid at the top.

oblate A category of dependent person attached to the temples of the gods.

obol A weight of metal in ancient Greece, equivalent to one-sixth of a drachma.
obsidian A volcanic glass that was used in making tools.
obverse The "heads" side of a coin; this side of a coin often, but not always, contains a portrait bust.
ocarina A wind instrument, often oval in shape, with finger holes and a projecting mouthpiece.
ocher A powdery form of iron-rich earth or clay widely used as a pigment.
octant A navigational device used for measuring angles to a celestial body as a way to calculate position, with a calibration of 45 degrees.
odeion A Greek roofed hall used for musical performances
oenology The science of making wine.
offering formula A text inscribed on some funerary goods to magically provide sustenance for the deceased in the afterlife.
offering table A place where Egyptian priests or family members could place provisions for the deceased, often in the shape of a cone-shaped loaf of bread on a table.
***oikistes* (pl. *oikistai*)** The founder of a Greek *apoikia*, responsible for establishing the city walls and distributing land among its settlers.
oikonomia A Greek word translating roughly to "household regulation," from which the English word *economy* derives.
***oikos* (pl. *oikoi*)** In Greece and the ancient Near East, a great household, typically a temple, palace, or large estate, that controlled the labor, production, and consumption of its many members, most of whom were not related; a basic economic unit.
oligarchy A form of government in which rule resides jointly in the hands of a few people, usually the wealthiest and most powerful.
***olla* (or *aula*)** A deep, round-bottomed Roman vessel used for boiling stews or porridge.
omen Any event in nature that provides insight into the future.
onomastica Catalogues of things arranged under their kinds, not alphabetically.
opening of the mouth ceremony Funerary ritual that enabled the deceased to breathe, eat, and talk in the afterlife.
***oppidum* (pl. *oppida*)** A type of fortified town that was developed before the Roman Iron Age in western Europe and was a center of residential, administrative, commercial, and industrial activities
oracle bones Bones of animals, typically shoulder blades (usually of oxen), and also turtle shells that were heated to produce cracks, which were analyzed by those seeking to divine the future.
oracle A person, such as a priest, through whom a god is believed to speak.
oratory The art of public speaking.
orature Oral literature in ancient Africa.
orchestra A flat, circular area in which much of the action of a Greek drama occurred, situated between the spectators' seating area and the stage.
order The three ancient Greek styles of building design.
ore A naturally occurring mineral from which metals can be extracted.
orrery A mechanical model that reproduces the movements of heavenly bodies.
orthogonal planning City plan in which the perpendicular axes of streets create square city blocks.
orthostat An upright stone or slab used by architects in buildings.
osteomyelitis Bacterial infection of the bones and bone marrow.
ostracon (pl. ostraca) A fragment of pottery, typically carrying an inscription or drawing.
outcastes A person in ancient India who had no caste or had been ejected from a caste for violation of customs and rules.
outlier A language geographically detached and possibly remote from the range of the languages closely related to it.
outrigger A float attached by spars, or poles, to a watercraft.
overdying Successively dying a thread with individual colors until the desired color is reached.
overtone series In music, a number of higher notes produced simultaneously above a lower continuous drone.
oxidize To combine with oxygen.
pack animal An animal used to carry loads on its back.
paedagogus In ancient Rome, an educated slave who served as a tutor in ancient Rome.
paidotribēs In ancient Greece, a gymnastics teacher, working on physical fitness and the vigorous games that formed the basis of public competition and prepared young men for war.
palaestra Facility for training in wrestling and boxing in ancient Greece.
palanquin A litter or carriage body on poles, carried on the shoulders of men or women.
paleoclimatologist A scientist who studies long-term changes in climate on the earth throughout the planets four-billion-year existence
paleographic Having to do with ancient writings.
paleopathologists Scientists who study disease in prehistoric populations through examination of skeletal and tissue remains, coprolites, and works of art.
palette A flat stone tray, often decorated with carved designs, upon which colored minerals (such as malachite or hematite) were ground to make cosmetics.
palisade A fence made of upright stakes or posts set very closely together; a stockade.
pallium A rectangular woolen mantle worn by lower-class Romans.
panchayat In India, a council at the village level, responsible for dealing with local crime and punishment.

panegyric Laudatory written or oral poem.
pankration An event in ancient Greece that combined elements of boxing and wrestling.
pantheistic Relating to the worship of all gods.
pantheon The group of gods worshipped by a particular culture.
papyrus A tall aquatic plant used mainly by the Egyptians to make a writing material resembling paper.
parapegma A calendar that lists annual celestial events, such as the rising and setting of specific stars or constellations on given days of the year; a star calendar.
parrhesia In ancient Greece, frank or open speech, a cherished Athenian principle.
passage tomb A tomb where the burial chamber is reached through a low passage; secondary chambers may lead off from the main chamber.
pastoral nomadism An economic lifestyle that revolves around entire families or kin groups following domesticated animals during yearly cycles.
pastoral poetry Poetry that presents an idealized portrait of country life, often concerning the love between shepherds and shepherdesses.
pastoralism The breeding, tending, and exploitation of domestic herd animals as a principal means of livelihood for a community or society.
paterfamilias In ancient Rome, the male head of a household.
pathogen Any agent capable of causing disease.
patria potestas The legal authority (including the power of life and death) of a Roman head of household over his family (including slaves and other dependents).
patriarch A male head of a family.
patrician The upper social class of Rome, consisting of those who held social, political, and economic power.
patrilineal Descent traced through the male ancestors.
patrilocal A residence pattern in which married couples live with or near the husband's family.
patronus A Roman of wealth and status who extended his patronage and protection to one or more lower-status clients.
pavimentum Concrete foundation of a Roman road.
Pax Romana Term used to describe the relative peace and stability that the Romans imposed on their empire.
payment in kind The offering of crops, animals, and textiles, and other goods instead of money to pay taxes or a debt.
peat Partially carbonized plant matter, usually found in bogs.
pectoral A breastplate or breast covering.
pederasty An erotic relationship common in Greek culture between a youth (usually between the onset of puberty and the full growth of the beard) and an adult man.
pediment The triangular section just below a sloped roof, which may contain decorative or sculptural features.
peltast A Greek lightly armed infantry soldier.
pemmican A mixture of dried meat, dried berries, and rendered fat.
pentameter A poetic meter that has five feet per line.
pentecontor A 50-oared ship, rowed by arranging 25 oarsmen on each side of a vessel.
peplos A loose gown worn over a tunic by the ancient Greeks.
peret The "growing season," one of three seasons in the Egyptian calendar, based on the stages of the Nile's transformation.
perioikoi In ancient Greece, people from neighboring towns, especially those subject to the people of Sparta.
***periplous* (or *periplus*; pl. *periploi*)** In ancient Greece, a narrative of discovery containing details of navigation, such as ports and coastal landmarks.
peristyle An open area or courtyard surrounded by columns.
permafrost Permanently frozen ground.
petasos A hat with a broad, floppy brim worn by the ancient Greeks.
petroglyph An image that is carved or pecked into a rock surface with a hard stone or some other tool.
phalanx A rectangular formation of heavy infantry, densely arrayed so that each man's shield protected both himself and his neighbor to his left.
pharmaceutical Having healing properties.
pharmacology The study of drugs, especially their effects.
phonetic Having to do with the sounds of languages.
phonogram Written symbol used to express a sound.
phratry A kinship group found in many Greek cities.
phyle (pl. phylae) One of the main divisions of the citizen body in most ancient Greek cities; in ancient Athens the 10 phylae provided the organizational basis for many government functions.
physis Greek word for "nature"; can refer to the overall state of the physical body and its health and well-being.
pictograph Picture symbol representing by way of an illustration a person, idea, object, activity, event, or place.
pietas A sense of duty, one of the Roman virtues.
pilaster A rectangular column that projects from a wall to which it is attached.
pile weave Weaving that produces raised loops rather than a flat surface.
piles A beam of timber driven into the ground to be part of a foundation for a building.
***pilum* (pl. *pila*)** The standard missile weapon of the ancient Roman legionnaire, similar to a javelin.
pips Small fruit seeds.
pit house An ancient form of dwelling consisting of a pit excavated in the earth and roofed over.
pitch accent In language, the form of accentuation in which the accented syllable does not receive additional emphasis (as in English) but instead is pronounced at a musical pitch different from the rest of the word.
pitched roof A two-sided, sloped roof.

pithoi Large terra-cotta jars used for storage in ancient Greece and Rome.

placebo effect The effect seen when patients improve as a result of their positive expectations about the treatment rather than as a result of the treatment itself.

placer deposits Glacial deposits that contain valuable minerals, especially gold.

plain weave A technique of passing weft threads alternately over and under the warp threads.

plaiting Braiding a number of strips of leaf to create one long strip for use in a basket or mat.

plano-convex A shape comprising five flat sides, each one forming a plane, and one side curved upward, or convex.

plaza Large open-air area for public gatherings, created by the enclosure of buildings or mounds.

plebeian In Roman society, a commoner.

plinth An architectural support or base, such as small stands for statues and larger platforms for entire buildings.

plowshare The metal blade of a plow.

pneumatics The study of the mechanical properties of gases.

pneumoconiosis A disease of the lungs caused by inhalation of other irritating particles in the environment.

polestar Known as Polaris, the star that hangs above the North Pole and is a useful navigational guide at night.

poliomyelitis Severe viral infection that affects the spinal cord and brainstem and can lead to muscle wasting and partial or complete paralysis.

polis (pl. poleis) A ancient Greek city-state.

polity A politically organized unit.

pollen analysis A type of analysis that studies pollen that has survived for many thousands of years in waterlogged or acid conditions in the soil to gain a picture of plants growing in the vicinity the sample was taken from.

polychrome Multicolored.

polyculture The practice of planting several different crops in the same place, such as growing wheat among the trees of an orchard or lentils between the rows of vines in a vineyard.

polygamy The practice of marrying more than one spouse.

polyglot A person who speaks several languages and, hence, a place where several languages are widely spoken.

polygyny The practice of having two or more wives.

polyreme A large, multi-oared warship.

polytheism A religious system based on the belief in and worship of multiple gods.

pomerium A ritual boundary that separated the sacred space of the Roman city from the nonsacred world beyond.

pommel A knob on the part of a bladed weapon that is held in the hand.

pontifex maximus The chief religious figure in ancient Rome.

porcelain A white, hard, almost transparent ceramic coated with colored glazes.

pornai Prostitutes in ancient Greece.

port of trade Place where emissaries from central places trade and exchange goods.

portico A porch with regularly spaced columns, or colonnades, often surrounding the sanctuary of a temple.

portoria Customs duties.

post mast A simple mast made of one long timber.

post Vertical timber joined to a ship's keel at the bow (stem) and the stern (sternpost) to receive the hull planking.

post-and-beam construction An important early architectural design in which vertical posts, made of wood or stone, support horizontal beams anchoring the walls and roof; also called "post and lintel."

potsherd A fragment of a clay vessel or other object.

potter's wheel A circular platform that spins, on which wet clay is shaped by a potter's hands.

pozzolana Hard volcanic stone that went into Roman *caementum*, or cement, helping to make the walls of Roman buildings impervious to fire and moisture.

praetentura The quarters of elite troops within a Roman camp or fortification.

praetor In the government of ancient Rome, officials who held imperium, or the authority to lead an army and the power of life and death over citizens, and who were in charge of litigation and courts of law.

Praetorian Guard The Roman emperor's private military troops.

praetorium The headquarters of a Roman camp or fortification, built to house the legionary commander and the unit's symbolic banners.

precentor A person who leads worshippers in singing or chanting prayers.

precession The movement of an axis of a rotating body, causing it to "wobble" slightly in its orbit.

primogeniture The legal right of inheritance belonging to the first-born child, most often the eldest son.

proconsul A Roman consul whose imperium was continued after his year in office as a promagistrate.

***proletari,* (pl. *proletarii*)** People in ancient Rome who owned no property.

pronominal A term use to describe the nature of a pronoun.

propylon A porchlike structure that typically served as an entrance to the grounds of temples in ancient Greece.

prothesis A ceremony in which the corpse was laid out for mourning at home.

protohistoric Historical era immediately preceding the emergence of writing.

protolanguage An ancestral or root language, the basis for a family of languages.

provenance Place of origin.

proyet The period when the waters of the Nile receded, literally meaning "the emergence."

prytaneion A Greek city hall.

***prytanis* (pl. *prytaneis*)** Member of the executive committee presiding over the Athenian *boulē*, or citizens' council.

psephismata Decrees, that is, decisions of the Assembly in Athens that pertained to a specific situation and did not establish a permanent law.

pseudepigraphic Having a false title.

publicani Wealthy partners in Roman companies that invested large sums in bidding for state contracts to collect taxes or operate facilities like state-owned mines.

pueblos Native American communal dwellings built in cliff faces.

pulmentarium In ancient Rome, stew or porridge made of grains or beans.

pulque An alcoholic beverage made by ancient Mesoamericans from the fermented juice of various agave plants, such as the maguey.

purdah An Indian woman's garment that covers the entire body.

pututu Traditional Andean musical instrument made by drilling a large seashell at its point to make a mouthpiece.

pylons Large gates with two abbreviated pyramids on each side.

pyrotechnology The process of transforming a raw material such as clay into its final form using fire.

Pythagorean theorem A technique for finding the length of a side of a right triangle if the other two sides are known, based on the fact that the area of the squares made from any two sides have a known relationship to that made by the remaining side ($a^2 + b^2 = c^2$, where c is the hypotenuse).

qanat An irrigation system of underground tunnels developed by ancient Persians.

quadratum A building technique in which blocks of dressed stone were fastened to a concrete wall to form a regular facing.

quaestor In the government of ancient Rome, an official who handled financial matters: collecting customs or duties at ports and rent for Rome's public lands, running the city's treasury, and helping a provincial governor administrate his province.

quay A wharf built parallel to the shoreline.

quern A smooth stone used as a surface for grinding grain.

quetzal A bird indigenous to Guatemala with feathers greatly favored for making ancient ceremonial garments.

quinoa A pseudograin, consisting of the seeds of a herb from the goosefoot family and used by ancient Mesoamericans in making bread.

quinquireme A large multi-oared vessel; the oars are thought to have been arranged in sets of three, with two men pulling each of the top two oars.

quotidian Relating to common, everyday life.

radiocarbon dating (carbon-14 dating) A method that relies on the carbon-14 isotope (a specific form of carbon), which has a predictable rate of decay over time, to date historical artifacts based on the amount of carbon-14 remaining within a particular sample

raised relief A form of stone carving where the background is cut away, leaving the figures to stand out from the surface of the stone.

raja Indian title of nobility.

rampart A raised fortification resembling a wall and surrounding a township or other area to be protected.

rebate A continuous rectangular recess along the top or bottom edge of the face of stonework.

recession agriculture A way of scheduling agricultural production by planting crops after the recession, or receding, of annual floodwaters in a river valley.

reciprocity Type of exchange that takes place between two individuals when neither is dominant.

rede A Germanic word meaning "leadership" or "governance," especially if favored by the gods.

regent Someone who rules in a monarch's stead, especially when the monarch is a child.

regimen Lifestyle, largely diet and exercise, prescribed by ancient Greek physicians to treat ill health.

reincarnation The rebirth of a soul into a new human being (or other creature).

relics Objects venerated by Christians, often fragments of a saint's body or objects related to a saint's martyrdom or life.

relief Artwork that projects outward from a flat background; a coin, with its raised forms, is a common example of relief work.

rendered Melted; used in connection with animal fats melted for use as fuel.

repoussé A method for creating designs in relief on metal by hammering on the reverse side.

retentura The quarters of ordinary soldiers and cavalry, placed at the rear of a Roman fort or camp.

retiarius Gladiator armed with a net; from the Latin for "net."

reticulum A pattern of stones or bricks laid into a wall in regular, rectangular blocks.

retting A process in which fibers that make up the stems of certain plants, such as jute and flax, are detached from their woody core by soaking the fibers in water for several days.

reverse The "tails" side of a coin, with a wide range of design types and images.

revetment A decorative thin slab of stone, or facing, on a wall.

rhetor In ancient Rome, a teacher of public speaking.

rhetoric The study of principles and techniques that aid in the effective presentation and defense of a line of reasoning; also simply eloquence in speaking.

rhizome An elongated, underground (or underwater) horizontal stem from which roots and shoots emerge.

rhizotomoi Pharmacists or herbalists (literally "root cutters") in ancient Greece.

rites of passage Rituals used within a community to mark the transition of individuals from one status to another, including weddings, funerals, and rituals of initiation.

river ordeal A method used in the ancient Near East to reach a verdict when all else failed; the accused was thrown into a river, being judged innocent if he or she survived and guilty if drowned.

rock gong A large rock that produces a resonant tone when struck.

Romanitas A sense of belonging to a great empire felt by many of the conquered peoples of the Roman Empire.

Romanization The process of culturally changing foreigners into Romans.

rondo A piece of music that has a central theme repeated between contrasting sections.

rope stretchers Ancient Egyptian land surveyors who used essentially modern surveying tools to remeasure individual property lines on the farmland washed free of all distinguishing features by the annual Nile inundation.

rudder A large paddle at the rear of a vessel that is manipulated in order to steer the vessel.

rudus Mixture of components such as sand, soil, clay, or concrete, which is used as a foundation for a Roman road.

runes Form of writing in ancient Germany and medieval Scandinavia.

rushes Marsh plants with hollow stems.

rushlight A type of early candle, consisting of the pith of a stalky plant stem soaked in oil.

sacred barks Boats that carried the shrines of the gods in ancient Egypt.

sakkia An Egyptian animal-powered waterwheel.

salient A segment of the wall that projects outward from the wall.

salting A method of drying and preserving food.

san An ancient Chinese jacket.

sand-core technique Threads of molten glass are wound around a shaped core of sand; after the glass hardens, the sand is removed.

sapper Engineer used to undermine or dismantle walls.

saqiya A waterwheel powered by a domestic animal, used to collect water in buckets and raise it to an irrigation ditch or container, used in ancient Egypt and the Near East.

sarcophagus A coffin made of stone, often decorated with relief sculpture.

sari A long, wrapped Indian garment.

sarisa The long Macedonian spear, an innovation of Philip of Macedon.

sarongs Long pieces of cloth that are wrapped around the body.

saros cycle A period of about 18 years after which eclipses of the sun and moon reoccur.

***sastras* and sutras** Books of rules for conduct that formed the foundation for ancient Indian law.

satire Verse, prose, or a combination of the two that with humor, and sometimes harshness, criticizes bad behavior, hypocrisy, and other failings of society.

satrap A political office in the Persian Empire and later in the eastern kingdoms ruled by the successors of Alexander the Great.

satrapy A Persian province, administered by a royally appointed governor, who was known as a satrap.

Saturnian A native Roman poetic meter that was composed of two feet separated by a caesura, or pause, and that fell out of fashion in the late third century B.C.E.

satyr play An ancient Greek farce on a mythological subject, with a chorus representing satyrs, deities that have characteristics of horses or goats.

satyr A mythological creature that is usually part man and part goat, known for excessive drinking and lechery.

savanna A flat tropical or subtropical grassland.

scale armor Armor named for its resemblance to fish scales and made by sewing small oblongs of bronze or iron to a linen or felt shirt.

scale In music, a series of notes differing in pitch, varying with the frequency of vibration.

scarab A beetle used as a charm to ward off evil.

scarification Deliberate scarring of skin to create decorative patterns.

schenti A fabric loincloth or skirt.

schistosomiasis Parasitic infection acquired by immersion in water containing a certain species of worm; infection can result in fever, fatigue, serious anemia, and even liver damage.

scop Anglo-Saxon bard.

scoria Light volcanic ash that was used to extend concrete and make it capable of supporting longer arches and vaults.

scribe A man of letters in the ancient world who was capable of writing and who often worked as a teacher, a copyist, or a public official in the capacity of a clerk.

script A handwritten language.

scrivener A professional copyist or scribe.

scutum A rectangular or cylindrical shield.

scytale An encryption device consisting of rods and leather straps.

seal A carved piece of stone pressed into moist clay to leave an image that would be preserved when the clay was fired.

secondary burial Burial (or reburial) of bones from which the flesh has already decomposed. This practice implies that the corpse was originally buried elsewhere or exposed aboveground deliberately to reduce it to bones.

sedentary pastoralism A herding economy practiced by people living in permanent settlements.

sedentism A culture's shifting from living in nonpermanent settlements to living in permanent settlements.

sediment core A sample of layers of sediment, taken from lake bottoms or dry lands using a long cylinder, for the purpose of studying past environmental or human conditions

sedimentary rock Rock formed from sediment that has drifted down and settled in a seabed.

seine A fishing net that hangs vertically in the water via floats at the top and weights at the bottom.

seismic Relating to an earthquake.

selvedge Edge of a textile created by the looping of the weft around the warp.

senator The highest-ranking Roman class, consisting essentially of former magistrates. Their wealth lay in land, since they were banned from engaging in trade.

senyu In ancient Egypt, a weight in silver equal to one-half deben, or 1.75 ounces.

sepulchre A tomb.

serf A category of dependent person attached to the soil.

sericulture The breeding and raising of silkworms.

serpentine A soft, blue-green stone, sometimes used by the Olmec as an apparent substitute for more valuable jade.

sesterti (pl. sestertii) A Roman coin, made of silver or bronze, equal to one-fourth of a denarius.

sexagesimal In a mathematical system, relying on the base number 60.

sexireme A ship with six rows of oarsmen.

sextant A navigational device used measuring angles to a celestial body as a way to calculate, with a calibration of 60 degrees.

***shabitib* (pl. *shabitii*)** Small figure placed in an Egyptian tomb used as a substitute workman in case the spirit of the deceased is called on to do work in the afterlife.

shaduf A tool for irrigation made of a long branch or pole on a frame, with a bucket at one end and a counterweight at the other, allowing the operator to lower the bucket into the water and then easily raise it out with the help of the counterweight.

shaman A person who acts as intermediary between the natural and supernatural worlds, using magic or sorcery for purposes of healing, divination, and control over natural events.

shed rod A stick that separates warp threads into over-and-under groups.

sheet bronze Bronze that has been beaten or compressed into a thin sheet, which can then be fashioned into tubular and other shapes.

shemu The "drought season," one of three seasons in the Egyptian calendar, based on the stages of the Nile's transformation.

shinty A game resembling field hockey and dating to ancient times in the British Isles.

sibbe An ancient Germanic clan.

sickle sword A sword with a blade that curves so that it resembles the sickle used in harvesting crops.

sidelock of youth A long ponytail, worn to one side by youngsters.

sidereal Having a relation to or based on the stars.

silt Sand or earth, usually fine grained, carried by flowing water and then deposited.

singlet A loose shirt made of one layer of cloth.

sirocco A warm, moist Mediterranean wind.

sistrum (pl. sistra) An ancient Egyptian hand-held percussive musical instrument consisting of a handle and a U-shaped frame with crossbars holding loose rings that would jangle or tinkle when the instrument was shaken.

***situla* (pl. *situlae*)** A bronze vessel, similar to a bucket.

skene A rectangular building with one to three doors at the rear of the Greek stage, often representing a house, palace, military tent, cave, or other enclosure.

***skyphos* (pl. *skyphoi*)** A deep, two-handled cup.

slag What remains after ore is smelted and metal is removed.

slash-and-burn agriculture The practice of felling and burning trees to clear land for planting.

slip A thick clay-based liquid coating applied to the surface of a ceramic vessel, either for decorative purposes or to make the vessel surface less porous.

smallpox A highly contagious and deadly viral disease that produces fever and skin eruptions.

smelting A method of separating metal from surrounding rock or soil through heating or mixing with chemicals; also the process of heating and transforming mineral ores into more refined and usable finished metals and alloys.

social stratification The division of people into classes; from the word *strata,* meaning "layers."

socket ax A battle-ax with a bronze or iron head possessing a socket that slips over the end of the ax's handle to which the head is fastened with a rivet.

soil resistivity testing Detecting changes in the electrical resistance of the soil in order to find the remains of structures hidden beneath the ground.

solar calendar A calendar that bases a year on the time it takes the earth to complete one revolution around the sun.

solar year A year based on the time it takes the earth to complete one revolution around the sun; a calendar year of 365 days.

solar zenith passage The day of the year when the sun passes directly overhead and casts no shadow on vertical objects.

solstice The point at which days are longest or shortest, depending on the earth's tilt to its orbital plane. The winter solstice occurs in December in the Northern Hemisphere and in June the Southern Hemisphere, and the summer solstices are the reverse.

sophistēs A sophist, or professional teacher of rhetoric in ancient Greece; literally "professional wise person."

sorghum A cereal grain crop.

sound box On a stringed instrument, the hollow shell that amplifies the sound of the strings.

souterrain Underground chambers lined with stone.

spar A pole used for support on a watercraft.

speakers of the laws Legal specialists in the Persian Empire who explained the ins and outs of the law to those involved in court cases as well as helping to conduct those cases.

spear thrower Also called by its Aztec name, *atlatl,* a weapon used as an extension of the thrower's arm to add force and speed to a hurled spear or dart.

spelt A kind of wheat (*Triticum aestivum spelta*).

sphere of influence and **sphere of interest** A means of reserving a portion of territory from the political interference of another state; *interest* is assumed to be a less significant claim than *influence.*

spillway A channel carrying water around an obstruction.

spindle whorl A circular object that weights a spindle for spinning to improve rotation.

spindle A pointed stick about 12 inches long, used for spinning.

sprang Stretchy fabric woven of intertwined warp threads only.

squinch A small arch built across the interior angle of two walls.

stadion A term denoting both the rectangular ground upon which the Greeks ran in competition and the name of a race covering one length of this track.

stalactites Mineral deposit, often shaped like a spike, hanging down from the ceiling of a cavern.

stalagmites Mineral deposit, often shaped like a spike, pointing up from the floor of a cavern.

standard A wooden pole surmounted by an image used to represent a town or province in Egypt.

stasis A political faction in Greece, or the strife caused by such a faction.

statics The branch of mechanics dealing with weights in static equilibrium.

statumen Mixture of stones used as a foundation for a Roman road.

steganography A writing system used for hidden messages; the message is literally hidden from readers other than the intended recipient.

stela (pl. stelae) A carved stone slab, usually installed vertically and used to commemorate an event or person.

steppe A vast treeless grassland

stepped fret A zigzag form resembling a mountain, especially the terraced mountainsides of the Andes—a prominent feature in later Andean art and a symbol of prestige.

stereometry The measurement of solid figures or volumes.

stoa A narrow hallway often found in the commercial districts of Greek towns, with an open colonnade, where merchants set up shops.

stola The long garment worn by married Roman women over the tunic.

strategos "General," one of the few elected officials in democratic Athens, with authority that often extended beyond military matters.

stratification Division of people into social groups or classes

strut Bar used to draw weight down to a central point.

stucco A fine plaster used to cover walls.

stupa A dome-shaped mound serving as a Buddhist shrine.

stylus An instrument, often made of reed, used by the ancients for incising or inscribing on clay or wax tablets.

suasaria In Roman rhetoric, an argument made to justify or condemn a course of action.

subligaculum Also called a *campestre,* a garment worn under the tunic and toga as underwear and as a sports garment.

subsistence farming The practice of agriculture that provides enough food to eat without an excess for sale.

suffets Nonroyal magistrates who were granted control over a Punic city-state.

sumptuary laws Laws designed to limit excessive consumption or use of luxury goods.

sunk relief A form of stone carving where the background is left as it is and the figures are carved into the stone.

supernova A star's explosion, producing an exponential increase in its luminosity.

surface mining The process of harvesting useful stone and metals at above-ground sites, such as hillsides, and where drilling underground is not necessary or desirable.

swastika A pattern resembling a cross with each arm bent at a right angle, an ancient Hindu symbol (also used by Buddhists and Jains); the term is derived from the Sanskrit word for "well-being."

swidden An area cleared for temporary cultivation by cutting and burning the vegetation.

sykophantes In the legal system of ancient Athens, a class of professional prosecutors.

syllabary A written set of symbols that represent syllables.

sympathetic magic Magic that looks to achieve its ends through imitation of the desired results.

symposium A drinking party for Greek aristocrats featuring wine, games, poetry, and conversation.

synodic cycle The lunar phase cycle of 29.5 days.

synoecism In ancient Greece, the amalgamation of villages and towns into a larger unit.

synoikiai In ancient Greece, blocks of apartment buildings.

syntax The grammatical arrangement of words in a sentence.

syssitia In ancient Greece, military-style messes or eating clubs to which every Spartan citizen belonged.

syumuu In ancient Egypt, the dry season from March to July, literally meaning "the drought."

t'un-t'ien Military colonies set up by the ancient Chinese.

tabby weave A type of weave in which a single thread from the weft passes over and under one warp thread at a time.

tablinum A "home office" for the head of household in a Roman home.

taboos Practices or objects that are forbidden or banned because of social custom or religious practices.

talent The largest unit of weight and money in the ancient world, variously defined as a man's weight in gold or the amount of gold one man could carry; in ancient Greece, a specific weight of metal equivalent to 60 minas, or 6,000 drachmas.

tallow Animal fat.

Talmud The Jewish book of law and scriptural commentary.

talud-tablero A system of construction generally associated first with the city of Teotihuacán in ancient Mesoamerica; facades are formed by vertical panels alternating with sloped and diagonal ones.

tang A narrow projection by which a tool, typically a knife, is attached to its handle.

tanning The process of drying, curing, and dyeing leather for use in clothing, armor, and shoes.

taper A slender candle.

taproot A primary root that sends out offshoots.

tarentine A thin, almost transparent white gown worn by the ancient Greeks.

taro A large-leaved plant that is typically cooked as a vegetable or ground into flour.

tartan A cloth woven in a plaid or checked pattern.

tebenna A short, semicircular woolen mantle worn by the Etruscans and which was the forerunner of the Roman toga.

techne Greek term meaning "art," "craft," or "expertise" and the root of such words as *technical* and *technology.*

tectonic plate One of seven major pieces of the earth's crust that moves slowly over the mantel

tell An ancient mound built up from the remains of earlier settlements.

templum Any sacred area (not necessarily a building) in which ancient Roman priests could conduct rituals of augury, or foretelling of the future.

teosinte The plant from which early Americans bred maize, or corn.

terra sigillata Ornate red pottery favored in and around the Roman Empire.

terrace A "step" cut into the slope of a hill, providing a flat place for farming or building.

terra-cotta A hard fired clay used in pottery, sculpture, and building decoration.

tessera (pl. tesserae) One of the small pieces of stone, ceramics, or glass used in making mosaics.

tetrachord The building block of Greek melodic theory, consisting of four notes, with the top and bottom note forming an interval of a fourth.

tetradrachm In ancient Greece, coin equal to four drachms, issued under several different weight standards.

tetrarchy Rule by four people.

thalassocracy Maritime dominance or supremacy.

thatch Roofing made of grasses or leaves.

theocracy A government or political system based on the rule or religious authority of a god or gods and their human representatives (such as kings and priests), as found in the ancient Near East.

theriac A medicine used by the ancient Romans as an antidote to poison and a cure-all or preventative against numerous diseases.

thermae Public bathhouses, found in all Roman cities.

thermoluminescence A process of measuring the age of an object, often used for ceramic objects between 10,000 and 300 years old to determine their authenticity.

thermopolium A shop in an ancient Roman city where people could buy hot wine and food.

tholia A high, pointed hat worn by ancient Greek women.

tholos A circular building used for religious purposes in ancient Greece.

thronos A solid, upright chair with armrests, usually found in ancient Greek temples or palaces.

throwing knife Multibladed weapon without a solid hilt and with one plain, flat side and one decorated or embossed side.

tidal bore A wave that travels from the ocean up a river.

tinfoil A thin sheet of tin used as a wrapping.

titulus crucis The *elogium* (headboard) attached to the cross above someone who has been crucified, stating the offense the person committed; specifically, the headboard above Jesus, with the inscription *Jesus of Nazareth, King of the Jews.*

toga The rounded, woolen mantle worn by Roman citizens.

Torah The Jewish book of scripture, generally referring to the first five books of the Old Testament.

torque Circular bar worn around the neck as jewelry by ancient Celts and Germans.

torsion catapult A launching device that derives its power from the twisting of ropes or wooden elements of the frame.

transhumant pastoralism A system in which some members of the community migrate with herds to distant pastures on a seasonal basis while most remain sedentary and focus on agricultural activities.

transliterate To reproduce in English letters the sound of a word's original pronunciation in another language.

transmigration The movement of a dead person's soul into the body of an already existing living person.

trapeza A four-legged table used by the ancient Greeks.

trappings Clothing, jewelry, and symbols of office.

trepanning An ancient European medical practice that consisted of sawing or drilling a hole in the skull to treat head or psychological disorders.

tribe Group of people related by lineage, kin, or clan with or without centralized leadership.

tribon A coarse, dark-colored wrap worn by the ancient Greeks.

tribulum A device to thresh grain, consisting of a heavy board with flints or small wheels on its underside.

tribunal The raised platform at one end of a basilica from where a judge or other magistrates presided over a hearing or tried legal cases.

tribune An elected representative of the plebeians of Rome.

tribute Goods, labor, or payment offered to the ruling classes, usually by obligation, in exchange for their rulership.

triclinium A Roman dining room containing three couches on which men reclined to eat.

trilithon A megalithic structure made of two large vertical stones supporting a horizontal stone laid across the top.

trireme An ancient ship with three rows of oars on each side.

trittys Political division in Athens consisting of several contiguous demes.

trypanosomiasis A disease caused by parasitic single-celled organisms generally transmitted by insect bites; the form popularly known as "sleeping sickness" is transmitted by tsetse flies.

tsetse fly A fly that spreads diseases among cattle and humans, including sleeping sickness.

tsunami A giant wave or series of waves created by earthquakes, volcanic eruptions, or other major impact to an ocean.

tubers Rounded roots, such as the potato, that grow underground.

tufa Soft volcanic rock that was frequently used as a filler or as facing stone in Roman buildings.

tumbaga An alloy of gold and copper used by the ancient Peruvians.

tumulus (pl. tumuli) An artificial mound built, in ancient Europe, usually over the remains of the dead; also called a *barrow.*

tundra A vast, cold, treeless plain characteristic of arctic and subarctic regions.

tunic A T-shaped garment with openings at the top for the head and arms.

turf Sod; a mat of grass and its roots.

tuyere Nozzle through which air is delivered into a furnace.

twill Fabric threads interwoven to give the cloth a parallel diagonal, diamond shape or herringbone ridges on the surface.

typhoon A hurricane occurring in the western Pacific region.

typology Within the discipline of historical linguistics, the characteristic of surface structural similarity.

***tyrannos* (pl. *tyrannoi*)** In ancient Greece, sole ruler without hereditary claim to the throne; the word sometimes has negative connotations but less so than the English word *tyrant.*

Tyrian purple An ancient dye made from the secretions of marine snails and very highly valued throughout the ancient Mediterranean world.

Tzolkin Mayan sacred calendar based on a 260-day ritual cycle.

unguent A medicinal or cosmetic ointment.

univira A matron who had the honorable distinction of having married only once in her life and not having divorced.

untouchables People without caste in India, the lowest social group.

urbs Latin word for "city."

ushabtis In ancient Egypt, small figurines that were buried with the dead to accompany them into the underworld and work for them in the afterlife.

uttariya A scarf that covered the upper body, worn by ancient Indians.

vallus Ancient Roman reaping machine pulled by an animal and used to cut off the heads of wheat stalks and drop them in a container.

varna Associated with Hinduism; the name in India for the original social division of people into four main groups, which in turn contain thousands of subdivisions.

vassal A person, nation, or group that is dependent on or subordinate to another.

vault An arched brick or stone ceiling or roof.

Vedic laws Legal codes based on religious texts, such as the sacred writings of Hinduism.

vela A linen awning covering a Roman theater; sometimes called a *velarium.*

vellum A special kind of leather used to make sheets for writing. In general this was more prestigious and expensive than papyrus.

venatio Beast hunts that were conducted as a spectator sport in ancient Roman amphitheaters.

venator Hunter in a staged wild-animal hunt in the Roman arena.

veneer Thin strips of decorative wood applied to the surface of an object to hide a wood of less aesthetic value or to mask imperfections.

vestal virgins The priestesses of the Roman hearth goddess, Vesta, who were required to be virgins and entrusted with keeping a sacred flame burning in Vesta's temple.

vigesimal Referring to a number system based on 20.

vihara In Indian architecture, a small building consisting of cubicles arranged around a central courtyard, used by monks and visitors to meditate and do penance.

villa A self-sufficient community, including a residential building, gardens, workshops, and cultivated fields.

viticulture The science of growing grapes.

vivisection The cutting open of a living being for the investigational or diagnostic purposes.

vizier In ancient Egypt, the highest-ranking government official after the pharaoh.

volute A type of spiral scrollwork.

votive Given or done in fulfillment of a vow or pledge.

wabet The workshop in which bodies were embalmed before burial in ancient Egypt.

warp In weaving, the threads that run lengthwise.

warp-weighted loom A rectangular, upright loom with the warp hanging from the top crossbar and anchored by weights on the free ends.

wattle and daub A method of building construction that involves a wooden lattice structure covered with packed mud, clay, and other materials.

wedge To stamp on clay to remove air pockets and impurities.

weft In weaving, the threads that run crosswise.

weir trap A cone-shaped wicker basket with an internal funnel.

weld A plant used to make yellow dye.

well-field system During the Chinese Zhou Dynasty, the territory controlled by a duke and divided into nine equal portions arranged in a square; the commoners worked all the land, but the produce of the center square belonged to the duke.

were-jaguar An Olmec sculptural figure combining human and jaguar traits.

wet nurse A woman who nurses another woman's infant in exchange for wages.

whorl A pulley that helps to rotate a spindle.

wick A short length of cloth or fiber that draws fuel oil from a reservoir by capillary action and then can be burned to provide a steady light.

wickerwork shield A shield made from woven reeds or twigs supported by a wooden frame.

wisdom literature Ancient Egyptian texts that consist of either instructions or philosophical dialogue.

woad A plant used to make blue dye.

wuxing The five elements of ancient Chinese philosophy and science: fire, earth, water, wood, and metal.

xenia Greek word usually denoting the relationship between host and guest.

xenos Greek word meaning, variously, "foreigner," "stranger," or "guest-friend."

xoanon One of a set of wooden cult objects venerated in ancient Greece for the deities that they represented.

yakshi In India, a female supernatural being who guards the earth's mineral treasures.

yang In Chinese philosophy, the form of energy that supposedly is hard, bright, active, and "male."

yaws A bacterial skin infection marked by red skin eruptions and joint pain.

yin In Chinese philosophy, the form of energy that supposedly is soft, dark, receptive, and "female."

zaliths Members of an assembly who governed an Etruscan city-state.

zenith The point on the celestial sphere directly above the place on which the observer stands and opposite the zenith.

ziggurat In ancient Mesopotamia, a pyramid-shaped tower rising in stages of decreasing size to a shrine at the top.

zooarchaeology A field of science that has to do with uncovering, identifying, and interpreting animal remains in archaeological contexts.

zoomorphic Having animal attributes or an animal form.

zori A Japanese sandal that resembles modern flip-flops.

	AFRICA	THE MIDDLE EAST
prehistory – 10,000 B.C.E.	**Ca. 2 million years ago:** *Homo erectus* emerges and spreads to Asia and Europe **ca. 1 million–500,000 years ago:** *Homo erectus* gains the ability to make fire **ca. 200,000–100,000 years ago:** Homo sapiens emerges and spreads to Europe and Asia. **ca. 27,500–ca. 25,000 B.C.E.:** Date of the earliest-known rock art in Africa, found in eastern and southern Africa and produced by the San.	**ca. 10,000 B.C.E.:** Emergence of Natufian culture in the Middle East, to the west of the Euphrates River; establishment of the town of Abu Hureyra in present-day Syria; earliest firm evidence of domesticated dogs from a grave in Palestine. **ca. 11,000 B.C.E.:** As the glaciers retreat, fields of wild grain begin to appear in the Near East.
10,000 B.C.E. – 5000 B.C.E. (continues)	**ca. 11,000 B.C.E.:** Beginning of the African Humid Period, a period of warmer and wetter weather on the African continent. **ca. 9000 B.C.E.:** New Stone Age begins in Egypt. **ca. 8500 B.C.E.:** The harpoon is developed in present-day Sudan, allowing for the exploitation of deepwater fish. **ca. 7700 B.C.E.:** Nile Valley forms part of the Fertile Crescent. **ca. 7500 B.C.E.:** Egyptians first begin using reed boats; earliest-known African pottery is produced in the Sahara. **ca. 6000 B.C.E.:** Onset of dry conditions begins the desertification of the Sahara.	**ca. 10,000 B.C.E.:** Hunter-gatherers begin to domesticate the goat. **ca. 9000 B.C.E.:** The New Stone Age begins in Mesopotamia. **ca. 8000 B.C.E.:** Agriculture begins in the Near East; farmers use sticks to scratch up the earth to plant grains; thick beer ("drinkable bread") first brewed in Mesopotamia by the Sumerians; clay tokens first used for counting purposes in Mesopotamia. **ca. 7700 B.C.E.:** Milk from ewes (sheep) used widely as a food source in Near East. **ca. 7500 B.C.E.:** Reed boats come into use in Mesopotamia. **ca. 7000 B.C.E.:** Emmer wheat becomes a major food crop in portions of the Middle East.

Chronology by Region

ASIA AND THE PACIFIC

ca. 42,000 B.C.E.: The first seafaring colonists arrive in Australia from the Asian mainland.

ca. 28,500 B.C.E.: Seafaring colonists from Australia or the Asian mainland arrive in New Guinea.

ca. 27,000 B.C.E.: The first people arrive on the islands of Japan over land bridges or ice from the Asian mainland.

ca. 13,000–300 B.C.E.: Jōmon Period of Japan.

---

ca. 9000 B.C.E.: By this date people in Siberia and central Asia are using bones and skins from animals such as mammoths to build shelters.

ca. 7000 B.C.E.: Tropical horticulture begins in New Guinea.

ca. 6500 B.C.E.: Farming starts on the Indian subcontinent.

ca. 6400 B.C.E.: Pengtoushan in China is the oldest-known site of rice cultivation in Asia.

ca. 5500 B.C.E.: Beginning date for the earliest paintings in India, found on large stones and rock faces, mostly in central India.

ca. 5400–ca. 5200 B.C.E.: The Yellow River region in China provides the earliest evidence for the domestication of chickens in Asia.

EUROPE

ca. 1,000,000??–ca. 8,000 B.C.E.: Paleolithic Period.

ca. 34,000 B.C.E.: Beginning of the Aurignacian culture in the region of present-day Bulgaria, Hungary, and France.

ca. 25,000 B.C.E.: First human settlements in what is now Spain.

ca. 24,000 B.C.E.: First evidence of cold food storage and preservation, discovered in eastern Europe.

ca. 10,500 B.C.E.: Würm Glacial Age ends; ice withdraws so that humans can move into northern Europe.

---

ca. 9500 B.C.E.: Ice sheets start to melt in Europe.

ca. 8000–ca. 4000 B.C.E.: Mesolithic Period.

ca. 7200 B.C.E.: Sheep domesticated in the area of present-day Greece.

ca. 7000–ca. 2000 B.C.E.: Neolithic Period; emergence of agriculture, sometimes called the Neolithic Revolution.

ca. 6500 B.C.E.: Ancestor of cattle first domesticated in the region of present-day Yugoslavia.

THE AMERICAS

ca. 18,000–ca. 3,000 B.C.E.: The first Americans migrate from Siberia over the Bering Sea Land Bridge, now the Bering Strait, into present-day Alaska, though this date remains uncertain.

ca. 10,500 B.C.E.: Date assigned to early Clovis points (stone tools such as arrowheads, named after site in New Mexico where the first such points were found) at Monte Verde site in Chile.

ca. 10,200 B.C.E.: Dogs domesticated by earliest Americans.

---

ca. 9,500 B.C.E.: Date assigned to the first-discovered Clovis points in New Mexico; Clovis culture formed.

ca. 9200–ca. 8000 B.C.E.: Folsom tradition spreads across North America.

ca. 9000 B.C.E.: Bison herds cover the Great Plains of North America; first civilizations develop in the Arctic North.

ca. 8000 B.C.E.: First Americans arrive in South America; Archaic Age begins in North America, with dramatic changes in the landscape cause by receding of glaciers.

ca. 7000 B.C.E.: First cultivation of corn, or maize; agriculture begins to develop in the Americas.

	AFRICA	THE MIDDLE EAST
10,000 B.C.E. – 5000 B.C.E. (continued)		**ca. 6500 B.C.E.:** A primitive plow called the *ard* is used in the Near East. **ca. 6000 B.C.E.:** Production of wine begins in Mesopotamia and along the eastern shore of the Mediterranean Sea.
5000 B.C.E. – 4000 B.C.E.	**ca. 5000 B.C.E.:** Egyptians first build canals and dikes to irrigate crops. **ca. 4500 B.C.E.:** Start of cattle herding in the Sahara. **ca. 4400 B.C.E.:** First evidence of use of horizontal loom, depicted on Egyptian pottery.	**ca. 5000 B.C.E.:** People in the valleys surrounding the Tigris and Euphrates rivers domesticate cattle and begin to build irrigation systems for crops. **ca. 4500 B.C.E.:** Permanent settlement is established at Ur in Mesopotamia; clay tokens are first used for accounting purposes in Mesopotamia. **ca. 4300 B.C.E.:** Turntable for pottery making is invented in Mesopotamia. **ca. 4200 B.C.E.:** Copper mining begins in the area of modern-day Oman.
4000 B.C.E. – 3000 B.C.E.	**ca. 4000 B.C.E.:** Beginning date for the cultivation of yam along the Niger River. **ca. 3600 B.C.E.:** Beginning of Bronze Age in Egypt. **ca. 3500 B.C.E.:** Egyptians develop complete number system. **ca. 3100 B.C.E.:** Egyptian hieroglyphic writing emerges.	**ca. 4000 B.C.E.:** Earliest copper objects appear in the ancient Near East. **ca. 3500 B.C.E.:** The Sumerians begin crafting tools out of bronze, a mixture of copper and tin, initiating the Bronze Age, which begins to reach its height in about 2000 B.C.E.; Sumerians also start to use wheeled vehicles pulled by animals. **ca. 3400 B.C.E.:** Earliest form of cuneiform script is devised to record the language used by the ancient inhabitants of Uruk in southern Mesopotamia.
3000 B.C.E. – 2000 B.C.E. (continues)	**ca. 3000 B.C.E.:** Egyptians begin to mine copper and develop the first crude paper, made of papyrus; Sahara Desert begins to form in North Africa. Berbers arrive in North Africa. **ca. 2920 B.C.E.:** The start of Egypt's First Dynasty, uniting Upper and Lower Egypt. **ca. 2650 B.C.E.:** The first pyramid, the Step Pyramid, built by Imhotep in Egypt. **ca. 2575 B.C.E.:** The Great Pyramid of Cheops is constructed. **ca. 2400–ca. 1500 B.C.E.:** Kingdom of Karmah in Nubia.	**ca. 2800 B.C.E.:** The sickle is invented by farmers in Sumer. **ca. 2750 B.C.E.:** The Phoenician city of Tyre emerges as a great sea power. **ca. 2500 B.C.E.:** Beginning of the Iron Age in the ancient Middle East. **ca. 2400 B.C.E.:** The Babylonians first use the abacus for computation; Sumerians first use "positional notation," where numbers take their value depending on their position in a numerical group. **ca. 2350 B.C.E.:** The Old Akkadian Empire begins rule of Mesopotamia.

ASIA AND THE PACIFIC	EUROPE	THE AMERICAS
		ca. 6000 B.C.E.: The Coahuiltecan culture forms in Texas; North American population groups become more settled, and cultural differences begin to emerge.
ca. 5000 B.C.E.: Longshan culture emerges in China. **ca. 4500 B.C.E.:** China domesticates the water buffalo.	**ca. 5000 B.C.E.:** Southeast European plains populated by agriculturalists. **ca. 5000–ca. 900 B.C.E.:** Rock faces in Alps carved with figures of animals, warriors, and buildings. **ca. 4500–ca. 3500 B.C.E.:** Europeans begin to use pottery with linear ornamentation. **ca. 4350 B.C.E.:** Horses first domesticated in Europe and used for power.	**ca. 5000 B.C.E.:** Cochise culture forms in Arizona and New Mexico. **ca. 4800 B.C.E.:** Peoples from the Central American mainland become the first inhabitants of the Caribbean. **ca. 4300 B.C.E.:** A variety of cotton is produced in the area of present-day Mexico.
ca. 4000 B.C.E.: The people of the Indus Valley in India are cultivating a wide variety of crops, including dates, mangos, wheat, barley, and peas, using irrigation systems to water the crops.	**ca. 3400–c. 1600 B.C.E.:** Earliest evidence of wheeled vehicles in Europe (from a grave in Poland). **ca. 3200–c. 1600 B.C.E.:** The "Iceman," equipped with a cast copper ax, dies while crossing the Alps near the present-day Italian-Austrian border. **ca. 3100–c. 1600 B.C.E.:** Construction of Stonehenge megaliths in England.	**ca. 4000 B.C.E.:** First permanent shelters constructed in the North American Midwest; corn is domesticated in Mexico; llamas and alpacas are domesticated in the region of present-day Peru.
ca. 3000 B.C.E.: People in the Indus Valley begin to weave fabric out of cotton; the Chinese begin to manufacture silk. **ca. 2900 B.C.E.:** In China the mythical emperor Fu Xi develops the concept of yin and yang, fundamental to the practice of ancient Chinese medicine and the Chinese view of nature. **ca. 2700 B.C.E.:** Mythical Chinese emperor Shennong develops the principles of acupuncture; tea is first used as a beverage in China. **ca. 2600 B.C.E.:** Long-distance trade, particularly in luxury goods, develops among the nations of Southeast Asia; the major Indian cities of Harappa and Mohenjo Daro are founded. **ca. 2300 B.C.E.:** Rice from the Indus Valley is introduced in northern China. **ca. 2296 B.C.E.:** Chinese astronomers make the first recorded sighting of a comet.	**ca. 3000 B.C.E.:** The ox-drawn plow first used in Europe **ca. 2800 B.C.E.:** Emergence of the Aegean Sea civilizations on Minoa and Crete, precursors of the Greeks. **ca. 2800 B.C.E.–ca. 700 B.C.E.:** Bronze Age, marked by use of bronze tools. **ca. 2500 B.C.E.:** Horses are introduced to Ireland. **ca. 2400 B.C.E.:** People of the Beaker culture begin migration from Spain to France, Germany, and Britain.	**ca. 3000 B.C.E.:** Early Alaskans begin to construct permanent villages; artwork produced by Native Americans begins to appear; Andes peoples of South America first cultivate potatoes; adobe pyramids built at Caral and El Aspero in modern-day Peru. **ca. 2600 B.C.E.:** First temple mounds are constructed in Peru. **ca. 2500 B.C.E.:** North Americans begin to make pottery; village cultures become predominant in the Americas. **ca. 2475 B.C.E.:** Maize is domesticated and becomes a staple crop.

	AFRICA	THE MIDDLE EAST
3000 B.C.E. – 2000 B.C.E. (continued)		
2000 B.C.E. – 1000 B.C.E.	**ca. 2000 B.C.E.:** Date assigned to the remains of cities in Mauritania, Africa's oldest cities. **ca. 2000–ca. 1000 B.C.E.:** Emergence of Bantu language and its spread throughout much of Africa in what is called the Bantu Migration. **ca. 1700 B.C.E.:** Date of the world's oldest mathematical document, on Egyptian papyrus. **ca. 1400 B.C.E.:** Africa passes directly from the Stone Age to the Iron Age, skipping the Bronze Age important in other world cultures. **ca. 1380 B.C.E.:** Egyptians complete construction of a canal linking the Nile River and the Red Sea. **ca. 1323 B.C.E.:** Death of Egypt's King Tutankhamen.	**ca. 2000 B.C.E.:** The Epic of Gilgamesh, written in cuneiform, is the world's oldest epic poem; its story of a great flood and an ark is believed to be the origin of the story of Noah's flood narrated in the biblical book of Genesis. **ca. 1800 B.C.E.:** First taboos against eating pork develop in the Near East. **ca. 1850 B.C.E.:** Judaism is founded by Abraham, a Mesopotamian prince. **ca. 1750 B.C.E.:** Babylon's king Hammurabi dies. **ca. 1700 B.C.E.:** Syria and Palestine develop the first alphabet; windmills first used by Babylonians. **ca. 1275 B.C.E.:** Beginning of the 40-year-long Israelite migration from Egypt to the Near East, commonly called the Exodus and recorded in the Old Testament book of the same name. **ca. 1141 B.C.E.:** The Jewish Ark of the Covenant is seized by the Philistines. **ca. 1124 B.C.E.:** Nebuchadnezzar I becomes king of Babylon.
1000 B.C.E. – 500 B.C.E.	**ca. 1000–ca. 100 B.C.E.:** The kingdom of Kush flourishes in Sudan. **ca. 800 B.C.E.:** North African city of Carthage founded by the Phoenicians. **ca. 600 B.C.E.:** The Sahel, south of the Sahara Desert, emerges as the site of numerous cities along an east-west trading route; Phoenician seafarers circumnavigate Africa. **ca. 580 B.C.E.:** Africans first produce iron, in Meroë.	**961 B.C.E.:** The Great Temple of Jerusalem is constructed under the leadership of King Solomon. **ca. 800 B.C.E.:** Babylonian astronomers discover how to predict lunar eclipses. **ca. 700 B.C.E.:** Cities in the Near East build aqueducts to provide water to their populations. **ca. 689 B.C.E.:** The Assyrians destroy the city of Babylon, but the city is rebuilt and in the next century is one of the great cities of the world. **ca. 600 B.C.E.:** The religion Zoroastrianism found by Zoroaster in Persia. **ca. 587 B.C.E.:** The Great Temple of Jerusalem is destroyed by Nebuchadnezzar; temple is rebuilt ca. 516 B.C.E.

ASIA AND THE PACIFIC

ca. 2205 B.C.E.: The Chinese become the first civilization to mill grain; sheep, oxen, dogs, pigs, and goats first domesticated in China.

---

ca. 2000 B.C.E.: Horses are first tamed by nomads on the Asian steppes.

ca. 1750 B.C.E.: In India two major historic cities, Harappa and Mohenjo Daro, collapse.

ca. 1500 B.C.E.: Aryan nomads arrive in India from the steppes of Eurasia, bringing with them cattle and sheep; Chinese begin to use vehicles drawn by horses.

ca. 1400 B.C.E.: China domesticates first poultry, the jungle fowl from Malaya.

ca. 1300 B.C.E.: Date assigned to the first evidence of Chinese writing.

ca. 1100 B.C.E.: The Chinese invent the crossbow and the kite and begin using ice for refrigeration.

ca. 1045 B.C.E.: Zhou Dynasty founded in China; the dynasty will last until approximately 256 B.C.E.

---

ca. 1000 B.C.E.: Polynesian expansion across the Pacific Ocean reaches Samoa and Tonga.

ca. 876 B.C.E.: The concept of zero first introduced in India.

ca. 700 B.C.E.: China introduces the concept of crop rotation.

ca. sixth century B.C.E.: Confucianism developed in China by philosopher Confucius (Kong Fuzi).

ca. 600 B.C.E.: The Upanishads, texts of Hinduism, are compiled in India.

ca. 565 B.C.E.: The Chinese philosopher Laozi founds the religious philosophy of Daoism.

ca. 528 B.C.E.: The religion of Buddhism wins its first adherents in India.

EUROPE

---

ca. 2000 B.C.E.: Seafarers from Crete and Phoenicia adopt sails and masts on ships.

ca. 1600 B.C.E.: Arrival of the Greeks in the Aegean region.

ca. 1500–ca. 1000 B.C.E.: Emergence of Celtic cultures in central Europe and the Balkans.

ca. 1470 B.C.E.: Minoan civilization in the Mediterranean Sea destroyed by volcanic eruption.

ca. 1200–ca. 800 B.C.E.: Hallstatt A and B cultures, of the Bronze Age, flourish in the region around present-day Austria.

ca. 1100 B.C.E.: Collapse of Mycenaean civilization; Iron Age begins in Europe, marked by the use of iron tools.

ca. 1100–ca. 750 B.C.E.: Greek Dark Ages.

---

ca. Eighth–seventh centuries B.C.E.: Homer writes/compiles Greek epics *The Iliad* and *The Odyssey.*

ca. 800–ca. 500 B.C.E.: Halstatt C and D cultures, of the Iron Age, arise in the region around present-day Austria.

ca. 776 B.C.E.: First ancient Olympic Games held in Greece.

ca. 753 B.C.E.: Traditional date of the founding of Rome, although archaeologists have found graves in Rome dating to at least a century earlier.

ca. 650–ca. 500 B.C.E.: Etruscan dominance of Rome, ending with Roman rebellion against Etruscans.

ca. 600 B.C.E.: Capitoline temple built in Rome.

ca. 525 B.C.E.: The Greek philosopher Pythagoras declares that the earth is round.

ca. 509 B.C.E.–ca. first century B.C.E.: Roman Republic.

ca. 508 B.C.E.: Beginning of democracy in Greece.

THE AMERICAS

---

ca. 2000 B.C.E.: Arctic ancestors of the Inuit begin to use small tools, especially the harpoon.

ca. 1800 B.C.E.: People in Peru first make pottery.

ca. 1600–ca. 1300 B.C.E.: Mounds constructed by peoples along the Mississippi River; best-known mound is Poverty Point.

ca. 1500–ca. 400 B.C.E.: Olmec civilization arises and flourishes in Mesoamerica.

ca. 1200 B.C.E.: The ancient ball game, the oldest-known game in the Americas, originates with the Olmec civilization.

---

ca. 1000 B.C.E.: Archaic Age ends in North America; cultivation of corn is introduced to North America from Mexico.

ca. 900–ca. 200 B.C.E.: The Chavín culture thrives in Peru.

ca. 800 B.C.E.: Pottery making emerges in Alaska; the temple center of Chavín de Huántar is established in Peru.

ca. 650 B.C.E.: The Maya begin using smoke to cure diseases.

	AFRICA	THE MIDDLE EAST
500 B.C.E. – 250 B.C.E.	**ca. 300 B.C.E.:** Carthaginians attain height of power and influence as traders and shipbuilders; date assigned to Namoratunga, a cluster of stone pillars in Kenya that may have served as a calendar; museum and Great Library are founded at Alexandria, Egypt. **ca. 280 B.C.E.:** Ptolemy II of Egypt completes a canal between the Mediterranean Sea and the Red Sea. **ca. 264 B.C.E.:** Beginning of the Punic Wars between Rome and Carthage.	**ca. 420 B.C.E.:** The Nabataeans establish a kingdom at Petra, in present-day Jordan. **ca. 311 B.C.E.:** The start of the Seleucid Empire, which rules Babylonia and Syria.
250 B.C.E. – 0	**ca. 250 B.C.E.:** Dromedaries are introduced into Egypt. **ca. 200 B.C.E.:** Formation of kingdom of Axum in northern Ethiopia. **ca. 146 B.C.E.:** Carthage falls to the Roman invaders, marking the end of the Third Punic War.	**ca. 66–ca. 73 B.C.E.:** The first great revolt of the Jews of Judea against the Romans, during which legions under Titus destroyed Jerusalem, looting and burning Herod's Temple. **37 B.C.E.:** Herod the Great is made king of Judea by the Romans. **7 B.C.E.:** Jesus of Nazareth born in Bethlehem; historians arrive at this date based on astronomical records.
0 – 250 C.E.	**ca. 100s C.E.:** The Bantu use iron utensils for cooking, iron spearheads for hunting, and iron hooks for fishing. **ca. 150 C.E.:** Kingdom of Meroë goes into decline from competition with the rival kingdom of Axum. **ca. 200 C.E.:** Kingdom of Ghana, a major gold producer, flourishes.	**33 C.E.:** Jesus Christ is condemned to death and crucified in Jerusalem; Christian religion founded. **ca. 50:** Farmers in Near East (and China) first begin using silos for grain storage. **67:** The apostle Paul, the leading member of the new Christian faith, is executed on June 29. **132–135:** The second (sometimes called the third) Jewish revolt against the Roman Empire; after this revolt the emperor Hadrian roots out Jews and Judaism from Judea and bars Jews from Jerusalem. **ca. 224:** Sassanian Dynasty begins in Persia and will rule until 651.

ASIA AND THE PACIFIC

ca. 475 B.C.E.: Beginning of the Iron Age in China.

ca. 400 B.C.E.: The Chinese become the first to use catapults in warfare.

ca. 301 B.C.E.: Nomadic tribes invade parts of northern China; Chinese construct a massive irrigation system to relieve flooding in river basins in Sichuan.

ca. 300 B.C.E.–ca. 300 C.E.: Yayoi Period in Japan; religion called Shinto may have originated during this period, though the matter is disputed.

---

ca. 221 B.C.E.: Qin Dynasty founded in China; country united.

ca. 202 B.C.E.: Han Dynasty begins in China.

ca. 101 B.C.E.: Using a compass for the first time, Chinese seafarers arrive on the eastern coast of India.

---

ca. 6 C.E.: People in China who want jobs as government officials have to take a civil service examination.

ca. 31: Earliest description of a Chinese horizontal waterwheel.

ca. 80: A massive migration of Asians moves westward with horses and cattle to join the Iranians and Mongols to become the Huns.

ca. 100: Japan imports rice for cultivation from China.

ca. 105: China develops the first paper made from fibers.

ca. 200: Japan invades and subdues Korea.

EUROPE

ca. 500 B.C.E.: Portions of Greece become the first to use coins.

ca. 480 B.C.E.–ca. 1 C.E.: La Tène culture, a Celtic Iron Age culture, emerges in the area of modern-day Switzerland, and the Celts expand through much of Europe.

ca. 457–ca. 429 B.C.E.: The "Golden Age" of Athens under the rule of Pericles.

ca. 450 B.C.E.: Celts arrive in the British Isles.

ca. 440 B.C.E.: The first textbook of geometry written by the Greek Hippocrates of Chios.

ca. 323–ca. 31 B.C.E.: Hellenistic Period of Greece.

ca. 312 B.C.E.: Construction on Roman Appian Way begins.

ca. 270 B.C.E.: Rome brings all of Italian Peninsula under its authority.

---

ca. 250 B.C.E.: Greek mathematician Archimedes calculates value of pi and develops the screw for pumping water.

ca. 170 B.C.E.: Rome builds the world's first paved streets.

58–51 B.C.E.: Julius Caesar subdues Gaul (France) in the name of the Roman Empire.

1st century B.C.E.–476 C.E.: Roman Empire.

55 B.C.E.–43 C.E.: Roman Empire invades Britain twice, and Roman domination and influence grow through trade and other interactions; city of London founded.

60s: First revolts against Roman rule by Germanic and Celtic tribes.

64: Great Fire destroys much of Rome; first persecutions of Christians.

75–77: Roman conquest of Britain is complete.

ca.138–ca. 192: Period of the so-called Antonine plague, a series of epidemics in the Roman world, including two notable outbreaks in 165 and 180.

167: The first Barbarian attacks on Rome.

THE AMERICAS

ca. 500 B.C.E.: Adena culture of the North American Midwest reaches its peak; date of the Maya story of creation, the Popol Vuh; the Cuspisnique build roads exclusively with walls.

ca. 400 B.C.E.: The Mayans begin using jugs with spouts.

ca. 400 B.C.E.–150 C.E.: Preclassic Period of Mayan civilization.

---

ca. 200 B.C.E.–ca. 600 B.C.E.: The Nazca create hundreds of earth drawings, or geoglyphs, that can been seen only from the air.

ca. 100 B.C.E.: Hopewell societies, especially in Illinois and Ohio, flourish; pottery from Peru and Ecuador shows the presence of facial ulceration, scarring, and malformation of the mucous membranes among the pre-Inca, an indication of epidemic *leishmaniasis*.

---

ca. 1 C.E.: Hohokam culture forms in U.S. Southwest; Toltec city of Teotihuacán founded.

ca. 50 C.E.: The city of Teotihuacán establishes control in the valley of Mexico; construction of the Pyramid of the Sun begins.

ca. 100–600: The Moche people flourish in northern Peru.

ca. 150–650: Classic Period of Mayan civilization.

250 C.E. – 500 C.E.

AFRICA

343 C.E.: King Ezana of Axum is converted to Christianity by Egyptian missionaries.

ca. 350: Kingdom of Axum defeats kingdom of Kush.

439 C.E.: Vandals capture the city of Carthage and establish a kingdom.

THE MIDDLE EAST

ca. 370: The Sassanian Dynasty attains the height of its power under the leadership of Shāpūr II.

ca. 460: Famine strikes the Sassanian Empire.

ASIA AND THE PACIFIC

ca. 280 C.E.: China is reunified under the Western Jin Dynasty.

ca. 300–ca. 538: Kofun Period in Japan.

ca. 320: Northern India unified by the Gupta Dynasty.

ca. 375 C.E.: Stirrups are invented in China.

ca. 450: The Chinese invent ink, made from lampblack.

EUROPE

313: Emperor Constantine I of Rome converts to Christianity and declares it the official religion of the empire.

330: Foundation of Constantinople by Emperor Constantine I of Rome.

ca. 360: Invasion of Europe by the Huns.

391: Roman emperor Theodosius I makes Christianity the sole legal religion of the Roman Empire.

410: Rome besieged by Visigoths under the command of Alaric.

ca. 430: Angles and Saxons from Denmark invade the eastern portion of Britain; the bubonic plague strikes Europe for the first time.

455: Vandals sack Rome.

476: The Roman Empire falls when the last of the Roman emperors in the West, Romulus Augustus, is deposed and not replaced.

THE AMERICAS

ca. 400 C.E.: The sacred site of Serpent Mound is created by the Hopewell culture in present-day Ohio.

General Bibliography

GENERAL

Adas, Michael, ed. *Agricultural and Pastoral Societies in Ancient and Classical History.* Philadelphia: Temple University Press, 2001.

Bahn, Paul G. *The Atlas of World Archaeology.* New York: Checkmark Books, 2000.

Bauer, Susan Wise. *The History of the Ancient World: From the Earliest Accounts to the Fall of Rome.* New York: W. W. Norton, 2007.

Bogucki, Peter. *The Origins of Human Society.* Malden, Mass., and Oxford, U.K.: Blackwell Publishers, 1999.

Clark, J. Desmond, and Steven A. Brandt, eds. *From Hunters to Farmers.* Berkeley: University of California Press, 1984.

Nagle, D. Brendan. *The Ancient World: A Social and Cultural History,* 6th ed. Upper Saddle River, N.J.: Prentice Hall, 2006.

Scarre, Christopher. *The Human Past: World Prehistory and the Development of Human Societies.* London: Thames and Hudson, 2005.

AFRICA

Boonzaier, Emile, ed. *Cape Herders: History of Khoikhoi of Southern Africa.* Athens: Ohio University Press, 1997.

Connah, Graham. *African Civilizations: An Archaeological Perspective,* 2nd edition. Cambridge, U.K.: Cambridge University Press, 2001.

Davis, R. Hunt Jr., ed. *Encyclopedia of African History and Culture.* Vol. 1: *Ancient Africa (Prehistory to 500 CE).* New York: Facts On File, 2005.

Ehret, Christopher. *An African Classical Age: Eastern and Southern Africa in World History, 1000 B.C. to A.D. 400.* Charlottesville: University Press of Virginia, 1998.

Ehret, Christopher. *The Civilizations of Africa: A History to 1800.* Oxford, U.K.: James Currey, 2002.

Ehret, Christopher. *Sudanic Civilization.* Washington, D.C.: American Historical Association, 2003.

Hall, Martin. *Farmers, Kings, and Traders: The People of Southern Africa, 200–1860.* Chicago: University of Chicago Press, 1990.

Phillipson, David W. *African Archaeology,* 3rd edition. Cambridge, U.K.: Cambridge University Press, 2005.

Schoenbrun, David. *A Green Place, a Good Place: Agrarian Change, Gender, and Social Identity in the Great Lakes Region to the 15th Century.* Portsmouth, N.H.: Heinemann, 1998.

Strigner, Chris, and Robin McKie. *African Exodus: The Origins of Modern Humanity.* New York: Henry Holt, 1997.

Vansina, Jan. *How Societies Are Born: Governance in West Central Africa before 1600.* Charlottesville: University of Virginia Press, 2004.

Vansina, Jan. *Paths in the Rainforests: Toward a History of Political Tradition in Equatorial Africa.* Madison: University of Wisconsin Press, 1990.

Vogel, Joseph O., ed. *Encyclopedia of Precolonial Africa: Archaeology, History, Languages, Cultures, and Environments.* Walnut Creek, Calif.: AltaMira Press, 1997.

EGYPT

Baines, John, and Jaromir Malek. *Cultural Atlas of Ancient Egypt.* New York: Facts On File, 2000.

Bard, Kathryn, ed. *Encyclopedia of the Archaeology of Ancient Egypt.* London and New York: Routledge, 1999

Bunson, Margaret R. *Encyclopedia of Ancient Egypt,* rev. ed. New York: Facts On File, 2002.

David, Rosalie A. *Handbook to Life in Ancient Egypt,* rev. ed. New York: Facts On File, 2003.

Grimal, Nicolas-Christophe. *A History of Ancient Egypt.* Translated by Ian Shaw. Cambridge, Mass.: Blackwell, 1992.

Hornung, Erik. *History of Ancient Egypt: An Introduction.* Translated by David Lorton. Ithaca, N.Y.: Cornell University Press, 1999.

Hornung, Erik. *The Secret Lore of Egypt.* Translated by David Lorton. Ithaca, N.Y.: Cornell University Press, 2001.

Hornung, Erik, Rolf Krauss, and David A. Warburton. *Ancient Egyptian Chronology.* Leiden, Netherlands, and Boston: Brill, 2006.

Lichtheim, Miriam. *Ancient Egyptian Literature: A Book of Readings.* Berkeley: University of California Press, 2006.

Loprieno, Antonio. *Ancient Egyptian: A Linguistic Introduction.* New York: Cambridge University Press, 1995.

Manley, Bill. *The Penguin Historical Atlas of Ancient Egypt.* London and New York: Penguin Books, 1996.

Quirke, Stephen, and Jeffrey Spencer. *The British Museum Book of Ancient Egypt*. New York: Thames and Hudson, 1992.

Redford, Donald B., ed. *The Oxford Encyclopedia of Ancient Egypt*. Oxford and New York: Oxford University Press, 2000.

Shaw, Ian, ed. *The Oxford History of Ancient Egypt*. Oxford, U.K.: Oxford University Press, 2000.

Simpson, William Kelly, ed. *The Literature of Ancient Egypt: An Anthology of Stories, Instructions, and Poetry*. New Haven, Conn., and London: Yale University Press, 2003.

THE MIDDLE EAST

Aruz, Joan. *Art of the First Cities: The Third Millennium BC from the Mediterranean to the Indus*. New York: Metropolitan Museum of Art, 2003.

Bertman, Stephen. *Handbook to Life in Ancient Mesopotamia*. New York: Facts On File, 2003.

Bryce, Trevor. *The Kingdom of the Hittites*. Oxford, U.K.: Oxford University Press, 2005.

Due, Andrea, and M. Chesi. *The Atlas of the Bible Lands: History, Daily Life and Traditions*. New York: Peter Bedrick, 2001.

Frankfort, Henri. *The Art and Architecture of the Ancient Orient*, 5th ed. New Haven, Conn.: Yale University Press, 1996.

Kuhrt, Amelie. *The Ancient Near East, c. 3000–330 BC*. London: Routledge, 1995.

Leick, Gwendolyn. *Who's Who in the Ancient Near East*. London: Routledge, 2002.

Postgate, J. N. *Early Mesopotamia: Society and Economy at the Dawn of History*. London: Routledge, 1992.

Potts, D. T. *The Arabian Gulf in Antiquity*. Vol. 1: *From Prehistory to the Fall of the Achaemenid Empire*. Vol. 2: *From Alexander the Great to the Coming of Islam*. Oxford, U.K.: Clarendon Press, 1990.

Roaf, Michael. *Cultural Atlas of Mesopotamia and the Ancient Near East*. Oxford, U.K.: Equinox, 1990.

Snell, Daniel C. *Life in the Ancient Near East, 3100–332 BC*. New Haven: Yale University Press, 1998.

Wilkinson, T. J. *Archaeological Landscapes of the Near East*. Tucson: University of Arizona Press, 2003.

ASIA AND THE PACIFIC

Auboyer, Jeannine. *Daily Life in Ancient India: From 200 BC to 700 AD*. Translated by Simon Watson Taylor. London: Phoenix, 2002.

Chang, K.C. *Art, Myth, and Ritual: The Path to Political Authority in Ancient China*. Cambridge, Mass.: Harvard University Press, 1983.

Di Cosmo, Nicola. *Ancient China and Its Enemies: The Rise of Nomadic Power in East Asian History*. Cambridge, U.K.: Cambridge University Press, 2002.

Drège, Jean-Pierre, and Emil Bührer. *The Silk Road Saga*. New York: Facts On File, 1989.

Habu, Junko. *Ancient Jomon of Japan*. Cambridge, U.K.: Cambridge University Press, 2004.

Higham, Charles F. W. *The Bronze Age of Southeast Asia*. Cambridge, U.K.: Cambridge University Press, 1996.

Higham, Charles F. W. *Encyclopedia of Ancient Asian Civilizations*. New York: Facts On File, 2004.

Lewis, Mark Edward. *The Early Chinese Empires: Qin and Han*. Cambridge, Mass.: Harvard University Press, 2007.

Lilley, Ian, ed. *The Archaeology of Oceania: Australia and the Pacific Islands*. Malden, Mass.: Blackwell, 2006.

Loewe, Michael. *Everyday Life in Early Imperial China: During the Han Period, 202 BC–AD 200*. Indianapolis: Hackett, 2005.

Loewe, Michael, and Edward L. Shaughnessy, eds. *The Cambridge History of Ancient China: From the Origins of Civilization to 221 BC*. Cambridge, U.K.: Cambridge University Press, 1999.

Possehl, Gregory. *The Indus Civilization: A Contemporary Perspective*. Walnut Creek, Calif.: Altamira, 2002.

Sinor, Denis, ed. *The Cambridge History of Early Inner Asia*. Cambridge, U.K.: Cambridge University Press, 1990.

Thapar, Romila. *Early India: From the Origins to AD 1300*. Berkeley: University of California Press, 2002.

EUROPE

Aldhouse-Green, Miranda J. *Dying for the Gods: Human Sacrifice in Iron Age and Roman Europe*. Stroud, U.K.: Tempus, 2001.

Audouze, Françoise, and Olivier Buchsenschutz. *Towns, Villages, and Countryside of Celtic Europe: From the Beginning of the Second Millennium to the End of the First Century BC*. London: B. T. Batsford, 1992.

Bogucki, Peter, and Pam J. Crabtree. *Ancient Europe 8000 B.C.–A.D. 1000: An Encyclopedia of the Barbarian World*. New York: Charles Scribner's Sons, 2004.

Castleden, Rodney. *The Stonehenge People. An Exploration of Life in Neolithic Britain, 4700–2000 BC*. New York: Routledge, 1990.

Cunliffe, Barry W. *The Oxford Illustrated Prehistory of Europe*. Oxford, U.K. and New York: Oxford University Press, 1994.

Cunliffe, Barry W. *The Ancient Celts*. Oxford, U.K. and New York: Oxford University Press, 1997.

Fowler, Brenda. *Iceman: Uncovering the Life and Times of a Prehistoric Man Found in an Alpine Glacier*. New York: Random House, 2000.

Glob, P. V. *The Bog People: Iron Age Man Preserved*. Ithaca, N.Y.: Cornell University Press, 1969.

Harding, Anthony F. *European Societies in the Bronze Age*. Cambridge, U.K.: Cambridge University Press, 2000.

Hedeager, Lotte. *Iron-Age Societies: From Tribe to State in Northern Europe, 500 BC to AD 700*. Malden, Mass., and Oxford, U.K.: Blackwell, 1992.

James, Simon. *The World of the Celts*. London and New York: Thames and Hudson, 1993.

Laing, Lloyd Robert. *The Archaeology of Celtic Britain and Ireland, c. 400–1200 AD*. Cambridge, U.K.: Cambridge University Press, 2006.

Malone, Caroline. *Neolithic Britain and Ireland*. Stroud, U.K.: Tempus, 2001.

McIntosh, Jane. *Handbook to Life in Prehistoric Europe*. New York: Facts On File, 2006.

Moffat, Alistair. *Before Scotland: The Story of Scotland before History*. London: Thames and Hudson, 2005.

Piggott, Stuart. *Ancient Europe: From the Beginnings of Agriculture to Classical Antiquity: A Survey*. Edinburgh, U.K.: University Press, 1965.

Scarre, Christopher. *Exploring Prehistoric Europe*. New York: Oxford University Press, 1998.

Waldman, Carl, and Catherine Mason. *Encyclopedia of European Peoples*. New York: Facts On File, 2006.

Wells, Peter S. *The Barbarians Speak: How the Conquered Peoples Shaped Roman Europe.* Princeton, N.J.: Princeton University Press, 1999.

GREECE

Adkins, Lesley, and Roy Adkins. *Handbook to Life in Ancient Greece.* New York: Facts On File, 2005.

Camp, John. *The Archaeology of Athens.* New Haven, Conn.: Yale University Press, 2001.

Camp, John, and Elizabeth Fisher. *Exploring the World of the Ancient Greeks.* London: Thames and Hudson, 2002.

Cartledge, Paul. *The Cambridge Illustrated History of Ancient Greece.* New York: Cambridge University Press, 2002.

Finley, M. I. *The Ancient Greeks*, 2nd ed. New York: Penguin, 1991.

Garland, Robert. *Daily Life of the Ancient Greeks.* Westport, Conn.: Greenwood Press, 1998.

Green, Peter. *Ancient Greece: A Concise History*, 2nd ed. New York: Thames and Hudson, 1980.

Lassieur, Allison. *The Ancient Greeks.* New York: Franklin Watts, 2004.

Pedley, John G. *Greek Art and Archaeology*, 3rd ed. Upper Saddle River, N.J.: Prentice Hall, 2002.

Sacks, David. *Encyclopedia of the Ancient Greek World*, rev. ed. by Lisa R. Brody. New York: Facts On File, 2005.

Shuter, Jane. *Life in Ancient Athens.* Chicago: Heinemann Library, 2005.

Sparkes, Brian A., ed. *Greek Civilization: An Introduction.* Malden, Mass.: Blackwell Publishers, 1998.

Taylor, Pat. *The Ancient Greeks.* Chicago: Heinemann Library, 2007.

ROME

Adkins, Lesley, and Roy Adkins. *Handbook to Life in Ancient Rome.* New York: Facts On File, 2004.

Aldrete, Gregory S. *Daily Life in the Roman City: Rome, Pompeii, and Ostia.* Westport, Conn.: Greenwood Press, 2004.

Alston, Richard. *Aspects of Roman History, AD 14–117.* New York: Routledge, 1998.

Bunson, Matthew. *Encyclopedia of the Roman Empire*, rev. ed. New York: Facts On File, 2002.

Chrisp, Peter. *Ancient Rome.* New York: DK Publishing, 2007.

Coulston, Jon, and Hazel Dodge, eds. *Ancient Rome: The Archaeology of the Eternal City.* Oxford, U.K.: Oxford University School of Archaeology, 2000.

Hodge, Susie. *Ancient Roman Art.* Des Plaines, Ill.: Heinemann Library, 2006.

Jay, David. *Ancient Romans.* Brookfield, Conn.: Copper Beech Books, 2000.

Kleiner, Fred S. *A History of Roman Art.* Belmont, Calif.: Thomson Wadsworth, 2007.

Nardo, Don. *Ancient Rome.* San Diego: Kidhaven Press, 2002.

Ramage, Nancy, and Andrew Ramage. *Roman Art: Romulus to Constantine*, 4th ed. Upper Saddle River, N.J.: Pearson Prentice Hall, 2005.

Reece, Katherine. *The Romans.* Vero Beach, Fla.: Rourke Publishing, 2006.

Rees, Rosemary. *The Ancient Romans*, rev. ed. Chicago: Heinemann Library, 2006.

THE AMERICAS

Adams, Richard E. W., and Murdo J. MacLeod, eds. *The Cambridge History of the Native Peoples of the Americas.* Vol. 2: *Mesoamerica.* New York: Cambridge University Press, 2000.

Calloway, Colin G. *One Vast Winter Count: The Native American West before Lewis and Clark.* Lincoln: University of Nebraska Press, 2003.

Coe, Michael D., and Rex Koontz. *Mexico, From the Olmecs to the Aztecs*, 5th ed. New York: Thames and Hudson, 2002.

Evans, Susan Toby. *Ancient Mexico and Central America: Archaeology and Culture History.* New York: Thames and Hudson, 2004.

Foster, Lynn V. *Handbook to Life in the Ancient Maya World.* New York: Facts On File, 2002.

Josephy, Alvin M. Jr. *500 Nations: An Illustrated History of North American Indians.* New York: Grammercy, 2002.

Mann, Charles C. *1491: New Revelations of the Americas before Columbus.* New York: Knopf, 2005.

Moseley, Michael E. *The Incas and Their Ancestors: The Archaeology of Peru*, rev. ed. New York: Thames and Hudson, 2001.

Pohl, John M. D. *Exploring Mesoamerica.* New York: Oxford University Press, 1999.

Salomon, Frank, and Stuart B. Schwartz. *The Cambridge History of the Native Peoples of the Americas*, Vol. 3: *South America.* New York: Cambridge University Press, 1999.

Silverman, Helaine, ed. *Andean Archaeology.* Malden, Mass.: Blackwell Publishing, 2004.

Thomas, David Hurst. *Exploring Ancient Native America: An Archaeological Guide.* New York: Routledge, 1999.

Trigger, Bruce G., and Wilcomb E. Washburn, eds. The *Cambridge History of the Native Peoples of the Americas.* Vol. 1: *North America.* New York: Cambridge University Press, 1996.

von Hagen, Adriana, and Craig Morris. *The Cities of the Ancient Andes.* New York: Thames and Hudson, 1998.

Index

Locators in boldface indicate main entries. Locators followed by *f* indicate figures. Locators followed by *m* indicate maps.

C

D

F

L

M

N

P

S

U

V